Oxford Dictionary of National Biography

Volume 5

Oxford Dictionary of National Biography

IN ASSOCIATION WITH

The British Academy

From the earliest times to the year 2000

Edited by

H. C. G. Matthew

and

Brian Harrison

Volume 5
Belle–Blackman

OXFORD
UNIVERSITY PRESS

OXFORD

UNIVERSITY PRESS

Great Clarendon Street, Oxford OX2 6DP

Oxford University Press is a department of the University of Oxford.
It furthers the University's objective of excellence in research, scholarship,
and education by publishing worldwide in

Oxford New York

Auckland Bangkok Buenos Aires Cape Town
Chennai Dar es Salaam Delhi Hong Kong Istanbul Karachi
Kolkata Kuala Lumpur Madrid Melbourne Mexico City Mumbai Nairobi
São Paulo Shanghai Taipei Tokyo Toronto

Oxford is a registered trade mark of Oxford University Press
in the UK and in certain other countries

Published in the United States
by Oxford University Press Inc., New York

British Library Cataloguing in Publication Data
Data available

Library of Congress Cataloging in Publication Data
Data available: for details see volume 1, p. iv

ISBN 0-19-861355-5 (this volume)
ISBN 0-19-861411-X (set of sixty volumes)

Text captured by Alliance Phototypesetters, Pondicherry
Illustrations reproduced and archived by
Alliance Graphics Ltd, UK
Typeset in OUP Swift by Interactive Sciences Limited, Gloucester
Printed in Great Britain on acid-free paper by
Butler and Tanner Ltd,
Frome, Somerset

LIST OF ABBREVIATIONS

1 General abbreviations

AB	bachelor of arts		BCnL	bachelor of canon law
ABC	Australian Broadcasting Corporation		BCom	bachelor of commerce
ABC TV	ABC Television		BD	bachelor of divinity
act.	active		BEd	bachelor of education
A$	Australian dollar		BEng	bachelor of engineering
AD	*anno domini*		bk *pl.* bks	book(s)
AFC	Air Force Cross		BL	bachelor of law / letters / literature
AIDS	acquired immune deficiency syndrome		BLitt	bachelor of letters
AK	Alaska		BM	bachelor of medicine
AL	Alabama		BMus	bachelor of music
A level	advanced level [examination]		BP	before present
ALS	associate of the Linnean Society		BP	British Petroleum
AM	master of arts		Bros.	Brothers
AMICE	associate member of the Institution of Civil Engineers		BS	(1) bachelor of science; (2) bachelor of surgery; (3) British standard
ANZAC	Australian and New Zealand Army Corps		BSc	bachelor of science
appx *pl.* appxs	appendix(es)		BSc (Econ.)	bachelor of science (economics)
AR	Arkansas		BSc (Eng.)	bachelor of science (engineering)
ARA	associate of the Royal Academy		bt	baronet
ARCA	associate of the Royal College of Art		BTh	bachelor of theology
ARCM	associate of the Royal College of Music		*bur.*	buried
ARCO	associate of the Royal College of Organists		C.	command [identifier for published parliamentary papers]
ARIBA	associate of the Royal Institute of British Architects		*c.*	*circa*
ARP	air-raid precautions		c.	*capitulum pl. capitula*: chapter(s)
ARRC	associate of the Royal Red Cross		CA	California
ARSA	associate of the Royal Scottish Academy		Cantab.	Cantabrigiensis
art.	article / item		cap.	*capitulum pl. capitula*: chapter(s)
ASC	Army Service Corps		CB	companion of the Bath
Asch	Austrian Schilling		CBE	commander of the Order of the British Empire
ASDIC	Antisubmarine Detection Investigation Committee		CBS	Columbia Broadcasting System
ATS	Auxiliary Territorial Service		cc	cubic centimetres
ATV	Associated Television		C$	Canadian dollar
Aug	August		CD	compact disc
AZ	Arizona		Cd	command [identifier for published parliamentary papers]
b.	born		CE	Common (*or* Christian) Era
BA	bachelor of arts		cent.	century
BA (Admin.)	bachelor of arts (administration)		cf.	compare
BAFTA	British Academy of Film and Television Arts		CH	Companion of Honour
BAO	bachelor of arts in obstetrics		chap.	chapter
bap.	baptized		ChB	bachelor of surgery
BBC	British Broadcasting Corporation / Company		CI	Imperial Order of the Crown of India
BC	before Christ		CIA	Central Intelligence Agency
BCE	before the common (*or* Christian) era		CID	Criminal Investigation Department
BCE	bachelor of civil engineering		CIE	companion of the Order of the Indian Empire
BCG	bacillus of Calmette and Guérin [inoculation against tuberculosis]		Cie	Compagnie
BCh	bachelor of surgery		CLit	companion of literature
BChir	bachelor of surgery		CM	master of surgery
BCL	bachelor of civil law		cm	centimetre(s)

Cmd	command [identifier for published parliamentary papers]
CMG	companion of the Order of St Michael and St George
Cmnd	command [identifier for published parliamentary papers]
CO	Colorado
Co.	company
co.	county
col. *pl.* cols.	column(s)
Corp.	corporation
CSE	certificate of secondary education
CSI	companion of the Order of the Star of India
CT	Connecticut
CVO	commander of the Royal Victorian Order
cwt	hundredweight
$	(American) dollar
d.	(1) penny (pence); (2) died
DBE	dame commander of the Order of the British Empire
DCH	diploma in child health
DCh	doctor of surgery
DCL	doctor of civil law
DCnL	doctor of canon law
DCVO	dame commander of the Royal Victorian Order
DD	doctor of divinity
DE	Delaware
Dec	December
dem.	demolished
DEng	doctor of engineering
des.	destroyed
DFC	Distinguished Flying Cross
DipEd	diploma in education
DipPsych	diploma in psychiatry
diss.	dissertation
DL	deputy lieutenant
DLitt	doctor of letters
DLittCelt	doctor of Celtic letters
DM	(1) Deutschmark; (2) doctor of medicine; (3) doctor of musical arts
DMus	doctor of music
DNA	dioxyribonucleic acid
doc.	document
DOL	doctor of oriental learning
DPH	diploma in public health
DPhil	doctor of philosophy
DPM	diploma in psychological medicine
DSC	Distinguished Service Cross
DSc	doctor of science
DSc (Econ.)	doctor of science (economics)
DSc (Eng.)	doctor of science (engineering)
DSM	Distinguished Service Medal
DSO	companion of the Distinguished Service Order
DSocSc	doctor of social science
DTech	doctor of technology
DTh	doctor of theology
DTM	diploma in tropical medicine
DTMH	diploma in tropical medicine and hygiene
DU	doctor of the university
DUniv	doctor of the university
dwt	pennyweight
EC	European Community
ed. *pl.* eds.	edited / edited by / editor(s)
Edin.	Edinburgh

edn	edition
EEC	European Economic Community
EFTA	European Free Trade Association
EICS	East India Company Service
EMI	Electrical and Musical Industries (Ltd)
Eng.	English
enl.	enlarged
ENSA	Entertainments National Service Association
ep. *pl.* epp.	*epistola(e)*
ESP	extra-sensory perception
esp.	especially
esq.	esquire
est.	estimate / estimated
EU	European Union
ex	sold by (*lit.* out of)
excl.	excludes / excluding
exh.	exhibited
exh. cat.	exhibition catalogue
f. *pl.* ff.	following [pages]
FA	Football Association
FACP	fellow of the American College of Physicians
facs.	facsimile
FANY	First Aid Nursing Yeomanry
FBA	fellow of the British Academy
FBI	Federation of British Industries
FCS	fellow of the Chemical Society
Feb	February
FEng	fellow of the Fellowship of Engineering
FFCM	fellow of the Faculty of Community Medicine
FGS	fellow of the Geological Society
fig.	figure
FIMechE	fellow of the Institution of Mechanical Engineers
FL	Florida
fl.	*floruit*
FLS	fellow of the Linnean Society
FM	frequency modulation
fol. *pl.* fols.	folio(s)
Fr	French francs
Fr.	French
FRAeS	fellow of the Royal Aeronautical Society
FRAI	fellow of the Royal Anthropological Institute
FRAM	fellow of the Royal Academy of Music
FRAS	(1) fellow of the Royal Asiatic Society; (2) fellow of the Royal Astronomical Society
FRCM	fellow of the Royal College of Music
FRCO	fellow of the Royal College of Organists
FRCOG	fellow of the Royal College of Obstetricians and Gynaecologists
FRCP(C)	fellow of the Royal College of Physicians of Canada
FRCP (Edin.)	fellow of the Royal College of Physicians of Edinburgh
FRCP (Lond.)	fellow of the Royal College of Physicians of London
FRCPath	fellow of the Royal College of Pathologists
FRCPsych	fellow of the Royal College of Psychiatrists
FRCS	fellow of the Royal College of Surgeons
FRGS	fellow of the Royal Geographical Society
FRIBA	fellow of the Royal Institute of British Architects
FRICS	fellow of the Royal Institute of Chartered Surveyors
FRS	fellow of the Royal Society
FRSA	fellow of the Royal Society of Arts

FRSCM	fellow of the Royal School of Church Music
FRSE	fellow of the Royal Society of Edinburgh
FRSL	fellow of the Royal Society of Literature
FSA	fellow of the Society of Antiquaries
ft	foot *pl.* feet
FTCL	fellow of Trinity College of Music, London
ft-lb per min.	foot-pounds per minute [unit of horsepower]
FZS	fellow of the Zoological Society
GA	Georgia
GBE	knight or dame grand cross of the Order of the British Empire
GCB	knight grand cross of the Order of the Bath
GCE	general certificate of education
GCH	knight grand cross of the Royal Guelphic Order
GCHQ	government communications headquarters
GCIE	knight grand commander of the Order of the Indian Empire
GCMG	knight or dame grand cross of the Order of St Michael and St George
GCSE	general certificate of secondary education
GCSI	knight grand commander of the Order of the Star of India
GCStJ	bailiff or dame grand cross of the order of St John of Jerusalem
GCVO	knight or dame grand cross of the Royal Victorian Order
GEC	General Electric Company
Ger.	German
GI	government (*or* general) issue
GMT	Greenwich mean time
GP	general practitioner
GPU	[Soviet special police unit]
GSO	general staff officer
Heb.	Hebrew
HEICS	Honourable East India Company Service
HI	Hawaii
HIV	human immunodeficiency virus
HK$	Hong Kong dollar
HM	his / her majesty('s)
HMAS	his / her majesty's Australian ship
HMNZS	his / her majesty's New Zealand ship
HMS	his / her majesty's ship
HMSO	His / Her Majesty's Stationery Office
HMV	His Master's Voice
Hon.	Honourable
hp	horsepower
hr	hour(s)
HRH	his / her royal highness
HTV	Harlech Television
IA	Iowa
ibid.	*ibidem*: in the same place
ICI	Imperial Chemical Industries (Ltd)
ID	Idaho
IL	Illinois
illus.	illustration
illustr.	illustrated
IN	Indiana
in.	inch(es)
Inc.	Incorporated
incl.	includes / including
IOU	I owe you
IQ	intelligence quotient
Ir£	Irish pound
IRA	Irish Republican Army

ISO	companion of the Imperial Service Order
It.	Italian
ITA	Independent Television Authority
ITV	Independent Television
Jan	January
JP	justice of the peace
jun.	junior
KB	knight of the Order of the Bath
KBE	knight commander of the Order of the British Empire
KC	king's counsel
kcal	kilocalorie
KCB	knight commander of the Order of the Bath
KCH	knight commander of the Royal Guelphic Order
KCIE	knight commander of the Order of the Indian Empire
KCMG	knight commander of the Order of St Michael and St George
KCSI	knight commander of the Order of the Star of India
KCVO	knight commander of the Royal Victorian Order
keV	kilo-electron-volt
KG	knight of the Order of the Garter
KGB	[Soviet committee of state security]
KH	knight of the Royal Guelphic Order
KLM	Koninklijke Luchtvaart Maatschappij (Royal Dutch Air Lines)
km	kilometre(s)
KP	knight of the Order of St Patrick
KS	Kansas
KT	knight of the Order of the Thistle
kt	knight
KY	Kentucky
£	pound(s) sterling
£E	Egyptian pound
L	lira *pl.* lire
l. *pl.* ll.	line(s)
LA	Lousiana
LAA	light anti-aircraft
LAH	licentiate of the Apothecaries' Hall, Dublin
Lat.	Latin
lb	pound(s), unit of weight
LDS	licence in dental surgery
lit.	literally
LittB	bachelor of letters
LittD	doctor of letters
LKQCPI	licentiate of the King and Queen's College of Physicians, Ireland
LLA	lady literate in arts
LLB	bachelor of laws
LLD	doctor of laws
LLM	master of laws
LM	licentiate in midwifery
LP	long-playing record
LRAM	licentiate of the Royal Academy of Music
LRCP	licentiate of the Royal College of Physicians
LRCPS (Glasgow)	licentiate of the Royal College of Physicians and Surgeons of Glasgow
LRCS	licentiate of the Royal College of Surgeons
LSA	licentiate of the Society of Apothecaries
LSD	lysergic acid diethylamide
LVO	lieutenant of the Royal Victorian Order
M. *pl.* MM.	Monsieur *pl.* Messieurs
m	metre(s)

m. *pl.* mm.	membrane(s)		ND	North Dakota
MA	(1) Massachusetts; (2) master of arts		n.d.	no date
MAI	master of engineering		NE	Nebraska
MB	bachelor of medicine		*nem. con.*	*nemine contradicente*: unanimously
MBA	master of business administration		new ser.	new series
MBE	member of the Order of the British Empire		NH	New Hampshire
MC	Military Cross		NHS	National Health Service
MCC	Marylebone Cricket Club		NJ	New Jersey
MCh	master of surgery		NKVD	[Soviet people's commissariat for internal affairs]
MChir	master of surgery		NM	New Mexico
MCom	master of commerce		nm	nanometre(s)
MD	(1) doctor of medicine; (2) Maryland		no. *pl.* nos.	number(s)
MDMA	methylenedioxymethamphetamine		Nov	November
ME	Maine		n.p.	no place [of publication]
MEd	master of education		NS	new style
MEng	master of engineering		NV	Nevada
MEP	member of the European parliament		NY	New York
MG	Morris Garages		NZBS	New Zealand Broadcasting Service
MGM	Metro-Goldwyn-Mayer		OBE	officer of the Order of the British Empire
Mgr	Monsignor		obit.	obituary
MI	(1) Michigan; (2) military intelligence		Oct	October
MI1c	[secret intelligence department]		OCTU	officer cadets training unit
MI5	[military intelligence department]		OECD	Organization for Economic Co-operation and Development
MI6	[secret intelligence department]		OEEC	Organization for European Economic Co-operation
MI9	[secret escape service]			
MICE	member of the Institution of Civil Engineers		OFM	order of Friars Minor [Franciscans]
MIEE	member of the Institution of Electrical Engineers		OFMCap	Ordine Frati Minori Cappucini: member of the Capuchin order
min.	minute(s)		OH	Ohio
Mk	mark		OK	Oklahoma
ML	(1) licentiate of medicine; (2) master of laws		O level	ordinary level [examination]
MLitt	master of letters		OM	Order of Merit
Mlle	Mademoiselle		OP	order of Preachers [Dominicans]
mm	millimetre(s)		op. *pl.* opp.	opus *pl.* opera
Mme	Madame		OPEC	Organization of Petroleum Exporting Countries
MN	Minnesota		OR	Oregon
MO	Missouri		orig.	original
MOH	medical officer of health		OS	old style
MP	member of parliament		OSB	Order of St Benedict
m.p.h.	miles per hour		OTC	Officers' Training Corps
MPhil	master of philosophy		OWS	Old Watercolour Society
MRCP	member of the Royal College of Physicians		Oxon.	Oxoniensis
MRCS	member of the Royal College of Surgeons		p *pl.* pp.	page(s)
MRCVS	member of the Royal College of Veterinary Surgeons		PA	Pennsylvania
MRIA	member of the Royal Irish Academy		p.a.	per annum
MS	(1) master of science; (2) Mississippi		para.	paragraph
MS *pl.* MSS	manuscript(s)		PAYE	pay as you earn
MSc	master of science		pbk *pl.* pbks	paperback(s)
MSc (Econ.)	master of science (economics)		*per.*	[during the] period
MT	Montana		PhD	doctor of philosophy
MusB	bachelor of music		pl.	(1) plate(s); (2) plural
MusBac	bachelor of music		priv. coll.	private collection
MusD	doctor of music		pt *pl.* pts	part(s)
MV	motor vessel		pubd	published
MVO	member of the Royal Victorian Order		PVC	polyvinyl chloride
n. *pl.* nn.	note(s)		q. *pl.* qq.	(1) question(s); (2) quire(s)
NAAFI	Navy, Army, and Air Force Institutes		QC	queen's counsel
NASA	National Aeronautics and Space Administration		R	rand
NATO	North Atlantic Treaty Organization		R.	Rex / Regina
NBC	National Broadcasting Corporation		r	recto
NC	North Carolina		r.	reigned / ruled
NCO	non-commissioned officer		RA	Royal Academy / Royal Academician

RAC	Royal Automobile Club		Skr	Swedish krona
RAF	Royal Air Force		Span.	Spanish
RAFVR	Royal Air Force Volunteer Reserve		SPCK	Society for Promoting Christian Knowledge
RAM	[member of the] Royal Academy of Music		SS	(1) Santissimi; (2) Schutzstaffel; (3) steam ship
RAMC	Royal Army Medical Corps		STB	bachelor of theology
RCA	Royal College of Art		STD	doctor of theology
RCNC	Royal Corps of Naval Constructors		STM	master of theology
RCOG	Royal College of Obstetricians and Gynaecologists		STP	doctor of theology
RDI	royal designer for industry		*supp.*	supposedly
RE	Royal Engineers		suppl. *pl.* suppls.	supplement(s)
repr. *pl.* reprs.	reprint(s) / reprinted		s.v.	*sub verbo* / *sub voce*: under the word / heading
repro.	reproduced		SY	steam yacht
rev.	revised / revised by / reviser / revision		TA	Territorial Army
Revd	Reverend		TASS	[Soviet news agency]
RHA	Royal Hibernian Academy		TB	tuberculosis (*lit.* tubercle bacillus)
RI	(1) Rhode Island; (2) Royal Institute of Painters in Water-Colours		TD	(1) *teachtaí dála* (member of the Dáil); (2) territorial decoration
RIBA	Royal Institute of British Architects		TN	Tennessee
RIN	Royal Indian Navy		TNT	trinitrotoluene
RM	Reichsmark		trans.	translated / translated by / translation / translator
RMS	Royal Mail steamer		TT	tourist trophy
RN	Royal Navy		TUC	Trades Union Congress
RNA	ribonucleic acid		TX	Texas
RNAS	Royal Naval Air Service		U-boat	*Unterseeboot*: submarine
RNR	Royal Naval Reserve		Ufa	Universum-Film AG
RNVR	Royal Naval Volunteer Reserve		UMIST	University of Manchester Institute of Science and Technology
RO	Record Office		UN	United Nations
r.p.m.	revolutions per minute		UNESCO	United Nations Educational, Scientific, and Cultural Organization
RRS	royal research ship			
Rs	rupees		UNICEF	United Nations International Children's Emergency Fund
RSA	(1) Royal Scottish Academician; (2) Royal Society of Arts			
RSPCA	Royal Society for the Prevention of Cruelty to Animals		unpubd	unpublished
			USS	United States ship
Rt Hon.	Right Honourable		UT	Utah
Rt Revd	Right Reverend		*v*	verso
RUC	Royal Ulster Constabulary		v.	versus
Russ.	Russian		VA	Virginia
RWS	Royal Watercolour Society		VAD	Voluntary Aid Detachment
S4C	Sianel Pedwar Cymru		VC	Victoria Cross
s.	shilling(s)		VE-day	victory in Europe day
s.a.	*sub anno*: under the year		Ven.	Venerable
SABC	South African Broadcasting Corporation		VJ-day	victory over Japan day
SAS	Special Air Service		vol. *pl.* vols.	volume(s)
SC	South Carolina		VT	Vermont
ScD	doctor of science		WA	Washington [state]
S$	Singapore dollar		WAAC	Women's Auxiliary Army Corps
SD	South Dakota		WAAF	Women's Auxiliary Air Force
sec.	second(s)		WEA	Workers' Educational Association
sel.	selected		WHO	World Health Organization
sen.	senior		WI	Wisconsin
Sept	September		WRAF	Women's Royal Air Force
ser.	series		WRNS	Women's Royal Naval Service
SHAPE	supreme headquarters allied powers, Europe		WV	West Virginia
SIDRO	Société Internationale d'Énergie Hydro-Électrique		WVS	Women's Voluntary Service
			WY	Wyoming
sig. *pl.* sigs.	signature(s)		¥	yen
sing.	singular		YMCA	Young Men's Christian Association
SIS	Secret Intelligence Service		YWCA	Young Women's Christian Association
SJ	Society of Jesus			

2 Institution abbreviations

All Souls Oxf.	All Souls College, Oxford
AM Oxf.	Ashmolean Museum, Oxford
Balliol Oxf.	Balliol College, Oxford
BBC WAC	BBC Written Archives Centre, Reading
Beds. & Luton ARS	Bedfordshire and Luton Archives and Record Service, Bedford
Berks. RO	Berkshire Record Office, Reading
BFI	British Film Institute, London
BFI NFTVA	British Film Institute, London, National Film and Television Archive
BGS	British Geological Survey, Keyworth, Nottingham
Birm. CA	Birmingham Central Library, Birmingham City Archives
Birm. CL	Birmingham Central Library
BL	British Library, London
BL NSA	British Library, London, National Sound Archive
BL OIOC	British Library, London, Oriental and India Office Collections
BLPES	London School of Economics and Political Science, British Library of Political and Economic Science
BM	British Museum, London
Bodl. Oxf.	Bodleian Library, Oxford
Bodl. RH	Bodleian Library of Commonwealth and African Studies at Rhodes House, Oxford
Borth. Inst.	Borthwick Institute of Historical Research, University of York
Boston PL	Boston Public Library, Massachusetts
Bristol RO	Bristol Record Office
Bucks. RLSS	Buckinghamshire Records and Local Studies Service, Aylesbury
CAC Cam.	Churchill College, Cambridge, Churchill Archives Centre
Cambs. AS	Cambridgeshire Archive Service
CCC Cam.	Corpus Christi College, Cambridge
CCC Oxf.	Corpus Christi College, Oxford
Ches. & Chester ALSS	Cheshire and Chester Archives and Local Studies Service
Christ Church Oxf.	Christ Church, Oxford
Christies	Christies, London
City Westm. AC	City of Westminster Archives Centre, London
CKS	Centre for Kentish Studies, Maidstone
CLRO	Corporation of London Records Office
Coll. Arms	College of Arms, London
Col. U.	Columbia University, New York
Cornwall RO	Cornwall Record Office, Truro
Courtauld Inst.	Courtauld Institute of Art, London
CUL	Cambridge University Library
Cumbria AS	Cumbria Archive Service
Derbys. RO	Derbyshire Record Office, Matlock
Devon RO	Devon Record Office, Exeter
Dorset RO	Dorset Record Office, Dorchester
Duke U.	Duke University, Durham, North Carolina
Duke U., Perkins L.	Duke University, Durham, North Carolina, William R. Perkins Library
Durham Cath. CL	Durham Cathedral, chapter library
Durham RO	Durham Record Office
DWL	Dr Williams's Library, London
Essex RO	Essex Record Office
E. Sussex RO	East Sussex Record Office, Lewes
Eton	Eton College, Berkshire
FM Cam.	Fitzwilliam Museum, Cambridge
Folger	Folger Shakespeare Library, Washington, DC
Garr. Club	Garrick Club, London
Girton Cam.	Girton College, Cambridge
GL	Guildhall Library, London
Glos. RO	Gloucestershire Record Office, Gloucester
Gon. & Caius Cam.	Gonville and Caius College, Cambridge
Gov. Art Coll.	Government Art Collection
GS Lond.	Geological Society of London
Hants. RO	Hampshire Record Office, Winchester
Harris Man. Oxf.	Harris Manchester College, Oxford
Harvard TC	Harvard Theatre Collection, Harvard University, Cambridge, Massachusetts, Nathan Marsh Pusey Library
Harvard U.	Harvard University, Cambridge, Massachusetts
Harvard U., Houghton L.	Harvard University, Cambridge, Massachusetts, Houghton Library
Herefs. RO	Herefordshire Record Office, Hereford
Herts. ALS	Hertfordshire Archives and Local Studies, Hertford
Hist. Soc. Penn.	Historical Society of Pennsylvania, Philadelphia
HLRO	House of Lords Record Office, London
Hult. Arch.	Hulton Archive, London and New York
Hunt. L.	Huntington Library, San Marino, California
ICL	Imperial College, London
Inst. CE	Institution of Civil Engineers, London
Inst. EE	Institution of Electrical Engineers, London
IWM	Imperial War Museum, London
IWM FVA	Imperial War Museum, London, Film and Video Archive
IWM SA	Imperial War Museum, London, Sound Archive
JRL	John Rylands University Library of Manchester
King's AC Cam.	King's College Archives Centre, Cambridge
King's Cam.	King's College, Cambridge
King's Lond.	King's College, London
King's Lond., Liddell Hart C.	King's College, London, Liddell Hart Centre for Military Archives
Lancs. RO	Lancashire Record Office, Preston
L. Cong.	Library of Congress, Washington, DC
Leics. RO	Leicestershire, Leicester, and Rutland Record Office, Leicester
Lincs. Arch.	Lincolnshire Archives, Lincoln
Linn. Soc.	Linnean Society of London
LMA	London Metropolitan Archives
LPL	Lambeth Palace, London
Lpool RO	Liverpool Record Office and Local Studies Service
LUL	London University Library
Magd. Cam.	Magdalene College, Cambridge
Magd. Oxf.	Magdalen College, Oxford
Man. City Gall.	Manchester City Galleries
Man. CL	Manchester Central Library
Mass. Hist. Soc.	Massachusetts Historical Society, Boston
Merton Oxf.	Merton College, Oxford
MHS Oxf.	Museum of the History of Science, Oxford
Mitchell L., Glas.	Mitchell Library, Glasgow
Mitchell L., NSW	State Library of New South Wales, Sydney, Mitchell Library
Morgan L.	Pierpont Morgan Library, New York
NA Canada	National Archives of Canada, Ottawa
NA Ire.	National Archives of Ireland, Dublin
NAM	National Army Museum, London
NA Scot.	National Archives of Scotland, Edinburgh
News Int. RO	News International Record Office, London
NG Ire.	National Gallery of Ireland, Dublin

NG Scot. — National Gallery of Scotland, Edinburgh
NHM — Natural History Museum, London
NL Aus. — National Library of Australia, Canberra
NL Ire. — National Library of Ireland, Dublin
NL NZ — National Library of New Zealand, Wellington
NL NZ, Turnbull L. — National Library of New Zealand, Wellington, Alexander Turnbull Library
NL Scot. — National Library of Scotland, Edinburgh
NL Wales — National Library of Wales, Aberystwyth
NMG Wales — National Museum and Gallery of Wales, Cardiff
NMM — National Maritime Museum, London
Norfolk RO — Norfolk Record Office, Norwich
Northants. RO — Northamptonshire Record Office, Northampton
Northumbd RO — Northumberland Record Office
Notts. Arch. — Nottinghamshire Archives, Nottingham
NPG — National Portrait Gallery, London
NRA — National Archives, London, Historical Manuscripts Commission, National Register of Archives
Nuffield Oxf. — Nuffield College, Oxford
N. Yorks. CRO — North Yorkshire County Record Office, Northallerton
NYPL — New York Public Library
Oxf. UA — Oxford University Archives
Oxf. U. Mus. NH — Oxford University Museum of Natural History
Oxon. RO — Oxfordshire Record Office, Oxford
Pembroke Cam. — Pembroke College, Cambridge
PRO — National Archives, London, Public Record Office
PRO NIre. — Public Record Office for Northern Ireland, Belfast
Pusey Oxf. — Pusey House, Oxford
RA — Royal Academy of Arts, London
Ransom HRC — Harry Ransom Humanities Research Center, University of Texas, Austin
RAS — Royal Astronomical Society, London
RBG Kew — Royal Botanic Gardens, Kew, London
RCP Lond. — Royal College of Physicians of London
RCS Eng. — Royal College of Surgeons of England, London
RGS — Royal Geographical Society, London
RIBA — Royal Institute of British Architects, London
RIBA BAL — Royal Institute of British Architects, London, British Architectural Library
Royal Arch. — Royal Archives, Windsor Castle, Berkshire [by gracious permission of her majesty the queen]
Royal Irish Acad. — Royal Irish Academy, Dublin
Royal Scot. Acad. — Royal Scottish Academy, Edinburgh
RS — Royal Society, London
RSA — Royal Society of Arts, London
RS Friends, Lond. — Religious Society of Friends, London
St Ant. Oxf. — St Antony's College, Oxford
St John Cam. — St John's College, Cambridge
S. Antiquaries, Lond. — Society of Antiquaries of London
Sci. Mus. — Science Museum, London
Scot. NPG — Scottish National Portrait Gallery, Edinburgh
Scott Polar RI — University of Cambridge, Scott Polar Research Institute
Sheff. Arch. — Sheffield Archives
Shrops. RRC — Shropshire Records and Research Centre, Shrewsbury
SOAS — School of Oriental and African Studies, London
Som. ARS — Somerset Archive and Record Service, Taunton
Staffs. RO — Staffordshire Record Office, Stafford

Suffolk RO — Suffolk Record Office
Surrey HC — Surrey History Centre, Woking
TCD — Trinity College, Dublin
Trinity Cam. — Trinity College, Cambridge
U. Aberdeen — University of Aberdeen
U. Birm. — University of Birmingham
U. Birm. L. — University of Birmingham Library
U. Cal. — University of California
U. Cam. — University of Cambridge
UCL — University College, London
U. Durham — University of Durham
U. Durham L. — University of Durham Library
U. Edin. — University of Edinburgh
U. Edin., New Coll. — University of Edinburgh, New College
U. Edin., New Coll. L. — University of Edinburgh, New College Library
U. Edin. L. — University of Edinburgh Library
U. Glas. — University of Glasgow
U. Glas. L. — University of Glasgow Library
U. Hull — University of Hull
U. Hull, Brynmor Jones L. — University of Hull, Brynmor Jones Library
U. Leeds — University of Leeds
U. Leeds, Brotherton L. — University of Leeds, Brotherton Library
U. Lond. — University of London
U. Lpool — University of Liverpool
U. Lpool L. — University of Liverpool Library
U. Mich. — University of Michigan, Ann Arbor
U. Mich., Clements L. — University of Michigan, Ann Arbor, William L. Clements Library
U. Newcastle — University of Newcastle upon Tyne
U. Newcastle, Robinson L. — University of Newcastle upon Tyne, Robinson Library
U. Nott. — University of Nottingham
U. Nott. L. — University of Nottingham Library
U. Oxf. — University of Oxford
U. Reading — University of Reading
U. Reading L. — University of Reading Library
U. St Andr. — University of St Andrews
U. St Andr. L. — University of St Andrews Library
U. Southampton — University of Southampton
U. Southampton L. — University of Southampton Library
U. Sussex — University of Sussex, Brighton
U. Texas — University of Texas, Austin
U. Wales — University of Wales
U. Warwick Mod. RC — University of Warwick, Coventry, Modern Records Centre
V&A — Victoria and Albert Museum, London
V&A NAL — Victoria and Albert Museum, London, National Art Library
Warks. CRO — Warwickshire County Record Office, Warwick
Wellcome L. — Wellcome Library for the History and Understanding of Medicine, London
Westm. DA — Westminster Diocesan Archives, London
Wilts. & Swindon RO — Wiltshire and Swindon Record Office, Trowbridge
Worcs. RO — Worcestershire Record Office, Worcester
W. Sussex RO — West Sussex Record Office, Chichester
W. Yorks. AS — West Yorkshire Archive Service
Yale U. — Yale University, New Haven, Connecticut
Yale U., Beinecke L. — Yale University, New Haven, Connecticut, Beinecke Rare Book and Manuscript Library
Yale U. CBA — Yale University, New Haven, Connecticut, Yale Center for British Art

3 Bibliographic abbreviations

Adams, *Drama* — W. D. Adams, *A dictionary of the drama*, 1: *A–G* (1904); 2: *H–Z* (1956) [vol. 2 microfilm only]

AFM — J O'Donovan, ed. and trans., *Annala rioghachta Eireann / Annals of the kingdom of Ireland by the four masters*, 7 vols. (1848–51); 2nd edn (1856); 3rd edn (1990)

Allibone, *Dict.* — S. A. Allibone, *A critical dictionary of English literature and British and American authors*, 3 vols. (1859–71); suppl. by J. F. Kirk, 2 vols. (1891)

ANB — J. A. Garraty and M. C. Carnes, eds., *American national biography*, 24 vols. (1999)

Anderson, *Scot. nat.* — W. Anderson, *The Scottish nation, or, The surnames, families, literature, honours, and biographical history of the people of Scotland*, 3 vols. (1859–63)

Ann. mon. — H. R. Luard, ed., *Annales monastici*, 5 vols., Rolls Series, 36 (1864–9)

Ann. Ulster — S. Mac Airt and G. Mac Niocaill, eds., *Annals of Ulster (to AD 1131)* (1983)

APC — *Acts of the privy council of England*, new ser., 46 vols. (1890–1964)

APS — *The acts of the parliaments of Scotland*, 12 vols. in 13 (1814–75)

Arber, *Regs. Stationers* — F. Arber, ed., *A transcript of the registers of the Company of Stationers of London, 1554–1640 AD*, 5 vols. (1875–94)

ArchR — *Architectural Review*

ASC — D. Whitelock, D. C. Douglas, and S. I. Tucker, ed. and trans., *The Anglo-Saxon Chronicle: a revised translation* (1961)

AS chart. — P. H. Sawyer, *Anglo-Saxon charters: an annotated list and bibliography*, Royal Historical Society Guides and Handbooks (1968)

AusDB — D. Pike and others, eds., *Australian dictionary of biography*, 16 vols. (1966–2002)

Baker, *Serjeants* — J. H. Baker, *The order of serjeants at law*, SeldS, suppl. ser., 5 (1984)

Bale, *Cat.* — J. Bale, *Scriptorum illustrium Maioris Brytannie, quam nunc Angliam et Scotiam vocant: catalogus*, 2 vols. in 1 (Basel, 1557–9); facs. edn (1971)

Bale, *Index* — J. Bale, *Index Britanniae scriptorum*, ed. R. L. Poole and M. Bateson (1902); facs. edn (1990)

BBCS — *Bulletin of the Board of Celtic Studies*

BDMBR — J. O. Baylen and N. J. Gossman, eds., *Biographical dictionary of modern British radicals*, 3 vols. in 4 (1979–88)

Bede, *Hist. eccl.* — *Bede's Ecclesiastical history of the English people*, ed. and trans. B. Colgrave and R. A. B. Mynors, OMT (1969); repr. (1991)

Bénézit, *Dict.* — E. Bénézit, *Dictionnaire critique et documentaire des peintres, sculpteurs, dessinateurs et graveurs*, 3 vols. (Paris, 1911–23); new edn, 8 vols. (1948–66), repr. (1966); 3rd edn, rev. and enl., 10 vols. (1976); 4th edn, 14 vols. (1999)

BIHR — *Bulletin of the Institute of Historical Research*

Birch, *Seals* — W. de Birch, *Catalogue of seals in the department of manuscripts in the British Museum*, 6 vols. (1887–1900)

Bishop Burnet's History — *Bishop Burnet's History of his own time*, ed. M. J. Routh, 2nd edn, 6 vols. (1833)

Blackwood — *Blackwood's [Edinburgh] Magazine*, 328 vols. (1817–1980)

Blain, Clements & Grundy, *Feminist comp.* — V. Blain, P. Clements, and I. Grundy, eds., *The feminist companion to literature in English* (1990)

BL cat. — *The British Library general catalogue of printed books* [in 360 vols. with suppls., also CD-ROM and online]

BMJ — *British Medical Journal*

Boase & Courtney, *Bibl. Corn.* — G. C. Boase and W. P. Courtney, *Bibliotheca Cornubiensis: a catalogue of the writings … of Cornishmen*, 3 vols. (1874–82)

Boase, *Mod. Eng. biog.* — F. Boase, *Modern English biography: containing many thousand concise memoirs of persons who have died since the year 1850*, 6 vols. (privately printed, Truro, 1892–1921); repr. (1965)

Boswell, *Life* — *Boswell's Life of Johnson: together with Journal of a tour to the Hebrides and Johnson's Diary of a journey into north Wales*, ed. G. B. Hill, enl. edn, rev. L. F. Powell, 6 vols. (1934–50); 2nd edn (1964); repr. (1971)

Brown & Stratton, *Brit. mus.* — J. D. Brown and S. S. Stratton, *British musical biography* (1897)

Bryan, *Painters* — M. Bryan, *A biographical and critical dictionary of painters and engravers*, 2 vols. (1816); new edn, ed. G. Stanley (1849); new edn, ed. R. E. Graves and W. Armstrong, 2 vols. (1886–9); [4th edn], ed. G. C. Williamson, 5 vols. (1903–5) [various reprs.]

Burke, *Gen. GB* — J. Burke, *A genealogical and heraldic history of the commoners of Great Britain and Ireland*, 4 vols. (1833–8); new edn as *A genealogical and heraldic dictionary of the landed gentry of Great Britain and Ireland*, 3 vols. [1843–9] [many later edns]

Burke, *Gen. Ire.* — J. B. Burke, *A genealogical and heraldic history of the landed gentry of Ireland* (1899); 2nd edn (1904); 3rd edn (1912); 4th edn (1958); 5th edn as *Burke's Irish family records* (1976)

Burke, *Peerage* — J. Burke, *A general [later edns A genealogical] and heraldic dictionary of the peerage and baronetage of the United Kingdom* [later edns *the British empire*] (1829–)

Burney, *Hist. mus.* — C. Burney, *A general history of music, from the earliest ages to the present period*, 4 vols. (1776–89)

Burtchaell & Sadleir, *Alum. Dubl.* — G. D. Burtchaell and T. U. Sadleir, *Alumni Dublinenses: a register of the students, graduates, and provosts of Trinity College* (1924); [2nd edn], with suppl., in 2 pts (1935)

Calamy rev. — A. G. Matthews, *Calamy revised* (1934); repr. (1988)

CCI — *Calendar of confirmations and inventories granted and given up in the several commissariots of Scotland* (1876–)

CCIR — *Calendar of the close rolls preserved in the Public Record Office*, 47 vols. (1892–1963)

CDS — J. Bain, ed., *Calendar of documents relating to Scotland*, 4 vols., PRO (1881–8); suppl. vol. 5, ed. G. G. Simpson and J. D. Galbraith [1986]

CEPR letters — W. H. Bliss, C. Johnson, and J. Twemlow, eds., *Calendar of entries in the papal registers relating to Great Britain and Ireland: papal letters* (1893–)

CGPLA — *Calendars of the grants of probate and letters of administration* [in 4 ser.: England & Wales, Northern Ireland, Ireland, and Éire]

Chambers, *Scots.* — R. Chambers, ed., *A biographical dictionary of eminent Scotsmen*, 4 vols. (1832–5)

Chancery records — chancery records pubd by the PRO

Chancery records (RC) — chancery records pubd by the Record Commissions

CIPM	*Calendar of inquisitions post mortem*, [20 vols.], PRO (1904–); also *Henry VII*, 3 vols. (1898–1955)
Clarendon, *Hist. rebellion*	E. Hyde, earl of Clarendon, *The history of the rebellion and civil wars in England*, 6 vols. (1888); repr. (1958) and (1992)
Cobbett, *Parl. hist.*	W. Cobbett and J. Wright, eds., *Cobbett's Parliamentary history of England*, 36 vols. (1806–1820)
Colvin, *Archs.*	H. Colvin, *A biographical dictionary of British architects, 1600–1840*, 3rd edn (1995)
Cooper, *Ath. Cantab.*	C. H. Cooper and T. Cooper, *Athenae Cantabrigienses*, 3 vols. (1858–1913); repr. (1967)
CPR	*Calendar of the patent rolls preserved in the Public Record Office* (1891–)
Crockford	*Crockford's Clerical Directory*
CS	Camden Society
CSP	*Calendar of state papers* [in 11 ser.: *domestic, Scotland, Scottish series, Ireland, colonial, Commonwealth, foreign, Spain* [at Simancas], *Rome, Milan,* and *Venice*]
CYS	Canterbury and York Society
DAB	*Dictionary of American biography*, 21 vols. (1928–36), repr. in 11 vols. (1964); 10 suppls. (1944–96)
DBB	D. J. Jeremy, ed., *Dictionary of business biography*, 5 vols. (1984–6)
DCB	G. W. Brown and others, *Dictionary of Canadian biography*, [14 vols.] (1966–)
Debrett's Peerage	*Debrett's Peerage* (1803–) [sometimes *Debrett's Illustrated peerage*]
Desmond, *Botanists*	R. Desmond, *Dictionary of British and Irish botanists and horticulturists* (1977); rev. edn (1994)
Dir. Brit. archs.	A. Felstead, J. Franklin, and L. Pinfield, eds., *Directory of British architects, 1834–1900* (1993); 2nd edn, ed. A. Brodie and others, 2 vols. (2001)
DLB	J. M. Bellamy and J. Saville, eds., *Dictionary of labour biography*, [10 vols.] (1972–)
DLitB	Dictionary of Literary Biography
DNB	*Dictionary of national biography*, 63 vols. (1885–1900), suppl., 3 vols. (1901); repr. in 22 vols. (1908–9); 10 further suppls. (1912–96); *Missing persons* (1993)
DNZB	W. H. Oliver and C. Orange, eds., *The dictionary of New Zealand biography*, 5 vols. (1990–2000)
DSAB	W. J. de Kock and others, eds., *Dictionary of South African biography*, 5 vols. (1968–87)
DSB	C. C. Gillispie and F. L. Holmes, eds., *Dictionary of scientific biography*, 16 vols. (1970–80); repr. in 8 vols. (1981); 2 vol. suppl. (1990)
DSBB	A. Slaven and S. Checkland, eds., *Dictionary of Scottish business biography, 1860–1960*, 2 vols. (1986–90)
DSCHT	N. M. de S. Cameron and others, eds., *Dictionary of Scottish church history and theology* (1993)
Dugdale, *Monasticon*	W. Dugdale, *Monasticon Anglicanum*, 3 vols. (1655–72); 2nd edn, 3 vols. (1661–82); new edn, ed. J. Caley, J. Ellis, and B. Bandinel, 6 vols. in 8 pts (1817–30); repr. (1846) and (1970)
DWB	J. E. Lloyd and others, eds., *Dictionary of Welsh biography down to 1940* (1959) [Eng. trans. of *Y bywgraffiadur Cymreig hyd 1940*, 2nd edn (1954)]
EdinR	*Edinburgh Review, or, Critical Journal*
EETS	Early English Text Society
Emden, *Cam.*	A. B. Emden, *A biographical register of the University of Cambridge to 1500* (1963)
Emden, *Oxf.*	A. B. Emden, *A biographical register of the University of Oxford to AD 1500*, 3 vols. (1957–9); also *A biographical register of the University of Oxford, AD 1501 to 1540* (1974)
EngHR	*English Historical Review*
Engraved Brit. ports.	F. M. O'Donoghue and H. M. Hake, *Catalogue of engraved British portraits preserved in the department of prints and drawings in the British Museum*, 6 vols. (1908–25)
ER	The English Reports, 178 vols. (1900–32)
ESTC	*English short title catalogue, 1475–1800* [CD-ROM and online]
Evelyn, *Diary*	*The diary of John Evelyn*, ed. E. S. De Beer, 6 vols. (1955); repr. (2000)
Farington, *Diary*	*The diary of Joseph Farington*, ed. K. Garlick and others, 17 vols. (1978–98)
Fasti Angl. (Hardy)	J. Le Neve, *Fasti ecclesiae Anglicanae*, ed. T. D. Hardy, 3 vols. (1854)
Fasti Angl., 1066–1300	[J. Le Neve], *Fasti ecclesiae Anglicanae, 1066–1300*, ed. D. E. Greenway and J. S. Barrow, [8 vols.] (1968–)
Fasti Angl., 1300–1541	[J. Le Neve], *Fasti ecclesiae Anglicanae, 1300–1541*, 12 vols. (1962–7)
Fasti Angl., 1541–1857	[J. Le Neve], *Fasti ecclesiae Anglicanae, 1541–1857*, ed. J. M. Horn, D. M. Smith, and D. S. Bailey, [9 vols.] (1969–)
Fasti Scot.	H. Scott, *Fasti ecclesiae Scoticanae*, 3 vols. in 6 (1871); new edn, [11 vols.] (1915–)
FO List	*Foreign Office List*
Fortescue, *Brit. army*	J. W. Fortescue, *A history of the British army*, 13 vols. (1899–1930)
Foss, *Judges*	E. Foss, *The judges of England*, 9 vols. (1848–64); repr. (1966)
Foster, *Alum. Oxon.*	J. Foster, ed., *Alumni Oxonienses: the members of the University of Oxford, 1715–1886*, 4 vols. (1887–8); later edn (1891); also *Alumni Oxonienses … 1500–1714*, 4 vols. (1891–2); 8 vol. repr. (1968) and (2000)
Fuller, *Worthies*	T. Fuller, *The history of the worthies of England*, 4 pts (1662); new edn, 2 vols., ed. J. Nichols (1811); new edn, 3 vols., ed. P. A. Nuttall (1840); repr. (1965)
GEC, *Baronetage*	G. E. Cokayne, *Complete baronetage*, 6 vols. (1900–09); repr. (1983) [microprint]
GEC, *Peerage*	G. E. C. [G. E. Cokayne], *The complete peerage of England, Scotland, Ireland, Great Britain, and the United Kingdom*, 8 vols. (1887–98); new edn, ed. V. Gibbs and others, 14 vols. in 15 (1910–98); microprint repr. (1982) and (1987)
Genest, *Eng. stage*	J. Genest, *Some account of the English stage from the Restoration in 1660 to 1830*, 10 vols. (1832); repr. [New York, 1965]
Gillow, *Lit. biog. hist.*	J. Gillow, *A literary and biographical history or bibliographical dictionary of the English Catholics, from the breach with Rome, in 1534, to the present time*, 5 vols. [1885–1902]; repr. (1961); repr. with preface by C. Gillow (1999)
Gir. Camb. opera	*Giraldi Cambrensis opera*, ed. J. S. Brewer, J. F. Dimock, and G. F. Warner, 8 vols., Rolls Series, 21 (1861–91)
GJ	*Geographical Journal*

Gladstone, *Diaries* — *The Gladstone diaries: with cabinet minutes and prime-ministerial correspondence*, ed. M. R. D. Foot and H. C. G. Matthew, 14 vols. (1968–94)

GM — *Gentleman's Magazine*

Graves, *Artists* — A. Graves, ed., *A dictionary of artists who have exhibited works in the principal London exhibitions of oil paintings from 1760 to 1880* (1884); new edn (1895); 3rd edn (1901); facs. edn (1969); repr. [1970], (1973), and (1984)

Graves, *Brit. Inst.* — A. Graves, *The British Institution, 1806–1867: a complete dictionary of contributors and their work from the foundation of the institution* (1875); facs. edn (1908); repr. (1969)

Graves, *RA exhibitors* — A. Graves, *The Royal Academy of Arts: a complete dictionary of contributors and their work from its foundation in 1769 to 1904*, 8 vols. (1905–6); repr. in 4 vols. (1970) and (1972)

Graves, *Soc. Artists* — A. Graves, *The Society of Artists of Great Britain, 1760–1791, the Free Society of Artists, 1761–1783: a complete dictionary* (1907); facs. edn (1969)

Greaves & Zaller, *BDBR* — R. L. Greaves and R. Zaller, eds., *Biographical dictionary of British radicals in the seventeenth century*, 3 vols. (1982–4)

Grove, *Dict. mus.* — G. Grove, ed., *A dictionary of music and musicians*, 5 vols. (1878–90); 2nd edn, ed. J. A. Fuller Maitland (1904–10); 3rd edn, ed. H. C. Colles (1927); 4th edn with suppl. (1940); 5th edn, ed. E. Blom, 9 vols. (1954); suppl. (1961) [see also *New Grove*]

Hall, *Dramatic ports.* — L. A. Hall, *Catalogue of dramatic portraits in the theatre collection of the Harvard College library*, 4 vols. (1930–34)

Hansard — *Hansard's parliamentary debates*, ser. 1–5 (1803–)

Highfill, Burnim & Langhans, *BDA* — P. H. Highfill, K. A. Burnim, and E. A. Langhans, *A biographical dictionary of actors, actresses, musicians, dancers, managers, and other stage personnel in London, 1660–1800*, 16 vols. (1973–93)

Hist. U. Oxf. — T. H. Aston, ed., *The history of the University of Oxford*, 8 vols. (1984–2000) [1: *The early Oxford schools*, ed. J. I. Catto (1984); 2: *Late medieval Oxford*, ed. J. I. Catto and R. Evans (1992); 3: *The collegiate university*, ed. J. McConica (1986); 4: *Seventeenth-century Oxford*, ed. N. Tyacke (1997); 5: *The eighteenth century*, ed. L. S. Sutherland and L. G. Mitchell (1986); 6–7: *Nineteenth-century Oxford*, ed. M. G. Brock and M. C. Curthoys (1997–2000); 8: *The twentieth century*, ed. B. Harrison (2000)]

HJ — *Historical Journal*

HMC — Historical Manuscripts Commission

Holdsworth, *Eng. law* — W. S. Holdsworth, *A history of English law*, ed. A. L. Goodhart and H. L. Hanbury, 17 vols. (1903–72)

HoP, *Commons* — *The history of parliament: the House of Commons* [1386–1421, ed. J. S. Roskell, L. Clark, and C. Rawcliffe, 4 vols. (1992); 1509–1558, ed. S. T. Bindoff, 3 vols. (1982); 1558–1603, ed. P. W. Hasler, 3 vols. (1981); 1660–1690, ed. B. D. Henning, 3 vols. (1983); 1690–1715, ed. D. W. Hayton, E. Cruickshanks, and S. Handley, 5 vols. (2002); 1715–1754, ed. R. Sedgwick, 2 vols. (1970); 1754–1790, ed. L. Namier and J. Brooke, 3 vols. (1964), repr. (1985); 1790–1820, ed. R. G. Thorne, 5 vols. (1986); in draft (used with permission): 1422–1504, 1604–1629, 1640–1660, and 1820–1832]

IGI — *International Genealogical Index*, Church of Jesus Christ of the Latterday Saints

ILN — *Illustrated London News*

IMC — Irish Manuscripts Commission

Irving, *Scots.* — J. Irving, ed., *The book of Scotsmen eminent for achievements in arms and arts, church and state, law, legislation and literature, commerce, science, travel and philanthropy* (1881)

JCS — *Journal of the Chemical Society*

JHC — *Journals of the House of Commons*

JHL — *Journals of the House of Lords*

John of Worcester, *Chron.* — *The chronicle of John of Worcester*, ed. R. R. Darlington and P. McGurk, trans. J. Bray and P. McGurk, 3 vols., OMT (1995–) [vol. 1 forthcoming]

Keeler, *Long Parliament* — M. F. Keeler, *The Long Parliament, 1640–1641: a biographical study of its members* (1954)

Kelly, *Handbk* — *The upper ten thousand: an alphabetical list of all members of noble families*, 3 vols. (1875–7); continued as *Kelly's handbook of the upper ten thousand for 1878* [1879], 2 vols. (1878–9); continued as *Kelly's handbook to the titled, landed and official classes*, 94 vols. (1880–1973)

LondG — *London Gazette*

LP Henry VIII — J. S. Brewer, J. Gairdner, and R. H. Brodie, eds., *Letters and papers, foreign and domestic, of the reign of Henry VIII*, 23 vols. in 38 (1862–1932); repr. (1965)

Mallalieu, *Watercolour artists* — H. L. Mallalieu, *The dictionary of British watercolour artists up to 1820*, 3 vols. (1976–90); vol. 1, 2nd edn (1986)

Memoirs FRS — *Biographical Memoirs of Fellows of the Royal Society*

MGH — Monumenta Germaniae Historica

MT — *Musical Times*

Munk, *Roll* — W. Munk, *The roll of the Royal College of Physicians of London*, 2 vols. (1861); 2nd edn, 3 vols. (1878)

N&Q — *Notes and Queries*

New Grove — S. Sadie, ed., *The new Grove dictionary of music and musicians*, 20 vols. (1980); 2nd edn, 29 vols. (2001) [also online edn; see also Grove, *Dict. mus.*]

Nichols, *Illustrations* — J. Nichols and J. B. Nichols, *Illustrations of the literary history of the eighteenth century*, 8 vols. (1817–58)

Nichols, *Lit. anecdotes* — J. Nichols, *Literary anecdotes of the eighteenth century*, 9 vols. (1812–16); facs. edn (1966)

Obits. FRS — *Obituary Notices of Fellows of the Royal Society*

O'Byrne, *Naval biog. dict.* — W. R. O'Byrne, *A naval biographical dictionary* (1849); repr. (1990); [2nd edn], 2 vols. (1861)

OHS — Oxford Historical Society

Old Westminsters — *The record of Old Westminsters*, 1–2, ed. G. F. R. Barker and A. H. Stenning (1928); suppl. 1, ed. J. B. Whitmore and G. R. Y. Radcliffe [1938]; 3, ed. J. B. Whitmore, G. R. Y. Radcliffe, and D. C. Simpson (1963); suppl. 2, ed. F. E. Pagan (1978); 4, ed. F. E. Pagan and H. E. Pagan (1992)

OMT — Oxford Medieval Texts

Ordericus Vitalis, *Eccl. hist.* — *The ecclesiastical history of Orderic Vitalis*, ed. and trans. M. Chibnall, 6 vols., OMT (1969–80); repr. (1990)

Paris, *Chron.* — *Matthaei Parisiensis, monachi sancti Albani, chronica majora*, ed. H. R. Luard, Rolls Series, 7 vols. (1872–83)

Parl. papers — *Parliamentary papers* (1801–)

PBA — *Proceedings of the British Academy*

Pepys, *Diary*	*The diary of Samuel Pepys*, ed. R. Latham and W. Matthews, 11 vols. (1970–83); repr. (1995) and (2000)
Pevsner	N. Pevsner and others, Buildings of England series
PICE	*Proceedings of the Institution of Civil Engineers*
Pipe rolls	*The great roll of the pipe for . . .*, PRSoc. (1884–)
PRO	Public Record Office
PRS	*Proceedings of the Royal Society of London*
PRSoc.	Pipe Roll Society
PTRS	*Philosophical Transactions of the Royal Society*
QR	*Quarterly Review*
RC	Record Commissions
Redgrave, *Artists*	S. Redgrave, *A dictionary of artists of the English school* (1874); rev. edn (1878); repr. (1970)
Reg. Oxf.	C. W. Boase and A. Clark, eds., *Register of the University of Oxford*, 5 vols., OHS, 1, 10–12, 14 (1885–9)
Reg. PCS	J. H. Burton and others, eds., *The register of the privy council of Scotland*, 1st ser., 14 vols. (1877–98); 2nd ser., 8 vols. (1899–1908); 3rd ser., [16 vols.] (1908–70)
Reg. RAN	H. W. C. Davis and others, eds., *Regesta regum Anglo-Normannorum, 1066–1154*, 4 vols. (1913–69)
RIBA Journal	*Journal of the Royal Institute of British Architects* [later *RIBA Journal*]
RotP	J. Strachey, ed., *Rotuli parliamentorum ut et petitiones, et placita in parliamento*, 6 vols. (1767–77)
RotS	D. Macpherson, J. Caley, and W. Illingworth, eds., *Rotuli Scotiae in Turri Londinensi et in domo capitulari Westmonasteriensi asservati*, 2 vols., RC, 14 (1814–19)
RS	Record(s) Society
Rymer, *Foedera*	T. Rymer and R. Sanderson, eds., *Foedera, conventiones, literae et cuiuscunque generis acta publica inter reges Angliae et alios quosvis imperatores, reges, pontifices, principes, vel communitates*, 20 vols. (1704–35); 2nd edn, 20 vols. (1726–35); 3rd edn, 10 vols. (1739–45); facs. edn (1967); new edn, ed. A. Clarke, J. Caley, and F. Holbrooke, 4 vols., RC, 50 (1816–30)
Sainty, *Judges*	J. Sainty, ed., *The judges of England, 1272–1990*, SeldS, suppl. ser., 10 (1993)
Sainty, *King's counsel*	J. Sainty, ed., *A list of English law officers and king's counsel*, SeldS, suppl. ser., 7 (1987)
SCH	Studies in Church History
Scots peerage	J. B. Paul, ed. *The Scots peerage, founded on Wood's edition of Sir Robert Douglas's Peerage of Scotland, containing an historical and genealogical account of the nobility of that kingdom*, 9 vols. (1904–14)
SeldS	Selden Society
SHR	*Scottish Historical Review*
State trials	T. B. Howell and T. J. Howell, eds., *Cobbett's Complete collection of state trials*, 34 vols. (1809–28)
STC, 1475–1640	A. W. Pollard, G. R. Redgrave, and others, eds., *A short-title catalogue of . . . English books . . . 1475–1640* (1926); 2nd edn, ed. W. A. Jackson, F. S. Ferguson, and K. F. Pantzer, 3 vols. (1976–91) [see also Wing, *STC*]
STS	Scottish Text Society
SurtS	Surtees Society
Symeon of Durham, *Opera*	*Symeonis monachi opera omnia*, ed. T. Arnold, 2 vols., Rolls Series, 75 (1882–5); repr. (1965)
Tanner, *Bibl. Brit.-Hib.*	T. Tanner, *Bibliotheca Britannico-Hibernica*, ed. D. Wilkins (1748); repr. (1963)
Thieme & Becker, *Allgemeines Lexikon*	U. Thieme, F. Becker, and H. Vollmer, eds., *Allgemeines Lexikon der bildenden Künstler von der Antike bis zur Gegenwart*, 37 vols. (Leipzig, 1907–50); repr. (1961–5), (1983), and (1992)
Thurloe, *State papers*	*A collection of the state papers of John Thurloe*, ed. T. Birch, 7 vols. (1742)
TLS	*Times Literary Supplement*
Tout, *Admin. hist.*	T. F. Tout, *Chapters in the administrative history of mediaeval England: the wardrobe, the chamber, and the small seals*, 6 vols. (1920–33); repr. (1967)
TRHS	*Transactions of the Royal Historical Society*
VCH	H. A. Doubleday and others, eds., *The Victoria history of the counties of England*, [88 vols.] (1900–)
Venn, *Alum. Cant.*	J. Venn and J. A. Venn, *Alumni Cantabrigienses: a biographical list of all known students, graduates, and holders of office at the University of Cambridge, from the earliest times to 1900*, 10 vols. (1922–54); repr. in 2 vols. (1974–8)
Vertue, *Note books*	[G. Vertue], *Note books*, ed. K. Esdaile, earl of Ilchester, and H. M. Hake, 6 vols., Walpole Society, 18, 20, 22, 24, 26, 30 (1930–55)
VF	*Vanity Fair*
Walford, *County families*	E. Walford, *The county families of the United Kingdom, or, Royal manual of the titled and untitled aristocracy of Great Britain and Ireland* (1860)
Walker rev.	A. G. Matthews, *Walker revised: being a revision of John Walker's Sufferings of the clergy during the grand rebellion, 1642–60* (1948); repr. (1988)
Walpole, *Corr.*	*The Yale edition of Horace Walpole's correspondence*, ed. W. S. Lewis, 48 vols. (1937–83)
Ward, *Men of the reign*	T. H. Ward, ed., *Men of the reign: a biographical dictionary of eminent persons of British and colonial birth who have died during the reign of Queen Victoria* (1885); repr. (Graz, 1968)
Waterhouse, *18c painters*	E. Waterhouse, *The dictionary of 18th century painters in oils and crayons* (1981); repr. as *British 18th century painters in oils and crayons* (1991), vol. 2 of *Dictionary of British art*
Watt, *Bibl. Brit.*	R. Watt, *Bibliotheca Britannica, or, A general index to British and foreign literature*, 4 vols. (1824) [many reprs.]
Wellesley index	W. E. Houghton, ed., *The Wellesley index to Victorian periodicals, 1824–1900*, 5 vols. (1966–89); new edn (1999) [CD-ROM]
Wing, *STC*	D. Wing, ed., *Short-title catalogue of . . . English books . . . 1641–1700*, 3 vols. (1945–51); 2nd edn (1972–88); rev. and enl. edn, ed. J. J. Morrison, C. W. Nelson, and M. Seccombe, 4 vols. (1994–8) [see also *STC, 1475–1640*]
Wisden	*John Wisden's Cricketer's Almanack*
Wood, *Ath. Oxon.*	A. Wood, *Athenae Oxonienses . . . to which are added the Fasti*, 2 vols. (1691–2); 2nd edn (1721); new edn, 4 vols., ed. P. Bliss (1813–20); repr. (1967) and (1969)
Wood, *Vic. painters*	C. Wood, *Dictionary of Victorian painters* (1971); 2nd edn (1978); 3rd edn as *Victorian painters*, 2 vols. (1995), vol. 4 of *Dictionary of British art*
WW	*Who's who* (1849–)
WWBMP	M. Stenton and S. Lees, eds., *Who's who of British members of parliament*, 4 vols. (1976–81)
WWW	*Who was who* (1929–)

Belle, Alexis-Simon (1674–1734), portrait painter, was born on 12 January 1674, in the rue du Bac, Paris, and baptized on 17 January at St Sulpice, Paris, the second child but only son of Jean Belle (1636/1641–1703), portrait painter, and Anne Malguy (d. 1705). He trained initially with his father, then became a pupil in the early 1690s of François de Troy, one of the painters at the exiled court of James II at St Germain-en-Laye.

Belle's career at St Germain started about 1698–1701, a period of peace between France and England, when it was easy for British travellers to cross the channel carrying with them small portraits of the prince of Wales (James Edward Stuart, Stuart claimant to the British throne), and his sister Princess Louise Marie. Troy, by then the only painter still working for James II, was commissioned to produce more portraits than he could manage and invited Belle, his most able pupil, to collaborate. During these three years they produced many copies of Troy's portraits of which over twenty-five are now known, mainly of the prince of Wales. Belle became so busy that when he won the prix de Rome in August 1700 he preferred to continue his Jacobite commissions than to travel to Italy.

Belle also produced some original compositions, the earliest of which seem to date from 1698, when the prince of Wales was ten and Princess Louise Marie was six (priv. colls.). In 1699 he produced a large allegorical portrait showing the former as a guardian angel, leading his sister under the protection of cherubim (Royal Collection). At about the same time he also painted *Mary of Modena* (Sizergh Castle, Cumbria). On 12 November 1701, when he married the miniature painter Anne Chéron (c.1663–1718), he described himself as 'peintre ordinaire du Roy d'Angleterre'. James II had died in September of that year, but Belle continued to work for his son.

War was renewed between France and England in 1702, and in the years that followed Belle replaced Troy as the official painter of the Jacobite court, where he and his wife quickly became integrated into the British community and where he settled permanently. Chiefly he concentrated on producing portraits of James Stuart and his sister, some of them copied as miniatures by his wife, to be smuggled into Britain. Belle also worked for various Jacobite courtiers and the nuns of the English Augustinian convent in Paris. By 1705 he was doing so well that he was able to invest annually in the government 'rentes'.

Belle was elected to the Académie Royale de Peinture et Sculpture in August 1703 when he submitted a number of portraits including a three-quarter-length portrait of his former master, *François de Troy* (Château de Versailles); he exhibited nine portraits in the Salon the following year. Three portraits showed members of the court at St Germain and two showed James Stuart and his sister. The demand for portraits of James Stuart was so great that by 1706 he was employing a small atelier to help him. One of these portraits, engraved by Le Roi, first brought the painter's name to the attention of the British public.

Belle's most significant composition from this period is a whole-length portrait of James Stuart, dated 1703 (Collège des Écossais, Paris). It shows him in armour standing beside the channel, on which several warships can be seen. He is pointing towards the cliffs and castle of Dover and is accompanied by a page in Polish costume. A similar three-quarter-length painting was produced by Troy in 1704 (Parham House, Sussex), without either the page or the view of Dover. These two portraits were frequently copied and it seems that Belle continued to copy Troy's portrait as well as his own until approximately 1707. Belle also made several copies (examples are in the Scottish National Portrait Gallery, Edinburgh, and priv. coll.) of a small portrait of Princess Louise Marie by Troy (National Portrait Gallery, London) which dates from these years.

Belle's most famous portrait of James Stuart was painted in 1712 during the negotiations for the treaty of Utrecht, just before James was obliged to leave St Germain for Lorraine. He is portrayed in military costume inside a tent (Gov. Art Coll.). This portrait quickly became the standard image of the exiled Jacobite claimant to the throne and was copied many times. In an engraving of the portrait by François Chéreau that was widely circulated in England and Scotland Belle was described as 'peintre de S. M. Brit'. This portrait was paired with Belle's portrait of Princess Louise Marie (c.1710, Sizergh Castle) which was engraved posthumously by Chéreau in 1713.

Belle remained at St Germain after the departure of James Stuart and produced portraits of some of the diplomats associated with the treaty of Utrecht. In 1714 he was invited by James Stuart to join his court at Bar-le-Duc, where he continued to produce portraits of the Jacobite exiles. He also painted James Stuart in profile (Gov. Art Coll.) and in the robes of a knight of the Garter (lost), a work known through an engraving by Marie-Nicolle Horthemels and which resulted in commissions for similar portraits from the other Jacobite Garter knights.

By this time Belle's reputation as a portraitist was assured in Great Britain and in the years 1716–19 he received many commissions from English and Scottish Jacobites in exile after the rising of 1715. By then James Stuart lived in Italy, but in the winter of 1717/18 he employed Belle to make copies of the first portrait of him to be painted in Rome, by Antonio David.

During the 1720s Belle worked increasingly for French patrons. His numerous portraits of the French court and nobility included *Louis XV* (Château de Versailles). The many contemporary engravings after his work give some indication of his status in France. He continued also to receive commissions from Jacobites in Paris; in 1724 he signed himself 'pictor regis Britann' on a portrait of James Stuart's sister-in-law, Marie-Charlotte Sobieska (Walters Art Gallery, Baltimore). A project for Belle to make copies in 1727 of a portrait by David of James Stuart's wife, Maria-Clementina Sobieska, seems to have come to nothing, but in 1731 Belle did make two copies of each of David's portraits of James Stuart's two sons.

As a court portraitist Belle worked in the style developed in France by Troy, Hyacinthe Rigaud, and Nicolas de Largillière, though his greatest debt was to Troy, his former master. His portrait of James Stuart as a Garter knight was influenced by Benedetto Gennari's portrait of James

II. Belle might not have been very original in his compositions, but he was praised for his exceptional skill in accurately reproducing a likeness of his subject. About twenty-five of his Jacobite portraits are known to have survived, in addition to the much larger number that show the exiled Stuart family.

Belle's first wife died in April 1718 and on 12 January 1722 he married the engraver Marie-Nicolle Horthemels (1689–1745); they had two sons (1722, 1726) and a daughter (1730). His elder son was the history painter Clément-Louis Belle. Belle continued to live with the Jacobite community at St Germain, where he owned two properties, until his death at his home in the rue du Four, Paris, on 21 November 1734. He was buried on 22 November in St Sulpice, Paris.

EDWARD CORP

Sources F. Camus, 'Alexis-Simon Belle, portraitiste de cour', *Bulletin de la Société de l'Histoire de l'Art Français* (1990), 27–70 · E. Corp, *The king over the water: portraits of the Stuarts in exile after 1689* (2001) · F. Camus, 'Alexis-Simon Belle, peintre de Jacques III et des Jacobites', *Revue de la Bibliothèque Nationale*, 46 (1992), 50–57 · D. Nairne, diary, NL Scot., MS 14266 · Royal Arch., Stuart papers · Nairne MSS, Bodl. Oxf., MSS Carte · R. Sharp, *The engraved record of the Jacobite movement* (1996)
Likenesses A.-S. Belle, self-portrait, oils, 1730, Musée National du Château de Versailles, France · J.-N. Tardieu, engraving, 1744 (after self-portrait by A.-S. Belle, 1730), Bibliothèque Nationale de France, Paris, France
Wealth at death approx. 100,000–120,000 livres: F. Camus, 'Alexis-Simon Belle, portraitiste de cour'

Belle, Dido Elizabeth (*b. c.*1763, *d.* in or after 1794), protégée of the first earl of Mansfield, was the illegitimate daughter of Sir John *Lindsay (1737–1788), a captain in the Royal Navy. Her mother was a black slave of African origin, possibly called Belle, whom Lindsay had taken prisoner in a Spanish vessel in the West Indies and brought to England, where Dido was born.

Dido Belle's historical significance relates to her unusual position as a black girl taken into the care of William Murray, first earl of Mansfield (1705–1793). Mansfield was the uncle of Sir John Lindsay and he seems to have welcomed Dido into his household as a playmate and later companion for his great-niece, Lady Elizabeth Murray (*c.*1763–1823), whom Lord and Lady Mansfield had adopted. Dido lived with the family at their house in Bloomsbury Square until 1780 and then at Kenwood House. She held a position balanced between family member and servant and was in charge of the dairy and poultry yard. Her familiarity with Lady Elizabeth Murray shocked Thomas Hutchinson when he attended a family dinner in 1779: 'A Black came in after dinner and sat with the ladies and after coffee, walked with the company in the gardens, one of the young ladies having her arm within the other' (Adams, 10). Mansfield was fond of Dido and provided her with an education, an allowance, and gifts.

A portrait of Dido Belle with Lady Elizabeth Murray, attributed to Johan Zoffany, shows an attractive woman with dark skin, a long, straight nose, and large, dark eyes. Dido wears outmoded masquerade dress associated with black servants and the exotic while Elizabeth is shown in contemporary fashion. Thus Zoffany has suggested the

Dido Elizabeth Belle (*b. c.*1763, *d.* in or after 1794), attrib. Johan Zoffany, *c.*1780 [left, with Lady Elizabeth Murray]

relative ambiguity of status between the two sitters in the portrait. Hutchinson's description of Dido was biased by his racial opinions: 'her wool was much frizzled in her neck, but not enough to answer the large curls now in fashion. She is neither handsome nor genteel—pert enough' (Adams, 10).

As lord chief justice from 1756 to 1788 Mansfield had jurisdiction over cases involving slaves and the presence of Dido Belle as his ward made some planters sceptical about his judgments. Indeed, Mansfield's judgment of the case of James Somerset (22 June 1772) was popularly and erroneously believed to emancipate slaves in England. Mansfield himself was aware that the Somerset case merely prevented planters from forcibly returning slaves resident in England to the West Indies. Acknowledging the continued legality of slavery in England, Mansfield carefully stated Dido's freedom in his will of 17 April 1782.

Dido Belle was well looked after by the Mansfield family and was financially secure. Sir John Lindsay had no legitimate heirs and in 1788 he left Dido and his son John £1000 in trust. After Lord Mansfield's death in 1793, she received an annuity of at least £100 and a lump sum of £500. Lady Margery Murray also left Dido £100. Dido changed her name to Davinier in 1794, presumably on marriage.

REYAHN KING

Sources G. Adams, 'Dido Elizabeth Belle, a black girl at Kenwood: an account of a protegée of the 1st Lord Mansfield', *Camden History Review* (1984), 10–14 · F. Shyllon, *Black people in Britain, 1555–1833* (1977), 40–41 · E. Heward, *Lord Mansfield* (1979), 145, 161–2 · R. King, 'Ignatius Sancho and portraits of the black élite', *Ignatius Sancho: an African man of letters*, ed. R. King (1997), 32–3
Archives Kenwood House, London, Iveagh bequest, account books · priv. coll., Murray Mansfield MSS
Likenesses attrib. J. Zoffany, double portrait, *c.*1780 (with Lady Elizabeth Murray), Scone Palace, earl of Mansfield collection [*see illus.*]

Belleman, John. *See* Belmaine, Jean (*fl.* 1546–1559).

Bellême, Robert de, earl of Shrewsbury and count of Ponthieu (*bap. c.*1057, *d.* in or after 1130), magnate, was the second, but eldest surviving, son of Roger de *Montgomery (d. 1094), vicomte of the Hièmois in Lower Normandy and earl of Shrewsbury, and his wife, Mabel de Bellême (d. 1077), daughter of Guillaume Talvas, lord of Alençon, from whom Robert gained his occasional name of Robert Talvas ('the Shield'). His mother's family held extensive property in northern Maine and the border region to the south of Normandy, where the dukes could not always impose their authority, and his father successfully asserted her claims to the entire inheritance of that family, thus accumulating widespread estates both inside and outside Normandy and handing on to Robert complex allegiances to the dukes of Normandy, counts of Maine, and kings of France.

Early life Robert was baptized at Sées by Thierry de Mathonville, abbot of St Evroult, before the abbot's departure for the Holy Land about 1057. He can be found attesting charters before the Norman conquest of England in company with his father and elder brother, Roger. In 1073 he was knighted by William I at Fresnay, during a campaign by which the king sought to enforce the overlordship of Maine which he had won in 1063; and in 1077–8, like many of the younger generation of Norman nobles, Bellême joined the first rebellion by the king's eldest son, Robert Curthose. His mother, Mabel, was killed in December 1077 and Robert, together with other members of the family, witnessed a confirmation to Troarn made in her memory. It appears that shortly thereafter there was a division of family interests, with Robert taking responsibility for the family's holdings in northern France and his father, Roger, taking up residence in England with his new wife and other sons. Robert probably did not inherit his mother's lands outright, for his father retained an interest in his first wife's property; but he certainly seems to have been in day-to-day control during the 1080s. He received a memorandum from his father about routine matters of tenure, for example, and in 1086 he can be found judging two lawsuits involving tenants of the family's French lands. His relations with the king were good, for William the Conqueror arranged Bellême's marriage to Agnes, the heir of the small, but strategically important, county of Ponthieu, to the north-east of Normandy; and in 1087, when news reached him of William's death, Robert was on his way to visit the king in Rouen to discuss important business. Bellême, anxious about the uncertainty which attended a changeover of power, immediately returned home and, like other Norman nobles, expelled the garrisons which the king had placed in his castles.

Normandy, 1087–1096 In 1088 Robert de Bellême was among the foremost of the conspirators who attempted to replace William II (William Rufus) as king of England with his elder brother, the new duke of Normandy, Robert Curthose, and he joined the forces fighting against William Rufus at the siege of Rochester Castle. When the attempted coup failed Robert returned to Normandy in the company of the youngest son of William I, Count Henry, and was arrested on his arrival by agents of Robert Curthose. Bellême was imprisoned at Neuilly l'Évêque, while Curthose made an expedition to assert Norman authority in Maine. Robert's father, Roger de Montgomery, then returned to Normandy to prepare the family's castles to defy the duke. On his return from Maine, Robert Curthose took one of those castles, St Céneri, near Alençon, and blinded its commander, Robert Quarrel, as a reprisal. Robert de Bellême was then released, but the duke granted the castle of St Céneri to Robert Giroie, a man whose family had a series of grudges against Robert de Bellême and his kin. In this manner the duke might be said to have secured a points victory over the powerful Montgomery–Bellême family.

In the subsequent unsettled conditions of Duke Robert's reign, Robert de Bellême's activities were singled out by the historian Orderic Vitalis as among the most anarchic and self-seeking; but those activities were nearly always undertaken in support of the duke or in defence of his family property. In 1089 he was among Curthose's counsellors in dealing with the proposed marriage between Foulques, count of Anjou, and Bertrade, the niece of the count of Évreux. Then, in November 1090, he played a prominent part in putting down the rebellion among the citizens of Rouen, despite an earlier setback in his relations with the duke when Curthose granted the castle of Exmes (which had formed part of the *vicomté* of the Hièmois and had therefore been held by Robert's father) to Gilbert de l'Aigle. In the early 1090s the extensive property accumulated by Bellême's paternal ancestors also came under attack from ambitious local lords. In the Hièmois, where much of the Montgomery patrimony lay, Robert's estates were attacked by the Grandmesnil family and their relatives the Courcys.

These quarrels, which probably had their origins in long-standing disputes, were given added impetus by the conflict between Robert Curthose and William Rufus. When Robert de Bellême besieged his enemies at Courcy in 1092 he did so with the support of the duke, which implies that the Courcy family had declared for King William. In the same year Robert fought with the duke against the rebellious Ascelin Goel during the siege of Bréval, where his skill in devising new siege machinery was particularly useful. Meanwhile, the more southerly of Robert's lands, which had been the property of his mother's family, the lords of Bellême, had come under attack from a second cousin, Geoffroi, count of Mortagne. Geoffroi, whose family had been consolidating an area of land just beyond the Norman border which would later become the Perche, claimed the Bellêmois region by right of inheritance from his mother and made repeated raids on the area. Geoffroi's failure to make progress in seizing the area is an indication of Bellême's military ability and the effectiveness of his fortifications. Orderic Vitalis repeatedly mentions the thirty-four castles held by Robert and the place-name element *la motte* is common on the borders between Normandy, the Perche, and Maine.

In the early months of 1092 Bellême lost control of an important part of his mother's family estates, the town of Domfront in the Passais, which was seized by Count

Henry (the future Henry I); this usurpation must have done much to sour relations between Robert and Henry, with whom he had previously worked well during the Rouen rebellion. Henry used Domfront as a base to raid his brother's duchy and entered into alliance with Manceau lords who were anxious to throw off the authority of the Norman duke. Among his close associates was Robert Giroie, the castellan of St Céneri, which Robert de Bellême had lost in 1089. Now that Giroie had allied himself with the enemies of the duke, Bellême attacked St Céneri, repossessing in 1092 the castle which had been taken from him by Curthose in 1089. Giroie then established himself in a new castle at Montaigu, from which he proceeded to attack the Bellême lands. Ducal forces were summoned to restore order; Montaigu was taken and ordered to be razed; but as part of the settlement the family property of Robert Giroie was restored to him by the duke. These estates, which lay around Échauffour, near the abbey of St Evroult, had been in the hands of the Montgomery–Bellême family since the rebellion and forfeiture of Giroie's father in the early 1060s. This conciliatory treatment of Giroie, coupled with the loss of revenues involved in the return of Giroie's inheritance, alienated Robert de Bellême and in 1094 he changed his allegiance from Robert Curthose to William Rufus. The death of Roger de Montgomery in July of that year removed the only influence which could keep Robert loyal to the duke, and the Anglo-Saxon Chronicle records that the family castles of Le Houlme and Argentan were in the hands of William Rufus's men by the summer of 1094, with Argentan under the command of Robert's younger brother, *Roger the Poitevin [see under Montgomery, Roger de], who had already served as a trusted agent of King William in the north of England. Robert Curthose was saved only by the timely intervention of Philippe I of France, who joined Curthose in a campaign up through the Sées corridor into Normandy to recover the castles. The success of this and other attempts by William Rufus to win over Bellême and the rest of the Norman baronage may have contributed to Curthose's decision to join the expedition to the Holy Land in 1096. Robert de Bellême was then left free to work with the king of England, to whom Robert Curthose mortgaged the duchy in September 1096.

Years of success, 1096–1102 Robert de Bellême worked well with the new master of Normandy, whose military designs made the services of a competent soldier such as Robert particularly welcome. In 1097–8 Bellême served with William Rufus's forces in the Vexin and was responsible for the design of the first castle at Gisors. Then, when the king attempted to renew Norman control in Maine, Robert's military experience, fortification skills, and local knowledge must have made him the obvious candidate as *princeps militiae* ('military commander'). His contribution on the Manceau front involved the establishment of forward positions and fortifications at Ballon and culminated in the capture of the count of Maine, Helias de La Flèche. In the summer of 1098 the king rewarded Bellême for his achievements by permitting him, upon payment of £3000, to succeed to the English lands of the Montgomery

family, after the death of his younger brother, Hugh de *Montgomery, earl of Shrewsbury. Robert had thus reconstituted the great cross-channel honour established by his father; and a further sign of the king's confidence was the grant of the castle of Tickhill in the West Riding of Yorkshire in the late 1090s.

In 1100 Robert de Bellême attained the zenith of his power when he acquired the county of Ponthieu as the inheritance of his wife, Agnes; but his fortunes were to go into decline from this point, after the accession of Henry I to the kingdom of England and the return of Duke Robert Curthose to Normandy. Bellême accepted Henry as the new king of England in August 1100, but received no acknowledgement from the king, who retained his hold on Robert's town of Domfront. By the time Curthose tried to assert his claims to the English crown at Alton in 1101, Bellême was again supporting the duke. Orderic Vitalis says that the king spent the next year collecting evidence against Bellême and in 1102 he was accused on forty-five counts in the king's court. Robert fled the king's presence and refused another summons to the court, fortifying his castles in England to defy the king and making an alliance with the Welsh kings, while his brother Arnulf de *Montgomery sought help from the Irish. Henry then proceeded to pick off Robert's castles, one by one, until his newest fortification at Bridgnorth was taken, whereupon Robert sued for peace. Robert and his brothers, Roger the Poitevin, lord of extensive lands in Lancashire, north Yorkshire, and East Anglia, and Arnulf, lord of Holderness and castellan of Pembroke, were banished from the kingdom and their lands declared forfeit.

Return to Normandy, 1102–1112 From 1102 onwards Robert de Bellême's activities were confined to the French side of the channel. When his wife died in 1105 or 1106 he stopped using the title count of Ponthieu and his young son, Guillaume Talvas, took control of the county, leaving Robert to concentrate on the traditional Montgomery–Bellême lands. The years before the duke, Robert Curthose, lost the duchy to his brother Henry I in 1106 were as disturbed as those in the early 1090s, and initially Robert de Bellême found himself at war with the duke, who had agreed to support the king against Robert. Bellême's brother Arnulf betrayed a centre of family power at Alménêches to the duke and Robert was forced to burn the nunnery there (despite the abbess being his sister Emma) in order to expel the ducal forces. Eventually he defeated the duke and a formidable array of the Norman aristocracy in a pitched battle which took place near Exmes, probably in 1103. As a result Robert Curthose came to terms with Robert de Bellême, confirming him in his lands and extending his power by granting him rights over ducal demesne, including the castle at Argentan and the forest of Gouffern, as well as some sort of authority over the bishopric of Sées. Thereafter Bellême supported the ducal cause and Orderic Vitalis describes how he and his nephew, Guillaume, count of Mortain, who had also been exiled from England, made war on the supporters of Henry I in Lower Normandy.

Robert de Bellême was under considerable pressure during this period both from the local lords of the Hièmois and from his old enemies, the counts of Mortagne; and late in 1105 he made a journey to England, where he attempted to come to terms with the king. He also entered into relations with the counts of Anjou, whose influence in Maine (where Robert had considerable property) was on the increase. In March 1106 Robert and his son were at Marmoutier, in the lands of the counts of Anjou, and in May he was fighting with the heir to Anjou, Geoffroi Martel, at the siege of Candé. By September, however, he was back in Normandy and at the battle of Tinchebrai he commanded the rear of Curthose's forces, a role which probably contributed to his unique survival among the duke's commanders. After failing to persuade Helias, count of Maine, to support further resistance to King Henry, Bellême presented himself in November 1106 at Henry's first Norman court and was allowed to retain all his hereditary estates, giving up only the property he had acquired from ducal demesne. He even remained in office as the vicomte with jurisdiction over Argentan, Exmes, and Falaise, perhaps because Henry had insufficient men to guarantee continuity of administration; and in 1110 Robert was among the witnesses to a renewal of the treaty of Dover.

Imprisonment and death Between 1110 and 1112 Robert de Bellême became involved in the unrest in southern Normandy, encouraged by the new overlord of his Manceau lands, Foulques, count of Anjou, who had become count of Maine after the death of his father-in-law, Helias, in 1110. King Henry brought a series of charges against Robert and, on the grounds that he had failed to answer them, seized him at Bonneville-sur-Touques on 4 November 1112 while he was visiting the royal court as an envoy from the French king, Louis VI. Bellême was sentenced to close confinement, first at Cherbourg and then at Wareham. His lands were declared forfeit and his maternal family stronghold of Bellême granted to Rotrou of Mortagne, his long-standing rival, in 1113. Although King Louis of France demanded the release of his former envoy in 1118, and Robert's son Guillaume Talvas, count of Ponthieu, succeeded in regaining the Norman property in 1119, Robert was never released and he was still alive at Wareham in 1130. His obituary was celebrated at the family foundation of St Martin of Sées on 8 May, but the year of his death is unknown.

Character and family relations Robert de Bellême's military ability is unquestioned, despite the remarks of Orderic Vitalis that he feared open battle and preferred to lurk behind his fortifications. He gave useful service both to Curthose at Rouen and Bréval and to William Rufus in the Vexin and Maine; his help was clearly not unwelcome to the count of Anjou in the siege of Candé; and he maintained the Norman pressure on the Welsh during his tenure of the earldom of Shrewsbury. His chief talent seems to have lain in the siting and fortification of castles, of which he raised many in Normandy. He built a fortified centre at Fourches, near Falaise, and moved there the inhabitants of nearby Vignats; and he made a similar

change in England, by moving the inhabitants of Quatford to Bridgnorth. He also raised a castle known as Château Gontier, at La Courbe, above the River Orne, which dominates the Houlme region. He acted as castellan of Tickhill, Yorkshire, built the castle for William Rufus at Gisors, and improved the fortifications of a series of castles in northern Maine at William's request. He seems to have undertaken all his military responsibilities in a thoroughly professional manner, which aroused the hostility of chroniclers. He was clearly prepared to mobilize every resource, even those of the church, in the forwarding of his military plans. He used the tenants of the abbey of St Evroult, for example, to demolish the castle of Montaigu, though Orderic Vitalis says he had no rights to their labour; and he appropriated the revenues of the bishopric of Sées. So strained were his relations with the church that Serlo, bishop of Sées, excommunicated him and went into exile in England, followed by his archdeacon, John, and the abbot of Sées, Ralph d'Escures.

Defects within Bellême's personality also contributed to the poor reputation he acquired through his treatment of the church. Numerous atrocities are attributed to him, such as the burning of the church of Tournai where civilians were sheltering and the murder of his godson, though many of these stories come from later and biased sources. He is alleged to have preferred to keep his captives for torture and mutilation rather than to accept ransom as was customary in the warfare of the period. There are many contemporary references to his prisons and prisoners, and the conduct of Rotrou, count of Mortagne, who made his will and sent a messenger to his mother upon hearing that he was to be handed over to Robert, certainly implies that Bellême's prisoners did not expect to be released.

None the less Bellême practised the conventional pieties. He confirmed benefactions made by his family to Shrewsbury Abbey and La Sauve Majeure and issued a general confirmation to the abbey of St Vincent of Le Mans. During the very difficult year of 1092 he gave the church of St Léonard in Bellême to the abbey of Marmoutier and secured a royal confirmation of his act. After his recapture of St Céneri in the same year he allowed relics from the church there to be taken to the family foundation of St Martin of Sées and he granted the monks of Marmoutier exemption from tolls in his lands. He even attempted to remonstrate with the ecclesiastical authorities about the imposition of an interdict, referring the matter to the noted canonist, Ivo of Chartres, whose diplomatic refusal to intervene survives in his letter collection.

Robert de Bellême probably spent little time in England, despite the great increase in his wealth brought about by his succession to the earldom of Shrewsbury; but he witnessed a series of English royal charters in 1101 and received jointly with other lords with Welsh connections a letter from Archbishop Anselm regarding their conduct towards Bishop Wilfrid of St David's. Robert was responsible for the fortification of the Bridgnorth site and also built another castle at Carreghofa, in Powys. He is also credited with the introduction of Spanish bloodstock into the Welsh marches in an effort to improve the quality of horses available to the Normans.

Bellême's marriage to Agnes, the elder daughter of Gui, count of Ponthieu, was arranged before 1087, but may not have taken place until about 1092, perhaps because of the age of Agnes. Their union was neither long-lasting nor successful and Agnes left Robert, probably shortly after the birth of their only child, Guillaume Talvas, and returned to Ponthieu; but despite the lurid story of marital collapse given in Orderic Vitalis's ecclesiastical history (Ordericus Vitalis, *Eccl. hist.*, 4.300), there are no signs of discord between Robert and his father-in-law, Count Gui, with whom he judged a plea in the ducal court at Rouen in 1093. Robert witnessed a charter given by Gui, apparently on his deathbed, and it may be that Agnes returned to Ponthieu in the later 1090s to act on her father's behalf because of his advanced age. She probably took her son with her since he does not attest Robert's acts until 1106. Only one act of Agnes as countess of Ponthieu is known and she must have died in 1105 or 1106, when Robert ceased to use the title count of Ponthieu. Robert was the father of another son, Andrew, who attests one of his brother Guillaume's acts, but Andrew's mother is unknown.

The chroniclers have given Robert de Bellême an appalling reputation, though his actions as a man of violence and an oppressor of the church were probably little worse than those of his contemporaries. He was faced with an enormous task in trying to hold together his family's extensive lands, which lay in very unstable regions, and it proved to be impossible without the support of an effective ruler. Although Bellême was a capable soldier and an efficient administrator, it was his misfortune that he lacked political judgement, as his support of Robert Curthose and failure to establish satisfactory relations with Henry I indicate.   KATHLEEN THOMPSON

Sources Ordericus Vitalis, *Eccl. hist.* · *Willelmi Malmesbiriensis monachi de gestis regum Anglorum*, ed. W. Stubbs, 2 vols., Rolls Series (1887–9) · Gaufridus Grossus, 'Vita S. Bernardi Tironensis', *Patrologia Latina*, 171 (1854), 1363 · *ASC*, s.a. 1098, 1102, 1104–6, 1112–13 [text E] · C. Brunel, ed., *Recueil des actes des comtes de Ponthieu* (1930) · 'Livre blanc de Saint-Martin de Sées', *Bibliothèque de l'Évêché, Sées* · l'Abbé Barret, ed., *Cartulaire de Marmoutier pour le Perche* (1894) · K. Thompson, 'Robert of Bellême reconsidered', *Anglo-Norman Studies*, 13 (1990), 263–86 · C. W. Hollister, 'The campaign of 1102 against Robert of Bellême', *Studies in medieval history presented to R. Allen Brown*, ed. C. Harper-Bill, C. J. Holdsworth, and J. L. Nelson (1989), 193–202 · M. Chibnall, 'Robert of Bellême and the castle of Tickhill', *Droit privé et institutions régionales: études offertes à Jean Yver* (1976), 151–6 · K. Thompson, 'Orderic Vitalis and Robert of Bellême', *Journal of Medieval History*, 20 (1994), 133–41
Wealth at death Norman property was in hands of son: Ordericus Vitalis, *Eccl. hist.*, 6.224

Bellenden, Adam (*c.*1572–1648), bishop of Dunblane and of Aberdeen, was the son of Sir John *Bellenden (*d.* 1576) of Auchnoul, lord justice clerk 1547–72, and his third wife, Janet Seton, and the half-brother of Sir Lewis *Bellenden, also lord justice clerk. He studied at the University of Edinburgh from 1586, graduated MA on 1 August 1590, and continued in the capital for some time after. He participated in the presbytery's weekly exercise of doctrine, obtaining a testimonial from it on 12 June 1593, and was ordained minister of Falkirk, Stirlingshire, five weeks later on 19 July.

Bellenden married Jean Abercromby on 17 February 1595; the couple had ten children, many of whom predeceased them both. In April 1597 Bellenden was evicted from his manse and denied his stipend by Lord Livingstone in retribution for the presbytery of Stirling's pursuit of Lady Livingstone for Catholicism. The presbytery's response was to elect him moderator, in spite of his inability to attend. In 1598 he was suffering from illness and depression, and the following year he remained absent from Falkirk, but he appears to have been back in his charge by 1600.

In 1602 Bellenden attended the general assembly of the kirk, and was one of the ministers who met on 10 January 1606 at Linlithgow to support fellow ministers facing trial for declining royal authority in spiritual matters as a result of attendance at the illegal Aberdeen assembly of 1605. At a meeting of ministers and nobles at Linlithgow in December 1606 Bellenden urged that it should not be regarded as a general assembly, but, after it had risen, the crown declared it to have been one. In 1609 he attended a convention of ministers and bishops at Falkirk which failed to resolve matters in dispute. In November 1614 Bellenden was suspended from the ministry, but on 18 January 1615 the sentence was lifted and he was enjoined 'to wait more diligently on his flock in preparing them for communion' (*Fasti Scot.*, 1.205).

Bellenden demitted his charge at Falkirk in July 1616 and was then appointed to the bishopric of Dunblane, although he had hitherto been firmly opposed to episcopacy, and had been one of forty-two ministers who signed in 1606 a protest to parliament against its reintroduction. He was consequently criticized for accepting this preferment. Translated to the bishopric of Aberdeen in 1635, he was succeeded at Dunblane by James Wedderburn in 1636. In 1638, in common with all Scottish bishops, he was deprived of his see on the abolition of episcopacy in Scotland by the Glasgow general assembly. He fled to England, where his wife died some time before 19 October 1639, and he was admitted to the rectory of Porlock in Somerset in July 1642. He died at Porlock in February 1648 and was buried there on 4 March.

A. B. GROSART, *rev.* ALAN R. MacDONALD

Sources *Fasti Scot.*, new edn, 1.205; 7.330–31, 338 · D. Calderwood, *The history of the Kirk of Scotland*, ed. T. Thomson and D. Laing, 8 vols., Wodrow Society, 7 (1842–9) · Register of the presbytery of Stirling, NA Scot., CH2/722 · T. Thomson, ed., *Acts and proceedings of the general assemblies of the Kirk of Scotland*, 3 pts, Bannatyne Club, 81 (1839–45) · J. Forbes, *Certaine records touching the estate of the kirk in the years MDCV & MDCVI*, ed. D. Laing and J. Anderson, Wodrow Society, 19 (1846) · J. Row, *The history of the Kirk of Scotland, from the year 1558 to August 1637*, ed. D. Laing, Wodrow Society, 4 (1842) · D. Laing, ed., *A catalogue of the graduates ... of the University of Edinburgh*, Bannatyne Club, 106 (1858) · R. Lippe, ed., *Selections from Wodrow's biographical collections: divines of the north-east of Scotland*, New Spalding Club, 5 (1890)

Bellenden [Bannatyne], **John** (*c*.1495–1545×8), poet and translator, may have been born in Lothian. He was probably a younger son of Patrick Bellenden (*fl.* 1486–1520), steward to Margaret Tudor, and Marion Douglas (*fl.* 1490–1542), nurse to James V. He belonged to a family prominent in royal service throughout the sixteenth century and his parentage also linked him firmly to the Douglas kin. Bellenden was educated at St Salvator's College: he matriculated at the University of St Andrews in 1508 and gained his licentiate in 1512; under university rules this means that he must have been born in the last decade of the fifteenth century. After taking his degree Bellenden became *clericus expensarum* (clerk of expenses) in the household of James V, from August 1515 to August 1522, which involved keeping the accounts of the household and preparing them for presentation to the exchequer. His departure from this post coincides with the return of the duke of Albany, the governor, and he was probably a casualty of factional interests.

Bellenden is then absent from the records until September 1528. On the 14th he gained the position of canon of Ross and rector of Lumlair. On the 4th he also appears as a 'servitour and secretar' to Archibald Douglas, earl of Angus, defending him, his brother, and his uncle against charges of treason before parliament (*Acts of the Parliaments of Scotland*, 1814–44, 2.322–4). As James V was determined on revenge against the Douglases for his confinement during the last years of his minority, Bellenden's defence of his patron was dangerous, but he secured a remission for his treasonable activity in April 1529 (Livingstone, 2, no. 56).

Bellenden regained his place at court through his literary skills rather than political intrigue. He is now best known for his translations rather than his poetry. The lesser of the former is his version of the first five books of Livy's *History of Rome*, complete by 1534, when Bellenden received payment for it from the king. His other translation was more localized. Bellenden prepared two major vernacular versions of Hector Boece's *Scotorum historia* (1527): the first, commissioned by the king, survives in manuscript, and was finished in 1531; the other was printed by Thomas Davidson in Edinburgh *c*.1536, and it may also be the 'new cronikle' presented to James V in 1533 (Paul, 6.97). Neither version is an entirely reliable witness to Boece's text, and while the two versions are obviously connected, not least by intermediate manuscripts, they are far from identical. The second one is more critical of the church, and more overtly favourable towards the Douglases; it also varies from the original Latin in different ways. While the title page of the print asserts that the chronicles have been 'newly correckit' by Hector Boece, the exact nature of the relationship between Boece and Bellenden remains unclear. Many of Bellenden's alterations may be of his own devising, since they do not appear in the 1574 edition of the *Scotorum historia*, nor do they correspond with Boece's style. Nevertheless, Bellenden's translation was highly influential on the way in which the Scots regarded themselves.

Bellenden's contemporary Sir David Lindsay describes him as a 'plant of poetry' (Lindsay, line 51), but only a limited sample of his poetry survives. Three of his poems are connected to his translations and are addressed to the king. The first appears as 'The Ballat apon the Translation' in manuscript, and is revised later for print as 'The Proheme of the History'. The second is 'The Proheme of the Cosmographe', which is attached to the published translation of Boece, and also appears in the Bannatyne manuscript. The third, 'The Proloug apoun the Traduction of Titus Livius', precedes the translation of Livy. The last surviving poem, 'Baner of Petie', is preserved in the Bannatyne manuscript, and is an allegorical piece about the incarnation.

After he received preferment to the archdeaconry of Moray in August 1533, Bellenden seems to have written little. About 1538 he exchanged this post for the precentorship of Glasgow. In 1542 he was elected rector of the university, and he was re-elected in 1543 and 1544. In 1545 he went to Rome, presumably to defend in person his claim to the precentorship. As there is no record of his ever returning to Scotland, it seems likely that he died there, some time before 10 November 1548, when his prebend of Lumlair passed to his nephew, John Kincaid.

NICOLA ROYAN

Sources E. A. Sheppard, 'John Bellenden', in *The chronicles of Scotland compiled by Hector Boece*, ed. W. Seton and E. C. Batho, trans. J. Bellenden, 2, STS, 3rd ser., 15 (1941), 411–61 • E. A. Sheppard, 'Studies in the language of Bellenden's Boece', PhD diss., U. Lond., 1937 • T. van Heijnsbergen, 'The interaction between literature and history in Queen Mary's Edinburgh: the Bannatyne manuscript and its prosopographical context', *The Renaissance in Scotland: studies in literature, religion, history, and culture offered to John Durkan*, ed. A. A. MacDonald and others (1994), 183–225 • S. Mapstone, 'Shakespeare and Scottish kingship: a case history', *The rose and the thistle: essays on the culture of late medieval and Renaissance Scotland*, ed. S. Mapstone and J. Wood (1998), 158–89 • *The Bannatyne manuscript*, ed. W. T. Ritchie, 4 vols., STS, new ser., 22, 23, 26; 3rd ser., 5 (1928–34) • D. Lindsay, 'The testament and complaynt of … Papyngo', in *The works of Sir David Lindsay*, ed. D. Hamer, 1, STS, 3rd ser., 1 (1931) • J. M. Anderson, ed., *Early records of the University of St Andrews*, Scottish History Society, 3rd ser., 8 (1926) • M. Livingstone, D. Hay Fleming, and others, eds., *Registrum secreti sigilli regum Scotorum / The register of the privy seal of Scotland*, 1–2 (1908–21) • J. M. Thomson and others, eds., *Registrum magni sigilli regum Scotorum / The register of the great seal of Scotland*, 11 vols. (1882–1914), vol. 3 • J. B. Paul, ed., *Compota thesaurariorum regum Scotorum / Accounts of the lord high treasurer of Scotland*, 2–8 (1900–08) • G. Burnett and others, eds., *The exchequer rolls of Scotland*, 13 (1891); 17 (1897)

Archives Longleat, Bath MSS, MS *Chronicles of Scotland* • Morgan L., MS *Chronicles of Scotland*, MS 527 • NA Scot., MS *Chronicles of Scotland*, RH 13/10 • NL Scot., MS *Chronicles of Scotland*, MS Adv. 33.4.15 • NL Scot., MS *Chronicles of Scotland*, MS 5288 • NL Scot., MS *Chronicles of Scotland*, MS 2766 • NL Scot., MS *Chronicles of Scotland*, MS 3146 • NL Scot., MS *Chronicles of Scotland*, MS 21244 • NL Scot., Bannatyne MS, MS Adv. 1.1.6 • Trinity Cam., MS *Chronicles of Scotland*, MS 0.3.21 • U. Edin., MS *Chronicles of Scotland*, MS Laing III.205 • UCL, MS *Chronicles of Scotland*, MS Angl. 1

Bellenden, Sir John, of Auchnoul [of Auchinoul] (*d.* 1576), judge and legal writer, was the eldest son of Thomas Bellenden of Auchinoul (*d.* 1546), director of the king's chancery and justice clerk; his mother's name is unknown. He had two brothers, Patrick Bellenden of Evie and Stennes, and George, chantor of Glasgow; and an illegitimate half-brother, another George. He also had two sisters, Katherine (through whose marriage to the Edinburgh burgess Robert Craig he became the uncle of Thomas Craig of Riccarton) and Agnes. Through his paternal aunt Katherine, Bellenden was related to her second husband Francis Bothwell, a lord of session, and also to their son Adam Bothwell, bishop of Orkney. He himself was married thrice: first, by 22 February 1550, to Margaret (or Marion) Scott (d. c.1554), widow of George Henryson of Fordell and a lady of the household of Mary of Guise; then in 1554 to Barbara Kennedy; and finally on 14 January 1565 to Janet Seton. There were children from all three marriages, including Adam *Bellenden, who became bishop successively of Dunblane and Aberdeen, and Lewis *Bellenden, who succeeded his father as justice clerk.

It is possible that Bellenden should be identified with a determinant at the University of St Andrews in 1517 recorded as Johannes Ballantyn, though there was a licentiate with a similar name in 1512. Nothing else can be said of his education and study abroad cannot be discounted. On 17 January 1543 he was appointed director of chancery and custodian of the quarter seal. He appears on a college of justice sederunt as justice clerk as early as 16 November 1546, succeeding his father in that office. A royal letter formally mandating him as justice clerk for life was composed on 25 June 1547. By then he had the funds to lend 2000 merks to Matthew Hamilton of Mylburn for expenses in France. In December 1553 he was a commissioner for discussing good rule in the borders with English commissioners; their deliberations resulted in a new codification of border laws. Knighted by 1 April 1554, in October 1556 he received a mark of royal favour in the form of the grant to him for life of the office of clerk of coquet for Edinburgh. He was employed by Mary of Guise, the queen regent, as a mediator with the protestant lords of the congregation, but he soon joined the reformers and was said by Knox to have been one of those who fled during a French attack in Edinburgh in October 1559.

Bellenden demonstrated his legal knowledge and practical experience when in 1560 he co-authored, with the clerk register James McGill of Nether Rankeillour, a treatise called *Discours particulier d'Ecosse* (it is not known whether the treatise was originally written in French or later translated). Written at the behest of Mary of Guise for transmission to her daughter Mary, queen of Scots, and the latter's husband François II, it provided them with a brief survey of Scottish administration. An unusual work, composed to meet a special need, it places a particular emphasis on the basic laws of tenure governing the crown estates, the role of the major royal financial and judicial officers, and the law of treason, and concludes with a description of the major treason cases of the recent past. It is likely, given his experience of the subject, that Bellenden was principally responsible for the sections concerning crime and criminal jurisdiction. That experience was put to further use when in December 1560 he

undertook a judicial role within the kirk session of Edinburgh's Canongate.

Bellenden appears to have been close to the young Queen Mary on her arrival in Scotland, and in 1561 he supported her right to worship by Roman Catholic rites in her private chapel. In August that year he was sworn a member of the privy council and in December he was appointed one of the commissioners for the adjustment or 'modification' of the stipends of the reformed clergy. The queen also showed her favour by attending the marriage celebration of one of Bellenden's daughters, held near Edinburgh in October 1564. This was almost certainly the wedding of Marion to John Ramsay of Dalhousie, for which Bellenden contracted to pay a dowry of 3500 merks. The following May he succeeded in persuading the duke of Châtelherault to acquiesce in the queen's plan to marry Henry, Lord Darnley. That August a letter from Mary and Darnley was sent to Holyrood Abbey on Bellenden's behalf, ordering the immediate acknowledgement of Bellenden's appointment as heritable justiciar and bailie of the barony and regality of Broughton and the burgh of Canongate. This office was granted to him by Robert Stewart, commendator of the abbey and the queen's half-brother, for whom Bellenden had stood caution in December 1554.

Bellenden's connections with Orkney, through his aunt Katherine's third husband, Oliver Sinclair of Pitcairns, and through Bishop Adam Bothwell, did more to link him to Robert Stewart, later earl of Orkney. Having been granted the temporality of the bishopric on 22 March 1559, ahead of Bothwell's elevation, from 1560 Bellenden was in dispute with Bothwell over pensions he believed he was owed. The dispute turned violent, and in June 1562 Bothwell agreed to pay his cousin 400 merks annually, while as a final settlement in 1564 he granted Bellenden lands in Birsay. Shortly thereafter Bellenden leased them back to the bishop. Despite some later claims on Stronsay, Bellenden's main interest thereafter in Orkney was through his brother Patrick and through his connection with Robert Stewart. There is evidence of much co-operation between them in the 1560s, and Bellenden became guardian of Stewart's son Henry.

In October 1565 Bellenden was one of the cautioners for James Douglas, fourth earl of Morton, guaranteeing that he would surrender Tantallon Castle to the nominees of Mary and Darnley. His own relationship with the queen suffered, however, when in April 1566 he was suspected of complicity in the murder of David Riccio, Mary's secretary for French affairs. His brother Patrick had been present at the killing and Bellenden fled temporarily from Edinburgh, but he does not appear to have been directly involved and on 18 May was permitted to purge himself. In February 1567 depositions in regard to Darnley's murder were taken in his presence, and he acted as a witness in the process whereby the fourth earl of Bothwell divorced his wife, prior to marrying the queen. Having attended James VI's coronation on 25 July, Bellenden read the queen's commission and administered the oath of regency to the earl of Moray on 22 August. That same month he was appointed as one of a parliamentary commission to consider the proper jurisdiction of the reformed 'trew Kirk'. He also showed his loyalty to the new regime by appearing on the regent's side at the battle of Langside in May 1568.

Following Moray's murder, Bellenden was present when the fourth earl of Lennox was elected regent on 21 September 1570. His name is found in 1570 in a list of protestant notables, and in 1571 he was nominated a commissioner to meet English representatives at the border. In August 1572 he appears to have gone to France to negotiate on the regent's behalf during the siege of Edinburgh Castle, and in October he was called upon to frame an answer to the demands of the besieged 'castilians'. A year later he acted for Regent Morton in negotiating an agreement at Perth with the Huntly and Hamilton factions, ending the Hamiltons' involvement in the civil war. His protestant credentials were underlined when he was nominated by parliament to a commission set up in 1575 to 'put in forme the ecclesiastical policie and ordour of the governing of the kirk as they sall find maist aggreabill to the trewth of goddis word' (*APS*, 1567–92, 89).

Bellenden remained concerned with the borders throughout his career. In October 1573 he was appointed coadjutor and administrator to Francis Stewart, later first earl of Bothwell, as commendator of Kelso Abbey, and late in July 1574 he attended a muster of the lieges at Peebles. Maintaining his links with Orkney, he concluded an agreement with Robert Stewart on 17 September 1568, whereby he received Stewart's lands in the barony of Kerse in Lothian in exchange for his own Orkney estates; a separate agreement covered bishopric lands in Shetland in which Bellenden had an interest. When Bellenden died, on 6 October 1576, he left an estate valued at £5900 13s. 5d. Scots.   JOHN FINLAY

Sources commissary court of Edinburgh, manuscript register of testaments, NA Scot., CC8 · manuscript books of sederunt, NA Scot., CS1 · manuscript acts of the lords of council and session, NA Scot., CS6 · register of deeds, NA Scot., RD1 · R. K. Hannay, ed., *Acts of the lords of council in public affairs, 1501–1554* (1932) · *APS* · John Knox's *History of the Reformation in Scotland*, ed. W. C. Dickinson, 2 vols. (1949) · J. Anderson, ed., *Calendar of the Laing charters* (1899) · *Reg. PCS*, 1st ser., vols. 1–3 · M. Livingstone and others, eds., *Register of the privy seal of Scotland*, 7 vols. (1908–66) · A. I. Dunlop, ed., *Acta facultatis artium universitatis Sanctiandree, 1413–1588*, 2, Scottish History Society, 3rd ser., 55 (1964) · *CSP Scot., 1547–81* · *Scots peerage*, 2.63–8 · G. Donaldson, *Reformed by bishops* (1987) · M. G. Kelley, 'The Douglas earls of Angus: a study in the social and political bases of power in a Scottish family from 1389 to 1557', PhD diss., U. Edin., 1973 · T. I. Rae, *The administration of the Scottish frontier, 1513–1603* (1966) · T. van Heijnsbergen, 'The interaction between literature and history in Queen Mary's Edinburgh: the Bannatyne manuscript and its prosopographical context', *The Renaissance in Scotland: studies in literature, religion, history, and culture offered to John Durkan*, ed. A. A. MacDonald and others (1994), 183–225 · P. D. Anderson, *Robert Stewart, earl of Orkney, lord of Shetland* (1982) · NA Scot., Bellenden MSS, no. 1100 · M. Lynch, *Edinburgh and the Reformation* (1986) · P. G. B. McNeill, ed., 'Discours particulier d'Escosse, 1559/60', *Miscellany II*, ed. W. D. H. Seller, Stair Society, 35 (1984) · *Book of the Old Edinburgh Club*, 10.129
Archives NL Scot., letters and papers

Wealth at death £5900 13s. 5d. Scots—in Scotland: NA Scot., CC 8/8/6, fol. 190

Bellenden, Sir Lewis, of Auchnoll (1555×7–1591), administrator and judge, was the eldest son of Sir John *Bellenden of Auchnoul (d. 1576) and his second wife, Barbara, daughter of Sir Hugh Kennedy of Girvanmains and Dame Jane Stewart, Lady Methven. Lewis was born between 1555 and August 1557, when he and his mother were granted a charter of certain lands in the Canongate, Edinburgh. Adam *Bellenden, bishop of Dunblane and of Aberdeen, was his younger half-brother. Lewis's formal education was primarily Scottish; he matriculated at the University of St Andrews in 1571 and graduated BA 1573 and MA 1575. He also studied abroad, in a letter of procuratory dated 28 April 1575 appointing factors to administer his estate while he travelled to 'the parts of France and others beyond [the] sea for learning of virtue and good letters' (National Register of Archives for Scotland, Roxburghe Papers, item 1938).

Bellenden succeeded his father in the crown office of justice clerk on 15 March 1577 (his paternal grandfather had also been justice clerk), and was knighted shortly after August that year. He was one of the Ruthven raiders with the earl of Gowrie in August 1582, being described as one of the more 'violent' members of the group. Subsequent political intrigue brought him into the manoeuvrings of John Maitland of Thirlestane and the master of Gray against Chancellor Arran in 1585. He was also an ambassador to England at this time, and supported the cause of the earl of Angus and the other 'banished lords' against Arran. Returning to Scotland in May, Bellenden was prominently involved in Arran's downfall in November 1585. In October 1589 he accompanied James VI on his voyage to Norway to marry Anne of Denmark, and stayed with the royal couple in Denmark until the spring of 1590. He proceeded thence to England to receive Elizabeth I's wedding gifts for James and his bride and returned to Scotland in April.

Bellenden maintained his place at court primarily by virtue of his social connections, personal wealth and, as a Lothian nobleman, his proximity to the royal court. He was the last of the hereditary office-holders to be tolerated by James VI in an important administrative post. Thanks to his position as justice clerk—and probably as a means of training him for it—he was given dispensation in 1578 to attend the proceedings of the court of session, the highest civil court in Scotland, although he was still a minor. In July 1584 he became a judge ordinary of the court of session.

Bellenden controlled extensive property and financial interests in and around Edinburgh, Linlithgow, and Haddington, some of them consisting of secularized lands formerly pertaining to Holyrood Abbey and the Dominican nunnery of Sciennes. He also held lands in Orkney, Wigtownshire, Kirkcudbrightshire, Peeblesshire, and Stirlingshire, while in 1586 he acquired the barony of Ochiltree in Ayrshire. A number of his territories between Edinburgh and Leith were conjoined for him as the barony of Broughton in July 1587. He also possessed a large house in the Canongate, Edinburgh. In 1586 he purchased the Linlithgow estate of his kinsman Robert Denniston, a procurator fiscal of the Edinburgh commissary court who in May 1589 was appointed conservator of the Scottish nation at Campveere, in the Netherlands. Bellenden raised much capital in the late 1580s, some of it secured by mortgages on portions of his estate. Such resourceful financial activities enabled him simultaneously to support the career of relatives such as Denniston, promote the cause of Scottish foreign trade and other government projects, and augment his own landholdings. Bellenden was particularly well placed to exploit the system of judicial and administrative fines, penalties, and escheats, commonly called feudal casualties, that the crown sold as patronage to augment royal revenues. As justice clerk he had foreknowledge of these feudal privileges becoming available to the crown. Such rights were often given as 'gifts' by the king to crown officials, who could quickly sell them on to kinsmen and other interested parties for cash, often at a significant profit.

Raised as a protestant, Bellenden was active on behalf of the reformed church and was often an important intermediary in the religious politics of his day. In 1587 he procured the support of the clergy in appropriating the landed remains of former ecclesiastic houses to the crown. He was also a member of the parliamentary commission of 1587 to settle the 'life-rents' or salaries and pensions of the clergy. However, in striking contrast to Bellenden's relatively modest public life as a judge, courtier, and royal official, his death was the subject of lurid rumour, as preserved by the gossipy John Scot of Scotstarvit: 'By curiosity, he dealt with a warlock called Richard Graham (well known in the annals of sorcery,) to raise the devil, who having raised him in his own yard in the Canongate, he was thereby so terrified, that he took sickness and thereof died' (Scot, 131). Although this report is anecdotal, it is possible that Bellenden experimented with a form of Neoplatonism, which may have involved elements of 'diablerie'; he could have been introduced to the topic either by his kinsman Mark Ker, Lord Newbattle, who may have encountered the subject while studying at Padua, or by another kinsman, Adam Bothwell, bishop of Orkney, whose extensive library contained books related to such matters. Certainly Bellenden died unexpectedly in his early thirties on 27 August 1591, in Edinburgh, leaving a young widow and an underage son. His testament, recorded on 25 December 1591, lists residual goods and debts owed to him (primarily rentals from the estates) amounting to £2900 Scots, exclusive of the value of his lands; debts owed by him were £2293 Scots.

Bellenden was first married in February 1580 to Giselle or Geilis, a daughter of Sir James Forrester of Corstorphine, near Edinburgh; she died not long after their marriage. He married his second wife, Margaret, daughter of William, sixth Lord *Livingston, in July 1581. They had three sons, James, William, and John, and two daughters, Margaret and Anna. James succeeded to his father's estate but died young in 1606. William and John became landed proprietors in Ulster. Scotstarvit further reports that Bellenden left Margaret Livingston a very wealthy widow, but that her second husband, Patrick Stewart, second earl of Orkney, spent the greater portion of her fortune and abandoned her in the Canongate to live in poverty. She died some time after 21 March 1620.   R. R. ZULAGER

Sources NRA Scotland items, NRA Scotland, Roxburghe family muniments, 1197, 1938, 1939 · register of deeds, NA Scot., RD1/xi/262–5; RD1/xxxii/395b; RD1/xl/30b · U. Edin. L., MS La.II.2 · G. Brunton and D. Haig, *An historical account of the senators of the college of justice, from its institution in MDXXXII* (1832) · Lord Hailes, *A catalogue of the lords of session* (1794) · *CSP Scot.*, 1574–93 · J. Scot, *The staggering state of Scottish statesmen from 1550 to 1650*, ed. C. Rogers (1872) · J. M. Anderson, ed., *Early records of the University of St Andrews*, Scottish History Society, 3rd ser., 8 (1926) · E. J. Cowan, 'The darker version of the Scottish Renaissance: the Devil and Francis Stewart', *The Renaissance and Reformation in Scotland: essays in honour of Gordon Donaldson*, ed. I. B. Cowan and D. Shaw (1983), 125–40 · private information (2004) [J. Ballantyne] · Edinburgh testaments, NA Scot., CC8/8/22/192 · GEC, *Peerage*
Archives U. Edin. L., corresp. and MSS
Wealth at death £2900 Scots (excl. lands) in goods and debts owed to him; £2293 Scots in debts he owed: NA Scot., Edinburgh testaments, CC8/8/22/192

Bellenden, William (*c.*1550–1633?), political theorist, was born in Lasswade, near Edinburgh, the son of John Bellenden of Lasswade, who also held properties in Pendreich, Stirlingshire, and at St Leonards in Edinburgh. He registered himself as 'noble' on matriculating at the University of Paris in 1568 (rector's book, fol. 14v). He apparently proceeded to legal studies, as he is later heard of as an advocate in Paris. This was in the summer of 1584 when he visited James VI of Scotland, having been described the previous year as a 'Papist in Paris', employed as tutor to the son of the earl of Lennox, Lord Aubigny, that is Esmé Stewart; he also acted as negotiator for the duke of Guise. His visit to the Scottish king was an occasion when he distributed sums of money out of Queen Mary's French dowry to win support for her cause. He reported on his activities to Archbishop James Beaton of Glasgow, now King James's Paris envoy, and also to Rome, still further arousing English suspicions. His Catholic connection roused concern in the kirk, which cited Bellenden to appear before it.

At some point James decided to appoint Bellenden his master of requests, though a letter in French, which Irving saw, pointed out to the king Bellenden's awkward situation as beneficed in Scotland but living in France. In 1606 we find him, theoretically at least, attached to James's household when the king became king of Great Britain. Previous to this he was servitor to Beaton, the ambassador. In April 1603, when Beaton drew up his will, he made Bellenden an overseer for the new foundation of the Scots College at Paris. Already at that date he was master of requests in ordinary to the Scottish king. There is no doubt that Bellenden's published works would have been pleasing to the king as he adopted a radically royalist view of government. His first book may have been issued in 1606, for a manuscript only of his verses in honour of the union of the crowns of 1603 exists in the Cecil archives. The first surviving book is *Ciceronis princeps: rationes et consilia bene gerendi formandique imperii* (Paris, 1608). Like many men of the Renaissance, Bellenden was a thorough-going Ciceronian, and his experience had also made him a thorough royalist. He assiduously excerpted from Cicero's works that author's views on kingly rule, concluding that the faults of princes should be overlooked as laws were not applicable to them, the makers of laws. Virtues, however, were to be encouraged in the person of the king. His *Ciceronis consul, senator, senatusque Romanus illustratus* (Paris, 1612) is dedicated to James VI and I. Cicero is again the principal source, though Bellenden shows familiarity with other Latin authors. His *De stata prisci orbis in re politica religione et litteris* appeared in Paris in 1615 with a variant the following year. It describes a primitive harmony upset by Cain's murder of Abel, and goes on to delineate Hebrew history and that of the pagans. The latter overlooked the three grounds of state government, a single doctrine of the deity, one religion only professing this doctrine, and worship rituals to match. The second part of this publication, written in 1610, celebrated Prince Henry before his early death.

All Bellenden's works are orderly in arrangement. He could also produce Latin verse, as he did for the wedding of Charles I and the French princess Henrietta Maria, *Caroli primi et Henricae Mariae epithalamium et panegyricum carmen et elogia* (Paris, 1625). His last major work was long in preparation, and was intended to celebrate Pliny and Seneca as well as Cicero. Its title was *De tribus luminibus Romanorum libri sexdecim* (1633 and 1634), published in Paris after Bellenden's death by his priest-nephew, and dedicated to Prince Henri Bourbon, archbishop of Metz. It goes into some detail over the history of Rome, and Cicero himself does not appear until book 8. There is much learned reference to Greek literature as well as Latin. This work was much admired and much plagiarized in the eighteenth century. Samuel Parr, for instance, issued a new edition of Bellenden in 1787, and supplied three English luminaries (Burke, Fox, and Lord North) in place of Bellenden's Romans. The exact date of his death, probably in Paris, remains unknown but was probably before August 1633.   JOHN DURKAN

Sources *CSP Scot., 1581–5; 1593–5* • *Calendar of the manuscripts of the most hon. the marquis of Salisbury*, 24 vols., HMC, 9 (1883–1976), vols. 18, 24 • J. D., 'Bellenden, William', *The dictionary of seventeenth-century British philosophers*, ed. A. Pyle (2000), vol. 1, pp. 81–2 • *Liber protocollorum M. Cuthberti Simonis*, ed. J. Bain and C. Rogers, Grampian Club (1875) • *Protocol book of Gilbert Grote*, ed. W. Angus, Scottish RS (1914), no. 157 • rector's book of Paris University, Bibliothèque Nationale, MS Lat. 9955, fol. 14*v* • D. Irving, *Lives of Scotish writers*, 1 (1851), 147–57

Bellenden, William, **first Lord Bellenden of Broughton** (1604/5–1671), Treasury official, was the only son of Sir James Bellenden of Broughton (*d.* 1606) and his wife, Elizabeth Ker (*d.* 1656). He succeeded to his father's estates in 1606. Bellenden took the royalist side during the civil wars. Seeking to procure arms, ammunition, and shipping from Amsterdam in 1648, he detected among exiled English royalists the desire that the war effort could be accomplished 'without the assistance of the Scotis … that

perfidens mercenarie Nation' (Bellenden to the earl of Lanerick, 9 July 1648, National Archives of Scotland, Hamilton MS GD 406/1/2418). Following the restoration of the monarchy, he was not only made a privy councillor, but also formally appointed treasurer-depute in April 1661 and on 10 June of that year created Lord Bellenden of Broughton. Having warned the earl of Lauderdale as early as May 1661 that 'you have many enemyes heir' (*Lauderdale Papers*, 1.98), he became one of Lauderdale's most frequent correspondents during the 1660s. When the decision was taken to place the Scottish treasurership in commission in 1668, Bellenden was appointed one of the commissioners. However, acknowledging himself to be one who 'cannot doe things by halfes' (ibid., 1.260), and suffering from increasingly poor health, Bellenden was latterly regarded by Lauderdale as 'ane old fretfull man' ('Letters from John, second earl', 172). Criticized for repeatedly disrupting Treasury business by 'suearing & railing at a prodigious rate, [and] Hectoring & threatening striking' (*Lauderdale Papers*, 2.124), he eventually resigned from the commission in December 1670 and was replaced by Charles Maitland, Lord Halton, on 17 February 1671. Although he remained a privy councillor, he did not survive long thereafter, dying later that year. He was buried in St Martin-in-the-Fields, London, on 6 September 1671. He had never married. In April 1671 he had disinherited his sister Margaret, bequeathing his title and fortune instead upon his first cousin twice removed John Ker, second son of the earl of Roxburghe. This settlement was confirmed by royal charter on 12 December 1673.   CLARE JACKSON

Sources GEC, *Peerage* • *The Lauderdale papers*, ed. O. Airy, 3 vols., CS, new ser., 34, 36, 38 (1884–5) • 'Letters from John, second earl of Lauderdale, to John, second earl of Tweeddale', ed. H. M. Paton, *Miscellany … VI*, Scottish History Society, 3rd ser., 33 (1939), 111–240 • NA Scot., Hamilton MSS, GD 406/1/2418 [Bellenden to earl of Lanerick, 9 July 1648] • BL, Lauderdale MSS, Add. MSS 23116–23131 • NL Scot., Yester MSS 7003, 7023 • A. L. Murray, 'The Scottish Treasury, 1667–1708', *SHR*, 45 (1966), 89–104 • *Scots peerage*
Archives BL, letters to earl of Lauderdale, etc., Add. MSS 23116–23131 | BL, letters to Sir Edward Nicholas, Egerton MSS 2534–2536, *passim* • Buckminster Park, Grantham, corresp. with second earl of Lauderdale • NL Scot., Yester MSS

Bellerby [née Parker], **(Mary Eirene) Frances** (1899–1975), poet and novelist, was born on 29 August 1899 at St Aidan's House, Summerhill Road, St George, Bristol, the younger of the two children of Frederick Talbot Parker (*d.* 1954), Anglo-Catholic clergyman, and his wife, Marion Eirene, *née* Thomas (1868/9–1932), nurse, daughter of a Bristol solicitor and his wife. Her father was English and her mother Welsh. She was brought up in Bristol where she attended Mortimer House School, Clifton, from 1908 to 1919. She was a popular pupil, outstanding academically, and a superb athlete. In August 1915 her brother Jack was killed in action and his loss affected her all her life.

On leaving school Frances had a series of voluntary and paid jobs: veterinary assistant (she was always passionate about animals), teacher, journalist, research assistant, and parish duties. She also joined the Neighbours, a fellowship for social services founded by the economist John

Rotherford Bellerby (1896–1977) and described by her in a tract and a novel, *The Neighbours* (1931) and *Shadowy Bricks* (1932). As the sole remaining child she found her parents oppressive and was stifled by her father's religious discipline although she shared his capacity for zealous idealism in whatever she undertook.

Frances began keeping a commonplace book of readings and observations in 1925. Her first published works were a volume of essays, *Perhaps?* (1927), and a novella, *The Unspoiled* (1928). By this time she was living in London where she worked as drama critic for the *Bristol Times and Mirror*. She married John Rotherford Bellerby (1896–1977), university teacher, author, and economist, on 9 December 1929. A person who delighted in physical activities, she found it particularly hard to deal with the disabilities with which she was afflicted in adult life. In 1930 she fell and began to suffer recurrently from a spinal injury. When her mother committed suicide in 1932 Bellerby became estranged from her father, haunted by the breakup of her family. Her marriage faltered from the mid-1930s, ending in divorce about 1948, and she moved to a cottage in Cornwall in 1940.

Primarily remembered for her poetry (she wrote poems from the age of three), Bellerby published five collections in her lifetime: *Plash Mill* (1946) (named after her home in Cornwall), *The Brightening Cloud and other Poems* (1949), *The Stone Angel and the Stone Man* (1958), *The Stuttering Water and other Poems* (1970), and *The First-Known and other Poems* (1975). Two volumes of her selected poems were introduced in 1970 and 1986 by Charles Causley and Robert Gittings respectively. Bellerby's poetry has an intense, visionary quality and deals with nature, memory, and loss. This is also true of her prose. Her best-known novel, *Hath the Rain a Father?* (1946), addresses the social and psychological consequences of bereavement after the First World War, and this is the focus of a number of stories in her three collections: *Come to an End and other Stories* (1939), *The Acorn and the Cup with other Stories* (1948), and *A Breathless Child and other Stories* (1952). Her *Selected Stories* (1986) was introduced by Jeremy Hooker.

In 1950 Bellerby was diagnosed as having breast cancer and treated with operations and excruciating X-ray therapy. While her work was published in many magazines and anthologies, and she received a pension from the civil list for her services to literature in 1973, Bellerby, who was an intensely private person, became increasingly reclusive. In 1951 she moved to Devon and finally settled in Goveton, near Kingsbridge, living at Upsteps Cottage. After her father's death in 1954 she began her autobiography but abandoned it because of the pain it caused her. In 1957 she contracted arterial claudication, a circulatory disorder which made it difficult for her to walk. The cancer recurred in 1973 and she died of breast cancer and ankylosing spondylitis on 30 July 1975.

A Quaker since 1934, Bellerby instructed in her will that her body be donated to research and that her ashes be scattered near her place of death without flowers or any kind of ceremony. In her obituary Charles Causley wrote: 'The death … of Frances Bellerby … has robbed contemporary poetry of a unique and distinguished voice. To read her, is to be in the presence of a true original' (Causley).

NATHALIE BLONDEL

Sources R. Gittings, 'Biographical introduction', in *Selected poems by Frances Bellerby*, ed. A. Stevenson (1986), 9–43 [incl. bibliography] · N. Blondel, '"It goes on happening": Frances Bellerby and the Great War', *Women's fiction and the Great War*, ed. S. Raitt and T. Tate (1997), 151–73 [incl. bibliography] · priv. coll., Gittings MSS · J. Hooker, introduction, in F. Bellerby, *Selected stories* (1986), 7–12 · J. Hooker, *The poetry of place* (1982), 130–36 · private information (2004) · C. Causley, *The Times* (7 Aug 1975) · A. Born, 'Variations of light: the prose and poetry of Frances Bellerby', *Report and Transactions of the Devonshire Association*, 120 (1988), 67–79 · b. cert. · d. cert.
Archives Frances Bellerby estate, MSS · University of Exeter | NRA, priv. coll., Gittings MSS, research papers for his Bellerby work, incl. his notes and some of her MSS
Likenesses photograph, repro. in F. Bellerby, *Selected poems*, ed. A. Stevenson (1986), cover · photographs, Exeter archive?
Wealth at death £12,130: probate, 10 Oct 1975, *CGPLA Eng. & Wales*

Bellers, Fettiplace (*b.* **1687**, *d.* in or before **1750**), philosophical writer and playwright, the son of John *Bellers (1654–1725) and Frances, *née* Fettiplace (*d.* 1717), was born on 23 August 1687 in the parish of St Andrew's, Holborn. His parents were Quakers, his father being the author of several tracts, largely on the employment of the poor and on prison reform, anticipating John Howard in some aspects of the latter.

In 1732 Bellers came for the first time into public notice with the performance and subsequent printing of an anonymous tragedy titled *Injur'd Innocence*, in some measure derived from Sir William Davenant's *Unfortunate Lovers* (1649). The play was staged at the Drury Lane Theatre and appeared six times, on 3, 4, 5, 7, 8, 9 February, with the performances on the 5th and 9th being for the author's benefit. Bellers may have felt some degree of satisfaction, despite the short run of his play, as the final performance was graced by the presence of the prince and princess royal. That he was not greatly pleased at the fate of his tragedy is painfully clear from the tenor of his remarks in his preface to the printed play. There he wrote about the treatment his play received,

> For, as its short life, in the representation, had been prophesy'd, *they* [those who staged it] thought, it seems, that neither the disadvantages all tragedy must necessarily labour under from the *present state* of the *stage*, nor a want of proper *scenes*, and *dresses*, and regular *rehearsals* to mellow and perfect the *action*, were, of themselves, sufficient to prevent its success, but, in aid to all these, if the *author* is not much mis-inform'd, they did their utmost, by themselves and their emissaries, to decry it in all places where their judgments would pass.

Some ten years before he saw his tragedy performed Bellers had written the outline of a work, *Of the Ends of Society*, which appeared posthumously in 1759. There is some evidence from the archives of the Royal Society that he had withdrawn from the society on 12 April 1752, having been elected a fellow on 30 November 1711, and admitted 17 April 1712. However, there is also evidence in the advertisement to his *Delineation of Universal Law* (1750) that Bellers was dead when it was published, conflicting with the evidence from the Royal Society archives. It is not known for what reasons, in the absence of published work of any kind, he was admitted to the Royal Society as early as he was. Possibly, as with others, it was on the basis of known work in progress.

For some twenty years, from about 1730 to its publication in 1750, Bellers was engaged in what must be termed his *magnum opus*, *A Delineation of Universal Law*, which contained five books: 'Of law in general', 'Of private law', 'Of criminal law', 'Of the laws of magistracy', and 'Of the law of nations'; there was a second edition in 1754 and a third in 1759. The work has been both praised and adversely criticized, one critic deploring the extreme length of time productive of so little of commensurate value.

ARTHUR SHERBO

Sources DNB · A. H. Scouten, ed., *The London stage, 1660–1800*, pt 3: 1729–1747 (1961), 187–9

Bellers, John (1654–1725), political economist and cloth merchant, was probably born in Philpot Lane, near Gracechurch Street, London, the eldest of three children of Francis Bellers (1616–1679), merchant and Quaker, and his wife, Mary Read. His father was from Alcester, Warwickshire, and, besides accumulating substantial wealth as a merchant and trader after his migration to London in 1650, was an early and active member of the Society of Friends (or Quakers). John Bellers was raised a Quaker and remained an active member of the Society of Friends throughout his life.

Early life Apprenticed as a cloth merchant, and regularly referred to as such in early records, John Bellers began his public life and his lifelong involvement with social policy in 1680, when he was appointed treasurer of the Box Fund—an employment fund established by the six weeks meeting (the most important of the regular London Quaker committee meetings established as part of the reorganization of the sect in the 1670s). During the next fifteen years Bellers served as correspondent for Yorkshire under the auspices of the meeting for sufferings, and on the weekly second day's morning meeting, which had responsibility for the publication of Quaker writings and for collecting anti-Quaker material. His active participation in the society is also evidenced by Bellers's prosecution for riotous assembly in 1684 and again in 1685.

John Bellers married a fellow Quaker, Frances Fettiplace (d. 1717), at Cirencester meeting-house in 1686. Frances was the daughter of Giles and Mary Fettiplace, and it was through her that John became lord of the manor of Coln St Aldwyns, in Gloucestershire. John and Frances had six children, the first two while they lived in London—Fettiplace *Bellers (1687) and Mary (1689)—and the next four while they lived at The Grange, Chalfont St Peter, Buckinghamshire—Elizabeth (1690–1717), Theophila (1692), who died soon after birth, Francis (1693–1717), and Theophila (1695).

Proposals for a college of industry By 1685 Bellers's involvement with social policy had become more substantial. In that year he contributed to the purchase of 10,000 acres of land in Pennsylvania for the resettlement of French Huguenots displaced by the revocation of the edict of Nantes. But his most significant contributions came in the 1690s, and were as a result of his writing rather than his direct involvement with philanthropic enterprises. In 1695 he published his *Proposals for Raising a Colledge of Industry of All Usefull Trades and Husbandry*. And while many of his later writings are equally innovative, it is for this first piece that Bellers is best remembered. In it, he advocates the establishment of free-standing, co-operative communities in which no money would be needed and all middlemen eliminated. The pamphlet describes the college as a mixed agricultural and manufacturing settlement wherein 300 people, 200 of them labourers and craftspeople, would live and work. It would be, in Bellers's words, an 'Epitome of the World', with the addition that children would be educated and the elderly and ill looked after. Such colleges would be run in a rather paternalistic manner by people able to contribute at least £100 to the original foundation; but both in their organization and the expectation that each college should be free-standing and self-sustaining they prefigure many nineteenth-century experiments in co-operation. More than this, contained within the description of the colleges is a substantial critique of the nature of value, which had a profound impact on both Robert Owen (who had 1000 copies of the pamphlet reprinted in 1817, ensuring its continued importance for nineteenth-century writers) and Karl Marx, who refers to Bellers at least four times in *Das Kapital* and describes him as a 'veritable phenomenon in the history of political economy' (K. Marx, *Capital*, trans. B. Fowkes and D. Fernbach, 3 vols., 1976–81, 1.619). What Bellers advocated and what Marx adopted was a pure form of a labour theory of value. In Bellers's words, the college 'will make labour and not money, the standard to value all necessaries by'. More than this, in his *Proposals* he asked 'if one had a hundred thousand acres of land, and as many pounds in money, and as many cattle, without a labourer, what would the rich man be, but a labourer?' (Clarke, 54).

In part, Bellers derived his ideas from the broader English tradition of radical social criticism. The influence of mid-seventeenth-century figures such as Samuel Hartlib can be clearly discerned. But more importantly, what Bellers achieved in his *Proposals* was a dynamic fusion between a Quaker emphasis on hard work and self-reliance, and the contemporary preoccupation with the establishment of workhouses and similar institutions for the employment and housing of the poor. The intellectual context out of which Bellers's college evolved must include the work of John Cary, the Bristol merchant and political economist, whose *Essay on the State of England* (1695) contained proposals for establishing large regional workhouses, and who helped to establish the Corporation of the Poor at Bristol in 1696. It must also include the London philanthropist Thomas Firmin, whose employment scheme was such a significant feature of social policy thinking in the 1680s and 1690s, and the slightly earlier Sir Matthew Hale (1609–1676), whom Bellers quotes at length in the introduction to the second edition of the *Proposals*.

More than this, the wider European context had a signifi-cant impact on Bellers's views. He looked to the German pietist school and college at Halle, Germany, established by August Herman Francke, as one model for his own institutions.

Wider influence The 1690s witnessed a wide range of social policy experiments and a series of attempts to reform the old poor law (spearheaded by the Board of Trade). It also saw the development of the societies for the reformation of manners and the Society for Promoting Christian Knowledge (all concerned with reforming society). Bellers was both a part of this set of initiatives and an active con-tributor to contemporary thinking. The first edition of the *Proposals* was addressed to the Society of Friends, but the second edition (1696) was addressed to parliament. He also served as an assistant in the London Corporation of the Poor, re-established in 1698. And over the next thirty years Bellers regularly used his publications to popularize his ideas, and more particularly his plan for a college of industry, to a broad, non-Quaker audience.

In this, Bellers had only limited success. But he did man-age to interest the Quaker community in his scheme. The original pamphlet had been scrutinized by the second day meeting prior to publication, but it was not until 1698 that the yearly meeting in London recommended the scheme to the monthly and quarterly meetings around the coun-try. There is some evidence to suggest that the Quaker workhouse at Bristol, established in 1696, owed its origin to Bellers's pamphlet, although the Bristol experiment also shared personnel, in the character of Thomas Callow-hill, with the contemporaneous Bristol Corporation of the Poor. In 1698 the six weeks meeting in London commis-sioned a report on poverty among London Quakers which concluded that there were '184 aged people most of them capable of some work and 47 children', and that the estab-lishment of a college of industry was practical (Hitchcock, xv). After an unsuccessful attempt to obtain a private act of parliament, the six weeks meeting raised £1888, a lease was taken on half of a building in Clerkenwell, and neces-sary repairs were undertaken.

This initiative resulted in the establishment of the Quaker workhouse at Clerkenwell in 1702. The Quaker workhouse was never as radical as Bellers's vision, but it did house, clothe, and employ poor Quaker children and adults for the rest of the eighteenth century. More import-antly, and much more radically for an eighteenth-century workhouse, the institution at Clerkenwell also educated the children of wealthier Quakers, and provided house-room to elderly fee-paying residents. To the extent that the workhouse population reflected and served the whole of the Quaker community, it did go some way towards realizing Bellers's ambitions. More than this, it was recog-nized as a radical departure by other eighteenth-century commentators. John Wesley, for instance, used the oppor-tunity of a visit to the Quaker workhouse in 1744 to sound out the early Moravian activist Richard Viney's views on the practicality of establishing a 'community of goods' (Viney's diary, fol. 29).

The Quaker workhouse at Clerkenwell gradually evolved into the Friends' school at Saffron Walden, in which form it still survives. But Bellers was an active par-ticipant in the administration of the house throughout his life, and while it was never the free-standing co-operative envisaged in the 1695 *Proposals*, it did have a significant practical impact on the development of eighteenth-century social policy.

Other writings and death The *Proposals for a Colledge of Indus-try* has received the greatest attention from historians, but Bellers's other writings are equally striking. He expanded his views to consider more general issues of education, employment, and trade, as well as the treatment of crim-inals, in his *Essays about the Poor, Manufactures, Trade, Plant-ations, & Immorality* (1699). In this pamphlet he returns to the proposal for colleges of industry, but sets them in a more substantive intellectual context, and includes an argument for the absolute abolition of the death penalty. Prior to this, Quaker commentators had continued to allow the death penalty as an appropriate punishment for murder. Bellers creates a more consistent pacifist argu-ment, and in the process became the first European advoc-ate of the abolition of capital punishment, predating Cesare Beccaria (1738–1794) by some six decades.

Ten years later Bellers also published *Some Reasons for an European State, Proposed to the Powers of Europe* (1710), in which he advocates the establishment of an annual 'Con-gress, Senate, Dyet or Parliament' to settle disputes, and the creation of a 'General Council or Convocation of all the different Religious Perswasions in Christiendom, (not to dispute what they differ about, but) to settle the general principles they agree in'. In part, this was simply a reflec-tion of a broader advocacy of Quaker pacifism, and can be seen as an extension of the ideas of writers such as Wil-liam Penn, a lifelong friend and co-religionist of Bellers, whose own pamphlet *Towards the Present and Future Peace of Europe* (1693) is similarly concerned with avoiding inter-national conflict. But what sets Bellers's work apart is the direct and practical nature of his proposals, and, as with his ideas for a college of industry, his ability to put con-temporary institutions, in this case convocations and par-liaments, to new and radical uses.

The breadth of Bellers's ambitions is also evident in *An Essay towards the Improvement of Physick* (1714), in which Bel-lers advocates the creation of what can only be described as a comprehensive national health service. Local doctors were to be appointed and a series of specialist and regional hospitals created to care for the health of the poor. In itself this is not overwhelmingly radical, and in many ways simply prefigures the infirmary movement of the mid-eighteenth century. But Bellers adds to this the advocacy of a thorough reform of medicine itself, and a justification for his plans which appeals to the infirmities of the rich. Each of his hospitals was intended to provide both education and a natural laboratory for furthering of medical 'science'. Thorough autopsies, the creation of new specialisms, and the scouring of the globe for new and effective medicines were to characterize Bellers's system, while the administration was to be centralized in order to facilitate the dissemination of the discoveries which Bellers felt would flow from his new institutions.

Beyond these major proposals, Bellers also wrote a series of lesser pamphlets and broadsheets, each of which expressed a broad and impassioned concern for the poor and for the maintenance of peace. Besides writing several more pamphlets specifically about poverty, including *An Essay for Imploying the Poor to Profit* (1723) and *An Abstract of George Fox's Advice and Warning to the Magistrates of London in the Year 1657 concerning the Poor* (1724), he also wrote on education and on the conduct of elections. In his *Essay towards the Ease of Election of Members of Parliament* (1712) he proposed that alcohol and bribery be eliminated from polling for parliament. In what he would have seen as a similar vein, he also wrote extensively on religious matters, addressing both the Society of Friends and the established church.

And finally, towards the end of his life, Bellers became involved in visiting prisons and agitating for the improvement of prison conditions. One of his last published works was *An Epistle to Friends of the Yearly, Quarterly, and Monthly Meetings, concerning the Prisons, and Sick, in the Prisons and Hospitals of Great Britain* (1724). This was followed by a broadside entitled *To the Criminals in Prison* (n.d.), which he apparently distributed to inmates on his round of visits to the prisons of London.

Bellers had become a member of the Royal Society in 1718, and was a correspondent and friend of Sir Hans Sloane and William Penn. In many respects he was at the heart of a broad intellectual community which reached to the highest levels in British society, and which spanned the Atlantic. It was a community desperately concerned with the social problems of an increasingly urban and industrial society. But John Bellers was by far the most radical and innovative thinker among this group of reformers. And while historians, and to some extent his contemporaries, have tended to ignore his contributions and insights, there can be little doubt that he represents an important facet in early eighteenth-century thinking.

John Bellers died in London on 28 April 1725 as a result of a persistent internal disorder. He was buried in the Quaker burial-ground, Bunhill Fields, London.

TIM HITCHCOCK

Sources G. Clarke, ed., *John Bellers: his life, times and writings* (1987) · A. R. Fry, *John Bellers, 1654–1725 (a memoir)* (1931) · D. W. Bolam, *Unbroken community: the story of the Friends' school, Saffron Walden, 1702–1952* (1952) · W. C. Braithwaite, *The second period of Quakerism*, ed. H. J. Cadbury, 2nd edn (1961) · T. Hitchcock, ed., *Richard Hutton's complaints book: the notebook of the steward of the Quaker workhouse at Clerkenwell, 1711–1737*, London RS, 24 (1987) · diary of Richard Viney, 1744, BL, Add. MS 44935 · 'John Bellers' will', *Journal of the Friends' Historical Society*, 12 (1915), 103–8
Archives RS Friends, Lond., notes and transcripts of writings
Wealth at death see will, 'John Bellers' will'

Bellers, William (*fl.* **1752–1773**), landscape painter and engraver, was probably the son of a William Bellers (*b.* 1703?) who matriculated at the University of Oxford on 9 April 1734 as 'illuminator' and 'privilegiatus', the first epithet referring to his profession as a limner or painter. William Bellers junior is known for his engravings and paintings of landscapes, particularly those of the Lake District, which form the greater part of his work (though he also painted and etched landscapes in Birmingham, Derbyshire, Hampshire, and Sussex, as well as coastal scenes), and he was one of the most active designer–publishers of the period. He produced topographical landscapes in crayons and chalks as well as oil, and is noted to have worked in the manner of George Lambert.

Bellers contributed over sixty landscapes to the exhibitions of the Free Society of Artists between the years 1761 and 1773, several of these concentrating on the effects of sunset, moonlight, and storm. He engraved some of his own drawings and paintings, the first, *View of Derwent Water towards Borrodale*, being published in 1752 (British Museum department of prints and drawings). The publication and exhibition of his landscapes helped establish the Lake District as a principal focus for the fashionable appreciation of picturesque landscape in the later eighteenth century. The rights to the plates were sold to Robert Sayer and John Boydell about 1766 and 1769 respectively. Boydell reissued a series of eight of Bellers's scenes in 1774, having them engraved by Simon François Ravenet the elder, Johann Sebastian Müller, Jean-Baptiste Chatelain, Charles Grignion, Pierre-Charles Canot, and James Mason (a set of which is in the collection of the British Museum department of prints and drawings).

Bellers's own engravings made up only a part of his business as a printseller. He regularly advertised the sale of old-master prints and drawings in the 1750s and 1760s in periodicals such as the *Gentleman's Magazine*. In 1762 he was selling prints in London at Poppins Court, Fleet Street. It is possible that he inherited the business from William Bellers of Oxford, who dealt in prints in Oxford and Cambridge, and was supplied by Arthur Pond. Nothing is known of his marital status or education, and suggestions that he himself was a drawing master appear to be unfounded. He lived in Poppins Court from 1752 until 1773. In 1774 the land tax registers recorded that his house was unoccupied. His name does not appear on any of the burial registers of the local parishes for those years, and he is not known to have left a will.

R. E. GRAVES, *rev.* NICHOLAS GRINDLE

Sources E. Croft-Murray, 'Catalogue of British drawings in the British Museum', vol. 2, BM, department of prints and drawings · T. Clayton, *The English print, 1688–1802* (1997) · P. Bicknell, *Beauty, horror and immensity: picturesque landscape in Britain, 1750–1850* (1981) · T. Mortimer, *The universal director* (1763) · GL, MS 11316/221 · Graves, *Soc. Artists* · IGI · L. Lippincott, 'Arthur Pond's journal … 1734–1750', *Walpole Society*, 54 (1988), 220–333 · archive material, Courtauld Inst., Witt Library · K. M. Sloan, 'The teaching of non-professional artists in eighteenth-century England', 2 vols., PhD diss., U. Lond., 1986 · Foster, *Alum. Oxon.* · Waterhouse, *18c painters* · Mallalieu, *Watercolour artists* · *Anecdotes of painting in England, 1760–1795 … collected by Horace Walpole*, ed. F. W. Hilles and P. B. Daghlian (1937), 88
Archives GL, land tax assessments for city of London

Bellesmains, John. *See* Canterbury, John of (*c.*1120–1204?).

Bellew, Harold Kyrle (1855–1911), actor, the youngest son of John Chippendale Montesquieu *Bellew (1823–1874), popular preacher and public reader, and his wife, Eva Money, was born at Prescot, Lancashire, on 28 March 1855. He was educated at the Royal Grammar School, Lancaster, and, though originally intended for the army, he drifted into the navy, and for some time served on the training ship *Conway*. He left this for the merchant service, in which he remained intermittently for several years. He then spent four years in Australia, and on 26 October 1873 he married Eugénie Legrand (*b. c.*1854) in St Patrick's Cathedral, Melbourne. The following year he made his first appearance as an actor, at Solferino, New South Wales, playing Eglinton Roseleaf in T. J. Williams's farce *Turn Him Out*.

Bellew returned to England in August 1875, and almost immediately secured an engagement with Helen Barry. His English début was at the Theatre Royal, Brighton, on 30 August, as Lord Woodstock in Tom Taylor's *Lady Clancarty*, when he performed as Harold Kyrle, the name by which he was known until the end of 1878. After moving to London he made his first appearance in the capital at the Park Theatre, Camden Town, in October 1875, as Roseleaf in *Turn Him Out*, and was next engaged at the Haymarket Theatre, where he was seen in January 1876 as Paris in *Romeo and Juliet*, with Adelaide Neilson. He made his first notable success there in February 1877, when he played Belvawney in W. S. Gilbert's comedy *Engaged*. The following year he supported Adelaide Neilson as leading man in *Measure for Measure*, *Twelfth Night*, and other plays.

In December 1878 Bellew was engaged by Henry Irving for the opening of his Lyceum management, and in September 1879 he joined Marie Litton's company at the Imperial Theatre. In the next few years he achieved his greatest success in comedies, notably playing Jack Absolute in *The Rivals* and Charles Surface in *The School for Scandal*; his Orlando in *As You Like It* was widely regarded as one of his best efforts. He also toured the provinces with his own company before leaving for New York in 1885. His first appearance there was at Wallack's Theatre, as Hubert in *In his Power*, and he remained in America for the next two years, performing chiefly in old comedy parts.

After his return to London in 1887 Bellew began a long artistic association with Cora Urquhart Brown-Potter at the Gaiety Theatre. That autumn they formed a company, which toured for ten years through England, Australia, America, South Africa, and the Far East; their repertory included such plays as *Antony and Cleopatra*, *Romeo and Juliet*, *Camille*, *She Stoops to Conquer*, *As You Like It*, *La Tosca*, and *David Garrick*. Brief appearances in London during this period were made, among others, in three plays of his own composition: *Hero and Leander*, at the Shaftesbury (June 1902), *Francillon*, at the Duke of York's (September 1897), and *Charlotte Corday*.

At the termination of his partnership with Mrs Brown-Potter, Bellew performed at the Criterion (November 1898) with Charles Wyndham, in *The Jest* by Murray Carson and Louis N. Parker, but soon rejoined Irving at the Lyceum (April 1899), where he appeared as Olivier in Sardou's *Robespierre*. Later in the year he returned to Australia, and interested himself in mining ventures, which proved profitable. From January 1902, when he was once more at Wallack's Theatre, New York, until his death he was associated entirely with the American stage. His new parts, which were few, included Raffles, in the play of that name (1903), and Richard Voysin in *The Thief* (1907).

Bellew was an actor of ease and distinction, with a beautiful voice, handsome, clear-cut features, and a courtly bearing. He died of pneumonia while on tour at Salt Lake City, Utah, on 2 November 1911, and was buried in a cemetery on the Boston Post Road, New York.

J. PARKER, *rev.* NILANJANA BANERJI

Sources B. Hunt, ed., *The green room book, or, Who's who on the stage* (1906) · J. Parker, ed., *The green room book, or, Who's who on the stage* (1907–9) · D. Hines and H. P. Hanaford, *Who's who in music and drama* (1914) · W. Browne and E. de Roy Koch, eds., *Who's who on the stage, 1908* (1908) · *The Theatre*, 3rd ser., 6 (1882), 263–6 · *The Theatre*, 4th ser. 30 (1897), 308 · *M. A. P.* (13 Sept 1902) · *New York Dramatic Mirror* (8 Nov 1911) · *The Stage* (9 Nov 1911) · *New York Dramatic News* (18 Nov 1911) · M. E. Bancroft and S. Bancroft, *Recollections of sixty years* (1909) · Adams, *Drama* · C. E. Pascoe, ed., *The dramatic list*, 2nd edn (1880) · m. cert.

Likenesses portrait, *c.*1901, repro. in *Harper's Weekly*, 45 (1901), 784, 1107 · portrait, *c.*1902, repro. in *Critic*, 40 (1902), 43 · portrait, *c.*1902, repro. in *Harper's Weekly*, 46 (1902), 60 · portrait, *c.*1904, repro. in *Bookman*, 18 (1904), 467 · photograph, repro. in *The Theatre* (Nov 1882) · photograph, repro. in *The Theatre* (Dec 1897) · portrait, repro. in *New York Dramatic Mirror* · portrait, repro. in *New York Dramatic News*

Bellew, Henry Walter (1834–1892), army medical officer, born at Nusserabad in India on 30 August 1834, was the son of Captain Henry Walter Bellew of the Bengal army, assistant quartermaster-general attached to the Kabul army in the First Anglo-Afghan War and the disastrous retreat of 1842. He trained at St George's Hospital, London, and was admitted a member of the Royal College of Surgeons in 1855. He served in the Crimean War during the winter of 1854–5, and on 14 November 1855 was appointed assistant surgeon in the Bengal medical service, becoming surgeon in 1867 and deputy surgeon-general on 14 November 1881. He went to India in 1856, and was at once appointed to the corps of guides on the Punjab frontier, but was soon afterwards ordered to join Major Henry Lumsden on his mission to Kandahar, and he was serving in Afghanistan during the Indian mutiny.

Bellew rendered important services to the government by his local knowledge during the Ambela campaign, and as civil surgeon at Peshawar he became well known among the frontier peoples, whose language he spoke, and with whose manners and feelings he was familiar. In 1869 Lord Mayo employed him as interpreter with the amir, Sher Ali, during the durbar at Ambala.

In 1870 Bellew married Isabella Jane, daughter of Major R. Guthrie MacGregor of the Royal Artillery and sister of General Sir George MacGregor; they had two daughters and one son, Robert Walter Dillon, who subsequently served in the 16th lancers. Bellew's wife survived him.

In 1871 Bellew accompanied Sir Richard Pollock on a political mission to Sista, and during 1873–4 he was attached to Sir Douglas Forsyth's embassy to Kashgar and Yarkand.

In 1873 he was made CSI, and after acting as sanitary commissioner for the Punjab he was appointed chief political officer at Kabul. The cold and hardships he endured at the siege of Sherpur brought on an illness which obliged him to leave his post. He retired from the service with the rank of surgeon-general in November 1886.

Bellew belonged to the school of dedicated Anglo-Indian officials who helped to build up and consolidate the British empire in India by acquiring a thorough knowledge of indigenous customs and modes of thought. He was passionately fond of oriental studies, and possessed the ability to learn languages with great ease. His views on the history of these languages did not meet with general approval, but the numerous works he wrote and his services to ethnography, grammar, and lexicography deserve acknowledgement. As sanitary commissioner of the Punjab, in the towns and villages he explained and popularized hygienic practices and preventive medicine. As an explorer he supplied data on previously little-known regions. As a political officer on the Punjab frontier he gained the confidence of the local rulers as well as of their subjects.

Bellew's publications included *Journal of a Political Mission to Afghanistan in 1857* (1862), *A Grammar and Dictionary of the Pukkhto or Pukshto Language* (1867), *Afghanistan and the Afghans* (1879), *A New Afghan Question, or, Are the Afghans Israelites?* (1881), and *The History of Cholera in India from 1862 to 1881* (1885). Bellew died at the Chalet, Farnham Royal, Buckinghamshire, on 26 July 1892, and his body was cremated at Brookwood crematorium.

D'A. POWER, *rev.* JAMES FALKNER

Sources *Army List* · *The Times* (29 July 1892) · *Indian Lancet* (1896) · T. D., *Journal of the Royal Asiatic Society of Great Britain and Ireland* (1892), 880–84 · *Hart's Army List* · Kelly, *Handbk*
Likenesses bust, United Service Museum, Simla, India
Wealth at death £20,868 4s. 10d.: probate, 4 Oct 1892, *CGPLA Eng. & Wales*

Bellew [*formerly* Higgin], **John Chippendale Montesquieu** (1823–1874), popular preacher and public reader, was born at Lancaster on 3 August 1823. He was the only child of an infantry officer, Captain Robert Higgin (*d.* 1853) of the 12th regiment, who had married in 1822 a daughter of John Bellew of Castle Bellew, co. Galway. On attaining his majority in August 1844 he assumed his mother's family name, probably because of her distinguished descent from the O'Brien earls of Thomond.

After attending Lancaster grammar school, Higgin was entered in 1842 as a student at St Mary's Hall, Oxford. Here he gained a reputation as an effective speaker at the Oxford Union; his aptitude for oratory influenced him in the choice of a clerical career. After ordination in 1848 he was appointed to curacies at St Andrew's, Worcester (1849), and Prescot, Lancashire (1850). In 1851 he travelled to India, where he was chaplain of St John's Cathedral in Calcutta from December 1852 to 1855. During this time he wrote for the *Morning Post* and edited the *Bengal Hurkaru*. In 1855 he returned to England, and in the autumn of that year he was appointed assistant minister of St Philip's, Regent Street, London. In 1857, he became the minister of St Mark's, St John's Wood, where he remained until October 1862, when he became the incumbent of Bedford Chapel, Bloomsbury.

During the late 1850s and early 1860s, he built up a reputation as one of the most popular preachers in London, becoming as well known as Charles Spurgeon. Some of his success was no doubt due to his impressive appearance: he was nearly 6 feet tall, with an 'expansive forehead', and eyes which were described as 'very fine, large, dark, and luminous'. Perhaps the most striking feature of his physical appearance was his 'extraordinary profusion of hair', which had turned from black to iron-grey during his residence in India (Rennie, 1.287–8). Among his contemporaries, opinions on his oratory varied: an admirer, impressed by the 'singular and liquid sweetness' of his voice, was full of praise for the 'fervid earnestness of his manner' and the 'sacred tone' of his discourse (Rennie, 1.297, 306). But another commentator, although he acknowledged that Bellew was 'a master of one of the three Rs—reading', nevertheless ascribed 'no inconsiderable portion of his success to his hair, which he wears in the most melodramatic fashion' (*Cartoon Portraits*, 51). Another contemporary described his sermons rather disparagingly as 'somewhat graceful mosaics' (*Athenaeum*, 862). In private life, he seems to have been an entertaining companion, very fond of music, and devoted to children, of whom he and his wife, Eva Money, had four; one son, Harold Kyrle *Bellew (1855–1911), became an actor. A contemporary commented that Bellew had 'a disregard for conventionalities and an unaffected love of easy life, like an old French abbé, in his airy, defiant, gallant, philandering way' (ibid.). Much of his leisure time was devoted to writing: besides many of his sermons, he also published *Shakespeare's Home at New Place, Stratford-upon-Avon* (1863), a novel, *Blount Tempest* (3 vols., 1865), and an anthology of English poetry, *Poets' Corner* (1869).

In 1868, Bellew converted to Roman Catholicism, the faith of his mother, for reasons which remain obscure; on 13 August 1870 he relinquished Anglican holy orders. Subsequently he devoted most of his time to public readings, by which he often raised money for Roman Catholic charities (and possibly also his own livelihood). His readings were said to equal those of Fanny Kemble and Charles Dickens, and his performance of Thomas Hood's 'Bridge of Sighs' to rival that of Thackeray. Julia Cartwright Ady, the art historian, attended one of his readings at the pavilion in Brighton in the year of his conversion, and noted that he 'reads very well but exaggerates rather, as all those people do'. The programme included Southey's 'The Curse of Kehama' and an extract from *Nicholas Nickleby*. But the readings and the travel involved were exhausting for Bellew; two expeditions to America in rapid succession were probably responsible for his death, which took place at 16 Circus Road, St John's Wood, on 19 June 1874. He was buried at Kensal Green cemetery.

ROSEMARY MITCHELL

Sources *The Tablet* (27 June 1874), 815 · *The Athenaeum* (27 June 1874), 862 · Ward, *Men of the reign* · Boase, *Mod. Eng. biog.* · E. Rennie,

Traits of character: being twenty-five years' literary and personal recollections, 2 vols. (1860) · F. Waddy, *Cartoon portraits and biographical sketches of men of the day* (1873) · *A bright remembrance: the diaries of Julia Cartwright, 1851–1924*, ed. A. Emanuel (1989) · *CGPLA Eng. & Wales* (1875)

Archives NL Scot., letters to William Blackwood & Sons · Shakespeare Birthplace Trust RO, Stratford upon Avon, letters to E. F. Flower and Samuel Phelps · U. Edin. L., corresp. with James Halliwell Phillipps

Likenesses Mayall, carte-de-visite, *c*.1860, NPG · R. W. Thrupp, carte-de-visite, *c*.1860, NPG · F. Waddy, mechanically reproduced caricature, 1872–3, repro. in F. Waddy, *Cartoon portraits and biographical sketches of men of the day* (1873), following p. 50 · D. J. Pound, line engraving (after photograph), BM; repro. in D. J. Pound, *The drawing room portrait gallery of eminent persons* (1859) · Southwell Bros., carte-de-visite, NPG · woodcut, NPG

Wealth at death under £450: probate, 30 Nov 1875, *CGPLA Eng. & Wales*

Bellewe [Bellew], **Richard** (*fl.* 1575–1585), compiler of legal cases, supposedly of Irish origin, was entered at Lincoln's Inn in London on 5 June 1575, and its arms appear in one of his books. Nothing more apart from his printed works is now known. In 1578 he published in Norman French *Ascun Nouel Cases*, a collection of law cases from the reigns of Henry VIII, Edward VI, and Queen Mary, familiarly known as *Brooke's New Cases*, *Little Brooke*, or *Bellewe's Cases tempore Henry VIII*. The work had six more editions by 1625. The cases were selected from Sir Robert Brooke's *La graunde abridgement* (1573) and arranged chronologically. Bellewe was the editor and compiler of this rare volume, though probably not the author of the summaries. A more usable edition of 1651, translated into English by John March, rearranged the collection alphabetically under subject headings.

In 1585 Bellewe brought out *Les ans du Roy Richard le Second*, a further compendium of cases taken from the abridgements of Statham, Fitzherbert, and Brooke, and now sometimes referred to as *Bellewe's Cases tempore Richard II*. William Dugdale in *Origines juridiciales* (1666) describes this latter volume as 'the Year-book of Richard II', implying by his citation of this volume alone that it was the sole legal authority then extant for the reign. A dedication of the new collection to the 'Benchers, Vtterbarresters and Students of Lincolnes Inne' claims that the 'good liking' shown the earlier work provoked Bellewe to produce a second volume, this time with the cases arranged alphabetically by subject matter rather than by year. It too is written in French. The rarity of *Brooke's New Cases* and of March's translation occasioned the reprinting of both books under one cover in 1873.

CHARLES R. FORKER

Sources D. M. Walker, *Oxford companion to law* (1980) · Allibone, *Dict.* · W. Dugdale, *Origines juridiciales, or, Historical memorials of the English laws* (1666) · *DNB* · *STC, 1475–1640* · W. P. Baildon, ed., *The records of the Honorable Society of Lincoln's Inn: admissions*, 1 (1896)

Bellin, Samuel (1799–1893), printmaker and draughtsman, was born at Doctors' Commons, London, on 13 May 1799, the son of John Bellin, of Burnt House in Chigwell, Essex. His earliest training was under the Huguenot engraver James Basire the younger (1769–1822), and

between 1828 and 1834 he completed his artistic education in Rome. There he mixed with young artists such as J. M. W. Turner and Frederick Catherwood and was loosely associated with the studio of the Danish sculptor Bertel Thorvaldsen (1768–1844). While in Rome he concentrated on making copies of many notable old master paintings and, according to *The Athenaeum*, displayed 'a wonderful facility for rapid and accurate drawings' (*The Athenaeum*, 6 May 1893, 579). During this stay he also made preliminary pencil drawings for his *Panoramic View of Rome* (1835), which, engraved on three plates, is an early example of his lifelong preference for large-scale work. This panoramic engraving does, however, differ from the majority of Bellin's œuvre, as it was one of the few prints he executed after his own drawing.

On his return to London, in 1834, Bellin began as a line engraver and specialized in reproducing the paintings of many of the leading artists of the day. These included Holman Hunt, Frederick Stone, and Charles Eastlake, whose *Aged Friars* (1851), issued in various proof states and priced between 3 and 10 guineas, illustrates Bellin's typical publishing strategy. He quickly extended his range to include mezzotint portrait prints, such as *The Late John Rickman Esq.* (1843), after S. Lane, or *Henry Phillpotts, Bishop of Exeter* (1867), which are notable for their effective combination of tonal mezzotint with additional line or stipple engraving. Bellin was chiefly acclaimed for his sophisticated mezzotint reproductions of sentimental genre scenes, such as Sarah Setchel's *The Momentous Question* (n.d.) or Charles Lucy's *Cromwell at Hampton Court* (1866); often these originals were described as 'much improved in the process of translation' (*The Athenaeum*, 6 May 1893, 579). Although he did occasionally exhibit plates at the Royal Academy and Suffolk Street, Bellin was probably best known for his illustrations in the *Art Union* periodical and his many reproductive engravings published by Agnew, Lloyd Brothers, or Graves & Co.

Throughout a long and prolific career Bellin earned respect both as an artist and as a man of charity and compassion, especially towards more unfortunate artists. Indeed, from his earliest days in Rome he was evidently a sociable man who enjoyed the benefits of participating in the artistic community. Accordingly he was one of the first members of the Graphic Society, an artists' conversazione established in 1833, where he played an active part in the meetings held at University College, Gower Street, and contributed work to many of the monthly exhibitions. He also developed close friendships with Sir Edwin Landseer, C. R. Leslie, and other leading artists whose work he reproduced.

After retiring around 1870 Bellin moved from Camden Town, an area where many engravers lived and worked, to the more genteel setting of Regent's Park Road. After having lived a quiet and abstemious life he died at home, on 29 April 1893, at the age of nearly ninety-four. A representative selection of his work is held in the Victoria and Albert Museum.

LUCY PELTZ

Sources J. Agnew, *Report on the records of the Graphic Society in the custody of the Royal Academy of Arts*, HMC (1974) · *The Athenaeum* (6

May 1893), 579 • Boase, *Mod. Eng. biog.* • Bryan, *Painters* (1903–5) • R. K. Engen, *Dictionary of Victorian engravers, print publishers and their works* (1979) • Graves, *Artists* • Graves, *RA exhibitors* • Graves, *Soc. Artists* • *The Times* (27 Jan 1894), 10 • J. Turner, ed., *The dictionary of art*, 34 vols. (1996) • *Catalogue of engravings registered by the Printsellers' Association, from its establishment in 1847 to 1863 inclusive* [1865]

Wealth at death £57,190 7*s*. 2*d*.: probate, 15 June 1893, *CGPLA Eng. & Wales*

Belling, Charles Reginald (1884–1965), electrical engineer and manufacturer, was born on 11 May 1884 at Fore Street, Bodmin, Cornwall, the son of Samuel Thomas Belling, a dentist, and his wife, Maria, *née* Harry. Charles Belling, known to all as C. R. B., was educated at Burts Grammar School, Lostwithiel, and at Crossley School, Halifax. He attended technical college at Derby and Chelmsford. From 1903 to 1906 he was apprenticed to Crompton & Co. Ltd, of Chelmsford, remaining on their staff until 1909, when he joined Ediswan Electric Company Ltd, of Ponders End, Hertfordshire, to supervise the production of arc lamps, auto-transformers, and Bastian electric heaters. By 1912 Belling felt he had enough experience to set up on his own as a manufacturer of electric heaters. With just £150 of his own capital and £300 from two colleagues, Belling took on a local boy and a fitter from Ediswans and began equipping a small shed in Lancaster Road, Enfield, ready to begin work on a firebar that would revolutionize electric fire design. Rather than adapt the workings of the Bastian heater, which consisted of a resistance spiral inside a quartz tube, Belling hit on the idea of winding a resistance wire on the front face of a strip of fireclay, which would allow the wire to work at high temperatures and the heat to be thrown forwards. On the back of this success, Belling began to develop a new electric geyser which could deliver instant boiling water at a rate of 3 pints a minute. He clearly anticipated the declining need for coal in the home, and with full order books, a move to larger premises was now essential. During the summer of 1913, just one year after taking the plunge, Belling moved to Derby Road, Edmonton, and set about producing his second brochure devoted exclusively to a range of about a dozen fires.

Profits from Belling's first balance sheet of £3500 on sales of £11,000 must have come to the attention of the Admiralty, for, when war was declared and Lloyd George announced that it was 'business as usual', Belling was called on to switch production to heating and cooking equipment for submarines as well as supplying ovens for canteens. The war not only provided Belling with increased turnover and profits, but also offered the opportunity to buy out his two partners, who were no longer able to commit themselves to the firm. This freed Belling to oversee a period of expansion and diversification that continued virtually unchecked until 1939. The inter-war years saw the company establish itself as one of the leading suppliers of electrical appliances to the British domestic market. The year 1919 saw the introduction of the first modern cooker—the Modernette—followed by the first imitation coal fire and the forerunner of a range of Baby Belling cookers that were to grace countless bedsits over the following decades. By 1924, soaring sales persuaded Belling to buy a 10 acre site at Enfield, and in 1935 he formed the private limited company of Belling & Co. Ltd, because he had 'got a bit sick of paying super tax on works extensions, etc.' On the eve of war, the Enfield site accommodated 500 workers engaged in producing cookers and 50,000 fire units a year.

The Second World War again saw Belling & Co. shift production to wartime requirements. Flexibility and innovation allowed emphasis to be placed on the manufacture of hand and rifle grenades, trench mortar sights, and fuel jettison tanks. This ability to confront new challenges stood the company in good stead in the boom years following the war as the high price of competitive fuels and the Clean Air Act saw the swing towards electricity gain momentum.

Belling married, on 19 March 1946, Cicely Edith (*b*. 1906), daughter of William Ernest Williams, a railway goods manager. There were no children. By 1955, Belling again found he was short on factory space and he decided to buy a new 30 acre site at Burnley and to move all fire production there, leaving the Enfield works free to concentrate on the production of all types of cookers. By the time of Belling's death in 1965, the company owned 70 acres of freehold property and over 1 million square feet of production space, and had some 3500 workers on its payroll. Belling was immensely proud that he had built up the business entirely out of profits, and that the firm was able to remain a private company. In spite of insisting that all employees had the right to decide whether or not to become a member of a trade union, relations with the thirteen unions represented in the two factories were generally cordial. This is partly explained by the pension fund and profit-sharing schemes Belling had introduced, which were a major factor in securing the loyalty of the workforce. The royal warrant received by the company in 1962 (its golden jubilee year) was for Belling the highest seal of approval anyone could bestow.

Yet, in spite of buoyant sales, Belling remained acutely aware of the shortage of qualified technical staff who had the capability of converting original ideas into practical applications. He had long pioneered the idea of technical training colleges, a move designed primarily to prevent other countries 'exploiting our brains'. In his will, Belling set aside £1 million for a technical school to be built on the 60 acres lying to the side of Owls Hall Farm, his home in Enfield, in the hope of bridging the deep divide between pure research and its shop floor application. That said, Belling's autocratic style and his propensity to promote from within ultimately stifled the company's chances of further development after his death.

Charles Belling died on board the *Empress of England* on 8 February 1965 while cruising in the Bahamas. He left the bulk of his estate, worth over £2.5 million, to his wife. His cousin, Richard Eric Belling, who had been groomed as the future director of the company, was the other main beneficiary.   Barbara Trompeter

Sources G. Jukes, ed., *The story of Belling, 1912–1962* (1962) • trade literature, Sci. Mus., 1912, 1935 • b. cert. • m. cert. • d. cert.

Likenesses bronze bust, 1962; last known at Bridge Works, Enfield · bronze bust, 1962; last known at Burnley Works, Lancashire
Wealth at death £2,845,459: probate, 22 March 1965, *CGPLA Eng. & Wales*

Bellinger, Francis (d. 1721), physician, was educated at Brasenose College, Oxford. He was admitted a licentiate of the Royal College of Physicians, London, on 29 March 1708, practising first at Stamford, Lincolnshire, and afterwards in London. He was an original member of the Spalding Society on its establishment in 1712. He was the author of *A discourse concerning the nutrition of the foetus … with an appendix … on the food of children newly born, and the management of the milk of women* (1717) and *A treatise concerning the small-pox* (1721). He died in September 1721.

[ANON.], *rev.* PATRICK WALLIS

Sources Foster, *Alum. Oxon.* · Munk, *Roll* · Nichols, *Lit. anecdotes*, 6.29, 71 · P. J. Wallis and R. V. Wallis, *Eighteenth century medics*, 2nd edn (1988)

Bellingham, Sir Edward (d. 1550), lord deputy of Ireland, was the eldest son of Edward Bellingham, a gentleman of Erringham in Sussex, and Jane, daughter of John Shelley of Michelgrove in the same county. Raised in the household of the duke of Norfolk, Bellingham served in Hungary with Sir Thomas Seymour, and with the earl of Surrey at Boulogne. While lieutenant of the Isle of Wight in 1545, he was instrumental in repelling the French attack on the island. He was a member of parliament for Gatton in 1544 and a member of the privy council of Edward VI. In June 1547 he was dispatched to Ireland to serve as captain-general, with overall military command. At Waterford he joined forces with Lord Deputy St Leger and they proceeded to invade Leix (Laois) and Offaly and proclaimed the Gaelic lords O'More and O'Connor to be traitors. Bellingham was subsequently knighted and promoted marshal of Ireland.

In October 1547 Bellingham was granted leave to repair to England. In December Sir William Brabazon, with Bellingham's connivance, mounted an attack on St Leger's governance as a result of which the privy council recalled St Leger. On 22 April 1548 Bellingham was appointed lord deputy of Ireland. The following day he was appointed a commissioner of the prerogative court and of the court of wards. He served as lord deputy from 21 May 1548 to 29 December 1549. His immediate concern upon his arrival in 1548 was the prosecution of a war against MacGillapatrick O'More and Brian O'Connor and their followers in Leix and Offaly. He led a hosting into O'More's country and established Fort Protector. He also decimated MacCoughlan's lordship. He was responsible for the construction of fortresses at Dangan and Ballyadams in Offaly and Leix, and he stationed a garrison at Leighlin Bridge in co. Carlow in order to exercise control over the Kavanaghs. He was the first deputy to organize a defence system for the midlands which radiated outwards from the two fortresses in Leix and Offaly, connecting them with a string of lesser forts at Nenagh and Athlone. He divided the three lordships of the Kavanaghs, O'Byrnes, and O'Tooles into three administrative districts which were to be under the surveillance of English seneschals backed by bands of soldiers. By late 1549 he had laid the basis of a fortified frontier around the expanded pale.

Bellingham also effectively exercised his authority as deputy beyond the midlands. When in December 1548 the earl of Desmond refused to comply with Bellingham's summons to appear in Dublin, the deputy travelled to Desmond's castle and escorted him to Dublin where he formally pardoned the earl. In June 1549 he summoned the earl of Tyrone and several other lords of Ulster to Dublin to settle disputes in the province. Similarly he arbitrated in cases concerning the Burkes of Clanricarde and others. He established a mint in Dublin Castle, though it was short-lived, and he is credited with having placed purveyance on a more regular footing. He enjoyed extended vice-regal powers, being entrusted with specific responsibility for implementing the government's religious policy, and he was zealous in his pursuit of religious conformity. With the demise of his patron, Protector Somerset, Bellingham was recalled and departed for England on 16 December 1549. He was in poor health and died in England the following year.

Traditionally portrayed as bellicose and ruthless, Bellingham is now regarded as a great deal more lenient and accommodating in his dealings with recalcitrant Gaelic lords than he pretended to be. Continuities are identified between his policies and those of St Leger. Attention is also drawn to his reputation among the pale population as one of the most generous and unexacting governors of the century. Stanihurst described him as 'a man very well learned, grave and wise … stout and valiant … [who] did very worthily direct his government … magnanimous and courageous … feared for his severity, and beloved for his integrity' (*Holinshed's Chronicles*, 6.323–4).

MARY ANN LYONS

Sources PRO, state papers, Ireland, Edward VI, SP 61 · *CSP Ire.*, 1509–73 · *Holinshed's chronicles of England, Scotland and Ireland*, ed. H. Ellis, 6 (1808) · R. Cox, *Hibernia Anglicana, or, The history of Ireland from the conquest thereof by the English to the present time*, 1 (1689) · C. Brady, *The chief governors: the rise and fall of reform government in Tudor Ireland, 1536–1588* (1994) · C. Lennon, *Sixteenth-century Ireland: the incomplete conquest* (1994) · S. G. Ellis, *Ireland in the age of the Tudors* (1998) · J. Morrin, *Calendar of the patent and close rolls of chancery in Ireland, of the reigns of Henry VIII, Edward VI, Mary, and Elizabeth*, 1 (1861) · R. Lascelles, ed., *Liber munerum publicorum Hiberniae … or, The establishments of Ireland*, 2 vols. [1824–30], pt 2 · J. L. J. Hughes, ed., *Patentee officers in Ireland, 1173–1826, including high sheriffs, 1661–1684 and 1761–1816*, IMC (1960) · J. Haydn, *The book of dignities: containing rolls of the official personages of the British empire* (1851) · T. W. Moody and others, eds., *A new history of Ireland*, 10 vols. (1976–96), vols. 3, 9 · B. Bradshaw, *The Irish constitutional revolution of the sixteenth century* (1979) · J. T. Gilbert, R. M. Gilbert, and J. F. Weldrick, eds., *Calendar of the ancient records of Dublin*, 18 vols. (1889–1922), vol. 1 · visitation of Westmorland, BL, Harleian MS 1435
Archives NL Ire., corresp. [microfilm] | BL, visitation of Westmorland, Harleian MS 1435 · PRO, state papers, Ireland, Edward VI, corresp. relating to his term of office in Ireland, SP 61

Bellingham, John (1770–1812), assassin, was born in St Neots in Huntingdonshire, the younger child and only son of a London land surveyor and miniature painter and his wife, Elizabeth Searbrow, of St Neots gentry stock. His

John Bellingham (1770–1812), by Denis Dighton, pubd 1812

father became mentally ill in 1779, and died a year later. At fourteen Bellingham was apprenticed to a Whitechapel jeweller but proved 'perverse and troublesome' and eventually ran away. In 1787 he sailed as a subaltern on a merchantman that was wrecked.

In 1793 Bellingham established himself as a tradesman in Oxford Street but was gazetted bankrupt in 1794. Later he became a commercial agent, and in 1804 was arrested for debt in Archangel. He accused the local authorities of improper detention and made repeated appeals for help to the British consul and ambassador. They did not act, since the case was one for the Russian authorities alone. Finally released in October 1809, he returned to England, determined to gain redress.

After Bellingham's return from Russia he married Mary-Anne, daughter of John Neville, a Dublin merchant. The pair settled in Liverpool; Bellingham practised as an insurance broker and his wife as a milliner. They had two children. Preoccupied with efforts to gain redress from the British government, however, Bellingham abandoned his family and moved to London.

Persistent calls for justice were unavailing and, exasperated by his lack of success, Bellingham decided upon the extreme course of assassinating the prime minister, Spencer Perceval—a crime carried out, with pistols, coolly and

deliberately, in the lobby of the House of Commons on 11 May 1812. Tried on 15 May, he was found guilty of murder and executed three days later in London. Before, during, and after the trial Bellingham remained calm and collected, showing no signs of fear or remorse. He felt fully justified in acting as he did, asserting that true blame attached to those who had refused to listen to his grievances.   MICHAEL J. TURNER, rev.

Sources D. Wilson, *The substance of a conversation with John Bellingham* (1812) · *The trial of John Bellingham* (1812) · *The Times* (12 May 1812) · *The Times* (13 May 1812) · *The Times* (16 May 1812) · *The Times* (18 May 1812) · *The Times* (19 May 1812) · D. Gray, *Spencer Perceval: the evangelical prime minister, 1762–1812* (1963)
Archives BL, corresp. and papers, Add. MS 48216
Likenesses D. Dighton, etching, pubd 1812, NPG [*see illus.*]

Bellingham, Richard (1591/2–1672), colonial governor, was the son of William Bellingham, esquire (*c*.1555–1620), of Bromby Woods, Lincolnshire, and Frances Amcotts. He matriculated, aged seventeen, from Brasenose College, Oxford, on 1 December 1609, but did not proceed to any degree, and entered Lincoln's Inn in 1612. By 1622 he had married Elizabeth (*d.* in or before 1641), daughter of Samuel Backhouse of London, and by 1628 they were residing at Boston, Lincolnshire, where they had children buried in 1628 and 1629; a son, Samuel, was their only child who lived to marry. Bellingham was serving as recorder of Boston at the time of his children's deaths. John Cotton was at the height of his ministerial fame at Boston when Bellingham arrived there, and so Bellingham's decision to sail for New England in 1634 was undoubtedly influenced by Cotton's migration the year before.

Within a year of his arrival in New England, Bellingham was elected deputy governor of Massachusetts Bay Colony, and held high office every year thereafter. He served as assistant in 1636–9 and 1642–52; treasurer in 1637; deputy governor in 1640, 1653, and 1655–65; and governor in 1641, 1654, and 1665–72. He also held several offices at county and town level. After the death of his first wife, on 9 November 1641 Bellingham married Penelope Pelham (*d.* 1702), sister of Herbert Pelham, who had arrived in New England just two years earlier. (As a magistrate, Bellingham took the highly unusual step of officiating at his own wedding.) They had seven children, only one of whom lived to adulthood. Bellingham resided in Rowley for a few years in the 1640s and early 1650s, although he certainly would have maintained a residence in Boston, where he would have spent a substantial part of the year fulfilling the duties of colonial office. In 1667 or 1668 he fell from a boat in the Charles River, and was rescued by Angola, a free black man. Bellingham rewarded Angola with a grant of 30 acres of land.

Bellingham died in office as governor at Boston, aged eighty-one, on 7 December 1672, at which time Samuel Sewall noted that he was the last patentee, that is, the last survivor in New England of those who had obtained the charter for the Massachusetts Bay Company. His estate was one of the largest probated in New England by that date, totalling £3244 3s. 7d., of which £2864 was real estate at Boston and Winnisimmett. Bellingham was survived by his wife and their son Samuel, and Samuel's daughter, who was not expected to marry. For this reason he bequeathed most of his estate as an endowment for various Congregational ministers. John Winthrop portrayed Bellingham as a very contentious man, indicating that Bellingham and Richard Saltonstall frequently found themselves in a minority of two, at odds with the rest of the Massachusetts Bay magistrates. Bellingham tended to side with the lower house of the legislature, which did not appeal to Winthrop's more elitist leanings. A competent and respected leader, Bellingham was never out of colonial office over a span of nearly four decades.

ROBERT CHARLES ANDERSON

Sources R. C. Anderson, G. F. Sanborn, and M. L. Sanborn, eds., *The great migration: immigrants to New England, 1634–1635*, 1 (Boston, MA, 1999) · M. L. Sanborn, 'Angola and Elizabeth: an African family in the Massachusetts Bay Colony', *New England Quarterly*, 72 (1999), 119–29 · R. E. Wall jun., *Massachusetts Bay: the crucial decade, 1640–1650* (1972) · Foster, *Alum. Oxon.* · S. Freeman, *The probate directory, or, An assistant to probate courts, executors, administrators, and guardians*, 2nd edn (1803), vol. 9, pp. 303–5
Wealth at death £3244 3s. 7d.: 20 Dec 1692, inventory, S. Freeman, *The probate directory, or, An assistant to probate courts, executors, administrators, and guardians*, 2nd edn (1803), vol. 9, pp. 303–5

Bellings, Richard (*c.*1603–1677), politician and historian, was the eldest son of Sir Henry Bellings, landowner, of Kilessin, and his wife, Maud. The Bellings were an established Old English family with extensive landholdings, estimated in the 1660s to amount to almost 5000 acres, in counties Dublin, Wicklow, and Kildare. His grandfather Richard Bellings was solicitor-general of Ireland from 1576 to 1584, while his father served as sheriff of co. Kildare in 1616 and 1618, and in 1628 acted as Viscount Falkland's emissary to England, defending his stewardship as lord deputy. During this time Sir Henry earned a formidable reputation for rapacity and unscrupulous behaviour. He was credited with the execution of over eighty rebels in 1618 alone, and in 1633 he was subjected to proceedings in the Star Chamber and a fine of £2000 for collusion in a fraudulent trial.

Sir Henry Bellings conformed to the state church but his wife remained a Catholic. Richard Bellings subsequently adhered to his mother's religion, although his education at Lincoln's Inn, to which he was admitted on 4 September 1619 after previous education in a Dublin grammar school, suggests that during his early years he may have followed his father in conforming. While a student in London, Bellings became an accomplished poet and wrote his best-known poetic work, the sixth book to the *Arcadia* of Sir Philip Sidney; it was published in Dublin in 1624 and was incorporated into many subsequent editions of the *New Arcadia*. In July 1631 he married Margaret (*c.*1609–1635), daughter of Richard Butler, Viscount Mountgarret, and Margaret, daughter of Hugh O'Neill, second earl of Tyrone. They had four children: Richard, Henry, Mary, and Joan. Margaret died in August 1635.

During the 1630s Richard Bellings found that, as a Catholic, he was debarred from the type of office-holding that he and other members of the Old English community saw as commensurate with their wealth and social eminence.

The burgeoning crisis in the three Stuart kingdoms after 1640 ultimately opened the door to a political career of great importance. In March 1641 Bellings was elected to the House of Commons of the Irish parliament as MP for the borough of Callan, probably owing to the influence of the earl of Ormond, with whom he had developed a personal friendship, and to whom he was related by marriage. His parliamentary career was short. Following the rebellion of 1641 he was appointed by the Commons to the commission to treat with the Ulster rebels in November. However, Old English participation in the rebellion exercised a gravitational pull on Bellings. He was probably present at the stage-managed meeting between the lords of the pale and the Ulster rebels at the hill of Crofty which resulted in an overt union between the two groups. His father-in-law's assumption of leadership of the Catholic community in arms in south Leinster and east Munster towards the end of 1641 also inevitably exerted an influence on Bellings. He may in fact have acted as commander of a Catholic force which attempted to take the Boyle stronghold, Lismore, some time before Christmas 1641 and on 22 June 1642 he, together with forty other Catholic MPs, was expelled from the House of Commons and was indicted for rebellion.

Bellings co-operated closely with Nicholas Preston, Viscount Gormanston, the *de facto* leader of the pale lords in rebellion, and was a central figure in the establishment of the confederate Catholic association in the summer and autumn of that year. He occupied the important post of secretary to the supreme council of the confederate Catholics from the association's foundation until his departure from Ireland at the beginning of 1645 as ambassador to various continental powers. He resumed this position on his return to Ireland in October 1645 until the declaration of the first Ormond peace in August 1646 and was secretary of the association again in 1648–9.

Bellings was at the heart of the dominant clique in confederate politics, which included the confederate president, his father-in-law, Mountgarret, and other prominent members of a Butler network of influence such as Donough McCarthy, Viscount Muskerry, the earl of Castlehaven, and Gerald Fennell, which organized the first confederate–royalist truce in September 1643. It was he who undertook to provide the papal representative, Pierfrancesco Scarampi, with a detailed memorandum attempting to modify his opposition to the cessation of hostilities. This document, with its litany of Catholic woes prior to 1641, remains interesting not only in itself but also as a useful counterpoint to the markedly different analysis of these years which Bellings later produced in his great historical narrative. From 1643 he was an active supporter of attempts to negotiate a peace which would allow for the dissolution of the confederate association and the re-establishment of royal government. Bellings's interest in this regard was substantially influenced by the growing importance of his friend James Butler, earl (and later marquess and duke) of Ormond, who was appointed lord lieutenant of Ireland in November 1643, and who was to emerge as the principal royalist negotiator with the confederates. Even in his official correspondence with Ormond, Bellings sometimes allowed a personal note to intrude on his observations, although he was evidently not quite so reliable a source of internal information on confederate affairs for the lord lieutenant as Fennell.

In 1644 Bellings was awarded the freedom of Waterford city and on 1 January 1645 he sailed from Galway as a confederate ambassador, heading first to Paris. He then proceeded to Italy, hearing in Florence of the appointment of a papal nuncio to Ireland. Bellings was deeply shocked and anxious at this news as his brief had been to solicit money and arms, not enhanced papal representation in Ireland which might be expected to make the conclusion of the peace negotiations more difficult. Neither in Genoa, nor Florence nor Venice did Bellings acquire any substantial assistance for the confederate cause and although the pope did offer about £12,500 this was given into the sole custody of the nuncio, Giovanni Battista Rinuccini. Bellings returned to Paris with Rinuccini where a lesser sum for the assistance of the confederates was also entrusted to the nuncio and the two men returned to Ireland from La Rochelle, narrowly avoiding capture by a protestant privateer in the process. Blown west of Waterford, the party finally made landfall in Kenmare in October 1645. Bellings returned to Kilkenny and was responsible for the organization of the unsatisfactory (in Rinuccini's eyes) ceremonial reception of the nuncio by the confederate government. Already the nuncio had conceived a distrust of Bellings and this blossomed over the course of the next year into a passionate and mutual animosity.

The first Ormond peace, secretly signed on 28 March 1646, was strongly supported by Bellings. Its delayed publication in August opened the prospect of the restoration of his personal estates, which were mostly situated outside confederate quarters, but the opposition of Rinuccini and the national synod of clergy swiftly overturned the settlement. Bellings was imprisoned and was probably exposed to some danger of summary execution. The failure of the clerical-inspired offensive on Dublin, however, witnessed a change in confederate policy and he was released from captivity and attended the first general assembly of 1647. His masterly description of this assembly in his later history of the confederate era is one of the highlights of that compelling narrative but so highly slanted as to render it very untrustworthy. Bellings and others were personally exonerated of perjury of the confederate oath in this assembly but to his intense disappointment the clerical rejection of the Ormond peace itself was endorsed. Bellings never reconciled himself to this decision and in the course of 1647 was prepared to plot secretly against the new confederate executive in an attempt to keep Ormond from leaving Ireland.

The catastrophic confederate defeats at Dungan's Hill in August and Knocknanuss in November 1647 created a new political scenario and at the second assembly of that year Bellings returned to the supreme council in the teeth of Rinuccini's passionate opposition. He was a strong supporter of the Inchiquin truce of May 1648 and supported the winning side in the subsequent confederate civil war. This victory ushered in the second Ormond peace, of January 1649, which Bellings fervently welcomed, and he was an important element of the royalist coalition which opposed Cromwell in 1649.

In 1650 Bellings fled to the continent and lived in Paris for most of the 1650s under the pseudonym Kingston. He published two pamphlets in Paris in 1652 and 1654 defending himself against accusations by Nicholas French and John Punch of betrayal of the Catholic cause. In 1655 he travelled to Poland with Viscount Muskerry but was back in Paris by November 1656. He accompanied Ormond on part of his secret journey to England two years later and was included in Charles II's declaration of 1660. In December 1661 he was involved in the drafting of the 'loyal formulary' or 'remonstrance' which declared that spiritual allegiance to Rome did not compromise a Catholic's temporal loyalty to kings, who were declared to be God's lieutenants on earth. This failed to gain the support of the majority of the Irish clergy and was condemned by the Vatican. Bellings was restored to 4500 acres of land as a result of the Act of Settlement of 1662 and the following year he travelled to Rome in a failed attempt to achieve an acceptable solution to the intractable problem of the dual loyalty of Irish Catholics. In the 1660s his eldest son, Richard, was knighted and appointed secretary and master of requests to Queen Catherine.

During the 1670s Bellings composed a history of the confederate era which both exonerated his party in the controversies of the 1640s and offered itself as a commentary on the similar developments occurring in the early 1670s. Although it must be approached with great caution, it remains a source of central importance for this period. In addition it establishes Bellings as one of the greatest prose stylists in English of seventeenth-century Ireland: indeed with some justice he could be considered in this regard as the Irish Gibbon. The history was not published during his lifetime.

Bellings was a man of great intellectual gifts, ably discharging a wide variety of tasks. His religious affiliation, however, restricted the parameters of his activity for most of his career. The exception was the 1640s, and his political importance during this period has recently been recognized. His literary output, on the other hand, remains unjustly neglected. In terms of personality, he evidently had a certain talent for making enemies as well as important friends: Rinuccini cordially detested him, as did Thomas Preston, the confederate general, and he took full revenge on both in his history. Despite the resigned and philosophical note which pervades this text, he evidently nurtured these animosities until the end of his life. He died in September 1677 at Crehelpe in co. Wicklow, and was buried the same month in Mulhuddart, co. Dublin.

TADHG Ó HANNRACHÁIN

Sources *History of the Irish confederation and the war in Ireland … by Richard Bellings*, ed. J. T. Gilbert, 7 vols. (1882–91) • B. O'Ferrall and D. O'Connell, *Commentarius Rinuccinianus de sedis apostolicae legatione ad foederatos Hiberniae Catholicos per annos 1645–1649*, ed. J. Kavanagh, 6 vols., IMC (1932–49), vol. 1, pp. 302, 304, 426, 498, 502, 660,

680–83, 697–705, 718–21, 732; vol. 2, pp. 139, 228, 259, 268, 281, 307, 341, 357, 389, 403, 605, 633, 782, 801, 803; vol. 3, pp. 146, 170, 210, 300; vol. 4, pp. 16, 20, 160 • B. McGrath, 'A biographical dictionary of the membership of the Irish House of Commons, 1640–41', 2 vols., PhD diss., TCD, 1997, vol. 1, pp. 63–4 • R. Gillespie, 'The social thought of Richard Bellings', *Kingdoms in crisis: Ireland in the 1640s, essays in honour of Dónal Cregan*, ed. M. Ó Siochrú (2001), 212–28 • M. Ó Siochrú, *Confederate Ireland, 1642–1649: a constitutional and political analysis* (Dublin, 1999), 12, 49, 65–7, 103, 106, 116, 126–35, 153, 164, 169, 181, 194, 203, 219–20, 266 • [J. Lodge], ed., *Desiderata curiosa Hibernica*, 2 (1772), 151–479 • Bodl. Oxf., MSS Carte, 17, fols. 15r–16v, 440v; 18, fol. 176r • B. McGrath, 'Parliament men and the confederate association', *Kingdoms in crisis: Ireland in the 1640s, essays in honour of Dónal Cregan*, ed. M. Ó Siochrú (2001), 102 • J. Morrin, ed., *Calendar of the patent and close rolls of chancery in Ireland*, 3 vols. (1861–3), vol. 3, pp. 647–8 • *CSP Ire.*, 1615–25, 127, 246; 1633–47, 26–31; 1666–9, 126 • J. Lodge, *The peerage of Ireland*, rev. M. Archdall, rev. edn, 7 vols. (1789), vol. 1, p. 180; vol. 4, p. 67 • S. H. Bindon, *The historical works of the Right Reverend Nicholas French* (1846), vol. 2, p. 103 • *The whole works of Sir James Ware concerning Ireland*, ed. and trans. W. Harris, rev. edn, 2 (1764), 165 • Biblioteca Apostolica Vaticana, Vatican City, MS Barberini Lat. 8626 • [T. Carte], *The life of James, duke of Ormond*, new edn, 6 vols. (1851), vol. 6, pp. 526–9 • G. Aiazzi, *The embassy in Ireland of Monsignor G. B. Rinuccini*, trans. A. Hutton (1873), 251–2, 348–9 • [U. de Burgh, earl of Clanricarde], *Letter-book of the Earl of Clanricarde, 1643–47*, ed. J. Lowe, IMC (1983), 76–9, 120–28, 133, 146 • D. Cregan, 'The confederate Catholics in Ireland: the personnel of the confederation, 1642–49', *Irish Historical Studies*, 29 (1994–5), 507, 510–12 • D. F. Cregan, 'Irish Catholic admissions to the English inns of court, 1558–1625', *Irish Jurist*, 5 (1970), 110 • J. Ohlmeyer, 'Irish recusant lawyers during the reign of Charles I', *Kingdoms in crisis: Ireland in the 1640s, essays in honour of Dónal Cregan*, ed. M. Ó Siochrú (2001), 79, 80

Archives BL, imperfect copies of his *History of the late warre in Ireland*, Add. MSS 4763, 4819 • TCD, MS 747

Bellman, Sir (Charles) Harold (1886–1963),

building society manager, was born in Paddington on 16 February 1886, the second son of Charles Henry Bellman, coach-builder, and his wife, Ellen Clemens, both of Cornish origin. After attending a higher-grade school in Kilburn until the age of fourteen he entered the Railway Clearing House near Euston in 1900. An early and lasting cultural influence was Wesleyan Methodism. He also, as a young man, served with the 3rd County of London imperial yeomanry. Bellman's talent for organization became apparent during the First World War, when he served as principal assistant in the establishment department of the Ministry of Munitions.

In 1918, having formed a friendship with Gilbert Lane, secretary of the Abbey Road and St John's Wood Permanent Building Society, he was invited to join its board of management. When Lane died in 1921, Bellman succeeded him as secretary. When Bellman joined the society it was little known outside the borough of Paddington in which it was situated. Bellman studied minutely every aspect of the work—the processes of borrowing and lending, the duties of clerks, cashiers, and surveyors—and made many innovations and improvements. He appointed agents and pioneered a policy of opening branches. He overhauled the publicity, wrote the prospectus himself, and advertised in the national press. Home-ownership through thrift became for him a conviction.

The inter-war years witnessed both rising incomes and a

Sir (Charles) Harold Bellman (1886–1963), by Lafayette, 1929

continuing shortage of houses to let, and these conditions led to the growth of the building society movement. There was a strong flow of funds into building societies, not least the Abbey Road. Its assets, which in 1919 were £750,000, rose to £8 million in eight years, and advances rose from about £150,000 to over £3 million.

During these years the board was strengthened by new directors. Sir Josiah Stamp (1880–1941) became president in 1926, and Bellman took great trouble to make the annual meeting a memorable occasion, inviting a prominent person, usually a cabinet minister, to be the chief speaker. In 1932 the society's new building in Baker Street, with its lofty belled tower, was opened by the prime minister, James Ramsay MacDonald. In 1944 the society merged with the National Society to form the Abbey National, with assets of £80 million and Bellman as chairman and joint managing director. After four years he gave up his executive post, but he remained chairman until his death.

Bellman's activities were not confined to his own society. As early as 1922 he formed the Metropolitan Building Societies Association, composed of some fifty societies, and became its first honorary secretary, then its chairman. In 1923 he was elected to the council of the central organization, the National Association of Building Societies; from 1933 to 1936 he served as its chairman, in succession to Sir Enoch Hill (1865–1942). In 1934 the Building Societies Institute for training building society staff was founded, with Bellman as the first president. From 1934 until 1938 Bellman was president of the International

Union of Building Societies and presided with great distinction over two conferences: at Salzburg in 1935 and at Zürich in 1938. By this time, influence in the building society movement had become worldwide; he was especially highly regarded in the USA.

The years in which Bellman served as chairman of the National Association were stormy: he tried to secure the co-operation of the 374 societies for the common purpose of adopting a new code of ethics and procedure, but was frustrated by the old-established societies. In consequence, those societies assenting to the new code dissolved the National Association in 1936 and formed the new Building Societies Association. Bellman remained its chairman for another year. Some fifty societies, however, splintered off and founded their own national organization. The split was healed only in 1940 after public anxiety about alleged irregularity by a Yorkshire society in the 'borders' case' had led to the passing of the Building Societies Act of 1939. This embodied in the main the code of ethics and procedure which the dissenting societies had rejected and which all societies now had to accept. The Building Societies Association then became the authoritative voice of the whole movement. Although Bellman retired from the chair in 1937 he remained on the council until 1956, when he was made a vice-president.

Bellman had a dignified presence and perfect articulation. He had first learned to speak in the Sunday school and the guild attached to the Wesleyan chapel in Fernhead Road, Paddington, which he claimed had been the strongest influence in his life as a boy. In 1911 Bellman married Kate, daughter of Edwin George Peacock, of Brondesbury Park. They had been at school together, but it was their common interest in the choir and the social life of the chapel which ripened their friendship. When she died in 1959 Bellman presented a window to the new Fernhead Road Chapel in her memory. They had two sons and a daughter.

In addition to his chapel activities, Bellman undertook a wide range of public duties, serving as chairman of Clayesmore, the boys', and Queenswood, the girls', public schools. He was chairman and treasurer of the National Children's Home, chairman of several hospitals, and a member of the Ministry of Health's Central Housing Advisory Committee and of numerous departmental committees. He was president of the Aldwych Club (1935-6) and of the Advertising Association (1939); and as a member of the court of governors of the London School of Economics took a special interest in its department of business management. He was chairman of the Hampstead and Marylebone bench of magistrates and a vice-lieutenant of Middlesex. In the war of 1939-45 he served as a major in 22nd Middlesex battalion Home Guard. He wrote some dozen books—four of which became standard works in the building society world: *The Building Society Movement* (1927), *The Silent Revolution* (1928), *The Thrifty Three Millions* (1935), and *Bricks and Mortals* (1949). He was appointed MBE in 1920 and knighted in 1932. He was a chevalier of the Légion d'honneur, an officer of the Australian order

of merit, and an honorary LLD of the American University, Washington (1939).

Gardening was Bellman's chief relaxation; he cultivated azaleas and prize-winning roses and chrysanthemums. He died at Guy's Hospital, London, on 1 June 1963.

GEOFFREY SHAKESPEARE, rev. ROBERT BROWN

Sources H. Bellman, *Cornish cockney* (1947) · H. Bellman, *The thrifty three millions: a study of the building society movement and the story of the Abbey Road Society* (1935) · E. J. Cleary, 'Bellman, Sir Charles Harold', *DBB* · E. J. Cleary, *The building society movement* (1965) · S. J. Price, *Building societies: their origin and history* [1958] · *The Times* (3 June 1963) · *WWW* · H. Bellman, *Bricks and mortals: a study of the building society movement and a study of the Abbey National Society* (1949) · E. C. L. Butler, *The Building Societies Institute, 1934-1978* (1980) · J. Brace, 'A statistical analysis of building societies', *Journal of the Royal Statistical Society*, 94 (1931) · d. cert.
Likenesses Lafayette, photograph, 1929, NPG [*see illus.*] · J. Gunn, portrait, Abbey National Building Society, Baker Street, London
Wealth at death £67,351 11s. 0d.: probate, 2 Aug 1963, *CGPLA Eng. & Wales*

Bello, Sir Ahmadu [*formerly* Ahmadu Rabah], **sardauna of Sokoto** (**1910–1966**), premier of Northern Nigeria, was born at Rabah, a small riverain town upstream of Sokoto, one of ten half-brothers and fifteen half-sisters born to his father, Ibrahim Rabah, the district head. Both parents were Sokoto Fulani, though his maternal grandmother was a daughter of Ibrahim Dabo, emir of Kano (r. 1819-46). His paternal grandfather was Abubakar Atiku, the seventh sultan of Sokoto (r. 1873-7). 'Sardauna', the title by which he was later universally known and which he preferred to all others awarded him, was one of the senior traditional Fulani titles in Sokoto, restricted to scions of the ruling family. It glosses as 'captain of the royal bodyguard'.

Ahmadu Rabah, as he was then known, learned Arabic and the Koran from a local religious *malam* or teacher. Aged ten, he was sent to the Sokoto provincial school and in 1926 to the Katsina Training College. The college, opened only in 1922, was designed to enable emirate Muslim students to observe their religious principles and upbringing while at the same time learning to become teachers in the new English-language based secondary schools. The college was to become 'the Eton of the North', and so influential were its alumni that when the first cabinet of Northern Nigeria was formed in 1951, nearly every minister was an old Katsina College boy. A prefect and a hard-working student, Ahmadu was also a keen cricketer and captained the college team at Eton fives, introduced by one of the first British tutors at the college, S. J. Hogben. In later years he was invited to play fives at Eton College; in return he hosted the Eton fives team in Nigeria. During his premiership he was frequently to be found enjoying fives with members of the northern politico-administrative élite, urging his cabinet to play also—'quick exercise for stiff Ministers', he would explain.

On finishing at Katsina College in 1931 Ahmadu was appointed to the new Sokoto middle school, teaching English and geometry and being in charge of games. In 1934 he was, at only twenty-four, turbanned district head of

Rabah. There were still no schools in the outlying districts, so, in addition to tax-collecting and encouraging agricultural improvements, Ahmadu spent his spare time teaching local children. To keep up his English in a town where no other Nigerian spoke it, he borrowed the *Illustrated London News* from a district officer who used to visit Rabah on tour.

Promotion in the Sokoto native administration (local government) came in 1938 when Ahmadu was posted to the boom town of Gusau, on the new railway line from Zaria, to supervise the work of a dozen subordinate district heads. He was appointed to the sultan's council and given the title sardauna. He became involved in 'war work', including grain purchases, recruitment of labour, and organizing patrols on the frontier with Dahomey. Intrigue played its part, too, but following his conviction for tax embezzlement he appealed to the supreme court and was acquitted. He did not return to Gusau but became the sultan's councillor for police and prisons.

Unlike his political peers Obafemi Awolowo and Nnamdi Azikiwe, the sardauna was essentially a native administration man. He had no higher education or professional training. It was not until 1948 that he travelled outside Nigeria, to England on a British Council study tour of local government, and only in 1949 did he visit the Nigerian capital, Lagos. With party politics imploding on Nigeria following the 1946 constitution, the sardauna was elected a member for Sokoto in 1949. He became president of the literary society turned political party, the Northern Peoples Congress (NPC), and after the 1951 election he was appointed minister of works for the north. He soon added community development and the powerful portfolio of local government. Under the 1954 federal constitution he became premier of the Northern Region. Again unlike his regional counterparts, he never sought to move to Lagos, content to leave the prime ministership to his NPC vice-president, Abubakar Tafawa Balewa. Significantly, he publicly referred to Tafawa Balewa as 'my able lieutenant'.

Fortunately for the north, its political leadership was in strong and safe hands during the critical years from 1951 to 1960. Determined that the region—larger than the west and east together in population and land—should play its full role in the federal government despite its backwardness in Western education, the sardauna rejected the southern politicians' motion of 1953 in the house of representatives that Nigeria should become self-governing in 1956, and substituted the words 'as soon as practicable' (*Debates of the House of Representatives*, 31 March 1953, 985 ff.), meaning when the north was ready to assume its role in the manning and management of the federation. To this end, the sardauna instituted a vigorous programme of northernization of the regional bureaucracy, with priority of appointment going first to a northerner, then, if none was available, to a European on contract, and only finally to a Nigerian from the other regions. This policy was implemented through crash programmes to train northerners for the civil service, in which the Institute of Administration at Zaria (called 'my baby' by the sardauna)

was the region's flagship. Northernization did not endear the sardauna to the south, nor did his threat to secede unless the north was given what he saw as its fair share and proper place. Because of his impeccably aristocratic (his great-grandfather was Shehu Usman dan Fodio, founder of the Sokoto empire *c*.1810) and religious (he traced his lineage to the Prophet Muhammad) pedigree, he was able to carry the traditional northern rulers with him in his change-within-continuity reforms. He remained premier of the Northern Region after Nigerian independence in 1960, keeping a vigilant eye on the national policies formulated in Lagos.

The sardauna was appointed CBE in 1953. Advanced to KBE in 1959, he took the name of his revered ancestor Sultan Bello. His memoir, *My Life*, appeared in 1962. Though ghosted, it represents a major statement. In 1963 he became the founding chancellor of Ahmadu Bello University. He had married Hafsatu (1920–1966) of Sokoto, daughter of the waziri, Abdulkadir Macido, in 1932. They had no children but the sardauna was survived by three daughters born to his fourth wife, Amina, whom he married in 1940. In 1934 he had also married Kande and then Amiru. Both were divorced in 1938. He married Jabbo in 1952. Despite not bearing him any children, Hafsatu remained his senior wife throughout.

A giant in every sense and an aristocrat in every way, 'distinguished in appearance and conspicuously well dressed in the many-coloured splendour of the Northern robes' (*DNB*), the sardauna held centre stage. With the ready vanity of a prima donna and a thunderous temper as quick to deflate as to erupt, he was no sufferer of fools. 'They say that I am proud and impatient', he wrote. 'Who would not be, with all the responsibilities that have been placed upon me?' (Bello, 238). Yet laughter, friendship, and generosity came easily to him. As leader of the NPC, he enjoyed huge popularity in the north. A devout Muslim who frequently undertook the pilgrimage to Mecca, his personal leadership of the Islamic conversion campaign among northern animists nevertheless did not win him uncritical support, even from the clerics. He had the gift of portraying himself as the northern culture-hero, rich in allusion to the history of his ancestors in establishing the Fulani empire and ever ready with a Hausa proverb or allegory. In the military coup of 15 January 1966 the sardauna and his wife Hafsatu were murdered: they were shot at State House. He was buried at the sultan's house in Unguwar Sarki, Kaduna. For many in the south, his assassination was the symbolic elimination of the feared northern political domination.

Death spared the sardauna the need for any decision over when to retire from party politics and compete for the sultanship of Sokoto, for which both his ancestry and his achievements rendered him pre-eminently eligible. In 1968 the award of grand commander of the federal republic of Nigeria (GCON) was posthumously conferred. On his success in creating Northern Nigeria there is no dissent: without his strong and unifying leadership in the 1950s, there would have been no such polity. On his contribution to Nigerian unity, debate continues. To understand the sardauna, it is not possible to isolate his activities and attitudes from the mood of his time and the whole context of 150 years of Nigerian history. His legacy remains a palpable one.   A. H. M. KIRK-GREENE

Sources personal knowledge (2004) · *DNB* · A. Bello, *My life* (1962) · J. N. Paden, *Ahmadu Bello: sardauna of Sokoto: values and leadership in Nigeria* (1986) · C. S. Whitaker, *The politics of tradition: continuity and change in Northern Nigeria, 1846–1966* (1970) · C. S. Whitaker, 'Three perspectives on hierarchy: political thought and political leadership in Northern Nigeria', *Journal of Commonwealth Political Studies*, 3 (1965), 1–19 · R. L. Sklar, *Nigerian political parties: power in an emergent African nation* (1963) · B. Sharwood Smith, *'But always as friends': Northern Nigeria and the Cameroons, 1931–1957* (1969) · G. Bell, *An imperial twilight* (1989) · B. J. Dudley, *Parties and politics in Northern Nigeria* (1968) · A. T. Clark, *A right honourable gentleman* (1991) · L. S. Adamu, *Hafsatu Ahmadu Bello* (1995) · A. H. M. Kirk-Greene, 'His eternity, his eccentricity, or his exemplarity? A further contribution to H. E. the African head of state', *African Affairs*, 90 (1991), 163–87 · A. H. M. Kirk-Greene, *Mutumin Kirkii: the concept of the good man in Hausa* (1974)

Archives FILM IWM FVA, documentary footage |SOUND Nigeria Broadcasting Company, Kaduna, Nigeria

Likenesses photograph, 1959, Hult. Arch. · M. Fiévet, portrait, *c*.1960 · photographs, ministry of information, Lagos, Nigeria · photographs, ministry of information, Kaduna, Nigeria · photographs, repro. in Bello, *My life* · portrait, Lugard Hall (Legislative Building), Kaduna · publicity hand mirror, priv. coll.

Belloc, (Joseph) Hilaire Pierre René (1870–1953), poet and author, was born on 27 July 1870 at La Celle St Cloud, near Paris, the younger child of Louis Marie Belloc (1830–1872), barrister, and his wife, Elizabeth Rayner (Bessie) *Parkes (1829–1925), daughter of Joseph *Parkes, a prosperous solicitor from Birmingham, and his wife, Eliza. Louis Belloc was French (although with Irish blood from his maternal grandfather, Armand Swanton); his father Hilaire was a well-known portrait painter. Bessie's family was both wealthy and cultivated—her father founded the Reform Club—and she grew up among eminent Victorians. She became a Roman Catholic as a young woman and Cardinal Manning was among her friends.

Hilaire Belloc was born just before the outbreak of the Franco-Prussian war; a few weeks later the family retreated to England, having taken the last train out of Paris. When the Bellocs returned to the family home after the war they found that it had been wrecked and pillaged by Prussian soldiers. Belloc would have been too young to remember this episode, but accounts of it would have fuelled his lifelong prejudice against all things German. When he was only two years old his father died, and Bessie Belloc and her two children (the older, Marie, became the well-known novelist Mrs Belloc *Lowndes) moved to London. She had inherited enough family money to be comfortably off, but lost most of it when she entrusted it to an incompetent stockbroker. Thereafter the family were never far from genteel poverty, though Belloc did not realize this for several years; the loss of what he liked to think of as a considerable fortune was a cause of enduring resentment. The Bellocs then settled at Slindon in Sussex, a county he came to love and celebrate in his writings. He spent holidays in France and throughout his life preserved a sense of Anglo-French identity. He grew up to be a prolific and respected English writer but his French origins

(Joseph) Hilaire Pierre René Belloc (1870–1953), by Emil Otto Hoppé, 1915

gave him an unusual and sometimes disconcerting view of English life and society.

Education and early career Belloc attended the Oratory School, Birmingham, between 1880 and 1887; it had been founded by John Henry Newman and the aged cardinal occasionally appeared before the boys, but Belloc had no high regard for him. After he left school his characteristic energy and restlessness made it hard for him to settle to a career; in succession he attempted to train for the French navy, to become a farmer, and then a draughtsman. In 1891 he travelled across the United States, walking much of the time, financing himself by making drawings and selling them. He was bound for California on a romantic mission to see Elodie Agnes Hogan (1868–1914), an Irish-American girl he had met and with whom he had fallen in love when she was visiting London with her mother and sisters the previous year. The journey was inconclusive, though they eventually married. Belloc spent most of 1892 doing his military service in the French army as an artilleryman; this was necessary if he wished to retain French nationality, though a few years later he opted to become a British subject. It was a severe but highly formative experience, which gave him a lifelong interest in military matters. It also made him aware that he was by now more of an Englishman than a Frenchman; he was known to his comrades as 'l'Anglais' and later wrote, 'I had come into the regiment faulty in my grammar and doubtful in accent, ignorant especially of those things which in every civilization are taken for granted but never explained in full' (*Hills and the Sea*, 1930, 89). The experience is said to have left his spoken French with soldierly turns of phrase which could be an embarrassment on formal occasions.

After he returned from France, Belloc was admitted to Balliol College, Oxford, with the financial support of his sister and her fiancé. Belloc loved Oxford, and particularly Balliol, as he later recalled in one of his best-known poems, 'To the Balliol Men Still in Africa'. He became a star performer in debates at the Oxford Union and was awarded a first in modern history in 1895. After he graduated he applied for a prize fellowship at All Souls College, which would have given him a financially secure niche in Oxford—without any teaching duties—for the next few years, while becoming established in an academic or legal career. He was over-optimistic about his chances in the highly competitive examination, and he was not successful; his aggressive and argumentative demeanour had already made him enemies in the small world of the university. He took this disappointment very hard, and thereafter lost no opportunity to mock and ridicule 'dons' and 'pedants', just as the loss of family money lay behind his attacks on the 'rich', though he enjoyed the company of rich people and was always ready to cultivate them.

Early publications and marriage   For a while Belloc hung on in Oxford, making money by tutoring and giving extension lectures, while unsuccessfully applying for academic posts. He was also launching himself as a writer, and it was in this early phase of his career that, beginning with *The Bad Child's Book of Beasts* in 1896, he started to produce the comic and satirical verse which for many readers is the best-known and most enjoyable part of his *œuvre*. In the same year he published *Sonnets and Verse*, a collection of sonnets and lyrical poems which are classical in form but romantic in spirit, and are at their best when they are most compressed and epigrammatic. Henceforth he made his living by his pen, and as a man of immense energy, versatile talents, and wide reading, he worked in many genres. *Danton* (1899) was the first of a long series of studies in French and English history.

For five years Belloc had corresponded with Elodie Hogan, and he had never doubted his love for her, which took the form of what his biographer A. N. Wilson has called 'a chivalric ardour' (Wilson, 67). Elodie, a very devout (and painfully scrupulous) Catholic, was unsure whether to marry or to become a nun; eventually she entered a convent to try out the religious life, but the experiment showed that she was not suited to it. Belloc crossed the Atlantic again and married Elodie at Napa, California, in June 1896. It was to be a happy marriage, but Belloc, restless and constantly needing money to support his growing family, was often away from home on lecture tours which took him all over England, with occasional trips to the United States. There were, too, the walking holidays, alone or with male companions, which provided material for books and essays. In 1897 Elodie gave birth to a son, Louis, the first of their five children.

Belloc eventually realized that he would never get a college fellowship in Oxford, and in 1899 the family moved to London, to a rented house at 104 Cheyne Walk, Chelsea. In 1900 he met G. K. *Chesterton whom he strongly influenced. Belloc's literary career was taking off, though finances were always precarious, and he began producing a stream of books and articles. His energy was prodigious; he had a sharp, dogmatic intelligence, and there were few subjects on which he did not have strong opinions. In 1902 he published *The Path to Rome*, which remains one of his most attractive and popular books; it tells the story of the author's solitary walk—in effect a personal pilgrimage—from Toul in Lorraine, where he had done his military service, to Rome. It is full of entertaining reflections about the people he met and Sternean digressions on whatever came into his mind on the journey. It also shows his capacity to convey physical experience vividly, as, for instance, in the account of crossing the Alps, when he was lost in a snowstorm. Belloc wrote many other books in this vein of reflective pedestrianism, describing journeys through France and England and further afield. *The Four Men: a Farrago* (1912) is one of the best of them, a semi-fictional account of a walk through Sussex with three invented companions. Pedestrianism came into Belloc's many historical studies; he was particularly interested in military history, and before writing about a battle he liked to traverse the battlefield on foot. In 1904 he published *Emmanuel Burden*, the first of a series of satirical novels about Edwardian political and social life (some of them illustrated by Chesterton).

A public personality and Catholic apologist   In the Edwardian era Belloc acquired a public literary personality: a lover of wine and beer, of songs and male companionship, of walking and sailing, who was at home on both sides of the channel. J. B. Morton wrote, 'His wit was French but his humour English. … He was profoundly moved by the beauty of the English landscape, but preferred the French way of living' (Morton, 3–4). In 1906 Belloc and his family left London for Sussex, where he had bought King's Land, a rambling brick house in Shipley, near Horsham (parts of it dating from the fourteenth century); it was his home for the rest of his life, though his constant journeying meant that he was seldom there for long at a time.

Most famously, Belloc became known as a polemical apologist for the Roman Catholic church, which he regarded as the only source of sanity and order in the world. He was an important influence on the small Roman Catholic community in England, giving them a new self-confidence, insisting that though they might seem to be a vulnerable minority in an offshore protestant island they were really part of the universal church with its centre in Rome. Although Roman Catholicism was central to Belloc's life and his writings, these reflect little of the serenity and hope of faith. His religion was a disciplined matter of the will and the intelligence, but his subjective stance to the world was a sad, stoic acceptance of the blows of fate, more pagan than Christian in spirit. It informs some of his best writing, such as the reflections on exile and death at the end of *The Four Men*, and much of his poetry. The epigram 'The False Heart' is characteristic:

I said to Heart, 'How goes it?' Heart replied:
'Right as a Ribstone Pippin!' But it lied.

Liberal MP In 1906 Belloc entered politics as Liberal MP for South Salford, placing himself on the radical wing of the party. It was to be an unsatisfactory and disillusioning experience, for he was never at ease with the practice and assumptions of the British parliamentary system and turned sharply against it after he left the House of Commons in 1910. He was outraged by the Marconi scandal of 1913, in which members of the Liberal government, including David Lloyd George, chancellor of the exchequer, were accused of improper trading in the shares of the Marconi Company. It was a complex business, never fully resolved, but Belloc had no doubt of the ministers' guilt. In 1911 he founded a weekly journal, the *Eye Witness* (later the *New Witness*) in collaboration with Cecil Chesterton, G. K.'s younger brother, a fierce crusading journalist whose temperament and beliefs were akin to his own. Following an imprudent article on the Marconi affair in the *New Witness* Cecil Chesterton appeared in court charged with criminal libel, was found guilty, and fined. This episode deepened Belloc's bitterness.

Belloc believed that true democracy was feasible only in small communities such as the Greek city state or the Swiss canton, and that in large modern societies it inevitably degenerated into oligarchy. He had originally described himself as a republican and, despite his Catholicism, supported the ideals of the French Revolution; later he shifted towards a belief in absolute monarchy, or, in effect, dictatorship, as he expounded in *The House of Commons and Monarchy* (1920). In 1912 he published a critique of modern society, *The Servile State*, which attacks both capitalism and socialism. His thesis is that modern civilization combines notional political freedom with economic slavery, since most people possess little or no property, and property is essential for both freedom and well-being. He opposed recent legislation imposing employers' liability and compulsory national insurance, since it reinforced a society divided by status, where the proletariat are essentially dispossessed. Belloc's ideal was a society of peasant proprietors or craftsmen, negotiating with each other by free contract, where property is widely distributed and not concentrated in a few hands. *The Servile State* is forceful and lucid though repetitive, and its ideas were later developed in the distributist movement in which Belloc and G. K. Chesterton were active in the 1920s.

Wife's death, the war, and post-war publications Belloc was shattered when Elodie died (probably of cancer) early in 1914. He treasured her memory for the rest of his life, turning her room at King's Land into a shrine which was never opened, and always wearing black. J. B. Morton recalled him thus:

> The black clothes, black tie and old-fashioned, stiff, stick-up collar made him look like the Frenchman of my boyhood. But the ruddy complexion and the broad, square shoulders and massive body gave him the look of an English farmer. (Morton, 26)

The outbreak of the First World War strengthened Belloc's attachment to France, a Catholic nation at the heart of civilization in conflict with protestant Germany, or 'Prussia', as he liked to call it; he regarded the Catholic south Germans and Austrians as at best misguided, at worst renegades. During the war he was much in demand as a commentator on military affairs, and this work temporarily restored his finances. But his grief over Elodie was extended when his eldest son, Louis, an airman, was reported missing in action and was later confirmed as dead; a further blow was the death of Cecil Chesterton in December 1918 from an illness contracted on active service.

Belloc entered the post-war period 'an unhappy and a disappointed man', in Morton's words (Morton, 118); to his existing resentments were added disgust with public affairs and sorrow at personal losses. Two books from the 1920s develop some of his basic ideas. *Europe and the Faith* (1920) sets out a mythologized reading of European history: true civilization has been preserved by the Latin Catholic nations as the legacy of Rome, with France the senior partner; Belloc is hostile to the protestant nations and ignores the Orthodox ones. The Roman Catholic church has continued and transformed the Roman empire; he argues 'that the Catholic Church which accepted it in its maturity caused it to survive, and was, in that origin of Europe, and has since remained, the soul of our Western civilization' (p. 163). England, which Belloc loved, was a special case; it had been a province of the empire but was lost to the barbarians; then it was redeemed by a thousand years of communion with Christian Rome. *Europe and the Faith* is a work of personal myth-making, written with passion and energy, rather than of accurate historiography.

In *The Jews* (1922) Belloc argues that the Jews are an essentially alien people who cannot be successfully assimilated in Christian societies; he refers to the Jews with respect and even admiration and denies that he is antisemitic. There is no doubt, though, that that was the case, as is evident from his novels and references in his essays and verse. He rejects any suggestion of persecuting or expelling the Jews and proposes that they should be recognized as a special community, with the rights and responsibilities of resident foreigners; this is, in effect, an extension of the ancient institution of the ghetto. Despite its conciliatory tone, the book is offensive as well as unconvincing; it reflects not just personal prejudice but Belloc's adherence to the attitudes of the French right, evident in his lifelong belief in the guilt of Dreyfus. The deepest cause of his antisemitism seems to have been the ancient Christian hostility to the Jews as deicides.

Belloc's qualities as a writer are much more happily expressed in two other books of the 1920s. *The Cruise of the 'Nona'* (1925) is in the relaxed, digressive vein of travel writing first evident in *The Path to Rome*. It recalls a voyage which he made round the coast of England in his small boat on the eve of war in 1914. *Belinda* (1928) is a romantic novella subtitled 'A Tale of Affection in Youth and Age'; it has a fairy-tale setting in early Victorian England and is written in a sparkling pastiche of the minor fiction of the period. It possesses a delicate charm and tenderness, and is quite unlike most of his writing.

Last years In his final years Belloc was a public figure with many friends and admirers, in the Catholic world and outside it; in his personal life, though, he was lonely, and increasingly wearied by having to turn out books for money. His desolation deepened during the Second World War when his son Peter died on active service in the Royal Marines. After a stroke in 1942 his health declined and he became senile within a few years. Many of Belloc's numerous books are now forgotten, though some remain immensely readable as biography and history, and others are significant contributions to early twentieth-century debates about politics and social organization; developments in the Roman Catholic church since the Second Vatican Council (1962–5) have made his writings about religion very dated, and his antisemitism has been universally rejected. But as he remarked in an essay on Gibbon, whom he detested as a historian because of his anti-Christian content but loved as a writer, 'A writer's business is to write' (*A Conversation with an Angel*, 1928, 24). And at his best he wrote extraordinarily well; in some of his travel writing and personal narratives he is a master of prose; as a serious poet he is minor but memorable and sometimes haunting; and his comic verse is splendid—it remains in print and is frequently quoted.

Hilaire Belloc died on 16 July 1953 at the Mount Alvernia Nursing Home, Guildford, Surrey, from shock and burns following a fall at King's Land when he was trying to put a log on a fire. He was buried at West Grinstead, Sussex, on 20 July 1953.   BERNARD BERGONZI

Sources R. Speaight, *The life of Hilaire Belloc* (1957) • A. N. Wilson, *Hilaire Belloc* (1984); repr. (1986) • *DNB* • J. B. Morton, *Hilaire Belloc: a memoir* (1956) • E. Jebb and R. Jebb, *Testimony to Hilaire Belloc* (1956) • G. K. Chesterton, *The autobiography of G. K. Chesterton* (1936) • M. H. Markel, *Hilaire Belloc* (1982) • P. Cahill, *The English first editions of Hilaire Belloc* (1953)
Archives BL, corresp. and papers [microfilm copies] • Boston College, Massachusetts, corresp. and papers • Marquette University Memorial Library, literary MSS • NYPL, literary papers • Ransom HRC, letters and literary MSS • U. Reading L., corresp. • University of Notre Dame, Indiana, diary and sketchbooks | BL, corresp. with G. K. Chesterton and F. A. Chesterton, Add. MS 73190, fols. 1–113 • BL, corresp. with Sir Sydney Cockerell, Add. MS 52704 • BL, letters to Luvain Oldershaw, RP2157 [copies] • BL, letters to the Society of Authors, Add. MS 56668 • BLPES, letters to the Fabian Society • Bodl. Oxf., corresp. with Sibyl Colefax • Bodl. Oxf., letters to William Montgomery Crook • Bodl. Oxf., letters to H. A. L. Fisher • Bodl. Oxf., letters to J. L. Hammond • Bodl. Oxf., letters to Gilbert Murray • Bodl. Oxf., letters to Elizabeth Wansborough • CAC Cam., corresp. with Duff Cooper; corresp. with Sir W. J. Haley • Castle Howard, North Yorkshire, letters to Lord Carlisle • Cumbria AS, Carlisle, letters to Lord Howard of Penrith • FM Cam., letters to Wilfrid Scawen Blunt • Georgetown University, Washington, DC, Lauinger Library, corresp. with Hames Murray Allison and Elsie Allison; letters to his daughter Elizabeth; corresp. with Sir Arnold Lunn • HLRO, corresp. with Herbert Samuel • King's Lond., Liddell Hart C., corresp. with Basil Liddell Hart • L. Cong., Lippincott MSS • LUL, corresp. with Duckworth & Co. • NL Scot., letters to Sir John Richmond • NRA, priv. coll., letters to Sir Norman Moore • Princeton University, New Jersey, letters and postcards to Maria Hornor Lansdale • priv. coll., letters to Lord Carlisle • U. Aberdeen, letters to Malcolm Vivian Hay • U. Edin. L., corresp. with Charles Sarolea • U. Reading L., corresp. with Nancy Astor • University of Bristol Library, corresp. with Penguin Books •

W. Sussex RO, letters to Wilfrid Scawen Blunt | SOUND BL NSA, performance recordings
Likenesses M. Beerbohm, caricature drawing, c.1906, Yale U. • A. L. Coburn, photogravure, 1908, NPG • T. R. Annan & Sons, photograph, 1910, NPG • E. Gill, drawing, 1910, repro. in Jebb and Jebb, *Testimony to Hilaire Belloc* • I. Hamilton, photograph, 1910 • portraits, 1910–39, repro. in Speaight, *The life of Hilaire Belloc* • G. C. Beresford, two photographs, c.1913, NPG • E. O. Hoppé, photograph, 1915, NPG [*see illus.*] • J. Gunn, group portrait, oils, 1932, NPG • D. Pollen, chalk drawing, 1932, NPG • D. Pollen, lithograph, 1932, repro. in Wilson, *Hilaire Belloc* • J. Gunn, oils, 1939 • J. Gay, vintage bromide print, 1948, NPG • F. Brangwyn, sanguine drawing, c.1950, Museum and Art Gallery, Dundee • J. Gunn, oils, 1950, Oxford Union • B. Partridge, drawing, NPG; repro. in Wilson, *Hilaire Belloc* • B. Partridge, pencil caricature, NPG; repro. in *Punch* (17 Aug 1927) • print (after D. Low), NPG; repro. in *Supplement to The New Statesman* (17 April 1926)
Wealth at death £7451 8s. 3d.: probate, 16 Sept 1953, *CGPLA Eng. & Wales*

Bello Fago, Robert de. *See* Beaufeu, Robert de (*d.* in or before 1219).

Bello Fago, Roger de. *See* Beaufou, Roger (*d.* 1309).

Bellomont. For this title name *see* Bard, Henry, first Viscount Bellomont (1615/16–1656).

Bellot, Hugh (1542–1596), bishop of Bangor and of Chester, was the second son of Thomas Bellot, esquire, of Great Moreton, Cheshire, and Burton, Denbighshire. The Bellots were an ancient family whose original home was in Norfolk but who moved to Cheshire in the reign of Henry VI as a result of the marriage of John Bellot to Katherine, daughter and heir of Ralph Moreton of Great Moreton. Hugh Bellot was educated at Cambridge University, where he matriculated as a pensioner of Christ's College on 21 May 1561. He graduated BA in 1563/4 and became MA in 1567, when he migrated to Jesus College, Cambridge, of which he was a fellow from 1567 to 1573. He was a proctor of the university in 1571, when he had to deal with a number of drunken townsmen. He was a contemporary and friend of a number of students at Cambridge later to become prominent figures in the Welsh church, including William Morgan, Edmwnd Prys, Gabriel Goodman, and Richard Vaughan. The eighteenth-century antiquary Philip Yorke in *The Royal Tribes of Wales* claimed that Bellot participated in the translation of the Bishops' Bible (1568), but his name is not included in Archbishop Matthew Parker's list of contributors.

Bellot was probably ordained at Ely since he served as chaplain to Richard Cox, bishop of that diocese. He became rector of Tyd St Giles, Cambridgeshire, and was rector of Doddington-cum-Marsh, Isle of Ely (1572–3). He proceeded DD in 1579, and in that year was collated vicar of Gresford, Denbighshire, and in 1584 rector of Caerwys, Flintshire, both livings in the diocese of St Asaph, where his former Cambridge associate William Hughes was then bishop. He was also on good terms with Gabriel Goodman, dean of Westminster, who may have helped him attain some of his preferments. His elevation to the episcopate, however, he probably owed to the circumstance that his brother Thomas was Lord Burghley's steward. He was elected bishop of Bangor on 3 December 1585 and consecrated at Lambeth on 30 January following. He also held the deanery of Bangor *in commendam* until his resignation on 29 May 1593. He remained bishop of Bangor until translated to Chester on 25 June 1595.

Bellot's Bangor registers, which have been published in summary form, survive from 14 May 1586 to 14 April 1595. He seems to have been a conscientious bishop, who gave preferment to a number of able men, many of them Cambridge graduates like himself. In 1592 a relatively large proportion of the clergy in his diocese—43 out of 154—were listed as preachers. Among those whose progress he advanced were Henry Rowland (bishop of Bangor), Richard Parry (bishop of St Asaph), Lancelot Bulkeley (archbishop of Dublin), and his brother Cuthbert. He was, however, accused by one of his clergy, Dr Prydderch, who had been presented to the rectory of Llanbeulan in 1587 by the crown, of selling benefices in his gift. But as Bellot had refused him institution, Prydderch may be suspected of having been prejudiced. Although most of his ordinations were held at Bangor, Bellot conducted a number outside his diocese, especially during the first two years of his episcopate: at Doddington (1586); Jesus College, Cambridge (1586); and Gresford (three times, 1586–7). Many of those ordained appear to have been intended for English dioceses.

Bellot served as a member of the council in the marches. He was also singled out for thanks by Dr William Morgan, who, in the dedication to his Welsh Bible (1588), referred to the bishops of St Asaph and Bangor as having 'more especially endeavoured to promote this work. They have both of them lent me books for which I asked'—no small boon at that time—'and have condescended to examine, weigh and approve of this work'. Although Bellot was a considerable scholar, justifiable doubt has been expressed about how much Welsh he knew. He was, admittedly, bishop of Bangor, the most Welsh of dioceses, but seems to have been brought up in Cheshire.

Bellot had the reputation of being a severe persecutor of Roman Catholics, but the only tangible evidence of that survives from July 1592. Along with two justices of assize and others, he took part in the examination at Beaumaris of a Roman Catholic priest, William Davies, which caused a great stir in the diocese of Bangor. Davies was found guilty, but was not executed until after his second trial in 1593.

In 1595 Bellot was translated to Chester, where he took the opportunity to create his brother Cuthbert archdeacon of Chester. Bellot never married; according to tradition he was such a misogynist that he would never admit a female into his family. He died at Tŷ Bellot, Denbighshire, on 13 June 1596 and was buried in the parish church of Wrexham, although his funeral was solemnized at Chester Cathedral on 22 June. In his will he bequeathed three volumes of divinity to Jesus College, Cambridge. A life-sized effigy and monument were erected to him in the south window of the chancel at Wrexham by Cuthbert Bellot. The effigy is recumbent, showing a figure in post-Reformation vestments, continuing the tradition from medieval tombs, but with modifications reflecting Reformation changes. The Latin inscription records Bellot's merits: 'singularem in Deum pietatem, vitae integritatem, prudentiam et doctrinam' ('his singular godly piety, his integrity, practical wisdom and learning in life').   GLANMOR WILLIAMS

Sources *CSP dom.*, *1581–97* · Cooper, *Ath. Cantab.* · A. O. Evans, *Memorandum on the legality of the Welsh Bible* (1925) · W. P. Griffith, *Learning, law and religion: higher education and Welsh society, c.1540–1640* (1996) · *Fasti Angl.* (Hardy) · G. Ormerod, *The history of the county palatine and city of Chester*, 2nd edn, ed. T. Helsby, 3 vols. (1882) · *Correspondence of Matthew Parker*, ed. J. Bruce and T. T. Perowne, Parker Society, 42 (1853) · A. I. Pryce, *The diocese of Bangor in the sixteenth century* (1923) · D. A. Thomas, *The Welsh Elizabethan Catholic martyrs* (1971) · D. R. Thomas, *Esgobaeth Llanelwy: the history of the diocese of St Asaph*, rev. edn, 3 vols. (1908–13) · K. R. Wark, *Elizabethan recusancy in Cheshire*, Chetham Society, 3rd ser., 19 (1971) · F. O. White, *Lives of the Elizabethan bishops of the Anglican church* (1898) · G. Williams, *Wales and the Reformation* (1997) · B. Willis, *A survey of the cathedral church of Bangor* (1721) · P. Yorke, *The royal tribes of Wales*, new edn, ed. R. Williams (1887) · will, PRO, PROB 11/88, sig. 72 · R. C. Barnett, *Place, profit and power: a study of the servants of William Cecil, Elizabethan statesman* (1969) · *DNB*

Archives NL Wales, Bangor episcopal registers

Likenesses effigy, Wrexham parish church

Bellot, Thomas (1806–1857), naval surgeon and philologist, was born on 16 March 1806 at Manchester, where his father, after whom he was named, was a practising surgeon in Oldham Street. The father, a native of Derbyshire, gave evidence in 1818 to a House of Lords committee on Peel's factory bill. His mother, Jane, was the daughter of Thomas Hale of Darnhall, Cheshire, author of *Social Harmony*, who claimed to be related to Sir Matthew Hale. Thomas Bellot was at Manchester grammar school from 1816 to 1820, and later became a pupil of Joseph Jordan, a well-known medical practitioner in Manchester. In February 1828 he became MRCS and in 1831 began the service as a naval surgeon in which he spent most of his life.

Bellot's first appointment was as assistant surgeon on the sloop *Harrier*, where he joined in several boat attacks on pirates in the Strait of Malacca. In 1835 he joined the *Leveret*, and served against the African slave trade until 1839. On this expedition he was one of the party that boarded the slave brig *Diogenes*, and had charge of the wounded prisoners until they were transferred to the hospital at Mozambique. He next served for three years with the *Firefly* off the West Indies. In 1843 he went with the *Wolf* to the coast of China. During his absence, without his knowledge, he was elected FRCS *honoris causa* on 6 August 1844. In 1849 he had medical charge of the *Havering*, which took 365 convicts to Sydney. Cholera broke out, but Bellot showed great firmness and judgement in dealing with the situation. Some scientific maps and specimens sent by him to the Admiralty from Labuan were forwarded to the Museum of Economic Geology.

Bellot's last outward voyage was in November 1854, when he joined, as surgeon, the flagship *Britannia*, which conveyed Vice-Admiral Dundas to the Black Sea as commander of the fleet. Bellot was assigned the care of the sick at the naval hospital of Therapia on the Bosphorus, as one of the chief hospital surgeons, and returned to Britain in March 1855 in charge of invalids. His adventurous life, even for a naval surgeon, affected his health, and during his stay in the West Indies he had two attacks of yellow fever. He died at 37 Greek Street, Stockport, on 25 June 1857, and was buried in the churchyard of Poynton, Cheshire.

Somewhat unusually for a naval surgeon, Bellot was an honorary member of several learned societies. The classical learning he received at school was increased by study in his scanty leisure. He translated the aphorisms of Hippocrates and of Galen on the hand (1840). His interest in philology led him to study oriental literature. In the intervals on half pay he visited many European cities, attended the lectures of H. H. Wilson at Oxford, made the acquaintance of Christian Bunsen, and was a friend and disciple of Franz Bopp. Bellot's work on the *Sanscrit Derivations of English Words*, printed at Manchester in 1856 by subscription, was effectively a comparative dictionary, in which a number of English words were traced to their source. The illustrations range over a wide field of philological knowledge, including Chinese.

Bellot had studied the language and antiquities of China, and bequeathed his collection of Chinese books and bronzes to Manchester Free Library. An article by him on the best method for learning Chinese was published in *Notes and Queries* (1st ser., 1854, 10.168).

W. E. A. AXON, *rev.* ANDREW LAMBERT

Sources Boase, *Mod. Eng. biog.* · *Manchester grammar school register* (1874) · *Handbook to the public libraries of Manchester* (1877) · *Catalogue of the library of the Manchester Medical Society* (1866) · private information (1886)

Bellows, John Thomas (1831–1902), printer, lexicographer, and archaeologist, born at Carthew House, Church Street, Liskeard, Cornwall, on 18 January 1831, was the elder of the two sons of William Lamb Bellows (1798–1877), schoolmaster, of Bere Regis, Dorset, and his wife, Hannah Stickland (1790–1874), daughter of John Stickland, bailiff and Wesleyan preacher, of Eastholme, Wareham, Dorset. John's parents later became Quakers. John was educated at his father's school in Camborne until he was apprenticed, aged fourteen, to a local printer. At twenty he moved to Gloucester, working as a foreman printer until he started his own business.

In 1872, needing premises for his new steam printing press, Bellows developed a site at Eastgate, Gloucester, using the excavation as an opportunity for archaeological research. Against advice, he dug down, finding Roman pottery and a section of the Roman city wall. Later evidence confirmed his projected line of the entire city wall. He saved the 'Birdlip grave group' and gave this, together with his collection of Samian and Roman fragments and coins, to Gloucester Museum. Malcolm Watkins, the city's archaeologist, called him 'a genuine pathfinder' (Charity, 118).

In January 1863 Bellows's Norwegian fiancée was seriously ill. In *A Winter Journey from Gloucester to Norway* he describes his dangerous journey to her home in Arendal,

John Thomas Bellows (1831–1902), by H. W. Watson, 1891

unhappily arriving just after her death. The bulkiness of the Danish dictionary he used on his travels led to his creation of a French pocket dictionary: 'one cannot unpack a portmanteau for the sake of a word' (J. E. Bellows, 5).

For the next ten years Bellows worked unstintingly as a lexicographer while continuing his printing business. Professor Max Müller, the philologist, helped him to produce his English *Outline Vocabulary for the Use of Students of the Chinese Language* (1868). He mastered the French language and with the aid of the Beljame brothers (Paris) produced the first French pocket dictionary in 1873, dedicated to the philologist Prince Lucien Bonaparte. The book contained 340,000 words, measured 4¾ x 2¾ inches, and was printed by hand in diamond type on specially thin paper; 6000 copies sold rapidly, and thirty reprints were made between 1915 and 1947. *The Times* called it 'a gem of typographical art' (J. E. Bellows, 6), and Mark Twain referred to it in 'The church of the gratis lesson'.

In January 1869 Bellows married Elizabeth Earnshaw (1841–1932), daughter of Mark Earnshaw, surgeon, of Clitheroe, Lancashire. There were nine children, whose early lives are described in letters to his American friend and correspondent Oliver Wendell Holmes.

During the Franco-Prussian War (1870) Bellows spent one month as a commissioner for the Quakers, travelling the war zone on horseback, wagon, and foot, to assess the needs of the populace. He describes his journey in *The*

Track of the War around Metz. Deeply committed to the Society of Friends, Bellows used their plain speech and wore Quaker dress to the end of his life. The austerity of this tall and distinguished figure was tempered by his warmth and irrepressible humour. His independence of mind and un-Quakerly views were expressed in his pamphlets.

In 1892, aged sixty, Bellows accompanied an Australian Friend to the Caucasus to aid a group of persecuted Russian pacifists. In Moscow the travellers visited Count Lev Tolstoy, who was sympathetic to their project. Bellows and Tolstoy formed a close friendship, corresponding for several years. The two Friends travelled into the mountains. Negotiating hazardous roads, and threatened by armed robbers, they reached the remote settlements of the Stundists and Dukhobors. 'Don't be uneasy on our account … we are under a higher protection than the police', John wrote to his wife (*Letters and Memoir*, 178). On returning to Moscow, he and Tolstoy, with others, arranged for many Dukhobors to emigrate to Canada.

Despite further travels the business continued to thrive: Bellows was an inventive employer, too, producing Bellows's cylindrical rapid wages calculator, and a series of concentric calculators for metric conversion. In 1901 he made his final journey, to America, to receive an honorary degree of MA at Harvard, with the citation 'English Quaker, authority on Roman antiquities in Britain, delightful essayist and learned lexicographer'. After returning home he developed heart failure and died of cardiac asthma at his country home, Upton Knoll, Upton St Leonards, Gloucestershire, on 5 May 1902. He was interred in Painswick burial-ground, Gloucestershire, on 9 May 1902.   KATE CHARITY

Sources [E. Bellows], *John Bellows: letters and memoir* (1904); repr. (1905) · J. T. Bellows, *A winter journey from Gloucester to Norway* (1867) · J. T. Bellows, *The track of the war around Metz and the fund for non-combatant sufferers* (1870?) · J. E. Bellows, *John Bellows and his French dictionary* (1948) · K. Charity, *A many-sided man: John Bellows of Gloucester* (1993) [incl. bibliography] · *DNB* · E. Bellows, letter on *DNB* article, *The Times* (7 Dec 1916)
Archives City of Gloucester Museum, collection · Glos. RO, business, family, and personal MSS · RS Friends, Lond., papers
Likenesses H. W. Watson, sepia photograph, 1891 [see illus.] · P. Bigland, oils, 1901, City Art Gallery, Gloucester
Wealth at death £19,648 12s. 2d.: probate, 11 July 1902, *CGPLA Eng. & Wales*

Bellucci, Antonio (1654–1726). *See under* Venetian painters in Britain (*act.* 1708–c.1750).

Belmaine, Jean (*fl.* 1546–1559), royal tutor, is of uncertain origins. He probably came to England from France in the wake of the French persecutions of religious evangelicals after the edict of Fontainebleau (1540). He certainly had Calvinist sympathies: his corrections to Edward VI's French exercises show he was deeply affected by the cruelty of the French authorities who cut out the tongues of heretics before burning them to stop them from testifying to their faith. He entered the service of the Tudor court as a protégé of Sir John Cheke, who had become Prince Edward's chief tutor in 1544. Appointed Edward's French tutor on 25 September 1546 at an annual salary of 40 marks, Belmaine began his teaching duties on his royal pupil's ninth birthday (12 October 1546). By the following February, at the funeral of Henry VIII, he had become a gentleman of Edward's chamber. Under his tuition the prince began 'to learne Frenche with a great facilité even at hys first entre', according to Cox (Nichols, 1.lxxviii), and by December he had progressed sufficiently under Belmaine's tuition to write a letter in French to his sister, the Princess Elizabeth. He could not yet converse in French with the new French ambassador in February 1547, but by 1550 he was speaking 'bon langaige françois' with his French visitors (Loach, 13).

Belmaine may have originally entered the service of the Tudor court as Princess Elizabeth's French tutor. Upon his appointment as Edward's French tutor, his salary was backdated to the preceding 25 March, and at the same time his former salary of 4d. per day was transferred to 'the eldest groom with my Lady Elizabeth' (*LP Henry VIII*, 212, no. 199/74). These facts imply continuing service rather than a new appointment and suggest a transfer from Elizabeth's household to Edward's. Some have detected Belmaine's supervision in the translations Princess Elizabeth produced between 1544 and 1546 as new year presents for Katherine Parr and Henry VIII: English translations of Marguerite de Navarre's *Le miroir de lâme pécheresse* and of Calvin's *Institution de la religion Chrestienne* (Book 1), and French translations of Queen Katherine's own *Prayers and Meditations* and of Erasmus's *Dialogus fidei*. After his appointment as Edward's French master, Belmaine almost certainly continued to tutor Elizabeth as well. His French translation (from the Greek) of St Basil the Great's epistle to St Gregory Nazianzen on the solitary life, for instance, strongly suggests a continuing interest in the princess, both personal and pedagogical. Designed to console Elizabeth at a time when she was herself 'en lieu solitaire', he pedantically explains why he refuses to use the French spelling conventions that had been recently introduced, and he teasingly refers to the difficulties of finding anything worth translating that Elizabeth had not already read. Both comments suggest a teacher's close familiarity with his pupil's studies.

After the death of Henry VIII Belmaine openly began to tailor Edward's schoolwork to encourage his pupil's enthusiasm for evangelical Christianity. Several of the young king's exercise books still exist, each bearing corrections in Belmaine's own hand. In the earliest of them (late 1547 – early 1548), he set Edward the task of collecting sentences from the Bible on the subject of idolatry and translating them into French (Cambridge, Trinity College, MS R.7.31). He completed a second such exercise, this time a collection of French biblical sentences on justification by faith, on 2 December 1548 (BL, Add. MS 9000). He then immediately (13 December 1548) launched into a third, a French treatise attacking papal supremacy, which he finished on 31 August 1549 (CUL, MS Dd 12.59). The dedications of all three exercises to Edward's uncle, Protector Somerset, show that Belmaine's attempts to inculcate reformed religious ideals along with French language fluency were part of a concerted and authorized campaign aimed at educating a champion of the reformed religion.

Belmaine not only brought his own strong evangelical convictions to this task, but also drew upon his relationships with continental—particularly Genevan—reformers. His sole remaining letter, written to Calvin from Greenwich Palace on 29 May 1552, suggests an apparently extensive correspondence and intellectual exchange. In it Belmaine refers to previous correspondence with his 'très cher frère', thanks Calvin for the 'petit traité' he had sent to Belmaine, reports that the new prayer book would be published in November, and promises to send his own French translation of it to Calvin as soon as possible thereafter. In closing, he sends greetings to 'tous mes bons amis' in Geneva, particularly to the printer Robert Estienne, and to his son Henry, who had fled to Geneva in 1551 to escape persecution in Paris ('Lettre de Jean Belmaine à Calvin'). This letter, which accompanies an exchange of texts, provides an important context for Belmaine's own translation work at the Tudor court. His translations of such works as the second Edwardian prayer book (1553) and of Queen Katherine Parr's *Lamentation of a Sinner* (1548?) were not mere language exercises. Rather, they were probably designed for an audience of continental reformers. Belmaine circulated the important documents of the Edwardian reformation abroad, and he likewise received and circulated important continental texts at the English court. In these efforts he was encouraged by Cheke and Cranmer (whom he mentions in his letter to Calvin) and by William Cecil, to whom he sent his translation of Katherine Parr's *Lamentation*. Whether or not Belmaine was personally responsible, this pattern of exchange may well explain how Princess Elizabeth's translation from Marguerite de Navarre, *A Godly Medytacyon of the Christen Sowle*, reached Wesel, where John Bale printed it in April 1548.

By the middle of Edward's brief reign, Belmaine's part in the king's instruction seemed to be paying material as well as spiritual dividends. The privy council recognized his efforts with a reward of £50 in 1550, and with a lucrative twenty-one-year lease on property in Somerset in 1551. By January 1551 he was feeling settled enough in his position to apply for a patent of denization, which was granted on 11 June. Another lucrative lease, this time on property in Southampton, followed in 1552. Perhaps it was at this relatively settled time in his life that he married Sir John Cheke's niece, Jane Alington, with whom he had a daughter, Elizabeth. The match made him not only the nephew of his patron, but also a nephew by marriage of William Cecil, who had married one of Cheke's sisters.

This period of stability and success abruptly ended with Edward VI's death. Belmaine makes a last appearance as 'Frenche Skoolemaster' at Edward's funeral in 1553 (Ord, 389), then disappears permanently from the royal household. His annuity, awarded to him 'for life' by Henry VIII, went unpaid during Queen Mary's reign, so he may well have emigrated to escape religious persecution. On 27 June 1559, as one of her first acts as queen, Elizabeth restored Belmaine's annuity, together with all arrears due to him, as a recognition of 'his service to Edward VI and the present queen' (*CPR, 1558–75*, vol. 1, no. 94). He did not resume court service, however, and this record may represent no more than a brief appearance in England to settle his financial affairs. In June 1568, as perhaps another sign that he had emigrated, the privy council awarded a new lease on his Somerset property to two of Elizabeth's yeomen, even though Belmaine's lease still had four years to run. GORDON KIPLING

Sources *APC, 1550–54* · 'Lettre de Jean Bellemain à Calvin, 1552', *Bulletin Historique et Littéraire* [Société de l'Histoire du Protestantisme Français], 15 (1866), 203–5 · J. Belmaine, 'Le livre des prieres ecclesiastiques et administration des sacremens et aultres ceremonies et facon de faire dont on use en l'eglise d'Angleterre', 1553, BL, Royal MS 20 A.xiv · J. Belmaine, 'Epistle of St Basil the Great to St Gregory Nazianzen on the solitary life', *c*.1550, BL, Royal MS 16 E.i · *CPR, 1550–53; 1558–75* · Edward VI, 'A l'encontre de la primauté du pape', 1549, CUL, MS Dd 12.59 · Edward VI, 'Sensuit un recueil des principales places de la Sainte Escriture, qui traitent de foy en Dieu nostre pere, et createur: traduites d'Angloys en Francoys', 1548, BL, Add. MS 9000 · Edward VI, 'Sentences de la Sainte Escriture qui accordant à la réformation de l'ydolatrie', 1547?, Trinity Cam., MS R.7.31 · S. E. James, *Kateryn Parr: the making of a queen* (1999) · *LP Henry VIII* · J. Loach, *Edward VI*, ed. G. Bernard and P. Williams (1999) · D. MacCulloch, *Tudor church militant: Edward VI and the protestant Reformation* (1999) · A. R. Maddison, ed., *Lincolnshire pedigrees*, 1, Harleian Society, 50 (1902) · G. Masson, 'Jean Bellemain', *Bulletin Historique et Littéraire* [Société de l'Histoire du Protestantisme Français], 15 (1866), 138–45 · *Literary remains of King Edward the Sixth*, ed. J. G. Nichols, 2 vols., Roxburghe Club, 75 (1857) · C. Ord, 'Sir Edward Waldegrave's account of the burial of King Edward VI', *Archaeologia*, 12 (1796), 334–96 · Queen Katherine Parr, 'La complainte de lame pecheresse', trans. J. Belmaine, 1548?, BL, Royal MS 16 E.xxviii · Queen Katherine Parr, 'La complainte de lame pecheresse', trans. J. Belmaine, 1548?, Hatfield House, Hertfordshire, Cecil papers, no. 314

Archives BL, Add. MS 5464 · BL, Royal MSS, 16 E.i, 16 E.xxviii, 20 A.xiv · CUL, MS Dd 12.59 · Hatfield House, Hertfordshire, Cecil papers · Trinity Cam., MS R.7.31

Belmeis [Beaumais], **Richard de** (d. 1127), administrator and bishop of London, came (according to one of L. C. Loyd's less fully proven attributions) from Beaumais-sur-Dive in Calvados. Beaumais was in the Hièmois, and Belmeis first appeared in England as a rear-tenant of Roger de Montgomery, vicomte of the Hièmois and first Norman earl of Shrewsbury (d. 1094): he can plausibly be identified with the Richard who held of Helgot (one of Roger's more important vassals) a small manor at Meadowley in southeast Shropshire, near Morville, where the earl's chaplains held land, and also 2 hides at Preen, a few miles away. His name occurs in dubious documents in the Shrewsbury cartulary purporting to describe transactions of the years before 1102, and the annals of Winchester describe him as a clerk of Robert de Bellême, son of Roger and third Norman earl of Shrewsbury. His actual office was perhaps that of steward of the Montgomery lands in both Shropshire and Sussex: in a later charter for Shrewsbury Abbey he is called *dapifer* of Shropshire. Orderic once calls him *vicecomes Scrobesburiae*, translated by Chibnall as 'viceroy of Shropshire' (Ordericus Vitalis, *Eccl. hist.*, 6.144–5).

Henry I defeated and expelled Earl Robert in 1102; he allowed the earldom to lapse, but its tasks were soon carried out by Belmeis, who was addressed as a royal functionary in Sussex as early as Michaelmas 1102 and very soon afterwards began twenty years or more of royal duty in Shropshire, although again his title is unclear. One version of the *Brut y tywysogyon* (*Brenhinedd y Saesson*) describes him in 1109 as 'seneschal to the king in Shrewsbury' who 'held authority over the county of Shrewsbury' (*Brenhinedd*, 107, 119); the Red Book of Hergest calls him 'Richard the steward' in 1109, and under 1111 records that he was 'the man who was holding the king's place and directing it at Shrewsbury' (*Brut: Hergest*, 62, 75); Peniarth MS 20 calls him 'officer to the king at Shrewsbury', in 1109, and two years later states that Belmeis 'held the king's place' (*Brut: Peniarth MS 20*, 29, 36). But it is clear that he was based at Shrewsbury, and exercised in Shropshire all the varied powers that would be vested in a steward as a great lord's factotum.

Belmeis was doubtless fairly continuously in Shropshire during the next five years, for he received or attested no firmly datable royal instruments before 1108, when he was appointed to the see of London; he was not priested until shortly before his consecration, which took place at Pagham on 26 July 1108, with some haste because the king wished to dispatch him quickly to the distant Welsh border for the conduct of business. His best-evidenced activity in Wales followed his return to the border in 1109: he reacted with skill to the abduction at Cenarth Bychan in 1109 of Nest, daughter of Rhys ap Tewdwr and wife of Gerald of Windsor, by Owain ap Cadwgan ap Bleddyn of Powys, inciting Madog and Ithel, sons of Rhiryd ap Bleddyn, to dispose of their kinsman Owain. At one stage in the complicated sequel, he returned lands to Madog, a step taken, according to the Red Book of Hergest, 'not out of love for him, but because he knew the ways of the people of that land, that they were all of them slaying one another' (*Brut, Hergest*, 75)—an enduring truth, doubtless perceived in the service of the Norman earls. Apart from intrigues at the evanescent Welsh courts, his chief activity in Shropshire concerned the earls' great foundation, the abbey of St Peter at Shrewsbury. He also left an enduring mark on Wenlock Priory, refounded by Earl Roger, and he indirectly determined the political geography of south Shropshire until the nineteenth century: about 1110 he created the extensive immunity of the priory, to which the borough of Wenlock later succeeded.

After his consecration Belmeis witnessed numerous documents issued by Henry I, among the most notable being the writs that separated the jurisdictions (1108), created the see of Ely (1109), defined the privileges of various (mostly English) monastic houses, disposed of the Beauchamp inheritance (1114—a matter of much interest in the west midlands), and notified the consecration of St Albans Abbey (1115). No detailed itinerary of the bishop's movements can, however, be compiled from these and other indications. He also actively defended the special position of his primatial superior: as early as 1109, during a vacancy at Canterbury, he received from Thomas (d. 1114), archbishop-elect of York, a profession of obedience to Canterbury, before he joined in Thomas's consecration. In his diocese he was active chiefly in London: he secured privileges for the churches of the capital, and used his episcopal and other revenues to continue the great work

of reconstruction of St Paul's, begun by his predecessor Maurice (d. 1107) after the fire of 1087, though his powers waned in face of the magnitude of the task. In Essex he endowed the Augustinian priory of St Osyth, the first prior of which, William de Corbeil (d. 1136), was promoted to Canterbury in 1123, when Belmeis was among his consecrators, and was probably his backer.

In Shropshire Belmeis gave to the church and took from it. He granted his 2 hides at Preen to Wenlock Priory; after some dispute a priory dependent on Wenlock was established at Preen. However, he attempted to convert to his own right some prebends of St Alkmund's, Shrewsbury, which were properly his only for life; other prebends there were granted to him by Henry I, and after his death regranted by the king to the bishop's nephew, also Richard, who used them to endow the new abbey of Lilleshall. Another nephew, William, became dean of St Paul's, and a third, Philip, was ancestor of the families of Zouche, Pembridge, and Vernon, all of Tong, Shropshire; the later Belmeis family descended from Philip's and Richard's youngest brother, Robert. Between 1123 and 1126 Belmeis, attacked by paralysis, resigned his charge in Shropshire; on 16 January 1127 he died at St Osyth's. The inscription under his marble tomb there was recorded by John Weever in 1631.

Belmeis's career was an early demonstration of the fact that a capable man could proceed easily, and with no loss of competence, from baronial service to the king's. As his tombstone said, he was 'per totam vitam laboriosus' (Weever, 607–8)—in three different contexts: as a civil servant involved with royal policy, as the bishop of a diocese containing England's capital, and as a border lieutenant mastering the Welsh. In both London and Shrewsbury he showed his skill from the outset. As an ecclesiastic he seems to have been very much of his time—there is a hint of at least one bastard son; as an administrator he must rank close behind Roger of Salisbury himself. R. W. Eyton's reference, in a rare literary flight, to his 'sumptuous and viceregal pride' (Eyton, 2.191) is by no means sufficient; we must add not only the characteristic Norman mixture of liberality and its prerequisite, acquisitiveness, but also loyalty, adaptability, and versatility.

J. F. A. MASON

Sources *Willelmi Malmesbiriensis monachi de gestis pontificum Anglorum libri quinque*, ed. N. E. S. A. Hamilton, Rolls Series, 52 (1870) · *Eadmeri Historia novorum in Anglia*, ed. M. Rule, Rolls Series, 81 (1884) · *Radulfi de Diceto … opera historica*, ed. W. Stubbs, 2 vols., Rolls Series, 68 (1876) · T. Jones, ed. and trans., *Brut y tywysogyon, or, The chronicle of the princes: Peniarth MS 20* (1952) · T. Jones, ed. and trans., *Brut y tywysogyon, or, The chronicle of the princes: Red Book of Hergest* (1955) · T. Jones, ed. and trans., *Brenhinedd y Saesson, or, The kings of the Saxons* (1971) [another version of *Brut y tywysogyon*] · *Reg. RAN*, vol. 2 · U. Rees, ed., *The cartulary of Shrewsbury Abbey*, 2 vols. (1975) · R. W. Eyton, *Antiquities of Shropshire*, 12 vols. (1854–60), vol. 2, pp. 191–201 · *VCH Shropshire*, vols. 2–3 · J. F. A. Mason, 'The officers and clerks of the Norman earls of Shropshire', *Transactions of the Shropshire Archaeological Society*, 56 (1957–60), 244–57 · J. A. Green, *The government of England under Henry I* (1986) · F. C. Suppe, *Military institutions on the Welsh marches: Shropshire, 1066–1300* (1994), 91–2 · L. C. Loyd, *The origins of some Anglo-Norman families*, ed. C. T. Clay and D. C.

Douglas, Harleian Society, 103 (1951) · J. Weever, *Ancient funerall monuments* (1631), 607–8

Belmeis [Beaumais], **Richard de** (*d.* 1162), bishop of London, was the son of Walter de Belmeis and nephew of Richard de *Belmeis, bishop of London from 1108 to 1127. He owed his career and his prominence mainly to family influence, as one of no fewer than six known sons and nephews established by Richard de Belmeis as members of the chapter of St Paul's Cathedral, some of them in the higher offices. While still a minor he was appointed archdeacon of Middlesex by his uncle, who entrusted the duties of the office to a custodian. In the time of Gilbert the Universal, bishop of London from 1128 to 1134, Belmeis made an unsuccessful claim to the archdeacon's office, but the custodian's rights were upheld by the bishop, and it was not until 1138 that Belmeis was restored to the archdeaconry and ordained deacon. He had taken the opportunity to promote his own case when he went to Rome as an envoy of the party of the dean of St Paul's, who was then his cousin William, in the long dispute in the cathedral chapter between 1136 and 1138 over the election of Anselm, abbot of Bury St Edmunds and nephew of Anselm of Canterbury, as bishop of London. In Shropshire, where his uncle had won favour with the king as sheriff and viceroy, the king conferred on Belmeis one of his uncle's most valuable benefices: a prebend in St Alkmund's, a collegiate church of secular canons in Shrewsbury, which as a royal foundation was in the king's gift. As dean of St Alkmund's, Belmeis, together with his brother Philip, the heir of the secular possessions of his family in Shropshire, founded the abbey of Lilleshall in Shropshire. With the permission and confirmation of all the royal and ecclesiastical authorities concerned, he suppressed St Alkmund's and endowed the new foundation with his own prebend—forming the lion's share of St Alkmund's possessions—and with the remaining prebends when they fell vacant. It was out of prudence rather than opportunism that he secured the approval of King Stephen as well as of Stephen's adversaries, the Empress Matilda, and her son Henry. The abbey was founded for a colony of Augustinian canons from Dorchester, following the strict observances of Arrouaise in Flanders, who were finally established at Lilleshall between 1145 and 1148.

In the spring of 1152 Belmeis was elected bishop of London. The vacancy of more than a year after the death on 29 September 1150 of his predecessor Robert de Sigillo, a sequence of letters by his relative Gilbert Foliot, bishop of Hereford, in support of him, and further information from the chroniclers combine to show that he did not succeed without difficulty to the episcopal see of London. He was canonically elected by the chapter of St Paul's where his family and relatives were still strongly represented, and there is no indication of any dissension, but for some reason the pope became involved in the process, and the king seems to have resented the election. According to John of Salisbury, Stephen demanded £500 for the right of free election. On 20 September 1152 Archbishop Theobald of Canterbury ordained Belmeis priest, and on 28 September he consecrated him bishop in Canterbury. But this was not the end of Belmeis's troubles. On his election he had bestowed his archdeaconry on Ralph de Diceto, but as a result of his involvement in the election the pope claimed the right to fill this vacancy, and appointed John of Canterbury, a clerk to Archbishop Theobald who later became archbishop of Lyons. This problem remained unsolved until John was appointed treasurer of York, probably in December 1153. It is widely assumed that Belmeis's episcopate was overshadowed by this difficult start. What is known for certain of his years as bishop amounts to very little. But there is no reason to doubt that after so many years as canon and archdeacon he knew how to administer a diocese. Letters that John of Salisbury wrote in the name of Archbishop Theobald show Belmeis as a busy judge and as party in lawsuits, though mainly in cases which went on appeal to the pope and thus necessitated John's letters. It is also known, from the difficult negotiations involved, that Belmeis founded and endowed the dignity of a treasurer in his cathedral chapter. Late in life he was handicapped by a stroke. Being heavily in debt, he had difficulties in finding someone to look after his affairs. He died on 4 May 1162. FALKO NEININGER

Sources *Radulfi de Diceto ... opera historica*, ed. W. Stubbs, 1: 1148–79, Rolls Series, 68 (1876), xxi–xxvi, 250–52, 295–6, 301, 304, 306 · M. Chibnall, 'The Abbey of Lilleshall', *VCH Shropshire*, 2.70–80, esp. 70–1 · F. Neininger, ed., *London, 1076–1187*, English Episcopal Acta, 15 (1999) · *Letters and charters of Gilbert Foliot*, ed. A. Morey and others (1967), nos. 99–103, 109, 113, 139–40 · *The letters of John of Salisbury*, ed. and trans. H. E. Butler and W. J. Millor, rev. C. N. L. Brooke, OMT, 1: *The early years, 1153–1161* (1986), nos. 2, 7, 11, 14, 68, 70–76, 84, 113 [Lat. orig. with parallel Eng. text] · *The Historia pontificalis of John of Salisbury*, ed. and trans. M. Chibnall, rev. edn, OMT (1986), 88–9 · C. N. L. Brooke, 'The earliest times to 1485', *A history of St Paul's Cathedral and the men associated with it*, ed. W. R. Matthews and W. M. Atkins (1957), 1–99, 361–5, esp. 28–9 · *Fasti Angl., 1066–1300*, [St Paul's, London], 2, 15, 32 · R. W. Eyton, *Antiquities of Shropshire*, 12 vols. (1854–60), vol. 8, pp. 212–27 · M. Gibbs, ed., *Early charters of the cathedral church of St Paul, London*, CS, 3rd ser., 58 (1939) · C. N. L. Brooke, *The medieval idea of marriage* (1989), 84–7 · M. Richter, ed., *Canterbury professions*, CYS, 67 (1973), no. 97 · Dugdale, *Monasticon*, new edn, 6/1.262–6 · *Reg. RAN*, vol. 3 · A. Saltman, *Theobald, archbishop of Canterbury* (1956)

Beloe, Robert (1905–1984), educationist, was born in Winchester on 12 May 1905, the eldest of the four sons (there were no daughters) of the Revd Robert Douglas Beloe (1868–1931), headmaster of Bradfield College, Berkshire, and his wife, (Margaret) Clarissa, the daughter of the Revd Prebendary John Trant Bramston, of Winchester College. Throughout his life his career was marked by the twin interests of education and the Church of England. He was educated at Winchester College and at Hertford College, Oxford, where he obtained a second-class honours degree in modern history in 1927.

There followed a brief apprenticeship in teaching—at his father's old school, then at Eton, and finally (as some preparation for the very different realities of popular education) at an elementary school in Reading. Beloe married in 1933 Amy, daughter of Captain Sir Frank Stanley Di Rose, second baronet, with whom he had a son and two daughters. In 1931 he had joined the ranks of educational administration as a trainee in Kent, and three years later he was promoted to Surrey, to which the central twenty-five years of his career were devoted. In 1939 he became deputy education officer, and one year later chief education officer.

Beloe was therefore well placed to become a central member of that significant group of chief education officers who were responsible for putting into effect, in the years after the Second World War, the provisions of the Education Act of 1944 designed by R. A. Butler. The two decades during which Beloe presided over the provision of public education in Surrey represented the high-water mark of the influence of enlightened administrators working amicably with elected councillors. Such influence by local government officers was to be much eroded in the closing decades of the twentieth century. He was among the first to make detailed plans for the expansion of secondary education, which required both the abolition of all fees for secondary school pupils and the provision of secondary education for all pupils over the age of eleven.

The urgent requirements of expansion and building, the traditional respect in which the county grammar school had been held since the act of 1902, and the prevailing orthodoxies inherited from the 1930s made it inevitable that the majority of secondary school pupils would be directed into secondary modern schools while the more academic minority would enjoy the undoubtedly superior provision of the grammar schools. Surrey was rich in such schools. Beloe's own preference was for a form of common or comprehensive schooling for pupils between the ages of eleven and thirteen, at which point more definitive choices could more appropriately be made. Although this preference did not prevail, he did ensure—as educational expectations and performance rose—that good opportunities for some of the pupils excluded from the grammar schools were provided within the secondary modern schools. Socially and economically Surrey was a well-favoured area, and the development of the bilateral school (essentially a secondary modern school with a grammar school stream within it) was a distinctive mark of Beloe's years in that county.

Such a development, in a county warily suspicious of innovation, furnished a natural bridge to the more dramatic growth of comprehensive schooling which was to be so pronounced a feature of the educational history of the 1960s. Beloe himself had little interest in some of the more ambitious claims made for comprehensive education, and little sympathy with their ideological roots. His concern was for the individual (pupil or teacher or colleague) and with the extension to him or her of the advantages enjoyed by those who came, like himself, from a privileged background.

One measure of these advantages in post-war Britain was access to an appropriate public examination attesting educational success for those pupils choosing to stay on at school for at least one extra year beyond what was at that time the legally imposed school-leaving age. Beloe's introduction of the GCE (general certificate of education, as it had been constituted in 1951) into the secondary modern

schools of Surrey was an index of the determination of parents, teachers, and pupils to enlarge the scope of that examination. It was nevertheless acknowledged that the GCE had weaknesses, which became more obvious as it was opened to less academic pupils.

Beloe had been a member since 1947 of the Secondary Schools Examination Council, the national body then responsible for policy on such matters, and it was therefore particularly appropriate that in 1958 he should be appointed chairman of a committee of that council charged with reviewing the provision of school examinations. The Beloe report of 1960 enjoys a place in educational history and led to the introduction five years later of the certificate of secondary education (CSE) which was intended to meet the needs of pupils across a wide range of ability. That examination was designed to be determined by the curriculum provided in each school, to be controlled very largely by teachers, and to provide an acceptable alternative to the GCE. Its success and popularity created problems—inherent in the provision of two separate examinations for sixteen-year-old pupils—and in 1988 (fifteen years after the minimum school-leaving age had been raised to sixteen) the two examinations were merged in the general certificate of secondary education (GCSE). The CSE, the principal national monument to Beloe's career, represented an important transition and epitomized many of the liberal values of the decade in which it was born.

In 1959 Beloe, to the surprise of many, was appointed as the (first) lay secretary to the archbishop of Canterbury. In that discreet capacity he served for ten years two archbishops, G. F. Fisher and A. M. Ramsey. He was appointed CBE in 1960 and was made in 1979 an honorary DCL of the University of Kent. He was a member of many committees and other bodies, including the royal commission on marriage and divorce (1951–5). His recreations included travel and gardening. Beloe died at his home, the Hill House, Queens Road, Richmond, Surrey, on 26 April 1984. He was survived by his wife.   H. G. JUDGE

Sources *The Times* (30 April 1984) · *Education* (4 May 1984) · private information (1990) · personal knowledge (2004) · *CGPLA Eng. & Wales* (1984)
Archives LPL, corresp. and papers, incl. letters to Ramsey | Bodl. Oxf., corresp. with Lord Monckton
Likenesses photograph, 1984, repro. in *The Times*
Wealth at death £73,325: probate, 13 Aug 1984, *CGPLA Eng. & Wales*

Beloe, William (1758–1817), writer and translator, was born in Norwich on 18 February 1758, son of William Beloe (*d.* 1791), a tradesman, and his wife, Hannah Hedslup (*c.*1721–1803). His early education in Norwich was followed by several years in Yorkshire under the care of the Revd Matthew Raine at Hartforth, and then four years at Samuel Parr's Stanmore School. In *The Sexagenarian* Beloe gives what was widely regarded as an extremely unfair picture of the unnamed but easily identifiable Parr and his school. In 1818 the *Monthly Review* reported that Parr had urged Beloe's departure from Stanmore after a deputation from the other boys had pressed for this. He went on to Corpus

Christi College, Cambridge, where he was admitted sizar in 1774, matriculated in 1776, and received his BA in 1779.

Following his ordination as deacon in February 1780, Beloe became curate of Taverham in Norfolk; he was ordained priest in May 1782. In the meantime Samuel Parr had become headmaster of Norwich Free School and invited Beloe, whom he later described as 'this worthless man' (Johnstone, 1.60), to become under-master. Beloe, who later represented himself as having been unwilling to take on this life of subservience to one 'from whose severity and waywardness, much mortification and uneasiness had formerly been experienced' (Beloe, *Sexagenarian*, 1.169), was appointed in January 1780 and resigned in December 1783. By then he had published his first poem, 'Ode to Miss Boscawen'.

On 12 August 1780 Beloe married Mary Anne Rix (*d*. after 1817), daughter of William Rix of London, at St Peter Mancroft, Norwich. On leaving Norwich, he moved to London with his family and became master of Emanuel Hospital, Westminster. Several more publications followed, including *The Rape of Helen, from the Greek of Coluthus* (1786), *Poems and Translations* (1788), *Incidents of Youthful Life, or, The True History of William Langley*, a children's book (1790), and his translation of Herodotus (1791); this last was often reprinted. In June 1792 he was elected FSA.

In 1793 the *British Critic* launched itself as a conservative review journal claiming a vital socio-political function at a time when, as Beloe later put it, 'the contagion of the French Revolution had … infected our purer atmosphere' (Beloe, *Sexagenarian*, 1.296). Beloe and the Revd Robert Nares, as assistant editor and editor respectively, were joint proprietors of the *British Critic* with the booksellers Francis and Charles Rivington; the Rivingtons were entitled to 50 per cent of the profits and Beloe and Nares shared the other 50 per cent, Beloe with a two-fifths share and Nares three-fifths. Beloe continued to write for the journal until the end of its first series in 1813.

Two years after the establishment of the *British Critic* Beloe published both his translation of *The Attic Nights of Aulus Gellius* and *Miscellanies: Consisting of Poems, Classical Extracts, and Oriental Apologues*. In 1796 he became rector of All Hallows, London Wall, where he remained until his death, and in 1797 a prebendary of Lincoln. During these years he published a number of works, including his poem *Julia, or, Last Follies* (1798) and two anonymous prefaces to volumes of the *Gentleman's Magazine*. Altogether he published in the magazine more than twenty of these prefaces, together with other miscellaneous pieces in verse and prose, between 1796 and 1816.

In 1803 came the high point of Beloe's career, 'the great object of [his] ambition' (Beloe, *Anecdotes*, 1.vi): appointment as under-librarian at the British Museum after presenting 'an Instrument, signed by the Archbishop of Canterbury, the Lord Chancellor, & the Speaker of the House of Commons' (BM, central archives, minutes of committees, C2236, 5 Aug 1803). Here he began his *Anecdotes of Literature and Scarce Books*, published in six volumes between 1806 and 1812. His position was short-lived, however; in 1806 it emerged that James Deighton, a printseller, had stolen from the museum £1500 worth of engravings by Rembrandt and others. Beloe was held to have been negligent and the museum's trustees dismissed him. He remained permanently bitter about being deprived of his ideal job, blaming his difficulties, with characteristic self-flattery, on his 'too easy disposition to believe every man honest who appeared so' (Beloe, *Sexagenarian*, 2.130) and considering that he had 'not the smallest occasion for self-reproach' (Beloe, *Anecdotes*, 6.viii).

Following the completion of publication of *Anecdotes*, Beloe's health began to decline, and in March 1817 he suffered a seizure and paralysis. He lingered for three weeks and died on 11 April 1817 at his house in Kensington Square, and was buried in his own church of All Hallows. He was survived by his wife and their four sons and one daughter.

Shortly after his death Beloe's greatest literary row blew up with the publication in 1817 of *The Sexagenarian*. As the supposed editor, Thomas Rennell, who was anxious to escape blame for the 'passages which have been deemed objectionable', explained in a postscript to the second edition, the autobiography

> was printed under the inspection of its real author; and *to the very last sheet*, was revised and corrected by HIMSELF—and had his life been spared for one month longer, the work would have been sent out into the world upon his whole and sole responsibility. (Beloe, *Sexagenarian*, 2.388)

It was 'the ungrateful and calumnious attack' on Parr that caused much of the trouble, but there was considerable disagreement (*Monthly Review*, 198). The *Monthly*'s comment that

> bedaubing himself with his own praise, he mingles with nauseating doses of self-applause a disgusting (if not a due) portion of flattery of those who are distinguished by rank and power, and who appear to be in any way likely *to do him service* (ibid., 192)

represents one side; the other may be seen in the *British Critic*'s view that Beloe was charitable to his contemporaries and that the 'few instances only … of spleen or ill humour' were justified (*British Critic*, 63). A few years before his death Beloe had congratulated himself on having 'passed through a career so long and so perilous, without being seriously implicated either in personal or literary hostilities' (Beloe, *Anecdotes*, 6.xv); if this was unlikely during his lifetime, it was certainly untrue after his death.   ANTONIA FORSTER

Sources Nichols, *Lit. anecdotes*, 9.94–6 · Venn, *Alum. Cant.* · *GM*, 1st ser., 87/1 (1817), 371–2 · *Annual Biography and Obituary*, 3 (1819), 29–72 · J. Johnstone, 'Memoirs', in *The works of Samuel Parr … with memoirs of his life and writings*, ed. J. Johnstone, 1 (1828) · minutes of committees, BM, C2236, 5 Aug 1803 · W. Beloe, *The sexagenarian, or, The recollections of a literary life*, ed. [T. Rennell], 2nd edn, 2 vols. (1818) · *British Critic*, new ser., 8 (1817), 47–63 · *Monthly Review*, new ser., 85 (1818), 192–203 · W. Beloe, *Anecdotes of literature and scarce books*, 6 vols. (1807–12) · W. Field, *Memoirs of the life, writings and opinions of the Rev. Samuel Parr*, 2 vols. (1828) · J. F. Waller, ed., *The imperial dictionary of universal biography*, 3 vols. (1857–63) · H. W. Saunders, *A history of the Norwich grammar school* (1932) · indenture document setting up *British Critic*, LMA · J. M. Kuist, *The Nichols file of the*

Gentleman's Magazine: attributions of authorship and other documenta-
tion in editorial papers at the Folger Library (1982) • *DNB* • parish register, Norwich, St Peter Mancroft, 21 Feb 1758 [baptism]
Archives BL, letters, as sponsor, to Royal Literary Fund, loan 96
Wealth at death see will, PRO, proved June 1819

Beloff, Max, Baron Beloff (1913–1999), historian, was born
on 2 July 1913 at 21 York House, Fieldway Crescent, Islington, London, the elder son in a family of five children of
Simon Beloff, general merchant, and his wife, Marie, *née*
Katzin. Nora *Beloff and Anne Ethel Beloff-*Chain [*see
under* Chain, Sir Ernst Boris] were his younger sisters. His
parents were Orthodox Russian Jews who had emigrated
to Britain in 1903. He was brought up speaking English as
his first language in a multilingual household, his parents
speaking Russian to one another, and also Yiddish and
German. He also spoke fluent and grammatical French
(though with an accent and a sentence structure that was
Churchillian rather than Parisian), as a result of a year in
Switzerland.

Education and early career Beloff was educated at the progressive King Alfred School in Hampstead (where his sister Renee was later a teacher) before attending St Paul's
School, London, where he showed a particular aptitude
for classics and history. After six months in Germany and
Danzig he went to Corpus Christi College, Oxford, as a
scholar, where he read history. He won the Gibbs scholarship in modern history in 1934, graduated with first-class
honours in modern history in 1935, and was elected a
senior demy at Magdalen College in the same year. He
then studied for a B.Litt. on seventeenth-century English
history, with G. N. Clark as his supervisor. In 1937 he
became a junior research fellow at Corpus Christi College.
On 19 March 1938 he married Helen (*b.* 1915/16), daughter
of Samuel Dobrin, barrister; they had two sons.

Beloff was appointed an assistant lecturer in history at the University of Manchester, specializing in
seventeenth-century history, in the summer of 1939. He
served in the Royal Corps of Signals in 1940–41, and was
invalided out, returning in 1941 to Manchester, where he
added American history to his teaching. In 1946 he
returned to Oxford as Nuffield reader in the comparative
study of institutions, holding a fellowship at Nuffield College from 1947. In 1957 he was elected Gladstone professor
of government and public administration, with a fellowship at All Souls College.

History and politics Beloff was a teacher of and writer on
politics in the old British tradition, treating politics from
the point of view of a historian, both of political developments and of political thought. For his 'intellectual autobiography', he chose the title *An Historian in the Twentieth
Century* (1992). He disliked the concept of 'political science' as it was conceived in the United States and copied in
Britain, and was disliked by many of its practitioners at a
time when even some groups of British historians copied
the French school, the Annalistes, in the search for a
value-free 'hard' and 'scientific' history. But the subtitle of
his autobiography—'Chapters in intellectual autobiography'—revealed the anomaly of his position. Few historians of his generation thought of themselves consciously

Max Beloff, Baron Beloff (1913–1999), by Sydney O'Meara, 1976

as 'intellectuals', a concept which seemed more akin to
the use of the term 'intelligentsia' for a recognizably separate class of politically minded, educated, and politically
and culturally active persons in Russian and Soviet
society.

Whether as a historian of events, of structures, or of
ideas, Beloff was profoundly bound to the written word.
Unlike some of his contemporaries, he was not tempted
into public debate either on radio or on television. The
range of his writings revealed his belief in the ability of
the trained intellect to range across topics of government
and politics, political thought, modern and contemporary
history, and international affairs. Nor did he restrict himself to English and American history. He was as much at
home with the detailed monograph as with the popular-
ization of history; his *Thomas Jefferson and American Democracy* (1948) and *The Age of Absolutism* (1954) were excellent
examples of the kinds of book called into existence by the
development of secondary education following the 1944
Education Act.

Beloff's two-volume study of British imperial decline,
Imperial Sunset, 1897–1942 (1969 and 1989), showed him
embracing the new concentration under younger historians on the multi-biographical approach to the political
decision makers, though his abandonment after twenty
years of what was originally intended to be a three-
volume work showed that he found the enormous expansion of personal data required by this approach uncongenial. His method was always the condensation of data
into a single, scaled-down vision. The Breughelian accumulation of numbers of individual scenes into an enormous canvas was not something which appealed to him.
His writings on international politics reflected the same
development. His earliest work, *The Foreign Policy of the
Soviet Union, 1936–1941* (1949), a two-volume monograph,
and for decades the standard work on the subject, developed out of his work as a historical adviser to a Chatham
House study group. His later works—*Foreign Policy and the
Democratic Process* (1955), *New Dimensions in Foreign Policy*
(1961), and *The United States and the Unity of Europe* (1963)—

were essentially contributions to the debate on democracy and foreign policy provoked by dissident western voices in the first full decade of the cold war, dealing as they did with concepts and positions rather than with narrative expositions.

Later career Beloff retained his ability to write history, especially to re-examine events in the history of his own times, until the end. But from 1970 onwards his main energies were drawn into resisting the nationalization of university education begun under Anthony Crosland and continued throughout the 1970s. In 1974 he abandoned Oxford (though retaining a fellowship at St Antony's College, from 1975 to 1984) to become the first principal of the University College of Buckingham, a privately financed institution of higher learning set up to show what university education could become if freed from direction from and financial dependence upon the government of the day. He saw it successfully established, and its independence guaranteed; the college was awarded a royal charter, enabling it to award degrees, in 1983, four years after Beloff's retirement. His success made him a hero to the new toryism of Margaret Thatcher, winning him a knighthood in 1980 and a life peerage, as Baron Beloff, in 1981. But Mrs Thatcher's government proved in practice to be at least as dirigiste in matters of higher education as its Labour predecessor; Beloff opposed dirigisme of any kind, and swiftly broke with the Conservative Party and remained a trenchant critic of its university policy until his death.

In later years Beloff became an outspoken opponent of the European Union, and in particular of continental federalist ideas. He compared the parliamentary vote on the Maastricht treaty with the French national assembly voting for Pétain and the Vichy regime, and in 1996 published *Britain and the European Union: Dialogue of the Deaf*, in which he argued that British membership of the European Union was incompatible with the survival of its tradition of liberal constitutionalism. He also engaged in numerous other controversies, ranging from what he considered the harmful consequences of Britain's premature abandonment of its imperial role to the quality of performances by the Royal Shakespeare Company. A month before his death he again sparked controversy by comparing the rise of Tony Blair to that of Adolf Hitler.

A short, pugnacious man, Beloff 'was never able to participate easily in conversations without serious intellectual content, and could strike those who came into contact with him as impatient and forbidding' (*The Times*); he was nevertheless generous in assisting younger scholars. He was elected a fellow of the British Academy in 1973, held honorary doctorates from Pittsburgh University (USA), Bishop's University (Canada), Bavdoin College (USA), the University of Aix-Marseilles (France), and Manchester, Oxford, and Buckingham universities, and was an honorary fellow of Mansfield and Corpus Christi colleges, Oxford. He died of heart failure at St Thomas's Hospital, Lambeth, London, on 22 March 1999, and was survived by his wife and their two sons. A commemoration was held in the Codrington Library, All Souls College, on 19 June 1999.

Assessment Beloff was a historian by training; but his concept of history was resolutely bound by concepts of national history and national historiography, expanded to take in the concept of 'European history'. He never crossed the boundary into international history. He wrote of the foreign policies of nations, not of the interplay between the actions of nations. He never entered the history of wars and their origins. He did not write on the history of international movements and institutions, apart from the old Commonwealth. Nor did he tackle the history of international law as the attempt to embody and formulate the conventions and compacts necessary to any kind of multinational arrangement. He matured under a particular stage of British historiographical development, learned from some of the great names, including Sir George Clark, Maurice Powicke, and Denis Brogan, and he read extensively and almost avariciously the works of his successors. Perhaps his most striking book of essays was entitled *The Intellectual in Politics and other Essays* (1970). He was pre-eminently a political intellectual of a recognizably European type among historians. He attracted a good deal of ill-natured carping from among those writers on politics who felt disadvantaged in the face of his historical knowledge. But his achievements were solid, and his books will continue to repay those for whom content is more important than the style of the moment. There are those who have tried to link his achievements with the Jewish community in Britain. But although he never made any attempt to disguise his Jewish origins, and played his part in Jewish academic institutions such as the Wiener Library, he wrote as a British and European intellectual, and not as a self-proclaimed member of the Jewish community, and his allegiance was primarily to the tradition of Oxford University scholarship.

D. CAMERON WATT

Sources M. Beloff, *An historian in the twentieth century* (Yale, 1992) · *The Times* (24 March 1999) · *Daily Telegraph* (24 March 1999) · *The Guardian* (25 March 1999) · *The Independent* (26 March 1999) · *Daily Telegraph* (30 March 1999) · *WWW* · private information (2004) · personal knowledge (2004) · b. cert. · m. cert. · d. cert.
Likenesses photograph, 1973, repro. in *The Times* · S. O'Meara, photograph, 1976, Hult. Arch. [*see illus.*] · photograph, 1983, repro. in *Daily Telegraph* (24 March 1999) · N. Libbert, photograph, repro. in *The Guardian* · photograph, repro. in *The Independent*

Beloff, (Leah) Nora (1919–1997), journalist, was born on 24 January 1919 at 65 Oakwood Court, Kensington, London, the middle of five children (two sons and three daughters) of Simon Beloff and his wife, Marie, formerly Katzin. Her elder brother Max, later Lord *Beloff (1913–1999), was Gladstone professor of government and administration at Oxford University and founding principal of Britain's first private university at Buckingham. Her other brother, John, became professor of psychology at Edinburgh University. One of her sisters was a headmistress, and the other, Anne Ethel Beloff-*Chain [*see under* Chain, Sir Ernst Boris], a biochemist, was married to Sir Ernst Boris *Chain

(1906–1979), who won a Nobel prize for his work on peni-cillin. Her parents, Simon and Marie, had changed their name from Rabinovich on emigrating to England from Belorussia a decade before Nora was born. Her father built a prosperous export business trading in chemicals. Her mother, a graduate of St Petersburg University, was a Zion-ist and worked for a charity that taught skills to the Jews of eastern Europe to prepare them for life in Palestine. Her father was also a benefactor to institutions of higher edu-cation there.

Although Nora was named after the emancipated hero-ine of Ibsen's *En dukkehjem* ('A Doll's House'), she did not inherit her mother's commitment to feminism or to Zion-ism. Of the one she wrote: 'I have never been much identi-fied with women's liberation causes'; and of the other: 'I took exception to the whole idea of belonging to a select tribe and shrunk from the rituals of the synagogue.' She was educated at the King Alfred School, a progressive school in Hampstead, and at Lady Margaret Hall, Oxford, where she read history. On graduating in 1940 she was employed by the Foreign Office intelligence department, but she moved to the British embassy in Paris in 1944. After the Second World War she stayed in Paris with Reu-ters, then became the Paris correspondent of *The Economist* before transferring to the same role for *The Observer* in 1948. She first attracted attention during the Algerian war with some reports on the torture of women rebels by French soldiers. She was on *The Observer* for nearly thirty years, moving on from Paris to cover the cold war from Washington and Moscow until, in 1964, she was appoin-ted as the first female political correspondent of a British newspaper.

Beloff's editor, David Astor, to whom she remained close despite frequent disagreements over policy, described her as 'a pure journalist of courage and inde-pendence. Her loyalty was to the truth.' She pursued her perception of the truth with a terrier-like tenacity that made her some powerful enemies, including the prime minister. By June 1966 Harold Wilson was instructing col-leagues to deny Beloff interviews (R. H. S. Crossman, *The Diaries of a Cabinet Minister*, 3 vols., 1975–7, 1.552). He seems to have kept a file of her articles, and two years later David Astor became aware that Wilson thought *The Observer* was pursuing a personal vendetta against him, Astor having allegedly instructed Beloff to write hostile stories (*The Observer*, 25 May 1969, 7). Wilson became so exasperated by Beloff's exposure of divisions within the Labour Party that he summoned Astor to Downing Street in an effort to get her dismissed. He even hinted that the government was keeping her under surveillance. She courted more unpopularity when she revealed Trotskyist infiltration of the Labour Party in the late 1960s and 1970s. Although she was later shown to have been right, she suffered scorn and ridicule at the time, some of it from her own office col-leagues.

Beloff was a tiny woman who seemed to be in a perpet-ual hurry. She had been present at most of the great events of the post-war world, which gave her a rare per-spective on British domestic politics and a wider frame of reference than her younger colleagues in the political lobby had: an advantage she took no pains to hide from them. She did not suffer fools gladly, among either politi-cians or journalists, and did not allow any loose comment to go unchecked. She would harangue politicians on the telephone if she thought they were acting dishonourably or not telling the truth; not surprisingly, some tried to avoid her. Having experienced the war and the nuclear tensions of the post-war period and reported on the suffer-ing of those living under communist rule, she knew that politics had a profound effect on people's lives and scorned a younger generation of political writers who treated it as a comical game.

Perhaps because of this apparently superior air, and because she was a woman in a traditionally male environ-ment, Beloff became a victim of newspaper gossip col-umns, the attacks culminating in Auberon Waugh's cruel jest in *Private Eye* that she had slept with the entire cabinet. 'Ballsoff', to use her sobriquet in the satirical magazine, successfully sued for libel, but lost a more celebrated case when she claimed breach of copyright over a memo, reporting a lunchtime conversation with a senior politic-ian, which had been leaked to *Private Eye*. The action was regarded in legal circles as ill judged and set a damaging precedent for freedom of the press.

Beloff was never a professional journalist in the trad-itional sense—she had no shorthand, could barely type her own stories, and left it to others to translate her idio-syncratic use of the English language into a form that readers could follow. She exchanged stories with her opposite number on the *Sunday Times* to make sure that neither was scooped by the other—a practice that brought the managing editor of *The Observer* near to apoplexy when it came to light. She never came to terms with *The Observer* after David Astor's retirement in 1975 and left in a typic-ally bizarre fashion after proposing in a letter to the news-paper's owners that they should change the new editor—then posting it in an envelope addressed to the editor him-self.

Her energy and crusading valour undimmed, Beloff travelled widely in Europe, highlighting the persecution of Soviet Jews and getting herself arrested in Georgia and expelled from Yugoslavia. She caused controversy in her later years as a public defender of the Serbs in post-Tito Yugoslavia. She was the author of five books, the first of which, *The General Said No*, was a vivid account of Britain's abortive bid for European entry in 1963. Two were on British politics: *Transit of Britain* (1973), an analysis of Brit-ain's changing role in the post-war world, and *Freedom under Foot* (1976), a polemic against Michael Foot for his support, as Labour's employment secretary, for a trade union closed shop in newspapers. *No Travel Like Russian Travel* appeared in 1979, and her last book was *Tito's Flawed Legacy* (1985), in which she claimed that Britain's wartime support for the partisan leader had been influenced by communist infiltration of British security services.

Beloff once wrote:

I prefer male company and enjoy the fact that the political and diplomatic world in which I live is almost entirely male

... I have found that men, either because they are gallant or because they are intimidated, tend to be nicer to women than to each other.

Even so, it was a source of amazement to her colleagues and friends when on 8 March 1977, at the age of fifty-eight, she suddenly married the gifted but somewhat shambolic sports editor of *The Observer*, (George) Clifford Philip Makins (*b.* 1923/4). They were together for thirteen years before he died in 1990. She once wrote of herself: 'Journalism was obviously the right choice. I had three of the necessary qualifications: inexhaustible stamina, insatiable curiosity and a thick skin.' She had all these qualities in abundance, especially the last. For all her quirks and obsessions, she enjoyed one of the most distinguished careers of any twentieth-century woman in British journalism. She died of a pulmonary embolism and Hodgkin's disease at the Royal Free Hospital, Camden, London, on 12 February 1997.   DONALD TRELFORD

Sources W. Millinship, *The Independent* (15 Feb 1997), 18a–f · D. Astor, *The Guardian* (15 Feb 1997), 19a–h · personal knowledge (2004) · private information (2004) [family] · E. Pace, *New York Times* (23 Feb 1997), sect. 1, p. 39 · *Washington Post* (18 Feb 1997), 'Metro' section · b. cert. · m. cert. · d. cert.

Likenesses photograph, repro. in *The Guardian*

Belper. For this title name *see* Strutt, Edward, first Baron Belper (1801–1880).

Belsham, Thomas (1750–1829), Unitarian minister, was born in Bedford on 15 April 1750, the eldest son (of four) and the eldest child (of eight) of the Revd James Belsham (*d.* 1770) and his wife, Ann(e) Woodward (*d.* 1780), eldest child of Thomas Woodward, a Bedford brewer. The elder Belsham had been dissenting minister at Bishop's Stortford from 1735 to 1748; on moving to Bedford he assisted at the Bunyan Meeting and was pastor at Newport Pagnell until 1763. The fourth son and child of the marriage, William *Belsham (1752–1827), became a well-known historian.

Thomas Belsham studied happily with John Aikin (1713–1780) at Kibworth in 1757–8, just prior to Aikin's departure for Warrington Academy, and for eight years with John French at Ware and Wellingborough, where his education was certainly better than he later allowed. In 1766 he entered Daventry Academy, then headed by Caleb Ashworth (1722–1775); Thomas Robins (1732–1810) was divinity tutor and Ashworth's successor in 1775. While Belsham was open to a wide range of influences in the relatively easy-going theological circumstances of mid-century, he became a member of the Independent (Congregationalist) church in Daventry, of which Ashworth was the minister, in 1768.

On completion of his course in 1770 Belsham was chosen assistant tutor at Daventry, first in Greek, then in mathematics, logic, and metaphysics, holding the post until July 1778, when he became minister to the Independent congregation at Worcester. His success there and his growing reputation led to invitations from other congregations, but only in 1781, on Robins's retirement, was he prevailed upon to return to Daventry as divinity tutor and as minister of the Independent congregation.

Thomas Belsham (1750–1829), by Henry Howard, exh. RA 1809

While Belsham's orthodoxy remained unquestioned, his diaries betray a steady move towards heterodoxy, and by 1789 he had abandoned Arianism (which posited a subordinate divinity for Christ, in contrast to the equality of divine persons envisioned in orthodox trinitarianism) for the unitarian position on the humanity of Christ; his consequent resignation from Daventry and from his pulpit in June of that year caused a sensation in the dissenting world.

Belsham was quickly offered the posts of professor of divinity and resident tutor at New College, Hackney, founded in 1786, and embarked on a course of increasing theological and political radicalism. When the college was closed because of financial and disciplinary difficulties in 1796—Belsham blamed the extremity of its radicalism on the youthful quest for certainty in a world governed by probability—he was left with only his pulpit at the Gravel Pit Chapel, for which he was chosen, with some difficulty, in April 1794 after Joseph Priestley (1733–1804) resigned to emigrate to the United States; for a time Belsham added a school to his responsibilities. In 1805 he succeeded John Disney (1746–1816) at Essex Street, founded by Theophilus Lindsey (1723–1808) in 1774 and established as the most fashionable of the Unitarian chapels in the capital.

Gradually abandoning his earlier, rather formulistic introspection, Belsham translated his growing confidence into a new role as an aggressive Unitarian apologist. His début as a polemical writer came in 1798 with an attack on William Wilberforce's *Practical View of the Prevailing Religious System* (1797), which made him a marked man among evangelicals and other orthodox believers, and he gleefully returned the many assaults on him in a slashing, witty controversial style that, despite excesses, still makes for good reading. Deservedly the most remembered of his sallies was a comment on the bitter exchange between Priestley and Archdeacon (later Bishop) Samuel Horsley (1733–1806), that each retired from the field with what he most sought: Priestley with his victory and Horsley with his mitre. Belsham was primarily responsible for the publication in 1808 of an 'improved' translation of the New Testament, largely from an earlier translation (based on Johann Jakob Griesbach's recently established text) by William Newcome (1729–1800), archbishop of Tuam, which called forth many attacks. So too did his translation and commentary on the epistles of St Paul, published in 1822, while an appendix on the progress of Unitarianism in America included in his biography of Lindsey (1812) created a furore in the United States.

W. J. Fox (1786–1864) said that Belsham had 'a mind of great force, but not of the highest order', persuasive to the understanding but deficient in imagination (Fox, 249). He was an authoritative synthesizer and transmitter of unitarian and necessarian ideas advanced by Priestley and Lindsey, a tireless publicist who dominated the second generation of Unitarianism as a continuous denomination. His *Elements of the Philosophy of the Mind* (1801) was long the standard textbook for the metaphysics and psychology drawn from David Hartley (1705–1757) and Priestley. Belsham was sympathetic to German historical criticism and rejected many parts of the Bible, including the account of creation in Genesis, but he disliked German theology and, despite repeated efforts, confessed his failure to penetrate Kant's intentions.

Belsham was a tireless advocate of extended toleration and of the civil rights of dissenters. He distrusted missionary effort and, true to his Independent background, opposed most denomination-wide organizations, though in 1791 he had been instrumental in establishing the Unitarian Society for distributing books, with (characteristically) a stringent and much contested anti-Arian definition of membership. A persisting measure of sympathy toward establishment, increasing doubts about improving the lot of the poor, and an inclination to give credit to government for good intentions caused uneasiness in some of his younger contemporaries, whose radicalism had outstripped his old-fashioned Foxite whiggism.

Belsham never married; his usual geniality was not without flaws—at any rate, he did not make life easy for Thomas Madge (1786–1870), who was his assistant at Essex Street after 1825 (Belsham and Madge to J. H. Bransby, 6 and 28 Feb 1826). He was vastly corpulent; a wit unkindly asked, 'Is it possible *that* man really believed in the resurrection of *that* body?' (Gordon, 287), and, when he preached at Chowbent, in Lancashire, a hole had to be cut in the wall to allow him to enter the pulpit. Belsham suffered much from ill health in his later years, though his mind remained clear to the end, despite a series of apoplectic seizures. He died at Hampstead on 11 November 1829 and was buried in Bunhill Fields, London, in the tomb of his friends Theophilus and Hannah Lindsey.

R. K. WEBB

Sources J. Williams, *Memoirs of the late Reverend Thomas Belsham* (1833) · [W. J. Fox], 'On the character and writings of the Rev. T. Belsham', *Monthly Repository*, new ser., 4 (1830), 73–88, 162–72, 244–53 · A. Gordon, *Addresses biographical and historical* (1922), 283–310 · H. L. Short, 'The founding of the British & Foreign Unitarian Association', *Transactions of the Unitarian Historical Society*, 16 (1975–8) [suppl.] · J. Hunter, *Familiae minorum gentium*, ed. J. W. Clay, 1, Harleian Society, 37 (1894)

Archives Harris Man. Oxf., notes, lectures, sermons | N. Yorks. CRO, corresp. with Christopher Wyvill

Likenesses H. Howard, oils, exh. RA 1809, DWL [*see illus.*] · H. Meyer, engraving (after H. Howard), Harris Man. Oxf.

Wealth at death under £3000: estate duty registers, 1829, PC 4/745

Belsham, William (1752–1827), political writer and historian, was born in Bedford, the fourth son of the Revd James Belsham (*d.* 1770), dissenting minister, and Ann(e) Woodward (*d.* 1780), daughter of Thomas Woodward, a Bedford brewer. His eldest brother, Thomas *Belsham, later became a prominent Unitarian minister. Keenly interested in politics, Belsham was hostile to the Fox–North coalition in 1783, friendly towards Lord Shelburne, and an admirer of William Pitt until he opposed the repeal of the Test Act in 1788. He launched his career as an author in 1789 with a volume entitled *Essays, Philosophical, Historical and Literary*, published anonymously by Charles Dilly, another dissenter from Bedfordshire. The essays were pleasant, discursive, and miscellaneous, but owed most of the attention they received to Belsham's comments on other writers. James Boswell, though regretting Belsham's nonconformist sympathies, quoted approvingly from the essay on dramatic criticism and conceded that the essays showed 'much reading and thinking, and good composition' (Boswell, *Life*, 1.389 n.). Essay 18, 'Strictures on Walpole's catalogue of royal and noble authors', complained that Horace Walpole sacrificed judgement to 'a fanciful and affected turn of thinking' (Walpole, 31.293–4). In essay 10, 'On the study of metaphysics', Belsham attacked Vicesimus Knox, who had condemned that discipline as idle and useless, fit only for mere speculation; Knox subsequently complained to Boswell that Dilly ought not to encourage his authors to attack each other. Several of the remaining essays reflected Belsham's religious views. He demanded repeal of the Test Act, dismissing those 'malevolent and senseless bigots' who maintained it (essay 41), wrote cogently on unitarianism, which 'seems to advance with accelerated force and vigour' (essay 23), disliked ecclesiastical establishments (essay 28), and gave an ecstatic welcome to the early days of the French Revolution, maintaining that 'in that short space of time … since the National Assembly was convened, more has been accomplished for the glory and happiness of the community than could previously have been imagined possible' (essay 40). Essay 23, on the African slave trade, which he denounced as 'the height of moral and political depravity', was reprinted in 1790 as a separate pamphlet.

In 1791 Belsham published a second volume of essays, which included a severe attack on Edmund Burke's *Reflections on the Revolution in France*, which Belsham considered 'dangerously calculated to soothe the pride, to dazzle the imagination, and to inflame the ambition of kings'. Thereafter he published prolifically. His *Examination of an Appeal from the New to the Old Whigs* (1792) insisted that the Society for Constitutional Information, in promoting Thomas Paine's *Rights of Man*, did not endorse all Paine's views, and added incautiously, 'the French nation having very wisely retained the monarchical form of government' (Goodwin, 178 and n.). His *Remarks on the Nature and Necessity of a Parliamentary Reform* (1793) deplored the extravagance of both Paine and Burke, and commended the Society of Friends of the People, to which he belonged, as a moderate alternative. Pamphlets on the poor laws and on the peace of Amiens followed in 1797 and 1802. In 1800 and 1801 he was involved in an exchange with Herbert Marsh, later bishop of Peterborough, whose *History of the Politics of Great Britain and France* had maintained that the French were the aggressors in the revolutionary wars. Belsham's *Remarks* (1800) was answered by Marsh's *Vindication*, which in turn provoked Belsham's *Reply* (1801).

The later part of Belsham's life was devoted to the writing and updating of his history, which began in 1793 as *Memoirs of the Kings of Great Britain of the House of Brunswic-Lunenberg [sic]* and finished as *A History of Great Britain from 1688 to 1820* (1805–24). Lord Macaulay predictably placed Belsham among 'wretched historians' (*Letters of Thomas Babington Macaulay*, 5.279). Belsham confined himself largely to political narrative, depending heavily on published parliamentary debates and sources in print, but he wrote soberly, pursuing an impeccably radical whig and dissenting line. He helped to establish the pattern of a hostile interpretation of the reign of George III, 'distinguished by a strange and dreadful fatality' and starting with the baneful intrigues of Lord Bute and the princess dowager. He was convinced of the growing influence of the crown, deplored the injustice of the American War of Independence, and denounced George III as a 'sullen and malignant bigot'. He died at Portland Place, Hammersmith, Middlesex, on 17 November 1827.

JOHN CANNON

Sources *GM*, 1st ser., 98/1 (1828), 274–5 · H. Butterfield, *George III and the historians* (1957) · *VCH Bedfordshire* · Boswell, *Life*, 1.389n. · R. W. Davis, *Dissent in politics, 1780–1830: the political life of William Smith, MP* (1971) · *The letters of Thomas Babington Macaulay*, ed. T. Pinney, 5 (1981), 279 · Walpole, *Corr.*, 31.293–4 · A. Goodwin, *The friends of liberty: the English democratic movement in the age of the French Revolution* (1979) · *The correspondence and other papers of James Boswell relating to the making of the Life of Johnson*, ed. M. Waingrow (1969), vol. 2 of *The Yale editions of the private papers of James Boswell*, research edn (1966–) · J. Williams, *Memoirs of the late Reverend Thomas Belsham* (1833)
Archives Beds. & Luton ARS, letters to Samuel Whitbread

Belsky [*née* Owen], **Margaret Constance** (1919–1989), cartoonist and illustrator, was born in Wareham, Dorset, on 20 June 1919. Her father, Albert Edward Owen (*c*.1880–*c*.1958), was an Australian engineer of Welsh/Irish ancestry who came to the UK about 1917 after being wounded at Gallipoli. Her mother, Margaret Constance Davies-Bunton (*c*.1880–*c*.1958), was British and a good amateur painter. Known as Cooee (an Australian call) to her family and friends, Margaret had three younger brothers—John, Archibald, and Michael—and a younger sister, Dinah. She was educated at a Parents' National Educational Union school in West Moors, Dorset, and studied at Bournemouth School of Art (*c*.1936–9) under Charles Henry Collins Baker. In the late 1930s, while still a student in Bournemouth, she won a *Punch* cartoon competition and went on to study illustration and engraving under E. W. Tristram at the Royal College of Art (1940–44). Here she met a Czech soldier, Franta Belsky (1921–2000) (later a celebrated sculptor, president of the Society of Portrait Sculptors, and governor of St Martin's School of Art), and they were married in Newport, Monmouthshire, on 20 June 1944.

During the war Margaret Belsky worked as an art teacher in Dorset and began to draw cartoons regularly when Franta, on the recommendation of his fellow countryman Walter Trier (cartoonist, illustrator, and cover artist of *Lilliput* magazine), showed her work to Kaye Webb, assistant editor of *Lilliput*, in 1943. Her first drawing, based on an idea by her husband, was published in the magazine in December 1944, signed 'Belsky' but with Czech accents on the letters e and y. The letter B of the signature contained a C in the upper and an F in the lower loop (for Cooee and Franta)—Franta signed his work in the same way. As a freelance artist Margaret later contributed regular illustrations, cartoons, and caricatures to various publications including *Strand* magazine, *Punch*, *Guardian*, *John Bull*, *Financial Weekly*, and the *Sunday Graphic* (until it closed in 1960).

Early in 1951 Belsky joined the staff of the *Daily Herald* as its first-ever pocket cartoonist, thereby also becoming the first woman to draw a daily (six times a week) front-page cartoon for a national newspaper. Over the next nineteen years she produced more than 6500 cartoons for the *Herald* under the titles 'Belsky's Breakfast Cartoon' or 'As Belsky Sees It'. She continued to work for the paper after it was renamed the *Sun* in 1964 but left in 1969 when it was taken over by Rupert Murdoch. She then joined the *New Statesman*, drawing topical cartoons (1970–72), and also contributed to the *Sunday People*.

Belsky had a loose, expressive, drawing style and, after roughing out her work in pencil, drew in pen and ink on half imperial size sheets cut into four with a penknife. 'Pinkish' (her own description) in her politics, her jokes often made fun of dogs and tory ladies and she regarded herself modestly as 'the poor man's Osbert Lancaster'. Belsky also believed she had a large nose and no chin: 'When I was a child I chewed gum to try and develop my chin. So all the faces I draw have huge noses and no chins' (Bateman, 40). Of medium height, she had brown hair and brown eyes. Her favourite spokesmen were two tramps discussing economics and she often incorporated faces of her friends in her drawings. She also illustrated children's books—including eight titles by A. Oates as well as R. Brown's *Chubb on the Trail* (1976), E. Ramsbottom and J. Redmayne's *Colour* (1978), and P. Arnold and P. Scott-Kay's *The Gay Way Workbook* (1980)—designed jackets for Penguin, and drew for advertising. Margaret Belsky died of cancer at her home at 4 The Green, Sutton Courtenay, Oxfordshire, on 26 January 1989. She was cremated in Oxford.   MARK BRYANT

Sources private information (2004) [Franta Belsky] · M. Bryant, *Dictionary of twentieth-century British cartoonists and caricaturists* (2000) · M. Bryant and S. Heneage, eds., *Dictionary of British cartoonists and caricaturists, 1730–1980* (1994) · M. Bateman, *Funny way to earn a living: a book of cartoons and cartoonists* (1966) · T. S. Matthews, *The Independent* (1 Feb 1989) · *The Times* (2 Feb 1989) · *Daily Telegraph* (30 Jan 1989) · T. Baistow, *The Guardian* (30 Jan 1989) · A. Horne, *The dictionary of 20th century British book illustrators* (1994)
Archives priv. coll., scrapbooks, original drawings, photos · University of Kent, Canterbury, Centre for the Study of Cartoons and Caricature | FILM TV interview 1969 (details not found)
Likenesses M. C. Belsky, self-portrait, caricature, repro. in Bateman, *Funny way to earn a living* · photographs, priv. coll.
Wealth at death £9337: probate, 22 May 1989, *CGPLA Eng. & Wales*

Belson, John (*c*.1625–1704), historian and religious controversialist, was born at Stokenchurch, Buckinghamshire, the eldest son of Augustin Belson (*c*.1606–1684) and Elizabeth Cursonn (*b. c*.1606). The Belsons were an ancient Roman Catholic family with estates in Brill and Aston Rowant. The brother of John Belson's great-grandfather was the martyr Thomas *Belson. The Belson family suffered much under the anti-Catholic penal laws of the seventeenth and eighteenth centuries. John was probably educated abroad like his brothers who went to Douai. The Berkshire Record Office possesses a manuscript poem in Latin addressed to Charles I at the outbreak of the civil war written by John when he was a student. In 1653 he married Clare Gage, with whom he raised a family.

Belson had a modest private income from his estates and devoted himself to historical studies. He moved in a circle which included Catholic writers such as Thomas White, Thomas Blount, John Austin, and John Sergeant. During many years he collaborated with Thomas Blount on the *Chronological History of England*, a work that was never finished. In 1662 he published *Tradidi vobis, or, The traditionary conveyance of faith cleer'd, in the rational way, against the exceptions of a learned opponent*. It is a detailed exegesis and defence of the *Dialogues* of William Rushworth (edited and partly written by Thomas White) and as such it is one of the many contributions to the contemporary controversy about the authority of the scriptures versus the authority of the church. As letters by Belson to members of his family and friends show, he lived in France for extended periods: from about 1680 to 1681 he lived in Abbeville. In the late 1670s he was involved in the controversy about the oath of allegiance. Belson took the oath and defended his decision in an apologia. From about 1684 he and his wife lived in King Street, in St James's, Westminster. Belson died in London in 1704, possibly in December.   J. BLOM and F. BLOM

Sources Berks. RO, D/EBt/Q26/1–2, 7, 9, F66–81 · Bodl. Oxf., MS d.d. Barrett a.3 · *The correspondence of Thomas Blount (1618–1679): a recusant antiquary*, ed. T. Bongaerts (1978) · D. Krook, *John Sergeant and his circle: a study of three seventeenth-century Aristotelians* (1993) · G. H. Tavard, 'Scripture and tradition among seventeenth-century recusants', *Theological Studies*, 25 (1964), 343–85 · *VCH Oxfordshire*, 3.40 · M. A. H. Stapleton, *A history of the post-Reformation Catholic missions in Oxfordshire: with an account of the families connected with them* (1906), 263–6 · Gillow, *Lit. biog. hist.*, 1.180 · C. Dodd [H. Tootell], *The church history of England, from the year 1500, to the year 1688*, 3 (1742), 458 · J. Gillow and R. Trappes-Lomax, eds., *The diary of the 'blue nuns' or order of the Immaculate Conception of Our Lady, at Paris, 1658–1810*, Catholic RS, 8 (1910), 324
Archives Berks. RO, corresp., theological and antiquarian MSS, family papers · Bodl. Oxf., family MSS, MS d.d. Barrett

Belson, Thomas (*bap.* 1563, *d.* 1589), Roman Catholic martyr, was baptized on 14 December 1563 in the parish church of Aston Rowant, Oxfordshire, the third son and sixth and youngest child of Augustine Belson (*d.* in or before 1601), landowner, and Margaret Scarneinge (*d.* after 1612). A wealthy landowner with properties on the Oxfordshire–Buckinghamshire border, Augustine Belson was churchwarden at Aston Rowant in 1553, but refused to conform to the Elizabethan church settlement and became a determined recusant after 1559. To avoid the heavy fines and confiscation of property imposed on him, as head of the family, under the penal laws, he conveyed much of his freehold land to his three young sons. In 1575 he moved to Ixhill Lodge in Buckinghamshire, where the magistrates were more lenient to Catholics, but the family soon became known for receiving priests. During one raid a pursuivant reported that, although the priest escaped, he had found a box with a false bottom containing the Belsons' church things and books.

Thomas Belson grew up in this intense world of secrecy and danger. A former servant of the Belson family, arrested for praising Edmund Campion, confessed that in 1581 he was drawn 'to absent himselfe from churche by the speciall perswacon of Thomas and William Belson, who … sayed that it was rather a hell than heven to come to churche' (PRO, SP 12/173/29). Nothing is known of Thomas Belson's early education, but the breadth of his reading emerges in the Latin sonnet that he drafted in a family commonplace book and the inventory of his goods includes a Greek testament and a Hebrew psalter. In 1580, described as a gentleman aged sixteen, he matriculated from St Mary's Hall, part of Oriel College, Oxford, and three years later, in February 1583, supplicated for his BA but, like many Catholics, never graduated to avoid taking the oath of supremacy. Instead, he continued his studies at the English College at Douai, then in exile in Rheims.

Until he left Oxford, Belson was financially independent but in April 1583 he transferred all his properties to his brother William, thus evading the penalty for studying abroad—confiscation of all his possessions. During his year at Douai College he took no steps towards ordination and was described as a layman on his departure for England in April 1584. Nothing is known of his activities until June 1585, when he was imprisoned in the Tower of London with those helping the recently converted Philip Howard, first earl of Arundel, in his attempt to leave for Rheims. He was described as 'conveying intelligence between Bridges the priest and others beyond the seas and some in this realm, by unknowen means' (*Miscellanea II*, 261, 264). Bridges was Arundel's chaplain and helped plan his secret departure. However, in April 1585 Arundel was arrested on board ship, betrayed by Bridges, who was a secret apostate and Sir Francis Walsingham's spy.

Belson spent nearly two years in the Tower. In November 1586 he was sentenced to be banished the realm upon bonds, but was still there in March 1587, when his dying brother Robert willed that Thomas 'whensoever he shall come owte of prison wherein he nowe is shall at all times being unmaryed have meate drinck and lodging at Ixhill as often and as longe as he shall lyke to come thither to take it' (PRO, PROB 11/70, sig. 40). On his release he continued liaising between Catholics in Rheims and England (he was described as a conveyor of letters from beyond the seas during his second trial), and his father shrewdly transferred his remaining lands to avoid paying the bond should Belson be caught returning to England.

There is no record of Belson's movements until midnight on 18 May 1589, when he was arrested at the Catherine Wheel Inn in Oxford, together with two priests who had been with him at Douai, George Nichols, whom he thought of as his spiritual father, and Richard Yaxley, and a servant at the inn, Humphrey Prichard. The four men were taken on horseback to London, where they were tortured and interrogated but revealed nothing. After six weeks they were sent back to Oxford (in a wagon since they were now incapable of riding), tried, and found guilty. All four were executed in Longwall, Oxford, on 5 July 1589, the two priests hanged, drawn, and quartered for treason, Belson and Prichard hanged as felons. On the scaffold Belson embraced the bodies of the priests, declaring that he was very happy to suffer with them and be presented before God in such good company. The brutality of the executions shocked the local population, making them reluctant to aid the pursuivants; it was twenty years before another priest was executed in Oxford. Within a year eyewitness accounts of their execution were published in Rome, Paris, and Madrid. Belson was beatified on 22 November 1987. CHRISTINE J. KELLY

Sources C. Kelly, *Blessed Thomas Belson: his life and times, 1563–1589* (1988) • Bodl. Oxf., MS d.d. Barrett a.2 • state papers domestic, Elizabeth, PRO, SP 12 • *Miscellanea, II*, Catholic RS, 2 (1906) • will, PRO, PROB 11/70, sig. 40 [Robert Belson] • parish register of Aston Rowant, Oxfordshire [baptism] • BL, Lansdowne MS 61, no. 47
Archives Bodl. Oxf., Barrett papers, leases, deeds of gift, account books
Wealth at death £2 7s.: inventory, 1591, Oxf. UA, Hyp.B.10. Inventories, A–B (this includes only his clothes and books in his possession)

Belstead. For this title name *see* Ganzoni, (Francis) John Childs, first Baron Belstead (1882–1958).

Belt, Thomas (1832–1878), geologist, was born at Newcastle upon Tyne, the son of a seedsman in Brigg market. He was educated at a private school there, run by John Storey, a secretary of Tyneside Naturalists' Field Club. From his early youth Belt was an enthusiastic student of natural history; he became a member of the club in 1850, and contributed to its *Transactions*. In 1852 he left England for the Australian gold-diggings, and, with three brothers, worked as a miner. Between 1853 and 1860 he visited several mining districts and pursued his geological investigations. He became a member of the Philosophical Institute of Victoria and contributed in 1857 a paper on the origin of whirlwinds. In 1861 he published *Mineral veins, an enquiry into their origin, founded on a study of the auriferous quartz veins of Australia*.

In 1862 Belt returned to England with a high reputation and established himself in London as a consultant mining engineer. He was a fellow of the Geological Society and a corresponding member of the Philadelphia Academy of Natural Sciences. Soon afterwards he went to Nova Scotia as superintendent of the Nova Scotian Gold Company's mines. At about this time he married Jane Stephenson; they had at least one son. A few years later, back in Britain, he examined the quartz rocks of north Wales in a vain search for gold. From 1868 to 1872 he conducted the mining operations of the Chontales Gold Mining Company in Nicaragua. His observations of that country's geology, flora, and fauna were described in his book *The naturalist in Nicaragua: a narrative of a residence at the gold mines of Chontales and journeys in the savannahs and forests* (1873).

Between 1873 and 1876 Belt went several times to Siberia and the southern steppes of Russia. From his knowledge of the terrain in North America, Russia, and Wales, Belt developed an interest in the glacial period. He ascribed the formation of boulder clays and other outwash sediments in Europe to the action of ice flowing from Greenland, likewise the extinction of the great mammals and probably of Palaeolithic man, arousing controversy with his numerous articles on this topic. In 1878 he went to Colorado to fulfil a professional engagement but succumbed to fever and died at Kansas City on 21 September 1878, leaving a widow and a son, Anthony Belt.

SIDNEY LEE, *rev.* ANITA McCONNELL

Sources *Journal of Science*, 3rd ser., 1 (1879), 143–4 • *Nature*, 18 (1878), 570 • T. Belt, *The naturalist in Nicaragua* (1874) • R. Welford, *Men of mark 'twixt Tyne and Tweed*, 1 (1895), 250–54 • CGPLA Eng. & Wales (1879)
Archives NHM, corresp. • U. Newcastle, Hancock Museum, papers relating to Northumberland plants | CUL, letters to Charles Darwin
Likenesses engraving, repro. in Welford, *Men of mark*
Wealth at death under £2000: resworn probate, Sept 1879, CGPLA Eng. & Wales (1878)

Beltz, George Frederick (1774–1841), genealogist, was born on 9 August 1774, the eldest son and second of seven children of George Nicholas Beltz of St George's, Bloomsbury, coal merchant, and his wife, Elizabeth (d. 1796), only child of Samuel Gutteridge of Purley, Berkshire. From 1797 or earlier until 1816 he was employed as clerk to Sir Isaac Heard, Garter king of arms. He was admitted to the Inner Temple in 1810. He became gentleman usher of the scarlet rod of the Order of the Bath and Brunswick herald in 1814, in succession to Sir Isaac Heard, and held both appointments until his death. In 1813 he was secretary to the mission sent to invest the emperor of Russia with the Order of the Garter, and in 1814 he performed a similar office at the investiture of the emperor of Austria. After being Portcullis pursuivant from 1817 to 1822 he was appointed Lancaster herald. In 1826 he was made a companion of the Royal Guelphic Order, of which order he was honoured with knighthood in 1836.

Beltz, who was an executor for the widow of David Garrick, wrote a memoir of Mrs Garrick in the *Gentleman's Magazine* for November 1822, and he contributed papers on archaeological subjects to the *Gentleman's Magazine* (1822), to the *Retrospective Review* (1823), and to volumes 25, 27, and 28 of the *Archaeologia* of the Society of Antiquaries (1833–9). A fellow of the Society of Antiquaries (from 1807), he was elected to the society's council in 1837. Many of the elaborate pedigrees in Sir R. C. Hoare's *History of South Wiltshire* were compiled by him. He also assisted his cousin (their mothers were half-sisters) and clerk George William Collen, who was appointed Portcullis pursuivant in 1841, in the editing of the 1840 and 1841 editions of Debrett's *Peerage*.

Beltz was a first-class scholar and genealogist, and he and Sir Isaac Heard were on friendly social terms with William Beckford and frequent visitors at Fonthill. In 1817, on Heard's instructions, Beltz investigated the pedigree of William Radclyffe, Rouge Croix. As a result, in 1820 Radclyffe was prosecuted for forgery, fined £50, and sentenced to three months in prison. As well as exposing Radclyffe's imposture and forgery, Beltz exposed the imposture of Sir Samuel Egerton Brydges, bt, to the barony of Chandos of Sudeley. His *Review of the Chandos peerage case adjudicated 1803 and of the pretensions of Sir Samuel Egerton Brydges Bart to designate himself per legem terrae Baron Chandos of Sudeley*, published in 1834, revealed the emptiness of the pretensions and listed relevant documents which had vanished or suffered obliterations and additions. Beltz's reputation as a scholar and genealogist was confirmed by his *Memorials of the Order of the Garter from its Foundation to the Present Time*, published in 1841, the year of his death. He was attacked by his last illness while on a tour on the continent and died unmarried at Basel, Switzerland, on 23 October 1841 of abdominal typhus; he was interred in the cemetery of the parish of St Peter there. Sir Isaac Heard left a large proportion of his manuscripts jointly to Beltz and another of his assistants, James Pulman, with remainder to the survivor. Beltz left his own manuscripts to Pulman, who left Heard's, Beltz's, and his own manuscripts to the College of Arms in 1859. The collection comprises 219 manuscript volumes.

THOMAS WOODCOCK

Sources *GM*, 2nd ser., 17 (1842), 107 · W. H. Godfrey, A. Wagner, and H. Stanford London, *The College of Arms, Queen Victoria Street* (1963), 141 · A. Wagner, *Heralds of England: a history of the office and College of Arms* (1967), 426, 428–9, 452–6, 458–61, 464–5, 468–71, 495, 498–9, 526 · H. Stanford London, 'Lives of the heralds', MS and typescript, priv. coll. · A. R. Wagner, *The records and collections of the College of Arms* (1952) · will
Archives Coll. Arms, collections, corresp., and papers · CUL, pedigrees and genealogical notes | BL, letters to Philip Bliss, Add. MSS 34569–34573, *passim* · Bodl. Oxf., corresp. with William Beckford · Coll. Arms, Ebblewhite MSS · Derbys. RO, letters to Sir Roger Gresley · Dorset RO, letters to Thomas Rackett · U. Nott. L., corresp. with the fourth duke of Newcastle

Belzoni, Giovanni Battista (1778–1823), performing artist and Egyptologist, was born on 5 November 1778 in Padua, the son of a barber, Giacomo Belzoni, and his wife, Teresa. He went to Rome aged sixteen to prepare himself for monastic orders; he claimed also to have studied hydraulics. The French invasion of Rome in 1798 caused him to leave the city and become, he said, 'a wanderer' (Belzoni, 3.iii). His wanderings took him north, eventually into France and Germany, it seems mainly as a pedlar of religious objects. By the end of 1802 he was in the Netherlands and soon afterwards arrived in England. He was now twenty-four years old, a magnificent 6 feet 6 inches tall, and of great strength, a handsome man with blue eyes, dark hair, and a fresh complexion. In 1803 he married Sarah, probably *née* Banne [see Belzoni, Sarah (1783–1870)], a woman of great courage and fortitude, who was to accompany him on most of his travels, and embarked on a theatrical career. On Easter Monday 1803 a Sadler's Wells playbill announced the first appearance in England of the 'Patagonian Sampson', to present 'the most extraordinary specimens of the Gymnastic Art' (Fagan, 101). On an iron frame, itself weighing over 100 pounds, Belzoni carried eleven persons about the stage. He also acted the giant in *Jack the Giantkiller* to the dwarf of the famous clown Grimaldi. From playbills his career over the next nine years can be followed about the British Isles, and to Ireland, at fairs and theatres, often as strongman, but also as actor, conjuror, or designer of dramatic scenic effects produced by hydraulics. In 1812 Belzoni spent some months performing in Spain and Portugal, but next year was back in England, his last known performance there taking place in Oxford on 26 February 1813.

Belzoni travelled again to Iberia, this time accompanied by Sarah. By early 1815 they were in Malta, planning to go to Constantinople, where showmen were always welcome. But in Malta, Ismael Gibraltar, an agent of Mehmet Ali, pasha of Egypt, was recruiting engineers and industrialists to help modernize that country. Belzoni persuaded Gibraltar he could build a water-wheel which, with one ox, could lift as much water as four in the traditional Egyptian machine. In June 1815 Belzoni arrived in Egypt, but a year later, though he had fulfilled his promise, for political reasons the pasha rejected both wheel and inventor, and Belzoni found himself left almost destitute.

But this misfortune heralded his third and greatest career. The traveller John Lewis Burckhardt wished to present to the British Museum the famed colossal granite head of Ramses II, then known as the Young Memnon, which lay broken from its body at Thebes (Luxor), but had neither the money nor the engineering ability to move it. However, at this time Henry Salt had just arrived as British consul-general, also with a patriotic desire to benefit the British Museum, and prepared to share the cost, while Belzoni was eager to supply the physical means. Success was uncertain, for others had tried to move the huge weight in vain. Accompanied by Sarah, Belzoni set forth on 30 June 1816, and with levers, a cart on rollers, and great perseverance, in two weeks moved the head from its temple to the edge of the Nile. While awaiting a boat strong enough to

Giovanni Battista Belzoni (1778–1823), by Maxim Gauci, pubd 1821

transport it, he went south to Nubia and attempted to excavate the buried temple at Abu Simbel. Lack of money halted him, and he returned to embark the Memnon. The head is now a central feature of the British Museum's Egyptian collection. Belzoni was next employed by Salt to excavate at Thebes, but, frustrated by the machinations of his French rivals, returned to Abu Simbel, this time with Salt's sanction as well as his money. Sarah, indignant, was left behind; Belzoni's companions were Salt's secretary, Henry Beechey, two naval officers on half pay, Captains Irby and Mangles, an interpreter, Yanni d'Athanasi, and a janizary, Giovanni Finati. The locals became intransigent and it was Belzoni's party who eventually dug down to the door of the temple, and Finati who was the first to enter. Back again at Thebes, there were yet greater triumphs. Perseverance and mechanical ingenuity enabled him to remove great stones or cliffs of sand, but discovering the previously unknown required more: experience, acute observation—and luck. Belzoni possessed all three. Within twelve days he uncovered four new tombs in the Valley of the Kings, the most important being that of Seti I, in which lay a wonderful alabaster sarcophagus, now in Sir John Soane's Museum in Lincoln's Inn Fields.

Unlike his rival excavators, Belzoni's chief desire was for fame, not profit. He now fell out with Salt, whom he feared would, as his employer, assume the glory he felt should be solely his. Taken aback, but with typical generosity, Salt agreed that Belzoni should henceforth use his

funding as being 'under his auspices', rather than 'in his employ', and Belzoni appeared satisfied.

Belzoni next discovered the entrance to the second pyramid at Giza, which many had believed to be a solid mass. Later he excavated for himself at Thebes and travelled with Beechey to the Red Sea to establish the location of the ruins of the ancient city of Berenice. In November 1818 he went south to remove from Philae, for William John Bankes, the obelisk which now stands at Bankes's Dorset mansion, Kingston Lacy. Back in Thebes, Belzoni was attacked by French excavators and failed to gain redress in law. Having made a last journey, to the Little Oasis, and believing, wrongly, he had found the temple of Jupiter Ammon, Belzoni quitted Egypt in September 1819.

In Italy his native Padua, to which Belzoni presented two statues, struck a medal in his honour. The 'celebrated traveller' reached England in March 1820. Lionized by London society, he quickly wrote his *Narrative of the Operations and Recent Discoveries within the Pyramids, Temples, Tombs and Excavations in Egypt and Nubia* (1820), which went into several English editions and was also published in France and Italy. This, the first such account, is fascinating, but marred by his insinuations that Salt tried to steal his glory, which, repeated more openly to his friends, did the consul's reputation lasting harm. Usually mild mannered, Belzoni was possessed of an unfortunate jealousy and suspicion, which led him to accuse others beside Salt, including, once, his publisher and friend John Murray, of intriguing against him.

Belzoni was desperate that nobody should identify him with the Patagonian Sampson, for he now claimed a status he feared his past would diminish, but, ever a showman, he rented the Egyptian Hall in Piccadilly for a year and staged an exhibition of the tomb of Seti I. Two rooms were presented full size, while models showed the entire tomb. It was a wild success; on the first day 1900 people paid their half crowns to enter 'Belzoni's Tomb'. But Belzoni desired new fame. In 1823, leaving Sarah in Morocco, he set out to find the source of the Niger. Many explorers had tried and failed and Belzoni, too, was to pay with his life. In Benin he fell ill with dysentery and was carried down to Gwato (the port of Benin), where he died on 3 December 1823. He was buried on the same or the following day beneath a tree, and a wooden tablet requested that, 'every European visiting this spot will cause the ground to be cleared and the fence repaired if necessary'. When Richard Burton went there in 1862, old men still remembered the giant stranger, but all traces of the grave were gone.

Belzoni's efforts acquired for the British Museum many of its finest Egyptian antiquities. His sometimes rough methods and lack of documentation of finds fill modern archaeologists with horror, yet he was actuated by a desire to increase knowledge of ancient Egypt, and is thus a true pioneer in the field. Benjamin Haydon's words are a fitting epitaph:

Belzoni is a glorious instance of what singleness of aim and energy of intention will accomplish. He was a man with no single pretension to calculate on attaching his name to

Egypt, but by his indomitable energy he has attached Egypt to his name for ever.   (Mayes, title page)

PETA RÉE

Sources G. B. Belzoni, *Narrative of the operations and recent discoveries within the pyramids, temples, tombs and excavations in Egypt and Nubia* (1820) • S. Mayes, *The great Belzoni* (1959) • J. J. Halls, *The life and correspondence of Henry Salt*, 2nd edn, 2 vols. (1834) • G. Finati, *Narrative of the life and adventures of Giovanni Finati*, ed. and trans. W. J. Bankes, 2 vols. (1830) • R. F. Burton, 'Giovanni Battista Belzoni', *Cornhill Magazine*, 42 (1880), 36–50 • *Life of Benjamin Robert Haydon, historical painter*, ed. T. Taylor, 3 vols. (1853) • B. Fagan, *The rape of the Nile* (1977)
Archives BM, department of Egyptian antiquities • BM, department of prints and drawings • Bristol City Museum and Art Gallery • Sir John Soane's Museum, London | Dorset RO, W. J. Bankes MSS
Likenesses R. H. Norman, watercolour, 1803, BM • A. Van Assen, etching, pubd 1804 (after drawing by J. Parry), BM, NPG • T. J. Wells, medal, 1818, BM • W. Brockedon, oils, *c*.1820, NPG • M. Gauci, lithograph, pubd 1821, repro. in G. B. Belzoni, *Narrative of the operations and recent discoveries within the pyramids*, 2nd edn (1821), frontispiece [*see illus.*] • W. Brockedon, pencil and chalk, 1823, NPG • W. Brockedon, sketch, 1824, BM • F. C. Lewis, chalk manner engraving, pubd 1824 (after W. Brockedon), BM • G. Cruikshank, engraving (after drawing), BM • J. Thomson, stipple, BM, NPG; repro. in *European Magazine and London Review*, 82 (1822), facing p. 99 • group portrait, etching (*Five remarkable characters*), BM

Belzoni, Sarah (1783–1870), traveller, was born (probably Sarah Banne) in January 1783 in Bristol. Nothing is known of her before her marriage in 1803 to Giovanni Battista *Belzoni (1778–1823), the actor, strongman, and, later, Egyptologist. She travelled, and possibly worked with him, all over the British Isles, and in 1815 accompanied him to Egypt. There she lived with him in tombs or temples and on small boats on the Nile, or alone with the local people. They had no family.

Mrs Belzoni loyally followed her husband whenever she could, but she also had a life of her own. She spent many, often lonely, weeks, sometimes months, with the local women, writing of her life with them and of their way of life in 'Mrs Belzoni's trifling account of the women of Egypt, Nubia and Syria', published in her husband's *Narrative of the Operations and Recent Discoveries … in Egypt and Nubia* (1820). Hers was the first such record, and covered a greater variety of people than Sophia Lane Poole's later, more erudite study in *The Englishwoman in Egypt* (1844).

In 1816 at Aswan and Abu Simbel, Sarah visited the women of the chiefs. The aga of Aswan, she said, like other Egyptian men, treated his women with the greatest contempt, although always behaving to her 'not only with respect, but even with humility' (Belzoni, 410). She described the women's relationships, rooms, possessions, and dress, finding the Nubian women more kind and civil with less of the 'invidious jealousy and covetousness the Arab women possess' (ibid., 413). On their return to Luxor, Belzoni left her in an Arab house on her own with 'about twenty Arab words in my mouth' (ibid., 416) and no interpreter. All the village women came to look at her and, when she suffered a long and severe attack of ophthalmia, to help her. In June 1817 she rejoined Belzoni at Philae as he was setting off to enter the temple at Abu Simbel. She wished to go too, but he insisted she remain on the island.

'Had I been there,' she said, 'I should have helped to remove the sand as well as them … and claimed as much merit' (ibid., 418). Instead she camped on top of the temple with their Irish servant. The village women came daily to look, talk, and trade antique beads for modern ones.

In January 1818 Sarah persuaded Belzoni to let her visit the Holy Land. She arrived in Jerusalem in mid-March to witness the last days of Passion week. In May she joined the Jordan pilgrimage, rejecting other European travellers as she 'made it an invariable rule to be independent of everyone, that it might not be said, if it had not been for … *us*, she could not have gone on' (Belzoni, 424). However, she then travelled with Lord Belmore's party to Nazareth, but returned to Jerusalem on her own, staying in the shepherds' black tents and in a common caravanserai. She determined to enter the great Muslim temple—barred to both Christians and women. Dressed as a man she achieved her purpose, in mid-June 1818, but quickly left Jerusalem lest the adventure be discovered and she be punished.

In November 1818, back at Luxor, while Belzoni was at Philae collecting an obelisk for William Bankes, she lived in a tomb again and saved the famed Seti I's tomb from flood damage. Reunited with Belzoni, she settled at Rosetta while Belzoni went off to the Libyan desert. Here she amused herself with several pets, including chameleons, and by distributing Bibles. The Belzonis left Egypt in 1819.

On their return to London in 1820 after some months on the continent, Sarah helped Belzoni with his Egyptian exhibition (1820–21) and finally travelled to Morocco with him to bid him farewell as he set off south in 1823 for Benin and his death. She continued to promote his achievements, living on a meagre income for another forty-five years, in England and from 1833 in Brussels. She organized an exhibition in London of his models and drawings of Seti's tomb, but it was unsuccessful and closed in 1825. In 1828 she tried but failed to publish his lithographs of the tomb. In 1851 she was awarded a small civil-list pension in recognition of Belzoni's service to the nation. Although there was 'nothing remarkable in her person or manners', Sarah was said to have 'a sensible and intrepid cast of features' (Smith). She died in Bellozanne Road, Jersey, in the Channel Islands, on 12 January 1870, aged eighty-seven. Sarah Belzoni's account, while it is somewhat 'trifling', personal, and unorganized, reveals a valiant, enterprising woman who had exceptional experiences for her day.

DEBORAH MANLEY

Sources S. Belzoni, 'Mrs Belzoni's trifling account of the women of Egypt, Nubia and Syria', in G. B. Belzoni, *Narrative of the operations and recent discoveries within the pyramids, temples, tombs and excavations in Egypt and Nubia* (1820), 441–83 • S. Mayes, *The great Belzoni* (1959) • L. Montobbio, *Giovanni Battista Belzoni: la vita i viaggi le scoperte* (1984) • J. T. Smith, *A book for a rainy day, or, Recollections of the events of the years 1766–1833* (1845) • C. Clair, *Strong man Egyptologist* (1957)
Archives Bristol City Museum and Art Gallery

Bembridge [*née* Kirkland; *other married name* Harrison], **Sarah** (*c*.1794–1880), Primitive Methodist travelling preacher, was born at Mercaston, Derbyshire, the daughter of Rowland Kirkland (*d.* 1813). The family were Wesleyan Methodists of farming stock, and preaching services were held for a number of years in their home. Sarah was particularly affected as a child by the preaching of the Wesleyan William Bramwell. The Wesleyans withdrew from Mercaston, but when the Primitive Methodists visited the area the preaching services began again. Sarah started on the road to conversion following a visit by Hugh Bourne, co-founder of Primitive Methodism, in 1811. William Clowes, the other founder, preached there in 1813 and she received her first membership ticket. Her father and two brothers died of smallpox in the summer of 1813. She started to preach in 1813 or 1814, taking her first service at Sutton on the Hill, where a Gypsy boy was so impressed that he virtually constituted himself as her publicity agent.

Sarah Kirkland engaged in missions with other Primitive Methodist preachers throughout Staffordshire and Derbyshire, including camp meetings. However, at Christmas 1815, at the request of Robert Winfield, she was the first Primitive Methodist missioner to enter Nottingham, where she met with considerable success. She was 'taken out' as an itinerant by Hugh Bourne in February 1816, and paid 2 guineas a quarter, and she took part in many of the early Primitive Methodist missions, especially in the north midlands—Cheshire, Derbyshire, and Nottinghamshire. The Vale of Belvoir was notorious for its persecution of Primitive Methodist preachers, but Sarah Kirkland does not seem to have suffered. The novelty of a young female preacher always drew great crowds and in consequence she received many invitations to take services, travelling into Leicestershire and Lincolnshire.

Sarah Kirkland married John Harrison (1795/6–1821), a fellow itinerant, at Bingham, Nottinghamshire, on 17 August 1818 and they worked together in the midlands, although John was often ill. In 1819 the Harrisons were appointed as missionaries to Hull, a stronghold of early Primitive Methodism, mainly through the influence of a Mr and Mrs Woolhouse, who entreated the Primitive Methodist authorities for preachers. William Clowes laboured there alone until the Harrisons arrived. Sarah Harrison had an immediate impact, drawing crowds too great to be accommodated in the preaching house, so she often preached in the open air in Hull and made missionary trips to other areas, including the city of York. Primitive Methodist work in Hull progressed so greatly that a chapel was built in Mill Street; she preached at its opening services in September 1819. John Harrison's health failed in November 1819 and it seems that she undertook his duties as well as her own until he recovered somewhat, but he again overtaxed his strength. As she was now pregnant, they both retired in May 1820 and returned to Mercaston, where their son, a sickly child, was born. John Harrison died suddenly on 22 July 1821, aged twenty-five.

After she became a widow, the society in Hull asked Sarah Harrison to return as an itinerant, but she remained at Mercaston, tending a small dairy farm and serving as a local preacher. Although commonly regarded as the first female itinerant of Primitive Methodism, she was never actually stationed by the connexion, as she retired before the first conference. In February 1825 she married William Bembridge (*d.* 1880), a fellow local preacher. Following their marriage, friends asked the Bembridges to go to Hull, but they refused and continued their ministry as local preachers and class leaders in Mugginton, Derbyshire, until his death in January 1880. Sarah Bembridge was taken ill after conducting services at Somercotes and Alfreton, Derbyshire, and died at the home of Mr and Mrs Calladine of Alfreton on 4 March 1880, soon after the arrival from Mercaston of her daughter, Mary Sherlock. She was buried in Mugginton churchyard beside William Bembridge. A memorial service was held at Mercaston Chapel and the erection of a memorial tablet was planned. Sarah Bembridge was described as 'calm, modest, capable, tender' (Kendall, 176), with a 'respectable speaking ability' (*Primitive Methodist Magazine*, 1881, 424).

E. DOROTHY GRAHAM

Sources *Primitive Methodist Magazine*, 62 (1881) · G. Herod, *Biographical sketches of some of those preachers whose labours contributed to the origination and early extension of the Primitive Methodist Connexion* [n.d., *c.*1855] · H. Bourne, journals, JRL, Methodist Archives and Research Centre · J. Walford, *Life and labours of ... Hugh Bourne*, 1 (1855) · H. B. Kendall, *The origin and history of the Primitive Methodist church*, 2 [n.d., *c.*1906] · records, Notts. Arch.
Likenesses portrait (in old age), repro. in Kendall, *Origin and history of the Primitive Methodist church*, vol. 1, p. 177
Wealth at death under £100: administration, 7 May 1880, CGPLA Eng. & Wales

Bemrose, William (1831–1908), writer on wood-carving and ceramics, was born at Derby on 30 December 1831, the second son in a family of three sons and one daughter of William Bemrose of Derby, founder in 1827 of the printing and publishing firm of William Bemrose & Sons of Derby and London. His mother was Elizabeth Ride of Lichfield. His elder brother, Henry Howe Bemrose (1827–1912), was Conservative member of parliament for Derby from 1895 to 1900 and was knighted in 1897.

After education at King William's College in the Isle of Man, Bemrose, like his brother Henry, joined his father's business, which passed to the management of the two brothers on their father's retirement in 1857, and grew rapidly in all directions. In 1858 Bemrose married Margaret Romana (*d.* 1901), only daughter of Edward Lloyd Simpson of Spondon, with whom he had five sons and one daughter. Although always active in the printing business, Bemrose pursued many other interests. In middle life he became a director of the Royal Crown Derby porcelain works, and thus helped to revive an important local industry.

Bemrose travelled and studied varied forms of art, on which he wrote with much success. Practising in early life wood-carving, fret-cutting, and modelling in clay, he compiled useful manuals on these subjects for the instruction of amateurs, which were well illustrated and circulated widely. The chief of these was his *Manual of Wood-Carving* (1862), the first work of its kind in England, which reached a twenty-third edition in 1906. This was followed by several other instructional works on wood-carving, marquetry, and paper mosaic work. Meanwhile Bemrose's association with the local pottery led him to publish three authoritative works on china. The first, with A. Wallis, was *The Pottery and Porcelain of Derbyshire* (1870), followed by his own *Bow, Chelsea and Derby Porcelain* (1898) and *Longton Hall Porcelain* (1906).

Bemrose was also a clever amateur painter in oils and watercolour. He collected pictures, china, and objects of vertu, especially rare specimens of Egyptian art, which he acquired on visits to the East. In 1885 he published a sumptuously illustrated and finely printed *Life and Work of Joseph Wright. A Descriptive Catalogue of Porcelain and other Art Objects* in his own collection was published in 1898. He also wrote on technical education and archaeological and topographical subjects. In 1905 he was elected a fellow of the Society of Antiquaries. Bemrose played an active part in local affairs of Derby, and was for many years chairman of the Railway Servants' Orphanage. In 1903 Bemrose married as his second wife Lilian, daughter of William John Cumming MRCS of Matlock, and widow of Alderman William Hobson of Derby, proprietor of the *Derbyshire Advertiser*. He died on 6 August 1908 at Bridlington, Yorkshire, while on a short holiday, and was buried at the new cemetery, Derby.   S. E. FRYER, *rev.* CLIVE D. EDWARDS

Sources *The Times* (8 Aug 1908) · *Derby Express* (8 Aug 1908) · H. H. Bemrose, *The house of Bemrose, 1826–1926* (1926) · *CGPLA Eng. & Wales* (1908)

Wealth at death £92,393 13*s.* 5*d.*: probate, 28 Aug 1908, *CGPLA Eng. & Wales*

Ben, James (*d.* 1332), bishop of St Andrews, is of unknown origins; the only clues to his background are provided by the style he used on his seal when archdeacon of St Andrews, where he is described as being 'of Edinburgh', and a dispensation for his illegitimacy, granted at the time of his provision to the see of St Andrews. He seems to have graduated from an unknown university before 1299, when, if the identification is correct, he was the canon of Moray who accompanied David Murray to the papal curia for the latter's provision to the see of Moray. He also held benefices in Cruden and Glasgow, before becoming archdeacon of St Andrews between 1323 and 1325. He was one of the clerks in a team of Scots envoys sent to negotiate with the English at York in 1320 and was again employed as an envoy in discussions with the French leading to a renewal of the Franco-Scottish alliance in 1326. Between July 1326 and early 1329 he was probably a resident envoy of Robert I at the curia. Certainly he seems to have been one of those with primary responsibility for negotiating the lifting of the excommunication of the king (15 October 1328), and perhaps also for gaining the papal grant of the rites of coronation and unction for the Scottish monarchy (June 1329), which had been blocked by English pressure during the previous two centuries. Following the death of William Lamberton, bishop of St Andrews, on 20 May 1328, Ben was elected to the see on 19 June, although he was then still absent at the curia. (The election may not

have been without dispute, since a rival, Alexander Kinninmund, apparently challenged Ben's provision.) Having been given papal permission to return to Scotland in October of that year, Ben arrived early in 1329. Robert I died on 7 June 1329, but it was not until November 1331 that his son and successor, David II, was crowned, and Ben thus became the first bishop formally to crown and anoint a Scottish king. Within a few months, however, Edward Balliol's forces invaded from England. After the Scottish defeat at Dupplin Moor on 11 August 1332 Ben (unlike several other bishops) refused to acknowledge Balliol as king and instead went into exile in Flanders. He died at Bruges just over a month later, on 22 September, and was buried at Echkot, near Bruges.   NORMAN H. REID

Sources D. E. R. Watt, *A biographical dictionary of Scottish graduates to AD 1410* (1977), 36–8 · D. E. R. Watt, ed., *Fasti ecclesiae Scoticanae medii aevi ad annum 1638*, [2nd edn], Scottish RS, new ser., 1 (1969), 293 · A. Theiner, *Vetera monumenta Hibernorum et Scotorum historiam illustrantia* (Rome, 1864), no. 253 · D. L. Galbreath, 'Scottish seals from the continent', *SHR*, 27 (1948), 127–41

Wealth at death 2000 florins and one ring left as legacy to the Pope: Theiner, *Vetera monumenta*

Benazech, Charles [*pseud.* Frieselheim] (**1767/8–1794**), portrait and history painter, was born in London, the son of the engraver and draughtsman Peter Paul *Benazech (1730?–1798). In 1782, at the age of fifteen, he went to Rome, and in October 1783 to Florence, where on 11 January 1784 he was elected to the Florentine Academy. His self-portrait, of *c.*1790, is in the Uffizi Gallery, Florence. On his way home from Italy he stayed for a time in France, at Paris, where he studied under Greuze. There he witnessed the outbreak of the French Revolution, from which he took the subjects of four pictures, sympathetic to Louis XVI, by which he became known: *The Address of Louis XVI at the Bar of the National Convention*; *The Separation of Louis XVI from his Family*, in which—alone among artists of the time—he emphasized Louis's Catholic piety; *The Last Interview between Louis XVI and his Family*; and *Louis XVI Ascending the Scaffold*. These were engraved by Luigi Schiavonetti and published by Colnaghi; impressions of the last three of these engravings are in the British Museum and the Royal Collection. His other paintings included *The Last Interview between Charles I and his Children*, engraved by T. Gaugain, some subjects from the poets, and several good portraits. He exhibited at the Royal Academy in 1790 and 1791, when his address was 19 Porter's Street, Newport Market: a theatrical scene and two history paintings in 1790, and three portraits in 1791. He engraved a few plates in aquatint, including the *Couronnement de la rosière*, in which he attempted to imitate the manner of P.-L. Debucourt; some of his own portraits; and two of Henri IV, king of France, and the duc de Sully, after Pourbus, which are signed with the fictitious name of Frieselheim. Two of his portraits are in the Louvre, Paris. Benazech died, apparently unmarried, in London on 24 May 1794.   R. E. GRAVES, *rev.* A. NISBET

Sources Redgrave, *Artists* · D. Bindman, *The shadow of the guillotine: Britain and the French Revolution* (1989) [exhibition catalogue, BM, April 1989 – August 1989] · J. Ingamells, ed., *A dictionary of British*

and Irish travellers in Italy, 1701–1800 (1997) · Waterhouse, *18c painters* · L. Binyon, *Catalogue of drawings by British artists and artists of foreign origin working in Great Britain*, 4 vols. (1898–1907), vol. 1, pp. 97–8 · H. Hammelmann, *Book illustrators in eighteenth-century England*, ed. T. S. R. Boase (1975) · G. Meissner, ed., *Allgemeines Künstlerlexikon: die bildenden Künstler aller Zeiten und Völker*, [new edn, 34 vols.] (Leipzig and Munich, 1983–)

Likenesses C. Benazech, self-portrait, oils, *c*.1790, Uffizi Gallery, Florence, Italy

Benazech, Peter Paul (1730?–1798), engraver and watercolour painter, is said to have been born in England. In 1746 he was apprenticed to the landscape engraver Francis Vivares for £20, and he continued to work for Vivares after the expiration of his apprenticeship, producing, for instance, two views of Charenton and *The Handsome Cook Maid*, after François Boucher. After further training in Paris he worked both in that city and in London as a draughtsman and engraver. His engravings, tastefully executed, consisted chiefly of landscapes and marine subjects, the best being those after Christian Dietrich and Joseph Vernet, now in the British Museum.

Benazech also worked for other printsellers, notably Thomas Jefferys, for whom he engraved a *General View of Richmond* (1755), after Peter Tillemans, and a number of American views, including *A View of the City of Quebec* (1761), after General Wolfe's aide-de-camp, Captain Hervey Smyth. He also engraved a series of anatomical plates, a series of seven scenes from the Seven Years' War, and, in conjunction with Canot, four plates showing engagements between the English and French fleets, after Francis Swaine. Besides these he engraved *Peasants Playing at Bowls*, after Adriaan van Ostande, and views in England after Chatelain and Brooks. Benazech exhibited with the Society of Artists in 1761 and 1762. In Mortimer's *Universal Director* (1763) he was listed as a landscape engraver living in Tottenham Court Road. His last dated plate was *The Tomb of Vergil*, after Hugh Dean, engraved in 1783.

The name of Benazech's wife is not known, but their son was the painter and engraver Charles *Benazech (1767/8–1794), who was a pupil of Greuze in Paris. Benazech senior died in Exeter between 23 November and 4 December 1798. TIMOTHY CLAYTON and ANITA MCCONNELL

Sources G. Meissner, ed., *Allgemeines Künstlerlexikon: die bildenden Künstler aller Zeiten und Völker*, [new edn, 34 vols.] (Leipzig and Munich, 1983–) · W. S. Sparrow, *British sporting artists: from Barlow to Herring* (1922), 55 · C. Du Peloux, *Répertoire biographique et bibliographique des artistes du XVIIIe siècle français*, 2 vols. (1930–41), vol. 1 · R. Portalis and H. Béraldi, *Les graveurs du dix-huitième siècle*, 1 (Paris, 1880), 157–8 · D. Bindman, *The shadow of the guillotine: Britain and the French Revolution* (1989) [exhibition catalogue, BM, April 1989 – August 1989] · R. Portalis, *Henri-Pierre Danloux: peintre de portraits et son journal durant l'émigration (1753–1809)* (1910) · catalogue of the National Maritime Museum's print collection · will, PRO, PROB 11/1315, sig. 757

Benbow, John (1653?–1702), naval officer, was born in Shropshire, the son of William and Martha Benbow. The details of his reputation, birth, family, and lineage have been extensively and inconclusively debated. The astrologer Partridge recorded the exact date of his birth as noon on 10 March 1653 (BL, Egerton MS 2378, fol. 29*b*). Although

John Benbow (1653?–1702), by Sir Godfrey Kneller, 1701

this date has sometimes been accepted as the year of his birth, no other documentary support for it survives and the inscription on his tomb reports that he was in his fifty-second year in 1702. There are two contending theories about his parentage, both of which lack convincing documentation, and which are sometimes conflated. One maintains that he was born to a couple in Newport, Shropshire, among whose relations was one John Benbow (1565–1625), a deputy clerk in chancery who had been granted arms in 1584. His nephew, also John Benbow (1609–1651), was a captain in the parliamentary army, changed his allegiance, and, perhaps, became a colonel in the king's army. He was captured at the battle of Worcester, tried at court martial by order of the council of state for having changed his allegiance, and executed in the cabbage patch under the walls of Shrewsbury Castle as an example of the fate of a renegade (H. Owen and J. B. Blakeway, *History of Shrewsbury*, 2 vols., 1825, 1.469, 2.391; *CSP dom.*, *1651*, 421–2, 457). This theory has linked the admiral with the landed gentry, a coat of arms, and the romance of the civil war.

The opposing theory ties Benbow to another set of parents, who were also named William (*b*. 1615, *d*. after 1664) and Martha, but who were from a separate, perhaps distantly connected, line of the Benbow family in the parish of St Mary, Coton Hill, Shrewsbury. This William Benbow, like his father before him, was a burgess of Shrewsbury, owned the tannery at Coton Hill, and lived in the dwelling adjoining it. This theory is related to the erroneous tradition that the admiral was a working-class tanner's son who ran away to sea.

According to an account in the *Historical and Political Mercury* (1703) Benbow attended the free school in Shrewsbury and was later apprenticed to a waterman on the River Severn. If he had followed a typical pattern, he would have completed his apprenticeship about 1673 and gone to sea.

Mediterranean engagements The first documented fact of Benbow's life is dated 30 April 1678, when he entered the navy as a master's mate on board the *Rupert* (64 guns, Captain Arthur Herbert), fitting out at Portsmouth. In the *Rupert* he went out to the Mediterranean, where Herbert served with the rank of vice-admiral under the commander-in-chief in the Mediterranean, Admiral Sir John Narborough. In these waters the *Rupert* captured an Algerine warship, which was brought into the Royal Navy as the *Tiger*. Benbow was engaged in some other smart actions with Algerine corsairs, and so far won the goodwill of his captain that when Herbert became acting commander-in-chief on the station, on Narborough's return to England, he appointed Benbow master of the *Nonsuch* on 15 June 1679. The *Nonsuch* (Captain George Rooke) continued at Tangier and on the African coast, under the successive command of Rooke, Cloudesley Shovell, and Francis Wheler, then young captains, all of whom became flag officers. All were afterwards able to testify to their high opinion of Benbow, and to push his fortune. On 8 April 1681 the *Nonsuch* captured an Algerine warship, the *Golden Horse*, which had been engaged by the *Adventure* (Captain William Booth). *Nonsuch* arrived towards the end of the action at dusk and when she showed her colours at dawn, the Algerine surrendered without firing a shot. A dispute arose between the two ships' companies over sharing the prize money and apparently the *Nonsuch*'s men indulged in rude witticisms at the expense of the *Adventure*'s. Benbow repeated some of these, reflecting on Captain Booth's conduct, which came to Booth's knowledge. He brought Benbow to a court martial and, the fault being proved, with the saving clause that he had 'only repeated those words after another', Benbow was sentenced to forfeit three months' pay, 'to be disposed of for the use of the wounded men on board the *Adventure*'; and likewise to 'ask Captain Booth's pardon on board his Majesty's ship *Bristol*, declaring that he had no malicious intent in speaking those words; all the commanders being present, and a boat's crew of each ship's company' (minutes of the court martial, 20 April 1681, PRO, ADM 1/5253). The three months' pay, amounting to £12 15s., appears duly checked against his name in the *Nonsuch*'s pay-book.

In the following August Captain Wheler was superseded by Captain Wrenn and the ship returned to England. Shortly after his return from the Mediterranean Benbow appears to have married Martha (*d.* 1722), a woman with the same name as his mother and whose maiden name, like hers, is unknown. Their first child was born shortly thereafter. Like so much of the Benbow family information, the dates and places of birth and marriage for his wife as well as the birth dates of their children are poorly documented and often disputed.

Soon after *Nonsuch* was paid off on 9 November 1681 Benbow appears to have left the navy, but returned to sea in a merchant vessel, sailing between London, Bristol, and ports in Italy and Spain. About this time his family lived in the parish of St Dunstan and All Saints, Stepney, where another son, Solomon (who died in infancy), was baptized in 1686. In the same year Benbow owned and commanded a ship named the frigate *Benbow*, in the Levant trade. In May 1687 he was reported to be in command of a merchant vessel, the *Malaga Merchant*, and in her to have made a stout and successful defence against a Salé rover. The story that he cut off and salted down the heads of thirteen Moors who were slain on the *Benbow*'s deck, that he carried these trophies into Cadiz, and displayed them to the magistrates in order to claim head-money, is not in itself improbable, though told with much grotesque exaggeration (J. Campbell, *Lives of the British Admirals*, 4 vols., 1779, 3.335), and is to some extent corroborated by the existence of a Moorish skull-cap, made of finely plaited cane and mounted in silver, bearing the inscription 'The first adventure of Captain John Benbo, and gift to Richard Ridley, 1687'. Ridley was the husband of one of Benbow's sisters, and about 1825 the skull-cap was still in the possession of his descendants.

In home waters Benbow did not re-enter the navy until after the revolution, and his first recorded commission, dated 1 June 1689, was as third lieutenant of the *Elizabeth*, then commanded by Captain David Mitchell. On 20 September he was appointed captain of the *York*, on 26 October was transferred to the *Bonaventure*, and again on 12 November to the *Britannia*. He may have owed this rapid promotion to Admiral Herbert, whose star was at this time in the ascendant; possibly, during the critical months of the revolution, he had been in Herbert's service and had piloted the fleet which landed William III in Torbay, but there is no evidence for this.

From the *Britannia* Benbow was appointed master attendant of Chatham Dockyard; early in March 1690 he was removed to Deptford in the same capacity, and he continued to hold that office for the next six years, although frequently relieved from its duties and employed on particular service. In the summer of 1690 he was master of the *Sovereign*, bearing the flag of Lord Torrington, and acted as master of the fleet before and during the unfortunate battle of Beachy Head. During the preliminary investigation of the royal commission in July 1690 Benbow's evidence, as a specialist in navigation and pilotage, strongly favoured Torrington, but he did not testify at the court martial in December. Benbow was still in the *Sovereign* during the summer of 1691, and in the summer of 1692 was again master of the fleet under Admiral Russell, on board the *Britannia*, where he worked closely with Captain David Mitchell, who served as Russell's first captain, and Josiah Burchett, who was Russell's clerk. On receiving the news that the French fleet was at sea, secretary of state Lord Nottingham had urged Russell to sail immediately from the Nore. Taking advantage of wind and weather Russell made a courageous decision, possibly with

Benbow's advice as master of the fleet, to risk taking the Gull Passage inside the Goodwin Sands to the Downs, where the Dutch squadron and remainder of the fleet lay at anchor. Benbow served as master of the fleet through the subsequent actions at Barfleur and La Hogue. After the battle of La Hogue he returned to his duties as master attendant at Deptford and, for a brief period, was on loan to the dockyard at Portsmouth, where he was needed in connection with repairs to the fleet (Merriman, 37). It had been already ordered that while he was serving afloat his pay as master was to be made up to that of master attendant at Deptford. An order was now issued for him to be paid as master attendant in addition to his pay as master, presumably in direct acknowledgement of special services in the conduct of the fleet. In May 1692 he was elected an elder brother of Trinity House.

In September 1693 Benbow was again appointed away from his dockyard to command, jointly with second engineer of the ordnance Thomas Phillips, a flotilla of a new class of bomb vessels ordered to attack St Malo. With Benbow directing operations in *Norwich* (48 guns, Captain Josias Crow), the bombardment began on the evening of 16 November, and continued irregularly until the evening of the 19th, when a large fireship was sent in. It was intended to lay this vessel alongside the town walls, but she grounded at some little distance, where she was set on fire and exploded. Even so, the damage done was considerable. While withdrawing, Benbow's forces captured and disabled the fort on nearby Quince Rock, taking captured prisoners and artillery to Guernsey. Despite these achievements Benbow was much dissatisfied with the result, and brought the commander of the bomb vessel *Mortar* (Captain Henry Tourville) to a court martial for disobedience in not going in closer; he was not, however, able to procure a conviction as his mortars proved defective. In September 1694 he was again appointed to a similar flotilla under Vice-Admiral Shovell, intended to act against Dunkirk. The bomb vessels were to be supported by a number of 'machines'. As the term was used in these years, it applied to a small merchant vessel, often a fishing smack, converted into something like a fireship, but one which exploded rather than burnt. In preparing and employing these particular vessels in 1694 Benbow worked closely with Willem Meesters, the principal storekeeper of the ordnance, who accompanied him at sea as his technical adviser during operations. Together they exercised absolute control over the commanders of the bomb and machine vessels and their weapons. The attacking squadron was covered by the fleet from the Downs, commanded by Shovell, and the attempt was made on 12 and 13 September. Although Benbow himself had made soundings of the approaches to the harbour, his vessels were unable to enter after the French had blocked the entrance and the weather became stormy. After leaving Dunkirk Benbow bombarded Calais from the bomb-ketch *Kitchen* on 27 September, destroying several houses, but once again the tide and wind prevented getting into close range. After returning to the Downs with the fleet, Benbow resumed his duties at Deptford Dockyard and in December concentrated on organizing a convoy for a fleet of merchant vessels sailing to Cadiz. In the spring of 1695 it was resolved to make a further attempt with the machine vessels. In March 1695 Benbow was appointed commander-in-chief of his majesty's ships then on the coast of France. In early April his squadron captured a number of French merchant ships and brought them in as prizes. In June 1695, on Lord Berkeley's recommendation, the lords justices recommended Benbow to the king for the first vacant flag and to have the pay of a rear-admiral. Meanwhile, the Admiralty ordered Benbow to command the *Northumberland* (70 guns). His fourteen-year-old son, John *Benbow, soon joined the ship as a volunteer, shortly before the ships sailed with allied ships under Berkeley and Dutch Lieutenant-Admiral Philips van Almonde for St Malo, where they hoped to hinder further privateering operations from that island. On Berkeley's signal Benbow shifted from the *Northumberland* to the galley *Charles*, in which he broke his broad pennant to direct the inshore operations of ten English and Dutch warships, nine English bomb vessels, and seventeen small boats and vessels. Arriving off St Malo on 4 July, they immediately opened fire. They kept this up until dark, renewed it the next morning, and continued until evening, when they drew off, without any decisive result, several houses having been knocked down or set on fire, while on the side of the assailants some of the bomb vessels were shattered or sunk. In a council of war held the next day it was resolved that as much had been done as could be hoped for. Benbow, with eight bomb vessels and seven or eight frigates, was sent along the coast to attack Granville, which he shelled for some hours, on 8 July, leaving it in flames after firing 900 bombs.

Benbow gave up his command on the return of the fleet to the Downs under odd circumstances. His relationship with his immediate superior had become tense, for while Berkeley was criticized for timidity in the failure of the attack on Dunkirk, Benbow had won widespread fame for his fearless inshore attacks with bomb vessels. 'Benbow is quitting his ship', wrote Lord Berkeley on 23 July. 'I cannot imagine the reason. He pretends sickness, but I think it is only feigned' (*CSP dom.*, 1695, 26). On the 28th he again wrote:

> As to Captain Benbow, I know of no difference between him and me, nor have we had any. He has no small obligation to me, but being called in some of the foolish printed papers 'the famous Captain Benbow', I suppose has put him a little out of himself, and has made him play the fool, as I guess, in some of his letters. I will not farther now particularize this business, but time will show I have not been in the wrong, unless being too kind to an ungrateful man. (*CSP dom.*, 1695, 5)

Notwithstanding this, however, Benbow's conduct was warmly approved of; the Admiralty ordered him 'to be paid as rear-admiral during the time he has been employed this summer on the coast of France ... as a reward for his good service' (Admiralty minutes, 12 Sept 1695, PRO, ADM 3/12). During this period Benbow had been strongly supported by the lords justices over Berkeley's criticisms, but in August 1695 the lords justices and the Admiralty were attempting to resolve an issue over conflicting orders for admirals Rooke and Russell, when additional misunderstandings arose over the amount of Benbow's half pay when he was not employed at sea and whether he should be considered a captain or a rear-admiral. In December 1695 Benbow was appointed to the grand committee of sixty men to oversee the plans for Greenwich Hospital, but the issue was not resolved until 1 May 1696. At that point the Admiralty appointed Benbow commander-in-chief of the squadron before Dunkirk as 'rear-admiral of the blue for the duration of this present expedition', flying his flag in the *Suffolk* (70 guns), and he was ordered to stretch as far northward as he thought 'convenient for the intercepting of Bart's squadron and protecting the English and Dutch trades expected home northabout'. The orders to look out for the Dunkirk privateer squadron under Jean Bart were repeated more than once (Admiralty minutes, 15 May and 29 July 1696, PRO, ADM 3/12; Japikse, 1.1.189) as Bart was reportedly cruising in the North Sea to attack allied shipping, sailing in the area between Dunkirk, Dogger Bank, and Norway. Benbow's efforts were unavailing. In the middle of September he did, indeed, manage to get a distant view of the object of his search, but Bart easily escaped into Dunkirk, owing to the fouled bottom of the slower English ships. Benbow returned to the Downs, and in December 1696 was appointed to command the squadron in the Soundings, in the flagship *Duke*, for the protection of the homeward-bound trade. His operations between March and August 1697 marked the last English naval expedition of the war. During this period his squadron cruised in the western approaches to the channel, bringing in safely the West Indian and Virginian merchant fleets. He made a close observation of the French fleet at Brest in July, returning to the patrol operations with the Dutch ships under Rear-Admiral Philips van der Goes off Dunkirk until the end of the war in September 1697.

In June 1696 Benbow signed a three-year lease on Sayes Court, a house belonging to John Evelyn near the dockyard at Deptford. Six months later Evelyn wrote to an acquaintance, 'I have let my house to Captain Benbow, and have the mortification of seeing everyday much of my former labours and expenses there impairing for want of a more polite tenant' (letter to Dr Bohun, 18 Jan 1697; *Diary and Correspondence*, 1 June 1696 and 18 Jan 1697). A year later, in January 1698, Tsar Peter of Russia arrived to study British shipbuilding and seamanship and William III provided Sayes Court to him and his entourage. Three months later, when Peter left London to tour the countryside, Benbow asked for reparation to be made him from the Treasury in order to reimburse Evelyn and to recover his own personal losses, complaining that the Russians left the house in so bad a condition he could scarcely describe it, with 'much of the furniture broke, lost or destroyed'. In response to Benbow's petition Sir Christopher Wren surveyed the damage and reported, among other things, that much on the property was 'entirely ruined'.

The Treasury subsequently allowed payment of £350 9s. 6d. in compensation for the damage done (*Calendar of Treasury Books*, 1697–1702, 158–9). Among the personal belongings that Benbow lost were 'twenty fine paintings' and 'several fine draughts and other designs relating to the Sea'.

On the West Indies station On 9 March 1698 the Admiralty appointed Benbow commander-in-chief of the king's ships in the West Indies, with special orders to hunt down the pirates. His sailing was delayed until November. On the first leg of the outward passage, from Portsmouth to Madeira, Benbow provided protection against the Salé warships for the *Paramore* (Captain Edmond Halley), just beginning her first expedition to observe magnetic variation in the north Atlantic. Benbow did not reach Barbados until February 1699. Thence he proceeded towards the Spanish main in his flagship *Gloucester* (60 guns), and by a threat of blockading Cartagena induced the governor to restore two English merchant ships which he had detained to form part of a projected expedition against the Scottish colony at Darien. Benbow's action virtually put an end to this, and preserved the colonists for the time. This result seems to have been displeasing to the home government, and in June stringent orders were sent to Benbow and the governors in the West Indies 'not to assist the Scotch colony in Darien' (Admiralty minutes, 21 June 1699, PRO, ADM 3/13), which soon failed. The rest of the year was occupied in ineffectual efforts to persuade or constrain the Spanish commandants at Porto Bello, or Santo Domingo, to restore some ships which had been seized for illicit trading, and in a vain attempt to induce the Danish governor of St Thomas to give up some pirates who had sheltered themselves under the Danish flag. He afterwards ranged along the coast of North America as far as Newfoundland, scaring the pirates away for the time, but failing to capture any, and towards the summer of 1700 he returned to England. He was almost immediately appointed to the command in the Downs. At the time the Admiralty made this appointment, it also confirmed the commission that Benbow had given his son, John, the previous March and appointed him lieutenant in the *Maidstone* (24 guns). Benbow continued in the Downs through the spring and summer of 1701, operating under Admiral Sir George Rooke. In April he had been promoted to rear-admiral of the red and in July vice-admiral of the blue, flying his flag in the *Breda* (70 guns). In that uneasy period of peace a major concern for the English government was the Spanish silver fleet, soon expected to arrive from America. English merchants were concerned about their investments in goods valued up to £500,000, while the government feared that the French might divert the fleet and seize its cargo to support war preparations. Benbow's secret instructions authorized him to find the ships of the Spanish *flota* and then 'to seize and bring them to England, taking care that no embezzlement be made', even though it risked war with France and Spain (Japikse, 2.3.477–9). On 2 September off the Isles of Scilly, Rooke detached Benbow's squadron from the main fleet, on receiving the news that the French fleet under Château-renault had sailed from Brest and was apparently searching for the Spanish *flota*. For protection against the French squadron Benbow's ten ships were escorted on their way to the West Indies to a point beyond the usual cruising range of the French ships by the squadrons under Rear-Admiral Sir John Munden and the Dutch ships under Lieutenant-Admiral Baron van Wassenaer. Benbow's squadron arrived at Barbados on 14 November and proceeded on to Nevis and then to Jamaica, arriving in mid-December. For several months Benbow remained at Jamaica, and on 8 May 1702 he was joined by several vessels with Captain William Whetstone, who assumed the local rank of rear-admiral under Benbow. On 7 July Benbow received news that the allies had declared war on France and Spain and, within a few days, detached Whetstone with six ships to look for the French squadron under Admiral Ducasse off Port St Louis in Hispaniola, where it was anticipated he would call on his voyage en route to Cartagena. The English expected that he would make arrangements for the *asiento* there and prevent English and Dutch trade on that coast. Shortly after Whetstone departed Benbow and the remainder of his squadron sailed directly towards Cartagena, hoping that either his detachment or Whetstone's would encounter Ducasse. Whetstone arrived off Hispaniola after Ducasse had departed and Benbow's ships eventually sighted the French squadron on 30 August, off Cape Santa Marta. It consisted of four ships of from 68 to 70 guns, one of 40, and three transports, all under the command of Ducasse. The English force consisted of seven ships of from 50 to 70 guns, but was much scattered, and with light winds the commanders could not show great alacrity in closing. It was four in the afternoon before the ships were in any collected order, and a partial engagement, lasting a couple of hours, was ended by nightfall. Benbow had intended that the *Defiance* (64 guns, Captain Richard Kirkby) would lead the line of battle, but finding that Kirkby would not, or could not, maintain his station, Benbow issued a new line of battle, placing his flagship, the *Breda* (70 guns), in the lead. The *Breda*, closely followed by Captain George Walton in the *Ruby* (50 guns), kept company with the French all night, and was well up with them at daybreak, but the other ships did not close during the whole day. The 1st of September and three following days brought no more resolution to the different captains of the squadron. Only Walton and Captain Samuel Vincent of the *Falmouth* were able to support the admiral in his continued attempts to bring Ducasse to action, and for some time these three sustained the fire of the whole French squadron. The *Ruby* was disabled on the 3rd, and ordered to make the best of her way to Port Royal. At two in the morning the action resumed as a wind came up and all the ships were temporarily able to close the flagship from positions 2 or 3 miles astern. About three in the morning Benbow's right leg was broken by a chain-shot and he was carried below. Captain Kirkby of the *Defiance* came on board and urged him to give up the chase. All the other captains being summoned on board concurred, in a paper that was drafted by Kirkby

and signed by all. In this they reported their views that after six days of battle the squadron lacked enough men to continue and that there was little chance of a decisive action, since the men were exhausted, there was a general lack of ammunition, the ships' rigging and masts were badly damaged, and the winds were generally variable and undependable. The captains jointly recommended to the admiral that their squadron not engage the French squadron immediately, but keep company with them throughout the night, observe them, and if wind and weather improved, try their strength once again against Ducasse. The wounded Benbow

> who having seen the cowardly behaviour of some of them before, had reason to believe that they either had a design against him or to be traitors to their country if an opportunity happened that the French could have destroyed the Admiral, (Benbow's deposition, court martial proceedings, PRO, ADM 1/5263)

ordered his squadron back to Jamaica and imprisoned the captains pending trial by court martial.

Shortly after the ships returned to Port Royal, Jamaica, Acting Rear-Admiral Whetstone also returned with his squadron, after a 62-day cruise off the coast of Hispaniola. Soon after the return to port Captain Thomas Hudson of the *Pendenis* died on board his ship. The remaining captains, on Benbow's orders, were remanded to the court martial board convened on board the *Breda* on 19–23 October 1702. Benbow delegated his normal responsibilities of presiding over the court to Whetstone, but nevertheless was present and appears to have played a dominant role in the proceedings. As a result, the court condemned captains Richard Kirkby of the *Defiance* and Cooper Wade of the *Greenwich* to be shot to death for breach of orders, neglect of duty, and for the 'ill signed paper and consultation … which obliged the Admiral … to give over the chase and fight' (court martial report, PRO, ADM 1/5263). John Constable of the *Windsor* was found guilty of breach of orders and drunkenness and ordered to be cashiered from the service upon return to England. The court martial board ordered Samuel Vincent of the *Falmouth* and Christopher Fogg of the *Breda* both cashiered for joining in signing the six captains' resolution, but, on Benbow's declaration that these two had fought bravely, the lord high admiral later remitted their sentence and they returned to service. Most of the court's sentences were deferred until 'her Majesty's pleasure be known therein'. After consideration in January 1703 the queen declined to hinder the sentences on Constable, Kirkby, and Wade, who were returned to England as prisoners. Constable remained imprisoned until Queen Anne pardoned him in 1704; Kirkby and Wade were shot on board the *Bristol* (Captain Edward Acton) in Plymouth Sound on 16 April 1703.

The Benbow legend Meanwhile, on 15 November 1702, Benbow had died at Port Royal, Kingston. The cause of death, as Whetstone reported, was:

> the wound of his leg which he received in battle with Monsieur Du Casse, it never being set to perfection, which malady being aggravated by the discontent of his mind, threw him into a sort of melancholy which ended his life as before. (Whetstone to Burchett, PRO, ADM 1/2641)

He was buried the following day in the chancel of St Andrew's Church, Kingston. Some time later a marble slab was laid over the grave, emblazoned with a coat of arms and inscribed:

> Here lyeth the Body of John Benbow, Esq., Admiral of the White, a true pattern of English Courage, who lost his life in Defence of his Queene & Country, November the 4th, 1702, In the 52nd year of his age, by a wound in his Legg. Received in an Engagement with Monsr. Du Casse; being Much Lamented.

Before news of his death reached London the secretary of state, Lord Nottingham, wrote to Benbow in January 1703 that the queen was 'extremely well pleased with your conduct and much offended with the baseness of those officers who deserted and betrayed you' (23 Jan 1703, PRO, SP 44/209). The draft instructions were approved by the cabinet on 19 January (*CSP dom.*, 1702–3, 546–7) and show that at that time Benbow was about to be promoted to vice-admiral of the white and that the government was planning for him to transport troops to Newfoundland for an attack on the French colony at Placentia.

Benbow's will provided for his wife, Martha, and five surviving children: John, William, Richard, Martha, and Katherine. The exact value of his estate cannot be determined, but he intended to provide an annuity of £70 for his wife from a £2500 mortgage he held on a property named Greenlands in Hambleton, Buckinghamshire, and to give a minimum of £1000 to each of his children when they reached the age of twenty-one, with a surplus being divided equally among his sons. Additionally, his widow applied for and received an annual pension of £200 until her death at Deptford in December 1722.

Among Benbow's surviving children, John, who had served in the navy with his father until about 1700, had joined a merchant vessel, was shipwrecked, and, after returning to England, died in 1708 without children, and was buried in the Benbow family tomb in St Nicholas's, Deptford Green, where a monument to his memory was erected. William Benbow (1690–1728/9) was clerk of storekeeper's accounts at the Navy Office from June 1711 to December 1723 and died without children. The youngest, Richard (*b.* 1696?), appears to have been preceded by two other children with the same name who died in infancy. He married Elizabeth Cowley in 1714, and it is only through them that direct descent from the admiral with the Benbow family name could be established, although no children have been identified. The eldest daughter, Martha (1684?–1719?), married Thomas Stringer and then Samuel Robinson. The youngest daughter, Catherine (1694?–1744), kept house for her mother until her death and then moved to Milton House near Abingdon, Berkshire, the Calton family property on which her father may have held the mortgage. There in 1723 she married the lord of the manor, Paul Calton, and it was from him about 1742 that John Campbell acquired Benbow family information that he later published and whose accuracy has been disputed.

Admiral Benbow is linked directly with the 1584 coat of arms granted to John Benbow (1565–1625) of Newport, Shropshire, in three instances: his tomb in Kingston, Jamaica; his son's memorial in St Nicholas's, Deptford Green; and on a 1679–80 silver alms dish presented to the church of St Blaise, Milton, by his daughter Catherine. There is no evidence to prove that the admiral was entitled to the arms by direct unbroken male descent nor is there evidence that he assumed and used them in his own lifetime, without licence making a minor alteration in the older arms, as was not unknown at that time. It is clear, however, that at least Benbow's daughter Catherine allowed the use of the arms on the alms dish, on her brother's memorial, and on her father's gravestone.

In the years that followed Benbow's death controversy slowly developed over the engagement off Santa Marta. The decision of the court martial was the first to be published, as *An Account of the Arraignments and … Transmitted from Two Eminent Merchants at Port Royal* (1703). Two years later supporters of Richard Kirkby and Cooper Wade sought to discredit Benbow by publishing *An Account of the Transaction between Admiral Benbow and Monsieur Du Casse* (1705). Admiralty secretary Josiah Burchett, in his authoritative *Transactions of War at Sea* (1720, p. 598) thought Benbow had made errors both in dealing with his captains and in allowing an acting rear-admiral to conduct a court martial, a power reserved to vice-admirals. While Bishop Burnet omitted any mention of the incident in his *History of my Own Time* (1734), other influential writers of the period, such as Thomas Lediard in *A Naval History of England* (1735, p. 734) and John Campbell in *Biographia Britannica* (1747, 1.687) and *Lives of British Admirals* (4.222) praised Benbow's courage and fighting spirit. Typical of the view at that time, a monument by the sculptor John Evan Thomas was erected in 1843 by public subscription in St Mary's Church, Shrewsbury, commemorating 'a skillful and daring seaman whose heroic exploits long rendered him the boast of the British Navy and still point him out as the Nelson of his times'. The dramatic story of Benbow's last fight had become one of the great legends of the English fighting sailor, immortalized in contemporary ballads and prints. Later in the nineteenth century the Benbow legend was recalled in Tennyson's poem 'The Captain', the names of a 74-gun ship of the line (1813) and two battleships (1885 and 1913), as well as in the evocative name for a public house that Robert Louis Stevenson chose for a chapter in his romantic adventure novel *Treasure Island* (1883)—'The Old Sea Dog at the Admiral Benbow'.

In their attempts to counteract the then very popular Benbow legend, naval historians in the late nineteenth and early twentieth centuries were particularly critical of Benbow. Perhaps the most critical of all was Sir John Knox Laughton, who in the *Dictionary of National Biography* article of 1885 concluded:

> The exact narration of Benbow's history may cause some wonder as to his high reputation. For in no instance where he commanded was any success over the enemy obtained, and his engagement with Du Casse was the most disgraceful event in our naval records.

Laughton's work was certainly a step forward in using

manuscript evidence to correct popular history, but in doing so he became an advocate of one distinct interpretation. Since Laughton's time, further evidence has come to light which suggests other interpretations. Nevertheless, Benbow's early life and family background remain unclear. In his naval career, the leading flag officers of the day repeatedly showed their respect for his abilities as a fearless fighting officer as well as for his great skill as a pilot and navigator. The debate over the 'mutiny' of Benbow's captains in the action off Cape Santa Marta has been previously seen as either a cowardly desertion by the captains or, alternatively, as a reaction caused by Benbow's lack of proper leadership. For a deeper understanding of these events, one needs to put them in the context of the exhausting effect that a running six-day battle had on all involved. The conditions of the battle also need to be taken into consideration: light and variable winds, diminishing ammunition, battle-damaged ships, a French squadron bent on carrying out its mission and not being led astray to fight a battle, English ship captains with serious professional doubts about obtaining a decisive victory, the established practice by which captains advised an admiral, and an admiral bent on having his way and proving his case shortly after the Admiralty had cashiered Rear-Admiral Sir John Munden from the service—although acquitted by a court martial—for not having been aggressive enough with his squadron. Taken together, the interacting pattern of these complex factors suggests that the events of September 1702 show that common assumptions among naval officers about the conduct of battles at that time were only beginning to develop into what they would become a century later.

JOHN B. HATTENDORF

Sources J. B. Hattendorf, ed., 'Benbow's last fight: documents relating to the battle off Cape Santa Marta', *The naval miscellany*, 5, Navy RS, 125 (1984), 143–206 • W. A. Benbow, *Brave Benbow: the life of Vice-Admiral John Benbow, 1653–1702*, 5th edn (1992) • G. Callender and C. J. Britton, 'Admiral Benbow: fact and fiction', *Mariner's Mirror*, 30 (1944), 123–43, 200–19 • *CSP col.*, vol. 21 • *CSP dom., 1691–1703* • PRO, ADM 1/5253, 1/5263, 3/12, 3/13, 6/3–6 • *Correspondentie van Willem III en van Hans Willem Bentinck*, ed. N. Japikse, 5 vols. (The Hague, 1927–37) • Pitcairn-Jones, 'Ship histories', NMM [card file] • NMM, Sergison MSS, SER/136 • D. J. Lyon, *Sailing navy list* (1994) • *The Sergison papers*, ed. R. D. Merriman, Navy RS, 89 (1950) • *Diary and correspondence of John Evelyn*, ed. H. B. Wheatley and W. Bray (1906)
Archives Shrops. RRC, material relating to him | PRO, Admiralty papers
Likenesses English school, group portrait, oils, 1692–3 (with Ralph Delavalle and Thomas Phillips, c.1692), NMM • G. Kneller, oils, 1701, NMM, NPG [*see illus.*] • J. E. Thomas, medallion relief bust, 1843, St Mary's Church, Shrewsbury
Wealth at death approx. £7500: will, PRO, PROB 11/469, fol. 47; repr. in Benbow, *Brave Benbow*, 196–7

Benbow, John (1681?–1708), traveller, was the son of Vice-Admiral John *Benbow (1653?–1702) and his wife, Martha (*d*. 1722). On 29 June 1695 he was appointed a volunteer on board HMS *Northumberland*. He did not remain long in the Royal Navy and in February 1701 sailed as fourth mate of the *Degrave*, a merchant ship of 700 tons bound for India. In Bengal the captain and first mate died and Benbow was thus second mate when the ship began her homeward

voyage late in 1702. In going out of the Hooghly River the *Degrave* grounded heavily, and began leaking badly when out to sea. With the pumps going constantly they reached Mauritius in a couple of months, but rashly started again for the Cape without having identified the leak. In imminent danger of sinking, the crew decided to make for the nearest land, which was the southern tip of Madagascar, where they ran the ship ashore.

On reaching land the men were almost immediately made prisoners by the local king, and encountered other stranded Europeans, including two Scottish captains, Drummond and Stewart. Assisted by these men, the *Degrave's* crew boldly took the king hostage, with his wife and a nephew, and set off east across the country to the territory of another king, known as King Samuel, but were pursued and duped into giving up their hostages. Foreseeing the outcome, Benbow, with Drummond, Stewart, and some others, slipped away under cover of darkness. The following day all those who remained were massacred, with the exception of some boys, one of whom, Robert Drury, spent about fifteen years on the island before escaping to tell his story in *Madagascar, or, Robert Drury's Journal* (1729).

Benbow, Drummond, and Stewart reached Fort Dauphin (Tôlañaro) on the south-east coast and were given hospitality by King Samuel for some months. Benbow and some others then travelled north up the east coast, but he returned after a year to Fort Dauphin, where he grew sweet potatoes and lived on them until the arrival in December 1706 of a Dutch ship, *Ter Aa*, whose crew 'found the son of the deceased English Admiral Benbow, who was dressed in the same way as the natives there, and lived as intimately with them as if he were a native of the country' ('To the seventeen at Amsterdam', 9 Feb 1707, Leibbrandt, 310).

Benbow wrote an account of his experiences which was accidentally burnt in manuscript in his brother's house near Aldgate, London, in 1714, but an account he gave to his Dutch rescuers has been preserved in the Dutch archives at the Cape of Good Hope. Benbow himself did not long survive his repatriation, dying at Deptford on 17 November 1708. He was buried in the Benbow family tomb in St Nicholas's, Deptford Green, where a monument was erected to his memory.

J. K. LAUGHTON, *rev.* NEIL RENNIE

Sources H. C. V. Leibbrandt, *Précis of the archives of the Cape of Good Hope. Letters despatched, 1696–1709* (1896), 310–12 • R. Drury, *Madagascar, or, Robert Drury's journal, during fifteen years captivity on that island* (1729) • W. Duncombe, 'An account of William Benbow, son to the admiral', *GM*, 1st ser., 39 (1769), 171–2 • H. Owen and J. B. Blakeway, *A history of Shrewsbury*, 2 (1825), 394 • W. A. Benbow, *Brave Benbow: the life of Vice-Admiral John Benbow, 1653–1702*, 5th edn (1992) • A. W. Secord, *Robert Drury's journal and other studies* (1961) • will, PRO, PROB 11/511, sig. 238 • private information (2004)

Benbow, William (*b.* 1784, *d.* in or after 1852), radical and publisher, was born at Middlewich, Cheshire. He learned the trade of a shoemaker, but was a dissenting preacher in Newton, Manchester, by the time that he commenced his political activities in 1808. In December 1816 he was delegated by the Lancashire radicals to liaise with ultra-radical elements in London. It seems likely that he was fully aware of the Spa Fields conspiracy of that month, and his association with the Spencean revolutionary group in London dates from about that time. He also associated with Sir Francis Burdett and William Cobbett, and acted as agent in Lancashire for the *Political Register*. He represented the Manchester Hampden Club at the convention called by Major John Cartwright in January 1817 and was an organizer of the Blanketeers' march. After plans for a revolutionary government involving him were exposed later that month, Benbow prepared to flee to the United States, but he was arrested in May and detained for the remainder of the year.

After a brief spell in Manchester, mainly promoting a plan to destabilize the economy through the circulation of forged banknotes, Benbow joined Cobbett in America. Benbow was responsible for disinterring the bones of Thomas Paine, though it was Cobbett who brought them back to England. Benbow returned to Manchester in December 1819 to resume insurrectionary activity, but moved to London early the following year. From a shop in the Strand he established himself as a major radical bookseller, a leading supporter of Queen Caroline, and also a publisher of bawdy and obscene literature. He was arrested for caricaturing George IV in May 1821 and was detained without trial for eight months, during which time his first wife died and his business collapsed. He resumed on a smaller scale in 1822, and was immediately prosecuted, unsuccessfully, for a pirated edition of Byron's *Cain*. A further unsuccessful prosecution for obscenities published in his *Rambler's Magazine* followed in July 1822. He quarrelled furiously with Cobbett, and with the radical publisher Robert Carlile about his pirated editions of Paine and pornographic publications.

During the quieter political climate of the mid-1820s Benbow concentrated on publishing pornography. After further imprisonment in 1827, possibly for debt, he changed his business to that of coffee- and beer-house keeper. The 'Institution of the Working Classes', his premises at 8 Theobalds Road, Holborn, became an important centre for metropolitan radicals, especially the National Union of the Working Classes, co-operators, and female radicals (led by Benbow's second wife). His insurrectionary views were undiminished in the reform crisis, but his lasting contribution to radicalism was made in his pamphlet of January 1832, *Grand National Holiday and Congress of the Productive Classes*. In it Benbow argued the case for a simultaneous general strike and radical convention. Neither of these ideas was original: he leaned heavily on Spencean thinking in his development of the strike proposal, while the idea of a national convention as a radical alternative to parliament had been a staple of English reform since the 1780s. Benbow's anti-establishment invective and cogency were remarkable, however, and *Grand National Holiday* went through three large editions and continued to be read well into the 1840s.

Benbow is most easily characterized as an insurrectionary conspirator and opponent of the 'old corruption', whose political work constituted a significant stage in the evolution of a self-consciously working-class radicalism. However, his career after the famous pamphlet was anticlimactic and was marked by several unsuccessful publishing ventures, by quarrels with fellow radicals over his financial probity, and by his trenchant opposition to the influence of Robert Owen. Benbow espoused the cause of working-class co-operation against what he claimed was Owen's patronizing and anti-democratic attitude, and in doing so he achieved some influence. In all, though, these were inauspicious circumstances in which to develop further his career as a radical reformer, even after he had ceased issuing libertinist literature. In 1834 his business failed and he turned first to shoemaking and then greengrocery to earn a living. He reactivated his links with Lancashire during the anti-poor law and Chartist agitations, and was arrested there in August 1840 and charged with sedition. In all he spent two years in prison, where, in the words of a prisons inspector, 'time seems to have abated nothing of his warmth in the cause of Republicanism' (PRO, HO 20/10). Released in 1841, he returned to London and a precarious career as a Chartist lecturer. His last public appearance of any kind was on the platform of a meeting of the Finsbury Manhood Suffrage Society in October 1852. The date and circumstances of his death are unknown.   MALCOLM CHASE

Sources I. Prothero, 'Benbow, William', *DLB*, vol. 6 • I. McCalman, *Radical underworld: prophets, revolutionaries, and pornographers in London, 1795–1840* (1988) • I. Prothero, 'William Benbow and the concept of the "general strike"', *Past and Present*, 63 (1974), 132–71 • prison inspector's report, 1 Jan 1841, PRO, HO 20/10
Likenesses J. L. Marks, 1820, BM

Bendall, Cecil (1856–1906), Sanskritist, was born on 1 July 1856 in Islington, London, the youngest son in a family of six sons and three daughters of Robert Smith Bendall (*d.* 1863/4), a tradesman in London, and his wife, Elizabeth Kay, daughter of William Holmes. He was educated at the City of London School (1869–75), gaining a Carpenter scholarship in 1871. On the initiative of the progressive headmaster, Edwin Abbott Abbott, Bendall, who had shown a talent for languages, was taught Sanskrit from 1872/3 by George Frederick Nicholl, afterwards professor of Arabic at Oxford. In 1875 he entered Trinity College, Cambridge, with a Broderers' Company scholarship, and soon won a Sanskrit exhibition also. In 1877 he migrated as a scholar to Gonville and Caius College; he graduated BA in 1879 in the first class of the classical tripos, and then became a fellow of Caius (1879–86). During seven years' residence in the university he read Sanskrit with Edward Byles Cowell, professor of Sanskrit, whose influence decided the direction of his career. After graduating, he turned his whole attention to Sanskrit; in the summer of 1879 he attended Theodor Benfey's lectures at Göttingen on the Veda and on Avestan, and in 1881 gained a first class in the Indian languages tripos at Cambridge. That October he began lecturing on Sanskrit to classics students and to Indian Civil Service candidates studying at Cambridge. He had already published his first work, an annotated abridgement of the *Megha-Sutra*, with translation (*Journal of the Royal Asiatic Society of Great Britain and Ireland*, new ser., 12, 1880, 286–311), and in 1883 he completed the *Catalogue of the Buddhist Sanskrit Manuscripts in the University Library of Cambridge*, which had been initiated by Cowell. In the introduction Bendall showed systematically for the first time how palaeography determined the age of Sanskrit manuscripts.

In 1882 Bendall moved to London to become senior assistant in the department of oriental manuscripts and printed books in the British Museum. He held the post until his retirement, through ill health, in 1898. While at the museum he catalogued both the Sanskrit and Pali books (1893) and the Sanskrit manuscripts (1902). He was from 1883 a member of the Royal Asiatic Society of Great Britain and Ireland and from 1884 a member of its council. He was a contributor to its *Journal*. He frequently read papers at the meetings of the International Congress of Orientalists, and was delegate for his university in 1899 and 1902. He also held the chair of Sanskrit at University College, London, from 1885 to 1903.

With the aid of grants from the Worts fund at Cambridge Bendall twice visited Nepal and northern India to acquire manuscripts for Cambridge University Library. On his first visit (1884–5) he obtained some 500 Sanskrit manuscripts and discovered nine historical inscriptions, one of great importance for the early chronology of Nepal; he described the trip in his *Journey of Literary and Archaeological Research in Nepal and Northern India* (1886). His second visit (1898–9) resulted in the acquisition of some ninety manuscripts (see *Journal of the Royal Asiatic Society of Great Britain and Ireland*, 1900, 162–4).

At Esher on 19 July 1898 Bendall married a French woman, Georgette, daughter of Georges Joseph Ignace Jung, and widow of G. Mosse of Cowley Hall, Middlesex; they had no children. She became a member of the Royal Asiatic Society in 1901, was author of *Practical Lessons in Cookery for Small Households* (1905), and died on 24 December 1910 at her sister's home in Paris.

In 1901 Bendall returned to Cambridge, having succeeded Robert Alexander Neil as university lecturer and lecturer to the Indian Civil Service board. In 1902 he became curator of oriental literature in the university library. On Cowell's death in 1903 he was elected professor of Sanskrit and was made honorary fellow of Caius in 1905. By this time Bendall had become recognized throughout Europe as a scholar of the first rank. He was a sound textual critic, an expert in Indian palaeography and epigraphy, and a vigorous and clear teacher. His special interest was the Sanskrit literature of Mahayana Buddhism, and his *magnum opus* was his edition of the Śikshāsamuccaya (1897–1902), an important compendium of Mahayana doctrine, which he made from a unique manuscript and an early Tibetan version; he was engaged with W. H. D. Rouse on its translation at his death.

Bendall was slight and delicate, but had a bright and kindly personality, and was self-disciplined but sympathetic towards others. His chief interests from childhood on were music, especially that of Palestrina, Bach, and Handel, and the religious architecture of both Britain and India, as well as English literature. In late 1905 he had to go to Liverpool for surgery. He died on 14 March 1906 at 96 Princes Road, Liverpool, and was buried on 19 March in the Huntingdon Road cemetery, Cambridge. By his will he left books and a unique palm-leaf manuscript of the *Tantrakhana*, a collection of Indian folklore, to Cambridge University. His residuary estate after his wife's death was assigned to the foundation of a prize for Sanskrit at Caius and the formation there of an oriental lending library for undergraduates. Part of his valuable musical collection was acquired by the Fitzwilliam Museum.

W. B. OWEN, *rev.* R. S. SIMPSON

Sources H. T. Francis, *In memoriam: Cecil Bendall* (privately printed, Cambridge, 1906) · E. J. Rapson, 'Cecil Bendall', *Journal of the Royal Asiatic Society of Great Britain and Ireland* (1906), 527–33 · *Cambridge Review* (26 April 1906), 334 · *The Times* (15 March 1906), 10d · *The Times* (20 March 1906), 10a · *The Times* (18 June 1906), 4d · Venn, *Alum. Cant.* · J. Venn and others, eds., *Biographical history of Gonville and Caius College*, 2: 1713–1897 (1898), 429 · J. Venn and others, eds., *Biographical history of Gonville and Caius College*, 4 (1912), 131 · WWW, 1897–1915 · C. Bendall, *Journal of the Royal Asiatic Society of Great Britain and Ireland* (1900), 162–4 [letter] · private information (1912)
Archives CUL, corresp. · CUL, collection of his non-duplicate books and oriental palm-leaf MSS · King's Cam., letters to Oscar Browning | FM Cam., collection of music
Likenesses sepia drawing, Institute of Oriental Studies, Cambridge
Wealth at death £1588 6s. 6d.: probate, 28 April 1906, *CGPLA Eng. & Wales*

Bendings, William (*d. c.*1197), justice, first appears in the royal financial records of 1170/71. According to Gerald of Wales, he was sent to Ireland by Henry II in 1176 as one of four envoys, of whom two were to remain with the viceroy, Earl Richard fitz Gilbert de Clare, and two were to return, bringing with them Raymond Fitzgerald. However, in changed circumstances following Earl Richard's death, all the envoys returned to England, leaving Fitzgerald in Ireland. In 1178 Bendings was acting as a royal justice in Yorkshire. The following year, after the resignation of the justiciar, Richard de Lucy, a redistribution of the circuits of the general eyre was carried into effect. In place of the six circuits then existing, the country was divided into four, to each of which, except the northern circuit, five justices were assigned, three or four of the number being laymen. Bendings was one of six justices assigned to the northern circuit and led by Ranulf de Glanville, who became justiciar shortly afterwards. In November 1179 Bendings is named as a royal justice in a fine made at Westminster. In 1182–4 he acted as sheriff of Dorset and Somerset, the two counties being united under his single jurisdiction. Bendings was outlived by his wife, Gunnora, and by at least one son, Adam. He had almost certainly died before 1196/7, for in that year his son Adam started to account for the debts William had incurred as sheriff of Dorset and Somerset.   J. M. RIGG, *rev.* JOHN HUDSON

Sources Pipe rolls · Giraldus Cambrensis, *Expugnatio Hibernica / The conquest of Ireland*, ed. and trans. A. B. Scott and F. X. Martin (1978) · L. Landon, ed., *The cartae antiquae: rolls 1–10, printed from the original in the custody of the master of the rolls*, PRSoc., 55, new ser., 17 (1939) ·

J. C. Davies, ed., *The cartae antiquae: rolls 11–20, printed from the original in the Public Record Office*, PRSoc., 71, new ser., 33 (1960) • D. M. Stenton, ed., *Pleas before the king or his justices*, 4 vols., SeldS, 67–8, 83–4 (1952–67) • *Chronica magistri Rogeri de Hovedene*, ed. W. Stubbs, 2, Rolls Series, 51 (1869), 191

Bendish [*née* Ireton], **Bridget** (1649/50–1726), granddaughter of Oliver Cromwell, was the daughter of Henry *Ireton (*bap.* 1611, *d.* 1651), parliamentarian army officer and regicide, and his wife, Bridget *Fleetwood (*bap.* 1624, *d.* 1662), daughter of Oliver *Cromwell, lord protector. Her mother married General Charles Fleetwood in 1652, and after her death Bridget lived with her stepfather at Stoke Newington, Middlesex, until, aged nineteen, she was licensed on 24 August 1669 to marry Thomas Bendish (*bap.* 1645, *d.* 1707) of Gray's Inn. Two of their sons and a daughter reached adulthood. Bendish had been admitted to Gray's Inn on 2 July 1666 as the son and heir of Thomas Bendish, a member of the Independent congregation at Great Yarmouth, Norfolk, who had served as bailiff in 1656. He was called to the bar by order of the reader on 2 August 1673.

Bridget and Thomas Bendish took up residence in Southtown, adjacent to Great Yarmouth, where he owned salt marshes and a saltworks on Cobholme island. In 1672 he was charged with landing coal from the vessel of a non-burgess on the west side of the haven without the permission of Yarmouth's bailiffs and in contravention of the town's privileges. Bridget's politics may well have been sympathetic to the whig exclusionists: in May 1685 she apparently aided the escape of her brother, Henry Ireton, who had been arrested for complicity in the Rye House plot upon his return to England in April 1685. Following his recapture and imprisonment, she was allowed access to him in Newgate in November and December 1685. In 1689 the Revd Rowland Davies visited Bendish's house 'and saw all his contrivance to make salt' (*Journal of Rowland Davies*, 31). In 1694 Bridget was introduced to Queen Mary by Archbishop Tillotson and reputedly promised a pension.

Thomas Bendish died on 27 April 1707, leaving his wife in charge of the business. Bridget was always determined to defend her family heritage. In 1719 a local dissenting minister, Samuel Say, wrote in *The character of Mrs B[ridget] B[endish] grand-daughter of Oliver Cromwell written in the year 1719, on occasion of the closing words of Lord Clarendon's character of her grandfather* that he was 'a brave wicked man'. This work, which was not published until after Bridget's death, portrayed her as a rigid Calvinist of uncertain temper, with a strength of will and physical courage rarely paralleled. According to Say she laboured incessantly in her own household, on her husband's farm, and at his saltworks, yet was always noted for dignity of mien and the charm of her conversation. She was reputed to bear a physical resemblance to her grandfather, of whose reputation she was an ardent champion. Say recorded an incident when Bridget was travelling to London in a public coach when a fellow passenger, in conversation with a companion, spoke lightly of the protector. Bridget not only inveighed against the offender for the rest of the journey, but on alighting in London snatched another passenger's sword from its sheath and challenged the slanderer to fight her there and then. Bridget died early in 1726 and was buried in Great Yarmouth. Her will was proved at Norwich consistory court in the same year.

SIDNEY LEE, *rev.* STUART HANDLEY

Sources M. Noble, *Memoirs of the protectoral house of Cromwell*, 2 vols. (1787) • 'Owd Soul', 'Mistress Bridget Bendish', *East Anglian Magazine*, 6 (1946–7), 544–7 • *A miscellany*, Norfolk RS, 22 (1951), 9–33 • J. L. Chester and J. Foster, eds., *London marriage licences, 1521–1869* (1887), 114 • BL, Add. MS 19118, fols. 54–63 • IGI • GM, 1st ser., 35 (1765), 357–8 • *Journal of the Very Rev. Rowland Davies*, ed. R. Caulfield, CS, 68 (1857), 31 • *CSP dom.*, 1685, 394, 417 • T. Barton and M. A. Farrow, *Index of wills proved in the consistory court of Norwich, 1687–1750*, Norfolk RS, 34 (1965), 24 • P Gauci, *Politics and society in Great Yarmouth, 1660–1722* (1996), 124 • J. Granger, *A biographical history of England, from Egbert the Great to the revolution*, 4th edn, 4 vols. (1804), vol. 3, p. 17n. • 'Ireton, Henry', HoP, *Commons, 1690–1715* [draft]

Bendish, Sir Thomas, second baronet (1607–1674), diplomat, was the eldest son of Sir Thomas Bendish (*c.*1568–1636) of Bower Hall, Steeple Bumpstead, Essex, and his wife, Dorothy (*d.* in or after 1635), daughter of Richard Cotts or Cutts. He matriculated as a fellow-commoner from St John's College, Cambridge, in the Easter term of 1624 and was admitted to the Middle Temple on 13 May 1626. On 16 October the following year he married, at Barkway, Hertfordshire, Anne (*d.* 1649), daughter of Henry Baker of Shoeberry, Essex. Following his father's death on 26 March 1636 he succeeded as second baronet.

On the outbreak of civil war Bendish supported the king and in 1643 he published a proclamation against the associating of counties by parliament. He was imprisoned in the Tower of London until 1644 and his estates were sequestered. On his release he was fined £800 and banished from Essex; his movements remained restricted until 1646. However, he seems to have been rehabilitated in public society by the following year, when he was appointed 'Ambassador, Consul or Agent' to Turkey 'upon a desire of the Company of Merchants trading to the Levant Seas' (*JHL*, 8.694) and under a commission of the great seal with a salary of £2000.

Bendish left for Constantinople with his wife, five of his daughters, and at least one of his sons. *En route* he stopped off for a long period in Italy, where his eldest daughter married a Leghorn merchant, Philip Williams. Bendish's eventual arrival in Constantinople was not without incident: his predecessor, Sackville Crowe, refused to accept his appointment and had to be forcibly removed by boat after Bendish bribed key officials in the Ottoman administration to accept his documents. Charles I, who may have signed Bendish's credentials under duress, appears eventually to have acquiesced in his appointment: in 1648 he sent him a bed—a traditional royal gift to ambassadors in Turkey. Bendish's allegiance in the later stages of the English civil war is not clear but he was furnished with both letters patent from Charles I and a commission from parliament.

Much of Bendish's time was spent reorganizing the English communities resident in Constantinople, Smyrna (Izmir), and Aleppo and removing the factionalism he had inherited from his predecessor. He managed to improve the profitability of the company in Turkey by reducing the level of corruption among merchants and local suppliers. In 1648 he secured the Capitulations (the written consent of the Ottoman sultan to trade in Ottoman territory which bestowed on the English community various privileges of status and residence), with gunboat diplomacy, bringing a small merchant fleet towards the sultan's administrative centre in a demonstration of England's naval power. He also had to tour the slave entrepots of Constantinople buying English slaves to free them. This was often the only way to secure a successful outcome to the frequent acts of piracy in Ottoman waters.

Bendish survived the turmoils of the Commonwealth, withstanding an attempt by a royalist sympathizer, Henry Hyde, to assume charge in 1650, and efforts by disgruntled merchants to have him declared a traitor in 1651 by suggesting that he had carried out an illicit correspondence with the young Charles II. He also had to contend with administrative instability in the Ottoman Porte (seat of government) as chief ministers were replaced frequently and the authorities in Constantinople tried to keep control over the widening empire. Bendish, who proved an able administrator and excelled at manipulating the Ottoman system to the company's advantage, executed both commercial and political policy for his two masters: the Levant Company and the Commonwealth. He secured free passage for English ships in Ottoman waters, free power over the disposal of goods by English merchants, and customs exemptions. But he also worked to protect the English from Venetian and Ottoman pressure during the Cretan war, to deal with increasing complaints of Ottoman piracy in Mediterranean waters and to defend British naval policy in the region, most notably Admiral Robert Blake's campaign against Tunis.

Bendish suffered personal tragedy and hardships during his residence: one of his two sons, Thomas, was drowned in 1649 when his ship, the *Talent*, was attacked by the French. His wife died of plague in Constantinople later the same year. And in 1651 Bendish had the distinction of being the first English ambassador to be imprisoned in Turkey. He was placed in shackles at the order of the shaikh-ul-Islam or grand mufti, the leading religious cleric in the Ottoman hierarchy, when he refused to remove the consul of Smyrna over a commercial dispute involving a relative of the mufti.

In 1652 the Commonwealth authorities decided to replace Bendish with a close associate of Oliver Cromwell, Richard Salway. Salway could not travel immediately and Bendish prevented the interim agent, Richard Lawrence, from being presented at the Porte, arguing that he did not have sufficient experience or clout to deal with merchant business or renew the Capitulations. When Salway asked to be relieved of his commission because it did not pay well Lawrence was recalled to England and Bendish was reconfirmed in his position.

Bendish was then involved in an ambitious but unsuccessful project to provide Cromwell with Arab stallions, to be transported through Aleppo. He also played a mediation role in protestant efforts to encourage the Ottoman authorities to allow Transylvania more autonomy while continuing to protect it against Catholic Habsburg aspirations. It is not clear how far this last policy had Cromwell's approval.

Bendish's links with the Levant Company grew during his residence in Constantinople. Two of his sons took up posts locally, John (the eldest) at the embassy in Constantinople and Andrew as a factor in Smyrna. John appears to have returned to London to work for the company there and to manage his father's estate but Andrew continued to work in the Levant after his father left Constantinople, possibly securing a post in Cairo. An unnamed son of Bendish (possibly John) also worked for the company in Surat under the protection of George Oxinden in 1666. Two of Bendish's daughters also married company members. His second daughter, Abigail, married a Smyrnan merchant after breaking off her engagement to a senior administrator at the embassy, James Modyford. The youngest, Anne, married Sir Jonathan Dawes, the treasurer's assistant at the embassy, who stayed on as adviser to Bendish's successor before becoming a financier to the crown.

Immediately after the Restoration, Charles II decided that he needed a stalwart royalist in Constantinople. Bendish's successor, the earl of Winchilsea, recognizing Bendish's administrative ability, tried to secure a position for him as agent in Cairo. When he failed Bendish returned to England, taking his dead wife's body back with him for reburial at the family home of Bower Hall, Steeple Bumpstead. After a lengthy and acrimonious battle with the Levant Company over expenses he died at his home in 1674, leaving his estate to his son John. He was buried at Steeple Bumpstead.   LIANE SAUNDERS

Sources PRO, SP 97/17 · BL, Harleian MS 6210, fols. 42–51 · Essex RO, D/DLf 01–049 · *Newes from Turkie* (1648) · T. Bendish, *A brief narrative and vindication of Sir Thomas Bendish* (1660) · M. Naima, *Tarihi*, trans. Z. Danişman, 6 vols. (Istanbul, 1969) · Venn, *Alum. Cant.* · GEC, *Baronetage*, 1.62–3 · Herts. ALS, D/P. 13/1/9, 22 · G. M. Bell, *A handlist of British diplomatic representatives, 1509–1688*, Royal Historical Society Guides and Handbooks, 16 (1990) · A. C. Wood, *A history of the Levant Company* (1935) · *Essex Notebook*, 11 (1885), 127 · JHL, 8 (1645–6) · Bodl. Oxf., MS Rawl. A. 14 · BL, Add. MSS 15750; 40700, fol. 135

Archives Essex RO, Chelmsford, corresp. and papers · PRO, estate papers, SP 97/17 | Bodl. Oxf., MSS Rawl.

Bendlowes, William (1516–1584), serjeant-at-law and law reporter, was the son of Christopher Bendlowes of Great Bardfield, Essex, and Elizabeth, daughter of John Rufford. He was educated at St John's College, Cambridge (c.1530), Thavies Inn, and Lincoln's Inn, where he was admitted in 1534 and called to the bar in 1539. In his early years at the bar he practised as an attorney of the common pleas, and is named in a case of 1540 acting for Matthew Parker, the future archbishop. This circumstance, taken together with his keen interest in the forms of pleading, raises the possibility that he was trained in the office of Nicholas Rokewode, the chief protonotary, which was located in

Lincoln's Inn gateway. He became a reader of his inn in 1549, and served for four years as treasurer.

In 1553–4 Bendlowes enjoyed a brief parliamentary career as member for three Cornish constituencies in succession, and about this time he became recorder of Thaxted in Essex. His call to the order of the coif came in 1555, when he was created serjeant with his fellow bencher William Rastell and five others. His patrons on this occasion were Cuthbert Tunstall, bishop of Durham, and Edmund Bonner, bishop of London, and it is well known that he favoured the Marian religious regime. On the accession of Elizabeth I, when a projected call of serjeants failed, Bendlowes found himself for a few months the only practising serjeant in England; it was the only time such a thing ever occurred, and a fact of which he was proud. Nevertheless, although his known religious inclinations did not prevent him from being continued as an assize commissioner by Elizabeth I until 1567, they did bar his promotion to a permanent judgeship or office. He therefore remained in private practice for the rest of his life, acquired a high reputation for learning, and by the time of his death, though not a queen's serjeant, was the acknowledged leader of the common pleas bar.

Bendlowes is still known for his reports of cases, which run from 1534 to 1579. They consist largely of Latin pleadings with relatively short French annotations, and constitute, in effect, an annotated book of entries. This unusual but restricted format suggests that they were not originally intended for publication, and does not entitle them to a particularly high estimation, though they had an enormous circulation in manuscript. A fair copy in the Bodleian Library (MS Rawl. C.728), which belonged to the serjeant's son and was said to have been 'composed' by the serjeant in 1573, was submitted for the judges' approval in 1601 with a view to publication. In fact the reports were not printed until 1661, though some extracts appeared as appendices to Ashe's *Epieikeia* (1609) and to the 1633 edition of Keilwey. A better text was printed in 1689, under the editorship of Serjeant Rowe, as *Les reports de Gulielme Benloe serjeant del ley*. This version was known in the profession, somewhat misleadingly, as *Old Benloe*, presumably because it was nearer to the vulgate manuscript texts than the *New Benloe* of 1661, where the text was mixed with cases from the time of James I and Charles I.

Bendlowes inherited land at Bardfield and built Great Bardfield Place, an enterprise commemorated by a cornerpost inscribed 'W. B. mense Aprilis a° Dñi 1564', a shield of arms of Bendlowes impaling Palmer, and an inscription mentioning that he was for a time the only serjeant-at-law in England. His wife, Eleanor, was the daughter of Sir Edward Palmer of Angmering, Sussex, and widow of John Berners of Finchingfield. His only son, William (*d.* 1613), followed his father to Lincoln's Inn and became a bencher. He was ancestor of Edward Bendlowes [*see* Benlowes, Edward] the poet.

Bendlowes the serjeant probably retired about 1579, when his reports cease, though it was noted that 'Father Benloos … did put a short case' when Chief Justice Anderson was installed in 1582 (Cooper, *Ath. Cantab.*, 1.496). He died on 19 November 1584 and was buried on 3 December at Great Bardfield, Essex, where there is a monumental brass with a lengthy inscription; his own effigy was badly defaced by 1740 and has been missing since 1836. There is a fine portrait dated 1564, in which Bendlowes is wearing the scarlet robes and white coif of his order, in St John's College, Cambridge. Bendlowes founded a free grammar school and almshouses in Great Bardfield, and left money to provide clothing for local children and doles to the poor. He also bequeathed 40s. to Serjeants' Inn, Fleet Street, though an inscription which his son placed beneath his arms in the chapel window there in 1596 stated that he had given £50 towards the chapel, adding that he wrote reports of cases which were still in use.

J. H. Baker

Sources HoP, *Commons, 1509–58*, 1.416–17 • L. W. Abbott, *Law reporting in England, 1485–1585* (1973) • Baker, *Serjeants* • Cooper, *Ath. Cantab.*, 1.495–7 • W. C. Metcalfe, ed., *The visitations of Essex*, 1, Harleian Society, 13 (1878), 347, 459 • W. Dugdale, *Origines juridiciales, or, Historical memorials of the English laws*, 3rd edn (1680), 331 • Bodl. Oxf., MS Rawl. C. 728 • P. Morant, *The history and antiquities of the county of Essex*, 2 (1768), 442 • N. Salmon, *The history and antiquities of Essex* (1740) • C. F. Smith, 'William Bendlowes of Great Bardfield Place', *Essex Review*, 27 (1918), 113–22 • will, PRO, PROB 11/67, sig. 10 • BL, Stowe MS 586, fol. 59*v*
Likenesses oils, 1564, St John Cam. • brass, Great Bradfield Church, Essex

Benedict [Benedict of Peterborough] (*c.*1135–1193), abbot of Peterborough and royal councillor, is first recorded at the event that shaped his life, as an eyewitness to the murder of Thomas Becket in his cathedral church at Canterbury on 29 December 1170. A monk of Christ Church at this time, Benedict was the first custodian of Becket's tomb when it was made accessible to pilgrims in April 1171, and made what was both the earliest and the definitive collection of the saint's miracles. To serve as an introduction to this, he wrote an account of the martyrdom ('The passion of St Thomas'): this is known only from fragments embedded in *Quadrilogus*, a later compilation. The first recensions of both the 'Passion' and the 'Miracles' existed by mid-1174. Benedict became chancellor of Becket's archiepiscopal successor, Richard of Dover (*d.* 1184), in 1174, and as such proclaimed the statutes of the Council of Westminster in May 1175. In the same year he became prior of Canterbury, the head of the community under the archbishop. His tenure of this office was short, for on 29 May 1177 he was elected abbot of Peterborough, on the king's nomination, and was consecrated by the archbishop of Canterbury. He is recorded as reluctant to leave, and in a sense he never did leave, Canterbury. He made Peterborough a centre of Becket's cult; he used as altars two paving stones stained with the martyr's blood, took with him several other relics, and created a chapel—open to pilgrims—at the gate to the monastic precinct. He returned regularly to Canterbury: he was present in August 1183, when the bishop of Rochester swore fealty to the prior and convent, and in February 1187, when the king came to pray at Becket's tomb, while in the disputed election to the archbishopric in December 1184 the king used him as an intermediary in dealings with the chapter.

As abbot of Peterborough Benedict was a vigorous administrator, concerned to build both the intellectual and material capital of his monastery. He brought from Canterbury a valuable book collection, which included classics and theology, but was particularly rich in canon law. Among this collection was a book that has survived and bears the heading 'Gesta Henrici II Benedicti Abbatis' (BL, Cotton MS Julius A.xi, fols. 3–112). A literal translation of the heading, which is not contemporary with the text, represents Abbot Benedict as the author of the chronicle. Stubbs showed that he was certainly not the author, and the work is now attributed to Roger of Howden (d. 1201/2). On his accession Benedict discharged debts which totalled 1500 marks, and redeemed plate and other goods that had been pawned. He completed the nave of the church, built a new gatehouse to the abbey precinct, and other monastic buildings, including a new hall. He set up a new demesne manor at Biggin Grange near Oundle, by means of a firm assertion of his lordship, 'for many saw the force of his arms in this transaction' (Historiae Anglicanae, 100). The abbey's other manors were taken in hand, and farmed directly.

Abbot Benedict's energy also found an outlet on the national stage, particularly after the accession of Richard I, whose special intimate he is said to have been. He attended Richard's coronation on 3 September 1189, and for several months thereafter was almost continuously at court, at Canterbury in late November and early December 1189, and at Rouen and Lyons-la-Forêt in March and April 1190. During this period he assiduously collected charters in support of the abbey's privileges, obtaining twenty of these in all. Returning to England in the summer of 1190, he served as head of a panel of justices itinerant. He also served on a number of occasions as a papal judge-delegate, including a case heard at Northampton on 14 October 1192 between the archbishop of York and the bishop of Durham. The Peterborough Abbey chronicler, Robert of Swaffham, states that, during the absence of the king in the east, Abbot Benedict was a close ally and counsellor of the chancellor, William de Longchamp (d. 1197); and he credits Benedict also with the idea that to secure the king's ransom from captivity the chalices of the clergy should be melted down. Early in June 1193 the king nominated Benedict to be one of those to go to Germany to escort him home. There is no record of his going, and possibly he was unfit to travel, for he died on 29 September 1193. He was buried at Peterborough, and the earliest of the abbots' tombstones in the abbey (now the cathedral) church has long been identified as his.

EDMUND KING

Sources J. Sparke, ed., *Historiae Anglicanae scriptores varii*, 2 vols. (1723) · C. R. Cheney and B. E. A. Jones, eds., *Canterbury, 1162–1190*, English Episcopal Acta, 2 (1986) · C. R. Cheney and E. John, eds., *Canterbury, 1193–1205*, English Episcopal Acta, 3 (1986) · D. M. Smith, ed., *Lincoln, 1186–1206*, English Episcopal Acta, 4 (1986) · A. Gransden, *Historical writing in England*, 1 (1974) · F. Barlow, *Thomas Becket* (1986) · D. Knowles, C. N. L. Brooke, and V. C. M. London, eds., *The heads of religious houses, England and Wales*, 1: 940–1216 (1972), 34,

61 · R. W. Eyton, *Court, household, and itinerary of King Henry II* (1878) · L. Landon, *The itinerary of King Richard I*, PRSoc., new ser., 13 (1935) · E. King, *Peterborough Abbey, 1086–1310: a study in the land market* (1973) · A. Duggan, *Thomas Becket: a textual history of his letters* (1980), 192–5
Likenesses marble effigy on monument, c.1195, Peterborough Cathedral

Benedict Biscop [St Benedict Biscop] (c.628–689), abbot of Wearmouth and scholar, was born about 628 of a noble Northumbrian family, named in the life of Bishop Wilfrid by Stephen of Ripon (Eddius Stephanus) as Baducing. Bede provides the chief narrative for his life in the *Historia abbatum*, which may be supplemented by information from the anonymous life of Biscop's successor Ceolfrith. Since he was given the name Biscop (bishop), his parents must have been Christians and it is possible that he may have possessed a Romano-Christian ancestry although he is named as an Angle by Bede. At some unspecified point Biscop acquired the cognomen Benedict, presumably out of his devotion to St Benedict of Nursia rather than to Pope Benedict II (r. 684–5). He entered the household of King Oswiu as a thegn.

Travels to the continent, 653–668 In 653, at the age of twenty-five, Biscop decided to forsake secular ambition and wealth, leave his kinsfolk, and travel to Rome. On his journey he passed through Canterbury and met Wilfrid at the court of King Eorcenberht of Kent. With royal permission, the two travelled to Lyons where Wilfrid was persuaded to stay by Archbishop Dalfinus. Benedict Biscop travelled on to Rome where he lodged at the monastery of St Andrew on the Caelian Hill, where Gregory the Great had been abbot.

Biscop returned to England for a stay of some years and gained the support of Oswiu's son, Alchfrith, king of Deira, whose wish to visit Rome in the company of Biscop was prevented by his father. Biscop then departed to the continent for a more prolonged visit, c.665–668. He stayed at the monastery of Lérins in southern Gaul for two years, a period which saw him tonsured and was to be of great significance for his future career. During this time Lérins underwent important changes which were inaugurated by the arrival of Aigulf, from the monastery of Fleury, to become the new abbot. Abandoning its commitment to the eremetic life, Lérins adopted a mixed rule for the communal life inspired by the reforms inaugurated by St Benedict and St Columbanus. These reforms had spread through the Merovingian kingdoms of Francia from the monastery of Luxeuil and were in evidence in other monasteries in the Rhône valley. Although it is not quite clear where Biscop's visit fits into this pattern of events, monasticism in Frankish Gaul exercised a profound impact on the rest of his ecclesiastical career.

Biscop intended to spend the remainder of his life at Lérins but in 667 he returned to Rome for his third visit. This visit coincided with the arrival of Wighard, archbishop-elect of Canterbury, who died at the papal court before he could be consecrated. Pope Vitalian then appointed Theodore of Tarsus as his successor, with Hadrian to serve as Theodore's assistant. Biscop was enjoined to abandon his monastic life at Lérins and return to England to act as an interpreter for Theodore and Hadrian. On their way to England in the winter of 668–9, Biscop and Theodore spent approximately six months with Agilbert, bishop of Paris (and formerly of the West Saxons) and former patron of Wilfrid, whose abbey at Jouarre observed the mixed Benedictine and Columbanian rule. This short visit allowed Biscop to gain further opportunities of studying the customs prevalent in Merovingian monasteries.

Monastic foundations, Roman influences, and death Biscop arrived in Canterbury with Theodore in 669; he spent two years there ruling the monastery of St Peter and St Paul (later St Augustine's) before Hadrian's arrival. In 671 he returned once again to Rome to procure books on sacred literature and visited Vienne to acquire further texts. He returned to England in 672 and intended to join the court of King Cenwalh of the West Saxons whose friendship he had previously enjoyed. He planned the foundation of a monastery in Wessex, a kingdom marked by Frankish influence. The bishop under whom Biscop planned to settle was Agilbert's nephew, Leuthere, and Wessex was also an early outpost of Benedictine influence in Britain. Cenwalh's sudden death, however, caused Biscop to return to his native Northumbria where, with the help of King Ecgfrith, who provided him with 70 hides of land, he founded the minster of St Peter's at Wearmouth in 674, persuading Ceolfrith to join him and serve as prior.

Biscop spent the next few years building and equipping his new foundation. He imported Frankish stonemasons, recruited from his friend Abbot Torthelm, to build a church in the Roman style, the porch of which can still be seen. Glassmakers and other craftsmen were also imported from Frankish Gaul, not only to make the windows but also to teach local men their skills. Books bought at Rome and Vienne were added to the endowment and a rule for the community was drawn up based on that of St Benedict and on the customs of seventeen monasteries Biscop had visited in Gaul.

In 679 Biscop made a further visit to Rome in the company of Ceolfrith, returning with books, relics, calendars, and service books as well as the arch-chanter of St Peter's, Rome; this was John, the abbot of St Martin's basilica, who arrived to instruct the monks in the Roman liturgy. John brought with him the acts of the Lateran Council of 649 which had declared against those who believed that only one will operated in Christ. A manuscript of these acts was written at Jarrow. In addition to increasing the resources of the library at Wearmouth, Biscop also brought back a series of pictures of gospel scenes, and of incidents in the Apocalypse, which he intended to be set up in the church. This visit to Rome proved to be vital to the future development of Wearmouth as an ecclesiastical community because Biscop obtained from Pope Agatho a privilege limiting the degree of episcopal power over the monks and guaranteeing the freedom of abbatial elections from outside interference.

In 681 or 682 Biscop was granted a further estate of 40 hides by King Ecgfrith which he entrusted to Ceolfrith,

who was thereby able to found at Jarrow a sister community to Wearmouth, dedicated to St Paul. In 685 Biscop made a final visit to Rome, returning with yet more books, vestments, pictures, and fine silk cloaks. On his arrival in Northumbria he discovered that King Ecgfrith had been killed in battle by the Picts and that his own cousin, Eosterwine, to whom he had designated the governance of Wearmouth during his absence, had succumbed to the plague along with many of the monks. Ceolfrith and the other monks had selected the deacon Sigfrid to rule as abbot and their decision was ratified by Biscop. After he had used two of the silk cloaks he had brought back from Rome to purchase 3 hides of land on the south side of the Wear from King Aldfrith, Biscop's own health broke down and, along with Sigfrid, he was stricken with paralysis. He recognized the seriousness of his illness, and appointed Ceolfrith abbot of the joint community of Wearmouth–Jarrow. His final address to the brethren, given on his deathbed, emphasized the need for the community to keep to his eclectic rule, to preserve the large library which he had established, and to ensure that they elected as abbot a man distinguished by his spirituality and teaching, according to the rule of St Benedict, rather than by his membership of a particular family. Biscop's devotion to this cause was such that, according to Bede, he decreed that he would rather see his foundation revert to a wilderness than that his brother, a layman, should succeed him as abbot. He died on 12 January 689 and was buried in the church of St Peter at Wearmouth; Ceolfrith succeeded him as abbot. Biscop's cult developed early; Bede composed a homily assessing his virtues and stressing the need for a man to abandon his family for the sake of salvation. The cult received additional stimulus in the tenth century when Æthelwold, bishop of Winchester, transferred Biscop's relics to Thorney; Glastonbury also claimed, with little foundation, to possess his relics. His feast is celebrated on the anniversary of his death.

Achievement In some ways Benedict Biscop's career resembles that of Bishop Wilfrid: both were aristocrats who travelled extensively in Francia and Italy, acquiring knowledge of continental monastic customs as well as books and other treasures. Biscop, however, was ultimately more detached from the world than Wilfrid. His contribution to Anglo-Saxon Christianity lay not in episcopal organization or miracle working, but in the life of monasteries: in scholarship, liturgy, architecture, and the spread of the Benedictine rule.

Biscop's chief contribution to scholarship lay in the foundation of the monastic library at Wearmouth–Jarrow, which was ultimately expanded by his successor, Ceolfrith. This library consisted of a wide range of classical and patristic literature in addition to musical scripts, books on monastic practice, and monastic sacramentaries. These influences helped the monks to perfect both the Italian uncial and the Irish minuscule scripts; they also provided the basis for the learning, unparalleled in his generation, of Wearmouth–Jarrow's most famous inhabitant, Bede. Biscop's chief contribution to the liturgy lay in his ability to secure the services of John the

Arch-Chanter who, according to Bede, taught the monks the practice of singing throughout the year which was the established custom in Rome. His instructions for the performance of the rite were written down and copied by other foundations. In the field of monastic architecture, Biscop was responsible for the construction of substantial stone buildings to house large numbers of monks. At Wearmouth the floors were surfaced with powdered brick in the Roman manner, while evidence from both communities suggests that church and public buildings were arranged around a cloister.

While most seventh-century monasteries followed mixed rules, the evidence suggests that at Wearmouth–Jarrow the Benedictine rule was observed quite closely. Although Bede tended to minimize the impact of Wilfrid, it may have been that powerful bishop's influence that lay behind Biscop's preference for the strictest of the monastic rules. Wilfrid had brought a copy of the rule to Northumbria by 666 and, like Biscop himself, had strong contacts with Frankish monasteries of the Columbanian tradition, which had refined Benedictine observance. Bede's emphasis on Rome in his account of Biscop's career obscured the abbot's position in a continental monastic network which, while originating in Rome (whence Gregory the Great's *Dialogues* had spread knowledge of Benedict even to England), was by the mid-seventh century most strongly centred in a series of northern Frankish and Burgundian monasteries.

Biscop's appearance at the head of the list of abbots in the possibly eighth-century *Liber vitae* of Durham, which may have been a Wearmouth–Jarrow manuscript, testifies to his role in fostering and developing Christian culture in Northumbria and bringing the early Anglo-Saxon kingdom into close contact with the Mediterranean world. His preoccupation with the preservation of learning, commitment to the works and customs of Rome, and the protection of the monastic life from the encroachments of the world make him in some ways a precursor of Bede.

S. J. COATES

Sources 'Historia abbatum auctore anonymo', *Venerabilis Baedae opera historica*, ed. C. Plummer, 1 (1896), 388–404 [Vita Ceolfridi] · 'Historia abbatum auctore Baeda', *Venerabilis Baedae opera historica*, ed. C. Plummer, 1 (1896), 364–87 · Bede, *Hist. eccl.*, 4.18; 5.19, 21, 24 · *Willelmi Malmesbiriensis monachi de gestis pontificum Anglorum libri quinque*, ed. N. E. S. A. Hamilton, Rolls Series, 52 (1870), 328–9 · *Bedae venerabilis opera: pars 3, opera homiletica*, ed. D. Hurst, 1 (1955), 13 · F. Wormald, ed., *English kalendars before AD 1100*, 1, HBS, 72 (1934), 30, 44, 58, 72, 86 · P. Wormald, 'Bede and Benedict Biscop', *Famulus Christi: essays in commemoration of the thirteenth century of the birth of the Venerable Bede*, ed. G. Bonner (1976), 141–69 · E. Fletcher, *Benedict Biscop* (1981) · P. Meyvaert, 'Bede and the church paintings at Wearmouth–Jarrow', *Anglo-Saxon England*, 8 (1979), 63–77 · E. Stephanus, *The life of Bishop Wilfrid*, ed. and trans. B. Colgrave (1927), chap. 3 · M. B. Parkes, *The scriptorium of Wearmouth-Jarrow* (1982) · [A. H. Thompson], ed., *Liber vitae ecclesiae Dunelmensis*, SurtS, 136 (1923), 8 · R. J. Cramp, 'Monastic sites', *The archaeology of Anglo-Saxon England*, ed. D. M. Wilson (1976), 201–52

Benedict Chelydonius. *See* Chelidonius, Benedict (*d.* 1521).

Benedict of Gloucester. *See* Gloucester, Benedict of (*fl.* c.1150).

Benedict of Norwich. *See* Norwich, Benedict (*fl.* 1340).

Benedict of Ramsey [Master Benedict] (*d.* in or after **1211**), ecclesiastic and administrator, was one of King John's royal clerks. He first appears as a clerk in John's household, in the office of seal bearer, *c.*1189–94. He was among John's supporters whom William de Longchamp, bishop of Ely (*d.* 1197), excommunicated in January 1192, after the bishop had lost his posts as chancellor and justiciar and fled from England the previous autumn. Roger of Howden's chronicle quotes Longchamp as charging that Benedict had 'presumed to bear the king's seal contrary to the statute of the king and of the realm and to our prohibition' (*Chronica … Hovedene*, 3.154).

After Richard I's return from crusade in 1194 John joined his entourage and no longer maintained an independent household, and it is not known whether Benedict remained with him during Richard's last years. But he appears early in King John's reign as a clerk in the royal household and at the exchequer. In June 1200 John wrote to his justiciar commanding him to find 'our beloved clerk Master Benedict' an income of 40s. Benedict had custody of Barking Abbey, Essex, in 1200 and of Ramsey Abbey, Huntingdonshire, during the vacancy of 1201–2. In December 1205 King John ordered Benedict 'our exchequer clerk' to have certain London houses; and in 1208 he approved his appointment as vicar of the church of Houghton, probably in Huntingdonshire. Benedict fades from the records after May 1211. At that time the king commanded the custodian of Ramsey Abbey to hand over to Benedict the heir and possessions of Master Ivo of Wistow, properties he had earlier claimed in lawsuits: a house at Ramsey and land at Burwell, Cambridgeshire. Benedict also held a quarter of a knight's fee of the honour of Gloucester in Somerset. Earlier scholars conflated Master Benedict, the royal clerk, with another Master Benedict, also known as Benedict of *Sawston, clerk of the bishop of London, who was named precentor of St Paul's in 1204 and elected bishop of Rochester in 1214.

RALPH V. TURNER

Sources Pipe rolls, 2, 4–5, 7, 11–12 John · *Chronica magistri Rogeri de Hovedene*, ed. W. Stubbs, 4 vols., Rolls Series, 51 (1868–71) · Pipe rolls, 1 John [memoranda roll] · W. H. Hart and P. A. Lyons, eds., *Cartularium monasterii de Rameseia*, 3, Rolls Series, 79 (1893) · H. Hall, ed., *The Red Book of the Exchequer*, 2–3, Rolls Series, 99 (1896), vols. 2–3 · M. Gibbs, ed., *Early charters of the cathedral church of St Paul, London*, CS, 3rd ser., 58 (1939)

Benedict, Sir Julius (**1804–1885**), conductor and composer, was born at Stuttgart, Germany, on 27 November 1804 (in some nineteenth-century reference works the date was given incorrectly as 24 December 1804), the son of a rich German Jewish banker. At the Stuttgart Gymnasium he received a thorough general education and showed exceptional ability in all his studies. His musical talents were fostered by J. C. L. Abeille, with whom he

Sir Julius Benedict (1804–1885), by Lock & Whitfield, pubd 1881

studied piano and theory. By the age of twelve he was considered a virtuoso pianist, and his father made no objection to his pursuing a musical career. However, he remained at the *Gymnasium* until, in 1819, he was sent to study with Hummel, who had just resigned the position of Kapellmeister in Stuttgart to take up a similar post in Weimar, and he accompanied Hummel on a visit to Beethoven. At his father's wish, Benedict became a pupil of Weber in Dresden in February 1821, and went with him to Berlin for the production of *Der Freischütz* in June that year. There he had the first of many meetings with Felix Mendelssohn, and, as his 1850 book on the composer relates, was deeply impressed by the thirteen-year-old's abilities.

In September 1823 Benedict travelled to Vienna with Weber for the première of *Euryanthe*, and was present at his meeting with Beethoven in Baden on 5 October. When Weber quit Vienna a month later he left Benedict, of whom he thought highly, to supervise further performances of *Euryanthe*, and shortly afterwards the impresario Barbaja appointed Benedict Kapellmeister of the German opera at the Hoftheater. In 1825 he accompanied Barbaja on a journey through Germany and Italy to Naples, where he became conductor at the San Carlo and Fondo theatres. His first opera, *Giacinta ed Ernesto*, was produced at the San Carlo in 1829, but roused little interest; a second opera, *I Portoghesi in Goa*, was better received, perhaps because it leaned rather towards the style of Rossini than that of Weber, but it was a failure in Stuttgart when it was performed during Benedict's visit there in 1831, and did not obtain success elsewhere.

In 1834 Benedict travelled to Paris, but soon, encouraged by Maria Malibran, went to London, which was to be the focus of his activities for the rest of his career. He quickly obtained a post as conductor of the Italian Opera at the Lyceum, and made his London début as an opera composer with a revised version of his one-act operetta *Un anno ed un giorno*, which had been performed shortly before in Naples. In 1838 he was engaged by Alfred Bunn as conductor at Drury Lane, where, in the same year, he produced his first English opera, *The Gipsy's Warning*. He wrote two more works for the same company, *The Bride of Venice* (1843) and *The Crusaders* (1846), neither of which enjoyed particular success; he directed the premières of many highly successful operas by other composers, such as Balfe's *The Bohemian Girl* and Wallace's *Maritana*. In 1848 he conducted the performance of Mendelssohn's *Elijah* in which Jenny Lind made her first appearance as an oratorio singer. Shortly thereafter he gave a lecture on Mendelssohn, published in 1850 as *A Sketch of the Life and Works of the Late F. Mendelssohn-Bartholdy*. He was Jenny Lind's accompanist at the beginning of her extensive American tour, but relinquished this role to her future husband, Otto Goldschmidt, in 1851. In London he resumed his conducting activities at Her Majesty's Theatre, and in 1855 founded a vocal association which he directed for ten years.

Among these multifarious activities Benedict found time to edit a significant edition of Beethoven's piano music (1858) and in 1860 to produce a revised Italian version, with newly composed recitatives, of Weber's *Oberon*, in conjunction with its original librettist, J. R. Planché. In the same year his cantata *Undine* was given its première at the Norwich festival, of which he conducted every meeting from 1845 to 1878. His most successful opera, *The Lily of Killarney*, based on Dion Boucicault's popular play *The Colleen Bawn*, was composed in 1862 for the Pyne–Harrison Opera Company, for which Balfe wrote many of his later works. His last opera, *The Bride of Song*, was produced two years later. In the meanwhile, for the Norwich festival, he had composed a cantata, *Richard Coeur de Lion*, in 1863, and he followed this with *The Legend of St Cecilia* in 1866. He later wrote the oratorio *St Peter* (1870) and the cantata *Graziella* (1882) for the Birmingham festival. His symphony in G minor, op. 101, was composed for the Crystal Palace concerts in 1873. Other music includes two piano concertos, four concert overtures, and incidental music to *Romeo and Juliet*, as well as many smaller instrumental and vocal works. Benedict was a fine pianist, combining the 'calm and clarity' of Hummel with the 'fullness and fire' of Weber (Schilling, 553), and wrote idiomatically for the instrument; though much of his output of piano music consists of occasional pieces written for immediate profit. For many years he accompanied at the Monday Popular Concerts, and he directed the Liverpool Philharmonic Society from 1876 to 1880.

Benedict, a naturalized Englishman, was knighted in 1871, and in 1874 was made a knight commander of the order of Franz Joseph by the Austrian emperor, and of the order of Frederick by the king of Württemberg. He was twice married; his first wife was Adèle Jean, his second, Mary Comber Fortey (*b.* 1857/8), whom he married in 1879. One of his last major achievements was his book *Carl Maria von Weber* (1881), an important source of information about the composer. He kept up his teaching and conducting activities until the end, but in later years was in financial difficulties, and a testimonial fund, with royal patronage, was established. Referring to this, an article in the *Musical Times* in 1884 remarked:

> In reviewing the fifty years of Sir Julius Benedict's career in this country, during which music has grown from an aristocratic luxury to a popular necessity, it must be recollected that he has ever been one of the most active agents in its progress; for as executant, composer, teacher, lecturer, and writer he has made a name which will be permanently enrolled in the annals of art. (*MT*, 25, 1884, 144)

On 18 March 1885 Benedict caught a severe cold in Manchester and was seriously ill for a while with bronchitis and heart disease. After rallying sufficiently to resume teaching he died suddenly at his London home, 2 Manchester Square, at eight o'clock in the morning on 5 June 1885. His burial took place at Kensal Green cemetery on 11 June. CLIVE BROWN

Sources G. Schilling, ed., *Encyclopädie des gesammten musikalischen Wissenschaften*, 1 (1835), 552–4 · *Allgemeine musikalische Zeitung*, 33 (1831), 187 · A. Bunn, *The stage: both before and behind the curtain*, 3 vols. (1840) · *MT*, 25 (1884), 144, 330, 397–9, 469 · *MT*, 26 (1885), 385–6 · *CGPLA Eng. & Wales* (1885) · 1879 marriage registers index, freebmd.rootsweb.com [Dec 1879, Marylebone 1a 1102] · census returns, 1881
Archives Royal College of Music, London, autograph of symphony in G minor and collection of letters
Likenesses C. Baugniet, lithograph, pubd 1844 (after his watercolour drawing), BM · Fradelle & Marshall, woodburytype carte-de-visite, *c.*1876, NPG · C. Baugniet, watercolour drawing, BM · E. Edwards, photograph, NPG; repro. in L. Reeve, ed., *Men of eminence*, 2 (1864) · F. G., process block caricature, BM · Lock & Whitfield, woodburytype photograph, NPG; repro. in T. Cooper, *Men of mark* (1881) [*see illus.*] · Spy [L. Ward], chromolithograph caricature, NPG; repro. in *VF* (27 Sept 1873) · T. B. Wirgman, pencil drawing, Royal College of Music, London · lithograph, Musikhistorisches Museum, Frankfurt am Main, Germany · lithograph (*Fashionable music*), BM
Wealth at death £6440 1*s.* 1*d.*: probate, 23 July 1885, *CGPLA Eng. & Wales*

Benefield [Benfield], **Sebastian** (1568/9–1630), Church of England clergyman and divine, was born at Prestbury, near Cheltenham, Gloucestershire, and went to school in Cheltenham. His long career at Oxford began when he was admitted scholar of Corpus Christi College on 30 August 1586, aged seventeen. He graduated BA in 1589 (25 June), became a probationer fellow on 16 April 1590, and proceeded MA in 1593 (3 April). Following ordination he was licensed to preach, becoming a well-known and frequent preacher; one of his earliest publications was a sermon at the university church (24 March 1610), commemorating the accession of James I. A number of his special or occasional sermons from this period survive. He was appointed rhetoric reader of his college in 1599 and the following year received his BTh, and was also admitted

collegiate reader of the sentences. On 12 May 1608 he proceeded DTh.

Anthony Wood commented on Benefield's developing reputation that not only was he identified as 'a person for piety, strictness of life, and sincere conversation incomparable', but also 'so noted an humanitian, disputant, and theologist, and so well read in the fathers and schoolmen, that he had scarce his equal in the university' (Wood, *Ath. Oxon.: Fasti*, 1.488). He took an active role in university politics. As deputy vice-chancellor in 1611 he intervened in the bitterly contested election for the presidency of St John's College between William Laud and John Rawlinson. Using a pre-election ploy to prevent Laud from winning, Benefield deprived four of the non-graduate fellows (three of whom were pro-Laudian) of their right to vote, but the move proved unsuccessful. He had attracted the attention of George Abbot, master of University College, and it was Abbot's authority as vice-chancellor and later as archbishop of Canterbury that helped his advancement, a benefit Benefield acknowledged. For a short time he acted as one of the archbishop's chaplains.

The high point of Benefield's academic career came in 1613 with his selection as Lady Margaret professor of divinity. Calvinism remained the dominant orthodoxy at Oxford and, as Wood noted, Benefield 'was accounted no mean lover of the opinions of John Calvin, especially as to the points of predestination, which is the cause why one calls him a downright and doctrinal Calvinist' (Wood, *Ath. Oxon.: Fasti*, 1.488). He had already published a major theological work explicitly condemning the anti-Calvinist views of the growing school of English Arminians. His *Doctrinae Christianae sex capita*, published at Oxford in 1610, was based on a series of lectures delivered at the divinity school. Appended to it was an answer to a book by Humphrey Leech, *A Triumph of Truth* (1609), which upheld an anti-Calvinist view of works of supererogation or perfection like chastity and poverty. Benefield firmly defended the Calvinist doctrine that salvation belonged solely to the elect chosen by God, denying that they could fall finally or totally from grace. This view is also found in one of his collected *Eight sermons publikely preached in the University of Oxford, the second at St. Peter's-in-the-East, the rest at St. Mary's Church, begunne in the year 1595* (1614). The same Calvinist proposition was expounded in another course of lecture–sermons published abroad, *De perseverantia sanctorum* (1618). Similarly Calvinist in slant were the dozen sermons entitled *The Sinne Against the Holy Ghost Discovered and other Christian Doctrines Delivered* published in 1615.

Benefield had his detractors as Wood made clear: 'Some have blasted him (I know not upon what account) for a schismatic, yet Dr. Ravis, sometimes B. of London, and of honourable memory, approved him to be free from schism, and much abounding in science' (Wood, *Ath. Oxon.: Fasti*, 1.488). His most scholarly work was a three-volume *Commentarie or Exposition* upon part of the text of the minor prophet Amos. The tomes appeared at intervals (1613, 1620, 1629), each based on a course of sermons, scholastic and dry, but practical—'the lawfull use of things indifferent'. A forty-year academic career ended in 1626 when he resigned the Lady Margaret chair and:

> receded to the rectory of Meysey Hampton near to Fairford in Glocestershire, which he had long before obtained by his predecessor's guilt of simony, where he spent the remaining part of his days (about 4 years) in great retiredness and devotion. (ibid., 487–8)

The only vignette of Benefield comes from the same pen: 'The truth is, he was a sedentary man, and of great industry, and so consequently (as 'tis observed by some) morose, and of no good nature.' He died in the rectory of Meysey Hampton on 24 August 1630 and was buried in the chancel of the church five days later.　　　JOHN S. MACAULEY

Sources DNB · Wood, *Ath. Oxon.: Fasti* (1815), 487–9 · Foster, *Alum. Oxon.* · N. Tyacke, *Anti-Calvinists: the rise of English Arminianism, c.1590–1640* (1987) · A. Milton, *Catholic and Reformed: the Roman and protestant churches in English protestant thought, 1600–1640* (1995) · T. Fowler, *The history of Corpus Christi College*, OHS, 25 (1893) · *Reg. Oxf.*, 2/1–3

Benese, Richard (d. **1547**), Augustinian canon and surveyor, can probably be identified with the rector of Woodborough in Wiltshire, a benefice in the king's gift to which he was admitted in 1511, and which financed his study of canon law at Oxford. After five years' study at the university, he supplicated to proceed to BCnL on 6 July 1519. By this time he had resigned his benefice, and subsequently became an Augustinian canon at Merton Priory, Surrey. He was a succentor there in February 1530, figuring prominently in the election of the new prior. His closest friend at the priory was Thomas Paynell, the writer of a medical treatise and a prodigious translator and humanist. Benese himself wrote a mathematical treatise entitled *This boke sheweth the maner of measurynge of all maner of lande, as well of woodlande, as of lande in the felde, newly invented and compyled by Syr Rycharde Benese, canon of Marton Abby*. This was printed by James Nicholson, in Southwark, probably in 1537 (Bodl. Oxf., MS Tanner 773; Bodl. Oxf., MS Ashmole 1638), and there were subsequent editions, perhaps in 1550 and 1553, and then again in 1563 and about 1565.

Noting that sellers overestimated the size of the land they were selling and buyers underestimated, Benese set out to devise geometric rules for the accurate measuring of land to be sold. Casting scorn on traditional irregular modes of measuring, such as using ears of barley corn, he recommended the standard artificer's London rule of a square foot using a cord set in bees' wax, a method employed by the prophet Zacharias. Instructions with square tables were also provided for the measurement of irregular pieces of timber, stone, pavements, and glass, and for converting sums from the mark to the now more widely used pound. The preface to Benese's work was written by Paynell, who places it in the noble, learned scientific tradition of geometry that had enabled the Egyptians to calculate the rise and fall of the Nile, and Archimedes to measure altitudes and the motions of the planets. Paynell even claimed that God, when creating the firmament, used geometric principles.

Although Benese's treatise would have been useful for a monastery with frequent boundary disputes with lay landlords, its importance in facilitating the selling of monastic property was immediately recognized. Its printing in 1537 coincided the following year with the largest transaction of landed property, timber, stone, and glass in English history as the religious houses passed into the hands of the crown and its supporters. The usefulness of Benese's treatise and his skills in geometry, surveying, and calculation were acknowledged in the royal preferments that followed the dissolution of Merton Priory, which he signed with seventeen other canons on 16 April 1538. Three days earlier the first of hundreds of carts arrived to take the stone from the priory, which along with the broken pieces of sculpted angels, was used to build the foundations of Henry VIII's new palace of Nonsuch. Benese was responsible for supervising the dismantling of the priory; he was the surveyor, based at Hampton Court, placed in charge of the king's works and responsible for building works in Surrey and the fortification of castles in Kent; and on 16 September 1538 he was made paymaster for the repairing and building of the king's houses of Hampton Court and Nonsuch, with responsibility for the payment of wages to the labourers who were bringing to a close the rebuilding of Hampton Court and starting the construction of Nonsuch. Much of the money he handled came from the sale of monastic property which Benese had greatly facilitated, and he and Paynell, who was similarly employed, showed what was certainly a robustly down-to-earth attitude towards the fate of their hapless brother monks; it is perhaps significant that in the preface to Benese's treatise on measuring, Cain is described as the first exponent of geometry.

The crown showed its gratitude to Benese. In October 1535 he was first described as king's chaplain (a post also held by Paynell in 1541) and made precentor of Hereford Cathedral by royal grant on 24 December 1538. In April 1539 he and Paynell were given crown pensions, and crown preferments followed for Benese, including: the rectory of Beckington on 7 August 1540; All Hallows, Honey Lane, London, in October of the same year (to which he was succeeded in 1545 by Paynell); and in 1542 Long Ditton in Surrey, formerly in the gift of Merton Priory. On 20 January of the latter year, described as a member of the king's chapel, he was given the prebend of Farndon-cum-Balderton in Lincoln Cathedral. He still held the post of surveyor of the king's works at Hampton Court in April 1545 when he was responsible for levying and paying five hundred pioneers to accompany Henry VIII's army to Boulogne, captured by the duke of Suffolk in September 1544. That Henry VIII was able to hold on to this city until his death was due to heavy financial investment of profits from the sale of monastic property, and the building of defences for which Benese was partly responsible. He still held the post of king's surveyor in February 1546, but he made his will in November of that year, requesting burial in Long Ditton churchyard, Surrey, and died in January 1547.　　　JONATHAN HUGHES

Sources *This boke sheweth the maner of measurynge of all maner of lande, as well of woodlande, as of lande in the felde, newly invented and compyled by Syr Rycharde Benese, canon of Marton Abby,* Bodl. Oxf., MS Tanner 773; MS Ashmole 1638 · *LP Henry VIII*, vols. 13–21; *addenda* 1/2 · Emden, *Oxf.*, 4.41–2, 437–8, 728–30 · J. Dent, *The quest for Nonesuch* (1962) · H. M. Colvin and others, eds., *The history of the king's works*, 3–4 (1975–82) · will, PRO, PROB 11/31, sig. 47
Wealth at death see will, PRO, PROB 11/31, sig. 47

Benet of Canfield. *See* Fitch, William (1562–1610).

Benet, John (*d.* 1458), composer, has left about twenty compositions whose style proclaims him to have been a slightly younger contemporary of John Dunstaple, perhaps a close disciple. Nothing is known of his parentage or birth and very little of his life. He may have been a vicar-choral at Lincoln Minster from 1437 to 1441. It is likely that he was the John Benet of London, clerk, who in 1443 was appointed master of the six choristers of St Anthony's Hospital in London. A John Benet, very probably the same man, was listed in 1448–9 as an existing member of the Confraternity of St Nicholas, the London guild of parish clerks, to which several known composers and their wives belonged; his wife, Agnes, is also named. The indenture of 1443 suggests that Benet was by then approaching the end of his career, while a citizen's will of 1449 implies that the mastership of St Anthony's had by then become vacant. Benet apparently lived for several years more, however, for his will was proved on 4 December 1458. He does not seem to have been wealthy. He lived in the parish of St Benet Fink, London (the parish of St Anthony's Hospital), but probably died in Southwark and was buried in St Olave's, Southwark; his executors were his widow, Elena, who must have been his second wife, and John Weston.

Benet's motet *Lux fulget ex Anglia|O pater pietatis|[Salve Thoma]*, a complex large-scale composition honouring St Thomas of Hereford, has plausibly been connected with Hereford Cathedral, which was dedicated to the saint and contained his tomb. The likely occasion for the motet would seem to be the centenary in 1420 of St Thomas's canonization. Dunstaple was a canon of Hereford, and there is certainly a close stylistic relationship between his music and that of Benet, who was one of the last practitioners of a form brought to its apogee by Dunstaple, the mathematically proportioned isorhythmic motet. Three examples survive from Benet's pen; the other two are in honour of St Mary Magdalen and St Alban respectively, which may suggest connections with Magdalen College in Oxford and St Albans Cathedral.

The rest of Benet's works are all settings of items from the ordinary of the mass, and include an entire five-movement mass cycle and fragments of two more. The first is not based on chant, but relies on a repeated and varying motto in the tenor, with similar beginnings to each movement in the upper voices; its authorship is sometimes allotted to Lionel Power or Dunstaple. Of the incomplete cycles, one also employs motto openings and the other is based on a tenor plainsong. Both these methods of construction were taken up by continental masters,

and Benet holds an important place as one of the early creators of the mass cycle, the leading musical form of the fifteenth and sixteenth centuries. He has also left a remarkable four-voice canonic Kyrie.   BRIAN TROWELL, *rev.*

Sources B. Trowell, 'Some English contemporaries of Dunstable', *Proceedings of the Royal Musical Association*, 81 (1954–5), 77–92 [incl. work list, pp. 91–2] · B. Trowell and A. Wathey, 'John Benet's *Lux fulget ex Anglia–O pater pietatis–Salve Thoma*', *St Thomas Cantilupe, bishop of Hereford: essays in his honour*, ed. M. Jancey (1982), 159–80 · C. Barron, 'The expansion of education in fifteenth-century London', *The cloister and the world: essays in medieval history in honour of Barbara Harvey*, ed. J. Blair and B. Golding (1996), 219–45 · GL, commissary wills, 9171/5, fol. 263v · B. Trowell, 'Benet, John', *New Grove* · R. Bowers, 'Music and worship to 1640', *A history of Lincoln Minster*, ed. D. Owen (1994), 47–76

Benet, William (*d.* 1533), diplomat, from the diocese of Salisbury, was the younger brother of Dr Thomas Benet (*d.* 1558), a canon of Salisbury and of St Paul's, London, and nephew of John Benet, merchant taylor of the city of London. By 1521, when he was admitted to Doctors' Commons, he was doctor of civil law. His university is unknown but was probably Oxford. By October 1522 Benet was active as a canon lawyer at the legatine court of Cardinal Wolsey. He represented Wolsey in other capacities, for instance, at the abbatial election at Glastonbury in 1525 that selected Richard Whiting. In that year he became a canon of St Paul's, London, and, at some point, a prebendary of Wells. He held a number of other benefices, including Marnhull in Dorset. His highest ecclesiastical appointment was to the archdeaconry of Dorset, in his native diocese, in 1530. By that time he was busy about the matter of the king's attempt to divorce Queen Catherine.

Initially one of three envoys sent to Rome in late 1528—he got no further than Lyons—Benet was appointed Henry VIII's resident ambassador to Rome on 20 May 1529. There he remained, except for one brief break in late 1531, until Henry rebelled against the pope in 1533. Benet arrived at Rome on 16 June 1531, while a special legatine court of cardinals Wolsey and Campeggi had begun to hear the marriage suit in England. The new ambassador swore 'a hundred times' that no judgment would be given in England (*LP Henry VIII*, 4 (3), no. 5725). The news that Catherine had appealed from the legatine court he tried, unsuccessfully, to keep from papal officials. When, on 15 July 1529, Pope Clement VII 'avoked' (that is, recalled) the English proceedings to Rome, Benet suggested to Wolsey that the document be intercepted, but the papal curia shrewdly issued multiple copies. With the marriage suit removed from England to Rome, the diplomatic ground had shifted.

From early in 1530 Benet had a twofold task: to delay proceedings at the Roman rota and to have the case returned to England. In early June, in a private meeting with Clement, he urged delay and the pope agreed to a summer adjournment. When ordered by the king to tell the pope that he would appeal to a general council, Benet wisely demurred. And when told to present the pope with the king's claim that no Englishman should be cited out of

England, he also demurred, but a displeased king remonstrated with him and, at length, Benet presented this 'custom' to the pope, who was so irritated that he refused to meet Benet at that time except in the presence of others. Still dissatisfied, Henry, in a letter of 6 December 1530, implied that his representatives in Rome were not 'entire Englishmen' but 'Englishmen papisticate' (*LP Henry VIII*, 4 (3), no. 6760). The king criticized Benet once again, in the autumn of 1531, for being remiss in his duties and not entirely credible. There the matter remained: the postponement of proceedings having limited success and the attempt to remove the suit to England having none. With the enactment of the Act in Restraint of Appeals (April 1533) and the declaration by Archbishop Cranmer's court (23 May) that Henry's marriage to Catherine was null, Benet's mission to Rome lost its purpose.

Benet left Rome in August 1533. On his return journey he was stricken with fever and died at Susa in the Piedmont on 26 September. On the following day a local official made unsuccessful attempts to investigate Benet's belongings with a view to seizing them. Although the official based his claim on Benet having died intestate, a will was produced in the prerogative court of Canterbury, bearing the incomplete date '12 December 15—', quite possibly 1531, when Benet was briefly back in England. It was proved on 11 May 1534. He made bequests to Marnhull church and for the repair of the prebendary of Litton's house at Wells, and left the unspecified residue of his estate to his brothers and sisters.

Benet's personal sympathies appear to have been with Queen Catherine. While in England in late 1531, he sent her the message that he was sorry that he had to take the king's side but that she had no better servant than he and that he prayed that she would continue as queen. On one occasion, he confided to the pope that he personally regretted that Henry had thrown the world into confusion over a flight of fancy. When he learned of Benet's death, Pope Clement mourned him as a man poorly treated by his king.   F. DONALD LOGAN

Sources *LP Henry VIII*, vols. 4–6 · *Fasti Angl., 1300–1541*, [Salisbury] · *Fasti Angl., 1300–1541*, [St Paul's, London] · *Fasti Angl., 1300–1541*, [Bath and Wells] · PRO, PROB 11/25, fol. 91r–v · G. de C. Parmiter, *The king's great matter: a study in Anglo-papal relations, 1527–1534* (1967) · J. J. Scarisbrick, *Henry VIII* (1968) · G. D. Squibb, *Doctors' Commons: a history of the College of Advocates and Doctors of Law* (1977)
Wealth at death see will, PRO, PROB 11/25, fol. 91r–v

Benett, Etheldred (1775–1845), fossil collector and geologist, was born on 22 July 1775 at Pyt House, Tisbury, Wiltshire, the eldest daughter of Thomas Benett (*c.*1729–1797) and Catherine Darell (*d.* 1780). Her eldest surviving brother, John (1773–1852), was a deputy lieutenant and magistrate for Wiltshire and a whig MP for Wiltshire from 1819 to 1852. His wife's brother, Aylmer Bourke Lambert (1761–1842), an original fellow of the Linnean Society and well known as a botanist and geologist, encouraged Etheldred and her sister Anna Maria to study natural history. Etheldred took up the newly fashionable study of fossils, while her sister took up botany. Evidence of Etheldred's activity dates from July 1809, when William Cunnington

Etheldred Benett (1775–1845), by unknown artist, 1837

(1754–1810), naturalist and antiquary of Heytesbury, saw 'Miss Bennett's collection' (Cunnington MSS). Etheldred visited Cunnington in November the same year, and by 1810 she was in contact with James Sowerby (1757–1822), artist and naturalist of London, then busy on his project to illustrate British fossils. From then on she acted as a clearing-house for palaeontological and geological investigations throughout Wiltshire, though these were sometimes interrupted by electioneering for her brother in the often sordid provincial politics before the Reform Act of 1832.

Benett started corresponding with G. B. Greenough (1778–1855), first president of the Geological Society, in 1813. In 1815 she sent the society a sketch of a measured section of the quarry at Chicksgrove, one of the first recorded in Britain. She had obtained the section from the quarry foreman. In 1816 she sent drawings of new fossil sponges from the Warminster Greensand. Sowerby soon reproduced her section (without permission) in *Mineral Conchology*. By 1817 she was in correspondence with Gideon Mantell, the discoverer of ancient fossil reptiles in Sussex. She was also soon in correspondence with William Buckland at Oxford University and, from 1829, with Samuel Woodward in Norwich.

Never having married, Benett was able, thanks to her financial independence, to gather high-quality specimens of fossils. She obtained these mostly through local collectors, from whom she purchased material from the many quarries then actively worked throughout Wiltshire. She also gathered fossil material on summer holidays to the Dorset coast. She distributed duplicate material to museums all over the country and further afield, making many donations to the Bristol Institution, the Geological Society of London, and the British Museum. Her fine personal collection became a first port of call for visiting geologists, who used it to study the strata exposed in her area, as did Charles Lyell in 1826. Inspired by this activity and by Mantell's publication of his *Catalogue of the Organic Remains of Sussex* (1829), in 1831 Benett published her similarly unillustrated 'Catalogue of the organic remains of Wiltshire' in *Ancient Wiltshire* by her friend Sir Richard Colt Hoare. This work also contained her sister's list of local plants. The same year she reissued the fossil catalogue as a separate publication, adding newly prepared plates for illustration. 'This little work … of mere local interest' she dedicated to Greenough. Her disclaimers reveal the difficulties she saw for any female geological author. These later gave some the false impression that her 'Catalogue' of 1831 had not been properly published, when in fact it was widely distributed.

Benett's devotion to Wiltshire fossils, which had 'largely contributed' to Sowerby's 'text book', was fêted by Murchison, the president of the Geological Society ('Address', 373). In her 'Catalogue' she gave names to a number of valid new species and genera, and illustrated others, like Richard Owen's *Ichthyosaurus trigonus*, named later by experts she had consulted. She published another book in 1833, on the genealogy of her ancestor William Wake, archbishop of Canterbury, from whose family she had acquired her unusual Christian name. In 1836, when she was made a member of the Imperial Natural History Society of Moscow, she angrily discovered that her diploma was for 'Dominum [Master] Etheldredus Benett'. The British Museum also had thanked 'Etheldred Benett Esq.' for her book on fossils, though she had presented it in person to one of the librarians, 'telling him it was written by myself'. Such episodes led her to believe that 'scientific people in general have a very low opinion of the abilities of my sex' (letter to Samuel Woodward, 12 April 1836, Castle Museum, Norwich).

On 11 January 1845 Benett died at her home, Norton House, Norton Bavant, Wiltshire. She was buried at Bavant parish church on 18 January. Her wonderful collection of fossils, her best memorial, was sold. The best portions are now in the Academy of Natural Sciences, Philadelphia; a smaller portion remains in Leeds City Museum. The greatest treasures in her collection were specimens of *Trigoniid* bivalves from the Portlandian of Tisbury. These showed that 'soft parts' could be petrified. This first demonstration that muscle and gill parts could be preserved in fossils caused a sensation when announced by Edward Charlesworth in 1848. Extant specimens of her collection held in Philadelphia also reveal that Benett was one of the first to sieve for microfossils. Barred from the Geological Society by her sex, she was one of the earliest to demonstrate why such discrimination was short-sighted.

H. S. TORRENS

Sources [G. A. Mantell], *London Geological Journal*, 1 (1846), 40, 128 · H. S. Torrens and others, 'Etheldred Benett of Wiltshire, England, the first lady geologist—her fossil collection in the Academy of Natural Sciences of Philadelphia, and the rediscovery of "lost" specimens of Jurassic Trigoniidae … with their soft anatomy preserved', *Proceedings of the Academy of Natural Sciences of Philadelphia*, 150 (2000), 59–123 · E. E. Spamer and others, 'Recovery of the Etheldred Benett collection', *Proceedings of the Academy of Natural Sciences of Philadelphia*, 141 (1989), 115–80 · M. R. S. Creese and T. M. Creese, 'British women who contributed to research in geological sciences', *British Journal for the History of Science*, 27 (1994), 26–7 · H. Wansey and R. C. Hoare, *The history of modern Wiltshire*, 3/2: Hundred of Warminster (1831), 78, 117–27 · R. C. Moore and N. D. Newell, dedication, in L. R. Cox and others, *Mollusca 6: Bivalvia*, 3 vols. (1969–71), pt N of *Treatise on invertebrate paleontology*, vol. 1, N1–N2, 21 · HoP, *Commons* · GM, 2nd ser., 23 (1845), 220 · J. Murray, 'The late Miss Bennet [*sic*] the geologist', *Mining Journal*, 18 (1848), 54 · E. E. Spamer and A. E. Bogan, 'Where is *Polypothecia* Benett, 1831?', *Journal of Palaeontology*, 67 (1993), 156–7 · W. Smith, *Geology of England: William Smith's claims* (1818) · parish register (birth), Tisbury, 22 July 1775 · parish register (baptism), Tisbury, 29 July 1775 · parish register (burial), Norton Bavant, 18 Jan 1845 · Devizes Museum, Cunnington MSS · Castle Museum, Norwich, Woodward MSS, letter to S. Woodward, 12 April 1836 · 'Address to the Geological Society by the president', *Proceedings of the Geological Society*, 1/25 (1826–33), 362–86

Archives Academy of Natural Sciences, Philadelphia, specimens · Leeds City Museum, specimens | Castle Museum, Norwich, S. Woodward archive · NL NZ, Turnbull L., G. A. Mantell archive · UCL, Greenough archive

Likenesses silhouette, 1837, Castle Museum, Norwich [*see illus.*]

Wealth at death see will, proved 1845, Wilts. & Swindon RO (413/368)

Benezet, Anthony [*formerly* Antoine] (1713–1784), educational reformer and abolitionist, was born on 31 January 1713 in St Quentin, Picardy, France. In 1715 his wealthy protestant parents, Jean Étienne Benezet (1683–1751) and Judith de la Méjenelle (1693–1765), fled to Rotterdam to escape religious persecution, bribing the border guard with a bag of gold. After three months the Benezets relocated near London, where they spent the next sixteen years. Jean Étienne changed his name to John Stephen and became a successful merchant. Anthony, the second of thirteen children, received a liberal education, probably at the Friends' school in Wandsworth. Anthony Benezet's early work experience began at a counting-house, but this job held too many temptations for the budding Quaker. He instead bound himself to a cooper, but was too frail for the physical labour. By 1731, when the Benezet family emigrated to Pennsylvania, Benezet had established close ties to London Quakers who recommended the young man to Philadelphia Friends.

In March 1736 Benezet married Joyce Marriot (1713–1786), a Philadelphia Quaker minister. The couple had two children who died in infancy, Mary (*b.* 1737) and Anthony (*b.* 1743). Benezet continued to search for meaningful employment in America, selling commodities with his brothers and briefly running a manufacturing business. Finally, in 1739, Benezet found his true calling as an educator. He began teaching in Germantown, Pennsylvania, and later at the Quaker school in Philadelphia. Benezet developed a teaching philosophy that highlighted personal development, piety, and virtue. He authored several primers and a book that stressed the importance of a well-rounded education. Benezet's greatest achievement as an educator lay in his commitment to teaching children who had no access to traditional schools. In 1750 Benezet offered evening classes to black people; in 1755 he taught at the first Philadelphia secondary school for girls; by 1770 he convinced Quakers to build a free day school for African Americans. Notable black students included the religious leader Absalom Jones and prominent businessman James Forten. Benezet's close work with African Americans led him to state that black people had 'as great a variety of talents as … whites' (Vaux, 30).

Benezet is most noted for a brand of abolitionism that challenged assertions of innate black inferiority. At first, in an epistle seeking to eradicate slaveholding among Quakers, Benezet argued that 'if we continually bear in mind the royal law of doing to others as we would be done by, we shall never think of bereaving our fellow creatures of that valuable blessing liberty'. Slavery, Benezet held, was inconsistent with both 'Christianity' and 'common justice' (Brookes, 475). His later anti-slavery tracts circulated in America, England, and the continent. *A Short Account of that Part of Africa Inhabited by the Negroes* (1762) was translated into French and German. *Some Historical Account of Guinea* (1772) convinced abolitionist leader Thomas Clarkson to begin his fight against slavery. Benezet's abolitionist circle of correspondents included Benjamin Franklin, Abbé Raynal, Granville Sharp, John Wesley, and John and Samuel Fothergill. Active in Philadelphia's anti-slavery societies, Benezet helped secure emancipation in Pennsylvania.

Benezet's wide range of social interests led him to advocate and write about temperance, pacifism, and American Indian reform. He took a particular interest in a group of Acadian exiles, even bringing them blankets from his home. Benezet died on 3 May 1784 of a stomach disorder, and was buried the following day. Charitable to the end, he willed his estate to support the education of African Americans and Indians. Contemporaries noted the large numbers of Philadelphians who mourned his passing, including many black citizens. Benezet continued to influence people even after his death. Thus in 1787 he appeared to Benjamin Rush in a dream that convinced the well-known doctor to free his slave. Benezet had always declined having his portrait taken, saying his 'ugly face shall not go down to posterity' (Brookes, 50). But despite his homely appearance, an acquaintance noted that Benezet's countenance wore 'the stamp of a peaceful soul and the repose of a good conscience' (Brookes, 131).

CARLA GERONA

Sources G. S. Brookes, *Friend Anthony Benezet* (1937) · R. Vaux, *Memoirs of the life of Anthony Benezet* (1817) · W. Armistead, *Anthony Benezet: from the original memoir, revised, with additions* (1859) · N. S. Hornick, 'Anthony Benezet: eighteenth-century social critic, educator and abolitionist', PhD diss., University of Maryland, 1974 · W. C. Kashatus, 'A reappraisal of Anthony Benezet's activities in educational reform', *Quaker History*, 78 (1989), 24–36 · R. A. Bruns, 'A Quaker's antislavery crusade: Anthony Benezet', *Quaker History*, 65 (1976), 81–92 · N. S. Hornick, 'Anthony Benezet and the Africans' school: toward a theory of full equality', *Pennsylvania Magazine of History and Biography*, 99 (1975), 399–421 · W. W. Hinshaw, *Encyclopedia of American Quaker genealogy*, ed. [T. W. Marshall and others], 7 vols. (1936–50), vol. 7
Archives Haverford College, Haverford, Pennsylvania · Hist. Soc. Penn. · RS Friends, Lond., collection of Indian treatises, letters, papers · Swarthmore College, Swarthmore, Pennsylvania
Likenesses portrait (posthumous), Harvard U., Houghton L.; repro. in Brookes, *Friend Anthony Benezet*
Wealth at death approx. £700: will, Brookes, *Friend*, 165–7

Benfield, Paul (1741–1810), financier in India, was baptized on 25 January 1741 in Cheltenham, Gloucestershire. He was the eldest son of John Benfield (*d.* in or before 1767), carpenter and joiner, of Cheltenham, and of his wife, Anne, daughter of the Revd Stephen Cull of Cranham in the same county. In 1763 the directors of the East India Company described Benfield as 'having been regularly bred an Architect, Surveyor and draughtsman' and as having a good 'knowledge in Fortification and other Branches of the Mathematicks' (Love, 2.600). They gave him a commission as lieutenant in the company's Madras army and the appointment of assistant engineer and civil architect. In 1765 he transferred to the civil service as a writer. In his early service he earned a good reputation for his building work, but showed the turbulence and factiousness that was to mark the rest of his career. Between 1769 and 1774 he was twice dismissed from the service, reinstated, but again suspended.

Madras was a settlement transformed by British success in the long series of wars in which the East India Company had both fought off the French and intervened decisively in the politics of southern India. The outcome of the wars was that a British client, Muhammad Ali Khan, Walajah, usually known as the nabob of Arcot, had become titular nawab of the Carnatic with claims to exercise authority over much of south-eastern India. For the effective exercise of that authority he needed continuing British support, for which he had to mobilize large sums of money. Providing this money opened lucrative opportunities for many British people, among whom Benfield became preeminent. Acting as banker to the nawab was to make Benfield a great fortune and to earn him notoriety as the most unscrupulous of the British 'nabobs'.

Benfield's career as a banker began in the early 1770s. He specialized in raising money from Indian banking businesses and from his fellow Europeans at high rates of interest and passing it on at even higher rates, 20 per cent or more. His first venture in large-scale moneylending was to enable the raja of Tanjore, whose territory the nawab of the Carnatic wished to absorb, to raise a large sum to buy off an attack in 1771. Two years later Benfield gave his support to the nawab, who had succeeded in conquering Tanjore with British help and needed money to pay off the obligations that he had incurred in doing so. The equivalent of at least £800,000 seems to have been advanced and more was lent over the next two years. The nawab's method of repayment was to allocate the taxation of certain of his districts to Benfield, a large part of what was owed being secured on the revenue of the recently conquered Tanjore. British support for the nawab's conquest of Tanjore was not, however, approved by the directors of the East India Company and a new governor, Lord Pigot, was sent out to Madras in 1775 with orders to restore the raja of Tanjore. This restoration put Benfield's loans at risk. Having failed to persuade Pigot to make special provision for him, Benfield resorted to the desperate step of joining—with other British people at Madras whom Pigot had alienated—in a plot to depose the governor by force. The coup was duly executed on 29 August 1776 and Pigot died in confinement shortly afterwards.

News of these events caused an uproar in Britain. Benfield was ordered home. Both the nawab of the Carnatic and the raja of Tanjore were aware of the importance for them of decisions taken in Britain and did their best to influence such decisions by appointing agents. It was Benfield's misfortune that the raja chose as his agent William Burke, who was to interest his kinsman and close friend Edmund Burke in what appeared to be the wrongs inflicted on Tanjore. The Burkes did their best to publicize what they saw as Benfield's iniquities. Benfield left claims to repayment behind him in India amounting to about £500,000. To protect his interests he tried to build up a parliamentary interest. In 1780 he became MP for the small borough of Cricklade by spending money on a scale which nearly got him unseated for bribery, and fanciful allegations were made that eight other MPs also owed their election to him. He held the seat until 1784. The government of Lord North evidently regarded him as of sufficient political significance to be worth supporting in his campaign to get back to India. In the face of Edmund Burke's passionate denunciations of him as 'a destroyer of countries' (*Writings and Speeches*, 132), Benfield was permitted to return to Madras in 1781.

Benfield remained in India for another seven years, seeking favours from successive governors of Madras, who generally regarded him as a dangerous intriguer. His Indian clients also found him difficult. The nawab's son reminded him of how in frustration at not getting his way Benfield 'sat upon a China Pot in the Nabob's garden from early in the Morning until 4 o'clock in the afternoon, exposed to all the scorching heat of the sun' and how 'you tore your waistcoat and beat your own breast' (Amir ul-Amira to Benfield, 19 Aug 1785, BL OIOC, H/290, fol. 250). In 1788 Benfield was again suspended and was permitted to return home, showing 'symptoms of Hypochondriasis' (Love, 3.397).

By 1788, however, events in Britain had gone in Benfield's favour. The administration of William Pitt had taken the highly contentious decision of ordering that all established claims of the nawab of the Carnatic should be paid off from a fund in India. Benfield, described by Burke as 'a criminal, who long since ought to have fattened the region's kites with his offal', was entitled to recover more than £500,000 (*Writings and Speeches*, 544–5, 632). Fearful of being arrested for debt in Britain, he went from India to France until he could secure a seat in parliament (for Malmesbury) in 1790. Having transferred part of his fortune to Britain, he then set himself up in great style. On 7 October 1793 he married Mary Frances (*d.* 1828), daughter of Henry Swinburne, with whom he had a son and two daughters. He spent £125,000 on the estate of Woodhall in Hertfordshire, £35,000 on property that established his control over the borough of Shaftesbury, which he represented in parliament from 1793 until 1802, and £16,000 on a London house.

Unhappily for him, Benfield tried to improve his fortune by entering into a partnership in a banking business with Walter Boyd. Benfield's role was to supply capital rather than to take an active role in managing the bank. Boyd was extremely ambitious, and Boyd and Benfield became the main contractor both for the British government's borrowing to fight revolutionary France and for the loans to Austria which the government guaranteed. For a time the bank prospered, but by 1797 it had overreached itself and could not meet its obligations. On 8 March 1799 Boyd, Benfield & Co. was wound up and the partners were declared bankrupt the following year, Boyd complaining that Benfield's 'Temper, Disposition, Habits and Pursuits' made him an impossible person with whom to do business (Boyd, 17).

Benfield's English property had been mortgaged for loans from the government in efforts to keep the bank afloat and was sold up. Loans had also been taken out on the security of Benfield's assets which were still in India. There was controversy between him and Boyd about the extent of his wealth still in India, but Benfield insisted that it had all gone to support the bank (*The Case of Paul Benfield*, 2). Benfield did, however, have money owing to him from Boyd in France. At the peace of Amiens he went there to try to secure it, but was interned when the war was resumed. He remained in Paris 'destitute of pecuniary resources, and literally wanting all the comforts of life' until his death in April 1810, when his funeral expenses—he was buried in Paris—had to be paid by subscription (*Memoirs of … Wraxall*, 4.94–5). After the war the French property was recovered for his wife and children.

P. J. Marshall

Sources J. D. Gurney, 'The debts of the nawab of Arcot, 1763–1776', DPhil diss., U. Oxf., 1968 · HoP, *Commons, 1754–90* · HoP, *Commons, 1790–1820* · *The writings and speeches of Edmund Burke*, ed. P. Langford, 5: *India: Madras and Bengal, 1774–1785* (1981), appx C, 629–33 [Paul Benfield] · S. R. Cope, *Walter Boyd: a merchant banker in the age of Napoleon* (1983) · *A short account of Mr Benfield's conduct in India* [n.d., 1780?] · *The case of Paul Benfield esq., partner in the house established in London under the name of Boyd Benfield and Company* (1803) · W. Boyd, *Letters to the creditors of the house of Boyd Benfield and Company* (1803) · BL OIOC, Benfield MSS, MS Eur. C 307 · letter, Amir ul-Amira to P. Benfield, 19 Aug 1785, BL OIOC, H/290, fol. 250 · *The historical and the posthumous memoirs of Sir Nathaniel William Wraxall, 1772–1784*, ed. H. B. Wheatley, 5 vols. (1884) · H. D. Love, *Vestiges of old Madras, 1640–1800*, 4 vols. (1913) · biographical memorandum, BL OIOC, O/6/11, fols. 143–5 · *GM*, 1st ser., 63 (1793), 861 · *GM*, 1st ser., 80 (1810), 493 · *GM*, 1st ser., 98/2 (1828), 188

Archives BL OIOC, corresp. and papers, MS Eur. C 307 · BL OIOC, Home misc. series, corresp. relating to India | Bodl. Oxf., corresp. with Lord Macartney

Wealth at death very indigent: Cope, *Walter Boyd*, 161; *GM*, 80

Bengal, nawabs of (*act.* 1756–1793), rulers in India, were formally the *subahdars*, or governors, of a Mughal province. In reality they were rulers of what since the early eighteenth century had been an effectively autonomous Bengal. That autonomy was to be lost to the British during their lifetimes.

Estimates of the date of birth of **Siraj ud-Daula** (*d.* 1757) vary from 1729 to 1738. He was the son of Zain al-Din Ahmad Khan (*d.* 1748) and of his wife, Amina Begam (*d.*

1760), daughter of Alivardi Khan, nawab of Bengal since 1740, who in 1752 or 1753 had declared Siraj ud-Daula to be his heir. On Alivardi's death on 10 April 1756 Siraj ud-Daula succeeded to a territory, including Bihar as well as the historic area of Bengal, which had been brought by his predecessors under a relatively centralized administration, owing only a nominal allegiance to the Mughal emperors, the formal source of the nawabs' authority. Bengal was a prosperous province, yielding a high return in taxation and with a vigorous commerce. By 1756 its external trade by sea was largely in the hands of European merchants operating out of privileged coastal enclaves. The East India Company and its servants were the dominant European merchants and the British town of Calcutta was the major foreign enclave.

Within a few months of his accession Siraj ud-Daula decided to bring pressure on the British at Calcutta. He evidently wished to curb the immunities which they enjoyed and to force them to make a fiscal contribution commensurate with their wealth. The British prevaricated, and the nawab forced the issue with an attack on the city, which he captured in June 1756. A number of British prisoners subsequently perished in the dungeon called the 'black hole', an episode for which the nawab seems to have been in no way responsible.

The victory at Calcutta was to be a short-lived one. British troops and warships were dispatched from Madras under the command of Robert Clive to recover the settlement, which they duly did in February 1757. This reverse left Siraj ud-Daula vulnerable to a coalition of enemies within Bengal, who began to intrigue against him. The opposition which nawabs of Bengal habitually faced at the beginning of their reigns seems to have been exacerbated by fear and dislike for a headstrong, violent young ruler, whose 'quarrel and enmity with all the people, whether high or low, nobles or lords, exceeded all limits' (*Tarikh-i-Bangala*, 131). The plotters were aided and abetted by the British army. Most of the nawab's commanders deserted him on the field of Plassey on 23 June 1757, leaving the victory to Clive. Siraj ud-Daula fled, but was killed by his enemies on 2 July. He left a widow, Lutfunessa, and a young daughter. He had a fine *imambara*, or hall, for celebrating Muharram built at his capital at Murshidabad.

Mir Jafar Ali Khan (*c*.1691–1765), the leading conspirator against Siraj ud-Daula, succeeded him. Symbolically for the future, he was placed on his throne by Robert Clive. Son of an Arab, Sayid Ahmad Najafi, he was a recent immigrant into Bengal, of good birth but 'an almost uneducated soldier' (Khan, 8). He had married Shah Kanum (*d.* 1766), half-sister of the nawab Alivardi Khan, whom he served as military commander, and had two other wives, Babbu Begam (*d.* 1808) and *Munni Begam (1723?–1813).

In return for British help in the plot that brought him the throne, Mir Jafar was obliged to cede some territory around Calcutta, to confirm and strengthen British commercial privileges, and to make huge public and private payments as rewards and indemnities to his British allies. In other respects, he evidently assumed that he would rule his dominions as his predecessors had done. This was

not to be. Although Clive had a personal regard for him, his authority was quickly eroded. Parts of his revenues were claimed by the British to clear his debts to them, the British army took over the defence of Bengal against incursions from northern India, and a British resident posted to the nawab's capital at Murshidabad actively intervened in court politics.

Relations between the nawab and his British protectors broke down completely. He resented their interference and they regarded him as incompetent to govern, a view shared by Indian contemporaries, one of whom reported that he talked of matters of state 'with the incoherence and insensibility of a man loitering his time in a tippling shop' (*Sëir mutaqherin*, 2.272). In October 1760 Henry *Vansittart, the British governor who had replaced Clive, insisted that Mir Jafar must cede territory to the East India Company and hand over his government to a minister of their choice. Mir Jafar preferred to give up his throne and went to live in Calcutta.

The man chosen by the British to be the effective minister became the new nawab. He was called **Mir Kasim Ali Khan** (*d.* 1777), probably the son of Mir Razi Khan and son-in-law of Mir Jafar through his marriage to his daughter Fatima Begam. Mir Kasim had already proved himself to be an effective administrator before his succession. His strategy as nawab seems to have been to accept the domination of the British in the coastal regions of lower Bengal, including the outright cession of territory to them, but to try to restrict their interference elsewhere and to be ruler in the fullest sense over the rest of Bengal and Bihar. To reduce British influence, he moved his capital to Monghyr in Bihar. There he enforced his own will on the administration, dismissing most of those who had held office under his predecessors, greatly enhancing the revenue that remained under his control, and reforming his army.

Mir Kasim's hopes of an effective independence from the British were to prove vain. Supporters of Clive who were still in India were never reconciled to his promotion and worked against him. Trade was, however, the issue on which relations with the British broke down. With the crippling of the nawabs' power after Plassey, private British merchants from Calcutta and their Indian partners and subordinates extended their trade throughout Bengal. This was a serious challenge to the nawabs' authority, since British merchants refused to pay their duties or to accept the jurisdiction of local officials and intruded into trades reserved for the government. Vansittart was willing to reach a settlement with the nawab, but his council overruled him. Local conflicts about trade and jurisdiction developed into a full-scale war in 1763. As British troops moved against him, Mir Kasim withdrew into northern India, killing numbers of British personnel and Indian notables who had fallen into his hands, acts of revenge which left him with a reputation for brutality. Mir Kasim was given support by the wazir of Oudh and by the Mughal emperor, but their combined army was defeated by the British at the battle of Buxar on 23 October 1764. The last challenge to British control of Bengal had been beaten off, and Mir Kasim was to spend the rest of his life in exile until his death from dropsy at Delhi on 7 June 1777.

When the British formally declared war on Mir Kasim on 7 July 1763, they proclaimed that Mir Jafar was again nawab of Bengal. The office had lost most of its credit and was to become of even less account on Mir Jafar's death from leprosy at Murshidabad on 5 February 1765, when he was succeeded by his eldest surviving son, Najm ud-Daula. The succession was formally confirmed by the East India Company, who took on themselves the appointment of the ministers to manage the government for the young nawab. On 12 August 1765, by a direct grant from the Mughal emperor, the company took over the major part of the nawabs' functions. The company became *diwans*, or administrators, of the finances of Bengal. The revenues of the province now belonged to them. The nawabs were to be guaranteed a fixed tribute and were to retain the remainder of their functions, the *nizamat*, or responsibility for defence and criminal justice.

Najm ud-Daula reigned for little more than a year. On his death on 8 May 1766 another young son of Mir Jafar, Saif ud-Daula, succeeded, again for a short period. He died on 10 March 1770, to be succeeded by the even younger **Mubarak ud-Daula** (1757/8–1793), aged eleven or twelve, the son of Mir Jafar by Babbu Begam.

Mubarak ud-Daula's reign was to last for more than twenty years, during which the office of nawab lost all its significance. The nawabs had long since been deprived of their military functions with the disbanding of their army; when Warren Hastings became governor of Bengal in 1772, he began to regulate their judicial responsibilities and he greatly reduced the nawab's tribute. In 1791 the company's courts took over complete responsibility for the criminal law from the nawab. Mubarak ud-Daula lived out his life in his palace at Murshidabad, until 1787 under the close supervision of a British resident. In addition to his principal wife, Fais-un-Nisa, he had a number of other wives, with whom he had twelve sons and thirteen daughters. Like his predecessors, Mubarak ud-Daula was a generous patron of religious festivals, Hindu as well as Muslim. He died in Murshidabad on 6 September 1793, heavily in debt.　　　　　　　　　　　　　　　　　P. J. MARSHALL

Sources A. M. Khan, *The transition in Bengal, 1756–1775: a study of Saiyid Muhammad Reza Khan* (1969) · G. H. Khan, *A translation of the Seïr mutaqherin, or, View of modern times, being an history of India*, trans. M. Raymond, 4 vols. (Calcutta, 1902); repr. · *Calendar of Persian correspondence: being letters, referring mainly to affairs in Bengal, which passed between some of the company's servants and Indian rulers and notables*, 11 vols. (1911–69) · J. H. Tull Walsh, *A history of Murshidabad District* (1902) · A. C. Roy, *The career of Mir Jafar* (Calcutta, 1953) · N. Chatterjee, *Mir Qasim* (Allahabad, 1935) · S. C. Hill, *Bengal in 1756–1757*, 3 vols. (1905) · *The Tarikh-i-Bangala-i-Mahabatjangi*, trans. A. Subhan (Calcutta, 1982) · J.-N. Sarkar, *The history of Bengal*, 2 (Dacca, 1948) · N. Majumdar, *Justice and police in Bengal, 1765–1793* (1960)
Archives BL, Warren Hastings papers, Add. MSS 29122–29123 · BL OIOC, East India Company records, letters [translations] · National Archives of India, New Delhi, Persian records
Likenesses gouaches (after G. Farington?), BL OIOC, V&A · portrait (Mir Jafar Ali Khan), repro. in H. N. Sinha, ed., *Fort William–India House correspondence*, 2 (1957) · portrait (Mir Kasim Ali Khan), repro. in R. R. Sethi, ed., *Fort William–India House correspondence*, 3 (1968) · portraits (Siraj ud-Daula; Mir Jafar Ali Khan; Mir Kasim Ali Khan; Mubarak ud-Daula), repro. in Walsh, *History of Murshidabad District*
Wealth at death large state treasury; Siraj ud-Daula · 5 lakhs of rupees [over £100,000]; Mir Jafar Ali Khan · destitute; Mir Kasim Ali Khan · £120,000 in debt; Mubarak ud-Daula: *Fort William–India House correspondence*, vol. 11, 1789–92, ed. I. B. Banerjee (Delhi, 1974), 498

Benger, Elizabeth Ogilvy (*bap.* 1775, *d.* 1827), historian and novelist, was baptized at West Camel, Somerset, on 15 June 1775, the only child of John Benger or Benjey, and his wife, Mary, *née* Long. Her father gave up trade in Wells, Somerset, to enter the navy as a purser in 1782, moving with his family to Chatham, where they stayed (apart from two years in other ports) until 1797. According to her friend and memorialist Lucy Aikin, Elizabeth Benger soon showed 'an ardour for knowledge, a passion for literary distinction' but both her sex and her social standing 'debarred her from the most effective means of mental cultivation' (Aikin, 1); apparently, her thirst for reading matter drove her to read the open pages of books in booksellers' windows. Her parents were persuaded to let her learn Latin at the age of twelve in a local boys' school, and in the next year she published a poem, *The Female Geniad*, with the consent of her father who 'contemplated her literary progress with delight and with pride' (ibid., 2).

It appears that Benger's father planned to pay for his daughter's education, but his death in 1796 left his family destitute. In 1797 they moved to Devizes, to be near friends and family. However, hungry for literary society, Benger persuaded her mother to move to London in 1802, where she built up a circle of literary acquaintances through friends including Jane and Anna Maria Porter, Sarah Wesley, and Lady de Crespigny; her circle eventually included George Gregory, Elizabeth Hamilton, John Aikin, Anna Laetitia Barbauld, Lucy Aikin, the painter Robert Smirke, Elizabeth Inchbald, and Joanna Baillie. By the time of her death, Benger had achieved a modest reputation as a literary hostess; it seems the novelist Edward Bulwer-Lytton met his future wife, Rosina Wheeler, at one of her parties. This achievement was facilitated by her attractive and vivacious personality. Her appearance, however, left something to be desired: although 'a tall, dark woman with fine dark eyes', she was almost 'a female George Dyer' (Martin, 141) in her dress (an allusion to the notoriously slovenly and eccentric poet, who was, ironically, for a time in love with Elizabeth Benger).

Nevertheless, Elizabeth Benger's extraordinary enthusiasm for literary lions exposed her to some ridicule: after attending a party at the Aikins' in May 1812, where Wordsworth was present, Henry Crabb Robinson recorded unkindly that 'Miss Benger was ludicrously fidgety until she was within hearing' of the poet (Morley, 1.83). In April 1800 Charles Lamb described in a letter to Coleridge how he had arrived home one afternoon to find his sister Mary closeted with 'one Miss Benge, or Benjey—I don't know how she spells her name' who would not leave until they promised to come to tea the next day. The Lambs found her at her lodgings 'up two pairs of stairs in East Street', where she apparently sounded them out on a variety of subjects, including metaphysics, poetry, and Hannah More's recently published *Strictures on Female Education* (1799), but the Lambs were largely unresponsive (*Letters of Charles and Mary Lamb*, 1.198–9). Other literary celebrities were more welcoming of Benger's advances: she disguised herself as a maid in order to make the acquaintance of Elizabeth Inchbald, who became a close friend. According to Lucy Aikin, Germaine de Staël described her as the most interesting woman she had met during her visit to England.

Possibly in emulation of Elizabeth Inchbald, Elizabeth Benger originally hoped to make her name as a playwright but, after several disappointments, she turned to poetry, publishing a poem entitled *The Abolition of the Slave Trade* in 1809. This was followed by two novels, published anonymously, *Marian* (1812) and *The Heart and the Fancy, or, Valsinore* (1813). This latter work is uneven and melodramatic, suggesting that the author was better supplied in the first of the qualities named in the title than the second: while her enthusiasm for philanthropic causes—such as the abolition of slavery and prison reform—is very evident, the plot is muddled and unoriginal and the characters are largely one-dimensional. Both novels feature eccentric, enthusiastic, and kind-hearted spinsters who may be self-portraits. Despite its shortcomings, *The Heart and the Fancy* was favourably reviewed in the *Gentleman's Magazine* and translated into French in 1816.

Meanwhile, Elizabeth Benger had abandoned fiction in favour of publications more suited to her talents. Proficient in German, she translated a volume of Klopstock's letters, published in 1814 with a short introduction. Two biographies followed, *Memoirs of the Late Mrs Elizabeth Hamilton* (1818) and *Memoirs of John Tobin* (1820). In 1821—possibly inspired by Lucy Aikin's court histories—Benger published the *Memoirs of the Life of Anne Boleyn*. Although dominated by the moralistic objectives of the 'philosophical' historian—Benger claimed that Boleyn's career 'exemplified the vanity of human ambition' (preface, iii)—this historical biography is surprisingly critical in approach to its sources; Benger's emphasis on the queen's support of early protestant reformers such as Latimer has been vindicated by later research. Her next work, *Memoirs of the Life of Mary, Queen of Scots* (1823), a balanced but sympathetic biography, was the first account of this queen to cover fully her early life in France; it included several previously unpublished letters. It was followed by *Memoirs of Elizabeth Stuart, Queen of Bohemia* in 1825.

In the following year, Elizabeth Benger's health began to fail. She was collecting materials for a biography of Henri IV of France at the time of her death on 9 January 1827. Her determined struggles to cultivate a literary career and make her living exhibit the difficulties confronted by the woman writer of the Romantic period; in her historical biographies of royal women she helped to pioneer a field much worked by other nineteenth-century women writers, such as the Strickland sisters and Mary Anne Everett Green.   ROSEMARY MITCHELL

Sources IGI • L. Aikin, 'Memoir of Miss Benger', in P. H. Le Breton, *Memoirs, miscellanies, and letters of the late Lucy Aikin* (1864), 1–70 • *Quarterly Biographical Magazine*, 1/1 (1828), 125–8 • Blain, Clements & Grundy, *Feminist comp.*, 81–2 • J. Todd, ed., *A dictionary of British and American women writers, 1660–1800* (1984), 45 • *The letters of Charles and Mary Lamb*, ed. E. W. Marrs, 3 vols. (1975–8) • *Henry Crabb Robinson on books and their writers*, ed. E. J. Morley, 1 (1938) • M. E. Martin, ed., *Memories of seventy years* (1883), 141–7 • *The Athenaeum* (1 March 1884), 280–81 • review of 'The heart and the fancy', *GM*, 1st ser., 84/1 (1814), 159–60

Likenesses stipple, 1823 (after T. C. Wageman), BM, NPG; repro. in *La belle assemblée* (1823) • T. Woolnoth, stipple, 1825 (after T. C. Wageman), BM, NPG; repro. in *Ladies' Monthly Musèum* (1825)

Wealth at death see Aikin, 'Memoir'

Benham, James (1820–1885). *See under* Benham, John Lee (1785–1864).

Benham, John Lee (1785–1864), stove manufacturer, was the second son of Avery Benham (*b.* 1753), a whitesmith of Reading, Berkshire, where he was probably born. In 1791 Avery moved to London, where he set up in business as A. Benham & Son, tinplate workers, of Commerce Row, Blackfriars Road. John worked for his father until 1817, when he bought an ironmonger's shop in Edward Street (which soon after became part of Wigmore Street), Marylebone, all manufacturing being done by his father. His first wife having died after giving birth to the second of two children, he married in 1818 Jane Kirkpatrick, from an old and well-connected Scottish family. A daughter, Emily, survived from his first marriage; five sons and two daughters were born of the second.

The nondescript area north of Oxford Street was being rapidly covered by large and elegant new houses for the gentry, complete with the new stoves and cooking and bathroom appliances designed for comfortable living. Benham was well aware of his market; he advertised his fancy lamps for the forthcoming coronation of George IV in *The Times* (14 July 1821), and in 1827 in *John Bull*; he advertised in the *Morning Post* his portable shower bath for use in the bedroom, which he patented in 1830. In 1824 he took over premises formerly occupied by the bishop of Chichester, on the corner of Wigmore and Welbeck streets. The family occupied the upper part of the house and showrooms were laid out on the ground floor. Workshops were installed in the basement and cellars, though Benham had to weather opposition to this supposed desecration of a former bishop's palace. The Benhams' first and third sons, **James Benham** (1820–1885) and Frederick (*c.*1826–1891), went straight from school into the business, the second son, Edward, settled in Essex where he started a printing business in Colchester and was proprietor of the *Essex County Standard*. The junior sons, Augustus (*b. c.*1826) and John (*c.*1830–1899), were put into a coppersmithing business, but it could not support both of them, and John joined his brothers in his father's business. By 1848 James was married, to Eliza Horsey; they had at least two children.

The enlarged showrooms encouraged Benham to diversify beyond the domestic market. From the 1840s he secured several major contracts to fit up kitchens, most famously in 1841 that of the Reform Club. The entire cooking apparatus, made to the requirements of its chef Alexis Soyer, was manufactured at Wigmore Street. Benham was employing forty-four men by 1851, the year that he won medals for his extensive displays at the Great Exhibition. He was successful at the Paris exhibitions of 1855 and 1867, and the London Exhibition of 1862. When workshop space became inadequate for the ninety-three men labouring to fulfil his orders, he took over two adjacent houses, with land on which he built a fine modern factory. Much of the trade centred on the extremely successful range of 'combined' cooking apparatus designed by Samuel Hazard Huntly, who was Benham's works manager from about 1850. A single fire heated one or more ovens, supplied steam to the boiling pans and hot water for washing up, and in certain instances, for laundries and hot baths. The arrangement was so efficient that, under test at the Royal Artillery barracks, Woolwich, all the food for 663 men, including their bread, was cooked, and hot water delivered for washing up, from 3¾ oz of coal per head per day, which worked out at a cost of 8d. per head per annum, a remarkably small sum, even allowing for the low cost of coal and the simple meals. By 1876 similar stoves were in use throughout the country, in twelve military barracks, sixty workhouses, twenty-two hospitals, several schools, and some of the larger West End department stores. When the Admiralty decided that henceforth sailors should have bread rather than pre-baked ship's biscuit, Huntly designed a compact stove with one furnace heating four ovens and four boiling pans; between 1859 and 1876 Benhams stoves were put into eighty-four ships of the British navy and some seventy other foreign and commercial vessels. Benhams' peak of success was 1874, when the partners, James, Frederick, and John, made a profit of over £15,000, much of which they prudently reinvested.

John Lee Benham, whose ability and drive had underpinned this success, died at 19 Wigmore Street, London, on 10 March 1864. A Baptist, he was involved in many religious and philanthropic activities and his judgement and advice were widely sought. Seven Benhams had joined the new Bloomsbury Baptist Chapel at its opening in 1848, participating actively and generously in Baptist missionary, educational, and poor relief projects. James served as the first treasurer; from 1864 he was also steward in charge of its building fabric, and he rose to be senior deacon.

Huntly had departed and the firm was going through difficult times when James Benham died suddenly at 50 Wigmore Street, London, on 15 June 1885. Unwisely, the combined stoves were abandoned in favour of large boilers and steam appliances but the directors lacked experience in costing these and the heart of the West End was ill suited to their noisy manufacture. Losses were continuing to mount when Frederick Benham, a man of charm and humour but unable to impose order, died in 1891, whereupon Benhams was formed into a private company. John's son Stanley J. Benham joined the business in 1892 and was appalled at the inefficiency and drunkenness accepted on the shop floor.

By the early years of the century the various directors were eager to sell the Marylebone leases and cancel their losses. The old company was quietly liquidated and a new one having the same name was formed with Stanley Benham and his cousin Walter Benham (d. 1908) as managing directors. Benhams' prosperity was restored by commissions to refit the galleys of warships prior to the First World War. They subsequently absorbed various smaller companies, the first of which, Johnson and Ravey, brought with it the royal warrant which surprisingly Benhams had not been given for their work on the royal yacht in 1898. The business continued under the command of various members of the Benham family and was absorbed into the Thorn Group after the Second World War.

ANITA MCCONNELL

Sources S. J. Benham, *Under five generations: the story of Benham and Sons Ltd* (1937) · F. Bowers, 'The Benhams of Bloomsbury', *Baptist Quarterly*, 29 (1981–2), 64–76 · *The Freeman* (19 June 1885) · F. Bowers, 'Benham, James', *DBB* · *London Directory* (1791–1820) · census returns, 1841, 1851, 1861, 1871 · *CGPLA Eng. & Wales* (1864) · *CGPLA Eng. & Wales* (1885) · d. cert. · d. cert. [James Benham]
Likenesses photograph, repro. in Benham, *Under five generations* · photograph (James Benham), repro. in Bowers, 'Benham, James'
Wealth at death under £20,000: probate, 2 April 1864, *CGPLA Eng. & Wales* · £60,209 19s.—James Benham: probate, 20 July 1885, *CGPLA Eng. & Wales*

Benham, William (1831–1910), Church of England clergyman and author, was born on 15 January 1831 at West Meon, near Petersfield, Hampshire, where his grandfather and his father, James Benham, successively held the position of village postmaster. He was educated until 1843 at the village school, built by the rector, Henry Vincent Bayley, who made him his secretary and taught him Greek and Latin. At his death in 1844 Bayley left instructions that the boy's education should be continued—he was therefore trained as a schoolmaster at St Mark's College, Chelsea, under Derwent Coleridge. Among other places, he then taught at the Blue Coat School, Westminster, and as a private tutor. Then by his own exertions and the help of Archdeacon Bayley's family he was enabled in 1856 to attend the theological department of King's College, London, where the influence of F. D. Maurice permanently affected his religious position in the direction of attempted engagement with intellectual trends outside the church, such as evolutionism. In 1857 he was ordained deacon, and priest in 1858. He was appointed divinity tutor and lecturer in English literature at St Mark's, Chelsea, still under Derwent Coleridge, and remained there until in 1864 he became editorial secretary to the Society for Promoting Christian Knowledge and professor of modern history at Queen's College, Harley Street, in succession to F. D. Maurice. At the same time he engaged in Sunday ministerial work as curate of St Lawrence Jewry, under Benjamin Morgan Cowie. On 4 January 1862 he married Louisa Marian Engelbach (1831/2–1870), daughter of Lewis Edward Engelbach, esquire.

Meanwhile Benham's preaching attracted the attention

of Archbishop Longley, who made him in 1867 first vicar of the newly formed parish of Addington, where the archbishop resided. The health of the primate was giving way. Benham assisted him as his private secretary during the anxious period of the first Lambeth conference in 1867, and was with him at his death in 1868. Partly to vindicate Longley, he entered the periphery of the Colenso controversy by seeking to publicize what he regarded as the true views of the conference against misrepresentations by Archbishop Robert Gray, who sought to claim its support for all his actions against Bishop Colenso of Natal. Comparative leisure at Addington enabled Benham to increase his literary work. He produced *The Church of the Patriarchs* in 1867 and an edition of William Cowper's poetry in 1870 (followed by one of his letters in 1884), worked on a commentary on the New Testament, and published in 1873 his well-known *Companion to the Lectionary* (new edn, 1884).

For Tait, Longley's successor in the archbishopric, Benham developed 'a love that was filial in its nature … a case of genuine hero-worship' (*Church Times*). Tait gave him the Lambeth degree of BD, made him one of the six preachers of Canterbury, and in 1872 bestowed on him the important vicarage of Margate. Here Benham restored the parish church, was chairman of the first school board of the town, and made the Church Institute a centre of intellectual and spiritual life. He lectured there on church history and also on Charles Dickens, of whose liaison with Nelly Ternan he handed down the first clear hints to posterity after having become a confidant of hers at Margate. He now resigned his Queen's College chair, but remained on the college council. After the death of his first wife, in August 1870, he married Caroline Elizabeth Sandell (*b.* 1839/40) of Basing, Hampshire, on 9 January 1872. She outlived him.

As Benham complained of overwork at Margate (aggravated by his disputes with the Irvingists), in 1880 Tait made him vicar of Marden, and in 1882 he was appointed rector of St Edmund the King with St Nicholas Acons, Lombard Street, a benefice he held until his death. There Benham suffered from attacks by low-churchmen. His curate, at least, was accused of saying prayers for the dead at Lombard Street. *The Record* conceded in an obituary (5 August 1910) that he was 'never a High Churchman in the modern sense'. Benham wrote that 'the Tractarian movement was an inestimable boon to English religion, in spite of all its errors' (*Treasury*, 1, 1902–3, 548). He had sought to play a mediatory role in the affair of C. H. Collette's attack on J. H. Newman. His personal letters, however, show very limited sympathy for Anglo-Catholicism. His own view of Lombard Street was: 'Our ritual is not very high. I moderated it as much as I could when I came there first, but continued what I felt able to fall in with, and so kept my congregation together' (Fulham MSS, F. Temple MS 22, fol. 349). At St Peter, London docks, on the other hand, he had been appalled in 1874 by a service full of interpolated mumblings and strange gestures—'simply the mass', he complained to the archbishop (Tait MS 203, fol. 328). He deplored Christopher Wordsworth's degree of hostility to both Romans and nonconformists; to a large extent, his own position was equal tolerance of both. Tait, when asked Benham's party, thought that 'on the whole he belonged to the Benhamist school' (*The Guardian*). A later archbishop, Randall Davidson, considered: 'People might or might not agree with him in opinion. They could hardly fail, if they knew him well, to respect and even love him as a man' ('Foreword' to *Letters of Peter Lombard*, iv).

Benham made St Edmund's Church a preaching centre of exceptional intellectual force and impartiality; *Lombard Street in Lent* (1894), the title of a course of addresses by various preachers, presented the kind of sermon which he thought a city church should supply in order to attract the businessman in the lunch hour. In 1888 Archbishop Benson made him honorary canon of Canterbury, and in 1898 Hartford University, USA, granted him the degree of DD. He was Boyle lecturer in 1897, and rural dean of East City from 1903 until his death.

Benham's literary activity was always great. He collaborated with Randall Davidson on the *Life of Archbishop Tait* (1891), having already (1879) edited the memoirs of Catherine and Craufurd Tait, his wife and son. Benham also edited the series of cheap reprints entitled the Ancient and Modern Library of Theological Literature and contributed substantially to the series English Cathedrals. But the characteristic work of the last twenty years of his life was the lightly written series of miscellaneous paragraphs which he contributed to the *Church Times* week by week under the heading 'Varia' and with the signature of Peter Lombard, edited after his death by his daughter Ellen Baxter as *Letters of Peter Lombard* (1911). Benham's long involvement with the Society for the Propagation of the Gospel was unfortunately overshadowed in his last years by some bitterness arising from the death of another of his daughters by his first marriage, Marian, in an accident (in which Benham considered her superiors to have been negligent) during missionary work in India in 1902. He died at his home, 32 Finsbury Square, London, of heart failure on 30 July 1910, and was buried at Addington churchyard (near Archbishop Tait) on 4 August.

JULIAN LOCK

Sources DNB · WWW · LPL, Tait MSS · LPL, Fulham MSS, F. Temple MSS, MS 22, fols. 346–52 · E. D. Baxter, 'Memoir', in W. Benham, *Letters of Peter Lombard*, ed. E. D. Baxter (1911) · R. Davidson, 'Foreword', in W. Benham, *Letters of Peter Lombard* (1911) · W. Benham, 'Preface', in W. Benham, *Henry Callaway, MD, DD: first bishop for Kaffraria, his life-history and work* (1896) · *Treasury*, 1 (1902–3), 1043–8 · *The Guardian* (5 Aug 1910) · *Church Times* (5 Aug 1910) · *The Times* (1 Aug 1910), 11 · *The Record* (5 Aug 1910) · A. M. G. Stephenson, *The first Lambeth conference, 1867* (1967) · C. Tomalin, *The invisible woman: the story of Nelly Ternan and Charles Dickens*, new edn (1991), 229–31 · census returns for Marden, Staplehurst, Kent, 1881, PRO, RG 11/6925, fol. 15 · CGPLA Eng. & Wales (1910) · IGI · m. cert. [Louisa Marian Engelbach] · d. cert. [Louisa Marian Engelbach]

Archives Birmingham Oratory, J. H. Newman MSS · BL, letter to Sir T. Acland, Add. MS 44092 · BL, Gladstone MSS, Add. MS 44516 · LPL, Benson MSS · LPL, Davidson MSS · LPL, Longley MSS, vol. 8 · LPL, Tait MSS · LPL, Fulham MSS, corresp. with Bishop F. Temple

Likenesses Mason & Co., photograph, 1867–72, LPL, MS 3063, fol. 61 · photograph, 1870–72, LPL, MS 2445, fol. 14 · S. A. Walker, photograph, 1877, LPL, MS 2154, fol. 17 · photograph, *c.*1880, repro.

in Tomalin, *The invisible woman*, facing p. 241 • Elliott & Fry, photograph, repro. in *The Guardian* • Russell, photograph, repro. in *ILN* (6 Aug 1910)

Wealth at death £16,899 18s. 2d.: probate, 31 Aug 1910, CGPLA Eng. & Wales

Benhyem, Hugo de. *See* Bennum, Hugh of (d. 1281/2).

Bening, Levina. *See* Teerlinc, Levina (d. 1576).

Benisch, Abraham (1811–1878), Hebraist and newspaper editor, was born to Jewish parents at Drossau, a small town 8 miles south-west of Klattau in Bohemia. About 1836 he studied surgery at Prague University where, with other Jewish students, he formed an organization for re-establishing Jewish independence in Palestine; the group's ideology was a precursor of Zionism. By 1838 Benisch was studying at Vienna University, where, with others, he formed a secret society, Die Einheit, which had the same aim. He gained a PhD, and in 1841 went to London with a letter of recommendation from the house of Rothschild. His goal was to gain the support of Sir Moses Montefiore and other leading British Jews for his Palestine settlement scheme, but they rejected it. He never entirely abandoned the idea, and started a career within Anglo-Jewry as a journalist, scholar, writer, publicist, polemicist, apologist, and person active in various Jewish organizations. 'A typical enlightened Jew from central Europe, a *maskil*' (Cesarani, 9), he co-edited in 1841 a Jewish paper, the *Voice of Jacob*. He worked as an author and tutor. In 1854 he edited and purchased another Jewish paper, the *Hebrew Observer*. In 1855 he arranged its merger with the *Jewish Chronicle* (founded in 1841) and was thereafter the latter's proprietor and editor until 1868.

Initially assisted only by his wife, Henrietta, Benisch increased the circulation of the *Jewish Chronicle* and by early 1858 had brought it from loss into profit. In the early 1860s he was involved in speculation and 'puffed' some companies in the *Chronicle*. With the recession it went into debt and new ownership. Benisch, in ill health and financial difficulty, was replaced as editor by his deputy, Michael Henry. Following Henry's accidental death in June 1875, Benisch again edited the *Chronicle*, and he continued to do so until his own death. As editor he favoured a moderate orthodoxy and he campaigned on various Jewish issues, including the admission of Jews to parliament; he wrote about the Board of Deputies of British Jews, and the Mortara case—the abduction in 1858 by the archbishop of Bologna of a Jewish boy, causing international Jewish and protestant protest—and he continued to advocate settlement in Palestine. He also penned anti-Christian and anti-conversionist polemic. The *Chronicle* was an influential forum for communal debate, and also a Jewish voice to the *goyim*. The major controversy during Benisch's second period as editor was about the Eastern question and especially the 1876 Bulgarian massacres. Benisch, like most of Anglo-Jewry before this episode, supported the Liberal Party. However, most Jews, including Benisch, favoured the Ottoman Turks against their oppressed Balkan Orthodox Christian subjects, and for this they were criticized by British atrocitarians, most notably Gladstone. Benisch corresponded with and twice met Gladstone, in October 1876 and May 1877 (in 1875 he had sent Gladstone a copy of his book *Judaism Surveyed*, published in the previous year), but Gladstone continued his criticism of 'Judaic sympathies'. David Cesarani has commented, 'Benisch wanted to have his cake and eat it: he wanted to defend the right of Jews to have a special sympathy for fellow Jews abroad while rejecting any criticism of that right' (Cesarani, 64).

Benisch helped to form the Jewish Board of Guardians (1859), the Society of Hebrew Literature (1870), the Anglo-Jewish Association (1871), and the Biblical Institute (later merged into the Society of Biblical Archaeology); and he supported Jewish education and the Jews' College, London. He published numerous works—some reprinted from his *Chronicle* articles and his lectures—on biblical studies, biography, travel, and defence of Judaism, including a translation of the Old Testament with the Hebrew text (1851), an elementary Hebrew grammar (1852), *Scripture History: Simply Arranged for the Use of Jewish Children* (1853), *Bishop Colenso's Objections to the Historical Character of the Pentateuch and the Book of Joshua* (1863), and *Why I should Remain a Jew* (published posthumously). He died, of kidney and bladder disease, following an operation for stone in the bladder, at his home, 13 Brownswood Park, Green Lanes, South Hornsey, London, on 31 July 1878.

SIDNEY LEE, *rev.* ROGER T. STEARN

Sources *The Athenaeum* (10 Aug 1878), 180 • D. Cesarani, *The Jewish Chronicle and Anglo-Jewry, 1841–1991* (1994) • private information (1885) • D. Feldman, *Englishmen and Jews: social relations and political culture, 1840–1914* (1994) • Boase, *Mod. Eng. biog.* • Gladstone, *Diaries* • C. Roth, ed., *Encyclopaedia Judaica*, 16 vols. (Jerusalem, 1971–2) • I. Singer and others, eds., *The Jewish encyclopedia*, 12 vols. (1901–6), vol. 3 • H. C. G. Matthew, *Gladstone, 1875–1898* (1995) • R. T. Shannon, *Gladstone and the Bulgarian agitation, 1876* (1963) • *BL cat.* • *Diaries of Sir Moses and Lady Montefiore*, ed. L. Loewe, 2 vols. (1890); facs. edn in 1 vol. (1983) • d. cert.

Wealth at death under £18,000: probate, 22 Aug 1878, CGPLA Eng. & Wales

Benison, Ann. *See* Fenwick, Ann (1724–1777).

Benjamin, Arthur Leslie (1893–1960), composer and pianist, was born on 18 September 1893 in Sydney, Australia, the son of Abram Benjamin and his wife, Amelia (whose maiden name may also have been Benjamin). His father worked on the stock exchange. Benjamin began his career as a pianist at the age of six. He studied at Bowen House preparatory school, Brisbane, then at Brisbane grammar school. During his teens he worked as a demonstrator at a Brisbane piano store; visiting Europe with his parents, he saw his first opera in Brussels.

In 1911 Benjamin went to the Royal College of Music, London, and studied composition with Charles Villiers Stanford, with whom he shared an admiration for Brahms; he studied fugue with Frederick Bridge. After gaining a scholarship in 1912 he stayed until 1915, when he joined the Royal Fusiliers, later transferring to the Royal Flying Corps.

Arthur Leslie Benjamin (1893–1960), by Lida Moser, 1953

After the war Benjamin returned to Sydney, where he taught the piano at the New South Wales State Conservatorium. Back in London in 1921, he composed, taught, and adjudicated, winning in 1924 the Carnegie award for composition with his first published work, a string quartet. In 1926 he became a piano professor at the Royal College of Music; his pupils included Benjamin Britten, William Blezard, Ivan Clayton, Irene Kohler, and Joan and Valerie Trimble. As an adjudicator for the Associated Board he visited Latin America and the Caribbean, where he was influenced by local dance rhythms. His *Jamaican Rumba* (1938) has had a popular worldwide reputation ever since: on the strength of it he received a yearly barrel of rum from the Jamaican people.

Benjamin wrote film music from the 1920s onwards, for example 'Waltz' and 'Hyde Park Gallop' for *An Ideal Husband* (1947). In Alfred Hitchcock's *The Man Who Knew Too Much* (1955) he is seen rehearsing his own cantata at the Royal Albert Hall, and later listening in the audience at the performance. He also wrote for a documentary on the ascent of Everest (1953). As a concert pianist he performed his own concertino in 1926, conducted by Henry Wood. He gave the première of Constant Lambert's piano concerto in 1931, with Lambert conducting.

The first of Benjamin's five operas, *The Devil Take Her*, was performed at the Royal College of Music in December 1931, and again in 1933–4 with the Vic Wells company under Sir Thomas Beecham. His second, *Prima Donna* (1933), was produced at the Fortune Theatre in 1949 and revived at the Royal College of Music in 1968. In 1940 Benjamin became conductor of the Canadian Broadcasting Corporation orchestra, with which he stayed for five years. While in Vancouver he composed his first symphony. At the same time he was a resident lecturer at Reed College, Portland, Oregon.

After returning to London, Benjamin resumed teaching at the Royal College of Music. On an Arts Council commission he wrote the longest and most serious of his operas, *A Tale of Two Cities* (1950), which was broadcast three times on BBC radio's Third Programme in 1953. The New Opera Company gave the first stage production at Sadler's Wells in 1957; a year later it was broadcast on BBC television. Meanwhile his fourth opera, *Mañana*—the first opera commissioned for television by the BBC—was screened on 1 February 1956. At his death Benjamin's final opera, *Tartuffe* (1957–60), was finished in short score, with just a few pages orchestrated; this was completed by Alan Boustead, who conducted the New Opera Company at Sadler's Wells in the 1964 première.

A colourful and warm-hearted man, Benjamin liked to dress casually in an open-necked shirt worn loosely outside his shorts. He was a Savile Club member; his hobbies included cooking (assisted by his Jamaican manservant), theatre, bridge, and nude sunbathing, which he undertook in the seclusion of his Hampstead bungalow garden. He spent many winters in Jamaica, travelling both ways on a banana boat.

Benjamin admired above all Brahms—his proudest possession was a signed photograph—and Puccini, whose dramatic technique and orchestration he emulated. He stood at a large draughtsman's desk in the window of his living room to orchestrate. His professionalism he attributed to the example of his close friend Ralph Vaughan Williams. While insisting that he did not teach composition, he was glad to advise young composers, including Richard Stoker and Alun Hoddinott. He considered Benjamin Britten a genius, and his opera *Peter Grimes* a masterpiece, but he disliked Beethoven's 'Pastoral' symphony— 'Damned cuckoos!' he exclaimed, according to one pupil.

In 1956 the Worshipful Company of Musicians awarded Benjamin the Cobbett medal for composition. His individual approach took in all styles, and like his antipodean successors Malcolm Williamson and Barrington Phelung, he made no distinction between light and serious.

Latterly Benjamin developed a heart condition, but enjoyed the resulting daily glass of brandy 'on doctor's orders'. He died at the Middlesex Hospital, London, on 10 April 1960, eight days after the American première of *A Tale of Two Cities* at the State College, San Francisco. He was cremated at Golders Green on 14 April; his ashes were scattered on the crocus lawn there.   RICHARD STOKER

Sources D. Arundell, 'Arthur Benjamin's operas', *Tempo*, 15 (1950), 15–18 · R. Stoker, 'Remembering Arthur Benjamin', *RCM Magazine*, 90/1 (1994), 11–17 · R. M. Shafer, 'Arthur Benjamin', *British composers in interview* (1963), 47–52 · C. Cliffe, 'Benjamin's *Tartuffe*', *MT*, 105 (1964), 819–20 · *The Times* (11 April 1960) · J. Schaarwachter, *Die britische Sinfonie, 1914–1945* (Cologne, 1995) · P. J. Pirie, 'Benjamin, Arthur', *New Grove* · N. Goodwin, 'Benjamin, Arthur', *New Grove dictionary of opera* (1992) · personal knowledge (2004) · private information (2004) [William Blezard, Angela Escott] · M. V.

Searle, *John Ireland: the man and his music* (1979) • R. Stoker, *Open window—open door* (1985) • *WW* (1956–9) • *WWW, 1951–60* • *Who's who in music* • Burke, *Peerage* (1935); (1950) • J. O. Ward, ed., *The concise Oxford dictionary of music*, 2nd edn (1964) • H. Rosenthal and J. Warrack, *The concise Oxford dictionary of opera*, 2nd edn (1979) • records, Golders Green crematorium, London NW11 • *CGPLA Eng. & Wales* (1960) • Royal College of Music, London, archives

Archives BL, music manuscripts, deposit 1996/13 |FILM BFI NFTVA, documentary footage |SOUND BL NSA, performance recordings

Likenesses photograph, 1935, Royal College of Music, London • L. Moser, bromide print, 1953, NPG [*see illus.*] • F. Otley, photograph, c.1955, Boosey and Hawkes, London

Wealth at death £24,167 0s. 6d.: probate, 27 July 1960, *CGPLA Eng. & Wales*

Benjamin, (Thomas) Brooke (1929–1995), mathematician and physicist, was born on 15 April 1929 at 5 The Laund, Wallasey, Cheshire, the eldest of the three children of Thomas Joseph Benjamin (1884–1960), solicitor and high-court registrar, and his wife, Ethel Mary (1900–1975), daughter of Henry Brooke, engineer, of Meols, the Wirral, Cheshire, and Mary Meadows, granddaughter of Sir William Brown. His father, who served with distinction in the First World War, was energetic but strict, and his mother more sympathetic and artistic; she was a good amateur pianist. At home and at his local primary school in Wallasey, which he attended between the ages of five and seven, Benjamin was early recognized as being exceptionally intelligent. When he was eight he was sent away, as was customary, to a preparatory boarding-school, where he was very unhappy though he shone scholastically. In 1939 he enrolled at Wallasey grammar school but, owing to the wartime bombing of Merseyside, the family moved to Mold, in north Wales, where the children attended the Alun county school. Among his hobbies at this time was constructing radio sets. In 1943 the family returned to Wallasey, where Benjamin became ill and was diagnosed with diabetes. His school years were spent partly at home, where school work was brought to him by his companions. He developed musically, saving up to buy a second-hand violin and writing a number of musical compositions, notably a string quartet (1948) and a piano quintet performed at a concert in Wallasey when he was sixteen. Despite his irregular school attendance he was strongly recommended by the discerning headmaster, Mr Allen, for a place at Liverpool University, to which he was admitted in 1947; he graduated BEng with first-class honours in 1950. He was active in the Liverpool University Music Society and conducted numerous performances in Liverpool and elsewhere, frequently of his own compositions. He helped to found the Liverpool Mozart Orchestra, and regularly conducted it. By this time he had also developed a strong social and political awareness, and spoke often in public as a pacifist and independent.

Faced with a decision between music and science as a profession, Benjamin chose science. In 1951 he was granted a Rotary foundation fellowship to study electronics at Yale University, where he gained an MEng in 1952. At the death of George VI he gave a local broadcast which won public praise. While at Yale he was approached by a

(Thomas) Brooke Benjamin (1929–1995), by unknown photographer

medical researcher who instructed him how to inject himself with insulin in the precise amounts needed to counterbalance and widen his food intake. This treatment considerably improved his health and energy. After a short visit to the University of California, Berkeley, he befriended a Norwegian sea captain and returned to England on a cargo vessel via Manila and Singapore. He was accepted as a research student at King's College, Cambridge, in October 1952. There, with A. M. Binnie FRS, he devised ingenious and accurate new experiments to study cavitation in fluid flow. He also took a leading part in the musical activities of the college. In 1955 he was elected to a research fellowship at King's, which was subsequently twice renewed. In 1958 he was appointed assistant director of research jointly in the engineering department and in the department of applied mathematics and theoretical physics (DAMTP). An important development was when, unable to obtain other experimental facilities, and believing strongly that experiment and theory should go hand-in-hand, he turned to G. K. Batchelor, then head of the DAMTP, whom he persuaded to convert the basement at the department into a fluid mechanics laboratory. Among the significant experiments done there was Benjamin's discovery, together with his student J. E. Feir, of the essential instability of a regular train of water waves when the water depth exceeds a certain critical value. The analysis of this phenomenon, done by Benjamin, has much wider implications in physics, and has become known as the Benjamin–Feir instability.

While at Cambridge Benjamin published many other

penetrating researches of a similar kind, having especially to do with the instabilities of different types of fluid motions. In 1967 he was promoted to a readership in hydrodynamics. On 9 July 1956 he married Helen Gilda-Marie Rakower Ginsburg (*b.* 1927), an American and a graduate of Stanford University, who had met him during his visit to Berkeley in 1952 and followed him to England. They had three children: Lesley, Joanna, and Peter. By 1970 the marriage had broken down and it was dissolved in 1974.

During the latter part of his time at Cambridge Benjamin became convinced that in order to understand certain fluid instabilities, particularly the annular flow between rotating cylinders, studied experimentally by G. I. Taylor, and the phenomenon of vortex breakdown behind the wings of aircraft, it was necessary to master the French school of nonlinear analysis, to which he accordingly devoted much attention. As a result of his studies he wrote a series of seminal papers in which he made theoretical predictions that were later confirmed by experiment. In 1970 Benjamin was appointed to a professorship at the University of Essex, where he set up the Fluid Mechanics Research Institute. Its explicit objective was to promote collaboration between mathematicians and experimentalists in fluid mechanics research. In this it was outstandingly successful, publishing over ninety research reports and attracting able visitors, especially mathematicians, from overseas. Benjamin also played a moderating role in the student unrest at the University of Essex in 1974, giving good and sympathetic advice to the students and even visiting them in gaol. In order to avoid violence during a student demonstration he marched at their head. While at Essex he met his second wife, Natalia Marie-Thérèse Court (*b.* 1944), whom he married on 25 February 1978. The marriage was supremely happy. A daughter, Victoria, was born in 1982.

Lacking ongoing support for his laboratory at Essex University, in 1978 Benjamin applied for and was subsequently appointed to the Sedleian chair of natural philosophy at Oxford, with a fellowship at Queen's College. He occupied the chair from 1980 until his death from lung cancer in 1995. During that time he held an appointment as adjunct professor at Pennsylvania State University, which he visited annually and which held a conference in honour of his sixtieth birthday in April 1989. At Oxford he had at first to do experiments in his own house, but later when he was joined by T. Mullin from London University he was granted facilities in the physics department. Ever concerned for students, he argued publicly for an overhaul of the system of degrees, supporting the option of a general degree, carrying equal prestige, for those students not intending to pursue an academic career. He also led a campaign against the Conservative government's policy towards the universities, which in his view tended to harm them and to underestimate their contribution to the country's economy. To this end he founded the National Conference of University Professors and was its first president. He supported the International Centre for Theoretical Physics in Trieste for its work for third-world young scientists.

Benjamin received many honours, including the Lewis F. Moody award from the American Society of Civil Engineers in 1966, and election to the Royal Society of London (1966), where he was twice a member of council and in 1992 gave the Bakerian lecture, entitled 'The mystery of vortex breakdown'. In 1969 he was awarded the William Hopkins prize of the Cambridge Philosophical Society. In 1993 he was elected a foreign member of the French Academy of Sciences. He received honorary degrees from the universities of Liverpool, Bath, and Brunel.

Benjamin, known to his friends as Brooke, was tall, modest, and always polite. Among his colleagues he inspired great admiration, affection, and loyalty. With a quiet sense of humour, he was inwardly sensitive and imaginative. In his later years he took to writing poetry to express his inner reactions to everyday occurrences. He never sought publication, though his poems can be moving and show both imagination and originality of form. He was justifiably proud that despite taking a leading part in many activities he made no known enemies. He died on 16 August 1995 at Oxford, survived by his wife, Natalia, their daughter, Victoria, and the three children of his first marriage, and was cremated at Oxford crematorium on 23 August.
        M. S. LONGUET-HIGGINS

Sources report on the correspondence and papers of Thomas Brooke Benjamin, FRS (1929–1995) by the National Cataloguing Unit for the Archives of Contemporary Scientists, University of Bath, NCUACS 63/1/97, Bodl. Oxf. · reports from Fluid Mechanics Research Institute, 1970–78, University of Essex · registrar's certificate of career, 1 Nov 1950, U. Lpool · private information (2004) [Helen Benjamin, sister; Natalia Benjamin, widow; G. Morrison] · *Liverpool Daily Post* (15 April 1954) · *Essex County Standard* (2 April 1971); (31 March 1972) · *Institute of Mathematics and its Applications*, 31 (1995), 184–5 · *The Times* (2 Sept 1995) · J. Hunt, 'Professor T. Brooke Benjamin', *The Independent* (28 Aug 1995) · m. cert. [Helen Gilda-Marie Ginsburg] · m. cert. [Natalia Marie-Thérèse Court]

Archives Bodl. Oxf., corresp. and MSS · priv. coll.

Likenesses photograph, *c.*1950, repro. in *The Times* · photograph, *c.*1950, repro. in Hunt, 'Professor T. Brooke Benjamin' · photograph, 1980, West Freedom Railway, Wisconsin · photograph, 1991 · double portrait, photograph, 1992 (with his daughter Victoria) · photograph, 1992 · photograph, 1993 · photograph, RS [*see illus.*]

Wealth at death under £145,000: administration with will, 15 Dec 1995, *CGPLA Eng. & Wales*

Benjamin, Judah Philip (1811–1884), barrister and politician in the United States of America, was born on 11 August 1811. His parents, Philip and Rebecca Benjamin, London shopkeepers, were Sephardic Jews of British nationality, who, in 1807, sailed from England to make their home across the Atlantic in St Croix, in the West Indies, an island then belonging to Great Britain but subsequently ceded to Denmark. Here Benjamin was born, the first son of seven children, and lived until 1813. He was thus by birth a British subject, as was recognized fifty-five years later, when he was called to the English bar, and as is attested by a statement in his own handwriting in the books of Lincoln's Inn.

In 1813 Benjamin's parents removed from St Croix to

settle in Fayetteville, North Carolina, and later in Charleston. After attending a school at Fayetteville, he was entered at Yale College at the age of fourteen, but left it in mysterious circumstances three years later (1828) without taking any degree. In 1828 he went to New Orleans and entered an attorney's office. He was called to the bar on 16 December 1832. In 1833 he married Natalie St Martin, a Roman Catholic Creole to whom he was teaching English; she was a spectacular and sensuous beauty. From 1844, she and their daughter, Ninette, lived mostly in Paris. For some time he was engaged in studying law, in taking pupils, and in compiling a digest of cases decided in the local court. This, the first of his works, was originally intended for his own private use, but after its utility had been proved among those to whom, with his accustomed generosity, he lent it, he extended its scope, and, along with his friend Thomas Slidell, published it in 1834 as *A digest of reported decisions of the supreme court of the late territory of Orleans, and of the supreme court of Louisiana*. It was the first collection of the peculiarly complicated law of New Orleans, derived from Roman, Spanish, French, and English sources, and to his early study of this composite body of law Benjamin probably owed that knowledge of different juristic systems which afterwards distinguished him in England. In 1840 he was a member of the firm of Slidell, Benjamin, and Conrad, and the volume of work was such that he left to Slidell the preparation of the second edition of the digest, called for that year. He did a leading business in planters' and cotton merchants' cases. His arguments in the *Creole case* (1842), on insurance claims arising from an insurrection of slaves on shipboard, excited much admiration, and were printed. A United States commission was appointed in 1847 to investigate the chaos of Spanish land titles under which the early speculators in California claimed, and Benjamin was retained as counsel, receiving a fee of $25,000. He returned to New Orleans, and in the December term 1848 was admitted counsellor of the supreme court. His practice, which from that time lay chiefly in Washington, though large, was by no means so lucrative as that he was to have in England, for he never made more than £16,000 a year there along with the other members of his firm, while at the English bar his income was for two or three successive years £15,000.

During this time Benjamin took a keen interest in politics. For a time he had been a whig, and when that party broke up he joined the democrats. He was elected a senator for Louisiana to the United States senate (the first practising Jew to be a senator) in 1852 and again in 1857, having for his colleague John Slidell. Subsequently, when a commissioner of the Confederate states, he was seized by the federal warship *San Jacinto*, on board the British ship *Trent*. Benjamin made a great impression in the senate becoming with Slidell the leader of the 'Buchaneers', moderates attempting to maintain the Union, but with slavery. When South Carolina seceded Benjamin cast in his lot with the south, bidding farewell to the senate in a famous speech on 31 December 1860, and formally resigning on 4 February 1861. When Jefferson Davis

formed his provisional government of the Southern Confederacy in the same month, Benjamin was included in the cabinet as attorney-general. He became a close friend of Varina, Davis's wife. In August he became acting secretary of war, and continued in this office until the reconstruction of the cabinet in February 1862, when he became secretary of state, an office which he retained until the final overthrow of the Confederate forces. Benjamin's exertions in the discharge of his official duties were so great as almost to break down even his iron strength. He had the reputation of being 'the brains of the Confederacy', and Davis fell into the habit of sending to him all work that did not obviously belong to the department of some other minister. Beginning work at his office at 8 a.m. he was often occupied until one or two o'clock next morning. The autocratic character of Davis's administration, and the secrecy often observed in the debates of the house of representatives, made it doubtful how far Benjamin was responsible for the many arbitrary measures which marked the conduct of the war by the Confederates. Some of the orders he issued were, however, undoubtedly harsh. On 25 November 1861, for example, he ordered that persons found burning bridges in Tennessee should be summarily tried by court martial and executed, and that no one who had borne arms against the government should be liberated on parole. In spite of the high opinion Davis had of him, some of his measures were sharply opposed in congress, and the severe criticism evoked by his conscription law led to his being appointed instead secretary of state. As such he was generally blamed for the part he took in raising a loan from France. On the failure of the commissioners sent to Fortress Monroe to treat for peace, Benjamin made a spirited speech at a meeting held at Richmond, urging the liberation of all slaves who would join the ranks of the army, and declaring that his own slaves had asked to be allowed to fight.

On the fall of the Confederacy Benjamin fled from Richmond and headed south, at one point posing as a Jewish galley cook. He was later indicted for conspiracy in the assassination of Lincoln.

After an adventurous voyage, Benjamin landed in Southampton in August 1865 almost penniless. With the exception of a small sum of under £3000 remitted to England, all his fortune was lost or confiscated. A small portion of his real estate was indeed overlooked in the confiscations, but this was not sold until 1883. On the confiscation of his property his friends bought in his law library. He entered as a student at Lincoln's Inn on 13 January 1866, and at once began the study of English law in the pupil-room of Charles Pollock. He was dispensed from the usual three years of studentship, and was called to the English bar on 6 June 1866 at the age of fifty-five, joining the northern circuit. Here he was befriended by J. R. Quain and John Holker, then leaders of the circuit, but for some time got little practice. Misfortune seemed to attend him wherever he went. What little was saved from the wreck of his property in America he lost in Messrs Overend and

Gurney's failure in 1866, and he was compelled to resort to journalism for a livelihood.

In 1868 appeared Benjamin's work on the contract of sale (*Benjamin on Sales*), a classic upon this subject in English law. Its success was immediate and complete both in England and America. A second edition appeared in 1873, and a third, the revision of a portion of which was Benjamin's last task before his health gave way, was brought out in 1883. His practice now grew rapidly. He was already a 'Palatine silk' for the county of Lancaster, and although he met a slight check by the refusal of his application for the rank of queen's counsel, when, in January 1872, a large number of juniors received silk, it was soon retrieved. A few months later, in arguing *Potter v. Rankin* in the House of Lords, he so impressed Lord Hatherley that he shortly afterwards received a patent of precedence. It was said that embarrassment at his Confederate career led him to refuse to be sworn as a queen's counsel. His patent, however, carried with it by courtesy the privileges of that rank. After a time he ceased to practise at *nisi prius*, where, though his addresses to juries were very able, he failed in cross-examination and the general conduct and strategy of a case. His forte lay in argument, especially on colonial appeals before the privy council, where his great knowledge of systems of law other than the English gave him an advantage over purely English lawyers. Henceforward he appeared often before the courts sitting in banc or in equity cases, and at length only took briefs below the privy council and House of Lords on a special fee of 100 guineas. He had a great faculty for argumentative statement, and would put his case at once fairly and yet so that it seemed to admit of no reply. Naturally he objected to being interrupted by the court. Once in the House of Lords, so he told the story, he heard a noble lord on some proposition of his ejaculate 'Nonsense!' Benjamin stopped, tied up his brief, bowed, and retired; but the Lords sent him a public conciliatory message, and his junior was allowed to finish the argument. His power of stating his own case probably was the cause of the very sanguine character of the opinions he gave on cases laid before him. Among his best known arguments were those in *Debenham v. Mellon*, *United States of America v. Wagner*, and *United States of America v. Rae*, the *Franconia* case—one of his rare appearances in a criminal court—and the Tichborne appeal to the House of Lords.

Latterly Benjamin suffered from diabetes and weakness of the heart. He had built himself a house in the avenue d'Iéna, in Paris, where his wife and daughter lived, and he constantly went there, living only a bachelor life in London, and frequenting the dining and billiard rooms of the Junior Athenaeum. In 1880 he received an injury through a fall from a tramcar in Paris, and, on going there as usual at Christmas 1882, was forbidden to return to work. So unexpected was this by him that he had to return many briefs. His retirement caused deep regret. He was entertained at a farewell banquet in the hall of the Inner Temple on 30 June 1883. He said on this occasion that in giving up his work he gave up the best part of his life, and that at the English bar he had never felt that anyone looked on him as an intruder. To commemorate this occasion, an engraving was published by W. Rolfe, after a portrait by Piercy.

From this time Benjamin's health failed fast, and he died on 6 May 1884 at his house, 41 avenue d'Iéna, Paris, from the effects of diabetes. He was buried under the name Philippe Benjamin in the family grave of the Bousignacs in Père Lachaise, Paris; in 1938 an inscription added his full name. By his will, made on 30 April 1883, and proved 28 June 1884 by the executors, his friends John George Witt and Lindsey Middleton Aspland, of the common law bar, he left of his total personalty of £60,000 legacies to his sisters in New Orleans, his brother Joseph, his nephew and five nieces, his wife, Natalie, and his daughter, Ninette, wife of Captain Henri de Bousignac of the 117th regiment of the French line, and to avoid questions of domicile he declared his intention to reside until his death in Paris.

Benjamin was regarded by his British contemporaries as rather a characteristic Southerner. He was skilful at games, and used to say of himself that he loved to bask in the sun like a lizard. Though on compulsion he would work into the small hours, he preferred to put off his dinner until late in order to complete his work before it, and he claimed that to rise and work early in the morning was impossible to him. To the last he retained his loyalty to the lost cause of the Southern Confederacy, and was always generous to those who had suffered for it. He left no memoirs, his habit being to destroy private documents.

J. A. HAMILTON, rev. H. C. G. MATTHEW

Sources E. N. Evans, *Judah P. Benjamin* (1988) · *The Times* (9 May 1884) · *Law Journal* (10 May 1884), 307 · *Law Journal* (5 July 1884), 415 · R. D. Meade, *Judah P. Benjamin* (1943)
Likenesses W. Rolfe, engraving (after Piercy) · portrait, Historic New Orleans Collection, 533 Royal Street, New Orleans · wood-engraving, NPG; repro. in *ILN* (17 May 1884)
Wealth at death £60,221 9s. 1d.: probate, 28 June 1884, *CGPLA Eng. & Wales*

Benlowes, Edward (1602–1676), poet, was born on 12 July 1602, the son of Andrew Bendlowes (*c.*1582–1612) and Philippa Gage (*b. c.*1576), who came from a well-known Catholic family of Framfield in Sussex. Edward was the first of their family of five sons and two daughters. The Bendloweses were descended from Christopher Benlowes (or Bendlowes; Edward himself avoided the alternative spelling) of an old Yorkshire family, Catholic in religion. In the earlier part of the sixteenth century Christopher Benlowes moved to Essex and settled at Great Bardfield, where he accumulated considerable wealth and property and achieved such importance for himself and his family that he was granted a coat of arms. His descendants established themselves in a mansion in nearby Finchingfield, which came to be known as Brent Hall.

Two of Benlowes's brothers were sent abroad for a Catholic education at Douai but Edward remained at home and was privately tutored; he then went up to St John's College, Cambridge, as a fellow-commoner in the Easter term of 1620 and matriculated on 8 April. He remained at St

Edward Benlowes (1602–1676), by Francis Barlow, pubd 1652

John's for about two years. Then, according to the fashionable custom of wealthy young gentlemen, he continued his education by going to one of the inns of court in London, where he was admitted to Lincoln's Inn on 30 January 1622; there he remained for about a year. Now having reached his majority he was ready to manage the family estates. About this time he abandoned the Catholic faith, against which he railed for the rest of his life.

In 1627 Benlowes determined to make the grand tour, and in September he began his journey, first visiting Brussels and the Low Countries. Benlowes continued his journey up the Rhine, visiting southern Germany, then made his way to Austria, and eventually to Venice and the great cities of Italy. He returned home early in 1630 and settled once more at Brent Hall.

Benlowes lived in the style that his wealth easily afforded him. Never married, he was able to devote himself to lavish patronage of the arts, especially of poetry. His affectionate generosity toward Phineas Fletcher led to the publication of Fletcher's *Purple Island* (1633), a beautiful edition which Fletcher dedicated to Benlowes. Moreover Benevolus (the anagram that Benlowes devised from his name) befriended Francis Quarles and almost certainly provided him with copies of the two Jesuit emblem books *Pia desideria* and *Typus mundi* to which Quarles's *Emblemes* (1635) is indebted. Benlowes probably acquired

books such as these during his continental journey and he bestowed many of them, with numerous other gifts, including two globes, on St John's College. Benlowes delighted in emblem books, rich engravings, fine bindings, metaphysical conceits, and witty expressions of all kinds, including obscure puzzles and anagrams. He had acquired a rolling press that he installed in Brent Hall, on which he was able to produce plates of exquisite beauty to embellish the works of his friends and his own major work, *Theophila, or, Loves Sacrifice* (1652).

During the civil war Benlowes was on the royalist side; yet he deeply distrusted the Laudian church—though not its ceremonial—and feared that King Charles and his bishops were growing more and more tolerant of Catholics. But Benlowes also abhorred the plainness of puritan worship. He was naturally disposed toward serenity and quietness and he tried to remain aloof from the conflict that surrounded him but he was unlucky enough to be a great landowner in a parliamentary stronghold. After the king surrendered at Oxford in June 1646, which marked the end of the first civil war, Benlowes, who had so far seen no action, joined Sir Charles Lucas and other passionate royalists in the second civil war, which culminated in the siege of Colchester, where the royalists met defeat on 27 August 1648. Benlowes's participation in this last-ditch struggle is unclear, though at some point he was commanding a troop of cavalry. His part in the war was slight but was enough for him afterwards to be heavily fined and forced to part with considerable sums of money to parliament. At the same time he was under increasing strain to remain current with his numerous charities, benefactions, endowments, and payments of annuities.

Benlowes's most important occupation during the civil wars was the composition of his epic poem on the soul's desire for and subsequent union with God. He had already written commendatory verses for *The Purple Island* and also for Quarles's *Emblemes*, as well as a Latin echo poem (praised by James Howell) in denunciation of the pope, *Papa perstrictus* (1645); he would continue to write occasional verse after completing (and then revising and expanding) his monumental *Theophila*.

Benlowes's long poem has much in common with Joseph Beaumont's *Psyche, or, Loves Mysterie* (1648, 1652). Beaumont, deprived of his fellowship at Peterhouse, Cambridge, after the parliamentary visitation in 1643, retreated to Hadleigh, Suffolk, not far from Benlowes's Essex mansion, where he wrote of the sufferings of Psyche, who longed for union with the divine soul. Benlowes surely knew Beaumont's poem and probably the poet himself; whether he modelled his Theophila on Psyche—or whether the influence may have worked in reverse, or whether there may have been some kind of mutual attachment—we cannot certainly know. Yet *Theophila* possesses a similar kind of exuberant incoherence and extravagant wit, with similar general aims. Benlowes writes in his long preface:

> if actions of magnanimity and fidelity advancing moral
> virtue merit the title of heroic, much more may Theophila, a
> combatant with the world, hell, and her own corruptions,

gain an eternal laurel; whose example and precepts, well followed, will without doubt bring honour, joy, peace, serenity, and hopes full of confidence.   (Saintsbury, 1.320)

The text contains thirteen cantos, numbered in sequence, but there are Latin translations of cantos 1, 2, 7, and 9, so that the total number is seventeen; canto 7 in Latin is placed at the end. The stanzaic form is also curious for Benlowes adopts an awkward three-line stanza with a common end rhyme in each stanza and with lines, respectively, of ten, eight, and twelve syllables. The volume was sumptuously produced and it included as many as twenty-five engraved plates by Hollar, Thomas Barlow, and others. No two copies are quite the same, however, for Benlowes, making use of his rolling press at Brent Hall, personally bound up each one as a particular presentation copy.

Benlowes had little time remaining to enjoy his country estates, diminished though they had now become, for Brent Hall was totally consumed by fire in 1653. For a time he lived with his niece and her husband, Philippa and Walter Blount, in Mapledurham, Oxfordshire. But in 1667, pursued by his creditors, he was taken away and imprisoned briefly in Oxford. He remained in Oxford, mainly in solitude and considerable need, spending most of his time reading in the Bodleian Library, until his death in Oxford on 18 December 1676, when 'he marched off in a cold season … whereupon, by a collection of money among certain scholars, who knew what he had been, he was decently buried' in St Mary's Church, Oxford (Wood, *Ath. Oxon.: Fasti*, 2.359).   P. G. STANWOOD

Sources H. Jenkins, *Edward Benlowes, 1602–1676: biography of a minor poet* (1952) [incl. bibliography] · G. Saintsbury, ed., *Minor poets of the Caroline period*, 3 vols. (1905), 1 · Wood, *Ath. Oxon.: Fasti* (1820) · T. Baker, *History of the college of St John the Evangelist, Cambridge*, ed. J. E. B. Mayor, 2 vols. (1869) · K. J. Höltgen, 'Catholic pictures versus protestant words? The adaptation of the Jesuit sources in Quarles's *Emblemes*', *Emblematica*, 9 (1995), 221–38 · K. J. Höltgen, 'Francis Quarles and the Low Countries', *Anglo–Dutch relations in the field of the emblem*, ed. B. Westerweel (1997), 123–48 · E. Roditi, 'The wisdom and folly of Edward Benlowes', *Comparative Literature*, 2 (1950), 343–53 · C. Hill, 'Benlowes and his times', *Essays in Criticism*, 3 (1950), 143–51 · Venn, *Alum. Cant.*, 1/1
Likenesses S. Walter, oils, 1650, St John Cam. · D. King, engraved miniature, 1658, Bodl. Oxf.; repro. in *On St Paul's Cathedral* [broadsheet] · F. Barlow, etching, BM, NPG; repro. in E. Benlowes, *Theophila, or, Loves sacrifice* (1652), frontispiece [*see illus.*]

Benmohel, Nathan Lazarus (1803–1869), university teacher, was born in Hamburg, Germany, son of Rabbi Elieza Lazi (1741–1841), presiding judge, or *dayan*, of Posen, and the united congregations of Altona, Hamburg, and Wandsbeck. His mother was the daughter of Rabbi Todros Munk of Posen. Benmohel arrived in Dublin about 1827, accompanied by his elder brother, Alexander Lazarus, formerly secretary and preacher in the Portsmouth Jewish community, and Alexander's wife, Rosa.

After private tuition and matriculation, he entered Trinity College, Dublin, on 6 February 1832; he won prizes for answering in Hebrew in 1835 and three times in 1836. Having subscribed to the Thirty-Nine Articles of the Church of England, he graduated BA in 1836. Benmohel was the first person of the Jewish faith to graduate from a British university open only to Anglicans. In June 1846 he took his MA degree. He taught German at Trinity College from 1839 to 1842, deputizing for the professor of French and German during illness, and appears to have taught Hebrew privately. He finished in 1830, but never published, a work entitled 'Orthographia Hebraeo Anglicana', and was the author of a number of scholarly translations from the Hebrew. In 1851 he read a paper to the Royal Irish Academy, published in the proceedings of the academy, on 'etymological criticism'. His certificate of entry into Trinity College, his master's diploma, and two letters written by him were displayed at the Anglo-Jewish Historical Exhibition in London in 1887.

In spite of his descent from a rabbinical and communally minded family, Benmohel acquired a reputation for unorthodoxy and for being very lax in observance. He held no office in the Dublin congregation, and appears to have had little to do with his co-religionists. He died at Sandycove, Dublin, on 22 December 1869. Although he had conformed some time after entering Trinity College, he was allowed to be buried on the periphery of the Jewish cemetery at Ballybough out of respect for his sister-in-law, to whom he had frequently expressed his wish to be buried there.   DOREEN BERGER

Sources L. Hyman, *The Jews of Ireland: from the earliest times to the year 1910* (1972) · J. Salmon, 'Jews in Ireland', *Belfast Evening Telegraph* (29 Sept 1915) · L. Huhner, 'The Jews of Ireland: an historical sketch', *Transactions of the Jewish Historical Society of England*, 5 (1902–5), 226–47, esp. 241 · E. N. Adler, *Miscellanies of the Jewish Historical Society*, 6 vols. (1925–62) · I. Singer and others, eds., *The Jewish encyclopedia*, 12 vols. (1901–6) · TCD · P. H. Emden, *Jews of Britain: a series of biographies* (1944) · Boase, *Mod. Eng. biog.*
Wealth at death £200: administration, 16 March 1870, *CGPLA Ire.*

Benn, Sir Anthony (1569/70–1618), lawyer and judge, was the first son of Robert Benn, a linen draper of St Nicholas Cole Abbey, London. He matriculated at Broadgates Hall, Oxford, in January 1584 at the age of fourteen, and took a BA degree in 1587, having in the meantime been enrolled at the Middle Temple in 1583. Called to the bar there in 1594, he was raised to the bench and appointed autumn reader in 1612, when he lectured on forcible entries (8 Henry VI c. 9). He married Jane, daughter of John Evelyn of Kingston and Godstone, Surrey, about 1601, and in 1605 bought the house and manor of Norbiton Hall, Surrey, from his father-in-law. In 1610 he was appointed recorder of Kingston.

Jane Benn's uncle, George Evelyn, was a six clerk in chancery, the court in which Anthony had become a leading advocate by the mid-1610s, and during the controversy that erupted when Sir Edward Coke accused Lord Chancellor Ellesmere of committing the offence of *praemunire* by issuing chancery injunctions, which stayed causes that were being heard in the common-law courts, Benn wrote a fulsome manuscript defence of the position of chancery. While acknowledging that the court was disliked by some because its procedures differed from those of the common-law courts, Benn argued that the laws of nature and reason were older than, and transcended, any national laws. He also defended the equitable powers of the chancellor by associating them with those of the king, who was the fountain of justice. Indeed, this treatise includes a phrase 'God before all and all after the king' (BL, Stowe MS 177, fol. 198), which formed the title of another, more extensive, manuscript tract that Benn composed, probably between 1610 and 1618. With the financial worries of James I and the controversy surrounding Bate's case and the crown's attempt to increase revenue through impositions clearly in mind, Benn wrote that the absolute prerogative of the crown 'carries with it Caesar's superscription and must be left to Caesar himself'. 'Ragion di stuto' ('God before all and all after the king', Wrest papers), or reason of state, was essential to governing, and there was no doubt, according to Benn, that the common law lacked the power or the means to arrest the sovereign arm and absolute will of the king. It was 'most certain that when a prince prest by necessity seems to doe somethinge against the lawe yet it is not against Justice because through him and by his support the law receaves life and Continewance' (ibid.). Although he explicitly denounced tyranny, Benn held that the king was a 'mixt' person between God and man.

No doubt in part owing to his political views, but also apparently enjoying the patronage of the duke of Buckingham as well as that of Ellesmere, and allegedly willing to pay for promotion, Benn obtained the position of recorder of London in 1617 and was knighted in the same year. A speech that he gave when introducing the new lord mayor of London again reflects his high view of the powers of the crown. According to Chamberlain, Benn was expelled from commons at the Middle Temple in January 1618 for giving offence to Chief Justice Sir Henry Montagu, but—cut short as it was by his death later the same year—Benn's tenure as recorder was otherwise unremarkable, and he might be allowed to slip quietly out of history if it were not for the fact that he wrote a large number of nonprofessional essays, many of which survive in manuscript at the Bedfordshire Record Office. Clearly inspired by Montaigne, but much more prolix and self-contradictory than the similar work of Sir Francis Bacon, these expressed his private opinions on more than seventy separate topics including: debt, going to law, judges and justice, the duty of subjects, religion, the passions, trembling, health, life and death, learning, schoolmasters, age and youth, wealth and poverty, colonies, friendship, love, marriage, and advice to his daughter, Annabell.

Benn may have been the lawyer Ben Jonson had in mind in his 'Epigram to the Counsellor that Pleaded and Carried the Cause', and he was the dedicatee of E. Howes's *Abridgement of English Chronicles* (1618), but little else is known about the intellectual circles in which he mixed. The works themselves refer frequently to Seneca, Tacitus, and Plutarch, as well as to moderns such as the French legal writer Bodin. His perspective combines neo-Stoical scepticism about the extent of human capacity to know or act on truth with a certain degree of sentimentality, and he had the habit of always looking at a question from more than one angle. He thought that 'Of all our vanities, our imaginations are the most irksome and most foolish' (will). In his essay 'Discretion' he resolved that he would carry himself 'outwardly for public reverence according to that the present tymes require but within my heart only I will judge of the truth of things as they are, not as they personate' ('Essays of Sir Anthony Benn', fol. 10v). Men were all too likely to overrate the truth of their own opinions, and though Benn admired those who spoke up for their country, he also thought that they needed to be careful that their words did not cause the 'multitude' to become unruly. Moderation and the maintenance of order required submission to the prince in the same way that he advised his daughter to submit to her husband. Yet, while Benn's political opinions are often authoritarian, he also believed that justice should be tempered with equity and mercy. Although he could be patriarchal, and decried the way in which women sought to bring lawsuits so that they would be able to hear their own voices in court, he advised husbands to be kind to their wives, and he clearly had a deep love and affection for his own family. His will, which was written in June 1618, expresses the 'hartie desire to God' that his children would 'truly and hartely love each other even as wee their parents have loved them'. He died on the following 29th of September, and was buried in All Saints' parish church, Kingston, where his wife erected a monument to his memory that depicts him in his lawyers' robes.

CHRISTOPHER W. BROOKS

Sources W. R. Prest, *The rise of the barristers: a social history of the English bar, 1590–1640* (1986) · *CSP dom.*, 1611–18, 448, 518, 564, 584 · *VCH Surrey*, 3.504, 510 · BL, Stowe MS 177 [Benn's treatise on proceedings in chancery], fols. 190–98 · 'God before all and all after the king', Bedfordshire county RO, Wrest papers, L 48/49 · 'Essays of Sir Anthony Benn, knt, recorder of London', Bedfordshire county RO, Wrest papers, L 28/46 · BL, Lansdowne MS 157 [speech of Anthony Benn, recorder of London, at the installation of the lord mayor, 27 Sept 1617], fols. 110ff. · will, PRO, PROB 11/132, sig. 97 · *Advice to Amabella … Sir Anthony Benn to his daughter*, ed. B. Carroll (Clayton, Victoria, 1990) · *Report on the manuscripts of the late Reginald Rawdon Hastings*, 4 vols., HMC, 78 (1928–47), vol. 4, p. 16 · *Poems of Ben Jonson*, ed. I. Donaldson (1975), 180 · Foster, *Alum. Oxon.* · H. A. C. Sturgess, ed., *Register of admissions to the Honourable Society of the Middle Temple, from the fifteenth century to the year 1944*, 3 vols. (1949)

Archives BL, speech at the installation of the lord mayor, Lansdowne MS 157, fols. 110ff. · BL, treatise on proceedings in chancery, Stowe MS 177, fols. 190–98 | State Library of Victoria, Melbourne, 'Advice to Annabell'

Likenesses effigy, Kingston upon Thames parish church

Wealth at death wealthy; provided marriage portion of £2000 to daughter: will, PRO, PROB 11/132, sig. 97

Benn, Sir Ernest John Pickstone, second baronet (1875–1954), publisher and libertarian, was born in Ferncliffe Road, Hackney, London, on 25 June 1875, the eldest child of the four sons and two daughters of Sir John Williams *Benn, first baronet (1850–1922), publisher and Liberal member of parliament, and his wife, Elizabeth (d. 1928), daughter of John Pickstone of Hyde, Cheshire. He was the elder brother of William Wedgwood *Benn, first Viscount Stansgate. Ernest Benn was educated at a local dame-

Sir Ernest John Pickstone Benn, second baronet (1875–1954), by Sir William Orpen, 1928

school and then at the Central Foundation School, Cowper Street, City Road, London; his time there was interrupted by an eighteen-month exchange visit, from 1890, to Paris, where he attended the Lycée Condorcet. In 1891 he joined the family firm of Benn Brothers Ltd, founded by his father in 1880 to publish the *Cabinet Maker*. This journal, declared the father, 'was the cornerstone, but the bricks for the House that Benn built have been collected and well and truly laid by my eldest son' (J. Benn, 8). By the turn of the century Ernest Benn had taken effective control of Benn Brothers 'because of his father's preoccupation with other matters' (Shaw, 281), and the business developed rapidly; the *Hardware Trade Journal* and other trade papers were acquired, others were newly launched. On 3 January 1903 he married Gwendoline Dorothy (*d.* 1966), youngest daughter of Frederick May Andrews of Edgbaston, Birmingham; they had three sons and two daughters.

Benn succeeded to the baronetcy, and to formal management of the firm, on his father's death in 1922. In 1923 he founded the book publishing company of Ernest Benn Ltd, introducing in the late 1920s the Augustan Poets and Benn's Sixpenny Library as the precursors of the paperback. In 1926, with the construction for £150,000 of new premises at Bouverie House, he said that he had 'put the trade press into its proper place in the heart of Fleet Street' (J. Benn, 9).

In 1927 Benn sponsored what became the Boys' Hostels Association, of which the prince of Wales became patron, to provide residential clubs for homeless boys in London. He was president of the National Advertising Benevolent Society (1928), the Readers' Pensions Committee (1933),

the Royal Commercial Travellers' Schools (1935), and the Advertising Association (1935). In 1932 he became high sheriff of the county of London. From 1934 until 1949 he was chairman of the United Kingdom Provident Institution, a position which took much of his time and where his major contribution was a significant improvement in staff conditions and relations.

In the First World War Benn served as a voluntary civil servant at the Ministry of Munitions and later at the Ministry of Reconstruction; he also became honorary chairman of the trade organization commissioners. He was appointed CBE in 1918. In 1916–18 he wrote three books advocating collaboration between government, business, and trade unions in the management of industry. This represented his early collectivist political views. But, his son later claimed, his growing impatience with 'the ways of bureaucracy' (J. Benn, 10), during the war years, and a five-week visit to the United States in 1921, led him to radically alter his views and to embrace a full-blooded individualism.

In 1925 Benn wrote *Confessions of a Capitalist*, a classic exposition of the view that 'successful and conscientious businessmen were public benefactors through the employment they provided and the wealth they created' (Shaw, 282). He also epitomized the libertarian position, criticizing the process whereby 'Day by day, in a well-meaning effort to ease somebody's little trouble, we take away a little bit of discretion or liberty from the rest of the 40 millions of us' (Freeden, 267). Benn made the promotion of such views the central cause of his life.

In 1926, with Sir Hugh Bell, Benn founded the Individualist Bookshop. As leader of the Friends of Economy from 1931 he attacked what he saw as excessive public expenditure. He began a weekly magazine, *The Independent*, in 1933, but this lasted only for a short time. Benn had been a Liberal until 1929 but in that year he publicly supported the Conservatives because of what he considered to be their sounder position on individualism.

The increased government controls brought about by the outbreak of the Second World War revitalized the individualist movement. The Individualist Bookshop, which had closed in 1934, was reopened in 1941 and Benn wrote a large number of pamphlets as part of a sustained campaign, which continued after the war, against any move towards a state-planned economy or a reduction in personal liberty. Between 1916 and 1953 he wrote some twenty books on these subjects; he also wrote libertarian feature articles for scores of newspapers and journals at home and overseas, and contributed for many years a weekly column, 'Murmurings of an individualist', to *Truth*. In 1951 he protested over compulsion in the national census, and was prosecuted for refusing to fill in his form.

Sir Stephen King-Hall wrote of Benn that 'he was a most warm-hearted generous man, who while publicly proclaiming the principles of undiluted *laissez-faire* … privately followed the dictates of his great humanity' (J. Benn, 12). He believed in his role as paternalist employer and philanthropist, concerned for his workers' welfare and contributing to many causes and charities. His son suggested that Benn could be a stubborn man, with a strong belief in his own correctness. This both typified his approach to his political causes and at times caused difficulties for his family to whom he was 'apt to dictate' (ibid.). Benn died at Oxted and Limpsfield Hospital, Oxted, Surrey, on 17 January 1954.

DERYCK ABEL, rev. MARC BRODIE

Sources J. Benn, 'Foreword', in D. Abel, *Ernest Benn: counsel for liberty* (1960) · E. J. P. Benn, *Happier days: recollections and reflections* (1949) · S. Higgins, *The Benn inheritance: the story of a radical family* (1984) · C. Shaw, 'Benn, Sir Ernest John Pickstone', *DBB*, vol. 1, pp. 280–84 · *The Times* (18 Jan 1954) · M. Freeden, *Liberalism divided: a study in British political thought, 1914–1939* (1986) · Burke, *Peerage* · *CGPLA Eng. & Wales* (1954)
Archives U. Warwick Mod. RC, books, cuttings, diaries, etc.
Likenesses W. Orpen, oils, 1928, priv. coll. [see illus.] · photographs, repro. in D. Abel, *Ernest Benn: counsel for liberty* (1960)
Wealth at death £101,413 11s. 5d.: probate, 27 Feb 1954, *CGPLA Eng. & Wales*

Benn, George (1801–1882), historian, was born on 1 January 1801 at Tandragee, co. Armagh, the fourth of six children of John Benn (1767–1853), a brewer. His obituarist noted that George attributed his unionist sympathies to the fact that he was born on the day the Act of Union came into force. In 1809 the family moved to Belfast and he was educated at Belfast Academy and privately. In 1816 he entered the college side of the Belfast Academical Institution, established in 1814 by Presbyterians as both a school and a college. He won gold medals in logic (1817) and moral philosophy (1818) and won the faculty prize in 1819 and 1821. The prize-winning essay for 1819 was an account of the parish of Belfast, which was published anonymously in an expanded form in 1823 as *The History of the Town of Belfast with an Accurate Account of its Former and Present State*. Its form owes much to the county descriptions by Walter Harris and Charles Smith for the Physico-Historical Society in the mid-eighteenth century and to the Royal Dublin Society's county statistical surveys of the early nineteenth century.

George and his elder brother Edward (1798–1874) set up a distilling business at Downpatrick before moving to an estate purchased by their father at Glenravel, co. Antrim, in 1835. In 1842 John Benn built Glenravel House, where George lived until moving to Fortwilliam Park in Belfast in 1875. Described as 'genial' by his obituarist, George was also retiring and most of the management of the estate fell to Edward Benn, who was responsible for the smelting of iron ore found on the estate in 1851 and commercially extracted after 1866. Edward founded three hospitals in Belfast, which George also endowed, and contributed to the building of York Street non-subscribing Presbyterian church.

While at Glenravel, George corresponded with a number of local antiquarians, most prominently William Reeves, later bishop of Down and Connor, and Classon Porter, the non-subscribing minister at Larne. His interest at this time was in the history of co. Antrim. In the 1850s he resumed his interest in Belfast with a number of articles in the *Ulster Journal of Archaeology* (founded in 1853) on both Belfast and Ulster token issues.

In 1858 Benn approached a London-based Ulster historian, William Pinkerton, with a number of queries on the history of distilling in Ireland, on which he contributed articles to the 1858 and 1859 issues of the *Ulster Journal of Archaeology*. Pinkerton replied enthusiastically, claiming his interest in antiquities had first been awakened by reading at the printers the proof sheets of Benn's 1823 history of Belfast. The correspondence continued until Pinkerton's death.

In 1862 Pinkerton was approached by the publisher Marcus Ward to write a history of Belfast, but he fell ill in 1868 and was unable to complete it. Benn acquired Pinkerton's papers and intended to put them into a form suitable for publication but this proved impracticable. Pinkerton's research was not sufficiently advanced and, living in London, he had little opportunity to consult local sources such as the Belfast corporation book, lost in the eighteenth century and rediscovered by Benn in 1864.

In 1871 Benn began writing a history of Belfast himself. He drew on the expertise of his friends Reeves and Porter and received offers of help from others such as the Ulster historian George Hill. On Reeves's recommendation he contacted William Hennessy, recently appointed to the staff of the Dublin Public Record Office, who provided material from that source. Benn also acquired material from the London Public Record Office through Hans Hamilton, then engaged on preparing calendars of the Irish state papers. In 1877 George Benn's *History of the Town of Belfast from the Earliest Times to the Close of the Eighteenth Century* was published by Marcus Ward. It met with considerable critical acclaim—Hennessy, for example, wrote 'I think you have managed to do an almost impossible thing, namely to create a history for an unhistoric town' (Benn MSS, PRO NIre., D3113)—but it was not a financial success, a fact which Ward attributed to the depressed state of trade in Belfast.

In 1878 Benn began collecting material for a supplementary volume which would carry the history to 1870. By 1879 he was almost blind and the volume had reached only 1810, with histories of the main Belfast families. The enlarged *History* appeared in 1880. Unlike the original volume, the supplement was not based on archival materials but on local reminiscences and accounts of prominent families supplied by their living representatives.

Benn, who never married, spent his last years in poor health, and he died at Fortwilliam Park, Belfast, on Sunday 8 January 1882 as a result of a 'bronchial attack' which had begun the previous Friday. He was buried in the city cemetery on Wednesday 11 January.

RAYMOND GILLESPIE

Sources *Northern Whig* (9 Jan 1882), 5 · *DNB* · PRO NIre., Benn MSS, D3113
Archives PRO NIre., corresp. and papers · TCD
Wealth at death £5743 12s. 3d.: probate, 17 March 1882, *CGPLA Ire.*

Benn, John Meriton (1908–1992), educationist and civil servant, was born on 16 July 1908 at 231 Manchester Road, Burnley, Lancashire, the third of the five children of Ernest Benn (1871–1935), leather merchant, and his wife, (Emily) Louise, *née* Hey (1879–1957). John Benn was educated at Burnley grammar school and Christ's College, Cambridge (1926–30), where he was a scholar and took a degree in French and German, with a first class in French. He became a teacher at Exeter School (1931–4), Lektor at Halle University (1934), and then a teacher at Regent Street Polytechnic secondary school, London (1935). In the same year he published a school text of *Practical French Proses*. On 18 April 1933 he married Valentine Rosemary Seward (1910–1998), daughter of William Seward. They had two daughters, Diana and Susan.

In 1935, at the very early age of twenty-seven, Benn became a divisional inspector of schools in Northern Ireland, and moved to Londonderry. This was a determining event for him, as he lived in Northern Ireland for the rest of his life, and became an outstanding public servant there. As an inspector he was immersed in the strengths and weaknesses of Ulster public elementary schools. The children left school at fourteen, classes of over fifty children were commonplace, parents had to pay for all books, there were no school meals, and there was virtually no school transport. Benn recalled that most rural schools had no artificial lighting and very often no running water, and that the teachers laid and lit the fires in the morning. And yet, he insisted, there was often first-class education in progress, and he admired many of the teachers he encountered. But the system was frugal and old-fashioned, and once the 1944 Butler proposals for England and Wales were known, the case for radical change in Northern Ireland was overwhelming.

In 1944 Benn ceased to be a school inspector, moved to Belfast as a principal in the Ministry of Education for Northern Ireland, and emerged as the administrative driving force in adapting the Butler Education Act so that universal secondary education was provided for in Northern Ireland, building partly on the private secondary school system which had run parallel to the elementary schools. The separate Roman Catholic schools were retained, and were substantially grant-aided. During the next twenty years, thanks to greatly increased exchequer funding, a completely new network of secondary schools was created and the old secondary schools became high-standard selective grammar schools. The facilities which had been lacking before the war became commonplace. A secondary-school examination system, fully compatible with the system in England and Wales, was introduced. The Ulster College, which evolved later into the University of Ulster, was established. Benn, who became assistant secretary in 1951, senior assistant secretary in 1959, and permanent secretary in 1964, had a gift for steady constructive action, and without him the changes in Northern Ireland would have been far less effectively made.

In 1969, as one of the responses to the tensions that had erupted in 1968, Benn was appointed the first Northern Ireland commissioner for complaints (or ombudsman), dealing with allegations of unfair practices by local and public bodies. For this post he was ideally suited by temperament and background, and he held it until 1973. It was coupled with the post of Northern Ireland parliamentary commissioner for administration in 1972–3. He gave much time and thought to individuals, and was adept at reconciling conflicting interests. After retirement he was chairman of the Northern Ireland schools examination council (1974–81); pro-chancellor of Queen's University, Belfast, and chairman of the senate (1979–86); chairman of the board of governors of Rupert Stanley College of Further Education (1986–91); and chairman of the board of governors of Sullivan Upper School, Holywood (1987–9).

Throughout his life Benn was interested in people. He was immensely sociable, and relished nothing better than exercising his skill as a raconteur and enjoying the pleasure of good company. He showed a remarkable gift for understanding ordinary human problems. When he summed up fraught discussions on Irish issues, which he was often asked to do, he was wonderfully fair and illuminating. His integrity, ability, and goodwill were unmistakable. At St Mark's, the Church of Ireland parish at Dundela, Belfast, he was a regular worshipper, church warden, and expert bellringer. He was also an enthusiastic and successful actor with his local dramatic society, the Holywood players. His contribution to society in Northern Ireland was recognized by his appointment as CB in 1969 and the award of an honorary degree of LLD by Queen's University in 1973. He died at 75 Church Road, Holywood, co. Down, on 16 September 1992, and was cremated at Roselawn crematorium, Belfast, following a funeral service in the church of St Philip and St James, Holywood, on 18 September. He was survived by his wife and two daughters. ARTHUR GREEN

Sources *The Independent* (21 Oct 1992) • C. Macmahon, 'John Meriton Benn', *Queen's Letter* (Oct 1992) • C. Palley, citation for LLD, 1973, Queen's University • *WWW*, 1991–5 • personal knowledge (2004) • private information (2004) [S. Pearson, D. Hetherington] • b. cert. • m. cert. • d. cert.
Archives priv. coll., letters and other papers
Likenesses bust, Ulster Museum, Belfast • photograph, repro. in *The Independent* • photographs, priv. coll.
Wealth at death £70,000: probate, 18 Feb 1993, *CGPLA NIre.*

Benn, Sir John Williams, first baronet (1850–1922), publisher and politician, was born at Hyde, Cheshire, on 13 November 1850, the eldest child of the Revd Julius Benn (1826–1883), Congregational minister, and his wife, Ann Taylor (d. 1890). The family settled in Stepney in the East End of London when Benn was nine and he attended a small private school there before beginning work, at the age of eleven, as an office boy. At seventeen he moved to a wholesale furniture house. He was attending an art school at night, and in 1868 became a junior draughtsman for the firm, and then quickly chief designer. He was made a junior partner in 1873. On 1 July 1874 he married Elizabeth (Lily; d. 1928), the youngest daughter of John Pickstone, of Silver Hill, Hyde. They had two daughters and four sons.

In 1880 Benn resigned his partnership and launched his own furniture design journal, the *Cabinet Maker*. Although forming the foundation of what was to become a thriving

Sir John Williams Benn, first baronet (1850–1922), by Sir George Clausen, 1906

publishing firm, the journal struggled early on, and to support it Benn, a natural performer, began a successful part-time career providing illustrated lecture entertainments at various clubs and halls.

In 1889, in the first London county council (LCC) election, Benn stood for East Finsbury. In his election address he called for municipal control of gas and water supply, of liquor licences, and of markets; he supported council housing, the abolition of the privileges of the city corporation, and a fairer local taxation system. He assured his electorate that 'if elected, I shall be found among the party of progress' (East Finchley election address, 1889, National Liberal Club Collection, Bristol University Library). He was easily elected, and remained on the council until his death. Benn has been described as a 'classic radical' (Thane, 246). By 1893 Beatrice Webb could identify him as one of the inner group of Progressives 'who direct the parliamentary and political policy of the County Council' (The Diary of Beatrice Webb, 2: 1892–1905, ed. N. Mackenzie and J. Mackenzie, 1983, 34). His major target was élitism and corruption in local government, particularly within the City of London. He fought for the reform and public ownership of London's tramways and other utilities through much of his long period of LCC membership. He concerned himself above all with the tramways, successfully advocating the electrification of the system, and less successfully the large-scale construction of subways at busy junctions (the underpass which carries road traffic from Waterloo Bridge to Kingsway survives as a memorial to Benn's ambitions).

Benn was adopted as the Liberal parliamentary candidate for the St George-in-the-East and Wapping constituency at the 1892 general election. He campaigned for social reform, often recalling the work of his father as a missionary in the area. He said that he aspired 'to the honour of being the member for the back streets' (Higgins, 27), and was elected with a comfortable majority but lost the seat in the 1895 election by just four votes. The 1895 campaign became extremely bitter, after personal attacks were made on Benn and, as 'restraint and calculation were never strong points in his vivacious character' (Gardiner, 190), he responded in kind. In counter-suits of electoral malpractice following the election, he lost, and was banned from being a candidate in St George's for seven years. He stood unsuccessfully for Deptford in 1897 and Bermondsey in 1900. At a by-election in 1904 he won the seat of Devonport, which he held until January 1910. That December he unsuccessfully contested Clapham.

Benn was chairman of the LCC in 1904–5 and leader of the Progressives on the council from 1907 to 1918. In his last years, as the only remaining original member, Benn was widely known as the 'Father' of the council (The Times, 11 April 1922). He was knighted in 1906 and made a baronet in 1914. Benn was tall and distinguished in his looks and was said to have a 'breathless interest in life' (Gardiner, 473). He was a man of great passion and enormous vitality, often extremely impulsive. He died on 10 April 1922 at his home, Stone Wall, Limpsfield, Surrey. He was buried at Limpsfield church on 13 April. His eldest son, Ernest John Pickstone *Benn (1875–1954), politician, succeeded to the baronetcy. Another of his sons, William Wedgwood *Benn (1877–1960), was created Viscount Stansgate and was the father of Anthony Wedgwood Benn (b. 1925), politician.   MARC BRODIE

Sources A. G. Gardiner, John Benn and the progressive movement (1925) · Burke, Peerage · WWW, 1916–28 · The Times (11 April 1922), 16d · S. Higgins, The Benn inheritance: the story of a radical family (1984) · R. Jenkins, Tony Benn: a political biography (1980) · P. Thane, The foundations of the welfare state (1982)

Archives HLRO, corresp. with his son W. W. Benn · NL Scot., corresp. with Lord Rosebery

Likenesses G. Clausen, portrait, 1906, Guildhall Art Gallery, London [see illus.] · four photographs, repro. in Gardiner, John Benn, facing pp. 32, 298, 468 · photograph, repro. in The Times, 18

Wealth at death £7375 10s. 10d.: probate, 20 June 1922, CGPLA Eng. & Wales

Benn, Margaret Eadie Wedgwood [née Margaret Eadie Holmes], **Viscountess Stansgate** (**1897–1991**), religious campaigner, was born on 7 June 1897 in Paisley, the elder daughter of Daniel Turner Holmes (1863–1955), the son of a tailor and steeplejack and himself a schoolmaster, lecturer, and Liberal MP for Govan (1911–18), and his wife, Margaret (d. 1953), daughter of Peter Eadie, sometime provost of Paisley. Religion and politics were the two themes running through her life. Rejecting her parents' agnosticism—her father had left the Irvingites—as a girl of six or seven she became an Episcopalian, attending church alone and finding religion a 'great comfort' (Stansgate, 22). Still unschooled and illiterate at the age of seven, she was belatedly educated at St Columba's School, Kilmalcolm, and, after her family moved to London following the 1911 election, at St Mary's, Lancaster Gate—which she left because its high-church headmistress made the girls pray against disestablishment—and at a school in Holland Park. She developed a passion for learning. She followed her father's Liberalism and by the age of twelve was a feminist. She and her mother were non-militant suffragist members of the National Union of Women's Suffrage Societies. She rode in Hyde Park, 'came out' shortly before the First World War, left school in 1915, took a secretarial course, worked in the new Ministry of Labour, and was confirmed an Anglican. After the war her parents refused her request to study for a theology diploma at St Hugh's College, Oxford, and she considered becoming a nun. Instead, on 17 November 1920 she married William Wedgwood *Benn (1877–1960). They had four sons, one of whom died at birth.

Following her marriage—she wrote later that they were strongly mutually attracted but not in love—Margaret Wedgwood Benn loyally supported her husband's political career and also, following his example, became teetotal. They sent their sons to public school so that they should be able to 'deal with the Tories' (Stansgate, 58). She later wrote in her autobiography, 'My main interest was, and is, theology' (ibid., 70), and while a young mother she studied the subject as an external non-examination student at King's College, London, learning Greek and Hebrew, and she met and formed a lasting friendship with the Congregationalist Elsie Dorothea Chamberlain. She long campaigned for the ordination of women, in 1922 clashing with Randall Davidson, archbishop of Canterbury, and in 1928 she was a founder of the interdenominational Society for the Ministry of Women. In 1927 with her husband she joined the Labour Party, and in the 1920s and 1930s they travelled extensively, visiting the USSR, the Near East, and the United States, where she met Henry Ford. During the Second World War she worked under the chaplain's department with servicewomen. She influenced her husband (created Viscount Stansgate in 1942), who was air secretary in the 1945 Labour government, to appoint in 1946 Elsie Chamberlain, who had become a Congregational minister, as the first female RAF chaplain. Long 'deeply ecumenical' (ibid., 50), Lady Stansgate in 1948 attended as an Anglican delegate the inaugural assembly of the World Council of Churches in Amsterdam. She protested against the limitation of the Anglican communion and Archbishop Fisher's refusal to allow Anglicans to participate in the conference communion, celebrated according to the reformed rite. This led her to join the Congregationalists, whose puritan principle of local church autonomy she continued to defend. She travelled with Stansgate, attending conferences of the Inter-Parliamentary Union, of which he was president, and met foreign leaders including Eisenhower, Ben Gurion, Ho Chi Minh, and Zhou Enlai.

After her husband's death in 1960 Lady Stansgate considered entering the ministry. With Elsie Chamberlain she refused to compromise and agree to the formation of

the United Reformed church (Congregationalists and Presbyterians, 1972) and together they led the Nottingham-based 'rump', the Congregational Federation, of about 300 churches. Lady Stansgate was its first president. Like many keen Christians, she was fascinated by and sympathetic to Judaism and Jews, and was a Zionist. She was a vice-president of the Council of Christians and Jews. Her Hebrew studies reinforced her faith, and she was appreciated by Hebrew scholars. She helped raise funds in Britain for the Hebrew University in Jerusalem. In 1975 the library at Mount Scopus was named after her, and in 1982 she was made an honorary fellow of the Hebrew University. She was formidable, kind, charming, and committed. Her sight failed, she suffered a series of strokes, and she died on 21 October 1991 at Goldsborough Nursing Home, 40–42 Goldsborough Road, London. Her autobiography, *My Exit Visa*, was published posthumously with a postscript appreciation by her son the Labour politician Tony Benn.

ROGER T. STEARN

Sources M. Stansgate, *My exit visa* (1992) · *The Times* (23 Oct 1991) · *Daily Telegraph* (22 Oct 1991) · *The Guardian* (23 Oct 1991) · *The Independent* (22 Oct 1991) · Burke, *Peerage* · WWW [W. W. Benn] · CGPLA Eng. & Wales (1992)
Likenesses E. Hamilton West, photograph, repro. in *The Guardian*
Wealth at death £639,824: probate, 1992, CGPLA Eng. & Wales

Benn, William (1600–1681), clergyman and ejected minister, was born in November 1600 at Egremont, Cumberland, the son of John Benn (d. 1620) and his wife, Ann, daughter of John Goodwyn. He was educated at St Bee's School and Queen's College, Oxford, but took no degree. During the 1620s he was curate of Wokingham, Berkshire, then chaplain to Helena, marchioness of Northampton, at Redlynch, Somerset.

Benn was chosen rector of All Saints', Dorchester, by the town corporation (possibly with some opposition), on 12 July 1629, and inducted on 11 August. The rectory was worth only £28 a year, but Benn's stipend was later supplemented out of the £100 a year assigned to the Dorchester clergy from the corporation's purchase of the parsonage of Seaton, Devon. Benn was somewhat overshadowed at Dorchester by his more famous colleague, John White (who is said to have invited Benn to the town), but he gained an even more uncompromisingly puritan reputation than White. Parishioners complained of his longwinded sermons, and of his looseness in using the Book of Common Prayer. He was also accused of being less charitable towards the poor than his predecessors, and of being haughty and distant in his manner. In 1634 Benn refused to read the Book of Sports, but seems to have escaped official censure. He preached regularly at the county gaol, for which he was granted £10 a year by a Dorset sessions order in 1631; he is also said to have built a chapel at the gaol, largely at his own expense. The name of his first wife is unknown, but among their children were three daughters who married ministers subsequently ejected in 1662. On 19 May 1641 Benn married as his second wife Prothesy Pinney at St Mary Arches, Exeter.

During the civil war Benn preached vigorously against

the king, but when a royalist army threatened Dorchester in August 1643 he fled to London, where he was for a time assistant to John White at Lambeth. At the end of the war he returned to his former parish, where to begin with he received better remuneration than he had been given before the war—an augmentation of £50 a year from the committee for plundered ministers, and then another £60 a year after the town bought the impropriation of the neighbouring parish of Fordington. He was a member of the committee of triers and ejectors in Dorset in 1646, and was one of the lecturers at Shaftesbury in the following year. After White's death in 1648 Benn preached in the other two Dorchester churches until a successor was appointed, and continued to assist Samuel Gower in them in the 1650s while still ministering to his own parish.

When required to take the engagement to the Commonwealth in 1650, Benn did so only in a modified and virtually meaningless form. By now he was moving away from the mainstream Presbyterianism that both he and White had embraced during the war, and formed a 'gathered church' within his parish, whose members alone were admitted to communion. During the protectorate he was an assistant to the commissioners for ejecting scandalous ministers, and in January 1655 was one of the clergy asked by the council to help them in observing a special day of prayer.

At the Restoration Benn was immediately presented at Dorset's summer assizes for not using the Book of Common Prayer. He was imprisoned but soon released, and not until he refused the oaths required by the 1662 Act of Uniformity was he deprived of his living at All Saints'. From then until the end of his life Benn was one of the ejected clergy, sometimes preaching legally, sometimes illegally. He was briefly imprisoned after the discovery of the 1663 northern plot, but soon resumed preaching to a conventicle in Dorchester. When the Five Mile Act forced him to leave the town in 1665 he preached at Maiden Newton, still in the county, and was preaching at Fordington, just outside Dorchester, by 1669. On 1 May 1672, under the declaration of indulgence, he was licensed to preach as a congregationalist at the house of Philip Stansby, a former mayor of the borough.

Also in 1672 a pamphlet appeared entitled *The Judgment of Mr. Francis Bamfield ... together with Mr. Benn's Sober Answer to the Same*, an exchange between Benn and Francis Bampfield, another ejected minister. Benn temperately rejected Bampfield's argument that the sabbath should be observed, as by the Jews, on Saturday rather than Sunday. Benn died early in 1681 and was buried on 7 March of that year at All Saints' Church in Dorchester. He is said to have been able to read without spectacles even at the age of eighty, and to have prayed in his study seven times a day.

After Benn's death his friend Joshua Churchill, another Dorchester congregationalist minister, helped to see a collection of his sermons through the press under the title *Soul Prosperity* (1683). A preface by John Owen commended Benn's fifty years of 'painful, faithful, and successful labour in the Vineyard of Christ'. The thirteen sermons take the form of a series of meditations on a text from 3 John: 2. They are straightforward, full of practical, spiritual counsel, and avoid controversial matters that might get an ejected minister into trouble (they must have been composed after 1669). Benn left other papers which Churchill said that he would publish if the sermons found acceptance, but none seems to have appeared.

DAVID UNDERDOWN

Sources Calamy rev. · C. H. Mayo, ed., *Municipal records of the borough of Dorchester, Dorset* (1908) · Dorset RO, Dorchester records · D. Underdown, *Fire from heaven: the life of an English town in the seventeenth century* (1992) · *An abridgment of Mr. Baxter's History of his life and times*, ed. E. Calamy (1702) · Wood, *Ath. Oxon.*, new edn, 3.1273 · *William Whiteway of Dorchester: his diary, 1618 to 1635*, Dorset RS, 12 (1991) · DNB
Archives JRL, sermons | Dorset RO, Dorchester corporation records
Likenesses J. Caldwall, line engraving, NPG

Benn, William Wedgwood, first Viscount Stansgate (1877–1960), politician, was born on 10 May 1877 at Hackney, London, a younger son of Sir John Williams *Benn, first baronet (1850–1922), publisher and politician, and his wife, Elizabeth Pickstone (d. 1928). His eldest brother was Sir Ernest John Pickstone *Benn, the publisher and libertarian. William Wedgwood Benn was educated at the Lycée Condorcet, Paris, and at University College, London, where he obtained a first in French (1898) and later became a fellow (1918). He worked for some years in his father's publishing business. Deeply influenced by social conditions in the East End of London, and associated with the London Progressive Party, of which his father was leader within the London county council, Benn was a lifelong radical nonconformist. He was soon adopted as Liberal candidate for his father's former seat of St George's, Tower Hamlets, and became a member at the general election of 1906. He gained experience at the Treasury, Board of Education, and Admiralty as parliamentary private secretary to Reginald McKenna. After retaining his seat at both general elections in 1910, Benn became a junior lord of the Treasury and a singularly active politician, serving as Liberal whip for 1910–15. In 1912 he successfully organized relief of suffering during the dock strike and two years later, when war broke out, he became chairman of the organizing committee of the National Relief Fund.

In October, when over £2 million had already been raised, Benn answered an inner call and resigned this post to apply for active service. Despite his short stature, he secured a commission in the Middlesex yeomanry. He took part in the fierce fighting on the heights above Suvla Bay in August 1915, during the Gallipoli campaign, and later became an observer with the Royal Naval Air Service; he participated in the pinpoint bombing of the Baghdad railway. Among his other exploits was to be rescued from a sinking aeroplane in the Mediterranean, and to be aboard an improvised aircraft-carrier sunk by shore batteries at Castelorizo. He also commanded a party of French sailors in guerrilla activities against the Turks and served in authorized privateering in the Red Sea, before returning to Britain to qualify as a pilot.

After refusing the office of chief whip from the hand of

William Wedgwood Benn, first Viscount Stansgate (1877–1960), by Olive Edis, 1920

India with a seat in the cabinet, and was sworn of the privy council.

Benn occupied this high, but exposed, position for the next two years under fairly constant attack. The controversial political trial at Meerut, of Indian communists accused of a 'conspiracy' against the government, was about to commence, having been authorized by his predecessor. And the report of the Indian statutory commission under Sir John Simon, published in June 1930, was in course of preparation. Against this background Benn authorized the viceroy, in October 1929, to make the historic declaration that the legitimate goal of Indian aspirations was dominion status. Simon's concurrence was not obtained and a short but bitter parliamentary debate ensued, in which Benn defended his action with courage. When Lloyd George denounced him as a 'pocket edition of Moses' he retorted, 'But I never worshipped the golden calf' (*Hansard 5C*, 231, 1929, 1321). In 1930 the Indian leader M. K. Gandhi initiated a successful campaign of civil disobedience, directed against the salt tax, and Benn ultimately felt compelled to order his arrest. Gandhi was released the following year for talks with the viceroy which resulted in the Delhi pact, but by the time he arrived in London for the second round-table conference, Benn was out of office. On the formation of the 'national' government in August 1931 he had remained loyal to the Labour Party, and was decisively defeated at the ensuing general election. He was again defeated in November 1935 as a candidate for Dudley.

Benn used this period of enforced parliamentary inactivity to make, with his wife, a journey round the world by almost every known means of transport: an extensive visit to the United States was followed by travels through the Far East, Japan, Mongolia, Siberia, and Moscow.

At a by-election in 1937 Benn was returned as member for the Gorton division of Manchester. On the outbreak of war in 1939 he enlisted as a pilot officer in the Royal Air Force, where he rose to the rank of air commodore. He was again mentioned in dispatches, and though officially grounded was known to have taken part in air operations. In January 1942 he was called to the House of Lords as first Viscount Stansgate: the peerage was expressly granted to strengthen Labour representation in the upper house. He was vice-president of the Allied Control Commission in Italy, 1943–4.

In the Labour government of 1945 Stansgate became secretary of state for air. The following year he was entrusted by the foreign secretary, Ernest Bevin, with the conduct in Cairo of the abortive negotiations for a revision of the Anglo-Egyptian treaty. Later that year, however, Stansgate, who was nearly seventy, was one of a number of older ministers dropped from the government to make way for younger blood.

In 1947 Stansgate became president of the interparliamentary union, and he held this position for ten years with universal esteem. In the House of Lords he became the authentic voice of liberalism. His persistence

Lloyd George, Benn returned to service in Italy and was eventually seconded to the Italian army to organize and participate in the first parachute landing of a secret service agent behind the enemy lines. His distinguished war record was recognized with many honours: he was twice mentioned in dispatches, appointed to the DSO, awarded the DFC, was made a chevalier of the Légion d'honneur, received the Croix de Guerre, the Italian war cross, and the Italian bronze medal for valour. He later published an account of his wartime experiences, which was modestly entitled *In the Side Shows* (1919). On 17 November 1920 he married Margaret Eadie (1897–1991) [*see* Benn, Margaret Eadie Wedgwood], daughter of Daniel Turner Holmes, Liberal member for Govan, Lanarkshire, from 1911 to 1918. There were four sons of the marriage, of whom the youngest died at birth.

At the general election of 1918, his former constituency having been redistributed, Benn was returned as member for Leith, a seat which he held through three more general elections and for nine years of intense parliamentary activity. A supporter of Asquith just this side of idolatry, Benn chafed under the leadership of Lloyd George. He found himself increasingly voting with the Labour Party, applied for membership of that party in 1927, and resigned his seat. The next year he was returned at a by-election as member for North Aberdeen, and held the seat in the general election of 1929. His transfer of allegiance had proved timely, and in Ramsay MacDonald's second administration he became secretary of state for might cause temporary annoyance, and once Lord Hailsham carried a motion that 'the noble lord be no longer heard', but Stansgate's patent sincerity, his complete freedom from malice, and his natural modesty of manner, made many admirers. While his perpetual effervescence, buoyancy, and wit conveyed an impression of the gay cavalier, 'Wedgy Benn' was really the happy warrior, a man of profound ethical conviction, with a great love for his fellow human beings.

Stansgate was taken ill in the Palace of Westminster on 16 November 1960 while waiting to speak. He had closed the previous day's proceedings with some brief observations on the importance of continued friendship with India. He was taken to Westminster Hospital, where he died on 17 November 1960. His eldest son, a flight lieutenant who was awarded the DFC, had died in 1944 of injuries received in action. His second son, Anthony Neil Wedgwood (Tony) Benn (b. 1925), was elected Labour member for Bristol South East in 1950. Though he sought to renounce the succession, he was held to be disqualified from the Commons after his father's death. He headed the poll at the ensuing by-election in May 1961 but was again ruled disqualified, and so began a protest that resulted in the 1963 Peerage Act, which made possible the renunciation of a hereditary peerage. Having duly disclaimed his title, Benn was returned, unopposed, for Bristol South East in August 1963. He went on to become postmaster-general in the Labour government of 1964, entered the cabinet as minister of technology in 1966, and was a candidate for the Labour leadership in 1976 and 1988. The viscountcy remained in abeyance.

LESLIE HALE, *rev.* MARK POTTLE

Sources W. W. Benn, *In the side shows* (1919) · W. W. Benn and M. Benn, *Beckoning horizon: the story of a journey round the world* (1935) · *The Times* (18 Nov 1960) · personal knowledge (1971) · K. Harris, *Attlee* (1982) · Burke, *Peerage* (1999) · *CGPLA Eng. & Wales* (1961) · m. cert. · d. cert. [Margaret Eadie Benn]
Archives HLRO, corresp. and papers | BL OIOC, corresp. with Lord Halifax, MS Eur. C 152 · BL OIOC, corresp. with Sir Frederick Sykes, MS Eur. F 150 · HLRO, letters to Herbert Samuel · HLRO, letters to David Lloyd George · King's Lond., Liddell Hart C., corresp. with Sir B. H. Liddell Hart · NA Scot., corresp. with Lord Lothian · NRA, priv. coll., corresp. with Lord Irwin · Women's Library, London, corresp. with Eleanor Rathbone
Likenesses W. Stoneman, photograph, 1917, NPG · O. Edis, photograph, 1920, NPG [*see illus.*] · T. Cottrell, cigarette card, NPG
Wealth at death £37,888 10s. 9d.: probate, 1 Aug 1961, *CGPLA Eng. & Wales*

Bennelong (*c.*1765–1813), Aboriginal visitor to England, belonged to the Wangal band of the Eora people, who lived on the southern shore of Port Jackson, between what is now central Sydney and Parramatta. He was sometimes called Wolarawaree and also Ogultroyee. Following the British settlement of January 1788 he was one of a number of local men who became well acquainted with the invaders. As Watkin Tench, one of the officers, remarked, 'His powers of mind were far above mediocrity' (Fitzhardinge, 160), and he led the way in coming to terms with the British. He was vain and quick-tempered, but also a loyal friend, a comedian, gentle with children, and with no hint of cowardice.

Bennelong (*c.*1765–1813), by James Neagle, pubd 1798

From the beginning of settlement the governor, Arthur Phillip, tried to maintain good relations with the Aborigines. Finding that they kept their distance at first, he ordered the capture of several men with the hope that they might be a means of mediation with their own people. Bennelong was brought to headquarters in November 1789. He managed to escape in May 1790, but by that time he had learned a good deal about his captors and had also freely taught Phillip and other officers about his own language and culture. He afterwards regarded Phillip as his friend and often lived at Government House, dining at the governor's table. In 1790 a hut was built for him on what is now Bennelong Point.

Bennelong was clearly impressed with European artefacts, especially blankets, which resembled the possumskin rugs which were highly prized ritual items among his people. He was also inspired by what he understood of Phillip's authority among the settlers and by the significance of Government House within the refashioned landscape at Sydney Cove. Power to remake the land, according to Aboriginal belief, belonged to ancestral figures, inhabitants of the dreaming, and Bennelong seems to have thought of Phillip in these terms. The name Be-anna, or Father, which he used for the governor, suggests a wish to create ties of spiritual kinship within the new religious dispensation existing at Sydney Cove. So does his request that his wife, Barangaroo (d. 1790x92), be allowed to give birth at Government House. Places of birth and burial were of vital importance for spiritual identity. The child, Dilboong, was in fact born at the government hospital, but following her early death she was buried in the governor's yard. Bennelong persuaded the governor to participate in such family ceremonies.

In December 1792 Bennelong sailed with Phillip for England, where he is said to have been presented to the king; he returned with the second governor, John Hunter, in September 1795. He had taken a second wife, Gooroobarooboloo, before Barangaroo's death, but she had since found another husband. Bennelong now hoped to spread English ideas of civility among his own people, but his authority among them had waned and with Phillip gone he no longer cut such a significant figure among the

Europeans. However, he proved his daring yet again in 1796, by sailing to Norfolk Island.

Bennelong died at Kissing Point, near Sydney, on 3 January 1813 and was buried in the garden of James Squire's inn nearby. A son born after his return from England was educated, apparently to an impressive standard, and baptized Thomas Walker Coke, but died in 1823 aged about twenty. Many young Aboriginal men and women have taken advantage of culture and artefacts brought from Europe to enhance their authority among their own people. This was Bennelong's ambition, and his extraordinary imagination, together with the dramatic circumstances of first settlement in Australia, make his case especially significant.   ALAN ATKINSON

Sources D. Collins, *An account of the English colony in New South Wales*, 2 vols. (1798–1802) · W. Tench, *Sydney's first four years: being a reprint of 'A narrative of the expedition to Botany Bay' and 'A complete account of the settlement at Port Jackson'*, ed. L. F. Fitzhardinge (1979) · A. Atkinson, *The Europeans in Australia: a history*, 1: *The beginning* (1997) · I. McBryde, *Guests of the governor: Aboriginal residents of the first Government House* (1989) · *Sydney Gazette* (9 Jan 1813) · F. Péron, *Voyage de découvertes aux terres australes*, 1 (1817)
Likenesses watercolour, *c*.1790, Watling Collection · watercolour, 1790–99, State Library of New South Wales, Australia, Dixson Galleries · J. Neagle, engraving, pubd 1798, National Library of Australia, Canberra [*see illus.*] · engraving, repro. in Collins, *Account of the English colony*, p. 439

Bennet, Abraham (*bap.* **1749**, *d.* **1799**), Church of England clergyman and natural philosopher, was baptized in Taxal, Cheshire, on 20 December 1749, the son of Abraham Bennet, schoolmaster, of Whaley Lane, Cheshire, and his wife, Ann Fallowes of Cheadle. He appears to have been the eldest child, with at least one brother, William. On 5 April 1774 he married Jane Fallowes (presumably related to his mother's family); they had two sons and six daughters. In September 1775 he was ordained in London and appointed to Derbyshire curacies, first at Tideswell, and the next year at Wirksworth at a doubled annual stipend of £60, where he remained for the rest of his life; Bennet also taught at Wirksworth grammar school. He became domestic chaplain to the duke of Devonshire at nearby Chatsworth, and perpetual curate at Woburn and librarian there to the duke of Bedford. For the last three years of his life he also held the living of Fenny Bentley in Derbyshire.

Bennet maintained links with local natural philosophers, including Josiah Wedgwood at Etruria, Joseph Priestley at Birmingham, and Erasmus Darwin at Derby, who encouraged him to begin a weather diary to record atmospheric electricity, a principal interest of Darwin and other electrical experimenters such as Priestley and Benjamin Franklin. In September 1786 Bennet sent Priestley an account of an electrometer (soon published in the *Philosophical Transactions of the Royal Society*) that could detect such electricity using the repulsion of thin gold leaves in an earthed glass bottle, 5 inches high, with a flat brass cap. Atmospheric electricity could be gathered by putting a candle on the cap or connecting it to a kite during lightning storms. This robust device, used in Birmingham, Etruria, and London, proved popular. In December

1786 Bennet described using the electrometer with marble and metal plates to condense electricity in the manner set out in 1782 by Alessandro Volta. Such an instrument had been outlined by Darwin in 1778 before it received a fuller treatment in Volta's paper.

In May 1787 Bennet published extracts from his electro-meteorological diary in the *Transactions*, along with a detailed account of his new device to make weak atmospheric electricity detectable by repeated doubling using brass plates as condensers. He gathered atmospheric electricity from a candle flame (or, if it was raining, from an umbrella handle) onto a Leyden jar, then brought the jar indoors to charge the electrometer cap. After earthing a varnished brass plate on the cap, Bennet would lift it off the electrometer with an insulating mahogany handle, making the leaves in the electrometer separate. Then he would bring the plate into contact with another varnished plate, earth the latter, and separate them, giving a charge to the second plate of the same sign and size as that initially given to the top of the electrometer. Touching this plate to the electrometer cap while the first plate also sat on it and was grounded doubled the initial charge on the cap. The agile Bennet could double the charge twenty times in about forty seconds. Darwin lauded Bennet's process to Franklin in May 1787, and in 1788 the natural philosopher William Nicholson of London mechanized the process, using a winch to turn a metal disc round a central metal ball. Bennet claimed he had been on the point of mechanizing his own apparatus when Nicholson announced his scheme to the Royal Society.

In 1789 Bennet was elected a fellow of the society. With support from Darwin, Wedgwood, and Priestley, he published at Derby new accounts of what became known as Bennet's electrometer and doubler in *New Experiments on Electricity* (1789). He endorsed the French theory that atmospheric electricity stemmed from the evaporation of water through solar heat. Following trials in the 1770s by the natural philosopher Georg Lichtenberg of Göttingen, Bennet worked on 'adhesive electricity', making dust figures on the surface of an electrified resin cake. The expert potter Wedgwood helped Bennet to fix these figures by covering the cake with powdered enamel, then baking it, thus potentially allowing the effects of atmospheric electricity on such figures to be recorded. In autumn 1789 Bennet worked with Darwin to test whether iron filings became more magnetic when mixed with dilute sulphuric acid, and whether inflammable air were magnetic. In both cases Bennet decided in the negative. For these experiments he suspended a magnetic needle within a glass jar from a spider's thread, a sensitive device that could also be used to detect wind currents. He published his results in the *Transactions* in early 1792. In November 1795 Bennet sent an account of an earthquake to the Royal Society, and suggested an electrical cause of such phenomena. In December 1795 he signed a Derby petition against Jacobinism and in support of the war with France. He died in Wirksworth after a severe illness, and was buried on 9 May 1799.   SIMON SCHAFFER

Sources A. Bennet, *New experiments on electricity* (1789) · A. Bennet, 'Description of a new electrometer', *PTRS*, 77 (1787), 26–34 · A. Bennet, 'An account of a doubler of electricity', *PTRS*, 77 (1787), 288–96 · *The letters of Erasmus Darwin*, ed. D. King-Hele (1981) · J. L. Heilbron, *Electricity in the 17th and 18th centuries: a study of early modern physics* (1979) · A. Bennet, 'A new suspension of the magnetic needle', *PTRS*, 82 (1792), 81–98 · *Derby Mercury* (23 May 1799) · *IGI* · P. Elliott, 'Abraham Bennet', *Notes and Records of the Royal Society*, 53 (1999), 59–78
Archives Derby Local Studies Library
Likenesses oils, St Mary's Church, Wirksworth, Derbyshire

Bennet, Benjamin (*c.*1674–1726), Presbyterian minister, was born at Wellsborough, a hamlet in the parish of Sibson, near Market Bosworth, Leicestershire, the son of Robert Bennet (*d.* 1686), a substantial tenant farmer of the Hall House, Wellsborough, and his wife, Patience Somerfield (*d.* 1718). His father died in 1686 leaving him grazing ground and the meadow that he rented, together with £100 in money or stock, but Bennet determined on the ministry. 'A dangerous Illness he had while young, contributed to make the most serious Impressions on him', and he met regularly in private prayer with other young persons among whom he awakened 'a serious Concern for their Souls' (Worthington, 25). He was educated for the nonconformist ministry at John Woodhouse's academy at Sheriffhales, Shropshire.

On the removal of John Sheffield to Southwark in 1697, Bennet succeeded him as minister of the Presbyterian meeting at Temple Hall, which adjoins Wellsborough. He was ordained with three other ministers at Oldbury, Shropshire, on 30 May 1699. Following the death in February 1700 of Richard Gilpin, minister of Close Gate meeting, Newcastle upon Tyne, Bennet was invited to succeed him. Thomas Bradbury had become Gilpin's assistant on Timothy Manlove's death in August 1699. Bradbury had hopes of being chosen as Gilpin's successor, or at least as co-pastor, but the congregation preferred Bennet, who was related to Manlove, with Bradbury as his assistant. After about three years Bradbury left to become assistant to the Revd John Galpin at Stepney. According to the 1715 'Evans list', Bennet had a very substantial meeting of 700 hearers and was assisted in turn by Nathaniel Fancourt, who departed to Salisbury in 1719, William Wilson, and finally Samuel Lawrence (1693–1760), his successor. Bennet baptized the poet Mark Akenside in 1721, who later attended Wilson's school. Bennet was married, but nothing is known of his marriage except that his wife died in 1718 and that he had a daughter, who subsequently married Lemuel Latham.

During the winter of 1713–14, with fears of a return of the Stuarts on the death of Queen Anne, Bennet preached a series of sermons published as *Several Discourses Against Popery* (1714). His major controversial work, *A Memorial of the Reformation* (1717), was planned originally as a 'few Sheets' to introduce a sermon preached on King George's coronation 'connecting former with later Deliverances'. The *Memorial* was intended not as a history of the Reformation, but 'to celebrate Providence in our National Deliverances, among which that grand Deliverance from Popery'

(Preface, unpaginated). It contained, however, some original details, such as Judge Jeffreys's visit to Newcastle in 1683. The partiality of the account and Bennet's treatment of such controversial subjects as the civil war and the execution of Charles I drew him into a controversy with the Anglican divine Zachary Grey following the publication of the second edition in 1721, which carried the account to 1719 and was dedicated to Lord Barrington. Grey published anonymously three works ridiculing Bennet's efforts: *Presbyterian Prejudice Display'd* (1722), *A Letter of Thanks to Mr. Benjamin Bennet* (1723), and *A caveat against Mr Benjamin Bennet … proving from some of his late performances, how little qualify'd he is, to be either an historian, or critick* (1724), but Bennet in his *Defence of the 'Memorial of the Reformation'* (1723) had the better of the historical argument.

Bennet published his *Irenicum* (1722) as a result of the controversy among dissenters over the Trinity. Although Bennet was orthodox in doctrine, he defended the right of private judgement in matters of conscience, arguing that although certain doctrines can be regarded as fundamental, 'Thousands, I doubt not, we shall find in Heaven at last, who had but very dark and confused Notions of some Articles … and some who had no Notions at all of them' (Bennet, 57). The work created a great sensation and John Atkinson, Independent minister at Stainton, Westmorland, published a reply.

Bennet's most celebrated work was *The Christian Oratory, or, The Devotion of the Closet Display'd* (1725), intended to provide a directory of meditations on various subjects for the Christian in his 'oratory' or place of retirement. It had gone through six editions by 1760, including a very cheap subscription edition in 1756, and was also translated into Dutch. After Bennet's death Lemuel Latham published the *Second Part of 'The Christian Oratory'* (1728) from Bennet's manuscript remains. By the early nineteenth century the whole had been abridged and revised as the dissenter's *Whole Duty of Man*, edited by Charles Atmore (1811), and in America as *Devout Meditations from the Christian Oratory* (1819). It was this work which established Bennet's reputation and explains the later interest in his life. He published a volume of *Occasional Hymns* (1722), a collection largely derived from others, but including twenty-one of his own.

Bennet 'had an excellent Talent at managing an Argument … in its utmost Force and Strength … He was a very close indefatigable Student', devoting fifty, sometimes sixty, hours a week to study (Worthington, 27). In 1726 his congregation built a new meeting-house in Hanover Square, Westgate Street, Newcastle, but Bennet did not live to see it opened. He died of a fever at Newcastle on 1 September 1726, having fallen ill the day before the new meeting-house was due to open. DAVID L. WYKES

Sources I. Worthington, *A sermon occasion'd by the death of the Reverend … Benjamin Bennet* (1727) · 'A sketch of the life and character of the Rev. Benjamin Bennet, author of "The Christian oratory": extracted from his funeral sermon, preached by the Rev. J. [*sic*] Worthington 1726', *Protestant Dissenter's Magazine*, 5 (1798), 361–5 · J. T[oulmin], 'Biography: a review of the life, writings and character of the Rev. Benjamin Bennet, of Newcastle upon Tyne', *Monthly Repository*, 2 (1807), 341–5, 453–9 · D. Bogue and J. Bennett, *A history* *of the dissenters from the revolution in 1688 to the year 1808* (1810), 3.429ff. • biographical account of Benjamin Bennet, DWL, Walter Wilson MS F1, fols. 325–36 • J. Evans, 'List of dissenting congregations and ministers in England and Wales, 1715–1729', DWL, MS 38.4 • W. Turner, *A short sketch of the history of protestant nonconformity and of the society assembling in Hanover-Square, Newcastle* (1811) • R. Welford, *The church and congregation of the Divine Unity, Newcastle upon Tyne* (1904) • will and inventory, Leics. RO, 1686/60; PR/I/88/73 [R. Bennet] • parish register (marriage), 29 June 1658, Newtown Linford [R. Bennet and P. Somerfield] • B. Bennet, *Irenicum, or, A review of some late controversies about the Trinity, private judgment, church authority, etc.* (1722)

Archives Congregational Library, London, MS sermons
Likenesses J. Pine, line engraving, NPG; repro. in J. T[oulmin], 'Biography', 341
Wealth at death £50: U. Durham L., archives and special collections; Durham probate records A145; administration, 1729

Bennet, Christopher (1617–1655), physician, born in Somerset, was the son of John Bennet of Raynton in that county. He matriculated from Lincoln College, Oxford, on 7 December 1632, aged fifteen, graduated BA on 24 May 1636, and proceeded MA on 24 January 1639. He did not graduate in medicine at Oxford but was incorporated MA at St Catharine's College, Cambridge, and graduated MD there in 1646. On 11 September of the same year he was admitted a licentiate of the College of Physicians, London, on 16 July 1647 a candidate, and on 7 December 1649 a fellow of the college, where he was censor in 1654. Bennet practised first at Bristol (for how long is not known) and afterwards in London, where he acquired a considerable reputation.

Bennet was best known for his *Theatri tabidorum vestibulum* (1654), a treatise on consumption, the disease which eventually killed him. From its title and from certain allusions the treatise was apparently intended to be the introduction to a larger work. It examines various forms of wasting disease, dealing more with what would be now called pathology than with treatment, in which it was quite traditional. The work is notable for the constant reference to cases observed, 'explanatory histories', and to dissections, not to classical authorities, which make the treatise stand out as an example of the Baconian method applied in medicine. The book was republished a number of times after Bennet's death, and was translated into English in 1720. His edition of *Health's Improvement, or, Rules for Preparing All Sorts of Food* by Thomas Muffett was published in 1655.

Bennet's life was cut short by consumption at the age of thirty-eight. He died in London on 30 April 1655, and was buried on 2 May in the church of St Gregory by Paul.

J. F. PAYNE, rev. PATRICK WALLIS

Sources Foster, *Alum. Oxon.* • Venn, *Alum. Cant.* • Munk, *Roll* • A. Kippis and others, eds., *Biographia Britannica, or, The lives of the most eminent persons who have flourished in Great Britain and Ireland*, 2nd edn, 2 (1780), 193 • Wood, *Ath. Oxon.* • B. Harey, *Bustorum aliquot reliquiae*, BL, Sloane MS 2149
Likenesses P. Lombart, line engraving, BM, NPG; repro. in C. Bennet, *Theatri tabidorum vestibulum* (1654), attached to prefix

Bennet, Edward Armstrong (1888–1977), psychiatrist, was born on 21 October 1888 in Poyntzpass, co. Down, Ireland, the younger of twin sons, and last of the five children born to William Boyd Bennet (d. 1897), farmer, and his wife, Marion, *née* McCaldin (d. 1933). On his father's death the family moved to Belfast, where Edward Bennet (Eddie) attended Campbell College. At the age of sixteen he entered Trinity College, Dublin, taking an honours degree and medal in philosophy in 1908. After further studies he read theology at Ridley Hall, Cambridge, in 1912, and was ordained in the Church of England in September 1913. He worked for a year in a deprived Liverpool parish, but at the outbreak of war in 1914 he volunteered as an army chaplain. Serving in France, he was awarded the Military Cross for gallantry at Thiepval in 1916; later he was posted to Mesopotamia. After the war Bennet returned to Trinity College to study medicine, attracted from the first to psychiatry. Qualifying in 1925, he joined the staff of the Tavistock Clinic in London, then the pioneering centre for psychotherapy. On 21 December 1926 he married Annie Flora Newbery (*née* Wylie; d. 1952), daughter of the Revd Alexander Wylie, of Edinburgh, and widow of Dr Theodore Newbery. They lived at 2 St Katharine's Precinct in Regent's Park, where their two sons were born.

Bennet's work expanded within the developing field of psychotherapy: his clinical work extended to the West End Hospital for Nervous Diseases; he also lectured there, as well as at the Tavistock Clinic and in Trinity College, Dublin. Bennet was already contributing to medical and psychiatric literature, and Trinity College conferred his MD in 1930, and in 1939 honoured him with the ScD. In 1938–9 he was chairman of the medical section of the British Psychological Society. Significant among the events of these years was his meeting with Professor C. G. Jung, who visited London in 1935 to lecture at the Tavistock Clinic. Already familiar with Jung's published work, Bennet now sought closer understanding of his thought from Jung himself, and visited him in Zürich from time to time until the outbreak of war in 1939; so began a friendship which lasted until Jung's death.

During the Second World War Bennet served in the Royal Army Medical Corps from 1939 to 1942 as command psychiatrist to South-Eastern command, and from 1942 to 1945 as consultant in psychiatry to India and Burma command with the rank of brigadier. Here he contributed much to the psychiatric service in India, and many of his contacts with Indian psychiatrists continued after the war when he was appointed consulting psychiatrist to the Commonwealth Relations Office. After returning to civilian life in 1946 he took up his former hospital work and private practice, and renewed his contact with Jung. In 1948 he was appointed senior physician in psychotherapy at the Maudsley Hospital, London, where his responsibilities included postgraduate clinical teaching and lecturing at the Institute of Psychiatry. In this capacity his presentation of Jung's analytical psychology was appreciated, as no formal teaching on Jung's work had previously been given.

Bennet's background of philosophy and theology disposed him to value Jung's approach over that of other approaches current in the 1930s (notably that of Freud). Jung's ideas formed the theoretical ground for his clinical approach, and he described these succinctly in many of his writings. He was particularly influenced by the idea that there is a creative potential in most mental disturbance, and that people can be helped through their difficulties on to a more fulfilling life. This is in contrast to the medical view of mental disturbance as an illness, a regrettable occurrence which must be disposed of.

Bennet had a busy and successful clinical psychiatric practice. He would see people from Britain and other countries with a wide range of psychiatric disorders. Because of this, he would adapt his treatment method to the person in front of him, and was not limited to the techniques of psychotherapy and analysis. Occasionally he would use drugs, although drugs influencing depression, for example, were still fairly rudimentary; he would also, rarely, recommend electro-convulsive therapy.

For most of the patients referred to him psychotherapy was the preferred treatment. Bennet used no couch in his consultations, and his interviews followed no preconceived procedure, but were informal dialogues in which the patient's problems, dreams, or other material were discussed. The course of treatment varied with each patient, and with the nature of their problem, sometimes developing into a long analysis, but not always. Many people came to him seeking a specifically Jungian analysis. Some of these were people in mid-life, or older, whose problems led them to search for personal development; others were younger doctors who came to him for training analysis, and there was a smaller group who similarly came to him for training from abroad. Bennet possessed a profound capacity for human understanding and empathy and, in the course of analysis, his warm responsiveness to the needs of his patients influenced and helped them.

After retiring from his hospital appointments in 1953 Bennet continued the personal psychotherapy central to his work in private practice. His lecturing also continued for a number of years. He served on two BMA committees: the hypnotism subcommittee in 1953, and the drug addiction committee from 1955 to 1961. In 1954 he was a member of the archbishop of Canterbury's commission on spiritual healing. He was elected a foundation fellow of the Royal College of Psychiatrists in 1971. His contributions to medical and psychiatric literature had continued throughout his career and reflected the broad medical base of his work, most of them concerning the recognition, treatment, or social aspects of psychoneuroses. His book *C. G. Jung* was published shortly before Jung's death in 1961. His later book *What Jung Really Said* (1966) was based on the exposition of Jung's work which he presented in his lectures at the Maudsley Hospital.

In appearance Bennet was of slight build, his voice and manner gentle, humour never far away. Within lay a quiet firmness of character that found expression in the steady gaze of his eyes. In conversation he was an attentive listener, perceptive of what was important in people's lives. The course of his life brought him a wide circle of friends; he deeply valued companionship, and he was a generous and genial host, amusing and well informed.

On 10 May 1958 he had married Frances Eveline,

younger daughter of Ida and the Revd R. F. R. Routh. He died on 7 March 1977 of pneumonia at their home in St Katharine's Precinct, survived by his wife and his two sons. His ashes were buried in the Bennet family grave in Poyntzpass churchyard, co. Down. GLIN BENNET

Sources personal knowledge (2004) · private information (2004) · b. cert. · m. certs. · d. cert. · H. V. Dicks, *Fifty years of the Tavistock Clinic* (1970) · E. A. Bennet, *Meetings with Jung* (1985) · *BMJ* (19 March 1977), 782 · *The Lancet* (2 April 1977), 763 · *CGPLA Eng. & Wales* (1977)
Archives Carl Jung Archives, Zürich
Likenesses portrait, repro. in *BMJ*
Wealth at death £42,694: probate, 23 May 1977, *CGPLA Eng. & Wales*

Bennet, George (1750/51–1835), Hebraist and Presbyterian minister; details of his upbringing and parents are unknown. He passed a great portion of his life in the study of Hebrew and he was well acquainted with the learning of the rabbis, who were in his opinion more accustomed, if not better able, than Christian commentators to interpret the Hebrew Bible. One of the principal contributors to the *British Critic*, Bennet reviewed from time to time the works of some of the most celebrated English divines, and as a young man he became acquainted with many eminent theologians of his day. He was minister of a small congregation in Carlisle, and he corresponded on intimate terms with Isaac Milner, dean of Carlisle, and his brother Joseph the historian, with archdeacons William Paley, William Markham, and Edward Nares, and with bishops Beilby Porteus and Samuel Horsley. It was the learning and power of writing displayed in his criticisms of their works which induced Horsley and others to enquire of Archdeacon Nares, then editor of the *British Critic*, the name of the reviewer to whom they were indebted for such able and luminous articles. In 1796 Bennet published *A display of the spirit and designs of those who, under the pretence of reform, aim at the subversion of the constitution and government of this kingdom*, an attack on defenders of the French revolution. Four years later there appeared his *Olam Hanashamoth* which Horsley, seldom forthcoming with his praise, warmly commended in his *Hosea* (1801). In the following year Bennet received an honorary DD from Harvard College, Boston. Despite pressure from his friends Bennet refused to take Anglican orders and moved instead to become minister at Strathmiglo, Fife, a position secured for him by the earl of Mansfield on the request of Archdeacon Markham, his brother-in-law. Bennet died at Strathmiglo in 1835, aged eighty-four.

JAMES MEW, *rev.* PHILIP CARTER

Sources *N&Q*, 6th ser., 7 (1883), 334–5 · Watt, *Bibl. Brit.* · W. Orme, *Bibliotheca biblica* (1824) · review, *British Critic*, 11 (1798), 326–8 · C. T. Ramage, *Drumlanrig Castle and the Douglases* (1876)

Bennet, Henry (*fl.* 1561), translator, probably of Calais, published in 1561, at the press of John Awdelay, a volume of translations from the German reformers. The book is divided into two parts; the first contains Philip Melanchthon's life of Luther, Luther's declaration of his doctrine before the emperor Charles at Worms, and an oration of Melanchthon's at Wittenberg, given in place of his usual 'grammatical' exposition of the epistle to the Romans, after a short 'intimation' of the news of Luther's death. This part is prefaced by a dedication to Thomas, Lord Wentworth, dated 18 November 1561. The second part has a similar dedication to Lord Mountjoy, dated 'the last of November' 1561, and consists of a life of John Ecolampadius by Wolfangus Faber Capito, an account of his death by Simon Grineus, and a life of Ulrich (Huldreich) Zwingli by Oswald Miconius; the last two are in the form of letters. The two parts were published together. The translations are careful and idiomatic, and the quotations of Ecolampadius from Homer and Euripides are turned into English verse.

Bennet may be identical with the 'doctour Bennet' who was part of the audience who greeted Cardinal Wolsey on his arrival in Calais in July 1527.

RONALD BAYNE, *rev.* CHRISTOPHER BURLINSON

Sources STC, 1475–1640 · J. G. Nichols, ed., *The chronicle of Calais, in the reigns of Henry VII and Henry VIII to the year 1540* (1846) · Tanner, *Bibl. Brit.-Hib.*

Bennet, Henry, first earl of Arlington (*bap.* 1618, *d.* 1685), politician, was baptized at Little Saxham, Suffolk, on 6 September 1618, the second son of Sir John Bennet (1589–1658), landowner, of Dawley, Harlington, Middlesex, and Dorothy, daughter of Sir John Crofts of Little Saxham. He was educated at Westminster School until 1635 and then went up to Christ Church, Oxford; he graduated BA in 1639, proceeded MA in May 1642, and gained the reputation of a scholar and poet. John Sheffield, duke of Buckingham, later wrote that few were 'so well versed in the classic poets … [and] I never knew any man apply them so properly on any subject whatsoever, and without any pedantic affection' (*Works of … Buckingham*, 2.84–8).

Royalist, exile, and diplomat Bennet was thought to be destined for the church but the civil war intervened and in 1643 he entered the service of George, Lord Digby, secretary of state to Charles I. 1644 was the occasion of his only known military action, as a volunteer in a skirmish at Andover, in which he gained the scar on the bridge of his nose that he bore for the rest of his life. In later years he was prone to emphasizing his contribution to the royal cause by placing a black plaster over the scar, to the amusement of many satirists. Bennet continued in the army until its return to Oxford in November 1644 and then acted as courier for various royal notables, visiting Paris, Rome, and Dublin. He came into frequent contact with the marquess of Ormond, Queen Henrietta Maria, and Charles, prince of Wales. With the collapse of royal fortunes in Ireland, Bennet finally joined the exiled court at St Germain in September 1647.

By the following year Bennet had proved personable enough to be appointed secretary to James, duke of York. He soon joined Henrietta Maria's faction and was regarded as a creature of her lord chamberlain, Henry, Baron Jermyn. After Charles II returned from Scotland in 1651, however, Bennet shifted his position and sought to join the king's party. He found favour with Charles II, who wrote to the duke of York in 1654 that he was 'full of duty

Henry Bennet, first earl of Arlington (*bap.* 1618, *d.* 1685), by Sir Peter Lely and studio, *c*.1673

and integrity' (*Letters … of Charles II*, 30). When Charles left France in 1654 Bennet remained behind with James, who regarded him coolly as entirely the king's man. Bennet made two lengthy visits to the king's court at Cologne and saw the king installed at Bruges in 1656 before returning to James in Paris. Bennet and the rest of James's entourage joined the king's court in September 1656 and, after an unsuccessful court intrigue against one of James's followers, Sir John Berkeley, Bennet was knighted in March 1657 and sent on a diplomatic mission to Spain. There he discovered the Spanish courtier's formality, which stayed with him for the rest of his life. According to contemporary rumour he was also first attracted to the Catholic church during this period.

Bennet was still in Madrid at the time of the restoration of Charles II in May 1660 and did not return to England until April 1661, almost too late to obtain office in the new administration. He was immediately associated with the faction led by George Digby, now earl of Bristol, which included the king's mistress the countess of Castlemaine, and which opposed the powerful lord chancellor, Sir Edward Hyde, soon created earl of Clarendon. Clarendon, who had known and disliked Bennet in exile, viewed him as a rival and tried to prevent his advancement but in

August 1661 Bennet was made keeper of the king's privy purse, an appointment which brought him into close contact with Charles II. He used his position to advantage and on 15 October 1662 succeeded in replacing Sir Edward Nicholas, Clarendon's ally, as secretary of state for the south.

Secretary of state Bennet held the secretaryship until 11 September 1674, the longest serving secretary of the reign. Under Charles II a secretary of state needed to be a master of foreign and domestic affairs, a defender of government policies in parliament (the office also began to be involved in managing the House of Commons), and a gatherer of news and intelligence from all quarters. His proximity to the king enabled Bennet to have a significant influence on policy and he was certainly more interested in the opportunity to engage in high politics than the more mundane administrative aspects of his post. Bennet was nevertheless interested in efficient government and although not himself a great innovator he promoted talented men such as Sir Joseph Williamson, his undersecretary, and gave them a free hand in undertaking reforms.

By virtue of his position Bennet was also a privy councillor, and he added a number of other posts to his name, becoming a justice of the peace, postmaster-general (1667–77), a commissioner for trade (1668–72), and lord lieutenant of Suffolk (1681–4). He also served as MP for Callington from June 1661 to March 1665, but to no great effect. He seems to have spoken rarely in the Commons although he did serve on a number of committees, including that for explaining the Act of Settlement in Ireland in 1664 (taking a share of Irish lands in the process) and the committee for Tangier in 1665. He left the Commons for the House of Lords on being created Baron Arlington on 14 March 1665.

Arlington's craving for power was moderated by a fear of failure and a genuine timidity in his character which made him ever cautious, and his advice to the king was always circumspect. Thus, although he was personally in favour of religious toleration, particularly for Roman Catholics, he also thought it too risky, both for himself and the government, to express this fact openly. He warily supported the religious policies of Charles II, was certainly involved in the abortive declaration of indulgence of 1662, and returned to similar proposals in 1665 and 1672. Arlington, however, was always motivated less by his own religious sensibility than by a desire to keep religious dissenters quiet and raise cash through the issuing of licences to nonconformist ministers. He was less concerned with men's souls and more with an ordered society and money. In his own religious life, while he undoubtedly became pro-Catholic, possibly due to his preference for social order, grandeur, and stateliness (he always felt something of a parvenu), he did not risk converting during his active political career, had no trouble in taking all of the required oaths, and refrained from declaring his actual religious beliefs until his dying moments.

At court Arlington was notorious for remaining silent at council and cabinet meetings, having stated his views privately to the king beforehand. When required, however, he could display an admirable fluency and although some thought him arrogant, one foreign ambassador wrote that he was 'the most polite and obliging minister that the English court has' (CSP Venice, 1671–2, 67). Even Clarendon was forced to admit that he sometimes had a winning way, although he used his skills corruptly 'to make himself acceptable to any man who loved to hear himself commended and admired' (Scrope and Monkhouse, 3.lxxxii). He frequented the king's leisure parties and was himself a generous host. According to John Evelyn 'there is no man more hospitably easy to be withall than my L: Arlington' (Evelyn, 3.591). He was not above trying to influence the king's choice of mistress. In 1663 he intrigued with the duke of Buckingham to set up the maid of honour Frances Stuart as a royal mistress. Armed with 'a great number of fine maxims and some historical anecdotes' (Hamilton, 151), he apparently merely amused Frances with his pompous attempts to pimp for the king. Trying to keep all his options open, his hypocrisy was exposed on one occasion in 1666 when he was lamenting to Clarendon the 'many great miscarriages by the license of the court, and how much his majesty suffered thereby' (Life of ... Clarendon, 2.301–2). At that moment the king entered the room and enquired what they were discussing. Clarendon, much to Arlington's chagrin, frankly informed Charles, whereupon Arlington swiftly turned the matter into 'raillery' and diverted the king from any 'serious reflections' on the matter of his lifestyle, leaving Clarendon looking somewhat foolish (ibid.).

In the 1660s Arlington was responsible for furthering the careers of a number of men. Apart from Sir Joseph Williamson two others stand out: Thomas, Lord Clifford, who soon became a rival, and William Temple, one of Arlington's team of diplomatic contacts. In fact Arlington's clients eventually inhabited most of the major embassies of Europe: Temple in The Hague, William Godolphin in Madrid, Robert Southwell in Lisbon, John Trevor and Ralph Montagu in Paris. One client of Arlington claimed that of all the 'great men of England, there is none that endeavours to raise those he takes in to favour [more] than my Lord Arlington, and on that score, he is more to be made one's patron than my Lord Chancellor [Clarendon]' (Pepys, 8.185–6). By 1677, however, it was claimed that he was 'unfortunate ... in those he has advanc'd, proving ungratefull most of them' (Evelyn, 4.119).

In foreign affairs Arlington was generally in favour of a pro-Spanish, anti-French policy. He was suspected of being less than enthusiastic about the Anglo-Dutch War of 1665–7, particularly as in the middle of the conflict, on 16 April 1666, he married a Dutch aristocrat, Isabella (bap. 1633, d. 1718), daughter of Lodewyck van Nassau, heer van Beverweerd. Isabella, described by Evelyn as 'goodnatured, & obliging' (Evelyn, 4.118), brought Arlington some important connections: her father was an illegitimate son of Prince Maurice of Orange and cousin to William II of Orange, and was the Dutch envoy to England in 1660–

62, and her sister was married to the duke of Ormond's son, the earl of Ossory. The couple's only child, Isabella, nicknamed Tata by her affectionate father, was born in 1667. During the war Arlington set out to prove his usefulness by attempting, with the help of his clients Clifford, Williamson, and William Coventry, to manage the House of Commons and obtain supply, essential to financing the war. An anonymous pamphlet of 1669 claimed that in his early attempts at management Arlington was willing to 'give promises of this or that place, [and] telleth out ready money to these hirelings who engage to betray their country for it' (*English Historical Documents*, 8.235). His part in the notorious division of the fleet in 1666 was a major blot on his career. As secretary of state he was responsible for the intelligence that led to the English admirals dividing their forces and the earl of Albemarle attempting to fight the Dutch with only part of the fleet on 1–4 June. Although the faulty intelligence which began the whole incident could be laid at Arlington's door Clarendon's subsequent attempt to foist most of the blame on him was both malicious and misleading. The real problem lay in the divided command and other strategic errors made during the campaign, and Arlington's guilt was far less than that of the admirals.

The king's leading minister With the conclusion of the war Arlington found himself in a powerful position and turned on the duke of Buckingham, who was always more of a rival than an ally. Buckingham's involvement with astrologers and republicans, revealed by a helpful Arlington to Charles II, infuriated the king and led to Buckingham's brief incarceration in the Tower in 1667. Arlington also promoted the removal of Clarendon from office, although he was reluctant to pursue the matter much beyond this, fearing the consequences for his own safety should he set a precedent. He therefore stood back and allowed Buckingham to take the lead in calling for impeachment and pursuing Clarendon into exile. With the downfall of Clarendon, and Buckingham revealed as unreliable, Arlington reached his greatest influence. He shared Dutch concerns about French aggression in Spanish Flanders, and consequently backed a series of diplomatic moves that led to the alliance in 1668 between the British and the Dutch, soon joined by Sweden, known as the triple alliance. Its creation was to Arlington's credit and it was the most popular policy with which he had yet been associated. Britain and the Dutch republic agreed to assist one another should they be invaded, some concessions were to be made by Spain to French interests and a frontier created between Flanders and the republic. There is some claim that the triple alliance also brought a resentful Louis XIV to the negotiating table and resulted in the French–Spanish treaty of Aix-la-Chapelle. Almost as soon as the treaty was signed, however, it was undermined by Charles II's pro-French designs.

It became clear in 1669 that Charles had determined on a French alliance. Fearful of being seen as an obstruction to his master's plans, and apparently exasperated with the attitude of the Dutch and the Spanish, Arlington soon shifted his ground. He subsequently led the negotiations

with the French, being fully aware of the proposals for the king to become a Catholic and the English and French to attack the Dutch, and although some doubted his loyalty to the plan, Charles II did not. The king wrote to his sister Henriette Anne:

> I can say no more for him than I have already done, only that I think, being upon the place and observing everybody as well as I can, I am the best judge of his fidelity to me and what his inclinations are. And, if I should be deceived in the opinion I have of him, I am sure I should smart for it most. (*Letters … of Charles II*, 239–40)

Arlington appears to have refused Louis XIV's cash bribes (although not his presents), but he did eventually throw caution to the winds and become a signatory to the secret treaty of Dover in June 1670.

Although Arlington had misgivings about another war with the Dutch and seems (as did Charles II) to have tried to delay it for as long as possible, he supported the declaration of indulgence which immediately preceded it. Issued on 16 March 1672, the declaration suspended all the penal laws against nonconformists, including Catholics. In Arlington's opinion it provided a useful means of keeping nonconformists peaceable during the coming war, and when the whole design began to go awry in 1673 he advised the king to withdraw it. He later claimed that he was present during the formulation of the declaration, 'but as soon as I was convinced … it was contrary to law, I was the first man that advised to desist from what was tenable by law' (Cobbett, *Parl. hist.*, 4.653).

When the Third Anglo-Dutch War began in March 1672 Arlington had reached the peak of his career and was publicly rewarded for his services by promotion in the peerage to earl of Arlington and Viscount Thetford on 22 April 1672 and was made a knight of the Garter on 15 June 1672. He became even more closely connected with the king when his five-year-old daughter was betrothed on 1 August 1672 to Henry *Fitzroy, later duke of Grafton, second son of Charles II and the countess of Castlemaine. The war quickly began to go against England, the French land campaign soon appeared too successful for English interests, and it appeared that the French might come to an agreement with the Dutch. Arlington and Buckingham consequently were sent on a mission to Louis XIV. The former's presence was the more important in French eyes; he was 'an other self' to Charles II, aware of 'his most secret intentions and designs and [one who] possesses his confidence, his esteem and his friendship in the highest degree that a good subject could desire' (marquis de Croissy, quoted in Barbour, 191–2). Although the treaty of Heeswick was signed on 6 July 1672 reaffirming the Anglo-French alliance, the mission was not in the end a success, for it kept England in an increasingly unpopular war.

Arlington's rivalry with his ministerial colleagues remained intense. In particular he fell out with his former client Clifford on the latter's promotion to lord treasurer in November 1672, a post Arlington had always coveted. It was later alleged that this slight caused Arlington to reveal the secret treaty of Dover to the earl of Shaftesbury but there is little evidence for this. In 1673 the House of

Commons refused to consider supply for the war until the declaration of indulgence was withdrawn. Arlington, ever the pragmatist, advised compliance and may even have counselled the king to make his own separate peace with the Dutch. Parliament followed up its success with the Test Act, designed to force out any closet Roman Catholics. When Clifford, a Catholic, resigned from the Treasury Arlington was once again denied the post, Sir Thomas Osborne, later earl of Danby, being appointed. He was also foiled in his hopes for a dukedom and rumours began to circulate that his power was waning.

Declining powers, death, and reputation Rumours of Arlington's decline gathered pace in 1674 when the House of Commons attacked the king's ministers. On 14 January Buckingham appeared before the Commons and blamed Arlington for the regime's policies. The following day an impeachment was launched against Arlington, accusing him of promoting popery, advising war and government by an army, and working for his own self-aggrandizement and fortune. Arlington surprised everyone by his skilful defence, winning over a vengeful House of Commons with his subtle verbal dexterity. He denied all the charges, somewhat disingenuously claiming, 'As to my engrossing all affairs … 'tis not my nature so to do, and that I bear as uneasily as any man the burthen of my employment, and that I should think myself happy, could I with conveniency retire' (*CSP dom.*, 1673–5, 105). Some thought he 'gave so good an acc[oun]t of himselfe, that he not only wiped off all that dirt the Duke of Bucks had cast upon him … But gave the Howse a very good impression of his partes & capacitye for business' (Airy, 1.163). After his performance, when it was evident that he would survive, it was rumoured that his friends in the Commons even deliberately strove for an impeachment so that Arlington could be brought off as gloriously as possible. This brush with the forces of parliament, however, was too much for Arlington and he sought the quieter waters of a court post. He sold his secretaryship to Sir Joseph Williamson for £6000 and became lord chamberlain of the king's household in September 1674. He wrote that resigning from the secretary's office had delivered him of such a 'burthensom Imployment … [of] almost Twelve years, with more labour and Envy than I would willingly undergo, or indeed can support in my declining Age' (*Arlington's Letters*, 2.479).

In his new and less onerous post Arlington no doubt planned to spend more time cultivating his image as a patron of literature and the arts. Evelyn noted that in his later years Arlington 'never plays, but reades much, having both the Latine, French & Spanish tongues in perfection' (Evelyn, 4.118). The philosopher Thomas Hobbes was one who sought his patronage, dedicating the manuscript of 'Behemoth' to him. Arlington's London residence, Arlington House, near St James's Park, was extensively damaged in a fire in September 1674 to the loss of £40,000 to £50,000, but his country house, Euston Hall in Suffolk, remained as a monument to his grandeur. Purchased in 1666, over the years a lavishly grand house in the French style was constructed there, with gardens planned by Evelyn and Sir Samuel Morland, interior frescoes by Antonio Verrio, and a library 'full of excellent bookes' (Evelyn, 4.121). It was at Euston in 1671 that Charles II and his new mistress, Louise de Kéroualle, were alleged to have held a mock wedding and consummated their relationship during one of Arlington's lavish house parties.

In the mid-1670s Arlington skirted the fringes of opposition policies in response to the increasing power of the lord treasurer, Danby, whose rise he bitterly resented. He sought the friendship of the now outcast Shaftesbury and tried to use his still extensive network of clients to damage Danby. His efforts to gain credit by promoting a marriage between William of Orange and the duke of York's eldest daughter, Mary, however, annoyed most of the principal parties and his mission to the Netherlands to negotiate with William on this and other matters in November 1674 was a failure. It was said that he was also supporting the cause of the ambitious duke of Monmouth and rumour had it in January 1675 that he would be appointed lord lieutenant of Ireland in order to get him out of the way. Although Arlington stood aloof from attacks on Danby in the Lords in 1675 Charles II became convinced that he was supporting the unsuccessful impeachment attempt against the lord treasurer in the Commons in 1675 and consequently, although he hurled 'himself at all doors in the effort to re-enter affairs' (marquis de Ruvigny, quoted in Barbour, 253), his influence declined still further. His promotion of the duchess of Mazarin as a new mistress for the king in 1675–6 also proved a disappointment. He was probably happy to see the downfall of Danby in 1679 but his involvement, if any, is obscure and he regained none of his former power. During the crisis over the possible exclusion of the Catholic James from the succession in 1679–80 Arlington was something of a neutral figure. He remained friendly with Shaftesbury and Monmouth but was apparently one of the sponsors of a regency solution, and then voted against the Exclusion Bill in November 1680. In the early 1680s he sometimes became a focal point for factional infighting as a man whose power might, even at this late stage, return if the king so willed it. As lord chamberlain he remained a significant presence at court and in 1681 his wife was appointed groom of the stole to the queen.

Arlington retained the office of lord chamberlain under James II but, after a brief illness, he died on 28 July 1685 at Arlington House, leaving his estate to his wife, son-in-law, and daughter. On his deathbed he called for a Catholic priest but did not want his belated conversion known until after his death. James II was reported to have remarked with some disgust that he knew Arlington had been 'long wavering, but [for] feare of loosing his places [he] did not think it convenient to declare himself' (Evelyn, 4.476). He was buried in the south chapel of the church of St Geneviève, Euston Hall.

Clarendon wrote that Arlington was 'a man bred from his cradle in the Court, [who] had no other business in the world than to be a good courtier' (Scrope and Monkhouse, 3.lxxxi). Even a more sympathetic contemporary agreed that 'after all he was rather a subtle courtier, than an able Statesman' (*Works of ... Buckingham*, 2.87). Early historians took a negative view of his career, condemning him as dull and pompous, a backstairs intriguer not only lacking the talent but indeed the courage to bring him to real greatness. In modern times, however, Arlington's career has been reassessed. Well educated, cultivated, and fashionable, he sometimes found the rowdy atmosphere of Charles II's court distasteful but was politician enough to stoop low and play the game in order to gain power. An intelligent and shrewd man, he was tactful, civil, and ingratiating to his superiors, generous and obliging to his clients and social inferiors, and talented enough to work his way to the top. He was, moreover, well aware of the 'inconstancy of the country [so that he] proceeds very deliberately in dealing with serious matters ... and so while ripe in consultation he is correspondingly slow in execution' (*CSP Venice*, 1671–2, 68–9). 'Patience and shuffle againe' (Bodl. Oxf., MS Carte 221, fol. 52), he once said of an unsuccessful attempt to manage parliament, and this became his motto for life in general, his lengthy career attesting to his success as the court politician of his age.

ALAN MARSHALL

Sources *The right honourable the earl of Arlington's letters to Sir W. Temple, bart and to the several ambassadors to Spain*, ed. T. Bebington, 2 vols. (1701) • T. Brown, *Miscellanea Aulica, or, A collection of state treatises, never before published* (1702) • F. A. M. Mignet, ed., *Négociations relatives à la succession d'Espagne sous Louis XIV*, 4 vols. (Paris, 1835–42) • V. Barbour, *Henry Bennet, earl of Arlington, secretary of state to Charles II* (Washington, 1914) • M. Lee, *The cabal* (Urbana, IL, 1965) • R. Hutton, *Charles the Second: king of England, Scotland and Ireland* (1989) • Evelyn, *Diary* • *Works of John, earl of Mulgrave, marquess of Normanby, and duke of Buckingham*, 2 vols. (1729) • G. de F. Lord and others, eds., *Poems on affairs of state: Augustan satirical verse, 1660–1714*, 7 vols. (1963–75) • A. Hamilton, *Memoirs of Count Gramont*, ed. A. Fea (1906) • *The letters, speeches and declarations of Charles II*, ed. A. Bryant (New York, 1968) • C. MacCormick, ed., *The secret history of the court and reign of Charles the Second by a member of his privy council*, 2 vols. (1792) • Bodl. Oxf., MS Carte 221 • *English historical documents*, 8, ed. A. Browning (1953) • *CSP Venice, 1671–2* • R. Scrope and T. Monkhouse, eds., *State papers collected by Edward, earl of Clarendon*, 3 vols. (1767–86) • *The life of Edward, earl of Clarendon ... written by himself*, 2 vols. (1857) • Pepys, *Diary* • Cobbett, *Parl. hist.* • *CSP dom., 1660–85* • O. Airy, ed., *Essex papers*, CS, new ser., 47 (1890) • C. E. Pike, ed., *Selections from the correspondence of Arthur Capel, earl of Essex, 1675–1677*, CS, 3rd ser., 24 (1913) • H. Forneron, *Louise de Keroualle, duchess of Portsmouth, 1649–1734*, 2nd edn (1887) • J. P. Ferris, 'Bennet, Sir Henry', HoP, *Commons, 1660–90* • R. Hutton, 'The making of the secret treaty of Dover', *HJ*, 29 (1986), 297–318 • *Seventh report*, HMC, 6 (1879) • P. Milton, 'Hobbes, heresy and Lord Arlington', *History of Political Thought*, 14 (1993), 501–46 • *The works of Sir William Temple, bart, to which is prefix'd, the life and character of the author, written by a particular friend: never before publish'd with his works*, 2nd edn, 2 vols. (1731) • C. Macleod and J. M. Alexander, eds., *Painted ladies: women at the court of Charles II* (2001) [exhibition catalogue, NPG, 11 Oct 2001–6 Jan 2002; Yale U. CBA, 25 Jan – 17 March 2002] • *The autobiography of Sir John Bramston*, ed. [Lord Braybrooke], CS, 32 (1845) • GEC, *Peerage*, new edn • memorial, church of St Genevieve, Euston Hall, Suffolk • will, PRO, PROB 11/381, fol. 130

Archives BL, corresp., Add. MSS 16272, 34077–34079, 34330–34341, *passim* • BL, letter-book with dukes of Monmouth, Buckingham, and Halifax during their embassy in France and Low Countries • N. Yorks. CRO, corresp. • NL Scot., corresp. and papers • Northants. RO, corresp. and papers • Suffolk RO, Bury St Edmunds, accounts for paving London house | BL, corresp. with Sir Edward Dering, Stowe MSS 744–745, *passim* • BL, letters, etc. to Lord Essex, Stowe MSS 200–212 *passim* • BL, letters to Sir Edward Nicholas, Egerton MSS 2534–2535, 2537 • BL, letters to Sir John Robinson, Egerton MS 3349 • BL, corresp. with Sir W. Vane, Add. MS 16272 • Bodl. Oxf., corresp. with duke of Ormond, MSS Carte • Folger, letters to duke of Montagu as master of the great wardrobe • Leics. RO, cooresp. with Lord Winchelsea • PRO, state papers (foreign and domestic) for the reigns of Charles II and James II • Sheff. Arch., corresp. with Sir Thomas Osborne, etc. • W. Yorks. AS, Leeds, letters to Sir John Reresby • Yale U., Beinecke L., letters to earl of Carlingford

Likenesses P. Lely and studio, oils, *c.*1673, NPG • P. Lely and studio, oils, other version, *c.*1673, Euston Hall, Suffolk [*see illus.*] • P. Lely and studio, oils, other version, *c.*1673, Longleat House, Wiltshire • P. Lely and studio, oils, 1676, Christ Church Oxf. • line engraving, 1679 (after P. Lely, 1676), BM, NPG; repro. in Guillim, *Heraldry* (1679) • J. Houbraken, line engraving, pubd 1789 (after P. Lely), BM, NPG • group portrait, oils (after G. Netscher), Euston Hall, Suffolk

Wealth at death substantial; estates in Suffolk, Norfolk, Middlesex, and London to daughter and her husband (duke and duchess of Grafton); wife to receive £10,000 raised by sale of Arlington House and lands, plus manor of Tottenham, all goods and chattels within her chamber at Somerset House, London, for life; nephew Henry Bennet to receive titles and interests in several offices incl. excise, etc. granted by Charles II, plus £350 owed by earl of Ranelagh from lands in Ireland; various other leases, bonds, and debts, household goods, and plate left; also holdings on timber to be sold within forests and £30,000 promised on marriage of duke of Grafton to his daughter to pay off his debts; residue to duke of Grafton, incl. pension and arrears due from treasury: will, PRO, PROB 11/381, fol. 130

Bennet, Henry Grey (1777–1836), politician, was born on 2 December 1777, the second of three sons and fourth of eight children of Charles Bennet, fourth earl of Tankerville (1743–1822), of Chillingham Castle, Northumberland, and his wife, Emma (1752–1836), daughter and coheir of the London banker Sir James Colebrooke, first baronet, of Gatton, Surrey. He was educated at Eton College (1788–92), served five years in the 1st foot guards, and entered Lincoln's Inn in 1798, and Peterhouse, Cambridge, in 1799 before graduating MA in 1801. Between interludes as assistant to William Drummond, envoy at Naples, and captain of militia volunteers, he was called to the bar in 1803, and afterwards practised on the western circuit. The political diarist Thomas Creevey described him in 1805 as 'most amiable, occasionally most *boring*, but at all times most upright and honourable' (Maxwell, 1.36).

Bennet, whose father had retreated from public life after two spells as postmaster-general, shared the political ambitions of his brother Charles Augustus Bennet (1776–1854): both belonged to the whiggish Brooks's Club. Bennet's first election as MP for Shrewsbury in 1806 was invalidated, not before he had signalled hostility to George III's dismissal of the 'ministry of all the talents'. His advocacy of Catholic emancipation courted defeat in 1807. Before regaining his seat in 1811 he travelled to Spain to view the theatre of the Peninsular War. He faced no contest for his parliamentary seat after 1812. In the Commons he joined the opposition 'mountain' led by Samuel Whitbread, whom he revered, although his closest associates were his fellow lawyers Creevey and Henry Brougham. His maiden speech, ostensibly a conventional attack on placemen, was directed at the prince regent, who, provoked by Bennet's championship of his estranged wife, labelled him 'factious' (Aspinall, 134). Bennet shunned the 'constitutional' opposition leaders as deviants from Foxite principles, but his *bête noire* was Robert Stewart, Viscount Castlereagh, leader of the house, with the home secretary Henry Addington, first Viscount Sidmouth, a close second. His quest for 'a cheap government under a reformed parliament' (*Hansard 2*, 7, 1822, 1313) meant frequent tirades against army estimates, civil list extravagance, and taxes. He assailed other reactionary regimes sanctified by Napoleon's final defeat, before which he toured the continent. He condemned post-war curtailment of civil liberties, and support for parliamentary reform involved him in metropolitan politics, but he disappointed whigs and radicals alike. After the Peterloo massacre of August 1819 he sought an inquiry into the manufacturing districts' plight. His outspoken defence of Queen Caroline in 1820–21 led to his portrayal among her champions in an engraving by Francis Holl after Abraham Wivell. The radical *Black Book* (1823) commended him:

> Always at his post. Supports Mr [Joseph] Hume nobly. Tells the Collective Wisdom home truths. Calls for useful papers and documents. Shames the rogues ... Great ... as the labours of Mr Hume have been, it may be doubted whether all his exertions can be put in competition with the single act of Mr Bennet in obtaining an accurate return of the salaries, offices and emoluments of the honourable Members. (J. Wade, 2.139)

Bennet's efforts 'to diminish the sum of human misery' (*Hansard 1*, 39, 1819, 118), adorn the history of English criminal law. No retributory institution, prison, hulk, penal colony, or penitentiary adequately combined punishment with reformation: he and his select committees exposed them, but to little avail. The inquiry into metropolitan policing which he initiated, prompted by Sir Samuel Romilly, caused such a furore in 1816 that ten years elapsed before constructive legislation emerged, although Bennet, having previously piloted the abolition of gaol fees, overthrew statutory rewards for informers on felony in 1818. Other abuses that he confronted included flogging, callous capital punishments, confusion of political prisoners with felons, the despotism of colonial governors, the plight of lunatics and child chimney sweeps, and corrupt licensing. He was sometimes taken in by unscrupulous petitioners.

On 15 May 1816 Bennet married Gertrude Frances (*d.* 23 Jan 1841), daughter of Lord William Russell. They had one son and three daughters. The abrupt termination of his public career, ascribed to the death from consumption of his only son six months after that of one of his daughters, in 1824, was followed by a curative continental trip in the spring of 1825. His public reputation at home was ruined by the threat, albeit averted, of criminal prosecution for importuning a young male servant at Spa in August 1825. This accounts for his remaining in exile, and giving up his seat in parliament the following year. He and his wife resided in a villa near Lake Como in Italy until his death on 29 May 1836. Bennet's disgrace explains his subsequent pathetic submission to criticism of his parliamentary endeavours, themselves often misreported. The author of several pamphlets, and a fellow of the Royal Society, Bennet kept a political diary from 1806, now lost, though extracts were published in the nineteenth century and one volume (for 1821) has come to light.   ROLAND THORNE

Sources HoP, *Commons* · L. Radzinowicz, *A history of criminal law and its administration from 1750*, 5 vols. (1948–86) · BL, Holland House MSS, Add. MSS 51749, 52017 · Bennet's MS diary for 1821, HLRO · Mitchell L., NSW, Macarthur MSS, J. Macarthur to his father, 12 June 1825, MLA 2911 · *The Creevey papers*, ed. H. Maxwell, 2nd edn, 2 vols. (1904) · A. Aspinall, ed., *Letters of Princess Charlotte* (1949) · *Hansard* · *GM*, 2nd ser., 6 (1836), 558 · Burke, *Peerage* · *The Eton register*, 8 vols. (privately printed, Eton, 1903–32) · W. P. Baildon, ed., *The records of the Honorable Society of Lincoln's Inn* [incl. *Admissions*, 2 vols. (1896), and *Black books*, 6 vols. (1897–2001)] · Peterhouse college register, Cambridge
Archives HLRO, MS diary for 1821 | BL, Holland House MSS, Add. MSS 51749, 52017 · BL, letters to Robert Peel and others
Likenesses F. Holl, stipple, pubd 1823 (after A. Wivell), BM, NPG
Wealth at death £7000: PRO death duty registers, IR 26/1440/552; will, PRO, PROB 11/188/516

Bennet, Sir John (1552/3–1627), judge, was the second son of Richard Bennet of Clapcot, Berkshire, and his wife, Elizabeth Tesdale (*b.* 1535). His parents were step-brother and step-sister by the third marriage of Elizabeth's father, Thomas, a prosperous farmer from Abingdon, Berkshire, to Richard's widowed mother, and there were nine children of the marriage. Bennet was probably first educated at Abingdon School, of which his family were benefactors, and then attended Oxford University. He matriculated at Christ Church in 1573, received the degrees of BA in 1577 and MA in 1585, and was elected a proctor in April 1585. In 1589 he was given a dispensation to take the degrees of BCL and DCL together, having qualified for the DCL with three dissertations on family law. In 1590 he was admitted as an advocate in the court of arches.

Having completed his professional education, Bennet began his judicial career in York, probably through the influence of Archbishop John Piers, previously dean of Christ Church. By September 1589 he had been appointed chancellor of the diocese and joint commissary of the exchequer court, which had responsibility for probate. As chancellor he was a commissioner for ecclesiastical causes in the province of York, and retained this office until 1620. He was also appointed to the prebend of Langtoft in 1591, which he held until 1608. These provincial posts by no means satisfied Bennet's ambitions, and in June 1596 he wrote to Cecil expressing dissatisfaction with York and asking for advancement. Meanwhile his career continued to develop. He acted as legal adviser to the commission appointed to negotiate with the Scots for a new treaty, signed on 5 May 1597, reorganizing the security of the Anglo-Scottish border, and earned high praise for his knowledge and diligence. Two years later he was appointed to the council of the north. This resulted in friction with the council's deputy secretary, John Ferne, who complained of Bennet claiming precedence over him. Distinctions bestowed on Bennet while in York included appointment as a justice of the peace, honorific admission to Gray's Inn in 1599, and the freedom of York in 1601. On 15 April 1603 he made a speech of welcome to James I when he passed through the city on his way to receive the English crown, and on 23 July 1603 he was knighted. While at York, Bennet suffered a personal misfortune in the death of his wife, Anne Weeks of Salisbury, whom he had married on 29 May 1586. She died on 9 February 1602, leaving him with four sons and two daughters, and was buried with a memorial in York Minster.

Bennet found a wider role in public affairs as a member of parliament. In 1597 he served for Ripon, and was a member of two legal committees and a committee on the malting industry. In the parliament of 1601 he was a member for York and spoke in support of the Act of Uniformity, claiming that there were some 1300 recusants in Yorkshire. He also contributed to the debate on monopolies, supporting the royal prerogative but attacking the salt monopoly. Bennet again represented Ripon in 1604. His experience in negotiating with the Scots may well have been one of the reasons why he was one of two civil lawyers appointed to the commission on the Union to consider the legal problems arising from the union of England and Scotland. He was also active in defending the ecclesiastical courts, and unsuccessfully opposed a bill prohibiting the residence of married men with their families in the colleges of Oxford and Cambridge.

In 1604 the centre of Bennet's activities moved to London, when he was appointed judge of the prerogative court of Canterbury, which administered the archbishop's testamentary jurisdiction, and in the same year became a full member of Doctors' Commons. However, he retained his post of commissary in York until 1609, and that of chancellor until 1624. Further offices soon followed. In 1605 he became a member of the high court of delegates, which heard appeals from the ecclesiastical and admiralty courts. In 1605 he was appointed to the court of high commission, and was reappointed in successive commissions in 1608, 1611, 1613, and 1620. His purchase of the manors of Harlington and Dawley, in Middlesex, in 1607 showed his rapidly growing wealth and social status. The following year he was made a master in chancery, one of the senior officials in the court of chancery, and in May 1609 he took part in a debate before the king, in which he defended rights of the ecclesiastical courts against the courts of common law. In 1611 he received a place on the council of Queen Anne, wife of James I. He was one of the commissioners appointed in 1613 to hear the case for the annulment of the marriage of the earl and countess of Essex. By early 1617 his aspirations had soared to such a level that it was reported that he had made an unsuccessful offer of £30,000 for the post of lord chancellor.

Bennet took an active interest in the University of Oxford, and on 5 November 1611 he was asked by Sir Thomas Bodley to act as fund-raiser and overseer of building work for the Bodleian Library. His strategy for raising money, proposed on 1 April 1612, was efficient and effective, and by 1619 he had collected over £5000. Bodley died

in January 1613, making Bennet one of his executors. Bennet was also one of the first governors of Pembroke College, which was founded with money left by his uncle, Thomas Tesdale. In the parliament of 1614 he represented the University of Oxford. Although he served on a number of committees, his participation was interrupted on 12 May 1614 by the death of his second wife, Elizabeth. She was the daughter of Sir Thomas Lowe, mayor of London and governor of the Merchant Adventurers, in which Bennet was an investor.

It was not long before Bennet remarried; his third wife was Leonora (d. 1638), daughter of Adriaan Vierendeels of Antwerp. She had been married twice previously, and was probably one of the Flemish community gathered around the church of the Austin friars, London. It was said that she was a large, over-dressed woman, who dominated her husband. No doubt it was this link with the Low Countries that led to Bennet being appointed, in April 1617, as special ambassador to the Archduke Albert, governor of the Netherlands. His mission was to seek the punishment of the author of a work entitled *Corona regia*, which attacked James I, and although he obtained only a token response, Bennet gained considerable credit by his endeavours.

Bennet was again MP for the University of Oxford in 1621, when he was said to be sixty-eight. Parliament was bent on investigating grievances, and soon turned its attention to abuses in the judiciary. The fall of Francis Bacon swiftly followed, and in April Bennet's career also met with sudden catastrophe, when he was accused in the committee of courts of exacting bribes and excessive fees for making grants of administration of intestates' estates. His chief accuser was Richard Kilvert, a proctor in the prerogative court of Canterbury, who made no less than twenty-nine accusations against him. On 20 April a debate on how to deal with Bennet's case was held in the Commons, from which Bennet was absent on a plea of ill health. The issue was important, as it raised the question of the respective roles of the two houses in trying a delinquent member of parliament. It was finally decided that he should be expelled from the house, that the Commons should rule on the issue of fact, and that the case should then be referred to the Lords. It was agreed that he should be placed under house arrest, since he was too ill for prison. On 30 May Bennet was brought to the bar of the House of Lords and charged, but claimed that he could account for all but £4000 of the moneys that had passed through his hands. He was allowed time to prepare his defence, was bailed on the sum of £20,000, and was ordered to repay £1000 still in his hands from Sir Thomas Bodley's legacy to the University of Oxford. Of this amount, £450 was never recovered by the university.

When parliament reconvened it had more pressing matters to consider, and took no further action. In the following June proceedings were commenced in the Star Chamber; in November, since Bennet's counsel had produced only a weak defence, it was decreed that he should be fined £20,000, imprisoned in the Fleet, and permanently disabled from holding office. This was reduced in July 1624 to the fine only. In his disgrace, Bennet wrote a meditation on the Fifty-First Psalm, published in 1625 under the title *The Psalme of Mercy*, with a dedication to the puritan divine John Downame. He died on 15 February 1627 at his house in Warwick Lane, in the parish of Christ Church, Newgate, London, and was buried in the parish. His wife Leonora survived until 1638.

Bennet's personality shows several opposing qualities. In religion his leanings were towards puritanism, as witnessed by the dedication to him of books by two puritan writers. The first of these was *A Counterblast Against a Masked Companion* (1603) by Thomas Bell, and the second was *Justinian the Emperor Defended* (1616) by Richard Crakanthorpe. At the same time he was obliged by his official position to defend the church courts and to stand up for the royal prerogative in parliament, in opposition to the general puritan viewpoint. He was well liked by his colleagues, although there are a few indications that subordinates saw him in a different light. Even in his disgrace his ability and learning were unquestioned, but there is nothing to suggest that he had any of the wider intellectual interests which redeemed Bacon's reputation. Indeed, the extent of his profiteering from his post so overshadowed Bacon's misdemeanours that it was said, 'Sir John Bennet hath made my Lord Chancellor an honest man' (PRO, SP 14/120/107). Had this not nullified his achievements, Bennet might have been remembered as an able judge, parliamentarian, and diplomat, and a generous benefactor of the University of Oxford.

At his trial it was stated that Bennet had ten children and forty grandchildren. This may have included children-in-law, since only the six children of his first wife have been traced. In spite of the set-back of his disgrace, the family continued to prosper, his eldest son, John, being the father of Henry, first earl of Arlington.

Sir Thomas Bennet (1592–1670), civil lawyer, was the second, and most professionally successful, son of Sir John Bennet; his mother was Sir John's first wife, Anne Weeks. He was born in York on 5 December 1592. Destined for his father's profession, he matriculated at All Souls College, Oxford, in 1613, graduated BCL in 1615, and was awarded the degree of DCL in 1624. He may have been admitted to Gray's Inn in 1617. He joined Doctors' Commons in 1624, and obtained full membership in 1626. While pursuing his career as an advocate in the London courts, he was appointed to the court of delegates, and was also a commissioner for piracy in London in 1633, 1635, and 1638. He became a master in chancery in 1635. In the civil war he seems to have leaned towards royalism, but then made his peace with parliament. He may have been one of those expelled from Oxford in 1648 for not submitting to the parliamentary visitors, but in the same year he was listed as having been discharged from sequestration. Although in February 1649 an information was laid claiming that he had been an active royalist, he continued as master in chancery during the interregnum. Following the Restoration he was knighted on 21 August 1661, the year after his cousin Sir Thomas Bennet of Babraham, Cambridgeshire, was created a baronet. At the time of his death on 27 June 1670 he was living on his estate at Salthrop, Wiltshire. He left a daughter, Mary, from his first marriage to Charlotte, daughter of William Harrison of London, and a son, Thomas, from his second marriage to Thomasine, daughter of George Dethick. Thomasine appears to have predeceased him. His career was typical of the generation of lawyers who lived through the disruption of the civil war and adapted to changing political circumstances to ensure professional survival.

SHEILA DOYLE

Sources B. P. Levack, *The civil lawyers in England, 1603–1641* (1973), 45, 47–8, 55, 80, 142, 167, 174, 182, 209–10, 228 · A. E. Preston, *The church and parish of St Nicholas, Abingdon* (1929), pl. facing pp. 412, 438–46, 455 · *Hist. U. Oxf.* 4: *17th-cent. Oxf.*, 138–40, 145, 151, 154, 197–8, 667 · HoP, *Commons, 1558–1603*, 1.428 · *JHC*, 1 (1547–1628), 172, 204, 208, 229, 237, 268, 274, 286, 296, 326, 342–3, 350–51, 580, 583–4, 586–8, 590–91 · *State trials*, 2.1146–54 · L. Rostenberg, *The minority press and the English crown* (1971), 153–5 · *The Chamberlain letters*, ed. E. M. Thomson (1966), 96, 180, 353 · *Calendar of the manuscripts of the most hon. the marquis of Salisbury*, 9, HMC, 9 (1902), 257, 363 · *CSP dom.*, 1611–18, 449; 1619–23, 465; 1623–5, 303 · M. A. E. Green, ed., *Calendar of the proceedings of the committee for advance of money, 1642–1656*, 1, PRO (1888), 91 · M. A. E. Green, ed., *Calendar of the proceedings of the committee for compounding … 1643–1660*, 5 vols., PRO (1889–92), 1019 · *Collins peerage of England: genealogical, biographical and historical*, ed. E. Brydges, 9 vols. (1812), vol. 4, p. 125 · *DNB* · *Le Neve's Pedigrees of the knights*, ed. G. W. Marshall, Harleian Society, 8 (1873), 145

Archives Bodl. Oxf., corresp. and papers

Wealth at death very wealthy in early 1621; manors of Harlington and Dawley, Middlesex, and Salthrop, Wiltshire; house in London; allegedly had access to at least £30,000 cash; in 1621, transferred Wiltshire property to son William; fined £20,000 in 1624; family retained Middlesex property; subject retained London house at death: *VCH Middlesex*, 3.262–4 · £2000 cash; estate of Salthrop—Sir Thomas Bennet: will, PRO, PROB 11/334, sig. 175

Bennet, John (*fl.* **1599–1614**), composer, was probably born in the north-west of England. The preface to his *Madrigals to Four Voices* (1599), the contents of which Bennet describes as 'the first fruits of my simple skill', declares his indebtedness to the volume's dedicatee, 'the right worshipful Ralph Assheton Esq', a justice of the peace in the counties palatine of Lancaster and Chester. In 1601 he contributed to *The Triumphs of Oriana*, the collection of madrigals in honour of the aged Queen Elizabeth.

Despite his very modest output, Bennet was one of the most wide-ranging English composers of his generation. For instance, while 'Eliza, her name gives honour' (presumably a tribute to the queen) is a dignified consort song for singer and four viols, composed in an archaic, early Elizabethan style, Bennet's six contributions to Thomas Ravenscroft's *A Brief Discourse* (1614) are bluff and humorous, one of them, 'A borgens [bargain's] a borgen', setting a text written in a west-country dialect. Between these stylistic extremes come the four simple psalm settings and prayer for the queen that Bennet provided for William Barley's *The Whole Book of Psalms* (c.1599). Bennet's sole surviving piece of church music is a verse anthem, 'O God of gods', for soloists, choir, and viols, later described in James Clifford's *The Divine Services and Anthems Usually Sung in his Majesty's Chapel* (1663) as 'for the king's inauguration'; it was presumably composed on the accession of James I in 1603.

However, Bennet is best known for his volume of seventeen madrigals. Again his stylistic range is notable, especially for a collection of pieces all limited to four voice parts. Thus while one, 'I languish to complain me', blends a measured pre-madrigalian manner with some true madrigalian pathos, others display an impressive command of the light canzonet manner introduced into English music by Thomas Morley, some also showing awareness of the newer, more serious trends being revealed in the works of Thomas Weelkes and John Wilbye. Bennet is best known for his ebullient *Oriana* contribution, 'All creatures now are merry minded'; yet there is equal cause for gratitude for pieces from his 1599 volume such as the mercurial narrative madrigal 'Thyrsis, sleepest thou?' and the touchingly intimate 'Weep, O mine eyes'. Nothing more is known of Bennet after his contribution to *A Brief Discourse*.   DAVID BROWN

Sources J. Bennet, *Madrigals to four voices* (1599), preface · *New Grove* · E. H. Fellowes, *The English madrigal composers*, 2nd edn (1950)

Bennet [Bennett], **John** [*alias* William Freeman or Hill; *called* the Golden Farmer] (*d.* **1690**), thief, of unknown parentage, is at present visible only in the last year of his life. On 9 September 1689 the authorities had—or thought they had—him in Newgate prison and advertised in the *London Gazette* for witnesses to come forward to identify the notorious thief, the Golden Farmer. They knew him under two of his aliases, William Freeman alias Hill, housebreaker, 'aged between 50 and 60 years of age' (*London Gazette*, 9 Sept 1689).

For whatever reason, Bennet was free within a few weeks and on the afternoon of 16 October 1689 he was among those who broke into the house of an Essex magistrate, Charles Palmer, at Gray's Thurrock, stealing over £400 worth of goods. Seven men had attacked the house and four, including Bennet, entered, tying up the magistrate and his servants, forcing Palmer's wife, Elizabeth, at gunpoint to lead them to the valuables in the house, and overcoming some soldiers from a nearby blockhouse who came to investigate the disturbance. On 26 February 1690 he and others robbed the house of Thomas Bird in Ware, Hertfordshire, stealing £500 worth of goods.

However, later that year he was informed against by one of his fellow gang members, who reported other crimes and named his chief accomplices: one Marshal, Jenkins the barber, and 'Old Mobb'. Bennet went into hiding but his betrayer's wife and sister, Elizabeth Holt and Anne Holland, found him by following his wife. On 26 September he was drinking at the Rose and Crown ale house in Dorset Gardens in St Bride's when they came in with a warrant to arrest him for a robbery. In the disturbance that followed, with the two women shouting 'stop thief, a highwayman', a soldier, Charles Taylor, tried to detain him. Bennet shot him in the stomach with a double-shotted pistol and fled; Taylor died of his wounds two days later. Bennet took refuge in Southwark, where he was discovered soon after. Chased by a group of butchers, he shot one of his pursuers, who also later died of his wounds, but he was finally cornered and knocked down by brickbats.

He was committed to Newgate on 23 October, 'accused upon oath for having committed several Robberies upon the Highway and severall Burglaries' and for Taylor's murder (CLRO, SF374, gaol calendar). Again, advertisements were placed in the *London Gazette*, identifying him as 'William Netherway, alias Freeman, alias Bennet, but commonly known by the name of The Golden Farmer, a tall red faced Man, his Face full of Pimples, above 50 years of Age, his Head shakes' (*London Gazette*, 23 Oct 1690).

They also had in custody two of his accomplices, and the advertisement charged the three men with highway robbery on Bagshot and Hounslow heaths and between Edmonton and Enfield—that is, on roads to the south, west, and north of London—and housebreaking in Middlesex, Hertfordshire, and Essex. Elizabeth Palmer came forward and identified Bennet as one of the men who had broken into her house (though she knew him as William Newman, alias Nethway), while Thomas Bird was also bound over to testify against him. Bennet was tried and convicted at the Old Bailey on 18 December 1690 for the Essex housebreaking and for Taylor's murder. Awaiting execution, he showed remorse for his crimes, but insufficient to satisfy the ordinary (the prison chaplain): pressed to make recompense to the victims of his crimes, he asked what more could he give than the law taking his life. The ordinary explained that 'he Paid his Life to the Justice of the Law; it made no Satisfaction nor Recompense to those he had despoil'd of their Estates' (Smith). He must not regard his charity to the poor from the profits of theft as acceptable to God. He was hanged on Fleet Street, near the site of Taylor's murder, on 22 December 1690. On 26 December his body was hanged in chains on Bagshot Heath, Surrey. His death was commemorated in a ballad, *The Golden Farmer's Last Farewell*, in which the condemned man acknowledged his involvement with 'a gang of robbers, notorious hardy highwaymen who did like ruffians reign' and bade farewell to his accomplice Old Mobb. Within the year Richard Awson, alias Old Mobb, had followed Bennet to the gallows, accused by a fellow gang member, Anthony Dunn, 'as being menconed in their Maties proclamacon for being a Notorious Highwayman' (LMA, MJ/SR 1783, gaol calendar).

The ordinary of Newgate's account and the Old Bailey trial report concur that Bennet was the Golden Farmer. However, his identity became lost when Captain Alexander Smith linked the nickname of the Golden Farmer to the name of **William Davis** (*d.* 1689), reputed highwayman, in his *The History of the Lives of the most Noted Highwaymen* (1714), a best-seller which had reached its fifth edition by 1719–20 as *A Compleat History*. Smith's William Davis took his nickname from his practice of always settling his debts in gold. In the account provided by Smith and elaborated on by later Grub Street hacks, Davis was born into a farming family near Wrexham in Denbighshire and moved to Chipping Sodbury in Gloucestershire, where he married the daughter of a wealthy innkeeper with whom he had eighteen children. He later settled near Bagshot Heath, Surrey, living a double life as a respectable farmer and busy highwayman, unsuspected by his neighbours, for over forty years. The many robberies attributed to Davis by Smith are characterized by cunning, repartee, and ruthlessness, often involving a sort of rough-and-ready justice against social stereotypes ripe for their come-uppance—a canting Quaker, a tinker, a greedy lawyer, a dim gentleman, a magistrate. Once Davis confided to a wealthy grazier that there were highwaymen about and asked him to hide some money for him. In hiding the money, the grazier inadvertently showed Davis where he had concealed 50 guineas of his own. Soon Davis announced that since nobody would take the trouble to rob either of them that day, he would be obliged to rob the grazier himself. On another occasion, he held up Anne Monck, duchess of Albemarle, on Salisbury Plain. Having been the well-known scold Nan Clarges before her marriage, it is not surprising that she obstinately refused to hand over anything. Infuriated, Davis forcibly removed her rings while at the same time reproaching her for her painted face.

According to Smith, Davis was a master of disguise, which helps explain why he went undetected among his neighbours. One anecdote recounts that Davis, having paid 70 guineas rent to his landlord, caught up with him later in full disguise and took back his money; the landlord never suspected that he had been robbed by his own tenant. Later accounts claimed that Davis may have given up highway robbery for some years as his farming business (and according to one version a corn-chandler's shop in Thames Street, London) prospered. He robbed again when he needed money to buy adjacent farmland. The same later accounts claimed that Davis was shot in the back as he escaped from a hold-up and was taken to the King's Arms at Bagshot, where his identity was revealed to his astonished neighbours.

Smith certainly knew something of the real Golden Farmer. Though he presented Davis as a man who worked alone, he recorded his association with Old Mobb (in his life of the latter). His account of the pursuit of the Farmer is reasonably true to the actual event. Smith gave Davis's date of execution, in his sixty-fourth year, in Fleet Street, as 20 December 1689; almost exactly a year out from Bennet's. Smith evidently conflated William Davis (one of several men of that name who appears in the sessions records in the 1680s and 1690s), who was convicted of burglary at the Old Bailey sessions in December 1689, with the real Golden Farmer, John Bennet, convicted in December the following year. Smith may have known that he had misidentified the Golden Farmer. However, historical accuracy was not a high priority in Smith's picaresque accounts of highwaymen's lives.   BARBARA WHITE

Sources L. B. Faller, *Turned to account: the forms and functions of criminal biography in late seventeenth- and early eighteenth-century England* (1987) · *The proceedings on the king and queens commissions of peace, and oyer and terminer, and gaol delivery … at Justice-Hall in the Old Bayly* (10–17 Dec 1690) · S. Smith, *A true account of the behaviour, confession, and last dying speeches of the 15 criminals that were executed on Monday the 22th [sic] of December 1690* (1690) · *LondG* (9 Sept 1689) · *LondG* (23 Oct 1690) · London sessions roll, December 1690, SF 374 · coroner's inquest on Charles Taylor, 1690, CLRO, LSP 1690/4; examinations of William Palmer and Elizabeth Palmer, CLRO, LSP 1690/5 · *The*

Golden Farmer's last farewell [n.d., 1691?] · *The proceedings on the king and queens commissions of peace, and oyer and terminer, and gaol delivery … at Justice-Hall in the Old Bayly* (11–14 Dec 1689) · Middlesex gaol delivery roll, September 1691, MJ/SR 1783 · privy council register, PRO, PC2/72, fols. 23–4 · C. G. Harper, *Half hours with the highwaymen* (1908) · C. Johnson, *A general history of the lives and adventures of the most famous highwaymen, murderers, street robbers, etc.* (1734) · G. C. B. Poulter, 'Golden Farmer': the inn and the highwayman (1934) · J. L. Rayner and G. T. Crook, eds., *The complete Newgate calendar*, 5 vols. (privately printed, London, 1926) · A. Smith, *A complete history of the lives and robberies of the most notorious highwaymen, footpads, shoplifts, and cheats*, ed. A. L. Hayward (1926) · N. Luttrell, *A brief historical relation of state affairs from September 1678 to April 1714*, 6 vols. (1857) · *The Portledge papers: being extracts from the letters of Richard Lapthorne … to Richard Coffin*, ed. R. J. Kerr and I. C. Duncan (1928) · J. Beattie, *Policing and punishment in London, 1660-1750* (2001)

Likenesses portrait (*The Golden Farmer and the Tinker*), repro. in Smith, *Complete history*

Bennet, John (1657–1686), writer, was born on 28 October 1657 in the parish of St Margaret, Westminster, the son of John Bennet and Jane Gavell. He was educated at Westminster School before proceeding to Christ Church, Oxford, where he matriculated on 20 October 1676. He took his BA degree in June 1680. In the same year that he took his MA degree he published *Constantius the Apostate* (1683). This was one of the many replies to *Julian the Apostate* (1682), a carefully controversial tract written by the Revd Samuel Johnson, chaplain to the whig leader and reputed republican Lord William Russell. By rehearsing the lives of the early Christians under the fourth-century apostate emperor Julian, and his subsequent death, Johnson advocates the exclusion of James, duke of York, from the succession, defending resistance, sanctioning active disobedience, and even condoning tyrannicide: 'saints own no allegiance to their Prince', Dryden concluded in his hostile portrait of Johnson, who appears as Ben-Jochanan in *The Second Part of Absalom and Achitophel: a Poem* (1682). Bennet in his reply identifies the Arian Constantius as a truer parallel than Julian to the case of a Catholic sovereign of England; adopting Johnson's method, he attempts to show that Constantius's orthodox subjects recognized the duty of passive obedience to a heretic emperor. Bennet's soggy prose fails to ground his argument—'the nature of the thing will not allow me to make any proof from History that it was so, but I don't question to make it more than probable it would have been so, if there had been occasion' (Bennet, *Constantius*, 11)—but Johnson thought his reasoning worthy of a special refutation (*Julian's Arts*, 1683, published 1689). Bennet afterwards studied medicine. He died of a violent fever on 6 October 1686, and was buried in Christ Church Cathedral, Oxford.   JONATHAN PRITCHARD

Sources Wood, *Ath. Oxon.*, new edn, 4.201–2 · Wood, *Ath. Oxon.: Fasti* (1820), 372, 386 · *The life and times of Anthony Wood*, ed. A. Clark, 3, OHS, 26 (1894), 18 · *Old Westminsters*, 1.74; suppl. 1.14 · J. Welch, *The list of the queen's scholars of St Peter's College, Westminster*, ed. [C. B. Phillimore], new edn (1852), 178 · R. A. Beddard, 'Tory Oxford', *Hist. U. Oxf.* 4: 17th-cent. Oxf., 863–906 · *The poems of John Dryden*, ed. P. Hammond, 4 vols. (1995–2000), 2.49–51 [ongoing] · BL, Add. MS 41804

Bennet, John (c.1670–1750), Church of England clergyman, may have been a member of the family of that name settled at Hexworthy near Launceston, Cornwall, over many generations. He was admitted sizar at Queens' College, Cambridge, as 'of Cornwall' on 7 September 1693, proceeding BA in 1697 and MA in 1726. He is said by Charles Wesley, who met him on 13 July 1744, to have claimed to be a contemporary of Wesley's father, but, since the latter must have been at least ten years older and was at Exeter College, Oxford, their acquaintance could not have been at university. Bennet was ordained deacon at Exeter on 19 September 1697 and priest on 16 March 1700, being licensed thereafter in 1705 to the perpetual curacy of North Tamerton, Cornwall, which he retained until his death and to which he added Tresmere in 1720 and Laneast in 1731.

For much of his life Bennet appears to have been an ordinary country parson of no particularly distinctive views, farming his glebe and associating with the local gentry, but late in 1742 he experienced an evangelical conversion after hearing George Thomson of St Gennys preach on salvation by faith. Subsequently he entertained Whitefield and Wesley on their preaching tours and, like them and Thomson, he peregrinated, and as a result he would incur the wrath of the Methodist-hating bishop of Exeter, George Lavington, who required him in a judgment given on 18 July 1749 to confine his preaching to his own parishes on pain of ecclesiastical censure. Bennet may have continued his itinerant work, but we do know that, whether he did so or not, with Thomson he continued to welcome Whitefield and John Wesley, the latter recording in his journal on 27 August 1750 that Bennet, though still ministering, was 'full of days and by swift steps removing into eternity' (*Journal of … John Wesley*, 3.492). Bennet lived for less than two months after this, and was buried at North Tamerton on 13 October 1750.

ARTHUR POLLARD

Sources G. C. B. Davies, *The early Cornish evangelicals, 1735–60* (1951) · *The journal of the Rev. John Wesley*, ed. N. Curnock and others, 8 vols. (1909–16); repr. (1938), vol. 3, pp. 132, 181, 309, 492–3 · *The journal of the Rev. Charles Wesley*, ed. T. Jackson, 1 [1849], 369

Bennet, John (1715–1759), Methodist preacher and Independent minister, was born on 1 March 1715 in Whitehough, near Chinley, Derbyshire, the younger son of William Bennet (*c*.1677–1766), farmer, and his wife, Ann (*d*. 1752). Raised as a presbyterian, he was educated at a school in Chapel-en-le-Frith, where he acquired proficiency in Latin and Greek, intending to become a dissenting minister or attorney. However, after a short period in 1732 at the dissenting academy in Findern, Derbyshire, he became a justices' clerk in Sheffield until 1737, and then commenced work as a carrier between Sheffield and Macclesfield.

On 1 January 1742 Bennet experienced a religious conversion through the influence of David Taylor, an evangelical preacher formerly in the service of the family of Selina Hastings, countess of Huntingdon. From March 1743 he began to preach and built up a network of religious societies in Derbyshire, Cheshire, and south-east Lancashire, which soon became part of the Methodist organization led by John Wesley. As one of Wesley's leading preachers he attended the first Methodist conference in 1744, and in 1748 promoted the system of quarterly meetings to oversee the local Methodist circuits (groups of societies).

Relations with Wesley, however, became strained as a result of Bennet's marriage on 3 October 1749 to Grace *Murray (1715–1803), the widow of a Newcastle ship's captain and daughter of Robert Norman of Newcastle upon Tyne, since Wesley claimed that Grace was already contracted to marry himself. Bennet developed Calvinistic views and by the beginning of 1754 had broken with Wesley, followed by some of his societies, notably at Bolton. Bennet continued to be a travelling preacher, hoping at first to obtain aid from George Whitefield and his Calvinistic Methodist Connexion. Failing to achieve this, he was licensed as a dissenting preacher in January 1754, had a meeting-house built for him at Warburton in Cheshire, and on 9 November 1754 was ordained as an Independent minister. Although he also continued to preach elsewhere, ill health probably curtailed his activities.

Bennet was among the better educated of the early Methodist preachers and more sober than some in his attitude to supernatural phenomena. He was of a somewhat anxious and dependent temperament, especially when faced with persecution. He died in Chinley on 24 May 1759 and was buried in the presbyterian graveyard there. He left five sons, one of whom, William, became an Independent minister in London. His wife returned to Methodism later in life and died in Chapel-en-le-Frith on 23 February 1803.

HENRY D. RACK, *rev.*

Sources Bennet MSS, JRL · S. R. Valentine, *John Bennet and the origins of Methodism and the evangelical revival* (1997) · W. Bennet, *Memoirs of Mrs Grace Bennet* (1803) · J. Augustin Léger, *John Wesley's last love* (1910) · *The diary of James Clegg of Chapel en le Frith, 1708–1755*, ed. V. S. Doe, 3 vols., Derbyshire RS, 2–3, 5 (1978–81) · H. D. Rack, 'Survival and revival: John Bennet, Methodism and the old dissent', *Protestant evangelicalism in Britain, Germany and America, c.1750–1900*, ed. K. G. Robbins (1990) · Drew University, Madison, New Jersey, John Bennet MSS, Methodist Research Collection · C. Warhurst, diary, Man. CL, MS 185, box 1 · J. S. Simon, *John Wesley and the advance of Methodism* (1925)
Archives Drew University, Madison, New Jersey, Methodist Research Collection · JRL, corresp., diaries, and sermons
Likenesses Bentley, engraving, JRL, Grace Bennet MSS; repro. in Valentine, *John Bennet*, frontispiece

Bennet, Joseph (bap. **1627**, d. **1707**), nonconformist minister, elder son of Joseph Bennet (*d*. 1635), curate of Warbleton, Sussex, and Anne (*bap*. 1600), daughter of Thomas Lord, rector of that parish, was baptized there on 19 November 1627. He was educated at Tonbridge School and St John's College, Cambridge, where he was admitted sizar on 30 June 1645 and graduated BA in 1649. He was ordained by the fourth London classis on 1 May 1651 and was for a time chaplain to Sir John Wollaston at Highgate, Middlesex. On returning to Sussex he served as a preacher at Hooe and Burwash and in 1658 his uncle Thomas English presented him to the rectory of Brightling, where he was instituted on 14 July.

After the Act of Uniformity, although neighbouring clergy pressed him to conform, Bennet withdrew from his living, where his successor was installed on 14 February 1663. He continued to live in the parish, probably in a house opposite the church, where he kept a school until it was dispersed by the plague in 1665. At this point the new incumbent (his uncle John Lord, vicar of Salehurst) abandoned Brightling, but Bennet remained and ministered to his former parishioners, who died in great numbers. He is said to have 'resigned himself and his family to the care of Divine Providence and none of them were visited, though he went daily among those that were' (Calamy, 2.682). Earlier that year, on 3 April 1665, he married Elizabeth (b. c.1645), daughter of Florice Cooke, vicar of Mountfield; they had four sons and a daughter.

In spite of the Five Mile Act Bennet stayed in Brightling and continued to take in pupils. In April 1672, following the declaration of indulgence, he was licensed as a presbyterian teacher at his own house. After the withdrawal of the indulgence he was on several occasions brought before the Lewes archdeaconry court, but his friends always rescued him. In 1685 he was accused of high treason for preaching at a service of thanksgiving for the reported success of Monmouth's rebellion, but was saved from prosecution by the intervention of influential friends. He was able to prevent his congregation from addressing their thanks to King James for the declaration of indulgence. After the Toleration Act he lived in Burwash, where he kept a school, travelling to preach to a congregation at Hellingly. From 1690 onwards he received an annual grant from the Common Fund set up by London dissenters to assist impecunious ministers. In 1696 he moved to Hastings, where he continued to minister to a presbyterian congregation until blindness and loss of memory obliged him to retire.

Calamy, who knew Bennet's son, gives a very full account of this minister, who:

> passed through the world with a character as unstained as most men. His zeal was not laid out in little matters but in promoting practical religion … He had a great tenderness towards vagabonds … He never entered into discussion with them without giving them something. He had great satisfaction in considering that worldly regards had not influenced him, but only the word of God and an unbiassed conscience. (Calamy, 2.681–3)

By his will dated 25 April 1700 Bennet left property in Brightling and Pevensey, and bequeathed all his books to his eldest son, Joseph, then minister of the presbyterian congregation at Newington Green, Middlesex, requesting that he should give 'three or four of the smaller divinity books' to his sister and to each of his three brothers (E. Sussex RO, W/A 47/73). Bennet died in November 1707 and was buried on 1 December at All Saints', Hastings. His wife survived him.   JEREMY GORING

Sources E. Calamy, ed., *An abridgement of Mr. Baxter's history of his life and times, with an account of the ministers, &c., who were ejected after the Restauration of King Charles II*, 2nd edn, 2 vols. (1713), vol. 2 · *Calamy rev.* · A. Gordon, ed., *Freedom after ejection: a review (1690–1692) of presbyterian and congregational nonconformity in England and Wales* (1917) · J. J. Goring, *Church and dissent in Warbleton, c.1500–1900* (1980) · E. Sussex RO, PAR 361/1/1/3, 424/1/1/2, 477/1/1/1, 501/1/1/1 · will, E. Sussex RO, W/A 47/73 · Common Fund minute books, 1690–1707, DWL · BL, Add. MS 39330, fols. 186, 189v · Venn, *Alum. Cant.*

Wealth at death books to eldest son: will, E. Sussex RO, W/A 47/73

Bennet, Robert (d. 1617), bishop of Hereford, was the son of Leonard Bennet of Baldock, Hertfordshire, and his wife, Margaret Langley. Having matriculated as a pensioner at Trinity College, Cambridge, in Easter term 1563, Bennet proceeded BA in 1566–7 and was admitted as a minor fellow in September 1567. He became a major fellow in April 1570, took an MA the same year, and served as university preacher in 1576. He was incorporated at Oxford in 1572. At Cambridge Bennet was a keen sportsman and fine racket player. Later, after taking his BTh in 1577, contemporaries called him 'Erudito Benedicte' as, by now, 'he would tosse an Argument in the Schools, better than a Ball in the Tennis-court' (Harington, 139). In 1572 he had opposed the university statutes as redrafted by John Whitgift, the master of Trinity, and in 1578 he collaborated with his fellow collegian William Whitaker in a Latin translation of John Jewel's *A Replie unto M Hardinge's Answeare* (1565): Whitaker made the translation and Bennet supplied a Latin preface.

Bennet left Cambridge in 1583 to become master of the hospital of St Cross, Winchester, where in concert with Thomas Bilson, warden of Winchester College, he set about eradicating Catholic recusancy. This made Bennet enemies but also brought him to the favourable attention of William Cecil, Lord Burghley, who made him one of his chaplains. When a number of senior church positions became vacant in the autumn of 1594 Bennet and Bilson both sought promotion. Burghley offered the deanery of Windsor to Bilson, who turned it down in the hope of something better. Meanwhile Bennet complained to Burghley that he was unwilling to be buried at St Cross 'amongst beggers' such as the bedesmen of the hospital, particularly as a number of his own pupils had been 'advanced to the highest callinges in this church' (Lansdowne MS 77, fol. 38). In March 1596 Bennet was appointed to Windsor when the incumbent dean, William Day, was made bishop of Winchester.

Bennet remained at Windsor for seven years, during which time he continued as master of St Cross. He was sworn registrar of the Order of the Garter in April 1596 and was a member of the high commission from October 1597. His increased exposure to the court occasioned controversy, however. During much of 1596–7 he laboured unsuccessfully to resist the queen's order that he alienate a lease belonging to St Cross, and in 1598 he turned down the bishopric of Salisbury, the offer being conditional on the making of a further alienation. In the process Bennet was so derogatory of the man appointed, the queen's personal candidate Henry Cotton, that he earned a sharp rebuke from Sir Robert Cecil for his 'medling' (PRO, SP 12/268/60). Nevertheless, in January 1603 he was elected bishop of Hereford. Bennet, it seems, lobbied for the position, most notably through a court sermon in Lent 1602 which was 'very well liked' by some but dismissed by others as 'all needle-worke' (*Letters of John Chamberlain*, 1.147); also significant was the patronage of Cecil.

Once installed at Hereford, Bennet made his priority the

suppression of Catholic recusancy. His preferred instrument was a diocesan commission of the kind that Burghley had granted him at Winchester in 1584–5. Yet despite repeated appeals during 1604–10 Bennet was unsuccessful in persuading James I, Cecil (now earl of Salisbury), and Archbishop Richard Bancroft to grant one. Meanwhile his health was faltering, and from 1605 Bennet complained of periods of 'continued sickness and lameness' due to the 'cold and rheumatic' climate of the border country (*Salisbury MSS*, 16.93). In 1610 he sought unsuccessfully the vacant bishopric of Worcester. Thereafter Bennet became prominent among the Jacobean episcopate in sponsoring evangelical activity, most notably a combination lecture licensed at Leintwardine from 1612, and in tackling low clerical standards. He ousted absentee ministers, usually licensed curates in person, presided over diocesan visitations in 1612 and 1615, and during 1614–15 embarked on a vocational training programme for non-preaching ministers in the diocese. Bennet also laboured to win over the scruples of nonconformist ministers, but not at any price: to Thomas Pierson, puritan lecturer at Leintwardine, Bennet remarked that 'he would not loose his byshoprick for my sake' (Fincham, 259).

Bennet was known at Cambridge for his good looks, and James I reportedly said of him that 'if he were to chuse a Bishop by the aspect, he would chuse him of all the men he had seen, for a grave reverent and pleasing countenance' (Harington, 138). He died on 25 October 1617 and was buried in his cathedral, having bequeathed the unusually large sum of £500 for his burial expenses. Bennet had also selected the preacher for the service, designed his own monument in white alabaster (the effigy remains), and specified in his will how much cloth should be used and at what price for the cloak of each relative participating at the ceremony. He laid down that his tomb was to be erected 'in the church of the choir, behind the seat of his wife' (Wood, *Ath. Oxon.*, new edn, 2.846). The name of his wife is unknown, and his heir was the son of his brother John, another Robert Bennet.

WILLIAM RICHARDSON

Sources K. Fincham, *Prelate as pastor: the episcopate of James I* (1990) • Venn, *Alum. Cant.*, 1/1.134 • F. O. White, *Lives of the Elizabethan bishops of the Anglican church* (1898) • J. Harington, *A briefe view of the state of the Church of England* (1653) • *Calendar of the manuscripts of the most hon. the marquis of Salisbury*, 24 vols., HMC, 9 (1883–1976), vols. 11, 14–17, 19 • state papers domestic, Elizabeth I, PRO, SP 12/12/60 • J. Berlatsky, 'The Elizabethan episcopate: patterns of life and expenditure', *Princes and paupers in the English church, 1500–1800*, ed. R. O'Day and F. Heal (1981), 111–27 • *The letters of John Chamberlain*, ed. N. E. McClure, 2 vols. (1939) • Wood, *Ath. Oxon.: Fasti* (1815), 191–2 • Wood, *Ath. Oxon.*, new edn, 2.845–6 • P. Collinson, *The religion of protestants* (1982) • J. Eales, *Puritans and roundheads: the Harleys of Brampton Bryan and the outbreak of the English civil war* (1990) • BL, Lansdowne MS 77, fol. 38 • W. H. Rylands, ed., *The four visitations of Berkshire*, 1, Harleian Society, 56 (1907), 70
Archives BL, Lansdowne MSS 39, 40, 45, 46, 54, 77, 80 • Bodl. Oxf., Ashmole MS 1162 • Herefs. RO, administrative papers • PRO, corresp., SP 12, vols. 177, 260, 261, 268, 286; SP 14, vols. 14, 16, 44, 48, 52, 53; SP 15, vol. 36 • Worcs. RO, administrative papers
Likenesses alabaster effigy, Hereford Cathedral

Wealth at death lavish burial: Berlatsky, 'Elizabethan episcopate', 123, 126 n. 74 • will, PRO, PROB 11/122

Bennet [Bennett], **Robert** (*d.* 1687), clergyman and ejected minister, is a figure whose birth and parentage remain unknown; he may have come from Derbyshire, as the *Dictionary of National Biography* suggested. He matriculated at Magdalene College, Cambridge, in 1631, graduating BA in 1635 and proceeding MA in 1638. His one published book designated him BD on the title-page, but there is no other indication that he had received this degree. In 1645 Bennet was vicar of Hayes, Middlesex. In 1648 he was a chaplain to Philip, Lord Wharton, a staunch parliamentarian opponent of Charles I and a patron of ministers of puritan outlook. In 1648 Lord Wharton presented Bennet for the position of rector of Waddesdon, Buckinghamshire, to which he was admitted on 21 September. According to the Waddesdon parish registers Bennet had a wife, Margaret, a daughter of the same name (*bap.* 1653), and a son, Gervase (*bap.* 1651). In 1654 Bennet was an assistant to the Buckinghamshire commission.

In 1661, after the Restoration, Bennet was ejected from Waddesdon because of nonconformity, and the living of Waddesdon, which consisted of three rectories, was given to John Ellis. Ellis had already in 1658 been presented to one of these rectories by Lord Wharton, but, according to Edmund Calamy the younger, Ellis 'scrupled to take the title upon him, and only preach'd every other Lord's-Day, in his Turn' (Calamy, *Abridgement*, 2.107). Bennet performed the other parish duties and allowed Ellis one half of the income. After Ellis, who conformed to the Restoration Church of England, received all three Waddesdon rectories, he gave £55 annually to Bennet. However, writing to Lord Wharton in 1678, Bennet complained that Ellis was two years in arrears in his payments to him, and in another letter of the same year Bennet refers to an agreement he had made with Ellis and considers that in case of Ellis's death he would still have some title to this income. In 1663 Bennet travelled to Caen, France, at the behest of Lord Wharton, in order to investigate difficulties that had arisen in connection with Lord Wharton's children and their tutor, Theophilus Gale, and report back to his patron.

In 1666 Bennet was described as living in Snelston, Derbyshire, where his son, Gervase, lived. By the summer of 1668 he was back in Buckinghamshire. In 1669 he was reported as preacher to a conventicle of some thirty or forty men and women 'but of ordinary quality' which had been meeting since the previous June at the manor house in Whitchurch where Bennet and his wife lived (Broad, 42). At the same time he was reported to be teaching a conventicle consisting of about two hundred people which met in private houses at Thame, Oxfordshire. In 1672, under the terms of the declaration of indulgence he was licensed as of Waddesdon and as a presbyterian. Thereafter he preached for some years at Aylesbury, Buckinghamshire, where he was in 1674, and at Abingdon, Berkshire, where his daughter was reported as living in 1678. It was there that he died on 6 April 1687.

Bennet was the author of *A Theological Concordance of the*

Synonymous Terms in the Holy Scriptures, published in 1657, an alphabetically arranged work that gathered relevant biblical references under 'Morally or Theologically significant' scriptural words and some terms drawn from theology, such as 'assurance', 'atonement', 'banish', and 'baptize'. The work was designed as a way of taking 'the shortest cut to knowledge', and consequently useful for students and 'private Christians' as well as for the learned. Appended to it was a list of scripture references outlining 'the Promises of the Covenant'.

DEWEY D. WALLACE, JUN.

Sources Calamy rev. • E. Calamy, ed., *An abridgement of Mr. Baxter's history of his life and times, with an account of the ministers, &c., who were ejected after the Restauration of King Charles II*, 2nd edn, 2 vols. (1713), vol. 2, p. 107 • DNB • Venn, *Alum. Cant.* • A. G. Mathews, 'The Wharton correspondence', *Transactions of the Congregational Historical Society*, 10 (1927–9), 53–65 • G. L. Turner, *Original records of early nonconformity under persecution and indulgence*, 3 (1914) • J. Broad, ed., *Buckinghamshire dissent and parish life, 1669–1712*, Buckinghamshire RS, 28 (1993) • IGI • R. Bennet, *A theological concordance of the synonymous terms in the holy scriptures* (1657)
Archives Bodl. Oxf., Bodleian MSS 322, 351 • Bodl. Oxf., Rawlinson letters, vols. 51, 53 • Bodl. Oxf., Willis MS 12.81

Bennet, Sir Thomas (1592–1670). *See under* Bennet, Sir John (1552/3–1627).

Bennet, Thomas (1645–1681), grammarian, was born at Windsor, Berkshire, the son of Henry Bennet of Binfield, Berkshire. He was a queen's scholar at Westminster School. He matriculated as a plebeian at Christ Church, Oxford, on 19 July 1662, was elected a student in the same year, and graduated BA in 1666 and MA on 3 April 1669, whereupon he became corrector at the university press. In 1669 he corrected the proofs of the first book of John Fell, dean of Christ Church, and was nominated by him architypographer, an officer who oversaw the workmanship of the press's productions and was, according to William Laud who drew up the original statute, to be 'thoroughly acquainted with Greek and Latin literature and deeply learned in philological studies' (Carter, 31). Bennet, thinking the appointment secure, did not go round cap in hand to the masters as was usual. Even Fell, though most powerful in the university, failed to prevent convocation's rejecting Bennet and electing a relative nonentity, Norton Bold, and Fell's second attempt to secure the post for Bennet also failed, in October 1671.

In 1673 Bennet published *Many useful observations by way of comment out of antient and learned grammarians on Lilly's Grammar*, which became known as the Oxford grammar or sometimes as Dr Fell's grammar. From its first edition in 1527 the Latin grammar of William Lily had been largely used in teaching classics, especially in the new grammar schools. In the words of John Twells, a schoolmaster of Newark writing in 1683, what Bennet did for Latin grammar was to make 'the Rules of *Lilie's Propria quae maribus*, and *As in praesenti* … more easie and infinitely more compleat' (Twells, sig. B7v). Twells called him the '*Oxford* Grammarian' and, apparently unaware of Bennet's death two years earlier, hoped he would 'speedily apply both his Head and Hand' to remedy 'the grand

Inconveniences of *Quae genus* and *Syntax*' (ibid., title-page, sig. B7v).

Following his second rebuff by the university, Bennet became ordained. He was appointed to two livings in Berkshire—Steventon in 1675 and Hungerford from 1678 until 1679. He died at Hungerford in August 1681 and was buried there.   JENNETT HUMPHREYS, *rev.* EVELYN E. COWIE

Sources Foster, *Alum. Oxon.* • P. Sutcliffe, *The Oxford University Press: an informal history* (1978) • N. Barker, *The Oxford University Press and the spread of learning, 1478–1978* (1978) • *Printing and publishing at Oxford: the growth of a learned press, 1478–1978* (1978) [exhibition catalogue, Bodl. Oxf.] • W. Money, *A historical sketch of the town of Hungerford* (1894) • C. Smyth, *Church and parish* (1955) • J. Twells, *Grammatica reformata* (1683) • C. Brown, *A history of Newark-on-Trent* (1907) • M. L. Clarke, *Classical education in Britain, 1500–1900* (1959) • D. S. White, *The teaching of Latin* (1941) • W. A. L. Vincent, *The grammar schools, 1660–1714* (1964) • H. Carter, *A history of the Oxford University Press*, 1: *To the year 1780* (1975)

Bennet, Thomas (1673–1728), Church of England clergyman and religious controversialist, was born on 7 May 1673 in Salisbury, the son of Thomas Bennet, gentleman. He was educated at the free school in Salisbury from 1680 to 1688, when, at the age of fifteen, his prodigious learning earned him a place as sizar at St John's College, Cambridge. He matriculated on 31 May 1689 and graduated BA (1693), MA (1696), and DD (1715). He was elected fellow in 1694 and held that position until 1705. He was ordained deacon by Bishop Henry Compton on 8 March 1696 and priest on 19 June 1698. His whig principles were evident in the Hebrew verses he composed on the death of Queen Mary that were published in the university collection in 1695.

The foundations of Bennet's career were his elocution, his voice, and his prowess as a preacher. In 1700 he travelled to visit a friend, John Rayne, rector of St James's, Colchester, but arrived to find him dead. Bennet undertook the duty of preaching Rayne's funeral sermon and so impressed his audience that they successfully persuaded Bishop Compton to choose Bennet as Rayne's successor. Though the income of St James's, Colchester, was modest, with his talents Bennet raised it, from gifts and subscriptions, to £300 a year. He left Colchester when the appointment of other strong preachers to livings in the town eroded his income.

In 1711 Bennet accepted the appointment of deputy chaplain to Chelsea Hospital, Middlesex. Soon afterwards he preached the funeral sermon for Mr Erington, lecturer of St Olave's, Southwark, and again his talents won him the support of the congregation in his election to the post of lecturer. In 1715 he accepted the appointment of morning preacher at St Lawrence Jewry, Gresham Street, under Dr Mapletoft. It seems likely that Bennet's preferment so early in the reign of George I was due to his whig principles and to the patronage of Benjamin Hoadly. On 4 April 1717 he was appointed by the dean and chapter of St Paul's Cathedral to the living of St Giles Cripplegate, which carried an income of £500 a year. In his first few years as rector Bennet resorted to a lengthy and exhausting lawsuit to recover tithes on peas and beans, which amounted to £150 a year. In 1721 he installed a new clock on the steeple. In 1717 he married Elizabeth Hunt of Salisbury, a widow and 'a gentlewoman of great merit' (Chalmers, 463), with whom he had three daughters.

Bennet's talents as a preacher combined with his energies as a controversial author. Some of his publications addressed the issue of the separation of dissenters and nonjurors from the church. At Cambridge he wrote *An Answer to the Dissenters Plea for Separation* (1699), which by 1711 had run through five editions. He followed this, in 1702, with *A Discourse of Schism*, which claimed that schism was a sin and that dissenters were responsible for it; he also claimed that the Toleration Act of 1689 did not justify schism by dissenters. This tract drew the attention of three dissenting ministers in Essex, who contradicted it, stimulating Bennet to publish, in 1703, *A Defence of the Discourse of Schism* and *An Answer to Mr Shepherd's Considerations on the Defence of the Discourse of Schism*. Bennet's defence of the Church of England was further expressed in *A Confutation of Popery* (1701), and in *A Confutation of Quakerism* (1705). The latter work was sufficiently popular for Bennet to extract sections from it, entitled *A discourse on the necessity of being baptised with water and receiving the Lord's supper, taken out of the confutation of Quakerism*, for those who could not afford either the money to buy, or the time to read, the whole book. The separation of the nonjurors was the subject of Bennet's attack, in 1716, entitled *The Non-Jurors Separation from the Public Assemblies of the Church of England*, which asserted that the nonjurors' separation was as sinful a schism as that of dissenters.

Bennet also expressed the views of leading Anglicans in his determination to insist on the liturgy rather than extempore prayer, which was held to lead to nonconformity. His *Devotions, viz confessions, petitions, intercessions and thanksgivings, for every day in the week, and also before, at, and after the sacrament, with occasional prayers for all persons whatsoever* was published in 1705. These prayers were the subject of a number of jibes and led him to publish, in 1708, *A Brief History of Joint Use of Precomposed Set Forms of Prayer*, *A Discourse of Joint Prayer*, and *A Paraphrase with Annotations upon the Book of Common Prayer*. It was typical of Bennet's prolific pen that he published three tracts to respond to his opponents.

Bennet was also anxious to defend the traditional interests of the church. In 1711 he published *The rights of the clergy of the Christian church, or, A discourse shewing that God has given and appropriated to the clergy authority to ordain, baptise, preach, preside in church prayer, and consecrate the Lord's supper*; ironically, given Bennet's career, this attacked the claims of the laity to the right to elect their own pastors. In 1715 he published an *Essay on the XXXIX Articles*, which attacked the freethinker Anthony Collins's *Priestcraft in Perfection*. Bennet's defence of orthodoxy was also effected in *A Discourse of the Ever-Blessed Trinity in Unity* (1718), which attacked Samuel Clarke's work.

Bennet had a complete understanding of Hebrew and other eastern languages, and in 1726 he published *A Hebrew Grammar*, which earned him a reputation far greater than that achieved by his polemical writing. He was a tall, imposing man with a haughty manner. He died on 9 October 1728, of apoplexy, in the rectory at St Giles Cripplegate, and was buried in his church two days later.

WILLIAM GIBSON

Sources A. Chalmers, ed., *The general biographical dictionary*, new edn, 3 (1812), 460–65 • Venn, *Alum. Cant.* • G. Hennessy, *Novum repertorium ecclesiasticum parochiale Londinense, or, London diocesan clergy succession from the earliest time to the year 1898* (1898) • J. Ecton, *Liber valorum et decimarum* (1728) • A. E. Daniell, *London city churches* (1896) • *DNB*

Bennet, William (1746–1820), bishop of Cloyne and antiquary, was born in the Tower of London on 4 March 1746, the son of Robert Bennet. He was educated at Harrow School, where he made the acquaintance of Dr Samuel Parr, Gilbert Wakefield, and Sir John Parnell: his friendship with Parr lasted until Bennet's death. He afterwards attended Emmanuel College, Cambridge, where he graduated BA in 1767, and proceeded MA in 1770 and DD in 1790. Bennet was ordained deacon on 21 May 1769 and priest on 9 June 1770. In 1773 a fellowship was conferred upon him, and for many years he was the chief tutor at the college. During this period he compiled a register of Emmanuel College. Among his pupils were John Fane, later tenth earl of Westmorland, and Charles Manners-Sutton, the future archbishop of Canterbury. On 24 September 1791 he married Frances, daughter of the Revd Nathaniel Mapletoft, of Boughton in Northamptonshire, and his wife, Anna Maria, only daughter of Charles, fifth Viscount Cullen.

On his appointment as lord lieutenant of Ireland in 1790, Westmorland nominated his old tutor as his chaplain. Bennet's promotion was then assured, and it came quickly. From 12 June 1790 to 1794 he held the see of Cork and Ross, and was then translated to the more lucrative bishopric of Cloyne: he was enthroned by proxy on 1 July 1794. It was at one time proposed to appoint Bishop Bennet to an English see, and he was put in nomination for the provostship of Trinity College, Dublin, to be held *in commendam* with his bishopric. The latter plan was vigorously opposed by Edmund Burke, and Bennet's candidacy failed. In his last years Bennet was resident mainly in London: Richard Mant often saw him at Manners-Sutton's table at Lambeth. A noted pulpit orator, he preached frequently on behalf of city charities. His exertions while preaching a charity sermon at St Michael, Cornhill, exacerbated by a recent attack of gout, are supposed to have hastened his death. He died at Montagu Square, London, on 16 July 1820, and was buried in the church at Plumstead, Kent; a monument to his memory was erected in Cloyne Cathedral.

Like Berkeley and Woodward before him, and Brinkley after him, Bennet enhanced the scholarly reputation of the bishops of Cloyne during the last century of the see's separate existence. An exact classical scholar, he was best-known as an antiquary. He was elected FSA in 1790, but does not seem to have contributed to the *Archaeologia*. His favourite pursuit was to trace the Roman roads in Great Britain. He shared this interest with the Revd Thomas Leman, whom he appointed chancellor of Cloyne (1796–1802), and together they visited most Roman roads and stations. Bennet communicated his knowledge widely. Daniel and Samuel Lysons, in their advertisement to the *Magna Britannia* (1806–22), their topographical description of Britain, acknowledged their indebtedness to him. His paper 'On the Roman architecture and castrametation' appeared in R. Polwhele's history of Cornwall; and to J. Nichols's history of the antiquities of Leicestershire he contributed some remarks on the county's Roman roads, as well as an account of the Jewry wall of Leicester.

Within the Irish church Bennet's episcopate spanned the transition from high Georgian latitudinarianism to the post-union era of episcopal reform and evangelical revival. Though himself a traveller like Pococke of Ossory earlier, and an antiquary like his contemporary Percy of Dromore, he yet identified with the new influences in the church's life through 'his long and persistent advocacy of the Bible Society' (Phillips, 3.290). His monument records his ten years as vice-president of the British and Foreign Bible Society (while ignoring, at the height of the 'Bible controversy' in Ireland, his having held a like office in the Hibernian Bible Society). Bennet's clergy pointed also to his courtesy, simplicity of spirit, and philanthropy of heart; and Cotton concluded: 'He was reckoned an elegant and profound scholar, an able preacher, and a good man' (Cotton, 1.234).

W. P. COURTNEY, *rev.* ALAN R. ACHESON

Sources R. Mant, *History of the Church of Ireland*, 2 (1840), 718–20 · H. Cotton, *Fasti ecclesiae Hibernicae*, 2 (1848), 304–6; 2nd edn, 1 (1851), 234 · W. M. Brady, *Clerical and parochial records of Cork, Cloyne, and Ross*, 3 (1864), 82, 126–9 · C. A. Webster, *The diocese of Cork* (1920), 325–9 · W. A. Phillips, ed., *History of the Church of Ireland*, 3 (1933), 290 · Venn, *Alum. Cant.*
Archives Bodl. Oxf., continental travel diary · Bodl. RH · Emmanuel College, Cambridge, William Bennet's book | BL, corresp. with Lord Hardwicke and others · Northants. RO, letters to Mapletoft family · TCD, letters to James Sandiford
Likenesses attrib. G. Stuart, *c.*1787–1793, Emmanuel College, Cambridge · monument, Cloyne Cathedral, co. Cork

Bennet, William (*b.* 1767?, *d.* in or after 1833?), organist and composer, was born at Combeinteignhead, Devon, where his father, the organist at St Andrew's Church, Plymouth, and a descendant of an old Devon family, had inherited an estate. Bennet's first music teachers were Hugh Bond and William Jackson of Exeter, but he later went to London, where he studied under Johann Christian Bach and had piano lessons from Johann Schroeter. He was an excellent pianist, and was known for his extempore performances on the organ. He was appointed organist of St Andrew's Church, Plymouth in 1793 and may still have been serving there in 1833. Bennet is said to have been the first to introduce the grand piano to Plymouth, and his performances helped to bring about the decline in popularity of the harpsichord. His compositions include *Six Songs and a Glee* (1799), anthems, organ music, songs, and solo piano pieces, as well as *The Collects of the Church of England*, and a new version of the Psalms in four parts with accompaniments for piano or organ. He wrote an anthem for the coronation of George IV in 1820. All his music fell into early obscurity.

In 1797 Bennet married the daughter of John Debell (or Deball) of Guildford. Nothing is known about his later life.

W. B. SQUIRE, *rev.* ANNE PIMLOTT BAKER

Sources J. D. Brown, *Biographical dictionary of musicians: with a bibliography of English writings on music* (1886) · [J. S. Sainsbury], ed., *A dictionary of musicians*, 2 vols. (1824) · [Clarke], *The Georgian era: memoirs of the most eminent persons*, 4 (1834). 547

Bennett, Alfred Rosling (1850–1928), electrical engineer, was born on 14 May 1850 in Islington, London, the son of John Richard Bennett. He had at least one brother. He was educated at a private school, and later at the Bellevue Academy, Greenwich. His original leanings were towards railway engineering, and he maintained an interest in the subject all his life, but his first appointment in 1869 was to the Indian government telegraph department in Karachi, on whose behalf he visited Baluchistan, Mesopotamia, and Turkey, receiving special mention for his proficiency in the testing of land line and submarine cables.

In 1873 he returned to England and became electrician to the Highton Battery Company, which worked the battery and other patents of the Revd Henry Highton. In 1877, only two years after Alexander Graham Bell had invented the telephone, Bennett set up the first experimental overhead telephone line in England, linking the Queen's Theatre in Long Acre and the Canterbury Music Hall, in London, for a demonstration of Varley's musical telephone. Soon afterwards, he engaged in research which resulted in his filing patents for the telephonic translator (1880), the caustic alkali and iron battery (1881), and a telephone transformer (1881).

Bennett entered the service of the National Telephone Company in 1883, becoming general manager and chief engineer for Scotland and north-west England from 1886 to 1890. During this time he was responsible for the installation of the first incandescent lamps in Scotland, and the first electric lighting in a coal mine, near Hamilton. After short periods as general manager and chief engineer of the Mutual and the New Telephone companies he set up in practice in 1893 as a consulting telephone and telegraph engineer, in which capacity he acted as consulting engineer to the telephone departments of Guernsey (1896–1921) and Glasgow (1900–04), as well as Portsmouth, Hull, Brighton, and Swansea (1900–11). He was the originator of, and vice-chairman of the executive council for, the Edinburgh International Electrical and Engineering Exhibition of 1890. His last work was the reorganization of the telephone system in Malta. From 1891 on, Bennett published books and papers on both telephony and railways. He was a member of the Institution of Electrical Engineers and a vice-president of the Institution of Locomotive Engineers.

Bennett was unmarried. He spent the winter of 1927–8 in Malta, and had only been back in England for a few days when he succumbed to bronchitis and died on 24 May 1928, at Smedley's Hydropathic Establishment, Matlock, Derbyshire. He was buried at Darley Dale cemetery, Matlock. His obituarist in *Locomotive* noted that 'death brought to a close an interesting and useful life'. Bennett was known for his remarkable energy, great sincerity, and

Alfred Rosling
Bennett (1850–
1928), by Elliott &
Fry, pubd 1907–9

charm, and was always ready to acknowledge merit in others. H. W. D., obituarist, writing in the *Transactions* of the Newcomen Society (Bennett had been a member since 1921), commented on his remarkable memory, and described him as 'a man of genial breezy temperament, a strong individualist, and one who made friends wherever he went.'   RONALD M. BIRSE, *rev.* BRIAN BOWERS

Sources *Journal of the Institute of Electrical Engineers* (1928), 1233–4 · *Electrical Trades Directory* (1903), x–xi [biographical entry] · *Locomotive*, 34 (June 1928), 177 · *Locomotive*, 34 (July 1928), 235–6 · *Journal of the Institution of Locomotive Engineers*, 5/18 (1928), 448 · H. W. D., *Transactions* [Newcomen Society], 7 (1926–7), 151–2 · d. cert. · CGPLA *Eng. & Wales* (1928)
Likenesses Elliott & Fry, photograph, pubd 1907–9, NPG [*see illus.*] · photograph, repro. in *Electrical Trades Directory* · photograph, repro. in *Locomotive*, 34 (July 1928), 235
Wealth at death £9115 14s. 0d.: probate, 25 July 1928, CGPLA *Eng. & Wales*

Bennett, Alfred William (1833–1902), botanist and publisher, was born on 24 June 1833 at Clapham, Surrey, the second son of William Bennett (*d.* 1873), tea dealer and botanist, and his wife, Elizabeth (*d.* 1891), author of religious books for the Society of Friends. His father was interested in education and apart from the winter of 1841–2, which the family spent at the Pestalozzi School at Appenzell in Switzerland, Bennett was taught at home. He later attended classes at University College, London, and graduated BA from the University of London with honours in chemistry and botany (1853). He proceeded MA in 1855 and gained his BSc in 1868.

On leaving college Bennett became tutor to the family of the banker Gurney Barclay. In 1858 he married Katherine, the daughter of William Richardson of Sunderland, and started business as a bookseller and publisher. He was one of the first publishers to use photography for illustrating his books, whose topics ranged from alpine scenery to Yorkshire abbeys. For a time about 1860 he was both proprietor and editor of the weekly journal *Friends*; he later wrote on pre-Foxite Quakerism (1894). Among other works Bennett published were poems by John Leicester Warren, afterwards third Baron de Tabley, and his own

parents. Bennett also prepared the original catalogue of the Lindley Library following its purchase by the Royal Horticultural Society in 1867.

In 1868 Bennett gave up his business and became a lecturer on botany at Bedford College and St Thomas's Hospital, London. He remained there until 1896 and was described as 'an excellent and painstaking teacher, and a careful examiner' (Baker, 157). He also had an interest in the higher education of women and opened his house to enable several female students to attend Bedford College. From 1870 to 1874 he was biological sub-editor for the newly established journal *Nature* and was also botanical reviewer and writer for *The Academy*. Bennett became a fellow of the Linnean Society in 1868. He briefly served as assistant editor of the society's publications during 1873–4, but was 'grossly careless in his reporting' (Gage, 67). About this time he also wrote several papers on flower-fertilization and began his studies of the order Polygalaceae (milkworts) which allowed him to contribute a synopsis of the Indian species for J. D. Hooker's *Flora of British India* (1872) and also of the more numerous Brazilian species for the *Flora Brasiliensis* published by Martius (1874).

Bennett's knowledge of the German language enabled him, with the assistance of William Thiselton-Dyer, to translate the third edition of the *Lehrbuch der Botanik* by F. G. Julius von Sachs as the *Textbook of Botany, Morphological and Physiological* (1875). This had a great influence on the teaching of botany, 'turning it away from lectures … to courses on anatomy and physiology' (Baker, 157). Bennett also translated and edited the *Lehrbuch* by Professor Otto Thome, which was published as *Textbook of Structural and Physiological Botany* in 1877 and 1885. Throughout his life he made numerous botanical contributions to scientific periodicals and published *Mycological Illustrations* (1871) with W. Wilson Saunders and Worthington G. Smith.

An early love of natural history, walking, and flowers led to a tour of Switzerland in 1875 that resulted in Bennett's translation of J. Seboth's *Alpenpflanzen nach der Natur gemalt* as *Alpine Plants* (1879–84), and of a work by K. W. von Dalla Torre as *Tourists' Guide to the Flora of the Austrian Alps* (1882, 1886). In these and his own *The Flora of the Alps*, published in 1897 with the coloured plates taken from David Wooster's *Alpine Plants* (1872), Bennett endeavoured to improve and widen the available illustrations of alpine plants.

In 1879 Bennett became a fellow of the Royal Microscopical Society, and thereafter confined his research to cryptogamic plants, especially the freshwater algae. He revised the section on cryptogams for the fourth edition of Henfrey's *Elementary Botany* (1884) and dealt with all the groups containing chlorophyll for the joint *Handbook of Cryptogamic Botany* with G. R. Milne Murray (1889), which has been recognized as his 'most valuable original work' (Baker, 157).

Bennett served on the council of the Royal Microscopical Society and became editor of its publications in 1897. He died suddenly from heart disease, collapsing on the top of an omnibus at Oxford Circus, London, on his way home from the Savile Club to his home in Regent's Park, on 23 January 1902. His wife had predeceased him and he was buried next to her at the Quaker burial-ground in Isleworth, on 28 January; they had no children.

R. J. CLEEVELY

Sources J. G. Baker, *Journal of the Royal Microscopical Society* (1902), 155–7, portrait · *Proceedings of the Linnean Society of London*, 114th session (1901–2), 26–7 · *Journal of Botany, British and Foreign*, 40 (1902), 113–15 · A. T. Gage, *A history of the Linnean Society of London* (1938) · Desmond, *Botanists*, rev. edn · *Gardeners' Chronicle*, 3rd ser., 31 (1902), 85 · F. A. Stafleu and R. S. Cowan, *Taxonomic literature: a selective guide*, 2nd edn, 1, Regnum Vegetabile, 94 (1976), 171 · *WWW* · J. Britten, 'Biographical index of British and Irish botanists', *Journal of Botany, British and Foreign*, 41 (1903), 2nd suppl., 345 · *Nature*, 65 (1901–2), 34 · *The Garden*, 61 (1902), 81–2

Archives NHM, drawings · RBG Kew, letters | NHM, plant specimens · RBG Kew, plant specimens

Likenesses Maull & Fox, platinum cabinet print, Linn. Soc. · photograph, repro. in *Journal of the Royal Microscopical Society* (1902), 154 · portrait, Hunt Library, Pittsburgh, Pennsylvania

Wealth at death £10,829 0s. 11d.: probate, 12 March 1902, CGPLA Eng. & Wales

Bennett, Anna Maria (d. 1808), novelist, was probably the daughter of David Evans of Merthyr Tudful, Glamorgan, who has been described as a customs officer and a grocer. She was briefly married to Mr Bennett, a custom house officer. Other than this, her origins are obscure. After moving to London, she met Admiral Sir Thomas *Pye (1708/9–1785), while working in a chandler's shop. She became his housekeeper and mistress in Tooting, Surrey, and had at least two children with him, Thomas Pye Bennett and Harriet Pye Bennett. Her daughter became the famous actress Harriet Pye *Esten (1761?–1865). It seems that, aside from writing, Anna Bennett was instrumental in launching and perpetuating her daughter's acting career.

In 1785, after Pye's death, Anna Bennett (sometimes mistakenly called Agnes) was permitted to dedicate her first novel, *Anna, or, The Memoirs of a Welch Heiress*, to the princess royal. The whole impression of the work, though published anonymously, was sold on the day of publication, and by 1805 it had gone through four editions. The novel was twice translated into French, first by Dubois Fontenelle, apparently in 1784 (though this must be an error, unless the translation was from the manuscript in advance of the English press), and secondly in 1800. Anna Bennett's second novel, again published anonymously, was *Juvenile Indiscretions* (1786); it was attributed at first to Fanny Burney, and translated into French the same year. In 1789 her third novel, a reworking of Richardson's *Clarissa*, entitled *Agnes de Courci: a Domestic Tale*, was published; it too was popular enough to be translated. A fourth novel, entitled *Ellen, Countess of Castle Howel*, was issued from the Minerva Press on 12 March 1794 with an 'Apology' prefixed, which indicated 'the greatest Distress, both of Mind and Circumstances' (Bennett, 1.3). It was noticed in the *Monthly Review* (14, 1794, 74). *The Beggar Girl and her Benefactors* was published in seven volumes in 1797; it was supposedly based on existing characters at Tooting and was dedicated to the duchess of York, near whom Anna Bennett then lived. *The Beggar Girl* was very popular, and had some distinguished admirers. Coleridge copied four of

Anna Bennett's titles onto the flyleaf of his *Conciones ad populum* (1795), and added 'all by the authoress of *The Beggar Girl*, the best novel me judice since Fielding. I should like therefore to see the others' (Blakey, 54). By 1806 Anna Bennett's popularity was immense. She produced a new novel that year in six volumes called *Vicissitudes Abroad, or, The Ghost of my Father*; 2000 copies were sold on the first day, although the price was 36s.

Another work by Anna Bennett was published posthumously in 1816, under the title of *Faith and Fiction, or, Shining Lights in a Dark Generation* (5 vols.). She is also credited with the authorship of two French novels, *L'orphelin du presbytère* (1816); and *Beauté et laideur* (1820), but these were apparently portions of *Faith and Fiction*, translated. In 1822 Defauconpret translated *Ellen de Courci*; and in 1853 an attempt was made by W. Strange, of Lovel's Court, Paternoster Row, to reprint *Anna* in penny numbers, but only two numbers were printed. Anna Maria Bennett died at Brighton on 12 February 1808; her body was taken to London, where it was met at The Horns, Kennington Common, on 21 February by a large circle of friends.

JENNETT HUMPHREYS, *rev.* REBECCA MILLS

Sources J. F. Fuller, 'A curious genealogical medley', *Miscellanea Genealogica et Heraldica*, 4th ser., 5 (1912–13), 244–7 · Highfill, Burnim & Langhans, *BDA* · Blain, Clements & Grundy, *Feminist comp.* · J. Todd, ed., *A dictionary of British and American women writers, 1660–1800* (1984) · J. Shattock, *The Oxford guide to British women writers* (1994), 37 · T. Gilliland, *The dramatic mirror, containing the history of the stage from the earliest period, to the present time*, 2 (1808), 756 · J. Aikin, *Athenaeum: a Magazine of Literary and Miscellaneous Information*, 3 (1808), 391–2 · *European Magazine and London Review*, 53 (1808), 156 · *ESTC* · Watt, *Bibl. Brit.*, vol. 1 · *IGI* · A. M. Bennett, 'Apology', *Ellen, countess of Castle Howel: a novel*, 2nd edn, 1 (1805) · D. Blakey, *The Minerva Press, 1790–1820* (1939)

Likenesses K. Mackenzie, stipple (after T. Braine), BM, NPG; repro. in *Ladies' Monthly Museum* (1804)

Bennett, (Enoch) Arnold (1867–1931), writer, was born at Hope Street, Burslem, Staffordshire, on 27 May 1867.

Family, education, and early life Arnold Bennett was the eldest child in a family of three sons and three daughters—three other children died in infancy—of Enoch Bennett (1843–1902) and Sarah Ann (1840–1914), eldest daughter of Robert Longson, who started life as a weaver in Glossop and moved to Burslem in 1860, where he set up a tailor's shop. According to his son, Enoch had been an ambitious child, who, by the age of ten, was earning 2d. an hour teaching in 'a sort of night school'. Unable to pursue either an academic or a legal career, Enoch took up pottery, and by the age of twenty-two had become a master potter. On his marriage in 1866, his business having failed, he set up as a draper and pawnbroker. Four years later his father died, leaving him some money with which he articled himself to a solicitor, and in 1876 he himself qualified as a solicitor.

Arnold Bennett's early years were beset by his father's financial worries. Nevertheless the Bennett family, Wesleyans though they were, encouraged musical and artistic activities. They were also bookish. From 1877 Bennett attended the endowed school, Wedgwood Institute, Burslem, transferring in 1882 to Newcastle under Lyme middle

(Enoch) **Arnold Bennett** (1867–1931), by Howard Coster, 1929

school. He stayed there for only a year, but in that time was fortunate to be taught French by a gifted master who instilled in him a love of French language and literature that was to last a lifetime. Alone of his class, in 1882 he passed the Cambridge junior local examination, which would have qualified him to go on to Newcastle under Lyme high school, and thence in all probability to university. But in 1883, at the age of sixteen, Bennett left school and began work in his father's office at Piccadilly, Hanley. Here he divided his time between rent collecting and other menial tasks by day, all of them unpaid, and at night studying for his matriculation. His father intended a legal career for him but Bennett repeatedly failed his examinations. He did, however, master Pitman's shorthand, and in March 1889, having borrowed the train fare from his mother, he set off for London, to take up a clerical post with a firm of solicitors, Le Brasseur and Oakley.

In the days since leaving school Bennett had begun to contribute light journalistic articles on such subjects as tramlines and coffee houses to the *Staffordshire Sentinel*. Once settled in London he began to write more seriously. His first success came with a story, 'A Letter Home', published in the *Yellow Book* (July 1895). Bennett, who had become devoted to the fiction of George Moore, now resolved to write a novel modelled on Moore's naturalistic mode. 'Life being grey, sinister, and melancholy, the novel must be grey, sinister, and melancholy' (*DNB*). The novel, to which Bennett had given the title 'In the Shadow', was sent to the publisher John Lane, who asked John Buchan to report on it. Buchan's favourable comments led to the publication in 1898 of what was now called *A Man from the North*. By then Bennett had long given up his legal work. In 1893 he had become assistant editor of the weekly journal *Woman*, and three years later he was made editor-in-chief.

During this period he began the practice of regular journalism and reviewing which in later years brought him considerable sums of money as well as hostility from a younger generation of writers.

Professional writer In 1900 Bennett felt sufficiently confident of his future as a writer to resign as editor of *Woman*. He also left London to set up house at Trinity Hall Farm, near the village of Hockliffe in Bedfordshire, where he installed his parents and younger sister. Here, already the author of two pot-boilers, *Journalism for Women* (1898) and *Polite Farces for the Drawing Room* (1899), he finished writing *Anna of the Five Towns*, on which he had begun work in 1896, immediately after selling his first novel. The novel was completed in 1901 and published more or less alongside *The Grand Babylon Hotel* in 1902. Bennett, who had become friendly with the writer Eden Phillpotts, followed him in deciding to keep a journal, although Bennett's journals owe rather more to the Goncourt brothers in their scrupulous recording of the details of financial transactions. He was thus able to note that although *The Grand Babylon Hotel* helped to make his name—it was the first of his books to be reviewed in *The Times*, and remained in print up to the twenty-first century—it did not fill his purse. He did not of course know that it was going to prove so phenomenal and long-lasting a best-seller, but he quickly realized that he had sold it far too cheaply. The mistake forced him to recognize the value of a good literary agent. Fortunately, one was to hand. At the end of 1901 Bennett had been introduced to J. B. Pinker by H. G. Wells, with whom he was on friendly terms. By the time Bennett set off for France, which he did at the end of 1902, Pinker had agreed to act as agent for his work, an agreement which not only led to a lifelong friendship between the two men but eventually made Bennett one of the highest-paid authors of his age.

It was almost certainly Bennett's desire to be recognized as a serious artist that prompted his move to Paris at the end of 1902. There, and in a house at Fontainebleau, he lived for the next ten years. During this period he married in July 1907 Marie Marguerite Soulié (b. 1874); they were to have no children. In France Bennett developed and widened his expertise as a dedicated man of letters. There were dramatic collaborations with Phillpotts, articles for *T. P.'s Weekly*, and further pot-boilers, including *The Truth about an Author* (1903), *A Great Man* (1904), and *Sacred and Profane Love* (1905). Bennett may have intended the last of these to be a serious study of sexual passion, although it reads as though an unconscious parody of the school of Elinor Glyn.

Yet to these years belong also *Whom God hath Joined* (1906), *The Old Wives' Tale* (1908), and the first volume in the Clayhanger trilogy (1910). These works between them justly established Bennett as a major exponent of realistic fiction. At the same time he maintained his output of lighter fiction, including most memorably *The Card* (1911), and he also produced a steady stream of literary journalism. In this regard, the short pieces he wrote about books under the pseudonym Jacob Tonson, which were published at regular intervals between 1908 and 1911 in A. R.

Orage's *New Age*, deserve mention. These pieces initiated the type of brief literary essay, aimed at the general 'cultivated' reader, which later writers such as J. B. Priestley and V. S. Pritchett took up, and which was perfectly adapted for weekly journals. In 1911 Bennett visited America, which led to *Those United States* (1912). The visit was a financial success; Bennett sold the serial rights of his projected novel, *The Price of Love*, to *Harpers* for £2000 (it was published in novel form in England in 1914), eight essays to *Metropolitan* for £150 each (they were later gathered together as *The Author's Craft*, 1914), and the American rights of a hastily planned fourth volume of Clayhanger for £3000. Bennett was accompanied on his voyage over by Edward Knoblock, an American dramatist whom he had first met in London at the Author's Club in May 1911. Bennett, keen to learn more of the craft of writing for the theatre, collaborated with Knoblock on a play entitled *Milestones*. This, together with other plays successfully produced for the stage, including *The Great Adventure* (1913; a dramatization of his 1908 novel *Buried Alive*), brought him yet further fame and money. In 1912 he returned from France to England. He now bought himself a yacht, *Velsa*, and soon bought a Queen Anne country house at Thorpe-le-Soken, Essex, which he furnished at considerable expense.

Later years During the First World War Bennett busied himself as a public servant and public man, furthering the war effort. In 1915 he produced a book, *Over There*, derived from his experiences when sent to France. Three years later, when in 1918 Lord Beaverbrook was made minister of information, Bennett was put in charge of propaganda in France. He devoted considerable energies to the work, but misgivings about the war reveal themselves in his fine novel *The Pretty Lady* (1918). In *Lord Raingo* (1926) he memorably anatomizes the kind of public figure with whom war work had brought him increasingly into contact. His introduction to the catalogue which accompanied a showing of Paul Nash's work as a war artist, held at the Leicester Galleries in 1924, provides further evidence of Bennett's less than wholly enthusiastic endorsement of the war. That he should have been asked to write the catalogue also testifies to Bennett's lively and enduring interest in the visual arts. Further evidence of this is to be found in the introduction he wrote in 1919 for a catalogue of an exhibition of modern paintings organized by Osbert, Sacheverell, and Edith Sitwell at the Mansard Gallery, London. The previous year he had agreed to help stand the losses of the distinguished quarterly *Art and Letters*, which published work by Modigliani, Gaudier-Brzeska, T. S. Eliot, Ezra Pound, Wyndham Lewis, Herbert Read, and Aldous Huxley.

After the war Bennett gave up the house in Essex. Following the legal separation from his first wife in 1921, he lived in London with Dorothy Muriel Cheston (*b*. 1891), an English actress, first in George Street, Hanover Square, later in Cadogan Square. Their daughter, Virginia, was born in 1926. During these years Bennett, by now a friend of cabinet ministers and newspaper moguls, including Beaverbrook, went on publishing novels and plays. The latter were for the most part inconsiderable and even unperformed. The best of his post-war novels are *Riceyman Steps* (1923), *Lord Raingo* (1926), *Accident* (1929), and *Imperial Palace* (1930). For much of the 1920s he was famously the highest-paid literary journalist in England, contributing a weekly column to the *Evening Standard*, advertisements for which were splashed on the sides of London omnibuses. At the very end of 1930 he and Dorothy went on holiday to France, where he unwisely drank local tap water. By the time they returned to England in the third week of January 1931, Bennett was already ill; influenza was at first suspected, but it was from typhoid fever that he eventually died in his flat at 97 Chiltern Court, Clarence Gate, Regent's Park, London, on the night of 26 March 1931. He was cremated at Golders Green, Middlesex, in April 1931.

Achievement and reputation Arnold Bennett was a prolific and highly successful author in a wide variety of modes. As essayist, dramatist, occasional travel writer, author of short stories, and, above all, of novels, he profited in most senses of the word from the fact that his career coincided with the pre-eminence of the printed word in cultural life. Yet his very success alienated younger writers suspicious of the professionalism on which he prided himself. Bennett for them exemplified the popular as opposed to the good. They saw him as a man whose concern for his pocket far outweighed concern for the novelist's art. This view of Bennett is most famously advanced in Ezra Pound's poem *Hugh Selwyn Mauberley* (*Life and Contacts*) (1919), where a Mr Nixon, met aboard 'the cream gilded cabin of his steam yacht', advises the poem's writer-protagonist always to

Consider
Carefully the reviewer.

The line-break and thus pause between the words 'Consider' and 'Carefully' may well have been intended to mime the stratagems by which Bennett attempted to conquer his stutter. More importantly, the bathos of the conclusion indicates that Mr Nixon has no interest in art's considerations. Nixon indeed offers further advice:

And give up verse, my boy,
There's nothing in it.

Pound may have wanted not merely to impugn Bennett, but to present a more generalized cameo of the kind of author whom he saw as selling out to commercial interest. Yet in some aspects Bennett's profile matches that cameo to perfection. He used his journal to record at each year's end the number of words he had written in the previous twelve months and the amount of money their publication had brought him. And certainly a good deal of his writing was made to order. As a journalist he became an accomplished space-filler, a master of the *feuilleton*. His plays, lively though their dialogue is, have not worn well; the same may be said of many of his novels, especially those written with an eye to the market in crime and detective fiction, such as *Teresa of Watling Street* (1904). *The Loot of Cities* (1905) is a collection of stories which owes much to that fictional anti-hero of the 1890s, Raffles. Bennett came to call these and other such novels 'fantasias'.

His final fiction in this mode, *The Strange Vanguard*, appeared as late as 1928. Bennett confided in his journal that when reading the proofs of the novel's opening chapters he found them to be 'very good—brilliant'; there is a temptation to believe that after years of efficiently supplying the fiction market with entertainments, whatever critical judgement Bennett may once have had was by now quite eroded.

Yet from *A Man from the North* (1898) right through to *Imperial Palace* (1930) Bennett could produce fictional work of rare distinction. He began as a novelist obedient to the requirements of realism, and he remained loyal to them as he remained loyal to his early hero, George Moore. Bennett often praised the scrupulous attention which he felt that Moore in the 1880s had directed towards the ordinary lives he had studied in several novels, of which perhaps the most important for Bennett was *A Mummer's Wife* (1885). His admiration for this novel is recorded in various journal entries of the 1890s, most significantly perhaps in the remark that Moore is the only English novelist who can stand comparison with the major French realists. *A Mummer's Wife*, which in some ways reads like an English version of a novel by Zola, is set in part in that area which Bennett was to make his own. But in one all-important respect he goes beyond his master. Bennett brings far greater understanding to his studies of the five towns than Moore was capable of. While *Anna of the Five Towns*, the first of Bennett's novels to be set in the Potteries, undoubtedly owes something to Moore's example, the imaginative sympathy of his portrait of the young woman for whom the novel is named extends well beyond Moore's range. It also gives the lie to another familiar criticism of Bennett, first voiced by Virginia Woolf: that while he was capable of describing the bricks and mortar out of which a house is built, he was unable to imagine the life within. Anna Tellwright is a most convincing study of a girl trapped in joyless family circumstances who struggles to do her best for others. Her escape into a loveless marriage is made entirely credible.

From the beginning Bennett was clearly alert to issues which preoccupy other novelists of the period, especially women's rights, and the 'new woman'. Hence he produced two important novels which turn on married infidelity and divorce. The first of these, *Leonora* (1903), is marred by the convenient suicide of the heroine's erring husband; this spares her the full pain of the divorce proceedings for which the novel seems to have been preparing us. The second, *Whom God hath Joined* (1906), is a minor masterpiece in its anatomy of a failing marriage. All through his career, indeed, Bennett showed remarkable insight into the plight of women caught in marriages or by emotional circumstances which bring them little satisfaction but which they nevertheless try to manage in ways that allow them some freedom. This ability shows itself in another excellent work, *The Price of Love* (1914). On the other hand, as with most of his would-be liberated male contemporaries, Bennett could only cope with suffragettism by condescending to it in a genially jokey manner, as he does in *The Lion's Share* (1916).

By then, with *The Old Wives' Tale* and the Clayhanger trilogy behind him, Bennett's major work was done. These novels, important though they are, and impressively though they testify to his thoroughgoing realism, suffer from his habitual recourse to invocations of 'the riddle at the heart of life' or 'life's melancholy'—phrases which testify to a rather debilitating pessimism, and which caused D. H. Lawrence explosively to protest that tragedy should be a great kick at misery. Moreover, the second novel in the trilogy, *Hilda Lessways*, suffers from the fact that the eponymous heroine is one of Bennett's least convincing female characters; and while the concluding novel, *These Twain*, marks something of a recovery, especially in its detailed study of a provincial marriage, it is the first novel, *Clayhanger* itself, that is fit to set beside *The Old Wives' Tale*. These two ambitious novels most memorably concentrate Bennett's great virtues of patient, scrupulous narrative, together with his ability to accumulate a convincing account of intertwined lives and circumstance, in a place to which he gave lasting identity through his term 'the five towns'. He can justly be thought of as one of the finest of all regional novelists.

In common with Lawrence and other writers of his age Bennett felt deeply divided about his origins. The Potteries had nurtured him and he turned to them for nearly all his finest work. Yet he clearly felt that in order to become a writer he needed to escape from the environment in which he had grown up. This is explored in the finest of all his short stories, 'The Death of Simon Fuge', which formed part of his collection *The Grim Smile of the Five Towns* (1907).

The Pretty Lady is a much underrated study of England during the war years, especially in its sensitive feeling for the destructive frenzy that underlay much apparently good-hearted patriotism. However, with *Mr. Prohack* (1922) Bennett might seem finally to have succumbed to the temptation to turn out nothing but undemanding fictional entertainments. The novel's hero, in his untroubled and unquestioning acceptance of the postwar world as it is, including the thousands of unemployed war veterans who throng London's streets, is a monster of complacency, although that is not what Bennett intended. But even then Bennett was not done. *Riceyman Steps* is a remorseless study of miserliness. Its protagonist, Henry Earlforward, a second-hand bookseller, is constitutionally incapable of generosity—he even sells his wife's previous wedding-ring so he can buy her a cheaper one. (He gives her the change.) Henry's death from stomach cancer reads not merely as symbolically appropriate, but suggests that Bennett was responsive to the then fashionable theories of Homer Lane (an American psychologist who worked in London between 1918 and 1925) and others who proclaimed the psychosomatic basis of all forms of illness.

Bennett liked to keep abreast of new ideas and fashions. When T. S. Eliot was working on *Sweeney Agonistes* he consulted Bennett about what he called 'jazz rhythms'. And *Accident* (1929), a novel which turns on a train crash, for at least half its length tries to ponder the meanings of those cracks and divisions opening up in post-war society for which the general strike, although it is never mentioned, provides the most troubling evidence. Significantly, Bennett began writing the novel in 1926. However, in the latter half of *Accident* he dissolves the mood of ominous danger which he has so skilfully built up in the opening pages. He thus leaves it to Edward Upward in 'The Railway Accident' (1928) and Evelyn Waugh in *Vile Bodies* (1930) to develop the potential for dystopic fables of a society about to go smash which *Accident* begins. The limits of Bennett's realism perhaps lie in his cautious assumption that as things are, so they must be. Nevertheless, at its finest, Bennett's work has rightly commended itself to successive generations of readers and is certain to continue to do so.   JOHN LUCAS

Sources *The journals of Arnold Bennett*, ed. N. Flowers, 3 vols. (1932–5) · *Letters of Arnold Bennett*, ed. J. Hepburn, 1–3 (1966–70) · D. Barker, *Writer by trade: a view of Arnold Bennett* (1966) · M. Drabble, *Arnold Bennett: a biography* (1974) · J. Hepburn, ed., *Arnold Bennett: the critical heritage* (1981) · *Letters of Arnold Bennett*, ed. J. Hepburn, 4 (1986) · Mrs A. Bennett [M. Bennett], *Arnold Bennett* (1925) · [M. Bennett], *My Arnold Bennett* (1931) · D. C. Bennett, *Arnold Bennett: a portrait done at home* (1935) · *DNB* · F. Swinnerton, *Swinnerton: an autobiography*, [new edn] (1937) · R. Pound, *Arnold Bennett: a biography* (1952) · K. E. Roby, *A writer at war* (1972) · F. Swinnerton, *Arnold Bennett: a last word* (1978) · J. Lucas, *Arnold Bennett: a study of his fiction* (1974) · *CGPLA Eng. & Wales* (1931)
Archives BL, journal, Add. MS 59841 · Harvard U., Houghton L., journal · Hunt. L., letters, literary MSS · NRA, corresp. and MSS · NRA, priv. coll., MSS, notes, and corresp. with Edward Garnett · Ransom HRC, notebooks and MSS · Stoke-on-Trent City Museum and Art Gallery, corresp. and papers · U. Cal., Berkeley, Bancroft Library, corresp. and literary MSS · UCL, corresp. and MSS · Yale U., Beinecke L., letters and papers | BL, letters to Mrs Cheston, Add. MS 60391 H · BL, letters to C. F. G. Masterman and Lucy Masterman, Add. MS 62111 · BL, letters to Michael Morton, Add. MS 59877 · BL, letters to Ivor Nicholson and Miss Head, RP2848 [copies] · BL, letters to F. F. Rosher, RP2614 [copies] · BL, corresp. with Society of Authors, Add. MS 56668 · BL, corresp. with Marie Stopes, Add. MS 58497 · BLPES, letters to A. G. Gardiner · Bodl. Oxf., letters to Richard Blaker · Col. U., Rare Book and Manuscript Library, corresp. with Edward Verrall Lucas · CUL, letters to Richard Bennett · HLRO, corresp. with Lord Beaverbrook · HLRO, corresp. with Herbert Samuel · JRL, letters to Basil Dean · Keele University Library, letters to W. W. Kennerley and Tertin Kennerley, verses, and papers · NL Scot., letters to Sir John Richmond · Stoke-on-Trent City Museum and Art Gallery, letters to Annie Truscott Wood · TCD, letters to Thomas Bodkin · U. Leeds, Brotherton L., letters to Pauline Smith · UCL, letters to André Gide · University of Arkansas, Fayetteville, special collections, corresp. with Frank Swinnerton · University of Rochester, New York, Rush Rhees Library, corresp. with Edward Knoblock | SOUND BL NSA, documentary recording
Likenesses M. du Mayne, watercolour, 1891, City Museum and Art Gallery, Stoke-on-Trent · H. Furniss, three pen-and-ink drawings, c.1910, NPG · A. L. Coburn, photogravure, 1913, NPG · W. Rothenstein, chalk sketch, 1920, City Art Gallery, Stoke-on-Trent · M. Beerbohm, caricature, 1922 (with H. G. Wells), AM Oxf. · W. E. Tittle, pencil drawing, 1923, NPG · K. Shackleton, chalk drawing, c.1925, Stoke-on-Trent Art Gallery · D. Low, chalk caricature, 1926, NPG · G. C. Beresford, two photographs, 1927, NPG · B. Partridge, ink-and-watercolour caricature, 1928, NPG; repro. in *Punch* (21 May 1928) · H. Coster, two photographs, 1929, NPG [*see illus.*] · E. Kapp, chalk drawing, 1929, Barber Institute of Fine Arts, Birmingham · W. Nicholson, ink caricature, Stoke-on-Trent Art Gallery · OWL, mechanically reproduced caricature, NPG; repro. in *VF* (2 April 1913) · B. Partridge, pencil caricature, NPG; repro. in *Punch* (21 May 1928) · T. Spicer-Simson, plasticine medallion, NPG · cigarette card, NPG · print (after D. Low), NPG; repro. in *New Statesman* (30 Jan 1926)
Wealth at death £40,551 18s. 2d.: probate, 19 June 1931, *CGPLA Eng. & Wales*

Bennett, Charles, fourth earl of Tankerville (1743–1822). *See under* White Conduit cricket club (*act. c.*1785–1788).

Bennett, Charles (1870–1949), athlete, the third son and fifth child of Henry Bennett and his wife, Peggy Kerley, was born on 28 December 1870 on a farm at Shapwick, near Wimborne, Dorset, where his father worked as a labourer. Nothing is known of his childhood; he later worked as a railway engine driver at Bournemouth Central Station. He made his track début at the Amateur Athletics Association (AAA) championships in 1895, representing Portsmouth Harriers, and finished fourth in the 4 miles. After joining the more prestigious Finchley Harriers in London he enjoyed many successes at the top level, taking over as Britain's leading amateur distance runner after Fred Bacon and George Crossland were banned for accepting appearance money in 1896. He won three consecutive AAA 4 mile titles (1897–9) and was also the AAA champion at 10 miles (1899) and at 1 mile (1900). He was an unusually versatile athlete: as well as setting a British three-quarter mile record he won the British title at 10 miles. He also excelled over the country and was the southern counties' cross-country champion for three successive years (1898–1900), he won the national championship in 1899, and in the first international cross-country race against France in Paris in 1898 he was placed third.

One week after claiming the AAA 1 mile title Bennett won the 1500 metres at the 1900 Olympic games in Paris and celebrated his victory with a visit to the Folies Bergère. His winning time of 4 min. 6.2 sec. was said to be a world record, but clearly many runners had passed the 1500 metres mark in a faster time during the course of a 1 mile race. A week later Bennett led Great Britain to victory in the Olympic 5000 metres team race, and again his winning time of 15 min. 20.0 sec. was a world record. In between these two races he was placed second in the 4000 metres steeplechase. His achievement—two gold and one silver Olympic medal and two world records—has been one of the most underrated performances by a British track and field athlete at the Olympic games. On his return from Paris a defeat by the Olympic 800 metres champion, Alfred Tysoe, in a challenge match over the three-quarter mile distance at Manchester led to Bennett's retirement from the sport a few months before his thirtieth birthday.

During his athletic career Bennett had continued to live and train in Dorset, where, from around 1892, he was the landlord of the Crown Hotel, Wimborne. He later took over the Dolphin Hotel at Kinson, near Bournemouth, and after a spell as the gardener at a sanatorium near Ringwood he bought a 12 acre smallholding at Kinson, where he spent the rest of his life. He was married. He died in Boscombe Hospital, Hampshire, on 9 March 1949.

                                                IAN BUCHANAN

Sources *British Society for Sports History Newsletter* (spring 1992) [interview with subject's daughter] · I. Buchanan, *British Olympians: a hundred years of gold medallists* (1991) · b. cert. · *CGPLA Eng. & Wales* (1949)

Wealth at death £2,442 4s. 0d.: probate, 30 June 1949, *CGPLA Eng. & Wales*

Bennett, Charles Henry (1828–1867), illustrator, was born on 26 July 1828 at Tavistock Court, Covent Garden, London, the son of Charles Bennett and his wife, Harriet. He seems to have been self-taught as a draughtsman on wood, but by 1855 his sketches were appearing in *Diogenes*, a comic paper, and the *Comic Times*. In 1856 his 'Studies in Darwinesque development' and the 'Shadows' series of caricatures in Henry Vizetelly's *Illustrated Times* became very popular. His drawings were also engraved on wood for the *Illustrated London News* in 1857 and 1866, and the *Cornhill Magazine* in 1861, and he worked for other popular papers, including *Good Words* in 1861, *London Society* from 1862 to 1865, and *Comic News* between 1863 and 1865, as well as various children's papers including *Every Boy's Magazine* from 1864 to 1865, and *Beeton's Annuals* in 1866.

Bennett illustrated several books, the most famous of which was his edition of Bunyan's *Pilgrim's Progress* (1859), published by Longmans thanks to the help of Charles Kingsley. He also illustrated the *Fables of Aesop* (1858), *Proverbs with Pictures* (1858–9), *London People Sketched from Life* (1863), and *Quarle's Emblems* (1861), which were engraved by Joseph Swain and Edmund Evans. A collection of his earlier illustrations was published as *Character Sketches, Development Drawings, and Original Pictures of Wit and Humour* (1872). He also wrote and illustrated many books for children, including *Nine Lives of a Cat* (1860), *The Adventures of Young Munchausen* (1864), *The Sorrowful Ending of Noodledo* (1865), and *Lightsome and the Little Golden Lady* (1866). In collaboration with Richard Doyle, he illustrated *Fairy Tales* (1865) by Mark Lemon, editor of *Punch*.

Bennett joined *Punch* in February 1865, contributing over 230 drawings in the two years before his death, the most famous of which were his parliamentary drawings for the 'Essence of Parliament' series. His last illustration for *Punch* appeared on 23 March 1867, the famous sketch showing Lord John Russell as a cock crowing on an 1832 Easter egg. One of the original members of the Savage Club, Bennett was popular at *Punch* for his good humour and high spirits.

Although very successful, Bennett's work was not well regarded by his contemporaries—Henry Vizetelly described him as a 'poor draughtsman' (Vizetelly, 388–9)—and his caricature portraits, with large heads and tiny bodies, came to seem old-fashioned. He signed his sketches in the corner with the figure of an owl, later carrying a 'B'in its beak. He died on 2 April 1867 at his home, 2 Caversham Road, Kentish Town, London, after a long illness. He was buried on 8 April at Brompton cemetery. To raise money for his widow, Elizabeth, and eight children, his colleagues at *Punch* put on a benefit entertainment on 11 May 1867 at the Adelphi Theatre, including the first public performance of Arthur Sullivan's comic operetta *Cox and Box*, starring the *Punch* illustrators Sir John Tenniel and George Du Maurier. This was repeated at the Theatre Royal, Manchester, on 29 July 1867.

ANNE PIMLOTT BAKER

Sources J. Swain, 'Charles Henry Bennett', *Toilers in art*, ed. H. C. Ewart (1891), 189–208 · S. Houfe, *The dictionary of 19th century British book illustrators and caricaturists*, rev. edn (1996) · R. K. Engen, *Dictionary of Victorian wood engravers* (1985) · M. H. Spielmann, *The history of 'Punch'* (1895) · G. White, *English illustration, 'the sixties': 1855–70* (1897) · E. de Maré, *The Victorian woodblock illustrators* (1980), 153–4 · H. Vizetelly, *Glances back through seventy years: autobiographical and other reminiscences*, 1 (1893), 388–9 · Boase, *Mod. Eng. biog.* · *The Times* (29 April 1867) · A. Watson, *The Savage Club* (1907) · IGI · d. cert. · *CGPLA Eng. & Wales* (1867)

Likenesses C. H. Bennett, self-portrait, engraving, repro. in Ewart, ed., *Toilers in art*, 201 · C. H. Bennett, self-portrait, watercolour, repro. in Spielman, *History of 'Punch'*, 526 · carte-de-visite, NPG

Wealth at death under £200: administration, 10 May 1867, *CGPLA Eng. & Wales*

Bennett [née Rawlings], **Crystal-Margaret** (1918–1987), archaeologist, was born on 20 August 1918 in Alderney, the third of five children of George Rawlings, a soldier, and his wife Elizabeth (née Jennings). Educated at La Retraite Convent School and then Bristol University, where she received a bachelor's degree in English, she married Philip Roy Bennett (1907–1986), a draughtsman, in 1940. He was an Anglican, and she converted from Roman Catholicism to the Church of England on his account. Their only child, Simon, was born in 1945, and they divorced in 1946.

Bennett's archaeological career began in 1954 at the Institute of Archaeology, University of London, where she took the postgraduate diploma in the archaeology of the Roman provinces in the west and later the diploma in Palestinian archaeology under Kathleen Kenyon. After directing two excavations at Roman sites in England she joined Kenyon's pioneering excavations at Jericho in Palestine in 1957.

In 1958, while taking part in excavations at Petra in Jordan, Bennett became interested in the Iron Age Edomite site of Umm al-Biyara in the centre of Petra. At the time little was known about the Edomites, the Iron Age inhabitants of southern Jordan, so she undertook excavations there between 1960 and 1965. Umm al-Biyara was an almost inaccessible rock massif; even donkeys were unable to climb it, and all water and supplies had to be carried by hand (or dropped by helicopter). The Edomites became the prime focus of her research from then on; she also excavated the Edomite sites of Tawilan (1968–70, 1982) and Busayra, the probable capital of Edom (1971–4, 1980). Her results considerably revised the generally accepted chronology of Edom, clearly dating Edomite pottery to the seventh century BC, rather than to the thirteenth century BC as previously thought. Although she published regular preliminary reports on her excavations in academic journals, she did not produce a final report for any of these sites. After her death this work passed to younger colleagues for completion.

Bennett was assistant director of the British School of Archaeology in Jerusalem from 1963 to 1965, and director from 1970 to 1980. After the Six Day War of 1967 and Israel's occupation of the West Bank it became difficult to cross from Jerusalem to Jordan, which affected the British School's archaeological work in Jordan. In 1970 she therefore set up at her own expense an office in Amman which acted as a base for British excavations in Jordan. In 1975 she was asked by the Jordanian department of antiquities to direct a rescue excavation on Amman citadel, prior to the building of a new museum. This work lasted three long seasons, the final results being published after her death by her assistant director. Bennett's experiences in Jordan convinced her that there was a real need for a permanent British archaeological body in the country, and together with Kenyon she persuaded the British Academy to found and fund the British Institute at Amman for Archaeology and History. Bennett served as its first director from 1980 to 1983.

Bennett was tall, well-built, provocative, and energetic, although late in life illness confined her to bed for long periods, even during excavations. At a politically difficult time she managed to remain friends with Israelis and Arabs, and was never shy of using her close friendship with the Jordanian royal family to solve seemingly intractable bureaucratic problems. She was generous to younger scholars, helping them to establish their own archaeological projects. She was made an OBE in 1980 for services to archaeology in Jordan and was awarded an honorary degree of DLitt by Trinity College, Dublin, in 1983. After a short retirement in Cyprus, she died of liver disease at her home, Tolbury House, Bruton, Somerset, on 12 August 1987, and was buried at Bruton on 17 August 1987.

PIOTR BIENKOWSKI

Sources G. Talbot, 'Crystal-M. Bennett, O.B.E., D.Litt., F.S.A.: an appreciation', *Levant*, 19 (1987), 1–2 · P. Bienkowski, 'Bennett, Crystal-Margaret', *Oxford encyclopedia of archaeology in the Near East*, ed. E. M. Meyers, 1 (1997), 298 · personal knowledge (2004) · private information (2004) [Simon Bennett]
Archives British School of Archaeology, Jerusalem, collection of artefacts from excavations at Umm el-Biyara · Liverpool Museum, archives of excavations at Umm el-Biyara, Tawilan, and Busayra · Liverpool Museum, collection of artefacts from excavations at Tawilan and Busayra
Likenesses photographs, Liverpool Museum, Bennett's excavation archives
Wealth at death £69,394: probate, 15 Oct 1987, *CGPLA Eng. & Wales*

Bennett, Donald Clifford Tyndall (1910–1986), air force officer and politician, was born on 14 September 1910 in Toowoomba, Queensland, Australia, the fourth and youngest son and youngest of the five children of George Thomas Bennett of Brisbane, cattle estate owner, and his wife, Celia Juliana Lucas. His sister died in early childhood. He was educated at Brisbane grammar school and enlisted in the Royal Australian Air Force.

In 1931 Bennett was posted to England on a short-service commission in the Royal Air Force. He resigned in 1935 to join Imperial Airways, having successfully passed the examinations for a civil navigator's licence (first class) and both wireless operator's and ground engineer's licences.

Donald Clifford Tyndall Bennett (1910–1986), by Walter Stoneman, 1943

In 1938 he gained the world's long-distance record for seaplanes in a flight from Dundee in Scotland to Alexandra Bay in South-West Africa. In 1935 he married Elsa, daughter of Charles Gubler, jeweller, of Zürich; they had a son and a daughter.

In 1940, as flight superintendent of the Atlantic Ferry service, Bennett flew the first of thousands of American-built aircraft to the British Isles, a feat never before attempted in winter. Despite his technical brilliance and outstanding capacity for work, his relationship with his civilian masters was difficult and he returned to the RAF in 1941. He was posted to Leeming, Yorkshire, to command 77 squadron operating Whitley bombers and in April 1942 to 10 squadron, also at Leeming. During an attack on the *Tirpitz* in a Norwegian fjord his Halifax was shot down. After bailing out he escaped on foot to Sweden to be repatriated to Britain, where he was immediately awarded the DSO.

When the Air Ministry ordered Bomber Command to create an élite target-finding force Bennett was the obvious choice to command it. Promotion followed swiftly and as air officer commanding 8 group his Pathfinder force successfully mastered the identification and marking of chosen targets. In 1943 he was accorded the rank of air vice-marshal. Although regarded by many as the architect of the efficiency of Bomber Command, his relationship with other long-serving bomber group commanders was not without friction. Few had any recent operational experience and most were reluctant to release their best crews to 8 group.

In 1945, having resigned his commission, Bennett was appointed chief executive of British South American Airways, a new airline founded by shipping interests. His policy of operating only British aircraft involved dependence upon a converted bomber, the Lancastrian, until the Avro Tudor was ready for service. The deficiencies of the airport facilities, together with the inexperience of the youthful crews, took their toll in accidents. In 1948, following the unexplained disappearance of a Tudor *en route* to Bermuda, the minister for civil aviation, Lord Nathan, grounded the remainder, pending an investigation. Convinced that the Tudor was perfectly airworthy, Bennett angrily denounced the minister to the national press. In the ensuing furore he refused to resign and was dismissed.

Almost at once the Russian blockade of road, rail, and river routes to West Berlin provided Bennett with an opportunity to prove the Tudor's merits. He founded Airflight, based at Langley, near Slough, equipping two Tudors as oil tankers and personally flying 250 sorties to Berlin. In May 1949 he registered a new company, Fairflight, based at Blackbushe, Hampshire. Charter flights to the Middle East and Far East were carried out before the company was sold in 1951.

At the invitation of Sir Archibald Sinclair, leader of the Liberal Party, Bennett stood for Middlesbrough West at a by-election in May 1945. He was unopposed but at the general election shortly afterwards he lost the seat to the Labour candidate. In 1948 he unsuccessfully contended North Croydon, and, in 1950, Norwich North. Thereafter the Liberal Party's enthusiasm for the European Economic Community and its defence policies alienated Bennett, whose upbringing was founded on pride in the empire and the merits of imperial preference. He left the Liberal Party in 1962 and five years later polled about 500 votes as a National Party candidate at a by-election in Nuneaton, Warwickshire. Although not a member of the National Front, he supported some of its policies, such as the voluntary repatriation of immigrants, when he organized, in 1969, the Association of Political Independents and, later, the independent democratic movement. He joined the National Council of Anti-Common Market Organizations and was its chairman from 1973 to 1976. From 1946 to 1949 he was chairman of the executive committee of the United Nations Association of Great Britain and Northern Ireland. His most notable publication, *The Complete Air Navigator* (1931), ran through many editions until 1967. He also wrote *The Air Mariner* (1938) and *Pathfinder* (1958), among other books. He was appointed CBE (1943) and CB (1944). The Russian government awarded him the order of Alexander Nevsky in 1944. For services to aviation he was awarded the Johnston memorial trophy in 1937 and 1938, and the Oswald Watt medal in 1938 and 1946. Bennett died on 15 September 1986 at Wexham Hospital, Buckinghamshire.

ARCHIE STEWART JACKSON, *rev.*

Sources D. C. T. Bennett, *Pathfinder: a war autobiography* (1958) · *The Times* (17 Sept 1986) · personal knowledge (1996)
Likenesses W. Stoneman, photograph, 1943, NPG [*see illus.*] · photograph, priv. coll. · photograph, Hult. Arch.

Bennett, Edward Hallaran (1837–1907), surgeon, born on 9 April 1837 at Charlotte Quay, Cork, was the youngest of the five children, all sons, of Robert Bennett, recorder of Cork, and Jane Hallaran, the daughter of William Saunders Hallaran, a physician of Cork with an interest in mental disease who wrote on insanity. His grandfather James Bennett was a physician in Cork, and another kinsman, James Richard Bennett, was a distinguished teacher of anatomy in Paris in the 1820s. His brother Robert served all through the Crimean War and retired with the rank of major-general.

Bennett was educated at Hamblin's School in Cork, and then at the Academic Institute, Harcourt Street, Dublin, whose headmaster was the Revd Daniel Flynn. Bennett entered Trinity College, Dublin, in 1854, and graduated in 1859 with the degrees of BA, MB, and the newly established MCh. He continued his surgical career in Dublin at the school of physic, Trinity College, and at Dr Steevens' Hospital, the Meath Hospital, the Richmond Hospital, and Sir Patrick Dunn's Hospital; in 1863 he became a fellow of the Royal College of Surgeons in Ireland. The following year he proceeded MD and was appointed university anatomist in Dublin University, a post that carried with it the office of surgeon to Sir Patrick Dunn's Hospital. On 20 December 1870 Bennett married Frances, the daughter of Conolly Norman of Fahan, co. Donegal, and a cousin of the alienist Conolly Norman; they had two daughters.

In 1873, on the death of Robert William Smith, Bennett was appointed professor of surgery in Trinity College and curator of the pathological museum. He held these posts, together with his appointment as surgeon to Sir Patrick Dunn's Hospital, until 1906. Bennett also held numerous appointments of distinction in Ireland; in 1880 he was president of the Dublin Pathological Society; from 1884 to 1885 he served as president of the Royal College of Surgeons in Ireland; from 1897 to 1900 he was president of the Royal Academy of Medicine in Ireland; from 1897 to 1906 he represented the University of Dublin on the General Medical Council; and from 1902 to 1905 he was surgeon to the lord lieutenant, the earl of Dudley. In 1900 he was made an honorary fellow of the Royal College of Surgeons in England (his photograph with signature is in the album of honorary fellows).

Bennett assembled a remarkable collection of fractures, dislocations, diseases, and surgery of bones in the Pathological Museum of Trinity College, Dublin. The collection was begun by his predecessor, R. W. Smith, and was developed by Bennett into one of the most important collections of its kind in Europe. He spent years in compiling a catalogue furnished with notes and clinical histories, but it remained unfinished. Bennett frequently published communications and reports dealing with the surgery and pathology of bones. In 1880 he described for the first time at the Cork meeting of the British Medical Association, and in 1881 at the Dublin Pathological Society, the fracture at the base of the metacarpal bone of the thumb which was previously unrecognized and which became universally known as 'Bennett's fracture'. Its significance lies in the fact that, unless skilfully treated, it leads to arthritic changes at the base of the thumb with consequent pain and disability. As an operating surgeon, Bennett was one of the earliest in Ireland to adopt the antiseptic technique of Lister. As a teacher, he was forcible and practical, and able to enlighten the driest subject with touches of humour.

Bennett died on 21 June 1907 at his residence, 26 Lower Fitzwilliam Street, Dublin, and was buried at Mount Jerome cemetery in Dublin. He was survived by his wife and one daughter, Norah Mary. HAROLD ELLIS

Sources V. G. Plarr, *Plarr's Lives of the fellows of the Royal College of Surgeons of England*, rev. D'A. Power, 1 (1930) • D. Coakley, *Irish masters of medicine* (1992), 205–12 • M. Rang, *Anthology of orthopaedics* (1966), 95–7 • *DNB* • *CGPLA Eng. & Wales* (1907) • *WWW*
Likenesses G. Jerrard, photograph, 1881, Wellcome L. • photograph, 1900, RCS Eng. • O. Sheppard, relief bust on bronze panel, TCD • bronze medallion, TCD, manuscript department • bronze roundel, Royal College of Surgeons in Ireland, Dublin
Wealth at death £12,266 16s. 5d.: Irish probate sealed in London, 23 July 1907, *CGPLA Eng. & Wales* • £17,136 5s. 6d.: resworn probate, 17 July 1907, *CGPLA Ire.*

Bennett, Edward Turner (1797–1836), zoologist, was born in Hackney, Middlesex, on 6 January 1797, the son of Edward Turner Bennett and his wife, Lucy. He was the elder brother of the botanist John Joseph *Bennett (1801–1876). He practised as a surgeon in Portman Square, having been a pupil at the anatomy school operated by the surgeon Joshua Brookes. Bennett was interested in zoology and became a prominent member of the Zoological Club of the Linnean Society. In 1828 he became vice-secretary of the newly founded Zoological Society of London, whose secretary, Nicholas Aylward Vigors, seems to have been his patron. Indeed, it has been claimed that some of Vigors's works were ghost-written in part by Bennett (Mitchell, 128–9).

In 1833 Bennett was himself elected secretary of the Zoological Society. He was extremely diligent and enriched the collection of living animals with many new specimens, notably four giraffes in 1836. His attention to the routine work of the zoological gardens and the society's museum was exemplary, and he carefully supervised the publication of the society's *Proceedings* and *Transactions*. His gift of 218 volumes was the effective nucleus of the society's library. Some idea of the general magnitude of his services can be gleaned from the decline in its fortunes during the decade and a half that followed his death.

Bennett wrote *The Tower Menagerie* (1829) and edited *The Gardens and Menagerie of the Zoological Society Delineated* (2 vols., 1830, 1831), to which Vigors, Broderip, Wallich, and Yarrell also contributed; in addition he contributed many papers to the *Proceedings* and *Transactions* of the Zoological Society and to other natural history periodicals of his

time. He was working on an edition of Gilbert White's *Natural History of Selborne* at the time of his early death. He never married, and died on 21 August 1836 at Bulstrode Street, London. J. C. EDWARDS

Sources Zoological Society of London Archives • H. Scherren, *The Zoological Society of London: a sketch of its foundation and development* (1905) • *DNB* • P. Chalmers Mitchell, *Centenary history of the Zoological Society of London* (1929)

Bennett, Elizabeth (d. 1582). *See under* Essex witches (*act.* 1566–1589).

Bennett, Sir Ernest Nathaniel (1868–1947), politician and journalist, was born on 12 December 1868 in Colombo, Ceylon, the only son of the Revd George Bennett (1830–1897), a Church of England clergyman and schoolmaster, and his wife, Elise (d. 1911), daughter of Captain Fewson HEICS. George Bennett was the second son of Thomas Bennett, a cobbler or shoemaker of Roseacre, near Kirkham, Lancashire, graduated from Trinity College, Dublin (BA, 1849), and was rector of Rede, near Bury St Edmunds, Suffolk (1885–96). He was described as being 'strongly Tory'.

Ernest Bennett was educated at Durham School (1881–5), becoming a king's scholar, a school monitor, and captain of the rugby fifteen. Briefly at Wadham College, Oxford, in 1885, then scholar (1885) of Hertford College, Oxford, he gained firsts in classical moderations, *literae humaniores* (BA, 1889), and theology (1890), and won the senior Hall-Houghton Greek testament prize. He became a fellow of Hertford (1891–1915), and was a lecturer of Wadham, Pembroke, Lincoln, and Hertford colleges. In 1900 he published *Christianity and Paganism in the Fourth and Fifth Centuries*, a short book based on his lectures to honours theology men.

Bennett travelled in Palestine and elsewhere, and in 1896 he explored the island of Socotra with James Theodore Bent (1852–1897). An ambitious man, Bennett wanted to make his name as a journalist before entering politics. In 1897, as a *Times* assistant correspondent, he reported the insurrection in Crete. In his February 1898 *Blackwood's* article 'Amongst the Cretan insurgents', Bennett, in the tradition of Victorian war correspondents, described his adventures and narrow escapes from death under fire. He praised the Turks, and condemned the Cretan insurgents as barbaric 'ruffians' who massacred their prisoners of war. He also, in what was to be a recurring theme of his writings, denounced wartime 'alleged atrocities'.

In the 1898 long vacation Bennett went as correspondent of the Liberal *Westminster Gazette* to report the Sudan reconquest. He described himself as a 'non-journalistic amateur, who, in order to go through the campaign, has secured a permit to act as a correspondent' (Bennett, *The Downfall of the Dervishes*, 77). He reported the battle of Omdurman (2 September 1898) and its immediate aftermath. Like other correspondents, he rushed out a book on the campaign, *The Downfall of the Dervishes* (1898). As an imperialist, he condemned the Mahdist regime and praised the reconquest. However, he criticized the killing of wounded Mahdists. He also criticized, unnamed but identifiable, Bennet Burleigh, the veteran *Daily Telegraph* war correspondent. Bennett in his January 1899 *Contemporary Review* article 'After Omdurman' condemned the killing of Mahdist wounded, looting, and the treatment of the Mahdi's corpse and tomb as 'a return to the barbarism of the Middle Ages'. His allegations 'created such a stir' (Churchill, 1004), made him 'one of the most talked of men in England' (Gaskell, 85), and provoked rebuttals from (among others) Burleigh in the *Daily Telegraph* and *Khartoum Campaign, 1898* (1899). Burleigh denounced Bennett's allegations as 'unwarranted and untruthful libels … inaccuracy and sensationalism' (Burleigh, 337, 339). The hostile response apparently surprised Bennett. He hoped to stand as a Liberal parliamentary candidate at the next election, and he wrote to C. P. Scott that he feared no constituency would listen to someone who by Burleigh's and others' 'disgraceful' attacks had been misrepresented as a 'traducer' of British imperial forces (Spiers, 122). When, in 1899, the government proposed a money grant to Kitchener, Scott opposed it on the issue of the Mahdi's remains and the treatment of the wounded. Bennett gave Scott information, but asked him not to quote him in the house.

In 1899 Bennett went to the Second South African War and joined, as an orderly, a Royal Army Medical Corps volunteer ambulance train attached to Lord Methuen's command. Like some other volunteers he donated his pay to the Widows' and Orphans' Fund. He witnessed the aftermath of the battles of Belmont, Graspan, and Magersfontein. He left in 1900 and later that year published *With Methuen's Column in an Ambulance Train*, a short, impressionistic, and opinionated work, bound in the fashionable khaki, in which he criticized Uitlanders, especially 'German Jews', Kipling, and 'amateur critics at home', and praised the British soldiers. In May 1900 he was commissioned second lieutenant in the 1st (Oxford University) volunteer battalion, Oxfordshire light infantry, and in 1902, as temporary lieutenant, he commanded the Oxfordshire Volunteers in the Orange River Colony. By 1912 he shared the view that the war had been engineered by 'cosmopolitan financiers'.

In 1906, asserting his belief in 'the creed of Radicalism' and campaigning largely on the free trade issue, Bennett was elected Liberal MP for the Mid or Woodstock division of Oxfordshire. He was especially committed to the cause of Congo reform, though he also spoke on the auxiliary forces and other issues. In 1909 he was appointed parliamentary private secretary to Sir Edward Strachey, bt, of the Board of Agriculture and Fisheries. Bennett was defeated in both 1910 elections. Relatively radical, he favoured land reform and criticized Grey's conduct of foreign policy. In *Problems of Village Life* (1914) he attacked the 'chains of Feudalism' and the drink trade, and demanded land nationalization. He was honorary treasurer of the Land Nationalization Federation. Meanwhile he continued part-time soldiering with the volunteers of the Oxfordshire light infantry, as a lieutenant from March 1903 and a captain from August 1904. He was an Oxfordshire JP from 1909 to 1936.

In 1911, with authorization as a *Manchester Guardian* reporter, Bennett visited the Turkish army during the Turco-Italian war in Libya, leaving in 1912. His reports and his *With the Turks in Tripoli* (1912) were pro-Turkish and anti-Italian. In the First Balkan War of 1912 he accompanied the Turkish army, and acted as press censor in Thrace. In the first year of the First World War he was a British Red Cross commissioner in Belgium, France, and Serbia. Later he was attached to the staff of 11th (reserve) infantry brigade, admiralty intelligence division, headquarters of 9th army corps (1917) and headquarters of the army of the Rhine (1919). On 4 October 1915 he married Marguerite Wilhelmina, eldest daughter of H. G. Kleinwort, of Wierton Place, near Maidstone, Kent. They had two sons and one daughter.

Bennett was one of the first former Liberal MPs to defect to Labour, joining the Independent Labour Party in 1916. He unsuccessfully contested West Wiltshire (1918), Banbury (1922 and 1923), and South-West St Pancras (1924). Apparently sharing the leftist reaction against Versailles and the war, in 1921 he translated *The German Army in Belgium: the White Book of May 1915*, German propaganda attempting to justify their killing of Belgian civilians. In May 1929 he was elected for Central Cardiff, and in 1930 he was knighted. Opinions of Bennett differed. Hugh Dalton wrote in 1930 that Bennett was 'a talkative and unatmospheric fool—audibly and visibly half a Liberal who, by his continual intervention, creates suspicions against himself' (Pimlott, 109–10). In 1931 he supported Ramsay MacDonald's National Government and became one of thirteen National Labour MPs. In 1932 he went to India as a member of the (Lothian) Indian franchise committee, and in 1933 he was a British delegate to the League of Nations assembly. From October 1932 to December 1935 he was assistant postmaster-general. He was on various committees, including (from 1939) the select committee on national expenditure, and was chairman of the Near and Middle East Association. He was a member of the archbishops' committee on church and state, and of the governing body of the Church in Wales. By 1937 he had acquired his home called Cwmllecoediog, Aberangell, Montgomeryshire, and had an entry in Burke's *Landed Gentry*.

Bennett had three predominant political concerns: anti-communism, improving relations with Germany, and a pro-Arab, anti-Zionist policy for Palestine. A member of the Anglo-German Fellowship, in letters to the press and elsewhere he condemned the Versailles treaty as 'harsh, vindictive, indefensible' (Griffiths, *Fellow Travellers of the Right*, 256), advocated appeasement of Nazi Germany, and condemned the Franco-Soviet pact (1935), and he voted in support of the Munich agreement in October 1938. In 1937 he condemned Italian reprisals in Abyssinia. His predominant political concerns led him in 1939 to associate with extreme right-wing and antisemitic groups, and to join Captain Archibald Maule Ramsay's clandestine Right Club. He deplored the British declaration of war in 1939, and voted for Chamberlain at the Norway debate (May 1940). In late 1939 and early 1940 he was prominent among those MPs advocating a negotiated peace with Germany, and he worked with the parliamentary peace aims group. On 22 May 1940 he was one of a delegation of MPs who asked Lloyd George to appeal for a negotiated settlement: Lloyd George refused. Bennett retired from parliament in June 1945.

At Oxford Bennett was influenced by the psychical research of F. W. H. Myers, 'a veritable inspiration' (Bennett, *Apparitions*, xviii). In 1894 he joined the Society for Psychical Research and from 1901 he was on its council. He attended séances and investigated various alleged paranormal phenomena, sometimes exposing fraud. He believed that, despite fraud and trickery, there were genuine paranormal phenomena, including 'telepathy from the dead' (ibid., 376), and called for further research. He claimed that he once witnessed at a séance 'the production of a complete, visible and tangible figure' (Bennett, *Apollonius*, 79). He published *Apollonius, or, The Present and Future of Psychical Research* (1927) and *Apparitions and Haunted Houses: a Survey of Evidence* (1939). His interest in the field continued: early in 1942, for example, he investigated for the society an alleged poltergeist case at the Clarence Nursing Home, Malvern, in which, reportedly, a kitchen poker detached itself from its hook, rose in the air, and flew some 10 or 12 feet. Bennett died at Amberfield, Chart Sutton, near Maidstone, Kent, on 2 February 1947. He was survived by his wife.   ROGER T. STEARN

Sources *The Times* (4 Feb 1947), 7 • R. Griffiths, *Patriotism perverted: Captain Ramsay, the Right Club and British anti-Semitism* (1998) • R. T. Stearn, 'Ernest Bennett and war', *Soldiers of the Queen*, 105 (2001) • *WWW, 1941–50* • T. H. Burbidge, ed., *Durham School register*, 3rd edn (1940) • *WWBMP*, vol. 2 • J. Foster, *Oxford men, 1880–1892: with a record of their schools, honours, and degrees* (1893) • Kelly, *Handbk* (1942) • Burke, *Gen. GB* (1937) • Burke, *Peerage* (1931) • *Army List* (1900–20) • R. Griffiths, *Fellow travellers of the right: British enthusiasts for Nazi Germany, 1933–9*, pbk edn (1983) • Crockford (1885–92) • E. Gaskell, *Oxfordshire leaders: social and political* [n.d.] • Burtchaell & Sadleir, *Alum. Dubl.* • E. N. Bennett, *The downfall of the dervishes: being a sketch of the final Sudan campaign of 1898* (1898) • E. N. Bennett, 'After Omdurman', *Contemporary Review*, 75 (1899), 18–33 • E. N. Bennett, *Apollonius, or, The present and future of psychical research* (1927) • E. N. Bennett, *Apparitions and haunted houses: a survey of evidence* (1939) • B. Burleigh, *Khartoum campaign, 1898, or, The re-conquest of the Soudan* (1899) • E. M. Spiers, ed., *Sudan: the re-conquest reappraised* (1998) • J. M. MacKenzie, ed., *Popular imperialism and the military, 1850–1950* (1992) • [S. Morison and others], *The history of The Times*, 3 (1947) • R. S. Churchill, ed., *Winston S. Churchill*, companion vol. 1/2 (1967) • *CGPLA Eng. & Wales* (1947) • R. Haynes, *The Society for Psychical Research, 1882–1982: a history* (1982) • *The political diary of Hugh Dalton, 1918–1940, 1945–1960*, ed. B. Pimlott (1986) • *Jackson's Oxford Journal* (6 Jan 1906) • *Jackson's Oxford Journal* (13 Jan 1906) • *Jackson's Oxford Journal* (27 Jan 1906) • *Hansard 5C* (1906–9) • *Hansard 5C* (1938), 339.558; (1940), 360.1361 • J. Oppenheim, *The other world: spiritualism and psychical research in England, 1850–1914* (1985) • d. cert.

Archives BLPES, letters to E. D. Morel, MOREL/F8/7 • JRL, letters to *Manchester Guardian*

Likenesses photograph, c.1908, repro. in Gaskell, *Oxfordshire leaders*, facing p. 85

Wealth at death £8549 4s. 7d.: probate, 26 June 1947, *CGPLA Eng. & Wales*

Bennett, Gareth Vaughan (1929–1987), ecclesiastical historian, was born on 8 November 1929 at 19 Valkyrie Road, Westcliff-on-Sea, Essex, the only child of Roy Charles Frederick Bennett, a London shipping clerk, and his wife, Kathleen Beryl Vaughan (d. 1981). A lonely child, he was educated at private schools in Essex before gaining a place at the Royal Grammar School, Guildford, in 1941, completing his schooling at Southend High School for Boys after Easter 1943. Declared unfit for national service, he went to Christ's College, Cambridge, in 1948, and gained a first class with distinction in part two of the history tripos. He became Lloyd student in 1951 and Allen scholar in 1953 before taking his PhD in May 1954 under Norman Sykes, whose memorial volume he later edited. His thesis on White Kennett won the Thirlwall prize in 1955 and was published in 1957. In 1954 Bennett was appointed assistant lecturer at King's College, London. Encouraged by the dean, Eric Abbott, he was accepted for ordination and spent two summer vacation terms at Westcott House, Cambridge, where he found Robert Runcie, the vice-principal, a source of support. He was ordained deacon at Michaelmas 1956 and priest in the following year, serving his part-time curacy at Prittlewell under the ailing Archdeacon Ellis Norman Gowing, who had earlier prepared him for confirmation. While at King's he continued his eighteenth-century studies, eventually publishing a reassessment of Francis Atterbury (*The Tory Crisis in Church and State*) in 1975. He gave the Birkbeck lectures at Trinity College, Cambridge, and was awarded the DLitt by Cambridge University in 1987. A collection of papers was published posthumously in 1988 (*To the Church of England*).

In June 1959 Bennett became dean of divinity at New College, Oxford, where he revived chapel life and proved an able pastor to undergraduates. In 1961 he was appointed to a Wiccamical prebend in Chichester Cathedral, a link he greatly valued. He served as college librarian from 1963 and sub-warden in 1968, and was junior proctor of the university from 1973 to 1974. In 1975 he was elected as university proctor to the general synod, and in this capacity brought historical perspectives to bear on the controversial issues of the day. He was elected to the standing committee and in 1987 to the Crown Appointments Commission. In 1977 his mother moved to Oxford, which precipitated his moving out of New College. Two years later he resigned as chaplain, hoping the college would support the appointment of a younger theologian. He remained fellow and tutor in history.

After Runcie became archbishop of Canterbury in 1980, he frequently called on Bennett to prepare speeches and sermons, encouraging him to expect an ecclesiastical appointment; he hoped that this might help him out of Oxford, where he was becoming increasingly frustrated. However, by the beginning of 1987 Bennett felt such preferment unlikely in a church dominated by the 'liberal establishment' (Carpenter, 339). Invited by Derek Pattinson, synod general secretary, to write the traditionally anonymous preface to *Crockford's Clerical Directory for 1987–8*, he outlined what he saw as a crisis of Anglican identity. The publication on 3 December 1987 created a media sensation, primarily on account of unguarded comments on Runcie's leadership and accusations of ecclesiastical nepotism. Several leading churchmen attacked the author—John Habgood, archbishop of York, accusing him of 'sourness and vindictiveness' (Oddie, 100) and of hiding under the cloak of anonymity. Hounded by the press, Bennett realized that he had been 'bloody foolish' (Carpenter, 352) in misjudging the situation. He attended a college feast in Cambridge on 4 December and returned to his house at 15 Moody Road, Oxford, on the following day. He was found dead in his car on 7 December by his New College colleague John Cowan, and Harold Cooper, a neighbour. His cat was found dead in the house. The requiem eucharist, concelebrated by three diocesan bishops, was held in New College on 15 December 1987, and Bennett was cremated at Oxford crematorium on the same day. A verdict of suicide by carbon monoxide poisoning was returned on 16 March 1988, the Oxford coroner noting that Bennett did not have the resilience to match the pressure from the media (*Church Times*, 18 March 1988). He left the residue of his estate to Pusey House, where he had been a governor, a bequest that helped to secure its future.

Had it not been for these tragic last days, Bennett would have been remembered as a conservative but unpartisan high-churchman who had contributed to a revival of interest in the eighteenth-century church, but who had been passed over for academic and ecclesiastical preferment. He was also regarded as an open, hospitable, and pastorally sensitive chaplain. At the same time Bennett, who was unmarried, was a lonely man and was apparently unable to form close friendships; he could also be irritating, vain, and self-centred. His death, which some thought the result of hounding by the liberal establishment, took on a symbolic importance for many Anglican conservatives. The Crockford affair was undoubtedly a bitter blow to Runcie, and perhaps a factor in preventing Habgood's preferment from York to Canterbury.

MARK D. CHAPMAN

Sources G. Rowell, Memoir, in G. Bennett, *To the Church of England* (1988), 1–17 • private information (2004) [P. Ursell, principal of Pusey Oxf.; G. Rowell, bishop of Gibraltar in Europe] • H. Carpenter, *Robert Runcie: the reluctant archbishop* (1996), 327–59 • W. Oddie, *The Crockford's file: Gareth Bennett and the death of the Anglican mind* (1989) • B. McHenry, *Church Times* (18 Dec 1987) • *Church Times* (18 March 1988), 1 [report on coroner's verdict] • G. Rowell, 'Funeral sermon', in G. Bennett, *To the Church of England* (1988), 253–6 • b. cert. • d. cert.

Archives priv. coll., diaries, letters, and papers • Pusey Oxf., academic and sermon notes

Likenesses M. Noakes, pencil drawing, New College, Oxford

Bennett, George John (1800–1879), actor, was born at Ripon, Yorkshire, on 9 March 1800, the son of George Bennett, a long-standing member of the Norwich theatre company. After a short spell in the navy (1813–17) he made his début as an actor at King's Lynn, Norfolk, in 1818. Following work in different provincial towns he became a member of the Bath company in 1820, then in 1822 went to London. He made an unsuccessful début at Covent Garden on 27 January 1823 as Richard III. On 23 July 1824, at the Lyceum (then the English Opera House), he created the part of Conrad in the first presentation in England of

George John Bennett (1800–1879), by William Sharp, pubd 1831 (after G. F. Stroehling) [as Cassius in *Julius Caesar*]

Der Freischütz, or, The Seventh Bullet, a rendering by Logan of Weber's famous opera. In 1830 he joined the Covent Garden company, and made a noteworthy appearance as Hubert in *King John* to the Constance of Fanny Kemble. He remained at Covent Garden through the successive managements of Charles Kemble, Laporte, and W. C. Macready, playing such characters as Grindoff in Pocock's *The Miller and his Men*, Macduff, Master Walter in Sheridan Knowles's *The Hunchback*, and Caliban in Macready's revival of *The Tempest* (October 1838). He then accompanied Macready to Drury Lane, where he worked for the duration of the latter's management (4 October 1841 to 14 June 1843).

On 27 May 1844 Samuel Phelps and Greenwood began their memorable campaign at Sadler's Wells. Bennett joined them, and remained with them during the eighteen years over which the management extended. He left the stage when Phelps retired in 1862. He then took up photography professionally and became established in his new career in Chepstow. The name of his wife is not known, but his two daughters, Rosa and Julia Bennett (Mrs Barrow), played with success at minor theatres. Bennett wrote two plays: *Retribution, or, Love's Trials*, in five acts, was successfully produced at Sadler's Wells on 11 February 1850, the principal parts being taken by Phelps, Henry Marston, A. Younge, the author, and Isabella Glyn, and the drama *The Justiza* was produced by Charlotte Cushman at Birmingham. *A Pedestrian Tour through North Wales* (1838) is also said to be his work. Bennett died at Edmonton on 21 September 1879 and was buried at Nunhead cemetery.

JOSEPH KNIGHT, rev. KATHARINE COCKIN

Sources Adams, *Drama* • Hall, *Dramatic ports.* • Genest, *Eng. stage* • G. J. Bennett, *A pedestrian tour through north Wales* (1838) • Boase, *Mod. Eng. biog.* • *The Era* (29 July 1879)

Likenesses W. Sharp, lithograph, pubd 1831 (after G. F. Stroehling), BM, NPG [*see illus.*] · thirteen prints, Harvard TC

Bennett, George Macdonald (1892–1959), chemist, was born in Lincoln on 25 October 1892, the youngest of the three children of the Revd John Ebenezer Bennett (*d.* 1906), teacher and Baptist minister, and his wife, Hanna Martha (*d.* 1932), daughter of William Grange, a farmer in Hertfordshire. He was named after the novelist and children's writer George MacDonald (1824–1905), a friend of his father. In 1893 his father moved to a living in Hackney, and about 1899 to Clacton-on-Sea, where he ran a private boarding-school.

Bennett was a pupil at the school for ten years. The science teacher, who took over the running of the school when J. E. Bennett died, was Harold Picton, a pupil of William Ramsay. Under Picton's influence Bennett developed a liking for chemistry and decided to take it up as a career. He obtained a London University exhibition in 1909 and entered East London (later Queen Mary) College as an internal student, subsequently obtaining a scholarship in chemistry. In 1911 he took an external BA degree, and in the following year he was awarded first-class honours in chemistry. He then began research in organic chemistry but in 1913 he obtained an open exhibition at St John's College, Cambridge, becoming a foundation scholar in the following year. In 1915 he obtained a first class in chemistry in part two of the natural science tripos and became a research assistant to William Pope, with whom, and with C. S. Gibson, he made important contributions in the field of explosives and war gases. Notably, he carried out the first experiment for making mustard gas from disulphurdichloride and ethylene, work which led to his sustained interest in sulphur chemistry.

In 1918 Bennett left Cambridge to take up a post in industry, where he worked on the commercial production of citric acid from cane sugar. He was unhappy there, however, and in 1921 became a senior demonstrator in the chemistry department of Guy's Hospital medical school. In 1924 he became lecturer in organic chemistry in the University of Sheffield, where he built up an enthusiastic research team. In 1931 he was appointed to the university's Firth chair of chemistry.

In 1938 Bennett became professor of organic chemistry at King's College, London, and was in charge of the chemistry department when the college was evacuated to Bristol at the outbreak of war in 1939. There, in addition to his teaching and administrative duties, he carried out studies on the mechanism of aromatic nitration which were of great importance in relation to the development of explosives. King's College returned to London in 1943 but in 1945 Bennett left academic work to become the government chemist. Despite a serious heart condition he undertook much administrative work and actively encouraged the development of links with industry and other government departments. He also maintained a close contact with the academic world through the University of London, the Chemical Society, and the Royal Society, and he

George Macdonald Bennett (1892–1959), by Walter Stoneman

was especially concerned in the development of new experimental techniques such as X-ray diffraction, X-ray fluorescent spectroscopy, and gas chromatography.

Bennett obtained the degrees of PhD (London, 1924) and ScD (Cambridge, 1932). He was a fellow of St John's College, Cambridge (1917–23), and was elected a fellow of Queen Mary College in 1939 and FRS in 1947. In 1948 he was appointed CB. He generously devoted his time to the service of chemistry, and was a member of the council of the Chemical Society (1929–32), honorary secretary (1939–46), and vice-president (1948–51); he was a member of the council of the Royal Institute of Chemistry (1949–51) and its vice-president (1951–3). He was also a member of the council of the Faraday Society (1946–8) and honorary secretary of the Chemical Council (1945–51).

Bennett was a scrupulous and conscientious scientist. Reserved in nature, he could show tremendous excitement when research investigations were going well. He was rigorous in his dealings with students, and only the hard worker received his fullest support. He was a prolific reader but his main interest was always chemistry and apart from walking he had few outdoor activities. His contributions to chemical knowledge ranged over a wide field and he was author or joint author of some ninety publications, most of which appeared in the *Journal of the Chemical Society*.

Bennett suffered a severe heart attack in 1953, after

which he did little beyond his official duties at the Government Laboratory. In 1918 he had married Doris, daughter of James Laycock MPS, of Fulham; they had no children, and when she died in 1958 he was devastated. Bennett died on 9 February 1959 at his home, 74 Kingsmead Avenue, in Worcester Park, Surrey, after a further heart attack. He left the bulk of his estate to Dr Barnardo's Homes.　　　　　　　　　　R. L. Wain, rev. K. D. Watson

Sources R. D. Haworth, *Memoirs FRS*, 5 (1959), 23–36 · E. E. Turner, *Proceedings of the Chemical Society* (1959), 197–200 · *The Times* (11 Feb 1959), 14 · P. W. Hammond and H. Egan, *Weighed in the balance: a history of the laboratory of the government chemist* (1992)
Likenesses W. Stoneman, photograph, RS [*see illus.*] · photograph, repro. in *Memoirs FRS* · photograph, repro. in *The Times* · photograph, King's Lond., department of chemistry
Wealth at death £26,916 19s. 9d.: probate, 21 April 1959, *CGPLA Eng. & Wales*

Bennett, Sir **Henry Honywood Curtis-** (1879–1936), barrister, was born on 31 July 1879 at Brentwood in Essex, the son of Sir Henry Curtis-Bennett (1846–1913), chief metropolitan magistrate, and his wife, Emily Jane Hughes-Hallett (1855–1942), daughter of a Kent solicitor. He was the most celebrated of the three lawyers who bore the double-barrelled name, and in the second of the generations which did so; the Bennetts from whom he was descended on his father's side were mainly men of the cloth. He was educated at Radley College and Trinity College, Cambridge, where he won blues for cycling in 1899, 1900, and 1901; in later life his sporting interests were expressed in his stewardship of the British Board of Boxing Control, his captaincy of the village cricket team at Boreham in Essex, and regular attendance at the cup final.

Curtis-Bennett was called to the bar by the Middle Temple in 1902 and appointed a KC in 1919 and a bencher in 1926. During the First World War, in which for health reasons he was unable, though willing, to serve, he first was briefed for the defence in several spy cases, then, in a career volte-face from 1917 to 1919, was engaged by the War Office's contra-espionage department to cross-examine suspected spies (including Mata Hari). His knighthood in 1922 was conferred for his work in the secret service. As was still a custom of the time for king's counsel, he entered the House of Commons. He represented Chelmsford in the Conservative interest from 1924 to 1926. Less attuned to the Commons than to the courts, he applied for the Chiltern Hundreds when his wife sued him for divorce. She was Elsie Eleanor Dangar, daughter of Albert Augustus Dangar, landowner of Baroona, New South Wales; they had married on 4 April 1903. After the divorce, on 15 August 1929 he married his long-standing mistress, (Lilian) Mary Jeffries, daughter of William Charles Jeffries, of independent means.

Known as Harry, Curtis-Bennett was the epitome of the fashionable silk, specializing in criminal cases at a time when these still commanded the headlines in the press, when and no doubt because the penalty for murder was hanging. No lawyers' lawyer, he was a consummate trial performer and fearsome cross-examiner. His entry into the courtroom with his clerk Hollis in attendance carrying his book, papers, and coloured pencils, the traditional tools of the advocate's trade, as well as his favourite lozenges, was a piece of pure theatre. He gave a phrase (now obsolete) to the vocabulary of the bar, 'doing a Curtis', which originally meant submitting optimistically no case to answer to the judge, but with an eye on the jury, who might later dismiss the case. It later came to mean any manoeuvre of ingenuous guile. He appeared for the defence in some of the most celebrated trials of the age, in particular for Mrs Edith Thompson in the Thompson and Bywaters murder case (1922), and for Lord de Clifford in a manslaughter case arising out of a car accident in 1935, the last occasion on which a peer was tried by his fellows in the House of Lords. In 1922 he unsuccessfully defended Herbert Armstrong, a solicitor, hanged for the murder of his wife. He held part-time judicial appointments as deputy chairman (1923–35) and chairman (1935–6) of Essex quarter sessions and recorder of Chelmsford from 1929 to 1935.

In his youth Curtis-Bennett was a handsome man with striking aquiline features. His loves were France, fast cars, and food. And his convivial nature (he was a member of the Garrick and Beefsteak clubs, and the RAC) and love of good living (he became an *habitué* of the Colchester oyster feast) increased his figure to proportions that justified his sobriquet as the Falstaff of the bar. He was a favourite of the after-dinner speech circuit, the occupational hazard of lawyers, where his qualities of fluency and wit were highly valued. During his lifetime Harry was lent by his mother (who had inherited it from her husband) a country seat, Boreham Lodge in Essex, where he used to keep a donkey in a field opposite. His dogs Judge and Jury were buried in the grounds of the house.

In 1936, to his contemporaries' surprise, Curtis-Bennett accepted the full-time judicial appointment of chairman of the county of London sessions, with his eye on the more senior post of the recordership of London, but his judicial career was nipped in the bud. Like his father and brother, he suffered from heart trouble; and like theirs, his death was a public one. He was replying to the toast of the guests at a dinner of the National Greyhound Racing Society at the Dorchester Hotel, Park Lane, London, on 2 November 1936, when he collapsed and died instantaneously. As his brother Sir (Francis) Noel Curtis-Bennett (1882–1950), who was present, said, his death was 'magnificent in one sense … he went out with a joke on his lips'. He was buried in the churchyard at Kelvedon, Essex. He had a son and a daughter with his first wife: the son, Frederick Henry Derek Curtis-Bennett (1904–1956), sought to emulate his father—not always a wise ambition for sons—and had himself a distinguished legal career as a silk.

Michael Beloff

Sources E. Grice, *Great cases of Sir Henry Curtis Bennett KC* (1937) · R. Wild and D. Curtis-Bennett, *Curtis: the life of Sir Henry Curtis-Bennett, K.C.* (1937) · E. A. Bell, *These meddlesome attorneys* (1939), 155–8 · S. Curtis-Bennett, *The Curtis-Bennett chronicle* (1998) · Venn, *Alum. Cant.* · m. certs.
Likenesses Lafayette, photograph, repro. in Wild and Curtis-Bennett, *Curtis*, facing p. 64 · Maull & Fox, photographs, repro. in Wild and Curtis-Bennett, *Curtis*, frontispiece and facing p. 64 ·

H. Stiles and R. Stiles, photograph, repro. in Wild and Curtis-Bennett, *Curtis*, facing p. 64

Wealth at death £35,030 9s. 5d.: probate, 5 Feb 1937, *CGPLA Eng. & Wales*

Bennett, Jack Arthur Walter (1911–1981), literary scholar, was born on 28 February 1911 at Auckland, New Zealand, the eldest son of Ernest Bennett, foreman shoemaker, and his wife, Alexandra Corrall. Both parents were born in Leicester in the 1880s: Ernest worked in shoe manufacturing, and emigrated to New Zealand in 1907; Alexandra followed in 1908. Bennett's younger brother Norman was born in 1916. Bennett was educated at Mount Albert grammar school in Auckland, where he won a Lizzie Rathbone scholarship to Auckland University College. The most important influence on his work while he was at Auckland was that of Philip Sidney Ardern. While undergraduates, Bennett and his friend James Bertram founded and edited a controversial literary magazine, *Open Windows*, intended to introduce New Zealand readers to the larger world of literary modernism.

In 1933 Bennett left for Merton College, Oxford, with a postgraduate scholarship, having taken a first class in the Auckland MA examination. He completed the Oxford BA English course (medieval and philological option) in 1935, with a first class, and at once, with Kenneth Sisam as his supervisor, embarked on a doctoral thesis 'Old English and Old Norse studies in England from the time of Francis Junius till the end of the eighteenth century'. He took his DPhil in 1938; in the same year he was elected to a junior research fellowship at Queen's College, Oxford.

In 1937 Bennett married a pupil at Oxford, Edith Bannister; the marriage was annulled in 1949. At the outbreak of war in 1939 Bennett was in the United States. He stayed there until September 1945, working for the Ministry of Information, and becoming head of the research division of British information services. He returned to Queen's College late in 1945 and took up teaching for the English faculty. In 1947 he was elected to a tutorial fellowship at Magdalen College, where his colleague in teaching English was C. S. Lewis. In 1951 he married as his second wife Gwyneth Mary Nicholas (d. 1980), the daughter of Archibald John Nicholas, a civil servant; they had two sons. Bennett soon began to help C. T. Onions, who was also at Magdalen, to edit his journal *Medium Aevum*; he succeeded Onions as sole editor in 1956 and continued until 1980. In 1964 he succeeded C. S. Lewis as professor of medieval and Renaissance English at Cambridge; in the same year he became a fellow of Magdalene College, and in 1968 was made the keeper of the old library at Magdalene.

Bennett's first substantial publications were editions of medieval texts: *The Knight's Tale* (1954), and *Devotional Pieces in Verse and Prose from MS Arundel 285 and MS Harleian 6919* (1955). Also published in 1955 was his edition (with H. R. Trevor-Roper) of *The Poems of Richard Corbett*. His three books on Chaucer occupied him intermittently for the following twenty years. *The Parlement of Foules: an Interpretation* appeared in 1957, *Chaucer's Book of Fame* in 1968, and (based on the Alexander lectures given at Toronto in 1970–71) *Chaucer at Oxford and at Cambridge* in 1974. *Early Middle*

Jack Arthur Walter Bennett (1911–1981), by unknown photographer

English Verse and Prose, a volume of annotated selections which Bennett edited with G. V. Smithers, appeared in 1966.

From the 1950s until the early 1970s Bennett was also much involved, as general editor, with the Clarendon Medieval and Tudor series of annotated texts, to which he himself contributed two of the later volumes: *Gower* (1968) and *Piers Plowman* (1972). From 1972 to 1976 he published four sets of *Supplementary Notes on 'Sir Gawain and the Green Knight'* and in 1980 a short book, *Essays on Gibbon* (this was not such a radical departure as it might seem, since his interest in Gibbon went back to his doctoral thesis of over forty years before). Bennett's last completed book, *Poetry of the Passion* (1982), examined poetic treatments of Christ's passion from the Old English *Dream of the Rood* to *The Anathemata* of David Jones. Also in 1982 appeared a volume of Bennett's uncollected essays; edited by Piero Boitani and published in Rome, it was called *The Humane Medievalist and other Essays*.

Bennett left unfinished at his death a large work which had engaged him for many years—the medieval volume intended for the Oxford History of English Literature. Entitled *Middle English Literature*, this was completed and edited by Douglas Gray and published in 1986. *Medieval Studies for J. A. W. Bennett*, a volume of essays by pupils and friends, edited by Peter Heyworth and intended for Bennett's seventieth birthday, appeared too late for him to see it in 1981.

Although Bennett was unquestionably one of Britain's leading literary medievalists, his interests were by no means confined to the middle ages. The seventeenth century was a favourite period, and he was surprisingly well read in American literature. Erudite, imaginative, sensitive, his work as a whole was nourished by his curious and highly independent reading in all periods and by a wide and discriminating experience of the arts, especially painting.

Bennett was made a fellow of the British Academy in 1971. In 1976 he held a visiting fellowship at the Australian National University, and was elected a corresponding fellow of the Medieval Academy of America, and an honorary foreign member of the American Academy of Arts and Sciences. In 1978 he was elected to an emeritus fellowship of the Leverhulme Trust, and in 1980 was awarded the Sir Israel Gollancz prize of the British Academy.

Bennett had long suffered from cardiac asthma; some months after his wife's death in March 1980 he was on his way to New Zealand, and had stopped at Los Angeles, when he died suddenly on 29 January 1981. He was buried in Cambridge beside his wife. He had been a devout Roman Catholic.   EMRYS JONES, *rev.*

Sources N. Davies, 'Jack Arthur Walter Bennett, 1911–1981', *PBA*, 68 (1982), 481–94 · *Magdalen College Record* (1979) · P. L. Heyworth, ed., *Medieval studies for J. A. W. Bennett* (1981) · private information (1990) · personal knowledge (1990)

Archives NL NZ, Turnbull L., corresp. and papers

Likenesses photograph, repro. in Davies, 'Jack Arthur Walter Bennett' · photograph, British Academy [*see illus.*]

Wealth at death £143,235: probate, 2 Sept 1981, *CGPLA Eng. & Wales*

Bennett, James (1774–1862), Congregational minister, was born in east London on 22 May 1774. His early education there he considered a waste of time and he was set to work with an overbearing tradesman. He moved to Bath and was converted there on 13 August 1792, under Methodist influence. He began to preach in the neighbourhood on 24 December 1792. On 17 October 1793 he entered the academy at Gosport under the tuition of David Bogue (1750–1825). He began work as a Congregational minister at Romsey, Hampshire, in February 1796 and was ordained there on 5 April 1797. In 1797 he married Sarah Comley, the daughter of John Comley of Romsey and his wife, Katharine, and the granddaughter of Risdon Darracott (1717–1759). Their eldest child was the physician Sir James Risdon *Bennett (1809–1891). While at Romsey, Bennett became one of the founder members of the London Missionary Society, preaching its annual sermon in 1804. He saw the first missionary ship, the *Duff*, sail from Spithead for Tahiti on 10 August 1796. He travelled in Scotland with Robert and James Haldane in some of their evangelistic tours and helped to gather a Congregational church at Aberdeen. He moved in August 1813 to Rotherham, where he was tutor in the college and pastor of the church at Masborough. In November 1828 he moved to London, where, first in Silver Street and then in Falcon Square, he exercised his ministry.

Bennett was well thought of by contemporaries on account of his diligence, his high ideals and attractive character. His interests were varied. Zeal for evangelical orthodoxy led him to spark off the Manchester Socinian controversy in 1824 with its subsequent court actions over the right of churches to enjoy charitable bequests that had originally been conditional on the profession of the Calvinism which they had abandoned. It was the same concern that moved Bennett to engage in controversy with the deist Robert Taylor (1784–1844). He was one of the founders of the Congregational Union of England and Wales in 1831, and chairman in 1840. He was also a member of the council of the London Missionary Society, and came much into contact with its missionaries, both while they were prosecuting their studies and after they engaged in active work. Among those who in their younger days were members of his church was David Livingstone (1813–1873). Bennett continued throughout his life to be an active participant in local evangelization.

Bennett was a voluminous author. He contributed many articles to journals such as the *Eclectic Review* and the *Evangelical Magazine*. Of the thirty-four titles that he published his historical studies are of most interest. Together with David Bogue he published a *History of Dissenters from … 1688 to … 1808* (4 vols., 1808–12; 2nd edn, 2 vols., 1833), with an additional volume of his own on developments down to 1838 (1839). His aim as a historian was frankly didactic, to teach 'with the voice of examples and facts'. He sought to explain and justify the principles of dissenters and to celebrate the achievements of their leaders. His concentration on the dissenters' contribution to the growth of religious liberty makes him one of the proponents of the whig interpretation of history. His memoir of Risdon Darracott, *The Star of the West* (1815), and the *History of the Church in Silver Street, London* (1842) are still useful.

Bennett resigned his ministry in 1860 and died at 49 Gibson Square, Islington, on 4 December 1862, aged eighty-eight; he was buried at Abney Park cemetery.

      W. G. BLAIKIE, *rev.* R. TUDUR JONES

Sources S. McAll, *Memorials of … James Bennett, D. D.* (1863) · E. J. Evans and W. F. Hurndall, eds., *Pulpit memorials* (1878) · *Congregational Year Book* (1863) · J. Bennett, *The star of the west* (1815) · K. W. Wadsworth, *Yorkshire United Independent College* (1954) · 'Memoir of Rev. James Bennett', *Evangelical Magazine and Missionary Chronicle*, [3rd ser.], 5 (1863), 141–6 · R. Lovett, *The history of the London Missionary Society, 1795–1895*, 2 vols. (1899) · J. G. Miall, *Congregationalism in Yorkshire* (1868) · T. S. James, *The history of the litigation and legislation respecting Presbyterian chapels and charities in England and Ireland between 1816 and 1849* (1867) · A. Peel, *These hundred years: a history of the Congregational Union of England and Wales, 1831–1931* (1931)

Likenesses C. Baugniet, lithograph, pubd 1845, BM · T. Blood, stipple (after J. Renton), BM, NPG; repro. in *Evangelical Magazine* (1818) · photograph, repro. in Evans and Hurndall, *Pulpit memorials* · stipple and line engraving, NPG

Wealth at death under £5000: probate, 13 Jan 1863, *CGPLA Eng. & Wales*

Bennett, James (1785–1856), topographer, was born at Falfield in the parish of Thornbury, Gloucestershire, on 10 May 1785, the eighth of the thirteen children of John Bennett, a yeoman farmer. He was sent to school at Stone, and was then apprenticed to George Robbins of Bath, printer.

After a brief spell as a printer in Whitefriars, London, Bennett returned to Gloucestershire as overseer of printing for the *Gloucester Journal*. In 1810 he became a printer and bookseller at 139 High Street, Tewkesbury. In 1823 he married Anna Maria (*d.* 1846), daughter of John Phillips, alderman. They had five children, one of whom, Charles James Bennett, survived his father. As churchwarden, Bennett helped restore the abbey church of Tewkesbury in 1828. In 1830 he published his *History of Tewkesbury* (abridged as a *Guide* in 1835), which remains an authoritative work (republished 1976). Also in 1830 Bennett brought out the first part of the *Tewkesbury Register and Magazine*, a useful annual which was continued until 1849. He continued in business until 1851, when he retired, having become a person of substance in the town. He died at Tewkesbury on 29 January 1856.

THOMPSON COOPER, *rev.* H. C. G. MATTHEW

Sources GM, 2nd ser., 45 (1856), 317 • Boase, *Mod. Eng. biog.* • J. G. Nichols, 'Notes', *Tewkesbury Register*, 2 (1850) • C. R. Elrington, introduction, in J. Bennett, *History of Tewkesbury* (1976)

Bennett, James Gordon (1795–1872), newspaper editor and publisher, was born on 1 September 1795 in Old Town (later called New Mill), Keith, Banffshire. Catholic farmers in a protestant community, his parents' names are unknown, but Bennett claimed descent from ninth-century Saxon freebooters and Benoits of Normandy. His siblings included two sisters, Margaret and Anne, and a younger brother, Cosmo. Bennett left home at fifteen to attend Blair College, an Aberdeen seminary, for four years, but rejected a religious vocation. Cosmo joined the priesthood, and James, who believed that his own Catholicism provoked whippings at school, blamed his brother's death at the age of twenty-three on the church. Well read in the Bible, Bennett idolized Lord Byron and Robert Burns, absorbed Scott, Rousseau, and Thomas Paine, and spent stretches of the five years between seminary and his departure for America in 1819 on pilgrimages to historical and literary shrines. Ben Franklin's autobiography so intrigued him that on meeting a friend bound for the United States, he vowed to 'see the place where Franklin was born' (Carlson, 3).

After emigrating in 1819, Bennett taught bookkeeping in Halifax, Nova Scotia, then reached Boston in January 1820. A romantic pilgrim again, he sighed at freedom's shrines, spending hours at Bunker Hill and other sites, gushing odes to 'thy blessings, blue-eyed liberty' (Carlson, 33). Sentimental but unemployed, he took work as a proofreader for printers until heading to New York in 1822 and encountering Aaron Willington. The owner of the *Charleston Courier* lured him to South Carolina in 1823 with the promise of journalistic fame. Instead of celebrity, Bennett found literary fellowship and learned the importance of news-gathering from Willington's use of harbour boats to speed news from arriving ships. Having decided that other careers paid more than journalism, he returned to New York city in 1824; but this led to pursuits which did not pay well—lecturing on political economy and opening a commercial school. He soon returned to journalism,

first as an editorial assistant for the *New York National Advocate*, then for the *New York Courier*, which he briefly owned before resuming his writing.

In 1826, when Noah of the *Morning Enquirer* made him a Washington correspondent, Bennett's distinctive writing and reporting style first gained acclaim. He later credited his reading of Walpole's letters in 1828 as a key influence, but even before 1828 his work displayed qualities later described by Frederic Hudson, the first historian of American journalism and long-time managing editor of Bennett's *Herald*, as having brought a new French style to journalistic writing, full of dash and vigour and contrasting with a heavier, more argumentative British style. J. Parton referred to his 'almost inexhaustible fund of French vivacity' (Parton, 392). Bennett also attributed his literary 'force, brevity, spirit' to scripture reading, but surely his style stemmed also from Greek and Roman classics, plus his passion for Scott's Waverley novels and the poetry of Byron. These influences did not always urge brevity but spawned such purple prose as that which celebrated the inauguration of President Andrew Jackson, when Bennett crowed in 1829, 'The welkin rang with music and the feeling plaudits of the populace; beauty smiled and waved her kerchief' (*New York Enquirer*, 6 March 1829, 1) and 'the Genius of our country breathed a living defiance to the world' (ibid.). Noah's newspaper had become the *Courier and Enquirer* and Bennett's lively reporting helped its circulation climb. When anti-Jackson forces gained control in 1832, Bennett left and started his own dailies: *The Globe*, which lasted briefly in New York, and the *Philadelphia Pennsylvanian*, which also failed in 1833 without financial support from Jacksonian democrats.

On 6 May 1835 Bennett launched his *New York Herald*, a penny paper joining eighteen others in the city, including Ben Day's successful *New York Sun*, and such sixpenny papers as the *New York Post*. He soon led revolutionary changes that transformed journalism from passive news-receiving by printer–editors to active news-gathering by a reporting corps that grew from lone police reporters to the sixty-three correspondents Bennett would disperse to cover the civil war. He promised independence from political parties and 'facts on every public and proper subject, stripped of verbiage and coloring' (*New York Herald*, 6 May 1835). By 1858 *Harper's Weekly* concluded, 'No American journal at the present time can compare with it in point of circulation, advertising, or influence. Its most bitter assailants concede to it unrivaled sagacity and enterprise in the collection of news' (*Harper's Weekly*, 2/80, 10 July 1858, 433). Parton, an admiring biographer of the *New York Tribune*'s Horace Greeley and, like the editors of *Harper's*, no friend of Bennett, regretted in 1866 that 'It is impossible any longer to deny that the [city's] chief newspaper is the *New York Herald*' (Parton, 379). According to Parton, Bennett surpassed Greeley and Henry Raymond of the *New York Times* because both were distracted by noble causes while the *Herald* focused on news-gathering. Greeley, often designated America's greatest journalist, admitted that his rival 'had an unerring judgment of the pecuniary value of news. He knew how to pick out of the events of the day the subject that engrossed the interest of the greatest number of people' (*New York Tribune*, 3 July 1872).

That Bennett knew what readers wanted—Raymond swore the Devil advised him each evening—was agreed. The implications were controversial. Contemporaries and historians weighed his accomplishments against his shortcomings or ignored the former to scorn the latter. Yes, he succeeded in gaining the most readers, but at what price? Even as a one-man band, publishing, editing, and reporting the news single-handed in the earliest days, he provoked controversy. Already greying at the age of forty, lean and hard from long hours and missed meals, Bennett had scant time for vices with his 5 a.m. to 11 p.m. working days. Yet he paused to pick fights, fixing rivals in his cross-eyed gaze, denouncing the *Sun*'s 'dirty and indecent police reporters' as 'the garbage of society' (*New York Herald*, 16 May 1835). Greater excesses would ignite the 'Moral War' against Bennett in 1840, when competitors called him a 'moral pestilence' with 'ghoul-like propensity' and 'infamous blasphemer'. *Herald* coverage of the great Wall Street fire of 1835 inspired Parton to trumpet, 'American journalism was born amid the roaring flames' (Parton, 396), but the story that most roused his critics came in 1836 with the discovery of a prostitute's scorched corpse. Bennett interviewed Madame Townsend, the brothel proprietor, in arguably the first consciously journalistic interview, and lavished observational detail on the remains of Helen Jewett. The victim's body 'looked as white, as full, as polished as the purest Parian marble. The perfect figure, the exquisite limbs, the fine face, the full arms, the beautiful bust, all, all surpassed in every respect the Venus de Medici' (*New York Herald*, 12 April 1836). Presses kept running to meet the demand for his sensational reports, and rivals cried 'buzzards' and 'vampires'.

The clergy objected to Bennett's predilection for exploiting sexual indiscretions of protestant pastors, which he justified to counter press hypocrisy toward priestly peccadilloes. He elaborated in 1836 on an Episcopalian cleric's seduction of a widow, separating such words as 'ecstasy', 'clasped', 'bust', and 'screamed' with strings of asterisks, and the next day published a notice offering to reward any woman who 'will set a trap for a Presbyterian parson, and catch one of them flagrante delicito [*sic*]' (*New York Herald*, 8 March 1836). Contrary to Isaac Pray, his first biographer and defender, Bennett went beyond writing 'petticoats' rather than 'inexpressibles' and 'legs' rather than 'limbs'. His personal journalism was never more vulgar than when he was writing of Henrietta Agnes Crean, the piano teacher of Irish heritage in the Warren and Crean Lynch families who became his wife on 6 June 1840. Their first meeting inspired him to delineate for subscribers her 'most magnificent' figure, and his editorial excesses continued unblushingly through their wedding and the birth of James Gordon Bennett junior on 10 May 1841. Mrs Bennett subsequently lived in Europe, educating their son and a daughter, Jeannette, there. Another daughter died during infancy, and another son, Cosmo, at the age of five. When not crossing the Atlantic for visits, Bennett was left to his long hours at the *Herald*.

The readership of the *Herald* was growing, and Bennett led the race for news, buying pilot boats in 1837 to greet ships and co-operating with the new pigeon express in 1838. He booked passage on the first transatlantic steamer that year, and signed six correspondents to report from Europe, then added more in Canada, Mexico, and Texas on his return. In 1841 a Washington staff was initiated, and when the *Herald* occupied a new plant in 1842, its presses could print 60,000 copies daily. Frederic Hudson ran the paper when Bennett toured Europe again in 1843—when in Dublin he was verbally assaulted by Irish repeal leader Daniel O'Connell—and 1846, but Bennett personally pushed the expansion of the *Herald*'s news-gathering resources. Earlier growth spurred financial coverage more reliable than its rivals, and full-time reporters were assigned to society, religion, sports, and other news previously given sporadic attention. The Mexican war and the California gold rush of 1849 confirmed the *Herald*'s superiority in rapid coverage.

While continuing to attack abolitionists who would end slavery, Bennett reported extensively in 1859 on the African slave trade, blaming black republicans. While condemning the raid on Harper's Ferry, *Herald* reports of John Brown's gaolhouse interrogation portrayed him as heroic. While opposing Lincoln's candidacy in 1860, Bennett permitted Henry Villard to give friendly treatment to his campaign. Opposing conflict until it exploded in 1861, Bennett then backed the Union cause and splurged an unprecedented half a million dollars for the most extensive coverage of the civil war. An editor for Greeley's *Tribune* griped of lagging behind, 'obliged to copy' from the *Herald*. In 1862 the paper ran the entire roster of the Confederate army. Despite long resistance to emancipation, Bennett came to accept it. He supported Lincoln's re-election in 1864 and favoured Liberal reconstruction policies.

At the age of seventy in 1866, with circulation at 90,000, Bennett relinquished control to his son, spending some time at the *Herald* each week. Young Bennett would finance Henry Stanley's expedition to find Dr Livingstone and a second African adventure. Dividing time between his country home and a town house, the senior Bennett still marked notations on newspapers delivered to him, editorializing as late as 2 June 1871 on the pretentious wedding of Boss Tweed's daughter. His health prevented a European trip in the spring of 1872, and on 21 May he received the last sacrament and rejoined his natal church. Hudson came to his bedside after a stroke on 25 May, but his death on 1 June 1872 at home at 425 Fifth Avenue, New York city, was unattended by family members. Only his son returned from Europe for the funeral. He was buried at Greenwood cemetery, Brooklyn. His great rival, Greeley, who served as pallbearer with other famous editors, had the last word, noting that 'He developed the capacities of journalism in a most wonderful manner, but he did it by degrading its character. He made the newspaper powerful, but he made it odious' (*New York Tribune*, 3 June 1872). If so, as *Harper's Weekly* had observed, 'No one can seriously deny the merit of the *Herald* without impugning the judgment or the morals of the community' (*Harper's Weekly*, 2/80, 10 July 1858, 433).   WARREN T. FRANCKE

Sources *New York Herald* (6 May 1835–3 June 1872) · O. Carlson, *The man who made news* (1942) · J. Parton, 'The *New York Herald*', *North American Review*, 102 (1866), 373–419 · *Harper's Weekly*, 2 (1858), 433–4 · I. Pray, *Memoirs of James Gordon Bennett and his times* (1855) · *The life and writings of James Gordon Bennett* (1844) · F. Hudson, *Journalism in the United States from 1690 to 1872* (1873), 408–56 · J. L. Crouthamel, 'James Gordon Bennett, the *New York Herald*, and the development of newspaper sensationalism', *New York History*, 54 (1973), 294–316 · W. T. Francke, 'Investigative exposure in the nineteenth century', PhD diss., University of Minnesota, 1974
Likenesses M. Brady, engraving (after his photograph), repro. in *Harper's Weekly* (10 July 1858) · engraving, repro. in Pray, *Memoirs of James Gordon Bennett* · wood-engraving, NPG; repro. in *ILN* (10 Aug 1872)
Wealth at death a multi-millionaire: Carlson, *The man who made news*

Bennett, Sir James Risdon (1809–1891), physician, eldest son of James *Bennett DD (1774–1862), nonconformist minister, and his wife, Sarah Comley, was born at Romsey, Hampshire, on 29 September 1809. He was educated at Rotherham College, Yorkshire, of which his father became principal; at the age of fifteen he was apprenticed to Thomas Waterhouse of Sheffield, and in 1830 he went to Edinburgh University, where he graduated MD in 1833. He then spent some time on the continent with Lord Aberdeen. On his return to England in 1837 he settled in London and became physician to the General Dispensary, Aldersgate Street; he also lectured on medicine at the Charing Cross Hospital medical school and at Grainger's private school of medicine. In 1843 he was appointed assistant physician to St Thomas's Hospital, and in 1849 full physician. On the foundation of the City of London Hospital for Diseases of the Chest in 1848 he was appointed physician to that institution; from 1843 to its dissolution in 1857 he acted as secretary to the Sydenham Society. He took an active interest in the work of the Religious Tract Society and the London Missionary Society. In 1875 he was elected FRS.

Bennett married on 8 June 1841 Ellen Selfe, daughter of the Revd Henry Page of Trowbridge, Wiltshire: of nine children born to them three boys and three girls survived; one son, Selfe Bennett, followed him into the medical profession. The Bennetts settled in London's Finsbury Square. For many years Bennett enjoyed a good position as a consultant, especially in connection with chest diseases, having been one of the first to introduce into this country the use of the stethoscope, which, though popular in the USA and Europe, had hitherto been ignored in England. In 1876 he was elected to the office of president of the Royal College of Physicians, London, and he was knighted in 1881. In later years his opinion was frequently sought by those in the government, and he was well known in the City of London as a consultant in life insurance cases. In 1881 Bennett moved to 22 Cavendish Square, Marylebone, where he died on 14 December 1891, survived by his wife.

Bennett published *The Nature and Treatment of Diseases of the Ear* (1837), a translation of Kramer's text; an essay on acute hydrocephalus, which obtained the Fothergillian gold medal of the Medical Society of London in 1842 and which was published as *The Causes, Nature, Diagnosis and Treatment of Acute Hydrocephalus* (1843); and in 1872 *Cancerous and other Interthoracic Growths*—the Lumleian lectures at the Royal College of Physicians.

J. B. NIAS, *rev.* ANITA MCCONNELL

Sources *The Times* (16 Dec 1891), 5f · private information (1901) · Munk, *Roll* · *The Lancet* (2 Jan 1892), 64–5 · *BMJ* (19 Dec 1891), 1336 · P. H. P. S., *PRS*, 51 (1892), xli–xliii · *ILN* (5 March 1881), 220 · *ILN* (26 Dec 1891), 826 · d. cert.
Likenesses F. Piercy, chalk drawing, 1899, RCP Lond. · L. S. Breslau, pastel drawing, 1908 (after F. Piercy), RCP Lond.
Wealth at death £17,441 14s. 0d.: probate, 5 Feb 1892, *CGPLA Eng. & Wales*

Bennett, (Nora Noel) Jill (1929?–1990), actress, was born, possibly on 24 December 1929, in Penang, Malaya, the only child of (James) Randle Bennett, an owner of rubber plantations, and his wife, Nora Adeline Beckett. Her death certificate claims that she was born in 1931, but she was reticent about her date of birth. In *Who's Who* she wrote that she was born in 1929. When war broke out in 1939 her mother took her to England. Her father was taken prisoner by the Japanese, and neither Jill nor her mother saw him again for five years. In England she attended several boarding-schools, including Priors Field, Godalming, Surrey, where, she claimed, she was good at games, French, riding, and the history of art. She was expelled at the age of fourteen. She also showed an early talent for ballet, but at fifteen decided to be an actress and was accepted by the Royal Academy of Dramatic Art, London, which she attended in 1944–6. She made her stage début in 1947 in *Now Barabbas* (Bolton's Theatre and, later, Vaudeville Theatre).

In 1949 Bennett was given one speaking part and walk-ons with the Shakespeare Memorial Theatre Company at Stratford upon Avon, where she met Godfrey *Tearle (1884–1953), a fine actor, who was more than forty years her senior. From then until his death, they had what she called 'a passionate friendship'. In her book, *Godfrey: a Special Time Remembered* (written with Suzanne Goodwin in 1983), she makes it clear that he was the great love of her life. She later married twice, both times to playwrights. In 1962 she married Willis Hall, the son of Walter Hall. Willis Hall wrote, among other things, *The Long, the Short and the Tall*. The marriage was dissolved in 1965, and in 1968 she married (as his fourth wife) John James *Osborne (1929–1994), the son of Thomas Godfrey Osborne, copy-writer in an advertising agency. John Osborne was the author of *Look Back in Anger* (1956), which started a new kind of drama in England, known as the kitchen sink drama. They were divorced in 1977. There were no children of either marriage, though she had two miscarriages when married to Osborne. Osborne's hostile picture of her in *Almost a Gentleman* (1991) is unrecognizable to those who knew her well.

Bennett had a long and successful career in theatre, films, television, and radio. Her first parts in London were as Anni in *Captain Carvallo*, directed by Laurence Olivier (St James's, 1950), and Iras in both *Antony and Cleopatra* and

Caesar and Cleopatra in the Sir Laurence Olivier season, also at the St James's Theatre (1951). From 1955 she was much in demand, mostly in the West End, notably as Helen Eliot in *The Night of the Ball* (New Theatre, 1955), Masha in *The Seagull* (Saville, 1956), and Isabelle in *Dinner with the Family* (New, 1957). In December 1962 she began her important association with the Royal Court Theatre, as Hilary in *The Sponge Room* and Elizabeth Mintey in *Squat Betty*. In 1965 she made the first of her three appearances there in a play by her future husband, John Osborne, as Countess Sophia Delyanoff in *A Patriot for Me*. She was also in the film versions of Osborne's *Inadmissible Evidence* and *The Charge of the Light Brigade* (both 1968). Osborne wrote *Time Present*—based on her relationship with Godfrey Tearle—for her in 1968, and in it, as Pamela, she won the Evening Standard and Variety Club awards for best actress. Her final Osborne play (also at the Royal Court, and subsequently at the Cambridge Theatre) was *West of Suez* (1971). She was a memorable Hedda Gabler in 1972, and Fay, in Joe Orton's *Loot*, in 1975 (both at the Royal Court), and she was highly successful in a revival of Sir Terence Rattigan's *Separate Tables*, in which she played the contrasting emotional cripples Mrs Shankland and Miss Railton Bell (Apollo, 1977). This was followed by leading parts in successive seasons at the Festival Theatre, Chichester, in 1978 and 1979, which included Miss Tina in *The Aspern Papers*. Other personal successes included Gertrude in *Hamlet*—in the opinion of the director, Anthony Page, the best Gertrude he ever saw

(Royal Court, 1980)—and the wife in August Strindberg's *Dance of Death* (Manchester Royal Exchange, 1981).

Bennett's films included *Lust for Life* (1956), Joseph Losey's *The Criminal* (1960), *The Nanny* (with Bette Davis, 1965), *Britannia Hospital* (1982), and Bernardo Bertolucci's *The Sheltering Sky* (1990). Her many television credits included *The Heiress*, *The Three Sisters*, *Design for Living*, and *Rembrandt* (all 1970), Alan Bennett's *The Old Crowd* (1979), and John Mortimer's *Paradise Postponed* (1986).

No conventional beauty, Bennett considered herself ugly. She was in fact extremely attractive, elegant, petite, blonde, and blue-eyed, with a distinctively turned-up nose, flared nostrils, strong teeth, and a small, amusingly jutting chin. She had quick intelligence and wit, and her laughter was companionable and infectious, but needed to be won. She often indulged in extravagant behaviour, which could be embarrassing. She wrongly believed that she was a failure in her relationships with men. Her friendships were many and long-lasting. For instance, Anthony Page was a friend and colleague for over thirty years, and Lindsay Anderson, the film director, for longer still—as was her loving and much-loved secretary, Linda Drew.

Bennett adored acting but, being sensitive and nervous, preferred the cloistered security of rehearsal, the passionate search for character and motive, and the trusting relationship with her directors to the exposure of performance. When, however, she felt utterly secure in her part,

(Nora Noel) Jill Bennett (1929?–1990), by Patrick Procktor, 1972

in the play, and in her colleagues, she could be superb. She committed suicide on 5 October 1990 at her home, 23 Gloucester Walk, Kensington, London, by taking an overdose of sleeping-pills, having tried unsuccessfully to do so a month previously. Her relationship with a Swiss businessman, Thomas Schoch, had foundered and her ever-present sense of failure had finally overcome her.

DULCIE GRAY, rev.

Sources J. Bennett and S. Goodwin, *Godfrey: a special time remembered* (1983) · J. Osborne, *Almost a gentleman* (1991) · private information (1996) [L. Drew, A. Page] · *The Times* (6 Oct 1990) · d. cert. · *WW* · personal knowledge (1996)
Likenesses P. Procktor, portrait, 1972, priv. coll. [*see illus.*] · photographs, Hult. Arch.

Bennett, John (*c*.1550–1625), Jesuit, was a son of Hugh John Bennett, gentleman, of Bryn Canathan, Cwm, Holywell, Flintshire. Bennett received his early education in St Asaph. At some unknown date he abandoned his country because he 'had thoroughly apprehended the malice of the heretical depravity which by that time bore sway over the whole kingdom' (Foley, 4.498) and travelled to the continent. Having attended the English College, Douai, and perhaps moved with it to Rheims in 1578, he was ordained in Cambrai on 29 March 1578; he was sent to England on 2 May 1580. He worked throughout Wales but primarily in the north. In 1582 Sir Thomas Mostyn arrested him at Gloddaith, Caernarvonshire, and conveyed him to William Hughes, bishop of St Asaph. Through argument and offers of ecclesiastical offices the bishop sought to win Bennett to the established church. Bennett's refusal resulted in his imprisonment. Arraigned at different times between 1582 and 1584 at Holywell, Wrexham, Bewdley, and finally before the council of the marches in Ludlow, Bennett was examined about his beliefs and his ministry with Catholics. He was tortured but was never condemned to death: all his arraignments occurred before Elizabeth's law declaring the return of Catholic priests to the realm to be treason (27 Eliz. c. 2, 1584–5). While he was being moved to Ludlow, Bennett was lodged in a room allegedly haunted by evil spirits, whom, through his prayers and exorcisms, he expelled. In late 1584 or early 1585 he was transferred to a prison in London; on 24 September 1585 he was exiled, arriving at the English College in Rheims on 8 October. On 6 September 1586 he entered the Society of Jesus in Verdun. In 1590 he was in Paris. In October of the same year he returned to the realm despite threats of severe punishment if he ever set foot in the country again. His decision was probably the result of Henry Garnet's request for a Welsh speaking preacher. He landed at Shields, near Newcastle, and apparently set off immediately for Wales.

Little is known about Bennett's subsequent work. With the possible exception of 1593 when one catalogue listed him at Verdun (perhaps completing tertianship, the final year of Jesuit formation), he worked in Wales for almost all his life

with great pains and diligence in the continual exercise of his apostolical functions, assisting for the most part the poor or meaner sort of person, who about Holywell, and

elsewhere in North Wales, flocked to him in such multitudes to receive the spiritual cordials and divine food which he freely and copiously ministered to them. (Foley, 4.500)

He attended the famous gathering of Jesuits at Baddesley Clinton in October 1591 but departed before the raid. On 8 September 1603 he pronounced his final vows as a spiritual coadjutor 'near London'. Some time in late 1624 or early 1625 he begged permission from his Jesuit superior to go to London to work among the victims of the plague then raging there. He died in that service on 8 September 1625.

THOMAS M. McCOOG

Sources T. M. McCoog, *English and Welsh Jesuits, 1555–1650*, 2 vols., Catholic RS, 74–5 (1994–5) · T. M. McCoog, ed., *Monumenta Angliae*, 1–2 (1992) · H. Foley, ed., *Records of the English province of the Society of Jesus*, 7 vols. in 8 (1875–83) · T. F. Knox and others, eds., *The first and second diaries of the English College, Douay* (1878) · G. Anstruther, *The seminary priests*, 1 (1969) · D. A. Thomas, *The Welsh Elizabethan Catholic martyrs* (1971) · T. M. McCoog, 'The Society of Jesus in Wales; the Welsh in the Society of Jesus: 1561–1625', *Journal of Welsh Religious History*, 5 (1997), 1–27

Bennett, Sir John (1814–1897), watchmaker and politician, was born on 15 October 1814, the son of John Bennett (*d*. 1829/30) of Stockwell Street, Greenwich, watchmaker, and his wife, Elizabeth Sinnock Bennett, and the elder brother of George Weedon Bennett and William Cox *Bennett. He was educated at Colfe's Grammar School, Lewisham. Following the death of his father he assisted his mother in running the business at Greenwich, but by 1847 he was established on his own account as goldsmith and watchmaker at 65 Cheapside, London, an address the firm occupied for the rest of its existence. Bennett married on 19 August 1843 Agnes, daughter of John Willson; she died on 26 October 1889. They had a son and two daughters: the elder daughter, Alice, married Sydney John Cockerell, and was the mother of, among other children, Sir Sydney Carlyle Cockerell and Douglas Bennett Cockerell. A long relationship with Aimée Guilbert (1842–1931) produced seven children, the first born in 1866 and the last in 1884.

Bennett promoted his business vigorously by advertising in media such as the Great Exhibition catalogue and Kelly's directories, by the use of gimmicks including a time ball operated electrically from Greenwich and a public clock with figures of Gog and Magog (later acquired by the Henry Ford Museum in Dearborn, Michigan), and by frequent lectures, at which a pedlar's licence permitted him to sell direct to his audience. Records of Bennett's dealings with the Royal Observatory indicate that initially he was engaged in general repair work and supply of sundries. Later he became primarily a retailer and his use of foreign manufacturers provoked some hostile comment, though he also used British suppliers, including V. Kullberg. The connection with the Royal Observatory ceased in November 1849, when the astronomer royal, G. B. Airey, asked his assistant to retrieve all instruments 'from Mr Bennett, as I will have no more to do with him', but this did not stop Bennett continuing to describe himself as maker to the Royal Observatory. Bennett's involvement with the business ceased shortly after it became a limited

Sir John Bennett (1814–1897), by unknown engraver, pubd 1879

company in 1889; it continued to operate until 1940. As well as running his own business Bennett had pronounced views on the watch and clock trade in general. His lectures advocating systematic methods of manufacture along Swiss lines, including the use of female labour, aroused hostility among English craftsmen and led indirectly to the formation in 1858 of the British Horological Institute to protect their interests. Ironically Bennett was one of the original members of the institute's council.

Bennett's involvement with City of London local politics began with his election as common councilman for Cheap ward in 1860. He retained this office until 1888, when he retired, and was deputy for the ward, 1874–7. As a common councilman his readiness to consider municipal reform set him at odds with his colleagues: he was the only member to oppose petitioning against the London Government Bill of 1884. On 20 October 1871 he was elected sheriff of London and Middlesex in the place of Richard Young, who had died before he could take office, and served for the remainder of the term. During his shrievalty he was knighted on 14 March 1872, in commemoration of the queen's earlier visit to St Paul's Cathedral to give thanks for the recovery of the prince of Wales from typhoid fever. Bennett twice stood, unsuccessfully, as candidate for alderman of Cordwainer ward, in 1873 and 1875. On 4 June 1877 he was elected alderman of Cheap ward by a margin of one vote (one of his opponent's votes was later found to be invalid). Petitions were presented for and against his election, and at a subsequent scrutiny it was alleged that eight who had voted for Bennett had temporarily rented property solely in order to qualify themselves to vote. One of the eight admitted that this was the case,

but the recorder ruled that this did not invalidate his vote. His opponent then withdrew and Bennett was declared elected. On 27 July the court of aldermen voted by nineteen to nil, with two abstentions, that Bennett was not a person fit and proper to discharge the office of alderman. Bennett was elected again on 11 August and refused again on 25 September by sixteen votes to two, elected a third time on 3 October and refused a third time on 16 October. Following the third refusal the aldermen exercised their right to make an appointment to the vacancy and on 23 October appointed Edgar Breffit, who had been defeated by Bennett in the latter two elections. On the wider political scene, Bennett served on the school board for London as member for the City of London in 1872–3 and 1876–9, and for Southwark in 1885–8; he also stood unsuccessfully for the City in 1873, 1879, and 1882. He three times stood unsuccessfully for parliament—at Greenwich in 1873, Maldon in 1874, and Wiltshire (Cricklade) in 1886—on the first two occasions as a Liberal and on the third as an independent Liberal.

Bennett's 'mother' livery company was the Spectaclemakers, of which he was made free by redemption on 31 October 1849, and to the livery of which he was admitted on 24 June 1865. He was also a liveryman of the Clockmakers' and Loriners' companies, and master of the Loriners in 1877–8. His involvement with livery companies did not prevent his adopting a critical attitude towards them: in Archer's *History of the Haberdashers' Company* he is quoted as saying that 'like the fly in the treacle pot', the companies 'could not move for wealth'.

In the 1851 census Bennett is shown as living at 65 Cheapside, but by 1861 his residence was in Dulwich Common where he had 'a little box', as he put it. Later he lived at The Banks, Mountfield, Sussex, and Druid's Glen, Chislehurst. About 1889 he got into serious financial difficulties, although apparently did not, as some have suggested, become bankrupt. The contents of Druid's Glen were ordered to be sold, and he retired to Hastings. He died of bronchitis at 135 London Road, St Leonards, on 3 July 1897 and was buried at Mountfield. In his will made 1 May 1891 and proved on 1 February 1898 he named Aimée Guilbert as sole beneficiary 'in grateful acknowledgement of the incessant kindness I have received from the said Aimée Guilbert for upwards of a quarter of a century'.

Bennett was a flamboyant personality who seems to have aroused in his contemporaries varying degrees of ridicule, hostility, and admiration: members of the Cockerell family described him as 'abominable' and 'something of a monster'. His flamboyance extended to his dress and public appearances: he used to appear in the lord mayor's show mounted on a white horse and dressed in black velvet jacket and broad-brimmed hat, to applause which sometimes exceeded that for the lord mayor. A *Vanity Fair* cartoon of 1883 by 'Spy' shows him thus attired, but mounted on a bay: the accompanying text refers to his unexaggerated collection of scruples and remarkable head of hair, and suggests that it might have been his ability to 'captivate the fair' that led to his difficulties with the court of aldermen. A profile in *The Hornet*, 3 April 1872, hints at a pronounced cockney accent, employed in the promotion of his business and himself.

RICHARD HARVEY

Sources Boase, *Mod. Eng. biog.* · A. B. Beaven, ed., *The aldermen of the City of London, temp. Henry III–[1912]*, 2 vols. (1908–13) · Court of Aldermen, Corporation of London, *Report of the proceedings of the Cheap ward election* (1877) · W. Blunt, *Cockerell: Sydney Carlyle Cockerell, friend of Ruskin and William Morris, and director of the Fitzwilliam Museum, Cambridge* (1964) · I. W. Archer, *The history of the Haberdashers' Company* (1991) · J. Foster, *The peerage, baronetage, and knightage of the British empire for 1881*, [2 pts] [1881] · records, CUL, RGO 6/722 · *City Press* (19 April 1884), 5 · *CGPLA Eng. & Wales* (1898) · d. cert.

Likenesses Pet, chromolithograph caricatures, NPG; repro. in *Monetary Gazette*, 13 Dec 1876, 21 July 1877 [supplement] · Spy [L. Ward], cartoon, repro. in *VF* (13 Jan 1883) · caricature, NPG; repro. in *The Hornet* (3 April 1872) · wood-engraving, NPG; repro. in *Walter Pelham's Illustrated Journal*, 1 (20 Dec 1879) [*see illus.*]

Wealth at death £463 19s. 6d.: probate, 1 Feb 1898, *CGPLA Eng & Wales* · £88 9s. 6d.: administration with will, 14 Sept 1899, *CGPLA Eng. & Wales*

Bennett, John Hughes (1812–1875), physician and physiologist, was born on 31 August 1812 at Exeter, Devon, the only son of John Stokes Bennett (1773–1829), Exeter freeman, actor, and musician, and his wife, Julia Hughes (1783–1854), an actress, daughter of Richard Hughes (d. 1815), who owned many theatres, including Sadler's Wells in London. Bennett was educated at Exeter grammar school and Mount Radford School, Exeter, but he also owed much to his mother's literary and artistic influence, which shaped his skills as a writer, teacher, and debater.

In 1829 Bennett became apprenticed to William Sedgwick, a surgeon in Maidstone. In the penultimate year of the five-year apprenticeship he began medical duties at dispensaries in north London under guidance from William Kingdon, consultant surgeon in London and long-standing friend of the Hughes family. In 1833 Bennett, encouraged by Kingdon, enrolled as a medical student at the University of Edinburgh, Scottish medical education being considered superior to that in England. While still a student Bennett published two papers, and in his final year was elected president of the Royal Medical Society and the Royal Physical Society of Edinburgh, and a vice-president of the Anatomical and Physiological Society. He graduated MD in 1837, receiving a gold medal.

Following graduation Bennett spent two years studying in Paris and founded there the English Medical Society, becoming its first president. In 1839 he continued his postgraduate studies in Germany, principally at Heidelberg and the Charité Hospital in Berlin. He returned to Paris in 1841 to study the use of the microscope under Alfred Donné. Fluent in French and impressed by Parisian methods of clinical study, Bennett was elected to the Anatomical Society of Paris.

Returning to Edinburgh in 1841, Bennett began lecturing on histology, giving a series of microscopical demonstrations illustrating anatomy, physiology, pathology, and the diagnosis of disease. He was the first in Britain to give this practical instruction systematically and was instrumental in increasing awareness of the importance of the microscope in the clinical investigation of disease. Lectures on pathology and the practice of physic followed, with emphasis on fuller examination by students of both patients and specimens, to achieve a reasoned diagnosis. In 1841 Bennett published his treatise on cod-liver oil, based on his studies in Germany. The reintroduction of cod-liver oil as a beneficial therapeutic agent is credited to Bennett who also used it successfully in the treatment of tuberculosis, on the management of which he was an authority. He was elected in 1842 to fellowships of the Royal College of Physicians of Edinburgh and the Royal Society of Edinburgh. His appointment as pathologist to Edinburgh Royal Infirmary followed and in 1845 he became a lecturer in medicine at the university medical school. On 22 August 1844 Bennett married Jessie Samuel (1824–1906), niece of the Revd Dr Alexander Simpson (later moderator of the Church of Scotland). They had five children—a son who became a consultant neurologist in London and four daughters, a circumstance which perhaps explains Bennett's support of the admission of women to read medicine. He was a connoisseur of fine art and music, and an accomplished singer.

In the eight years following graduation Bennett published thirty-eight papers; the most important, 'A case of hypertrophy of the spleen and liver in which death took place from suppuration of the blood', appeared in the *Edinburgh Medical and Surgical Journal* of 1 October 1845. This celebrated paper described the first recorded case of leukaemia. Rudolf Virchow in Berlin published the second case of the disease independently six weeks later and some controversy, initiated by others, ensued over the priority of discovery. This question was resolved by Virchow's statement that Bennett had observed a case of 'indubitable leukaemia' some months prior to his own observations. In 1852 Bennett published *Leucocythemia, or, White Cell Blood*, an authoritative collection of cases.

Bennett was appointed editor of the *London and Edinburgh Monthly Journal of Medical Science* in 1846 and later became its proprietor. He sold the journal in 1849 to the publishers Sutherland and Knox, but it returned to Bennett's proprietorship some years later, to be sold again to the same publishers. His able management made it a lucrative property. These transactions and the earlier financial support from his maternal grandfather permitted Bennett to pursue his interests in academic medicine without needing to engage extensively in private medical practice.

In 1848 Bennett was appointed to the chair of the Institutes of Medicine. With characteristic vigour he taught clinical physiology and pathology, precisely illustrated by diagrams and specimens, and trained students in accurate observation and sound reasoning. He enjoyed a particularly high reputation as a lecturer, his system of instruction becoming a model for other teaching institutions. In 1855 he was a candidate for the Edinburgh chair of the practice of physic. The appointment at that time was controlled by the city council as patrons of the university. Transference from the Institutes of Medicine to the practice of physic was regarded as somewhat customary and those who had taken this route included William Cullen, James Gregory, and William Alison. This was not to be repeated; after an intense political contest, Thomas Laycock from York was elected. Disappointed though he was, Bennett continued his teaching and clinical work with undiminished energy and was active in university matters. Although he was sometimes judged by others to be confrontational, and despite attempts to discredit him, the medical and therapeutic advances he initiated were acknowledged as a successful challenge to outdated treatments and views. Unsurprisingly, he was not universally popular, but his intellect and logic, his oratory and literary mastery combined to establish him as a bold and determined reformer in clinical medicine. Criticized at times for outspokenness and impatience, Bennett encouraged those who, like himself, were frustrated by the inadequacy or lack of beneficial therapies. His most valuable therapeutic work was in the treatment of pneumonia and tuberculosis. His work helped to reduce substantially the mortality of uncomplicated pneumonia and he condemned the treatment of tuberculosis patients which confined them to overheated rooms with doses of cough mixtures and applications of leeches, with occasional general bleeding. It was principally Bennett who overthrew the common practice of bloodletting.

Bennett was an indefatigable writer, publishing 105 papers, many of importance. The principal results of his work are published in *Clinical Lectures on the Principles and Practice of Medicine*, of which five editions appeared from 1850 to 1868, with six American editions and translations into French, Russian, and Hindi. His *Textbook of Physiology* (1871, 1872), published simultaneously in Edinburgh and the USA, was also translated into French, and he had the rare distinction in 1879 of having his 'Restorative treatment of pneumonia' translated and published in Japanese.

Bennett's formerly robust health deteriorated progressively from 1871, despite recuperative winter visits to the south of France. In 1873 he was elected a member of the French Académie de Médecine and was granted special recognition by the government to practise medicine in France. He was a fellow or member of numerous scientific societies in Europe and the USA.

In the year of his death Edinburgh University honoured Bennett with the degree of LLD. Ill health forced his resignation in 1874; he died at Norwich on 25 September 1875, nine days after surgery to remove a stone by lateral lithotomy, and was buried on 30 September in Dean cemetery, Edinburgh. He was survived by his wife and children.

In 1901 one of Bennett's daughters, Harriet Cox, wife of an Edinburgh member of parliament, donated substantial funds to the university to establish the John Hughes Bennett Laboratory in his memory.   G. J. PILLER

Sources parish register, St David's, Exeter, 1812–13, Devon RO · testimonials in favour of John Hughes Bennett, M.D., candidate for the situation of pathologist and superintendent in the Royal Infirmary Edinburgh, 1841, U. Edin. L., special collections division · J. D. Comrie, *History of Scottish medicine*, 2nd edn, 2 (1932) · A. Logan Turner, *Story of a great hospital: the Royal Infirmary of Edinburgh, 1729–1929* (1937) · W. S. Craig, *History of the Royal College of Physicians of Edinburgh* (1976) · J. G. McKendrick, *Edinburgh Medical Journal*, 21 (1875–6), 466–74 · *The Lancet* (2 Oct 1875), 504 · *The Lancet* (9 Oct 1875), 533–4 · *BMJ* (9 Oct 1875), 473–8 [incl. list of publications] · *BMJ* (27 July 1901), 223–4, 229–30 · *Boston Medical and Surgical Journal*, 93 (1875), 509–12 · *The Scotsman* (27 Sept 1875) · *Proceedings of the Royal Society of Edinburgh*, 9 (1875–8), 15–17 · C. Newman, *The evolution of medical education in the nineteenth century* (1957) · D. Arundell, *The story of Sadler's Wells, 1683–1964* (1965) · R. Virchow, *Cellular pathology*, trans. F. Chance (1863); repr. (1971) [Ger. orig., *Die Cellularpathologie*, 2nd edn (1859)] · J. G. McKendrick, *The story of my life* (1919) · CCI (1876) · old parochial register, General Register Office for Scotland, Edinburgh · DNB

Archives U. Edin., department of biomedical sciences · U. Edin. L., lecture notes · U. Glas. L.

Likenesses E. Bosse, oils, 1847, U. Edin., department of physiology · W. Brodie, bust, 1875, U. Edin., Old College · P. MacGillivray, bronze relief, 1901, U. Edin., department of physiology · W. Hole, etching, NPG; repro. in W. Hole, *Quasi cursores: portraits of the high officers and professors of the University of Edinburgh at its tercentenary festival* (1884) · H. W. Kerr, oils (after photograph), Royal College of Physicians, Edinburgh, Great Hall · photograph, Wellcome L.

Wealth at death £12,169 3s. 5d.; plus property at 1 Glenfinlas Street, Edinburgh, and Edendarrock, Tarbet, Loch Lomond: confirmation, 3 Jan 1876, CCI

Bennett, John Joseph (1801–1876), botanist, was born at Tottenham, Middlesex, on 8 January 1801, the son of Edward Turner Bennett and his wife, Lucy. He was educated at Enfield grammar school, where his schoolfellows included the poet John Keats and the actor John Reeve; the latter fought for Bennett in return for help with arithmetic. Bennett then went as a student to the Middlesex Hospital and was admitted a member of the College of Surgeons in 1825. He settled in a house in Bulstrode Street, Cavendish Square, with his older brother, Edward Turner *Bennett, and for some time both brothers practised as surgeons. While so engaged, they became acquainted with John Edward Gray, who was then helping his father, Samuel Frederick Gray, prepare *Natural Arrangement of British Plants* (1821). Both brothers assisted with the work, as acknowledged by the plant genus *Bennettia* (although this later had to give way to De Candolle's *Saussurea*, 1810, in priority). Following the death of his brother in 1836, Bennett supervised the final stages of printing of, and wrote a preface for, an edition of Gilbert White's *Natural History of Selborne* on which his brother had been working.

In 1827 Bennett became associated with Robert *Brown. In September of that year the trustees of the British Museum arranged that the herbarium and library of Sir Joseph Banks, of which Brown had a life possession, should be transferred to the museum. Brown was appointed under-librarian on his own terms, with an assistant. In November 1827 Bennett was appointed Brown's assistant, and thenceforward he devoted his life to botany. The two men spent the winter of 1827–8 in moving the Banksian collection from Banks's house at Soho Square, London, to Montague House, the first home of the British Museum. For eight years Brown and Bennett did everything, even the merest drudgery, to maintain Banks's botanical collection as a scholarly resource. In 1828 Bennett was elected fellow of the Linnean Society, and of the Royal Society in December 1841. From 1840 to 1860 he served the Linnean Society as secretary efficiently but rather too much under the conservative influence of Brown. On his resignation Thomas Bell testified to his 'devotion to the society's interest' (*Proceedings of the Linnean Society*, 1888–90, 32). Bennett served as a vice-president of the society in 1860–72.

In 1843 Banks's botanical collections were removed from Montague House to Smirke's new British Museum building. Robert Brown died in 1858, and on his death a strong effort, by no means the last, was made to transfer the entire botanical collections to the Royal Botanic Gardens, Kew, where the herbarium was rapidly becoming important through the munificence of George Bentham and the enterprise and aspirations of Sir William J. Hooker and his son, Joseph D. Hooker. After a long parliamentary inquiry it was decided that the collections should not be transferred to Kew. Anxiety resulting from this inquiry told upon Bennett, who had taken Brown's place as keeper of the botanical department, and he sought relief by a two months' residence on the continent in 1859; in the next year he suffered illness for three months, but a still longer holiday in Scotland and the north of England restored him in great measure. In 1870 he retired from the British Museum, and in 1871 he moved to Sandrock, Maresfield, Sussex, where he died from heart disease on 29 February 1876. He bequeathed Robert Brown's herbarium, which had been passed to him as private property, to the museum. His widow, Anne, whom he had married on 1 April 1839, bequeathed three Linnean medals, also the property of Brown, to the Linnean Society in her husband's name.

Bennett was singularly kind, quiet, and retiring. He published only seven papers, mostly describing new west African plants sent to him by his friend W. F. Daniell (1817–1865). He was interested, however, in the pharmacological properties of plants and some of his taxonomic work included descriptions of poisons and suchlike. His most important contribution to science is his chief share in Bennett and Brown's *Plantae Javanicae rariores* (4 pts., 1838–52), based on Thomas Horsfield's collection of more than 2000 species gathered in Java between 1811 and 1819. To Horsfield's disappointment Bennett and Brown succeeded in dealing with only fifty plants, admittedly with great care and scholarship, between 1821 and 1852. In 1852 John Lindley referred to this 'Herculean labour', and stated that it was Horsfield's misfortune to have placed his collection into the hands of a gentleman whose procrastination was 'fortunately unparalleled in the annals of natural history' (*Gardeners' Chronicle*, 26 June 1852). Bennett shared Brown's high standards and reluctance to publish. As an example of Bennett's care in small matters, reference may be made to his account of the Upas tree from Java, said to kill everything within a few yards' radius, and his separation of fact and fiction concerning it. He edited for the Ray Society *The Miscellaneous Botanical Works of Robert Brown* (1866–8), making valuable scattered material conveniently available.

When S. F. Gray named a genus after the Bennett brothers, he inadvertently made it impossible to use the form *Bennettia* elsewhere. Hence *Bennettia* Miquel (1858) has been renamed Bennettiodendron Merrill (1927), and *Bennettia* R. Brown (1852) is a synonym of *Cremostachys* Tulasne (1851). The fossil genus *Bennettites* Carruthers (1870) was also named in J. J. Bennett's honour, together with the fossil group Bennettitales.

WILLIAM T. STEARN

Sources *Journal of Botany, British and Foreign*, 14 (1876), 97–105 · A. T. Gage and W. T. Stearn, *A bicentenary history of the Linnean Society of London* (1988), 43, 66, 162 · CGPLA Eng. & Wales (1876)
Archives Croydon Natural History Society · NHM · RBG Kew
Likenesses E. U. Eddis, oils, c.1862, Linn. Soc. · H. Weekes, busts, BM, Linn. Soc. · engraving (after photograph, 1859), repro. in *Journal of Botany, British and Foreign*, frontispiece · lithograph, BM · portrait, repro. in Gage and Stearn, *A bicentenary history*, 66, pl. 106
Wealth at death under £4000: probate, 22 March 1876, CGPLA Eng. & Wales

Bennett, Sir John Wheeler Wheeler- (1902–1975), historian and expert on international affairs, was born on 13 October 1902, at Keston, in Kent, the youngest in the family of three sons (the first of whom died in childhood) and one daughter of John Wheeler Wheeler-Bennett (1840–1926), a wealthy merchant in the City of London, and his wife, Christina Hill McNutt, of Truro, Nova Scotia. He went to a preparatory school in Westgate, Kent, where, in April 1916, he was shell-shocked in an air raid, an experience which left him with a severe stammer. He only overcame this handicap after fifteen years of effort, and with the aid of Lionel Logue, who also treated George VI. He completed his education at Malvern College but further ill health prevented him from going as intended to Christ Church, Oxford. Instead he became unpaid personal assistant to General Neill Malcolm, who had been head of the British military mission in Berlin immediately after the armistice and who encouraged him to deepen his knowledge of international affairs, in particular to concentrate on the situation in Germany.

Wheeler-Bennett started to work in the publicity department of the League of Nations Union, and in 1924, while still a fairly impecunious young man, he established his own information service on international affairs, with a fortnightly *Bulletin of International News*. He also inaugurated a series of authoritative studies on contemporary international problems. The first of these, *Information on the Problem of Security*, was published in 1925. He became closely involved with the Royal Institute of International Affairs (Chatham House), whose chairman was Malcolm, and in 1929 he produced on its behalf the first of a new series of annual *Documents on International Affairs*, which he continued to edit until 1936. It was a major contribution to the subject.

In 1929 Wheeler-Bennett was persuaded by Malcolm to go to Germany and make a special study of conditions there. He rented a small stud at Fallingbostel on the Lüneburg Heath, not far from the training headquarters of the German army Olympic riding team. He met conspicuous figures like Franz von Papen, who was to become German chancellor in 1932. In Berlin he established himself in the Hotel Kaiserhof, well placed for access to the foreign ministry and a social centre for many important people, including the leaders of the Nazi party. He cultivated the acquaintance of leading Germans of various shades of opinion, including the minister of defence and the president of the Reichsbank. His most valuable friendship was with Heinrich Brüning, who became chancellor at the end of March 1930. During the crisis which led to his downfall in May 1932 Wheeler-Bennett saw him every night. To the end of his life he retained loyal affection for the ex-chancellor though he may have underestimated the authoritarian, nationalist traits in Brüning's policies. Wheeler-Bennett's many contacts in Berlin gave him a first-hand experience, unrivalled by any other historian, of the collapse of the Weimar republic. He ran considerable risks in helping Brüning to flee the country. At the end of June 1934, during the so-called Röhm purge, his rooms at the Kaiserhof were ransacked. He believed that he would have been killed, had he not been called away to visit Neill Malcolm in Switzerland. He did not return to Germany until 1945.

Wheeler-Bennett saw himself as an 'unofficial channel of communication between leading German politicians (excepting Nazis) and London'. His work in Germany was approved by Sir R. G. Vansittart, the head of the British Foreign Office. Many Germans regarded him as a well-connected Englishman whose good opinion might be useful in relations with the British government. He made an open foray into diplomacy in November 1932, when he sent a letter to *The Times* suggesting a scheme for disarmament, to which he believed he had obtained the agreement of the German chancellor, von Papen. The Foreign Office was sceptical about the latter's good faith, and Wheeler-Bennett was reproved for his action.

It was after he left Germany that Wheeler-Bennett really began to write history. His first major work was a biography of Germany's ill-starred president, *Hindenburg: the Wooden Titan*, published in 1936. It combined careful scholarship with unique personal knowledge of the events which had led to the collapse of the Weimar republic. He then began what some historians regard as his finest book, *Brest-Litovsk: the Forgotten Peace*. The importance of the eastern front in the First World War had already impressed him when writing *Hindenburg*, and one of his earliest military acquaintances in Germany had been General Seeckt, the architect of the German victory at Gorlice in 1915. Wheeler-Bennett interviewed the major German participants in the peace negotiations, the former Austrian foreign minister, Count Czernin, and, most remarkable of all, some of the Bolshevik actors in the drama. He travelled to the Soviet Union in 1935 and talked to Bukharin, Kamenev, Radek, and others, most of whom were soon to perish in the purges. Two years later he visited Trotsky in Mexico. The book appeared in 1938. By then war clouds were gathering in Europe and Wheeler-Bennett was greatly exercised by the German threat to Czechoslovakia. He deplored the Munich agreement. It caused him later to write his vivid account *Munich: Prologue to Tragedy*, which appeared in 1948. Soon the German threat came nearer home, and Wheeler-Bennett, physically unfit for military service, threw himself into political warfare. As personal assistant to the British ambassador in Washington he travelled widely in the USA putting the British point of view. He helped to establish the British information services in New York, and later was posted to Washington in the political warfare mission, where he worked closely with the American office of war information. In May 1944 he was back in London in the political intelligence department, ending as assistant director-general. During these years he was often called to advise on the British attitude towards Hitler's opponents in Germany, many of whom he knew personally. He opposed any bargain, partly because he doubted their capacity to carry out effective resistance, but mainly because he feared that a new 'stab-in-the-back' legend might again give German nationalists an excuse for the failure of their disastrous policies. He attended the Nuremberg war crimes trials as an adviser to the British prosecution team, and he was also appointed British editor-in-chief of the captured archives of the German foreign office.

In 1945 Wheeler-Bennett married Ruth Harrison, daughter of Alvin Daniel Risher, inventor and scientist, of Charlottesville, Virginia, USA; they had no children. They settled down near Oxford at Garsington Manor, former abode of Lady Ottoline Morrell, which again became a notable centre of hospitality. There he forged close links with Oxford University. He taught at New College and he was elected a member of the Christ Church senior common room. In 1950 he became a founding fellow of St Antony's College, an international graduate centre for the study of recent history and politics. He returned to the writing of German history, and in 1953 published *Nemesis of Power*, a study of the German army in politics, from the collapse of the Wilhelmine Reich to Hitler's defeat in 1945. It was a literary and historical *tour de force* which aroused indignation as well as admiration. He honoured the bravery of those who resisted the Nazis, but pointed out the errors of Hitler's conservative opponents and the responsibility which the German army leaders bore for the Second World War. The main conclusions of the book have stood the test of time.

Wheeler-Bennett then turned to the task of writing the official biography of King George VI. A staunch monarchist, he enjoyed personal contacts with many royal houses and was able to put these to good use. He had a remarkable facial resemblance to the Kaiser, and would often joke about it. The book appeared in 1958 and in the following year the queen appointed him KCVO, as well as historical adviser to the Royal Archives. In 1962 he published the authorized biography of John Anderson, Viscount Waverley. At the suggestion of Harold Macmillan, his publisher as well as a close friend, he decided to write a history of the political settlement after the Second World War. Here again, he was able to draw on a wealth of personal knowledge and reminiscences. The result was *The Semblance of Peace* (1972), which he wrote in collaboration with

Anthony Nicholls. In his final years he devoted himself to writing his autobiography; the first two volumes give a vivid picture of his life in Europe and America. Lord Avon, whom he had always admired, asked him to write his biography but his health, never robust, deteriorated and he died in a London hospital on 9 December 1975.

Wheeler-Bennett was an expert on international relations, an adviser and informant to governments, and a pioneer in the art of writing contemporary history. His best works were based on rigorous historical scholarship and top-level oral evidence. Despite a certain weakness for purple prose, his books attracted the general reader as well as the specialist. He benefited much from the advice and friendship of Sir Lewis Namier, whom he had helped financially at the outset of his career.

Wheeler-Bennett possessed a great personal charm which assisted him to gain access to the mighty, but it also illuminated the lives of many others—numerous young scholars in Britain and America where he taught at the universities of Virginia, New York, and Arizona. For them he was always accessible and unstintingly generous of his time. He was a great 'club man' and universally popular wherever he dined.

He was appointed OBE in 1946, CMG in 1953, and GCVO in 1974. He was also a fellow of the Royal Society of Literature (1958), of the Zoological Society (1973), and of the British Academy (1972), and an honorary DCL of Oxford University (1960).   A. J. NICHOLLS, rev.

Sources J. Wheeler-Bennett, *Knaves, fools and heroes* (1974) • J. Wheeler-Bennett, *Special relationships* (1975) • J. Wheeler-Bennett, *Friends, enemies, and sovereigns* (1976) • A. Bullock, 'John Wheeler Wheeler-Bennett, 1902–1975', *PBA*, 65 (1979), 799–833 • personal knowledge (1986) • private information (1986)
Archives St Ant. Oxf., Middle East Centre, papers relating to German affairs | BL OIOC, corresp. relating to Lord Waverley, MS Eur. F 207 • Bodl. Oxf., corresp. with Lord Monckton
Likenesses Lord Charteris of Amisfield, bronze bust, St Ant. Oxf. • J. Pannett, portrait; known to be in family possession in 1986
Wealth at death £90,354: probate, 6 Feb 1976, *CGPLA Eng. & Wales*

Bennett, Louise [Louie] (1870–1956), suffragist, trade unionist, and pacifist, was born in Temple Road, Temple Hill, near Dublin, the eldest of five daughters and five sons of an auctioneer and antiques valuer called Bennett and his wife, Susan Boulger, daughter of an army officer. Her family were prosperous protestants who had lived in Ireland since the late eighteenth century.

Educated at an English boarding-school and at Alexandra College, Dublin, and then in Bonn where she studied music, Louie Bennett at first lived the life of a cultivated lady with literary pretensions. She wrote two novels, *The Proving of Priscilla* (1902) and *A Prisoner of his Word* (1908). She was forty years old when she started on her serious life's work of social intervention to which she then devoted herself with total commitment for the next forty years. In August 1911 she founded the Irishwomen's Suffrage Federation, becoming its first secretary. It was also at that time and in joint pursuance of that cause that she met her lifelong companion Helen Chenevix—one of the first women

graduates from Trinity College, Dublin. Together they worked to link the various Irish suffrage societies.

It was the bitter labour conflicts in Dublin in 1913 that awakened Louie Bennett to full realization of the desperate situation of Irish women workers—'the slaves of slaves'—who were very near starvation level. She founded the Irish Women's Reform League and thereafter became the leading activist and organizer in the cause of economic justice and human dignity for the sweated women workers of Ireland. Starting with the printing trade and then the laundry workers, Louie Bennett fought decade after decade not just for better wages but also for improved sanitation, ventilation, light, heat, shorter hours, and paid holidays—all to 'humanize' industrial working life. Louie Bennett was a co-operative socialist, believing in workers' control and a minimum equal living wage for both men and women. Although born a 'lady', she was a familiar sight standing on the picket line with girl strikers in the rain.

Louie Bennett's other cause was pacifism. Although converted to the cause of Irish independence by the Easter rising in 1916, she herself always insisted on non-violent struggle—in this agreeing with the murdered Francis Sheehy Skeffington and with 'A. E.' (George William Russell). Her commitment to pacifism made her unpopular both with belligerent pro-Britons and with militant Irish nationalists. Her pamphlet, *Ireland and a People's Peace* (1918), advocated both national self-determination and international co-operation, criticizing Sinn Féin both for its failure to see the importance of international interdependence and for its violence. In it she argued that 'No revolution is permanently achieved by violence: such violence, even in the name of freedom, is tyranny.' Between 1920 and 1922 Louie Bennett participated in efforts to end the Irish civil war by negotiation and in 1921 she went to Washington to give evidence before the American commission on conditions in Ireland.

In Dublin in 1926 Louie Bennett presided over the congress of the Women's International League for Peace and Freedom, of which she had been a founder member since 1915 and whose international president, Jane Addams, was the woman Louie Bennett admired most in the world. In 1928 she wrote an article in the *Irish Statesman* supporting Litvinov's call to the League of Nations for general and immediate disarmament. And when appointed the first ever woman president of the Irish Trades Union Congress in 1932, she was prescient enough to warn her hearers of the dangers of Fascism.

After the partition of Ireland, Louie Bennett continuously tried to keep every channel of friendly contact open between south and north, working to establish the basic co-operative links of transport, communications, power lines, and drainage. Her hope was to see a peacefully reunited, federal Ireland. The last cause she worked for in her old age was the outlawing of nuclear weapons.

Louie Bennett was of middle height with shrewd, twinkling dark brown eyes expressive of her humour, liveliness, and strength of feeling. She was a thoughtful, forceful speaker who exuded dignity and determination. When she died at her home in Killiney, near Dublin, on 25 November 1956 at the age of eighty-six she was called the best-loved woman in Dublin.   SYBIL OLDFIELD

Sources R. M. Fox, *Louie Bennett, her life and times* (1957) · R. C. Owens, *Smashing times: a history of the Irish women's suffrage movement, 1889–1922* (1984) · L. Bennett, *Ireland and a people's peace* (1918), 16 · *Pax et Libertas* (1926–7) [articles on and by Louie Bennett] · L. Bennett, 'Women of Europe, when will your call ring out?', *Ius Suffragii* (1 March 1915) · *The Times* (27 Nov 1956), 13
Likenesses photographs, repro. in Fox, *Louie Bennett*
Wealth at death £3570: probate, 6 Feb 1957, *CGPLA Éire*

Bennett, Mary (1813–1899). *See under* Saunders, John (1811–1895).

Bennett, Peter Frederick Blaker, Baron Bennett (1880–1957), industrialist, was born on 16 April 1880 at Dartford, Kent, the eldest son of Frederick Charles Bennett, a carpenter, and his wife, Annie Eliza Blaker. When Bennett was twelve the family moved to Birmingham, where he was educated at Five Ways grammar school of the King Edward's Foundation. A convinced Christian like his father, who had been a YMCA organizing secretary, Bennett was brought up as a Methodist and was an active worker in his younger years, a Sunday school superintendent, and a teetotaller.

On leaving school, Bennett worked for a time with an electrical company in India. The course of his business career was set in 1903, when he joined the Electrical Ignition Company of Sparkbrook, makers of sparking plugs, trembler coils, and switches. As sales manager Bennett met the motor factor Albert Thomson in 1905 and in 1907, with Thomson's backing, set up Thomson-Bennett Ltd to manufacture products similar to those of the Sparkbrook firm. The new business began on a small scale, as Bennett described it in *British Industries*, 'four white-washed walls, my signature and the little money I had scraped together' (Bennett, 143–4). Thomson-Bennett began making magnetos, but only for specialized purposes as a result of the virtual monopoly on the car magneto maintained by the German Bosch company.

The outbreak of the First World War underlined the seriousness of this dependence on German supplies and British manufacturers such as Joseph Lucas, British Thomson-Houston (BT-H), and Morris and Lister, eventually under Admiralty control, endeavoured to develop magnetos and to rationalize and expand production. (The Admiralty's concern was for aero-engine magnetos for the Royal Naval Air Service.) It was in this context that Bennett's business skills found the environment in which to expand and mature, when his company was taken over by the older and much larger Joseph Lucas Ltd in the early months of the war. The latter, founded in 1875, employed about four thousand in 1914, in comparison with the Thomson-Bennett workforce of about a hundred. Harry Lucas had seen the need for British-made magnetos, vital to the development of mechanized armed services, and for this reason he acquired Bennett's small firm with its specialist production.

Bennett's wartime role was on the home front, where he was appointed chairman of the two bodies set up to co-ordinate magneto producers, the Aero Magneto Manufacturers' Association and the British Ignition Apparatus Association. Bennett was remembered by A. P. Young of BT-H as 'a humble and kindly man with a keen business brain', with whom 'right from the start we established a friendly relationship' (Young). Within the Lucas concern Thomson-Bennett was run as a separate business under Bennett as managing director.

In the early post-war years the Lucas board suffered internal disputes, which opened the way for Bennett to join Harry Lucas in 1920 as one of two managing directors. In the following year Oliver Lucas was made a director and he and Bennett became joint managing directors in 1923. Oliver, born in 1891, had been educated at King Edward's School and had then gone into the family firm, where his skill as a motorist proved of considerable practical use. His war service resulted in the development of the 'OL' signalling lamp for the army. Despite the eleven-year difference in age, the partnership of Bennett and Oliver Lucas was crucial for the inter-war growth of Joseph Lucas and the development of Bennett as a leading entrepreneur in the motor component industry, although his qualities and capabilities would have brought him to prominence whatever the external circumstances of his career.

The Bennett–Lucas partnership from the early twenties was described by Nockolds as one of the most remarkable the motor industry has ever seen. Oliver Lucas brought to it his technical skill and good commercial judgement, while Bennett's significant contribution lay not in his early technical experience, but in the strength of his main interest, the expansion of the company. Though the two differed widely in their personal interests and beliefs, within the company the outstanding feature of their partnership was their unanimity in business decisions. As Bennett expanded his public life and Oliver Lucas immersed himself in the technical details of engineering development, their partnership was increasingly supported by Bertram Waring as company secretary.

Bennett came to play a major role in public life in Birmingham and on the national scene. He was a member of the British delegation to Ottawa in 1932, president of the Birmingham chamber of commerce, 1932–3, of the Society of Motor Manufacturers and Traders, 1935–6, and of the Federation of British Industries during the crucial period 1938–40, which included the 1939 negotiations with the German Reichsgruppe Industrie. In 1940 Bennett succeeded Neville Chamberlain as Unionist member for Edgbaston. Rearmament and war brought numerous official appointments, such as membership of the panel of industrial advisers to the Ministry of Supply, 1938–9, and the chair of the Automatic Gun Board, 1941–4. The war also proved the long-term value of the decision of Bennett and Oliver Lucas to set up CAV-Bosch in 1931, without which a deficiency in supplies of fuel-injection equipment might well have paralleled that in magnetos in the First World War.

In the house Bennett commanded respect by his moderation and modesty, speaking only on what he knew, in a

quiet and persuasive manner. This was especially important during his term of office as parliamentary secretary to
the Ministry of Labour and National Service, 1951–2. Bennett resigned on health grounds in 1952, rejoining Lucas
as joint managing director with Waring in August of that
year. His great partner in business, Oliver Lucas, had died,
from overwork, four years earlier, prompting Bennett's
comment that he had lost his lifelong friend and colleague.

Bennett was a generous public benefactor, donating
£10,000 to the Birmingham Children's Hospital in 1936
and the same amount to Lucas employees' hard luck fund
two years later. He was knighted in 1941 and raised to the
peerage in 1953. He married Agnes, daughter of Joseph
Palmer, in 1905; there were no children of the marriage.
Bennett's wife had a distinguished record of social service
and she provided guidance and encouragement throughout his career. For recreation Bennett turned to sport,
rugby giving place to golf and tennis, and he was an enthusiastic walker. He remained with Lucas until his death at
his home, Ardencote, 18 Luttrell Road, Four Oaks, Warwickshire, on 27 September 1957. Great figures of industry, especially the motor industry, attended his funeral on
2 October (the Rootes brothers, Sir Leonard Lord, and Sydney Guy) and his memorial service, at which the Federation of British Industries (Sir Norman Kipping), Jaguar
Cars (Sir William Lyons), ICI, the Dunlop Rubber Company, the Standard Motor Company, and Vauxhall Motors
were represented.   RICHARD A. STOREY

Sources H. Nockolds, *Lucas: the first hundred years*, 2 vols. (1976–8) ·
DNB · P. Bennett, 'Men in industry, I: Mr Peter Bennett', *British
Industries*, 23 (1939), 143–4, 163 · *The Times* (30 Sept 1957) · A. P.
Young, 'My struggling years', Modern Records Centre, A. P. Young
MSS, MS 242/BIo/8, chap. 6, 'An industry is born' · d. cert. · *CGPLA
Eng. & Wales* (1957)
Archives U. Birm. L., papers
Likenesses J. Gunn, drawing, *c*.1940, Confederation of British
Industry, London · W. Stoneman, photograph, 1948, NPG ·
J. Gunn, oils, Joseph Lucas Industries Ltd, Birmingham
Wealth at death £312,353 4*s*. 9*d*.: probate, 8 Nov 1957, *CGPLA Eng.
& Wales*

Bennett, Richard (1608–1675), colonial governor, was the
nephew of the early Virginia merchant Edward Bennett,
and may have been the Richard Bennett baptized in Somerset on 6 August 1609, the son of Thomas Bennett,
though this is not certain. He went to Virginia in the 1620s
to work with his uncle Edward Bennett, who was a major
planter and merchant in the colony. Because of his wealth
and connections he held office from an early age, serving
as a representative to the house of burgesses for the first
time in 1629. He sat on the governor's council regularly
from 1639. By 1638 he had married Anne Utie, who had
travelled to Virginia in 1620 with her young son, following
her husband John Utie. Bennett settled in Nansemond
county, a centre for those with puritan inclinations.
Because early Virginia included a number of settlers with
such leanings and the government tolerated some dissent, the Bennett family's position was not at first problematic. As the political and religious situation in England
polarized in the 1640s, however, the government became
less tolerant of those it came to perceive as critics of monarchy. Despite his association with these views, Bennett
continued to serve as a councillor under Governor William Berkeley. In 1642 he signed a letter to New England
seeking ministers of a more congenial religious sensibility for the pulpits in his region. Berkeley soon hounded
the men who answered this call out of the colony. In 1648
or 1649 Bennett led a migration of puritans into Maryland.
The new protestant governor of Maryland, William Stone,
invited these families to relocate there as part of his commitment to increase the population of Lord Baltimore's
sparsely settled and highly vulnerable province. Bennett
retained his extensive landholdings in Virginia, however.
He was residing in Maryland when Governor Berkeley,
upon hearing of the execution of Charles I, proclaimed
Charles II. This act put Virginia at odds with the authority
of the new Commonwealth of England. As a result, in
early 1652 a fleet arrived carrying a commission naming
Bennett one of five men to oversee the 'reduction' of Virginia. Because two of the commissioners had been lost at
sea, Bennett, another long-time Chesapeake resident William Claiborne, and ship's captain Edward Curtis took
charge. The surrender of Virginia was easily negotiated,
the colonists having learned of Charles's defeat at Worcester and of the successful reduction of Barbados by a
second fleet in the interim. The commissioners and the
house of burgesses then selected Bennett governor. He
and Claiborne, interpreting their commission very
broadly, travelled to Maryland to 'reduce' that province as
well. Although they soon reinstalled Stone as governor,
they would later intervene again on behalf of the lord protector, though without a new commission from Cromwell. In 1655 he left the office of governor in order to travel
to England to battle Baltimore's claim to Maryland. In
November 1657 he and Samuel Matthews came to terms
with Baltimore, signing an agreement that effectively permitted Baltimore to keep his colony. Bennett returned to
Virginia in 1658, resuming his seat on the council. At the
Restoration he was able to maintain his position of prominence in the colony, sitting on the council and serving as
a major-general of the militia. The travelling evangelist
William Edmundson converted him to Quakerism in
1672. He made his will in March 1675 and it was proved in
April that year. In it he left his sizeable estate to various
relatives, to a number of Quakers, and to the poor of his
parish.   CARLA GARDINA PESTANA

Sources J. B. Boddie, *Seventeenth century Isle of Wight County, Virginia*
(1938); repr. (1959) · B. C. Steiner, *Maryland under the Commonwealth:
a chronicle of the years 1649–1658* (1911) · B. M. Levy, 'Early puritanism
in the southern and island colonies', *Proceedings of the American
Antiquarian Society*, new ser., 80 (1961), 69–163 · M. N. Browne, 'Governor Richard Bennett', *Maryland Historical Magazine*, 9 (Dec 1914),
307–15 · E. C. Papenfuse and others, eds., *A biographical dictionary of
the Maryland legislature, 1635–1789*, 2 vols. (1979–85) · J. W. Raimo,
*Biographical directory of American colonial and revolutionary governors,
1607–1789* (1980) · J. Butler, 'Two 1642 letters from Virginia puritans', *Proceedings of the Massachusetts Historical Society*, 84 (1972), 99–
109 · R. M. Jones, *The Quakers in the American colonies*, new edn
(1966) · J. Horn, *Adapting to a new world: English society in the
seventeenth-century Chesapeake* (1994)

Wealth at death prominent major landowner with sizeable estate; bequeathed 5600 acres; also parcels of unstated size; main estate went to nephew and namesake; also gave away £70 sterling, and many thousand pounds of tobacco: *New England Historical and Genealogical Register*, 48 (1894), 114–15

Bennett, Richard Bedford, Viscount Bennett (1870–1947), prime minister of Canada, was born at Hopewell Hill, Albert county, New Brunswick, on 3 July 1870, the eldest of the three sons and two daughters of Henry John Bennett (1842–1905), shipbuilder and later general merchant at Hopewell Cape and his wife, Henrietta Stiles (1844–1914), a schoolteacher, daughter of Captain Daniel Stiles of Hopewell Hill, 8 miles to the west of the cape. His mother was a staunch Wesleyan Methodist, her husband an easy-going, occasionally bibulous, Baptist.

Family and early life Henrietta Stiles's Methodism became the supreme law in the Bennett family, with its strong emphasis on work, diligence, and self-denial. Make sure, John Wesley had said, that you don't waste time with

> silly unprofitable diversions. You have always something better to do … Do it as soon as possible. No delay! … And do it as well as possible. Do not sleep or yawn over it. Put your whole strength to the work.   (J. Wesley, 'The use of money', *The Works of John Wesley*, ed. A. C. Outler, 1985, 273–9)

Then followed Wesley's further rule, 'Save all you can' (ibid.). And curb wilfulness, which is the main source of sin, including smoking, drinking, and dancing. By this abstemious life, having earned and saved all you could, you then gave away as much as you could to society, to the needy, to good causes. These were the lessons that Henrietta taught Richard, her eldest son. Bourgeois to the core, they inculcated a way of life that was austere, sober, hardworking, and socially conservative. If charitable to the outer world, Henrietta's Methodism was exacting to the inner self. Those moral principles would guide R. B. Bennett all his life.

Something else came from Bennett's mother: ambition. Aim high, she said. Young Bennett had to memorize Longfellow's 'Ladder of St Augustine':

> The heights by great men reached and kept
> Were not attained by sudden flight,
> But they, while their companions slept,
> Were toiling upward in the night.

Henrietta Bennett's ambition for her eldest son came probably from frustrated hopes for her husband. Henry Bennett's training was in shipbuilding in his father's yard at the cape; by the mid-1870s the shipyards there, and in the maritime provinces of Canada generally, were having a difficult time and Henry Bennett had to turn himself into a general merchant and farmer. He was not very successful at either. R. B. Bennett's penury started early in life and he never forgot it. 'I'll always remember', said he in 1934, 'the pit from which I was digged and the long uphill road I had to travel. I'll never forget one step' (J. S. Stewart to Alice Millar, Bennett's private secretary, 27 Sept 1947, Bennett MSS).

After attending Fredericton Normal School in New Brunswick, Bennett started work as a schoolteacher when

Richard Bedford Bennett, Viscount Bennett (1870–1947), by Walter Stoneman, 1930

he was sixteen years old, and for the next four years, from 1886 to 1890, he eked out a living teaching at Douglastown, a lumber village on the Miramichi River in northeastern New Brunswick. But he saved enough to put himself through law school at Dalhousie University, Halifax, in 1890–93. He did remarkably well, eschewing all but work, study, and debating. His record was sufficiently remarkable that Dalhousie's dean of law, R. C. Weldon, also MP for Albert county, 1887–96, in the Canadian House of Commons, recommended Bennett to a fellow Conservative, Senator James Lougheed of Calgary. Lougheed was looking for an able young lawyer and possible junior partner. At this point, 1896, Bennett had taken up a law practice in Chatham, New Brunswick, on the Miramichi, his familiar territory. But the call of western opportunity was strong and in January 1897, his law books preceding him, young Bennett, tall, lean, and twenty-six years old, got off the Canadian Pacific Railway train in Calgary, Alberta. It was bitterly cold, with a thin skiff of snow holding down the dirt and dust of the streets; Calgary was a cow town of some 4000 people, new, raw, and as Bennett added in letters back to New Brunswick, with not all that much business.

Bennett was a very eastern looking denizen of Calgary. He dressed meticulously. He was not like the local Calgary lawyers, but then he never was one to emulate the crowd. He took the world on his own terms, with his own standards of what an able, upright, advocate should, or should not, do. He neither drank nor smoked. He did not swear;

his expletive nearest to swearing was 'Blast!' He had a vigorous and retentive mind; he worked like a horse, long hours with little or no play; there was in fact only a little play in him.

The Loughheed–Bennett practice went slowly at first; but by 1900 Calgary was expanding, with land, farming, ranching (and by the 1920s oil). Bennett's reputation grew with it as an honest, versatile, clever, and persistent lawyer; he took silk in 1905 and by 1914 had an extremely busy and profitable practice, and with a substantial clutch of business ventures and investments as well.

Conservative politician Bennett was by this time well into Conservative politics. A vigorous, not to say voluble, debater, not afraid of challenges, confident, perhaps too confident, of his own mind and opinions, he took on the Alberta Liberal establishment. He was elected first in 1898 for Calgary West to the territorial legislature at Regina. After Alberta's creation as a province in 1905, with its new capital in Edmonton, he was put forward by friends in 1909 for the new 41-seat Alberta legislature. In that election the Liberals took thirty-seven seats; there was one socialist and three Conservatives. Of this narrow and unpromising opposition he was soon the spokesman, giving the Liberal government no quarter. In 1911 he ran in the Canadian general election for Calgary West and won. That rare being, a successful western Conservative, he was now a formidable voice, though not one brought easily under party discipline.

Bennett's views on Canadian railways, tariffs, on Canada's proper position within the British empire, were in advance of those of the Conservative Party leader, Robert Borden. To his old friend Max Aitken, now in London contemplating entry into British politics, Bennett wrote on 13 November 1910:

> Your problem is how best to serve the Empire. It is too bad that such erroneous ideas should prevail in England about Canada and the Empire. I am convinced that the real crisis in the life of our Empire is now upon us. If the Empire is to endure the self-governing nations which compose it must in some way be federated. Unless there is a recognition of common interests, common traditions, & above all common responsibilities and obligations, and that too within the lifetime of this generation, independence is inevitable not of Canada alone but of all the nations that now make up the Empire. In Canada the situation is really acute.
> (Beaverbrook MSS, vol. 66)

That prescient letter sums up much of Bennett's imperial ideas then and later.

Bennett was a restive back-bencher in the Canadian House of Commons. He was never much of a follower, ready to quarrel with party leaders on what he felt were important issues of principle. But he was so able a parliamentarian, so valuable an assistant, that Borden took him to England in 1915 as adviser, and on a tour of the battlefields of France. Both men came home dissatisfied with British conduct of the war. In October 1916 Bennett was appointed director of the Canadian National Service, an inventory of Canada's male population. In his view this was not a prelude to conscription but an effective substitute for it, rationalizing manpower in all aspects of war,

army, industrial production, and farming. He wanted to make sure that useful farmers and workers were not sent needlessly off to the western front. Like Borden, he was still confident that Canada's war effort could go forward without conscription. But the battle of Vimy Ridge in April 1917 changed that. The Canadian army lost 10,000 men in that battle and that April produced only 4000 recruits. Bennett believed that the war now required conscription though still not at the expense of sacrificing Canada's farm labour.

Bennett was chagrined that the prime minister, Robert Borden, did not appoint him to the senate in February 1918, something that Bennett believed he had been promised. That humiliation—for so he regarded it—was partly assuaged by his being appointed minister of justice in 1920 under a new Conservative prime minister, Arthur Meighen, Borden having retired from politics owing to ill health. But in the general election of December 1921 the Meighen government was defeated and Bennett with it. Just then he was called to England on an appeal in one of his cases at the judicial committee of the privy council.

Return to law practice Bennett was already thinking of moving to England, losing interest in his Calgary law practice. But when his partner, Sir James Loughheed, with a minimum of consultation and arrangement, arbitrarily chose to use Bennett's absence in England to dissolve the old partnership, Bennett, after an acrimonious exchange of cables, returned from England in high dudgeon. He went straight to Calgary and established his own law firm. It would fare much better than his old partnership with Loughheed. That accident of circumstance would keep him in Canada for the eventful next seventeen years.

Bennett was by this time a millionaire. In 1925 he had an annual income from professional fees and business of some $90,000. He was elected to the House of Commons in the general elections in 1925 and in 1926, and Meighen appointed him minister of finance in 1926 during Meighen's brief three-month tenure as prime minister. Meighen then resigned the leadership of the Conservative Party, and the party for the first time called a national convention, set for Winnipeg in October 1927, to select a new leader.

In the meantime Bennett had to deal with his serious responsibilities for the E. B. Eddy Company, a huge match and pulp and paper conglomerate that stretched along the Quebec shore of the Ottawa River for 2 miles. Bennett owned just over half of Eddy's 3000 shares. How that came to be went back to Bennett's days on the Miramichi in the 1890s. One of his acquaintances was Jennie Shirreff, some nine years older than Bennett. She had trained as a nurse in Boston, and in 1894 in Halifax married E. B. Eddy, a 67-year-old widower who had created the Eddy Company. Eddy died in 1906 and his widow inherited his control of the company. The Quebec government demanded succession duties on such a scale that Jennie Shirreff Eddy needed expert legal advice and at once. She called on Bennett, whom she knew had the tough legal skills she needed. Eddys was also profitable: dividends in 1907 were 14 per cent and in 1910 reached 50 per cent. Bennett was drawn into the company more and more, becoming the senior legal adviser, and was so influential that when Mrs Eddy died in 1921 she left 500 shares to him and 1007 shares to her brother. The latter died in 1926 and left his shares to Bennett who now held 1508 shares, at that time worth about $1.5 million.

The Winnipeg convention of October 1927 elected R. B. Bennett leader of the Conservative Party. He was now leader of the opposition. He set about getting rid of some of the more important corporate commitments, directorships especially, that would get in the way of political responsibilities. Eddys was sold to Bryant and May, the English company, late in 1927; many of Bennett's other directorships, and some substantial blocks of stock, were given up in 1928. It was a good time to be unloading stock!

Prime minister of Canada, 1930–1935 The depression that followed the 1929 crash made it easier for the Bennett Conservatives to win the general election of July 1930. The Liberal regime of Mackenzie King was defeated partly by issues arising from the gathering force of the worldwide economic dislocations. Bennett promised measures that would cure those effects on the Canadian economy and would push Canadian exports into the markets of the world. A strikingly successful businessman and politician, he was listened to and believed. He and his party won the election of July 1930 with 137 seats in the 245-seat House of Commons. He was sworn in as prime minister, minister of external affairs, and minister of finance on 7 August 1930. He had now to deliver on his promises to the Canadian electorate. It was not going to be easy.

There was an early session of parliament in September 1930 to provide emergency funds for the unemployed. Bennett, his party, and the public expected orthodox solutions to Canada's problems in the world economic crisis. He went to the Imperial Conference in London later that autumn, where he urged an economic union of the British empire, with free admission of empire natural products into the British market, in return for what would be, presumably under certain conditions, free entry of British goods into the Canadian market. The Ottawa economic conference of 1932, called and presided over by Bennett, was to be the capping stone of this policy. It did not work all that well. Britain was not ready to exclude foreign wheat and lumber, and Canadian manufacturers were unwilling to allow free admission of British goods. What emerged were complex bilateral treaties between different segments of the empire. Nevertheless, trade between Canada and the rest of the empire rose considerably; Canadian exports rose by 51 per cent over the next two years, most of the increase being between Canada and Great Britain.

In 1931 and 1932 the judicial committee of the privy council reversed policies of many years' standing. The privy council's rulings in Canadian constitutional cases for half a century had favoured the provinces in legal battles with the central government. Now with new questions of jurisdiction, aviation, and radio broadcasting, the privy council gave the federal government control over

them. Bennett acted. The Canadian Radio Broadcasting Commission was established in 1932, the immediate predecessor of the Canadian Broadcasting Corporation. The following year he appointed Lord Macmillan as royal commissioner to examine the possibility of establishing a central bank, the Bank of Canada. This was done in 1934 in the teeth of the resistance of the Canadian private chartered banks.

In 1935, with the depression still grinding down the country, exports still languishing, and conditions in the prairies truly desperate, Bennett went much further. Overcoming resistance within his own cabinet and his party, he established the Prairie Farm Rehabilitation Act, and, more dramatically, the Employment and Social Insurance Act, the latter the centrepiece of what came to be called the Bennett New Deal. This social legislation, as the name suggests, was inspired superficially by the Roosevelt New Deal in the United States, but its social core was the Methodist Bennett of old. When asked about it, he would pull out his speeches in his first days as an MP in 1911, or his address on becoming party leader in 1927. This leftish social legislation did not sit well with older members of the party, particularly the business elements from Montreal and Toronto. Moreover, to the electorate as a whole it seemed like a last-minute conversion, for Bennett had to have an election in 1935. On top of those questions, the Conservative Party was weakened by the defection of H. H. Stevens, one of Bennett's ablest and most popular ministers, whose royal commission on price spreads was revealing how big business was systematically undercutting the small businessman.

Thus came the election of 14 October 1935, which Bennett fought boldly and lost. Probably no government would have survived five years of the depression of the 1930s. But he took the defeat much to heart, especially its devastation of the Conservative Party in the House of Commons. With 30 per cent of the popular vote, the Conservatives took only 16 per cent of the seats; the Liberals, with 45 per cent of the popular vote, took 71 per cent of the seats. So the Conservatives in 1935 elected only 40 members, the Liberals 173, others 32.

Bennett was not well. In March 1935 he had been diagnosed with atrial fibrillation of the heart. He might then have resigned, but the forthcoming election and the defection of Stevens put him squarely on his mettle, and he carried on despite the heavy drain on his hitherto superabundant energy. Indeed as leader of the opposition from 1935 to 1938, he was still one of the most vital and vigorous members of the House of Commons. Finally, however, in March 1938 he resigned the leadership of the Conservative Party.

Retirement, peerage, and death A private tragedy now was upon him. In May 1938 Bennett's sister Mildred died of breast cancer in a New York hospital. She was only forty-nine years old. Mildred had been the light of his life. Born in 1889, three years after Bennett had left home, a surprise baby to her mother, Mildred was always something more than a sister to him. He had looked after her education and as she grew into an attractive young woman, she became his hostess and companion. She had qualities that Bennett lacked. She loved a party, she could dance, she liked champagne; she had what men called charm, that is, vivacity, a sense of humour, tact, and a willingness to listen. She had also great political sagacity, and she had much to do with Bennett's victory in the 1930 election. Mildred had the moral sweep of Shaw's Candida and her death stunned her brother. Bennett shut himself up in his suite in the Château Laurier, reading aloud the book of Ruth, 'And Ruth said, Intreat me not to leave thee, or to return from following after thee, for whither thou goest, I will go … ought but death part thee and me.'

Bennett had been a bachelor all his life, but certainly not a misogynistic one. There had been ladies who wanted him, and after Mildred's marriage in 1931 to W. D. Herridge, Canadian minister to the United States, he had certainly wanted at least one lady, a rich and handsome Montreal widow, Hazel Kemp Colville. After two years she broke off relations. Bennett would not have been the most tractable of husbands: gifted, energetic, honest, generous, with integrity beyond the reach of most businessmen of his time, he could also be temperamental, autocratic, and impatient. Mildred knew how to handle him, and also his long-serving secretary, Alice Millar; few others did.

In the autumn of 1938 Bennett decided he would live in England. His ample means allowed him to buy a substantial 60 acre property at Juniper Hill, Mickleham, Surrey, next to that of Max Aitken, now Beaverbrook. He moved his books and effects from Ottawa and Calgary to England, and after effecting at some expense those very necessary Canadian improvements, central heating and substantial new plumbing, he came to settle in at Juniper Hill, not unhappily. He had things to do; there was his house, garden, and grounds; after the war started he was recruited by Beaverbrook to help at the Ministry of Aircraft Production, and there was an abundance of charities. He was also a justice of the peace, and occasionally sat on the local bench at Dorking. His social life was considerable and he commuted back and forth from Mickleham to London by chauffeur-driven car. In June 1941 he was made Viscount Bennett of Mickleham, Calgary, and Hopewell, the result of Beaverbrook's lobbying with Churchill. In the House of Lords he was not a viscount *fainéant*; his not infrequent interventions were usually pertinent and informed.

In 1944 Bennett was diagnosed with diabetes and from then on had to take insulin every day. He loved chocolates and never stinted his food. He always claimed sugar did not ruin families: alcohol did. He also liked his hot baths and had his butler to help. On 26 June 1947 he had been in London all day; it was warm. Epps, his butler, was sent off for the evening; Bennett would not bathe that night. But he changed his mind, and died in his bath of a heart attack. He was buried on 30 June at St Michael's, Mickleham.

Bennett had considerable gifts: a quick intelligence, a tenacious memory, enormous energy, and a huge appetite for work. As prime minister he took on too much; he was rarely satisfied with the work and functioning of his colleagues, and would often say so with his mordant wit and sarcastic style. That did not always endear him to his associates. His style of dress, formal and stiff whether in Calgary or Ottawa, suggested he was rich even before he became so. In the depression years in Canada it was easy to cartoon him as crass, wealthy, overbearing, and unfeeling. While that had some truth in it some of the time, it was a gross distortion of his real character. His reputation has suffered ever since, in many respects unjustly. He gave his best to Canada at a very difficult time and was ill rewarded for it. P. B. WAITE

Sources University of New Brunswick, Fredericton, R. B. Bennett MSS · HLRO, Beaverbrook papers · NA Canada, Sir Robert Borden collection · Public Archives of Nova Scotia, Edgar Rhodes MSS · president's office correspondence, Dalhousie University Archives, Halifax, Nova Scotia, Canada, A148–151 · NA Canada, Arthur Meighen collection · Lord Beaverbrook [M. Aitken], *Friends* (1959) · J. Gray, *R. B. Bennett: the Calgary years* (1991) · P. B. Waite, *The loner: three sketches of the personal life and ideas of R. B. Bennett, 1870–1947* (1992) · E. Watkin, *R. B. Bennett* (1963) · L. A. Glassford, *Reaction and reform: the politics of the conservative party under R. B. Bennett, 1927–1938* (1992) · *CGPLA Eng. & Wales* (1947)

Archives University of New Brunswick, Fredericton | HLRO, corresp. with Lord Beaverbrook · NA Canada, Sir Robert Borden MSS · NA Canada, J. W. Dafoe MSS · NA Scot., corresp. with Lord Elibank · Queen's University, Kingston, Ontario, Grant Dexter MSS · U. Birm. L., Neville Chamberlain MSS | SOUND BL NSA, current affairs recording

Likenesses W. Stoneman, photograph, 1930, NPG [*see illus.*] · K. Forbes, oils (in privy council uniform), New Brunswick Museum, Saint John, New Brunswick, Canada · photographs, National Archives, PA117652, PA117659, PA117666 · photographs, Glenbow Archives, Calgary, Canada

Wealth at death £878,795 13s. 2d.: probate, 15 Aug 1947, *CGPLA Eng. & Wales*

Bennett, Robert (1605–1683), parliamentarian army officer and religious radical, was born in Hexworthy, Lawhitton, Cornwall, the eldest son of Richard Bennett esquire and his wife, Mary, daughter of Oliver Clobery of Bradstone, Devon. He matriculated from Exeter College, Oxford, on 13 December 1622 and left after taking his BA in 1624; during 1622 he was also enrolled at the Middle Temple. He seems to have played no active part in public affairs until 1642, when he responded to a request from the parliamentarian deputy lieutenants to recruit a company of foot soldiers and to muster them at Torrington on 22 August. He was commissioned a captain and served with the earl of Stamford until after his defeat at the battle of Stratton on 16 May 1643, after which, he recorded in his diary, 'I lost my trunk with all my musters and accounts and all my former orders, all my apparel, and 15lbs in money' (Coate, *Cornwall*, 71). Bennett was sent with what was left of his company to strengthen the garrison at Barnstaple and was present at its surrender to Prince Maurice on 2 September 1643. He then moved to Plymouth and during the winter lull to his home. There he was surprised by a group of royalist marauders who so frightened his wife that she miscarried and subsequently died. He fled to the Bristol Channel and thence to south Wales, where he served with colonels John Poyer and Rowland Laugharne at the siege of Tenby. In July 1644 he answered a call to return to Devon, where he was promoted colonel of a foot regiment, and he served out the remainder of the war in the south-west, having the satisfaction of taking the surrender of Pendennis Castle, the last royalist stronghold in the west, on 15 August 1646.

By then Bennett was one of the most energetic members of the county committee and in the later 1640s he was both a garrison commander (at St Michael's Mount) and a 'local boss' (Woolrych, 174). In 1648 he was instrumental in breaking up a royalist uprising in Cornwall, first by negotiating (where officers of the New Model Army had failed) the surrender of Pendennis, whose garrison had gone over to the king (though he ended their mutiny only by 'frantic borrowing' to pay off their arrears; Stoyle, 116) and then by a ruthless operation at Penzance in which many insurgents were killed and many more arrested. His interrogations of fifty-eight of the prisoners are still to be found in the papers he was later to brick up in a chimney, where they remained hidden for 200 years.

At some point in the 1640s Bennett became a committed Baptist with strong millenarian leanings and during 1648 he became firm friends both with Colonel Hardress Waller, with whom he corresponded throughout the latter's long tour in Ireland in the 1650s, and with Major-General Thomas Harrison, the future fifth monarchist. John Moyle, a former close ally on the Cornish county committee, complained about Bennett's refusal to attend a fast day in June 1648 because of his strict separatist leanings.

On 3 April 1649 Bennett acted as *custos* at the quarter sessions at Truro and made a passionate justification of the regicide (subsequently published as *King Charles's Trial Justified by Colonel Robert Bennett*, 1649). This was a defence both of popular sovereignty and of a radical providentialism, and he called for 'a public peace upon a foundation of equal justice' and for a peace built upon 'this sure cornerstone under God' (Bennett, 4, 6). His garrison duties were extended to include St Mawes as well as St Michael's Mount, and his role in civil administration reinforced. When the crown lands were sold off in 1650 he used his debentures to acquire both the manor of Tintagel and the honour of Launceston, including the ancient castle and the town gaol. In October 1651 Bennett was returned at one of the Rump Parliament's rare by-elections as MP for West Looe. In the last eighteen months of the Rump he divided his time between Westminster and west Cornwall. He made some notable speeches, denouncing his fellow MPs for their failure to address the needs of the poor, served on the important committee to consider (sympathetically) the army petition of 13 August 1652, and chaired the committee that investigated presbyterian complaints against the propagators of the gospel in Wales, bringing in a report in the final days of the parliament exonerating the propagators.

After Cromwell violently ended the life of the Rump on 20 April 1653 Bennett was one of its few members to give him unstinted support, and he was one of the thirteen men chosen to serve on the interim council of state that debated what to do next. He thus played an active part in the selection of the nominated assembly which first met on 4 July, being one of its members. Bennett was elected to serve on its first council of state. His behaviour thereafter was a little erratic. He sought leave to return to Cornwall to attend to his own affairs, but was only away briefly. Bennett was one of the most active of all members of the assembly in terms of appointment to committees, but he was also one of the most lax attenders at the council of state, and he was dropped when it was re-elected on 1 November. Within parliament, Bennett was always to be found on the radical wing, being added to the committee that was to recommend the abolition of chancery on a day when the radicals were in control, and being a teller on the motion for the outright abolition of the rights of private (gentry) patronage over livings in the state church.

Bennett was bitterly disappointed at the precipitous end to the nominated assembly, and he was at best a hesitant supporter of Cromwell as lord protector. He wrote Cromwell a strikingly forthright admonitory letter in June 1654, warning him of the 'laxness of some in authority' and the 'iron rigour' of others (Folger Shakespeare Library, Add. MS 483, fol. 114). His support was dependent on the maintenance of religious liberty. Thus he was willing to serve under him as a JP in Devon and Cornwall, as a member of the commission for ejecting scandalous ministers, and as a member of parliament. He was returned for Launceston and for Looe in 1654, but defeated (probably at the instigation of Major-General Disbrowe) in 1656. His papers show him as very active in protecting radical evangelists. Bennett was himself a lay preacher, and he was suspicious of all who claimed any special authority by virtue of ordination. He entertained the visionary Anna Trapnel at Lawhitton during a tour she made of the west in 1656. He had a complex relationship with the Quakers, securing George Fox's release without penalty from Launceston gaol, and being praised by Fox, but being deeply troubled by some of their teachings—especially that 'the Second Coming of Christ and day of Judgement … is already past' (ibid., fol. 177). Bennett's papers contain an anguished debate with a friend about the defection of 'sister Cornish' from the Baptists to the Quakers.

In 1659 Bennett was once more returned to parliament, where he gave grudging support to Richard Cromwell, but when the protectorate fell he took his seat in the restored Rump, but refused to take part in the remaining bodies set up by the army as it desperately sought to stave off the Restoration. In 1660 he retired to Cornwall and kept himself to himself. Occasionally, because he was a prominent dissenter, his house was searched but nothing was ever found. Bennett died at home and was buried in Lawhitton on 7 July 1683. He was a man who was pragmatic in his politics but utterly convinced in his separatist and chiliastic religious faith: efficient, pragmatic, determined, honest, egalitarian, godly, visionary—he epitomizes the puritan dimension of the English revolution.   JOHN MORRILL

Sources M. Coate, *Cornwall in the great civil war and interregnum, 1642–1660* (1933) · A. Woolrych, *Commonwealth to protectorate* (1982) · M. Stoyle, *West Britons* (2002) · I. Gentles, *The New Model Army in England, Ireland, and Scotland, 1645–1653* (1992) · D. Underdown, *Pride's Purge: politics in the puritan revolution* (1971) · B. Worden, *The Rump Parliament* (1976) · S. Roberts, *Recovery and Restoration in an English county: Devon, 1646–1670* (1985) · *Diary of Thomas Burton*, ed.

J. T. Rutt, 4 vols. (1828), vols. 3–4 • T. Masson, *The life of John Milton* (1877), vol. 4 • M. Coate, 'The diary of Colonel Thomas Bennett', *Devon and Cornwall Notes and Queries*, 18 (1934–5), 251–9 • R. Bennett, *King Charles's trial justified by Col. Robert Bennett* (1649) • G. Fox, *The west answering the north* (1657) • A. Trapnel, *The cry of a stone* (1656) • Foster, *Alum. Oxon.*

Archives BL, Add. MS 12098 • Folger, family, military, and business corresp. and papers | Bodl. Oxf., Tanner MSS

Bennett, Sarah (1797–1861), governess, was born at Spalding, Lincolnshire, on 4 March 1797; her mother was the daughter of a tradesman, her father an architect and builder. Her father died aged thirty-eight, leaving a family of eight children and a ruined business. Sarah, the eldest daughter, was seven at the time of her father's death, and was sent by her godfather, a solicitor at Spalding, to his sister's school at Camden House, Kensington, London, to be educated as a governess, then the main respectable occupation for impoverished ladies. She worked for a number of wealthy families, and seemed to be establishing a stable career. In 1817, however, her former Camden House teachers moved to Spalding and invited Sarah to assist them in running their new school, which she dutifully did for eight years, until the school closed. She then returned to work in private families, entering on her last and longest engagement in 1827 with the daughters of a general. When her situation concluded in 1837, she moved to Melton Mowbray, where much of her family lived, to open a private school, for day and boarding scholars, with a friend, Miss Baldwin.

Sarah Bennett's stress in education was on religious instruction—hence the title of the memoir published in 1862 after her death, *The Christian Governess*. While not against an education in the social graces, she refused to include dancing, which she dismissed as 'ungodly', in her curriculum, publishing a short pamphlet, *Worldly Amusements* (which can be found in the appendix of the 1862 memoir), explaining her objections. She believed that dancing encouraged vanity and frivolity and discouraged domesticity among young girls, and that it was particularly injurious for the lower orders. Her educational methods, however, were not severe: instead she stressed love, example, firmness, careful attention to religious duties, and punctuality. She tried to enliven lessons by means of anecdote, and to cater for different levels of ability. She also encouraged her elder pupils to engage in charitable work, as she did, in visiting the poor. An Anglican with strong evangelical convictions, she raised funds for a school in Larne, co. Antrim, where protestants and Catholics were educated together, in the hope of ridding Ireland of 'Popery' (Bennett, 94), and she sought to convert Jews (through the Society for Promoting Christianity amongst the Jews and the London Philojudaean Society). She was also a supporter of the temperance movement, publishing a pamphlet, *The Snare: its Danger* (apparently in the late 1830s, and included as an appendix to the 1862 memoir). When she retired in 1852, with hearing and sight impaired, the school closed. She spent much time visiting former pupils as well as family, and continued her charitable activities, including work with blind people for which she learned to read with Moon's embossed characters. Moon type (based on the Latin alphabet, invented in 1845 by William Moon of Brighton) was especially useful for older, newly blind people for whom Braille was too difficult to feel, and proved beneficial as her own sight deteriorated.

Sarah Bennett exemplified Hannah More's (1745–1833) ideal of the dutiful and virtuous middle-class single woman, timid and yet resolute in her faith, always busy, a dedicated philanthropist of the poor and teacher of young ladies, for whom the appearance of being learned was anathema. Her letters (a selection of which are included in the 1862 memoir) give only vague hints of the difficulties encountered by governesses in fitting into a new family. The extent of her correspondence to former pupils, family, and missionaries (profits from the memoir were dedicated to the Church Missionary Society) gives an indication of the esteem in which she was held, especially as a role model for young ladies in similar straitened circumstances. Her memoirist, her nephew the Revd George Bright Bennett (1830–1890), records that after a full working life dedicated to serving others, Sarah Bennett had accumulated only enough to ensure a small annual income, which may explain her itinerant life, staying with friends and family, once the school closed. She died at Nuneaton on 12 March 1861 in the home of a former pupil, and was buried in Birmingham's Anglican cemetery, in her brother's family vault. JANE MCDERMID

Sources G. B. Bennett, *The Christian governess: a memoir and a selection of the correspondence of Miss Sarah Bennett, late of Melton Mowbray* (1862) • *CGPLA Eng. & Wales* (1861)

Likenesses engraving, repro. in Bennett, *The Christian governess*, frontispiece

Wealth at death under £800: probate, 18 April 1861, *CGPLA Eng. & Wales*

Bennett, Sir Thomas Jewell (1852–1925), journalist and newspaper proprietor, was born on 16 May 1852, at Elm Road, Wisbech, Cambridgeshire, the son of John Thomas Bennett, solicitor's clerk, and his wife, Charlotte Mary Galopin Chabert. He entered journalism early in life, beginning his apprenticeship on the paper of the Cambridgeshire fenland, the *Isle of Ely and Wisbech Advertiser*. After a move to Carlisle his career in provincial journalism peaked when he became assistant editor of the *Western Daily Press* in Bristol. This was followed by a stint in Fleet Street working on *The Standard* as a leader writer.

As was becoming increasingly common, Bennett journeyed overseas in 1884 to work in the English newspaper press of the empire, proceeding to Bombay, the principal city in western India, where he was to remain for seventeen years. He worked initially for the *Bombay Gazette* as associate editor and leader writer for eight years. Henry Curwen, a close personal friend, was the editor of the influential English newspaper the *Times of India*, and upon Curwen's death in 1892 Bennett succeeded to the editorship and to Curwen's principal proprietary interest in the paper. At first he ran the paper in partnership with Curwen's business manager, Charles Kane, and after the latter's death in 1894 became its sole proprietor. Bennett was responsible for the consolidation, modernization, and expansion of the paper, making it the premier newspaper publishing house in India. He set up new machinery at the offices, acquired land from the Bombay Improvement Trust, and erected new buildings. More significantly, using his professional connections in England, Bennett strengthened the paper's staff. He brought from London a master printer, F. M. Coleman, and his brother; and the publishing company that they formed, Bennett, Coleman & Co., still operated a century later. He also utilized his Bristol press connections to bring over British writing staff, including Lovat Fraser and Stanley Reed, both of whom subsequently became editors of the paper. His decision to bring across such aggressive, imaginative, and professional journalists was a boon for the development of the newspaper press in India. Fraser (editor, 1901–7) was the leading journalist of his time, winning from the viceroy, Lord Curzon, the assurance that the *Times of India* was the first newspaper in Asia. Though Bennett left India in 1901, he continued to guide the fortunes of his company from England. (The company passed into Indian ownership in 1946.)

In directing the policy of his paper, Bennett demonstrated sound and cautious judgement, and his support for the raj was discriminating. While recognizing the gravity of the increasing political unrest in western India which was encouraged by B. G. Tilak, for instance, he was nevertheless alive to the political and economic problems of the Indian community and worked steadfastly for Indian political advancement and to enhance amity between the races. He wrote largely on Indian topics, and championed Indian grievances with regularity and compassion. On leaving India he was presented with an address of thanks by 3000 agricultural workers from Gujarat for the persistence with which he had brought their grievances before the government. He was nominated by the Bombay government as a fellow of Bombay University, but for the most part declined direct participation in the university's affairs in order that he might retain his journalistic independence. Similarly, he only accepted company directorships, for example, of the Bombay, Baroda and Central India Railway, after his retirement.

Back in Britain, Bennett was a JP for Kent, and in December 1910 unsuccessfully contested the Brigg division of Lincolnshire as a Unionist. He was returned for the Sevenoaks division of Kent in December 1918, and held the seat until December 1923. In parliament he spoke chiefly on Indian issues, and occasionally on domestic, Irish, and African empire affairs. He was a vehement critic of racism in the empire, as was demonstrated by his spirited speech against the racist tenor of the Commons debates in July 1920 on the Hunter committee report into the unrest in India in 1919 and in particular into the massacre of unarmed civilians at Amritsar. Bennett stressed the importance of taking account of the broad interests of India and the feelings and expectations of her people. British rule, he affirmed, was not founded on brute force alone but on sympathy, generosity, and co-operation: 'Unless we get the sympathy and goodwill of the people of

India our task is ended or will be ended in a short time,' he remarked. Though his reasoned support for the coalition government's censure of General Dyer's action at Amritsar brought him into trouble with the 'diehard' element in his constituency, he held his ground and was rewarded when a party meeting expressed its entire confidence in him.

Bennett's aversion to reaction and racism was complemented by his desire for Indian political advancement, and he hoped that even after becoming a self-governing nation India would remain an integral part of the British Commonwealth. Thus he was a warm supporter of the Montagu–Chelmsford reforms of 1919. He spoke vigorously in defence of the Government of India Bill during its successive readings in the Commons, and served as a member of the joint select committee on the bill, and subsequently on the joint standing committee on India. Outside parliament he continued to work on Indian issues, often contributing to the columns of *The Times*. Bennett was one of the first back-bench Conservatives to advocate publicly the policy of ending the party's support for the coalition government led by Lloyd George, a policy later adopted at the famous Carlton Club meeting in 1922.

On 1 August 1917 Bennett married the forty-year-old Elena Brooke-Jones, daughter of Thomas Brooke-Jones, mining engineer, of Ferrol, Spain. She was active in the Unionist organization. Bennett was described as a widower at this time, though nothing is known of a former marriage. They made their home at Harwarton House, Speldhurst, Kent, and at 38 Hans Place, London. A member of the Church of England, Bennett represented the diocese of Rochester on the national assembly of the Church of England. In 1902 he had been awarded the silver medal of the Society of Arts for a paper on the British connection with the Persian Gulf, and in 1903 he was made a CIE. He was knighted in 1921. After a period of ill health Sir Thomas Bennett died from heart failure on 16 January 1925 at 38 Hans Place. The funeral was held at Speldhurst church, Kent. His widow, who survived him by more than twenty-five years, served on the national assembly of the Church of England from 1930.

CHANDRIKA KAUL

Sources *The Times* (17 Jan 1925) · *The Times* (6 June 1919) · *WWBMP*, vol. 3 · *Hansard 5C* (1918–22), esp. vol. 131 · *WWW* · S. Natarajan, *A history of the press in India* (1962) · K. Balakrishnan, 'The Times of India— 150 years on', 1988, Times of India offices, New Delhi, India · A. Tikekar, 'A galaxy of editors', *Times of India* (28 Oct 1988), 6–7 · b. cert. · m. cert. · d. cert. · Burke, *Peerage* (1924)
Wealth at death £52,878 13s. 2d.: administration with will, 17 March 1925, *CGPLA Eng. & Wales*

Bennett, Sir Thomas Penberthy (1887–1980), architect and public servant, was born on 14 August 1887 at 39 Kensal Road, London, the elder child and only son of Thomas William Bennett (d. 1901), clerk for the London and North Western Railway (LNWR), and his wife, Ann Frances Hodge, *née* Penberthy. He was educated at St Augustine's church school, Kilburn. When his father died in 1901 he entered the drawing office of the LNWR at Euston, where he began his architectural training. He studied architecture at evening classes of the Regent Street Polytechnic under A. E. Richardson and won several prizes there. He obtained a place at the Royal Academy Schools, where he won a year prize for sculpture. He learned to draw at Heatherley's atelier, was a good watercolourist, and played the piano and organ well.

In 1911 Bennett left the LNWR for the architect's office of the Office (later Ministry) of Works: the chief architect said that he could not possibly be more of a nuisance inside the office than he had been knocking at the door. He qualified ARIBA in 1912 and FRIBA in 1922. When war broke out in 1914 he enlisted but was called back to supervise the construction of hutting in France and Wales. There he learned the value of good site management and labour relations. On 19 August 1916 he married Mary Langdon Edis (1883/4–1976), portrait painter, daughter of Charles Vessey Edis, a retired clerk.

In 1919 Bennett joined the firm of Méwès and Davis as chief assistant. He could have had a partnership there but, after eighteen months, left to set up his own practice with J. D. Hossack. At the same time he became head of the school of architecture and building at the Northern Polytechnic. He entered this field with great energy, and had become a recognized authority on technical education when in 1929 he resigned to devote more time to his practice. During the next ten years Bennett built a mass of buildings; large scale flats, of which he built many, including those at Westminster Gardens, Marsham Street, Eyre Court, Finchley Road, Hillcrest, Hampstead, and the Avebury estate at Bethnall Green, and public authority housing, offices, stores and suburban shops, banks and cinemas, the Saville Theatre in Shaftesbury Avenue, and establishments for the Royal Navy. Many of these were designed with the help of Morris W. Linslade, his son Philip, and W. Bonham Galloway.

Bennett's reputation as an architect came from sound contract management and financial control rather than from innovation or refinement in design. He was not an 'architects' architect', and held the view that good architecture comes from good building backed by sound administration, and, in his case, from unbounded faith in his own judgement. His self-confidence brought many clients. His ability to assess the potential of a site, prepare alternative sketch plans, produce carefully worked out figures of costs and likely returns, and to complete his building on time made him popular, particularly with developers. As a clear-thinking, determined, and efficient architect he was without equal.

In 1940 Lord Reith called Bennett to the Ministry of Works to be controller of bricks. In 1941 he became director of works and played an important part in the construction of hospitals, airfields, ordnance factories, and naval and prisoner-of-war camps. In 1944 Lord Portal invited him to oversee contracts for the production of the temporary housing programme. Bennett returned to private practice at the end of the war. In 1947 he was invited by Lewis Silkin to become chairman of Crawley New Town. He had already made a name as independent chairman of the Board of Trade boot and shoe working party

(which reported in 1945), and Crawley was a new challenge which once more exercised his flair for organization. Such was his success that in 1951 Lord Dalton, who had succeeded Silkin, asked him to be chairman of Stevenage New Town, the appointments to run concurrently. At Stevenage, Bennett found irreversible planning difficulties which he was unable to resolve and he resigned in 1952.

In 1960, with Crawley almost completed, Bennett retired from public life but continued with his practice. He became consultant to the partnership in 1967. He was appointed CBE in 1942, knighted in 1946, and appointed KBE in 1954. Of medium height and strongly built with a straight back, he walked with a measured tread. His voice was authoritative. He appeared to look neither to left nor right when speaking. A firm mouth contributed to a somewhat brusque manner. He was a keen golfer, and a proud life president of the Highgate Golf Club. When over ninety he was still playing, 'but only twice a week, apart from practice'. His only son, Philip Hugh Penberthy Bennett CBE, succeeded his father as senior partner in T. P. Bennett & Son in 1967, before retiring in 1980. Thomas Bennett died at his home, The Sycamores, 19 North Road, Highgate, London, on 29 January 1980.

GONTRAN GOULDEN, *rev.* KAYE BAGSHAW

Sources *The Times* (31 Jan 1980) · *RIBA Journal*, 87 (April 1980), 29 · *Building*, 9 (Feb 1980) · *Architects' Journal* (6 Feb 1980) · RIBA BAL, biographical file · personal knowledge (1986) · b. cert. · m. cert. · d. cert. · *CGPLA Eng. & Wales* (1980)

Archives RIBA BAL, MSS, BeT/1/1 | RIBA BAL, archives, RIBA/SPR/1

Wealth at death £686,280: probate, 7 March 1980, *CGPLA Eng. & Wales*

Bennett, William Cox (1820–1895), journalist and author, born at Greenwich on 14 October 1820, was the younger son of John Bennett (d. 1829/30), a watchmaker there, and his wife, Elizabeth Sinnock Bennett, and younger brother of Sir John *Bennett. He was educated at Greenwich in the school of William Collier Smithers, but when he was nine he was compelled, by the death of his father, to remain at home to assist his mother in business. Bennett took much interest in the affairs of his native borough, and succeeded in effecting several useful reforms. In 1868 he proposed Gladstone to the Liberals of the borough as their candidate, and played an important part in organizing his successful election campaign. He was subsequently an important link between Gladstone and the very radical Liberal association in Greenwich. In 1869 he gained the degree of LLD from the University of Tusculum. He was a member of the London council of the Education League. In 1869 and 1870 he was employed on the staff of the *Weekly Dispatch* as a leader writer and art critic, and subsequently he contributed to the London *Figaro*. He edited six issues of *The Lark* (1883–4), a periodical collection of songs, ballads, and poems; he also published a number of his own poems in the tradition of radical patriotism, and *Prometheus the Fire-Giver* (1877). His *Songs for Sailors* (1878) were set to music by J. L. Hatton. A diabetic, he died on 4

March 1895 from pneumonia at his home, 4 Eliot Cottages, Blackheath, and was buried at Nunhead cemetery on 8 March.   E. I. CARLYLE, *rev.* H. C. G. MATTHEW

Sources *The Times* (8 March 1895) · Boase, *Mod. Eng. biog.* · *Men and women of the time* (1895) · *Biograph and Review*, 2 (1879), 125–7 · *Biograph and Review*, new ser., 1 (1882), 57–9
Archives Bodl. Oxf., corresp. with Sir Henry Taylor · NL Scot., letters to John Stuart Blackie · NL Scot., letters to William Blackwood & Sons · NL Scot., letters to George Combe and poems · Yale U., Beinecke L., letters to Fred Locker-Lampson
Likenesses Byrne & Co., photograph, repro. in *ILN* (16 March 1895), 319c

Bennett, William Henry (1855–1920), Congregational minister and biblical scholar, was born on 22 May 1855 at 1 Conduit Street, Paddington, London, the son of William Emmanuel Bennett, draper, and his wife, Emily Brice. He was educated at the City of London School under E. A. Abbott, and proceeded to Lancashire Independent college, Manchester, in 1873. Although a near contemporary at the college, J. P. Kingsland, recalled Bennett's kindly disposition, he also remarked upon 'the extreme difficulty he experienced in writing a sermon for Sermon Class. I have often wondered whether he succeeded later in writing a passable sermon!' (Kingsland, 176). There was clearly some improvement, for at his death Bennett was remembered by a friend as one who spoke 'home to the conscience and to the heart', though another noted that 'his pulpit style was not what the ordinary congregation regarded as popular' (*Manchester Guardian*, 28 Aug 1920). While in Manchester, Bennett graduated from the University of London with second-class honours in mathematics in 1875 and an MA in that subject in 1876. From 1878 to 1882 he was at St John's College, Cambridge, on leave from Lancashire College. He gained his Cambridge BA with first-class honours in the theological tripos in 1882, and proceeded MA in 1885. He won a number of prizes and was elected a fellow of his college, the first Free Churchman to be thus honoured in Cambridge. In 1902 he became LittD Cantab., as well as DD at the University of Aberdeen, where the ceremony was somewhat disturbed by younger graduands.

Meanwhile, in 1884, Bennett had been appointed professor of Hebrew, church history and New Testament at Rotherham Independent college, and on 31 March 1885 he married Annie, daughter of R. J. Wibley, grocer, of Market Hill and Hurst, Cambridge, at Victoria Road Congregational Church, Cambridge. They had two daughters. While at Rotherham, Bennett lectured in Hebrew at Firth College, the predecessor of the University of Sheffield, and from 1888 to 1913 he was professor of Old Testament exegesis at Hackney College, London, assuming in addition the identical role at New College, London, from 1891. Recalling his own appointment to New College, A. E. Garvie described Bennett as 'the soul of magnanimity in welcoming and working with me as Principal for some years', remarking that 'on the Senate of London University he surprised many as a "man of affairs"' (Garvie, 230–31). Bennett served as dean of the faculty of theology, and as examiner to the universities of London, Wales, Manchester, and

William Henry Bennett (1855–1920), by James Russell & Sons, pubd 1907–9

Bristol. Garvie further considered that the demands of the principalship of Lancashire Independent college, which, on the retirement of Walter F. Adeney, Bennett accepted in 1913, probably shortened his life; certainly the management of the college during the First World War imposed added burdens upon him.

Bennett enjoyed excellent relations with colleagues and students alike, though he never courted popularity and could be self-deprecating. When it was suggested to him that he might consider becoming principal of Mansfield College, Oxford, he replied, 'They need a popular preacher and a man of the world, and I am neither' (*British Weekly*, 9 Sept 1920, 443). Modest himself, he knew how to prick the pretensions of the pompous.

While at Hackney and at New colleges, Bennett collaborated with Adeney on *The Bible Story Re-Told for Young People* (1897), *A Biblical Introduction* (1899), and *The Bible and Criticism* (1912). An example of Bennett's wry humour occurs in his introduction to the 1912 volume. In the wake of the 'Downgrade' controversy which was orchestrated by the Baptist C. H. Spurgeon, Bennett wrote, '"Higher Criticism" forms and expresses judgments as to the date, authorship, and mode of composition of a book. When Mr. Spurgeon expressed such judgments he was a "Higher Critic"' (p. viii). In 1887, when the controversy was at its height, and in response to the *British Weekly*'s question, 'Are Nonconformists departing from the faith?', Bennett suggested that there were changes of terminology rather than of substance, and that for the most part nonconformists remained evangelical in doctrine.

Bennett was the sole author of *The Mishna as Illustrating the Gospels* (1884), and *A Primer of the Bible* (1897). He contributed the volumes on Chronicles (1894) and Jeremiah 21–52 (1895) to the Expositor's Bible, those on Genesis and Exodus to the Century Bible, and Joshua, a new translation, illustrated and 'with colours exhibiting the composite structure of the book', to *The Polychrome Bible* (1899). This was followed by *Joshua and the Conquest of Palestine* (1904). In 1907 his *Religion of the Post-Exilic Prophets* appeared. Here Bennett introduced the prophets in chronological order and then expounded their teaching in relation to the standard themes of dogmatics. While he admitted that a new reformation of theological thought, comparable with that of the sixteenth-century Reformation, was required, he considered that the scholarship of the time, both biblical and scientific, was too much in a state of flux for any such enterprise to succeed. In 1909 his *Old Testament History* appeared, followed by *The Moabite Stone* (1911), *The Historical Value of the Old Testament* (1911), *The Value of the Old Testament for To-Day* (1914), and (for young people) *The Bible: its Place in the Christian Life* (1918).

Though pre-eminently concerned with the Old Testament (he was the first president of the Society for Old Testament Study, from 1917 to 1920), Bennett also published *The Life of Christ According to St Mark* (1907), in which he sought to reproduce the impression of Christ which would be gained by a reader who had no other source of knowledge of Jesus than this gospel. Bennett also contributed the volume on the general epistles, James, Peter, John, and Jude, to the Century Bible, and published a pamphlet on *The Congregational Churches* (1910). Among his other writings are articles in *Encyclopaedia biblica*, *Encyclopaedia Britannica*, *Hastings Dictionary of the Bible*, the Expositor's Bible, and chapters in *Faith and Criticism* (1893) and *Christianity and Civilization* (1910). Bennett died aged sixty-five on 27 August 1920 at Lancashire College, and was survived by his wife.

Bennett was a 'believing critic': P. T. Forsyth described him as one who taught the Old Testament in the spirit of the New. Over and above his careful if not earth-shaking studies of biblical texts and themes, his contribution lay in keeping his head and helping others to find their feet in the wake of the 'higher criticism'. It is not wildly speculative to surmise that but for the work of scholars such as Bennett and his Manchester colleagues, the Wesleyan J. H. Moulton and the Primitive Methodist A. S. Peake, the reaction against biblical criticism and towards fundamentalist literalism would have been much stronger than it proved to be in Britain. The words with which Bennett and Adeney concluded the preface to their *Biblical Introduction* epitomized their work as a whole:

> The authors of this volume trust that it may help its readers to a truer understanding of the sacred Scriptures, and to a fuller appreciation of their unique importance; and may confirm them in the evangelical recognition of the supreme authority of the Bible as interpreted and applied by the Holy Spirit for the spiritual life. (Bennett and Adeney, *Biblical Introduction*, vii)

ALAN P. F. SELL

Sources Venn, *Alum. Cant.* · *Congregational Year Book* (1921), 102 · St John Cam., Sandys Tutorial Admissions MSS · *The Times* (2 Sept 1920) · *Manchester Guardian* (28 Aug 1920) · *British Weekly* (2 Sept 1920) · *British Weekly* (9 Sept 1920) · *Cambridge Independent Press* (4 April 1885) · *Aberdeen Daily Journal* (1 April 1902) · J. P. Kingsland, 'Lancashire College sixty-five years ago', *Transactions of the Congregational Historical Society*, 14 (1940–44), 173–80 · A. E. Garvie, *Memories and meanings of my life* (1938) · W. B. Glover, *Evangelical nonconformists and higher criticism in the nineteenth century* (1954) · J. W. Rogerson, *The Society for Old Testament Study: a short history, 1917–1992* (1992) · W. H. Bennett and W. F. Adeney, *The Bible and criticism* (1912) · W. H. Bennett and W. F. Adeney, *A biblical introduction* (1899) · *CGPLA Eng. & Wales* (1920)

Likenesses James Russell & Sons, photograph, pubd 1907–9, NPG [*see illus.*] · photograph, repro. in *Congregational Year Book*, following p. 102

Wealth at death £3477 15s. 4d.: probate, 15 Nov 1920, *CGPLA Eng. & Wales*

Bennett, William James Early (1804–1886), Church of England clergyman and author, was born on 15 November 1804 at Halifax, Nova Scotia, the eldest son of William Bennett, a major in the Royal Engineers, and his wife, Mary, daughter of James Early. Educated at Westminster School (1816–23) and Christ Church, Oxford (1823–6), from 1826 to 1828 he acted as an assistant master at Westminster School. He was ordained deacon on 2 March 1828 and priest on 6 June 1830, and served as an assistant curate in three west London parishes: St Peter, Vere Street (1828–30); Holy Trinity, Marylebone (1830–33); and All Souls, Langham Place (1833–6). From 1836 to 1843 he was minister of the Portman Chapel. During this time he acquired a considerable reputation as a preacher, and in 1840 the bishop of London, Charles Blomfield, appointed him priest-in-charge of the important new district of St Paul's, Knightsbridge.

At St Paul's, Bennett immediately set about building a new church: the architect was Thomas Cundy (1790–1867). The first stone was laid on 6 November 1840 and the building was consecrated on 30 June 1843, when Bennett became the first incumbent of the new living. Within a few years he had persuaded his wealthy congregation to help him build a new church in Pimlico, then a poor part of the parish. The architect was again Thomas Cundy, assisted on this occasion by William Butterfield. The new church of St Barnabas was hailed by supporters as the most complete architectural expression of Anglo-Catholic and ecclesiological ideals yet built. It was widely denounced by the enemies of those ideals. The bishop of London had already complained about practices at St Paul's before St Barnabas was consecrated on 11 June 1850. In September there were anti-ritualist riots outside St Paul's; the police had to guard the church and parsonage day and night. The situation was further inflamed by the re-establishment of the Roman Catholic hierarchy in England and by the notorious letter, with its references to Bennett's innovations, which Lord John Russell, one of his parishioners, sent to the bishop of Durham to denounce 'papal aggression'. Bennett was lampooned in *Punch*, and Lord Ashley told a great meeting, 'I would rather worship Lydia on the banks of the river than with a hundred surpliced priests in the gorgeous temple of St. Barnabas' (E. Hodder, *The Life and Work of the Seventh Earl of Shaftsbury, KG*, 1892, 433). When Bishop Blomfield demanded his resignation, Bennett obeyed out of deference to his episcopal authority and resigned the incumbency on 4 December 1850. Blomfield was accused of having sacrificed an exemplary parish priest to the clamour of popular opinion, a charge which, according to his son, depressed him until his death seven years later.

The dowager marchioness of Bath, who had been a

William James Early Bennett (1804–1886), by Francis Holl, pubd 1854 (after George Richmond, 1851–2)

member of Bennett's congregation at Portman Chapel, appointed him to the vicarage of Frome Selwood in Somerset. He took possession of the benefice in January 1852, despite anti-ritualist opposition, with the support of the bishop of Bath and Wells. One of Bennett's first major undertakings in his new living was to restore the fine medieval parish church, which had been neglected and left in a bad state of repair. The extensive restoration work was finally completed in 1866 at considerable cost. Bennett also greatly increased the number of church services, celebrating holy communion and reciting morning and evening prayer daily. In 1867 he told the royal commission on ritual that out of a parish of 5000 (3000 of whom were dissenters or non-churchgoers) at least 20 people attended each of the daily services. On Sundays there were at least 80 at the early holy communion, with 500 at matins and 1000 at evensong.

In that year the arch-protestant Church Association brought a prosecution against Bennett over some injudicious words which he had included in a pamphlet entitled *A Plea for Toleration in the Church of England in a Letter to Dr Pusey* (1867). These included a reference to 'the real, actual, and visible Presence of our Lord upon the Altars of our parish churches'. Pusey—who wrote to Gladstone that the existence of the whole high-church body was threatened by the prosecution—persuaded him to change this phrase to 'the real and actual Presence of our Lord under the form of bread' in a third edition published in 1868. Despite this change the Church Association went ahead with the prosecution of Bennett on a charge of heresy. The dean of arches, Sir Robert Joseph Phillimore, at first declined to entertain the charges, but was ordered to consider them

by the privy council. Phillimore, who based his judgment on the amended wording of the third edition of the pamphlet, decided on 23 July 1870 that the defendant had not broken the law of the church. The Church Association appealed to the judicial committee of the privy council, but on 8 June 1872 Phillimore's judgment was upheld. Bennett was not represented at these proceedings by counsel, since he refused to recognize the authority of the privy council over the church.

Bennett's troubles at St Paul's and St Barnabas, together with his skirmish with the Church Association, were the almost inevitable result of his strong Anglo-Catholic convictions. He was one of the first Anglican priests to reintroduce the use of long-forgotten Catholic ceremonies and ornaments into parish churches, insisting that these were justified as the symbolic expression of vital but neglected sacramental doctrines. Eucharistic vestments, which he waited to introduce at Frome until 1865 when he judged his people were ready, were the visible expression of his belief in a sacrificial priesthood and in the doctrine of the real presence of Christ in the consecrated bread and wine. Bennett had no doubt that such teachings and practices were fully in accordance with scripture and the mind of the Church of England. He judged that some Catholic practices, such as the use of altar lights, could be introduced lawfully because they were not forbidden by the Church of England; other practices which were unlawful, such as the reservation of the consecrated host in an aumbry or tabernacle, had to be foregone even though desirable. He used only the holy communion service of the Book of Common Prayer with no interpolations, although he allowed space for private devotions.

Bennett's refusal to recognize the authority of the privy council in ecclesiastical affairs stemmed from his belief in the separation of church and state: in 1850, following the Gorham judgment, he had preached two sermons in which he argued that the sovereignty of the monarchy had passed to a House of Commons which was no longer exclusively Anglican in its membership. Consequently the church should seek full control over her own affairs and freedom from state interference. In tandem with his disestablishment views, Bennett was firmly committed to the Church of England as the sole true representative of the Catholic church in England. He was firmly opposed not only to the restoration of the Roman Catholic hierarchy in 1850 but to any Roman Catholic presence in England at all; equally he held that the Church of England had no right to establish herself in Roman Catholic countries. When he was abroad in a Roman Catholic country he would attend mass, even though he had to remain content with making a spiritual communion.

Bennett was above all an outstanding parish priest who belonged to the notable post-Tractarian generation of clerics that succeeded in translating Anglo-Catholic principles into pastoral practice. In addition to church restoration and the reform of worship he was intensely concerned with Christian education. In all of his parishes he built and rebuilt schools. He was constant in his attention to catechizing children at evensong on Sundays—Prince Albert had twice attended to observe him catechize at St Paul's. He was also a popular and lucid preacher. At Frome, as in Pimlico, he was intensely concerned for the welfare of the poor. A dispensary was opened, provident clubs instituted, and a home for factory girls established, together with a crèche for the children of working mothers. The parish was divided into districts in which the clergy visited homes assiduously.

Bennett was not an original theologian; his contribution to the Anglo-Catholic movement was as an effective publicist of its ideals in a large number of writings, many of which are collections of sermons. Among these are *The Principles of the Book of Common Prayer Considered* (1845), *The Church, the Crown and the State: their Junction and their Separation* (1850), *A Farewell Letter to his Parishioners* (1851), *The Old Church Porch* (1854–62), and 'Some results of the Tractarian movement of 1833' in *The Church and the World: Essays and Questions of the Day in 1867*, ed. O. Shipley (1867).

Bennett married Mary Concetta Franklin (*d.* 1879), the eldest daughter of Sir William Franklin, principal inspector-general of army hospitals, at Marylebone on 21 August 1828; they had one son, William Henry Bennett, who died in 1854, and three daughters, one of whom died in infancy. Bennett continued to work in his parish and to take part in services until three days before his death, at the vicarage at Frome, on 17 August 1886. He was buried on 21 August near the grave of Bishop Ken, on the south side of the chancel in Frome church.   PETER DAVIE

Sources F. Bennett, *The story of W. J. E. Bennett ... and of his part in the Oxford church movement of the nineteenth century* (1909) · Blomfield letter-books, LPL, Fulham MSS, vols. 383, 384, 395, 396 · 'Royal commission on ... the course of public worship: first report', *Parl. papers* (1867), 20.719, no. 3951 · H. P. Liddon, *Life of Edward Bouverie Pusey*, ed. J. O. Johnston and others, 4th edn, 4 vols. (1894–8), vol. 3 · A. Blomfield, *A memoir of Charles James Blomfield, with selections from his correspondence*, 2nd edn (1864) · J. Bentley, *Ritualism and politics in Victorian Britain* (1978) · *London: the cities of London and Westminster*, Pevsner (1973)
Archives LPL, corresp. · LPL, *Directory for the celebration of holy communion and English mass book* | LPL, Bath MSS · LPL, Fulham MSS · LPL, Longleat MSS
Likenesses F. Holl, engraving, pubd 1854 (after G. Richmond, 1851–2), AM Oxf., Hope collection [*see illus.*]
Wealth at death £7725 16s. 1d.: resworn probate, Feb 1887, *CGPLA Eng. & Wales* (1886)

Bennett, William Mineard (1778–1858), miniature painter, was born in Exeter, Devon, and baptized on 2 November 1778 at St Thomas's, Exeter, one of at least two sons of William Bennett, who worked for the Exeter Bank, and his wife, Mary. He was apprenticed to Abraham Ezekiel, an Exeter engraver, but he chose miniature painting rather than engraving as his profession and moved to London, where he became a pupil of Sir Thomas Lawrence before establishing a successful practice as a miniature painter and portrait painter in oil. A lifelong passion for music was pursued in a professional capacity at this early stage in his career, and he made several appearances at public concerts in Bath from 1806 to 1808 as well as publishing some of his own musical compositions. His début on the London stage was made as Paul in *Paul and Virginia*,

a musical after-piece performed at the Haymarket Theatre, but he then opted to make portrait painting his primary occupation.

Bennett exhibited at the Royal Academy between 1812 and 1835 and then settled in Paris. He enjoyed the patronage of the duc de Berri and of Louis-Philippe, who decorated him in recognition of his work for him. Such was his financial success that in 1844 he was able to retire to Exeter, where he died, apparently unmarried, on 17 October 1858 at his home, 2 Hill's Buildings, St Sidwells. Two of his self-portraits in oil on canvas are in the Royal Albert Memorial Museum and Art Gallery, Exeter.

R. E. GRAVES, *rev.* V. REMINGTON

Sources *GM*, 3rd ser., 5 (1858), 647–8 · *Monthly Mirror* (Feb 1808), 75–9 · MS letter from W. M. Bennett to T. Bennett, Royal Albert Memorial Museum and Art Gallery, Exeter, 8 Nov 1830 · T. L. Ormiston, *Parish register of St Thomas's, Exeter, 1541–1837*, 4 vols. (1934), vol. 3 · D. Foskett, *Miniatures: dictionary and guide* (1987), 417, 426, 491 · B. S. Long, *British miniaturists* (1929), 27 · L. R. Schidlof, *The miniature in Europe in the 16th, 17th, 18th, and 19th centuries*, 1 (1964), 75 · Graves, *RA exhibitors* · *CGPLA Eng. & Wales* (1858)
Archives Royal Albert Memorial Museum and Art Gallery, Exeter, letters to his father and brother
Likenesses W. M. Bennett, self-portrait, 1808, repro. in *Monthly Mirror*, facing p. 75 · S. Freeman, stipple, pubd 1808 (after W. M. Bennett), BM, NPG · W. M. Bennett, self-portrait, exh. RA 1812 · W. M. Bennett, self-portrait, oils, 1815–32, Royal Albert Memorial Museum and Art Gallery, Exeter
Wealth at death under £6000: probate, 22 Oct 1858, *CGPLA Eng. & Wales*

Bennett, William Robertson Russell [Billy] (1887–1942), comedian, was born in Glasgow, the son of John Bennett who partnered Robert Martell in the Bennett and Martell slapstick comedy act which was quite well known in the 1890s and Edwardian years. Billy Bennett made his youthful first appearance as the rear end of a cow and spent a period as an acrobat, but was not keen to emulate his father and enlisted in the army. He then returned to the stage as a burlesque comic, but re-enlisted for the duration of the First World War. He served in the 16th lancers, winning the Distinguished Conduct Medal, the Military Medal, and the Belgian Croix de Guerre.

It was only in 1919 that Bennett really began his popular career as a 'cod' monologist. He had gained some experience as a 'canteen comic', appearing with Mark Lupino in the Shellfire Concert Party, which proved invaluable in honing his forceful style. Like many comedians of the era he also had experience with the Fred Karno troupe. By the early 1920s he was a welcome fixture in the top rank of variety theatres throughout the country, and appeared at royal command variety performances in 1926, 1933, and 1934. With his famous billing of 'almost a gentleman', his forthright, raucous delivery, and the almost surreal mode of his parodies, Billy Bennett was an outstanding comedian in the inter-war years. A burly figure, with a bulging face sporting an 'Old Bill' moustache, he paraded in ill-fitting 'masher' togs, the shrunken jacket and dickey struggling to reach the floppy trousers and cumbersome boots. Thus attired he bellowed accusingly at his audience in a 'turbulent baritone' (Fisher, 31), martial in resonance and betraying a trace of the Lancashire of his early upbringing. Victorian monologues—facile rhyming narratives on social issues or tales of imperial derring-do, associated with writers such as George R. Sims, Robert Service, and Milton Hayes—were still often performed on the stage, and, in his early years, Billy Bennett's lampoon may have followed a genuine recitation by an unfortunate thespian. Whether it was 'The Green Tie on the Little Yellow Dog', 'Christmas Day in the Cookhouse', or 'The Charge of the Tight Brigade', Bennett adhered tenaciously to the story-line, but then brought to the yarn a beguiling combination of fantasy and earthiness, the keen-edged snap of the rhyme ramming home the awful pun or the unblushing annotation. A line such as 'The little sardines had gone into their tins and pulled down the lids for the night' (from the unlikely annals of 'The Sailor's Farewell to his Horse'), or the question raised in 'The League of Nations'—'can a bandy-legged gherkin be a straight cucumber's child?'—offer some hint of his sub-Carrollian 'nonsense' quality. Sometimes he was moved to trumpeting a song, such as 'She was poor, but she was honest', or a version of 'The Road to Mandalay' with a tattoo motif. George Formby was to take on some of the saucy flavour of the Bennett melody, and Tommy Cooper and Ron Moody, in their monologue parody mien, and Ken Dodd in the more grotesque extremes of his humour, were to echo his comic lines.

With the coming of radio, in 1930 Bennett evolved a black-face minstrel cross-talk act 'Alexander and Mose', first with James Carew and then with Albert Whelan; the act was best known for Bennett's debonair singing and the signature tune 'The Jolly Brothers'. This earned Bennett another royal command appearance, with Carew, in 1931. His last stage appearance was in Blackpool in May 1942, just weeks before his death, at 17 Queensway, Blackpool, on 30 June. Ever the enemy of the genteel on stage, as far as is known Billy Bennett in his private life was the reverse of his brash public persona. He was unmarried and appears to have led a quiet, serious, and uneventful existence off the stage, held in esteem and affection by family and friends.   ERIC MIDWINTER

Sources J. Fisher, *Funny way to be a hero* (1973) · E. C. Midwinter, *Make 'em laugh: famous comedians and their worlds* (1979) · R. Busby, *British music hall: an illustrated who's who from 1850 to the present day* (1976) · Theatre Museum Collections, London · d. cert.
Archives FILM BFI NFTVA, performance footage | SOUND BL NSA, documentary footage · BL NSA, performance footage
Likenesses photographs, Hult. Arch. · portrait, Theatre Museum, London · portrait, Jerwood Library of the Performing Arts, London, Mitchenson and Mander Collection

Bennett, Sir William Sterndale (1816–1875), composer, was born at 7 Howard Street, Sheffield, on 13 April 1816, the third child and only son of Robert Bennett (1788–1819) and his wife, Elizabeth, *née* Donn (1791–1818). Bennett's grandfather, John Bennett (1754–1837), was a bass lay clerk in the choir which at that time served the Cambridge colleges of King's, St John's, and Trinity. His father was organist of Sheffield parish church from 1811, a piano teacher trained in Logier's method of instruction, and the composer of a few published songs, including *Six Melodies to*

Sir William Sterndale Bennett (1816–1875), by London Stereoscopic Co., late 1860s

Original Poetry (1815), settings of words by his friend William Handley Sterndale, the son of a Sheffield surgeon, after whom Robert Bennett named his son. Bennett's mother was the daughter of James *Donn, curator of the botanic gardens at Cambridge and author of *Hortus Cantabrigiensis* (1796). On 7 May 1818 Bennett's mother died, shortly after giving birth to a third daughter, who survived only a few days. On 11 January 1819 Robert Bennett married Harriet Blake (1794–1828) of Sheffield, but a few months later, on 3 November 1819, he himself died of tuberculosis. Bennett and his two sisters, Marianne Ellen (1813–1857) and Emily Agnes (1814–1852), were therefore brought up by their paternal grandparents in Cambridge, and were all baptized at St Edward's Church, Cambridge, on 19 March 1820.

Musical education As a child Bennett showed exceptional musical promise. He received piano lessons from the daughter of the chief music-seller in Cambridge, and on 17 February 1824, aged seven, was admitted as a chorister in King's College chapel. In the spring of 1826 he was introduced to the Revd Frederick Hamilton, superintendent of the Royal Academy of Music, who was on a visit to friends in Cambridge. As a result, on 7 March 1826, at the age of nine, Bennett entered the academy, being the first student to be accepted as a boarder without expense. He received instruction on the violin, initially his principal study, from Pietro Spagnoletti and Antonio James Oury, and on the piano from William Henry Holmes and later Cipriani Potter. Charles Lucas was his first teacher in harmony and counterpoint. In July 1828 he was awarded a prize for progress in harmony, and his first surviving composition, an exercise in canon, dates from that year. On 6 September 1828 he played one of Dussek's piano concertos at an academy concert. In April 1829 he failed to win a student competition to set the words of a 'Fairy Chorus' to music, but he gained a bronze medal for general progress in the summer prize-giving. A serious illness in December 1829 was a check to his advancement, and in the summer of 1831 he was reproved by the academy examiners 'for his diffidence with respect to composition' (Bennett, 21). The unsatisfactory report which he took home to his grandparents had an effect: his interest in the piano revived and he was promoted to William Crotch's class in harmony.

In the autumn term of 1831 Bennett experimented with extended composition for the first time, completing on 15 October the string quartet in G major, wo 17, which was composed for private performance with fellow pupils. On 3 December 1831 he surprised the academy with an accomplished performance of Hummel's piano concerto in A♭ major, op. 113, given in the presence of the pianist and composer John Field. Bennett's compositional skills now developed rapidly, and his symphony no. 1 in E♭ major, wo 20, completed on 6 April 1832, was performed at an academy concert at the Hanover Square Rooms on 16 June 1832. Ambitious in scale and confidently orchestrated, the symphony follows the Mozartian models advocated by Crotch, but shows the composer striving to find an individual style and experimenting with audacious chromaticisms. At the annual prize-giving on 26 June Bennett was awarded a silver medal. At this time Crotch resigned as principal of the academy and his place was taken by Cipriani Potter, who became Bennett's teacher in composition. Potter's appointment was a direct stimulus on the compositions that brought Bennett to public notice and launched him on his career. By the end of October 1832 he had completed his first piano concerto, op. 1, which received its first public performance at Cambridge town hall on 28 November 1832, with himself as soloist and an orchestra consisting of his fellow pupils. Many of the features of his mature concerto style were already present in this work: energetic tuttis contrasting with lyrical passages, economical scoring, and a technically brilliant solo part. At its first London performance, at an academy concert at the Hanover Square Rooms on 30 March 1833, the concerto attracted considerable favourable critical attention, and Bennett was summoned to perform it at Windsor Castle before William IV and Queen Adelaide on two occasions in April 1833. It was published in June 1833 at the academy's expense by a leading London music publisher, Cramer, Addison, and Beale. At a further performance at the Hanover Square Rooms, on 26 June 1833, it made a great impression on Mendelssohn, then on his third visit to England, and he invited Bennett to visit Germany, not as a pupil but as a friend. Thus, within the space of a few months, Bennett found his status transformed from that of an unknown student to that of a prodigy.

Early successes Success encouraged the composition of further orchestral works, including an overture, *The Tempest*, wo 22 (1832), the symphony no. 2 in D minor, wo 23 (1833), the piano concerto no. 2 in E♭ major, op. 4, dedicated to Potter and first performed by the academy on 24 May 1834, the overture *The Merry Wives of Windsor*, wo 25, performed by the Society of British Musicians with Bennett conducting on 8 December 1834, the symphony no. 4 in A major, wo 28 (a third symphony was unfinished), which was first performed on 5 January 1835 by the Society of British Musicians (conducted by the composer), and the piano concerto no. 3 in C minor, op. 9, first performed on 16 May 1835. From April 1834 to April 1835 Bennett held the position of organist at St Ann's, a chapel of ease to Wandsworth parish church, and he is recorded as having played the viola in the orchestra for the Handel festival held in Westminster Abbey in June and July 1834. On 11 May 1835 he created a sensation with his début at the Philharmonic Society, when he played his second piano concerto. He was soon a familiar figure to London audiences, performing both his own works and those by others at concerts of the academy, the Society of British Musicians, and the Philharmonic Society, so much so that in 1835 he was described as 'one of our principal performers' on the piano (Hogarth, 420).

In October 1835 *Six Studies in the Form of Capriccios*, op. 11, was published in London by Coventry and Hollier, marking the beginning of a fifteen-year relationship with the firm. The overture *Parisina*, op. 3 (1835), was published in a piano duet arrangement in March 1836. In May 1836, at the expense of Henry Broadwood, Bennett visited the lower Rhine music festival at Düsseldorf in the company of Carl Klingemann and J. W. Davison, and was present at the production of Mendelssohn's *Paulus*. The invitation to visit Leipzig, where Mendelssohn was now conductor of the Gewandhaus Orchestra, was renewed. Mendelssohn declared to the English composer Thomas Attwood, in a letter of 28 May 1836, 'I think him [Bennett] the most promising young musician I know, not only in your country, but also here …' (Bennett, 41). On Mendelssohn's advice, Bennett and Davison sailed up the Rhine to Mainz, and Bennett conceived the idea for his most popular orchestral work, the overture *The Naiades*, op. 15, cast in a similar mould to Mendelssohn's *The Hebrides*. Dedicated to the Royal Academy of Music, the overture was completed in the summer of 1836 at Grantchester, near Cambridge, and first performed at a trial concert of the Philharmonic Society conducted by Ignaz Moscheles on 20 January 1837.

Mature works The end of Bennett's period as a student was marked by the first performance of his unpublished piano concerto in F minor, wo 32, at the academy prize concert on 1 July 1836. The period following, up to his marriage in 1844, was the most intensely creative of his life, and many of his finest works date from it. Aided by the prospect of a legacy on his twenty-first birthday from his maternal grandfather, James Donn, he was able to spend eight months in Leipzig, from October 1836 to June 1837, where he became friends with Robert Schumann and Ferdinand David, made the acquaintance of many German musicians, and established a lifelong relationship with the music publishing firm of Friedrich Kistner, which in December 1836 published his *Three Musical Sketches*, op. 10, *Six Studies*, op. 11, and *Three Impromptus*, op. 12 (all of which had previously been published in England), and went on to produce authoritative editions of most of his published works. Bennett made his début at the Leipzig Gewandhaus on 19 January 1837, playing his third concerto, and on 13 February he conducted the first German performance of *The Naiades*. Schumann was moved to comment in his review of the third concerto, '… were there many artists like Sterndale Bennett, all fears for the future progress of our art would be silenced' (Schumann, 214). During his stay in Leipzig he revised *Parisina*, and it was performed at the Gewandhaus on 6 March 1837. He also completed the piano sonata, op. 13, dedicated to Mendelssohn, the *Three Romances*, op. 14, and the fantasia, op. 16, dedicated to Schumann, who in return dedicated his *Études symphoniques*, op. 13 (1837), to Bennett. Bennett was never Mendelssohn's pupil, but the two composers submitted their works to each other for comment and approval.

Leaving Leipzig on 11 June 1837, Bennett returned home via Mainz and Rotterdam, and arrived in London by 14 July. There he began to take private pupils and was given a class at the academy. In 1838 he was elected to membership of both the Garrick Club and the Royal Society of Musicians, and he also became an associate of the Philharmonic Society. The fourth piano concerto in F minor, op. 19, composed in the summer of 1838, was performed by the academy on 26 September 1838. A second long visit to Leipzig took place from October 1838 to March 1839 and saw the performance at the Gewandhaus on 17 January 1839 of the fourth concerto, incorporating a new slow movement, a lyrical barcarole, which immediately 'created a great enthusiasm' (letter to J. W. Davison, Bennett, 77) and became one of Bennett's best-known pieces. On 24 January the newly composed overture *Die Waldnymphe*, op. 20, received its first performance, also at the Gewandhaus, conducted by Mendelssohn. In Leipzig Bennett composed *Three Diversions*, op. 17, for piano duet, which he played with Mendelssohn, and the *Allegro grazioso*, op. 18. Back in London, on 22 August 1839 he signed an agreement with Coventry and Hollier to compose an opera on a tale of Sir Walter Scott, the libretto to be written by George Linley. However, the libretto was never completed and no music for it has survived. Another unfinished work, the oratorio *Zion*, had been begun in Germany, and ten movements were completed between 1839 and 1844. Two choruses were later used in *The Woman of Samaria*, op. 44. Towards the end of 1841 Bennett became engaged to Mary Anne Wood (1825–1862), a former piano student at the academy and the daughter of Commander James Wood of the Royal Navy.

Another visit to Germany, from January to March 1842, enabled Bennett to meet Louis Spohr, and in Kassel on 7 January 1842 he performed his caprice in E major for piano and orchestra, op. 22, with a quartet accompaniment in which Spohr played first violin. The caprice was repeated at the Leipzig Gewandhaus on 17 January 1842. After returning to London Bennett continued to build up his career as a teacher, pianist, and conductor, and also as an advocate of neglected earlier music. His series of editions of eighteenth- and early nineteenth-century keyboard music, *Classical Practice*, which appeared from 1839 onwards, made available works otherwise difficult to obtain in England. In 1843 he established the first of a series of Classical Chamber Concerts, featuring solo piano music by such composers as Bach, Handel, Scarlatti, Mozart, Beethoven, Clementi, Spohr, and Mendelssohn, as well as his own works.

Teaching and conducting Bennett's marriage at Southampton on 9 April 1844 to Mary Anne Wood, and the subsequent birth of three children, Charles Sterndale in 1845, James Robert in 1847, and Elizabeth Donn in 1848, meant that he had to concentrate on earning a living through teaching, leaving himself less time for composition. In 1844 he was a candidate for the Reid professorship of music at Edinburgh University, but was unsuccessful, despite impressive testimonials from Mendelssohn and other leading musicians. In March 1845 Bennett and his family moved from 42 (later no. 92) Upper Charlotte Street to 15 Russell Place, Fitzroy Square (now 19 Fitzroy Street), where they lived until 1859, when a move was made to 50 (now no. 47) Inverness Terrace, Bayswater. On 1 May 1848 Bennett delivered an inaugural lecture at the newly established Queen's College, London, where he gave regular lessons in harmony. For his pupils at the college he composed the *Preludes and Lessons*, op. 33, a series of short technical studies in all the major and minor keys, which was published in 1853 and widely used as teaching material well into the twentieth century. Also in May 1848 he broke off his connection with the Philharmonic Society following a protracted argument with Michael Costa over a performance of *Parisina*. On 15 June 1848 the final version of his piano concerto in A minor, wo 48, begun in 1841, was performed at his annual benefit concert. More compressed in form and intimate in expression than the previous five concertos, its reception was mixed and this last concerto remained unpublished. The rift with the Philharmonic Society, the death of Mendelssohn the previous year, which had affected him deeply, and increasing pressure of work led to a breakdown of Bennett's health in August 1848.

In 1849 Bennett founded the English Bach Society, in which he played a leading role, conducting the first performance of the St Matthew passion in England in 1854 and preparing the first English edition (choral parts 1858, vocal score 1862). From 1851 he published his works with Leader and Cock, maintaining for the rest of his life a mutually supportive business relationship with James Lamborn Cock. The only significant work to appear in the early 1850s, and one which demonstrates his mastery of large-scale design, was the sonata duo, op. 32, composed for the cellist Alfredo Piatti, and first performed by the composer and the dedicatee at a Classical Chamber Concert on 16 March 1852. The esteem in which Bennett was held in Germany is reflected in the offer made to him of the conductorship of the Gewandhaus in 1853, which he declined owing to his teaching commitments in London. On 4 March 1856 he was elected professor of music at Cambridge University. For his MusD degree, awarded on 30 June 1856, he composed the impressive anthem for double choir, 'Lord, who shall dwell in thy tabernacle?', wo 57. At Cambridge Bennett introduced reforms to the system of awarding music degrees, insisting that candidates should take the degree of bachelor of music before proceeding to the doctorate and instigating *viva voce* examinations, and he did much to encourage musical performances by members of the university. Also in 1856 he succeeded Richard Wagner as sole conductor of the Philharmonic Society, an appointment which he held until 1866, and which consolidated his position as the most important English conductor of the period. These appointments, however, meant the end of his career as a concert pianist.

Late works Most of Bennett's major later works were composed in response to important commissions, often at speed and under great pressure, their success reflecting his skill at tailoring a work to a particular audience. The light-hearted pastoral cantata *The May Queen*, op. 39, with libretto by Henry Fothergill Chorley, was composed for the Leeds festival of 1858 and anticipates some of the stylistic features found in the operettas of his pupil Arthur Sullivan. For the opening of the International Exhibition of 1862 he composed the suitably grand *Exhibition Ode*, op. 40, designed for performance with a choir and orchestra numbering 2400, to a libretto by Alfred, Lord Tennyson. The *Cambridge Installation Ode*, op. 41, was written as a formal welcome ode to celebrate the installation of the duke of Devonshire as the new chancellor of Cambridge University the same year. For the jubilee concert marking the fiftieth anniversary of the Philharmonic Society, also in 1862, Bennett produced the elegant overture *Paradise and the Peri*, op. 42, which contains some of his most beautiful music and is a symphonic poem in all but name, based on the poem from Thomas Moore's *Lalla Rookh* (1817). His last symphony, in G minor, op. 43 (1864, revised 1867), was also composed for the Philharmonic Society and remains faithful to classical models in its form and delicate orchestration, with a songlike romanza as its slow movement. The sacred cantata *The Woman of Samaria*, for the Birmingham festival of 1867, followed in the tradition of Mendelssohn's *Elijah* (1846), but deliberately eschewed any attempt to compete with it by concentrating on lyricism rather than on the dramatic aspects of the story. Both *The May Queen* and *The Woman of Samaria* passed into the repertories of many amateur choirs and continued to be popular into the early decades of the twentieth century.

On 17 October 1862 Mary Bennett died at Eastbourne after a long illness, a severe blow from the effects of which Bennett is said never to have recovered. In August 1863 he visited Germany again after an absence of twenty years, travelling to Düsseldorf, Bonn, Mainz, Frankfurt am Main,

and Cologne. In January 1865 he returned to Leipzig, where he conducted the first German performance of his last symphony (op. 43) at the Gewandhaus on 15 January 1865. In the autumn of 1865 he moved to 38 Queensborough Terrace, and the following year acquired an adjacent property, 18 Porchester Terrace, in which he lived from 1870 to 1873. With Otto Goldschmidt he produced *The Chorale Book for England* (1863, supplement 1865), a collection of old German chorale melodies set to translations of German hymn texts by Catherine Winkworth. In 1866 he was appointed principal of the Royal Academy of Music, and his arduous duties, in addition to his other commitments, left him no time for composition. He received the honorary degrees of MA from Cambridge (October 1867) and DCL from Oxford (22 June 1870), was awarded the Beethoven gold medal from the Philharmonic Society (7 July 1867), and was knighted at Windsor on 24 March 1871. In August 1871 he visited the Beethoven festival at Bonn with J. W. Davison. His last works, the programmatic piano sonata *The Maid of Orleans*, op. 46 (1873), which was quickly taken into the repertories of several leading pianists, and the uncompleted music to Sophocles' *Ajax*, show signs of a late resurgence of his creative powers. In March 1872 he received a public testimonial in St James's Hall, and at the same time a scholarship at the academy was founded in his honour by subscription. On 29 September 1873 he moved from Porchester Terrace to 66 St John's Wood Road.

Bennett held a central position in English musical life from the mid-1830s to his death and is regarded as the leading English composer of the early Victorian period. His music was well received in both England and Germany and his overtures *The Naiades* and *The Wood-Nymphs* were regularly performed in Leipzig. At the Royal Academy of Music he taught a whole generation of British composers, his pupils including Joseph Parry, W. S. Rockstro, William Shakespeare, Alice Mary Smith, and Arthur Sullivan. He was regarded as one of the best pianists of his day, and his finest works are those for, or including, the piano. Rejecting the superficial virtuosity of many of his contemporaries, he developed a style acknowledged to be peculiarly his own, essentially classical in nature, but with reference to a multiplicity of influences from his own performance repertory. The technical difficulties of his most interesting solo piano works, such as the sonata, op. 13, the fantasia, op. 16, and the exuberant *Suite de pièces*, op. 24 (1841), probably his finest work for his own instrument, meant that they were overshadowed by less demanding and more popular works such as the *Three Musical Sketches*, op. 10, the *Rondo piacevole*, op. 25 (1842), and *Genevieve*, wo 42 (1839). His overtures are some of the earliest examples of concert overtures by an English composer. In addition to the works mentioned above, Bennett wrote many other short piano pieces, a sextet for piano and strings, op. 8 (1835, revised 1844), a chamber trio for piano, violin, and cello, op. 26 (1839), two sets of songs with English and German words, op. 23 (1842) and op. 35 (1855), other sacred and secular songs, several partsongs, another eight anthems, eleven hymn tunes, and some Anglican chants.

His editions of works by other composers included Handel's *Acis and Galatea* (1847), Beethoven's piano works, piano trios, and violin sonatas (1850–66), Bach's *Das wohltemperierte Clavier* (1852–66), and Mendelssohn's piano works (1855–61).

Gentle, sensitive, and retiring in character, but vivacious in movement, Bennett shunned self-publicity and was indifferent to the financial worth of his own music. He was a sympathetic teacher and was well liked by his students. He was 5 feet 7 inches in height and slender in build, and his head was large in proportion to his body.

Bennett was taken ill on 24 January 1875 and died at his home, 66 St John's Wood Road, London, at a quarter past twelve on 1 February 1875. He received the honour of burial in Westminster Abbey on 6 February 1875.

ROSEMARY FIRMAN

Sources J. R. Sterndale Bennett, *The life of William Sterndale Bennett* (1907) · N. Temperley, 'Bennett, Sir William Sterndale', *New Grove*, 2nd edn · W. T. Freemantle, *Sterndale Bennett and Sheffield* (1919) · R. Williamson, *William Sterndale Bennett: a descriptive thematic catalogue* (1996) · R. Williamson, 'William Sterndale Bennett (1816–75) and his publishers', PhD diss., U. Nott., 1995 · F. G. E. [F. G. Edwards], 'William Sterndale Bennett, 1816–1875', *MT*, 44 (1903), 306–9, 379–81, 523–7 · A. O'Leary, 'Sir William Sterndale Bennett: a brief review of his life and works', *Proceedings of the Musical Association*, 8 (1881–2), 123–45 · C. V. Stanford, 'William Sterndale Bennett, 1816–1875', *Musical Quarterly*, 2 (1916), 628–57; repr. in C. V. Stanford, *Interludes: records and reflections* (1922) · W. Spark, *Musical memories*, 2nd edn (1888) · B. Walker, *My musical experiences*, new edn (1892) · R. Williamson, 'Sterndale Bennett's lost piano concerto found', *Journal of the Royal Musical Association*, 119 (1994), 115–29 · G. Hogarth, *Musical history, biography and criticism* (1835) · R. Schumann, *Music and musicians: essays and criticisms*, ed. and trans. F. R. Ritter, 1st ser., 6th edn (1877)
Archives Bodl. Oxf. · Royal Academy of Music, London, MSS · Sheff. Arch., letters and papers · W. Yorks. AS, Leeds, letters and papers | priv. coll. · priv. coll. · priv. coll.
Likenesses J. W. Childe, watercolour, *c.*1832, Royal Academy of Music, London · A. F. Pecht, portrait, 1839 · T. C. Wageman, watercolour, *c.*1840, priv. coll. · C. Baugniet, lithograph, 1844, BM, NPG · London Stereoscopic Co., carte-de-visite, 1866–9, NPG [*see illus.*] · J. E. Millais, oils, 1873, priv. coll. · L. A. Malampré, marble bust, 1875, Cutlers' Hall, Sheffield · T. Smith, medallion, 1875?; copy, memorial tablet, Sheffield Cathedral · T. O. Barlow, mezzotint (after J. E. Millais), BM, NPG · E. Edwards, photograph, NPG · D. J. Pound, stipple and line engraving (after photograph by J. J. E. Mayall), NPG · Weger, stipple and line engraving (after photograph), BM · oils, King's Cam. · photographs, priv. coll.
Wealth at death under £8000: probate, 15 March 1875, *CGPLA Eng. & Wales*

Benninck, Levina. *See* Teerlinc, Levina (d. 1576).

Bennis [*née* Patten], **Eliza** (1725–1802), Methodist leader, was born in Limerick. Little is known of her background except that her family were Presbyterian and that her father died when she was eighteen. Two years later she married Mitchell Bennis (d. 1788), who in 1769 was master of the corporation of Saddlers. The marriage was apparently a happy one: her husband was described as a 'tender and affectionate partner' (*Christian Correspondence*, 244) and Bennis, following her spiritual conversion, worried that her husband and children were 'idols set up in … the place that God should have' (ibid., 285).

For much of her early life Bennis was troubled by a sense of spiritual emptiness: 'I saw I was not right', she remembered, 'yet thought that I was not as bad as many' (*Christian Correspondence*, 266). When Robert Swindells, the first Methodist missionary to visit Limerick, preached there on 17 March 1749, she went to hear him. She was 'much affected' (ibid., 267) and shortly afterwards became the first member of the Methodist society in the city. Although she continued for some years to be troubled by 'unbelief' (ibid., 282) and by self-doubt, her conversion marked the beginning of a wholehearted and energetic commitment to the consolidation and expansion of Methodism.

As a member of the local congregation Bennis took charge of class and band meetings and ultimately assumed a leadership role within the society. In 1769 she successfully petitioned the Methodist conference for the appointment of a preacher to Limerick—the earliest example, according to C. H. Crookshank, 'of the voice of the people being heard in connection with a preaching appointment' (Crookshank, *History of Methodism*, 229). Under her supervision, the society in Limerick flourished: in 1772 she reported that

> the select band in particular, and the society in general, are much stirred up … the class-meetings are lively; the prayer meetings … are revived; the public congregation is in general much larger, and a deeper seriousness and spirit of enquiry observable. (*Christian Correspondence*, 55)

From 1768 Bennis spent much of her time in Waterford, involving herself in the affairs of the society there. In 1770 she informed Wesley that 'the people here go on at a poor rate, nor do I think it likely to be otherwise until they have a stationed preacher; they desired me to mention this, and would thank you to think of them' (Crookshank, *History of Methodism*, 237). Wesley acceded to her request and in 1772 acknowledged her success in building up the society in Waterford, going on to commission her to re-establish order in Limerick, where the society was currently in disarray. She continued to report to Wesley on the state of Methodism in Waterford and Limerick, interesting herself not only in spiritual questions but also in more practical matters: noting that a wealthy Mr T— had joined the Waterford society, she remarked that 'God does graciously throw in a rich person here and there, to bear the needful expenses of his poor followers' (*Christian Correspondence*, 55).

Bennis's incessant zeal and ability to inspire are suggested by the Methodist preacher John McGregor, who, recalling their association in Limerick, described her as his 'golden spur', and asked,

> Whose parlour can I now turn into a study? What woman will throw away her work, to meditate and converse with me on the things of God? … Who will now counsel, instruct, or admonish me? … Who will thrust me into the jail, among the malefactors; to the barracks, amongst the soldiers; to sick beds, and distressed souls? This have you often done, when I was able, but not always willing. (*Christian Correspondence*, 245)

In 1773 Bennis had rejoiced that 'the Lord has blessed my husband's industry far above our expectation' (*Christian Correspondence*, 76), but some unspecified 'trials' (ibid., 297) resulted in a decline in the family's fortunes and led her and her husband to leave Limerick for Waterford. Widowed in 1788, Bennis later emigrated with her family to Philadelphia, where she died in June 1802.

ROSEMARY RAUGHTER

Sources Christian correspondence: being a collection of letters written by the late Rev John Wesley … to the late Mrs Eliza Bennis, with her answers (1809) · C. H. Crookshank, Memorable women of Irish Methodism in the last century (1882) · C. H. Crookshank, History of Methodism in Ireland, 1 (1885) · D. Hempton and M. Hill, 'Women and protestant minorities in eighteenth-century Ireland', Women in early modern Ireland, ed. M. MacCurtain and M. O'Dowd (1991), 197–211

Bennis, George Geary (1790/1793–1866), librarian and author, was born in Corkamore, co. Limerick. After some years as a grocer in Limerick he settled for a time in Liverpool, and while there appears to have become a Quaker. His first work was The Principles of the one Faith Professed by All Christians (1816). He moved to London, and in 1823 he settled in Paris, where a third edition of his Principles was printed in 1826. He also published the Traveller's Pocket Diary and Student's Journal and a Treatise on Life Assurance. He travelled on the continent; but from 1830 to 1836 he was the director of a librairie des étrangers in Paris, founded by Bossange and Renouard. Afterwards he acted as an insurance agent, and in addition was librarian to the British embassy. He was also at one time the editor of Galignani's Messenger. While in France he ceased to be a member of the Society of Friends, but always professed an attachment to their principles.

Most of Bennis's property was lost during the coup d'état of 1852, soon after which he retired. He received the decoration of the Légion d'honneur in 1854. He was said to have been nearly burnt to death by the great fire which destroyed the government bakeries during the Crimean War; the fire also led to the loss of most of his valuable library. He was still able, however, to found a free library in his native city, to which he left over 10,000 volumes. A collection of coins which he had made was stolen between the time of his death and the arrival of his executor, Edward Bennis of Bolton. He died on 1 January 1866 in Paris, and was buried there; but by his own desire no tombstone was placed on his resting-place.

W. E. A. AXON, rev. NILANJANA BANERJI

Sources J. Smith, ed., A descriptive catalogue of Friends' books, 2 vols. (1867); suppl. (1893) · J.-M. Quérard, Littérature française contemporaine (1842) · J.-M. Quérard, France littéraire (1827) · L. G. Vapereau, Dictionnaire des contemporains (1858) · private information (1885)

Bennum, Hugh of (d. 1281/2), bishop of Aberdeen, probably took his name from Benholm in Kincardineshire. His father's name may have been Hugh. Having become a canon of Aberdeen, Bennum had by November 1266 been promoted to be chancellor of the diocese. In 1271 or 1272, following the death of Bishop Richard Potton, Bennum was elected to succeed him. He went to the papal curia to obtain confirmation, and was consecrated at Orvieto by Gregory X between 27 March and 23 July 1272. Having returned home, he was probably one of the Scottish bishops who attended the Council of Lyons in 1274. He was

several times appointed by the pope to investigate the fitness for office of men elected to be bishops. Abetted by the locally influential Alexander Comyn, earl of Buchan, Bennum was apparently an active diocesan, who began the rebuilding of Aberdeen Cathedral and also attended a number of provincial church councils, at one of which he is said to have presided. He died between 30 April 1281 and 17 June 1282, when a successor was provided to his see. According to one account he perished in an unexplained ambush; according to another he died of a streaming cold.

HENRY SUMMERSON

Sources D. E. R. Watt, A biographical dictionary of Scottish graduates to AD 1410 (1977), 39–40 · J. Dowden, The bishops of Scotland … prior to the Reformation, ed. J. M. Thomson (1912), 106–8

Benoist, Anthony [Antoine] (1721?–1770), draughtsman and engraver, probably born at Tracy le Mont, near Noyon, France, was the son of Jean-Isaac Benoist, one of a family of artists living in the region of Picardy. The progress of his career makes it likely that he was born before 1721, the date generally given. The engraver and printseller Claude Du Bosc brought him to England as a youth to work on the plates to his two-volume Military History of the Late Prince Eugene of Savoy and of the Late John Duke of Marlborough (1736). His print of The Taking of Oczakow 13 July 1737 by the Russians was probably published at this time. In June 1741 he was in Paris, where he published a portrait of Louis XV after Nicholas Blakey and a drawing book of landscapes. By spring 1742 he was back in London, where he etched on two plates a remarkably detailed view entitled The Grand Procession of the Scald Miserable Masons, recording a spoof parade on the Strand of mock freemasons on 27 April, the same day as the genuine masons processed to their annual feast. Of this print George Vertue noted:

> Twas drawn & Engravd Etch'd by A Benoist from Paris who having stayd here about a Year & half returnd again.—he also painted very well & sometimes employd his time that way—this print is made in two plates well & truly drawn with the prospect of Somerset house palace and that part of the Strand—Benoist staid not long in Paris—returnd again to London. (Vertue, Note books, 6.197)

He probably remained in London until France declared war in March 1744. During this stay he was one of the engravers employed by the Bowles brothers to engrave Hayman's designs for Vauxhall Gardens and thus became the first engraver of a game of cricket (1743). He also engraved six of the set of twelve large plates published by Joseph Highmore after his paintings illustrating Richardson's Pamela (1745).

In Paris between 1744 and 1747 Benoist designed and engraved a series of plates illustrating the battles of Fontenoy, Lauffeld, and other French victories over the allies, together with a view of the place Louis le Grand (1747). This burst of patriotic enterprise ceased with the treaty of Aix-la-Chapelle and at some point Benoist returned to England, where he produced numerous topographical and architectural prints and portraits (including those of victorious British admirals) and plates for books such as Smollett's History of England. As he had announced in the inscription on The Grand Procession, Anthony Benoist was also a drawing-master and in 1763 Beauvais, another drawing-master and a dealer in prints and drawings, was lodging at Benoist's house opposite Long's Court in St Martin's Lane, London. In that year Benoist engraved a view of the town and citadel of Le Palais on Belleisle after Dominic Serres. He was living in the parish of St Giles-in-the-Fields, Westminster, at the time of his death, apparently unmarried, in August 1770.

TIMOTHY CLAYTON and ANITA McCONNELL

Sources G. L., 'Benoist, Antoine', Thieme & Becker, *Allgemeines Lexikon*, 9.130 · R. Portalis and H. Béraldi, *Les graveurs du dix-huitième siècle*, 1 (Paris, 1880), 160 · will, PRO, PROB 11/960, sig. 323 · C. le Blanc, *Manuel de l'amateur d'estampes*, 1 (Paris, 1854), 270 · Y. Sjöberg and F. Gardey, eds., *Inventaire du fonds français: graveurs du XVIIIe siècle* (1977), 2.331–4 · Vertue, *Note books*, 6.197–8 · 'Catalogue of prints and drawings', www.nmm.ac.uk, 31 Jan 2001 · *Public Advertiser* (8 Jan 1763) · *Engraved Brit. ports.*

Wealth at death modest: will, PRO, PROB 11/960, sig. 323

Benolt, Thomas (*d.* 1534), herald and diplomat, may have been born at Rouen; his mother's maiden name was Meautis, but his father's identity is not known. It was with Calais, however, that the family had its strongest links; Benolt is generally thought to have been a native of Calais, while his brother John, a priest, became secretary of the town. Their uncle John Meautis was secretary of the French language to Henry VII and Henry VIII. Thomas Benolt, too, took up royal service, but the attribution to him of pursuivantships under Edward IV and Richard III is unreliable; his first definite appointment was as Windsor herald on 6 May 1504. On 20 November 1510 he was promoted to Norroy king of arms, and on 30 January 1511 to Clarenceux king of arms.

Benolt's knowledge of French made him an obvious choice for foreign employment, either on his own or attached to embassies. His first known mission was to France in 1505. In the next reign he accompanied the earl of Surrey when the latter took precautions against Scottish invasion in the autumn of 1512, and in August 1513 he took part in the Thérouanne expedition. According to Hall, it was Benolt's urging 'in God's name set forward' that won the victory of the 'battle of the Spurs' on the 16th (*Hall's Chronicle*, 550). Thenceforward he was employed almost continually abroad, being in France in 1514, 1515, every year from 1518 to 1522, and again in 1524, 1529, and 1533; he was in Scotland in 1516, 1517, and every year from 1519 to 1526; in Germany in 1519; and in Spain in 1528 and 1529. Towards the end of his life he wrote, 'It was the pleasure of the king my master to send me often … beyond the sea, whereas I was as much without the realm as within' (Wagner, *Heralds of England*, 161).

If some of Benolt's commissions could be as routine as buying wine for Cardinal Wolsey, others were of considerable sensitivity, such as his orders to defy Charles V at Burgos in 1528, jointly with the French herald Guienne. Guienne failed to carry this off; Benolt on the other hand was praised by the emperor. He also managed to avoid being put to death on Wolsey's orders for having declared war without authority, by taking an alternative route home and getting to the king first. 'After that time', says Hall,

'the King mistrusted him [Wolsey] ever after' (*Hall's Chronicle*, 745). Benolt was clearly a safe pair of hands, one of perhaps only two heralds (the other being his predecessor as Clarenceux, Roger Machado) who were ever used for really important missions. Henry VIII showed his favour to Benolt by various grants: a wardship in 1510, the reversion of the office of bailiff of Boston in 1517, and the surveyorship of the lands supporting the garrison of Berwick in 1522. He was also on the pension list of the king of France following the peace of 1514, and was given a gold chain by the emperor (perhaps the one of 108 links mentioned in his will).

Benolt can be found participating in ceremonies in England when he was in the country, from the funeral of Henry VII in 1509 to the coronation of Anne Boleyn in 1533. On being appointed Clarenceux he had delegated his domestic functions of granting arms, making visitations, and conducting funerals to Thomas Wriothesley, Garter king of arms. But in 1530, not being sent abroad, he sought to take these back, which Wriothesley resisted, and an acrimonious controversy ensued which threatened the whole future of the office of arms. Benolt in the end brought the king round and obtained a commission under the great seal to carry out visitations. In the following years he visited in person or by deputy throughout his southern province, including south Wales. He may also have had the permission of Norroy to visit Lancashire and Cheshire. His victory ensured not only the survival of the English heralds, but also the creation of the entire body of visitation records by them over the next 150 years.

Benolt married twice. His first wife was Margaret (*d.* 1526), widow of Henry Arnold and daughter of Richard White of Kent, with whom he had no children. His second wife was Mary, daughter of Laurence Fermor of Minster Lovell, Oxfordshire, with whom he had a son, who probably died young, and two surviving daughters. He owned a house in London within the priory of St Helen, Bishopsgate, and also one in Chiswick, Middlesex, besides a manor in Gillingham, Kent.

'Absent and sick' (Coll. Arms, partition book, fol. 42) at Easter 1534, Benolt died on 8 May, and was buried in St Helen, Bishopsgate. In his will, made on 24 April, he mentions his swans in the fens near Boston, his gold chains, plate, furred gowns, and second-best tabard. To Thomas Hawley, then Carlisle herald, he left nearly 100 itemized heraldic manuscripts and books, directing that they were afterwards to pass from Clarenceux to Clarenceux. This provision was not honoured, though a number of the manuscripts survive at the College of Arms, including his own visitation records. Benolt's widow later married Richard Buckland.   ROBERT YORKE

Sources A. Wagner, *Heralds of England: a history of the office and College of Arms* (1967) · A. R. Wagner, *Heralds and heraldry in the middle ages*, 2nd edn (1956) · F. Lambarde, 'Clarenceux Benolt', *Miscellanea Genealogica et Heraldica*, 5th ser., 8 (1932–4), 257–9 · M. Noble, *A history of the College of Arms* (1805), 111–15 · officers of arms, Coll. Arms, vol. 2, pp. 351–79 · W. H. Godfrey, A. Wagner, and H. Stanford London, *The College of Arms, Queen Victoria Street* (1963), 80–81 · *LP Henry VIII*, vols. 1–7 · *Hall's chronicle*, ed. H. Ellis (1809) · will, PRO, PROB 11/25, quire 14 · A. R. Wagner, *The records and collections of the College* of Arms (1952) • J. E. Cox, ed., *The annals of St Helen's, Bishopsgate, London* (1876) • Coll. Arms, scrapbook, pp. 32–3; Heralds vol. 3; MS H.20; partition book (*temp.* Henry VIII) • T. Philipott, *Villare Cantianum, or, Kent surveyed and illustrated* (1659)

Archives BL, corresp., Cotton MSS | Coll. Arms, MSS A.17, D.13, G.2, 2 G.4, 1 H.7, H.18, H.20, L.6 *bis* (part), Muniment Room 5/25

Likenesses drawing of brass, 1600–25, BL, Harley MS 1099, fol. 71 • J. Anstis, drawing of brass, 1700–44, Coll. Arms, officers of arms, vol. 2, p. 378 • A. D. Macquin, painting on vellum of brass, 1793, Coll. Arms, scrapbook, pp. 32–3 • T. Fisher, drawing of brass, *c.*1800, Coll. Arms, scrapbook, pp. 32–3; repro. in *Parish of St Helen* (1924), pl. 39 • drawing of brass, *c.*1800, S. Antiquaries, Lond.; repro. in M. Reddan and A. W. Clapham, eds., *The parish of St Helen, Bishopsgate*, 1, Survey of London, 9 (1924), pl. 38

Wealth at death owned swans, gold chains, plate, furred gowns and nearly 100 manuscripts and books: will, PRO, PROB 11/25, quire 14

Bensley, Robert (1741/2?–1817), actor, was probably born in 1741 or 1742, for his gravestone at Stanmore church records his age at death as seventy-five, and no other reliable record of his origins and early life exists. In his youth he may have attended Westminster School and spent time either as a lieutenant of marines or as a captain in the army in North America, where he took part in military theatricals. There are also reports that he acted with Roger Kemble's and Stanton's touring companies before moving to London.

In 1765 Bensley came to the notice of David Garrick, who offered him his first appearance at Drury Lane on 2 October, as Pierre in Thomas Otway's *Venice Preserv'd*—a role that remained in his repertory for the next thirty years. A letter from Garrick to Bensley dated 28 August 1766 commended him for his industry during a season at Liverpool's own Drury Lane theatre, in which Bensley had acted eight parts, and also contained Garrick's admission that he had considered him 'naturally inclined to indolence' (*Letters*, 2.536). Having thus proved his worth, Bensley was rewarded with a number of roles for Garrick during the 1766–7 season at Drury Lane, among them Edmund in *King Lear*, Buckingham in *Richard III*, and Aboan in Thomas Southerne's *Oroonoko*. In 1767 he moved to Covent Garden, an engagement that lasted for eight seasons, until 1775 (a spell in Bristol in 1772 led to his acquiring a share in the Bristol playhouse). He played mostly supporting roles but did take a handful of leads (Tamerlane and Macbeth in 1769; Julius Caesar in 1773). For the 1775–6 season he returned to Drury Lane, where he remained, alternating with summer seasons at the Haymarket, until his retirement in 1796. He had at least fifty roles in his repertory at the start of his stint at Drury Lane, and took on at least half that many again in the course of his career. In addition to 'the stock roles of the fond parent, the considerate guardian, the reserved noble, and the austere moralist' (Highfill, Burnim & Langhans, *BDA*), these included major parts such as Iago, Prospero, and Mark Antony.

Bensley's best role was that of Malvolio in *Twelfth Night*. His portrayal was uniquely praised by Charles Lamb, writing some five years after the actor's death, as 'magnificent', with its 'air of Spanish loftiness' (Park, 55). Lamb concluded that the actor conveyed a pathos, dignity, and tragic grandeur not usually associated with the part,

while noting Bensley's deficiencies: 'his voice had the dissonance, and at times the inspiriting effect of the trumpet' and his gait 'was uncouth and stiff' (Park, 53). But he none the less admired his lack of affectation and avoidance of tricks: being 'totally destitute of trick and artifice', Bensley 'seized the moment of passion with the greatest truth, like a faithful clock, never striking before the time; never anticipating or leading you to anticipate'. His strengths were those of tact, discretion, and understatement, as he 'betrayed none of the *cleverness* which is the bane of serious acting' (ibid.). Elsewhere, however, Bensley was the subject of sharp criticism, which targeted his clumsy and awkward movement, his monotonous, nasal delivery, and his unprepossessing appearance. His 'glassy and protuberant' eyes which maintained a 'uniform goggle' were remarked upon, and he was characterized as stiff and bombastic, a representative of the theatrical tradition which Garrick (who reportedly labelled him 'Roaring Bob') was working hard to supplant (Highfill, Burnim & Langhans, *BDA*). Francis Gentleman observed that 'his person is slight, his features contracted and peevish, his deportment falsely consequential, his action mostly extravagant, and his voice rather harsh' (Gentleman, 2.491). Despite these disadvantages, Bensley was a dependable presence at Drury Lane until his retirement on 6 May 1796, marked by a final benefit in which he played opposite Sarah Siddons in Arthur Murphy's *The Grecian Daughter*.

Bensley lived for another twenty years, and possibly worked for a time either as paymaster or as barrackmaster at Knightsbridge barracks. He had married Francina Augustina Cheston at St Stephen's, Bristol, on 8 September 1772, and from 1777 to 1796 they lived in Charlotte Street, Bedford Square, Bloomsbury. In 1809 his uncle Sir William Bensley died, leaving him a substantial inheritance which afforded him financial security during the last years of his life. Bensley was at Stanmore, Middlesex, when he died on 12 November 1817, and he was buried at Stanmore church. Mrs Bensley was named as the sole beneficiary in his will, although the couple may have had a daughter, Elizabeth, who married Charles Bowen at St George's, Hanover Square, on 24 May 1802.

ROBERT SHAUGHNESSY

Sources Highfill, Burnim & Langhans, *BDA* • *The letters of David Garrick*, ed. D. M. Little and G. M. Kahrl, 2 (1963) • R. Park, ed., *Lamb as critic* (1980) • F. Gentleman, *The dramatic censor, or, Critical companion*, 2 vols. (1770)

Likenesses J. H. Mortimer, group portrait, oils, 1768, Garr. Club • E. Edwards, sketch, 1777, Harvard U. • G. Dance, sketch, 1814, Harvard U. • W. Daniell, etching, pubd 1814 (after G. Dance, 1795), BM, NPG • S. De Wilde, oils (as Harold in *The battle of Hastings*), Garr. Club • S. De Wilde, oils (as Oakley in *The jealous wife*), Garr. Club • R. Dighton, drawing (as Prospero in *The tempest*), Garr. Club • J. Roberts, pencil drawing, Garr. Club • C. J. Sayers, caricature, etching, NPG • prints, BM, NPG

Bensley, Thomas (*bap.* 1759, *d.* 1835), printer, was christened on 17 December 1759 at St Martin-in-the-Fields, the son of Thomas Bensley (*d.* 1789), printer, of Swan Yard, Strand, London, and his wife, Ann, *née* Trubshaw. He was apprenticed to his father on 1 March 1774, being freed on 6

March 1781 and cloathed in the livery of the Stationers' Company the next month. His marriage to Mary (her last name is unknown) probably took place in Hillingdon on 15 September 1788. He worked for his father, and on the latter's death in 1789 succeeded to the business in Bolt Court, Fleet Street, London. One of his earliest works was the first edition of Gilbert White's *Natural History of Selborne* (quarto, 1789). He was soon recognized as a fine printer, and was commissioned by Robert Bowyer to print (with type designed by Bowyer and cut under Bensley's direction) his edition of Hume's *History of England*, which was issued in parts from 1793 to 1806. Later Thomas Macklin, the printseller who established the Poets' Gallery in Fleet Street in competition with the Boydells' Shakspeare Gallery, commissioned Bensley to print a folio edition of the Bible (7 vols., 1800–16), embellished with engravings after the 'most eminent artists', and printed in a bold type cast by Joseph Jackson. He also printed many editions of William Cowper's *Poems*. T. F. Dibdin, in his *Bibliographical Decameron* (1817, 2.397–401), lists several more works finely printed by Bensley, and includes an engraved portrait of the printer showing his strong features. Like the other fine printers of the time he also produced run-of-the-mill work, as evidenced in his printing of the sermons of William Huntington, the Coalheaver Saint and minister of the Providence Chapel in Gray's Inn Road, of which the keenly religious and charitable printer was a trustee and where five of his children were baptized (Benjamin 1793, thought to have died in infancy, Benjamin 1796, Sarah 1801, Elizabeth 1805, and Thomas 1808). In 1822 he printed and partly edited Huntington's *Posthumous Letters*.

Bensley was entrusted with several of the earliest books for the Roxburghe Club, the club's second work, Cutwode's *Caltha poetarum* (quarto, 1815), being described as 'the prettiest of the early books' (Barker, 67). This was followed by *A Roxburghe Garland* (duodecimo, 1817), presented by James Boswell the younger, Bancroft's *The Glutton's Feaver* (quarto, 1817), and J. H. Markland's edition of *Chester Mysteries* (quarto, 1818). It is notable that all four predated the disastrous fire of 1819, after which his fine output appears to dry up.

Bensley worked for more than forty-five London publishers, printing for most of them no more than one or two publications: fine large works for Thomas Macklin, Rudolph Ackermann, and Paul Colnaghi, all mainly printsellers, for example, and smaller works for most of the others. His principal publishers were Joseph Johnson, Vernor and Hood, Longmans, and Cadell and Davies. For about seven years from 1797 he was printer at the Clarendon Press in association with William Dawson and J. Cooke, and again from 1812 to 1816 in association with Cooke and Collingwood. He worked on the 'Bible side', printing Bibles and Books of Common Prayer in English and Welsh.

Unlike William Bulmer and John M'Creery, Thomas Bensley was ready to embrace innovations in printing practice. In 1794 he claimed to have 'discovered an entire new method of printing in gold, in the most beautiful style' (English, 12). In the first decade of the nineteenth century Bensley actively supported, both financially and with practical trials, the efforts of Friedrich Koenig to develop steam-driven printing machinery, the printers George Woodfall and Richard Taylor later also supporting the project. Dibdin writes that 'After great toil, and proportionally heavy expense, Mr. Bensley has completed the establishment of a *self-working press*, which prints on *both sides* of the sheet by one and the same operation—and throws off 900 copies in an hour!' (Dibdin, 2.400), and goes on to point out the threat to employment of such *steamification*. Using this press Bensley was able, in April 1811, to perfect sheet H of the *New Annual Register* for 1810. In 1807 he printed John Thomas Smith's quarto *The Antiquities of Westminster*, for which the author produced an experimental lithographic plate, the first known lithographic book illustration.

Bensley was a prominent printer, binding thirty apprentices between 1782 and 1813. From 1805 to at least 1811 he was also the secretary of the committee of London master printers, who were at that time negotiating wages with the journeymen compositors and pressmen, during the years of financial pressure resulting from the Napoleonic wars.

On 5 November 1807 Bensley's warehouse in Bolt Court was burnt, supposedly 'occasioned by boys letting off fireworks' (*GM*, 77, 1807), and the sheets of several valuable works were destroyed, including 700 copies of Smith's *Antiquities of Westminster*, a quarto edition of Thomson's *The Seasons*, and a fine edition of Juvenal. The printing office itself was unaffected, but on 26 June 1819 his premises extending from Bolt Court to Gough Square were burnt out, although the steam press escaped relatively lightly and was brought back into use. Bensley's son Benjamin (b. 1796) had set up in business in Nelson Square, Southwark, in 1819, and it may be that Bensley joined him there while the printery in Bolt Court was being re-established; by 1821 Benjamin was working with his father in Bolt Court. Another son, Joseph, had joined his father and brother in 1818. The 1825 edition of James Morgan Cobbett's *Letters from France* carries the imprint 'Printed by Mills, Jowett & Mills (late Bensley), Bolt Court, Fleet Street', and for a few years from 1824 imprints show the address of Bensley's printing shop to have been Crane Court, Fleet Street. His son Benjamin had established business in Andover by 1829, moving to Woking by 1841, and continuing to print for William Cobbett and London publishers. In the middle 1820s Bensley moved his residence to Clapham Rise, London, where William Bulmer had retired some years earlier. He died there on 11 September 1835.   PETER ISAAC

Sources *GM*, 2nd ser., 6 (1836), 100–02 · H. V. Marrot, *William Bulmer, Thomas Bensley: a study in transition* (1930) · *GM*, 1st ser., 84/2 (1814), 541–4 · *GM*, 1st ser., 77 (1807), 1072 · *GM*, 1st ser., 89/1 (1819), 575 · T. F. Dibdin, *The bibliographical decameron*, 2 (1817), 397–401 · I. Maxted, *The London book trades, 1775–1800: a preliminary checklist of members* (1977), 18–19 · W. B. Todd, *A directory of printers and others in allied trades, London and vicinity, 1800–1840* (1972), 15–16 · N. Barker, *The publications of the Roxburghe Club, 1814–1962* (1964) · M. Twyman,

Lithography, 1800–1850 (1970), 29–30 • L. English, 'ESTC and the library of the Royal Society of Arts', *Factotum: Newsletter of the XVIIIth-Century Short Title Catalogue*, 37 (Sept 1993), 11–12 • *IGI*
Archives priv. coll., minutes of the Master Printers
Likenesses portrait, repro. in Dibdin, *Bibliographical decameron*, 401

Bensly, Robert Lubbock (1831–1893), Hebrew, Syriac, and biblical scholar, born at Eaton, near Norwich, Norfolk, on 24 August 1831, was the second son of Robert Bensly of Eaton, and his wife, Harriet Reeve. Educated in Eaton at a private school (where he began the study of Hebrew), and King's College, London (1848–51), he matriculated in 1851 at Gonville and Caius College, Cambridge; he was a scholar there from 1852 to 1855, and graduated second class in the classical tripos in 1855. He was college lecturer in Hebrew from 1861 to 1889, and was fellow of the college from 1876 until his death. In 1857 he gained the Tyrwhitt university scholarship for Hebrew. He studied from 1855 to 1860 at German universities, at Bonn and then at Halle, where he became the pupil of Rödiger, especially in Syriac. From 1864 to September 1876 Bensly was under-librarian at Cambridge University Library, and from 1887 until his death he was Lord Almoner's professor of Arabic.

Semitic studies had not flourished at Cambridge during Bensly's student career. He often told of his persistent but fruitless attempts to induce one of the Arabic professors, Theodore Preston, an obdurate absentee, to deliver lectures. In 1870 Bensly joined the Old Testament Revision Company, of which he was a regular and valued member, conservative in his minute scholarship yet unbiased by traditional authority. In 1875 he edited *The Missing Fragment of the Latin Translation of the Fourth Book of Ezra* (2 Esdras), which he had found in the communal library at Amiens. He also published, on the occasion of the orientalists' congress in 1889, *The Harklean Version of Hebrews 11: 28–13: 25*.

After his stay in Germany, Bensly lived permanently in Cambridge, but during his time there he made two visits to Egypt. The latter was to visit Mount Sinai, to assist in the decipherment of the important Syriac palimpsest of the gospels. This had been previously discovered by Mrs A. S. Lewis; but its identity and importance were first pointed out by Bensly and his pupil, F. C. Burkitt, who together examined Mrs Lewis's photographs. The manuscript was published in 1894 by Cambridge University Press.

Bensly's strong point as an orientalist was his exhaustive knowledge of Syriac literature. His scholarship was distinguished by painstaking and minute accuracy, which explained the small amount of his published work. His edition of the fourth book of Maccabees was in hand for twenty-seven years, and was published with additional material by W. E. Barnes in 1895. Bensly's only other separate work was the *Epistles of St Clement in Syriac*, also published posthumously at Cambridge, in 1899, and edited from the unique manuscript which, twenty-three years before, he himself had brought to light.

Bensly married at Halle, on 14 August 1860, Agnes Dorothee, daughter of Baron Eduard von Blomberg, who, with three children, survived him. His eldest son, Edward von Blomberg Bensly (1863–1939), was professor of classics in Adelaide University from 1895 to 1905, and professor of Latin at University College, Aberystwyth from 1905 to 1919. Robert Bensly died three days after his return from the east, on 23 April 1893 at his home, 2 Gresham Road, Cambridge. He was buried at Eaton. His friends and pupils raised a memorial fund, and purchased and presented as a separate collection to the university library his oriental books and adversaria, to which his widow added his manuscript collection.

CECIL BENDALL, *rev.* ROGER T. STEARN

Sources H. T. Francis, *In memoriam R. L. Bensly* (1893) • J. Venn and others, eds., *Biographical history of Gonville and Caius College*, 2: 1713–1897 (1898) • personal knowledge (1901) • private information (1901) • Boase, *Mod. Eng. biog.* • Venn, *Alum. Cant.*
Archives CUL, notes
Wealth at death £21,298 1s. 0d.: resworn probate, May 1894, *CGPLA Eng. & Wales* (1893)

Benson [married name McDowall], **Ada** (1840–1882), headmistress and educationist, was born on 27 November 1840 at Winson Green, Birmingham, sixth of the eight children of Edward White Benson (1800–1843), chemical manufacturer, and his wife, Harriet (*née* Baker). Their mother's death in 1850 left the six surviving orphans unprovided for, and they were separated into the care of friends and relatives; Ada and her elder sister Eleanor Bowes Benson (1833–1890) settled after an interval with Mary Sidgwick, widow of their father's cousin, the Revd William Sidgwick, at Rugby, in 1852. Ada's eldest brother, Edward White *Benson, the future archbishop of Canterbury, was a master at Rugby School. He supervised her care and education, and there was a close affinity and likeness, both physical and temperamental, between them in spite of an age difference of eleven years. Ada told him she meant to work hard to gain financial independence, and Edward wrote: 'Do not kill yourself for my sake', such was her conscientiousness and the delicate state of her health. At Rugby Ada had the advantage not only of her brother Edward's proximity but also of the Sidgwick family governess, Frances Greene, and the company of her young cousin Mary (Minnie) Sidgwick, a light-hearted girl of her own age. At seventeen Ada went to Miss Martine's school at Brighton, but still suffered poor health despite the bracing climate.

In 1859 Edward Benson married Minnie Sidgwick, and became founding master of Wellington College. Now approaching nineteen, Ada had had enough of schooling, but Edward wished her to learn more before taking up teaching. A compromise was struck whereby Ada went to Dresden, with a curriculum set by Edward and based on the German language and literature, to receive regular lessons from a male tutor. She was to devote no more than two and a half hours daily to music. She taught English and music to the family she lived with and, notwithstanding discouragement from home, published her German translation of John Ruskin's *King of the Golden River* in 1861. Her letters home show increasing homesickness, and exhortations from Edward did not help. Her health broke

Ada Benson (1840–1882), by unknown artist

introduced. Ada embraced the ideals of true religion, good manners, and sound learning. At Norwich the GPDSC wanted scripture teaching kept undenominational. Ada thought otherwise, and undertook the teaching of scripture to the whole school herself. Edward Benson approved making both Latin and German compulsory, provided the girls were well grounded in the subjects. He also urged Ada to delegate. Within months her health broke down again: the harsh East Anglian winter was blamed. Before her resignation became effective she had been elected headmistress of the company's new school at Oxford, and she served out the summer term at Norwich while paying a deputy to begin preparations there. Edward Benson was present on opening day, 3 November 1875, at Oxford, as he had been at Norwich. The building was the Judges' Lodging in St Giles ('the Judges ruin the school and me' she wrote), and the school opened with twenty-nine pupils; this figure rose rapidly, necessitating a move in 1877, which Ada could not oversee because her health broke down again. Her doctor sent her abroad, where she kept in close touch until July 1879, when she resigned.

Ada's breakdowns are never explicitly described. The evidence points to some form of psychosis, which was rife in the family. Only incapacitating illness could have induced her to give up at this time. In the ensuing period of uncertainty she thought of joining an Anglican sisterhood, an idea first mooted in 1871, but her brother was adamantly opposed to this. The problem was resolved by her marriage to Andrew McDowall (b. 1839/40), secretary to the GPDSC, on 27 December 1879. After a miscarriage, which she greeted with relief, Ada immediately became pregnant again, at the age of forty. Her daughter was christened in 1881, when Ada was fighting depression and too weak to attend. When, on 2 February 1882, Ada successfully applied for the post of headmistress of the new Bedford high school Andrew McDowall agreed reluctantly; Eleanor was 'confounded' and Edward 'horror stricken'. Ada's husband kept their London house, hired a nurse, and moved to Bedford.

The new Bedford school opened in unfinished buildings on 8 May 1882, with forty-three girls and four mistresses: two from Norwich, one from North London Collegiate School, and one former Norwich pupil who had gone on to Oxford and Somerville. Ada's first prospectus boasted a laboratory, and she introduced a gymnasium and the services of a drill sergeant. The 1882 timetable, in her own hand, survives. She also gave her girls homework timetables. Between her appointment on 2 February and the opening date she interviewed all staff and pupils. Her organization of the entire project, including boarding houses, was piloted through the board of governors in good time, and the results lasted for the next twenty-five years.

Ada Benson went to Bedford full of ideas and energy; her health restored, her hopes high for the new school, and expecting that its convenient location would make it a centre for all of Britain. Her daughter was nine months old. Her husband soon agreed to give up the London

down, and she returned to Wellington in January 1861, her brilliance clouded. Not until 1864 was Ada well enough to set up school with Eleanor. Sydney Lodge, Surbiton, opened in January 1866, and had no pupils for a year; when the school closed on Eleanor's marriage in 1872 to Thomas *Hare they were turning pupils away.

Ada Benson did not enjoy the Surbiton experience among those she described as: 'the *vulgarest* people … rolling in riches'. She shook off the dust of 'detestable Surbiton' on a continental tour of some eight months' duration in charge of a young lady, Edith Johnson, to whose father Ada submitted written reports. A diary she kept from August 1872 to April 1873 shows they visited only one school: for boys, and by mistake. Ada returned to England and was elected headmistress of Norwich high school, the first school outside London set up by the Girls' Public Day School Company (GPDSC), on 17 December 1874. When Ada saw the proposed premises, their size and location did not satisfy her. She telegraphed London to propose Churchman House, and when London demurred she replied that if the company would not take it, she would do so herself. The school opened in Churchman House on 22 February 1875 with 61 pupils, rapidly increasing to 150.

The GPDSC's model for this and subsequent schools was the North London Collegiate School of Miss Buss: Ada spent ten days there before going to Norwich. Ada's models were, with her brother's constant advice, Rugby and Wellington. There were no 'governesses', but 'mistresses', along the lines of the boys' 'masters'. At the Oxford school she later headed, a prefect system was house. On 11 October 1882, ten days after the birth of a son, Ada died at St Giles, Lansdowne Road, Bedford, of puerperal peritonitis. She was nearly forty-two. She had been able to devote little more than one full term to the Norwich and Bedford foundations, while in the years 1875–9, centred on Oxford, she had been there for only about half the time. Before taking on Oxford she had been considered for the mistress-ship of Girton College, Cambridge, but was runner-up; perhaps her authoritarian ways would not have been appropriate there. She left her stamp on the GPDSC schools, in which girls of strongly differing social backgrounds were educated together. Her work established models, raised the status of women teachers, and supplied from among her own pupils the qualified women who would take her work further in the next generation. Eight of her thirteen assistants, and eight of her pupils, were to become headmistresses.

RUTH PRYOR

Sources H. S. Benians, 'The forgotten Benson', 1973, Girls' Public Day School Trust · J. Godber and I. Hutchins, eds., *A century of challenge: Bedford high school, 1882 to 1982* (privately printed, Bedford, 1982) · V. E. Stack, ed., *Oxford high school … 1875–1960* (1963) · K. M. Westaway, ed., *Seventy-five years: the story of Bedford High School, 1882–1957* (1957) · J. Sondheimer and P. R. Bodington, eds., *The Girls' Public Day School Trust, 1872–1972: a centenary review* (1972) · M. F. Hunt, 'Secondary education for the middle class girl: a study of ideology and educational practice, 1870 to 1940, with special reference to the Harpur Trust Girls' Schools, Bedford', PhD diss., U. Cam., 1984 · J. S. Pedersen, *The reform of girls' secondary and higher education in Victorian England: a study of elites and educational change* (1987) · A. C. Benson, *The life of Edward White Benson*, 1 (1900) · A. C. Benson, *Genealogy of the family of Benson* (1895) · *CGPLA Eng. & Wales* (1883) · b. cert. · m. cert. · d. cert.

Archives Bodl. Oxf. | Bedford high school, Bedford · E. F. Benson Society, London · Friends of the Girls' Public Day School Trust, London

Likenesses portrait, repro. in K. M. Westaway, ed., *A history of Bedford High School*, 1 (1932), facing p. 23 · portrait, Bedford high school [*see illus.*]

Wealth at death £1482 15s. 1d.: administration, 31 March 1883, *CGPLA Eng. & Wales*

Benson, Arthur Christopher (1862–1925), writer and university teacher, was born on 24 April 1862 at Wellington College, the son of Edward White *Benson (1829–1896), first headmaster of the college and later archbishop of Canterbury, and his wife, Mary, *née* Sidgwick (1841–1918). He was the brother of Edward Frederic *Benson, Robert Hugh *Benson, Mary Eleanor *Benson, and Margaret *Benson. In 1874 he won a scholarship to Eton College from Temple Grove, a preparatory school in East Sheen; in 1881 he went on to King's College, Cambridge, where he was a scholar and took a first in the classical tripos in 1884.

The formative influences upon Benson were essentially ecclesiastical. Between the ages of ten and twenty-one his home was in the cathedral close, first at Lincoln and then at Truro. He retained a love of church music and ceremony, and although his Christianity became theologically liberal and distinctly unorthodox, he remained definitely 'on the side of the things it stands for' (*Diary*, ed. Lubbock, 1913, 139.52). Having an archbishop for a father sharpened the sense that he ought to achieve something in life. But

Arthur Christopher Benson (1862–1925), by Sir William Nicholson, 1924

what? He returned to Eton as a master in 1885, a post he was to hold for eighteen years, yet despite his obvious success at schoolmastering he had no real interest in it, and was largely bored by the grind of classical teaching and the dominance of the games ethos. Even the compensation that he found in being surrounded by attractive boys was marred by his consciousness of their propensity for masturbation: a dreaded and disastrous 'moral evil', deeply troubling to him, 'the dark shadow on the life of a schoolmaster, his most anxious and saddest preoccupation' (A. C. Benson, *The Schoolmaster: a Commentary*, 1902, 1908, 148–9).

Benson nurtured, however, a real ambition for a literary career, and began by writing poetry. He completed an impressive two-decker biography of his father in 1899, and throughout his life he wrote or edited upwards of sixty books. These included relatively serious literary studies of Rossetti, Fitzgerald, and Pater (between 1904 and 1906), but his output mostly consisted of essays, quietly reflective and homiletic, and quasi-autobiographical stories, popular with a genteel, middle-class readership. They were the kind of books which got bad reviews but made him a lot of money, books happily and obsessively churned out between tea and dinner—'a thousand pages in his sight / were but an evening gone' (Benson, *Final Edition*, 24). Such titles as *The House of Quiet* (1904), *From a College Window* (1906), and *Beside Still Waters* (1907) speak for themselves. Benson himself acknowledged their essential vapidity ('sauce without meat'). The complacent fluency, daintiness, and over-written tepid sentiment lent themselves easily to parody, most notably in Max Beerbohm's 'Out of Harm's Way' (*A Christmas Garland*, 1912, 21–30); but *At a Safe Distance* was also tellingly suggested as a possible future title.

Meanwhile, as a result of Queen Victoria's understandable indifference to Alfred Austin, Benson became an unofficial laureate of the court at Windsor. This led to the writing of the famous words of 'Land of Hope and Glory' as a coronation ode for King Edward VII in 1902, fitted to what Benson called Elgar's 'wizard-like music' (*Diary*, ed. Lubbock, 1902, 19.157). He became a fellow of Magdalene College, Cambridge in 1904, his court connections having enabled him to retire from Eton to Cambridge on appointment as joint editor (with the second Viscount Esher) of the first three volumes of *The Letters of Queen Victoria, 1837–1861*, which appeared in 1907.

In appearance Benson was a tall, upright figure of considerable bulk (weighing 16 stone when he was sixty), with shaggy fair hair going grey, a ruddy complexion, a heavy moustache, blue eyes, and bushy eyebrows. He was, in his own description, 'like the cornet-player of a German Band'. Invariably he dressed in grey flannel with a double-breasted jacket. He loved to observe life, but was a reluctant participator. He could feel warm affection for boys and young men (among them George Mallory and Dadie Rylands), but was totally unable to come to terms with physical intimacy of any kind. This fastidious self-withholding apparently precipitated a nervous breakdown as an undergraduate (November 1882), when a chastely loved schoolfriend gave in to 'immorality' with someone else, and ruined Benson's relationship with him. He never married; in fact, he never even contemplated it. 'My own emotions do not scorch,' he wrote, 'they merely shine and ripple like the waters of a lake' (*Diary*, ed. Lubbock, 1907, 94.15–16). And: 'I don't want to claim or to be claimed—I want nothing but a cordial camaraderie—and thus a whole range of [sexual] problems mean nothing to me' (ibid., 1916, 159.45). In any case: 'the Head of a College can hardly hope to inspire undergrads with romantic passion' (ibid., 1924, 175.26). So he concentrated on entertaining the young men to lunch, talking amusingly, and perhaps taking them for a cycle ride afterwards.

The real love affair of Benson's life was with Magdalene College, where after eight years he became president in 1912 and master in December 1915, a post he held until his death. The college was at a very low ebb indeed when he joined it (at the invitation of his old colleague S. A. Donaldson, who had just been appointed master). But he rapidly supplied the courageous inspiration and the generous benefactions needed to brighten and improve it, to establish indeed a 'New Magdalene'. 'He built, he adorned, he financed and he reigned' (Benson, *Final Edition*, 126). He was helped crucially by gifts totalling over £60,000 from an American admirer living in Switzerland, Mme de Nottbeck. Benson promoted lively and genial teaching, his most notable protégé being I. A. Richards. He encouraged 'modern' subjects, not only English and history, but science, archaeology, and music. He also widened the range of school connections, and supplied good sense and forward-looking understanding to governing body debate. Above all, he was friendly and helpful towards a large proportion of the undergraduates. As master he was kindly, benevolent, and richly humoured, certainly, but he was also radical, analytical, combative, egotistical, and despotic. In short, he was a figure quite unrecognizable from most of his writings. As he himself put it, 'in my books I am solemn, sweet, refined; in real life I am rather

vehement, sharp, contemptuous, a busy mocker' (*Diary*, ed. Lubbock, 1913, 142.31).

If, on the whole, Benson could hold these two aspects of personality together—the quietistic scribbler and the activating leader, the generously companionable but finally unapproachable man—there was a price to pay. Twice (in 1907–8 and 1917–22) he descended into prolonged and terrible depression, diagnosed as neurasthenia. He struggled to make sense of it in his diary, but even his facility with words was eventually crushed by the enervating, baffling unintelligibility of it all (*Diary*, ed. Lubbock, 1917, 166.48).

Benson died in the Old Lodge at Magdalene on 17 June 1925 and was buried at St Giles's cemetery, Huntingdon Road, Cambridge. Of all of his writings, it is his diary which may give him enduring significance. Begun in 1897 when he was thirty-five years old, it is well over 4 million words long, and runs to 180 volumes. Two edited selections have appeared—Percy Lubbock's a year after Benson's death, and, more recently, David Newsome's in 1981. The diary remains an important document for understanding late Victorian (public) schoolmastering, the Edwardian literary scene, and Cambridge in the first quarter of the twentieth century. Benson was one of the most charismatic, intelligent, and culturally influential dons Cambridge has ever seen.   R. Hyam

Sources D. Newsome, *On the edge of paradise: A. C. Benson, the diarist* (1980) · E. H. Ryle, *Arthur Christopher Benson: as seen by some friends* (1925) · P. Cunich and others, *A history of Magdalene College, Cambridge, 1428–1988* (1994) · *The diary of Arthur Christopher Benson*, ed. P. Lubbock (1926) · F. McD. C. Turner, *A. C. Benson* (1992) · E. F. Benson, *Final edition: informal autobiography* (1940) · D. Newsome, ed., *Edwardian excursions: from the diaries of A. C. Benson, 1898–1904* (1981) · R. Hyam, 'A. C. Benson: on the edge of hell?', *Cambridge Review* (5 Dec 1980), 56–9 [review article] · private information (2004) · *DNB*

Archives Bodl. Oxf., corresp. and literary MSS · Borth. Inst., corresp. · CUL, corresp. and MSS · Harvard U., Houghton L., corresp. and literary papers · Magd. Cam., diaries and MSS · Magd. Cam., corresp. · University of Iowa Libraries, Iowa City, special collections, corresp. and MSS | BL, corresp. with Sir Sidney Cockerell, Add. MS 52705 · BL, letters to Mary Gladstone, Add. MS 46244 · BL, letters to W. E. Gladstone, Add. MSS 44502–44525 · BL, corresp. with Macmillans, Add. MSS 55021–55022 · BL, letters to Charles E. Sayle, Add. MS 51290 · Bodl. Oxf., letters to Lewis Harcourt · Borth. Inst., corresp. with Lord Halifax · CAC Cam., corresp. with Lord Esher · Elgar Birthplace Museum, Worcester, corresp. with Sir Edward Elgar · JRL, letters to Charles Fairfax Murray · King's AC Cam., letters to Oscar Browning · King's AC Cam., letters to G. H. W. Rylands · King's AC Cam., letters to W. J. H. Sprott, MAC · LPL, letters to E. W. Benson · LPL, corresp. with Randall Thomas Davidson · LPL, letters to J. A. L. Riley · LUL, letters to Austin Dobson · Magd. Cam., letters to Geoffrey Madan · NA Scot., corresp. with H. W. Hope · Ransom HRC, corresp. with John Lane · Royal Society of Literature, London, corresp. with Royal Society of Literature · Society for Psychical Research, London, corresp. with Sir Oliver Lodge · Trinity Cam., letters to Sir Henry Babington Smith · U. Durham L., archives and special collections, letters to Sir Harold MacMichael · U. Leeds, Brotherton L., letters to Edmund Gosse · U. Sussex Library, special collections, letters to Kingsley Martin · W. Sussex RO, letters to L. J. Maxse

Likenesses M. Beerbohm, cartoon, 1908, Magd. Cam. · R. E. Fuller Maitland, oils, 1911, Magd. Cam. · Vandyk, photograph, *c*.1911, NPG · W. Nicholson, oils, 1924, FM Cam. [*see illus.*] · H. Abbot, group portrait, photograph (with his brothers Edward Frederic Benson and Robert Hugh Benson), NPG; *see illus.* in Benson, Robert Hugh (1871–1914) · Spy [L. Ward], lithograph caricature, NPG; repro. in *VF* (4 June 1903) · memorial roundel (south transept window), Rye parish church, East Sussex

Wealth at death £112,440 10s. 7d.: probate, 11 July 1925, *CGPLA Eng. & Wales*

Benson, Christopher (1788–1868), Church of England clergyman, was born on 16 January 1788, at Cockermouth, the son of Thomas Benson, solicitor. He went to Eton College and then in 1804 obtained a scholarship at Trinity College, Cambridge, where he took his BA degree in 1809 and his MA in 1815. After being ordained he spent some years as a curate at St John's, Newcastle upon Tyne, and St Giles-in-the-Fields, London. In 1817 he was select preacher at Cambridge, and delivered a course of sermons on baptism, which he subsequently printed; two years later he published *A Chronology of our Saviour's Life*. Benson rapidly earned a high reputation as a preacher, and in 1820 he was selected as the first lecturer under John Hulse's bequest at Cambridge. Benson's lectures, which were dedicated to the masters of Downing and St John's colleges, went through many editions, and he was again appointed in 1822. The second volume is dedicated to Granville Hastings Wheler, of Otterden Park, Kent, heir to the munificent Lady Betty Hastings, who had presented Benson to the vicarage of Ledsham in 1822. In the meantime he had been elected fellow of Magdalene College, Cambridge, and in 1825 he became canon of Worcester, holding the canonry until his death. He successively held the livings of Lindridge and Cropthorne, and was from 1827 to 1845 master of the Temple.

Benson belonged to the broader evangelical school, and a series of 'Discourses upon tradition and episcopacy', preached in the Temple Church in 1839, criticized the views of the Oxford Tractarians—a term which Benson seems to have been one of the first to attach to Pusey, Newman, and their friends. These discourses (afterwards published), in which he argued against the apostolical authority of the Fathers, and condemned the prominence assigned to tradition, led him into a controversy with the Revd F. Merewether, then rector of Cole Orton. He published a number of other theological works. Benson died on 25 March 1868 at Woodfield, Ross, Herefordshire, and was survived by his wife, Bertha Maria. He is to be distinguished from his namesake who attended Queen's College, Oxford, and was vicar of Brampton.

LEWIS SERGEANT, *rev.* H. C. G. MATTHEW

Sources Venn, *Alum. Cant.* · Boase, *Mod. Eng. biog.*
Archives Inner Temple, London, papers · LPL, letters | LPL, corresp. with William Howley
Likenesses etching, NPG · oils, Inner Temple, London
Wealth at death under £30,000: probate, 27 May 1868, *CGPLA Eng. & Wales*

Benson, (Gertrude) Constance, Lady Benson (1864–1946). *See under* Benson, Sir Francis Robert (1858–1939).

Benson, Edward Frederic (1867–1940), novelist, was born at Wellington College on 24 July 1867. He was the third son of Edward White *Benson (1829–1896), headmaster of Wellington College and subsequently archbishop of Canterbury, and his wife, Mary Sidgwick (1841–1918). He was a younger brother of Arthur Christopher *Benson (1862–1925), Mary Eleanor *Benson (1863–1890), and Margaret *Benson (1865–1916), and an elder brother of Robert Hugh *Benson (1871–1914). He was educated at Temple Grove School, Sheen, at Marlborough College, and at King's College, Cambridge, where he was exhibitioner (1888) and scholar (1890), and secured first classes in both parts of the classical tripos (1890, 1891). His first book, *Sketches from Marlborough*, was published while he was at Cambridge.

Benson worked in Athens for the British School of Archaeology (1892–5) and in Egypt for the Society for the Promotion of Hellenic Studies (1895). His first novel, *Dodo*, was published in 1893 and was a runaway success. From 1895 to 1918 he lived in London and devoted himself to writing, much of his work being published in fashionable magazines. From 1918 he lived for the greater part of each year at Lamb House, Rye, Sussex, which had been the home of Henry James.

Benson described himself as uncontrollably prolific: he published at least ninety-three books, excluding collaborations. Benson's writings fall into three groups: novels of social satire, reminiscences, and horror stories. Most famous among his social satires are the novels of manners, especially the 'Mapp and Lucia' novels, which include *Queen Lucia* (1920), *Lucia in London* (1927), and *Miss Mapp* (1922); they are set both in London and in 'Tilling', a fictionalized Rye, and are said to be *romans-à-clef* (as also are the *Dodo* novels, where Dodo is believed to be a portrait of Margot Tennant, later Lady Oxford). These novels remain witty and penetrating social studies. A BBC dramatization, entitled *Mapp and Lucia*, combined with an omnibus publication of the complete novels, entitled *Make Way for Lucia* (1977; 1986), revived interest in Benson's work, and increased his popularity with a wider audience. Another group of his social satires deals with university life, examples being, *The Babe, BA* (1897), *David Blaize* (1916), and *Colin II* (1925); these novels are less successful.

Benson's books of reminiscences, such as *As we were* (1930), *As we are* (1932), and *Final Edition* (1940), have value as sources for social history and personal anecdote, as he excelled in creating vivid pictures of the atmosphere of the times, and this was a quality also displayed in his biographical studies of Edward VII and Queen Victoria. In one of his books of family recollections Benson claims for himself a retentive, observational memory, even of things hardly noted at the time; and this was perhaps his most remarkable quality, displayed in his non-fiction and fiction alike. His stories of horror and the supernatural have remained consistently popular. Early horror novels, such as *The Luck of the Vails* (1901), and *The Room in the Tower* (1912), are characterized by lavish descriptions and psychological tension. *Visible and Invisible* (1923), *Spook Stories* (1928), and *More Spook Stories* (1934) are more coldly unemotional excursions into the realm of ghosts and marvels.

Benson never married and many of his novels suggest that he had a generalized dislike of women. He lived alone in Rye and continued writing until his death. He was mayor of Rye from 1934 to 1937 and a JP. He was elected an honorary fellow of Magdalene College, Cambridge, in 1938 and was appointed OBE. He died in University College Hospital, London, on 29 February 1940, and was buried in the Rye cemetery after a funeral conducted by the bishop of Chichester. The E. F. Benson Society was founded in London in 1984, and publishes a journal, *The Dodo*, semi-annually. SAYONI BASU

Sources E. F. Benson, *Final edition: informal autobiography* (1940) · *The Times* (1 March 1940) · *TLS* (9 March 1940) · J. Aiken, foreword, in *The collected ghost stories of E. F. Benson*, ed. R. Dalby (1992) · J. Adrian, 'Introduction', in E. F. Benson, *Desirable residences* (1992) · H. Vickers, 'Introduction', in E. F. Benson, *Final edition* (1988) · B. Masters, *The life of E. F. Benson* (1991) · R. F. Kiernan, *Frivolity unbound: six masters of the camp novel* (1990) · A. Downend, 'Benson, E. F., 1867–1940', *The 1890s: an encyclopedia of British literature, art, and culture*, ed. G. A. Cevasco (1993) · D. Newsome, *On the edge of paradise: A. C. Benson, the diarist* (1980) · DNB
Archives Bodl. Oxf., corresp. and literary papers · NRA, corresp. and literary papers · U. Cal., Los Angeles, corresp. and literary papers | BL, corresp. with Society of Authors, Add. MS 56669 · Bodl. Oxf., letters to members of the Lewis family, papers · U. Reading L., corresp. with the Bodley Head Ltd
Likenesses H. Coster, photographs, c.1936, NPG · H. Abbott, group portrait, photograph (with his brothers Arthur Christopher Benson and Robert Hugh Benson), NPG; *see illus. in* Benson, Robert Hugh (1871–1914)
Wealth at death £79,382 18s. 3d.: probate, 17 May 1940, CGPLA Eng. & Wales

Edward White Benson (1829–1896), by Sir Hubert von Herkomer, 1890

Benson, Edward White (1829–1896), archbishop of Canterbury, was born on 14 July 1829 at 72 Lombard Street, Birmingham, the eldest of the eight children of Edward White Benson (1800–1843), chemical engineer and manufacturer, and his wife, Harriet Baker (d. 1850). His father was a strong evangelical with Yorkshire roots and his mother, from a Manchester Unitarian family, had converted to the Church of England before their marriage in August 1826. Benson was baptized on 31 March 1830 in St Martin's Church, Birmingham. When his father became manager of the British Alkali Works at Stoke, near Droitwich, the family moved first to Ivy Cottage in Wychbold and later to Brook House, nearer the factory. The failure of the business in 1842 proved a great strain on his father's health and he died the following year. The business partners gave his widow an annuity, as well as a small house within the deserted factory on Birmingham Heath.

Education and early career, 1840–1858 In 1840 Benson entered King Edward's School, Birmingham, under the chief mastership of James Prince Lee, for whom he quickly developed what he called a 'perfectness of affection', and whose influence, particularly in the close textual study of the classics, was vital in his intellectual formation. At school he met J. B. Lightfoot, who became a lifelong friend; both boys were intellectually precocious and spent much time discussing theology. He developed a keen interest in liturgy and ritual, which he retained for the rest of his life and which shaped his religion, this being, according to his son, 'not mystical, but of a disciplinary and liturgical type' (Benson, *Trefoil*, 253). In 1845 one

of Benson's father's partners offered to take him into business, whereupon his mother asked the advice of William Jackson, his father's half-brother and fellow of Worcester College, Oxford, who offered, together with his mother's brother, J. B. Sidgwick, to pay the school expenses.

After a holiday tutorship in Scotland, Benson entered Trinity College, Cambridge, in October 1849, having been elected to a sub-sizarship, but was forced to live in conditions of relative poverty. Lightfoot had entered Trinity the previous year and fell under the influence of B. F. Westcott, whom he and Benson had known as a senior boy at King Edward's. In his second year at Cambridge, Benson also became a private pupil of Westcott's, and this developed into a close and lasting friendship. It has been suggested by Hinchliff (*God and History*, chap. 7) that this 'triumvirate' was one of the most creative and influential partnerships in late nineteenth century religious life. In May 1850 Benson's eldest sister died of typhus fever in Birmingham, and on his return home he found his mother also dead. This left him virtually penniless, but again relatives came to his help and he was supported through Cambridge by William Jackson as well as by his cousin, Christopher Sidgwick. On returning to Trinity he was befriended by the bursar, Francis Martin, who soon became a friend and benefactor to the whole family. Benson's Cambridge career was characterized by scholarly and liturgical seriousness, although he displayed a lighter side, founding the Ghostlie Guild (later Psychical Society) with Lightfoot, Westcott, and F. J. A. Hort. Although he never achieved the highest academic honours, lacking the originality of his closest friends, he nevertheless won a silver cup in 1851 for a speech on George Herbert, came out senior optime in mathematics, was placed eighth in the classical tripos, and won the senior chancellor's medal.

In the autumn of 1852 Benson was offered a part-time mastership at Rugby School by E. M. Goulburn, which would allow sufficient leisure to read for a fellowship at Trinity. He accepted, and shortly after his appointment lodged with his cousin, Mary Sidgwick, who was looking after his younger sister, Ada *Benson. Among her own children were Henry, who became professor of moral philosophy at Cambridge, and Mary (known as Minnie; 1841–1918), who, although only twelve years old, he vowed to marry. They announced their engagement on her seventeenth birthday in 1858 and were married by Frederick Temple, headmaster of Rugby from 1857, on 23 June 1859 in Rugby church. Temple became a close friend, and sponsor to the first of their six remarkable children. Mary became Benson's most trusted confidante, as well as a support through his frequent periods of depression, although from her own private account it appears that she was a victim of frequent bullying and remained afraid of Benson throughout their marriage. While he felt in constant need of love and affirmation he found it difficult to express his feelings publicly, and both his wife and his children found him austere and distant. Writing of his parents, A. C. Benson 'wondered if they ever *really* loved. Certainly I never remember them seeking each other's company or wanting to be alone together' (Newsome, *Paradise*, 15).

In 1852 Benson took the fellowship examination at Trinity, but was placed behind Lightfoot and Hort and failed to get elected. The following year he was successful, although he never took up residence. He took his MA in 1853, his BD in 1862, and his DD in 1867. Later in his life he was select preacher at Cambridge on six occasions and at Oxford twice. He was ordained deacon by letters dimissory from the bishop of Ely on 9 January 1854 in Bury church by Prince Lee, who had become the first bishop of Manchester. It was at this time that he made his first serious theological studies, publishing two articles on Hippolytus and beginning his reading of Cyprian, which was to occupy him for the rest of his life. In 1857 he was ordained priest at Ely, and in the same year he was offered a lectureship at Trinity, although he declined, chiefly because it would have meant deferring his marriage. Earlier A. P. Stanley had tried to press Benson's name as the 'best Cambridge man of fit age and the like' (Davidson and Benham, 1.207) for the post of domestic chaplain to A. C. Tait, who had just been appointed to London, although he was not chosen. However, in 1858, on Temple's recommendation, Benson was appointed by Prince Albert to the headmastership of Wellington College, which had been established to perpetuate the memory of the duke of Wellington. At the prince's desire he toured Germany to survey continental methods of education.

Wellington and Lincoln, 1858–1877 Although the school was set up to offer almost gratuitous education to the orphans of army officers, Benson succeeded in creating one of the great public schools of England, his 'seminary of sound learning and religious education' (Benson, *Life*, 1.163) inspired by the example of Thomas Arnold. Benson fought hard battles, both over finances and over the improvement of academic standards (pressing hard for the study of classics and university entrance), and he also devoted considerable energy to his work in the chapel, preaching sermons every Sunday, many of which were published in *Boy Life, its Trials, its Strength, its Fulness* (1874). Although no ritualist, he paid the finest attention to liturgical detail and translated many ancient hymns in the rather idiosyncratic hymn book. It was at Wellington, too, that he developed his rigorous regime of work, relying on less than six hours' sleep. He appears to have inherited something of his father's puritanism, which led him to despise 'irresponsible enjoyment as tending to relax the moral fibre' (Benson, *Trefoil*, 58). Throughout his life he found it nearly impossible to relax and he had an almost pathological dislike of waste, as his son, Arthur, commented: 'He would have liked to be comfortable, but didn't know how—his fear of waste was so strong' (Newsome, *Paradise*, 16). As a schoolmaster, although he was respected by many of his pupils both at Rugby and Wellington, he ruled largely by fear, frequently displaying a lack of self-control, particularly during periods of depression, which could lead to undue severity in punishment. One of his pupils wrote in 1864: 'We thought we hated him, because he had a violent temper; he would turn perfectly white sometimes when flogging a boy; and we thought he toadied to people of title' (Newsome, *Wellington College*, 158). However, it was at Wellington that Benson learned self-control, and in later life his depression manifested itself in self-reproach and a feeling of deep inadequacy.

Benson's success at Wellington as well as in his subsequent career depended to a great degree on help from his wide network of friends, many of whom were of quite different opinions. He spent much time, for instance, with Charles Kingsley, rector of nearby Eversley. In 1866 Benson appointed John Wordsworth as a sixth-form master, and got to know his father, Christopher, then archdeacon of Westminster. They soon became close friends. C. W. Penny, Benson's colleague at Wellington, considered this to be the first step on Benson's rapid rise to Canterbury. On becoming bishop of Lincoln in 1869 Christopher Wordsworth appointed Benson as an examining chaplain; he preached at Wordsworth's first ordination and in July 1870 he was installed as prebendary of Heydour-cum-Walton. He meanwhile formed a friendship with Wordsworth's daughter Elizabeth. Temple's appointment as bishop of Exeter caused a storm throughout the church because of his earlier contribution to *Essays and Reviews*. Although Wordsworth led the opposition, Benson came to the defence of his friend, writing a weighty letter to *The Times* on 22 October 1869. At the same time he wrote to Wordsworth offering to resign his examining chaplaincy. Wordsworth threw the letter in the fire and within months Temple had also appointed Benson as an examining chaplain. The year 1871 had proved a particularly difficult one for Benson at Wellington and he vowed to move on. Following the death of Francis Massingberd he was offered the chancellorship of Lincoln Cathedral and was installed on 28 December 1872.

The move to the medieval chancellery soon led Benson into a deep depression. He escaped through frenetic activity, which included the founding and endowment of a theological college, the Cancellari Scholae. He also started night schools for mechanics from neighbouring villages and introduced Lenten lectures. He reintroduced daily matins in a restored chapel in the cathedral. His establishment of a society for mission priests, under the title Novate Novale, led to a general mission in Lincoln in 1876, which proved 'a real epoch in his life' (Benson, *Life*, 1.379). While at Lincoln he declined the offers of the Hulsean professorship at Cambridge in 1875 and the bishopric of Calcutta in 1876, though with much soul-searching. He became an honorary chaplain to the queen in 1873, and from 1875 to 1877 was a chaplain-in-ordinary.

Bishop of Truro, 1877–1883 On 15 December 1876 an order in council had created the new diocese of Truro, which comprised the archdeaconry of Cornwall of the diocese of Exeter. After some deliberation Benson accepted Disraeli's offer of the bishopric and was consecrated at St Paul's on 25 April 1877, having been presented by Wordsworth and Temple together. He was enthroned in St Mary's Church, Truro, on 1 May 1877. His immediate task was to establish an identity for the diocese. To this end he brought with him A. J. Mason, as diocesan missioner, and G. H. Whitaker, who was given the role of establishing a theological college. No episcopal palace had been provided, but Benson was able to convert Kenwyn vicarage, near Truro, for the purpose, giving it the Cornish name Lis Escop ('bishop's court'). Such quaint antiquarianism characterized Benson's episcopate, and later he gave each of the canons' stalls the title of a Cornish saint. He devoted considerable energy to the study of Cornwall's Celtic tradition as well as its more recent history of nonconformity. He also applied his genius for construction, founding a girls' school (in part under the influence of his sister Ada, a pioneer of the girls' high school movement), organizing the Sunday school work of the diocese, and ensuring the continued success of the diocesan conference which had been established by Temple. After the conference of 1877 a committee was set up to look into the question of a cathedral for the diocese, and by 1880 work had begun on building the first new English cathedral since the Reformation on the site of (and incorporating parts of) St Mary's Church. As archbishop, Benson was to consecrate the cathedral on 3 November 1887.

Throughout his life Benson was always more at home in ecclesiastical matters than in affairs of state, and he devoted extraordinary energy to the seeming minutiae of liturgy, history, or even dress. It was said by many that he looked the part of a bishop, dressed to perfection in a linen rochet copied from a Holbein picture. At Truro he devised the service of nine lessons and carols, and worked hard at liturgies for special occasions. He took pains over the pastoral care of his often badly endowed and demoralized clergy, at one point taking a six-week holiday duty at

Davidstowe (his longest period as a parish priest). He found the building up of a new diocese immensely satisfying, and his diaries are far less introspective during this period. However, although relatively happy he continued to suffer from fits of depression, which were exacerbated in February 1878 by the death from meningitis of his eldest son, Martin, a brilliant scholar at Winchester. He never fully came to understand this death and on his sixtieth birthday he still felt 'inexplicable grief' every day: 'to see into that will be worth dying' (Benson, *Life*, 2.268).

Benson did not have a seat in the House of Lords while at Truro, his wider church involvement being limited to convocation and to membership of the ecclesiastical courts commission, to which he was appointed by Archbishop Tait in 1881. The commission's report, published in 1885, concluded, largely through the researches of William Stubbs, bishop of Oxford, that the archbishop or bishop could sit in judgment upon ritual or doctrinal matters, a finding which Benson was later to put into practice. While in London he stayed at Lambeth Palace, and it was here that he was recognized by Tait as being a possible successor, a man who 'will come forward and do a great work' (Davidson and Benham, 2.592).

Archbishop of Canterbury, 1883–1896 At the death of Tait on 3 December 1882 there was no natural successor among the senior bishops. It seems that the queen's advice to appoint Benson (who had been close to the prince consort) was followed by Gladstone, who, having previously sounded out R. W. Church, dean of St Paul's, offered him the primacy on 16 December. Since Benson was known to be a tory, the appointment was censured by some in the Liberal Party. Gladstone defended himself by claiming that Benson's decision to go specially to Cambridge to vote for the Conservative candidate the month before Tait's death proved that he was not interested in worldly power, and furthermore his time at Truro had shown that he was primarily interested in ecclesiastical rather than political affairs. Gladstone also thought it important to have a young man as archbishop because of the many challenges faced by the church. Benson's appointment was confirmed in Bow church on 3 March 1883, and he was enthroned in Canterbury Cathedral on 29 March. He retained R. T. Davidson, Tait's son-in-law, as his chaplain. Davidson became a close friend and confidant, especially over questions of preferment.

In the House of Lords, Benson worked closely with Chancellor Lewis Dibdin, pressing for bills to reform patronage as well as to make it easier to remove incumbents from livings. It was not until after his death, however, that these measures were passed by parliament. His most important reform in the organization of the church was the setting up of a house of laymen, which first met on 16 February 1886 and which paved the way for more complete synodical government. His trust in an increasingly educated population to make their own decisions was also displayed in the secular sphere, and on occasion he entered directly into the political debate. In an influential and controversial speech delivered in the House of Lords on 8 July 1884 in favour of the extension of the franchise, which Gladstone described as 'an historical event' (Gladstone to Benson, 9 July 1884; Gladstone, *Diaries*, 11.172), Benson claimed that it was vital to 'elevate the people', since it encouraged 'the principle of independence upon which so much of progress depended' (*Hansard 3*, 290, 1884, 442–3). Similarly, in 1893 he supported the creation of parish councils.

Although Benson had published many volumes of sermons and had a reputation as a lively and inspiring preacher, he was far less confident in public speaking. He was overawed by the House of Lords, and his parliamentary performance was characterized by an unsubtle nervousness stemming from a fear of criticism and conflict. While he came across as publicly affable and witty he also demanded unquestioning obedience and deference. His son remarked that no one was 'ever wholly at ease with him, because he could not stand aside and watch tolerantly another mind working on different lines from himself' (Benson, *Trefoil*, 256). As archbishop he spent as much time as he could at Addington Palace, near Croydon, and regularly attended worship and preached in the parish church. It was here that he suffered his deepest depressions and periods of self-doubt, and frequently sought refuge in study, returning to his book on Cyprian as often as possible. He also used his remarkably outspoken diary as a safety valve. At Lambeth, however, where he was more fully involved in the business of state, he was far less often ill or depressed.

In the years following 1884 Benson was involved in refounding the mission to the Eastern churches, and in his primary charge (*The Seven Gifts*) to his diocese in 1885 he enunciated his principles for 'missions of maintenance', and he urged his missionaries A. J. Maclean and W. H. Browne to do everything within their power to build up existing churches rather than to absorb them into the Church of England. His general approach to mission elsewhere, as exemplified in his many sermons and addresses to missionary societies, was to build up 'native' churches rather than to transplant Englishness abroad. In reconstituting the bishopric of Jerusalem in 1887, a move which provoked a vigorous reaction from Henry Liddon, he was also careful not to be seen to be making any efforts at proselytizing Orthodox Christians. In 1888 he gave the inaugural address to the third Lambeth conference, where cultural differences were discussed (for instance over the question of polygamy). He was clear, however, that the conference was in no sense competent to make decisions for the whole of the Anglican communion. He was keen on establishing new missions (such as that in Korea) and also saw his role as a mediator in helping solve schism in colonial churches, especially that in Natal, which was sharpened after the death of J. W. Colenso.

One event that shook Benson's whole archiepiscopate and which perhaps gave him more notoriety than anything else was the trial of Edward King, bishop of Lincoln. King had been accused of ritualism in 1887, and a petition was presented to the archbishop by the Church Association on 2 June 1888. In response Benson revived the archiepiscopal court (which was itself of dubious authority, having sat only once since the Reformation). Stubbs, who acted as one of five episcopal advisers, considered that it was not a court but 'an archbishop sitting in his library' (W. H. Hutton, *William Stubbs*, 1906, 210). Nevertheless the judicial committee of the House of Lords felt he had the jurisdiction, and the case opened on 12 February 1889. The process was long and drawn out, the bulk of the evidence being heard a year later. The archbishop reserved his judgment on 25 February 1890 and set about detailed research into the history of liturgy, apparently convinced that the antiquity of a practice would prove its legitimacy. Judgment was postponed because of the death of his eldest daughter, Nelly [*see* Benson, Mary Eleanor], and was eventually given on 21 November 1890 and found generally in favour of King. With the exception of the mixed chalice and the sign of the cross at blessing and absolution, all the other practices (such as facing east during the prayer of consecration or the singing of the Agnus Dei) were permitted. The judgment was favourably regarded by the Anglo-Catholic *Church Times* as making 'considerable progress in the acceptance of Catholic truth', and Dean Church regarded it as the 'most courageous thing that has come from Lambeth for the last two hundred years' (R. W. Church, *Life and Letters of Dean Church*, ed. M. C. Church, 1895, 349). The decision was upheld by the judicial committee the following year.

Benson's own position with regard to ritual, however, is difficult to gauge. He seems to have had a profound respect for symbolism (to the extent of inviting the freemasons to the laying of the foundation-stone of Truro Cathedral), but felt it improper to mimic the ways of any other church. Here as elsewhere he adopted the principle of 'elasticity', which exasperated many of his contemporaries. He said of himself while at Wellington: 'I am myself neither High, nor Low, nor Broad Church, though I hear myself consigned by turns to all—as often to one as to another' (Benson, *Life*, 1.179).

Benson was convinced of the importance of establishment, and in 1891 he spoke on the subject at the church congress at Rhyl, when Welsh disestablishment was becoming a live issue after its formal adoption by the Liberal Party in the February of that year. By 1893 matters were growing more pressing with a suspensory bill having been brought before parliament, which would pave the way for disestablishment. He organized and chaired a large meeting held in the Albert Hall, London, on 16 May 1893 in defence of the national church, and addressed it in passionate terms, resting his case on the recent revival of the established church in Wales and its achievements in the fields of education and pastoral duty. A year later, on 17 May 1894, the bishops issued a manifesto against the suspensory bill which attacked the 'dismemberment' of the Church of England. Concerted opposition in Wales was organized by A. G. Edwards of St Asaph and John Owen of St David's. The Disestablishment Bill fell with the Liberal government in 1895.

Benson's opinion of the Roman Catholic church appears to have been affected both by his study of Cyprian and by his idea that the Church of England should be free from any outside influence, a point he emphasized in his first visitation charge. In 1894, however, he was approached by the French priest Fernand Portal, a friend of Lord Halifax, who had made a study of Anglican orders. After an initial informal interview at Addington, Portal was received by Pope Leo XIII, who appeared anxious to write to the English archbishops. As a cautious preliminary he urged his secretary of state, Cardinal Rampolla, to write privately to Benson, the letter being conveyed personally by Halifax and Portal to Benson on 28 September 1894. Benson was unsympathetic to the general drift of the letter, his major objection resting in the matter of the royal supremacy, as well as Portal's one-sided observations of English church life. His suspicions had earlier been aroused by Cardinal Vaughan's speech, delivered shortly before the interview, which called for unqualified submission to the pope before any possibility of reconciliation. Benson's reaction caused Halifax profound dismay, and a different response could possibly have affected the constitution of the Vatican commission on Anglican orders, which in the end was composed solely of Roman theologians. The encyclical 'Satis cognitum' was issued on 29 June 1896 and was followed by the bull *Apostolicae curae* on 13 September, which declared Anglican orders utterly null and void.

Benson made his initial response during his short but energetic tour of Ireland, where he claimed the bull was 'a new instance to-day of defiance of history perfectly in accord with all we knew of Rome' (Benson, *Life*, 2.623). On his journey back to England he set about work on a reasoned reply, in which he defended the catholicity of Anglican orders. Breaking his journey at Hawarden on 10 October 1896 he discussed the matter with Gladstone for three hours. The following morning, 11 October 1896, he attended the early celebration of holy communion in Hawarden parish church, returning later for morning prayer, where he died of heart failure during the confession. His body was conveyed to Canterbury on 14 October, where the funeral was held on 16 October, the first archbishop to be buried in his own cathedral since Pole. His wife and four of their children, Arthur Christopher *Benson, Edward Frederic *Benson, Margaret *Benson, and Robert Hugh *Benson, survived him. He left a completed manuscript of *Cyprian: his Life, his Times, his Work*, which was published the following year, and in 1900 his notes for *The Apocalypse* (1900) were worked into a book by his daughter, Margaret.

Assessment Benson was undoubtedly a child of his time, displaying, like many of his friends, an extraordinary faith in the power of education to help men and women reach mature judgements. Similarly, like his lifelong friends Westcott and Lightfoot, he placed his trust in the authority of antiquity, and often sought refuge in detailed historical scholarship, which may perhaps have led to an ecclesiasticism which evaded some of the pressing social, religious, and economic problems of the time. Though by nature conservative in his opinions, he nevertheless sought to extend the popular voice in church and state. In

his dealings with the churches of the Anglican communion he was in part responsible for laying the foundations for the development of the principle of provincial autonomy, first formulated by his beloved Cyprian, which ensured that each province could respond distinctively to its specific cultural needs. In his personal life Benson found it difficult to express his emotions and display affection, and he was subject to violent mood swings and extended periods of depression. His portraits show a Victorian gentleman with long white hair and staring eyes.

MARK D. CHAPMAN

Sources A. C. Benson, *The life of Edward White Benson*, 2 vols. (1900) · J. A. Carr, *The life-work of Edward White Benson* (1898) · A. C. Benson, *The trefoil* (1923) · W. Benham and R. T. Davidson, *Life of Archibald Campbell Tait*, 2 vols. (1891) · A. Westcott, *Life and letters of Brooke Foss Westcott*, 2 vols. (1903) · E. F. Benson, *As we were* (1930) · A. C. Benson, *Memories and friends* (1924) · D. Newsome, *A history of Wellington College, 1859–1959* [1959] · D. Newsome, *On the edge of paradise: A. C. Benson, the diarist* (1980) · J. F. Coakley, *The church of the East and the Church of England: a history of the archbishop of Canterbury's Assyrian mission* (1992) · P. Hinchliff, *God and history: aspects of British theology, 1875–1914* (1992), chap. 4 · J. Overton and E. Wordsworth, *Christopher Wordsworth, bishop of Lincoln, 1807–1885* (1888) · B. Masters, *The life of E. F. Benson* (1991) · D. Williams, *Genesis and Exodus* (1979) · D. Newsome, *Godliness and good learning* (1961) · G. Battiscombe, *Reluctant pioneer: a life of Elizabeth Wordsworth* (1978) · G. I. T. Machin, *Politics and the churches in Great Britain, 1869 to 1921* (1987) · Gladstone, *Diaries* · Boase, *Mod. Eng. biog.*

Archives BL, corresp. and papers relating to printing of prayer book · Bodl. Oxf., corresp. with ecclesiastics, Add. MS 49457 · Bodl. Oxf., corresp. · Lincs. Arch., personal book of Lincoln chapter minutes as chancellor · LPL, corresp. and papers · Trinity Cam., diaries, notebooks, and typescript copies of corresp. | BL, corresp. with Arthur James Balfour, Add. MS 49788, *passim* · BL, corresp. with Lord Carnarvon, Add. MS 60834 · BL, letters to G. L. Craik, Add. MS 61895 · BL, letters to Lord Cranbrook, Add. MS 62537 · BL, corresp. with W. E. Gladstone, Add. MS 44109 · BL, corresp. with Macmillans, Add. MS 55109 · BL, letter to Sir John Stainer, Add. MS 62121 · BL, corresp. with Lord Stanmore, Add. MS 49209 · Bodl. Oxf., letters to Sir Henry Wentworth Acland · Bodl. Oxf., corresp. with Samuel Bickersteth, MS Eng d 3056, *passim* · Bodl. Oxf., letters to Sir William Harcourt · Bodl. Oxf., corresp. with Lord Kimberley · Bodl. Oxf., corresp. with George Ridding · CKS, letters to Lord Stanhope · Cornwall RO, letters to Saltram Rogers, vicar of Gwennap, Cornwall · Cornwall RO, corresp. mainly relating to Truro diocese · LPL, corresp. with Randall Thomas Davidson, archbishop of Canterbury · LPL, papers relating to Lambeth conference · LPL, corresp. with Lord Selborne · LPL, corresp. with A. C. Tait · LPL, corresp. with Frederick Temple, bishop of London · LPL, corresp. with Christopher Wordsworth · NRA Scotland, letters to Lord Aberdeen · Pusey Oxf., letters to H. P. Liddon · Wellington College, Berkshire, corresp. and papers relating to Wellington College

Likenesses Mayall, photograph, 1867, repro. in Benson, *Life of Edward White Benson*, frontispiece · S. Laurence, oils, 1872, priv. coll. · Harrison, photograph, 1876, repro. in Benson, *Life of Edward White Benson*, vol. 1, p. 377 · A. B. Joy, marble bust, 1885, LPL; similar plaster and bronze busts, NPG · H. von Herkomer, oils, 1890, LPL [*see illus.*] · plaster death mask, 1896, NPG · T. Brock, marble effigy on monument, 1899, Canterbury Cathedral · A. B. Joy, medallion on memorial, 1899, Rugby School chapel, Warwickshire · W. E. Miller, oils, 1900, Trinity Cam. · F. Argall, photograph, NPG · Barraud, photograph, NPG; repro. in *Men and Women of the Day*, 2 (1889) · W. & D. Downey, photographs, NPG · Elliott & Fry, photograph, NPG · Fradelle, photograph, NPG · F. C. Gould, pen-and-pencil caricature, NPG · Lock & Whitfield, photograph, NPG · London Stereoscopic Co., photograph, NPG · H. Pinker, bust, Wellington College, Berkshire · Russell & Sons, photograph, NPG ·

F. Sargent, pencil drawing, NPG · C. W. Sherborn, etching (after H. T. Wells), BM · Spy [L. Ward], chromolithograph caricature, NPG; repro. in *VF* (30 July 1887) · E. Walker, photograph (after Mayall), NPG · etching (after H. T. Wells), NPG · portrait, repro. in T. Cooper, *Men of mark: a gallery of contemporary portraits* (1880) · portrait, repro. in *Edgbastonia*, 3 (1883) · portrait, repro. in *Dignitaries of the church* (July 1889) · portrait, repro. in *Church Portrait Journal*, 1 (1880) · portrait, repro. in *Church Portrait Journal*, 4 (1883) · portrait, repro. in *St. Paul's* (March 1884) · portraits, repro. in *ILN* (6 Jan 1877–17 Oct 1896)

Wealth at death £46,396 5s. 3d.: probate, 4 Dec 1896, *CGPLA Eng. & Wales*

Benson, Sir Francis Robert [Frank] (1858–1939), actor and theatre manager, was born at Eden House, Tunbridge Wells, Kent, on 4 November 1858, the third son and fourth child of William Benson (1816–1887), a barrister and justice of the peace of Alresford, Hampshire, and his wife, Elizabeth Soulsby (d. 1892), the daughter of Thomas Smith of Colebrooke Park, Tonbridge. William Arthur Smith *Benson, the designer, and Godfrey Rathbone *Benson, later Baron Charnwood, were among his brothers.

Youthful sports and acting Although Benson claimed viking ancestry, his family is traceable to eighteenth-century Quakers. He spent an idyllic, rural childhood before attending Darch's Preparatory School in Brighton (from 1867). In 1871 he went to Winchester College, where he preferred sports to academics, but was attracted to Shakespeare and played female roles. Sports still predominated when he went to New College, Oxford, in 1878, but he created a stir in 1880 when he mounted a successful production of Aeschylus's *Agamemnon*. Presented in Greek and with Benson as Clytemnestra, the production was repeated for three performances at St George's Hall, London, an enterprise witnessed by Henry Irving and Ellen Terry (the latter particularly fostered Benson's early career). His Oxford days were also typified by his triumph in winning the inter-varsity 3 mile race against Cambridge in 1881 in fifteen minutes and five seconds.

The success of *Agamemnon* persuaded Benson his future lay in the theatre and, on leaving Oxford, he presented *Romeo and Juliet* for a single performance at the Imperial Theatre, London, in July 1881. In addition to playing Romeo, Benson attempted to manage every aspect of the production. The result was amateurish and financially disastrous, although some perceived histrionic potential in Benson himself. Indeed, this early effort epitomizes Benson's whole career: his own limited acting and managerial capabilities, his abundant enthusiasm, and his ensuing financial woes, which resulted in someone else bailing him out. On this occasion his father provided £500, an act he was to repeat frequently.

Benson's determination to become a professional actor was founded on a minimal understanding of acting or of the theatre, but he possessed an almost arrogant conviction he could improve conditions. However, for a few months he did study stage-fighting, dancing, boxing, and elocution with various tutors, notably Hermann Vezin, the last in an attempt to improve his always problematic voice. Then, in June 1882, the supportive Ellen Terry invited him to participate in a private reading of *Much Ado*

Sir Francis Robert Benson (1858–1939), by Reginald Grenville Eves, 1924

about Nothing, with Irving as Benedick, Helen Faucit as Beatrice, and Benson as Don Pedro.

Shortly afterwards Benson obtained his first professional engagement, playing Paris in *Romeo and Juliet* with Irving and Terry at the Lyceum Theatre (2 September 1882). His performance, despite Benson's own confidence, was inauspicious, and Terry had to persuade Irving to retain him. When no further roles materialized, Benson was told he would profit from working with a provincial touring company, advice which fundamentally dictated the remainder of his career.

Founding his own company Benson joined the Manchester Shakespearian company of Charles Bernard and Annie Alleyn in December 1882. After a few weeks' trial he failed to impress and was advised to quit the stage. Undeterred, early in 1883 he joined Walter Bentley's touring company, which performed Shakespeare and classic comedies in the north of England and Scotland. After a few months Bentley decamped for financial reasons, and Benson, still the novice, arrogantly took over the company, although not without his father's substantial financial assistance. The new F. R. Benson company began its first tour on 5 May 1883 at the Public Hall in Airdrie, Lanarkshire, still presenting Shakespeare and old comedies. The tour eventually lost £450. However, Benson did attempt some innovations, largely as a result of seeing the Meiningen company at Drury Lane in 1881. Although circumstances made application of the Meiningen theories difficult, he tried to present concerted scenes, ensemble acting, and a coherent stage picture. During his career he became notorious for conducting protracted rehearsals, oblivious to the needs of ordinary mortals. His objectives were to perform constantly as many of Shakespeare's plays as possible, changing the programme frequently so that no play predominated. Additionally, his actors were trained in speaking blank verse. He believed that a play should not be adapted merely to serve star performers, and that scenery should be simple and subordinate to dramatic interest.

More provincial touring followed, posing its own difficulties. Benson perceived the need for a circuit of towns for his company's visits, although it was difficult to keep the company stable. People constantly joined and then moved on (although some, such as the excellent low comedian George R. Weir, stayed permanently with Benson). Salaries were negligible and the lure of the London stage was irresistible. All, however, remained loyal old Bensonians, and it is significant that in 1920, for example, no fewer than seventy old Bensonians were playing prominent parts in London. Those who remained on several occasions made financial sacrifices cheerfully in order to keep the venture afloat: such was the loyalty Pa, as Benson was dubbed, inspired.

Indeed, the concept of provincial touring inherently courted financial strains as people and baskets of costumes and sets were transported from town to town. But Benson gradually built up his stock of properties so that he was able to stage virtually any play anywhere as he knocked on virtually every door in the country. In November 1899 a fire at the Theatre Royal, Newcastle, destroyed the company's possessions entirely, a loss from which Benson never really recovered (although on that occasion Irving and George Alexander generously loaned costumes so that Benson could fulfil his engagements). Eventually, by the early 1900s, there were several Benson companies, each with a designated area of the country ('north', 'south', 'midland') to cover. And there was the occasional trip overseas, such as that led by Matheson Lang to the Caribbean in 1904.

A significant aspect of a visit to any town were the games Benson and his company would play against the locals: cricket, soccer, water polo, and other sports were played with equal zest as occasion demanded. This habit endeared them to the provinces but incurred metropolitan disdain. There is the apocryphal tale of a young actor who, asked by Benson whether he could play Rugby, assumed Benson meant the sport, not the role (in *The Merry Wives of Windsor*). Benson did believe acting demanded physical fitness, and he once played hockey in the morning, and then performed Henry V and Macbeth later the same afternoon and evening.

Marriage to Constance Early in his touring ventures (December 1884) Benson met an actress performing as Constance Fetherstonhaugh. Her father was Captain Morshead Fetherstonhaugh Samwell (1827–1864), and he had died shortly before her birth in India on 26 February 1864. **(Gertrude) Constance Benson** (1864–1946) was above average height, and had a slight build and a high, quick voice. Against the wishes of her mother, Anna, who died three months before Constance's wedding day, she

had become an actress, beginning her career with bit parts at Irving's Lyceum. She and Benson married on 24 July 1886 and enjoyed a largely happy marriage which produced two children, Eric William (1887–1916) and Brynhild Lucy (*b*. 1888). Apart from acting, Constance designed costumes and discovered her vocation in teaching the students attached to the company. Indeed, she was closer to the company than her husband and loved company gossip. When she became too old to sustain leading roles she began her own acting school in London, and one of her early pupils was John Gielgud. She clearly had many strengths, which she drew upon to cope with Benson's many eccentricities. However, she could not tolerate his affair in 1921 with an actress, Geneviève Smeek, also known as Townsend (*d*. 1 May 1927), and they separated, though they did not divorce. Constance wrote an autobiography, *Mainly Players: Bensonian Memories* (1926), two novels, *The Chimera* (1928) and *Cuckoo Oats* (1929), and a handbook on acting, *One Hundred Practical Hints for the Amateur* (n.d. [1930]). Lady Benson outlived her husband by six years and died on 19 January 1946.

Benson and Stratford upon Avon Benson's provincial reputation grew rapidly, and in 1886 he was asked to direct a one-week spring festival at the Memorial Theatre, Stratford upon Avon, which was the beginning of a long and successful association. The festival week had been established only in 1879 and had not been marked by noteworthy productions. But Benson's zealous, missionary passion for Shakespeare coincided with the ideals of the festival's founder, Charles E. *Flower (1830–1892), the Warwickshire brewer. Benson was seen as a responsible director who could pick a good company, although his early work at Stratford was disdained by London managers and ignored by the capital's press.

The first season began modestly enough on 24 April 1886 with *Hamlet*, and included *Othello*, *Richard III*, and Sheridan's *The Rivals*. Of these *Richard III* was deemed the best. Other plays in the Shakespearian canon were added with successive festivals, and eventually, in his thirty years' association with Stratford, Benson produced all Shakespeare's plays with the exception of *Titus Andronicus* and *Troilus and Cressida*. The most frequently staged were *Hamlet*, *The Merchant of Venice*, and *The Merry Wives of Windsor* (twenty festivals each), followed by *The Taming of the Shrew* and *Twelfth Night* (17), *As You Like It* (16), *Henry V* (16), and *Richard II* (14). Several plays, however, received only a solitary production.

Benson preferred plays which gave him the opportunity to perform athletically: for example, in 1891 as Caliban in *The Tempest*, he hung upside down from a tree while keeping a fresh fish in his mouth. It was this sort of athletic trait which led Max Beerbohm in 1900 to characterize Benson's *Henry V* as a good form of cricket but not acting, a characterization which stuck, much to Benson's detriment. But that overlooks such achievements as introducing the little-performed *Timon of Athens* to Stratford in 1892, the never highly popular *Coriolanus* in 1893, and a lavish and archaeologically accurate *Antony and Cleopatra* in 1898. He was particularly good as Coriolanus and Antony, although Constance was less secure as Cleopatra. 1899 saw the production of the complete folio version of *Hamlet*, which was performed over an afternoon and evening, with Benson restoring large, unfamiliar portions of the play. Novel, too, was Benson as a beardless Lear for the 1902 festival. By the middle of the 1900s he had staged thirty of Shakespeare's plays and the festival lengthened in duration (the 1903 festival, for example, comprised six plays in two weeks, the 1906 festival eighteen plays in three weeks). A summer season of three to four weeks was instituted in 1910 and became a regular feature. All this received due recognition when in 1910 Stratford conferred the freedom of the borough on Benson, the first actor so distinguished since David Garrick in 1769 (the city of Cork followed suit in 1931).

Ironically, from 1910 onwards Benson's relationship with Stratford became more uneasy, largely because of the financial difficulties he invariably incurred, but also because there was a sentiment to replace Constance, who was becoming too old for the female leads she insisted on performing. Benson soldiered on for a few more years until the First World War finally took its toll. His last attenuated Stratford season was in the spring of 1916.

Benson on the London stage The provinces and Stratford were never enough for Benson, and he always yearned to make his mark in London. So he presented his first London season at the Globe Theatre in 1889, beginning on 19 December with *A Midsummer Night's Dream*, which ran for a then record 110 performances. He added *The Taming of the Shrew*, *Hamlet*, and *Othello* to form a four-play repertory, but this policy, essential to his artistic vision, succeeded only in confusing a public unfamiliar with such a notion. The season ended less successfully than it might have done, and Benson, typically, lost money. He did not return until February 1900, when he took the Lyceum for four months. He presented the *Henry V* so disdained by Beerbohm, along with seven other plays, including *A Midsummer Night's Dream*, a complete *Hamlet*, and the production considered to be his best, *Richard II*. Again, the season ticket and repertory policy displeased audiences, as did Benson's methods of staging, which were less sumptuous than the elaborately pictorial Shakespeare given by Herbert Beerbohm Tree at Her Majesty's. Subsequently West End seasons followed—at the Comedy (1901), Adelphi (1905), St James's (1910), Shaftesbury (1914), Court (1915), and St Martin's (1920). Additionally, Benson's company appeared regularly at 'outer' theatres—the Coronet (Notting Hill), Hammersmith, and Wimbledon—until the late 1920s. Benson also toured Canada and the United States in 1913–14, sometimes to appreciative audiences, but he was mauled by the critics in Chicago. He did, however, receive an honorary LLD degree from McGill University in Montreal in recognition of his services to the theatre.

Further recognition was the knighthood conferred on Benson by George V, during the Shakespeare tercentenary performance given at Drury Lane on 2 May 1916, when he appeared as Julius Caesar. Still in costume, he was knighted in the royal box with a sword borrowed from a local armourer, the first instance of an actor being knighted in a theatre.

War, decline, death, and reputation While Benson staged patriotic performances of *Henry V* during the early war years, he desperately wanted to make a practical contribution, but he was rejected for active service because of his age. However, while his wife directed a canteen for soldiers in France, Benson drove an ambulance and received the Croix de Guerre for rescuing wounded men on the firing line. Both Benson and Constance grieved deeply for their son, Eric, when he was killed in action in September 1916.

After the war, Benson's fortunes declined sharply. He made his last appearance at Stratford in 1919, and then toured South Africa in 1921–2. On his return he toured the provinces giving farewell performances, and found time to write a book of genial if vague reminiscences, *My Memoirs* (1930), and the brief handbook of advice about the acting profession, *I Want to Go on the Stage* (1931). He made what was to be his last appearance on stage, as Dr Caius in *The Merry Wives of Windsor*, at the Winter Garden on 26 December 1932. When Benson was injured by a bicyclist in Bradford in March 1933, his career was finally ended. He was, by now, living in much reduced financial circumstances and was awarded a civil-list pension of £100 in July 1933. He remained a solitary but gentle, courteous old man and, a husk of his former self, lived out his days eccentrically in lodgings at 18 Holland Road, Kensington, London, where he died of broncho-pneumonia and a kidney infection on 31 December 1939. A small private funeral followed on 4 January 1940, attended by Lady Benson and the family; his body was cremated the same day at Golders Green crematorium. However, the theatrical profession was out in force to honour Benson at a memorial service held at St Martin-in-the-Fields on 12 January 1940.

By the time of his death, Benson, and whatever innovations and contributions he had made, had been superseded. It is true he was never a great actor: Richard II, Petruchio in *The Taming of the Shrew*, and Caliban were probably his best roles. His noble Roman appearance with his aquiline nose lent physical distinction to other roles, but he could become easily bored by his own performances and was notorious for 'ponging' or extemporizing blank verse (albeit expertly). His great talent was for nurturing other actors, teaching them with his wife, affording them opportunities, and creating a theatrical nursery, and for bringing Shakespeare to countless provincial towns; perhaps his greatest contribution was laying a solid foundation for theatrical performances at Stratford.

J. P. WEARING

Sources J. C. Trewin, *Benson and the Bensonians* (1960) · F. Benson, *My memoirs* (1930) · C. Benson, *Mainly players: Bensonian memories* (1926) · H. Pearson, 'Sir Frank Benson', *The last actor-managers* (1950), 33–40 · *The Times* (1 Jan 1940) · D. Rostron, 'F. R. Benson's early productions of Shakespeare's Roman plays at Stratford', *Theatre Notebook*, 25 (1970–71), 46–54 · R. Ellis, *The Shakespeare Memorial Theatre* (1948) · J. C. Trewin, *Shakespeare on the English stage, 1900–1964* (1964) · M. Mullin, ed., *Theatre at Stratford-upon-Avon: a catalogue-*

index to productions of the Shakespeare Memorial/Royal Shakespeare Theatre, 2 vols. (1980) · S. Beauman, *The Royal Shakespeare Company: a history of ten decades* (1982) · *Who was who in the theatre, 1912–1976*, 4 vols. (1978) · BL OIOC [birth of Gertrude Constance Benson] · d. cert. · *CGPLA Eng. & Wales* (1946) [Gertrude Constance Benson]

Archives JRL, corresp. with Robert Donat | FILM BFI NFTVA, propaganda footage (Hepworth Manufacturing Company) | SOUND BL NSA, documentary recording

Likenesses J. C. Smith, photograph, *c.*1906, NPG · H. Rivière, oils, 1910, Shakespeare Memorial Picture Gallery, Stratford upon Avon · R. G. Eves, oils, 1924, NPG [*see illus.*] · W. Stoneman, photographs, 1924–34, NPG · R. G. Eves, oils, 1927, Theatre Museum, London · Mrs A. Broom, photograph, NPG · Chancellor & Son, photogravures, NPG · W. J. Morgan, oils, University of Newcastle, Callaghan, New South Wales, Australia, Michael R. Booth Theatre Collection · photographs, repro. in Trewin, *Benson and the Bensonians* · photographs, repro. in Pearson, *The last actor-managers* · photographs, repro. in Benson, *My memoirs* · photographs, repro. in Benson, *Mainly players* · photographs (Gertrude Constance Benson), repro. in Trewin, *Benson and the Bensonians* · photographs (Gertrude Constance Benson), repro. in Benson, *My memoirs* · photographs (Gertrude Constance Benson), repro. in Benson, *Mainly players* · print (after H. Van Dusen), NPG

Wealth at death £9433 3*s.* 8*d.*—Gertrude Constance Benson: probate, 1946, *CGPLA Eng. & Wales*

Benson, George (1699–1762), Presbyterian minister and theologian, was born on 1 September 1699 at Great Salkeld, Cumberland, the sixth of seven children born to Joseph Benson (*d.* 1722) and his wife, Isabel Moorehouse (*d.* 1718); he was baptized on 7 September in the parish church, a not uncommon practice among dissenters at that time. His father was the grandson of John Benson, a Londoner who had settled in Kendal, Westmorland, late in the reign of Elizabeth I. His grandfather George Benson (1618–1692) was an ejected minister who founded the congregational church at Cockermouth and was licensed to preach at his houses in Kendal and Nether Kellett.

Educated in the parish school, which had been rebuilt and reinvigorated by William Nicolson (1655–1727), rector of Great Salkeld and later bishop of Carlisle, the younger George Benson was reportedly able to read the New Testament in Greek by the age of eleven. In 1716 he entered the academy at Whitehaven, headed by Thomas Dixon, and a year later, with support from the Presbyterian Fund, matriculated from the University of Glasgow, where he remained until 1721. Towards the end of that year he settled in London, where he was taken into the household of Edmund Calamy (1671–1732), the celebrated nonconformist historian and minister. Benson preached in Chertsey and in London, and in 1722, through Calamy's good offices, settled in Abingdon, Berkshire, where he was ordained on 27 March 1723. On 14 March 1726, at All Hallows Bread Street, London, he married Elizabeth Hills (*d.* 1740), a widow from London.

At his ordination Benson espoused traditional Calvinism, but, consistently with his declaration that 'I wou'd as soon give up my Bible, as ye Right of private Judgment' (G. Benson to G. Fothergill, 28 Dec 1726, Benson MSS), he developed doubts about predestination. He defended his new Arminian understanding of God's providence in *The Doctrine of Predestination Review'd … in a Letter to a Friend*

George Benson (1699–1762), by unknown artist

(1729) and forbade republication of three 'practical discourses' published earlier as guides to the young. As his congregation disapproved of the change, he resigned in 1729. He had considered practising medicine—a common resort either as a supplement to the ministry or a substitute for it—but accepted the pulpit at King John's Court, Southwark. In 1740 he succeeded William Harris as minister at Crutched Friars, Poor Jewry Lane, London. He subsequently turned down a unanimous invitation to join his friend Samuel Bourn in the pastorate at New Meeting, Birmingham, an offer that perhaps resulted from his having married, on 22 June 1742 at the parish church of St Martin, Birmingham, Hannah (*bap.* 1706, *d.* 1754), daughter of William Kettle, a prominent member of New Meeting. There were no children of either of his marriages. Benson regularly took young men into his household to oversee their preparation for the ministry.

In his sketch in *Biographia Britannica* Joseph Towers recorded that Benson's fellow students thought him dull and unlikely to be heard from, but he more than made up for his lack of originality of mind by remarkable industry. His most important theological works were his paraphrases of the epistles, in 'imitation of Mr. Locke's manner'. In his last years John Locke had undertaken paraphrases, with extensive interpretive notes, of the epistles of St Paul. Pursuing these studies for his own purposes, he was subsequently persuaded to permit their publication, done posthumously, beginning with Galatians and proceeding through 1 and 2 Corinthians, Romans, and Ephesians (1705–7, collected edition 1707). James Peirce, the controversial Arian minister in Exeter, followed Locke's model with paraphrases of Colossians, Philippians, and

Hebrews; the last three chapters of Hebrews were completed by Peirce's colleague Joseph Hallett III, and the whole was published in 1733. Benson, following Locke's (and Peirce's) example and format, brought out Philemon and 1 Thessalonians (1731), 2 Thessalonians (1732), 1 Timothy and Titus (1733), and 2 Timothy (1734); he then turned to the seven so-called Catholic epistles: James, 1 and 2 Peter, 1, 2, and 3 John, and Jude. The Pauline paraphrases were republished in a single volume in 1752, the Catholic epistles in 1756. To some of the paraphrases were appended 'dissertations' on particular points in the text, for example on 'the kingdom of God' and on 'the man of sin' (which he thought signified the pope); several of these essays were republished in later collections of tracts.

In the essay on inspiration (1 Timothy), and again in the introduction 'on the unity of sense' to the collected Pauline epistles, Benson deplored ambiguity, which allowed mystics and enthusiasts, as he put it in the treatise on inspiration, 'more easily [to] bend such texts to their humours or fancies, inclinations or wishes; and prove, as established, doctrines by them which could otherwise never be proved, or established'. Rather, the first principle of interpretation should be that 'no text of Scripture has more than one meaning', to be discovered just as one would seek out the sense of Homer or any other ancient writer, by constant re-examination and debate. In the same spirit he declared, in *A Summary View of the Evidences of Christ's Resurrection* (1754), his concern to 'settle the harmony' (p. i) of seemingly conflicting biblical accounts.

This positivist outlook underlay Benson's certainty that history, 'an easie and agreeable method', had advantages for religious instruction far beyond 'that of systems, institutions, or apostolical canons ... [for] no evidence strikes the public mind like public and undoubted fact' (Benson, *First Planting*, iii). His *History of the First Planting of Christianity* (1735; 2nd edn 1752) was based on Acts and the epistles and, in addition to his own studies, on Josephus, on *Miscellanea sacra* (1725) by John Shute, first Lord Barrington, and on *The Credibility of Gospel History*, then appearing from the pen of Nathaniel Lardner. It traces in two large volumes, with a third of appended essays and indexes, the spread of Christianity among the Jews, gentiles, and idolatrous gentiles from AD 33 to 63. His similarly based life of Christ was published posthumously in 1764.

Benson published a number of shorter apologetical or polemical works, of which probably the most widely admired was *The Reasonableness of the Christian Religion as Delivered in the Scriptures* (1743, 1746, 1759), an account of an imaginary dialogue that serves as a reply to the then scandalous *Religion not Founded on Argument* (1742) by the deist Henry Dodwell the younger. Of particular note is *A Brief Account of Calvin's Burning of Servetus for an Heretic*, published as four letters in the *Old Whig* in early 1738 but omitted from the two-volume reprinting of that periodical and republished with revisions as a pamphlet in 1743; in it, as he did often, he called for the free exchange of ideas, however erroneous, as well as for the separation of church and state. This extensive and varied display of scholarship and argument secured Benson's reputation in religious circles

in England and on the continent. For all their differences, he was respected by leading Anglicans, including Archbishop Herring, Joseph Butler, and Benjamin Hoadly; Edmund Law, the latitudinarian master of Peterhouse and later bishop of Carlisle, was a close friend.

The University of Aberdeen conferred a DD on Benson in 1744, but plans for a similar honour from the University of Glasgow were derailed because of doubts about his doctrinal soundness; one of the professors 'spoke of him with Abhorrence as an avowed Socinian' (D. Fordyce to G. Benson, 20 Aug 1746, Benson MSS). The accusation is not easy to support, despite the assertion to that effect by one mid-Victorian memorialist (W. in Jones, *Bunhill Memorials*). To be sure, Benson shared his reliance on private judgement with the broad range of those he called 'rational Christians'. He seemed to approach the possibility of universal salvation and (in *Second Thoughts Concerning the Suffering and Death of Christ*, 1748) rejected, as did unitarians, the orthodox conception of Christ's death on the cross as a propitiatory sacrifice. Moreover, at Crutched Friars his assistant (as with William Harris before him) was the great dissenting polymath Nathaniel Lardner, until Lardner's frail health forced his resignation in 1751. There is no suggestion in Lardner's surviving letters to him that Benson held the unitarian (or Socinian) position that Christ was not God but a man, albeit with a divinely conferred mission; Lardner had come to that view by 1730, but his *Letter on the Logos* was published only in 1759 and then under a pseudonym. Open avowal of such a theology was certain to offend most congregational opinion at the time and, moreover, ran a serious legal risk, as the privileges of the Toleration Act of 1689 did not extend to deniers of the Trinity; reticence would be understandable. Whatever may have passed between the two friends in conversations, it seems unlikely that Benson ever moved openly beyond his undoubted Arianism: the belief that Christ, while divine, was created and subordinate to God the Father.

Benson was a regular participant in a group that over many London winters met weekly to discuss theological and biblical issues. The extensive archive of letters written to him by correspondents throughout England and Scotland reflects his key position and high personal standing in the dissenting community. His patronage as manager of the Presbyterian Fund from 1740 to 1762 and, after 1758, as a trustee of Dr Daniel Williams's Trust was valued, as was his role as a mentor to the young. He was involved in endless efforts to secure and distribute books, his own and others', and his views on theological matters were sought by ministers isolated not only by distance from the capital but by their heterodoxy.

A collection of Benson's sermons was published in 1747. Shortsightedness made preaching difficult for him. As was common among ministers who shared his outlook, his method of preaching was to examine critically the text he had chosen, illustrate its doctrinal points, and enforce the duties that followed. This he did, said Thomas Amory, afternoon preacher at the congregation in Carter Lane, 'with great seriousness, and with a plain and honest freedom', but 'his natural temper prevented his excelling in a warm and pathetic address to the passions of his hearers' (Amory, xiii–xiv). His evident piety and righteousness, however, went far to compensate for the lack of what was coming to be seen as a popular style. In his funeral sermon Edward Pickard, the high Arian minister at Carter Lane, enforced the point: as providence had created

> various dispositions and tastes amongst men, so it shows the care of the Head of the christian church, that his ministers should be so differently furnished, as that the whole flock may have that food dispensed to them which is most suited … to their mental constitution; to their growth in knowledge, piety, faith, and goodness.   (Pickard, 32)

Benson retired from Crutched Friars in January 1762 and continued to work on his life of Christ almost to the end, which came suddenly at his house in Prescot Street, Goodman's Fields, London, on 6 April 1762. In his will he left £100 to the Presbyterian Fund and another £100 to the Widows Fund, for the widows and orphans of ministers. Ebenezer Radcliff (1731?–1809), Benson's assistant and successor at Crutched Friars, delivered an oration at the interment in Bunhill Fields, London. The memoir by Thomas Amory appears as a preface to Benson's *History of the life of Jesus Christ* (1764).   R. K. WEBB

Sources T. Amory, 'Memoir of the life, character, and writings of the author', in G. Benson, *The history of the life of Jesus Christ, taken from the New Testament* (1764), iii–xix • [J. Towers], 'Benson, George', *Biographia Britannica, or, The lives of the most eminent persons who have flourished in Great Britain and Ireland*, ed. A. Kippis and others, 2nd edn, 1 (1778) • E. Pickard, *The character and reward of the good and faithful servant: a sermon preached at Crutched Friars, London, April the 18th, 1762, on occasion of the death of George Benson, D.D.* (1762) • A. G. Loftie, *Great Salkeld: its rectors and history* (1900) • *Calamy rev.* • bishops' transcripts of Great Salkeld parish registers, 1662–1863, PRO • W. B. Bannerman, ed., *The registers of All Hallows, Bread Street, and of St John the Evangelist, Friday Street, London*, Harleian Society, register section, 43 (1913), 121 • parish register, Birmingham, St Martin's, 22 June 1742, PRO [marriage] • J. A. Jones, ed., *Bunhill memorials* (1849) • J. Locke, *A paraphrase and notes on the epistles of St Paul …*, ed. A. W. Wainwright (1987) • J. Peirce, *A paraphrase and notes on the epistles of St Paul … after the manner of Mr Locke* (1733) • E. Calamy to G. Benson, 31 Jan 1723, JRL, Benson collection, iii, B111/51 • G. Benson to G. Fothergill, 28 Dec 1726, JRL, Benson collection, General, B116/193 • D. Fordyce to G. Benson, 20 Aug 1746, JRL, Benson collection, v, B/113/103 • F. G. James, *North country bishop: a biography of William Nicolson* (1934) • O. M. Griffiths, *Religion and learning: a study in English Presbyterian thought from 1662 to the foundation of the Unitarian movement* (1936) • W. Wilson, *The history and antiquities of the dissenting churches and meeting houses in London, Westminster and Southwark*, 4 vols. (1808–14) • W. D. Jeremy, *The Presbyterian Board and Dr. Daniel Williams's Trust; with biographical notes of the trustees* (1885) • W. Turner, *Lives of eminent Unitarians*, 2 vols. (1840–43)

Archives BL, corresp. and papers, Add. MSS 5157, 6033, 6210–6211, 6269 • JRL, corresp. • Lancs. RO, corresp.

Likenesses J. Macardell, mezzotint, repro. in Benson, *The history of the life of Jesus Christ*, frontispiece • oils, DWL [*see illus.*]

Benson, Gervase (d. 1679), Quaker leader, lived at Haygarth in Sedbergh, Yorkshire, and Kendal, Westmorland; he also had a house at Borratt in Sedbergh. A notary public before 1640, and later commissary of the archdeaconry of Richmond at Kendal, Benson was the first ecclesiastical lawyer to join Kendal corporation, which was dominated by mercers. Elected in December 1640, he became an alderman in April 1641, an unusually rapid promotion.

Early in the civil war the Kendal corporation was subordinated to divisions within the Westmorland gentry between ardent royalists and neutrals. Benson revealed his own political inclinations on 9 May 1644 when he tried unsuccessfully to commit the town to parliament by inviting Lancashire parliamentarian forces to Kendal; however, it was the Scottish invasion of Cumbria in September that brought Kendal under parliamentarian control. Whether or not the Scots' arrival had any influence over his election as mayor of Kendal at Michaelmas 1644, Benson leapfrogged two more senior corporation men into the mayoralty. Thereafter he became a county JP in his own name, despite doubts that he had enough land in Westmorland to qualify, a measure of his rising importance. He was known as Colonel Benson in 1645, and was in command of local forces in the town's small garrison, but recent research has not confirmed twentieth-century claims that he served in the New Model Army. In March 1646 he helped to organize a presbyterian classis in Westmorland.

Benson was driven out of Kendal during the second civil war. However, after parliament's victory he and other parliamentarian aldermen became more prominent in a county and regional administration purged of royalists, and he became known in London. From this local power base Benson and his allies used the 1650 oath of engagement to attack royalist and conservative members of Kendal corporation; their reports prompted the House of Commons in October to remove corporation men who had not taken the oath. The resort to an outside authority not only challenged the town's charter but also suggests that Benson had enjoyed only minority support in the corporation.

While Benson evidently favoured the republic it is not clear how far his religious tenets had moved by late 1650, and his signature to a cleric's augmentation in July 1651 does not suggest he was then a sectarian. Nevertheless a year later, on 6 June 1652, George Fox visited a gathered church at Sedbergh led by Benson, whenceforth the colonel is counted a Quaker. He tried to shield James Naylor in the latter's trial at the Westmorland sessions on 11 January 1653, and later that year he advocated Quaker tenets in public debates in Kendal. Benson's sectarianism found little support among his corporation colleagues, who were busy imprisoning Quakers, and they excluded him in September 1653. In the meantime the corporation and local clerics had begun a pamphlet war against Quakers, to which Benson would answer in 1655. He must have been one of the first Quakers to be removed from office on the grounds of religion, though after his dismissal from Kendal corporation he was for some time still able to protect Quakers through his place in county and national affairs.

The dominance of George Fox in Quaker history has probably undervalued the contribution of Gervase Benson to the early years of Quakerism. Benson was one of the founders of the Friends, and remained involved in the affairs of the notable Quaker Fell family of Swarthmore into the 1670s. He is credited with important early missionary work in London in 1653, and with Quaker fundraising campaigns. He spoke for northern Quakers in organizational matters, on occasion in opposition to Fox. Benson also had a special interest in tithes. In the autumn of 1653 he and others lobbied parliament for the anti-tithe cause, and with effect: a division in parliament on 10 December 1653, which favoured the abolition of tithes, precipitated the demise of the Nominated Parliament. His wife, Dorothy (d. 1656), whom Benson had married before June 1652, was equally active, and, with her neighbour Anne Blaykling, she was imprisoned at York by December 1653 for a period of at least a month. Benson's youngest son, Emanuel, was born during this imprisonment. Gervase wrote against tithes in 1655, and his *Cry of the Oppressed* (1656) also publicized Quakers who were persecuted for non-payment of tithe. He was again among those who petitioned parliament over tithe in 1659. Benson's legal training and probate office made him particularly valuable to Quakers on trial, and in dealing with oaths, especially in probate. He contributed in 1655 to a printed discussion of Quaker difficulties with the oath of abjuration.

Benson buried Dorothy at their house at Haygarth on 28 February 1656, and in 1660 he married Mabell, widow of John Camm of Camsgill. After the Restoration, he was credited by the Friends with effective intervention over oaths with Anglican probate officials. He published two books on the issue of oaths, in 1669 and 1675. By about 1678 he had moved back to Kendal; he died there and was buried in the Quaker burial-ground on 5 May 1679. His will, made in 1678, mentions his wife, and three sons and five daughters. C. B. PHILLIPS

Sources Cumbria AS, Kendal, Kendal corporation archives, esp. Book of Record, apprenticeship register 1645–1789, chamberlains' accounts, records of mayors' elections, papers listed by HMC · C. B. Phillips, 'Colonel Gervase Benson, Captain John Archer and the corporation of Kendal, c.1644–c.1655', *Soldiers, writers and statesmen of the English revolution*, ed. I. Gentles and others (1998), 183–201 · C. B. Phillips, 'County committees and local government in Cumberland and Westmorland, 1642–1660', *Northern History*, 5 (1970), 34–66 · B. Nightingale, *The ejected of 1662 in Cumberland and Westmorland* (1911) · N. Penney, ed., 'The first publishers of truth': being early records, now first printed, of the introduction of Quakerism into the counties of England and Wales (1907) · W. C. Braithwaite, *The beginnings of Quakerism*, ed. H. J. Cadbury, 2nd edn (1955) · D. Boulton, *Early friends in Dent* (1986) · M. K. Peters, 'Quaker pamphleteering and the development of the Quaker movement, 1652–1656', PhD diss., U. Cam., 1996 · C. H. Firth and G. Davies, *The regimental history of Cromwell's army*, 2 vols. (1940) · M. E. Hirst, *The Quakers in peace and war* (1923) · J. Besse, *A collection of the sufferings of the people called Quakers*, 2 vols. (1753)

Wealth at death £22 16s. 2d.; probate bond in £500: probate inventory, 8 Aug 1679, Lancs. RO, Archdeaconry of Richmond wills, Kendal Deanery

Benson, Godfrey Rathbone, first Baron Charnwood (1864–1945), politician and writer, was born at Langtons, Alresford, Hampshire, on 6 November 1864, the fourth son of the six children of William Benson (1816–1887), barrister, and his wife, Elizabeth Soulsby (d. 1892), daughter of Thomas Smith, of Colebrooke Park, Tonbridge. The actor–manager Sir Francis Robert (Frank) *Benson and the designer William Arthur Smith *Benson were his brothers.

Benson was educated at Winchester College and Balliol College, Oxford. He obtained a first class in *literae humaniores* (1887) and was appointed lecturer in philosophy at Balliol. He worked in close association with R. L. Nettleship, the second volume of whose *Philosophical Lectures and Remains* (containing the well-known lectures on the *Republic* of Plato) he edited in 1897.

In 1892 Benson was elected as the Liberal member for the Woodstock division of Oxfordshire, but held the seat only until the next election in 1895. He unsuccessfully stood for St Pancras West in 1900 and Worcestershire West in 1906. He was called to the bar by the Inner Temple in 1898. On 11 May 1897 he married Dorothea Mary Roby (1876–1942), daughter of Roby Thorpe of Nottingham, and granddaughter of A. J. Mundella. The marriage brought Benson significant wealth and political connections. They had two sons, the younger of whom died in infancy, and two daughters. As *The Times* noted, as a member Benson 'never took strongly to life in the House of Commons. The House of Lords probably suited his temperament better' (5 Feb 1945, 6) and he was elevated in June 1911 as Baron Charnwood of Castle Donington, Leicestershire. He was initially a strong supporter of home rule and later of imperial federation and national service. He 'was happier perhaps when dealing with questions outside the range of party politics, in supporting Lord Cromer and Lord Curzon in their opposition to woman suffrage' (ibid.). He did much social, charitable, and municipal work, serving as chairman of the council of the Charity Organization Society, president of the National Institute for the Deaf, chairman of quarter sessions, a deputy lieutenant for Staffordshire, and mayor of Lichfield.

Benson's deepest interests were religious and intellectual, and, partly through his friendship with Randall Davidson and H. M. Burge, he was closely associated with various causes connected with the Church of England. In 1930 he edited a volume of Burge's *Discourses and Letters*. His own personal views on religion were set out in a very candid study of St John's gospel, *According to St. John* (1926), and, in revised form, in *A Personal Conviction* (1928). His biography of Abraham Lincoln (1916) was widely praised for its 'originality … keen analysis and literary facility' (Thomas, 209–10) and it changed the historical approach to Lincoln's life, with an emphasis on interpretation of the acts of his administration rather than idolatry. He also published *Theodore Roosevelt* (1923).

Benson died at his home, 5 Cadogan Court, Draycott Avenue, London, on 3 February 1945, and was buried at Kingston, near Lewes, Sussex, on 7 February. He was succeeded by his son, John Roby (1901–1955), who, as an ophthalmic surgeon, did valuable research in space perception. Benson's elder daughter, Antonia, married as her second husband Sir Cyril John Radcliffe, and the other, (Eleanor) Theodora Roby Benson, became a novelist and writer of books on travel.

HUMPHREY SUMNER, rev. MARC BRODIE

Sources *The Times* (5 Feb 1945) · *The Times* (6 Feb 1945) · personal knowledge (1959) · private information (1959) · Burke, *Peerage* · J. B. Wainewright, ed., *Winchester College, 1836–1906: a register* (1907) · B. P. Thomas, *Portrait for posterity: Lincoln and his biographers* (1947) · P. M. Angle, *A shelf of Lincoln books: a critical, selective bibliography of Lincolniana* (1946) · D. Charnwood, *Call back yesterday* (1937) · CGPLA Eng. & Wales (1945)
Archives Richmond Local Studies Library, London, letters to Douglas Sladen
Likenesses W. Stoneman, photograph, 1920, NPG
Wealth at death £27,342 17s. 0d.: probate, 8 June 1945, *CGPLA Eng. & Wales*

Benson, Henry Alexander, Baron Benson (1909–1995), accountant, was born in Johannesburg on 2 August 1909, the son of Alexander Stanley Benson, solicitor, and his wife, Florence Mary, *née* Cooper. He was educated at St John's College preparatory school in Johannesburg before being moved (Benson believes because of a shortage of cash for school fees) to Parktown high school. The strongest influences on his early life seem to have been his preparatory school teacher, Miss Thomas, a firm disciplinarian who drummed into the young Henry the need always to attain the highest possible standard, and his mother, who seems to have shared similar priorities. The lasting contribution of his father, a warm but at times irascible character, arose from a passionate belief in the proper use and elocution of the English language.

Benson's mother was the daughter of Francis Cooper who joined his two elder brothers as a partner in Cooper Brothers & Co. about 1871 [*see* Cooper family]. She brought her son to England when he was fourteen years old for a family visit. With time on their hands, they visited the office of Cooper Brothers for what turned out to be a rather sticky meeting, with nobody having much to say. In desperation, the senior partner, his mother's cousin (son of the youngest of the four initial Cooper brothers) Stuart Cooper, said 'Well, Florence, if you want this lad to come here when he has finished school, we will take him.' Florence thought this a capital idea and Henry commenced articles in London a couple of months after his seventeenth birthday in October 1926. The usual premium of 500 guineas was waived because of the family connection and his uncle, Sir Francis D'Arcy Cooper, made Henry an allowance of £250 a year during his training. Benson passed eleventh in the intermediate examination and fourth (out of 1088 candidates) in the final examination of the Institute of Chartered Accountants in England and Wales (ICAEW), and qualified as a chartered accountant in 1932. Continuing nepotism, coupled with fierce ambition and ability, produced an annual salary of £250 (£25 more than was paid to other newly qualified staff) and accelerated promotion to salaried partner two years later at the age of twenty-five, on £1000 a year.

Following the outbreak of war, Benson obtained a commission as second lieutenant in the Grenadier Guards through the good offices of his uncle and Viscount Trenchard. The guards' rigid, unswerving discipline, attention to detail, and determination that anything undertaken should be as good as human endeavour could make it, made an impression on Benson which remained with him throughout his life. One of his early duties was to patrol the terrace on the side of Windsor Castle where the two princesses slept. In 1942 he was promoted to major and moved to the Special Operations Executive, a branch of the services engaged in all kinds of undercover work. He was promoted to colonel in 1944 and, a year earlier, plucked temporarily from his battalion and seconded to the Ministry of Supply to advise on the reorganization of the accounts of the Royal Ordnance factories. These were found to be in a chaotic state and Benson accepted the appointment of director of factories (accounts) giving him executive authority over a staff of about 10,000. In a successful endeavour to inculcate the need for order and discipline, Benson toured the factories in battledress tapping the floor with his swagger stick for emphasis or using it to point out anything he did not like. He admits to being tough with staff; anyone who did not pull his weight was replaced by some means or another, and everyone who seemed capable of doing the job and complying strictly with the manuals was promoted.

Leaving the army as an acting brigadier, Benson returned to Coopers on 1 January 1946 full of enthusiasm to expand the firm rapidly, partly through the application of military-type disciplines. This determination was shared by another relatively young partner, Sydney John Pears, but not the still senior partner, Stuart Cooper. Following the resignation of Francis D'Arcy Cooper as senior partner in 1923 to become vice-chairman (later chairman) of Lever Brothers, Coopers had gone through a fairly quiet period. Stuart Cooper's health was patchy and, in Benson's and Pears's estimation, he failed to put into the firm the required work and energy. After some difficult meetings in 1946, Stuart Cooper agreed to retire. Pears and Benson immediately undertook a radical overhaul of the organizational framework, with separate departments established to deal with audit, tax, executorship work, liquidation and receivership, registration and share-transfer work, costing and organization, secretarial work, and investigations. Another key initiative was for Benson, drawing on his experience in the ordnance factories, to write an audit manual setting out precisely the procedures for all audit work carried out for clients, for use within the firm.

There then began a period of rapid growth which gave rise to tinges of jealousy among some of Coopers' more staid competitors. Benson later admitted that the firm was partly to blame, being insufficiently sensitive to the attitude of colleagues within the profession. Hostility was to some extent ameliorated by the decision of Coopers to share with the rest of the profession their experience in the development of improved auditing standards through the publication, in 1966, of *Cooper's Manual of Auditing*, drawn from the original audit manual Benson had written for internal use. This became the standard work used by students and practitioners in the UK and overseas. Another major step in the early 1960s, again under the direction of Benson and Pears, which significantly enhanced the growth of the firm, was the establishment of a management consultancy arm, Coopers being the first of the major accounting firms to branch out into this field. The UK firm grew from 173 staff in 1945 to 2207 staff when Benson retired thirty years later. The numbers in the international firm rose from 239 to 18,386 over the same period, and offices worldwide increased more than fortyfold from 8 to 332. A key trigger for international growth was a chance telephone call from the senior partner of Lybrand, Ross Brothers and Montgomery, in 1956. It seems that this American firm was keen to divest itself of its London and Paris offices, thereby gifting Coopers $40,000 worth of work. While more than pleased to take on these activities, Benson and Pears pressed Lybrand for, and achieved agreement to, the establishment of an international network of firms practising under a common agreement and to common standards. The international firm of Coopers and Lybrand was launched on 1 January 1957 and, from 1973, all firms within its network practised worldwide under this new label until the merger with Price Waterhouse in 1998.

Benson also became heavily involved in running the accountancy profession following election to the ICAEW council in 1956. He was the third member of his family to hold the office of president in 1966, following in the shoes of great-uncles Arthur *Cooper (1883–4) and Ernest *Cooper (1899–1901) [see under Cooper family]. A presidential speech implored members of the Chartered Accountants' Students Society 'to remember that we have the privilege of belonging to a private organisation which serves the public interest'. Probably his most significant contribution as president was in the creation of the Accountants' International Study Group—a collaboration between the ICAEW, the Canadian Institute of Chartered Accountants, and the American Institute of Certified Public Accountants—with the remit to study major accounting problems and issue an agreed statement upon each of them. This initiative was a further manifestation of his developing belief of the value of uniformity in accounting matters, growing out of his wartime experiences in the ordnance factories and in recognition of the increasingly international nature of large accounting firms. Leading from this, as the need for more rigorous, worldwide accounting standards and procedures became accepted, Benson was the driving force in the formation of the International Accounting Standards Committee in 1973. As chairman from 1973 to 1976, he oversaw the issuing of standards designed to improve the quality and comparability of corporate disclosures through harmonizing financial reporting requirements throughout the world.

Following the Second World War, Coopers made the policy decision that its senior partners should set aside a part of their time for government work. It is unlikely that the firm was behaving in a purely altruistic manner, and there is no doubt that Cooper Brothers & Co. and its partners obtained significant financial benefits both directly in the

form of government engagements and indirectly in the high public profile that they enjoyed. Benson's appointments to a bewildering variety of committees and public bodies are summarized in six pages of an appendix to his autobiography, *Accounting for Life*. His achievements caused the obituary correspondent to *The Times* to conclude that 'Few men outside Whitehall can have had more influence on public affairs in postwar Britain'. Immediately after the war he was invited to advise the new Labour government on housing production while, in 1953, he was made deputy chairman of the Fleck committee on the organization of the National Coal Board, later becoming deputy chairman of the NCB. Many other appointments quickly followed, including studies of Northern Ireland's railways, the New Zealand fruit trade, and the transformation of coal into oil, chemicals, and gas (the Wilson committee). In 1963 he was invited by the chancellor of the exchequer to examine the impact of tax on companies' turnover, in effect the precursor to the introduction of VAT. Immediately following his retirement from Coopers, he was invited by his friend Gordon Richardson, the governor of the Bank of England, to serve as his industrial adviser (1975–83). Between 1976 and 1979, Benson chaired the royal commission on legal services, whose mammoth report included the recommendations that individual solicitors or firms should be permitted a restricted right to advertise, and that the Law Society should be responsible for taking action in cases of sub-standard professional work. From 1974 to 1979 he also served as a director of the Industrial and Commercial Finance Corporation.

Benson was appointed CBE in 1946 in recognition of his work at the Ministry of Supply, with his further government service producing a knighthood in 1964, appointment as GBE in 1971, and a life peerage in the 1981 new year's honours list. He subsequently sat in the House of Lords as a cross-bencher, speaking frequently on industrial issues and on the incidence of fraud in the European Union. In 1983 he was elected an honorary master of the bench at Inner Temple. In the following year he was made an honorary freeman of the Worshipful Company of the Chartered Accountants in England and Wales. In 1985 he was elected to the Accounting Hall of Fame by Ohio State University, USA, and in 1986 he was made a freeman of the City of London.

Benson appears to have had a miserable time when, 'raw and unsophisticated, [he] first came to wet and foggy London from warm and sunny South Africa'. That apart, his entire life was happy, exciting, and enjoyed to the full. His explanation for his enjoyment as well as his success was a willingness to work hard. Indeed, he became restive and uncomfortable when not fully occupied. His history of the firm (1954) noted that the original Cooper brothers were not easy taskmasters; he was no different. The level of commitment which he expected at the Ministry of Supply was carried over into his professional life. He once observed that, to find out what a man could do, you put him under strain. His address to the Chartered Accountants' Students Society in 1966 stressed, in addition to hard work, the virtues of single-mindedness, independence, humility, loyalty, and trustworthiness. His stern demeanour cloaked both a keen sense of humour and a deeply seated concern for humanity. The latter was well illustrated at the end of the Second World War when he was sent to Cairo by the Special Operations Executive in order to close down force 133, which controlled the under-cover and resistance operations in Greece and the Balkans. Concerned about the families of Greek patriots who had died helping force 133, Benson successfully negotiated a fund of £200,000 from the Treasury, in those days a substantial amount of money, to ease their burden.

The limited amount of time Benson devoted to recreation was also exploited to the full. His hobbies were gardening, tennis, sailing, golf, and shooting, inheriting from Sir Francis D'Arcy Cooper the shooting rights of the Drovers estate near Chichester, Sussex. He was also sufficiently interested in racing to work closely with the sixteenth duke of Norfolk, a personal friend, to put up a new stand at Ascot in the 1960s, thereafter becoming a member of the Jockey Club.

Benson married Anne Virginia, daughter of Charles Macleod, a tea planter, on 2 September 1939. They had three children: Peter (b. 1940) and twins Michael and Phyllida (b. 1943). In the family tradition, Peter Benson became a partner in Coopers and Lybrand in 1971. Benson's wife, Ginny, accompanied her husband on many of his trips and described herself, in a paper written at the time of Henry's retirement, as his 'bag and baggage'; also 'as a Cooper's wife and latterly a C & L wife'. This lifestyle did not come as a surprise; her future husband's proposal for marriage, offered in a taxi cab bound for King's Cross Station, was accompanied by a stated list of priorities among which the firm came first. She seemed entirely comfortable with this arrangement, which did not preclude the existence of strong family ties, as reflected in the continuance of family holidays with their children, after they had grown up, and their grandchildren. Lord Benson died on 5 March 1995 at Chichester in Sussex; he was survived by his wife and three children.　JOHN RICHARD EDWARDS

Sources E. Jones, 'Benson, Henry Alexander, Lord Benson (1909–), accountant', *DBB*, 1.287–8 • G. Holmes, 'Sir Henry Benson moves on from Coopers', *Accountancy* (May 1975), 46–7, 50 • G. Holmes, 'Obituary: Lord Benson', *Accountancy* (April 1995), 17 • H. Benson, *A history of Cooper Brothers & Co., 1854–1954* (1954) • H. Benson, *Accounting for life* (1989) • private information (2004) [Hon. Peter M. Benson] • *The Times* (7 March 1995) • WWW
Likenesses photograph, repro. in *The Times*
Wealth at death £2,625,167: probate, 10 May 1995, *CGPLA Eng. & Wales*

Benson, Ivy (1913–1993), band leader, was born at the Malt Shovel, 26 Lowerhead Row, Holbeck, Leeds, a public house owned by her grandparents, on 11 November 1913. She was the only daughter and third child of Douglas Rolland Benson (1890–1977), a musician, and his wife, Mary Jane Mead; their first son, Thomas, born in 1911, died of diphtheria in 1914, and Douglas, born in 1912, died of a heart attack following rheumatic fever in 1929.

Ivy, a pupil at St Luke's School, Beeston Hill, Leeds, took piano lessons from the age of five, and at nine she made her first broadcast on the BBC's *Children's Hour* on 2LO. A

year later she won a talent contest at the Leeds Empire singing 'Yes, we have No Bananas' and was presented with a doll's house by the music-hall star Florrie Forde. Her father, known as Digger, a trombonist in the pit orchestra at the Leeds Empire, played several instruments and taught his daughter to play the clarinet. In spite of teaming her up on the piano with a banjo-playing colleague and billing her as Baby Benson, he hoped she would choose a classical career, but on hearing a Benny Goodman record Ivy knew she wanted to play jazz.

On leaving school at fourteen Ivy won a scholarship to Leeds College of Art, but was unable to attend because there was insufficient money to keep her there. After taking a job at the clothing store Montague Burton's for 15s. a week, she saved enough to buy her first alto saxophone. At fifteen she joined Edna Crowdson's Rhythm Girls, and a summer season in Bridlington resulted in a chance meeting with the songwriter and music publisher Reg Connelly, who was to have a big influence on her career, starting with an engagement at a London club where she was heard by Teddy Joyce, the leader of the group Teddy Joyce and the Girlfriends.

In 1937, as a featured soloist with the Girlfriends, Ivy toured in a show entitled *Radio Rodeo*, and when Teddy Joyce died shortly before the outbreak of the Second World War she formed her own band, auditioning successfully for the revue *Meet the Girls* (starring Hylda Baker). With the male musicians disappearing into the armed forces, the impresario Jack Hylton booked the Ivy Benson band into Covent Garden, which was converted in 1940 into a ballroom. In 1943, with Hylton's help, the band was given the job of a BBC house band based in Bristol where the girls were visited by Queen Mary and broadcast at all hours of the day and night to the troops overseas. In October of that year Ivy plus the strings and rhythm sections of her twenty-strong line-up made their first records for EMI at their Abbey Road studios, the brass and saxophones being rejected because of poor intonation. Nevertheless, that same year the band was on peak form in a feature film for British National, *The Dummy Talks* starring Jack Warner and Claude Hulbert, with Ivy playing herself in a speaking role.

In 1944 the Ivy Benson band topped the bill at the London Palladium for six months, and following VE-day in 1945 it was the first group of entertainers to be invited by Field Marshal Montgomery to join the victory celebrations in Berlin. A further accolade was a live broadcast from Hamburg immediately following George VI's speech on Christmas day 1945. The band then embarked on a punishing schedule of tours for the Entertainments National Service Association and was soon top of its ratings. In between overseas tours, it headlined at variety theatres and was resident for summer seasons at Butlin's holiday camps.

It was at Butlin's in Filey that Ivy met Caryll Stafford Clark (b. 1916/17), a theatrical producer and the son of Caryll and Mundy, a double act from the *Crazy Gang Show*. She and Clark were married at Caxton Hall on 19 October 1949, but the marriage lasted just two years. Ivy married for the second time on 6 September 1957, while the band was resident for one of sixteen summer seasons spent at the Villa Marina on the Isle of Man. When her husband, (Berthold) Brantley (Brant) Callaway (b. 1914), of the US air force, returned to the United States in 1963, Ivy, refusing to leave her elderly parents or her band, was divorced for desertion.

Ivy continued to front her band for another couple of decades, eventually reducing to a ten-piece as big bands lost out in popularity to the guitar-based groups. In 1977 she was the subject of the television programme *This is your Life*; following this burglars broke into her house in Chiswick, mugging her father, Digger, who as a result of the attack died a few months later. Ivy finally called it a day in 1982, although in 1983 she celebrated her seventieth birthday by re-forming her band for an appearance on the Russell Harty television show. During her retirement in Clacton-on-Sea she entertained the holidaymakers at local hotels by playing the electronic organ.

In 1984 a play based on Ivy Benson's life, *The Silver Lady*, by Liane Aukin, was staged at the Birmingham Repertory Theatre, and in 1988 she was the subject of a BBC television documentary named after her signature tune, 'Lady be Good'. Also in 1988, she was awarded an honorary fellowship by Leeds Polytechnic, formerly the Leeds College of Art, the only honour to be bestowed on one of the most popular stars of the 1940s. She died in the Clacton and District Hospital, Clacton-on-Sea, on 6 May 1993, and was cremated in Clacton-on-Sea on 13 May.   SHEILA TRACY

Sources personal knowledge (2004) · private information (2004) [M. Ayres] · *The Times* (8 May 1993) · *The Stage* (3 June 1993) · *The Independent* (10 May 1993) · *Daily Telegraph* (7 May 1993) · *The Guardian* (10 May 1993) · *Daily Mail* (7 May 1993) · b. cert. · m. certs. · d. cert.
Archives SOUND BL NSA, interview, N464/02 · BL NSA, performance recording
Likenesses H. Hammond, group portrait, photograph, 1952, NPG [*see illus.*] · photograph, repro. in *The Times*
Wealth at death under £125,000: administration, 17 Dec 1993, *CGPLA Eng. & Wales*

Benson, Sir John (1812–1874), architect and civil engineer, was born at Collooney, co. Sligo, the only son of John Benson. He attended the Royal Dublin Society's School of Architectural Drawing and worked for the office of public works on a number of buildings, including the Dominican church and convent in Sligo and the restoration of Markree Castle. In March 1846 he was appointed county surveyor for the west riding of Cork, moving the following month to the east riding. During the period of the famine of 1847 he superintended considerable relief works, including roads and many bridges. In 1849 he married Mary Clementina Pyne, daughter of John Smith, a member of the 56th regiment; they had no children.

In 1851 Benson was promoted to be city surveyor of Cork and architect to the corporation. He was also appointed engineer to the Cork harbour commissioners and designed the Victoria deep water quay. He built up a considerable practice as an engineer and architect, accepting both public and private commissions. Some thirty bridges were replaced under his direction following the disastrous floods of 1853, and the Victoria Bridge, Sligo (1852), Cork waterworks (1858), St Patrick's Bridge, Cork (1861), and several buildings in the city, including the magistrates' court and St Vincent's Church, were designed by him. His prize-winning design for the buildings to house the Irish Industrial Exhibition in Dublin brought him into the public eye. He personally superintended their erection and was honoured by the receipt of a knighthood at the opening of the exhibition on 12 May 1853.

Benson was also involved in railway construction in the Cork area as engineer to the Rathkeale and Newcastle Railway, as engineer-in-chief and architect to the Cork and Passage Junction Railway, as engineer to the Cork and Limerick Railway, and as a director of the Cork and Kinsale Railway. He was elected a member of the Institution of Civil Engineers in 1862. He resigned his posts in 1873. During the last two years of his life he suffered increasingly from ill health and moved with his wife to London, where he died at his home, 15 Alexander Square, Brompton, South Kensington, on 17 October 1874.

G. V. BENSON, *rev.* R. C. COX

Sources PICE, 40 (1874–5), 251–3 · *Annual Register* (1874), 168 · *The Constitution* [Cork] (23 Oct 1874) · J. Sproule, ed., *The Irish Industrial Exhibition of 1853* (1854) · *Irish Builder* (1 Nov 1874) · *The Times* (21 Oct 1874) · B. O'Donoghue, 'The office of county surveyor: origins and

Ivy Benson (1913–1993), by Harry Hammond, 1952 [centre, with her band]

early years', *Transactions of the Institution of Civil Engineers of Ireland*, 117 (1992–3) • *ILN* (31 Oct 1874) • d. cert.

Benson, Joseph (1749–1821), Wesleyan Methodist minister, was born at Melmerby, Cumberland, on 25 January 1749, the son of John Benson (*d.* 1769), a landowner, and his wife, Isabella Robinson (*d.* 1779). His father, intending him to enter the church, placed him in the care of the local Presbyterian minister, from whom he received a classical education.

Benson's biographer states how, as a youth, he was 'serious and thoughtful, and so attentive to his books, that he could rarely be prevailed upon to amuse himself with his school fellows' (Macdonald, 7–8). At the age of sixteen he became a teacher at Gamblesby. During 'a conversation with a cousin', Joshua Watson, Benson was 'made sensible of [his] alienation from God'. Having gone through 'horrid agony' during which 'satan thrust sore at me' (*Methodist Magazine*, 1821, 295), he underwent an evangelical conversion in 1765. In December of that year he journeyed to Newcastle in the hope of meeting John Wesley. On finding that Wesley had gone to London he travelled there, only to find that again he had missed the Methodist leader. The two men finally met at Bristol, where Wesley, being impressed with Benson, made him classical tutor at Kingswood School. While in this position he began preaching, first to the local colliers. In 1769 he entered St Edmund Hall, Oxford, but his Methodist leanings prevented his being ordained by the bishop of Worcester. Depressed, he continued preaching in Wiltshire where, as he remarked, 'the Lord scattered my doubts, and showed me more clearly the way of salvation by faith in Christ' (Stevens, 1.518). In 1769 Benson served as headmaster of the countess of Huntingdon's college at Trefeca in Wales. Shortly after his appointment John Wesley reissued a minute first declared at the conference of 1744 stating: 'We have leaned too much toward Calvinism'. The countess opposed this and declared that anyone who did not wholly disavow it should leave the college. Benson, Arminian in theology, defended the minute and was dismissed.

In 1771 Benson was received on trial as a preacher at the Bristol conference and admitted into full connection at the Leeds conference of the following year. From that date he 'thenceforward for half a century, occupied the most important posts of English Methodism' (Stevens, 1.517). As a preacher he was charismatic and authoritative:

> So powerful was his word, that his immense congregations were moved not only to tears, but to loud wailing, so that he was compelled to kneel down in the course of his sermons, to allow the people to relieve their minds by acts of devotion, when he arose and resumed his discourse. (Treffry, 120)

Although frequently troubled by malaria Benson usually preached four times daily, holding a meeting for the society in the evening. Benson married Sarah Thompson at Leeds in 1780. They had at least two sons, one of whom, Samuel, wrote a four-volume manuscript life of his father, which at present cannot be traced.

In 1780 Thomas Coke had accused Benson of holding heretical views. An exchange of letters having failed to resolve the matter, Wesley referred it to a committee,

Joseph Benson (1749–1821), by T. Blood (after John Jackson)

which exonerated Benson, both men cordially shaking hands at the conference of that year. In 1794–5, during the dispute whether lay preachers could administer the sacrament, Benson revealed his pro-Anglican principles by supporting the 'old plan', by which Methodist preachers were not to administer sacraments. He was instrumental at the conference of 1795 in appealing for acceptance of the 'plan of pacification'. He was president of the Methodist conference in 1798 and 1810, and served as secretary of the conference in 1805 and 1809. Benson, leader of the 'high-church' Methodists, opposed the separation of Methodism from the established church.

In 1803 Benson became the editor of the *Methodist Magazine*, a position he held until his death. 'As a writer he was correct, perspicuous, and argumentative' (*Methodist Magazine*, 1821, 703), and he was also well acquainted with Hebrew, Latin, and Greek. In addition he edited collected editions of the works of John Fletcher (1806–8) and John Wesley (1809–13), and wrote a biography of the Revd John William Fletcher (1804). His other publications include a commentary on Old and New testaments (1810), one of four biblical commentaries published within fifty years of Wesley's death which made a significant contribution to Methodist biblical studies. His apologetic and polemic works include *A Defence of the Methodists, in Five Letters Addressed to the Rev Dr Tatham* (1793), *A Further Defence of the Methodists* (1793), *A Vindication of the People called Methodists* (1800), and his *Inspector of Methodism Inspected* (1803).

Benson died in London on 16 February 1821; and was buried in the burial-ground adjoining the City Road Chapel. In character he was solemn, devout, and earnest. As the Revd J. Robinson Gregory remarked, Benson was not only 'the foremost scholar and author of the Conference, but he was also one of the most impassioned of preachers, a notable revivalist' (Townsend and others, 1.390).

SIMON ROSS VALENTINE

Sources J. Macdonald, *Memoirs of the Rev. Joseph Benson* (1822) · R. Treffry, *Memoirs of the Rev. Joseph Benson* (1840) · M. W. Jones, 'Pulpit, periodical and pen: Joseph Benson and Methodist influence in the Victorian prelude', PhD diss., University of Illinois, 1995 · H. J. Downey, 'The Bristol dispute of 1794–5 ... with an assessment of the role of Joseph Benson', PhD diss., U. Edin., 1957 · *The journal of the Rev. John Wesley*, ed. N. Curnock and others, 8 vols. (1909–16) · S. R. Valentine, 'Wesley's successor: Joseph Benson', *Methodist Recorder* (28 Jan 1999), 14 · *Methodist Magazine*, 44 (1821), 223–4, 295–301, 702–3 · J. Bunting, 'Biographical sketch of the character of the late Rev Joseph Benson', *Wesleyan Methodist Magazine*, 45 (1822), 7–13, 73–9, 141–6 · A. Stevens, *The illustrated history of Methodism*, 2 vols. (1873–4) · W. J. Townsend, H. B. Workman, and G. Eayrs, *A new history of Methodism*, 2 vols. (1909)
Archives JRL, Methodist Archives and Research Centre, corresp. and papers · Wesley College, Bristol, letters and draft notes
Likenesses J. Holloway junior, line engraving, pubd 1804, BM, NPG · T. Blood, stipple (after J. Jackson), BM, NPG [*see illus.*] · portrait, repro. in *Commentary on the Bible* (1810), frontispiece · portrait, repro. in Macdonald, *Memoirs of the Rev. Joseph Benson*

Benson, Margaret (1865–1916), Egyptologist and religious philosopher, was born on 16 June 1865 at Wellington College, Berkshire, the fourth of the six children of Edward White *Benson (1829–1896), archbishop of Canterbury (1882–96), and his wife, Mary (1841–1918), daughter of the Revd William Sidgwick, of Skipton, Yorkshire, and sister of the philosopher Henry *Sidgwick. Margaret's academic, if not her literary achievements, exceeded those of her more famous brothers, Arthur Christopher *Benson, Edward Frederic *Benson, and Robert Hugh *Benson. Her mother was notable as a 'spiritual counsellor' to younger women, and tended to romantic involvements with them. Her sister was the social worker Mary Eleanor *Benson.

Benson was educated at Truro Girls' High School from its founding in 1879 to July 1883. That October she entered Lady Margaret Hall, Oxford, where she read philosophy and political economy. She was extremely happy there. Her drawings, as well as her youth, delighted John Ruskin. Her supervisor, G. W. Gent, later described her intelligence as 'remorseless', observing that he had looked for, but could not discern, the 'feminine difference'. In June 1886, in the women's examination, she tied for first place in England; after which she went to live at home, to help with dinner parties at Lambeth Palace. Here she met—and quarrelled with—some formidable contemporaries, including the composer Ethel Smyth. She produced two books during this time: *Capital, Labour, Trade and the Outlook* (1891) and a ladylike piece of anthropomorphism about her pets (1895).

In 1895, thwarted, restless, and increasingly frustrated by chronic low-grade illness, Benson found an outlet in Egyptology. She obtained permission to excavate the Temple of Mut, situated between Karnak and Luxor. With a companion, Janet Gourlay, she spent the winters of 1895 and 1896 there. In 1897 she wrote for the *Edinburgh Review*, discussing contemporary books on Egypt and describing her own excavation. By 1899 she and Janet Gourlay had produced a fine account of the latter, *The Temple of Mut in Asher*. In 1900 the archaeologist P. E. Newberry, who admired her crisp prose, asked her if she would collaborate on his monumental history of Egypt. She declined: it would be, she explained, a 'free choice' not a call 'by God'. Instead, between 1900 and 1904, she produced a witty and hostile polemic against Christian Science, opposed the rationalism of Robert Blatchford in *The Clarion*, a socialist weekly paper, edited a number of her father's works, and helped her brother to write their father's biography.

Margaret Benson involved herself in theology, particularly as it bore on the field of women's higher education. From 1902 to 1904 she was on the council of Lady Margaret Hall. In 1904 she organized the St Paul's Biblical Association as part of the Oxford and Cambridge vacation terms scheme. The association became a forum at which women met to give and discuss papers, and to hear leading theologians. This grew into the archbishop's diploma in theology, which still exists. In 1904 she used the association to set up an ambitious lecture series in biblical study from the women's branch of King's College at Kensington. The courses met a real need, finding 292 subscribers in their first year.

Benson's theological concerns dovetailed with her work on Hegel. She spent fifteen years writing a book, aimed at 'the average man', which used philosophical discursive tools to argue that it was reasonable to postulate the existence of a merciful God. The result, called *The Venture of Rational Faith*, appeared in 1908, a year after a mental breakdown, with attendant loss of faith, caused her to be confined, first in an asylum at St George's Convent, Wivelsfield, Sussex, and from November 1907 to 1912 at The Priory, Roehampton, Surrey. She suffered severe depression with occasional delusions, though generally remained quite lucid. From late 1912 she lived quietly under supervision in a private house, The Rowans, 27 Lingfield Road, Wimbledon. In 1913 she produced an extraordinary collection of semi-autobiographical prose-poems, *The Court of the King*, many of which have Egyptian settings. She died at The Rowans on 13 May 1916, and was buried on 16 May at Addington Park, Croydon. She never married.

Margaret Benson was fiercely handsome, with heavy-lidded eyes, whose shadows became very pronounced in later life. Absolute in temperament, she had a strong, lucid intelligence, and great thwarted organizational ability. She attempted a self-immolatory patience for which she was unsuited, and was arguably the casualty of her attempts at self-suppression.

JESSICA MARTIN

Sources A. C. Benson, *Life and letters of Maggie Benson* (1917) · A. C. Benson, *The life of Edward White Benson*, 1 (1900) · G. M. Watkins and M. R. Pryor, 'The feminine difference: a life of Maggie Benson', 1982 · B. Askwith, *Two Victorian families* (1971) · B. Masters, *The life of E. F. Benson* (1991) · Wellington College records · d. cert.
Archives Bodl. Oxf. · King's Lond. · Lady Margaret Hall, Oxford · LPL · Magd. Cam. · Trinity Cam.
Likenesses J. Thomson, photograph, 1893, repro. in Benson, *Life and letters of Maggie Benson*, facing p. 150 · F. Argall, photograph, 1898 (with mother), repro. in Benson, *Life and letters of Maggie*

Benson, facing p. 268 · H. W. Barnett, photograph, 1906, repro. in Benson, *Life and letters of Maggie Benson*, frontispiece

Wealth at death £4636 7*s.* 7*d.*: administration, 16 June 1916, *CGPLA Eng. & Wales*

Benson, Margaret Jane (1859–1936), botanist and palae-ontologist, was born on 20 October 1859 in London, the sixth of the nine children of William Benson, architect and civil engineer, and his wife, Edmunda, daughter of landscape painter James Bourne. The family moved to Norton House, Hertford, in 1871.

Margaret received her early education at home, where she was tutored by her older sister Henrietta until she was able to continue on her own. Her father, long interested in natural history, gave her a thorough introduction to field botany, and her mother, a successful flower painter, taught her how to paint. When she was nineteen she spent a year at Newnham College, Cambridge, studying classics. She also took the Cambridge higher local examination, but before continuing her studies earned some necessary money by teaching for seven years as assistant mistress in Exeter high school.

Margaret entered University College, London, in 1887 and took a first-class BSc degree in botany in 1891. Supported by a Marion Kennedy research studentship (1892–3) she went on to postgraduate research under F. W. Oliver of University College. Her detailed investigation of the embryology of catkin-bearing plants, particularly birches, was carried out in part at Newnham College; the study was later considered a classic. She received a DSc (London) in 1894.

In 1893 Margaret was appointed head of the newly founded department of botany at Royal Holloway College (then a wholly female establishment) where she had already held the post of senior lecturer in botany and zoology for four years. From then until her retirement in 1922 she worked with tremendous energy, enthusiasm, and what has been described as wonderful dogged determination to establish botanical studies at the college on a solid foundation. To investigate the best in laboratory equipment she took a term's leave of absence in 1897, and, with her friend, the botanist Ethel Sargant, visited several outstanding European botanical laboratories including that of Eduard Strasburger in Bonn. She also began planning and stocking what became an excellent botanical garden as well as a museum and herbarium.

Margaret's research in palaeophytology, work involving the analysis and interpretation of complex sections of often tiny structural features, was inspired by the ongoing investigations of D. H. Scott of the Jodrell Laboratory. She began about 1902, when the technique of cutting fossil sections for microscopic examination was still in its infancy. Most of her slides she prepared herself, working at a small lapidary bench with a gas-powered cutting machine in a shed in the college grounds. Her detailed studies of spore-producing bodies and ovules in the seed ferns, among the earliest of the seed plants, were valued contributions to the understanding of the development of the seed habit, a key event in the evolution of plant life. Also especially notable were her investigations of early

Margaret Jane Benson (1859–1936), by Maull & Fox, *c.*1911

Palaeozoic herbaceous plants and some of the earliest of the true ferns. She was soon recognized as a very able palaeobotanist, and her findings, published in about twenty original papers, were quickly incorporated into the textbooks.

An enthusiastic traveller and collector, Margaret brought back much botanical material from frequent visits to Europe and the Middle East. She also collected on a visit to Australia in 1905–6 and on a trip to Australia, Java, and India in 1914–15. In 1912 the University of London recognized her research and the overall standing of her department by conferring on her the title of university professor. She had been elected a fellow of University College in 1898. In 1904, when, after four years of stalling, the Linnean Society opened its fellowship to women, she was one of the first fifteen admitted.

After retiring in 1922 to her family home in Hertford Margaret occupied herself with parish and domestic concerns, but also kept in touch with Royal Holloway College. Pleasant and genial, she was always a welcome visitor in the botany department. She returned briefly to technical work in 1932, urged by D. H. Scott to bring out some unpublished results. Her last contribution was made at the 1935 Botanical Congress in Amsterdam. She died at 32 Wood Lane, Highgate, Middlesex, on 20 June 1936 at the age of seventy-six. Funeral rites were at All Saints' Church, Hertford, on 23 June.   MARY R. S. CREESE

Sources E. M. Blackwell, *Proceedings of the Linnean Society of London*, 149th session (1936–7), 186–9 · *Nature*, 138 (1936), 17 · [A. B. White and others], eds., *Newnham College register, 1871–1971*, 2nd edn, 1 (1979), 64 · D. H. Scott, *Studies in fossil botany*, 2nd edn, 2 vols. (1908–9) · D. H. Scott, *Studies in fossil botany*, 3rd edn, 2 vols. (1920–23) · *Chronica Botanica*, 3 (1937), 159–60 · *The Times* (22 June 1936) · *CGPLA Eng. & Wales* (1936)

Archives Royal Holloway College, Egham, Surrey, letters; papers

Likenesses Maull & Fox, photograph, *c*.1911, Linn. Soc. [*see illus.*] · A. de B. Footner, pencil and wash, 1927, Royal Holloway College, Egham, Surrey · engraved collotype, Linn. Soc. · photographs, Royal Holloway College, Egham, Surrey

Wealth at death £10,540 13*s*. 0*d*.: probate, 21 Dec 1936, *CGPLA Eng. & Wales*

Benson, Martin (1689–1752), bishop of Gloucester, was born on 23 April 1689 at Cradley, Herefordshire, the son of the Revd John Benson (1652?–1713), rector of Cradley, and his wife, Catherine Martin (*d*. 1725). He entered Charterhouse in 1703, from where he went to Christ Church, Oxford, matriculating on 1 July 1706, and graduating BA in 1712 and MA in 1713. He became a student of Christ Church in July 1712, lecturer in Greek in 1714 and in rhetoric in 1715, and was a tutor between 1714 and 1716. During this period he entered the church, being ordained deacon by John Potter, bishop of Oxford, on 21 February 1714, and priest by Bishop George Smalridge, dean of Christ Church, on 12 March 1715. Benson left Oxford to accompany Thomas Fermor, Baron Leominster, on the grand tour, during which he met George Berkeley in Italy and Thomas Secker in France. These meetings marked the beginning of lifelong friendships with both clergymen and Secker later married Benson's sister Catherine.

In the 1710s Benson's politics appear to have been tory; at Christ Church he was tutor to Edward Harley, later third earl of Oxford. However, by 1720 he had formed a close friendship with Edward Talbot, the son of the whig bishop of Salisbury and the brother of Charles, the future lord chancellor, and soon he was being described by Thomas Hearne as 'a most vile Whig' (*Remarks*, 7.287). None the less, a continuing reputation for toryism prevented his appointment as the first regius professor of modern history at Oxford in 1724. After Benson's death there were suggestions that he may have shared the theological liberalism that characterized much of the Talbot circle—if he did, it probably extended no further than a dislike of the Athanasian creed, although he certainly favoured a revision of the liturgy along the lines attempted in 1689. It was the Talbot family who provided Benson with most of his early preferment: a prebend of Salisbury in 1720, the archdeaconry of Berkshire in 1721, and a prebend of Durham in 1724. In 1727 he was presented to the rectory of Bletchley in Buckinghamshire by Browne Willis and, on the accession of George II, he was made a royal chaplain. The following year, on the occasion of a royal visit to Cambridge, he received the degree of DD.

Towards the end of 1734 Benson was offered the bishopric of Gloucester. This was probably intended in part as a sop to his patron, Lord Chancellor Talbot, whose nominee, Thomas Rundle, had been finally defeated by the

Martin Benson (1689–1752), by John Vanderbank, 1732

opposition of Bishop Gibson following a long public controversy. At first Benson refused the offer, but he was later persuaded to change his mind and he was consecrated on 19 January 1735. He soon found himself drifting into opposition to the Walpole ministry, alienated by its religious and political policies. In 1736, along with most of his episcopal colleagues, he opposed the Quaker Tithe Bill and afterwards wrote to Gibson, informing him that, in order to preserve his independence, he had resolved to 'banish every desire & thought' of translation to a wealthier see (Hunt. L., Gibson papers, MS 24). Benson also blamed the ministry for the failure to send bishops to the American colonies and he reopened public debate on the subject after many years of silence when, in a sermon before the Society for the Propagation of the Gospel in February 1740, he highlighted the damage done to the church in America through the lack of a resident episcopate. It was not, however, until 1739 that Benson, together with his brother-in-law Secker, first opposed the ministry on a political question. Thereafter Benson intermittently voted against the government on issues such as the Anglo-Spanish treaty of 1739—the convention of El Pardo—and place and pension bills. Even after the fall of Walpole he continued to oppose the court occasionally, noting that 'it was measures and not ministers I desired to see changed' (BL, Add. MS 39311, fols. 49–50).

Benson thought it his duty to attend the House of Lords regularly to safeguard the interests of the church, but he was also a vigorous and active diocesan bishop, conducting a visitation every three years during his tenure and confirming in the diocese in most years. In response to the failings of his archdeacon, who was almost ninety years old at the time of Benson's consecration, he reinvigorated the office of rural dean—'this … ancient & … regular form of Government', as he described it (BL, Add. MS 39311, fols. 49–50)—and he used the newly appointed deans to visit parochially all churches, chapels, and parsonages within the diocese. In addition, Benson undertook a great deal of work for colleagues who were ill or infirm. In 1737 he performed a visitation and confirmation at York for the aged Archbishop Blackburne, and subsequently he regularly ordained and confirmed for Bishop Chandler during his annual periods of residence in Durham as a prebendary.

Shortly before his death Benson referred to himself as 'a censurer of the present times', complaining of 'a most unbounded licentiousness of all sorts' (BL, Add. MS 39311, fols. 55–6). In fact, his concern about the corruption of manners and disregard for things sacred was long-standing, and in particular he feared that the very nature of the English people was being changed by 'that poison which is called Gin' (ibid., fols. 49–50).

Benson's archidiaconal and episcopal charges are preserved in the British Library, but he published only three occasional sermons during his lifetime. This meagre output may account for his relative neglect by later generations, but in pastoral terms he was among the best of eighteenth-century bishops, not only diligent but also innovatory in responding to the problems that he faced. He was certainly held in high regard by his contemporaries. On his death the *Gloucester Journal* commented that to say of him 'all that he deserves … is almost impossible' (*GM*, 432). Even Alexander Pope was an admirer, writing in 1738:

> Ev'n in a Bishop I can spy Desert,
> *Secker* is decent, *Rundel* has a Heart;
> Manners with Candour are to *Benson* giv'n,
> To *Berkley*, ev'ry Virtue under Heav'n.
> (Pope, 2.70–73)

In June 1752 Benson fell ill, having ridden from Gloucester to Bath to visit Bishop Butler during his final illness and then back again to the north of his diocese to confirm. He died in Gloucester on 30 August 1752 and was buried, 'without any funeral pomp … according to his own direction' (*GM*, 432), in Gloucester Cathedral on 15 September.

STEPHEN TAYLOR

Sources BL, Berkeley MSS, Add. MSS 39311, 39313 • *The autobiography of Thomas Secker, archbishop of Canterbury*, ed. J. S. Macauley and R. W. Greaves (1988) • archives, Christ Church Oxf. • Hunt. L., Gibson papers • *GM*, 1st ser., 22 (1752), 432 • A. Pope, *One thousand seven hundred and thirty eight: a dialogue something like Horace* (1738) • *Remarks and collections of Thomas Hearne*, ed. C. E. Doble and others, 11 vols., OHS, 2, 7, 13, 34, 42–3, 48, 50, 65, 67, 72 (1885–1921), vols. 5, 7, 10–11 • S. Taylor, 'The bishops at Westminster in the mid-eighteenth century', *A pillar of the constitution: the House of Lords in British politics, 1640–1784*, ed. C. Jones (1989), 137–63 • *The manuscripts of his grace the duke of Portland*, 10 vols., HMC, 29 (1891–1931), vol. 7 • Benson to Lord Harley, 20/2/1717, BL, Add. MS 70373, fols. 78–9 • *Manuscripts of the earl of Egmont: diary of Viscount Percival, afterwards first earl of Egmont*, 3 vols., HMC, 63 (1920–23), vol. 2 • S. Taylor, 'Whigs, bishops and America: the politics of church reform in mid eighteenth-century England', *HJ*, 36 (1993), 331–56 • Bishop Gibson to ?, PRO, SP 35/50/1, 2 June 1724 • *Samuel Johnson, president of King's College: his career and writings*, ed. H. Schneider and C. Schneider, 4 vols. (1929) • T. Herring, letter to William Herring, 10 June 1743, U. Nott. L., PWV/120/45 • S. L. Ollard and P. C. Walker, eds., *Archbishop Herring's visitation returns, 1743*, 5 vols., Yorkshire Archaeological Society, 71–2, 75, 77, 79 (1928–31) • *Tory and whig: the parliamentary papers of Edward Harley, third earl of Oxford, and William Hay, MP for Seaford, 1716–1753*, ed. S. Taylor and C. Jones (1998) • PRO, LC 3/64, 108 • Bristol RO, EP/A/10/1/8 • A. C. Fraser, *Life and letters of George Berkeley* (1871) • E. B. Fryde and others, eds., *Handbook of British chronology*, 3rd edn, Royal Historical Society Guides and Handbooks, 2 (1986) • Venn, *Alum. Cant.*, 2/1 • Foster, *Alum. Oxon.* • parish register, Cradley, 25 April 1689, Herts. ALS [baptism] • *IGI*

Archives Berks. RO, visitation notebook as archdeacon of Berkshire, R/D/80/17 • BL, corresp., Add. MS 39311 • BL, sermons and charges, Add. MS 39313

Likenesses J. Vanderbank, oils, 1732; Christie's, 7 Jan 1981, lot 7 [*see illus.*] • J. Vanderbank, oils, 1735, Christ Church Oxf. • J. Richardson, oils, c.1739, Bishop's House, Gloucester • G. Vertue, line engraving, 1739 (after J. Richardson), BM, NPG • plaster medallion, 1891 (replica; after W. Whitley), Scot. NPG

Wealth at death £400 each to two executors: *Autobiography of Thomas Secker*, ed. Macauley and Greaves, 31

Benson, Mary Eleanor [Nelly] (1863–1890), social worker and writer, was born on 16 October 1863 at Wellington College, Crowthorne, Berkshire, the elder daughter of the four sons and two daughters of Edward White *Benson (1829–1896), later archbishop of Canterbury, and his wife, Mary, *née* Sidgwick (1841–1918). Arthur Christopher *Benson (1862–1925), Edward Frederic *Benson (1867–1940), and Robert Hugh *Benson (1871–1914) were her brothers, and Margaret *Benson her younger sister. She was educated at Truro Girls' High School and Lady Margaret Hall, Oxford (1881–3), where she took the equivalent of a second in modern languages. In 1887 she published an article on the poet George Crabbe in *Temple Bar*.

On going down from Oxford Nelly Benson (as she was known) had planned to concentrate on literature and art but, feeling overpowered by a passionate desire to 'do something for the poor', she turned to social work. Anxious to help the poorest women and girls to help themselves, she felt especially addressed by the struggle of 'respectable' girls to stay 'respectable'. No friend to socialism, Nelly Benson did not consider structural alternatives to the British economic system that might diminish, or even abolish, extreme poverty, concentrating instead on personal intervention in particular cases. She was a voluntary, unpaid social worker rather than a pioneer of the emerging new profession. She did play a pioneering role, however, as honorary treasurer, in helping to establish the Women's University Settlement in Southwark, 1886–7, out of which courses in social work were later to develop at the London School of Economics. Her own personal approach to social work may be seen in the posthumous *Streets and Lanes of the City* (1891), printed privately for her friends. The book gives a detailed account of Nelly Benson's emotionally draining commitment to help the daughter of an alcoholic mother, among other cases.

Nelly Benson's writings include a schoolchildren's *History of Russia* up to the abolition of serfdom (1885), a novel entitled *At Sundry Times and in Divers Manners* (1891) about the growth of a woman's commitment to Christianity, and a long, surprisingly conservative article in the *Nineteenth Century* (28, 1890, 616–26), 'In Defence of Domestic

Mary Eleanor Benson (1863–1890), by Hills & Saunders, c.1893

Service', in which she disputed the servants' need for two hours' leisure a day: 'They do not need or desire exercise and … as for going to entertainments … it would be giving them leisure such as hardly any of their class enjoy, and leisure that they have not yet learnt to use'. That article was, admittedly, defensive polemic in answer to Mrs Francis Darwin's vigorous attack on the life endured by domestic servants published in the *Nineteenth Century* the previous August.

On 21 October 1890 Nelly Benson contracted diphtheria, almost certainly from an infection afflicting the local poor, and died on 27 October at her home, Addington Park, Croydon. She was buried at Addington church on 29 October. Her family, in her memory and according to her wish, made a bequest to supply the training, outfit, and convalescence or holiday of poor girls in Lambeth, the first preference being given to her own Bible class girls (a clear indication that she did recognize the girls' need for recuperation and holidays after all). The Women's University Settlement established a nurseship for the poor in Southwark as her memorial.

Nelly Benson had a complex, even enigmatic personality: lively, humorous, yet depressive; enormously active and physically vigorous yet often prostrated by chronic illness; intensely sympathetic to poor women yet also extraordinarily unimaginative at times as to how the light fell for them; in some ways a 'new woman', in others deeply conservative. She was the only child not to be afraid of her father—or not to seem so—but she was careful to project for him an acceptable image of a good daughter that in

turn produced a memoir of her by him in the preface to *Streets and Lanes of the City* which her siblings found unrecognizable. Her brother A. C. Benson presented her very differently in his preface to *At Sundry Times*. Like her extraordinary mother, who was a Christian version of Virginia Woolf's Mrs Ramsay, Nelly Benson's most passionate relationships were with women, above all with the composer Ethel Smyth, whom her father could not tolerate. It is probable that her most real self is to be found in that correspondence. SYBIL OLDFIELD

Sources A. C. Benson, *The life of Edward White Benson*, 2 vols. (1899) · E. W. Benson, 'Memoir', in M. E. Benson, *Streets and lanes of the city* (privately printed, London, [1891]) · A. C. Benson, 'Memoir', in M. E. Benson, *At sundry times* (1891) · A. C. Benson, *Life and letters of Maggie Benson* (1917) · E. F. Benson, *Our family affairs, 1867–1896* (1920) · G. Bailey, ed., *Lady Margaret Hall* (1923) · B. Masters, *The life of E. F. Benson* (1991) · Boase, *Mod. Eng. biog.*

Likenesses Hills & Saunders, photograph, c.1893, repro. in E. F. Benson, *Mother* (1925), facing p. 184 [*see illus.*] · photograph (aged about twenty-six), repro. in Benson, *At sundry times*, frontispiece

Wealth at death £2624 6s. 11d.: resworn administration, Jan 1891, CGPLA Eng. & Wales (1890)

Benson, Sir Reginald Lindsay [Rex] (1889–1968), army officer and merchant banker, was born on 20 August 1889 at 16 South Street, Mayfair, London, the second of the five children of Robert Henry *Benson (1850–1929), merchant banker and art collector, and his wife, Evelyn Mary (1856–1943), daughter of Robert Stayner *Holford (1808–1892), art collector and MP, of Westonbirt, Gloucestershire, and Dorchester House. He had two brothers and two sisters and was educated at Ludgrove School, Wokingham, at Eton College, where he was captain of cricket and president of Pop, and at Balliol College, Oxford.

Benson's career as a soldier began in 1909 when, having overcome his father's opposition, he left Oxford after only a year and entered into an attachment with the Life Guards. In 1910 he was gazetted a subaltern in the 9th Queen's Royal Lancers. Impatient to join the regiment he could not bear to wait for its imminent return from South Africa and so paid for the journey out by working as a stoker on a Union Castle steamer. In 1913 he was appointed aide-de-camp to the viceroy of India, Sir Charles Hardinge; he was able to score some notable polo victories in India, in the same year winning the coveted Calcutta cup with fellow aide-de-camp John Astor, against a team of Indian princes.

Rex Benson rejoined his regiment, which formed part of the 2nd cavalry brigade, in France in August 1914; he survived the battle of the Aisne despite, he wrote to Hardinge, having 'had two horses shot, and my pipe taken out of my mouth by a shrapnel bullet' (private information). After serving at Ypres and then Messines, where he and three others defended the regimental aid post (housing the wounded) for forty-six hours under continual fire from the Germans who were within 50 yards, he was awarded one of the first Military Crosses. In May 1915, during the second battle of Ypres, he was severely gassed and wounded by a bullet that destroyed the brachial artery and the nerves of his right arm, after which he endured numerous operations at Dorchester House, which was turned into a hospital for the duration of the war.

From there, with his arm still in a sling, Benson was sent officially as liaison officer with the *ministère de la marine* in Paris but unofficially as representative of the head of the secret service (MIIC). This involved some curious work with the head of the French *sûreté*. After service in Ireland during the 1916 uprising he returned to France as liaison officer with General Franchet D'Esperay, commanding the *groupe des armées du nord*, and then with Marshal Petain at the French headquarters at Compiègne. The success of his role was acknowledged by the French, who awarded him the Croix de Guerre and made him a member of the Légion d'honneur. After the armistice he became chief of the British Mission and was attached to the staff of Sir Henry Wilson at the peace conference. While in France he had also been appointed to the DSO and mentioned four times in dispatches.

Promoted major in 1920 Benson next accepted the post of military secretary to the governor of Bombay, Sir George Lloyd, and in 1922 he helped to organize the highly successful official tour of the prince of Wales, for which he became MVO. On his return home that year he resigned his commission and was almost immediately entrusted with a covert mission by Lloyd George to try to reopen trade with post-revolutionary Russia. He was given a large cargo of tea, among other basic commodities, and sent to Batumi without possessing a word of Russian. It turned out to be a language it was then much safer not to know: his Russian-speaking companion, Tommy Carr, was flung into gaol, leaving Benson, dressed as a Russian, to travel across country to Moscow. Undaunted he proceeded to sell £10,000 of goods, hiding the payment in banknotes inside his boots. He was searched at the Russian–Polish frontier but, fortunately, not asked to remove his boots. The Bank of England duly honoured the bundle of notes without question, even though they appeared somewhat worn and full of holes.

Benson's father, however, decided that such escapades were no substitute for a career and that Rex should learn the business of banking at the family firm of Robert Benson & Co. In 1924 the partnership was reconstituted to include Rex Benson and his two brothers and, after his father's death in 1929, Benson set about trying to modernize the firm and improve its profitability. The Bensons' personal and banking exposure to US securities was large at the time of the Wall Street crash, with the result that their investment management business—the mainstay of the firm—faded to nothing, and the whole office sat idle. Despite this Rex Benson and his brothers refused to make any staff redundant, indeed they rewarded them with bonuses for having worked so well during a trying period.

Conditions improved, however, to the extent that by 1934 the firm had recovered almost all of its lost capital as the performance of its stable of investment trusts had improved. In 1928 Benson had been given by his father a dormant investment trust, the English and New York, to revitalize. Its capital of £750,000 plummeted in the depression but by 1935 Benson, through hard work and enthusiasm coupled with the skill and experience of his chosen co-directors, had increased its capital to £1.35 million. He also made many business trips to North America, where he vigorously exploited the firm's long-standing connections and developed underwriting and new-issue business. He was, in the words of a colleague at Bensons, 'a devil for work', and in 1936 he succeeded his elder brother Guy as chairman of Robert Benson & Co. In November 1932 he married Leslie, formerly wife of the publisher Condé Nast, and daughter of Albert Volney Foster, investment banker, of Lake Forest, Illinois. They raised a daughter from her previous marriage and their two sons.

In September 1939, though aged fifty and despondent at the outbreak of another war, Benson served as liaison officer to the French First Army until the evacuation from Dunkirk. He was appointed chairman of the inter-allied timber commission in 1940, and then in 1941 he became, with the rank of colonel, military attaché at the British embassy in Washington, under Lord Halifax. The appointment owed much to his excellent high-level connections in America and, with a brief to try to persuade America to enter the war on the allied side, he immediately undertook a series of speaking engagements throughout the country. Wherever Benson went he knew people, but he always knew more by the time he left. He possessed a delightful way of getting on with everybody—literally from the lift operator to the chairman or prime minister.

After the war Benson returned to the chairmanship of Bensons and oversaw the resurgence of its investment banking business. The problem of inadequate capitalization was resolved in 1947 by merging with the Lonsdale Investment Trust, a quoted public company, to form Robert Benson Lonsdale & Co. (RBL) under his chairmanship. He continued to concentrate on the firm's American investment holdings, remembering his father's adage, 'to keep on the inside track with management', by travelling over twice a year to see brokers and directors of companies in which RBL had an interest. Although he had no formal training or technical expertise, he was an astute banker; he was adept at identifying investment opportunities, especially in smaller North American companies, and at finding the talent to run them. He valued people and excelled in personnel management. Despite the increase in staff at Bensons he continued to know everyone who worked for him. As Jim Deacon, a long-serving commissionaire, pointed out, 'I don't work for Sir Rex, he works for me'. He was decisive, sometimes too impulsive, and an excellent communicator.

In 1958 Benson was knighted for his contribution to the work of the English Speaking Union, of which he had been honorary treasurer for thirty-three years and joint deputy chairman since 1957. He was a trustee of, and instrumental in starting, the Winston Churchill Memorial Trust, for which he personally met the development cost in the early years. To these and the many other organizations and projects with which he was involved he brought a strength of purpose, an inexhaustible enthusiasm, and an endearing modesty: he never spoke of his many exploits or achievements because his mind was entirely focused on the future and on what he could do next. Whether it was international polo—he played to a 7 handicap and picked, purchased, and managed the ponies for the British teams; or sheep farming—he improved the stock at his farm in Singleton, Sussex, to win two championships at the royal show in 1960 and 1968—he devoted himself with unquenchable energy and panache to the task at hand.

Benson possessed a talent for friendship. His bright blue eyes would sparkle with high spirits and a wide smile would crease his aquiline features as he entered a room. His warmth and gaiety were exhilarating and he was wonderful company. He played the piano impeccably by ear, often singing songs by Cole Porter, whom he had known well in Paris at the end of the First World War.

Under Benson's chairmanship RBL achieved growth and greater profitability, and it moved up the league table of City issuing houses. In March 1959 he retired from the chairmanship aged seventy, but he remained on the board until 1961. He thus oversaw the merger that year between Robert Benson Lonsdale and Kleinwort Sons & Co. to form Kleinwort Benson Lonsdale Ltd, of which he was a director. Sir Rex Benson died suddenly from a heart attack, while on board an aeroplane awaiting take-off at Naples airport, on 26 September 1968. He was survived by his wife.   JEHANNE WAKE

Sources J. Wake, *Kleinwort Benson: a history of two families in banking* (1997) [incl. C. Sebag-Montefiore, 'R. H. Benson as a collector', 480–87] · C. Norman, 'Sir Rex Benson', *The 9/12th Royal Lancers' Regimental Journal* (1968), 73 · *Kleinwort Benson Magazine* [house journal of Kleinwort Benson, City of London] (winter 1965–6), 16 · *DNB* · *CGPLA Eng. & Wales* (1969) · private information (2004) · d. cert.
Archives King's Lond., Liddell Hart C., corresp. and papers
Likenesses J. S. Sargeant, portrait, 1910, priv. coll. · O. Birley, portrait, 1937, priv. coll. · S. Elwes, portrait, 1959, priv. coll. · E. Halliday, portrait, 1968, Kleinwort Benson Group, 20 Fenchurch Street, London
Wealth at death £289,959: probate, 4 March 1969, *CGPLA Eng. & Wales*

Benson, Richard Meux (1824–1915), Church of England clergyman and theologian, was born on 6 July 1824 at Bolton House, Russell Square, London, the second son of Thomas Starling Benson (1775–1858) and his third wife, Elizabeth (d. 1859), only child of Richard Meux. He was baptized at St George's, Bloomsbury. His father was the high sheriff of Surrey and rented a succession of country houses where he could occupy himself in hunting, shooting, and fishing. Shortly after Richard's birth the family moved from Camberwell to Sanderstead Court, near Croydon, soon moving to North Cray Place, Kent. In 1833 they moved to Sketty Park, near Swansea, and eventually settled in 1839 at the Manor House, Teddington, Middlesex. Mrs Benson's father owned a noted London brewery and claimed royal descent from Anne, sister of Edward IV. The strong evangelical faith in which she raised her sons had been nurtured in her upbringing among the influential evangelicals known as the Clapham Sect.

Mrs Benson allowed Henry Roxby, her eldest son, who was to become a general and colonel of the 17th lancers, to be educated at Harrow School, but Richard was educated at home by tutors. In 1841 he spent the summer in Germany with his half-sister Sarah Benson and the following year they spent the winter in Rome, where they quickly made friends among the intelligentsia. Benson's fluent Italian enabled him to converse easily with Pope Gregory XVI in a private audience and to develop his theological acumen in conversations with leading theologians.

Benson went up to Christ Church, Oxford, in October 1844. When he arrived the Oxford Movement—which had already attracted him—was in crisis. E. B. Pusey, regius professor of Hebrew, was still prohibited from preaching in the cathedral of which he was a canon and Newman's conversion to Roman Catholicism was impending. Benson was indifferent to outward success and came under Pusey's influence at this time of apparent débâcle. Benson remained a loyal disciple of Pusey throughout his life. In 1846 Pusey nominated him to a studentship, and he was admitted on 24 December along with his friend H. P. Liddon; he retained his studentship until death. He took his BA degree (second class in *literae humaniores* and mathematics) in 1847. In 1848 he won the Kennicott Hebrew scholarship and was ordained deacon by Bishop Samuel Wilberforce, becoming assistant curate of St Mark's, Surbiton. He was ordained to the priesthood in 1849 and graduated MA in the following year.

In 1850 Benson accepted the college living of St James, Cowley, a sparsely populated parish extending from the eastern side of Oxford to the small village of Cowley. The prayer and study that accompanied his pastoral work enabled him to pioneer a form of ministry through which he would exercise great influence as a spiritual guide for half a century. After immersing himself in Ignatian spirituality, Benson led the first retreat for Anglican clergy at Cuddesdon in July 1858. He was also preparing to pioneer an unprecedented form of missionary endeavour in India, a brotherhood that would bear witness to native people by living the ascetic life among them. As he was about to sail plans were announced to develop Cowley Common as a suburb of Oxford, and at the urging of Bishop Wilberforce he agreed to remain in order to serve the new population.

Within a few years Benson emerged as the key figure in a movement to found an Anglican religious order for men, to which John Keble had given impetus in a sermon of July 1863. Several orders for women had been founded in the previous two decades. In the spring of 1865 an American priest, C. C. Grafton (later bishop of Fond du Lac), who had been attempting to found a community with O. S. Prescott, came to Oxford to participate. Benson was successful in obtaining the approval of Bishop Wilberforce for 'a Congregation of Priests and Laymen, giving up the world, living by simple rule and devoting ourselves to prayer, study and mission work' (Woodgate, 64). Grafton and Benson were joined by S. W. O'Neill and they spent 1866 establishing the life of the community. The Society of St John the Evangelist came into being when the three priests made their life vows of poverty, celibacy, and obedience on 27 December and Benson was elected superior. In 1868 the community moved into the mission house at 16 Marston Street, Oxford. In 1870 the parish was divided and Benson became the vicar of the new parish of Cowley St John.

Benson did not imitate a traditional model of the religious life, but crafted a synthesis. The ordered life of liturgical prayer and community was derived from the Benedictine heritage, and the emphasis on solitary prayer in the cell and asceticism from the contemplative orders. But the mobility and availability for evangelistic and pastoral work reflected the charisms of the Society of Jesus and the modern apostolic congregations.

In the next two decades Benson exhibited the full range of his extraordinary versatility. Fully active as the pastor of a rapidly expanding parish, he was at the same time establishing the society on the foundation of a monastic theology and spirituality, the power and originality of which is evident in *The Followers of the Lamb* (1900) and the addresses and commentary on the rule of life in *Instructions on the Religious Life* (1927, 1935, 1951) and *The Religious Vocation* (1939). His influence spread not only through his preaching, retreats, and immense correspondence but also through parochial missions. This was a form of ministry that he had pioneered from 1862, adapting methods developed by the Lazarist Fathers in France in the eighteenth century, and those of Robert Aiken and Richard Twigg, Anglican priests who used revivalist techniques to encourage 'Catholic' churchmanship. In his writing he especially devoted himself to spiritual commentary on scripture and the liturgical year, notably *Bible Teachings* (1875), *Spiritual Readings* (1879–82), and *The Final Passover* (1884, 1893–5).

Benson was a small, wiry man of formidable stamina, with an ascetic's indifference to comfort or appearance. Although his personal reserve and prophetic intensity could be intimidating, he was known for a rich and sardonic sense of humour and the remarkable tenderness he could show. His letters reveal a wide and cultivated mind with a lively interest in current affairs, literature, poetry, music, and history. In his preaching he habitually soared to heights where few could follow, but in the more intimate setting of retreat the immediacy of his inspiration and his spiritual passion made an indelible impression on his hearers. His monastic experience and his absorption of patristic theology and the writings of the mystics gave rise to an uncompromising insistence on orthodoxy as a living reality that could only be appropriated through prayer and worship. Benson's loyalty to the Church of England was undeviating, but his critique of the entire system of Christendom that had been inaugurated under Constantine was very radical. He believed that a renewed apostolic Christian community could emerge only from the disintegration of Christendom, and criticized political schemes for disestablishment as partial and unrealistic. Much of his motivation for foreign mission stemmed from his hope that the younger churches could forge more authentic expressions of Christianity.

Benson was resistant to some of the later developments of the Oxford Movement. His unwavering focus on spiritual conversion excluded sympathy with Christian socialism. Developments in biblical criticism did not impress him; he mordantly referred to *Lux mundi*, the volume of essays edited by Charles Gore in 1889, as *Lux mundana*, worldly light.

In 1870 Benson went to the USA to establish a branch of the society in Boston; work in India began in 1874 and in South Africa in 1883. By 1884 the society had attained maturity, and its rule and statutes were formally approved by Bishop Mackarness of Oxford, who accepted the position of visitor. Two years later Benson relinquished his responsibilities as vicar.

The era of his leadership drew to a close in 1890 when Benson resigned as superior. Administration of the society had become complex and he had reservations about the institutional development of religious life. He left for a long mission tour in India and then Canada, finally settling in Boston in 1892, where he was to stay until recalled to Cowley in 1899. His later years bore fruit in *The War Songs of the Prince of Peace* (1901), a spiritual commentary on the psalter. He continued to be active in preaching and retreat conducting for several years until the onset of blindness and crippling rheumatism curtailed his ministry. He died at the mission house in Oxford on 14 January 1915, and was buried two days later in the cemetery adjoining the parish church of St Mary and St John.

MARTIN L. SMITH

Sources M. V. Woodgate, *Father Benson of Cowley* (1953) · M. Smith, *Benson of Cowley* (1980) · *DNB* · *Letters of Richard Meux Benson*, ed. G. Congreve and W. H. Longridge (1916) · *Further letters of Richard Meux Benson*, ed. W. H. Longridge (1920) · P. F. Anson, *The call of the cloister: religious communities and kindred bodies in the Anglican communion*, 4th edn (1964) · A. M. Allchin, *The silent rebellion* (1958)
Archives Society of St John the Evangelist, St Edward's House, London, corresp. and papers | Borth. Inst., corresp. with Lord Halifax
Likenesses L. Carroll [C. L. Dodgson], photograph, *c.*1856, NPG · photographs, Society of St John the Evangelist, St Edward's House, London

Benson, Robert, Baron Bingley (*bap.* **1676**, *d.* **1731**), politician, was baptized on 25 March 1676 at Wakefield All Saints, Yorkshire, the second child and only son of Robert Benson (*d.* 1676) of Wrenthorpe, Yorkshire, and his wife, Dorothy (*d.* 1696), the daughter of Tobias Jenkins of Grimston, Yorkshire. His father was described by Sir John Reresby as a man of mean extraction and of little worth, but he was in fact a county attorney who served as clerk of the peace for the West Riding and then clerk of the assizes for the northern circuit before becoming an official of Lord Treasurer Danby and a parliamentary candidate. At his death he was worth anything between £1500 and £3000 per annum. Benson's mother remarried in 1680; her new husband was Sir Henry Belasyse.

After entering Christ's College, Cambridge, in 1691 Benson embarked on a grand tour in 1693, and in 1694 was in Italy, where he signed the register at Padua University. In 1702 he was returned to parliament for Thetford, Norfolk, on the interest of his erstwhile brother-in-law Sir John Wodehouse, bt, who had married his elder sister,

Elizabeth (*d.* 1701). Benson married, at St Giles-in-the-Fields, London, on 21 December 1703, Lady Elizabeth Finch (*c.*1676–1757), the eldest daughter of Baron Guernsey, later first earl of Aylesford. In 1705 his uncle Tobias Jenkins stood aside for him at York, and he continued to represent the city in parliament until his elevation to the peerage. Away from politics he pursued an interest in architecture, and between 1700 and 1710 designed Bramham Park, West Riding of Yorkshire.

In the Commons, Benson eschewed extremes, espousing a moderate toryism. As such he was an obvious candidate for office in Harley's incoming ministry, and became a lord of the Treasury (10 August 1710); when his chief was made earl of Oxford, Benson was appointed chancellor of the exchequer and a privy councillor (14 June 1711). He was a key spokesman for the government in the Commons during the following two sessions. On 21 July 1713 he was raised to the peerage as Baron Bingley, of Bingley, Yorkshire, a creation which led to much carping about his lowly origins and want of a coat of arms. His peerage precluding a Treasury office, in December 1713 he was appointed ambassador-extraordinary to Spain. However, he never left England, and in February 1714 was present to take his seat in the Lords. He lost office after the Hanoverian succession. An inveterate speculator in South Sea stock, having been on the company's first board of directors, during the South Sea Bubble he probably lost money owing to a mistaken belief that the falling stock would soon recover its upward momentum. He joined the opposition led by Lord Cowper (1720–23) to the whig ministry, and continued in opposition until 1730, when he spoke in the Lords in favour of the treaty of Seville. He was rewarded with the post of treasurer of the household, but held it only for a year, as he died, 'of a pleurisy and a fever' (Boyer, 41.411), on 9 April 1731. He was buried on 14 April in St Paul's chapel, Westminster Abbey.

Bingley's only legitimate child, Harriet, inherited a reputed £100,000 in cash and her father's landed property. A few months after his death she married George Fox, later Baron Bingley (1762). Bingley also bequeathed £7000 to his 'natural' daughter, Mary Johnson, and £400 per annum to Anna Maria, the wife of Sir John Burgoyne. Since Bingley's godson, John Burgoyne, was the ultimate beneficiary if his daughters should fail to produce an heir, it has been speculated that Burgoyne was Bingley's natural son, but this must remain conjecture.

STUART HANDLEY

Sources 'Benson, Robert', HoP, *Commons* · will, PRO, PROB 11/643, sig. 86 · *Memoirs of Sir John Reresby*, ed. A. Browning, 2nd edn, ed. M. K. Geiter and W. A. Speck (1991), 90–106 · *The Wentworth papers, 1705–1739*, ed. J. J. Cartwright (1883), 133–348 · IGI · *The manuscripts of the earl of Dartmouth*, 3 vols., HMC, 20 (1887–96), vol. 1, pp. 325–6 · C. Jones, 'The new opposition in the House of Lords, 1720–1723', *HJ*, 36 (1993), 309–29 · A. Boyer, *The political state of Great Britain*, 41 (1731) · *Yorkshire: the West Riding*, Pevsner (1959) · *Westminster Abbey Register*, Harleian Society, 54, 331 · *Manuscripts of the earl of Egmont: diary of Viscount Percival, afterwards first earl of Egmont*, 3 vols., HMC, 63 (1920–23), vol. 1, p. 11 · H. R. F. Brown, *Inglesi e scozzesi all'università di Padova dall'anno 1618 sino al 1765* (Venice, 1922)

Archives PRO, family and estate papers, C107/31, 56, 89–90, 169 | Staffs. RO, letters to Lord Dartmouth · W. Yorks. AS, Leeds, Lane-Fox MSS
Likenesses A. von Behn, vellum, 1704, V&A
Wealth at death £100,000: HRC, 1731, p.19

Benson, Robert (1797–1844), judge and local historian of Salisbury, was born in the cathedral close, Salisbury, on 5 February 1797, the youngest son of the Revd Edmund Benson (*d.* 1835), vicar of Salisbury Cathedral, and his wife, Anne Hunt Grubbe. He was educated at a private school in Salisbury and at Trinity College, Cambridge, where he graduated BA in 1818 and MA in 1821. After being called to the bar at the Middle Temple in 1821, he practised in the equity courts. In 1823 he went to Corsica as one of the commissioners to carry into effect the bequests of the Corsican patriot General Paoli, and published *Sketches of Corsica* (1825) on his return.

Benson was elected deputy recorder of Salisbury in 1829 and became recorder in 1836. In 1837 he published his best-known work, *Memoirs of the Life and Writings of the Rev. Arthur Collier*, a contemporary expounder of Bishop Berkeley's metaphysical doctrine. In 1843 his *History of Salisbury* was published as a volume in Richard Colt Hoare's History of Modern Wiltshire series, with Robert Benson and Henry Hatcher, of Salisbury, as joint authors. Hatcher had objected to Benson taking credit, since he had contributed only 16 pages out of 600. A pamphlet war ensued.

Benson died unmarried at the house of his only surviving sister in the cathedral close, Salisbury, on 21 June 1844. He was buried in the cathedral with the other members of his family. THOMPSON COOPER, *rev.* HUGH MOONEY

Sources GM, 2nd ser., 22 (1844), 323 · *BL cat.* · H. R. Luard, ed., *Graduati Cantabrigienses*, 6th edn (1873), 33
Archives Bodl. Oxf., drawings of buildings in Oxfordshire and Wiltshire · Wilts. & Swindon RO, autobiographical and family history papers | Bodl. Oxf., corresp. with Sir Thomas Phillipps

Benson, Robert Henry [Robin] (1850–1929), merchant banker and art collector, was born on 24 September 1850 at Fairfield House, Fairfield, near Manchester, the eldest of three children of Robert Benson (1814–1875), merchant banker, and his wife, Eleanor (1824–1883), daughter of Vice-Admiral Constantine *Moorsom. He was educated at Eton College and at Balliol College, Oxford, where he was a notable athlete and gained a blue.

In January 1873 Benson was admitted to the Inner Temple to read for the bar, but before starting pupillage he was sent by his father to Boston in October 1874 to learn about the family firm's American business, in the aftermath of the financial crash of 1873. The sudden death of his father brought him home and on 19 January 1875 he and his younger brother Constantine became partners in the City mercantile and banking firm of Robert Benson & Co. They soon discovered that the firm was in no position to withstand the losses incurred by the financial failure of several major creditors, its precarious condition having been masked by lapses in accounting procedures. On 16 June 1875 the firm's failure was announced, leaving Robin and his brother with little of their once substantial inheritance.

Although the Bensons had left the Society of Friends in 1836, it was with the help of old Quaker connections that in the autumn of 1875 Robin Benson was able to enter into a partnership with the banker John Cross (who was briefly married to the novelist George Eliot at the end of her life). The new firm of Cross, Benson & Co. subsequently engaged in the business of investment, principally in American securities for private clients. Benson proceeded to build up a sound, profitable, niche business in financing railways in the American west, and he amassed a large personal fortune through identifying Chicago and the mid-west as a growth area; at that time, during the depression after the 1873 crash, the City viewed 'Yankee' rail stocks with suspicion and Benson thus bought cheaply before renewed demand in 1879 caused prices to surge higher. He also invested in mid-western railroad and land development companies through his brother, who was based in St Paul. Cross retired in 1883, when the firm became Robert Henry Benson & Co.; it reverted to Robert Benson & Co. in the following year.

Robin Benson had a forging role in the creation of the investment trust industry through two friends, Robert Fleming and Alexander Henderson, later Lord Faringdon; they sat on the boards of each other's trusts and unofficially acted together to invest in railways in the United States and South America. In 1889 Benson founded the Merchants' Trust which, with a capital of £2 million, largely concentrated on American railway investments, though it also invested in southern African ones. His involvement in the financing of southern African railways and mining development increased when, after the Jameson raid, his brother-in-law Albert *Grey, later fourth Earl Grey, was appointed administrator of Rhodesia and replaced Cecil Rhodes as chairman of the Chartered Company. Benson knew Cecil Rhodes and, concerned about the potential for an abuse of power, was instrumental in the separation of the concessionary and financial functions of the Chartered Company. Robert Benson & Co. managed the £1 million flotation to form the Charter Trust and Agency Company, which managed the financial side of the business and of which Robin Benson was a director. He sat on many other boards, including those of several infant electricity companies, as the finance of technological innovation in electrical power and machinery attracted his interest, and he was also chairman of the Anglo-American Telegraph Company.

On 7 July 1887, Benson married Evelyn Mary (1856–1943), daughter of Robert Stayner *Holford (1808–1892), MP and art collector, of Westonbirt, Gloucestershire, and Dorchester House, and they had three sons and two daughters. After his marriage he devoted increasingly more time to interests not directly concerned with banking. The foremost of these was his collection of Italian pictures, which was of outstanding importance. Benson had begun to collect works of art before his marriage under the guidance of William Graham, a noted collector, and his earliest Italian acquisitions were in 1884 with the purchase from the dealer Martin Colnaghi of *Portrait of a Collector* by Mario Basaiti, *Madonna and Child*, attributed to Mainardi, and A

Triumphal Procession with Prisoners by Andrea Schiavone. From this modest beginning the collection built up by Benson and his wife grew into one that David Lindsay, twenty-seventh earl of Crawford and earl of Balcarres, himself a discerning collector, called the finest personal and the finest specialized collection he had come across. Confined to pictures from the fourteenth and fifteenth centuries, it included four panels by Duccio di Buoninsegna, as well as works of old masters ranging from Bellini, Giorgione, and Botticelli to Correggio, Titian, and Veronese.

During the First World War, the bank's business was reduced to a holding operation. This meant that Benson was able to write about economic policy, preparing for Arthur Balfour *A Résumé of War Finance* (1916); he also pondered business conditions after the war and published a booklet in 1918 advocating the creation of a central bank to 'do for the lock-up capital in Government Securities what the Bank of England does for the Bill Market' (Benson, 47). After the war he realized that his firm could only survive with increased capitalization. In 1924, therefore, Benson brought his three sons into the partnership and recapitalized the firm by consigning a major portion of his early Chinese porcelain and pottery collection for sale at Christies in July 1924. He converted the partnership into a limited company in 1926, but on the death of his brother-in-law Sir George Holford, long a sleeping partner in the firm, the large Holford share of the firm's capital had to be realized by his estate. Benson nevertheless replenished the shortfall in the capital—but only through the sale of his picture collection. Joseph Duveen had long coveted the collection and it was sold to him *en bloc* for $4 million in 1927. Robin Benson left a permanent record of the Italian collection in his illustrated *Catalogue of Italian Pictures Collected by Robert and Evelyn Benson* (1914), as he did for another family collection sold in 1926, *The Holford Collection at Westonbirt* (1924) and *The Holford Collection, Dorchester House* (1927). The pictures later found a home in major galleries throughout the world.

Benson had long been active in public life, serving as a trustee of the National Gallery from 1912 and also as a trustee of the Tate Gallery. He was a member of the council of the Victoria and Albert Museum and joined the executive committee of the National Art Collections Fund in 1903, the year of its foundation, and became treasurer in 1906, the year he was actively engaged in saving Velázquez's *Rokeby Venus* for the nation. He was also one of the pillars of the Burlington Fine Arts Club, contributing largely to its periodical exhibitions, and he wrote the introduction to the 1893 exhibition, 'Luca Signorelli and his school'. He frequently lent pictures of his own and, through his brother-in-law, from the Holford collection, to exhibitions at the major galleries.

During Benson's later years he neglected the City for the attractions of family life. He rented Buckhurst Park, Withyham, Sussex, from Lord De La Warr for twenty-four years and considerably improved it entirely at his own expense. The only sign that he remembered the financial difficulties of his youth was that he wished his capital to remain liquid and not tied up in maintaining an estate—a sensible approach during a time of agricultural depression. He was musical, and as a patron of the Royal College of Music he would arrange for a college quartet to play at Buckhurst house parties and invite his guests to sing and play in what one called 'a real orgy of music'. He was an affectionate father, delighting in the company of his five children and keen to do all he could for them.

A slim, dark-haired man of middle height with a neat, fine beard, he was good-looking and possessed of a quiet charm that could have enabled him to slide effortlessly through life if he had been less conscientious and intellectually agile. He carried his learning lightly and was full of enthusiasm about books, ideas, art, rose champagne, and philosophical debate. He was tolerant in his judgement of others, incapable of malice, but hated meanness. During a visit to Paris he bought an expensive present and was furious to be charged extra for the string required to tie the parcel.

Benson died of a paralytic stroke on 8 April 1929 at his London home, Walpole House, on Chiswick Mall, and was buried in the churchyard at Westonbirt, Gloucestershire. The firm suffered very badly from the Wall Street crash and the onset of the depression, but Benson's three sons, including Sir Reginald Lindsay (Rex) *Benson, played a key role in its subsequent recovery.   JEHANNE WAKE

Sources J. Wake, *Kleinwort Benson: a history of two families in banking* (1997) [incl. C. Sebag-Montefiore, 'R. H. Benson as a collector', 480–87] · R. H. Benson, *State credit and banking* (1918) · private information (2004) · b. cert. · d. cert. · *CGPLA Eng. & Wales* (1929)
Archives CUL, corresp. with Lord Hardinge · Harvard University, near Florence, Italy, Center for Italian Renaissance Studies, letters to B. Berenson · Kleinwort Benson archives, 20 Fenchurch Street, London, Kleinwort Benson MSS · U. Durham, Earl Grey MSS
Likenesses W. Richmond, portrait, 19th cent., priv. coll. · P. de Laszlo, portrait, 20th cent., priv. coll. · J. S. Sargent, portrait, 20th cent., priv. coll.
Wealth at death £116,481 6s. 3d.: probate, 26 June 1929, *CGPLA Eng. & Wales*

Benson, Robert Hugh (1871–1914), Roman Catholic priest and writer, was the fourth son and youngest child of Edward White *Benson (1829–1896) and his wife, Mary Sidgwick (1841–1918), a second cousin. He was born on 18 November 1871 at Wellington College, of which his father was the first headmaster. In 1872 Edward Benson was appointed chancellor of Lincoln Cathedral and moved to Lincoln; in 1877 he became bishop of the new diocese of Truro, and in 1882 archbishop of Canterbury, from which date the Bensons had Lambeth Palace and Addington Court, near Croydon, for their homes. These romantic surroundings ever coloured the imagination of Robert Hugh Benson, and he inherited, and early displayed, a highstrung and dramatically responsive temperament. He was also hopelessly spoiled and indulged as a child. His brothers included Arthur Christopher *Benson, later master of Magdalene College, Cambridge, and also the writer Edward Frederic *Benson. His sisters were Mary Eleanor *Benson and Margaret *Benson.

In 1882 Benson went to a preparatory school at Clevedon, Somerset, and in 1885 gained a scholarship at

Robert Hugh Benson (1871–1914), by H. Abbott [centre, with his brothers, Arthur Christopher Benson (left) and Edward Frederic Benson (right)]

Eton College, where he stayed until 1889. Not idle, he yet showed no interest in study, nor any remarkable religious sense, but ended by winning the Hervey prize for a poem on Father Damien. At Wren's collegiate establishment, a crammer where he prepared unsuccessfully for a year for the Indian Civil Service, *John Inglesant* (1880) by J. M. Shorthouse made a lasting impression on him. In October 1890 he went up to Trinity College, Cambridge, graduating BA in 1893. He was only moderately successful in classics, but he began theology, as he had decided to take holy orders. Wagner, Swedenborgianism, mesmerism, and climbing in the Alps were among his interests.

Prepared for the diaconate by Charles John Vaughan, dean of Llandaff, Benson was ordained deacon in 1894, not without a sharp mental struggle due, seemingly, to a fear of the irrevocable. After a retreat in which Father Basil Maturin, still an Anglican, gave him much spiritual and intellectual help, he was ordained a priest in the Church of England (1895), and until the autumn of 1896 he worked in the Eton mission at Hackney Wick among poor people who loved him more than he liked them. After his father's death in October 1896 he went to Egypt, whence Anglicanism 'seemed provincial'. From May 1897 until June 1898 he was curate at Kemsing, near Sevenoaks, but fled, for discipline, to the Community of the Resurrection at Mirfield, Yorkshire. Benson's views about the sacraments developed fast, but some lectures by Charles Gore, then superior of the community, unsettled him: he began to see no alternative but authority or scepticism.

In 1903 Benson returned to his home and in September of that year was received into the Roman communion at Woodchester, Gloucestershire. Given his background, he was regarded as 'the supreme catch of a convert from the very arms of Canterbury' (Masters, 206). However, his family felt the conversion made him 'smug and insufferably pontifical' (ibid., 162), however much they continued to love him.

Benson had already written *The Light Invisible*, a very popular semi-mystical fiction (1903); in 1904 appeared *By what Authority?*, a vivid story of the Elizabethan religious revolution. The months from November 1903 to June 1904 were spent at San Silvestro, Rome, and, after ordination as a Roman Catholic priest in 1904, he returned to England, and at Llandaff House, Cambridge, read theology and wrote *The King's Achievement* (1905) on Henry VIII, *The Queen's Tragedy* (1906) on Mary Tudor, and *The History of Richard Raynal, Solitary* (1906), fiction disguised as history, being an account of a hermit in Henry VI's reign. He migrated in 1905 to the rectory, Cambridge, and there wrote novels of modern life: *The Sentimentalists* (1906), *The Conventionalists* (1908)—studies of rather abnormal, and also of very average, temperaments; *A Mirror of Shalott* (1907), *The Papers of a Pariah* (1907)—studies of Roman Catholic ritual as from without; and *The Lord of the World* (1907), a sensational description of the coming of Antichrist. Lesser works of this period were *A City Set on an Hill* (1904) and *An Alphabet of Saints* (1905).

Benson bought and quaintly adorned an old house at Hare Street, Buntingford, Hertfordshire, where he lived from 1908 until his death, carving, embroidering, gardening, entertaining friends, and writing. The books belonging to this period were: *The Necromancers* (1909) on spiritualism, *A Winnowing* (1910), *None other Gods* (1910), *The Coward* (1912), *Come Rack, Come Rope* (1912), *An Average Man* (1913), *Oddsfish* (1914) on Charles II, *Initiation* (1914), a study of pain, and *Loneliness* (1915). He also printed some sermons, *The Religion of the Plain Man* (1906), *Christ in the Church* (1911), *The Friendship of Christ* (1912), and *Paradoxes of Catholicism* (1913), four short religious plays, as well as some war prayers and poems.

Perhaps the most unfortunate friendship of Benson's life was with the writer Frederick *Rolfe (Baron Corvo). The two proposed to collaborate on a life of Thomas Becket. However, not only did Rolfe prove impossible to work with, but Benson 'was advised that it was hardly suitable to have his name coupled on the title-page with a Venetian pimp and procuror of boys' (Masters, 207). In the event, the life of Becket appeared in 1910 under Benson's name alone. Rolfe is said to have cruelly satirized Benson in *The Desire and Pursuit of the Whole* (1934).

Benson was immensely popular as a preacher, although his manner was violent owing to his stammer, and his voice shrill. However, his brother E. F. Benson referred to his 'tumultuous eloquence' and to the 'flawless, flame-like delivery of his sermons' (Masters, 207). Benson visited Rome and America more than once, preaching and lecturing, had a vast correspondence, and poured forth press articles on innumerable subjects; but he lacked leisure, patience, and health to deal adequately with his materials. *By what Authority?*, at once well documented, vigorous, and tender, and *None other Gods*, with strong characterization, varied incident, and many mystical touches, not superadded to but expressed through the normal, were perhaps the best specimens of his two styles of writing. But his astounding vitality was infused into all his books; the charm of his boyish enthusiasm won him a welcome everywhere; his friendships were warm; but they were none too lasting when he lost interest, save within his family where the influence of his mother remained paramount with him. Athirst for experience, he used fully every lesson he had learned, yet his piety remained childlike and his faith fierce. In 1911 he was made private chamberlain to Pius X.

Benson's death was due to pneumonia supervening on false angina, and to the ruin of his nervous system by feverish yet systematic overwork. He died at Bishop's House, 250 Chapel Street, Salford, on 19 October 1914, in the presence of his brother Arthur Christopher Benson, to whom he was devoted. He bequeathed his house in Hare Street to the church as a residence for archbishops of Westminster. A morbid side to Benson's nature was manifest in his will. This gave elaborate instructions for burial in a tomb which could be opened from the inside, in case he was entombed while still alive.

One of the most high profile converts to Roman Catholicism of his day, Benson was a Catholic author of suggestive power. Discussing his conversion, the *Catholic Who's Who* noted that few had converted 'with so high a sense of responsibility and so entire a devotion of … time and interests to the service of the Church'.

C. C. MARTINDALE, rev. ROBERT BROWN

Sources C. C. Martindale, *The life of Monsignor Robert Hugh Benson* (1916) • A. C. Benson, *Hugh* (1914) • private information (1927) • *WWW* • Venn, *Alum. Cant.* • B. Masters, *The life of E. F. Benson* (1993) • F. C. Burnand, ed., *The Catholic who's who and yearbook* (1910) • CGPLA *Eng. & Wales* (1915)
Archives Bodl. Oxf., corresp., diary, family corresp., literary MSS, literary papers, and sermons | Archives of English Dominican Province, Edinburgh, 63 letters to Elizabeth Anstice Baker • CUL, letters to Lord Hardinge • LPL, corresp. with Randall Thomas Davidson • U. Edin. L., corresp. with Charles Sarolea • U. Glas., letters to D. S. MacColl • U. St Andr. L., corresp. with Wilfrid Ward
Likenesses H. Abbott, group portrait, photograph, NPG [*see illus.*]
Wealth at death £16,905 3s. 9d.: administration, 22 Feb 1915, CGPLA *Eng. & Wales*

Benson, Samuel Herbert (1854–1914), advertising agent, was born on 14 August 1854 at 7 Somerset Street, Marylebone, Middlesex, the son of Samuel Miles Benson, solicitor, and his wife, Phillipa, daughter of James Bourne of Lincolnshire. Benson began training for the law but at sixteen changed his mind and passed the entrance examination for the Royal Navy. His active service took him to various points of conflict in west Africa, to Gallipoli, and

Samuel Herbert Benson (1854–1914), by unknown photographer

samples, exchangeable coupons, and London buses disguised as cocoa pods, causing a surge in demand which delighted Rowntrees. In 1899 he moved the agency to a new three-storey block in Tudor Street and in 1909 to its best-known home, Kingsway Hall, the first office building in the new thoroughfare of Kingsway.

In the spring of 1899 Benson organized the Advertisers' Exhibition at the Niagara Hall in London, with eye-catching electric signs and a phonograph player—still very much a novelty. The inaugural lunch was attended by all the great Fleet Street newspaper magnates, advertisers, and their agents. Benson clashed memorably with Sir George Newnes of *Strand Magazine*, but his challenging assertion that newspapers and magazines would wither without advertising and not the other way round proved true. But the confrontation raised the old controversies over reliable circulation figures and commission charges.

Benson brought new ideas into the advertising world; his two booklets, *Wisdom in Advertising* (1901) and *Force in Advertising* (1904) were widely read by the industry's practitioners. From 1905 his biennial handbook, *Benson's Facts*, presented data on press and outdoor publicity. He believed that a study of the market should precede product development and that advertising campaigns should have definite objectives, rather than simply announce existing products. His attempt to set up an organization, the Association of Advertising Agents, failed, however, as there was no agreement on who might join or how to exclude the many charlatans who sullied the profession's name. Benson was thought to pay the best wages in London, rewarding his staff for loyalty and ability. Though somewhat remote and autocratic by nature, his temper often frayed by recurring pain in his injured leg, he took a personal interest in the welfare of his staff and assisted their families in time of trouble. Benson also found time in 1899 to be a founder of the war employment bureau, which provided work for the wives of reservists called up to fight in the Second South African War.

After being struck by a bus in Fleet Street in November 1913 Benson was found to be suffering from an incurable disease of the gall bladder, from which he died at his home, Beechgrove, Sydenham Hill, London, on 21 July 1914. He was buried on 24 July at All Saints' Church, Hertford. He was survived by his wife. His son, Philip de Gylpin Benson (1881–1931), was the first president of the Institute of Practitioners in Advertising (1927), but when he died there was no one in the family to succeed him and the firm passed into other hands, and later became part of Ogilvy Benson Mather. GORDON PHILLIPS

to Suez during the campaign against Arabi Pasha in 1882. There he was severely bitten by a poisonous insect, had to be invalided home, and spent three years on crutches, employed as secretary to several Admiralty committees, before he decided to resign from the navy.

In 1882 Benson married Mary Ann Phillips, daughter of a naval paymaster; they had three sons and two daughters. In 1885 he set up the Express Courier Corps, an organization of messenger boys, but Post Office opposition compelled him to disband it. He then undertook a series of managerial posts: from 1886 with the Normal Company, fish processors, at Aberdeen; from 1889 with John Lawson Johnston at his Bovril works at Clerkenwell, London; then briefly in France.

When the owners of Bovril invited Benson to become their advertising agent he admitted to knowing no more of the subject than most businessmen, but he had the foresight to see the part that skilful advertising might play in business practice. He accepted the invitation, entering into his new profession with dignity and purpose, and, in a milieu where sharp practice and outright fraud were commonplace, he earned a reputation for integrity. From its inception in 1893, with the prestigious Bovril company on his books, his agency held the front rank. Among his more innovative schemes were his thirteen full-page advertisements depicting topical events of 1896–7 such as the Jameson raid and the budget, in which he introduced, incidentally yet forcefully, three well-known branded goods. The 'Cocoa War' which he orchestrated on behalf of Rowntrees was even more colourful, introducing free

Sources S. Pigott, *OBM, a celebration: one hundred and twenty-five years in advertising* (privately printed, London, 1975) · T. R. Nevett, *Advertising in Britain: a history* (1982) · E. Field, *Advertising: the forgotten years* (1959) · E. S. Turner, *The shocking history of advertising!* [1952] · G. Edgar, *Mr S. H. Benson: a character sketch* (1909) · P. Hadley, *The history of Bovril advertising* [n.d., 1970?] · D. Hindley and G. Hindley, *Advertising in Victorian England, 1837–1901* (1972) · *Printer's Ink* (1888) · *Advertising World* (July 1914) · *The Times* (22 July 1914) · T. R. Nevett, 'Benson, Samuel Herbert', *DBB* · b. cert. · d. cert. · *CGPLA Eng. & Wales* (1914)

Archives History of Advertising Trust, Raveningham, Norwich, Ogilvy Benson Mather (OBM) collection
Likenesses caricature, repro. in Hadley, *History of Bovril advertising*; *Vanity Fair* type · photograph, repro. in *Advertising World* [*see illus.*]
Wealth at death £17,478 17s. 1d.: probate, 21 Aug 1914, *CGPLA Eng. & Wales*

Benson [*married name* Anderson], **Stella** (1892–1933), writer, was born at Lutwyche Hall, Wenlock Edge, Shropshire, on 6 January 1892, the younger daughter and third child of Ralph Beaumont Benson (1862–1911), landowner, of Lutwyche Hall, and his wife, Caroline Essex (1861–1934), second daughter of Richard Hugh Cholmondeley, rector of Hodnet, later of Condover Hall, Shropshire, and younger sister of the novelist Mary Cholmondeley. Benson spent an isolated, lonely, and sickly childhood in the care of a succession of nannies, and she watched uncomprehendingly as her parents' marriage deteriorated because of her father's alcoholism and womanizing. She found consolation in her dog Pepper, in a secret 'imaginary world filled with imaginary people' (Grant, 19), and in her diary, begun in 1901 and kept throughout her life. Attempts to have her educated foundered, always ending 'in illness and great nervous unhappiness' (Roberts, 14). She was educated at home, then at a private school at Hindhead, Surrey, and in 1906–7 at a boarding-school in Eastbourne. In 1910 she attended a girls' school in Freiburg, Germany. Despite her frailty, she fared better with travel, spending a happy seventeen months in Switzerland and the south of France from 1910 on, before sailing to the West Indies for the winter of 1913–14, the latter experience providing material for her first book, *I Pose* (1915).

Benson's experiences leading up to and during the early part of the First World War working for suffragists' organizations and for charities in the East End of London also contributed material for this 'post-impressionist' novel. Its originality lies in its radical subversion of the traditional closure of romance in marriage: Benson has the suffragette heroine defiantly hurl a bomb at a church altar. After the financial success of this effort (which netted her £60) Benson wrote another novel set in the East End, *This is the End* (1917), that centres on unrequited love and conveys a broad range of attitudes towards the war as well. During the latter years of the war Benson continued to work for the Charity Organization Society, though she satirized members' self-righteous attitudes in her third novel, *Living Alone* (1919), and then worked for the war effort as a gardener in Berkshire.

In 1918 for health reasons Benson voyaged to the USA, and travelled from New York to California. After a year there working at various odd jobs she felt so alienated by the vulgarity of America that she decided in December 1919 to travel to Hong Kong, where she taught at an Anglican boys' school, and then to Peking (Beijing), where she worked in a medical institute.

In China, where she would spend much of the rest of her life, Benson met James Carew O'Gorman Anderson (1893–1946), known as Shaemus, who was employed by

Stella Benson (1892–1933), by Cuthbert Julian Orde, 1929

the imperial Chinese maritime customs service. She married him in London on 27 September 1921, exactly one year after meeting him. There were no children of the marriage. They spent their honeymoon making the daring journey between New York and California in a Model T Ford, affectionately named Stephanie. All the while Stella worked on a fourth novel, *The Poor Man* (1922), which included satirical treatment of her first stay in California that provoked outrage among some Californian friends.

Though Benson was often depressed in China, partly because of the narrow-minded colonial mentality and partly because of marital difficulties, she was quite productive as a writer. Along with three more novels, she began to publish whimsical and amusing short stories, and well-regarded travel books (*The Little World*, 1925; *Worlds within Worlds*, 1928). With her novel *The Far-Away Bride* (1930; published in the UK as *Tobit Transplanted* in 1931) she achieved both popular success and critical acclaim, winning the A. C. Benson silver medal of the Royal Society of Literature and, more important to her, the French Femina Vie Heureuse prize in 1932. This carefully crafted novel develops the theme that most obsessed her—loss of identity and resulting isolation—in tracing the plight of the White Russians exiled in Manchuria.

On returning alone to England in January 1932 Benson found herself a literary celebrity. She had her portrait drawn by Wyndham Lewis, and renewed her friendship with, among other writers, Virginia Woolf, who described her as:

> quiet, as controlled, white, drawn as usual, also deaf: with steady honest eyes … a very weak but persistent voice; she coughs; & then goes on with a mild persistent patience. She is bleached; even her blue eyes are bleached. But at the same time she's practical; realistic. … All this serious, weary, intent. (*Diary of Virginia Woolf*, 117–18)

By August she was off to rejoin her husband, Shaemus, now in Hong Kong. In Hong Kong she helped organize a successful campaign against its system of licensed prostitution. With him on a visit to Hongay in Tonkin, French Indo-China, she contracted pneumonia and died in hospital at Baie d'Along, near Haiphon, on 6 December 1933. She was buried on 7 December in the French cemetery on the Île de Charbon, near Hongay.

Collections of Benson's poems and short stories and an unfinished novel about colonial life were published posthumously. L. P. Hartley wrote of the novel *Mundos* (1935) that '[Stella Benson's] talent never found more brilliant expression than in the haunting, disturbing cadences of her swan song' (Grant, 293). It seems probable that had she lived she would have surpassed her already notable achievement.

Stella Benson had a unique ability to blend fantasy and reality, especially evident in her earlier novels and in her short stories. Her impish humour and wicked wit, frequently directed towards a satirical end, masked an underlying compassion. Benson's novels (especially her later more realistic ones) and stories often treat serious social issues and reflect her travails as a twentieth-century woman: supporting female suffrage, witnessing the tragedy of the First World War, and living in a hostile, volatile colonial setting. Despite her very modern, ironic treatment of the theme of individuals lost, isolated, and alienated in strange and frightening situations, she has not garnered much contemporary critical attention, and deserves reappraisal.   GEORGE MALCOLM JOHNSON

Sources DNB · *The Times* (8 Dec 1933) · J. Grant, *Stella Benson: a biography* (1987) · G. M. Johnson, 'Stella Benson', *British short-fiction writers, 1915–1945*, ed. J. H. Rogers, DLitB, 162 (1996), 22–31 · R. M. Bedell, *Stella Benson* (1983) · R. E. Roberts, *Portrait of Stella Benson* (1939) · P. Bottome, *Stella Benson* (1934) · J. Gawsworth [T. I. Fytton Armstrong] and others, *Ten contemporaries: notes toward their definitive bibliographies* [1933] · J. A. Collins, 'Two lesser literary ladies of London: Stella Benson and Virginia Woolf', in J. A. Collins, *The doctor looks at literature: psychological studies of life and letters* (1923) · S. Benson, *Some letters of Stella Benson, 1928–1933*, ed. C. Clarabut (1978) · *The diary of Virginia Woolf*, ed. A. O. Bell and A. McNeillie, 4 (1982) · *CGPLA Eng. & Wales* (1934) [Hong Kong]
Archives BL, additional papers · BL, corresp., Add. MSS 59659–59660 · CUL, diaries and papers · Harvard U., corresp. · L. Cong., corresp. · Mills College, Oakland, corresp. · NYPL, corresp. · Ransom HRC, corresp. · U. Leeds, corresp. · U. Lpool, corresp. · University of Chicago, corresp. | BL, corresp. with Macmillans, Add. MS 54972 · BL, letters to Sydney Schiff and Violet Schiff, Add. MS 52916 · NYPL, letters, mainly to Donald B. Clark
Likenesses C. J. Orde, oils, 1929, priv. coll.; repro. in Grant, *Stella Benson* [see illus.] · W. Lewis, drawing, 1932, NPG · C. J. Orde, watercolour, 1934, NPG · C. J. Orde, drawings, priv. coll.
Wealth at death £5939 6s. 3d.: English administration with will, resworn in Hong Kong, 10 Aug 1934, *CGPLA Eng. & Wales*

Benson [*name in religion* Boston], **William** (d. 1549), abbot then dean of Westminster, is said to have been born at Peterborough, though his name in religion implies that he was originally from Boston, Lincolnshire. As a monk of Peterborough Abbey he appeared as witness in a Star Chamber case in 1518. Following Abbot Kirkton's death in 1528 Boston was a candidate for the succession. He had, meanwhile, studied at Cambridge, proceeding BTh in 1521 (or 1526/1527) and DTh in 1528. He may at first have lodged in the Benedictine hostel (Buckingham College), but he was affiliated to Clare College. At the university he formed lasting friendships with Cranmer, Hugh Latimer, and other reformers. In 1530 he was one of the Cambridge doctors to whom the king's great matter was referred; he voted with the majority against the validity of the marriage. On 21 March 1531 he was elected abbot of Burton upon Trent, and on 30 April 1532 he was summoned to parliament, the first head of his house to sit in the Lords. Greater distinction soon followed: on 10 April 1533 he was elected abbot of Westminster, the first outsider to rule there for over 300 years. His advancement was evidently engineered by Cromwell, who in his turn received favours from his client. The new abbot offered Cromwell £20 for the king's permission to appoint a steward of his own choosing, simultaneously inviting Cromwell to accept the office. Boston took personal control of several of the obediences (posts of responsibility in the monastery), accounting as keeper of the new work for the financial years 1532–4, as cellarer and keeper of the lady chapel 1535–6, and treasurer by 1536 to 1537. This was in line with recent practice at Westminster and other Benedictine houses.

Boston's first appearance on the national stage was as celebrant of Anne Boleyn's coronation mass on 1 June 1533. On 10 September following he assisted at Princess Elizabeth's baptism at Greenwich. In 1534 he was one of the commissioners to administer the oath of succession. He unsuccessfully tried to persuade More to adapt his conscience to the oath, and More was in his custody for four days before being transferred to the Tower. In 1536 Boston presided over an exchange of property with the crown, which deprived the abbey of much of its estate in Westminster in return for less valuable lands of the dissolved priory of Hurley, Berkshire. In July of the same year the king confirmed instructions from Cromwell which relaxed the monastic rule at Westminster relating to absences from the house, entertainment of women at the abbot's table, and religious instruction. In all these respects Boston's regime may be seen as a studied rundown of the abbey's discipline and economy. In 1539 he gave his opinion that priests should marry, and supposed that the cup might be given to the laity as originally practised. Boston surrendered his house to the crown on 16 January 1540, but remained in informal charge of the church, pending its reconstitution as a secular cathedral. He asked to be freed from his duties because of 'dyverse most grevouse dyseases' (PRO, SP 1/157, fol. 59). But when the new foundation was erected on 17 December 1540 Benson (having now reverted to his family name) was appointed dean, with several of his former monks in his chapter. Because there was now a bishop to be accommodated in the former abbot's house Benson had to move into the second residence in the precinct (hitherto the prior's). He continued to hold property at Peterborough. When the deanery there fell vacant in 1543 Benson was recommended by Sir Edward North for a canonry should one become vacant by promotion, but this did not occur.

On 20 February 1547 Benson took part in Edward VI's coronation as deputy for the absent Bishop Thirlby; as dean he assisted the archbishop as the abbots had done before, bringing each item of regalia from the altar—an honour which has ever since belonged to the dean of Westminster. On 1 July 1547 he was dispensed from residence at his deanery and other benefices (though none other is known) for all but three months, however comprised, in a year, and allowed to receive payments as if resident. Despite this he appears to have lived more or less permanently at Westminster, as he had previously done. His administration (so far as the written record bears witness) was untidy. It was to be said that his death was hastened by the depredations of Protector Somerset. Certainly Somerset and his brother Lord Seymour received generous leases of Westminster property and other favours from the dean and chapter. But whatever his anxieties about the church's finances Benson's own seem to have been secure. He had retained a monastic pension of £110 16s. 8d. as well as his decanal stipend, worth a minimum of £232 10s. a year. His pecuniary bequests totalled over £600. In addition to the deanery house he had a country residence at Belsize, Middlesex, and private houses in Long Ditch, Westminster, and at Peterborough. He left the Long Ditch house and all his books to Hugh Latimer. Other bequests were made to Martin Bucer, Paul Fagius, Cranmer, and Thirlby. Benson died at Westminster between 10 and 23 September 1549 and was buried in the chapel of St Blaise in the abbey, from which his monument has long been lost.   C. S. KNIGHTON

Sources E. H. Pearce, *The monks of Westminster* (1916), 189–90 · *LP Henry VIII*, vols. 5–7, 10–11, 14, 17–18 · *CPR, 1547–8*, 86; *1548–9*, 159 · W. T. Mellows, ed., *Peterborough local administration: the last days of Peterborough monastery*, Northamptonshire RS, 12 (1947), xvi, 71 and n. 5, 79, 88 · W. T. Mellows, ed., *Peterborough local administration: the foundation of Peterborough Cathedral, AD 1541*, Northamptonshire RS, 13 (1941), xxvi, xxvii, xliv · I. S. Leadam, ed., *Select cases before the king's council in the star chamber, commonly called the court of star chamber*, 2, SeldS, 25 (1911), 131–3 · M. Bateson, ed., *Grace book B*, 2 (1905), 95, 137, 143 · R. S. Sylvester and D. P. Harding, eds., *Two early Tudor lives* (1962), 238 · D. MacCulloch, *Thomas Cranmer: a life* (1996), 20, 136, 369, 613 · Westminster Abbey, muniments, MS 33313; MS LXXXIII · C. S. Knighton, ed., *Acts of the dean and chapter of Westminster*, 1 (1997), esp. xxxvii–xxxviii · [W. Camden], *Reges, reginae, nobiles* (1600) · PRO, state papers domestic, Henry VIII, SP 1/157, fol. 59 [LPH, 15.70] · PRO, PROB 11/32, fols. 290–291v · B. Harvey, *Living and dying in England, 1100–1540: the monastic experience* (1993)
Archives Westminster Abbey, account book of his expenses as abbot; MSS
Likenesses portrait in illuminated initial, 1542 (of William Benson?), Westminster Abbey muniments, MS LXXXIII
Wealth at death over £600 in cash; also houses in Westminster and Peterborough: will, PRO, PROB 11/32, fols. 290–291v

Benson, William (*bap.* 1682, *d.* 1754), politician, architect, and literary critic, was baptized on 17 March 1682 at St Leonard's Church, Bromley by Bow, Middlesex; he was the eldest of fourteen children of William Benson (1640/41–1712), a wealthy iron merchant of Bromley by Bow, and Martha (1659/60–1722), daughter of John Austin, a London jeweller. William Benson senior was knighted on 8 December 1706, when sheriff of London, and assumed arms he had no right to bear (Marshall).

Early in the reign of Queen Anne young Benson made a continental tour which included Hanover and Stockholm. On 8 October 1707 he married Eleanor (*d.* 1722), only child of Joseph Earle, a Bristol merchant, receiving thereby a settlement of £10,000 jointly from his father and father-in-law, with which he bought estates in three southern counties, became sheriff of Wiltshire (1709–10), and shortly afterwards built Wilbury House, a villa in the Palladian style near Amesbury, Wiltshire. Colen Campbell illustrated the house in *Vitruvius Britannicus*, volume 1 (1715), saying it was 'invented and built' by Benson himself. H. M. Colvin adds: 'Even if this was polite flattery, Benson was clearly an architectural patron with advanced ideas' (Colvin, *Archs.*).

Benson was a whig. In 1711 he published a letter attacking the tory MP Sir Jacob Bankes for advocating passive obedience to monarchs. Bankes was of Swedish birth; Benson depicted the miseries of the Swedes after their liberties were surrendered to arbitrary power; the Swedish ambassador protested; Benson was summoned before the privy council but not prosecuted. It was said that his pamphlet sold 100,000 copies in several languages. Benson contested Shaftesbury and Minehead (Bankes's seat) unsuccessfully in 1713, but was returned as MP for Shaftesbury in 1715, having ensured popularity by engineering a piped water supply to that town from one of his estates. He demonstrated further hydraulic skill by greatly improving the fountains in George I's gardens at Herrenhausen.

Favoured by the king, Benson superseded the octogenarian Christopher Wren as surveyor of the king's works on 26 April 1718. Bribery was alleged, but Benson might have been appointed because Wren was thought old-fashioned, whereas his successor was a pioneer of up-and-coming Palladianism—as he showed by appointing Colen Campbell to his staff. However, Benson's surveyorship was high-handed, disastrous, and brief. He dismissed his ablest subordinates, quarrelled with his officials, and antagonized the Treasury. In January 1719 he reported that the House of Lords' chamber was in imminent danger of collapse: seemingly a clumsy stratagem by which he hoped to gain permission to pull down both houses and replace them with a Palladian palace designed by Campbell and himself. The Lords obtained a second opinion, and discovered that their house was not ready to fall, and that the shoring up already undertaken by Benson had made things more dangerous. They procured Benson's dismissal, and he surrendered his patent on 17 July 1719. To add to his troubles, he lost his parliamentary seat on a petition alleging bribery, and his wife, who had borne four sons and three daughters, died on 5 February 1722.

Benson was still in sufficient favour at court to obtain the lease of a wharf in Scotland Yard, said to be worth £1500 p.a., the assignment of a large debt due to crown in Ireland, and, on 16 November 1717, the reversion of the post of auditor of the imprests in the exchequer. (His surveyorship, with all perquisites, was probably worth less than £1000 p.a.) He had a hand in the building of Stourhead House, designed by Campbell for Benson's brother-in-law Henry Hoare. His last architectural work was the design, with Campbell in 1723, of a Palladian chancel for the parish church of Quarley, Hampshire; but he may have influenced the classical landscaping at Stourhead by Hoare's son Henry (1705–1785). At an unknown date Benson married a woman named Elizabeth, with whom he had a son and a daughter. In the 1727 parliamentary election he stood for Shaftesbury, received only four votes, and thereupon cut off the town's water supply.

Benson diverted himself with literary criticism. His *Essays* (1724–5) on the first two books of Virgil's *Georgics*, with 'Notes critical and rustick', dwells on Dryden's shortcomings as translator and poet, and argues that Virgilian husbandry could work in England (an opinion refuted in Jethro Tull's *Horse-Hoeing Husbandry*, 1733). Benson's *Letters Concerning Poetical Translations* (1739) praises Virgil at the expense of Homer and contains good close criticism of Milton's versification. His monument to Milton in Westminster Abbey (1737), with a self-regarding inscription, aroused the ridicule of Pope and Johnson. His commissioning William Dobson to translate *Paradise Lost* into Latin for a fee of £1000 aborted Dobson's plan to do the same for Pope's *Essay on Man*. Unsurprisingly he was mocked by Pope in both versions of *The Dunciad*. Benson also wrote a 'Prefatory discourse' to a sumptuous new edition (1741) of the metrical Latin psalter of Arthur Johnston (1587–1641).

In 1734 Benson sold Wilbury to his nephew Henry Hoare for £14,000 and retired to Wimbledon. On 20 August 1735 he succeeded to the lucrative office of auditor of imprests. Papers in a legal case of 1745 state that he was out of his mind and unable to transact business between September 1741 and December 1742. In his last years he had an unconquerable aversion to books. He died at Wimbledon on 2 February 1754 and was buried on 9 February in his family's vault at St Leonard's Church, Bromley by Bow; his wife survived him. He left a large fortune to his only surviving son, John Aislabie Benson, together with at least £14,600 to other legatees.   JAMES SAMBROOK

Sources H. M. Colvin and others, eds., *The history of the king's works*, 5 (1976), chap. 5 · Colvin, *Archs.* · C. R. Ashbee, ed., *The parish of Bromley-by-Bow*, Survey of London, 1 (1900), 8 · *Report of the Lords committees, containing a resolution relating to W. Benson* (1719) · Nichols, *Lit. anecdotes*, 2.137–9; 9.492 · HoP, *Commons, 1715–54* · J. C. Sainty, ed., *Officers of the exchequer: a list* (1983), 139 · R. C. Hoare, *The history of modern Wiltshire*, 2 (1826), 103–5 · *William Benson ... and Stephen Whateley ... the case of the appellants* (1745) · D. Lysons, *The environs of London*, 2 (1795), 68 · will, PRO, PROB 11/812, fols. 350r–351r · J. Redington, ed., *Calendar of Treasury papers*, 5, PRO (1883), 416 · W. A. Shaw, ed., *Calendar of treasury books*, 31/2, PRO (1960), 14; 32/2 (1957), 571–2, 619, 633 · *Le Neve's Pedigrees of the knights*, ed. G. W. Marshall, Harleian Society, 8 (1873), 494 · *Wren Society*, 7 (1930), 190, 193, 203–4, 212–20 · K. Woodbridge, *Landscape and antiquity: aspects of English culture at Stourhead, 1718 to 1838* (1970), 18–21 · *London Magazine*, 23 (1754), 92

Wealth at death £14,600 total bequests; plus residuary estate inherited by only surviving son: will, PRO, PROB 11/812, fols. 350r–351r

Benson, William Arthur Smith

Benson, William Arthur Smith (1854–1924), metalwork designer, was born at 6 Sussex Square, Paddington, Middlesex, on 17 October 1854, the eldest in the family of four sons and two daughters of William Benson (1816–1887), barrister, and his wife, Elizabeth Soulsby, daughter of Thomas Smith of Colebrook Park, Tonbridge, Kent. Among his brothers were Francis Robert *Benson, actor, and Godfrey Rathbone *Benson, first Baron Charnwood. Educated first at Darch's Preparatory School, Brighton, Sussex, and afterwards at Winchester College, he entered New College, Oxford, in 1874. In 1876 he decided to be an architect, the following year becoming articled to Basil Champneys. By chance he became acquainted with Edward Burne-Jones and his circle, through whom he also met William Morris.

Benson remained with Champneys until 1880, but it soon became clear that architecture would never be his chief preoccupation. Instead, with memories of boyhood visits to his uncle, William Arthur Smith, 'a great worker with his hands' (W. A. S. Benson, ix), who introduced the lad to lathes and elementary mechanics, Benson began to consider a career in handicrafts. 'The long and short of it is', he wrote to his mother, 'I must make something or be miserable' (ibid., xxii). With the encouragement of Burne-Jones and Morris, and a modest financial backing from his father, he established a business to manufacture domestic articles in metal to be designed by himself and made, in part, with specially constructed tools and machinery.

Benson's first workshop opened in 1880 at North End Road, Fulham, where a few men operated foot-powered lathes for turning metal. This was eventually moved to a purpose-built factory, Eyot works, at St Peter's Square, Hammersmith. The enterprise proved so successful that Benson, now nicknamed 'Brass Benson', established a showroom in 1887 at 82 and 83 New Bond Street. He married on 26 October 1886 Venetia Margaret, daughter of the landscape painter, Alfred William *Hunt. They had no children. The firm's range, much of it in combinations of copper and brass, gradually increased to include numerous patterns of gas and electric lamp fittings, furniture decorations, and tea-kettles. The business was converted into a limited liability company named W. A. S. Benson & Co. Ltd in 1901, and was sold upon Benson's retirement in 1920.

Those who knew Benson only as 'a rather dreamy artist' were astounded upon visiting his factory (W. A. S. Benson, xxvi). This advocate of the 'intelligent education of the hand and eye' had after all shown himself to be a resourceful manufacturer. Success lay in the fact that his products were fashionably artistic as well as affordable. Nor did Benson let indifferent health interfere with many other projects and interests. In 1884 he became a founder member of the Art Workers' Guild. The Arts and Crafts Exhibition Society, which held its inaugural exhibition in 1888, came into being through his initiative. After William Morris's death in 1896, Benson also became the first chairman of William Morris & Co. Decorators Ltd.

Benson's books, *Elements of Handicraft and Design*, *Rudiments of Handicraft*, and *Drawing: its History and Uses*, were published respectively in 1893, 1919, and posthumously in 1925. He died after only three days' illness on 5 July 1924 at his cottage, Castle Cottage, in Manorbier, Pembrokeshire. JOHN CULME, rev.

Sources W. A. S. Benson, *Drawing: its history and uses* (1925) [incl. memoir of the author by W. N. Bruce] · *The Times* (9 July 1924) · F. Benson, *My memoirs* (1930) · J. C. Trewin, *Benson and the Bensonians* (1960) · M. Collins, introduction, in M. Whiteway and P. Reeves, *W. A. S. Benson, 1854–1924: an exhibition of his metalwork* (1981) [exhibition catalogue, Halsam and Whiteway, London, 1–24 Dec 1981] · *CGPLA Eng. & Wales* (1924) · b. cert. · m. cert. · d. cert.
Wealth at death £17,385 15s. 4d.: probate, 20 Oct 1924, *CGPLA Eng. & Wales*

Benstede, Sir John (d. 1323), administrator, probably took his name from Binsted near Alton, in a part of Hampshire where he later had property. He may have been identical with the man of his name who was ordained acolyte in March 1286, but the first certain record of him is as a royal clerk, on 15 December 1291. From the first he was employed in the king's wardrobe; he presented the hanaper accounts in 1293, and having accompanied Edward I on his Welsh campaign in 1295, was promoted on 20 November to be controller of the wardrobe, a post that carried with it the position of confidential secretary to the king and keeper of the privy seal. He served in Scotland in 1296, and in 1297 went with the king to Flanders, having the great seal, too, in his keeping. He had temporary custody of the great seal again in 1299 and 1305, as well as being entrusted with a number of state documents. By this time he had become an important royal councillor; many chancery acts are recorded as having been authorized by the king 'on the information of J. de Benstede', and in 1301 he was one of the small group on whose advice the Statute of Escheators was issued. In the following year Edward I himself referred to Benstede as one who 'stays continually by his side' (*CClR, 1296–1302*, 602). He served in war as well as peace, being in Scotland in 1301, 1303, and 1304, in the last instance drawing a banneret's wages, while in 1305 he went to France on diplomatic missions, first to Gascony and then to Lyons. As a clerk he was rewarded with a number of livings, including prebends at Ripon and Salisbury and the deanery of the royal free chapel of Tetenhale, Staffordshire. On 25 September 1305 he was appointed chancellor of the exchequer, but he remained close to the king, with whom he was at York in 1306 and Lanercost in 1307.

Following the accession of Edward II Benstede left the exchequer on 20 August 1307, but resumed office in the wardrobe, becoming its keeper on 1 October following. But although he was almost unique among the servants of the dead king in being trusted by the latter's son, he had resigned his new post by 2 October 1308, when he was appointed a justice of the common bench. His name appears subsequently in a number of fines, indicating that he sat at Westminster; that he is not named in reports must reflect his lack of legal training. At about the same time that Benstede became a judge he abandoned his clerical orders, and by 1311 had married and taken knighthood. His wife was Petronilla (d. 1342), daughter and coheir of Henry Grapenell and widow of John Fitzjohn, who brought her second husband the Essex manor of Stanbridge. Benstede also acquired estates in Devon, centred on Ermington hundred, Hampshire (where he farmed Alton from Queen Margaret), Essex, Cambridgeshire, Hertfordshire, and other counties. He had two sons, Edmund, born in July 1312, and Guy.

Benstede continued to be employed by Edward II, primarily as a diplomat, though he also acted as a commissioner of oyer and terminer in several counties, usually in counties where he held lands; early in 1311 he went to the curia to seek papal support for the king against the ordainers, while in the following year he was sent to summon the earls of Lancaster, Hereford, and Warwick to appear before the king, specifying that they were to come without horses and arms. At about this time he fell very ill, so much so that the earl of Pembroke petitioned for the wardship of his heir, but he recovered, and in 1315 went on an embassy to Aquitaine to raise money for the Scottish war. In 1318 he was an ambassador to Scotland, and in 1319 went once more to the curia, this time to press for the canonization of Thomas of Hereford (d. 1282), which took place in the following year. No doubt it was because of advancing years that on 16 October 1320 he was replaced on the bench by William Hurle. Still alive on 5 June 1323, Benstede was dead by 20 December of that year. He was probably buried in the church of Benington, Hertfordshire, which he appears to have substantially rebuilt, and where he and Petronilla may still be commemorated by defaced effigies. Following Benstede's death, his widow showed her resourcefulness in the measures she took to keep her considerable wealth out of the hands of thieves, by pretending to deposit it in a chest in the treasury of St Albans Abbey, to which she also made gifts of plate and a jasper altar-top. HENRY SUMMERSON

Sources C. L. Kingsford, 'John de Benstede and his missions for Edward I', *Essays in history presented to Reginald Lane Poole*, ed. H. W. C. Davis (1927), 332–9 · Tout, *Admin. hist.*, vol. 2 · Chancery records · J. Topham, *Liber quotidianus contrarotulatoris garderobae: anno regni regis Edwardi primi vicesimo octavo* (1787) · *Registrum epistolarum fratris Johannis Peckham, archiepiscopi Cantuariensis*, ed. C. T. Martin, 3, Rolls Series, 77 (1885) · *Gesta abbatum monasterii Sancti Albani, a Thoma Walsingham*, ed. H. T. Riley, 3 vols., pt 4 of *Chronica monasterii S. Albani*, Rolls Series, 28 (1867–9), vol. 2, pp. 365–6 · J. C. Davies, *The baronial opposition to Edward II* (1918), 158–9 · *Registrum Henrici Woodlock, diocesis wintoniensis, AD 1305–1316*, ed. A. W. Goodman, 2, CYS, 44 (1941), 963 · M. Prestwich, *War, politics, and finance under Edward I* (1972), 272 · *CClR, 1296–1302*, 602; 1302–7, 319; 1307–13, 340 · *CPR, 1321–4*, 294 · *Calendar of the fine rolls*, PRO, 3 (1912), 258, 277–8, 280 · *Calendar of chancery warrants*, 1: 1244–1326 (1927), 370
Likenesses effigy (of Sir John Benstede and his wife), Benington church, Hertfordshire

Wealth at death over £113 8s. 2d.: *Calendar of the fine rolls*, 258, 277, 278; *CClR*, 1302–7, 319; *Calendar of chancery warrants*, 370

Bensusan, Samuel Levy (1872–1958), journalist and author, was born on 29 September 1872 at Dulwich, London, the second of five children of Jacob Samuel Levy Bensusan (1846–1917), feather merchant, and Miriam (1848–1926), the daughter of Moses Levy Bensusan and his wife, Emily. His parents were Orthodox Sephardi Jews of Spanish descent whose ancestors had held high office in the courts of the kings of Spain; one of them, Samuel Ha Levi, the poet, married into the Bensusan family. Levi was incorporated into the family name, and changed to the European Ashkenazi Jewish spelling in the nineteenth century.

Educated at the City of London School and Greater Ealing School, Bensusan then became articled to Bentwich, a firm of City solicitors. Distressed at the severity of sentences handed down to defendants, Bensusan sought a change of career in journalism. His frequent visits as a child to the Crystal Palace to hear concerts under the baton of August Manns and Sir George Grove, and piano tuition from Professor Schiermacher, laid the foundation for an understanding of music that enabled him to secure the post of music and drama critic on the *Gentlemen's Journal* (1893–4) and the *Illustrated London News*. Commissions came from *Pick Me Up*, *Vanity Fair*, and the *Daily Sketch* for interviews and reviews. In 1896 Bensusan wrote an article on the mistreatment of performing animals. Published in the *English Illustrated Magazine*, it became a *cause célèbre* taken up by James Milne of the *Daily Chronicle*. In due course an act of parliament was passed protecting these creatures.

Several trips to Spain, Portugal, Italy, and Morocco proved a useful source of income in further articles supplementing Bensusan's regular work. The list of publications for which he wrote was steadily growing. Taking up the editorship of the *Jewish World* (1897–8), he asked two of his friends to contribute, Israel Zangwill to write a serial for the paper and Soloman J. Soloman to design the cover. In 1899 Bensusan rented a farmhouse at Asheldham in the marshlands of Essex for shooting and other country pursuits. It was a move that was to influence his writing for the rest of his life. Articles began to appear in *Today*, the *Daily Sketch*, and the *Daily Chronicle* on country life; and studies on Spanish artists and the impressionist painter Camille Pissarro in the *Windsor* and *Black and White* magazines. In 1904 he published his first book, *Morocco*, with illustrations by A. S. Forrest, an authoritative account of life in that country.

In 1902 the début of *In Japan*, a ballet by Bensusan adapted from his story 'DéDé' published in the *Daily Sketch*, was performed at the Alhambra. It met with some success and was featured at La Scala six months later. He then went on to write a ballet scenario, *Torio*, for Adline Genée. In 1907 the publisher T. and E. Jack brought out a series called Masterpieces in Colour. There were thirty-eight volumes on the great artists with coloured plates of the artists' work. Seven were written by Bensusan and one by Lucien Pissarro, who had married Bensusan's elder sister Esther on 11 August 1892. In 1900 Bensusan had a liaison with a Miss Fanny Barfoot, and a son was born to her on 14 December 1900. Bensusan accepted responsibility for the care and education of the boy, who was named Paul Selby, the surname being based on Bensusan's initials.

A move in 1906 to Brick House, a 50 acre farm at Duton Hill near Great Easton in the rural uplands of Essex, opened up new avenues in his writing career. Studying methods of farming, he began to write on the subject and became the agricultural correspondent for the *New Statesman*. This led to his being asked by Lord Lee to take over the running of the press department at the Board of Agriculture and Fisheries in 1919. He left in 1921 disagreeing with the introduction of the Corn Production Act of that year. On 1 November 1909 he married Marian Lallah Prichard (1883–1964), the daughter of Russell Prichard, a civil servant. There were no children.

Brick House Farm was a haven in which Bensusan could write without interruption. It was also a place to meet the good and the great. Lady Warwick's home at nearby Easton Lodge was the venue for many gatherings of people from all walks of life and the Bensusans were a part of the coterie that Lady Warwick gathered around her. Among neighbours that the Bensusans counted as friends were H. G. Wells; R. D. Blumenfeld, editor of the *Daily Express*; Conrad Noel, the 'Red Vicar' of Thaxted; and, living in a cottage at Monk Street owned by Bensusan, Gustav Holst.

Between 1904 and 1925 Bensusan published twenty books ranging from children's stories to works on beekeeping, art, and travel, and country tales. His output was prodigious. In 1924 he received a commission to write the 25,000 word guidebook for the British Empire Exhibition in five days, a feat that he accomplished. As well as regular columns under his own name, he wrote articles in the name of Lady Warwick for the *Daily Sketch* and other newspapers. There were several autobiographies that he ghostwrote, including those of the Earl and Lady Warwick. The major part of his work, however, was the twenty-four volumes of short stories and six plays (1912–55) that tell of the life and times of the people of his beloved Essex. Written for the most part in dialect, and based on the people and places around the Dengie peninsula, they provide an invaluable picture of rural life at the beginning of the twentieth century. His prose was much admired by his peers such as Hardy, Wells, and Kipling. Kipling wrote to him saying how much he liked his tales: 'when all agriculture is run by gentlemen and ladies out of London offices they would stand as a record' (S. L. Bensusan, *A Marshland Omnibus*, 1954, flyleaf). His works are some of the finest of English descriptive literature. *A Marshland Omnibus*, a collection of tales from the twenty-four books, is a fine example of Bensusan's literary skills. There were three novels written during this period, *A Child of Chance* (1932), *Joan Winter* (1933), and its sequel, *Maurice Dravidoff* (1934). Bensusan read a selection of his short stories on BBC radio from 1938 to 1952, including a tribute to Thomas Hardy, whom he had known and regularly visited at Max Gate. He died at Belfield Nursing Home, 1 Hollington Park Road, St Leonards, Sussex, on 11 December 1958.

LAWRENCE PETERS

Sources University of Essex, Colchester, Albert Sloman Library [S. L. Bensusan] • m. cert. • m. cert. [Jacob Samuel Levy Bensusan to Miriam Levy Bensusan] • private information (2004) • b. cert. [Paul Selby] • J. Bensusan-Butt, letter, 19 Nov 1993, priv. coll. [nephew of S. L. Bensusan] • S. L. Bensusan, diaries, University of Essex, Colchester, Albert Sloman Library • *CGPLA Eng. & Wales* (1959)
Archives University of Essex, Colchester, Albert Sloman Library, corresp., diaries, and papers | Essex RO, Chelmsford, letters to J. W. Gilmer • UCL, letters to Moses Gaster
Likenesses photographs, *c.*1910–1950, University of Essex, Colchester, Albert Sloman Library
Wealth at death £20,869 7s. 6d.: probate, 29 April 1959, *CGPLA Eng. & Wales*

Bent, Geoffrey (1932–1958). *See under* Busby Babes (*act.* 1953–1958).

Bent, (James) Theodore (1852–1897), traveller and antiquary, born at Baildon, Yorkshire, on 30 March 1852, was the only child of James Bent of Baildon and Margaret Eleanor, eldest daughter and coheir of James Lambert of Baildon. He was educated at Malvern Wells, then at Repton School. He matriculated on 8 June 1871 from Wadham College, Oxford, and graduated BA in 1875. He entered as a student at Lincoln's Inn on 14 November 1874, but was not called to the bar.

On 2 August 1877, at Newtownbarry House, co. Wexford, Ireland, Bent married Mabel Virginia Anna, second daughter of Robert Westley Hall-Dare of Theydon Bois, Essex, and Newtownbarry. Bent possessed considerable linguistic abilities, and he and his wife, who also enjoyed travelling, spent part of each year abroad. After early visits to San Marino (1877 and 1878) and Italy (1879 and 1880) he produced minor books. His *Cyclades, or, Life among the Insular Greeks* (1885), published after he spent two winters in the islands, was a more serious work. Much of the years 1885, 1886, and 1887 he passed in Karpathos, Samos, and Thasos, where he began archaeological work, contributing articles to the popular press and the *Archaeological Journal*, the *Journal of Hellenic Studies*, and the *Journal of the Anthropological Institute*. The Turkish authorities prevented his removing to England marbles and monuments from Thasos, but the inscriptions from his impressions were published in 1887. The winter of 1888–9 he spent on the coast of Asia Minor, trying to identify the site of the city of Lydae in Caria, and that of Caesarea. The inscriptions which he collected from the sites of these cities and from those of Patara and Myra were published in the *Journal of Hellenic Studies* (vol. 10) and were reprinted in 1889. In the same year Bent visited the Bahrain Islands in the Persian Gulf, where his observations and excavations led him to conclude that the Phoenicians originated there.

In 1891 Bent went to southern Africa to undertake what was to be his most famous, or indeed infamous, work. In 1872 the traveller Karl Mauch had brought to the notice of Europeans the existence of stone structures, including the spectacular Great Zimbabwe, then called the Zimbabwe ruins, on the southern tip of the high plateau which divides the Limpopo and Zimbabwe rivers. Bent was the first European to investigate the site in any detail, publishing in 1892 his *Ruined Cities of Mashonaland*. The book was enthusiastically received at the time and reached its third edition in 1895, but both his methods and his conclusions came in for trenchant criticism from professional archaeologists and other scholars. His amateur methods damaged sites and artefacts, and his 'sketchy records' (Caton-Thompson, 88) made it impossible in some instances to establish where he had found artefacts, or the state of structures when he arrived. His removal of the best examples of the famous soapstone birds at Great Zimbabwe has been particularly criticized. Worse than his methods was his conclusion that the sites were constructed by a northern race coming from Arabia and akin to the Phoenicians. There seems to have been no sound empirical foundation for this belief, which rested largely on the assumption that African people were too primitive to have sustained a society which required and could construct such complex buildings. It also reflected ideas of the importance of cultural diffusion which were to gather popularity in the next century. Although doubts were cast on Bent's thesis by professional archaeologists Randall-McIver (1906) and particularly Caton-Thompson (1931), who dated the structures to the middle ages and attributed their building to local Shona people, Bent's conclusions, and the similar conclusions of others such as Hall (1905) who followed him, that the structures were of great antiquity and non-local construction, were consonant with the ideology of the prevailing political regime, and they retained popular currency long after they had been discredited by the scholarly community. Even those who disavowed his conclusions continued to use his nomenclature for the site, for example using his name 'the Acropolis' for part of Great Zimbabwe.

A four-month journey in Ethiopia in 1893 provided material for Bent's *The Sacred City of the Ethiopians* (1893). His impressions of inscriptions added materially to knowledge of Ethiopian antiquities. In the same year he edited the Hakluyt Society's *Early Voyages and Travels in the Levant*. He and his wife undertook seven journeys in the southern Arabian peninsula from 1893 to his death. Bent added much to European knowledge of the Hadhramaut country, the mountainous area backing the Gulf of Aden, but his attempts to penetrate the Mahri district were unsuccessful. In November 1896 he traversed Socotra and explored the little-known country within 50 miles of Aden. His last journey was through parts of southern Arabia in 1897.

Bent died on 5 May 1897 at his home, 13 Great Cumberland Place, London, just four days after his return from his last journey. The whole party had gone down to malarial fever, which in Bent's case led to pneumonia and his death. He was buried at Theydon Bois, Essex. His wife (d. 1929) was herself an intrepid traveller who accompanied her husband on most of his explorations. After his death she published, as Mrs Theodore Bent, accounts of their Arabian journeys in the *Geographical Journal* (12, 1898, 41–

63) and, with her husband as co-author, *Southern Arabia* (1900, reprinted 1994). Her important and early photographs enliven both works.   ELIZABETH BAIGENT

Sources *The Times* (7 May 1897) · G. Caton-Thompson, *The Zimbabwe culture: ruins and reactions* (1931) · D. Randall-McIver, *Mediaeval Rhodesia* (1906) · B. M. Fagan, *Southern Africa during the iron age* (1963) · M. Hall, '"Hidden history": iron age archaeology in southern Africa', *A history of African archaeology*, ed. P. Robertshaw (1990), 59–77 · Burke, *Gen. Ire.* · Foster, *Alum. Oxon.* · *WWW* · *CGPLA Eng. & Wales* (1897) · *DNB* · R. N. Hall, *Great Zimbabwe, Mashonaland* (1905) · *GJ*, 15 (1900), 295 [notice of book] · *GJ*, 16 (1901), 101 [review]
Archives RBG Kew, papers relating to Hadramaut · U. Lond., Institute of Classical Studies, notebooks concerning travels in Arabia
Likenesses photogravure, repro. in M. V. A. Bent, *Southern Arabia* (1900) · portraits, repro. in J. T. Bent, *The ruined cities of Mashonaland* (1892), 18
Wealth at death £26,861 7s. 8d.: probate, 18 Aug 1897, *CGPLA Eng. & Wales*

Bent, Sir Thomas (1838–1909), premier of Victoria, Australia, born at Penrith in New South Wales on 7 December 1838, was the eldest child of five sons and three daughters of James and Maria (*née* Toomey) Bent. His father had been transported for housebreaking; his mother was a free immigrant from co. Clare, Ireland. In 1849 the family moved to Fitzroy in the Port Phillip district (later Victoria) where James Bent worked as a contractor and Thomas attended St Mark's Anglican school. Two years later the family moved to Moorabbin where James set up a market garden and Thomas's formal education ended when he left school at the age of thirteen to work with his father. He exhibited his enterprising spirit early on, starting a small market garden in 1859 and taking his produce to market in a rough cart. In 1861 he became rate collector for the district of Brighton.

Bent entered public life in 1863 when he was elected to the Moorabbin Road board district (after 1874 known as the shire of Moorabbin). He entered the Victorian parliament in 1871 when, to general surprise, he defeated the highly respected retiring member, George Higinbotham, for the legislative assembly seat of Brighton. It was subsequently revealed that Bent had used the position of rate collector to stack the electoral rolls. He represented the constituency with one short interval throughout his career. In 1874 he resigned his position as rate collector on being elected to the Brighton borough council. He was thus on both the Brighton and Moorabbin councils and was the district's legislative assembly member (MLA).

From the outset Bent demonstrated that he was a force to be reckoned with, and early in 1880 he was responsible for bringing down the government of Graham Berry. He held the public works portfolio in the short-lived government of James Service (March–August 1880) and in mid-1881 joined the government of Sir Bryan O'Loghlen as minister for railways. His term was characterized by his uninformed interference in the day-to-day running of the railways and by his introduction of a Railway Construction Bill which the press dubbed the 'bribery bill'. It provided for a railway in every electorate and gave Bent considerable power in the house as each member sought to secure the line for his district. O'Loghlen's government

Sir Thomas Bent (1838–1909), by John Lockwood, *c.*1907

lasted until March 1883, when for a time Bent led the opposition; but his temperament was little suited to such a task. In October 1887 he was defeated by one vote as candidate for the office of speaker of the assembly. Almost immediately afterwards he was elected chairman of the first railways' standing committee, and in that capacity for two years did much solid work. In 1892 he was elected speaker, and held the office (for which he had few qualifications) for nearly two years.

Bent was obsessed with real estate and in 1873 began speculating in land. Never one to do things on a small scale, he seriously stretched his resources and by the early 1880s was in severe financial difficulty. No sooner had he recovered than he began again and between 1887 and 1893 was engaged in the 'land boom'. At first this brought him a huge fortune, on paper at least; but by 1893 he was all but ruined. His land-booming activities became public, he was thrown out by the electors of Brighton, and from 1894 to 1900 he eked out a living milking cows at Port Fairy. He made two unsuccessful attempts to come back, at South Melbourne in 1896 and at Port Fairy in 1897, before being again elected for Brighton in 1900. This time he used voters' certificates to stack the rolls.

On 10 June 1902 Bent joined William Irvine's ministry as minister for railways and works, and was heavily involved in the great railway strike of May 1903. On Irvine's retirement Bent became premier (February 1904). His ministry lasted over four years, and in that period passed much valuable legislation, but in December 1908, six months after being made KCMG, he failed to survive a vote of no confidence. John Murray became premier and immediately announced a royal commission into the land transactions of Bent's cabinet. He emerged with general credit.

Bent married twice: first, in 1860, Elizabeth Hannah Hall (b. 1839), who died within a year leaving no children. In 1864 he married Elizabeth Huntley (d. 1903). Their first daughter, Elizabeth Hannah (b. 1866), as Elizabeth Bleazby became a Brighton councillor and was one of Victoria's first female councillors. A second daughter, Gertrude Huntley (b. 1868) died in infancy. Bent died on 17 September 1909 at his home, Huntley, Bay Street, Brighton. He was still a councillor for both Moorabbin and Brighton and the MLA for Brighton. After a state funeral on 19 September he was buried at Brighton cemetery.

Rough and uncultivated, shrewd and strong, Bent was certainly an interesting and remarkable figure. His methods were unorthodox, often unprincipled, and, towards the end, quite eccentric; but he had an uncanny ability to sum up others and to turn a situation to advantage.

MARGARET GLASS

Sources M. E. Glass, *Tommy Bent: 'Bent by name, bent by nature'* (1993) · W. Bate, *A history of Brighton* (1963) · M. Cannon, *The land boomers* (1977) · A. Deakin, *The crisis in Victorian politics, 1879–1881*, ed. J. A. La Nauze and R. M. Crawford (1957) · E. H. Sugden and F. W. Eggleston, *George Swinburne: a biography* (1931) · R. L. Wettenhall, *Railway management and politics in Victoria, 1856–1906* (Canberra, 1961) · *Brighton Southern Cross* (18 March 1871) · *Brighton Southern Cross* (25 March 1871) · *Brighton Southern Cross* (19 Oct 1872) · *Brighton Southern Cross* (13 Sept 1873) · *Brighton Southern Cross* (20 June 1874) · *Brighton Southern Cross* (4 July 1874) · *Brighton Southern Cross* (19 July 1875) · *Brighton Southern Cross* (15 June 1874) · *Brighton Southern Cross* (18 Sept 1909) · *The Argus* [Melbourne] (20 July 1872) · *The Argus* [Melbourne] (21 Aug 1882) · *The Argus* [Melbourne] (10 Oct 1882) · *The Argus* [Melbourne] (9 Oct 1902) · *The Argus* [Melbourne] (10 Feb 1904) · *The Argus* [Melbourne] (13 Jan 1909)
Likenesses J. Lockwood, photograph, c.1907, State Library of Victoria, Melbourne [*see illus.*] · M. Baskerville, statue, c.1913, intersection of Hampton Street, Bay Street, and Nepean Highway, Brighton, Australia · portrait (in robes of speaker), Billila, Brighton, Australia
Wealth at death A$35,000—valuation, excl. his residence

Bentall family (*per.* 1904–1993), department store owners, came to prominence with **Leonard Hugh Bentall** (1875–1942), who was born on 2 September 1875 at Holly Lodge, Orchard Road, Kingston upon Thames, Surrey, the second of the two sons and third of the four children of Frank Bentall (1843–1923), draper, of Kingston upon Thames, and his wife, Laura, daughter of George Dowman, a pharmacist, of Southampton. He was educated at New College, Eastbourne, and Forest House, Woodford, and considered becoming an engineer.

Instead, on leaving school in 1894 Bentall followed his brother George into the family drapery business, started by Frank Bentall in 1867 when Kingston was still a small market town, and worked in the shop for a short time before spending two years employed at Jones and Higgins in Peckham, followed by a year with Peter Jones in Chelsea, gaining experience before returning to Kingston. On 5 February 1902 Leonard Bentall married Winifred Ivy Smith (1879/80–1953), youngest child of Edward Smith JP,

clothing manufacturer, of Bewdley, Worcestershire. They had two sons, Gerald Chalmers Bentall and (Leonard Edward) Rowan Bentall [*see below*], and four daughters. At the end of the 1890s the firm bought several adjacent shops and knocked them down in order to build a new department store, which opened in 1904. By 1907 there were departments selling china and glass, stationery, silver, beds, and toys, and there was a Moorish tea-room, with 'Sesame' doors which opened automatically.

When Frank Bentall retired in 1909, the annual turnover was £60,000. He handed the business over to his sons, and Leonard became general manager. The name of the business was changed from Frank Bentall to Bentalls in 1912. George left the business in 1917, but Leonard continued the expansion, buying up more properties and opening new departments, and in 1925 he converted the business into a private limited company. In the inter-war years Kingston grew rapidly as a prosperous London suburb, and the opening of the Kingston bypass in 1927 helped to make it into a major shopping centre for Surrey and west London, able to compete successfully with the West End. In 1927, to celebrate the store's diamond jubilee, Bentall opened the Tudor restaurant (formerly the vicarage) in the main store, featuring murals by Herman Cawthra showing scenes from Kingston's history. A large covered car park was built opposite the entrance to the store in order to attract the wealthier middle classes. In 1926 Bentall had decided to install his own generator in the basement to provide power for the store, and he was able to introduce the latest electrical gadgets such as electronic calculating machines and power sunblinds. In the 1930s he continued to add departments, including a food hall, a theatre booking agency, a travel bureau, and a building department selling new houses.

From 1930 to 1935 a new Bentalls store was built, in order to bring all the new departments under one roof, while business continued in the old store as building work went on underground. The architect, Maurice Webb of Sir Aston Webb & Sons, designed a steel-frame building faced with bricks and Portland stone which extended for 750 ft along Wood Street and 230 ft facing Clarence Street (the latter the site of Frank Bentall's original shop). The façade of the new building was modelled on the William and Mary wing of nearby Hampton Court Palace, designed in the seventeenth century by Sir Christopher Wren. Escalators were installed and many of the store's fittings came from Gamages in Oxford Street, which had recently closed. Webb also designed a new furniture depository for Bentalls, in the Italian Renaissance style, and a drawing of it was exhibited at the Royal Academy in 1936.

From the start, Bentall was interested in publicity and in the 1930s, under the publicity director Eric Fleming, who had been recruited from Gamages, Bentalls began to stage a number of exhibitions and other special attractions. In 1930 Albert Sadler and his Palm Court Orchestra were engaged to play in the Tudor restaurant, and in 1932 *Bluebird*, the racing car in which Sir Malcolm Campbell broke the world land speed record, was on display. When the transatlantic liner the *Queen Mary* was built, Bentall not only created a special window display but also organized school trips to Southampton to see it. One of the more sensational attractions was the Swedish diver Anita Kittner, who twice a day dived 63 ft from the top of the store into a pool of water. The food exhibition in the new food hall in November 1933 attracted 35,000 visitors, while the sewing exhibition in 1933 was attended by the Lancashire cotton queen. The store also hosted a schoolboys' hobbies exhibition, and a bonny baby competition, judged by the customers, as well as fashion shows. Every year Bentalls bought the floral displays from the royal box at Ascot to decorate its foyer. All this publicity, and the slogan 'Why go to the West End—when there's Bentalls of Kingston', was successful, and the expansion continued, so that the number of employees grew from 1000 in 1925 to 2000 in 1946.

Leonard Bentall devoted a lot of attention to his staff and their well-being. In 1925 he started a bonus scheme for employees who invested in the business and he introduced a pension fund in 1929. There was a staff clinic and food parcels were delivered by its matron to those who were ill. When he and his wife returned from a world tour in 1937, the staff put on a welcome-home ball in the store. Bentall was brought up in a Congregationalist household and was active in the Congregational church all his life. He devoted much time and energy to charitable causes, in particular the Warehousemen, Clerks' and Drapers' School in Purley for the children of textile workers. He was president of the appeal which raised £52,000 for a second school in Addington, and from 1924 he was chairman of the after-care committee, which helped to place the school-leavers in business, mainly in the textile trade. He was on the committee, and was later trustee and chairman, of the Steadfast Sea Cadet Corps at Kingston from 1911 to 1936, and he also built cottages at Mill Hill for the Linen and Woollen Drapers' Cottage Homes, helped to raise money for the Kingston YMCA in 1927, and was treasurer of the Roberts Marine mansion, a convalescent and holiday home for shop assistants in Bexhill, Sussex. Bentall was elected a JP in 1925. An enthusiastic cricketer and golfer, his other interest was gardening, and he created a magnificent garden at his home in Cobham. He died on 24 December 1942 at Oakwood Court, Givons Grove, Leatherhead, Surrey, and was buried at Dorking cemetery in Surrey.

Both sons of Leonard and Winifred Bentall made a career with the firm. The elder son, **Gerald Chalmers Bentall** (1903–1971), department store owner, was born at Glendon Lodge, Fassett Road, Kingston upon Thames, Surrey, on 17 February 1903. Educated at Tonbridge School, he joined Bentalls in 1922 and was appointed a director in 1925, when the firm became a limited company. He became general manager in 1928. As a territorial, he was called up at the outbreak of the Second World War, but was released from the forces in order to help his father run the store; he succeeded his father as chairman and managing director in 1942. Bentall's first marriage, which took place on 30 April 1930 to Edith Marjorie Shouler (*b.* 1906/7), ended in divorce and on 2 March 1945 he married

his second wife, Marjorie Sydney Meller (*b.* 1909/10), a department store welfare officer. They had one son. This marriage also ended in divorce.

Gerald was faced with heavy death duties following Leonard Bentall's death, and in 1946 the business was converted into a public company. He began to expand the number of stores in 1947, when he bought Bentall & Sons Ltd in Worthing, Sussex, founded by his great-uncle Charles Bentall in 1875. The business grew to include stores in Ealing and Tunbridge Wells. He was appointed CBE in 1950, and on 8 October 1959 he married his third wife, Sybil Gladys Brett (*b.* 1897/8). He retired as managing director in 1963 and as chairman in 1968, and died on 17 September 1971 at his home, Witley Park, Brook, Godalming, Surrey. His ashes were interred on 22 September at Dorking cemetery in Surrey.

Leonard Bentall's younger son, **(Leonard Edward) Rowan Bentall** (1911–1993), department store owner, was born on 27 November 1911 at Ferney, 23 Lovelace Road, Surbiton, Surrey. Educated at Eastbourne College, he joined Bentalls in 1930. His father arranged for him to spend a year working at Harrods in 1933, after a plan to send him to Macy's, in New York, was cancelled because of the international financial situation. He was appointed a director of Bentalls in 1936. On 15 September 1937 he married Adelia Elizabeth Hawes (1916–1986), daughter of Edgar David Hawes, company director, of Southgate, London. They had three sons and two daughters. In 1940 he joined the East Surrey regiment as a private and was later commissioned into the Royal Welch Fusiliers. He served in the Eighth Army at El Alamein, in Sicily, and the mainland of Italy, and took part in the Normandy landings in 1944.

On demobilization in 1946 Rowan Bentall became merchandise director of Bentalls and in 1947 he made a six-week tour of the United States, visiting thirty-eight stores. Much impressed by what he saw, he recorded his impressions in a booklet, *My American Tour* (1947). Like his father, he took a particular interest in publicity, with advertising campaigns such as the 'June bride' in 1951, promoting the idea that everything for a wedding and a couple's future home could be bought in the store, and 'Italy in Kingston' in 1955. He became deputy chairman of Bentalls in 1950, and after his brother's heart attack in 1963 he became managing director. Under his chairmanship, which lasted from 1968 to 1978, the turnover of the group doubled, and in 1973 he opened a new store in Bracknell, Berkshire. He published a history of the firm, *My Store of Memories*, in 1974. On 23 June 1987 he married Katherine Christina Allan (*b.* 1935/6), a physiotherapist.

Bentall died at his home, Hill House, Buckholt Road, Broughton, near Stockbridge, Hampshire, on 24 July 1993. He was buried on 30 July in the churchyard of St Andrew's parish church, Chippenham, Wiltshire. In 1982 his eldest son, L. Edward Bentall (*b.* 1939), became chairman, the fourth generation to head the family business, which was still widely known as Bentalls of Kingston upon Thames. Bentalls stores continue to trade at Kingston and Bracknell at the start of the twenty-first century.

ANNE PIMLOTT BAKER

Sources C. Herbert, *A merchant adventurer, being the biography of Leonard Hugh Bentall, Kingston upon Thames* (1936) • P. E. Firth, *The men who made Kingston: a history of Bentalls of Kingston upon Thames, 1867–1995* (1995) • R. Bentall, *My store of memories* (1974) • H. H. Perkins, *The rise of Bentalls: over 80 years of progress, 1867–1951* (1951) • B. Lancaster, *The department store: a social history* (1995) • D. Jeremy, 'Bentall, Leonard Hugh', *DBB*, 1.292–5 • A. Adburgham, *Shops and shopping, 1800–1914*, 2nd edn (1981) • *The Times* (18 Sept 1971) • *The Times* (22 Oct 1971) • *The Times* (28 July 1993) • *The Times* (31 July 1993) • *WWW* • private information (2004) • m. cert. [Leonard Hugh Bentall] • d. cert. [Leonard Hugh Bentall] • b. cert. [Gerald Chalmers Bentall] • m. cert. [Marjorie Sydney Meller] • m. cert. [Sybil Gladys Brett] • d. cert. [Gerald Chalmers Bentall] • b. cert. [Rowan Bentall] • m. cert. [Adelia Elizabeth Hawes] • m. cert. [Katherine Christina Allan] • d. cert. [Rowan Bentall] • b. cert. [Adelia Elizabeth Hawes] • d. cert. [Adelia Elizabeth Hawes]

Likenesses E. Cooper, portrait, *c.*1969 (Gerald Chalmers Bentall), Bentalls store, Kingston • A. E. Cooper, portrait (Leonard Hugh Bentall), repro. in Jeremy, 'Leonard Hugh Bentall' • K. Dannatt, photograph (Leonard Hugh Bentall), repro. in Herbert, *Merchant adventurer*, frontispiece • W. R. Dick, bronze statue (Leonard Hugh Bentall), over entrance to Bentall's store, Kingston; repro. in Firth, *Men who made Kingston*, 48 • W. S. Stuart, photograph (Leonard Hugh Bentall), repro. in Firth, *Men who made Kingston*, 48 • double portrait, photograph (Gerald Chalmers Bentall and Rowan Bentall), repro. in Firth, *Men who made Kingston*, 156 • double portraits, photographs (Gerald Chalmers Bentall and Rowan Bentall), repro. in Herbert, *Merchant adventurer*, 54 • photograph (Rowan Bentall), repro. in Herbert, *A merchant adventurer*, 56 • photograph (Rowan Bentall), repro. in *The Times* (31 July 1993) • photograph (Rowan Bentall), repro. in Firth, *Men who made Kingston*, 156

Wealth at death £167,100 7*s*. 6*d*.—Leonard Hugh Bentall: probate, 7 May 1943, *CGPLA Eng. & Wales* • £406,637—Gerald Chalmers Bentall: probate, 13 Oct 1971, *CGPLA Eng. & Wales* • £2,547,307—Rowan Bentall: probate, 15 Sept 1993, *CGPLA Eng. & Wales*

Bentall, Gerald Chalmers (1903–1971). *See under* Bentall family (*per.* 1904–1993).

Bentall, Leonard Hugh (1875–1942). *See under* Bentall family (*per.* 1904–1993).

Bentall, (Leonard Edward) Rowan (1911–1993). *See under* Bentall family (*per.* 1904–1993).

Benthall, Michael Pickersgill (1919–1974), theatre director, was born at 29 Hertford Street, Mayfair, London, on 8 February 1919, the son of Sir Edward Charles Benthall (1893–1961), director of the Reserve Bank of India, and his wife, the Hon. Ruth McCarthy, *née* Cable, daughter of Ernest *Cable, Baron Cable. He was educated at Eton College and at Christ Church, Oxford; he played Claudio in the Oxford University Dramatic Society's production of *Much Ado about Nothing* in 1938. While at Oxford he met Robert Murray *Helpmann (1909–1986), the charismatic ballet dancer, ten years Benthall's senior, and the two began a lifelong homosexual relationship. After spending just one year in residence, Benthall left Oxford in 1938 without taking a degree and became a professional actor, performing at the Old Vic and at the Regent's Park Open Air Theatre. When the Second World War broke out in 1939 he joined the Royal Artillery, was mentioned in dispatches, and rose to the rank of major by the time he was demobilized in 1946.

Already in 1944 Benthall had assisted Tyrone Guthrie on his production of *Hamlet* for the Old Vic Company and had written two ballet scenarios for Helpmann at Sadler's Wells, *Miracle in the Gorbals* and *Adam Zero*. After the war he directed operas, including *Turandot* (1947) and *Aida* (1948) at Covent Garden, and embarked on his career as director of Shakespeare, for which he is now best remembered. He joined the Shakespeare Memorial Theatre at Stratford upon Avon under the directorship of Barry Jackson, who encouraged a fresh approach to the staging of Shakespeare, nurturing the talents of young directors such as Benthall and Peter Brook. Benthall's most notable production of this period was his staging of *Hamlet* in 1948, with the main role being played alternately by Helpmann and Paul Scofield in a Victorian Gothic setting. Scofield's performance, which Kenneth Tynan regarded as the best Hamlet he had ever seen, portrayed Hamlet as a petulant adolescent, sometimes thrashing on the floor in frustration. In 1950 Benthall was invited to New York, where he directed *As You Like It*, and in 1951 was asked by Laurence Olivier to direct him and his wife, Vivien Leigh, in *Antony and Cleopatra* and Shaw's *Caesar and Cleopatra* in London. In the same year he staged *The Tempest* at Stratford, with Michael Redgrave playing Prospero.

In 1953 Benthall was appointed artistic director of the Old Vic, with which he had worked in the past, on *Hamlet* in 1944 and on a memorable production of Goldsmith's *She Stoops to Conquer* in 1949, set against a backdrop of Rowlandson's cartoons. At the Old Vic he embarked on an ambitious 'five-year plan' to stage all thirty-six plays in the Shakespeare first folio. This not only provided the British capital with a reliable source of Shakespearian performance, maintaining the Old Vic as the potential source for the future National Theatre; it also revived neglected plays such as *Troilus and Cressida* and *Titus Andronicus*, which have subsequently become staples of Shakespeare production. Some of the productions were notable, not least for attracting great names of British theatre to the Old Vic (Ralph Richardson as Timon of Athens in 1956, John Gielgud and Edith Evans in *Henry VIII* in 1958) and for the publicity-seeking but not very convincing casting of the film actress Ann Todd as Lady Macbeth (1954) and the comedian Frankie Howerd as Bottom (1957). More importantly the productions launched or established the careers of several young performers, most notably Richard Burton, John Neville, Keith Michell, and Judi Dench who went straight from drama school to playing Ophelia. To lend unity to this massive Shakespeare project, Benthall got his designer James Bailey to create a permanent set, consisting of three Palladian arches and balconies. This proved too restrictive, and was abandoned after the first season.

The Old Vic's programme was easily overshadowed by its rival, the Shakespeare Memorial Theatre Company at Stratford, with its fresh and imaginative approach to Shakespeare. Under Benthall, the Old Vic developed an image of being worthy rather than challenging, especially when the direction of plays such as *The Tempest* and *Antony and Cleopatra* was entrusted to Helpmann. After the end of the five-year plan, Benthall introduced other classics of the European theatre into the repertory, but, since the Old Vic was now in the public mind the London home of Shakespeare, these were often not well attended. The high point of Benthall's remaining years at the Old Vic was playing host to Franco Zeffirelli's flamboyant production of *Romeo and Juliet* in 1961, the year Benthall resigned from the Old Vic.

Benthall then directed abroad in New York, Lisbon, and Tokyo, most memorably with Katharine Hepburn in the New York production of *Coco* in 1969. Despite being an innovative force in Shakespearian direction, Benthall has no entry in most standard reference works on the theatre. Castigated at the time for the subsequently more fashionable tendency to give greater importance to visual elements of a production than to the delivery of language, and overshadowed in the public mind by more radical directors such as Peter Brook and Peter Hall, he was nevertheless highly regarded by his actors. Claire Bloom declared him to be her favourite director, and one of his most famous protégées, Judi Dench, called him 'a wonderful director who was never really appreciated' (Dench, 200). He died at the Royal Free Hospital, St Pancras, London, of chronic liver failure and micronodular cirrhosis on 6 September 1974.   MICHAEL PATTERSON

Sources *The Times* (9 Sept 1974) · G. Rowell, *The Old Vic Theatre: a history* (1993), 145–50 · P. Roberts, *The Old Vic story* (1976), 138–9 · J. Dench, 'A career in Shakespeare', *Shakespeare: an illustrated stage history*, ed. J. Bate and R. Jackson (1996), 197–210 · K. Tynan, 'Claire Bloom in the limelight', *New York Times* (14 Dec 1952) · J. Parker, ed., *Who's who in the theatre*, 15th edn (1972) · b. cert. · d. cert.
Archives Theatre Museum, London, corresp. and papers
Wealth at death £360,640: probate, 18 March 1975, *CGPLA Eng. & Wales*

Bentham, Edward (1707–1776), university professor, fifth son of the Revd Samuel Bentham (*c.*1681–1733), a minor canon of Ely, and his wife, Philippa Willen (*c.*1681–1747), was born in the college at Ely on 23 July 1707, and baptized in the cathedral on 21 August 1707. After singing as a chorister at Christ Church, he entered Corpus Christi College, Oxford, on 28 March 1724, and studied under the care of his cousin John Burton, later vice-provost of Eton College. In 1730 he was briefly vice-principal of Magdalen Hall, Oxford, and the next year was elected fellow of Oriel. He graduated MA in 1732, and was appointed to a tutorship at the college, a post held for twenty years in which he established his reputation as one of the most diligent undergraduate divinity teachers in Oxford. In 1743 he took his BD degree, and was collated to the prebendal stall of Huntingdon in Hereford Cathedral on 22 August. He proceeded DD in 1749, and in 1754 became canon of the first prebend at Christ Church, Oxford (presented 27 April, installed 9 June), also acting as subdean. Bentham was a moderate high-churchman, but a court whig, and it endeared him to the Pelham government if less to the university. As Archbishop Herring of Canterbury told Newcastle on 30 April 1753, 'I find the best of our Oxford friends think his Majesty can't do a better thing for that place, than to give this worthy man this particular preferment' (BL, Add. MS 32731, fol. 395). On 22 June 1754 Bentham married Elizabeth Bates (*d.* 1790), daughter of Theophilus Bates of Alton, Hampshire.

On the death of Dr John Fanshaw, regius professor of divinity, Bentham was eventually persuaded by Archbishop Secker and other friends to accept the chair, and in 1763 exchanged his existing canonry for the more junior fifth prebend annexed to the professorship (presented 2 June, installed 9 June). 'I am sorry for poor Bentham', wrote Secker to the archbishop of York on 31 May 1763, 'but I am glad for the University' (T. Secker to R. H. Drummond, 31 May 1763, Borth. Inst., MS Bp C. & P. VII (20c/68)). His brother James *Bentham (1709–1794) saw the move as a step to another office but Bentham remained in the post for the rest of his life. He took his professorial duties seriously. With Secker's encouragement, he started a course of lectures in divinity in 1764 for intending ordinands, reading three lectures each week during term time without exacting any fee for attendance, 'a striking innovation' as R. Greaves has called it (*Hist. U. Oxf.* 5: *18th-cent. Oxf.*, 406). The year's sixty to seventy lectures formed one continuous course. Surviving undergraduate notes make clear that Bentham was not attempting his own *summa* of Anglican doctrine and history, or trying in divinity to rival Blackstone in law. The lectures had a practical edge appropriate for their audience, down to offering guidance on legal questions they might encounter in their parishes. Bentham urged a close familiarity with biblical languages to facilitate close textual study of scripture for 'the Transcribers were not certainly inspired by the Holy Ghost … often they might be nodding' (Hall, Bodl. Oxf., MS top. Oxon. c.226, fol. 135). The notes on the lectures confirm his doctrinal orthodoxy, and his rehearsal of all the usual objections to those outside the Church of England. Oxford was Bentham's world, and he never missed one term's residence from matriculation to his death. He supported Lord North's government in the last few years of his life, delivering an oration on the latter's installation as chancellor in 1773. He offered a defence in Latin of government policy in *De tumultibus Americanis* (1776), and anonymously attacked Burke for his criticisms of the university's loyalty during the American crisis in *The honor of the University of Oxford defended against the illiberal aspersions of E—d B—e esq.* (1776).

Bentham published widely, wrote well, and was not afraid to speak out for the Hanoverian regime in tory Oxford during George II's reign. His *Letter to a Young Gentleman of Oxford* (1749) recalled members of the university to abide by their oaths of allegiance and abjuration following the Jacobite rising and public disturbances in the city during 1748. The sequel, *A Letter to a Fellow of a College*, was an essay in pragmatic, moderate politics reminding the university of the benefits it enjoyed under the existing regime, in which Bentham was not frightened to strike an anti-French, anti-Catholic note. He claimed that liquor was the lifeblood of Jacobitism among undergraduates and called on dons to enforce discipline more rigorously.

His *bête noire*, William King, the principal of St Mary Hall, subsequently lampooned him as:

> Half a casuist, half lawyer, half Courtier, half Cit,
> Half Tory, half Whig (may I add, half a Wit?)
> (Ward, 173)

Bentham's philosophical works ranged widely and had student needs in mind. His *Introduction to Moral Philosophy* (1745) offered a clear summary of contemporary discussions and included a lengthy list of topics with recommended reading on each one. His *Reflections upon the Nature and Usefulness of Logick* (1740) was a succinct examination of old and new approaches to the subject, although *An Introduction to Logick (Scholastick and Rational)* (1773) was a rather pedestrian text. He moderated Locke's dismissal of scholastic logic by preferring not to condemn the subject as wholly unworthy of academic attention. His principal theological writings were *De studiis theologicis praelectio* (1764) and *Reflections on the Study of Divinity* (1771). They upheld his moderate, orthodox line.

One commentator, the antiquary William Cole of Cambridge, who claimed acquaintance with Bentham, suggested his limitations. According to Cole's sneering account, Bentham was 'a good husband and father, and an excellent brother, but as poor a creature, both in conversation, manner, and behaviour, as I have generally met with' (*DNB*) and was unworthy of the biographical account called for by a correspondent to the *Gentleman's Magazine*, probably James Bentham of Ely (*GM*, 1st ser., 50, 1780, 187). Bentham died at Christ Church, Oxford, on 1 August 1776, aged sixty-nine, and was buried in Christ Church Cathedral on 8 August 1776. His wife survived him, together with their son and daughter; she died on 26 May 1790.

NIGEL ASTON

Sources *GM*, 1st ser., 46 (1776), 386 · *GM*, 1st ser., 50 (1780), 187 · Foster, *Alum. Oxon.* · Venn, *Alum. Cant.* · *Fasti Angl.* (Hardy), 2.511 · *Fasti Angl., 1541–1857*, [Bristol], 88, 98 · W. R. Ward, *Georgian Oxford: university politics in the eighteenth century* (1958) · *Hist. U. Oxf.* 5: *18th-cent. Oxf.* · E. G. W. Bill, *Education at Christ Church, Oxford, 1660–1800* (1988) · *The memoirs of the life of Edward Gibbon*, ed. G. B. Hill (1900), 80 · J. Boswell, *Life of Johnson*, ed. R. W. Chapman, rev. J. D. Fleeman, new edn (1970), 693 · Nichols, *Lit. anecdotes*, 8.450 · archives, Christ Church Oxf. · Ely Cathedral registers · *IGI* · *Monthly Chronicle* (1790), 399 · A. Chalmers, ed., *The general biographical dictionary*, new edn, 4 (1812), 475 · Boswell, *Life*, 2.445, 530 · H. Hall, notes on Bentham's lectures, Bodl. Oxf., Henry Hall MSS, MS Top. Oxon. c. 226 · *DNB*

Archives Borth. Inst., MS Bp C. & P. VII (20c/68) | BL, Newcastle MSS, Add. MSS 32731, fol. 397; 32732, fol. 505; 32857, fol. 101; 35590, fol. 75; 54225, fol. 59; 5864 B., fols. 35, 120 · Bodl. Oxf., notes on Bentham's lectures by Henry Hall (1749–1839), MS Top. Oxon. c. 226 · Bodl. Oxf., Rawl. MSS · CUL, letter-books of James Bentham, Add. MS 2960

Bentham, Ethel (1861–1931), physician and politician, was born on 5 January 1861 at 82 King William Street, City of London, one of at least two daughters of William Bentham, an inspector and later general manager of the Standard Life Assurance Company, and his wife, Mary Ann Hammond. She grew up in Dublin, where she was educated at Alexandra School and College. With her mother she visited the slums of Dublin on charitable missions, and what she saw there inspired her to become a doctor, as

a means of helping the poor. She began her training at the London School of Medicine for Women at the age of almost thirty, and gained her certificate in medicine in 1893. She qualified in midwifery at the Rotunda Hospital for Women in Dublin, became LRCP LRCS (Edinburgh) and LRFPS (Glasgow) in 1894, and studied in Paris and in Brussels, where she achieved the degree of MD in 1895. After a brief spell working in London hospitals she went into general practice in Newcastle upon Tyne with Dr Ethel Williams, whom she had met as a student in London.

In 1909 Bentham moved to London, where she continued in general practice; she lived in Holland Park. A commitment to the suffrage movement was increasingly overtaken by her involvement in labour politics, and from March 1910 she sat on the executive of the Women's Labour League, chairing the committee regularly from 1912 onwards; she also held office in the Fabian Society. When the Women's Labour League was absorbed into the Labour Party in 1918, Bentham came top of the women's ballot in elections to the national executive committee (of which she was a member from 1918 to 1920, 1921 to 1926, and 1928 until her death). She represented Golborne ward on Kensington borough council from 1912 to 1925, as part of a small but determined Labour group on that Conservative local authority. She was one of the first cohort of women to serve as magistrates, working particularly in the children's courts, and sat on the Metropolitan Asylums Board. After standing unsuccessfully on three previous occasions, she was returned as Labour MP for East Islington in 1929, at the age of sixty-eight. She spoke in the House of Commons on a few occasions only, usually on matters relating to her experiences as a doctor and a magistrate, and she introduced a bill on married women's nationality in November 1930.

Bentham's most significant work was in the field of infant welfare. In 1911 she was a major force behind the founding of a pioneering baby clinic in North Kensington, as a Women's Labour League memorial to Margaret MacDonald and Mary Middleton. In an area with the highest infant mortality rates in London, the clinic at 12 Telford Road (from 1924 at 92 Tavistock Road) aimed to provide preventive medicine for mothers and babies, as well as to treat sick children—a task which often brought it into conflict with the local council. It built up a loyal following and thrived as an independent institution until taken over by the borough council in 1936. Bentham, the clinic's medical officer, underwrote its expenses and was responsible for much of its administration. A baby hospital to complement the clinic's work was established at 127 Ladbroke Road in 1919; this institution later moved to 1 Ladbroke Square. The surgical ward in the hospital was named the Ethel Bentham ward after her death.

Bentham was unmarried and had no children. Her social circle in London was largely female in composition and socialist in outlook. Her close friends and associates included Marion Phillips and Mary Longman (who lived in her house at 74 Lansdowne Road), and Mrs Pember Reeves, whom she helped with research for the report, *Round about a Pound a Week* (1913), which concerned women in

Lambeth. She was brought up an Anglican but became a member of the Quaker meeting at Friends' House in London in 1920, and she engaged in social work through the Society of Friends. She died at her home at 110 Beaufort Street, Chelsea, London, on 19 January 1931, of heart failure following influenza—the first woman to die while a member of parliament—and was cremated three days later at Golders Green, Middlesex. C. V. J. GRIFFITHS

Sources *The Labour who's who* (1927) · *WWW* · *The Times* (23 Jan 1931) · *The Lancet* (24 Jan 1931) · *Daily Herald* (20 Jan 1931) · Women's Labour League MSS, Labour Party Archives, London · annual reports of The Baby Clinic, 1919–38, Kensington Central Library, London · minutes of council, royal borough of Kensington, Kensington Central Library, London · C. Collette, *For labour and for women: the Women's Labour League, 1906–1918* (1989) · L. Middleton, ed., *Women in the labour movement: the British experience* (1977) · P. Hollis, *Ladies elect: women in English local government, 1865–1914* (1987) · L. V. Marks, *Metropolitan maternity: maternal and infant welfare services in early twentieth century London* (1996) · private information, RS Friends, Lond. [RS Friends, Lond.] · *DLB* · b. cert. · d. cert. · *CGPLA Eng. & Wales* (1931)

Archives Labour History Archive and Study Centre, Manchester, archives of the labour party, LP/WLL

Likenesses photograph, June 1929, repro. in P. Brookes, *Women at Westminster* (1967)

Wealth at death £8552 5s. 9d.: probate, 26 March 1931, *CGPLA Eng. & Wales*

George Bentham (1800–1884), by Lowes Cato Dickinson, exh. RA 1871

Bentham, George (1800–1884), botanist, was born in Stoke, near Plymouth, on 22 September 1800, the third of five children of Samuel *Bentham (1757–1831) and Maria Sophia Fordyce (1765–1858). His parents were both active in intellectual circles. Samuel Bentham, a naval engineer and inventor, travelled widely on government service in Russia before becoming inspector-general of naval works in 1796. Maria Bentham was very interested in botany and accompanied her husband on tours of inspection, making notes (her father, George *Fordyce, was a physician who wrote on various topics, including agriculture). A formidable lady, she impressed the American botanist Asa Gray with her knowledge of southern European plants when the latter met her in 1839, and in her nineties she started a correspondence in *The Times* about the proper guns to use in the Crimean War. She also edited her husband's papers for publication after his death.

Europe and education Bentham showed the same mental calibre as his parents from a very early age. In 1805 the family moved to St Petersburg for two years, during which time he showed great proficiency in languages, learning Russian and French, and some German, Latin, and Swedish (the latter during an unexpected stay in Sweden). They returned to England when war broke out and lived mainly at Hall Oak Farm, in Frognal, West Hampstead, later acquiring a summer home between Gosport and Alverstoke close to Portsmouth. They remained interested in Russian affairs, and in 1812 Bentham and his sisters translated accounts of the fighting during Napoleon's invasion for an English magazine. In 1814 his father was pensioned off, and the family went to live in France. They were frequently on the move, at times travelling in a small caravan, with a library and piano in one of the vans—on one occasion they were mistaken for a travelling circus. Bentham had a succession of tutors and, for a few months in 1818, attended the faculty of theology at Montaubon, where he recorded learning from Benedict Prevost about the continuity of life and the *scala naturae*. In 1820 his father bought an estate of some 2000 acres at Restinclières, near Montpellier, for which Bentham acted as manager with considerable success. His uncle Jeremy *Bentham (1748–1832) sent friends and amanuenses, including J. S. Mill and Richard Doane, to the estate to learn French.

In 1816 Bentham's older brother Samuel (b. 1799) died after falling from a swing. The brothers had been very close and the accident affected George considerably, and also changed his prospects in that it was decided that he should become a barrister and perhaps succeed to the chambers of his uncle, Jeremy Bentham, the philosopher and jurist, in London. However, in 1817 Bentham became enthusiastic about botany when he was able to identify plants near Angoulême. He found interesting similarities between Lamarck's and Candolle's *Flora Française* (3rd edn, 1805) and Jeremy Bentham's ideas about classification in general, and subsequently worked for five years translating and supplementing an appendix to Jeremy Bentham's *Chrestomathia* which appeared in 1823 as *Essai sur la nomenclature et la classification*. His uncle's arguments about the logic of nomenclature, tabulation, and arrangement influenced him greatly thereafter. By now very attracted by botany, he met some of the great names in this subject, including J. E. Smith and W. J. Hooker, during a brief trip to Britain in 1823. In 1825 he spent three months with

George Walker Arnott collecting in the Pyrenees, his only extensive fieldwork. His first original publication, *Catalogue des plantes indigènes des Pyrénées et du Bas Languedoc*, appeared in 1825 to critical acclaim.

Lawyer and leisured botanist The Benthams moved back to England in 1826 and George became Jeremy Bentham's secretary and amanuensis, at the same time reading for the bar at Lincoln's Inn without his uncle's knowledge. Living with his uncle in London was apparently not easy for the younger man, not least because there was no piano in the house and the elder Bentham would have only one person to dinner at a time. During this period Bentham edited and partly rewrote his father's papers on naval administration. His next major work was *Outline of a New System of Logic* (1827), which was largely in the form of a criticism of Whateley's *Logic*; however, the publishers went bankrupt, and Bentham did not act to save the book from being pulped. As a result the book was barely noticed, and only later was it realized that he—and not Sir William Hamilton—had been the first to quantify the predicate. In several other articles Bentham presented opposite views to his uncle. His paper on codification attracted the attention of Brougham, Hume, and O'Connell, and suggestions on the larceny laws drew a complimentary letter from Peel. A pamphlet on the law of property, dealing with the Registration Bill of 1831, showed the same mastery of detail that was afterwards so conspicuous in his botanical writings. He nevertheless continued his botanical studies, snatching half an hour at Lambert's herbarium or the British Museum on his way to his chambers, and in 1828 he was made a fellow of the Linnean Society of London. In 1830 he became honorary secretary of the Horticultural Society and was elected to the Athenaeum. Bentham was up for election to the Royal Society in the same year, but Robert Brown persuaded him, along with other scientists, to withdraw his name in protest at a royal duke's becoming president rather than a man of science (Bentham was finally elected in 1862). Called to the bar in 1831, his analyses of legal situations were exemplary, yet his first (and last) brief as junior council in 1832 was a disaster; he was so nervous that he cut short what he had to say.

When Bentham's father and uncle died (in 1831 and 1832 respectively), he inherited a share of 2 Queen Square Place, in Bloomsbury, and soon after went to live there. On 11 April 1833 at Kentchurch near Hereford, he married Sarah Laura Brydges (*d.* 1881), youngest daughter of the diplomatist Sir Harford Jones Brydges, and decided to devote his time to botany: 'finding that there was little likelihood of our having any family, and that my wife's wishes were very moderate, … and that I need not toil for our support, I determined to give up the law, to devote myself entirely to botany' (Bentham, *Autobiography*, 415). John Lindley suggested that Bentham work on the Labiatae, and between 1832 and 1836 his revision of this difficult family appeared and was immediately recognized as a classic piece of work. At the same time he played

a major role in the Horticultural Society, especially in discharging its debt of £22,000. He worked on the Horticultural Society collections, including those of Robert Schomburgk and Carl Theodore Hartweg; 800 of the 2230 species he described in *Plantae Hartwegianae* (1839–1857) were new to science.

In 1842 the Benthams moved to Pontrilas House in Herefordshire, near Kentchurch Place, where Sarah Bentham's sister, Lucy Scudamore, lived. They were happy in the country and Bentham became a JP, although he was increasingly concerned about his wife's health. He continued his botanical work, helping to distribute the massive collections made by employees of the East India Company and arranging Charles Morgan Lemann's large herbarium of some 30,000 species before its move to Cambridge University. In 1849 he began a long association with Richard Spruce, describing many of the new species collected by him in the Amazon as well as ticketing and distributing his collections. The Benthams usually spent some months in the summer travelling on the continent; in 1846 they went as far as Odessa and Nizhniy Novgorod. Bentham customarily took botanical books on these trips, visited local botanists, and studied the local flora. Informal accounts of some of these visits and meetings were sent to W. J. Hooker, who published anonymous extracts in the *Companion to the Botanical Magazine* and *London Journal of Botany*. In the early 1850s Bentham's income proved insufficient to maintain his herbarium (103,000 sheets representing 50,000–60,000 species), and a library of about 1200 volumes, and in 1854 he arranged to move the collection to the Royal Botanic Gardens at Kew in four large railway trucks. For a while, at least, he retained ownership, the sole condition being that it should be accessible to the public. At the same time he moved back to London. It was an unsettling time for him, and his correspondence with close colleagues such as Asa Gray and Joseph Decaisne virtually ceased between 1854 and 1856; he thought of giving up botany, considering himself only an amateur, but was dissuaded by his friends.

The Linnean Society and *Genera plantarum* Bentham's life settled into a routine after he found a London flat at 91 Victoria Street, and in 1861, his final residence, a house at 26 Wilton Place, Knightsbridge. He pursued the same quiet timetable every day: at nine he caught the train to Kew, where he worked in the herbarium from ten to nearly four in the afternoon; on his return home he wrote up the work done during the day, and then dined; he never took lunch and saw only intimate friends. This regular course of life was varied by a two-month holiday every autumn, in the country or abroad. Between 1862 and 1874, while president of the Linnean Society, he devoted each Thursday to its affairs. He was its longest-serving president after Sir J. E. Smith, but resigned in a dispute over a by-law change (although he had been talking about leaving for some time previously). His anniversary addresses gave valuable summaries of progress in botany and zoology, as well as providing support for Darwin. Both during and before his presidency he took considerable interest in the society's publications, indexing volumes and even rewriting manuscripts, but towards the end of his tenure he allowed meetings to become rather stereotyped, with little discussion. He surprised some fellows by his grasp of business affairs, and his clarity of expression was much valued by Hooker and others for drawing up reports.

With a routine established, Bentham's botanical publications became substantial. In 1858 his *Handbook of the British Flora* appeared. It was the result of several years' work—on occasion he even shaved by candle-light to have an hour to study his plants before breakfast. The introduction to the *Handbook* was very important, being used again, only slightly modified, to set out a recommended botanical procedure in the Colonial Floras—the series describing the plants of the British empire written at Kew in the nineteenth century. In 1858 and 1859 he delivered a series of papers to the Linnean Society on conceptual matters arising from the *Handbook*. The discussion on species, intended for publication, was delayed while he pondered the ideas set out in Charles Darwin's *Origin of Species*, which concerned matters that he thought were hypothetical; Bentham's work appeared in 1861 (after much encouragement from his friends), although part of the manuscript, which still exists, remained unpublished. His *Handbook*, as revised by Hooker (5th edn, 1887), remained in print until the Second World War; an edition with line illustrations by Walter Fitch (1863–5) was also popular, and 'painting one's Bentham' remained in vogue into the 1920s.

Hooker considered Bentham to be an amateur, although remarkably gifted and well known and much liked by botanists throughout Europe (Bentham's circle of acquaintances was very wide). Hooker thought Bentham would not put himself out for the cause of science as a true professional would, and Bentham also refused to discuss philosophical botany, claiming that he had never been taught it, yet in 1858 Bentham finally committed himself to writing the *Genera plantarum* (1862–83) with Hooker. Bentham disliked the idea of joint work, but believed that he and Hooker agreed enough on taxonomic principles to make collaboration possible. Hooker had many administrative duties, and Bentham consequently wrote just under three-quarters of this great work, an estimated 1,199,500 words. During this time Bentham also published the *Flora Hongkongensis* in 1861 and then wrote the *Flora Australiensis* (1863–78), in which he was much helped by Ferdinand Mueller at Melbourne, who forwarded his own extensive collections of Australian plants to Kew. Work on the Australian flora and on the *Genera plantarum* took most of Bentham's energy during the last twenty years of his life, and he cut back still further on his social activities. This retreat from social engagements was accelerated by the failure of his wife's health in 1872; from that time until her death in 1881 she was a semi-invalid. Bentham's health gave way shortly after the appearance of the final part of *Genera plantarum* in 1883. He became bedridden, refusing visitors and even being read to, and died at home in Wilton Place

on 10 September 1884. He was buried in Brompton cemetery, in the same grave as his wife, who had died on 15 July 1881 after a fall the previous October.

Influence and character As a botanist Bentham was noted for his accurate descriptions based on personal observations, careful assessment of the limits of species and genera, and caution in discussing matters that he considered to be theoretical or hypothetical. Even in his early *Outline of a New System of Logic* he evinced dislike of the use of inference and analogy in argument and was wary of induction. He believed that theory and hypothesis tended to involve these suspect processes. Thus he interpreted plant morphology narrowly, restricting it largely to the outside of the organism. He was sceptical about the value of developmental and anatomical studies in systematics. Microscopical work involved aspects of form and anatomy that could not readily be seen, and he felt proponents of such studies were over-inclined to invoke theory. He paid considerable attention to plant terms, again preferring those that had minimal theoretical connotations, and distrusted the use of homology in systematic studies, largely because of its theoretical and speculative implications.

Bentham's general approach to systematics remained similar throughout his life, despite his cautious acceptance of the idea of evolution in the 1860s. In an address to the British Association in 1874 he claimed that evolution meant that varieties, species, and orders were distinguishable only in degree, but this is little different from his position in practice prior to 1859. He consistently argued that species should be broadly delimited, and although his *Handbook* was faulted by some as being too extreme in this direction, his practice was close to that of Hooker and many other botanists who had access to large collections and studied plants over a wide geographical area. Even the way in which he visualized relationships remained constant. In 1857 he compared relationships in plants to a more or less wooded landscape, and in 1873 to the massings of foliage of the branches of trees seen from above. Relationships could be demonstrated for only a few generations, so ancestors (the branches of the trees) were necessarily speculative. Massings of foliage in a tree crown and massings of trees in a landscape differ only in scale.

The *Genera plantarum* is the one publication for which Bentham (and Hooker) is most remembered, the three volumes still being in almost daily use at large herbaria worldwide. However, although Bentham and Hooker's system is thought of as a 'natural' classification, an unpublished introduction (in Bentham's hand, with annotations by Hooker) challenges this interpretation. There, and in a paper, 'Memorandum on the principles of generic nomenclature', that he wrote in 1857, he speaks of conflict between science and 'language' (that is, convention). Indeed, in some of his own papers he discarded his own classification when discussing the biogeographical relationships of plants, suggesting that his scheme acknowledged the dictates of convention. Bentham and Hooker constrained their ideas of botanical relationship by the largely conventional major groupings they accepted and their division of these groupings in such a way as to make the whole classification readily memorable. The overall scheme of classification in the *Genera plantarum*, in fact, is profoundly ambiguous even if the descriptions, based on close observation, are precise.

In adulthood, Bentham was slim, just under 6 feet tall, and his hair had a dash of white; as he aged, his aspect became rather forbidding, and pronounced furrows developed between his piercing eyes—a far cry from the plump young boy called 'Devonshire dumpling'. He blamed his shyness and lack of self-confidence on his lack of formal education. The long sojourn in France as a boy did not help; revealingly, in 1838 his friend Alphonse de Candolle described him as a 'métis des deux pays' (mongrel of two countries). As a youth, he much enjoyed dancing, although he characterized himself even then as being cold and passive; he was always fond of music (he played the piano) and singing. Those who penetrated his reserve found him a good friend with a large store of anecdotes about Europe in the early part of the nineteenth century. Bentham was a compulsive diarist, his first surviving diary dating from February 1811. He sent long, journal-like letters to his family when he was travelling in England in 1823, and later letters (many now lost) to his sister, Mary, in France. From 1830 to his death, his diary is continuous, with annual summaries of his finances from 1856 onwards; an uncompleted autobiography dates from the last years of his life, a period in which he became quite melancholy.

Bentham received many honours. They included a royal medal of the Royal Society in 1859 and an LLD from Cambridge in 1874; in both cases he needed Hooker's reassurance before he accepted them. He was also a corresponding member of the Institut de France. On being gazetted CMG in 1879, he characteristically noted that he had 'no claims to the distinction[;] it annoys me much and I have written to remonstrate' (Linn. Soc., Diary, 24 May 1879). At all times an extremely reserved man, he was characterised in the *Gardeners' Chronicle* as 'one of our greatest scientific worthies ... but of whom none but a few students have had the opportunity of knowing much'.

Bentham was comfortably off. As far as can be ascertained, his income was £878 in 1856, and for the last decade of his life it ranged between £1460 and £1676. Although he was paid for some of his botanical writings, his maximum annual income from these was £191 (in 1867). He himself paid for a number of publications. Most notably, he guaranteed Hooker against loss from the printing of their *Genera plantarum*, and he paid for several volumes of Hooker's *Icones plantarum*. There was controversy over his will, and because of the Statute of Mortmain the bulk of his estate, some £20,000, went to his great-niece, Mary Louisa Wallon; among other bequests, Kew Gardens received some £7200, now part of the Bentham–Moxon Trust. The mounted lens that Bentham used, the gold pen with which he wrote the *Genera*

plantarum (its nib had broken just before his death), and a table that had belonged to Jeremy Bentham (in which the latter kept a tame mouse) also went to Kew.

P. F. STEVENS

Sources *George Bentham: autobiography, 1800–1834*, ed. M. Filipiuk (1997) · B. D. Jackson, *George Bentham* (1906) · G. Bentham, diary, RBG Kew · *Gardeners' Chronicle*, new ser., 22 (1884), 368–70 · *GM*, 1st ser., 103/2 (1833), 364–8 [obit. of the Rajah Rammohun Roy]
Archives Conservatoire et Jardin Botanique de la Ville de Genève, Geneva · Fondation Augustin de Candolle, Geneva · Linn. Soc., corresp., diary, and papers · RBG Kew, corresp. and papers | Harvard U., Arnold Arboretum, letters to Asa Gray · RBG Kew, corresp. with Sir William Hooker · RBG Kew, corresp. with William Munro · RBG Kew, corresp. with Sir Ferdinand von Mueller · RBG Kew, corresp. with Richard Spruce · Royal Botanic Gardens and National Herbarium of Victoria, South Yarra, letters to Sir Ferdinand von Mueller
Likenesses C. Leblanc, watercolour, 1834, Linn. Soc. · L. Dickinson, oils, exh. RA 1870, Linn. Soc. · G. Wallich, photograph, *c*.1870, RBG Kew · L. Dickinson, oils, exh. RA 1871, Linn. Soc. [*see illus.*] · C. Leblanc, drawing (aged thirty-four), Linn. Soc. · drawing (aged ten), Linn. Soc.
Wealth at death £23,513 8*s*. 8½*d*.: probate, 11 Dec 1884, *CGPLA Eng. & Wales*

Bentham, James (1709–1794), antiquary and Church of England clergyman, was born in Ely, probably on 10 March 1709, and baptized at Ely Cathedral on 17 March. He was the third son of the Revd Samuel Bentham (*c*.1681–1733), registrar of Ely Cathedral and vicar of Witchford, and of his wife, Philippa Willen (*c*.1681–1747). The family, of Yorkshire origin, was strongly clerical, and James Bentham was the sixth priest in continuous descent from Thomas Bentham, bishop of Lichfield (1559–78). The Benthams formed a tight clan, centred on Ely and Cambridge. Although their enthusiasm for obtaining good livings did not pass unnoticed, they were acknowledged to be modest in disposition, orthodox in faith and life, but somehow eccentric.

James Bentham enjoyed a sound education at Ely grammar school (*c*.1718–1726) and Trinity College, Cambridge (1727–31), even if it was less distinguished academically than that of his elder brother Edward *Bentham (1707–1776), fellow of Oriel College, Oxford, and eventually regius professor of theology at Oxford and canon of Christ Church. Bentham was ordained priest on 20 May 1733. He became vicar of Stapleford, Cambridgeshire, in 1733, a living which he resigned in 1736 in favour of a minor canonry at Ely, which henceforth remained his home, despite later preferments in Norfolk and Bedfordshire. His attachment to his native city helps to explain the unusual mixture of his interests: cathedral music, the drainage of the fens and driving turnpike roads through them, and the study of medieval architecture, focusing on Ely Cathedral. This last enthusiasm was perhaps inspired by Bishop Tanner, the distinguished antiquary, who was a prebendary of Ely from 1713 to 1723/4 and became a great friend and patron of the Bentham family. A further stimulus to the idea of writing the history of the cathedral was provided by the collections made by his father as registrar. The project was evidently well under way by 1756, when Bentham circulated printed lists of the dignitaries of the church, both to elicit corrections and to advertise the book. Eight years later the text seems to have been virtually complete, although the volume was not published until 1771. A major problem was finding sufficient patrons not only to subscribe to the book but to pay for the fifty engraved plates with which it is illustrated; Bentham's pertinacity secured both. Once published, the book enjoyed great success. A second edition, enlarged by a memoir of the author and some other material, was published in 1812 and a further supplement and notes in 1817. As William Cole commented, 'Church works, especially such great cathedrals, are never quick in their execution but, when finished, surprise by their majesty and grandeur' (Walpole, 1.210).

Cole, in a private note, however, questioned how 'so good a book should come from such Idiot appearance' (Davis, 122), and other contemporaries were quick to suspect that the book owed much to hidden hands. In 1783 an article in the *Gentleman's Magazine* claimed that the section on medieval architecture had been written by the great poet and antiquary Thomas Gray, but Bentham could demonstrate from Gray's own letter that he had contributed only the analysis of Romanesque ornament. The truth seems to be that Bentham, behind his unassuming exterior, was adept at extracting the most from colleagues, whether William Cole or his brother Edward. The latter was a key figure in checking the text, both for content and for style; William Cole did likewise, contributing in particular the biographies of the bishops. James *Essex, the architect and antiquary of Cambridge, contributed his ideas as to the architectural history of the cathedral, as well as measuring masterly surveys of the fabric in elevation and in section to illustrate the text. Finally, Bentham's brother Joseph, printer to the University of Cambridge, saw the volume through the press as his swansong.

The success of the book was due to the way it combined both a history of the cathedral establishment, listing dignitaries and tombs, on the lines established by William Dugdale in his *History of St. Paul's Cathedral*, with a broader view, setting Ely in a national context. Bentham prefaced the Ely material by lengthy essays on the conversion of the English and the development of ecclesiastical architecture, giving the early period an unusual prominence, devoting to it four times the number of pages describing the high Gothic. While Christopher Wren's pithy comments on the origins of medieval architecture had been published in *Parentalia* in 1750 and Samuel Warburton and Thomas Warton had written summaries of the subject, Bentham was the first to trace a coherent history of the development from Saxon to Romanesque, or Norman, to Gothic. His arguments, for example on the use of stone rather than wood for major Saxon churches, carry conviction through the extensive quotation of contemporary sources and through their balance and common sense.

Bentham's other writings lacked the same broad scope and public acclaim. In 1757 he published a series of 114 queries addressed to the 'principal inhabitants and gentlemen of the county', shrewdly pointing out how defective communications were throughout the Isle of Ely and how they created ill health and unemployment. This initiative won support and subscriptions from local magnates, such as the bishop and Lord Hardwicke, and led to the establishment in 1769 of a turnpike road between Cambridge and Ely. In 1778 Bentham returned to print to encourage further improvement in fen drainage, in particular by the enclosure of the 1300 acres of Grunty Fen, some 3 miles south of Ely. Again he combined enthusiasm for economic advantage with awareness of the social improvements that should follow.

Bentham was not only interested in the liturgical and historical aspects of his beloved cathedral. During the major restoration works undertaken from 1757 by James Essex, it was Bentham who acted as clerk of works. He particularly promoted the moving of the choir to the far east end, his enthusiasm evidently overcoming any antiquarian scruples about the rearrangement of tombs and the destruction of the Romanesque pulpitum which the project involved. In his defence, the reordering was carried out in 1770–71 with some sensitivity, the fourteenth-century stalls carefully moved, the tombs reset in the aisles, and the remains of seven Saxon notables entombed in the choir walls reverently reinterred in Bishop West's chapel.

Bishop Mawson of Ely, who was Bentham's constant patron in both his historical research and in the embellishment of the cathedral, gave him two successive livings in Norfolk: Wymondham and Feltwell, St Nicholas. The next bishop, Edmund Keene, preferred him to another Norfolk living, Northwold, in 1774, which he was happy to surrender five years later in favour of the second prebend, held some sixty years before by Bishop Tanner. In 1783 Bentham was appointed to the living of Bow Brickhill in Bedfordshire, which again had an antiquarian link through Browne Willis. In 1767 Bentham had been elected a fellow of the Societies of Antiquaries. His personal life proved less serene. His first wife, Elisabeth Sutton, died in 1748 after only two years of marriage, and their daughter Elisabeth also died young. His second marriage, in 1752, to Mary Dickens (*b. c.*1717) of Ely was ended by her death in 1781 and Mary, his daughter by this marriage, also predeceased him, aged seventeen. Only three of the children of James and his siblings lived to maturity; they included James's only son, another Revd James Bentham, born in 1755. Bentham died at Ely on 17 November 1794, aged eighty-five, and was buried in Ely Cathedral on 22 November. Though frail and housebound towards the end, he had continued alert in mind, adding further to his collections on medieval architecture. Some of his papers are now in Cambridge University Library but the objects he gathered have been scattered beyond trace.

T. H. COCKE

Sources Walpole, *Corr.* · W. Davis, ed., 'Mr. Cole's unpublished notes on the Rev'd James Bentham's "History and antiquities of the cathedral church of Ely from 673 to the year 1771"', *An olio of bibliographical and literary anecdotes and memoranda*, new edn (1817), 109–26 · J. Bentham, *The history and antiquities of the conventual and cathedral church of Ely* (1771) · J. Bentham, *The history and antiquities of the conventual and cathedral church of Ely*, ed. J. Bentham, 2nd edn (1812) · W. Stevenson, *A supplement to the first edition of Mr Bentham's* *history and antiquities of the cathedral and conventual church of Ely* (1817) • Nichols, *Lit. anecdotes*, vol. 3 • J. Frew, 'James Bentham's *History of Ely Cathedral*: a forgotten classic of the early Gothic revival', *Art Bulletin*, 62 (1980), 289–92 • Venn, *Alum. Cant.* • register of baptisms, marriages, and burials, Ely Cathedral, CUL • *DNB*

Archives BL, Add. MSS 2944–2959, 2961–2962 • BL, corresp., Add. MSS 5804–5860, *passim* • CUL, collections relating to Ely Cathedral, letter-book | Bodl. Oxf., corresp. with Charles Lyttleton relating to Gothic architecture [nineteenth-century copy] • Bodl. Oxf., letters to William Stukeley • CUL, letters, etc., relating to drainage of Cambridgeshire fens and navigation of the Cam

Likenesses I. Facius, stipple (after drawing by T. Kerrich), BM, NPG; repro. in Bentham, *History and antiquities of the conventual and cathedral church of Ely*, frontispiece

Bentham, Jeremy (1748–1832), philosopher, jurist, and reformer, was born on 4 February 1748 in Church Lane, Houndsditch, London, the eldest of the seven children of Jeremiah Bentham (1712–1792), attorney, and Alicia Woodward Whitehorne (d. 1759), the eldest daughter of Thomas Grove, a mercer of Andover, and Alice Woodward. He was baptized on 14 February at St Botolph's, Aldgate. Of his siblings, only his youngest brother, Samuel *Bentham (1757–1831), survived early childhood, and his mother died when Jeremy was eleven.

The various branches of the Bentham family were descended from a common ancestor, Thomas Bentham (c.1513–1579), who was born at Sherburn in Yorkshire and became bishop of Coventry and Lichfield in 1559. The bishop's grandson, Francis Bentham (d. 1670), a draper from Stafford, migrated to London, and established the London branch of the family. Francis's son, Bryan (b. 1627), was Bentham's great-great-grandfather, and his son, also Bryan (b. 1657), was master of the Clothworkers' Company.

Bentham's grandfather (1685–1741) and father, both named Jeremiah, were prosperous attorneys in London with extensive investments in property, some of which may have been acquired through the grandfather's marriage in 1706 to Rebecca Tabor, a member of a well-established Essex family. Bentham's father had numerous interests in the City of London and, for example, was involved for more than fifty years in securing the future of the Sir John Cass Charity located in Aldgate. At his death a silver cup, commemorating his father's service, was presented by Bentham to the trustees in accordance with his father's will.

Less is known of Bentham's mother, Alicia Whitehorne, who was a young widow when she met Jeremiah Bentham at Buckholt Acres, a place of entertainment near Epping Forest. Jeremiah fell deeply in love, disappointing his parents, who had greater ambitions for their son. Alicia was a kindly woman whose early death deprived Bentham and his younger brother of an important source of family affection which his father's second marriage to Sarah Abbot (*née* Farr), the widow of John Abbot, a clergyman and fellow of Balliol College, Oxford, did not provide. Alicia's own mother, Alice Woodward, was the daughter of William Woodward (c.1640–1703), rector of Baughurst in Hampshire. Alice Woodward latterly lived with other

Jeremy Bentham (1748–1832), by Henry William Pickersgill, 1829

Grove relatives on an estate at Browning Hill, near Reading. The house had an extensive library, much loved by the young Bentham, which had been established by his grandmother's brother, Thomas Woodward, a London bookseller. His paternal grandmother resided mainly in a country house at Barking, Essex, which the Bentham family often visited at weekends.

Early life and education Bentham's upbringing and early education was dominated by his father, who sought to develop his talents and produce not only an attorney like himself but also a future lord chancellor of England. Bentham was undeniably precocious, and his intellect was encouraged by his father in a way that resembled the education of John Stuart Mill a generation later. He began to learn Latin at the age of three, and while at Oxford in 1761 (aged twelve or thirteen) was translating for his father the first book of Cicero's *Tusculanae disputationes*. Through his father's friendship with William Markham, then headmaster of Westminster School, he was enrolled there at the age of seven in 1755. He became a king's scholar, before leaving for Queen's College, Oxford, in 1760 at the age of twelve. He was unhappy at both institutions. Not only was he much younger than the other pupils, he was also small in stature, and physically weak. He had many interests, such as music (he became proficient on the violin, harpsichord, piano, and organ), natural science, and reading, and played battledore (a kind of badminton). But for the most part he was isolated and lonely, living under the crude and often unreasonable authority of his father. In this early period he became thoroughly familiar with the classical authors and the Bible. By the age of ten he could write in both Greek and Latin, and he acquired a reputation at school for writing verses in these languages. He was also known as 'a little philosopher', and, when pushed and prodded by his father, he would reluctantly display his precocity.

At the age of sixteen in 1764 Bentham took the degree of BA, and in 1767 MA. According to Thomas Southwood Smith in his lecture delivered over Bentham's remains in 1832, he was the youngest graduate known at either Oxford or Cambridge. Following the route mapped out by his father, Bentham then turned to the study of law. In 1763 he took his place as a student in the court of king's bench, Westminster Hall, and was admitted to Lincoln's Inn. He returned to Oxford to attend the lectures given by William Blackstone, first Vinerian professor of English law, which were eventually published as the *Commentaries on the Laws of England* (1765–9). Like his colleagues he first attempted to take notes, but was soon prompted to reflect critically on what he had heard. In Blackstone he found a notable opponent against whom he wrote a series of works at different periods throughout his life. Early, unfinished, and unpublished writings, like the 'Elements of critical jurisprudence', from which his major early work on Blackstone, the 'Comment on the commentaries' (unpublished until 1928), was itself an unfinished digression, owed much to the systematic arrangement which Blackstone gave to English law.

In 1769 Bentham was admitted to the bar and moved from chambers in the Middle Temple to Lincoln's Inn, where he continued to live until the death of his father in 1792, when he inherited the family home at Queen Square Place, Westminster. Through his father's remarriage in 1766, he acquired two stepbrothers, one of whom, Charles *Abbot (1757–1829), became speaker of the House of Commons and later Lord Colchester. Although Bentham and Abbot became political allies, especially over the project for the panopticon prison, they were never close friends, and Bentham actively disliked his stepmother. Mainly for this reason, he continued to live in chambers at Lincoln's Inn. Nevertheless, despite assistance from his father, he did not actively engage in the practice of law, and it seems that Charles Abbot rather than Bentham himself took up the sort of career envisaged by his father.

Early writings Despite his essentially tory and Anglican upbringing, Bentham soon became a child of the Enlightenment. Even at a young age he had considerable philosophical ambitions. He drew on such writers as John Locke, Charles-Louis Secondat, baron de Montesquieu, David Hume, Joseph Priestley, Claude-Adrian Helvétius, Jean le Rond d'Alembert, and Cesare Beccaria, and produced work of undoubted originality. He sought to develop a new logic of the will to supplement what he called Aristotle's logic of the understanding. His writings on language, eventually called the theory of fictions, represented an important departure from the earlier work of Locke and his followers in the eighteenth century. Although he took the idea of utility as the foundation of morals from Hume, he gave the principle a more prescriptive dimension and linked it more closely with pleasure and pain.

By the early 1770s Bentham wrote at length on numerous topics under headings such as 'Preparatory principles' and 'Elements of critical jurisprudence'. These works were never completed and remain among the voluminous collection of his manuscripts at University College, London. His friendship with the political writer John Lind, whose family had professional dealings with Jeremiah Bentham, and who had returned to England in 1772 following a period in the service of the king of Poland, led to a number of collaborative efforts, including Bentham's work on Blackstone. Bentham took some material from his 'Comment on the commentaries' on the nature of government and political obligation, and published it anonymously in 1776 as *A Fragment on Government*. This slim volume examines a few paragraphs in the *Commentaries* and offers a masterly analysis of Blackstone's failure to think systematically about crucial themes concerning government. While Bentham was content to point out the confusions in Blackstone's thought without developing his own ideas at any length, he none the less gave the first formulation of the principle of utility as the foundation of his system as well as some indication of the direction of his thought on themes such as sovereignty, the social contract, submission, resistance, and fictions.

Bentham's main ambition, however, was to create a complete code of laws which he eventually called the *pannomion* (from the Greek meaning 'all the laws'). He worked on various parts of the *pannomion* throughout his life but never managed to bring it to completion. Much of his writing during this period focused on penal law, stimulated perhaps in 1777–8 by the competition announced by the Oeconomical Society of Bern for a 'Plan of legislation on criminal matters'. The theoretical starting point was Montesquieu's insights into crime, punishment, and liberty in books 6 and 12 of *De l'esprit des lois* (1748), Beccaria's great work on crime and punishment, *Dei delitti e delle pene* (1764), the fourth volume of Blackstone's *Commentaries*, and William Eden's recent and influential work, *Principles of Penal Law* (1771). Bentham's writings were highly original, partly because he sought to create a philosophical system which he could bring to bear on hitherto largely emotive issues of crime and punishment. Some of this material appeared in the chapters on punishment and offences in *An Introduction to the Principles of Morals and Legislation* (written in the 1770s, printed in 1780 but not published until 1789). Other aspects of his writings on penal law were first published in two of the recensions of Bentham's works prepared by Étienne Dumont, *Traités de législation civile et pénale* (1802) and *Théorie des peines et des récompenses* (1811). These works were to establish Bentham's reputation as the most important European writer on crime and punishment after Beccaria.

At this early stage in his long career Bentham devoted much time to thinking and writing. But his life was more active and engaged than this account of his early philosophical work would suggest, and this was partly due to the close connection between his philosophical theory and the strategy of reform which emanated from it. For example, his interest in crime and punishment was stimulated not only by his reading but also by the crisis caused by the end of transportation to America due to the War of Independence, by the unsatisfactory state of the prison hulks on the Thames, and by the failure of the widespread use of capital punishment to deter crime. Bentham first entered this debate with his pamphlet *A View of the Hard Labour Bill* (1778). This has been credited with some influence on the seminal Penitentiary Act of 1779, which had been introduced by reformers such as Charles Bunbury, Gilbert Elliot, and William Eden, with Blackstone and the prison reformer John Howard providing assistance in drafting the act. Bentham wrote lengthy, detailed comments on each clause of the act, employing his method of using the detailed examination of laws and institutions as an instrument of reform.

At the time of the American War of Independence, Bentham supplied material for several pamphlets written by Lind attacking the ideas of the noted dissenting clergyman Richard Price. The occasion enabled Bentham to clarify his thinking about liberty. He realized that there were two distinct ideas of liberty, one negative and the other more positive. By the former he meant simply acting as one pleased without restraint or constraint from any other person or institution such as government. This simple idea of liberty as the absence of coercion was, he believed, often confused with the idea of civil liberty which depended on the authority of the state to protect the individual from the interference of others in society. This latter idea of liberty required positive action through legislation and its enforcement. So as not to confuse the two ideas, he called the second 'security', which he then made the main object of the civil law and an important component of both his utilitarian system and his later constitutional theory.

During the 1770s Bentham developed numerous interests: he corresponded with Joseph Priestley on chemical experiments; published in 1774 an English translation of Voltaire's *Le taureau blanc*; worked on a translation of the first volume of *Les Incas* by Jean François Marmontel; and by the end of the decade was revising for publication a rough translation of *The Usefulness of Chemistry* by a Swedish chemist, Torbern Olaf Bergman. In the middle of all this activity he fell deeply in love with Mary (Polly) Dunkley (*b.* 1757) from Colchester, whom he met during a visit to Lind's sisters. Dunkley, the orphaned daughter of an Essex surgeon, lacked a fortune, and Bentham's father strongly opposed the relationship. For a time Bentham considered supporting himself by writing, but he abandoned his plan and the relationship eventually ended.

Russia Bentham's relationship with his brother was always close, but it developed as Samuel grew up into a devoted concern for his welfare. In 1778 at the age of twenty-one, having also attended Westminster School, Samuel completed an apprenticeship to William Gray, master shipwright, first at Woolwich and then at Chatham, and sought to follow a career as a naval architect. The two brothers shared numerous interests and a common temperament, both being full of creative energy. But Samuel could not find a satisfactory outlet for his proposals and schemes in Britain and considered going to India. Bentham despaired at the thought of losing his only close friend and relative: 'O my Sam, my child, the only child I shall ever have, my only friend, my second self, could you bear to part with me?' (*Correspondence of Jeremy Bentham*, 2.222). A plausible alternative to India was Russia, which had increasingly become an object of attention to British entrepreneurs and travellers. Catherine II, empress of Russia since 1762, had a growing reputation in Britain as an enlightened ruler, committed to reform and the advancement of talent.

Both Benthams came to believe that in Russia their talents would not go unrecognized, and Bentham hoped that his special gifts for legislation and codification might be noticed by Catherine and her circle. The brothers began to cultivate every friend and acquaintance connected with Russia. Their father, however, was not initially in favour of the plan. He approached a Mr Randal, senior partner in a firm of shipbuilders, to obtain a post for Samuel, but by this time the brothers were strongly committed to their project and had amassed some eighty letters of reference and introduction to smooth Samuel's path. Among these were several written by William Petty, earl of Shelburne (created marquess of Lansdowne in 1784), to whom Samuel was introduced through Bentham's legal acquaintance, the exchequer judge Francis Maseres. This contact was to bear fruit for both brothers, and Bentham kept Shelburne informed of Samuel's activities by sending him excerpts from Samuel's letters. Samuel left Britain in August 1779 to begin an odyssey in Russia which lasted for nearly twelve years until his return in May 1791.

Bentham's close association with Shelburne began in July 1781 when Shelburne visited him at his chambers in Lincoln's Inn. Shelburne borrowed a copy of *A Fragment on Government* and invited Bentham to spend part of the summer at Bowood, his country house. After some hesitation Bentham visited Bowood and established a relationship with Shelburne which lasted for many years. He depicted his involvement with Shelburne and his family over the next eight years as among the happiest days of his life. Accepted into this highly intellectual household at the centre of national politics, he enjoyed the conversation and took part in the domestic life of a great country house. There he met and fell in love with Caroline Fox (*b.* 1767), a niece of Lady Shelburne. Although they enjoyed each other's company, and met later on several occasions, Bentham's offer of marriage in 1805 was politely refused. Bentham advised Shelburne on numerous topics, and secured several offers of assistance for his brother and himself. He made numerous important contacts through the Lansdowne circle, most importantly his introduction to Dumont and the development of his relationship with the legal reformer Samuel Romilly, whom he had previously met.

At this time Bentham was also preparing to travel to Russia to join his brother. He began the arduous journey in early August 1785 and in February 1786 arrived in Krichev in the Crimea, where Samuel was in the service of Prince Grigory Aleksandrovich Potyomkin. The two brothers were joyfully reunited after a separation of five and a half years. Bentham's period in Russia (approximately twenty months until his departure in the autumn of 1787) revealed some differences in temperament between the two brothers. If Samuel was gregarious and sociable, Jeremy tended towards introversion. While Samuel travelled extensively throughout Russia, Jeremy hardly left the tiny village of Zadobrast, several miles from Krichev, where he lived in a cottage assigned for Samuel's use, not even to see Catherine pass through Krichev in January 1787, or to visit St Petersburg or Moscow. Bentham found in his Russian retreat the opportunity for uninterrupted intellectual activity. He worked on penal and civil codes, and produced a French version of what would eventually become his *Rationale of Reward* (1825). In early 1787 he wrote *Defence of Usury*, a critique of Adam Smith's reluctance to advocate free trade in money in *An Inquiry into the Nature and Causes of the Wealth of Nations* (1776). The *Defence* was prompted by a report that the British government was about to issue new restrictions on rates of interest. It was dispatched to his good friend George Wilson for publication, and eventually became a highly influential economic essay.

The most important work of this period was inspired by Samuel, who had devised a scheme of an 'inspection house', a circular building with an observation post in the centre from which a few skilled craftsmen could supervise the work of unskilled men. Bentham saw numerous possibilities in Samuel's invention, particularly its application to prisons, hospitals, and schools, as well as to industrial enterprises. He wrote a series of letters during 1786, entitled *Panopticon: or, the Inspection-House*, which were sent to London but which were not published until 1791.

French Revolution When Louis XVI announced in autumn 1788 that he would call a meeting of the estates-general for May 1789, Bentham, who had returned from his journey to Russia in February 1788, like many Britons, became fascinated by the unfolding events in France. His connection with Lansdowne's circle, which now included Dumont (who had become tutor to one of Lansdowne's sons in 1785) and Romilly, placed him in a good position to use the marquess's contacts to advance various projects in France. He had already attempted to make contact with noted *philosophes*, such as d'Alembert, André Morellet, and François Jean, marquis de Chastellux, and had made a useful friendship with Jacques-Pierre Brissot, whom he had met through François-Xavier Schwediauer.

In the summer of 1788 Dumont and Romilly visited Paris for two months, where Dumont met Honoré-Gabriel Riqueti, comte de Mirabeau. That autumn Bentham drafted a number of essays dealing with the situation in France, including an open letter to Mirabeau criticizing the decision to employ the constitution of 1614 for the estates-general, and another short essay criticizing the defence by the Breton nobility of that arrangement. The latter essay represents Bentham's first collaborative effort with Dumont, to whom Romilly had given the essay to correct Bentham's French.

The major work begun at this time was his 'Essay on political tactics', a comparative study of French and English parliamentary procedure. At the same time Bentham composed an essay on representation which was linked to this work on legislative procedure. He received strong encouragement from Lansdowne, who invited Bentham to use the extensive library in Lansdowne House (his London residence), discussed numerous issues with him, and put him in contact with leading figures in France. Bentham rekindled his earlier brief correspondence with Morellet by sending him (via Lansdowne's son John Henry Petty, Lord Wycombe) a manuscript of the 'Essay on political tactics' to see if he might oversee a translation. Another copy was sent to Madame Necker. Bentham had hoped that it might be published in French before the estates-general met, but that hope was soon dashed. Although Morellet had found a translator, little progress was made on it, and Bentham began to lose interest. Only a brief article listing six principles concerning parliamentary debate was published by Mirabeau in the *Courier de Provence*, and even then without acknowledging Bentham as the author.

Two other works received greater recognition in France. During 1790 Bentham was mainly living at Dollis's Farm in Hendon, Middlesex, where he had stayed since returning from Russia (though he kept his chambers in Lincoln's Inn). In April, with Bentham and Dumont working in adjacent rooms in Lansdowne House under the supervision of the marquess himself, he addressed a letter to the president of the national assembly and sent a hundred copies of a French version of the first part of 'Draught of a new plan for the organization of the judicial establishment in France'. The letter appeared in the *Journal de Paris* and instalments of the 'Draught' in Mirabeau's *Courier de Provence*. Bentham heard little about the fate of this work, however, until October 1791, when he learned that Jean-Philippe Garran de Coulon, a member of the national assembly, had cited Bentham's work, praised it highly, proposed that a committee of the national assembly should examine the 'Draught', and that Bentham should be invited to communicate his ideas on civil law. When Bentham learned of these proposals, he sent Garran copies of his 'Essay on political tactics', an extract from 'Panopticon' in French (prepared by Dumont), a promise to send the English version, and an offer to establish a panopticon prison in France. On 13 December 1791 Garran showed Bentham's extract from 'Panopticon' to the assembly, which voted to mention Bentham's offer in the *procès-verbal*, with a recommendation that a committee should examine the extract and that it should be printed.

Meanwhile, events in France did not favour the adoption of Bentham's ideas and plans. Following the death of Mirabeau and the increasing violence, the Lansdowne circle tended to become disillusioned with the revolution. During 1792 numerous French refugees were sent by Dumont, Romilly, and the political reformer Benjamin Vaughan to Bentham at Queen Square Place, which he had inherited on the death of his father. In October, Bentham, together with other reformers and philanthropists, was made an honorary citizen of France. In accepting the honour Bentham mentioned the refugees and called for greater tolerance of those who opposed the new regime.

Bentham's writings for France achieved no immediate results. No proposal was adopted and no panopticon prison appeared in revolutionary Paris. Bentham's experience with France revealed in a dramatic way the difficulties of adapting complex arguments and proposals to changing political circumstances. Even arrangements for translating and publishing his writings became problematic. The French Revolution also affected Bentham personally. For the first time, albeit in essays he never published and could even have forgotten, he adopted radical principles in favour of representative government, near-universal suffrage, the secret ballot, and annual assemblies. But he soon reacted strongly against the course of the revolution. One essay of this later period was Bentham's denunciation of the declaration of rights of man and the citizen, published posthumously in English as 'Anarchical fallacies' and containing Bentham's famous remark that natural rights were 'simple nonsense' and natural and imprescriptible rights, 'nonsense upon stilts'. Not until 1809–10 did Bentham begin to write in favour of radical parliamentary reform in Britain, and not publicly until the *Plan of Parliamentary Reform* appeared in 1817.

The French Revolution by no means absorbed all Bentham's attention at this time. In 1789, urged by George Wilson and others, he finally published *An Introduction to the Principles of Morals and Legislation*. He merely added a final chapter in the form of a 'Concluding note' in which he briefly indicated a range of issues contained in the question 'What is a law?'. These issues were dealt with at length in a further work, written in 1780–82 (just after *An Introduction to the Principles of Morals and Legislation* was printed) but left unpublished until 1945, and eventually called *Of Laws in General*, when it was republished in 1970 as part of the new *Collected Works of Jeremy Bentham*. Bentham may have decided to publish the *Introduction* following the appearance in 1785 of William Paley's *Principles of Moral and Political Philosophy*, which bore a superficial resemblance to Bentham's book in its use of the idea of utility. But Bentham was also aware of the imperfections of his own work. It was written as an introduction to a penal code which remained unfinished and unpublished. The discussions of the psychology of human action (the logic of the will) and the principle of utility, though profound and revolutionary, were highly compressed. The 'Concluding note', and the previous chapter on the distinction between penal and civil law and on the demarcation line between private ethics and the sphere of legislation, were brief indications of Bentham's thinking which had not yet been brought to fruition.

The first six chapters of the *Introduction* have often been taken as a concise statement of Bentham's principle of utility. They contain several important aspects of the utilitarian doctrine, such as the emphasis on the classification and measurement of pleasure and pain, the belief that utility is the only principle which can provide an objective foundation for morals and legislation, as opposed to other principles such as moral sense, common sense, understanding, rule of right, fitness of things, law of nature, law of reason, right reason, natural justice, natural equity, good order, truth, and the doctrine of election. Nevertheless, this brief work fails to capture the full meaning of Bentham's principle which emerges in other works, especially the emphasis on secondary principles such as security and equality, which indirectly advance the greatest happiness; and the emphasis on equal distribution, captured in part in John Stuart Mill's dictum (Mill, *Utilitarianism*, 5.36), taken from Bentham's *Rationale of Judicial Evidence*, that 'everybody to count for one, nobody for more than one'.

Panopticon prison Bentham's trip to Russia, his involvement in the Lansdowne circle, and the French Revolution had led to his involvement in other issues apart from philosophical jurisprudence. For example, he wrote a series of letters, published in the *Public Advertiser* in May and June 1789, entitled 'Letters of Anti-Machiavel', criticizing the hostile attitude towards Russia adopted by the Pitt administration. In 1793 he published *A Protest Against Law Taxes* attacking a move by the Irish chancellor of the exchequer to impose a tax on legal judgments. But the most important and absorbing of his interests at this time became the panopticon prison project. The panopticon letters, written in Russia, were partly stimulated by an announcement in the *St James' Chronicle* that transportation would soon be resumed, and that plans for a new house of correction in Middlesex were being solicited. The letters were sent to Bentham's father and to George Wilson in England, but neither were as enthusiastic about the plan as the two brothers. The letters remained unpublished for several years after Bentham's return from Russia, in spite of the interest in the project in France.

One attempt to build the panopticon stemmed from Lansdowne's initiative in August 1790 in sending a copy of the unpublished letters to Sir John Parnell, chancellor of the Irish exchequer. Parnell was favourably impressed, and by the end of the year the book was being printed in two parts, while Bentham actively prepared several postscripts. However, by the spring of 1791 Parnell's initial enthusiasm had greatly diminished, and with the failure of the French initiative Bentham began to concentrate his attention on building the panopticon prison in London.

A number of other factors led Bentham to take this course. On his return from Russia at the age of forty, and his involvement with Lansdowne and his circle, Bentham began to come to terms with his own personal ambitions. In August 1790 he wrote a long letter to Lansdowne accusing him of a betrayal of faith in not returning him to parliament for one of his pocket boroughs. Perhaps Bentham was upset that his stepbrother Charles Abbot had already been offered a seat. Perhaps it was simply frustration at the lack of success of his own projects. 'Do you really then think me', he wrote to Lansdowne, 'incapable of every thing but proposing impracticable projects, and throwing out odd ideas that would not have occurred to any body else? Is *good* ... absolutely synonymous to *impracticable*?' (*Correspondence of Jeremy Bentham*, 4.167). Lansdowne replied by saying that he had been unaware of Bentham's parliamentary ambitions, and had thought that Bentham had placed great value on his independence. He also promised that he would bring him into parliament at the first opportunity, a promise that Bentham did not take seriously.

With the return of Samuel from Russia in May 1791 to an uncertain future, Bentham began to see the panopticon project as the vehicle for realizing the ambitions of them both. When he sought to establish the panopticon in Ireland, he did not envisage himself as the contractor–governor. In November 1791, however, in a letter to William Pitt he suggested that he might develop the panopticon scheme himself. His brother was also to be closely involved, and within a month of his return to England Samuel began to devote himself to the panopticon project. When Bentham inherited Queen Square Place and sufficient funds to live comfortably there, he continued to press on with panopticon when there was no obvious financial reason to do so. In moving into his father's house, he seemed to take on his father's ambitiousness for himself, and QSP, the nickname the Bentham brothers had used to refer to their father, appeared ubiquitously at the top of virtually every letter Bentham subsequently wrote.

In the long silence following his letter to Pitt, during which time the two brothers installed a model of the panopticon in a room in Queen Square Place, Bentham began to win over political allies, such as Reginald Pole Carew, William Wilberforce, and Sir Charles Bunbury. By May 1792 the home secretary, Henry Dundas, had taken an interest in the project and in September visited the display at Queen Square Place. Despite Dundas's approval little happened for nearly a year. In May 1793 Bunbury, who was one of the commissioners appointed under the 1779 Penitentiary Act with the power to acquire land, spoke in the House of Commons about the scandals surrounding transportation to Botany Bay, the state of the hulks and gaols, and recommended Bentham's plan to the government, as one where 'well regulated prisons calculated to reform offenders, and to convert the dissolute and idle into good and industrious subjects, would be provided at a cheaper rate than vessels in the Thames' (Semple, 109–10). Dundas and Pitt eventually visited Queen Square Place together in July and asked the two brothers to make the appropriate arrangements to proceed with their plans.

For the first time Bentham saw a clear road ahead. But he could not have realized how far the war with France would absorb the energies of leading figures. Nor could he have foreseen the legal complexities in which he would

soon be enmeshed. Bentham thought that with the votes of two of the three commissioners under the act of 1779, Bunbury and Thomas Bowdler, the scheme might go ahead on the Battersea site which had been selected for a prison in 1782. But John Reeves, a legal adviser to the government, argued that a new act would be necessary, as the 1779 act applied to a public institution to be run by public officers, and not to one privately run, as Bentham envisaged. Thus the land at Battersea Rise could not be compulsorily purchased under the act.

Bentham then approached the two owners of the Battersea Rise site to see if they might sell the land without compulsion. The freehold on which George John, second Earl Spencer, held long leases was owned by the see of York. Bentham wrote to his father's friend and his own old headmaster at Westminster School, William Markham, then archbishop of York, from whom he received a cautious response. From Earl Spencer he received determined opposition to any plan to deprive him of this land.

The new bill was introduced by Dundas in May 1794 with the sole purpose of securing the land for the prison. But Spencer's faction in parliament opposed the bill, and inserted an amendment so that alternatives to the Battersea Rise site might be selected. Bentham was told that the bill had been passed on condition that the Battersea Rise site was not selected, and thus Bentham met with a serious rebuff from Spencer. To complicate matters, Spencer was appointed at this time to the post of first lord of the Admiralty, and Samuel's appointment as inspector-general of naval works in 1795 brought him into close and friendly contact with the Spencer family.

The Penitentiary Act of 1794 gave the Treasury the task of acquiring the land and negotiating the contract. But many of those sympathetic to Bentham's project had moved on to other posts, especially Dundas, who was by then wholly absorbed in the war with France as secretary at war, and Evan Nepean, who became secretary to the Admiralty. Those who were responsible for implementing the act, George Rose and Charles Long together with a number of others, who might be regarded as 'Pitt's men', were unenthusiastic or even hostile to the project. Others who might have come to Bentham's assistance favoured other principles of management and architecture.

Negotiations concerning various locations for the prison ran into numerous difficulties, as few wanted a prison on or near their estates, and the whole idea of public inspection depended on the prison being situated on an accessible and convenient site. For a brief period, when Long offered Bentham the Salisbury estate at Millbank, and Bentham actually acquired the land in November 1799, it seemed that the project would go forward. But Pitt resigned in 1801 without authorizing the prison, and the Addington administration kept Bentham waiting until 1803 before saying that the government was unwilling to fund the project. The Treasury considered panopticon again in 1811–12, when Bentham was still willing to be governor, but in October 1813 he finally gave up all hope and accepted £23,000 in compensation.

Economics, administration, and the poor laws The panopticon prison scheme absorbed a good deal of Bentham's time between his early forties and mid-sixties, and might have broken a less resourceful person. Yet he managed not only to generate an extraordinary amount of activity and correspondence to advance the scheme from one year to the next but also to pursue a number of other projects to which he devoted equal enthusiasm and energy. During 1796 and 1797, partly stimulated by the scarcity and increasing expense of food and the growing debate about the treatment of the poor in England, he began to write at length on poor relief, and composed a number of works which, mainly through Edwin Chadwick, had some influence on the reforms of the nineteenth century. He opposed proposals to abolish poor relief and replace it with private charity; for Bentham, a reliance on private charity would almost certainly lead to the death of many impoverished people. He supported the public provision of relief but, in order to avoid excessive expenditure and the decline of incentives to work, he insisted that those unable or unwilling to work for their own subsistence should not be better off than those who did. In addition, he extended the panopticon idea to encompass a system of 'industry houses' run by a joint-stock company to house the indigent and make provision for them to labour and through labour to acquire the virtues of frugality, sobriety, and industry. The industry houses would also be used to provide a range of welfare services for the working poor. Part of this material was published in a series of articles in Arthur Young's *Annals of Agriculture* in 1797–8.

A number of Bentham's writings on financial administration and political economy were produced during the 1790s and early 1800s. Partly owing to the struggles over panopticon, he had numerous friends with whom he could share his ideas or discuss their own ideas and projects. Pole Carew, for example, sent him his 'Ideas on financial reform' in 1798, while Bentham was developing his own thoughts on similar topics. Bentham came into contact with Patrick Colquhoun, whose works on the police and other statistical studies he greatly admired. He assisted Colquhoun in drawing up various bills, including the Thames Police Bill, which was enacted in 1800. Bentham also wrote extensively on economic policy and public finance. Among his most important writings were the 'Manual of political economy', written between 1793 and 1795, covering numerous topics in economics; *Supply without Burthen, or, Escheat Vice Taxation* (1795), which advocated the confiscatory taxation of remote inheritances; *A Protest Against Law Taxes* (1795), calling for the abolition of all taxes on legal proceedings; and 'Circulating annuities' (1799–1800), 'Paper mischief' (1800–01), and 'The true alarm' (1801), works intended to show the effects of the unlimited issue of notes by country banks. He also wrote an essay entitled 'Defence of a maximum', which criticized Charles Long's argument against the establishment of a maximum price for grain. Another work, 'Institute of political economy' (1800–01), attempted to define both the science and the art of political economy. Few of these essays were published, and many were hardly known

prior to W. Stark's edition of *Jeremy Bentham's Economic Writings* (3 vols., 1952–4).

Bentham's status as an economist has never been fully explored. His early *Defence of Usury* reflects the influence of Adam Smith, whom he frequently praised as a great thinker. Classical economists, such as James Mill, David Ricardo, and John Stuart Mill, might be considered among Bentham's followers, but his idea of utility and related concepts also influenced neo-classical economists, such as W. S. Jevons and F. Y. Edgeworth. Economic ideas appear in many of his writings, and he was probably the first to see the importance of using the language and concepts of economics in place of highly emotive religious, moral, and political ideas. Such thinking lay behind his approach to punishment in *An Introduction to the Principles of Morals and Legislation*. The writings on panopticon and the poor laws reveal a different dimension of Bentham's use of economics. Here, in detailed considerations of management, accountability, and financial administration, he laid the foundations for the more politically oriented examination of bureaucracy in such later writings as *Constitutional Code* which he began in 1822.

Dumont's recensions The publication in Paris in 1802 of the first of Dumont's recensions of Bentham's writings, *Traités de législation civile et pénale*, brought Bentham's ideas for the first time before a wide audience. Estimates in 1830 that 50,000 copies of the various recensions were sold in Europe and 40,000 in Spanish translation in Latin America testify to the importance of Dumont's work in giving Bentham an international reputation. The three-volume *Traités* contained numerous writings taken from Bentham's manuscripts, such as those on civil law concerned with justice and 'Indirect legislation' on the prevention of crime, which were not fully published in English until after his death, when they were retranslated for the Bowring edition of his *Works* (1838–43). The two important works on reward and punishment, written by Bentham in the late 1770s and early 1780s, appeared for the first time in Dumont's second recension, *Théorie des peines et des récompenses* (1811), and were then published in English as the *Rationale of Reward* (1825) and the *Rationale of Punishment* (1830), a half-century after they were written.

In *Tactique des assemblées législatives, suivie d'un traité des sophismes politiques*, published in 1816, Dumont used Bentham's manuscripts to create the substantial essay on the organization of legislative assemblies of which Bentham himself gave a brief indication in his 'Essay on political tactics' (1791). In addition, Dumont included a version of Bentham's writings on political fallacies in this recension, from which and with the use of the original manuscripts Peregrine Bingham later produced *The Book of Fallacies* (1824). Dumont published two other recensions, a work on evidence, *Traité des preuves judiciaires* (1823), and another on judicial organization, *De l'organisation judiciaire, et de la codification* (1828). In 1829–30 a substantial three-volume edition of the *Œuvres de J. Bentham, jurisconsulte anglais*, was published in Brussels, and it was reissued in 1832 and 1840. However much Bentham may have complained that

Dumont's versions were not his own, he was grateful to Dumont for what he could not achieve alone, a growing international reputation based on highly readable editions of his works.

Law and law reform Bentham devoted much time between 1803 and 1806 to writing about evidence and the related subject of judicial procedure. With the formation of the Grenville–Fox ministry in 1806, several of Bentham's friends joined the government, including Romilly, who became solicitor-general, and Lord Henry Petty, who became chancellor of the exchequer. The new government was supposedly sympathetic to reform, and Lord Grenville himself proposed the initiation of the reform of the system of civil justice in Scotland. Although the administration was dismissed in March 1807, the new government, with Lord Eldon reinstated as lord chancellor, indicated that it would press on with the reform of the Scottish courts.

Bentham published *Scotch Reform* in 1808 with a further edition in 1811. Although he was not encouraged to follow up his proposal to prepare a draft code for Scotland, his friend Francis Horner suggested some amendments to the Scotch Judicature Bill, based on Bentham's ideas. In 1808 Bentham printed another work on judicial procedure, the 'Summary view of the plan of a judicatory, under the name of the court of Lords' delegates', and circulated it widely among members of the House of Lords. This work was connected with *Scotch Reform*, but both represented only a small portion of the manuscripts Bentham actually wrote on these subjects.

Bentham's writings on evidence took longer to come to fruition. James Mill worked on some of the manuscripts between 1808 and 1811, when what was published posthumously in the Bowring edition as 'An introductory view of the rationale of evidence' was partially printed. Bentham's major work on evidence was edited by the youthful John Stuart Mill and published in five volumes in 1827, a task so difficult and demanding that it may have contributed to Mill's mental crisis which began soon afterwards. In these writings Bentham attacked what he called the 'technical' system of evidence and adjective law which was employed in England and which, in his opinion, led to obscurity in the law and unnecessary expense, delay, and corruption. Bentham recommended the 'natural' system of procedure where all parties were heard, all evidence admitted, cross-examination encouraged, and increased powers given to courts to obtain evidence.

Radicalism As Bentham saw how little an impact his ideas on law reform actually were having, and as he reflected on the enormous amount of time and money he had invested in the panopticon project, he eventually was converted to political radicalism as the only means to achieve reform. For much of his career he had believed that he could deal directly with governments, that his proposals would receive a fair hearing, and that they might be adopted and enacted into law. The question of whether reform depended on the form of government was not a serious issue in his early writings. His brief flirtation with radicalism at the time of the French Revolution was soon abandoned. In 1809 he began to think seriously about parliamentary reform, including such radical doctrines as universal suffrage, the secret ballot, annual parliaments, and a representative system based on equal electoral districts, and he wrote at length on these and related topics. Some of the reasons for his adopting the radical mantle have already been mentioned, such as the failure of panopticon and his proposals for law reform. In addition, for the first time in fifteen years, political reform had become a topic of public debate, and Bentham shared in this renewed interest. At this time he also became close friends with James Mill, and they may have persuaded each other to advocate parliamentary reform.

Bentham's first public declaration of his radical position came only with the appearance of his *Plan of Parliamentary Reform* in 1817. Although Bentham's style was widely criticized, the work itself was favourably received. In 1818 he was thanked by a public meeting of Westminster householders for his support for radical principles. Thomas Wooler then brought out a popular edition which first appeared in instalments in his periodical, *Black Dwarf*, and was then reprinted as a book. In 1819 the *Plan* was followed by *Bentham's Radical Reform Bill*, which in turn became his 'Election code' when eventually incorporated into the *Constitutional Code*.

Bentham's reluctance to publish his radical views between 1809 or 1810 and 1817 was based partly on fear of prosecution. During the decade between 1815 and 1825, he developed radical critiques of the law (*Truth versus Ashurst*, written in 1792, published in 1823; *Indications Respecting Lord Eldon*, 1825; and *Observations on Mr Secretary Peel's House of Commons Speech, 21st March, 1825*, published in 1825), religion (*Church of Englandism and its Catechism Examined*, 1818; *Not Paul but Jesus*, published under a pseudonym, Gamaliel Smith, in 1823; and *Analysis of the Influence of Natural Religion on the Temporal Happiness of Mankind*, also published under a pseudonym, Philip Beauchamp, in 1822), and economy in government (*Defence of Economy Against the Right Honourable Edmund Burke*, written in 1810 but published in 1817; *Defence of Economy Against the Right Honourable George Rose*, written in 1810 but published in 1817). Bentham often published these against the advice of friends and colleagues, and had to choose radical publishers such as the Hunts, Richard Carlisle, and William Hone who were willing to face prosecution. He also developed a close relationship with Francis Place, whom he met through James Mill in 1812, and with whom he made contact with other writers deeply involved in radical politics, such as John Wade, Thomas Hodgskin, and William Thompson. Place and Bentham also co-operated in a number of radical schemes such as the Parliamentary Candidates Society in 1831.

Education and philosophy Bentham's interest in education stemmed from many sources, not least from his dissatisfaction with his own education in classical languages and religion. His *Church of Englandism* was probably conceived originally as an appendix to his book on education,

Chrestomathia (*chrestos* meaning useful and *mathos*, knowledge or learning), and in it he attacked the National School Society, an Anglican body, for insisting on a major role for religion in the education of the poor. Bentham was also attracted to the monitorial system of education, whereby a master taught the older pupils and they in turn taught the others. Bentham agreed with Mill and Place that this system would be a means of providing inexpensive education for all children. But while the Anglican church paid lip service to the Madras system of Andrew Bell, Mill, Place, and the philanthropist Edward Wakefield favoured the system devised by Joseph Lancaster, which was non-sectarian in design, and opened the possibility of schools for all.

Although Bentham gave considerable credit to Bell as well as to Lancaster in *Chrestomathia*, he clearly wanted to exclude religion from his Chrestomathic school. The proposed exclusion was probably one reason for the failure of the school, as some potential backers would not support it without a religious foundation. The idea of the school was suggested by Place to Wakefield in the autumn of 1813. It was designed to provide secondary education for children of the 'middling ranks' (tradesmen and those of similar status) for whom no suitable education was available. Mill and Bentham readily joined the project, and Bentham generously offered a portion of his garden as a site for the school. Even though he was initially enthusiastic about locating the school in his garden, others expressed doubts that he would accept that arrangement once he had begun to consider the idea more carefully. David Ricardo had nearly completed negotiations in 1817 for a site in the centre of Leicester Square, when local shopkeepers threatened legal proceedings to prevent building there. Despite their hesitation the trustees of the school then returned to Bentham, and, as anticipated, protracted negotiations took place for two years between 1818 and 1820, when the project was finally abandoned. In conjunction with the development of plans for the school, Bentham began writing about education in spring 1814 in the work entitled *Chrestomathia*. The first edition was printed and privately circulated in 1815 with an edition actually published in 1816. In 1817 part II of the work was published containing an 'Essay on nomenclature and classification', which Bentham's nephew George *Bentham, the future botanist, translated into French and published in Paris in 1823.

Bentham's educational theory emphasized subjects such as mathematics, physical science, modern languages, economics, law, and music, as opposed to classical languages and religion, the staple diet of most schools at the time. If he favoured 'useful' learning, he was not narrow in his conception of what subjects were useful. It is worth noting that most of Bentham's important writings on logic and language were produced between 1813 and 1815, just as he was writing *Chrestomathia* and involved in the Chrestomathic school. Furthermore, after George Bentham completed his French edition of the extract from *Chrestomathia* on classification, he turned to Bentham's writings on logic and produced a work entitled

Outline of a New System of Logic (1827), based in part on Bentham's ideas and published at Bentham's expense. A version of Bentham's writings on logic and language was published in the Bowring edition and became well-known in the twentieth century in the edition prepared by C. K. Ogden, *Bentham's Theory of Fictions* (1932). When one considers the philosophical material on language and classification in *Chrestomathia*, together with the writings on logic and language, plus such works as *Table of the Springs of Action* (printed in 1815 and published in 1817), in which he developed further his account of the logic of the will, the material on ethics under the heading of 'Deontology' written mainly between 1814 and 1816, the writings on fallacies (first published by Dumont in the second volume of *Tactique des assemblées législatives, suivie d'un traité des sophismes politiques*, 1816), and the substantial writings on evidence written between 1802 and 1812, it is clear that at the end of the panopticon project Bentham turned for a second period in his life to intensive work on philosophical and related issues and produced a major body of writings apart from the philosophical writings of the 1770s.

Legislation   At an early age Bentham decided that if he had a genius for anything, it was for legislation. His early writings were directed at producing a penal code and ultimately a complete code of laws. He later pursued more systematically his career in codification (a word he invented) in a series of offers to leaders of various states. As chronicled in detail in *Papers Relative to Codification and Public Instruction* (1817), his codification odyssey began with a letter to the American president, James Madison, on 30 October 1811, the reply to which, owing to the intervening war with Britain, was not sent by Madison until May 1816. Meanwhile, working through Dumont, Bentham made contact with Dumont's fellow Genevan, Albert Gallatin, who had pursued a successful political career in the United States and travelled to London in April 1814 as an American representative to negotiate an end to the hostilities between Britain and the United States. Gallatin thought that Pennsylvania would be most sympathetic to Bentham's efforts at codification, and he wrote a letter of recommendation which Bentham sent with his own letter to the governor, Simon Snyder. In December 1816 Snyder placed Bentham's offer and Gallatin's letter before the legislature, but nothing came of this initiative.

Bentham then made contact with the American minister in London, John Quincy Adams, and they met on several occasions in spring 1817 before Adams left London in June to take up his post as secretary of state. Adams was to take with him copies of *Papers Relative to Codification and Public Instruction*, as well as 'Circulars' on codification and public instruction, and copies of the recently published *Chrestomathia* and *Plan of Parliamentary Reform*, which were to be sent to various officials and to each of the state governors. If a legislature agreed to accept Bentham's offer to codify the laws, Adams was to send other works by Bentham to the governor for use by the legislature. Bentham also drafted a series of letters 'to the Citizens of the several American United States' which he hoped would be widely circulated.

Adams did as he was asked, and Bentham eventually received news that his circular letters had appeared in a number of newspapers in the United States. In October 1817 he received a letter from William Plumer, governor of New Hampshire, who promised to present Bentham's offer to the legislature at its next meeting in June 1818, after which a committee was set up to consider it. Bentham also heard that it had been received by De Witt Clinton, governor of New York. But no state actually accepted Bentham's offer. Bentham believed that this was because most members of legislatures were lawyers and antagonistic to the threat to their livelihoods implicit in the codification of the law. The codification movement did not develop until later in the nineteenth century. The only example of partial success at this time was by the lawyer and diplomat Edward Livingston, who drafted a penal code for the state of Louisiana, based on Bentham's ideas, and then revised it for the federal government, but neither body adopted the code.

Bentham also pursued the possibility of codifying the laws of Russia and Poland, offering his services to Alexander I in January 1814. He redoubled his efforts in June of that year, when Alexander and Prince Adam Jerzy Czartoryski, whom Bentham had met during an earlier visit to Britain in 1789–91, went to London. Czartoryski hoped to assist in the restoration of the kingdom of Poland with Alexander as sovereign and himself as viceroy. He presented Bentham's letter to Alexander at the Congress of Vienna in April 1815. Alexander replied by telling Bentham that he would instruct the commission for the compilation of the laws, established in 1801, to direct its questions to him and by sending him a gift of a gold ring. Bentham was not impressed with this suggestion and returned the ring, explaining that he neither expected payment nor wished to answer specific questions, but wanted to draft a complete code for Russia which could then be accepted or rejected. With hopes dashed for becoming a legislator for Russia, he still believed that his offer might be accepted in Poland; but Alexander passed over Czartoryski when appointing a viceroy, and Bentham was again disappointed.

More promising than the United States, Russia, or Poland was Geneva, where in May 1817 two commissions were appointed to draw up a new penal code and a code of criminal procedure. Dumont was a member of the commission for the penal code and wanted the code based on Bentham's ideas. Bentham, however, wanted to draft the codes himself, and after much correspondence and a visit by Dumont to Bentham, one code, based firmly on Bentham's principles, if not drafted by him, was completed, but never adopted.

Early liberalism Bentham's efforts at codification eventually became part of his involvement with early liberalism, especially in Spain, Portugal, Greece, and Latin America. This involvement began in 1820 when the liberal government in Spain came to power, and Bentham began to work in conjunction with two disciples, Edward Blaquiere,

whom he met in 1813, and John Bowring, who was introduced to Bentham in 1820 by Blaquiere and who soon became an important figure in many aspects of his life. Blaquiere and Bowring were early visitors to Spain under the new regime, where they made contact with leading politicians and journalists and encouraged them to correspond with Bentham. Among his correspondents were José Canga-Argüelles, the finance minister, Augustin Argüelles, the minister of the interior, Count Toreno, deputy to the Cortes, to whom Bentham addressed his *Letters to Count Toreno on the Proposed Penal Code* (1822), José Joaquín de Mora, the editor of *El Constitucional*, who translated some of his writings into Spanish, and Toribio Núñez, librarian of the University of Salamanca, who published recensions of Bentham's writings, *Espiritu de Bentham ó sistéma de la ciencia social, ideado por Jeremías Bentham* (1820) and *Principios de la ciencia social ó de las ciencias morales y politicas por el jurisconsulto Inglés Jeremías Bentham* (1821).

Bentham was not entirely happy with the new government. When a law was passed by the Cortes in 1820 limiting freedom of speech and discussion, which led to the arrest and imprisonment of Mora, Bentham responded with *On the Liberty of the Press and Public Discussion* (1821); and when the Cortes approved a new customs tariff, Bentham wrote, in conjunction with Bowring, a strong tract on the advantages of free trade, *Observations on the Restrictive and Prohibitory Commercial System* (1821). In spite of his involvement with a number of Spaniards, and his acquiring a reputation as an early icon of liberalism, he never received what he sought most: an invitation to codify the laws of Spain. Although the Cortes approved a plan in October 1820 to build panopticon prisons throughout Spain, it was not until 1863 that one was established. With the fall of the liberal regime in 1823, all hopes for codification in Spain were lost.

In Portugal, however, where a new constitution based on the Spanish constitution of 1812 had been established in 1820, prospects appeared brighter. His 'Letter to the Portugueze nation' (included in *Three Tracts Relative to Spanish and Portugueze Affairs*, 1821) was translated into Portuguese. In 1821 a consignment of his books was received by José da Silva Carvalho, a member of the council of regency and later minister of justice, who presented these to the Portuguese Cortes, which on 13 April 1821 ordered them to be translated. Bentham then wrote again to the Cortes in November 1821 making a formal offer to produce penal, civil, and constitutional codes. The Cortes accepted Bentham's offer, and he proceeded almost immediately to draft material for *Constitutional Code*, and worked on related penal, civil, and procedure codes throughout the 1820s. Unfortunately, as in Spain, the regime fell. Although Bentham's efforts were not rewarded, the intensive work on codification in his last decade owed a good deal to the stimulus provided by the invitation from the Portuguese Cortes.

When the liberal governments in Spain and Portugal fell in 1823, Blaquiere and Bowring turned their attention to Greece, where the war against the Turkish empire had been waged since 1821. The two established the London

Greek Committee with Bowring as secretary, and Bla-quiere was sent to Greece in March 1823 to observe conditions and present a manuscript of Bentham's 'Observations' on the Greek constitution of 1822 to the Greek government. Although the main object of the London Greek Committee was to raise and supervise a major loan for the fledgeling government, it also sponsored an expedition to Greece, led by Lord Byron and Colonel Leicester Stanhope, later the fifth earl of Harrington. Stanhope took with him an early manuscript draft of *Constitutional Code* which he presented to the Greek government in April 1824. He also established several newspapers which published brief extracts from Bentham's works. Nevertheless, even the westernized Greeks, like the future prime minister Alexander Mavrokordatos, were too absorbed in their struggle for survival to do more than thank Bentham for his efforts on their behalf. Many of these letters and testimonials from Spain, Portugal, Greece, and eventually Latin America were then printed in 'Codification proposal' (1822) and its supplements (1827 and 1830).

One of Bentham's important writings of the early 1820s, which was not published until 1995, was first entitled 'Emancipation Spanish', and then 'Rid yourselves of Ultramaria'. This work followed Bentham's early pamphlet written for France, 'Jeremy Bentham to the national convention of France' (1793, published as *Emancipate your Colonies!* in 1830), but developed at length a highly sophisticated analysis of the disutility of colonies to both the mother country (in this case Spain) and the colonies themselves.

During the 1820s Bentham also cultivated several leaders of the newly independent countries of Latin America in the hope of providing codes, if they were desired. He opened a correspondence with Bernadino Rivadavia, later chief minister of Buenos Aires, when he went to Paris in 1818, and they met in London in 1820. When Rivadavia returned to Buenos Aires, he drew up a system of rules for the legislature based on Bentham's ideas. José del Valle, who was a member of the provisional government of Central America in 1821–2, secretary of foreign and domestic affairs of the Mexican empire in 1822, and a member of the ruling triumvirate of Central America in 1823–4, sought Bentham's help in 1826 in drawing up a civil code for Guatemala, and soon became a devoted disciple. Among other disciples in Latin America was Francisco de Paula Santander, vice-president of Colombia 1821–8, and subsequently president of New Grenada. In 1825 in the absence of the president of Colombia, Simón Bolívar, Santander issued a decree that Bentham's principles of legislation should be taught by professors of law. This was opposed by the Roman Catholic church, and following Bolívar's return in 1826, though Bentham thought him to be a disciple following a flattering letter received in 1822, he issued a decree in 1828 proscribing Bentham's texts in the universities. In spite of numerous followers throughout Latin America, from Argentina and Chile to Mexico, and the widespread use of his works, especially Dumont's recensions and translations of these into Spanish, Bentham was never invited to draft a legal code for any of the new states of Latin America. Nevertheless, there is no doubting his considerable influence on those who did establish the legal and political systems in these countries.

Last decade The last decade of Bentham's life was highly productive on numerous levels. New editions of his early works, such as *An Introduction to the Principles of Morals and Legislation* and *A Fragment on Government*, as well as of Dumont's recensions were published. A number of the Dumont volumes were translated into English. Bentham was also surrounded by numerous friends, associates, and secretaries, who assisted him in publishing his various works. He now possessed a considerable international reputation, and many writers, politicians, and revolutionaries were eager to meet him and involve him in their various activities. Some of these ventures were new, as his attempts to assist the young unofficial ambassador from Tripoli, Hassuna D'Ghies, in overthrowing the government in Tripoli with the assistance of John Quincy Adams and the American government. This led to one of Bentham's most important political essays, 'Securities against misrule', concerned with the question of how to introduce political liberty into an absolute Muslim state. Other ventures were a continuation of long-standing concerns with codification and law reform. For example, he managed to publish the first of three volumes of *Constitutional Code* in 1830, and print most of the second volume. He also published a collection of papers on political and administrative reform in 1830, entitled *Official Aptitude Maximized; Expense Minimized*. None of the other codes were completed, though Richard Doane, his former amanuensis, produced versions of a procedure code and the whole of the constitutional code for the Bowring edition.

During the 1820s Bentham continued to advance the cause of law reform in Britain, and his papers contain considerable correspondence with a wide variety of political figures, including Henry Brougham, Sir Robert Peel, and Daniel O'Connell. Towards the end of the decade he attempted to establish a Law Reform Association which would include political figures who would not support radical political reform, but who none the less might lend their names to the urgently needed reform of the law. When the opportunity arose, he continued to press for reform. He intervened in the movement to reform land law and attempted to influence the real property commission of 1828, beginning with his review of *Observations on the Actual State of the Law of Real Property* by James Humphreys (1826), which appeared in the *Westminster Review* in 1826 and was subsequently published as a pamphlet in 1827. Among his last writings on the reform of judicial organization and procedure were *Equity Dispatch Court Proposal* (1830) and *Lord Brougham Displayed* (1832).

Bentham's interest in radical reform did not diminish. In 1823 he established and funded the *Westminster Review* as an organ of radical reform to oppose the tory *Quarterly Review* and the whig *Edinburgh Review*. Bowring became the editor, and although Longman & Co. initially agreed to publish the new journal, the firm withdrew because of the journal's radical position. A new publisher was found, and the journal was successfully launched. News that the Reform Bill was successful was eagerly brought to Bentham on 5 June 1832, the day before he died, and though he was 'quite speechless and powerless', according to George Bentham, he understood the news and was happy to receive it.

After the journey to Russia to join his brother, Bentham seldom travelled abroad. He made a brief trip to Paris in 1802 following the publication of Dumont's *Traités de législation* and returned in 1825 to obtain treatment for a skin problem (a kind of eczema) which had been troubling him. He received a warm welcome from many distinguished French writers and politicians. Bowring recorded that when he visited a French court the lawyers rose to greet him, and the president seated him at his right hand. He also visited his old friend the marquis de Lafayette, with whom he had been corresponding for many years, latterly via an attractive courier, the author Frances Wright. During the revolution of 1830 Bentham addressed the French in several works, arguing against the adoption of a second legislative chamber and against the use of the death penalty. He wrote as a 'fellow citizen' rather than as an Englishman. In February 1832 Bentham was reunited with another old friend, the French statesman Talleyrand, first introduced to him by Dumont in 1792. According to Bowring, who arranged the dinner at Queen Square Place, Talleyrand regarded Bentham as a genius from whom much had been stolen without acknowledgement, but who remained as rich as before.

During his last years, Bentham established a routine which he followed until shortly before his death. For many decades his main activity consisted of writing, and he would regularly write and revise up to twenty foolscap folios each day. He was assisted in this work by a number of young men who eventually went on to distinguished careers of their own, though often in the professions Bentham himself had so vigorously opposed, such as the law and the church. These 'reprobates', as he called them, would join him for the first half of his evening meal, when he often entertained a single or at most two or three guests. They would then depart so that Bentham and his guests could carry on their conversation. Apart from the summers spent at Forde Abbey between 1814 and 1818, he stayed mainly at Queen Square Place. Although he referred to his abode as the Hermitage and himself as the Hermit, he was not reclusive, but jealously guarded his time. He frequently took exercise and developed a kind of jogging which enabled him to exercise in a shorter time than his customary walks. He also enjoyed gardens and flowers and often walked in his own substantial garden, which contained Milton's house. His love of music remained throughout his life, and his home could boast the numerous musical instruments which he played.

Death and the auto-icon Bentham died on 6 June 1832 at 5.30 in the afternoon at his residence in Queen Square Place. According to Bowring, he died with his head on Bowring's bosom and grasping his hand; no one else seems to have been present. In another account by George Bentham, he simply breathed his last in the presence of Bowring, Doane, the social reformer Edwin Chadwick, and himself. He had continued to write up to a month before his death, and had made careful preparations for the dissection of his body after death and its preservation as an auto-icon.

As early as 1769, when he was just twenty-one years old, he made a will leaving his body for dissection to a family friend, the physician and chemist George Fordyce, whose daughter, Maria Sophia (1765–1858), married Samuel Bentham. Bentham's main object was to advance the study of anatomy, and he is credited with drafting the legislation which formed the basis of the Anatomy Act of 1832. In 1824, following the publication in the *Westminster Review* of Southwood Smith's article entitled 'Use of the dead to the living', encouraging people to leave their bodies for dissection, Bentham began to entertain the idea of experimenting with the preservation of a human head. There is some evidence of consultations with John Armstrong and Edward Grainger of the Webb Street school of anatomy and medicine. During this period he considered the idea of a public dissection of his body and its subsequent preservation. A paper written in 1830, instructing Southwood Smith to create the auto-icon, was attached to his last will, dated 30 May 1832.

On 8 June 1832, two days after his death, invitations were distributed to a select group of friends, and on the following day at 3 p.m. at Webb Street school of anatomy and medicine, Southwood Smith delivered a lengthy oration over Bentham's body. Many friends, including Brougham, James Mill, and the historian George Grote, attended, and the audience was impressed by a violent thunderstorm which interrupted the proceedings. The printed oration contains a frontispiece with an engraving of Bentham's body partly covered by a sheet, made from a drawing by Henry William Pickersgill. The oration was a remarkable tribute to Bentham and his work, and Southwood Smith subsequently followed Bentham's instructions. Following dissection, the skeleton was wired together, and the head was preserved by placing it under an air pump over sulphuric acid and simply drawing off the fluids. The preservation of the head was successful in producing a head as hard as that produced in New Zealand by the indigenous people upon which Bentham based his own plan, but the face had lost all expression and was deemed unsuitable for display. A wax head was then made by Jacques Talrich, a physician who had taken up anatomical modelling with great success. Talrich based the wax head on several sources, including the bust of Bentham executed in 1828 by P. J. David d'Angers (now in Senate House Library, University of London), the painting of Bentham by Pickersgill (now in the National Portrait Gallery), and the silhouette on the mourning rings made by John Field. Some of Bentham's own hair was placed on the wax likeness, and the skeleton, padded out with straw and cloth, and wax head were carefully assembled by Southwood Smith in Bentham's own clothes, seated in a chair, with his familiar walking stick, Dapple. Bentham's own 'Auto-icon; or, Farther uses of the dead to the living ... From the MSS. of Jeremy Bentham' fared less well than the auto-icon itself. Printed for the Bowring edition, it was excluded from the published version (with only a few copies surviving) as tending, in Bowring's eyes, to diminish rather than enhance Bentham's posthumous reputation.

During the period the auto-icon was in Southwood Smith's possession, little is known of its use or even of its location. When he gave up his consulting rooms in Finsbury Square in 1849–50, he offered it to University College, London. On behalf of the council, Brougham quickly accepted the offer, but the correspondence indicates that the auto-icon was not at Finsbury Square but at 36 Percy Street, the home of Margaret Gillies, an artist and intimate friend of Southwood Smith, who was also leaving her house. Even at University College the auto-icon was not prominently displayed until after the Second World War (during which it was evacuated to Hertfordshire), when it was placed in its familiar location in the South Cloisters.

There was more to Bentham's will than the auto-icon. As he had no children and Samuel Bentham had died in 1831, Queen Square Place was inherited by his nephew George Bentham and two of his sisters. Bowring, however, had been made sole executor of the will with instructions to produce and publish an edition of his writings. George Bentham had never liked Bowring. He shared with Mill, Place, and others the view that Bowring had acquired great power over Bentham's affairs which he preserved through flattery. George Bentham complained that Bowring was profligate in his expenditure on the new edition of Bentham's writings, the final result being a loss of £6000. He was also dissatisfied with other aspects of Bowring's management of the estate, especially as he was supposed to inherit what remained after Bowring's expenditure. When Jeremy Bentham had received £23,000 in compensation from the government after the failure of the panopticon prison project, he invested £10,000 in a quarry and cement firm, Grellier & Co., which went bankrupt in 1817. A further £10,000 had been invested in Robert Owen's cotton mills at New Lanark, with Bentham becoming the owner of a sixth-share of the firm. Bowring was about to settle for £7000 from the New Lanark investment, but George Bentham filed a bill in chancery and won a decision for £10,000. Nevertheless, he was unable to limit expenditure on the edition to the £2000 referred to in Bentham's will.

Despite the expense of producing Bentham's *Works*, the new edition did little for his reputation. Its eleven volumes were printed in a virtually unreadable two-column format with very small print. Bowring's biography of Bentham, which occupies the last two volumes of the edition, was poorly written and appears a hastily assembled collection of parts of letters and various anecdotes. Important works, such as the three books on religion, were excluded. With a few exceptions, those works produced from manuscript were poorly edited with numerous mistakes not only in transcription but also in the arrangement of the various texts. What appeared to be new in the Bowring edition were often English translations of the Dumont recensions. The remedy for these deficiencies is now in progress with a new edition in approximately fifty volumes with an additional fifteen volumes of correspondence.

Although historians have questioned Bentham's influence on the major reforms in government during the nineteenth century, his standing as a philosopher and jurist increased throughout the twentieth. He is widely regarded as the founder of modern utilitarianism, which remains an important theme in contemporary moral and political philosophy. Bentham's positivist account of law has replaced that of his disciple, John Austin, as the more subtle, complex, and authoritative theory in this tradition, and he is generally recognized as one of Britain's greatest jurists. His theory of democracy has replaced that found in James Mill's *Essay on Government* and J. S. Mill's *Considerations on Representative Government*, and is now regarded as the classic utilitarian alternative to modern theories of participatory democracy. Among economists he is credited with important contributions to classical economics and especially with his insistence on the value of extending economic concepts to the fields of law and politics. He is also widely regarded as the founder of welfare economics, the creator of the theory of marginal utility, and the first exponent of cost–benefit analysis.

F. ROSEN

Sources *The collected works of Jeremy Bentham*, ed. J. H. Burns, J. R. Dinwiddy, F. Rosen, and P. Schofield (1961–) · J. Bentham, *An introduction to the principles of morals and legislation*, ed. J. H. Burns and H. L. A. Hart (1970) · J. Bentham, *Of laws in general*, ed. H. L. A. Hart (1970) · J. Bentham, *A comment on the commentaries and A fragment on government*, ed. J. H. Burns and H. L. A. Hart (1977) · J. Bentham, *Constitutional code, volume 1*, ed. F. Rosen and J. H. Burns (1983) · J. Bentham, *Chrestomathia*, ed. M. J. Smith and W. H. Burston (1983) · J. Bentham, *Deontology together with a table of the springs of action and article on utilitarianism*, ed. A. Goldworth (1983) · J. Bentham, *First principles preparatory to constitutional code*, ed. P. Schofield (1989) · J. Bentham, *Securities against misrule and other constitutional writings for Tripoli and Greece*, ed. P. Schofield (1990) · J. Bentham, *Official aptitude maximized; expense minimized*, ed. P. Schofield (1993) · J. Bentham, *Colonies, commerce and constitutional law: rid yourselves of Ultramaria and other writings on Spain and Spanish America*, ed. P. Schofield (1995) · *'Legislator of the world': writings on codification, law, and education*, ed. P. Schofield and J. Harris (1998) · J. Bentham, *Political tactics*, ed. M. James, C. Blamires, and C. Pease-Watkin (1999) · J. Bentham, *Writings on the poor laws, 1*, ed. M. Quinn (2001) · J. Bentham, *Rights, representation and reform: nonsense upon stilts and other writings on the French Revolution*, ed. P. Schofield, C. Pease-Watkin, and C. Blamires (2002) · *The correspondence of Jeremy Bentham*, ed. T. Sprigge and others, [11 vols.] (1968–), in *The collected works of Jeremy Bentham* · *The works of Jeremy Bentham*, ed. J. Bowring, 11 vols. (1838–43), esp. vols. 10–11 · *Jeremy Bentham's economic writings*, ed. W. Stark, 3 vols. (1952–4) · S. Ikeda, M. Otonashi, and T. Shigemori, eds., *A bibliographical catalogue of the works of Jeremy Bentham* (1989) · A. T. Milne, ed., *Catalogue of the manuscripts of Jeremy Bentham in the library of University College, London*, 2nd edn (1962) · B. Parekh, ed., *Jeremy Bentham: critical assessments*, 4 vols. (1993) · I. R. Christie, *The Benthams in Russia, 1780–1791* (1993) · J. Semple, *Bentham's prison: a study of the panopticon penitentiary* (1993) · F. Rosen, *Jeremy Bentham and representative democracy: a study of the constitutional code* (1983) · F. Rosen, *Bentham, Byron, and Greece: constitutionalism, nationalism, and early liberal political thought* (1992) · *George Bentham: autobiography, 1800–1834*, ed. M. Filipiuk (1997) · J. Dinwiddy, *Radicalism and reform in Britain, 1780–1850* (1992) · T. S. Smith, *A lecture delivered over the remains of Jeremy Bentham* (1832) · C. F. A. Marmoy, 'The "auto-icon" of Jeremy Bentham at University College, London', *Medical*

History, 2 (1958), 77–86 · R. Richardson and B. Hurwitz, 'Jeremy Bentham's self image: an exemplary bequest for dissection', *BMJ* (18 July 1987), 195–8 · J. H. Burns, 'Bentham and the French Revolution', *TRHS*, 5th ser., 16 (1966), 95–114 · J. H. Burns, 'Bentham and Blackstone: a lifetime's dialectic', *Utilitas*, 1 (1989), 22–40 · M. Mack, *Jeremy Bentham: an odyssey of ideas, 1748–1792* (1962) · R. D. C. Black, 'Bentham and the political economists of the nineteenth century', *Bentham Newsletter*, 12 (1988), 24–36 · M. Quinn, 'Jeremy Bentham on the relief of indigence: an exercise in applied philosophy', *Utilitas*, 6 (1994), 81–96 · M. Sokol, 'Jeremy Bentham and the real property commission of 1828', *Utilitas*, 4 (1992), 225–45 · W. L. Twining, *Theories of evidence: Bentham and Wigmore* (1985) · L. J. Hume, *Bentham and bureaucracy* (1981) · E. Halévy, *La formation du radicalisme philosophique*, 3 vols. (Paris, 1901–4), trans. M. Morris as *The growth of philosophic radicalism* (1928) · C. Fuller, ed., *The old radical: representations of Jeremy Bentham* (1998)

Archives BL, corresp. and papers, Add. MSS 29806–29809, 33537–33564, 37520 · King's Cam., letters and papers · Queen's College, Oxford, notes on William Blackstone's lectures · Trinity Cam., corresp. and papers · UCL, corresp. and papers · UCL, project | Balliol Oxf., letters to David Urquhart · Bibliothèque Publique et Universitaire, Geneva, Dumont Archive · BL, corresp. with Jabez Henry and others relating to international law, Add. MS 30151 · BL, letters to John Tyrrell, Add. MS 34661 · BL, letters to Nicholas Vansittart, Add. MS 31235 · Bodl. Oxf., corresp. with Sir Francis Burdett · Bodl. Oxf., letters to William Wilberforce · DWL, letters to Henry Crabb Robinson · NRA, priv. coll., letters to Reginald Pole Carew

Likenesses T. Frye, oils, *c*.1761, NPG · British school, oils, *c*.1790, UCL · W. H. Worthington, line engraving, pubd 1823, BM, NPG; repro. in Bentham, *Introduction to the principles* · P. J. David (D. D'Angers), marble bust, 1828, U. Lond.; bronze copy, UCL · H. W. Pickersgill, oils, 1829, NPG [*see illus.*] · J. Field, silhouette, *c*.1830, NPG, UCL · D. D'Angers, bronze medallion, UCL · A. Geddes, oils, Queen's College, Oxford · H. W. Pickersgill, oils, second version, UCL · J. Thomson, stipple (after W. Derby), BM; repro. in *European Magazine* (1823) · J. Watts, crayon drawing, Queen's College, Oxford · portrait, UCL

Bentham, Joseph (1593/4–1671), Church of England clergyman, graduated BA from Pembroke College, Cambridge, in 1615 and proceeded MA in 1618; nothing is known about his early life. Ordained a priest at Peterborough on 21 September 1617, he was appointed vicar of Weekley, Northamptonshire, by Sir Edward Montagu on 24 February 1618 and was assimilated into a moderate puritan brotherhood sponsored by the magnate, which focused its public activity on the Kettering lecture. Before 1619 he married; his wife's name was Martha, and they had eight children. Bentham attracted interlopers from other parishes to hear him preach at Weekley, and in 1630 and 1635, encouraged by fellow ministers Robert Bolton and Nicholas Estwick, dedicated to the now Lord Montagu and his children collections of sermons preached at the lecture, respectively entitled *The Societie of the Saints* and *The Christian Conflict*. Bishop William Piers of Peterborough in 1630 introduced regulation of the lecture to exclude what he regarded as disruptive puritan elements: Bentham was high on the list of those permitted to continue. Montagu transferred him to his benefice of Broughton on 24 December 1631 on the recommendation of Bolton and Estwick.

The crux of Bentham's puritan stance was a form of Calvinist predestinarianism which stated that church and society were sharply polarized between the godly exponents of true religion and the ungodly adherents of Satanic error. The godly were distinguished by their preference for a word-centred piety expressing itself in numerous practices supplemental to basic parish observance, an ethical stringency, and a preoccupation with achieving an assurance of their elect status. The main thrust of his divinity was to establish that, since the English church was basically Calvinist–evangelical and sabbatarian, the godly posed no threat to hierarchical order but simply functioned as an orthodox spiritual élite. The ungodly denounced them as puritans but Bentham was proud to own the sobriquet by which he understood 'practising Protestants; such men who daily reade the Scriptures, pray with their families, teach them the way to heaven', avoid sin and:

> spend the Lord's daies holily in hearing God's Word, prayer, meditation, conference, singing of Psalmes, meditation of the creatures, are merciful to the poore, diligent in their particular Callings, frame their lives according to God's will revealed in his Word. (*Societie*, 29)

Thus the apparent aggressiveness of the underpinning divinity was moderated in its application; this applied equally to the requirement that the godly should shun their anti-religious counterparts socially. The final impossibility of distinguishing sheep from lambs and the potentially disruptive effect of such divisions on normal social intercourse led him to a more moderate position: 'To hate the sin and love the person is a charitable Christian hatred' (ibid., 31).

Bentham's recommendation of obedience to Laudian policies should not be taken to imply sympathy with their content. His encouragement of conformity was far from strident and stemmed partly from a desire to prevent the godly from molestation by the courts; about 1636 his own platform—the Kettering lecture—was abolished. He defended a Calvinist orthodoxy against Laudian 'malignant spirits' (*Conflict*, foreword) who, he alleged, threatened right doctrine when they emphasized the antinomian implications of puritanism, and imposed altar-based ceremonies which he claimed had no religious value. His sabbatarianism ran clean contrary to the Book of Sports. However, divine precept forbade the deferential subject's criticism of his prince—there is no record of his refusing to read the Book of Sports, and he was careful to advertise Charles I's godliness. Parliament's was the central role in redressing the nation's grievances. An emergent split in the Northamptonshire godly ranks caused by the issue of ceremonial conformity was deliberately obscured.

Early in the 1640s Bentham wrote an obsequious life of Montagu as the ideal godly private and public man, which remained in manuscript. During the civil war parliament expelled him from Broughton and following the death of his royalist patron he took refuge with the courtier Sir Thomas Tirringham at Lower Winchendon, Buckinghamshire. In 1657 he repaid Tirringham with the dedication of *Chorotheologon, or, Two Briefe but Usefull Treatises*, which addressed the nature of the ministry and the question of 'mixed dancing'. His wife, Martha, was buried on 30 December 1658, and on 2 January 1660 he married a widow, Elizabeth Brooks. Following Charles II's Restoration Bentham was reinstated at Broughton. He published two further books, *The Right of Kings by Scripture* (1661) and *A Disswasive from Error* (1669). He died at Broughton, aged seventy-seven, on 16 April 1671 and was buried three days later in the chancel of his church. His will enjoined that his corpse be carried by six Kettering lecturers, the preacher exhort the congregation to order and obedience, and alms be distributed annually on the day of Charles's return. His second wife survived him.   J. FIELDING

Sources P. Lake, '"A charitable Christian hatred": the godly and their enemies in the 1630s', *The culture of English puritanism, 1560–1700*, ed. C. Durston and J. Eales (1996), 145–83 • A. J. Fielding, 'Conformists, puritans and the church courts: the diocese of Peterborough, 1603–1642', PhD diss., U. Birm., 1989, 25–6, 150, 151, 158, 187, 199, 227–8, 269 • H. I. Longden, *Northamptonshire and Rutland clergy from 1500*, ed. P. I. King and others, 16 vols. in 6, Northamptonshire RS (1938–52), vol. 2, pp. 73–5 • *DNB* • Northants. RO, Peterborough diocesan records, archdeaconry of Northampton wills, 4th ser., 2.67 • J. Bentham, 'Character and life of Edward, Lord Montagu', *c.*1642–1645, Northants. RO, MS 186 • E. S. Cope, *The life of a public man: Edward, first Baron Montagu of Broughton, 1562–1644* (1981), 2–3, 204–5, 141–3, 51–2, 74–6

Bentham, Samuel (1757–1831), naval architect and inventor, was born in London on 11 January 1757, the youngest of the seven children of Jeremiah Bentham (1712–1792), an attorney, and his wife, Alicia Woodward Whitehorne (*d.* 1759), the eldest daughter of Thomas Grove, an Andover mercer. The philosopher Jeremy *Bentham (1748–1832) was their eldest child, and he and Samuel were the only two children to survive infancy. The brothers had a particularly close relationship. Both had exceptionally fertile and inventive minds, and a passion for reform and improvement in their several fields of endeavour; many projects were shared and there was a constant exchange of ideas throughout their lives.

Early years and education Samuel Bentham was sent to Westminster School in 1763 but, having an intelligence that was more practical than academic, he did not follow his brother to Oxford. Instead he was apprenticed in 1771 to William Gray, a master shipwright at Woolwich and later at Chatham. Bentham studied mathematics, grammar, and chemistry alongside the technical skills associated with shipbuilding. His inventive nature was already in evidence during his apprenticeship: aged sixteen he impressed the commissioners of the navy with a model of a ship's pump of his own design. On completion of his apprenticeship in 1777, Bentham's talents and ambition spurred him to hope for more than an ordinary shipwright's place. Without influence or connections, however, he was uncertain exactly how to further his career. For almost two years he continued to glean knowledge in the dockyards, pursuing his mathematical studies at the Royal Naval Academy, Portsmouth, and in 1778 going to sea with Lord Keppel's fleet as a volunteer. Eventually, in 1779, he decided to seek a suitable post in Russia. Jeremy was in favour of such a trip, as he saw it as a possible

Samuel Bentham (1757–1831), by Henry Edridge, *c.*1795–1800

opportunity to interest the empress, Catherine the Great, in his own ideas on law reform.

Russia, 1780–1791 Furnished with many letters of recommendation and introduction, Samuel Bentham set out in August 1779. He crossed the frontier into Russia in February of the following year, going first to Moscow and then on to St Petersburg, where there was a sizeable English community. He made contact with many Russians and with the British ambassador Sir James Harris; Dr John Grieve, physician to the Russian army, found him 'an uncouth young man' (Farington, *Diary*, 3.701), but other contemporary accounts record that his easy-going and charming personality made him a wide circle of friends. In the spring of 1780 Bentham was offered a position as director or surveyor-general of shipbuilding by Chernyshev, head of the Russian admiralty, which he turned down because the proposed salary was inadequate, and because he had hoped for more freedom to experiment in shipbuilding at the government's expense. Bentham spent the rest of 1780 observing the shipbuilding industry and other commercial ventures. He perceived that much profit could be made by the instigation of improvements in trade in various commodities, but as such purely commercial enterprises required capital, which he lacked, he was unable to take advantage of the opportunities. He made further contacts, most notably with Catherine's favourite, Prince Grigory Aleksandrovich Potyomkin.

Being particularly interested in the employment of European workmen, Potyomkin was predisposed to be impressed by Bentham, whom he authorized to travel freely throughout the Russian empire, inspecting and reporting on natural resources and on the improvements which could be made in the use of those resources. In February 1781 Bentham embarked on a tour which lasted for almost two years. Besides visiting industrial centres, mines, and quarries, he was occupied in preparing plans, models, and prototypes of various inventions, ranging from a planing machine to an amphibious vessel, essentially a boat mounted on a wheeled chassis. His tour took him through Siberia as far east as the border with China, where he learnt about the trade in fur with Alaska. He eventually returned to St Petersburg in October 1782.

Bentham's prospects for employment were now significantly improved. His spoken and written Russian was fluent, he had amassed considerable knowledge about commercial and industrial enterprises, and he had given ample demonstration of his technical abilities. However, in Russia as in England, there was once again some delay in finding a suitable post. In the end it was Potyomkin who determined the course of Bentham's future. He asked for a written memorandum of Bentham's travels, and that account was shown to the Catherine the Great, who was impressed and interested. Yet events moved slowly, and it was not until the spring of 1783 that Bentham met the empress; in May he submitted to her a formal offer of his services, and in September he was taken into service and attached to the department of hydraulic works. In December 1783 Potyomkin, believing Bentham's talents to be wasted there, offered him employment at the naval base at Kherson on the northern shore of the Black Sea, with the army rank of lieutenant-colonel. Bentham left St Petersburg to enter Potyomkin's service in the following March; the portrait which he commissioned at this time shows him in his Russian uniform.

Bentham was based on Potyomkin's estate at Krichev in the Crimea, which included a thriving industrial centre comprising manufactories of glass and leather, as well as products such as rope and sailcloth required by the shipyard which had been established at Kherson in 1779. His main assignment was to establish a shipyard for the construction of river transports; large vessels were to be built in pieces and assembled hundreds of miles downriver at Kherson. He was given complete freedom to experiment in the building of all kinds of ships, in the erection of machinery of his own invention, and in industrial processes such as steel making. Potyomkin also had plans to build up a Black Sea naval base at Sevastopol in the Crimea, with which Bentham was to be involved. Samuel's main difficulty was the lack of skilled assistants; with his brother's help, he made several attempts to recruit men from England, with partial success. Alongside his other duties, Samuel also had command of a battalion of infantry, whom he was to train as marines. Throughout his time in Russia, Bentham attempted to interest people in his brother's works, although with little success. In February 1786 Jeremy himself paid an extended visit to Krichev, but he did not actively attempt to promote his own works in Russia. Indeed, when Catherine the Great visited

Krichev, Jeremy did not even attempt to meet her; he departed in the autumn of 1787.

In early 1786, having impressed Potyomkin with his shipbuilding abilities, Samuel Bentham was commissioned to build a fleet of special vessels for the empress's southern tour, planned for 1787. For this he invented, among other craft, a multi-unit river transport consisting of a series of articulated vessels which the Bentham brothers called the 'vermicular'. From his earliest arrival at Krichev, Bentham had been making suggestions to Potyomkin about the better organization of the factories, and in early 1786 he was given official responsibility for their management. Bentham's preoccupation with the management of the unskilled labourers in the factories of Krichev led him to draw up plans for a 'central inspection house', an idea usually associated with his brother. Although the initial idea was Samuel's, Jeremy spent much of his time in Russia developing the idea and writing a series of letters describing the principle and the building, letters later published as *Panopticon*.

The unexpected sale of Potyomkin's estate in spring 1787 was one of two events which abruptly changed the course of Bentham's Russian career; the second was Turkey's declaration of war on Russia in August 1787. The Crimea had been annexed by Russia four years previously; the Turks, however, had a fortress at Ochakov on the estuary of the River Dnieper, and the bay of the Dnieper, known as the Liman, was a crucial site when hostilities broke out, as Turkish possession of Ochakov hampered Potyomkin's plans for a Black Sea Fleet. In October a small-scale engagement proved inconclusive. Bentham meanwhile was preparing a fighting flotilla out of a motley assortment of pleasure barges and other unsuitable ships, which were ready by early 1788. One of his flotilla's key features was the mounting of the ordnance on the principle of non-recoil, which meant that much larger guns could be installed on small ships. Bentham was given command of one division of the flotilla; the campaign for the Liman began in June, and the Russians were victorious, although their fleet was fewer in number. Bentham himself played a modest part in the Russian victory, suffering no more than a singed eyebrow in battle. His contribution was recognized by his promotion to colonel, and the bestowal of a knighthood of the Russian order of St George, whereupon he adopted the title of brigadier-general. His later attempt to have the non-recoil principle adopted in the Royal Navy failed, as sundry trials proved beyond doubt that it did not work.

After the battle at Ochakov, Bentham exchanged his regiment of infantry for one of cavalry in Siberia, where he still had hopes of undertaking some profitable trade. From February 1789 he travelled in Siberia and commanded his battalions. Ever concerned with making improvements, he established a regimental school there near the border with China. In June 1790 he returned to Moscow, partly to consult Potyomkin about various schemes, and partly to take a long overdue leave of absence in England. In January 1791 he left Russia, fully intending to return. In the event, he did not do so for four-teen years, a delay that can be explained by several factors. On the death of their father in March 1792, Jeremy inherited his house in Westminster, which meant that the brothers now had ample means to pursue their schemes, particularly their plans for a 'panopticon' prison. The out-break of war with France in 1793 also encouraged Samuel to hope that he might obtain a technical post in naval administration. However, once again an office commensurate with his talents proved elusive. In the meantime, both Jeremy and Samuel spent much time and effort promoting the panopticon scheme. Samuel patented planing and sawing machines for its design, and the brothers built a model panopticon in their workshop, which excited much attention, although the scheme ultimately failed.

Inspector-general of naval works, 1796–1807 Samuel Bentham was still hoping for a suitable post in naval administration, and in 1795 he applied to the Admiralty, offering to make a tour of the dockyards for the purpose of suggesting improvements. His offer having been accepted, he formally resigned from the Russian service. His main aims in this new role were to increase efficiency and economy. In March 1796 the post of inspector-general of naval works was created for Bentham. This was an Admiralty appointment, but its remit intruded into preserves hitherto ruled by the Navy Board; the post and its holder were therefore inevitably destined to add to the existing friction between the two departments. Although the salary was far below that which Bentham could have hoped for had he returned to Russia, he took the post, as 'the improvement of the naval service of his *own* country had been the object of his ambition from his boyhood' (Bentham, *Life*, 103). Bentham himself stipulated the specifications of the new post, one of the most important of which was the concept of individual responsibility, a notion at the time unprecedented in the civil department: although Bentham was to have assistants, he alone would ultimately be responsible for decisions made. Furthermore, all proposals from Bentham to the Navy Board were to be submitted in writing, and all reasons for his proposals were likewise to be documented.

Bentham married on 26 October 1796 in Westminster Maria Sophia (1765–1858), daughter of George *Fordyce, a Scottish physician. They had five children: Mary Louisa (1797–1865), Samuel (1798–1816), George *Bentham (1800–1884), the renowned botanist, Clara (1802–1829), and Sarah (1804–1864). Bentham also had at least three illegitimate daughters (Alicia and Sophia Burton, and Elizabeth Gordon), about whom little is known except that he made some attempts to support them financially. Bentham's wife was a tireless assistant to him at all stages of his career, accompanying him on official trips to the dockyards and helping him write reports for the Navy Board. She also dealt with payments made to the illegitimate daughters.

In pursuit of reform, a commission of inquiry into fees, perquisites, gratuities, and emoluments had produced a report on the dockyards in 1788. Many of its recommendations had emanated from the senior naval lord, Sir Charles Middleton (later Lord Barham), to whose annoyance they were then shelved. In February 1801 the earl of St Vincent took over as first lord of the Admiralty. St Vincent had previously imposed a severe discipline on the Mediterranean Fleet and now sought to impose a similar regime on the dockyards in order to eliminate waste, corruption, and abuse of privilege. Shipboard discipline was not, however, readily applied to dockyard business, and he therefore supported Samuel's reforms, which incorporated many of Middleton's earlier proposals.

Bentham's ideas for improvement covered every aspect of dockyard organization, including the size of the dock basins, the layout of various offices, and measures to minimize the risk of fire in the yards. At Portsmouth he enlarged the basin and built two new deep docks, so that larger vessels could be repaired and refitted without first being stripped of their stores and armaments. He adopted the idea first proposed by George St Lo, commissioner for Chatham Dockyard in 1703–12, for a floating caisson, across which heavy traffic could pass, instead of dock gates. He recruited James Sadler to design the navy's first steam engine, which from 1799 powered the woodworking machines by day and pumped out the dry-dock reservoir during the night. In 1803 his bucket-ladder steam dredger began work in Portsmouth harbour and other dredgers were soon at work in the Thames and the Medway.

Samuel Bunce (who had already worked on the panopticon project) was hired as the navy's first salaried architect; he was succeeded by Edward Holl. The draughtsman Samuel Goodrich was promoted to a new post as mechanist, and he, with Joshua Field, adapted the designs of Marc Isambard Brunel for block-making machinery. Built by Henry Maudslay between 1802 and 1806 at a cost of £54,000, the block mills were the first steam-powered manufactory in any dockyard. Now celebrated as the first use of machine tools for mass production, the block mills had a devastating effect on the workforce: ten unskilled men could oversee a production which by 1808 had risen to 130,000 blocks annually, displacing 110 skilled workers and saving £17,000. This was part of a general reduction of manpower, supplemented by ejecting the elderly and infirm men. As for practical shipbuilding, Bentham constructed seven small experimental vessels on quite new principles, which meant that the vessels were both stronger and cheaper to build; although the response to these vessels was somewhat unenthusiastic, some features of his designs were later to become standard.

Bentham's correspondence with the Navy Board reveals frequent conflict during his eleven years in the post. Bentham did not disguise his lack of respect for the board, and he was not prepared to be conciliatory or to compromise. He frequently alienated the board with his exhaustive reports and proposals, and they did not take kindly to his charges of incompetence and inefficiency and viewed him as a hindrance. In pursuit of efficiency and economy, Bentham rode roughshod over the vested interests of both workmen and the board. His institution of a timber master in each yard to oversee the receipt, conversion, and employment of every single piece of timber used, a proposal designed to minimize wastage and to end the customary free purloining of 'chips' or offcuts, was unpopular with the men, the merchants, and the board. Similarly Bentham's reorganization of the system of apprenticeships, again intended to improve efficiency, backfired and led to a lessening in the supply of boys to be apprenticed, and a drop in the standard of their instruction.

Return to Russia and final years In 1805 Bentham was sent back to Russia when the British government mistakenly believed that the tsar was willing to allow British warships to be built at Archangel, to overcome the shortage of oak timber in England. On Bentham's arrival in St Petersburg he found that no arrangements had been made. However, he was able to pursue various private enterprises and he supervised the erection of a wooden panopticon at Ochta (which was destroyed by fire in 1818). On his way back in 1807, he inspected the covered slip at Karlskrona, and he may have been responsible for introducing similar structures in British dockyards. During his absence the naval commissioners of revision recommended that the inspector-general should become a member of the Navy Board, with the title of civil architect and engineer, and the office of inspector-general was abolished in October 1807, a decision which Bentham discovered on his return in November.

Back in England, Bentham continued to produce designs, including a cast-iron piled river wall at Sheerness, and developments to caissons, which he patented in 1811 and 1812. While he had been in Russia, John Rennie had submitted a highly critical report on the naval dock facilities. Arguments with Rennie and with the board led to Bentham's dismissal in 1812, though he left with a pension of £1000 plus £500 expenses, a sum twice his previous salary. He published an account of his achievements as inspector-general, *Services Rendered in the Civil Department of the Navy*, in 1813. In 1814 Bentham moved to France with his family for reasons of health, finance, and his children's education. Some stages of the journey to the south of France were made in a multi-purpose vehicle of Bentham's design, complete with sleeping quarters—a vehicle which caused some embarrassment to his daughters. The family eventually settled at the Château de Restinclières, near Montpellier, in 1820. Here, as ever, Bentham was full of schemes for improvement: he imported agricultural machinery as yet unknown in that part of France, and installed a system of irrigation on his land, which led to a lawsuit brought by disgruntled local residents. This dispute was one of the factors which drove the family back to England in 1826. The latter years of Bentham's life were mostly spent writing various works detailing his achievements in naval management and engineering, and even in the last few months of his life he was involved in experiments for the navy. He died on 30 April 1831 at 2 Lower Connaught Place, London; the cause of death was said to be 'exhaustion' rather than any specific illness (*George Bentham*, 365). After his death his wife, Maria, prepared his biography, including a full list of his publications; her account of his career attempted to gain wider recognition for his achievements, recognition which was somewhat sparingly bestowed during his lifetime. A recent judgement credits him with a remarkable range of interests, noting that 'his small department was the seed from which ultimately grew the great civil engineering and architecture departments of Admiralty' (Coad, 53). CATHERINE PEASE-WATKIN

Sources M. S. Bentham, *The life of Brigadier-General Sir Samuel Bentham, KSG* (1862) · *The collected works of Jeremy Bentham: correspondence*, ed. J. H. Burns, J. R. Dinwiddy, F. Rosen, and P. Schofield, 1–2: *The correspondence of Jeremy Bentham* (1968–2000) · *George Bentham: autobiography, 1800–1834*, ed. M. Filipiuk (1997) · I. R. Christie, *The Benthams in Russia, 1780–1791* (1993) · R. Morriss, 'Samuel Bentham and the management of the royal dockyards, 1796–1807', *BIHR*, 54 (1981), 226–40 · J. G. Coad, *The royal dockyards, 1690–1850* (1989) · S. Sebag Montefiore, *Prince of princes: the life of Prince Potemkin* (2000) · R. F. Cairo, 'Samuel Bentham: forgotten shipbuilder and engineer — parts 1–5', *Nautical Research Journal*, 23/3–4 (1977); 24/1,3 (1978); 25/1 (1979) · J. Coad, 'Bentham, Sir Samuel', *Biographical dictionary of civil engineers in Great Britain and Ireland*, ed. A. W. Spempton and others (2002) · R. Morriss, *The royal dockyards during the revolutionary and Napoleonic wars* (1983) · R. Morriss, 'St Vincent and reform, 1801–1804', *Mariner's Mirror*, 69 (1983), 269–90 · W. J. Ashworth, '"System of terror": Samuel Bentham, accountability and dockyard reform during the Napoleonic wars', *Social History*, 23 (1989), 63–79

Archives BL, family corresp. and MSS, Add. MSS 33537–33564 · UCL, school of Slavonic and east European studies, papers relating to Russia | BL, corresp. with Lord Spencer · NMM, navy board in-letters and orders

Likenesses H. Edridge, ivory miniature, after 1776, V&A · ink silhouette, c.1778, BL, Bentham papers, vol. XX, Add. MS 33556, fol. 3 · Russian school, oils, 1784, NMM · H. Edridge, ivory miniature, c.1795–1800, NPG [*see illus.*] · J. F. Skill, W. Walker, and E. Walker, group portrait, pencil and wash, 1855–8 (after design by J. Gilbert; *Men of science living in 1807–1808*) · W. Walker and G. Zobel, engraving, 1862 (after group portrait by J. F. Skill, W. Walker, and E. Walker, 1855–8), NPG · W. Walker, engraving (key to group portrait by J. F. Skill, W. Walker, and E. Walker), repro. in W. Walker, ed., *Memoirs of the distinguished men of science of Great Britain living in the years 1807–8* (1862), frontispiece

Bentham, Thomas (1513/14–1579), bishop of Coventry and Lichfield, was born in Sherburn, Yorkshire, to unknown parents. Nothing is known of his education before he graduated at Oxford in February 1544 at the relatively late age of thirty. He held a fellowship at Magdalen College from 1545 and proceeded MA in 1547. He became known as a theologian and as one learned in Latin, Hebrew, and Greek and took his BTh degree in 1552. By now the Magdalen fellowship contained a number of committed evangelicals, including John Foxe, Laurence Humphrey, and three future Elizabethan bishops besides Bentham himself. In 1554 Bentham was one of several fellows removed for their protestant proclivities (in his own case for an act of sacrilege) by the college visitor, Bishop Stephen Gardiner of Winchester.

Exile, return, and elevation Bentham travelled to Zürich and remained there from April to October 1554. Shortly afterwards he moved to Basel and registered there as a student for the year 1555–6. He seems to have lived with John Bale and other English exiles in the Clarakloster. He became preacher to the exiles in Basel, but in 1557 transferred to Frankfurt, where he acted as one of the eight official arbiters in the quarrel between Robert Horne and Thomas Ashley. William Whittingham praised his impartiality. Bentham declined to become an officer in the church at Frankfurt. During that year, because of his renown as a Hebrew scholar, he received an invitation from Geneva to co-operate on the Geneva Bible; he answered the call and was received as a member of John Knox's congregation on Monday, 29 November. At some time between then and January 1558 he married a fellow exile, Maud or Mathilda Fawcon of Hadleigh, Suffolk, who was perhaps one of Roland Taylor's congregation. Shortly afterwards he returned to England with his family and by the summer of 1558 was chief pastor to the secret protestant congregation in London. What little is known of the early protestant church in the capital (outside John Foxe's work) comes from Bentham's letter of 17 July 1558 to Thomas Lever, former comrade in exile and future archdeacon of Coventry, describing some of the martyrdoms at which he had been present. His courage in attending some of the public burnings, to the point of openly protesting against them from the crowd, earned Bentham the acclaim of contemporaries and of later historians.

Royal commissioner and bishop of Coventry and Lichfield Bentham's high preferment under Elizabeth was scarcely in doubt. In August 1559 he was appointed one of the commissioners for the royal visitation which was made responsible for implementing the settlement of 1559. He and Alexander Nowell, future dean of St Paul's, were the only two clerics seconded to the formidable array of protestant laymen, headed by the marquess of Northampton, who processed through the dioceses of Coventry and Lichfield, Oxford, Lincoln, and Peterborough. Whatever Elizabeth's reservations about appointing the returned exiles to senior positions within the church, it was probably the steady support of Sir William Cecil and Sir Nicholas Bacon that secured for Bentham the bishopric of Coventry and Lichfield. He was consecrated on 24 March 1560 and preached at court the same day. It seems probable that Bentham remained in London for the time being, and did not assume control of his diocese until late May or early June. Thereafter he established his official residence at Eccleshall Castle, Staffordshire, using the see's rectory of Hanbury as a summer residence. During February and March 1561 he was again in London, overseeing his legal and financial affairs.

Problems as bishop Bentham faced enormous problems during his episcopate—of residence, finance, control, and conformity—for which his scholarly and impecunious background had left him ill-equipped. By 1560 there were three episcopal residences nominally available to him, but in fact there was considerable doubt as to where he could live: the Coventry palace had been leased out for ninety-nine years by Bishop Richard Sampson in Henry VIII's reign; Christopher Grene and Christopher Bayne had a pretended title to Hanbury, which resulted in a lengthy legal suit; and even Bentham's right to possession

of the castle, manor, and lordship of Eccleshall was early challenged by Humphrey Swinnerton and George Blount. Not only did this mean that Bentham had nowhere to house his family, but it also worsened his financial predicament. He wrote to the queen on 9 September 1560, seeking a release from the payment of first fruits or some part of them:

> Or els he shall be able neither to pay any part of his detts, whiche to hym is great greyfe, neither to mak necessary provision for house kepyng, nor to kepe any howse at all, whiche he iudgeth wyll redowne moche to the slaunder of the gospell. (NL Wales, MS 4919 D, fol. 39)

Bentham's letters reveal the strength of his connections at court. He followed up his appeal for financial relief by lobbying support among influential friends such as Sir William Cecil, Walter Haddon (master of requests), Katherine Ashley (Elizabeth's former governess), and Alexander Nowell. He was forced to raise loans among the wealthy citizens of Coventry, using Thomas Lever as an intermediary, but found his own lack of local connections a difficulty. He frequently borrowed from his brother-in-law Ralph Egerton, a leading member of the London Haberdashers' Company. Trips to the capital became a financial necessity: as he wrote in February 1561, 'althoughe I have nothyng here to lyve upon, yett thorowe myne acquayntance in London I can nowe and then borowe somethyng to helpe me, whiche in the countree I can not doo' (NL Wales, MS 4919 D, fol. 76). For at least the first year of his episcopate a high proportion of his time was taken up by his financial predicament and resulting legal suits. Of the letters that he is known to have sent, some 114 (46 per cent) concerned money or the lands attached to his see, and a further thirty-seven (11 per cent) mentioned his financial problems. In April 1561 he appealed to Sir Clement Throckmorton for help in legal processes, including a case before the Star Chamber, concluding, 'I pray you of your helpe that I may the rather folowe my vocation, whitche ys my cheyfe desyre as knowethe god' (ibid., fol. 90). His successor, William Overton (not always a reliable witness), reported that Bentham died heavily in debt, suggesting that these worries persisted throughout his episcopate, and that his efforts to find a solution were ultimately unsuccessful.

Men whom Bentham regarded as friends were not slow to criticize him for not exercising his pastoral charge as well as he might—through administering a true, fatherly discipline and reforming the church. It was his additional misfortune that his colleagues, and especially the former exiles, had such high expectations of him as a man of conviction who had braved the fires of Marian London. Bentham certainly saw himself as misunderstood, and with some justification. His self-defence, contained in a letter of 2 October 1560, conjures up a picture of a well-meaning man, beset on all sides by financial and legal problems beyond his control:

> I heare say that I am moche slaundered of negligence, coldnes and weaknes, whith maney other grevous faults. Whereunto I say nothyng, but wyshe theym that slaunder me yf they wold do more and better in my place. ... I believe

they never felt suche a burden as I am compelled to beare dayle. Beyng so many wayes vexed as I am and havyng so litell helpe & comfort as I fynd, no marveyle yf I satisfy not all mens expectation, for indede I do not content myselffe. (NL Wales, MS 4919 D, fol. 54)

Attempted solutions Bentham did, however, attempt to address the twin problems of control and conformity, and did so within a framework of fatherly discipline. While his efforts were scarcely a resounding success, they were certainly vigorous. His task was made the more difficult because several of the most populous communities—for example, Lichfield, Bakewell, Eccleshall, Shrewsbury, and Wolverhampton—were outside his jurisdiction and consequently remained strongholds of Roman Catholicism. Bentham concerned himself in particular with the affairs of Staffordshire and Shropshire. Clergymen who neglected their cures or who clung to the old religion were brought before him for correction, as were men and women who were offending against the laws of the church. Bentham seems to have heard such cases in a court of audience at Eccleshall rather than in the more remote consistory court of Lichfield. His injunctions of 1563 show that he tried to revive the role of the rural dean both in the organization of parish clergy and in pastoral care. He also delegated some duties to able and trustworthy preachers and clergymen such as Thomas Ashton, first master of Shrewsbury School, and Robert Aston, rector of Mucklestone and vicar of Sandon, Staffordshire. Most notably he gave Thomas Lever quasi-episcopal standing in the diocese.

The archdeacon of Coventry was by right 'archidiaconus major' within the diocese, but Lever's preeminence stemmed principally from his hallowed status among the returned Marian exiles and from Bentham's respect for him. The bishop's only caution to Lever was that the enthusiastic protestant congregation in Coventry should not burn itself out through its enthusiasm but should remain steadfast in the faith. Bentham entrusted Lever with the selection of suitable ordinands. It has been suggested that he was only too relieved to load some of the tedious and tortuous work of administration onto someone else's shoulders, and it is certainly Lever rather than Bentham who emerges as the dominant figure in the diocese with regard to initiatives for administrative reform and the organization of the clergy. Credit should nevertheless be given to Bentham for encouraging the expansion of the role of the rural dean in pastoral care and also for using the services of able men wisely to administer and serve the far-flung communities of this huge diocese.

Bentham bemoaned the poor quality of his diocesan clergy and the fact that he was forced to retain the services of many who resisted the protestant settlement of 1559. After the initial deprivations of Catholic clergy only a few more lost their livings, despite the fact that not many subscribed to the oath of supremacy. This was probably due to a severe shortage of new recruits to the ministry and to Bentham's reluctance to leave parishes totally unmanned. Bentham did rid himself of some of the more

notorious Catholics from high positions, notably Anthony Draycot, Marian chancellor of the diocese and persecutor of protestants in the late reign. But he continued to work with Richard Walker (appointed in 1547) as his archdeacon of Derby, instructing him carefully to enforce the visitation articles. Leaving the archdeaconry of Coventry to Lever and that of Derby to Walker, Bentham concentrated on reforming the archdeaconries of Shropshire and Stafford, where resistance to the new settlement seems to have been particularly strong.

Recusancy remained a persistent problem throughout Bentham's episcopate and was reflected in the harshness of his injunctions of 1565. His travels through these archdeaconries revealed that most of their churches still retained their altars late in 1560 and had had 'theyr images reserved and conveyd away … hopyng and lookyng for a newe day as may be thereby coiectured' (NL Wales, MS 4919 D, fol. 58). Bentham ordered George Torperlaye, archdeacon of Shropshire, to visit the churches of his jurisdiction, to remove the remaining images, and to present to himself for discipline the names of any who resisted. There are signs that he found particularly objectionable those clergy who picked those aspects of both the old and the new religions which most appealed to them but would not commit themselves fully to either. Henry Techoo, vicar of Monford, Shropshire, was brought before him for correction as one who 'beare ii faces in one hood, to marry & love Images etc.' (ibid., fol. 58). While circumstances prevented the bishop from introducing a wholly reformed clergy, he attempted to attract more able clergymen to fill vacancies and tried to influence the choices made by patrons; he also chose well-qualified preachers when faced with opportunities for the exercise of his own patronage.

Bentham's enthusiastic organization of the preaching activities of his clergy under his own leadership prompted Roger Morrice to describe him as 'a preaching Bishop' who gave the lie to Queen Elizabeth's quip that 'when shee had made a Bishop shee had mar'd a preacher' (Morrice MSS, no. 9, 41). Bentham approved of the prophesyings established within his diocese, and when he was required in 1576 by Archbishop Grindal to comment upon them responded that he saw them as 'not only profitable both for the ministers & the people, but also very necessary … to increase learning in the simple & ignorant, & to continue the same clear in the Learned' (LPL, MS 2003, fol. 5). With this went an indulgent attitude towards conscientious nonconformists, whom Bentham regarded as offering a truly pastoral ministry (a stance apt to incur severe criticism from the higher authorities). In 1565 the curate of Measam, a village near Ashby-de-la-Zouch, was presented for not wearing the surplice; but when two elderly parishioners testified that they had been converted by the preacher's painful travail Bentham reportedly discontinued the case against him.

It must have been with some relief that Bentham turned to his commission to translate the books of Daniel and Ezekiel for the Bishops' Bible of 1568. This was one task for which he was eminently suited. The later years of his episcopate are poorly documented.

The man and his significance Little is known of Bentham's private life, though his professional career clearly affected it. He had six children. Something is known of two of them. Thomas, who was born during his father's episcopate and was still at university at the elder Thomas's death, was educated at Merton College, Oxford, proceeded MA in 1581, and had a career in the church which included a Lichfield prebend (in which he was installed before his father's death) and the rectories of Chichester and Hockliffe. The bishop's younger son, Benjamin (born about 1566), followed his brother to Merton and held a fellowship there from 1585 to 1598. One of this name served a cure in Lichfield diocese. Bishop Bentham died at Eccleshall, Staffordshire, on 21 February 1579; a monumental tomb displaying his effigy stands in the chapel of the episcopal palace at Eccleshall. His wife survived him but she and her children were not well provided for, and his possessions had to be sold on his death to cover his considerable indebtedness—£1100 to the crown and £250 to the bishopric.

Thomas Bentham's importance lies first of all in his activities as a theologian and a scholar and then as the bishop and chief pastor of a large midlands diocese in the early years of the Elizabethan religious settlement. Bentham is also notable as author of a large number of letters (118 surviving *in extenso* and 114 in paraphrase), which reveal a good deal about him as both man and reformer, as well as about the difficult circumstances of his episcopate and his responses to them. For many years his reputation was that of a weak figure who failed both to impose a reformed discipline on his diocese and to exercise control over nonconformist protestant clergy. It was once believed to have been Bentham who admonished the Shropshire preacher William Axton for refusing to conform and then deprived him when he refused to compromise, but it is now known that it was Bentham's successor William Overton who dealt thus with Axton in 1582. However, more recent work has reassessed Bentham's effectiveness as bishop. While his labours at Coventry and Lichfield were only moderately effective, the evidence suggests that Bentham was a committed pastor who found himself out of his depth in his remote, rural, and resistant diocese, but persevered in his efforts to solve its problems.

ROSEMARY O'DAY

Sources letter-book of Thomas Bentham, NL Wales, MS 4919 D · M. R. O'Day, 'Thomas Bentham: a case study in the problems of the early Elizabethan episcopate', *Journal of Ecclesiastical History*, 23/2 (1962), 137–59 · 'The letter-book of Thomas Bentham, bishop of Coventry and Lichfield, 1560–1561', ed. R. O'Day and J. Berlatsky, *Camden miscellany, XXVII*, CS, 4th ser., 22 (1979) · J. Berlatsky, 'Marriage and family in a Tudor elite: familial patterns of Elizabethan bishops', *Journal of Family History*, 3 (1978), 6–22 · R. O'Day, 'Cumulative debt: the bishops of Coventry and Lichfield and their economic problems, c.1540–1640', *Midland History*, 3 (1976), 77–93 · J. Berlatsky, 'Thomas Bentham and the plight of Elizabethan bishops', *Historical Magazine of the Protestant Episcopal Church*, 43 (1974), 317–40 · P. Collinson, *The Elizabethan puritan movement* (1967) · 'Letters of Thomas Wood, puritan, 1566–1577', ed. P. Collinson, *BIHR*, special suppl., 5 (1960) [whole issue] · C. Cross, *Church and people, 1450–1660* (1976) · queen's remembrancer, ecclesiastical miscellanea, PRO, E 135/9/6 · queen's remembrancer, special commissions of inquiry, PRO, E 178/2092 · M. Bateson, ed., 'A collection of original letters from the bishops to the privy council, 1564', *Camden miscellany, IX*, CS, new ser., 53 (1893) · Lichfield Joint RO, B/V/1/2; B/V/1/4; B/A/1/15 · M. C. Loftus, ed., 'Strange news from Staffordshire', *Staffordshire Catholic History*, 1 (1961) · C. Martin, *Les protestants anglais réfugiés à Genève, 1550–1560* (Geneva, 1915) · H. Robinson, ed. and trans., *Original letters relative to the English Reformation*, 1 vol. in 2, Parker Society, [26] (1846–7) · LPL, MS 2003 · W. N. Landor, 'Staffordshire incumbents and parochial records, 1530–1680', *Staffordshire Historical Collections*, 41 (1915) · B. Usher, '"In a time of persecution": new light on the secret protestant congregation in Marian London', *John Foxe and the English Reformation*, ed. D. Loades (1997), 233–51 · Wood, *Ath. Oxon.*, new edn, 1.442–3 · H. Gee, *The Elizabethan clergy and the settlement of religion, 1558–1576* (1898) · *The diary of Henry Machyn, citizen and merchant-taylor of London, from AD 1550 to AD 1563*, ed. J. G. Nichols, CS, 42 (1848)

Archives Lichfield Joint RO, MSS · NL Wales, letter-book, MS 4919 D · PRO, E 135/9/6; E 178/2092 | BL, Lansdowne MSS · DWL, Morrice MSS

Likenesses bas-relief effigy on table tomb, Eccleshall church, Staffordshire

Wealth at death £1100 in debt to crown; £250 in debt to see: 1583, Bishop William Overton's statement, PRO E 135/9/6

Bentinck, Lord (William) George Frederic Cavendish-Scott- [*known as* Lord George Bentinck] (1802–1848), politician and sportsman, was born on 27 February 1802 at Welbeck Abbey, Nottinghamshire, the fifth child and second surviving son of William Henry Cavendish-Scott-Bentinck, fourth duke of Portland (1768–1854), and his wife, Henrietta (*d.* 1844), eldest daughter and coheir of Major-General John Scott of Balcomie, Fife. (William) John Cavendish-Scott-*Bentinck, the fifth duke, and Lord Henry William Cavendish-Scott-*Bentinck were his brothers.

Early life, the army, and parliament Bentinck was sent neither to school nor to university but picked up a patchy education in the intervals of roaming freely about Welbeck where he gained his sporting skills as a brilliantly daring horseman, a good shot, cricketer, and oarsman. In 1820 he joined the 9th lancers as a cornet, quickly showing his pugnacious temperament in a quarrel with his equally touchy superior officer, Captain Ker. A duel in Paris was prevented only by the intervention of his uncle George *Canning (who had married his mother's younger sister Joan). Plainly unsuited to peacetime military life, he was wafted into politics in 1822 as Canning's private secretary and would have accompanied his uncle to India as his military secretary if Lord Londonderry's suicide had not opened Canning's way to the foreign secretaryship. In 1828, now a half-pay major in the 2nd Life Guards, he succeeded his uncle Lord William Bentinck as MP for King's Lynn, a borough where the family had much influence and for which he sat uninterruptedly until his death. He greatly admired Canning and behaved in exemplary Canningite fashion after Canning's death: he refused to support Wellington's ministry after William Huskisson and the Canningites resigned from it in 1828, voted for Catholic emancipation in 1829, and generally supported the Reform Bill. His independence and close friendships with Edward *Stanley (later fourteenth earl of Derby) and

Lord (William) George Frederic Cavendish-Scott-Bentinck (1802–1848), by Samuel Lane, c.1836

the fifth duke of Richmond led him in 1834 into the 'Derby Dilly' for which he acted as an unofficial whip. Like most of its members, he was soon absorbed into the Conservative opposition; he consistently supported Sir Robert Peel but refused office, offered to him through Stanley, when Peel formed his ministry in 1841. In these years he was punctilious in his own way in attendance in the Commons but so addicted to his hunting that he would take the 7 a.m. South Western train to Andover, hunt all day with Thomas Assheton Smith's great pack, the Tedworth, and return to the house in the evening wearing leathers and top-boots and 'a light-coloured zephyr paletot' over his pink coat.

'The Leviathan of the turf' Politics came a very poor second to Bentinck's growing interests in racing. His father, who had won the Derby with Tiresias in 1819, detested betting but paid most of Bentinck's losses of £13,000 on the St Leger in 1826 'without a single observation … Neither promise was asked for nor reproach made,' though the duke bought him the estate of Muirkirk in Ayrshire in the hope of distracting his son from racing. On another occasion, Bentinck is reported to have said: 'Never mind the money; my mother will let me have the amount'. Such indulgence, even if exceptional, was also dangerous. He had an ample income of £18,000 a year, most of it from life interests, but little capital. This lack was partly remedied by his brothers' guarantee of a credit of £100,000 on Drummond's Bank when Bentinck went into partnership with his cousin, the diarist Charles *Greville. After some successes, notably Preserve's victory in the One Thousand

Guineas in 1835, the partnership broke up in a bitter quarrel when a minor racing incident provoked Bentinck to 'a vehemence and ferocity' which astounded Greville, who also disliked the subterfuges designed by Bentinck to lengthen the odds on horses he was backing. One such practice, much used later, was to enter his yearlings for many races, despite heavy costs in inevitable forfeits, in order to mislead other owners and the bookmakers about his intentions. The elder John Day was his trainer at Danebury, near Stockbridge, until 1841 when, after serious differences arising from Bentinck's justifiable suspicions of the Days' deceptions, he moved his horses to Goodwood. There, by the generosity of Richmond and with John Kent the elder and his son, also John Kent, as his trainers, he carried on breeding, training, and racing operations on an unrivalled scale. He was a generous but exacting employer, sending long and detailed instructions to the Kents when not requiring their attendance at Harcourt House. He left his mark on Goodwood, indeed he virtually controlled it: he had enclosures made in order to improve viewing conditions and charged for entry to them; he presented the valuable Waterloo shield, built two long-distance courses and created the Halnaker Park gallop after felling large numbers of the duke's great trees, levelling banks at huge expense and relaying 16,000 tons of turf. At the height of his activities, he owned over 200 horses at Goodwood and other lesser establishments, the best being Elis who won the St Leger in 1836 and Miss Elis, victorious in the Goodwood Cup and Stakes on successive days in 1845; Grey Momus who took the Two Thousand Guineas in 1838 and Firebrand the One Thousand Guineas in 1842; and his outstanding filly Crucifix who as a three-year old won the One Thousand and Two Thousand Guineas and the Oaks in 1840. Crucifix was the dam of Surplice who, no longer in his ownership, won the Derby in 1848. To Disraeli's vivid biographical account of Bentinck's chagrin it may be added that Bentinck had cleared £11,000 by betting on Surplice.

The 1845 season was Bentinck's most successful: 36 horses, in his colours of sky-blue jacket and white cap, won 58 of the 195 races in which they started, and, according to John Kent jun., his overall and prodigious winnings were close on £100,000, of which only some £17,000 came from prize money. Lacking the capital of owners such as the duke of Grafton, the earl of Jersey, John Bowes, and Colonel Jonathan Peel, he had to bet heavily and successfully—the 'great coups' for which he was known as 'a very dangerous customer' among the bookmakers—in order to meet huge running costs of £45,000 a year by 1845. Betting was an essential aspect of his racing. In a sport swarming with swindlers and rogues of all kinds, his maxim evidently was to fight fire with fire. Some of his practices were distinctly sharp. He would put out misleading statements about his horses' health and performances in training or early races; he once threatened to withdraw a horse—Elis from the St Leger—unless he could back the animal at 12 to 1; and the means by which he secured long odds on Red Deer to win the Chester Cup in 1844 clearly involved a degree of deceit. The evidence of much more unscrupulous conduct, such as bribing other owners' jockeys or ordering his own to lose races, is circumstantial and unspecific; it derives notably from men with whom he had quarrelled—Greville and the Days—none of whom published their charges during his lifetime. Greville's verdict that Bentinck had made for himself 'a peculiar code of morality and honour' which allowed a certain measure of 'deceit and falsehood' may well be right (*Greville Memoirs*, 28 Sept 1848). Like nearly all owners, he took the view that his horses were investments for his own profit, regardless of how his plans might affect the public. While some of his chicaneries were shared by most owners, including Stanley and Greville, and affected seriously others who were not blameless, his temperament led him to practise them systematically. The need to gamble successfully brought out flaws in his character: intensely competitive, strong-willed, and self-reliant, he had a quick and unforgiving temper. His not unreasonable view that 'Squire' Osbaldeston had behaved dishonourably in winning money from him at Lord Wilton's Heaton Park meeting led to a duel on 14 April 1835. They met at twelve paces at 6 a.m. at Wormwood Scrubs. Bentinck fired first and in the air; Osbaldeston, a crack shot, then put a bullet through his opponent's hat, Bentinck's second, George Anson, pleasantly remarking: 'I did not think you were so bad a shot, Squire.' The two men were reconciled several years later, but Bentinck rebuffed all efforts to end his quarrel with Charles Greville.

Racing was now poised for its commercial expansion brought about by the railways but suffered from seriously inadequate administration: the Jockey Club, its competence restricted to Newmarket, Epsom, and Ascot, was weakened by divisions and by its withdrawal in 1842, to Bentinck's fury, of its claims to adjudicate on horse-race betting. Bentinck was keenly interested in improvements such as the expulsion of defaulters from courses, flag starts, punctual times for races, and the numbering of horses. He devised a code of racing rules in 1844. And he was a near-pioneer of 'vanning' horses: in 1836 his specially built high van, padded inside and drawn by six post horses, took Elis and the Drummer from Goodwood to Doncaster in three days, not only saving long and debilitating walking but enabling Elis to win the St Leger and Bentinck to obtain long odds when it seemed that the horse would not be able to get to the course in time. Within a few years he and others were making heavy use of the railways for such transportation. As a reformer of racing, he was best known to the public for his leading part in exposing Abraham Levi Goodman's ingenious scheme to win the Derby in 1844 with Running Rein, in reality an over-age four-year-old named Maccabeus. Funds raised to thank him for his exertions, after the court case of *Wood v. Peel* before Baron Alderson in July 1844 had proved the fraud, were used at his wish to provide the nucleus of the Bentinck Benevolent Fund for the widows and children of deserving trainers and jockeys.

It was in the courts that Bentinck made his most important contributions to purifying the turf. In *Bentinck v. Connop* (1843) before Lord Denman, he lost his suit for the recovery of entry money of £150, the defendant relying on the statute of 1676 (16 Charles II c. 7) which enacted that no action in horse-racing could be maintained to recover more than £100. Effectively, the courts would neither recognize gambling transactions nor enforce their settlement. Bentinck's prominence made him the main target for unscrupulous opponents in the racing world, who exploited the chaotically obsolete laws concerning betting. Between July and December 1843 J. T. and C. H. Russell took out *qui tam* writs against Bentinck and twelve others, including Greville, Colonel Peel, Anson, and Sir William Gregory, under 9 Anne c. 14 for winning or losing sums of over £10 in contravention of the statute. The sums conceivably recoverable under the thirty-four writs amounted to nearly £500,000 inclusive of moneys payable to the informers, of which Bentinck's six writs stood to lose him £62,500. He was the strategist behind moves to foil what he called 'the Infernal Alliance' of the Russells. The sporting interest in parliament was quickly mobilized. Richmond's Gaming Actions Suspension Continuation Act repealed the penalties on horse-race betting while select committees of both houses investigated the gaming laws. These moves gave some protection for the future but could not retrospectively affect the case of *Russell v. Bentinck* involving a claim for £12,000 (a bet of £3000 won of John Day and treble that sum in penalty), which was tried before Baron Parke and a jury at Guildford on 8 August 1844. Bentinck's victory ended all such actions.

Crisis over the corn laws, 1846 Bentinck's short, turbulent, but influential political career has no parallel in British history. Pitched unwillingly into the leadership of the protectionist cause in the Commons in April 1846 some three months after Peel's plan for repeal of the corn laws was known, he suffered at first from the grave disadvantage that he was wholly inexperienced at this level: before February 1846 he had never spoken in a major debate although he had taken an active part in 1845 in defence of the landed interest as a member of John Bright's select committee on the game laws, subjecting witnesses who were critical of the laws to searching and well-informed cross-examination. With his indifferent education, he was ill-matched against opponents of the calibre of Peel, Russell, and Cobden, and even contemplated bringing a lawyer into parliament to put the protectionist case on his behalf. But apart from his high station, he possessed other advantages. He was wholly fearless and no respecter, as was already evident, of persons or feelings. Over 6 feet tall, with a handsome, refined face framed by a light beard and auburn hair, he was a commanding figure invariably dressed in a long black frock coat, dark-blue or black double-breasted velvet waistcoat, dark trousers with bootstraps, and a gold waistcoat and neck chain ornamented with a large turquoise. His high-pitched, weak voice was often helped by doses of quinine; he always pronounced 'Rome' as 'Room', 'wonder' as 'woonder'.

Bentinck was transparently sincere in believing that protectionism was right both in principle and policy. He regarded the Conservatives' electoral victory in 1841 and the modified protection given by Peel's corn law of 1842 as committing the party and government to a policy which was now threatened by Peel's new course. He had been unswervingly loyal to Peel and had taken no part in earlier protectionist mutinies. 'I keep horses in three counties', he is reported to have said, 'and they tell me that I shall save 1500 *l.* a year by free trade. I don't care for that. What I cannot bear is "being sold".' He convinced himself that Peel must make 'atonement' for breaking the unwritten code of aristocratic honour. More practically, he believed, as he told Stanley (20 January 1846), that if one section of the aristocracy—Peel and his followers—went in for 'political lying and pledge-breaking', the legitimacy of aristocratic predominance would be gravely damaged. These views, combined with a dogmatically contractarian outlook, energetic single-mindedness, and an insistence on political consistency, formed the explosive imperatives of his politics. In August 1846, during the evening after the third day's racing at Goodwood, he abruptly sold his entire breeding and racing establishment to the Hon. Edward Mostyn for the ludicrously low sum of £10,000, the bargain to include his jockey Little Kitchener who weighed 3 stone 4 lb, and 'old Bay Middleton', the stallion who sired the Derby winners of 1846 and 1851. Uncompromising and authoritarian, he could be vindictive in his combativeness. His ferocious attacks on Peel and his 'paid janissaries' and 'renegades', most notoriously the unjust charge on 8 June 1846 that Peel had 'hunted' Canning to his early death, increased the already high temperature of debate in the Commons. Although his probity and reforming reputation were vindicated on the two occasions when opponents—Lord Lyndhurst in August 1846, Lord John Russell in June 1848—accused him of bringing into politics the disreputable methods of the turf, he readily admitted that if Lyndhurst used the rapier, he himself wielded the broadsword and the bayonet, as in his censure of Prince Albert for giving the crown's personal sanction to corn-law repeal. His style, consciously different from Peel's nuanced pragmatism and the equivocal passivity of his own leader Stanley, emphasized the protectionists' commitment to clear-cut policies; and his methods had the desired effects of implicating his party in his hostility to the 'Arch Traitor' and of perpetuating the schism among the Conservatives. He stamped on every attempt at reconciliation, notably Lyndhurst's improbable 'grand junction ministry' of July 1846 in which he was to be chancellor of the exchequer. His mission was to purify the Conservative Party by removing all taint of Peelism. Benjamin *Disraeli saw him as a modernized whig of 1688. He called himself a 'disciple' of Pitt, whom he saw as far from holding 'the cold blooded Philosophy of the Political Economists'—a political lineage reasonable in a former Canningite and with the added attraction of reaching back well beyond Peel (Disraeli to C. E. de Michele, 19 Oct 1847, *Letters*).

Bentinck made up for inexperience by readiness to take advice, most conspicuously from Disraeli who quickly made himself his lieutenant and whose 'political biography' of 1852, despite its flawless hero and its calculated silences, is an indispensable source for the protectionists'

strategies between 1846 and 1848, the more so given the dearth of Bentinck's papers: these were available to Disraeli but many were apparently destroyed by Portland, though he kept some of his son's letters to him. Bentinck may not have known Disraeli when he peremptorily refused in 1834 to accept him as a fellow candidate at King's Lynn. Their acquaintance began in 1842 when Bentinck gave Disraeli a half interest in a filly called Kitten which proved worthless. The friendship of 'the Jockey and the Jew' was unlikely and unclouded. The vital trappings of landownership at Hughenden were supplied by Bentinck and his brothers with a loan of £25,000. Disraeli advanced considerably under Bentinck's patronage and repaid it by real admiration at the time: he described Bentinck privately to Lord John Manners as 'the only head of decision & real native sagacity, that we possess' and noted his increasing maturity as a politician (Disraeli to Manners, 26 Dec 1847, *Letters*). Others whom Bentinck consulted were J. C. Herries, Thomas Baring, and the 'railway king' George Hudson, while Richard Burn of Manchester, editor of the *Commercial Glance*, and H. C. Chapman, a Liverpool shipowner and protectionist, provided much commercial and political information. Of a piece with the modernity of his interests in railways (he was a major shareholder in the London and Birmingham Railway), agricultural improvement, and navigation and drainage schemes for King's Lynn and the fens was his keen interest in the newspaper press, and he maintained particularly close links with C. E. de Michele, proprietor of the *Morning Post*.

Leading the protectionists, 1846–1847 The protectionist movement, primarily agrarian but involving shipping and colonial interests as well as commercial elements in the City of London, Liverpool, and elsewhere, with writers such as Archibald Alison, Charles Neave, and William Aytoun in *Blackwood's Edinburgh Magazine*, the contributors to the *Quarterly Review* under J. W. Croker's editorship, and the lively satirists of *Fraser's Magazine* to conduct a vigorous defence of protectionism on historical, social, political, and economic grounds, presented a formidable ideological challenge to whiggism, radicalism, and Peelite Conservatism. Protectionists saw themselves as heirs of a broadly Pittite governing ethic. Paternalistic, patriotic, and anti-radical, they believed in a responsive state which, through its tariff and taxation policies, arbitrated between the needs of society and government. Their organicist system aimed at class integration; insisting on the interdependence of consumers and producers, they wanted to promote home and colonial markets for British manufactures as against the free-traders' emphasis on export-led growth dependent on foreign demand. Bentinck fully shared these views, rejecting only the populist protestantism of many protectionists.

By insisting in his first major speech on 27 February 1846 that Peel's policies amounted to 'a great commercial revolution' which would damage domestic industry, shipping, and the colonies as well as agriculture, Bentinck tied his party to defending protection on the broadest grounds. His cast of mind was strictly practical: 'I never read or mean to read a tract in all my life, Puseyite or other', he told Manners in 1847. He defended the corn laws pragmatically, arguing that their success had boosted farmers' confidence and generated agricultural improvement, and producing as a metaphor for his elaborate calculations about increased yields from applying guano (as to whose good quality as a fertilizer he was right). As a riposte to Peel, he argued that domestic production had more than kept pace with population growth. His handling of the statistics with which his speeches were loaded doubtless owed something to his racing experiences but also reflected his efforts both to match Peel's and Cobden's economic expertise and to convince a statistics-obsessed public. By his relentless exposure of the weaknesses in Peel's case that the Irish subsistence crisis required repeal, his accusation that Ireland was a mere pretext, and his claim that Irish agriculture would be an early victim of free imports, he cast further serious doubts on Peel's motives and judgement, at least among protectionists. Two-thirds of Peel's party turned against him in the Commons. Bentinck's tactics in the complex preparations for bringing Peel down on the Protection of Life (Ireland) Bill were skilful: he kept lines open to the whigs in unsuccessful negotiations for a moderately protectionist whig government in April–May 1846; and in refusing Disraeli's advice to oppose the Irish Coercion Bill *ab initio* but holding the ministry to the alleged urgency of the measure, he put the irreconcilable protectionists in as strong a moral position as was possible. Revenge was now not the prime consideration. He feared, as he told his father (9 June 1846), that Peel might appeal as prime minister to the country and cause 'a terrible division of the Conservative ranks … Out of office I think for a long time he will be nobody'. On 25 June he and seventy protectionists joined Peel's other opponents in defeating the government on the Irish bill.

Bentinck soon showed that his forte did not lie solely in destructive opposition. His programme of February 1847 for famine-stricken Ireland, centring on his ambitious railways scheme and including endowment of the Roman Catholic church, tenants' compensation, and taxes on absentee landlords, was a remarkable venture in constructive unionism and social engineering. The railway plan, by which Treasury loans of up to £16,000,000 repayable over thirty years were to be made to railway companies, was designed both to give employment to over a fifth of those half a million people currently employed on 'unproductive' public works and to provide Ireland with a modern transport system as a necessary stimulus to British capital investment. These social and economic objectives were linked to broader political considerations. The Union and the dominance of landownership in Britain were to be buttressed by identification with a thriving Irish economy reinvigorated in its social base and hooked into the British market. Although he received warm initial support from the so-called 'Irish party' of whigs, tories, and nationalists, his plan was wrecked by the eventual collapse of Irish unity, whig and Peelite economic orthodoxy, and the fears of many of his own followers at the consequences of defeating the whig government.

Although Bentinck had put forward his railway scheme as non-partisan, Russell was right to make it an issue of confidence. It was a question, as Bentinck told his father (19 February 1847), of 'whether Lord John Russell or I were to govern Ireland'.

Bentinck was convinced that beyond the agrarian heartland which remained solidly protectionist in the general election of 1847, much support was waiting to be tapped in the urban and commercial worlds. He accepted that the *status quo ante* 1846 was not immediately realizable. The fiscal policy in his election manifesto (24 July 1847), a deliberate reply to Peel's Tamworth apologia, called for a 'revision and equalization of taxation' to put the overtaxed agriculturist 'on a fair footing with the Manchester manufacturer'. Excise duties would be abolished and replaced by revenue duties on foreign agricultural and manufactured products; free colonial imports would be allowed; and 'the mischievous and absurd restrictions' of Peel's Bank Charter Act of 1844 would be dealt with. This programme was designed to appeal both to landlords and farmers and to urban shopkeepers and small capitalists, and it foreshadowed Disraeli's ingenious proposals after 1849. With some 230 MPs the protectionists formed the largest single party, but Bentinck did not last long as its leader in the Commons. He had made his freedom to vote as he thought right on religious questions a condition of becoming leader, and he was disgusted by the No Popery cry raised in 1847 by many of the party including the whips, William Beresford and Charles Newdegate, with whom he was often at loggerheads. The same elements' resistance to the Jewish Disabilities Bill, he told Disraeli (14 November 1847) was 'the tea table twaddling' of 'a pack of Old Maids' when 'the greatest Commercial Empire of the World is engaged in a life & death struggle for existence'. Consistently with his support for religious toleration and his loyalty to Disraeli, he spoke and voted for the bill on 17 December 1847. On 23 December, he resigned as leader without waiting, as he told J. W. Croker, to be 'cashiered', temporarily bitter at the degeneration of 'the great Protectionist Party' into 'a "No Popery", "No Jew" Party'.

Ill health and death Overwork, the result of taking too much on himself, his habit of eating nothing after a light breakfast until he dined late at night at White's, and recurrent, depressing bouts of influenza had damaged his health, as he recognized. Yet he continued as, in Manners's phrase, 'the bulwark of the [protectionist] cause' and with a considerable body of support. Against the drive for further instalments of free trade, the protectionists' well-organized resistance at least bought time for endangered interests to adapt to new terms of trade. Bentinck's massive labours, often eighteen hours a day between February and May 1848 as chairman of the select committee on sugar and coffee plantations, finally allowed the bargain to be struck with Russell in August by which British-grown sugar was protected by a 10s. differential duty until 1854; and his vigorous defence of the shipping interest helped to secure a year's postponement of repeal of the navigation laws.

At the end of the 1848 session Bentinck went down on 11

September to Welbeck, and two days later saw the Derby winner Surplice beat Stanley's Canezou to win the St Leger at Doncaster. On 21 September 1848 he set out to walk the 5 miles from Welbeck to stay with Lord Manvers at Thoresby. Last seen standing by a water-meadow gate, his head down as if reading, he died on the way of a heart attack. Curious local rumours of suicide or murder were dispelled by the autopsy which revealed 'congestion over the whole system', emphysema of the lungs, and a large muscular heart with the appearance of 'irregular contraction'. He was privately buried on 29 September in the family vault in St Marylebone Old Church. British merchant ships in the Thames from London Bridge to Gravesend, in Liverpool, and in French and Dutch ports hoisted their flags at half-mast in tribute. He was a proud and inaccessible man with few close friends outside his own family, notably his younger brother Henry. He never married. The only record of his relations with women is Greville's unconfirmed but presumably knowledgeable testimony that he was once desperately but unrequitedly in love with Caroline, duchess of Richmond. He died intestate, and his father's provisions for him—a life interest in £50,000 in 3½ per cent stock, some £700 a year from the North Lynn estate, and a share in a settlement worth £6600—reverted to the family.

'The Strafford of the 19th Century' Whether 'the wild Bird', as Stanley called him (26 December 1847) when congratulating him on his freedom, would have been politically successful if he had lived longer was doubted later by Stanley and Disraeli. He might well have returned to racing. *The Times* (23 September 1848) acknowledged his formidable quality as an opposition leader but saw him as 'a political moralist, not a statesman'. Lord John Manners memorably described him to Disraeli in 1850 as 'the Strafford of the 19th Century'. Disraeli, perhaps more questionably, described his biography as 'the portraiture of an English Worthy'. Bentinck was chiefly responsible for Peel's fall, the permanent division of Peel's party, and the successful launching of a protectionist party which defended important interests and expressed traditional social and political ideals against progressive liberalism. Its landed leadership, personified by him, Derby, and Richmond, was as effective as the concessionary strategies of the whigs and Peel in prolonging aristocratic dominance. Victorian parliamentary government, with its classic conflictual base, owed much to him.

ANGUS MACINTYRE

Sources B. Disraeli, *Lord George Bentinck: a political biography* (1852) • *Benjamin Disraeli letters*, ed. J. A. W. Gunn and others (1982-), vols. 4-5 • *The Croker papers: the correspondence and diaries of … John Wilson Croker*, ed. L. J. Jennings, 3 (1884), 127-66 • R. Stewart, *The politics of protection: Lord Derby and the protectionist party, 1841-1852* (1971) • A. Macintyre, 'Lord George Bentinck and the protectionists: a lost cause?', *TRHS*, 5th ser., 39 (1989), 141-65 • F. W. Fetter, 'The economic articles in *The Quarterly Review* and their authors, 1809-1852', *Journal of Political Economy*, 66 (1958) • F. W. Fetter, 'The economic articles in *Blackwood's Edinburgh Magazine* and their authors, 1817-1853', *Scottish Journal of Political Economy*, 7 (1960), 85-107, 213-31 • *The Greville memoirs, 1814-1860*, ed. L. Strachey and R. Fulford, 8 vols. (1938), vol. 6., pp. 105-22 • J. Kent, *Racing life of Lord George Cavendish Bentinck, and other reminiscences*, ed. F. Lawley (1892) • M. Seth-Smith, *Lord Paramount of the Turf: Lord George Bentinck, 1802-1848* (1971) • E. Eadie, 'The structure and organization of English horse-racing, 1830-1850', DPhil diss., U. Oxf., 1990 • N. Gash, 'Lord George Bentinck and his sporting world', *Pillars of government and other essays on state and society, c.1770 – c.1880* (1986) • U. Nott. L., Portland MSS

Archives U. Nott. L., corresp. and papers | BL, corresp. with John Wilson Croker, Add. MS 41129 • BL, letters to Stanley Lees Giffard, Add. MS 56368 • BL, corresp. with Sir Robert Peel, Add. MSS 40416-40600, *passim* • Bodl. Oxf., letters to Benjamin Disraeli, earl of Beaconsfield • Bodl. Oxf., Charles Eastland de Michele MSS • Cambs. AS, letters to Millicent Sparrow • Lpool RO, letters to Lord Stanley • PRO, corresp. with Stafford Canning, FO 352 • W. Sussex RO, letters to duke of Richmond

Likenesses R. Westmacott, statue, 1835, Calcutta • S. Lane, oils, c.1836, NPG; copies by E. Belli, Jockey and Carlton clubs [*see illus.*] • E. H. Baily, marble bust, 1842, Russell-Cotes Museum, Bournemouth • C. B., lithograph, pubd 1848 (after daguerreotype), BM, NPG • T. Campbell, marble bust, 1848, NPG • J. B. Hunt, stipple and line engraving, pubd 1848 (after photograph by Claudet), NPG • T. C. Hine, monument, 1849, Market Place, Mansfield, Nottinghamshire • line engraving, pubd 1849 (after Count D'Orsay), BM • T. Campbell, bronze statue, 1851, Cavendish Square, London • E. Belli, portrait (after Lane); known to be at Welbeck in 1936 • Count D'Orsay, bust; formerly at Hughenden Manor, Buckinghamshire • J. Doyle, two drawings, Hughenden Manor, Buckinghamshire • attrib. R. J. Lane, lithograph (after Count D'Orsay, 1840), BM • R. J. Lane, lithograph (after Count D'Orsay, 1848), BM, NPG • T. C. W., lithograph, BM, NPG • caricature drawings, BM • oils, Hughenden Manor, Buckinghamshire

Wealth at death Muirkirk estate in Ayrshire; father's provisions of life interest of £50,000 in 3½ per cent stock, £700 p.a. from North Lynn estate, and share in a settlement valued at £6600 reverted to family

Bentinck, Hans Willem [William], **first earl of Portland** (1649-1709), diplomat and politician, was born on 20 July 1649 NS at Diepenheim in the eastern Netherlands, the fifth of nine children of Berent Bentinck (1597-1668), lord of Diepenheim and *drost* (sheriff) of Deventer, and his wife, Anna van Bloemendaal (1622-1685), daughter of Hans Hendrik van Bloemendaal, *drost* of Vianen. The Bentincks were members of the old nobility of Gelderland and Overijssel, but as a younger son Hans Willem could not expect to inherit the family estates. He was thus fortunate to be chosen in 1664 as a page of Prince William III of Orange, and it was principally at the Orange court in The Hague that the next twenty-four years of his life were spent.

Confidant to William of Orange Bentinck was fifteen when he arrived in The Hague, the prince a year younger and already an orphan. Both were isolated figures and it was natural that they should have become friends. Moulded by a common Calvinist upbringing, they shared a taste for the aristocratic pursuits of hunting and military exercises, as well as for the gentler pleasures of art collecting and landscape gardening, and their views on foreign policy developed in tandem. Bentinck was one of the young gentlemen attending William when he travelled to Middelburg in September 1668 to be installed as first noble by the states of Zeeland, and two years later he was part of the larger entourage which accompanied the prince on

Hans Willem Bentinck, first earl of Portland (1649–1709), studio of Hyacinthe Rigaud [original, 1698–9]

his first visit to England. The main purpose of the journey—a purpose only partially achieved—was to obtain repayment of debts owed to William by his uncle Charles II; but the prince also visited Cambridge and Oxford, whose universities conferred honorary degrees on him and some of his companions, including Bentinck.

In February 1672, with the threat of a French invasion looming over the Dutch Republic, the states general appointed William III captain- and admiral-general, and when the threat became a reality in June the prince was raised to the office of stadholder in the provinces of Holland and Zeeland. Bentinck was by now the prince's chamberlain and regarded as one of his inner circle of advisers. He already had several years' experience as a cornet in the prince's Horse Guards, and in the ensuing war against France (1672–9) he proved himself to be a courageous soldier as well as William's loyal servant. Promoted major in 1672 and colonel two years later, he nursed the prince when in 1675 he succumbed to smallpox (contracting the disease himself in the process) and fought in the battle of St Denis, near Mons, in August 1678 while peace was being negotiated at Nijmegen. It was, however, as a diplomat that Bentinck's most important early work was done. Following the Anglo-Dutch treaty of Westminster, signed in February 1674, William hoped for English support in his struggle against France and with this in mind Bentinck was sent to London in June 1677 as the prince's special envoy. Instructed to gauge Charles II's willingness to support the republic in seeking favourable peace terms with France, Bentinck found the king predictably non-committal. However, with the help of Thomas Osborne, earl of Danby, Charles's lord treasurer, who opposed the

French, he broached successfully the subject of an Orange–Stuart marriage and obtained royal approval for William's request to visit England in the autumn. The visit duly took place and, on 4 November, Orange was married to the Lady Mary, elder daughter of James, duke of York. No doubt the event prompted Bentinck to consider the matter of his own marriage. Among those accompanying the new princess of Orange when she arrived at The Hague in December were her childhood friends Elizabeth and Anne Villiers, daughters of Sir Edward and Lady Frances Villiers, her former governess. Their brother was Edward *Villiers, later first earl of Jersey (1655?–1711). Just two months later, in February 1678, Bentinck married the younger sister, Anne (1659/1660?–1688). Their first child, Mary, was born in 1679 and a son, Willem, in 1681; five more children (a son and four daughters) followed over the next seven years.

Bentinck's growing influence within the stadholder's circle was accompanied by the acquisition of land and titles. In December 1674 he had bought the estate of Zorgvliet, near The Hague, which now became his family home; in 1674 he was appointed *drost* of Breda, with an annual salary of 2000 guilders, and in 1675 *drost* of Lingen. William granted him the lordship of Drimmelen in 1676 with the right to sit in the states of Holland as a member of the nobility, while in 1683 Bentinck purchased the lordships of Rhoon and Pendrecht, near Rotterdam, for 154,000 guilders, and was promoted sergeant-major-general of cavalry. The same year saw him once again in London as the prince's envoy, ostensibly to congratulate Charles II on the collapse of the Rye House assassination plot, though really to further William's strategy of drawing England out of the orbit of Louis XIV. Bentinck warned of the dangers posed by French aggrandizement in Alsace, Luxembourg, and the Spanish Netherlands, but the king was not to be shaken from his belief in the 'bonnes intensions de la France' (Japikse, 1.1.15). Nor, despite considerable efforts, was he able to win over the new king, James II, when he was sent to England for a third time in the summer of 1685. James's request in June for the loan of six Scottish and English regiments in Dutch service to assist in suppressing Monmouth's rising in England and Scotland was quickly and efficiently met by the states general, with Bentinck taking charge of the transportation of the troops across the North Sea. He followed in person a month later, carrying instructions to offer the military services of William himself against the rebels; and, after three weeks of negotiations with the pro-Dutch Laurence Hyde, earl of Rochester, and other ministers, he was able on 17 August 1685 os to sign a declaration renewing all existing treaties between England and the Dutch Republic. The king duly acknowledged his obligations to William and the states general, 'nos bons amis, alliez et conféderez' ('our good friends, allies, and confederates'; J. Ferguson, ed., *Papers Illustrating the History of the Scots Brigade in the Service of the United Netherlands*, 1, 1899, 539), but he was not willing to match their assistance with any comparable gesture of support for the republic, and relations between London and The Hague quickly cooled. A lasting entente between the houses of Stuart and Orange seemed unattainable and as he returned to Holland Bentinck had to content himself with more modest achievements. He now had a network of contacts in English political circles and he had gained experience in matters of logistics. Both would soon be needed again.

The revolution of 1688 Precisely when William of Orange made his decision to intervene directly in English affairs by mounting an armed invasion of the country is unclear: possibly as early as 1686, more likely in April or early June 1688. What is certain, however, is that Bentinck played a key role in every aspect of the planning and execution of the enterprise. By now the leading member of William's inner triumvirate of advisers—the others were Gaspar Fagel, grand pensionary of Holland, and the soldier diplomat Everard van Weede van Dijkveld—Bentinck was, in Bishop Burnet's phrase, 'the person that was most entirely trusted and constantly employed by him' (*Bishop Burnet's History*, 3.311). From late 1687 Bentinck's secret correspondents in Britain (Henry Sidney and James Johnstone among others) kept William informed of events there: the progress of the queen's pregnancy, the likely outcome of the king's attempt to pack parliament, the state of his relations with Louis XIV. Even his private secretary, Jacob van Leeuwen, was dispatched to London on the eve of the invasion to report on James's military and naval preparations.

At the same time, Bentinck's diplomatic experience was put to use in a series of important negotiations with the Dutch Republic's north German neighbours. Their co-operation was vital in order to reinforce the eastern frontier of the state while part of its forces were engaged in the descent on England, and while the disputed succession to the archbishopric of Cologne threatened to bring French troops within striking distance of Dutch territory. Talks about joint defence had already taken place in July 1686, when he accompanied William to Cleves for a meeting with Frederick William, elector of Brandenburg, and with the death of the veteran elector in May 1688 Bentinck was immediately sent to Berlin to congratulate his successor, Frederick III, and to take the negotiations further. It proved a difficult assignment, not least because the elector's first minister, Danckelmann, favoured the French rather than the imperial candidate for the see of Cologne. Bentinck had personal tragedy to contend with, too. The death of his eldest son, the seven-year-old Willemtie, and the serious illness of his wife forced him to return to The Hague in June. By late July, however, he was in Germany once more; and though he failed to win over the elector of Hanover, he succeeded (after a series of secret meetings at Celle) in reaching agreements with Brandenburg, Lüneburg, Wolfenbüttel, and Hesse for the hire of 12,000 troops to secure the republic's German border and the middle Rhine.

It was not only in Germany that Bentinck's powers of persuasion were called for. Returning to Holland in June and again in August, he had meetings with three of Amsterdam's burgomasters, although more than a month was to pass before they and other major towns in the Netherlands were ready to declare their support for the stadholder's invasion plans. British opinion, too, had to be wooed. With his network of agents in Britain, Bentinck had been given the task earlier in the year of arranging the distribution of an important propaganda pamphlet, *Their highness the prince and princess of Orange's opinion about a general liberty of conscience*, and had encountered some difficulties. His English correspondents complained that there were insufficient copies of the piece and that outside court circles its impact was limited. But he learned from experience and the production in the autumn of the prince's *Declaration … of the Reasons Inducing him to Appear in Armes in the Kingdome of England* was much more efficiently handled. Drafted by Fagel, who discussed its content at length with Bentinck and with William himself, it was printed secretly and in bulk, all 60,000 copies being kept under seal at Bentinck's quarters in The Hague and then delivered to his agents in Britain, with orders 'to disperse none of them till the prince be landed' (Japikse, 1.2.619). The distribution of a shorter manifesto, addressed to the officers and men of King James's navy, was also Bentinck's responsibility, and he even devised the banners, with their motto 'Pro religione et libertate', that were to fly from the mastheads of the invasion fleet.

Finally, as an experienced staff officer Bentinck was given responsibility during the latter part of 1688 for co-ordinating the land and sea forces involved in the invasion. On 15 August he and the secretary of the Admiralty of Amsterdam, Job de Wildt, drew up a detailed estimate for provisioning and clothing an army of 16,000 men and 4000 horses. They oversaw the building of twenty-one new warships and ensured the availability of suitable transport vessels, especially for the cavalry. From mid-September onwards Bentinck was in frequent consultation with the commanders of the fleet, determining its sailing formation (a diagram of this, drawn by Bentinck himself, survives among his papers), considering potential landing-places on the north-east and south coasts of England, and instructing Admiral Arthur Herbert, the supreme commander, to avoid combat as far as possible. Bentinck personally supervised the embarkation of troops at Hellevoetsluis and was with the fleet at the end of October when its first attempt to set sail was prevented by storms. After attending a council of war on board Herbert's flagship on 11 November, he paid a last visit to his ailing wife at The Hague and rejoined the expedition as it put to sea two days later.

After landing in Tor Bay on 5/15 November, the entire force disembarked within forty-eight hours, thanks to Bentinck's planning. He himself commanded a cavalry regiment, one of the few contingents to see action during the army's advance on London. His men encountered a company of Irish horse near Wincanton in Somerset and suffered a few casualties. But, as his correspondence with Admiral Herbert shows, Bentinck never doubted that the invasion would win support in England and that it would prevail. 'Nos affaires publiques vont de mieux à mieux' ('Our public business is going better and better'), he wrote from Newbury on 10 December in a letter which also reveals his deep private grief on learning of the death of his wife (Japikse, 2.3.80). Three days later he was informed of James II's flight, and by 18 December Dutch troops were in control of London, with Bentinck's regiment stationed in Richmond and Wimbledon. In such rapidly changing circumstances his ideas about the constitutional objectives of the invasion naturally changed too. A few days earlier he had told Henry Hyde, second earl of Clarendon, that William had no designs on the English crown: to suggest otherwise was 'the most wicked insinuation that could be invented' (*Correspondence of Henry Hyde, Earl of Clarendon*, ed. S. W. Singer, 2 vols., 1828, 2.215). Yet with James out of the country—he finally sailed for France on 22 December—the throne was effectively vacant, and during the next three weeks Bentinck was reported to be active in urging the initially hesitant prince to seize the opportunity now presented to him ('Verbaal … Engeland, 1689, … door Mr Nicolaas Witsen' in J. Scheltema, *Geschied- en letterkundig mengelwerk*, 6 vols., 1817–36, 3.147, 159–60). He discussed the matter also with leading whigs such as Burnet and Herbert, communicating to William their view that he and his wife should become joint sovereigns. It was in these terms that the Convention Parliament formally offered the crown to William and Mary on 13 February 1689, and their willingness to accept it owed a good deal to Bentinck's influence.

Widening responsibilities William III was generous in rewarding those who had sustained his cause during the invasion of England. An act of naturalization for Bentinck and his children was passed by parliament on 8 April 1689 and the following day he was created earl of Portland, Viscount Woodstock, and Baron Cirencester. He was introduced into the House of Lords on 15 April, and in early May was given the estate of Theobalds in Hertfordshire. At court he was appointed groom of the stole, first gentleman of the bedchamber, treasurer of the privy purse, and privy councillor, receiving apartments adjoining the king's in the palaces of Whitehall, Kensington, and Hampton Court. Portland's duties in his English offices were in some ways similar to those he had undertaken for the past two decades at The Hague. In daily conference with the king, he remained his closest adviser and secretary, the intermediary between William and the British political nation, and the person to whom the bulk of state correspondence was addressed. But there were also important differences. For one thing, the strands of policy which he now co-ordinated were more numerous and complex, embracing the domestic politics not only of the United Provinces but of the whole British Isles as well, in addition to the foreign affairs of the grand alliance in its Nine Years' War against France (1689–97). Moreover, with the death of Fagel in December 1688 and Dijkveld's return to the Netherlands eleven months later, Portland's position in the political entourage of the stadholder-king was unrivalled—and would remain so until the rise of Keppel and Heinsius later in the 1690s.

As first the Dutch Republic and then England declared war on France and James II's landing at Kinsale threatened counter-revolution from the west, Portland's main preoccupations during the spring and summer of 1689 were logistical. He was the principal organizer of the first allied expedition to Ireland: Marshal Schomberg, who commanded the invasion force, referred to him as effectively William III's war secretary. Early in August he inspected the troops at Chester before their embarkation, and in the same month he is mentioned as one of the four members of William's cabinet council, dealing with naval strategy. The expedition, however, had little success outside Ulster, and by December William had decided to take personal command of the next Irish campaign, sending Portland to the Netherlands to secure Dutch support. That support could by no means be taken for granted. Resentment was growing about the use of Dutch resources to fight British wars and in some quarters there were fears that William III's position as king was making him too powerful as stadholder in the republic. In December 1689 Amsterdam challenged his right of selecting its *schepenen* (aldermen) by sending the nominations not, as was usual, to William himself but to the provincial court of justice at The Hague; and when Portland arrived in the United Provinces in January 1690 he found himself lampooned in the public prints (one caricature showed him as an over-mighty English lord riding roughshod over Dutch freedom and trade) and attacked by the Amsterdam delegation in the states of Holland, who proposed barring him from his seat in the assembly on the grounds that he was now in the service of a 'foreign prince' (*An Account of the Passages in … the States of Holland … Concerning the Earl of Portland's Exclusion*, 1690, 4–5). Portland, however, ignored these attacks and by rallying the majority of the delegates against the anti-Orangists of Amsterdam he eventually reached a compromise with the city over the appointment of its magistrates in March. In the meantime, he was active on several other fronts too—conferring with ministers of the grand alliance at The Hague, hiring troops from the republic's north German neighbours to augment the Dutch army in the Low Countries, and securing the transport vessels, artillery, tents, and other equipment needed for William's forthcoming Irish campaign.

Portland returned to London early in April 1690 and two months later embarked with the king for Ireland. Promoted at his own request to the rank of lieutenant-general, he commanded his regiment of Dutch cavalry at the battle of the Boyne, entered Dublin five days later, and witnessed the subsequent capitulation of Waterford and Duncannon. His most significant contribution to the Williamite reconquest of Ireland, however, was diplomatic rather than military. After his initial victories and James II's flight to France, William had demanded the unconditional surrender of the Jacobite forces. But his failure in August to take Limerick weakened his position and during the following months he was persuaded by Portland and Ginckel (commander of the allied forces in Ireland after the king's return to England) to adopt a more conciliatory stance. During October Portland had talks in London with John Grady, representing the Jacobite peace party, and in his correspondence with Ginckel during the following winter and spring he repeatedly urged that favourable terms be offered to the Irish so that the war could be ended quickly and allied forces released for service in the Low Countries. Portland's cavalry (though not Portland himself) fought at Aughrim in July 1691, when the Jacobites were decisively defeated, and three months later the second siege of Limerick ended in a negotiated surrender. Reflecting the conciliatory tactics adopted by Portland and Ginckel, the treaty of Limerick (3 October 1691) included articles granting a measure of toleration to Irish Catholics and restoring lands to those who submitted to William and Mary—though both concessions were later jettisoned when the treaty came before the fiercely protestant Irish and English parliaments. As Portland soon learned, anti-Catholic legislation was the price to be paid for the Irish parliament's financial support of the continental war, and securing that support remained the first priority of his management of Irish affairs for most of the 1690s.

But if Ireland had to be taken in hand, so too did post-revolution Scotland. From March 1689, when the Scottish Convention Parliament met, William III delegated supervision of Scottish affairs largely to his confidant, while Portland relied in turn on the advice of William Carstares, the king's chaplain, whom he had known when Carstares was living as an exile in Holland during the 1680s. Portland's control of Scottish affairs was thus considerable and Burnet was not alone in considering that for much of the 1690s 'he had that nation ... wholly in his hands' (H. C. Foxcroft, ed., *A Supplement to Burnet's 'History of my Own Time'*, 1902, 415). He supported George Melville, first earl of Melville, as William's first secretary of state for Scotland, managed the ministerial reshuffles of 1692 and 1695–6 (bringing first James Johnstone and then Lord John Murray to power), and rode out the storms raised by the massacre of Glencoe and by the mismanagement of the Company of Scotland trading to Africa and the Indies. Even after his formal retirement from public office in 1699 he was still active in ensuring support for the ministry of the William Douglas, first duke of Queensberry, and Archibald Campbell, tenth earl of Argyll. Yet Portland never once set foot in Scotland and, no doubt for this reason, his grasp of the peculiarities of Scottish politics remained superficial. Like Carstares he aimed to reconcile what he took to be the country's rival religious parties—presbyterian and episcopalian—but he underestimated the importance of magnate groups driven by personal ambition.

The Nine Years' War and English politics Compared with his role in Irish and Scottish affairs, Portland's involvement in English politics developed more gradually. This was partly because William III relied at first on George Savile, first marquess of Halifax, for advice in this sphere, but also because Portland's own principal concern after the Irish campaign of 1690 was with the conflict in continental Europe. Every year from 1691 to 1697 he spent the spring and summer months with the king in the Low Countries, either on campaign or employed in the diplomacy and strategic planning that accompanied the fighting; while he was abroad he kept up a correspondence

with ministers in London about naval strategy and the co-ordination of Dutch and English fleet movements. Simply crossing the North Sea had its dangers: in January 1691 the yacht carrying William and Portland became fog-bound in icy waters off the Dutch coast and they spent sixteen hours in an open rowing-boat before reaching land at Goeree. Six months later Portland was with the allied army at Anderlecht, manoeuvring to prevent French forces from taking Halle; and in the two subsequent campaigns he fought at the indecisive battles of Steenkerke (3 August 1692 NS) and Landen (29 July 1693 NS), where he was wounded. In June 1695 he commanded a cavalry troop which routed French forces seeking to capture the supply lines of the allied camp at Beselare and—more importantly—brought his experience as a staff officer to bear on the meticulous preparations which preceded the siege of Namur. For the allies recapturing this town was one of the great successes of the land war and when the citadel surrendered on 1 September 1695 NS it was Portland who took charge of the defeated commander, Marshal Boufflers, arrested in retaliation for the imprisonment of Dutch garrisons at Diksmuide and Deinze a few weeks earlier.

Portland's military duties may have diverted his attention from English domestic politics for a while, but the larger demands of war soon made involvement in English affairs essential. From his network of informers in Europe he had been receiving intermittent intelligence of Jacobite activities since 1689, and early in May 1692 a flurry of reports confirmed that a French invasion to restore James II was imminent. Portland, who was in Holland at the time, was sent back to London with orders to co-ordinate counter-measures and an elaborate plan for arresting Jacobite suspects in the capital. In the event, the French fleet was defeated by a combined Anglo-Dutch force off Barfleur (19/29 May) and Portland spent the next three months discussing a projected counter-invasion of France—first at a council of war held in Portsmouth, then in correspondence with Daniel Finch, second earl of Nottingham, secretary of state (whose preference for a 'blue water' strategy at the expense of the Flanders land campaign he strongly opposed), and later in a further council at Nieuwpoort in Flanders. By September this project had been abandoned, but Portland continued to take responsibility for Britain's internal security. In 1694 he was supervising the reimbursement of spies, and in June considered a plan from Sir William Trumbull 'for preventing correspondence with France' (U. Nott. L., Portland MS PwA 1436). Then, in February 1696, after receiving repeated intelligence of a Jacobite plot to assassinate William III and initiate a general uprising backed by French arms, he persuaded the king to protect himself and organized the arrest and interrogation of the conspirators.

Portland did not, however, support the whig ministry's efforts to exploit the assassination scare for political advantage. When on 26 February 1696 the House of Lords debated the association with its confirmation of William as 'rightful and lawful king', Portland supported the proposal of the duke of Leeds (formerly Danby) to substitute a less controversial phrase, referring only to his 'right by law to the crown of this realm' (A. Browning, *Thomas Osborne Earl of Danby*, 1951, 1.533). But if Portland was not a party politician (as his parliamentary voting record earlier in the 1690s confirms), he was well aware of the indispensable part which parliament now played in the English political system. He regularly attended debates in the upper house and early in 1693 conveyed to William III the advice of Sir William Temple to approve the Triennial Bill (advice which the king at first ignored). It was at this time, too, that Robert Spencer, second earl of Sunderland, initiated an important correspondence with Portland, persuading him of the need for effective management of parliament in order to ensure support for the king's foreign policy. Together the two earls persuaded William III to make the ministerial changes which in the course of 1693 and 1694 brought the whig junto to power, and until Sunderland's fall from power at the end of 1697 they worked in tandem to establish a court interest in parliament, Sunderland distributing favours to MPs while Portland secured royal approval of appointments. For much of the 1690s, moreover, he exercised considerable patronage within the diplomatic service.

Inevitably there was resentment in Britain over the authority which Portland as a foreigner now exercised in the nation's affairs and over his growing wealth and status. 'Mynheer Benting … now rules over us', complained one pamphleteer, portraying him as the leader of a 'Cabal of Dutchmen' intent on subordinating British interests to those of the Netherlands ([N. Johnston], *The Dear Bargain*, 1688, 1690, repr. *Scarce and Valuable Tracts … Lord Somers*, ed. Sir W. Scott, 10, 1813, 374, 376), while in London coffee-houses there was talk of the fortune he was supposedly making from the sale of offices. William III's rejection of the place bill in January 1694 was attributed to Portland's malign influence (he had voted, and probably spoken, against the bill when it was first considered in the Lords a year earlier), and the Commons promptly passed a resolution condemning whoever had recommended the veto as 'Enemies to your Majesty and your kingdom' (*JHC*, 11.71–2). In April 1695 Portland was accused—without justification, it was later shown—of accepting a substantial bribe from the East India Company to influence legislation in its favour, and the king's attempt, a few months later, to grant him the Welsh lordships of Denbigh, Bromfield, and Yale provoked such an outcry in parliament about the prospect of a 'Dutch Prince of Wales' and of Britain becoming a 'colony to the Dutch' ([Robert Price], *Gloria Cambriae*, 1702, repr. *Scarce and Valuable Tracts … Lord Somers*, 11.387, 391), that William, on Portland's own suggestion, decided to withdraw the grant. Informing the Commons in January 1696, he added that he would 'find some other Way of shewing my Favour to him' (*JHC*, 11.409) and within a few months had given his confidant lands scattered across eight English counties.

Like other royal favourites, moreover, Portland was accused of sexual as well as political corruption. To Jacobite writers especially, William III was a usurper, presiding over 'a Court full of vice', and Portland was consequently portrayed as his 'bardash' or 'he-bedfellow' (*Poems on Affairs of State: Augustan Satirical Verse, 1660–1714*, 7 vols., 1963–75, 5.38, 60, 153, 221). It was a portrayal prompted by political opposition and xenophobia, and it should be said that there is no factual evidence of a homosexual relationship between him and the king. The charge seems never to have been made by Dutch pamphleteers before 1689; and even after that date, when it became one of the clichés of anti-court satire in England, it was not mentioned by any of those who had the opportunity to observe the royal household at first hand—including the younger Constantijn Huygens, who was quite frank about the sexual activities of courtiers. Not least, Portland's own shocked reaction to rumours later fabricated around William's friendship with Arnold Joost van Keppel was hardly the response of a man likely to condone sodomy, still less to practise it himself.

That Portland benefited materially from the king's favour cannot of course be doubted. Royal generosity combined with the salaries of office to make him a rich man—reputedly 'the richest subject in Europe' (*Memoirs of the Secret Services*, 62) by the time he was fifty. And as a man accustomed to managing his own wealth, he had a sound understanding of the changes in public finance which were occurring in England in the mid-1690s. He kept up a regular correspondence at this time with Charles Montagu, the reforming chancellor of the exchequer, and during 1696 was able to play an important part in resolving the monetary crisis which threatened to undermine the allied war effort. With the army in Flanders close to being disbanded for lack of money to pay soldiers and suppliers, Portland was ordered in late July back to London, where he sought to instil new energy into Charles Talbot, duke of Shrewsbury, and his fellow ministers and plunged into a series of urgent discussions with city financiers. He secured a loan of £20,000 from London Jewish lenders, and by 15/25 August could report a further £200,000 from the Bank of England—sufficient, as William III acknowledged, to 'bring us indeed into winter quarters' (Horwitz, 182).

But it was not sufficient for another full campaign. Exhaustion on both sides led to the opening of peace talks at Rijswijk (Ryswick) in May 1697, and when these became deadlocked William III decided to bypass the formalities by employing Portland to deal directly with a representative of Louis XIV. An approach was made to Marshal Boufflers, with whom Portland had become friendly after the fall of Namur and whose military rank he now shared, having been promoted general of horse in June. The two men met on 8 July NS at the village of Brucom, near Halle, midway between the opposing armies, and in a series of conversations held over the next three weeks were able to reach agreement on two specific points: first, that Louis would undertake not to assist William's enemies (implicitly including James II); and second, that he would withdraw his demand that a general amnesty be granted to the Jacobites. More generally the talks created an atmosphere of trust between the two monarchs and thus paved the way for the formal treaties, signed on 10/20 September 1697 at Rijswijk. Peace had at last been made made, and

Sunderland complimented Portland on 'being the instrument of it' (Sunderland to Portland, 10 Aug [1697], U. Nott. L., Portland MS PwA 1267/1–2).

Diplomacy and disillusion Although the treaties of 1697 brought one war to an end, they provided no security against the outbreak of another, threatened by the likely death of Carlos II, the childless king of Spain. Like Louis XIV, William III recognized that European peace depended on solving the problem of the Spanish succession and Portland spent much of his time and energy over the next three years in search of a settlement. In some ways, this was the zenith of his career, the point at which he became unmistakably a diplomat of European standing, as famous and respected in Paris as in The Hague and the German courts—and even, briefly, in London. Yet it was also a time when Portland experienced growing personal disillusion with his situation at court, eventually deciding in April 1699 to resign his offices and retire from public life. He had first told William of his wish to retire in the spring of 1697, giving as his reason 'les bontez que Vostre Majesté a pour un jeune homme' ('the kindesses which your majesty has for a young man') and their damaging effect on the king's reputation (Japikse, 1.1.197–9). The young man was Keppel, whose rise to favour during the 1690s had been viewed by Portland with mounting unease. Keppel may not have posed much of a threat to Portland's handling of royal policy: as the French ambassador to London was told in his instructions of March 1698, the new favourite had not until recently been involved in important matters of state. But he was unquestionably a serious rival for the king's friendship. So different in manner—Portland reserved and discreet, Keppel 'open and free in his conversation' (*Memoirs of the Secret Services*, 68)—the two men, in Burnet's words, 'grew ... to hate and oppose one another in everything; by which the king's affairs suffered much' (*Bishop Burnet's History*, 4.413). William was aware of their rivalry and sought to reassure his older confidant. In February 1697, a few weeks after Keppel had been raised to the peerage as earl of Albemarle, Portland was made a knight of the Garter—'to shew', as secretary Vernon noted, that 'he is still preferred a step above him' (J. Vernon, *Letters Illustrative of the Reign of William III*, ed. G. P. R. James, 3 vols., 1841, 1.209). In the following month he was appointed ranger of Windsor Great Park, with use of the lodge and an annual salary of £1500. Finally in June, when Portland pleading illness had retreated to Brussels, the king made use of a mutual friend, the prince de Vaudemont, to coax him back to his public duties.

By July the crisis of confidence between Portland and his sovereign had passed, or at least moderated. After negotiating with Boufflers he rejoined the king at the palace of Het Loo in Gelderland; and in October, shortly before returning to London, he was in The Hague holding discussions with the imperial ambassador, Auersperg, about the problem of the Spanish succession. This was now the first priority of William's foreign policy and was the reason for Portland's appointment in January 1698 as ambassador to France, with secret instructions to sound Louis XIV 's'il n'y auroit pas moien de trouver des expédiens pour prévenir une guerre que la mort du Roy d'Espagne sans enfans pouroit causer' ('whether some expedients could not be found to prevent a war breaking out on the death without issue of the king of Spain'; Japikse, 1.1.219). The embassy was as outwardly grand as the previous year's talks at Brucom had been modest and informal. The earl travelled with eighty servants and ninety carriage and saddle horses, and was joined by a distinguished entourage that included his own eldest son, Henry, Lord Woodstock, accompanied by his tutor, the Huguenot scholar Paul de Rapin-Thoyras, and, as secretary of legation, the poet Matthew Prior. The French were impressed by such magnificence and not least by the ambassador himself. 'Poli aux autres, fidèle à son maître, adroit en affaires' ('Courteous to others, faithful to his master, skilful in negotiation') was Saint-Simon's favourable estimate of Portland (*Mémoires*, ed. Y. Coirault, 8 vols., 1983–8, 1.413), while Hyacinthe Rigaud's portrait, for which he sat when in Paris, is equally sympathetic, the most vivid and humane of the various likenesses of him painted during his lifetime. In the serious business of the embassy, his initial demand, that James II and his court be removed from St Germain, was met with a blunt refusal. But better progress was made on the question of Spain. A series of meetings with Pomponne and Torcy moved cautiously towards the principle of a partition of the empire, while Portland proposed that the inheritance should pass to the young electoral prince of Bavaria, Joseph Ferdinand. No agreement was reached, but there was sufficient common ground for Count Tallard to be sent at the end of March on a return mission to London in order to continue negotiations directly with William III.

Portland himself returned to London in June. His role in the peace-making of 1697 combined with the personal success of his French embassy had made him a celebrated figure. In January 1698 he had been granted a lucrative estate in the parish of St Anne, Westminster, and now there was talk of new honours, even of a diplomatic mission to Madrid. Instead, however, he withdrew to the Netherlands, accompanying the king to Het Loo, where they were joined by Tallard and the Dutch grand pensionary Heinsius. Within weeks a draft treaty had been agreed, leaving most of the Spanish possessions to the Bavarian candidate. Ministers in London were informed of the terms by Portland towards the end of August, and on 24 September 1698 he and Tallard signed what was soon to be known as the first partition treaty. It proved, however, to be a short-lived solution. The death of the electoral prince in February 1699 necessitated a fresh round of talks, conducted now in London, in which Portland struggled to defend the Austrian candidate's claim to Spain and the Spanish Netherlands against the rising demands of Tallard on behalf of the dauphin. On 21 April os, while these negotiations were still in train, Portland informed the king once again of his determination to retire. His reasons, about which he said little, no doubt had to do with what William called his 'blind jealousy' of Albemarle (Macaulay, 6.2896). He was tired of the factions and intrigues which now divided the court, but it is likely that his decision was motivated by political as well as personal considerations. The fall of Sunderland in December 1697 had meant the collapse of their joint system of parliamentary management, as a series of weak ministries failed to sustain royal policy against a vigorous country opposition. Successive votes to reduce the strength of the armed forces, including in 1699 the disbanding of Portland's own regiment of Dutch horse, weakened his position in the negotiations with Tallard and deepened his sense of disillusion. 'I am so weary of the world', he wrote to Prior in March, 'that if there were cloisters in our religion I believe I should withdraw to one' (Grew, 359). Despite the king's efforts to dissuade him, Portland resigned his offices at court and in the army and was succeeded in June as groom of the stole by Henry Sidney, earl of Romney. In his diplomatic role, however, he was considered irreplaceable. 'Le bien et le repos de toutte l'Europe' ('The peace and well-being of all Europe'), William insisted (Japikse, 1.1.338), depended on his negotiation with Tallard, which continued during the summer at The Hague and later in London. Finally, on 21 February 1700 os, he and the French ambassador signed the second partition treaty, by which Spain's Italian lands were left to the Dauphin Louis and the rest of the Spanish empire to the Habsburg Archduke Charles.

Retirement　To some of his contemporaries the earl's prospects in retirement seemed bleak. 'My Lord Portland's *entre-deux* is a jest', wrote his former secretary Prior, 'and will give him all the uneasiness of a cast favourite without the quiet of a country gentleman' (L. G. Wickham Legg, *Matthew Prior*, 1921, 99). As a fallen courtier, he was indeed vulnerable to the continuing attacks of the country opposition in parliament. In December 1699 a hostile parliamentary committee reported on the various grants of confiscated Irish land made by William to his officers and friends, including the huge Clancarty estates given in 1697 to Portland (and then transferred to his son, Lord Woodstock); and in April 1700 the king was forced to consent to an Act of Resumption, placing all the property in the hands of public trustees. By this time, reports of the second partition treaty had come to the attention of parliament, provoking criticism both of its terms and of the king's failure to consult the privy council before concluding it. With William's permission Portland defended the treaty in the House of Lords on 15 March 1701, naming the English ministers with whom it had been discussed and inadvertently revealing the existence of the first treaty. The Commons' reaction was to vote for his impeachment and that of lords Somers, Orford (Edward Russell), and Halifax (Charles Montagu). There was delay and confusion, however, in drawing up the charges. In an atmosphere of growing tension between the two houses and of rising public agitation over parliament's failure to respond to the immediate threat posed by France's invasion of the Spanish Netherlands, the case against the four peers collapsed. On 24 June, Portland's impeachment was dismissed by the Lords because no articles had been exhibited against him.

Such attacks on Portland and the king probably had the effect of drawing them more closely together once more. They corresponded and continued to meet from time to time, especially during the last winter of William's life. On his deathbed, according to Burnet, he 'called for the earl of Portland, but before he came his voice quite failed, so he took him by the hand and carried it to his heart with great tenderness' (*Bishop Burnet's History*, 4.560). Even in the new reign, Portland's political activities continued to be noticed and his opinions to carry weight. As a Calvinist sympathetic to the fate of the Camisards during the revolt which broke out in the Cévennes in 1702, he conferred with the Dutch states general in 1704 about ways to assist them, while in 1706, at the height of the war against France, he was among those subscribing to a loan of £250,000 to the emperor. He still attended the House of Lords and his diplomatic advice continued to be sought, notably by Marlborough and Godolphin, for whom he served as an informal means of communication with the Dutch Republic.

For all his political awareness, however, the main focus of Portland's life during his last decade was on his family and estates. At Chiswick on 12 May 1700, almost twelve years after the death of his first wife, he married Jane Martha (1672–1751), widow of John Berkeley, third Baron Berkeley of Stratton, daughter of Sir John and Lady (Jane) Temple of East Sheen, and niece of Sir William Temple, the diplomat. Over the next nine years six children were born—four daughters and two sons—joining the children of his first marriage, who had been cared for during the 1690s by his sister Eleonora. The growing Bentinck household divided its time between Whitehall and Windsor, while summers were spent at Zorgvliet in Holland. In 1701 Portland arranged the grand tour of his eldest son, Lord Woodstock, who was married in 1704 to Lady Elizabeth Noel, daughter of Wriothesley Noel, second earl of Gainsborough, and his countess, Katherine Greville. He had once said that he would take his son away from England so 'that he might not learn debauchery in that country' (Grew, 203). Yet he evidently became reconciled to his adopted country, and it is striking that of his twelve surviving children no fewer than nine married into English noble or gentry families, and only two into those of the Netherlands.

On the death of William III, Portland's office as ranger of Windsor Great Park was given, through the influence of the Marlboroughs, to Edward Seymour, and with it went the use of the Windsor lodge. Portland then rented Bagshot Park from the earl of Arran for three years, before in 1706 acquiring Bulstrode in Buckinghamshire, where he devoted much of his energy to transforming and extending the gardens. He was a noted connoisseur of trees and plants and was well read in French and Italian garden literature. At Zorgvliet he had created a garden famous for its orangery and exotic plants, of which an illustrated catalogue was compiled, the *Codex Bentingiana*. Appointed in 1689 as superintendent of the royal gardens (a post that he continued to hold until William III's death), he had played a leading role in the design and development of the gardens of Het Loo and Dieren in Gelderland, working subsequently with George London and William Talman on those of Hampton Court and Windsor and absorbing French styles of garden design during his embassy to Paris in 1698. His own gardens at Bulstrode were thus not purely Dutch in character but a blend of Dutch and French, adapted to the English landscape. Their most idiosyncratic feature, a wilderness with winding paths, looked forward to the taste of the next generation.

Portland was at Bulstrode when he died of pleurisy on 23 November 1709, a month after the birth of his youngest daughter, Barbara. He was buried ten days later in the chapel of Henry VII at Westminster Abbey. Valued at over £850,000 on his death (Grew, 416), his English possessions passed to his son Lord Woodstock, created first duke of Portland in 1716; his Dutch estates, worth 1,562,670 guilders (£142,000), went to Willem, the eldest son of his second marriage and later an influential adviser of Prince William IV of Orange and his wife, Anne, daughter of George II. Portland's widow survived him by more than forty years and was appointed governess to the daughters of George II.

Looking back over Portland's career, what is immediately striking is the extraordinary range of his responsibilities—military and naval, diplomatic, financial, political, even horticultural—and the consistency and tenacity with which he undertook them. Driven by Calvinist convictions and undeniably ambitious for power and wealth, he was energetic, straightforward, and loyal: in Temple's judgement 'the best Servant I have ever known in Prince's or private family' (*The Works of Sir William Temple*, 2 vols., 1720, 1.401). As his extensive correspondence shows, moreover, he was capable not only of executing royal policy but of shaping it too. His initially limited command of the English language, his natural coldness and reserve, and his unwillingness to ingratiate himself—all of which he freely acknowledged—led some of his British contemporaries (and some historians since) to underestimate him. He was nicknamed 'the wooden fellow' (H. L. Snyder, ed., *Marlborough–Godolphin Correspondence*, 1975, 3.1215), dismissed as 'so dull an animal' (*Bishop Burnet's History*, 4.412n.). Yet such views were superficial. Those who knew him better respected him. And abroad, in France, the Netherlands, and Germany, where his accomplished French was the language of diplomacy, he was widely admired—'a model of grace … a dextrous negotiator and a finished gentleman' (Macaulay, 6.2804). In the end, he should be seen not simply in a Dutch or British context but as an international figure, a crucial player in William III's defence of the liberties of Europe.

HUGH DUNTHORNE and DAVID ONNEKINK

Sources M. E. Grew, *William Bentinck and William III* (1924) · *Correspondentie van Willem III en van Hans Willem Bentinck*, ed. N. Japikse, 5 vols. (The Hague, 1927–37) · U. Nott. L., Portland MSS, PwA 1–2870, Pw2A 1–29, PwV 50 · P. Grimblot, ed., *Letters of William III and Louis XIV and their ministers*, 2 vols. (1848) · P. C. Molhuysen and P. J. Blok, eds., *Nieuw Nederlandsch biografisch woordenboek*, 10 vols. (Leiden, 1911–37) [s.v. Bentinck] · GEC, *Peerage*, new edn · *Bishop Burnet's History* · J. P. Kenyon, *Robert Spencer, earl of Sunderland,* *1641–1702* (1958) · S. B. Baxter, *William III* (1966) · J. Carswell, *The descent on England: a study of the English revolution of 1688 and its European background* (1969) · J. I. Israel, ed., *The Anglo-Dutch moment: essays on the Glorious Revolution and its world impact* (1991) · T. B. Macaulay, *The history of England from the accession of James II*, new edn, ed. C. H. Firth, 6 vols. (1913–15) · H. Horwitz, *Parliament, policy and politics in the reign of William III* (1977) · P. W. J. Riley, *King William and the Scottish politicians* (1979) · P. Hopkins, *Glencoe and the end of the highland war* (1986); rev. edn (1998) · J. G. Simms, *Jacobite Ireland, 1685–1691* (1969) · J. D. Hunt and E. de Long, eds., *The Anglo-Dutch garden in the age of William and Mary* (1988) [special double issue of *Journal of Garden History*, 8/2–8/3 (1988)] · Portland–Heinsius correspondence, Nationaal Archief, The Hague, Archief Antonie Heinsius 3.01.19: 2189 · J. R. Jones, *The revolution of 1688 in England* (1972) · *DNB* · J. G. Simms, 'Williamite peace tactics, 1690–1691', *War and politics in Ireland, 1649–1730*, ed. D. W. Hayton and G. O. Brien (1986), 181–201 · W. Troost, *William III and the treaty of Limerick, 1691–1697* (Leiden, 1983) · J. Childs, *The Nine Years' War and the British Army, 1688–1697: the operations in the Low Countries* (1991) · *Calendar of the manuscripts of the marquis of Bath preserved at Longleat, Wiltshire*, 5 vols., HMC, 58 (1904–80), vol. 3 · *Report on the manuscripts of Allan George Finch*, 5 vols., HMC, 71 (1913–2003) · *CSP dom.*, 1689–1702 · C. Kirby, 'The four lords and the partition treaty', *American Historical Review*, 52 (1947), 477–90 · P.-E. Schazmann, *The Bentincks: the history of a European family* (1976) · *State papers and letters addressed to William Carstares*, ed. J. M'Cormick (1774) · W. H. L. Melville, ed., *Leven and Melville papers: letters and state papers chiefly addressed to George, earl of Melville … 1689–1691*, Bannatyne Club, 77 (1843) · A. J. Veenendaal, ed., *De briefwisseling van Anthonie Heinsius*, vols. 1–9 (1976–88) · *Memoirs of the secret services of John Macky*, ed. A. R. (1733) · *Journaal van Constantijn Huygens den zoon, 1688–1696* (1876) · W. Scott, ed., *A collection of scarce and valuable tracts … Lord Somers*, 2nd edn, 10 (1813) · W. Scott, ed., *A collection of scarce and valuable tracts … Lord Somers*, 2nd edn, 11 (1814)

Archives BL, corresp. and papers, Egerton MSS 1704–1756 · BL, Add. MSS 4236, 15892, 15902, 20806, 21505, 28942, 29547, 29592, 32681, 34515, 38499, 40060, 40771–40774, 40777, 41823, 46528, 50842, 57861, 61118, 61153, 61419, 61471 · U. Nott. L., corresp. and papers | BL, Egerton Charters 103–105, 8305 · BL, Egerton MSS 3324, 3522 · BL, letters to Herbert, Egerton MS 2621 · BL, corresp. with Lord Lexington, Add. MS 46525 · BL, letters to Jean Robethon, Stowe MSS 222–223, *passim* · BL, corresp. with Sir William Trumbull · BL, letters to Prince De Vaudemont, Add. MS 24205 · BL, corresp. with James Vernon · BL, corresp. with James Vernon the elder and Sir Joseph Williamson, Add. MS 69955 · Cumbria AS, Carlisle, letters to Lord Lonsdale · Leics. RO, corresp. with earl of Nottingham · Longleat House, Wiltshire, corresp. with Matthew Prior · NA Scot., corresp. with Melville, GD26 · Nationaal Archief, The Hague, Archief Antonie Heinsius, corresp. with Antonie Heinsius, 3.01.19: 2189 · NL Scot., corresp. with Tweeddale, MSS 14407–14408 · Northants. RO, corresp. with duke of Shrewsbury · Surrey HC, letters to Lord Somers, 371/14/K/1–26

Likenesses C. J. van Ceulen, oils, 1659, Amerongen Castle, Utrecht · J. F. van Douven, double portrait, oils, 1676 (with William of Orange), Amerongen Castle, Utrecht; repro. in Grew, *William Bentinck*, frontispiece · C. Netscher, oils, *c.*1680, Welbeck Abbey, Nottinghamshire · G. Kneller, oils, 1697, Welbeck Abbey, Nottinghamshire; copies at Middachten Castle, Gelderland, Rhoon, and Amerongen Castle, Utrecht · H. Rigaud, sketch for oil portrait, 1698, Louvre, Paris; repro. in Schazmann, *The Bentincks*, 144 · H. Rigaud, oils, 1698–9, Welbeck Abbey, Nottinghamshire; copy, Middachten Castle, Gelderland · studio of H. Rigaud, oils, *c.*1698–1699, NPG · studio of H. Rigaud, oils, 1698–9, NPG [*see illus.*] · S. du Bois, oils, 1702?, Middachten Castle, Gelderland · S. du Bois, oils, 1702, Welbeck Abbey, Nottinghamshire; copy, Indio, Devon · J. Houbraken, engraving, 1702 (after S. du Bois, 1702?), repro. in Grew, *William Bentinck*, 302 · attrib. C. Netscher, group portrait, oils, 1706 (with family); formerly at Welbeck Abbey, Nottinghamshire · J. Dringen, oils, Indio,

Devon • W. Faithorne, group portrait, mezzotint (*The impeached lords*), BM • C. Jervas, oils, Broadlands, Hampshire

Wealth at death English possessions valued at over £850,150; possessions in the Netherlands valued at 1,562,670 guilders or £142,000: BL, Egerton MS 1708, Nov 1709; Grew, *William Bentinck*, 416

Bentinck, Sir Henry John William (1796–1878), army officer, youngest son of Major-General John Charles Bentinck and his wife, Helena, daughter of Frederick Christian Rynhart Ginkel, fifth earl of Athlone, was born on 8 September 1796. He entered the Coldstream Guards as an ensign on 25 March 1813, advancing to lieutenant in the regiment and captain in the army on 18 January 1820. Curiously, until 1820, entries in the Army Lists showed him as 'Hon', apparently a clerical error for 'Henry'. On 2 February 1820, Bentinck became adjutant of the 1st battalion, retaining that appointment until he was promoted captain in the regiment and, by purchase, lieutenant-colonel in the army on 16 May 1829, without previously being major. He had married Renira Antoinette, daughter of Admiral Sir James Hawkins Whitshed, on 10 March 1829. On 23 November 1841, Bentinck was promoted colonel and appointed aide-de-camp to the queen. At about this time, he transferred to the 2nd battalion on its return from Canada. He progressed to major in the regiment on 9 November 1846 and, on 22 August 1851, to lieutenant-colonel by purchase.

Thus far, Bentinck had seen no active service. However, he was appointed brigadier-general in command of the guards brigade in the duke of Cambridge's 1st division with Lord Raglan's 'eastern army' (the Crimean expeditionary force) on 21 February 1854, the day before leaving England for Malta, Turkey, Bulgaria, and, at length, the Crimea. He was promoted major-general on 20 June and ceased thereby to be aide-de-camp to the queen. On 20 September he decisively ordered the brigade to advance uphill across the River Alma to carry the Russian artillery and infantry defences on Kourgane Hill, which dominated the post-road and barred the way to Sevastopol. Once the allies had begun siege operations from upland to the south of Sevastopol, he helped to repulse a strong Russian sortie on 26 October, the day after his brigade had been engaged on the plain of Balaklava after the charge of the light brigade. During the battle of Inkerman (5 November), when enemy troops attacked again, Bentinck was severely wounded in the right arm, as his brigade fought fiercely around the Sandbag Battery on the British right. Promoted local lieutenant-general on 22 January 1855, he replaced Sir George Cathcart (killed at Inkerman) in command of the 4th division; until 1 June, however, the after-effects of his wound and subsequent illness prevented him from taking effective control. He relinquished command on 10 October 1855, after the main part of Sevastopol had fallen, before returning to England. On 11 October he became colonel of the 28th foot, an appointment he retained until his death.

For his services in the Crimea, Bentinck received the war medal and four clasps (Alma, Inkerman, Balaklava, and Sevastopol) and the Sardinian and Turkish medals,

and was made a knight second class of the Mejidiye and commander of the Légion d'honneur. He was appointed KCB on 5 July 1855, and the award was made at British headquarters before Sevastopol on 27 August 1855 by Lord Stratford de Redcliffe, British ambassador to Turkey. Bentinck was promoted lieutenant-general on 2 April 1860, having surrendered his temporary rank in the Crimea, and served as groom in waiting to the queen until he was promoted general on 8 December 1867. He died at 22 Upper Grosvenor Street, London, on 29 September 1878 and was buried in Kensal Green cemetery on 5 October.

In the Crimea, Bentinck reminded Lieutenant A. M. Earle of 'a stud-groom' (Pemberton, 55) and another, anonymous, officer pronounced him 'the biggest fool ever' (Hibbert, 198), not unusual condemnations of a commander by disgruntled junior officers. Bentinck appears to have been conscientious, if uninspiring. He was not responsible for the initial, disjointed advance of the Scots fusiliers at the Alma, but he did direct the final, successful assault, which a captured Russian general described as 'trop majestueux' in execution. At Inkerman he displayed considerable personal bravery and ordered several important counter-attacks.　　JOHN SWEETMAN

Sources Army List • J. F. G. Ross-of-Bladensburg, *The Coldstream guards in the Crimea* (1897) • J. F. G. Ross-of-Bladensburg, *A history of the Coldstream guards* (1896) • W. B. Pemberton, *Battles of the Crimean War* (1962) • C. Hibbert, *The destruction of Lord Raglan* [1961] • CGPLA Eng. & Wales (1878) • DNB

Likenesses D. J. Pound, stipple and line engraving (after photograph by Watkins), NPG

Wealth at death under £7000: probate, 29 Oct 1878, *CGPLA Eng. & Wales*

Bentinck, Lord Henry William Cavendish-Scott- [*known as* Lord Henry Bentinck] (1804–1870), sportsman and politician, was born on 9 June 1804, the fourth son of William Henry Cavendish-Scott-Bentinck, the fourth duke of Portland (1768–1854), and his wife, Henrietta (*d.* 1844), elder daughter and coheir of Major-General John Scott of Balcomie, Fife. Lord Henry was educated at Christ Church, Oxford, where he took a second class in classics in 1826. His early life was devoted to fox-hunting. He was an intrepid horseman, but rather than join the fashionable set of fast Meltonian fox-hunters, Bentinck rode to hunt; his passion was the study and breeding of hounds. As Henry Chaplin wrote, he was 'the best brain ever given to hounds' (Londonderry, 198). His career as master of fox hounds began at the Rufford (Nottinghamshire), where he was master from 1834 to 1836. He was master of the Burton in Lincolnshire from 1842 to 1862. Like his brother Lord George Bentinck [*see* Bentinck, Lord (William) George Frederic Cavendish-Scott-] he was a fanatic, devoting obsessive energy and considerable wealth to hunting as his brother did to racing. At the Burton, he hunted six days a week, riding 30 miles or more to the meet from his home, at Welbeck Abbey in Nottinghamshire, each day. In winter he never saw Welbeck by daylight, except on Sundays; and Sundays he spent throwing balls to test the young hounds. His method of hunting, detailed in his treatise, *Foxhounds and their Handling in the Field* (*William*

Goodall's Method) (reprinted, ed. Viscount Chaplin, 1922), was to let hounds alone, leaving them to work out the fox's line for themselves, rather than the huntsman interfering to 'cast' hounds on to the line of the fox. This was practicable in a country like the Burton, where the mounted field was small and manageable, and Lord Henry, who never hunted hounds himself, exercised iron control over his huntsman.

Lord Henry was drawn into politics during the struggle over the corn laws in 1846, when his brother Lord George Bentinck led the protectionist opposition to Peel. He won North Nottinghamshire for the protectionists in the by-election (March 1846) occasioned by the promotion of Lord Lincoln to Peel's cabinet; the duke of Portland owned over 35,000 acres in the county and Lord Henry was also supported by Lincoln's estranged father, the duke of Newcastle, owner of a further 35,000 acres. After the sudden death of Lord George Bentinck in 1848, Henry Bentinck carried out his brother's political wishes, guaranteeing the loan of £25,000 which Lord George had pledged to Disraeli for the purchase of Hughenden, and, in 1849, campaigning vigorously for Disraeli's leadership.

Capable of great generosity, Henry Bentinck was, like his brother George, proud, stubborn, and prone to bitter quarrels. His feud with his elder brother (William) John Cavendish-Scott-*Bentinck, Lord Titchfield, who succeeded as fifth duke of Portland in 1854 (the eldest brother had died in 1824), led to Lord Henry's resignation as member for North Nottinghamshire in March 1857. He was succeeded in the seat by his brother-in-law, J. E. Denison. Disraeli appointed Denison speaker in 1857, much to Lord Henry's annoyance, but when Portland (who was a Peelite) proceeded to call in his loan to Disraeli, Bentinck hastened up to London to borrow money to ease the pressure on Disraeli. In 1860 he quarrelled with Disraeli too. 'Let me at least know on what ground I am deprived the friendship which was the pride and consolation of my life', Disraeli implored him; it seems more than likely that his plea went unanswered (Blake, 422–3).

After his retirement from parliament, Bentinck devoted himself once more to sport—hunting, deerstalking (at which he excelled, perfecting his aim by practising in summer with a pea-shooter), and salmon-fishing. In summer he played world-class whist at the Portland Club; he invented the call for trumps at whist known as Blue Peter. He was unmarried. He died suddenly at Tathwell Hall, his home on Henry Chaplin's estate near Louth in Lincolnshire, on 31 December 1870, and was buried in Tathwell church, Louth. The cause of death was heart failure, following a hard day's shooting.   JANE RIDLEY

Sources Marchioness of Londonderry [E. H. Chaplin Vane-Tempest-Stewart], *Henry Chaplin: a memoir* (1926) · Duke of Portland, *Memories of racing and hunting* (1935) · 'Lord Henry Bentinck: a memoir', *Baily's Magazine*, 19 (1870–71), 288–93 · R. Blake, *Disraeli* (1966) · *Benjamin Disraeli letters*, ed. J. A. W. Gunn and others (1982–), vol. 5 · Boase, *Mod. Eng. biog.*
Archives Notts. Arch., corresp. and papers relating to stables and kennels at Welbeck and Burton | Bodl. Oxf., letters to Benjamin Disraeli · Bodl. Oxf., Hughenden MSS · W. Sussex RO, letters to duke of Richmond
Likenesses R. Dighton, engraving, repro. in Duke of Portland, *Memories of racing and hunting* · photograph, repro. in Marchioness of Londonderry, *Henry Chaplin*
Wealth at death under £500,000: probate, 19 Jan 1871, CGPLA Eng. & Wales

Bentinck, John Albert (1737–1775), naval officer and inventor of mechanical devices, was born on 29 December 1737, the second son of William, Count Bentinck (1704–1774) and Countess Charlotte Sophie of Aldenburg (1715–1800), and grandson of Hans Willem *Bentinck, first earl of Portland. His parents separated when he was about a year old and he never knew his mother. He went to sea at the age of fourteen in the *Centurion*, and in June 1753 he sailed to Newfoundland as midshipman in the *Penzance* (44 guns).

On 21 July 1757 Bentinck was appointed third lieutenant of the *Arc de Ciel*, and on 9 August third lieutenant of the *Nottingham*. He joined the *Dorsetshire* (70 guns) as fourth lieutenant on 6 February 1758 and took part in the capture of the *Raisonnable* on 12 May. He was appointed commander of the sloop *Fly* on 18 May and joined the squadron covering Marlborough's landing at St Malo. Off Emden in September he took the extraordinary step of arresting his superior officer, Captain Henry Angel, for an alleged sexual relationship with his lieutenant, but the allegations were later withdrawn. On 17 October Bentinck was promoted captain of the *Dover*, which he joined on 9 March 1759, on Baltic convoy duty, before moving to the frigate *Niger* (32 guns) on 27 October. In April 1760 the *Niger* captured the *Brocanteur*, a French brig laden with sugar and indigo, and retook the merchant ship *York*. She came across the French ship *Diadème* (74 guns), escorting storeships to Martinique, on 16 May and tailed and harried her until the next day, when Bentinck was obliged to break off the engagement to repair damage to his ship. Off Ushant on 25 May the *Niger* had the good luck to capture the privateer *Jason* (8 guns), and, on another cruise on 27 November, she took the *Epreuve* (14 guns).

In August 1762 Bentinck got into trouble for ignoring his orders to cruise off Bordeaux, and going off in search of prizes, and was superseded in the command of the *Niger*, 'not only on account of his own ill conduct but as an example to deter other officers from behaving in the like manner' (minutes of the Admiralty board, 24 Aug 1762, PRO, ADM 3/70). But his considerable 'interest' ensured his career was not damaged, and on 1 November 1762 he was appointed to the *Anson*, and very shortly afterwards to the *Torbay*, in which he finished the war.

On 17 July 1763 Bentinck married Renira de Tuyll (1744–1792), daughter of John, Baron de Tuyll de Serooskerken, and their son William (1764–1813), who became an admiral, was born the next year. After about eighteen months of marriage Bentinck wrote to Rousseau, introducing himself and his wife as readers of *Emile* and asking him to offer some advice to Renira, who 'cannot bear the shortest separation' (Le Blond, 2.64)—a serious problem for the wife of a sailor. The great *philosophe* obliged, and

John Albert Bentinck (1737–1775), by Mason Chamberlin, 1775 [left, with his son William Bentinck]

subsequently became godfather to the Bentinck's first daughter, Sophie. They also had two more daughters and another son.

His father's influence with the duke of Newcastle ensured that Bentinck was elected unopposed as MP for Rye in 1761. In 1765 he switched his allegiance to the Rockingham whigs and got himself appointed to the *Dragon* on 6 May 1766. But he took little part in politics and spoke only once in the house, on 6 March 1765, during a debate on discovering longitude at sea. He also paid little attention to his constituents, and lost his seat in 1768, the same year he succeeded his brother as a count of the Holy Roman empire.

Bentinck's greatest success was as an inventor and designer of improvements to many mechanical devices, especially those for use in ships. His improved pulley blocks were, he claimed, lighter, smoother-running, cheaper, and more durable than previous types. 'Bentinck shrouds' were developed to support the masts more securely, and other innovations in rigging and sails were represented by the Bentinck boom and by triangular mainsails simply known as Bentincks. He also devised an ingenious method for determining the trim of a ship, a new capstan, an improved plough, and a machine for pulling up trees which he christened 'Archimedes'. Several of his nautical improvements were given trials in British ships, but Bentinck's most important innovation was the Coles–Bentinck pump, which he developed in collaboration with William Coles between 1767 and 1774. A much more efficient and reliable version of the standard chain-pump, it was adopted for use in all Royal Navy ships.

Bentinck was elected a fellow of the Royal Society on 20 June 1765. In October 1773 Benjamin Franklin came to his ship at Portsmouth, the *Centaur* (74 guns), which he had commanded since 25 October 1770, to test the theory of stilling waves by pouring oil onto the sea. Bentinck died suddenly on 23 September 1775. Two years later he was praised by James Fordyce in his highly influential *Addresses to Young Men* as a man of 'much knowledge and

many liberal acquirements' and a 'masculine character in an uncommon degree' (J. Fordyce, *Addresses to Young Men*, 1777, 2.226).   RANDOLPH COCK

Sources corresp. of Count Bentinck, 1752–9, BL, Egerton MS 1727 · copy of the scheme book of the late John Albert Bentinck esq., NMM, SPB/33 · commission and warrant books, PRO, ADM 6/18, 19, 20 · minutes of the admiralty board, 24 Aug 1762, PRO, ADM 3/70 · L. B. Namier, 'Bentinck, John', HoP, *Commons, 1754–90* · U. Nott. L., third duke of Portland MSS, Pw F673–716 · T. J. Oertling, *Ships' bilge pumps: a history of their development, 1500–1900* (1996) · A. Le Blond, *Charlotte Sophie, Countess Bentinck: her life and times, 1715–1800*, 2 vols. (1912) · *Annual Register* (1775) · W. H. Smyth, *The sailor's wordbook: a dictionary of nautical terms* (1867) · captains' letters, PRO, ADM 1/1489–1496

Archives NMM, notebook, SPB/33 | BL, corresp., mainly with father, Count William Bentinck, Egerton MS 1727 · U. Nott. L., letters to his father, W. Bentinck · U. Nott. L., letters to third duke of Portland and other MSS

Likenesses M. Chamberlin, oils, 1775, NMM [*see illus.*]

Bentinck, (William) John Cavendish-Scott- [*formerly* Lord John Bentinck], **fifth duke of Portland** (1800–1879), recluse, son of William Henry Cavendish-Bentinck, fourth duke (1768–1854), who in 1795 assumed the additional surname of Scott by royal licence, and Henrietta (d. 1844), eldest daughter and coheir of Major-General John Scott of Balcomie, Fife, was born in London on 17 September 1800. Lord (William) George Frederic Cavendish-Scott-*Bentinck and Lord Henry William Cavendish-Scott-*Bentinck were his brothers. Known as Lord John Bentinck, he served in the army from 1818, becoming lieutenant and captain in the Grenadier Guards in 1830. On the death of his elder brother, William Henry Cavendish-Scott-Bentinck (4 March 1824), he succeeded as marquess of Titchfield, and also replaced him as tory MP for King's Lynn, serving until 1826, when he gave place to his uncle, Lord William Bentinck. He succeeded to the dukedom on 27 March 1854, but did not take the oaths and his seat in the House of Lords until 5 June 1857. From 1859 until his death he was deputy lieutenant for Nottinghamshire. As head of the Portland family, he nominated a trustee to represent the Harley family on the British Museum trust. Throughout life he was an adherent of the tory party, but did not distinguish himself as a debater in either house of parliament. The turf and the management of his large estates chiefly occupied his time, particularly the grounds of Welbeck Abbey: his hothouses and greenhouses were reputed the best in the kingdom. Among the extensive building works, which were unfinished at his death, were a series of tunnels and a suite of underground rooms, including a chapel and a ballroom. In the 1830s he courted the singer Adelaide Kemble, but thereafter lived an isolated life, unmarried, seeing little or no society. It was rumoured that he even refused to allow the workpeople engaged on the improvements to his estates to show any sign of recognition on meeting him. His reputation as an eccentric recluse was posthumously enhanced by the publication of the memoirs of his relative Lady Ottoline Morrell. He was a munificent donor to various charities, while his constant building programmes provided much employment. He died on 6 December 1879 at Harcourt House, 19 Cavendish Square, London, and was buried on

(William) John Cavendish-Scott-Bentinck [Lord John Bentinck], **fifth duke of Portland** (1800–1879), by Richard Dighton

the 12th at Kensal Green cemetery with the utmost simplicity. As his younger brother, Henry William, had died without male issue on 31 December 1870, the title devolved upon the duke's cousin, William John Arthur Charles James Cavendish-Bentinck.

J. M. RIGG, *rev.* K. D. REYNOLDS

Sources GEC, *Peerage* · Boase, *Mod. Eng. biog.* · D. J. Bradbury, *Welbeck and the fifth duke of Portland* (1989) · *Men, women and things: memories of the duke of Portland* (1937)
Archives U. Nott. L., corresp. and papers | Northumbd RO, corresp. with William Sample · Notts. Arch., letters to William Cripwell and Charles Neale · U. Durham L., letters to Maria, Lady Grey · U. Nott. L., letters to sixth and seventh viscounts Galway · U. Nott. L., letters relating to building work at Hyde Park Gardens
Likenesses R. Dighton, drawing; Sothebys 24 Nov 1977, lot 134 [*see illus.*] · portrait, Royal Collection
Wealth at death under £1,500,000 effects in England: probate, 12 March 1880, *CGPLA Eng. & Wales* · £185,083 11s. 1d. effects in Scotland: 31 March 1880, *CCI*

Bentinck, Margaret Cavendish [*née* Lady Margaret Cavendish Harley], **duchess of Portland** (1715–1785), collector of art and natural history specimens and patron of arts and sciences, was born on 11 February 1715 in London, the only surviving child of Edward *Harley, later second

earl of Oxford (1689–1741), and his wife, Henrietta Cavendish *Harley (1694–1755), daughter of John *Holles, duke of Newcastle upon Tyne (1662–1711), and Lady Margaret Cavendish (1661–1716). The marriage of Margaret's parents in 1713 had been eagerly sought by the bridegroom's father, Robert *Harley, first earl of Oxford. The bride brought with her great wealth, along with the Cavendish estates.

Margaret Harley soon became a favourite of the literary circle surrounding the Harleys. Matthew Prior addressed verses to her when she was five beginning, 'My noble, lovely, little Peggy', which have often been described as the finest poem to a child in English. As an infant Margaret was painted with her mother by Bernard Lens III (1681–1740), who subsequently gave her art lessons. To her marriage, on 11 June 1734, to William Bentinck, second duke of Portland (1709–1762), she brought a dowry of £20,000, about half the value of her husband's estates. Her parents had considered many offers made to them for her hand, and fixed on Portland as the candidate least prone to fashionable vices. Fortunately for the marriage, the duke, unlike Margaret's father and two sons, managed to avoid ruinous expense.

The couple settled at Bulstrode, near Gerrards Cross in Buckinghamshire, where the duchess paid special attention to the gardens. For the next fifty years she devoted her time and energy, and much of her wealth, to the formation of an immense collection embracing natural history, in its broadest sense, and the fine arts, stored at Bulstrode. It was, eventually, the largest in Britain, and possibly in Europe, exceeding that of Sir Hans Sloane deposited in the British Museum. She developed a passion for botany and cultivated the friendship of the plantsman Philip Miller (1691–1771) and the botanical illustrator Georg Dionysius Ehret (1708–1770), who produced for her many of his most notable paintings of British plants. She also employed John Lightfoot (1735–1788), the naturalist, as chaplain and librarian. Together they created a herbarium, now at Kew. One of her special interests lay in seashells: through Peter Collinson (1694–1768) she obtained drawings of American shells by William Bartram (1739–1823). Her fondness for botany also brought her into contact with Joseph Banks and Daniel Solander, who visited her after their return from Cook's first voyage. The duchess kept bees and hares, as well as maintaining an aviary and a menagerie.

To care for her five surviving children (a daughter was to die aged sixteen), the duchess employed Elizabeth Elstob (1683–1756), the pioneering Anglo-Saxon scholar, as governess from 1739 until her death. From the age of seventeen Margaret had been on close terms with Elizabeth Robinson (1720–1800), better known as Mrs Montagu, 'Queen of the Blues'. Together they engaged in many pursuits, intellectual and social, until their relationship declined about 1753. Another friend was the poet Edward Young (1683–1765), for whom the duchess tried unsuccessfully to obtain a deanery from the duke of Newcastle. Young was likewise unable to persuade her into admiring the novels of his friend Samuel Richardson; late in life she

Margaret Cavendish Bentinck [Lady Margaret Cavendish Harley], **duchess of Portland** (1715–1785), by Joseph Brown, pubd 1861 (after Christian Friedrich Zincke, 1738)

expressed her much greater delight in Fanny Burney's work *Cecilia* (*Diary and Letters*, 2.254).

Mary Delany (1700–1788) was a close friend from youth. Through Mary's brother, who lived near Wootton Hall, Northampton, the duchess met and generously befriended Jean Jacques Rousseau who took refuge there for a few months in 1766–7. She sent him plants and books, and in September 1766 he joined her on an expedition to the Peak District in search of wild plants. After the death of the duke in 1762 and of her own husband in 1768, Mrs Delany passed every summer at Bulstrode, where in 1772 she devised her method of cutting flowers in paper, allegedly deceiving the duchess with her initial collage into taking it for a real geranium. The two women botanized and ornamented a grotto at Bulstrode with an ever-increasing collection of shells. The duchess spent her winters in London, where she created a 'museum' of natural curiosities at her house in the Privy Garden, Whitehall. She also made Mrs Delany an interest-free loan of £400 to enable her friend to buy a house in London.

The most famous item in the duchess of Portland's huge collection was acquired in 1784, when she bought the so-called 'Portland vase', from Sir William Hamilton. She paid £2000 for the vase and three other items; sold at her death, it was bought back by the third duke for £1029. The vase was loaned in 1810 to the British Museum, where it remains.

The duchess died at Bulstrode after a short illness on 17 July 1785. Mary Delany was left to the kindness of George III and Queen Charlotte, who had often visited Bulstrode,

as well as receiving the duchess at Windsor. The duchess's huge collection of works of art and virtu was disposed of at a sale in 1786 lasting thirty-eight days. The aim was to recoup the family fortunes, drained by the electioneering expenses of her elder son and the high living of the younger. Four of the duchess's children survived to adulthood: Elizabeth (1735–1825) married Thomas *Thynne, later first marquess of Bath (1734–1796), and was lady of the bedchamber to Queen Charlotte; Henrietta (1737–1827), married George Grey, later fifth earl of Stamford (1737–1819); the statesman, William Henry Cavendish Cavendish-*Bentinck, third duke of Portland (1738–1809), married Lady Dorothy Cavendish (1750–1794), daughter of the fourth duke of Devonshire; and Edward Charles (1744–1819) married Elizabeth Cumberland (*d.* 1837).

PAT ROGERS

Sources *The autobiography and correspondence of Mary Granville, Mrs Delany*, ed. Lady Llanover, 1st ser., 3 vols. (1861) · *The autobiography and correspondence of Mary Granville, Mrs Delany*, ed. Lady Llanover, 2nd ser., 3 vols. (1862) · S. Harcstark Myers, *The bluestocking circle: women, friendship, and the life of the mind in eighteenth-century England* (1990) · *Calendar of the manuscripts of the marquis of Bath preserved at Longleat, Wiltshire*, 5 vols., HMC, 58 (1904–80) · *The correspondence of Edward Young, 1683–1765*, ed. H. Pettit (1971) · A. Dobson, 'Prior's Peggy', *Rosalba's journal and other papers* (1915), 95–128 · Walpole, *Corr.* · *Diary and letters of Madame D'Arblay*, ed. [C. Barrett], 2 (1842) · *The correspondence of Jonathan Swift*, ed. H. Williams, 5 vols. (1963–5) · A. S. Turberville, *A history of Welbeck Abbey and its owners*, 2 vols. (1938–9) · Madame D'Arblay [F. Burney], *Memoirs of Doctor Burney*, 3 (1832) · J. Lees-Milne, *Earls of creation: five great patrons of eighteenth-century art* (1962) · *Elizabeth Montagu, the queen of the blue-stockings: her correspondence from 1720 to 1761*, ed. E. J. Climenson, 2 vols. (1906) · D. E. Allen, *The naturalist in Britain: a social history*, 2nd edn (1994) · A. B. Shteir, *Cultivating women, cultivating science: Flora's daughters and botany in England, 1760–1860* (1996)

Archives U. Nott. L., corresp. and papers | BL, letters to Thomas Birch, Sir Hans Sloane, and others · Hunt. L., Montagu MSS

Likenesses B. Lens, double portrait, *c.*1717 (with her mother) · M. Dahl, pastels, *c.*1723; formerly at Welbeck Abbey · C. F. Zincke, enamel miniature, 1738, Welbeck Abbey · J. Brown, engraving, pubd 1861 (after enamel by C. F. Zincke, 1738), NPG [*see illus.*] · T. Hudson, portrait; fomerly at Welbeck Abbey

Bentinck, Ruth Mary Cavendish- [*née* Ruth Mary St Maur] (**1867–1953**), women's suffragist and socialist, was born in Tangier on 21 October 1867, the illegitimate daughter of Edward Adolphus Ferdinand *St Maur, Earl St Maur (1835–1869), eldest son of the twelfth duke of Somerset [*see under* St Maur, Edward Adolphus], and Rosina Elizabeth Swan (*d.* 1872), daughter of a bricklayer and a Gypsy. Shortly after her birth she and her mother were brought to England. In 1869 her father died of a lung tumour, and Rosina and her children (she had given birth to a son, Richard Harold, in 1869) came under the care of the duke and duchess of Somerset. In 1872 Rosina married François Tournier of Bordeaux, but died shortly afterwards of consumption. The children became the informally adopted wards of their Somerset grandparents (the relationship was also acknowledged in their surname, St Maur), living with them mainly at Bulstrode Park in Buckinghamshire, Stover Lodge in Devon, and in London. Although suffering the social stigma of illegitimacy, Ruth received a good private education and was introduced into aristocratic society.

In 1885 the duke died, leaving Ruth St Maur a fortune of £80,000, and she went to live with her aunt, Lady Guendolen Ramsden, in Upper Brook Street, Mayfair. She began to take an interest in social questions at this time, and in the condition of the poor. In 1887 she made her début in society, creating a stir by her combination of wealth, striking good looks, and outspoken wit, which did much to overcome the disadvantages of her birth. In the course of her first season she met, and on 8 August 1887 married, (William George) Frederick Cavendish-Bentinck (1856–1948), barrister, a great-grandson of the third duke of Portland. The young couple received the castle on Brownsea Island as a wedding present; they travelled widely in Europe and the Mediterranean, and after a period of financial difficulty consequent on the death of Frederick's father, settled at 78 Harley Street, a house owned by Frederick's wealthy benefactor and cousin Lucy, Lady Howard de Walden. They continued to travel and to visit widely among friends and relatives, meeting both royalty and Fabian socialists.

Ruth Cavendish-Bentinck grew increasingly active politically, becoming involved with a girls' club in the East End of London, supporting the Bryant and May matchgirls' strike, and helping Beatrice Webb with the reform of the poor law. She came to know Beatrice and Sidney Webb closely, and was a friend of Keir Hardie and R. B. Cunninghame Graham, as well as many other socialists. She contributed to such papers as the *Socialist Review* and the *Labour Leader*, and took a strong radical line over such matters as the Second South African War and Lloyd George's budget, as well as being a confirmed anti-vaccinationist. Her labour movement activities involved her particularly with the Women's Trade Union League, and later the National Federation of Women Workers, and in 1911 she helped Ben Tillett organize the dockers' strike. At the same time she continued to move in high society, although she did not always meet with its approval, particularly on the part of her husband's family (her husband remained a lifelong Conservative). Her attitudes in this respect always remained contradictory.

Ruth Cavendish-Bentinck also became increasingly active in the campaign for women's suffrage. In this she was to some extent following in family tradition: Caroline Norton, the campaigner for married women's rights, was a great-aunt, and Lady Guendolen Ramsden was also a supporter of women's suffrage. Ruth Cavendish-Bentinck's main sympathies came to lie with the militant Women's Social and Political Union, and she frequently spoke publicly and demonstrated on their behalf, on one occasion parading between sandwich-boards outside the House of Commons. However, she herself was never actually arrested for militant action, and she did maintain friendly relations with non-militants. In 1913, with Florence de Fonblanque, she founded the Qui Vive Corps, which was intended to be a sort of suffragist 'flying squad', with its own uniform (brown with a green cockade and badge). Members were pledged to turn out at any time to support suffrage activity, but without the use of militant tactics. It is unclear how active this organization proved to be.

In 1909 Ruth Cavendish-Bentinck established the Cavendish-Bentinck Library as a subscription library for suffragists, collecting not only feminist classics and works of antiquarian interest, but up-to-the-minute publications such as Havelock Ellis's *Studies in the Psychology of Sex* (the future Lord Rhondda, being unable because of censorship to buy a copy, had to ask his daughter, a member of the Cavendish-Bentinck Library, to borrow it for him). The library eventually became part of the Women's Service Library (now the Women's Library), and Ruth Cavendish-Bentinck maintained an active interest in it until her death.

In the First World War, Ruth Cavendish-Bentinck campaigned for women's war work, although she was highly critical of the war mentality; her elder son was severely wounded at Mons. After the war she became an enthusiastic supporter of the Soviet Union, especially in the 1930s, when she joined with Beatrice Webb in demonstrating the necessity and legitimacy of the Moscow trials; the Nazi–Soviet pact of 1939–41 appears to have shaken her confidence in Stalin only briefly. In the Second World War she and her husband had to move out of their Harley Street house into a flat, but otherwise suffered little. Despite differences in temperament and politics they had been a devoted couple. However, after the war her husband's health declined, and he died in 1948. Ruth Cavendish-Bentinck survived him by five years, dying at her home, 36 Harley House, Marylebone Road, London, on 28 January 1953. She was survived by four children (a fifth had died in infancy); her elder son eventually became the eighth duke of Portland and was succeeded by his brother Victor Frederick William Cavendish-*Bentinck (1897–1990). DAVID DOUGHAN

Sources J. Colville, *Strange inheritance* (1983) · *The Times* (3 Feb 1953) · autograph letter collection, Women's Library, London · library committee minutes, Women's Library, London · Viscountess Rhondda [M. H. T. Mackworth], *This was my world* (1933), 127 · *The Times* (2 Feb 1953) · m. cert. · d. cert. · Burke, *Peerage* (1939)

Archives Women's Library, London, corresp.; minutes of library committee

Likenesses photograph, repro. in Colville, *Strange inheritance* · photograph, Women's Library, London

Wealth at death £38,258 14s. 10d.: probate, 12 March 1953, CGPLA Eng. & Wales

Bentinck, Victor Frederick William Cavendish- [known as Bill Bentinck], **ninth duke of Portland** (1897–1990), diplomatist and businessman, was born on 18 June 1897 at 16 Mansfield Street, London. He was the younger son and third of the four children of (William George) Frederick Cavendish-Bentinck (1856–1948), barrister, who managed the ducal family's Marylebone estate, and his wife, Ruth Mary Cavendish-*Bentinck (1867–1953), who was the illegitimate daughter of Edward Adolphus Ferdinand *St Maur, Earl St Maur [see under St Maur, Edward Adolphus, twelfth duke of Somerset], a son of the duke of Somerset, and was reputed to have Gypsy blood. Bill Bentinck was educated at Wellington College, but left at seventeen without making a mark and in August 1916 was appointed honorary attaché at the British legation at Christiania (Oslo). In 1918 he enlisted and trained with the household

Victor Frederick William Cavendish-Bentinck [Bill Bentinck], ninth duke of Portland (1897–1990), by Bassano, 1947

brigade but saw no active service. He entered the diplomatic service in 1919, missing the chance of university education, and was posted as third secretary to the legation at Warsaw. It was as ambassador at Warsaw twenty-seven years later that he ended a diplomatic career in which he achieved special distinction as chairman of the wartime joint intelligence committee (1939–45). In 1922 he began work in the Foreign Office and took charge of administrative arrangements for the Lausanne conference before moving to the embassy in Paris as second secretary. There in 1924 he contracted a marriage that soon cast a shadow over a very promising career. His wife, Clothilde, was the daughter of James Bruce Quigley, a lawyer from Kentucky; her lifestyle was extravagant and she had a talent for quarrelling with other diplomatic wives. Bentinck was a conciliator by nature, though well able to fight his corner. His tall, stooping figure and rather myopic look belied the resolution he displayed in a crisis.

Back in the Foreign Office in 1925, Bentinck served in the League of Nations department and had a useful role at the Locarno conference. He was promoted first secretary and sent back to Paris in 1928; but, as his domestic problems worsened, assignments grew shorter and further from the 'inner circle': Athens in 1932 was followed by Santiago in 1933. In 1937, however, he was recalled to the Foreign Office as assistant in the Egyptian department and there acquired experience of handling military matters. In the summer of 1939 his wife left without warning for the USA, taking their two children—a boy and a girl.

Her departure coincided with the high point of his diplomatic career, when the Foreign Office, which had been reluctant to pool intelligence with the armed services, appointed him chairman of the joint industrial council and he found himself, as a civilian and relatively junior, reporting to the chiefs of staff. His perceptiveness and tact enabled him to overcome service rivalries and weld the joint industrial council into a highly effective instrument. He was appointed CMG in 1942 and promoted counsellor to head the newly created services liaison department of the Foreign Office.

Despite wartime success, Bentinck's diplomatic career was doomed. He had formed a close friendship with a Canadian, Kathleen Elsie, widow of Arthur Richie Tillotson and daughter of Arthur Barry of Montreal, but his absent wife refused to divorce him. He explained his difficulties to the Foreign Office, which persuaded him in July 1945 to take the key post of ambassador to Poland, a country which had fallen under Soviet control. The communist-dominated government did its utmost to sabotage his mission and in February 1947 the Foreign Office withdrew him and applied to Brazil for his *agrément* as ambassador. In March his suit for divorce came before the court and was exploited by his wife to discredit him. The resultant publicity obliged the Foreign Office to withdraw the request for *agrément*. He then resigned, thus forfeiting his pension under Treasury regulations. The Court of Appeal finally granted his divorce and in July 1948 he married Kathleen Tillotson.

Bentinck had lost no time in finding remunerative work as vice-chairman of the committee of industrial interests in Germany, becoming chairman in 1949. In addition to advancing the interests of major British companies such as Unilever, he formed close connections with leading German companies, such as Bayer AG. He promoted the German and Belgian nuclear industries and was awarded a high German decoration (Bundesverdienstkreuz). On the death of his elder brother in 1979, he became the ninth duke of Portland; but he inherited neither land nor capital, since the entail had been broken eight years previously by the seventh duke. His son, William, had died of heart failure in 1966, leaving no children. When he himself died at his home, 21 Carlyle Square, Chelsea, London, on 30 July 1990, the dukedom created in 1716 became extinct.   ROBERT CECIL, *rev.*

Sources P. Howarth, *Intelligence chief extraordinary: the life of the ninth duke of Portland* (1986) · *The Times* (31 July 1990) · personal knowledge (1996) · private information (1996)
Likenesses Bassano, photograph, 1947, NPG [*see illus.*]
Wealth at death £352,414: probate, 19 Oct 1990, *CGPLA Eng. & Wales*

Bentinck, William Henry Cavendish Cavendish-, third duke of Portland (1738–1809), prime minister, was born on 14 April 1738, the eldest son of William Bentinck, second duke of Portland (1709–1762), courtier and landowner, and his wife, Lady Margaret Cavendish Harley (1715–1785), the only daughter and heir of the second earl of Oxford [*see* Bentinck, Margaret Cavendish, duchess of Portland]. Styled marquess of Titchfield until his father's

William Henry Cavendish Cavendish-Bentinck, third duke of Portland (1738–1809), by Sir Thomas Lawrence, completed 1792

death, he was educated at Westminster School from 1747 to 1754 and at Christ Church, Oxford, from 1755 to 1757. In 1755 he informally assumed the additional surname of Cavendish (which he already bore as a forename), but he did not obtain a royal licence legally to adopt the name until 5 October 1801. From December 1757 to October 1761 he made a grand tour of Poland, Germany, and Italy. Shortly before his return home he was elected MP for Weobley on the interest of his brother-in-law Lord Weymouth. He made no mark in the Commons, and his political career did not commence in earnest until he succeeded to the dukedom on 1 May 1762, aged only twenty-four.

The making of a Rockingham whig, 1762–1782 Portland's father, a court whig, had not been an active politician. The young duke, in contrast, was desperate to prove his credentials as an opponent of the alleged increase in royal power in the new reign. Portland's association with the opposition to George III caused distress to his mother, who was a close friend of the wife of Lord Bute, the royal favourite. Such differences over politics were exacerbated by discord about financial arrangements. The dowager duchess retained a life interest in a considerable portion

of her son's inheritance. She insisted on remaining in residence at Bulstrode, in Buckinghamshire, and Portland therefore made his seat at Welbeck, in Nottinghamshire; but he was denied clear control of estate management for many years.

Portland had joined the faction of disaffected whig peers, headed by the duke of Newcastle. His correspondence at this time demonstrates a deep antagonism to Bute and an eagerness for the return to influence of the great aristocratic whig families. He was immensely proud of his ancestry: his great-grandfather William Bentinck, first earl of Portland, had played a key role in the revolution of 1688–9, and his grandfather had been rewarded with a dukedom at the Hanoverian succession. Portland's connection with the grand whiggery was further confirmed by his marriage, on 8 November 1766, to Lady Dorothy Cavendish (1750–1794), the only daughter of William *Cavendish, fourth duke of Devonshire, and his wife, Charlotte Boyle, Baroness Clifford. They had four sons and two daughters. The eldest son did not share his father's enthusiasm for public service, but the second, Lord William Henry Cavendish-*Bentinck, was more ambitious and pursued a distinguished career as a soldier, diplomatist, and colonial administrator.

In 1765 Portland was rewarded for his loyalty to the whig opposition with appointment to the office of lord chamberlain in the ministry of the second marquess of Rockingham. The post was not congenial, and he found little satisfaction in arranging the details of life at court. When the Rockingham ministry fell in March 1766, Portland was eager to quit and feared that his credibility as a whig would be damaged if he continued to serve the court. Reluctantly succumbing to party pressure, he agreed to remain in office as a potential link with the incoming ministry of William Pitt, first earl of Chatham. Portland thus became a victim of Rockingham's unrealistic scheme to manipulate the Chatham ministry from without. When the Rockinghamite bluff was called by the dismissal of Lord Edgcumbe as treasurer of the household, it fell to Portland to conduct various negotiations as a counter-campaign. On 27 November, after some farcical manoeuvres, he led a small band of fellow whig peers into resignation; however, crucial figures chose to remain with Chatham. The Edgcumbe affair had a lasting effect on Portland. He was determined that he would never again accept an office that was merely ceremonial, and he became deeply antagonistic to Chatham and his admirers, believing them guilty of perverting the true whig cause. Conversely, his political connection and personal friendship with Rockingham became unshakeable. Wholeheartedly embracing Rockingham's high-minded and exclusive political style, Portland gradually abandoned his ageing mentor, Newcastle. From the late 1760s onwards Portland actively promoted the transformation of whiggery from the coalition-hungry mentality of the 'old corps', as exemplified by Newcastle, to the rather power-shy pride of Rockingham and his coterie. The party's insistence that Rockingham should assume the premiership in any prospective coalition proved a stumbling block to power but conversely gave coherence to the opposition. Although Portland, who was even more averse to public speaking than Rockingham, contributed nothing more than mute votes to the party's profile in the House of Lords, he nevertheless gave strong organizational support, not least by jeopardizing his limited fortune in costly electoral campaigns. His influence assisted the return of seven MPs at the 1768 election and that of another member at a by-election shortly afterwards. This was the high point of Portland's electoral endeavours, and yet it contained within it the seeds of disaster.

At the general election Portland had taken it upon himself to counter the influence of Sir James Lowther in Cumberland and Westmorland, acting as the aristocratic figurehead for widespread local resentment. Portland's leverage was based on grants of property in the region that had been made to his great-grandfather by William III. But Lowther discovered technical flaws in one of these grants and successfully applied to the crown to be leased the disputed land himself. This attack on Portland's property was based upon the legal maxim that the elapse of time was no obstacle to reviving dormant claims of the crown (*nullum tempus occurrit regi*). The speed with which Lowther's demand was accepted by the Treasury was taken as further proof of the hostility of the court to the whig aristocracy, and the fact that Lowther was Bute's son-in-law gave fuel to the myth of secret influence. Portland became a whig martyr, and his case prompted a successful campaign to place a statutory time-limit on such disputes over crown property. For political and procedural reasons the new legislation was not made retrospective. Portland was therefore left to battle on against Lowther in the courts. The cost of his eventual victory, nearly ten years later, together with other financial constraints, forced Portland to sell off all his property in the north-west. Inherited debts and his mother's longevity all contributed to Portland's monetary problems, but it must also be conceded that he lavished expenditure on estate improvements and was too open-handed with impecunious friends and relatives.

High office, 1782–1783 After nearly sixteen years in opposition Portland returned to government with Rockingham in 1782. He was given the difficult responsibility of serving in Ireland as lord lieutenant. The Irish patriots, galvanized by British failure to prevent American independence, were determined to exact a greater degree of self-government for the Dublin parliament. Portland was rapidly convinced that demands for legislative independence could not be resisted, and he suggested a policy of offering generous terms in return for a thorough renegotiation of the Anglo-Irish relationship. He also had great hopes of establishing a whig party in Ireland on the Rockinghamite model. He tried to persuade Lord Shelburne, his departmental superior at the Home Office, that commissioners should be appointed to negotiate a final settlement. Portland anticipated that by proceeding in this manner it would be possible to create ties of mutual respect and obligation between English whigs and Irish patriots. Shelburne and George III were opposed to Portland's scheme, partly out of a realistic assessment of its likely failure, but also in accordance with their joint policy of undermining Rockinghamite control of the ministry. Thus extensive concessions were made to Ireland without any of the reciprocal benefits for which Portland had piously hoped. He subsequently pursued a vague and abortive scheme to negotiate a federal union, but he was disappointed at the first attempt and did not remain in office long enough to revive the initiative.

Portland, who was predisposed to mistrust Shelburne as Chatham's political heir, had been well aware of the interminable cabinet wrangles which had dogged the Rockingham ministry. The government was already on the verge of collapse when Rockingham died in July 1782. George III appointed Shelburne as prime minister, to the disgust of the Rockinghamites, most of whom, including Portland, resigned immediately. Somewhat to the duke's surprise, the party chose him to succeed as leader. As a landed aristocrat with an impeccable record of party loyalty, the decision in favour of Portland made good sense. Although Charles James Fox had a better claim in terms of parliamentary abilities, he was considered unsuitable as the official head of a party that was based on aristocratic influence.

The balance of parliamentary forces made it impossible for the Shelburne ministry to survive against the combined forces of the Rockinghamites, led by Fox in the Commons, and the supporters of the former premier, Lord North. The formation of the Fox–North coalition owed a great deal to Portland's efforts. He sanctioned this alliance with former enemies by arguing that with the end of the American war their major disagreement over policy had ended, while justifying the balance within the coalition as demonstrated by the apportionment of places. Most of the efficient offices went to Rockinghamites, whereas the Northites were compensated with a greater share of the lesser places. It was a condition of the coalition that Portland should become first lord of the Treasury, and it was further insisted that the king should approve the entire cabinet list at the outset of the ministry's formation. Portland was responsible for conducting the awkward and acrimonious discussions with George III on this subject. The king finally acquiesced in April 1783 but privately resolved to destroy the coalition at the first opportunity. Although Portland, in his later ministerial career, developed an excellent working relationship with the king, at this time their mutual mistrust was too great.

Portland was the official head of the Fox–North coalition, but many observers doubted his ability to live up to the role of prime minister. It was not simply that he lacked the confidence of the king: there were other practical limitations upon his authority. Successful predecessors in the premiership had customarily held the twin offices of first lord of the Treasury and chancellor of the exchequer. But the chancellorship could be held only by a member of the Commons, and Portland as a peer was restricted to holding the Treasury alone. His chancellor, moreover, was the ineffective Lord John Cavendish. For leadership in the Commons, Portland was utterly dependent on Fox.

The ministry survived its first parliamentary session without much difficulty, enjoying an unassailable majority. This circumstance impeded the king from obtaining any alternative ministerial arrangement, though he nevertheless pursued various confidential soundings. In the meantime he tried to make life uncomfortable for Portland, for example, by opposing proposals for the payment of the prince of Wales's debts. This may have been an attempt to precipitate the duke's resignation, but Portland chose instead to negotiate a cautious compromise. By the summer of 1783 Portland seemed to have established himself in office, and he faced the coming session with sufficient confidence to bring forward ambitious legislation. A bill to reform the East India Company had been drafted by Edmund Burke and other party members. With the approval of Portland and Fox, this was presented to the Commons, where it passed comfortably through its early stages without any significant disapproval from the king. When the bill came before the Lords, however, George III used his personal influence against it. Having already negotiated a secret deal with the younger William Pitt to form a new ministry, the king authorized Lord Temple to declare that anyone voting for the India Bill would incur lasting royal enmity.

Portland was faced with an extremely awkward situation. It was by no means clear how best to counter such rumours. To attack them directly might make the damage worse, and there were also traditional restraints on bringing up such a subject in parliamentary debate. The India Bill itself was proving unpopular. Criticism focused on the proposed creation of a new supervisory commission to be appointed, in the first instance, by parliament. Portland believed that the alternative of allowing royal nomination of commissioners would have contravened the whig principle of preventing any increase in the influence of the crown. Opponents of the bill persuasively argued that the real motive for granting parliament the right to nominate the commission was political greed. The India Bill was portrayed as a cynical attempt to confirm the coalition's hold on power through the creation of a new source of patronage.

Portland failed to rise to the daunting challenges of persuading the Lords of the merits of the India Bill and countering the king's unconstitutional interference. The duke's speeches were lacklustre, and he also contrived to bungle the management of parliamentary procedure. After the loss of key divisions on 15 and 17 December, the coalition was summarily dismissed. Pitt was unable to command a majority in the Commons but refused to resign in the face of repeated defeats. When a general election was held in the spring of 1784 many supporters of the Fox–North coalition were defeated. This reflected both the loss of patronage consequent upon a fall from

government and the unpopularity of Fox, North, and Portland.

Head of the whig party, 1784–1790 The failure of the Fox–North coalition had the perverse consequence of enhancing Portland's status and reputation. Once again the duke was a whig martyr. He was so firmly identified with the constitutional crises of 1782–4 that it became impossible to conceive of the return to power of the whigs without his reinstatement at the Treasury. Portland also worked hard to make himself indispensable to the party, a task that was made simpler by the easing of his financial difficulties with the death of his mother in 1785. He was able to resume occupation of his splendid London residence at Burlington House, which he had earlier vacated in the interests of economy. This not only provided a venue for party meetings but also became a centre of whig electoral organization. Although his status as the aristocratic head of the party was unchallenged, Portland was not on good terms with all sections of the party. Innately conservative, he opposed parliamentary reform and the repeal of the Test and Corporation Acts. The duke had little in common with the rakish and radical elements within the whig opposition. He particularly disapproved of Richard Sheridan and was distressed by the recurrent scandals which surrounded the prince of Wales and his set. In 1787 Portland opposed bringing the issue of the prince's debts before parliament. A breach with the prince ensued, and this had serious repercussions at the outbreak of the regency crisis in November 1788.

The apparent madness of George III gave strong grounds to hope that the prince would be made regent and empowered to appoint a new ministry. The fact that Portland and the prince were not on speaking terms created a great deal of initial confusion within the whig party. The situation was made worse by Fox's absence from the country upon a continental tour. Sheridan tried to exploit this political vacuum, and it was rumoured that he had used his personal influence with the prince to secure the promise of a cabinet place. This was entirely unacceptable to Portland. Sheridan continued to hold sway until Fox returned in late November and was able to bring about a reconciliation of Portland and the prince. Thereafter it was clear that Portland and Fox would dominate any ministry appointed under a regency. The king's recovery dashed such hopes, however, and the whig party was in danger of collapsing under the disappointment. But party morale was boosted by the diligence of Portland and William Adam, who made extensive preparations for the general election of 1790. The whig party had never previously attained such a level of co-ordinated electoral activity, with centrally organized funds and even a few agents dispatched to the localities. A revival in whig fortunes was also reflected in spirited attacks on ministerial foreign policy in the new parliament.

Reactions to the French Revolution, 1790–1792 The resurgence of the Fox–Portland whig party was soon undermined by repercussions from the French Revolution. When Edmund Burke launched his assault on the British supporters of the French Revolution in his famous *Reflections*, Portland refused to endorse his conduct. Although privately sympathetic to the conservative ideology which Burke propounded, the duke refused to give him public countenance. He was further alienated by Burke's denunciation of Fox in the Commons on 6 May 1791 and was particularly disgusted by Burke's *Appeal from the New to the Old Whigs*, published in November 1791. Portland believed that this pamphlet gave a false and damaging impression of the extent of whig sympathy for radical ideas. On the other hand the duke was deeply disturbed by the formation of the Association of the Friends of the People in April 1792, a pro-reform pressure group within the party. He organized resistance to the reformers by holding a meeting of conservative whigs at Burlington House on 29 April 1792, on the eve of a Commons debate on a motion for parliamentary reform. Fox was disappointed by Portland's departure from the old Rockinghamite position of treating parliamentary reform as an open question within the party. Portland in return was exasperated by Fox's refusal to prevent the divisive actions of the Friends of the People. Further disagreements arose over the royal proclamation of 21 May against seditious writings. Portland supported the proclamation as a necessary response to Painite radicalism, whereas Fox opposed it as an attack on civil liberty.

The growing rifts within the opposition encouraged the Pitt ministry to hold out tantalizing offers of individual rewards and vague hints of a wider coalition. Portland countered these cynical attempts to divide him from Fox by paying particular attention to the machinations of Lord Loughborough, an ambitious party member whose aim was to become lord chancellor. Pitt used Loughborough as a go-between for various tentative discussions, but he found that Portland stuck fast to the precondition that Fox should be included in any coalition. During July and August 1792 Portland and Fox proved the insincerity of ministerial motives by engineering an independent approach to the king by the hapless duke of Leeds. When Leeds suggested in a private interview with the king that a coalition of Pitt and Fox might be formed with himself as a neutral head of the Treasury, George III not only dismissed the scheme as hare-brained, but also let slip that he had already forbidden his ministers from making anything more than complimentary gestures to the whig opposition. Thus Pitt's duplicity was exposed to the satisfaction of many members of the party. During the course of these complex negotiations Portland rejected an offer of the Garter in order to demonstrate the disinterested nature of his support for the government's anti-radical measures. He did, however, accept nomination to the vacant chancellorship of Oxford University, feeling that this honour did not carry the same political overtones. He was duly installed at a private ceremony at Bulstrode in October.

The break with Fox, 1792–1794 The deteriorating situation in France and the prospect that Britain might be sucked into war brought renewed strain to the relationship between Portland and Fox. In the winter of 1792–3 a bitter struggle was waged for the soul of the whig party. Portland's conduct was vilified as weak and indecisive by those who agreed with Burke on the necessity of a crusade against revolutionary France. The memoirs of Lord Malmesbury and Sir Gilbert Elliot, published in the nineteenth century, have long distorted historical interpretations of Portland's conduct, but the duke's alleged weakness is far less evident if his unpublished correspondence is analysed. Instead he seems to have been politically astute in refusing to break prematurely with Fox. His public silence on Fox's conduct was certainly frustrating. After a series of inconclusive private meetings between Portland and the so-called alarmists, Elliot took it upon himself to announce in the Commons on 28 December that the political connection between Portland and Fox was now at an end. He attributed the breach to Fox's recent declarations for parliamentary reform and to his official recognition of the French republic. Elliot made his announcement without authority and even pre-empted a more moderate statement that was planned to be made during the same debate by Portland's son Lord Titchfield. Elliot was forced into retracting his statement in a speech on 31 December, which was followed by Titchfield's declaration that Portland would only support measures in defence of the constitution, such as the proposed Alien Act, but could give no general confidence to ministers. Portland stuck to this position even after the French declaration of war, making one of his rare parliamentary speeches on 12 February, in which he promised to give firm support to the war while continuing to criticize and oppose the government as and when necessary. This policy of trying to hold the middle ground between the opposing wings of the party was also evident during March 1793, when Portland succeeded in preventing a provocative vote of thanks being proposed at the Whig Club. The original version had thanked Fox for his recent conduct; Portland supported a less explicit form of words and urged his supporters to attend the meeting. This well-intentioned compromise was insufficient to prevent a secession from the club led by Burke, Elliot, and other conservative whigs. This was the first public action of what became known as the 'third party'.

Portland was now faced with the task of reuniting his followers within the whig party with those who had seceded. Only twenty-eight members of the whig party had joined the third party in 1793, and Portland recognized the real danger that a premature separation from Fox would leave the radical wing of the whig party with a larger base of support than it deserved. Portland adopted a gradualist approach, refusing to condemn the seceders and delaying his separation from Fox for as long as possible. Fox made no concessions to Portland's difficulties: he openly countenanced the Friends of the People and continued vigorously to oppose the French war. In the wake of the allied evacuation of Toulon in December 1793 Portland decided that a breach with Fox was now unavoidable. He was also encouraged by friendly approaches from William Windham, the effective head of the third party. In January 1794 Portland made a formal declaration of his separation from Fox. Under the leadership of Portland and Windham the conservative whigs gave their support to the Pitt ministry but continued to refuse unsatisfactory offers of individual preferments. This grouping had more than sixty supporters in the Commons and enjoyed the allegiance of grandees such as Fitzwilliam and Spencer in the Lords. The political weight of the Portland whig party was sufficient to persuade Pitt to alter his approach. After protracted negotiations the duke secured a handsome coalition in July 1794.

The Portland whigs gained five cabinet places and a welter of honours for loyal supporters. The strategy which many of the alarmists had denounced as weak and indecisive secured a far greater share of power than anyone could have imagined. Portland's aims had remained consistent throughout: to deny Pitt the cheap acquisition of opposition support while offering limited co-operation with anti-revolutionary policies. Also, by repeatedly giving Fox the benefit of the doubt Portland was able to win the support of a larger number of whigs than he would have gained by a precipitate separation. Without the advantages of oratorical prowess or dynamic leadership Portland had achieved a significant share of political power for himself and his fellow aristocratic whigs.

Home secretary, 1794–1801 As home secretary in Pitt's ministry Portland devoted himself to the details of administration and played a significant role in countering domestic radicalism. He made effective use of the domestic secret service and condoned new repressive legislation. Never shirking the use of military force against the civilian population, he adopted a hard line on the distress caused by the serious food shortages from 1795 onwards. He maintained that only the free market could prevent the onset of famine. Food shortages would only be increased by any attempt to lower food prices artificially. Popular attempts to fix prices or to force local sales would simply encourage hoarding and deter future production. Portland was ideologically opposed to the neo-mercantilist policies that were sometimes raised in the cabinet: he condoned the state purchase of grain only out of dire necessity in 1795, and with great reluctance accepted the need for time-limited import bounties on rice and grain in 1800. He conspicuously promoted the government's campaign in favour of increased consumption of brown bread and consistently denied the existence of cynical conspiracies among the mercantile élite to raise food prices. Food shortages, he maintained, were caused by actual scarcity and not by hoarding. Such opinions, which were promulgated through official letters and proclamations, made him an unpopular figure in the press.

Portland also had departmental responsibility for Irish affairs, and it had been a condition of the coalition in 1794 that Fitzwilliam, who was his closest political ally, should be made lord lieutenant. This proved disastrous. There were delays in making the changeover, during which time damaging rumours circulated in Britain and Ireland about the likely consequences of Fitzwilliam's appointment.

When the new viceroy arrived in Dublin in January 1795 there was a crisis already brewing. Fitzwilliam made matters worse by ill-considered alterations in government personnel and a precipitate endorsement of the campaign for Catholic emancipation. Portland was taken aback by the speed of Fitzwilliam's actions and failed to give strong enough leadership to prevent the situation from spiralling out of control. Fitzwilliam had failed to adhere to certain preconditions about government patronage, which had been negotiated before his departure. Portland contented himself with chastising Fitzwilliam on this score while remaining silent on the Catholic question. He expected, not unreasonably, that Fitzwilliam would await the mature deliberations of the British cabinet before proceeding to initiate a serious change in government policy. Portland's misjudgement was disastrous. Fitzwilliam construed silence as approval and allowed legislation to come before the Irish parliament without even dispatching a copy of the draft bill for prior vetting by the cabinet. Such reckless and improper conduct left Portland with little alternative than to propose Fitzwilliam's immediate recall on 21 February.

Many whigs denounced Portland for betraying his friend and changing his mind on the Catholic question. The Foxites took particular delight at the duke's discomfort. The Fitzwilliam episode could easily be assimilated into whig mythology about Pitt's duplicity. Although Portland emerged from the affair with little credit, the accusations that he betrayed his friend and changed his mind on the Catholic question cannot be substantiated. Portland did not act firmly enough to restrain Fitzwilliam, but he could not have foreseen that the viceroy would act in such a headstrong manner. Having taken the painful decision to recall Fitzwilliam he did his best to soften the blow by offering to resign from the Home Office as a demonstration of friendship. This was on condition that Fitzwilliam continued to support the ministry. Portland even managed to secure a promise from the king that Fitzwilliam would, at the very least, be given a place in cabinet. George III, who had been horrified at the viceroy's conduct, agreed only out of respect for what he regarded as Portland's principled and dignified stance. These peace offerings were rejected out of hand by Fitzwilliam, and his friendship with Portland was terminated. The duke was deeply wounded by this outcome, but he sincerely believed that Fitzwilliam had been led astray by ambitious members of the Irish opposition and had therefore failed to perceive the need for compromise with Pitt's longstanding supporters in Ireland. As for Catholic emancipation, Portland had never given it public sanction, and in his earlier private correspondence with Fitzwilliam had even expressed disapproval of more minor reforms in favour of Catholics. He considered the Anglican establishment in church and state to be an essential part of British rule in Ireland and viewed emancipation as a prize to be deferred until a lasting solution was devised for Anglo-Irish relations. In the aftermath of the Irish rising of 1798, when the negotiation of a parliamentary union became government policy, Portland went only so far as to concede that emancipation might follow, but should never precede, unification.

The Irish union, 1799–1800 Portland's most significant contribution to the passage of the union has long been obscured from view. Only in the 1990s, with the release of Home Office secret service papers, was it possible to trace how the British government bribed Irish MPs into voting their parliament out of existence. A number of vouchers for payment, which survive among these assorted papers, can be linked with Portland's official bank account at Drummonds and with scattered references in collections of official and private correspondence. The chain of evidence proves that British secret service money was used, at Portland's direction, to extend the increasingly strained resources of the administration in Dublin. After the failure of the union at the first attempt in 1799 it was vital to prevent a second humiliation. A total of £30,850 was sent to Ireland between October 1799 and May 1800. The sending of this money to Ireland was in flagrant breach of the British and Irish Civil List Acts. It was intended to cover up the transactions by gradually repaying the deficit on the British secret service through the annual surplus on the Irish civil list, which automatically reverted to the British crown.

Secret service money was used in Ireland for three main purposes: paying government supporters, funding a propaganda campaign, and purchasing seats in parliament. This formed a hidden counterpart to the overt campaign to buy support by promoting some unionists to key legal and ecclesiastical offices and promising peerages and financial compensation to others for loss of privileges. Perhaps the most important function of secret funds was to establish annuities above and beyond those currently available on the civil list. Sixteen Irish members were granted secret annuities ranging from £300 to £1000 a year. This secret list was to be reduced as quickly as possible by offering official sinecures and pensions as soon as they became available. Portland's concurrence in this illegal policy was vital to the successful passage of the Irish union. In the early months of 1800 a number of government supporters were wavering under the combined pressure of hostile public opinion and the temptation to change their votes in return for money from the anti-unionists, who had raised a large sum by subscription. Access to secret funds allowed the Dublin administration to firm up the unionist vote and prevent damaging defections from an unpopular cause.

The legislation for union did not include Catholic emancipation for fear of alienating influential government supporters. After the passage of the union, however, Pitt decided to make the granting of emancipation an issue of confidence with George III. When the king vetoed emancipation in February 1801 Portland chose not to resign with Pitt and other leading members of the cabinet. He preferred to support the crown's prerogative and considered it his duty to promote stability in government. In order to assist Henry Addington in forming his new ministry Portland made an immediate offer to change department. It

had not yet dawned on him that the deficit in the Home Office secret service account would come to light when he changed office. Circumstances worsened when the king fell ill during February and March. After his recovery George III had lost all memory of the arrangement to repay the money out of the Irish civil list. For a time it appeared that Portland would be held personally responsible for the shortfall, and it took a blunt reminder from Pitt to the king for the arrangement to be reinstated. In the meantime Portland's successor at the Home Office, Thomas Pelham, was cajoled into falsely signing to the existence of the missing funds. The duke could then take up his new office as lord president of the council in July 1801. Until the secret service papers were made available, historians had wrongly assumed that Portland had selfishly delayed changing departments in order to arrange repayment of money borrowed from official funds to cover personal debts.

An establishment figurehead, 1801–1809 During the crisis over Catholic emancipation the various strands of Portland's political development since 1794 may be seen as converging towards the 'toryism' which dominated the remainder of his political career. Although no clearly defined tory party existed at this juncture, many of the ideological elements of toryism were evident in Portland's political attitudes. Hostile to parliamentary reform and Catholic emancipation, the duke was also a proponent of strong, even reactionary, government, not to mention being a loyal supporter of the royal prerogative. Irish politics had played no small part in this evolution, which may be traced from his disillusionment with the Irish whigs from 1795 onwards and mirrored by growing respect for ultra-protestants such as Lord Clare. Above all, Portland had come to view himself as a servant of the crown. This was indeed a far cry from the whiggism of his earlier career, and this transformation was a precondition for his ensuing role as an elder statesman and establishment figurehead.

Portland had also developed a profound respect for Pitt's abilities. As the Addington ministry appeared incapable of coping with the returning prospect of war, the duke lobbied the king for the reinstatement of Pitt. It is a mark of how far Portland had shifted from his former whig sympathies that he welcomed the royal veto on Fox, whom Pitt had hoped to include within his new ministry of 1804. The consequent decision of Grenville also to refuse coalition marked an important stage in the development of allegiances that were to dominate politics after Pitt's death. Portland had already decided that he would have no truck with the Grenville–Fox opposition and was exceedingly disappointed, like many of Pitt's supporters, that Grenville would not serve under his former chief. In the broader coalition which Pitt had originally envisaged, there would have been no room for Portland, but in this narrowly based ministry he was retained as lord president of the council. In January 1805 he gave up his place to Addington but remained in the cabinet without portfolio; he resigned after Pitt's death the following year.

The formation of the so-called 'ministry of all the talents' in 1806 excluded a number of former Pittites, such as George Canning, Spencer Perceval, Lord Castlereagh, and Lord Hawkesbury (the future Lord Liverpool). After a period of indecisive manoeuvring they chose Portland as their nominal leader. He lent a degree of respectability to this loose connection of disgruntled politicians and his presence helped mitigate their internal rivalries. Portland had no personal following in the Commons, his party having dwindled to nothing during the years of coalition. His political importance derived solely from his record of loyalty to Pitt and his excellent relationship with George III. When the king clashed with the talents ministry over Catholic relief in 1807 he called on Portland to save him, and the duke unwisely accepted the offer to become first lord of the Treasury. Longstanding illnesses—the gout and the stone—together with his advancing age made Portland totally unfit for the task. He delegated virtually all Treasury business to his chancellor, Spencer Perceval, and made little attempt to co-ordinate government policy in his capacity as prime minister. This was a government of separate departments, which conspicuously lacked the kind of leadership that Pitt had provided. After eighteen months, latent rivalries among Portland's ministers began to surface, prompted by military reverses in the Iberian peninsula and by sensational accusations of corruption against the duke of York and his mistress.

Disturbed by the ministry's poor performance in the face of these and other difficulties, George Canning privately informed Portland that he would resign as foreign secretary unless there was a cabinet reshuffle. Between March and September 1809 a complicated series of negotiations took place. One plan emerged whereby Canning was to be placated by removing Castlereagh from the war department and replacing him with Lord Wellesley. Portland hoped to retain the services of both Canning and Castlereagh. He was anxious that Castlereagh should not be alarmed by any premature disclosure of Canning's wishes. Those involved in these clandestine discussions were therefore sworn to silence. Differing interpretations of the reshuffle gradually emerged as more people were let into the secret. Worst of all, the timing of the disclosure to Castlereagh was bungled. It was deemed impolitic to inform him of his demotion while he was preparing a large-scale military expedition to Walcheren. After its departure in July, Portland expected Castlereagh's stepuncle Lord Camden to begin preparing his mind for the impending change. This seemed an obvious channel of communication because of their family ties and because Camden would probably need to resign as lord president in favour of his nephew. But Camden's nerve failed him and his pride intervened. Portland therefore promised to undertake the unpleasant duty himself. He was prevented from doing so by a rapid deterioration in health. On 11 August he suffered a life-threatening seizure while travelling in his coach to Bulstrode. His immediate survival did not, however, preclude an increasingly frenetic search for a replacement prime minister.

In what rapidly became a contest for the succession between Canning and Perceval, the former overplayed his hand. When the failure of the Walcheren expedition became known on 2 September, Canning insisted on Castlereagh's immediate removal. Portland refused to countenance this and, under pressure from his family, accepted Perceval's suggestion that the best course of action was to resign so that the ministry could be comprehensively restructured. He tendered his resignation at a private interview with the king on 6 September. Canning proceeded to implement his threatened resignation and Castlereagh therefore learned details of the secret campaign against him. Portland's ministry ended in confusion and disgrace with Canning and Castlereagh fighting a duel on Putney Heath on 21 September. The duke gave public support to the new prime minister, Perceval, by agreeing to remain in cabinet without office.

Portland did not long survive the political crisis which had brought down his ministry, and he died at Bulstrode on 30 October 1809 after undergoing an operation to remove a kidney stone. He was buried in St Marylebone Church on 9 November 1809. He left debts of over £500,000. His eldest son, the fourth duke, set about paying off these debts by selling property, including Bulstrode, and by adopting a more rigorous approach to the management and improvement of his remaining estates. Understandably, he had no taste for the expensive game of party politics that had helped ruin his father's finances.

Historical reputation Portland's historical reputation has undergone significant change in recent years. Beyond the superficial portrayals of a weak dullard, mostly derived from the poisoned assessments of disaffected contemporaries, can be perceived the intelligent brain of an adroit politician. Portland freely acknowledged his shortcomings as an actor on the political stage: his shyness of public speaking and his refusal to pander to popular clamour for the sake of political advantage. His political career was nevertheless significant. As Rockingham's right-hand man he helped establish the serious reputation of the aristocratic whig party, and he dutifully carried on the fight against royal influence during his ill-fated ministry of 1783. He further contributed to the whig cause by enhancing the respectability and organizational competence of his party during long years of opposition. These achievements were reflected in the paramount importance accorded to him by the Burkean alarmists after the outbreak of the French Revolution. In refusing to bow to their premature demands to separate from Fox, the duke eventually obtained significant power for himself and his supporters. He used his ministerial influence to defend aristocratic privilege and the traditional constitution. Although this was not a departure from values that he had long maintained to be truly whiggish, his outright rejection of all shades of reform gave him no common ground with the Foxites. Portland's period at the Home Office, albeit distinguished by administrative vigour, was highly reactionary in its consequences. It was therefore entirely appropriate that he should emerge, in his final years, as a tory figurehead. Crippling ill health and irreconcilable colleagues made for an unhappy and disastrous return to the highest office in government. The glaring shortcomings of his second ministry, however, should not be allowed to obscure the considerable achievements of his long and varied career.   DAVID WILKINSON

Sources D. Wilkinson, 'The political career of William Henry Cavendish-Bentinck, third duke of Portland, 1738–1809', PhD diss., U. Wales, Aberystwyth, 1997 • D. Wilkinson, 'The Fitzwilliam episode, 1795: a reinterpretation of the role of the duke of Portland', *Irish Historical Studies*, 29 (1995), 315–39 • D. Wilkinson, 'How did they pass the union? Secret service expenditure in Ireland', *History*, new ser., 82 (1997), 223–51 • D. Wilkinson, 'The Pitt–Portland coalition of 1794 and the origins of the "tory" party', *History*, new ser., 83 (1998), 249–64 • A. S. Turberville, *A history of Welbeck Abbey and its owners*, 2 vols. (1938–9) • F. O'Gorman, *The rise of party in England: the Rockingham whigs, 1760–1782* (1975) • F. O'Gorman, *The whig party and the French Revolution* (1967) • L. G. Mitchell, *Charles James Fox and the disintegration of the whig party, 1782–1794* (1971) • D. Gray, *Spencer Perceval: the evangelical prime minister, 1762–1812* (1963) • GEC, *Peerage* • HoP, *Commons, 1754–90*

Archives Duke U., Perkins L., letters • Hants. RO, papers • Notts. Arch., household accounts • NRA, priv. coll., official papers, PRO 30/58 • U. Nott. L., corresp. and papers | Arundel Castle, letters to duke of Norfolk • BL, corresp. with James Adair, Add. MSS 50829–50830, 53800–53815 • BL, letters to second earl of Chichester, Add. MSS 33100–33112 *passim* • BL, corresp. with Charles James Fox, Add. MSS 47560–47561 • BL, letters to Sir James Willoughby Gordon, Add. MS 49476 • BL, corresp. with Lord Grenville, Add. MS 58934 • BL, letters to Thomas Grenville, Add. MSS 41855, 42058 • BL, corresp. with second earl of Hardwicke, Add. MS 45030 • BL, corresp. with third earl of Hardwicke, Add. MSS 35349–35707 *passim* • BL, letters to fifth duke of Leeds, Add. MSS 28060–28067 • BL, corresp. with earls of Liverpool, Add. MSS 38191–38566 *passim* • BL, corresp. with duke of Newcastle, Add. MSS 32948–33116 • BL, corresp. with Lord North, Add. MS 61862 • BL, corresp. with second earl of Nottingham, Add. MS 38716 • BL, letters to second Earl Spencer • BL, corresp. with Lord Wellesley, Add. MSS 37283–37309 *passim* • BL, corresp. with William Windham, Add. MS 37845 • BL, letters to Charles Yorke, Add. MS 35638 • BL, corresp. with Charles Philip Yorke, Add. MSS 45041–45042 • Bodl. Oxf., corresp. with William Beckford • CKS, letters to William Pitt • Cumbria AS, Carlisle, letters to Lord Lonsdale • Devon RO, letters to John Simcoe • Hants. RO, letters to James Harris, first earl of Malmesbury • Hants. RO, corresp. with William Wickham • NA Scot., letters to Sir James Grant • NA Scot., corresp. with Lord Hopetoun • NA Scot., corresp. with Lords Melville • NAM, corresp. with Sir George Nugent • NL Ire., letters to John Forbes • NL Scot., corresp. with Lord Balcarres • NL Scot., corresp. with seventh marquess of Tweeddale • NMM, letters to Lord Sandwich • Northants. RO, Milton MSS, papers of fourth Earl Fitzwilliam • NRA Scotland, priv. coll., letters to William Adam • NRA, priv. coll., letters to Thomas Butterworth Bayley • NRA, priv. coll., letters to Spencer Perceval • PRO, letters to William Pitt, PRO 30/8 • PRO NIre., corresp. with Lord Castlereagh • Royal Arch., letters to George III • Sandon Hall, Staffordshire, Harrowby Manuscript Trust, corresp. with Lord Harrowby • Sheff. Arch., corresp. with Edmund Burke • Sheff. Arch., corresp. with Earl Fitzwilliam • Sheff. Arch., letters to Lord and Lady Rockingham • Suffolk RO, Bury St Edmunds, letters to duke of Grafton and earl of Euston • TCD, corresp. with Sir John Pratt • U. Nott. L., corresp. with duke of Newcastle • W. Yorks. AS, Leeds, letters to George Canning

Likenesses J. R. Smith, mezzotint, pubd 1774 (after B. West), BM, NPG • J. Sayers, caricature, etching, pubd 1783, NPG • J. Murphy, mezzotint, pubd 1785 (after J. Reynolds), BM, NPG • T. Lawrence, oils, completed 1792, Bristol Corporation [see illus.] • G. Romney, oils, c.1794–1797, Christ Church Oxf. • B. West, oils, 1814, Examinations Schools, Oxford • M. Pratt, oils, National Gallery of Art, Washington DC • J. Singleton Copley, drawing, Metropolitan Museum of Art, New York • J. Singleton Copley, group portrait, oils

(*The collapse of the earl of Chatham in the House of Lords, 7 July 1778*), Tate collection; on loan to NPG • caricatures, BM, NPG

Wealth at death debts of approx. £520,000; income in the region of £17,000 p.a.: Wilkinson, 'Political career'

Bentinck, Lord William Henry Cavendish- [*known as* Lord William Bentinck] (**1774–1839**), army officer, diplomatist, and governor-general of India, was born on 14 September 1774 at Burlington House in London, the second son of William Henry Cavendish Cavendish-*Bentinck, third duke of Portland (1738–1809), and Lady Dorothy Cavendish (1750–1794), only daughter of William Cavendish, fourth duke of Devonshire.

Education and early career, 1774–1803

Bentinck was born into a pre-eminent aristocratic family. His father was a key figure in the whig party; he led it through the turbulent 1790s and twice served as prime minister (in 1783 and in 1807–9). Yet the family's political importance was not matched by its economic resources. The duke of Portland was a poor businessman, and the family's estates fell deeply into debt. There was no family fortune upon which Bentinck could depend, and consequently many of his career decisions hinged on his need for a secure income.

Bentinck began his education in 1781 at the Revd Dr Samuel Goodenough's school at Ealing, Middlesex. About seven years later he enrolled at Westminster School, London, and in 1791 was commissioned ensign in the 2nd (Coldstream) guards. With his family influence promotions and plum postings came quickly, and it seems that his family's finances sufficed to underwrite the costs of his commissions. He was promoted captain in the 2nd light dragoons in 1793, and with the outbreak of war with France he joined the duke of York's forces in Flanders as an aide-de-camp. In 1794 he purchased a lieutenant-colonelcy in the 24th light dragoons and accompanied it to Ireland, where he remained until 1798. Although he later championed Catholic emancipation, he considered the Irish rude and violent.

In 1796 Bentinck was returned as MP for the rotten borough of Camelford in Cornwall, which he soon exchanged for the family controlled seat in Nottinghamshire. Despite being repeatedly returned as MP for Nottinghamshire (1796–1803, 1812–14, 1816–26), he made little impact in the Commons, partly because of his frequent absences from the country, but also because of his apparent dislike of public speaking. He also spent some time in 1798–9 studying privately with General Jarry, the former intendant at the military academy in Berlin, who soon opened the school that eventually became the Royal Military College at Sandhurst, Berkshire.

Following the outbreak of the War of the Second Coalition in 1799, Bentinck went to northern Italy, where he served for two years as liaison officer with the Austro-Russian forces. He was initially attached to the Russian general Suvorov, but when the latter withdrew into Switzerland, Bentinck transferred to General Bellegarde's Austrian forces and was present at the battle of Marengo in 1800. He apparently enjoyed these two years in northern Italy; he lived a rakish life and consorted with dancers, and there is some evidence that he contracted a sexually

Lord William Henry Cavendish-Bentinck (1774–1839), by Sir Thomas Lawrence, 1804

transmitted disease. He returned to London in June 1801, only to be sent to General Abercromby in Egypt, where he was to command the cavalry. However, he arrived too late to see action, and he decided to return to Britain via the Balkans. He was appalled by the despotism and barbarism there (which he associated with oriental rule), and his whig sensibilities were offended by what he saw as an almost universal disregard for personal and property rights.

Soon after returning to Britain, Bentinck married, on 19 February 1803, Lady Mary Acheson (d. 1 May 1843), the second daughter of Arthur, first earl of Gosford; apparently it was a happy and loyal marriage. She exerted great influence on Bentinck: he was a secretive man and she became his principal confidante, her evangelical Christianity dovetailing with his own evolving ideas of imperial trusteeship. They had no children.

Madras, 1803–1807 In 1802 Bentinck's father lobbied Prime Minister Addington to make Bentinck the governor of Madras, and despite some opposition from the East India Company and the Board of Control, the nomination went through. Bentinck hoped that at the very least he could hold office until 1812 and save £100,000; better yet would be succession to Bengal, a promotion his father also worked to achieve. Their plans failed, however, when news reached London of a mutiny of Indian troops at Vellore on 10 July 1806. This mutiny, in which 114 British officers and other ranks and more than 350 Indians were killed, prompted the East India Company to order the immediate recall of Bentinck and Sir John Cradock, the

local commander-in-chief. Bentinck never fully recovered from the disgrace of his recall.

The introduction of new uniforms and dress codes was the immediate cause of the mutiny. The Sepoys refused to obey the new codes, insisting that these violated their religious and caste customs. Yet some evidence suggests a deeper conspiracy: Vellore was home to the family and heirs of Tipu Sultan, the ruler of Mysore who had resisted British rule in the late eighteenth century. There were rumours that the mutineers were but part of a broader movement aimed at expelling the British. Whatever its origins, the mutiny was deeply unsettling to British officials, for it revealed just how precarious was their grip on India. A scapegoat was required: Bentinck had neither instigated nor approved of the changes to the Sepoys' costume, yet it was widely believed that he had failed to intervene once it became apparent that the army's discipline was crumbling.

The Vellore mutiny tended to overshadow Bentinck's initiatives and achievements. The duke of Wellington's campaigns against the Marathas were substantially aided by the alacrity with which Bentinck had provided logistical, military, and political support. Contact with Thomas Munro and others led Bentinck to champion the *ryatwari* system of land revenue settlement (which called for settling with the individual cultivator) rather than a *zamindari* settlement such as that introduced into Bengal (which rested on granting proprietary rights to large tax farmers and landholders in return for their payment of a sum to be fixed in perpetuity). He also had to contend with an unusually hostile presidency council as well as discontent in the army and civil service. That he overcame such opposition is indicative of his tenacity. At the same time, however, it confirmed him in his mistrust of the company's bureaucracy, and this, when he returned to India, justified his decision in many instances to disregard the opinions and advice of those around him.

Corunna and Sicily, 1808–1815 Having been promoted major-general in 1805, in July 1808 Bentinck joined the staff of the British army in the Peninsula under Sir Harry Burrard. He was soon sent as an envoy to the Spanish supreme junta to negotiate the details of Anglo-Spanish co-operation. But the rapid French advance overtook his efforts, and he rejoined Sir John Moore's forces in time to command a brigade at the battle of Corunna. He was praised for his conduct then, one of the few occasions when he commanded troops in battle. He then returned to Britain, where Spencer Perceval, the incoming prime minister, was seeking allies to shore up his shaky government. Perceval, eager for the support of the Portland whigs, tempted Bentinck with the office of secretary at war, but he declined. Perceval then offered to send him to the Peninsula as Wellington's second in command. Bentinck refused, mainly for fear that he could be easily superseded by officers senior in rank. Meanwhile, he experimented with agricultural improvement in the marshlands near King's Lynn in Norfolk, which nearly bankrupted him.

In 1811 the foreign secretary, Marquess Wellesley, appointed Bentinck envoy to the court of the Two Sicilies.

Bentinck concurrently held a commission as commander-in-chief in the Mediterranean. Owing to Sicily's resources and its proximity to France, Spain, and Italy, the British government viewed it as an ideal base for British operations in the Mediterranean. They hoped that once Bentinck had re-established order there, he would assist British operations in Spain and Portugal. However, he had other ideas. Sicily was the first stage in his wider plans for an independent and united Italy. His solution to Sicilian civil strife was to introduce sweeping constitutional changes. Sicily was ruled by a Bourbon dynasty, recently expelled from Naples. Ferdinand IV and Queen Maria Caroline hoped to use Sicily as a springboard to recapture Naples. This brought them into conflict with a deeply entrenched local aristocracy, which had indicated some willingness to forgo their medieval rights and obligations. By playing on their nationalist feelings, Bentinck hoped to convince these nobles of the merits of constitutional reform. Despite some misgivings, he was given London's political blessing and some financial support. Ferdinand resigned in favour of his son, and Maria Caroline, who referred to Bentinck as the *bestia feroce* and who was determined to frustrate what she feared were British designs on Sicily, was eventually expelled from the island. A parliament was established and a constitution drafted, modelled on Britain's, and foisted by Bentinck on the Sicilians. His political manoeuvres in Sicily exasperated Wellington and others, who were awaiting his assistance. It was not until the summer of 1812 that he sent a force of 7000 to Catalonia, and not until 1813 that he took personal command of the expedition.

As Napoleon's empire began to disintegrate, Bentinck sought and was given permission in February 1814 to land a force in northern Italy to operate with the Austrians. He again alarmed his political masters by attempting to initiate a popular uprising in Italy. He took Genoa on 19 April 1814 and proclaimed a republic. His address to the Genoese opened with 'Warriors of Italy! only call and we will hasten to your relief, and then Italy by our united efforts shall become what she was in her most prosperous period and what Spain now is' (Boulger, 49). When news of this speech reached London, Lord Castlereagh complained 'how intolerably prone he is to Whig revolutions' (*Supplementary Despatches*, 9.64). Yet Bentinck's attempts to kindle a nationalist uprising in Italy were, at least in the short run, unsuccessful. He exaggerated the strength and resilience of nationalist aspirations in Italy, and the other European monarchies were unwilling to tolerate such political experiments. The British government, under pressure from the Austrian foreign minister Prince Metternich, after Bentinck's further constitutionalist intervention in Piedmont, in April 1815, finally replaced him with Sir William A'Court, who was committed to restoring the pre-war status quo. For the second time Bentinck was recalled in disgrace.

Interlude, 1816–1828 Following the conclusion of the war in Europe, Bentinck in 1816 retrieved his Nottinghamshire seat. He appears to have had little political weight, at least in parliament, as his attendance was patchy, and his political affiliation unclear. He favoured the suspension of habeas corpus in June 1819, but supported Roman Catholic relief, burgh reform, and Henry Brougham's demand for inquiry into the abuse of charitable foundations. He spent most of his time at his country seat of Downham Market, Norfolk. He became involved in local affairs and served as commissioner for drainage and navigation in the fens. Most winters were spent on the continent, where costs were lower and the weather better for Lady William's health. He continued to declare that he was a Pittite and a follower of George Canning, yet his identification with reform agendas stretched, and in some cases severed, his links with mainstream Pittites. However, he was not suited to semi-retirement. His finances were in poor shape (his fenland experiments had by the mid-1820s put him £80,000 in debt), and his recall from Madras continued to rankle. He badgered his contacts in London for an opportunity to return to India. In 1819 he turned down an appointment to Madras when he was told that he could not be governor and commander-in-chief. In 1822 there was talk of making him governor-general, but this was quashed by Canning and Prime Minister Liverpool, as his appointment would not materially strengthen the government. His name was again raised in 1825, when the East India Company toyed with recalling Lord Amherst on account of the disasters of the First Anglo-Burmese War (1824–6). Wellington thought otherwise; not only did he defend Amherst's conduct of the war, but he insisted that Bentinck 'must be rejected by the government at all events' (Wellington to Liverpool, 10 Oct 1825, Wellington MS WP 1/830/10). However, opportunity came in 1827. The directors of the company were still favourably disposed towards him (though this was waning); Liverpool, who had blocked his earlier appointment, had died; Wellington was out of office, and Canning was prime minister between April and August 1827. Yet it was by no means certain: Canning might have been Bentinck's political ally in the past, and they were related by marriage (Canning had married Bentinck's sister), but he was still reluctant and only approached Bentinck after five others had declined.

In the meantime, Bentinck had been elected MP for King's Lynn in 1826 on the strength of his landholdings and local ties. He resigned the seat on setting off for India, but retained control over it and passed it on to his nephew, Lord George Bentinck.

Governor-general in India, 1828–1835 Bentinck's subsequent fame rested largely on his achievement as governor-general in India from 1828 to 1835, and especially his sweeping social, economic, and political reforms which, as some have argued, laid the foundations for modern India. This was expressed by the inscription that Thomas Babington Macaulay added to the statue of Bentinck erected in Calcutta in 1835, part of which described Bentinck as a person

> Who infused into Oriental despotism the spirit of British
> freedom:
> Who never forgot that the end of government is the
> happiness of the governed:
> Who abolished cruel rites:

Who effaced humiliating distinctions:
Who gave liberty to the expression of public opinion:
Whose constant study it was to elevate the intellectual
    and moral character of the nations committed to his
    charge.

Bentinck went to India under much pressure to restore the East India Company's finances, which had been harmed by over a decade of war. Moreover, he knew that if it appeared that he was failing to meet these objectives, he could count on little support in either the government or the company. Wellington, who became prime minister, was apprehensive about what Bentinck might do, and changes in the company's court of directors meant that their support was not unqualified. Wellington opined that Bentinck 'did everything with the best intention, but he was a wrong-headed man, and if he went wrong he would continue in the wrong line' (Law, 2.56). *The Times* described Bentinck as a 'perfectly honest and well-meaning man but the most inflexible of all descendants from a Dutch forefather' (*The Times*, 22 Oct 1829). To bolster his position Bentinck quickly imposed economies, in some cases even when he feared their consequences. His popularity among the British in India plummeted as his retrenchments bit deeper, though many of the cutbacks for which he was blamed had been initiated by his predecessor, Lord Amherst; Bentinck's reputation as a ruthless cost-cutter continued long after his departure from India. One officer reported that 'it is my firm belief that he will, as Governor General, depart from our shores without one friendly heart to say "God Bless Him"' (*East India United Service Journal*, 7, 1835, 7).

Bentinck's task was made even more difficult by his administrative heavy-handedness. He mistrusted most Calcutta officials, and rather than deal with those with whom he disagreed, he sought out those who were less likely to challenge him. One example of his policies was his closure of the lock hospitals (hospitals for prostitutes with venereal diseases) of the Bengal army in 1830. He had initially favoured such hospitals, and it was in Madras during his governorship that they were first introduced. But by 1830 he had concluded that lock hospitals were morally suspect, and ineffective against the spread of disease. Most surgeons and military commanders disagreed, yet he disregarded their opinions and quoted only the few who opposed lock hospitals.

One of the most controversial measures pursued by Bentinck was his imposition of the court's orders to reduce *batta* (field pay) for the army. Three months before it was ordered, he wrote to one of the company's directors that 'I dread as much touching any civil or military allowance as much as a magazine of gunpowder' (Bentinck to Loch, 12 Aug 1828, U. Nott. L., PwJf 1202). He was pilloried in the Indian press and delegations were sent to lobby the government and the court in London. There were even rumours that a fire in the Allahabad magazine had been deliberately set by disgruntled officers. Some officers refused Bentinck's invitations to dinner; others attended for fear that they would otherwise be punished. 'They all thought it better to swallow his dinner than lose their commissions' (Note by Dalhousie, 16 Dec 1830, NA Scot., GD 45/5/59). Bentinck did not relent: *batta* was reduced; and while tensions within the army subsided, his reputation with the army was irretrievably damaged.

By the end of the century Bentinck's reputation as the Clipping Dutchman had given way to one as reformer and modernizer of India. He described India 'as a great estate, of which I am the chief agent, whose principal business is to improve the condition of the tenantry and to raise the revenues' (*Correspondence of … Bentinck*, 1.333). India needed western skills, education, and an end to superstitious and barbaric traditions. Hence, he advocated opening India to European colonization. Their capital would partly redress the chronic shortage of disposable capital while their skills improved output. This was rejected by both the company and the government, neither of which wanted a potentially troublesome settler population. However, Bentinck had some successes, including the abolition of suttee, a well-publicized campaign against the thugs, reforms to the land revenue system in the North-Western Provinces, enhanced employment opportunities for Indians in the company service, the abolition of Persian as an official language (English became the sole official language of government), the abandonment of government support for traditional schools in favour of an exclusively western-based curriculum, and the establishment of a medical college to train Indians in western medicine.

These reforms should not be exaggerated, nor intent confused with consequence, nor accounted for simply by reference to some overarching ideological or ethical position. Bentinck's enthusiasm for Macaulay's plan to put all government educational funding behind western education, rather than have a mixture of traditional and western as previously, has often been cited as proof of his plans to remake Indian society. Although this legislation was undoubtedly a useful indicator of contemporary attitudes, its immediate impact should not be overestimated, as the government actually funded very few school places. In the case of suttee, Bentinck's pragmatism was clear in his decision to ban it only after surveying officers of Sepoy regiments to determine whether such legislation would be viewed with alarm by the Sepoys, whose loyalty he had learned not to take for granted. And on at least one occasion he echoed the racist opinions which were becoming more prevalent: he rejected a lieutenant for a staff appointment because his mother was Indian.

There are also some questions as to whether Bentinck was responsible for all the ideas and decisions with which he has been credited. Much of his thinking on Britain's military position and policies in India actually originated with General Sir Samford Whittingham, one of his most trusted informants. In at least one of his minutes, Bentinck lifted not only the idea but also its exact wording from a letter from Whittingham.

Bentinck left India in 1835, having stayed longer than he had planned. Both his health and that of Lady William had suffered, and his popularity in India was only just starting to recover. He had introduced important changes to

British rule, of which arguably the most important was a more forward-looking sense of trusteeship. He had also managed to save enough to get himself out of debt on his return home. Yet much of the optimism that he inspired was shattered by the outbreak of the Indian mutiny in 1857.

Final years, 1835–1839 As was customary with returning governor-generals, Bentinck was offered a peerage. He refused it, partly because he had no heirs to inherit it and partly because he wished to pursue parliamentary politics from the House of Commons. In February 1836 he was elected MP for Glasgow, and again in the 1837 general election, though with a slim margin (2768 votes to his closest rival's 2732). He campaigned on a radical reform platform: notably, franchise extension, the ballot, and opposition to the corn laws and church rates. However, his energy in this campaign was not carried over into parliament, where he was again an infrequent participant. Both he and his wife were sickly, and they preferred to spend their time in Paris. He even tried to give up his seat, and he requested Melbourne, the prime minister, to reoffer him the peerage. Melbourne refused, so Bentinck reluctantly kept his Glasgow seat until a few days before his death. Like other whigs, he did not consider supporting some Liberal or even radical causes incompatible with his profiting from 'Old Corruption'. In addition to his large military and civil salaries, he held lucrative sinecures, notably the clerkship of the pipe in the exchequer (£1131 p.a.) for life. John Wade commented in his *Extraordinary Black Book* (1832), 'look at this nobleman's offices, emoluments, and localities, and then think of the incongruities tolerated under the system'.

Having fallen very ill the previous month, Bentinck died in Paris on 17 June 1839. The autopsy pointed to circulatory problems; these may have first begun in India. His body was brought back to England, and in keeping with his wishes it was given a small private funeral followed by burial on 26 June in the family vault of the dukes of Portland at Trinity Chapel, Marylebone, Middlesex.

Bentinck in retrospect Historians have disagreed on Bentinck's impact, partly because of their different emphases on the various stages of his career. Those who focused on him as governor-general generally agreed that he was personally responsible for the sweeping changes in British India; some even described his term as a watershed, attributing to him the responsibility for ushering in an 'age of reform'. In the words of Cyril Philips, 'Bentinck in his day was the man who did the greatest honour to Europe in Asia' (*Correspondence of … Bentinck*, 1.xlvi). Yet those who looked at his earlier career, and particularly his idiosyncratic and ultimately futile efforts to set Italy ablaze, tended to be harsher in their evaluation. Charles Webster dismissed Bentinck as a 'brilliant and unbalanced egoist, all the more dangerous because he was also imbued with a species of idealism' (C. Webster, *The Foreign Policy of Castlereagh*, 1.75). More charitable assessments of his years in Italy were offered by Denis Mack Smith and Harry

Hearder, though both admitted his unrealistic expectations.

Agreement was also lacking over the source of his political and social views. Some scholars such as Manazir Ahmad and Eric Stokes (the latter in *The English Utilitarians and India*) have explained Bentinck's enthusiasm for reform in terms of utilitarian influences—to support this position they pointed to Bentinck's contacts with Jeremy Bentham and his oft-quoted comment to James Mill: 'I am going to British India, but I shall not be governor-general. It is you that will be governor-general' (*Correspondence of … Bentinck*, 1.xv). Others such as George Bearce have positioned Bentinck within an English liberal tradition. One can question whether there is much to be gained by trying to account for Bentinck's actions in terms of a particular ideological position, for not only was he prone to snap decisions, but people close to him noted that he was not a systematic thinker. John Rosselli conceded this point, but by treating Bentinck's career in its entirety, and by tracking the interaction of ideas and actions through Madras, Italy, the Norfolk fens, India, and Glasgow, he concluded that there was a set of core ideas at work on Bentinck, which included a slow but steady transition from the whiggism of Edmund Burke to the constitutional liberalism of the mid-nineteenth century, a heady dose of evangelicalism, and a paternalistic view of society that justified the autocratic measures that imperial rule often required.

DOUGLAS M. PEERS

Sources J. Rosselli, *Lord William Bentinck: the making of a liberal imperialist, 1774–1839* (1974) · *The correspondence of Lord William Cavendish Bentinck, governor-general of India, 1828–1835*, ed. C. H. Philips, 2 vols. (1977) · D. M. Peers, *Between Mars and Mammon: colonial armies and the garrison state in India, 1819–1835* (1995) · J. Rosselli, *Lord William Bentinck and the British occupation of Sicily, 1811–1814* (1956) · H. Hearder, *Italy in the age of the Risorgimento, 1790–1870* (1983) · D. M. Smith, *A history of Sicily* (1968), vol. 3 · *GM*, 2nd ser., 12 (1839), 198–200 · *The Times* (20 June 1839) · J. C. Marshman, 'Lord William Bentinck's administration', *Calcutta Review*, 1 (1844), 337–71 · D. C. Boulger, *Lord William Bentinck* (1892) · M. Ahmad, *Lord William Bentinck* (1978) · C. D. Hall, *British strategy in the Napoleonic war, 1803–15* (1992) · D. M. Peers, 'Sepoys, soldiers, and the lash: race, caste, and army discipline in India, 1820–1850', *Journal of Imperial and Commonwealth History*, 23 (1995), 211–47 · E. Stokes, *The English utilitarians and India* (1959) · C. E. Barrett, 'Lord William Bentinck in Bengal, 1828–1835', DPhil diss., U. Oxf., 1954 · Fortescue, *Brit. army* · C. H. Philips and M. D. Wainwright, eds., *Indian society and the beginnings of modernisation, c.1830–1850* (1976) · HoP, *Commons* · J. L. Clive, *Thomas Babington Macaulay: the shaping of the historian* (1973) · G. D. Bearce, 'Lord William Bentinck: the application of liberalism to India', *Journal of Modern History*, 28 (1956), 234–46 · T. J. Hope, 'The journey of an English aristocrat through the Balkans in 1801: the travel diaries of Colonel Lord William Bentinck, M.P.', *Revue des Études Sud-Est Européennes*, 12 (1974), 551–60 · *Supplementary despatches (correspondence) and memoranda of Field Marshal Arthur, duke of Wellington*, ed. A. R. Wellesley, second duke of Wellington, 15 vols. (1858–72) · E. Law, Lord Ellenborough, *A political diary, 1828–1830*, ed. Lord Colchester, 2 vols. (1881) · R. E. Frykenberg, 'New light on the Vellore mutiny', *East India Company Studies*, ed. K. A. Ballhatchet and J. Harrison (1986) · U. Southampton L., Wellington MSS · NA Scot., Dalhousie muniments · Burke, *Peerage*

Archives BL, corresp. and papers, Add. MS 36730 · BL OIOC, Home misc. series, corresp. relating to India · McGill University, Montreal, McLenna Library, minutes relating to composition and organization of Indian army · U. Nott. L., corresp. and papers | All

Souls Oxf., corresp. with Sir Charles Vaughan · BL, corresp. with Lord Bathurst, loan 57 · BL, corresp. with Lord Castlereagh, Add. MS 43073 · BL, corresp. with Sir H. W. Dalrymple, Add. MS 50827, *passim* · BL, Fagan MSS · BL, Liverpool MSS · BL, letters to Sir John Moore, Add. MS 57540 · BL, letters to Sir Arthur Paget, Add. MS 48396 · BL, corresp. with Sir P. K. Roche, Add. MS 49490, *passim* · BL, corresp. with Lord Wellesley, Add. MSS 13633–13635, 37284, 37292–37293, *passim* · BL OIOC, Amherst MSS · Ches. & Chester ALSS, Combermere MSS · Cumbria AS, Carlisle, Graham MSS · JRL, Clinton MSS · JRL, letters to William Murray · Leeds RO, Canning MSS · NA Scot., corresp. with Lord Dalhousie · NA Scot., Dalhousie muniments · NAM, corresp. with Sir Frederick Maitland · NAM, Moore MSS · NL Scot., corresp. with first earl of Minto · PRO, Colchester MSS · PRO, corresp. with Andrew Snape Douglas, PRO 30/7 · PRO, Ellenborough MSS · PRO NIre., corresp. with Lord Castlereagh · Royal Arch., Melbourne MSS · Trinity Cam., Macaulay MSS · U. Southampton L., corresp. with Sir Arthur Wellesley

Likenesses T. Lawrence, oils, 1804, priv. coll. [*see illus.*] · R. Fagan, watercolour miniature, 1814–15 · J. A. D. Ingres, pencil drawing, 1816, Musée Bonnat, Bayonne, France · B. Thorvaldsen, marble bust, 1816, U. Nott. · W. Heath, engraving, 1823 (*The patriotic dinner*), repro. in M. D. George, *Catalogue of political and personal satires* (1952), vol. 10, pp. 366–7 · H. Bone, enamel, 1828 (after T. Lawrence), Welbeck Abbey, Nottinghamshire · W. Read, stipple, 1828, BL OIOC · J. Atkinson, pencil-and-ink drawings, *c*.1833, NPG · T. Phillips, oils, 1835, Government House, Madras, India · R. Westmacott, statue, 1835, Calcutta, India · G. H. Phillips, mezzotint, pubd 1838 (after T. Phillips), BL OIOC, NPG · oils, *c*.1839, Welbeck Abbey, Nottinghamshire · D. Hardy, oils, 1914 (after T. Lawrence), Victoria Hall, Calcutta, India · H. R. Cook, stipple (after T. Lawrence), BM, NPG, NAM; repro. in *Military Panorama* (1812–13), facing p. 399 · C. Motte, lithograph (*The Bengal Boombah among the tombs*), repro. in M. D. George, *Catalogue of political and personal satires* (1952), vol. 11, p. 329 · B. Thorvaldsen, plaster bust, Thorvaldsen Museum, Copenhagen, Denmark

Bentinck, Winifred Anna Cavendish- [*née* Winifred Anna Dallas-Yorke], **duchess of Portland** (1863–1954), bird protectionist and philanthropist, was born at Murthly Castle, Perthshire, on 7 September 1863, only daughter of Thomas Yorke Dallas-Yorke (*b*. 1826), formerly Dallas, of Walmsgate, Lincolnshire, and his wife, Frances Perry (*d*. 1912). She married William John Arthur Charles James Cavendish-Bentinck, sixth duke of Portland (1857–1943), at St Peter's, Eaton Square, on 11 June 1889. As chatelaine of Welbeck Abbey, the duchess was a prominent society figure.

The duchess became involved in the protection of birds from 1891, eschewing the fashionable use of plumes taken from wild birds. She had her own hats trimmed with feathers taken from domestic fowl on the Welbeck estate, to show that these could be as becoming as those of birds of paradise and egrets. It was the slaughter of breeding egrets (and the consequent death in the nest of their young) to supply so-called osprey plumes which led to the foundation of the Society for the Protection of Birds. The duchess was the first and longest-serving president of the society, being elected in 1891 and serving until her death. Since she moved in court circles she may have been influential in Queen Victoria's confirming in 1899 an order prohibiting the military from wearing 'osprey' plumes and the society's being awarded a royal charter in 1904. Her standing at court is shown by the fact that Queen Victoria stood sponsor in person for her daughter, Victoria, born

on 27 February 1890; from 1913 to 1925 she was mistress of the robes to Queen Alexandra.

The duchess's concern for the plight of captive wild birds was given practical force on a motor tour of Spain before the Second World War, according to I. H. R. in *The Times* (9 Aug 1954, 9). So horrified was she by the overcrowded conditions of songbirds in cages fixed to the walls of a tenement building that she sent her courier to buy the birds and liberate them. Then she discovered that the other side of the building contained as many cages and realized that the position was hopeless. However, she did have contacts and spoke to the king of Spain when she returned to Madrid. Despite his sympathy and promise of legislation, the Spanish Civil War started before legislation could be passed.

The duchess was also active on behalf of the Royal Society for the Prevention of Cruelty to Animals (RSPCA): she was a vice-president for many years and president of the ladies committee of the RSPCA, and took a particular interest in education, organizing Bands of Mercy and then the Animal Defenders Corps. She was knowledgeable about horses, campaigning against the trade in decrepit horses to continental Europe and towards the end of her life launching an appeal for the improvement in the treatment of horses in Nigeria. At Welbeck Abbey she kept a stable for old horses, especially pit ponies from the Nottinghamshire coalfield.

In the year of the duchess's marriage her husband won a large sum of prize money with two racehorses, and at his wife's suggestion the greater part of this was used to build the Welbeck almshouses, which were popularly known as The Winnings. Her concern for the disadvantaged in the local community was further evidenced in her active support for the mining community, which included payments for the medical treatment of miners and the organization of cookery and sewing classes for their daughters. In such affection did the community hold her that the Nottinghamshire Miners Welfare Association, on behalf of the miners, their wives, and children, petitioned the king that an honour be conferred on 'that angel, our beloved Duchess' on the occasion of his silver jubilee; as a result, she was made a dame of the British empire on 3 June 1935. She was also a dame of justice of the order of St John of Jerusalem, to which she gave long service. Her marriage to the duke of Portland, which lasted fifty-four years until the duke's death in 1943, was described in her obituary as 'an ideally happy union' (*The Times*, 31 July 1954). They had a daughter and two sons, the elder of whom succeeded as seventh duke. The duchess died early on 30 July 1954 at Welbeck Abbey.   NICHOLAS HAMMOND

Sources N. Hammond, 'Conservation and sister organisations: Royal Society for the Protection of Birds', *Enjoying ornithology*, ed. R. Hickling (1983), 158–64 · *The Times* (31 July 1954) · I. H. R., *The Times* (9 Aug 1954) · *Bird Notes*, 36 (1954) · GEC, *Peerage* · Burke, *Gen. GB* · d. cert.

Archives Lincs. Arch., family MSS

Likenesses photographs, Royal Society for the Protection of Birds Library, The Lodge, Sandy, Bedfordshire

Wealth at death £87,859 0s. 4d.: probate, 21 Oct 1954, CGPLA Eng. & Wales

Bentine [*formerly* Bentin], **Michael** (1922–1996), comedian, was born on 26 January 1922, in Watford, Hertfordshire, the second of two sons of Adan (later Adam) Bentin, aeronautical engineer, and his wife, Florence (*d.* 1949), daughter of James Dawkins, a Southend Water Board official. His paternal grandfather was Don Antonio Bentin Palamerra, vice-president of Peru for eight years and president-elect on his death. He added the final 'e' to his name when he went into show business after the war. When he was a child a botched tonsillectomy left him with a profound stammer that was not cured until he was sixteen and a schoolboy at Eton College. In the Second World War he was at first turned down by the RAF, despite repeated applications, because of his father's Peruvian nationality. He was playing Lorenzo in *The Merchant of Venice* at the Open Air Theatre, Regent's Park, when he was arrested as a deserter; the RAF had accepted him at last but had failed to inform him. He was, he said later, 'the first British serviceman to be arrested in doublet and hose for 400 years' (*The Independent*, 28 Nov 1996). He wanted to fly, but inoculation with a faulty serum nearly cost him his life and left him with poor eyesight. He spent the war as an intelligence officer and was deeply distressed when, as he saw it, the psychic gifts he had inherited from his father gave him hideous foreknowledge of those who would be killed as he briefed air crew on their missions; he saw their heads as skulls.

Part of Bentine's work as an intelligence officer with the RAF was to organize forward airfields as the allies advanced through France and into Germany. As such, he was one of the first British officers to enter Belsen. This affected him deeply. The Nazis, he concluded, were 'pure evil'. After the war he had a minor breakdown and was unable to stop weeping for a time. Bentine left the RAF a junior officer, but more than fifty years later his memorial service in the actors' church, St Paul's, Covent Garden, was attended by three air marshals, and he was roared to his rest by the RAF red arrows aerobatics team streaming coloured smoke as they flew in formation over central London. He had helped to raise millions of pounds for the RAF Benevolent Fund.

After the war Bentine and his friend Tony Sherwood—they called themselves Sherwood and Forrest—played the Windmill Theatre, London, a temporary refuge for budding former service comedians. Sherwood left, and Bentine and his brother Philip were fooling around with a broken chair at home; Philip pretended it was a machine-gun and within minutes they had found a hundred uses for it. It became the basis of black-bearded Bentine's surreal solo act. Later, it gave him a star spot in the West End show, *Starlight Roof*. A plunger on his wild black hair enabled him to impersonate a trolley-bus, among other things. This led to four years' work in the West End, with an appearance at a royal command performance, and seasons at the London Palladium and in the London production of the *Folies Bergère*.

Bentine was one of the founder members of *Crazy People* (later to become *The Goon Show*) on radio in 1951. It was a show peopled by surrealist characters, and it quickly

Michael Bentine (1922–1996), by unknown photographer, 1992

acquired a massive cult following and exercised enormous influence on subsequent radio and television comedy. Bentine played Osric Pureheart, inventor of the permanently submergible submarine and other unique artefacts. He pulled out of *The Goon Show* after two series (forty-three shows), because, he said, its original conception had changed. Bentine then made *The Bumblies*, a show that appealed both to children and to adults, for the BBC, and he later made other children's shows, including *Potty Time* and *Madabout*, for BBC television. After working in America and Australia for two and a half years he returned to Britain to launch a series of brilliant comic fantasies on television with *It's a Square World*, which ran from 1960 to 1964, and won the grand prix de la presse at Montreux in 1963 (the first BBC show to win an award at the Swiss television festival). In one episode he hired a Chinese junk, dressed his actors as a Chinese crew, and bombarded the houses of parliament with plastic cannon balls until parliament appeared to sink. 'Do any of you gentlemen speak English?', enquired an officer from a river police launch. At other times he fired the BBC television centre into space, raided it with whooping 'Red Indians', and pretended to torpedo it. After scorching a brick he was sent a memorandum by a BBC executive that said: 'Under no circumstances is the BBC Television Centre to be used for the purposes of entertainment'. His effect on BBC staff can be measured by an incident about eighteen months after he had shot the last *Square World* episode. A gang wielding baseball bats and wearing balaclavas raided the BBC's pay office. As they made their getaway, preparing to batter their way through the barrier, one of the BBC guards opened it, gave them a cheery wave and shouted, 'When will it be on, Mr Bentine?'

Bentine was a gifted restorer of Victorian paintings, a collector of jade, an amateur astronomer, and an expert on—and with—all kinds of weaponry, from sabres to sub-machine guns, though after the war he determined he would never shoot another living creature. In 1998, *Ghost Force*, Ken Connor's 'secret history of the SAS', disclosed that in the mid-1960s, Bentine, by then a combat firearms instructor on special consultation to the armed forces and the police, was invited to a shooting demonstration at Paddington Green police station. Connor described how he drew a .44 Magnum with a 12-inch barrel and began rapid fire. 'When the smoke cleared', Connor wrote, 'every single target had been blasted apart'. The author went on to say that, 'As much as anyone, he deserves the credit for promoting the idea of a counter-terrorist force within the SAS' (Connor, 204–5).

Bentine pioneered the use of hovercraft to open up areas of Peru that were unreachable even by waterways, and was made a comandador del merito for that and his work in organizing relief after Peru's devastating floods in 1970; he was appointed CBE by the queen in 1995. He represented Prince Charles at Peter Sellers's funeral. He wrote no fewer than three autobiographies: *The Long Banana Skin* (1975), *The Door Marked Summer* (1981), and *The Reluctant Jester* (1992). He also wrote five novels, four books describing his psychic experiences, and five children's books. Bentine was a compendium of seemingly contradictory ideas and decidedly odd notions, of recondite knowledge and technical skills. He had the insatiable curiosity and meticulous grasp of detail of a good research scientist and engineer; he also possessed an awareness of human folly that made him burn with anger at its cruelties and shake with laughter at its absurdities. It was this that put him at the cutting edge of radio and television comedy for more than two generations.

Bentine's first marriage, to Marie Barradell on 9 August 1941, ended in divorce on 20 January 1947. His second wife, Clementina Theresa Gadesden Stuart-McCall, was a ballet dancer. They married on 14 February 1948. Two daughters, Elaine, sole child of his first marriage, and Marylla, elder daughter of his second marriage, both died of cancer in the 1980s. His eldest son, Stuart, was killed in a light-aircraft crash in 1972. Bentine himself died from prostate cancer on 26 November 1996, in Walton on the Hill, Tadworth, Surrey. He was cremated at Leatherhead, Surrey. He was survived by his wife, Clementina, his son Richard, and his daughter Serena.   DAVID NATHAN

Sources M. Bentine, *The reluctant jester* (1992) · M. Bentine, *The long banana skin* (1975) · D. Nathan, *The laughtermakers* (1971) · K. Connor, *Ghost force* (1998) · private information (2004) [C. Bentine, R. Bentine] · *The Times* (28 Nov 1996) · *The Independent* (28 Nov 1996) · *Daily Telegraph* (28 Nov 1996)
Likenesses photographs, 1949–77, Hult. Arch. · photograph, 1992, Rex Features, London [*see illus.*] · photograph, repro. in *The Times* · photograph, repro. in *The Independent* · photograph, repro. in *Daily Telegraph*

Bentley, Adam of (*fl.* 1230–1246). *See under* Moneyers (*act. c.*1180–*c.*1500).

Bentley, Catharine [*name in religion* Magdalen Augustine] (**1591–1659**), abbess and translator, may have been the younger sister of Ann Bentley who entered the same convent on 3 May 1611, aged twenty-two; nothing further is known of her family. She took vows at the English convent of the Poor Clares at Gravelines, France, on 3 November 1610, aged eighteen, adopting the name Sister Magdalen Augustine. In 1619 she was one of eleven nuns who left Gravelines for Aire, in the province of Artois, to set up a secondary branch of the convent there. She became abbess of the nunnery at Aire and died, at the age of sixty-eight, on 1 July 1659, 'having been very vertuous, charitable, and devout' (Hunnybun, 38).

Bentley seems to have been involved with translations of religious works. A group of interconnected texts related to St Clare appeared in print around 1621–2, mostly associated with Douai, and one of them names Magdalen Augustine as the translator behind it. In addition, in 1635 there appeared *The History of the Angelicall Virgin Glorious St. Clare ... Extracted out of the R. F. Luke Wadding his Annalls of the Freer Minors Cheifly by Francis Hendricq and now Donne into English, by Sister Magdalen Augustine, of the Holy Order of the Poore Clares in Aire, Printed by Martin Bocart at Douai.* As the title-page states the text is a translation of Hendricq's 1631 abridgement of Wadding's work. The translator dedicates the work to Queen Henrietta Maria from her 'Beads-women' at Aire, and adds a preface to the reader stressing that Clare was 'Of Feminine Sex, but Masculine virtue' (p. 3).

While the evidence that Bentley was involved in these translations seems strong, Luke Wadding himself, writing within the lifetime of all involved, credited them not to her but to Catherine Magdalen—that is Bentley's colleague Elizabeth Evelinge. The problem seems insoluble, although it has been suggested that it is evidence of collaborative translation practices (Allison, 37).

MATTHEW STEGGLE

Sources W. M. Hunnybun, 'Registers of the English Poor Clare Nuns at Gravelines ... 1608–1837', *Miscellanea, IX*, Catholic RS, 14 (1914), 25–173 · A. F. Allison, 'Franciscan books in English, 1559–1640', *Biographical Supplement*, 3/1 (1955), 16–65 · O. Valbuena, introduction to M. Augustine, [C. Bentley], *The history of the angelic virgin glorious S. Clare*, www.wwp.brown.edu/texts/rwoentry.html [Renaissance women online], Sept 1999 · www.wwp.brown.edu/texts/rwoentry.html

Bentley, Charles (**1805/6–1854**), watercolour painter, was born in Tottenham Court Road, London, the son of a master carpenter; he may possibly be identified with Charles, the son of Thomas and Mary Bentley, baptized at St James's, Paddington, on 24 August 1806. He was apprenticed to the engraver Theodore Fielding about 1819 and spent some time with Newton Fielding in Paris, where he is known to have engraved the work of R. P. Bonington, whose style was an influence on Bentley's own in terms of colour, composition, and line. From 1827 he made a meagre living by engraving and illustrating. He was elected an associate of the Society of Painters in Water Colours on 10 February 1834 and a full member on 12 January 1843, and he exhibited a total of 209 works between 1834 and 1854. He accompanied his close friend William Callow—whom he first met as a fellow pupil with the Fieldings—on several sketching trips, including a tour of Normandy in 1841. This area of France had special appeal for Bentley, but his most frequent subjects were breezy scenes off the coast of England. A reviewer in *The Athenaeum* noted that 'He has indeed few compeers in the delineation of water in movement' (13 June 1846).

Critics commented on a similarity of manner in the sea pieces of Bentley and Callow, but the development of their careers was very different: while Callow prospered, Bentley was often swindled by opportunistic picture dealers and always in financial difficulty. Bentley shared a home and studio with Callow at 20 Charlotte Street, London, from 1843 until 1846 when he returned to his previous address at 11 Mornington Place, Hampstead Road, where he died suddenly of cholera on 4 September 1854, aged forty-eight, leaving a widow, Eliza, and an aged mother in very poor circumstances.

An obituarist in *The Athenaeum* observed that 'In marine landscapes, and other subjects of the kind, he may be ranked between Messrs. Copley Fielding and Callow' (9 Sept 1854). A studio sale was held at Christies on 16 April 1855. *Fishing Boats* and *Dunluce Castle, Ireland* are two of seven examples of his work in the Victoria and Albert Museum. The British Museum has *Sailing Barge Near Dover* on permanent loan from the Royal Society of Painters in Water Colours. *Shipping off Scarborough*, now in the collection of the National Maritime Museum, Greenwich, was shown in the exhibition 'Masters of the sea' in 1987. Provincial locations for work by Charles Bentley include Blackburn Museum and Art Gallery; Birmingham Museum and Art Gallery; Oldham Art Gallery; Leeds City Art Gallery; Laing Gallery, Newcastle; and Newport Museum and Art Gallery.   JAN REYNOLDS

Sources F. G. Roe, 'Charles Bentley', *Walker's Quarterly* [whole issue], 3 (1921) · W. Callow, *William Callow, RWS, FRGS: an autobiography*, ed. H. M. Cundall (1908), 86, 109 · J. Reynolds, *William Callow* (1980), 3, 65, 67, 78, 81, 87, 97 · J. Reynolds, 'Glorious light', *Collectors Guide*, 46/9 (April 1993), 28–31 · *The Athenaeum* (13 June 1846), 610 · *The Athenaeum* (9 Sept 1854), 1091 · Redgrave, *Artists*, 2nd edn, 37 · J. L. Roget, *A history of the 'Old Water-Colour' Society*, 2 (1891), 238–40 · d. cert. · IGI

Wealth at death under £300: Roe, 'Charles Bentley'

Bentley, Charlotte Eliza (1915–1996), nurse and nursing activist, was born on 15 December 1915 at 63 Portland Court, Great Portland Street, London, the daughter of John Richard Bentley, hosier, and Charlotte Emma Redard. After education at a Swiss convent school and secretarial training Bentley trained as a nurse at the Royal Free Hospital, London, from 1943 to 1946, and there became a student political activist at a time when nursing was considered a vocation above politics. As national chairman of the Student Nurses' Association she campaigned for probationer nurses studying for the state registration examinations to be recognized as students rather than as hospital employees. This did not endear her to the hospital authorities, for whom probationers were a valuable supply of cheap labour on the wards. In 1948 she was appointed sister-in-charge of a new outpatients' department at Lambeth General Hospital, a former London county council hospital, to which she brought the different standards and practices of the teaching hospitals.

Bentley's attention soon turned to raising the status of state-enrolled nurses, a grade of assistant nurses created by the 1943 Nurses' Act, who were widely regarded as inferior to their state-registered colleagues. In 1955 she was elected general secretary of the National Association of State Enrolled Assistant Nurses, despite the concern of some members that a state-registered nurse should be appointed to the post rather than an enrolled nurse. An appeal to members for funds ensured that her first year's salary was paid, but she accepted the challenge of making the association financially viable, as well as ceaselessly campaigning on behalf of her members. While often finding it necessary to adopt a confrontational approach to those hospitals and matrons whom she considered unjust to enrolled nurses she also attempted to build bridges between senior figures in the nursing hierarchy, nurse educators, and state-registered and state-enrolled nurses at all levels. For many years she organized 'all-grade' tours for nurses to the Netherlands, Spain, and Switzerland, during which social contact could help to break down professional barriers. On such social occasions she was considered an erudite companion whose learning was tempered by a keen sense of humour.

Bentley enlisted the support of Dame Irene Ward, MP for Tynemouth, to sponsor successfully a private members' bill in 1961 to remove from the title of state-enrolled nurses the word 'assistant', which she considered demeaning and derogatory. National conferences of enrolled nurses were organized to raise their professional profile. She also argued that enrolled nurses should be allowed to manage hospital wards. With sponsorship from the *Nursing Mirror* she established a scholarship for enrolled nurses to encourage practical nursing skills. She herself was appointed MBE for her services to nursing.

In 1970 the National Association of State Enrolled Nurses was absorbed by the Royal College of Nursing, despite the prejudice previously shown by the college towards enrolled nurses. Bentley became an official of the college, still dominated by an ethos that saw the nursing profession as a vocation and enrolled nurses as belonging to an inferior grade. Although herself a state-registered nurse Bentley continued to champion enrolled nurses in her new role as section secretary of the enrolled nurses' section of the Royal College of Nursing. Her outspoken, sceptical, strongly held views were not always popular with her colleagues at the college; an avowed agnostic, she alienated many by her principled refusal to attend college religious services, just as previously she had refused to attend church services held at the annual conferences of the National Association of State Enrolled Nurses. On retiring from the Royal College of Nursing in 1977 she became secretary of the nursing sub-committee of the Edwina Mountbatten Trust, charged with administering project grants to advance nursing, midwifery, and health-visiting in the United Kingdom and the Commonwealth.

Though a campaigner for the rights of enrolled nurses Bentley was keen to preserve the distinction between state-registered and state-enrolled nurses, as she believed that there was a place for the more practical, skills-oriented nurse alongside the more academically trained nurse. While welcoming the setting up in 1983 of one register for all nurses under the aegis of the United Kingdom Central Council for Nursing, Midwifery and Health Visiting she did not support the later cessation of enrolment of pupil nurses for the enrolled sections of the register, nor the encouragement given to enrolled nurses to convert to registered general nurses. Nevertheless she had done much toward breaking down the barriers within the nursing profession that ultimately tended towards the extinction of the enrolled nurse.

In retirement Bentley suffered from Parkinson's disease. She remained unmarried, and died of old age on 20 March 1996 at 37 Elsworthy Road, Camden, London. Her body was cremated. KEVIN BROWN

Sources *The Times* (17 April 1996) · *The Times* (27 April 1996) · private information (2004) · Royal College of Nursing Archives, Edinburgh, National Association of Registered Nurses, archives · enrolled nurses' minutes, Royal College of Nursing Archives, Edinburgh · b. cert. · d. cert.
Likenesses photograph, repro. in *The Times* (17 April 1996)
Wealth at death £332,846: probate, 24 June 1996, *CGPLA Eng. & Wales*

Bentley, Derek William (1933–1953), victim of a miscarriage of justice, was born on 30 June 1933 at 13 Surrey Row, Blackfriars Road, Blackfriars, London, the third of five surviving children of William George Bentley (1905–1974), an engineer, and his wife, Lilian Rose (1903–1976), daughter of William Cooper and his wife, Sarah. Bentley, the survivor of a pair of twins, was born into a respectable working-class family. He was legally borderline feeble-minded, with a mental age variously estimated as between nine and twelve years and an IQ of 66–77. He was rejected for national service as mentally sub-standard. He was ill co-ordinated, epileptic, and totally illiterate. He attended several state schools but received little education and left Ingram Road School in July 1948, immediately after his fifteenth birthday. A timid person, he kept many pets, including cats, dogs, and a chicken. He was particularly attached to his elder sister **Iris Pamela Bentley** (1931–1997), born on 5 August 1931, also a surviving twin, with whom he was dug out of house rubble during the blitz.

At fifteen Bentley was convicted of petty theft and sentenced to twenty-one months at the Kingswood approved school near Bristol. After his release he was mentally disturbed, and refused to leave the house for over six months. He worked as a furniture remover, then as a dustman before being downgraded to road sweeper. He was ultimately dismissed as even this proved beyond him.

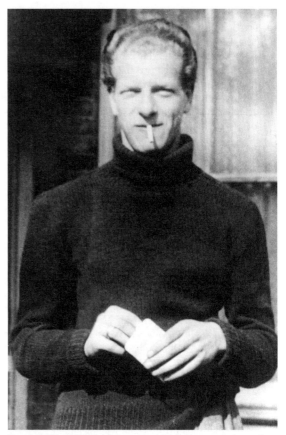

Derek William Bentley (1933–1953), by unknown photographer, 1952

When arrested for murder he was unemployed, and almost certainly unemployable.

On the night of 2 November 1952 two figures, identified in court as Derek Bentley and Christopher Craig, were seen entering a warehouse in Croydon. The police arrived and trapped the youths on the roof. Detective Constable Fairfax climbed up and seized Bentley, placing him under arrest. Police witnesses claimed—but both defendants steadfastly denied—that Bentley shouted 'Let him have it, Chris!'—an instruction which, even supposing it had been said, 'was on any showing ambiguous' (as the Court of Appeal observed in 1998). Craig, the dominant male leader, fired a revolver, and Fairfax received a graze on the shoulder and let go of a cowed Bentley, who made no effort to escape. Craig fired several more shots, one of which killed Police Constable Miles. Craig then dived off the roof in a futile effort to kill himself.

Bentley's defence was not well handled. In a two and a half day trial no defence witnesses were called on his behalf, and neither the details of his mental incapacity nor the fact of his being on prescribed medical drugs was revealed. The judge, Lord Chief Justice *Goddard, was a domineering man who acted in a partisan manner. He created an atmosphere which led to a verdict of guilty by the use of emotional language and behaviour, prematurely used the word 'murdered', muzzled a defence witness, and helped prosecution witnesses; his summing up was also biased and lacked proper direction to the jury. Both Bentley and Craig were found guilty, the former with a jury recommendation for mercy. Craig at sixteen was too young to hang but Bentley was sentenced to death.

Bentley appealed but Goddard refused to add his recommendation for mercy to that of the jury. The appeal was rejected, despite apparently valid legal grounds being available. The home secretary, Sir David Maxwell Fyfe, refused to recommend that the queen exercise the prerogative of mercy. In the House of Commons, Sydney Silverman's attempt to get this decision debated was refused, the speaker ruling that only after Bentley had been executed could it be discussed. There was a widespread feeling of disquiet that Bentley, who was dimwitted, had no record of violence, had no gun, had not fired the shot, and had been under police arrest for fifteen minutes before the fatal shooting, was to hang. Petitions and letters, and even a delegation of MPs, failed to alter Maxwell Fyfe's decision. Bentley was executed at Wandsworth prison at 9 a.m. on 28 January 1953 while an angry crowd waited outside.

There is little doubt that the home secretary was wrong in refusing to commute the sentence of death. Clemency can normally be exercised for any one of the following reasons: youth; mental problems; a jury recommendation for mercy; widespread or strong local public opinion; the principle that if the leading actor cannot be executed then neither should any associate; and the existence of more than a scintilla of doubt about the evidence. Bentley met each criterion. Maxwell Fyfe's advisers recommended clemency but he remained obdurate to the end.

Despite a broken marriage to Stewart Dingwall and a twenty-three-year battle against cancer, Bentley's sister Iris devoted her life to campaigning for a pardon for him. In 1966 his body was disinterred from the grounds of Wandsworth prison and reburied in Croydon cemetery on 4 March. Initially a headstone was not permitted; in July 1994 it was allowed, after a dispute about the wording. The tombstone bears the words 'A victim of British justice'. In 1991 Peter Medak's film *Let him have it* revived the general public's interest. In 1992 Iris achieved a police re-examination of the case, but the home secretary refused to take further action. A new home secretary, Michael Howard, granted a rather strange partial pardon on 29 July 1993, which admitted it had been wrong to execute but maintained the guilty verdict. During the 1990s linguistic evidence emerged that suggested police witnesses had lied; and Police Constable Claude Pain, who claimed he had been on the warehouse roof at the time, but was never called as a witness, maintained that police witnesses had perjured themselves and the fatal words 'Let him have it, Chris' had never been uttered. Iris Bentley died on 22 January 1997 at St George's Hospital, Tooting, and was buried on 31 January at Croydon cemetery.

In 1997 the case was one of the earliest examined by the Criminal Cases Review Commission for a suspected miscarriage of justice. The commission determined that it merited referring back to the Court of Appeal to reconsider the verdict. This time the court decided that the conviction was unsafe and quashed it on 30 July 1998. The lord chief justice, Lord Bingham, ruled that Goddard's summing up had been 'a highly rhetorical and strongly-worded denunciation of both defendants and of their defences. The language used was not that of a judge but of an advocate (and it contrasted strongly with the appropriately restrained language of prosecuting counsel)'. The appeal court noted that Bentley's appeal had mistakenly not complained about Goddard's summing up, for it was questionable if it 'would have been thought acceptable even by the standards prevailing at the time' (Court of Appeal judgment in *R. v. Bentley*, 30 July 1998).

This was one of the most controversial British criminal trials of the twentieth century. It affected public opinion, causing many supporters to reconsider the desirability of capital punishment; it raised the issue of parliament's inability to discuss matters of royal prerogative; it is a case that is regularly cited as an example of the irreversibility of the death penalty should the verdict be later called into question; and it is a shocking reminder that state criminal justice systems can sometimes be barbarous and fail with disastrous consequences. KEVIN B. BUCKNALL

Sources Court of Appeal judgment in *R v. Bentley (Derek William)*, 30 July 1998, Criminal Division, case no. 9707533 S1 • H. M. Hyde, *Trial of Christopher Craig and Derek William Bentley* (1954) • M. J. Trow, *Let him have it, Chris: the murder of Derek Bentley* (1992) • I. Bentley and P. Dening, *Let him have justice* (1996) • W. G. Bentley, *My son's execution* (1957) • *The Guardian* (24 Jan 1997) • *The Independent* (28 Jan 1997) • D. Pannick, 'A woman who refused to accept injustice', *The Times* (11 Feb 1997) • B. Levin, 'Judgement on Lord Goddard', *The Times* (8 June 1971) • D. Yallop, *To encourage the others* (1990) • R. T. Paget and S. S. Silverman, *Hanged—and innocent?* (1953) • 'Clarke erred on Bentley pardon', *The Times* (8 July 1993) • 'Partial pardon fails to satisfy family of hanged Bentley', *The Times* (31 July 1993) • A. Smith, *Lord Goddard: my years with the lord chief justice* (1959) • b. cert. • d. cert. • inscription on gravestone, Croydon cemetery
Archives FILM BFI NFTVA, *Thames reports*, Thames television, 3 Sept 1991 • BFI NFTVA, *Storyline*, 11 Feb 1995 • BFI NFTVA, documentary footage
Likenesses photographs, 1952, Hult. Arch. [*see illus.*]

Bentley, Edmund Clerihew (1875–1956), writer, was born in London on 10 July 1875, the eldest son of John Edmund Bentley, a civil servant in the queen's bench office, and his wife, Margaret Richardson Clerihew. He was at St Paul's School in the days of Frederick Walker, and formed there his lifelong friendship with G. K. Chesterton. He was a member of the history eighth, newly created by Walker, and won a history exhibition at Merton College, Oxford. He fell in love with the college at once and quickly and gratefully absorbed the spirit of Oxford. At the Oxford Union he was an effective debater in a quiet and scholarly style and became president in 1898. John Simon, F. W. Hirst, and John Buchan were among his friends; he knew Hilaire Belloc slightly, but it was not until later that he became close friends with him. His interests during his Oxford years were not confined to political and intellectual discussion: he was captain of the Merton boat club,

Edmund Clerihew Bentley (1875–1956), by Hugh Goldwin Riviere, 1915

but gave up rowing in his fourth year in order to work for his degree. One great disappointment of his life was his failure in 1898 to obtain a first in history.

In 1898 Bentley went down from Oxford and read for the bar. He did well in his examinations at the Inner Temple, London, became a pupil in William Hansell's chambers in 1900, and was called to the bar in 1902. One of his closest friends recorded that Bentley had all the qualifications of a successful barrister except the legal mind. On the other hand, he had from his schooldays onwards been active with his pen. At St Paul's he had been a contributor to *The Debater*, founded by his friend Lucian Oldershaw; at Oxford he had written regularly for *Isis* and for *The J. C. R.*, the magazine in which Belloc's *Lambkin's Remains* first appeared. While still in chambers he wrote light verse for *Punch* under the critical eye of Owen Seaman, and by the end of 1899 he was a regular contributor to *The Speaker*, the Liberal weekly edited by J. L. Hammond.

On 14 June 1902 Bentley married Violet Alice Mary (1878/9–1949), fourth daughter of General Neil Edmonstone Boileau, of the Bengal staff corps. They had one daughter and two sons, of whom the younger, Nicolas [*see* Bentley, Nicolas Clerihew (1907–1978)], went on to illustrate his father's books, as well as many others. Bentley's marriage was one of the reasons for his decision in 1901 to become a professional journalist and to join the staff of the *Daily News*. Its editor was Rudolph Chambers Lehmann, a good Liberal, a strong opponent of the Second South African War, and a great oarsman. Thus Bentley felt

thoroughly at home in his new work and with his new colleagues, among whom were Herbert Paul, H. W. Massingham, and Harold Spender. The owner of the *Daily News* was George Cadbury, who, as a Quaker, was regarded by Bentley as a serious-minded nonconformist, but still commendable: 'if all business men were Quakers, I do not think we should be any the worse off' (Bentley, *Those Days*). Nevertheless, Lehmann fell out with the Cadbury family on a matter of principle, 'and journalism knew him no more'. Lehmann was succeeded by A. G. Gardiner, under whom Bentley in due course became deputy editor. In that capacity he was faced at times with critical decisions and he confessed that he enjoyed the experience. When the *Daily News* was amalgamated with the *Morning Leader*, Bentley felt that he was no longer in sympathy with Liberal journalism and in 1912 he joined the *Daily Telegraph*, with which he remained for twenty-two years.

Had Bentley confined his activities to leading articles, he might well have been little known and gradually forgotten. In fact, his name is linked with two highly individual achievements: he added a new word to the language and he wrote what Chesterton once described as the finest detective novel of the century. As he sat in the science class at St Paul's at the age of sixteen, the following lines came into his head:

> Sir Humphrey Davy
> Abominated gravy.
> He lived in the odium
> Of having discovered Sodium.

Such was the beginning of what Chesterton called the 'severe and stately form of free verse known as the Clerihew'. Sir Humphrey soon had a number of companions, and their lives were entered into a notebook with appropriate sketches by Chesterton. Bentley chose to drop his surname for the occasion and *Biography for Beginners* by E. Clerihew, with illustrations by G. K. C., was published in 1905. The book did not have an immediate success, but in Bentley's own words, 'in course of time it seemed to find its way into the hands of connoisseurs of idiocy everywhere'. *More Biography* followed in 1929; *Baseless Biography*, with illustrations by the author's son Nicolas, in 1939; finally *Clerihews Complete* appeared in 1951. It should be noted that the drawings of Clerihew in the illustrations are themselves caricatured portraits of the author.

In 1910 Bentley thought of a new kind of detective story. Like all boys of his generation he had revelled in the Sherlock Holmes series; but Holmes's eccentricities and his reputed infallibility irritated him and he conceived the notion of a detective's convincing solution being proved wrong in the end. The result of his meditation was *Trent's Last Case*, published as one of Nelson's two-shilling novels in 1913. It was a best-seller immediately, and was published in the USA as *The Woman in Black*: amid the torrential output of detective stories in that period, it still holds its distinctive place. Bentley's later books are *Trent's Own Case*, written with H. Warner Allen (1936); *Trent Intervenes* (sixteen short stories, 1938); and *Elephant's Work* (1950).

Bentley was happy in, and proud of, his profession as a journalist. At the outbreak of the Second World War he returned to the *Daily Telegraph*; but the worlds that he loved best—Oxford in the nineties and pre-1914 Fleet Street—had vanished and he recalled them nostalgically in *Those Days* (1940). Bentley died at his home, 10 Porchester Terrace, Paddington, on 30 March 1956.

SYDNEY C. ROBERTS, *rev.* MICHAEL J. TOLLEY

Sources E. C. Bentley, *Those days* (1940) · N. Bentley, *A version of the truth* (1960) · G. Ewart, introduction, in *The complete clerihews of E. Clerihew Bentley* (1981) · WWW
Archives Bodl. Oxf., corresp. with publishers | BL, corresp. with G. K. Chesterton and F. A. Chesterton, Add. MS 73191, fols. 1–242 · BL, corresp. with Society of Authors, Add. MS 56669 · Bodl. Oxf., letters to J. L. L. Hammond · W. Sussex RO, corresp. with Oswald Barron |SOUND BL NSA, 'Edmund Bentley', BBC Radio 3, 16 June 1981, NP5124R
Likenesses H. G. Riviere, charcoal drawing, 1915, NPG [*see illus.*] · H. Coster, photographs, *c.*1936, NPG
Wealth at death £4523 11s. 4d.: probate, 27 June 1956, *CGPLA Eng. & Wales*

Bentley, Elizabeth (*bap.* 1767, *d.* 1839), poet, was baptized on 26 November 1767 at All Saints', Norwich, the only child of Daniel Bentley (*bap.* 1735, *d.* 1783), a journeyman cordwainer, and his second wife, Elizabeth Lawrence, the daughter of a Norwich cooper. Most of what is known of Bentley's life comes from a letter of 23 July 1790, addressed to her patron and first editor, the Revd John Walker, and included among the prefatory materials to both her volumes of verse. She reports that her father, having received a good education himself, taught her reading, spelling, and writing but never gave her 'the least idea of grammar'. When she was ten, her father suffered a stroke that disabled him from working as a shoemaker. He hawked garden produce for a living until being made bookkeeper to the London Coach, only a few months before he died, aged forty-eight.

Two years after her father's death, Bentley discovered in herself 'an inclination for writing verses', and although she 'had no thought nor desire' for them to be seen by anyone, her mother showed them to acquaintances, who encouraged her (*Genuine Poetical Compositions*, sigs. A3v–A4r).

So impressed was William Cowper with 'the Norwich maiden's' 'strong natural genius', that he not only subscribed to her first volume, *Genuine Poetical Compositions, on Various Subjects* (1791), but compared her verse with Mary Leapor's of forty years before, discerning 'more marks of true poetical talent' than he had observed 'in the verses of any other male or female, so disadvantageously circumstanced' (Hayley, 3. 295–6). The list of 1935 subscribers includes peers, gentry, members of parliament, clergymen, Cambridge dons, surgeons, attorneys, and such literati as Cowper, Elizabeth Carter, Elizabeth Montagu, and Hester Chapone. Bentley appears in the frontispiece portrait as a robust, broad-faced girl with a snub nose, crisply neat in a starched cap and neckerchief. Dedicated by permission to 'William Drake, Jr., Esq., M.P.', the volume announces itself as designed to fund an annuity for the author and her mother. As we might expect, there are odes to 'Benevolence', 'Content', and 'Chearfulness', as

Elizabeth Bentley (*bap.* 1767, *d.* 1839), by unknown engraver, pubd 1820 (after Joseph? Clover)

well as concluding 'Lines, Addressed as a Tribute of Gratitude to the Subscribers in General', in which Bentley regrets that she cannot 'follow where seraphic MILTON led' (line 20). Since her 'lot' has been 'fix'd' to 'sing in humbler strain', she must make do with the self-effacing modesty suitable for a poet of plebeian origins, 'content to be the last and lowest of the tuneful train' (*Genuine Poetical Compositions*, lines 30–32). In spite of her frequent reliance upon Popean rhymed couplets, Bentley most often evokes a Cowperian mood, inviting her readers to 'quit the bustling town, where busy, anxious care your bliss destroys', to pursue instead 'the country's joys' ('On a Summer Morning', lines 20–24). 'On Cruelty to Animals' and 'On the Abolition of the African Slave-Trade' are notably compassionate contributions to contemporary debates.

After the success of this volume, Bentley kept a small boarding-school in the London Road. Except for occasional poems in the *Norfolk Chronicle*, a small collection of verses for children, sold for a shilling, and a short ode on Nelson's victory at Trafalgar (reprinted in her second volume), she published nothing until *Poems; being the Genuine Compositions of Elizabeth Bentley* in 1821. Dedicated to John Wodehouse, lord lieutenant of Norfolk, this collection represents her as more than ever a local poet and elegist. The frontispiece portrait represents her as thoughtful and hollow-cheeked, in a shawl and frilled cap and collar.

Bentley died at Doughty's Hospital in the parish of St Saviour's, Norwich, an almshouse for aged poor men and women, on 13 April 1839 and was buried at St Stephen's, Norwich, on 17 April. In her will she bequeathed to Seth

William Stevenson, of the firm of printers who had published her work, the sum of £10, and the residue of her estate, to cover funeral expenses, to Elizabeth Lawrence Whiting. DONNA LANDRY

Sources E. Bentley, *Genuine poetical compositions, on various subjects* (1791), preface • E. Bentley, *Poems; being the genuine compositions of Elizabeth Bentley, of Norwich* (1821), preface • W. Hayley, *The life and posthumous writings of William Cowper*, 4 vols. (1806) • parish register, Norwich All Saints (baptisms), 1739–70 • parish register, Norwich St Stephen's (baptisms and burials), 1710–81, 119 • d. cert.

Likenesses stipple, pubd 1820 (after drawing by J.? Clover), NPG [*see illus.*] • Miss Buck, engraving (after T. Bassett), repro. in Bentley, *Genuine poetical compositions*

Wealth at death under £100; £10 to Seth William Stevenson; residue to Elizabeth Lawrence Whiting: will, 1839, ANW W.65 f.94–95, Norfolk RO, Norwich

Bentley, George (1828–1895), publisher and writer, was born at Dorset Square, London, on 7 June 1828, the eldest surviving son of the publisher Richard *Bentley (1794–1871) and Charlotte, daughter of Thomas Botten, and nephew of the printer and author Samuel *Bentley (1785–1868). George Bentley grew up in the midst of one of the most prominent mid-Victorian printing and publishing families. Educated first at a boarding-school in Elliott Place, Blackheath, Kent, run by the Revd John Potticary, a nonconformist minister (Benjamin Disraeli had been a pupil there two decades previously), Bentley completed his schooling at King's College, London University, and then, at the age of seventeen, entered his father's firm. For a few years thereafter he was adventurous enough to travel abroad, residing in Rome at the time the French occupied the city in 1849, but his lifelong asthma eventually confined him to the London area, or to such health resorts as Bath, Tenby in south Wales, and Weston-super-Mare.

Bentley's partnership with his father, whose business was declining steeply, did not run smoothly in the 1850s. George Bentley befriended a number of younger authors, notably Wilkie Collins, whose books the firm published and which George Bentley reviewed favourably in *Bentley's Miscellany*. On at least one occasion Richard Bentley was offended that Collins had consulted with the son instead of the father about business matters. But George Bentley was not entirely absorbed by the office: on 16 June 1853 he married Anne, daughter of William Williams of Aberystwyth, moving then from his bachelor's quarters to a home in Regent's Park, London. In May 1854 their only child, Richard, was born, and six years later the family moved to Upton Park, near Slough, where they were to reside for the remainder of their lives.

In 1856–7 Bentley took time off from business, perhaps on furlough during the firm's near-brush with bankruptcy. Once he returned, however, he played an increasingly prominent role, and grew to know every aspect of the printing and publishing business, from advertising to contracts. Among other things, he appreciated the power of vivid bindings: no other firm, Michael Sadleir observes, 'went in so thoroughly and so persistently … for all the panoply of glitter and colour' that bespoke 'prosperity, confidence, and peace' (Sadleir, 1.xxiv). Guinevere Griest

suggests that the gold stamping and brilliant hues helped the staff of Mudies, working in the gloomy catacombs of stacks, to select a Bentley title whenever a customer asked for an unspecified 'good' novel. A genial, kindly employer, who 'had every one's good word, and … had a good word for every one' (*The Athenaeum*, 8 June 1895) and who loved especially the writings of Charles Lamb and William Hazlitt, Bentley ran a firm that eventually prospered. He became especially adept in two branches of production: editing and publishing fiction.

In 1860 the publisher John Maxwell had started up a new magazine, *Temple Bar*, inculcating 'thoroughly English sentiments—respect for authority, attachment to the Church, and loyalty to the Queen' (*Wellesley index*, 3.386) for the comfortably-off, John Bullish middle classes. It featured two continuing serial fictions and a variety of miscellaneous articles, and was initially edited by George Augustus Sala, who about 1863 purchased the magazine from Maxwell. Circulation began at 30,000, dropping to 11,000 by 1866. In January of that year Bentley's firm bought out Sala for £2750. Edmund Yates, who had succeeded Sala as editor, resigned on 7 July 1867, and after a fruitless search for an outside successor George Bentley became editor by November 1867 (ibid., 3.388–9). He upgraded the quality of the writing, selected fiction that could be effectively serialized, folded in *Bentley's Miscellany* after Harrison Ainsworth had almost run it into the ground, and turned *Temple Bar* into 'one of his three most valuable literary properties' (Gettmann, 148). Among the British authors Bentley commissioned were Thomas Adolphus Trollope and his younger brother Anthony Trollope, Rhoda Broughton, Mrs Henry Wood, Sheridan Le Fanu, Charles Reade, Henry Kingsley, Robert Louis Stevenson, George Gissing, Arthur Conan Doyle, Maarten Maartens, and Henry James. But Bentley ranged much further afield, introducing his readers to works by Honoré de Balzac and Alphonse Daudet; Anton Chekhov, Ivan Turgenev, and Lev Tolstoy; and Hans Christian Andersen. He was also a skilled and tactful facilitator of many late-Victorian memoirs and translations of such signal works of scholarship as Theodor Mommsen's *History of Rome* and Ernst Curtius's *History of Greece*. Author of occasional papers, George Bentley collected them for private circulation (*After Business*, 1883); he also composed a 'Sketch of Dr. Maginn' for an 1860 edition of Maginn's *Shakespeare Papers* and a quarter-century later published a lecture, *The Rock Inscriptions in the Peninsula of Sinai* (1886). He became a member of the Stationers' Company and a fellow of the Royal Geographical Society.

George Bentley was also an influential and knowledgeable publisher of fiction. An advantage for a printing and publishing firm to owning a magazine was that material might be purchased for, and reimbursed by sales of, the periodical, and then republished in volumes for the general public and the circulating libraries. This synergy fuelled Bentley's business throughout the 1870s and 1880s. Although in the 1850s Richard Bentley had tried to cut the price of three-volume novels from 31s. 6d. to 10s.

6*d*., and thus to break the control that commercial lending libraries exercised over the marketing of fiction, the experiment was not successful; so in 1864 Bentleys bought a share in Mudies limited liability company and from the 1860s on the firm became a principal supplier of three-deckers to the library trade. During that period George Bentley relied on many female readers for recommendations, including Maria Featherstonehaugh, Mrs G. W. Godfrey, Lady Dorchester, Mrs Gertrude T. Mayer, and Adeline Sergeant. Geraldine Jewsbury was especially shrewd and indefatigable; though Bentley complained that she turned down too many manuscripts, she was often very accurate about how daring a book could be and still be acquired by Mudies, Smiths, and other circulating libraries.

But George Bentley increasingly chafed at the aesthetic, moral, and commercial restrictions of the three-volume novel—920 pages with 21.5 lines per page and 9.5 words/line, he specified in 1883 (Gettmann, 232). Though he thought of himself as a conserver of mid-Victorian decencies and was uncomfortable with those such as George Gissing who transgressed boundaries, nevertheless Bentley agreed with Arthur Mudie and others who by the mid-1880s were decrying the stultifying effect of the prolix three-decker, republished almost immediately in a cheaper one-volume format that threatened all profits for publisher, author, and circulating library.

Having set Richard Bentley & Son on a profitable course after his father's death in 1871, by the mid-1880s Bentley was himself ready—sometimes—to share authority with his son Richard, and to withdraw from the day-to-day office management. He commissioned George Devey, an architect specializing in half-timbered 'Old English' mansions for the Rothschilds, to build The Mere on land adjacent to Upton Park, Paxton's first suburban residential development, laid out in 1843. With double walls and glazing to keep out the damp and cold, tall brick chimneys, and luxuriant landscaping, the house was a refuge from the fierce cost-cutting competition of late Victorian publishing. There Bentley continued to indulge in his favourite hobby, meteorology, and to guide a firm that was resolutely old-fashioned in its practices. Richard Bentley & Son was, for instance, the last publisher to hold an annual trade dinner, sometimes at the Albion tavern, sometimes in the hall of the Stationers' Company, and in the final years at the Hotel Metropole.

By 1894 no one wanted the three-decker. Bentley tried to drift on by issuing fiction in transitional formats—two volumes or a 6*s*. octavo printed in small tightly leaded type. But such expedients failed and did not interest him. After a winter spent in search of health, he returned to The Mere in spring enfeebled and uncertain whether any novel could be issued in multiple volumes. On 29 May 1895, a little before midnight, he succumbed to an attack of angina pectoris. He was survived by his wife.

Burial in the churchyard of the Norman church of St Laurence, Upton, on 5 June, was strictly a private ceremony. The estate was valued for probate at over £86,000. Four years later the firm was valued at £20,000 for stock, copyright, and goodwill; but Richard Bentley, more engaged by the firm's history than by its future, sold out in 1898 to Macmillans for only £8000.

ROBERT L. PATTEN

Sources R. A. Gettmann, *A Victorian publisher: a study of the Bentley papers* (1960) · M. Sadleir, *XIX century fiction: a bibliographical record based on his own collection*, 2 vols. (New York, 1969) · G. L. Griest, *Mudie's circulating library and the Victorian novel* (1970) · *Wellesley index*, vol. 3 · G. Bentley, letter, *The Times* (8 Dec 1871) · R. Bentley jun., *Some stray notes upon Slough and Upton* (1892) · R. Bentley jun., *Leaves from the past* (1896) · A. Ingram, *Index to the archives of Richard Bentley & Son, 1829–1898* (1977) · M. Turner, *Index and guide to the lists of the publications of Richard Bentley & Son, 1829–1898* (1975) · *The Academy* (8 June 1895) · *The Athenaeum* (8 June 1895) · 'The late Mr George Bentley', *The Bookman*, 8 (1895), 104–5 · *The Times* (31 May 1895) · 'The house of Bentley', *The Bookseller* (7 Sept 1898), 854–5 · *DNB* · M. Plant, *The English book trade* (1939) · 'Bentley, Richard (1794–1871)', *DNB* · 'Bentley, Samuel', *DNB* · N. P. Davis, *The life of Wilkie Collins* (1956) · C. Peters, *The king of inventors: a life of Wilkie Collins* (1991) · P. D. Edwards, *Dickens's 'young men'* (1997) · *The life and adventures of George Augustus Sala*, 2 vols. (1895) · E. H. Yates, *Edmund Yates: his recollections and experiences*, 2 vols. (1884) · A. Trollope, *Letters*, 2 vols. (1983) · W. H. Scheuerle, 'Temple Bar', *British literary magazines*, ed. A. Sullivan, [3]: *The Victorian and Edwardian age, 1837–1913* (1984), 403–7 · R. P. Wallins, 'Richard Bentley', *British literary publishing houses, 1820–1880*, ed. P. J. Anderson and J. Rose, DLitB, 106 (1991), 39–52 · *Buckinghamshire*, Pevsner (1994) · W. F. Monypenny, *The life of Benjamin Disraeli*, 1 (1910) · R. Blake, *Disraeli* (1966) · S. Bradford, *Disraeli* (1982) · S. Weintraub, *Disraeli* (1993)
Archives U. Cal., Los Angeles · University of Illinois, Urbana-Champaign, diary and corresp. | BL, letters to W. E. Gladstone, Add. MSS 44393–44506 *passim* · Hove Central Library, Sussex, corresp. with Lord Wolseley · NL Wales, letters to Johnes family · NL Wales, corresp. with Lady Llanover
Likenesses wood-engraving (after F. M. Sutcliffe), NPG; repro. in *ILN* (8 June 1895)
Wealth at death £86,088 17*s*. 5*d*.: probate, 27 June 1895, *CGPLA Eng. & Wales*

Bentley, Iris Pamela (1931–1997). *See under* Bentley, Derek William (1933–1953).

Bentley, Sir John (*bap.* 1703, *d.* 1772), naval officer, was, according to a privately printed life by 'R. B.' (1921), baptized at St Leonard's, Deal, Kent, on 27 December 1703, the second surviving son of William Bentley (1660–1719) and Sarah, *née* Ballard (1666–1738). His elder brother, Thomas (1701–1739), is stated to have died a naval captain, though it may be that he was in fact the master of a merchant ship. John Bentley entered the navy as a lieutenant's servant (perhaps in the late 1710s), but despite his outstanding potential he was not commissioned until 28 March 1732. Prior to this he may have served in the *Grafton* at the battle of Passaro (1718), in the *Torbay* about 1720, in the *Falmouth* (confirmed by his passing certificate, PRO, ADM 107/3, fol. 166), and in 1728 in the *Grafton* once more. From 1734 he is thought to have been lieutenant in the fireship *Poole*. In the rather discreditable battle of Toulon (11 February 1744) he was a lieutenant of the *Namur*, Admiral Thomas Mathews's flagship, and in view of his personal gallantry he was immediately afterwards promoted to command the hospital ship *Sutherland*. On 1 August 1744 he was posted into the *Burford* (70 guns), and a few months later he was sent home as a witness on the courts martial which rendered the years 1745–6 notorious.

In spring 1747, when Admiral George Anson took command of the Channel Fleet, Bentley was chosen to be his flag captain in the *Prince George*, and was with him in the battle off Cape Finisterre on 3 May. When the fleet returned to England, and Anson hauled down his flag, Bentley was transferred to the *Defiance* (60 guns) in which he shared in Edward Hawke's victory in the Bay of Biscay (14 October 1747). He engaged, among others, the mighty *Tonnant* (80 guns) 'within pistol shot three-quarters of an hour, in which time we shot away his mizen topmast' (PRO, ADM 51/282). Bentley afterwards, during the peace, successively commanded the *Invincible*, the yacht *Royal Charlotte*, and the *Barfleur* at Portsmouth, and in 1757 he was a member of the court martial on Admiral John Byng.

In the following year Bentley was again in command of the *Invincible*, one of the finest 74-gun ships in the service, which he had himself helped Anson to capture from the French. She was under orders to proceed to Louisbourg with Admiral Edward Boscawen, when, on 19 February, weighing from St Helen's, her rudder jammed, and she grounded heavily on the Dean Sand. In the evening it came on to blow very hard, and the ship became a complete wreck. Bentley, with his officers, was acquitted of all blame by the consequent court martial, and he was shortly afterwards appointed to the *Warspite* (74 guns), which through summer 1759 was in the Mediterranean with Boscawen, and at the defeat of the French squadron, under La Clue Sabran on 18 August. Next day, when the ships that had sought refuge in Lagos Bay were captured or destroyed, it was by Bentley's exertions that the *Téméraire* (74 guns), which had been run ashore, was brought off and added to the strength of the British navy.

In September Bentley was sent to England where he was presented to the king and knighted. Still in the *Warspite* he was then ordered to join Hawke in the blockade of Brest. It was thus his peculiar fortune, after sharing in the defeat of La Clue, to be very noticeably present also in the great victory of Quiberon Bay (20 November 1759). When Hawke finally sailed for England in January 1760 he left the fleet, by now much afflicted with scurvy, under Bentley's command. Later in that year Bentley was again attached to the Grand Fleet under Hawke, but the victories of 1759 had minimized the action of the navy in European waters, and Bentley's further service afloat was uneventful. In 1761 he was appointed to a commissionership of the navy, but he resigned it on being promoted to his flag on 28 December 1763. He held no further command, but became a vice-admiral in October 1770.

According to R. B.'s *Life* Bentley had retired to a property at Buckland, near Dover, where he remained until his death, unmarried, on 3 January 1772 (not 14 December 1772 as stated in John Charnock's *Biographia navalis*). He was buried at St Andrew's, Buckland, and his will, in which he left numerous bequests to friends, cousins, and godchildren, was proved on 19 February.

J. K. LAUGHTON, *rev.* RUDDOCK MACKAY

Sources N. A. M. Rodger, *The wooden world: an anatomy of the Georgian navy* (1986) · R. F. Mackay, *Admiral Hawke* (1965) · R. F. Mackay, ed., *The Hawke papers* (1990) · G. J. Marcus, *Quiberon Bay* [1960] · W. L. Clowes, *The Royal Navy: a history from the earliest times to the present*, 3 (1898); repr. (1996) · PRO, ADM 51/282, 107/3, fol. 166 · will, PRO, PROB 11/974, fol. 322 · R. B., *Life of Sir John Bentley* (1921) [privately printed study] · *GM*, 1st ser., 42 (1772), 46

Archives PRO, Admiralty records, incl. those relating to courts martial

Bentley, John Francis (1839–1902), architect, was born at Doncaster on 30 January 1839, the third surviving son of Charles Bentley, wine merchant, and his wife, Ann, daughter of John Bacchus of that town. He received his education partly at home and partly at a private school in Doncaster. In boyhood he made a model from memory of St George's Church, Doncaster, after its destruction by fire in February 1853, and when George Gilbert Scott began the rebuilding in October 1853, Bentley frequented the fabric and rendered some services to the clerk of works. In 1854 he acted as voluntary superintendent in the restoration of Loversall church, Yorkshire, and there tried his hand at carving. His father, who deprecated the artistic career on which his son had set his heart, placed him for a short time, early in 1855, with Sharpe, Stewart & Co., a firm of mechanical engineers at Manchester; but in August 1855 Bentley entered on a five years' indenture with the building establishment of Winslow and Holland in London. The next year his father died, and Richard Holland, a partner of this firm, placed him (1857) in the office of Henry Clutton (1819–1893), an architect in extensive domestic and ecclesiastical practice, who had joined the Church of Rome. Bentley took the same step in 1862, taking the baptismal name Francis. In 1860, though invited by Clutton to join him in partnership, he preferred the risks of independence. In 1862 he took chambers at 14 Southampton Street, Covent Garden.

While waiting for commissions, Bentley continued the sketching and modelling which had already occupied his evening leisure, and often made for other architects designs for work in stone, metal, wood, stained glass, and embroidery. Works designed by him were shown at the exhibitions of London (1862) and Paris (1867). These included stained glass made by the firm of Lavers and Barraud (after 1868 Lavers, Barraud, and Westlake), and metalwork made by Hart & Son. He designed over forty organ cases for his friend the distinguished organ builder T. C. Lewis. For St Francis's Church, Notting Hill (the scene of his own baptism by Cardinal Wiseman), he designed the stone-groined baptistery, font, and porch, as well as the altars of St John and the Blessed Virgin (with paintings by his friend N. H. J. Westlake), a jewelled monstrance in the Byzantine style (now in the City of Birmingham Art Gallery), and at a later date the high altar. In 1866 he undertook for the poet Coventry Patmore the adaptation of an old Sussex house, Heron's Ghyll, near Uckfield (now Temple Grove preparatory school). His work betrayed from the first conscientious anxiety for perfection and soundness of construction. His own experience of entering the competition for a new church at Heigham, Norfolk, in 1858 led him to regard architectural competitions as inimical to art.

John Francis Bentley (1839–1902), by William Christian Symons, 1902

In 1868 Bentley received the commission for the seminary of St Thomas at Hammersmith (built 1876–88; since 1893 the Convent and High School of the Sacred Heart), one of his best works, and in the same year transferred his office to 13 John Street, Adelphi. In 1870 he designed the altar and reredos of the church of St Charles, Ogle Street, Marylebone. In 1887–8 Bentley built in the style of the Renaissance (but with a Gothic chapel) the large preparatory school (St John's) in connection with Beaumont College (now closed) at Old Windsor. For some years (beginning in 1874) he spent much thought and labour on the internal decoration and furniture of Carlton Towers, Selby, Yorkshire, for Lord Beaumont. On 6 October 1874 he married Margaret Annie (1857–1939), daughter of Henry J. Fleuss, a painter, of Düsseldorf (later art master at Marlborough College); they had four sons and seven daughters, of whom one son and one daughter died in infancy, and the remainder survived him.

For thirty years Bentley was engaged at intervals on the church of St Mary of the Angels, Moorhouse Road, Bayswater, where he designed additional aisles, a baptistery, various chapels, and furnishings. Apart from Westminster Cathedral, only five churches were erected to Bentley's designs. The church and presbytery of St Mary at Cadogan Street, Chelsea (1877–9), and the church of Our Lady of the Holy Souls at Bosworth Road, Kensal New Town (1881–2), are simple examples of Bentley's brick construction. In 1886–7 he built the unfinished portion of Corpus Christi Church, Brixton Hill, in Early Decorated style. The fine church of the Holy Rood at Watford, his Gothic

masterpiece, was, with its schools and presbytery, in hand from 1889 to 1900. Bentley's fifth church was for the Church of England. The commission for St Luke's, Chiddingstone Causeway, Kent (built 1897–8), came to him on the recommendation of John Singer Sargent.

For the Redemptorist Fathers, Bentley did varied work at Bishop Eton, Liverpool, and Clapham. To the church of Our Lady of Victories at Clapham (his own parish church) he added a fine lady chapel (1883–7), a transept, stained-glass windows, and a monastery, completed in 1893. For the church of St James, Spanish Place, London, he designed several altars and some glass. In 1898–9 he built with stone and red brick in the early fifteenth-century style the convent of the Immaculate Conception for Franciscan nuns at Bocking, near Braintree. The screen and organ case of St Etheldreda's, Ely Place, Holborn, are from his designs. Bentley also had commissions from the Church of England. In 1893–4 the two City churches of St Botolph came under his care. For St Botolph without Bishopsgate he provided external repair as well as internal decoration (1889–94), and for that at Aldgate he designed numerous embellishments (1888–93), notably the fine cornice of angels bearing the shields of the City companies. Similar works were done at St Mark's, North Audley Street. For St John's Church, Hammersmith (designed by his old friend William Butterfield), he schemed a morning chapel, organ case, and some decorations.

In 1894 came the great opportunity of Bentley's life. Cardinal Vaughan called upon him to design the Roman Catholic cathedral of Westminster. The conditions laid upon the architect were that the church should have a nave of vast extent giving an uninterrupted view of the high altar; that the design should be such that the fabric could be erected comparatively quickly, and the decoration added later; and that rivalry with the nearby Westminster Abbey should be avoided. Vaughan was thinking of an Early Christian basilica, but Bentley won him over in favour of the Byzantine style. Bentley perceived that his design should be preceded by special foreign study, and though not in robust health set out in November of the same year for a tour of Italy. After visiting Milan (especially for Sant' Ambrogio), Pavia, Florence, Rome (where the work of the Renaissance disappointed him), Perugia (which with Assisi delighted him), and Ravenna, he came at last to Venice, where cold and fatigue compelled him to rest before he could study St Mark's. His natural wish to proceed to Constantinople was frustrated by the prevalence there of cholera, and after returning to London in March 1895 he was ready by St Peter and St Paul's day (29 June) for the laying of the foundation-stone.

The cathedral is outwardly remarkable for its tall campanile and its bold use of brick and stone. The design is throughout marked by the greatest simplicity, largeness of scale, and avoidance of trivial ornament. Internally the vast nave consists of three bays measuring 60 feet square and each surmounted by a concrete dome. A fourth bay nearest the nominal east forms the sanctuary, and beyond it is an apse. The nave is flanked on each side by an aisle;

outside the aisles are the many chapels. When first opened for worship, and before any progress had been made with the marble decorations, the interior effect was a triumph of pure form. The construction was remarkable, Bentley having set himself to avoid any structural materials but brickwork, masonry, and concrete. 'I have broken', he said, 'the backbone of that terrible superstition, that iron is necessary to large spans' (Howell, 1982, 90). The cathedral was praised by Richard Norman Shaw as 'beyond all doubt the finest church that has been built for centuries' (*Architectural Review*, 10, 1901, 171). At the time of Bentley's death in 1902 the whole fabric of the building was complete, except for the final 50 feet of the campanile, but only a part of the marble revetment of one chapel had been installed. The first great ceremony held in the cathedral was Vaughan's requiem, on 25 June 1903. It was consecrated in 1910. The marble decoration is largely complete, but comparatively little of the mosaic decoration has been carried out.

In 1898 Bentley was summoned to the United States to advise on the design and construction of the Roman Catholic cathedral at Brooklyn, for which he prepared a Gothic scheme, which remained unexecuted. After being seized in November 1898 with paralytic symptoms, which in June 1900 affected his speech, he died on 2 March 1902 at his residence, 3 The Sweep, Old Town, Clapham Common, the day before his name was to be submitted to the Royal Institute of British Architects for the royal gold medal. He was buried in the cemetery of St Mary Magdalen's Church, Mortlake. His third son, Osmond, succeeded, in partnership with J. A. Marshall, to the architectural practice, and his eldest daughter, Winefride de l'Hôpital, wrote her father's biography.

PAUL WATERHOUSE, rev. PETER HOWELL

Sources W. de l'Hôpital, *Westminster Cathedral and its architect* (1919) · P. Howell, ed., 'Letters from J. F. Bentley to Charles Hadfield [2 pts]', *Architectural History*, 23 (1980), 95–137; 25 (1982), 65–97 · T. J. Willson, 'John Francis Bentley: a memoir', *RIBA Journal*, 9 (1901–2), 437–41 · *The Builder*, 82 (1902), 243–4 · *Building News*, 82 (1902), 339 · H. Ricardo, 'John Francis Bentley', *ArchR*, 11 (1902), 155–64 · *RIBA Journal*, 9 (1901–2), 164, 219, 279 · *Catalogue of the drawings collection of the Royal Institute of British Architects: B* (1972), 73–6 · J. Browne and T. Dean, *Building of faith* (1995) · *Dir. Brit. archs.* · W. W. Scott-Moncrieff, *John Francis Bentley* (1924) · R. Bentley, *Some leaves from the past* (1896) · *CGPLA Eng. & Wales* (1902)

Archives RIBA BAL, letters to Charles Hadfield · Westm. DA, letters to W. C. Symons

Likenesses O. Bentley, photograph, 1896, NPG · R. de l'Hôpital, oils, c.1899, Westminster Cathedral · R. Le Brun, oils, c.1899, Westminster Cathedral, London · W. C. Symons, oils, 1902, NPG [*see illus.*] · O. Bentley, photograph, repro. in de l'Hôpital, *Westminster Cathedral*, frontispiece · H. McCarthy, medallion on memorial, church of the Holy Rood, Watford · photograph, repro. in *Building News*, 56 (1890), 720 · photograph, repro. in de l'Hôpital, *Westminster Cathedral*, pl. XLV · silhouette, repro. in de l'Hôpital, *Westminster Cathedral*, pl. XLIV

Wealth at death £5961 13s. 9d.: administration with will, 24 March 1902, *CGPLA Eng. & Wales*

Bentley, John James (1860–1918), journalist and football administrator, was born at Chapel Town, Turton, Lancashire, on 14 June 1860, the third of four sons of John Bentley, a grocer, and his wife, Ann Beavan. Turton was only a small village but what may have been the first football club in Lancashire was formed there in 1872 when John Charles Kay, son of the local squire, returned from Harrow School and put together a team which played on a pitch behind the row of terraced houses where Bentley lived. By the time he was fourteen John was playing alongside his elder brothers, Tom and William; at twenty he was the club's captain, and shortly afterwards he became secretary and treasurer. His strength as a wing-half also won him selection for Bolton Association and for Lancashire. He stopped playing at the relatively early age of twenty-five but was involved with the sport at the highest level for the rest of his life.

The early part of Bentley's professional career was as a clerk for the London and North Western Railway Company in Bolton and then as a clerk to the Bolton school board. In 1882 he set up in business on his own in the emerging profession of accountancy and on 21 September that year married Betsy (1862/3–1917), daughter of Richard Entwistle, a builder from Blackpool. Their relationship was not broken until her death thirty-five years later. They had three daughters and a son, Harry, who died at the age of two in December 1892. Bentley had begun sending in reports of Turton's matches to local newspapers while still playing, adopting as his *nom de plume* Free Critic. In 1884 he began writing regularly for the *Bolton Cricket and Football Field*, and two years later he became assistant editor of the *Athletic News*. Sports writing was a growing branch of journalism and Bentley learned the job as he went along. He helped to transform the *Athletic News* from a twopenny weekly with a circulation of about 10,000 in 1886 to a penny paper with a circulation of nearly 200,000 by 1900 and a readership of many more. He was editor from 1895 to 1900.

In 1885 Bentley became secretary of Bolton Wanderers and in 1888 he was one of those to whom William McGregor wrote proposing what became the Football League. He served on the league's management committee for the next thirty years. By the middle of the 1890s he was combining the roles of referee, journalist, editor, Football Association (FA) councillor, and president of the Football League. In 1905 he became the first league official to become a vice-president of the FA. By this time he held a wide variety of other positions within the game and must have been one of the most powerful figures in English football. It caused no surprise when he became chairman of Manchester United in 1908 after the restructuring of the club following financial mismanagement; he later filled the position of club secretary between 1912 and 1916.

Bentley was a staunch defender of the professional player, although he supported the setting of a maximum permissible wage. He believed that professional football had to be run on business principles but thought that there should be no direct profit to individuals. His short hair and clipped moustache gave him an autocratic air, and although he was no orator (his many journalistic words were eminently unquotable) he was an influential leader of the sport during its most formative phase. He died at Fairhaven, near Blackpool, on 2 September 1918 and was buried in Turton cemetery, next to his wife and son. TONY MASON

Sources A. Gibson and W. Pickford, *Association football and the men who made it*, 4 vols. [1905–6] • S. Inglis, *League football and the men who made it: the official centenary of the Football League, 1888–1988* (1988) • T. Mason, *Association football and English society, 1863–1915* (1980) • T. Mason, 'Sporting news, 1860–1914', *The press in English society from the seventeenth to nineteenth centuries*, ed. M. Harris and A. Lee (1986) • b. cert. • m. cert.
Wealth at death £865 13s. 7d.: probate, 7 Nov 1918, *CGPLA Eng. & Wales*

Bentley, Joseph Clayton (1809–1851), engraver and painter, was born in Bradford, Yorkshire, the third son and fifth child of Greenwood Bentley (1777–1858), a well-known Bradford solicitor, and Jane, the daughter of Robert Stockdale, gentleman, of West Marton, Skipton, Yorkshire. He began his artistic career as a landscape painter, and was a founder member of the Bradford Artists' Society of Painting and Sculpture (1827). In 1832 he went to London, where he studied engraving under Robert Brandard. He never entirely abandoned painting, however, and occasionally exhibited at the British Institution (1833–51), the Royal Academy (1846–52), the Royal Hibernian Academy (1856), the Society of British Artists, and in provincial exhibitions. His exhibited works were mainly views of Yorkshire, painted with great freedom of hand and showing a nice feeling for colour.

Bentley enjoyed a successful career as an engraver, largely on account of his ability to meet deadlines. Many of his plates were executed for the publications of the publishing firms of Fisher and Virtue, notably S. C. Hall's *The Gems of European Art* (1846), published by Virtue, for which he engraved *The Fountain* after Francesco Zuccarelli and *A Sunny Day* after Aelbert Cuyp; these were republished in the *Art Journal* (1868). Some of his best works are the plates after pictures in the Robert Vernon collection in the National Gallery, London, which he produced for the *Art Journal* from 1849: these included *The Brook by the Way* after Gainsborough, *Lake Avernus* after Richard Wilson, *The Valley Farm* after Constable, *The Windmill* after John Linnell, *The Way to Church* after Thomas Creswick, and *The Wooden Bridge, Port of Leghorn*, and *Sea-Shore in Holland*, all after Sir Augustus W. Callcott. Bentley's engravings are not of the highest quality, but they do show considerable artistic feeling. His hard work undermined his already fragile health and brought on tuberculosis; he died at his home in Perry Vale, Sydenham, Kent, on 9 October 1851, leaving a widow and two children. There are examples of his work at Cartwright Hall, Bradford; the National Gallery of Ireland, Dublin; the Oblastní Galerie, Liberec, Czech Republic; and the Victoria and Albert Museum, London (*Woodland Scene with a Startled Heron*). DELIA GAZE

Sources *Art Journal*, 14 (1852), 15 • B. Wood, 'Some old Bradford artists', *Bradford Antiquary*, 2 (1890–95), 198–209 • W. Cudworth, 'Old Bradford lawyers: the Bentley family', *Bradford Antiquary*, 2 (1890–95), 65–71 • B. Hunnisett, *An illustrated dictionary of British steel engravers*, new edn (1989) • B. Hunnisett, *Steel engraved book illustration in England* (1980) • H. M. Cundall, *A history of British water colour painting*, 2nd edn (1929) • T. Fawcett, *The rise of English provincial art: artist, patron and institution outside London, 1800–1830* (1974) • L. Lambourne and J. Hamilton, eds., *British watercolours in the Victoria and Albert Museum* (1980) • G. Meissner, ed., *Allgemeines Künstlerlexikon: die bildenden Künstler aller Zeiten und Völker*, [new edn, 34 vols.] (Leipzig and Munich, 1983–) • Wood, *Vic. painters*, 3rd edn • *DNB* • J. Johnson, ed., *Works exhibited at the Royal Society of British Artists, 1824–1893, and the New English Art Club, 1888–1917*, 2 vols. (1975)

Bentley, Nathaniel [nicknamed Dirty Dick] (1735?–1809), eccentric, was the son of a successful City of London merchant and shopkeeper who received an education 'equal to his situation as a gentleman' (*History of the Extraordinary Dirty warehouse*, 6). After the death of Bentley's mother, details of whom are unknown, his father married a woman of considerable property to provide a new source of revenue for his hardware business. Bentley's stepmother was a dissenter and encouraged his father to give up the Church of England for the nonconformist faith. Previously Bentley's father had provided his local Anglican church, St Katharine Cree, with a gift of a bell to be rung on his birthday during his lifetime. On his father's death in 1760 Bentley inherited 'a good fortune' (ibid., 8) which he used to embellish his existing reputation as 'the beau of Leadenhall-Street' well known for his fine manners and dress. In 1764 he visited Paris where he participated in high society, met Louis XVI, and was identified as the best dressed and mannered English gentleman. On his return to London, Bentley maintained his reputation for refinement when in public, and remained a patron of Vauxhall and Ranelagh Gardens until the early nineteenth century.

However, Bentley's celebrity now rested less on his fine dress than on the squalor in which he was said to live at his business premises, the so-called 'dirty warehouse' at 46 Leadenhall Street. Several pamphlets published at the turn of the century claimed that the shop had not been cleaned since his father's death, and speculated on the existence of a dining room that had been shut up following the death of Bentley's fiancée shortly before their marriage. Bentley's appearance and mannerisms also attracted considerable attention. Unwashed and dressed in shirt sleeves and an ill-powdered wig, he refused offers for his house to be cleaned claiming that its notoriety was good for trade. Certainly his reputation attracted a number of female visitors intrigued by rumours of his miserliness, the infamous 'blue room', and his supposed habit of sleeping in a coffin. In fact the majority emerged to speak of the gentlemanliness beneath the grime, politeness being 'his ruling passion'. At a time when refinement was a highly valued indicator of status and character, Bentley's quixotic personality proved fascinating for many commentators who speculated on his rejection of appropriate conduct and on the true meaning of politeness:

> Thou art ('tis said) a very comely man,
> Of polish'd language, partial to the fair,
> Then why not wash thy face, and comb thy matted hair?
> (*European Magazine*, January 1801, quoted in *History*, 18)

In February 1804 Bentley left 46 Leadenhall Street when the lease expired. The move prompted several new biographies which offered readers an intimate tour of the 'dirty warehouse' and further speculated as to the reasons for Bentley's behaviour, with particular attention being given to his strict upbringing, desire for independence, and parsimony. Thereafter Bentley lived in Jewry Street, Aldgate, until 1807 and then at Leonard Street, Shoreditch, for a further year before he took up as a beggar and travelled the country. After a brief period at Musselburgh, Midlothian, he moved to nearby Haddington where he died, unmarried, from fever in 1809.   PHILIP CARTER

Sources DNB · *The history of the extraordinary dirty warehouse in Leadenhall Street; together with the memoirs of its eccentric inhabitant, Nathaniel Bentley, esq.* (1803) · *Authentick memoirs of the life of the celebrated Nathaniel Bentley, esq., commonly called Dirty Dick* (1802) · *The olde port wine house of Dirty Dick* (c.1900) · *The dirty old man, Dirty Dick* (1880) · H. Wilson, *Wonderful characters*, 1 (1821), 166–80
Likenesses I. Mills, etching, BM, NPG · R. Page, engraving, repro. in Wilson, *Wonderful characters*, vol. 1, facing p. 166 · prints, NPG
Wealth at death £400: Wilson, *Wonderful characters*, vol. 1, p. 179

Bentley, Nicolas Clerihew [Nicholas Clerihew] (1907–1978), cartoonist and author, was born at 75 Dartmouth Park Hill, Highgate, Middlesex, on 14 June 1907, the youngest in the family of one daughter and two sons of Edmund Clerihew *Bentley (1875–1956), writer, and his wife, Violet Alice Mary (1878/9–1949), daughter of General Neil Edmonstone Boileau, of the Bengal staff corps and something of an eccentric: of him, Bentley wrote: 'of all my immediate relatives whom I never had a chance to meet, the General, who died twelve years before I was born, is the one I would most like to have known, and knowing, I feel equally sure, would have loved' (Bentley, *Version of the Truth*, 29).

Nicholas Bentley (he later dropped the 'h' from his first name) was sent to University College School in Hampstead, London, and left it, no scholar, at seventeen. He was already visiting the National Gallery to study painting, and knew he was going to be some kind of artist. The illustrated books in his father's library included works by Caran d'Ache and Gustave Doré, which he enjoyed before he could read. He enrolled in 1924 at the Heatherley School of Fine Art, London, known to be good for teaching illustration. The joint principal was Iain Macnab, who became important in Bentley's development. Bentley described him as a genius, both for the way he gave students confidence in themselves and, in particular, for how he insisted on practising observation, which became the sure foundation of Bentley's own success as an artist. Bentley seems to have been observant from childhood, but after learning from Macnab he wrote, 'One's eye is never off duty'.

Bentley left Heatherleys after a comparatively short time, and became a clown (unpaid) in a circus. He had always been fond of dressing up, especially with his father's friends the Chestertons—and getting inside the skin of somebody else is as much the business of the illustrator as of the actor. He worked as a clown for six weeks, and then for a short time took part as an extra in films. His experiences in the ring and on the stage are reflected in several of his early cartoons.

In 1926 Bentley worked on the London underground during the general strike and sold his first drawing to his

Nicolas Clerihew Bentley (1907–1978), by Howard Coster, 1953

godfather, G. K. Chesterton, but it is not known what it was. In 1928 he was illustrating a diary in a trade paper, *Man and his Clothes*: clothes always interested him, and he always drew them with great skill. He was then offered a job by Jack Beddington, the director of Shell publicity, and joined a group which included Edward Ardizzone, Barnett Freedman, Rex Whistler, Arthur Elton, John Betjeman, Peter Quennell, and Robert Byron; the American poster artist Edward McKnight Kauffer also became a close friend. In his autobiography, *A Version of the Truth* (1960), he wrote: 'the three years I spent with Jack Beddington were decisive, not so much for Shell as for me ... I ... would certainly not be the sort of man I am if I had never felt Jack's influence' (Bentley, *Version of the Truth*, 139). Bentley's friendship with Beddington was deep but he was not fond of advertising. Rescue came from Hilaire Belloc, an old friend of his father's, who asked him to illustrate his *New Cautionary Tales* (1930). Bentley took Belloc's memorable advice, delivered on a visit to Shell-Mex House:

> If you don't get out of here pretty soon, my boy, you'll be tied to the chariot wheels of commerce for the rest of your life! ... Where's it going to get you? Clear out of it while you can, my boy!   (ibid., 142–3)

The collaboration led him to illustrate, with equal success, several comic books by J. B. Morton (Beachcomber of the *Daily Express*), Damon Runyon, and others, as well as anthologies, sometimes compiled by himself. The twelfth book bearing Bentley's name as illustrator, also written by him, was *Ready Refusals, or, The White Liar's Engagement Book*. The text consists of a quotation for every day of the year, collected by Bentley from an astonishing range of authors, and sets down in his own words 'an invitation resistance that is proof against every effort of the most insultingly charitable hostess'. The first published collection of Bentley's cartoons, culled from *The Bystander*, *Punch*, and *Men Only*, was *Die? I Thought I'd Laugh!* (1936); but he was already as much of a writer as he was an artist.

On 17 October 1934 Bentley married Barbara Mary Hastings (1908–1989), the daughter of Sir Patrick Gardiner *Hastings, the most famous QC of his day; their only child, Arabella (Bella), was born in 1943. During the Second World War Bentley illustrated several books for children, including two written by his wife: *Lobby Lobster* (1943), with eight full-page illustrations beautifully conceived in full colour, not just in line with colour added; and *Mustapha Monkey* (1945), with many illustrations, among the best he ever did, but all in line.

Before the war Bentley had been a prison visitor at Wormwood Scrubs prison and in 1938 became an auxiliary fireman. During the war he served with the London Fire Brigade, and had grim experiences in the London blitz, vividly described in *A Version of the Truth*. He worked in the Ministry of Information throughout the war, first in the home intelligence and later in the publications and films divisions. After the war he continued to draw for books, newspapers, magazines, and advertisers, and also wrote three thrillers, all published by Michael Joseph and later as paperbacks by Penguin. In 1950 he joined the publishing firm of André Deutsch, for whom he had illustrated George Mikes's best-seller *How to be an Alien* in 1946: he became not only Deutsch's partner but a lifelong friend.

Working as a publisher enabled Nicolas Bentley to go on drawing without being forced to over-produce. Between 1952 and 1954 he drew regular cartoons for the weekly *Time and Tide*, and after that for the daily *News Chronicle*. Between 1958 and 1962 he drew over 600 'pocket cartoons' for the *Daily Mail*, published about 2 inches wide from much larger drawings. He finally found the strain of this work too great, and gave it up as a regular commission.

Bentley had an outstanding ability to catch likenesses. His faces are clearly real people he has observed, both rich and poor, old and young, women and children as well as men, and even dogs and cats. Some portraits may be called cruelly accurate, but they are never savage. He also drew many portraits, in black and white line, of famous people, for various papers, including over sixty for the *Sunday Telegraph*, which began publication in March 1964. When aged over sixty-four, he began drawing for *Private Eye*, at that time the most youthful of Britain's adult satirical weeklies. His cartoon of the royal family sitting in 1972 for a group photograph (reproduced in *Nicolas Bentley Drew the Pictures*, 1990) is accurate, funny, and devastating.

The source of Bentley's inspiration is man himself: man, proud man, especially when dressed in a little brief authority. He became the first artist in England of recent times to get away with loud laughter at certain aspects of death and the church—perhaps from natural irreverence and also because they gave him the opportunity to use pleasing areas of solid black. More usually he showed the gentler, more pleasant face of life. His pretty girls, whether vacuous or intelligent, are enchanting, and his housewives, chars, couturiers, schoolgirls, Wren officers, cellists, and hockey players are never mere caricatures: they are honest portraits of individuals we all know. The people of England in the mid-twentieth century live on in all his pages.

Towards the end of his life Bentley moved out of London and settled down in a converted village school at Downhead, near Shepton Mallet, Somerset. Though becoming elderly, he retained a youthful appearance—slim, shy, and friendly. He died at the Royal United Hospital, Bath, on 14 August 1978. His wife survived him.

RUARI McLEAN

Sources *Nicolas Bentley drew the pictures*, ed. R. McLean (1990) [incl. bibliography and over 114 pp. of illustrations] · *DNB* · personal knowledge (2004) · private information (2004) [A. Deutsch, D. Athill, Bella Bentley (Mrs Jones)] · N. Bentley, *A version of the truth* (1960) · b. cert. · m. cert. · d. cert. · M. B. Grimsditch, 'Nicolas Bentley', *The Artist* (Sept 1938)
Archives Bodl. Oxf., corresp. and literary papers
Likenesses H. Coster, photograph, 1953, NPG [*see illus.*] · A. Deutsch, photograph, repro. in McLean, ed., *Nicolas Bentley drew the pictures*
Wealth at death £37,875: administration, 22 June 1979, *CGPLA Eng. & Wales*

Bentley, Phyllis Eleanor (1894–1977), novelist, was born on 19 November 1894 at Victoria House, Stanley Road, Halifax, Yorkshire, the fourth child and only daughter of Joseph Edwin Bentley (1855–1926), master dyer and finisher, and his wife, Eleanor Kettlewell (1859–1949), daughter of Thomas Kettlewell, representative of a cloth-manufacturing firm in Huddersfield, Yorkshire. She was educated at the Princess Mary High School for Girls, Halifax, and, from 1910, at Cheltenham Ladies' College, where she studied for an external London University degree. In 1914 she was awarded a first-class pass degree, an indication that she should have taken the honours degree that was at that time forbidden to women students.

After her years at Cheltenham, Bentley returned to Halifax. Her autobiography *'O Dreams, O Destinations'* (1962) recalls the dilemma of the educated woman living in the parental home without income or independence in the early years of the twentieth century. She came under strong pressure to 'stay out of a man's job' and help her mother with domestic tasks, but in 1915 she took a teaching post in a boys' grammar school. She was an unsuccessful schoolteacher, in particular unable to keep order, and after six months of misery returned home. After an unsettled period of two years she became a volunteer at a new, progressive child welfare clinic in Halifax, and her work with working-class women and their children awakened her political conscience. She combined volunteer work with a rigorous programme of reading and self-education, and her political and religious convictions gradually shifted from Conservative and Church of England to socialist and humanist.

In 1918 Bentley moved to London to work as a munitions clerk. After the war she returned to Halifax with a strong sense of herself as a 'surplus woman', both personally and professionally. Convinced from an early age that she was unattractive to men, she was inhibited by shyness and had never considered marriage an option. Instead, she determined to 'reform injustice, banish iniquities, dismiss hate … by presenting human character in story' (Bentley, 107). A librarian friend taught her the Dewey decimal system, and she spent the next six years cataloguing books in local libraries while working on a novel in the evenings. In 1922 *Environment* was published. Set in her native West Riding of Yorkshire, it was the first of many novels in which she saw her own district as a microcosm of the world and expressed her strong belief that only through understanding and conciliation could troubles be cured. Partly autobiographical, its story was that of a young woman struggling for education and fulfilment in the fictional Yorkshire town of Hudley. It was damned with faint praise by reviewers, but, undeterred by lukewarm notices, she slowly mastered the techniques of crafting fiction. Over the next three years she managed to save £700 from the modest sales of *Environment*, subsequent short stories, and contributions to the *Yorkshire Post*. In 1926, during the general strike, the family textiles business foundered, but, by giving up her savings, she managed to keep it afloat. Her father died from a heart attack in 1926, which Bentley attributed to the stress of impending bankruptcy, and from then on she had the responsibility of supporting her widowed mother, who lived to be ninety. In 1929 *Carr* was published, the imaginary biography of Philip Joseph Carr, a west Yorkshire manufacturer, written by his granddaughter. This novel was more favourably received by the critics: the *Times Literary Supplement* commended her for overcoming the difficulties of the fictional biography. It was Bentley's first experiment with historical regional fiction, and two years later she achieved her great success with *Inheritance* (1932), a chronicle of the Oldroyd family and their mill from the time of the Luddites to the closing of the mill in 1930. The sequels *The Rise of Henry Morcar* (1946), *A Man of his Time* (1966), and *Ring in the New* (1969) carried the chronicle of the Oldroyds up to 1968. The entire series became a television serial. These novels and all her subsequent ones were published by Victor Gollancz.

Inheritance brought Bentley to prominence both in Britain and in the United States. During the early 1930s she was befriended by Winifred Holtby and Vera Brittain, both of whom invited her to London and introduced her into literary circles. In 1934, 1936, 1939, and 1941 she visited the United States on lecture tours, on which she was promoted as a regional novelist. Her only novel set outside Yorkshire, *Freedom's Farewell* (1936), about the fall of the Roman empire and written as a protest against the rise of Hitler and Mussolini, was not a success. In 1941 she published *The English Regional Novel*, a survey of regional fiction from 1840 to 1940, with special emphasis on Charlotte Brontë, George Eliot, Thomas Hardy, and Arnold Bennett. In January 1941 Bentley braved London in the blitz to work there for the American division of the British Ministry of Information, taking a small flat in Bloomsbury. The position was an acknowledgement of her fame in the

United States, and in 1944 she crossed the Atlantic on government business, risking the perils of submarines, to work with the British information service in New York. From 1945 until 1949 her time was occupied with nursing her invalid mother, and she was unable to write. After her mother's death in 1949, she worked prodigiously, producing volumes of short stories, her autobiography in 1962, several historical children's books, a short biography, *The Brontës* (1947), *The Brontës and their World* (1969), and detective stories for American magazines. She also contributed many reviews and articles to various journals, for years writing a fortnightly column of fiction reviews in the *Yorkshire Post*. She was also a vigorous supporter of local arts activities, particularly amateur dramatics, and was active on many committees.

During the fifties Bentley became aware that her popularity was on the wane, as, with the arrival of the Angry Young Men on the literary scene, the working class was replacing the middle class as the material for novels. Her later fiction, such as *Crescendo* (1958), did not enjoy the success of her Oldroyd series. However, in later life she achieved recognition as an accomplished writer. Leeds University awarded her an honorary DLitt in 1949, in 1958 she became a fellow of the Royal Society of Literature, and she was appointed OBE in 1970. She died at her home, Ing Royde, Broomfield Avenue, Halifax, on 27 June 1977.

KATHERINE MULLIN

Sources *DNB* • P. Schlueter and J. Schlueter, eds., *An encyclopedia of British women writers* (1988) • P. Bentley, *'O dreams, O destinations': an autobiography* (1962) • D. L. Kirkpatrick, ed., *Reference guide to English literature*, 2nd edn, 1 (1991) • Blain, Clements & Grundy, *Feminist comp.* • *CGPLA Eng. & Wales* (1978)
Archives Saddleworth Museum and Art Gallery, Oldham, letters • W. Yorks. AS, Calderdale, corresp., diary, literary notebooks, papers, and scripts | JRL, letters to *Manchester Guardian* • Royal Society of Literature, London, letters to Royal Society of Literature • UCL, letters to Arnold Bennett • W. Yorks. AS, Bradford, corresp. with Bradford English Society
Likenesses photographs, repro. in Bentley, *'O dreams, o destinations'*
Wealth at death £29,930: probate, 6 Jan 1978, *CGPLA Eng. & Wales* • £1740: further probate, 22 March 1978, *CGPLA Eng. & Wales*

Bentley, Richard (*bap.* 1645, *d.* 1697), bookseller, was baptized on 18 December 1645 at Barton on the Heath, Warwickshire, the son of Thomas Bentley. Nothing further is known of his childhood or his parents' circumstances, but when Bentley was apprenticed for the term of eight years to James Magnes in March 1659, his father was described as 'gent.'. Magnes, of Russell Street, Covent Garden, was a member of the Merchant Taylors of London, but worked in the book trade. After his apprenticeship Bentley seems to have stayed on in the business as a journeyman and after the death of Magnes in 1678 went into partnership with his master's widow. When she died in July 1682, her part of the stock was left to her daughter Susanna, whose name appeared with Bentley's in the imprint of publications until 1689. In 1684 Bentley was made free of the Stationers' Company, and only then was he able to register titles in the Stationers' register under his own name. Throughout his career, Bentley worked from the address that Magnes had used, the Post House (or Office) in Russell Street. In August 1689 Bentley acquired a lease on a house in King Street, Covent Garden, and married Katherine Davis (d. 1699) on 13 February of the following year. The couple had at least three children, Dawbenny, Richard, and Thomas, all three baptized in the local church of St Paul's, Covent Garden.

Bentley published mainly, but not exclusively, novels and plays, which led John Dunton, a fellow stationer, to call him 'novel Bentley' (Mandelbrote, 56). He had varying percentages of shares in the copyright of many literary works such as Milton's *Paradise Lost* and *Paradise Regained* and some of Shakespeare's plays. Bentley often made up collections of novels or plays, which were sometimes no more than a reissue with a new title-page of unsold publications from the time when he and Magnes worked together. He frequently published works in association with other members of the book trade, owning only a part share in the rights. In one instance Bentley fell foul of the authorities over Gabriel de Brémond's *Hattige*, a satire on the conduct of Charles II, but the work was published nevertheless with a false imprint in 1680 and incorporated into one of Bentley's collections, *Modern Novels*, in 1692.

Bentley died at King Street very shortly after his will was drawn up on 15 June 1697 and was buried in St Paul's Church, Covent Garden, on the 23rd of the same month. Probate was granted on 16 July 1697 to Katherine, whom Bentley had named executor and guardian of Dawbenny and Thomas; Richard junior presumably died before his father. Katherine sold the copyrights that Bentley had held on his publications and part of the stock to Richard Wellington, but kept the shop going until she herself died; she was buried on 16 September 1699. The one surviving child of the marriage, Dawbenny, died in May the following year. Administration of Katherine's estate was granted to Anna Davis, her sister. The shop passed into the hands of Edmund Rumball, a former apprentice of Bentley, who went into partnership with Wellington, bringing Bentley's assets back together again.

MARJA SMOLENAARS

Sources G. Mandelbrote, 'Richard Bentley's copies: the ownership of copyrights in the late 17th century', *The book and its customers, 1450–1900*, ed. A. Hunt, G. Mandelbrote, and A. Shell (1997), 55–94 · D. F. McKenzie, ed., *Stationers' Company apprentices*, [2]: 1641–1700 (1974), 105 · W. H. Hunt, ed., *The registers of St Paul's Church, Covent Garden, London*, 1–4, Harleian Society, register section, 33–6 (1906–8) · H. R. Plomer and others, *Dictionaries of the printers and booksellers who were at work in England, Scotland and Ireland, 1577–1775* (1910–32); repr. (1977) · will, PRO, PROB 11/439, sig. 135 · administration, PRO, PROB 6/75, fol. 156r · parish register, Westminster, St Peter, 13 Feb 1690 [marriage]

Wealth at death see will, PRO, PROB 11/439, sig. 135

Bentley, Richard (1662–1742), philologist and classical scholar, was born on 27 January 1662 at his maternal grandparents' house at Oulton, Yorkshire, the second child of Thomas Bentley (*bap.* 1637, *d.* 1675), a yeoman farmer, and his wife, Sarah (*bap.* 1642, *d.* in or after 1684), the daughter of Richard Willies and his wife, Ann. His paternal grandfather, James Bentley, born at Heptonstall,

Richard Bentley (1662–1742), by Sir James Thornhill, 1710

settled in Methley, the parish of his wife, Jane Crabtree. He is said to have been a civil war royalist captain and died a prisoner at Pontefract. Methley borders on Rothwell parish, which included Oulton, and also Woodlesford, where Thomas Bentley may have owned property. Bentley was baptized at Rothwell on 6 February 1662. He had four siblings: James, Ann, Joseph, and Mary. Thomas Bentley of Oulton was also the father of Elizabeth Eltringham's illegitimate child Thomas.

Education and early career After learning Latin accidence from his mother, Bentley was taught by Paul Greenwood at Methley day school and by John Baskerville at Wakefield grammar school. When his father died in April 1675, Bentley's grandfather Richard Willies, a builder, assumed responsibility for his education. Admitted as a subsizar to St John's College, Cambridge, on 24 May 1676, and tutored by Joseph Johnston, he was awarded a Dowman scholarship in November 1678 and subsequently a Constable one. He graduated BA on 23 January 1680, being ranked sixth in the first class (actually third, three of those above him being the honorary nominees of the vice-chancellor and the two proctors), and proceeded MA in 1683.

In 1682 St John's, having no vacancy for another Yorkshire fellow, nominated Bentley master of Spalding School in Lincolnshire—or possibly Francis Johnson of Ayscoughfee Hall nominated him after he tutored his son (E. H. Gooch, *A History of Spalding*, 1940, 205–6, 255). Bentley soon left Spalding and on 1 January 1683 became tutor to James Stillingfleet, whose father Edward was dean of St Paul's Cathedral. Over the next six years Bentley took advantage of Dean Stillingfleet's outstanding library to consolidate his knowledge of the classics and scripture. Before he was twenty-four he compiled his 'Hexapla' (now BL, Add. MS 11357), a 300-leaf quarto book, whose parallel columns, written very small, index alphabetically every word in the Hebrew Bible, with its equivalents in different Latin and Greek translations, and also in Aramaic and Syriac texts.

In 1689 Bentley, accompanying James Stillingfleet, was admitted as a commoner to Wadham College, Oxford, and incorporated MA on 4 July. Henry Compton, bishop of London, ordained him deacon on 16 March 1690, and Edward Stillingfleet, now bishop of Worcester, soon made him his chaplain. Always interested in metrics, Bentley collated manuscripts of the Greek metrist Hephaestion. He negotiated for Oxford University to buy Isaac Voss's magnificent library and regretted the university's 'falling so in their price' (Bentley to Edward Bernard, 20 Sept 1690, *Correspondence*, 1.9). Leiden University secured it for £3000.

Bentley also worked on Lucretius: unaware of Voss's superior manuscripts, he missed making the discoveries reserved for Karl Lachmann in 1850, but his valuable annotations—left, like much of his work, for posthumous publication—were printed in Gilbert Wakefield's Glasgow edition of 1813. He embarked on two prohibitively time-consuming editions: one was of fragments of the Greek poets, from which his collection of Callimachus was published by Johann Georg Graevius in 1697; the other was a three-volume lexicon of 'Hesychius, Suidas, Etymologicon, all in one page, after the manner of Walton's Polyglott', with a supplementary volume of other lexicographers (Bentley to Bernard, 1690, *Correspondence*, 1.10). Bentley worked most on Hesychius, where he reckoned on correcting 'about five thousand faults' (*Works*, 2.292).

Letter to Mill and Boyle lectures Bentley's first published work instantly made his reputation. His Latin letter to John Mill, principal of St Edmund Hall, Oxford, was printed in June 1691 as a 98-page appendix to the *editio princeps* of the *Historia chronica* by John Malalas of Antioch (*c*.480–*c*.570). Mill edited the chronicle from a Bodleian manuscript; Humphrey Hody of Wadham College wrote the prolegomena. Malalas becomes valuable when he reaches the sixth century, but that did not interest Bentley; so his letter, which Mill pressed him to compose, took up instead historical and literary topics that Malalas's references suggested. These include the oracular names of Orpheus, monotheist verses misattributed to Sophocles, lost plays of Euripides, forgotten rules of anapaestic verse, trees native to Crete, Hesychius's lexicography, the original tragedian Thespis, the poet Ion of Chios, Greek verse fragments, and the formation of Greek names.

The chronicler's own name was at issue: having exposed Hody's ill-informed objection to the termination -*as* instead of -*a*, Bentley refuted Hody's unconvincing response, in which Hody pointedly prayed to write without arrogance and bitterness. This argument, which was published in the edition, between two chaplains of Stillingfleet's, achieved some notoriety; but the brilliance of Bentley's letter impressed scholars throughout Europe, both Graevius and Ezechiel Spanheim calling Bentley England's bright and rising star.

Bentley began editing Manilius's *Astronomica*, perhaps in this connection consulting Isaac Newton's *Principia* and obtaining from Newton a preliminary reading-list 'sufficient for understanding my book' (*Correspondence of Isaac Newton*, 3.156). Newton may have prompted Bentley's nomination in February 1692 as the first Boyle lecturer; but one of the trustees, Bishop Thomas Tenison, already knew him, as possibly did another, John Evelyn, who later became a close friend. Robert Boyle had bequeathed £50 per annum for eight sermons 'proving the Christian religion against notorious Infidels, *viz*. Atheists, Theists, Pagans, Jews, and Mahometans'. Noting that Boyle put atheists 'in the very first place as the most dangerous enemies', Bentley observed that 'not one English Infidel in a hundred is any other than a Hobbist; which I know to be rank Atheism in the private study and select conversation of those men, whatever it appear to be abroad' (Bentley to Bernard, 28 May 1692, *Correspondence*, 1.39–40). Accordingly he devoted his course of lectures (between 7 March and 5 December 1692) to atheists.

Having dismissed atheism as a way of life, Bentley proceeded to confute atheistic theory: first from the faculties of the soul, without which sense, perception, and motion would be impossible; next from the structure of human bodies, which cannot always have subsisted and whose origin must be divine, not some astrological or natural or random process; lastly from the world or universe, whose matter—even granting the impossible, that it always subsisted and moved—could never have fallen into any system, let alone this one, whose order and beauty evince its divine origin.

Sermon 7 is particularly interesting for its use of Newton's gravitational theory to prove that atoms in an Epicurean chaos could never simply by reciprocal attraction convene to form the present system. Before publishing that sermon Bentley sent Newton several queries, answered in four letters (10 December 1692 – 25 February 1693), in which Newton expresses his pleasure in his *Principia*'s being used to 'work wth considering men for the beleife of a Deity' (*Correspondence of Isaac Newton*, 3.233). The published sermons, which had greatly impressed their hearers, were frequently reprinted.

John Moore, bishop of Norwich, whose famous library Bentley used, ordained him priest in September 1692; on 8 October he was instituted prebendary of Worcester. On 23 December 1693 he was appointed keeper of the king's libraries; his patent was dated 12 April 1694, and he assumed custody of the St James's Palace library in May. He was reappointed Boyle lecturer in 1694; he intended to publish the sermons, whose precise topic is unknown, but never did—to the displeasure of Tenison, who became archbishop of Canterbury in 1695.

In 1695 Bentley was made chaplain-in-ordinary to William III. On 4 September he was instituted rector of Hartlebury, Worcestershire, pending James Stillingfleet's becoming eligible three years later. On 30 November the

Royal Society elected him a fellow: he served on its council in 1697 and paid his subscription regularly but, on the evidence of the minutes, was barely an active member. In January 1696 he moved from Stillingfleet's house to the librarian's quarters at St James's, where he hoped Lord Marlborough would 'obtain for me a new ground room' to shelve the books (Bentley to Evelyn, 22 Feb 1696, *Correspondence*, 1.114). In *A Proposal for Building a Royal Library* (1697) he pointed out the advantages of 'a free library' with funds to acquire collections, but the necessary legislation could not be introduced.

Having received 'a *civil denial*' when he applied to Tenison for a Lambeth doctorate (Bentley to Evelyn, 29 Jan 1695, *Correspondence*, 1.92), Bentley was in due course created DD at Cambridge. His sermon at the commencement, 'On revelation and the messias' (5 July 1696), was directed against deists and subsequently published. On 10 July the university authorized him 'to purchase types from abroad for the new printing house' (McKenzie, 2.1), a most important initiative to revive Cambridge publishing, which had languished in the hands of private printers. The vice-chancellor's accounts tend to support Bentley's later claim that the press was 'projected and founded solely by myself' (Bentley to Thomas Bateman, 25 Dec 1712, ibid., 2.448). His eminence may be gauged from the London club he formed: 'Sir Christopher Wren, Mr. Lock, Mr. Newton, &c., (and I hope when in Town Mr Evelyn) are to meet here once or twice a week in the Evening' (Bentley to Evelyn, 21 Oct 1697, ibid., 1.152).

Dissertation upon the Epistles of Phalaris The controversy over the respective merits of the ancients and the moderns took on new life in England towards the end of the century. When Sir William Temple affirmed 'that the oldest Books we have are still in their kind the best', he cited Aesop's fables and the letters of the Sicilian tyrant Phalaris (W. Temple, 'An essay upon the ancient and modern learning', 58, in *Miscellanea: the Second Part*, 1690). His assertion that only Phalaris could have represented the distinctive passions and actions in the letters was cited in a new edition by the Hon. Charles Boyle, the late chemist's undergraduate nephew. It was prepared under Dean Henry Aldrich's auspices as the customary gift-book for members of Christ Church, Oxford, on new year's day 1695.

Boyle had wanted a king's library manuscript collated: his London bookseller Thomas Bennet neglected his instructions, but eventually, after Bentley assumed custody of the library, the manuscript was borrowed for some days in May 1694 until recalled by Bentley, who was leaving London. The collator, George Gibson, had time enough but completed only a third of the manuscript, and Bentley was surprised to find Boyle's preface accuse him of denying its further use—'out of his singular humanity' (*Phalaris*, *Epistolæ* [1695], sig. a4*v*). Moreover, when Bentley explained, Boyle refused to retract.

Behind the ill feeling at Christ Church lay Bennet's report that Bentley had called the epistles spurious—as

scholars had occasionally suspected. William Wotton had wanted Bentley's proofs of this for his critique of Temple's antimodernist stance, *Reflections upon Ancient and Modern Learning* (1694); but Bentley lacked time to compose them. However, for the enlarged second edition (May 1697) he quickly wrote, as a letter addressed to Wotton, his 150-page *Dissertation upon the Epistles of Phalaris*. After outlining the uncertain chronology of 'The age of Phalaris', he advanced sixteen arguments proving that historically and stylistically the letters could not have been written by their purported author; likewise the letters ascribed to Themistocles, Socrates, and Euripides, and Aesop's fables. Bentley also told his version of the royal manuscript story.

Temple had no answer to Bentley's arguments, but Christ Church took up the cudgels and published in March 1698 *Dr. Bentley's Dissertations on the Epistles of Phalaris, and the Fables of Æsop, Examin'd* (known as the *Examination*). This 300-page *jeu d'esprit*, equally entertaining and misleading, was written mostly by Francis Atterbury, helped by George Smalridge and others. They successfully convinced polite readers that Bentley had treated Boyle and Temple 'clownishly, and unlike either a gentleman or a scholar' (Smalridge to Walter Gough, 22 Feb 1698, Nichols, *Illustrations*, 3.268–9). Even Henry Dodwell, the chronologist, told Bentley:

> I can hardly think you did expect so much could have been said against you in a cause wherein you were so confident, by so young a Gentleman, in a part of Learning to which you had so particularly addicted yourself. (H. Dodwell to Bentley, 14 May 1698, Bodl. Oxf., MS Cherry 23, fol. 56*v*)

Bentley promised to refute the *Examination* 'with that clearness and fulness in every particular, great and little, both in points of Learning and points of Fact, that the Authors will be ashamed' (Bentley to Evelyn, 21 April 1698, *Correspondence*, 1.167). Early in 1699 he published his second *Dissertation*, four times the length of the first and treating only Phalaris (other bogus letters and Aesop being reserved for another volume, which never appeared). After an extensive preface and introduction, the sixteen arguments are reprinted and four more added; each is followed by a detailed refutation of the *Examination*'s objections.

Most arguments are chronological: cities, artefacts, terms, and expressions in the letters postdate Phalaris; so do stage tragedies, even epistles themselves. Moreover, the Attic dialect and currency values are incongruous in Sicily, the subject matter is absurd, and ancient writers never mention the letters. Bentley's 'clearness and fulness' is always impressive; he eschews scholarly jargon and multiplies his proofs, some from evidence hidden in corrupt texts.

Bentley's *Dissertation* was unanswerable; however, Christ Church produced its irrelevant and rancorous *Short Account of Dr Bentley's Humanity and Justice* (1699), and William King mocked 'Bentivoglio' in his intermittently amusing *Dialogues of the Dead* (1699). Bentley's philology destroyed a complacent humanist illusion of familiarity with the ancient world. Sir William Temple's having 'written to Kings, and They to Him' might not after all have 'qualified him to judge how Kings should write' (F. Atterbury and others, *Examination*, 92). And even kings, it seemed, were restricted to the language of their age and country. However, as a work of genius Bentley's *Dissertation* was not alone: Jonathan Swift's *Tale of a Tub* and *Battle of the Books* (published together in 1704 but dating from 1697) transcended other contributions to the controversy and refocused in a highly original way the essential concern with creativity and criticism.

Trinity College and Horace After Edward Stillingfleet died in March 1699, Bentley, who composed his monumental inscription, tried unsuccessfully to have the bishop's library bought for St James's or the Royal Society. On 21 December 1699 Bentley was named master of Trinity College, Cambridge, where some much needed reforms were anticipated. He was installed on 1 February 1700, having resigned his Worcester prebend on 4 January. The fellows resented an outsider's appointment, and Bentley showed his concern for the mastership's income by obtaining £170 due to his predecessor.

Bentley had been 'cross't & defeated' in his affection for Joanna Bernard (*bap.* 1665, *d.* 1740), the daughter of Sir John Bernard (or Barnard) of Brampton, Huntingdonshire, and his first wife, Elizabeth St John, who had died in Joanna's infancy. The 'alteration in my Circumstances' gave him 'some hope that a Proposal of that kind may be now better entertaind by You & your Relations, than formerly it was' (Bentley to Joanna Bernard, 6 Aug 1700, Trinity College, Cambridge, MS R.17.31, item 145). They were married in St George's Chapel, Windsor, on 4 January 1701—after at least one 'delaying scruple' of hers (Bentley to Joanna Bernard, 23 Nov 1700, *Diary … of Edward Rud*, appendix, 36). By all accounts it was a very happy marriage. They had four children: Elizabeth, Joanna, William (who died soon after birth), and the writer and artist Richard *Bentley (*bap.* 1708, *d.* 1782). Joanna married Denison Cumberland; Elizabeth married Humphrey Ridge.

In November 1700 Bentley, the senior graduate among college heads not chosen previously, was elected vice-chancellor. He was collated archdeacon of Ely on 12 June 1701, receiving with that office the livings of Haddenham and Wilburton, Cambridgeshire, and membership of convocation's lower house. At Trinity he made changes—in scholars' and fellows' elections and seniority, and in library finances—that were desirable in themselves but objectionable to senior fellows, whose role in decisions he disregarded. His justifiable but increasingly expensive repairs to the master's lodge culminated in a staircase costing £350: for two years the fellows resisted payment, but they capitulated on 20 December 1704 after Bentley withheld the college preacherships that they needed before holding church preferments.

In 1706 Bentley began three important building projects: an observatory for the first astronomy professor, Roger Cotes; a laboratory for the first chemistry professor,

John Francis Vigani; and a remodelling of the chapel costing £6000, which depleted the fellows' incomes and required domestic economies. Bentley's first clear breach of integrity, on 1 October, was electing the disreputable nephew of the vice-master, Wolfran Stubbe, as a supernumerary fellow. His expulsion of two fellows on 5 April 1708 initiated a new series of arbitrary acts.

Bentley was extraordinarily generous to continental scholars—for example, in his long critical letters in summer 1708 to Ludolph Küster on Aristophanes and to Tiberius Hemsterhuys on Julius Pollux and Greek comic metres. He provided John Davies's edition of Cicero's *Tusculan Questions* (1709) with a 94-page appendix on textual emendations. His *Emendations in Menander and Philemon* (1710), correcting Jean Le Clerc's worthless edition of the poets' fragments, was published in the Netherlands under the pseudonym Phileleutherus Lipsiensis. Through his efforts Cambridge University Press produced some remarkable books: Küster's Suidas (1705), edited with Bentley's assistance; Bentley's own edition of Horace (1711); and the splendid second edition of Newton's *Principia* (1713), commissioned and distributed by Bentley and superintended by Roger Cotes.

The *Principia* was a massive undertaking: over five years separated 'a specimen of the first sheet' and the book at last 'happily brought forth' (Bentley to Newton, 10 June 1708 and 30 June 1713, *Correspondence of Isaac Newton*, 4.518, 4.413). Bentley's Horace took longer still: less than a year for the text, but nearly seven for the textual notes, during part of which he stopped work altogether. In 1713 a second edition was printed in Amsterdam and a small edition in Cambridge with short notes, prepared by his nephew Thomas Bentley, who became a fellow of Trinity in the following year. A few days after its initial publication Thomas Hearne observed, on 29 January 1712, 'Dr Bentley's Horace is much condemn'd for the great Liberty he hath taken in altering the text' (*Remarks*, 3.273), and pamphlet attacks soon followed.

With more than 700 changes from the vulgate, this was indeed 'unlike any edition of a Latin author ever before given to the world' (Monk, 1.316). Few of Bentley's conjectures are accepted, but many of his accepted emendations began as conjectures before he found support in manuscripts consulted for his notes. Confident in his own divination, Bentley emended 'anything inconsistent with the harmonious measures of classical poetry' (Pfeiffer, 154). Yet, even where his solutions are wrong, Bentley's grasp of textual problems and the learning he brings to bear on them are quite extraordinary. The much quoted note on *Odes*, book 3, ode 27, line 15—'To us reason and common sense are better than a hundred codices'—significantly continues, 'especially with the added testimony of the old Vatican codex'.

First trial and *Remarks* on Collins In December 1709, after a year resisting Bentley's redistribution of their dividends, the fellows of Trinity looked to higher authority on the advice of Edmund Miller, a barrister holding the physic fellowship. On 18 January 1710 Bentley—having declared,

'From henceforward, farewell peace to Trinity College' (Monk, 1.243–4)—expelled Miller on the questionable grounds that he was not a doctor of medicine. The fellows petitioned as college visitor John Moore, now bishop of Ely. Bentley published a letter to Moore, dated 13 February, criticizing 'the scandalous Lives, Insufficiency in Learning, and seditious Practices of most of this Gang' (R. Bentley, *The Present State of Trinity College*, 1710, 8).

The fellows published six replies and presented Moore with fifty-four articles of accusation, which they also published. Having boasted that his whig politics upset the fellows, Bentley nevertheless courted the new tory administration, whose secretary of state, Henry St John, was related to Joanna Bentley, as was Queen Anne's new favourite, Abigail Masham. Bentley failed to obtain a royal letter in his favour; however, when he eventually received on 21 November Moore's demand that he answer the articles, he stopped the process with a petition to the queen as the true visitor of Trinity College.

The original college statutes had made the bishop of Ely visitor, but Queen Elizabeth's new statutes named none, in effect making the crown visitor. However, in the fortieth Elizabethan statute—the very one concerning a master's deprivation—the bishop of Ely is named. Secretary St John referred the question to the attorney- and solicitor-general; on 29 May 1711 they reported that Bentley was answerable to the bishop under the fortieth statute but could challenge that in court.

Bentley wrote to the earl of Oxford, the lord treasurer, on 12 July asking that the queen vacate the fortieth statute and send commissioners to Trinity. Oxford referred the matter to the lord keeper and crown lawyers, who determined in January 1712 that Bentley was answerable to the bishop. Bentley dedicated his edition of Horace to Oxford, and the treasurer, solicited also by the fellows, counselled patience. Eventually on 18 April 1713 the ministry authorized Moore to proceed—since the fellows were applying to the court of queen's bench, which later ruled Moore should show cause for not proceeding.

Meanwhile an opportunity to defend the church was presented by *A Discourse of Free-Thinking*, in which the deist Anthony Collins denounced 'pious fraud' and claimed that the gospel recommended freethinking. The most formidable response was Bentley's *Remarks upon a Late Discourse of Free-Thinking* (1713), written as a letter to 'FH' (Francis Hare) under Bentley's old pseudonym Phileleutherus Lipsiensis and comprising thirty-three remarks on the first half of Collins's *Discourse*. The exposure of Collins's ignorance and misprision begins in earnest with remark 7 on the *Iliad*, Collins's 'epitome of all arts and sciences': here Bentley, in partial anticipation of Friedrich August Wolf, observes that Homer's 'loose songs were not collected together' until the mid-sixth century BC (*Works*, 3.304). Remark 32, demonstrating that the Greek Testament is not invalidated by 30,000 variant readings in John Mill's edition of 1707, is particularly impressive.

Encouraged by Hare's *The Clergyman's Thanks to Phileleutherus* (1713), Bentley published a second part containing twenty remarks on the second half of Collins's *Discourse*. These turn Collins's complaints of mistranslation back on himself and ridicule his catalogue of illustrious freethinkers from Socrates to Cicero. A fragmentary third part of the *Remarks*, continuing with Cato, was added to the posthumous eighth edition of 1743. The work's success—Cambridge passed a grace thanking him on 4 January 1714—was welcome to Bentley in his legal predicament.

In mid-May, after various depositions and delays, Bentley's six-week trial on the fifty-four articles commenced at Ely House, London. But before the judgment later found in Moore's papers could be delivered against Bentley, the bishop, having caught cold at the sittings, died, on 31 July 1714. The policy of his successor, William Fleetwood—that any visitation he made would punish all delinquencies—induced some apprehensive fellows to accept Bentley's offered peace and frustrated a new petition by Miller, once more threatened with expulsion.

Whig politics and divinity professorship Bentley was a staunch Hanoverian. With the Jacobite army in England, his university sermon upon popery (5 November 1715) attacked 'the many, which adulterate and negotiate the word of God for their own lucre and advantage'. He traced this 'specific character of Popery' through 'their corruptions and cauponations of the Gospel', starting with 'their enhancing the authority of the vulgar Latin above the Greek original' (*Works*, 3.243, 246, 247). The propagator of 'suspected doctrines', who is 'but a *negotiator* for his partisans abroad', is clearly a type of Jacobite (ibid., 3.261). After the uprising failed, Bentley manoeuvred the passage on 16 October 1716 of Cambridge's congratulatory address, and his archidiaconal visitation charge of 11 December explained that all post-revolutionary preferments and rites (even baptism) would have been invalidated 'had the fortune of the sword fallen out contrary' (ibid., 3.282).

When the new archbishop of Canterbury, William Wake, encouraged another fellows' petition, Bentley cunningly sought his patronage for 'an edition of the Greek Testament exactly as it was in the best exemplars at the time of the Council of Nice' (Bentley to Wake, 15 April 1716, *Correspondence*, 2.503). This departure from the received text 'anticipated by a whole century the work of Lachmann and others' (Pfeiffer, 156). Bentley worked hard collating manuscripts, helped in Europe by Johann Jacob Wettstein and later by the young Trinity fellow John Walker. His subsequent *Proposals for Printing* (1720), with a specimen chapter (Revelation 22), reassured subscribers that 'in the sacred writings there's no place for conjectures or emendations' without manuscript authority (*Works*, 3.488).

While Bentley was commending his work to Wake, nineteen fellows petitioned the king on 18 May 1716 'to ascertain the visitorial power'. Bentley had constables bar Miller from college elections on 28 September and three days later broke with John Colbatch, the fellow who became his most persistent antagonist. On 26 October the fellows' petition was referred to the attorney-general, who did nothing. The following February Miller hurt their cause with *An Account of the University of Cambridge*, attacking the ecclesiastical and academic establishment (and Bentley) so violently that the university censured it.

When the regius professorship of divinity fell vacant Bentley contrived with three other electors to choose himself, and on 1 May 1717 delivered his praelection, a historical account of the disputed verse 1 John 5: 7, concluding against its authenticity. He anticipated the income of £600 per annum from the professor's Huntingdonshire rectories of Somersham, Pidley, and Coln: new improvements to Trinity lodge included a granary for his tithe wheat and malt, which he made the college buy. As professor he created three doctors of divinity when George I visited Cambridge on 6 October; another thirty-one waited until the following day. When Bentley demanded each pay an additional fee of 4 guineas, Conyers Middleton, among others, agreed on condition the king sanctioned it. Since that never happened and Bentley would not return the money, Middleton had him arrested for debt on 1 October 1718.

This exposed Bentley to the vindictive toryism of Vice-Chancellor Thomas Gooch and other college heads; for not appearing personally in the vice-chancellor's court, and other acts of contempt, he was sentenced to be deprived of his degrees and threatened with losing his professorship. When he did not make the required submission, the senate was assembled on 17 October to share responsibility for the sentence: 'the houses were very full, and there was the greatest appearance of scarlet that perhaps has ever been seen there in the memory of man' (*Diary … of Edward Rud*, 23). A grace confirming the deprivation passed by 108 votes to 50. Bentley petitioned the king as supreme visitor; the ministers, after interviewing Vice-Chancellor Gooch on 6 November, referred the business to a committee. A pamphlet war broke out, in which Arthur Sykes and John Byrom defended Bentley, while William Sherlock and Middleton attacked him.

Meanwhile, through Colbatch's efforts the fellows' petition of 1716 was recalled to council on 26 May 1719. Bentley disposed of it, however, by a bargain concluded with Miller on 5 December: the lawyer withdrew their petition (and his too) while Bentley, in 'by far the greatest malversation' charged against him, had the college pay Miller's costs of £528 and his own of £500 (Monk, 2.86). As for the vice-chancellor's threat to replace him as divinity professor, that was impossible without the master of Trinity's consent; so an attempt to invalidate his election was made at the king's bench. It failed in November 1720.

About that time, Middleton anonymously published *Remarks* upon Bentley's Greek Testament *Proposals*, and Bentley, thinking Colbatch responsible for this resentful attack, abused him as a 'cabbage-head' and lunatic in *Dr Bentley's Proposals … with a Full Answer to All the Remarks*, dated 31 December 1720. Colbatch disclaimed authorship and obtained a *Declaration of the Vice-Chancellor and Heads*, dated 27 February 1721, pronouncing Bentley's answer 'a most virulent and scandalous libel'. Middleton acknowledged his authorship shortly afterwards in *Some farther Remarks*.

The king's bench, Terence, and Milton On 30 November 1719 Bentley persuaded the college seniors to condemn Middleton's recent pamphlet, *A True Account of the Present State of Trinity College*, and pay for a libel action against him. On 24 November 1720 the king's bench sentenced Middleton to beg Bentley's pardon and pay his substantial costs. That same day, in the vice-chancellor's court, Colbatch was seeking redress for *Dr Bentley's Proposals … with a Full Answer*. Bentley, summoned to appear on 17 January 1722, contrived to be engaged in his duties as royal chaplain, then by a king's bench rule stopped the vice-chancellor's proceedings (which were later dropped). Colbatch in a substantial pamphlet, *Jus academicum*, denied the court's authority over the university. Bentley accordingly moved the king's bench on 20 April to consider *Jus academicum* contempt.

The whig ministers had little interest in saving Colbatch from the indignant judges: after anxious months of attendance, and a week in prison, on 16 May 1723, 'I was fined 50^{li} to be imprisond till I paid it and give security for my good Behavior during the Year' (Colbatch, fol. 101r). When Middleton foolishly reflected on the judges in his preface to *Bibliothecae Cantabrigiensis ordinandae methodus* (1723), Bentley prosecuted him too, and on 20 June he received the same sentence. Bentley's most important king's bench action—for the restoration of his degrees—had commenced in May 1722: the court condemned the university's proceedings on 7 February 1724; Bentley's degrees were restored on 26 March.

Bentley's son Richard, who at the age of ten had been admitted to Trinity as his father's pupil, was elected a fellow in 1723, aged fifteen. On 11 March 1725 Richard succeeded his father as keeper of the king's libraries. Bentley continued to stay at Cotton House, where the books from St James's had been moved; he was on hand, in his night-gown, to rescue the Alexandrian codex from the disastrous fire there in 1731.

Francis Hare's edition of Terence appeared in mid-1724 without acknowledgement that Hare had learned its novel feature, metrics, from Bentley. Resenting his erstwhile friend's ingratitude, Bentley rapidly prepared his own edition, published early in 1726. The text, which he reckoned to have corrected in 1000 places, was transformed through Bentley's awareness of a variety of metres where previous critics had imagined poetic licence. He stated his principles in a concise introduction and placed metrical marks throughout the text. Unfortunately he added a hastily prepared edition of Phaedrus, to anticipate one by Hare, and Hare exposed its weaknesses in his acrimonious *Epistola critica* (1726).

Bishop Fleetwood had died in 1723. His successor, Thomas Green, expressed readiness to hear Colbatch and others' complaints, and on 30 April 1728 five eminent lawyers pronounced he had sufficient jurisdiction. Bentley took the initiative: with nine senior fellows he petitioned the king, then early in 1729 he published a supporting pamphlet, *The Case of Trinity College*. However, a council committee determined against interfering, and on 1 April Green cited Bentley to answer the charges. That summer Bentley worked hard to complete his Greek Testament—an answer to the charge that he passed 'an irreligious life'—but the task was too great.

In March 1730 Bentley was offered and refused the deanery of Lincoln. For two years during king's bench proceedings he had Green prohibited from acting. However, on 11 May 1731 the court declared Green visitor by virtue of the original statutes—but therefore wrongly described in the citation as 'visitor specially appointed by the 40th statute of Elizabeth'. So the prohibition continued. Bentley petitioned the king unsuccessfully, and to avoid further petitions Green, financed by Colbatch, appealed the king's bench decision to the House of Lords.

In January 1732 Bentley published his edition of *Paradise Lost*. He 'had made emendations upon Milton' as early as 1726 (*Private Journal*, 1.188); however, about 1730 he was encouraged by Queen Caroline and quickly completed his work. Successive reprintings had corrupted Milton's text, but Bentley's preface alleged 'such monstrous Faults, as are beyond Example in any other printed Book' (sig. a2r), for which he blamed an interfering editor. This hypothesis required he deny the existence of the manuscript he had consulted. His nephew Thomas complained 'he can't forbear talking of Milton, & I can't bear the nonsense & absurdities he puts upon him' (Hale, 26). His nephew Richard, a Trinity fellow since 1728, corrected the proofs; he tried to dissuade Bentley from publication.

Having collated carelessly and neglected authoritative editions, Bentley failed to correct Milton's text. What raised an outcry, however, were his 800 emendations in the margin (plus some seventy expulsions of text in brackets) and his notes defending this virtual rewriting. Bentley's audacity certainly stimulated interest in Milton's text, and some scholars have thought his notes show 'a great gift for getting hold of the right thing—by the wrong end' (C. Ricks, *Milton's Grand Style*, 1963, 14).

Second trial, Homer, and Manilius On 8 May 1732 the Lords upheld Green's appeal by twenty-eight votes to sixteen. 'Bishop Sherlock spoke allmost 2 hours on purpose to tire the House, for many that would have voted for us was tired and had made appointments &c. went out, for they satt till almost 7 oclock' (Joanna Bentley to Joanna Cumberland, 11 May 1732, *Diary … of Edward Rud*, appendix, 44). After comparing each accusation with the statutes, which took until February 1733, the Lords permitted Green to try Bentley on twenty of the sixty-four articles. The trial began on 13 June, and Bentley's defensive plea was entered ten days later. The protracted proceedings ended on 27 April 1734 with Green's sentencing Bentley to be deprived of the mastership.

However, the fortieth statute required that the vice-master execute the sentence. Having persuaded John Hackett to resign that office, Bentley appointed his friend John Walker. When Walker ignored the bishop's mandate, Colbatch on 10 March 1735 petitioned the House of

Lords to compel him. When the Lords declined to interfere, he sought a mandamus from the king's bench. It proved impossible to contrive a phrasing the judges would accept. A month after the third attempt failed Bishop Green died, on 18 May 1738. Though safe from expulsion, Bentley had not done with the law: as archdeacon of Ely he prosecuted Colbatch for unpaid procurations, and a year and a half later, in January 1740, the consistorial court awarded him 6s. plus £20 costs.

During the judicial delays Bentley had found time to annotate Homer's text for an edition that would correct the versification. As early as 1713 he had the brilliant idea that hundreds of hiatuses would disappear if the obsolete digamma (pronounced as 'w') were restored. His discovery, unappreciated until the nineteenth century, was praised by Samuel Clarke, commenting on *Iliad*, book 16, line 172 in his edition of 1729–32. Soon after 23 March 1739, when the vice-chancellor's court met in Trinity lodge—since Bentley caught cold easily—to sentence the atheist Tinkler Ducket, a paralytic stroke disabled Bentley from his work on Homer.

Bentley's edition of Manilius, which he had prepared in the early 1690s, appeared in 1739, seen through the press by his nephew Richard. Bentley's genius for interpretation and emendation was especially well suited to this 'superlatively difficult text badly transmitted and deeply interpolated, and moreover concerned with a recondite subject' (Brink, 77). A. E. Housman called the edition 'a greater work than either the Horace or the Phalaris' (Housman, 28).

Bentley's wife died early in 1740 and was buried at Brampton on 25 January. Thereafter his daughter Joanna Cumberland spent much of her time at Trinity lodge, where her widowed sister Elizabeth Ridge already lived. Joanna's son Richard recorded some affectionate anecdotes of his grandfather in his *Memoirs* (1806). Bentley was nearly confined to his chair and left college business to Walker, but only a month before his death he examined for the Craven scholarships. He first smoked tobacco in his old age, and enjoyed port. He worked for most of the day in his study, in his nightgown, as he always had, wearing 'a hat with an enormous brim, as a shade to protect his eyes' (Monk, 2.401).

Bentley died in the master's lodge at Trinity College on 14 July 1742 of what 'is said to have been a pleuritic fever' (Monk, 2.413). Most dignitaries of the university and town attended his funeral five days later; Philip Yonge, later bishop of Norwich, gave the oration. He was buried on the same day in the college chapel; his grave is on the north side of the communion rails, under a small stone, whose inscription omits his mastership. His will, dated 29 May 1741 (PRO, PROB 11/715–722, proved 10 August 1742), divided his estate among his family: his son Richard, Elizabeth (shortly married to James Favell), Joanna, and her children. Its gross value, £6500, was less than might be expected: Bentley said he 'had lost £4,000 in the South Sea' (*Private Journal*, 1.624); furthermore, his son had no profession and 'occasioned him considerable expense' (Monk, 2.415). He left his Greek manuscripts to Trinity and the rest of his library to Richard, his nephew and executor.

The greatest scholar Four months before Bentley died Pope published *The New Dunciad*, which perpetuated in 'Aristarchus' the popular caricature of Trinity's master as overweening pedant. The turmoil Bentley caused ought not to obscure his raising, especially through careful examining, of the college's academic standards. As a critic he was too far ahead of his time to be appreciated. Yet textual criticism flourished through his influence at Cambridge. Jeremiah Markland's 'critical taste and skill were formed' on Bentley's model (Monk, 2.59). Richard Porson, whose *Letters to Travis* (1788–90) imitated 'that immortal *Dissertation*' (Euripides, *Medea*, ed. Porson, note on ll. 139–40n), 'is said to have cried with delight' on finding Bentley had anticipated his emendations in Aristophanes (H. R. Luard, 'Porson', *Cambridge Lectures*, 1857, 153). Among the so-called Porsonians, James Henry Monk stands out for his magnificent biography of Bentley, first published in 1830 and still unrivalled 170 years later.

Richard Cumberland's edition of Lucan (1760) included his grandfather's emendations; here 'Bentley did much more than anyone else, but less than he ought to have done', and mistakenly tried to expel all the poet's repetitions (Lucan, *Bellum Civile*, ed. Housman, 1926, xxxii). The bulk of Bentley's unpublished work had to wait until the nineteenth century—most significantly his notes on the *Iliad*, included in Christian Gottlob Heyne's edition (1802–22), and his New Testament materials, edited as *Critica sacra* by Arthur Ayres Ellis (1862).

Bentley's historical criticism, though disregarded in England, was taken up in Germany by Wolf—who outlined Bentley's life in his *Literarische Analekten* (1816)—and Gottfried Hermann. Through the enthusiasm of 'the great Germans who had made themselves his disciples' (Brink, 138), scholars since mid-Victorian times have appreciated the full range of Bentley's work. His command of Latin, Greek, and biblical studies was prodigious, and his grasp of critical principles—visible even in his rashness and inevitable errors—has confirmed him as 'the greatest scholar that England or perhaps Europe ever bred' (Housman, 12). HUGH DE QUEHEN

Sources A. T. Bartholomew and J. W. Clark, *Richard Bentley, D.D: a bibliography* (1908) · J. H. Monk, *The life of Richard Bentley, DD*, 2nd edn, 2 vols. (1833) · *Works*, ed. A. Dyce, 3 vols. (1836) · *The correspondence of Richard Bentley*, ed. C. Wordsworth, 2 vols. (1842) · *The diary (1709–1720) of Edward Rud*, ed. H. R. Luard (1860) · J. Colbatch, diary and letters, 1719–28, Trinity Cam., MS B.17.4 · R. C. Jebb, *Bentley* (1882) · C. O. Brink, *English classical scholarship: historical reflections on Bentley, Porson, and Housman* (1986) · R. Pfeiffer, *History of classical scholarship from 1300 to 1850* (1976) · D. F. McKenzie, *The Cambridge University Press, 1696–1712*, 2 vols. (1966) · E. J. Kenney, *The classical text* (1974) · A. E. Housman, *Selected prose*, ed. J. Carter (1961) · J. E. B. Mayor, *Cambridge under Queen Anne* (1911) · *The private journal and literary remains of John Byrom*, ed. R. Parkinson, 2 vols. in 4 pts, Chetham Society, 32, 34, 40, 44 (1854–7), vol. 1 · *Remarks and collections of Thomas Hearne*, ed. C. E. Doble and others, 11 vols., OHS, 2, 7, 13, 34, 42–3, 48, 50, 65, 67, 72 (1885–1921) · *The correspondence of Isaac Newton*, ed. H. W. Turnbull and others, 7 vols. (1959–77) · *Fasti Angl., 1541–1857*, [Ely] · will of Richard Willies, 17 July 1684?, York registry · Nichols, *Illustrations* · M. Hunter, *The Royal Society and its fellows, 1660–1700: the morphology of an early scientific institution*, 2nd edn (1994) · J. K. Hale, 'Thomas Bentley to Dr. Pearce', *Turnbull Library Record*, new ser., 14 (1981), 23–31 · *CSP dom.*, *1699–1700*, 324 · W. A. Shaw, *Calendar of treasure books, 1742–5*, 846 · G. D. Lumb, ed., *The registers of the parish church of Rothwell*, part 1: *1538–1689* (1906) · E. H. Fellowes and E. R. Poyser, *Registers of St George's Chapel, Windsor* (1957)

Archives BL, corresp. and papers, Add. MSS 5831–5832, 5834, 5845, 5848, 6194, 6209, 6457, 6911 · CUL, notes and papers · Trinity Cam., corresp. and MSS | BL, Royal MSS, notes for edition of *Manilius* · Bodl. Oxf., letters to Edward Barnard

Likenesses J. Thornhill, oils, 1710, Trinity Cam. [*see illus.*] · T. Hudson, oils, 1749 (after J. Thornhill), Trinity Cam. · L. F. Roubiliac, marble bust, 1756, Trinity Cam. · R. W. Buss, oils (after J. Thornhill), V&A · J. Downman, oils (after copy of painting by J. Thornhill, 1710), NPG · J. Downman, pencil drawing (after J. Thornhill), FM Cam. · G. Vertue, engraving (after J. Thornhill), repro. in M. Manilius, *Astronomicon*, ed. R. Bentley (1739) · oils (after J. Thornhill, 1710), NPG · oils (after J. Thornhill), St John Cam. · plaster cast (after marble bust by L. F. Roubiliac, 1756), LPL · terracotta sculpture (after marble bust by L. F. Roubiliac, 1754), BM

Wealth at death £6521 5s. 2d.—total receipts · £5422 12s. 11d.—total disbursements · £1098 12s. 3d.—surplus: 'A full and true account of the estate and other effects of the late Dr Bentley' (Trinity Cam., Add. MS a.197, no. 9), signed by R. Bentley, Denison Cumberland, Joanna Cumberland, James Favell, and Elizabeth Favell (legatees and residuary legatees) on 15 April 1747

Bentley, Richard (*bap.* 1708, *d.* 1782), writer and artist, was baptized on 3 June 1708 at All Saints', Cambridge, the youngest of the four children and only surviving son of Dr Richard *Bentley (1662–1742), master of Trinity College, Cambridge, and his wife, Joanna Bernard (*bap.* 1665, *d.* 1740), daughter of Sir John Bernard of Brampton, Huntingdonshire. A precocious child, he entered Trinity College at the age of ten, matriculated at eleven, and at fifteen was simultaneously granted a BA (as a junior bachelor) and elected a fellow. In 1725 Dr Bentley transferred to his son his keepership of the king's libraries, with a remuneration of £200 per annum for life. Outraged by this nepotism, the fellows at Trinity College in 1725 denied young Bentley the Craven scholarship, though in 1727 he received both an MA and a lay fellowship. On 23 October 1731 a fire destroyed part of the Cottonian and king's libraries at Ashburnham House, London; Bentley, in residence at the time, received some of the blame and eventually resigned.

On 17 June 1733 Bentley married Susanna Vavasor Durell at (or of) Stevenage, Hertfordshire, a niece of Dr Robert Freind, headmaster of Westminster School, London, and soon became entangled in a lawsuit over her mother's estate. William Cole and Horace Walpole refer to Bentley's imprudence and irresponsibility about money in these early years, as well as his father's disappointment that his son had not become a scholar like himself. Dr Bentley remarked that 'Tully had his Marcus' and implied, in the words of his son, that 'the sons of heroes are loobies' (Walpole, *Corr.*, 9.105, 227). Despite the unkind comparison, which made him desultory and resentful, Bentley in later years strongly defended his father against detractors. Dr Bentley bequeathed the bulk of his estate to his daughters and his personal library to a nephew. In 1745, three years after his father's death, the younger

Bentley no longer held any position at Trinity College. He spent two or three years in France, probably, as Cole suggests, to escape creditors.

In 1750 Bentley met Horace Walpole. Writing to George Montagu, in condemnation of Dr Bentley's cruelty and arrogance, Walpole asserted that the younger Bentley had 'more sense, judgment, and wit, more taste and more misfortunes than sure ever met in any man' (Walpole, *Corr.*, 9.105). Having remarried in the late 1740s (his second wife's name is unknown), Bentley moved with his growing family into a cottage at Teddington, near Strawberry Hill, Walpole's house in Twickenham, Middlesex. He joined Walpole and John Chute to form a committee on taste to renovate Strawberry Hill in the Gothic style. He produced innovative architectural drawings for Strawberry Hill, painted landscapes and allegorical designs, and made ingenious illustrations for the first anthology of Gray's poems, *Designs by Mr. R. Bentley, for Six Poems by Mr. T. Gray* (1753). But his financial embarrassments and occasional lassitude soon exasperated Walpole; in late 1753 Bentley fled to Jersey to escape his creditors. After his return to Teddington in 1756, he collaborated with Walpole for another four years.

Bentley's work at Strawberry Hill included illustrations for Walpole's *Memoirs of King George II* (*c.*1752–*c.*1756; pubd 1822) and *Fugitive Pieces* (*c.*1753–*c.*1757; pubd 1758, incomplete and without illustrations); he published several poems and a half-dozen satires; and he contributed to the Strawberry Hill Press a translation into English (1757) of Paul Hentzner's *Itinerarium … Angliae* and an edition (1760) of Lucan's *Pharsalia* with his father's notes. After his final break with Walpole in 1760, he wrote longer literary pieces: the *Epistle to Lord Melcombe* (1763); a comedy called 'The Wishes, or, Harlequin's Mouth Open'd', performed in 1761 (Hunt., MS Larpent Plays 199); a tragedy, *Philodamus* (1767), and a mock-heroic poem entitled *Patriotism*, published first in five and then in six cantos (1763, 1765). Bentley's literary works, particularly his plays or longer satires, sometimes seem laboured. His attacks on John Wilkes and the duke of Newcastle, enemies of the earl of Bute, flattered George III but reaped for Bentley only a small pension from the king, irregularly paid.

During ten years of friendship with Walpole and Gray, and later during his acquaintance with Melcombe, Halifax, and Bute, Bentley attracted only transitory public attention. Neglected, embittered, and poor, he withdrew from society in the late 1760s. He died on 23 October 1782 at his home near New Palace Yard, Abington Street, Westminster, London, and was buried in the churchyard at Teddington. His widow continued to receive his pension from the king; he was also survived by two sons and three daughters.

Bentley's architectural designs, less restrained than Chute's, fuse rococo eccentricity and Gothic form. His designs for Gray's poems were deemed by Hanns Hammelmann to be 'a turning-point in British decorative art' (Hammelmann, 14). Their complement of visual puns and pictorial allusions to other works of art gives the interplay of the sister arts an unexpectedly provocative coherence.

Walpole referred to them enthusiastically in his correspondence; Gray felt embarrassed over his small output of poetry and asserted that his verses were 'only subordinate, & explanatory to the Drawings' (T. Gray, *Correspondence of Thomas Gray*, ed. P. Toynbee and L. Whibley, 3 vols., 1971, 1.371). In 'Stanzas to Mr. Richard Bentley' he wrote that when the artist bid 'the pencil answer to the lyre', he 'fix'd' each 'transitory thought' with 'a lasting essence' and awakened to 'local Symmetry' the idea of each poem (Gray, 98). Bentley's unique pictorial enrichment of the poems enlarges yet refines traditional articulations of *ut pictura poesis* and anticipates the book illustrations of William Blake. His finest work, whether in the graphic or literary arts, reveals a fertile genius, an energetic imagination, and an ebullient, incisive wit. Nearly all of his architectural elevations, paintings, and original drawings for book illustrations are in the Lewis Walpole Library, Yale University, Farmington, Connecticut.

LOFTUS JESTIN

Sources L. Jestin, 'Richard Bentley the younger (1708–1782): a critical biography', PhD diss., Yale U., 1985 • L. Jestin, *The answer to the lyre: Richard Bentley's illustrations for Thomas Gray's poems* (1990) • Walpole, *Corr.* • *The works of Horatio Walpole, earl of Orford*, ed. R. Walpole and M. Berry, 5 vols. (1798) • J. H. Monk, *The life of Richard Bentley, DD*, 2nd edn, 2 vols. (1833) • R. Cumberland, *Memoirs of Richard Cumberland written by himself* (1806) • BL, Add. MSS 32903, fols. 414–414v; 35399, fols. 207–208v; 35586, fol. 212; 36031, fol. 81; 36125, fols. 232, 232v; 38202, fols. 37–8, 272–272v; 38203, fol. 195; 38205, fol. 34; 38206, fols. 50–51; 38209, fol. 349; 38210, fols. 69–70; 38213, fols. 278–9; 38214, fols. 113, 113v, 231, 231v; 38215, fol. 76; 38217, fols. 16, 255; 38470, fol. 324 • Venn, *Alum. Cant.* • Nichols, *Lit. anecdotes* • *GM*, 1st ser., 1 (1731), 379, 454 • *GM*, 1st ser., 52 (1782), 540 • E. Brydges, *Restitutes…*, 4 vols. (1816) • *DNB* • J. Thorne, *Handbook to the environs of London*, 2 vols. (1876) • *IGI* • *The complete poems of Thomas Gray*, ed. H. W. Starr and J. R. Hendrickson (1966); repr. (1972) • H. Hammelmann, *Book illustrators in eighteenth-century England*, ed. T. S. R. Boase (1975), 14

Archives Yale U., Farmington, Lewis Walpole Library, corresp., drawings • Yale U. CBA, wash drawing | BL, letters to earl of Liverpool, Add. MSS 38202–38217, 38470, *passim*

Likenesses J. G. Eccardt, oils, *c.*1752, NPG; commissioned by H. Walpole • J. Heath, line engraving, 1798 (after J. G. Eccardt), BM, NPG; repro. in R. Berry, ed., *The works of Horace Walpole*, vol. 2, p. 436

Wealth at death £600 p.a., incl. pension of £500 from the king and £100 from the customs: Cumberland, *Memoirs*, 160; Walpole, *Corr.* (1937–83), vol. 24, pp. 276–7

Bentley, Richard (1794–1871), printer and publisher, was born near Fleet Street in London on 24 October 1794, the youngest but one of the children of Edward Bentley (*b.* 1753), publisher and principal of the accountant's office in the Bank of England, and Anne Nichols, daughter of a confectioner living opposite Islington church. Though not related to seventeenth- and eighteenth-century publishers with the same surname, Bentley grew up from the cradle among printers, publishers, and authors. His father and maternal uncle John Nichols (1745–1826) jointly owned and published the *General Evening Post*; Nichols also published and wrote for the *Gentleman's Magazine* and composed antiquarian compilations. From 1803 Bentley attended St Paul's School, where he became close friends with Richard Harris Barham, later minor canon of St

Richard Bentley (1794–1871), by Charles Baugniet, 1844

Paul's Cathedral, author under the pen-name Thomas Ingoldsby, and Bentley's literary adviser.

After leaving school Bentley worked for a time in his uncle's Red Lion Court office, learning the craft and business of printing. Then in 1819 he joined with his older brother Samuel *Bentley (1785–1868) in a printing business, located first in Dorset Street, Salisbury Square, and afterwards in Shoe Lane. This firm, the first to pay artistic attention to wood-engraved illustrations, became arguably the finest printers in London. Established in business, Bentley married Charlotte, daughter of Thomas Botten; their eldest surviving son was George *Bentley (1828–1895), afterwards his father's partner and successor.

Henry Colburn, an opportunistic and unscrupulous publisher, had the Bentley firm produce his books; by the late 1820s his printing bill was running at more than £3000 annually, and he was about to dispose of his business. To protect the firm's investment, Richard agreed on 31 August 1829 to sell his interest in the printing business to his brother, and by the terms of an agreement on 3 June 1829 to become Colburn's partner. Bentley brought £2500, took 'upon himself all the active part of the business', and was to receive two-fifths of the profits, while Colburn, reserving to himself certain properties, brought the rest of his investments and copyrights and was to receive three-fifths of the profits, guaranteed to be at least £10,000.

From the beginning the partners' working relationship soured; among other causes of friction, according to his office manager, Edward Morgan, Colburn's accounts were so 'carelessly kept' (Morgan), that it took over two years to ascertain a balance. Meanwhile Colburn and Bentley launched four series of books: a National Library of General Knowledge (25 August 1830–29 February 1831), which failed after 55,750 copies of fourteen titles had been printed; the Juvenile Library (April to October 1830), which lost £900; a Library of Modern Travels and Discoveries, which never got into print; and the Standard Novels, an enormously successful series of monthly one-volume reprints at 6s. each which began in February 1831 and concluded in 1854 with volume 126. The first inexpensive reprints of Jane Austen's fiction appeared in 1833 as numbers 23, 24, 28, and 30 of the Standard Novels. Many other novels in this series were written by American authors, and most incorporated authorial changes or additions that allowed Colburn and Bentley to claim that these editions reproduced 'the texts finally approved by their authors'. Between 1829 and 1832 Colburn and Bentley had 107,070 books printed, exclusive of the Standard Novels, and had 31,845 of these remaindered or wasted (pulped). Among their best-sellers were Bulwer's *Paul Clifford* and *Eugene Aram*, Disraeli's *The Young Duke*, and four silver-fork novels by the prolific Catherine Gore. The firm also spent £27,000 'puffing' their own publications in advertisements and in periodicals they owned.

In autumn 1831 Morgan concluded that Colburn's debts exceeded £18,000, and that a Mr Willis, one of the firm's employees, had appropriated more than £700 of the cash which retailers had remitted. Colburn sold or mortgaged his shares in several periodicals to keep the firm solvent, and from May until August 1832 Bentley, no longer on speaking terms with his partner, negotiated through Morgan what he characterized as 'a kind of patchwork' settlement (Morgan). On 1 September 1832 Bentley purchased Colburn's share for £1500, bought stock and copyrights for a further £5500, and bonded Colburn not to publish any new books within 20 miles of London. Colburn immediately violated the spirit if not the letter of the agreement; eventually Bentley received a substantial further sum to release Colburn from exile. Thereupon Colburn moved to 13 Great Marlborough Street, where he continued in business, imitating Bentley's Standard Novels and sometimes publishing Bentley's authors. Bentley meanwhile hired several of Colburn's former staff, including Morgan, who served him faithfully until he retired on 31 March 1858; also G. Dubourg, William Shoberl, Charles Ollier, Eliza Ketteridge, and John Pickersgill, brother of the portraitist Henry William Pickersgill RA (1782–1875). Within a few years, having made successful hits with Edward Bulwer's *Last Days of Pompeii* and William Harrison Ainsworth's *Rookwood*, Bentley proposed to buy the *Monthly Magazine* in order to compete with Colburn's successful *New Monthly Magazine*.

Over a weekend late in October 1836, Morgan, who disliked the *Monthly* (an 'old harridan … little better than a Fleet St. walker'), came up with a proposal for a new 2s. 6d. periodical 'devoted to humorous papers by popular writers'. Bentley, 'almost frantic with approbation', at first adopted Morgan's suggestion for a title, *The Wits' Miscellany*. But after hearing objections from Dickens and his friends, the publisher switched to *Bentley's Miscellany*, prompting Barham's quip, 'Why go to the other extreme?' and Theodore Hook's observation that the title was ominous: 'Miss-sell-any' (Patten, *Cruikshank*, 2.51). On 4 November 1836 Bentley signed an agreement to hire Charles Dickens to edit the periodical at £20 monthly and for a further 20 guineas 'to furnish an original article of his own writing, every monthly Number, to consist of about a sheet of 16 pages' (*Letters of Charles Dickens*, 1.649–50). At the same time Bentley paid George Cruikshank £50 for the use of his name as illustrator, contracted to pay 12 guineas for a monthly etching, and subjected the artist to a £100 penalty should he draw anything for Colburn. The first numbers of the new magazine, which from February contained the instalments of *Oliver Twist* as Dickens's 'original article … monthly', proved very popular, even though conservatives such as Barham disliked the novel's 'Radicalish tone' (*Life and Letters*, 2.24); sales rose and Dickens even received bonuses. But by autumn Dickens and Bentley were fighting over editorial prerogatives. Dickens threatened to resign on several occasions—Morgan thought that Dickens's 'feelings of discontent' could be attributed to 'the meddling agency' of John Forster (Morgan). But Cruikshank and Barham as intermediaries managed to reconcile the co-editors, and Bentley acceded to a total of nine agreements restating, in Dickens's favour, the terms upon which Bentley would purchase Boz's editorial services and Dickens's next two novels. The final break with the 'Burlington Street Brigand' (*Letters of Charles Dickens*, 1.619) came in February 1839, and at that point Ainsworth took over as the magazine's editor. Within a few years Ainsworth and Cruikshank too had severed relations with Bentley because of editorial and financial disputes, partly stemming from the very success of their enterprises, which were governed by contracts that did not allow sufficiently for additional remuneration and enhanced editorial control.

During the 1830s and 1840s Bentley was at the top of his form. A 'serious-minded craftsman-booklover' (Sadleir), Bentley offered good value and well-produced books. As his business prospered (in 1839 Bentley had amassed a nest-egg of about £6000), he enjoyed hosting *Miscellany* dinners at the Red Room at New Burlington Street, where 'all the very *haut ton* of the literature of the day' gathered, Thomas Moore recorded in his *Journal* (5.2023, 21 Nov 1838). Bentley was publishing leading British authors: Henry Luttrell, Moore, Isaac Disraeli and his son Benjamin, Theodore Hook, Frances Trollope, and Caroline Norton. He also had virtually a monopoly on American authors: the Standard Novels eventually printed twenty-one by James Fenimore Cooper. And with taste and discernment Bentley picked outstanding continental writers: Alphonse de Lamartine, the vicomte de Chateaubriand, Louis-Adolphe Thiers, François Guizot, Leopold von Ranke, and Theodor Mommsen.

But Bentley was also slow and often imitative of other publishers, and he had a strong bourgeois streak that prompted him to stand upon his proprietorial and editorial dignity, even when he lost contributors through his stubbornness. Moreover, he repeatedly overreached: symbolically, in obtaining in 1833 an appointment as 'publisher in ordinary to his majesty' (the firm never published anything for William IV or Victoria over sixty-five years); practically, especially in the 1840s and 1850s, when he tried to launch major periodicals. A 6*d*. weekly newspaper, *Young England*, which began on 4 January 1845, enjoyed the assistance of the Hon. George Smythe (the original of Coningsby) and Lord John Manners, to no avail; it failed after fourteen issues. A decade later, *Bentley's Quarterly Review*, a 6*s*. quarterly appearing one month before the venerable *Quarterly Review* to try to steal its market, started bravely on 28 February 1859 with John Douglas Cook, later successful as editor of the *Saturday Review*, as editor and Lord Robert Cecil as political editor. By 8 June, when he discontinued the venture, Bentley to his 'extreme regret and mortification' (Bentley to Cook, 31 May 1859, Gettmann, 146) had lost £640.

In the later 1840s Bentley became increasingly rash, 'more self willed and impulsive', says Morgan. Barham retired in 1843; lacking any steadying hand, Bentley found himself adrift in a cut-throat market with inadequate resources and many losing properties. The circulation of *Bentley's Miscellany* dropped by two-thirds; Mrs Gore thought the magazine nothing but 'hashed mutton': 'your procession of authors', she told Bentley on 2 May 1847, 'wants an elephant at its head' (Gettmann, 143–4). Competition from Routledge and Colburn forced Bentley to reduce the price of his Standard Novels to unprofitable levels. To stay solvent, he sold the *Miscellany* to Ainsworth for £1700 in October 1854 with the proviso that the transfer of ownership could 'scarcely be known to the outer world' (ibid., 24); he off-loaded 17,730 volumes to a Belfast remainder dealer for £525; and, his mind 'clouded over with adversity' according to Morgan, he beseeched his commercial authors to buy back their copyrights. The firm's debts to family members, authors, and suppliers were so great that its stock, copyrights, stereo plates, steel etchings, and bound volumes were sold in three auctions: 26–7 February 1856; 14 July 1856; and 18–22 July 1857. Nevertheless, Bentley's affairs remained in such bad shape that the printers William Clowes and G. A. Spottiswoode were appointed inspectors of the firm. Although their supervision nominally ended on 31 March 1858, some debts ran for decades beyond that date. Bentley suffered a further, grievous blow in 1857: he lost about £16,000 as a consequence of the Lords' decision to void British copyright in American authors.

The 1860s ushered in an upswing in Bentley's fortunes. Geraldine Jewsbury, who became a 'decisive' and enterprising publisher's reader for the firm at this time (R. Bentley, 'Diary', 3 March 1859), recommended Mrs Henry Wood's racy novel *East Lynne*; it went through four editions in six months in 1861. Bentley was still then so strapped for funds he had to publish on half-profits, however, so he reaped no huge gains. While in his dyspeptic moments Bentley believed that grasping writers were convinced that 'Publishers drink their claret out of authors' brains' (ibid., 24 Sept 1859), and that some of his printing industry colleagues conspired against him, he was still held in high repute by the Stationers' Company, which elected him upper warden on 6 July 1861. On 27 January 1866 Bentley purchased *Temple Bar* from George Augustus Sala for £2750; Edmund Yates edited it for two years, then George Bentley took over, merging it with *Bentley's Miscellany*, repurchased from Ainsworth for a mere £250. From the start, *Temple Bar* was a money-maker; but on the other side of the ledger, Bentley gained prestige while losing considerable money issuing Peter Cunningham's complete edition of Horace Walpole's *Letters*.

In 1867 a severe accident at Chepstow railway station left Bentley shaken and enfeebled. He relinquished management to his son and spent the next four years in fragile health, during which time he knitted up the ravelled ends of old friendships and revisited former triumphs. A reissue of Barham's *Ingoldsby Legends* with a specially commissioned frontispiece by George Cruikshank, to whom he was now reconciled, heartened the old man. On 10 September 1871 Bentley died at Ramsgate.

Bentley was remembered variously by his contemporaries. *The Bookseller* on 3 October 1871 eulogized his 'fine taste' and 'integrity' but added that 'his judgment was at times warped by his predilections, and he frequently overestimated the value of works offered him'. The American historian W. H. Prescott, who broke with Bentley in the 1850s, noted his 'tricky spirit' (Gettmann, 107), and Dalton Barham wrote to his daughter Caroline that Bentley was determined 'to judge for himself in all matters of literary taste' (*Life and Letters*, 2.108–9, 20 Oct 1840). Una Pope-Hennessy's oft-quoted assessment of Bentley's character, 'purblind and mean of soul', is certainly overwrought (Pope-Hennessy, 83). Because Bentley's quarrels with Dickens have been so frequently retold from Dickens's standpoint, Bentley's reputation has suffered, even though in those protracted contretemps Bentley had, as Dickens's biographer Edgar Johnson concedes, 'the law on his side at every stage of their contention' (Johnson, 1.252). Bentley's major contributions to nineteenth-century publishing are the Standard Novels—freshly revised texts of major contemporary authors made affordable for the middle class; *Bentley's Miscellany* and *Temple Bar*; the quality of his author list and of his book manufacture; his introduction of high-calibre international writers to British readers; and his founding of a family publishing firm that lasted through two further generations.

ROBERT L. PATTEN

Sources R. A. Gettmann, *A Victorian publisher: a study of the Bentley papers* (1960) • R. L. Patten, *Charles Dickens and his publishers* (1978) • E. S. Morgan, 'A brief retrospect', 4 July 1873, University of Illinois, Bentley MSS • R. Bentley sen., 'Recollections of Edward Bentley [and early life]', *The archives of Richard Bentley & Son, 1829–1898* (1976) [microfilm] • R. Bentley, 'Diary', *The archives of Richard Bentley & Son, 1829–1898* (1976) [microfilm] • M. Sadleir, *XIX century fiction: a bibliographical record based on his own collection*, 2 vols. (New York, 1969) • R. L. Patten, *George Cruikshank's life, times, and art*, 2 vols. (1992–6) • R. P. Wallins, 'Richard Bentley', *British literary publishing houses, 1820–1880*, ed. P. J. Anderson and J. Rose, DLitB, 106 (1991), 39–52 • *The letters of Charles Dickens*, ed. M. House, G. Storey, and others, 1 (1965) • J. Forster, *The life of Charles Dickens*, 3 vols. (1872–4) • E. Johnson, *Charles Dickens: his tragedy and triumph*, 2 vols. (1952) • G. Bentley, letter, *The Times* (8 Dec 1871) • *GM*, 5th ser., 1 (1868) • *The Bookseller* (3 Oct 1871) • *The Bookseller* (7 Sept 1898) • *The life and letters of … Richard Harris Barham*, ed. R. H. D. Barham, 2 vols. (1870) • W. G. Lane, *Richard Harris Barham* (1967) • T. Moore, *Journal*, ed. W. S. Dowden, 5 (1988) • A. Ingram, *Index to the archives of Richard Bentley & Son, 1829–1898* (1977) • M. Turner, *Index and guide to the lists of the publications of Richard Bentley & Son, 1829–1898* (1975) • M. Plant, *The English book trade* (1939) • U. Pope-Hennessy, *Charles Dickens* (1946) • 'Bentley, George', *DNB* • 'Bentley, Samuel', *DNB* • 'Nichols, John', *DNB* • 'Pickersgill, Henry William', *DNB* • 'Smythe, George Augustus Frederick Percy Sydney', *DNB* • K. Chittick, *Dickens and the 1830s* (1990)

Archives BL, corresp., accounts, and papers, Add. MSS 46560–46682, 59622–59651 • Bodl. Oxf., corresp., diaries, and papers • Boston PL, corresp. • Hunt. L., letters • NL Scot., corresp. • U. Cal., Los Angeles • University of Illinois, Chicago | Bodl. Oxf., letters to Benjamin Disraeli • Essex RO, Chelmsford, corresp. with G. D. Warburton • Harvard U., Houghton L., corresp. with W. H. Prescott • NL Wales, corresp. with Lady Llanover

Likenesses C. Baugniet, lithograph, 1844, NPG [*see illus.*] • J. Heath, line engraving (after J. G. Eccardt), BM, NPG; repro. in *The works of Horatio Walpole, earl of Oxford*, ed. R. Walpole and M. Berry, 5 vols. (1798) • photograph (after oil painting), repro. in Gettmann, *Victorian publisher*

Wealth at death under £9000: probate, 20 Oct 1871, *CGPLA Eng. & Wales*

Bentley, Robert (1821–1893), botanist and pharmacognosist, was born at Hitchin, Hertfordshire, on 25 March 1821, the son of William Bentley, solicitor, and his wife, Jane. He was apprenticed to William Maddock, a druggist at Tunbridge Wells, where he began the study of botany. He then became assistant to the chemists Bell & Co. in Oxford Street, London, and, on the establishment of the Pharmaceutical Society, became one of the first associates. He attended the lectures of Anthony Todd Thomson on botany and materia medica. For some years Bentley studied at the King's College medical school, whence he qualified as a member of the Royal College of Surgeons in 1847. He became a fellow of the Linnean Society in 1849. In the same year he was appointed lecturer on botany at Middlesex Hospital and professor of botany to the Pharmaceutical Society where, from 1851, he was also professor of materia medica. He later became professor of botany at King's College (1859) and at the London Institution. For ten years he edited the *Pharmaceutical Journal*, in which almost all of his original papers were published.

In retrospect, the most far-reaching aspect of Bentley's career was with the school of pharmacy of what became the Royal Pharmaceutical Society of Great Britain. As professor of botany and then of both botany and materia medica he played a key role in the development of the new field of pharmacognosy as a scientific discipline. This, distinct from medical botany, focused on the identification, collection, and description of crude drugs as well as on the determination of the effects of climates, soils, and other circumstances on the medicinal activity of plants. Bentley also saw pharmacognosy as contributing to the introduction of new medicinal plants into Britain, such as those from North America. He published a number of textbooks, but of particular importance is the authoritative *Medicinal Plants* (1876–80) written with Henry Trimen in four volumes. It immediately became and has remained a standard work.

Bentley also took an active part in the affairs of the English Church Union, serving for some years on the council. He died at his home, 91 Warwick Road, Earls Court, on 24 December 1893, and was buried at Kensal Green cemetery.   G. S. BOULGER, rev. J. K. CRELLIN

Sources O. Corder, 'Robert Bentley', *Pharmaceutical Journal and Transactions*, 3rd ser., 24 (1893–4), 559–60 · *Chemist and Druggist* (15 Jan 1874) · E. J. Shellard, 'A history of British pharmacognosy, part 1: the long beginning, 1842–1890', *Pharmaceutical Journal*, 226 (1981), 108–11 · private information (2004) · *Proceedings of the Linnean Society of London* (1893–4), 28 · C. Knight, ed., *The English cyclopaedia: biography*, 6 vols. (1856–8) [suppl. (1872)]

Likenesses H. J. Whitlock, carte-de-visite, NPG · wood-engraving (after photograph by Martin & Sallnow), NPG; repro. in *ILN* (6 Jan 1894)

Wealth at death £4988 4s. 4d.: probate, 18 Jan 1894, CGPLA Eng. & Wales

Bentley, Samuel (1785–1868), printer and antiquary, was born on 10 May 1785, the eldest surviving son of Edward Bentley (b. 1753), publisher and principal of the accountant's office at the Bank of England, and his wife, Anne Nichols, only sister of the printer and historian John Nichols (1745–1826). Bentley was educated at St Paul's School alongside his nephew John Bentley, and upon leaving school was apprenticed to his maternal uncle, who in 1766 had been taken into partnership by the printer William Bowyer. Nichols was a fine scholar who inherited his patron's estate when Bowyer died in 1777, and who took into partnership his own son John Bowyer Nichols. With Bentley's father, Edward, John Nichols published the *General Evening Post*; on his own he printed, published, edited, and contributed articles to the *Gentleman's Magazine*. Thus Samuel Bentley was able to learn from his father, uncle, and cousin the commerce and craft of publishing and also the art of antiquarian scholarship. His industriousness and excellent mind earned him a partnership in the firm of Nichols, Son, and Bentley in April 1812 (Turner, 4). Bentley edited his uncle's *Literary Anecdotes of the Eighteenth Century* (1812–16) and Robert Surtees's *History … of Durham* (1816–40), and in 1816 he edited and wrote Latin prefaces for *Concio de puero Jesu*, composed by Desiderius Erasmus; the work was dedicated to the headmaster of St Paul's.

In 1819 Bentley left Nichols, whose business continued as John Nichols & Son, to join his younger brother Richard *Bentley (1794–1871) in inaugurating the printing and publishing firm of S. and R. Bentley, located in Dorset Street, Salisbury Square, London. This enterprise rapidly established itself as among the best printers in London. Samuel Bentley became skilled at integrating woodcuts into the text before other printers concerned themselves with relief illustration, and he had a fine eye for design and for accuracy. Benjamin Disraeli once said that if he had to choose between two editions, he would unhesitatingly pick the one printed by Bentley.

In 1825 Samuel Bentley married. Four years thereafter Richard Bentley negotiated his withdrawal from his brother's firm in order to enter into partnership with an over-extended publisher, Henry Colburn. Colburn owed the Bentleys a large printing bill; it was hoped that Richard Bentley would be able through his active management of Colburn's business to repay the debt. Samuel Bentley continued primarily as a printer, especially of historical subjects and books published by his brother. Childless himself, Bentley took his nephew John as junior partner, and in later years the firm expanded to become Bentley, Wilson, and Fley, with larger quarters at Bangor House, Shoe Lane. He kept up with technological improvements, travelling to Paris to inspect the type foundry Firmin-Didot.

The *chef d'œuvre* of Samuel Bentley's production is usually regarded as the *Excerpta Historica*, a quarterly periodical reissued as a royal octavo in 1831. This compilation was the fruit of many years of research in which Bentley was assisted by notable antiquaries: Sir Nicholas Harris *Nicolas (1799–1848); Sir Charles George *Young (1795–1869), Garter king of arms; William Henry *Black (1808–1872); and Sir Thomas Duffus *Hardy (1804–1878), deputy keeper of the Public Record Office from 1861. Bentley continued to transcribe, edit, and publish ancient documents; in 1836 he printed for private circulation *An abstract of charters and other documents contained in a cartulary of the abbey of St. Peter, Westminster, in the possession of S. Bentley* (BL, 7709. bb. 34). He also helped Sir Nicholas Harris Nicolas prepare for private publication the *Scrope and Grosvenor Controversy* (1832; BL, 708 i.5). 'Nothing', Sir Nicholas wrote, 'could be more delightful to me than the cordial co-operation I have received from you throughout the work, or more useful than the numerous suggestions with which you have favoured me.' But deciphering this decayed manuscript in the dark rooms of the Tower severely injured Bentley's eyesight, and by April 1853 blindness compelled him to abandon business, discontinuing the firm.

Bentley retired to Croydon with his wife, and contrived to enjoy himself. He was a good musician, interested in old English music, and had been an accomplished painter whose portrait of his father, Edward, earned praise from Daniel Maclise. He was also interested in architecture and languages, being particularly adept at translating Norman French. He died at North End, Croydon, on 13 April 1868, and was interred in the cemetery there. He was survived by his wife.   ROBERT L. PATTEN

Sources R. Bentley sen., 'Recollections of Edward Bentley [and early life]', *The archives of Richard Bentley & Son, 1829–1898* (1976) [microfilm] · *GM*, 5th ser., 1 (1868) · M. Turner, *Index and guide to the lists of the publications of Richard Bentley & Son, 1829–1898* (1975) · A. Ingram, *Index to the archives of Richard Bentley & Son, 1829–1898* (1977) · *DNB* · *BL cat.* · *National union catalog*, Library of Congress · R. A. Gettmann, *A Victorian publisher: a study of the Bentley papers* (1960) · *CGPLA Eng. & Wales* (1868)

Archives BL, corresp. and business papers, Add. MSS 15951, 24865, 34188, 37966, 46566–46567, 46652, 46681 · Bodl. Oxf., corresp. · U. Cal., Los Angeles · University of Illinois | Bodl. Oxf., letters to Sir Thomas Phillipps · LPL, letters to John Bowyer Nichols

Wealth at death under £14,000: probate, 6 May 1868, CGPLA Eng. & Wales

Bentley, Thomas (1690/91–1742), classical scholar, the son of James Bentley, grandson of Thomas Bentley of Woodlesford, near Oulton, Yorkshire, and nephew of Richard *Bentley, 'was brought up at St Paul's School in London'. He entered Trinity College, Cambridge, on 19 December 1707, aged sixteen, graduated BA (1711), MA (1715), and was elected a fellow of the college. In 1713 he published a small edition of Horace, which was in fact an annotated edition of a text by his uncle Richard, dedicated to Lord Harley, son of the earl of Oxford. Alexander Pope, in an offensive note to the edition of 1735, referred to this dedication, and declared that a couplet in the *Dunciad* (2.205–6), typically understood to refer to the uncle, actually applied to Thomas.

> Bentley his mouth with classic flatt'ry opes
> And the puff'd orator bursts out in tropes.

In 1718 Bentley published his *M. T. Ciceronis De finibus bonorum et malorum libri quinque et paradoxōn liber unus. Emendavit, notisque illustravit Thomas Bentley, A.M., Trin. Coll. Camb. socius.* As he declined or neglected to take orders, he lost his fellowship about 1723. Instead he was appointed librarian of Trinity College, and proceeded to his LLD degree in 1724. In 1725–6 he was abroad on a literary excursion to examine and collate manuscripts which might assist his uncle in the projected edition of the Greek New Testament. Bentley consulted manuscripts at Paris, Rome, Naples, and Florence, and took part in the collation of the celebrated Vatican manuscript, his notes on which were afterwards (1784) submitted to Charles Godfrey Woide for use in his valuable *Novum testamentum Graecum e codice MS. Alexandrino* (1786). In addition to this work, Bentley spent much of his time in Paris and Rome collating Greek manuscripts of Plutarch, with a view to the publication of an edition of that author, to which his health rendered him unequal. In 1741 he published his handsome edition of the hymns of Callimachus, *Callimachi hymni et epigrammata: quibus accesserunt Theognidis carmina* (1741), which was for some time mistakenly ascribed to his uncle. His edition of Caesar, with notes of his own and of his friend James Jurin, appeared in 1742. Bentley died suddenly on 28 May 1742, at Clifton. The *Gentleman's Magazine* (1786) confuses Thomas Bentley with his cousin Richard Bentley, rector of Nailston from 1745 to 1786, and a literary executor of their famous uncle.

ARTHUR H. GRANT, rev. PHILIP CARTER

Sources Venn, *Alum. Cant.* • Nichols, *Lit. anecdotes*, 4.491–2 • Nichols, *Illustrations*, 2.222 • *GM*, 1st ser., 56 (1786) • T. Bentley, 'Introduction', *Q. Horatius Flaccus* (1713) • J. H. Monk, *The life of Richard Bentley* (1830) • S. T. Coleridge, *Biographia literaria, or, Biographical sketches of my literary life and opinions*, 2 vols. (1817)
Likenesses P. L. Ghezzi, etching (after his portrait), BM, NPG

Bentley, Thomas (1731–1780), porcelain manufacturer, was born on 1 January 1731 at Scropton, Derbyshire, the elder son of Thomas Bentley. His father was a Presbyterian, which may account for Bentley's late baptism on 18 February 1736 at St Paul's Church. He was educated at the Presbyterian Collegiate Academy at Finderne, Derbyshire, until he was sixteen, when he was indentured to a Manchester textile merchant.

When he was twenty-three Bentley toured France and Italy and learned fluent French and Italian, before settling in Liverpool as a textile and, later, general merchant. Here his business prospered greatly. In 1754 at All Saints' Church, Chesterfield, he married Hannah, daughter of James Oates; she died in childbirth in 1759. Concerned with the restricted educational opportunities for dissenters, Bentley was a founder trustee of the celebrated Warrington Academy. He also co-founded the Octagon Chapel in Liverpool and wrote its non-sectarian liturgy. Though Liverpool was a centre of the slave trade Bentley opposed it, and his posthumous influence may have impelled the potter Josiah *Wedgwood to join the anti-slavery movement of the late 1780s.

In 1762 there occurred a meeting important in the history of English ceramics. Josiah Wedgwood travelled from his Staffordshire factory to Liverpool on business and fell ill. His doctor Matthew Turner brought his friend Thomas Bentley to visit the patient and Wedgwood was captivated. Bentley's classical education, languages, and elegant manners were attributes that Wedgwood lacked. The latter's letters have largely survived, and vividly express his pleasure in Bentley's friendship and admiration for his capabilities.

Wedgwood soon took the opportunity to propose a partnership. However, Bentley, who had taken Samuel Boardman as a partner in 1764, did not agree immediately. He was prosperously settled in Liverpool, whereas Wedgwood's future prospects were uncertain. However, he helped Wedgwood, who was deeply involved in the project for the Trent and Mersey Canal, by writing a pamphlet and advising on promotional tactics. When, in 1768, Wedgwood had his leg amputated, Bentley went to Staffordshire to help to run the factory until he recovered. After tentative discussions in 1767 and 1768, the partnership was finalized on 10 August 1769 but for the decorative ware only, as Wedgwood was already in partnership with his cousin Thomas for 'useful' (table) wares. At the opening of Wedgwood's factory at Etruria, Staffordshire, beside the canal, six 'first day's vases' were made, with Wedgwood throwing the vases and Bentley working the potter's wheel.

In 1769 Bentley moved to Great Newport Street in London to undertake the management of the Wedgwood showrooms and establish a ceramic enamelling studio at Little Cheyne Row, Chelsea. In 1770 a large service painted there so pleased the Empress Catherine of Russia that she ordered a huge dinner service of 952 pieces, each depicting a different British scene. Though this was strictly 'useful' ware, Wedgwood offered Bentley a half share in 'this superb commission'. Nothing of the kind had previously been attempted in England, and Bentley's support in supervising and training as many as thirty-three previously semi-skilled painters, and finding illustrations for them to copy, must have been invaluable to Wedgwood. The service was successfully completed in 1774, and was displayed in new showrooms in Greek Street, Soho, causing a sensation. Catherine paid £2700 for it immediately.

Bentley's education and gracious manners were ideal in

welcoming the queen and exacting metropolitan customers, and his erudite circle of friends played a part in Wedgwood's connections with connoisseurs such as Sir William Hamilton or the sculptor John Flaxman; but his most essential role was in alerting Wedgwood to the importance of the fashionable neo-classical interior decoration of Robert Adam, for whom Wedgwood made innovative chimney-piece plaques at 20 St James's Square, Westminster, in 1773. In consequence, Wedgwood's pieces reflected this new and influential decorative style, years before his competitors abandoned the outmoded rococo fashions.

On 22 June 1772 Bentley married Mary Stamford (d. 1797) at All Saints, Derby. In 1776 he revisited France for several weeks, partly to report on French taste, and kept detailed notebooks, one of which was rediscovered and printed in 1977. Bentley also wrote a biography of the canal designer Brindley, and articles in the *Gentleman's Magazine* on the education of women, inland waterways, and the cultivation of waste land.

In 1776 Bentley moved to Turnham Green, near Chiswick, Middlesex, for country air. He is reported to have had several illnesses, but none seemed life-threatening, so his sudden end on 26 November 1780, officially of a seizure, was a devastating blow to Wedgwood. He had lost both an invaluable partner and an irreplaceable friend. Bentley was buried at St Nicholas's Church, Chiswick, on 2 December 1780.

The wares representing the Wedgwood and Bentley partnership were auctioned by Christie and Ansell in December 1781, fetching £2152 6s. 6d., half of which went to Bentley's widow. She was also executor of his will, proved in January 1781. In it no figure is given for his estate from the Bentley and Boardman partnership.

Bentley appears frequently in all biographies of Josiah Wedgwood, but owing to the loss of almost all of his voluminous correspondence, his personal character seems shadowy, and his importance in the history of Georgian ceramics is often underestimated. However, the period of the Wedgwood and Bentley partnership, 1769 to 1780, is by common consent the high-water mark of Wedgwood's production, in which he developed his black basaltes and created the Adam-inspired jasper ware with white classical figures with which he is most associated. Bentley's contribution in advising, encouraging, and occasionally criticizing was incalculable.   ALISON KELLY

Sources G. B. Roberts, 'Ceramics' unsung hero', *Transactions of the English Ceramic Circle*, 15 (1993–5) · J. Boardman, *Bentleyana* (1851) · T. Bentley, *Journal of a visit to Paris, 1776*, ed. P. France (1977) · R. Bentley, *Thomas Bentley* (1927) · E. Meteyard, *The life of Josiah Wedgwood, from his private correspondence and family papers*, 2 vols. (1865–6) · R. Reilly, *Josiah Wedgwood, 1730–1795* (1992) · K. E. Farrer, *Letters of Josiah Wedgwood*, 3 vols. (1903–6)
Likenesses W. Caddick, portrait, 1766, repro. in F. Falkner, *The Wood family of Burslem* (1912), no. 101, pl. 27 · J. Smith, Wedgwood jasper medallion, c.1773, Man. City Gall.; copy, NPG · attrib. W. Hackwood, Wedgwood jasper medallion, c.1778, Wedgwood Museum, Barlaston, Staffordshire · attrib. W. Hackwood, Wedgwood jasper medallion, c.1780 (after his medallion), Wedgwood Museum, Barlaston, Staffordshire · Wedgwood medallion, c.1780, Wedgwood Museum, Barlaston, Staffordshire · J. F. Rigaud, oils, Lady Lever Art Gallery, Wirral, Cheshire; copy in Wedgwood Museum, Barlaston, Staffordshire · T. Scheemakers, marble bas-relief, St Nicholas's Church, Chiswick, Middlesex · oils, Walker Art Gallery, Liverpool · oils, Wedgwood Museum, Barlaston, Staffordshire

Bentley, Walter Owen (1888–1971), designer and racer of motor cars, was born on 16 September 1888 at 78 Avenue Road, Hampstead, London, the youngest in the family of six sons and three daughters of Alfred Bentley, retired businessman of London, and his wife, Emily Waterhouse. After leaving Clifton College at sixteen and a premium apprenticeship (1905–10) with the Great Northern Railway at Doncaster, he raced motor cycles and cars, and worked as a driver and mechanic for the National Motor Cab Company.

In 1912 Bentley acquired, with his brother Horace Milner Bentley, the London agency of three French cars, Buchet, La Licorne, and Doriot, Flandrin et Parant. At their premises off Upper Baker Street he then made a major contribution to the development of the internal combustion engine, originating the use of aluminium for pistons. Commissioned in 1914 and attached to the Royal Naval Air Service, he designed two rotary aero-engines, BR1 and BR2, which were successfully fitted to the Sopwith Camel and Snipe respectively. In 1919 he was appointed MBE.

In that year, with F. T. Burgess and Harry Varley, Bentley designed, built, and marketed a 3 litre engine and car, aimed at the top of the market, with a high performance for fast, sporting touring. He subsequently designed 4, 6, and 8 litre engines. Speed and endurance record breaking and long-distance racing were the surest forms of testing and advertising. 'We were in racing, not for glory and heroics but strictly for business.' Paradoxically, his 'Bentley boys', among them Woolf Barnato, son of the South African diamond millionaire, provided the British motor industry with its most glamorous episode. The works-entered team won the twenty-four hours' race at Le Mans in the years 1927–30.

Bentley's company was chronically underfunded and development costs always outran returns. Financial disaster was temporarily averted when Barnato put his money in and replaced Bentley as chairman in 1926, but the Wall Street crash in 1929 (the first year in which the company showed a profit) exposed the vulnerability of the luxury car market. In 1931 the company was bought, to Bentley's chagrin, by its rival, Rolls-Royce, Bentley's service contract being among the assets acquired. He had no part as a designer in the new subsidiary, Bentley Motors (1931). He felt 'a hostage—a dangerous ex-enemy confined (with all the comforts) to my Elba'. His contract expired, he moved to Lagonda in 1935, dangerously returning to the precarious world of the fast car. There he improved the Le Mans 4 litre and introduced a new V 12 twelve-cylinder.

During the Second World War Bentley worked with Lagonda on aircraft and tank components. After the war Lagonda announced a 2 litre car to be sold as Lagonda-Bentley. Rolls-Royce was swift to establish in the courts that its purchase of the trademark Bentley over-rode its contract with him, which had banned his own use of his

Walter Owen Bentley (1888–1971), by unknown photographer, 1969

name for ten years only. The car was then marketed as 'Lagonda, designed under the supervision of W. O. Bentley', but the volume of orders could not be met owing to the post-war shortage of steel. The firm was sold to David Brown and Bentley's engine was used in the Aston-Martin DB2 developed in its successors.

Taciturn, precise, a perfectionist engineer, but with little skill in a boardroom, Bentley was, by his own account, unresponsive and over-sensitive to criticism, dependent always on the riches of others whom he could not control. Though not easily approachable, he inspired enthusiasm, lasting devotion, and, increasingly, historic reverence.

Bentley married three times. On 1 January 1914 he married Léonie, daughter of (St George) Ralph Gore, ninth baronet. She died in the influenza epidemic of 1919. His unsuccessful second marriage, to which he never referred, was to Audrey Morten Chester Hutchinson. After a divorce he married on 31 January 1934 Margaret Roberts (*b.* 1892?), daughter of Thomas Roberts Murray, mechanical engineer, and divorced wife of Charles Alan Hutton. There were no children from these marriages. Bentley died at the Nuffield Nursing Home, Woking, on 13 August 1971.   H. G. PITT, *rev.*

Sources *The Times* (14 Aug 1971), 14f · *The Times* (17 Aug 1971), 12h · *The Times* (21 Aug 1971), 12h · *The Independent* (10 July 1990) · W. O. Bentley, *W. O., an autobiography* (1958) · W. O. Bentley, *The cars in my life* (1961) · W. O. Bentley, *My life and cars* (1967) · J. M. L. Frostick, *Bentley, Cricklewood to Crewe* (1980) · A. F. C. Hillstead, *Those Bentley days* (1953) · V. L. P. Davis, *W. O. Bentley, MBE: summary of his life and work* (1988) · *WWW* · b. cert. · m. certs. · d. cert.

Likenesses Dave, photograph, 2 Oct 1968, Hult. Arch. · photograph, 1969, Sci. Mus., Science and Society Picture Library [*see illus.*]

Wealth at death £3121: administration with will, 22 Oct 1971, *CGPLA Eng. & Wales*

Benton, Sir John (1850–1927), civil engineer, was born on 5 August 1850 at Sheriffhaugh, Banffshire, the second son of John Benton, of Sheriffhaugh, and his wife, Mary, daughter of Alexander Hay, of Edintore. He was educated at Aberdeen, attended lectures at the university, and in 1869 became a pupil of William Smith, a civil engineer, in Aberdeen. In 1870 he entered Edinburgh University, but in 1871 he became one of the first students of the Royal Indian Engineering College at Cooper's Hill, Englefield Green, Surrey, which was opened in that year. In 1873 he was appointed a second-grade assistant engineer in the Indian public works department, assigned to the Punjab. He was promoted to executive engineer, fourth grade, in 1881, to third grade in the same year, to second grade in 1885, and to first grade in 1892. During this period he had charge of heavy constructional work on the improvements and extensions to the network of canals irrigating the area around Lahore. Benton married, in 1885, Margaret Forsyth, daughter of Robert Dick, provost of Rothes, Moray; they had two daughters, and a son, who was killed in the First World War.

In 1897 Benton became a superintending engineer and his services were lent to the government of Burma. Fresh from the Punjab canals he found irrigation in Burma in a primitive state, weirs being made of stakes and stones instead of masonry and brickwork; but by originality and resource, as well as by refusing to tolerate incompetence, he effected great reforms. On the Mandalay Canal, his first work, opened in 1902, when he found that the standardized 10 foot openings could not take the amount of drift brought down by the floods, he substituted 40 foot openings, a practice which he followed later in the Shwebo and Ye-u canals, the former of which was opened in 1906. In the Thapaugaing Aqueduct, spanning a flood-swept ravine, he converted the walls into folding shutters, so that the flood water might safely sweep over the whole structure. He remodelled the canals in the Kyaukse district, and improved the Meiktila Lake works. He remained in Burma for five years, was made a chief engineer in 1900, and was created a CIE in 1902.

At the end of 1902 Benton returned to the Punjab in order to succeed Sidney Preston (with whom he had earlier been associated in his work there) as chief engineer and secretary to government. He retired under the age limit in August 1905, but in January 1906 he was recalled by the viceroy, Lord Curzon, and appointed, in succession to Preston, inspector-general of irrigation for all India.

In these later periods of service Benton undertook two projects of the greatest importance, the Triple Canals scheme and the upper Swat Valley Canal. The former doubled the fertile area in the Punjab by distributing the surplus waters of the Jhelum across the province. The scheme, sanctioned in 1905 and completed in 1917 at a cost of £8 million, was the largest irrigation work hitherto carried out in India and served as an example for subsequent achievements. It was described by Benton in a paper read before the Institution of Civil Engineers in November 1915, for which he received a Telford medal.

Benton's second irrigation scheme was located nearer the Afghan frontier. He tapped the Swat River at Chakdara by a canal, which he carried in a tunnel more than 2 miles long, known as the Benton Tunnel, under the Malakand Pass through the mountain barrier above Dargai. This extension more than doubled the area formerly served by the Swat River Canal. The fall of 400 feet from the mouth of the tunnel into the Dargai valley provided power for the electrification of the Nowshera–Dargai railway as well as for local purposes.

Benton was created KCIE in 1911 and retired finally in 1912. He was elected a member of the Institution of Civil Engineers in 1893, and was a member of its council from 1906 to 1908. He died at his home, Westcroft, 49 Silverdale Road, Eastbourne, Sussex, on 29 August 1927. He was survived by his wife.

E. I. CARLYLE, rev. ANITA McCONNELL

Sources The Times (31 Aug 1927) · PICE, 225 (1927–8), 353–4 · d. cert. · CGPLA Eng. & Wales (1927)
Archives CUL, corresp. with Lord Hardinge
Wealth at death £34,172 19s. 5d.: probate, 12 Oct 1927, CGPLA Eng. & Wales

Benton, Mary Sophia (1855–1944), headmistress, was born at Wennington, Hornchurch, Essex, on 23 December 1855, the daughter of Aaron Benton, a farmer, and his wife, Sophia Elizabeth, née Julian. She was educated at home by a governess until the age of nine, then at a boarding-school, where the curriculum was confined to subjects considered 'ladylike'. Her own aspirations were already higher than this, and she demanded that her parents remove her. The subsequent years she spent in a school in Germany and working as a governess in France, which left her with a lifelong love of French and German language and literature. In 1875 she went from her home in Essex as one of the earliest students to Newnham College, Cambridge, where she remained for a year but took no tripos examination. As a student she had already adopted the masculine dress which was to remain her style throughout life, despite the alleged efforts of Miss Anne Jemima Clough, Newnham's principal, to encourage her to adopt more conventional attire.

From Newnham, Mary Benton began her lifelong association with the Girls' Public Day School Company (later Trust). For a year she taught at St John's Wood high school; then she spent a few months teaching at Bath high school. Three years at Chelsea (later Kensington) high school were followed by six years at Oxford high school. Finally, in 1886, she returned to her first school, renamed South Hampstead high school, where she remained for the next thirty-two years.

Morale at South Hampstead had sunk after a difficult period. With characteristic energy and determination Mary Benton transformed it into one of the foremost girls' schools in London. She particularly encouraged girls to specialize in languages and the sciences. Most girls were required to study three languages, including German, and it was not until 1917, after protests from parents, that she modified this requirement. The jubilee magazine of 1926 claimed that the majority of degrees taken by Mary Benton's old girls were in scientific subjects, an unusual achievement for the time. Her own teaching subjects, as well as French and German translation, were geography and scripture; she was a familiar sight walking round the school carrying a globe. A special chair was reserved for her in each classroom so that she could pay regular visits to classes which interested her.

Mary Benton was short and well built, vigorous and forthright in speech and manner. Her masculine dress (tailored suit, plain shirt, and collar and tie), her severe hairstyle, and her deep voice led the assistant secretary of the trust to refer to her as 'the brigadier-general', and her younger pupils to feel in great awe of her. But she had a keen sense of humour and genuine respect for every one of her pupils, and as they grew older their awe developed into affection, which for many lasted long past their schooldays. On one occasion, she qualified a ruling that jewellery might not be worn by announcing that any girl who wished her friends to know what jewellery she possessed might bring a list to be pinned on the form notice board. Of awkward parents, she said, 'I always receive them standing, it's easier to get rid of them.'

Mary Benton was a well-known figure in Hampstead life, and served on several local committees, including the Red Cross and the Secondary Schools' Patriotic Union. Her administrative gifts found an outlet beyond the school in the committees of the Head Mistresses' Association, of whose general committee she was twice chairman, in 1903–5 and 1906–7. She was a public supporter of the National Society for Women's Suffrage. She spent the first few years of her official retirement teaching in a primary school until a pension problem was sorted out. Finally she moved to Cadnam in the New Forest, where it was said that she acted as unofficial headmistress of the village. She continued to take a lively interest in world affairs and in her school and all its former pupils. She died on 28 May 1944 of cancer in St John's Nursing Home at Rownhams, Southampton; her funeral was at Southampton crematorium.

ELAINE KAYE

Sources P. R. Bodington, The kindling and the flame (1976) · South Hampstead High School Magazine (1926) · South Hampstead High School Magazine (1927) · South Hampstead High School Magazine (Jan 1945) · L. Magnus, The jubilee book of the Girls' Public Day School Trust, 1873–1923 (1923) · folder of letters about Miss Benton, Croydon high school, GPDST MSS · GPDST Council Minutes · [A. B. White and others], eds., Newnham College register, 1871–1971, 2nd edn, 1 (1979), vol. 1 · Newnham College Roll Letter (1945) · J. Kamm, Indicative past: one hundred years of the Girls' Public Day School Trust (1971) · N. Glenday and M. Price, Reluctant revolutionaries (1974) · b. cert. · d. cert.
Likenesses J. Inglis, portrait, 1918–19, South Hampstead high school, London

Bentwich [née Franklin], **Helen Caroline** (1892–1972), local politician, was born on 6 January 1892 at 29 Pembridge Gardens, Notting Hill, London, the fifth child and second daughter (there were also four sons) of Arthur Ellis Franklin (1857–1938), merchant banker, and his wife,

Caroline, *née* Jacob (1863–1935), members of the Anglo-Jewish élite. Hugh Arthur *Franklin (1889–1962) was an elder brother; Herbert *Samuel, first Viscount Samuel was her uncle; and Rosalind *Franklin was her niece. Her parents were involved in Jewish communal and general charitable work, and their example inspired her. Educated at St Paul's Girls' School and at Bedford College, University of London, she took up social work. On 7 September 1915 she married, at the West London Synagogue, Norman de Mattos *Bentwich (1883–1971); the marriage proved childless.

After the wedding Helen Bentwich accompanied her husband to Cairo, where he was employed as a British civil administrator and law lecturer. She worked first in a hospital as a voluntary aid detachment nurse and then as confidential secretary in the ministry of finance. Her husband, meanwhile, had joined the British army, serving on the Palestine front, where he reached the rank of major. In summer 1916 Helen Bentwich returned to London, becoming a forewoman in the munitions factory at Woolwich arsenal. Convinced that its female workforce was overworked and underpaid, she attempted to form a trade union and was either dismissed outright or compelled to resign. She then became the able and highly regarded organizer of the Women's Land Army in the home counties.

In January 1919 Helen Bentwich rejoined her husband, who from 1920 to 1931 was attorney-general in the mandate government of Palestine. In addition to acting as his hostess she immersed herself in community activities, organizing nursery schools for Jewish and Arab children, supervising Jewish girls working on the land, and forming an arts and crafts centre. From 1921 until 1930 she served as honorary secretary of the feminist-inclined Palestine Council of Jewish Women. Her letters home during this period in Palestine, which she drew upon in *Mandate Memories* (1965) co-written with her husband, were published in 1999.

In 1931, at the end of Norman Bentwich's period in office, the couple returned to England, maintaining homes in Hampstead, London, and in Sandwich, Kent. They also kept a residence in Jerusalem, for from 1932 until 1951 Norman was professor of international law at the Hebrew University. A stalwart member of the Labour Party, Helen Bentwich stood unsuccessfully at a parliamentary by-election in Dulwich, south London, in 1932. Defeated, again, standing for Harrow at the general election of 1935, she found her true calling on the London county council (LCC), having been co-opted onto its education committee in 1934. Three years later she was elected to the LCC as member for North Kensington, which she represented until 1946, when she became member for Bethnal Green North-East; from 1955 until she retired in 1965 she represented Stoke Newington and Hackney North. She became chairman of the education committee in 1947, serving in that capacity until 1950, and promoted the establishment of comprehensive secondary schools. She took a particular interest in the development of evening institutes. In 1949 she was made an alderman, became

vice-chairman of the LCC in 1950, and was elected chairman for the session 1956–7. An obituarist trivialized her as merely 'a very decorative chairman' (*The Times*), but she was in truth a considerably active, successful, and respected one, known for her energetic commitment, administrative capabilities, and forceful, even combative, style. A highlight of her term of office was her official four-day visit to Paris as the guest of the municipal authorities. In 1965 she was appointed CBE for political and public services.

Helen Bentwich was connected with many organizations, chiefly of an educational or cultural nature. She was a governor of Bedford College, the Central School of Arts and Crafts, Dartford Physical Education College, and King Edward's School, Witney. She was a trustee of the London Museum and the Whitechapel Art Gallery and a member of the Burnham committee, the Council of Industrial Design, the Army Educational Advisory Board, and the National Advisory Council for the Training and Supply of Teachers. She also served as president of the Brady Clubs and Settlement, an initiative for youth in east London started by her mother. Her husband took great pride in her achievements and was unfailingly supportive. She shared his interest in Zionist endeavours in Palestine, in the welfare of refugees from Nazism, and in that of the so-called Falashas (the Judaic Ethiopians). In the 1930s she was a full-time organizer of the Movement for the Care of Children from Germany, and with her husband visited several countries on behalf of refugees. The couple paid several visits to Jewish inhabitants of Ethiopia, and she was planning another at the time of her death.

Helen Bentwich survived her husband by just twelve months, dying at her home, Hollycot, Vale of Health, Hampstead, London, on 26 April 1972. Likening the 'redoubtable Bentwiches' to the Webbs 'in so many ways', the future life peer Lord Mishcon observed on learning of her passing that it was 'difficult to imagine how one could go on living without the other' (*Jewish Chronicle* 5 May 1972). Inter alia, she left bequests to the Brady Clubs and Settlement, the West Central Jewish Club and Settlement, with which she had long been associated, the Friends of the Hebrew University, and the London Labour Party. Her unfinished autobiography was published posthumously in 1973.

HILARY L. RUBINSTEIN

Sources N. Bentwich, *My 77 years: an account of my life and times, 1883–1960* (1962) · C. Bermant, *The cousinhood: the Anglo-Jewish gentry* (1971) · V. Mishcon, *Jewish Chronicle* (5 May 1972) · *The Times* (28 April 1972) · A. E. Franklin, ed., *Records of the Franklin family and collaterals* (1935) · will, 1 Sept 1963 · b. cert. · m. cert. · d. cert. · N. Bentwich and H. Bentwich, *Mandate memories, 1918–1948* (1965) · H. C. Bentwich, *If I forget thee: some chapters of autobiography, 1912–1920* (1973) · H. C. Bentwich, *Tidings from Zion: Helen Bentwich's letters from Jerusalem, 1919–1931*, ed. J. Glynn (1999)
Archives Women's Library, London, corresp., diaries, notebooks, and papers | LMA
Likenesses photograph (in old age), repro. in *Jewish Chronicle*
Wealth at death £100,705: probate, 3 July 1972, *CGPLA Eng. & Wales*

Bentwich, Herbert (1856–1932), lawyer and Zionist leader, was born on 11 May 1856 at 57 Church Lane, Whitechapel,

London, the youngest of three children (he had a brother and a sister) of Marks, or Mattos (Mattathias), Bentwitch, a jeweller who had immigrated from Peiser in Russian Poland, and his wife, Rosa, or Rose, daughter of Godfrey Levy, a prominent figure in Bedford. He was brought up in Spital Square, Bishopsgate, in the City of London; the family name (as on his birth certificate) was originally spelt Bentwitch. Marks Bentwitch, like his father and paternal grandfather, was a qualified rabbi; with other members of the family, his parents also settled in Britain, providing Herbert Bentwich with a firm grounding in Jewish law and lore. Godfrey Levy, a campaigner for Jewish rights, in whose household the young Herbert often spent his holidays, provided his grandson with a role model of the ideal Anglo-Jewish gentleman, imbued with a deep and genuine English patriotism while remaining a proudly loyal Jew. A sickly child, Herbert Bentwich was educated in London: initially at Woodman's, a Christian-run private school in Bishopsgate; from 1866 to 1869 at a Jewish boarding-school in Edmonton headed by a respected Hebraist and Talmudist, Henry Naphtali Solomon; and from 1869 to 1872 at the Whitechapel Foundation, a long-established grammar school where he was a brilliant pupil and where his profound interest in the present and future status of world Jewry, which prompted his passionate attachment to the Zionist cause, was already evident.

Determined upon a career as a lawyer, in 1872 Bentwich entered University College, London, then the only British institution of higher learning which permitted Jews and other non-Anglicans to take degrees. There he obtained the Hollier Hebrew scholarship and gained first prize for English law as well as for jurisprudence. Having graduated bachelor of laws with honours in 1877, he completed his articles with Emmanuel and Simmons, in Finsbury Circus, London, with whom he had begun in 1873, and then set up in practice on his own as a solicitor in the City. He soon became a specialist in copyright law, his expertise in that field honed in a series of actions he fought on behalf of the art publishers Raphael Tuck & Sons: he described his relative, Sir Adolph Tuck, as his best friend. He took an active part in the work of the Incorporated Law Society, was appointed to the London Chamber of Arbitration, and in 1926 formed an English branch of the Society of Jewish Jurisprudence. He had always yearned to become a barrister, but financial and family circumstances precluded further study until 1901. He was admitted to the Inner Temple in 1903, and practised on the south-eastern circuit. But he swiftly proved ill-suited for the cut and thrust of the bar, and contented himself instead with owning and editing the *Law Journal*, which he acquired in 1908. With his predecessor as editor, Lewis Edmunds KC, he wrote a definitive work on the law of designs, and, with W. H. Stoker KC, one on the Military Service Acts.

On 14 December 1880, in the Borough New Synagogue, London, Bentwich married Susannah (Susie; *b.* 1861/2), daughter of Joseph Solomon, a leather dresser of Bermondsey who had immigrated from Vienna with his Prague-born wife. The Bentwichs, who had nine daughters and two sons, lived in London, first in Kilburn, and

from 1892 in St John's Wood. Susie Bentwich, a talented pianist, died on 19 May 1915 and was buried in Willesden cemetery.

Herbert Bentwich first became involved in Jewish communal affairs in 1875, when he did voluntary work for Anglo-Jewry's principal charity, the Jewish Board of Guardians. In 1876 he became honorary secretary of a group which organized free lectures for Jewish working men. In 1877 he assumed the honorary secretaryship of the Stepney Jewish schools, and in 1878 of the education committee of Jews' College. Simultaneously a proud Englishman and a proud Jew, he believed passionately that Jewish exclusivity was intended by God for some higher purpose and that the thirst for social parity with non-Jews at the expense of religious observance threatened to undermine western Jewry. In 1880, aiming to combat assimilation and intermarriage, he launched an abortive campaign to establish Jewish denominational schools among the middle-class Jews of north London. In 1883 he was elected to the board of St John's Wood synagogue and shortly afterwards he successfully urged the formation of Sunday school classes in Hebrew and the tenets of Judaism for members' children. The system was swiftly imitated by three other London synagogues. In 1892 he helped to found the Hampstead synagogue, a torchbearer of modern, moderate Orthodox Judaism—as was reflected in its mixed choir of male and female voices and other modifications to the traditional liturgy and ritual. He belonged to the Society of Wanderers, a group of intellectuals centring on the eminent rabbinic scholar Solomon Schechter and including Moses Gaster, the *haham* (effectively the chief rabbi of the Spanish and Portuguese Jews in England), who strove to promote Judaism as a relevant force.

In 1891 Bentwich attended a mass meeting held at the Great Assembly Hall, Mile End, against the background of intensifying tsarist antisemitism, in support of the Chovevei Zion ('Lovers of Zion') movement which aimed to settle deprived and persecuted Jews in agricultural colonies in Palestine. Deeply affected, Bentwich was propelled into Zionist activism. Thus later that year he was among the founders of the Maccabeans under the presidency of his wife's brother, the artist Solomon Joseph Solomon RA, known to his family as Toddy. In 1894 he became a vice-chief of the Chovevei Zion movement and commander of its so-called Western Tent. He aroused considerable comment in the spring of 1897 when he led twenty-one Jewish 'pilgrims', including the writer Israel Zangwill, on a tour of Palestine. That initiative was extravagantly praised by Theodor Herzl who, as Bentwich hastened to point out, misinterpreted it as a 'national enquiry commission' rather than the tour of ancient holy sites and new settlements that it actually was. Since he remained officially wedded to the Chovevei Zion philosophy, which stopped short of the quest for a legally secured Jewish national home, he ignored Herzl's insistence that he attend the inaugural Zionist Congress held at Basel in 1897. Yet he was rapidly moving in a Herzlian direction, as articles by him in the *Nineteenth Century Review*

(October 1897) and the *Fortnightly Review* (December 1898) testify.

In 1898 Bentwich convened a conference of 8000 English Zionists at Clerkenwell town hall, London, to which Herzl sent a spokesman. Delegates decided to affiliate their groups to the newly created World Zionist Organization. Most Anglo-Jewish leaders, men of Bentwich's milieu, stood aloof. That same year he became foundation chairman of the English Zionist Federation, and he also attended the second Zionist Congress at Basel, which entrusted him with the task of drawing up the statutes of the Jewish Colonial Trust and the Anglo-Palestine Bank. He also advised on the constitution of the Jewish National Fund. In 1899 he attended the third Zionist Congress, and chaired the annual conference of the English Zionist Federation in St Martin's Hall, Long Acre, London, when Herzl was the keynote speaker. Herzl frequently visited his home, as did Zionist activists and prominent non-Jewish sympathizers. Bentwich's unabashed display of dual loyalty was remarkable in a Jew of his milieu. He named his country house at Birchington, Kent, purchased in 1900, Carmelcourt, in evocation of Mount Carmel in Palestine, and on Jewish festivals proudly hung the Zionist flag. Carmelcourt became the almost legendary venue for lively gatherings of Jewish intellectuals.

In 1901 Bentwich was elected to the Board of Deputies of British Jews, and in 1902 he investigated the degraded status of Romanian Jewry at the behest of the London-based Russo-Jewish committee. Concluding that the true solution was Romanian Jewry's migration to Palestine, he urged his fellow deputies, with the pugnacity for which he was renowned, to campaign for British government intervention with the Romanian authorities, but in vain. His strident pleas for uncompromising opposition by the board to the Aliens Act of 1905 were also unavailing. Concerned for the welfare of indigent Jewish newcomers to Britain, he formed a London branch of the international Jewish fraternal organization B'nai B'rith, serving as its foundation president and providing legal aid for arriving foreign Jews denied entry by immigration officials.

Bentwich flounced out of the English Zionist Federation in 1909 when Leopold Jacob Greenberg beat him by one vote for its vice-presidency. From 1905 to 1919 he was grand commander of the order of Ancient Maccabeans, a British-based Jewish friendly society with branches in Palestine. Hoping to create an agricultural settlement of British Jews there, he organized in 1911 the Maccabean Land Company, which acquired the historical site of Gezer, but the project foundered. He was honorary president of the Zionist societies of London and Cambridge universities, and in 1913 attended the Zionist Congress in Vienna. He wrote a typically belligerent defence of Zionist aims in response to a critique by 'an Englishman of the Jewish faith' (almost certainly the publicist and historian Lucien Wolf); the exchange appeared in the *Fortnightly Review* during the latter half of 1915. As head of the order of Ancient Maccabeans he took a prominent role, with Nahum Sokolow, Chaim Weizmann, and others, in the

conferences and negotiations with Whitehall that led to the Balfour declaration of 1917. Representing B'nai B'rith, he attended the Paris peace conference as a member of the committee of Jewish delegations which demanded civil equality for central and eastern European Jewry. In 1920 his son Norman de Mattos *Bentwich (1883–1971) was appointed attorney-general of Palestine.

The following year Bentwich travelled to Palestine, reburying his wife on Mount Scopus (the Mount of Olives) in Jerusalem. Three daughters had emigrated to Palestine, and henceforth he visited that country annually. During these latter years he lived on weekdays in London at a bachelor flat near the editorial offices of the *Law Journal* in Essex Street, socializing on weekends at Carmelcourt. In 1929 he settled in Palestine, for so long his homeland of the mind. He died at his home in the Jerusalem suburb of Rehavia on 25 June 1932 and was buried beside his wife. Not the least interesting of several noteworthy relatives was an Australian cousin, Lizzie Bentwich, the mistress of General Sir John Monash; Bentwich left her a token legacy.   HILARY L. RUBINSTEIN

Sources M. Bentwich and N. Bentwich, *Herbert Bentwich: the pilgrim father* (Jerusalem, 1940) · N. Bentwich, *My 77 years: an account of my life and times, 1883–1960* (1962) · *The Times* (27 June 1932) · *Jewish Chronicle* (1 July 1932) · copy of will, with 10 codicils, 1 Dec 1915, priv. coll. · G. Alderman, *Modern British Jewry* (1992) · N. Rose, *Chaim Weizmann: a biography* (New York, 1986) · C. Weizmann, *Trial and error: the autobiography* (1950) · b. cert. · m. cert. · *CGPLA Eng. & Wales* (1932)

Archives Central Zionist Archives, Jerusalem, Herbert Bentwich papers

Likenesses L. Pilichowski, oils, priv. coll. · S. J. Solomon, oils, bequeathed to the World Union of Jewish Students · plates, repro. in Bentwich and Bentwich, *Herbert Bentwich*

Wealth at death £11,392 7s. 9d.: probate, 10 Oct 1932, *CGPLA Eng. & Wales*

Bentwich, Norman de Mattos (1883–1971), colonial official and exponent of Jewish ideals, was born in London on 28 February 1883, the elder son and second of eleven children of Herbert *Bentwich (1856–1932) and his wife, Susannah, daughter of Joseph Solomon, leather merchant, and sister of Solomon J. Solomon, painter. His father, a solicitor, was an active member of the Anglo-Jewish community who brought up his family in the fervent belief that Israel had a continuing religious mission to fulfil, while his mother stressed the universal values of music and art. The Hebrew scholar Solomon Schechter was a great friend of his father. He attended St Paul's School whence he went as major scholar to Trinity College, Cambridge. He read classics, winning the Yorke essay prize twice, and rabbinics under Solomon Schechter. He obtained first classes in both parts of the classical tripos (1903 and 1905). In 1905 he took up law with the Whewell scholarship and was called to the bar by Lincoln's Inn in 1908.

In 1912 Bentwich entered the Egyptian ministry of justice as inspector of native courts. In 1915 he joined the British army in Egypt (Camel Transport Corps) and took part in the conquest of Jerusalem, which earned him the rank of lieutenant-colonel, an MC, and appointment as

Norman de Mattos Bentwich (1883–1971), by Elliott & Fry, 1950

OBE (1918). In 1915 Bentwich married Helen Caroline Franklin (1892–1972) [*see* Bentwich, Helen Caroline], daughter of Arthur Ellis Franklin, banker and company director. There were no children.

In 1918 Bentwich became legal secretary to the British military administration in Palestine and after the establishment of the mandatory government in 1922 he became the country's first attorney-general. Bentwich's wife was the niece of Lady Samuel, wife of the then high commissioner, Sir Herbert Samuel. In Zionist politics Bentwich was moderate, working for Arab–Jewish understanding and a bi-national state. But with the conflict between the two nations steadily intensifying, the government was bound to find a Jewish attorney-general a political embarrassment, however reconciling his personal views might be. In 1929 Bentwich clashed with a subsequent high commissioner, Sir John Chancellor, over plans to prevent the sale of 'Arab land' to Jews. Unfortunately, the Colonial Office supported Chancellor. Bentwich was put on paid leave, and then detained in London under the pretext of 'giving temporary assistance to the Legal Department of the Colonial Office' (Shepherd, 113). Bentwich was offered promotion in the service outside Palestine, and, when he declined, was retired from the colonial service in 1931.

In 1932 Bentwich was appointed professor of international relations at the Hebrew University of Jerusalem. His inaugural lecture, 'Jerusalem, city of peace', was interrupted by students who opposed his pacifying approach and had to be continued under police protection. The terms of the chair provided that the holder would lecture during only one of the two terms of the year and otherwise be free to work in the field of international relations where he wished. He made full use of these opportunities. Thus, when the Nazi persecutions began, he became one of the foremost fighters for the rescue of the oppressed. He travelled to all countries, pleading with governments and investigating possible places of refuge. He became director both of the League of Nations high commission for refugees from Germany (1933–5) and of the Council for German Jewry.

During the Second World War Bentwich served in the Ministry of Information in London, and for a time in the Air Ministry. He lectured for the government, especially in the United States. In 1943 he went to the Middle East and to Ethiopia where he advised the emperor on the treaties to be concluded with Great Britain. During the following years he was engaged, as chairman of the Anglo-Abyssinian Society, in furthering Ethiopia's claim for the recovery of Eritrea, and attended the Paris conference of 1946 as a member of the Ethiopian delegation. In addition he took up the cause of the Falashas, an Ethiopian tribe who consider themselves Jews, but are not recognized as such by Israel and most Jewish communities.

Bentwich was chairman of the National Peace Council (1944–6) and in the post-war period had a major part in securing restitution and compensation for the victims of Nazi persecutions. In 1951, having reached the statutory age, Bentwich retired as professor at the Hebrew University, and was elected a member and vice-chairman of its board of governors. Work for the university now became his main concern. Since its foundation the Hebrew University had been to him the symbol of Jewish renaissance and of all the causes he served probably this was nearest to his heart. He was president of the London North-Western Reform Synagogue from 1958 until his death.

Bentwich was the author of nearly thirty books on subjects ranging from Judaeo-Greek civilization to international law, refugees, and the rebirth of Israel. These included a major biography of Solomon Schechter. He was awarded honorary doctorates from the universities of Aberdeen (1942), Melbourne (1938), and Jerusalem (1956). He was always ready to help others, indefatigable in the causes he had taken up, and deeply committed to what he considered right. He sometimes wondered whether his life had perhaps lacked a certain 'one-pointedness' and had been too much divided between different worlds. But however this may be, all divisions were overcome and reconciled by his gentle personality and his spirit of service.

Between 1919 and 1931 Helen Bentwich had documented the social life of the mandate in letters home. Norman Bentwich quoted these extensively in *Mandate Memories, 1918–1948* (1965), and in 1999 the letters themselves were published. Helen Bentwich was active in local government in London in her later career, and served as a Labour councillor. She was chair of the London county council (1956–7) and was appointed CBE in 1965.

Bentwich died in London on 8 April 1971 and according to his wish was buried in Jerusalem on Mount Scopus. Helen Bentwich died in 1972.

WALTER ZANDER, rev. ROBERT BROWN

Sources N. Bentwich, *My 77 years: an account of my life and times, 1883–1960* (1962) · *The Times* (10 April 1971) · *The Times* (28 April 1972) · personal knowledge (1986) · private information (1986) · N. Shepherd, *Ploughing sand: British rule in Palestine, 1917–1948* (1999) · B. Wasserstein, *The British in Palestine: the mandatory government and the Arab-Jewish conflict, 1917–1929* (1978) · B. Wasserstein, *Herbert Samuel: a political life* (1992) · *WWW* · *CGPLA Eng. & Wales* (1971)
Archives St Ant. Oxf., Middle East Centre, corresp. and MSS | Bodl. Oxf., corresp. relating to Society for Protection of Science and Learning · CUL, corresp. with Sir Herbert Butterfield · JRL, letters to the *Manchester Guardian* · U. Southampton L., corresp. with J. M. Shaftesley; corresp. and papers relating to Anglo-Jewish Association · U. Warwick Mod. RC, corresp. with Victor Gollancz
Likenesses Elliott & Fry, photograph, 1950, NPG [*see illus.*]
Wealth at death £45,885: probate, 20 Aug 1971, *CGPLA Eng. & Wales*

Benwell, John Hodges (1762–1785), genre painter, was born on 6 May 1762 at Blenheim Palace, Oxfordshire, where his father was under-steward to the duke of Marlborough. He was a pupil of a portrait painter named Sanders (possibly John Sanders; *fl.* 1750–1783), and he also studied in the Royal Academy Schools, which he entered on 25 March 1779 when his age was given as '17 6th next May' (Hutchison, 144), and won a silver medal in 1782. He afterwards taught drawing at Bath, and produced small oval drawings of fancy subjects in watercolour which he combined effectively with crayon in a unique manner. He was mainly a draughtsman and illustrator in these media but his works deteriorated with time. He returned to London and exhibited a classical subject at the Royal Academy in 1784: '*Glycaera at the Tomb of her Mother*, an illustration for Gessner's *Idylls*' (Graves, *RA exhibitors*, 1.183). His address then was 24 Henrietta Street, Covent Garden. He died prematurely of consumption in 1785, and was buried in St Pancras old churchyard. Several of his works were well known from engravings by W. Sharp and Bartolozzi. His drawing of *The Chevalier de Bayard* is in the Victoria and Albert Museum, London. Other examples of his work are in the British Museum and Manchester City Galleries.

R. E. GRAVES, rev. A. NISBET

Sources Redgrave, *Artists* · Waterhouse, *18c painters* · S. C. Hutchison, 'The Royal Academy Schools, 1768–1830', *Walpole Society*, 38 (1960–62), 123–91, esp. 144 · G. Meissner, ed., *Allgemeines Künstlerlexikon: die bildenden Künstler aller Zeiten und Völker*, [new edn, 34 vols.] (Leipzig and Munich, 1983–) · Graves, *RA exhibitors*

Benwell [*married name* Code], **Mary** (*fl.* 1761–*c*.1800), portrait painter, of whose parents nothing is known, is not known to be related to the painter John Hodges Benwell. She lived in Warwick Court, London, and worked in crayon, oils, and miniatures. She began exhibiting at the Incorporated Society of Artists in 1761 and at the Royal Academy in 1775, contributing regularly until 1791. She was elected an honorary member of the Society of Artists in 1769 with, among others, Catherine Read. About 1782 she married an army officer named Code, and purchased his promotion. After 1783 she was entered at both the Royal Academy and Society of Artists as Mrs Code. Her miniature *Portrait of Mrs. Bradney* (1772) is in the Victoria and Albert Museum, London. A self-portrait miniature (1779) was taken to Florence by Giovanni Fabbroni and given to the Uffizi on 2 March 1780. The British Museum and the National Portrait Gallery, London, have examples of engravings after her work, that by Richard Houston after her crayon portrait of Queen Charlotte (exh. Society of Artists, 1762) being of particular interest.

It is thought that her husband was sent to Gibraltar and died there. Mary Benwell is said to have retired to Paddington, Middlesex, about 1800.   TINA FISKE

Sources E. Edwards, *Anecdotes of painters* (1808); facs. edn (1970) · *Firenze e Inghilterra: rapporti artistici e culturali dal XVI al XX secolo* [exhibition catalogue, Palazzo Pitti, Florence, July–Sept 1971] · W. T. Whitley, *Artists and their friends in England, 1700–1799*, 2 vols. (1928) · G. Hall and others, *Summary catalogue of miniatures in the Victoria and Albert Museum* (1981) · Waterhouse, *18c painters* · B. Stewart and M. Cutten, *The dictionary of portrait painters in Britain up to 1920* (1997) · Graves, *Soc. Artists* · Graves, *RA exhibitors* · Redgrave, *Artists* · Bryan, *Painters* · J. Gould, *Biographical dictionary of painters, sculptors, engravers and architects*, new edn, 2 vols. (1839) · H. G. Adams, ed., *A cyclopaedia of female biography* (1857) · M. Pilkington, *A general dictionary of painters: containing memoirs of the lives and works*, ed. A. Cunningham and R. A. Davenport, new edn (1857) · D. Foskett, *Miniatures: dictionary and guide* (1987) · G. Meissner, ed., *Allgemeines Künstlerlexikon: die bildenden Künstler aller Zeiten und Völker*, [new edn, 34 vols.] (Leipzig and Munich, 1983–) · *DNB*
Likenesses M. Benwell, self-portrait, oils, 1779, Uffizi Gallery, Florence, Italy · H. Kingsbury, mezzotint, pubd 1779, BM

Benwell, William (*bap.* 1765, *d.* 1796), Church of England clergyman and classical scholar, was baptized at St Peter's, Caversham, Oxfordshire, on 10 April 1765, the second son of Henry Benwell (*bap.* 1722, *d.* 1787) and his wife, Mary Ackerman (*bap.* 1729, *d.* 1766). He was educated at Reading School where the headmaster was Dr Richard Valpy, who married his sister Mary in 1782. He was admitted to Trinity College, Oxford, in 1783 and became a close friend (and later executor) of Henry Headley, the poet. In his preface to *Select Beauties of Ancient English Poets* (1787), Headley wrote 'For assistance received I am solely indebted to my very dear friend, Mr Benwell'. Thomas Warton gave especial encouragement to both young men. In 1783 Benwell obtained the chancellor's prize for the best Latin verse. He took his BA degree in 1787 and received the chancellor's prize for the best English essay—'In what arts have the moderns exceeded the ancients?' He was also ordained deacon and appointed to the curacy of Sonning, Berkshire, in countryside which he loved and where he was highly regarded for his exemplary care of his parishioners and the excellence of his sermons. He obtained his MA degree in 1789, was elected a fellow of Trinity College in 1790, and soon afterwards he was ordained priest. As he was then appointed Greek lecturer and tutor he became resident in college in May 1791 and resigned the curacy.

During these years Benwell frequently visited the Old Rectory at Caversham where he assisted John *Loveday (1711–1789), the antiquary and traveller, many of whose anecdotes he recorded and from whose learning he benefited. In 1788 he became secretly engaged to Penelope Loveday (1759–1846), the eldest daughter of Loveday's third marriage, to Penelope Forrest. This was not revealed until after John Loveday's death in 1789 as the couple had thought marriage would not be countenanced owing to the difference in their ages. Benwell had been presented to the living of Hale in Lincolnshire, but never lived there. He resigned on being given the living of Chilton in Suffolk by William Windham, secretary of war, who was a family friend. The marriage finally took place in Milton, Wiltshire, on 20 June 1796, but lasted only eleven weeks, for it was while he was staying in his mother-in-law's house, prior to moving to Chilton, that Benwell succumbed to typhus fever which was raging in Milton. Although it was not his parish he had visited the sick constantly. He died on 6 September 1796 and was buried on the 14th, at St Peter's Church, Caversham. A memorial was erected in the church, and also at Chilton, where the parishioners had been greatly impressed by him, although he had never been resident. All reports of Benwell point to his devotion to duty, his attractive personality, and pleasant appearance, as well as his gentle and modest demeanour. His intellectual attainments culminated with an edition of Xenophon's *Memorabilia* which was published in 1804.

SARAH MARKHAM

Sources Loveday family MSS, priv. coll. · R. Valpy, ed., *Poems, odes, prologues, and epilogues* (1804) · S. Markham, *A testimony of her times* (1990) · *DNB* · parish register, 10 April 1765, St Peter's, Caversham [baptism]
Archives priv. coll., Loveday family MSS

Benyng, William. *See* Binning, William of (*d*. in or after 1258).

Benzie, Isa Donald (1902–1988), radio broadcaster, was born on 4 December 1902 at 157 Nithsdale Road, Glasgow, the daughter of Robert Marr Benzie, a chartered accountant, and his wife, Annie Young Lamberton. She attended the city's Laurel Bank School. In 1922 she went up to Lady Margaret Hall, Oxford, where in 1926 she secured an *aegrotat* degree in German.

In February 1927 Benzie joined the BBC as a secretary in the foreign department. Her point of entry in that early wireless world can be illuminated exactly: it was two months before the boat race was first broadcast and six months before the BBC took over the Proms. Fledgeling though it was, the BBC had already secured a firm place in the national affections with a variety of both speech and music programmes catering for the increasingly popular pastime of 'listening in'. The Daventry longwave transmitter, opened in 1925, enabled its services to reach virtually all parts of the country.

With a serious yet supple mind and good judgement, Benzie rose quickly. In 1933 she was appointed director of the foreign department—one of the first two women to become a head of department at the BBC. This 'pale, slim, enigmatic slip of a girl', as the famous radio reporter Jonah Barrington described her (*Sunday Express*), thereafter took responsibility for the BBC's entire panoply of non-technical links with other broadcasters: cultural relations, listening to the output of foreign stations to see whether any of it might be suitable for carrying on the

BBC, receiving at Broadcasting House a constant flow of visitors from abroad, and corresponding with broadcasters all over the globe. On 2 September 1937, a year after the BBC launched its television service, she married John Royston Morley, one of the first television producers. He was nine years her junior. They had one child, Teresa Priscilla Royston, but later divorced. She had to leave the BBC four months after her marriage because of the rule that prevailed in the Reithian era against husband and wife both being employed by the BBC. When the ban was lifted during the Second World War Benzie returned to the corporation as a talks producer. She spent twenty years (1943–64) producing talks on a variety of topics, mainly for the Home Service, showing an awareness of health, medical and psychological issues, and the increasing wish by some women to combine motherhood with career.

Lively, down-to-earth, and a clear thinker and communicator, Benzie was the key figure in the conception and birth of the *Today* programme. This began in October 1957 as a light-hearted morning miscellany for busy 'people on the move' (Ronald Lewin, head of Home Service planning, *Radio Times*, October 1957). It was Isa Benzie who first came up with the name *Today*, and she who first recognized the need for a personality presenter (Alan Skempton was the first, replaced after less than a year by Jack de Manio). Benzie was also the first editor of *Today*, although her official title was senior producer. She seized the initiative in running it:

> I should like the job of organising this programme. I can't see how it goes on the air without an organiser. It wants lots and lots of fresh ideas … The audience, to me, is typically on its feet, dressing, making packed lunches, cooking and eating—certainly before I am. Everything must exploit the virtues of brevity.   (BBC WAC, memo to Janet Quigley, 22 May 1957)

The sender and the recipient of this note were the programme's two midwives. (Quigley, chief assistant in the talks department, occupied the key management role.) The two women enjoyed a close friendship and long professional collaboration. They were born in the same year, went to the same Oxford college, and worked for the BBC at the same time. Furthermore, they worked in the same department for the BBC before the Second World War and for the same programmes after it. They were witnesses at one another's weddings.

After retiring in 1964, Benzie went to live in St Leonards on the Sussex coast. She died of acute pneumonia on 25 June 1988 in St Helen's Hospital, Hastings.

PAUL DONOVAN

Sources Isa Benzie to Janet Quigley, 22 May 1957, BBC WAC · P. Donovan, *All our todays: forty years of Radio 4's 'Today' programme* (1997) · *The Times* (13 July 1988) · b. cert. · m. cert. · d. cert. · m. cert. [J. Quigley] · J. Cain, *The BBC: 70 years of broadcasting* (1992) · *Wireless* (May 1936) · *Sunday Express* (24 Feb 1935)
Likenesses photograph, repro. in Donovan, *All our todays* · photograph, repro. in *Sunday Express*

Béoáed mac Olcáin (*d*. 520/24). *See under* Connacht, saints of (*act. c*.400–*c*.800).

Beoán [St Beoán, Bean, Mo Bhióc] (*supp. fl.* **1012x24**), bishop of Mortlach, was possibly of Irish origin. His feast day is celebrated on 16 December. He was the first bishop of Mortlach (Murthilach) and when the see was transferred to Aberdeen in 1136 by King David, Beoán was considered its founding bishop. There is, however, no contemporary witness to Beoán's elevation. The foundation charter in the registry of the deanery of Aberdeen claims that he was appointed bishop of Mortlach by King Malcolm II at the suggestion of Benedict VIII, who was pope from 1012 to 1024, but this charter is unlikely to be genuine. John Fordun records substantially the same tradition as the registry in the *Scotichronicon*.

Beoán's supposed Irish origins are obscure and he has been confused with at least one other identically named saint. This is the Beoán who appears under the hypocoristic form Mo Bheóc in the ninth-century *Félire Óengusso*. Suspiciously, his feast day is 16 December—the same as that of the Scottish bishop. The Irish Beoán is associated with Ard Camrois (Ard Cáinrois) near Wexford Harbour and Ros Caín in Connacht. Obviously enough, as *Félire Óengusso* was written before Bishop Beoán was born, they cannot be the same person. It is difficult to know when the confusion first arose. Johannes Molanus's revised text of Usuard's ninth-century martyrology, published in 1573, states that Beoán, the first bishop of Aberdeen, was born in Ireland. A note in Mícheál Ó Cléirigh's seventeenth-century martyrology of Donegal, although not in Ó Cléirigh's hand, makes the identification complete. The Scottish and the Irish Beoán are equated and Molanus is quoted as evidence.

Ironically then, an important Scottish bishop became confused with an obscure Irish saint and subsumed into his cult. Nothing is known of the bishop's origins and almost nothing about his career; even his feast day may have been borrowed from his Irish namesake.

ELVA JOHNSTON

Sources *Johannis de Fordun Scotichronicon genuinum*, ed. T. Hearnius, 5 vols. (1722) · C. Innes, ed., *Registrum episcopatus Aberdonensis*, 2 vols., Spalding Club, 13–14 (1845) · J. Molanus, *Usuardi martyrologium, quo Romana Ecclesia, ac permultae aliae utuntur* (Louvain, 1573) · *Félire Óengusso Céli Dé* / *The martyrology of Oengus the Culdee*, ed. and trans. W. Stokes, HBS, 29 (1905) · *Félire húi Gormáin* / *The martyrology of Gorman*, ed. and trans. W. Stokes, HBS, 9 (1895) · M. O'Clery, *The martyrology of Donegal: a calendar of the saints of Ireland*, ed. J. H. Todd and W. Reeves, trans. J. O'Donovan (1864)

Beorhtric (*d.* 802), king of the West Saxons, became king on the death of Cynewulf in 786. Whether he was Cynewulf's intended successor or an outsider who took advantage of a power vacuum is unclear. According to the Anglo-Saxon Chronicle, he was descended in the paternal line from Cerdic, but this claim, apparently held to confer legal title to rule in Wessex, may have been fabricated in some cases, and cannot always be relied upon. Beorhtric is the last of five kings who do not feature in the extant genealogies of the West Saxon kings.

Close and friendly relations with neighbouring Mercia are a feature of Beorhtric's reign. In 789 he married *Eadburh, one of the daughters of King *Offa of Mercia, and presumably entered into a formal alliance with Mercia at this time. Silver pennies were already being minted for Offa in Canterbury, and soon after the marriage a mint was opened in Wessex (possibly at Winchester, more probably at Southampton) and similar coins were produced in Beorhtric's name. Some time between 789 and 796 Beorhtric helped Offa to drive Ecgberht (later king of the West Saxons) out of England. Offa was probably the dominant partner in the alliance and he is recorded as granting lands in what is now Somerset, probably in 794, but Beorhtric clearly remained an independent king.

After the death of Offa in 796, Beorhtric and Eadburh appear to have maintained close contacts with her brother, *Ecgfrith [*see under* Offa], during his brief reign. The nature of Beorhtric's relationship with Ecgfrith's successor, Cenwulf (*d.* 821), is less clear. In 798 Beorhtric apparently agreed that Cenwulf's son, Cynehelm, should become the owner of the monastery at Glastonbury. It is hardly likely that Beorhtric agreed to this willingly, but the circumstances are obscure and the transaction does not necessarily imply a Mercian takeover of a larger area. West Saxon grants of land in Somerset continued to be made without reference to Mercia.

It was during Beorhtric's reign that the first viking ships landed on the shores of Wessex. The reeve, believing them to be traders, rode to meet them and ordered them to report to Beorhtric at his residence, whereupon they killed him.

Although Beorhtric is not recorded as a benefactor of monasteries, since his few surviving charters relate to transactions with laymen, this is probably just an accident of survival. Queen Eadburh also granted land in her own name, as well as witnessing charters of Beorhtric and of her brother, Ecgfrith. As a daughter of the most powerful Anglo-Saxon king of his time, she was probably both proud and influential. However, her appalling reputation in later years, when she was accused by, among others, Asser of tyranny, plotting against the king's friends, and poisoning various people—including Beorhtric himself— probably derives far more from hostile propaganda following the accession of Ecgberht, the enemy of both her husband and her father, and perhaps also from the inventions of Asser, than from her own conduct.

Ecgberht became king in 802 and it is highly unlikely that this happened by peaceful succession. His previous enmity with Beorhtric has already been mentioned. In its entry for 802, the Anglo-Saxon Chronicle states that Beorhtric and Ealdorman Worr died and Ecgberht succeeded, and then goes on to record an invasion by the Hwiccians across the northern border of Wessex, which was repulsed by the men of what is now Wiltshire, and which occurred 'that same day' (*ASC*, s.a. 800, *recte* 802, texts A, E). It is therefore clear that Beorhtric and Worr died on the same day, and the most likely reason for this is that they died by violence. Asser reports that after Beorhtric's death Queen Eadburh took countless treasures and fled across the sea to Francia where, like other Anglo-Saxon exiles, she took refuge at the court of the emperor, Charlemagne. The probability is that Ecgberht invaded Wessex with his followers, and that Beorhtric died on the battlefield. He was buried at Wareham.

HEATHER EDWARDS

Sources ASC, s.a. 786, 789, 800, 802, 839 [texts A, E] • AS chart., S 267, 268, 269, 270a, 148, 149, 150, 1692 • Alfred the Great: Asser's Life of King Alfred and other contemporary sources, ed. and trans. S. Keynes and M. Lapidge (1983) • P. Grierson and M. Blackburn, Medieval European coinage: with a catalogue of the coins in the Fitzwilliam Museum, Cambridge, 1: The early middle ages (5th–10th centuries) (1986) • English historical documents, 1, ed. D. Whitelock (1955) • S. Keynes, 'England, 700–900', The new Cambridge medieval history, 2, ed. R. McKitterick (1995), 18–42 • F. M. Stenton, 'The supremacy of the Mercian kings', Preparatory to 'Anglo-Saxon England': being the collected papers of Frank Merry Stenton, ed. D. M. Stenton (1970), 48–66 • F. M. Stenton, Anglo-Saxon England, 3rd edn (1971) • P. Wormald, 'Bede, the "Bretwaldas" and the origins of the "gens Anglorum"', Ideal and reality in Frankish and Anglo-Saxon society, ed. P. Wormald, D. Bullough, and R. Collins (1983), 99–129 • D. N. Dumville, 'Kingship, genealogies and regnal lists', Early medieval kingship, ed. P. H. Sawyer and I. N. Wood (1977), 72–104 • H. Edwards, The charters of the early West Saxon kingdom (1988)

Beorhtric [Brihtric] (d. in or before **1066**?), magnate, was the son of Ælfgar Mæw, who was prominent in the reigns of both Æthelred II (d. 1016) and Cnut (d. 1035). Beorhtric was among the richest magnates in the time of Edward the Confessor (d. 1066), with over 350 hides of land in Cornwall, Devon, Dorset, Gloucestershire, Wiltshire, and Worcestershire. He acquired Bushley, Worcestershire, from Lyfing, bishop of Worcester, and attested charters of Bishop Ealdred in the 1050s (AS chart., S 1406, 1409). Domesday Book mentions some of the men commended to Beorhtric, among them Dunning, a minor thegn with land in Devon, Gloucestershire, and Worcestershire, who was a benefactor of Winchcombe Abbey.

Beorhtric was patron both of the minster at Tewkesbury, Gloucestershire, and of the abbey at Cranborne, Dorset, founded by his grandparents, Æthelweard Mæw ('seagull') and Ælfgifu. Æthelweard, who was dead by c.1000, was allegedly related to the royal house. He may be identical with Æthelweard the Chronicler, ealdorman of the western shires (d. 998); or, given the large estate held by his grandson in Devon, a descendant of Ælfgar 'the king's kinsman in Devon' (AS chart., S 962 [text A]), who died in 962 and was buried at Wilton. Æthelweard's son, Ælfgar Mæw, who also gave land to Cranborne, attested charters of Æthelred II between 999 and 1009, and probably to 1014. In 1016 he fought on the Danish side at the battle of Sherston. Ælfgar's support for Cnut perhaps enabled him to preserve his lands through the upheaval of the Danish conquest and he may be the minister who attests charters of Cnut in 1019 and 1023 (AS chart., S 956, 960).

The name Beorhtric appears on charters of 1019 and 1026 (AS chart., S 953, 962) but the first attestations which may be those of Beorhtric son of Ælfgar appear in charters of Harthacnut in 1042 (AS chart., S 993–4). One of these is also attested by Ordgar, kinsman of Æthelred II, and Odda of Deerhurst, another possible descendant of Æthelweard the Chronicler and thus of the West Saxon kings. Thereafter Beorhtric (presumably the son of Ælfgar, though

there are other possibilities) attests the Confessor's charters fairly regularly between 1043 and 1065. He usually signs as minister or nobilis, but in 1061 (AS chart., S 1034) he and Ordgar's brother Ælfgar are described as consiliarii. Although the implications of this designation are unclear, it seems that they should be numbered among King Edward's councillors.

Most of Beorhtric's land passed after 1066 to Queen Matilda, which may account for Wace's romantic tale of how, as a young girl in Flanders, she fell in love with the handsome Englishman who had come on an embassy to her father and, because he spurned her, took revenge by persuading her royal husband to arrest him and confiscate his land. Beorhtric's actual fate is unknown. He may have died without heirs before 1066, leaving his land to be appropriated first by King Edward and then by the Conqueror, for Tewkesbury itself was originally given, perhaps as early as 1067, to William fitz Osbern, earl of Hereford, who died in February 1071. After Matilda's death in 1083, Beorhtric's lands reverted to the king and later became the core of the honour of Gloucester. In 1102 the community of Cranborne moved to Tewkesbury, which then became a Benedictine house; its twelfth-century Chronica provides the clues to Beorhtric's ancestry.

ANN WILLIAMS

Sources C. H. Bickerton-Hudson, 'The founders' book of Tewkesbury Abbey', Transactions of the Bristol and Gloucestershire Archaeological Society, 33 (1910), 60–66 • C. R. Hart, The early charters of eastern England (1966) • F. Michel, ed., Chroniques anglo-normandes: recueil d'extraits et d'écrits relatifs à l'histoire de Normandie et d'Angleterre, 3 vols. (Rouen, 1836–40) • A. Williams, 'A west-country magnate of the eleventh century: the family, estates and patronage of Beorhtric son of Ælfgar', Family-trees and the roots of politics, ed. K. S. B. Keats-Rohan (1996) • P. A. Clarke, The English nobility under Edward the Confessor (1994) • S. Keynes, An atlas of attestations in Anglo-Saxon charters, c.670–1066 (privately printed, Cambridge, 1993) • S. Keynes, The diplomas of Æthelred II, 'the Unready', 978–1016 (1980) • A. Farley, ed., Domesday Book, 2 vols. (1783), vol. 1 • Dugdale, Monasticon, new edn, vol. 3 • R. R. Darlington, ed., 'Winchcombe annals, 1049–1181', A medieval miscellany for Doris Mary Stenton, ed. P. M. Barnes and C. F. Slade, PRSoc., new ser., 36 (1962), 111–37 • S. Keynes, 'Regenbald the Chancellor [sic]', Anglo-Norman Studies, 10 (1987), 185–222 • A. Williams, 'An introduction to the Gloucestershire Domesday', The Gloucestershire Domesday, ed. A. Williams and R. W. H. Erskine (1989) • AS chart., S 953, 956, 960, 962, 993–4, 1034, 1406, 1409

Beorhtwulf. See Berhtwulf (d. 852?).

Beorn Estrithson, earl (d. **1049**), magnate, was the second son of Estrith, the sister of King *Cnut (d. 1035), and her Danish husband, Ulf, and thus a nephew of *Gytha [see under Godwine], wife of *Godwine, earl of Wessex (d. 1053). Like his paternal uncle Eilaf, earl of Gloucestershire under Cnut, Beorn made his career in England, receiving from Edward an earldom in the east midlands in 1045. His cousin Harold Godwineson was already earl of East Anglia and Beorn was probably under his command. In 1049 Beorn participated with earls Harold and Godwine in the muster of the English fleet in support of the campaign launched by the emperor Henry III against Baldwin of Flanders. When Swein Godwineson (d. 1052) fled from England in 1046, his property was divided between Harold and Beorn, who therefore opposed his reinstatement in 1049. In revenge, Swein tricked Beorn into riding with him to Bosham, dragged him on board a ship, and murdered him. Beorn was buried at Dartmouth (or Axmouth) but Earl Harold and some of the shipmen from London removed his body to Winchester, to lie beside Cnut, his uncle, in the Old Minster. Adam of Bremen presents the murder of Beorn as part of a revolt led by the sons of Earl Godwine against Beorn's brother Swein Estrithson, king of Denmark (1047–76), which also involved the expulsion from England of Asbjorn, brother of Swein and Beorn; but these are the jaundiced views of Swein himself, who had been refused English help against Norway in 1047–8. Asbjorn, who was presumably the youngest brother, led the fleet sent by Swein to support the English rebellion against William I in 1069. ANN WILLIAMS

Sources ASC, s.a. 1049, 1069–71 [texts D, E] · AS chart., S 1010, 1013, 1015, 1019, 1022–3 · F. Barlow, Edward the Confessor (1970) · A. Williams, 'The king's nephew: the family, career, and connections of Ralph, earl of Hereford', Studies in medieval history presented to R. Allen Brown, ed. C. Harper-Bill, C. J. Holdsworth, and J. L. Nelson (1989), 327–43 · John of Worcester, Chron., vol. 2 · Adam of Bremen, History of the archbishops of Hamburg-Bremen, ed. and trans. F. J. Tschan (1959), 92, 125 · A. Williams, '"Cockles amongst the wheat": Danes and English in the western midlands in the first half of the eleventh century', Midland History, 11 (1986), 1–22

Beornred (d. 797), archbishop of Sens and abbot of Echternach, went from Northumbria to the continent at an unknown date and was made abbot of the monastery of Echternach in 775, in succession to the second abbot, Albert. He was a relative both of Echternach's founder, Willibrord, and of Alcuin, who wrote his prose and verse lives of Willibrord for Beornred. The numerous surviving charters from Echternach provide most of the reliable dates for Beornred's life.

Beornred preceded Alcuin to the continent and, to judge from a letter-poem that probably dates from Alcuin's first visit there in the late 770s, had established himself as part of the court circle of the Frankish king Charlemagne by that time. There survive two poems by Alcuin addressed to Beornred (to whom he gave the pseudonym Samuel) and two letters, one accompanying the lives of Willibrord, the other asking if Beornred had had copied Alcuin's book of excerpts from John's gospel. Beornred played host at Echternach to another Anglo-Saxon, Willehad, at some point between c.782 and c.784, when the latter was forced to interrupt his missionary work among the Saxons by their revolt against Frankish overlordship.

In 785 or 786 Beornred was consecrated to the diocese of Sens, though he also retained the abbacy of Echternach until his death. Although a number of his predecessors had been archbishops, Sens's metropolitan status at this time was still unclear. Beornred appears in the sources variously as bishop and archbishop. He was certainly an ecclesiastic of some standing. A letter of 790 or 791 from Pope Hadrian I to Charlemagne reveals that Beornred had travelled to Rome, together with Rado, abbot of St Vaast, as a *missus* (envoy) of Charlemagne. He and Rado doubtless conveyed the questions which Hadrian's letter answered, chiefly concerning the condition of the Italian church.

Beornred died in 797 and was succeeded in his bishopric by Ragembert, and at Echternach by Ado. He was buried in the monastery of St Pierre-le-Vif, Sens.

MARIOS COSTAMBEYS

Sources W. Levison, England and the continent in the eighth century (1946) · E. Dümmler, ed., Epistolae Karolini aevi, MGH Epistolae [quarto], 4 (Berlin, 1895) · Alcuin, 'Carmina', Poetae Latini aevi Carolini, ed. E. Dümmler, MGH Poetae Latini Medii Aevi, 1 (Berlin, 1881) · L. Weiland, 'Monumenta Epternacensis: catalogus abbatum', [Chronica aevi Suevici], ed. G. H. Pertz, MGH Scriptores [folio], 23 (Hanover, 1874) · L. Duchesne, Fastes épiscopaux de l'ancienne Gaule, 2 (1899) · E. Gundlach, ed., 'Codex Carolinus', Epistolae Merowingici et Karolini aevi, 1 (1892), no. 97 · C. Wampach, Geschichte der Grundherrschaft Echternach im Frühmittelalter, 2 (Luxembourg, 1930)

Beornwulf (d. 826?), king of the Mercians, came to power after the deposition of King Ceolwulf in 823. The basis of his claim to the kingship is unknown (he may have been a descendant of the Beornred from whom Offa wrested the kingdom in 757). During his brief reign the long-standing Mercian domination of southern England rapidly disintegrated. His control over London, the principal Mercian trading port and mint, appears tenuous; only a single fragmentary London coin is attributable to him. In Kent a certain Baldred emerged as king; it is unknown to what extent he acknowledged Beornwulf's overlordship. In the same way as earlier Mercian rulers, Beornwulf was present at two synods of the Southumbrian church which took place at 'Clofesho' in 824 and 825 (AS chart., S 1434–6). The chronology of his downfall is rather uncertain, for the Anglo-Saxon Chronicle compresses the events of several years into a single annal; the sequence in the narrative of Roger of Wendover may be preferable. First, in 825, Beornwulf was defeated in battle at Ellendun (Wroughton, in modern Wiltshire) by King Ecgberht of Wessex. This was a serious blow to the military superiority on which the Mercian supremacy was based and seems to have encouraged the East Anglian kingdom to repudiate Mercian overlordship (until then the East Anglian mint had been the only one regularly striking coins for Beornwulf).

Beornwulf was killed by the East Angles, probably in 826 (he was still alive on 27 March in that year). Subsequently or simultaneously, King Ecgberht sent a West Saxon force to drive out Baldred and occupy Kent; as a result the peoples of Kent, Surrey, Sussex, and Essex, all of which had previously been subject to Mercia, submitted to Ecgberht's authority. Beornwulf was succeeded in Mercia by Ludeca (or Ludica), of unknown origin, who seems temporarily to have re-established Mercian control over East Anglia (the East Anglian mint struck coins for him and there is also one London coin in his name). But in 827 Ludeca and his five ealdormen were killed, probably by the East Angles, and the Mercian kingdom passed to Wiglaf. S. E. KELLY

Sources ASC, s.a. 825, 827 [texts A, E] · [Roger of Wendover], Rogeri de Wendoveri chronica, sive, Flores historiarum, ed. H. O. Coxe, EHS, 1 (1841), 275–6 · AS chart., S 1434, 1435, 1436 · S. Keynes, 'The control of Kent in the ninth century', Early Medieval Europe, 2 (1993), 111–32, esp. 119–20 · P. Grierson and M. Blackburn, Medieval European coinage: with a catalogue of the coins in the Fitzwilliam Museum, Cambridge, 1: The early middle ages (5th–10th centuries) (1986), 283,

292–3 • N. Brooks, *The early history of the church of Canterbury: Christ Church from 597 to 1066* (1984), 136–7, 352–3 n.22
Likenesses coin, BM

Berach mac Amargin (*fl.* late 6th–early 7th cent.). *See under* Connacht, saints of (*act. c.*400–*c.*800).

Berain, Katheryn of. *See* Katheryn of Berain (*c.*1540–1591).

Beranger, Gabriel (1729–1817), landscape draughtsman, was born at Rotterdam, in the Netherlands, of an emigrant French Huguenot family. In 1750 he moved to Dublin to join some of his relatives who had settled there earlier; nothing is known of his training, but his name appeared as the artist on a drawing of *The Round Tower of St Michael le Pole*, now in the Irish Academy. On 26 May 1756 he married his cousin Louise Beranger (*d.* 1782), and shortly afterwards he opened a print shop in the house on St Stephen's Green where his kinsman David Beranger (*d.* 1758) had kept a coffee shop. He became acquainted with several members of Dublin society who were then taking a great interest in Irish history and antiquities. Foremost among these were General Charles Vallancey (another Huguenot from Flanders) and William Burton Conyngham, who admired Beranger's artistic skills, his intellectual tastes, and his lively disposition.

During the 1760s Beranger was sketching standing and ruined buildings and other remarkable places in and around Dublin. He exhibited at the Society of Artists from 1763 to 1768, contributing landscapes, sea pieces, and 'medleys'. In 1769 he moved to South Great George's Street, where he continued to sell prints, taught drawing, and painted flowers and birds with great accuracy.

In 1773 Beranger and his antiquarian friends made the first of their tours through Ireland, starting with co. Wicklow. When Conyngham and others instituted the Antiquarian Society, Beranger and another artist, Angelo Bigari, made a tour of western Ireland in 1779 in order to make plans and drawings for the society. Beranger kept a diary of these often difficult travels through the wilder parts of the country, observing the customs and manners of both the Irish-speaking peasantry and the gentry. His drawings and descriptions of antiquities were transferred to several volumes intended for publication, most of which are now preserved in the Royal Irish Academy.

Beranger's wife died on 15 April 1782, and on 29 June he married Elizabeth Mestayer (*d.* 1802). His printselling business probably brought him little reward, and about 1783 Conyngham procured for him a post as assistant ledger-keeper in the exchequer office. In later years his circumstances were eased after he inherited part of a fortune amassed in India by his brother-in-law Colonel Mestayer. He died at the house of his friend Clarke in St Stephen's Green on 18 February 1817. Beranger and his first wife were both interred in the French burying-ground at St Stephen's Green; his second wife had been interred in Peter Street cemetery. As he had no children, Beranger bequeathed his property to the nieces of his second wife.

TIMOTHY CLAYTON and ANITA MCCONNELL

Sources W. G. Strickland, *A dictionary of Irish artists*, 1 (1913); repr. with introduction by T. J. Snoddy (1989), 56–9 • W. Wilde, *Memoir of Gabriel Beranger and his labours in the cause of Irish art and antiquities from 1760 to 1780* (1880)
Likenesses G. Beranger, self-portrait, crayon (after lithograph for *Kilkenny Archaeological Journal*), NG Ire. • lithograph, repro. in *Journal of the Royal Society of Antiquaries of Ireland* (1870–71) • portrait, repro. in Wilde, *Memoir of Gabriel Beranger*

Berchet, Peter [Pierre] (1659–1720), painter, was born in France and trained with the artist Charles de Lafosse. From the age of eighteen he was employed at the French court. He went to England in 1682 with the French architectural painter Jacob Rambour (*fl.* 1674–1721) to work for Antonio Verrio at Windsor Castle, returning after a year to France to work at Louis XIV's palace at Marly. Berchet was once again in England a year later, but then received a commission from William III to assist in the decoration of his new palace at Het Loo in the Netherlands, where he remained for fifteen months working under the direction of the architect Daniel Marot.

The revocation of the edict of Nantes in 1685 forced Berchet, a Huguenot, to seek refuge in England, where he remained for the rest of his life, working principally as a decorative painter in the houses of the nobility. His works included the decoration of the walls and ceiling of the staircase of Schomberg House, Pall Mall, for Mindhardt, third duke of Schomberg (des.), and an *Ascension* for the chapel ceiling of Trinity College, Oxford. His work was praised for its good draughtsmanship, 'pleasant colouring', and 'landskips glowering and warm' (Vertue, *Note books*, 1.87). In 1709 he was one of five artists invited to submit designs for the decoration of the dome of St Paul's Cathedral. He was probably a member of Sir Godfrey Kneller's academy, established in 1711, as Vertue noted that he 'drew in the academy very well both at London & at Paris' (ibid.).

Berchet became ill towards the end of his life and confined himself to painting small easel pictures, chiefly of a mythological character. His last painting was a 'Bachanal lightly frought & [with] much variety' (Vertue, *Note books*, 1.87), signed the day before his death in Marylebone, Middlesex, on 1 January 1720. He was buried in the church of St Marylebone, Middlesex. There are at least three known etchings after Berchet's designs, all with a musical theme, and a mezzotint of *Diana and Actaeon* after Berchet by John Smith.   KATHRYN BARRON

Sources E. Croft-Murray, *Decorative painting in England, 1537–1837*, 2 vols. (1962–70), vol. 1, p. 243; vol. 2, p. 319 • Vertue, *Note books*, 1.87 • *Wren Society*, 16 (1939), 108 • W. C. Smith, *A bibliography of the musical works published by John Walsh … 1695–1720* (1948), nos. 156, 221, 94; pl. 13 • T. Murdoch, ed., *The quiet conquest: the Huguenots, 1685–1985* (1985), 194, no. 277 [exhibition catalogue, Museum of London, 15 May – 31 Oct 1985]

Berchthun. *See* Berhthun (*d.* 733/40).

Berdmore, Samuel (1739–1802), headmaster, was born in Nottingham on 29 May 1739, the son of Thomas Berdmore, vicar of St Mary's, Nottingham, and his wife, Martha. He was educated on the foundation at Charterhouse School from 1749 until 1755, when he was admitted to

Jesus College, Cambridge. He graduated BA in 1759, winning the members' prize for a Latin essay, was elected a fellow of his college, and proceeded to the degree of MA in 1762. Ordained deacon in 1763 he was vicar of Whittlesford, Cambridgeshire, from 1763 to 1771. He was elected master of Charterhouse School on 17 April 1769, the first foundation scholar, or gownboy, to hold the office. On 6 June that year he married Maria Matthews (d. 1821) at St Philip's in Birmingham; their son Thomas was baptized in the chapel at Charterhouse on 3 June 1773.

As master Berdmore presided over a school whose fortunes had been restored by his predecessor, Lewis Crusius, and he ensured that the reputation and finances of the school were maintained. In addition to educating forty boys on the foundation, he took on about twenty boarders each year and made substantial alterations to his own living quarters to increase its capacity to house pupils. He continued the annual school play, and Addison's *Cato* was performed in 1770 and 1773 with Charles and Thomas Manners-Sutton in leading roles. He edited a collection of school orations, including some of his own composition, published as *Lusus poetici ex ludo literario apud ædes Carthusianas Londini* in 1791. He resigned as master on 10 May 1791 and retired to a house in Southampton Row, Bloomsbury, London. A member of the Unincreasable Club that met at the Queen's Head, Holborn, whose members included Isaac Reed, George Romney, and Richard Farmer, Berdmore was also a keen literary scholar and he published in 1801 *Specimens of Literary Resemblance in the Works of Pope, Gray, and other Celebrated Writers*, which he dedicated to his friend Peter Forster, rector of Hedenham, Norfolk. Following an accident in 1801 at Charterhouse on founder's day, 12 December, Berdmore developed an inflammatory fever and he died in Southampton Row on 20 January 1802. He was buried on 28 January in the Charterhouse and was survived by his wife.

THOMPSON COOPER, *rev.* S. J. SKEDD

Sources B. Marsh and F. A. Crisp, eds., *Alumni Carthusiani: a record of the foundation scholars of Charterhouse, 1614–1872* (1913), 118 · Venn, *Alum. Cant.* · A. Quick, *Charterhouse: a history of the school* (1990) · *IGI* · will, PRO, PROB 11/1369, sig. 82 · *GM*, 1st ser., 72 (1802), 94, 605 · N. Carlisle, *A concise description of the endowed grammar schools in England and Wales*, 2 vols. (1818) · W. H. Brown, *Charterhouse past and present* (1879) · Nichols, *Lit. anecdotes*, 2.72, 638

Archives BL, corresp. with Peter Forster, Add. MS 11278

Likenesses W. Nutter, stipple, pubd 1788 (after S. Shelley), BM, NPG

Wealth at death over £500—in annuities, stocks, and property: will, PRO, PROB 11/1369, fols. 196v–198r

Bere, Richard (c.1455–1525), abbot of Glastonbury, was a Benedictine monk of that house when he was made acolyte and subdeacon on 14 February 1478, suggesting that he was born c.1455. He was ordained deacon in 1479, but no record has been found either of his priesting or of his education, for both of which he may have been abroad. Absence may also account for the fact that he held no administrative office within the monastery before his appointment as abbot. He was certainly a priest by 1493 and was admitted DTh at Oxford in 1503.

Bere was nominated abbot of Glastonbury in November 1493 by Richard Fox, bishop of Bath and Wells, after the annulment of the election of Thomas Wason. The delay of two months until his installation may in part have been an assertion of episcopal strength after an election of which Fox did not approve, but the bishop's choice of Bere suggests prior knowledge of the man. His appointment in 1503 as head of the diplomatic mission to the Roman curia may have owed as much to Fox, as keeper of the privy seal, as to the king, to whom Bere had been host in 1498 when Henry VII was in the west country. The mission, originally to congratulate Pius III on his election to the papal throne, arrived in 1504 to congratulate his successor, Julius II. A second purpose was to confer the Garter on Guidobaldo de Montefeltro, duke of Urbino, whose support was then needed to promote a dispensation for the recently widowed Katherine of Aragon to marry her brother-in-law, Henry, prince of Wales. Bere's expenses, paid by his abbey, were at least £800. On his return Bere created a chapel in the north transept of the abbey church at Glastonbury in honour of Our Lady of Loreto, whose cult was then popular in Italy and was also taken up at Walsingham.

A detailed survey of abbey estates undertaken in Bere's name survives in four volumes (BL, Egerton MSS 3034, 3134; BL, Harley MS 3961; Society of Antiquaries, MS 653). The survey probably reflected his personal concern for the efficient administration of Glastonbury. His encouragement of the popular cult of St Joseph perhaps suggests business considerations alongside piety. His robust defence of the claims to ownership of relics of St Dunstan, which Archbishop Warham disputed in 1508, was probably occasioned by the removal of a shrine to a prominent place in the Edgar chapel. Both suggest his awareness that the history of his house was an important part of its continuing appeal, and from the beginning of his rule novices took names of saints and other figures from its illustrious past—an innovative practice at this date.

Erasmus considered Bere to have been sympathetic to the cause of humanistic scholarship, deferring to the abbot's opinion on his translation of part of the New Testament from the Greek. He also praised Bere's generosity to such scholars as Richard Pace. In that same spirit Bere endowed lectures in his monastery on early Christian texts—*lectura antiqui operis*. His household at Glastonbury included a French poet, a harper, and a maker of tapestries.

Loans of money made by Bere to the king and a wide cross-section of ecclesiastics, gentry, and merchants were as much a reflection of the financial status of his abbey as an expression of particular political interests. The abbot's planned appearance at Dover in 1522 to meet the emperor Charles V may be seen as an indication of friendly association with Wolsey; the cancellation of his name is likely to have been due to his age.

At Glastonbury Bere was remembered as a builder. Under his rule the central tower of the abbey church was saved from collapse, the Edgar chapel begun, and a crypt created under the twelfth-century lady chapel as the focus of the cult of St Joseph of Arimathea. Within the conventual enclosure he built lodgings for the visit of Henry VII and quarters for staff of the lady chapel. He also built almshouses in the outer court of the abbey. His initials are to be found in several other buildings with abbey connections, evidently a sign of his financial involvement.

Richard Bere died on 20 January 1525 and was buried in the south aisle of the nave of his abbey church under a marble slab near the Holy Sepulchre chapel, which he had built. He was remembered for the particular gift of a silver-gilt frontal for the high altar. Forty years after his death he was also remembered by a witness in a lawsuit as 'good, honest, virtuous, wise and discrete, as well as a grave man, and for those virtues esteemed in as great reputation as few in England at that time of his coat and calling were better accounted of' (Gasquet, 160).

ROBERT W. DUNNING

Sources register of Bishop Robert Stillington of Bath and Wells, Som. ARS, MS D/D/B, reg. 7 · H. C. Maxwell Lyte, ed., *Register of Bishop Richard Fox, bishop of Bath and Wells*, Somerset RS, 52 (1937) · H. C. Maxwell Lyte, ed., *Register of Bishop John Clerke, bishop of Bath and Wells*, Somerset RS, 55 (1940) · *The itinerary of John Leland in or about the years 1535–1543*, ed. L. Toulmin Smith, 11 pts in 5 vols. (1906–10), vol. 1 · *LP Henry VIII*, vols. 3–4 · Longleat House, Wiltshire, MS 10751 · F. A. Gasquet, 'Blessed Richard Bere', *Downside Review*, 9 (1890), 158–63 · Emden, *Oxf.*, 1.150 · B. André, *Historia regis Henrici septimi*, ed. J. Gairdner, Rolls Series, 10 (1858)
Wealth at death Glastonbury Abbey value well over £3300 p.a.

Bereblock, John (*fl.* 1557–1572), draughtsman, was born near Rochester and graduated BA from St John's College, Oxford, in 1561. In 1562 he wrote the official copy of the recently founded college's statutes. He was elected to a fellowship in 1561 and served as bursar in 1563/4, but soon after receiving his MA degree in 1566 he migrated to Exeter College, where he took up the post of dean. Having served, with Thomas Bodley, as senior proctor of Oxford University in 1569/70, he was allowed leave of absence to attend an unknown foreign university, and in 1572 he was awarded the degree of BCL. Nothing is known about his subsequent life.

Bereblock's main claim to fame rests on a set of drawings he made of Oxford's colleges and university buildings in connection with a visit by Queen Elizabeth and the earl of Leicester, chancellor of the university, in September 1566. Accompanied by a map and by a set of Latin verses composed by Thomas Neale, regius professor of Hebrew, they were hung up for several days at St Mary's, the university church, and were examined by the queen when she went there to hear disputations. She was later given a copy of the map, drawings, and verses, and, in an account of her visit probably written by Bereblock himself, she was said to have regarded the gift as 'the greatest and best she had ever received' ('Commentarii sive ephemerae actiones rerum illustrium Oxonii gestarum in adventu serenissimae principis Elizabethae' in the appendix to T. Hearne, *Historia vitae et regni Ricardi II*, 1729). Bereblock's drawings were presented to St John's College by a former member, William Nutburne, and were hung in the president's lodgings, but they were given in 1616 to

Sir Thomas Lake, secretary of state to James I, in recompense for money spent on repairing buildings in the front quadrangle, and their subsequent whereabouts are unknown. A copy, however, was given to the Bodleian Library by John More in 1630, and the drawings were published, along with Neale's verses, by the antiquary Thomas Hearne as an appendix to Henry Dodwell's *De parma equestri Woodwardiana dissertatio* (1713). In 1728 they were engraved in the margin of a reproduction of Ralph Agas's map of Oxford (1578), and they were published privately, with a scholarly introduction by Falconer Madan (*Collegiorum scholarumque publicarum academiae Oxoniensis topographica delineatio, auctore Thoma Nelo, cum figuris Johannis Bereblocci*), in 1882. According to William Laud, president of St John's and later archbishop of Canterbury, Bereblock also drew a map of Rochester, but no copy appears to survive today.

Judging from the manuscript of the St John's College statutes, Bereblock was a good calligrapher, but his drawings of Oxford are crude in style and not altogether accurate in detail. They depict all the colleges in existence in 1566, along with the two largest university buildings at that time: the divinity school and Duke Humfrey's Library, and the 'public schools' or lecture rooms which were later replaced by the old schools, now part of the Bodleian Library complex. They are the first surviving representation of all the colleges, and in many cases, including Oriel and Exeter colleges, they constitute the only extant record of buildings which disappeared in the great expansion and rebuilding of the university in the first half of the seventeenth century. For this reason, for all their artistic shortcomings, they are of great value to the historian and topographer.

GEOFFREY TYACK

Sources *Collegiorum scholarumque publicarum academiae Oxoniensis topographica delineatio, auctore Thoma Nelo, cum figuris Johannis Bereblocci* (1882) · W. H. Stevenson and H. E. Salter, *The early history of St John's College, Oxford*, OHS, new ser., 1 (1939) · C. W. Boase, ed., *Registrum Collegii Exoniensis*, new edn, OHS, 27 (1894) · Wood, *Ath. Oxon.: Fasti* (1815), 168 · Wood, *Ath. Oxon.*, new edn, 1.577

Bereford, Ralph (*d.* 1329), administrator and justice, appears to have come from Wiltshire, and to have taken his name from Barford near Downton, where he is later recorded as holding land. The Ralph Bereford recorded in 1316 as a landowner at Mollington, Barford St John, and elsewhere in Oxfordshire was probably a namesake. The future justice is first recorded in October 1294, in the service of the justice John Berewyk, with whom he continued to be associated for some years, but he was a royal clerk by November 1296, accompanying Edward I to Flanders in that capacity. In June 1298 he was presented to Colerne church in Wiltshire, suggesting that he had proceeded at least to minor orders. He then appears to have left the king's service for that of the bishop of Winchester (the lord of Downton hundred), being appointed in 1305 one of two overseers of episcopal manors and stewards of courts in Hampshire, Oxfordshire, Berkshire, Buckinghamshire, and Surrey. He seems to have remained steward of the bishopric until at least 1316, when, following the death of

Bishop Woodlock, he was appointed one of the two custodians of the diocese during the subsequent vacancy. He had links with Woodlock's successor, John Sandale, occurring as first witness to a charter of the latter in November 1318, but he was by then returning to the king's service, and acted as a justice of assize and gaol delivery and commissioner of oyer and terminer, most often in Hampshire.

On 20 November 1320 Bereford was appointed keeper of writs and rolls for the London eyre that opened on 14 January 1321. He conducted himself much like the other justices, taking a full and active part in judicial proceedings, and when the mayoralty was declared forfeit on 20 February, it was Bereford who acted as warden until a full-time warden was appointed three days later. During the 1320s he resumed work as a commissioner and justice in the south of England. That he was appointed to investigate Robert Lewer's attack on Odiham Castle in 1322, and to deliver Winchester gaol of a woman charged with assisting Roger Mortimer's passage from England in 1324, suggests that he was regarded as trustworthy by Edward II's regime. But he escaped involvement in the overthrow of that regime, and on 4 December 1327 was appointed a justice for an eyre to be summoned in Kent. The eyre was promptly cancelled, but on 3 September 1329 he was again appointed a justice itinerant, this time for Nottinghamshire. That eyre went ahead, but without Bereford's involvement, for on 22 October following another justice had to be appointed, 'in the place of Ralph de Berford, deceased' (CPR, 1327–30, 454). It is possible that he was buried in the parish church of Chute, Wiltshire, where he had founded a chantry in 1320. The terms of the foundation make no mention of wife or children, and his heir was probably the John Bereford named with Ralph in a fine of 1327; it is not known how the two men were related.

HENRY SUMMERSON

Sources Chancery records · Registrum Henrici Woodlock, diocesis wintoniensis, AD 1305–1316, ed. A. W. Goodman, 1, CYS, 43 (1940), pt 1, p. 20 · F. J. Baigent, ed., The registers of John de Sandale and Rigaud d'Asserio, bishops of Winchester, Hampshire RS, 8 (1897), 508 n. 2 · The registers of Roger Martival, bishop of Salisbury, 1315–1330, 3, ed. S. Reynolds, CYS, 59 (1965) · E. B. Fryde, ed., Book of prests of the king's wardrobe for 1294–5 (1962) · R. B. Pugh, ed., Abstracts of feet of fines relating to Wiltshire for the reigns of Edward I and Edward II, Wilts RS, 1 (1939) · C. R. Elrington, ed., Abstracts of feet of fines relating to Wiltshire for the reign of Edward III, Wilts RS, 29 (1974) · Registrum Simonis de Gandavo, diocesis Saresbiriensis, AD 1297–1315, ed. C. T. Flower and M. C. B. Dawes, 2 vols., CYS, 40–41 (1934) · H. M. Cam, ed., The eyre of London, 14 Edward II, AD 1321, 2 vols., SeldS, 85–6 (1968–9)

Bereford, Richard (fl. 1280–1318), administrator, probably took his name from Barford St John in Oxfordshire—in 1311 he alleged that he had been assaulted there and forced to take refuge in the church. He may have been connected with the justice Sir William Bereford, whose horse he was able to recognize when he saw it in Ireland in 1302. Richard Bereford is first recorded in 1280, when he was presented by the king to Wembworthy church in Devon. Four years later he was keeper of the bishopric of Salisbury during a vacancy, and in 1285, as a royal clerk, he was employed in the collection of a clerical twentieth in the bishoprics of Worcester and Hereford. His services brought him further benefices, including the church of Shenley in Hertfordshire in 1291.

On 8 June 1300 Bereford was appointed treasurer of the exchequer in Dublin, with a yearly salary of £40. From the first he was heavily involved in raising men, money, and victuals to support English campaigns in Scotland, and his responsibilities brought him into abrasive contact with some of the leading men in English Ireland, notably with Sir Geoffrey de Geneville, lord of Trim, whose liberties Bereford was inclined to override, and Geoffrey Morton, the litigious mayor of Dublin. He also had problems with some of his own subordinates, one of whom removed over £400 from the Irish exchequer and then tried to make the shortfall look like the treasurer's responsibility. In 1302 he was presented to the prebend of Killardry, Tipperary, in Cashel Cathedral, but although he is recorded as taking the fealty of the men of Dublin to Edward II on the latter's accession in 1307, he was replaced as treasurer on 24 January 1308.

Summoned back to England to render his accounts at the Westminster exchequer Bereford was at first unable to make the journey because he had been arrested at Geoffrey Morton's suit, and sentenced to imprisonment in Dublin Castle. Released on royal orders, he is recorded as presenting his accounts in 1309. He appears to have cleared himself, since in August 1310 he was appointed a justice to take assizes and deliver gaols in Essex and five other counties, and he was several times a commissioner of oyer and terminer in the years that followed. In September 1311 he attended parliament, one of a group of men, mostly justices, who were rebuked for leaving early. But on 11 May 1314 he was sent back to Ireland, this time as chancellor, and he retained that office, in a period of growing difficulties, until 23 February 1316. Thereafter he seems to have gone into retirement, passing out of public life so completely that in June 1318 another man was presented to his living of Shenley, in the mistaken belief that Bereford was dead. It is not known when he became so indeed.

HENRY SUMMERSON

Sources Chancery records · F. Palgrave, ed., The parliamentary writs and writs of military summons, 2/2 (1830), 56–7 · H. S. Sweetman and G. F. Handcock, eds., Calendar of documents relating to Ireland, 5 vols., PRO (1875–86), vols. 4–5 · J. T. Gilbert, ed., Historic and municipal documents of Ireland, AD 1172–1320, from the archives of the city of Dublin, Rolls Series, 53 (1870) · J. Mills and others, eds., Calendar of the justiciary rolls … of Ireland, 3 vols. (1905–56) · M. S. Arnold, ed., Select cases of trespass from the king's courts, 1307–1399, 1, SeldS, 100 (1985), 32 · H. G. Richardson and G. O. Sayles, The administration of Ireland, 1172–1377 (1963) · G. J. Hand, English law in Ireland, 1290–1324 (1967)

Bereford [Barford], **Sir William** (d. 1326), justice, was the son of Walter de Bereford, and probably took his name from Barford near Warwick, though by the middle of the thirteenth century the main family lands, held of the earl of Warwick, were at Langley in Sutton Coldfield. In 1287 property at nearby Wishaw was settled on William by his elder brother, Osbert de Bereford, a past sheriff of Warwickshire and Leicestershire, who seems to have died within a few years, leaving William as his heir. It was probably also in the 1280s that William married Margaret, the daughter of Hugh de Plessy and granddaughter of John de Plessy, seventh earl of Warwick, who brought him lands at Wittenham in Berkshire.

By 1285 Bereford was a pleader in the court of common pleas, and the purging of the royal justices in 1290 gave him the chance of judicial promotion. The roll of the Easter parliament of 1290 records Roger Brabazon, William Bereford, and Gilbert Rothbury as inquiring into the liberties of the prior of Tynemouth, who was accused before the parliament of encroaching on the rights of the king and the burgesses of Newcastle. Brabazon and later Rothbury were promoted to the reconstituted court of king's bench, but Bereford's experience equipped him for the common bench, and he first appeared there in Hilary term 1292, only to be moved at Michaelmas to one of the circuits of what proved to be the last countrywide eyre. In 1293 Eustace and John de Parles denounced him in the presence of magnates in the king's court ('in aula regis') for partiality in the administration of justice in Staffordshire, but his fellow justices satisfied the king of his innocence, and the brothers were sent to the Tower for publicly insulting a royal minister rather than presenting a formal complaint ('querela') against him.

At Trinity term 1294 Bereford returned to the common bench, where he was to remain for thirty-two years, standing second to John Mettingham and Ralph Hengham successively until his own appointment as chief justice on 15 March 1309. As a justice he sat in parliament among the lords and royal councillors, and in 1297 he was one of the councillors who reassured Humphrey (VI) de Bohun, earl of Hereford, and Roger (IV) Bigod, earl of Norfolk, that they would not suffer the king's 'rancour and indignation' for their opposition to his arbitrary measures when Edward returned from campaign in Flanders. A knight by 1302, in 1304 Bereford was commissioned to inquire into the break-in at the treasury at Westminster; in 1305 he was among the twenty-one English representatives appointed in parliament to confer with the same number of Scots on how to promote stability in Scotland; and in 1306 he was a commissioner of trailbaston on the northern circuit. On the accession of Edward II in 1307 he was given a leading role in the collection of *querelae* against Edward I's treasurer and chief minister, Walter Langton, bishop of Lichfield. In the following years he sat frequently at the exchequer on council business.

Perhaps because he had acquired property close to Wittenham, and a fishery below Shillingford Bridge, in the earl of Cornwall's honour of Wallingford, Bereford was associated with Piers Gaveston, Edward II's doomed favourite, when he obtained that earldom, and he was one of the executors of Gaveston's will. Only Bereford and three others were recorded as standing with the king against the barons who demanded Gaveston's banishment in 1308, so that their removal from the king's presence was demanded also. Neither this nor the stipulation in the baronial ordinances of 1311 that the chief justices should be appointed in open parliament seems in fact to have affected Bereford's career; nor did his receipt of robes from Thomas of Lancaster. In a parliament at York in 1318, which attempted to reform the royal household, he and Scrope, the chief justice of king's bench, were among royal ministers retained in office.

Bereford is chiefly notable as the most formidable and cantankerous of that first generation of lay lawyers who moved from pleading to presiding in the king's courts, and whose personalities can be known through the reports of their legal arguments in the year-books. He claimed special authority in the interpretation of the great statutes of Edward I's reign, and in 1310 gave the famous judgment that an entail as provided in 1285 should last until the third heir entered. He died in harness before 20 August 1326, holding estates in eight counties, and leaving a son and heir, Edmund, said to be aged twenty-eight and more. In the following year this Edmund, 'a king's clerk', was given licence to crenellate his house at Langley.   ALAN HARDING

Sources CIPM, 6, no. 748 · VCH Warwickshire, 4.238, 259, 5.190 · VCH Berkshire, 3.547, 4.387 · Chancery records · Baker, Serjeants · D. Crook, Records of the general eyre, Public Record Office Handbooks, 20 (1982) · RotP · J. C. Davies, The baronial opposition to Edward II (1918) · W. C. Bolland, Chief Justice Sir William Bereford (1924) · D. E. C. Yale, A centenary guide to the publications of the Selden Society, ed. G. H. Jones and others, 2nd edn, SeldS (1987) · T. F. T. Plucknett, The legislation of Edward I (1949)

Berengaria [Berengaria of Navarre] (c.1165–1230), queen of England, consort of Richard I, was the eldest daughter of Sancho VI, king of Navarre (1150–1194), and Sancha, daughter of Alfonso VII of Castile. She was born in Navarre, probably during the 1160s, her eldest brother being the future Sancho VII of Navarre. In 1190 *Richard I, recognizing Sancho VI as a valuable potential ally in his struggle against Raymond (VI), count of Toulouse, began negotiations for his marriage to Berengaria. He had first to pay off Philip Augustus of France, to whose sister Alice he had been betrothed since 1168. This he did in March 1191 while the two kings stayed in Sicily, on their way to Palestine on crusade. Richard's mother, *Eleanor of Aquitaine, who favoured the Navarrese alliance, had meanwhile escorted Berengaria to Sicily where she met Richard on 30 March 1191.

The royal fleet set off for Palestine on 10 April; Berengaria and Richard's sister Joan were driven onto the shores of Cyprus by a storm and threatened by its hostile ruler, Isaac Komnenos. Richard arrived on 6 May and rescued them (he later defeated Isaac and captured Cyprus), and on 12 May 1191 Berengaria was married to Richard at Limasol. She was then crowned queen of England by Jean, bishop of Évreux. A generous dower was settled on her: her father gave her important Pyrenean castles, while Richard assigned to her all his rights in Gascony south of the Garonne for Eleanor of Aquitaine's lifetime, and thereafter Eleanor's marriage portion in England and northern France. The political value of the match was demonstrated when in 1192 Sancho helped to quash a rebellion of some Gascon vassals supported from Toulouse, but for Richard, at least, this appears to have been nothing other than a marriage of convenience. He spent very little time with Berengaria and their union was childless.

The royal party finally reached Palestine in June 1191. Acre fell to Richard and his allies on 12 July and from late July until October Berengaria and Joan stayed in the royal palace at Acre. In the course of his highly successful campaigns Richard moved them to Jaffa, and then to Latrun for Christmas. At Michaelmas 1192 the king, having decided to leave Palestine, sent Berengaria's party ahead from Acre. After landing in southern Italy at Brindisi, they travelled to Rome where they were received honourably by the pope, Celestine III, and were given news of Richard's captivity in Germany. For fear of the emperor Henry VI, Richard's captor, they remained in Rome. Shortly after Richard's release (June 1193), they departed for Pisa and Genoa and then went by ship to Marseilles. From here they crossed Provence and the county of Toulouse on their way back to Poitou. Richard made no attempt to see Berengaria again until, following a warning from a hermit about the dangers of his unclean life, he suffered a serious illness. He and Berengaria were reunited at Le Mans on 4 April 1195, and were together at Poitiers for Christmas 1195, but no later meetings between them are recorded. Unlike Eleanor of Aquitaine, Berengaria was not at Richard's deathbed, and there is no evidence that she attended his funeral on 11 April 1199. But having passed inconspicuously through the 1190s as Richard's queen, Berengaria was now as his widow forced to come out of the shadows to defend her rights. This she did with tenacity and success.

Throughout John's reign Berengaria, with the full support of Pope Innocent III, struggled with the English king to obtain her dower payments. In response to political pressure, John offered to pay off her claim in 1201 and again in 1215, but in the interim honoured very few promises to her. Berengaria was offered a safe conduct to visit England in 1206, but did not take it up. However, after 1216 Henry III's minority government accepted its obligations towards her, and in the 1220s she received regular payments from the English exchequer. Meanwhile in 1203–4 Philip of France had seized Normandy, Maine, and Anjou from John. Eleanor's death in 1204 released her marriage portion for Berengaria; and in this matter the French king was more scrupulous than John. He bestowed the city and seneschalcy of Le Mans upon Berengaria in return for her surrender of lands and rights which included Falaise and Domfront. Berengaria settled in Le Mans for the rest of her days, and took an active role in running the city. She devoted herself to many works of piety, which included funding major building works at the cathedral of St Julien, and from 1220 assisting the new Franciscan friary in Le Mans. Her most important project was her foundation of the Cistercian abbey of L'Épau on land near Le Mans which was granted to her by the young Louis IX of France, a patron of the order, in 1228; and when she died on 23 December 1230 it was here that she was buried. Stylistic evidence suggests that the fine tomb effigy, depicting the queen crowned and recumbent, was fashioned almost immediately afterwards. Several contemporaries described Berengaria as both beautiful and prudent; more convincing is Richard of Devizes' view that she was more sensible than attractive. She emerges from the sources as an intelligent, pious, and quietly determined person, tenacious in adversity, an active ruler of her lands, well able to gain and use allies and defenders, and strikingly generous to the religious orders even by the standards of her day. She has the additional distinction of having been the only queen of England never to set foot on its shores.

ELIZABETH HALLAM

Sources E. Hallam, 'Bérengère de Navarre: les Plantagenets et les Capétiens', *La province du Maine*, 93 (1991), 225–37 · J. Gillingham, 'Richard I and Berengaria of Navarre', *BIHR*, 53 (1980), 157–73 · H. Chardon, 'Histoire de la Reine Bérengère', *Bulletin de la Société d'Agriculture, Sciences et Arts de la Sarthe*, 2nd ser., 10 (1863), 376–465 · L. Landon, *The itinerary of King Richard I*, PRSoc., new ser., 13 (1935) · R. Howlett, ed., *Chronicles of the reigns of Stephen, Henry II, and Richard I*, 1, Rolls Series, 82 (1884) · W. Stubbs, ed., *Gesta regis Henrici secundi Benedicti abbatis: the chronicle of the reigns of Henry II and Richard I, AD 1169–1192*, 2 vols., Rolls Series, 49 (1867) · *CEPR letters*, vol. 1 · *Chronica magistri Rogeri de Hovedene*, ed. W. Stubbs, 4 vols., Rolls Series, 51 (1868–71), vols. 3–4 · *The letters of Pope Innocent III (1198–1216) concerning England and Wales*, ed. C. R. Cheney and M. G. Cheney (1967) · T. D. Hardy, ed., *Rotuli litterarum patentium*, RC (1835) · *CPR, 1216–25* · *Chronicon Richardi Divisensis / The Chronicle of Richard of Devizes*, ed. J. T. Appleby (1963)
Likenesses tomb effigy, 1230–1239?, abbey of L'Épau, Le Mans, France; copy, plaster card, V&A
Wealth at death valuable estates in northern France

Berenger, Richard (*bap.* 1719, *d.* 1782), courtier and equestrian, was baptized on 17 December 1719 at St Martin-in-the-Fields, Westminster, the eldest of the three sons of Moses Berenger, a wealthy London merchant, and Penelope, youngest daughter of Sir Richard *Temple, third baronet (1634–1697), and Mary, *née* Knapp (*b.* after 1640, *d.* 1727). Little is known of his early life before he published in 1754 *A New System of Horsemanship*, a translation from the French of Claude Bourgelat's two-volume work. He followed this with *The History and Art of Horsemanship* (2 vols., 1771), which included a translation of Xenophon's celebrated treatise on horsemanship. Following George III's accession to the throne, Berenger was appointed gentleman of the horse to the king, on 22 December 1760. He held the post until his death, but lived beyond his means in later life and, to avoid his creditors, was confined for a while to his official residence in the King's Mews. The actor David Garrick enabled him to appease his creditors by giving him £300 and standing security for him for a further £500.

Berenger was well known in the London literary world, and he contributed a few poems to volume 6 of Robert Dodsley's *A Collection of Poems by Several Hands* (1758) and three essays to the periodical *The World*. Described by Dr Johnson as the 'standard of true elegance' (Boswell, 3.83), he was genial and gregarious; Hannah More summed him up as 'everybody's favourite' (Roberts, 1.74). He died in the King's Mews, London, on 9 September 1782.

W. P. COURTNEY, *rev.* S. J. SKEDD

Sources IGI · GM, 1st ser., 52 (1782), 455 · J. C. Sainty and R. O. Bucholz, eds., *Officials of the royal household, 1660–1837*, 2: *Departments of the lord steward and the master of the horse* (1998), 59 · J. Boswell, *The life of Samuel Johnson*, ed. J. W. Croker, rev. J. Wright, [another edn], 10 vols. (1835), vol. 3, p. 83; vol. 7, p. 100; vol. 8, pp. 66–7 · W. Roberts, *Memoirs of the life and correspondence of Mrs Hannah More*, 2nd edn, 4 vols. (1834), vol. 1, pp. 74, 77, 175 · J. Taylor, *Records of my life*, 2 vols. (1832), vol. 1, pp. 325–6 · *The private correspondence of David Garrick*, ed. J. Boaden, 2 vols. (1831–2), vol. 2, pp. 297–8, 364–5 **Archives** BL, corresp., Add. MS 59438 | BL, letters to Lord Camelford and Lady Camelford, Add. MS 69305 · BL, letters to Charles Jenkinson, Add. MSS 38209–38210, 38470 · PRO, letters to first earl of Chatham, 30/8

Beresford, Charles William de la Poer, Baron Beresford

(1846–1919), naval officer, was born at Baronstown, Dundalk, co. Louth, on 10 February 1846, the second son of the Revd John de la Poer Beresford, fourth marquess of Waterford (1814–1866), and his wife, Christiana (1820–1905), fourth daughter of Charles Powell Leslie MP, of Glaslough, co. Monaghan.

Early naval career He was educated at the Revd George Renaud's Bayford School, Hertfordshire (1855–7), by a tutor, the Revd David Bruce Payne, at Deal, and at Stubbington House, near Fareham, Portsmouth. He entered the *Britannia* as a naval cadet in December 1859, and in March 1861 was appointed to the *Marlborough*, 121 guns, flagship in the Mediterranean, one of the last built and finest of the old wooden line of battleships. He was rated midshipman in June 1862. He was transferred in July 1863 to the *Defence*, a new wooden hulled ironclad which he later described as 'a slovenly, unhandy tin kettle' (*Memoirs*, 1.41). After less than a year he was appointed as senior midshipman to the corvette *Clio*, 22 guns, in which he sailed to the Falkland Islands and round Cape Horn to Honolulu and Vancouver. In December 1865 he was transferred to the frigate *Tribune*, 31 guns, at Vancouver, promoted sublieutenant 1866, and in the following February transferred to the steam frigate *Sutlej*, flagship on the Pacific station. The following June he returned home in her and joined the *Excellent* gunnery school ship. After eight months in the royal yacht, *Victoria and Albert*, which gave him his promotion to lieutenant in October 1868, he was appointed to the frigate *Galatea* (captain, Prince Alfred, duke of Edinburgh), in which he made a voyage of two and a half years, visiting the Cape, Australia, New Zealand, Japan, China, India, and the Falkland Islands. In November 1872 he was appointed flag lieutenant to Sir Henry Keppel, commander-in-chief at Plymouth, and remained there until August 1874, when he was sent for a few months to the *Bellerophon*, flagship of the North American station.

Through the influence of his brother Lord Waterford, Beresford was Conservative MP for co. Waterford from 1874 to 1880, opposing home rule but supporting denominational education, and opposing abolition of naval flogging. In September 1875 he went as aide-de-camp to the prince of Wales on his tour in India and was promoted commander in November of that year. In May 1877, after a short period in the *Vernon* for torpedo instruction, he was appointed executive officer of the *Thunderer*, channel squadron, until April 1878. Beresford married, on 25 April 1878, the 'picturesque' Ellen Jeromina (*d.* 26 May 1922). Called Mina by her friends and Dot by her husband, she was the daughter of the late Richard Gardner, MP for

Charles William de la Poer Beresford, Baron Beresford (1846–1919), by Charles Wellington Furse, exh. RA 1903

Leicester, and his wife, Lucy, Countess Mandelsloh. Beresford and his wife had two daughters. Shortly after Beresford's marriage the prince of Wales requested that he be given command of his paddle yacht, the *Osborne*, a post which Beresford retained until November 1881. During these years, 1874–1881, he was known chiefly as a dashing sportsman, a friend of the prince of Wales, and a prominent popular figure in smart society.

The 'member for the navy' At the beginning of 1882 Beresford took command of the barque rigged screw gunvessel *Condor*, 3 guns, under Sir Beauchamp Seymour (afterwards Lord Alcester). At the bombardment of the Alexandria fortifications (11 July 1882), Beresford took the little *Condor* close in under Fort Marabout and she took the leading part in silencing its guns. Seymour signalled 'Well done, Condor' and the crews of the great ironclads cheered her. Aboard the *Condor* were the *Times* correspondent and the *Graphic* special war artist, Frederic Villiers. Beresford's role was fully reported. After the bombardment Beresford was sent ashore under Captain John Fisher and appointed provost-marshal and chief of police, and efficiently restored order. He was promoted captain and mentioned in dispatches for gallantry. 'Charlie B' became a national hero and celebrity, from then on much featured in the illustrated and other press, and later also on picture postcards. He was offered an appointment on the staff of the khedive and also as war correspondent of the *New York Herald*, but Sir Garnet Wolseley refused to release him. Beresford returned home to public adulation and royal congratulations, and remained on half pay until August 1884, when he was appointed to the *Alexandra*, to act on the staff of Lord Wolseley (as he now was) during the Gordon relief expedition. He afterwards commanded the naval brigade on the Nile, with which he took part in the battle of Abu Klea on 17 January 1885. He also commanded the expedition which went to the rescue of Charles William Wilson in the *Safieh*, when he kept his ship steadily engaged under heavy fire while his engineer, Benbow, repaired her disabled boiler (4 February). He was commended in the House of Commons, and described by Wolseley in his dispatch as 'an officer whose readiness and resource and ability as a leader are only equalled by his daring'. For these services he was made CB (1885).

Beresford came home in July 1885 and was elected Conservative MP for East Marylebone, London; he was re-elected in 1886. The prince of Wales, to whom he had become close, urged Lord Salisbury, on the formation of the 1886 Conservative government, to give him political office, but Salisbury appointed him fourth naval lord of the Admiralty under Lord George Hamilton. He secured the establishment of the naval intelligence department, but was a difficult colleague and early showed himself hostile to the policy of the board. He criticized the shipbuilding programme and the organization and pay of the intelligence department, and objected to the supreme authority of the first lord in naval administration. He resigned over the naval estimates in January 1888. Salisbury commented to the queen that he was 'an officer of great ability afloat, but he is too greedy of popular applause to get on in a public department. He is constantly playing his own game at the expense of his colleagues' (Bennett, 145). For the next two years he was 'member for the navy', a constant and outspoken critic of naval affairs in the House of Commons, demanding naval reforms and a stronger fleet. He contributed to the introduction of the 1889 Naval Defence Act and the Hamilton naval building programme.

The controversial commander and 'ass' During the period from 1889 to 1892 Beresford's and his wife's lives were darkened by a quarrel with the prince of Wales and the threat of public scandal. It stemmed from the prince's attempt to retrieve a highly indiscreet letter written in January 1889 by Frances, Lady Brooke, later countess of Warwick (1861–1938) [*see* Greville, Frances Evelyn], with whom Beresford had an affair in 1886–7 and who, in 1889, became the prince's mistress. Beresford and the prince were eventually formally reconciled, but their once warm relationship was replaced by resentment. In December 1889 Beresford was appointed to command the armoured cruiser *Undaunted* on the Mediterranean station, resigning his seat in parliament. He returned to England in June 1893 to take command of the Medway dockyard reserve until March 1896. In 1897 he was appointed aide-de-camp to Queen Victoria, and in September 1897 was promoted rear-admiral. From 1897 to 1900 he was Conservative MP for York. He continued to use the press to demand naval reform.

In 1898–9 Beresford visited China on an investigative mission for the Associated Chambers of Commerce—one of his indiscreet speeches led Salisbury to comment

'C.B. is an ass' (Bennett, 219)—and published his report, *The Break-up of China* (1899), advocating British reassertion of the 'open door', and Chinese reforms, and warning against the Russian threat. In January 1900 he was sent to the Mediterranean as second in command to Sir John Fisher, whose reforming zeal he shared. He earned a rebuke from the Admiralty after Arnold White in 1901 leaked to the *Daily Mail* a letter criticizing Admiralty policy. From very different backgrounds, Beresford and Fisher were both naval reformers with their own agenda, ambitious and sometimes unscrupulous rivals, and prima donnas. From 1900, through several incidents including Fisher's public reprimanding of Beresford, relations between them deteriorated into hostility. Thenceforth Beresford was apparently motivated largely by hatred of Fisher, whom he called 'the Mulatto', and whom he challenged for leadership of the navy. Their feud split the navy into the Fisherite 'Fishpond' and the Beresfordian 'Syndicate of Discontent', while others deprecated the dispute and its harmful results. In the following years, to some extent Beresford became the spokesman of, and was used by, others with their own naval agendas.

In February 1902, after returning to England, Beresford was elected MP for Woolwich. He was promoted vice-admiral in October 1902, and early in 1903 again left the House of Commons to take command of the channel squadron. He was made KCB in June 1903. In 1904 he opposed Fisher's proposal for fast armoured cruisers rather than battleships, and he favoured Arthur Pollen's controversial rangefinding apparatus rejected by Fisher and the Admiralty. In March 1905 he hauled down his flag, and two months later went to the Mediterranean as commander-in-chief, with the acting rank of admiral, to which he was promoted in November 1906.

From 1907 to 1909 Beresford was commander-in-chief of the Channel Fleet, then the principal fleet with fourteen battleships. His flagship was, ironically, the new battleship *King Edward VII* and he 'lived in great style' (Bennett, 283), attended by his Irish servants and his bulldog bitch Kora—with whom he was repeatedly photographed—and kept his motor car stowed amidships. In November 1907 he publicly reprimanded the Fisherite Sir Percy Scott for his insubordinate 'paintwork' signal. It was a time when, against the German threat, the naval forces in home waters were being gradually but radically reorganized by Fisher, first sea lord from 1904 to 1910; Fisher's 1905 promotion to admiral of the fleet dashed Beresford's hopes of succeeding him as first sea lord. Beresford opposed many of the changes, and relations between him and Whitehall became very strained; the gradual development of the Home Fleet as an independent command in peacetime, resulting in a significant diminution of his command, angered him. In March 1909, following McKenna's decision, he was ordered to haul down his flag and come ashore a year short of the normal term of command, the Channel Fleet being abolished as a separate command and absorbed into the enlarged Home Fleet. Beresford, greeted by cheering crowds at Portsmouth and London, next challenged the policy of the Admiralty and its organization of the fleets in a long polemical letter (dated 2 April 1909), particularly on the necessity for a war staff, to the prime minister, Asquith.

Politics and personalities played a major role. Beresford was a Unionist, Fisher a Liberal. Beresford accused Fisher of operating a system of espionage against him when he was commander-in-chief, Mediterranean, and ruthlessly crushing all opposition at the Admiralty. However, there were also solid professional reasons for the dispute. Beresford believed that Fisher's division of the forces destined to defend home waters into separate channel, home, and Atlantic fleets was potentially disastrous and that these forces should be under a single commander-in-chief who would manoeuvre and train them for war. Beresford alleged that the policy of scrapping obsolete warships had gone too far and left the navy with too few cruisers for trade route protection in war. Furthermore, there were not enough British destroyers suitable for work in the North Sea and they compared poorly with their potential German foes. Money spent on submarines was also wasted, they were purely defensive craft and not suited for an offensive fleet like that of the British. Beresford also asserted he had not received proper war plans from the Admiralty and that it was necessary to establish a real naval staff. Beresford's charges were referred to a subcommittee of the committee of imperial defence, composed of the prime minister, Crewe, Morley, Grey, and Haldane. Asquith defined the inquiry very narrowly, excluding the 1904–5 reforms. Beresford, McKenna (who put the Admiralty case), and others presented evidence. Beresford showed up very badly under Asquith's penetrating examination and he gave an impression of incompetence. The committee's report (published August 1909) on the whole vindicated the Admiralty, though in certain respects—notably that the Admiralty had insufficiently informed Beresford—it justified some of his criticisms. Beresford published his views in *The Betrayal* (1912). He was placed on the retired list in February 1911, and received the GCB the same year.

From 1910 to 1916 Beresford was MP for Portsmouth. He continued in parliament, the press, and elsewhere his campaign against Fisher and Fisher's changes. Although he gained some right-wing support, Balfour and other leading Unionists refused to support him. He supported the National Service League and compulsory military training, and co-operated with Roberts on the invasion controversy. He supported and was supported by the more extreme and largely Unionist Imperial Maritime League (the 'Navier League') which with his encouragement broke from the Navy League in 1908 and demanded Fisher's removal. Rebuffed by Northcliffe, Beresford was supported by the *Daily Express* and the *Standard*—H. A. Gwynne was probably his most important ally—both owned by Arthur Pearson, and by the *Morning Post*. In parliament he spoke vehemently but sometimes incoherently. He bitterly criticized Churchill (first lord of the Admiralty, 1911–15) for his autocratic methods and interference in professional naval matters, and in 1914 for his

apparent attempt to coerce the Ulster loyalists. In 1914 Beresford published his surprisingly non-controversial two-volume *Memoirs*, largely on his career to 1885. In 1915 he requested a peerage. Balfour and Bonar Law favoured this and Asquith, though disliking it, acquiesced. On 22 January 1916 Beresford was created Baron Beresford of Metemmeh and Curraghmore, co. Waterford.

Character and reputation Charlie B was one of the most remarkable personalities of his generation: colourful, idiosyncratic, maverick, brave, high-spirited, an enthusiastic sportsman, of noble birth, and with ample private means. He touched life at many points, and to the general public was the best-known sailor of his day. However, arguably there was truth in Lansdowne's criticism that 'there never was a more cheaply acquired reputation than his' (Williams, 135). Beresford was passionately devoted to the navy and to his country, but his love of publicity and impatience of control sometimes led him into conduct alien from the strict traditions of the navy. He was not an original thinker. In parliament and on the platform, while not strong in argument—the pro-Fisher Garvin called Beresford 'the great dirigible … the biggest of all recorded gas-bags' (Williams, 213)—he was a forceful speaker and was widely popular, usually confining himself to naval topics in which he was especially interested. Owing partly to his variety of interests and partly to his quarrels with authority, he had until late in life comparatively little sea experience, but from January 1900, when he hoisted his flag in the Mediterranean, aged nearly fifty-four, he was for the greater part of nine years continuously afloat. He was an able and active flag officer; and he commanded the most important British fleet with energy and ability, enhancing fighting efficiency, and devoting personal care to the welfare of his men.

There are however widely divergent opinions about Beresford. Many of his ideas were sound and full of common sense, but his actions and statements, particularly in later years, alienated others. He was ambitious to reach the highest naval position, and it was unfortunate that the last years of his command were clouded by personal antagonism with Fisher. An admirable host, in London and in general society, he enjoyed widespread popularity.

Beresford died of a cerebral haemorrhage while staying with the duke of Portland at Langwell, Berriedale, Caithness, on 6 September 1919. He had a state funeral in St Paul's Cathedral, followed by burial at Putney Vale cemetery, London, four days later. At his death his peerage became extinct.

V. W. BADDELEY, *rev.* PAUL G. HALPERN

Sources Admiralty records, 1927 · *The memoirs of Lord Charles Beresford*, 2 vols. (1914–27) · G. M. Bennett, *Charlie B: a biography of Admiral Lord Beresford of Metemmeh and Curraghmore* (1968) · A. J. Marder, *From the Dreadnought to Scapa Flow: the Royal Navy in the Fisher era, 1904–1919*, 5 vols. (1961–70), vol. 1 · R. F. MacKay, *Fisher of Kilverstone* (1973) · A. J. Marder, *The anatomy of British sea power*, American edn (1940) · J. T. Sumida, *In defence of naval supremacy: finance, technology and British naval policy, 1889–1914*, new edn (1993) · GEC, *Peerage* · S. W. Roskill, *Hankey, man of secrets*, 1 (1970) · P. Kennedy, *The rise of the Anglo-German antagonism, 1860–1914* (1980) · A. J. A. Morris, *The scaremongers: the advocacy of war and rearmament, 1896–1914* (1984) ·

R. Williams, *Defending the empire: the conservative party and British defence policy, 1899–1915* (1991)

Archives BL, corresp. and papers, Add. MS 50288, *passim* · BL, corresp. of him and his wife, Add. MSS 63116–63117 · Duke U., Perkins L., corresp. · Hunt. L., corresp. · NMM, notebook; corresp. | BL, corresp. with Arthur James Balfour, Add. MS 49713 · BL, corresp. with H. O. Arnold-Foster, Add. MS 50288, *passim* · BL, letters to Lord Gladstone, Add. MSS 46052–46060, *passim* · BL, corresp. with Lord Long, Add. MS 62407 · BL, corresp. with Sir H. Evan-Thomas, Add. MS 52504, *passim* · Bodl. Oxf., corresp. with Herbert Asquith · Bodl. Oxf., corresp. with H. A. Gwynne · Bodl. Oxf., corresp. with Lord Selborne · CAC Cam., corresp. with Lord Randolph Churchill · CAC Cam., letters to John De Robeck · CKS, letter to Aretas Akers-Douglas · CKS, corresp. with Sir J. C. Ardagh · Durham RO, letters to Lady Londonderry · Elgin Birthplace Museum, letters to Edward Edgar · HLRO, letters to R. D. Blumenfeld · HLRO, corresp. with Andrew Bonar Law · NAM, letters to Spencer Wilkinson · PRO, letters to Lord Kitchener, PRO 30/57; WO 159 · PRO NIre., corresp. with Edward Carson · Richmond Local Studies Library, London, corresp. with Douglas Sladen

Likenesses Violet, duchess of Rutland, lithograph, 1890, NPG · B. Stone, photographs, 1899, NPG · C. W. Furse, oils, exh. RA 1903, NPG [*see illus.*] · E. Lanteri, bronze bust, 1910, Crown Commissioners · M. Beerbohm, pencil and wash caricature, 1913, AM Oxf. · W. Stoneman, photograph, 1918, NPG · Barraud, photograph, NPG; repro. in *Men and women of the day*, 2 (1889) · Cloister, cartoon, NPG; repro. in *VF* (6 July 1899) · Maclure & Macdonald, chromolithograph (after photograph by London Stereoscopic Co.), NPG; repro. in *Pictorial World* (1882) · Spy [L. Ward], cartoon, NPG; repro. in *VF* (12 Aug 1876) · group portrait, oils (*The 'Safieh' in action at Wad Habeshi, 4 February* 1885), Curraghmore, near Portlaw, co. Waterford; repro. in Bennett, *Charlie B*, jacket · photographs, NPG

Wealth at death £13,122 11s. 0d.: probate, 29 Oct 1919, *CGPLA Eng. & Wales*

Beresford, Henry de la Poer, third marquess of Waterford (1811–1859), reprobate and landowner, was born on 26 April 1811 at 5 Mansfield Street, Marylebone, Middlesex, the second son of Henry de la Poer Beresford, second marquess of Waterford (1772–1826), and his wife, Lady Susanna Hussey Carpenter (1784–1827), daughter of the second earl of Tyrconnel. His elder brother and both his parents died before he was seventeen, and the young marquess, who was educated at Eton College (1824–9), became notorious for his wildness. (He returned to Eton in 1838 to steal the headmaster's whipping block, an exploit Waterford celebrated with an annual dinner.) He matriculated at Christ Church, Oxford, in 1829, but was invited to leave, and for the next decade he was to be found most frequently at the racetrack, on the hunting-field, or in the police courts. His favoured companions were young 'sporting men', prize-fighters, and prostitutes; powerfully built, rich, and with an uncontrolled sense of humour, it amused him to challenge passers-by to fight him, to break windows, to upset (literally) applecarts. He painted the Melton Mowbray toll-bar red; he fought a duel; he painted the heels of a parson's horse with aniseed and hunted him with bloodhounds. When, as frequently occurred, his activities landed him in court, he laughed at (and paid) the derisory fines which were designed to control the excesses of the working class, not those of the apparently limitlessly wealthy aristocracy. Waterford's reputation as a rowdy and boisterous ruffian led to his name being associated with Spring-Heeled Jack, the unknown figure who terrorized women in London in 1838.

The turning point in Waterford's life was the Eglinton tournament of 1839. He took an enthusiastic part as one of the thirteen knights in Lord Eglinton's attempt to revive ideas of chivalry among the tory aristocracy. The Knight of the Dragon (the sobriquet taken by Waterford) excelled his host's hopes by not only being so carried away in the mêlée that he had to be separated from his opponent, Lord Alford, by the knight marshal but also by falling in love at first sight with Louisa Stuart [see Beresford, Louisa Anne (1818–1891)], younger daughter of Charles *Stuart, Lord Stuart de Rothesay. The beautiful Louisa Stuart, like her sister Charlotte, Lady Canning, was celebrated as a model of pious, gentle, artistic womanhood; on the surface, she was the most unlikely match for Waterford. At the same time, the wooing of the pure, virtuous woman by the worldly, rough—if good-natured and kind-hearted—reprobate, and the reshaping of his character by the love of a good woman, represented an archetype of the chivalric ideal. After a courtship of three years, Waterford secured his lady's affections and the consent of her family, not least by the reform of his habits. The wedding took place on 8 June 1842 and the couple went immediately to his estate, Curraghmore, in co. Waterford, where they were to pass most of their happily married but childless life together.

Marriage ended Waterford's career in the police courts. Instead, he busied himself with the management of his estates, becoming in the process something of a model landlord. Resident on their estate in Ireland, the Waterfords worked long hours to attempt to relieve the worst effects of the famine on their tenants and neighbours. Despite generally good relations with his tenants, unrest in the region in 1848 led Waterford to fortify Curraghmore. He remained devoted to horses, of which he kept hundreds, and, if he no longer steeplechased, he continued to hunt with passion (six days a week during the season). His death came suddenly, on 29 March 1859, on the hunting-field, at Corbally, near Carrick-on-Suir: thrown from his horse, he broke his neck and died almost instantly. He was buried in the family mausoleum at Clonegam, close to Curraghmore. His title and estates passed to his brother.   K. D. REYNOLDS

Sources A. J. C. Hare, *The story of two noble lives*, 3 vols. (1893) · V. Surtees, *Charlotte Canning* (1975) · J. Lenox, *Fast life* (1859) · R. Nevill, *Sporting days and sporting ways* (1910) · M. Girouard, *The return to Camelot: chivalry and the English gentleman* (1981) · I. Anstruther, *The knight and the umbrella* (1963) · *Sporting Review*, 41 (1859), 239–40 · *Sporting Review*, 42 (1859), 232–4 · H. M. Neville, *Under a border tower: sketches of Ford Castle, Northumberland* (1896) · Boase, *Mod. Eng. biog.* · GEC, *Peerage* · G. F. Berkeley, *My life and recollections*, 2 (1865) · O. W. Hewett, *Strawberry fair: a biography of Frances, Countess Waldegrave, 1821–1879* (1956) · *The Times* (14 June 1837) · *The Times* (10 July 1837) · *The Times* (16 Sept 1837) · *The Times* (2 July 1838) · *The Times* (9 Oct 1838) · *The Times* (14 April 1840) · *The Times* (28 Nov 1840) · *The Times* (12 July 1841) · *The Times* (31 Oct 1843) · *The Times* (4 Aug 1845)

Likenesses H. Thornburn, miniature, repro. in Hare, *Story of two noble lives*; priv. coll. · L. Waterford, drawings, repro. in Hare, *Story of two noble lives*

Beresford, Jack [*formerly* Jack Beresford Wiszniewski] (1899–1977), oarsman, was born at 36 St Mary's Grove,

Jack Beresford (1899–1977), by unknown photographer, 1923 [on shore, left]

Chiswick, Middlesex, on 1 January 1899, the elder son and eldest of the three children of Julius Beresford Wiszniewski (b. 1868) and his wife, Ethel Mary Wood. His father, Julius, was taken to Britain from Poland by his governess at the age of twelve, and became a furniture manufacturer. Jack was educated at Bedford School, served with the Artists' Rifles in 1917, was commissioned in the Liverpool Scottish regiment, and was wounded in the leg in northern France in 1918. At school his sporting ambitions were directed at rugby, but prescribed physiotherapy of rowing a dinghy at Fowey, Cornwall, turned him to rowing. He then entered his father's business, and began working at the furniture factory Beresford and Hicks, of Curtain Road, London.

Beresford had an outstanding record as an amateur sculler and as an oarsman with Thames Rowing Club. He won the Wingfield sculls from 1920 to 1926, which made him amateur champion of England, and he won the diamond sculls at Henley royal regatta four times during that period. He made his international mark by winning a silver medal at the Olympic games in Antwerp in 1920, when he lost the single sculling title by one second to an Irish bricklayer from Philadelphia, John Brendan (Jack) Kelly. The two men, who in later years became friends, encapsulated the controversy of the day concerning amateur status. Before competing in the Olympics, Kelly's entry for the diamond sculls was refused. Kelly claimed that he never received the rejection letter, and the story spread that he was snubbed because, as a manual worker, the Henley stewards considered him to be a professional. Beresford, however, epitomized their view of an amateur oarsman prevalent at the time. He was sporting, displayed loyalty to his club, dressed for dinner, was well heeled, and when not in a boat was an ambassador for a gentlemanly way of life. He was fit and hardy, and a colleague remembered him as never wearing a waistcoat or an overcoat, whatever the weather. The real reason for Kelly's ban, however, was that his club, Vesper of Philadelphia, had been barred by the stewards in 1905 for sending for

the Grand Challenge Cup an eight who had received payment and been supported by public subscription. Kelly's family bricklaying company built many of Philadelphia's twentieth-century public buildings. His son Jack grew up to win the diamond sculls in 1947 and 1949, and his daughter Grace became the princess of Monaco.

From the beginning of his rowing career, Beresford displayed the tactical brilliance of a winner, assessing his opponents' capabilities and pacing his training, and usually his racing, to do just enough to beat them, although he clearly possessed the killer instinct which motivates a winner and a breaker of records. 'He was very vicious in the boat,' said Eric Phelps, his coach for the Berlin Olympics. 'He would give a sickly smile to the man next to him. He never knew what it was to pack up' (private information, E. Phelps).

Beresford's successes proved his worth in every type of boat—eights, fours, pairs, and sculls—the more remarkable because his rowing weight was normally just over 11 stone and he stood about 5 feet 10 inches, light and short as oarsmen go. He won the Philadelphia gold cup for the world amateur title in 1924 and 1925, and was given the Helms award for sculling in Los Angeles in 1926. He won four further medals in the next four Olympic games: gold in the single scull in Paris in 1924, silver in the British eight in Amsterdam in 1928, gold in the coxless four in Los Angeles in 1932, and his most celebrated gold in the double sculls with Leslie (Dick) Southwood in Berlin in 1936.

The Berlin medal was Beresford's finest moment. The first five of the seven Olympic titles had gone to the Germans, under the watchful eye of their chancellor, Adolf Hitler, who was presenting the medals. Beresford and Southwood were coached by the English professional Eric Phelps, who had an intimate knowledge of the German team. He had a new, light boat built for his charges by Roly Sims in two and a half days (although it was lost in suspicious circumstances on the German rail system and turned up in Berlin only shortly before their first race) and surmised that the German crew, strong favourites, lacked the stamina to complete the 2000 metre course if put under severe pressure.

The British crew lost in the first heat to the Germans, who crossed into their lane, but qualified for the final by winning a *repêchage*, or 'second chance' round, in champion form. In the final, both crews jumped the start after observing that the starter, Victor de Bisschop, was using a megaphone so large that he could see nothing once he raised it to his lips. The British led for 500 metres, then Willy Kaidel and Joachim Pirsch went ahead. Opposite Phelps's vantage point at 1800 metres the crews were level. Southwood shouted when the Germans wandered from their lane, and then Pirsch stopped rowing. Phelps's men had rowed them down, just as he predicted. Beresford's German nickname, the Old Fox, was vindicated. It was 'the sweetest race I ever rowed in', he said. His record of rowing medals in five consecutive Olympics was unsurpassed until 2000, when Steven Redgrave of Britain won his fifth consecutive gold in Sydney.

Beresford crowned his outstanding record at Henley of two wins in the Grand Challenge Cup (1923, 1928), two in the goblets (1928–9), one in the stewards' (1932), and four in the diamonds (1920, 1924–6) by coming out of retirement with Southwood for a new event in 1939, the invitation centennial double sculls. Their famous victory in Berlin inspired the stewards to introduce this class of boat, and the Thames Rowing Club men, aged forty and thirty-six respectively, won the final in a dead heat with the Trieste double G. Scherli and E. Broschi. The Italians were European champions and much heavier and younger than Beresford and Southwood, and the Thames men realized that they would have no chance should the stewards order a re-row. As soon as they had returned their boat to its rack in the boat tent, Beresford went over to where the Italians were lying exhausted and, in a superb act of gamesmanship, cheerily congratulated them on a great race. 'Do it again in half an hour?' he is reputed to have said (private information, L. Southwood). The Italians declined profusely, and honours remained even.

In 1940 Beresford married Mary Elizabeth, daughter of Robert Craske Leaning, a medical doctor. They had one son and one daughter. This marriage was dissolved and in 1958 he married Stroma Jean Margaret, daughter of the Revd Andrew Morrison; they had two daughters.

Beresford lived at Shiplake and was often seen sculling at Henley, but always competed for Thames Rowing Club, the Putney club for which his father, 'Old Berry', had a distinguished record as an oarsman and coach, including winning a silver medal in the 1912 Olympic games and several Henley medals. Jack was captain of Thames in 1928–9, a vice-president from 1936 to 1977, and president from 1970 to 1977. He devoted considerable efforts to coaching and sports administration, and he carried the flag as leader of the British team in the opening ceremony of the Berlin games. He managed rowing teams on tour in South America in 1947, for the empire games in 1950, and the Olympic games of 1952. He was a rowing selector from 1938 to 1954.

Beresford was a member of the British Olympic Council from 1936 and a member of the organizing committee of the Olympic games in 1948, as well as helping to coach the double scullers Bert Bushnell and Richard Burnell, who won a gold medal. He was awarded the gold medal of the International Rowing Federation in 1947, and the Olympic diploma of merit in 1949, after helping to organize the games in London and Henley-on-Thames in 1948. He was elected a Henley steward in 1946 and was on the committee of management for many years. He was connected with the National Playing Fields Association, the Greater London and South-east Sports Council, and served on the council of the Amateur Rowing Association for thirty-five years. He was a keen swimmer and beagler with the Farley Hill beaglers, and played the umpire in the film *Half a Sixpence*. He was rowing correspondent of *The Field* from 1966 to 1971. He was a member of the court of the Furniture Makers' Guild and a liveryman of the Painters' and Stainers' Company. He was made a freeman of the City of London in 1952 and appointed CBE in 1960.

Beresford was courteous both to colleagues and to younger oarsmen, although his competitive edge in a boat occasionally spilled into arrogance when dealing with lesser mortals on the bank. When over seventy he competed in the 4½ mile scullers head of the river race. He was shaken in his last years by a tragic accident at the national schools regatta at Pangbourne in 1969. On that occasion, aged seventy, he dived into the Thames from his umpire's launch to rescue a boy who had caught a crab during a race and had been swept out of his boat. Beresford, an expert swimmer, reached the boy under the surface but had to struggle with the victim's desperate attempts to cling to him. The boy was eventually drowned. His failure to overcome the boy's plight and the tricky currents troubled him for the rest of his life. He died at his home, Highlands House, Shiplake, on 3 December 1977, the morning after presiding cheerfully over the Thames annual dinner.

CHRISTOPHER DODD

Sources personal knowledge (2004) · private information (2004) [family, L. Southwood, E. Phelps] · C. J. Dodd, *The story of world rowing* (1992) · G. G. H. Page, *Hear the boat sing: the history of Thames RC and Tideway rowing* (1991) · *British Rowing Almanack* (1978) · E. Halladay, *River and Rowing Museum hall of fame biography* (1997) · *Regatta* (1988) [articles by Olympic oarsmen] · *Regatta* (1992) [articles by Olympic oarsmen] · *Regatta* (1996) [articles by Olympic oarsmen] · b. cert. · *The Times* (5 Dec 1977)

Archives FILM BFI NFTVA, sports footage · Keller Library, Henley-on-Thames, River and Rowing Museum, 'Tales of gold'

Likenesses Central Press, photograph, 1923, repro. in J. Huntington-Whiteley, ed., *The book of British sporting heroes* (1998) · photograph, 1923, Hult. Arch. [*see illus.*]

Wealth at death £73,566: probate, 10 March 1978, *CGPLA Eng. & Wales*

Beresford, James (1764–1840), writer, second son of Richard Beresford of Upham, Hampshire, and his wife, Sarah, was born at Upham on 28 May 1764. He was educated at Charterhouse School and at Merton College, Oxford, where he matriculated in March 1783. He graduated BA in 1786, MA in 1798, and was elected a fellow of his college. He became rector of Kibworth Beauchamp, Leicestershire (a college living), in 1812, and died there on 29 September 1840. His chief work was *The miseries of human life, or, The last groans of Timothy Testy and Samuel Sensitive, with a few supplementary sighs from Mrs Testy* (2 vols., 1806–7), which went through several editions and was held for a time to be a minor classic in the genre, praised by Walter Scott. He also wrote some translations of poetry and religious books which attacked Calvinism among the clergy, and contributed to the *Looker-on*. [ANON.], *rev.* H. C. G. MATTHEW

Sources *GM*, 2nd ser., 15 (1841), 548 · Foster, *Alum. Oxon.* · Allibone, *Dict.*

Beresford, John (1738–1805), politician, was born in Dublin on 14 March 1738, the fifth but second surviving son of Marcus Beresford, first earl of Tyrone (1694–1763), politician, and Lady Katherine Power (1701–1769), daughter and heir of James Power, third earl of Tyrone and, after 1767, Baroness de la Poer in her own right. Both his parents were members of the Irish protestant élite, their marriage

John Beresford (1738–1805), by Charles Howard Hodges, pubd 1790 (after Gilbert Stuart)

uniting the Beresford interest arising from personal and stewarded property in counties Kildare, Kilkenny, and Londonderry with the older and more substantial Power property in co. Waterford to create one of the most powerful landed interests in Ireland. Beresford was educated at Kilkenny School and at Trinity College, Dublin, graduating BA in 1758. In 1756 he had been admitted to Lincoln's Inn and he was called to the Irish bar in 1760, but he never practised. In November 1760 he married his first wife, Annette Constantia de Ligondes (d. 1770), daughter of the comte de Ligondes of Auvergne; they had four sons and five daughters. It was at this time that he purchased a house near Swords, co. Dublin, naming it Abbeville after his wife's birthplace in France. Four years after her death on 26 October 1770 he married on 4 June 1774 Barbara, daughter of Sir William Montgomery, first baronet, of Magbie Hill, Peeblesshire, a celebrated beauty of the day, immortalized in Sir Joshua Reynolds's *Graces*. This marriage produced three sons and five daughters, during which time Abbeville was extensively remodelled by James Gandon.

Beresford succeeded his elder brother as MP for co. Waterford at the general election in 1761, and he held the seat until his death in 1805. His political horizon, however, extended well beyond the confines of the county, of which he was made a deputy governor in 1763, the same year as his father's death. Helped on his way by Lord Townshend's search when lord lieutenant (1767–72) for supporters to replace the Ponsonby 'connection', Beresford quickly established serving the British government's interest in Ireland as the best course, both for himself and

his family and for the protestant élite as a whole. This led to a series of appointments: to the Irish privy council in 1768; as a commissioner of the revenue in place of John Ponsonby in 1770, supplemented in 1772 with the sinecure of taster of wines in the port of Dublin; and as first commissioner of the revenue in 1780.

By the time the Rockingham whigs took office in February 1782 Beresford had established himself as one of the most influential and powerful politicians in Ireland with an interest equal to that of the Ponsonbys. He was a highly effective administrator at the revenue and had set in train a series of reforms of revenue collection and of improvements in Dublin's architecture and street communication. He had also acquired sufficient weight, demonstrated by his political 'connection' of some twenty votes in the Irish Commons, to become a member of the informal Irish 'cabinet' of senior office-holders that traditionally advised the lord lieutenant. Finally the combination of his support of the British interest in Ireland, his administrative skill, and some carefully cultivated friendships with men such as John Robinson and William Eden had earned him the admiration of English politicians. In 1780, for example, following Beresford's visit to London to discuss the Irish legislation consequent upon the government's free trade measures, Lord North suggested, unsuccessfully, that Beresford be appointed chief secretary.

Although Beresford was treated coldly by the duke of Portland, Rockingham's lord lieutenant and a relative of the Ponsonbys, his political influence grew once Pitt had become prime minister. Proof of this was his appointment to the British privy council on 6 September 1786, which was comparatively rare for an Irishman. The principal reason for this was a personal friendship with the prime minister that had taken root when Beresford was in London between December 1784 and the summer of 1785 to discuss a new commercial relationship between the two countries; this friendship had matured subsequently, partly because Beresford was able to see both the British and the Irish points of view in the difficult conditions that prevailed after the establishment of the new Irish constitution in 1782. Indeed William Orde, a chief secretary at this time, once referred to Beresford's 'Anglicism' (Kelly, 86). The fact that Pitt called upon Beresford to persuade William Eden to negotiate the Anglo-French commercial treaty and that Lord Townshend asked him to use his influence with the prime minister to obtain a step in the peerage in 1787—requests that were successful on both counts—is ample evidence of the good relations between the two men.

Another reason for Beresford's growing influence was the longevity of his tenure of the revenue post, a position strengthened by his appointment as a commissioner of the Irish treasury in December 1793, which made him not only a permanent member of the Irish 'cabinet' but also a stronger magnet to aspiring politicians. However, the combination of his friendship with Pitt and his entrenched position at the revenue also led to charges of excessive power, criticism focusing on his brother William's progress in the Church of Ireland and the posts occupied by two of his sons. Beresford was undoubtedly sensitive to such accusations and although there is no doubt that revenue patronage was useful to him politically, he took every opportunity to justify his own conduct. He had done this in June 1782 in response to charges by George Ponsonby, stating that by comparison with the revenue regime of the latter's father, he had not created offices for political purposes, and he went out of his way in 1784 and 1785 to make public statements criticizing the misuse of revenue patronage. This formed the backdrop to the most dramatic event in Beresford's career: his dismissal from office by Earl Fitzwilliam, the lord lieutenant appointed by Pitt following the coalition with the Portland whigs in July 1794. Fitzwilliam's case, which drew on Portland's view, formed when he had been lord lieutenant in 1782, and that of Billy Ponsonby, the leader of the Irish whigs, was that Beresford's command of revenue patronage meant that he was 'filling a situation greater than that of the Lord-Lieutenant himself' and was considered to be 'King of Ireland' (*Correspondence*, 2.51, 82). To leave Beresford in office, Fitzwilliam said, would antagonize the whigs and make it impossible to win them over in support of Pitt's reconstructed government. Beresford was therefore notified that he would be dismissed from the revenue but could retain the salary of £2000 in recognition of his 'long and laborious' services (ibid., 58). The dismissal, however, never took practical effect. Beresford, supported by English politicians familiar with Irish affairs, made a personal appeal to Pitt for 'common justice' (ibid., 51). The prime minister responded by deciding that the dismissal broke the terms of an agreement made with Fitzwilliam on his appointment and that it presaged the triumph of the Ponsonbys and their whig friends. Fitzwilliam was therefore dismissed in March 1795 for this and other *faux pas* and Beresford was reinstated. Moreover, the reversal of fortunes did not end there: in the same month letters from Fitzwilliam to Lord Carlisle were made public in which Fitzwilliam referred to Beresford's 'mal-administration' and 'much imputed' corruption (ibid., 82). Beresford demanded a disavowal or explanation and when these were refused he challenged Fitzwilliam to a duel. This almost took place in London on Monday 29 June 1795, but was stopped at the very last moment by the intervention of a magistrate.

Beresford thus resumed his former positions in the revenue and the Irish cabinet, but was soon to confront the crisis in Irish politics engendered, in part at least, by the fact that Fitzwilliam's dismissal seemed to dash all hopes of further Catholic relief. As a loyal servant of government, he had supported concessions in 1778 and had probably given a silent support to the 1793 bill giving Catholics the vote, even though he was fully aware of the threat that the last measure posed to the protestant élite; indeed Beresford seems to have become an advocate of a reform of parliament that would increase the representation of that élite. There is also some evidence that he and another member of the Irish cabinet, Lord Fitzgibbon, played a part in persuading George III in 1795 that his consenting to Catholic relief would infringe his coronation oath. The

Irish rising of 1798 put thoughts about how best to preserve the protestant interest into a different context. Beresford, who served on the secret committee of the Irish House of Commons that investigated the rising, concluded with Pitt that a union was the only answer to a problem that he himself attributed, in part at least, to years of British mismanagement. Indeed, although he was by now plagued by gout, he played a notable part in shaping the union's commercial provisions in London and had an anonymous pamphlet on the subject published by the Irish government and distributed among ministers. Castlereagh believed that his 'important services on this most important of all measures' was a fitting climax to his contribution to Irish administration (*Correspondence*, 2.251–2).

Beresford took his seat in the imperial parliament at the age of sixty-two, in declining health, but he nevertheless remained a politician of consequence. He was still commissioner of the revenue and in February 1802 became a member of the Board of Trade. It was in these capacities that he advised the Addington government on the financial aspects of the union, fearing the worst if solely 'English ideas' were applied to them (*Correspondence*, 2.264). He was also the principal figure in the second marquess of Waterford's not insignificant group of five MPs and he was recommended to the government by the king, who believed that he and Beresford were of one mind in their opposition to Catholic relief. Despite these advantages Beresford was unsure of what role he should play in the new state of affairs. Initially he considered retiring from parliament, but in November 1801, following an autumn at Walworth, his seat in co. Londonderry, he chose instead to retire from the revenue with a pension of £2000. He subsequently bought a house in Bruton Street, London, to make parliamentary attendance easier. From the general election of 1802 until the fall of Addington in April 1804, however, Beresford appears to have tried to recapture his old role in Dublin rather than embarking on a new one in London. He was therefore 'an active and efficient member' of the privy council in Ireland, but despite the lord lieutenant's having unexpectedly appointed Beresford's son to the bishopric of Kilmore, he took little part in debate at Westminster (Aspinall, 188). Such was his behind-the-scenes activity that William Wickham, on leaving his post as chief secretary in January 1804, went out of his way to express 'sincere thanks for the very kind and friendly advice and assistance' that he had received from him (*Correspondence*, 2.270).

Beresford's preference for Dublin rather than London may have been due to misgivings about Addington's Irish policy and his loyalty to Pitt. Pitt's decision to oppose the government in the spring of 1804, however, and his personal request for support from Beresford led to a change of direction. He therefore responded to the call and rallied the Beresford MPs (as well as several others) to play their part in replacing Addington with Pitt. Furthermore the combination of the change of government with the appointment of John Foster—his former colleague in the Irish cabinet—to the chancellorship of the Irish exchequer, and the growing misgivings about direct rule, gave Beresford fresh ambitions. He therefore let it be known in 1804 and again in June 1805 that he would accept the offer of the more powerful post of chief secretary. The offer, however, was never made: partly because of his infirmity and partly because it was thought, in the words of the lord lieutenant, Lord Hardwicke, that 'his appointment would revive all the old clamour about the influence of his family; and it would look too much like a recurrence to the old system before the union' (Aspinall, 188). His health was certainly in decline and, having loyally supported Pitt in the Melville case and probably voted against Catholic relief in the 1805 session, he died at Walworth on 5 November 1805.

Assessments of Beresford have been influenced strongly by judgements such as that of Lord Hardwicke and those of Fitzwilliam and Portland before him, as well as by the contemporary Catholic view that the Beresfords as a whole represented the worst aspects of a protestant ascendancy. It was the last judgement that inspired Daniel O'Connell to lead the successful campaign in 1826 to oust a Beresford from the co. Waterford seat for the first time since 1757. In Beresford's case, however, the view that he was the chief beneficiary of a corrupt political system is unfair. His family certainly benefited from his influence, but Billy Ponsonby is alleged to have admitted that the case he and the deluded Fitzwilliam brought against Beresford in 1795 was political rather than moral, and that he knew Beresford to be 'a very honourable man and a good officer' (Kavanaugh, 303). Moreover, although two select committees that subsequently enquired into the management of the revenue board differed on whether the growth in the costs of collection, and therefore the reserves of patronage, were commensurate with the increase in revenue, neither found Beresford guilty of corruption. He is therefore best described as an efficient, effective, but not uncritical servant of British government in Ireland, who, while presiding over a considerable increase in the size of the revenue, supported his own interests to a no greater or lesser degree than was customary. It was in that capacity that he earned the enmity of those whose primary loyalty was to the English whigs, such as the Ponsonbys, and of those who felt that the protestant élite was best defended either by a strengthened ascendancy or by political equality for Catholics. As Dr Malcomson puts it: 'At bottom, he simply enjoyed solving problems, working hard, and reaping the rewards of his labours. Matters personal to himself were the only things he felt strongly about' (Malcomson, 359).   P. J. JUPP

Sources BL, Eden MSS · BL, Althorp MSS · BL, Hardwicke MSS · BL, Liverpool MSS · Keele University, Sneyd MSS · CKS, Camden papers · PRO NIre., Macartney MSS · PRO, Chatham MSS · PRO, Granville MSS · A. Aspinall, 'Beresford, John', HoP, *Commons, 1790–1820*, 3.187–8 · T. Bartlett, *Macartney in Ireland, 1768–72: a calendar of the chief secretaryship papers of Sir George Macartney* (1978) · *The correspondence of the Right Hon. John Beresford, illustrative of the last thirty years of the Irish parliament*, ed. W. Beresford, 2 vols. (1854) · D. Dickson, *New Foundations: Ireland, 1660–1800* (1987) · A. C. Kavanaugh, *John Fitzgibbon, earl of Clare* (1997) · J. Kelly, *Prelude to Union: Anglo-Irish politics in the 1780s* (1992) · A. P. W. Malcomson, *John Foster: the politics of the Anglo-Irish ascendancy* (1978) · T. W. Moody and others, eds., *A new history of Ireland*, 4: *Eighteenth-century Ireland, 1691–1800* (1986) · *DNB* · GEC, *Peerage*

Archives BL, corresp. with Lord Auckland, Add. MSS 34418–34460, *passim* · BL, corresp. with earl of Liverpool, Add. MSS 38210–38472, *passim* · Keele University Library, letters to William Eden · PRO, letters to William Pitt, PRO 30/8 · PRO NIre., corresp. with Lord Castlereagh · PRO NIre., corresp. with Sir Hugh Hill and G. F. Hill

Likenesses C. H. Hodges, mezzotint, pubd 1790 (after G. C. Stuart), BM, NPG [*see illus.*] · G. C. Stuart, oils, NG Ire. · F. Wheatley, group portrait, oils (*The Irish House of Commons, 1780*), Leeds City Art Galleries, Lotherton Hall, West Yorkshire · group portrait, oils, Curraghmore House, co. Wexford

Beresford, John Davys (1873–1947), novelist and essayist, was born on 7 March 1873 at the rectory, Castor, Northamptonshire, to an evangelically minded couple, the Revd John James Beresford (1822–1897), a Church of England clergyman, and his wife, Adelaide Elizabeth Morgan (b. 1836), of Welsh extraction. J. D., as he was known, was doted on by his mother, especially after, owing to the neglect of a nurse, he suffered the trauma of infantile paralysis at three and a half and was left permanently lame. His rather ascetic father viewed this affliction of his second son as an embarrassment and consequently neglected J. D.'s education, which he himself recalled as 'a very haphazard affair'. He did attend various schools, including Oundle in 1886 and notably the Peterborough King's School in 1887–9, but had no particular ambitions.

At sixteen Beresford lackadaisically accepted his father's suggestion that he become an architect, and for eight years he slaved as a draughtsman in London. At twenty-one he experienced a 'conversion' from religious orthodoxy to independent thinking and evolutionism. By 1901 he was making 'spasmodic efforts to write short stories'; another turning point occurred in 1903 when he read *Human Personality and its Survival of Bodily Death* (1903), a book by the psychical researcher F. W. H. Myers that sparked Beresford's fascination with abnormal psychology and led him to adopt permanently an idealist position. During that year he also married Linda Lawrence, *née* Brown (1872–1917), a former actress, though the marriage lasted only until about 1907 owing to his wife's infidelity and the couple's financial distress. However, in 1907 his fortunes improved when he began a long career as a reviewer, initially with the *Westminster Gazette* and later with the *Manchester Guardian*. He also began to publish idealistic short stories.

Beresford first achieved critical acclaim in 1911 with the publication of two novels indicative of two trends in his novel writing. *The Early History of Jacob Stahl* is an autobiographical *Bildungsroman* that deepens realism in the manner of Wells and Bennett by attending to unconscious motivation and the spiritual quest of the protagonist. The reviewers lauded it, along with the two other volumes, *A Candidate for Truth* (1912) and *The Invisible Event* (1915), comprising a trilogy, as a psychological masterpiece, and this acclaim placed him in the forefront of modern novelists. Beresford penned another thirty-seven novels in this vein of realism, notably *The House in Demetrius Road* (1914), *The Monkey Puzzle* (1925), *Seven, Bobsworth* (1930), and *Cleo* (1937).

After about 1924 these novels became increasingly concerned with the mystical awakenings of his protagonists.

Beresford's other novel of 1911, *The Hampdenshire Wonder*, is a speculative narrative, the first novel to consider seriously the consequences of an individual's reaching a higher evolutionary stage than his contemporaries. It earned the praise of the likes of G. B. Shaw and has since become an influential classic of scientific romance. Beresford gave play to this speculative aspect of his vision sporadically during his career, most notably in *Revolution* (1921), *What Dreams May Come* (1941), and *The Riddle of the Tower* (1944), but also in brief whimsical short stories, especially those collected in *Nineteen Impressions* (1918) and *Signs and Wonders* (1921).

Beresford's early successes drew him from the fringe into neo-Georgian literary circles, and he formed friendships with other writers including H. G. Wells, Dorothy Richardson, Katherine Mansfield, and especially Walter de la Mare. In May 1913 he married Beatrice Evelyn (Trissie) Roskams (1880–1975), boarding-house keeper, with whom he had four children, two of whom, Marcus (pseudonym Marc Brandel) and Elisabeth, became professional writers. From 1923 to 1927 the family sojourned in France, and in 1931 they settled in Brighton. By this time Beresford's marriage had begun to deteriorate, partly because of his increasing interest in unorthodox spiritual beliefs such as faith-healing, an interest not shared by his conventionally religious wife. In 1937 he met Esmé Wynne-Tyson, a writer on a similar spiritual quest, and in 1939 they began a fruitful collaboration, eventually totalling eleven books. In that year Beresford separated from his wife and he and Wynne-Tyson maintained a platonic relationship while living in a series of vegetarian guest houses. At one of these, Kildare, in Sydney Gardens, Bath, he suffered a stroke, and he died there in his sleep a week later, on 2 February 1947.

Since then Beresford has been almost completely neglected, but at the height of his fame in the mid-twenties he was considered by Frank Swinnerton and others as one of the most reflective lights, along with E. M. Forster, of the younger generation of Georgian realists, and the 'intellectual' among them. However, his goal to illustrate in fiction his fundamental principles, such as the spiritual rather than material nature of the universe, occasionally caused him to be overly didactic and practically guaranteed that he would never be a popular writer. This goal prompted him to eschew modernist experimentation, and that position lost him critical acclaim in the latter part of his career.

Beresford deserves attention for several reasons. He was one of the first and most knowledgeable of English novelists to explore in his fiction the 'new' dynamic psychologies of F. W. H. Myers, Henri Bergson, Freud, and Jung. His *God's Counterpoint* (1918) represents an early foray into the explicitly psychoanalytic novel. In several critical essays he articulated more clearly than his contemporaries the strengths and limitations of the use of the new psychology in fiction. He dealt equally perceptively with a number of other unpopular advanced ideas, some of which have since gained acceptability, including pacifism, vegetarianism, and faith-healing. His speculative novels remain particularly relevant because of their depiction of societies based on co-operative principles and their espousal of pacifism.

Beresford's life was often unsettled: he suffered from a sense of dividedness, and he was frequently harried by financial anxiety. Yet those who knew him commented most often on his gentleness, tolerance, compassion, kindness, and loyalty to friends, qualities buoyed by a wry sense of humour. He was intensely self-conscious, a quality he believed hampered his writing, despite his handsome appearance: he stood a full 6 feet tall, had an athletic physique, a face striking for its suggestion of deep contemplation, and piercing blue eyes.

GEORGE MALCOLM JOHNSON

Sources J. D. Beresford, 'Memories and reflections', 1947, priv. coll. · G. M. Johnson, *J. D. Beresford* (1998) · H. E. Gerber, 'J. D. Beresford: a study of his works and philosophy', diss., University of Pennsylvania, 1952 · B. Stableford, *Scientific romance in Britain, 1890–1950* (1985) · H. E. Gerber, 'J. D. Beresford: a bibliography', *Bulletin of Bibliography*, 21 (1956), 201–4 · A. Chevalley, 'J. D. Beresford', *The modern English novel*, trans. B. R. Redman (New York, 1925); repr. (1973) · F. Swinnerton, 'Oliver Onions and J. D. Beresford', *The Georgian literary scene: a panorama* (1935); rev. edn (1969) · R. Hoops, *Der Einfluss der Psychoanalyse auf die englische Literatur* (Heidelberg, 1934) · R. Brimley Johnson, 'J. D. Beresford', *Some contemporary novelists (men)* (1922); repr. (1970) · R. H. Ward, 'J. D. Beresford: artist in living', *Aryan Path*, 18 (1947), 212–14 · A. St J. Adcock, 'John Davys Beresford', *Gods of modern Grub Street* (1923) · S. J. Kunitz and H. Haycraft, eds., *Twentieth century authors: a biographical dictionary of modern literature* (1942) · private information (2004) [E. Beresford]

Archives Hunt. L., letters · NRA, priv. coll. · NYPL | BL, corresp. with Society of Authors, Add. MS 56669 · BL, letters to Jacques Brunius, Add. MS 61893 · Bodl. Oxf., letters to John Lane · NL Wales, letters to John Cowper Powys · U. Reading L., letters to R. L. Mégroz

Likenesses H. Wilson, drawing, 1928, repro. in *The Bookman*, Christmas supplement (1928) · R. Nelson, caricature, 1929, repro. in *The Bookman* (April 1929), 27 · Bassano, two photographs, 1932–9, NPG · C. Lowe, drawing, 1933, repro. in *The Bookman* (April 1933) · H. Coster, photographs, 1934, NPG · E. D. Hoppé, photograph, NPG · photographs, priv. coll.

Wealth at death £700: Esmé Wynne-Tyson, unpublished letter to Helmut Gerber, 11 Jan 1951, priv. coll.

Beresford, Lord John George de la Poer (1773–1862), Church of Ireland archbishop of Armagh, was a younger son of George de la Poer Beresford, second earl of Tyrone and first marquess of Waterford (1735–1800), and his wife, Elizabeth *née* Monck (c.1741–1816). He was born at Tyrone House, Dublin, on 22 November 1773, and was educated at Eton College and at Christ Church, Oxford, where he graduated BA on 30 April 1793, MA on 17 March 1796, and DD by diploma on 11 March 1805, on succeeding to the bishopric of Cork. He was ordained deacon on 2 April 1795 and priest on 17 December 1797. His first preferment was to the family rectories of Clonegam and Newtownlennan in the diocese of Lismore. He was presented on 23 December 1799 to the deanery of the cathedral church of St Macartan's, Clogher, and in 1801 became rector of Termonmaguirk in the diocese of Armagh. He was appointed on 20 February 1805 to the bishopric of Cork and Ross, from which he was translated to the see of Raphoe on 10 August

Lord John George de la Poer Beresford (1773–1862), by Sir Thomas Lawrence, c.1829

1807, and to that of Clogher on 25 September 1819. On 21 April 1820 he was created archbishop of Dublin, and was enthroned at Christ Church on 6 May following. On 23 May he was appointed a privy councillor in Ireland, and was translated to the archbishopric of Armagh and the primacy of all Ireland on 17 June 1822. On the death of the bishop of Clogher in 1850 that diocese was united to Armagh under the terms of the Church Temporalities Act (1833), a contentious statute whose opponents were highly critical of Beresford's conciliatory approach to government.

In 1829 Beresford became vice-chancellor of the University of Dublin, and continued in that office until his election to the chancellorship in 1851. He made munificent gifts to the library, erected a campanile in the centre of Front Square, Trinity College, Dublin, in 1853, at a cost of £3000, and presented £1000 that year towards founding a chair of ecclesiastical history, and a further £1000 in 1861 towards augmenting its income. He also gave more than £6000 to the college of St Columba, near Stackallan, co. Meath, which was opened in 1844 to furnish the gentry of Ireland with a school 'on the model of Eton'. The archbishop was for several years visitor and patron of St Columba's, with which he severed his official connection on 6 December 1853 owing to a disagreement with the warden, whose Tractarian views (in matters scarcely connected with St Columba's) Beresford regarded as extreme.

On Thursday 29 March 1855 Beresford celebrated his episcopal jubilee at the palace of Armagh, receiving an address from the clergy drawn up by Archbishop Richard Whately of Dublin. Beresford and Whately differed both in temperament and on some major matters of policy, the primate tending to look on the archbishop 'as the eighteenth upon the nineteenth century'. Beresford gave generous support to the Church Education Society, the Church of Ireland's riposte to the state national schools (which Whately ardently supported), though in time he came to see the latter as better than nothing, a perceived shift of allegiance that earned him some abuse. Beresford also opposed (successfully) Whately's plan for a school of divinity for clergy in Dublin that would have been only loosely associated with the university.

Beresford restored the cathedral of Armagh at an expense of nearly £30,000, and maintained the choral services by his own generosity. He gave liberally to clergy salaries, and during the 'tithe war' of the 1830s he intervened to save many of the clergy and their families from starvation. He was a Conservative in politics, and opposed the Roman Catholic Relief Bill of 1829, against which he seconded the motion of the archbishop of Canterbury in the House of Lords, arguing that it would 'transfer from Protestants to Roman Catholics the ascendancy in Ireland'. His speech on that occasion, one of his very few publications, was printed in 1829.

Beresford died, unmarried, on 18 July 1862 at Woburn, near Donaghadee, co. Down, the home of George Dunbar, who had married one of his nieces. His remains were taken to Armagh and buried on 30 July in the crypt of the cathedral he had restored. His funeral was attended by the Roman Catholic primate, Joseph Dixon, and Henry Cooke, the moderator of the general assembly of the Presbyterian church.   ARTHUR H. GRANT, *rev.* KENNETH MILNE

Sources H. Cotton, *Fasti ecclesiae Hibernicae*, 6 vols. (1845–78) · [J. H. Todd], ed., *A catalogue of graduates who have proceeded to degrees in the University of Dublin, from the earliest recorded commencements to … December 16, 1868* (1869) · Foster, *Alum. Oxon.* · W. A. Phillips, ed., *History of the Church of Ireland*, 3 vols. (1933–4) · R. B. McDowell, *The Church of Ireland, 1869–1969* (1975) · D. H. Akenson, *The Irish education experiment: the national system of education in the nineteenth century* (1970) · R. B. McDowell and D. A. Webb, *Trinity College, Dublin, 1592–1952: an academic history* (1982) · *Parliamentary Debates*, new ser., 21 (2 April 1829), col. 74 · D. Bowen, 'Lord John George Beresford', *New Divinity: a Church of Ireland Journal*, 3/1 (summer 1972), 93–102 · *Irish Ecclesiastical Gazette* (15 Aug 1862) · *Irish Ecclesiastical Gazette* (15 Nov 1862) · G. K. White, *A history of St Columba's College, 1843–1974* (1980) · *Annual Register* (1862)

Archives Armagh Public Library, primatial corresp. · Down and Connor and Dromore Diocesan Library, Kilkenny, corresp. relating to Down, Connor, and Dromore dioceses · NRA, priv. coll., corresp. relating to St Columba's College · NRA, priv. coll., ecclesiastical corresp. and papers · PRO NIre., corresp. and papers; corresp. and papers relating to his estates; papers relating to the Belfast Academical Institution · Representative Church Body Library, Dublin, corresp.; papers relating to clerical relief, patronage, tithes, etc. · St Canice's Cathedral Library, corresp. and papers relating to Ossory, Ferns, and Leighlin diocese · TCD, corresp. and papers relating to Trinity College Dublin and educational affairs | BL, corresp. with Sir Robert Peel, Add. MSS 40259–40605 · Exeter Cathedral Library, letters to Henry Phillpotts · LPL, letters to the bishop of Meath · Lpool RO, letters to fourteenth earl of Derby · PRO NIre., corresp. with Richard Mant · TCD, letters to J. H. Todd · U. Southampton L., letters to duke of Wellington

Likenesses E. U. Eddis, oils, 1822, Synod Hall, Armagh · T. Lawrence, portrait, c.1829, priv. coll. [see illus.] · C. Turner, mezzotint, pubd 1841 (after T. Lawrence), BM · G. S. Sandes, engraving, July 1857 (after S. C. Smith), Christ Church, Dublin · J. Doyle, chalk drawing, BM · J. Kirkwood, etching, NPG · S. C. Smith, oils, TCD · Walker, photograph, NPG · engraving (after T. Lawrence), Synod Hall, Armagh · wood-engraving, NPG; repro. in *ILN* (2 Aug 1862), 128

Wealth at death under £70,000: probate, 4 Dec 1862, *CGPLA Ire.*

Beresford, Sir John Poo, first baronet (1766–1844), naval officer and politician, was an illegitimate son of George de la Poer Beresford, earl of Tyrone and afterwards first marquess of Waterford, and brother of William Carr *Beresford, Viscount Beresford. He was educated at Catterick Bridge, Yorkshire. He entered the navy in 1782 on board the *Alexander*, under the protection of Lord Longford. Having served his full time, principally on the Newfoundland and West India stations, he was made lieutenant on 4 November 1790. He joined the frigate *Lapwing* in the Mediterranean, and while in her was specially employed on shore at Genoa and Turin, arranging the evacuation of British residents and running considerable risk in the revolutionary excitement, from which he escaped disguised as a peasant.

In 1794 Beresford was appointed to the *Resolution* (74 guns), bearing the flag of Rear-Admiral Murray, the commander-in-chief on the North American station, by whom, in November 1794, he was promoted to the command of the sloop *Lynx*. His successful protection of a convoy, a few weeks later, against two French ships of superior force, the energy and skill he displayed in rescuing the frigate *Thetis*, which had gone ashore, and the capture of a powerful French privateer, all within the next three months, won for him from the admiral an appointment to the frigate *Hussar* as acting captain, and he was sent, under the immediate orders of Captain Cochrane of the *Thetis*, to destroy some French store ships in Hampton Roads. On 17 May 1795 they met the store ships outside the Capes; there were five of them, all heavily armed, though still no match for the frigates. After a smart action, two of them were captured, the *Prévoyante* and the *Raison*, both nominally frigates, but under-gunned. None the less, the action was considered highly creditable, and Murray moved Beresford to the *Prévoyante*; but the Admiralty considered her too large for a first command, and appointed him to the *Raison*.

In the following year, on 25 August 1796, while carrying £200,000 in specie from Boston to Halifax, Beresford fell in with the *Vengeance*, a large French frigate upgunned to 52 18-pounders; the *Raison* was a 9-pounder frigate with 30 guns, including carronades. A running fight began. The *Vengeance*, damaged, dropped astern, and a lucky fog enabled the *Raison* to escape. In March 1797 the *Raison* captured a large and rich Spanish ship near the Bahamas, and drove another on shore; during the year she made several other prizes, and towards the end of it was sent home with a convoy, and was paid off.

Early in 1798 Beresford was again sent to the West Indies, in command of the frigate *Unité* in which, or afterwards in the *Diana*, he assisted in the capture of Surinam, St Martin, St Bartholomew, St Thomas, St John, Santa Cruz, and all the Swedish and Danish colonies, and returned home in charge of a convoy of some 200 vessels; the preliminaries of peace were signed shortly afterwards, and the *Diana* was paid off. On the renewal of the war in 1803 he was appointed to the frigate *Virginie*, which he commanded in the North Sea for more than a year. During this time constant cruising in bad weather rendered the *Virginie* no longer seaworthy, and Beresford was ordered to North America, to take command of the frigate *Cambrian*. In her he captured several privateers, and when, following the death of Sir Andrew Mitchell, on 26 February 1806, he had to act as senior officer of the station, his measures won the praise of the Halifax merchants.

In 1808 Beresford commanded the *Theseus* (74 guns), first in the channel, and afterwards, under Sir Richard King, off Ferrol, where the blockading squadron kept at sea for eight consecutive months. Beresford was then detached, in command of three ships of the line, to maintain the blockade of Lorient, and although driven off for a few hours on 21 February 1809 by the squadron under Willaumez, which had escaped from Brest, he continued to do this until March, when he joined the fleet under the command of Lord Gambier, and served with it during the operations in Basque roads. Early in 1810 the *Theseus* was paid off, and Beresford was appointed to the *Poitiers*, in which he was stationed for several months off Brest, as senior officer; he was afterwards sent to Lisbon, acting during the rest of the year in co-operation with the army under Wellington. In 1811 he was employed in the North Sea, in the Texel blockade, and in 1812, on the outbreak of the war with the United States, he was sent over to the coast of America. The service there, arduous and harassing, without much opportunity for distinction, lasted nearly two years, and during the second year he was authorized to bear a broad pennant as commodore. He was knighted in 1812.

Early in 1814 Beresford was appointed to the yacht *Royal Sovereign*, and on 24 April carried Louis XVIII to Calais. In May 1814 he was created a baronet, and attained the rank of rear-admiral on 4 June. In the following September he hoisted his flag in the *Duncan*, and was sent to Rio de Janeiro to carry home the prince regent of Portugal. The prince, however, decided not to return to Lisbon then, and Beresford, after receiving from him the order of the Tower and Sword, returned to England. In August 1819 he was made a KCB. From 1820 to 1823 he commanded at Leith and on the coast of Scotland, and on his leaving he was presented with the freedom of the city of Edinburgh. From 1830 to 1833 he commanded at the Nore. He became a vice-admiral on 27 May 1825, admiral on 28 June 1838, and in 1836 was created GCH.

From 1809 to 1812 and from 1814 to 1823 Beresford was tory MP for the marquess of Waterford's pocket borough, Coleraine, criticizing slave emancipation and opposing Roman Catholic relief. From 1823 to 1826 he represented Berwick, and from 1826 to 1832 Northallerton; re-elected for Coleraine in 1832, he was unseated on petition; in 1835 he was elected for Chatham, having served as a junior lord of the Admiralty between December 1834 and April 1835 in the brief administration of his friend, Sir Robert Peel. After this he lived in comparative retirement at his seat at Bedale in Yorkshire, where he died, after a long illness, on 2 October 1844.

Beresford married three times. On 22 June 1809 he married Mary (d. 1 July 1813), daughter of Captain Anthony James Pye Molloy RN; they had one son. On 17 August 1815 he married Harriet Elizabeth (d. 28 Feb 1825), daughter of Henry Peirse, of Bedale, Yorkshire; they had two sons and four daughters. On 26 May 1836 he married Amelia, daughter of James Baillie and widow of Samuel Peach; they had no children. Beresford had a highly successful career afloat, and was noted, in later life, for his good humour, generosity, and ready wit.

J. K. LAUGHTON, rev. ANDREW LAMBERT

Sources J. H. Briggs, *Naval administrations, 1827 to 1892: the experience of 65 years*, ed. Lady Briggs (1897) · D. Syrett and R. L. DiNardo, *The commissioned sea officers of the Royal Navy, 1660–1815*, rev. edn, Occasional Publications of the Navy RS, 1 (1994) · Burke, *Peerage* · *GM*, 2nd ser., 22 (1844), 646–8 · HoP, *Commons* · private information (1885)
Archives N. Yorks. CRO, corresp. and papers
Likenesses T. Hodgetts, mezzotint, pubd 1828 (after W. Beechey), BM, NPG · G. Hayter, group portrait, oils (*The House of Commons, 1883*), NPG

Beresford [*née* Stuart], **Louisa Anne**, **marchioness of Waterford** (**1818–1891**), watercolour painter and philanthropist, was born on 14 April 1818 at the Hôtel Charost, Faubourg St Honoré, Paris, the second daughter of Sir Charles *Stuart, later Baron Stuart de Rothesay (1779–1845), diplomatist. Her paternal grandfather was General Sir Charles *Stuart and her mother was Lady Elizabeth Margaret Yorke (1789–1867), the third daughter of Philip *Yorke, third earl of Hardwicke. Apart from a four-year interval (1824–8) when the family lived on their estate at Highcliffe, near Christchurch, Hampshire, her childhood, until 1830, was spent in Paris where her father occupied the position of British ambassador to the court of France. Both she and her elder sister, Charlotte *Canning (1817–1861), showed artistic talent. Louisa Stuart was taught to copy heads in chalk after French pictures and she drew from prints of the human figure. At the age of ten she copied a portrait by Joshua Reynolds with an artist called Shepherdson. The sisters, who were educated at home, also received lessons in landscape from a Mr Page.

In 1830 the family returned to England. After Charlotte's marriage to Charles Canning in 1835 and Louisa's presentation at court in the same year (when her beauty was widely acclaimed), she was taken on a tour to Rome and Naples (1836–7) where she copied enthusiastically in galleries. Her own marriage, to Henry de la Poer *Beresford, third marquess of Waterford (1811–1859), took place on 8 June 1842 at the Royal Chapel at Whitehall, London. To many the match seemed incongruous. Louisa Stuart was cultured, pious, and shy, while the marquess had a reputation for practical joking, appearances in police courts, and intrepidity on the hunting-field and racecourse. (They had met at Lord Eglinton's tournament in 1839, where Waterford was a principal knight.) Despite Waterford's 'rough

Louisa Anne Beresford, marchioness of Waterford (1818–1891), by Sir Francis Grant, 1842

manners' as Charlotte Canning described them (Surtees, *Canning*, 54), he was devoted to his wife and always encouraged her artistic work. Lady Waterford's married life, which was happy but childless, was spent at Curraghmore House, on her husband's large estate in co. Waterford, southern Ireland. Following his tragic death from a riding accident in 1859, she then moved to Ford Castle on his estate in Northumberland. In 1867, when her mother died, she inherited Highcliffe also and thenceforth divided her time between the two properties.

Three main interests dominated the marchioness's life: religion, philanthropy, and art. Her religious convictions (originally high church but from the late 1850s broader Church of England) permeated all her activities. At her instigation two chapels were built at Curraghmore, an infant school was founded, and a cloth factory established. During the great famine in Ireland in the 1840s, her efforts to relieve suffering led to a public acknowledgement in the House of Commons, and in 1848, when threatened with a local insurrection, she remained at Curraghmore for as long as Lord Waterford would allow. In 1850 her sister wrote cheerfully that 'Church and State, trades and commerce, manufactories, woods and forests, and home department, are all under her thumb' (Hare, 1.341).

She continued her reforming and charitable work at Ford—creating a model village and starting a temperance society—and also at Highcliffe.

Lady Waterford sketched constantly and pursued her interest in Italian Renaissance art (particularly the Venetian painters) during trips to northern Italy in 1858 and 1860. In colouring, breadth of design, and massiveness of figure, much of her work recalls the art of this period, though most was on a small scale and in watercolour. She was highly motivated, holding that art should be used 'in God's service' and concern itself with 'useful and good teaching' through parables and scenes from everyday life, as in the Bible (Hare, 3.462–3, 2.113). Thus, while her most ambitious work was on biblical and allegorical themes, there is a 'hallowing' quality (the word is her own) even in her genre compositions, and pictures of children, due largely to monumentality of style. As early as 1848, when *The Babes in the Wood* was published with ten designs by the artist, *The Spectator* commented that 'The children are noble as well as beautiful specimens of budding humanity: they belong to the same large mould with the children of Raphael' (18 Nov 1848, 1119). *Ford School, 'Standard One'* (*The Writing Lesson*; exh. Grosvenor Gallery, London, 1880; Bolton Museum and Art Gallery) illustrates the same characteristics in a picture of children executed much later at Ford. Similarly, there is a religious dimension in many of her rural genre scenes: *Pietro Ricci, a Fisherman at Sospello, Near Mentone* (*A Mentone Fisherman*; V&A), for instance, recalls Christ's injunction to the disciples to be fishers of men, while *The Sower* (exh. Grosvenor Gallery, London, 1881; V&A) gestures towards the parable of that name. Massive form is typical also of more serious subjects such as *Disciples Sleeping in the Garden* (*Sleeping Disciples*; exh. Amateur Artists, Burlington House, London, 1855; Tate collection) and *Relentless Time* (Royal Library, Windsor Castle). She illustrated numerous episodes from the life of Christ, including *Christ on the Mount of Olives* and *Christ Blessing the Little Children* (both British Museum, London), as well as the parables of the marriage supper and the good Samaritan. Her greatest achievement was the decoration (1862–83) of the new school at Ford with edifying, life-sized scenes from the Old and New testaments 'showing that faith must be taught and worked for' (Joicey, 10), using children and adults from the village as models. These were painted in watercolour on distempered paper which was pasted on calico and stretched on wooden frames.

As a result of her acquaintance with John Ruskin in the early 1850s, Lady Waterford's work became known to the Pre-Raphaelites. Dante Gabriel Rossetti described her as 'great in design' and John Everett Millais included her in an unfulfilled sketching club project of 1854. George Frederick Watts wrote that she was '*born* an artist greater than any England has produced' (Surtees, *Sublime and Instructive*, 4–5). John Ruskin himself, for many years her mentor, commented that 'she might have been a Paolo Veronese, had she been poor' (ibid., 5), his main criticisms concerning her lack of finish and attention to detail. Despite frequent acknowledgement of her talent, she remained humble and self-critical: 'I see myself just an amateur and

no more', she wrote (Hare, 3.392). Although her work appeared at a charitable exhibition of amateur artists in 1855, she did not exhibit at professional galleries until the 1870s, in which decade she was represented at the Dudley and Grosvenor galleries; in the 1880s she also contributed to the Royal Manchester Institution, the Royal Hibernian Academy, and the Society of Lady Artists. She was a patron (1865–76) and an honorary member (1887–91) of the Society of Lady Artists and also a member of the Dudley Gallery Art Society (1889–90).

The marchioness died at Ford Castle, Cornhill-on-Tweed, Northumberland, on 12 May 1891 and was buried on 19 May in the churchyard at Ford. The memorial on her grave was designed by Watts. Retrospectives of her work were held in 1891, 1892, 1910, and, more recently, in 1983.

CHARLOTTE YELDHAM

Sources A. J. C. Hare, *The story of two noble lives*, 3 vols. (1893) · V. Surtees, *Sublime and instructive* (1972) · V. Surtees, *Charlotte Canning* (1975) · C. Stuart, *A short sketch of the life of Louisa, marchioness of Waterford* (1892) · H. M. Neville, *Under a border tower: sketches of Ford Castle, Northumberland* (1896) · M. Joicey, *The Lady Waterford Hall and its murals* (1983) · H. Honour, 'A Victorian amateur artist: paintings by Lady Waterford', *Country Life*, 121 (1957), 664–6 · S. Erskine, 'The drawings of Lady Waterford', *The Studio*, 49 (1910), 283–6 · 'Lady Waterford's *Babes in the wood*', *The Spectator* (18 Nov 1848), 1118–19 · C. Wood, 'foreword', *Lady Waterford centenary exhibition* (1983) [exhibition catalogue, Lady Waterford Hall, Northumberland, 2 July – 10 Sept 1983] · *Louisa Anne, marchioness of Waterford* (1987) [David Ker Fine Art, London, Oct 1987, organized by D. Ker and W. Drummond] · exhibition catalogues (1878–82) [Grosvenor Gallery, London] · exhibition catalogues (1877); (1883); (1887–9) [Dudley Gallery, London] · exhibition catalogues (1882); (1884); (1887) [Royal Manchester Institution] · exhibition catalogues (1886–8); (1890) [Society of Lady Artists, London] · exhibition catalogue (1885) [Royal Hibernian Academy, Dublin] · exhibition catalogue (1855) [Amateur Artists, Burlington House, London] · GEC, *Peerage* · *CGPLA Eng. & Wales* (1891)

Archives Dorset RO, recollections of her childhood at Highcliffe Castle · Lady Waterford Hall, Ford, Northumberland

Likenesses W. H. Egleton, engraving, 1839 (after J. Hayter), BM, NPG · F. Grant, portrait, 1842, priv. coll. [*see illus.*] · F. Grant, oils, c.1845, NPG · J. R. Swinton, chalk drawing, 1851, Harewood House, West Yorkshire · W. Roffe, line engraving, NPG · W. Roffe, stipple, NPG · C. Spindler, oils (with sister), Musée Historique de la Ville de Strasbourg · R. Thorburn, miniature (with sister), Scot. NPG · R. Thornburn, miniature (with sister), Harewood House, West Yorkshire

Wealth at death £40,096 16s. 3d.: resworn probate, June 1892, *CGPLA Eng. & Wales* (1891)

Beresford, Marcus Gervais (1801–1885), Church of Ireland archbishop of Armagh, was second son of George De la Poer Beresford, bishop of Kilmore and Ardagh, and of Frances, daughter of Gervais Parker Bushe, and niece of Henry Grattan. He belonged to a family 'connected for generations with the highest dignity and power in the civil and ecclesiastical administration of Ireland' (*The Times*, 28 Dec 1885). He was born on 14 February 1801 at the Custom House, Dublin, then the residence of his grandfather, John *Beresford, the unionist politician, and received his education first at Dr Tate's school at Richmond, and afterwards at Trinity College, Cambridge, where he graduated BA in 1824, MA in 1828, and DD in 1840; he received an honorary DCL from Oxford in 1864.

On 25 October 1824 he married Mary (*d.* 1845), daughter of Henry L'Estrange of Moystown, and widow of R. E. Digby of Geashill. They had two sons and three daughters. On 6 June 1850 he married Elizabeth (*d.* 1870), daughter of James Trail-Kennedy of Annadale, co. Down, and widow of Robert George Bonford of Rahenstown, co. Meath.

Beresford was ordained deacon in 1824 and priest in 1825, and was preferred to the rectory of Kildallon, co. Cavan, in his father's diocese, which he held for three years. He was then appointed to the vicarages of Drung and Larah (both in the diocese of Kilmore), which he held until 1854, before being appointed archdeacon of Ardagh when that diocese was united to Kilmore in 1839 under the terms of the Church Temporalities Act of 1833. On the death of Bishop Leslie, who had succeeded Beresford's father in the see, he was appointed bishop of Kilmore and Ardagh. He was consecrated in Armagh Cathedral on 24 September 1854. Eight years later—in 1862—on the death of his cousin, Lord John George Beresford, Beresford was translated to the Irish primacy, and was enthroned in Armagh Cathedral. With the archbishopric he also held the bishopric of Clogher, which was united to the see of Armagh under the Church Temporalities Act. By virtue of his office Beresford was a member of the Irish privy council. He was on several occasions sworn a lord justice for the government of Ireland in the temporary absences of the viceroy.

In the stormy controversies provoked by Gladstone's measure for the disestablishment and disendowment of the Church of Ireland, as well as in the difficult task of remodelling the constitution of the church after disestablishment, Beresford earned the reputation of an ecclesiastical statesman. In the discussions on the Irish church that preceded the passing of the Irish Church Act, Beresford was among those who favoured a measure of reform, a policy which savoured too much of Erastianism to satisfy the more militant among Irish churchmen. Beresford had no place in the House of Lords during the debates on disestablishment (the Irish archbishops sitting in turn, and his brother archbishop, Richard Chenevix Trench, having the right for that session). But the primate played a large part in the negotiations. He was a ready debater, and proved an able chairman of the general synod over which he presided. His conservatism was seen to considerable effect in the discussion of prayer book revision, for he supported with his prestige those who (successfully) argued for minimal change.

Beresford died at the bishop's palace, Armagh, on 26 December 1885, and was buried in St Patrick's Cathedral, Armagh, on 1 January 1886.

C. L. FALKINER, *rev.* KENNETH MILNE

Sources J. B. Leslie, 'Clergy and parishes of Kilmore', RCB Library, Dublin, typescript, MS 51 · J. B. Leslie, *Clogher clergy and parishes* (1929) · *Irish Ecclesiastical Gazette* (2 Jan 1886) · Venn, *Alum. Cant.* · W. A. Phillips, ed., *History of the Church of Ireland*, 3 vols. (1933–4) · R. B. McDowell, *The Church of Ireland, 1869–1969* (1975) · P. M. H. Bell, *Disestablishment in Ireland and Wales* (1969) · D. H. Akenson, *The Church of Ireland: ecclesiastical reform and revolution, 1800–1885* (1971)

Archives CUL, corresp. and papers | BL, letter to Lord Cranbrook, Add. MS 62537 · Bodl. Oxf., letters to Disraeli · LPL, corresp. with A. C. Tait · NL Ire., letters to Lord Farnham

Likenesses S. C. Smith, portrait, 1854?; in possession of Beresford's eldest son in 1901 · S. C. Smith, oils, 1862 (after his father's portrait), Synod Hall, Armagh, Northern Ireland · J. R. Jackson, mezzotint etching and stipple, pubd 1866 (after S. C. Smith), NPG, NG Ire. · S. C. Smith, portrait (as bishop of Kilmore); in possession of Beresford's second son in 1908 · engraving, palace, Armagh, Northern Ireland · miniature, County Museum, Armagh, Northern Ireland

Wealth at death £91,022 15*s*. 3*d*.: probate, 10 Feb 1886, *CGPLA Ire.* · £21,532 in England: English probate sealed in Ireland, 25 Feb 1886, *CGPLA Ire.*

Beresford, William Carr, Viscount Beresford (1768–1854), army officer, was born on 2 October 1768, the illegitimate son of George de la Poer Beresford, earl of Tyrone, and later first marquess of Waterford in the Irish peerage (1735–1800). His mother has not been identified, although Thomas Creevey referred to the notion that he and his younger brother, John Poo *Beresford (1766–1844), seemed to be special objects of affection of Elizabeth, Lady Waterford (*née* Monck, *c*.1742–1816), and that they might have been hers before her marriage.

Education and early career Beresford attended schools at Catterick Bridge and York. At seventeen his father sent him to a military school at Strasbourg, then a common practice among the British élite. In August 1785 he was appointed ensign in the 6th regiment, which was sent to Nova Scotia during the following year for a routine tour. While hunting, Beresford's gun misfired and blinded his left eye. The extent of disfigurement seems to be disputed: some called it severe, or even ugly, while others referred to it as nominal.

Beresford was promoted lieutenant in the 16th foot in 1790 and captain unattached in 1791. In May 1792 he joined the 69th foot. The Horse Guards decided to send a force that included the 69th to the West Indies, but when the continental situation became more threatening Beresford and his regiment were ordered to serve as marines aboard the *Britannia* (100 guns) in the Mediterranean. Although British Mediterranean operations then often seemed disjointed, a spectacular opportunity, although it was not exploited effectively, arose when the British, invited by local anti-Jacobins, landed at the great French naval base of Toulon in August 1793. If the ministry had initiated a priority programme of sending large numbers of troops to southern France, a great beachhead might have been established, but instead Admiral Hood, commander of a small unsustainable force, including Beresford, entered Toulon. Beresford carried out his duties routinely until the republican forces, including Napoleon Bonaparte, stepped up their attack and forced the British to evacuate in December.

When Hood became aware of an insurrection led by General Pasquale Paoli on Corsica, he immediately sailed thither. The British attempted control of Corsica, and Beresford's regiment was engaged in some hard fighting. He commanded the storming party at the tower of Martella Point (the origin of the British Martello towers) and

William Carr Beresford, Viscount Beresford (1768–1854), by Sir Thomas Lawrence, c.1818

began to form a reputation as a fearless soldier. He was promoted brevet-major in March 1794 and returned to England. In recognition of his services he was promoted lieutenant-colonel of a new regiment recruited from the Irish estates of his father, but this was dispersed shortly after formation.

With the 88th foot, 1795–1807 In September 1795 Beresford received command of the famous 88th foot, the Connaught Rangers. Soon the 88th was assigned to the force commanded by Sir Ralph Abercromby, who received orders to sail to the West Indies. Thus Beresford came under the influence of another of the great military personages of the period, although Abercromby's command skills have been questioned. At Toulon, Beresford had been in the presence of David Dundas, Sir John Moore, and generals O'Hara and Mulgrave. His own style of command was then being formed and several of these men, especially Moore, were fine field commanders.

Admiral Sir Hugh Christian's fleet sailed with Abercromby's force to dislodge the French from the West Indies. *En route*, however, a mammoth storm, 'Christian's storm', broke up the expedition, so some of the 88th ended up in Jamaica, the Mediterranean, and English

ports. Beresford reassembled the regiment and commanded it at Jersey for about two years. Meanwhile, in 1799, as the campaign against Tipu Sultan in India was approaching a crisis, Beresford and the 88th sailed for Bombay, arriving in June 1800, and did garrison duty for several months. When Bonaparte led a powerful force to Egypt in 1798 the British government sent a force there under Abercromby. A supporting force under Sir David Baird, including Beresford and the 88th, left Bombay in December 1800. The 88th finally arrived at Quseir, in Egypt, and disembarked in June 1801. By then Nelson had destroyed the French fleet at Abu Qir Bay (1 August 1798), and Abercromby's force had landed and taken Cairo. Baird formed four brigades, of which Beresford commanded the first; the latter led the march across the desert toward Cairo, often at temperatures reaching 120 °F. By the time Baird's force arrived the British were already in control of most of Egypt, but the British victory added lustre to the reputation of Beresford and the other commanders. The 88th remained in Egypt until 1803 and returned to England with considerable fanfare. Success breeds promotions, and Beresford was breveted as colonel (1800) while still in Egypt and upon his return was advanced to the rank of brigadier-general.

Beresford's career fluctuated as he took part in expeditions that sometimes were ill-conceived and usually risky. Fortunately the first of these, the recapture of the Cape of Good Hope in January 1806, was successful. Baird commanded the force, with Beresford, commander of the 1st brigade, Ronald Ferguson, later Beresford's colleague in the Peninsula, and others. The 1806 Argentine expedition was a miserable failure. The phlegmatic Sir Home Popham somewhat whimsically planned the expedition, and Beresford, in command of the 88th and 74th foot, sailed with the fleet to the Argentine coast. Beresford took advantage of surprise and occupied Buenos Aires (27 June 1806) with his tiny force of 1200 men. The Argentine forces, under a French soldier of fortune, the Chevalier de Liniers, attacked the British and forced their surrender after three days of hard fighting. Beresford escaped from prison, joined British forces at Montevideo, and returned to England in 1807.

The government considered that despite his rather humdrum military record Beresford had administrative ability and so sent him to occupy Madeira, since the French and Spanish governments had allied to dismember Portugal. The prince regent, João, barely escaped from Lisbon late in 1807, as General Andoche Junot's forces approached Lisbon, and took up residence in Brazil. Beresford commanded the forces at Madeira and to some extent studied the Portuguese character and language. However, according to later observers he never could write Portuguese or French acceptably. His written style was awkward, and his convoluted syntax required his aides, such as Robert Arbuthnot and Henry Hardinge, to put correspondence in final form. Nevertheless, since there were few British functionaries fluent in Portuguese, Beresford developed linguistic skills that, while hardly expert, were better than those of other British officers.

With Wellesley in the Peninsula, 1808–1809 When the government ordered Sir Arthur Wellesley to land a force on the coast of Portugal in August 1808 Beresford obtained permission to leave Madeira and join him there. Previously Beresford had approached Lord Mornington about using his influence to have Beresford transferred to Wellesley's command, an arrangement that proved short-lived since Sir Hew Dalrymple, senior to Wellesley, soon took command. Beresford was appointed commandant of Lisbon, but he found it rather uncomfortable as he had to help implement the disgraceful and unpopular convention of Cintra (30 August 1808). He worked hard and received credit for negotiating with a strong hand the French evacuation of the fortress Elvas. After the principals of the 1808 campaign in Portugal—Wellesley, Burrard, and Dalrymple—were exonerated by a court martial Beresford completed his administrative duties. He received a command in Sir John Moore's forces stationed around Lisbon. He had been promoted to major-general in April 1808; he now took command of a division that marched toward Spain by way of Coimbra and Almeida, while Moore's other forces advanced by several other routes.

Moore lacked accurate intelligence and was greatly outnumbered, and Napoleon recognized a rare opportunity to defeat and perhaps destroy a British army. When Moore began to retreat toward Corunna, Beresford's force marched near the rear and often aided Paget in repulsing the French vanguard. When Moore reached Corunna, hotly pursued by Marshal Andoche Soult, he deployed his forces while British transports sailed to the harbour to evacuate the army. After Moore's death Hope assumed command and placed Beresford's and Rowland Hill's brigades as covering forces while the army embarked. The British army, including Beresford's men, downcast and physically wasted away, arrived at British ports under a deep shadow cast by the 1808 campaigns. Beresford's performance in administration and campaign was quite good, but whether the British would attempt further Peninsular operations was problematic.

Marshal of the Portuguese army, 1809–1811 Even before the second British expedition reached Portugal in the spring of 1809 the elevation of Beresford to marshal in the Portuguese army began to alter the equation of power. Portugal was weak, it was believed, not because the Portuguese soldiers were deficient in courage and ability, but because of the poor military establishment of the old regime. The Portuguese regency therefore requested the British government to send a British general and a cadre of officers to create a reformed army. Partly as Beresford had a background that included acquaintance with the language, he was chosen, although Sir William Napier later claimed that he could not read the letter from the regency appointing him marshal. Castlereagh selected Beresford after considering Sir John Murray, Sir John Doyle, and the marquess of Hastings, and Beresford's British rank was advanced to lieutenant-general. Moreover, from the beginning Beresford seemed to have the approval of Wellesley, then commanding British forces in Portugal. The

government promised to support Beresford's reforms by sending arms, ammunition, and clothing.

At the beginning of his role as marshal of the Portuguese army Beresford was quite successful. The Portuguese regency was weak, the prince regent was in exile, and the danger of another French invasion was high. Beresford's personality—demanding, complaining, threatening—was an asset as he began to reform the Portuguese army. He intimidated subordinates and was described as 'large, ill-tempered, and foul mouthed'. His style of command was rigorous to the point of harshness. Rifleman Harris, however, spoke of his fine appearance and bearing. R. B. Long, later an outspoken critic, wrote that his first impression of Beresford was favourable. Michael Glover has described him as 'an inspired choice' and the 'organism of victory'. Beresford ploughed into the task of shaping an effective Portuguese army, despite formidable handicaps. The country of 3 million inhabitants was impoverished, and military discipline was poor. He installed British officers whenever possible and a scattering of bright young Portuguese. He removed the worst of the corrupt officers and demanded strict discipline. On one occasion he made a speech to the troops against removing brass buttons and beating them into counterfeit coins; he promised a flogging to anyone whose greatcoat buttons were missing. He tried to impose a size requirement on recruits of 63 inches but was forced to come down to 58 inches and later to 55½.

Gradually in 1809 Beresford's stern methods began to produce a small but effective army that was trained on British lines and was potentially capable of being incorporated with British units. He suffered shortages of money, food, and clothing, but the Portuguese government could not supply his needs. Reluctantly the British government increased its subsidies, but officials in London doubted Portuguese soldiers ever becoming reliable fighting men. Yet Beresford's brilliance at organization began to emerge. He punished slackers and rewarded those who emerged as soldiers, and the result was the emergence of the Caçadores and other Portuguese units which, if not crack fighting forces, developed a modicum of fighting abilities. The first attempts to deploy them, however, early in 1809 were unsuccessful, and even though some Portuguese troops fought in the Oporto campaign, they were held to limited service. While Wellington led his forces into Spain to an unsatisfactory junction with the Spanish army to oppose the French at Talavera, Beresford remained in Portugal, and his energetic reforms began to produce Portuguese regiments that won the approval of Wellington and the British officers. As the Portuguese were attached to British brigades, the third French invasion of Portugal began in 1810, and Marshal André Masséna's forces began advancing against Wellington's forces at Busaco. The British forces were outnumbered, so Beresford's units were greatly needed. The performance of the Portuguese was excellent, and the Beresford reform system proved to be effective. Moreover, additional British officers joined him at Lisbon as Wellington's crucial fortifications at Torres Vedras stopped Masséna's advance. Beresford now enjoyed considerable popularity. He was made KB (16 October 1810) and on 19 October 1811 was made count of Trancoso in the Portuguese peerage, and grand cross of the Tower and Sword. He had reached the zenith of his career.

Decline of Beresford's career in Portugal, 1811–1822 Every British officer was subject to Wellington's influence, and Beresford often seemed to enjoy his special favour. Wellington confided, of all his generals, in Rowland Hill and Thomas Graham from time to time. Although he did not do so with Beresford he spoke approvingly of him. In early 1811 Hill, commander of Wellington's southern wing in Spain in 1810 and a model of caution and sound tactics, ill from an infectious fever, had to go home. On new year's day 1811 Wellington reluctantly ordered Beresford, next in seniority to Hill, to take command of his corps of 13,000 men which was soon increased to 18,000 infantry and 2000 cavalry. A peripheral operation at Campo Mayor (25 March 1811) indicated early in the campaign that Beresford was clumsy if not incompetent at field command. The 13th light dragoons drove the French cavalry beyond Campo Mayor, but Beresford's faulty intelligence resulted in poor orders, the escape of the enemy, and the raising of questions about his skills. Fortescue, Dickson, and Burgoyne all thought that Beresford lost a good opportunity there. Beresford's personal courage contrasted with his inability to manage troops on the battlefield. Moreover, a major confrontation with the enemy was developing beyond the Guadiana. Soult's army of the south, 24,000 strong—Beresford estimated it at 20,000 to 21,000—began moving northward from Andalusia, and the stage was set for the bloody battle of Albuera (16 May 1811).

The allied army at Albuera consisted of about 30,000 men, but many were the remnants of Joachim Blake's Spanish army and some Portuguese units; only 8000 were British, the 2nd division under General William Stewart and the 4th division under General Lowry Cole, as well as some cavalry under General R. B. Long. Beresford placed his forces in a low area near the bridge of Albuera, and Soult immediately began moving his main force to an undefended height on Beresford's right. Beresford ordered the 2nd division to move against the heights, but it was soon overwhelmed. He ordered a retreat, but the resilient Colonel Henry Hardinge, the quartermaster-general, decided on his own to order Cole's 4th division to attack the heights. The gallant move saved the day, although Beresford's overall performance and tactics have been described as 'beneath contempt' (*DNB*). Wellington said that another such battle would ruin them. Byron said, 'Oh, Albuera, glorious field of grief! … A scene where mingling foes should boast and bleed!' (G. G. Byron, *Childe Harold's Pilgrimage*, 1812, canto 1, section 43). Soult also took dreadful losses and retired to the south. Wellington arrived shortly afterwards to find Beresford completely dispirited, and his morbid attitude was apparent in his dispatch about the battle. Wellington ordered Beresford to destroy it and 'to write a victory' (Longford, 257).

He also withdrew Beresford from the command and directed him to resume training of the Portuguese army. Wellington then restored Hill to the command of the southern wing of the army, and Beresford went away to Calhariz. There he spent almost six months, virtually incommunicado and possibly suffering from nervous exhaustion. His career in Portugal continued to decline.

Beresford's career suffered inversely from the successes of the allied activities in the Peninsula. The political scene in Portugal resembled a caldera ready to explode. The Sousa family increased its influence in Portugal, in Brazil, and in London, but while the Conde de Linhares was pro-British at Rio, the Sousa faction in Portugal was generally anti-British, and Domingos de Sousa in London tried to play both ends against the middle. In politics in 1811 and afterwards Beresford lost his influence, and as Wellington took the offensive in 1812 Beresford joined the advance without any specific command. He fought well at Salamanca, where he was wounded. At this juncture the topic of Wellington's statements about Beresford's abilities came into view and even today pose something of a dilemma. Despite Beresford's chequered performance in the Albuera campaign of 1811, Wellington, toward the end of 1812, spoke of him as 'the ablest man I have yet seen with the army, the one having the largest views … [and] the only person capable of conducting a large concern' (*Supplementary Despatches*, 7.484). However, although Beresford rendered a great service in developing the Portuguese army his conduct of field operations was completely inadequate. Nevertheless Wellington advanced him to second in command in 1813, but he stationed him so that he could keep an eye on him and be in constant communication. Apparently Wellington's views of his subordinates varied from time to time in different contexts.

During the invasion of France, Beresford commanded the light, 3rd, 4th, 7th, and two Spanish divisions, but Wellington stayed right with him. In 1814, in the final action in the south of France, at Toulouse, Beresford expertly led his force against the eastern defences of the city, the French were forced out of the city, and peace was announced shortly afterwards. On 17 May 1814 Beresford was created Baron Beresford of Albuera and Dungarvan, co. Waterford, with a pension of £2000 for life and those of the next two successors in the peerage.

Meanwhile, Beresford's ties with the Portuguese government, already damaged by the infighting among the political factions, remained tenuous. He briefly returned to England in 1814, where Wellington unsuccessfully urged him to retire from Portuguese service. He returned to Lisbon, but no amount of coaxing could convince João to return from Rio. Beresford spent the next five years managing the army amid growing resentment from the ruling element of Portugal and shrinking funds for the army's maintenance. Eventually the Portuguese expelled the British from the army, and although Beresford twice went to Brazil to rally João's support—on his first visit in 1817 he had to suppress a rebellion in Rio—his role in Portugal ended when he was refused entry in 1822. Though twice during the civil wars he was asked to take command of the army he refused, and never revisited Portugal.

Political career and marriage Beresford returned to England soon after George IV ascended the throne, and joined some of his colleagues, including Hill, in pursuing tory politics intermittently in the House of Lords. From June 1811 to May 1814 he had been tory MP for co. Waterford on the interest of his legitimate brother, the second marquess, but his war service prevented him taking his seat. His undistinguished career in the Lords at least kept up his contacts with Wellington, and when the latter formed a government in 1828 Beresford became master-general of the ordnance, for which he was well suited. The ministry fell in 1830, and he was never again very active in politics. Thomas Creevey wrote of Beresford, 'such a low-looking ruffian in his air, with damned bad manners, or rather none at all [that] I defy any human being to find out that he is either a marshal or a lord' (HoP, *Commons, 1790–1820*, 191).

Beresford gained affluence from his military and political career. He was created Viscount Beresford of Beresford in Staffordshire on 28 March 1823 and purchased the ancestral estate of Beresford, Staffordshire, in 1824. He received lucrative stipends as governor of Cork (1811–20) and Jersey (1820–54), and from various colonelcies. According to John Wade's *Black Book* (1832) Beresford received in pay and emoluments £1182, as governor of Jersey £1100, and his parliamentary pension of £2000. He was promoted full general in 1825. His British and foreign honours included GCB (2 January 1815), GCM (1818), duke of Elvas in the Spanish peerage, and knight of San Fernando in Portugal. On 29 November 1832 he married a cousin, Louisa (d. 1851), daughter of William Beresford, first Baron Decies, archbishop of Tuam, and widow of Thomas *Hope, one of the wealthiest women in England. He purchased Bedgebury Park, Kent, and lived there for the rest of his life. His wife's son, Alexander James Beresford *Hope, attended to Beresford's affairs until the latter's death.

In the mid-1830s there was an acrimonious dispute between Beresford and Charles Ballard Long over Beresford's alleged mismanagement of the Albuera campaign, and Sir William Napier alleged that Beresford had overstated his own contributions. Beresford's ponderous defence in three long pamphlets, combined with Napier's rapier-like thrusts, caused many readers to believe that Beresford had blundered at Albuera and that his claims were inaccurate. Assuredly, Beresford, a brave if controversial soldier, made many great contributions in the Peninsula, but the 1811 campaign was not one of them. However, throughout his Peninsular career he enjoyed the confidence of Wellington, who understood his hypochondria, his harsh personality, and his tendency to blame subordinates when his projects failed. Yet his long life of service was largely admirable, and, on balance, he made great contributions to British successes in the Napoleonic wars.

Beresford died at Bedgebury Park, Kent, on 8 January 1854 and was buried at Kilndown church, Goudhurst,

Kent, on 17 January. He left no legitimate issue and his titles became extinct. He left his English estates to his stepson Alexander James Beresford Hope.

GORDON L. TEFFETELLER

Sources S. E. Vickness, *Marshal of Portugal: the military career of William Carr Beresford* (1976) · W. F. P. Napier, *History of the war in the Peninsula and in the south of France*, rev. edn, 6 vols. (1876) · Fortescue, *Brit. army* · C. W. C. Oman, *A history of the Peninsular War*, 7 vols. (1902–30) · W. C. Beresford, *Collecção das ordens do dia*, 6 vols. (1809–14) · F. A. de la Fuentes, *Dom Miguel Pereira Forjaz … during the Peninsular War* (1980) · A. Halliday, *Observations on the present state of the Portuguese army as organized by W. C. Beresford* (1811) · *The dispatches of … the duke of Wellington … from 1799 to 1818*, ed. J. Gurwood, new edn, 13 vols. (1837–9) · *Supplementary despatches (correspondence) and memoranda of Field Marshal Arthur, duke of Wellington*, ed. A. R. Wellesley, second duke of Wellington, 15 vols. (1858–72) · J. Philippart, ed., *The royal military calendar*, 1 (1815), 206–8 · A. I. Shand, *Wellington's lieutenants* (1902) · J. Wade, ed., *The extraordinary black book*, new edn (1832) · J. W. Cole, *Memoirs of British generals distinguished during the Peninsular War*, 2 vols. (1856) · *DNB* · *GEC, Peerage* · *The Creevey papers*, ed. H. Maxwell, 3rd edn (1905); rev. edn, ed. J. Gore (1963) · E. Longford [E. H. Pakenham, countess of Longford], *Wellington*, 1: *The years of the sword* (1969) · P. J. Jupp, 'Beresford, Sir William Carr', HoP, *Commons, 1790–1820*

Archives Hunt. L., letters · N. Yorks. CRO, corresp. and papers · NL Ire., letters relating to elections, MS 21767 | Arquivo Historico Militar, Lisbon · Arquivo Nacional da Torre do Tombo, Lisbon · Biblioteca Nacional, Lisbon · BL, corresp. with Sir James Willoughby Gordon, Add. MS 49485, *passim* · BL, corresp. with Lord Liverpool, Add. MSS 38241–38576, *passim* · BL, letters to earls of Liverpool, loan 72 · BL, letters to Sir Robert Peel, Add. MSS 40238–40528, *passim* · BL, corresp. with duke of Wellington, Add. MS 30106 · BL, letters to Sir Robert Wilson, Add. MS 30106 · NAM, letters to Sir Benjamin D'Urban, 7805/46 · PRO · PRO NIre., corresp. with J. G. Beresford, D 664 · PRO NIre., corresp. with Lord Castlereagh, D3030 · U. Southampton L., letters to duke of Wellington, MS 61

Likenesses D. A. De Sequeira, chalk drawing, c.1810, Museu Nacional de Arte Antiga, Lisbon · T. Heaphy, watercolour, 1813–14, NG Ire.; watercolour study, NPG · C. Turner, mezzotint, pubd 1814 (after W. Beechey), BM, NPG · T. Lawrence, oils, c.1818, Wellington Museum, London [*see illus.*] · J. Doyle, pencil and chalk caricature, 1829, BM · J. Cochran, stipple, pubd 1830 (after E. Kendrick), BM · R. Rothwell, oils, c.1831, NPG · F. Bromley, group portrait, mixed, pubd 1847 (*Peninsular heroes*; after J. P. Knight), BM, NPG · R. Sayers, oils, 1849; formerly United Service Club, London · E. Beresford, oils (after W. Beechey, c.1814), NPG

Wealth at death large fortune

Beresford, William Marcus Joseph (1797/8–1883), politician, was born in Ireland on 17 April 1797, or possibly in 1798 after the death of his father. He was the youngest in the family of two sons and two daughters of Marcus Beresford MP (grandson of Marcus Beresford, first earl of Tyrone and counsel to the Irish revenue commissioners), and his wife, Lady Frances Arabella, daughter of Joseph Leeson, first earl of Milltown. His father died on 16 November 1797. He was educated at Eton College and St Mary Hall, Oxford, where he took his BA in 1819.

In 1822 he was commissioned as lieutenant in the 9th (Royal) Dragoons, transferring to the 12th lancers in 1826. He served in the Lisbon expedition of 1826 and retired on half pay in January 1831 with the rank of major. For some years he lived on his estate at Ballinastow in co. Wicklow, where he was high sheriff in 1835. After contesting Waterford City in 1837, he was elected MP for Harwich in 1841. He kept this seat until 1847, when he became MP for North

Essex. In public life his guiding principles were protestantism and protectionism. He opposed the Maynooth Bill of Sir Robert Peel in 1845 and was made chief whip of the protectionist party early in 1846. As such he was responsible both for the retirement of Lord George Bentinck from its leadership in 1847, after his vote for Jewish emancipation, and for the resumption of the title 'Conservative' for his party in 1848. While initially suspicious of Benjamin Disraeli, he recognized his talents and served loyally under him from 1849. In Lord Derby's ministry he became secretary for war (February–December 1852) and was party manager in the following general election. Subsequent parliamentary inquiries into improper electoral practices involved him in some censure, and this enabled Disraeli, who never liked him, to make fresh arrangements for the management of the party in opposition. In 1859 Beresford headed a protest against the Derby ministry's Reform Bill but did not press his opposition to a vote. Defeat in the general election of 1865 ended his parliamentary career.

Under William IV and Victoria he held court appointments as groom of the privy chamber and from 1823 master of the tennis court. His several business interests included the chairmanship of the Northern Counties Union Railway and various directorships. A tall, rough, hot-tempered Irishman, given to profanity, Beresford was more popular with back-benchers than with his leaders. His encouragement to the tory press to take a strong protestant and anti-Peelite line contributed to the perpetuation of the 1846 disruption. He assisted nevertheless in keeping the protectionist party together in a difficult period, with few resources and little help from his leaders.

In 1833 he married Catherine, youngest daughter of George Robert Heneage, of Hainton Hall, Lincolnshire; they had two sons and a daughter. Beresford died at his home, 40 Eccleston Square, London, on 6 October 1883.

NORMAN GASH, rev.

Sources GM, 1st ser., 67 (1797), 990 • ILN (3 April 1852) • The Times (9 Oct 1883) • W. F. Monypenny and G. E. Buckle, The life of Benjamin Disraeli, 6 vols. (1910–20) • Benjamin Disraeli letters, ed. J. A. W. Gunn and others (1982–), vol. 4 • R. Stewart, The politics of protection: Lord Derby and the protectionist party, 1841–1852 (1971) • R. Stewart, The foundation of the conservative party, 1830–1867 (1978) • D. N. Gash, 'Major William Beresford: protectionist chief whip', Parliamentary History, 10 (1991), 183–93
Archives Bodl. Oxf., Hughenden MSS
Likenesses portrait, repro. in ILN (31 April 1852), 268
Wealth at death £20,569 12s. 11d.: probate, 23 Nov 1883, CGPLA Eng. & Wales

Berewyk, John (b. in or before 1252, d. 1312), justice, probably came from Berwick St John in Wiltshire, where he is known to have acquired property. He appears to have served as a clerk of the Westminster bench between 1273 and 1278, and in 1279–80 was entrusted with custody of the temporalities of the abbey of Bury St Edmunds and the see of Lincoln during vacancies. In June 1280 he was appointed to the senior clerical position of keeper of rolls and writs on the southern eyre circuit and he kept this post until 1289. During the same decade he performed a number of other tasks both for Edward I and for his consort, Eleanor of Castile, from 1284 until Eleanor's death in 1290 holding the responsible post of queen's treasurer and keeper of the queen's gold; Berewyk was sufficiently high in Eleanor's confidence to be appointed one of the executors of her will. When the two eyre circuits resumed work in 1292 Berewyk was appointed chief justice of the southern eyre circuit, and surviving reports show him at work, alone or with others, hearing civil pleas and occasionally quo warranto pleas as well.

Trouble in Wales and war with France led to the suspension of both circuits in 1294, but Berewyk was appointed chief justice of the two isolated eyres held in Cambridgeshire and the Isle of Ely in 1299 and in Cornwall in 1302. During one case heard in the former eyre he revealed some of the discussion that had taken place (apparently within the king's council) before the enactment of the statute De finibus earlier that year. Berewyk was also employed by Edward I in negotiations for truce and peace with France, and on a variety of confidential tasks connected with raising money for the king—a reporter present at the Cornish eyre censured his conduct and that of his colleague Henry Spigurnel in a criminal case in squeezing a fine out of a defendant as 'more for the king's profit than in accordance with the law' (Year Book 30–31 Edward I, 507).

Berewyk made extensive property acquisitions in Hampshire, Surrey, and Dorset and less extensive acquisitions in Essex, Norfolk, and Cambridgeshire. Some years before his death in 1312 he had granted some of these lands to Reynold of Haselden and his wife, Isabel, possibly Berewyk's sister, and to John Huse, the husband of their daughter Maud; and after his death several of his servants claimed they had also been granted lands by him just before his death, but they may have forged the charters concerned. An ordained cleric, Berewyk held a number of valuable livings, some concurrently, and his tenure of prebends in St Paul's, Salisbury, York, Lichfield, and Wells, as well as of the deaneries of Wimborne Minster and South Malling, is further evidence of his status as one of the most senior royal clerks of the latter part of Edward I's reign.

PAUL BRAND

Sources Chancery records • Common bench plea rolls, PRO, CP 40 • A. J. Horwood, ed. and trans., Year books of the reign of King Edward the First, 5 vols., Rolls Series, 31 (1863–79) • GEC, Peerage • CIPM, 5, no. 397
Wealth at death see CIPM, 5, no. 397

Berg, Peter von. See Henderson, Sir John (fl. 1632–1658).

Bergavenny. For this title name see Beauchamp, William (V), first Baron Bergavenny (c.1343–1411); Beauchamp, Joan, Lady Bergavenny (1375–1435) [see under Beauchamp, William (V), first Baron Bergavenny (c.1343–1411)]; Neville, Edward, first Baron Bergavenny (d. 1476); Neville, Frances, Lady Bergavenny (d. 1576); Neville, George, third Baron Bergavenny (c.1469–1535).

Bergel, Franz (1900–1987), biochemist, was born on 13 February 1900 in the Alsergrund quarter of Vienna, the younger child and second son of Moritz Martin Bergel, a

Hungarian immigrant and wine merchant, and his wife, Barbara Betty Spitz, daughter of a carpet manufacturer. He was educated at a *Realgymnasium* in Vienna and was called up into a cavalry regiment at the beginning of 1918. At the end of the war he returned to school, from which he went to the universities of Würzburg and Freiburg in Germany to study chemistry. He obtained his PhD in 1924 and published some first-class work on amino-acid oxidation.

In 1928, having begun a whirlwind affair with Luise Creszentia Antonie (Niddy) Impekoven, a popular solo dancer and wife of a professor at Freiburg University, Bergel eloped with her following her divorce. They married in 1930. From then until he went to Edinburgh in 1933 he was mainly occupied as a kind of manager–impresario for his wife in dance tours all over Europe, and in 1932–3 he acted in this capacity in an extended tour of Ceylon and Indonesia. The couple had one daughter, and were divorced in 1933, after which the child lived with her mother in Switzerland.

On Bergel's return to Freiburg in 1933 the National Socialists were already in power. He was totally opposed to national socialism and immediately decided to leave Germany, though at that time he was under no necessity to do so, since although he was of Jewish descent he was an Austrian citizen and not, therefore, subject to persecution. He went from Freiburg to Edinburgh, where, thanks to financial support from Hoffmann La Roche & Co. of Basel, he joined the laboratory of George Barger, professor of medical chemistry at the university. He did not at first find this very congenial, but in the summer of 1934 he was joined by A. R. Todd, who had been brought to Edinburgh from Oxford to carry out research on the structure (and eventual synthesis) of vitamin B1, of which a very small quantity was in Barger's possession. Todd and Bergel struck up an immediate and lasting friendship and worked together on vitamin B1, for which, in 1936, they developed an effective synthesis which permitted the commercial development of the vitamin by Hoffmann La Roche. When, in 1936, Todd moved to the Lister Institute of Preventive Medicine in London, Bergel moved with him (still supported by Hoffmann La Roche) and the two continued their joint work on vitamin E and the active principle of cannabis resin. Bergel was naturalized about 1938. Todd moved to Manchester in 1938 as professor of chemistry and Bergel to Welwyn Garden City, Hertfordshire, as director of the new research laboratories of Roche Products Ltd. There he worked on synthetic analgesics, cannabinoids, antibacterials, and vitamins. With the enforced wartime separation of Roche Products from the mother firm in Basel, he had to devote much time to the process control and development of vitamins and to the study of the various new vitamins that had been discovered. On 6 April 1939 he married for the second time. His wife was Phyllis Edith Shuell (*b.* 1904/5), the divorced wife of (Anthony) John Shuell (otherwise Shaw), and the daughter of John Thomas, of independent means. They had no children.

Bergel remained at Welwyn Garden City until 1952, when he succeeded G. A. R. Kon as professor of chemistry in the Chester Beatty Research Institute at the Royal Cancer Hospital, London—a post which he filled with great distinction until his retirement in 1966. He concentrated on cancer chemotherapy, enlarging Kon's programme of work on derivatives of 'nitrogen mustard' as possible chemotherapeutic agents. He also initiated and developed a substantial programme of research on the biochemical properties of tumours. He sought to exploit the emphasis of tumours on anabolic rather than catabolic pathways, and also to use enzyme therapy to deprive particular tumours of essential nutrients. In 1961 he published a comprehensive monograph, *Chemistry of Enzymes in Cancer*, in which he reviewed all that was known about the role of enzymes in cancer and the potential of some of them as therapeutic agents.

Bergel's outstanding contributions to cancer research are the more remarkable since he underwent a major operation for rectal cancer in 1957 which involved a colostomy; despite this handicap he continued his work and lived an active life. He was deputy director of the Chester Beatty Research Institute, serving on all its major committees and acting as dean from 1963 to 1966. He was an honorary lecturer at University College, London (1946–72), served on the council of both the Chemical Society and the Society of the Chemical Industry, and was chairman of the Co-ordinating Committee for Symposia on Drug Action. He was elected a fellow of the Royal Society in 1959.

Bergel was a kind, compassionate, and gentle man. Widely read, with an active interest in European languages, he was an engaging conversationalist and a talented amateur artist. Tall and handsome, he was very much a 'ladies' man', similar to the typical Austrian aristocrats of Franz Lehár's operettas. He retired to Bel Royal in Jersey, where he died on 1 January 1987.

A. R. TODD and C. S. NICHOLLS, *rev.*

Sources Lord Todd, *Memoirs FRS*, 34 (1988), 1–9 • *The Times* (13 Jan 1987) • m. cert. [Franz Bergel and Phyllis Shuell (Shaw)]
Archives Bodl. Oxf., Society for Protection of Science and Learning MSS

Bergenroth, Gustav Adolph (1813–1869), historian, was born at Treuburg, East Prussia, on 26 February 1813, the second of the five sons of Johann Friedrich Bergenroth, the town magistrate, and his wife, Johanna Dörk. At home and at school in Lyck he developed the discipline, self-reliance, and stamina which laid the basis of his life's work. After taking a degree in law at the University of Königsberg, he entered the Prussian judiciary in 1836 and occupied successive posts at Königsberg, Koszalin, Cologne, and Berlin while devoting his leisure to the study of economics and statistics. Having adopted the ideals of Saint-Simonian socialism, he took an active part in the Berlin revolution of 1848 and in the following year published a scathing attack on the Pomeranian landowner von Bülow-Cummerow. Following the defeat of the revolution, rather than accept relegation to an obscure provincial post, he decided on emigration to California in order to lay the foundations of an agricultural commune on socialist lines. At the end of an eventful journey (during which he contracted yellow fever, and was robbed of all his possessions), he reached San Francisco in the late summer of 1850 only to be struck down by cholera. A strong constitution and the devoted care of a stranger enabled him to survive. He settled on what was then the remote peninsula of Pillar Point, 20 miles south of San Francisco, where he intended to make his living as a trapper and seller of furs, using the skills he had acquired on earlier expeditions in the forests of Mazuria. He established his authority over a motley community of hunters, outlaws, and cattle-rustlers and was instrumental in setting up one of the first vigilance committees which, in the absence of official law enforcement, were taking upon themselves the duties of police and courts martial. His vivid account of this formative period of Californian history was later published in *Household Words* (15 November 1856).

Forced to abandon his utopian scheme for want of funds, Bergenroth returned to Europe in 1851 and spent the following years as a wandering scholar before finally settling at London in 1857 with the intention of making English history his life's work. His first subject was Wat Tyler, on whom he wrote for Sybel's *Historische Zeitschrift* in 1859. Having then chosen the Tudor period as his specialism, and finding the resources of the Public Record Office inadequate for the reign of Henry VII, he concluded that the missing key to Tudor history lay in the Spanish archives of Simancas, only recently (1844) opened to the public and virtually untapped by English historians. Hitherto only John Lingard had obtained at second-hand a few documents relating to the marriage settlement of Henry VIII and Katherine of Aragon. In the summer of 1860 Bergenroth set out on his own initiative and at his own expense for what was then the primitive village of Simancas, described by one of his visitors as 'a collection of wretched hovels half-buried in dust and sand' (Cartwright, 89–90). The graphic letters he wrote from Simancas over the following months to J. S. Brewer aroused wide interest when they were published in *The Athenaeum*, and as a result the master of the rolls, Sir John Romilly, was authorized to appoint him as official editor of the Spanish state papers in February 1861, though he did not receive a salary until a year later.

It was generally believed that the Simancas archives had been pillaged by Napoleonic troops, but Bergenroth found this to be false: cartloads of documents had been carefully removed to Paris, but the great majority had now been returned. In order to allay the suspicions of the Spanish authorities he had first to enlist the help of the Prussian, British, and French representatives at Madrid. Having with difficulty gained entrance to the archive, he found that most of the papers he had to transcribe were either illegible or written in ciphers to which the archivists themselves did not possess the key. He had no previous experience of deciphering but rapidly developed a remarkable talent for the task, to which he brought the instincts of a hunter, intense powers of concentration, and a zest for grappling with difficulty. The rigours of the following winter—in an unheated archive where even the ink froze over—did not daunt his enthusiasm. After a visit

to Simancas in the autumn of 1861 Brewer reported to Romilly that 'nothing but the strongest desire to do service to history could reconcile any man to so much hardship' (Cartwright, 89–90).

Bergenroth continued his investigations in the Aragonese archives at Barcelona, and at Madrid, Paris, and Brussels. In 1866 the first volume of the Spanish state papers was published, covering the years 1485 to 1509, with a long preface which included a fascinating account of the editor's work on the ciphers. A second and even longer volume covering the years 1509 to 1525 followed in 1866. Bergenroth's growing obsession with sensational aspects of private life became glaringly evident in a supplementary volume published in 1869, in which he cast doubt on the chastity of Katherine of Aragon and on the madness of her sister Juana 'the Mad', queen of Castile. He had meanwhile been amassing material for a monumental work of his own on Charles V and the papacy, but did not live to complete the task. Early in 1869 he contracted typhus at Simancas and was removed to Madrid where he died, unmarried, at the Fonda de los Principes on 13 February and was buried in the protestant cemetery of San Isidoro. He was attended in his final days by the young scholar Juan Facundo Riaño y Montero, the son-in-law of his friend Pascual de Gayangos; the latter succeeded him as editor of the Spanish state papers.

Romantic but methodical, impetuous but laborious, Bergenroth was an unusually contradictory character, unsurpassed in the pursuit and collection of data but deficient in a sense of proportion. In pioneering the investigation of the Spanish state archives for English records he not only wrote but made history. After his death the voluminous transcripts he had made for his work on Charles V, amounting to some 18,000 folio pages, were acquired from his mother by the British Museum, after prolonged haggling. The purchase was made on the recommendation of Sir John Acton, who commented that Bergenroth's 'power of detecting what was important and new was superior by far to his manner of using what he had obtained'. W. C. Cartwright's memoir of 1870, written in a style as colourful as its subject, reproduces the text of the letters from Simancas published in *The Athenaeum*. Bergenroth's brother Julius (1818–1896) represented Thorn in the Prussian parliament.

G. MARTIN MURPHY

Sources W. C. Cartwright, *Gustave Bergenroth: a memorial sketch* (1870) · R. Pauli, 'Bergenroth, Gustav Adolph', *Allgemeine deutsche Biographie*, ed. R. von Liliencron and others, 2 (Leipzig, 1875), 369–72 · C. Krollmann, *Altpreussische Biographie*, 1 (1941), 50 · *The Athenaeum* (20 Oct 1860), 517–18 · *The Athenaeum* (29 Dec 1860), 910–12 · *The Athenaeum* (17 Nov 1860), 673 · *The Athenaeum* (3 Nov 1860), 593–4 · *The Athenaeum* (1861), 51–3 · *Household Words* (15 Nov 1856), 409–16 · *Fraser's Mag.*, 74 (1866), 48–9

Archives BL, transcripts of state papers in Spain and in the public archives of Paris and Brussels, Add. MSS 28572–28597 | BL, Papers regarding purchase and requisition of MSS, 1871–3, fols. 1–95 · CUL, letters to Lord Acton · PRO, PRO 1/24–27

Berger, Francesco (1834–1933), music administrator, was born in London on 10 June 1834, the son of a Bavarian mother and a naturalized Italian father, a merchant from

Trieste. He studied music in Trieste with Luigi Ricci and Aegidius Karl Lickl, then went to Leipzig, where he learned piano with Felix Moscheles and composition with Moritz Hauptmann. In 1855 he settled in London and started practice as a conventional music 'professor', teaching young ladies the piano and accompanying singers. In later life his pupils included Marie Corelli and Sybil Thorndike. He published more than a hundred works for the piano, violin, and cello, and as many songs, duets, trios, and partsongs. 'The Band Passes' was a minor success, and, among his educational works, *Pretty Little Pieces for Pretty Little Players* drew on melodies from Weber, Verdi, and popular tunes. Other music included a mass and an opera, *Il lazzarone*. A youthful friendship with Charles Dickens and Wilkie Collins led to his providing incidental music to *The Frozen Deep* and *The Light House*, entertainments written by Collins and in which Dickens acted; Queen Victoria commanded a private performance of the latter. In 1864 Berger married Annie Lascelles, a contralto whose voice he described as being 'rich, mellow and of exceptional compass', who was admired by the queen and Prince Albert and for whom composers including Balfe, Wallace, and Macfarren wrote songs (Berger, 97, 97–8). She abandoned her career on her marriage. In 1868 Berger established the 'Après-midis Instrumentales'. From 1885 he taught at the Royal Academy of Music, and later also at the Guildhall School of Music.

There was no reason to expect that Berger's election to the Royal Philharmonic Society in 1859, as member in 1871, as director in 1880, and, crucially, as secretary from 1884 to 1911, would give an entirely new brand of vital leadership to that once distinguished institution. Seventy years after its establishment in 1813, the society was artistically and financially moribund, impervious to a new world of public concerts. Berger found new audiences, subscribers, and alternative sources of income. With legendary displays of obsequiousness he wooed prima donnas and virtuosos including Patti and Paderewski, countering inflated demands for fees (newly transformed by America and international agents) with similarly modern images of tradition and heritage, and offering medals in place of dollars. Attempting to discipline and maintain an orchestra (never possible for long in London), he built attractive programmes from the competing requirements of quality, popularity, and nationalism in an age of live repertory. Taking the society into profit within a decade earned him a modest cheque and testimonial, headed by the lord chief justice, to his 'indefatigable and self-denying zeal'. These feats of entrepreneurship, sustained without much faltering for a further twenty years, might have earned lasting fame and fortune in an easier business.

After 1911 Berger subsisted on pittances from teaching and nondescript journalism, presumably reduced by the collapse of the old drawing-room piano culture in which he had his roots. In 1930 he was granted £100 from the civil list 'in recognition of his services to music'. He published a tutor, *First Steps at the Pianoforte* (1894), and *Musical Expressions, Phrases and Sentences* (1921). He also wrote two books

of memoirs, *Reminiscences, Impressions and Anecdotes* (n.d. [1913?]) and 97 (1931). They give a vivid account of London's social musical life in Victorian and Edwardian times, with glimpses of the many musicians, including Wagner and Tchaikovsky, who visited London, and an admiring portrait of Dickens. Berger retained to the end of his long life an alert face with a neat beard and a high forehead, crowned in these last years with a shock of white hair. He died on 25 April 1933, at his home, 38 Hardwicke Road, Palmer's Green, London, at the age of ninety-eight.

CYRIL EHRLICH

Sources C. Ehrlich, *First philharmonic: a history of the Royal Philharmonic Society* (1995) • F. Berger, *Reminiscences, impressions, and anecdotes* [1913] • C. Tomalin, *The invisible woman: the story of Nelly Ternan and Charles Dickens*, new edn (1991) • Brown & Stratton, *Brit. mus.* • *Biographical dictionary of musicians*, rev. N. Slonimsky, 5th edn (1958); rev. edn pubd as *Baker's biographical dictionary of musicians* (1978) • *Riemann Musik-Lexikon*, ed. W. Gurlitt, 12th edn (1959–67) • F. Berger, 97 (1931) • *CGPLA Eng. & Wales* (1933) • d. cert.
Archives BL, Royal Philharmonic Society MSS, loan 48
Likenesses H. Furniss, pen-and-ink, NPG • photograph, repro. in F. Berger, 97 (1931), frontispiece
Wealth at death £788 7s. 11d.: probate, 20 May 1933, *CGPLA Eng. & Wales*

Berghe, Nikolaos van den. *See* Hill, Nicolas (d. 1555).

Bergmann, Walter Georg (1902–1988), composer and musician, was born on 24 September 1902 in the Lindenallee, Altona, Hamburg, Germany, the youngest of the three sons of Oskar Gustav Adolph Bergmann (1859–1936), a building engineer who worked for the German railways, and his first wife, Alice, née König (1874–1925), of Jewish ancestry. The family moved to Bremen, and then in 1909 to Halle, where he was educated at the *Stadtgymnasium*. He studied the piano and the flute at the Leipzig Conservatorium before enrolling as a law student at the University of Leipzig, and was awarded a doctorate of law by the University of Freiburg im Breisgau. In 1930 he married Marthel Kolb, a singer, but they separated in 1931 and were divorced in 1936. He was unable to marry his second wife, Margarete (Grete; 1904–1983), a gymnastics teacher, daughter of Hermann August Haase, a Halle businessman, in Germany because of the Nüremberg laws forbidding interracial marriages, but they had a daughter, Erica Helen, in 1932. He practised law in Halle until 1938, when he was barred from practising in Germany and was imprisoned for three months after acting as legal adviser to a Jewish firm.

After his release Bergmann managed to emigrate to England in March 1939, carrying two suitcases filled with music (including Purcell's fantasias), a flute, and a tenor recorder. He was followed by Grete and Erica in July: Bergmann and Grete were married in London on 6 September 1939. He was helped on his arrival by the Society of Friends, as his legal qualifications were of no use in England. After the fall of France in 1940 he was classed as an enemy alien and spent eight months interned on the Isle of Man. He then started work as a packer at Schotts, the music publisher, in December 1941, but when he was called for national service in 1944 he had to move to a munitions factory in King's Cross, where he worked as a fitter until the end of the war. He then returned as an editor to Schotts, where he remained until his retirement. He was naturalized in 1949.

In 1941 Bergmann met Michael Tippett, director of music at Morley College in Southwark, who asked him to come to Morley as accompanist for the college choir. Bergmann was one of several refugee musicians on the staff, including Walter Goehr and Matyas Seiber, as Tippett wanted Morley to be a haven for those who had been uprooted by the war. After a performance on 22 November 1941 of Purcell's *Ode for St Cecilia's Day* (1692), for which Bergmann used descant recorders for the trumpet parts, Tippett asked him to start recorder evening classes. It was these that kept recorder playing alive during the war. Tippett dedicated his second string quartet, first performed in 1943, to Bergmann. When Tippett heard the counter-tenor Alfred Deller sing in Canterbury and brought him to London, his first public performance, at a Morley College concert in October 1944, included Purcell's *Music for a While* in a new edition prepared for him by Bergmann, and Deller always subsequently used this edition. Bergmann was influential in launching Deller's solo career, and was his accompanist until 1950, when Deller formed his partnership with the lutenist Desmond Dupré. It was at Morley College that Bergmann developed his love of early English music, especially the work of Purcell. He was fascinated by the problem of Purcell's unfigured basses, and went on to prepare editions of a number of his vocal works for publication by Schotts, many in collaboration with Tippett. He was especially proud of his editions of the odes on the death of Henry Purcell by John Blow and Jeremiah Clarke.

Tippett left Morley College in 1951, and in 1952 Bergmann moved to the Mary Ward Settlement, and taught recorder classes there until it closed in 1960. He later taught at the City Literary Institute, and from 1966 at the Marylebone Institute. He played an important part in the recorder revival after the war, as one of those who refounded the Society of Recorder Players in 1946, as musical director of the London branch of the society for twenty years, and as a founder of the Recorder in Education summer schools at Roehampton in 1948 and tutor there until 1982. His legendary 'Golden rules for ensemble playing', first published in *Recorder News* in 1957, included maxims such as 'an ornament should be an embellishment and not an embarrassment', and 'thou shalt not play the little bit left over at the end'. Above all, through his position as an editor at Schotts he built up an extensive recorder catalogue of solo and ensemble music, editing much of it himself. He also arranged music of all styles and periods for amateur recorder players, trying out his arrangements on his evening classes first. He prepared editions of the recorder works of Barsanti, and discovered the twenty-four recorder sonatas of Schickhardt, preparing an edition for Faber Music, for whom he helped to establish a recorder list after he left Schotts. In 1952 he published a transposed version of Hindemith's recorder trio from *Plöner Musiktag* (1932), authorized by the composer.

Bergmann wrote several works for the recorder, the best known being the sonata for descant recorder and piano (1965), a lyrical piece influenced by Hindemith, first performed by Frans Brüggen, and the sonata for treble recorder and piano (1973). He was inspired by early English poetry, as in his *Pastorella* (1972) for sopranino recorder and soprano voice, a setting of a poem from John Attey's *First Book of Ayres* (1622), commissioned by Carl Dolmetsch for that year's Wigmore Hall recital; 'The Passionate Shepherd to his Love' (1971) to the text of Marlowe's 'Come live with me and be my love', for two counter-tenors, two recorders, and harpsichord; and *Four Lute Songs* (1973), settings of poems by Robert Herrick and others. Bergmann also wrote extensively for children, including *The Drummer Boy* (1968) for children's voices, recorders, percussion, and piano, and *Casey Jones* (1972), first performed by five hundred children in Stockport town hall.

Bergmann described himself as a professional musician whose hobby was music. A book of poetry, *Kristall der Sprache*, was published privately in 1971. He died of cerebral thrombosis and atherosclerosis on 13 January 1988 at 141 Walm Lane, Willesden Green, London, and was cremated at Golders Green six days later. He was survived by his daughter, Erica. ANNE PIMLOTT BAKER

Sources *Recorder News* (1937–9) · *Recorder News* (1950–63) · *Recorder and Music Magazine* (1963–88) · D. Richards, *Offspring of the Vic: a history of Morley College* (1958) · M. Hardwick and M. Hardwick, *Alfred Deller: a singularity of voice* (1968) · M. Tippett, *Those twentieth century blues* (1991) · I. Kemp, ed., *Michael Tippett: a symposium on his 60th birthday* (1965) · I. Kemp, *Tippett: the composer and his music* (1984) · J. Parkinson, 'Dr Walter Bergmann: musician. Hobby: music', *American Recorder*, 13/2 (May 1972), 40–41 · *Recorder and Music Magazine* (March 1988) · *Early Music*, 16 (1988) · *The Independent* (20 Jan 1988) · private information (2004) · m. cert. · d. cert. · *CGPLA Eng. & Wales* (1988) · *The Times* (15 Jan 1988) · *Recorder and Music Magazine* (Sept 1988) · A. Martin, *Musician for a while* (2002)

Archives priv. coll., diaries

Likenesses E. Seelig, photograph, repro. in *Recorder and Music Magazine* (Sept 1982), cover

Wealth at death £14,849: probate, 1 March 1988, *CGPLA Eng. & Wales*

Bergne, John Brodribb (1800–1873), civil servant and numismatist, was descended from a family originally of Auvergne, France, but settled in England since the French Revolution; he was born at Kensington. Having entered the Foreign Office in January 1817 he was for some time attached as clerk to the treaty department, of which he became superintendent on 1 July 1854. This part of the office was then, to some extent, remodelled, in order that the secretary of state might avail himself of Bergne's special knowledge and ability. No one, probably, could have occupied this post more efficiently than Bergne, who for many years was a trusted adviser of successive secretaries of state, and whose reputation as an authority on all matters connected with treaties extended far beyond English official circles. In 1865 he was a member of the commission appointed to revise the slave trade instructions. He remained the head of the treaty department until his death, at 21 Thurloe Square, Kensington, on 16 January 1873. He married Rebecca Gibbs and had at least two sons, the elder of whom, Sir J. H. G. *Bergne, followed him in the Foreign Office.

Although Bergne's name did not come prominently before the general public, the sterling services which his remarkable memory, accuracy, and judgement enabled him to render during the long years of his life in the Foreign Office were universally and cordially recognized by his colleagues. He made his mark not less as an antiquary and numismatist than as an important public servant. He was one of the founders in 1837 of the Numismatic Society, of which he was treasurer from 1843 to 1857, and was several times afterwards elected a vice-president. He was also a fellow of the Society of Antiquaries. As a numismatist he devoted his attention chiefly to Roman and English coins, his collection of which was dispersed after his death; many of the most valuable examples were bought for the British Museum at a Sothebys sale in May 1873. He wrote at least fourteen articles in the *Numismatic Chronicle*.   A. A. Brodribb, *rev.* H. C. G. Matthew

Sources *Numismatic Chronicle*, new ser., 13 (1873) · Boase, *Mod. Eng. biog.* · b. cert., John Henry Gibbs Bergne
Wealth at death under £20,000: probate, 13 Feb 1873, *CGPLA Eng. & Wales*

Bergne, Sir John Henry Gibbs (1842–1908), diplomatist, was born at 19 Hans Place, London, on 12 August 1842, the elder son of John Brodribb *Bergne (1800–1873), Foreign Office clerk, and his wife, Rebecca, *née* Gibbs. He was descended from a French family originally resident in Auvergne, which settled in England after the French Revolution. Educated at schools at Brighton and Enfield and at London University, where he graduated BA, he followed his father by entering the Foreign Office as a clerk in the diplomatic establishment after passing a competitive examination in 1861; he was appointed an assistant clerk in 1880, and promoted to be superintendent of the treaty department in 1881, an office in which he continued until 1894, when he became superintendent of the commercial department and examiner of treaties. He held this position for eight years, doing much valuable work in the development of the commercial department and particularly in the arrangement of its relations with the Board of Trade, and in introducing a more regular and complete system of reports on commercial and industrial subjects from diplomatic and consular officers in foreign countries. He was occasionally employed abroad on business which came within the sphere of his permanent work, and on which he possessed special knowledge. In 1875 he assisted the British agent before the international commission, which sat under article 22 of the treaty of Washington, to assess the amount to be paid by the United States to Great Britain in return for the fishery privileges accorded to the citizens of the United States under article 18 of that treaty; when the commission met at Halifax in 1877 he acted as secretary and protocolist to it. In September 1887 he was appointed secretary to Joseph Chamberlain's special mission to Washington to adjust certain questions relating to the North American fisheries. For his services he was made KCMG in 1888, having been made CMG in 1886.

In 1885 Bergne was second British delegate at the international copyright conference held at Bern, and signed the convention which was agreed there (9 September 1886). While at Washington in 1887 he was deputed to discuss the copyright question with the United States department of state. In May 1896, as British delegate to a conference at Paris, he signed the additional act to the international copyright convention of 1886. He was appointed a member of the departmental committee on trade marks in 1888, and was sent as British delegate to the conference on industrial property held at Rome in 1888, at Madrid in 1890, and at Brussels in November 1897 and again in 1900. From 1898 onwards he was constantly employed in the negotiations for the abolition of bounties on the export of sugar, and was one of the British delegates at the conferences held in Brussels on this question in 1899 and 1901; on 5 March 1902 he signed the convention concluded on the latter occasion. In 1903 he was appointed the British delegate on the permanent commission established under article 7 of that convention, and attended the various meetings of the commission, furnishing reports which were laid before parliament and which were marked by his usual power of terse, lucid explanation. He served as a member on the royal commission for the Paris Exhibition of 1900. He retired from the Foreign Office on a pension on 1 October 1902, but his employment on the special subjects of which he had an intimate knowledge continued. He was made CB in 1902 and KCB in the following year. In November 1908 he served as British delegate at the international copyright conference at Berlin.

Though scarcely an author in the ordinary sense of the term, Bergne rendered important services to the Society of Authors, of which he became a member in 1890; after his retirement from the Foreign Office he served on the committee of management and copyright subcommittee, and acted as chairman of the general committee (1905–7). He contributed articles on diplomatic topics to the *Quarterly Review*, *Blackwood's Magazine*, *The Spectator*, and other periodicals. He was also an accomplished mountaineer and well-known member of the Alpine Club from 1878 until his death, and a collector of oriental china.

Bergne married, in 1878, Mary à Court, daughter of the Revd S. B. Bergne; they had two sons, the elder of whom was killed in an accident near Saas Fee in Switzerland in January 1908. Bergne died of a chill at the Hotel Continental, Berlin, on 15 November 1908. His wife survived him.
                            T. H. Sanderson, *rev.* H. C. G. Matthew

Sources *The Times* (16 Nov 1908) · *Author* (1 Dec 1908) · W. E. Davidson, 'In memoriam: Sir Henry Bergne', *Alpine Journal*, 24 (1909), 499–501 · *FO List* (1909), 397 · b. cert.
Wealth at death £15,535 7s. 2d.: probate, 17 Dec 1908, *CGPLA Eng. & Wales*

Berhthun [St Berhthun, Berchthun] (d. **733/40**), abbot (probably of Beverley), was originally a deacon under John, bishop of Hexham and of York, now known as St John of Beverley. It was from Berhthun that Bede obtained much of the information respecting John's life and miracles which is contained in his history. The only biographical information about Berhthun which is certain from

Bede is that he had been John's deacon but was by 731 abbot of the monastery of 'Inderawuda' to which John had retired and where he was buried in 721; 'Inderawuda' was identified by later tradition, almost certainly correctly, as Beverley. Two at least of the stories which Berhthun told Bede are in the first person, and refer to miracles which John performed while bishop of York. There is no other contemporary evidence for Berhthun, but Folcard's life of John and other later sources assert that it was John who had founded the monastery and appointed Berhthun abbot, and that John had retired there on Berhthun's advice. They also suggest that Berhthun died in either 733 or 740. Although no formal record of his canonization seems to exist, the title of saint is given to him by early writers, and his name appears in the calendar under 15 May, the day of his death. After the fire at Beverley Minster in 1188, where he had been buried, Berhthun's remains were translated to a new tomb. His name, which is given by Bede as Bercthun, was probably Berhthun in Old English.

HENRY BRADLEY, *rev.* D. M. PALLISER

Sources Bede, *Hist. eccl.*, 5.2, 4 • J. Raine, ed., *The historians of the church of York and its archbishops*, 3 vols., Rolls Series, 71 (1879–94) • 'De S. Joanne Beverlacensi', *Acta sanctorum: Maius*, 2 (Antwerp, 1680), 167; 3 (1680), 500

Berhtwald [Brihtwald] (*c*.650–731), archbishop of Canterbury, was born about the middle of the seventh century, but neither the place nor the exact date of his birth is known. According to Bede, Berhtwald, although not to be compared with his predecessor Theodore, was none the less thoroughly read in scripture, and well instructed in ecclesiastical and monastic discipline. In 669 Ecgberht, king of Kent, gave the old Roman fort of Reculver to the church; within a decade a monastery had been established there and Berhtwald had become its abbot. A grant of land to Berhtwald as abbot, dated May 679, from Hlothere, king of Kent, is the earliest original Anglo-Saxon charter to have survived.

Two years after the death of Theodore, Berhtwald was elected archbishop of Canterbury, on 1 July 692. The delay is perhaps to be attributed to opposition to the election coming from the kingdoms of Mercia, Northumbria, and East Anglia where the preferred candidate for the job is likely to have been the Northumbrian bishop Wilfrid. Such opposition would also explain Berhtwald's decision to be consecrated in Francia by Godinus, archbishop of Lyons, on 29 June 693 and his subsequent journey to Rome to receive his pallium from Pope Sergius. Sergius, moreover, gave Berhtwald two letters: one addressed to the kings of Mercia, Northumbria, and East Anglia exhorting them to receive Berhtwald as 'primate of all England', the other to the English bishops, enjoining obedience to him as such. The authenticity of these letters is now generally accepted; earlier doubts based on the fact that the letters have been preserved only in the context of Canterbury's claims to the primacy of England in the late eleventh century are no longer considered to carry conviction.

As archbishop Berhtwald enjoyed a fruitful partnership with Wihtred, king of Kent. In 695 he attended a royal council at Bearsted in which laws were passed giving exemption from taxation to Kentish churches and prescribing the penalties to be exacted for various offences, ecclesiastical and moral. In 699 ordinances seemingly drawn up by Berhtwald, and confirmed by the king, gave further privileges to the church in Kent. These are, however, not to be confused with the so-called 'privilege of Wihtred', a ninth-century forgery that aimed to claim exemption for Kentish monasteries from all lay control.

In 702 Berhtwald presided at the council of Austerfield attended by Aldfrith, king of Northumbria, in order to try to resolve the long-standing dispute between the king and Bishop Wilfrid. The council failed to achieve its aims, but on the death of Aldfrith in 704, Berhtwald was at last able to find a compromise acceptable to all parties and agreed upon at the council of Nidd in 705. In the same year, 705, Berhtwald took measures for the division of the diocese of Wessex, by creating on the death of Hædde, bishop of Winchester, a new see at Sherborne. Shortly afterwards Berhtwald also established a new see for the South Saxons at Selsey.

An interesting letter has been preserved, in which Berhtwald addressed Forthhere, the successor of Aldhelm as bishop of Sherborne, imploring him to induce Beorwold, abbot of Glastonbury, to release a slave girl for a ransom of 300 shillings offered by her brother. Of at least equal, if not greater, interest is the letter addressed to Berhtwald by Waldhere, bishop of the East Saxons, written at the time of the proposed division of the see of Wessex. The interest here lies both in the deference displayed by Waldhere to Berhtwald and in the form of the letter, the earliest on parchment (originally tied closed) to have survived in the original in the West.

Berhtwald died on 13 January 731. According to Bede, he was buried near his predecessor Theodore inside the church of St Peter at Canterbury, the porch in which the first six archbishops had been buried being now quite full.   W. R. W. STEPHENS, *rev.* HENRIETTA LEYSER

Sources N. Brooks, *The early history of the church of Canterbury: Christ Church from 597 to 1066* (1984) • Bede, *Hist. eccl.*, 5.23

Berhtwulf [Beorhtwulf] (*d.* 852?), king of the Mercians, is usually regarded as the direct successor of King Wiglaf, although the *Passio sancti Wigstani*, which may be based on a ninth-century source, claims that Wiglaf's son, Wigmund, ruled in the intervening period. The circumstances of Berhtwulf's accession and the basis of his claim to the kingship remain obscure, though it is possible that he was a kinsman of Wiglaf's predecessor, *Beornwulf (*d.* 826?). The *Passio sancti Wigstani* gives a lurid but essentially credible account of dynastic politics in Berhtwulf's reign. Wigstan, son of Wigmund and grandson of Wiglaf, is said to have renounced the kingship in favour of the religious life. Subsequently, Berhtferth, the son of King Berhtwulf, asked for the hand of Wigstan's widowed mother, Ælfflæd, who was the daughter of the earlier King Ceolwulf (*r.* 821–3) and would have represented a potentially useful alliance for an aspiring king. Wigstan refused his consent, and was subsequently killed by Berhtferth (reputedly in

850); he was buried in the royal mausoleum at Repton, with his grandfather Wiglaf and the earlier King Æthelbald, and appears to have become the focus of an early cult, perhaps fostered by Berhtwulf's political opponents.

Like his predecessor Wiglaf, Berhtwulf seems to have reached an accommodation with the ruler of Wessex, the dominant power in southern England. During the early years of his reign the Mercian mint at London was revived, after apparently having ceased production for a decade or more. The dies for the first group of coins in Berhtwulf's name were the work of a Rochester die-cutter, who either worked in Mercia or supplied dies to Berhtwulf's moneyers. At this stage Kent was under West Saxon control, and it might be supposed that King Æthelwulf's permission would be required for such activity (for a short period the coins of Æthelwulf and Berhtwulf were virtually indistinguishable); on the other hand, there was a strong economic connection between Kent and the great Mercian port of London (*AS chart.*, S 88), and this might explain the numismatic contact. A convenient way to assess the relative strengths of the kingdoms of Wessex and Mercia is to look at the long-disputed territory around the upper Thames valley. Berhtwulf could dispose of land around Pangbourne in what is now Berkshire in 844, but the future King Alfred was born on a nearby West Saxon royal estate at Wantage in 849; either the disputed territory passed to Wessex in the course of the 840s, or there was an agreed division between the two old enemies (which may have taken place as early as Wiglaf's reign).

Fifteen charters in Berhtwulf's name survive, of which about two-thirds can be regarded as authentic; in proportion to the length of his reign, this indicates a far higher rate of charter production than was the case under his predecessor Wiglaf or his successor Burgred. The majority of the acceptable texts tend to be concerned with grants of privileges and exemption to churches and monasteries, in return for money, bullion, or the lease of ecclesiastical lands to grant to the king's thegns. One particularly interesting text describes the restoration to the church of Worcester of a number of estates which Berhtwulf, in the judgment of the Mercian witan, had stolen from the community and bestowed upon his men (*AS chart.*, S 192). These documents give the impression that Berhtwulf was anxious to build up his resources and to accumulate land with which to reward his followers. It seems likely that his position within Mercia was insecure, so that he needed to fight off challengers; the fact that he could not rely on the Mercian witan to support his depredations is a sign that he could not expect unconditional support from his subordinate nobles. But there was also an external threat in the shape of viking raids, which were becoming ever more of a problem on the English coasts. Thanks to its position, the Mercian heartland was relatively secure from these sea-borne pirates, although it is known that there was a devastating raid on the province of Lindsey in Berhtwulf's second year, and other raids on Mercian areas probably passed unnoticed by the West Saxon compilers of the Anglo-Saxon Chronicle. But the Mercian trading emporium at London was both a magnet to the raiders and very vulnerable. There was 'a great slaughter' there in 842; then in 851 a huge fleet (reputedly of 350 ships) sailed up the Thames and sacked the town. Berhtwulf came to meet the vikings with a Mercian army, but he was defeated and put to flight and it was left to the West Saxons to repel the raiders as they turned into Surrey.

Little is known of Berhtwulf's activities after this defeat. The three latest charters in his name (*AS chart.*, S 200–02) are all spurious. According to the Worcester chronicle he died in the thirteenth year of his reign (probably in 852) and was succeeded by Burgred (who was certainly king in 853). Berhtwulf probably had a son in addition to the (perhaps mythical) Berhtferth reputed to have murdered Wigstan: in two of his earlier charters (S 198, 205) a witness named Berhtric subscribes as 'the king's son'. Many of Berhtwulf's charters are also witnessed by his wife, Sæthryth, who (like a number of other Mercian queens) seems to have enjoyed a high status.   S. E. KELLY

Sources ASC, s.a. 841–2, 851 [texts A, E] · John of Worcester, *Chron.* · *AS chart.*, S 191–205 · S. Keynes, 'King Alfred and the Mercians', *Kings, currency and alliances: history and coinage of southern England in the ninth century*, ed. M. A. S. Blackburn and D. N. Dumville (1998), 1–46 · P. Grierson and M. Blackburn, *Medieval European coinage: with a catalogue of the coins in the Fitzwilliam Museum, Cambridge*, 1: *The early middle ages (5th–10th centuries)* (1986), 286, 291–3 · A. Thacker, 'Kings, saints and monasteries in pre-viking Mercia', *Midland History*, 10 (1985), 1–25, esp. 12–14 · D. W. Rollason, 'The cults of murdered royal saints in Anglo-Saxon England', *Anglo-Saxon England*, 11 (1983), 1–22, esp. 5–9

Berington, Charles (1748–1798), vicar apostolic of the midland district, was born at Stock Hall, near Chelmsford, Essex, the third of the four children of Thomas Berington, gentleman, of Moat Hall, Pontesbury, Shropshire, and his wife, Anne, daughter of a Mr Bates of Stock Hall. He was educated in classics at the English College, Douai (1761–5), and went to St Gregory's English College in Paris to study philosophy and divinity (DD 1776). Ordained in 1775, he served on the English mission at Ingatestone Hall in his native county between 1776 and 1784, before spending two years travelling in Europe as tutor to the young Thomas Joseph Giffard of Chillington. In March 1786 Bishop Thomas Talbot, vicar apostolic of the midland district, petitioned the Holy See to grant him a coadjutor in the person of Berington, who was accordingly appointed to that post. His brief to the see of Hierocaesarea, *in partibus infidelium*, was dated 12 May 1786, and he was consecrated at Longbirch, Staffordshire, on 1 August.

In 1788 Berington was elected a member of the Catholic Committee, which afterwards formed itself into the Cisalpine Club. He identified himself with the proceedings of this self-constituted body which, in its attempt to restore the privileges of the Catholic community in Britain, often appeared to reject the authority of the vicars apostolic as well as that of the court of Rome. In 1790 the Catholic Committee made strenuous efforts to obtain the translation of Berington to the London district on the death of Bishop James Talbot; but the choice of the Holy See fell upon Dr John Douglass. Several of the lay members of the committee went so far as to maintain that the clergy and laity ought to choose their own bishops without any reference to Rome, and to procure their consecration at the hands of any other lawful bishop. It was even proposed by them, after the nomination of Douglass, to pronounce that appointment 'obnoxious and improper' (Milner, 71 n.) and to refuse to acknowledge it. Berington, however, addressed a printed letter to the London clergy, resigning every pretension to the London vicariate, and thereupon the systematic opposition to Douglass was withdrawn.

Bishop Thomas Talbot died at Bristol on 24 February 1795, and Berington succeeded *per coadjutoriam* to the vicariate apostolic of the midland district. Berington was greatly disliked by the clergy who were loyal to the Holy See, however. The Revd Robert Plowden, who was chaplain of St Joseph's, Bristol, when Bishop Thomas Talbot died, went so far as to prevent Berington from saying mass in suffrage for the soul of the friend and prelate to whom he had been coadjutor.

The Holy See required of Berington, as an indispensable condition for the dispatch of the extraordinary faculties usually conceded to vicars apostolic, that he should renounce the condemned 'oath' and the 'blue books' of the Catholic Committee, and his subscription to them. This oath formed part of the Relief Bill proposed by the committee, who, surrendering the names 'Catholic' and 'Roman Catholic', designated themselves 'protesting Catholic dissenters'. The 'blue books', containing the protestation, the oath, and other documents issued by the committee, were so called from being stitched up in blue or rather purple covers. A long correspondence between Berington and Propaganda ensued before the bishop was persuaded to sign a satisfactory form of retraction. At last, after an interchange of letters for nearly three years, the bishop signed at Wolverhampton, on 11 October 1797, the retraction which was required of him. The papers containing the faculties were sent from Rome, and reached the hands of Bishop Douglass on 5 June 1798; but Berington died without having received them. While journeying on horseback from Sedgley Park to his residence at Longbirch, Staffordshire, he was taken suddenly ill, and his chaplain, the Revd John Kirk, had only just time to give him absolution before he died of apoplexy on the roadside on 8 June 1798. He was buried on 11 June in Brewood parish church, where his brother erected a memorial tablet.

An obituary in the *Gentleman's Magazine* praised his charm and learning, mentioning that Berington was

> a prelate whose amiable virtues gave an impressive charm to the truths of religion; a scholar of great classical taste, a man whose judgment was profound, whose manners were peculiarly conciliating, and whose hilarity of conversation rendered him the delight of society. (*GM*, 622)

Other Catholic obituaries, however, were critical of the important role he had played in the Catholic Committee. Thus Bishop John Milner wrote that although

> endowed with superior talents and the sweetest temper, he wanted the firmness requisite for the episcopal character in these times to stem the tide of irreligious novelty and lay influence, and so lent his name and authority to the oath and the 'blue books,' and to every other measure which his

fellow-committeemen deemed these might serve. (Milner, 94)

More critically, dismissing the suggestion that he write a biography of his friend, Joseph Berington mused that

> his moral character was great, and his natural talents excellent; but to the latter he had given no cultivation. Would you say, that he went to Douay young, where he applied little; that he removed to Paris, where he applied less; that he returned to England, where he did nothing; that he went abroad, and came back; that he was made bishop, lived a few years, and died? The part he acted as a member of the Cat[holic] Committee could not be mentioned, which was the only conspicuous part of his life, without giving offence, and, perhaps, provoking discussion. (J. Berington to J. Kirk, 14 Aug 1798, Birmingham Archdiocesan Archives, C1487)

THOMPSON COOPER, *rev.* JOHN SHARP

Sources Birmingham Roman Catholic archdiocesan archives, A and C series · J. Milner, *Supplementary memoirs of English Catholics* (1820) · C. Butler, *Historical memoirs of the English, Irish, and Scottish Catholics since the Reformation*, 3rd edn, 4 (1822) · Gillow, *Lit. biog. hist.*, vol. 1 · G. Anstruther, *The seminary priests*, 4 (1977) · J. Kirk, *Biographies of English Catholics in the eighteenth century*, ed. J. H. Pollen and E. Burton (1909) · W. M. Brady, *The episcopal succession in England, Scotland, and Ireland, AD 1400 to 1875*, 3 (1877) · B. Ward, *The dawn of the Catholic revival in England, 1781–1803*, 2 vols. (1909) · *GM*, 1st ser., 68 (1798), 542, 622 · E. Duffy, 'Ecclesiastical democracy detected [pt 2]', *Recusant History*, 10 (1969–70), 309–31 · E. Duffy, 'Ecclesiastical democracy detected [pt 3]', *Recusant History*, 13 (1975–6), 123–48

Archives Birmingham Roman Catholic archdiocesan archives, corresp.

Berington, Joseph (1743–1827), Roman Catholic priest and religious controversialist, was born on 16 January 1743 at Winsley, Herefordshire, the son of John Berington and his wife, Winefred Hornyold. From a prominent Catholic family, he was tutored for a year by his uncle Bishop John Hornyold; from 1754 he received his preparatory education at Esquerchin and then entered the English College at Douai on 12 August 1756. Berington always wished to pursue a literary life. Open to Enlightenment thought and influenced greatly by the growing empiricism and Gallican historical methodology of his teachers, he was ordained in 1770 and became professor of philosophy at Douai. In 1771 he was dismissed from teaching following the censure of his 'Theses ex logica et psychologia' by Alban Butler, another professor at Douai, for its anti-scholasticism and advocacy of sensationalism. He returned to England on 5 October 1772. The young priest resided briefly at his ancestral home, Winsley House, eventually took charge of the Wolverhampton mission, and in 1776 became chaplain to the Stapleton family at Carlton Towers, Carlton-juxta-Snaith, Yorkshire.

Berington rejected the more radical philosophical tendencies of his earlier opinions in *Letters on Materialism, and Hartley's Theory of the Human Mind, Addressed to Dr. Priestley* (1776). His 1780 advocacy of curricular reforms at Douai and *Letter to Dr. Fordyce in Answer to his Sermon on the Delusive and Persecuting Spirit of Popery*, denouncing established religion and appealing to toleration, continued both a theological liberalism which frightened the more conservative and a sharp criticism of an insular and combative Tridentine Catholicism. Berington learned German while

Joseph Berington
(1743–1827), by
unknown engraver

thick clouds which controversy has raised, it would then appear, that the Protestant Church of England and Catholics are divided by very thin partitions. (*The State and Behaviour of English Catholics*, 148)

His programme of political, social, and religious reform was furthered in a set of *Reflections Addressed to the Reverend John Hawkins* (1785) and in *The History of the Lives of Abeillard and Heloisa* (1787). His *History of the Reign of Henry II, and of Richard and John, his Sons* (1790) vindicated the character of Thomas Becket. The historical argumentation culminated in the much debated *The Memoirs of Gregorio Panzani, giving an account of his agency in England in the years 1634-5-6* (1793). This included a 'Supplement exhibiting the state of the English Catholic church. And the conduct of parties, before and after that period, to the present time'. In the preface to this last work the author announced his projected 'History of the rise, the greatness, and the decline of the papal power', a treatise never published but which J. Gillow identified in the later nineteenth century as still existing in manuscript form at Oscott College. Berington's shorter works during the same period, showing his affinities with Priestley, made common cause with religious dissenters and supported a public educational religious code capable of reaching all believers.

Through friendship and these historical and theological writings, Berington aligned himself with the lay Catholic Committee formed in 1782 and its more radical successor the Cisalpine Club (1792) led by Sir John Throckmorton. In 1786 the latter unsuccessfully pushed the vicars apostolic to accept the seventeenth-century statement *Roman Catholic Principles* which Berington had earlier attached to the Revd John Hawkins. In 1789 the committee proposed an oath of loyalty, eventually condemned by three out of the four vicars apostolic, and in its first (1789), second (1791), and third (1792) 'blue book' defended a standard Cisalpine interpretation of history similar to Berington's. Although expressing some reservations about the oath, in 1792 the controversial priest placed himself at the centre of the debate between some of the vicars apostolic and the clergy supporting the Cisalpine position. His 'Staffordshire creed' (*An Appeal to the Catholics of England by the Catholic Clergy of the County of Stafford*, 1792) defended the canonical rights of priests and argued that 'the Bishop of Rome [was] to be the *head*, supreme in *Spirituals* by divine appointment, supreme in *discipline* by ecclesiastical institution; but in the concerns of state and civil life, we believe him to be no governor, no master, no guide' (Duffy, 'Joseph Berington', 218). During these debates, the priest leaders of the oppositional side, Charles Plowden (*Considerations on the Modern Opinion of the Fallibility of the Holy See*, 1790) and John Milner (*The Divine Right of Episcopacy Addressed to the Catholic Laity*, 1791), supported by some of the vicars apostolic, attacked the Catholic Committee. In the following years, Plowden and Milner noted the affinities between Berington's thinking and that of medieval heretics, the ecclesiastical reformers of the Synod of Pistoia, and the French national assembly. They publicly and privately singled out his orthodoxy as suspect. Although

travelling on the continent (1783–5). Upon his return he served the small mission at Oscott, Handsworth, Staffordshire, where he was joined by his cousin Bishop Charles Berington, the coadjutor to Thomas Talbot, vicar apostolic of the midland district, both of whom would eventually protect him from severe ecclesiastical censure. While serving the mission, Berington attended social meetings at Barr with Joseph Priestley, Matthew Boulton, and James Watt. Miss Mary Anne Galton, afterwards Mrs Schimmelpenninck, witnessed these gatherings and described the erudite priest as a

> finished gentleman of the old school, and a model of ecclesiastical decorum of the church of ancient monuments and memories; his cold, stern eye instantly silenced any unbecoming levity either on religion or morality; his bearing was of a prince amongst his people, not from worldly position, but from his sacerdotal office, while his ancient and high family seemed but a slight appendage to the dignity of his character. His voice was deep and majestic, like the baying of a bloodhound; and when he intoned Mass, every action seemed to thrill through the soul. (Hankin, 36)

From 1780 to 1793 Berington entered into the struggle to win Catholic political freedoms with successive historical and theological publications severely criticizing medieval scholastic theology and the temporal power of the papacy. He also argued for 'reasonableness', universal toleration, the compatibility between Catholicism and English constitutionalism, and the need for the reform of the Roman church through the promotion of vernacular liturgy and a change in the discipline of a celibate priesthood. His most famous work, which appeared in 1780, was an account entitled *The State and Behaviour of English Catholics from the Reformation to the Year 1780, with a view of their present number, wealth, character*, in which he wrote:

> Of this, however, I am convinced, that, were certain obstacles removed, such as the views of interest, the animosity of party, the blindness of prejudice, and those

denied priestly faculties by the vicar apostolic of the London district, John Douglass, Berington accepted the invitation of John Throckmorton to become his chaplain and moved to his estate in Buckland, Berkshire, in May 1793. He continued exchanging his disagreements with Milner, and when the opposition party claimed ratification for its views from a series of reported miracles in Italy, Berington issued a vitriolic attack on Italian 'superstition', *An Examination of Events Termed Miraculous, as Reported in Letters from Italy* (1796). Douglass threatened suspension; Milner also responded in *A Serious Expostulation* (1797) and summarized many of the allegations which had occurred in the previous decade. Berington, refusing both to sign the creed of Pius IV because of its clause about exclusive salvation within the Catholic faith and to retract until Douglass affirmed his orthodoxy, finally accommodated himself, issued *A Letter to the Right Reverend John Douglass* (1797), and was temporarily reconciled. He then worked with the Staffordshire clergy to publish a more conciliatory *Exposition of our Sentiments* (1797), explaining the offending clauses in the 1791 creed. His explanation failed to mollify several of the vicars apostolic. Finally, when Milner claimed to present a true picture of Catholic England in his polemical *The History and Antiquities of Winchester* (1798), Berington agreed in some measure with Dr John Sturges's *Reflections on the Principles and Institutions of Popery* (1799). He summarized his lifelong convictions about civil liberty and papal authority by levelling a broadside attack on Milner's combative Catholicism in a letter to the *Gentleman's Magazine* (1st ser., 69, 1799, 653–4). Douglass withdrew Berington's faculties and publicly condemned his writings. Two years later, in 1801, the priest signed an unequivocal retractation, received his faculties and public rehabilitation, and the same year helped reconcile the Staffordshire clergy.

In his remaining years, apart from a printed compilation of prayers (1800), a few letters, and some manuscripts listed by Gillow, Berington published *The Faith of Catholics, confirmed by scripture, and attested by the fathers of the five first centuries* (1813, 1830; rev. edn, 3 vols., 1846). This work was based on the earlier *Roman Catholic Principles* and contained an important letter to Dr William Poynter, the vicar apostolic of the London district. His final work was the learned and still Cisalpine *A Literary History of the Middle Ages: comprehending an account of the state of learning, from the close of the reign of Augustus to its revival in the fifteenth century* (1814; repr. 1846 with introduction by William Hazlitt). Berington laboured as a priest at Buckland until his death there on 1 December 1827, and was buried under a prominently inscribed monument in the chancel of that church. The more moderate early twentieth century works of Bernard Ward and the factual groundwork laid by Eamon Duffy in studies in the 1970s have moved posterity's judgement of Berington beyond Milner's dominating and condemning interpretation. Yet, Berington still awaits a balanced study which places him in the context both of the Enlightenment and an Anglo-French orthodox theological and political tradition critical of Counter-Reformation Catholicism. J. P. CHINNICI

Sources E. Duffy, 'Joseph Berington and the English Catholic Cisalpine movement, 1772–1803', PhD diss., U. Cam., 1973 • E. Duffy, 'Ecclesiastical democracy detected [pt 1]', *Recusant History*, 10 (1969–70), 193–209 • E. Duffy, 'Ecclesiastical democracy detected [pt 2]', *Recusant History*, 10 (1969–70), 309–31 • E. Duffy, 'Ecclesiastical democracy detected [pt 3]', *Recusant History*, 13 (1975–6), 123–48 • E. Duffy, 'Doctor Douglass and Mister Berington: an eighteenth-century retraction', *Downside Review*, 88 (1970), 246–69 • G. Anstruther, *The seminary priests*, 4 (1977) • C. C. Hankin, ed., *Life of Mary Anne Schimmelpenninck*, 3rd edn, 2 vols. in 1 (1859), 36 • B. Ward, *The dawn of the Catholic revival in England, 1781–1803*, 2 vols. (1909) • B. N. Ward, *The eve of Catholic emancipation*, 3 vols. (1911–12) • Gillow, *Lit. biog. hist.* • M. Sharratt, 'Copernicanism at Douai', *Durham University Journal*, 67 (1974–5), 41–8 • F. C. Husenbeth, *The life of … John Milner* (1862)

Archives archives of the Roman Catholic archbishop of Westminster, London • Archivio Vaticano, Vatican City, archives of Propaganda Fide • Birmingham Roman Catholic archdiocesan archives, Birmingham, corresp. and papers • priv. coll. • Warks. CRO, corresp., especially with Throckmorton family | Archives of the bishop of Clifton, Clifton

Likenesses engraved silhouette, NPG [*see illus.*] • silhouette, repro. in *Laity's Directory* (1831)

Wealth at death £2000: will, PRO, PROB 8/221; Anstruther, *Seminary priests*, 29–30

Beriosova, Svetlana (1932–1998), ballet dancer, was born on 24 September 1932 at Kaunas, Lithuania, the daughter of Nicholas Beriozoff (1906–1996), dancer and ballet master, then a member of the Lithuanian State Ballet, and his first wife, Maria (d. 1941). Her grandparents had migrated to Lithuania from St Petersburg. Beriozoff, universally known (and addressed) as Poppa, was in 1935 invited to join René Blum's Ballet Russe de Monte Carlo, then in Paris, where he was joined by his wife and daughter. The latter was educated at local schools, including a Soho kindergarten during a visit to London with her parents in 1936, and was given early ballet lessons by her father. She became adept at languages, speaking Russian and French daily, later learning English (with much difficulty, she confessed), and having a conversational acquaintance with German, Italian, and Spanish.

On the outbreak of the Second World War in 1939 Beriozoff was on tour with the Blum company in the USA and sent for his wife and daughter to join him. This was accomplished with some difficulty, entailing an enforced detention as immigrant prisoners on Ellis Island, New York, which left the seven-year-old girl traumatized sufficiently to obliterate the experience from her subsequent memory. Having eventually been united with her father, she and her mother settled into a New York apartment while Beriozoff continued touring; it was Svetlana's first settled home. She was sent for regular schooling in local state schools, transferring at the age of ten to a special school for children of stage performers.

Beriosova had by then set her sights on a dancer's career despite its rigours, and in 1940 her father enrolled her in a newly opened school directed by two St Petersburg dancers from the former Diaghilev Ballets Russes, Anatole Wilzak and Ludmila Schollar, where Svetlana underwent a full ballet training, later supplemented by the distinguished Russian teacher Olga Preobrajenska in Paris. The

Svetlana Beriosova (1932–1998), by Baron, 1954 [with Michael Somes in *Rinaldo and Armida*]

New York training helped her to overcome the tragic loss of her mother, who died suddenly in 1941, and to establish a settled new relationship with a stepmother, Adeline Jeanne Rosalie, whom her father married after a few months. She had already begun some stage performances with Ballet Russe de Monte Carlo in New York, appearing at the age of eight as the child Clara in *The Nutcracker* and as the girl with the skipping rope in Massine's *Le beau Danube*.

Beriosova's professional adult début occurred in March 1947 as a guest in an end-of-term production by a ballet school (which was nevertheless of a high standard) billed as the Ottawa Ballet Company, dancing the Snow Queen and the Sugar-Plum Fairy in a complete *Nutcracker*, which brought her first enthusiastic press reviews. She returned to New York and to school lessons, which continued by correspondence when she accompanied her parents on tour. Her father was next invited, in the summer of 1947, to join a new company in Monte Carlo, later well known as the Grand Ballet du Marquis de Cuevas; Svetlana went with him and at the age of fourteen joined the company's *corps de ballet* as a salaried dancer.

Beriosova clearly paid heed to her father's advice in the furtherance of her career, but it is by no means clear that he was a major influence on her individual development. After nine months with the de Cuevas company, father and daughter were next invited to join the (English) Metropolitan Ballet, launched early in 1947 and gradually building a more than local reputation under the direction of Cecilia Blatch, which was bolstered by the arrival of the Beriozoffs. However, the teenage Beriosova, according to Blatch, 'isn't quite what we need at the moment but in a few months she'll be what everyone needs' (Franks, 23).

During 1948 Beriosova took her first leading roles, appearing in *Designs with Strings* by the American John Taras and then in the title role in *Fanciulla delle rose* by the South African Frank Staff, the first ballet created specifically for her. She was exposed to the rigours of touring in a still heavily rationed and often under-heated Britain, which no whit diminished her commitment and progress as a visibly great dancer in the making. Her image of striking physical beauty was now registering in the whole-hearted admiration of her audiences, who were captivated by her wide facial features with their high brow and Slavonic cheekbones, and a warmly generous smile to temper the touch of instinctive reserved aloofness in an already aristocratic, even regal, personality.

With the Metropolitan Ballet, Beriosova had her first modest success as Odette in act II of *Swan Lake* (the counterpart role of Odile in act III would not come until much later) during the company's climactic season at the former Scala Theatre in London; there she was seen by Ninette de Valois of the Sadler's Wells Ballet, who noted of her: 'Such poetry of emotion and feeling was rare in one so young. I hoped so much that one day she would be with us' (N. de Valois, *Come Dance with Me*, 1957, 178–9), expressing a hope that was soon fulfilled. Before that the schoolgirl dancer (she was pictured at her conventional lessons while in ballet costume in her dressing-room) was raised to journalistic celebrity status on a tour of Scandinavia with the Metropolitan company.

Late in 1949 the Metropolitan Ballet company was in the USA when Mrs Blatch, who had financed the company throughout from her own pocket, with no public subsidy, realized that her pocket was not bottomless, and was forced to close and disband her company—having been privileged, she commented, to bring to the fore and develop so great an artist as Svetlana Beriosova. The Beriozoffs too were in America at this time, involved in the tortuous process of acquiring United States citizenship. As soon as she heard of the Metropolitan's demise, however, de Valois immediately invited Beriosova to join Sadler's Wells Ballet in Britain, and the prospect this held of a reasonably secure career, dancing in a British classical style more suited to her than American athleticism, led to a change of mind in favour of seeking British nationality. Her father supported this decision, and in 1954 he became naturalized, followed by Beriosova in 1955.

Beriosova joined the Sadler's Wells Theatre Ballet in the rank of soloist. She made her début as a British ballerina on 20 May 1950 as Odette in act II of *Swan Lake*. In the view of many she was still too young to be considered a mature artist, but displayed true ballerina promise. She had to learn and rehearse eight roles new to her within three weeks, and happily settled down to a hard-working life with the company in London and on long regional tours, receiving friendly support on all sides.

Two years later Beriosova transferred to the main Sadler's Wells Ballet company (later the Royal Ballet) at Covent Garden, where she spent the rest of her career. She was promoted to official ballerina status (principal) in 1955, the year before the company received its royal charter. She danced all the great classical roles and enchanted audiences with the smooth serenity of her style, giving glimpses of hidden humour in such ballets as *Coppélia* (various dates), and *Jazz Calendar* (1968). Choreographers made new leading roles for her, notably that of Princess Belle Rose in John Cranko's original *Prince of the Pagodas* (1957), a major three-act production, and the role portraying the gentle, concerned dignity of Elgar's wife in Sir Frederick Ashton's *Enigma Variations* (1968). Ashton also cast her in the title role of his *Perséphone* (1961), where, as well as dancing superbly, she spoke the lines of André Gide's text in perfectly idiomatic French and with a beauty of feeling that remained unforgettable by all who heard her.

Off stage Beriosova lived modestly in a small but comfortable west London flat, entertaining her own circle of friends and keeping open house for fellow dancers in need of bed and board. Donald Macleary, her regular partner in the Royal Ballet for fourteen years, wrote of her: 'She was very caring and was always there if I had problems. It was difficult to return her kindness as she was a very strong and independent person. She loved books, painting, children and animals' (*The Guardian*, 16 Nov 1998). She was totally free of journalistic gossip until she surprised everyone by marrying, on 23 January 1959, (Mohammed) Masud Raza *Khan (1924–1989), a psychiatrist and psychoanalyst with a central London practice. He was the son of Fazaldad Khan, landowner. Those close to Beriosova blamed her husband for an adverse effect on her private persona, causing stress and weakening her self-reliance in a way that sadly led to her increasing dependence on alcohol. They had no children, and the marriage was dissolved in 1974. She continued to perform as before until, in 1975, she fell on stage while dancing the Tsarina in Kenneth MacMillan's *Anastasia*.

Beriosova immediately retired from performance, occasionally occupying herself with coaching other dancers in the great classical roles associated with her, a talent which was made abundantly evident by her part in Maina Gielgud's demonstration programme *Steps, Notes and Squeaks* (1978), but of which the Royal Ballet availed itself surprisingly little. Nor were any public honours accorded to her in the country of her adoption. In her last years she was confined to a wheelchair. She died of cancer at the Pembridge Palliative Care Centre, St Charles Hospital, Kensington, London, on 10 November 1998. Her funeral was held according to the Russian Orthodox rite to which she had been attached throughout her life; on 19 November her body was cremated. NOËL GOODWIN

Sources A. H. Franks, *Svetlana Beriosova* (1958) • *The Guardian* (12 Nov 1998) • *The Guardian* (16 Nov 1998) • *The Times* (13 Nov 1998) • *The Independent* (13 Nov 1998) • *Daily Telegraph* (17 Nov 1998) • A. Bland, *The Royal Ballet: the first 50 years* (1981) • M. Clarke, *The Sadler's Wells ballet: a history and an appreciation* (1955) • WWW • m. cert. • d. cert. • G. B. L. Wilson, 'Beriozoff at 75', *Dancing Times* (July 1981) • naturalization certificate, 21 Jan 1955, PRO, HO 334/387, BNA 36025 • naturalization certificate, 19 July 1954, PRO, HO 334/380, BNA 325216 [Nicholas Beriozoff]

Archives FILM BFI NFTVA

Likenesses Baron, photograph, 1954, Hult. Arch. [*see illus.*] • photograph, 1956, repro. in *The Independent* • photograph, 1960, repro. in *The Times* • photograph, 1967, repro. in *Daily Telegraph* • photographs, Royal Opera House Archive • photographs, Hult. Arch. • two photographs, repro. in *The Guardian* (12 Nov 1998)

Berisford, Charles (1830–1898), silk manufacturer, was born at Buglawton, Cheshire, the seventh of eleven children and fourth son of Isaac Berisford (1794–1854), tollkeeper turned farmer, and his wife, Alice, *née* Bonsall (1798–1860), formerly of Monyash. Charles started work when he was nine, presumably in textiles like his brothers. He was so small he had to stand on a stool to work. Later he was formally apprenticed, possibly to James Orme, silk throwster of Macclesfield, whose granddaughter he married, but more likely to a ribbon weaver (the trade he later adopted). He attended Sunday school, and then night school. Tradition has it that he extended his education by reading while at his loom.

In 1858 with his older brothers, William (1827–1879) and Francis (1829–1888), Berisford leased part of the Victoria silk mill on Foundry Bank in Congleton. It was a difficult time to start weaving silk, for Cobden's free trade treaty of 1860 virtually destroyed the British silk ribbon trade, as it allowed the entry of duty-free goods from France. The Berisfords turned to other silk small wares like ferrets (coarse tapes woven from floss silk and used as binding), Prussian or Paris bindings, galloons, and lutes.

In 1871 the three brothers entered into a formal partnership, calling themselves Berisford Brothers, silk manufacturers, but also carrying on a second business as silkmen, throwsters, and ribbon trimming manufacturers at Pool Street Mill, Macclesfield. In 1872 they bought the whole Victoria building at Congleton, on a mortgage paid off in 1893. In 1879 William died and Francis left the partnership to run the business at Macclesfield. By then the brothers had built a four-storey extension to the original mill and employed 110 people.

Charles Berisford married twice, but all that is known about his first wife is that she was the widow of a Captain Birchenhall. In 1861 Berisford married Sarah Ann Orme (1832–1910) of Sutton Lane Ends as his second wife. Of their seven children, three of the four sons were to enter the firm: Harry (1864–1936) in 1879, Philip Charles (1872–1945) in 1889, and Ernest Johnson (1875–1944) about 1893. David Birchenhall, his stepson by his first wife, became a partner in 1891, the firm being renamed Berisfords and Birchenhall. In 1892 they bought Parkside Mill, Prestwich, Manchester, and Birchenhall became its manager. There were also branches in London, Leeds, and Liverpool. Thus from its small beginnings the firm developed into one of the major ribbon and trimming manufacturers in the country. Until the year of his death Berisford retained an active interest in the firm, going to Manchester every Tuesday and Friday to buy cotton and to sound out the market. The firm's motto, 'The sapling has at length become a tree', was a fitting epitaph.

Physically frail from boyhood, Berisford lived a full and active life, 'an admirable example of those enlightened Victorian industrialists who to thrift and shrewdness added honesty in business and benevolence towards their work people' (*Berisfords: the Ribbon People*, 40). He was a trustee for the Methodist New Connexion chapel in Congleton (1871–84) and an 'Exhorter' for the chapel in Havannah. In 1884 he transferred to the Wesleyan Methodist chapel at Wragg Street, Congleton, and was instrumental in organizing and financing an enlargement of the premises. He was also a justice of the peace.

Berisford died at his home, Poplar Villas, West Road, Congleton, on 22 January 1898, and was buried at Astbury church. After his death his son Harry became chairman. In 1902 Philip Berisford moved to London to run that branch until he retired in 1924. Needing further accommodation to match expansion, in 1908 the Berisfords rented a mill at Derby to produce cotton bindings, and in 1913 they took over the small wares business of R. Thorp & Son of Macclesfield. The enlarged firm was incorporated as a limited company in 1916, known as Berisfords Ltd, a name it retained to its centenary in 1958 and beyond. The flexibility which characterized Charles's early success contributed significantly to the firm's survival between the wars. Berisfords was quick to innovate, introducing rayon in 1919 and producing bias binding in 1931 soon after the patent in the United States. NANCY COX

Sources C. Berisford Sebire and J. F. Sebire, *Berisfords, the ribbon people: the story of a family business* (1966) · private information (2004) · *Methodist Recorder* (27 Jan 1898) · *History, gazetteer, and directory of Cheshire*, F. White and Co. (1860) · *Slater's directory of Cheshire* (1890)
Archives priv. coll.
Likenesses oils?, Berisfords, Congleton, Cheshire
Wealth at death £7629 11s. 4d.: resworn probate, June 1898, CGPLA Eng. & Wales

Berkeley family (*per. c.*1200–1942). For members of this family *see* individual entries under Berkeley and related entries; for information on the family, *see* Berkeley, Sir Robert (*d.* 1220).

Berkeley, Charles, second Viscount Fitzhardinge of Berehaven (1599–1668), politician, was born on 14 December 1599 and baptized on 3 January 1600 at St Margaret, Lothbury, London, the eldest of five sons of Sir Maurice Berkeley (1576/7–1617) of Bruton, Somerset, and Elizabeth (*d.* 1626), daughter of Sir Henry Killigrew of Hanworth, Middlesex. His four younger brothers included Sir William *Berkeley (1605–1677), governor of Virginia, and the royalist general John *Berkeley, first Baron Berkeley of Stratton (*bap.* 1607, *d.* 1678). He also had two sisters, Margaret and Jane. Berkeley matriculated at Queen's College, Oxford, on 3 November 1615 but took no degree and returned to live at Bruton after his father's death. In 1622 or 1623 he was knighted at Beaulieu. On 6 September 1627 he married Penelope (*d.* 1689), daughter of Sir William

Godolphin of Godolphin, Cornwall, at St Breage, Cornwall. They had at least four sons—Maurice, third viscount (1628–1690), Charles *Berkeley, earl of Falmouth (*bap.* 1630, *d.* 1665), the favourite of Charles II, William *Berkeley (1639–1666), vice-admiral, and John, fourth viscount (1650–1712)—and one daughter, Jane (*fl.* 1645–1666).

The Berkeley family was one of the greatest landowners in eastern Somerset, with a seat at Bruton Abbey. Berkeley sat in six successive parliaments—for Somerset in 1621–2, Bodmin in 1624, 1625, and 1626, Heytesbury in 1628–9, and Bath in the Short Parliament of 1640. Between 1625 and 1637 he was one of ten deputy lieutenants for Somerset. In the disputes that divided the deputies in the 1630s he inclined to Sir Robert Phelips's 'country' party, though less so than his cousin, Sir Henry Berkeley of Yarlington. Berkeley led resistance to ship-money ratings on his home area in 1636, but he also had court interests, since he had taken part in the disafforestation of Frome Selwood Forest, near Bruton, from 1629 and was granted lands there in 1636. When the civil war broke out he was imprisoned in London by the parliamentarians but was later released. He became a commissioner for raising contributions in Somerset for the royal army and hosted the king at Bruton on 19 July 1644. In April 1645 Clarendon reported him aggrieved at not being on the prince of Wales's council of war despite being promised the controllership of the prince's household. Berkeley was at Exeter when the city surrendered to parliament in 1646, was imprisoned for three weeks, and was later fined £2000, though this was greatly reduced on condition he settle the revenues of three rectories in Somerset to support preaching ministers. His war-ravaged estate continued to be plagued by rioting in the disafforested parts, which delayed the completion of his composition until 1653. He entertained Sir John Berkeley and Sir John Ashburnham at Bruton in January 1648, when they were plotting to free the king, and was in prison again in May 1651 but otherwise stayed out of trouble during the interregnum.

After the Restoration, Berkeley was made a privy councillor on 7 June 1660, represented Heytesbury again in the Cavalier Parliament, and was comptroller of the household until 1662, then treasurer of the household until his death. He also had colonial interests in South Carolina, which he may have visited. On 28 September 1663 he was created MA at Oxford. The diarist John Evelyn dined at his London house three times between 1662 and 1666, including one occasion when the king and several courtiers gambled huge sums on dice. After his son Falmouth was killed in the naval battle off Lowestoft on 3 June 1665, Berkeley succeeded to his two Irish titles by virtue of a special remainder, taking his seat in the Lords by proxy on 23 May 1666 as Baron Berkeley of Rathdowne and Viscount Fitzhardinge of Berehaven. He made no discernible impression on his contemporaries: Pepys and Burnet, who both despised Falmouth, and Clarendon, who was equally scathing about both Falmouth and Sir John Berkeley, barely mention him. The state papers afford little more insight and it is not always clear which relate to him and which to Falmouth, though he appears to have been as greedy for land, money, and honours as every other Restoration courtier. He died 'of a short apoplecticall distemper' (Wood, *Ath. Oxon.*, 2.272) at Whitehall on 12 June 1668 and was buried on 26 June at Bruton.

ANDREW WARMINGTON

Sources GEC, *Peerage*, vol. 5 · J. Collinson, *The history and antiquities of the county of Somerset*, 3 vols. (1791) · *CSP dom.*, 1647–52; 1661–8 · T. G. Barnes, *Somerset, 1625–1640: a county's government during the personal rule* (1961) · Wood, *Ath. Oxon.*, new edn · W. A. Shaw, ed., *Calendar of treasury books*, 1, PRO (1904) · M. A. E. Green, ed., *Calendar of the proceedings of the committee for compounding … 1643–1660*, 1, PRO (1889) · M. A. E. Green, ed., *Calendar of the proceedings of the committee for advance of money, 1642–1656*, 3 vols., PRO (1888) · Clarendon, *Hist. rebellion* · Evelyn, *Diary* · D. Underdown, *Somerset in the civil war and interregnum* (1973) · *DNB* · W. A. Shaw, *The knights of England*, 2 vols. (1906) · will, PRO, PROB 11/328, fols. 2v–3r
Wealth at death considerable; left unspecified lands in England and Ireland plus monetary bequests worth £4000: will, PRO, PROB 11/328, fols. 2v–3r

Berkeley, Charles, earl of Falmouth (*bap.* 1630, *d.* 1665), courtier, was baptized on 11 January 1630 at Bruton Abbey, Somerset, the second son of Charles *Berkeley, second Baron Berkeley of Rathdowne, second Viscount Fitzhardinge of Berehaven (1599–1668), politician, and his wife, Penelope (*d.* 1689), daughter of Sir William Godolphin of Godolphin, Cornwall. William *Berkeley (1639–1666) was his younger brother. He was tutored by Hugh Cressy, the former chaplain of Thomas Wentworth, earl of Strafford, and Lucius Cary, second Viscount Falkland. During the civil wars his family was strongly royalist, and afterwards he was sent to serve the exiled Stuart court. In 1652 his uncle, Sir John (later first Baron) *Berkeley, used his influence as governor to James, duke of York, to secure the youth a commission as a cavalry officer under the command of that prince. He remained in York's employment until the Restoration—first in the French and then in the Spanish armies, where he saw considerable action—and became his groom of the stole and one of his closest friends. In 1660 he returned to England with his master, who ensured him several honours from the newly restored Charles II. These included a knighthood, the post of lieutenant-governor of Portsmouth, and the receipts from mooring fees levied on the Thames below London Bridge. The latter provided him with the income needed to purchase a house beside the bowling green at Whitehall, and York also secured his election as MP for New Romney, Kent, in 1661. Nevertheless, his most nefarious recorded act was to claim that he had enjoyed the favours of York's new wife, Anne Hyde, in an effort to dissolve the marriage, which many considered a disaster, and to defame her father, Edward, the king's new chief minister. This attempt to 'protect' his patron was, to say the least, both ill-considered and tactless, though seemingly had little effect on the favourite's relationship with either the king or his brother. The episode bears testimony to one who could be coarse in conversation, but Berkeley was to marry for love, as his own bride came from an impoverished royalist family. She was a famous beauty, Mary (1645–1679), daughter of Colonel Hervey Bagot of Pipe Hayes, Warwickshire, whom he married on 18 December 1664.

At court Berkeley became associated with the faction led by George Digby, second earl of Bristol, and Sir Henry Bennet, and was friendly with the king's mistress, Barbara Villiers, countess of Castlemaine. In 1662 that faction became an important part of the government, and Berkeley received Bennet's post of keeper of the privy purse when the latter was promoted. But it was during the next year that observers noticed that King Charles himself had become so fond of Berkeley that he was now one of the principal royal favourites, and perhaps the greatest. In July 1663 he was raised to the Irish peerage as Baron Berkeley of Rathdowne and Viscount Fitzhardinge of Berehaven and would have received an English title had the king not been conscious of hostility to his courtiers in the English House of Commons. However, in March 1665 he was granted the English titles Baron Botetourt of Langport and earl of Falmouth, as part of the honours bestowed when war was declared against the Dutch. The newly created earl volunteered for service in the royal fleet, and was killed by a cannon shot in the first battle, off Lowestoft on 3 June. On 22 June he was given a hero's funeral in Westminster Abbey, where he was buried. As his marriage had produced a single daughter, the earldom and his English barony became extinct; however, his father inherited his Irish titles by special remainder. Falmouth's widow married Charles Sackville, later sixth earl of Dorset and fourth earl of Middlesex, in 1674, and lived until 1679.

The king was more distressed by Falmouth's death than by that of any other person except his own sister, and it seems certain that the earl would have received further advancement had he lived. Even so, it may be doubted that he would have made a greater impact upon the course of history. No known portrait of him survives, and his character is almost as faintly recorded. He had no outstanding gifts, of intelligence, learning, or good looks, and was never employed for any important administrative, political, or diplomatic office. Instead he managed the privy purse, retained his post at Portsmouth, sat upon the committee for Tangier, and was sent upon polite diplomatic errands. He performed these minor tasks diligently, although he hated writing letters. He had no political aims and did not lead a faction, although he sought lesser posts for a few clients. If he had one trait of potential consequence it was his fondness for France, which led him to encourage efforts to ally with that country, but the international situation made these futile during his lifetime. His popularity with the royal brothers derived, indeed, from the fact that he was a devoted servant and affable companion who was content to further their wishes. His unpopularity with the more high principled of the English derived from the same qualities, for he indulged or encouraged what they considered to be the king's lechery and laziness. His prominence in his time and his lack of consequence for it both derive ultimately from his pleasant mediocrity.

RONALD HUTTON, *rev.*

Sources C. H. Hartmann, *The king's friend: a life of Charles Berkeley, Viscount Fitzhardinge, earl of Falmouth, 1630–1665* (1951) · B. D. Henning, 'Berkeley, Charles II', HoP, *Commons, 1660–90*, 1.630–31 · correspondance politique (Angleterre), French ministry of foreign affairs, Quai d'Orsay, Paris · GEC, *Peerage* · Pepys, *Diary* · CKS, Sackville papers · state papers Charles II, PRO, SP 29
Archives CKS, corresp. and papers

Berkeley, Craven Fitzhardinge (1805–1855), politician, seventh and youngest son and eleventh of the twelve children of Frederick Augustus, fifth earl of Berkeley (1745–1810), of Berkeley Castle, Gloucestershire, and of Mary (1766/7–1844), daughter of William Cole, was born in London, at Berkeley House, Spring Gardens, on 28 July 1805. During the early part of his career he was for a time captain in the 2nd Life Guards. Immediately after the passing of the Reform Bill, however, in 1832, a new path in life was marked out for him. On 10 December 1832 Cheltenham returned him without opposition as its first representative under the new order.

A staunch Liberal throughout his career, Berkeley was personally very popular with his constituents. His second return was in January 1835, when he defeated the other Liberal candidate by a majority of 386. In August 1837 he defeated a conservative by a majority of 334. In July 1841 he was at the head of the poll with a net majority of 109. On 5 July 1847, when the Health of Towns Bill was under consideration in committee, Berkeley indiscreetly said in the House of Commons that Cheltenham showed a greater mortality rate than any other place of the same size in England. On 30 July 1847 he was thereupon for the first time defeated, by a majority of 108. On 28 May 1848, however, the successful candidate, Sir Willoughby Jones, bt, was unseated upon petition, and on 28 July 1848 Berkeley was elected, being returned by 1028 votes. On 24 August this election was also declared void, on the ground that some of the voters had been supplied with refreshments. Incapacitated by that decision from sitting in parliament until after the next dissolution, Berkeley had to bide his time until July 1852, when, with an aggregate of 999 votes, he was for the sixth and last time returned as MP for Cheltenham.

On 15 July 1842, Berkeley fought a duel with Captain Boldero MP, in Osterley Park, Middlesex. Their encounter arose out of some words uttered by Captain Boldero with reference to the queen, which Berkeley, regarding as disrespectful to the sovereign, immediately called upon him to retract. Each of them fired twice without effect. Once before Berkeley had taken part, as a second, however, not as a principal, in a hostile encounter of a less seemly character. This was when, on 3 August 1836, he guarded the door of a bookseller's shop at 215 Regent Street, London, while his brother Grantley *Berkeley attacked James Fraser, the proprietor. Berkeley married twice; first, on 10 September 1839, Augusta Jones (*d*. April 1841), daughter of Sir Horace St Paul, bt, and widow of George Henry Talbot, half-brother of John, sixteenth earl of Shrewsbury; and secondly, on 27 August 1845, Charlotte, fourth daughter of General Denzil Onslow, of Stoughton, Huntingdonshire, and widow of George Newton, of Croxton Park, Cambridgeshire. Berkeley's daughter of his first marriage, Louisa Mary, married, on 3 April 1872, Major-General Gustavus H. L. Milman RA, and on 27 August 1882 became Baroness Berkeley, succeeding to the barony on the death of her uncle, Thomas Moreton Fitzhardinge, who refused to avail himself of the decision of the House of Lords on the alleged marriage of his father. Berkeley's stepdaughter, Augusta Talbot (*b*. 1832?), the only surviving child of his first wife's first marriage, was a ward in chancery, and, on attaining her majority, was to come into possession of £80,000. On the death of her mother, nine years previously, she, being both a Roman Catholic and an heiress, was confided by the court of chancery to the guardianship of her near relations and co-religionists, the earl and countess of Shrewsbury, who in September 1850 had placed their ward in the convent in Taunton, Somerset. Berkeley learned soon afterwards that she was there not as a pupil but as a postulant who would in all probability take the veil, and peremptorily interposed by presenting petitions to parliament and to the lord chancellor, in each of which documents charges were directed against the earl and countess and the spiritual advisers of the young heiress. Public opinion meanwhile was exasperated against the Catholics by reason of the establishment of their new hierarchy, and much excitement was aroused, which subsided when Augusta Talbot married, on 22 July 1851, the duke of Norfolk's younger brother, Lord Edward Fitzallan Howard, who eighteen years afterwards was summoned to the House of Lords as Lord Howard of Glossop. Berkeley's health declined as he approached his fiftieth birthday, and he went abroad in the hope of recovery. However, his condition worsened rapidly and he died on 1 July 1855 at Frankfurt am Main.

CHARLES KENT, *rev.* H. C. G. MATTHEW

Sources Boase, *Mod. Eng. biog.* · G. F. Berkeley, *My life and recollections*, 4 vols. (1865–6) · GEC, *Peerage* · J. Goding, *Norman's history of Cheltenham*, rev. edn (1863) · T. D. Fosbroke, *An original history of the city of Gloucester* (1819)

Berkeley [*formerly* Bergtheil; *née* Dunington], **Edith** (1875–1963), marine biologist, was born on 1 September 1875 in Tulbagh, Cape of Good Hope, the older daughter of Alfred Dunington, civil engineer, and his wife, Martha Treglohan (*c*.1837–*c*.1927). Having spent her early childhood abroad, and having had private tutors in the Cape, India, and Australia, she returned to England to attend a Quaker school (from about 1885) before going on to Wimbledon High School for Girls (1889–94). Edith Dunington entered the medical school, University College, London, in 1895, but soon gave up medicine for science. A lively, attractive, and serious student with an aptitude for research, she worked in Sir William Ramsay's chemistry laboratory. Attending W. W. R. Weldon's zoology course, she developed an interest in Polychaeta, a complicated class of marine worms. In 1900 she became a science teacher at a girls' school in Kensington, London.

On 26 February 1902, at Godstone, near East Grinstead in Sussex, Dunington married the agricultural chemist Cyril Jonas Bergtheil (1878–1973), son of the late Louis

Michael Bergtheil and Alice Collins. The couple soon sailed for Bihar, Bengal, India, where Cyril, as imperial bacteriologist, was to work on indigo cultivation. Their only daughter, Alfreda, was born there in 1903. Despite her scientific training, Edith, like other dependent colonial wives, had to give up her own interests; she served as the medical factotum to villagers in the district.

The Indian climate proved detrimental to Edith's health and in 1912 the Berkeleys (the couple had Anglicized their surname) left the subcontinent. *En route* for England they visited Canada. They may have spent a short time back in England, but in 1914 they bought a pig farm in the Okanagan valley of British Columbia, where they lived for the next two years. In 1916 Edith Berkeley was hired by the department of zoology and botany, University of British Columbia, the first woman to be employed there in a scientific position. Cyril Berkeley taught bacteriology at the same university before accepting a temporary post at San Diego.

In 1919 Edith Berkeley gave up her university position to become a volunteer investigator at the Pacific Biological Station at Nanaimo, Vancouver Island. At the time marine biology was a rapidly developing scientific field but in Canada there were few paid positions for non-university researchers. The station provided research facilities for volunteer investigators, and the Berkeleys' financial security enabled them to devote their lives to scientific research. As there were few polychaete experts in North America, Edith was inundated by samples and requests for identifications and in 1930 Cyril gave up his research on the chemical activities of marine bacteria to help her.

Between 1923 and 1961 Edith Berkeley was sole author of eleven papers—establishing one new genus, fifteen new species, and eight new varieties of polychaetes. Her collaborative work with Cyril, between 1930 and 1964, produced thirty-four joint publications in which they established four new genera, forty-three new species, one subspecies, seven varieties, and one new name. Edith Berkeley was senior author on all of the joint papers, which were published in journals such as *Nature*, *Proceedings of the Zoological Society*, the *Canadian Field Naturalist*, and *Contributions to Canadian Biology*. In addition to her polychaete research, she also acted as mentor to a number of young scientists. She was often seen cultivating her rhododendron garden and also read widely. She died from a stroke on 25 February 1963 at Nanaimo, where she was buried.

Edith Berkeley entered the field of marine biology when the discipline was becoming increasingly professionalized. Yet, without an advanced degree, she became one of the foremost experts of this scientific field. Four species of polychaetes were named after her and her husband. In 1971 an issue of the *Journal of the Fisheries Research Board of Canada* was dedicated to them. The Royal Horticultural Society named a rhododendron hybrid Edith Berkeley and in 1969 the University of British Columbia's department of zoology inaugurated the annual Edith Berkeley lectures.   MARIANNE GOSZTONYI AINLEY

Sources C. Berkeley, *My autobiography* (privately printed) • M. G. Ainley, 'Marriage and scientific work in twentieth-century Canada: the Berkeleys in marine biology and the Hoggs in astronomy', *Creative couples in the sciences*, ed. H. Pycior and others (1996), 143–55 • private information (2004) [Dr Mary Needler Arai] • C. J. Stevenson, 'Edith and Cyril Berkeley: an appreciation', *Journal of the Fisheries Research Board of Canada*, 28/10 (Oct 1971), 1363–4 • D. Peck, 'The Berkeleys: octogenarian couple recall active life', *Nanaimo Daily Free Press* (17 Jan 1959) • W. A. Clemens, 'Edith Berkeley', *Journal of the Fisheries Research Board of Canada*, 20 (1963), 1349–52 • M. H. Pettibone, 'Type-specimens of polychaetes described by Edith and Cyril Berkeley', *Proceedings of the United States National Museum*, 119 (1967), 1–23 • m. cert.
Archives NHM • Smithsonian Institution, Washington, DC, National Museum of American History, type specimens of polychaetes described by Edith Berkeley and Cyril Berkeley
Likenesses portrait, priv. coll.

Berkeley [*née* Frinsham], **Eliza** (1734–1800), literary editor, was born at the vicarage of White Waltham in Windsor Forest, the eldest daughter of the Revd Henry Frinsham (*d.* 1745) and Elizabeth (*d.* 1754), youngest daughter of Francis *Cherry, of Shottesbrooke House, Berkshire. The fullest source of biographical information available for Eliza Berkeley is her own extensive preface to her edition of her late son's *Poems* (1797).

Eliza Berkeley inherited her passion for learning from her father, whom she remembered as a generous, hospitable man who took 'incessant pains' that his daughters received a good Christian education (Berkeley, preface to *Poems*, 567). Eliza and her sister were brought up in the vicarage at Waltham, 'a very old barn, with small rooms on each side' (ibid., 170). Here Eliza showed an early capacity for reading and writing, sending innumerable letters to her friends, and composing two sermons when she was eleven. She and her sister attended Mrs Sheeles's school in Queen Square, London. After their father's death their mother removed them from the school, believing that women should not be too learned if they were to be marriageable, telling Eliza that 'you will never get a husband; you hold yourself up as a dragon, and men like quiet wives' (ibid., 112). Elizabeth Frinsham was conscious of the necessity of prudence in guarding her daughters' financial future. Her grandfather, William Cherry, had lost a great deal of his money in the South Sea Bubble, and the burning of the family mansion at Cliefdon further reduced his fortune. Suitors nicknamed Francis Cherry's three beautiful daughters Black Cherry, Duke Cherry, and Heart Cherry, the last alias designated to Elizabeth.

Despite her mother's warnings, the young Eliza was not to be deterred from her scholarly pursuits. At the age of seventeen she started to keep a diary to record the changing patterns of her life. She had an early interest in biographies, telling her mother, after reading a memoir of a prelate, that 'she thought she could write a better life of him herself!' (Berkeley, preface to *Poems*, 422). Eliza's friends were generally at least five or ten years older, as she believed that she could not learn much from girls her own age. She learned French, Spanish, and Hebrew and 'always took her Spanish Prayer-Book with her to Church' (*GM*, 70/2, November 1800, 1114). When Eliza was twenty years old her mother died, leaving her daughters a large fortune, variously described as a few thousands (Berkeley, preface to *Poems*, 278) and as £80,000 (ibid., 477). She and her sister took a house at Windsor. Eliza was married on 24 March 1761 to the Revd George Berkeley (1733–1795), son of the philosopher Bishop George *Berkeley. They had two sons, George Monck *Berkeley (1763–1793) and George Robert Berkeley (1767–1775).

Eliza was a devout Christian throughout her life. She approved of her husband's belief in the political role of the clergy in teaching 'inferior traders, farmers and labourers, soldiers and sailors, to learn their duty to their king and country … to "honour the king" and so obey GOD' (Berkeley, preface to *Sermons*, 20). She describes how she witnessed her husband's 'metamorphosing a *democrat into a good subject*' (ibid.) and viewed the passing of regular weekday prayers in the country as a cause of the 'lamentable decay of Christian piety' and 'ignorance of the lower ranks' (ibid., 22). Her husband's livings during the first ten years of their marriage were Bray, Acton, and Cookham, and at each she visited all new mothers within 2 or 3 miles and brought gifts of snuff, tea, and sugar to the needy in local workhouses. In her published writings Eliza presents herself as a loyal, hardworking, and efficient wife who assisted her husband in his studies as well as running the family home, distinguishing herself as a 'steward' rather than a mere 'housekeeper' (Berkeley, preface to *Poems*, 520). As well as knowing the Bible 'by heart from end to end' (ibid., 416) she read widely in polite literature, enjoyed the works of Romaine and Hervey, and was an enthusiastic admirer of Lord Monboddo's *Ancient Metaphysics* (ibid., 49).

Eliza's devotion to her sons became the focus of her life, and a major source of her creative energy. She oversaw the boys' prayers daily and taught them their lessons with a mixture of strong discipline and tender love. In 1771 Dr Berkeley became prebendary of Canterbury and the family went to reside at The Oaks, the boys attending King's School. On 15 April 1775 George Robert, aged nearly nine, died of an infectious fever. George Monck thus became the sole care of his parents, who guarded his safety with anxious solicitude. He was educated at Eton College, and during his time there he and his mother corresponded almost daily. He then went up to St Andrews University, accompanied by his parents, who lived there for all three years of his time as a student.

George Monck Berkeley's death on 26 January 1793 left his parents desolate. Eliza wrote that her vital love of knowledge had continued 'until she lost her idol. It is not yet quite extinct; the flame is out, but the embers glow a little' (Berkeley, preface to *Poems*, 572). Eliza suffered two further bereavements in swift succession. Her husband died in January 1795 and her sister in January 1797. Eliza dated the postscript to her son's poems 'January, fatal month, 1797'.

While the last decade of Eliza Berkeley's life was undoubtedly filled with sorrow, it also witnessed her most productive period in literary terms. She published her son's poems in 1797 and a selection of her husband's sermons in 1799, printing only 200 copies, 'As it is not the intention of the editor, that any of these excellent sermons should go to the pastry-cooks or chandlers shops' (Berkeley, preface to *Sermons*, 26). The copy in the British Library contains an indignant exclamation added to the title-page in her own, firm hand, 'What horrid paper, when the best was ordered'. While she described herself as a 'feeble, unlettered Female pen' (ibid., 1–2), she admitted that was 'addicted to scribbling' (Berkeley, preface to *Poems*, 488). Her memoirs are entertaining and original in style, demonstrating a vigorous and often inventive attitude to language: 'The Editor, when unexpectedly hearing of any base or worthless person, or action, has ever been addicted to utter her indignation in a word of her own composing, if she thought no dictionary afforded one sufficiently strong' (ibid., 225). A reviewer of the *Poems* in the *Gentleman's Magazine* commented:

> we are not to arraign the *garrula senectus* of Maternal Piety … We have accompanied Eliza Berkeley through 630 quarto pages of large and handsome type, which are 460 pages more than the poems occupy, besides a postscript by the same parental hand. Every writer has a peculiar character of manner and style. Mrs. B. writes as she talks. Anecdote is her forte; and the sentiments she intersperses are of the antient, but not less valuable, cast.   (*GM*, 67, January 1797, 403)

Another reviewer welcomed Eliza Berkeley's anecdotal style as an important new contribution to the increasingly popular genre of biography:

> Anecdote is comprized in biography; but one is the cream, and the other is the mass. It is of little import to the publick of what days a man was born, married, and buried, or by what gradations he attained eminence, however great his character, or useful his life.   (*GM*, 67, August 1797, 664)

Eliza Berkeley's 'Preface' is an eccentric text that is arguably more revealing of its author than of its subject, the life and rather indifferent poetry of George Monck. She is often sharp-tongued and forthright in tone but always witty and elegant in style. She refers to herself throughout the text in the third person, as 'the Editor', 'Mrs Berkeley', or 'Mr Berkeley's Mother' and seems particularly self-conscious of her own role in forming her son's life:

> The Editor, at length getting sight of most of the sheets at once, is confirmed in what she suspected; that she has been guilty of tautology, of Egotism, or rather *Editorism*. It is said of the excellent Lord Chancellor Clarendon, that, in his incomparable History of the Rebellion, the Chancellor of the Exchequer is too often introduced.   (Berkeley, preface to *Poems*, 523)

She writes of the difficulty of placing herself in the background when she, 'the most resolute of all females', was '*necessarily*' one of the 'principal actors' in her son's life (ibid., 523–7). Eliza explains that her zealous attention to her son's education is driven by 'violent love', telling him, 'Your mother's delight is in *learning*, not *teaching*. I wish to God you had your mother's rage for knowledge: it would be a happy thing for you' (ibid., 572).

Eliza Berkeley was connected with the bluestocking circle and particularly admired the learning of Elizabeth Montagu and Elizabeth Carter, regretting that she did not have the wealth or independence to exert her own ambitions fully. She was also associated with the writer and poet Catherine Talbot (1721–1770), who had been intimately attached to George Berkeley before his marriage to Eliza. Eliza only discovered this some time after she had married and took pride in the fact that the three friends conducted a harmonious relationship. After her husband's death, Eliza found Catherine Talbot's courtship letters among his papers, including two moving love poems, which Eliza published in an article explaining the history of the affair in order to 'soothe some' and 'warn others— especially parents' ('A singular tale of love in high life', GM, 66, August 1796, 631–2).

While Eliza Berkeley presented herself as a moral stoic in her published work, her unpublished letters present a more complex character who sometimes found the pressures of personal sacrifice and family relationships too much to bear. Among the Berkeley papers in the British Library there is a letter from Eliza to her husband written in 1777 in which she complained of mistreatment by his mother, 'satan', who had deprived her of her husband's love, and others written at the same time in which she expressed anger at a scandal involving her husband and another woman. She also complained that little money was left them except her settlement, which had not been equal to her fortune (BL, Add. MS 39312, fol. 1). However, it is her profound love for her son, or 'sun', as she called him, that forms the overarching theme of her private and her public writings. After a difficult few years in which she was embroiled in legal disputes surrounding her husband's will, Eliza Berkeley died at Kensington in November 1800. According to her wishes, her body was conveyed to Cheltenham, where on 13 November she was buried in the same tomb as her son.   ELIZABETH EGER

Sources E. Berkeley, preface, in Poems by the late George-Monck Berkeley … with a preface by the editor, ed. E. Berkeley (1797) · E. Berkeley, preface, in Sermons by the late Rev. George Berkeley, ed. E. Berkeley (1799) · BL MSS, Berkeley papers · GM, 1st ser., 60 (1790); 63 (1793); 65–70 (1795–1800) · A new catalogue of English authors: with complete lists of their publications and biographical and critical memoirs, 1 (1799) · S. Harcstark Myers, The bluestocking circle: women, friendship, and the life of the mind in eighteenth-century England (1990) · DNB · IGI

Archives BL, papers | BL, letters to Charles Poyntz

Berkeley, Elizabeth, countess of Warwick (c.1386–1422), magnate, was the daughter of Thomas, fifth Baron Berkeley (1353–1417), and Margaret (1360–c.1392), daughter and heir of Warin de Lisle. In September 1392 an agreement was drawn up with Thomas *Beauchamp, earl of Warwick (d. 1401), for her to marry the earl's son and heir Richard *Beauchamp (d. 1439). The marriage took place before 5 October 1397, and Elizabeth became countess of Warwick when her husband was granted livery of the earldom in 1403. As the only child of Thomas Berkeley and Margaret de Lisle, Elizabeth was a considerable heiress. From her mother she inherited the Lisle and Tyes baronies with their principal estates concentrated in Wiltshire, Berkshire, Oxfordshire, and the south-west; her mother died c.1392, and these lands were held by her father by the tenure of courtesy of England until his own death in 1417, when Elizabeth succeeded to them. During her lifetime most of Elizabeth's lands kept their own identity under

her own receiver, and receipts were paid to the keeper of her household.

Elizabeth was also heir-general to the Berkeley estates, but the castle, manor, and hundred of Berkeley and certain other manors had been entailed to the male line by her great-grandfather in 1349. She and her husband were not willing to accept this entail at her father's death on 13 July 1417, and this refusal initiated one of the longest lawsuits in England which was not concluded until 1609. The heir male was Elizabeth's cousin, James *Berkeley. At the time of Thomas's death James was in Dorset, while Elizabeth and her husband were either at Berkeley or at Wotton under Edge, well placed to seize the entailed manors and also Thomas's records. Difficulties arose over carrying out Thomas's inquisition post mortem, and it was only on 1 December 1417 that the entailed lands were adjudged to James. His tenure of the lands was however by no means secure. Elizabeth was holding Berkeley Castle in 1420–21; James however succeeded in taking possession of Wotton by July 1421. At that time Elizabeth and James appeared before the king's council (the earl was in France), and Elizabeth presented her complaint against James. Earlier mediation involving Joan Beauchamp, Lady Bergavenny, had taken place, but no settlement was reached by the council. James by then had secured the backing of Humphrey, duke of Gloucester, which put him in a stronger position. In fact it was only after Elizabeth's death that the earl and James reached a settlement, in 1425, which established peace between them until the earl's death in 1439.

A considerable amount is known about Elizabeth's daily life as a result of the survival of her household accounts for 1420–21. The autumn and winter were spent at Berkeley, but at the end of March Elizabeth and her daughters travelled to Walthamstow in Essex to join her husband, and they spent two months there before the earl's return to France. Apart from a rapid journey to Wotton, presumably on business, she remained in London until her appearance before the council in July after which she travelled west to Salwarpe near Worcester. The accounts give details of the structure and organization of the household, the exercise of hospitality, costs and consumption of food, and standards of living.

Elizabeth died on 28 December 1422, and was buried at Kingswood Abbey. Her husband provided in his will for a marble tomb to be built over her grave. The inscription described her as the daughter and heir of Thomas, Lord Berkeley and Lisle. She and the earl had three daughters: Margaret was born in 1404 and married John Talbot, afterwards earl of Shrewsbury, in 1425; Eleanor was born in 1408, and married Thomas, Lord Ros, some time after 17 December 1423, and, after his death in 1430, Edmund Beaufort, later duke of Somerset, before 7 March 1438; and Elizabeth was born c.1417 and married George Neville, Lord Latimer, before February 1437.

Elizabeth's daughters renewed their claim to the entailed Berkeley estates after their father's death in 1439, and the 1440s witnessed litigation and violence. Margaret, countess of Shrewsbury, was especially energetic in pressing the claim, and it was as a result of her action that Lady Berkeley was committed to prison at Gloucester in 1452 where she died soon afterwards. After the death of James, Lord Berkeley, eleven years later, Margaret carried on the dispute with William, Lord Berkeley. After her own death in 1467 her grandson Thomas, Lord Lisle, challenged Lord Berkeley to a military solution, but was killed at the ensuing battle of Nibley Green in 1470.

JENNIFER C. WARD

Sources J. Smyth, *The Berkeley manuscripts: the lives of the Berkeleys … 1066 to 1618*, ed. J. Maclean, 3 vols. (1883–5) • C. D. Ross, 'The household accounts of Elizabeth Berkeley, countess of Warwick, 1420–1', *Transactions of the Bristol and Gloucestershire Archaeological Society*, 70 (1951), 81–105 • A. Sinclair, 'The great Berkeley law suit revisited, 1417–39', *Southern History*, 9 (1987), 34–50 • W. Dugdale, *The baronage of England*, 2 vols. (1675–6) • *Thys rol was laburd and finished by Master John Rows of Warrewyk*, ed. W. Courthope (1859); repr. as *The Rous roll* (1980) • N. H. Nicolas, ed., *Proceedings and ordinances of the privy council of England*, 7 vols., RC, 26 (1834–7), vol. 2 • *CIPM*, 15, 17, 20 • *CPR, 1348–50; 1396–9; 1416–22* • *Calendar of the fine rolls*, PRO, 14 (1934) • *CClR, 1413–19*

Archives Berkeley Castle, muniments | PRO, Longleat MSS

Berkeley, Elizabeth. *See* Burnet, Elizabeth (1661–1709).

Berkeley, Lady Elizabeth. *See* Elizabeth, margravine of Brandenburg-Ansbach-Bayreuth (1750–1828).

Berkeley, George, eighth Baron Berkeley (1601–1658), nobleman, was born at Low Leyton, Essex, on 7 October 1601, son of Sir Thomas Berkeley (1575–1611) and Elizabeth Carey, later *Chamberlain (1576–1635) [see under Carey, Elizabeth], daughter of George *Carey, second Baron Hunsdon (1546/7–1603) [see under Carey, Henry, first Baron Hunsdon], and his wife, Elizabeth *Carey, Lady Hunsdon (1552–1618). Having spent his childhood in Warwickshire, where he was a scholar of Dr Philemon Holland of Coventry, and of Henry Ashwood, on 26 November 1613 he succeeded his grandfather Henry Berkeley, seventh Baron Berkeley (1534–1613), who had recently ended the 192-year legal feud over the estates with the Lisle family and their heirs, including the crown. Due to this and Henry's extraordinary profligacy, the once vast estate had been reduced to twenty-five manors covering about 11,000 acres, mainly in Gloucestershire, with a rental value of some £1200 per year. With difficulty, Lady Berkeley prevented the rapacious earl of Northampton from acquiring her son's wardship, and on 13 April 1615, Berkeley married Elizabeth (b. 1604), daughter and coheir of Sir Michael Stanhope, thereby acquiring estates worth £1503 per year in Suffolk and Middlesex. Berkeley, described by his steward, the antiquarian John *Smyth of Nibley, in 1618, as 'full of ingenuity, quick of apprehension and sweet of nature' (Smyth, *Lives of the Berkeleys*, 2.437), continued his education. Having matriculated from Christ Church, Oxford, on 10 June 1618, he entered the college as canon-commoner in 1619 and graduated MA on 18 July 1623. That year his elder son, Charles, was born; a daughter, Elizabeth (1624–1661), and younger son, George *Berkeley, later first earl of Berkeley (1626/7–1698), followed. Berkeley lived mainly

in London, entrusting the management of his estates to Smyth, but he also travelled extensively; he left England in 1626, was near Turin in May 1627 and in France in 1632–3.

By 1631, if not earlier, Berkeley had become bitterly estranged from his wife and he may even have produced another family elsewhere; Smyth's papers contain one thunderous letter—unsigned and undated but in the style of the formidable dowager Lady Berkeley—reproaching her son for squandering his inheritance and bringing scandal on the family. She herself disposed of patrimonial lands worth £11,000, much of it to her own kin, and in December 1633 Berkeley's debts totalled nearly £18,000 against annual revenues of about £6275 from lands in Gloucestershire, Leicestershire, Middlesex, Sussex, Norfolk, Suffolk, London, and elsewhere. Berkeley was also highly litigious. In Trinity term 1632 alone he had fourteen ongoing lawsuits and he was continuously at odds with the inhabitants of Slimbridge and Frampton, Gloucestershire, over the 300-acre New Grounds which had been created when the Severn changed its course about 1610.

In the two elections of 1640 Berkeley, at the bidding of courtier friends, unsuccessfully promoted pro-court candidates for Gloucestershire. On 27 January the following year he lost his elder son, Charles, who drowned while crossing the English Channel. In October 1642 he tried to gather some leading local gentlemen—who all became royalists—to consult on the war but, although he too inclined to royalism, he avoided commitment, remaining at his home in St John's parish, Clerkenwell, Middlesex, throughout, while John Smyth the younger, who had succeeded his father as steward in 1641, tried to hold the Berkeley interest together. His occasional appearances in the Lords at this time were usually on matters of personal concern, although he was also present on 10 August 1644, when it was resolved that no peer could sit in the house unless he took the covenant. After the fall of Berkeley Castle in September 1645, he fought against the Gloucestershire county committee's desire to demolish it, claiming that he had sustained losses of £20,000 in the war (including £3000 worth of damage to the castle itself) and that it could not be rebuilt even for £100,000. With difficulty, this was achieved: the Lords told the Commons that he had 'suffered so deeply for his adhering to the Parliament' (*CSP dom.*, 1645–7, 236). However, the depredations continued and the same year Smyth estimated that his debts totalled £20,000 and were growing at £3000 per year. The inhabitants of Slimbridge and Frampton reasserted control of the New Grounds, despite parliament's repeated orders confirming Lord Berkeley in possession. On 22 September 1646 Berkeley was among peers protesting against the vote that both houses would dispose of the king's person as they saw fit, and on 8 September 1647 he was among seven lords whom the Commons impeached for high treason. They were briefly imprisoned, then bailed in January 1648, but no more was heard of the matter after the Lords debated it on 2 February. Lord Berkeley thereafter disappears entirely from the records until his death in the parish of St John, Clerkenwell, on 10 August 1658, and subsequent burial in Cranford church, Middlesex; the fate of his estranged wife is unclear.

ANDREW WARMINGTON

Sources J. Smyth, *Lives of the Berkeleys* (1883), vol. 2 of *The Berkeley manuscripts*, ed. J. Maclean (1883–5) · Gloucester Public Library, Smyth of Nibley MSS, esp. 2, 3, 4 · GEC, *Peerage*, new edn, vol. 3 · J. Smyth, *A description of the hundred of Berkeley* (1885), vol. 3 of *The Berkeley manuscripts*, ed. J. Maclean (1883–5) · *JHL*, 6–8 (1643–6); 10 (1647–8) · *CSP dom.*, 1627–8; 1645–7 · I. H. Jeayes, *Descriptive catalogue of the charters and muniments in the possession of the Rt. Hon. Lord Fitzhardinge at Berkeley Castle* (1908) · T. D. Fosbroke, *Berkeley manuscripts: abstracts and extracts of Smyth's Lives of the Berkeleys* (1821) · *JHC*, 4 (1644–6) · J. H. Cooke, 'The great Berkeley law suit of the 15th and 16th centuries', *Transactions of the Bristol and Gloucestershire Archaeological Society*, 3 (1878–9), 304–24 · H. P. R. Finberg, *Gloucestershire studies* (1957)
Archives Gloucester Public Library, Smyth of Nibley MSS
Likenesses D. Mytens, oils, Berkeley Castle, Gloucestershire

Berkeley, George, first earl of Berkeley (1626/7–1698), politician, was the second, but eldest surviving, son of George *Berkeley, eighth Baron Berkeley (1601–1658), and Elizabeth (b. 1604), daughter and coheir of Sir Michael Stanhope; his elder brother, Charles, died while crossing the channel in January 1641. He may have followed his father as a canon-commoner at Christ Church, Oxford, but he did not take a degree. On 11 August 1646, at Morden, Surrey, he married Elizabeth (d. 1708), eldest daughter and coheir of John Massingberd, treasurer of the East India Company. They had two sons and six daughters, including Lady Henrietta *Berkeley. This marriage was the result of the disastrous state to which the patrimony had been brought by the profligacy of his predecessors and the effects of the civil war—his steward, John Smyth, had advised him in 1645 that finding a rich wife was vital to preserving an estate which would soon be worth 'less than your great-great-grandfather yearly expended in livery cotes and badges' (Gloucester Public Library, Smyth of Nibley MS XI, fol. 36). It also began a lifetime's close involvement in trade and colonial matters.

Although Berkeley took far more interest than his father in the estates and in local as well as national politics, he spent most of his time in London, especially after 1660. He was named a JP in Gloucestershire in 1655 and was elected for the shire in the protectorate parliaments in 1654 and 1656. Both elections were disputed between conservative county gentry and the radicals who dominated county life at the time, but Berkeley stood apart from these squabbles. He was named to the committee of trade on 30 January 1656 and was quite active in the Commons between April and June 1657. He succeeded his father on 10 August 1658.

In 1660 Berkeley promoted in the Lords the restoration of Charles II, moving for a supply to be voted, and he was one of the commission which went to The Hague and invited Charles to return. James, duke of York, said that Berkeley 'hath so much endeard himself to me by his services to the King my father and the King my brother and

my selfe with so much honour and success' (Jeayes, 325). Berkeley strongly and successfully promoted the candidatures of Sir Matthew Hale and of Sir Baynham Throckmorton in the Gloucestershire elections for the Convention and Cavalier parliaments (1660 and 1661 respectively). He became a knight of the Bath and joined the council for foreign plantations in 1661. In 1663 he was a founder member of the Royal African Company and was elected a fellow of the Royal Society. In 1667 he was added to the council of trade and sworn of the privy council. He joined the Board of Trade and Plantations in 1678, then became governor of the Levant Company in 1680 and master of Trinity House in 1681, as well as a member of the East India Company; speeches made to these institutions were published in 1681.

Berkeley was well known to Evelyn, who called him 'my old and noble friend' (*Diary of John Evelyn*, 708), and to Pepys, who often encountered him on trade and colonial matters. Both mention his fine country house, Durdens, near Epsom. He also inherited residences in St John's parish, Clerkenwell, and Cranford, Middlesex. Berkeley comes across as intelligent—his *Historical Applications and Occasional Meditations* (1666) went through several editions and was translated into French (1667)—but coarse, arrogant, and unscrupulous. His touchiness emerged in a long-running squabble over precedence with Lord De La Warr between 1660 and 1679, and was also exemplified by his writing in 1660 that he would not have any superior commander in the Gloucestershire horse regiment. On one occasion, Wren told Pepys, Berkeley creamed off £800 from the £1500 paid by wine licensees to the duke of York to surrender bad licences.

By 1677 the family fortune had been secured and Berkeley's personal estate was then worth £26,000, including £8000 in East India Company stock. On 11 September 1679 he was created Viscount Dursley and earl of Berkeley. He was sworn of the privy council for the second time on 17 July 1678, and for a third time on 21 July 1685. He also became *custos rotulorum* for Gloucestershire in 1685 and in Surrey in 1689. When James II fled, Berkeley was among those lords who assembled at the Guildhall on 11 December 1688 and constituted themselves a provisional government until the arrival of the prince of Orange. Sources differ as to whether or not William III reappointed him to the privy council; certainly, Berkeley had not taken up arms for him. Although never a party politician, he used his influence on the whig side in his later years and had always inclined to toleration for dissenters. He died, aged seventy-one, on 10 October 1698 and was buried at Cranford. He was survived by his wife, and succeeded by his elder son, Charles Berkeley (1649–1710).

ANDREW WARMINGTON

Sources GEC, *Peerage*, new edn, vol. 3 · *CSP dom.*, 1660–69 · *The diary of Samuel Pepys*, ed. R. N. G. Braybrooke (1825), esp. vols. 2–3 · Gloucester Public Library, Smyth of Nibley MSS, esp. II, III, XI · W. R. Williams, *The parliamentary history of the county of Gloucester* (privately printed, Hereford, 1898) · N. Luttrell, *A brief historical relation of state affairs from September 1678 to April 1714*, 1 (1857) · I. H.

Jeayes, *Descriptive catalogue of the charters and muniments in the possession of the Rt. Hon. Lord Fitzhardinge at Berkeley Castle* (1908) · *JHC*, 7 (1651–9) · *The diary of John Evelyn*, ed. E. S. De Beer (1959) · Glos. RO, Berkeley of Berkeley Castle papers, D 225 · A. R. Warmington, *Civil war, interregnum and Restoration in Gloucestershire, 1640–1672* (1997) · Wing, *STC*
Archives Gloucester Public Library, Smyth of Nibley MSS
Likenesses M. Beale, oils, after 1679, Berkeley Castle, Gloucestershire · T. Athow, wash drawing, AM Oxf. · N. Dixon, miniature, Berkeley Castle, Gloucestershire · J. B. Du Four, silver medal, BM
Wealth at death entire estate bequeathed to elder son: will, PRO, PROB 11/448, sig. 245

Berkeley, George (1685–1753), Church of Ireland bishop of Cloyne and philosopher, was born at or near Kilkenny on 12 March 1685. His father, William Berkeley (*d.* in or after 1734), who later held a military commission, was a gentleman farmer descended from a Staffordshire family related to the earls of Berkeley; he owned the property of Dysart, further down the River Nore near Thomastown, where Berkeley grew up. Berkeley's mother, a great-aunt of General James Wolfe, has been tentatively identified as Elisabeth Southerne, daughter of a Dublin brewer and on her mother's side a descendant of James Ussher (Luce, 23).

Early years For three and a half years from July 1696 Berkeley received a classical schooling in Kilkenny at what was then the Duke of Ormonde's School, whose former pupils included Jonathan Swift and William Congreve. A friendship established there with his fellow scholar Thomas Prior, his subsequent Dublin agent, is documented through an extensive correspondence that is important for Berkeley's biography. He left school in January 1700 and entered Trinity College, Dublin, as a pensioner, signing the matriculation register just after his fifteenth birthday; he was elected Erasmus Smith exhibitioner in 1701 and scholar the following year, and graduated BA in spring 1704. He was fortunate to go through college at a time when Dublin society still showed the effects of the great efflorescence of new learning associated with William Molyneux, the friend and correspondent of John Locke, and the Dublin Philosophical Society. The scholastic philosophy of the Laudian curriculum competed with reading in the Cartesian and atomist traditions and the writings of Locke.

Berkeley had an unbounded interest in the natural world. His recollections of his boyhood exploration of the Cave of Dunmore near Kilkenny were written up a few years later for the inaugural meeting (10 January 1706) of a society for natural history and the sciences—probably a college club—a constitution for which survives among his papers. After graduating he prepared an elementary textbook in which he explored the basis of arithmetical notation and the principal arithmetical processes as functions of that notation, explaining these without resort to algebraic or geometrical techniques. He published this in 1707 as *Arithmetica*, jointly with a further set of studies entitled *Miscellanea mathematica* dedicated to Molyneux's son Samuel, and indicated that mathematics had been his primary interest for three years. He probably took pupils in the

George Berkeley (1685–1753), by John Smibert, 1730

subject while awaiting an opening as a junior fellow. A vacancy arose in 1706 and it is no coincidence that Berkeley published these texts before the fellowship competition in June 1707. He secured the election and his London publisher, Churchill, was one of those to send congratulations. A month later he took his MA.

Fellow of Trinity College, Dublin Berkeley's tutorial responsibilities appear to have been light, but from 1709 to 1712 and from 1721 until his resignation in 1724 he accepted further occasional duties from time to time as librarian, junior dean, Greek lecturer, divinity lecturer, senior proctor, and Hebrew lecturer. On 19 February 1709 he was ordained deacon, and a year later priest, in the college chapel by St George Ashe, bishop of Clogher and vice-chancellor of the university. Ashe shared Berkeley's interests in mathematics and the new philosophy. Berkeley's ordination to the priesthood, at the normal interval from ordination as deacon, so incensed Archbishop William King, who was visiting England, that he ordered a prosecution in the ecclesiastical court. King represented it as an infringement of his diocesan jurisdiction, but was probably smarting from recent criticism by Berkeley; he had not contested the diaconal ordination the previous year. The matter blew over. These early years of Berkeley's professional career are important for a second friendship and another source of a lifelong correspondence: this was with Sir John Perceval, later first earl of Egmont, a landowner, privy councillor, and something of a colonial nationalist.

Two early pieces not published in Berkeley's lifetime have attracted later scholars. 'Of infinites', read to the reconstituted Dublin Philosophical Society on 19 November 1707, shows Berkeley's continuing absorption with mathematics and an evident indebtedness to Locke. An untitled homily delivered, while still a layman, in the college chapel on 11 January 1708 addresses the problem of how people can respond to the prospect of a future state they cannot conceive; this problem Berkeley derived directly from Locke and continued to address within a Lockean framework, notwithstanding the contrary suggestion of A. A. Luce (*Works*, 7.11–12) and others. There followed a productive period in which his most famous and revolutionary philosophical publications went through their first editions. *An Essay towards a New Theory of Vision* (1709), a work of lasting importance in the psychology of perception, was transitional between Berkeley's already informed interests in mathematics and natural philosophy and a growing independence of mind in metaphysics and epistemology. Part one of *A Treatise Concerning the Principles of Human Knowledge* (1710) is the classic exposition of his philosophy of immaterialism as an antidote to infidelity, prefaced with an influential essay in the philosophy of language; part two was later lost in manuscript, with other papers, in Italy. The first work was dedicated to Perceval, the second to the same earl of Pembroke as had formerly been Locke's patron. Pembroke had been the outgoing lord lieutenant and the galvanizing power behind the Dublin Philosophical Society when Berkeley wrote his paper in 1707.

In response to actual and reported criticisms, Berkeley recast his philosophy in a more popular form as a debate between the established new philosophy and his own in *Three Dialogues between Hylas and Philonous* (1713). In the same period he delivered three highly theoretical sermons on passive obedience in the college chapel, revising them for publication (1712) to counteract allegations of Jacobitism. Berkeley's defence of moral absolutes was too refined for many in practical politics. He sought to reconcile an obligation not to resist the rightful ruler with an obligation to follow conscience in not fulfilling an order to do wrong, though it might precipitate adverse personal consequences whose acceptance was 'passive obedience'. The rumours lingered, but Berkeley put out a firmly anti-Jacobite tract for the tory side, *Advice to the Tories who have Taken the Oaths*, in 1715. He would support the loyalist cause in letters to the *Dublin Journal* in 1745–6, when he also armed a local militia at his own expense.

After 1712 Berkeley kept his fellowship for another twelve years but spent only three of them in Dublin. In January 1713 he obtained leave to visit England, under a misapprehension about the likely benefits of English weather in curing an 'ague'; by September he had negotiated the first in a succession of two-year leaves, by royal authority, that saw him through the decade. He moved widely and easily in London cultural circles. Dublin contacts provided introductions to persons with connections in church or state, while curiosity about his philosophical theories attracted leading literary figures. Edward Southwell, secretary of state for Ireland, helped Berkeley establish a personal friendship with Pembroke, and he was cordially received by his compatriots Richard Steele and Jonathan Swift. Steele was soon to launch *The Guardian* and recruited Berkeley to combat the growing tide of freethinking. Berkeley contributed about a dozen essays, for which he prepared by eavesdropping in London coffee houses. Removed from the relatively sheltered environment he had previously known, he was apt to see moral and spiritual degradation everywhere, and whether he always put the best construction on the sophisticated conversation of the metropolis cannot now be established. Steele's bookseller Jacob Tonson undertook the publication of *Three Dialogues*, which Berkeley dedicated to a recent acquaintance and kinsman, Lord Berkeley of Stratton. At the same time Berkeley undertook compilation of the three-volume *Ladies Library* (purporting to be 'by a Lady') for Tonson, for which Steele wrote a preface. This quite heavily edited set of readings on social convention, the family, and religion was intended to better women's education and social standing, and went through six editions in Berkeley's lifetime. In the same literary culture he met Joseph Addison and the Scriblerian circle round Alexander Pope and John Arbuthnot. With Addison, despite political differences, he developed a particular rapport, accompanying him to the opening night of *Cato* in April 1713. His admiration for Pope was reciprocated and through Pope he was introduced to Richard Boyle, Lord Burlington, whose architectural and other artistic enthusiasms he shared. Addison, Pope, and Arbuthnot humoured Berkeley in his philosophical opinions without being convinced by them. He visited George Smalridge in Oxford and soaked up the music and theatre there. Swift secured for him introductions at court, including one to Charles Mordaunt, earl of Peterborough—another link with the age of Locke. Berkeley was recruited as his chaplain in October 1713 when Peterborough was dispatched to attend the coronation of the king of Sicily.

Most of the party never went beyond northern Italy. Berkeley was awed by the public buildings and churches of Paris, and while there studied the paintings and statuary of the Louvre. Letters to Perceval and Prior show that a significant meeting with the philosopher Nicolas Malebranche was arranged, and there is no reason to think that it did not occur. Berkeley had closely studied Malebranche's metaphysics, deriving both positive and negative lessons from it; and critics of Berkeley, especially in France, had begun to associate the two philosophies, though Berkeley himself repudiated the connection. Elsewhere on his travels, he commented on the open gambling of the priests at Lyon. 'The opera here is magnificent enough, but the music bad' (*Works*, 8.76). He spent new year crossing the Alps, a perilous trip 'in open chairs'. At Turin and Genoa he was disappointed with the colleges and bookshops:

I … do not find that learning flourishes among them. Nothing curious in the sciences has of late been published in Italy. Their clergy for the most part are extremely ignorant;

as an instance of it, they showed me in the library of the Franciscans in this town a Hebrew book, taking it to be an English one.   (ibid., 8.79)

Leghorn was worse: 2000 priests, none of them worth talking to. The climate suited him, but the countryside was not what the Roman poets had led him to expect:

England is a more poetical country, the spring there is forwarder and lasts longer, purling streams are more numerous, and the fields and groves have a cheerfuller green … England has the most learning, the most riches, the best government, the best people, and the best religion in the world.   (ibid., 8.84)

Berkeley returned by way of Paris and the Low Countries a few months before the Jacobite rising gave him a less sanguine view of the British situation. By May 1716, with powerful patrons, he confidently expected the living of St Paul's, Dublin, but the lords justices successfully opposed it. So apparently did Robert Molesworth, although Berkeley had been on cordial terms with Molesworth's eldest sons, his companions from Genoa to Paris in 1714. The rival candidate, the Revd Duke Tyrrell, wrote to Molesworth portraying Berkeley as someone 'highly esteemed' by the Jacobites, 'a creature of Dean Swift', and committed to 'the Tory interest' (Berman, 84). Bishop Ashe came to the rescue, employing Berkeley to travel with his son, St George Ashe the younger, and thus he found himself, with sword and pistol, making another winter alpine crossing. They were in Italy for four years (1717–20). In Rome and elsewhere they studied art, architecture, and antiquities, and in travelling further afield Berkeley felt a greater affinity than previously with the region's classical past. This time he was more impressed with the scenery, particularly round Naples and later on Ischia, where he was seriously ill. He was scornful of the idle Neapolitan aristocracy. He twice climbed Vesuvius when activity was threatening, and a report of his observations went to the Royal Society. An incomplete set of richly detailed journals survives. In the summer of 1717 they reached the heel of Italy, and Berkeley was dismayed at the poverty. He investigated the activity and folklore of the tarantula. Later in the year they crossed to Sicily, where the remains of Hellenic culture were more to his taste. He studied the natural history and met the Cartesian philosopher Tommaso Campailla (1668–1740). For much of 1720 they were in Florence, securing copies of art works that cost them great delays, and spent time in the company of the Scottish painter John Smibert. They returned to Rome in November.

Berkeley was back in London early in 1721, and in Dublin for the new college session that year, when he qualified for the degrees of BD and DD. He had attained senior fellowship while abroad in 1717. He returned with the manuscript of *De motu*, written during the journey home in an unsuccessful bid for a prize of the Académie des Sciences at Paris. Without giving overt expression to immaterialism, this work presents an account of natural philosophy that is compatible with the immaterialist position. Arriving back in the wake of the South Sea investment crisis, he also wrote and published *An Essay towards Preventing the*

Ruin of Great Britain (1721), an important piece of early economic literature, condemning the rush to acquire wealth through paper speculation instead of building it upon a solid base of manufacture, trade, and 'industry'. The failure of the South Sea shares was for Berkeley the symptom, not the substance, of the malady, which lay in the abandonment of generations of moral and religious tradition. The freethinkers and their secular values were the nation's undoing.

Although Berkeley undertook additional duties, his final years at Trinity College were subject to uncertainty about his future career. His links with the Ashes were terminated through the death of both father (1718) and son (1721). He was by now in favour with the duke of Grafton, the lord lieutenant, who as one of the lords justices had opposed his earlier preferment. Berkeley set his heart on the sinecure deanery of Dromore and secured a patent for it. The bishop of Dromore, however, claimed the right of appointment and installed his own nominee. Berkeley instituted legal proceedings financed by the Grafton administration, but as the months dragged on lost confidence in the outcome. Meanwhile by May 1722 he had resolved to emigrate permanently to Bermuda, with or without the deanery income. He planned to set up a college for the moral regeneration of the American colonies before they were overrun by popish missionaries from the Hispanic countries. In May 1724 he was awarded the rich deanery of Derry and relinquished his college living. He was installed in the new position but never took up residence. It carried financial obligations and he needed to cover for his intended absence. He concluded his affairs in Dublin that summer.

The Bermuda project   The proposed college was intended to train colonists and native Americans in equal numbers, the former to bring a 'reformation of manners' to their own communities and augment the protestant priesthood, the latter to convert the indigenous population to 'religion, morality, and civil life' (*Works*, 8.127). Although Berkeley was in earnest on both counts, his health was still a consideration: he believed Bermuda had the best climate in the world and an ideal economy, and he had Elysian visions of its topography. Much of his information came from out-of-date travellers' reports, but in June 1723 he found himself in receipt of a providential windfall. He was named co-executor and joint residuary legatee of the estate of Esther Van Homrigh, Swift's tragic Vanessa. There were, however, debts and a protracted lawsuit to settle and a fair portion of the estate was lost in costs. The affair does not seem to have soured Berkeley's relations with Swift, who probably neither had nor sought any claims on the estate, and the executors suppressed the Vanessa correspondence; Swift wrote to Lord Carteret, the new lord lieutenant, in September 1724, inviting him to encourage Berkeley's designs.

The next four years, spent mostly in London, were chaotic. Administrative problems over the Van Homrigh estate and the deanery were compounded by dilatory or unreliable agents. John Smibert, who had settled in London, would guide the sale of Vanessa's art collection. At the end of 1724 Berkeley published *A proposal for the better supplying of churches in our foreign plantations, and for converting the savage Americans to Christianity*, arguing the moral urgency of the project. He was addressing an Anglican public and bizarrely dismissed what he called 'the two presbyterian colleges of New England, which have so long subsisted to little or no purpose' as evidence that 'where Ignorance or ill Manners once take place in a Seminary, they are sure to be handed down in a Succession of illiterate or worthless Men' (*Works*, 7.354). He ignored the parlous state of the College of William and Mary at Williamsburg which already existed for purposes similar to his own, but that institution became indirectly the beneficiary of the mood of support for Berkeley's venture, attracting reform and investment to put it on the sounder footing that his own lacked. In the short term, however, his proposal caught the public imagination. By June 1725 he had a royal charter for 'St Paul's College in Bermuda'. He had discovered a dormant endowment that controlled vacant land in Bermuda reserved for educational purposes and had this written into the specification. In reissuing the *Proposal* to publicize the charter he instituted collection procedures for subscribers. He deleted the offensive reference to Harvard and Yale and extended his canvass to liberal Scots presbyterians. Hearing of the government's income impending from land sales on St Kitts, he lobbied hard for this to be put to the service of the college. George I approved of the St Kitts scheme and instructed Robert Walpole to prepare a petition from the Commons for its implementation, which was overwhelmingly carried. The utopianism of the venture is captured in verses penned by February 1726 that Berkeley published only long afterwards in *A Miscellany* (1752): Europe was in decay but a new golden age was dawning; time would play out its final act, as 'Westward the Course of Empire takes its Way'.

With the accession of George II, Berkeley was in favour with the intellectual Queen Caroline, and to keep the royal interest sweet he attended for a time regular but fruitless salons which she organized with himself, Thomas Sherlock, Samuel Clarke, and Benjamin Hoadly. Ever since the publication of the *Principles* he had sought to have Clarke on his side philosophically and probably met him on his first stay in London, but Clarke always dogmatically dismissed Berkeley's philosophy; churchmen with whom he formed closer contacts at various times included the future bishops Benson, Conybeare, Secker, and (despite philosophical differences) Butler. Another lady with whom Berkeley established a strong intellectual kinship was Anne (1700/01–1786), daughter of John Forster, former chief justice of the common pleas at Dublin. They married, probably in London, on 1 August 1728, and sailed together soon afterwards. Two children were born in America, the first of whom was still living at Berkeley's death, the other dying in infancy; five others were born after their return, of whom two were alive at Berkeley's death. Anne Berkeley lived to eighty-five, dying at Langley, Kent, on 27 May 1786.

Although £20,000 of public money was now formally earmarked for the Bermuda college, no account was ever established, or date set, for its use. The ministry, reluctant converts to the scheme, were repeatedly warned by merchant interests that it was impracticable, a criticism Berkeley ascribed to the commercial values he opposed and to sectarian opposition to the established church; but even within the largely sympathetic Society for Promoting Christian Knowledge to which he was elected in 1725, those with first-hand knowledge of the American colonies and missions raised serious doubts. To prevent a threatening decline in private support, Berkeley sailed for Newport, Rhode Island, with a small advance party on 6 September 1728; this included Smibert, who painted several well-known portraits of Berkeley and of his party before settling for life in Boston. The journey was hazardous and protracted. They made an unscheduled landfall on the Virginia coast about the turn of the year and were officially received at Williamsburg before reaching Rhode Island on 23 January 1729. By the spring Berkeley had bought a farm of 96 acres at Middletown 'with two fine groves and winding rivulet upon it' (*Works*, 8.194), whose produce would support the college. He employed slaves and was apparently indifferent to the institution of slavery provided that it was humane, seeing the moral need rather as one of conversion and baptism. He built a new house, Whitehall, which is now maintained as a historic site although the adjoining farmland has given way to urban development.

Berkeley often preached at Newport in the winter and in remoter outposts in the summer. The strongest and longest friendship he established among New England churchmen was with Samuel Johnson (1696–1772) of Stratford, Connecticut, a refugee from Calvinism who later became first president of King's College, New York (later Columbia University), and lent support to Berkeley's philosophy through his *Elementa philosophica* (1752) and other writings. Throughout his career Berkeley had little time for dissenters, although he abhorred the use of violence against them. The religious tolerance characteristic of Rhode Island induced a degree of ecumenicism in his social practice that was not always maintained in the pulpit. Reports of growing infidelity in English society, to which he was always liable to give credence, were fuelled by the continuing bad faith of the government in failing to lodge the funds he considered legally his. This was a factor in his writing *Alciphron*, a set of dialogues located notionally in England, but drawing much of the landscape description from Rhode Island, which was to sell well and stimulate controversy after his return. In this, theist and immaterialist combine their defences against a medley of intellectual trends (derived primarily but not exclusively from Locke, Bernard Mandeville, and the third earl of Shaftesbury) that Berkeley regarded as obstructive to religion. The work includes Berkeley's second foray into moral philosophy. Increasingly through 1730 he received reports that his funding would not come. Facing the reality in early 1731, he arranged a speedy return, via Boston and Cambridge, Massachusetts. He was in London with his family on 30 October 1731 and, despite the failure of his own scheme, had some part in the discussions of those planning the development of Georgia.

Berkeley had made two strategic errors before embarking for the New World, which no amount of long-distance communication through intermediaries could remedy. He left Britain when the funds had been only voted and not paid, and he held out for an impossibly distant off-shore location against the advice of knowledgeable friends of the enterprise. When he embarked for Rhode Island he was already considering relocating the college there. After arriving and testing local opinion he decided he had misjudged the country and the mores of the people. He wrote to friends, confidentially, that he now thought Rhode Island the better location, but dared not broach the matter with government until the money was in the bank. Rumours circulated which he felt obliged to deny, but the tide of opinion had changed and he had lost his chance.

How much hard support, both unconditional and conditional, Berkeley received for the Bermuda project is uncertain. He had promises as prospective teachers from three fellows of Trinity College named in the charter; Robert Clayton may have been a fourth before his elevation to a bishopric. Smibert was probably another teaching recruit, given that Berkeley's detailed architectural designs include provision for a school of fine art. A posthumous anecdote, derived from Oliver Goldsmith, that connects John Christopher Pepusch with a planned post in music is more problematic. Thomas Blackwell, the Aberdeen classicist, recorded having discussions with Berkeley in London but declined a position, and there is evidence that some members or former members of Edinburgh's Rankenian Club were approached, from a sympathy for Berkeley's philosophy they had shown in correspondence. In addition Berkeley had firm or provisional commitments from potential colonists with no teaching ambitions. His widow reported to the *Biographia Britannica* that of the planned 'circus' of houses for gentlemen, 'many had been actually bespoken, and the Dean had been requested to superintend the building of them'. As for donations, records survive of £5065 in twenty-eight personal subscriptions (*Works*, 7.361), which Berkeley offered back to all who were identifiable and alive on his return. Not all accepted them back. The residue he put to related purposes, sending books to Harvard and Yale, and discharging a mortgage loan drawn on his deanery account which freed him to make over both Whitehall and the farm to Yale. In 1733 he presented an organ to Trinity Church, Newport, Rhode Island.

Bishop of Cloyne Berkeley had intended to return to Derry if the Bermuda project foundered, but could not do so without dispossessing his deputy of the deanery house and ousting the curates who were carrying out his duties. He resumed the acquaintance and friendship of former supporters in London but faced hostility from influential whigs in both London and Dublin, including the Hoadly brothers, who considered him a visionary. Sympathetic friends like Perceval, on the other hand, lobbied to find

him at least some token preferment, to scotch the slanders against him. Exhausted by the American business and in poorer health, he sought a less strenuous deanery consistent with a scholar's life. His letters make regular reference to 'cholic' and 'gout'. While taking time to mull over his future Berkeley prepared new editions of his early philosophical writings, giving a sharper edge in all of them to the attack on freethinking and launching a significant new salvo in the campaign by returning to his former interests in mathematics and natural philosophy. *The Analyst* (1734) is a sustained critique of Newton's influential theory of fluxions, a theory Berkeley considered incoherent and a disservice to mathematics, but one which, if unchecked, might reinforce prevailing views on the divisibility of matter and support infidelity. The work generated wide interest and opposition among professional mathematicians, his most formidable critic being Colin MacLaurin of Edinburgh. Later scholarship has been divided: some consider that Berkeley got the mathematics right, some that he misconstrued Newton's purpose, and some both.

Berkeley was appointed bishop of Cloyne in January 1734 and consecrated in St Paul's Church, Dublin, on 19 May. This extensive minor see in a predominantly Roman Catholic part of rural Ireland included in its bounds both Perceval and Burlington estates. Despite the unsought and perhaps unwanted elevation, Berkeley judged it compatible with his needs and once again went into a position without fully exploring its finances. He settled to eighteen years of diligent pastoral work, refusing opportunities of further preferment. The return to Ireland was something of a culture shock:

> We in this island are growing an odd and mad people. We were odd before, but I was not sure of our having the genius necessary to become mad. But some late steps of a public nature give sufficient proof thereof. (*Works*, 8.244)

Travelling grew difficult and he depended increasingly on visitors and correspondents for news, both political and literary. Soon after his settlement he established a spinning school:

> The children begin to find a pleasure in being paid in hard money; which I understand they will not give to their parents, but keep to buy clothes for themselves … I am building a workhouse for sturdy vagrants, and design to raise about two acres of hemp for employing them. (ibid., 8.245)

He also planted flax on the sizeable episcopal estate. By 1741 over 100 agricultural day-labourers were employed under his wife's supervision.

In writings from *The Querist* (1735–7) to *A Word to the Wise* (1749) Berkeley condemned the English exploitation of the Irish economy and argued for the full integration of the Catholic population into the economic life of the country for the benefit of all parties; but he had no sympathy for the historical claims of a distinctive Gaelic culture. He advocated the development of a self-sufficient economy, complete reform of the banking system, and the introduction of a paper currency. His home became an artistic centre: he bought art works and musical instruments, involved family and visitors in painting and performing, and for a time in the 1740s employed a resident music teacher. The region lacked medical services and severe distress over the winter of 1739–40 led to widespread disease. Berkeley dispensed what advice he could, and somewhat later provided for 'a few strolling sick' (*Works*, 8.289). In 1744 appeared one of his most controversial works. *Siris* is a reconciliation of medicine with metaphysics, best known for its advocacy of the medicinal value of tar water, a native American preventative distilled from pine resins. Having conducted his own experiments Berkeley made specific claims for its beneficial effect in alleviating fevers, gout, scurvy, and dropsy. In trying to understand the cosmical principles that might explain this he conceived the possibility, which others took up with greater alacrity, that its properties might be those of a universal panacea, operating as condensed light. *Siris* had exceptional sales, primarily as a home medicine guide, for a few years and was translated into most western European languages, but its medical claims also provoked criticism. Of several editions separately set in both Dublin and London in 1744, the second London edition was kept in standing type through five separate issues of 1000 or more copies each.

The philosophy of immaterialism Berkeley was a person of deep piety and spirituality and a good patristic scholar, but has no claim to eminence or originality as a theologian. The little evidence that survives of his preaching shows a preference for straightforward biblical homilies with a conventional moral message, although his mode of delivery appears to have had some impact. His brilliance lay in his philosophical writing, and in the style almost as much as the content. Immaterialism is a philosophy that sees minds or spirits as the only ultimate existents. It does not dispute that there is an objective world order, independent of any individual mind and subject to the laws of nature, or that humans in respect of their corporeal nature need a sufficient understanding of these laws to function effectively in a context in which one bodily object remains spatially external to any other; but it challenges the 'absolute' existence of this or any other corporeal nature, abstracted from dependence upon mind. So Berkeley does not deny the common-sense reality of the natural world and the events occurring within it. These are a fact of experience, and he can enforce the distinction between the real and the imaginary by the same practical criteria as anyone else. His novelty lies not in challenging the existence of physical bodies, which he agrees with his critics would be a mark of lunacy, but in an analysis of what that existence consists in, namely in being perceived ('*esse* is *percipi*', *Principles*, section 3) or being capable of being perceived. They are the sum total of actual and potential experiences or, adapting the term given particular currency by Locke, 'ideas'. But these ideas are not chance or random: they are ordered and therefore caused, and inasmuch as they are actual experiences there are beings whose experiences they are. Minds are thus involved both as agents and as percipients, with the divine mind as the overall agent of the order within which created minds function. Agents and their acts are not perceptible and are not subject to this analysis of the existence of perceptibles. We are aware of our own agency by direct consciousness and of other agents by immediate inference.

In holding that the only ultimate agency is that of minds, while believing that there is a graduated scale of such minds from merely sentient to fully rational, Berkeley shared common assumptions of his day. Even in denying that there is also secondary or derived power in physical nature, if this means power vested in something other than minds, he was not significantly out on a limb. His distinctive thesis, that this ontology makes a second substance or 'matter' redundant to any theoretical account of the physical world, and that the accounts given of such a substance are incoherent, emerges (as his surviving early notebooks show) out of his wrestlings with the metaphysics of Cartesian and Newtonian science. Although he greatly respected Newton's genius he saw Newtonianism, when read literally, as running into paradox and contradiction from its commitment to absolute time and space and the infinite divisibility of the physical world, and from this he went on to consider the whole of the contemporary matter theory. In the *Principles* (sections 60–65) he admitted the intricate structures discernible by the microscope as evidence of the systematic character of the natural design and of the laws that enable us to turn nature successfully to human use, but he rejected theories that additionally postulated material and moving parts of bodies below the perceptual threshold of any sentient being whatever. That, in his view, would involve the imperceptible having perceptible qualities.

Developing the critique further in *De motu*, Berkeley argued that when physical science is reinterpreted within a theocentric framework, abstract forces such as gravity and attraction are unnecessary. While mathematical hypotheses have a practical application in mechanics, the only motion that is actually subject to laws is the perceptible effect—never the cause, or even the instrument—of change. From *Alciphron* onwards he increasingly stressed that natural philosophy may embody hypotheses with no literal experiential content, which serve only as verbal instruments to direct our practice. *Siris* admits a role for chemical particles in discussing the 'virtues' of particular treatments, but it is not clear how far these are theoretical entities and how far they are in principle perceivable: their theoretical standing in relation to the laws of nature seems to be acceptable to him as a means of predicting practical effects, so long as they are not made substantial by being credited with genuine power or activity. He even comes round to allowing the terminology of 'secondary' or 'instrumental' causes in referring to the status of aether or light, but the sense in which it is a mediate instrument is one relative to the humans who may harness it. Objectively considered, causation remains both spiritual and immediate.

While Berkeley showed increasing ingenuity as his

philosophy matured—not least in finding accommodations with Newtonianism—it is the early foundations of his immaterialism that have continued to attract most interest and comment. His *New Theory of Vision* is a study in the visual perception of distance in the sense of externality or 'outness'; of relative distance or magnitude; of relative placings in terms of higher and lower, before and beyond; and shape. Taking each in turn, Berkeley shows how we have to learn to interpret visual cues and eye sensations, and how, for doing so, we are crucially dependent on correlations between a changeable vision and a stable touch. We are not equipped with the instinctive geometry for which many contemporaries argued. Vision provides 'signs' consisting in appearances of shaped colour of variable intensities. Their interpretation becomes sufficiently habitual that we think we see the tangible world in which we live and move that these come to 'suggest'; but in fact we are reading the visual ideas like a language in which signifier and signified are only contingently associated, to the point where we are unaware of the transition in thought. There are no data actually common to any two senses: we do not through sight and touch perceive a shape or size that is common to both. The common world we come to believe in is a mental construct. Berkeley inferred that a man born blind who subsequently acquired sight would not immediately identify by vision the shapes appropriate to the sphere and cube he knew by touch, and afterwards considered himself vindicated by the experimental work of William Cheselden. In the *Principles* he extended his account to the objects of all the senses, including touch, to insist on the mind-dependence of everything perceptible.

Berkeley regularly reinforced his case with a critique of the distinction between what Locke had called 'primary' and 'secondary' qualities. Berkeley believed the prevailing philosophy had shown that colour, sound, taste, and smell are in the mind, although it was hardly consistent with his own position to accept the grounds upon which that was based; then, because any extension, shape, and size that we see are inextricably tied to a colour seen, these are in his view similarly relative to the perspective and condition of the perceiver, so that all the objects of vision, and of other senses by analogy, are mental. In some writings (for example, *Principles*, sections 11–12) he attacked the distinction between primary and secondary qualities in a form that conflates the views of Locke and Malebranche. But the fact that the distinction was drawn in different ways by Berkeley's time helps explain why many who shared his opinion that only minds are active nevertheless found the rejection of matter unacceptable. Samuel Clarke, for whom secondary qualities like colour were unreal—another idiosyncratic reading—estimated that Berkeley's philosophy would destroy the whole of natural philosophy, an understandable reaction if one sees the reduction of primary qualities to the status of secondary qualities as the reduction of everything quantifiable in nature to an illusion. Berkeley's view was precisely opposite: the 'matter' that he rejected had lost all reality by being deprived of secondary qualities and had become

an unobservable fiction of the philosophers, whereas he had removed the mystery of a world beyond experience and turned it into something familiar and fully describable. It was in this sense that he promoted his philosophy as the antidote to scepticism.

Most of the errors Berkeley claimed to detect in the science of the day he traced to incoherences arising from false abstraction—from misconstruing the ability of the mind to draw distinctions of reason as if it were an ability to conceive an order of things separable from all context in experience. An influential application of, and support for, this false abstraction he found in Locke's semantic theory as he understood it: namely, that the same words retain a common signification on different occasions by standing for a common idea that is abstracted from the particularizing details and circumstances of different individuals, thus giving credence to the possibility of a pure science of matter and motion, shape and space. For Berkeley, Lockean abstraction is a self-contradictory process. His alternative view, that words signify indifferently any individual in a class, involves an idiosyncratic use of 'signify' that would permit the same word never to have the same signification on successive occasions, or for different contributors to the same conversation. While signification in Berkeley's sense remains forever variable, definition (which is purely verbal) is constant. He nevertheless retained the Lockean ideal of words standing for determinate ideas in the exact sciences, but he qualified it in important respects. As early as the *New Theory of Vision* (section 147), the 'proper objects of vision' that constitute a 'universal language of nature' not only function as the signs of a tangible world but also 'regulate our actions' in matters affecting 'our preservation and well-being', and 'all the transactions and concerns of life'. In the introduction to the *Principles* (sections 19–20), he allowed that words may stand for ideas they no longer call to mind, and that by habituation they may come to have an influence on action or feeling equivalent to that of the former ideas. His model here was algebra. The influence may operate upon us through the mere authority of a name, like 'Aristotle' or (in an important discussion that survives in manuscript) 'St Paul', which for good or bad reasons has acquired a force in excess of any ideas we may actually have. By the time of *Alciphron*, he was prepared to loosen the link with ideas further and allow to some words, in both natural philosophy and theology, a use that could not be made individually intelligible. They could still be employed in framing beliefs that have practical applications, whether in relation to a revealed mystery or to a scientific theorem. The assumption that language is primarily a series of learnt associations nevertheless remains paramount for preserving the language metaphor to describe the organized character of experience that Berkeley never abandoned.

Since immaterialism does not contest the existence but only the status of the natural world, its implications are speculative rather than practical. There is, however, one point at which speculation and practice converge, namely in religion. Berkeley believed his philosophy sounded the death knell of atheism as well as scepticism, and this was his overriding purpose. His theism rests on a conventional design argument without the impediment of a metaphysics of matter. This constitutes the climax to the argument of the *Principles*, but the evidence of design is anticipated from an early stage in the work; Berkeley already assumes a divine existence in his depiction of the language of nature. In *Alciphron* the emphasis is different, for strategic reasons: the fact that experience functions as a language becomes the sole basis of the design argument itself, since language without controlling intelligence is inconceivable.

Death and reputation Berkeley was deeply affected by the death of his youngest son, William, in 1751. In August 1752 he left with his remaining family for an extended visit to Oxford, where his second son, George (1733–1795), who later attained a reasonable eminence in the Anglican church, had recently matriculated at Christ Church. By collating tenantry and parish records it is possible to show that the Berkeleys took a house at or near no. 7 Holywell Street (Tipton and Furlong); claims made on behalf of another Holywell address are a twentieth-century fabrication. A generation later the suggestion was that Berkeley had applied to resign his bishopric but the king had refused, permitting him instead to reside where he wished. Any truth behind this may relate to a period in the 1740s when Berkeley seems to have contemplated the development in or near Oxford of a self-supporting spiritual retreat (*Works*, 7.151–2, 155; 8.287); it came to nothing because of the illness of his eldest son, Henry. In 1752 the intention seems to have been simply to be close for the time being to George. Impressed with the decorum of Oxford students, he accepted his son's expensive lifestyle with equanimity. Berkeley died in his lodgings during tea on Sunday 14 January 1753, while his wife was reading to him from the epistle for the burial service. He had stipulated a simple funeral, and he was buried in Christ Church Cathedral on 20 January. An inscription commissioned by his widow was composed by William Markham, subsequently archbishop of York.

Already recognized at his death as one of Ireland's leading men of letters, Berkeley won few philosophical converts. His older contemporary Arthur Collier reached an immaterialist philosophy independently. In Ireland itself Peter Browne and Robert Clayton responded obliquely to aspects of Berkeley's philosophy, and James Arbuckle published a pleasant satire. The most ardent Irish advocates of Berkeley's philosophy would turn out to be professional metaphysicians—the natural philosopher Richard Kirwan in his *Metaphysical Essays* (1809) and the lawyer Henry O'Connor in his *Connected Essays and Tracts* (1837). Berkeley's importance was scarcely recognized at Trinity College except as a subject for biography until W. A. Butler wrote about him in the *Dublin University Magazine* in 1836; others remained more critical. Only in the twentieth-century scholarship of A. A. Luce and David Berman has Berkeley's true stature been fully appreciated. In the north, John Young (1781–1829) at the Belfast Academical Institution showed above-average understanding of his

system. The Irish literary perception of Berkeley's work has been influenced by the poet W. B. Yeats.

On the British side Berkeley's views have always attracted interest and comment, though often ill-informed. They gained additional currency in his lifetime through the dispassionate reporting of the encyclopaedist Ephraim Chambers and through an intermittent debate from 1747 to 1752 in the columns of the *Gentleman's Magazine*. Some of the strongest support as well as the most considered criticism in the eighteenth century came from Scotland, but it was directed to particular topics, not least the theory of vision and, later, Berkeley's economic writings. The Rankenians whom he tried to recruit for the Bermuda project probably included George Turnbull and one or two close associates like William Wishart who were attracted to Berkeley's theological voluntarism; later members of the club like MacLaurin were professionally hostile to immaterialism on perceived scientific grounds. Another Scot, William Dudgeon, used Berkeley's immaterialism to support a deist programme in several writings, most explicitly in *A Discourse Concerning the Immediate and Necessary Dependence of All Things upon the Deity* (c.1734); Dudgeon's opponent Andrew Baxter, on the other hand, felt the need to re-establish a Newtonian basis for theism by challenging Berkeley's conflation of idea and object. Adam Smith modelled his essay 'Of the external senses' almost entirely on the *New Theory of Vision*. Turnbull's pupil Thomas Reid at one time accepted Berkeley's philosophy without altogether understanding it, and spent much of his career trying to get it out of his system. William Porterfield's critique of Berkeley's optical theory was an important influence on the development of the Scottish response to immaterialism. David Hume was probably the first to extrapolate themes from Berkeley to advance a purely secular philosophy, a tradition continued later by J. S. Mill and by twentieth-century writers on phenomenalism. The Scottish philosopher A. C. Fraser was the first Berkeley scholar of international calibre.

The apparent failure of the phenomenalist programme—the attempt to reduce individually identifiable objects to a determinate set of *sensa*, or statements about objects to a determinate set of statements about *sensa*—has been widely seen as entailing the failure also of Berkeley's theocentric immaterialism. Arguably, however, the very attempt to give an analysis of physical objects was itself an error of abstraction, and Berkeley should not have fallen into the paradox of admitting that 'we eat and drink ideas, and are clothed with ideas' (*Principles*, section 38). On an immaterialist account it is the whole process of food-eating or clothes-wearing—not the food and the clothes in isolation—that depends upon a sustaining mind. A bigger imponderable, which Berkeley never adequately addressed, is whether his system gave him the wherewithal to individuate and identify distinct minds. He attracted the sobriquet of an 'idealist' in the eighteenth century, but this is misleading if taken, as it has been, to represent him as a precursor of Kant and post-Kantian idealist philosophies. Berkeley had no theory that the mind structures reality in the idealist sense, and no residual hankering for a transcendent order of anything but self-conscious agents.   M. A. STEWART

Sources *The works of George Berkeley*, ed. A. A. Luce and T. E. Jessop, 9 vols. (1948–57) · Berkeley MSS, TCD · Berkeley MSS, BL · letter book of Samuel Molyneux, 1707–1709, civic archives, Southampton, D/M 1/2 · Society for Promoting Christian Knowledge archives, London · Society for the Propagation of the Gospel archives, London · *The manuscripts of the earl of Buckinghamshire, the earl of Lindsey … and James Round*, HMC, 38 (1895), 294 [C. Godwin to C. Gray, 6 Dec 1752] · A. Kippis and others, eds., *Biographia Britannica, or, The lives of the most eminent persons who have flourished in Great Britain and Ireland*, 2nd edn, 5 vols. (1778–93), 2.247–62; 3, *corrigenda et addenda*, sig. *d1–2 · D. Berman, *George Berkeley: idealism and the man* (1994) · A. C. Fraser, *Life and letters of George Berkeley, DD* (1871) · A. A. Luce, *The life of George Berkeley, Bishop of Cloyne* (1949) · C. J. McCracken, *Malebranche and British philosophy* (1983) · *Berkeley and Percival: the correspondence of George Berkeley, afterwards bishop of Cloyne, and Sir John Percival, afterwards first earl of Egmont*, ed. B. Rand (1914) · E. S. Gaustad, *George Berkeley in America* (1979) · K. T. Hoppen, *The common scientist in the seventeenth century* (1970) · J. Ingamells, ed., *A dictionary of British and Irish travellers in Italy, 1701–1800* (1997) · I. C. Tipton and E. J. Furlong, 'Mrs George Berkeley and her washing machine', *Hermathena*, 101 (1965), 38–47 · M. Atherton, *Berkeley's revolution in vision* (1990) · H. M. Bracken, *The early reception of Berkeley's immaterialism, 1710–1733*, rev. edn (1965) · C. G. Caffentzis, *Exciting the industry of mankind: George Berkeley's philosophy of money* (2000) · J. Foster and H. M. Robinson, eds., *Essays on Berkeley* (1985) · A. C. Grayling, *Berkeley: the central arguments* (1986) · R. Jakapi, 'Emotive meaning and Christian mysteries in Berkeley's *Alciphron*', *British Journal for the History of Philosophy*, 10 (2002), 401–11 · P. H. Kelly, 'Ireland and the critique of mercantilism in Berkeley's *Querist*', *Hermathena*, 139 (1985), 101–16 · R. G. Muehlmann, *Berkeley's ontology* (1992) · P. J. Olscamp, *The moral philosophy of George Berkeley* (1970) · R. E. Savage, 'Natural philosophy and mathematics in the philosophy and theology of George Berkeley', MPhil. diss., Lancaster University, 2000 · M. A. Stewart, 'Abstraction and representation in Locke, Berkeley and Hume', *The philosophical canon in the 17th and 18th centuries*, ed. G. A. J. Rogers and S. Tomaselli (1996), 123–47 · M. A. Stewart, 'Berkeley and the Rankenian Club', *Hermathena*, 139 (1985), 25–45 · P. Walmsley, *The rhetoric of Berkeley's philosophy* (1990) · K. P. Winkler, *Berkeley: an interpretation* (1989) · DNB
Archives BL, papers, Add. MSS 39304–39316 · TCD | BL, corresp. with first and second lords Egmont, Add. MSS 46997–47014, *passim* · Society for Promoting Christian Knowledge archives, London · Society for the Propagation of the Gospel archives, London
Likenesses J. Smibert, group portrait, 1730 (*Bermuda group*), Yale U. Art Gallery; version, TCD · J. Smibert, oils, 1730, NPG [*see illus.*] · oils, *c.*1734, LPL · J. Latham, oils, *c.*1745, TCD; repro. in R. W. Houghton, D. Berman, and M. T. Lapan, *Images of Berkeley* (1986), 89 · W. Skelton, line engraving, 1800 (after Vanderbank), NPG · J. Brooks, mezzotint (after Latham), BM, NPG · J. Smibert, oils (in his thirties), repro. in *Works*, ed. Luce and Jessop, frontispiece · line engraving, NPG · oils, TCD

Berkeley, George (1693?–1746), politician, was the fourth and youngest son of Charles, second earl of Berkeley, and his wife, Elizabeth, the daughter of Baptist Noel, Viscount Campden, and the sister of Edward, first earl of Gainsborough. He was admitted to Westminster School on the foundation in 1708, and was elected a scholar of Trinity College, Cambridge, in 1711, where he graduated MA in 1713. He became MP for Dover in 1720, and represented the town in the two following parliaments. On 28 May 1723 he was appointed master keeper and governor of St Katharine's Hospital in London, a post which he held for life. Initially a supporter of the Walpole government, Berkeley

changed his allegiance to Pulteney following the dismissal of his brother Lord Berkeley, first lord of the Admiralty, on the accession of George II. At the 1734 general election he was returned as MP for Hedon, Yorkshire.

On 26 June 1735 Berkeley married Henrietta *Howard (*c.*1688–1767), the daughter of Sir Henry Hobart and the widow of Charles Howard, ninth earl of Suffolk. Lady Suffolk was celebrated for being a former mistress of George II; her marriage with Berkeley took place on 1 July 1735, nine months after the breakdown in relations with the king. According to his sister Lady Elizabeth *Germain, Berkeley had long admired his new wife. Writing to Dean Swift on 12 July 1735, Lady Germain described Lady Suffolk as

> indeed four or five years older than he; but for all that he has appeared to all the world, as well as to me, to have long had (that is, ever since she has been a widow, so pray do not mistake me) a most violent passion for her, as well as esteem and value for her numberless good qualities.

Court commentators were more confused by Lady Suffolk's reasons for choosing Berkeley. Lord Hervey described him as

> neither young, handsome, healthy, nor rich, which made people wonder what induced Lady Suffolk's prudence to deviate into this unaccountable piece of folly: some imagined it was to persuade the world that nothing criminal had ever passed between her and the king, others that it was to pique the king. If this was her reason, she succeeded very ill in her design. (Hervey, 2.10)

Berkeley died on 29 October 1746.   PHILIP CARTER

Sources A. N. Newman, 'Berkeley, Hon. George', HoP, *Commons, 1715–54* · John, Lord Hervey, *Some materials towards memoirs of the reign of King George II*, ed. R. Sedgwick, new edn, 3 vols. (1952) · GEC, *Peerage*, new edn
Archives Hunt. L., corresp.

Berkeley, Sir George (1819–1905), colonial governor, born on the island of Barbados, West Indies, on 2 November 1819, was the eldest son of General Sackville Hamilton Berkeley, colonel of the 16th regiment of foot, who had served at the capture of Surinam in 1804, of the Danish islands of St Thomas, St John, and St Croix in 1807, and of Martinique in 1809, and was descended from a branch of the family of the earls of Berkeley. His mother was Elizabeth Pilgrim, the daughter of William Murray, of Bruce Vale estate, Barbados. He entered Trinity College, Dublin, on 3 July 1837, and graduated BA in 1842. Soon afterwards he returned to the West Indies, where he remained for most of his active life.

On 11 February 1845 Berkeley was appointed colonial secretary and controller of customs of British Honduras, where he was also *ex officio* member of the executive and legislative councils. While still serving in that colony he was chosen in 1860–61 to administer temporarily the government of Dominica, and on 8 July 1864 was appointed lieutenant-governor of the island of St Vincent. During his tenure of office in 1867 an act to amend and simplify the legislature substituted a single legislative chamber for the two houses which had been in existence since 1763.

Berkeley was acting administrator of Lagos from

December 1872 to October 1873, when he was appointed governor-in-chief of the west Africa settlements (Sierra Leone, the Gambia, Gold Coast, and Lagos). The Gold Coast and Lagos soon became a separate colony (24 July 1874), and Berkeley was recalled to allow the appointment at a reduced salary of a new governor of Sierra Leone and the Gambia. While on his way home in June 1874 he was offered, and accepted, the government of Western Australia, but did not take up the appointment, being sent instead to the Leeward Islands as governor-in-chief. There he remained until 27 June 1881, when he retired on a pension. He was created CMG on 20 February 1874, and KCMG on 24 May 1881.

Berkeley died unmarried in London on 29 September 1905 at his home, 10F Hyde Park Mansions, Marylebone Road, and was buried in Kensal Green cemetery.

CHEWTON ATCHLEY, rev. LYNN MILNE

Sources Colonial Office List (1905) • The Times (2 Oct 1905) • WWW, 1897–1915 • D. P. Henige, Colonial governors from the fifteenth century to the present (1970)
Archives Bodl. Oxf., corresp. with Lord Kimberley
Wealth at death £54,474 6s. 6d.: probate, 20 Oct 1905, CGPLA Eng. & Wales

Berkeley, Sir George Cranfield (1753–1818), naval officer and politician, was born on 10 August 1753, the second son and last of the four surviving children of the eight born to Augustus, fourth earl of Berkeley (1716–1755), army officer, and Elizabeth (1719/20–1792), daughter of Henry Drax, MP for Charborough, Dorset, lady of the bedchamber to the princess of Wales. George attended Eton College from 1761 to 1766 before joining the royal yacht Mary under his cousin Rear-Admiral Augustus Keppel, then appointed to carry Princess Caroline Matilda to Denmark, where she was to be made queen. Berkeley served as her page. In 1767 he joined the Guernsey (50 guns), flagship of Commodore Sir Hugh Palliser's Newfoundland squadron. Berkeley received instruction from First-Lieutenant John Cartwright and Master Joseph Gilbert. Gilbert (later master of James Cook's Resolution) and Cartwright (later founder of the radical Society for Constitutional Information), took special interest in Berkeley's education and for two years he assisted in surveys of Newfoundland and the Gulf of St Lawrence.

In 1769 Berkeley was appointed to the Alarm (32 guns), under Captain John Jervis (later earl of St Vincent), and served with him and others in the Mediterranean until 1774. Berkeley was promoted lieutenant in September 1772. Following an abortive candidacy at Cricklade in 1774, Berkeley ran in his brother's interest for a Gloucestershire county seat in 1776. The Berkeleys and dukes of Beaufort long contested county control, and the costs of the election, which Berkeley lost, were more than £50,000. In 1778 Keppel gave Berkeley a lieutenancy on the Victory (100 guns). Berkeley supervised a gundeck during the battle of Ushant in July 1778 and led those charging Sir Hugh Palliser, the rear squadron commander, with failure to follow orders and secure a victory. The 'Keppel–Palliser affair' resulted in Palliser's Admiralty resignation, great

embarrassment to the government, and division in the officer corps that took a generation to heal. In September Berkeley received his first command appointment, the Pluto (8 guns). During the channel invasion in August 1779 he commanded the Firebrand (8 guns) and served as aide to Vice-Admiral Molyneux, Lord Shuldham, Plymouth commander. Berkeley's talent and energy induced Shuldham to recommend his promotion but the Admiralty refused because of Berkeley's politics. He was, however, appointed to the sloop Fairy (14 guns) in early 1780 and sent to Newfoundland. With his cousin, Captain George Keppel, Berkeley captured an American packet, the Mercury (8 guns), on 3 September. On the ship was Henry Laurens, latterly continental congress president, who was travelling to The Hague to negotiate a loan. The capture led George III to declare war against the Netherlands. Rear-Admiral Richard Edwards, Newfoundland governor, ordered the cousins to exchange ships on 12 September and promoted Berkeley captain on 15 September. In 1781 Berkeley participated in the second relief of Gibraltar and served again on the Newfoundland station. Berkeley took command of the Recovery (32 guns) in January 1782 and served in Vice-Admiral Samuel Barrington's squadron that engaged a French convoy off Ushant from 20 to 22 April, capturing most of it and two ships of the line. Berkeley received command of one, the Pegase (74 guns), in August. While preparing to sail for Jamaica in September he was approached on his ship by a volunteer, William Cobbett (later a great champion of radicalism). Berkeley convinced the young man that he should return home, and Cobbett wrote that he 'happily escaped, sorely against my will, from the most toilsome and perilous profession in the world' (Cobbett, 14–16).

In April 1783 Berkeley was elected to parliament on the death of Sir William Guise. In his first role, with the St Albans congress of country gentlemen, he sought to reconcile his cousins William Pitt and Charles Fox, and the failure led him to support Pitt unstintingly. Berkeley represented Gloucestershire for twenty-seven years and became an important naval MP. Elected on family interest, and not Admiralty patronage, he was free to vote his conscience. His vocal attacks on Henry Addington's administration elevated him to the position of leading naval opposition member in parliament, courted by Pitt, Fox, and the Grenvilles. He married on 23 August 1784 Emilia Charlotte (1762–1832), daughter of General Lord George *Lennox, son of the second duke of Richmond, and Lady Louisa Ker, daughter of the fourth marquess of Lothian. The couple had three daughters and two sons. Berkeley maintained very close relationships with his children, his brother and sisters, and his wife's family. His sister described his marriage as 'a pattern of domestic happiness scarcely to be equalled' (Craven, 1.75). During assignments overseas Berkeley's family accompanied his flagship. They maintained homes in Sussex at Wood End, near the Lennox estates of Stoke and Goodwood, and in London's Portugal Street. Berkeley's marriage, and that of his sister, brought him three influential brothers-in-law:

Charles, fourth duke of Richmond, Henry, third Earl Bathurst, and George Grenville, first marquess of Buckingham.

In 1789, having commanded the *Magnificent* (74 guns) for three years, Berkeley was appointed surveyor-general of the ordnance, an office he held until 1795. On the 1793 declaration of war with France he was appointed to the *Marlborough* (74 guns), and he later had an important share in the victory of 1 June 1794. His ship was one of six that broke the French line. The *Marlborough* dismasted two ships of the line, causing them to strike; she was totally dismasted, and had 132 men killed and wounded. Berkeley was wounded severely in the head and leg, and recovered ashore. The fleet received the thanks of parliament and Berkeley was one of fourteen captains, of twenty-six in the fight, to receive the gold medal. From 1795 to 1797 he commanded the *Formidable* (98 guns) and served off Brest, Cadiz, Ireland, and the Texel. In 1798 Berkeley commanded the Sussex sea fencibles and on 14 February 1799 he was promoted rear-admiral. During that year and the next he led squadrons in the Channel Fleet, and he held the advanced post from May to August 1800 when St Vincent instituted the close blockade of Brest. After retiring, because of chronic gout, in August, Berkeley increased his involvement in parliament, especially upon the March 1801 advent of Addington's administration.

In December 1804, on being appointed inspector of sea fencibles by Henry Dundas, Lord Melville, Berkeley began an exhaustive, fourteen-month survey of Britain's sea coast fortifications—the period in which Napoleon was expected to launch an invasion. Berkeley became a vice-admiral on 9 November 1805. William Pitt's death in January 1806 brought to power the Grenvillites and Foxites and, in April, family ties undoubtedly aided Berkeley's appointment to the North American command. It was under his direct orders that the incident between the *Leopard* (50 guns) and the *Chesapeake* (38 guns) took place on 22 June 1807, on account of the *Chesapeake*'s taking British deserters on board. The attack was a cause of the Anglo-American War (1812–14). Though the public, and some in government, applauded Berkeley's actions, the ministry recalled him and he returned to Britain in April 1808. In December he was appointed commander-in-chief on the coast of Portugal. In this, his final post, Berkeley rendered Britain his most important services. Directing all naval support to the Anglo-Portuguese army, first under Sir John Cradock and from April 1809 under Wellington, Berkeley provided remarkable co-operation. Nearly all the men, horses, weapons, equipment, money, and provisions required by Wellington arrived in Berkeley's ships or in convoys escorted by his ships. The squadron performed a major role in the French defeat in Iberia. In early 1809 Spanish and Portuguese irregulars in Galicia and northern Portugal, supported by Berkeley's frigates with arms, ammunition, and marines, debilitated the corps of marshals Nicolas Soult and Michel Ney, and enabled Wellington to defeat Soult at Porto in May. Four months later Berkeley secured, outfitted, and carried away a powerful

Spanish squadron at Ferrol, preventing its use by Napoleon. Throughout the campaign Berkeley exhibited such indefatigable zeal in support of operations that Wellington wrote 'His activity is unbounded, the whole range of the business of the Country in which he is stationed, civil, military, political, commercial, even ecclesiastical I believe as well as naval are objects of his attention' ('Some letters', 30–31). In time he acknowledged the importance of Berkeley's contributions. On 31 July 1810 he was promoted admiral, and was appointed lord high admiral of Portugal by its prince regent.

In October 1810 Berkeley placed gunboat squadrons on the Tagus, held fortifications with thousands of seamen and marines, and manned the army's signal stations in the lines of Torres Vedras. The retreat of Marshal André Masséna's army on 5 March 1811 ended French attempts to conquer Portugal. Berkeley's large squadron, and larger merchant fleet, had ensured a continuous flow of reinforcements and provisions for the armies and Lisbon civilians. His logistical preparations for the 1812 campaign provided Wellington with the forces and supplies to realize his operational vision, resulting in the captures of Ciudad Rodrigo and Badajoz, and the victory at Salamanca. These led Soult to raise the Cadiz siege and placed the allies on the strategic offensive for the remainder of the war. Wellington, who had difficulties with naval support after Berkeley's supersession, summarized their relationship in late 1811: 'I have always found the Admiral not only disposed to give us every assistance in his power, but to anticipate and exceed our wishes in this way' and 'It is impossible for 2 officers to be on better terms than we are' (*Dispatches*, 5.388). In July 1812 Berkeley sailed for Britain on his flagship, the *Barfleur* (98 guns), and retired altogether from active and indeed from public life. A young James Graham described how the Berkeleys' departure from Lisbon 'has created such a gap in society here that it has lost all its charms' (*Life and Letters*, 1.17). Berkeley, who was disappointed not to receive a peerage for his services, was made KB in 1813 and GCB in 1815. Throughout his life he maintained a close friendship with, and the patronage of, William Jenner and chaired the parliamentary committee that gave Jenner full credit and remuneration for his discovery of the smallpox vaccination. Berkeley was also well known for his interest in the health of seamen.

The years of retirement were unkind to Berkeley, whose health began to fail. In 1813 he and his wife purchased a home in London at 14 South Audley Street, near Grosvenor Square, where he suffered a painful death from gout on 25 February 1818.   BRIAN MARK DE TOY

Sources B. De Toy, 'Wellington's admiral: the life and career of George Berkeley, 1753–1818', PhD diss., Florida State University, 1997 • Rice University, Houston, Texas, George Berkeley Collection • PRO, Admiralty papers • U. Southampton, Hartley Library, Wellington MSS • *The dispatches of … the duke of Wellington … from 1799 to 1818*, ed. J. Gurwood, 13 vols. in 12 (1834–9) • NMM, AGC 1/42 • T. Trotter, *Medicina nautica: an essay on the diseases of seamen*, 2nd edn (1804); repr. in *The health of seamen: selections from the works of Dr. James Lind, Sir Gilbert Blane and Dr. Thomas Trotter*, ed. C. Lloyd, Navy RS, 107 (1965) • 'Some letters of the duke of Wellington to his brother, William Wellesley-Pole', ed. C. Webster, *Camden miscellany, XVIII*, CS, 3rd ser., 79 (1948), 11–35 • *The life and letters of Sir James Graham*, ed. C. Parker, vol. 1 (1907) • *The beautiful Lady Craven: the original memoirs*, ed. A. M. Broadley and L. Melville, 2 vols. (1914) • W. Cobbett, *The progress of a plough-boy to a seat in parliament*, ed. W. Reitzel (1933) • E. A. L. Moir, 'Gloucestershire association for parliamentary reform, 1780', *Transactions of the Bristol and Gloucestershire Archaeological Society*, 75 (1956), 171–92 • HoP, *Commons, 1754–90* • *Burke, Peerage* • *The Eton register*, 8 vols. (privately printed, Eton, 1903–32) **Archives** Hispanic Society of America Library, order book kept on board HMS *Barfleur* • Metropolitan Toronto Reference Library, corresp. as commander-in-chief of the Halifax Station • NL Scot., letter-books and order books • NMM, letter-book • PRO, ADM papers • Rice University, Houston, Texas, Fondren Library • Rice University, Houston, Texas, Woodson Research Center, corresp. and naval orders • Warks. CRO, letter-book | Berks. RO, orders to J. C. Crawford • BL, letters to Lord Grenville, Add. MS 58987 • Hunt. L., letters to Grenville family • NMM, letters to Perkins Magra • NMM, letters to Charles Yorke • PRO, letters to William Pitt, PRO 30/8 • U. Southampton, Hartley Library, Wellington MSS **Likenesses** F. Cotes, oils, 1769, Berkeley Castle, Gloucestershire • O. Humphry, group portrait, oils, 1780, Berkeley Castle, Gloucestershire • T. Gainsborough, oils, 1784–6, Berkeley Castle, Gloucestershire • attrib. Miss Paye, miniature, 1804, Berkeley Castle, Gloucestershire • H. Birche, engraving (after T. Gainsborough), White's Club, London **Wealth at death** approx. £25,000: Warks. CRO, CR 114A/574, 1818, memo

Berkeley, George Monck (1763–1793), writer, was born at Bray in Berkshire on 8 February 1763, the eldest son of Eliza (*née* Frinsham) *Berkeley (1734–1800), literary editor, and the Revd George Berkeley (1733–1795), prebendary of Canterbury, and the grandson of George *Berkeley, philosopher and bishop of Cloyne. After receiving some elementary instruction at the King's School, Canterbury, he was sent, at the age of twelve, to Eton College. His mother, who published his *Poems* for private circulation in 1797, after his death, described him as exceedingly self-willed. He was endowed with a singularly unselfish disposition, and his precocity was such that he began to publish before he had left Eton. His father took him away from Eton when he was sixteen and was his tutor for two years, after which he sent him to the University of St Andrews, where he stayed for three and a half years. At the age of nineteen he was elected a corresponding member of the Edinburgh Society of Antiquaries. On leaving St Andrews he became gentleman commoner of Magdalen Hall, Oxford, on 2 December 1786, and was admitted a student of the Inner Temple on 21 May 1783. In 1787 he published *Nina*, a comedy in two acts, which his mother maintained he translated from the French in six hours. His next dramatic attempt, *Love and Nature*, a musical piece in one act, performed at Dublin Theatre in 1789 and published in 1797, was founded on Prior's *Emma and Henry* (a modernization of the *Nut Brown Maid*). In 1789 *Literary Relics* was published, a book containing miscellaneous literary items including an essay on the life of Swift, and samples of previously unpublished correspondence of Swift, Congreve, Addison, and Steele. In 1789 Berkeley visited Ireland, and was made LLB of Dublin University. While he was staying in Dublin he sought out Richard Brenan (the servant who attended Swift in his last moments), and settled a small pension on him. His health began to fail and he went for

the benefit of the sea air to Dover. Afterwards he moved to Cheltenham, where he died, unmarried, on 26 January 1793, after a short illness. Had his health permitted it, he would have been destined for the bar, and according to his mother, he had intended to write a work in defence of the Christian religion.   A. H. BULLEN, *rev.* REBECCA MILLS

Sources *Poems by the late George Monck Berkeley*, ed. E. Berkeley (1797) [with a 'Preface' by the ed.] • Foster, *Alum. Oxon.* • R. A. Austen-Leigh, ed., *The Eton College register, 1753–1790* (1921), 44 • D. E. Baker, *Biographia dramatica, or, A companion to the playhouse*, rev. I. Reed, new edn, rev. S. Jones, 1 (1812), 34–5 • 'Berkeley, Eliza', *DNB* • Nichols, *Illustrations*, 6.698 • *GM*, 1st ser., 67 (1797), 403–6 • *IGI* • *The works of George Berkeley*, ed. A. C. Fraser, 4 (1871), 356, 359 **Archives** BL, corresp., Add. MS 39312 | BL, letters to Charles Poyntz **Likenesses** W. Skelton, line engraving, pubd 1797 (after W. Peters), BM, NPG; repro. in *Poems by … George Monck Berkeley*

Berkeley, Gilbert (*d.* 1581), bishop of Bath and Wells, may have been a native of Lincolnshire. It seems unlikely that he was a member of the baronial Berkeley family, as has been suggested. He took deacon's orders as a member of Lincoln's Franciscan friary on 27 March 1535, and was priested on 18 December following, but was recorded at Northampton at the end of that year, while on 27 November 1538 he was at York when that city's Franciscan house was dissolved. In the following year he graduated BTh at Oxford. In spring 1547 he was admitted rector of Attleborough, Norfolk. The presentation was in the gift of the second earl of Sussex, who in 1553 was quick to declare for Queen Mary. Berkeley's religious position by this time clearly differed from his patron's, for in 1554 he was deprived and left England for Frankfurt, where he encouraged the Calvinist Bartholomew Traheron to publish his lectures on the Apocalypse.

Following his return from exile Berkeley became a royal chaplain and was then made bishop of Bath and Wells; he was consecrated on 24 March 1560, and the temporalities (valued at £533 1s. 3d.) were restored on 10 July. He found the finances of his diocese in a parlous state. His primary visitation revealed that many Roman Catholic lessees had fled abroad, leaving their tenancies in the hands of proxies for terms of up to twenty-one years. Faced now with the possibility of dispossession these threatened to sue the new bishop. Moreover his episcopal predecessor, Gilbert Bourne, had shortly before his deprivation granted long leases of three of the richest diocesan manors (Banwell, Westbury, and Wiveliscombe) to his own brother, Richard Bourne. Despite Elizabeth's professed belief that Berkeley was succeeding to a 'richly endowed' diocese, the incoming bishop could reasonably have regarded his new charge as a poisoned chalice. His gross income, at just under £1000 per annum, was less than half that of Bishop John Clerk only twenty years earlier, and a good deal less than half that of an average peer of the realm. Yet a bishop was expected to play an active part in county society, and in particular to maintain traditional standards of hospitality. As Berkeley himself complained, 'The world expecteth and our vocation is to be hospitales' (Heal, 257). To add still further to his difficulties, not only did he find his palace so dilapidated that he had to fell sixty-one trees to carry out necessary repairs, but portions of it were occupied by tenants on terms that left the bishop so little the master of his own house that he was even required to feed the horse of the lessee of the brewhouse.

Berkeley's problems included his relations with his own chapter, and especially with its dean, William Turner, a radical protestant of whose refusal to conform on the issue of vestments Berkeley several times complained to Sir William Cecil. Their conflict was resolved only by Turner's death in 1568. Perhaps it was to enhance his authority in his cathedral, as well as in the administration of his diocese, that on 23 or 27 August 1560, through an arrangement with Archbishop Matthew Parker, Berkeley had himself made chancellor of his own diocese, a position he retained until April 1562. But although he was not without care for the pastoral side of his office, so that in 1576 he expressed approval of prophesyings as a means of raising the standards of the parochial clergy, his energies, as recorded, were principally devoted to his financial problems.

In this Berkeley enjoyed mixed fortunes. An already weak position was further undermined in 1564 when he lost the manor of Kingsbury to the crown, for inadequate compensation. Of the eight remaining episcopal manors he found six leased out, and the two that remained were heavily encumbered. However, he was not ungenerously treated by the crown, for instance in being granted remission of subsidy payments owed by Bishop Bourne to the exchequer, and he also made considerable efforts to exploit his remaining resources, often provoking resentment in the process. Thus his relations with his cathedral city of Wells, where his revenues increased more than fivefold between 1566 and 1576, were consistently prickly. His exploitation of the opportunities to raise money presented by entry fines also sometimes shows him in an unsympathetic light, especially when he challenged leases over technicalities. Probably less contentious was his quadrupling his revenues from local lead mines. Like most Elizabethan bishops he had to cope with the demands of greedy laymen, both courtiers and local magnates. In 1578 he faced down the efforts of Lord Thomas Paulet to secure the tithes of West Monkton rectory, but four years earlier he would have capitulated to the queen's demands for the manor of Banwell for Lord Henry Seymour had not his chapter refused to accept them. His income varied from year to year, as did his expenses. The surviving evidence shows the former fluctuating between about £750 and nearly £1000; when his outlays are taken into account his net income was highest in 1573, when it totalled £764.

By the early 1570s Berkeley's health was declining—in 1571 Bishop John Jewel bequeathed him a walking stick, and a year later he complained of sciatica. He died at Wells of a 'lethargy' on 2 November 1581, and was buried in the cathedral. His tomb chest survives in the north chancel aisle. In his will, which he had approved two days before he died, he made small bequests to the poor of Wells, the cathedral choristers, and others, but left nearly all his property to Emme Smarthwett, a Yorkshirewoman. Sir

John Harington wrote of Berkeley that 'he was a good justicer, saving that sometimes being ruled by his wife he swerved from the rule of justice and sincerity' (Hembry, 102), and this reference, together with an inscription in the Folger Shakespeare Library's copy of the 1570 edition of John Foxe's *Acts and Monuments*, recording its purchase from 'Mr tenant who married Emme bishop Barclay's wife whose book this was being bishop of Bath and Wells', makes it clear that Berkeley and Emme Smarthwett had been man and wife. Perhaps Emme's status was disguised, even in the bishop's will, less in order to avoid the queen's disapproval of married prelates (exaggerated by historians in any case) than to conceal what was probably a social *mésalliance*.   JOHN FINES

Sources P. M. Hembry, *The bishops of Bath and Wells, 1540–1640* (1967) · Emden, *Oxf.*, 4.45 · Cooper, *Ath. Cantab.*, 1.446–7 · L. S. Colchester, ed., *Wells Cathedral: a history* (1982) · F. Heal, *Of prelates and princes: a study of the economic and social position of the Tudor episcopate* (1980) · J. Strype, *The life and acts of Matthew Parker*, new edn, 3 vols. (1821) · P. Collinson, *Godly people: essays on English protestantism and puritanism* (1983) · *Correspondence of Matthew Parker*, ed. J. Bruce and T. T. Perowne, Parker Society, 42 (1853) · *Fasti Angl.*, 1541–1857, [Bath and Wells] · will, PRO, PROB 11/63, fol. 340r–340v · private information (2004) [Brett Usher]

Berkeley, (George Charles) Grantley Fitzhardinge

(1800–1881), politician and sportsman, was born at Cranford House, Hounslow, Middlesex, on 10 February 1800, the sixth son of Frederick Augustus Berkeley, fifth earl of Berkeley (1745–1810), and the second legitimate son after the earl's marriage, on 16 May 1796, to Mary Cole (1766/7–1844). His mother, who went under the name of Miss Tudor until her marriage, when she took the title of countess of Berkeley, was the daughter of William Cole, a publican and butcher. His elder brother by three years, Thomas Moreton Fitzhardinge, had been declared earl of Berkeley by the decision of the House of Lords, and Grantley was for seventy years heir presumptive to the earldom.

After the death of the fifth earl, Grantley Berkeley's childhood was passed almost entirely at Cranford House, one of the dower houses settled by his father on the countess. His godfather, the prince regent, presented him with a commission in the Coldstream Guards in 1816, after a year's instruction at the Royal Military College, Sandhurst. He first joined his regiment in 1816 at the Tower of London, and was on duty during the next four or five years at St James's Palace and Windsor Castle, at Chatham and at Woolwich. Shortly after coming of age he retired upon half pay from the Coldstream Guards into the 82nd foot.

On 16 August 1824 Berkeley married Caroline Martha, youngest daughter of Paul *Benfield, the merchant, and in 1829 he settled down as a keen sportsman at Harrold Hall in Bedfordshire. Between 1810 and 1829 his eldest brother, William (to whom the late earl had left Berkeley Castle and the bulk of his large property), then known as Colonel Berkeley, was seeking to establish his claim to succeed his father, the fifth earl, in the earldom of Berkeley, and Grantley believed that Colonel Berkeley's cause (which he later denounced, after they quarrelled) might be advanced by the presence in parliament of himself and his three brothers, Maurice, Henry, and Craven. Maurice *Berkeley therefore entered parliament in 1831, and Craven *Berkeley and Grantley were, in December 1832, returned to the House of Commons, the latter as member for West Gloucestershire; Colonel Berkeley himself never established his claim, but he became Baron Segrave (1831) and Earl Fitzhardinge (1841).

For twenty years Grantley Berkeley held his ground as member for West Gloucestershire. He did so in the end not merely in spite of the earl, but in open defiance of him, standing successfully at five general elections; however, his defence of protection finally cost him the seat after a narrow defeat in 1852. His maiden work, *Berkeley Castle*, a historical romance in three volumes, was savagely reviewed in the August 1836 number of *Fraser's Magazine*. Accompanied by his brother Craven, on the afternoon of 3 August Berkeley went to the bookseller's shop at 215 Regent Street, London, kept by James Fraser, the publisher and proprietor of the magazine. Craven Berkeley posted himself on guard there at the shop door, and Grantley, who had a strong, athletic build, confronted the rather puny publisher, demanding from him the name of the anonymous critic. Failing to obtain this information, he felled his feeble antagonist with a blow, and then, standing over him, beat him savagely about the head and face with the butt-end of a heavy, gold-headed hunting-whip—with effects said to have lasted until Fraser's death five years later. The two Berkeleys were brought before the neighbouring police magistrate in Great Marlborough Street. Two actions were tried, on 3 December 1836, in the court of exchequer—one, *Fraser v. Berkeley*, for assault; the other, the cross-action, *Berkeley v. Fraser*, for libel—in each of them the damages being set at £6000. In the action for assault the plaintiff (Fraser) got the verdict, with £100 as his damages; while in the action for libel the plaintiff (Berkeley), though he also got the verdict, had to content himself with 40s. damages. On another occasion Berkeley had to pay £100 after assaulting a neighbour in a hunting dispute, and he also appeared before magistrates for cock-fighting.

On 5 August 1836, two days after the assault on Fraser, Berkeley fought a duel with the author of the anonymous review in *Fraser's Magazine*, Dr William Maginn (the editor of the magazine), in a secluded meadow near the Harrow Road. Three shots each were exchanged by the belligerents, without effect—Berkeley, reputed a marksman, blamed unfamiliar pistols. Berkeley ascribed the bitterness of the encounter (and of the offending review) to an earlier quarrel—over what he claimed was Maginn's 'vile' behaviour towards Letitia Landor. But, as a second, he claimed to have prevented five duels through negotiation, to enforce which he considered the duel a valuable institution.

On 3 May 1836 Berkeley obtained the appointment of a committee on the question of whether women should be admitted to the gallery of the House of Commons. In 1841, on the concession of the privilege, he received a piece of plate from grateful women. He opposed John Bright (successfully) over reform of the game laws and (unsuccessfully) over the abolition of West Indian slavery.

Grantley Berkeley's second publication appeared in 1839. This was *A pamphlet dedicated to the noblemen, gentlemen, and sportsmen of England, Ireland, and Scotland. In reply to a prize essay by the Rev. John Styles, D.D., on the claims of the animal creation to the humanity of man*. His only other novel, *Sandron Hall, or, The Days of Queen Anne*, was published in 1840. After his election defeat in 1852, Berkeley took no further part in public life and devoted his energies to field sports. He was a master both of stag- and of foxhounds. Four of his favourite animals were famous: his terrier Smike, his bloodhound Druid, his mastiff Grumbo, and his retriever Smoker. Even his tame cormorant Jack was for a long time noted as a wonder. He prided himself on having learned pugilism from Byron's instructor, John Jackson. Until well into middle age he retained coarse, rakish manners. He delighted in wearing at the same time two or three different-coloured satin under-waistcoats, and round his throat three or four gaudy silk neckerchiefs, held together by passing the ends of them through a gold ring. Even when he had come to be an old man, he piqued himself upon having been the last to cling to the flat cocked hat of polite life, known early in the century as the *chapeau bras*.

In 1854 Grantley Berkeley published his *Reminiscences of a Huntsman*, illustrated by John Leech. He subsequently crossed the Atlantic and produced in 1861 *The English Sportsman in the Western Prairies*, profusely illustrated. In 1865 he published the first half and in 1866 the second half of his autobiography in four volumes, entitled *My Life and Recollections*. His last work, *Fact Against Fiction* (2 vols., 1874), gave a practical account of the habits and treatment of animals.

The last years of Grantley Berkeley's life were embittered by the loss of his wife and their two sons (who died in 1865 and 1878). His wife, who was a Catholic, died on 13 February 1873, after a quarrel with her husband over religious questions: he claimed she had been 'perverted' by Jesuits. Grantley Berkeley died on 23 February 1881 at home at Dursley House, Poole, Dorset, and was buried five days later; beyond his reach as ever remained what had been dangling tantalizingly close for nearly seventy years—the earldom of Berkeley.

CHARLES KENT, *rev.* JULIAN LOCK

Sources G. F. Berkeley, *My life and recollections*, 4 vols. (1865–6) · Boase, *Mod. Eng. biog.* · *Annual Register* (1881), pt 2, p. 104 · Ward, *Men of the reign* · *The Times* (6 Aug 1836) · *The Times* (24 Feb 1881) · *The Times* (1 March 1881) · *Fraser's Magazine*, 14 (1836), 242–7 · *Fraser's Magazine*, 15 (1837), 100–43 · P. Leary, 'Fraser's Magazine and the literary life, 1830–1847', *Victorian Periodicals Review*, 24 (1994), 105–26 · M. M. H. Thrall, *Rebellious Fraser's* (1934) · N. Gash, *Politics in the age of Peel* (1953) · Burke, *Peerage* · CGPLA *Eng. & Wales* (1881)
Archives University of Rochester, New York | BL, corresp. with Sir Robert Peel, Add. MSS 40509–40603, *passim* · Bodl. Oxf., letters to Lord Beaconsfield · Lpool RO, letters to fourteenth earl of Derby · NL Scot., letters to William Blackwood & Sons · Som. ARS, letters to William Jolliffe

Likenesses G. Hayter, group portrait, oils, *c*.1833 (*The House of Commons, 1833*), NPG • G. Hayter, oils, *c*.1833, Berkeley Castle, Gloucestershire • J. Brown, stipple, 1865 (after photograph), NPG; repro. in Berkeley, *My life and recollections*, vol. 1, frontispiece • portrait, repro. in *ILN*, 78 (1881), 253 • portraits, repro. in Berkeley, *My life and recollections*

Wealth at death under £5000: probate, 11 April 1881, *CGPLA Eng. & Wales*

Berkeley, Lady Henrietta [Harriett] (*b.* in or after **1664**, *d.* **1706**), figure of scandal, was a younger daughter of George *Berkeley, first earl of Berkeley (1626/7–1698), and his wife, Elizabeth (*d.* 1708), daughter of John Massingberd. Little is known of her early life. But in 1682 Lady Henrietta (or Harriett, as she was known in her family) became a well-known figure of scandal when still a minor, and under eighteen, following the revelation of her love affair with Ford *Grey, Lord Grey of Warke (*bap.* 1655, *d.* 1701), the husband of her elder sister Mary. The intrigue seems to have begun in 1681 and continued for about fourteen months before it was discovered by Lady Henrietta's mother. Lady Berkeley forbade Grey from seeing Henrietta, and took her to the family seat at Durdans, near Epsom, where Lady Mary was also staying. However, Grey was invited to Durdans at the instigation of his wife, who was ignorant of the affair; Lady Berkeley, desperate to keep the matter secret from her daughter and husband, agreed to his coming. Grey arrived late one evening in August and stayed several days until his mother-in-law's protests finally succeeded in getting him to leave on 19 August. Later that night Henrietta fled the house, apparently aided by Robert Charnock, Grey's servant, and his wife, Anne.

During the following weeks Lady Henrietta Berkeley lived incognito at a series of lodging houses in London. One week after she absconded lampoons began to appear speculating on the cause of her disappearance. Her family, who wished to send her to a nunnery in France, offered a reward of £200 to anyone who could trace her whereabouts and placed advertisements calling for her return in the London press. Grey admitted to the Berkeleys that he had access to his lover, but refused to let them see her. Eventually the earl of Berkeley launched a lawsuit for unlawful seduction against Grey and his accomplices, which was brought before the court of king's bench on 23 November 1682. Henrietta herself appeared at the trial, but with her evidence the lord chief justice told her, 'You have injured your own reputation, and prostituted both your body and your honour, and are not to be believed' (*State trials*, 9.176). As the court was breaking up the earl attempted to take his daughter away with him, whereupon Henrietta announced that she was married to William Turner (Grey's servant). A scuffle broke out in the courtroom as she refused to return home and her father tried to seize her by force. For her own safety she was taken to the king's bench prison, accompanied by Turner, who reportedly lay with her there. After three days she was released. Grey and the other defendants were found guilty but escaped punishment as the matter was compromised early the next year. The trial attracted a great deal of publicity and the story of Lady Henrietta's affair

with her brother-in-law became the inspiration for Aphra Behn's *Love Letters between a Nobleman and his Sister*, the first part of which was published in 1684. After Grey, a leading whig and supporter of the duke of Monmouth, was implicated in the Rye House plot in June 1683 Lady Henrietta accompanied him into exile in the Netherlands. She travelled with him to Cleves, where it was rumoured that she was pregnant.

The rest of Lady Henrietta Berkeley's life remains a mystery. It is possible that she stayed in the Netherlands or joined Grey at his seat at Uppark, Sussex, on his return to England. Grey, earl of Tankerville from 1695, died in 1701 and in his will settled £200 a year on her. She died at Tonbridge, Kent, on 10 August 1706. By then her affair with Grey was stale news, and in recording her death the annalist Narcissus Luttrell confused her with her younger sister Elizabeth [*see* Germain, Lady Elizabeth]. Lady Henrietta left in her will bequests totalling £370, of which £100 was left to her niece Elizabeth Berkeley. Lady Mary survived both her husband and her sister, marrying, in 1712, Richard Rooth of Epsom; she died in May 1719.

DAVID TURNER

Sources C. Price, *Cold Caleb: the scandalous life of Ford Grey, first earl of Tankerville, 1655–1701* (1956) • *The trial of Ford Lord Grey of Werk … for unlawful tempting and inticing, the Lady Henrietta Berkeley* (1716) • A. Behn, *Love letters between a nobleman and his sister*, ed. J. Todd (1993) [first published 1684–7] • GEC, *Peerage*, new edn, vol. 2 • *State trials*, vol. 9 • will, PRO, PROB 11/489, sig. 165 [Lady Henrietta Berkeley] • will, PRO, PROB 11/462, sig. 176 [Ford Grey, earl of Tankerville] • will, PRO, PROB 11/463, sig. 40 [Ford Grey, earl of Tankerville] • will, PRO, PROB 11/467, sig. 208 [Ford Grey, earl of Tankerville] • N. Luttrell, *A brief historical relation of state affairs from September 1678 to April 1714*, 6 vols. (1857), vols. 1, 6

Wealth at death £370: will, PRO, PROB 11/489, sig. 165

Berkeley, (Francis) Henry Fitzhardinge (1794–1870), politician, fourth son of Frederick Augustus, fifth earl of Berkeley (1745–1810), and Mary Cole (1766/7–1844), of Wotton under Edge (whom the earl married on 16 May 1796), was born on 7 December 1794, and baptized on 18 March 1795. At sixteen Henry Berkeley, as he was known, was already a first-rate shot, and for several years afterwards was regarded as one of the best amateur boxers in the country. He was a subaltern in the South Gloucester militia, and served with his eldest brother, William Fitzhardinge, then Colonel Berkeley. In 1814 Henry was entered as a gentleman commoner at Christ Church, Oxford. He left the university without taking a degree, and went abroad for a few years travelling. Having achieved little in his early life, he eventually joined his three brothers in the House of Commons in August 1837, after coming second in the poll as an independent Liberal candidate for Bristol. At the next general election, June 1841, he was again returned for Bristol. From that time until his death he was invariably at the head of the poll by a large majority, and he retained the seat for thirty-two years until his death.

Berkeley was a frequent speaker in the Commons on various subjects, including support for the abolition of corporal punishment in the army. He was a leading parliamentary opponent of the temperance cause, and received a large testimonial from the licensed victuallers on 24 September 1856 in recognition of his advocacy. But he was best known as the champion of the introduction of the ballot into parliamentary elections. His first speech on this subject was made on 21 June 1842, when he seconded the motion of H. G. Ward, MP for Sheffield. The year before, in June 1841, George Grote, who had been for nine years champion of the ballot in the House of Commons, retired from parliament. Berkeley was a less eloquent, an equally devoted, but a more vivacious champion of the cause. His first substantive motion on the ballot was brought forward on 8 August 1848. He had frequently addressed the house before on a great variety of subjects, but never so effectively. He was seconded on the occasion by Colonel Perronet Thompson, and the resolution was carried on a division by 86 votes to 81. His motion on 24 May 1849, to bring in a bill, was defeated (85–136). He was in a minority of 55 in the next session, 7 March 1850; but the year afterwards, 8 July 1851, he carried his motion by a majority of 37. In 1853 he chaired the recently formed Ballot Society. Besides the ballot, Berkeley was also a supporter of the Maynooth grant and the plans for national education.

Although his championship of the ballot lasted over the next twenty years, Berkeley only once again obtained a majority, on 27 May 1862 (83–50). He endured his failures with admirable cheerfulness. His speeches upon these occasions were always listened to with enjoyment for the wit and humour with which his arguments in favour of the ballot were enforced. Yet his annual motion was eventually regarded by the house as a good joke rather than as an earnest attempt at legislation. Nevertheless Berkeley remained convinced that the eventual passing of the Ballot Act was certain, and, even towards the close of his life, that it was imminent. On 22 January 1869, a test ballot was adopted at Manchester, where Ernest Jones was chosen through the ballot box as a candidate for representing that city in parliament.

Berkeley married Elizabeth, widow of John Austin. He died at his London home, 1 Victoria Square, Pimlico, on 10 March 1870. A bill introducing the ballot was passed in 1872. CHARLES KENT, rev. MATTHEW LEE

Sources Boase, *Mod. Eng. biog.* · *A dictionary of contemporary biography* (1861) · *Men of the time* · *The Times* (12 March 1870) · G. F. Berkeley, *My life and recollections*, 4 vols. (1865–6) · *Dod's Parliamentary Companion* (1869) · M. Taylor, *The decline of British radicalism, 1847–1860* (1995)
Archives Glos. RO, corresp. on politics and naval patronage | BL, corresp. with W. E. Gladstone and Sir Robert Peel · Tyne and Wear Archives Service, Newcastle upon Tyne, letters to Joseph Cowen
Likenesses H. B. Hall, stipple, pubd 1839 (after J. W. Childe), BM, NPG · portrait, repro. in *Illustrated News of the World*, 3 (1859), 84

Berkeley, James, first Baron Berkeley (*c.*1394–1463), nobleman, born in Raglan, Monmouthshire, was the son of Sir James Berkeley and Elizabeth Bluet and claimant to the Berkeley barony. He was dubbed 'James the Just' by the family historian James Smyth. The castle and hundred of Berkeley, Gloucestershire, had descended in the direct line of the lords Berkeley from the early twelfth century.

By 1346 the value of the estate under Lord Thomas ('the Rich') had increased to £1150 p.a., and the marriage of his grandson Thomas to Margaret, daughter and eventual heir of Lord Lisle, added extensive properties in southern England. About 1400 this Lord Thomas ('the Magnificent'), the fifth baron (counting from a writ of summons issued to Thomas de Berkeley in 1295), commanded an income and retinue the size of a lesser earl, his household numbered upward of three hundred persons and was a centre of culture and patronage, and the family had a tradition of distinguished military service and high standing in national affairs. But Lord Thomas's sole child was his daughter Elizabeth *Berkeley, married to Richard Beauchamp, earl of Warwick. Though heir-general to all the Berkeley and Lisle estates, her claim to the castle and hundred of Berkeley with its twelve manors, along with one in Somerset, was barred by an entail made in 1349 which limited these to a male heir. This was Thomas's nephew James Berkeley. Such a division would have dismembered the Berkeley inheritance and undermined the family's local hegemony. Lord Thomas never resolved this dilemma; indeed he worsened it through his own indecision, on the one hand seeking to bypass the entail to favour his daughter, on the other rearing James at Berkeley Castle as his heir. James Berkeley probably married first a daughter of Sir John St John (he was certainly contracted to her, though there is some doubt as to whether the marriage actually took place), and second one of Sir Humphrey Stafford, but both women died young and their names are now unknown. In 1423 or 1424 he married Lady Isabel (*d.* 27 Sept 1452), widow of Henry Ferrers and daughter of Thomas (I) Mowbray, duke of Norfolk.

When Lord Thomas died on 13 July 1417 Elizabeth and her husband quickly seized Berkeley Castle and secured interim custody of it from Henry V. James Berkeley found it impossible to implement his claim to the entailed lands, for Warwick's occupancy was legally safeguarded while he was fighting with Henry in France. In 1420 Berkeley (who was summoned to parliament as a baron in the following year; this summons was held in the modern period to have created a new peerage) secured the backing of Humphrey, duke of Gloucester, then keeper of the realm in the king's absence, by a bribe of 1000 marks, while the countess of Warwick solicited support from her brother John, duke of Bedford. Each side sought to strengthen its claims by acts of self-help, involving armed confrontation and skirmishes around Berkeley. Fearing that the feud might grow, the council of the young Henry VI persuaded both parties to accept arbitration under heavy financial penalties, but only after a succession of awards had failed, and following Elizabeth's death in 1422 and Warwick's remarriage, was an abiding settlement agreed in 1425. By this Berkeley received Berkeley Castle and most of the entailed lands while the earl was given a life interest in seven manors and until his death in 1439 retained his wife's inheritance, the Lisle lands, 'by courtesy of England'. On this basis both sides lived in peace, though Berkeley, who had been knighted by the infant Henry VI in 1426, was forced to mortgage lands and goods 'and lived and died in far meaner part and condition than his ancestors' (Smyth, 2.48). In 1436 his income was assessed at no more than £333.

If James Berkeley looked to recover not only the lands held by Warwick but the Lisle inheritance in 1439 he was disappointed. For Warwick's daughters claimed their mother's inheritance and were backed by their husbands, John Talbot, earl of Shrewsbury, Edmund Beaufort, then earl of Dorset, and George Neville, Lord Latimer, all men of greater power than Lord James. Once again both sides agreed under heavy recognizances to abide arbitration, which eventually in 1448 awarded the disputed lands to the three coheiresses for life. This was not acceptable to Berkeley who resorted to force in 1450, precipitating a private war with Shrewsbury. In September 1451 Shrewsbury's son, Lord Lisle, captured Berkeley Castle, taking Berkeley and his sons prisoners, and forcing him to hand over the castle for two years as security. The countess likewise seized Isobel, Lady Berkeley, to prevent her from appealing to the king, thereby hastening her death. But in July 1453 Shrewsbury and Lisle were both killed at the battle of Castillon in Gascony. Berkeley now found the new earl of Shrewsbury more ready to compromise and his marriage to the earl's sister, Joan, signalled the end of the dispute, formalized by a final reconciliation with the old countess shortly before his death in Berkeley Castle in late November 1463. He was buried in the family chapel at Berkeley church where his tomb and effigy survive. The final contest was a duel fought between his son William *Berkeley and the new Lord Lisle, Thomas Talbot, with their followers, at Nibley Green on 20 March 1470 where Lisle was mortally wounded.

James Berkeley's lifelong struggle to secure his inheritance seems to have monopolized his energies, for he took no part in war or politics, often absenting himself from parliaments, and was only intermittently named on local commissions. Whether this effacement reflected his circumstances or his temperament is now impossible to say. As Smyth wrote, 'the power and malice of the adversaries of this Lord James kept him for the most part within doors like a prisoner from youth to age' (2.96). Undoubtedly his lack of political standing and influence handicapped him in his contest with such major figures as the earls of Warwick and Shrewsbury. Technically a lawsuit between the heir-general and the heir male, it was essentially a struggle for land and power in Gloucestershire, fought by political rather than legal or even military means. Lord James's tenacity and longevity procured the survival of the Berkeley barony but as a mere shadow of its former wealth and esteem.   G. L. HARRISS

Sources J. Smyth, *The Berkeley manuscripts*, ed. J. Maclean, 3 vols. (1883–5) · J. H. Cooke, 'The great Berkeley law suit of the fifteenth and sixteenth centuries', *Trans. Bristol and Gloucester Archaeological Society*, 3 (1878–9) · A. Sinclair, 'The great Berkeley law suit revisited, 1417–39', *Southern History*, 9 (1987), 34–50 · GEC, *Peerage* · A. J. Pollard, 'The family of Talbot in the fifteenth century', PhD diss., University of Bristol, 1968, 39–51 · R. A. Griffiths, *The reign of King Henry VI: the exercise of royal authority, 1422–1461* (1981), 572–3 · N. Saul, *Knights and esquires: the Gloucestershire gentry in the fourteenth century* (1981) · N. H. Nicolas, ed., *Proceedings and ordinances of the privy council of England*, 7 vols., RC, 26 (1834–7), vols. 2–3, 6 · CPR · CClR · D. Verey, *Gloucestershire*, 2: *The Vale and the Forest of Dean* (1970), 98–103

Archives Berkeley Castle, Gloucestershire, muniments
Likenesses alabaster tomb effigy, Berkeley church, Gloucestershire

Berkeley, James, third earl of Berkeley (1680–1736), naval officer, was the second son of Charles, the second earl (1649–1710), and Elizabeth Noel (d. 30 July 1719), sister of Edward, first earl of Gainsborough, and daughter of Baptist Noel, first Viscount Campden, and his third wife, Hester Wotton. On 2 May 1695, at about the age of fifteen, he was appointed a volunteer on board the *Centurion* (Captain John Price), and in March 1697 he moved to the *Monk* (Captain Robert Stapleton). He was commissioned third lieutenant in the *Boyne* (Captain Hovenden Walker), flagship of Vice-Admiral Matthew Aylmer in the Mediterranean, on 10 March 1699. Following the death, from smallpox, of his elder brother, Charles, in June 1699, he was styled Lord Dursley. In 1701, with the family's interest, he was elected a whig MP for Gloucester, but he was not returned in 1702. At about the age of twenty-one he was promoted captain and from 4 April 1701 he commanded the frigate *Sorlings*. After seven months he moved to the *Lichfield* (50 guns), in which he successfully cruised in the channel during the following two years. On 5 March 1704 he was appointed to command the *Boyne* (80 guns) in the Mediterranean and later that year, on 13 August, he was in Sir John Leake's squadron at the battle of Malaga, in which he distinguished himself by his resolution and bravery. In December 1704 he took command of the *Devonshire*, and at one point he embarked the prince of Hesse, James Stanhope, and Paul Methuen in preparation for the landing at Barcelona in August 1705. He was summoned to the House of Lords in his father's barony as Lord Berkeley of Berkeley, on 5 March 1705 but he continued to be known as Lord Dursley in the fleet. On 30 August 1706 he took command of the *St George*, and was again in the Mediterranean with Sir Cloudesley Shovell. With Byng's squadron he was prominently engaged in the siege of Toulon during August 1707. While returning to England with Shovell he witnessed the *Association*'s destruction on rocks off the Isles of Scilly on 22 October. The *St George* struck the same rocks as Shovell's ship, but the swell which beat the one ship to pieces washed the other to safety. On 3 January 1708 he was raised to flag rank as vice-admiral of the red at the age of twenty-eight, and presently he hoisted his flag on board the *Berwick* as second in command under Sir George Byng during the operations in the Forth and on the coast of Scotland in 1708. He was promoted to vice-admiral of the white on 21 December 1708, and to vice-admiral of the blue on 19 December 1709, and was actively employed in the channel from 1708 until May 1710, when he struck his flag; thereafter he was not employed at sea for several years.

After the death of his father on 24 September 1710 he became earl of Berkeley, and succeeded him also as lord lieutenant of Gloucestershire, and high steward of

Gloucester, from which, for party political reasons, he was removed in 1712. On 13 February 1711 he married Louisa Lennox (1694–1717), daughter of James *Stuart, first duke of Richmond and lady of the bedchamber to Caroline, princess of Wales. At the time of their wedding Swift, who had been chaplain to Berkeley's father, commented in a letter to Stella on the 'young rake' and his marriage, predicting that it would not last long, 'The chit is but 17 and ill-natured, covetous, vicious, and proud in extremes' (*Correspondence*, 4.221).

Following the death of Queen Anne the lords justices immediately appointed Berkeley to command the fleet of warships to escort George I from the Dutch coast, where he embarked the king on 27 September 1714; they arrived at Greenwich two days later. After the king's accession he was restored to the offices he had lost in 1712. On 18 September 1714, even before arriving in Britain, George I appointed him a lord of the bedchamber, a position bringing him a salary of £1000 a year. He was also appointed master (1715–19) and elder brother of Trinity House. On 16 April 1717 he was appointed first lord of the Admiralty and on the following day he was sworn of the privy council. He was made a knight of the Garter on 31 March 1718, and installed on 30 April, taking the place of the duke of Shrewsbury. On five occasions between 1716 and 1725 he served as one of the lords justices while the king was in Hanover.

In March 1719, during the short war with Spain, he was appointed commander-in-chief of the fleet in the channel, with Sir John Norris commanding in the second post. Both were lords commissioners of the Admiralty and Norris was senior on the list of admirals, but as first lord, Berkeley was his superior. He had also been appointed vice-admiral of Great Britain on 18 March 1718. These offices had previously been considered purely civil, giving no executive command; Berkeley was the first to hoist the lord high admiral's flag with the crown's permission.

After this, on 15 April 1719, Berkeley struck his flag and held no further command at sea. He remained at the Admiralty until he was dismissed in 1727. Contrasting him to Byng, Lord Hervey described him as:

> a man of great family and great quality, rough, proud, hard and obstinate, with excellent good natural parts, but so uncultivated that he was totally ignorant of every branch of knowledge but his own profession. He was haughty and tyrannical, but honorable, gallant, observant of his word, but equally incapable of flattering a prince, bending to a minister or lying to anyone he had to deal with. (Hervey, 1.37)

There is much suspicion that he was removed for political reasons. Horace Walpole later characterized him 'a boisterous, zealous whig seaman' (Walpole, 1.67) and, perhaps, George II recalled the suggestion made in the press in 1717 that Berkeley had been involved in a plot to deport him as prince of Wales.

At the end of May 1735 Berkeley left England because of poor health, and travelled to northern France with his friend, Lord Bolingbroke, who was his host for some

months. He died at Aubigny in France, a seat of the duke of Richmond, on 17 August 1736, and was buried at Berkeley alongside his wife, who had died on 15 January 1717.

JOHN B. HATTENDORF

Sources list of captains, 1688–1715, NMM, Sergison MS SER/136 · S. Martin-Leake, *The life of Sir John Leake*, ed. G. Callender, 2 vols., Navy RS, 52, 53 (1920) · register of commissions and warrants, PRO, Adm 6 · *The Byng papers: selected from the letters and papers of Admiral Sir George Byng, first Viscount Torrington, and of his son, Admiral the Hon. John Byng*, ed. B. Tunstall, 3 vols., Navy RS, 67–8, 70 (1930–32) · J. Charnock, ed., *Biographia navalis*, 6 vols. (1794–8) · John, Lord Hervey, *Some materials towards memoirs of the reign of King George II*, ed. R. Sedgwick, 3 vols. (1931) · H. Walpole, *Memoirs of King George II*, ed. J. Brooke, 3 vols. (1985) · *The correspondence of Jonathan Swift*, ed. H. Williams, 5 vols. (1963–5)
Archives BL, lists, plans, etc. relating to house and gardens at Cranford, Add. MS 69965 · University of Kansas, Lawrence, Kenneth Spencer Research Library, account books of income and expenditure | Glos. RO, corresp. with Christopher Bond relating to patronage
Likenesses G. Kneller, oils, 1710?, NPG · J. Faber, mezzotint, 1731 (after Kneller), BM, NPG; copies, Berkeley Castle, Gloucestershire · attrib. E. Seeman, oils, Berkeley Castle, Gloucestershire · oils, Melbourne Hall, Derby
Wealth at death no value given; estate left to son: will, PRO, PROB 11/679, 31v–32

Berkeley, John, first Baron Berkeley of Stratton (*bap.* 1607, *d.* 1678), royalist army officer and courtier, was baptized on 1 February 1607 at Hanworth, Middlesex, the fifth son of Sir Maurice Berkeley (1576/7–1617) of Bruton, Somerset, a well-connected but penurious gentleman who died when Berkeley was ten years old, and his wife, Elizabeth (*d.* 1626), daughter of Sir Henry Killigrew, teller of the exchequer to Queen Elizabeth, and the widow of Sir Jonathan Trelawny. Charles *Berkeley (1599–1668) and Sir William *Berkeley (1605–1677) were among his elder brothers. Educated at Queen's College, Oxford, where he graduated BA in 1625, Berkeley first came to prominence in 1637, when he was recommended by Lord Holland, as a person both 'discreet and judicious' (*CSP dom.*, 1636–7, 380), as ambassador to Sweden to propose a joint effort to reinstate the elector palatine. Berkeley's cause was not hindered by the fact that Sir Thomas Roe, who had previously undertaken negotiations between Gustavus Adolphus and the king of Poland, and to whom Holland sent his recommendation, was his own cousin. However, the embassy proved fruitless, and he returned from Sweden in July 1638. In the position, as he himself put it, of 'being unprovided with any satisfactory course of life' (*CSP dom.*, 1640–41, 205), he entered into an agreement with the clerk of the council, Sir William Beecher, to succeed if Beecher had leave to retire, but nothing came of it.

In 1639 Berkeley received a commission in the army against the Scots, and was knighted by the king at Berwick in July. In the following year he was elected to the Short Parliament. He did not cut a figure in the Commons, though as a courtier and cavalier officer he was presumably a strong supporter of the king. He was not re-elected to the Long Parliament. Implicated in the first army plot, revealed to the Commons in May 1641, he submitted to parliament in September, together with Daniel O'Neill.

The two men were held in the Tower while being interrogated in closed committee, and preparations were made for a trial, but Berkeley was eventually bailed and the outbreak of the civil war put a stop to proceedings.

When the king's standard was raised Berkeley made his way westwards and joined Lord Hertford at Sherborne. He was one of four royalist officers jointly commissioned as commander-in-chief of the king's forces in the west, though in practice, as commissary-general, he acted under the direction of Sir Ralph Hopton. He fought with distinction, especially at Stratton Hill in 1643, when the parliamentarian forces under Lord Stamford were put to flight. Berkeley pursued Stamford to Exeter, which he took after a combined landward siege and naval blockade. He made Exeter his headquarters and was appointed by Charles I as its governor. In the following year, however, his support for Hopton's campaign in Hampshire ended in defeat at the hands of Sir William Waller at Alresford. In 1645 Berkeley was promoted to be colonel-general of the royalist forces in Devon and Cornwall, and in this capacity led his troops into Somerset to besiege Taunton. But the advance into the west of the parliamentarian army under Lord Fairfax proved unstoppable. Exeter was invested in January 1646 and in April Berkeley was obliged to negotiate an honourable surrender.

Berkeley travelled to Paris to wait on Queen Henrietta Maria, of whom he was a great favourite. He was able to convince her of his influence with the parliamentarian generals and was sent back to England to act as an intermediary. In particular he seems to have enjoyed the confidence of Cromwell and Ireton. Whereas in the years immediately preceding the outbreak of war he had been quick to advocate violence in pursuit of political ends, he now displayed a more pragmatic side to his character, but was unable to effect a royal acceptance of *The Heads of Proposals*. However, he was sufficiently trusted to be called upon to assist Charles I's flight from Hampton Court in 1647. Despite this last exploit Berkeley was again employed in April 1648 as a messenger from the generals to the king, but fearing prosecution as a delinquent thought it wise to retire abroad.

On arriving in Paris in summer 1648 Berkeley was made governor of the young duke of York in the temporary absence of Lord Byron. Berkeley's ambition, enhanced by a misplaced self-confidence, soon propelled him into intrigue, his close family connection with Lord Jermyn determining his allies and enemies. In strategic matters his pragmatic streak was again visible in 1650 when he argued strongly for the royalist alliance with the Scots. But his principal concern seems always to have been self-advancement. In 1651 his dubious claim that Charles I had intended to appoint him master of wards brought him into conflict with Sir Edward Hyde, whose unsuccessful resistance to Berkeley's pretensions inaugurated a longlasting mutual enmity. He also felt it necessary to compose a defence of his own conduct in relation to Charles I's escape to Carisbrooke, to refute insinuations of treachery. Charles II accepted this account, without ever entertaining much personal regard for Berkeley.

In 1652, through Jermyn's influence, Berkeley succeeded Byron as master of the duke of York's household. At this point he was said to have converted to Roman Catholicism, but those who knew him well, and questioned his motives, had grave doubts. Sir Edward Nicholas assumed that Berkeley would have 'no greater proportion of religion than a creature of Lord Jermyn's is obliged to have' (*Nicholas Papers*, 1.171). In the duke's household Berkeley assumed full powers, styling himself 'intendant'. He promoted a marriage between his charge and the daughter of the duc de Longueville only to be thwarted by the French court, and enjoyed no better fortune in his own attempts to secure the hand of Lady Morton, governess of the Princess Henrietta. But he was secure in the good graces of the duke, whom he accompanied on various military campaigns in Flanders. In 1657 the king (prompted by the earl of Bristol) failed to persuade James to dismiss him, and following only a brief banishment Berkeley was received again at court and even raised to the peerage, in 1658, as first Baron Berkeley of Stratton at York's request. The immediate occasion of the contretemps of the previous year had been the duke's tardiness in leaving France to join his brother at Bruges, which was blamed on Berkeley's influence. The deeper cause was the factionalism at the exiled court, exacerbated by resentment at Berkeley's arrogance, and even suspicion that his old contacts with Cromwell and the army grandees had not been entirely relinquished.

After returning to England at the Restoration, Berkeley was rewarded with a place as a commissioner of the navy and several sinecures in Ireland, including that of lord president of Connaught, and in 1663 he was sworn a privy councillor. In 1665 he swapped his naval commissionership for a post in the Ordnance. Despite the fact that he had not yet paid off the debts previously incurred in royal service (he later claimed that he had lent Charles I and Charles II over £10,000, and was still owed £1500 in arrears of army pay) he began a spending spree, building a London house near Piccadilly, which according to John Evelyn cost some £30,000, and acquiring a country estate at Twickenham Park. During the Second Anglo-Dutch War he allegedly spent a further £1000 of his own money in defensive operations at Chatham and in Suffolk. Income from office could have guaranteed only a part of this expenditure, even if one accepts the tales (told by Pepys among others) that he had systematically abused his position in the duke of York's household for his own profit. His marriage, about 1659, to Christian(a) (*bap.* 1639, *d.* 1698), daughter of the wealthy East India merchant Sir Andrew Riccard, and widow of John Gayer and Henry Rich, Lord Kensington, seems also to have brought him an infusion of funds. None the less, his appointment in January 1670 as lord lieutenant of Ireland was a mixed blessing: in the long term the viceroyalty promised further financial rewards, as well as political influence, but in the short term it also involved further conspicuous expenditure to maintain an appropriately viceregal presence in Dublin Castle.

Berkeley was a provocative choice as lord lieutenant.

The suspicions of his own religious allegiance, deriving from rumours that he had converted to Rome in the early 1650s, were reinforced by the fact that he had a Catholic wife, and he did not help matters by choosing for his chief secretary Sir Ellis Leighton, another suspected Catholic convert, who had been associated with him in the duke of York's service. Worse still, from a protestant perspective, Berkeley and Leighton were known to be in close contact with prominent Irish Catholics, most notably Richard Talbot, the future Lord Tyrconnell.

Berkeley arrived in Ireland in April 1670. Under his government Catholics were accorded a substantial degree of religious toleration: priests and bishops operated openly and were recipients of the viceroy's favour; lawyers were permitted to practise, merchants to return to towns and engage in trade; some Catholics were even made JPs. There were, however, considerable difficulties in following through this policy: divisions within the Catholic interest in Ireland hampered Berkeley's efforts; Irish protestants like Lord Orrery, who still held important positions in local government, exploited their authority to harass Catholics in defiance of the viceroy's aspirations; and anti-Catholic interests in the English ministry also worked to undermine tolerationist policies. Moreover Berkeley's character was unsuitable for a role which demanded discretion: his over-confidence and bad temper made him impatient of opposition and liable to make enemies gratuitously. During a brief visit to London in summer 1671, for example, he quarrelled with Lord Windsor over an accusation that he had failed to keep a promise to find Windsor a regiment, and a duel would have ensued had ministers not intervened to protect the dignity of the king's representative. Berkeley's instincts were also authoritarian, and in one important respect his concern to advance royal authority worked against the king's policy. In November 1671, in response to royal instructions for the revision of municipal government in Ireland, he issued a set of rules for governing borough corporations: these increased central control over corporation membership, but by imposing the oath of supremacy and a non-resistance oath (in accordance with what Berkeley thought were the king's preferences) effectively excluded Catholics. Berkeley was later to claim that these provisions had been inserted by political enemies in England; whatever the truth of the matter, the new rules were ordered to be suspended in 1672, and in accordance with Charles II's declaration of indulgence Catholics were readmitted to corporate privileges. However, even after this setback Berkeley could not let borough corporations alone, and a quarrel with the lord mayor and aldermen of Dublin culminated in a viceregal purge of the municipal body of the city.

Berkeley's replacement by Lord Essex in spring 1672 was a consequence of political changes in England rather than a judgement on his viceroyalty. On the other hand it could not be said that he had enhanced his reputation, and he had to suffer inquiries into his administration by the committee for Irish affairs and by parliament. The suppression of the Connaught presidency also cost him dear, for unlike Orrery in Munster he received no monetary compensation, and in 1675 he was petitioning the king for the continuance of his previous income from the office in the form of a pension. Instead he was appointed the same year to go to the peace negotiations at Nijmegen. Preparations for departure were delayed by illness—an apoplectic fit, sustained in the council chamber—from which he recovered, and after spending a long period in France on diplomatic business he eventually reached Nijmegen in November 1676. But in the following May his health broke down again and he was obliged to return to England. Berkeley died at Twickenham on 28 August 1678 and was buried there on 5 September. He left three sons, Charles (d. 1682), John *Berkeley (1663–1697), and William (d. 1741), who in turn succeeded each other in the barony. Berkeley's account of the part he had played in the negotiations between the army grandees and King Charles I in 1646–7, and the king's flight, was eventually published in 1699 as *Memoirs of Sir John Berkeley*.   D. W. HAYTON

Sources GEC, *Peerage*, 2.147–8 · *DNB* · *CSP dom.*, 1636–78 · *CSP Ire.*, 1669–70 · Clarendon, *Hist. rebellion* · *Memoirs of Sir John Berkeley* (1699) · *The Nicholas papers*, ed. G. F. Warner, 4 vols., CS, new ser., 40, 50, 57, 3rd ser., 31 (1886–1920) · Evelyn, *Diary* · *The life of James the Second, king of England*, ed. J. S. Clarke, 2 vols. (1816) · Pepys, *Diary* · S. R. Gardiner, *History of the great civil war, 1642–1649*, 3 vols. (1886–91) · P. R. Newman, *Royalist officers in England and Wales, 1642–1660: a biographical dictionary* (1981) · R. C. Gabriel, 'Berkeley, Sir Maurice', HoP, *Commons, 1558–1603*, 1.432–3 · N. M. Fuidge, 'Killigrew, Henry', HoP, *Commons, 1558–1603*, 2.394–5 · N. M. Sutherland, 'Trelawny, Jonathan', HoP, *Commons, 1558–1603*, 3.525–6 · Foster, *Alum. Oxon.* · F. T. R. Edgar, *Sir Ralph Hopton: the king's man in the west (1642–1652)* (1958) · J. Miller, *James II: a study in kingship* (1978) · M. A. Creighton, 'The Catholic interest in Irish politics in the reign of Charles II', PhD diss., Queen's University, Belfast, 2000

Archives BL, memoirs, Add. MS 29869 | BL, letters to H. Coventry, Add. MSS 22548, 25119 · BL, Nicholas MSS, Egerton 2536 · BL, Osborne MSS, Egerton 3326

Likenesses G. Netscher, group portrait, 1676 (with his wife and son), Berkeley Castle, Gloucestershire · oils, Berkeley Castle, Gloucestershire

Berkeley, John, third Baron Berkeley of Stratton (1663–1697), naval officer, second son of John *Berkeley, first Baron Berkeley of Stratton (*bap.* 1607, *d.* 1678), and his wife, Christiana Rich, *née* Riccard (*bap.* 1639, *d.* 1698), succeeded to the title on the death of his brother Charles (1662–1682), captain of the *Tiger*. John had matriculated at Christ Church, Oxford, in 1677, and served as a volunteer in various ships between 1680 and 1684. During this period he was also convicted of killing one Ralph Tonycliff, but was pardoned in May 1684. He was appointed lieutenant of the *Bristol* on 14 April 1685 by special direction of James II, but within three months he was already complaining that he had not received a command, despite having been at sea for longer prior to gaining a captaincy than his late brother. He also obtained commissions in the army in 1685, becoming (in October) cornet and major of the third troop of John Churchill's Horse Guards regiment. He finally obtained the naval command he wanted on 9 July 1686 when he was appointed captain of the *Charles Galley*, part of the squadron sent to the Mediterranean under the command of the duke of Grafton. He returned to England in May 1688 and on 30 August was appointed captain of the *Mountagu*, part of Lord Dartmouth's fleet assigned to guard against invasion from the Netherlands. Berkeley quickly became one of the leaders of the Williamite conspiracy within the fleet. He was involved in a plot to kidnap Dartmouth and give the command of the fleet to Grafton, but this came to nothing. Dartmouth, however, was aware of his 'very pert' activities and that he 'infused strange notions into the seamen and a great part of the commanders', and therefore moved his ship next to his in order to keep a closer eye on him (*Dartmouth MSS*, 1.260–61). Even his original patron, James II, later described him as one of the 'most factious and disaffected officers of the navy' (Clarke, *Life of James the Second*, 2.233–4). However, the success of the revolution transformed Berkeley from conspirator into victorious patriot. He was moved to the *Edgar* on 27 November and became rear-admiral on 14 December 1688, despite his obvious lack of seniority. He remained aboard the *Edgar* until March 1689, and was vice-admiral of the red under Herbert at the battle of Bantry Bay on 1 May 1689, subsequently moving into Dublin Bay to defend it against the French. He commanded a squadron cruising in the mouth of the channel from October 1689 to January 1690. Berkeley held no command during the 1690 campaign, but commanded the *Saint Andrew*, with no flag, between January and October 1691. On 8 March 1692 he married Jane Martha (1672–1751), daughter of Sir John Temple of East Sheen, one of the maids of honour. He spent the campaigning season of 1692 in Flanders, commanding his regiment of horse, and returned to England in late September.

On 8 February 1693 Berkeley was appointed vice-admiral of the blue with his flag in the *Neptune*, rising to become admiral of the blue aboard the *Britannia* in the fleet of the joint admirals Killigrew, Delaval, and Shovell following Sir John Ashby's death in June 1693. However, his appointment, and the others made at the same time, caused so much disquiet—particularly because they overlooked Sir George Rooke and Sir Thomas Hopson—that they had to be reversed in September, with Berkeley dropping down to vice-admiral of the red. Berkeley's health at this time was poor, and he spent much of the summer ashore at Exeter. He was an expert witness in the House of Lords' debates on naval miscarriages over the winter of 1693–4, and took over the command of the second marine regiment from the disgraced Killigrew at the same time. Berkeley was back at sea in 1694, and was ordered by Admiral Russell to lead the naval forces supporting the projected attack on Brest by General Talmash's army. When the fleet entered Camaret Bay on 7 June and attempted to land on the following day, it was beaten off by strong opposition ashore; Berkeley had to content himself with the lesser prizes of bombarding Dieppe and Le Havre (12 and 16 July). He gave up his command on 27 August and spent the winter in London. Berkeley hoisted his flag again aboard the *Shrewsbury* on 12 June 1695 and commanded the fleet at the bombardment of St Malo (4

July) by bomb vessels under the immediate command of Captain John Benbow. William III was set on another attack on Dunkirk (Sir Cloudesley Shovell had unsuccessfully attempted this in the previous September), and despite his own grave doubts about the operation Berkeley commanded the attack on 1 August. He was particularly scathing about the use of 'machine vessels', regarding their inventor, William Meesters, as a duplicitous fraud, and the miserable failure of the attack seems to bear out Berkeley's assessment: 'he is certainly near akin to the father of falsehood', Berkeley wrote (Berkeley to Shrewsbury, 8 Aug 1695, *Buccleuch MSS*, 2.212). His fleet then moved on to bombard Calais on 17 August before he again retired for the winter. His domestic affairs were now in some confusion, with both the marquess of Normanby and the duke of Devonshire claiming that he had agreed to sell Berkeley House in London to them, and he spent much of the summer of 1696 requesting successive leaves to go back to London. Nevertheless, he commanded in chief from the end of May, when Rooke was recalled to London, and (after being delayed by the wind until the end of June) he led a series of raids on the French Biscay coast in the hope of diverting troops from the Flanders front. Berkeley finally left the fleet in August 1696, and never returned to it. Struck down with pleurisy, he died at the family seat in Twickenham on 27 February 1697, and was buried there on 5 March. His will bequeathed £5000 to his daughter Mary, who died in infancy; a codicil left £200 to Mrs Olive Bracegirdle, possibly his mistress, 'at present belonging to the new playhouse in Lincoln's Inn Fields' (PRO, PROB 11/437, fols. 202–5). A proprietor of Carolina and the Bahamas, Berkeley had also been groom of the stool and gentleman of the bedchamber to Prince George of Denmark, as well as one of the conservators of Deeping Fen.

Berkeley emerges from all of his correspondence as an arrogant, ambitious young man, always jealous of his own pretensions, and—as his part in the events of 1688 suggests—always heavily involved in the political arena. However, his personal bravery can not be questioned. As early as 1686 he responded to an attempt by the local mob to seize an English merchantman at Algiers by leaping off the breakwater into his boat, getting to the ship, cutting her anchor cable, and fighting off the natives. Ten years later, as he took up his last command, he was 'but too sensible how very much it is necessary to my own reputation that the fleet should attempt something this year upon my first arrival to the command of it … but without wings 'tis impossible to fly' (*Buccleuch MSS*, 2.351).

J. D. DAVIES

Sources PRO, ADM MSS · GEC, *Peerage* · N. Luttrell, *A brief historical relation of state affairs from September 1678 to April 1714*, 6 vols. (1857) · *Report on the manuscripts of his grace the duke of Buccleuch and Queensberry … preserved at Montagu House*, 3 vols. in 4, HMC, 45 (1899–1926), vol. 2 · *The manuscripts of the earl of Dartmouth*, 3 vols., HMC, 20 (1887–96), vol. 1 · *The manuscripts of the House of Lords*, 4 vols., HMC, 17 (1887–94) · *The manuscripts of the House of Lords*, new ser., 12 vols. (1900–77), vols. 1–2 · *CSP dom.*, 1689–97 · PRO, PROB 11/437, fols. 202–5 · *Report on the manuscripts of Allan George Finch*, 5 vols., HMC, 71 (1913–2003), vols. 2–3 · J. D. Davies, 'James II, William of Orange, and the admirals', *By force or by default? The revolution of 1688–1689*, ed. E. Cruickshanks (1989), 82–108 · R. C. Anderson, 'English flag officers, 1688–1713', *Mariner's Mirror*, 35 (1949), 333–41 · E. B. Powley, *The naval side of King William's war* (1972) · J. C. R. Childs, *The British army of William III, 1689–1702* (1987) · J. D. Davies, *Gentlemen and tarpaulins: the officers and men of the Restoration navy* (1991) · *DNB* · *The life of James the Second, king of England*, ed. J. S. Clarke, 2 vols. (1816)

Archives CKS, letters to Shovell and orders · PRO, ADM MSS

Likenesses M. Dahl, oils, Berkeley Castle, Gloucestershire

Wealth at death £5000 bequeathed to daughter; estate to brother: will, PRO, PROB 11/437, fols. 202–5

Berkeley [*née* Clivedon], **Katherine**, **Lady Berkeley** (*d.* 1385), benefactor, was the daughter of Sir John Clivedon, a knight of Somerset and Worcestershire, and his wife, Emma. After an unrecorded childhood, she became, about the mid-1330s, the second wife of Sir Peter Veel of Charfield and Tortworth, Gloucestershire, with whom she had two children: John who died in childhood and Joan who married Henry Moigne. Sir Peter died in 1343 and Katherine remarried in 1347; her new husband was the Gloucestershire magnate Thomas, third Baron Berkeley (*b. c.*1293), who had also been married before. She subsequently bore him four children, the sole survivor, John, later founding a cadet branch of the Berkeley family at Beverstone, Gloucestershire. Thomas died in 1361, and Katherine spent her second widowhood (which lasted for twenty-three years) on the Berkeleys' manor of Wotton under Edge, Gloucestershire, pursuing devotional projects including pilgrimage overseas, the making of gifts to the nearby Cistercian abbey of Kingswood, and the foundation of a chantry in Berkeley church in 1384.

Katherine's most distinctive achievement was the endowment of a grammar school in the borough of Wotton under Edge near her principal residence. It is the earliest known example in England of a small, fully endowed school, staffed by one master and offering free tuition in Latin grammar to all comers, of a pattern that became common in later centuries. There had been a grammar school in Wotton at least intermittently since the late thirteenth century, and this may have received earlier patronage from the Berkeley family, but Katherine put the school on a statutory and secure basis. By 1380 she had established links with a young clerk named John Stone who studied at university, probably under her patronage, graduated MA, and became her first schoolmaster. In 1384 she obtained royal licence to build a schoolhouse and endow a school, transferred sufficient property to support a schoolmaster and two scholars, and issued foundation statutes. The master was to be a chantry priest, saying mass each day in the manor house or parish church of Wotton, thus introducing the notion of the chantry grammar school which was widely copied in England down to the Reformation. He received an unspecified stipend in return for providing the two scholars with food and lodging, and teaching grammar without charge to them and to any others who came to be taught. The school holidays were fixed as from 21 December to 6 January,

Palm Sunday to Low Sunday, Pentecost week, and 1 August to 14 September.

Katherine's project coincided chronologically with William Wykeham's much larger school foundation, Winchester College (1382), but this may have been fortuitous since the two enterprises differed in scale and details. More potent influences may have included the possible earlier links between the Berkeley family and Wotton school, and the family's general interest in culture. Katherine's step-grandson Thomas, Lord Berkeley (1353–1417), employed John Trevisa and other scholars to translate Latin works into English, including Bartholomew the Englishman's encyclopaedia *De proprietatibus rerum*, Ranulf Higden's world history, *Polychronicon*, and Vegetius's military treatise *Epitoma rei militaris*. Katherine's Wotton foundation was not widely imitated until the 1440s and appears to have been an isolated initiative, albeit one that established a practical and easily reproduced form. She died on 13 March 1385 and was buried beside her second husband in Berkeley church, Gloucestershire; the tomb still bears their effigies. NICHOLAS ORME

Sources N. Orme, *Education in the west of England, 1066–1548* (1976), 190–99 · J. Smyth, *Lives of the Berkeleys* (1883), vol. 1 of *The Berkeley manuscripts*, ed. J. Maclean (1883–5), 346–56 · GEC, *Peerage*, new edn, 2.129–31 · W. P. Marett, ed., *A calendar of the register of Henry Wakefield, bishop of Worcester, 1375–95*, Worcestershire Historical Society, new ser., 7 (1972), 80–89 · N. Orme, *English schools in the middle ages* (1973), 184–90, 196–7 · J. Trevisa, *Dialogus inter militem et clericum*, ed. A. J. Perry, EETS, 167 (1925), lxv–cxxxiii

Likenesses tomb effigy, *c.*1385, Berkeley parish church, Gloucestershire

Berkeley, Sir Lennox Randal Francis (1903–1989), composer, was born on 12 May 1903 at Melford Cottage, Boars Hill, near Oxford, the younger child and only son of Captain Hastings George FitzHardinge Berkeley RN (1855–1934) (the eldest son of George Lennox Rawdon Berkeley, seventh earl of Berkeley) and his wife, Aline Carla (1863–1935), daughter of Sir James Charles Harris, former British consul in Monaco. His father did not succeed as eighth earl of Berkeley because Captain Berkeley's parents were unmarried until prior to the birth of their third son, who succeeded to the earldom. After early schooling in Oxford, Lennox Berkeley was educated at Gresham's School in Holt, Norfolk, St George's School in Harpenden, Hertfordshire, and Merton College, Oxford, where he coxed the college rowing eight and took a fourth class in French (1926). He became an honorary fellow of Merton in 1974.

Berkeley had shown no outstanding musical abilities at school (though a contemporary remembers him playing the piano with much flourishing of hands), but while at Oxford he had several of his compositions performed and eventually made up his mind to be a composer. In this he was supported by the young British conductor Anthony Bernard, who later conducted first performances of a number of Berkeley's early works.

On advice from Maurice Ravel, Berkeley went to Paris in the autumn of 1926 to study with Nadia Boulanger, and stayed with her for six years. For the first of these she allowed him to do nothing but counterpoint exercises, a

Sir Lennox Randal Francis Berkeley (1903–1989), by Nicolo Vogel

discipline which often reduced him to tears at the time, but for which he was to remain grateful all his life. He had works performed in Paris and London, and his *Polka for Two Pianos* (1934) was a notable success, inaugurating his ties with the publishers J. and W. Chester. But the BBC broadcast of his oratorio *Jonah* (1935) in 1936 and the Leeds festival performance of it the following year led many critics to look at him askance as a purveyor of modernism. From 1932 to 1934 he lived on the Riviera with his invalid mother.

In 1936 Berkeley met Benjamin Britten and the two became close friends, sharing a house in Snape, Suffolk, just before the Second World War. Although rather daunted by what he felt to be Britten's superior talent, Berkeley was able to find a distinctive voice in the *Serenade for Strings* (1939), the first symphony (1940), and the *Divertimento* (1943). From 1942 to 1945 he worked for the BBC, first in Bedford and then in London, as an orchestral programme planner. The authorities noted with dismay that when he was labouring on a commission his BBC work suffered, and he was happy to accept an appointment as professor of composition at the Royal Academy of Music in 1946. He remained in the post until 1968 and numbered many of the country's best composers among his pupils, including David Bedford, Peter Dickinson, William Mathias, Nicholas Maw, and John Tavener. On 14 December 1946 he married Elizabeth Freda, daughter of Isaac Bernstein, a retired shopkeeper. They had three sons, of whom the eldest, Michael Berkeley, became a composer.

Until he succumbed to Alzheimer's disease in the early 1980s, Berkeley produced a succession of works which made him many friends and earned him admirers in the musical community, even if he never became famous outside it. He wrote for performers such as the pianist Colin Horsley, the oboist Janet Craxton, and the guitarist Julian Bream, and he produced a considerable body of fine chamber music. He was particularly at home with the voice, and his vocal and choral works, such as *Four Poems of St Teresa of Avila* (1947), the *Stabat mater* (1947), and *The Hill of the Graces* (1975), show a love and understanding of words at least equal to Britten's. His four operas—*A Dinner Engagement* (1954), *Nelson* (1954), *Ruth* (1956), and *Castaway* (1967)—display at times an individual view of what constitutes opera, and one which critics and impresarios have not always shared; certainly he was not always fortunate with his librettists. But *Nelson* suffered from less than adequate performances in London and deserves to be revived. From the late 1960s Berkeley, like many composers, experimented with serial techniques and, though they never took over his music, he admitted that thanks to them his musical language had expanded. The third symphony (1969) is perhaps his most impressive exercise in this new vein. In the 1970s he still remained true to his principles of writing, with performance in mind and never *in vacuo*. When his last illness struck he was working on a fifth opera, *Faldon Park*.

In 1959 Berkeley said: 'I know quite well I'm a minor composer, and I don't mind that'. It is true that he was not an Arnold Schoenberg or an Igor Stravinsky. His music made no revolutionary claims, partly because revolutionaries have to be destroyers and Berkeley was too respectful of tradition to set about it with a hatchet. If his studies with Boulanger taught him to be at ease with counterpoint, they also inculcated a love of 'la grande ligne', which Boulanger had inherited from Gabriel Fauré. His music, like Fauré's, eschews surprises and, for the most part, grand gestures (though, again, *Nelson* showed what he could achieve in this more public, extrovert manner). His colleague Edmund Rubbra referred to his work as offering 'so much in sanity and honesty of purpose'. These attributes were in general misprized in the twentieth century, and Berkeley's refusal to jettison them meant that his reputation likewise matured without sudden surprises. He was notable for attending to the needs of the amateur: it is unusual, for example, to come across a flautist who has not at some time played his sonatina. But his larger works, though always expertly written, demand patience and close attention to be fully appreciated. Even if his music always remains basically tonal, it can sometimes be fierce and gritty, very often as a result of his essentially linear thinking. Perhaps too much has been made of the Frenchness of his music, and too often critics have used this as an excuse to deny his work profundity, but at the very least he managed to avoid the vapid pastoral meanderings of some of his English predecessors. The history of twentieth-century music may not have been greatly changed by his passing across it, but without him it would have been immeasurably the poorer. He was a man dedicated, as his pupil Peter Dickinson has said, to 'passing on the love of music as a spiritual imperative in a foreign, material age'. He was appointed CBE in 1957 and knighted in 1974. Among many other honours were the papal knighthood of St Gregory (1973), honorary membership of the American Academy and Institute of Arts and Letters (1980), honorary doctorates of music from Oxford University (1970) and City University in London (1983), and an honorary fellowship of the Royal Northern College of Music, Manchester (1976). He also served as president of the Performing Right Society (1975–83), the Composers' Guild of Great Britain (from 1975), and the Cheltenham festival (1977–83).

Berkeley was, above all, graceful: he had been a good tennis player in his youth and remained all his life a tireless walker. As with his music, there was no hint of otiose flesh, but rather of a strength which he was careful to hide beneath beautiful manners. As well as being a kind and approachable man, he was always quick to see the funny side of things. During his time with Boulanger, he and Igor Markevich were members of a mildly disruptive 'back row', while in later life an eye would twinkle in response to persons on committees who treated 'criteria' as a singular noun or interposed with, 'Mr Chairman, I have a trepidation about that one'. Although determined to do what he saw as his civic duty, he never courted public notice unless forced by the strength of his own opinions. He had become a Roman Catholic in 1928 (when he took the name Francis) and, in the wake of the Second Vatican Council, wrote in the press urging the retention of the Tridentine mass, since he believed the authorities were ignoring a legitimate desire expressed by a large body of the Roman Catholic laity. In private he wrote of those 'for whom the overthrow of the old tradition appears to be an end in itself', an end which, in religion as in music, he was unable to approve. Berkeley died in St Charles's Hospital, Ladbroke Grove, London, on 26 December 1989. His ashes were scattered at Cap Ferrat, France. A memorial service was held on 20 March 1990 at Westminster Cathedral.

ROGER NICHOLS, rev.

Sources P. Dickinson, *The music of Lennox Berkeley* (1988) · BBC WAC · *The Times* (27 Dec 1989) · personal knowledge (1996) · private information (1996) · private information (2004) [M. Berkeley, son] · *CGPLA Eng. & Wales* (1990)
Archives BL, setting of *Counting the beats*, Add. MS 52464 · Britten–Pears Library, The Red House, Aldeburgh, Suffolk, MSS
Likenesses J. Mendoza, portrait, 1977 · N. Vogel, photograph, NPG [*see illus.*]
Wealth at death £848,453: probate, 19 March 1990, *CGPLA Eng. & Wales*

Berkeley, Sir Maurice (c.1514–1581). *See under* Henry VIII, privy chamber of (*act.* 1509–1547).

Berkeley, Maurice Frederick Fitzhardinge, first Baron Fitzhardinge of Bristol (1788–1867), naval officer and politician, was born on 3 January 1788, the second illegitimate son of Frederick Augustus, fifth earl of Berkeley (1745–1810), and Mary (1766/7–1844), daughter of William Cole, publican and butcher, of Wotton, near Gloucester. He entered the navy in June 1802, and after six years' service, mostly in the West Indies and on the Newfoundland station, where his uncle, Vice-Admiral G. C. Berkeley, was then commander-in-chief, was promoted lieutenant on 9 July 1808. He was then appointed to the frigate *Hydra* (Captain George Mundy), employed on the east coast of Spain during the next eighteen months. In February 1810 he was appointed flag-lieutenant to his uncle at Lisbon, and in the autumn commanded a division of gunboats on the Tagus, co-operating with the troops holding the lines of Torres Vedras. He was promoted on 19 December 1810 to command the *Vestal*, in which he continued until the following November. He reached post rank on 7 June 1814, and from 1828 to 1831 commanded the frigate *Semiramis*, flagship at Cork.

In 1823 Berkeley married Lady Charlotte Lennox (1804–1833), daughter of the fourth duke of Richmond; after her death he married, in 1834, Lady Charlotte Moreton (1806–1881), daughter of the first earl of Ducie. He entered parliament in 1831 as whig MP for the family borough of Gloucester; defeated in 1833, when he became a naval lord, he regained the seat on leaving office, only to lose it again on resuming office in 1837. In 1839 he resigned his seat. In 1840–41 he commanded the *Thunderer* (84 guns), in the Mediterranean, and took part in operations on the coast of Syria, where he served under Commodore Charles Napier; he was involved in the bombardment of Acre, for which he was made a CB and received the gold medal. There his sea service ended, though he became, in course of seniority, rear-admiral on 30 October 1849; vice-admiral on 21 October 1856; and admiral on 15 January 1862.

In 1841 Berkeley regained his seat in parliament, which he retained until 1857. He served as a junior naval lord from 1846 to 1852, and then briefly as senior naval lord before leaving office with Lord John Russell's ministry. He returned as second naval lord under Sir James Graham in 1853, and served as first naval lord from June 1854 to November 1857, when a combination of the death of his elder brother, family business, the loss of his seat, and ill health led him to resign. As a naval lord Berkeley proved a reliable supporter of government. His resignation in 1839—over the whig policy of reduced manning to cover inadequate estimates—revealed a rare streak of independence. In office he was narrow-minded, authoritarian, and uninspired. During the Crimean War he was left to concentrate on raising men, strategic guidance being provided by Captain Baldwin Walker, the surveyor of the navy. Refused a command afloat, for which he applied in 1854 and 1855, and conscious of his limitations in the higher direction of war, Berkeley quarrelled with his friend Vice-Admiral Napier and with Rear-Admiral Lyons. After leaving office he retained his interest in manning, and advocated a defence system based on gunboats.

Berkeley was nominated a privy councillor in 1855, and was made a KCB on 5 July 1855 and GCB on 28 June 1861. His elder brother, who had been created Earl Fitzhardinge in 1841, died in 1857, and his titles became extinct. Admiral Berkeley then, under his father's will, succeeded to the vast family estate. He claimed the barony of Berkeley, but the queen objected to promoting a second illegitimate son of Lord Berkeley. He was, however, raised to the peerage on 5 August 1861 as Baron Fitzhardinge of Bristol.

He died at Berkeley Castle, Gloucestershire, on 17 October 1867. A man of limited abilities, more politician than admiral, Berkeley's only real contribution was on the issue of manning, where his authoritarian views did not endear him to the sailors. ANDREW LAMBERT

Sources A. D. Lambert, *The Crimean War: British grand strategy, 1853–56* (1990) · C. J. Bartlett, *Great Britain and sea power, 1815–1853* (1963) · A. D. Lambert, *The last sailing battlefleet: maintaining naval mastery, 1815–1850* (1991) · E. D. H. E. Napier, *The life and correspondence of Admiral Sir Charles Napier*, 2 vols. (1862) · J. Bromley, ed., *The manning of the Royal Navy* (1974) · O'Byrne, *Naval biog. dict.* · *Journals and correspondence of Francis Thornhill Baring*, ed. Thomas George, earl of Northbrook [T. G. Baring] and F. H. Baring, 1 (privately printed, Winchester, 1902) · *CGPLA Eng. & Wales* (1867) · GEC, *Peerage* · *GM*, 4th ser., 4 (1867), 819

Archives Berkeley Castle, Gloucestershire, corresp., memoranda, and papers | BL, corresp. with Sir Charles Napier and others · BL, corresp. with Charles Wood, Add. MS 49532, *passim* · Borth. inst., corresp. with Sir Charles Wood · Cumbria AS, Carlisle, Graham MSS · Glos. RO, corresp. with W. H. Hyett · U. Southampton L., Palmerston (Broadlands) MSS · W. Sussex RO, letters to duke of Richmond

Likenesses J. Brown, stipple, NPG; repro. in *Baily's Magazine*, 6 (1863), 217

Wealth at death under £60,000: probate, 23 Nov 1867, *CGPLA Eng. & Wales*

Berkeley, Miles Joseph (1803–1889), Church of England clergyman and naturalist, was born at Biggin Hall, near Oundle, Northamptonshire, on 1 April 1803, the second son of Charles Berkeley of Biggin Hall and his wife, Charlotte, daughter of James Munn of Blackheath and sister of the watercolour artist P. S. Munn. After attending Oundle grammar school he went, in 1817, to Rugby School, entering Christ's College, Cambridge, as a scholar in 1821. He graduated BA in 1825, proceeded MA in 1828, took holy orders, and became curate at Thornhaugh, in the see of Peterborough, in December 1826. He was ordained priest on 23 December 1827 and became curate at St John's, Margate, Kent, in February 1829.

Berkeley's zoological and botanical interests, fostered at Rugby, had been reinforced by Professor J. S. Henslow at Cambridge and by meeting R. K. Greville and Dugald Carmichael (of Appin) during summer field collecting at Loch Lomond in 1823 and Oban in 1824. Molluscan anatomy and algal systematics (especially marine) were his primary interests until about 1833. However, from about 1827 mycology and phytopathology became increasingly important—indeed, he was later called 'the Father of British mycology' (English, 43; 150).

On 28 January 1833 Berkeley married Cecilia Emma, daughter of John Campbell of Blackheath. An accomplished linguist and botanical artist, she subsequently helped much in both translation and illustration of Berkeley's publications. Berkeley was offered a small living as perpetual curate of Apethorpe and Wood Newton, near Wansford in Northamptonshire, and he and his wife immediately moved to King's Cliffe, Wansford, where they lived until 1868. In May 1868 Berkeley moved, as vicar of Sibbertoft, to near Market Harborough. Berkeley and his wife produced a family of fifteen, and intense labours were needed to support them all, since stipends were small. Thus, in addition to fulfilling professional and scientific commitments, Berkeley took pupils. Correspondence with W. J. Hooker and J. S. Henslow during 1839–40 indicates how successful was his 'school'. He also became rural dean of part of Northampton (June 1854) and of Rothwell (1871), as well as chaplain to the earl of Westmorland in December 1834.

Berkeley's first major mycological work was the volume on fungi (1836) in J. E. Smith's *English Flora*. His subsequent series of 'Notices of British fungi' appeared over a long period in the *Magazine of Zoology and Botany*, which became *Annals and Magazine of Natural History*; his early zoological works appeared in this same journal. From 1848 C. E. Broome (1812–1886) became closely involved with Berkeley's work and 'it is almost impossible for a modern mycologist to think of one without the other' (English, 152). Despite an already intensely busy life, between 1844 and 1856 Berkeley issued *The Decades of Fungi* and, alone or with Broome, described fungi from widespread locations including those from Darwin's *Beagle* voyage, Hugh Cuming's Philippine collections, and the Ceylon material from G. H. K. Thwaites.

In 1845–7 the government commission established to determine the cause of the Irish potato blight greatly involved Berkeley in its work. With his interests in plant health and disease he also emerged as a consistent contributor to the *Gardeners' Chronicle*, especially between January 1854 and 1857, when more than 170 articles on vegetable pathology appeared. In the latter year his comprehensive *Introduction to Cryptogamic Botany* appeared; it was heavy going but original, and remained influential for more than thirty years. Also influential was his *The Outlines of British Fungology* (1860), but his 1863 *Handbook of British Mosses* was less effective.

Throughout the 1860s Berkeley remained intensely busy, writing articles, providing information for other authors, checking colleagues' proofs, and refereeing for the *Gardeners' Chronicle*. He also received a number of awards (including the Royal Society's gold medal in 1863), and was appointed as British commissioner to the Hamburg Exhibition in 1869. Between 1865 and 1873 he described fungi of Fiji for *Flora Vitiensis* (Seemann). For some time he had assisted John Lindley in preparing papers for the *Journal of the Royal Horticultural Society*, and from 1866 to 1877 he was its editor. He also became botanical adviser (director) of the society. He was president of section D of the British Association (1868).

In 1879 increasing deafness caused Berkeley largely to retire from active science. He then presented his fungal herbarium (more than 10,000 species, 6000 new species, and 20,000 specimens in total), with his mycological books, to the herbarium at the Royal Botanic Gardens, Kew. He continued occasionally to botanize and to publish on British fungi in the *Annals and Magazine of Natural History* until 1884. All contemporaries comment on his imposing presence, enthusiasm, courtesy, kindness, intellect, and pioneering spirit. He was regarded as urbane and with encyclopaedic knowledge.

Berkeley was a fellow of the Linnean Society (1836) and

of the Royal Society (1879). He was also an honorary fellow of Christ's College, Cambridge (1883), of St Augustine's College, Canterbury, and of the Royal Horticultural Society. He died at Sibbertoft vicarage on 30 July 1889.

JAMES H. PRICE

Sources J. H. Price, 'Miles Joseph Berkeley and the publication of *Gleanings of British algae, 1832–1833', From Linnaeus to Darwin* [London 1983], ed. A. Wheeler and J. H. Price (1985), 89–127 · *Gardeners' Chronicle*, 3rd ser., 6 (1889), 141–2 · M. P. English, *Mordecai Cubitt Cooke: Victorian naturalist, mycologist, teacher and eccentric* (1987) · G. C. Druce, 'Northamptonshire obituaries: the Rev. Miles Joseph Berkeley', *Northamptonshire Notes and Queries*, 4 (1892), 25–37; 221–4 · H. N. Dixon, *Journal of the Northamptonshire Natural History Society and Field Club*, 5 (1890), 343–9 · G. M. [G. Murray], *Journal of Botany, British and Foreign*, 27 (1889), 305–8 · M. C. [M. Cooke], *Grevillea*, 18/85 (1889), 17–19 · G. Massee, 'Miles Joseph Berkeley, 1803–1889', *Makers of British botany*, ed. F. W. Oliver (1913), 225–32, pl. XVIII · NHM, department of botany, Berkeley MSS · E. C. Nelson, 'David Moore, Miles J. Berkeley and scientific studies of potato blight in Ireland, 1845–1847', *Archives of Natural History*, 11 (1983), 249–61 · 'Rev. M. J. Berkeley', *Gardeners' Chronicle* (4 March 1871), 271 · H. M. Clokie, *An account of the herbaria of the department of botany in the University of Oxford* (1964) · G. D. R. Bridson, V. C. Phillips, and A. P. Harvey, *Natural history manuscript resources in the British Isles* (1980) · F. C. Sawyer, 'A short history of the libraries and list of manuscripts and original drawings in the British Museum (Natural History)', *Bulletin of the British Museum (Natural History)* [Historical Series], 4 (1970–75), 77–204

Archives Linn. Soc., drawings, notes, and papers · NHM, department of botany, corresp. · NHM, corresp. and papers · NHM, watercolour collection of fungi, with MSS notes · Oxf. U. Mus. NH, specimens of British fungi · RBG Kew, mycological herbarium and index | Bath Royal Literary and Scientific Institution, letters to Leonard Blomefield · Bolton Museum, Lancashire, Mason collection, specimens · CUL, Borrer corresp. · Linn. Soc., J. E. Smith corresp. collection · Ludlow Museum, Thomas Salwey corresp. collection · NHM, department of botany, Broome corresp. · NHM, letters to members of the Sowerby family · NHM, higher plants [through collections of Babington, Borrer, Power, and Watson] · Pharmaceutical Society of Great Britain, London, materia medica collection · RBG Kew, letters to Sir William Hooker · Royal Botanic Garden, Edinburgh, collections of marine algae · U. Glas., algae from Margate, 1829 · U. Oxf., department of plant sciences

Likenesses J. Peel, oils, 1878, Linn. Soc. · engraving, 1892 (after photograph by Maull & Fox), repro. in Druce, 'Northamptonshire obituaries', 25 · E. Edwards, photograph, NPG; repro. in L. Reeve, ed., *Portraits of men of eminence in literature, science, and art, with biographical memoirs* (1864), vol. 2 · W. G. Smith, portrait, repro. in *Gardeners' Chronicle* (1879), 789 · photograph, Christ's College, Cambridge · portrait, RBG Kew · portrait, Carnegie Mellon University, Pittsburgh, Hunt Botanical Library · portrait, repro. in *Gardeners' Chronicle* (1871), 271 · portrait (after photograph), priv. coll.; repro. in English, *Mordecai Cubitt Cooke*, p. 151, fig. 9.1

Wealth at death £3625 3s. 9d.: resworn probate, Feb 1891, CGPLA Eng. & Wales (1889)

Berkeley, Randal Thomas Mowbray Rawdon, eighth earl of Berkeley (1865–1942), physical chemist and landowner, was born on 31 January 1865 at Ixelles, Brussels, the third son—but the only one born after his parents' marriage—of George Lennox Rawdon Berkeley (1827–1888) and his wife, Cécile (d. 1914), daughter of Edward Drummond, count of Melfort, in the French nobility, and divorced wife of Admiral Sir F. B. R. Pellew (1789–1861). He assumed the courtesy title Viscount Dursley in 1882, when his father took the title of seventh earl of Berkeley on the

death of his cousin, Thomas Moreton Fitzhardinge Berkeley, who by a family arrangement had not used the earldom to which he was entitled. On his father's death in 1888 Viscount Dursley assumed the title of eighth earl of Berkeley and in 1891 his right to the peerage was established.

Berkeley's parents lived abroad and he was educated in France before moving to England to be coached for the Royal Navy at Burney's academy, Gosport. In 1878 he joined the cadet training ship *Britannia* berthed at Dartmouth. From 1880 to 1887 he served in various ships, including a period on the China station, and also attended the Royal Naval College, Greenwich. While he was in the navy his interest in science and mathematics was stimulated, particularly by books he was lent by a chaplain in one of the ships on which he served. In 1887, finding naval discipline irksome, he resigned his commission in order to devote himself to science. The same year, on 9 November, he married Kate (d. 1898), daughter of William Brand, a landowner, and widow of Arthur Jackson, a composer and teacher at the Royal Academy of Music.

Berkeley studied chemistry for a short time at the Royal College of Science and also attended lectures in other subjects, including geology. A lecture on petrography aroused in him an interest in crystals and he began to study the relationship between crystalline form and chemical composition. However, a serious illness put an end to his work in London. In 1893 he moved to Foxcombe near Oxford and resumed his crystallographic work in the Christ Church laboratory, work which led to two short papers on the accurate determination of the densities of solids. (Real understanding of the relationship between crystalline form and chemical composition had to await the advent of X-ray crystallography.) In 1897, in association with Ernald Hartley, Berkeley conducted research into the electrolysis of glass. No publication resulted, but this work apparently turned Berkeley's attention to semi-permeable membranes and hence to osmotic pressure.

Berkeley built a private laboratory at Foxcombe in 1898 and began researches on the measurement of osmotic pressure. The work began in earnest in 1902 when he was joined by Hartley (who was his collaborator until 1916). At that time physical chemists were interested in the deviations of real solutions from the osmotic pressure equation of Van't Hoff (analogous to the ideal gas equation) and the possibility of expressing these by an equation similar to the van der Waals equation used for real gases. First, however, there were major difficulties to be overcome in order to obtain accurate experimental results; this was the goal Berkeley set himself.

Berkeley and Hartley designed and built an apparatus incorporating a semi-permeable membrane which was capable of measuring accurately osmotic pressures up to 150 atmospheres. They also measured osmotic pressures by the so-called indirect method, based on the lowering of the vapour pressure of a solvent by a solute. Initially there were considerable discrepancies between the results given by the two methods, but these were gradually reduced, almost to zero, by refinements of technique and the discovery and application of necessary corrections. Although much effort was also expended in trying to express the results by equations of the van der Waals type, with the benefit of hindsight it is apparent that such attempts were doomed.

Over the years additional workers were recruited to Foxcombe and the study of solutions was broadened to include diffusion and centrifugation, and there were further opportunities for constructing ingenious apparatus. However, August 1914 marked the start of the decline of the Foxcombe laboratory, as the team Berkeley had assembled dispersed to war work.

During the war years Berkeley himself acquired another interest: on the death of his kinsman Lord Fitzhardinge in 1916 he succeeded to the Berkeley estates in Gloucestershire. The castle was in a neglected state and he threw himself energetically into its restoration, acting as his own architect and clerk of works. But he never lost his interest in osmotic pressure and related phenomena; some research continued at Foxcombe throughout the war and the laboratory did not finally close until 1928. Even after the laboratory closed Berkeley was seeking new equations to express his old experimental results.

Berkeley was not prominent in the life of the scientific community, but he was elected FRS in 1908 and served on the council of the Chemical Society from 1914 to 1918. For many years his main interest outside science was golf, and he laid out a nine-hole golf course at Foxcombe. In 1936 he published *Sound Golf by Applying Principles to Practice*. On inheriting the Berkeley estates he became master of the Berkeley hounds; he took up hunting when he was over fifty and continued in the sport until 1927. On 8 November 1924 he married his second wife, Mrs Mary Emlen Lloyd (*d.* 1975), daughter of John Lowell of Boston, Massachusetts; they spent much time in California and in Italy. Berkeley died peacefully in his sleep at Berkeley Castle on 15 January 1942. There were no children by either marriage and the earldom of Berkeley ended with him.

JOHN SHORTER

Sources H. Hartley, *Obits. FRS*, 4 (1942–4) [incl. list of publications] · *DNB* · Burke, *Peerage* · 'Pellew, Sir Fleetwood Broughton Reynolds', *DNB* · *American Chemical Abstracts*, 1–29 (1907–35) [for summaries of Berkeley's scientific papers] · GEC, *Peerage*, new edn, 2.143–4, 14.88 · *Navy List* (1879)
Archives Glos. RO, priv. coll. · RS · Trustees of the Berkeley Castle muniments, corresp. and notebooks | MHS Oxf., corresp. with Frederick Jervis-Smith and letter-book · Nuffield Oxf., corresp. with Lord Cherwell
Likenesses W. Stoneman, photograph, 1939, NPG · W. Orpen, oils, Berkeley Castle, Gloucestershire · A. Rosenkrantz, portrait, Berkeley Castle, Gloucestershire · photograph, repro. in Hartley, *Obits. FRS*
Wealth at death £361,877 1s. 0d.: probate, 1942, Wales

Berkeley, Sir Robert de (*d.* 1220), baron, the eldest of the six sons of Maurice de Berkeley, on his father's death in 1190 paid to the king a fine of £1000, for livery of his inheritance, and to King John in 1199 a further 60 marks for confirmation of his title and a charter of fairs in his manor of Berkeley. In 1208 he was a justice on eyre at Derby.

Berkeley took a leading part in the struggle between John and the barons, and, after he had been included in the excommunication of the barons pronounced by Innocent III, Berkeley Castle and his other estates were seized. In 1216, however, shortly before John died, he visited the king, then at Berkeley Castle, under a safe conduct, and made his submission. The manor of Cam in Gloucestershire was then granted him for the support of his wife, Juliana, daughter of Robert de Pont de l'Arche and Maud, sister of William (I) Marshal, earl of Pembroke. In 1216, on Henry's accession, he was restored to his lands on payment of a fine of £966 13s. 4d., with the exception of the castle and lands of Berkeley.

In 1218 Berkeley married as his second wife Lucy, whose family is not known. He had no children with either wife.

Berkeley died on 13 May 1220, still dispossessed of his Berkeley *caput*, and was buried in a monk's cowl in the north aisle of St Augustine's Abbey, Bristol (now Bristol Cathedral), of which, along with Bradenstoke in Wiltshire, Stanley Priory in Gloucestershire, and the canons of Hereford, he had been a benefactor. He was succeeded by his brother Thomas, to whom Berkeley Castle was restored. His widow married Hugh de Gurney, and after her death she too was buried at St Augustine's. In addition to his religious benefactions Berkeley founded St Katherine's Hospital, Bedminster, near Bristol, as an Augustinian priory for a warden and poor brethren, and two chantries elsewhere.

Robert de Berkeley stands near the head of one of the most enduring lineages in the history of the English nobility. He and his immediate successors enjoyed baronial status, while all the lords of Berkeley from Thomas (*d.* 1321) received individual summonses to parliament, although the continuous history of the barony of Berkeley in the parliamentary peerage is usually reckoned to begin only with James *Berkeley, Baron Berkeley (*c.*1394–1463). James's son William *Berkeley (1426–1492) was created marquess of Berkeley by Henry VII, in an arrangement which seriously impoverished his family. That title died with him, however, and his successors remained Barons Berkeley until George *Berkeley (1626/7–1698), the ninth baron, was created earl of Berkeley in 1679. Uncertainties over the marital arrangements of the fifth earl, Frederick Augustus (*d.* 1810), resulted in extended litigation in the House of Lords, and in the creation successively of an earldom and a barony of Fitzhardinge (titles named from Robert de Berkeley's grandfather, *Robert fitz Harding) for two of the fifth earl's illegitimate sons, before the sequence of earls of Berkeley continued with the grandson of their father's younger brother. The eighth and last earl, Randal *Berkeley, died in 1942, but the barony of Berkeley has continued in the descendants of the fifth earl's heir general.

J. A. HAMILTON, *rev.* NIGEL SAUL

Sources J. Smyth, *Lives of the Berkeleys* (1883), vol. 1 of *The Berkeley manuscripts*, ed. J. Maclean (1883–5) · GEC, *Peerage*

Berkeley, Sir Robert (1584–1656), judge, was born in the parish of St Martin's, Worcester, on 26 July 1584, the second son of Roland Berkeley (1548–1611) and his wife, Catherine Heywood (*d.* 1629). There were sixteen children in

Sir Robert Berkeley (1584–1656), by George Powle (after unknown artist, 1633)

the family, of whom all but one reached adulthood, and Berkeley's father, a clothier, was sufficiently wealthy not only to provide an inheritance for his eldest son but also to leave Robert an estate at Spetchley, to the east of Worcester.

Berkeley entered the Middle Temple on 5 February 1601 and was called to the bar on 6 May 1608. While establishing himself in his profession, he continued to play an active role in the affairs of Worcester, being elected sheriff for the county in 1613, two years before his elder brother. From about this date until at least 1637 he was a justice of the peace for the county. He served as recorder of Worcester in 1621 and 1623, and was appointed to the council of the marches of Wales, which included Worcestershire in its jurisdiction, in 1623. He was elected MP for Worcester in 1621 and 1624. In 1637 he was placed on the commission to compensate those whose interests had been affected by a scheme to improve the navigability of the Avon.

Berkeley was meanwhile rising in the legal world. He became a bencher of his inn on 18 November 1625 and was reader for autumn 1626, choosing the topic of 'conditions'. On 28 February 1627 he was made a serjeant-at-law, then the highest order of counsel at the bar. The rings which, as was customary, he gave to his colleagues on this occasion are said to have borne the inscription *Lege, Deus & Rex* ('God and the king through law'). He was made a king's serjeant on 12 April 1627, and was knighted two days later. It was probably at about this time that he married Elizabeth (*b.* in or before 1612), daughter of Thomas Conyers of East Barnet; through her inheritance he acquired Church Hill House in East Barnet, later known as Trevor House.

The dissolution of parliament in 1629 was followed by the arrest of several MPs who had opposed Charles I, and Berkeley was one of the counsel for the king when habeas corpus proceedings were brought on their behalf. He achieved judicial rank when he was appointed a justice of the court of king's bench on 11 October 1632. In the following year he was made a commissioner for ecclesiastical causes in the province of Canterbury.

As a judge, Berkeley's duties included hearing cases at assizes. He rode the Norfolk circuit in the winters of 1633 and 1635; in summer 1635 and 1636 he covered the northern circuit, and he was on the midland circuit in 1639. The annoyances of circuit life are glimpsed in an incident in 1636 when Berkeley and his colleague Sir George Vernon took the economical hospitality provided by the sheriff of Lancashire as a deliberate insult, and proceeded to make his life difficult for the remainder of his year in office.

Meanwhile, opposition was increasing to the attempts of Charles I to raise money by means which did not require parliamentary approval, one of which was ship money. The payment of this duty by maritime counties was not new, but became widely unpopular when, in August 1635, it was extended to counties inland. Berkeley supported the charge on the two occasions, in 1635 and 1637, when the king asked the judges for their extrajudicial opinion as to its legality. In 1636 Richard Chambers, a London merchant with a history of opposition to the king's taxation policy, tried to raise the issue in the courts. The case came before Berkeley, who refused to hear it, saying that 'many things which might not be done by the rule of law might be done by the rule of government' (J. Rushworth, *Historical Collections*, 1721–2, 2.323–4). It was not long before a test case was brought, when in May 1637 John Hampden was cited to show why he should not pay his assessment of 20*s*. The case was heard in the court of exchequer chamber by all twelve judges, who delivered their judgments at intervals during the first half of 1638.

In his judgment, Berkeley fully accepted that the king had no right to impose taxes for ordinary purposes without the consent of parliament, 'If that were made the question, it is questionless, That he may not.—The people of the kingdom are subjects, not slaves, freemen, not villains [*sic*], to be taxed *de alto et basso*' (*State trials*, 3.1090). The last sentence was quoted by Sir Richard Hutton in his own judgment, and so has sometimes been attributed to him. Nevertheless, Berkeley betrayed a certain suspicion of parliament, suggesting that some members of recent parliaments had pursued 'sinister ends' (ibid., 1101). He endorsed the view that ship money was not a tax but a payment due in lieu of the service of building and equipping a ship. The king had a duty to make provision for the safety of the kingdom, and if he judged a danger to be imminent he had right to claim such a service from his subjects, without the delay and risk involved in recalling parliament,

> The law knows no such king-yoking policy. The law is … his instrument or means which he useth to govern his people by.—I never read nor heard, that *Lex* was *Rex*; but it is

common and most true, that *Rex* is *Lex*, for he is '*lex loquens*', a living, a speaking, an acting law. (ibid., 1098)

The judges found in favour of the king by a majority of seven to five, but refusal to pay continued to be widespread. Worcestershire, however, was relatively co-operative, perhaps through Berkeley's influence. Although such money as was collected was genuinely used for the purposes for which it was intended, there was a public perception that if ship money were accepted as a legal charge the king might declare an 'emergency' whenever he was short of funds, and so evade parliament. When the king was at last forced by events to summon parliament in 1640, it was not long before ship money and the judges who had ruled in favour of it were attacked. Impeachment proceedings were begun against all the surviving judges who had declared the duty to be legal, and in December 1640 they were bound in £10,000 each to answer the charges which were being prepared against them. They were also questioned as to whether Chief Justice Finch had tried to influence their decisions. Berkeley replied that only Croke, the strongest opponent of ship money, had been subjected to pressure.

On 13 February 1641, as Berkeley was sitting in the court of king's bench, he was seized by the usher of the black rod and carried off to prison. Articles of impeachment against him were presented to parliament on 6 July. Most of the eleven charges related to ship money, but a number of lesser issues were included. Among the matters alleged were suppression of evidence in favour of the independent soap-makers in their dispute with the official company, and support for Laudian clergy in cases at the Norwich assizes and Hertfordshire quarter sessions.

A statute declaring that ship money was not, and never had been, legal was passed in August 1641. Berkeley's trial, however, was repeatedly deferred. In the autumn of 1642 it was found that no judges were available to sit in the court of king's bench, and it was therefore agreed that he should temporarily resume his judicial functions. Berkeley behaved throughout with dignity and a degree of courage, and the proceedings against him do not seem to have been based on any animus against him as an individual. He was eventually brought to trial before the House of Lords on 8 September 1643. By this time the charges had been reduced to three, all relating to his rulings on ship money. He replied, surely with some irony, that 'he gave Judgement therein as he conceived the Law to be; but since he is enlight[en]ed by the Votes of both Houses of Parliament' (*JHL*, 6.209–10). Berkeley's sentence was given on 12 September. He was to be fined £20,000, disabled from holding office, and imprisoned during pleasure. However, as parliament was in urgent need of money, the imprisonment and half the fine were waived for prompt payment, the money being sent to support the western forces.

Berkeley retired to his home in Spetchley, but was not entirely able to escape the upheavals of the civil war. In 1651, shortly before the battle of Worcester, his house was burnt down by Scots from the royalist army. No doubt their objective was to prevent Cromwell using the building when he established his headquarters at Spetchley on 30 August, but they took the opportunity to do some looting on their own account. Berkeley took this misfortune stoically, and converted the stables into a residence. A deeper cause of distress was the conversion of his son, Thomas, to Catholicism, while in exile in Belgium. A partial reconciliation was eventually achieved, but on his death he left the Spetchley estate to his grandson, having made provision for Thomas by a separate settlement. Berkeley also had three daughters, from one of whom he seems to have become estranged, since she was left no money for mourning in his will.

Berkeley died on 5 August 1656. He was buried in Spetchley church, where he had previously erected a memorial to his parents, with a handsome monument incorporating his full-length effigy. He was remembered with gratitude in Worcester for contributing to the repairs to St Martin's Church in 1616, and for a small charity which he established. He is also said to have provided the money for the bell, known as Berkeley's bell, installed there in 1640. He was not, however, the founder of Berkeley's Hospital in Worcester, which was established by his grandson; neither, as is sometimes claimed, was he the owner of the house in Worcester known as King Charles's House.

Bulstrode Whitelock, writing from the puritan viewpoint, described Berkeley as 'a very learned Man in our Laws, and a good Orator and Judge, moderate in his ways; except his desires of the Court-favour' (*Memorials of the English Affairs*, 1732, 40 [41]). Although he was undoubtedly a strong royalist, there is no reason to suppose that his ship money judgment did not proceed from genuine conviction. He did his duty as he saw it, and made a significant contribution to the public life of the period, both nationally and in his native county.

SHEILA DOYLE

Sources *State trials*, 3.235–94, 825–1316 · W. R. Williams, *The parliamentary history of the county of Worcester* (1897), 94–5 · R. I. Nobel, 'Lions or jackals? The independence of the judges in Rex v. Hampden', *Stanford Law Review*, 14 (1962), 711–61 · D. L. Keir, 'The case of ship money', *Law Quarterly Review*, 52 (1936), 546–74 · T. Nash, *Collections for the history of Worcestershire*, 2 (1781–2), 358–61 · *VCH Worcestershire*, 3.511, 513–14, 525–7, 554; 4.104, 393 · *VCH Hertfordshire*, 2.338 · J. S. Cockburn, *A history of English assizes, 1558–1714* (1972), 271–2 · B. W. Quintrell, ed., *Proceedings of the Lancashire justices of the peace at the sheriff's table during assizes week, 1578–1694* (1981), 45 · D. Lloyd, *Memoires of the lives … of those … personages that suffered … for the protestant religion* (1668), 93–7 · Clarendon, *Hist. rebellion*, 3.209–10 · *CSP dom.*, 1644, 3–4 · will, PRO, PROB 11/258, sig. 324 · V. Green, *The history and antiquities of the city and suburbs of Worcester*, 2 (1796), 61, n. 1 · W. J. Jones, 'Berkeley, Robert', HoP, *Commons, 1558–1603*, 1.433 · C. H. Hopwood, ed., *Minutes of parliament of the Middle Temple* (1904–5), vol. 1, p. 410; vol. 2, p. 491

Archives BL, opinion in a law case, Add. MS 6672 · CUL · Harvard U., law school, MS 90 | BL, letter to J. Smyth, Add. MS 33588 · Inner Temple, London, MS Misc. 89

Likenesses Hollar, print, BL, Add. MS 32348 · G. Powle, etching (after unknown artist, 1633), BM, NPG [*see illus.*] · memorial effigy, Spetchley church, Worcestershire; repro. in Nash, *Collections*, before 361

Wealth at death £755 in legacies; estate at Spetchley, Worcestershire: will, PRO, PROB 11/258, sig. 324 · other Worcester property settled during lifetime

Berkeley, Robert (1713–1804), political writer, was the son of Thomas Berkeley of Spetchley Park, Worcestershire, and Mary Davis, of Clytha, Monmouthshire. He was the author of *Considerations on the Oath of Supremacy* and *Considerations on the Declaration Against Transubstantiation*, both addressed to Josiah Tucker, dean of Gloucester, with whom he had a regular and friendly correspondence. Berkeley's chaplain, Thomas Phillips, wrote his celebrated *History of the Life of Cardinal Pole* (1764) while at Spetchley. It is presumed that Berkeley himself published several other works, and that the Roman Catholic nobility and gentry were principally stimulated by him to petition the king in 1778. This was followed in May and June 1778 by the passage of Savile's Catholic Relief Bill.

Berkeley married first Anne Wyborne, of Flixton, Suffolk; secondly, Catharine, daughter of Thomas Fitzherbert, of Swinnerton, Staffordshire; and thirdly, Elizabeth, daughter of Peter Parry, of Twysog, in Denbighshire. Dying without children on 20 December 1804, he was succeeded in the family estates by his nephew, Robert Berkeley, of Spetchley.

THOMPSON COOPER, rev. PHILIP CARTER

Sources Burke, *Gen. GB* · J. Chambers, *Biographical illustrations of Worcestershire* (1820)

Berkeley, Walter of (d. c.1193), administrator, was one of a number of Anglo-Norman knights from south-west England who went to seek their fortunes in Scotland during the middle decades of the twelfth century. His parentage is unknown, but he was almost certainly named after the village of Berkley, near Frome, in Somerset. He arrived in Scotland with his brother Robert c.1165, immediately entered royal service, and was appointed to succeed Philip de Valognes as chief chamberlain of William the Lion c.1171. He held this office until his death, when it reverted to his predecessor. Walter of Berkeley was regularly at King William's court before and after his appointment, but almost nothing is known in detail about his important financial functions as chamberlain. Robert, who became lord of Maxton, Roxburghshire, probably by marriage to a native heiress, also frequently attended on William the Lion, often at Walter's side. Walter fought in William's campaigns against northern England in 1173–4, and in December 1174 was named among the twenty earls and barons of Scotland required to find hostages under the treaty of Falaise.

Royal favour had by 1182 brought Berkeley sizeable estates to be held for knight-service, most notably Inverkeilor, Angus, later the barony of Redcastle, and Newton, near Hawick, later the barony of Chamberlain Newton. Robert of London, a kinsman from Somerset, gave him property at St Boswells and the land of Plenmeller, near Haltwhistle, in the Scots king's liberty of Tynedale. Walter carried Scottish royal influence into the semi-independent province of Galloway, where he was endowed with the large lordship of Urr by Uhtred, son of Fergus, c.1170 and very likely built Urr's great motte-and-bailey castle, the most impressive of all surviving Scottish earthworks of this type. He was a benefactor of the Tironensian monks of Arbroath Abbey, and was reconciled shortly before his death with the Cistercian abbey of Holm Cultram, Cumberland, part of whose territory in Galloway he had engrossed. It is possible, though by no means certain, that he married first an unidentified lady who was the heir of Ardoyne, Aberdeenshire. Walter's (second?) wife, Eve, may have been a daughter of his patron Uhtred, lord of Galloway. She was subsequently married to Robert de Quincy, justiciar of Lothian, after whose death c.1200 she purchased land at Stenton, Haddingtonshire, and granted it to Melrose Abbey for the salvation of the souls of her two husbands and of her brother, Roland, perhaps Uhtred's son and successor of that name.

Walter and Eve had a son called John who must have died young, and Walter was succeeded by two daughters. Of these, Agatha surrendered her claims to Ardoyne in return for land in Laurencekirk, Mearns, after her marriage by c.1190 to Humphrey, son of Theobald de Adeville (probably Addeville, near St Lô, in Normandy). Humphrey took the surname of Berkeley, and from them descend nearly all the Scottish Barclays. The other daughter, of unknown name, carried Urr and Inverkeilor to her husband, Enguerrand de Balliol, probably a younger son of Eustace de Balliol (d. c.1208) of Bywell. The date of Walter's death is not recorded, but c.1193 can be inferred from the fact that his name then disappears from the witness-clauses of Scottish royal charters. KEITH STRINGER

Sources G. W. S. Barrow, *The Anglo-Norman era in Scottish history* (1980) · G. W. S. Barrow, ed., *Regesta regum Scottorum*, 2 (1971) · [C. Innes], ed., *Liber sancte Marie de Melros*, 2 vols., Bannatyne Club, 56 (1837) · A. C. Lawrie, ed., *Annals of the reigns of Malcolm and William, kings of Scotland* (1910) · G. W. S. Barrow, *The kingdom of the Scots: government, church and society from the eleventh to the fourteenth century* (1973) · R. C. Reid, 'The mote of Urr', *Transactions of the Dumfriesshire and Galloway Natural History and Antiquarian Society*, 3rd ser., 21 (1939), 11–27 · B. Hope-Taylor, 'Excavations at mote of Urr, interim report: 1951 season', *Transactions of the Dumfriesshire and Galloway Natural History and Antiquarian Society*, 3rd ser., 29 (1950–51), 167–72

Berkeley, William, marquess of Berkeley (1426–1492), magnate, the eldest son of James *Berkeley, first Baron Berkeley (d. 1463), and Isabel, widow of Henry Ferrers and daughter of Thomas (I) *Mowbray, duke of Norfolk, and Elizabeth Fitzalan, was born at Berkeley Castle. He accompanied Cardinal Beaufort to the peace negotiations at Calais in 1439, presumably as a member of his household, and was knighted shortly after his return. His adolescence was dominated by the great feud between the Berkeleys and the Talbots over the descent of the Lisle barony which Thomas, Lord Berkeley, had enjoyed in right of his wife and which had passed via his daughter Elizabeth to his three granddaughters, among whom the Berkeleys' most committed opponent was Margaret, wife of the first earl of Shrewsbury. In 1451 a settlement was reached which was very much in the Talbots' favour, and which included the requirement that William Berkeley should enter the household of the earl of Shrewsbury's son Lord Lisle as surety for his father's observance of the agreement. The dispute lapsed until the death of James, Lord Berkeley, in November 1463, but was reopened by William and came to a head in 1470 when Margaret's grandson and heir,

Thomas Talbot, Viscount Lisle, challenged Berkeley to battle during a period when royal authority had been defied by the rebellion of Warwick and Clarence. The challenge was accepted and the two forces met at Nibley Green, Gloucestershire, on 20 March, where Lisle was killed.

The costs which Berkeley incurred in pursuing the dispute made him vulnerable to royal pressure when the descent of the Mowbray duchy of Norfolk became an issue on the death of the last duke in January 1476, leaving a daughter, Anne, whom Edward IV chose as the wife for his second son, Richard. In May 1476, when the marriage was being planned but had not yet been effected, Berkeley agreed to surrender all his reversionary rights in the Mowbray inheritance to Prince Richard and his heirs, and, failing such heirs, to the king and his heirs male. In return Edward took over Berkeley's debts totalling £34,000. In April 1481, probably as an encouragement to make the formal conveyance of the inheritance, which he had not yet done, Berkeley was made a viscount. On 19 November 1481 Anne died, and her estates, instead of reverting to the heirs general, Berkeley and his cousin John, Lord Howard, were settled on her young widower.

On 28 June 1483, two days after his accession, Richard III, in response to a petition from Berkeley, cancelled the settlement and divided the Mowbray inheritance between Howard, who became duke of Norfolk, and Berkeley, who was made earl of Nottingham. It seems, however, to have been understood from the outset that Berkeley would make over his share to the king. The formal grant was not made until 23 October 1484, but the manors concerned were at Richard's disposal earlier in the reign. The agreement was voided by the king's death at Bosworth. Howard died in the same battle and the Mowbray title of earl marshal, which he had held, was granted by Henry VII to Berkeley during pleasure on 26 October 1485.

To the disgust of the family historian, who dubbed him 'William Waste-all', Berkeley, who was by now childless and likely to remain so, continued to use his lands to buy advancement under the new regime. On 19 February 1486 he granted William Stanley his share of the Mowbray lands in Wales and the march, presumably in return for Stanley's support in having the title of earl marshal made into a life grant on the same day. In December 1488 he granted the reversion of Berkeley itself to Henry VII should he die childless and was rewarded with the title of marquess the following month. Grants were made on similar terms to several of the king's courtiers, including Reynold Bray, Thomas Stanley, earl of Derby, Richard Willoughby, and Humphrey Talbot, and it was evidently at court where Berkeley now spent most of his time. In 1490 he leased a house in the sanctuary, Westminster, and lived there for the remainder of his life.

Berkeley married three times. His first wife, whom he married in 1466, was Elizabeth, daughter of Reynold West, Lord de la Warr, and Margaret, daughter of Robert Thorley. Berkeley repudiated her shortly afterwards, whereupon she appealed to Rome, but the dissolution was upheld and in November 1468 he married Joan, widow of

Sir William Willoughby and daughter of Sir Thomas Strangways and Katherine, daughter of Ralph Neville, earl of Westmorland. She died on 24 February 1485 and was buried in the Augustinian friary in London, where Berkeley himself was subsequently buried. His third wife was Anne, daughter of Sir John Fiennes, Lord Dacre, and Alice, daughter of Henry, Lord Fitzhugh. Berkeley died on 14 February 1492. His widow married Sir Thomas Brandon; she died on 10 September 1497 and was buried in St George's Chapel, Windsor. Berkeley had two children with Joan: Katherine and Thomas (*b.* 1470). Both died in 1475 or shortly afterwards, when negotiations were under way for Thomas's marriage to Mary, daughter of William Herbert, earl of Pembroke. Berkeley's heir was thus his brother Maurice. The two brothers had apparently been allies in 1470, when Maurice was granted an annuity for his support at Nibley Green, but Berkeley's land transactions from 1476 onwards were all at Maurice's expense, who inherited nothing at his brother's death. Only with the end of the male Tudor line at the death of Edward VI were the Berkeleys able to regain some of their alienated estates.

ROSEMARY HORROX

Sources *Chancery records* · *RotP* · GEC, *Peerage* · J. Smyth, *The Berkeley manuscripts: the lives of the Berkeleys … 1066 to 1618*, ed. J. Maclean, 3 vols. (1883–5) · R. Horrox and P. W. Hammond, eds., *British Library Harleian manuscript 433*, 4 vols. (1979–83) · A. Crawford, 'The Mowbray inheritance', *Richard III: crown and people*, ed. J. Petre (1985), 79–85 · R. A. Griffiths, *The reign of King Henry VI: the exercise of royal authority, 1422–1461* (1981) · PRO, PROB 11/9, fol. 88

Archives Glos. RO, Berkeley muniments | Glos. RO, letters to Viscount Lisle [copies]

Berkeley, Sir William (1605–1677), colonial governor, was born at Hanworth Manor, Middlesex, the son of Sir Maurice Berkeley (1576/7–1617) and Elizabeth Berkeley (*née* Killigrew; *d.* 1626), and brother of Charles *Berkeley, second Viscount Fitzhardinge of Berehaven (1599–1668), and of John *Berkeley, first Baron Berkeley of Stratton (*bap.* 1607, *d.* 1678). He attended grammar school and graduated BA from St Edmund Hall, Oxford, in 1626 and proceeded MA from Merton College in 1629. He entered the Middle Temple in 1627 before touring the continent. In 1632 he secured an appointment to the privy chamber of Charles I, which led to his association with a court literary circle known as 'the Wits', and to social connections that stood him well for the rest of his life. He wrote several plays, one of which—*The Lost Lady, a Tragi-Comedy* (1638)—was performed for Charles I and Henrietta Maria.

Service in the first and second bishops' wars (1639–40) won Berkeley a knighthood in 1639 even as it disillusioned him about the wisdom of royal policies. In the spring of 1641 he concluded that his usefulness at court was at an end and turned elsewhere for preferment. He toyed with the idea of moving to Constantinople, but abruptly decided that settling in Virginia held better prospects and in August 1641 purchased the office of governor from the incumbent, Sir Francis Wyatt. Thus began a transformation similar to those of other English immigrants who went out to the colony in search of personal fulfilment.

Berkeley landed at Jamestown in 1642 and set about

joining the ranks of the colony's planter élite. He acquired land west of Jamestown, where he built Green Spring House and conducted numerous agricultural trials as he searched for substitutes for tobacco and markets for them. Within five years he was exporting rice, spirits, fruits, silk, flax, and potash through an extensive network of commercial contacts. He also immersed himself in real estate development and the American Indian trade, which led to his interest in developing Jamestown and discovering land beyond the Virginia frontiers. By 1650 he was married as well. However, the identity of that wife and the duration of their marriage remain mysteries. Berkeley deepened his devotion to the colony. He became its chief promoter and saw its future prosperity as lying hand-in-hand with freedom from London's direction. Autonomy would enable it to thrive as a deferential, closely knit community with a diversified economy that was linked to free markets around the Atlantic rim. Such a Virginia, he thought, would benefit England and also profit him.

That thinking conformed to Berkeley's general view of government. He inherited a troubled colony in troubled times, and, as he quickly realized, he was largely on his own. His survival depended upon his ability to navigate between rival factions of Virginians while carrying out the king's commands. He plotted his course with a deftness that belied his inexperience of governing and determined to win leading planters by making common cause with them. To that purpose, he staunchly avowed Virginia's loyalty to the Stuarts after Charles I perished on the block. He put on a bold show when the parliamentarians came to subdue the colony but drew back at spilling blood and surrendered his government on 12 March 1652. Thereby he won terms that left Virginia's social and political establishment intact and largely free of outside meddling. He also favoured leading planters with lands and offices. His willingness to share power enabled the general assembly to grow into a miniature parliament, whereas he abetted a decentralization of authority between province and county and all but guaranteed an élite few an unlimited right of local rule.

The sudden death of Governor Samuel Mathews jun. in January 1660 opened the door to Berkeley's own restoration. Resuming his former place, he also resumed his designs for Virginia, which the interregnum had interrupted. Now, however, he realized they could not work without the financial backing of Charles II. Confident of his talents for persuasion and the logic of his arguments, he returned to England in 1661 in search of royal sanction for his schemes. Assured of a ready hearing at court and a seat on the newly created Council for Foreign Plantations, he lobbied publicly and privately for almost a year, drawing up at one point his *Discourse and View of Virginia*, which put forth prescriptions for Virginia's improvements. Charles II affirmed the concept of agricultural diversification and warmed to the possibility of limiting tobacco, but he refused any financial support. More critically, he rejected Berkeley's plea for free trade.

Berkeley sailed for Virginia in September 1662 steadfastly determined to implement his master's commandments but as he saw fit. That persistence was the first in a series of misjudgements and misfortunes that at last destroyed him. Diversification failed. Few of his fellow Virginians matched Berkeley's wealth, his technical competence, or his depth of commitment, and he could not convince the dubious to follow him. Their doubts only intensified as they paid the increased taxes that underwrote the effort. Diversification was largely abandoned in the late 1660s. As for the limitation on tobacco, Berkeley actually negotiated a so-called 'stint' which the proprietor of Maryland vetoed, while the crown eventually withdrew its tentative endorsement of the proposal.

Berkeley neither accepted nor acceded to Stuart imperialism, which he chose to ignore as far as possible. That misapprehension derived as much from misunderstanding as from arrogance. He appreciated none of the underpinnings of Restoration colonial policy. His experiences were not those of the architects of the navigation system. Then, too, the departure or demise of his friends at court left him few defenders in Whitehall by the 1670s. Charles II and his younger advisers owed him nothing, but they chose not to remove him until Nathaniel Bacon gave them a reason. The governor never reckoned for the loss of the Dutch trade, war with the Netherlands, the deterioration of peace with the Indians, the revival of proprietary land grants, or being undercut by the crown. Closure of foreign markets affected tobacco prices, whereas the Second and Third Anglo-Dutch wars jeopardized the welfare of Virginia in ways Berkeley was unable to forestall. He could slow, but not stop, the repeated frontier skirmishes that flared into open warfare in 1675. The renewed grant of much of northern Virginia to Henry Bennet, first earl of Arlington, and Thomas, second Baron Culpeper of Thoresway, threw certain land titles into question and caused Berkeley to mount an expensive effort to buy out the proprietors.

Berkeley turned peevish as he aged and the burdens of government bore heavier upon him. Poor health slowed him, making him rely upon a diminishing circle of intimates, especially his second wife, Frances Culpeper Stephens Berkeley, whom he wed in 1670. His method of governance failed to assure his goal of political harmony, and he was slow to punish the misrule of his favourites. Virginians who stood outside the reach of his bounty increasingly questioned his leadership, though none dared challenge him until disagreements over Indian policy drove Nathaniel Bacon to revolt.

The road to rebellion started in July 1675, when a party of Indians attacked an outlying plantation. On its face the incursion differed little from similar sporadic incidents that had been part of frontier existence for decades. However, this raid set off a series of murderous strokes and counter-strokes that quickly incited frontier colonists. Berkeley failed to discern the gravity of the situation, and by the spring of 1676 his authority was seriously undermined. A further challenge to public order came in April, when Nathaniel Bacon took command of an illegally assembled force of volunteer Indian fighters. Bacon ignored the governor's admonition against leading the volunteers. Angered by Bacon's indifference, Berkeley led a force of men and tried to head off his rash kinsman, but Bacon gave him the slip, and he returned to Jamestown still in a fury. He realized for the first time the precariousness of his situation and tried to regain his authority. He proclaimed Bacon a rebel, dissolved the general assembly, circulated a remonstrance, which justified his dealings with Bacon, and vowed to redress whatever grievances the voters had with him. Even so he seemed to doubt his faculties for controlling events because just two days before the new assembly convened, he asked his superiors to replace him.

The general assembly opened on 5 June 1676, amid fears of what would happen next. Voters returned Bacon as one of their burgesses, but there were uncertainties about his taking his seat. Those doubts were resolved following Bacon's capture, pardon, and subsequent return to his plantation upriver from Jamestown. Bacon was not present for the bulk of the session, during which the burgesses and councillors laid plans for taking the fight to the natives and addressed a variety of voter complaints. Just as the assembly completed its business, Bacon suddenly marched into the capital with 500 armed men and extorted a general's commission from the terrified legislators, whereupon he marched off to war on the Indians.

Now the contest between Berkeley and Bacon became a duel to the death over who would control Virginia. Berkeley again proclaimed his enemy a rebel and tried to catch him. He got little support and fled to a refuge across Chesapeake Bay when Bacon doubled back on him. At that juncture the rebel tried to establish his command of the colony. He publicly denounced Berkeley and played for popular support even as he sent a flotilla of ships across Chesapeake Bay to dislodge Sir William from his stronghold. Then he again marched off in search of Indians, though the only foe he found was a band of defenceless tributaries, which he easily scattered. Berkeley captured the men Bacon sent against him and regained his capital but, fresh from his 'victory', Bacon drove Berkeley from Jamestown, which he torched. His triumph was short-lived because sudden illness took him off and his death all but ended the rebellion.

News of the insurrection compelled the crown to dispatch troops, ships, and a commission to put down Bacon and to investigate the causes of the disturbances. One of those commissioners, Colonel Herbert Jeffreys, carried orders to supplant Berkeley. The rebellion ended before the force arrived in America, while the commission and the governor clashed. Berkeley gave way and in May 1677 he sailed across the ocean for the last time. Sick, and weakened by the crossing, he landed in London a broken man. The old governor had but one desire, which was to clear his name. There was no opportunity. He died on 9 July 1677 and was buried on 13 July at St Mary the Virgin, Twickenham.

Sir William Berkeley quit England for a chance at a new beginning in America. He reinvented himself into a Virginian, meaning that his colonial experiences soon gave greater definition to his character and existence than his English origins. Being governor uniquely allowed him to mark Virginia as others could not. That impression was both his accomplishment and his failure.

WARREN M. BILLINGS

Sources W. M. Billings, ed., *The papers of Sir William Berkeley, 1605–1677* [forthcoming] · R. C. Bald, 'Sir William Berkeley's *The lost lady*', *The Library*, 4th ser., 17 (1936–7), 395–426 · R. Beverley, *The history and present state of Virginia*, ed. L. B. Wright (1947) · W. M. Billings, 'The causes of Bacon's rebellion: some suggestions', *Virginia Magazine of History and Biography*, 78 (1970), 409–35 · W. M. Billings, 'Berkeley and Effingham: who cares?', *Virginia Magazine of History and Biography*, 97 (1989), 33–47 · W. M. Billings, 'Imagining Green Spring House', *Virginia Cavalcade*, 44 (1994), 84–94 · W. M. Billings, 'Sir William Berkeley and the Carolina proprietary', *North Carolina Historical Review*, 72 (1995), 329–43 · W. M. Billings, 'Sir William Berkeley and the diversification of the Virginia economy', *Virginia Magazine of History and Biography*, 104 (1996), 433–55 · W. M. Billings, 'The return of Sir William Berkeley', *Virginia Cavalcade*, 47 (1998), 100–10 · W. M. Billings, 'Sir William Berkeley', *Dictionary of Virginia*, ed. J. T. Kneebone, B. Tarter, and S. G. Treadway (1998), 1.454–8 · W. M. Billings, J. E. Selby, and T. W. Tate, *Colonial Virginia: a history* (1986) · J. Carson, *Bacon's rebellion, 1676–1976* (1976) · L. R. Caywood, *Green Spring plantation: archaeological report* (1955) · W. F. Craven, *The southern colonies in the seventeenth century, 1606–1689* (1949) · E. S. Morgan, *American slavery, American freedom: the ordeal of colonial Virginia* (1975) · R. L. Morton, *Colonial Virginia*, 2 vols. (1960) · W. E. Washburn, *The governor and the rebel: a history of Bacon's rebellion in Virginia* (1957) · S. S. Webb, *1676: the end of American independence* (1984) · T. J. Wertenbaker, *Virginia under the Stuarts* (1914) · T. J. Wertenbaker, *Torchbearer of the revolution: the story of Bacon's rebellion and its leader* (1940) · parish register, Twickenham, St Mary the Virgin, 13 July 1677 [burial]

Archives University of Virginia, Charlottesville, corresp. and papers relating to Bacon's rebellion | Hunt. L., letters to William Blathwayt

Likenesses P. Lely, oils, *c*.1661, Berkeley Castle, Gloucestershire · P. Lely, oils, *c*.1666, NMM · H. L. Montague, portraits, 1907 (after *Stratford portrait*) · portrait (*Stratford portrait*), priv. coll. · portrait (after portrait, now lost), North Carolina Department of Archives and History, Raleigh

Wealth at death wealthiest man in Virginia in his day; 17,000 acres of Virginia land; largest stately house in seventeenth-century Virginia; owned eighth share in the Carolina Proprietary; suffered losses of £10,000 through plundering during Bacon's rebellion

Berkeley, Sir William (1639–1666), naval officer, was the third son of Charles *Berkeley, second Viscount Fitzhardinge of Berehaven (1599–1668) of Bruton, Somerset, treasurer of the household to Charles II, and his wife, Penelope Godolphin (*d.* 1689). William Berkeley became lieutenant of the *Swiftsure* on 4 April 1661, serving aboard her until April 1662. Despite his inexperience, his subsequent promotion was rapid. He was captain of the *Assistance* from April to August 1662, then successively of the *Bonadventure*, *Bristol*, and *Resolution* before the outbreak of the Second Anglo-Dutch War. Regardless of his own merits, his rise was due primarily to the influence of two powerful patrons. His brother Charles *Berkeley, successively Lord Fitzhardinge and earl of Falmouth, was one of the closest friends of both the king and James, duke of York, the lord high admiral, and worked actively to advance Berkeley's

Sir William Berkeley (1639–1666), by Sir Peter Lely, c.1665–6

career. Sir John Lawson, the admiral commanding the Mediterranean Fleet in which Berkeley served from 1661 to 1664, saw the advancement of the young man as a means of enhancing his own connections at court. Berkeley's meteoric rise culminated in a knighthood on 12 October 1664 and his appointment as rear-admiral of the red squadron for the 1665 campaign, flying his flag in the *Swiftsure*. However, his conduct at the battle of Lowestoft on 3 June 1665 was called into question—it was alleged that he withdrew from the action after his brother's death, a charge enshrined by Marvell in the caustic verse:

Berkeley had heard it soon, and thought not good
To venture more of royal Harding's blood …
With his whole squadron straight away he bore,
And, like good boy, promised to fight no more.
(*The Second Advice to a Painter*, 1666)

Pepys observed 'it is strange to see how people do already slight Sir Wm. Berkeley … who three months since was the delight of the Court' (Pepys, *Diary*, 6.129). Despite the duke of York's apparent vote of confidence in appointing him vice-admiral of the white, he was subsequently implicated in the irregular plundering of prize goods from captured Dutch merchantmen, while Dutch sources suggest that the *Swiftsure* withdrew discreditably from an action with the *Luipaard* on 21 August 1665. Aware of these reflections on his conduct, he set out to prove himself in the 1666 campaign. Appointed vice-admiral of the blue, again in the *Swiftsure*, he led the van of the English fleet on the first day of the Four Days' Fight (1 June 1666), outran his squadron, and sailed too far into the Dutch fleet. He was killed and the *Swiftsure* taken. His embalmed body was put on public display in the Grote Kerk in The Hague before

being returned to England in August and buried in Westminster Abbey, where there is a monument to him. Despite the general opinion that Berkeley had died gallantly, Marvell and other rumour-mongers pursued him even in death:

And if the thing were true, yet paint it not,
How Berkeley (as he long deserved) was shot,
Though others that survey'd the corpse so clear
Say he was only petrified with fear.
(*The Third Advice to a Painter*, 1666)

Berkeley had never married, although in 1665 he proposed unsuccessfully to Sir John Lawson's daughter. He served as lieutenant-governor of Portsmouth in 1665–6, succeeding his brother Charles. He emerges from his letters as a lively, friendly young man, fully aware of his dependence on the patronage of others, supportive of and loving towards his family, and genuinely enthusiastic to make a success of his chosen career—an enthusiasm which eventually killed him. As he wrote to Charles Berkeley in June 1663:

I must assure you I think there is no so beggarly a trade as this if people serve truly and honestly, as I am resolved I will do, although I am never worth six pence. All my hope is on my dearest brother's kindness. (Centre for Kentish Studies, Fitzharding MS U.269/C.298)

J. D. DAVIES

Sources C. H. Hartmann, *The king's friend* (1951) · CKS, Fitzharding papers, MS U.269/C.298 · J. R. Powell and E. K. Timings, eds., *The Rupert and Monck letter book, 1666*, Navy RS, 112 (1969) · *The Tangier papers of Samuel Pepys*, ed. E. Chappell, Navy RS, 73 (1935) · PRO, ADM 10/15, p. 12 · G. de F. Lord and others, eds., *Poems on affairs of state: Augustan satirical verse, 1660–1714*, 7 vols. (1963–75), vol. 1 · *CSP dom., 1661–6* · Pepys, *Diary* · R. C. Anderson, 'Sir William Berkeley', *Mariner's Mirror*, 24 (1938), 238–9 · PRO, Admiralty MSS · register of burials in Westminster Abbey
Archives CKS, Fitzharding papers, MS U.269/C.298
Likenesses P. Lely, oils, c.1665–1666, NMM [*see illus.*]

Berkenhead, William (*bap.* **1648**, *d.* **1701**), Jacobite spy, was apparently born at Northwich in Cheshire and baptized there in Witton Chapel on 3 April 1648. His parents were Randolph Berkenhead, the earl of Derby's bailiff in Northwich, and his wife, Elizabeth Harcourt, one of the Harcourts of Wincham, near Northwich. His uncle was Sir John *Birkenhead. The family were royalists and prospered after the Restoration. In February 1676 Berkenhead was given a job in the customs, first as a landwaiter at Southampton and then, in February 1688, as surveyor at Dover. While at Southampton he married, about 1678, Frances Harwood. They had four children, only one of whom, Elizabeth, survived into adulthood. Frances herself is reported as having been dead 'some years' by 1696 (*Memoirs of … Ailesbury*, 2.396).

After the revolution of 1688 Berkenhead, though protestant, remained loyal to James II and used his position at Dover to help the first Jacobites cross secretly to France. He was caught and dismissed in May 1690 but the earl of Ailesbury then gave him the more important task of handling Jacobite correspondence with St Germain and establishing a route by which Jacobite messages and travellers could pass safely between London and the continent. A farm on Romney Marsh in Kent, tenanted by James Hunt, was the main staging post on the route. From the end of 1692 Berkenhead was continually ranging over the English section of the route, conveying letters and escorting important Jacobite travellers. From about the same time he also worked for the French as a naval spy, receiving his instructions direct from navy minister Pontchartrain.

Three or four times a year Berkenhead visited St Germain, either on escort or courier duty or for consultations with his superiors at the exiled court. He met James, the deposed king, and his queen, Mary of Modena, on many occasions and was well known to Lord Melfort and his secretary David Nairne. When William III's Queen Mary died in December 1694 it was Berkenhead who conveyed the news to St Germain. Having served as captain of a troop of the Southampton trained band, Berkenhead was usually called Captain Berkenhead. He also had several aliases. The earliest was South, corresponding to Melfort's North. Afterwards he used East, West, Baker, and Fish, and latterly, from mid-1695 on, Steel. For his services St Germain paid him an annual salary of £100 plus expenses.

Over the winter of 1695–6 when a combined English Jacobite rising and French invasion was being planned, Berkenhead's charges included Sir George Barclay, whom James II had commissioned to raise the Jacobites, and the duke of Berwick, James II's illegitimate son, who came over to encourage the rebels. Barclay was also plotting to assassinate William III. During the crackdown following the discovery of this plot Berkenhead was arrested and imprisoned in Newgate in April 1696. He escaped at the end of August after inviting the keeper to supper and drugging his wine. Having made his way via the Romney Marsh farm to France, he returned with French sailors the next day, Saturday 30 October, and kidnapped Farmer Hunt, who had turned anti-Jacobite informer.

In France James rewarded the now-exiled Berkenhead by appointing him his clerk of the kitchen in February 1697. In April 1701 Berkenhead was accompanying James and Mary to the spa town of Bourbon-Lancy when he was taken ill at Montargis. Having been put to bed in the royal castle, he converted to Roman Catholicism and died shortly after, on 14 April 1701 NS; he was buried in the chapel of the town cemetery the following day.

ANDREW I. M. DUNCAN

Sources *Memoirs of Thomas, earl of Ailesbury*, ed. W. E. Buckley, 2 vols., Roxburghe Club, 122 (1890) • R. Blackmore, *A true and impartial history of the conspiracy* (1723) • *CSP dom.*, 1696–7 • P. Burger, 'Spymaster to Louis XIV: a study of the papers of the Abbé Eusèbe Renaudot', *Ideology and conspiracy: aspects of Jacobitism, 1689–1759*, ed. E. Cruickshanks (1982), 111–37 • D. Nairne, diary, NL Scot., MS 14266 • letter-book of Lord Melfort, June–Dec 1692, BL, Add. MS 37661 • J. Redington, ed., *Calendar of Treasury papers*, 1, PRO (1868) • *Calendar of the Stuart papers belonging to his majesty the king, preserved at Windsor Castle*, 7 vols., HMC, 56 (1902–23), vol. 1 • U. Nott. L., Portland MSS, PWA 2494 • W. A. Shaw, ed., *Calendar of treasury books*, 5, PRO (1911); 8–9 (1923–31) • J. Macpherson, ed., *Original papers: containing the secret history of Great Britain*, 2 vols. (1775) • Nairne MSS, Bodl. Oxf., MS Carte 208 • *Calendar of the manuscripts of the marquis of Bath preserved at Longleat, Wiltshire*, 5 vols., HMC, 58 (1904–80), vol. 3 • *Report on the manuscripts of his grace the duke of Buccleuch and Queensberry … preserved at Montagu House*, 3 vols. in 4, HMC, 45 (1899–1926), vol. 2 • N. Luttrell, *A brief historical relation of state affairs from September 1678 to April 1714*, 6 vols. (1857) • M. Hopkirk, *The queen over the water* (1953) • parish registers, Witton Chapel, Ches. & Chester ALSS, 3 April 1648 [baptism] • parish registers, Montargis, archives de Loiret, Orléans, France [burial] • G. D. Squibb, ed., *The visitation of Hampshire and the Isle of Wight, 1686*, Harleian Society, new ser., 10 (1991), 70–71 • E. Grew and M. S. Grew, *English court in exile: James II at St Germain* (1911) • F. Madan, ed., *Stuart papers relating chiefly to queen Mary of Modena and the exiled court of king James II* (1889) • P. W. Thomas, *Sir John Berkenhead, 1617–1679: a royalist career in politics and polemics* (1969) • M. Cox, *A history of Sir John Deane's grammar school, Northwich* (1975) • *The parish registers of Holy Rhood, Southampton* (1978) • J. Garrett, *The triumphs of providence: the assassination plot, 1696* (1980) • J. M. Kaye, ed., *A God's House miscellany* (1984), 113

Wealth at death   property (if any) forfeit to state

Berkenhout, John (1726–1791), physician and writer, was born in Leeds on 8 April 1726 and was educated at the grammar school there. His father, a merchant and native of the Netherlands, in order to train him for a commercial career, sent him at an early age to Germany, to learn foreign languages. After spending some years there Berkenhout accompanied some English noblemen on a tour through Europe. On returning to Germany he stayed in Berlin at the house of his father's relative, Baron de Bielfeld, a man distinguished in politics and literature. Finding commerce distasteful, Berkenhout became a cadet in a Prussian infantry regiment, where he was speedily promoted ensign, and afterwards captain. In 1756, war having been declared between England and France, he left the Prussian service, and received a commission with the English 24th regiment foot.

At the close of the war in 1760 Berkenhout entered Edinburgh University to study medicine. While a student at Edinburgh he published in 1762 his *Clavis Anglica linguae botanicae linnaei*; a second edition of this botanical lexicon appeared in 1764. From Edinburgh Berkenhout proceeded to the University of Leiden; he was entered on the register on 13 May 1765, and took the degree of doctor of physic on 25 May 1766. He composed for the occasion a 'Dissertatio medica inauguralis de podagra', which was dedicated on publication to Baron de Bielfeld. On his return to England Berkenhout settled at Isleworth in Middlesex, and in 1766 published his *Pharmacopoeia medici*. He may have practised for a time at Bury St Edmunds, and he certainly practised as a physician at the county hospital in Winchester in 1782, and at the general hospital in Bath in 1783.

In 1769 the first volume of Berkenhout's *Outlines of the Natural History of Great Britain* appeared; the second volume followed in 1770, and the third in 1771. A revised edition in two volumes appeared in 1788 under the title *A Synopsis of the Natural History of Great Britain*. His next publication was of William Cadogan's *Dissertation on the Gout, Examined and Refuted* (1771). Berkenhout is known mainly for his *Biographia literaria* (1777). In the preface he acknowledges his indebtedness to George Steevens, the Shakespearian commentator, who supplied him with information concerning the lives of the poets. Throughout the work Berkenhout loses no opportunity of displaying his hostility to all systems of dogmatic theology, and is loud in his praises of Voltaire. The first volume of *Biographia* extends to the end of the sixteenth century; the work was never continued.

In 1778 Berkenhout was sent by the government with some commissioners to America to make contact with Richard Lee, an influential congressman. Congress would not allow the visitors to proceed beyond New York, but Berkenhout contrived to reach Philadelphia. Here he stayed for about a week without interference by the authorities; but at length suspicion arose that he was meeting some of the leading citizens and he was thrown into prison. He was returned to British lines when nothing could be proved against him. He rejoined the commissioners at New York, returned to England, and was rewarded with a pension for his services. In 1780 he published *Lucubrations on Ways and Means, Inscribed to Lord North*, a proposal for the imposition of certain taxes. Some of the suggestions contained in this pamphlet were adopted by Lord North, others subsequently by Pitt.

Berkenhout's *Essay on the Bite of a Mad Dog* appeared in 1783 and his *Symptomatology* in 1784. His last work was *Letters on Education to his Son at the University* (1790). In the letters Berkenhout comments severely on the 'Gothic system' of fagging in public schools, and complains, but not unkindly, of the obstinate adherence of British universities to ancient customs. Berkenhout died on 3 April 1791 at Besselsleigh, near Oxford, where he had gone for a change of air. He was buried there three days later.

Berkenhout was a versatile man. His deep knowledge of natural history, botany, and chemistry was coupled with an extensive acquaintance with classical and modern literature. He was familiar with the French, German, Swedish, Dutch, and Italian languages, was a good mathematician, and is said to have been skilled in music and painting. In addition to the works already mentioned he published *A Treatise on Hysterical and Hypochondriacal Diseases* (1777). In 1779 he edited a fourth edition of John Campbell's *Lives of the Admirals*, continuing Campbell's own narrative from 1727 to 1778.

A. H. BULLEN, rev. CLAIRE L. NUTT

Sources 'An account of Dr John Berkenhout', *European Magazine and London Review*, 14 (1788), 155–6 · *GM*, 1st ser., 61 (1791), 388, 485 · E. Peacock, *Index to English speaking students who have graduated at Leyden University* (1883) · 'A British physician and government agent in the revolution', *Annals of Medical History*, 3rd ser., 3 (1941), 353–4 · R. Howell, 'John Berkenhout: a portrait of an eighteenth century physician', *The Practitioner*, 220 (1978), 162–5 · *IGI*
Archives U. Mich., Clements L., journal of an excursion from New York to Philadelphia
Likenesses J. Wright, oils, *c*.1756, priv. coll. · T. Holloway, line engraving (after his portrait), BM, NPG · portrait, repro. in 'An account of Dr John Berkenhout'

Berki, Robert Nandor (1936–1991), political scientist, was born on 12 July 1936 in Budapest, the only child of Ferdinand Berki (1898–1987), a bank clerk, and his wife, Anna (1904–1977), a bank secretary. He went to the Catholic Piarista Convent School in Budapest in 1941 and stayed there until 1952. He then worked in the land redistribution department of the Hungarian government, and left it more than a year later to study music at a music academy in Budapest. During his two years there he concentrated

initially on classical music and then on jazz, and learned to play timpani and drum. On leaving the academy he earned his living working as a petrol pump attendant during the day and as a drummer in jazz bands in the evening. When the revolution broke out in Hungary in 1956 he left the country after narrowly avoiding arrest. After a few weeks in a refugee camp in Vienna he arrived in Britain on 20 February 1957. He spent some time in a refugee centre outside London, and moved first to 7 Hereford Square, South Kensington, and then to 17 Rosenau Crescent in Battersea. During this period he worked as a dispatch clerk at Harrods and attended evening classes to improve his English and prepare for his O and A level examinations. He cleared the latter with top grades and joined the London School of Economics in 1961 as a full-time student, securing an outstanding first in international relations three years later. He proceeded to Cambridge University the same year and completed his doctorate in 1967 on the thought of Hegel and Marx, under the supervision of E. H. Carr.

Berki was appointed lecturer in the department of politics at the University of Hull in 1967, becoming senior lecturer in 1975, reader in 1982, and professor of European political and social theory and director of the Institute of European Studies in 1984. As director, one of his great achievements was to set up a new four-year degree in transnational integrated European studies, under which Hull students spent some time at selected universities in four European countries and acquired a truly European education and orientation. He also organized regular symposia and colloquia, which brought together eminent European scholars and placed Hull on the academic map of Europe. He wrote six books, co-edited three, and wrote more than a dozen major articles. His books included *Socialism* (1975), *The History of Political Thought* (1977), *On Political Realism* (1981), *Insight and Vision: the Problem of Communism in Marx's Thought* (1983), *Security and Society* (1986), and *The Genesis of Marxism* (1988). He was a reflective and meditative rather than an analytical and argumentative thinker, taking little interest in conceptual analysis and academic debates beyond the minimum necessary for his work. From the start of his academic career until the end of his life he remained deeply interested in Hegel, Marx, socialism, the best ways to combine the pursuits of order and justice, and the interplay between moral idealism and political realism.

Berki rebelled against the sombre image and lifestyle of *homo academicus* and freely indulged his dominant passions for jazz and football. He set up with like-minded colleagues a Don Beat Jazz group which provided excellent entertainment at departmental events and gave him the opportunity to display and sharpen his drumming skills. When once asked how his drumming fitted in with his philosophical preoccupation with the dialectic, he took a drumstick and said, 'Listen, you will hear the dialectic at work' (personal knowledge). Football was his other great interest. As a boy he was a keen supporter of Ferencváros in Budapest and he regarded his visit to its home ground nearly thirty years later as one of the great pleasures of his life. On arriving in Britain he developed an affection for Everton Football Club and later for Hull City, of which he remained an enthusiastic supporter until his death. The hour and a half during which a soccer match was shown on television every Saturday evening was the most sacred for him, which no telephone call or colleague was allowed to disturb and which was invariably accompanied by cheese sandwiches and total domestic silence.

Berki married Etelka Taph (*b.* 1934), a fellow Hungarian whom he had first met at a jazz club in Stalintown, about 30 miles from Budapest, on 3 August 1962, when he was just under half way through his undergraduate education. He gave her the name Micà (meaning a little pussy cat), and that is how she was known to their friends. They had two sons and a daughter, and a stepdaughter from Micà's first marriage to John Höller, whom she had divorced in 1959.

Berki was a tall and well-built man with a long and receding forehead and deep reflective eyes that occasionally betrayed touches of sadness and insecurity. He led a highly ordered life in which everything had its assigned place and whose routine was rarely allowed to be disturbed. He once remarked that there was something of a German civil servant in him. He was a deeply religious man who rarely missed his Sunday mass, and counted the local priest among his close friends. He had a strong sense of what was due to him and to others, and both demanded the former and readily conceded the latter. He was just as easily upset when others were late for a meeting with him as when he was, and apologized when late for being 'immoral by a few minutes' (personal knowledge). He was a warm and kind man, with a strong sense of duty to his students, colleagues, and the university. He was complex, not easy to get to know, but capable of deep and generous friendship with those who broke through his reserve and respected the order and rhythm of his life.

Berki was a strong family man. Deeply devoted to his parents, he got his mother to join him in Britain in 1964 and his father in 1970, and looked after both until their deaths. He was very fond of his stepdaughter, who lived with him until her marriage and was a regular visitor thereafter. He adored and was highly protective of his wife, who did not settle down in Britain as easily as he had. Like many first-generation migrants he was keen that his three children should become an integral part of British society without losing their cultural roots and language. Berki died of a brain haemorrhage in Hull on 17 September 1991, and was survived by his wife, stepdaughter, and three children. He was buried at Chanterland's Avenue cemetery, Hull, on 19 September.   BHIKHU PAREKH

Sources *The Independent* (19 Sept 1991) · *The Independent* (27 Sept 1991) · *The Times* (1 Oct 1991) · personal knowledge (2004) · private information (2004)
Likenesses photograph, repro. in *The Times*
Wealth at death under £125,000: administration, 1992

Berkley, James John (1819–1862), civil engineer, son of James Berkley of Hampstead Heath, was born on 21 October 1819 at Holloway, London. He completed his education at King's College, London, and, in 1836, was articled to Mr

Wicksteed, civil engineer. Soon, however, he entered the office of G. P. Bidder, civil engineer, and then, in 1839, that of Robert Stephenson. Much of Berkley's knowledge of engineering and subsequent professional opportunities came from his relationship with Stephenson whose secretary, assistant, and report writer he was, and whose trusted associate and good friend he became.

In the period from about 1842 to 1849 Berkley worked on a number of railway projects in England with which Stephenson was associated, notably the Northampton and Peterborough lines, and then the Churnet valley and Trent valley lines of the North Staffordshire Railway. It was, however, in 1849 that Berkley received the appointment upon which his fame rests: chief resident engineer (1849–62) of the Great Indian Peninsula Railway (GIPR). Berkley's successes in that demanding position place him among the major railway engineers of the mid-nineteenth century: a position he might have consolidated by future accomplishments had not the rigours of his work in a trying, disease ridden environment shortened his life.

Approval to construct the GIPR in western India was eventually given in August 1849. Berkley was appointed in December 1849 after strong recommendations from Stephenson, the company's consulting engineer, and other prominent engineers. He arrived at Bombay in February 1850 and remained in India until ill health obliged him to return to England in November 1855 on a six-month furlough during which, on 9 April 1856, he was fêted at a grand function in London chaired by Stephenson and attended by many leading engineers and other luminaries. Stephenson provided the main address in which he praised Berkley highly for his accomplishments in India. Arriving back in Bombay in May 1856, Berkley stayed in western India until April 1861 when serious ill health forced him back to England and to his early death.

Berkley did the detailed planning for the GIPR and he supervised, through the large contract system he advocated, its initial constructions and early operation, tasks that required all his considerable technical, administrative, and social skills—and, in the event, physical exertion beyond that which he could sustain, since, as his contemporaries observed, his energy of mind exceeded his physical stamina. The GIPR formally opened its first line, the first in India, Bombay to Thana, in April 1853. When Berkley left India in 1861 the GIPR had 340 miles of its sanctioned 1266 miles in operation and much of the rest under construction.

Berkley supervised and often personally conducted the surveys that established the routes for the south-eastern and north-eastern lines of the GIPR. These lines had to cross the formidable mountain range known as the Western Ghats whose rugged terrain and abrupt ascent separate the narrow west coast lowlands from the higher plateau of inland, peninsular India. Berkley's careful work over many surveying seasons established that the best routes for the railway inclines were to be found at the Bhore (south-eastern line) and Thal (north-eastern line) Ghats. Further work laid out the precise alignments—

detailed in over 3000 maps and drawings for the Bhore Ghat alone—by which ascents within the unaided tractive powers of mid-nineteenth century steam locomotives could be achieved. Planning and building these two great railway inclines were major accomplishments of mid-nineteenth century engineering. Construction of the inclines (Bhore, 1856–63; Thal 1858–65) involved tens of thousands of workers, high levels of mortality, and a cost of some £70,000 per mile. Berkley spent extended, health shattering periods at the construction sites.

During his years in Bombay, Berkley participated in educational and other activities. He was active in the mechanics' institution, serving as both its vice-president and its president, and giving lectures, subsequently published, on the progress of the GIPR. The government of Bombay appointed Berkley one of the founding fellows and member of the governing senate of the University of Bombay in 1857. He became a justice of the peace in 1855 and a commissioner of the Bombay municipal board in 1857.

Berkley was a fellow of the Royal Geographical Society. He was elected a full member of the Institution of Civil Engineers in December 1855 to which, in 1860, his paper describing railways in western India was read on his behalf. The paper, subsequently published in the institution's *Minutes of Proceedings*, gained for Berkley a Telford medal and premium. He died at his home, Lichfield House, Lawrie Park, Beckenham, Kent, on 25 August 1862. He was survived by his wife, Louisa, their two sons, daughters, and his brother, Sir George Berkley (1821–1893), a well-known civil engineer.

After his death many colleagues testified to Berkley's accomplishments and pleasant temperament. The GIPR board of directors praised him and funded a commemorative tablet to be erected at a conspicuous spot on the Bhore incline. A sum of £3000 raised privately from the GIPR staff and others provided for a substantial monument over Berkley's grave in Camberwell old cemetery, London, and for the establishment (1869) of the James Berkley gold medal presented annually to a top civil engineering student at the University of Bombay.   IAN J. KERR

Sources *PICE*, 22 (1862–3), 618–24 · *The Engineer* (12 Sept 1862) · *Herapath's Railway Journal* (6 Sept 1862) · copy of the will of James John Berkley and related material, BL OIOC, series and file L/AG/34/29/354 · J. J. Berkley, 'On Indian railways: with a description of the Great Indian Peninsular Railway', *PICE*, 19 (1859–60), 586–624 · *Bombay Government Gazette* (23 Aug 1855) · *Bombay Government Gazette* (8 Nov 1855) · *Bombay Government Gazette* (29 May 1856) · *Bombay Government Gazette* (23 April 1857) · J. J. Berkley, *An address delivered at the annual meeting of the Bombay Mechanics' Institution, in the town hall on Saturday, 11 April 1857* (1857) · 'East Indian railways: dinner to Mr. Berkley', *The Engineer* (25 April 1856) · I. J. Kerr, *Building the railways of the raj, 1850–1900* (1995) · minutes of the board of directors of the Great Indian Peninsula railway, BL OIOC, L/AG/46/12/3 and 12/7, 7 Dec 1849, 19 Sept 1862 · gravestone, Camberwell old cemetery, London · *The Bombay University Calendar for the Year 1871–72* (1871) · J. J. Berkley, *Paper on the Thul Ghaut railway incline: read at the Bombay Mechanics' Institution, in the town hall on Monday, 10 December 1860* (1861) · *Bombay Almanac and Year Book of Direction, for 1851* (1851) · *CGPLA Eng. & Wales* (1862) · d. cert. · school alumni records, King's Lond.

Archives BL OIOC, letters to A. A. West, MS Eur. D 1184/9

Likenesses photograph or painting, repro. in S. N. Sharma, *History of the Great Indian Peninsula Railway*, 1 (1990) · stone effigy (on monument), Camberwell old cemetery, London

Wealth at death under £30,000: resworn probate, Oct 1864, *CGPLA Eng. & Wales* (1862)

Berkshire. For this title name *see* Norris, Francis, earl of Berkshire (1579–1622); Howard, Henry, twelfth earl of Suffolk and fifth earl of Berkshire (1739–1779).

Berksted, Stephen. *See* Bersted, Stephen (*b.* before 1220, *d.* 1287).

Berlemont, Gaston Roger (1914–1999), publican, was born on 26 April 1914 in the Middlesex Hospital, London, the son of Victorien (Victor) Aimé Berlemont (*d.* 1951) and his wife, Victorine Marie Potbon. His father ran the Restaurant Européen in Dean Street, and at the outbreak of the First World War he bought the pub next door, then called the Wine House, from a German fearing internment. The Berlemonts were in fact Belgian, though it suited them (and later their son) to allow people to think they were French. Gaston was one of six children, and attended the nearby St Anne's School, attached to the local parish church, until he left at fourteen to help his parents run the pub.

The pub, officially called Victor Berlemont until Watneys acquired the freehold after the war and renamed it the York Minster, was universally known as 'the French pub', or just 'the French'. It was an important part of Soho life from the 1920s, when Soho was almost a French *quartier* and the clientele included Edith Piaf, the boxer Georges Carpentier, and the ladies of the night known as *Fifis*. Prostitutes always made up a considerable portion of those drinking in the bar and 'used to come in here and have a half bottle of champagne, a Pernod or a Ricard', Gaston remembered (*The Independent*, 11 Nov 1999). During the Second World War the pub became even more closely identified with France, when it became a gathering place for the Free French forces. It became a valuable centre for communication, as Victor Berlemont maintained an unofficial register of the French who passed through London, so that escapees and their relatives could be put in touch. The story that General de Gaulle wrote his appeal to the French to resist the Nazis after a good lunch in the upstairs dining-room was a myth, but the general certainly visited the pub at least once. The visit was not a success: the English in the pub fell into awed silence and the Free French stood to attention, making a tense atmosphere while de Gaulle drank his glass of wine.

Gaston Berlemont, who married his first wife, Gladys Jean Linsell, in 1937 and had a son and a daughter, served in the RAF during the war, working as an interpreter during the north-west Europe campaign. In Belgium he met Agnès Gérarda Deschuymer (*b.* 1920/21), whom he married on 29 May 1947; they had a daughter. In 1951 Victor Berlemont died, and Gaston took over the pub, which he ran like a cross between a private club and a bank. He seldom refused a loan, advanced taxi fares for those who could no longer stand at the bar, and cashed cheques for those who knew perfectly well they would bounce. He had luxuriant handlebar moustaches, though 'not as fine as your father's', President de Gaulle told him when he spotted him in the crowd in April 1960 on an official visit to London (*The Independent*, 15 Nov 1999). He was gallant to women, and would kiss their hands and say 'Madame, I should like to see more of you' before doing a double take, as though mildly shocked at his own *double entendre* (*Daily Telegraph*, 3 Nov 1999). The bar boasted a wondrous water urn with twin taps that emitted a thin trickle of water for pastis or for the illegal absinthe that Gaston was said to keep for favoured customers. Beer was dispensed only in half-pint glasses, to discourage its consumption in favour of the more profitable wine that Gaston imported and bottled himself. Those who drank it included Dylan Thomas, who unconcernedly left a manuscript there one night, knowing it would certainly still be there in the morning, Brendan Behan, who was said to have displeased Gaston by eating his *bœuf bourguignon* with both hands, Augustus John, Max Beerbohm, Aleister Crowley, Theodora FitzGibbon, the 'two Roberts' (Colquhoun and MacBryde), Nina Hamnet, and Stephen Spender. Later customers were a roll-call of bohemian Soho: Daniel Farson, Henrietta Moraes, Francis Bacon, Lucian Freud, Caroline Blackwood, Tambimuttu, and the Bernard brothers (Jeffrey, Bruce, and Oliver).

In the 1950s, when Soho was threatened with redevelopment, Berlemont was chairman of the Soho Association, and helped set up the annual Soho festival; but he himself moved out to suburban Hendon, where he grew herbs and collected stamps. His second marriage having also ended in divorce, on 26 October 1967 he married Sylvia Humphreys (*b*. 1920/21), a clerical officer. He had an extraordinary memory for faces and occasions, and, though he might meet someone at a gathering well out of context for both parties, he would recall, if not the name, then at least the description of the lady with whom he had last seen that person. On 14 July 1989 the whole of Soho seemed to gather on the pavement of the French, not to celebrate the 200th anniversary of the fall of the Bastille, but to mark the day Gaston, aged seventy-five, had stylishly chosen to retire. He died in the Royal Free Hospital, Camden Town, London, on 31 October 1999, survived by all three of his wives and their children.   PAUL LEVY

Sources *Daily Telegraph* (3 Nov 1999) · *The Independent* (11–15 Nov 1999) · *The Times* (3 Nov 1999) · *The Guardian* (4 Nov 1999) · private information (2004) · b. cert. · m. certs. [Agnès Deschuymer, Sylvia Humphreys] · d. cert.
Likenesses portrait, repro. in *The Times* · portrait, repro. in *The Guardian* · portrait, repro. in *The Independent* · portrait, repro. in *Daily Telegraph*

Berlepsch, Emilie von [*née* Dorothea Friderika Aemilia von Oppel; *other married name* Emilie Harmes] (*bap.* **1755**, *d*. **1830**), author and traveller, was baptized on 26 November 1755 as Dorothea Friderika Aemilia von Oppel, at Gotha, Thuringia, daughter of Carl Georg von Oppel (*d*. 1760), lord of the manor of Wellerswalde, near Oschatz, Saxony, and vice-chancellor of the duchy of Saxe-Gotha, and Amalie, countess of Dönhoff (*d*. 1768), lady in waiting to the duchess of Saxe-Gotha. After her father died, her

mother married *Legationsrat* ('Counsellor') Friedrich Ulrich von Stirn, and, possibly because of the marriage, Emilie was placed under the guardianship of her uncle, Johann Siegmund von Oppel, at Weimar where she received a good private education. On 2 March 1772 she married at Weimar Friedrich Ludwig von Berlepsch (1749–1818), subsequently *Hofrichter* ('judge') at the court of the elector in Hanover. She lived there and in Schloss Berlepsch, near Göttingen, and at Weimar, where she became a devoted disciple of J. G. Herder, leader of the pre-Romantic movement in Germany. She moved in literary circles, publishing two slim volumes of poetry.

Wavering between elation and depression, Emilie von Berlepsch took refuge in Switzerland in 1793–5. The sublime landscape peopled by innocent shepherds, which she knew from literature, seemed to exist in reality, and she came to love the country as a peaceful idyll. Its invasion by France in 1798 roused her to violent protest. In *Einige Bermerkungen zur richtigern Beurtheilung der erzwungnen Schweitzer-Revolution* (1799) she gave 'a fairer assessment of the revolution imposed on Switzerland by force', and she vowed she would not visit the country as long as it remained occupied by French troops. Instead she decided to visit Scotland where she hoped to regain the paradise lost in the Alps. Again literature—this time Ossian and Burns, both admired by Herder—was her guide, and she also saw Britain as a bulwark against French imperialism. Her host was the Revd James Macdonald, a Hebridean and promoter of cultural exchange between Scotland and Germany, whom she had met at Weimar soon after her first marriage ended in divorce in 1795. She spent the winter of 1799–1800 in Edinburgh and toured the highlands the following summer with Macdonald. *Caledonia* (4 vols., 1802–4), dedicated to Herder, is her account of the country and her emotional response to it. She recalls passages from Ossian in Glencoe and is distressed to be unable to reach Staffa. In the first long notice in German given to Robert Burns, she praises him as a true poet according to Herder's criteria, a creative genius drawn from peasant stock. By her prose paraphrase in German of 'The Cotter's Saturday Night' she tries to win to the ranks of his admirers those put off by his dialect. She saw the highlanders as noble savages, and, although aware of their lack of development and poverty, was full of praise for their frugal life, discipline at work, thrift, and pride in their history—all reminiscent of the Swiss. Her observations on Edinburgh upper-class society centre on the role of women. Her long excursus on British women writers singles out Mary Wollstonecraft as a kindred spirit. She evidently knew Wollstonecraft's work thoroughly and draws to her the attention of a German public which had largely forgotten her. She claims the right of women to write books on any subject, hitherto a male preserve, and indeed her own work, she proudly remarks, was the first of its kind by a German woman.

Emilie von Berlepsch returned home disillusioned after Macdonald had refused to marry her. On 5 June 1801 she married the commoner August Heinrich Harmes (1762–

1839) from Mecklenburg with whom she lived by Lake Zürich from 1804 to 1817. Bad fortune and ill health drove the couple back to Mecklenburg-Schwerin where they lived precariously on the benefaction of the grand duke. She died at Lauenburg on the Elbe on 27 July 1830. *Caledonia* received some critical notice at the time, but later descriptions of Scotland, inspired by Scott's fiction, eclipsed her work, rather than claiming it as a forerunner. Interest in her was revived in the later twentieth century.

HANS UTZ

Sources H. Utz, 'Bern—die Liebeserklärung der Emilie von Berlepsch', *Berner Zeitschrift für Geschichte*, 49 (1987), 57–115 · A. Gillies, 'Emilie von Berlepsch and her *Caledonia*', *German life and letters*, 29 (1975), 75–90 · H. Utz, *Schotten und Schweizer—brother mountaineers: Europa entdeckt die beiden Völker im 18. Jahrhundert* (1995) · A. Gillies, 'An embarrassing visitor', in A. Gillies, *A Hebridean in Goethe's Weimar* (1969), 101–14 · R. Dawson, 'And this shield is called: self reliance', *German women in the 18th and 19th centuries*, ed. R. E. B. Joeres and M. J. Maynes (1986), 157–74 · A. Gillies, 'Emilie von Berlepsch and Burns', *Modern Language Review*, 55 (1960), 584–7 · P. Corrodi, 'Das Landgut Mariahalden bei Erlenbach', *Jahrbuch vom Zürichsee*, 18 (1958), 107–33

Likenesses V. Sonnenschein, etching on medal, repro. in E. von Berlepsch, *Sommerstunden* (1794)

Berlin, Sir Isaiah (1909–1997), philosopher and historian of ideas, was born on 6 June 1909 in Riga, Latvia, then part of the Russian empire, the son of Mendel Borisovitch Berlin (*b.* 1883), a prosperous timber merchant whose main business was supplying wooden sleepers for the Russian railways, and his wife, (Mussa) Marie, *née* Wolschonock. Berlin was an only child; an elder sister had been stillborn, and his mother had been warned that further pregnancies would threaten her life too. She had a very difficult childbirth as predicted, and Berlin's left arm was permanently damaged by the forceps of the attending doctor.

Family and education Berlin's parents were well-educated secular Jews; they spoke German as well as Russian, and their literary and musical tastes rubbed off on their son. So did their lack of interest in religious faith. Berlin's wider family, however, was devout; his grandparents and his cousins were Chabad Hassidim, and Berlin later took a wry pleasure in the fact that Menachem Schneerson, the 'Lubavitcher Rebbe', was a distant cousin.

During the First World War the family moved first to Andreapol to escape the German advance of 1915, and then in 1916 to Petrograd (the former St Petersburg, renamed at the start of the war). There Berlin saw the brutality of revolution at first hand. He was horrified by the spectacle of a mob hounding a policeman in the street, and dragging him off to his presumed death. In later years he maintained that his hatred of political violence had its origins in that experience, though it was very far from making him a pacifist.

Antisemitism was never far below the surface of the Soviet revolution, and it was a constant threat during the subsequent civil war. Nevertheless the Berlins fared no worse and no better than most other middle-class Russians who found their homes requisitioned and their lives threatened by the ubiquitous informers who hoped to

Sir Isaiah Berlin (1909–1997), by Lucinda Douglas-Menzies, 1988

advance themselves by denouncing their neighbours. They escaped the worst of the subsequent horrors of life in the Soviet Union by moving to Britain two years after the end of the First World War. Mendel Berlin was an Anglophile. He had supplied plywood to Britain during the war, and possessed assets in Britain. Taking advantage of the peace treaty between the Soviets and Latvia to return to Riga in 1920, Mendel Berlin moved on from there to Britain in early 1921. The family settled in Surbiton, a place whose domestic comfort and security epitomized for Mendel Berlin the virtues of the British. They moved to Kensington a year later, and subsequently to Hampstead. They were naturalized in 1929.

The eleven-year-old Berlin was faced with the need to learn English from scratch, and to catch up with his English classmates. He did so at a great pace, and in old age amused his listeners with a rendition of 'Daisy, Daisy' as he thought it must have sounded when sung by himself some seventy-five years before. He survived the rigours of the English preparatory school, went as a scholar to St Paul's School in west London, and in 1928 was elected to a scholarship at Corpus Christi College, Oxford. Although his scholarship was in classics, he was not an enthusiastic or talented student of the ancient languages. He therefore bypassed honour moderations, and gained a first in Greats in 1931; a year later he took another first in philosophy, politics, and economics. Even as an undergraduate he was a notable talker, and his rooms in Corpus were thronged with friends listening to and arguing with him. Soon after his death his lifelong friend Miriam Rothschild maintained that nobody really knew the pleasures of Berlin's mind and conversation who had not known him as a teenager. However that may be, it was during the next decade that he began to acquire his reputation as the most interesting conversationalist of his age.

Philosophy don In the autumn of 1932 Berlin was elected to a prize fellowship at All Souls. He was the first Jew to be elected in the college's 500-year history, and one of only a handful of Jews who held fellowships anywhere in Oxford. Among acknowledgements of the achievement were a letter of congratulation from the chief rabbi and an invitation to lunch at Waddesdon with Baron Rothschild. Until 1938 Berlin held his All Souls fellowship in combination with a lecturership in philosophy at New College; then from 1938 to 1950 he was a fellow in philosophy at New College, though absent for several years on war service. In comparison with All Souls, where he enjoyed the company of John Austin and Stuart Hampshire, Berlin found New College deeply boring. The one bright spot was meeting the visitors at the warden's lodgings, including as they did both Virginia Woolf—a cousin of H. A. L. Fisher—and Elizabeth Bowen. The former wrote a maliciously amusing account of their meeting, but their relations improved in due course; of Elizabeth Bowen he became a close friend: he visited her in Ireland, and carried on a vivid correspondence with her for many years.

As an undergraduate teacher in the formal sense, Berlin would have been harshly judged by a later age. He subsequently observed that he could not have been a member of any academic community more tightly structured than Oxford then was; the ability to pursue his own interests in his own way was indispensable. Nor would he have survived the departmental organization of American university life or cared for the early morning classes common in the United States. He was reluctant to leave his bed before mid-morning, and sometimes passed the time during tutorials playing with mechanical toys or with the wind-up gramophone that was much admired by generations of pupils. In spite of this seeming lack of interest in their work, most of his pupils, and by no means only the cleverest of them, found that they learned more philosophy from Berlin than from their more orthodox instructors. Indeed, he was recalled with particular affection by students who had been terrified by, or entirely uninterested in, philosophy. The undergraduates of the 1930s were the first among many generations of students who found Berlin an astonishingly generous teacher, and one who fuelled their imaginations as few others could. He was a rarity among university teachers in the later twentieth century in finding the young irresistible; until his mid-eighties he was endlessly available to naïve and vulnerable graduate students from all parts of the world, who would sit at his feet for an afternoon and leave transformed.

In the later 1930s Berlin was part of a small group of young and iconoclastic philosophers that included John Austin, Stuart Hampshire, and A. J. Ayer. They met in Berlin's rooms in All Souls and thrashed out their puzzles in debate. Berlin later regretted that they had been too introspective to publish their conclusions; their passion was for the excitement of the chase, and their chief desire to convince one another. Once they had settled a problem to their own satisfaction, they saw no reason to broadcast the answer. All were broadly in sympathy with what became the linguistic turn in philosophy but, as their later careers showed, were otherwise far from being of one

mind. Ayer was an early convert to logical positivism; Austin, Hampshire, and Berlin were not. A favourite move within logical positivism was to translate propositions that were felt to be epistemologically dubious into propositions felt to be more secure; statements about the past, about the future, about the contents of other minds, and about persisting material objects, were parsed as hypothetical propositions about verifiable facts of our own experience. Berlin published three original and powerful criticisms of this central tactic of logical positivism, 'Verification', 'Empirical propositions and hypothetical statements', and 'Logical translation'; the first appeared in 1939, the others in 1950. In showing that hypothetical statements were logically parasitic on the supposedly dubious assertions for which they were offered as less dubious translations, Berlin attacked positivism at its weakest point.

More importantly for Berlin's long-term future, Fisher and Gilbert Murray commissioned him in 1933 to write an account of the life and ideas of Karl Marx for the Home University Library. The project had already been turned down by the Webbs, Frank Pakenham, and Harold Laski, and it took Berlin a long time to finish the book. But *Karl Marx* (1939) was both a publishing success and a double landmark in Berlin's life. In the first place, it was one of the first works in English that treated Marx absolutely objectively—neither belittling the real intellectual power of his work, nor descending into hagiography. Second, it revealed Berlin's unusual talent as a historian of ideas—or more exactly as a biographer of ideas. Berlin was no admirer of Marx, and wholly deplored the political consequences of his ideas, but he entered into the intellectual world of Marx and his fellow revolutionaries as few biographers have known how to do. The five years of reading and reflection on the ideas and allegiances of the radical intelligentsia of nineteenth-century Europe that were needed for *Karl Marx* also furnished Berlin with many of the resources he later employed in his accounts of the Enlightenment and its critics, of Romanticism, and of the ideas of the Russian radicals whom he brought to wider notice in the 1940s and 1950s.

Berlin's capacity for friendship, and his liking for people from all sorts of places and social backgrounds, meant that he was constantly in demand as a guest in London as much as in Oxford. He was a particular favourite of Emerald Cunard and of her rival London hostess, Sybil Colefax. His more austere Oxford colleagues fretted that he was wasting his brain on high society, but Berlin was not deterred. His friends reflected his passions—for music, literature, and philosophy, as well as for the sheer variety of human temperament—and they also reflected his political allegiances. The German philosopher and sociologist Theodor Adorno, in exile in Oxford in those years, was saved by Berlin's friendship from despair at the philistine surroundings into which he had strayed. Berlin's ability to distinguish between personal affection and intellectual approval allowed him to enjoy Adorno's company while thinking that his ideas were mostly nonsense. One friendship that came to grief on the rising power of Nazism was with Adam von Trott, the glamorous German Rhodes scholar who took Oxford by storm in the early 1930s. Relations cooled when Berlin thought von Trott insufficiently hostile to Nazism, and they were never fully restored. Although Berlin was not yet the theorist of liberal Zionism nor the commentator on its ambiguous connections with secular forms of nationalism that he became, he was quick to notice and resent anything smacking of anti-semitism. He began to take a serious interest in Zionism only after a visit to Palestine in the summer of 1934. His travelling companion, John Foster, found Berlin moved to tears by his first encounter with a Jewish ticket inspector.

War service, Moscow, and Zionism The outbreak of the Second World War changed Berlin's life dramatically. At first, he was left stranded. Physically he was not fit for military service, and as a Latvian by birth he was suspect to the intelligence services, who vetoed his application for a humble desk job. In the summer of 1940 he was persuaded by Guy Burgess to join him in Moscow; quite who had authorized this proposal, if anyone, remains unclear. Subsequent events suggest that if it was not Harold Nicolson, it was Burgess himself, and that he had not even tried to persuade his superiors to endorse the scheme. Burgess and Berlin arrived in the United States after an unpleasant Atlantic crossing, and Burgess was promptly recalled to London. Berlin's subsequent efforts to get to Moscow were cut short by Stafford Cripps, the British ambassador in Moscow. Meanwhile, Berlin had begun to charm the political and newspaper élites of Washington and New York, to whom he was introduced by Felix Frankfurter, the supreme court justice whom Berlin had met in Oxford a few years earlier. Friends suggested to Lord Lothian, the British ambassador, that a job should be found for Berlin, and he was set to work analysing American press reports of the British war effort. This went so well that he was drafted to the British information office in New York. After a few weeks back in Britain to settle his affairs, he returned to the United States in January 1941, and spent the remainder of the war there.

After a year of this work, Berlin was transferred from New York to Washington, and for the remainder of the war drafted on behalf of Lord Halifax, who had succeeded Lothian as ambassador, a stream of dispatches for onward transmission to London. (A selection was published by H. G. Nicholas as *Washington Despatches, 1941–1945* in 1981.) They were much admired by Winston Churchill, among others. The ordinarily rather remote Lord Halifax—'a creature from another planet', in Berlin's recollection—was fond of his young colleague from All Souls and gave him his head. Through Frankfurter, Berlin met most of the democratic administration, along with coming young journalists such as Joseph Alsop, and the present and future publishers of the *Washington Post*, Philip and Katherine Graham, all of whom remained friends for life. Berlin walked with some skill the fine line between exact reporting and colouring the news to enhance the prospects of a desired policy. It was a skill he especially needed to preserve relations with Chaim Weizmann and other Zionist friends. He was happy to do what he could to keep doors in both the American and British governments open for his friends, but he was also acutely aware of Foreign Office doubts about Zionist aspirations. He took care neither to betray his friends nor to destroy his own usefulness by becoming an object of suspicion to his employers, although in 1943 he was instrumental in obstructing a joint British–American declaration against the establishment of a post-war Jewish state.

Immediately after the end of the war Berlin served for four and a half months in the Moscow embassy. It was a painful homecoming, notable for meetings with the two greatest Russian poets of the day, and for the realization that almost all his extended family had been murdered during the war. With Boris Pasternak his relations were friendly, although he struck Berlin as somewhat reserved; they discussed his plans for *Dr Zhivago*, and on a return visit ten years later Berlin was given a typescript copy of the finished novel. His encounter with Anna Akhmatova in Leningrad on the other hand was a meeting of minds, or of souls, unlike any other he ever experienced. It was a costly encounter for Akhmatova, who well knew that the secret police would have followed Berlin to her flat, and that she would suffer their attentions and the bullying of the Writers' Union in consequence. Berlin and Akhmatova talked all night, and Berlin became fully aware of the psychological, cultural, and intellectual disasters that Soviet communism had inflicted on Russia. The contrast between the cultivated, imaginative, and liberal world that might have existed in Russia and the world of the commissar and the secret policeman that Stalinism had created coloured everything he wrote thereafter. Akhmatova thought their meeting was a world-historical event, and Berlin regarded it as the most important event of his life. A later meeting in Oxford was less successful; predictably, Akhmatova thought Berlin had become a songbird in a gilded cage.

As the time for him to leave government service drew closer, Berlin was unsure what to do with himself. He fended off the enticements of Weizmann, Ben Gurion, and others who wanted him to make his home in what shortly became the independent state of Israel. He was enthusiastic about the creation of Israel, but was not always an admirer of what had been created. The existence of an independent Israel was a necessity for the Jewish people, but he was critical of many of its leading figures, and unhappy at how Israel had come into existence. He enormously admired his uncle by marriage, Isaac Landoberg, who by 1946 had changed his name to Yitzhak Sadeh and was a leader of the anti-British Jewish underground; a little later Sadeh became a leader of Jewish forces in the war that followed the partition of Palestine. On the other hand, Berlin disapproved of terrorism, and felt that he himself was far too English to make his home among Middle Eastern Jews. He always insisted on the importance of the existence of the state of Israel for Jews outside Israel. It liberated them. It may not have been clear to all readers of his essay 'Jewish slavery and emancipation' just what the connection was between the existence of a state that Jews anywhere in the world could regard as a second home and the freedom of Jews else-where; but Berlin himself certainly felt that the existence of Israel was an element in his conviction that he did not face a stark choice between assimilation and exclusion if he chose to stay in England.

Berlin remained a Zionist, but always a liberal Zionist. He was deeply loyal to his fellow Jews, but he deplored narrow tribalism. He never forgave Menachem Begin his membership of the Stern gang, and never forgave the Stern gang for its murders of British administrators and soldiers during the struggle for an independent state of Israel. He was utterly unforgiving of anyone who displayed antisemitic sentiments, but his loyalties were not in the usual sense nationalistic. The Israel to which he was devoted was a liberal, or social-democratic, state, not a theocracy; his last intervention in public life, very shortly before his death in November 1997, was to plead for Israelis to make the concessions needed to secure peace between themselves and the Palestinians.

Historian of ideas Towards the end of the war Berlin decided that if he was to remain in England and Oxford, it could not be as a post-war incarnation of the philosophy tutor he had been before the war. He did not at once abandon philosophy for the history of ideas, nor did he immediately abandon undergraduate teaching for a life of writing and lecturing. It was not until 1950 that he resigned his fellowship at New College and returned to All Souls. Indeed, he half-jokingly claimed that he had been sacked by an economical bursar of New College who had counted the philosophy tutors and decided that Berlin was one too many. But his intellectual tastes had changed; analytical sharpness for its own sake was no longer something he much valued. He turned to the history of ideas, political theory, and what may be termed 'cultural commentary'. The change was marked by the publication in 1953 of *The Hedgehog and the Fox*, a long essay (an expanded version of an article originally published in 1951) on Tolstoy's theory of history that made famous a hitherto obscure tag from Archilochus: 'The fox knows many things, but the hedgehog knows one big thing'. Tolstoy, on Berlin's view of the matter, was a fox who tried to turn himself into a hedgehog, a man whose genius lay in his understanding of the infinite variety of human character, and who drove himself almost mad by trying to cramp that genius into a single recipe for salvation.

In 1954 Berlin gave the Northcliffe lectures on 'A marvellous decade', which brought to an English audience the ideas of Herzen and Belinsky and other Romantic Russian radicals of the 1840s. Their impact on British intellectual sensibilities was indirect but powerful. On the one hand, the lectures demonstrated that liberalism could no longer be thought of as an Anglo-American possession presented to the world by John Locke and John Stuart Mill; on the other, they showed that the contrast between a naturally despotic Russia and a naturally liberal western Europe had to be given up. In the Soviet Union, Berlin's revelation of the Romantic, liberal Herzen was heretical; in Soviet ideology, Herzen was approved of as a populist, though criticized for the inadequate, pre-Marxist view that underlay his populism. The loathing with which Herzen would assuredly have greeted the Soviet regime was not something that Soviet commentators dwelt upon.

Berlin described himself as having abandoned philosophy in order to pursue the history of ideas. He habitually gave two different reasons for the change of intellectual allegiance. Sometimes he suggested that he had become bored with philosophy as practised in Oxford and Harvard. He often quoted the deflationary observation of C. I. Lewis: 'There is no a priori reason for thinking that the truth, once discovered, will necessarily prove interesting'. Berlin did not wish to spend his life accumulating boring truths. More often he said that he had come to believe that there was no progress in philosophy and that he had wanted to work in a field where he could expect to know more by the time he died than he had known when he started. Whether he made the transition that these explanations suggest is doubtful. He was not interested in the quotidian history that lay behind the ideas by which he was fascinated. It was bold ideas and original, quirky, and imaginative thinkers that interested him. When historically minded historians of ideas observed that ideas are transmitted by the derivative and the second-rate, Berlin did not turn to the study of the derivative and the second-rate. He rescued the intellectually second-rate from obscurity, but only when he found them interestingly underivative. It sometimes seemed to be out of justice that he rescued them; because they had had no impact he wished to bring them to the attention of their descendants.

What Berlin wrote was in that respect still philosophy rather than history, but he took seriously the old Thucydidean tag that history is philosophy teaching by examples, and he had a rare talent for linking the intellectual to the imaginative and the emotional. Ideas came to life in a process that he self-consciously understood as a re-enactment of the original author's thinking. It was therefore unsurprising that one of the writers in whom he took a keen interest was Giambattista Vico, the author of the *Scienza nuová*, whose discussion of *fantasia* was perhaps the first systematic account of the nature of historical and sociological interpretation. Vico argued that the historian's task was to rethink the thoughts of other cultures and other times, and Berlin concurred. The ideas in which Berlin was interested, particularly the central concepts of politics such as freedom, equality, and progress, are arguably such that they must be understood historically and comparatively in the light of the ways in which they have been understood in different societies and cultures. They are also pre-eminently ideas that take their colouring from the personality of the thinkers who explore them. Berlin's talent for gossip was the everyday social counterpart of an unusual talent for exploring the psychology of his favourite thinkers. Critics sometimes complained that Berlin projected more of himself than was quite proper onto the figures he most admired, but the effect was certainly to bring to life many neglected thinkers as well as to illuminate well-known ones in novel ways. It also meant that his natural form of expression was the lecture and the essay rather than the monograph; this gave him an entirely unjustified reputation for being reluctant to publish. In fact, he published a great deal, but often in fugitive journals and out-of-the-way places. The publication of his collected works from 1978 onwards showed just how ready he was to put pen to paper; the projected four volumes rapidly turned into several more than that.

Marriage, the Chichele chair, and Wolfson College Berlin enjoyed the company of women, but thought himself sexually unattractive, and believed until his late thirties that he was destined to remain a bachelor. All Souls was a luxurious bachelor society, and Berlin's affection for his mother was sufficient to suggest that he would neither be driven into marriage by the discomforts of single life nor lured into it by the need for stronger emotional attachments than the unmarried life provided. It was therefore somewhat to the surprise of his numerous friends that on 7 February 1956 he married Aline Elisabeth Yvonne Halban (b. 1914/15), the daughter of the banker Baron Pierre de Gunzbourg, of Paris. He thereby acquired three stepsons as well as a beautiful and well-connected wife whose accomplishments had included the women's golf championship of her native France. They established themselves in Aline's substantial and elegant house on the outskirts of Oxford (Headington House, nicknamed Government House by Berlin's more left-wing friends), and there they lived and entertained—or, as the same friends had it, held court—for the next forty years. Although he had embarked on marriage rather late, Berlin never ceased to recommend the married condition, and his happiness was a persuasive advertisement for what he preached.

In 1957 Berlin was elected to the Chichele professorship of social and political theory. The next twenty years were the high tide of his career. He was elected to the British Academy in the same year, and was vice-president from 1959 to 1961 and president from 1974 to 1978; he was a member of the board of directors of the Royal Opera House, Covent Garden, from 1954 to 1965, and again from 1974 to 1987, and a trustee of the National Gallery from 1975 to 1985. He had been appointed CBE for his wartime service in 1946, was knighted in 1957, and was appointed to the Order of Merit in 1971. These positions and honours, more than enough for most people, do not capture the richness of Berlin's existence, nor his impact on British, American, and Israeli social and cultural life. He was in constant demand as a lecturer; repeatedly he gave dazzling performances in settings obscure and famous. He characteristically described himself in self-deprecating terms as an intellectual taxicab: when he was hailed, he went. Yet even though he was a figure who seemed more at home in the streets of Jerusalem and New York than in the English countryside, he found Oxford indispensable, and never succumbed to the urgings of Israeli or American friends who thought he should abandon his phlegmatic and slow-moving English university for more adrenalin-charged environments. They failed to see that Berlin was not the cosmopolitan figure they thought; his

view was that most people need a base in some particular place and attachments to particular people and opinions if they are to understand other places, people, and opinions. Perhaps he was conscious of the insult of 'rootless cosmopolitan' that was the commonplace of Soviet anti-semitism; at all events, it was a rooted cosmopolitanism that he espoused.

Berlin's loyalty to Britain needed little theoretical explanation. He had arrived as a small boy; Britain was tolerant and friendly, and it was full of people for whom he felt affection. Although he was instantly at home in New York, or Washington, or Cambridge, Massachusetts, he had no reason to emigrate to places that he could visit as often as he liked without at the same time revising his political and personal allegiances. In any case, if it was a question of sheer pleasure, he preferred Italy to any other destination. He and Aline built a house overlooking Portofino, and from there he explored far and wide, frequently in search of half-forgotten bel canto operas that were being revived in out-of-the-way places.

In 1966 Berlin became president of Wolfson College. Under the name Iffley College, this had been a new and under-financed graduate college, created to provide a collegiate base for lecturers—largely in the sciences—who had no collegiate attachment, and to provide a community for graduate students who had hitherto been neglected in Oxford. From the Ford Foundation and the Wolfson Foundation he secured an endowment for the college. It was renamed Wolfson College in acknowledgement of the generosity of Sir Isaac Wolfson's foundation. Berlin toyed with the thought that 'St Isaac's' might be apt, but only privately. With these resources he secured from the architectural practice of Powell and Moya one of their best large-scale developments, a set of unflinchingly modern collegiate buildings running gently down to the River Cherwell, whose white concrete and granite starkness was not so much softened as heightened very elegantly by the lushness of the surrounding gardens and riverside. Berlin was a highly successful founding president, but he had never been enthusiastic about presiding over an established collegiate institution. He was an inventor rather than a manager. Nor did he expect to feel entirely at home in the institution he had created. Berlin wanted Wolfson College to be family-friendly; but All Souls and New College did not provide much training for a world in which married graduate students took this to mean that they should bring their babies to dinner in college. Berlin retired from Wolfson College in 1975, and returned to All Souls as a distinguished fellow.

Liberal intellectual Berlin remained a considerable figure on the intellectual scene. His years at Wolfson had coincided with the most contentious period of British and American post-war politics. The Vietnam War, and the extraordinary upheavals of 1968 in France, Germany, Czechoslovakia, and the United States, raised both old and new questions about the prospects of liberal politics. Berlin's inaugural lecture as Chichele professor, 'Two concepts of liberty', was second in fame only to *The Hedgehog and the Fox*, and had come to occupy a position in late twentieth-century liberalism rather like Mill's essay *On Liberty* a hundred years earlier. Its ambiguities and unclarities were explored for many years thereafter, but its simple assertion of the general priority of 'negative liberty'—the right to be left alone—over other goals, including those that Berlin summed up as 'positive liberty', was irresistible to most readers and intolerable to many. Written at a time when admirers of the Soviet Union were still insisting that it had achieved a higher form of liberty than the decadent West, 'Two concepts of liberty' was seized on by the critics of Soviet communism, and inevitably became entangled in the arguments between cold war liberals and their liberal and socialist critics.

Its place in the contemporary politics of the 1950s and 1960s aside, Berlin's liberalism remains difficult to characterize. There is a tension at its heart that Berlin never quite addressed. Berlin was famous for holding two views, the first being that the ends of human existence are many, not one, that they conflict with one another, and that there is no one best life, either for an individual—who must choose only one of the possible lives that may suit her or him—or for whole societies, which inevitably hold a particular set of cultural, social, political, moral, or religious allegiances and must accept that these bring with them gains and losses peculiar to them. An insistence on the plurality of social and individual goods is neither relativism nor scepticism; it is not the view that what is good depends on who and where one is, nor the view that there are no real goods or bads. Berlin thought that there were many genuine goods; he espoused pluralism. Yet he also held a second view, that liberty takes priority over all other values. On the face of it, this combination is incoherent. If there is no rationally defensible hierarchy of values, liberty cannot be at the summit of that hierarchy. There are many ways of softening the conflict between Berlin's liberalism and his pluralism; none is so obviously right that one can assume that it must be what he really thought.

Berlin's liberalism was not in the ordinary sense a political creed. In party terms, it was consistent with voting for any of the main parties in British politics, and implied an allegiance to none of them in particular. It was the defence of a set of cultural and psychological attachments rather than the defence of a particular set of political and legal arrangements to which he committed himself. It was in this way that his controversy with E. H. Carr over the possibility of a scientific history, and his attack on the idea of historical inevitability, were aspects of his liberalism, and the controversy a politically loaded one. Like the Romantics that he invoked in his Mellon lectures of 1965 (published in 1999 as *The Roots of Romanticism*), Berlin saw human beings as always unfinished creatures capable of new and unpredictable feats of invention. Like the Romantics, he thought it was impossible to write history from the detached perspective appropriate to physics or chemistry, and that it was absurd to pretend to do so. History was not a scientific experiment but a moral drama. E. H. Carr, who had been Berlin's chief target, complained that Berlin ignored the explanatory aims of historians altogether; this was an unfair jibe uttered in the heat of the controversial moment, but one that Berlin's emphasis on empathy and insight could easily provoke.

The models for Berlin's literary, cultural, and philosophical engagement were Russian: Belinsky, Herzen, and Turgenev in particular. Berlin translated Turgenev's *First Love* as early as 1950, and twenty years later he devoted his Romanes lecture of 1970 to Turgenev's *Fathers and Children*. It was an extraordinarily apt choice. By this time Berlin closely identified with Turgenev. Turgenev sympathized with the young radicals of the 1870s while thinking they were intolerably crude and fanatical; Berlin felt the same about their successors of the 1960s. Turgenev feared that his scepticism and caution in political matters might be mere cowardice; so did Berlin. Such anxieties were inevitably heightened by the political quarrels of the 1960s, when Berlin's many American friends took violently opposed sides on the Vietnam War and all of them expected him to side with them. Berlin had no qualms about describing himself as a 'cold war liberal', inasmuch as he had no doubt that the United States and what they represented were worth defending against the threat posed by the Soviet Union. His doubts about the Vietnam War were not high-principled; but as a matter of prudence, he was far from certain that American foreign policy was well advised.

Music, and other interests Berlin's talent for friendship means that a roll-call of those who thought of themselves as his good friends would embrace most of the musical world in Europe and the United States, just as it would embrace social and political theorists, philanthropists, journalists, diplomats, and politicians. Their affection for him is not surprising; their admiration for him is perhaps more so. Berlin's passion for music was unaccompanied by any technical proficiency; he could not play an instrument or read a score. He was, nevertheless, a friend of Stravinsky, and later a close friend of Alfred Brendel, who said that Berlin was a uniquely illuminating commentator on his performances. He had discussed music endlessly with Theodore Adorno before the war, and his first published essays were on musical performances. He often said that he could not imagine a world without music.

As in many other areas, Berlin's intuitive sense of the most important issue at stake was uncanny. He had, like anyone else, blind spots and antipathies; he did not care for Wagner, and disliked the cruelty that lurks in *Turandot* and *Tosca*. His affections lay with the operas of Mozart and Italian opera from Bellini to Verdi, rather in the way in which his non-operatic passions led him to Mozart and Schubert. The powerful feelings that music provoked made him a very influential trustee of the Royal Opera House, Covent Garden. His passion was above all for the music; 'prima la musica' was his operating principle, though it took quite exceptional performances to make him forgive cheap or tawdry productions. Among his achievements, one was to secure the services of Sir George Solti as musical director at Covent Garden, and more generally to encourage ambition in the house. As a trustee of the National Gallery he was almost equally invaluable.

When the controversial Sainsbury wing was being built, he played a vital role in soothing the bruised feelings of the trustees on one side, and their distinguished architect Robert Venturi on the other. Characteristically, what enabled him to do this was his discovery that the architect's wife was a Baltic Jew like himself. And he was an impressively fearless president of the British Academy; his intellectual distinction, and his long years of mingling with politicians, senior civil servants, and the rich and famous in the worlds of arts and letters gave him a unique immunity against whatever governments and administrators might try to impose.

Assessment Berlin was one of the most important historians of ideas in the twentieth century, perhaps because he was not in the usual sense a historian at all. It is at first sight somewhat puzzling that he was admired by historians and sociologists, to whom his unconcern for minute factual detail would, on the face of it, have not endeared him; but only a very few of them could bring themselves to complain that his broad-brush characterizations of movements of ideas in European history omitted much and misrepresented a good deal. The obvious explanation is that, even where one might on third or fourth reading come to think that Berlin's characterization of a thinker or a thought was seriously askew, readers were grateful for the stimulus provided by his fertile imagination. He started hares, flushed the historical coverts for overlooked quarry, and discovered strange, neglected species. By the same token, his success as a college president and his membership of so many governing bodies and committees might seem slightly surprising. He was an enthusiastic conspirator, and enjoyed getting his favoured candidates into positions for which they were not always entirely suited, but he was not one of nature's civil servants. He did not need to be, since those who were were sufficiently enchanted to carry out his plans. The same qualities kept him on good terms with the publishers who despaired of the books they had been promised, and the editors who received corrected proofs long after the last possible moment. This did not go along with a wholly relaxed attitude to his work. He had a capacity for tinkering with the wording of his texts that went far beyond the point of diminishing returns, and his self-deprecating estimate of his own abilities did not extend to an equal tolerance of criticism from others. He was notably thin-skinned. It must be said in mitigation that his critics were rarely very friendly; they were made fiercer by Berlin's own eminence and because political allegiances were as much at stake as academic reputations.

Berlin died at the Acland Nursing Home, 25 Banbury Road, Oxford, on 5 November 1997. He had been in less than perfect health for some time, but his final illness was brief. He was survived by his wife, Aline, and his three stepsons, and was buried in Oxford. Commemorations of his life and work were held in Oxford, London, and New York.   A. RYAN

Sources I. Berlin, *Personal impressions* (1980) · A. Ryan, ed., *The idea of freedom: essays in honour of Isaiah Berlin* (1979) · E. Margalit and A. Margalit, eds., *Isaiah Berlin: a celebration* (1991) · R. Jahanbegloo, *Conversations with Isaiah Berlin* (1992) · J. Gray, *Isaiah Berlin* (1995) · M. Ignatieff, *Isaiah Berlin: a life* (1998) · G. Dalos, *The guest from the future: Anna Akhmatova and Isaiah Berlin* (1998) · M. Lilla, *The legacy of Isaiah Berlin* (2001) · *The Times* (7 Nov 1997) · *Daily Telegraph* (7 Nov 1997) · *The Guardian* (7 Nov 1997) · *The Independent* (7 Nov 1997) · 'Three faces of Isaiah Berlin', *TLS* (29 May 1998) · M. Brock, 'Nine years with Isaiah Berlin', *Oxford Magazine*, Michaelmas (1997), 13–14 · *WWW* · Burke, *Peerage* · P. A. Hunt, *Corpus Christi College biographical register*, ed. N. A. Flanagan (1988) · personal knowledge (2004) · private information (2004) · naturalization details, PRO, HO 334/118/B987 · m. cert. · d. cert.

Archives Bodl. Oxf., papers · Bodl. Oxf., corresp. relating to east European refugees | Bodl. Oxf., corresp. with Sir William Clark · King's AC Cam., corresp. with A. E. Felkin · U. Warwick Mod. RC, corresp. with Richard Crossman | FILM BFI NFTVA, 'Tribute to Isaiah Berlin', BBC 2, 15 Nov 1997

Likenesses photograph, 1950, repro. in *The Guardian* · D. Hill, portrait, 1973, repro. in *The Independent* · L. Gowing, oils, 1982, NPG · L. Douglas-Menzies, photograph, 1988, NPG [*see illus.*] · S. Pyke, bromide print, 1990, NPG · photograph, 1990, repro. in *Daily Telegraph* · R. Avedon, bromide print, 1993, NPG · photograph, repro. in *The Guardian* · photograph, repro. in *The Times* · photographs, repro. in berlin.wolf.ac.uk//

Wealth at death £1,537,871: probate, 30 June 1998, *CGPLA Eng. & Wales*

Berlin, Sven Paul (1911–1999), artist and writer, was born on 14 September 1911 at 6 South Terrace, Fairlawn Park, Sydenham, in south-east London, the second of the three children of Karl Gustave Hermann Berlin (1885–1972), a Swedish paper merchant (and nephew of the explorer Sven Hedin) who brought his business to London in the early 1900s, and his wife, Mary Louisa (1882–1955), daughter of Joseph Hughes, the central figure of a literary coterie in late nineteenth-century London. In a family falling on hard times, education was piecemeal, but for young Sven it included a boarding-school at Kenley, Surrey, and the Crystal Palace School of Practical Engineering.

Berlin had no formal art education; he enrolled at the Beckenham school of art, but stayed for only six weeks. He then met Phyllis Groom (1910–1960), a trained ballet dancer in need of a partner to form an adagio dance team to tour the British music-hall circuit. She and the Zelia Raye School of Dancing taught Berlin the necessary skills and techniques required for this part ballet, part burlesque dance, and together as Sven and Helga they appeared on stage throughout the 1930s with such stars as the Crazy Gang, George Formby, and Max Miller. Berlin's first published work, 'The adagio dancer', appeared in the *Dancing Times* in 1929.

On 4 December 1937 Sven and Helga were married, in Bromley, Kent, and that same year they visited the Cornish artists' colony at St Ives. They gave up the stage so that he could become an artist, his lifelong ambition. He worked as a labourer to make ends meet and in his spare time endeavoured to make up for lapses in his education by studying philosophy with Dr Frank Turk of Exeter University and art with Arthur C. Hambley, then in charge of the Redruth and Camborne schools of art. He met the resident artists of St Ives and soon became one of their number. His son Paul was born in 1940, his daughter Greta (also an artist) in 1942.

Sven Paul Berlin (1911–1999), by Stanley Devon, 1952

Berlin lost his job in a tin mine when he registered as a conscientious objector on the outbreak of war, but he later joined the Royal Artillery, serving as a forward observer at the time of the Normandy landings in 1944. A series of letters sent back from the battle zones of northern France to the art critic Adrian Stokes was later reformulated into *I am Lazarus* (1961), a much praised account of the front-line soldier's life under fire. Meanwhile, still in the services, he wrote the first biography of Alfred Wallis (1855–1942), the St Ives rag-and-bone man whose naïve paintings of ships and harbours so strongly influenced the more sophisticated artists of the colony. It was published in 1949. When he returned to Cornwall after the war, he found his marriage in disarray and moved to a studio which he called 'The Tower'. He became one of the most active and colourful figures of the St Ives art community, painting, writing prolifically, and carving the severe granite of the region. His work appeared in nationwide exhibitions, including that celebrating the Festival of Britain in 1950, in which he was awarded second prize for sculpture.

But St Ives was undergoing an artistic sea change as a younger generation of artists supplanted the old school. Berlin became embroiled in a controversy which divided traditional and modern artists into rival factions. He formed the Crypt group with like-minded fellow artists John Wells, Bryan Wynter, Peter Lanyon, and others. He also helped to create the Penwith Society in 1949, but soon resigned when he clashed with the major figures of St Ives, Ben Nicholson and Barbara Hepworth, who wanted a much more modernist exhibition policy than that which the liberal Berlin had in mind. In 1953 he and Helga were

divorced, and on 21 May he married the artist Joy Fisher, *née* Barlow (*b.* 1925), who adopted the name Juanita. (She was Ishtar in his books, and was later known as Juanita Casey, the novelist.) With Juanita and their son Jasper, born in 1953, Berlin left Cornwall in a horse-drawn wagon and travelled to the New Forest, where he lived for nearly ten years among the gypsies near Lyndhurst. An important film of his work as a sculptor during this period was made by the director John Boorman, and Berlin collaborated with the Swedish actor and director Mai Zetterling on a film of the Spanish gypsies. Among those who visited him at this time were Robert Graves and Ralph Vaughan Williams.

In 1963 Berlin divorced Juanita and on 6 September married Julia Pamela Lenthall (*b.* 1944), a distant relative of Alfred Wallis. They moved first to the Isle of Wight and then, in 1975, to Wimborne in Dorset, where Berlin spent the rest of his life. After an important exhibition celebrating the St Ives artistic traditions at the Tate Gallery, London, in 1985 and, in 1993, the opening of the Tate St Ives gallery, Berlin's work, both visual and literary, enjoyed a revival of public interest, and the two extensive volumes of his autobiography, *Coat of many Colours* (1994) and *Virgo in Exile* (1996), together with the reissue of *Alfred Wallis, Primitive* in 1992, were among the last of his published works.

In an artists' community which included Barbara Hepworth, Ben Nicholson, Naum Gabo, Patrick Heron, and the potter Bernard Leach, it is a measure of Sven Berlin's stature that he remains one of the best known and remembered figures from those post-war days. The others may have been better artists and more formative innovators in a colony which was shedding the influence of the old school of representational or 'academy' art in favour of modernism and the abstract interpretation of the landscape in which they lived, but Berlin's art remained firmly anchored in the vigorous bohemianism of the old romantics, such as that of his friend Augustus John.

Berlin's best visual art was his sculpture, and he was able to carve delicate images from that most inhospitable stone, Cornish granite. His line drawings, too, showed an empathy with natural things, especially insects and small animals, and he illustrated a number of books on natural history. He published several semi-autobiographical books of a philosophical nature, but the poetry he wrote profusely was not collected or published in his lifetime. On 7 September 1962 he published *The Dark Monarch*, ostensibly a fiction set in an imaginary artists' colony. Eight days later it was withdrawn and pulped, after four successful writs for libel were served by those of his fellow artists who recognized themselves as the inhabitants of the 'fantasy' town of Cuckoo, a place that was transparently St Ives. In art circles *The Dark Monarch* remains one of the best-known unread books. It chronicles, in strong partisan language, the rift between the colony's artists and the causes of Berlin's self-imposed exile from St Ives.

Berlin believed himself to have been ostracized, not only by the art community of St Ives, but by the wider art establishment, but when he returned to St Ives forty years later to sign copies of his autobiography *Coat of many Colours*, he found old sins forgiven, his *enfant terrible* reputation more cherished than deplored, and his art enjoying something of a renaissance. In 1991 he declined an invitation to republish *The Dark Monarch* in its original form, saying (in *Virgo in Exile*) he 'did not want to be responsible for the forces it would release'. He was, by then, one of the last survivors of the post-war days.

Berlin spent his last years in Wimborne, stone-cutting, painting, and writing with undiminished energy, his last letters being written only a few days before he died of septicaemia in Poole Hospital on 14 December 1999, at the age of eighty-eight. He was buried in Holt cemetery, near Wimborne.　　　　JOHN PADDY BROWNE

Sources b. cert. · m. cert. [Phyllis Groom] · m. cert. [Joy Fisher] · m. cert. [Julia Lenthall] · d. cert. · personal knowledge (2004) · private information (2004) · S. Berlin, *Pride of the peacock* (1972) · S. Berlin, *Coat of many colours* (1994) · S. Berlin, *Virgo in exile* (1996) · *The Times* (16 Dec 1999) · *The Guardian* (4 Jan 2001) · *The Independent* (17 Dec 1999)

Archives priv. coll., letters · Tate collection, transcript of interview with TV South West | Book Gallery, St Ives, Cornwall, letters, many illustrated, to J. P. Browne | FILM BBC TV, *A portrait in time*, John Boorman (director) · BBC TV (National and South) · Southern TV, TVS and Meridian · British Movietone News | SOUND Sven Berlin reads his poems, privately recorded by John Paddy Browne in 1960s

Likenesses S. Devon, photograph, 1952, News International Syndication, London [*see illus.*] · S. Berlin, self-portraits, priv. coll. · photographs, priv. coll.

Wealth at death under £200,000: administration with will, 21 Feb 2000, *CGPLA Eng. & Wales*

(Louis) Hector Berlioz (1803–1869), by Pierre Petit, 1863

Berlioz, (Louis) Hector (1803–1869), composer and conductor, was born on 11 December 1803 in La Côte St André, in the département of Isère, France, the first of four children of Dr Louis-Joseph Berlioz and his wife, Marie-Antoinette-Joséphine, commonly known as Joséphine, the daughter of Nicolas Marmion of Grenoble. In adulthood he was 5 feet 4 inches tall, with striking looks which included an aquiline nose and deep-set, penetrating grey eyes surmounted by a broad forehead and a shock of auburn hair. His health was not robust, and he fluctuated between extremes of boisterousness and deep melancholia. These qualities were balanced by the wit and humour which reveal themselves in his *feuilletons* and letters. On 3 October 1833 he married Harriet *Smithson (1800–1854), an Irish actress with whom he had been infatuated for six years. The couple were separated by 1844, having had a son, although Berlioz cared for Harriet until her death on 3 March 1854, soon after which, on 19 October, he married his mistress, Marie Récio.

Berlioz became established in the public eye with the first performance of his *Symphonie fantastique* in Paris in December 1830. However, it was performances of his overtures *Les Francs-juges*, *Le roi Lear*, and *Waverley* during 1840 that first aroused public interest in London. During the next few years he travelled with much success to Germany and Russia before venturing to London in November 1847 at the invitation of the impresario Louis Jullien. Berlioz was offered a contract to conduct the opening season of opera at Drury Lane in December, with the promise of a much needed handsome salary and the expectation of a six-month engagement for six years. Jullien went bankrupt in April 1848, and although Berlioz conducted the full season he went unpaid. He turned his attention to organizing concerts which included his own music; the two grandest were at Drury Lane on 7 February and at the Hanover Square Rooms on 29 June 1848. He was very successful and earned much praise, but in the absence of the offer of a suitable position he returned to Paris. During this visit he started to compile his *Mémoires*, noting in the preface (dated 21 March 1848) that he had been received in England with much warmth and hospitality.

Berlioz paid four further visits to London. In 1851 it was as a member of the French section of the jury adjudicating the musical instruments at the Great Exhibition. This was a busy and arduous time, and Berlioz took his duties very seriously: but by the end of the exhibition he was the only one of the twelve jurors left in the music section, and he remained unpaid. He attended the service of the charity children held in St Paul's Cathedral on 5 June, a performance involving 6500 children's voices, which made a deep and lasting impression on him; as a result he added a part for unison children's voices in the then unperformed Te Deum. Before he returned to Paris on 28 July he had taken an apartment for the following summer season. A New Philharmonic Society was planned to promote new or hitherto unknown works of merit, and Berlioz was to be its director.

The 1852 season saw Berlioz's greatest success in London, and between 24 March and 9 June he conducted six concerts at Exeter Hall with an orchestra of 110, the largest ever gathered in London, and one concert at the Hanover Square Rooms. All included his own music alongside other repertory, except the fourth, which was the first London performance of Beethoven's ninth symphony, the 'Choral'. For this he had managed to arrange five rehearsals, which was considered a great achievement as English orchestras had already earned notoriety for the paucity of their rehearsal time. This work was repeated at the final concert, with excerpts from *La damnation de Faust* (1846); Berlioz's reputation as the world's leading conductor was secured.

If 1852 saw Berlioz's triumph, the season of 1853 witnessed a disaster for his ill-fated opera *Benvenuto Cellini* (1837) at Covent Garden. The second overture Berlioz wrote for the work, *Le carnaval romain*, had been well received in an all-Berlioz Royal Philharmonic concert, and rehearsals for the opera had been good. But on the opening night, 25 June, a very loud claque hissed the work from start to finish in protest at the encroachment of foreign works and artists into an Italian opera house. It was Berlioz's only failure in London, and he withdrew the work immediately.

Berlioz returned to London for the last time in 1855 to conduct two New Philharmonic Society concerts of his own works at Exeter Hall and one concert of mixed repertory at Covent Garden. Despite rehearsal difficulties, the concerts were successful and plans were initiated for the following season, but they were later abandoned. Berlioz died at 4 rue de Calais, Paris, on 8 March 1869 and was buried at Montmartre three days later.

The lack of a strong native tradition during Berlioz's visits helps to explain why London was more open to musical innovation than other European cities at this time, and accounts for the warmth with which Berlioz was received—warmth which was notably lacking in Paris. Berlioz held London and his British friends in great affection, and would have considered a permanent residence in the city had the opportunity presented itself. Although his visits were not the source of any great compositional activity, the effect of his successes on his morale was certainly a positive one; and his articles for the *Journal des débats* (substantially reprinted in 1950 by A. W. Ganz in *Berlioz in London*), give a lively and colourful account of London's music-making and his experience of it during those years.   DIANA BICKLEY

Sources A. W. Ganz, *Berlioz in London* (1950); repr. (Westport, CT, 1979); repr. (1981) • D. Cairns, *The making of an artist* (1989), vol. 1 of *Berlioz* • D. K. Holoman, *Berlioz* (1989) • J. Barzun, *Berlioz and the Romantic century*, 3rd edn, 2 vols. (1969) • H. Berlioz, *Memoirs*, trans. D. Cairns (1969) • *Correspondance générale: Hector Berlioz*, ed. P. Citron, 7 vols. (Paris, 1972–95) • *New edition of the complete works: Hector Berlioz*, [20 vols.] (1967–) • J. Langford and J. Graves, *Hector Berlioz: a guide to research* (1989) • H. Macdonald, 'Berlioz, (Louis-)Hector', *New Grove* • M. Wright, *A Berlioz bibliography: critical writing on Hector Berlioz from 1825 to 1986* (1988)
Archives Bibliothèque Nationale, Paris • BL, letters to his family, Add. MS 56237 • Musée Hector Berlioz, Côte St André, Isère,

France • NL Scot., corresp. and music | Morgan L., Sarah Fenderson collection • NL Scot., Cecil Hopkinson Berlioz collection • priv. coll.
Likenesses C. Baugniet, drawing, 1851 • P. Petit, photograph, 1863, Hult. Arch. [*see illus.*] • Guillet, lithograph (after drawing by C. Baugniet), Bibliothèque Nationale, Paris • drawing, repro. in Cairns, *Making of an artist* • portraits, repro. in Holoman, *Berlioz*

Bermingham, John, earl of Louth (c.1290–1329), magnate and justiciar of Ireland, was the eldest of at least four legitimate sons of Peter Bermingham of Tethmoy (d. 1308) and Ela, one of four daughters and coheirs of William de Odingsells of Maxstoke, Warwickshire, who had served in Ireland during the 1280s and had been justiciar in 1294–5. In 1308 John's marriage was granted to Richard de Burgh, earl of Ulster, the most powerful Anglo-Irish lord of the day, and he was betrothed to Matilda, one of the earl's daughters; Matilda was, however, chosen as the fairest by agents of the earl of Gloucester, and instead John married, before 1320, her sister Avelina (d. 1350). He inherited from his father Carbury-Tethmoy, on the borders of Offaly and Meath, together with property in Connacht and Tipperary. His mother brought him lands in Solihull, apparently his only English possession, which he sold at the time of his elevation to the earldom in 1319.

Peter Bermingham had been from 1289 a member of the circle of John fitz Thomas Fitzgerald, the future first earl of Kildare (d. 1316). Like his lord, Peter spent much of his career fighting the midland Irish. His slaughter of the leaders of the Ó Conchobhair dynasty (O'Connors) of Offaly at a banquet in 1305 is celebrated in one of the Middle English 'Kildare poems'; it was also cited by Domnall Ó Néill and other Irish as a typical example of settler perfidy in their Remonstrance to Pope John XXII in 1317. John Bermingham, who must have been close to full age in 1308, rapidly assumed his father's role. In 1310 he was associated with fitz Thomas in a dispute with the Lacy family, and in 1313–14 they led campaigns against the Irish of Offaly.

The Bruce invasion of Ireland from 1315 to 1318 catapulted Bermingham into the front rank of Irish magnates. He served in the early campaigns against Edward Bruce, and in 1317—ironically in view of later events—supported Roger Mortimer, lieutenant of Ireland, against the Lacys; Mortimer was also his neighbour as lord of Trim in Meath. In 1318 Bermingham commanded the hastily raised force that killed Bruce at Faughart near Dundalk (Louth). This victory brought splendid rewards. Bermingham visited England in 1319 and was granted the earldom and liberty of Louth in tail male, together with the manor of Ardee (Louth). In 1321 he was in England again, and was made justiciar of Ireland, an office he held until 1323. At the time of his appointment as justiciar, he entered into an indenture with Hugh Despenser the younger. But this was at the point when the Despensers suffered a brief eclipse, and the earl reached Ireland only after a detour to Normandy. In Ireland his government led an assault on Roger Mortimer's lands and tenants following Mortimer's escape from the Tower early in 1322. He sent a contingent of troops to support the king against the earl of Lancaster, and in August and September 1322, after Lancaster's defeat at Boroughbridge, he himself led a force that participated in the king's disastrous campaign against the Scots. His brother William acted as deputy justiciar during his absence.

In 1324 the earl of Louth was among the magnates who undertook, in a parliament at Dublin summoned by the new justiciar, John Darcy, to discipline their kinsmen and adherents and give offenders up to royal justice. In June 1326 he was present at the death of his father-in-law, the earl of Ulster, which was soon followed by the collapse of the Despenser regime in England. These unrelated events destabilized aristocratic society in Ireland. Louth was among several lords involved in disputes in Munster in 1326-7, into which he may have been drawn by the marriage of William Bermingham to Joan, widow of Richard de Clare, lord of Thomond (d. 1318). Unlike some others, notably James Butler and Maurice fitz Thomas Fitzgerald, who were advanced to the earldoms of Ormond and Desmond, he seems to have established no close links with the government of Roger Mortimer. He attended parliament at Dublin in May 1329, when further assurances about the maintenance of order were given by the magnates. On 10 June he was murdered at Braganstown, near Ardee, together with several members of his family and many followers, including, according to the Kilkenny annalist John Clyn, a renowned native Irish musician. Clyn states that the earl fell because 'all those of his county conspired against him, not wishing him to rule over them' (*Annals of Ireland*, ed. Butler, 20). Inquisitions taken by the Dublin government confirm that the assassination was the work of local men, several of whom held, or were to hold, high office in Louth. The creation of the liberty had put Bermingham over an area where there was a well-rooted gentry society, and where his family had no established position. While there is nothing to show that Roger Mortimer plotted his death, it seems probable that the perpetrators were aware that the earl lacked political support. Mortimer rapidly pardoned them, an act which may explain the presence among the charges laid against him in 1330 of the accusation that he had procured '200 charters of pardon for those who had killed magnates and others of the land of Ireland' (*RotP*, 2.53). Shortly before his fall, he added the liberty of Louth to his own possessions.

John Bermingham, whose career encompassed both the Irish frontiers and the court, and who first benefited from and then fell victim to the turbulence of Edward II's reign, left no sons. Ardee and other property was shared between his three daughters, but the male line of the Berminghams clung to Carbury-Tethmoy, where the earl in 1325 had given land to found a Franciscan house at Monasteroris. Although William Bermingham was executed amid further factional quarrels in 1332, his son Walter (d. 1350) followed in the earl of Louth's footsteps by serving as justiciar of Ireland in 1346-9. ROBIN FRAME

Sources *Chancery records* · PRO · J. F. Lydon, 'The Braganstown massacre, 1329', *Journal of the co. Louth Archaeological and Historical Society*, 19 (1977), 5-16 · R. Frame, *English lordship in Ireland, 1318-1361*

(1982) · *The annals of Ireland by Friar John Clyn and Thady Dowling: together with the annals of Ross*, ed. R. Butler, Irish Archaeological Society (1849) · J. T. Gilbert, ed., *Chartularies of St Mary's Abbey, Dublin: with the register of its house at Dunbrody and annals of Ireland*, 2, Rolls Series, 80 (1884) · B. Smith, 'A county community in early fourteenth-century Ireland: the case of Louth', *EngHR*, 108 (1993), 561-88 · *CEPR letters*, 2.209, 245 · *RotP* · E. Tresham, ed., *Rotulorum patentium et clausorum cancellariae Hiberniae calendarium*, Irish Record Commission (1828)

Bermingham, Michel (*b.* 1685), surgeon, was born in London in 1685 and became a member of the Academy of Surgery at Paris. He published *Some Documents in French and English Belonging to the Hospital of Incurables in Paris* (1720), *Manière de bien nourrir et soigner les enfants nouveau-nés* (1750), and a translation of the statutes of the doctors regent of the faculty of Paris. An account by him of an excision of the parotid glands (1736) is preserved among the Birch MSS (no. 4433, art. 155).

THOMPSON COOPER, *rev.* MICHAEL BEVAN

Sources P. J. Wallis and R. V. Wallis, *Eighteenth century medics*, 2nd edn (1988) · S. Ayscough, *A catalogue of manuscripts preserved in the British Museum hitherto undescribed*, 2 vols. (1782)
Likenesses portrait, repro. in H. Bromley, *A catalogue of engraved British portraits from Egbert the Great to the present time* (1793)

Bermingham, Patrick (*c.*1460-1532), judge, was a native of Ireland and succeeded to the estates of his brother John in 1483. His family had long-established connections with the law in Dublin, and several members studied at the inns of court for that purpose. One Philip Bermingham had served as chief justice of the king's bench in Ireland from 1474 to 1490. 'Patryk Byrmyngham de Hibernia' was admitted to Lincoln's Inn in the summer of 1478. He is recorded as keeping at least four terms, but resided certainly until 1486, when he was put out of commons for various unspecified offences; he was readmitted after paying a fine, but there is no further mention in the inn records and he probably returned to Ireland. By 1503 he was a clerk of the exchequer in Ireland, and in 1513 was appointed chief justice of the king's bench there. In 1521 he became chancellor of the green wax (or exchequer), but his office as chief justice was continued by a new patent. He was a leading figure in the council in Dublin, and was responsible for keeping order in the pale during one of its many periods of rebellion, in 1528, when the earl of Kildare was in England.

Bermingham must have died late in 1532, as his successor was appointed on 13 January 1533. Nothing is known of his marriage, but he left a son, William, who married Margaret, the daughter of Thomas St Lawrence, justice of the king's bench in Ireland. In 1504 one Patrick Bromygham acted as a mainpernor for Richard Goldyng, an Irish law student admitted to Lincoln's Inn in 1505, in connection with an outbreak of disorder in the inns of chancery, and was ordered not to leave the realm. This must have been a younger member of the family studying in England, probably the Burbigham, or Byrmynham, who appears in the Inner Temple records in 1506 and 1509. J. H. BAKER

Sources F. E. Ball, *The judges in Ireland, 1221-1921*, 1 (1926), 192-3 · S. G. Ellis, *Reform and renewal* (1986), 34, 39, 45, 218, 221, 223 · W. P. Baildon and R. Roxburgh, eds., *The records of the Honorable Society of*

Lincoln's Inn: the black books, 5 vols. (1897–1968) · PRO, C244/155/85 [case of 1505] · D. B. Quinn, 'Anglo-Irish local government, 1485–1534', *Irish Historical Studies*, 1 (1938–9), 354–81, esp. 359 · F. A. Inderwick and R. A. Roberts, eds., *A calendar of the Inner Temple records*, 1 (1896), 7, 15 · *LP Henry VIII*, 6, no. 105 (11, 16)

Bermingham, William (*d.* 1312), archbishop of Tuam, was the son of Meiler de Bermingham, lord of Athenry. In 1288, following the death of Stephen of Fulbourne, Bermingham was unanimously elected archbishop of Tuam by the Anglo-Irish chapter, thereby becoming the first Anglo-Irishman appointed to that see. He proceeded to Rome where he was first raised from sub-deacon's orders to deacon's before being ordained priest and consecrated as archbishop on 26 May 1289. He was dispensed of various irregularities, among them that he had held a church in the diocese of Cashel since his eleventh year. One of his first duties in his new office was to summon the clergy of his province to induce them to grant the king a tenth of their spiritualities. He was unsuccessful and wrote to the king in 1291 that his clergy found themselves too much impoverished to comply with the request. Bermingham's episcopacy was a stormy one and the judicial and papal records contain details of frequent disputes between him and his clergy.

In 1297 began Bermingham's celebrated quarrel with the Dominican friars of Athenry. The friars complained in the justiciar's court that the archbishop, through his archdeacon, had excommunicated certain members of their community and had issued a proclamation forbidding the people to give them food or alms, sell them anything, or enter their church. The justiciar recommended that the archbishop and the vicar-general of the Dominicans should settle the matter between them. There is no record of the settlement, however. The abbess of the convent of Kilcreevanty, Galway, also had cause to complain before the justiciar about the archbishop's violent exercise of his visitation rights. Bermingham was summoned to appear in Dublin in January 1308 but before this date he had left Ireland to travel to the papal court. His visit was to answer the charges of the dean of Annaghdown, who complained to Pope Boniface VIII in 1303 that the archbishop had seized the church of Annaghdown, keeping the see vacant and depriving the dean and chapter of their dignities and benefices. The dean also claimed that the archbishop committed many acts of simony, oppressed his subjects, and employed notorious malefactors. The diocese of Annaghdown had been kept vacant by archbishops of Tuam for many years; however, in 1308 the first bishop for fifty years was consecrated, implying that Bermingham was not successful at the papal court. Meanwhile, in his absence, yet another case (this time involving the archbishop and members of his family with the rape of two girls) was being heard before the justiciar. In the course of this case the archbishop was distrained by chattels, including sixty stud horses worth 24 marks. There is no evidence that Bermingham was suspended from office. He died in January 1312 and was buried in the abbey of Athenry, near his father, Meiler.

P. W. Joyce, *rev.* Margaret Murphy

Sources J. Mills and others, eds., *Calendar of the justiciary rolls … of Ireland*, 3 vols. (1905–56) · E. A. D'Alton, *History of the archdiocese of Tuam*, 1 (1928) · H. T. Knox, *Notes on the early history of the dioceses of Tuam, Killala and Achonry* (1904) · *CEPR letters*, 1.498–500 · J. A. Watt, *The church and the two nations in medieval Ireland* (1970) · S. Mac Airt, ed. and trans., *The annals of Inisfallen* (1951) · A. M. Freeman, ed. and trans., *Annála Connacht / The annals of Connacht* (1944); repr. (1970) · H. S. Sweetman and G. F. Handcock, eds., *Calendar of documents relating to Ireland*, 5 vols., PRO (1875–86)

Bernal, (John) Desmond (1901–1971), physicist, was born on 10 May 1901 at Brookswatson, Nenagh, co. Tipperary, eldest of the three sons and two daughters of Samuel George Bernal, a farmer of Limerick, and his wife, Elizabeth Miller, elder daughter of the Presbyterian minister in San José, California. The Bernal family can be traced back to Sephardic Jews in sixteenth-century Spain. Among their descendants in the nineteenth century several flourished in England, but Bernal's grandfather lived in Ireland. Bernal's father, Samuel, had run away to sea and farmed sheep in Australia before he settled to farming in Ireland.

Education and political sympathies There seems to have been little in the way of a bond between father and son, but a rewarding companionship between Elizabeth Bernal and her first-born. His mother was described by C. P. Snow as literary and cultivated (she attended lectures at Stanford University and the Sorbonne, and contributed articles to the *San Francisco Argonaut*), and it was her care for his education which meant that at the age of ten he was sent, with his brother Kevin, to Hodder, the preparatory school for Stonyhurst College. However, both boys were miserable at Stonyhurst, and their mother moved them to Bedford School, where some science was taught. Emmanuel College, Cambridge, awarded Bernal a scholarship in mathematics in 1919, so it was to Cambridge he went, and when he completed his undergraduate courses in 1923 he had been educated in England for twelve years. For the rest of his life he spoke with the voice of an educated member of the upper class.

Bernal brought with him to Cambridge, alongside his passion for science, a deep concern for the state of Ireland and a strong attachment to Catholicism which he viewed positively as a powerful hindrance to the Anglicization of his home country. Long before—he claimed at the age of ten—he had come to the conclusion that the answer to Ireland's problems lay with science. Living in both countries as a boy he had been made painfully aware of the striking contrast between the poverty of agricultural Ireland and the growing wealth of industrial England. Ireland, he believed, needed to attain economic as well as political independence from Great Britain. His enthusiasm for science was not, therefore, solely that of curiosity but more importantly out of concern for its wealth-giving applications. In this he proved steadfast, despite the revelations of the atom's dread powers. Among fellow students he soon became something of a legend—his encyclopaedic knowledge and his photographic memory, his articulate and persuasive speech, and his passion for what he held dear earned him the nickname Sage. C. P. Snow described

(John) Desmond Bernal (1901–1971), by Wolfgang Suschitzky, 1949

his 'shock of fairish hair gone wild' and 'beautiful, humorous, hazel eyes' (Snow, 19). He married (Agnes) Eileen (b. 1898/9), a former student of Newnham College and the daughter of Dr William Carr Sprague, on 21 June 1922, having just reached his majority, but not his graduation. In any event, his marriage did not cramp his amorous nature. In addition to his two sons, Michael and Egan, with his wife, he had Martin with Margaret Gardiner and (Susanna) Jane with Margot Heinemann.

The intellectual qualities that Bernal displayed as an undergraduate, one would have thought, would have endeared him to his college and university, but there were problems. His young Cambridge friends had influenced him in the direction of Marxism. The Irish national foundation of his political concern, they considered, was too narrow. H. D. Dickinson introduced him to the socialist society. His communist friend Allen Hutt lent him Marx's works. Bernal was soon converted and his faith in the Roman Catholic church weakened. Already in his pioneer work *The Social Function of Science* (1937) his admiration for Marx's writings and for the organization of science in the Soviet Union is evident. Twenty years later he was to sum up his view of Marx in the little work *Marx and Science* (1957). By that time he could look back on the Second World War as 'another world catastrophe brought about by the insane greed and violence of a decaying capitalism' (J. D. Bernal, *Marx and Science*, 42). On the bright side, though, both in China and in the 'People's Democracies of Europe', he declared, 'the age-old role of the landlords is over and the natural talents of the people can find expression'. With pride and confidence he pointed to the 800 million of them now living under socialism. The Soviet

intervention in Hungary was four years away, but Lysenko's destruction of Russian genetics had begun in the 1930s and proved to be a serious embarrassment to socialist scientists in Britain. In due course J. B. S. Haldane resigned from the Communist Party chiefly because of it, but in 1939 Bernal had attributed the controversy to the fact that Soviet science as it grew was only just finding out its philosophy, a process which he described as 'lively and at times almost violent' (J. D. Bernal, *The Social Function of Science*, 1939, 231, 237). Reports of the matter had been greatly exaggerated outside the Soviet Union, he thought, and it was misleading to describe the controversy as a revival of the old Weismann–Lamarck debate. Over the years Bernal became more critical, and in 1968 he was prepared to admit that Lysenko had ignored contemporary biology—Bernal had by then visited Lysenko and seen his work. But it was modern molecular biology and the discovery of the double helical structure of DNA that changed Bernal's mind. These developments were to him 'more materialistic and hence more Marxist than Lysenko's views' (J. D. Bernal, 'The material theory of life', *Labour Monthly*, 50, 1968, 326).

Judged by the natural sciences tripos examinations results Bernal did not excel, perhaps due to the extent of his interests outside the formal curriculum, and to his discovery of a passion for crystallography. Taught this subject by Arthur Hutchinson, Bernal decided to derive the 230 space groups using Hamiltonian quaternions. This enormous task took his attention away from the physics of Professor Rutherford, and a second class in the part two physics final examination was the result—a disappointment after his first in the part one in chemistry, geology, and mineralogy, but the work on the space groups deeply impressed Hutchinson. Through his recommendation Bernal was offered a position at the Davy–Faraday Laboratory at the Royal Institution in London, directed by Sir William Bragg.

Research in crystallography By natural inclination Bernal was a theoretician rather than an experimentalist, but Sir William, who with his son Lawrence had worked out the structure of diamond in 1913, wanted the structure of graphite determined. These two forms of carbon could be considered as prototypes for the dimensions of the carbon–carbon bond in aliphatic and aromatic compounds respectively. Introduced to the exact method of measuring diffraction intensities using the X-ray spectrometer, Bernal recoiled at the patience required—a whole day to measure only two reflections! The alternative was to use photographic film, not so accurate but much quicker. The snag was that he had to assemble his equipment himself from bits and pieces. Doggedly he persisted and the structure came out with a carbon–carbon distance of 1.42 Å in contrast to the distance for diamond of 1.54 Å. This work done, Bernal turned to methods of analysis. He popularized Paul Ewald's conception of the reciprocal lattice, gave a systematic account of rotation methods, and in 1926 published the very useful charts he had laboriously calculated for plotting the layer lines of diffraction patterns. The distances between these lines represent the reciprocal of distances separating scattering points in the crystal lattice. To make the photographic method easy to use he designed equipment that was marketed by a Cambridge company as the X-ray photogoniometer. Bernal also worked on the structure of metal alloys while at the Royal Institution—a subject with obvious industrial applications.

In 1927 Bernal returned to Cambridge on his appointment to the revived lectureship in structural crystallography. He was to remain there until 1938, becoming assistant director of research in 1935. Then he moved to the chair of physics, subsequently crystallography, at Birkbeck College, London, retiring in 1968. If his years at the Royal Institution were the most exciting and formative of his scientific life, the decade he spent in Cambridge was the most significant for our assessment of his contribution to science, for it was then that the foundations were laid for the tradition of research on the structure of biologically important compounds which we associate with Cambridge, where he made firm friends with several biochemists. There followed a productive collaboration with the outstanding experimentalist Dorothy Crowfoot (subsequently Hodgkin) and Isidore Fankuchen. Between 1931 and 1937 Bernal published his preliminary study of the crystallography of amino acids and oligopeptides, the structure of the carbon skeleton of sterols, the structure of water, and the first description of the diffraction patterns of protein crystals using the trick of bathing the crystals in their mother liquor; the latter two achievements gave the first glimpse of the world of molecular structure that underlies living things. The hope of creating a molecular account of the organic basis of life was born here.

For a number of reasons Bernal's plans for crystallography at Birkbeck College did not enjoy quite the same success. His substantial contributions to civil defence, Bomber Command and combined operations, during the war won him the medal of Freedom (with palms) from the United States but inevitably took him away from the college. Then, as the cold war began, he became a globetrotter—working indefatigably for world peace and for the socialist cause. The fact that he found time to write his ambitious and extensive 1000-page *Science in History* (1954), although greatly aided by Francis Aprahamian and Anita Rimmel, suggests that his enthusiasms now lay outside the laboratory, that the man who had been torn away from his research by the war could not again recover the urge and the patience he once showed for the structural analysis of the proteins. Having shipped off his equipment with Fankuchen to America when hostilities began, he lived to mourn the loss of his promising researches of the inter-war years. When the double helical structure of DNA was discovered his regret at not being in the story was evident, but he could take pride in the contribution of his department, for it was Sven Furberg who came from Norway in 1947 to work at Birkbeck, there establishing the three-dimensional structure of cytidine (pyrimidine plus sugar)—essential information for the solving of the structure of DNA.

Also in 1947 Francis Crick visited Bernal in his quest for a research position in biology, followed two years later by an enquiry from Rosalind Franklin for the same purpose. Bernal had by this time a grant from the Nuffield Foundation, and the Medical Research Council's secretary, Sir Edward Mellanby, assured Crick that an application supported by Bernal would be accepted automatically, but Bernal was out of the country. In the meantime the biophysicist A. V. Hill urged Crick to consider Cambridge. Likewise the physical chemist Charles Coulson advised Franklin to apply to King's College rather than Birkbeck. After the DNA research was completed she did move to Birkbeck and carry out her fine researches into viral RNA. It seems, therefore, that it was neither the lack of funds nor Bernal's politics that prevented him from re-establishing his pre-eminent place in the field of biomolecular structure after the war, but the opinion formed about his commitment to research on a day-to-day basis. Was he not a founder member of the World Federation of Scientific Workers and the World Peace Council? Snow described him at this stage as 'in continuous motion, scurrying from Birkbeck, the most recent scientific paper being corrected in the car to London airport, off to one of the socialist capitals, Moscow, Warsaw, Bucharest, or Peking' (C. P. Snow, 'John Desmond Bernal', *DSB*, 15, Suppl., 1978, 19).

Assessment To view Bernal's achievement by comparing it with the success of 1950s molecular biology, however, fails to reveal Bernal's vision of biomolecular structure. First it is not clear that he was interested in genetics, or in the nucleic acids as the genetic material. Had he not, in support of Lysenko, claimed that genetics had inherent weaknesses due to its design to serve capitalist aims? Second, he was fascinated by the mystery of the origin of life, an interest continued over many years, and leading to his full-length study *The Origin of Life* (1967). This subject raised the question of the level of organization at which life could be said to emerge. He envisioned a series of levels from the molecular to the organismic, and his focus was on organization at the *inter*-molecular level of colloids, membranes, and Aleksandr I. Oparin's coacervates. Thus his pioneer study with Fankuchen of tobacco mosaic virus crystals was directed chiefly to the behaviour of the molecules at varying degrees of hydration, rather than to the internal structure of the molecules themselves. This was very understandable at the time: in the absence of the electron microscope the interpretation of the diffraction intensities corresponding to distances between molecules was the only way to bridge the gap between the molecular and the cytological structures. Hence, on his return from war work to Birkbeck College he wrote to Fankuchen describing his hopes and explaining that 'the main idea is to link up the long-range forces with the biological systems' (Olby, 262).

Additionally, the data of the diffraction patterns of the tobacco mosaic virus were not those of a single crystal to which the standard methods of interpretation could be readily applied. They were, it later turned out, the transforms of the molecules rather than of the crystal lattice.

This explains why Bernal and Fankuchen experienced such difficulty in establishing the features of the unit cell. Nor was the pattern blessed with numerous spots, at least not enough of them to justify the use of the standard methods of analysis which Bernal preferred. As he was later to remark (1968):

> The picture of a helical structure contains far fewer spots than does that of a regular three-dimensional crystalline structure, and thus far less detailed information on atomic positions, but it is easier to interpret roughly and therefore gives a good clue to the whole. (Bernal, 'Material theory', 324)

He added that it may appear 'paradoxical that the more information-carrying methods should be deemed the less useful to examine a really complex molecule'. Here he implied, it seems, that as far as methods of analysis for the nucleic acids were concerned, he had 'backed the wrong horse'.

The theme running through Bernal's popular writing is one of developing science in the service of all mankind. Like Marx, Bernal saw science as part of the productive forces, not an abstract body of idealistic thought. Time was when science was the occupation of the curious supported by the wealthy. Now, he explained, it has become 'an industry supported by large monopolies and by the State' (Bernal, 'Material theory', xiii). The problem for Bernal was to set out the conditions under which science can be most successfully pursued and most advantageously deployed for the benefit of all. In *The Social Function of Science*—a truly prophetic work—he stressed the need for organized and planned research, for co-operation in research, for adequate documentation, and for the scientific study of scientific activity—what was to become the 'science of science'. Bernal wrote the book because he resented the inefficiency and frustration of scientific research on the one hand, and its diversion to base ends on the other. Later he was to turn to the history of science, for only with that knowledge, he claimed, could we hope to understand the significance of the institution of science and its relation to society. In 1937 he remarked that existing histories of science 'are little more than pious records of great men and their works' (Bernal, *Social Function*, 11). What is history, he asked, but the progressive unfolding of the productive relation between man and nature? It was therefore fitting that he should take his great work *Science in History* (1954) up to the post-war period. Viewed from the present Bernal's unfailing optimism for nuclear power, world energy supplies, antibiotics, synthetic fibres, massive irrigation to make the deserts bloom, and changing the course of rivers to suit man's needs, seems outdated and naïve. Yes, he admitted, agriculture has produced devastation, but only because of the 'predatory nature of capitalism' (Bernal, *Science in History*, vol. 3, 964). In truth, Bernal remained to the end a passionate visionary. He was elected to fellowship of the Royal Society in 1937, and was the Society's royal medallist in 1945. In 1953 he received the Lenin prize for peace, in 1965 an honorary fellowship of his Cambridge college, and in 1969 fellowship of Birkbeck College. He began to suffer from health problems in 1951. The severe stroke he suffered in 1963 increasingly limited his activities and after several further strokes he died on 15 September 1971 and was buried in London. ROBERT OLBY

Sources D. M. C. Hodgkin, *Memoirs FRS*, 26 (1980), 17–84 • M. Goldsmith, *Sage, a life of J. D. Bernal* (1980) • J. D. Bernal, 'My life at the Royal Institution, 1923–27', *Fifty years of X-ray diffraction*, ed. P. P. Ewald (1962), 522–5 • G. Werskey, *The visible college* (1978) • R. Olby, *The path to the double helix* (1994) • C. P. Snow, 'J. D. Bernal, a personal portrait', *The science of science*, ed. M. Goldsmith and A. Mackay (1966), 19–31 • m. cert. • *CGPLA Eng. & Wales* (1972)
Archives American Institute of Physics, College Park, Maryland • CUL, MSS • King's Lond., Liddell Hart C., account of work as scientific adviser, combined operations, in relation to D-Day • London School of Economics | Bodl. Oxf., letters to Dorothy Hodgkin and others • Bodl. Oxf., corresp. with Sir J. C. Kendrew • Bodl. Oxf., corresp. relating to Society for Protection of Science and Learning • King's Lond., Liddell Hart C., corresp. with Sir B. H. Liddell Hart • U. Leeds, Brotherton L., corresp. with W. T. Astbury
Likenesses W. Suschitzky, photograph, 1949, NPG [*see illus.*] • Ramsey & Muspratt, photographs, repro. in Hodgkin, *Memoirs FRS*
Wealth at death £48,288: probate, 18 Jan 1972, *CGPLA Eng. & Wales*

Bernal, Ralph (*d.* 1854), politician and art collector, was of Jewish descent and came from a family of Spanish origin. He was the only son of Jacob Bernal (*d.* 1811) of 7 Fitzroy Square, London, was born at Colchester, Essex, and was educated at Shacklewell School. He went up to Christ's College, Cambridge, in 1804, where he graduated BA (11th wrangler) in 1806, proceeding MA in 1809. He was first married, on 10 April 1806, to Anne Elizabeth, only daughter of Richard Samuel White of New Ormond Street, London. Anne died tragically from burns after her clothes caught fire on 10 July 1823, at Bryanston Square, London, soon after giving birth to a child. Ralph Bernal *Osborne (1808?–1882), politician, was their eldest son. He was to marry again, to a daughter of Dr Henry White RN, the surgeon of Chatham Dockyard, and to have further offspring.

In 1810 Bernal was called to the bar at Lincoln's Inn. After inheriting a large estate in the West Indies he abandoned the law for a political career, and held a seat in the House of Commons from 1815 to 1852, spending the phenomenal sum of £66,000 on contesting elections, an indication of his political zeal. He represented Lincoln from 1818 to 1820 and Rochester from 1820 to 1841. He was the member for Weymouth from 1841 to 1847, and then for Rochester again until he lost his seat in 1852. He was a prominent whig, and chaired parliamentary committees from 1833 to 1841 and 1847 to 1852. He spoke against the immediate prohibition of the slave trade early in his career in the House of Commons, his speech of 19 May 1826 being published in pamphlet form. He also contributed to other publications, both political and antiquarian.

Bernal became president of the British Archaeological Society in 1853. He was well known as a collector of glass, plate, ceramics, and miniatures, and formed a cabinet of a kind just becoming of interest to public museums. After his death from fever at his house, 93 Eaton Square, London, on 26 August 1854, the Society of Arts tried to persuade the government to buy the collection *en bloc* for the

South Kensington Museum (now the Victoria and Albert Museum), for which it was in many ways extremely suitable, but despite the energetic support of the curator, John Charles Robinson, to no avail, although some of the pieces were to reach the public collections. Two catalogues of the collection were issued, and it was sold at auction; there were over 4000 lots, which realized £70,000. The prices attained in 1855 were immense, although the pictures and ceramics were regarded as of little value by the critics of the *Art Journal*. Bernal himself had formed the collection with some judgement but comparatively little expense. HELEN DAVIES

Sources P. H. Bagenal, *Life of Ralph Bernal Osborne* (1884) · *GM*, 1st ser., 93/2 (1823), 92 · *GM*, 2nd ser., 42 (1854), 628 · Venn, *Alum. Cant.* · *Return of members of parliament* (1818–52) · *Fifty years of public work of Sir Henry Cole*, ed. A. S. Cole and H. Cole, 1 (1884), 289–90 · J. R. Planché, foreword, *Catalogue of the celebrated collection of … Ralph Bernal* (1855) [sale catalogue] · *Art Journal*, 17 (1855), 116, 153 · T. Wilson, 'The origins of the maiolica collections in the British Museum and the Victoria and Albert Museum, 1851–1855', *Faenza*, 1–3 (1985), 68–81 · H. E. Davies, 'Sir John Charles Robinson (1824–1913): his role as a connoisseur and creator of public and private collections', DPhil diss., U. Oxf., 1992 · AM Oxf., Robinson MSS · art referee reports, V&A · d. cert.
Archives Jewish Museum, Camden, letters to Reynolds · U. Southampton L., letters to J. C. Isaac · W. Sussex RO, letters to duke of Richmond
Likenesses J. Thomson, stipple, pubd 1822 (after A. Wivell), BM, NPG · G. Hayter, group portrait, oils (*The House of Commons, 1833*), NPG

Bernard. *See* Neufmarché, Bernard de (d. 1121x5?).

Bernard [Bernard Sapiens] (*fl. c.*865–870), cleric and traveller, was the subject of misidentifications in the early seventeenth century, being described as English by John Pits and as Scottish by Thomas Dempster; the latter asserts that Bernard had been abbot of Holywood in Dumfriesshire and attributes to him a history of Jerusalem from 970 to 1100, a work *Ad suffraganeos suos*, and a treatise *De bello sacro* in seven books. The history of Jerusalem does not exist, but seems to derive from a misunderstanding by Dempster of Pits's account of the *Itinerarium* written by Bernard Sapiens. The *De bello sacro* is the work of the twelfth-century Italian Bernardus Accoltus. The assertion that Bernard was English may be a false inference from extracts from Bernard's *Itinerarium* quoted by William of Malmesbury in his account of the first crusade in his *Gesta regum*. Dempster also claims that Bernard was present at the Council of Clermont in 1095, and was sent to Scotland to preach the first crusade; and he identifies him with Bernard, bishop of Antioch, who died in 1150.

In his *Itinerarium*, a brief account of his journey from Rome to Jerusalem, made during the pontificate of Nicholas I (*r.* 858–67), the author names himself as Bernard and says that he travelled with two monks, Theudemund and Stephanus. With papal permission they sailed from Taranto to Alexandria, then up the Nile to Cairo, and crossed the desert via Damietta and Ferama to visit the holy places, especially at Jerusalem and Bethlehem. He returned via Rome to the monastery of Mont-St Michel. Although some manuscripts date the work to 970, internal references to Pope Nicholas I, Patriarch Michael of Alexandria, and Louis II of Italy confirm the 870 date ascribed to it by William of Malmesbury. The Rheims manuscript of the *Itinerarium*, now destroyed but used by Mabillon in the late seventeenth century, stated that Bernard was born in France, but that sentence is not found in the four surviving manuscripts. The *Itinerarium* has been printed several times; English translations by Thomas Wright and J. H. Bernard were published in 1848 and 1893 respectively. DAVID GANZ

Sources 'Itinerarium Bernardi monachi Franci', *Itinera Latina*, ed. T. Tobler and A. Molinier, Publications de la Société de l'Orient Latin, série géographique, 1–2 (1879), 308–20 · *Clavis des auteurs Latins du moyen age*, 1 (1994), 236–8 · F. Avril and J.-R. Gabortt, 'L'Itinerarium Bernardi monachi et les pèlerinages d'Italie du sud pendant le haut moyen age', *Melanges de l'école française de Rome*, 79 (1967), 269–98 · T. Wright, ed., *Early travels in Palestine* (1848) · *The itinerary of Bernard the Wise*, trans. J. H. Bernard, Palestine Pilgrims' Text Society, 3 (1893) · J. Pits, *Relationum historicarum de rebus Anglicis*, ed. [W. Bishop] (Paris, 1619), 827 · T. Dempster, *Menologium Scoticum* (1622), 17 · L. d'Archery and J. Mabillon, eds., *Acta sanctorum ordinis sancti Benedicti*, 9 vols. (Paris, 1668–1701), vol. 4

Bernard (d. 1148), bishop of St David's, was, as Gerald of Wales described him, 'the first bishop to be translated to the diocese of St David's by royal power'. A Frenchman, he emerged to prominence first as a chaplain serving Henry I's queen, Matilda, and then as her chancellor. He was elected at the palace of Westminster on 18 September 1115 (by a group drawn from St David's who subsequently asked Ralph, archbishop of Canterbury, to consecrate him); Matilda expressed a wish to be present at his consecration. Bernard was ordained priest on the day of his election and on the following day he was consecrated bishop at Westminster Abbey, near the royal palace. In the *Brut y tywysogyon* it was noted that Henry I 'made him bishop in Menevia in contempt of the clerics of the Britons'. They could well take offence at the comparatively new procedure and at the bishop's nationality.

As a servant of Matilda, Bernard was brought into close contact with Henry I, whose friendship he enjoyed and with whom he was in great favour. At intervals, as he travelled with the court in England and Normandy, he attested the king's charters. After his consecration he remained in the royal entourage and carried out a number of commissions. In 1119 Henry I sent to the Council of Rheims his Norman bishops, and those English bishops who were with him in Normandy, including Bernard. In 1121 Bernard and the royal clerk, John of Bayeux, were given the task of shepherding a papal legate around England without allowing him to establish any claims over the English church. Bernard was assiduous in his attendance at ecclesiastical councils, and he frequently took part in the consecration of new bishops. He was always in touch with the men of power of his day. In 1123 William de Corbeil, archbishop of Canterbury, went to Rome for his pallium. Bernard was with him as his proctor; he was also commissioned to guard the king's interests. Thurstan, archbishop of York, was in the party, and the vexed issue of his obligation to accept the primacy of Canterbury was raised. In the debate that followed Bernard was a staunch defender of Canterbury's claims which, at that stage, he did not wish to challenge. But Canterbury's evidence was sadly flawed, and Thurstan emerged as the victor in that contest.

On the death of Henry I, Bernard accepted Stephen as king and continued to attest his charters until 1140. He then transferred his allegiance to the Empress Matilda, and was constantly in her entourage during 1141. In March 1141 he was one of the two episcopal supporters who presented her on her triumphal entry into Winchester Cathedral. He was drawn into the local affairs of the west midlands, where she had her strongest backing, attesting charters and confirming grants to St Peter's Abbey, Gloucester. After the death of Miles, earl of Hereford, at Christmas 1143, he was one of three bishops who intervened in the struggle between St Peter's, Gloucester, and Llanthony Secunda over the right to bury Earl Miles, and who drew up and sealed an agreement between the two communities.

At St David's Bernard proved himself an able bishop. He had ample experience of getting business done efficiently and a capacity to weigh up alternative policies. From 1119 until 1133 Urban, bishop of Llandaff, was prosecuting a claim to the eastern part of the diocese of St David's, Ystrad Tywi, Gower, Kidwelly, and Cantref Bychan. Urban made little headway until 1128, but over the next five years Bernard successfully defended the rights of his see. He founded a house of Augustinian canons at Carmarthen, though that involved the dispossession of the Benedictine priory there. He also gave land in Trefgarn to the Cistercians, who established there the community which later moved to Whitland. He reorganized the diocese, using the ancient kingdoms of Dyfed, Ceredigion, and Brycheiniog to form the archdeaconries of St David's, Cardigan, and Brecon; the disparate group of territories in the east, Gower, Kidwelly, Carnwyllion, Cantref Bychan, and Cantref Mawr, which defied rationalization, made up the archdeaconry of Carmarthen. His rural deaneries retained the familiar boundaries of smaller territorial units.

At St David's, Bernard restructured the community of long-established *claswyr*, the Welsh clerics who served the cathedral, imposing on them a stricter discipline and redistributing their finances. They included two of the sons of Bishop Sulien, Ieuan and Daniel, both of whom worked closely with him. With this group he had to integrate those Anglo-Norman clerics who formed his immediate circle during his thirty-three years as bishop. He was a good listener and could take into account the views of men of different traditions. He was much influenced by his new Welsh colleagues. He absorbed their traditions of St David and in 1119 he secured from the papacy some recognition, if not formal canonization, of the patron saint of his diocese. He also gave full weight to their case that St David's had been, in some sense, a metropolitical see. That rested on the view that St David had himself been an archbishop and on the fact that the bishop of St David's had consecrated bishops for other Welsh dioceses. It also rested on the view that in 'nation, language, law, habits,

judicial procedures and customs' the Welsh province differed from England.

During the 1120s Bernard canvassed the view that the status of St David's should be enhanced. In September 1125, at the Council of London, he offered an apology to the archbishop of York for the extreme terms in which he had challenged York's claim for independence in 1123. His reading of the Welsh past and of contemporary English ecclesiastical politics marched together. His moves in the 1120s produced no concrete result but in the later years of Innocent II's pontificate (1130–43) his campaign was renewed. Innocent and his successors, Lucius II and Eugenius III, were prepared to give the case serious consideration. In a garbled account of the Welsh church, Henry of Huntingdon recorded, whether as fact or mere rumour, that in recent memory the bishop of St David's had been given a pallium but had lost it immediately. Gerald of Wales did not make this claim explicitly, but he did record that Bernard sometimes had a primatial cross carried before him as he travelled through Wales. From north Wales Owain Gwynedd and his brother, Cadwaladr, offered their support, and Bernard was anxious to secure further endorsement from Simeon, archdeacon of Bangor. In England Archbishop Thurstan was informed that Eugenius was considering the claim, and the bishops of Norwich, Hereford, Ely, Exeter, Bath, and Winchester rallied to the archbishop's support. The issue was to be put to the council summoned to meet at Rheims at the end of March 1148, and Eugenius gave partial judgment later in the year, leaving the question of the future status of the see to be discussed in October, but Bernard died and the cause lapsed. Not the least important aspect of this conflict was that documents produced during its course were invaluable when Gerald of Wales pursued the same case for the enhancement of St David's at the end of the twelfth century. Bernard was certainly the ablest bishop to hold office in Wales in the twelfth century, and one of the most distinguished of the medieval bishops of St David's.   DAVID WALKER

Sources *Gir. Camb. opera*, vols. 2–3 · Giraldus Cambrensis, *De invectionibus*, ed. W. S. Davies (1920) · *Reg. RAN*, vol. 3 · A. W. Haddan and W. Stubbs, eds., *Councils and ecclesiastical documents relating to Great Britain and Ireland*, 1 (1869) · J. G. Evans and J. Rhys, eds., *The text of the Book of Llan Dâv reproduced from the Gwysaney manuscript* (1893) · G. T. Clark, ed., *Cartae et alia munimenta quae ad dominium de Glamorgancia pertinent*, ed. G. L. Clark, 6 vols. (1910) · Henry, archdeacon of Huntingdon, *Historia Anglorum*, ed. D. E. Greenway, OMT (1996) · *Hugh the Chanter: the history of the church of York, 1066–1127*, ed. and trans. C. Johnson (1961) · *Eadmeri Historia novorum in Anglia*, ed. M. Rule, Rolls Series, 81 (1884) · J. C. Davies, ed., *Episcopal acts and cognate documents relating to Welsh dioceses, 1066–1272*, 1, Historical Society of the Church in Wales, 1 (1946) · M. Brett, *The English church under Henry I* (1975) · R. R. Davies, *Conquest, coexistence, and change: Wales, 1063–1415*, History of Wales, 2 (1987) · F. Barlow, *The English church, 1066–1154: a history of the Anglo-Norman church* (1979)

Bernard [Bernard the Scribe] (*fl.* 1123–1130), administrator, came from a middle-ranking thegnly family in Cornwall, which, like many others, had suffered loss of estates and social depression as a result of the Norman conquest. His grandfather, Theodulf, had a modest estate in Cornwall; his father, Ailsi, was a master builder in Launceston; and his uncle, Brihtric, in 1084 held five small manors in Cornwall of the count of Mortain. Bernard had two brothers: the elder, Jordan, was a landowner near Launceston, and the younger, Nicholas, was another royal scribe. Both Bernard and Nicholas seem to have been unmarried, and Bernard may, like Nicholas, have become a canon of the Augustinian priory of Merton in Surrey. Jordan, however had a son, Peter of Cornwall, who became prior of Holy Trinity, Aldgate, and early in the thirteenth century made a vast collection of visions and revelations which throw some light on the family's history.

As a *scriptor* ('scribe') Bernard clearly set himself, with the help of his royal master and of his chancery superiors and colleagues, to recover through litigation what ancestral lands he could; and he also benefited from rewards from his patrons and satisfied clients. Some of his acquisitions probably went with his office. In Cornwall he had the land and revenues of Gisulf, the royal scribe who had perished in the wreck of the *White Ship* on 25 November 1120, a man whom Orderic Vitalis despised. The grant by the king of a vacant plot in Launceston Castle, 'between the well and the chapel', was for his lodgings. He also held in the castle the land of Ranulf the chancellor and an orchard. In Winchester he had a tenement in Parchment Street, which Count Stephen of Mortain relieved of a rent-charge, and in Busket Lane, by grant of William de Pont l'Évêque, sheriff of Hampshire and royal chamberlain, two tenements which had belonged first to the clerk Anselm and then to Gisulf. As he does not appear by name in either of the Winchester surveys, Bernard's tenure of property there probably lies between *c*.1110 and 1148. In London, similarly, by confirmatory charter of John of Bayeux, a royal chaplain and bastard son of Bishop Odo of Bayeux, he held land and houses which had been Gisulf's, together with a soke held of the archbishop of Canterbury, free of all service so long as he served in the royal court. But if he left the court he had to make specified payments to John. Further afield he had land in Northamptonshire, and in Normandy at Mathieu near Caen.

As scribes are not itemized in *Constitutio domus regis*, a guide to the royal household prepared for King Stephen, it would seem that the compiler regarded them as of relatively lowly status. But Bernard was on occasion, perhaps usually, attended by two or three squires, and he is always found in the company of ministerial colleagues of high standing in the court. He and his brother Nicholas divided their wealth between their eldest brother's family, the church of Launceston, and Merton Priory. Launceston inherited *inter alia* the silver-embossed ivory writing-case with silver ink-horn they had used in the king's service. The church converted it into a reliquary. Although he attested none of Henry I's charters, Bernard was a rather grand royal domestic servant. FRANK BARLOW

Sources J. H. Round, 'Bernard the king's scribe', *EngHR*, 14 (1899), 417–30 • R. W. Southern, 'King Henry I', *Medieval humanism and other studies* (1970), 206–33, esp. 225–8 • J. A. Green, *The government of England under Henry I* (1986) • M. Biddle, ed., *Winchester in the early middle ages: an edition and discussion of the Winton Domesday*, Winchester Studies, 1 (1976) • *Reg. RAN*, vol. 2

Bernard (*d.* 1330/31), administrator and bishop of Sodor, has been identified since 1726, but erroneously, with the Bernard of Linton, parson of Mordington, recorded in the Ragman rolls of 1296. In view of the rarity of the name Bernard and the place of his burial he is much more likely to have been the Bernard, abbot of Kilwinning, also named in those rolls. If so, he will have been forced out by the English, and may have retired to Arbroath, like Kilwinning a Tironesian abbey, where an English abbot, John, had been imposed. In 1308 Bernard appears in Robert I's earliest acts as Dom Bernard the chancellor and must have been in the king's following. By the end of 1308 Angus was in Robert's hands, and Abbot John was sent on his way in 1309. Bernard may have been abbot-elect for some months before being blessed into office in 1310, and he then went as ambassador to Norway; he returned in February 1312, ahead of Norwegian ambassadors who completed a treaty with Robert at Inverness on 29 October 1312.

During that year Bernard had acted decisively to revive the fortunes of his house, recovering lost revenues and other rights, a course he was to pursue more gently during the remainder of his abbacy. The great seal imposed few burdens before 1315, and of the sixteen known charters of 1312–13 no fewer than nine were for the benefit of his abbey. After 1314 the pace increased significantly, and drafts were retained to become, from 1318, the basis of rather haphazard enrolment. Many royal acts must have been dated by the chancellor's whereabouts (especially if at the abbey of Arbroath), but his clerks were probably secular, not regular. Although he is often assumed to be author of the Declaration of Arbroath of 1320, the skilled use of the papal *cursus* in that text points rather to a professional rhetorician. On the other hand, Walter Bower preserves fragments of Latin verse chronicles, including a poem by Bernard on the battle of Bannockburn, which he ascribes sometimes to Abbot Bernard, sometimes to a monk of his abbey; these would repay further study.

When the war with England was won, in the autumn of 1327, Bernard looked for his reward; by January 1328 he was bishop-elect of Sodor and he ceased to be chancellor (losing his fee of 200 merks annually) probably on 3 April 1328. Having been given £100 towards his election expenses as bishop, he was consecrated before 12 November 1328. He visited his cathedral on Man, but died perhaps in 1330, certainly well before 10 June 1331, when his successor was appointed at Avignon. Bernard was buried in the abbey of Kilwinning, where he probably died, suggesting that he had made his profession as a monk there some forty or fifty years before. A. A. M. DUNCAN

Sources G. W. S. Barrow and others, eds., *Regesta regum Scottorum*, 5, ed. A. A. M. Duncan (1988) • G. W. S. Barrow, *Robert Bruce and the community of the realm of Scotland*, 3rd edn (1988) • W. Bower, *Scotichronicon*, ed. D. E. R. Watt and others, new edn, 9 vols. (1987–98), vols. 6–7

Bernard, Agnes Morrogh [*name in religion* Mary Joseph Arsenius] (**1842–1932**), Roman Catholic nun, was born on 24 February 1842 at Cheltenham, Gloucestershire, the only child of John Morrogh (*d.* 1866), landowner, who changed his name to John Morrogh Bernard on inheriting the Bernard estates in co. Kerry in 1849, and his wife, Frances Mary Blount (d. 1888). After her birth the family moved to Cork, where they lived until 1849, when they went to live at Sheheree House on her father's inherited estate.

Agnes Morrogh Bernard was educated at home by her mother until 1854, when she was sent to Laurel Hill convent in Limerick, where she spent three years. She returned to Sheheree House for a year before finishing her education in the Convent of Dames Anglaises in Paris. While still a student she had felt herself drawn to religious life; her father, who was opposed to her joining a religious community, finally allowed her to enter a convent when she reached the age of twenty-one.

On 2 July 1863 Agnes Morrogh Bernard entered the noviciate of the Sisters of Charity in Dublin. She took as her religious name Mary Joseph Arsenius, and was known as Sister (later Mother) Mary Arsenius. After her profession in 1866 she took up teaching posts in Gardiner Street in Dublin, and later in King's Inns Street School. She was appointed to the Mountjoy Street convent in 1869 and subsequently to Lakelands Orphanage, where she remained in charge until 1877. Her various convent experiences included managing budgets, overseeing the laundry work of the Magdalen Asylum, and supervising building works within the convents—skills which were to be beneficial in her later work. On 24 April 1877 she was appointed reverend mother of a new convent in Ballaghaderreen in co. Mayo. In 1879 the convent borrowed money to build a national school in the convent grounds and from 1886 it also ran an industrial school.

In April 1891 Mother Mary Arsenius, with four other nuns, opened a convent in Foxford, co. Mayo, an area racked by poverty. The convent initially took over the local national school and, to provide some employment for the local people, she decided to set up a woollen mill, the Providence Woollen Mill. She received a loan of £7000 from the newly formed congested districts board, the function of which was to support projects that aimed to alleviate poverty in areas along the western seaboard of Ireland. Another loan was received in 1893 to provide training for workers. By 1899 the convent had received a further £7000 for technical training. This was spent not only on the factory workers but also on the instruction of local cottiers in gardening, poultry breeding, and improved farming methods. All her projects were carefully planned and skilfully managed.

Mother Mary Arsenius declared herself to be apolitical. During the months following the fall of Charles Stewart Parnell a number of the mill workers derided the parish priest for his anti-Parnellite stand. She was informed by the local hierarchy that these workers had to apologize for their behaviour or an interdict would be inflicted on those concerned. Mother Mary Arsenius made a public apology on the workers' behalf. Her other foray into public politics came during the war of independence when some of the mill workers became the victims of the Black and Tans in 1921: she had the culprits brought to justice despite threats of retaliation.

In 1898 Mother Mary Arsenius undertook the task of building roads in the area; through her scheme cart roads were built to the doors of 118 houses. In addition, she encouraged the local authorities to build labourers' cottages. She was also interested in the social and cultural life of the area, and supported the efforts of the Gaelic League to revive Irish language and culture.

In 1869 Mother Mary Arsenius had suffered a bout of eczema which developed into erysipelas; she was to endure ill health for the rest of her life. However, she remained active in her various projects up to her death. She died at the convent at Foxford on 20 April 1932, from a flu-related illness, and was buried in the graveyard there on 23 April. MARIA LUDDY

Sources D. Gildea, *Mother Mary Arsenius of Foxford* (1936) • M. B. Butler, *A candle was lit: the life of Mother Mary Aikenhead* (1953) • J. A. Glynn, 'Irish convent industries', *New Ireland Review*, 1 (1894) **Archives** Foxford Convent, co. Mayo, Republic of Ireland • Foxford Woollen Mills Museum, co. Mayo, Ireland | Dublin Diocesan Archives, Walsh MSS **Likenesses** photographs, Foxford Woollen Mills Museum, co. Mayo, Ireland • photographs, repro. in Gildea, *Mother Mary Arsenius*

Bernard, (William) Bayle (1807–1875), writer, was born on 27 November 1807 in Pleasant Street, Boston, Massachusetts, USA, the eldest son of the English actor–manager John *Bernard (1756–1828) and his third wife (née Wright). The family returned to England in 1820 and Bernard was educated at Uxbridge before working from 1826 to 1830 as clerk in the army accounting office. He made his acting début at the Queen's Theatre in 1826 as Young Marlow in Sheridan's *She Stoops to Conquer* and, at the time of his father's death in 1828, was 'sustaining a trivial situation in a minor theatre' to support his family (*The Times*, 27 Dec 1828, 3e).

Abandoning acting for authorship, Bernard wrote, during the course of his prolific career, 114 plays, almost all of which were performed, although less than half were published. He adapted for the stage works by Byron, Edward Bulwer-Lytton, Wilkie Collins, James Fenimore Cooper, Goethe, Victor Hugo, and Eugène Scribe, and wrote one of the earliest stage versions of *Rip Van Winkle*; but the bulk of his production was original, consisting of domestic, historical, and romantic dramas, and his most popular genre, farce and comedy. Among his most acclaimed plays were *His Last Legs*, *The Irish Attorney*, *The Man about Town*, and *The Nervous Man and the Man of Nerve*, all apparently produced between 1835 and 1840.

Bernard earned £3 for what was probably his first drama, *Casco Bay*, produced at the Olympic Theatre in 1827, and received, as an added incentive, another £2 on the hundredth night of its 140-night run. Bernard often employed American themes and popularized, in plays such as *The Kentuckian* and *The Irish Attorney*, the characters of the eccentric rural Yankee and the comic Irishman. His plays served as vehicles for such stage personalities as John Brougham, James Henry Hackett, Samuel Phelps, Tyrone Power, and Madame Vestris.

For almost half a century, Bayle Bernard was, as his

father had been, a fixture of literary, theatrical, and bohemian life in London, frequenting, in the late 1830s and 1840s, the Wrekin tavern near Drury Lane, 'time out of mind the favourite resort of authors, actors, poets, painters, and penny-a-liners' (*Life and Reminiscences*, 1.62). He was a member of the Dramatic Authors' Society and theatre critic for the *Weekly Dispatch*. His wife, Esther Gozina Bernard (*d.* 1910), was herself an author and essayist. They had one daughter.

In 1830 Bernard made a significant contribution to English theatre history by editing and publishing *Recollections of the Stage* (2 vols., 1830), based on his father's manuscripts to the year 1797. His own busy career prevented his completion of an edition of John Bernard's manuscripts pertaining to his years as actor-manager in America between 1797 and 1820; however, he did publish selections as 'Early days of the American stage', serialized in six instalments of *Tallis's Dramatic Magazine* (1850–51). He apparently made three different excerpted versions of his father's original manuscripts concerning America, two of which were edited by his widow and published as *Recollections of America, 1797–1811* (1887).

A year before his death Bernard published *The Life of Samuel Lover* (2 vols., 1874), a tribute to his long-time friend which contains both autobiographical detail and examples of Bernard's literary criticism, which was much praised by contemporaries. Passages such as his description and defence of Nicolò Paganini, his anecdotes of Tyrone Power and Charles Kean, and his account of Lover's American tour of 1846–8 are notable. The biography serves as a memoir of Bernard himself, who died of decay and exhaustion at 5 St Peter's Place, Brighton, on 5 August 1875. Richard Garnett summed up Bernard's character and achievements in this way: 'Bernard was a highly accomplished man, a prolific and efficient playwright, an excellent dramatic critic, thoughtful, studious, and interested in serious subjects' (*DNB*). PAGE LIFE

Sources B. Bernard, *The life of Samuel Lover*, 2 vols. (1874) • J. Bernard, *Retrospections of the stage*, ed. W. B. Bernard, 2 vols. (1830) • J. Bernard, *Retrospections of America, 1797–1811*, ed. B. Bernard (1887) • N. B. East, 'John Barnard, actor-manager: 1756–1828', PhD diss., University of Kansas, 1970 • *The Times* (9 Aug 1875) • *New York Times* (9 Aug 1875) • *New York Times* (23 Aug 1875) • *The life and reminiscences of E. L. Blanchard, with notes from the diary of Wm. Blanchard*, ed. C. W. Scott and C. Howard, 2 vols. (1891) • J. R. Stephens, *The profession of the playwright: British theatre, 1800–1900* (1992) • d. cert. • Boase, *Mod. Eng. biog.*, 1.256 • will • *DNB* • S. J. Kunitz and H. Haycraft, eds., *British authors of the nineteenth century* (1936)
Archives BL, letters as sponsor to the Royal Literary Fund, loan no. 96 • Harvard U., letters and MSS | BL, agreement with R. Bentley, Add. MS 46611 • BL, letter to R. Bentley, Add. MS 33964, fol. 445 • BL, agreements with H. Colburn and R. Bentley, Add. MS 46611 • BL, letter to J. W. Davison, Add. MS 43382, fol. 165 • Hist. Soc. Penn., letters, incl. to Skelton Mackenzie
Wealth at death under £2000: probate, 21 Oct 1875, *CGPLA Eng. & Wales*

Bernard, Bruce Bonus (1928–2000), photographer and picture editor, was born on 21 March 1928 at 7 Shepherd's Hill, Highgate, London, the second of three sons and third

of the five children (one of whom died in infancy) of Oliver Percy *Bernard (1881–1939), stage designer and architect, and his second wife, (Edith) Dora, *née* Hodges (1896–1950), an opera singer with the stage name Fedora Roselli. (Despite her exotic stage name and flamboyant character, she was the daughter of a London butcher, originally from Sussex.) The Bernards' marriage was later described by their eldest son, Oliver, in *Getting Over It* (1992), as consistently stormy and occasionally violent. Oliver Percy Bernard died in 1939 leaving his wife with debts; nevertheless she managed to send all three sons to public schools—Oliver to Westminster, Jeffrey *Bernard (1932–1997), later a journalist, to Pangbourne College, and Bruce to the more liberal Bedales. In 1946 Bernard was called up for national service, but objected on moral grounds; he was exempted on condition that he worked as a porter at the West London Hospital for Nervous Diseases. He was soon dismissed. In London he had by then become a habitué of Soho, introduced by his brother Oliver. (Bruce in turn introduced Jeffrey, and sometimes blamed himself for doing so.) Thereafter (with the exception of the years 1948–50, when he lived in Cornwall) he was a fixture of Soho life, frequenting in particular the York Minster (the 'French pub'), run by Gaston *Berlemont, and the Colony Room Club, run by Muriel Belcher.

Bernard enrolled at St Martin's School of Art, but partly through lack of confidence he destroyed most of his work, a habit which remained with him in later life, and failed to complete the course. He then took a series of temporary jobs, including in bakeries, on building sites, and backstage in theatres. Meanwhile he continued to paint and to study painting, but he also developed an interest in photography and its history. Having been stunned in 1950 by Francis Bacon's second exhibition at the Hanover Gallery, he became a close (though not lifelong) friend of the artist. He also formed a more enduring friendship with Lucian Freud (whom he had first met as a schoolboy); Freud painted or drew him on many occasions. Throughout the 1950s and early 1960s Bernard lived a precarious existence, living in rented lodgings at his best or in a Rowton house (a privately run doss-house) at his worst. He was, in his own words, 'as good as down and out' (*The Independent*, 3 April 2000) when in 1967 Germano Facetti offered him a job as a picture researcher for Purnell's part-work magazine *History of the Twentieth Century*. He immediately found his métier, and soon became picture editor for the series.

In 1972 Bernard joined the *Sunday Times* as picture editor. He enjoyed a good relationship with the newspaper's editor, Harold Evans, though Bernard 'was not exactly a team player, and his inability to suffer fools led to some memorable confrontations' (*The Times*, 1 April 2000). He featured work by rising stars such as Don McCullin, Eve Arnold, Ken Griffiths, and William Klein, and also introduced a magazine series, 'Photodiscovery', featuring little-known but striking photographs from the past. The series became a book, *Photodiscovery: a Century of Extraordinary Images, 1840–1940*, edited by Bernard and published in 1980. In the same year he left the *Sunday Times*, following changes in the editorial regime, and became a freelance editor and writer of illustrated books. These included *The Bible and its Painters* (1983); *Vincent by Himself* (1985), a selection of the artist's paintings and of extracts from his letters; *Queen of Heaven* (1987), featuring paintings of the Virgin Mary from the twelfth to the eighteenth centuries; and *Humanity and Inhumanity: the Photographic Journey of George Rodger* (1994). He wrote introductions for two books of Lucian Freud's paintings, *Lucian Freud* (1996) and *Nudes* (1997). His friendship with Francis Bacon was ended when the latter withdrew consent to a book, 'About Francis Bacon', which Bernard had already edited. (Bernard stubbornly refused to excise material to which Bacon had objected; the book remained unpublished.) He curated a number of exhibitions, including a National Portrait Gallery exhibition of John Deakin's work, 'The Salvage of a Photographer' (1984), and an exhibition at the Barbican of photographs from the Hulton collection, 'All Human Life' (1994). From the mid-1990s he built up a collection of photographs for James Moores, son of the Littlewoods founder, Sir John Moores. (The collection was named after him, and exhibited at the Victoria and Albert Museum in 2002–3.) He was also a photographer in his own right, and in 1995 had a well-received exhibition in Portobello Road, London. Among the photographs included was one of Leigh Bowery and Nicola Bateman nude on a bed, with alongside them Lucian Freud's as-then uncompleted painting of them, 'And the Bridegroom' (exh. Whitechapel Gallery, 1993).

Possessed of a temperamental and frequently melancholic disposition, Bernard 'dressed as if he had been unemployed for a very long time, entering a room defensively as if prepared for disillusion. To strangers, he seemed to exist in a perpetual state of disgruntlement' (Farson, 236). Yet he could be passionately friendly, and was much loved by his circle of friends. Lucian Freud's portrait of him in his studio (1992), which the artist used as the poster for his exhibition at the Whitechapel Gallery in 1993, caught him in characteristic mode: hands in pockets, clothes dishevelled, his face intense, thoughtful, and inquisitive. He viewed his late success with both wry detachment and anticipatory enthusiasm. 'It's amazing … after a lifetime with no money, I'm a millionaire, give or take a few hundred thousand' (*The Times*, 1 April 2000). His last book was *Century* (1999), a photographic survey of the twentieth century ('one hundred years of human progress, regression, suffering and hope', as he put it in his subtitle), 1120 pages long and 13 pounds in weight. Half a million copies were sold. By then Bernard was suffering from cancer. He was cared for by his partner of seventeen years, Virginia Verran, an artist. He died at his home, 31 Frederick Street, Camden, London, on 30 March 2000, and was survived by her. An exhibition of his photographs of five artists—Michael Andrews, Frank Auerbach, Francis Bacon, Lucian Freud, and Euan Uglow—was held at Tate Britain in 2002.　　　　ALEX MAY

Sources *The Guardian* (31 March 2000) • *The Guardian* (1 April 2000) • *Daily Telegraph* (31 March 2000) • *The Times* (1 April 2000) • *The Independent* (3 April 2000) • O. Bernard, *Getting over it* (1992) • D. Farson, *The gilded gutter life of Francis Bacon* (1993) • *The Guardian* (31 Aug 2002) • *The Guardian* (3 Sept 2002) • b. cert. • d. cert. **Likenesses** J. Deakin, photograph, 1955 (with Jeffrey Bernard and Terry Jones), V&A; repro. in *The Guardian* (31 March 2000) • L. Freud, etching, 1985, repro. in *Daily Telegraph*; exh. Hayward Gallery • L. Freud, oils, 1992, repro. in *The Times*; exh. Whitechapel Gallery • T. Glanville, photograph, 1999, repro. in *The Independent* **Wealth at death** £246,541: probate, 4 Sept 2000, CGPLA Eng. & Wales

Bernard, Charles (*bap.* 1652, *d.* 1710), surgeon, was born at Waddon, Surrey, and baptized on 7 August 1652, son of the Revd Dr Samuel Bernard (1590/91–1657) and his wife, Elizabeth (1608/9–1705). Francis *Bernard was his brother. Samuel Bernard had been vicar of Croydon for nineteen years until his ejection in 1644. On 7 August 1670 Charles Bernard was apprenticed to Henry Boone, surgeon, for seven years and on the completion of his apprenticeship he was admitted a freeman of the Barber–Surgeons' Company in December 1677. He was appointed assistant surgeon at St Bartholomew's Hospital on 13 November 1683 and elected full surgeon on 26 August 1686. Bernard became the leading surgeon of his day with an enviable reputation for his skill when operating. A notable success was Benjamin (later Bishop) Hoadly, whose leg he saved when other surgeons recommended amputation. Bernard's conservatism was well known and he acknowledged that with the imperfect knowledge of the time he had never seen a cure for breast cancer and that rapid dissemination of the disease inevitably occurred following surgical intervention. He shared the post of lithotomist at Bart's between 1693 and 1705. Bernard was appointed sergeant-surgeon on the accession of Queen Anne in 1702, a post he held until his death, and thereafter was usually known as Sergeant Bernard. In November 1696 he was elected a fellow of the Royal Society.

Bernard became an assistant of the Barber–Surgeons' Company, a member of the governing body, on 25 October 1697, an examiner of surgeons on 8 November 1700, and in 1703 was elected master. During his mastership he obtained the remission of a debt of £1000 owed by the company to the exchequer and had the sheriff of London dismissed for failing to supply the bodies of executed criminals for dissection. In turn the queen presented the company with a silver wine cooler for its fidelity and diligence in examining surgeons for the navy.

In May 1679 Bernard married Susanna Gardner and the next month was elected surgeon to the Charterhouse. With Susanna he had one son, Charles, and three daughters, Susan, Elizabeth, and Mary. Elizabeth married Ambrose Dickins, who was apprenticed to Bernard between 1702 and 1709 and who succeeded him as sergeant-surgeon. One daughter is known to have married William Wagstaffe, later physician at Bart's. Bernard, who was a tory and a high-churchman, firmly believed in the curative power of the 'royal touch' for scrofula.

Bernard died on 9 October 1710 at Longleat House, Wiltshire, where he had been on a visit to treat Thomas Thynne, Viscount Weymouth. Bernard was buried in the church of Longbridge Deverill. An effigy of him was later placed there but has since been destroyed. Thomas Hearne noted that

> last week died Mr Charles Bernard, Chief Chirugeon to the Queen, to the great Reluctance of all that were acquainted with him & to the Publick Loss of the whole Nation, he being the best and most successful Chirugeon in England; and he was withall a man of Integrity, of good Natural Parts, and of some considerable Learning. He had collected an Excellent study of Books, as also before him had his brother Dr Francis Bernard. (Prewer, 'Charles Bernard', 246)

In his will Bernard left his wife his three houses in the City and there were bequests to his children and his sister Jane. His brother Dr William Bernard was an executor. Bernard's library was auctioned at the Black Boy Coffee House on 22 March 1711. Swift, a friend of Bernard, attended the viewing and noted it in his *Journal to Stella*.   IAN LYLE

Sources R. R. Prewer, 'Charles Bernard and Edward Thwaites: two scholars at an amputation', *Journal of Medical Biography*, 1 (1993), 241–7 · R. R. Prewer, 'The Reverend Doctor Samuel Barnard: Doctor William Harvey prescribes again', *Journal of Medical Biography*, 4 (1996), 53–7 · N. Moore, *The history of St Bartholomew's Hospital*, 2 vols. (1918) · C. Wall, *A history of the Worshipful Society of Apothecaries of London*, ed. H. C. Cameron and E. A. Underwood (1963) · S. Young, *The annals of the Barber–Surgeons of London: compiled from their records and other sources* (1890) · private information (2004) [G. C. R. Morris, J. Burnby]
Archives BL, papers, Sloane MSS, misc. MSS 1684, 1694, 1770
Likenesses T. Murray, oils, *c.*1711, Worshipful Company of Barbers, London

Bernard, Sir Charles Edward (1837–1901), administrator in India, was born at 16 The Crescent, Clifton, Bristol, on 21 December 1837, the son of James Frogo Bernard MD and his wife, Marianne Amelia Lawrence, sister of John, first Lord Lawrence. He was educated at Rugby School and in 1855 accepted a cadetship at Addiscombe College; in 1856 he switched to the East India College at Haileybury, and passed out in 1857 at the head of the list for Bengal with prizes in mathematics, Persian, Hindustani, and Hindi. He married at Calcutta on 23 October 1862 Susan Capel, daughter of Richard Tawney, rector of Willoughby, Warwickshire.

Bernard's early service was in the Punjab and afterwards the Central Provinces, where he was secretary to two chief commissioners, Sir Richard Temple and Sir George Campbell (in 1893 he was to oversee the posthumous publication of the latter's memoirs). In 1871 he became the commissioner of Nagpur division, and for four years he was a member of the council of the lieutenant-governor of Bengal. In 1880 he was appointed judicial commissioner of the Central Provinces.

In 1881 Bernard became home secretary to the government of India and in 1882 chief commissioner of British Burma. Upper Burma was then still independent, but in November 1885 Lord Dufferin, largely at the urging of Bernard, sent in an army and deposed King Thibaw. Bernard applied his characteristic energy to governing the new territory, but was handicapped by his disregard for Burmese social and political institutions. As a liberal he put great faith in the civilizing nature of British ideals of law and order and attempted to superimpose on Upper Burma the wholly alien system of civil administration developed in British India. Resistance to British occupation was not easily crushed, and as guerrilla outbreaks continued throughout 1886 rumours spread in Calcutta that Bernard was not up to the job, a view fuelled by a series of critical reports in *The Times*. This however was not the official line and in 1886 Bernard was created KCSI.

In 1887 he was briefly the resident at Mysore and chief commissioner of Coorg, before returning to England in 1888 to become secretary to the department of revenue, statistics, and commerce at the India Office. In 1889 he compiled a comprehensive report on Britain's administration of India since the uprising of 1857, which was laid before parliament. He finally retired in 1901 after forty-three years' continuous service. His extraordinary breadth of experience (he had served in all of the Indian provinces except the North-Western Provinces) meant that for the last twenty of these years his advice was sought on numerous issues. He was more a man of common sense than of original or radical ideas and although a liberal, his opposition to illiberal acts, such as the Vernacular Press Act, was typically based on a pragmatic appreciation of their inutility rather than moral repugnance. He was popular with his colleagues and made remarkably few enemies during his career. The Bernard Free Library in Rangoon was built in his memory.

He died on a visit to Chamonix in France on 19 September 1901 and was buried there the next day. His wife survived him; of their eight children the eldest son, James Henry, followed his father into the Indian Civil Service and died of cholera together with his wife at Chinsura in Bengal in November 1907.

J. S. COTTON, rev. KATHERINE PRIOR

Sources *The Times* (3 May 1886) · *The Times* (6 May 1886) · *The Times* (23 Sept 1901) · *The Times* (25 Sept 1901) · S. Gopal, *British policy in India, 1858–1905* (1965) · C. H. T. Crosthwaite, *The pacification of Burma* (1912) · G. A. Solly, ed., *Rugby School register*, rev. edn, 1: *April 1675 – October 1857* (1933) · *East-India Register and Army List* (1858–60) · *Indian Army and Civil Service List* (1861–88) · BL OIOC, Haileybury MSS · ecclesiastical records, BL OIOC · F. C. Danvers and others, *Memorials of old Haileybury College* (1894) · CGPLA Eng. & Wales (1901)
Archives BL OIOC, letter-book relating to Burma, MS Eur. D 912 | BL, letters to Lord Ripon, Add. MS 43595 · BL OIOC, letters to Sir E. B. Sladen, Eur. MS E 290 · BL OIOC, letters to Sir H. T. White, Eur. MS E 254 · U. Edin. L., Keith MSS
Likenesses photograph, 1874 (with Sir Charles Bernard), BL OIOC
Wealth at death £20,173 15s. 11d.: probate, 21 Oct 1901, CGPLA Eng. & Wales

Bernard, Daniel (d. 1588), Church of England clergyman and scholar, was the son of Thomas *Bernard (d. 1582) [see under Bernard, John], and the nephew of John *Bernard. He is likely to have had a reformist upbringing since his father, vicar of Pyrton, Oxfordshire, and canon of Christ Church, Oxford, was deprived under Queen Mary and restored under Queen Elizabeth. Daniel became a student of Christ Church in 1560 and graduated BA in 1566. He was lecturer in dialectic there in 1567–9 and in rhetoric in 1569–70. In 1571 he became censor of the college in moral philosophy and in 1577 a canon of Christ Church. He was its treasurer in 1577 and 1582 and also became subdean in the latter year. Gilpin (an eighteenth-century chapter clerk) reported that he was 'severe' and 'expended a large sum of money in building a handsome wall on the east side of his garden which before was only fenced with a hedge' (Christ Church, Oxford, dean's register, DP i.a.1, 16, fol. 4v). Bernard finally graduated DTh in 1585, after two previous attempts when he neglected to carry out the prescribed exercises; he may have been granted his BTh at the same time. He was chaplain to Sir Thomas Bromley (who deputized for the chancellor, the earl of Leicester, during his absence in the Low Countries, 1585) and was vice-chancellor of Oxford in 1586/7. In 1586 he was awarded two college livings, Ardington, Berkshire, and Wath, Yorkshire. He donated a book to his college, Pierre Viret's De vero ministerio (Geneva, 1553). Bernard had died by August 1588, when his estate was subject to probate in the court of the chancellor of Oxford; it was ratified by the prerogative court of Canterbury in September. He was buried in the choir of Christ Church Cathedral without any memorial. He was survived by his wife, Suzanne. He was the author of a Latin sermon, Concionem ad clerum de obedientia erga principes et praefectos in Tit.ii.3, published in 1587.

MARGARET LUCILLE KEKEWICH

Sources Hist. U. Oxf. 3: Colleg. univ., 507 · Tanner, Bibl. Brit.-Hib., 97 · Wood, Ath. Oxon., new edn, 2.171, 232, 235 · Foster, Alum. Oxon., 1500–1714 [Daniel Bernarde] · B. Willis, A survey of the cathedrals of Lincoln, Ely, Oxford and Peterborough (1730), 449 · Reg. Oxf., 3.71 · PRO, PROB 6/4, fol. 72r · dean's register, Christ Church Oxf., DP i.a.1, 16
Wealth at death see will, PRO, PROB 6/4, fol. 72r

Bernard, Edward (1638–1697), mathematician and Arabist, was born on 2 May 1638 at Paulerspury, near Towcester, Northamptonshire, the elder child of Joseph Bernard (c.1609–1644), clergyman, and Elizabeth Lenche or Linche (d. in or after 1669) of Wyche, near Great Malvern, Worcestershire. He was baptized at Paulerspury, where his father is thought to have been curate, on 15 May 1638. Soon after his sister Anne's baptism on 1 September 1639, the family moved to the town of Northampton, where he showed early promise as a student. After his father's death when he was barely six, his mother sent him to live with an uncle in London, where in 1647 he was admitted to the Merchant Taylors' School. In June 1655, already 'very well versed in the classic authors' and—thanks presumably to the headmaster, William Dugard—'not unacquainted with Hebrew' (Smith, 4), he was elected Merchant Taylors' fellow and Sir Thomas White scholar at St John's College, Oxford, from where he matriculated the same year. Thomas Wyatt, one of the younger fellows, was his tutor.

Bernard was made a fellow of St John's in 1658, and graduated BA on 12 February 1659. Guided by Edward Pococke's lectures, he mastered Hebrew, Arabic, Syriac, and later Coptic; his personal library catalogue of 1658 already listed Arabic and Hebrew books (now Bodl. Oxf., Lat. misc. MS f.11, fols. 14–17). In 1661 he contributed Arabic verses to Epicedia academica Oxoniensis on the death of Princess Mary, and Edmund Castell asked him to join in preparing the Lexicon heptaglotton, which he declined. He then studied Hebrew privately with Isaac Abendana, and

mathematics with John Wallis; after proceeding MA on 16 April 1662, he became college reader in mathematics in 1663. The Oxford edition of Georgios Pachymeres' Epitome (1666) of Aristotle's Organon is said to have been prepared by Bernard for John Fell.

Bernard was college bursar in 1667, 1668, and 1672, and in 1667 was chosen university proctor. He graduated BD on 9 June 1668 and in December travelled to Leiden University to complete an Oxford-commissioned transcription of books 5–7 of the Conics of Apollonius of Perga, which survived only in Arabic versions. The Bodleian Library has Bernard's transcript (MS Thurston 1) and other materials for an edition with Latin translation and commentary, which he never completed. He also examined Leiden's oriental manuscripts bequeathed by Joseph Scaliger and, more recently, Levinus Warner. On 16 February 1669 he thanked Joseph Williamson for expediting a lucrative offer 'to go with Sir Hugh Cholmondely to Tangiers, which I readily accepted' (CSP dom., 1668–9, 197). But this scheme—like others for escaping Oxford—failed, and he returned to St John's. Fell commissioned him to edit Josephus, at which he worked intermittently for the rest of his life.

When Christopher Wren accepted the surveyorship of royal works in 1669, he appointed Bernard to deputize for him as Savilian professor of astronomy. Bernard believed 'books and experiments do well together', and he regretted Oxford's lacking 'a set of grinders of glasses, instrument-makers, operators, and the like' (Rigaud and Rigaud, 1.158–9). But his own interest was mainly in ancient mathematics and astronomy, and his lectures reflected that. He was incorporated BD at Cambridge in 1672 and could have pursued a career in the church: that year St John's presented him to the rectory of Cheam, Surrey, and the college president, Peter Mews, named bishop of Bath and Wells in November, made him his chaplain, also choosing him to preach at his consecration on 9 February 1673. However, Bernard resigned these preferments when on 9 April he succeeded Wren as professor of astronomy. That same day he was elected FRS, proposed by Henry Oldenburg. The society's council planned in 1674 to ask him for an experimental discourse, but he remained an inactive member for many years.

In 1673 Bernard sent Robert Boyle a specimen from his planned edition of al-Maydani's proverbs in Arabic and Latin, also promising a specimen of his work on the Psalms. However, a proposed new edition of all ancient mathematicians, promoted by Fell, engaged Bernard's resourcefulness and energy: he sought out printed books and manuscripts, and drew up a synopsis of materials for the planned fourteen volumes. The proposal's reception was disappointing—as Fell observed in his preface to Archimedes' Arenarius et dimensio circuli (1676), edited by John Wallis, with commendatory Latin elegiacs by Bernard—and the first volume, Bernard's edition of Euclid, proceeded no further than specimen proofs.

Bernard grew unhappy with his professorship and, having some experience of young noblemen from tutoring the earl of Lauderdale's nephew at Oxford in 1672, was recommended in 1676 by the earl of Arlington to tutor Charles II's sons, the dukes of Grafton and Northumberland, then living in Paris with their mother, the duchess of Cleveland. Unfortunately the mild, deferential Bernard was 'entirely unaccustomed to the arts of courtiers and sycophants' (Smith, 26–7). Humphrey Prideaux reported, 'My friend Mr. Bernard, who went into France to attend on the 2 bastards of Cleveland, hath been soe affronted and abused there by that insolent woman that he hath been forced to quit that imployment and return' (*Letters*, 58). Bernard bought books and studied manuscripts in Paris and made friends with learned men, including André Dacier, Daniel Huet, and Jean Mabillon. Thomas Gale, in his edition of Iamblicus's *De mysteriis* (1678), thanked Bernard for the collating he had done there.

On 8 October 1677 Bernard wrote to Williamson:

> The rigour of the long winter term so greatly afflicts me, that I find necessity of quitting the profession for one of like value but more sacred. To this alteration I humbly beg your favour … I am not weary of the friendship and favour I receive from the learned here, but am troubled that my ill health makes me useless. (*CSP dom.*, *1677–8*, 393)

At the end of the year he was hoping to go abroad again, as Princess Mary's chaplain in the Netherlands, but William Lloyd was appointed instead. Early in 1678 John Flamsteed, having learned that Bernard 'designed to leave your mathematicall for a Theologicall employment', thanked him for 'the motion of mee to be your successor' (*Correspondence of John Flamsteed*, 1.593, 599). But Bernard remained professor of astronomy, corresponding with Flamsteed on comets and other observed phenomena, and editing Josephus, of which he sent John Locke a specimen on 8 March 1679.

In March 1683 Bernard revisited Leiden for the auction of Nicholas Heinsius's library, and bought valuable books. He made or renewed the acquaintance of eminent scholars, including Johann Georg Graevius and Jakob Gronovius, and the burgomaster of Amsterdam, Nicholas Witsen, who gave him a manuscript Coptic dictionary. Finding oriental scholarship more flourishing and easily published in the Netherlands than England, Bernard sought Leiden's professorship of Arabic, vacant since Jakob Golius's death. Despite the encouragement of friends at the university, he was unsuccessful and returned to Oxford. In 1684 the Royal Society published Bernard's uncritical collections of ancient Arabic and Greek observations, 'The longitudes, latitudes, right ascensions, and declinations of the chiefest fixt stars' and 'The obliquity of the zodiac', and his own 'Observations of the solar eclipse July the 2. 1684' (*PTRS*, 1684, 14.567–76, 721–5, 747–8). On 30 October he proceeded DD.

Pococke's *Commentary on the Prophecy of Hosea* (1685) included Bernard's substantial appendix on ancient weights and measures, which he corrected and enlarged as *De mensuris et ponderibus antiquis* (1688). He contributed some notes to Fell's edition of Barnabas's *Epistle* (1685) and persisted with Josephus. Clement Barksdale rhymed:

> Savilian *Bernard*, a good Learned man
> Will give us his *Josephus* when he can.
> (C. B., 'Authors and books', 1685, Bodl. Oxf., Ashm. 1818 (61))

Book 1 and part of book 2 of the *Jewish War* were printed in 1687. Bernard published three works in 1689: *Orbis eruditi literarum*, an engraved sheet of alphabets deducing their Samaritan origin; *Etymologicon Britannicum* (in George Hickes's *Institutiones grammaticae*), proposing Russian, Slavonic, Persian, Armenian, and other sources for English words; and *Private Devotion*, a popular collection of prayers for different occasions and needs.

In 1690 Bernard published the late William Guise's edition of the Mishnaic *Zeraim*. The following year he issued a specimen page of Josephus's *Antiquities*, which he sent to Williamson, among others; the four and a half books he completed appeared posthumously in 1700. He resigned his professorship in 1691 after Mews presented him to the lucrative rectory of Brightwell, Berkshire, only 9 miles from Oxford, where he retained his house. Not surprisingly, he refused to stand for the Hebrew professorship after Pococke's death in September. For Henry Aldrich's edition of Aristeas's pseudepigraphic *Historia* (1692) he collected oriental *testimonia* concerning the Septuagint.

On 6 August 1693 Bernard married Eleanor Howell (*b.* 1667), 'descended from princes of Cardiganshire', in the parish of Brightwell (*Life and Times of Anthony Wood*, 3.429). He persuaded the Oxford University Press, of which he had been a delegate since 1691, to make Cyrillic types for the *Grammatica Russica* (1696) by Heinrich Wilhelm Ludolf, with whom he had corresponded. His proposals of 1694 for a catalogue, with alphabetical index, of manuscript books at Oxford, Cambridge, and other celebrated libraries in England and Ireland resulted, through the work of many scholars, in the *Catalogi manuscriptorum Angliae et Hiberniae* (1697), commonly known as 'Bernard's catalogue'. On 18 September 1696, despite poor health, he left with his wife for the auction of Golius's manuscripts in Leiden. On 6 October he successfully purchased two-thirds of them—including the celebrated Arabic Apollonius—for Archbishop Narcissus Marsh, who at his death in 1713 bequeathed them with his other oriental manuscripts to the Bodleian Library.

Bernard died from malnutrition and consumption, with severe dysentery, in Oxford on 12 January 1697, and was buried four days later in St John's College chapel, where his widow placed the monument he had chosen—a heart surmounted by his arms, with the inscription 'Habemus cor Bernardi' ('We have the heart of Bernard')—since relocated inside the entry from the front quadrangle to the chapel passage. She was his executor and heir to 'all my estate, goods, & books' (will, 17 Sept 1696, proved 23 April 1697). The Bodleian Library paid her £340 for valuable books and manuscripts, including Bernard's own unpublished writings. Other books were auctioned on 25 October 1697: the printed catalogue, *Bibliotheca Bernardina*, lists 1462 lots. The Bodleian's Bernard collections were augmented in 1756 by the manuscripts of his friend Thomas Smith, who wrote *Vita clarissimi et doctissimi viri, Edwardi Bernardi* (1704). Bernard published relatively little;

his papers and correspondence—with Smith, Graevius, Richard Bentley, and many others—show the true range of his erudition and his friendship.

HUGH DE QUEHEN

Sources T. Smith, *Vita clarissimi et doctissimi viri, Edwardi Bernardi* (1704) · G. J. Toomer, *Eastern wisedome and learning: the study of Arabic in seventeenth-century England* (1996) · *Hist. U. Oxf.* 4: 17th-cent. Oxf. · H. Carter, *A history of the Oxford University Press*, 1: *To the year 1780* (1975) · F. Madan, *Oxford literature, 1651–1680* (1931), vol. 3 of *Oxford books: a bibliography of printed works* (1895–1931); repr. (1964) · W. C. Costin, *The history of St John's College, Oxford, 1598–1860*, OHS, new ser., 12 (1958) · *The life and times of Anthony Wood*, ed. A. Clark, 5 vols., OHS, 19, 21, 26, 30, 40 (1891–1900) · Wood, *Ath. Oxon.*, 2nd edn · S. Higgins, *The Bernards of Abingdon and Nether Winchendon*, 1 (1903) · G. Baker, *The history and antiquities of the county of Northampton*, 2 vols. (1822–41) · *Remarks and collections of Thomas Hearne*, ed. C. E. Doble and others, 11 vols., OHS, 2, 7, 13, 34, 42–3, 48, 50, 65, 67, 72 (1885–1921) · Mrs E. P. Hart, ed., *Merchant Taylors' School register, 1561–1934*, 1 (1936) · *The correspondence of John Flamsteed, the first astronomer royal*, ed. E. G. Forbes and others, 3 vols. (1995–2001) · M. Hunter, *The Royal Society and its fellows, 1660–1700: the morphology of an early scientific institution*, 2nd edn (1994) · R. H. Adams, ed., *Memorial inscriptions in St John's College Oxford* (1996) · S. P. Rigaud and S. J. Rigaud, eds., *Correspondence of scientific men of the seventeenth century*, 2 vols. (1841) · [J. Locke], *Correspondence*, ed. E. S. de Beer, 1 (1976); 3 (1978) · *CSP dom.*, 1691–2, 48 · Foster, *Alum. Oxon.* · will, Oxf. UA, 1696, no. 4 · parish register, Paulerspury, Northamptonshire, 15 May 1638 [baptism] · *Letters of Humphrey Prideaux … to John Ellis*, ed. E. M. Thompson, CS, new ser., 15 (1875) · parish register, Brightwell, Wilts. & Swindon RO [Bishop's transcript] · Bodl. Oxf., MS Smith 14, fol. 209 · R. Boyle, *Works*, 6 (1772), 585
Archives Bodl. Oxf., MSS collection, accession nos. 8717–8886

Bernard [*married name* Latham], (**Marianne**) **Frances** [Fanny] (**1839–1926**), college head, was born on 12 February 1839 in Charlotte Street, Bristol, the second daughter and third of the nine children of James Frogo Bernard (1806–1878), a physician, and his wife, Marianne Amelia, daughter of Colonel Alexander Lawrence, of Clifton, and sister of John, the first Lord Lawrence, viceroy of India from 1863 to 1869. She was usually known as Frances, or Fanny.

After being educated at home by governesses, Fanny Bernard later spent some time in India during her uncle's viceroyalty and with her elder brother Charles *Bernard. On her return, she took some training at the Home and Colonial Training College for elementary school teachers. In 1875 she became the first mistress of Girton to be appointed through advertisement. Her social contacts weighed heavily in her favour, as a possible source of new students, but her appointment was against the expressed wishes of former students, whose preferred candidate was Louisa Lumsden, an Old Girtonian of honours degree status. She also inherited a number of disaffected students who had challenged Emily Davies, when mistress, as the personification of a remote and unyielding governing council in London; some regarded Marianne Bernard as the creature of Emily Davies. She was certainly unswervingly loyal to her employers but could argue her case firmly with the council when need arose.

With a background of public service on both sides of her family, Miss Bernard proved well prepared to accept the responsibility of running the college. Hers was a solitary and demanding task. Although she was totally responsible for the work and administration of the college, the council retained control of the finances, requiring her to account for every penny spent. Her routine work involved much general accounting, and the supervision of the buildings, grounds, and domestic staff, as well as organizing the courses followed by the students and negotiating the hours and payment of visiting lecturers from Cambridge University who taught them. The duty of chaperonage at these lectures frequently fell to the mistress herself. During a smallpox outbreak at the college in May 1878 she and a maid, both vaccinated for the purpose, took on all the nursing until a professional nurse arrived.

Tall and dignified, Marianne Bernard had a quality of detachment which some students resented as aloofness. Contemporaries, however, were impressed by her easy manner and unfailing courtesy. A member of the Church of England, she led the student body in daily prayers. She was a competent horsewoman, able to accompany her senior students on a brisk ride. During her term of office the college underwent considerable expansion and development. In 1880 two students, E. E. C. Jones and C. A. Scott, each achieved marks equivalent to first class honours in the tripos examinations. Two large building extensions were undertaken, bringing student numbers up to seventy (there were only sixteen in residence in 1875). Gradually the council agreed to transfer some of the mistress's responsibilities, Elizabeth Welsh becoming vice-mistress in 1880 and garden steward in 1883. By the summer of 1884, when she resigned, Fanny Bernard had effectively groomed her successor.

In August 1884, Miss Bernard left Girton to marry, as his second wife, Peter Wallwork Latham (1832–1923), Downing professor of medicine in Cambridge University. The Lathams lived until 1912 at 17 Trumpington Street, where past and present Girtonians were among the many guests entertained. As mistress she had taken students with her to 'at homes' and dinner parties; and her stories of India fired a number of them to undertake work there or elsewhere in the empire. Her younger sister, Letitia (1853–1927), was in 1876 Girton's first medical student and subsequently practised as a missionary doctor in Poona.

Mrs Latham played a characteristically active part on the council of Girton, to which she had been appointed in 1885, until increasing deafness limited her ability to do so. In 1913 she retired with her husband to 15 Royal York Crescent, Clifton, Bristol, next door to the house in which she had lived as a child, and she died there on 9 April 1926. Her portrait in the college hall (although painted long after she had left Girton), conveys well her alert and dignified presence, but not, perhaps, her innate kindness with young and old. It was typical of her capacity for self-effacement that no other likenesses or photographs of her are known.

BARBARA E. MEGSON

Sources K. T. Butler and H. I. McMorran, eds., *Girton College register, 1869–1946* (1948) · *Girton Cam.* · *Girton Review*, Easter term (1926), 2–3 · B. Stephen, *Girton College, 1869–1932* (1933) · B. Megson and J. Lindsay, *Girton College, 1869–1959: an informal history* (1961) · b. cert. · m. cert. · d. cert. · *CGPLA Eng. & Wales* (1926)

Archives Girton Cam., council papers
Likenesses F. Dodd, oils, Girton Cam.
Wealth at death £6399 8s. 7d.: probate, 28 May 1926, *CGPLA Eng. & Wales*

Bernard, Francis (*bap.* 1628, *d.* 1698), apothecary and physician, one of at least nine children of Samuel Bernard (1590/91–1657), vicar of Croydon, Surrey, and his wife, Elizabeth (1608/9–1705), was baptized at St John the Baptist, Croydon, on 28 September 1628. He was bound apprentice to John Lorrimer, citizen and apothecary of London, for eight years from Michaelmas 1645. He gained his freedom of the Society of Apothecaries on 6 October 1653 and became a liveryman nine years later. He married his wife, Anne, some time about 1654.

In May 1661 Bernard was elected apothecary to St Bartholomew's Hospital, where he gave fine service throughout the great plague of 1665. The journal of the governors of the hospital has on 28 September 1666 the entry:

> Forasmuch as it was now understood that the two doctors were remiss to officiate or procure theire business as it ought to bee. It was therefore thought fitt that Mr Barnard the Apothecary whose abillityes are well approved of should prescribe at the present for the patients in the said Doctors stead until further order.

This was followed by an entry on 23 December:

> … and whereas Francis Barnard, Apothecary, hath officiated and prescribed to the sick patients in their absence wherin hee hath bin exposed to adventure his life, for whose paynes itt is thought fitt that hee shall have £35 paid unto him being the like soome he hath yerely. (Whittet, *The Apothecaries in the Great Plague*, 18)

The manuscript book which Bernard used on his ward rounds is to be found in the Sloane manuscripts.

On 6 February 1678 Archbishop Sancroft conferred on Bernard a Lambeth MD, which he incorporated at Cambridge in the same year. In November 1678 Bernard was appointed assistant physician at St Bartholomew's, and after five years was elevated to physician. Having taken an examination, on 30 September 1680 he was made an honorary fellow of the Royal College of Physicians. Unusually, he continued to be on the court of assistants of the Society of Apothecaries and in August 1684 was elected renter warden, a post he declined to take. His name was, moreover, on the list of twenty-five assistants whose removal James II demanded in September 1687; only days later Bernard was accepted as one of the forty additional fellows created by the Royal College of Physicians under its new charter. From 1685 Bernard served as physician-in-ordinary to James II, which did not prevent him from pledging his loyalty to William III in 1696.

Bernard was by no means intimidated by his new colleagues at the college, but rather proved a thorn in their flesh. The college's powers had steadily declined during the interregnum: its finances were low, and in order to repair them and to extend its authority, it had instituted in 1664 a new grade of membership, that of honorary fellow. The college was dealt a further blow by the loss of its house in the fire of 1666. The physicians were, in addition, being increasingly challenged by the popular London apothecaries, who had stood by the people during the great plague. Furthermore, there was no doubt that the college was hidebound and unreceptive to new ideas, while the apothecaries were more willing to experiment with medicinal chemicals and new drugs from overseas. A vitriolic pamphlet war broke out between the two bodies. In 1687, with its new statutes, the college tried to bring the apothecaries to heel by fair means and foul.

Bernard was one of those who opposed the setting up of the college's dispensaries, realizing that the idea had become less a desire to help the poor than a way to bring the apothecaries into subservience. He was later represented as Horoscope in Sir Samuel Garth's poem, *The Dispensary*. Bernard refused to oppose the Apothecaries' Bill of 1694, under which the apothecaries successfully obtained exemption from all municipal offices and jury service. He also supported a Dutch licentiate, Joannes Groenevelt, who was accused of malpractice, but who was more probably disliked for medical innovation; and defended John Badger, who had been treated very shabbily by the college. Bernard even gave Badger, for the use of the Society of Apothecaries, a copy of the college's revised statutes of 1692, little different from those of 1687, which had penalized the apothecaries; and he transcribed a list of signatories willing to subscribe to the college's first dispensary.

Bernard refused to give his bond of £50 in December 1695, to stand by the officers of the college in the carrying out of what were deemed to be their duties; or in June 1697, to obey the insulting 'Statutes of English directions'. A paper of his in the Sloane manuscripts charges the ruling element of the college, from 1687 to 1696, with being secretive, arbitrary, high-handed, and irregular. In short, Bernard was thoroughly recalcitrant.

Bernard died on 9 February 1698; his wife erected a monument to him in St Botolph, Aldersgate, London. His will shows that he had quarrelled with his daughter Anne, as she had married Thomas Barkham without either his consent or his knowledge; that his other two daughters were unmarried; and that his son, 'having taken very wicked and ungracious courses', was to receive only £50 because of his 'drunken and lewd demeanour'. His wife, Anne, he seems to have loved, for he apologized that he was unable to bequeath more to 'so good and virtuous a wife as she hath been for above 43 years'.

Bernard's house in Little Britain, close to St Bartholomew's Hospital, held his impressive library. Besides Greek and Latin, Bernard appears to have had a good knowledge of French and Italian, and to have read widely in both literary and medical subjects. It seems that this love of books had been instilled early, as Samuel Bernard had particularly mentioned in his will that his books were to pass to his sons Francis, Samuel, and John. Francis's library was sold by auction soon after his death.

JUANITA BURNBY

Sources minutes of the Apothecaries' Society, GL, MS 8200/1, fol. 443; MS 8200/2, fol. 16 · BL, Sloane MSS, MS 1058; MS 502; MS 1895; MS 1815, fols 7v–13v · C. Wall, *A history of the Worshipful Society of Apothecaries of London*, ed. H. C. Cameron and E. A. Underwood (1963) · G. Clark and A. M. Cooke, *A history of the Royal College of Physicians of London*, 1–2 (1964–6) · will, 1657, PRO, PROB 11/269, sig. 446 [Samuel Bernard] · will, 1698, PRO, PROB 11/443, sig. 31 [Francis

Bernard] • T. D. Whittet, *The apothecaries in the Great Plague of London, 1665* (1970) • Foster, *Alum. Oxon.* • H. J. Cook, 'Medical innovation or medical malpractice?, or, a Dutch physician in London: Joannes Groenevelt, 1694–1700', *Tractrix*, 2 (1990), 63–93 • *Doctor Badger's vindication of himself, from the groundless calumnies and malicious slanders, of some London Apothecaries* (1701) [broadsheet] • Association oath roll, William III, PRO, C213/171/58 • T. D. Whittet, 'John Badger, apothecaryite', *Pharmaceutical Historian*, 3 (1973), 2–4 • *Walker rev.* • parish register, St John the Baptist, Croydon, 28 Sept 1628 [baptism]

Archives BL, Sloane MSS, corresp. and papers • McGill University, Montreal, Osler Library of the History of Medicine, notes and horoscopes | GL, Apothecaries' Society minutes

Likenesses W. Angus, line engraving, pubd 1817, NPG, Wellcome L. • F. Hagel, portrait, 1902 (*The past surgeons and physicians of St Bartholomew's Hospital*), Wellcome L. • engraving, Wellcome L. • line engraving, BM

Wealth at death £1150: will, PRO, PROB 11/443, sig. 31

Bernard, Sir Francis, first baronet (1712–1779), colonial governor, was born in July 1712, in Brightwell parish, Berkshire, the son and namesake of Anglican minister Francis Bernard (1660–1715) and his wife, Margery Winlowe (1682–1718). Following the death of his mother he was raised by an uncle. He was educated at Westminster School and from 1729 at Christ Church, Oxford, and received an MA degree in 1736. He also attended the Middle Temple and was admitted to the bar in 1737. Bernard practised law in Lincoln until 1758, when he left for America. His appointment as governor of New Jersey was less a reward for his competence than the gift of Viscount Barrington, leader of the dissenting interest in parliament, whose cousin Amelia Offley (*c.*1719–1778) Bernard married in 1741. They had eleven children, of whom six boys and four girls survived to adulthood, among them Thomas *Bernard, founder of the Society for Bettering the Condition and Improving the Comforts of the Poor, and Frances Elizabeth [*see* King, Frances Elizabeth], the philanthropist and author. As governor, Bernard reconciled feuding Quakers in East Jersey with Presbyterians in West Jersey, persuaded the province to support substantially the French and Indian War, negotiated a treaty with the Delaware Indians, and convinced the British government to allow the province to issue paper money.

A successful and confident Bernard assumed the government of Massachusetts on 2 August 1760. Determined to place himself above faction and base his 'administration on the broad bottom of the people in general' (Bernard MSS, 1.269), Bernard enjoyed considerable success in the first four years of his administration. He raised thousands of troops for defence of the frontiers while taking the province's part in opposing wartime embargoes on colonial shipping and the Sugar and Stamp Acts. He solicited funds to replace the Harvard College Library, destroyed in a fire in 1764, gave the college his own books, and designed the new building. However, he erred badly in appointing Lieutenant-Governor Thomas Hutchinson chief justice of the superior court almost immediately after his arrival, thereby alienating the powerful Otis family: James Otis sen. claimed that the two previous governors had promised him the post. James Otis jun. proceeded

Sir Francis Bernard, first baronet (1712–1779), by John Singleton Copley, 1776–9

to unify the Boston merchant community—which he represented in the writs of assistance and other cases where they were accused of violating British trade regulations—with the town meeting and legislature in opposition to the new imperial regulations and the governor who was obliged to enforce them.

While Bernard opposed these regulations himself, he considered it his duty to support royal policy and maintain authority in the town of Boston. In 1766 he vetoed the election of resistance leaders to the council; the next year he called for troops to protect the customs commissioners who had been frightened out of town by crowd harassment. After the troops arrived in 1768, Bernard criticized the town and province for failing to provide quarters for them according to the Quartering Act of 1766. In letters to newly appointed colonial secretary Lord Hillsborough, Bernard urged that the provincial council (elected each year by the outgoing council and the incoming house of representatives, subject to the governor's veto) be appointed by the crown as in the other royal colonies, as it had failed to support him in the exercise of his duties. Somehow the *Boston Gazette*, the leading resistance newspaper, acquired these letters and published them in April 1769. The legislature requested Bernard's removal, he himself asked to be relieved of his duties, and on 1 August 1769 he left Massachusetts for ever, amid public rejoicing.

Before his removal, Bernard received a baronetcy on 5 April 1769; later he was awarded a DCL degree from Oxford University in 1772. In 1774 his *Select Letters on the Trade and Government of America* was published. In these letters, written in 1764, he had proposed an ingenious plan whereby the colonies would be represented both in the

House of Commons and through the creation of a colonial life peerage. The fact that the colonies believed they could never be adequately represented in parliament was lost on him. Bernard lived out his last decade in retirement as a semi-invalid, first in Nether Winchendon, near Aylesbury, Buckinghamshire, and then in Aylesbury, where he died after repeated strokes on 6 June 1779. Although he never received the £1000 pension he requested and he resigned after briefly holding a commission for customs in Ireland worth half that amount, in his will he left substantial sums, ranging from £500 to £1500, to his eight surviving children. An able official in ordinary times, Bernard found himself trapped between British imperialists and colonial resisters. His proposals to revise colonial government so liberty and order could be reconciled were reviled as a conspiracy against American liberty. Bernard deserved better than his fate: to be blamed by both sides for his inability to compromise irreconcilable differences.

WILLIAM PENCAK

Sources C. Nicolson, *The 'Infamas govener': Francis Bernard and the origins of the American Revolution* (2001) · T. E. Higgins, *The Bernards of Abington and Nether Winchendon* (1903), vols. 1–2 · B. Bailyn, *The ordeal of Thomas Hutchinson* (1974) · J. J. Waters, *The Otis family in provincial and revolutionary Massachusetts* (1968) · C. S. Humphrey, 'Bernard, Francis', *ANB* · J. T. Adams, 'Bernard, Francis', *DAB* · Harvard U., Houghton L., Bernard MSS

Archives Harvard U., Houghton L., papers · L. Cong., letter-book | Massachusetts Archives, Boston, Massachusetts, MSS of Thomas Hutchinson, esp. vols. 25–7 · U. Mich., Clements L., corresp. with Thomas Gage

Likenesses J. Blackburn, oils, 1760, Wadsworth Atheneum, Hartford, Connecticut · J. S. Copley, oils, 1776–9, Christ Church Oxf. [*see illus.*]

Wealth at death extensive; many thousands of pounds to heirs plus other non-enumerated bequests: will

Bernard, Herman Hedwig (1785–1857), Hebrew scholar, whose early life is obscure, taught Hebrew at the University of Cambridge from 1830 until 1857. He died on 15 November 1857 in Fitzwilliam Street, Cambridge. Rather than teaching Hebrew simply as a tool of Christian exegesis of the Old Testament, Bernard was interested in rabbinic Judaism. This led him to write a book best described by its own title: *The main principles of the creed and ethics of the Jews exhibited in selections from the Yad Hachazakah of Maimonides, with a literal English translation, copious illustrations from the Talmud … and a collection of the abbreviations commonly used in rabbinical writings* (Cambridge, 1832). His last work, *The book of Job, as expounded to his Cambridge pupils, edited, with a translation and additional notes, by F. Chance* (1864), was published posthumously and was attacked for its long-windedness. Well regarded in his day, Bernard has since slipped into complete obscurity.

THOMPSON COOPER, *rev.* GERALD LAW

Sources *GM*, 3rd ser., 4 (1858), 112 · *N&Q*, 3rd ser., 5 (1864), 225 · Venn, *Alum. Cant.* · d. cert.

Bernard, Jeffrey Joseph (1932–1997), journalist, was born on 27 May 1932 at 11 Hampstead Square, London, the youngest of the three sons and the four surviving children of Oliver Percy *Bernard (1881–1939), stage designer and architect, and his second wife, (Edith) Dora Hodges (1896–

1950), an opera singer with the stage name Fedora Roselli. At birth he was given the name Jerry, but from childhood he was always known as Jeffrey. After attending a series of preparatory schools he was sent to Pangbourne Naval College, Berkshire, but was removed after two years at the request of the college commandant, as 'psychologically unsuitable for public school life' (*Daily Telegraph*, 8 Sept 1997). During the school holidays he had discovered the delights of Soho, where his brother Bruce Bonus *Bernard was studying at St Martin's School of Art. From that point on, as Bernard was to write in a spoof obituary of himself (published in *The Spectator* in 1978), 'he was never to look upward. It was here in the cafés and pubs of Dean Street and Old Compton Street that he was to develop his remarkable sloth, envy and self-pity' (*The Independent*, 6 Sept 1997).

Using the Coach and Horses public house as his base, Bernard worked erratically at a series of mainly artisan jobs, usually in the orbit of Soho, in the course of which he built up an impressive list of acquaintances and drinking companions, including Dylan Thomas, Francis Bacon, John Minton, Nina Hamnett, Dan Farson, and a motley company of the flotsam and jetsam of Soho and Fitzrovia. It was the poet Elizabeth Smart who persuaded him to take up journalism. She suggested a racing column in *Queen* magazine. Racing being his other passion in life next to drinking vodka, he accepted the challenge with alacrity. Before long he was writing for other publications, and within a year he had begun to be noticed in Fleet Street.

In 1973 Bernard was paid £30 for an article on alcohol addiction in the *New Statesman*, and this led to a series of articles for the magazine stretching to 1975, when he was poached by the *Spectator*. Thus began the *Low Life* column which ran for twenty-one years, and made his name. The column did not necessarily appear week in week out. The author was drinking heavily by now, with consequent deterioration of his health, and occasionally the *Spectator* was obliged to announce, in the absence of his contribution: 'Jeffrey Bernard is unwell.' This tag—chosen by Keith Waterhouse as the title of a play based on Bernard's life and writings, which, starring Peter O'Toole, became a West End hit and turned Bernard into something of a celebrity—gave him a not altogether justified reputation for being unreliable. Although he sometimes missed deadlines and his copy often had to be coaxed out of him, Bernard managed to produce some 1000 *Low Life* columns over the years, as well as numerous articles and columns for other papers, notably the *Sporting Life*, from which he was eventually dismissed for 'unpardonable behaviour' at a point-to-point dinner. But while several collections of his writings were published, he never wrote a book. He was essentially a sprinter rather than a long-distance runner.

Described by Jonathan Meades (in a *Tatler* review) as 'a suicide note in weekly instalments' (*The Times*, 8 Sept 1997), Bernard's column was an intensely personal letter to the reader. He was called the Boswell of Soho but really he wrote about himself—'a series of personal and, at times, embarrassing columns about his own wretched life', to quote his mock obituary again (*Daily Telegraph*, 8 Sept 1997). Apart from some Runyonesque set pieces—his account of cat racing at Battersea is a classic—he did not tell stories but simply rambled on, with each funny or profound (or funnily profound) thought leading to the next. The apparent effortlessness of his work led many to think it was produced by instinct, that Bernard was the writing equivalent of a naïve painter. In fact he knew exactly what he was doing. The appeal of his *Sporting Life* column, he once said, was that he was the first racing correspondent to take the part of the loser. The devastatingly yet selectively honest *Low Life* column, too, was about losing.

Bernard's ramshackle life furnished him with ample material. Living always in one room, he spent most of his waking hours in the pubs and clubs of Soho. He could grow irascible as the day wore on, but was otherwise a most engaging companion, with a surprisingly cultured mind. He married four times. His first wife was Mary Patricia (Anna) Grice, a market research interviewer. They married on 18 September 1951 but separated shortly thereafter; she died in 1959. On 13 November the same year Bernard married Jacqueline Sheelagh (Jacki) Ellis (b. c.1934), an actress; they were divorced in 1964. Bernard's third wife was Gillian Dorothy (Jill) Stanley (b. 1942/3), a seamstress and dressmaker; they married on 23 August 1966 and divorced in 1973. Bernard married, finally, on 15 May 1978, Sue Ashley (later Sue Gluck; b. c.1948), an advertising worker; they divorced in 1981. There was one daughter by his third marriage. Bernard also had numerous affairs. But drink, he said more than once (he recycled much of his material), was the other woman. Inevitably the raffish lifestyle took its toll. There were spells in the alcoholic ward. Pancreatitis developed into chronic diabetes. His right leg was amputated below the knee and he finished his days in a wheelchair. He died at his home, 45 Kemp House, Berwick Street, Soho, on 4 September 1997, of renal failure; he was cremated at Kensal Green. Most of the reprobates of Soho attended his funeral.   KEITH WATERHOUSE

Sources G. Lord, *Just the one: the wives and times of Jeffrey Bernard* (1992) · O. Bernard, *Getting over it* (1992) · *The Scotsman* (6 Sept 1997) · *The Independent* (6 Sept 1997) · *The Times* (8 Sept 1997) · *Daily Telegraph* (8 Sept 1997) · WWW [forthcoming] · m. cert. · d. cert. · personal knowledge (2004)
Archives *New Statesman* office, files 1973–1975 · *The Spectator* office, London, files 1976–1997 | FILM BFI NFTVA, *Arena*, BBC2, 10 Oct 1997 · BFI NFTVA, 'Reach for the ground', Channel 4, 3 June 1996 | SOUND BL NSA, 'A day in the life of Jeffrey Bernard', BBC, 9 Oct 1997, V 4050/2 · BL NSA, performance recording
Likenesses photograph, repro. in *The Scotsman* · photograph, repro. in *The Independent* · photograph, repro. in *The Times* · photograph, repro. in *Daily Telegraph* · photograph, Hult. Arch.

Bernard, John (d. 1554), religious writer, was a Yorkshireman by birth, probably from the West Riding. His parentage is unknown. He is first recorded in 1541, as a scholar of Queens' College, Cambridge. Having graduated there in 1544 he became Trotter's priest and then, in 1545, a fellow, before commencing MA in 1547. He was college bursar in 1550–51 and 1551–2. A supporter of religious reform, he was granted a licence to preach by the bishop of Ely on 20

December 1552, and though he must have risked deprivation after Queen Mary's accession in 1553, he was still a fellow when he died, shortly before administration of his will was granted on 7 March 1554.

That John Bernard was still a reformist at his death is shown by his literary remains, his *Oratio pia, religiosa, et solatii plena, de vera animi tranquillitate*, which his brother Thomas found in John's study after his death and published in 1568, with a dedication to Peter Osborne, lord treasurer's remembrancer of the exchequer. A faithful English translation by Anthony Marten, dedicated to William Howard, Baron Howard of Effingham, appeared in 1570 as *The Tranquillitie of the Minde*. According to Thomas Bernard, his brother wrote the *Oratio pia* early in Mary's reign, when the persecution of protestants was beginning. Supported by much classical and patristic learning, John Bernard pursues the question of 'where the true tranquillitie of the minde may be founde' (*Tranquillitie*, 35). His standpoint is firmly evangelical. Proclaiming a scripture-based religion, he rejects clerical celibacy and the doctrine of purgatory, and asserts that if no morally worthy priest is available to comfort those troubled in conscience, the latter should go instead to 'the lay man which is indued with the same giftes that are in a godly Minister' (ibid., 104r–v). Ultimately it is 'justification by faith from whence the true quietnesse of the mind doth growe' (ibid., 82). From this assurance comes Bernard's answer to those who ask why God suffers his elect to be afflicted by evil-doers and permits the wicked to flourish: he recommends neither flight nor armed resistance but rather penitence and prayer, 'putting our trust in the free goodnesse, mercy, and clemencie of God' (ibid., 107v).

Thomas Bernard (d. 1582), Church of England clergyman, shared his younger brother's radical religious views. Educated first at Eton College, he went on to King's College, Cambridge, in 1524, where he graduated in 1530 and proceeded MA in 1533. On 4 November 1546 he was appointed canon of the seventh prebend in Christ Church, Oxford, under Henry VIII's foundation charter. In the same year he became vicar of the college's living of Pyrton, in south-east Oxfordshire, where he was also able to lease the rectory. Rectory and vicarage together were worth nearly £40 per annum. Bernard may have owed these preferments to Archbishop Thomas Cranmer, whose chaplain he had become by 5 September 1547. He probably married about this time, and certainly implemented the reformation of his parish church, which was whitewashed within, received new books and furnishings, and had its altar replaced by a table for the Lord's supper. In March 1551 he received a preaching licence. After the accession of Queen Mary, Bernard 'suffer'd much … for being a protestant and a married man' (Wood, *Ath. Oxon.: Fasti*, 1.172). He was deprived of his canonry on 23 March 1554, and also lost his living of Pyrton to Dean Richard Marshall. But his fortunes revived after the accession of Elizabeth I. By 15 September 1559 he had been restored to his canonry, and he also recovered Pyrton, purging the church once more of Catholic accoutrements. He proceeded BTh at Oxford on 22 March 1567. A leading figure among the godly of Oxford, with his wife Edith (surname unknown) he had five sons, all of whom received biblical names: Daniel *Bernard; John (who succeeded his father as vicar of Pyrton); Samuel; Abel; and Joel. Thomas Bernard died on 30 November 1582 and was buried at Pyrton the next day. He and his wife, who died on 6 April 1607, are commemorated in the church by an alabaster cartouche.

HENRY SUMMERSON

Sources J. Bernard, The tranquillitie of the minde (1570); repr. (1973) • J. Bernard, Oratio pia (1568) • Cooper, Ath. Cantab., 1.250–51, 459 • Emden, Oxf., 4.27 • Venn, Alum. Cant., 1/1.140 • Foster, Alum. Oxon., 1500–1714, 1.115 • Wood, Ath. Oxon.: Fasti (1815), 172 • Parochial collections made by Anthony à Wood and Richard Rawlinson, ed. and trans. F. N. Davis, 3, Oxfordshire RS, 11 (1929), 241–2 • VCH Oxfordshire, vol. 8 • J. Strype, Ecclesiastical memorials, 2/2 (1822) • J. Strype, Memorials of the most reverend father in God Thomas Cranmer, new edn, 2 vols. (1812), vol. 1 • W. G. Searle, The history of the Queens' College of St Margaret and St Bernard in the University of Cambridge, 2 vols., Cambridge Antiquarian RS, 9, 13 (1867–71) • Fasti Angl., 1541–1857, [Bristol]

Bernard [Barnard], **John** (1756–1828), actor and theatre manager, was born at Portsmouth, Hampshire, the son of John Bernard, an Irish naval lieutenant, and his wife, Ann, the daughter of a naval post captain. His posthumous memoirs, Retrospections of the Stage (1830) and Retrospections of America, 1797–1811 (1887), excerpted from extensive manuscripts which apparently no longer exist, illuminate the life of strolling companies of the 1770s. They also chronicle the formative years of the American stage, of which he claimed to be a founder, and offer a wealth of anecdote about actors such as Charles Macklin and George Frederick Cooke and Americans such as Charles Brockden Brown, George Washington, and Thomas Jefferson. Bernard's energetic career was divided equally between Great Britain (1774–97) and America (1797–1820).

Bernard described himself as 'acting mad' (Retrospections of the Stage, 1.31), and he performed in amateur theatricals at the grammar school at Chichester. On 5 May 1773 he ran away from home and joined a succession of strolling companies, or 'itinerant corps' (Haslewood, 241), until chosen the following year by the prestigious Norwich company. He formed a partnership with and claimed to marry its leading actress, Mrs Cooper, 'a kind of Garrick in petticoats' (Bernard, Retrospections of the Stage, 1.120), whose stage reputation continued for another decade to surpass his own. 'Mr and Mrs Bernard' played with the Exeter and York companies, at Plymouth, and in Ireland, where Bernard, in 1783, had his first experience of theatre management. In 1777–8 and 1784–7 the couple were employed by John Palmer of the Bath theatre.

In 1787 Thomas Harris engaged Bernard for 'four years articles' at Covent Garden to 'sustain the business of Lee Lewis … including all the fops and eccentric gentlemen, with smart servants and feeble old men ad infinitum' (Bernard, Retrospections of the Stage, 2.110). He opened there as Archer in The Beaux' Stratagem. On 22 May 1789 Bernard appeared for his benefit in his afterpiece The British Sailor, or, The Fourth of June. In London he progressed from his earlier involvement in the Bath Catch Club to become first an honorary member of and then secretary to the Beefsteak Club, an activity he ranked in importance with his acting

career. He was also a member of the Anacreontic Society and founded in 1791 Strangers at Home, a convivial society for comedians.

Bernard became part-proprietor of the Plymouth theatre in 1788, and, with the patronage of the prince of Wales, secured management of the Brighton theatre in summer 1795 and the Guernsey theatre in 1795–6. Bad luck rather than bad management turned both efforts to failure and, with the incentive of the salary of £1000 offered him by Thomas Wignell, manager of the Chesnut Street Theatre in Philadelphia, Pennsylvania, Bernard sailed for America on 4 June 1797. 'Mrs Bernard' having left him in 1792, he had married in 1795 a Miss Fisher of the Guernsey company, who accompanied him to America and with whom he had three children.

Bernard, who played forty-eight different characters during his first season in America, brought to the country an eclectic acting style influenced by David Garrick, Charles Macklin, John Philip Kemble, the consummate coxcomb James Dodd, and the low comedian John Edwin. He possessed physical attributes well suited to comedy: an agile body, mobile facial features, and strikingly expressive, almost electric, eyes. While he was criticized early in his career for excessive playing to the gallery, he later earned praise for his thoughtful characterizations and his ability to exaggerate nature for comic effect without lapsing into caricature. He continued to play fops and fine gentlemen well into middle age, and became known for his low comic characters. Among his best parts were Daniel Brulgruddery, the comic Irishman in the younger George Colman's John Bull; Sir Peter Teazle in Sheridan's The School for Scandal; Lovegold in Fielding's The Miser; and Sheva in Richard Cumberland's The Jew, a role influenced by Charles Macklin's Shylock.

From 1797 until 1820 Bernard was engaged as actor or actor–manager successively at the Chesnut Street Theatre (1797–1803); the Federal Street Theatre, Boston (1803–11, 1816–20); the Green Street Theatre, Albany, New York (1813–16); theatres in Montreal and Quebec City (1810–18); and on numerous tours. The New York manager William Dunlap attempted without success to lure Bernard, 'a capital Comedian' (Diary, 1.131), from the Philadelphia theatre to become his acting manager. In 1806 Bernard's own recruiting efforts in London yielded both actors for the Boston theatre and a new wife, a Miss Wright (his second wife having died the previous year), with whom he had three more children, among them (William) Bayle *Bernard, writer.

The lack of success of Bernard's theatres at Albany, Montreal, and Quebec may be attributed to economic and political factors; but at the age of sixty, sometimes forced by ill health to cancel performances, he was still considered the first comedian of the American stage. His financial fortunes failed, but he succeeded in raising both the level of comic acting in America and the tastes and expectations of American audiences, and he influenced the American actors and managers who succeeded him. The 1818–19 season was his last as a member of a regular stock company in America.

Bernard returned to England in 1820. Letters to James Winston, co-manager at Covent Garden, indicate that he wished to enter management again. With characteristic optimism, he directed his waning energies to writing his memoirs. He died in London in reduced circumstances on 29 November 1828. PAGE LIFE

Sources J. Bernard, *Retrospections of the stage*, ed. W. B. Bernard, 2 vols. (1830) · J. Bernard, *Retrospections of America, 1797–1811*, ed. B. Bernard (1887) · N. B. East, 'John Bernard, actor-manager: 1756–1828', PhD diss., University of Kansas, 1970 · 'Boston Theatre', *Boston Weekly Magazine*, 1 (21 Dec 1816), 42 · 'Sketch of the life of Mr. John Bernard', *The Polyanthos*, 2 (April 1806), 3–15 · [J. Haslewood], *The secret history of the green rooms: containing authentic and entertaining memoirs of the actors and actresses in the three theatres royal*, 2nd edn, 2 vols. (1792) · Highfill, Burnim & Langhans, *BDA* · W. Dunlap, *History of the American theatre*, 2nd edn, ed. J. Hodgkinson, 3 vols. in 1 (1963) · *Diary of William Dunlap (1766–1839)*, 3 vols. (1930) · *The thespian dictionary, or, Dramatic biography of the eighteenth century* (1802) · W. C. Young, ed., *Famous actors and actresses on the American stage: documents of American theatre history*, 2 vols. (1975) · W. Van Lennep and others, eds., *The London stage, 1660–1800*, 5 pts in 11 vols. (1960–68)

Archives Harvard TC · Harvard TC, J. N. Bernard MSS · Hist. Soc. Penn. | Boston PL, playbills, etc. · Harvard TC, Early American Playbills collection · Harvard TC, William Bayle Bernard MSS · Hist. Soc. Penn., William Bayle Bernard MSS

Likenesses P. Marshall, oils, *c*.1789–1790, Garr. Club · S. De Wilde, oils, 1791, Garr. Club · H. Meyer, stipple, 1830, repro. in Bernard, *Retrospections of America, 1797–1811*, ed. Bernard, vol. 1, frontispiece · J. Corner, line engraving (after S. De Wilde), Garr. Club · S. Harris, stipple, repro. in 'Sketch of the life of Mr. John Bernard', plate · Maguire, engraving (after S. De Wilde), repro. in Bernard, *Retrospections of America, 1797–1811*, frontispiece · W. Ridley, stipple (after Barry), BM; repro. in J. Parson, ed., *The minor theatre* (1794)

Wealth at death destitute: Highfill, Burnim & Langhans, *BDA*; East, 'John Bernard'

Bernard, John Henry (1860–1927), Church of Ireland archbishop of Dublin and college head, was born on 27 July 1860 at Sooree, Beerbohm, Bengal, the eldest of the three children (one brother who died in infancy and one sister) of William Frederick Bernard (1825–1863), a civil engineer who worked in India for sixteen years and died there in 1863, and his wife, Martha Amelia (1833–1899), eldest daughter of Henry Humphrys, woollen merchant, of Dublin.

On his father's death, when Bernard was still just two years of age, his mother returned to Ireland with the children, and settled in Bray, co. Wicklow, where Bernard attended school for the first time at the small local Bray College, then for a few months at St John's College, Newport, co. Tipperary, before in 1875, only just over fifteen, entering Trinity College, Dublin. He graduated in 1880, with a first in both mathematics and philosophy, and won a fellowship in 1884. Although he won the fellowship in mathematics, his real interest was in theology and philosophy and he took holy orders in 1886; two years later he was appointed to Archbishop King's lecturership, the second post in the divinity school of Trinity College.

After failing as part of a group seeking reforms to the management of the college, Bernard moved away from college politics and resolved to devote his energies to the duties of his lecturership (which was converted into a professorship in 1906) and to literary activities. Under the influence of Sir John Pentland Mahaffy, his output was prodigious and wide-ranging. Between 1889 and 1918 he published well over a dozen books, on biblical scholarship, theology, Kantian philosophy, and the writings of Jonathan Swift. He proved to be an excellent and influential teacher as well. On 29 July 1885 Bernard married his cousin Maud Nannie, second daughter of Robert Bernard MD RN. They had two sons and two daughters.

Judged by Irish standards Bernard ranked as a high-churchman, and was attacked for his views by others within the general synod. In 1897 he was appointed treasurer of St Patrick's Cathedral, and in 1902 he accepted the deanery of St Patrick's. He took advantage of his position to invite visits from leading men in the Church of England. Unity and close relations between the two churches he always strove for. He had many friendships among prominent English churchmen, and he frequently preached at Westminster Abbey and was select preacher at Oxford and at Cambridge.

In his double capacity at St Patrick's and in Trinity College Bernard's influence reached its maximum. But he was 'clearly marked out for the episcopate by intellectual gifts and administrative abilities' (*The Times*, 30 Aug 1927, 13), and in 1911 he accepted the see of Ossory, resigning his professorship, and severing for a time his connection with Trinity College.

In 1915 Bernard was elected archbishop of Dublin by the bench of bishops of the Church of Ireland. He was one of the two representatives of the Church of Ireland at the convention called by the British government following the nationalist Easter rising of 1916, to consider a new constitution for Ireland. Bernard supported the recommendations of the majority of the convention on a scheme for self-government and was chosen, along with Viscount Midleton, to speak for the southern unionists on this in private negotiations with Lloyd George. When conscription was extended to Ireland in March 1917 and opposed by nationalists and the Roman Catholic church, Bernard sent out an urgent appeal hoping 'that "compulsory service" would be cheerfully accepted' (*The Times*, 30 Aug 1927, 13).

In 1919 the provostship of Trinity College was offered to Bernard, and it seemed that this would give perfect scope to his administrative abilities. But the new political arrangements made for a difficult time for the college for a number of years, and Bernard required all his skills to maintain its stability.

Bernard's writings covered a wide range of subjects. Philosophy first engaged his attention, and he collaborated with Mahaffy in the second edition of Mahaffy's book *Kant's Critical Philosophy for English Readers* (1889), contributing a commentary on the *Dialectic of the Pure Reason*, which had been left unnoticed in the first edition; and in 1892 he published independently the first English translation of the *Kritik of the Judgment*. But he soon abandoned metaphysics for scholarship, although his four volumes of sermons often show evidence of his philosophical training. Between 1890 and 1894 he edited and translated for the Palestine Pilgrims' Texts Society a number of itineraries of the Holy Land, from the originals by Eusebius and several early travellers. He made an important contribution to Irish liturgiology in an edition of the *Liber hymnorum*, published in collaboration with Robert Atkinson for the Henry Bradshaw Society (1898). Among several notable papers of Irish interest which appeared in the *Proceedings of the Royal Irish Academy* was one on the *Domnach airgid*, a Latin–Irish manuscript of the gospels, and another on the copy of St John's gospel in the Stowe missal (1893). His contributions to biblical scholarship included commentaries on the pastoral epistles (1899) and on 2 Corinthians (1903), and two posthumously published volumes in the *International Critical Commentaries* on the gospel according to St John (1928). Like all his writings, these contained sound scholarship, terseness and lucidity of statement, well-balanced judgement, and a decidedly conservative point of view.

Bernard received the honorary degree of DCL of Oxford University (1920) and of Durham University (1905), and the honorary DD degree of Aberdeen University (1906). He was an honorary fellow of Queen's College, Oxford (1919), and of the Royal College of Physicians, Ireland (1921), a privy councillor of Ireland (1919), president of the Royal Irish Academy (1916–21), and warden of Alexandra College, Dublin (1905–11). Bernard died at the provost's house, Trinity College, Dublin, from heart failure, on 29 August 1927 and was buried in the old churchyard of St Patrick's Cathedral on 1 September.

E. J. GWYNN, *rev.* MARC BRODIE

Sources R. H. Murray, *Archbishop Bernard* (1931) · J. H. Bernard, *The Bernards of Kerry* (1922) · N. J. D. White, *John Henry Bernard* (1928) · *The Times* (30 Aug 1927) · *The Times* (31 Aug 1927) · *The Times* (1 Sept 1927) · *WWW* · N. Mansergh, *The unresolved question: the Anglo-Irish settlement and its undoing, 1912–72* (1991)
Archives BL, corresp. and literary MSS, Add. MSS 52781–52784 · TCD, corresp., papers and notebooks · TCD, diaries | NL Ire., letters to Thomas Sadleir · NL Scot., corresp. with T. & T. Clark · PRO, letters to Lord Midleton, PRO 30/67 · TCD, letters to William Starkie
Likenesses photograph, c.1911, NPG

Bernard, John Peter (*d.* 1750), compiler of histories and biographer, was the son of James Bernard, a French protestant minister and author. He was educated at the University of Leiden and took degrees in arts and philosophy. By 1733 he was settled in London, where he earned his living by preaching, teaching literature and mathematics, and compiling for the booksellers. He is principally remembered for his contribution to the *General Dictionary, Historical and Critical* (10 vols., 1734–41) which expanded the 1710 translation of Pierre Bayle's *Dictionaire historique et critique*. Some idea of Bernard's share in this laborious undertaking may be gathered from his correspondence with the editor, Thomas Birch, now held at the British Library. As a result of his work on the dictionary Bernard was admitted a fellow of the Royal Society in January 1738. He died in the parish of St Marylebone, Middlesex, on 5 April 1750.

GORDON GOODWIN, *rev.* PHILIP CARTER

Sources *GM*, 1st ser., 20 (1750), 188 · Nichols, *Lit. anecdotes*
Archives BL, letters to Thomas Birch, Add. MSS 4301, 4475–4476

Bernard, Mountague (1820–1882), jurist and international lawyer, was descended from a Huguenot family which left France after the revocation of the edict of Nantes and who for several generations owned land at Montego Bay in Jamaica. He was the third son of Charles Bernard of Eden of that island, and his wife, Margaret, daughter of John Baker of Waresley House, Worcestershire, and was born at Tibberton Court, Gloucestershire, on 28 January 1820. Thomas Dehaney *Bernard was his brother. Educated at Sherborne School, he gained a scholarship at Trinity College, Oxford, where in 1842 he was awarded first-class honours in classics and a second in mathematics. He subsequently took the degree of bachelor of civil law and was elected to the Vinerian scholarship and fellowship. After studying in the chambers of Roundell Palmer (later Lord Selborne), he was called to the bar at Lincoln's Inn on 30 April 1846.

The same year Bernard was, with his friend Frederic Rogers, Lord Blachford, one of the founders of *The Guardian*, a high-church newspaper founded by Tractarians who sought to remain true to the English church after Newman's conversion to Roman Catholicism; and he acted for some years as its editor. He also found time for much historical reading, and for a wide study of legal systems. In 1859 he became the first holder of the Chichele chair of international law at Oxford, which had been set up by the Oxford University commissioners of 1854. It was a successful appointment in many ways, for Bernard was both a zealous advocate of the academic study of law, and an indefatigable helper in the details of university administration. Bernard was appointed assessor, or judge, of the university chancellor's court, and was instrumental in assimilating its procedure—previously the province of civilians—into the practice of the courts of common law. He also served on Gladstone's election committees in the contests for the university seat in 1859 and 1865.

However, the demand for Bernard's services was not confined to the precincts of the university. In 1866 he was secretary to the royal commission for investigating the nature of the cattle plague, and in 1868 he was a member of the commission on naturalization and allegiance, the report of which led to the abandonment by Great Britain of the time-honoured but by now inconvenient rule, 'nemo potest exuere patriam' ('no one can renounce the land of his birth'). In 1871 he went out to America as one of the high commissioners appointed to resolve the dispute between Britain and the United States regarding the *Alabama*, a Confederate cruiser built at Liverpool during the American Civil War. The commissioners signed the treaty of Washington, which defined the duties in international law of neutral states in times of war. Bernard continued to advise the British government on matters of international law as the *Alabama* case went to arbitration in Geneva, and in 1872 he helped to prepare the case of the British government, which was presented by Sir Roundell Palmer. Also in 1871 Bernard was sworn of the privy council and he became a member of the judicial committee of privy council. His appointment was implicitly criticized by Lord Cairns in the House of Lords, who suggested that Bernard,

Mountague Bernard (1820–1882), by unknown engraver

a high-churchman, had been appointed only so that he could sit in one controversial ecclesiastical case, *Sheppard v. Bennett*, in which a clergyman was accused of maintaining doctrines contrary to the articles of the church. However, Bernard was defended by Lord Ripon against the insinuation, and retained the support of Gladstone. He had also been elected, in 1870, to a professorial fellowship at All Souls College, Oxford, and had received the degree of DCL.

Owing to the increasing amount of time he was devoting to public employments, Bernard resigned his professorship in 1874, and was succeeded by T. E. Holland. Henceforth he lived chiefly in London or, being unmarried, with relatives at Overross near Ross in Herefordshire, staying only occasionally at All Souls. In 1876 he served on the royal commission for inquiring into the duties of commanders of British vessels with reference to fugitive slaves. Bernard, Sir Robert Phillimore, and Sir Henry Maine took a different view of international law from that held by their fellow commissioners; they believed that such law was not static but admitted of progressive improvement. This led them to conclude that modern rules of international law condemned slavery, and consequently that the British captain of a ship of war that was in the port of a state which allowed slavery was therefore justified in refusing to give up a slave taking refuge on his vessel.

In 1877 Bernard became a member of the University of Oxford commission under the Universities of Oxford and Cambridge Act of that year. After Lord Selborne resigned from the commission in September 1880, on his appointment for the second time as lord chancellor, Bernard replaced him as its chairman. In that position, he exercised great influence on the commission. Its work was immensely laborious and involved the reconciliation of the interests of the university on the one hand and the autonomy of the colleges on the other, as well as the preparation of complex statutes. Although he was accustomed to hard work throughout his life, Bernard found that he had never worked harder than in the preparation of the new statutes. The work seems to have overtaxed his strength, and he became seriously ill in the spring of 1882, just when the new statutes for Oxford had received the royal assent and when he had published *A Letter to the Rt Hon. W. E. Gladstone on the Statutes of the University of Oxford Commission*, which explained the changes to the wider public. After lingering for some months, Bernard died at Overross on 2 September 1882.

Bernard was accomplished in all branches of law, and his reputation as a master of the law of nations was as high on the continent and in America as it was in his own country. He was committed to promoting the exchange of ideas between international jurists from different countries, in order to help stimulate the study of comparative law and to harmonize the principles of international law, both public and private; and he was one of the original members of the Institut de Droit International, founded in 1873. He presided over its Oxford meeting in 1880 with much tact and dignity. As a professor he inclined rather to the historical than to the systematic exposition of his subject, dwelling by preference on the analysis of treaties, the character of politicians, and the by-play of diplomacy. His work, *An Historical Account of the Neutrality of Great Britain during the American Civil War*, published in 1870, was praised as being a pioneering history of a war from the point of view of an international lawyer.

MICHAEL LOBBAN

Sources Boase, *Mod. Eng. biog.* · Ward, *Men of the reign* · Holdsworth, *Eng. law*, vol. 14 · R. Palmer, first earl of Selborne, *Memorials. Part II: personal and political, 1865–1895*, ed. S. M. Palmer, 2 vols. (1898) · *DNB*
Archives BL, corresp. with W. E. Gladstone and memoranda, Add. MSS 44182–44620, *passim* · JRL, letters to E. A. Freeman · UCL, Brougham MSS
Likenesses E. E. Geoflowski, plaster bust, 1873?, Bodl. Oxf. · engraving, NPG [*see illus.*] · monument, All Souls Oxf.
Wealth at death £93,643 14*s*. 5*d*.: resworn probate, April 1883, *CGPLA Eng. & Wales* (1882)

Bernard [Barnard], **Nicholas** (*d.* 1661), Church of England and Church of Ireland clergyman, was admitted pensioner at Emmanuel College, Cambridge, on 24 May 1617. He graduated BA early in 1621, and proceeded MA and became a fellow of the college in 1624. That year he met James Ussher, bishop of Meath, who was on an extended visit to England. Following Ussher's return to Ireland and consecration as archbishop of Armagh, he ordained Bernard deacon and priest at St Peter's Church, Drogheda, on 24 December 1626. Bernard subsequently became Ussher's chaplain, and through the archbishop he obtained in 1627 the deanery of Kilmore, which he held *in commendam* with the vicarage of Ballintemple and the rectory of Keady. He was incorporated MA at Oxford on 15 July 1628 and at an unknown date received the degree of DD from Trinity College, Dublin.

In 1630 Bernard attempted to acquire the vicarage of Kildromfaton, by persuading the incumbent to resign in his favour and by applying for the living, with Ussher's support, to the bishop of Kilmore, William Bedell. Bedell opposed this application because he viewed pluralism as one of the most deadly and pestilent diseases in the church. Moreover, Bernard spoke no Irish and therefore could not minister effectively to this Gaelic Irish parish. Despite Bedell's opposition, Bernard obtained the living through a decree of the archbishop's prerogative court. Subsequently, Bedell wrote to Ussher that what Bernard sought was the wages and not the work. According to Bedell, Bernard responded to this opposition by contesting Bedell's visitation rights, and making accusations that Bedell had incurred a *praemunire* by holding a diocesan synod. In 1635 Bernard received a further *commendam*: the vicarage of St Peter's, Drogheda. As this living lay outside the diocese of Kilmore, Bedell once again questioned Bernard's pluralism and non-residency. This led Bernard to seek an exchange of his livings in the diocese of Kilmore with Henry Jones, dean of Ardagh. Bedell attempted to obstruct this exchange by petitioning the lord deputy, Sir Thomas Wentworth, but to no avail. In 1637 the exchange was made and Bernard became dean of Ardagh and prebendary of Dromaragh in the diocese of Dromore.

In 1640 Bernard acted as a spiritual counsellor to the disgraced bishop of Waterford, John Atherton. The days leading up to the bishop's execution are recounted in Bernard's first publication, *The penitent death of a woefull sinner* (1640), which detailed Atherton's repentance. Appended to it was Bernard's funeral sermon for the bishop, preached in St John's, Dublin, on 6 December, in which he examined the duties and qualities required in a minister. Following the outbreak of the 1641 rising, Bernard sent his family, of whom no details are known, to England, but saw it as his duty to remain in Ireland; he was left in charge of Archbishop Ussher's library in Drogheda. In 1642 Drogheda was besieged; Bernard recounted his experiences in a series of pamphlets including *A letter sent from Dr Barnard* (1641), *A true and perfect relation of all the several skirmishes* (1642), and *The whole proceedings of the siege of Drogheda* (1642).

In 1647 Bernard visited London and was incarcerated in the Fleet prison for attempting to preach without a licence at St Margaret's, Westminster, on 25 December. This sermon was later published as *The still-borne nativitie, or, A copy of an incarnation sermon* (1648). Bernard returned to Ireland some time before 1649 and he remained there following the siege and fall of Drogheda to Oliver Cromwell in September that year. As both churches in the town were destroyed he continued to preach in a private chapel. While he was preaching one Sunday that autumn, the floor of the chapel collapsed because of the weight of the congregation. In February 1650 he preached his farewell

sermons to his congregation at Drogheda on the subject 'Of comfort and concord'. These were included in the third edition of *The penitent death of a woefull sinner* in 1651. That year Bernard was recommended for the position of preacher to Gray's Inn; James Ussher was a member of this society and may have been involved in Bernard's selection. In 1655 Bernard was admitted as a member of the society without a fine. During the 1650s Bernard became a chaplain to Oliver Cromwell and also one of his almoners. It was in this capacity in 1656 that Sir William Roberts was ordered to pay Bernard £200 to defray the charges of James Ussher's recent funeral.

In the years following Ussher's death, Bernard fought in print with Peter Heylin over the archbishop's reputation. With his funeral sermon Bernard published a biography of the archbishop, *The life and death of the most reverend and learned father of our church, Dr James Ussher* (1656); his *The judgement of the late archbishop of Armagh and primate of Ireland* appeared in 1657. When attempts were made to have Heylin's response to these works publicly burnt, Heylin wrote to Bernard for assistance but Bernard denied any responsibility and refused to assist Heylin. In these publications and in *Certain discourses of Babylon, of laying on of hands, of the old form of words in ordination, of a set form of prayers, each being the judgement of the late archbishop of Armagh* (1659) Bernard attempted to establish a canon of Ussher's work. It has been argued that these, together with Bernard's account of Bishop Atherton, form a body of works that offered a critique on the policies and governance of the Church of Ireland in the 1630s. Thus Bernard has been described as the first and most prolific historian of the Church of Ireland of that decade.

On 16 July 1660 Bernard was presented by John Egerton, second earl of Bridgewater, to the rectory of Whitchurch-cum-Marbury, Shropshire, although he was not instituted there until 22 December. Bernard's accommodating religious opinions are evident in his last two publications, *Devotions of the ancient church in seaven pious prayers with seaven administrations* (1660) and *Clavi trabales* (1661). The latter contained a number of discourses by Ussher, Richard Hooker, Lancelot Andrewes, and Hadrian Saravia on the royal supremacy, episcopacy, the liturgy of the Church of England, and the novelty of the doctrine of resistance. Bernard died at Whitchurch-cum-Marbury on 15 October 1661 and was buried on 7 November at Whitchurch parish church.

CIARAN DIAMOND

Sources J. B. Leslie, *Armagh clergy and parishes* (1911) • H. Cotton, *Fasti ecclesiae Hibernicae*, 3 (1849) • Venn, *Alum. Cant.* • Foster, *Alum. Oxon.* • *The whole works of … James Ussher*, ed. C. R. Elrington and J. H. Todd, 17 vols. (1847–64), vols. 1, 15–17 • E. S. Shuckburgh, *Two biographies of Bedell* (1902) • J. D. McCafferty, 'John Bramhall and the reconstruction of the Church of Ireland, 1633–1641', PhD diss., U. Cam., 1996 • R. Buick-Knox, *James Ussher archbishop of Armagh* (1967) • *Report of the Laing manuscripts*, 1, HMC, 72 (1914) • *Report on the manuscripts of the late Reginald Rawdon Hastings*, 4 vols., HMC, 78 (1928–47), vol. 4 • *CSP Ire.*, 1625–47 • P. Heylin, *An intercourse of letters between P. Heylin and D. Barnard touching the intended burning of the book called 'Respondit Petrus'* (1658) • J. Foster, *The register of admissions to Gray's Inn, 1521–1889, together with the register of marriages in Gray's Inn chapel, 1695–1754* (privately printed, London, 1889) • R. J.

Fletcher, ed., *The pension book of Gray's Inn*, 1 (1901) · *DNB* · *Calamy rev.*, 396

Bernard, Oliver Percy (1881–1939), architect and designer, was born on 8 April 1881 at 2 Box Villas, Danby Street, Camberwell, London, the younger son (there were no daughters) of Charles Bernard (formerly Charles West; d. 1894), theatrical manager of Scottish descent, and his wife, Annie Allen, actress, of Glasgow. There was also another son from a previous marriage. Bernard was married first on 23 October 1911 to Muriel Theresa Lightfoot (b. 1884/5), singer, daughter of Jabez Lightfoot, manager of the Bengal and North Western Railway. This marriage, of which there were no children, was dissolved in 1924 and in the same year he married (Edith) Dora Hodges (1896–1950), an opera singer with the stage name Fedora Roselli, daughter of Joseph Hodges, butcher, of Tooting; they had three sons and two daughters, one of whom died in infancy. Oliver Bernard, poet and translator, was his eldest son; Bruce Bonus *Bernard (1928–2000), photographer, picture editor, and art critic, was his second; and Jeffrey Joseph *Bernard (1932–1997), journalist, was the youngest.

Bernard grew up at 8 Waterloo Road, London, a household kept by his father, containing, in Bernard's words, 'vague and violent people together, to whom parents had consigned a son who would have encumbered their travels' (*Cock Sparrow*, 11–12). On the death of his father in 1894, Bernard went to Manchester and found work as a 'property boy and paint-room drudge', educating himself by reading, among others, John Locke and John Ruskin, and practising drawing (*Cock Sparrow*, 35). He escaped from Manchester as cabin-boy in a tramp steamer, the *Manchester Commerce*, and, tiring of this, became a seaman in the Norwegian barque *Naja*, a terrifying experience recounted in his autobiography. He resumed scene painting in London, in the studio of Walter Hann, participating in the sporting scene as a boxer and billiards player. He travelled to New York in the autumn of 1905 and became principal scenic artist for Klaw and Erlanger, and later technical director for the Boston Opera Company. Here, and again in London, as resident scenic artist for the Grand Opera Syndicate at Covent Garden, he became frustrated by the conservatism of management with regard to production and scenery, and returned to America after the outbreak of the First World War, having been rejected for military service because of deafness. Determined to try again, he crossed back in the *Lusitania*, and survived its sinking on 7 May 1915. Early in 1916 he was commissioned as a camouflage officer in the Royal Engineers and served in France, Italy, and Belgium, reaching the rank of captain. He was awarded the MC and appointed OBE.

In 1919 Bernard returned to the London theatre, designing Wagner's Ring cycle for Sir Thomas Beecham in the 1921 Covent Garden season. Acting as consultant to the board of overseas trade, he worked on the British Empire Exhibition, Wembley, in 1924, as a designer of friezes, decorations, and displays. He designed a new system of lighting and stage planning for the Admiralty Theatre and staged the *Raid on Zeebrugge* and *Air Attack on London*. For the Paris 1925 exhibition, Bernard was technical director for the British government, but he achieved his greatest fame as consultant artistic director to the caterers J. Lyons & Co. For the Strand Palace Hotel, he designed in 1929 a spectacular entrance of reflective metal and concealed lighting, and other interiors for the Oxford Street, Coventry Street, and Strand Corner Houses, and in 1932 for the Cumberland Hotel, with many separate restaurants in each building, cleverly exploiting new materials and techniques in a popular decorative manner.

Bernard's knowledge of continental modern design was considerable. He displayed it in journalism, arguing that the future of architecture lay with engineers. In 1931 he was appointed consultant designer to Practical Equipment Ltd, manufacturers of tubular steel furniture. His architectural works date from the late 1930s and were mostly industrial buildings, notably the Supermarine aviation works, Southampton (1937).

Bernard was short in stature with a large head. His former secretary described him as 'amusing, utterly impossible, kind, and a bully'. Bernard died unexpectedly of peritonitis on 15 April 1939 at the St Thomas Home, Lambeth Palace Road, London. ALAN POWERS, *rev.*

Sources *CGPLA Eng. & Wales* (1939) · O. Bernard, *Cock sparrow* (1936) · O. Bernard, *Getting over it* (1992) · private information (1993) · b. cert. · m. certs. · d. cert.
Wealth at death £2950 1s. 1d.: administration, 24 June 1939, *CGPLA Eng. & Wales*

Bernard, Percy Ronald Gardner, fifth earl of Bandon (1904–1979), air force officer, was born some twenty minutes before his twin brother at Gillingham, Kent, on 30 August 1904, the eldest of the three children (the last of whom was a daughter) of Ronald Percy Hamilton Bernard (1875–1921), the great-grandson of the second earl of Bandon and a captain in the rifle brigade, and his wife, Lettice Mina, the daughter of Captain Gerald Cecil Stewart Paget, the son of Lord Alfred Paget, fifth son of the first marquess of Anglesey. Percy Bernard, invariably known as Paddy, lived during his childhood on the Theobald's Park estate in Hertfordshire, where his parents had been loaned a house by the eccentric Lady Meux. In the summer of 1914 he and his twin brother were sent to St Aubyn's preparatory school at Rottingdean, and four years later both boys entered Orange dormitory at Wellington College, where the elder was incorrectly referred to as Bernard minor throughout his schooldays. Although he showed promise as an athlete and rugger player he never excelled academically, and it was only after spending the summer of 1922 at a Norfolk crammer that he passed the entrance examinations to the Royal Air Force College at Cranwell.

In May 1924 Bernard became the fifth earl of Bandon on the death of his grandfather's cousin. The peerage, being Irish, did not carry with it a seat in the House of Lords. His inheritance was the estate of Castle Bernard in co. Cork, but the castle had been burnt down by Sinn Féin in 1920 and the fourth earl had deliberately made little financial provision for his successor. The saving grace was the £123,000 compensation paid by the governor for the destruction of the castle. From the viewpoint of the Royal Air Force the fact that Cadet Bernard was now the earl of Bandon had immediate significance and future value. The army and navy had counted men of title among their serving officers for generations, but it was unprecedented for a twenty-year-old peer of the realm to be making his career in the RAF, which was still struggling to retain its independence as the third service.

During the next two decades Bandon served as an instructor at Sealand, near Birkenhead. He was posted for five halcyon years to Egypt, where he became adjutant of 216 squadron and gained renown as the pilot of the first Vickers Victoria to fly non-stop from Khartoum to Cairo. At the outbreak of the Second World War he commanded 82 squadron; he was appointed DSO in 1940 and in 1941 became station commander at West Raynham. The following year he was posted to air headquarters India before joining headquarters, south-east Asia command. At the end of the Burma campaign, having already been mentioned three times in dispatches, he was honoured by the Americans, who awarded him the United States Army Air Force Distinguished Flying Cross for 'leadership and command' and the bronze star medal.

On his return to England Bandon became commandant of the Royal Observer Corps and revitalized their morale, which was low since wartime incentive had departed and their future was uncertain. He was air officer commanding no. 2 group of the British air forces of occupation, Germany, in 1950–51 and in 1953, as air officer commanding no. 11 group, had the responsibility for organizing the coronation fly-past over Buckingham Palace and the coronation review of the RAF at Odiham. After serving as assistant chief of air staff (training) he was appointed commander-in-chief of the 2nd allied Tactical Air Force in Germany, and in March 1957 he was officially reprimanded by the secretary of state for air, George Ward, for giving information to foreign pressmen that tactical atomic weapons would soon be stored in Europe. As commander-in-chief of the Far East air force from 1957 to 1960 he received a 'rocket' telegram from Earl Mountbatten of Burma in August 1959 after he had shrewdly realized the strategic importance to the RAF of the Indian Ocean island of Gan and virtually 'commandeered' it. His final posting was as commander allied air forces, central Europe (1961–3). He was promoted air chief marshal in July 1959 and placed on the retired list in February 1964. He was created CB (1945), CVO (1953), KBE (1957), and GBE (1961).

Throughout his distinguished career Bandon retained the *élan* of the pioneering days of the Royal Air Force, which was always his first love. He possessed moral courage to a high degree and had the gift of conveying to those around him, irrespective of rank, a sense of loyalty. Affectionately known as the Abandoned Earl, in his later years he epitomized the man that young airmen hoped a senior RAF officer would be. His qualities of leadership were acknowledged to be outstanding, but equally his schoolboy humour, his practical jokes, and his crude language, allied to his non-conformist attitude, were frequently resented, particularly by those who found it difficult to recognize his true ability.

On 28 February 1933 Bandon married (Maybel) Elizabeth, the second daughter of Raymond William Playfair, a banker, of Nairobi, Kenya. Two daughters were born before the marriage was dissolved in 1946. On 2 October of that year Bandon married Mrs Lois White, the daughter of Francis Russell, also a banker, of Victoria, Australia.

Bandon always found pleasure in fishing, particularly in the River Bandon, where salmon abounded, and in shooting, especially in the bogs where snipe and woodcock were to be found in the vicinity of Castle Bernard. He was also an enthusiastic gardener with considerable knowledge of rhododendrons. He died on 8 February 1979 at the Bon Secours Hospital in co. Cork, after a short illness. As there was no male heir the earldom became extinct.

MICHAEL SETH-SMITH, *rev.*

Sources *The Times* (23 Nov 1979) · private information (1986) · Burke, *Peerage* (1967) · *CGPLA Eng. & Wales* (1980)
Archives SOUND IWM SA, recorded lecture
Likenesses oils, *c.*1969, RAF College, Cranwell
Wealth at death £30,050: probate, 7 Feb 1980, *CGPLA Eng. & Wales*

Bernard, Richard (*bap.* 1568, *d.* 1641), Church of England clergyman and religious writer, was baptized on 30 April 1568 at Epworth, Lincolnshire, the son of John Bernard (*d.* 1592) and his third wife, Anne Wright. Encouraged by Isabel and Frances Wray, two daughters of Sir Christopher Wray, lord chief justice, he matriculated as a sizar at Christ's College, Cambridge, in 1592, graduated BA in 1595, and proceeded MA in 1598. He was living at Epworth in 1598 when he completed a translation of Terence, six editions of which, with both Latin and English texts, were published in his lifetime. Married by 1601, he and his wife had six children, Cannanuel (*b.* 1600/01), Besekiell (*bap.* 18 Oct 1602), Hoseel (*bap.* 30 April 1605), Masakiell (*bap.* 27 Sept 1607), Mary (*bap.* 24 Sept 1609), and Benjamin (*bap.* 11 Oct 1613, *bur.* 12 Oct 1613).

On 19 June 1601 Bernard was presented to the vicarage of Worksop, Nottinghamshire, by Richard Whalley, father of the future regicide Edward Whalley. For his parishioners as well as residents of Epworth and Gainsborough, Lincolnshire, he published *A Large Catechisme* (1602), an expanded version of the one in the Book of Common Prayer. Opposed to the surplice, he refused to conform as required by the canons of 1604 and was deprived on 9 April 1605. He went to Gainsborough, where he affiliated with William Brewster and John Robinson, and he was with them in 1606 when they and others convened at the home of Isabel Wray, now Lady Bowes [see Darcy, Isabel], to discuss conditions in the Church of England. The group split, with Arthur Hildersham opposing separation, whereas John Smyth established a separatist congregation and Bernard entered into a covenant with approximately 100 people from Worksop and the neighbouring parishes. Those who entered this covenant pledged not to hear 'dumb' ministers, to watch over each other, and to celebrate the Lord's supper.

Ætatis suæ 74

Vera Effigies RICH. BERNARD, vigilantis simi Pastoris de Batcombe Somset A 1641

W: Hollar Bohem, ad vivum del. London

Richard Bernard (*bap.* 1568, *d.* 1641), by Wenceslaus Hollar, pubd 1644

The archbishop of York, Tobie Matthew, persuaded Bernard to conform and return to his vicarage at Worksop in 1607. In June of that year Bernard completed his most influential work, *The Faithfull Shepheard*, a handbook for ministers that explains qualifications for the ministry, the proper means of entering it, the importance of catechizing, and expository techniques. He dedicated this book to Richard Montagu, dean of the royal chapel, who, Bernard said, had lovingly embraced him. His keen interest in catechizing was reflected the same year in the publication of *A Double Catechisme*, which contained a version of his *Large Catechisme* and a shorter one for 'the weaker sort'. With the encouragement of Archbishop Matthew he published several attacks on separatists, including *The Separatists Schisme*, which apparently is not extant, although it was refuted by Henry Ainsworth's *Counterpoyson* (1608), Smyth's *Paralleles, Censures, Observations* (1609), and Henry Robinson's *A Justification of Separation* (1610). Ainsworth dismissed Bernard as a rebel against the light who was more interested in disgracing others than in defending his own position, but Smyth acknowledged his popularity and provided details about his brief period as a separatist. Commenting on Bernard's comparison of himself with Naaman when he returned to the established church, Smyth charged that he was 'as chandgable as the Moone, as mutable as Proteus, [and] as variable as the Chamaeleon' (Smyth, 5). Although Robinson recognized

Bernard as a zealous preacher and writer, he deemed his zeal misplaced and dangerous, and accused him of violating his pledge never to attack the separatists.

How far Bernard had retreated from his brief embrace of separatism is manifest in *Christian Advertisements and Counsels of Peace* (1608), in which he denounced the separatists for their novelty, schism, abuse of scripture, and affinity with such ancient heretics as Donatists and Novatians. He defended the Church of England from charges of idolatry, repudiated congregational polity, and supported set forms of prayer. Yet he did not fully conform, for in 1608 and 1611 he was presented for refusing to use the sign of the cross in baptism. He was careful, however, to nourish his relationship with Matthew, to whom he dedicated *The Sinners Safetie* (1609), an exposition of 2 Peter 1: 10 on how to attain assurance of salvation, and *Plaine Evidences* (1610), an attack on Ainsworth and Smyth, whom he denounced as 'wavering Reeds, that are tossed too and fro with the winde of their owne fantasies, arising from the humorousnesse of an instable minde, violently forced with the passion of unruled affection' (p. 336). In 1610 he also published *Contemplative Pictures*, a series of meditations and precepts for behaviour dedicated to Edmund Sheffield, Lord Sheffield, president of the council of the north, and his family.

From Bishop James Montague, whom he had known at Cambridge, Bernard received a licence to preach throughout the diocese of Bath and Wells beginning in the summer of 1612. With Montague's blessing Philip Bisse, archdeacon of Taunton, purchased the advowson of Batcombe, Somerset, for one turn and presented the living to Bernard in November 1613. Throughout the rest of his career Bernard participated in combination lectures in eastern Somerset. He also continued to write, completing *Josuahs Resolution for the Well Ordering of his Household* (1612), which included a version of his *Double Catechisme* and a substantive introductory dialogue explaining how to reform a family. The following year he published *Two Twinnes*, the first part of which was a sermon on catechizing commissioned by Matthew and preached at Southwell, Nottinghamshire. In the second part he articulated the case for adequate clerical maintenance, the lack of which he adjudged 'base contempt' (p. 33). His interest in devotional material led to the publication of three works in 1616, *A Staffe of Comforth to Stay the Weake*; *Davids Musick*, an exposition of Psalms 1–3 which he wrote with Richard Alleine, his eventual successor at Batcombe; and *A Weekes Worke*, a handbook of piety couched in the form of a dialogue between the apostle John and 'the Elect *Lady*'.

Following Montague's transfer to the see of Winchester in 1616, Bernard cultivated good relations with his successor, Arthur Lake, to whom, in part, he dedicated *A Key of Knowledge* (1617). In this commentary on Revelation he provided a bibliography of the thirty-nine authors he had consulted, including William Perkins, John Bale, John Napier, Thomas Brightman, Theodore Beza, Thomas Aquinas, and the Jesuit Francis Ribera. His association with Lake paid off the same year when charges that he had not worn his graduate hood (a violation of canon 58) were dropped in the Wells consistory court after he claimed to have received the bishop's acquiescence. In an epistle to *A Key* he called on justices of the peace to search for Catholics, enforce recusancy laws, and be alert to the danger posed by 'Church-Papists', and a companion epistle called on Christ's 'soldiers' to *'avenge the bloud of the Saints upon Babylon, that whore of Rome'* (C3r). His growing concern with Catholicism is reflected as well in *The Fabulous Foundation of the Popedome* (1619), in which he argues that Peter was never at Rome and that papal power is void. A devotional work, *The Good Mans Grace* (1621), included a call to depart from 'Papisme' as well as atheism, heresy, and other perils. Catholicism, he contended in *The Seaven Golden Candlestickes* (1621), hinders the mystery of salvation. In this work he matched historical periods to the seven churches of Asia, beginning with the church of Ephesus, the apostolic period of Christianity. He likened the present era, which commenced with Elizabeth I's accession in 1558, to the church at Philadelphia, the penultimate stage in history; the last age, corresponding to the church of Laodicea, would culminate in the last judgment. Catholicism was again on his mind in *Looke beyond Luther* (1623), in which he averred that the protestants, unlike the Catholics, could trace their doctrines through history to the Bible. In *Rhemes Against Rome* (1626) he responded to the attack on protestantism in John or Roger Heigham's *The Gagge of the New Gospel* (1623) by refuting thirty-three Catholic tenets.

Bernard's most popular work, *The Isle of Man* (1627), reached its sixteenth edition in 1683. Some commentators have suggested that this allegory of the trial of sin and its confederates influenced John Bunyan, particularly his trial scene in *The Holy War*; both men felt it necessary to defend their use of allegory, partly by reference to Jesus's employment of parables. Earlier in 1627 Bernard had published *A Guide to Grand-Jury Men*, a handbook on witchcraft that condemned all witches, whether 'good' or evil, as being in league with the devil and deserving of execution. Yet he cautioned Christians not to attribute their afflictions, including strange diseases, to witches. He included remedies against witchcraft as well as guidelines for magistrates to examine and convict witches. While at Worksop he even claimed to have exorcized a demon.

Bernard's pastoral interest in women is reflected in *Ruths Recompence* (1628), a lengthy commentary on the book of Ruth, in sermon form, which he dedicated to Frances Rich, dowager countess of Warwick. He followed this with *The Bible-Battells* (1629), in which he examined the concept of just war, arguing that such must be undertaken in defence of country, religion, or liberty, and he also dealt with preparations for war and how to fight. Concern for the pedagogical needs of believers was never far from his mind. As he explained to Bishop James Ussher, members of his congregation gathered in the rectory after the Sunday morning service to hear him repeat the sermon and correct their notes, after which he catechized them, and in the afternoon he preached again. To aid church-goers he prepared another edition of the prayer

book catechism, *The Common Catechisme* (1630), eleven editions of which had been published by 1640, and a companion work, *Good Christian, Looke to thy Creede* (1630). His pastoral experience was the basis for *Christian See to thy Conscience* (1631), which offered remedies for consciences that were blind, superstitious, desperate, overly secure, or otherwise ailing.

In October 1634 Bernard was cited before William Piers, bishop of Bath and Wells, for nonconformity. Unlike his predecessors Matthew, Montague, and Lake, Piers cracked down, ordering Bernard to genuflect when entering a church, remove his hat during prayers, cease his practice of repeating sermons, use only the questions and answers in the prayer book catechism, without expansion, and stop catechizing in the midst of prayers. Against this background Bernard continued to write, completing a nearly 500-page volume, *The Ready Way to Good Works* (1635), which exhorted the faithful to build more hospitals, almshouses, and houses of correction, provide storehouses for grain, sell corn during times of dearth to lower the price, establish apprenticeships for children of the poor, and redeem captives. In this spirit he worked with the Dorchester minister John White to collect funds to relieve silenced ministers in the 1630s. His long-standing sabbatarian convictions were articulated in *A Threefold Treatise of the Sabbath*, which insisted that sabbath observance is required by the moral law. Composed in the 1630s, it was not published until 1641, after Laudian censorship crumbled. About 1635–6 he wrote to church elders and magistrates in the Massachusetts Bay Colony about their church practices and enfranchisement provisions, provoking a defence of congregational polity from seven of their congregations in 1639. Richard Mather published their defence in two tracts in 1643, *An Apologie of the Churches in New-England* and *Church-Government and Church-Covenant Discussed*.

As the 1640s dawned Bernard remained active, in part by working with the Dorset ministers John Talbott, vicar of Milton Abbas, and Robert Walstead, rector of Bloxworth, to circulate a petition against the etcetera oath. In one of his last works, *The Article of Christs Descension into Hell* (1641), he contended that after the crucifixion Christ's soul first went to heaven before subjugating the power of darkness; on this subject he identified with Thomas Bilson, whose interpretation was Lutheran rather than Calvinist. If Bernard wrote *A Short View of the Praelaticall Church of England* (1641), as historians traditionally assert, his views on polity were altering. The author defends presbyterian government, though allowing a modest role for reformed bishops who have pastoral charges and are subordinate to the church's authority. This work also urges a reform of ecclesiastical courts, the removal of popish remnants from the liturgy, and the termination of the *ex officio* oath. Bernard's pastoral and pedagogical concerns were again manifest in *The Bibles Abstract and Epitome* (1642). He died on 31 March 1641, and his successor at Batcombe, Richard Alleine, was installed on 18 March 1642. Two of his manuscripts lay unpublished until 1644: *Certaine Positions Seriously to bee Considered of* and *Thesaurus biblicus, seu, Promptuarium sacrum*, a concordance containing his portrait (by Wenceslaus Hollar) and a preface by John Conant. Throughout most of his career Bernard was an example of those godly protestants who practised as much nonconformity as they could within the established church, yielding to authority as necessary but willing to work with those bishops who appreciated his marked commitment to elevating the piety of his parishioners through preaching and catechizing.

Bernard's oldest son, Cannanuel, matriculated from Exeter College, Oxford, on 17 December 1619, graduated BA on 21 February 1623, proceeded MA on 1 July 1625, and was appointed rector of Pitney, Somerset, in 1624, and vicar of Huish Episcopi, Somerset, in 1625. He was sequestered from the latter in 1656, though he later returned and finally resigned the living in 1663. Bernard's fourth son, Masakiell, a clothier, went to New England with the puritan minister Joseph Hull in 1636, and his daughter Mary married the separatist Roger Williams on 15 December 1629 and emigrated with him in 1631.

RICHARD L. GREAVES

Sources Venn, *Alum. Cant.* · J. Smyth, *Paralleles, censures, observations* (1609) · K. Fincham, *Prelate as pastor: the episcopate of James I* (1990) · G. A. Moriarty, 'Bernard of Epworth, co. Lincoln', *New England Historical and Genealogical Register*, 113 (July 1959), 189–92 · *CSP dom.*, *1635*, 373 · H. Ainsworth, *Counterpoyson* (1608) · J. Robinson, *A justification of separation from the Church of England* (1610) · I. Green, *The Christian's ABC: catechisms and catechizing in England, c.1530–1740* (1996) · K. Fincham, 'Episcopal government, 1603–40', *The early Stuart church, 1603–1642*, ed. K. Fincham (1993), 71–91 · T. Webster, *Godly clergy in early Stuart England: the Caroline puritan movement, c.1620–1643* (1997) · Wood, *Ath. Oxon.*, new edn, 4.13 · Foster, *Alum. Oxon., 1500–1714*, 1.114 · *Walker rev.*

Archives Bodl. Oxf., MSS Rawl. letters 89, fol. 28*r* · DWL, Morrice MS J, fol. 42 · PRO, SP 16/278/51; 16/290/15; 16/467/63, 63.2 · Som. ARS, MS D/D/CA 204; 299, fols. 56*v*–58*r*, 75*v*; 309, fol. 52*r*

Likenesses W. Hollar, etching, NPG; repro. in R. Bernard, *Thesaurus biblicus* (1644) [*see illus.*]

Bernard, Sir Robert, fifth baronet (1740–1789), politician, was born early in 1740 at Brampton Park, Huntingdonshire, the only son and second child of Sir John Bernard, fourth baronet (1685 1766), of Brampton, a gentleman farmer, and Mary, daughter and coheir of Sir Francis St John, first baronet, of Longthorpe, Northamptonshire. The Bernard family had lived in Huntingdonshire for decades and acquired the family estate at Brampton Park in 1666. The first baronet, Sir Robert Bernard (*d.* 1666), was recorder of Huntingdon and served the borough in the House of Commons. Despite their support for the parliamentary cause in the civil war, the Bernards apparently remained faithful Anglicans. Robert Bernard was educated at Westminster School, and matriculated at Christ Church, Oxford, on 10 May 1758.

Bernard continued the family's interest in politics when he stood successfully for a county parliamentary seat in 1765 made available by the retirement of Lord Charles Greville Montagu. Because the Bernards were historically allied with the Montagu family, Bernard was nominated to the seat by George Montagu, fourth duke and seventh earl of Manchester. He soon affiliated with the parliamentary whig faction led by the marquess of Rockingham. In

December 1766 he succeeded his father as fifth baronet. During his term in the House of Commons, he rarely spoke, although he voted for measures advanced by the Rockingham and Chatham ministries. According to the other Huntingdonshire political power, John Montagu, fourth earl of Sandwich, Bernard became attracted to the reform notions of William Petty, second earl of Shelburne, although no correspondence between the two exists in the Shelburne papers. Bernard quarrelled with the duke of Manchester in late 1766, which caused a breach between the two. At the election of 1768 Bernard spent considerable sums campaigning for re-election against two candidates backed by Manchester and Sandwich, but lost by 138 votes.

Bernard travelled to London in 1769, where he joined supporters of the radical reformer John Wilkes, imprisoned for outlawry and denied a seat in parliament from Middlesex. When the Society of Supporters of the Bill of Rights was founded to collect funds for Wilkes, Bernard became a charter member. Later in 1769 Bernard assisted John Calcraft, Chathamite MP, and the Surrey distiller Sir Joseph Mawbey in soliciting funds for the society in Essex. When a vacancy occurred in the parliamentary borough of Westminster in 1770, Wilkes's radical party persuaded Bernard to stand for the seat. Nominated by William Dowdeswell, Rockingham's leader in the Commons, Bernard was elected without opposition. Once again, however, he maintained a low profile, making only one speech attacking stock jobbing in the next parliament. A petition signed by several thousand Westminster constituents concerning Wilkes's Middlesex election dispute was presented to George III by Bernard in November 1770. Reportedly, Bernard refused to kneel in the presence of the king.

Bernard's close confidant in the Bill of Rights Society, John Horne, precipitated a split with Wilkes over the use of the society's funds. Bernard joined Horne, John Sawbridge, and others by leaving the society to form the Constitutional Society in March 1771. The decision to oppose Wilkes led to Bernard's failure to win nomination for the Westminster seat at the next election in 1774. Meanwhile, Bernard co-operated with Horne and Sawbridge in opposing the powerful borough patron, the duke of Bedford. The reformers hoped their campaign would inspire a general revolt against the electoral influence of powerful patrons such as Bedford. The mayor of Bedford, one Cawne, agreed to admit into the corporation Huntingdonshire and London associates of Bernard's as non-resident freemen. When the duke of Bedford died in 1771, the corporation gave the duke's post of recorder to Bernard, and he retained this post until his death in 1789. At the 1774 elections in Bedford, Bernard's interest captured both seats, including one for his brother-in-law, Robert Sparrow. The administration of Frederick, Lord North, was able to remove Sparrow from the Commons when the election was challenged by Samuel Whitbread. Bernard's faction held the other Bedford seat in the 1780 and 1784 elections, however.

At the same time that Bernard became heavily involved

in Bedford politics, he joined Christopher Wyvill's association movement for parliamentary reform in 1780. As chairman of the Huntingdonshire association, Bernard circulated Wyvill's petition for shorter parliaments and reapportionment of seats based on population shifts. Bernard also helped to organize the petitioning movement in neighbouring Cambridgeshire. Attacks of gout curtailed his activities in the mid-1780s; he died from complications of this ailment on 2 January 1789 at Brampton Park and was buried there on 7 January. Because Bernard never married, his landed property, worth £14,000 (including the Huntingdonshire manors of Brampton Park, Houghton and Grafham), was left to his nephew, Robert Bernard Sparrow, the son of his sister Mary.

Bernard became part of the early political reform movement, mainly extra-parliamentary, in the 1760s. He demonstrated the ability to bridge the rural and urban environments to produce a national agenda for reform. A moderate by the standards of the time, Bernard agreed with more substantial reformers that the crown's influence should be diminished and that parliamentary reform was necessary to recover the historical integrity of the most important national institution. John Horne was Bernard's principal mentor once he arrived in London, yet Bernard proved capable of managing reform campaigns alone, as he did in Bedford. Typical of most early moderate reformers, Bernard represented a substantial, politically independent gentry family, whose political sensibilities recoiled in the evidence of corruption at the national as well as local levels.   DANIEL WEBSTER HOLLIS, III

Sources D. W. Hollis, 'Bernard, Sir Robert', *BDMBR*, vol. 1 · *VCH Huntingdonshire* · HoP, *Commons* · L. S. Sutherland, *The City of London and the opposition to government, 1768–1774: a study in the rise of metropolitan radicalism* (1959) · I. R. Christie, *Wilkes, Wyvill and reform: the parliamentary reform movement in British politics, 1760–1785* (1962) · *GM*, 1st ser., 59 (1789), 88 · Foster, *Alum. Oxon.* · will, PRO, PROB 11/1174, sig. 10

Archives Cambs. AS, Huntingdon, Manchester MSS

Wealth at death under £14,000 in real property: *GM*, 88

Bernard, Thomas (*d.* **1582**). *See under* Bernard, John (*d.* 1554).

Bernard, Sir Thomas, **second baronet** (**1750–1818**), philanthropist, was born at Lincoln on 27 April 1750, the son of Sir Francis *Bernard, first baronet (1712–1779), and Amelia (*c.*1719–1778), daughter of Stephen Offley. His ten siblings included the author and benefactor Frances Elizabeth (1757–1821) [*see* King, Frances Elizabeth], who later collaborated with her brother in works of poor relief. Spending some early part of his life in British North America, where his father was governor of Massachusetts, he was educated at a private school in New Jersey and began studies at Harvard University. The disturbed state of colonial politics forced him to abandon these to work as confidential secretary for his father. Shortly afterwards Bernard returned to England and secured the post of commissary of musters. Pursuing a legal career, he entered the Middle Temple and was called to the bar in 1780. Owing to a

speech impediment he preferred to specialize in conveyancing and began to amass a fortune which was augmented by his marriage, in May 1782, to Margaret (*d.* 1813), daughter and coheir of Patrick Adair.

Thus set up in life, Bernard retired from the law and devoted the best part of his later life to philanthropy, especially concerning the welfare of the poor. He took an active interest in the London Foundling Hospital and became a governor, and then, in 1795, treasurer, all the while involving himself in its day-to-day affairs and finances until ill health forced his retirement in 1806. Bernard was also concerned at the unwholesome working conditions of children in cotton factories and of apprentice chimney sweeps. Although most of his good works were carried out from his home in London, his concern with the conditions of the poor grew from experience on the family estate in the Vale of Aylesbury and the influence of traditional county society.

Bernard developed a remarkable range of charitable interests and energetically pursued these for the rest of his active life. He was much admired and respected by churchmen, politicians, and other reformers. From the 1770s on food prices tended to rise faster than wages and many were forced to apply for parish relief. Other problems emerged from changing working relations in town and country, while during the 1790s poor rates rocketed and famine threatened a number of private relief schemes. Bernard adopted the ideas of Count Rumford on soup kitchens and the economical nutrition of the poor and promoted these generally. In 1796, along with William Wilberforce, Shute Barrington, bishop of Durham, Frances Elizabeth King, and others, he established the influential Society for Bettering the Condition and Improving the Comforts of the Poor. The society's principal aim was to promote good practice in poor relief measures by means of propaganda. The society's *Reports* collected information respecting the poor, and the best way of relieving their hardship. A central aim of this work was always to enable the poor to better their own condition through applying justly administered assistance, rather than to discipline them or make them objects of dependence. Incentives and examples were preferred to compulsion and control, with Bernard opposed in general to workhouse principles. Instead self-help and independence were to be fostered amid the lower orders: 'Let us give effect to that master spring of action, on which equally depends the prosperity of individuals and of empires—THE DESIRE IMPLANTED IN THE HUMAN BREAST OF BETTERING ITS CONDITION' (Poynter, 92). Moral improvement stemming from evangelical Christianity was to play a major role in the self-betterment of the poor. Bernard published exemplary tales of working men and women who had, through acts of economy and thrift, hard work, and initiative, supported their own families. His *Short Account of Britton Abbot* (1797) was about a Yorkshire cottager who enclosed a plot of wasteland upon which he was able to support his wife and six children.

In the early nineteenth century Bernard participated in

national debate as controversy on poor-law reform gathered momentum. He was partly in agreement with Thomas Malthus, first, that scarce resources would ultimately limit the growth of population, and that the poor law encouraged some false expectations about rights to subsistence in times of hardship, thereby encouraging imprudence among sections of the poor. He would not, however, accept the radical argument that the poor law should be abolished or charity discouraged. Although he made some suggestions for improving poor law administration, chiefly in better record-keeping, he always wanted it locally administered and thought an intimate knowledge of the recipients of relief would make it more effective. Bernard did not favour the policy of a minimum wage for fear that this would upset established relations of society and ideas about benevolence and entitlement. In time he placed growing emphasis upon distinguishing moral traits inside the body of the poor and argued that improved habits of life helped the rural labourer more than any increase in wages. Essentially he sought to maintain the great principle of the Elizabethan poor law, but to adapt and improve its workings. His recommendations were largely conservative, piecemeal, and mainly derived from existing schemes and initiatives with evangelical morality always more influential than utilitarian calculation. When dearth again threatened in 1812–13 Bernard pressed schemes to create employment by encouraging new industry, especially fishing and the wider consumption of fish. After the war he campaigned against the salt tax, eventually persuading the chancellor of the exchequer to lower the duty on rock salt used for agricultural purposes.

There emerged from the work of Bernard and the Society for Bettering the Condition of the Poor a school for the indigent blind, the Cancer Institution, and the Fever Institution, alongside other initiatives. He was also interested in allotments, friendly societies, Sunday societies, schools of industry, medical charities, penny clubs, the aged poor, and schemes for the promotion of vaccination. A defender of the sabbath and an opponent of strong drink and lewd entertainments, he considered *The Beggar's Opera* and like plays to be profane and immoral. In 1801 he was appointed chancellor to the diocese of Durham by Shute Barrington and established a school at Bishop Auckland for promising students and the training of teachers. Teachers from this school being in high demand, he wrote to publicize the aims and teaching methods of his new school, later known as the Barrington School. Bernard consistently supported general education for the poor. Aside from the education of the poor, he supported the fine arts, establishing, at the suggestion of Count Rumford, the Royal Institution, Piccadilly, in 1800. Five years later he formed the British Institution for the Promotion of Fine Arts in the United Kingdom. He also set up the Albert Club, a meeting place for writers which excluded any gaming, drinking, and party politics. In 1801 the archbishop of Canterbury awarded Bernard the degree of MA for his work, in which year he also received an honorary LLD from the University of Edinburgh.

In 1810 Bernard succeeded to the baronetcy on the death of his brother. His first wife, Margaret, died on 6 June 1813, and he remarried on 15 June 1815; his second wife was Charlotte Matilda, youngest daughter of Sir Edward Hulse, second baronet. Both his marriages were childless. He died on 1 July 1818 and was buried in a vault beneath the Foundling Hospital chapel, London. His second wife survived him.   R. D. SHELDON

Sources J. Baker, *The life of Sir Thomas Bernard* (1819) · DNB · J. R. Poynter, *Society and pauperism* (1969)

Archives BL, letters

Likenesses S. W. Reynolds, mezzotint, pubd 1805 (after J. Opie), BM · oils (after J. Opie), Royal Institution, London · portrait, repro. in Baker, *Life*

Bernard, Thomas Dehany (1815–1904), Church of England clergyman, second son of Charles Bernard of Eden estate, Jamaica, the descendant of a Huguenot family, and his wife, Margaret, daughter of John Baker of Waresley House, Worcestershire, was born at Clifton on 11 November 1815. Mountague *Bernard was his brother. After private education he matriculated on 2 December 1833 from Exeter College, Oxford, and in 1837 was placed in the second class of the final classical school. He graduated BA in 1838, when he won the Ellerton theological prize with the essay 'On the conduct and character of St Peter'. In 1839 he was awarded the chancellor's prize for an English essay, 'The classical taste and character compared with the Romantic'. He proceeded MA in 1840. In 1841 he married Caroline (d. 1881), daughter of Benjamin Linthorne of High Hall, Wimborne. They had two sons and seven daughters. In 1840 he was ordained deacon and licensed to the curacy of Great Baddow, Essex. Ordained priest in 1841, he succeeded to the vicarage of Great Baddow, where he remained until 1846. After working for a short time as curate of Harrow on the Hill, he became in 1848 vicar of Terling, Essex, showing a keen interest in the cause of foreign missions. He was select preacher at Oxford in 1858, 1862, and 1882. In 1864 he delivered the Bampton lectures, published as *The Progress of Doctrine in the New Testament* (5th edn 1900). In later life, Bernard published several other works; though his greatest talents undoubtedly lay in parish work and administration, contemporaries admired his *Before his Presence with a Song* (1885) and *The Central Teachings of Jesus Christ* (1892).

Of strong evangelical sympathies, Bernard was appointed by Charles Simeon's trustees to the rectory of Walcot, Bath, in 1864. There Bernard's gifts of organization were called into play. He increased the church accommodation and built St Andrew's Church and schools. In 1867 the bishop of Bath and Wells collated him to a prebendal stall in Wells Cathedral; and next year the dean and chapter elected him to a residentiary canonry. He succeeded to the chancellorship of the cathedral in 1879, and from 1880 to 1895 represented the chapter in convocation. Bernard was as zealous a cathedral dignitary as he was an energetic town rector. He revived the cathedral grammar school, at his own cost provided buildings for it, established a high school for girls, and interested himself in the general parochial life of Wells. An evangelical whom all trusted, though unfettered by party conventions, Bernard was a frequent speaker at the Islington clerical meeting, the most important annual gathering of Anglican evangelicals in his day. He resigned Walcot in 1886, and went to live at Wimborne, Dorset. In 1901 he retired from his canonry, retaining only the unpaid office of chancellor. He died at his home, High Hall, Wimborne, on 7 December 1904. Bernard had gained a reputation as a scholar and a man of affairs, and as a wise counsellor in private and a clear, cogent teacher in public.

A. R. BUCKLAND, rev. I. T. FOSTER

Sources Record (9 Dec 1904) · Crockford · Foster, Alum. Oxon. · P. Schaff and S. M. Jackson, Encyclopedia of living divines and Christian workers of all denominations in Europe and America: being a supplement to Schaff-Herzog encyclopedia of religious knowledge (1887) · Allibone, Dict. · E. Stock, The history of the Church Missionary Society: its environment, its men and its work, 4 vols. (1899–1916)

Wealth at death £62,808 11s. 1d.: probate, 3 Jan 1905, CGPLA Eng. & Wales

Bernardi, John (1657–1736), army officer and Jacobite conspirator, was born at Evesham, Worcestershire, the son of Francis Bernardi (b. c.1627), a Genoese nobleman and agent at the court of Charles II, naturalized in 1675, and grandson of the Genoese diplomat Count Philip de Bernardi. The principal authority for Bernardi's life is his self-serving autobiography, written while a prisoner in Newgate and published in 1729. His father was such a stern disciplinarian, beating the boy for the slightest fault, that in 1670 he ran away to Packington Hall, the seat of Sir Clement Fisher, whose wife had previously sympathized with Bernardi's plight. Discovering the Fishers to be in London, Bernardi pursued them. He was well received and recommended to their relative Littleton Clent, a captain in John Fitzgerald's marine infantry regiment then in garrison at Portsmouth. Clent taught him the rudiments of soldiering but, when the regiment was disbanded late in 1673, Clent slipped Bernardi £20 and left him to fend for himself. He gravitated to London, caught smallpox, and, while in financial extremis, was sold into the Dutch army for £3 by his godfather and professional recruiter Colonel William Anselme. A private in Captain Philip Savage's company, Bernardi fought at the siege of Grave in October 1674 and was slightly wounded.

Bernardi was commissioned ensign in the Anglo-Dutch brigade on 23 January 1675. Later that year he was injured while separating two duelling officers, and he then lost the sight of an eye and was partially disabled in one arm at the siege of Maastricht in 1676. While convalescing, in 1677 he met and married a Dutch woman aged forty 'of considerable fortune' (Bernardi, 36); subsequently they had four children. On 26 June 1677 Bernardi was raised to lieutenant; on 10 January 1683 to captain-lieutenant; and on 7 November 1685 to captain. When, on 14 March 1688, James II ordered the Anglo-Dutch brigade into England, Bernardi, a loyalist and Roman Catholic, was among the 104 officers who obeyed. Rewarded with a captaincy in John Hales's infantry regiment, he remained constant to James during the revolution of 1688 and duly lost his commission. Bernardi departed first for St Germain-en-Laye,

where he left his wife and children, before following James to Ireland, landing in Bantry Bay on 1 May 1689. He was appointed major of Charles Macarthy More's regiment.

The death of Viscount Dundee at Killiecrankie on 27 July 1689 deprived the Scottish Jacobites of leadership, and Bernardi was dispatched as a military adviser to the marquess of Seaforth, whose expedition to Scotland landed on 20 May 1690. Little was achieved, and when news of the defeat at the Boyne reached Scotland Seaforth's troops were disbanded. Escorted by forty MacDonalds, Bernardi fled south to Edinburgh in late October 1690 and then to London, where he sold his horses to raise money for a passage to Ostend. While waiting ship at Colchester, he was arrested. Eighteen months of legal wrangling and the expenditure of 'some hundreds of pounds' (Bernardi, 85) ensued before the case against him was withdrawn.

A free man, in 1692 Bernardi settled down to live quietly and garden in a country house near Brentford in Middlesex. By this time he was a widower, his wife having died during 1689 while in France. According to the Short History, when his tenancy expired in December 1695 Bernardi travelled to London and encountered at a tavern, 'by accident' (Bernardi, 88), an old associate, Captain Ambrose Rookwood, an operative in the Jacobite assassination plot. By 22 February 1696 it was clear that the plot had been betrayed, and, in panic, Rookwood sought assistance from Bernardi: they were arrested at a tavern on Tower Hill on Sunday 23 February. This account was disingenuous. Bernardi had returned to France at some time between 1692 and 1695 before crossing to England from Calais in company with Rookwood in early February 1696. Bernardi was fully involved in the assassination plot and intended as a senior officer in one of the rebel regiments. While Rookwood was promptly tried and executed, no tangible evidence against Bernardi could be discovered, but he remained in prison without trial for the remaining forty years of his life. When the suspension of the Habeas Corpus Act lapsed in October 1696, a bill was introduced to sanction the imprisonment of Bernardi and five others for a further twelve months on the plea that more time was required to collect evidence. The act was renewed at the end of each year until 1702. Similar acts were passed on the accessions of Anne, George I, and George II, each bout of Jacobite activity further reducing the chances of Bernardi and his companions being either brought to trial or released. As the years crept by and his money haemorrhaged, Bernardi became decreasingly able to help himself, while those who might have assisted either died or lost interest. In 1712 he married again, and his wife, Abigail, bore him a further ten children, all of whom were brought up in Newgate. In an effort to provide for his offspring, as well as to publicize his case, Bernardi wrote his autobiography during 1728. Despite his hopeless situation and declining health exacerbated by his old wounds, he bore his fate stoically. He died in Newgate, aged either seventy-nine or eighty, on 20 September 1736.

T. F. HENDERSON, rev. JOHN CHILDS

Sources J. Bernardi, *A short history of the life of Major John Bernardi* (1729) • Raad van State (1928), Nationaal Archief, The Hague • C. Dalton, ed., *English army lists and commission registers, 1661–1714*, 6 vols. (1892–1904) • W. King, *The state of the protestants of Ireland under the late King James's government* (1730) • D. Nairne, diary, NL Scot., MS 14266, fols. 92, 103 • U. Nott. L., Portland MSS, PWA 2485 • Northants. RO, Shrewsbury (Montagu) papers, vol. 63, no. 44 • PRO, SP 35/77 and 78
Likenesses G. Vandergucht, line engraving (after W. Cooper), BM, NPG; repro. in Bernard, *Short history* • engraving, repro. in Bernardi, *Short history*

Bernardine of St Francis. *See* Eyston, John (1627–1709).

Bernays, Albert James (1823–1892), chemist, was born on 8 November 1823 at St Pancras, London, the son of Dr Adolphus Bernays (*d.* 22 Dec 1864), professor of modern languages at King's College, London, and his wife, Martha. He was educated at King's College School, and studied chemistry with C. Remigius Fresenius, and afterwards with Justus Liebig at Giessen, where he graduated PhD with a thesis on limonin, a bitter principle which he discovered in the pips of oranges and lemons. In 1845 Bernays began his career as an analyst and lecturer on chemistry in Derby, and became known for his interest in questions concerning food and hygiene. In 1851 he served as a juror for those classes at the Great Exhibition. In 1852 he published the first edition of *Household Chemistry*, a popular work, reissued under various titles. He also compiled *Notes for Students*, in various formats and editions.

In 1855 Bernays was appointed lecturer in chemistry at St Mary's Hospital, London, which he left in 1860 to take up a similar post at St Thomas's Hospital, where he remained until his death. Bernays was also public analyst to St Giles, Camberwell, and St Saviour's, Southwark, and was for many years chemist and analyst to the Kent Water Company and an examiner for the Royal College of Physicians. He was a genial man and a capable and popular teacher; he took a great interest in social matters generally, and gave more than a thousand free public lectures during his lifetime. His essay, 'The moderate use of alcohol, true temperance', was published in the *Contemporary Review* and reprinted with essays by others in *The Alcohol Question*. He also carried out investigations on the atmosphere of Cornish mines and on dangerous trades, and made inventions in water filtration. He was a fellow of the Chemical Society and of the Institute of Chemistry.

Bernays married Ellen Labatt, daughter of Benjamin Evans; she died on 6 February 1901. He died from bronchitis at his home, Acre House, Brixton, on 5 January 1892, and was by his own desire cremated at Woking.

P. J. HARTOG, rev. ANITA McCONNELL

Sources *The Times* (9 Jan 1892) • *The Times* (8 Feb 1901) • T. S. [T. Stevenson], *JCS*, 61 (1892), 488 • *Chemical News* (12 Feb 1892), 85 • *Nature*, 45 (1891–2), 258 • *BMJ* (16 Jan 1892), 148 • *The Analyst*, 17 (1892), 60
Likenesses W. Brockedon, pencil-and-chalk drawing, NPG
Wealth at death £12,081 2*s.* 8*d.*: resworn probate, March 1892, CGPLA Eng. & Wales

Bernays, Robert Hamilton (1902–1945), politician and diarist, was born in Stanmore, Middlesex, on 6 May 1902, the fourth child and third son of the Revd Prebendary Stewart Frederic Lewis Bernays (1867–1941), rector of Great Stanmore, and his wife, Lillian Stephenson (*d.* 1935). He was educated at Rossall School, Lancashire, from 1915 to 1920, taught briefly at Solihull, and went up to Worcester College, Oxford, as an exhibitioner in history in 1922, being awarded an *aegrotat* degree in 1925. A member of the Liberal Club, he was president of the Oxford Union in 1925. Having tried and failed to enter the Sudan political service while at Oxford, he became a journalist and later leader writer with the *News Chronicle*.

After standing unsuccessfully as Liberal candidate for Rugby in 1929, Bernays had more luck in Bristol North in 1931. There, despite his hurried adoption and advocacy of free trade, he was unopposed by a Conservative and won the seat with a 13,000 majority. Before his election he had collected material as *News Chronicle* special correspondent in India for his first book, a study of Gandhi, *Naked Fakir* (1933), while after entering the Commons he used his status as an MP to advantage by travelling throughout Europe as a highly paid journalist. His second book, *Special Correspondent* (1934), consisted largely of an account of the beginnings of the Nazi regime in Germany, which he had visited in 1933.

Politics and journalism did not always combine well, however. Bernays's decision in November 1933 not to follow his party leader, Sir Herbert Samuel, into opposition to the National Government cost him his job at the *News Chronicle*. Though something of an impoverished political orphan for the remainder of the 1931–5 parliament, Bernays obviously enjoyed politics and the company of politicians. His sense—however precarious—of being close to the centre of things emerges clearly in the diary he maintained and in his letters to his sister, Lucy, who was living in Brazil. These, in edited form and covering the years 1932 to 1939, were published in 1996. They plot not merely the career of a young and ambitiously earnest politician, but also the tensions and uncertainties of politics in the 1930s. In throwing off his free-trading Liberal Party hat, Bernays had invested heavily in the National Government's survival. Calculating correctly that the route to promotion lay in joining the National Liberals he did so, and reward, when it came, took the form of his being appointed parliamentary secretary to the minister of health in May 1937. In this way he became one of the band of non-Conservative MPs serving in Chamberlain's administration. But the beneficiary of one form of coalitionism in British politics became the casualty of another. Hard-working though Bernays was, he was dropped as soon as Churchill formed his coalition government in May 1940.

Serving thereafter as deputy commissioner for the southern civil defence region, Bernays made two decisions in April 1942. One was to join the army and take a commission with the Royal Engineers. The other was to marry, on 26 April, Nancy Britton (*d.* 1984), the daughter of a constituent. The couple had two sons, neither of whom have any memory of their father. At the age of forty-two, while a member of a parliamentary team visiting troops in the Mediterranean, he was killed in an air crash off Brindisi on 25 January 1945.

By 1945 there was not much future for National Liberalism, and had he lived to contest Bristol North in the general election of that year Bernays would doubtless have been defeated. His political career would probably have ended then anyway. Although his life was cut short, he should be remembered as both creature and chronicler of an unusual phase in national politics: the period of National Government. In life his achievements were considerable without being exceptional. As an unattached and amusing young man he featured in the pre-war London scene. In death, however, he left in his diary and letters one of the fullest and most colourful accounts of a distinct political regime. In common with other noted political diarists (Cuthbert Headlam, Harold Nicolson, Henry (Chips) Channon, and, most recently, Alan Clark) he never rose above junior office status. Perhaps that level offers the best vantage point for a diarist.   NICK SMART

Sources *The diaries and letters of Robert Bernays, 1932–1939*, ed. N. Smart (1996) · papers, priv. coll. [family possession] · *WWW*
Archives NRA, priv. coll., papers | BL OIOC, letters to Lord Reading, MSS Eur. E 238, F 118
Likenesses photographs, priv. coll.
Wealth at death £17,798 12s. 2d.: probate, 10 Oct 1945, *CGPLA Eng. & Wales*

Berners. For this title name *see* Bourchier, John, second Baron Berners (*c*.1467–1533); Wilson, Gerald Hugh Tyrwhitt-, fourteenth Baron Berners (1883–1950).

Berners, Josias (*d*. 1661x3), government official, was the son of William Berners, an armigerous London silk merchant, and Katherin Tailbois. His father's family had branches in Essex and Hertfordshire. A great-grandfather was Sir Thomas Courteis, one-time lord mayor of London.

In 1620 Berners entered Gray's Inn, at the instance of his uncle, Robert, counsellor at law, but does not appear to have been called to the bar. However, he acted as attorney or solicitor to the New River Company in his capacity as company steward, and *c*.1637 he was appointed clerk to the company. Although Berners was the king's preferred candidate for the post, his tenure was disputed by his predecessor in that office, William Lewen, who appears to have enjoyed the support of certain privy councillors, despite his expulsion by the company court on charges of fraud and embezzlement.

Having served the parliamentarian cause in a minor capacity during the 1640s, Berners was named as one of the judges to try Charles I, but does not appear to have attended the high court of justice. A prominent member of that bureaucratic class which flourished during the civil war and interregnum, he was appointed one of the contractors for sale of dean and chapter lands in 1649. The following year he was appointed to the commission for sequestration and compounding, which body later assumed the responsibilities of the parliamentary indemnity committee. In 1652 he became a commissioner for the removal of obstructions to the sale of crown, church, and delinquents' lands, and was appointed to the Hale commission on law reform.

Associated with ideologically republican figures such as Thomas Chaloner, Henry Neville, and James Harrington, Berners clearly opposed the Cromwellian protectorate. It was reported in 1654 that he had been elected to sit in the first protectorate parliament for Middlesex, but there is no evidence that he ever took his seat. He helped present parliament with a London petition against the regime in February 1659, and when the Rump was restored in May 1659 he was elected to serve on the council of state as one of ten non-MPs who joined the new executive and narrowly missed appointment as one of the new lords commissioners of the great seal in June. Berners became very active on the part of the restored Commonwealth, allying with Sir Arthur Heselrige and Thomas Scot against the military interest championed by Charles Fleetwood and John Lambert. He helped secure the Tower during the counter-coup of December 1659 and was re-elected to the council of state when the Rump was restored once more. The return of the secluded MPs in February 1660 led to his abrupt departure from public office. Noble has claimed that Berners owed his pardon at the Restoration to nothing more than the king's own clemency.

Berners was married twice, first to one Cotton, and second to Abigail Keighley. His will, dated 1 January 1661 and proved in December 1663, stated that Berners resided in Clerkenwell Close, in the parish of St James's, Clerkenwell, Middlesex. Berners left property in the City, Clerkenwell, Enfield, and Hertfordshire to his only surviving son, James, having appointed Christ's Hospital his residual heir.

James also inherited a Marylebone estate in Middlesex which his father had bought for £970 in 1654 from Sir Francis Williamson of Isleworth. Situated on what is now Oxford Street, this happy investment formed the basis of a family fortune which descended through the male line right down to the end of the nineteenth century. The family's ownership of the estate is commemorated in modern day Berners Street.   SEAN KELSEY

Sources G. E. Aylmer, *The state's servants: the civil service of the English republic, 1649–1660* (1973), 210–13 · H. Chauncy, *The historical antiquities of Hertfordshire* (1700); repr. in 2 vols., 1 (1826), 175, 316–17 · *The visitation of London, anno Domini 1633, 1634, and 1635, made by Sir Henry St George*, 1, ed. J. J. Howard and J. L. Chester, Harleian Society, 15 (1880), 68 · J. Foster, *The register of admissions to Gray's Inn, 1521–1889, together with the register of marriages in Gray's Inn chapel, 1695–1754* (privately printed, London, 1889) · court book of the New River Company, LMA, ACC 2558/NR 13/2 [fire damaged and badly disordered] · B. Rudden, *The New River: a legal history* (1985) · C. H. Firth and R. S. Rait, eds., *Acts and ordinances of the interregnum, 1642–1660*, 1 (1911), 268, 920, 1011, 1087, 1246, 1254; 2 (1911), 20, 38, 87, 120, 303, 310, 382–3, 471, 479, 581–2, 588–90, 668, 676, 702–3, 783, 809, 824, 830, 839, 949, 1082, 1122, 1139, 1273, 1290, 1308, 1327, 1373–4, 1432, 1436, 1438 · *CSP dom.*, 1636–7, 170, 554; 1637, 27 · Bodl. Oxf., MS Tanner 51, fols. 5, 161 · Bodl. Oxf., MS Tanner 52, fols. 78, 96, 154, 214, 229 · Bodl. Oxf., MS Tanner 63, fols. 10, 18, 35 · Bodl. Oxf., MS Tanner 66, fols. 234, 242, 246 · Burke, *Gen. GB* (1952), 167 · J. Slater, 'The Berners estate, St Marylebone', *Transactions of the London and Middlesex Archaeological Society*, new ser., 4 (1918–22), 33–55 · M. Noble, *The lives of the English regicides*, 1 (1798), 90 · PRO, PROB 11/312/271, 286b–287 [will of Josias Berners]
Archives Bodl. Oxf., Tanner MSS

Wealth at death property in the City of London, Clerkenwell, Enfield, Hertfordshire; estate in Marylebone, Middlesex, which cost £970 in 1654: will, PRO, PROB 11/312/271, fols. 286b–287

Berners [Bernes, Barnes], **Juliana** (*fl.* 1460), supposed author and prioress of Sopwell, cannot be authoritatively identified. The biography of Dame Juliana Berners has grown from a brief note on sig. f3jr of *The Book of Hawking, Hunting, and Blasing of Arms* (also known as the Book of St Albans), a collection of instructive material in prose and verse which was first printed by the anonymous so-called Schoolmaster Printer at St Albans in 1486, and reprinted in many later editions until the early seventeenth century. The second main item in the collection, a verse treatise on 'the manere of huntynge for all manere of bestys', of which part takes the form of instructions from a 'Dame' to her sons or charges, concludes:

> Explicit Dam Julyans
> Barnes in her boke of huntyng.

Later editions of the collection preserved the note in one form or another, but without any important expansion: in Wynkyn de Worde's edition of 1496, for example, it reads:

> Explicit dame Julyans Bernes doc-
> tryne in her boke of huntynge.
> (sig. e1jv)

No reference to an author is made in either surviving manuscript copy of the text (LPL, MS 491, and Bodl. Oxf., MS Rawl. poet. 143), although two manuscript versions of a small compilation of hunting-related lore which, in the printed volume, follows the *Boke of Huntyng*, conclude with related notes: in Cambridge, Magdalene College, Pepys Library, MS 1047, the material ends *Explicit Julyan Barne*, and in BL, Harley MS 2340, *Explicit J B*. It is of course possible that these notes themselves derived from the information made available in the printed *Book*.

Despite the sparseness of information in the printed colophons and the manuscript attributions, a biography of sorts has been concocted over the centuries. John Bale's sixteenth-century account of the printed edition of 1496 attributed all its parts (including a treatise on angling which was added by de Worde) to Juliana Barnes, and spoke of her, in laudatory terms, as alive in 1460. A copy of the 1486 edition, now in Cambridge University Library, contains a manuscript note in the hand of William Burton (1575–1645), historian of Leicestershire, identifying the author as 'Lady Julian Berners', daughter of Sir James Berners, of Berners Roding, in Essex, and prioress of the nunnery of Sopwell, near St Albans. The introduction to Joseph Haslewood's facsimile of the 1496 edition, published in 1810, although conceding that 'very few particulars' were available in genealogical records or in lists of the prioresses of Sopwell, greatly expanded this information and supplied a hypothetical pedigree and other details which effectively formalized Juliana Berners's existence.

It is difficult to be anything but sceptical about this account, and about its elevation of Juliana Berners to the status of author. The phrasing of the various manuscript and printed notes does not necessarily imply that the individual named in them was the author of the text or texts in question: she (or even he, if 'Dam Julyans' is perhaps a corruption of 'Daun Julyan'; only the early printed notes refer to the individual as a female) may simply have owned, compiled, commissioned, or copied the material. Orthographical variation in the relevant manuscripts and printed books furthermore means that it is impossible to confirm the name Berners, rather than Barnes or Bernes (even Bemes, in some sixteenth-century accounts), as the foundation for genealogical research. The formalizing of the name as Berners, and the association with the Essex family of that name, may have been in some way influenced by the reputation of John, Lord Berners, translator of Froissart and of other French texts. Similarly, the association with Sopwell may simply have been suggested by the proximity of this house to St Albans, where the earliest printed version of the *Book* appeared. Sopwell may have had some temporary notoriety in the late fifteenth century on account of an action in the court of arches brought by a deposed prioress against the archdeacon of St Albans, and it may also have had some reputed association with learned women: Dame Eleanor Hull worked there on some English translations of devotional texts. Whatever reasons might explain the invocation of Juliana Berners's name at the end of the 'boke of huntyng', the attribution of the text to a female author is not implausible. Parts of it are addressed to 'my chylde' and 'my dere sonnys' by their 'dame' (instructress or mother here, although in the context of a nunnery either the prioress or one of the inhabitants able to contribute financially to her upkeep), and it offers advice on matters and procedures specific to hunting in the context of instruction in the cultivation of 'gentle' behaviour. To argue that these subjects would have been unlikely interests for women is to overlook the evidence suggested by a text such as *Le menagier de Paris*, in which a husband instructs his young wife in the skills of both hunting and hawking.

JULIA BOFFEY

Sources *STC, 1475–1640*, nos. 3308–3318 [esp. no. 3308: *Here in thys boke afore ar contenyt the bokys of haukyng and huntyng with other plesuris dyverse as in the boke apperis and also of cootarmuris a nobull werke* (1486), facs. edn with introduction by W. Blades as *The boke of Saint Albans by Dame Juliana Berners: containing treatises on hawking, hunting, and cote armour* (1881); also no. 3309: *This present boke shewyth the manere of hawkynge, huntynge, and also of divysynge of cote armours* (1496), repr. with introduction by J. Haslewood as *The book containing the treatises of hawking, hunting, coat-armour, fishing, and blasing of arms* (1810)] • R. Hands, 'Juliana Berners and *The boke of St. Albans*', *Review of English Studies*, new ser., 18 (1967), 373–86 • R. Hands, *English hawking and hunting in the 'Boke of St. Albans'* (1975) • *Julians Barnes: Boke of huntyng*, ed. G. Tilander (1964) • W. Braekman, The treatise on angling in the "Boke of St Albans" (1496), *Scripta*, 1 (1980) • A. Barratt, *Women's writing in Middle English* (1992), 232–7 • A. Barratt, 'Dame Eleanor Hull: a fifteenth-century translator', *The medieval translator: the theory and practice of translating in the middle ages*, ed. R. Ellis and others (1989), 87–101 • Bale, *Cat.*, 1.611 • H. Chauncy, *The historical antiquities of Hertfordshire* (1700); repr. in 2 vols. (1826), vol. 1, p. 317 • Dugdale, *Monasticon*, new edn, 3.362–4 • W. C. Metcalfe, ed., *The visitations of Essex*, 1, Harleian Society, 13 (1878), 21 • *VCH Hertfordshire*, 1.345; 4.422–6 • A. L. Binns, 'A manuscript source of the *Book of St Albans*', *Bulletin of the John Rylands University Library*,

33 (1950–51), 15–24 · E. F. Jacob, 'The Book of St Albans', *Essays in later medieval history* (1968) [repr. from *Bulletin of the John Rylands Library*, 28 (1944)] · *Le menagier de Paris*, ed. G. E. Brereton and J. M. Ferrier (1981)

Archives BL, Harley MS 2340 · Bodl. Oxf., Rawlinson poet. 143 · LPL, MS 491 · Magd. Cam., Pepys Library, MS 1047

Bernham, David of (*d*. 1253), bishop of St Andrews, came of a family of prominent Berwick burgesses, probably immigrants from England in an earlier generation, and became a master (at which university is unknown) before joining the *familia* of Bishop William Malveisin of St Andrews about 1224. His extraordinary promotion to be the king's chamberlain, probably in 1235, the only clerical chamberlain before 1306, is to be explained by the king's need for cash to marry off his sister, and the prominence of David's brother, Robert, who became the first mayor in the new commune of Berwick, which was probably established in the 1230s. When Malveisin died in 1238 the choice of the chapter was almost certainly opposed at Rome by the king. A new election was ordered and David of Bernham, now precentor of Glasgow, the king's choice, was successful; he was consecrated by three Scottish bishops on 22 January 1240, about which time he gave up the office of chamberlain.

Bernham played little part in secular affairs during his episcopate and, although he participated in the inauguration of Alexander III on 13 July 1249, he was not involved in the coup against Alan Durward at Christmas 1251. His energies were devoted to the affairs of his diocese and of the church, stimulated by the legation of Otto, who held a council at Edinburgh in October 1239. The canon *Basilicarum* required the dedication of existing churches within two years, and between 6 May 1240 and 24 August 1249 Bernham conducted about 140 dedications, over 110 of them by October 1244. In addition he held a synod for Lothian archdeaconry in May 1242, promulgating an eclectic set of canons which drew on legislation of the legate Otto and of a number of English sees. There was surely a parallel synod for the rest of the diocese, and within weeks the second known provincial council of the Scottish church, held at Perth in his diocese in July 1242, probably issued the early canons in the collection of provincial canons. He held another diocesan synod at Perth on 2 June 1248, whose business is largely unknown.

The effectiveness of these synodalia and provincialia is unquantifiable, but their concern is undoubted. Residence, the provision of a vicar who must be a priest (as must any chaplains), the avoidance by clerics of secular office, trade, the passing of capital sentences, and the annual visitation of parishes by the archdeacon, are some of the matters covered. Perhaps the most important provincial canon was that laying down (as the Fourth Lateran Council of 1215 had required) a minimum stipend for vicars—a modest 10 merks annually. This applied to the whole Scottish church and seems to have been or become effective except, perhaps, in the poor fringe dioceses.

In 1241 Bishop Bernham had tried to attend the abortive council summoned by the pope to Rome; he was more successful in July 1245, when he attended the Council of Lyons, using the occasion to forward the canonization of Queen Margaret, whose cult had been promoted by kings William the Lion and Alexander II. The exact date of canonization about 1249 is not known, but the event was celebrated by a translation of her relics at Dunfermline Abbey on 19 June 1250, conducted by Bishop Bernham and six other bishops, in the presence of the king and his mother.

About this time Bernham and the other six bishops protested at the infringement of the liberties of the church by the king's council, apparently by an attack on some possessions of St Andrews Priory, but probably in other unrecorded episodes also. There are hints that the government of the king's minority encroached upon the generously wide jurisdiction of canon law, and the bishops, led by Bernham, took their grievances to the pope, who, on 31 May 1251, ordered an inquiry into the liberties of the Scottish church. It seems to have come to nothing.

Not all the evidence is favourable to Bernham, but it is rare that both sides of ecclesiastical controversy are known. The canons of St Andrews complained of his extortions, and he certainly supported the rival collegiate church of St Mary in the struggle to secure its revenues against opposition from the priory. He also resisted a number of papal provisions of Italians who would have drained wealth from parishes in his diocese. He was as tenacious of his rights as any medieval cleric, but as Bishop Bernham was the outstanding Scottish representative of a reforming generation, whose achievement in providing a literate clergy serving in well-provided kirks has been undervalued. He died at Nenthorn, Berwickshire, on 26 April 1253 and was buried in Kelso Abbey.

In spite of his concern for residence, David of Bernham was himself content to divert the revenues of Inchture, properly in the patronage of the priory, to support in the schools of Paris his nephew, **W. of Bernham** (*fl*. 1248–1256). More probably William than Walter, he may have been the son of William of Bernham, a Berwick burgess (*c*.1200–1250), and certainly came from that Berwick family, since Bishop Bernham was his uncle. His mother was called Ema. He studied at Paris, probably arts, in the 1240s, and regented there for two years, at latest in 1252–4. After a visit to Scotland, he went to Oxford to study law. He is unknown to sources in Scotland, yet held a number of parsonages there from which he drew the revenues which supported his studies. Thus he was absentee parson of Inchture when his mother told him that his uncle had given a pension of 60 merks therefrom to Peter of Ramsay, bishop of Aberdeen. Bernham went to the papal curia about 1248 to litigate unsuccessfully against this diversion, and was left with only 32 merks annually from this benefice; but he had others yielding a further 80 merks. He farmed or sold the teinds (tithes) which yielded such rich revenues, using relatives or clerks in neighbouring Scottish benefices as his agents, and his servants as go-betweens.

Bernham was no great scholar, but in the margins of the manuscript of William of Malmesbury's works which he owned, he copied in pencil all or parts of eighteen letters from Paris and Oxford, mostly written home, in connection with his affairs. They are all undated and mostly undatable (though one can be firmly attributed to July 1256), but they give an unequalled insight into the life of an absentee pluralist, into the difficulties of a university student and teacher in gathering his income, and into the use and abuse of teinds which his uncle's synodalia sought to regulate. These letters are the only claim of W. of Bernham to fame. A. A. M. DUNCAN

Sources J. Dowden, *The bishops of Scotland … prior to the Reformation*, ed. J. M. Thomson (1912), 12–13, 300–01 · D. E. R. Watt, *A biographical dictionary of Scottish graduates to AD 1410* (1977), 41–66 · M. Ash, 'David Bernham, bishop of St Andrews', *Innes Review*, 25 (1974), 3–14 · [J. Robertson], ed., *Concilia Scotiae*, 2 vols., (1866), vol. 1, pp. clxxxiii–vi, ccxcviii–ccciii; vol. 2, pp. 53–63 · C. Wordsworth, ed., *Pontificale ecclesiae S. Andreae* (1885) · N. R. Ker and W. A. Pantin, 'Letters of a Scottish student at Paris and Oxford, c. 1250', *Formularies which bear on the history of Oxford*, ed. H. E. Salter, W. A. Pantin, and H. G. Richardson, 2, OHS, new ser., 5 (1942), 472–91

Likenesses seal, U. Durham L., dean and chapter muniments, Misc. ch. 944, 987x, 1320

Bernham, W. of (*fl.* 1248–1256). *See under* Bernham, David of (*d.* 1253).

Bernhardt, Sarah Henriette Rosine (1844–1923), actress, was born, probably on 22 or 23 October 1844, in Paris, the first of the three daughters of Julie Bernhardt (*d.* 1876), a Jewish courtesan from Amsterdam. The identity of her father remains unknown, although he is sometimes given as Paul Morel, a naval officer from Le Havre; others believe him to have been the man the young girl thought of as her uncle, Edouard Ker-Bernhardt.

Sarah Bernhardt was not simply the most famous actress the world has seen; she was among the most gifted. Her talents were first established at the Comédie Française; later they were displayed in a carefully selected repertory of tested favourites whose range she augmented with controlled experiment. Working within the Romantic tradition, she created exciting entertainment out of wild emotion, yet never quite lost her ability to touch the heights and depths of tragic understanding. There had been other stars before her, but the scale of Bernhardt's success resulted from her ability to harness the resources of the modern world. She first realized this potential in London, and throughout her life regularly returned to the capital, where she mixed with an artistic élite that included Ellen Terry and Oscar Wilde, influencing countless British actresses whose theatrical tastes, for Ibsen and for 'problem plays', were often very different from her own. It was Bernhardt's ability to dominate the stage intellectually without forsaking physical elegance that set the technical challenge; recent scholars have shown, too, that in London, from start to finish, she held particular sway over the female members of her audience, for whom she offered a startling example of how to live an independent yet glamorous life.

For a female performer to maintain direction over her career required vision and tenacity. Bernhardt turned those qualities to further account by incorporating them within her performances, and by allowing them to

Sarah Henriette Rosine Bernhardt (1844–1923), by Histed

become part of her legend. An overall impression of self-determination, even in the most fragile of roles, accounts, in large part, for her enduring appeal.

Early career Bernhardt's life could easily have turned out differently: she was born into the *demi-monde*, the Parisian milieu of high-class prostitutes, wayward aristocrats, and bohemian artists. Her mother had two sisters: Rosine Berendt, another courtesan, who died of tuberculosis in 1873, and the more responsible Henriette, who played some part in bringing up Sarah and her siblings, Régine and Jeanne. Sarah, though, was educated away from home, at the Institution Fressard in Auteuil and at Grandchamp, an Augustine convent near Versailles. The move, by no means decisive, from *demi-monde* to theatre came in 1860, when she entered the Paris Conservatoire, where she was instructed by three magisterial figures—François Joseph Pierre Regnier, Jean-Baptiste François Provost, and Joseph Isidore Samson. Despite a disappointing second prize in the final competition she went on to the Comédie Française, and made an unremarkable début in the title role of Racine's *Iphigénie* in August 1862. After two more roles and a ferocious quarrel with an elderly *sociétaire* she moved to the Théâtre du Gymnase, where she tried out her skills in more popular genres. Yet her performances were still not particularly well received and her career prospects remained far from certain, a professional situation made all the more precarious by the birth of her son, Maurice, on 22 December 1864. The father, or so she later let it be known, was a Belgian aristocrat, Prince Charles Lamoral de Ligne, though Bernhardt brought the child up single-handedly.

France conquered In 1866 Bernhardt joined the Théâtre de l'Odéon, France's second national theatre; here she established an artistic rapport with the director, Félix Duquesnel. She made her official Odéon début as Armande in Molière's *Les femmes savantes* in 1867, and followed that with Anna Danby in *Kean* by Dumas *père*, and the *travesti* role of the troubadour, Zanetto, in *Le passant* by François Coppée. In February 1872 she scored massively as Doña Maria in Victor Hugo's *Ruy Blas*. Now established, she returned to the Comédie Française, where Emile Perrin had become director. A series of increasingly significant roles followed: Gabrielle in Dumas *père*'s *Mademoiselle de Belle-Isle* in November 1872, Junie in Racine's *Britannicus* in December, the title role in *Andromaque* in August 1873, and the lead in *L'étrangère* by Dumas *fils* in February 1876. In 1877 she again triumphed in Hugo, as a captivating Doña Sol in *Hernani*. She had played the minor role of Aricie in Racine's *Phèdre* in September 1873; in December 1874 she returned to the play, this time as its heroine. Superimposing herself on memories of Rachel Félix, whose Phèdre had been a pillar of self-recrimination, she portrayed a more forgiving woman whose languor invited audiences to sympathize with, even to desire, her erotic condition. Of all the parts Bernhardt played in her career, Phèdre, victim of her own passions, was the most absorbing, for actress and audiences alike.

International triumph In 1879 the Comédie Française appeared in London for a season. Advance publicity had already established Bernhardt as the company's most charismatic member, a reputation that she consolidated in ways that, though lucrative to her personally, were not always acceptable to the company's administrators: she exhibited her own sculptures, gave private recitals, and became a favourite in high society.

The London reception made it clear that here was too volatile, and too valuable, a talent to be contained within hierarchical confines, and Bernhardt took the irrevocable decision to move into the commercial market. In the spring of 1880 she tried out her repertory with seasons in London and Brussels before departing in October 1880 for America, where she opened in New York with *Adrienne Lecouvreur* by Eugène Scribe.

The first few years of Bernhardt's artistic independence were insecure, and her success became guaranteed only as she developed the idea of reviving proven vehicles associated with actresses from earlier periods. These she reinvigorated with her own modern personality: *Adrienne Lecouvreur* written for Rachel, *Frou-Frou*, by Meilhac and Halévy, in which Aimée Desclée had made her name, and the part for which Bernhardt is, even now, most remembered, Marguerite Gautier in Dumas *fils*'s *La dame aux camélias*, a role that was already nearly thirty years old when she first introduced it in 1881.

Many of Bernhardt's roles have it in common that an apparent emotional weakness turns out to be the precondition for some heroic act of self-sacrifice. By performing these parts with extravagant passion she converted a maudlin, even misogynistic, tradition into a theatrical experience that modern audiences could view with awestruck enjoyment. But the actress paid a price for her insistence that emotional intensity was the defining quality of femininity. Introversion, sub-textual motivation, the deeper psychological qualities that were being explored by contemporary dramatists, would never be fully available to her. This became overwhelmingly true once she had added a final ingredient to the theatre of sensuality—exotic spectacle. Her co-conspirator was the playwright Victorien Sardou. Together they devised a theatrical formula requiring exotic locations and dazzling costumes that served them well in a series of lavish melodramas: *Fédora* (1882), *Théodora* (1884), *La Tosca* (1887), *Cléopâtre* (1894), *Gismonda* (1897), *Spiritisme* (1897).

The first American tour had also seen the début of 'Sarah Barnum', a satirical nickname for the actress as a vibrant *entrepreneuse* whose manipulation of the publicity machine knew no limits, but who brought such wit and gaiety to the business of self-promotion that press and public were, for the most part, happily complicit. This provided the foundation for many later visits to America between 1886 and 1916. Bernhardt's appetite for travel was boundless. She went to Russia in 1881 and South America in 1886, and embarked on a world tour in 1891 which lasted until 1893. Bernhardt's London seasons became an established routine, and she visited annually throughout the 1890s—although this familiarity did her some damage among advanced critics, who became increasingly disrespectful. Bernard Shaw was the most notorious hammer of her reputation, but others such as William Archer could be equally unforgiving about her reliance on old-fashioned techniques.

Private life and management Bernhardt lived much of her private life in public. As the press, increasingly internationalized and intrusive, turned her life into myth, so audiences found it hard to resist making connections between her roles and her lifestyle. In April 1882 she married Aristidis Damala (1857–1889), a Greek diplomat, and tried unsuccessfully to launch him on an acting career; he died a miserable death from drug addiction in 1889. She also had semi-public relationships with a number of her leading men, including the actors Jean Mounet-Sully, Jeanne Richepin, and, a late liaison, Lou Tellegen (*b.* 1883). These only added to her aura. Surrounded by unusual pets (a cheetah, monkeys), a lifetime's collection of bizarre objects, and an entourage of devoted admirers, she presented a formidable face to the world. Bernhardt's consumption of its luxuries was conspicuous; and yet she was said to be sometimes possessed by fits of ungovernable rage, encouraging the contemporary diagnosis of neurasthenia. She seemed, as she no doubt intended, to be the archetype of *fin de siècle* womanhood.

Bernhardt did have her commercial and artistic failures: Lady Macbeth in 1884, a production of *Hamlet* in which she played Ophelia in 1886. These became more serious once she had entered into theatre management herself. Her most distinguished period as a manager lasted from 1893 to 1899, when she ran the Théâtre de la Renaissance; her subsequent tenancy of the vast Théâtre des Nations (renamed the Théâtre Sarah Bernhardt) was less consistently distinguished. Throughout the 1890s, though, she countered the inroads made by the new drama of Ibsen and the symbolists with an innovative range of plays: *Jeanne d'Arc* by Barbier, *Amphytrion* by Molière, *Magda* by Suderman, *La princesse lointaine* by Rostand, *Lorenzaccio* by de Musset. At an 1896 banquet in her honour she could boast that she had played 'one hundred and twelve roles, and created thirty-eight new characters, sixteen the work of poets'. In 1897 she introduced Rostand's *La samaritaine* and, in the same year, in a publicly orchestrated contest of divas, survived comparison with a younger rival when the far more naturalistic Eleonora Duse appeared in Paris.

Later career By 1900 Bernhardt was a cornerstone of France's national life as well as a citizen of the world. She had always been a notable patriot—opening up the Odéon as a convalescent hospital during the Franco-Prussian War, consorting with both sides during the commune, intervening in the Dreyfus affair. Patriotism infused her repertory too when, in March 1900, she took on the role of L'Aiglon, Napoleon's son, in a play by Rostand. *Travesti* was nothing new to her: early on she had endeared herself to audiences in *Le passant*; in May 1899 she performed Hamlet, to mixed reactions. In 1905 she experimented with playing the male lead to Mrs Patrick Campbell's princess in Maeterlinck's *Pelléas et Mélisande*.

Nevertheless the new century was demanding, not least because of a leg injury that led to amputation in 1915. In 1910 and 1911 Bernhardt appeared at the Coliseum music hall in London, where she performed extracts from *La Tosca* and *L'Aiglon* between animal acts and acrobatic turns and, remarkably, held her own. What looks like a severe decline in professional status can also be seen as part of her determination to keep abreast of modern developments: she made silent films and sound recordings, toured with Constant Coquelin, and was hailed as an inspiration by American suffragettes.

In 1914 Bernhardt was created a chevalier of the Légion d'honneur, and the outbreak of hostilities again found her eager to make her contribution. She introduced a patriotic entertainment, *Les cathédrales*, by Eugène Morand, and campaigned for the war effort in the United States. In later life she took time to write a novelistic autobiography, *Ma double vie* (1907), which was eventually followed by an autobiographical novel, *Petite idole* (1920), and an acting primer, *L'art du théâtre* (1923), in which she made partial peace with the Paris Conservatoire. Her final appearances were extraordinary, especially in Racine's *Athalie* in 1920 and in *Daniel* by Louis Verneuil, a play about a morphine addict, in which she made her last appearance in London. She gave her last performance of all on 29 November 1922 in Turin. On 26 March 1923 she died in the boulevard Pénère, Paris, and, after a fittingly grandiose funeral procession, was buried in the cemetery at Père Lachaise.

It is possible to judge the career of Sarah Bernhardt by the animosity it inspired: from Chekhov in Russia, from Shaw and others in England, from embattled reformers in her native city. Today, however, it seems more than ever important to see her, as her faithful audiences did, as a premonition, a symbol of what could be achieved by a woman who engaged with the modern world on its own terms.   JOHN STOKES

Sources E. Pronier, *Une vie au théâtre: Sarah Bernhardt* (1942) · G. Taranow, *Sarah Bernhardt: the art within the legend* (1972) · A. Gold and R. Fizdale, *The Divine Sarah* (1991) · R. Brandon, *Being divine: a biography of Sarah Bernhardt* (1991) · E. Aston, *Sarah Bernhardt: a French actress on the English stage* (1989) · J. Stokes, M. R. Booth, and S. Bassnett, eds., *Bernhardt, Terry, Duse: the actress in her time* (1988) · R. Hahn, *La grande Sarah* (1930) · J. Huret, *Sarah Bernhardt* (1899) · M. Rostand, *Sarah Bernhardt* (1950) · L. Verneuil, *La vie merveilleuse de Sarah Bernhardt* (1942) · S. Bernhardt, *Ma double vie* (1907) · M. Colombier, *Les mémoires de Sarah Barnum*, 10th edn (1883) [this is a satire on Sarah Bernhardt]
Archives Bibliothèque de l'Arsenal, Paris · Bibliothèque Historique de la Ville de Paris, Association de la Régie Théâtrale · Bibliothèque-Musée de la Comédie Française, Paris · Theatre Museum, London | FILM BFI NFTVA, documentary footage; performance footage · Cinémathèque Française, Paris · Museum of Modern Art, New York | SOUND BL NSA, performance recordings; documentary recordings · NYPL, New York Library for the Performing Arts · Phonothèque Nationale, Paris
Likenesses F. Nadar, photograph, *c*.1858 · J. Bastien-Lepage, portrait, 1879 · C. Beaton, pen-and-ink drawing, NPG · E. Clairon, oils (as Ruy Blas), Bibliothèque de la Comédie Française · E. Clairon, oils, Palais des Beaux Arts, Paris, France · Florian, wood-engraving (after J. van Beers), NPG · Histed, photograph, priv. coll. [*see illus.*] · J. Lomering, chalk drawing, NPG · portrait (after W. Nicholson), NPG · print (after photograph by F. Nadar), NPG

Bernher, Augustine (*d.* 1565), religious reformer, was Swiss by birth. He was educated by Johannes Wolff at the school belonging to Zürich's main church, the Grossmunster, where Heinrich Bullinger was the chief pastor.

Bernher had arrived in England by November 1548, one in a wave of Swiss reformers whose influence over the English church was profound. In the 1520s and 1530s a coalition of evangelical reformers (Bullinger among them) from the cities of northern Switzerland and the upper Rhine had begun to develop their own understanding of the spiritual nature of the presence of Christ in the eucharist. Standing in sharp opposition to the tenets of the Roman Catholic church, they also challenged many of the views promoted by Martin Luther and his followers. For the Swiss reformers salvation came by faith alone, which preaching generated. Bullinger had nurtured close links with English churchmen, including Archbishop Thomas Cranmer. Cranmer invited foreign divines to find refuge in England in 1548 (after the repressive interim of Augsburg), in the hopes of furthering the unity of an international protestant movement. Already an accomplished preacher, Bernher may have accompanied John à Lasco to England from Emden.

Bernher was well placed to continue the process of

redefining the English church through a Swiss lens. He rapidly entered the employ of Hugh Latimer, who was a frequent preacher before Edward's court. Bernher served as his amanuensis, a much needed office, for Latimer had never been in the habit of preparing his sermons in written form. He travelled with his master on his regular sermon tours, and in the 1550s they rode frequently between Baxterley in Warwickshire (where Latimer resided with his niece Mary and her husband, Robert Glover), and the Lincolnshire household of Katherine, duchess of Suffolk, who became Latimer's chief patron in the last years of his life, after he withdrew into an active retirement. On at least one of these tours they were accompanied by Thomas Lever, who preached with Latimer in Leicester.

The further development of the English Reformation was interrupted by the accession of Mary Tudor in 1553. Latimer and many other protestant leaders were soon arrested. Robert Glover followed two years later. Bernher now began a covert existence as a courier, shadowing Latimer and his friends (including Nicholas Ridley, former bishop of London, and John Careless of Coventry) from prison to prison, moving between London or Oxford and Baxterley. He smuggled pen, ink, and paper to them, and channelled their writings towards foreign printing presses. He recorded accounts of Latimer's and Ridley's disputations and examinations. Ridley and Careless begged 'Brother Austin' not to put himself in jeopardy. When John Jewel (the Elizabethan bishop of Salisbury) collapsed on the side of the road as he fled Oxford, Bernher rescued him, and brought him safely to London so that he could continue to the continent. Ridley marvelled at all Bernher accomplished. 'Brother Austin, you for our comfort do run up and down', and who paid his heavy expenses? 'God knoweth' (Coverdale, 72).

Bernher attended many of the Marian martyrs in their last moments at the stake (including the Glovers' neighbour Joyce Lewes, burnt in 1557). When Robert Glover was executed at Coventry on 19 September 1555, Bernher encouraged him until the end. Less than a month later Latimer and Ridley died at Oxford, and again the loyal Bernher assisted them to the last.

Some measure of the protection that allowed Bernher to bring relief to the prisoners and yet remain miraculously unscathed—his many escapes encouraged Ridley to compare him to Faust—came first from the duchess of Suffolk and other godly ladies, and later from the backing of wealthy London merchants. The Londoners formed their own illegal underground church, constituting a 'congregation of faithful persons concealed in London during the time of Mary, among whom the gospel was always preached, with the pure administration of the sacraments' (Robinson, *Zurich Letters*, 29). Theirs was not the only clandestine community, but it was among the most important. Organized along lines laid down during Edward's reign by John à Lasco, under Mary the congregation acted autonomously, in emulation of Bullinger's Zürich and Calvin's Geneva. They had elders and deacons, and they chose their own ministers 'by common consent'.

After Latimer's execution Bernher was elected to become one of a team of ministers, ultimately led by Thomas Bentham. In 'the midst of enemies' (ibid., 160) Bernher survived the last years of Mary's reign.

The London congregation was one of the seedbeds from which Elizabethan nonconformity sprang. Bernher, like many of the hotter sort of protestants, had an uneasy relationship inside the Elizabethan establishment. On 27 December 1558, only six weeks after the new queen's accession, preaching and public assemblies were banned by royal proclamation. Although the congregation 'had survived in the midst of the flames' (Robinson, *Zurich Letters*, 160), Elizabeth suppressed it. Lever informed Bullinger in the summer of 1559 that the London congregation had had to revert to its Marian custom of meeting in 'private houses' once more. Bernher and other 'zealous preachers of the gospel' (ibid., 30) left London for quiet districts where they were less hindered; they were particularly influential in western counties where they had originally been introduced by Latimer. Early in 1560 Bentham was raised to the bishopric of Coventry and Lichfield, and Bernher received several ecclesiastical preferments in that diocese, most notably the living of Southam, Warwickshire. Members of the London congregation stood surety for the payment of his first fruits.

At Southam, Bernher prepared Latimer's sermons for the press, with a dedication to the duchess of Suffolk. Latimer, he wrote, 'shed his heart's blood in the defence of the gospel' (Bernher, 323), developing a theme from Eusebius's description of the martyrdom of Polycarp in the second century AD that John Foxe fully exploited for his own great martyrological work, *Acts and Monuments*. Bernher probably also encouraged a panel style of preaching at Southam. A company of ministers, drawn from the surrounding area, took regular turns to preach on an assigned scriptural text as a means of increasing their own learning as they instructed the laity. The 'combination' lecture, as it came to be known in England, had been pioneered in Zürich. Southam's godly exercise, though subsequently the cause of disquiet among the authorities, was considered by radicals to be the best in the realm. Although it has usually been associated with a later incumbent, it seems reasonable to conclude that Bernher initiated it.

In the mid-1550s, about the time that Latimer died, Bernher married a 'dear and faithful loving Sister', named Elizabeth, a member of that spiritual kinship near Coventry to which they both belonged. Careless sent each of them a letter of congratulatory advice, and praised Bernher to his bride for being 'a most godly learned, gentle, loving, quiet, patient, thrifty, diligent' sort of husband (Cambridge, Emmanuel College Library, MS 260, fols. 237r–237v). Foxe printed Careless's letters, making his vision of Austin and Elizabeth a pattern for the conduct of all godly men and women who entered the state of matrimony.

Their union was broken by Bernher's premature death,

probably at Southam, in 1565. Londoners rallied once again to maintain his young children. Bernher's loss was an incalculable blow to Elizabethan nonconformity.

SUSAN WABUDA

Sources Bernher's letter-book, Bodl. Oxf., MS Bodley 53 · Emmanuel College, Cambridge, MS 260 · BL, Add. MS 19400 · A. Bernher, *The seven sermons of the reverend father, W. Hughe Latimer* (1562); repr. *Sermons by Hugh Latimer*, ed. G. E. Corrie, Parker Society, 22 (1844), 311–25 · M. Coverdale, ed., *Certain most godly, fruitful, and comfortable letters* (1564) · J. Foxe, *The second volume of the ecclesiasticall history, conteyning the acts and monuments of martyrs*, 2nd edn (1570), 1890, 2115–17 · J. Foxe, *Acts and monuments*, ed. G. H. Townsend, 8 vols. (1843–9), vols. 7, 8 · H. Robinson, ed. and trans., *Original letters relative to the English Reformation*, 1 vol. in 2, Parker Society, [26] (1846–7) · H. Robinson, ed. and trans., *The Zurich letters, comprising the correspondence of several English bishops and others with some of the Helvetian reformers, during the early part of the reign of Queen Elizabeth*, 2, Parker Society, 8 (1845) · 'The letter-book of Thomas Bentham, bishop of Coventry and Lichfield, 1560-1561', ed. R. O'Day and J. Berlatsky, *Camden miscellany, XXVII*, CS, 4th ser., 22 (1979) · Lichfield Joint RO, B/A/1/15 [Bentham's register] · *CPR, 1560–66* · J. Strype, *Ecclesiastical memorials*, 3 vols. (1822), vol. 3 · P. Collinson, *The Elizabethan puritan movement* (1967) · P. Collinson, 'Lectures by combination: structures and characteristics of church life in 17th-century England', *Godly people: essays on English protestantism and puritanism* (1983), 467–98 · 'Letters of Thomas Wood, puritan, 1566-1577', ed. P. Collinson, *BIHR*, special suppl., 5 (1960) [whole issue]; repr. in P. Collinson, *Godly people: essays on English protestantism and puritanism* (1983), 45–107 · D. MacCulloch, *Thomas Cranmer: a life* (1996) · A. D. M. Pettegree, *Marian protestantism: six studies* (1996) · B. Usher, 'Backing protestantism: the London godly, the exchequer and the Foxe circle', *John Foxe: an historical perspective*, ed. D. Loader (1999), 105–34 · B. Usher, '"In a time of persecution": new light on the secret protestant congregation in Marian London', *John Foxe and the English Reformation*, ed. D. Loades (1997), 233–51 · S. Wabuda, 'Henry Bull, Miles Coverdale, and the making of Foxe's Book of martyrs', *Martyrs and martyrologies*, ed. D. Wood, SCH, 30 (1993), 245–58 · S. Wabuda, 'Sanctified by the believing spouse: women, men and the marital yoke in the early Reformation', *The beginnings of English protestantism, 1490-1558*, ed. P. Marshall and A. Ryrie [forthcoming] · S. Wabuda, 'Shunamites and nurses of the English Reformation: the activities of Mary Glover, niece of Hugh Latimer', *Women in the church on the eve of the dissolution*, ed. W. J. Sheil and D. Wood, SCH, 27 (1990), 335–44

Berni, Aldo (1909–1997), restaurateur, was born on 14 March 1909 in Bardi in northern Italy, the youngest of three sons of Louis Berni, the owner of the Louis Café in Ebbw Vale, Monmouthshire, which served meals consisting of soup, a joint, and two vegetables. Aldo's elder brother, **Frank Berni** (1903–2000), restaurateur, had also been born in Bardi, on 30 October 1903. Louis Berni was certainly settled in Wales, but in an interview he gave in 1990 Aldo Berni claimed that his grandfather John (in some versions a member of an old Parma family whose forebears had been circus owners) had emigrated from Bardi to Merthyr Tudful in 1862. He said the family 'had long been caterers and are direct descendants of several of the kingpins behind the once vast network of Italian cafés, still known as the *bracchi*, throughout the Welsh mining valleys' (*The Independent*).

Aldo Berni went to Britain when he was sixteen, as Louis had the boys educated in Italy before sending for them to join the family business (their mother stayed in Italy). When the Second World War came, his brothers Frank

Aldo Berni (1909–1997), by unknown photographer

and Marco were interned. Aldo, who had a British passport, was called up but exempted to work at a nursery by day, while in the evenings he ran the business—a chain of about six unlicensed restaurants in the west of England. In 1943 Aldo and Frank bought their first licensed restaurant, Horts, the best-known restaurant in Bristol, specializing in oyster soup and Dover sole. Two years earlier Frank had married Lina Allegri, the daughter of another Welsh Italian café-owner, from Llanelli; they had two daughters. On 15 January 1947 Aldo married Esmé Neville de Clifford Clifton (1920/21–1995), daughter of Edward Hinton Clifton of Clifton, Bristol; they had one daughter.

The brothers added more eating-houses to their chain, and when food rationing finally ended in 1954 and the British public went beef mad, the Berni boom began, and they instituted the famous 7s. 6d. set menu of steak, chips, peas, bread roll and butter, and pudding or cheese. This limited menu meant that no trained chef was needed, and most of the normal kitchen staff could be dispensed with. The cooking facilities needed were simply a central grill and a deep-fryer. The only important member of staff was the manager, who looked after the money and hired and fired the waiters. Quality was controlled by giving every establishment a 'bible', a large manual of instructions with every detail of the operation spelt out. The brothers replaced tablecloths with place mats and saved, it was said, £700,000 a year in laundry bills. They disliked written contracts and did business on a handshake; few suppliers ever let them down. Unusually for a British catering business, they encouraged their customers to complain if the standards of the food or service faltered, and were concerned that their clientele should perceive Berni Inns as giving good value for money. The inns were mobbed by beef-hungry customers, and the brothers converted as many pubs as they could get their hands on.

The Berni Inns chain evolved and grew until it comprised 147 hotels and restaurants, including the New Inn at Gloucester, the Mitre at Oxford, and several in Japan. The biggest food chain outside the USA, it based its identity not just on the food and the brand name, Berni Inn, but on the furnishings and décor, which were intended to mimic the luxury of American steakhouses: red velvet, stout wooden chairs, and paper parasols for the puddings and the cocktails. Frank, the chairman of the company, was responsible for the strict cost controls that made the chain so profitable, while the more outgoing Aldo was the public face of the company. The Bernis were probably the first caterers to use management consultants in their business. Aldo was generous with his money and helpful to others entering business careers, and earned the gratitude of a large number of younger people. He and Frank took very little out of the business. Aldo continued to live in Bristol, in a four-bedroomed bungalow in Clifton (he spoke with a decided Welsh lilt, but was proud to call himself a Bristolian). He owned a Bentley, but drove it himself, and would do the washing-up if the machine broke down. A passionate golfer, he had a handicap of five, and was an avid reader, browsing in encyclopaedias in his leisure hours. He enjoyed good wine, good food (except for Indian), and dining out. The brothers became millionaires when they went public in 1962, but eight years later they sold out to Grand Metropolitan for £14.5 million. By then Frank Berni had already retired to the Channel Islands. Aldo Berni remained on close terms with Sir Maxwell Joseph of Grand Metropolitan, and continued in the business in a non-executive role until the late 1970s. Berni Inns were later sold to Whitbread, who amalgamated them into their own Beefeater chain in 1990. A contemporary and friend of Lord Forte, whose family had similar Italian roots, Berni said of the Fortes, 'They were talented; we were lucky' (*Daily Telegraph*).

Aldo Berni was, above all, a family man. Sprightly, teasing banter was a feature of Aldo and Esmé Berni's strong marriage, and he devotedly gave her part of his fortune. She died first, in 1995. When her will was published in May 1996, he was not surprised to learn that she left the bulk of her £4.8 million to a home for cats and dogs. About this time, he suffered a severe stroke, and moved into the Avon Gorge Nursing Home, North Road, Leigh Woods, Clevedon, Somerset, where he died on 12 October 1997. He was survived by his daughter and by both his brothers; Frank died at St Lawrence, Jersey, on 10 July 2000.

PAUL LEVY

Sources *Daily Telegraph* (17 Oct 1997) · *The Guardian* (17 Oct 1997) · *The Independent* (20 Oct 1997) · *The Times* (21 Oct 1997) · m. cert. · d. cert. · *Daily Telegraph* (12 July 2000) · *The Independent* (14 July 2000) · *The Times* (20 July 2000) · *The Guardian* (1 Aug 2000)
Likenesses photograph, repro. in *Daily Telegraph* (17 Oct 1997) · photograph, repro. in *The Guardian* (17 Oct 1997) · photograph, Bristol Evening Post [*see illus.*]
Wealth at death £1,226,425: probate, 2 April 1998, *CGPLA Eng. & Wales*

Berni, Frank (1903–2000). *See under* Berni, Aldo (1909–1997).

Berningham, Richard de. *See* Bernyngham, Sir Richard (*d.* in or after 1335).

Bernstein, Basil Bernard (1924–2000), sociologist, was born on 1 November 1924 at 189 Oxford Street, Mile End Old Town, London, the son of Bertram Bernstein, furrier, and his wife, Julia, *née* Park. He was originally named Bernard Basil, but reversed the order of his forenames. He was brought up in the East End of London and educated at Christ's Hospital, and in 1939 volunteered, although under age, for the Royal Air Force, serving as a bombardier in Africa. After the war he became a residential family case-worker at the Bernhard Baron Settlement in Stepney, east London. He subsequently claimed that it was his observations there that posed the problems which dominated his academic career.

In 1947 Bernstein registered for a diploma in social sciences at the London School of Economics, but rapidly transferred to sociology, in which he obtained a BSc. He kept himself by casual work, and followed this by training as a teacher at Kingsway Day College. Then for six years he taught general subjects at the City Day College in Shoreditch before becoming a research assistant in phonetics at University College, London, and taking in succession a higher degree in linguistics and a PhD. A first marriage ended in divorce, and on 22 November 1955 he married Marion Black (*b.* 1930/31), a clinical psychologist; they had two sons, Saul and Francis. In 1962 he moved to the Institute of Education, where he spent the rest of his career, becoming rapidly senior lecturer (1963–5), reader (1965–7), and, in 1967, professor. He was head of the sociological research unit from 1963 to 1990 and Karl Mannheim professor of sociology of education from 1979 to 1990.

Bernstein was described as 'marvellously impish' (*The Guardian*, 29 Sept 2000), and more prosaically as 'one of the best known and most influential of British sociologists' (Atkinson, 1). However, throughout his academic career he remained a controversial and often misunderstood scholar. This was partly because he addressed an area of great importance in the second half of the twentieth century: the relationship between formal institutions and the process of cultural transmission. It was also, partly, because his writings were often abstract, intricate, and lacking in lucidity. Yet these apparently negative characteristics arose directly from his dogged refusal to simplify processes which were genuinely complex, his determination to pursue models of strong explanatory value, and his concern (justified by the reception of his early work) that simplification resulted in dangerous distortion.

Bernstein started with the relationship between language and culture. Behind this concern lay an awareness that mass schooling in industrialized societies had not by the 1960s delivered the hoped-for cultural emancipation of working-class learners. Bernstein addressed the perceived gap between widespread practices in the culture of ordinary upbringing and the practices expected by schooling (and by successful and dynamic engagement with changing social pressures in later life). His exploration of this gap became increasingly sophisticated as his career developed. In his early work he explored the close link that he perceived between language use and cultural achievement, but he never committed himself to the view of simple 'working class linguistic deficit' that his detractors (and some of his supporters) attributed to him. Rather, he introduced, and increasingly refined, the concept of 'code' as a 'regulative principle, tacitly acquired, which selects and integrates *relevant meanings*, the *form of their realization* and *evoking contexts*' (Bernstein, *Pedagogy, Symbolic Control and Identity*, 1996, 111). Exploration of the nature of elaborated codes, typically found within education institutions, and restricted codes, typically found when there are direct relations 'between meanings and a specific material base' (Bernstein, 'Codes, modalities and the processes of cultural reproduction: a model', *Language and Society*, 10, 1981, 332), was central to his whole intellectual project.

Bernstein always insisted on a close relationship between his theoretical discussion and empirical evidence; however, most commentators felt that he became increasingly abstract throughout the 1980s and 1990s. What was clear, though, was that articulating his perception of a disjuncture between the culture of schooling and that of much of normal life addressed a major concern for many social theorists, so that his work was never restricted to the fields of linguistics or education within which it started. By moving discussion away from a concern with communication to deeper principles of knowledge structure, organization, and transmission, he converted a widely held and relatively simple transfer model of education to something much more elusive, subtle, and profound. This progress is charted in his four-volume series *Class, Codes and Control* (1971; 1973; 1975; 1990).

Unlike many 1960s British sociologists, Bernstein responded sympathetically to many of the concerns preoccupying continental European scholars, and was consistently critical but appreciative in his relationship with the work of Pierre Bourdieu; he also traced the origin of much of his thinking to the founders of sociology, particularly Durkheim. Among British contemporaries he valued especially the work of the linguist Michael Halliday. Thus he drew upon a range of academic traditions to form a synthesis that was entirely his own, stubbornly addressing a single and central issue for an industrial and post-industrial democracy, and its practical corollary. First, how does cultural transmission occur, and second, how can it be carried out without discrimination and exploitation? Bernstein retired in 1990, and he died from cancer on 24 September 2000, in London, survived by his wife and two sons.   CHRISTOPHER BRUMFIT

Sources *The Guardian* (27 Sept 2000) · *The Guardian* (29 Sept 2000) · *The Independent* (9 Oct 2000) · *The Times* (11 Oct 2000) · WWW · P. Atkinson, *Language, structure and reproduction* (1985) · b. cert. · m. cert. · *CGPLA Eng. & Wales* (2000)
Archives U. Lond., Institute of Education, corresp., notes, lecture notes, and papers
Likenesses photograph, repro. in *The Times* · photograph, repro. in *The Independent* · photograph, repro. in *The Guardian* (27 Sept 2000)
Wealth at death £268,762—gross; £267,662—net: probate, 27 Nov 2000, *CGPLA Eng. & Wales*

Bernstein, Sidney Lewis, Baron Bernstein (1899–1993), businessman, was born on 30 January 1899 at 14 Westbury Road, Ilford, Essex, the fourth of nine children of Alexander Bernstein (*c*.1860–1922), businessman, and his wife, Jane Lazarus. His father had moved with his brother Julius from Riga, Latvia, in the early 1890s. The brothers married

Sidney Lewis Bernstein, Baron Bernstein (1899–1993), by Howard Coster, 1934

two sisters, whose family had come from Riga rather earlier. Alexander Bernstein was a shoemaker by trade and in due course, as Sir Denis Forman relates, 'set up a boot factory when he made a lucrative contract to supply boots to the Boers in South Africa … When the Boer War broke out the boot contract collapsed and he was declared a bankrupt' (Forman, 160). With the aid of his family his next venture was the manufacture of carborundum wheels. He also bought land in Edmonton. This piece of land was ideal for shops, but he thought it needed something to entice shoppers. He thought a film theatre with live entertainment seemed most likely to do so. In 1908 he built the first of the Bernstein theatres, the Edmonton Empire, and ran it like a music hall. In this way the Bernsteins became involved in the entertainment industry.

Early years When his father died in 1922, Bernstein's family owned a small but significant group of about twenty film theatres. Bernstein (who was educated at the Highlands board school, Ilford, and the Cooper's Company School, Bow, London) became head of this family business. He let the property and related interests go and concentrated on the film theatre business. He also loved the live theatre, and went into partnership with Arnold Bennett to put on a successful series of plays at the Court Theatre in Sloane Square. Some years later he collaborated with Bovis the builders to put up the Phoenix Theatre in Charing Cross Road, in the design of which he played the determining role. The theatre opened in 1930 with Noël Coward's *Private Lives*. That went well, but the following productions were not a financial success. In the absence of plays which he considered suitable, Bernstein used the theatre to show films—René Clair's second talking film, *Le million*, was first shown there.

By 1932 Bernstein realized that the financial returns from 'legitimate' theatre were inadequate. He therefore continued to develop his main interest, the chain of film theatres. His Granada theatres were grandiose in style. He took a close interest in their architecture, in partnership with the Russian designer Theodore Komisarjevsky. The latter had been educated at the Imperial Institute of Architecture in St Petersburg, and had gone to England in 1919. The most important of Bernstein's theatres was the Granada in Tooting. It combined Moorish, Renaissance, and classical styles. It is now a listed building and represents a lasting monument to the co-operation between Bernstein and Komisarjevsky. Bernstein's interest in film led him to join a group of film buffs in founding the Film Society in 1924, whose purpose was to show to London audiences the best films from around the world, and particularly those from Russia. This brought him into contact with some of the intellectuals who were also interested in films, including George Bernard Shaw, H. G. Wells, John Maynard Keynes, Julian Huxley, Augustus John, James Agate, Jacob Epstein, T. S. Eliot, Wyndham Lewis, and Ivor Montague. Although he did not operate at their intellectual level, Bernstein was accepted by them, since he was charming, rich, and generous. His membership of the Film Society helped to establish his position in London's artistic community.

Later Bernstein also helped to promote the National Theatre. The idea of such a theatre had had its proponents since the days of David Garrick two hundred years before. Bernstein's work for the theatre brought him in touch with another congenial group of people, including Sir Bronson Albery, Sir Lewis Casson, Dame Sybil Thorndyke, and Geoffrey Whitworth. His interest in theatre design caused him after the war to be co-opted to the committee considering the logistics of the new theatre. But he came to grief over his insistence that a projection room for films and facilities for television should be provided in its design. He fell out with the then architect, Brian O'Rourke, and resigned in 1956.

On 26 November 1936 Bernstein married Zoë Patricia Farmar (1911/12–1972), journalist, daughter of Egbert Farmar, scholastics coach. There were no children of the marriage.

The war years, and Hollywood Bernstein's contribution to the war effort began in May 1940 when Winston Churchill appointed Alfred Duff Cooper as minister of information. The minister recognized the potential importance of film and appointed Bernstein as film adviser. The appointment was made against the advice of MI5, who regarded Bernstein as a security risk. Although Bernstein had a number of communist friends, there is no evidence that he himself ever was a member of the Communist Party. His only active participation in politics had been to stand as a Labour candidate for the Middlesex county council in Willesden at the end of the 1920s. He was elected and served from 1929 to 1936. Bernstein was by nature a doer rather than an adviser. His keenness to get results made him enemies as well as friends. But by the autumn of 1940 the films division was producing some of its best work, such as *London Can Take It*, intended to explain the British war effort to the American public. American broadcasters such as Quentin Reynolds and Ed Murrow recognized the importance of these films. Bernstein also acted as godfather for a number of patriotic films for home distribution, such as *In Which We Serve* (1942). In 1944 he became head of the film section of the psychological warfare division attached to Supreme Headquarters Allied Expeditionary Force, and soon his work was extended to the liberated parts of Europe.

During the war Bernstein's brother Cecil looked after the family's theatres very competently. When the war ended there were still no building permits for more film theatres. But Bernstein needed an outlet for his energies. Hence he and his friend Alfred Hitchcock decided to form a partnership for independent film production in Hollywood. This met Bernstein's need for an entrepreneurial role with a creative side. It also suited Hitchcock's quest for creative autonomy without unreasonable commercial interference. The two of them founded the Transatlantic Picture Corporation as their joint enterprise. Their first film was *Rope* (1948), based on a play by Patrick Hamilton. This was moderately successful. *Under Capricorn* (1949) was a flop. *I Confess* (1953) was an artistic but not a commercial success. In 1951 Hitchcock and Bernstein decided to dissolve the partnership. Hitchcock continued in Hollywood; Bernstein returned to London.

His first marriage having ended in divorce, Bernstein married, second, on 11 December 1954, Sandra Malone (1923–1991), daughter of Charles Malone, of Toronto. There were two daughters and a son of this marriage.

Granada Television 'We wish to become exclusive programme contractors for the Manchester–Liverpool station for seven days a week' (Moorehead, 216). So wrote Bernstein to the Independent Television Authority (ITA) on 20 September 1954. The authority had invited applications for the first group of programme contractors in August of that year. But Granada had in effect been applying to enter television for years. Ever since their first inquiry in 1948 the Bernsteins had been keeping up a regular, if one-sided, correspondence with the postmaster-general's office. After the Labour defeat in 1951, Bernstein had written to Herbert Morrison:

> I think you should know that my company have applied to the Postmaster-General for a licence to operate a commercial television station or sponsored television. I still think the country would be better off without it. However, if there is to be commercial television in this country, we think we should be in. (ibid., 215)

When the time came in the mid-1950s for Bernstein's application to be considered, his long-standing links with the Labour Party in fact caused the authority some hesitation. Some of the members feared that he might not be wholehearted in his loyalty to the system as laid down by parliament. In the event the authority decided that Granada would be run by competent people who could be relied upon to bring an enterprising television company into existence. The fact that Granada Television was a wholly owned subsidiary of Granada Theatres Ltd was not regarded as a drawback. On the contrary, the good reputation of that company gave the authority an assurance that it could rely on a well-run enterprise.

The way some of the independent television contractors went about the building up of the commercial channel confirmed the worst fears of critics of the introduction of the new service. By contrast Granada claimed that it would be showing items of unusual or topical interest and special programmes of intellectual or cultural value. Bernstein assured the press that there would be nothing boring. At the end of its first year Granada produced a volume of essays entitled *Year One* (1958), with an introduction by Sir Kenneth Clark, then chairman of the ITA. Clark wrote a foreword in which he admitted that he had not foreseen how much Granada would develop a character 'which distinguishes it most markedly from the other programme companies and the BBC' (*Year One*, 3).

In the meantime Bernstein had begun to establish himself and his company in Manchester. A site in Quay Street was bought in May 1955 and a self-contained centre was built. Bernstein's interest in architecture came into its own again. In the view of some of those who knew him best, Bernstein's architectural talent consisted in his attention to detail rather than an interest in a grand design. The Granada headquarters building was functional, but hardly added an architectural landmark to the Manchester street scene. Bernstein attracted an able group of younger producers and directors and put his stamp particularly on the news and current affairs output and on Granada's drama and social documentaries. He found himself in conflict with the Independent Television Authority, as much on matters of substance as on his attitude to the contractual relationship between Granada and the ITA. Most of the other programme contractors recognized that they were dependent on a public authority, and conducted their relations with the authority accordingly. Bernstein barely acknowledged the nature of the relationship. This view of the autonomy of Granada was also reflected in his attitude to its northern location. He would spend two or three days in Manchester, flying from Biggin Hill on a Tuesday. He did not think it necessary to appoint any directors who lived locally, although in later years he complied with the ITA's insistence that he should. Through the Granada Foundation and in other ways he extended carefully targeted patronage to institutions and causes in the north-west. It is a measure of the lack of confidence of the local authorities in the north-west in the 1950s and 1960s that they were very pleased with the contribution that Granada was willing to make to the regional scene.

It was in the field of current affairs that Bernstein's interests first clashed with the prevailing orthodoxies of broadcasting, established during the BBC monopoly. As Asa Briggs, the historian of the corporation, recounted:

> More intrepid than other broadcasting organisations, Granada deliberately broke new ground when, after consulting its lawyers, it broadcast programmes while the campaign at Rochdale [the by-election of February 1958] was in progress … two Granada producers had been dispatched to the town to talk over with local party agents provisional plans for by-election broadcasts, proposals which were leaked to the *News Chronicle* before reaching the head offices of the parties in London … The *New Statesman* claimed that it was 'to the credit of Granada Television that at Rochdale, it finally forced the machine men to grow up into the television age'. (Briggs, 238–9)

The other area into which Bernstein steered his television company was drama. During the 1960s Granada's output was consistently better than that contributed from elsewhere on independent television. He kept a close personal eye on the company's drama output. Like Bernard Shaw, who had been the great playwright of his youth, what Bernstein looked for in a play was a social statement. But plays had also to be well constructed. Having himself little or no experience of production, he engaged producers and directors. Philip Mackie was the first. When Bernstein invited him to join Granada, Mackie wrote: 'I see you are offering me the post of Head of Drama'. Bernstein replied, 'No, I'm asking you to be in charge of plays' (Moorehead, 266).

This correspondence illustrates Bernstein's approach to the management of Granada. His theory that you must never give people titles of any kind, or they get above themselves, contrasted markedly with the carefully structured BBC hierarchy where everyone had his or her title (and the commensurate brass plate). Bernstein regarded himself as the producer of everything the company put out; all the other staff were his assistants. This did not make for easy relations with the more independent members of the company. It originated in the personal way in which Bernstein had run his cinemas, essentially as the proprietor of a private company. He brought from Granada Theatres three assistants to Granada Television: his brother Cecil, his man of business Victor Peers, and his accountant Joe Wharton, who acted as company secretary. They were his intimates; all the rest were disposable. Even Sir Denis Forman, who soon became indispensable to Bernstein, took a long time to be accepted by this tightly knit management group.

The essentially personal way which Bernstein brought over from Granada Theatres also accounted for the manner in which he dealt with the financial crisis which arose in 1956. The initial losses of the company led Bernstein to make a working arrangement with Associated Rediffusion for the exchange of programmes and networking. The purpose was to protect Granada Television against heavy losses, pending the establishment of satisfactory advertising revenue. The ITA did not take cognizance of this agreement until 1959, by which time the financial crisis had been overcome. Sir Kenneth Clark and Sir Robert Fraser did not insist, as perhaps they should have done, on an independent scrutiny of the compliance of the agreement with section 5 (2) of the Television Act (1954). But then, as Bernard Sendall argued in his history of independent television in Britain, 'neither Wills (the chairman of Rediffusion) nor Bernstein were men who would with deliberation have acted in breach of the Act or of the contracts which were based on it' (Sendall, 199).

Wider fields By the 1960s the prosperity of what had by then become the Granada Group (of which Granada Television was a subsidiary) enabled Bernstein to branch out into other fields. Cinemas were turned into bingo halls; a successful television rental enterprise was built up by Alex Bernstein, Cecil's son; motorway service stations were introduced; and an effort was made to establish the company in publishing. Granada acquired McGibbon and Kee, Rupert Hart-Davis, and one half of Jonathan Cape, as well as the Panther and Paladin paperback imprints. The music publisher Novello was another exercise in diversification. At the end of Bernstein's chairmanship television provided only 16 per cent of the group's income. Nevertheless Bernstein's heart remained in television. Although under the ITA's rules he had to retire as chairman of the Granada Television board in his early seventies, he remained chairman of the Granada Group until his eightieth birthday in 1979.

Bernstein was raised to the peerage, as Baron Bernstein of Leigh (a life peer), by Harold Wilson in 1969. Although he attended the House of Lords from time to time he spoke rarely. He liked to run his own show and it may be that he found the rules of the upper house too constricting. He died of cerebral arteriosclerosis on 5 February 1993, at his London home, Flat 4, 26 St James's Place, Westminster. He was survived by the three children of his second marriage, his wife, Sandra, having predeceased him in 1991.

Bernstein was essentially a product of the second television age, when in 1955 the BBC monopoly was replaced by the duopoly of the BBC and commercial television companies operating under the control of the Independent Television Authority. Bernstein contributed significantly to the building of independent television in the public interest, which characterized British television between 1955 and 1990. This period may well come to be seen in retrospect as television's golden age. The expansion of the technological options and the pressure for their exploitation during the Thatcher years brought this golden age to an end sooner than Bernstein would have liked.

GEORGE WEDELL

Sources C. Moorehead, *Sidney Bernstein: a biography* (1984) · D. Forman, *Persona Granada* (1997) · B. Sendall, *Origin and foundation, 1946–62* (1982), vol. 1 of *Independent television in Britain* (1982–90) · A. Briggs, *The history of broadcasting in the United Kingdom*, rev. edn, 5 (1995) · *Year one: an account of the first year of operation of an independent television company in England* (1958) · personal knowledge (2004) · private information (2004) · *The Independent* (6 Feb 1993) · *The Independent* (9 Feb 1993) · *The Independent* (13 Feb 1993) · *The Times* (6 Feb 1993) · *WWW, 1991–5* · b. cert. · m. cert. · d. cert.
Archives BFI, business papers · IWM, papers relating to his appointment as films adviser to the ministry of information · Library of Granada TV Network, Quay Street, Manchester, personal MSS | Rice University, Houston, Texas, Woodson Research Center, corresp. with Julian Huxley | FILM BFI NFTVA, documentary footage
Likenesses H. Coster, photographs, 1934, NPG [*see illus.*] · photograph, c.1949, Hult. Arch. · N. Bentley, cartoon (*The Czar of Granada*), repro. in *The Independent* (6 Feb 1993) · Low, cartoon, repro. in *The Independent* (6 Feb 1993) · photograph, repro. in *The Times* · photograph, repro. in *The Independent* (6 Feb 1993)
Wealth at death £6,748,956: probate, 25 June 1993, *CGPLA Eng. & Wales*

Bernyngham [Berningham], **Sir Richard** (*d.* in or after 1335), administrator and justice, came of a family of minor landowners in the North Riding of Yorkshire which took its name from Barningham, some 10 miles north-west of Richmond. He was a younger son of Stephen Bernyngham and his wife, Juliana, and had at least two brothers and a sister. Richard's earliest recorded employment was in the service of John of Brittany, earl of Richmond—in 1290 he was twice the earl's attorney. By 1297 he was bailiff of Boston, Lincolnshire, of which the earl was lord, and by July 1299 bailiff of Richmond itself. In November 1309, by now a knight, he is recorded as steward of Richmond, an office he still held in August 1317. By this time, however, he was increasingly active in the king's service. He became a justice of assize, on 6 September 1313 being instructed to attend parliament instead of taking assizes in the northern counties; by 1320 he was being paid £20 per annum for expenses incurred in the latter capacity. In 1314 he was appointed a keeper of the peace in Yorkshire.

Bernyngham received a large number of other commissions, all in the north of England and most of them relating to Yorkshire. He was called upon to inquire into destruction by Scottish raids, to assess and collect taxes, to investigate allegations of malpractices by officials, to deliver gaols, and to conduct proceedings of oyer and terminer. In 1317 and 1318 he was commissioned to raise men for campaigns against the Scots. Between 24 October 1314 and 5 August 1320 he was seven times among the justices and royal councillors summoned to attend parliaments. On 6 July 1323 he became constable of Barnard Castle.

During the 1320s Bernyngham became increasingly associated with Sir Geoffrey Scrope, whose father had also been a servant of the earl of Richmond. He witnessed some of the deeds whereby Scrope built up his Yorkshire estate, while when Bernyngham was licensed to alienate lands in Middleton Quernhow, north-east of Ripon, to Jervaulx Abbey, in order to endow two priests to pray for his soul, the licence was obtained at the instance of Geoffrey Scrope. Behind these transactions there seems to have been a marriage alliance; the name of Bernyngham's wife is unknown, but it appears that he had two daughters, Joan and Katherine, and that the latter married Sir William Scrope, probably the justice's third son. Hence the arrangement of 1332 whereby Bernyngham settled lands at Barningham and its neighbourhood on himself for life, with remainder to Geoffrey Scrope. His estate appears to have been modest in extent, though Bernyngham had added to it, particularly at Barningham itself. The last commission of oyer and terminer to him was issued on 27 February 1328. He witnessed the grant of the advowson of Scruton church to Geoffrey Scrope at York on 29 January 1335, but then disappears from the records, so he probably died soon afterwards.

HENRY SUMMERSON

Sources *Chancery records* · F. H. Slingsby, ed., *Feet of fines for the county of York from 1272 to 1300*, Yorkshire Archaeological Society, 121 (1956) · M. Roper, ed., *Feet of fines for the county of York from 1300 to 1314*, Yorkshire Archaeological Society, 127 (1965) · R. P. Littledale, ed., *The Pudsay deeds*, Yorkshire Archaeological Society, 56 (1916) · C. T. Clay, ed., *Yorkshire deeds*, 5, Yorkshire Archaeological Society, 69 (1926); 7, Yorkshire Archaeological Society, 83 (1932) · F. Palgrave, ed., *The parliamentary writs and writs of military summons*, 2/3 (1834) · *RotS*, vol. 1 · *VCH Yorkshire North Riding*, 1.40–41 · A. S. Ellis, 'Yorkshire deeds [pt 3]', *Yorkshire Archaeological Journal*, 12 (1892–3), 289–308, esp. 295

Berridge, John (1717–1793), Church of England clergyman, was born on 1 March 1717 at Kingston-on-Soar, Nottinghamshire, the eldest son of John Berridge (*b.* 1686), yeoman, a substantial farmer and grazier, and his wife, Sarah (*née* Hathwaite), of Nottingham. He received initial education in Nottingham, but, having shown himself to be inept at farming, he was sent to Cambridge, where he matriculated in 1735; he entered Clare College on 12 June as Lord Exeter scholar (1735–9) and Freeman scholar; he graduated BA in 1739 and proceeded MA in 1742. Berridge was elected an Exeter fellow of his college in 1740, and a Diggons fellow in 1743; he became a foundation fellow in 1748, and continued to reside at Clare until 1757, usually reading fifteen hours a day. He vacated his fellowship on 1 June 1764.

Berridge was well known in the university as a scholar of distinction, with an entertaining wit. He was, however, inclined to rely for salvation on a Socinian combination of good works and faith, and for at least ten years he gave up private devotions altogether. Nevertheless on 10 March 1745 he was made deacon, on the title of his fellowship, at Buckden, Huntingdonshire, by the bishop of Lincoln (Bishop Thomas), and on 9 June he was ordained priest. From 1750 to 1755 he served as curate at Stapleford, near Cambridge, riding out from college. Believing that he had had no beneficial effect, spiritual or moral, on the parishioners, he resigned. Nevertheless he soon took the college living of Everton, Bedfordshire (with Tetworth, Huntingdonshire), to which he was instituted on 1 July 1755. He continued to live in college, however, and employed John Jones (1700–1770), a liberal clergyman, as resident curate. Following domestic disagreement, Jones resigned: an episode, hitherto overlooked, which may have had an important bearing on the degree and nature of Jones's adverse comments on Berridge's character both then and later.

Not long afterwards (apparently in December 1757), while reading his Bible, Berridge had a vivid experience of spiritual rebirth, which amounted to a classic 'evangelical' conversion. The altered emphases of his sermons soon bore fruit locally and by 1759 Berridge was itinerating widely in surrounding villages, preaching effectively to country people in field and barn, regardless of parochial boundaries, and sometimes inducing physical convulsions among his hearers. With Berridge emphasizing justification by faith alone, not only in rural but in university sermons (1759), the master of Corpus, Dr John Green, began printing lengthy refutations (1760). Archbishop Secker required Green to desist. Bishop Thomas, however, remonstrated with Berridge; but the indirect influence of Berridge's former college friend, Thomas Pitt (later Lord Camelford), effectively deterred the bishop from further opposition.

Although tall, with a direct manner and strong voice, Berridge had suffered from an asthmatic condition since early manhood. After nine years of preaching constantly on mid-week circuits, increasingly far afield, from 1768 to 1773 he was too unwell to itinerate. Moreover he had come to believe that his Arminian understanding of the gospel was less than fully scriptural. He became a convinced Calvinist, explaining his change of view in the relatively simple language of *The Christian World Unmasked* (1773). John Fletcher of Madeley claimed, in his learned *Fifth Check to Antinomianism*, to find high Calvinist beliefs in Berridge's book, but this view was not generally accepted. Berridge's changed understanding of scripture had been marked incidentally by his appointment, on Lady Huntingdon's recommendation (1768), as chaplain to the eleventh earl of Buchan.

As the years went by congregations at Everton began to dwindle; but after an improvement in Berridge's health, and the appointment, in 1782, of a good curate, Richard Whittingham (subsequently Berridge's first biographer) the church filled again. Moreover Berridge resumed annual visits to London, where he preached to large numbers at Whitefield's Tabernacle (the customary likeness of Berridge shows him preaching from its pulpit) and elsewhere. By early 1793, however, he was once more unable to travel and, overcome at last by asthmatic illness, he died at his vicarage in Everton on 22 January. Charles Simeon of Cambridge preached a funeral sermon to large numbers, before his burial on 27 January in Everton churchyard, where a tombstone with Berridge's own striking inscription, including 'Reader, art thou born again?', remains.

Berridge was one of the more remarkable leaders of the evangelical revival. Not only was he among the most gifted intellectually; he was an effective teacher of the relatively uneducated, to whom he devoted his mature ministry. At the same time he was a friend of such notables as Henry Venn, John Wesley, George Whitefield, John Thornton, Lady Huntingdon, and Charles Simeon. Berridge's sense of humour, which occasionally seemed carried to excess, and his use of homely language, appealed to many hearers, not least to readers of his writings, and those who sang his hymns. He remained unmarried because he felt, after due consideration, that bachelorhood was more suitable for those called to a roving ministry. In 1759 John Wesley wrote of Berridge that he was 'one of the most simple as well as one of the most sensible men' (Telford, 4.58). 　　J. S. REYNOLDS

Sources N. R. Pibworth, *The gospel pedlar* (1987) · S. A. Beveridge, *The story of the Beveridge families of England and Scotland* (1923) · T. M. Blagg and F. A. Wadsworth, eds., *Abstracts of Nottinghamshire marriage licences*, 2, British RS, 60 (1935) · W. J. Harrison and A. H. Lloyd, *Notes on the masters, fellows, scholars and exhibitioners of Clare College, Cambridge* (1953) · 'The late Rev. John Berridge', *Evangelical Magazine*, 1 (1793), 8–20 · R. Whittingham, ed., *Works of the Rev. John Berridge, with memoir*, 2nd edn, 1864 (1838) · C. H. E. Smyth, *Simeon and church order* (1940) · J. C. Ryle, *The Christian leaders of the last century* (1869) · M. L. Loane, *Cambridge and the evangelical succession* (1952) · A. S. Wood, 'John Berridge', *Evangelical Library Bulletin*, 24 (1960), 2–4 · F. W. B. Bullock, *Evangelical conversion in Great Britain, 1696–1845* (1959), 95–9 · E. Walker, 'John Berridge', *Bedfordshire Magazine*, 4 (1953–4), 245–8 · *The letters of the Rev. John Wesley*, ed. J. Telford, 4 (1931), 58 · will, proved, archdeaconry court of Huntingdon, 29 Jan 1793

Archives JRL, corresp. | DWL, John Jones MS 39.B.24

Likenesses J. Ogborne, stipple, pubd 1788, BM, NPG · J. Ogborne, engraving, 1792, repro. in Ryle, *Christian leaders*, p. 216 · engraving, repro. in Smyth, *Simeon and church order*, p. 180 · engraving, repro.

in Whittingham, ed., *Works of the Rev. John Berridge*, frontispiece · line engraving, BM, NPG; repro. in *Gospel Magazine* (1774)

Berriman, John (1691–1768), Church of England clergyman, was born in Bishopsgate Street in the parish of St Ethelburga, London, on 27 January 1691, the son of John Berriman, an apothecary in Bishopsgate, and Mary, daughter of William Wagstaffe of Farnborough, Warwickshire. He was the younger brother of William *Berriman and grandson of the Revd Charles Berriman of Ratley, Warwickshire, rector of Beddington, Surrey. He was put apprentice to a wire-drawer in Foster Lane, London; he later matriculated at St Edmund Hall, Oxford, on 11 May 1714, proceeding BA (11 March 1718) and MA (1720). He became lecturer at St Thomas the Apostle on 10 April 1719 and rector of New Timber, Sussex, in 1732. He was curate of St Swithin's, lecturer at St Mary Aldermanbury, and rector of St Olave, Silver Street, and St Alban, Wood Street, all in London; he was appointed to the last in 1744. In 1722 he published a sermon (on 1 Kings 21: 12–13) comparing Charles I to the case of Naboth's vineyard, and in 1741 he published the eight sermons he had delivered as the Lady Moyer lecture in 1739. This work notes 100 errors in the Greek manuscript of the epistles of St Paul. After his brother William's death Berriman edited his brother's sermons, which were published, together with a memoir, in 1751, and wrote a preface to Charles Wheatley's *Fifty Sermons* (1753). He died on 8 December 1768, in Islington, and was survived by his wife, Katherine, to whom he left over £1500 and a leasehold house in Craven Street, and £700 to be distributed in her capacity as executor. They had no children.   A. H. BULLEN, *rev.* ADAM JACOB LEVIN

Sources Foster, *Alum. Oxon.* · will, PRO, PROB 11/944, sig. 438 · *GM*, 1st ser., 38 (1768), 590 · Allibone, *Dict.* · E. Evans, *Catalogue of a collection of engraved portraits*, 1 [1836], 28 · IGI
Likenesses engraving (after portrait), repro. in Evans, *Catalogue of … engraved portraits*
Wealth at death over £2200; plus goods: will, PRO, PROB 11/944, sig. 438

Berriman, William (1688–1750), theologian, was born in London on 24 September 1688, the son of John Berriman, apothecary in Bishopsgate Street, London, in the parish of St Ethelburga, and his wife, Mary, daughter of William Wagstaffe of Farnborough, Warwickshire. His brother was John *Berriman and his grandfather was the Revd Charles Berriman of Ratley, Warwickshire, rector of Beddington, Surrey. Aged five or six he started studying at the grammar school at Banbury, Oxfordshire, where he continued for seven years, before going to Merchant Taylors' School, London, under Dr Shorting, in 1700. He matriculated as a commoner at Oriel College, Oxford, on 5 March 1705. He took up residence there on 21 June 1705 and graduated BA (2 November 1708), MA (2 June 1711), BD and DD (25 June 1722). There he mastered Greek, Hebrew, Chaldean, Syriac, and Arabic. Glocester Ridley, in his funeral sermon, remarked:

> Aware of the ridiculousness of that dangerous and troublesome acquisition, 'a little learning', he did not quit the university when yet but a novice there, and rush into the world to be a teacher of it, till he had formed his judgment

by the compleat circle of academical sciences, and the exercise of the school.   (Ridley, 11)

Berriman was ordained deacon at Oxford by Bishop William Talbot but continued in residence at the university until he was settled in London on 5 May 1712, at about which time he commenced his duties as curate at All Hallows in Thames Street. He was ordained priest on 12 December 1712 by Dr Philip, bishop of Hereford. He was chosen lecturer of St Michael Queenhithe on 22 July 1714, and at All Hallows on 12 July 1715, when he gave up his curacy. On the strength of his early writings, especially *A Seasonable Review of Mr. Whiston's Account of Primitive Doxologies* (1719) and the *Second Review* (1719), Dr Robinson, bishop of London, made him his domestic chaplain in April 1720, from which time Berriman resided at Fulham. On 26 April 1722 he was presented to the parishes of St Andrew Undershaft, Leadenhall Street, and St Mary Axe, whereupon he resigned his lectureship at Queenhithe. In 1723 Robinson died and bequeathed Berriman one fifth of his library. In 1723 and in 1724 Berriman delivered the Lady Moyer lecture, which was published in 1725, and in 1731 he published *A Defence of some Passages in the Historical Account of the Trinitarian Controversy*.

On 17 November 1724 Berriman married Mary Hudson, who outlived him. They adopted children, but they had none of their own. On 16 June 1727 he was elected fellow of Eton College, on the merit of his Lady Moyer lectures, and for the remainder of his life took special interest in the foundation. Eton also became his summer residence, and he turned down the offer of a prebendal stall in Lincoln because it would have forced him to resign his fellowship at Eton. Between 1731 and 1734 he was involved in a controversy with the rational dissenter Samuel Chandler, and his Boyle lectures were published in 1733. He wrote several other occasional sermons and tracts, including a sermon preached before the trustees of the American colony of Georgia (1741) and a *concio ad clerum*, delivered in London in 1742. He resigned his lectureship at All Hallows on 24 June 1745. He was a friend of George Dixon, later principal of St Edmund Hall, Oxford, and of Daniel Waterland.

Berriman died, in Fulham, on 5 February 1750, aged sixty-one; he was buried five days later at St Mary Axe. His brother published posthumously, together with a memoir, two volumes of his sermons, entitled *Christian Doctrines and Duties Explained and Recommended in 40 Sermons* (1751). Some correspondence of his, concerning the unlawfulness of a widower marrying his deceased wife's sister, originally appended to the first volume, was included in Charles Forster's work on the subject (1850).
                                           A. B. GROSART, *rev.* ADAM JACOB LEVIN

Sources J. Berriman, 'Memoir', in W. Berriman, *Christian doctrines and duties explained*, 2 vols. (1751) · G. Ridley, *A good Christian never dies* (1750) · will, PRO, PROB 11/776, sig. 38 · Foster, *Alum. Oxon.* · *Monthly Review*, 4 (1750–51), 470 · *Monthly Review*, 29 (1763), 21–2 · C. L. Shadwell, *Registrum Orielense*, 2 (1902), 13 · IGI
Archives Bodl. Oxf., 'Letter' to R. Dyer
Likenesses S. Ravenet, line engraving (after A. Philips), BM, NPG; repro. in Berriman, *Christian doctrines*, vol. 1, frontispiece

Wealth at death over £800, plus leasehold of five houses and one quarter of Towerhill estate: will, PRO, PROB 11/776, sig. 38 (1750)

Berrow, Capel (1715–1782), Church of England clergyman and theological writer, was born on 27 September 1715 and baptized on 4 October at Northill, Bedfordshire, the third of nine children of Capel Berrow (1673/4–1751), curate of Northill and chaplain to the first Earl Cowper, and his wife, Sarah (d. 1723). One of his younger brothers, Harvey *Berrow (bap. 1719, d. 1776), became a printer and newspaper proprietor in Worcester. He was educated at Merchant Taylors' School from 1728 until 1734, when he matriculated as a commoner from St John's College, Oxford. He graduated BA on 1 June 1738 and was incorporated MA at Christ's College, Cambridge, in 1758. He became curate of St Botolph, Aldersgate, in March 1741 and, later, of St Austin's; on 12 July 1744 he was chosen lecturer of St Benet Paul's Wharf. He published two sermons celebrating the suppression of the Jacobite rising of 1745.

In 1747 Berrow was presented to the rectory of Finningley, Nottinghamshire, from where he issued a number of theological treatises. The first was *Deism not Consistent with the Religion of Reason and Nature* (1751; 2nd edn, 1780), a robust refutation of deism that he wrote in response to the provocative pamphlet *Deism Fairly Stated* (1746), probably written by Peter Annet. His next work was *A Pre-Existent Lapse of Human Souls Demonstrated from Reason* (1762; new edn, 1766), which was principally a compilation of writings by theologians and philosophers on that subject. Dedicated to the archbishop of Canterbury, this work may have brought Berrow preferment, for he was presented to the rectory of Rossington in 1762. He was non-resident at Rossington and there is no evidence in the parish registers of his ever having been seen there. His published works were collected in 1772 in *Theological Dissertations*, dedicated to the Honourable Society of Judges and Serjeants, in Serjeants' Inn, to whom he was chaplain; among the seven pages of subscribers' names was that of Samuel Johnson. Berrow died, unmarried, on 5 October 1782.

A. B. GROSART, rev. S. J. SKEDD

Sources GM, 1st ser., 52 (1782), 503 · parish register, Bedfordshire, Northill, 4 Oct 1715 [baptism] · parish register, Bedfordshire, Northill, 16 Feb 1723 [burial: Sarah Berrow] · Foster, *Alum. Oxon.* · Venn, *Alum. Cant.* · C. J. Robinson, ed., *A register of the scholars admitted into Merchant Taylors' School, from AD 1562 to 1874*, 2 (1883), 70 · *N&Q*, 2nd ser., 11 (1861), 341–2, 417 · private information (2004) [A. Forster]

Berrow, Harvey (bap. 1719, d. 1776), printer and newspaper proprietor, was baptized on 26 May 1719 at St Mary the Virgin, Northill, Bedfordshire, the third son of Capel Berrow (1673/4–1751), a clergyman, and his wife, Sarah (d. 1723). His eldest brother, Capel *Berrow (1715–1782), achieved a measure of repute through his theological writings; his other brother, Richard, was an apothecary in Peterborough. On 3 February 1733 Berrow was apprenticed to Edward Say, a printer of Warwick Lane, London, and was made free of the Stationers' Company on 2 September 1740.

Some time after 1740 Berrow arrived in Worcester, probably to assist **Stephen Bryan** (c.1685–1748). Bryan, like Berrow, was the son of a clergyman and from 1699 to 1706 he had been apprenticed to Bennet Griffin, a London printer. He too was in his mid-twenties when he moved to Worcester and set up his press 'at the Sadler's next the Cross-Keys' in Sidbury, just south of the city boundary. Bryan was the city's first printer for a century and a half and the *Worcester Post-Man*, which he began publishing in June 1709, remains the country's longest surviving newspaper. Bryan's only known apprentice, William Parkes, whom he bound in 1710, went on to carve out a distinguished career as a printer in America, first in Maryland, then in Virginia. The founder's tory beliefs that continued to colour the paper for over two centuries are clearly revealed in two editions of 1720. On 8 January Bryan referred to the attendance of 'the two Lechmeres' at a local ceremony. The following week he responded to the criticism this casual, but almost certainly deliberate, description had unleashed, with an admission that he should have included the titles of two of England's leading whigs but also with an expression of amazement that 'so small a Fault' should have caused 'so great Umbrage'. Bryan died on 20 June 1748, prosperous and still a bachelor, and the paper he assigned to Berrow in March 1748, by then named the *Worcester Journal*, its fourth title, was an influential weekly with a wide circulation throughout the surrounding counties, very little local news, and only a few advertisements.

Just one week after printing his first edition (on 14 April 1748) Berrow moved the business from outside the walls into the heart of the city, near the Cross in the High Street. He also changed the day of publication from Friday to Thursday, explaining to his readers that a Thursday paper would enable him to include 'the most material occurrences' (*Berrow's Worcester Journal*, 9 Nov 1769) published in the London press on Tuesday nights and circulate this news before the arrival of the capital's newspapers on Fridays. On 11 October 1753 the paper's name was changed again when Berrow, angry at the publication of an identically named rival paper by Richard Lewis, a High Street bookseller with whig sympathies, added his own name to distinguish the established weekly. Berrow's attack on Lewis was launched via the pages of his newspaper, but the battle was short and one-sided: on 8 November he exposed Lewis as an untrained printer, on 15 November he lampooned him in verse, and on 20 December he accepted the hand of peace only after addressing 'Brother Dick' as 'The New Printer (as he calls himself.)' and expressing contempt for his dull efforts.

Berrow played a crucial role in the growth of Worcester's book trade, building on Bryan's solid success and using to the full his position as proprietor. Benefiting from developments which were fashioning Worcester into an elegant regional centre, he helped stimulate the reading habit by increasing the paper's local content, by including a greater range of material, and by displaying an ever increasing number of advertisements paid for by London businesses eager to tap such growing provincial markets, especially for books and patent medicines. He became a significant seller of books as well as stationery and patent medicines; and he diversified further by offering goods ranging from musical instruments to mustard seed, from shoe polish to snuff, and by selling tickets for plays, concerts, balls, and, above all, the lottery. He used his columns to advertise his growing stock and developed the network of agents set up by his predecessor to distribute it. Two of his apprentices went on to become master printers in the city; the third, his youngest son, Joseph, was still in training when his father died.

Berrow's career was not all success, however. At some point he had to face insolvency, but the only known reference to this lies in his will where, without entering into detail, he leaves three rings to his brother, Capel, his cousin, John, and James Andrew of London for their great kindness to him and his family, 'particularly at the Time of my Insolvency'.

On 21 October 1748, shortly after taking over from Bryan, Berrow married Margaretta Cooke (d. 1765) at Ampney Crucis, Gloucestershire. Six of their seven children were still living when Berrow died at the age of fifty-seven. According to his will, he had been 'weakly in body' for over a year and was buried in St Oswald's Hospital, Worcester, on 19 August 1776. He left the business to his eldest son, Harvey, on condition that out of it he paid each of his brothers and sisters an annuity. On 11 June 1777, less than a year after officially succeeding his father, the younger Harvey died after a short illness. Berrow's eldest daughter, Elizabeth, then took over the family concern until she handed on the reins to John Tymbs, whom she had married on 25 September 1779. Tymbs, a Worcester man, had returned to the city from London in the previous year. He printed his first edition on 23 December 1779 and went on to become the third of the newspaper's long-serving publishers in its first hundred years.

MARGARET COOPER

Sources Berrow's Worcester Journal (1753–79) · Worcester Journal (1748–53) · Worcester Post-Man (1713–21) · Weekly Worcester Journal (1725–48) · Worcester Post; or, Western Journal (1722–5) · will, 6 May 1775, Worcs. RO · Arber, Regs. Stationers · parish register, St Mary the Virgin, Northill, Bedfordshire, 26 May 1719 [baptism] · parish register, St Swithun's, Worcester, 14 March 1765 [burial] · parish register, St Oswald's Hospital, Worcester, 19 Aug 1776 [burial] · parish register, Ampney Crucis, Gloucestershire, 21 Oct 1748 [marriage] · parish register, St Michael-in-Bedwardine, Worcester, 20 June 1748 [death] · parish register, Leigh with Bransford, Worcestershire · parish register, St Mary the Virgin, Northill, Bedfordshire, 16 Feb 1723 [burial]
Wealth at death left farm in Suckley, Worcestershire; £4 p.a. to Worcester's new infirmary; heir to pay £15 p.a. out of business to two brothers and three sisters (for ten years; to youngest sister for twelve): will, 6 May 1775, Worcs. RO

Berry, Charles (1783–1877), Unitarian minister, was born on 10 November 1783 at Romsey, Hampshire, the third of four sons of the Revd John Berry (1757–1821), Independent minister at Shaftesbury (1778–80), Romsey (1780–94), and West Bromwich (1794–6), then classical tutor at Homerton College (1797–1800), minister at Camberwell (1800–12), and afternoon preacher at Carr's Lane, Birmingham (1812–17). Charles Berry was descended from James Berry

(fl. 1655), one of Cromwell's major-generals. Two of his brothers, Joseph (1782?–1864) and Cornelius (1788–1864), also became Independent ministers, the latter for fifty-three years at Hatfield Heath, Essex.

Charles Berry entered Homerton in 1799 to prepare for the Independent ministry; the next year his father was succeeded as tutor in classics, logic, and natural philosophy by Dr John Pye Smith (1774–1851), whom the younger Berry recalled assisting in chemical demonstrations. In 1802 Berry left Homerton in consequence of the embroilment of a number of students with the college committee over alleged insubordination and a possible complication of heresy. In 1803, at the age of twenty, he became minister of the Unitarian congregation at Great Meeting, Leicester, succeeding Robert Jacomb (d. 1832). Jacomb's predecessor, the Revd Hugh Worthington (1712–1797), served Great Meeting for fifty-six years, a term Berry had also reached when he retired in 1859.

Jacomb's Calvinism had alienated a number of members of Great Meeting; he had submitted his resignation, then withdrawn it and insisted on communicating only with the congregation, not with the vestry or trustees, among whom, as in many congregations, more advanced sentiments had taken hold. Berry's eventual appointment quickly improved the situation. He had a conciliatory and appealing personality, and his preaching, which dealt with issues of daily life in pithy and studiously simple language, was greatly admired. He was also said to have a fine singing voice, which on one occasion entranced the actress Dorothea Jordan (1762–1816) (Gardiner, 1.372–3).

The progress of Unitarian sentiments is shown by the large and appreciative audiences that attended Berry's doctrinal lectures. One such series early in his career, emphasizing the human nature of Christ, led the famous Leicester Baptist preacher Robert Hall (1764–1831) to reply, and Berry responded in turn. A modest man who published very little, Berry admitted that he was relieved when Hall decided against publication, releasing him from a similar necessity; he disarmingly conceded a degree of laziness, explaining that the labour of transcribing his shorthand manuscripts into written texts grew increasingly painful. He maintained a lifelong friendship with Hall and delighted to recall Hall's having been heard to say, in London, that 'he hoped, (indeed he thought,) Mr Berry would be saved, but he did not see how!!' (Berry, autobiographical fragment). As late as 1838 one young Leicester admirer could still record his appreciation of a similar set of lectures on old Priestleyan themes of the corruption of primitive Unitarian Christianity and the absurdity of the doctrine of original sin.

An accomplished scholar and mathematician, Berry conducted a highly successful school for thirty years from 1808. In 1819 Samuel Parr (1747–1825), who regularly met Berry on visits to Leicester, addressed to him a once-famous letter on methods of classical training, choosing him, Parr said, because his good sense, good manners, and 'more than usual capacity for good taste' made him an exception to the undisciplined curiosity and mischievous sectarianism of 'non-con sciolists' (Works, 8.481).

In 1810 Berry married Ann (1779/80–1870), daughter of Thomas Paget (1732–1814), a livestock breeder and latterly a banker in Leicester; her brother, also Thomas (1778–1862), was active in the management of the bank and a leader of the reformers in a staunchly tory town. Charles and Ann Berry had three sons and three daughters, one of whom died in infancy. Berry, who had preached a fascinating sermon in 1821 on the death of Queen Caroline, was himself active in reform politics, which triumphed in Leicester after the Municipal Corporations Act of 1835. He was also a founder of the Leicester Literary and Philosophical Society in 1835 and of the town museum, later the New Walk Museum. Berry died on 4 May 1877 at Olive Mount, Wavertree, near Liverpool, the house of Francis Hollins, a son-in-law, and was buried on 11 May in the chapel yard at Great Meeting. R. K. WEBB

Sources The Inquirer (19 May 1877) · Christian Life (12 May 1877) · Christian Life (9 June 1877) · Charles Berry MS, autobiographical fragment, Great Meeting chapel, Leicester · Records of Great Meeting, Leicester (registers, minute books) · R. E. Cotton, ed., The Nonconformist registers of the city of Leicester, Family History Library, Salt Lake City · E. Clephan, journal, Northumbd RO, Clephan papers · 'Dr Parr's letter to Mr Berry on the plan of teaching', The works of Samuel Parr ... with memoirs of his life and writings, ed. J. Johnstone, 8 (1828), 481–6 · W. Gardiner, Music and friends, or, Pleasant recollections of a dilettante, 3 vols. (1838–53) · A. Temple Patterson, Radical Leicester: a history of Leicester, 1780–1850 (1954) · A. Herman Thomas, A history of the Great Meeting, Leicester, and its congregation (1908) · Transactions of the Leicester Literary and Philosophical Society (1875), vol. 1 · J. Clephan, 'The "Great Meeting" revisited', The bud and the flower (privately printed, 1956), 26–7 · d. cert.

Wealth at death under £10,000: probate, 30 May 1877, CGPLA Eng. & Wales

Berry, Sir Edward, baronet (1768–1831), naval officer, was one of a large family left in straitened circumstances by the early death of his father, a merchant in London. Through the patronage of Lord Mulgrave, a former pupil of his uncle, the Revd Titus Berry of Norwich, and one of the lords of the Admiralty, the boy was in 1779 appointed as a volunteer to the *Burford* (70 guns) with Captain Rainier, then sailing for the East Indies, where she remained until after the end of the war in 1783. He was made lieutenant on 20 January 1794, as a reward, it was said, for bravery in boarding a French warship; he also, reportedly, distinguished himself on 1 June; but the first distinct mention of him is on his appointment to the *Agamemnon* with Nelson in May 1796. He quickly won Nelson's esteem, followed him to the *Captain* on 11 June, and, while Nelson was on shore conducting the siege of Porto Ferrajo, Berry, then first lieutenant, so commanded the ship as to gain his captain's praise. This special service won for him commander's rank, on 12 November 1796; but, while waiting for an appointment, he remained as a volunteer on board the *Captain*, and was thus present in the battle of Cape St Vincent, when he led the boarding of the *San Nicolas*.

Berry was posted on 6 March 1797 and, being in England in October, was taken to court by Nelson, who, on the king remarking on the loss of his right arm, promptly presented Berry as his right hand. It was agreed between them that, when Nelson hoisted his flag, Berry would be his flag-captain; and on 8 December Nelson wrote to him:

'If you mean to marry, I would recommend your doing it speedily, or the to-be Mrs Berry will have very little of your company, for I am well, and you may expect to be called for every hour' (*Dispatches and Letters*, 2.456). On 12 December 1797 Berry married his cousin Louisa, daughter of the Revd Dr Samuel Forster of Norwich. On 19 December he was appointed to the *Vanguard*, but the ship did not leave England until 10 April 1798. In the battle of the Nile Berry, as captain of the flagship, had his full share, and when Nelson was wounded caught him in his arms and saved him from falling. He afterwards published anonymously *An authentic narrative of the proceedings of his majesty's squadron under the command of Rear-Admiral Sir Horatio Nelson, from its sailing from Gibraltar to the conclusion of the glorious battle of the Nile, drawn up from the minutes of an officer of rank in the squadron* (reprinted from the *True Briton* and *The Sun* newspapers, with additions, 1798): this proved a valuable account.

Within a few days of the battle Berry was sent in the *Leander* with Nelson's dispatches. On 18 August 1798 the little 50-gun ship was met by the *Généreux* (74 guns) and captured after a stout defence, in which Berry received a severe wound in the arm. He was taken, with the ship, to Corfu, and did not reach England until the beginning of December. The news of which he was the bearer had been already received, but Berry was enthusiastically welcomed; he was knighted on 12 December 1798, and presented with the freedom of the City of London, in a gold casket valued at 100 guineas. Early in the spring of 1799 he was appointed to the *Foudroyant*, in which he arrived at Palermo on 6 June. On the 8th Nelson hoisted his flag on board, but afterwards, staying at Palermo, sent the *Foudroyant* to strengthen the blockade of Malta. Berry had thus the satisfaction of assisting in the capture of his former captor, the *Généreux*, on 18 February 1800 and of the *Guillaume Tell*, on 31 March, the last of the French ships which had been in the battle of the Nile. In the following June the *Foudroyant* carried the queen of Naples from Palermo to Leghorn; she presented Berry with a gold box set with diamonds, and a diamond ring. A few months later Berry left the ship and returned to England. In the summer of 1805 he was appointed to the *Agamemnon*, and joined the fleet off Cadiz, only just in time for Trafalgar; he had, however, no opportunity of special distinction in the battle, nor yet, the following year, on 6 February, in the action off San Domingo. The *Agamemnon* was put out of commission towards the end of 1806, and Berry was made a baronet (12 December 1806). He is said to have been the only officer in the navy, of his time, except Collingwood, who had three medals, having commanded a ship in three general actions, namely, the Nile, Trafalgar, and San Domingo. In 1811 he commanded the *Sceptre*, and in September 1812 changed into the *Barfleur*, which he took to the Mediterranean. In December 1813 until the peace, he commanded one of the royal yachts, and on 2 January 1815 was made a KCB. On 19 July 1821 he attained the rank of rear-admiral, but never hoisted his flag. His health was much harmed, and for several years before his death he was incapable of any active duties. He died at his residence in

Bath on 13 February 1831, and was buried at Bath. He left no children, and the baronetcy became extinct.

Berry was noted more for seamanship and courage than intellect. Shortly before Trafalgar, Nelson observed his ship joining the fleet: '"Here comes that damned fool Berry!" he laughed, "*Now* we shall have a battle"' (Pocock, 319).   J. K. LAUGHTON, rev. ANDREW LAMBERT

Sources D. Syrett and R. L. DiNardo, *The commissioned sea officers of the Royal Navy, 1660–1815*, rev. edn, Occasional Publications of the Navy RS, 1 (1994) • T. Pocock, *Horatio Nelson* (1987) • *GM*, 1st ser., 101/1 (1831) • *Naval Chronicle*, 15 (1805) • J. Marshall, *Royal naval biography*, 1 (1823) • *The dispatches and letters of Vice-Admiral Lord Viscount Nelson*, ed. N. H. Nicolas, 7 vols. (1844–6)

Archives NMM, log-books and letters from Lord Nelson | BL, corresp. with Lord Nelson, Add. MSS 34905–34930, *passim*

Likenesses W. Ridley, stipple, pubd 1779 (after W. Grimaldi), BM, NPG • G. Keating, mezzotint, pubd 1799 (after H. Singleton), BM • D. Orme, stipple, pubd 1799, BM, NPG; repro. in *Naval Chronicle* (1799) • W. Bromley, J. Landseer, and Leney, group portrait, line engraving, pubd 1803 (*Victors of the Nile*; after R. Smirke), BM, NPG • J. S. Copley, oils, 1815, NMM

Berry, (James) Gomer, first Viscount Kemsley (1883–1968), newspaper proprietor, was born on 7 May 1883 at 11 Church Street, Merthyr Tudful, the youngest of the three sons (all of whom became newspaper proprietors) of John Mathias Berry (*d.* 1917), an estate agent and Liberal alderman, and his wife, Mary Ann (*d.* 1922), the daughter of Thomas Rowe, of Pembroke Dock. Berry followed in the footsteps of the second son, William Ewert *Berry, first Viscount Camrose (1879–1954), and left school at fourteen to work on the *Merthyr Tydfil Times*. Eager to learn his trade, William worked for several south Wales newspapers, before moving on to London, where he launched a paper of his own, *Advertising World*. His only capital was £100 lent by his elder brother, (Henry) Seymour *Berry, Baron Buckland (1877–1928), whose business partner he became in 1902.

Ambitious and able, William Berry identified sport and leisure as an untapped and potentially lucrative field of magazine publishing. From the outset he planned for take-over and expansion. Gomer, on the other hand, was expected to fulfil the very specific tasks of promoting sales and selling advertising space. Nevertheless, the Berry enterprise proved remarkably successful, with sibling rivalry subsumed in a potent mixture of energy, entrepreneurialism, and—particularly in the case of the junior partner—honest endeavour.

In 1905 William and Gomer Berry sold *Advertising World* at an excellent profit. They bought a publishing house and started sundry periodicals, notably (in 1909) *Boxing*, of which sport William was a devotee. Their interests widened rapidly but they were discerning in their acquisitions. In 1907 Gomer Berry married Mary Lilian (*d.* 1928), daughter of Horace George Holmers of Brondesbury Park, London. They had one daughter and six sons: one son died young, and another was killed in action in 1944.

For well over three decades the Berry brothers pursued a common strategy, moving from specialist magazines back into the familiar world of the provincial press. High profit margins facilitated diversification, particularly after the First World War when their company invested in the fledgeling film industry as well as in more reliable revenue earners such as Kelly's directories. Large reserves of surplus capital also funded an early excursion into Fleet Street, with the wartime purchase in 1915 of a struggling *Sunday Times*, whose fortunes were swiftly restored through shrewd editorial direction and long overdue investment. In 1919 their purchase of the St Clement's Press brought control of the *Financial Times*, and with it a high City profile.

The year 1924 saw the foundation of Allied Newspapers (later Kemsley Newspapers), controlled by the Berry brothers and Sir E. M. Iliffe. The purpose of this group was to take over most of the Hulton papers from Lord Rothermere. These included the *Daily Dispatch*, the *Manchester Evening Chronicle*, and the *Sunday Chronicle*. During the years up to 1928 Allied Newspapers further acquired papers in Glasgow, Sheffield, Newcastle, Middlesbrough, and Aberdeen. They also bought the *Daily Sketch* and *Illustrated Sunday Herald* from Rothermere's Daily Mail Trust. In Cardiff, where they already held the *Western Mail* and the *Evening Express*, they acquired the *South Wales Daily News* and the *South Wales Echo*, merging the two morning and the two evening papers.

Newspapers apart, the group's biggest purchase was made in 1926: the Amalgamated Press from the executors of Lord Northcliffe. This great concern comprised a large number of non-political periodicals, ranging from the *Woman's Journal* to children's comic sheets. It included a powerful encyclopaedia and book section, which had been built up under Northcliffe's aegis, chiefly by John Hammerton and Arthur Mee. There were also printing works at Blackfriars and Gravesend and the Imperial Paper Mills, also at Gravesend. In 1927 paper supplies were further augmented by the acquisition of Edward Lloyd Ltd, one of the largest mills in the world.

The key acquisition—of a first-rate serious London daily newspaper—came in 1927 when the Berry–Iliffe group purchased the *Daily Telegraph*. William Berry assumed editorial control with a clear agenda for modernization and major sales growth, and within a decade circulation had risen sevenfold. Other less prominent national titles were accumulated throughout the inter-war period, but predominance at regional and local level remained a central tenet of company policy, and the firm held an almost monopolistic position across large swathes of the provincial press, particularly in south Wales. Nationally, Allied Newspapers and its subsidiary companies owned the best-selling quality daily and Sunday newspapers, and dominated the magazine market.

Not surprisingly, the triumvirate at the heart of this huge media conglomerate were all ennobled, their loyalty dutifully acknowledged by a grateful Conservative premier. Stanley Baldwin recommended Gomer Berry for a baronetcy in 1928, and in 1936 facilitated his elevation to the peerage. Lord Kemsley, as he was now known, shared his brother William's unequivocal belief in Baldwin's ability, effortlessly transferring his affections to Neville Chamberlain when the latter entered Downing Street in May 1937. Indeed Kemsley kept faith with the new prime minister's policy of appeasing the axis powers long after his brother (since 1929 Lord Camrose) had steered the *Daily Telegraph* towards an editorial position little short of hostile. Kemsley in contrast encouraged close contact with the German press, and as late as 27 July 1939 paid a fruitless visit to Hitler at Bayreuth. Such a blinkered approach to great-power relations rarely generated any serious tension between the two brothers, if only because Allied Newspapers had been dissolved in 1937. The families of Camrose, Kemsley, and Iliffe each expected to inherit a recognized raft of financial holdings: hence the decision to divide up the company.

Although ownership of the *Daily Telegraph* kept Camrose in the limelight, after 1937 Kemsley stepped out of his brother's shadow. He became chairman of Allied Newspapers, renamed Kemsley Newspapers six years later. Although much diminished, this was still the largest newspaper empire in Britain, boasting no fewer than six morning, seven evening, six weekly, and four Sunday titles nationwide. These included some of the provincial press's most popular—and sometimes most notorious—newspapers, notably the *Daily Record* in Glasgow and the *Daily Dispatch* in Manchester. In Fleet Street Kemsley owned the equally downmarket *Daily Sketch*, and also the *Sunday Graphic*. However, the jewel in the crown, and the newspaper he remains most closely associated with, was the *Sunday Times*. True to character, he would have left the paper in the hands of his brother had there not been a last-minute intervention by his second wife. Lady Kemsley recognized that, although the once moribund *Sunday Times* was by 1937 outselling *The Observer* by nearly 70,000 copies a week, a burgeoning middle-class market still remained largely untapped. Such insight reaped a rich reward, both in sales and in advertising revenue: circulation was then already 263,000, but over the next two decades it quadrupled.

Though he was short on vision, and bereft of political nous, Kemsley had a real strength in his financial ability. His brother had for over twenty years been editor-in-chief of the *Sunday Times*: hence the new owner's insistence on adopting a similar hands-on approach. So acquiescent editors often found themselves awaiting lengthy and ponderous leaders, dispatched from the penthouse office in the renamed Kemsley House (a further insight into the nature of the man is his insistence in 1937 that henceforth every title block should include the words 'a Kemsley newspaper').

Although they were very different newspapers, both the *Sunday Times* and the *Daily Sketch* embodied the complacent conservatism and Victorian certitudes of their proprietor. Kemsley was genuinely shocked by Chamberlain's fall from grace in May 1940, adjusting only slowly to a very different political climate and a very different party leader. After all, only ten months had passed since he had blithely reassured the Führer that Churchill could no longer be taken seriously; and yet, once Kemsley had made the appropriate psychological adjustment, all his newspapers became ardently pro-Winston, as could be seen in the excessive partisanship of the *Daily Sketch* throughout the 1945 election campaign. Three years earlier the *Sunday Times* not only upheld the prime minister's right to shut down the *Daily Mirror* should he so wish (as was threatened, after its publication of the notorious cartoon by Philip Zec), but even went so far as to congratulate Churchill on his opposition to the Beveridge report. Every evening at dinner Kemsley scrutinized the *Sketch*'s galley proofs, his blue pencil poised to censor even the slightest hint of criticism or dissent. A defeated and despondent Churchill insisted in October 1945 that there was now only one press baron he could still depend upon. Kemsley's reward had been a viscountcy in the 1945 resignation honours list.

The *Daily Sketch* was relaunched as the *Daily Graphic* in 1946, but its editorial policy remained staunchly anti-Labour. The paper's idiosyncratic view of the world reflected the prevailing preoccupations of its proprietor, a state of affairs that survived until the second Lord Rothermere purchased the title in 1952 and restored its former name. Throughout Labour's period in office Kemsley clashed repeatedly with both back-benchers and ministers. The early post-war years were marked by acrimony and litigation, with Kemsley Newspapers fighting a number of libel actions: in August 1946 the attorney-general, Sir Hartley Shawcross, was forced to apologize for using the phrase 'the gutter press'. Kemsley's deep antipathy towards Labour was a key factor in the setting up of the 1947–9 royal commission on the press; and when giving evidence he was perhaps less than frank about the level of proprietorial interference in editorial policy.

By the early 1950s the lifting of wartime restrictions had left the newspaper industry facing a harsher, more competitive climate. As the decade progressed, Kemsley's stifling formality and relentlessly autocratic style of management appeared increasingly outmoded. The stiff manner and equally stiff collars, the bespoke suits and silk ties, the private lift to the top floor, the chauffeured limousine, and the white-gloved flunkeys all signalled a creaking, old-fashioned newspaper operation. Kemsley's sons, three of whom worked on the *Sunday Times*, enjoyed the same privileges as their father. Nevertheless, circulation remained buoyant in the mid-1950s, despite fierce competition from a revitalized *Observer*. The Suez crisis late in 1956 marked a dramatic clash between the two newspapers, with David Astor wholly opposed to intervention and Lord Kemsley stoutly defending Anthony Eden's conduct throughout the whole sorry affair.

With hindsight, it is clear that Kemsley made a crucial strategic error in 1955 by withdrawing from the consortium awarded the first ITA franchise for weekend television in the midlands and the north. The later 1950s also saw the gradual break-up of Kemsley Newspapers, culminating in the sale of the *Sunday Times* in August 1959. Initially Kemsley envisaged selling off all his holdings other than his flagship paper, but he was advised that any serious bidder would insist on the inclusion of the principal revenue earner. The family's extravagant lifestyle and heavy tax bills, together with the prospect of crippling death duties, necessitated the sale of their remaining 40 per cent stake in the company. In the aftermath of a costly strike, and with his bloated enterprise clearly ripe for take-over, Kemsley was determined to get out while he could still demand a high price for his ordinary shares. A discreet approach to the Canadian newspaper and television proprietor Roy H. Thomson (later Lord Thomson of Fleet) culminated in the whole portfolio being offloaded for £5 million. Thomson had to borrow £3 million in the city in order to complete the deal. With piquant irony it was the substantial profits from his commercial television franchise in Scotland that guaranteed his creditworthiness.

Kemsley left 200 Gray's Inn Road with scarcely a backward glance. He sold his large London home, Chandos House, but retained Dropmore, an impressive country estate in Buckinghamshire. Here he lived with his second wife, Edith (d. 1976), the daughter of E. N. Merandon Du Plessis, of Constance, Flacq, Mauritius, whom he had married in 1931. Divorced from a Dutch diplomat, Cornelius Dresselhuys, and an impressive figure in her own right, the flamboyant and formidable Lady Kemsley was appointed OBE in 1953, later becoming a commander of the Légion d'honneur. She suffered from severe ill health for several years, but outlived her husband. Kemsley died in Monte Carlo on 6 February 1968. His eldest son, (Geoffrey) Lionel (b. 1909), became the second viscount.

Kemsley's only daughter, **(Mary) Pamela Gordon** [née Berry], marchioness of Huntly (1918–1998), the twin of Oswald, Kemsley's fifth son, was born on 13 June 1918 at Granville, Gerrards Cross, Buckinghamshire. She grew up at Kemsley's Buckinghamshire house, Farnham Royal, and was educated at North Foreland Lodge School, North Foreland, Kent. On 15 March 1941 she married Douglas Charles Lindsey Gordon, twelfth marquess of Huntly (1908–1987), premier marquess of Scotland: they had one son and one daughter. Huntly had inherited the title in 1937 from his great-uncle, the spendthrift eleventh marquess, who in 1922 sold the estate of Aboyne Castle, Aberdeenshire. Pamela's Kemsley wealth largely restored the Huntly family fortunes, enabling her husband to buy back the ruined castle and 900 acres. During the Second World War she drove ambulances in Aberdeen, and she was later active in charity work in the city. Encouraged by her father, from 1940 to 1959 she was a director of Aberdeen Journals, a Kemsley subsidiary. She also wrote a weekly column under the name of Mary Meldrum (a Huntly title). A motor-car enthusiast, she owned various unusual models; she also qualified as a pilot. She played bridge to international standard and represented Britain at canasta. Her marriage ended in divorce in 1965, and Huntly remarried in 1977. Their son, Granville Charles Gomer Gordon (b. 1944), became the thirteenth marquess. She died on 29 January 1998.   ADRIAN SMITH

Sources Viscount Kemsley [G. Berry], *Kemsley manual of journalism* (1950) · Viscount Camrose [W. Berry], *British newspapers and their* controllers (1947) · S. E. Koss, *The rise and fall of the political press in Britain*, 2 (1984) · 'Evidence taken on 27th May', *Parl. papers* (1947–8), 15.427, Cmd 7503 [royal commission on the press] · 'Royal commission on the press: report', *Parl. papers* (1948–9), vol. 20, Cmd 7700 · *The Times* (7 Feb 1968) · *Sunday Times* (11 Feb 1968) · R. H. Thomson, *After I was sixty* (1975) · D. Hart-Davis, *The house the Berrys built: inside the 'Telegraph', 1928–1986* (1990) · D. Hamilton, *Editor-in-chief* (1989) · DNB · GEC, *Peerage* · CGPLA Eng. & Wales (1968) · *Daily Telegraph* (3 Feb 1998) · Burke, *Peerage*, 1967, 1999 [Mary Pamela Gordon] · b. cert. [Mary Pamela Berry]

Archives HLRO, corresp. with Lord Beaverbrook · HLRO, corresp. with Viscount Davidson

Likenesses W. Stoneman, photograph, 1936, NPG · O. Birley, oils, News Int. RO · H. Carr, oils

Wealth at death £310,866: probate, 1968, *CGPLA Eng. & Wales* (1968) · £1,275,153—Mary Pamela Gordon, marchioness of Huntly: probate, 1998, *CGPLA Eng. & Wales*

Berry, Sir Graham (1822–1904), politician in Australia, was born at Twickenham, England, on 28 August 1822 to Benjamin Berry, a retired shopkeeper, and his wife, Clara, *née* Graham. After basic schooling, he was apprenticed to a draper; in 1846 he married the Scottish Harriet Ann Bencowe (1804–1868), and by 1849 had his own shop in Chelsea. He emigrated to Melbourne in 1852, establishing a general store and wine and spirit business in South Yarra.

In the turmoil following the gold rushes, however, radical politics claimed Berry. In 1854 he sat on one of the juries which acquitted rebel miners who had defied the government at the Eureka Stockade, Ballarat. Soon he became a capable speaker and political organizer, and, in the post-gold rush depression, a passionate advocate of protectionism to foster native industry and, perhaps especially as father of a large and growing family (there were eleven children, eight of whom survived, from his first marriage), to employ native youth. In 1860 he bought the *Collingwood Observer*. At his third attempt, he entered the legislative assembly in 1861, for East Melbourne, and then for Collingwood at the August general elections. He opposed the Radical Party's alliance with businessmen and pastoralists in the McCulloch ministry in 1863, and after the 1864 elections formed a small, disciplined, protectionist opposition. McCulloch's battle with the legislative council over tariff increases, however, forced Berry to support the government, and when he opposed McCulloch on a point of political strategy, Collingwood rejected him as a traitor at the January 1866 elections.

Berry moved to Geelong and became part owner of the *Geelong Register*, amalgamating it later with the *Geelong Advertiser*. He supported McCulloch's party when the battle against the council revived in 1867, but not until it ended did he succeed in re-entering the assembly, at the Geelong West by-election of October 1868. This success was clouded by his wife's death shortly beforehand, but next year he married Rebecca Madge, daughter of J. B. Evans of Geelong. After much hesitation, he joined the dissidents who helped defeat McCulloch in September 1869, and in January 1870 became treasurer in the Macpherson ministry. The government was defeated on his

Sir Graham Berry (1822–1904), by Barraud, pubd 1891

budget in April, but when McCulloch's next ministry fell in June 1871, Berry again became treasurer, and commissioner for trade and customs, under the famous Irish radical, C. G. Duffy, and passed a strongly protectionist tariff. In May 1872 this ministry fell; worse, allegations of scandal and nepotism had forced Berry to resign office shortly beforehand.

Opportunity suddenly reopened three years later, when the Kerferd ministry resigned, its following divided over fiscal policy. In August 1875 Berry became premier, chief secretary, and treasurer, proposing to meet the deficit solely with a land tax. Although defeated in October, when McCulloch, having helped overthrow Kerferd, rejoined him and became premier, Berry unleashed a campaign of parliamentary obstruction and popular agitation which united radical Victoria behind him and a land tax to 'burst up the great estates'. At the May 1877 elections, helped by an extensive new party organization and by Catholics who remembered Duffy, he won a resounding victory, and became once more premier, chief secretary, and treasurer.

The legislative council, dominated by landowners, had to accept Berry's land tax, but opposed a bill to make payment of members (a temporary measure first introduced in 1870) permanent. Berry 'tacked' it to the appropriations bill, which the council rejected in December; as public funds ran out, he dramatized the crisis on 'black Wednesday', 8 January 1878, by dismissing higher public servants wholesale, and some judges and magistrates; rumours circulated of even more revolutionary intentions. In April, however, compromise secured payment of members; Berry now concentrated on reducing the council's power to obstruct the assembly.

When the council rejected his first attempt, Berry went on 'embassy' to London in December 1878, with Professor C. H. Pearson as adviser, seeking imperial legislation to allow the assembly alone to reform the constitution. The Colonial Office, despite having recalled governor Sir George Bowen for supporting Berry during the crisis, did not exclude future intervention, but preferred a local settlement. Berry returned to a public triumph, claiming victory, but his party was divided about the embassy, his reform proposals, and other matters; the assembly denied his reform bill the necessary absolute majority by one vote. He then lost the elections of February 1880, in part because a recession, called the 'Berry blight', was commonly blamed on his actions. However, he defeated the Reform Bill of his successor, James Service, narrowly won another election in July, and resumed his former offices; eventually he passed a bill which, abandoning mechanisms for resolving disputes between the houses, merely made the council's electoral basis somewhat less undemocratic. Further radical defections brought down his government in July 1881.

At the 1883 elections Berry and Service won roughly equal minorities; as no outstanding issues now separated them, Service became premier and Berry chief secretary. This alliance produced much practical legislation, promoted agricultural development inland, and freed the railways and public service from political patronage. In February 1886 Berry resigned and, after attending the first meeting of the newly established but rather ineffective federal council, became Victoria's agent-general in London, and was immediately appointed KCMG. There he took a vigorous part in lobbying the imperial government to curtail French imperialism in the New Hebrides, especially at the colonial conference of 1887. Further honours followed: he was made chevalier of the French Légion d'honneur and awarded the order of the Crown of Italy.

In 1891 Berry returned to a Melbourne battered by economic depression, and to the unfamiliar politics of the Labor Party and the federation movement. He won East Bourke Boroughs in the April 1892 election and became treasurer in Shiels's ministry, turning in vain to the old protectionist panacea; the ministry fell in January 1893. In 1894 he became speaker until losing his seat in 1897. As his financial affairs, after unaccustomed affluence in the 1880s, had now suffered disaster, the assembly bought him an annuity of £500. Although elected to the federal convention in 1897, Berry was incapable of active participation; on 25 January 1904 he died of pneumonia at Balaclava, Melbourne, and was buried in Boroondara cemetery, Melbourne, after a public funeral. Lady Berry survived him, with her seven children and eight from his first marriage.

Berry provided a remarkable example of what a man of humble origins could achieve in colonial politics. A man of great emotional energy and a remarkable orator, he was unusual among colonial politicians for his appreciation of political organization; as a political strategist he had, in his heyday, no equal. His ambition and persistence through political setbacks and financial difficulties were harnessed to enlarging opportunities for ordinary people, and bringing wealth and power under democratic control. Conservative caricaturists mocked his tall, skinny frame and whiskers, and his problems with the letter H; in later years he polished his speech and style, filled out into a dignified figure, and acquired a public standing beyond mockery.

G. R. Bartlett

Sources A. Deakin, *The crisis in Victorian politics, 1879–1881*, ed. J. A. La Nauze and R. M. Crawford (1957) • A. Deakin, *The federal story: the inner history of the federal cause*, ed. H. Brookes (1944) • G. R. Bartlett, 'Berry, Sir Graham', *AusDB*, vol. 3 • G. R. Bartlett, 'Political organisation and society in Victoria, 1864–1883', PhD diss., Australian National University, 1964 • J. E. Parnaby, *The economic and political development of Victoria, 1877–1881* (1951) • J. Tregenza, *Professor of democracy: the life of Charles Henry Pearson* (1968) • J. A. La Nauze, *Alfred Deakin: a biography*, 1 (1965) • probate, Melbourne • R. Wright, *A people's counsel: a history of the parliament of Victoria 1856–1990* (1992) • C. G. Duffy, *My life in two hemispheres*, 2 (1898) • H. G. Turner, *A history of the colony of Victoria*, 2 (1904) • *Imperial Review* (June 1882) • *Imperial Review* (Oct 1886) • *The Argus* [Melbourne] (26 Jan 1904) • *The Observer* (26 Jan 1904) [Collingwood]

Archives State Library of Victoria, Melbourne | NL Aus., Deakin MSS

Likenesses Barraud, photograph, NPG; repro. in *Men and Women of the Day*, 4 (1891) [*see illus.*] • photograph, repro. in Wright, *A people's counsel*

Wealth at death £500: probate, Melbourne, Australia

Berry, Henry (1719/20–1812), civil engineer, was probably born at the village of Parr, near St Helens in Lancashire, and is thought to have spent his childhood there. No record of his birth survives, but his parents are known to have been buried at the Independent chapel in St Helens. Barry became a trustee of this chapel in 1742, the same year that he served as the overseer of the poor at Parr (he became the surveyor from 1743); and his name appears in local records until 1747. He probably left for Liverpool in that year and that city was his home for the rest of his life.

By 1750, aged thirty, Berry was clerk to Thomas Steers (d. 1750), a dock engineer employed by the corporation of Liverpool. He may have assisted Steers in a survey of the River Boyne in Ireland in 1748; and after Steers's death Berry took over as Liverpool's dock engineer, his first task being the completion of the Salthouse Dock opened in 1753. He retained this post until his retirement in 1789, but he was allowed leave of absence by his employers to pursue other tasks. Usually described as a surveyor or engineer, after his retirement Berry adopted the status of a gentleman. There is no evidence that he ever married.

In 1754 Berry surveyed Sankey brook with William Taylor, with a view to making it navigable for the transport of coal from pits east of Prescot to Liverpool. An enabling act was obtained in 1755, but the evidence suggests that soon afterwards Berry came to favour a canal rather than a river-improvement scheme, and that with the approval of only one of the undertakers, John Ashton, Berry constructed a canal in a somewhat secretive manner, to forestall possible opposition to the idea. This canal, 10 miles long with 9 pound locks, was completed by November 1757. It was the first substantial dead water navigation built in England, preceding the better known Bridgewater Canal by some years. The effectiveness of Berry's work on the Sankey probably inspired James Brindley and the duke of Bridgewater. Berry's success led to his employment on the Weaver navigation in 1758. He surveyed the river and proposed a canalization scheme. He was appointed one of the three undertakers but the collapse of Pickering lock near the mouth of the river was held to be his fault and he was dismissed from this position in 1760. As a result he was never thereafter employed on river improvement or canal schemes.

Berry continued to oversee the expansion of the Liverpool dock system. In 1756 he had constructed a graving dock on the west side of the dry basin (subsequently Canning Dock), and in 1765 he constructed two more. By 1771 he had completed the George Dock, by 1788 the Kings Dock, and he had begun the Queens Dock by his retirement in 1789. Other local work included an appointment to supervise the maintenance of Liverpool roads and pavements in 1766, the investigation of a bridge-building contract for a local turnpike trust in 1772, and a survey of the Mersey shoreline for the Board of Ordnance to site three forts. In 1774 the corporation of Hull formally approached the Liverpool corporation for permission to use Berry's services, and from 1774 until 1781 he was employed as the dock engineer at Hull, overseeing the construction of the largest commercial dock in the country. Since he remained at Liverpool, supervising the work by visits and letter, a resident engineer, Luke Holt, was appointed to assist him. In the 1780s Berry was also involved in the first unrealized schemes to bridge the Menai Strait.

Whether Berry continued to give advice after his retirement has not been ascertained. He died at Duke Street, Liverpool on 31 July 1812 in his ninety-third year. He was buried on 6 August at the same chapel as his parents at St Helens. His estate included property at Parr and houses in Duke Street, Kent Street, and Berry Street in Liverpool. After bequests to several Liverpool charities and ample provision for his housekeeper, Mary Pembridge, it passed to his nephews and nieces and their children.

K. R. Fairclough

Sources S. Harris, 'Henry Berry, 1720–1812: Liverpool's second dock engineer', *Transactions of the Historic Society of Lancashire and Cheshire*, 89 (1937), 91–116 • S. Harris, 'Further information concerning Henry Berry, 1720–1812', *Transactions of the Historic Society of Lancashire and Cheshire*, 90 (1938), 197–8 • T. C. Barker, 'The Sankey navigation', *Transactions of the Historic Society of Lancashire and Cheshire*, 100 (1948), 121–55 • T. S. Willan, 'The navigation of the River Weaver in the eighteenth century', *Chetham Society*, 3rd ser., 3 (1951), 53–6, 70, 80–83 • M. W. Baldwin, 'The engineering history of Hull's earliest docks', *Transactions* [Newcomen Society], 46 (1973–4), 1–12 • N. Ritchie-Noakes, *Liverpool's historic waterfront: the world's first mercantile dock system*, Royal Commission on Historical Monuments, suppl. ser., 7 (1984), 23–26 • T. C. Barker and J. R. Harris, *A Merseyside town in the industrial revolution: St Helens, 1750–1900* (1954); repr. with corrections (1993), 16–20 • M. Clarke, 'Thomas Steers',

Papers on dock engineers and dock engineering, presented at Merseyside Maritime Museum, 13 Feb 1993 · W. H. Aldcroft and M. J. Freeman, *Transport in the industrial revolution* (1983) · register of the Independent chapel of St Helens, 1711–1837, Society of Genealogists, London, LA/R 209 [transcript] · will, Aug 1812, Lancs. RO, WCW Henry Berry · private information (2004)

Wealth at death under £12,500: Harris, 'Further information'

Berry, James (*d.* 1691), parliamentarian army officer and major-general, was in the late 1630s employed as a clerk in an ironworks in the west midlands. He was a friend of the puritan divine Richard Baxter with whom he shared a house for some time. Baxter described him as 'a man, I verily think, of great sincerity before the wars, and of very good natural parts, and affectionate in religion' (*Reliquiae Baxterianae*, 57). According to Baxter, Berry helped persuade him to become a minister. In 1638 Berry wrote to Baxter from Shrewsbury a letter of godly exhortation, praying that God would 'enable you to that great work whereunto he hath called you' (*Correspondence of Richard Baxter*, 1.39). It was through Berry's offices that the ironmaster Richard Foley of Stourbridge (with whom Berry had lived) offered Baxter the post of schoolmaster at Dudley; and Berry went with Baxter to his ordination at Worcester in December 1638.

On the outbreak of the civil war Berry joined the forces raised by Oliver Cromwell in East Anglia, and by 1643 he had risen to the rank of captain-lieutenant in Cromwell's regiment. At Gainsborough that year he killed the royalist commander, Lord Charles Cavendish. Baxter claims that Berry became one of Cromwell's favourites, and that under his commander's influence Berry adopted more radical religious beliefs, embracing separatism and regarding 'the old puritan ministers [as] dull, self-conceited men, of a lower form' (*Reliquiae Baxterianae*, 57). Baxter also admitted, however, that 'he lived as honestly as could be expected in one that taketh errour for truth and evil to be good' (ibid., 57).

Berry fought for parliament throughout the first civil war and by 1647 was acting as a major in Colonel Twistleton's regiment stationed in the east midlands. He was heavily involved in the disputes between the army and parliament in 1647, and on occasion acted as a spokesman for the radical army agitators. He fought at the battle of Preston in August 1648 and was afterwards chosen to bring the news of the victory to parliament. During the late autumn of 1648 he was serving in Scotland, and he thus took no part in the events in London which culminated in the trial and execution of Charles I. He may have been with Cromwell in Ireland in 1649 and 1650, and certainly fought in Scotland throughout the early 1650s. In 1651 he was raised to the rank of colonel of horse. At some point during the early 1650s he settled at Lincoln, and around 1652 he bought the former palace of the bishops of Lincoln and established it as his main residence. In 1654 he was appointed to the Lincolnshire commission for the ejection of scandalous and insufficient ministers and schoolmasters.

In the spring of 1655 Berry was involved in the suppression of the abortive royalist uprising at Rufford Abbey in Nottinghamshire. In the autumn of that year he was appointed one of Cromwell's major-generals and given control of Herefordshire, Worcestershire, Shropshire, and north Wales. In January 1656 he was also made responsible for south Wales; thereafter he controlled the largest of all the major-generals' associations. During 1655 and 1656 Berry made at least six tours around his large area to supervise the taking of security from local royalists and the assessment and imposition of the decimation tax. His letters to Cromwell's secretary of state, John Thurloe, during these months reveal that, while he was strongly committed to the godly cause, his zeal was tempered with an underlying tolerance and a wry sense of humour. He reported to Cromwell in November that he had told the Welsh Fifth Monarchist Vavasour Powell that he 'came forth in the worke as sent of God' and the next month he commented that 'the eyes of good men are much upon us and greedily watch to see what good we will bringe forth' (Bodl. Oxf., MS Rawl. A 32, fols. 715–18, A 33, fols. 519–22). He also admitted, however, that he found his work as a major-general 'toylesome and tedious' (Bodl. Oxf., MS Rawl. A 32, fols. 793–6), and he frequently complained about the lack of support he received from the magistrates of his counties.

While the royalists of his association generally complied with the new security arrangements which he imposed upon them, a great many of them fell below the lower threshold for payment of the decimation tax. Berry also had dealings with a number of the religious and political radicals in his area who were opposed to Cromwell's government. In line with his own religious radicalism, he adopted a relaxed and lenient approach to their activities. He described the Powell's Fifth Monarchists to Thurloe as 'affectionate, tender-spirited people that want judgement' (Bodl. Oxf., MS Rawl. A 34, fols. 217–20). He also looked indulgently on the Quakers of his area, and released a number of them from Evesham gaol. According to one of them, Edward Bourne, he treated them very civilly and later told the Worcestershire justices that if they behaved peaceably they should be allowed the freedom to exercise their beliefs. It is possible that Berry himself may have been attracted to Quakerism by this point, for in 1657 George Monck complained to Cromwell that most of his regiment were members of the sect. In 1659 Berry appointed two Quakers who had been purged by Monck as cornets in his regiments, and another in his own troop, while his captain was also a Quaker.

Berry sat in the second protectorate parliament as MP for Worcestershire. He is not recorded as having spoken in either the debates on James Nayler in December 1656 or on the Decimation Bill in December 1656 and January 1657. He was, however, involved in a violent dispute with another member in November 1656 who had argued for the introduction of a hereditary element in the constitution; and like most of his fellow major-generals he almost certainly opposed the offer of the crown to Cromwell in the spring of 1657. Later that year he was appointed to the other house. Following Oliver Cromwell's death he supported the army in the power struggles which developed with Richard Cromwell and the restored Rump Parliament. After the secluded members had been readmitted to the Rump Parliament in early 1660 he was imprisoned for refusing to take an engagement to live peaceably. Monck distrusted him deeply, and after the Restoration he was imprisoned for some years in Scarborough Castle. In 1667 he refused an offer of release in exchange for an admission of guilt. He was eventually released in 1672 and probably settled in Stoke Newington in Middlesex, a manor owned by Charles Fleetwood. According to Baxter, 'being released he became a gardiner, and lived in a safer state than in all his greatness' (*Reliquiae Baxterianae*, 58); if so, Berry's work may have been market-gardening, of which Stoke Newington was a centre for supplying London. Edmund Calamy relates the story of Berry's regretting his part in the fall of the republic. Upon meeting the Presbyterian minister John Howe, Berry (who was then 'but in very mean circumstances') 'very freely told him, with tears running down his cheeks, if *Richard* had but at that time hang'd up him, and nine or ten more, the Nation might have been happy' (Berry and Lee, 271). Berry attended John Owen's congregation, alongside other old Cromwellians such as Disbrowe and Kelsey, and was remembered in the wills of both Disbrowe and Fleetwood. Berry's wife, Mary—of whom little else is known beyond her having been with him in the marches in 1656 and her petitioning for his release in 1663—died in 1681. Berry died in Stoke Newington on 9 May 1691.

CHRISTOPHER DURSTON

Sources J. Berry and S. G. Lee, *A Cromwellian major-general; the career of Colonel James Berry* (1938) · Thurloe state papers, Bodl. Oxf., MS Rawl. A · *Reliquiae Baxterianae, or, Mr Richard Baxter's narrative of the most memorable passages of his life and times*, ed. M. Sylvester, 1 vol. in 3 pts (1696) · PRO, Interregnum state papers, SP 18–28 · C. H. Firth and G. Davies, *The regimental history of Cromwell's army*, 2 vols. (1940) · N. Penney, ed., 'The first publishers of truth': being early records, now first printed, of the introduction of Quakerism into the counties of England and Wales (1907), 283 · DNB · C. H. Firth, *The last years of the protectorate, 1656–1658*, 2 vols. (1909) · *The autobiography of Richard Baxter*, abridged edn, ed. J. M. Lloyd Thomas (1931); new edn, ed. N. H. Keeble (1974), 16, 281 · B. Reay, *The Quakers in the English revolution* (1985), 90 · *Calendar of the correspondence of Richard Baxter*, ed. N. H. Keeble and G. F. Nuttall, 2 vols. (1991) · Greaves & Zaller, *BDBR*, 58–60
Archives Bodl. Oxf., Thurloe state papers, MS Rawl. A

Berry, James (1852–1913), hangman, was born at Heckmondwike, Yorkshire, on 8 February 1852, one of the large family of Daniel Berry, a woolstapler, and Mary Ann Berry (*née* Kelley), both Wesleyan Methodists. He attended Heckmondwike day school and a boarding-school, Wrea Green Academy, near Lytham. At sixteen years of age he ran away to go to sea but was brought home from Goole by his father. Employed variously as a bookkeeper, joiner, apprentice engineer, printer, weaver, and railway porter, he eventually became a police constable with Wakefield West Riding depot in 1873. He met his future wife, Sarah Ann Ackroyd, one year his junior, then joined the Bradford borough police force. They married on 6 April 1874, at Richmond Terrace Chapel, Horton, Bradford, and eventually had six children, three dying in infancy. He left the police force, starting a business as an egg and butter merchant, which failed. After doing some machine-shop work, he joined the Nottingham borough police force for a year, resigning after a dispute with a sergeant. On returning to Bradford he worked as a coal merchant, then a boot salesman, on poor pay.

In September 1883 the public executioner, William Marwood, whom Berry claimed to have met while a police officer, died. The generous fees, £10 per execution plus expenses (£5 for reprieves), led Berry to apply for the post. One of 1400 applicants, Berry initially failed, but the new hangman, Bartholomew Binns, proved an inept drunkard. In March 1884 Berry had successfully executed two prisoners at Edinburgh and he soon replaced the discredited Binns.

What became the notorious incident of 'The Man They Could Not Hang' occurred on 23 February 1885. John Lee was convicted for the murder of Miss Keyse at Babbacombe in 1884, and Berry attended Exeter prison to conduct the execution. Despite the trapdoors working on test, they failed to open three times with Lee on the drop. Attributed variously to 'divine intervention', rain-swollen woodwork, and wedging by another convict, the real cause was a faulty long hinge on the trapdoor which snagged on the drawbolt while bearing Lee's weight. Reprieved, Lee served a lengthy prison sentence.

An eight-year career saw Berry hang upwards of 131 convicted murderers in British and Irish gaols, including Thomas Orrock, Israel Lipski, Dr Phillip Cross, William Henry Bury, and Mary Ann Wheeler (Pearcey). He increasingly incurred Home Office displeasure as a result of levees at pubs, sale of ropes as souvenirs, and a few bodged executions. Berry complained that the near decapitation of convict John Conway at Liverpool in 1891 was caused by the interference of the prison doctor, Dr Barr, and he resigned. He published his reminiscences as *My Experiences as an Executioner* (1892). Official displeasure became manifest when a circular was issued instructing the prisons to decline his services if offered.

Berry went on the entertainment circuit, giving lantern slide shows and lectures on crime and punishment, and was billed as providing 'eccentric, excruciatingly continuous entertainment without vulgarity'. He ran a pub but drank too much and decided to become a pig farmer. Despite claiming to be anti-capital punishment, stating he had hanged more than one innocent person, he again applied for the executioner's post in January 1902, and was refused by the Home Office. He contemplated suicide, but was converted by a young evangelist and toured the country conducting religious meetings. The 'late executioner' attracted the curious and claimed many converts. He lived out his final years quietly with his wife in Bradford as a farmer. He died on 21 October 1913, at 36 Bolton Lane, Bradford, of heart disease, and was buried at Lidget Green cemetery, Bradford.

STEWART P. EVANS

Sources J. Atholl, *The reluctant hangman* (1956) · B. Bailey, *Hangmen of England* (1989) · J. Berry, *My experiences as an executioner*, ed. H. Snowden Ward (1892); repr. (1972) · B. Bailey, *Hanging in judgment* (1993) · S. Fielding, *The hangman's record, 1868–1899*, 1 (1994) ·

J. Atholl, *Shadow of the gallows* (1954) • PRO, HO 144/212/A48697 A–F • PRO, PCOM 8/191 • private information (2004) • b. cert. • m. cert. • d. cert.

Archives PRO, HO 144/212/A48697 A–F • PRO, PCOM 8/191

Berry, Sir John (*c.*1636–1690), naval officer, was the second son of Daniel Berry (*d.* 1653), vicar of Knowstone and Molland, Devon, and his wife, Elizabeth, *née* Moor. The sequestration of Daniel's living in 1646, followed by his death in comparative poverty in 1653, forced his sons to seek any employment they could, and John, along with his elder brother, entered the merchant service. By 1663 he had moved to the navy as boatswain of the *Swallow Ketch* in the West Indies, and on the promotion of her captain after the successful capture of a pirate, Berry was given command of her in October 1665 by Sir Thomas Modyford, governor of Jamaica. Modyford's kinship with George Monck, duke of Albemarle, and his own Devon connections, probably benefited Berry on his return to England in 1666. Albemarle, as joint admiral for the campaign of that year, gave him commissions successively for the *Little Mary* (February 1666) and the *Guinea* (in August), and during July he was in command of all the small craft and auxiliaries attending the fleet. Berry returned to the West Indies in April 1667 in command of the hired ship *Coronation*. Given command by the governor of Barbados, Lord Willoughby, of a squadron totalling twelve ships he blockaded St Kitts, taken by the French in the previous year. A joint Franco-Dutch force sailed to engage him, and in the battle of Nevis which followed in May, his squadron won a strategic victory which enabled the English to retake Antigua and Montserrat. He commanded the *Pearl* from November 1668 to January 1670 and the *Nonsuch* from January 1670 to July 1671, serving in the Mediterranean against the Barbary corsairs, before returning to home waters in the *Dover*. He commanded the *Resolution* throughout the Third Anglo-Dutch War; his relief of the duke of York's flagship at the battle of Solebay (28 May 1672) brought him his knighthood, and he also served in all the engagements of the 1673 campaign. He commanded the *Bristol* in the Mediterranean in 1675–6, taking her to Virginia in January 1677 to deal with 'Bacon's rebellion'. Discovering on his arrival that the rebellion had already been suppressed, Berry instead became involved in the tangled disputes and recriminations of the Virginia colonial leaders in its aftermath. He was intended to command the West Indies squadron mobilized in the French war scare of 1678, although in the end neither he nor his ship, the *Dreadnought*, sailed for that theatre. From 1680 to 1681 he commanded the *Leopard*, convoying trade in the Mediterranean and training the king's illegitimate son, Henry, duke of Grafton. Throughout these years, he also developed an alternative 'career' as a land officer, holding commissions as a captain in the marine regiment in 1672, Sir Walter Vane's regiment in 1673, and the Holland regiment of foot in 1684, and from June 1674 onwards he was governor of Deal Castle.

In April 1682 Berry was appointed to command the *Gloucester*, assigned to carry the duke of York to Scotland. On 6 May, following a serious error by her pilot, the ship was wrecked on the Lemon and Oar Sands 25 miles east-north-east of Cromer. Partly through Berry's efforts and determination to stay with his ship until the end, the duke and many of his retinue were saved, although 150 were lost. Within six weeks he had been appointed to command the *Henrietta*, and in 1683 was vice-admiral of the fleet sent out under George Legge, Lord Dartmouth to evacuate and demolish Tangier. During this time he became one of Samuel Pepys's chief sources of information about the allegedly poor state of the navy in general and the indiscipline of the Mediterranean Fleet in particular. Berry blatantly flattered Pepys, who in turn showed an awareness of a self-righteous streak in Berry; indeed, at several points in his career Berry displayed overt immodesty about his professional competence and good standing with the seamen. His close relationship with Pepys paid dividends in April 1686 with his appointment to the special commission to reconstruct the navy, a position which he held until October 1688 when he became comptroller of the victualling accounts. On 24 September 1688 he had been appointed rear-admiral of the fleet being mobilized to defend against William of Orange's invasion, flying his flag in the *Elizabeth*. Despite his ties to James II he was an active conspirator on William's behalf. He was involved in a plot to kidnap Lord Dartmouth, the admiral, and was said to be one of eight captains ready to defect to William. His stance may have been determined by a strongly anti-French and anti-Catholic attitude; he had refused to join the jury trying the seven bishops, and had bought up former monastic lands in Kent which (his will suggests) he worried might have been reclaimed by a resurgent Catholic church. Berry became vice-admiral of the fleet in December, but it was paid off shortly afterwards. He commanded at Sheerness over the winter of 1688–9 but was considered too ill for further service by the summer of 1689. He died at Portsmouth on 14 February 1690 and was buried at Stepney church.

Berry made his will on 2 February 1688. In it, he mentioned a wife, Rebecca (*c.*1644–1696), who married the apothecary Thomas Elton ten months after Berry's death and died on 26 April 1696. Her monument at Stepney church bears an inscription which ends:

> The same in low and high estate
> Ne'er vext with this ne'er moved with that
> Go ladies now and if you'd be
> As fair as great as good as she
> Go learn of her humility.

Sir John's will also mentions four brothers, Thomas (who held a number of naval commissions between 1672 and 1689), Robert, Anthony, and Nathaniel. Berry had a house at Mile End and lands in Middlesex and Kent, but he also bequeathed £5 to the poor of the parish in Devon where he was born.

J. D. DAVIES

Sources PRO, PROB 11/398, fol. 291v • PRO, ADM 10/15, p. 12 • J. D. Davies, *Gentlemen and tarpaulins: the officers and men of the Restoration navy* (1991) • J. D. Davies, 'James II, William of Orange, and the admirals', *By force or by default? The revolution of 1688–1689*, ed. E. Cruickshanks (1989), 82–108 • P. M. Cowburn, 'Christopher Gunman and the wreck of the *Gloucester*', *Mariner's Mirror*, 42 (1956), 113–26, 219–29 • *The Tangier papers of Samuel Pepys*, ed. E. Chappell,

Navy RS, 73 (1935) · S. S. Webb, *The governors-general: the English army and the definition of the empire, 1569–1681* (1979) · *CSP dom., 1666–90* · J. M. Collinge, *Navy Board officials, 1660–1832* (1978) · *Walker rev.*, 109 · PRO, Admiralty MSS · E. B. Powley, *The naval side of King William's war* (1972) · W. A. Shaw, *The knights of England*, 2 vols. (1906) · *DNB* · *Le Neve's Pedigrees of the knights*, ed. G. W. Marshall, Harleian Society, 8 (1873) · memorial inscription, Stepney church, Stepney, London · *N&Q*, 7th ser., 10 (1890), 451–2 · *N&Q*, 7th ser., 11 (1891), 189–90, 434–5

Wealth at death manor of West Langdon Abbey, Kent; lands in Walmer; house at Mile End: will, PRO, PROB 11/398, fol. 291*v*

Berry, Lizzie. *See* Kemp, Elizabeth (1847–1919).

Berry, Mary (1763–1852), author, was born on 16 March 1763 at Stanwick, North Riding of Yorkshire, a hamlet south-west of Darlington. The birth of her sister and life-long companion Agnes (1764–1852) followed just over a year later. According to one possibly unreliable account, their grandfather was a tailor in Kirkcaldy, Fife. Their father, Robert Berry (*d.* 1817), was the nephew of a Scottish merchant, Robert Ferguson (1690–1781), who traded in Broad Street, London, and having made a fortune of almost £300,000 was able to buy the estate of Raith, near Kirkcaldy. The nephew was 'bred to the law, with or without any intention of following the profession' (*Extracts*, 1.2), but never practised. In 1762 he married Elizabeth Seton, daughter of John and Elizabeth Seton. After giving birth to Mary and Agnes, his wife died in childbed in 1767, aged twenty-three, along with a third daughter. Meanwhile Robert Berry's younger brother, William (*d.* 1810), who had worked for a mercantile house, had ingratiated himself with his uncle. He married an heiress named Crawford who brought him a dowry of £5000 and produced two sons. The younger brother was installed in comfort at Raith and looked after Ferguson's Scottish affairs, while Robert had to content himself with an allowance of £300 a year and a 'melancholy' City residence in Austin Friars (ibid., 1.3). Eventually at his death Ferguson left William Berry (who assumed his surname in 1782) £300,000 in the funds, with an estate worth £4000 to £5000 per annum. Robert Berry received a bare legacy of £10,000, but his brother was apparently shamed into making him an annuity of £1000 a year.

At first the motherless children lived with their grandmother Elizabeth Seton (1719–1797) in Yorkshire, until they moved in 1770 to College House, on the riverside at Chiswick. Their friends from girlhood included the daughters of John Loveday (1711–1789), an antiquary whose wife was a cousin of their grandmother. Mrs Seton remained with Mary and Agnes up to the time that they left with their father in May 1783 for a prolonged stay on the continent. At this point Mary began to keep a regular journal, which she continued intermittently for the rest of her life. The party first visited Rotterdam before travelling through Belgium, and then proceeded up the Rhine as far as Basel. Their journey continued through Lausanne and Geneva into Savoy, and across the Alps by Mont Cenis. In Italy their itinerary for 1784 included two long stays at Rome and one at Naples, where they were presented to Queen Maria Carolina. At Florence they met the envoy Sir Horace Mann, the correspondent of Horace Walpole.

Mary Berry (1763–1852), by Anne Seymour Damer, 1793

Their return was made through Switzerland, with a second trip to the Chamonix valley, and the south of France before reaching Paris in March 1785. They arrived home in June.

The family took a house at Twickenham Common in 1788 and made the acquaintance of Horace Walpole, who described the daughters as 'the best informed and the most perfect creatures I ever saw at their age' (Walpole, *Corr.*, 34.24). At seventy years of age, their new friend risked incurring public scorn as a result of the attachment which soon developed between the Berry sisters and himself, but he was prepared to endure such ridicule. He showed them round Strawberry Hill on 14 July 1788, and began a correspondence full of intimate detail and personal gossip. In his letters both women are addressed as his 'twin wives', as Rachel and Leah, or as '*mes très chères Fraises*'. The elder is called 'Suavissima Maria' and the younger 'my sweet Lamb'; but it was Mary who seems to have inspired the stronger attraction and within weeks 'Albion's old Horace' was exchanging verses of high-flown compliment with her. According to a story passed on by Macaulay and Thackeray among others, Walpole offered marriage to both sisters in turn, but Mary herself denied this. She admitted only that he had once replied to a question by the duchess of Gloucester whether he would marry the elder, 'That is as Miss Berry herself pleases' (Walpole, *Corr.*, 11.xxiv). The relationship appears to have been one of amiable badinage and warm affection laced by a characteristic sexless flirtation on Walpole's side.

In the winter of 1789-90 the Berry family took a house at Teddington which Walpole had found for them. In the following summer he was 'most seriously house-hunting' for the Berrys in the vicinity of Marble Hill (Walpole, *Corr.*, 11.103); but he then decided to offer to them the use of his own secondary residence of Little Strawberry Hill, which had been occupied by the actress Catherine Clive (1711-1785) until her death. Adverse commentary in the press caused Mary at first to refuse the offer, but she eventually agreed. By this time the friendship had strengthened further, and Walpole had completed his *Reminiscences of the Courts of George I and II*, written 'for the amusement of Miss Berry and Miss Agnes Berry' (1789). At the end of the same year he also dedicated to the 'dear sisters' his description of Strawberry Hill, 'which they often made delightful by their company, conversation and talents'. In this period comparatively few letters survive from either sister to Walpole, but it is evident that each wrote to him regularly, in reply to individual messages or to what he called 'bigamy' letters addressed to both.

An even more important friendship was forged after Mary Berry first met the sculptor Anne Damer (1748-1828) in 1789. When Walpole died, Damer was to become his executor, residuary legatee, and the life tenant of Strawberry Hill. She engaged in regular correspondence with Mary, especially when either woman was travelling abroad, and left surviving notebooks for the period 1791-7 which were addressed to her friend. When Mary formed an attachment to General Charles *O'Hara (c.1740-1802), Damer served as confidante and intermediary. The couple became engaged about October 1795 and both parties enlisted Damer's support and advice. At first it was agreed that the engagement should be kept from Walpole, but eventually Mary revealed her secret. However, she was unwilling to accompany O'Hara when he returned to his post as governor of Gibraltar in November. Within a few months of their separation, the couple embarked on fierce mutual recriminations, and by the end of April 1796 Mary had finally rejected her suitor. The episode remained a painful memory for the rest of her life, even though she never saw O'Hara again.

The Berry family had taken a house in North Audley Street after their continental travels and the sisters remained there until 1824. They continued to use Little Strawberry Hill, which Walpole settled on them at his death in 1797. He also bequeathed his literary manuscripts to them, and it was Mary who edited the posthumous collection of *The Works of Horatio Walpole, Earl of Orford*, published in five volumes (1798), although her father was named as editor. Mary had composed a five-act comedy called *Fashionable Friends*, first performed privately at Strawberry Hill, which was eventually staged with a noteworthy cast at Drury Lane in 1802, but the play lasted only three nights. By that date she was able to make another visit to France, during the peace of Amiens, this time in the company of Mrs Damer. In the course of her stay she was presented to Mme Bonaparte, mother of the first consul, and met Napoleon briefly. Mary also renewed her acquaintance with Mme de Staël, whom she had known

since her visit to Lausanne in 1784. After a brief return to London, she embarked on another extensive tour with her father and sister between October 1802 and September 1803, wintering in Nice and coming home via Switzerland and Germany. She finally escaped the war-torn continent at a small port in Schleswig-Holstein.

In her middle years Mary Berry began to emerge as a more prominent literary figure. She edited four volumes of the letters of Mme du Deffand to Walpole (1810) and in 1819 she used unpublished materials to compose the life and letters of Rachel Wriothesley (1636-1723), wife of Lord William Russell. Her circle of acquaintants had extended to include figures such as Princess Caroline, Joanna Baillie, Sarah Siddons, the countess of Albany, Benjamin Constant, the duke of Wellington, and Talleyrand. Mary again visited Paris in 1816, and later in the year set out with her father and sister for a prolonged visit to Italy. It was while they were at Genoa that Robert Berry died on 18 May 1817. His brother's annuity now ceased and the Berry sisters were left to live on a reduced income. Mary returned to London in September 1818, and then made further visits to the continent, principally France and Italy, in 1819-21, 1822-3, 1828-9, 1829-30, 1834, and 1836.

In 1824 the sisters left their house in North Audley Street and took up residence in Curzon Street. Here they established a salon frequented by many prominent figures in society. Mary became a friend and correspondent of Thomas Babington Macaulay, but she was irritated by the famous attack he launched on Horace Walpole in the *Edinburgh Review* in 1833: her defence of her old friend was printed at the head of the sixth volume of Walpole's *Letters* (1840). Her literary fame had spread with the publication of *A comparative view of the social life of England and France from the Restoration of Charles the Second to the French Revolution* (1828) and its sequel *Social Life in England and France from the French Revolution in 1789 to that of July 1830* (1831). Late in the life of the Berry sisters, Thackeray was a regular visitor to Curzon Street, and he refers to Mary at the start of *The Four Georges* (1860) as an anonymous lady who had been familiar with many of the great personages in the previous century. Maria Edgeworth, Francis Jeffrey, and Sydney Smith were also among her close acquaintances. Anne Damer's death in 1828 left a gap in Mary's life, not wholly filled by the constant companionship of Lady Charlotte Lindsay (1770-1849), her most devoted friend in later years.

Agnes Berry died in January 1852 and was buried at St Peter's parish church, Petersham, Surrey. There was just time for Mary to be honoured with a presentation to Queen Victoria on 17 June. Five months later, on 21 November 1852, she died peacefully at 8 Curzon Street, aged eighty-nine. She was buried alongside her sister at Petersham; an inscription by the earl of Carlisle commemorating both sisters was placed on the tombstone.

Until recently Mary Berry lived in the shadow of Horace Walpole. Scholars have now drawn attention to her letters and journals, for the light they throw on women's history, but her own published books remain neglected. An introspective and often melancholy temperament shows through in all her writings, but it is her correspondence with figures such as Anne Damer and the scattered confessional passages of her journals which afford the greatest insight into her sensitive and somewhat wounded spirit. The picture she gives of English society from mid-Georgian to mid-Victorian, as well as French society in the same period, is richly detailed, and gains from its nuanced treatment of individuals such as Napoleon, Mme de Staël, and Princess Caroline. She liked the princess, but regretted that 'she has not a grain of common sense' (*Extracts*, 2.389). Mary was also an amateur artist of moderate attainment; a few of her sketches survive.

CHARLES KENT, *rev.* PAT ROGERS

Sources *Extracts of the journals and correspondence of Miss Berry*, ed. M. T. Lewis, 3 vols. (1865); repr. (1971) · *The Berry papers: being the correspondence hitherto unpublished of Mary and Agnes Berry, 1763–1852*, ed. L. Melville (1914) · Walpole, *Corr.*, vols. 11–12 · V. Surtees, ed., *The grace of friendship: Horace Walpole and the Misses Berry* (1995) · W. S. Lewis, 'Mary Berry's sketch book', *Rescuing Horace Walpole* (1978), 172–80 · P. Noble, *Anne Seymour Damer: a woman of art and fashion* (1908) · d. cert.
Archives BL, corresp., papers, and journals, Add. MSS 37726–37761 · Yale U., Farmington, Lewis Walpole Library, letters, notebook, and MS poem | Castle Howard, North Yorkshire, corresp. with Georgiana, countess of Carlisle · Devon RO, corresp. with Lady Morley · Lpool RO, corresp. with William Roscoe · Morgan L., letters to her sister · Trinity Cam., letters to Lord Houghton · Wellcome L., corresp. with Joanna Baillie · Yale U., Farmington, Lewis Walpole Library, Horace Walpole papers, sketchbook, letters, and documents
Likenesses A. S. Damer, bronze bust, *c*.1793, NPG · A. S. Damer, terracotta bust, 1793, priv. coll. [*see illus.*] · H. Robinson, stipple, pubd 1850 (aged eighty-six; after J. R. Swinton), BM, NPG · photograph, *c*.1850, Yale U., Farmington, Lewis Walpole Library · H. Adlard, stipple (after miniature by Miss Foldsone [Mrs Mee]), NPG · H. Adlard, stipple and line engraving (as a child with her sister; after J. Zoffany), NPG · P. Sandby, drawing (with Agnes Berry), Royal Collection · engraving, repro. in Walpole, *Corr.*, vol. 12 · miniatures, sketches, Yale U., Lewis Walpole Library
Wealth at death the two sisters enjoyed only a small income (approx. £700 p.a.) since death of their father in 1817

Berry, Ronald Anthony [Ron] (**1920–1997**), novelist, was born on 23 February 1920 at Lower Terrace, Blaen-cwm, at the top end of the valley of the Rhondda Fawr, Glamorgan, the son of George Thomas Berry (1896–1977), a colliery fireman, and his wife, Mary Ann, *née* Davies (1896–1972). Both his parents were Welsh-speaking but he had only a little of the language. His paternal grandfather, James Berry, had come to the Klondyke of the Rhondda from rural Oxfordshire in search of work. The family moved shortly after Ron Berry's birth to 17 and then 4 Michaels Road, and in 1947 to 8 Beynons Row, Blaen-cwm.

After leaving school at the age of fourteen, Berry followed his father into the local pits, working as a collier until the outbreak of the Second World War, during which he served in both the army and the merchant navy. An injury to his knee while playing for Swansea City in 1943 put an end to a promising career as a footballer and shortly afterwards he went absent without leave from the ordnance corps, only to be caught by the military police

on his own doorstep. A born rebel, he put a good deal of effort into 'ducking and dodging' (his habitual phrase), trying to keep out of authority's way, and remained sceptical of all systems and conventional behaviour throughout his life. He spent some years as a carpenter, a steelworker, and a navvy in Wales and England and, 'thick-set, pigeon-toed and peasant-fisted' (autobiography), took up professional boxing, but was often unemployed.

Berry married Ethel Irene (Rene) Jones (*b*. 1928) on 12 July 1947, and they had five children. He was prevented from finding regular work by chronic ill health, but began writing poems, essays, and stories. After a year at Coleg Harlech, a residential college of further education for mature students, and another at Shoreditch College, where he read avidly and honed his left-wing political views in endless argument with staff and fellow students, he returned to the Rhondda in 1955, settling in Treherbert, where he spent the rest of his life at 1 Ael-y-bryn. A gruff man, he remained profoundly suspicious of academic exegesis of his writing and was so disenchanted with politicians that he never once voted in a general election.

Back in the Rhondda, and while working during the day as assistant manager at the swimming baths, Berry wrote his first novel, *Hunters and Hunted* (1960), which was soon followed by *Travelling Loaded* (1963). The main characters in both novels are feckless and mainly concerned with sex, boozing, and drawing the dole. The world of drifting, libidinous, hedonistic labourers was one which Ron Berry was to make his own. The Rhondda of his stories is unlike that of any other Welsh novelist: it is economically more prosperous (before the closing of the mines), and its people are more sophisticated and less concerned with politics and religion than those of, say, Rhys Davies or Gwyn Thomas.

Berry's concern that the old communal values, among men who lived and worked in the same village, were beginning to wither during the post-war period was first expressed in *The Full-Time Amateur* (1966), in which social change proceeds apace as the affluent working class begin to buy cars and television sets, go to bingo, and take holidays abroad. Ron Berry saw himself as their chronicler, lovingly but sometimes caustically recording 'what remains of the past before it sputters out as garbled memory' (autobiography). This threnody for a doomed way of life centred on mining found its fullest expression in *Flame and Slag* (1968), a novel based on the journal of a dying miner whose poignant recollections of the old, coal-bearing Rhondda and its vibrant society are used as counterpoint to the brash ignorance and apathy of his children. Berry's novel *So Long, Hector Bebb* (1970), told in the words of the people closest to him, is a portrait of a second-rate boxer, the revoking of whose licence after a foul in the ring leads to his tragic end.

Despite the fact that five of his novels were published in London by such reputable firms as Hutchinson, W. H. Allen, and Macmillan, Ron Berry was virtually ignored by metropolitan critics and neglected in Wales. It was twenty-six years before his next novel was published.

When Dewi Joshua, the hero of *This Bygone* (1996), is declared redundant, it looks like the end of him and his community. Yet the working class in Berry's novels, for all their shortcomings, adapt, survive, and eventually thrive in changing conditions, so that his work is more a warmhearted affirmation of his belief in them than a rigorous critique. Above all, he drew an authentic portrait of proletarian Wales because he was born into it and never left it. His novels and stories will almost certainly be the last to be written from inside a way of life that is now passing from living memory.

The general indifference to Berry's work took its toll and, together with the osteoarthritis which plagued him, was largely responsible for his rather sour attitude and gruff manner, even towards those who tried to help him. With time on his hands and often short of money, he spent a good deal of his time fly-fishing and birdwatching. One of his last books, *Peregrine Watching* (1987), finely observed and rather less hyperbolic than the novels, was about the return of the peregrine falcon to the Rhondda. His financial difficulties were partially relieved when, in the 1970s, some of his writer friends were instrumental in obtaining a civil-list pension for him. His autobiography, *History is what you Live*, by turns sentimental, darkly humorous, and splenetic, was published posthumously, with an introduction by Dai Smith, in 1998, and his *Collected Stories*, edited by Simon Baker, appeared in 2000. The latter book revealed a short-story writer of considerable power and it is on this showing that Ron Berry's reputation seems likely to rest.

Berry died in East Glamorgan General Hospital, near Pontypridd, on 16 July 1997, and was cremated at Llwydcoed, near Aberdâr, six days later.   MEIC STEPHENS

Sources personal knowledge (2004) · private information (2004) [daughter] · R. Berry, *History is what you live* (1998) · unabridged autobiography, Ron Berry estate

Archives priv. coll., writing, letters, diaries, estate | SOUND University of Glamorgan, interviews by Dai Smith on video and audio tape · BBC documentary *The long road* · BBC documentary 'Ron Berry', *Read all about us*

Likenesses J. 'Chunks' Lewis, oils, *c.*1940, priv. coll. · B. Thomas, bronze bust, *c.*1960, priv. coll. · J. 'Chunks' Lewis, watercolour, *c.*1970, priv. coll. · portrait, priv. coll.

Berry, (Henry) Seymour, Baron Buckland (1877–1928), financier and coal industrialist, was born at 73 Lower Thomas Street, Merthyr Tudful, on 17 September 1877, the eldest of three sons of John Mathias Berry (d. 1917), JP, estate agent and valuer, of Gwaelod-y-garth, Merthyr Tudful, and his wife, Mary Ann (d. 1922), daughter of Thomas Rowe of Pembroke Dock. He was educated locally at Caedraw higher grade school and (as a pupil teacher) at Abermorlais School. He soon left teaching to join his father's business where he stayed for two decades. On 5 September 1907 he married Gwladys Mary, eldest daughter of Simon Sandbrook JP, of Hawthorns, Merthyr Tudful, and they had five daughters. Both he and his wife, as natives and long-term residents of the town, shared a deep interest in the fortunes of Merthyr.

Berry seems to have had no direct involvement with the coal industry until about 1916, at just under forty, when his name first appeared in the *South Wales Coal Annual*. In the next two years he became a major star in what was then the glittering industrial firmament of south Wales. The transformation was not fortuitous: as a protégé of Lord Rhondda, the dominant figure in the Welsh coal industry and trade, Berry had a head start owing to the long family connection through his father, who had several times acted as election agent for Rhondda (when still D. A. Thomas). The initial opportunity was soon greatly added to when Rhondda was persuaded by David Lloyd George to join the wartime government; this necessarily threw much more responsibility and control onto his industrial lieutenants and the shift was given a permanent status with Rhondda's death in July 1918. Once thus provided with the opportunities, Berry's remarkable business gifts flourished, especially in visualizing and negotiating mergers and acquisitions.

After a few years of relative quiet Rhondda had in 1916 launched a new offensive to expand his industrial empire, and in that single year it swallowed at least four major companies (Gwaun-cae-Gurwen; Celtic Collieries; North's Navigation; and D. Davis & Son). Closely involved were the two contemporaries described as Rhondda's protégés—H. S. Berry and the stockbroker Archibald Mitchelson—who 'are on the Boards of several of the companies of which Lord Rhondda is Chairman' (*South Wales Coal Annual*, 1917, 143). Already in 1916, when Rhondda became food controller, Berry was chairman of one of these companies (Celtic Collieries). With his main allies—Mitchelson and D. R. Llewellyn—the campaign of expansion was continued into the 1920s. At one stage on the boards of more than sixty companies, at the time of his death Berry still held a position on about twenty of the larger companies (including the massive steel company of Guest Keen and Nettlefolds, of which he became chairman in 1927). The process was one of financial engineering, but the motivation seems to have been production-orientated: consolidating the coal holdings of various undertakings and, especially, negotiating sales and distribution.

Raised to the peerage in 1926 Berry wished to choose as his title Baron Bwlch, but the authorities refused him Bwlch and he settled for Baron Buckland of Bwlch. It is probably a record of sorts that, despite being from a non-aristocratic family and an unfashionable industrial town, not only he but his two brothers, William Ewert *Berry and (James) Gomer *Berry (later Viscount Camrose and Viscount Kemsley, respectively), attained peerages. Perhaps no less remarkable for a strong-willed and powerful trio, they were mutually supportive: William Berry's first newspaper-owning venture of 1901 derived all of its capital (£100) from a loan by Seymour Berry, and William and his younger brother, also a newspaper tycoon, shared a joint bank account for three decades.

Berry trod a familiar path for Welsh industrialists, from Liberal to Conservative, but it was a Labour-controlled council which in 1923 made him a freeman of the borough in recognition of his many benefactions to Merthyr. Although the council disliked his politics it esteemed him for his civic virtue. He does not seem to have been directly involved in industrial relations, but he was reputed to have helped relieve unemployment distress in his native Merthyr by keeping open the G. K. N. ironworks at Dowlais and by buying a local colliery which was to have been dismantled.

At his country estate, Buckland, Bwlch, Brecknockshire, Berry enjoyed rural pursuits. He died there on 23 May 1928: death resulted instantly from a head injury while he was taking a customary early morning ride—his horse suddenly veered close to a telegraph pole, and he was dashed against it. His funeral service was held on 26 May at the Congregational church, Market Square, Merthyr, of which Berry had been a lifelong member. Vast crowds gathered along the route, in the town, and towards Pontypridd, where he was then cremated. He was survived by his wife and his five daughters, and the barony became extinct on his death. 　　　　　JOHN WILLIAMS

Sources *Western Mail* [Cardiff] (24 May 1928) · *Western Mail* [Cardiff] (28 May 1928) · A. P. Burnett and D. Wilson Lloyd, *The south Wales coalfield* (1921) · *South Wales Coal Annual* (1916–26) · A. Lewis, 'The story of Merthyr General Hospital', *Merthyr Historian*, 4 (1989), 104–30 · *Merthyr Tydfil: a valley community*, Merthyr Teachers Centre Group (1981), 401–5, 411–23, 429–31 · *The Times* (25 May 1928) · *Merthyr Express* (26 May 1928) · Burke, *Peerage* · H. Watkins, 'The magistrates and courts of Merthyr Tydfil, 1600–1977', *Merthyr Historian*, 4 (1989), 104–30 · b. cert. · d. cert.
Likenesses J. Gascombe, statue · photographs, repro. in Burnett and Wilson Lloyd, *The south Wales coalfield* · photographs, repro. in *Western Mail* (24 May 1928)
Wealth at death £1,116,447 14s. 9d.: probate, 8 April 1929, CGPLA Eng. & Wales

Sidney Malcolm Berry (1881–1961), by Howard Coster, 1950s

Berry, Sidney Malcolm (1881–1961), Congregational minister, was born on 25 July 1881 at Southport, Lancashire, the younger son of Charles Albert Berry (1852–1899) and his wife, Mary Agnes Martin. He was always proud to think of himself as a Lancastrian. His father was then becoming widely known as a minister to large and flourishing Congregational churches in Bolton and then at Queen Street, Wolverhampton, and a preacher of great power. His fame crossed the Atlantic, where the Plymouth Church, Brooklyn, invited him to succeed Henry Ward Beecher, an honour he declined, and in later years Sidney himself also declined a similar invitation.

Charles Berry's early death at forty-seven at Wolverhampton, while in the high tide of his ministry, greatly affected his young son, then eighteen. Berry determined to follow him into the Congregational ministry, and from Tettenhall College, Wolverhampton, went up to Clare College, Cambridge, to read history, in which he was in the second classes in part one (1902) and part two (1903). He went on to Mansfield College, Oxford (1903), then under the principalship of Andrew Martin Fairbairn. Mansfield College and its welfare always had a prime place in Berry's affections. He was chairman of the college council for twenty-five years.

Berry was ordained at the Oxted Congregational Church in Surrey in 1906, and in 1909 was called to Chorlton-cum-Hardy, Manchester, and then in 1912 to Carr's Lane Chapel, in the heart of Birmingham, a pastorate made famous by R. W. Dale. He married in 1907 Helen, daughter of John Logan JP of Cambridge, and they had two daughters.

Sidney Berry was now launched on a civic and national career in addition to the pastoral cares of his large congregation. In Birmingham he had his initiation into public life, while in the country his personal charm and wit as a preacher made him much sought after for the notable occasions of church life. To take him away from a great pastorate, as the Congregational Union of England and Wales successfully did in 1923, was thought by some to be a disservice to Congregationalism as a whole. But Berry was persuaded—perhaps in loyalty to his father's memory, who had declined a similar invitation in 1893—that he had a duty to serve as the union's secretary, and so he went to the Memorial Hall in London where he stayed until 1948. For Congregationalism it was a revolutionary period. The independency of the Congregational churches was gradually reshaping itself into a more centralized fellowship, which carried responsibility for one another's churches and for their ministers. The moderational system, started in 1919, had proved its worth, and the £500,000 given through the Forward Movement (1925) helped to raise the standards of stipends, as did the later creation of the Home Churches Fund (1948), which made the regular income for ministerial maintenance a responsibility of the local county unions. Berry also took his share in raising the post-war Reconstruction Fund of £500,000.

Sidney Berry saw his task mainly as a *pastor pastorum*, welcoming his fellow churchmen for consultation to the Memorial Hall as members of a family. In return he was welcomed in local churches with enthusiasm. He tended to gird under the routine of committee work and administration, but he had the gift of discerning the leadership of other people, and was adroit in using it.

Berry gave considerable study to the art and style of preaching, and his Warrack lectures, entitled *Vital Preaching* (1936), delivered to theological students in the universities of Aberdeen and Glasgow, are a fine exposition of his methods and one of the best examples of homiletical skill at work. He also wrote religious meditations for the London *Sunday Times*. Glasgow made him an honorary DD in 1936.

In public as well as church affairs Sidney Berry was the national leader of English Congregationalism from 1923 to 1948. He was moderator of the National Free Church Council (1934–7) and chairman of the Congregational Union (1947), supported the moves for a British Council of Churches (1942), and was present at the Lausanne faith and order meeting (1927) and at the World Assemblies at Amsterdam (1948) and Evanston (1954).

But Berry was no over-zealous ecumenist. He believed that his best service for the cause of church unity was to nurture the life and witness of the Congregational churches and, if possible, to foster their union with the Presbyterian Church of England. It was this union he worked for through all its set-backs over fifteen years from 1932 to 1947, and he would have rejoiced in the eventual union of the two churches as the United Reformed church in 1972.

Berry's secretaryship of the Congregational Union coincided with the economic and political crises which preceded the war of 1939–45. The grave unemployment in the industrial areas of the north and south Wales, where the strength of Congregationalism lay, threatened church stability, and from the Memorial Hall Berry organized much private relief in money and goods.

As a League of Nations man and a convinced supporter of collective security Berry had to face strong pacifist opposition from the younger generation of both ministers and laymen, who accused him of supporting the establishment rather than the Christian pacifist view. At the union assembly in Norwich in 1929 the whole three days' agenda was devoted almost entirely to disarmament and the problems raised by pacifism in the church. The dropping of the atomic bomb on Hiroshima in 1945 produced a further period of frustration and helplessness for the churches, whose only activity could be resolutions of protest.

A fresh career opened before him on his retirement in 1948 when Berry was elected minister-secretary of the reorganized International Congregational Council (1949) which, under him, became a well-organized body for consultation and fellowship. Until 1956 he roamed the world as an ambassador of goodwill to the Congregational churches, and their immense affection for him was shown at a banquet in his honour at the Hartford (Connecticut) assembly in 1958. Berry died in University College Hospital, London, on 2 August 1961.

CECIL NORTHCOTT, rev.

Sources *The Times* (3 Aug 1961) · R. Tudur Jones, *Congregationalism in England, 1662–1962* (1962) · A. Peel, *These hundred years: a history of the Congregational Union of England and Wales, 1831–1931* (1931) · private information (1981) · personal knowledge (1981) · *Congregational Year Book* (1900) · *Congregational Year Book* (1962) · *CGPLA Eng. & Wales* (1961) · E. Kaye, *Mansfield College, Oxford: its origin, history and significance* (1996)
Likenesses F. O. Salisbury, portrait, 1938, Memorial Hall, London, Congregational Library · H. Coster, photograph, 1950–59, NPG [see illus.]

Wealth at death £139,171 2s. 0d.: probate, 12 Sept 1961, *CGPLA Eng. & Wales*

Berry, William (1774–1851), genealogist, was employed from 1793 to 1809 as a writing clerk to the registrar of the College of Arms; in 1810 he brought out a work entitled *Introduction to Heraldry*. On his retirement from that post, he for some time resided in Guernsey, where he published *The History of the Island of Guernsey, Compiled from the Collections of Henry Budd* (1815). After returning to England, he resided at Doddington Place, Kennington, Surrey. His *Genealogia antiqua, or, Mythological and Classical Tables* (1816), dedicated to Lord Grenville, met with some success, and a second, improved edition appeared in 1840. He next published *Encyclopedia Heraldica, or, Complete Dictionary of Heraldry*, brought out in numbers between 1828 and 1840. It embraces the greater part of the contents of the works of Joseph Edmondson (d. 1786) and other writers, with much original matter. In 1832 he began to issue his *Genealogical Peerage of England, Scotland, and Ireland*; this was a carefully compiled family history, with beautifully engraved coats of arms, but it did not receive much support, and after the fourth number, which terminated with an account of the dukes of Rutland, no further parts were printed.

Berry was best known by his contemporaries for his county genealogies of Kent (1830), Sussex (1830), Hampshire (1833), Berkshire, Buckinghamshire, and Surrey (1837), Essex (1839), and Hertfordshire (1842). The three latter volumes were printed lithographically from the handwriting of the author. The first portion of *The County Genealogies, Kent*, was severely reviewed in the *Gentleman's Magazine*, which objected to Berry's calling himself on the title-page 'registering clerk in the College of Arms' (he was actually 'writing clerk'). He consequently brought an action for libel against Messrs J. B. Nichols & Son, the publishers of the magazine. The trial took place in the court of king's bench before Lord Tenterden on 1 November 1830, when, although Berry was represented by Henry Brougham, afterwards the lord chancellor, the jury, without hearing any rebutting evidence, almost immediately gave a verdict in favour of the defendants. Berry died at his son's residence, Spencer Place, Brixton, on 2 July 1851, aged seventy-seven, having survived his wife by two months.

G. C. BOASE, rev. MYFANWY LLOYD

Sources *GM*, 1st ser., 99/2 (1829), 99–101 · *GM*, 1st ser., 100/2 (1830), 409–16 · Watt, *Bibl. Brit.* · Allibone, *Dict.* · Boase, *Mod. Eng. biog.*
Archives BL, index to his Essex pedigrees, Add. MS 33527 · BL, pedigrees of English families, Add. MSS 15445–15450

Berry, William Ewert, first Viscount Camrose (1879–1954), newspaper proprietor, was born on 23 June 1879 at Gwaelod-y-garth, Merthyr Tudful, the second of the three sons of John Mathias Berry (d. 1917), an estate agent and a Liberal alderman, and his wife, Mary Ann (d. 1922), the daughter of Thomas Rowe, of Pembroke Dock. Leaving school at fourteen, Berry joined the *Merthyr Times*, moving on to neighbouring newspapers in order to widen his experience. Having learned his trade in local journalism, in 1898 he was appointed a City reporter on the *Investors' Guardian*. Unfortunately this lucrative post was short-lived, and a chastened Berry spent three months in the capital out of work before finally being taken on by the Commercial Press Association. Having spotted a gap in the magazine market, in 1901 Berry launched his first commercial venture, investing £100 borrowed from an equally ambitious elder brother, (Henry) Seymour *Berry (1877–1928), fledgeling industrialist and future Baron Buckland. At first the tyro owner–editor doubled up as *Advertising World*'s sole contributor. He was also the advertising manager, and the sub-editor: the printrooms of the valleys had clearly provided a thorough grounding in the mechanics of production. Confident of early success, Berry brought to London his younger brother (James) Gomer *Berry (1883–1968), who later became a press baron in his own right as Viscount Kemsley.

When after four years William Berry decided to sell *Advertising World*, he saw a substantial return upon his initial investment. Innate financial acumen ensured that the next publishing company was sufficiently diverse to satisfy the burgeoning market for sports and leisure magazines. A lifelong love of the ring was reflected in the time and effort William put in to the successful launch of *Boxing* in 1909. In 1905 he married Mary Agnes (d. 1962), eldest daughter of Thomas Corns; they had four sons and four daughters.

Although William and Gomer Berry enjoyed a remarkably harmonious working partnership, the elder sibling was always in the driving seat. In both Fleet Street and the City invidious comparisons were invariably made, with Gomer dismissed as narrow-minded, unimaginative, and a pale shadow of his profit-hungry brother. Nevertheless, it took both men to establish their partnership as a major newspaper chain. An insatiable seven-day demand for news from the western front after the outbreak of the First World War convinced them that the moment was right to acquire the *Sunday Times*. In 1915 the least distinguished of the quality Sundays had seen sales slump to about 20,000 a week—less than a tenth of *The Observer's* circulation. When Gomer succeeded William as editor-in-chief in 1937, the *Sunday Times* was outselling its historic rival by nearly 70,000 copies a week.

The purchase in 1919 of the St Clement's Press, and its City flagship the *Financial Times*, further raised the Berrys' profile. Not surprisingly, therefore, they were assiduously courted by the circle surrounding the then prime minister, Lloyd George. One consequence was that in 1921 William Berry became a baronet. By buying up a variety of ailing enterprises, Berry expanded his business interests to cover a wide spectrum of media activities, ranging from Kelly's directories to the Gaumont-British film studios. Yet the secret of his company's success remained its strong regional presence, with the 1920s marked by the relentless and ruthless acquisition of provincial titles. From 1922 to 1932 the Berrys and Lord Rothermere were in fierce competition to take over the nation's few surviving independent morning and evening newspapers. One consequence was a spate of closures and a severe reduction in the number of firms and titles. Both sides eventually agreed upon a crude division of regional influence, but neutrals judged Rothermere the loser. The latter made a

costly tactical error in selling the Hulton chain to Allied Newspapers, a consortium established in 1924 by the Berrys and the owner of the *Midland Evening Telegraph*, Sir Edward Iliffe. The Hulton titles included the *Daily Dispatch*, the *Manchester Evening Chronicle*, and the *Sunday Chronicle* (the *Sunday News* was later acquired and merged with the *Sunday Graphic*, bought shortly after the war). At the same time a subsidiary company, Allied Northern Newspapers, was establishing a major presence across the north of England, as well as in Glasgow and Aberdeen. The Berrys' enthusiasm for rationalization and cost-cutting was best illustrated in Cardiff, where the two morning and the two evening papers were merged, leaving the *Western Mail* as the dominant voice in south Wales.

By 1932 Rothermere's Associated Newspapers controlled seventeen daily and Sunday newspapers, and had a major interest in three others. However, his great rivals boasted twenty-seven titles, notwithstanding Iliffe's personal fiefdom in the midlands, as well as their ownership of Amalgamated Press, purchased from Lord Northcliffe's executors in 1926 under the nose of Rothermere, his younger brother. The latter's loss was the Berry brothers' gain: Amalgamated Press boasted over seventy magazines, a highly lucrative encyclopaedia and book section, and in south London three large printing works and paper mills. To consolidate what was intended as a wholly integrated publishing operation Allied Newspapers next acquired Edward Lloyd Ltd, then one of the largest paper mills in the world. Offsetting these profitable enterprises were the steel and coal holdings inherited after the eldest Berry brother, Lord Buckland, died as the result of a riding accident in 1928. Only two years earlier William had been forced to give up riding after he had suffered a similar accident.

The Berry brothers had in less than twenty-five years established a vast and diverse media conglomerate; and yet it was not until 1927 that they finally acquired a major London-based daily newspaper. The *Daily Telegraph* had been a great Victorian success story, setting high standards in its news reporting and attracting suburban middle-class readers. A commitment to solid tory values, plus a reputation for extensive coverage of both major sporting events and salacious court cases, ensured daily sales of nearly 300,000 by the early 1890s. By the late 1920s, however, sales had slipped to about 84,000, and the *Daily Telegraph* was in urgent need of modernization. Reluctant to invest, the paper's chief proprietor, Lord Burnham, suggested a quick sale to Allied Newspapers. Thus on 1 January 1928 William Berry at last assumed editorial responsibility for a 'quality' national newspaper with enormous potential. While retaining the *Telegraph's* unequivocal centre-right politics, Berry nevertheless made key editorial and personnel changes, as well as updating the paper's type and format. Not that these changes extended to the front page, which contained news for the first time only in April 1939. Sales slowly grew, and then doubled to 200,000 after the price was halved to 1d. on 1 December 1930. The *Daily Telegraph's* claim to be an up-market leader derived from its ability throughout the years of the National Government to gain readers without having to rely upon the gimmicks and special offers favoured by its more populist rivals. Within seven years circulation had reached 637,000, and on the eve of the Second World War it had increased to 750,000.

In October 1937 Berry took over the *Morning Post*, the *Telegraph*'s creaking and penurious rival. He paid only £150,000 for the title, but honoured the *Morning Post*'s multiple debts, and provided pensions as well as posts for over half of the displaced editorial staff. His sympathy for unemployed journalists, rooted in his own experience as a young man, belied his reputation as a tough entrepreneur. He genuinely disliked shedding staff, generously rewarding loyalty. Berry respected long service and technical expertise, hence his preference for well-established, experienced men in key editorial posts: Colin Coote was appointed editor of the *Daily Telegraph* in 1942 after many years at *The Times*, and was pleasantly surprised by the proprietorial light touch. Berry's generally sound judgement and reluctance to interfere contrasted sharply with his Fleet Street peers, not least his own brother.

In 1929, on the recommendation of Stanley Baldwin, Berry was elevated to the peerage, as Baron Camrose of Long Cross, and it is as Lord Camrose that he is better known. Antipathy towards Rothermere was a factor in Camrose's continued loyalty to the former prime minister, particularly when the Empire Crusade in 1930–31 threatened Baldwin's leadership of the Conservative Party. A close working relationship culminated at the time of the abdication in Baldwin choosing the *Daily Telegraph* rather than *The Times* as the unofficial conduit of ministerial opinion.

Camrose was similarly loyal to Neville Chamberlain, as indeed was Gomer Berry, by now Lord Kemsley. However, after the 1938 Czech crisis the two brothers would increasingly disagree over foreign policy, with Camrose encouraging the *Daily Telegraph*'s sceptical, even hostile, view of the Munich agreement. He urged Chamberlain to bring Winston Churchill back into government, calling for a much stiffer line towards Germany. Meanwhile Kemsley endorsed Downing Street's efforts to keep negotiating with the Nazi regime, going so far as to meet Hitler in Bayreuth as late as July 1939. Such profound differences over appeasement were not unduly damaging to Allied Newspapers, as the company had been amicably dissolved in 1937. Each partner needed a distinct raft of holdings to pass on to his heirs, and Camrose assumed sole control of the *Daily Telegraph*, the *Financial Times*, and Amalgamated Press. In consequence, his brother now became proprietor of the *Sunday Times*.

Whatever his views on foreign policy, Camrose was insistent that Neville Chamberlain should remain prime minister. Personal affection and patriotic duty meant acceptance of Chamberlain's request that he sort out press relations within a then chaotic Ministry of Information. However, he resigned as chief assistant to the minister as soon as he had cut a swathe through several layers of bureaucracy, and at the same time rendered himself redundant. Camrose was shaken by Chamberlain's

departure in May 1940, yet by that time he had already forged a close relationship with Churchill. Again loyalty brought reward, and he became a viscount in 1941, followed by his brother four years later. The *Daily Telegraph* supported Churchill, in and out of office, albeit not as slavishly as Kemsley's *Daily Sketch*. After July 1945, its circulation boosted by the war to about 1.4 million, the *Daily Telegraph* tested a Labour government increasingly sensitive to middle-class discontent. During this period Camrose acquired serialization rights for Churchill's wartime memoirs as well as negotiating their publication in the United States. Having secured Churchill a $1 million deal, Camrose then ensured that in June 1953 Fleet Street remained silent about the ageing premier's severe stroke.

Camrose himself wrote only one volume. An uninspiring and unenlightening text, advertised originally as a reference book, which in format it resembles, *British Newspapers and their Controllers* (1947) was Camrose's contribution to the debate initiated by the royal commission on the press (1947–9). Writing was no doubt a distraction from making money, as were sailing and motoring, his two principal hobbies once he had abandoned the saddle. Yet, for a man who appeared to take himself so seriously, Camrose appears to have been good company: witness his popularity as an after-dinner speaker and his appreciation of a good joke.

Viscount Camrose died in the Royal South Hampshire Hospital, Southampton, on 15 June 1954, and was cremated at Woking on the 18th. His eldest son, John Seymour Berry (1909–1995), inherited the title, and at the same time became deputy chairman of the *Daily Telegraph*. Again, however, the driving force was the second son, Michael Berry (made a life peer, Lord Hartwell, in 1968), who was editor-in-chief from 1954 until 1986, when the paper was sold in straitened circumstances to the Canadian media magnate Conrad Black. The family had offloaded Amalgamated Press as early as 1958. Thus, less than forty years after his death, William Berry's great media empire was no more.   ADRIAN SMITH

Sources Lord Hartwell, *William Camrose: giant of Fleet Street* (1992) • D. Hart-Davis, *The house the Berrys built: inside the 'Telegraph', 1928–1986* (1990) • S. E. Koss, *The rise and fall of the political press in Britain*, 2 (1984) • Viscount Camrose, *British newspapers and their controllers* (1949) • C. R. Coote, *Editorial: the memoirs of Colin R. Coote* [1965] • D. Hamilton, *Editor-in-chief* (1989) • J. Tunstall, *Newspaper power: the new national press in Britain* (1996) • *Daily Telegraph* archive, London • *CGPLA Eng. & Wales* (1954)

Archives *Daily Telegraph* archive, London, MSS • priv. coll., family archive | HLRO, corresp. with Lord Beaverbrook • HLRO, corresp. with J. C. C. Davidson • Nuffield Oxf., corresp. with Lord Cherwell

Likenesses O. Birley, oils, *c.*1933, NPG • H. Coster, photographs, *c.*1939, NPG • A. Richardson, memorial, 1956, St Paul's Cathedral • O. Birley, oils, *Daily Telegraph*, London • M. Codner, oils, *Daily/Sunday Telegraph* offices, London

Wealth at death £1,480,685 12s. 9d.: probate, 14 Sept 1954, *CGPLA Eng. & Wales*

Bersted, Stephen (*b.* before 1220, *d.* 1287), bishop of Chichester, derived his family name from Bersted, Sussex, part of the archbishop of Canterbury's estate at Pagham, 5 miles south-east of Chichester; nothing is known of his parentage. He studied at Oxford, where he was regent in theology in 1254, and he was a canon and prebendary of Chichester in 1247. As chaplain to Richard Wyche, bishop of Chichester, he must have been deeply affected by Henry III's vindictive treatment of the future saint at the time of Wyche's disputed election. After the baronial take-over in 1258 curbed such interference Bersted, despite being the poorest of the canons, was elected bishop of Chichester, in May or June 1262, and was consecrated on 24 September by Archbishop Boniface of Savoy. In May 1263, together with the bishops of Worcester and Lincoln, he assisted John Gervase, bishop of Winchester (who had also been in Wyche's circle), in the consecration of Henry of Sandwich as bishop of London. Bersted and his companions believed that the provisions of Oxford embodied what constituted good government, and supported the baronial opposition to the king. In March 1264 Bersted and the bishops of Worcester, London, and Winchester represented the barons in talks with Henry III at Brackley and Oxford, and promised that if the king would rule through natives, they would accept the condemnation of the provisions by Louis IX of France in the mise of Amiens (of January 1264). When these terms were rejected he took part at the Dominican priory of Oxford in the excommunication of opponents of the provisions. On 12 May 1264, while the opposing armies were preparing for battle at Lewes, Bersted and a party of friars met the king to propose a compromise allowing for arbitration on disputed points in the provisions by bishops and men of learning, but he was again rebuffed.

After Henry III's defeat Bersted's standing was such that in June he was made one of the triumvirate, with Simon de Montfort and Gilbert de Clare, earl of Gloucester, empowered to nominate the new royal council of nine. He incurred papal hostility, however, by rejecting the command of Guy Foulquois, cardinal-bishop of Sabina and papal legate, to appear before the cardinal at Boulogne, and by refusing to publish the sentence of excommunication against the Montfortians. Bersted was summoned to the parliament of January 1265, and was probably among the bishops who excommunicated opponents of Magna Carta and the new constitution in the following March, but, perhaps disillusioned by the quarrel between Montfort and Clare, he was thereafter no longer active in affairs. After Evesham, Bersted and other bishops were summoned *coram rege* to answer for their support of the king's enemies, and Cardinal Ottobuono, the papal legate, suspended him from office in April 1266, and ordered him to appear before the pope, a decision later deplored by the rebels holding out in Ely. Bersted was the last of the Montfortian bishops to receive the papal pardon on 26 November 1272. After his return to England he seems to have been present at the church council at London in January 1278, which complained about interference by a papal official in English testamentary jurisdiction, and to have attended the first council of Archbishop John Pecham at Reading in July–August 1279, which issued important church legislation. By then he was back in favour, for on 16 June 1276 Edward I attended the magnificent ceremony,

which reputedly cost £1000, at Chichester, in which Bersted assisted Archbishop Robert Kilwardby in the translation of the relics of St Richard of Wyche to a new shrine. No bishop's register has survived to indicate how he administered his diocese, but he is remembered for establishing a short-lived new town of Wardur at Sidlesham in Selsey, near Bersted, which was probably intended to provide Chichester with the harbour it lacked. An exceptionally simple man of great integrity, Bersted was blind in his latter years and died on 21 October 1287.

CLIVE H. KNOWLES

Sources Chancery records · *Ann. mon.*, vols. 2–4 · *The historical works of Gervase of Canterbury*, ed. W. Stubbs, 2: *The minor works comprising the Gesta regum with its continuation, the Actus pontificum and the Mappa mundi*, Rolls Series, 73 (1880) · W. D. Peckham, ed., *The chartulary of the high church of Chichester*, Sussex RS, 46 (1946) · F. M. Powicke and C. R. Cheney, eds., *Councils and synods with other documents relating to the English church, 1205–1313*, 2 vols. (1964) · Emden, *Oxf.* · *CEPR letters*, vol. 1 · E. B. Fryde and others, eds., *Handbook of British chronology*, 3rd edn, Royal Historical Society Guides and Handbooks, 2 (1986)

Berstede, Walter of. *See* Bursted, Sir Walter of (*fl.* 1253–1266).

Bertha (*b. c.*565, *d.* in or after **601**), queen in Kent, consort of Æthelberht, was the daughter of the Merovingian Frankish king Charibert (*d.* 567) who reigned from 561. She was married to the then pagan *Æthelberht (*d.* 616?), son of the king of Kent. 'He received her from her relatives [*parentes*]', wrote Bede, 'on condition that she be allowed to practise her … religion unhindered, with a bishop named Liudhard whom they had provided for her to support her faith' (Bede, *Hist. eccl.*, 1.25). Bede mentions Bertha only here. Last documented as receiving a letter in 601 from Pope Gregory I, Bertha predeceased her husband, or was repudiated: after Æthelberht's death in 616 after a reign of fifty-six years, so Bede says, 'his son Eadbald took his father's wife' (Bede, *Hist. eccl.*, 2.5), but this woman was not Bertha.

Bertha's marriage date is problematic. Gregory of Tours, writing before 580, suggests she was born after her father became king. Her mother was Charibert's wife, Ingoberg (*d.* 589), repudiated some time before his death: Bertha must therefore have been born by about 565. The *parentes* from whom Bertha was 'received' did not include her father. She probably married about 579, at the earliest. Gregory says that Bertha's mother was, 'I think', sixty-nine when she died, in 589. If so, Ingoberg produced Bertha when well over forty. Gregory did not call Æthelberht a 'king' at the time of his marriage, perhaps, *pace* Bede, as late as *c.*590. Both partners were then royal scions with prospects only.

Pope Gregory I's letters of 595–7 suggest the significant help he expected Merovingian rulers, and especially Queen Brunechildis, to give the mission to England. Bertha's role is less clear. Gregory's letter to her of 601 was perhaps suppressed by Bede to play down Bertha's influence, or, more likely, it was unknown to him (though he reproduced Gregory's letter to Æthelberht). Gregory encouraged Bertha, as queen (*regina*), to use her influence to further the faith. 'You must have [*debuistis*: perhaps translates as "should have"] inclined your husband's mind', and 'this must [*debuit*: perhaps "should"] not have been tardy or difficult for you' (*Gregorii magni registrum*, 9.35). Rather than criticizing Bertha's ineffectiveness, Gregory's ensuing comparison of Bertha with St Helena seems, rather, to urge her to still greater success. The classical topos of the woman persuading her man to virtue was borrowed from St Paul (1 Corinthians 7: 14). Pope Gregory also suggested it to a Lombard queen. Chlothild, Bertha's great-grandmother, was said to have persuaded King Clovis to convert. Queens themselves may have aspired to the role of salutary counsellor. For Bertha, this self-image would have been reinforced by her sense of lineage and by the influence of her own mother: Gregory of Tours, who knew her, calls Ingoberg 'a woman of great wisdom, … constant in … prayers and almsgiving' (*History of the Franks*, 9.26). Thus nurtured, perhaps Bertha did play a key part in persuading Æthelberht to convert, even before 596 (however much later his baptism).

Bertha was almost certainly the mother of Æthelberht's son *Eadbald, whose short-lived apostasy in 616 need not indict Bertha's failure to promote Christianity in Kent. She may also have been the mother of Æthelburh, who married Eadwine of Northumbria; but this is not proven by Bede's statement that Æthelburh, when she fled back to Kent after Eadwine's death in 633, sent her son and stepgrandson to 'her friend' King Dagobert in Francia (Bede, *Hist. eccl.*, 2.20). Kent was closely linked, in any event, with Merovingian Francia. The Frankish influence epitomized by Bertha's marriage, and strengthened by the mission she encouraged, is vividly evoked by a surviving gold medalet, perhaps found at St Augustine's, Canterbury, which was apparently struck for 'her' bishop Liudhard.

JANET L. NELSON

Sources Bede, *Hist. eccl.* · *Gregorii Turonensis opera*, ed. B. Krusch and W. Levison, MGH Scriptores Rerum Merovingicarum, 1/1 (Hanover, 1937–52) · Gregory of Tours, *The history of the Franks*, ed. and trans. L. Thorpe (1974) · *S. Gregorii magni registrum epistularum*, ed. D. Norberg (1982) · A. J. Mason, *The mission of St Augustine to England* (1897) · D. P. Kirby, 'Bede and Northumbrian chronology', *EngHR*, 78 (1963), 514–27 · J. M. Wallace-Hadrill, *Early Germanic kingship in England and on the continent* (1971) · I. N. Wood, *The Merovingian North Sea* (1983) · J. M. Wallace-Hadrill, *Bede's Ecclesiastical history of the English people: a historical commentary*, OMT (1988) · H. Mayr-Harting, *The coming of Christianity to Anglo-Saxon England*, 3rd edn (1991) · D. P. Kirby, *The earliest English kings* (1991) · L. Webster and J. Backhouse, eds., *The making of England: Anglo-Saxon art and culture, AD 600–900* (1991), 23 · S. Hollis, *Anglo-Saxon women and the church* (1992) · I. Wood, 'The mission of Augustine of Canterbury to the English', *Speculum*, 69 (1994), 1–17 · I. Wood, *The Merovingian kingdoms, 450–751* (1994)

Bertheau, Charles (1660–1732), Reformed minister, was born at Montpellier and educated partly in France and partly in the Netherlands. He was admitted to the ministry at the synod held at Vigan in 1681, and shortly afterwards became one of the pastors of the large church of Charenton, Paris. Here worshipped some of the most important Huguenots: 'Its pastors had something of the standing of bishops' (Prestwich, 178). The revocation of the edict of Nantes drove him out of France, and he went to England in 1685. In the following year he was chosen one of the pastors of the French church in Threadneedle Street, London, which adhered to the liturgy and ritual of French Calvinism. He occupied this post for forty-four years.

Contemporaries were impressed by Bertheau's memory and eloquence. Two volumes of his sermons were printed in the Netherlands in 1712 and 1730. Bertheau died in Threadneedle Street on 25 December 1732. He was unmarried, and his principal legatee, after individual bequests, including one of £400 to the poor of his congregation, was his nephew Charles Mercier, who inherited £1000.

F. T. MARZIALS, *rev.* GEOFFREY TREASURE

Sources *Bibliothèque Britannique*, 1 (1733) · E. J. Ciprut, 'Le premier grand temple de Charenton', *Bulletin* [Société de l'Histoire du Protestantisme Français], 114 (1968), 106–13 · *The archives of the French protestant church of London*, Huguenot Society Quarto Series, 50 (1972) · M. Prestwich, 'The Huguenots under Richelieu and Mazarin', *Huguenots in Britain and their French background, 1550–1800*, ed. I. Scouloudi (1987) · *GM*, 1st ser., 2 (1732), 1126 · J. G. de Chauffepié, *Nouveau dictionnaire historique et critique*, 4 vols. (1750–56), 1

Wealth at death £400 to poor of church; £1000 to nephew: will; GM

Berthelet [Berthelot], **Thomas** (*d.* 1555), printer, was probably of French origin, and perhaps related to Jacques Berthelot (*d.* 1541), bookseller at Caen from 1527 and at Rennes from 1539 to 1541. Thomas's name was spelt Berthelot by the College of Arms when granting him a coat of arms, which incorporated the fleur-de-lis. The *Dictionary of National Biography*'s identification of Berthelet with Thomas Bercula is likely to be mistaken. Clair identified the name as a Latin form of Barclay and takes it to refer to Thomas Barclay, servant to John Rastell.

The first mention of 'Berthelett', resident in the parish of St Dunstan, Fleet Street, London, is when he applied on 23 August 1524 for a licence to marry Agnes Langwyth, widow, at St Bride's, also in Fleet Street. On 27 September that year his first book, a small tract by the monk Galfredus Petrus of Bayeux, *Opus sane de deorum dearumque gentilium genealogia* (STC 19816.5) was printed 'at the sign of the Roman Lucrece', Berthelet's premises midway along Fleet Street. At this time printers were being warned against handling books labelled as heretical or seditious, and Berthelet was summoned before the vicar-general in March 1526 for printing *A Devout Treatise upon the Pater noster* and other works, without first submitting them for licence. He later reissued them, having obtained the necessary privileges. In 1528 he printed Thomas Paynell's translation of *Regimen sanitatis Salerni*, one of the most popular medical books, which was widely translated. Between 1531 and 1545 he printed all fifteen of Sir Thomas Elyot's works. Among his later publications were a few yearbooks of Edward III (1527–32; STC 9562, 9565) and Sir Anthony Fitzherbert's *La novel natura brevium* (1534; STC 10958), showing his familiarity with the legal world of Rastell and Pynson.

Berthelet may not have immediately succeeded Richard Pynson (*d.* 1530) as king's printer, for John Rastell printed the statutes of 21 Henry VIII during the closing months of

1529, but he was already holding that office by 22 February 1530 when he was granted the annuity of £4 that went with it. He held the office until Henry's death, printing all statutes and proclamations with exemplary skill and efficiency, and on one occasion being ordered to produce a proclamation immediately, if necessary setting the type himself. His account submitted for payment covering the period 9 December 1541 to 12 June 1543 details not only quantities and costs of proclamations but also special purchases of books for the king, with the style and price of binding. Also king's business were several works fostering uniformity in religion such as the Bishops' Book (1537; STC 5163) and the King's Book (1543; STC 5168), of which multiple editions had to be printed.

Following Henry's death in 1547 Berthelet did not seek to renew his patent as king's printer, which was taken up by the ardent protestant Richard Grafton under Edward VI. Berthelet was granted a coat of arms in 1549, and may have retired to live in his house in the adjacent parish of St Andrew, Holborn. He died in London on 26 September 1555, leaving a second wife, Margaret, and two sons: Edward, a lawyer of Lincoln's Inn, and Anthony, still a minor. His funeral, held at some point before 26 January 1556, was celebrated with great pomp, attended, as Machyn relates, by many priests, clerks, and mourners, and a concourse of his fellow craftsmen in the book trades, although it is not recorded where he was buried. His nephew Thomas Powell, who was free of the Stationers' Company in 1556, ran the business under Berthelet's name for several years. K. F. PANTZER, rev.

Sources E. G. Duff, *A century of the book trade* (1905) · A. W. Reed, *Early Tudor drama* (1926) · C. Clair, 'Thomas Berthelet, royal printer', *Gutenberg Jahrbuch* (1966), 177–81 · *STC, 1475–1640* · PRO, C 66/599, m. 17 · *LP Henry VIII*, 7.535 · BL, Add. MS 28196, fol. 3 · *The diary of Henry Machyn, citizen and merchant-taylor of London, from AD 1550 to AD 1563*, ed. J. G. Nichols, CS, 42 (1848), 95 · Arber, *Regs. Stationers*

Berthon, Edward Lyon (1813–1899), inventor of nautical aids and Church of England clergyman, was born in Finsbury Square, London, on 20 February 1813, the tenth child of Peter Berthon, an army contractor, who was reduced to comparative poverty by the wreck of a number of his ships and the end of the war in 1814. In 1828 Berthon was sent to Liverpool to study surgery under James Dawson (who had just taken over the practice of Berthon's maternal grandfather, Henry Park), where he continued for more than four years. At the end of this time, having become engaged to a niece of Mrs Dawson, he went to Dublin to finish his course at the College of Surgeons; but a violent attack of pneumonia, and, on his recovery, his marriage on 4 June 1834, seem to have ended his medical studies. He spent most of the next six years travelling in France, Switzerland, and Italy.

During this time Berthon occupied himself with mechanical experiments. While at Geneva on his wedding tour—he noted the date, 28 June 1834—he conceived the idea of applying the screw to nautical propulsion. To him it seems to have been absolutely new, and, as far as practical adaptation went, it was so. In the autumn of 1835 he

carried out experiments with twin screws on a model 3 feet long, and developed an effective two-bladed propeller. The model was sent to the Admiralty, which was interested only in full-scale practical trials and it was consequently returned. Berthon never filed a patent, but in 1838 he read of the 'invention' of the screw propeller by Francis Smith, and assumed that Smith had pirated the idea from his sketch in the Patent Office. In 1840 he met Smith and realized that his design was original, and the two men became friends.

By 1841 Berthon had made up his mind to take holy orders. He entered Magdalene College, Cambridge, as a fellow commoner. He wrote that he spent more time in painting than in studying mathematics, and, being married, refused to read for honours. He continued his mechanical experiments, especially with a small gauge for measuring the speed of ships, which he called a 'nautachometer', but which has been more commonly called 'Berthon's log'. By his experiments he rediscovered the hydraulic principle enunciated long before by Bernoulli, of the sucking action of a stream of water crossing the end, or a small orifice near the end, of a pipe. Such a pipe projecting below the bottom of a ship, and acted on by its motion through the water, was made to indicate the speed by the surface level of a column of mercury placed in the cabin. In 1845 Berthon graduated BA (MA 1849), and was ordained and appointed to the curacy of Lymington. From 1847 he was vicar of Holy Trinity, Fareham, Hampshire, where he remained for eight years, making the acquaintance of many naval officers, and continuing his experiments with the log on board the steamers running between Southampton and Jersey. The instrument was shown to be capable of great accuracy; but it was judged too delicate for sea service.

Meanwhile, Berthon devised an instrument for showing exactly the trim of a ship at any moment—that is, whether and how much and in which direction the keel was out of the horizontal—and another for indicating the number of degrees through which the ship rolled. But the most celebrated, the most practically useful of all his inventions, was the collapsible boat, the idea of which first occurred to him after the terrible wreck of the steamer *Orion* off Portpatrick on 29 June 1849. After overcoming many difficulties, he obtained an order from the Admiralty for it to be tried and reported on. The report was adverse, and Berthon, in disgust, resigned his living at Fareham in order to get away from ships and boats. He was shortly afterwards presented to Romsey, where Lord Palmerston was his parishioner; and for many years he devoted himself to the restoration of the church.

In 1873, at the instigation of Samuel Plimsoll, he returned to the design of collapsible boats, and this time with complete success. The invention was taken up by Admiral Sir William Robert Mends, the director of transports at the Admiralty, and before the end of the year Berthon had Admiralty orders of more than £15,000. The business rapidly expanded; several boats were taken by Sir George Nares to the Arctic in 1875; while eight of the first made were sent to Gordon at Khartoum. After a few years the business was converted into a company. In 1881–2 Berthon made a return voyage to the Cape of Good Hope in the Union Company's steamer *Spartan*, partly for the trip, and partly also to give a thorough trial to the trim and roll indicators. In 1885 he went to New York to promote the sale of the boats, but found the duty prohibitive. In his later years he wrote his reminiscences, *A Retrospect of Eight Decades* (1899). He died at his home, the vicarage, Romsey, on 27 October 1899, of a cold caught on a visit to Jersey. His wife had predeceased him many years earlier, leaving several children. Berthon's perseverance, his pursuit of an alternative career, and his wide-ranging interests, notably in astronomy, reflected the environment in which he worked. The collapsible boat made a significant contribution to life-saving and riverine exploration.

J. K. LAUGHTON, rev. ANDREW LAMBERT

Sources E. L. Berthon, *A retrospect of eight decades* (1899) · *CGPLA Eng. & Wales* (1899)
Likenesses two photographs, repro. in Berthon, *Retrospect*
Wealth at death £2584 8s. 1d.: probate, 9 March 1900, *CGPLA Eng. & Wales*

Berthoud, Sir Eric Alfred (1900–1989), oil executive and diplomatist, was born on 10 December 1900 in Kensington, London, the second son and third child in a family of four sons and two daughters of Alfred Edward Berthoud, of the private merchant bank Coulon, Berthoud & Co., and his wife, Hélène Christ, who came from a Swiss-Alsatian banking family. As a boy at Gresham's School, Holt, Norfolk, Berthoud was greatly helped by his headmaster, G. W. S. Howson, who in 1914 found ways to keep him at the school when his father's bank collapsed and his relatives proposed moving him to Switzerland. In 1918 he went up to Magdalen College, Oxford, where he played hockey for the university, did well at other sports, and took his degree in chemistry in 1922, paying his way with tutoring during vacation and further help from Howson. His father, an alcoholic, died in 1920.

After four years with the Anglo-Austrian Bank in Vienna and Milan (1922–6), Berthoud joined the Anglo-Persian Oil Company (later BP), serving in Paris (1926–9). In 1927 he married Ruth Tilston (d. 1988), daughter of Sir Charles Bright, electrical engineer and fellow of the Royal Society of Edinburgh, and granddaughter of Sir Charles Tilston Bright, also an electrical engineer. They had a son who died in infancy, and two more sons and two daughters. Berthoud then moved with the Anglo-Persian Oil Company to Berlin (1929–35) and back to Paris (1935–8). On leaving Germany he sent a detailed memorandum to the director of military intelligence in London on Hitler's military build-up. When war began he joined the petroleum division of the Ministry of Fuel and Power, and by November 1939 he was installed at the British legation in Bucharest. His colleagues included the eccentric Edmund Hall-Patch, who was later helpful to his career. Berthoud's instructions were to impede the supply of Romanian oil to Germany by non-violent means such as diplomatic pressure, pre-emptive buying, manipulating prices, and cornering railcars, barges, and tankers on the Danube. These

Sir Eric Alfred Berthoud (1900–1989), by Elliott & Fry, 1952

and other British activities in Romania worried the Germans for a time, but both German vulnerability and British ability to exploit it were exaggerated in London; Berthoud himself was in agreement with the policy, but realistic as to its effectiveness, compared with other factors outside British control. In January 1941, by which time Romania had effectively thrown in its lot with Germany, Britain broke off relations and the legation in Bucharest was closed. Berthoud spent the next four years in a variety of countries undertaking various tasks, all related to the objective of securing oil for the allies and denying it to the axis powers. One sensitive mission was to the USSR, to which he travelled three times by adventurous routes in 1941–2. He soon became convinced of the need to support the USSR by all possible means—this at a time when many in London were disinclined to spend scarce resources on what they saw as a hopeless cause.

In 1945 Berthoud was in charge of the economic division of the British element of the Allied Control Commission for Austria. He then worked on east European peace treaties, on problems affecting the Anglo-Persian Oil Company, and finally on the Marshall plan, where his superiors valued his hard work and negotiating skill. After a long spell as assistant under-secretary in the Foreign Office (1948–52), he could have moved up to the deputy under-secretary's seat, but preferred to go as ambassador to Denmark (1952–6), where he made many friends. As ambassador in Warsaw (1956–60) he sympathized with the strivings of the ordinary Polish people, while unconditionally condemning the regime. He was appointed CMG in 1945 and KCMG in 1954, and retired in May 1960. From

1969 he was deputy lieutenant of Essex. In retirement BP made him a non-executive director on certain of its regional boards. Among other things he was deeply involved in the United World colleges, the new University of Essex, and the Anglo-Polish round-table conferences.

With his athletic build, countryman's face, and ready smile, Berthoud was a more complex character than he looked. Only one-quarter British by blood, he was as proud of his continental connections as of his own compensating 'Britishness'. As an ambassador he exacted a degree of deference (and punctuality) which some found excessive. He could be thick-skinned and overbearing, but there was a vein of sensitivity in him too, nourished by a protestant faith which strengthened as he grew older. He and his family lived in a series of houses in Essex and finally in Suffolk, where he enjoyed cricket and country sports to the full. Berthoud died in Tunbridge Wells, Kent, on 29 April 1989, his wife having predeceased him by a year.

JULIAN BULLARD, rev.

Sources E. Berthoud, *An unexpected life* (privately printed, 1980) · W. N. Medlicott, *The economic blockade*, 2 vols. (1952) · *Documents on German foreign policy, 1918–1945: from the archives of the German foreign ministry, ser. D, 8: The war years, September 4 1939 – March 18 1940* (1954), 502ff · personal knowledge (1996) · private information (1996) · *CGPLA Eng. & Wales* (1989)
Likenesses Elliott & Fry, photograph, 1952, NPG [*see illus.*]
Wealth at death £343,172: probate, 27 June 1989, *CGPLA Eng. & Wales*

Bertie, Sir Albemarle, baronet (1755–1824), naval officer, was born on 20 January 1755. Although very close in age and following the same service, he was not a blood relative of Thomas Bertie, who was born Thomas Hoar. Having joined the navy as a youth, Albemarle Bertie was made lieutenant on 20 December 1777, and in the battle of Ushant (27 July 1778) was first lieutenant of the frigate *Fox*, which acted as a repeating ship. On 10 September, 120 miles SSW of Ushant, the *Fox* was captured by the much stronger French frigate *Junon* and all her surviving officers and men became prisoners of war. In January 1779, however, Bertie was able to return to England to give evidence at the trials of Keppel and Palliser, which told heavily against the latter.

Although promoted to commander on 3 June 1780, Bertie was unemployed until March 1782, when with a change of government he was made post captain (21 March) and given command of the frigate *Crocodile* in the channel. The date of his marriage has not been located, but it was after 4 June 1782, the date of a 'settlement made previously to my marriage' and mentioned in his will; his wife Emma (*d.* before 1824) was the daughter of James Modyford Heywood, esquire, of Maristow in Devon. In 1790 Bertie commanded the frigate *Latona*; in 1792–3 he commanded a ship of the line, the *Edgar* (74 guns), in the Channel Fleet under Lord Howe; and in 1794 he commissioned the *Thunderer* (74 guns), in which he had a small share of the battle of 1 June 1794. In 1795, still in the *Thunderer*, he was with Sir John Borlase Warren in the Bay of Biscay; then in rapid succession he commanded the

Renown, the *Windsor*, and the *Malta*, all based in the channel.

Bertie became rear-admiral of the white on 23 April 1804 and of the red on 9 November 1805. On 28 April 1808 he was promoted vice-admiral of the blue, and in that rank he was sent out as commander-in-chief at the Cape of Good Hope. Soon after becoming vice-admiral of the red on 31 July 1810 he overreached himself: in October, when an attack on Île de France (Mauritius) was being prepared by the East Indies squadron, on his own initiative he went in the frigate *Africaine* to join the expedition. This was a large joint operation, with military forces from India authorized by Lord Minto, the governor-general, and led by Major-General the Hon. John Abercromby. The troops were accompanied by twenty-one vessels under Vice-Admiral William O'Bryen Drury, commander-in-chief of the East India station, whose involvement contravened Minto's advice. Although both he and Bertie were vice-admirals, Drury's rank was of the blue, junior to Bertie's. Thus Drury had to cede the chief command to Bertie. The operation was a success, for the French naval force had been previously overpowered, and the surveys necessary to ensure a safe landing had been made. On shore the troops found no enemy capable of withstanding them, and the island surrendered on 3 December. Since Bertie's active share in the enterprise was extremely small, Drury was naturally furious that someone else should pluck his laurels from him, and he wrote with great bitterness to the Admiralty (8 November 1810), saying he considered himself 'insulted and injured' (*DNB*).

Bertie returned to the Cape, and shortly afterwards received orders to return to England, apparently largely because of a disagreement with the local commissioner of the navy. On his arrival he wrote to the secretary of the Admiralty (28 March 1811) requesting, almost demanding, a full inquiry into his official conduct. However, this was coldly refused. Drury meanwhile had died (6 March 1811), his promotion to vice-admiral of the white being gazetted on 1 August, before his death was known. Bertie's complaint lay dormant until a ministerial crisis in the following year, when the verdict of the outgoing Admiralty was immediately reversed, and (because of the capture of Mauritius rather more than his other services) he was created a baronet on 9 December 1812. His chosen coat of arms depicted three battering rams. However, he had no further command, and though he and his wife (who predeceased him) had two daughters, Emma and Louisa Frances, they had no sons; the title therefore did not succeed him. His final home was at Donnington in Berkshire. He became an admiral of the blue on 4 June 1814, was made KCB on 2 January 1815, achieved the rank of admiral of the white on 19 July 1821, and died on 24 February 1824.

STEPHEN HOWARTH

Sources *DNB* · will, PRO, PROB 11/1682, sig. 136 · D. Syrett and R. L. DiNardo, *The commissioned sea officers of the Royal Navy, 1660–1815*, rev. edn, Occasional Publications of the Navy RS, 1 (1994) · J. Burke and J. B. Burke, *A genealogical and heraldic history of the extinct and dormant baronetcies of England, Ireland, and Scotland*, 2nd edn (1841) ·

A. B. Sainsbury, *The Royal Navy day by day*, 2nd edn [n.d., *c*.1991] · C. N. Parkinson, *War in the eastern seas, 1793–1815* (1954) **Likenesses** Bartolozzi, Landseer, Ryder, and Stow, group portrait, line engraving, pubd 1803 (after R. Smirke), BM, NPG

Bertie, Charles (1640/41–1711), diplomat and treasurer of the ordnance, was the fifth son of Montague *Bertie, second earl of Lindsey (1607/8–1666), and his first wife, Martha (*bap.* 1605, *d.* 1641), daughter of Sir William *Cokayne of Rushton, Northamptonshire, and the widow of John Ramsay, first earl of Holdernesse. Bertie attended a school run by Dr Charles Croke at Amersham until December 1650, when Croke was reported to have 'given over school' (*Ancaster MSS*, 425). He then probably attended Westminster School as he was reported to have studied there under the eminent headmaster, Richard Busby. He entered the Middle Temple on 25 October 1658, but he seems to have completed his education with a sojourn abroad, arriving in Dieppe in July 1660, touring extensively in France in 1660–62, and visiting Geneva.

Bertie seems to have been set upon a diplomatic career and to this end he served in 1664–5 as attaché at Madrid under Sir Richard Fanshawe, who wrote to the king of his 'virtues and extraordinary qualities' (*Supplementary Lindsey MSS*, 269–70). Bertie acquired both a naval commission as a second lieutenant and an army commission as a captain in the Coldstream Guards in 1668. In 1670 he was travelling in northern Europe—visiting Denmark, Sweden, and possibly Danzig and Poland—and this may again have been with an eye to a diplomatic posting, for in March 1671 he was named envoy-extraordinary to Denmark. He departed in April and stopped in Hamburg on the way. After completing negotiations on reparations due for an attack on an English ship in the sound, he set out for home in February 1672. In July 1672 he was on board the *St Michaels*.

The appointment in 1673 of his brother-in-law Sir Thomas Osborne (later earl of Danby) as lord treasurer provided a new opportunity for Bertie, as in July he was named secretary to the Treasury. For the next six years he acted as Danby's trusted administrator. Also in 1673 Bertie purchased Uffington, 2 miles from Stamford, Lincolnshire. On 2 September 1674 Bertie married Mary (*c.*1650–1679), daughter of Peter Tryon, of Harringworth, Northamptonshire, the widow of Sir Samuel Jones (*d.* 1673), of Courteenhall, Northamptonshire. They had one son and one daughter. Mary Bertie died on 13 January 1679.

Bertie was keen to add to his offices, securing a reversion to the office of treasurer of the ordnance in 1675 and a reversion for the auditor of the receipt in the exchequer in 1676. In April 1675 he had failed to win a by-election at Grimsby, but he was successful in the Stamford by-election of February 1678. His most notable parliamentary action was to oppose the motion for Danby's impeachment and the production of evidence of French collusion with the opposition. Given his support for Danby, Bertie was unable to win the seat at the election following the dissolution of parliament in January 1679. With the opposition in full cry Bertie became embroiled in the attacks upon Danby, and particularly upon the distribution of secret service money for which he had been responsible since 1676. He was summoned before a House of Commons committee investigating secret service money in April, but he refused to divulge any information without the king's command. He maintained this stance when called to the bar of the Commons on 10 May and was committed to the custody of the serjeant-at-arms for his pains. He remained in custody until the dissolution of parliament in July 1679.

Bertie was appointed envoy-extraordinary to Germany in summer 1681. He left England in October, and so was conveniently out of the way when a new parliament reassembled later that month. He visited many German states before he was recalled after the dissolution of the third Exclusion Parliament, returning to England in June 1681. As luck would have it the death of the treasurer of the ordnance in August saw Bertie succeed to the reversion of that office. The accession of James II saw Bertie appointed to local office in both Boston and Stamford, and regain his parliamentary seat at the latter. He had also been building at Uffington, for Danby's son recorded in August 1687 that 'Uncle Charles has built himself a noble home' (*Buckinghamshire MSS*, 446).

Bertie seems to have retained royal favour during James's reversal of policy in 1687–8, remaining a JP and being nominated as a court candidate in the abortive elections envisaged for later in 1688. However, he was in Yorkshire with Danby during summer 1688 when plans were being laid for William of Orange's intervention in English politics. Bertie was sent down to London in October 1688, probably to remove royal suspicions. He was an important witness to the last days of James's rule, and was even seen as a possible mediator between James and Danby should the king seek to throw himself on the mercy of the northern lords. With James II's final departure Bertie was able to switch allegiance without difficulty because of his close connection with Danby, and he secured election to the convention of 1689. In the lower house he supported Danby's proposal that Mary should be the sole monarch, and consequently voted for the motion from the Lords that the throne was not vacant.

Bertie continued to sit for Stamford and retained his ordnance office, but with Danby (now marquess of Carmarthen) in government he hankered for a more important role. He attempted to succeed William Jephson as secretary to the Treasury in 1691, but was rebuffed. He spoke frequently in the Commons in 1691–3, usually on the tory side, but he had to be content with relatively small roles—assistant in the corporation for setting the poor to work (Carmarthen was the first governor) in 1691; secretary to the justice in eyre (his half-brother, James Bertie, earl of Abingdon), a post worth £600 p.a. in 1693; and commissioner for managing the Million Act in 1694. He signed the Association in 1696 but continued to vote with the tories, opposing the attainder of Sir John Fenwick later that year. When Carmarthen (now duke of Leeds) was finally removed from office in 1699 Bertie lost his ordnance office, but he was reinstated in 1702 following the accession of Queen Anne. He retained his post until dismissed in 1705, probably for supporting the tack of the Occasional Conformity Bill to a supply measure. Not surprisingly, he voted against the impeachment of Henry Sacheverell in 1710.

Although he continued to sit as an MP, Bertie's final years were plagued with ill health. Shortly before his death he wrote to Dr Sloane asking about treatment for a 'bad stomach' (BL, Sloane 4077, fol. 84) which had troubled him for nine months. He died on 22 March 1711 in his seventy-first year and was buried at Uffington.

STUART HANDLEY

Sources P. Watson, 'Stamford', HoP, *Commons, 1660–90*, 1.305–8 · P. Watson, 'Bertie, Hon. Charles', HoP, *Commons, 1660–90*, 1.639–43 · 'Bertie, Charles', HoP, *Commons, 1690–1715* [draft] · *The Ancestor*, 2, 181 · *The manuscripts of the earl of Buckinghamshire, the earl of Lindsey … and James Round*, HMC, 38 (1895), 367–75, 403–56 · C. G. O. Bridgeman and J. C. Walker, eds., *Supplementary report on the manuscripts of the late Montagu Bertie, twelfth earl of Lindsey*, HMC, 79 (1942), 186–368 · *The manuscripts of his grace the duke of Rutland*, 4 vols., HMC, 24 (1888–1905), vol. 2, pp. 57–119 · A. Browning, *Thomas Osborne, earl of Danby and duke of Leeds, 1632–1712*, 1 (1951), 390, 394, 412 · G. M. Bell, *A handlist of British diplomatic representatives, 1509–1688*, Royal Historical Society Guides and Handbooks, 16 (1990), 38, 150, 157 · H. C. Tomlinson, *Guns and government: the ordnance office under the later Stuarts*, Royal Historical Society Studies in History, 15 (1979), 68, 80, 225 · *CSP dom., 1671–1704* · W. A. Shaw, ed., *Calendar of treasury books*, [33 vols. in 64], PRO (1904–69), esp. vols. 5–7, 14, 17, 20 · *The parliamentary diary of Narcissus Luttrell, 1691–1693*, ed. H. Horwitz (1972) · GEC, *Peerage* · *Old Westminsters*, 1.83

Archives BL, corresp., Egerton MSS 3328–3354 · Bodl. Oxf., papers | BL, Danby papers, Egerton MSS · HMC, Lindsey MSS

Bertie, Francis Leveson, first Viscount Bertie of Thame (1844–1919), diplomatist, was born on 17 August 1844 at 48 Charles Street, Mayfair, the second son of Montagu Bertie, sixth earl of Abingdon (1808–1884), and his wife, Elizabeth Lavinia (d. 1858), only daughter of George Granville Vernon Harcourt MP, of Nuneham Courtenay, Oxfordshire. He was educated at Eton College, and entered the Foreign Office by competitive examination in 1863. There he progressed steadily up the professional ladder. From 1874 to 1880 he was private secretary to the Hon. Robert Bourke (afterwards Lord Connemara), parliamentary undersecretary of state for foreign affairs, and in 1878 he was attached to the special embassy of lords Beaconsfield and Salisbury to the Congress of Berlin. As acting senior clerk in the Eastern department from 1882 to 1885, years of crisis and tension in central Asia and the Near East, Bertie impressed his superiors with his industry and judgement. Four years later he gained substantive promotion to the rank of senior clerk, and in 1894 became one of the office's two assistant under-secretaries. But sensing that he had reached the peak of his official career in London, he began, after the turn of the century, to seek a post abroad. He had the backing of Edward VII, to whose circle he belonged, and with his assistance he was appointed ambassador to Italy in 1903 and to France in 1905. He retained the Paris embassy for the next thirteen years.

Francis Leveson Bertie, first Viscount Bertie of Thame (1844–1919), by Lucie Lambert, 1911

By the time of his transfer to Rome, Bertie was already well known for his hard work, firm resolve, and strong language. Short in temper as well as stature, he was punctilious of etiquette and prone to Rabelaisian outbursts when others failed to meet his rigorous standards. He was a man of great likes and even greater dislikes, easily offended and slow to forgive. Yet, at Paris, where his junior staff nicknamed him 'the Bull', he was also remembered for his geniality, coarse humour, and love of gossip. Neither the arts nor literature were of great interest to him and he engaged in few outside pursuits other than shooting and fishing. He nevertheless maintained great state at the Paris embassy, to which he claimed a hereditary title. One of his ancestors, Lord Norreys of Rycote, had been an envoy of Elizabeth I to the French court; and, on 11 April 1874, Bertie had married Lady Feodorowna Cecilia Wellesley (1840–1920), daughter of Henry *Wellesley, the first Earl Cowley, the British ambassador at Paris during the reign of Napoleon III. As if to affirm his right and status, on full-dress occasions Bertie would drive to the neighbouring Elysée Palace in a sumptuous coach ornamented with silver fittings and with his coat of arms upon its panels. His robust personality and independence of mind drew from Lord Vansittart, who served him at Paris, the tribute that he was 'not only a great ambassador—and therefore troublesome—but *the* very last of the great ambassadors' (Lord Vansittart, *The Mist Procession*, 1958, 53).

Bertie had, however, found it difficult to adjust to the part of envoy. During his last years at the Foreign Office he had exercised considerable influence in framing policy. He was instrumental in promoting the idea of an Anglo-Japanese alliance as a means of containing Russian ambitions in the Far East, and he fostered the careers of younger diplomats such as his cousin Sir Charles Hardinge. But he was soon bored by Rome and complained that as ambassador he was 'only a d—d marionette'. Matters were different at Paris. There he became identified with the transformation of the *entente cordiale* from a colonial settlement to a close working relationship which had all the appearances but, until 1914, few of the formal obligations, of an alliance. A practitioner of *Realpolitik*, Bertie initially saw in Britain's friendship with France a means of preventing the emergence of a hostile continental coalition. Later he came to regard it as a way of maintaining the balance of power in Europe against a potentially dominant Germany. Since the 1890s he had been increasingly critical of German diplomacy and he was one of the first Foreign Office officials to recognize the threat posed to Britain by the expansion of the German navy. He opposed any attempt to improve Anglo-German relations that might sap French confidence in the entente, and when in 1905 and 1911 Germany challenged French pretensions in Morocco he urged the British government to give full support to France. Meanwhile, he remained suspicious of the intentions of France's ally Russia, and was at first inclined to blame Russia and Serbia, rather than Germany and Austria-Hungary, for the war crisis of July 1914.

Sir Edward Grey, the British foreign secretary from 1905 to 1916, valued Bertie's advice and allowed him wide discretion in handling relations with the French. After the outbreak of the First World War he agreed that Bertie, who had been due to retire in 1914, should remain ambassador until the end of hostilities. But Bertie soon found himself bypassed by ministers and others engaged in military liaison and planning. Unable to exert his authority over the numerous British missions that emerged in Paris, he was drawn into a personal feud with Lord Esher, who posed as a representative of both the War Office and the prime minister, David Lloyd George. The latter had little respect for traditional diplomatic methods and evidently sympathized with Esher's claims that Bertie was ineffective and out of touch with French opinion. When, in April 1918, Bertie fell ill, Lloyd George initiated a political reshuffle involving Bertie's replacement by the secretary of state for war, the querulous Lord Derby. After returning by hospital ship to England, in June 1918, Bertie recovered slowly but, following an operation, died at 9 Mandeville Place, Marylebone, London, on 26 September 1919; he was buried three days later in the chancel wall of Thame parish church.

Bertie was created KCB in 1902, GCVO in 1903, GCMG in 1904, GCB in 1908, and a privy councillor in 1903. He also received the grand cordon of the French Légion d'honneur. He was raised to the peerage under the title of Baron Bertie of Thame in 1915, and advanced to a viscountcy on his retirement in 1918. He had one son, Vere Frederick (1878–1954), who succeeded him as second viscount.

KEITH HAMILTON

Sources K. Hamilton, *Bertie of Thame: Edwardian ambassador*, Royal Historical Society Studies in History, 60 (1990) · *The diary of Lord Bertie of Thame*, ed. A. G. Lennox, 2 vols. (1924) · C. Gladwyn, *The Paris embassy* (1976) · Z. S. Steiner, *The foreign office and foreign policy, 1898–1914* (1969) · b. cert. · m. cert.
Archives BL, corresp. and papers, Add. MSS 63011–63053 · Bodl. Oxf. · PRO, letter-books and corresp., FO 800/159–191 | Bodl. Oxf., corresp. with Herbert Asquith · Bodl. Oxf., corresp. with Lord Kimberley · CUL, corresp. with Lord Hardinge · HLRO, corresp. with David Lloyd George · Lpool RO, corresp. with seventeenth earl of Derby · NA Scot., corresp. with A. J. Balfour · NL Scot., corresp. with Lord Rosebery · PRO, Grey of Falloden MSS · PRO, Lansdowne MSS · PRO, Nicolson MSS
Likenesses L. Lambert, pastel drawing, 1911, Gov. Art Coll. [*see illus.*] · photograph, repro. in Lennox, ed., *Diary of Lord Bertie of Thame*
Wealth at death £15,803 1s. 1d.: probate, 28 Nov 1919, CGPLA Eng. & Wales

Bertie [*née* Willoughby; *other married name* Brandon], **Katherine, duchess of Suffolk** (1519–1580), noblewoman and protestant patron, was the daughter of William Willoughby, eleventh Baron Willoughby de Eresby, a baron whose holdings ran to some thirty manors in Lincolnshire (and almost as many in Norfolk and Suffolk), worth over £900 per annum. In the absence of any greater magnate Lord Willoughby provided a substantial presence in Lincolnshire's administration, and his profile was enhanced in 1516 when he married Lady Maria de Salinas [*see* Willoughby, Maria], a Castilian noblewoman and maid of honour to Katherine of Aragon, as his second wife. Katherine, born in 1519, was his only child. Following her father's death in 1526, her inheritance was contested by his brother, Sir Christopher Willoughby, and the resulting struggle threatened to undermine the stability of the shire, until the dowager Lady Willoughby marshalled support at court. Katherine's wardship was acquired in February 1529 by Henry VIII's brother-in-law, Charles *Brandon, duke of Suffolk.

Brandon was a man of enormous ambition. In 1515 he had secretly married Henry's sister Mary upon the death of her first husband, King Louis XII of France. With her he had a son, Henry, who was created earl of Lincoln in 1525. Brandon was rapidly developing a sphere of influence in East Anglia, based largely on his acquisition of the de la Pole estates, to which the addition of Katherine's lands would be crucial. At least initially, she may have been intended for young Lincoln (who, due to Henry's continued dynastic failures, was a potential heir to the throne). But Lincoln may have been sickly (he died in 1534), and rumours emerged from Anne Boleyn's household in 1531 that Suffolk seemed more interested in Katherine than he should be. Anne's venom was probably aimed at the French dowager queen, who bore her no good will, but there might have been some truth in the dart, for three months after Mary's death in 1533, Katherine (at the age of fourteen) became Brandon's fourth wife.

Despite the difference in their ages, Katherine's marriage to Brandon was successful. They had two sons, Henry *Brandon and Charles *Brandon [see under Brandon, Charles]. He moved aggressively to oust Sir Christopher from some of his holdings (though a full settlement of the Willoughby inheritance did not occur until Elizabeth's reign), and by adding former monastic property to Katherine's, Suffolk eventually became the greatest landowner in Lincolnshire, and its chief magnate. He played a decisive role in quelling the Lincolnshire rebellion in 1536, and built a fine residence at Grimsthorpe.

In terms of religion, Katherine was conventionally pious, and 'as earnest as any', according to Stephen Gardiner, the conservative bishop of Winchester, in the early years when she made him 'her gossip' (Acts and Monuments, 8.570). She was an official mourner in 1536 at the funeral of Katherine of Aragon (for whom she had been named). The duke seems to have held no strong religious views, but protestants increasingly joined or served his household, most notably Alexander Seton, his Scottish chaplain, who had to recant an evangelical sermon on justification by faith in 1541. Probably the turning point for Katherine came in her association at court with the circle of reformers who backed Queen Katherine Parr. Brandon's death on 22 August 1545 gave her autonomy, but also made her more vulnerable to court intrigue. She was nearly enmeshed with the queen when Gardiner and other conservatives attempted to destroy protestant leaders in the waning months of Henry's life.

Under Edward VI, Katherine's encouragement and inexhaustible purse helped to shape a new protestant culture. As she passed the Tower one day, Gardiner 'veiled' his bonnet to her from the window of his cell. She replied that 'it was merry with the lambs, now that the wolf was shut up' (Acts and Monuments, 8.570). Over a dozen books carried her coat of arms or were dedicated to her, including the Paraphrases of Erasmus and biblical translations by William Tyndale. When the duchess and William Cecil persuaded Katherine Parr to print her book The Lamentacion of a Sinner in late 1547, they hoped to influence parliament to lift the old Henrician restrictions upon Bible reading by women and the lower classes. For many theologians, the duchess was a bright mirror for womenkind, a reproach to all those who thought it was inappropriate for women to take the gospels in their hands. Working with Bishop Henry Holbeach, Katherine introduced protestant clergy into Lincolnshire livings. Most notably, she was responsible for inviting Hugh Latimer to preach at Grimsthorpe. Most of his sermons have survived because they were printed under her aegis. At Cambridge, her sons were taught by Martin Bucer, and leading theologians at both universities (including John Parkhurst and Laurence Humphrey) had reason to pay her homage.

Protestant divines rallied to offer the duchess condolences upon the death of both of her sons, hours apart, of the sweating sickness in 1551. The title to the duchy of Suffolk now reverted to the heirs of the French queen. But Katherine had her own inheritance to consider, and, most likely in 1552, she took as her second husband Richard

*Bertie (1517–1582), her gentleman usher (probably with Latimer presiding). They had two children.

After the accession of Queen Mary in 1553 and the restoration of Roman Catholicism, the duchess came under increasing pressure to embrace the new regime, not only because of her prominence, but because she came of Spanish stock. Gardiner asked Bertie if the duchess were 'now as ready to set up the mass, as she was lately to pull it down' (Acts and Monuments, 8.570). Katherine and her servants made their way to the continent at the beginning of 1555, and Bertie's story of their predicaments in exile, as they travelled in Wesel, Strasbourg, and Frankfurt, was incorporated into John Foxe's Acts and Monuments. Eventually a version of their 'calamity' became the subject of a popular Elizabethan ballad that continued to be sung into the eighteenth century. Guests of the Polish king at the time of Mary's death in 1558, they returned to England the following year.

Upon her return the duchess resumed her extensive patronage, which rapidly assumed a puritan cast that set her apart from Cecil and Elizabeth, who had had to make accommodations to Mary's regime to ensure the ultimate survival of English protestantism. In the years that followed, Katherine's correspondence with Cecil urged him to promote the true faith, and her relations with the queen were strained. The duchess held property in the autonomous parish of the Holy Trinity Minories in London, a jurisdictional loophole that served as a seedbed for puritan preachers. Account books for her household in Lincolnshire show that she employed Miles Coverdale as preacher and tutor to her children, and some of her protégés, including John Field, were outspoken critics of the Elizabethan church. One of her chaplains died in prison after reproaching Archbishop Edmund Grindal for not doing enough to remove popish ceremonies.

In 1580 the dedication of Field's translation of a work by Theodore Beza referred to the duchess's continual illness, and she died on 19 September that year. She was buried in Spilsby church, Lincolnshire, where a fine alabaster tomb commemorates her and her second husband, who died two years later. Her son Peregrine *Bertie, born in exile, was then declared Lord Willoughby in right of his mother. For thirty-five years she had been (according to Latimer's servant Augustine Bernher) the mainstay of preachers, a comfort to martyrs, and God's instrument for the spread of the gospel.

SUSAN WABUDA

Sources The acts and monuments of John Foxe, new edn, ed. G. Townsend, 8 vols. (1843–9), vol. 5, pp. 447–51, 553–61; vol. 8, pp. 569–76 · The most rare and excellent history of the dutchess of Suffolks (and her husband Richard Berties) calamity (1602) · Katherine Parr, The lamentacion of a sinner … put in print at the instaunt desire of the righte gracious ladie Catherin Duchesse of Suffolke (1547) · A. Bernher, dedicatory epistle, Sermons preached by … maister Hugh Latimer (1562) [repr. Sermons by Hugh Latimer, ed. G. E. Corrie, Parker Society, 22 (1844), 311–25] · P. Collinson, The Elizabethan puritan movement (1967) · N. M. Fuidge, 'Bertie, Richard', HoP, Commons, 1558–1603, 1.434–5 · C. H. Garrett, The Marian exiles: a study in the origins of Elizabethan puritanism (1938) · S. J. Gunn, Charles Brandon, duke of Suffolk, c.1484–1545 (1988) · E. W. Ives, Anne Boleyn (1986) · M. E. James, 'Obedience and dissent in Henrician England: the Lincolnshire rebellion, 1536',

Past and Present, 48 (1970), 3–78 · H. G. Owen, 'A nursery of Elizabethan nonconformity, 1567–72', *Journal of Ecclesiastical History*, 17 (1966), 65–76 · S. Wabuda, 'The woman with the rock: the controversy on women and Bible reading', *Belief and practice in Reformation England: a tribute to Patrick Collinson from his students*, ed. S. Wabuda and C. Litzenberger (1998), 40–59 · T. Watt, *Cheap print and popular piety, 1550–1640* (1991), 91–6

Archives Lincs. Arch., estate papers | Lincs. Arch., Ancaster deposits · PRO, corresp. with William Cecil, SP 12
Likenesses portrait, 1548, repro. in Gunn, *Charles Brandon, duke of Suffolk*, pl. 3 · H. Holbein the younger, chalk drawing, Royal Collection · alabaster bust, Spilsby; repro. in N. Pevsner and J. Harris, *Lincolnshire* (1964), pl. 77–8 · miniature (after Holbein), repro. in E. Read, *Catherine, duchess of Suffolk* (1962), frontispiece
Wealth at death extensive lands in Lincolnshire

Bertie, Montague, second earl of Lindsey (1607/8–1666), royalist nobleman and army officer, was the eldest son of Robert *Bertie, first earl of Lindsey (1582–1642), and Elizabeth Montagu (*bap.* 1586, *d.* 1654). He was educated briefly at Sidney Sussex College, Cambridge, where he was admitted as a fellow-commoner on 1 February 1623. He served as MP for Lincolnshire in 1624 and for Stamford in 1625–6. Early in life he also acted as captain of a troop of cavalry in the low countries. He was styled Lord Willoughby of Eresby in 1626—a name he bore until his father's death in 1642—and soon attracted royal favour: Charles I hunted and dined with him in May 1633, appointed him a gentleman of the privy chamber and warden of Waltham Forest in 1634, and awarded him a pension. His first wife, whom he married on 18 April 1627, was Martha, daughter of Sir William *Cokayne and widow of John Ramsay, earl of Holdernesse; she had been baptized in 1605 and died in July 1641, aged thirty-six. They had five sons and three daughters, among them Charles *Bertie (1640/41–1711), diplomat and civil servant.

In the summer of 1639 Bertie provided four companies of life guards for the king's first campaign against the Scottish covenanters, and as civil war approached he instinctively rallied to Charles, joining him at Hull in April 1642. He and his father obeyed the commission of array and raised a regiment of cavalry in Lincolnshire. He commanded the life guards at Edgehill. When his father was mortally wounded in the battle, Bertie made an unsuccessful attempt to rescue him and then voluntarily surrendered in order to attend him during his final hours. Lindsey, as he now became known, was imprisoned in Warwick Castle, and there wrote a *Declaration and Justification* in which he pledged his loyalty to the king, 'upon whose head this crown is by the law of nature and nations justly fallen' (*A Declaration and Justification of the Earl of Lindsey, now Prisoner in Warwicke Castle*, 1643, 4). He remained a prisoner there until his release in July 1643 as part of an exchange of prisoners. He immediately rejoined the king at Oxford and was sworn of the privy council in the following December. Appointed lieutenant-general of the King's regiment of foot life guards, he fought in the battles of Newbury, Cropredy Bridge, and Lostwithiel, as well as at Naseby, where he was wounded. Yet alongside these military activities he was regularly involved as one of the king's commissioners in successive peace treaties and was one of several moderate royalist peers who consistently urged Charles to reach an accommodation with parliament.

Lindsey was at Oxford when it surrendered in June 1646. He was among a select group of advisers whom the king summoned to attend him during the summer and autumn of 1647, and Charles appointed him one of his commissioners at the treaty of Newport between September and December 1648. Lindsey attended the king during his trial, and after the execution he and three other peers accompanied Charles's body to its grave at Windsor. He paid a high price for his royalist allegiance. His estates had been sequestered in May 1643, and in December 1646 he compounded under the Oxford articles at the rate of one tenth (or the value of two years' income). His composition fine was set at £4360 (subsequently reduced to £2100) and was not finally paid off until the summer of 1651.

Although according to Sir Edward Walker, Lindsey 'retired and lived privately' after the regicide (Bodl. Oxf., MS Ashmole 1110, fol. 174*v*), the council of state monitored his movements closely during the early 1650s, and in the wake of Penruddock's rebellion in 1655 he was temporarily placed under house arrest. Again, in August 1659, during Booth's rebellion the council intercepted Lindsey's correspondence and suspected his eldest son of complicity in the rising. Yet there is no evidence that Lindsey was involved in either of these royalist rebellions and he apparently avoided political affairs until the Restoration. Sadness continued to dog Lindsey's personal life. His second marriage, which began at some stage between 1646 and 1653, was to Bridget (1627–1657), daughter and sole heir of Edward Wray, groom of the bedchamber to Charles I, and Lady Elizabeth Norris, daughter and heir of the earl of Berkshire, and widow of Edward Sackville, son of the fourth earl of Dorset. Bridget died aged only twenty-nine, having given birth to three sons (of whom one died young and the eldest became Lord Norris in right of his mother) and a daughter.

After the return of Charles II Lindsey was again appointed a privy councillor; he also became lord lieutenant of Lincolnshire and was awarded the Order of the Garter. In addition he was admitted to his father's old office of lord great chamberlain, and he officiated in that capacity at the coronation of Charles II on 23 April 1661. Lindsey died at Campden House, Kensington, on 25 July 1666, and was buried at Grimsthorpe in Lincolnshire.

DAVID L. SMITH

Sources Lincs. Arch., Ancaster MS · state papers domestic, Charles I, PRO, SP16 · committee for compounding papers, PRO, SP23 · council of state papers, PRO, SP25 · state papers domestic, Charles II, PRO, SP29 · *JHL*, 4–10 (1628–48) · Bodl. Oxf., MSS Clarendon 27–33 · B. Whitelocke, *Memorials of English affairs*, new edn, 4 vols. (1853) · D. L. Smith, *Constitutional royalism and the search for settlement, c. 1640–1649* (1994) · *DNB* · GEC, *Peerage*, new edn, 8.19–21 · C. Holmes, *Seventeenth-century Lincolnshire*, History of Lincolnshire, 7 (1980) · P. R. Newman, *Royalist officers in England and Wales, 1642–1660: a biographical dictionary* (1981), 26
Archives Lincs. Arch., Ancaster MS
Likenesses S. Cooper, watercolour miniature, 1649, FM Cam.; version, 1657, FM Cam. · R. Dunkarton, mezzotint, pubd 1812, BM, NPG · R. Cooper, stipple (after A. Van Dyck), BM, NPG · W. Faithorne, line engraving (after A. Van Dyck), BM, NPG · portrait,

repro. in J. E. Doyle, *The official baronage of England*, 3 vols. (1886), 2.391

Bertie, Peregrine, thirteenth Baron Willoughby of Willoughby, Beck, and Eresby (1555–1601),

nobleman and soldier, was born on 12 October 1555 in Wesel, Cleves, the only son of Richard *Bertie (1517–1582), landowner and religious evangelical, and his wife, Katherine [*see* Bertie, Katherine, duchess of Suffolk (1519–1580)], noblewoman and protestant patron, daughter of William Willoughby, eleventh Baron Willoughby de Eresby, and his wife, Maria *Willoughby (*née* de Salinas). His mother was twelfth Baron Willoughby de Eresby in her own right, and the widow of Charles Brandon, duke of Suffolk. His parents left England in 1555 as a result of Mary I's restoration of Catholicism and he was named in commemoration of their peregrinations. These travels later took them to Strasbourg and Frankfurt-am-Main, both reformed strongholds.

Home life and early career, 1555–1586 The family finally settled in Poland, but, after they had been there for a year, Mary's sister, Elizabeth, succeeded as queen and the Berties returned to England. Care was taken to obtain letters of naturalization for Peregrine Bertie. In England, the Berties made their home at the Willoughby ancestral castle of Grimsthorpe in Lincolnshire. Richard Bertie was known for his humanist scholarship and his son was educated in Latin and grammar. Once in his teens Peregrine Bertie was sent to the household of his mother's close friend Sir William Cecil, principal secretary, to be educated in the ways of the court. There he fell in love with one of Cecil's wards, the orphaned Mary de Vere (*b.* after 1550, *d.* 1624), daughter of John de *Vere, sixteenth earl of Oxford, and his second wife, Margaret. Cecil possibly encouraged their courtship but it was opposed by both Bertie's mother and Mary de Vere's brother, Edward de *Vere, seventeenth earl of Oxford (1550–1604). Even so, between 25 December 1577 and 12 March 1578 the young couple wed, and their marriage was for many years a loving and happy one. Through this de Vere connection, Bertie became cousin by marriage to the prominent puritan John *Stubbe (*c.*1541–1590), as well as to a number of soldiers who later distinguished themselves in the war with Spain. Peregrine and Mary Bertie had five sons—Robert *Bertie, first earl of Lindsey (1582–1642), Peregrine, Henry, Vere, and Roger—and a daughter, Katherine (*d.* 1611).

The duchess of Suffolk died on 19 September 1580 and Bertie was recognized as heir to the barony of Willoughby de Eresby on 11 November. He formally took his place in the House of Lords on 16 January 1581 as Lord Willoughby of Willoughby, Beck, and Eresby. His father died on 9 April 1582. Also in 1582 Willoughby began what would be a long career of service to his queen and country, taking part in a mission led by Robert Dudley, earl of Leicester, to the provinces of the Netherlands, then in revolt against Philip II—cautiously and covertly supported by England.

In July 1582 Willoughby was sent as special ambassador to invest Frederick II of Denmark with the Order of the

Peregrine Bertie, thirteenth Baron Willoughby of Willoughby, Beck, and Eresby (1555–1601), by unknown artist

Garter. It was a relatively straightforward first mission for him, but that he was given sole charge of it, despite his youth and inexperience, suggests that Cecil (now Lord Burghley) had formed a high opinion of him. It also reflects his protestant zeal, which made him agreeable to the regime and its policy. Willoughby handled himself well, securing an agreement for the protection of English merchantmen in Danish waters. He remained in Denmark until 1 November at the latest.

By 1585 the Dutch revolt against Habsburg rule was in dire straits and in August England entered the war against Spain. English special ambassadors, Willoughby among them, were promptly dispatched to Henri of Navarre, leader of the Huguenots, to the German protestant princes, and to the Scandinavian kings. Willoughby went first to Wolfenbüttel, seat of the Lutheran Julius, duke of Brunswick-Wolfenbüttel, and then on to Denmark again, where he arrived in October 1585. He was charged with persuading Frederick, with whom he had an audience about 18 October, to send either men or money to Navarre and to aid the Dutch. For Bertie the issues were clear-cut and the appropriate course of action obvious: at one point he told the Danish chancellor, Nicolas Kaas de Torup, that, to help afflicted brethren, they had 'to use ordinary means and not to wait for miraculous deliverance' (*CSP for., Sept 1585–May 1586*, 255–7). The negotiations with the Danes were nevertheless prolonged. He filled his spare time with visits to Tycho Brahe's observatory to examine the new comet the astronomer had just discovered, evidence of an enduring scientific interest, later directed solely towards military science. Willoughby wanted to be in the Netherlands, fighting in the army led by Leicester and Sir John Norris. He bombarded Sir Francis Walsingham, principal secretary, with requests to be 'discharged of these services; for … I am fitter to follow a camp' (West, 25). He also wrote directly to Leicester on 25 October, declaring his intention to join the earl as soon as his embassy was concluded.

Finally, despite Frederick's reluctance to commit himself, in late December the king agreed to put diplomatic pressure on Philip to abandon the war and to send 2000 horse to aid the Dutch (a promise that was never kept). Willoughby was satisfied and made his farewell: he then sailed, not to England, but to Hamburg, where he found a ship for the Netherlands. He eventually arrived at Amsterdam on 12 March 1586.

The soldier, 1586–1588 Willoughby was prepared to serve as an ordinary volunteer in the Netherlands, but hoped to be given a command. Sir Philip Sidney, who commanded the English garrison in Flushing, was also acting governor of the strategically important port town of Bergen op Zoom. This office was in the gift of the states general of the United Provinces, but Sidney resigned it 'to my lord Willoughby, my very special friend' and this recommendation obtained Willoughby a Dutch commission as Bergen's governor by the end of March (West, 29). It was followed in May by two more commissions for the captaincy of 100 lancers and colonelcy of an eight-company regiment of foot.

Willoughby had been trained in the military arts and was a good jouster, but at this point he had no actual military experience and owed his appointments partly to his friends in high places. However, he was already a military patron in his own right: his followers included the experienced officer Sir William Drury and several members of the de Vere and Wingfield families, all his kin by marriage. Actual military experience was not necessary to have a military clientele; it was a reflection of social position. Indeed, Willoughby's appointment as governor of Bergen owed much to the fact that sixteenth-century military theory regarded noble birth as the prime quality for a commander—the Dutch leaders told one of Elizabeth's envoys that they 'wolde not moche esteme of englishe companies, if thei were not conducted by some honorable and nobleman of their counterie' (J. M. B. C. Kervyn de Lettenhove, ed., *Relations Politiques des Pays-Bas et de l'Angleterre sous le règne de Philippe II*, 11 vols., 1882–1900, 10.353). Willoughby turned out to be a competent general, with a strong grasp of the importance of logistics and siege-craft.

One reason why the nobility were preferred as military commanders was because they had private financial resources with which to supplement those of the state. Stubbe, by now Willoughby's secretary, warned him that 'Bergen-op-Zoom is but a cherry-fair', contrasting Holland in the Low Countries with the 'Lincolnshire Holland' 'that must cherish your honorable age' (*John Stubbs's 'Gaping Gulf'*, 126). It was difficult, however, for Willoughby to be

an effective commander without committing his own resources. That he was later in constant financial difficulties was chiefly due to his unswerving commitment to the cause for which he fought between 1586 and 1589.

Willoughby risked his life as well as his patrimony. He did not rest on the defensive, but used Bergen as a base for vigorous raiding of the Spanish lines and more than once took contingents from his garrison to join the field army. He was present at the battle at Zutphen (27 September 1586) in which Sidney was mortally wounded. Willoughby led the celebrated English cavalry charge: he unhorsed the general of the enemy horse and took him prisoner, then rode on, wielding his pole-axe. His 'plumes [were] pluckt awaie from his head, & his Armes bebattered with blowes', but he emerged safe and famous (Churchyard, 104).

Promotion came Willoughby's way the next year, after Leicester quarrelled with Norris and sent him home. However, Willoughby was not promoted to general in winter 1586–7: nor, when he succeeded Norris, was it as colonel-general of the horse, for Willoughby's friend, Robert Devereux, second earl of Essex, who held that command rather than Norris, remained in office until November 1587; and Norris was replaced on 14 June, not 4 January, 1587. Willoughby immediately had to co-operate with Leicester in attempting to relieve the siege of Sluys, a port besieged by Alessandro Farnese, duke of Parma, Spain's captain-general in the Low Countries, who was seeking bases for the 'invincible Armada', which would sail the following year. Sluys fell in late summer 1587, but the fault lay with Leicester, who resigned his command and went home for good in mid-December. Willoughby was the obvious choice to replace him and, despite protesting that his financial resources were inadequate, Elizabeth and her privy councillors insisted. Although his commission as lieutenant-general was not issued until 22 January 1588, from 4 December 1587 he was the queen's commander-in-chief in the Netherlands.

The general, 1588–1590 Leicester had thoroughly soured relations with the Dutch so Willoughby inherited a poisoned chalice. He had a seat on the United Provinces' council of state, but the locals were asserting themselves *vis-à-vis* the English and pruned his powers. There was also intrigue within the English forces: Willoughby named Drury to replace him as governor of Bergen, but this was overturned and Sir Thomas Morgan, a veteran of the Netherlands campaigns, was commissioned instead, thanks to his astute politicking with both the Dutch and Elizabeth. Willoughby was infuriated, but his inability to secure such a simple appointment suggests a lack of adeptness in the political side of a general's business.

In action, however, Willoughby was undoubtedly effective. In July 1588 ships under his command helped to prevent a juncture between Parma's army and the Armada, and captured a Spanish galleon. Then, in the autumn, the Spanish—'to win some reputation' back from the English—laid siege to Bergen (West, 43). Willoughby took personal command and led a vigorous defence which, in November 1588, after a two-month siege, obliged Parma to withdraw, having suffered his first defeat. This is probably the origin of one verse in the ballad of 'Brave Lord Willoughby':

> Then quoth the Spanish General,
> Come let us march away,
> I fear we shall be spoilèd all,
> If that longer we stay.
> For yonder comes Lord Willoughby,
> Of courage fierce and fell,
> He will not give one inch of way
> For all the devils in hell.

Elizabeth was delighted and wrote to him in her own hand: 'suppose not that your travail and labours are not accepted, and shall be ever kept in good memory' (Markham, 136).

Within six months, however, Willoughby had resigned (he relinquished command on 14 March 1589 but his resignation was not accepted until 30 July). This was partly because of continual political disputes with the Dutch states about each nation's share of the allied war effort. These led to both sides withholding their financial contributions, which in turn meant the soldiers suffered from lack of pay and provisions, and often mutinied. The garrison of St Geertruidenberg betrayed that important city to Parma in consequence. The troops were not English, but the governor was Willoughby's brother-in-law, Sir John *Wingfield (d. 1596). Vitriolic criticism by the states' leaders of Wingfield (and, by extension, of Willoughby) masked their anguish at the city's loss and their own poor handling of the crisis, but soured relations between English and Dutch. There were also personal reasons for Willoughby's resignation. He had spent £7689 of his own money during the siege of Bergen alone and by the end of 1588 had debts of over £4000, despite having already 'pawned his plate, silver vessell, and all his own and my Lady's jewels for £1200' (Bertie, 527). Both the English and Dutch governments paid him late or not at all. Thus £1500, owed him by the Dutch for his services up to June 1587, was not paid until July 1588. In later life he suffered repeatedly from fevers; it is likely that in the swampy Low Countries he picked up a strain of malaria, doubtless due to stress and overwork. Willoughby was only finally formally discharged from his command in August 1589.

Less than four weeks later, on 15 September, Willoughby was appointed general of the army Elizabeth was sending to Normandy to aid Henri de Navarre, who had now succeeded as Henri IV of France. With 4000 men Willoughby landed at Dieppe on 29 September and joined Henri who, with this reinforcement, marched on Paris. Willoughby actually led his men into one of the city's suburbs, but the king was obliged to withdraw. Unusually, Henri campaigned on into the winter, making maximum use of his English troops. By mid-January 1590 they had helped him capture five fortresses in less than three months. This was a remarkable success rate and surely owed much to Willoughby's powers of leadership; certainly the English showed great dash and courage in storming strong defences. However, the army was wrecked by illness and lack of supplies, even though Willoughby had, once more, dipped into his own purse to help his unfortunate troops. In December 1589 Elizabeth again wrote to him in her own hand: 'I bless God that your old prosperous success followeth your valiant acts; and joy not a little that safety accompanieth your luck'—but the treasury did not reimburse his expenses (Markham, 141). After the capture of the channel port of Honfleur on 14 January 1590, Willoughby sailed home with the remnants of his army, of which he reported to the privy council, 'more died from hunger and cold than in battle' (Bertie, 312).

When in 1591 Elizabeth decided to send another army to Normandy to co-operate with Henri, Willoughby was the obvious candidate to command it. However, 'worn out and ill', he declined the appointment and instead backed Essex, who did eventually obtain the command (Hammer, 97). He raised troops in Lincolnshire for the army his friend took to Normandy in 1592, but himself never commanded troops in the field again.

Later life and career, 1590–1601 Willoughby spent much of the first half of the 1590s travelling on the continent, visiting northern Germany again, as well as northern Italy. He did not return home permanently until summer 1596. He took the waters at various spa towns, so his health was probably one reason for his travels, but he maintained a steady correspondence with Essex, reporting on the most recent continental military developments. He also wrote a series of briefings on problems in the ordnance office for Essex when the earl sought the mastership of the ordnance. Essex then backed Willoughby's bid to be governor of Berwick and warden of the east marches, after the death in 1596 of the long-term incumbent, Henry Carey, first Lord Hunsdon.

English politics was increasingly polarized in the 1590s by Essex's dispute with Robert Cecil. Willoughby was clearly aligned with Essex and this may be why his suit to be governor of Berwick and warden was not successful until 13 March 1598. However, he was always on reasonably good terms with Cecil, perhaps reflecting that both had been raised by Burghley. Traditionally, Berwick was one of the two or three most important fortresses in the country, but the impending accession to the English throne of James VI of Scotland meant that it was becoming a military backwater: twenty years had passed since England mounted military operations north of the border. Still, it had one of the largest permanent military garrisons in England, and as the borders continued to be lawless and the site of much Anglo-Scottish tension, the position of governor and warden was an important one, albeit unlikely to necessitate actual campaigning. All this is presumably what made it desirable to Willoughby.

Soon after taking command Willoughby set about introducing the latest continental military practices to the garrison, which he felt had grown lackadaisical during long years of peace. He also tried to impose strong government on the marches. The result was great friction both in and around Berwick, but the local gentry's complaints to the privy council about Willoughby's policies were always dismissed. The regime was less sympathetic to his proposals for improvements to Berwick's fortifications. Nothing came of these, no doubt because it was obvious that strong fortresses on the borders with Scotland would soon be redundant. Willoughby was appointed to the queen's council of the north in August 1599.

In the wake of Essex's fall in 1601 Elizabeth wrote to Willoughby, assuring him of her pleasure that Berwick was 'ruled by a person of your reputation abroad and at home', and noting that 'we know how apt you are to hurt yourself by over much care and labour in our service' (West, 76). Clearly, his deeds of 1588 were still in the queen's 'good memory'. This expression of his sovereign's confidence pleased him, but Willoughby was in decline. He had suffered from ill health, taking two leaves of absence in 1600. On 25 June 1601 he died of fever at Berwick. He was not quite forty-six. His widow survived him by twenty-three years. The final years of their marriage had been difficult and they separated before 20 April 1600, with Lady Willoughby enjoying an allowance of £300 per annum. Before 2 June 1605 she married, as his first wife, Sir Eustace Hart of London but the couple separated shortly after. She probably died on 24 June 1624 at Hackney in Middlesex.

Willoughby's will of 6 August 1599 is full of strongly Calvinist statements. His six children were all legal minors (as they still were in 1601). He appealed to the queen to ensure that the guardianship of his heir, Robert Bertie, nineteen in 1601, was not abused (a common fate for wards). He named him as executor, despite his youth, appointing four assistants to help him and become executors for the younger children in the event of Bertie's death as a minor. Despite his problems with debts, Willoughby passed on a large body of lands to his sons, and bonds for £4000 to his daughter, Katherine, for her marriage portion. To his second son, Peregrine, he willed 'the dyamont which the French kinge gave me', and to Robert a 'chayne of gould' and medal given him by the elector palatine (PRO, PROB 11/98, sig. 58).

As Willoughby's will dictated, his body was taken by ship back to Lincolnshire and buried in the Willoughby chapel at Spilsby church on 21 or 22 July 1601. Katherine Bertie, who married Sir Lewis Watson in 1609, erected a monument to her father's memory in 1610. In the effigy he stands proud, in half armour with helm and gauntlets at his feet: an appropriate representation.

Character, ability, and place in history First and foremost Willoughby was a soldier, and his skill in the art of war won him considerable fame. The next generation, looking back, remembered him as 'one of the Queen's first swordsmen' (Naunton, 228). In his own time, Parma declared that 'never anie English man enterprized more boldlie to meete his enimies ... more bravelie encountered them, nor more painefullie pursued and fought them out neere and farr off' (Churchyard, 104). Henri IV praised him as 'noble of heart' and as 'discreet as he is valiant'. Even after Willoughby had left France, Henri wrote declaring 'the esteem that I have of your virtue and merit' (West, 54, 60).

Willoughby was also renowned among ordinary Englishmen. He was celebrated in at least three contemporary ballads: 'Lord Willobie's welcome home', 'Lord Willoughby's march', and the well-known 'Brave Lord Willoughby'. The first two do not survive but the last is often mined by historians for choice quotations. The 'stout behaviour of brave Lord Willoughby' is lauded, but what seems to have won him popular acclaim is his care for his men. The queen took for granted his prodigal expenditure to keep her soldiers armed, clothed, and fed, but they appreciated it. He probably did not actually obtain 'a pension of eighteen-pence a day' for his French veterans and Elizabeth may not have 'quit and set them free' of 'all cost and charges ... all for the sake of brave Lord Willoughby', yet this captures accurately his concern for his soldiers' welfare. This was also his strength as a commander. He never evinced great tactical or strategical sophistication, but his character and powers of leadership were exceptional. In the ballad he is made to cry to his infantry:

Do you prove true to me
And I'll be foremost in the fight

and, indeed, he consistently led from the front. The hero of Zutphen was not simply a hard-charging warrior. At Bergen he mastered Parma, who for ten years had taken every fortress he besieged. Willoughby's papers on the ordnance office were not just cribs for Essex, but outlined reforms that would achieve improvements in 'the supply and distribution of munitions' (Hammer, 236). His plans for updating the fortifications of Berwick, including a detailed sketch in his own hand, are further testimony to his mastery of the technical aspects of the art of war.

What Willoughby disliked was administrators and courtiers, and he preferred the life of a soldier: the governorship of Berwick, although an administrative post, was still combined with military duties. Sir Robert Naunton remarked how 'as he was a great soldier, so ... [he] could not brook the obsequiousness and assidiuity of the court' (Naunton, 229). Willoughby allegedly contrasted himself with career courtiers, stating 'that he was none of the *Reptilia*', being unable 'to creep and crouch' (Hammer, 335). In a painting by Federico Zuccaro from the late 1570s he appears as a dashing young courtier, but in portraits of the late 1580s and 1590s, he is shown as a general and Christian soldier. His rejection of those who sought false economies in the national war effort, as 'contrary to sound judgment & weale publicque', was one reason why he supported Essex in his factional dispute with Cecil (ibid., 373). Willoughby stamped down on corruption in the Berwick garrison after his appointment, suggesting an intolerance of financial manipulation. He himself averred: 'I ambitiously affect not high titles, but round dealing, desiring rather to be a private lance with indifferent reputation than a colonel general spotted or defamed' (Wilson, 88). In October 1596 Essex briefly wanted Willoughby to seek the mastership of the ordnance, but he refused, arguing that only Essex had the political power to carry out the necessary reforms. This was probably true, but his strongly articulated view that 'none but a Hercules can cutt of Hidra's heades of ignorance, or an Alexander unloose a Gogon's knott of ill customes and abuses' reveals how he regarded administrative work: action never daunted him (BL, Egerton MS 1943, fol. 86r).

This did not mean that Willoughby was not valued by his queen and her privy councillors. Their preference for him to command in 1589 (and even 1592), despite his own reservations is a good indication of the respect they had for Willoughby's talents. Elizabeth regularly wrote salutations of letters to him in her own hand, customarily beginning 'Good Peregrine'. The letters are by turns encouraging and affirming, but also have that tone of hectoring (and even punning) affection that Elizabeth used to those she was fond of. In late 1594 she wrote to him, then on his travels, implying it was time he returned to duty, but concluding:

> Interpret this our plainness … to our extraordinary estimation of you; for it is not common with us to deal so freely with many; … not doubting but you have with moderation made trial of these your sundry peregrinations, as you will find as great comfort to spend your days at home. (West, 62)

Her letter after Essex's rising assuring him of her favour likewise demonstrates her enduring esteem for 'good Peregrine'. It is notable that his heir succeeded to his barony and estates immediately, rather than become a ward. Willoughby, for his part, reciprocated; in his will he left a gold cup or jewel worth £100 to the queen as 'a small token or remembrance of that loyalty and duty which allwayes I have offererd towardes her majestie' (PRO, PROB 11/98, sig. 58). Earlier Sidney had left his 'best swoord' to Essex, but had willed to Willoughby 'an other swoord the best I have' (Hammer, 53).

That Willoughby consistently deferred to Essex, ten years his junior, ultimately reflects a relative lack of ambition. As one historian notes, he was 'at heart oddly diffident' (Wilson, 88). Willoughby was ultimately less interesting than Essex, yet he ended his days in peace while the latter ended on the block. Essex overreached himself, striving for personal greatness, whereas Willoughby recognized his limitations and preferred to work within them, serving his sovereign and the greater good of the kingdom. However, while Willoughby's career path seems to epitomize the changes taking place in English aristocratic attitudes, he personally subscribed to the traditional values of chivalry and nobility, which Essex consciously attempted to embody; but the machinations of political bureaucracy were alien to him. He preferred the life of a soldier to that of a government administrator.   D. J. B. TRIM

Sources J. West, *The brave Lord Willoughby: an Elizabethan soldier* (1998) • P. E. J. Hammer, *The polarisation of Elizabethan politics: the political career of Robert Devereux, 2nd earl of Essex, 1585–1597* (1999) • *John Stubbs's 'gaping gulf' with letters and other relevant documents*, ed. L. E. Berry (1968) • C. G. Cruickshank, *Elizabeth's army* (1946); 2nd edn (1966) • R. B. Wernham, *After the Armada: Elizabethan England and the struggle for western Europe, 1588–1595* (1984) • T. Borman, 'Untying the knot? The survival of the Anglo-Dutch alliance, 1587–97', *European History Quarterly*, 27 (1997), 307–37 • G. Bertie, *Five generations of a loyal house* (1845) • J. L. Motley, *History of the United Netherlands: from the death of William the Silent to the Twelve Years Truce, 1609*, 4 vols. (New York, 1879–80) • C. R. Markham, *The fighting Veres: lives of Sir Francis Vere … and of Sir Horace Vere … Baron Vere of Tilbury* (1888) •

C. Wilson, *Queen Elizabeth and the revolt of the Netherlands* (1970) • S. L. Adams, 'The protestant cause: religious alliance with the west European Calvinist communities as a political issue in England, 1585–1630', DPhil diss., U. Oxf., 1973 • C. Read, *Lord Burghley and Queen Elizabeth* (1960) • *DNB* • R. Naunton, '"Fragmenta regalia", or, Observations on the late Queen Elizabeth, her times and favourites', *Memoirs of Robert Cary and Fragmenta regalia*, ed. W. Scott (1806) • *Report on the manuscripts of the earl of Ancaster*, HMC, 66 (1907) • *Calendar of the manuscripts of the most hon. the marquis of Salisbury*, 24 vols., HMC, 9 (1883–1976), vols. 4–11 • T. Churchyard, *A true discourse historicall of the succeeding governors in the Netherlands* (1602) • *CSP for., Jan 1581–Dec 1582; Sept 1585–July 1589* • LPL, MSS 654, 659 • J. Orlers, *Den Nassauschen Laurencrans … (Leiden, 1610)* • S. Adams, ed., *Household accounts and disbursement books of Robert Dudley, earl of Leicester, 1558–1561, 1584–1586*, CS, 6 (1995) • BL, Egerton MS 1943 • pipe office, declared accounts, PRO, exchequer, E 351/240–41 • exchequer of receipt, auditors' patent books, PRO, exchequer, 403/2453 • signet office, PRO, SO 3/1 • will, PRO, PROB 11/98, sig. 58 • Nationaal Archief, The Hague, Archief van de staten-generaal, 5881, 12536 • Nationaal Archief, The Hague, Archief van de raad van staate, 1524/i • Nationaal Archief, The Hague, Regeringsarchieven van de geünieerde Provinciën, 1:93 • *Recueil des lettres missives de Henri IV*, ed. B. de Xivrey and J. Gaudet, 9 vols. (1843–76), vol. 3 • Cinq cents de Colbert, Bibliothèque Nationale, Paris, MS 466 • J. Bruce, ed., *Correspondence of Robert Dudley, earl of Leicester*, CS, 27 (1844) • GEC, *Peerage*

Archives BL, papers, Egerton MS 1943 • Lincs. Arch., corresp. and papers | BL, Cotton MSS, corresp. and papers, Titus D.L. ii; c. vii • BL, Harley MSS, corresp. • Grimsthorpe Castle, Lincolnshire, earl of Ancaster's MSS • Hatfield House, Hertfordshire, Cecil papers, Cecil MSS • LPL, papers of Anthony Bacon • PRO, state papers France, SP 78 • PRO, state papers Holland, SP 84

Likenesses N. Hilliard, miniature, *c.*1600, V&A • funerary monument, 1610, parish church, Spilsby, Lincolnshire • F. Zuccaro, oils, Grimsthorpe Castle, Lincolnshire • oils, Grimsthorpe Castle, Lincolnshire [*see illus.*] • oils, Drummond Castle, Tayside region; version, attrib. H. Custodis, Rockingham Castle, Northamptonshire • oils, allegorical portrait, Grimsthorpe Castle, Lincolnshire; version, priv. coll. • portraits, repro. in West, *Brave Lord Willoughby*

Wealth at death see will, PRO, PROB 11/98, sig. 58

Bertie, Richard (1517–1582), landowner and religious evangelical, was the eldest son of Thomas Bertie (*d.* 1555), of Bearsted, Kent, and his wife, a member of the Say family of Shropshire. In February 1534 he was admitted to Corpus Christi College, Oxford, aged sixteen. Having graduated BA in 1537, he became a probationary fellow of Magdalen, but left in 1539.

Bertie found employment in the household of Lord Chancellor Thomas Wriothesley, who in 1538 had employed his father, a distinguished architect, and where his own skill in languages and his ready wit were valuable assets. Eventually he entered the service of Katherine [*see* Bertie, Katherine (1519–1580)], the widow of Charles Brandon, duke of Suffolk, possibly owing to her growing reputation for her patronage of protestants. As dowager duchess, Katherine maintained large households in London and her native Lincolnshire, so sizeable that they were tantamount to small courts. Bertie became her gentleman usher, a trusted man of affairs who dealt with a multiplicity of business on her behalf. And after the sudden deaths of her two sons, her only heirs, of the sweating sickness in 1551, Bertie became her second husband, probably in the following year.

With the restoration of Catholicism under Mary Tudor,

Bertie and his wife eventually realized that flight was their best course of action. In June 1554 Bishop Stephen Gardiner of Winchester summoned Bertie to discuss their religion, asking him if the duchess were ready 'to return from a new to an ancient religion' (*Acts and Monuments*, 8.570). Unlike other protestants, including their friend William Cecil, Katherine and Bertie refused to temporize or accommodate with the regime. Too prominent to hide in England, Bertie went abroad almost immediately to prepare the way. The duchess and their infant daughter followed with a small retinue (including their fool) at the beginning of 1555. They moved in increasing destitution from Wesel, to Strasbourg and Frankfurt, and at length they came to Poland, where they were the guests of King Sigismund Augustus. At every stage Bertie's facility with Latin (as well as French and Italian) helped them out of dangerous predicaments. In later years, he shared his story with Foxe, whose account of their wanderings has done more than anything else to preserve Bertie's memory. At the end of Elizabeth's reign, an extremely popular ballad incorporated some of the main features of his story, and portrayed Bertie and Katherine as models of protestant heroism, telling how, for instance, the duchess:

> ... for the love of God alone,
> her Land and Goods she left behind:
> Seeking still for that precious Stone,
> the Word and Truth so rare to find:
> She with her Nurse, Husband, and Child,
> In poor array their sighs beguil'd.
> (Watt, 92)

In the years that followed their return to England in 1559, Bertie wrote an answer to John Knox's *Monstrous Regiment of Women* for private circulation in manuscript. With Cecil, he represented Lincolnshire in the parliament of 1563, and he served as a tireless local official in many capacities, not least as sheriff of Lincolnshire 1564–5. In 1564 he was in Cambridge for Elizabeth's progress, and was granted an honorary degree.

Uncharacteristically for the Tudor period, Bertie has remained almost completely overshadowed by his wife. He continued to serve her interests, especially in attempting to gain recognition of her claim to the barony of Willoughby of Eresby, which she wished to enjoy as the sole heir of her father, William Willoughby, eleventh Lord Willoughby. In fact Bertie aspired to hold the title himself, in his wife's right, and in 1570 made a formal claim to that effect, which was placed before the queen two years later, but went no further. At the same time, in order to refute objections to his relatively humble origins, an elaborate pedigree was constructed for him, tracing his descent from the lords of 'Bertieland in Prussia', who were said to have come to England with the Saxons in the fifth century. The peerage claim was only resolved upon Katherine's death in 1580, when their son Peregrine *Bertie, who was so named from his having been born in exile, was granted the title. Bertie died at Bourne nineteen months after Katherine, on 9 April 1582. They were buried at Spilsby.

SUSAN WABUDA

Sources *The acts and monuments of John Foxe*, new edn, ed. G. Townsend, 8 (1849), 569–76 · *The most rare and excellent history of the dutchess of Suffolks (and her husband Richard Berties) calamity* (1602) · N. M. Fuidge, 'Bertie, Richard', HoP, *Commons, 1558–1603*, 1.434–5 · C. H. Garrett, *The Marian exiles: a study in the origins of Elizabethan puritanism* (1938), 11, 87–9 · T. Watt, *Cheap print and popular piety, 1550–1640* (1991), 91–6 · Emden, *Oxf.*, 4.45–6 · J. H. Round, 'The Willoughby d'Eresby case and the rise of the Berties', *Peerage and pedigree: studies in peerage law and family history*, 1 (1910), 1–54; facs. edn (1970)

Archives Lincs. Arch., accounts and papers · LPL, papers relating to the protestant exiles at Wesel

Likenesses alabaster bust on tomb, Spilsby; repro. in Pevsner, *Lincolnshire*, p. 77–8, 680 · portrait, repro. in E. Read, *Catherine duchess of Suffolk* (1962), facing p. 168

Bertie, Robert, first earl of Lindsey (1582–1642), naval officer and royalist army officer, was the eldest son of Peregrine *Bertie, thirteenth Baron Willoughby of Willoughby, Beck, and Eresby (1555–1601), and Mary (d. 1624), daughter of John de *Vere, sixteenth earl of Oxford. An early biographer, David Lloyd, claims that he was born in London on 16 December 1572 and that he was Queen Elizabeth's godson. The year of his nativity was probably 1582, however, as he was a minor in 1601, and his funeral monument records that he died in 1642 aged sixty. Admitted to Corpus Christi College, Cambridge, in 1594, he did not take his degree. Lloyd alleges that he served at Cadiz in 1596, and that he received in the town's marketplace a knighthood from the expedition's commander, the second earl of Essex, his godfather, but he was not then aged fourteen, and no other source mentions that he was dubbed. Likewise, there is no evidence that he subsequently accompanied the seventh earl of Shrewsbury on a diplomatic mission to Paris, as Lloyd supposes, and Bertie could not have served on the third earl of Cumberland's privateering voyage to the West Indies in 1598 or on an embassy to Denmark that same year, as he was then touring France, from where he sent regular reports in Latin and French to his father. Lloyd's claim that he subsequently observed the fortifications at Brill, one of England's two cautionary towns in the United Provinces, is more plausible, as from the spring of 1599 Brill's garrison was commanded by Bertie's kinsman, the renowned Sir Francis Vere. Lloyd adds that Bertie played a valiant part in Vere's victory over the Spanish at Nieuwpoort in July 1600, leading several attacks in person and sustaining no injury, although he was unhorsed three times.

Following his father's death Bertie returned to England in September 1601. However, as the settlement of his estate was in the hands of trustees during his minority, he was soon free to complete his education abroad. By July 1602 he was in northern Italy (and so cannot have participated in the capture of the great carrack off Portugal in June 1602, as Lloyd maintains). While touring Italy the new Lord Willoughby was urged by a friend to consider marriage to Dorothy, daughter of George, fourth earl of Huntingdon, an approach which he ungraciously rebuffed, and not even the offer of a £3000 dowry would change his mind. Some time after he returned to England in 1604 Willoughby concluded a match with Elizabeth

Robert Bertie, first earl of Lindsey (1582–1642), by Cornelius Johnson

Montagu (*bap.* 1586, *d.* 1654), daughter of Edward Montagu of Boughton, a wealthy Northamptonshire landowner who was ennobled in 1621. On 6 January 1605, on the occasion of the creation of Prince Charles as duke of York, Willoughby was made a knight of the Bath. Shortly thereafter he was granted honorary admission to Gray's Inn, and accompanied the embassy sent to ratify the peace with Spain led by the lord high admiral, the earl of Nottingham, returning to England via Paris in the summer.

In October 1611 Willoughby wrote to congratulate Christian IV of Denmark, brother-in-law to James I, on his recent military success over the Swedes and to offer his services to Christian, who authorized him to raise and command 1500 men. The troops were embarked in May 1612, but probably saw little action as most of them had perished from sickness before the end of the summer. Following the conclusion of peace Willoughby returned to England. On 14 May 1614 he was granted parliamentary leave of absence, 'being not well and in physic' (*Hastings MSS*, 4.248), and was still sick in December. He had recovered sufficiently by October 1615 to engage in a brawl with the second Lord Norreys at Bath, which resulted in the death of one of Willoughby's servants. In December 1618 it was rumoured that he was being considered for appointment as lord deputy of Ireland, and that his backers included the queen, who was grateful for the military assistance he had afforded her brother Christian IV. He languished without employment, however, except at a local level, until June 1624, when he secured the colonelcy of one of the four regiments raised to assist the Dutch. Later that year his regiment formed part of the

force under Prince Maurice which unsuccessfully attempted to relieve Breda.

Willoughby had returned to England by March 1626 when, in consequence of the death without direct male heir of Henry de Vere, eighteenth earl of Oxford, he laid claim to the earldom of Oxford. His petition to the House of Lords was rightly refused in favour of the heir male, Robert de Vere, but as a sop to his pride and in acknowledgement of his claims as heir-general the Lords awarded him the hereditary office of lord great chamberlain, which had previously been held by the earls of Oxford. Thus aggrandized, Willoughby took his seat in the upper house in April. Following parliament's dissolution Willoughby was sent to Portsmouth to take charge of a fleet which was being prepared against Spain. Poorly manned and provisioned, Willoughby's ships sailed in October, but they sustained severe storm damage on the outward journey and were compelled to return home. News of Willoughby's premature return was greeted with dismay by the lord high admiral, the duke of Buckingham, but Willoughby exonerated himself by producing certificates signed by the navy's senior masters demonstrating that his ships had sailed in an unseaworthy condition. In the following November he was offered the command of all four English regiments in the Dutch service, which were about to be transferred to the Danes. Willoughby refused the commission, pleading his pressing domestic affairs and secretly hoping that he would instead be appointed lord president of Munster in succession to Buckingham's recently deceased elder brother, Sir Edward Villiers. He was not offered this position, however, as Buckingham wished to make use of his military skills in the forthcoming war with France. On 22 November 1626 he was created earl of Lindsey, apparently without purchase, and in the following year he was appointed vice-admiral of the fleet which accompanied Buckingham to the Île de Ré. In August he was reported to have been dispatched with a squadron to St Malo to prevent the French from relieving their beleaguered forces. On 15 February 1628 he was appointed to the council of war established to advise Buckingham and the king, and on 20 July he was sworn of the privy council. He was present at Portsmouth when Buckingham was murdered in August, interrogating the duke's assassin, John Felton, immediately after the event, and subsequently replaced Buckingham as head of the fleet which the duke had assembled to relieve the Huguenots of La Rochelle. On anchoring off La Rochelle he found the harbour entrance so heavily defended that his captains resisted his best efforts to persuade them to force a passage, a failure which resulted in the city's capitulation in October. He returned to England where, held blameless by Charles I, he took his place on the Board of Admiralty, which had been appointed during his absence.

In January 1629 Lindsey was made lord lieutenant of his native Lincolnshire, where he had been a deputy lieutenant since 1612. On 18 April 1630 he was elected a knight of the Garter, being installed on 5 October following. Some time during the early 1630s Lindsey petitioned to be appointed either lord deputy of Ireland or lord high admiral, but had to make do with temporary appointment as lord high constable in 1631 and 1634. In June 1632 he was admitted a councillor of the New England Company. Later that year the king authorized Lincolnshire's sewer commissioners to enter into negotiations with Lindsey and his partners, Sir Robert Killigrew and Robert Long, to drain large tracts of the county's fens in return for part of the recovered land.

In May 1635 Lindsey's previous naval experience led to his appointment as admiral of the first of the ship money fleets, with instructions to force a confrontation with France over England's claims to sovereignty over its surrounding seas. In the event, he spent five fruitless months chasing the French around the channel. His failure irritated the king, but Lindsey remained confident, not only that he would command successive ship money fleets but that he would be permitted to behave in all respects like a lord high admiral of England. He was therefore devastated when in March 1636 Charles appointed in his stead the youthful Algernon Percy, tenth earl of Northumberland, and over the next ten months he failed to attend most meetings of the admiralty commission.

Lindsey was appointed a member of a new council of war in May 1637. On 30 March 1639, with war against the Scottish covenanters imminent, he was appointed governor of Berwick, the office held by his father forty years earlier. He entered Berwick in April, but obtained leave in September to return south to attend to his personal affairs, and in the following January he surrendered the governorship. In May 1640 he petitioned the Short Parliament in connection with fen drainage, on which he claimed to have spent nearly £50,000. Fourteen thousand acres, mainly consisting of former common, had been allotted to him by the crown, but the fens commoners resented the loss of traditional grazing ground and refused to allow him quiet possession of his gains. By the time the Long Parliament met Lindsey's enemies had been joined by the fourth earl of Lincoln, who protested that he had lost 2000 acres as a result of the drainage scheme. Lindsey therefore sought to achieve statutory recognition of his claims, but although his bill received a second reading in the Lords on 5 August 1641 it failed to emerge from committee.

Lindsey was a regency commissioner during the king's absence in Scotland in August 1641. In the months preceding the outbreak of civil war his loyalty to the king's person ensured that he was viewed with suspicion by many in parliament. When on 11 January 1642 Charles informed the Lords that he would appoint Lindsey to command a detachment of the city's trained bands to wait on both houses, the offer was spurned in favour of a force under Philip Skippon. One month later the Commons deprived Lindsey of his Lincolnshire lieutenancy and divided control of the county's militia between the earl of Lincoln and Lord Willoughby of Parham. Despite these affronts Lindsey continued to sit in the Lords, where he voted to prevent the kingdom from being placed in a posture of defence (2 March), against the militia ordinance (5 March), and against a joint declaration by both houses (7 March).

At the beginning of April he was granted twenty days' leave of absence, but he failed to return to Westminster and instead joined the king at York. There Charles reappointed him lord lieutenant of Lincolnshire, with orders to take control of the county's magazine. When news of this reached parliament Lindsey was declared to be 'a public enemy to the state and an incendiary between the King and his people' (6 June). Three days later, on learning that Lindsey was about to enter Lincolnshire, the Commons asked the Lords to issue a warrant for his arrest.

Lindsey signed the declaration of 15 June 1642, which avowed that the king had no intention of waging war on parliament. He headed the list of Lincolnshire's commissioners of array of 14 July, and by 1 August had been appointed lieutenant-general of the king's army. According to Clarendon, however, he 'took little delight' (Clarendon, *Hist. rebellion*, 6.356, n. 1) in this latest command after Charles's nephew Prince Rupert arrived in the royal camp. When the parliamentarian army was encountered at Edgehill on 23 October 1642 Charles turned to Rupert for advice in deploying his forces, ignoring Lindsey altogether. Finding himself effectively deprived of command, and unhappy with the army's disposition, Lindsey declared that 'since he was not fit to be a general, he would die a colonel in the head of his regiment' (ibid., 366). He was as good as his word. During the ensuing battle he led his regiment on foot and was felled by a shot in the thigh. He and his son were subsequently taken prisoner. Carried to a barn in a neighbouring village on the same day, he slowly bled to death for want of medical treatment. He was buried in his family's vault at Edenham, Lincolnshire. He bequeathed to his eldest son, Montague *Bertie (1607/8–1666), debts amounting to £13,438. His widow, who bore him nine sons and five daughters, survived until 30 November 1654.

ANDREW THRUSH

Sources D. Lloyd, *Memoires of the lives … of those … personages that suffered … for the protestant religion* (1668) · *Report on the manuscripts of the earl of Ancaster*, HMC, 66 (1907) · *Report on the manuscripts of his grace the duke of Buccleuch and Queensberry … preserved at Montagu House*, 3 vols. in 4, HMC, 45 (1899–1926), vols. 1, 3 · *The manuscripts of his grace the duke of Portland*, 10 vols., HMC, 29 (1891–1931), vol. 9 · *Report on the manuscripts of the late Reginald Rawdon Hastings*, 4 vols., HMC, 78 (1928–47), vols. 2, 4 · *Calendar of the manuscripts of the most hon. the marquis of Salisbury*, 11, HMC, 9 (1906); 17 (1938) · *Fourth report*, HMC, 3 (1874) · *The letters of John Chamberlain*, ed. N. E. McClure, 2 vols. (1939) · *CSP dom.*, 1603–41 · *Report of the Deputy Keeper of the Public Records*, 46 (1885), appx 2 · G. Lipscomb, *The history and antiquities of the county of Buckingham*, 4 vols. (1831–47) · *Letters of John Holles, 1587–1637*, ed. P. R. Seddon, 1, Thoroton Society Record Series, 31 (1975) · K. Lindley, *Fenland riots and the English revolution* (1982) · L. Stone, *The crisis of the aristocracy, 1558–1641* (1965), 779 · 'Records of the council for New England', *Proceedings of the American Antiquarian Society* (1867) · Lincs. Arch., Ancaster papers · GEC, *Peerage* · Venn, *Alum. Cant.*

Archives Borth. Inst., Rhodesian papers · Lincs. Arch., papers **Likenesses** J. Houbraken, wash drawing, AM Oxf. · C. Johnson, oils, Warwick Castle [*see illus.*] · R. van Voerst, line engraving (after G. Geldorp), BM, NPG

Bertie [*formerly* Hoar], **Sir Thomas** (1758–1825), naval officer, the fourth son of George Hoar of London and formerly of Middleton Era, co. Durham, was born in

Stockton-on-Tees on 3 July 1758 and was educated privately at Christ's Hospital, London. Although very close in age and following the same service, he was not a blood relative of Albemarle Bertie. (Sir Nicholas Nicolas mistakenly records two letters from Nelson to Thomas Bertie as being to Albemarle Bertie; *The Dispatches and Letters of Vice Admiral Lord Viscount Nelson*, 2.458, 3.1–2.) Thomas Hoar joined the navy in 1773, and in the frigate *Seahorse* sailed to the East Indies as messmate of both Horatio Nelson and Thomas Troubridge, with whom he maintained a close friendship until their deaths. After the *Seahorse* he served with Sir Edward Hughes in the *Salisbury*, and with Captain Joshua Rowley in the *Monarch*. He was made lieutenant on 21 May 1778 and less than six weeks later participated in the battle of Ushant (27 July). Hoar is credited with introducing the lifebuoy into naval service during the summer of 1778: following successful experiments at Spithead, 'much to the satisfaction of Captain Rowley', the device soon spread throughout the fleet.

In December 1778 Hoar followed Rowley to the *Suffolk*. The ship joined Admiral John Byron's squadron at St Lucia, seeing action at Grenada (6 July 1779). On 18 and 19 December 1779 Hoar distinguished himself in two boat actions close to the shore of Martinique, fulfilling his orders (with the loss of only one man) to destroy two enemy ships that were on the rocks, while under close fire from the local militia. In March 1780 he again followed Rowley to the *Conqueror*, now as first lieutenant. In that capacity he was in Rodney's three actions with de Guichen (17 April, 15 and 19 May 1780). Hoar continued with Rowley from July 1780 until made commander (10 August 1782), receiving the sloop *Duc d'Estisac* (16 guns) at Port Royal as his first command. He remained in command until the ship was paid off in England in August 1783.

On 20 May 1788 Hoar married Catherine Dorothy Bertie (*d.* before 1825) of Low Layton, Essex, whose surname he assumed in accordance with the terms of the will of her father, Peregrine (a descendant of the Bertie family ennobled as the earls of Lindsey). It was thus as Captain Bertie rather than Captain Hoar that he was advanced to post rank on 22 November 1790, receiving the frigate *Leda* as his first command in the rank of captain. His re-employment came about because of tension between Spain and Britain, arising in 1789 from Spain's claiming Vancouver Island, discovered by Captain James Cook in 1778. Unfortunately for Bertie the Anglo-Spanish differences were resolved shortly before his appointment, and as soon as the news reached Britain his ship was decommissioned.

Bertie remained unemployed until 1795, when he was sent out to the West Indies in command of the *Hindostan* (54 guns), but after a severe attack of yellow fever at Port-au-Prince he was obliged to return home in October 1796. The following year Bertie commanded the *Braakel* (54 guns), and was a member of the court martial trial of Captain John Williamson, who was charged with and found guilty of misconduct in command of the *Agincourt* during the battle of Camperdown (11 October 1797). In October

1797 Bertie was appointed to the *Ardent* (64 guns), whose captain (Richard Rundel Burges) had been killed in action at Camperdown. Despite her relatively small armament the *Ardent* was a spacious vessel: in a letter of congratulation Nelson called her 'the finest man-of-war upon her decks that I ever saw' (Nicolas, 3.2). While captaining the *Ardent* Bertie is credited with improving her armament by making the carriages of her 42-pound carronades 2 inches lower. The weapons could then be worked and run out by fewer men, and also recoiled less, proportionately increasing the power of their shot. As with the lifebuoy, this improvement was adopted by all ships so armed.

For three years Bertie served in the *Ardent* in the North Sea, first under Admiral Viscount Duncan; some authorities state that he was with Duncan at the surrender of the Dutch fleet in the Texel in August 1799 (*New Biographical Dictionary*). Thereafter he served under Vice-Admiral Andrew Mitchell and Vice-Admiral William Dickson, before coming under the command of Admiral Sir Hyde Parker, baronet, for the expedition into the Baltic in 1801. The *Ardent* was assigned to Nelson's division, and played an important part in the battle of Copenhagen (2 April): four of the Danish fleet, large and small, surrendered to Bertie, who lost 130 men killed and wounded. The following morning Nelson visited the severely damaged *Ardent* and personally thanked Bertie, his officers, and the surviving ship's company for their efforts; later Bertie received the thanks of parliament as well.

On 9 April 1801 Parker transferred Bertie to command the *Bellona* (74 guns), whose captain—Thomas Boulden Thompson—had lost a leg in the battle. Bertie and the *Bellona* stayed in the Baltic with Nelson until July, then returned to England before joining the blockade of Cadiz. With the signing of the short-lived peace of Amiens (25 March 1802), the ship was sent to the West Indies and was paid off in the following June.

War recommenced on 16 May 1803 and Bertie was appointed to the *Courageux* (74 guns, captured from the French in 1761), but after only a few months family matters obliged him to give up the command. His next appointment was surely a poignant one for him: in December 1805 he was given command of the *St George* (90 guns), in which Nelson, by then just a few weeks dead, had sailed to Copenhagen in 1801. Bertie remained in this ship, based in the English Channel, until his promotion to rear-admiral of the blue (28 April 1808), thereafter returning to the Baltic, where he was actively engaged for nearly two years, until illness forced him to strike his flag on 19 February 1810.

Although expressing himself willing to serve again whenever the need should occur, he saw no more active service. However, his automatic rise through the ranks of flag officers continued: he became rear-admiral of the white on 31 July 1810 and of the red on 1 August 1811. In June 1813 he was knighted, and also received royal permission to accept and wear the insignia of the Swedish order of the Sword, awarded that same month. He became vice-admiral of the blue on 4 December 1813, of the white on 4

June 1816, and of the red on 19 July 1819. His last promotion, to admiral of the blue, came on 27 May 1825, only seventeen days before his death on 13 June 1825.

From the details of his will Thomas Bertie comes across as a pious man to whom family and friendships were intensely valuable. His interment was to be 'quite plain and without affectation'. His wife having predeceased him, he took great pains to ensure an appropriate bequest to each of those who were dear to him. If he had children, none survived, for none is mentioned in his careful list. This included the distribution of his wife's jewellery together with gifts of money, mourning rings, and ivory toothpick cases bearing either her picture or his mother's hair to family members, clothes and a year's wages to his faithful servant Martin Spearing, and £100 to 'my dear friend Sir James Saumarez'. In a striking combination of domestic detail and romantic grandeur he left his brother William the same sum of money, a mourning ring, his gold watch, his 'four volumes of the Dictionary of Arts and Sciences', five letters he had received from 'my dear friend the late Lord Viscount Nelson', his insignia of the Swedish knighthood, and a gold ring containing 'the hair of my valued friend the said Lord Viscount Nelson'. Nor was this any random snippet of hair: Bertie specified that it was the forelock which Nelson 'used to wear and hang over his head to conceal the wound he received at the battle of the Nile [1–2 Aug 1797]'. Fully alive to the historical as well as the sentimental value of these items, Bertie directed that they should be 'preserved in the family as heirlooms and transmitted to their descendants' (will, PRO, PROB 11/1701, sig. 356).   STEPHEN HOWARTH

Sources DNB · D. Syrett and R. L. DiNardo, The commissioned sea officers of the Royal Navy, 1660–1815, rev. edn, Occasional Publications of the Navy RS, 1 (1994) · will, PRO, PROB 11/1701, sig. 356 · A new biographical dictionary of 3000 cotemporary [sic] public characters, British and foreign, of all ranks and professions, 2nd edn, 3 vols. in 6 pts (1825) [admiralty library microfiche of British biographical archive] · H. J. Rose, A new general biographical dictionary, ed. H. J. Rose and T. Wright, 12 vols. (1853) [admiralty library microfiche of British biographical archive] · A. B. Sainsbury, The Royal Navy day by day, 2nd edn [n.d., c.1991] · The dispatches and letters of Vice-Admiral Lord Viscount Nelson, ed. N. H. Nicolas, 7 vols. (1844–6), vol. 2–3

Likenesses Page, stipple, pubd 1811 (after Lea), NPG

Wealth at death substantial; bequests of £100 to two individuals; also money and jewellery: will, PRO, PROB 11/1701, sig. 356

Bertie, Vere (1638×40–1681), judge, was the fourth son of Montague *Bertie, second earl of Lindsey (1607/8–1666), and his first wife, Martha (*bap.* 1605, *d.* 1641), daughter of Sir William *Cokayne of Rushton, Northamptonshire, and the widow of John Ramsay, first earl of Holdernesse. He entered the Middle Temple on 29 January 1655 and was called to the bar on 10 June 1659. He was made an honorary MA of Oxford on 8 September 1665 upon the visit of the second earl of Manchester to the university.

Bertie's legal career was assisted by his kinship with Sir Thomas *Osborne (1632–1712), who in 1653 had married his sister, Bridget. A few months after Osborne assumed the lord treasurership, Bertie was named on 20 January 1674 a king's counsel and became a bencher of his inn three days later. On 4 June 1675 he was made a baron of the exchequer, as a result of which he became a serjeant-at-law, his patrons being Danby and his brother Robert Bertie, third earl of Lindsey. He was transferred to the court of common pleas on 15 June 1678, but his tenure of office was cut short when he was removed on 29 April 1679 along with several other judges a month after the fall of Danby from office, and only a few days after showing a marked scepticism of the evidence of William Bedloe which was used to convict Nathaniel Reading of stifling the king's evidence against the Catholic lords imprisoned in the Tower.

Bertie died on 23 February 1681, 'having but three or four days illness, and the doctor said he had only a cold. He has left no will' (*Portland MSS*, 3.371). He died unmarried, but he did leave a will, made as early as 1670, which named his brothers Richard and Charles as executors and consisted of a few relatively small bequests to his family. He was buried on 5 March 1681 in the Temple Church, London.   STUART HANDLEY

Sources Baker, Serjeants · Sainty, Judges · Sainty, King's counsel · H. A. C. Sturgess, ed., Register of admissions to the Honourable Society of the Middle Temple, from the fifteenth century to the year 1944, 1 (1949), 155 · Register of burials at the Temple Church, 1628–1853 (1905), 24 [with introduction by H. G. Woods] · will, PRO, PROB 11/365, sig. 41 · Foss, Judges, 7.56–7 · The manuscripts of his grace the duke of Portland, 10 vols., HMC, 29 (1891–1931), vol. 3, p. 371 · HoP, Commons, 1660–90 · GEC, Peerage

Bertie, Willoughby, fourth earl of Abingdon (1740–1799), politician, the son of Willoughby Bertie, third earl of Abingdon (1692–1760), and his wife, Anna Maria (*d.* 1763), daughter of Sir John Collins, was born on 16 January 1740 at Gainsborough, Lincolnshire. He was educated at Westminster School and at Magdalen College, Oxford, where he graduated MA in 1761. During the 1760s he travelled extensively on the continent, with lengthy stays in Geneva (where he is reputed to have come under the influence of the city's republican politics) and Rome. John Wilkes and James Boswell were among those he met; the former accompanied him on a visit to Voltaire.

Bertie succeeded his father as fourth earl in 1760 and took his seat in the House of Lords on 6 February 1761. He did not attend the house again until late in the 1765–6 session and became a frequent participant in its affairs only from 1770. He exerted influence on parliamentary elections in Oxfordshire, especially Oxford, and in Berkshire, both the county constituency and the boroughs of Abingdon and Wallingford. He consolidated his control over both seats at Westbury, Wiltshire, during the 1760s. He thus came to lead a small group of MPs that included his brother Peregrine, a captain in the navy, and Samuel Estwick, a pamphleteer. On 7 July 1768 Abingdon married Charlotte Warren (*bap.* 1749, *d.* 1794), the youngest daughter of Admiral Sir Peter Warren and Susanna Delancy of New York. They had seven children, three sons and four daughters.

Although he came from a tory family background, Abingdon's politics are best described as those of an independent who co-operated with the Rockingham whig and Chathamite opposition parties of the 1770s and early

1780s. He gave sporadic support to the Chatham administration during 1767 and 1768, but it was only during the 1770s that he gained his reputation as an eccentric and at times radical opponent of the North administration: Lord Charlemont once referred to him as 'a man of genius, but eccentric and irregular almost to madness' (McCulloch, 1). In his first speech in the upper house in 1770, he seconded an opposition motion for an increase in the number of seamen. Thereafter, he opposed the North administration on virtually every issue that came before parliament.

By 1775 Abingdon had emerged as one of the upper house's most vocal critics of the administration's American policies. His speeches were sometimes judged eccentric, as when in 1780 he opposed the address in reply to the king's speech (which included congratulations on the birth of a thirteenth child) by wondering if that number of royal children could be supported by an empire likely to be shorn of thirteen of its colonies. The earl also had a fondness for seeing his words in print, writing pamphlets and often sending copies of his speeches and protests to the newspapers. His 1777 pamphlet *Thoughts on the letter of Edmund Burke, esq. to the sheriffs of Bristol on the affairs of America* was his most important publication. Burke's *Letter*, published after the 1776–7 parliamentary session, sought to justify the Rockingham whigs' secession from parliament as a means of dramatizing their opposition to the ministry's American policy. Burke, however, did not disavow the Declaratory Act (passed by the first Rockingham administration in 1766) which claimed that parliament could legislate for the colonies in all cases whatsoever. Abingdon not only sought to justify his own conduct in continuing to attend the Lords, where he could at least hope to modify ministerial measures; he also argued against the unbounded parliamentary supremacy implicit in the Declaratory Act. Parliament had, he argued, exceeded its authority when it had sought to legislate for the colonies without their consent. Moreover, the idea that parliament's authority was unlimited was as dangerous to Britons as to Americans: 'The dagger uplifted against the breast of America, is meant for the heart of Old England' (Smith, 230). Burke, who had worked with Abingdon to promote petitions against the war in 1775, wrote to the earl in an attempt to prevent the pamphlet's publication. Abingdon refused and the relationship between the two men was never repaired. The pamphlet exposed divisions within the opposition; it also had a strong impact in America where Robert Morris circulated it and arranged for its publication with the endorsement of the Pennsylvania council as a means of raising American morale during the Valley Forge winter of 1777–8. The pamphlet went through seven editions in England.

After North's resignation in March 1782, Abingdon supported the second Rockingham administration (March–July 1782) and then that of his friend the earl of Shelburne. Declining the vice-treasurership of Ireland for himself, he successfully solicited a place for Samuel Estwick. Abingdon also created a minor sensation in the early days of the Shelburne administration by proposing that a bill be brought in to make clear Britain's continuing control over Ireland's external relations. Though unsupported by any other peer, news of his speech occasioned negative reaction in Ireland. Abingdon supported with vote and voice Shelburne's peace preliminaries in February 1783. When the coalition of Charles James Fox and Lord North forced Shelburne from office, Abingdon became a fierce opponent of the coalition, seeing it as an attempt, as he wrote to Shelburne, to create a new despotism based on 'that Hellish Doctrine of an Omnipotency of Parliament' (9 Dec 1783, Bowood House, Bowood MSS). He was the opposition's first speaker against the coalition's India Bill in the great debate of 15 December 1783, although characteristically he failed to concert his tactic of proposing questions to the judges with anyone except Shelburne (who did not attend). The rest of the opposition ignored his suggestion.

After the coalition's fall, Abingdon generally supported the younger Pitt, while hoping for Shelburne's return to office; he voted with ministerial forces during the Regency crisis of 1788 and later opposed the French Revolution (contrary to the description of his politics in the *Dictionary of National Biography*). To Abingdon, events across the channel bore no comparison to those of 1688 in England and he continued to regard France as the national enemy. Sometimes, however, he voted against administration measures, as when he opposed the Seditious Meetings Bill in 1795. Curiously for one often regarded as a radical, he saw efforts to limit the slave trade as dangerous concessions to Jacobinism, and in both 1792 and 1799 he voted against such attempts. His fondness for publicity got him into trouble in 1794. Publishing a speech he had given in the Lords against what he saw as the venal tendencies of attorneys, he singled out by name one Thomas Sermon (whom he had once employed). Publication deprived Abingdon of the protection of parliamentary privilege, and Sermon sued for libel. Abingdon, representing himself, was found guilty on 12 January 1795, sentenced to three months' imprisonment, and fined £100.

Abingdon was also a figure of significance on the London music scene. As a patron, he helped to organize the Bach–Abel concerts with his brother-in-law Giovanni Gallini and was involved in efforts to bring Haydn to England. J. C. Bach and Haydn were among the composers who dedicated works to Abingdon and to members of his family. The earl was also a composer. He set to music a number of literary pieces as well as his own lyrics. Very occasionally his political and musical interests converged, as when in 1783 he set to music a glee entitled 'Lord North in the Suds'. He was also noted by contemporaries as an accomplished flautist.

Abingdon died on 26 September 1799 and was buried at Rycote, his Oxfordshire home. His wife had predeceased him and their third but only surviving son, Montague Bertie, succeeded as fifth earl of Abingdon.

WILLIAM C. LOWE

Sources D. McCulloch, 'The musical oeuvre of Willoughby Bertie, 4th earl of Abingdon (1740–99)', *Royal Musical Association Research Chronicle*, 33 (2000) · P. H. Smith, ed., *English defenders of*

American freedoms, 1774–1778 (1972) · Bowood House, Wiltshire, Bowood MSS · *The correspondence of Edmund Burke*, 3, ed. G. H. Guttridge (1961) · Cobbett, *Parl. hist.*, vols. 16–31 · *Political Magazine* (1780–84) · *The manuscripts and correspondence of James, first earl of Charlemont*, 1, HMC, 28 (1891) · I. R. Christie, *The end of North's ministry, 1780–82* (1958) · C. Bonwick, *English radicals and the American Revolution* (1977) · A. S. Turberville, *The House of Lords in the age of reform, 1784–1837* (1958) · GEC, *Peerage*, new edn · *GM*, 1st ser., 69 (1799), 903 · *DNB* · IGI

Archives Bodl. Oxf., corresp. and papers | priv. coll., Bowood MSS, letters to Lord Shelburne
Likenesses J. F. Rigaud, double portrait, oils, 1792 (with daughter), priv. coll.; auctioned 1983 · M. Benedetti, stipple, pubd 1800 (with music masters; after J. F. Rigaud), BM, NPG · T. Gainsborough, oils (unfinished), priv. coll.; formerly at Wytham Abbey from 1797 to 1956

Berton, William. *See* Barton, William (*d.* after 1382).

Bertorelli, Joe [Giuseppe Domenico] (1893–1994), restaurateur, was born on 10 June 1893 at Bergazzi di Bardi, Piacenza, Liguria, Italy, the youngest of the four sons of Lazzaro and Marianna Bertorelli. By the time of his birth his father and three elder brothers were already living and working in London, where Lazzaro had a job building barrel organs and ran a boarding-house much frequented by Italians passing through on their way to Wales. In 1911 Giuseppe joined his family in London and worked as a waiter, but in the following year he joined an elder brother in New York, working as a waiter and chef in the otherwise all French-speaking kitchen at the Plaza Hotel. In 1916 he became an American citizen, calling himself Joe Bertorelli, and during the First World War he worked in an armaments factory (stomach disorders kept him from active service). He married Maria Bertorelli (1898–1978), a girl he had known in Italy, in 1917, and they had three sons. While working at the Plaza, he came into contact with many of the stars of the nearby Metropolitan Opera; he particularly admired Enrico Caruso, who was generous with his tips. He also developed his lifelong passion for opera.

In 1922 Bertorelli returned to England and joined the family restaurant business, which consisted at first of a café at Shoreditch, and another at Waterloo Bridge, selling pies, mash, and sausages. (Italians had taken over much of London catering on all levels from the French, who had returned home to fight during the war.) Next they acquired a five-table place in Charlotte Street, Fitzrovia, frequented by chauffeurs who, noticing the food the brothers cooked for themselves, asked for the same fare, thus establishing the dishes of northern Italy on the menu. Premises at Shepherds Bush Green soon followed, and the Charlotte Street café was expanded into a 100-seat restaurant. Joe opened a branch in Edgware Road and, in 1928, a restaurant in Queensway called the Monte Carlo, which, during the Second World War, 'used swan in pies and corned beef in bolognese. The staff ate horsemeat' (*Daily Telegraph*, 21 Sept 1994).

Bertorelli became a British subject in 1936. He dealt with anti-Italian feeling by putting up a sign in the window of the Monte Carlo saying 'My three sons are serving in the British Army'. After the war he began the practice of

importing barrels of wine from Italy and France and bottling it in the Charlotte Street cellar. In 1948 the family branched out into making ice cream, and for many years they supplied Fortnum and Mason and Harrods; the business was eventually sold to Lyons in 1966.

The Bertorelli brothers had a conservative set of business rules—not to borrow money, to keep prices low and service fast, and to avoid family disagreements by confining the running of their businesses to the men, keeping the women out of their financial affairs. But they were progressive in other ways, being among the first in the catering trade to give their staff a weekly day off. This resulted in a very loyal workforce in an industry plagued by rapid turnover of staff. Proof of this was the age of the waiters at Charlotte Street: by 1984, when the restaurant finally closed (leaving a blue plaque to mark the place where it stood), some of them seemed as old as the century. Indeed, Bertorelli's *Times* obituary mentioned a cook 'still peeling garlic well into his eighties' (1 Oct 1994). At the height of their success there were six Bertorelli restaurants in the capital, and, from the time when their customers included Augustus John and his bohemian artist friends to their later incarnations as places that provided affordable meals to students, Bertorelli restaurants had in common crisp white napery, pale green walls, and elderly waiters. The business empire declined in the 1960s as fewer and fewer of the younger generation of Bertorellis wanted to join it, and in the 1990s the two restaurants bearing the name ceased to have any connection with the family. In 1976, at the age of eighty-three Joe Bertorelli handed the business over to his eldest son and devoted himself to gardening and to visiting Italy. His wife died in 1978; he died, aged 101, on 12 September 1994 at Abercorn House, Hawley, Surrey.

Bertorelli was not the founder of his family business, nor, contrary to received wisdom, were the Bertorellis the first to serve Italian food in Britain, but, by his longevity, he survived into an age when restaurants became interesting as social phenomena, and it was he, rather than his father or brothers, who became the representative of the clan, and emblematic of the Italians who did so much to improve the standard of eating out in Britain.

PAUL LEVY

Sources personal knowledge (2004) · *Daily Telegraph* (21 Sept 1994) · *The Times* (1 Oct 1994) · *The Guardian* (8 Oct 1994) · d. cert. · naturalization certificate, 19 March 1936, PRO, HO 334/227/B2. 620 · d. cert. [Maria Bertorelli]
Likenesses photograph, repro. in *The Times*
Wealth at death under £125,000: probate, 7 Feb 1995, CGPLA Eng. & Wales

Bertram, Charles Julius (1723–1765), literary forger, was born in London, the son of a silk dyer who moved with his family to Copenhagen at an unknown date. Nothing else is known of his family or educational background, other than that he had a brother who died at sea in 1752. Bertram obtained the position of English teacher at the school for naval cadets, styling himself in 1746 'professor of the *English* tongue in the Royal Marine Academy of *Copenhagen*'. Little is known of his life beyond what can be gleaned from his correspondence with the antiquary William Stukeley. In one of these letters he thanked Stukeley for including a short autobiography, reflecting that:

it were enough to excite a Narration of my own past Life, but that it has run thro' so narrow a short Channel I blush to make it known, one of the most happy, as well as notable, occurrences in it being thus highly favoured with your most desirable Correspondence. (Bertram to Stukeley, 10 Nov 1747, Bodl. Oxf., MS Eng. lett. b.2, fol. 9.)

Bertram had penned his first letter to Stukeley on 23 August 1746, asking for further information about his books, especially on Celtic history, and inviting a literary correspondence. He vacillated over sending the letter, and Stukeley did not receive it until 11 June 1747, but replied immediately. In his next letter Bertram announced that he had

at present in my Possession, a copy of an old Manuscript Fragment (and am in hopes of getting the original) called Ricardi Monachi Westmonasteriensis comentariolum Geographicum de situ Britanniae & Stationum quas Romani ipsi in ea Insula aedificauerunt. It seems to me to have been part of a greater Treatise … compiled out of Beda [*sic*], Orosius, Pliny, &c. & some Authors quite unknown; it is pity it is so tenuous, consisting only of four sheets & an half in Quarto, the half of Parchment on which is depicted in colours the Islands of Britain, but in a manner peculiar to this Author. (Bertram to Stukeley, 1747, Bodl. Oxf., MS Eng. lett. b.2, fols. 7–8)

This letter also contained a reference vouching for Bertram from his 'great friend and patron' Hans Gramm, 'privy-counsellor, and chief librarian to his *Danish* Majesty: a learned gentleman, who had been in England' (Stukeley, 12).

Bertram and Stukeley's correspondence continued over the next sixteen years, concerning various antiquarian subjects; it revealed Bertram's antiquarian interest in barrows and standing stones, and his fine illustrative skills. But the main subject of their letters was the purported manuscript by Richard of Westminster. On Stukeley's solicitation, Bertram sent him 'in letters, a transcript of the whole: and at last a copy of the map: he having an excellent hand in drawing' (Stukeley, 14). The forgery was essentially a 'medieval' history of ancient Britain composed by Bertram from genuine classical sources, followed by an 'Itinerary' collected from fragments supposedly left by a Roman general. With the assistance of Mr Widmore, librarian to Westminster Abbey, Stukeley discovered that there had in fact been a fourteenth-century monk at the abbey, Richard of Cirencester, known author of the 'Speculum historiale de gestis regum Angliae' (ibid., 5–6). Stukeley showed a facsimile of the manuscript, supposedly copied out by Bertram, to David Casley, keeper of the Cottonian Library, who stated that it was of fourteenth-century origin. Bertram's forgery was thus lent credibility by a fortuitous association with an authentic medieval chronicler.

Even without this lucky stroke, Bertram's promotion of his forgery was subtle and intelligent. It is likely he was assisted in its creation by studying the works of modern antiquaries such as William Camden, Alexander Gordon, and John Horsley, all of whose books he mentions in his letters. The weakest link was his refusal to divulge either the owner of the supposed manuscript (who, he claimed, had stolen it from a library in England) or to agree to Stukeley's wish to purchase it for the British Museum. Stukeley encouraged Bertram to publish the manuscript, and it eventually appeared in 1757, cleverly printed alongside two genuine early medieval texts by Gildas and Nennius, as *Britannicarum gentium historiae antiquae scriptores tres*. The same year Stukeley published an abridged account of the itinerary with its accompanying map. As he explained, 'we learn from the present work now happily preserved, the completest account of the Roman state of Brittain, and of the most antient inhabitants thereof; and the geography thereof admirably depicted in a most excellent map' (Stukeley, 8).

It is conceivable that Bertram's motive was fame, though he claimed his only interest was that of 'serving my Native Country' (Bertram to Stukeley, 5 March 1759, Bodl. Oxf., MS Eng. lett. b.2, fol. 66*r*). It is possible Bertram was a compulsive liar, a teasing player of games, or simply a frustrated academic. He told Stukeley how 'future Ages will venerate the Memory of those deserving Men, when the very Names of their ungrateful Contemporaries will be quite forgotten' (ibid.). Another letter to Stukeley included a suspicious-sounding account of an old doctor who possessed a medicine that 'cures all Diseases arising from the Heart … in a most surprising manner'. Bertram offered to send the potion to Stukeley, asking him 'if all this you find to be true, and you can best judge, I shall rejoice more, that I am thus employed to serve my Country this way, than by recovering ten MSS' (Bertram to Stukeley, 12 May 1749, Bodl. Oxf., MS Eng. lett. b.2, fol. 24*r*). Stukeley ignored this offer, and he must also have had some suspicions over the medieval manuscript, for Bertram asserted in 1756 that if Richard 'was not the real Author, who was, & what Ends could they serve therein? or what Advantage reap from such an undertaking? for my Part, I declare I can't conceive any' (Bertram to Stukeley, 11 Dec 1756, Bodl. Oxf., MS Eng. lett. b.2, fol. 48). He certainly sought professional advancement by his forgery, asking Stukeley to broker his election to the Royal Society and the Society of Antiquaries, informing him that this would assist his career in the royal household. In 1756 Stukeley arranged for the Society of Antiquaries to elect him an honorary fellow.

In 1762 Bertram lost his teaching position in the academy, though he continued to be on good terms with Prince William of Hesse-Cassel, grandson of George II, to whom he had become tutor of English in 1757. In December 1762 Bertram told Stukeley 'I am disgusted here, and should be glad to end my Days in my native Country' (Bertram to Stukeley, 5 Dec 1762, Bodl. Oxf., MS Eng. lett. b.2, fol. 79*v*). Having served the king of Denmark for sixteen years, and with an aged mother to support, he was 'fed up with continual Hopes, and without the least Probability of seeing my Circumstances bettered' (Bertram to Stukeley, 16 Sept 1763, Bodl. Oxf., MS Eng. lett. b.2, fol. 82*r*). It appears Bertram never married, and he died, without returning to England, in 1765, the same year as Stukeley, for whom he had always shown great affection 'as my Father and Friend' (Bertram to Stukeley, 16 Oct 1753, Bodl. Oxf., MS Eng. lett. b.2, fol. 37v). Bertram had published two books on English grammar, *Rudimenta grammaticae anglicanae* (1750) and *The Royal English–Danish Grammar* (1753), as well as a philosophical collection, *Ethics from Several Authors* (1751), various translations of English works into Danish and German, and an illustrated volume on the Danish army. He had also sought Stukeley's assistance for a history of King Canute, though this was never published. A list of his manuscripts, medals, antiquities, paintings, and rare books, the sale of which he hoped would raise money, shows his enthusiasms as both a collector and a historian (Bertram to Stukeley, 16 Sept 1763, Bodl. Oxf., MS Eng. lett. b.2, fols. 82v–83).

Although there were those who from the start suspected the manuscript of being either a medieval or a modern forgery, or considered the material in it to be largely derivative, Richard of Cirencester's *De situ Britanniae* was accepted by many as genuine, and was utilized in various histories of Roman Britain. Bertram's spurious names for Roman stations even appeared in the Ordnance Survey maps. The manuscript was republished in the second volume of Stukeley's *Itinerarium curiosum* in 1776, and in 1809 Henry Hatcher published anonymously an English translation, *The Description of Britain*. Any claims Richard of Cirencester had to authenticity were demolished, however, by B. B. Woodward, royal librarian at Windsor Castle, in an essay published in the *Gentleman's Magazine* in 1866–7. He showed how Bertram used Latin words (such as *statio* for a Roman 'station' and *supplementum* for a 'supplement' or appendix) in ways which would have had no meaning in the Roman or medieval periods, and how his style and terminology differed from that appearing in Richard of Cirencester's genuine extant work, and also its palaeographic inaccuracies. The *Dictionary of National Biography* in 1885 described Bertram as 'the cleverest and most successful literary impostor of modern times', and his name sits comfortably alongside those other great eighteenth-century forgers Thomas Chatterton, William Henry Ireland, and James Macpherson (whose *Ossian* poems were also supported by Stukeley as authentic Celtic works).

DAVID BOYD HAYCOCK

Sources C. Bertram, letters to Dr Stukeley, Bodl. Oxf., MS Eng. lett. b.2 · W. Stukeley, *An account of Richard of Cirencester, monk of Westminster, and of his works* (1757) · S. Piggott, 'William Stukeley: new facts and an old forgery', *Antiquity*, 60 (1986), 115–22 · B. B. Woodward, 'A literary forgery: Richard of Cirencester's tractate on Britain', *GM*, 4th ser., 1 (1866), 301–7, 617–24 · R. W. Shirley, 'The map that never was', *Map Collector*, 53 (1990), 8–13 · M. Jones, *Fake? The art of deception* (1990), 25, 66 · DNB

Archives Bodl. Oxf., letters and papers, MS Eng. lett. b.2; Top. gen. e 66–68, g 1; Eng. misc. d 451

Bertram, Roger (*c*.1195–1242), baron and justice, was descended from the William Bertram who was granted the barony of Mitford in Northumberland in the reign of Henry I. Roger was the son of another William Bertram and his wife, Alice, the daughter of Robert de Umfraville of Prudhoe; a minor when his father died in 1199, his wardship was granted first to William Brewer, but later, at the end of 1205, to Peter de Brus, who undertook to pay 1300 marks for it. Bertram came of age about 1215, and, like most of the northern baronage, joined the rebellion against King John. In January 1216 his lands in Northumberland were granted to the loyalist Philip of Oldcotes, and although Bertram was one of the northerners said to have proposed negotiations with King John in May that year, he did not return to the king's allegiance until after the battle of Lincoln; his lands were restored to him on 24 July 1217, though a price of £100 was set upon Mitford Castle. In the event the issue of price was irrelevant for several years, because Oldcotes persistently refused to surrender Mitford, even though Bertram had much influential support in the north. Only in August 1220, under intense pressure from the central government, did Oldcotes give way; Bertram had to give a charter promising faithful service, and surrender his son as a hostage into the keeping of the bishop of Durham, before he could take possession of Mitford. But he was pardoned the £100 ostensibly due to the exchequer for the return of his castle, in consideration of the long time he had had to wait for this.

Roger Bertram appears to have been eager to prove his loyalty to the new regime. Already on 15 June 1220 he had been present at York as a witness to Henry III's promise to marry his sister Joanna to Alexander II, king of Scots. In 1221 he was active against the earl of Aumale in the north, and in 1224 he took part in the siege of Bedford Castle. On 4 July, while the siege was in progress, he was rewarded for his services by being pardoned money due from the previous year's scutage. An assessor and collector of the fifteenth of 1225 in Northumberland, he went on the expedition to Brittany of 1230, while in 1237 he formed part of the escort deputed to bring the Scottish king to York, and on 25 September witnessed the treaty of peace agreed upon there by kings Henry and Alexander. He acted several times as a royal justice. In 1225 he was appointed to take assizes of novel disseisin and deliver gaols in Northumberland, and he was subsequently commissioned to take assizes and deliver gaols in that county on a number of occasions in the late 1220s and during the 1230s. A justice itinerant in Cumberland in 1227, he went on eyre in the northern counties in 1234–5, and in 1237 was appointed to hear pleas in the bishopric of Durham, an appointment later modified to a commission of gaol delivery. Notwithstanding these judicial activities, in 1241 it was alleged that he and his men had been poaching in the king's forest, and that the king's servants trying to protect their master's interests were hampered by a confederacy between Bertram and his fellow Northumberland baron, the chief justice of the forests north of the Trent, Robert de Ros (*d. c*.1270) of Wark; it had been agreed that Bertram's son was to marry Ros's daughter, while Ros's son was to marry Bertram's daughter (it is not clear whether these unions actually took place). Bertram was later reported to have been amerced for his offence before the king at Windsor. Nevertheless, in September 1241 Ros was instructed to give Bertram deer from the royal park with which to stock his own park in Northumberland.

Bertram's wife, who was called Agnes, and whom he had married by 1224, was presumably the mother of the son and daughter whose marriages were provided for in the alliance with Robert de Ros. Roger Bertram died in 1242, before 24 May. He was probably buried in the church of Brinkburn Priory, which had been founded by his great-grandfather William Bertram, and where his grandfather, another Roger Bertram, had obtained licence to be buried. His heir was his son, also Roger *Bertram.

HENRY SUMMERSON

Sources Chancery records (RC) • PRO • Pipe rolls • Curia regis rolls preserved in the Public Record Office (1922-), vol. 16, pp. 282-6 • [W. Page], ed., The chartulary of Brinkburn Priory, SurtS, 90 (1893) • J. C. Holt, The northerners: a study in the reign of King John (1961) • D. A. Carpenter, The minority of Henry III (1990) • D. Crook, Records of the general eyre, Public Record Office Handbooks, 20 (1982) • I. J. Sanders, English baronies: a study of their origin and descent, 1086-1327 (1960) • GEC, Peerage • patent rolls, PRO, C 66/18, 66/19, 66/20 • CPR, 1232-47, 298

Bertram, Sir Roger (1224-1272), baronial leader, was the son of Roger *Bertram (c.1195-1242). He did homage for his lands in Northumberland and elsewhere on attaining his majority on 28 June 1246. He married Ida, probably his second wife, about 1252. He performed military summonses for Henry III in Wales, Scotland, and Aquitaine from the 1240s to the 1260s. In 1257, for an unknown reason, the king ordered the temporary confiscation of his estates; he was again before royal justices in 1261. He joined Simon de Montfort's party at the outbreak of the barons' war, probably motivated by hatred of William de Valence, Henry III's half-brother. A knight-banneret, according to the chronicler Rishanger, he was among the prisoners captured at Northampton by the king on 5 April 1264, whereupon his castle at Mitford and other lands were seized and entrusted to William de Valence. Released by the victory of Lewes (13 May 1264), his lands were restored on 14 June. His nephew Sir Norman d'Arcy, another rebel captured at Hull, was released about the same time. Granted remission of his Jewish debts in October 1264, Bertram was one of the eighteen barons summoned to Simon de Montfort's parliament on 14 December 1264, but is not further mentioned.

Bertram's retinue numbered at least two knights. His style of life outstripped his means and he was considerably in debt to Jewish moneylenders even in 1253. His main debt (400 marks) was sold to William de Valence in 1257 and by 1262 Bertram began alienations to him which eventually depleted his estates. He was 'recently deceased' in April 1272. Shortly afterwards, his heir, his daughter Agnes (who had married one of Peter de Montfort's sons about 1253) alienated the remainder of the Bertram barony to the queen, who had bought his debts. Bertram's widow, Ida, married Robert de Neville of Raby, co. Durham. He was also survived by a bastard son, Thomas.   J. H. ROUND, rev. H. W. RIDGEWAY

Sources Chancery records • A descriptive catalogue of ancient deeds in the Public Record Office, 6 vols. (1890-1915), vols. 2-5 • CIPM • C. Roberts, ed., Excerpta è rotulis finium in Turri Londinensi asservatis, Henrico Tertio rege, AD 1216-1272, 2, RC, 32 (1836), 266 • Ann. mon., 4.450 • [W. Rishanger], The chronicle of William de Rishanger, of the barons' wars, ed. J. O. Halliwell, CS, 15 (1840), 125 • [W. Illingworth], ed., Rotuli hundredorum temp. Hen. III et Edw. I, RC, 2 (1818), 20, 23 • [W. Page], ed., The chartulary of Brinkburn Priory, SurtS, 90 (1893) • J. Hodgson, A history of Northumberland, 3 pts in 7 vols. (1820-58), pt 2, vol. 2, pp. 34-41 • A history of Northumberland, Northumberland County History Committee, 15 vols. (1893-1940), vol. 7, pp. 230-32

Bertram, Walter (d. 1495/6), merchant and provost of Edinburgh, is first recorded in 1464. He received payments for expensive cloth sold to James III in 1473 and by 1477 was clearly wealthy, as he bought the lands of Normangills in Lanarkshire from David Lindsay, earl of Crawford. His links with the royal household as a prominent merchant led to royal favour in the late 1470s, and he was confirmed in his lands and appointed to the important roles of custumar, bailie, and chamberlain of Berwick, regained from England in 1461.

Bertram frequently attended parliament as a burgh commissioner representing Edinburgh from 1478 and he was elected to the influential committee of the articles on three occasions in the crisis of 1482-3. On 4 August 1482, before the dukes of Albany (James III's brother, who was seeking to control the government) and Gloucester—and with 20,000 English soldiers outside his city—Bertram, as provost of Edinburgh, promised that, if requested, the city would repay all the dowry payments made by Edward IV to James III as part of the marriage alliance of 1474. It was the price of an English withdrawal. On 29 September Bertram took part with Albany in the 'siege' of Edinburgh Castle, by which the king ended the two-month confinement imposed on him by rebellious nobles. Subsequent events, however, suggest Bertram was not a supporter of Albany, for he had been replaced as provost by 16 November and was omitted from a list of burgesses in a grant of Leith's customs to Edinburgh. On 29 January 1483, as the king began to regain his power after Albany's retirement to Dunbar, James III granted Bertram and his wife an annuity of £40 Scots for his services, particularly in the king's release from captivity. This was renewed in 1489, when it was specifically stated to be compensation for damage perpetrated by Albany.

Bertram married Elizabeth Cant (d. after 1498) before 4 November 1477. He died between 27 August 1495 and 3 August 1496 following a career in which he had been one of the very few members of the Scottish burgess estate to make an important mark on the political stage. He was succeeded by Andrew Bertram.   ROLAND J. TANNER

Sources M. D. Young, ed., The parliaments of Scotland: burgh and shire commissioners, 2 vols. (1992-3) • G. Burnett and others, eds., The exchequer rolls of Scotland, 8-10 (1885-7) • CDS, vol. 4 • J. M. Thomson and others, eds., Registrum magni sigilli regum Scotorum / The register of the great seal of Scotland, 11 vols. (1882-1914), vol. 2 • APS, 1424-1567 • T. Dickson, ed., Compota thesaurariorum regum Scotorum / Accounts of the lord high treasurer of Scotland, 1 (1877)

Berwick. For this title name see Hill, William Noel-, third Baron Berwick (1773-1842).

Berwick, Edward (b. 1753/4, d. in or after 1819), Church of Ireland clergyman and writer, was born in co. Down, the son of Duke Berwick. He entered Trinity College, Dublin, on 12 June 1770, aged sixteen, and gained a scholarship in 1773. Berwick came to notice in the following year through his successful resistance to certain arbitrary regulations of the new college provost, Major Hely Hutchinson, MP for Cork, who forbade the students to take a public part in electoral matters, while expecting them to vote for parliamentary candidates of his own nomination. Hutchinson's appointment was regarded by many younger members of the college as a government placement, for which reason it was resented and seen as potentially damaging to standards of academic life. Dubbed Harlequin Prancer, Hutchinson was the object of a number of squibs, some of which (appearing between 1774 and 1776) were collected and edited by Robert Dodsley, under the pseudonym Nathan ben Saddi, as *Pranceriana*. In 1775 Berwick, along with several other non-complying students, was deprived of his scholarship, ostensibly because he had failed to reside in college as regularly as the statutes demanded. He appealed to the college's visitors—the archbishops of Armagh and of Dublin—and after a hearing which occupied three days, in the course of which Hutchinson admitted that his 'unexceptionable character entitled him to every indulgence', Berwick was reinstated by the archbishop of Armagh, Richard Robinson. Referring to this trial one of the authors in Dodsley's collection wrote:

> Proud of imagin'd arbitrary sway,
> Prancer long dream'd he safely might display
> Imperial pow'r, accountable to none,
> Fear'd like a German monarch on his throne.
> Subservient to his will the board conven'd,
> Submissive, loyal; Berwick was arraign'd,
> Condemn'd, depriv'd, a convict on record;
> Three rebels only disobeyed their lord.
> But Robinson and justice interfer'd,
> Revers'd the sentence, and the victim spar'd.
> (*Pranceriana*, 2nd edn, 1784)

Berwick subsequently took holy orders and was presented by Bishop Percy of Dromore to the vicarage of Tullylish in co. Down; from there, in 1795, he was preferred to the vicarage of Leixlip, near Dublin, and to the rectory of Clongish, co. Longford, on the presentation of the earl of Moira (subsequently marquess of Hastings), who made Berwick his domestic chaplain.

A friend of Sir Walter Scott, Berwick provided considerable help in Scott's edition of the works of Jonathan Swift. In 1810 he published the *Life of Apollonius of Tyana, from the Greek*, and, in 1811, *A Treatise on the Government of the Church*. In the following year he dedicated to his patron (dating his preface from Esker, near Leixlip) the *Lives of Marcus Valerius, Messala Corvinus, and Titus Pomponius Atticus*. His patron, when marquess of Hastings, commissioned him to edit a number of letters to and from John Bramhall, a seventeenth-century archbishop of Armagh; these had come into the possession of the marquess through the Rawdon family. The preface to this work is dated 'Lurgan, 1 Jan 1819'. Details of Berwick's death and burial are unknown.   LEWIS SERGEANT, *rev.* PHILIP CARTER

Sources N. ben Saddi [R. Dodsley], *Pranceriana: a select collection of fugitive pieces*, 2nd edn, 2 vols. (1784) • Burtchaell & Sadleir, *Alum. Dubl.* • C. Maxwell, *A history of Trinity College Dublin, 1591–1892* (1946) **Archives** NL Scot., letters to Walter Scott • TCD, letters to Joseph Cooper Walker

Berwick upon Tweed. For this title name *see* Fitzjames, James, duke of Berwick upon Tweed (1670–1734); Fitzjames, Honora, duchess of Berwick upon Tweed (1675–1698) [*see under* Sarsfield, Patrick, Jacobite first earl of Lucan (*d.* 1693)].

Besant [*née* Wood], **Annie** (1847–1933), theosophist and politician in India, was born at 2 Fish Street Hill in the City of London on 1 October 1847, the only daughter of William Persse Wood (*d.* 1852), underwriter, and his wife, Emily Roche Morris (*d.* 1874). Other relatives were Matthew Wood (1768–1843), lord mayor of London; William Page Wood, Lord Hatherley (1801–1881); Katharine Wood, wife of Captain W. O'Shea and later of C. S. Parnell; and Sir Henry Trueman Wood, her elder brother. The Woods came from Devon, but Annie's grandfather, as a younger son, went to Ireland and settled in Galway. His son, Annie's father, studied medicine at Trinity College, Dublin, where he married Emily, who came of an Irish family whose fortunes had declined. In 1845 they returned to London, where William's family connection secured him a City post. He and Emily had three children; the first two, Henry (1845–1929) and Annie, survived. When Annie was five years old her father died. Although her prosperous Wood in-laws offered support, Emily chose to see Henry through Harrow School without help. She rented a house near the college and took in boys as boarders. There was no room for a precocious little girl, so in 1856, when a wealthy spinster, Ellen Marryat (sister of Captain Frederick Marryat, author of boys' adventure stories), offered to educate Annie, Emily accepted, though she knew how keenly her daughter would feel the separation.

Education, marriage, and loss of faith Miss Marryat had a 'perfect genius' for teaching (Besant, *Sketches*, 16). The children she educated in a handsome, sunny house near Charmouth in Dorset were encouraged to learn from observation and experience. Because her father had made a fortune planting sugar, she had always been accustomed to affluence and social position. Consequently, besides Latin, French, history, and geography, Annie absorbed the unshakeable self-confidence of an English gentlewoman, together with the sense of duty towards others less fortunate than herself that was the evangelical Miss Marryat's guiding principle. Religion was to be Annie's chief preoccupation, recreation, and study, but she was not attracted to Miss Marryat's plain and serviceable faith, preferring ritual. At sixteen, when Miss Marryat dismissed her, she was intensely devout; in her own words, the very stuff of which fanatics were made. She was prevented from converting to Roman Catholicism only by a prior commitment to the Oxford Movement; Edward Pusey, Henry Liddon, and John Keble ruled her faith, while her imagination was engaged by the esoteric practices discussed by the fathers of the church. Their works were in Harrow School Library, where she studied by herself in the brief interval between returning to her mother and her marriage in Hastings parish church on 21 December 1867 to the Revd Frank Besant (1840–1917), son of William Besant, a wine merchant. He was seven years older; an

Annie Besant (1847–1933), by Hayman Selig Mendelssohn

impecunious, parsimonious, stiff-necked young man from Portsea, whose evangelicalism was approvingly described as 'serious' (one of his five brothers became the writer Sir Walter Besant). Digby, their first child, was born on 16 January 1869, followed by Mabel on 28 August 1870.

In 1872 Lord Hatherley, now lord chancellor, preferred Frank Besant to the living of Sibsey, an agricultural parish in Lincolnshire. The marriage was already under strain from the—to Annie—horrid inevitability of a third pregnancy which, she argued, was beyond their means and a result of her having fallen out with God, whose failure to spare Mabel from a near fatal illness in 1871 she regarded as unjust. In vain she sought a remedy for her distress at losing her faith in the works of orthodox theologians, while an appeal in person to one of her heroes earned her a rebuke. 'You have read too much', E. B. Pusey told her (Besant, *Sketches*, 66). She turned for sympathy to the former vicar of Healaugh, Charles Voysey, whose appeal to the privy council against a sentence of deprivation for unorthodoxy had been upheld at a hearing on 11 February 1871 presided over by 'Pontius' Hatherley. Voysey, now head of a 'theistic' church in London, introduced her to the freethinker Thomas *Scott, who encouraged her to write a pamphlet, which he published in 1872 as *On the Deity of Jesus of Nazareth*, by the wife of a beneficed clergyman. Fearful that this might put his own living at risk, in the summer of 1873 Frank Besant issued an ultimatum: Annie was to be seen to take holy communion regularly at Sibsey or she was to leave. 'Hypocrisy or expulsion', Annie wrote, 'I chose the latter' (Besant, *Autobiography*, 99). In 1874 she moved to London.

A freethinker: Bradlaugh and birth control Annie Besant existed in London on the small allowance awarded to her under a deed of separation dated 25 October 1873 that gave her custody of Mabel, and by what she earned from writing articles in favour of freethought commissioned by Thomas Scott. Digby stayed with his father, who continued vicar of Sibsey until his death in 1917. In 1875 Charles Bradlaugh, president of the National Secular Society, gave her a job writing for the freethought newspaper, the *National Reformer*, and encouraged her to speak in public (her first attempt had been behind locked doors, from the pulpit of Sibsey church). Soon she was second only to Bradlaugh in her ability to fill the halls of science up and down the country. 'What a beautiful and attractive and irresistible creature she was then', the Irish journalist T. P. O'Connor wrote, 'with her slight but full and well-shaped figure, her dark hair, her finely chiselled features … with that short upper lip that seemed always in a pout' (*T. P.'s Weekly*, 21 Aug 1903). Her other asset was her voice, which Beatrice Webb described as 'the voice of a beautiful soul' (*Diary*, 4.305).

For the next eleven years Mrs Besant and Bradlaugh, who was fourteen years older, were close and affectionate colleagues. As Ajax she wrote a weekly column, 'Daybreak', in the *Reformer* about current affairs, while research for lectures such as 'The gospel of Christianity v. the gospel of freethought' and 'The atonement' (of which she disapproved) called for the kind of theological knowledge possessed by a clerk in holy orders. As bishop, Bradlaugh demanded excellence. On 20 January 1877 they set up the Freethought Publishing Company, promising that 'All that we publish we shall defend' (*National Reformer*, 4 March 1877). In March the publishing company invited prosecution under the Obscene Publications Act of 1857 by reissuing Charles Knowlton's treatise on birth control, *The Fruits of Philosophy* (1877). Bradlaugh and Besant aimed to establish the right to circulate information about a subject that, if mentioned at all, was referred to as neo-Malthusianism. At the trial on 18 June 1877 Mrs Besant conducted her own defence; the first woman publicly to endorse 'checks' on conception. In her evidence she stressed that such measures would help to relieve poverty. The pamphlet was judged to be calculated to deprave public morals, but Besant and Bradlaugh were exonerated from any corrupt motive in publishing it. Besant soon produced her own advice, *The Law of Population* (1878), which sold thousands over the years. But she stood condemned as shameless by the public, and on 18 May 1878 Frank Besant succeeded in an action to reclaim Mabel on the grounds that Annie's views made her unfit to bring up a young girl. Mabel and Digby were reconciled to their mother later on; Frank Besant never was. His vocation ruled out any question of divorce.

In 1879 Annie Besant was tutored in science by Edward Aveling, and matriculated at London University for a science degree, with which she did not proceed.

From 1880 to 1886 Annie Besant was caught up in the bitter struggle over Bradlaugh, as an atheist, taking his seat in parliament as MP for Northampton. Her approach to politics, always radical, grew more extreme. In 1884 a new recruit to the freethought movement, Edward Aveling, introduced her to socialist ideas; they began appearing in *Our Corner*, the literary magazine she had just launched. Its art critic after 1885 was George Bernard Shaw, who introduced her to the Fabian Society. In March 1885 she became a member of its executive. When she saw how repressive the Liberal government was in containing unrest in Ireland and among the unemployed in London she also offered her support to the Marxist Social Democratic Federation. These moves upset Bradlaugh, who regarded socialism as a disruptive foreign doctrine. In November 1887 he was further infuriated by her attempt to involve him in the agitation against the Metropolitan Police commissioner's decree closing Trafalgar Square to demonstrations. On Sunday 13 November Annie Besant led one of many processions starting in the East End that aimed to force the square. Her plan, to get arrested in order to test the law, was frustrated when the police, recognizing her, removed her from the vicinity of the violent clashes for which the incident was known as 'bloody Sunday'. She joined W. T. Stead, William Morris, H. M. Hyndman, John Burns, Jacob Bright, and others in the Law and Liberty League, the aim of which was to uphold the right of free speech. In the summer of 1888 its journal, *The Link*, of which she was editor, carried the first account of the strike by the match-girls employed by Messrs Bryant and May to improve their pay and conditions. Besant helped them form a union, the first for women only. In the next two years, by means of publications to which she was connected as editor or contributor—*The Link*, *Our Corner*, *Justice*, *The Commonweal*, *National Reformer*—she became a major figure in the organization of unskilled workers, referred to as the 'new unionism'. She published *Why I am a Socialist* and *Modern Socialism* (1886). By then it seemed the striking and effective personality she had become must find a role in politics. She hoped to stand for the newly founded London county council, but women were excluded. In 1889 she was top of the poll for the London school board when she won Tower Hamlets on a socialist platform. Hard work earned her the gratitude of her 'constituents' and the respect of her opponents on the board. In middle-class eyes her reputation, so badly damaged by her association with Charles Bradlaugh, was on the mend. But she refused a second term.

Theosophy In 1888 Besant's investigations into what she called the obscure side of consciousness—dreams, hallucinations—convinced her that 'there was some hidden thing, some hidden power' which it was her destiny to find (Besant, *Autobiography*, 309). She was disillusioned with other means of improving the human condition, not excepting socialism. In 1889 she put her large house at 19 Avenue Road, St John's Wood, at the disposal of Helena Petrovna Blavatsky, Russian co-founder of the Theosophical Society and author of the celebrated *Isis Unveiled* (1877) and *The Secret Doctrine* (2 vols., 1888). The society, which

Madame Blavatsky and an American colonel, Henry Steele Olcott (1832–1907), founded in New York in 1875, had its headquarters at Madras. According to Madame, India was open to spiritual regeneration, as was another country under British rule—one for which Annie Besant had a special feeling—Ireland. The origins of the Theosophical Society were to be found 'in a group of Superhuman Men, Teachers, Masters, Adepts whose universal knowledge of evolution … constitutes them the wise Initiators and Guides of all movements designed to influence profoundly the growth of the world', a disciple wrote (Ransom, 1). Among these teachers were mahatmas who communicated from their sanctuary in the Himalayas. Besant's acceptance of this new discipline profoundly changed her attitude and beliefs, and astonished her former colleagues. Because Blavatsky held that birth control was incompatible with reincarnation, Besant withdrew all copies of her *Law of Population*. Celibacy was another requirement of Madame's which seemed to contradict what had gone before—the world supposed Annie and Bradlaugh had been lovers. It may have been so; however, in her *Autobiographical Sketches* she revealed that, because her mother preferred her to be innocent, her wedding night had shocked and humiliated her; some thought the harm done to her pride then was never forgiven or repaired.

'Theosophists appear to me to have sought to rehabilitate a kind of Spiritualism in Eastern phraseology', Bradlaugh wrote in the *National Reformer* (30 June 1889), believing as he did that many of their allegations were erroneous and their reasoning unsound. Though Annie was offended, she was devastated by his death on 30 January 1891, aged only fifty-eight. Four months later, while she was lecturing in America, Madame Blavatsky also died. She had appointed Mrs Besant 'in the name of the Master, Chief Secretary of the Inner Group of the Esoteric Section, and Recorder of the Teachings' (Farquhar, 268). W. B. Yeats, who was briefly a member of the society at this time, reported that the esoteric section concerned itself with magic.

India On 16 November 1893 Mrs Besant was welcomed to India by Colonel Olcott, president founder of the Theosophical Society. Olcott hoped she would help him administer the many branches established since 1882, when he and Blavatsky moved into the former maharaja's palace on the banks of the River Adyar at Madras. Besant's progress towards Adyar was marked by such enthusiastic crowds that she was encouraged into breaking a taboo—she called on them to throw off the foreign yoke. The government of India had long since made it clear that theosophists must not engage in politics, a rule that Olcott scrupulously observed. Besant's speeches caused the vernacular press to hail her as the long-awaited leader against the raj. Rebuked by *The Times* (5 February 1894) for inflammatory remarks, she was called to order by Colonel Olcott. He and she also differed in the emphasis they placed on existing forms of belief: he was an enthusiast for Buddhism, she immersed herself in Hindu religion and culture. As long as he lived Olcott presided at Adyar, while

Besant made her home for six months every year at Benares, the sacred Hindu city. She adopted Indian dress, white sari and white sandals (the Hindu mourning colour): she was in mourning for the wrong British rule had done to India.

For the next fourteen years Mrs Besant was apparently content to carry on her work of regeneration in the field of education. In 1897, in Benares, she founded the Central Hindu College—monastery and English public school combined—where boys observed the Hindu way of life while becoming familiar with Western ideas. She published her own translation from Sanskrit of the sacred text the *Bhagavad Gita* (1895). According to her its most important lesson was that 'union with divine life may be achieved and maintained in the midst of worldly affairs' (A. Besant, *The Bhagavadgita*, 1895, Preface), a call to social duty which Miss Marryat must have approved.

In 1909, when Colonel Olcott died, the masters chose Mrs Besant to succeed him when she moved to Adyar. As president she reinstated Charles Webster Leadbeater, a former Anglican clergyman, who had resigned from the Theosophical Society in 1906 after charges of perversion—which were never proved—were brought against him. Leadbeater was an observant traveller on the astral plane and wrote many books describing his experiences. He and Besant collaborated to produce *Occult Chemistry* (2nd edn, 1919), when they used clairvoyance to examine atoms. Leadbeater was responsible for the discovery on the seashore at Adyar in 1909 of the fourteen-year-old Brahman boy Jiddu Krishnamurti, whom Mrs Besant brought up as the reincarnation of the World Teacher. Her failure to follow her own advice and keep this discovery secret caused many defections from the society, and was the reason why the Central Hindu College, where a personality cult focused briefly on the boy, ultimately passed from her control (it became the Hindu University).

Olcott's death in 1909 enabled Besant to re-enter Indian politics, where she poured her superabundant energy into campaigning for self-government by means of newspapers she controlled—*The Commonweal* and *New India*—and in lectures such as *India Bond or Free?* (1926). In 1913 she joined the Indian National Congress. In 1915 she proposed to its executive committee that a network of home rule leagues be set up across the country. While at the outbreak of the 1914–18 war most Indian politicians, including Gandhi, the rising star, called a truce in their opposition to the raj, Besant did not, proclaiming 'England's need is India's opportunity' (*New India*, August 1914). In 1916 the tragedy of the Dublin Easter rising incited Mrs Besant to new heights of ferocity and contempt. In May 1917 the viceroy, Lord Chelmsford, bowed to Anglo-Indian demands and interned her at Ootacamund. The historic announcement made at Westminster on 20 August 1917 promising 'the progressive realisation of responsible government in India' (*Hansard 5C*, 97, 1917, col. 1695) secured her release, when all India celebrated. Shortly afterwards the secretary of state, Edwin Montagu, granted her an interview at Viceregal Lodge at which she told him of her long-standing efforts to counter racial discrimination and

advised him on his future course. 'If only the Government had kept this old woman on our side', he lamented in his diary; 'if only she had been well handled from the beginning' (Montagu, 58–9). On 26 December 1917 she became the first woman president of the 32nd Indian National Congress meeting at Calcutta. It was the summit of her influence, which thereafter declined. She did not get on with Gandhi, whose new method of passive resistance she denounced, and in 1919 she was reviled when she miscalculated her response to the massacre by British soldiers of civilians at Amritsar in the Punjab. But in the 1920s she continued to attend those occasions when the two sides met to discuss the future. Her last official appointment—a token one—was in 1928 when she was named a member of the Nehru committee to draft an agreed constitution.

In this last decade, as president of the Theosophical Society, Besant visited branches all over the world, taking to the aeroplane with enthusiasm. Her support for Leadbeater and his Liberal Catholic church, for which she was visitor, remained a source of controversy. She presided at an annual camp in Holland when the coming of the World Teacher was proclaimed. In 1929 Krishnamurti's repudiation of this role was the blow that effectively ended her career. She retired to Adyar where she was much loved and, as her consciousness declined, faithfully looked after. She died there on 20 September 1933 and was cremated on the shore.

ANNE TAYLOR

Sources A. W. Besant, *Autobiographical sketches* (1885) • A. W. Besant, *Annie Besant: an autobiography*, 2nd edn (1908) • A. Taylor, *Annie Besant: a biography* (1992) • *Chancery records* • C. Bradlaugh, 'The Queen v. Bradlaugh and Besant', *National Reformer* (10 June 1877) [transcript in full] • PRO, HO 144/204 • *National Reformer* (1875–89) • *Bernard Shaw: the diaries, 1885–1897*, ed. S. Weintraub, 2 vols. (1986) • E. Royle, ed., *The Bradlaugh papers* (1975) • J. Ransom, *A short history of the Theosophical Society, 1875–1933* (1938) • A. H. Nethercot, *The first five lives of Annie Besant* (1961) • A. H. Nethercot, *The last four lives of Annie Besant* (1963) • J. N. Farquhar, *Modern religious movements in India* (1915) • E. S. Montagu, *An Indian diary*, ed. V. Montagu (1930) • *The diary of Beatrice Webb*, ed. N. MacKenzie and J. MacKenzie, 4 vols. (1982–5) • b. cert. • deed of separation, 25 Oct 1873 • will extract, Principal Registry of the Family Division, London, G29/94-05-00803

Archives PRO, Bloody Sunday, HO 144/204 • Theosophical Society, Adyar, Chennai (Madras), India • U. Leeds, Brotherton L., pamphlets | BL, letters to George Bernard Shaw, Add. MS 50529 • BL OIOC, corresp. with David Graham Pole, MS Eur. F 264 • BLPES, corresp. with Fabian Society • CAC Cam., letters to W. T. Stead • National Secular Society, London, Bradlaugh MSS • National Secular Society, London, Bradlaugh Bonner MSS • NL Scot., letters to Patrick Geddes • NL Scot., letters to R. B. Haldane • PRO, papers relating to Regina v. Bradlaugh and Besant | SOUND BBC WAC

Likenesses photographs, *c.*1927, NPG • Klein & Peyerl, photograph, 1933, NPG • postage stamp, 1947?, India • Barraud, photograph, NPG; repro. in *Men and Women of the Day*, 4 (1891) • H. S. Mendelssohn, photograph, NPG [*see illus.*] • bust, probably Theosophical Society, Varanasi, India • photographs, Adyar Archives, Madras, India • photographs, repro. in Besant, *Autobiographical sketches* • statue, Madras, India

Wealth at death £3510 11*s.* 9*d.*—in England: resworn, probate, 1934, *CGPLA Eng. & Wales* • Rs131,647 7*s.* 0*d.*—gross in India • Rs62,961 7*s.* 0*d.*

Besant, Sir Walter (1836–1901), writer and campaigner for authors' rights, was born on 14 August 1836 at 3 St

George's Square, Portsea, the fifth child and third son in a family of six sons and four daughters of William Besant (1800–1879), a wine merchant of Portsmouth, and his wife, Sarah Ediss (1807–1890), daughter of a builder and architect, of Dibden near Hythe, who married in 1825.

Walter Besant's introduction to literature was through his father's books, which included plays, eighteenth-century novels, Scott, and the works of Dickens then available. Besant's early education was varied. At nine he was taught the classics by a perpetual curate who had had the distinction of being mentioned in the *Memoirs of Harriette Wilson*. In 1851 he was sent as a boarder to Stockwell grammar school, then affiliated to King's College, London—a suitable choice for someone expected to become an Anglican clergyman. He enjoyed Stockwell and left in the summer of 1854 as school captain laden with academic prizes.

Besant entered King's College, London, in October 1854; though he distinguished himself in classics, mathematics, and divinity, it proved a miserable but formative year. His naturally liberal temperament was alienated by the college's thoughtless orthodoxy and poor teaching. He spent much of his free time wandering around the City, an experience that laid the foundation for his lifelong interest in London's history. The year also proved disturbing: he was tempted by the raucous night life of the casinos, the Coal Hole, and the Cider Cellars. He was tempted but did not fall, explaining his preservation as being due to his naïvety, his appearance (he was only 5 feet 6 inches tall and suffered from asthma and eczema), and his myopia. In 1855 he moved to Christ's College, Cambridge, which was then being transformed by reforming fellows such as Gunson and Wolstenholme. Here he found broader views and a greater sense of community. His near-contemporaries included Seeley, Skeat, and Calverley. Seeley introduced him to the writings of Coleridge, Carlyle, and Maurice, and these almost certainly confirmed Besant's doubts about Anglican orthodoxy.

Some of Besant's contemporaries regarded his graduation in the mathematical tripos as eighteenth wrangler in 1859 as a poor reflection of his abilities, but Besant always argued with typical modesty that being bracketed with Calverley for his college's English essay prize was the distinction he really treasured. After a few months trying to make a living from journalism, Besant accepted a post as mathematics master at Leamington College; he was expected to be ordained and become chaplain to the college. An alternative offer of the job of senior professor at the Royal College, Mauritius, provided an escape from both England and its church. Besant spent the next six and half years socializing, climbing, and writing. College life was made difficult by frequent conflicts between its rector and the professors; in time the rector was removed and Besant invited to take over. By then, however, he was on leave in England and disinclined to return.

Besant had spent much of his free time in Mauritius studying French literature and, in addition to writing his first (rejected) novel, he produced a series of essays which he published under the title *Early French Poetry* (1868), the first of his many books and articles on French culture and history. In June 1868 Besant was appointed secretary to the Palestine Exploration Fund (PEF), a paid post which he held for eighteen years. The PEF brought him into contact with scholars, publishers, and military men—including Edward Palmer, professor of Arabic at Cambridge, with whom he wrote *Jerusalem: the City of Herod and Saladin* (1871). Besant was also involved in 1877 in the investigation of the Shapira forgery. In order to provide the PEF with a steady income Besant organized a system of local societies spread throughout the country; he also set up a small society for the translation and publication of ancient accounts of pilgrimages to the Holy Land. The PEF gave Besant a financial security from which he could launch a career in authorship without, in his own words, 'dependence on the pen, and the pen alone' (W. Besant).

In 1874 Besant married Mary Garrat Foster Barham (b. 1849/50), with whom he had four children. His family life was happy and he extended this to include care for his nephew, Digby, the son of his younger brother the Revd Frank Besant and his estranged wife, Annie *Besant.

In October 1869 James Rice, unsuccessful barrister, historian of the turf, and editor of *Once a Week*, published an unacknowledged, uncorrected article by Besant. Besant protested; Rice made a fulsome apology and asked for more contributions. Rice had devised the plot of a novel on which he invited Besant to collaborate. The result, *Ready Money Mortiboy*, was initially serialized in *Once a Week* and was published as a three-volume novel in July 1872; it proved a steady seller (140,000 copies by 1902). Between 1872 and 1882 the partnership, as well as numerous short stories, produced nine novels that appeared first in serial form, then in three volumes, and then in series of progressively cheaper one-volume editions. Most successful of all was *The Golden Butterfly* (1876), which had sold some 300,000 copies by 1912. Rice provided more than plots: he also acted as Besant's unpaid literary agent. On Rice's death in 1882 Besant became, to use his own words, 'a novelist with a free hand' (W. Besant); he also found himself needing an agent. In appointing A. P. Watt to that job in 1883, Besant became one of the earliest major writers to employ a professional literary agent. The majority of his solo fictions were either concerned with current social conditions or were historical novels set in the seventeenth or eighteenth centuries. The latter benefited from his precise sense of period and place. Besant's most famous novel was his first: *All Sorts and Conditions of Men*, serialized in *Belgravia* from January to December 1882 and published in three volumes in October 1882. The story of two lovers bent on social reform in the East End of London caught the public imagination and the novel continued to sell for decades (250,000 copies by 1905). Besant managed to produce on average a three-decker novel per year until his death; in addition he wrote essays, Christmas books, collections of short stories, and plays (many in collaboration with Walter Herries Pollock).

Later in his writing career Besant developed a new line in the popular history of London. He published *London* in

1892, and followed this with other studies (*Westminster*, 1895; *South London*, 1898; *East London*, 1901). This interest culminated in 1894 when he was invited by A. and C. Black to undertake a multi-volume, modern version of Stow: *The Survey of London*. The project was significantly underfunded by the publisher, relied too much on Besant's talents and money—both already hopelessly overstretched—and was later seriously compromised by London county council's even more ambitious project. Ten volumes were finally issued, all posthumously, between 1902 and 1912.

Besant was a highly clubbable man, an energetic organizer, and an instinctive reformer. He became a freemason in 1862 as a member of the Quatuor Coronati lodge; freemasonry appealed to Besant as 'a religion which requires no priest'. He joined the Savile Club in 1873; he became a member of the Athenaeum in 1887. He helped organize the Rabelais Club (1880–89). In 1884, taking up an idea Charles Leland (Hans Breitmann) had tried in Philadelphia, Besant initiated the Home Arts Association, which established evening schools through the country to promote handicrafts. In 1897 Besant helped to found the Women's Central Bureau of Work which, despite his dislike of the 'new woman', was devised to help middle-class women into employment. In his writings and public speaking Besant campaigned for sweatshop workers in the East End, for the poor in the parish of St James's Ratcliffe, the Ragged School Union, the London Hospital, free public libraries, and the work of the Salvation Army. Besant must be one of the few social critics who witnessed one of his ideas taking literally concrete form. In *All Sorts and Conditions of Men* he had envisaged a Palace of Delight in the East End devoted to working-class recreation. Using *All Sorts* as, Besant claimed, a textbook, Sir Edmund Hay Currie combined the Beaumont bequest and £20,000 from the Drapers' Company with money raised from the public to fund the building of the People's Palace on the Mile End Road, opened by Queen Victoria on 14 May 1887. The palace had a 4000-seat concert hall/ballroom, a library, a gymnasium, a swimming-bath, a winter garden, an art school—and a technical school supported by the Drapers. Besant chaired the library committee, ran the literary club, and edited the *Palace Journal*. Despite great achievements, all did not go well. Finally the Drapers took over, and later the palace became the East London Technical College and then a college of London University. Concerned to cultivate better understanding with North America, Besant worked in the last two years of his life for the Atlantic Union. In 1895 he was knighted for his charitable work.

Besant was the prime mover in establishing the first successful collective organization for authors in Britain: the Society of Authors. He chaired the initial meeting on 28 September 1883 and it was he who drew up the plans. By 18 February 1884 a general meeting had been called, a prospectus issued, and fourteen vice-presidents and sixty-eight ordinary members had been enrolled. Perhaps Besant's greatest contribution in this formative period was to get Tennyson to become the society's first president, a morale-boosting coup which helped put the society on the map. Despite this, its growth was slow and Besant had to work tirelessly to encourage collective action in support of copyright law reform, the protection of literary property, and the promotion of the writing profession. For the last Besant had characteristically utopian hopes: he saw the society as a cross between the Académie Française and a self-regulating professional body. But he could not limit membership nor stop hopeful but hopeless writers paying for vanity publication. Although later Besant relinquished leadership of the society, his commitment to it increased. In 1890 he established the society's journal, *The Author*, and 'conducted' it (the Dickensian verb is significant) until his death. In 1892 he helped found the Authors Club and he was always to be found in the press promoting with vigorous hyperbole the rights and dignity of authorship. He summarized his views on authorship in *The Pen and the Book* (1899).

Amid rampant authorial egos, Besant was a touchingly self-denying figure: more than once he dipped into his own pocket to finance the Society of Authors; at society dinners he would often be found sitting near the bottom of the table. This modesty he also applied to his own writings which, one suspects, he did not believe would last. Despite advocating the retention of copyright, Besant tended to sell his own as soon as he could. Besant died of Bright's disease at his house, Frognal End, Hampstead, London, on 9 June 1901 and was buried in the burial-ground off Church Row in Hampstead.   SIMON ELIOT

Sources W. Besant, *Autobiography of Sir Walter Besant* (1902) • A. D. Besant, *The Besant pedigree* (1930) • R. E. Besant, 'The Portsea Besants', typescript, 1981, priv. coll. • S. Eliot, 'Sir Walter, sex and the SOA', *Reconstructing the book*, ed. Bell, Eliot, Hunter and West (Burlington, 2001) • S. Eliot, 'His generation read his stories: Walter Besant, Chatto and Windus, and *All sorts and conditions of men*', *Publishing History*, 22 (1987), 25–67 • V. Bonham-Carter, *Authors by profession*, 2 vols. (1978), vol. 1 • m. cert.
Archives Hunt. L., letters and literary MSS • NRA, corresp. and literary papers • Palestine Exploration Fund, London, papers as secretary of Palestine Exploration Fund • Princeton University Library, New Jersey, corresp. and papers, mainly with Chatto and Windus • Royal Literary Fund, London, letters as sponsor | BL, letters to Society of Authors, Add. MS 56863 • DWL, letters to Henry Allon • NL Scot., corresp. with Blackwoods • NYPL, A. P. Watt archives • U. Leeds, Brotherton L., letters to Edward Clodd • U. Reading, Chatto and Windus archives • University of Bristol Library, letters to James Baker • University of North Carolina, Chapel Hill, Wilson Library, A. P. Watt archive
Likenesses A. J. Stuart Wortley, double portrait, oils, 1882 (with Rice), NPG; on display at Boddwyddan Castle • D. A. Wehrschmidt, oils, 1887, Christ's College, Cambridge • Barraud, photograph, 1888, NPG; repro. in *Men and Women of the Day*, 1 (1888) • G. Frampton, relief bust on memorial, 1904, Victoria Embankment, London • intaglio print, repro. in Besant, *Autobiography*, frontispiece • photograph, repro. in *Hampstead Independent Journal*, 1/4 (June 1951), 6 • photographs, repro. in Besant, *Besant pedigree*
Wealth at death Books fetched £589 9s. 6d., 24–25 March 1902: BL, S.–C.S.1216 • £8812 19s. 7d.: PRO, A-B wills and admons, 1901.1

Besicovitch, Abram Samoilovitch

Besicovitch, Abram Samoilovitch (1891–1970), mathematician, was born at Berdyansk, on the Sea of Azov, on 24 January 1891, the fourth child of the family of four sons and two daughters of Samoil Abramovitch Besicovitch and his wife, Eva Ilinichna Sauskan. The family was descended from Karaite Jews, a breakaway sect who accepted the written but not the oral Jewish tradition. Samoil Besicovitch was a jeweller but, after losses by theft, he gave up his shop and became a cashier. All the children were talented and studied at the University of St Petersburg, the older ones in turn earning money and helping to support the younger. Abram Besicovitch graduated in 1912, one of his teachers having been A. A. Markov, who encouraged him to research in probability.

The last university to be opened before the revolution in Russia was at Perm near the Ural Mountains, established in 1916 as a branch of the University of St Petersburg. In 1917 it became autonomous, and Besicovitch became a professor in the school of mathematics. After Soviet power was established in Perm the university developed rapidly; at the end of the summer of 1918 the Perm Physics and Mathematics Society was founded and started to publish a journal.

The Russian civil war brought severe hardship in 1919. In 1917 the Japanese mathematician S. Kakeya had posed the following problem:

Let U=AB be a unit segment in the plane. We are to move U from its original position AB so as to bring it back to its original position with its end points reversed, so that the final position is BA, and during this motion U should sweep out the least possible area.

In the winter of 1919, when there was no fuel, Besicovitch worked on, and solved, another essentially equivalent problem. He held his feet in a box filled with straw to keep warm, and came to the conclusion that the switching of the end points of U can be done within an arbitrarily small area. On the strength of this work he was elected in 1920 to a professorship at the University of Leningrad.

In the early 1920s Besicovitch was offered a Rockefeller fellowship to work abroad, but his repeated requests to accept this offer were refused by the Soviet authorities. In 1924 he made plans to leave Russia illegally. Originally it was intended that three academics, A. A. Friedmann (famous for his theory of the expanding universe), J. D. Tamarkin, another mathematician, and Besicovitch should be smuggled out together. Friedmann's wealthy father supported the operation, but Friedmann dropped out at the last minute, and died a few months later of typhoid; Tamarkin and Besicovitch crossed safely into Latvia.

From Latvia, Besicovitch proceeded to Copenhagen, where he used the Rockefeller fellowship to work with Harald Bohr on almost periodic functions. While there Besicovitch visited Oxford, staying for some months in New College with G. H. Hardy who was quick to see his great analytical powers and secured for him a lectureship in the University of Liverpool for 1926. At the earliest opportunity in 1927 Cambridge appointed him a lecturer in the university, in 1928 he became Cayley lecturer, and in 1930 he was elected a fellow of Trinity College; he remained a fellow to the end of his life. He was naturalized in 1931.

In 1916 Besicovitch had married a mathematician, Valentina Vitalyevna, daughter of Vitaly Doynikov, an administrator. She remained in Russia when he left. There were no children and the marriage was dissolved in 1926. A friend from Perm days, Mariya Ivanova, widow of a mathematician, Aleksandr Denisov, settled in England, and on 5 December 1928 Besicovitch married her elder daughter, Valentina Aleksandrovna, then aged seventeen. They had no family and it was the children of his friends who, throughout his life, enjoyed his affection.

Besicovitch participated enthusiastically in Cambridge academic and social life. He organized his family life so that he could dine in the masculine setting of high table every evening, and drink port after dinner in the senior common room with bachelors G. H. Hardy and J. E. Littlewood and other Trinity intellectuals. As college lecturer he took a great personal interest in the undergraduates, and in the early 1940s when Winchester public school (which specialized in high-grade mathematics teaching) sent to Trinity an amazing crop of undergraduates which included Freeman Dyson, James Lighthill, and Michael Longuet-Higgins, who were joined by Tony Skyrme from Eton College, Besicovitch was heard to boast proudly that they now had several students of the calibre of Littlewood. He was elected FRS in 1934 and was Sylvester medallist of the Royal Society in 1952. He received in 1930 the Adams prize of the University of Cambridge for his work on almost periodic functions, and in 1950 the De Morgan medal of the London Mathematical Society.

Throughout his life Besicovitch maintained a great interest in mathematical problems of all kinds. Over many years at Cambridge he ran, for the pleasure and benefit of undergraduates, a weekly 'contest problem': he read and annotated the solutions submitted and his announcement that they had provided perfect solutions encouraged several young mathematicians to develop their analytical powers. He described himself as an expert in the 'pathology' of mathematics. If someone put forward a conjecture which Besicovitch suspected to be untrue, he would keep worrying until he had produced a counter-example.

Bessi (the name by which he was affectionately known to colleagues and students) was a superb lecturer and supervisor. Even in a full lecture class he could make analysis very personal by picking out a student (without the slightest trace of malice), leading that student to give the obvious answer to a problem, and then progressing gently to a contradiction, showing that the problem was much deeper than appeared at first sight. Those who experienced him as a teacher gained a clearer and more thoughtful attitude to mathematics.

Besicovitch's book, *Almost Periodic Functions* (1955), originated in his work with Harald Bohr in 1924–5. He wrote more than 120 papers, shedding new light on many questions in analysis and the classical theory of functions—he was more likely than many to solve problems which seemed intractable. Few mathematicians, facing such problems, can rid themselves of preconceived ideas about the nature of the solution and possible methods of obtaining it, but Besicovitch could keep an open mind and envisage unexpected results. He was a master of intricate construction which could reveal paradoxical truths. He did not strive after abstractions and generalities; he was a problem-solver, not a system-builder. His formal statements had to be in the notation of analysis; the underlying mental pictures were geometrical, often expressible in simple language. This is well illustrated by his work on fractional dimensions, which has led to the extraordinarily fruitful development of fractals in the hands of Benoît Mandelbrot. A point having no magnitude (Euclid) is of dimension 0. A straight segment is of dimension 1; so is the circumference of a circle. The inside of a circle or the surface of a sphere has dimension 2. In 1919 Hausdorff defined dimensions of fractional order. A suitably sparse set of points on a line could have a measure of dimension (say) one half. The idea could be extended to sets of points, curves, and other figures in space.

For a long time Besicovitch was the author or joint author of nearly every paper on the subject, and hence Mandelbrot decided to use the term Hausdorff–Besicovitch dimension to denote the dimension of a fractal. Pathological sets of points such as Weierstrass curves which are continuous but not differentiable at all points, the set of points belonging to a random walk, sets defined by Cantor, Koch, and others, can all be assigned a fractal dimension. Neither Hausdorff nor Besicovitch dreamed that their ideas would be of practical use in the real world. It was Mandelbrot who drew attention to the many occurrences of fractals in nature—shapes of coastlines, mountainous landscapes, clusters of stellar matter, turbulence, percolation, polymer chains, and so on; he initiated a new field which grew with extraordinary rapidity.

Besicovitch was exceptionally gentle as an oral examiner of doctoral students, and if he saw that a student was getting into trouble with one of the other examiners he would search out a method of intervening which would put the student at his ease. Since he spoke Russian at home, Besicovitch's command of English remained stationary from his early days at Cambridge. For him the definite and indefinite articles were superfluous. His individual words were usually correct—it was their assembly and arrangement which were unusual, although he always managed to convey the intended meaning correctly.

Besicovitch remained very suspicious of the Soviet Union. In the early 1930s his good friend the distinguished physicist Peter Kapitza was working at the Mond Laboratory, and used to return to Russia every summer. Besicovitch disapproved strongly of these return visits, and warned Kapitza that he would go back to Russia once too often, which is exactly what happened: on one such visit the Soviet authorities refused to grant Kapitza an exit visa (but provided him with a superb laboratory and excellent facilities).

'A mathematician's reputation rests on his bad proofs' was one of Besicovitch's surprising aphorisms. He wished to convey the idea that the originator of a result in mathematics usually establishes it by long and complicated proofs. It is later, less original workers who undertake the process of simplification. About professors at English universities he said: 'No one is elected to a professorship unless he has been respectable for at least three years. Once he has become respectable, he no longer produces creative work.' Nevertheless, at the age of fifty-nine, in 1950, he succumbed to the temptation of succeeding J. E. Littlewood, the first holder of the Rouse Ball chair at Cambridge. A colleague remembered that on his thirty-sixth birthday Besicovitch, thinking that his own creative resources were drying up, proclaimed that he had had four-fifths of his life. Reminded of this on his appointment to the chair, Besicovitch sent a postcard in reply: 'numerator was correct!'.

After his retirement in 1958 Besicovitch remained active in teaching and research and spent eight successive years as visiting professor in the United States. He then returned to live in Trinity College. Towards his eightieth year his health failed and he died in the Evelyn Nursing Home, Cambridge, on 2 November 1970.

CYRIL DOMB

Sources J. C. Burkill, *Memoirs FRS*, 17 (1971), 1–16 · S. J. Taylor, *Bulletin of the London Mathematical Society*, 7 (1975), 191–210 · C. Domb, 'Of men and ideas (after Mandelbrot)', *Physica*, D, 38 (1989), 67–70 · B. B. Mandelbrot, *Fractals, form, chance and dimension* (1977) · B. B. Mandelbrot, *The fractal geometry of nature* (1982) · private information (2004) · d. cert. · m. cert. · *DNB*
Archives Trinity Cam., MS notes and additions made to the work of Piero Sraffa | Trinity Cam., corresp. with Harold Davenport
Likenesses H. A. Freeth, drawing, 1952, Trinity Cam. · E. Coxeter, oils, 1956, Trinity Cam. · portrait, repro. in Burkill, *Memoirs FRS*
Wealth at death £35,086: probate, 10 Jan 1971, *CGPLA Eng. & Wales*

Bess of Hardwick. *See* Talbot, Elizabeth, countess of Shrewsbury (1527?–1608).

Bessborough. For this title name *see* Ponsonby, William, second earl of Bessborough (1704–1793); Ponsonby, Frederick, third earl of Bessborough (1758–1844); Ponsonby, Henrietta Frances, countess of Bessborough (1761–1821); Ponsonby, John William, fourth earl of Bessborough (1781–1847); Ponsonby, Frederick George Brabazon, sixth earl of Bessborough (1815–1895); Ponsonby, Vere Brabazon, ninth earl of Bessborough in the peerage of Ireland and first earl of Bessborough in the peerage of the United Kingdom (1880–1956).

Besse, Antonin (1877–1951), entrepreneur and benefactor, was born on 26 June 1877 at Carcassonne in southern France, the third son and fourth child in the family of four boys and three girls of Pierre Besse, leather merchant, and his wife, Marie Bonnafous. In failing health Pierre Besse moved his family to Montpellier, where he died in 1884.

Besse attended the local *lycée* but failed his *baccalauréat*, and after four years' military service he joined a coffee-exporting firm in Aden in 1899. He later set up in business in Aden on his own, keeping himself fit with tennis, swimming, and mountaineering. In 1908 he married Marguerite Hortense Eulalie Godefroid, who came from a wealthy Brussels family, with whom he had a son and a daughter. She contributed money from her private fortune and kept

Antonin Besse (1877–1951), by unknown photographer

the firm's books. Besse began trading in a wide variety of products, from hides and skins to incense, exploiting the huge demand from churches and mosques. In the seven years to 1914 his annual profits increased twentyfold.

After 1918 Besse opened offices in London and Marseilles, and added steamships to his extensive fleet of dhows. Two years later the errors of a partner left him with large debts. When his creditors threatened to bankrupt him he won an agreement to repay in instalments. This setback was compounded when, in 1922, his wife divorced him. The financial wranglings were acrimonious and long drawn out, and left him with a further massive overdraft, not finally paid off until after his death. In 1923 he married, as his second wife, an employee, Hilda Florence Crowther (1890–1981), daughter of Thomas Crowther, a businessman and his wife, Margaret Leitch, with whom he had two sons and three daughters.

Besse was small, roundish, and keen on creature comforts: his own generator for electricity, the best chef in Aden, a piano and gramophone for his beloved classical music, and hundreds of books, which he devoured while making extensive notes and reading aloud whenever possible. He had a good eye for nature and a quick and exceptionally receptive mind. Those admitted to his hospitality on the roof of his apartment over the business premises in Aden were enchanted by the Arabian Nights atmosphere of luxury. He impressed even hardened travellers such as Freya Stark and Evelyn Waugh, the former dubbing him 'a wonderful man who lets life play upon him as if he were an instrument responsive to all its variations' (Stark, 41).

Besse had a natural empathy for the Eastern mind and spoke fluent, if idiosyncratic, Arabic. However, he showed scant consideration for his expatriate staff; the men were not paid well and they seldom stayed for long. He could be mean with money and would travel second class on European railways. Despite his many failings he and his second wife were devoted to each other, regularly occupying their respective desks in the office. His son and daughter from his first marriage also kept in touch with him.

In 1923 Besse became an agent for Royal Dutch-Shell, distributing oil products throughout the Red Sea area. His vast local knowledge and attention to detail allowed him to hold his own against very powerful American rivals. He later acquired other commercial agencies, entered the sugar- and pilgrim-transporting trades, and even made money out of waste paper. The world depression of 1929–33 hit him badly but his firm soon recovered. His 1937 venture, Arabian Airways Ltd, was one of his very few business failures. The next few years were the most successful in the firm's history; in 1940, however, he injured his back very seriously in an aircraft crash, and this much reduced his energies while inflicting great physical pain. In France during the German occupation, he succeeded in returning to Aden via New York, Colombo, and Bombay. He had already placed all his business interests at the disposal of the British government.

After 1945 Besse started up new ventures in Aden and Ethiopia but as he approached his seventieth year he spent increasingly long periods away from the firm, his son Tony taking the reins. Having made a number of benefactions in the Near East, during 1947 he proposed the establishment of an educational foundation to encourage personal initiative and independence of thought. His approach to the French authorities was rebuffed on bureaucratic grounds, and he at once turned to Britain, where soundings were made on his behalf. The foundation of a college in an existing university seemed the most practicable plan, and Oxford was finally chosen.

Although in the spring of 1948 Besse had a severe stroke he was able to visit Oxford incognito, and that September the university's congregation approved the proposal of a donation of £1,500,000 for a postgraduate college, one third of the students to be French nationals. Although his name was initially kept secret the chosen title was St Antony's College. Besse earmarked £250,000 of this benefaction to help the less well-endowed Oxford colleges to improve their teaching and other facilities. A former Anglican convent in Woodstock Road was acquired and Frederick William Deakin appointed the first warden. Besse was also generous to Gordonstoun School, whose spartan regime chimed with his view of what the wimpishly-inclined younger generation really needed.

In the new year honours of 1951 Besse, a French national, was created an honorary KBE for public services in the British colony of Aden. Shortly afterwards Oxford University offered him an honorary doctorate of civil law, which was conferred at a private ceremony in June of the same year. Shortly afterwards, at Gordonstoun, Besse was taken gravely ill with thrombosis and double pneumonia. He died there on 2 July 1951, and was buried near the family retreat at Le Paradou, outside Toulon.

T. A. B. CORLEY

Sources D. Footman, *Antonin Besse of Aden* (1986) • *The Times* (4 July 1951) • *The Times* (14 July 1951) • *Financial Times* (9 July 1951) • F. Stark, *The coast of incense* (1953), 41 • E. Waugh, *When the going was good* (1946), 152–7 • T. Hickinbotham, *Aden* (1958), 32–5 • C. H. Johnston, *The view from Steamer Point: being an account of three years in Aden* (1964), 200, 214–15 • private information (2004) [M. Besse, T. E. Allbeury] • *CGPLA Eng. & Wales* (1952)
Archives Bodl. Oxf., corresp.
Likenesses photograph, repro. in *The Times* (4 July 1951) • photograph, St Ant. Oxf. [*see illus.*]
Wealth at death £496,042 12s. 6d. in England: Aden probate sealed in England, 12 Jan 1952, *CGPLA Eng. & Wales*

Besse, Joseph (1683–1757), historian of Quakerism, was born at Billericay, Essex, the son of Joseph Besse. In 1716 he married Hannah Dehorne (*d.* in or before 1757), daughter of George Dehorne of Colchester; they had six children. Besse worked as a schoolmaster in Colchester in the early part of his life. He undertook paid work for the meeting for sufferings (the executive body of the Society of Friends, which met weekly in London), compiling and editing works for publication and for the archives. From 1730 he was also employed to catalogue and sort books belonging to the central archives and library of the society. From 1746 to 1748 he was the recording clerk of the society, the senior paid official at national level. His work was integral to the foundation of the Quaker reputation for thorough record-keeping and the maintenance of a comprehensive library.

Besse's greatest single achievement, and still an invaluable source, was his *Collection of the Sufferings of the People called Quakers* (2 vols., 1753). The yearly meeting of Friends had taken a decision, in 1727, to undertake a more systematic record of their sufferings, and one of Besse's paid tasks was to gather and have bound together the manuscript records of these events. He was then commissioned, working with the advice of a committee, to produce *An Abstract of the Sufferings of the People Call'd Quakers*. Three volumes were published between 1733 and 1738, covering the period 1650–66. Besse had five more volumes prepared in manuscript when it was decided, in 1741, to publish the whole in two folio volumes. Although the *Sufferings* are not as comprehensive as has been generally assumed they range well beyond the British Isles in content and are a much more important source for Quaker history than the title implies, consolidating the material available in over 200 printed titles for the period up to 1689.

In addition Besse edited the important first collection of the works of William Penn (2 vols., 1726), writing for this publication the first biographical account of Penn. Besse's collection was more comprehensive in its scope than those of other early collections of the writings of Quaker authors and included some of Penn's secular writings, such as his political essays. Joseph Smith credits Besse as author, editor, or compiler of a further thirty-six titles, two of them in Latin. Most of these works were, in effect,

official publications of the society and they included several contributions to the Quaker campaign against tithes as well as other answers to anti-Quaker publications; some are anonymous and the attributions are not always certain. Apart from his authorship of controversial literature Besse was responsible also for *The Life and Posthumous Works of Richard Claridge* (1726) and for editing *An Account of the Life, Travels and Christian Experiences … of Samuel Bownas* (1756), both major works which confirmed Besse's place in the first rank of eighteenth-century Quaker authors. After the death of his wife, at Chelmsford, Besse moved to Ratcliffe, London, where he died on 25 November 1757. He was buried in the Quaker burial-ground at Ratcliffe.

DAVID J. HALL

Sources *DNB* • 'Dictionary of Quaker biography', RS Friends, Lond. [card index] • J. Smith, ed., *A descriptive catalogue of Friends' books*, 1 (1867) • [N. Penney?], 'The story of a great literary venture', *Journal of the Friends' Historical Society*, 23 (1926), 1–11 • A. Littleboy, 'Devonshire House reference library: with notes on early printers and printing in the Society of Friends', *Journal of the Friends' Historical Society*, 18 (1921), 1–16, 66–80 • *The papers of William Penn*, ed. E. B. Bronner and D. Fraser, 5 (1986) • W. C. Braithwaite, *The second period of Quakerism*, ed. H. J. Cadbury, 2nd edn (1961)
Archives RS Friends, Lond., administrative archives and manuscript collections

Bessell, Peter Joseph (1921–1985), politician and businessman, was born on 24 August 1921 at Elm Bank Nursing Home, Bath, the only son of Joseph Edgar Bessell, tailor, and his wife, Olive Simons Hawkins. His parents divorced in 1926 and Bessell was brought up by his father. Educated at Lynwyd School, Bath (1928–37), he took on his father's business at the latter's death in 1940. Having commenced a career as a Congregational lay preacher in 1939 he registered as a conscientious objector at the outbreak of the Second World War, only to de-register in 1942 and lecture for the Ministry of Information. He married Joyce Margaret Thomas in 1942; she died five years later.

Bessell married Pauline Colledge, with whom he had two children, in 1948; he sold his father's business and moved to Paignton, Devon, where he established his own dry cleaning firm. He became prominent in the Torbay area, particularly through organizing Paignton's coronation pageant, which led to his selection as Liberal candidate for Torquay for the 1955 general election. Bessell had first joined the Liberals in 1945, probably as a natural consequence of his religious nonconformism, but had no political experience before his selection. He saved his deposit and within months raised the Liberal vote by 10 per cent at a by-election, his brash showmanship making a significant contribution to the Liberals' best English by-election performance since the war.

Bessell moved to Bodmin in 1956 and was quickly adopted as the constituency's Liberal candidate. His organizational ability and modern, go-ahead image reinvigorated the Liberal Association and broadened its appeal beyond its traditional, nonconformist support. He cut the Conservative majority in Bodmin in 1959 and won the seat by more than 3000 votes in 1964. Despite this success the contradictions which destroyed his career were already becoming evident. He cultivated the support of

Isaac Foot, symbolically visiting his grave after his election was declared in 1964, and continued his preaching and his membership of the Brotherhood Movement, of which he was president in 1967–8. Behind his public image, however, his private life was shambolic. His Paignton business had collapsed and Bessell used his parliamentary office to try, unsuccessfully, to broker an ambitious range of Anglo-American business deals. Senior Liberals ensured that he did not lose his seat through bankruptcy as he lurched from one financial crisis to another. Self-confessedly a promiscuous womanizer, he boasted of affairs with his parliamentary secretaries.

Bessell was a hard-working MP, speaking for the Liberals on a wide range of economic and industrial issues and sitting on select committees on procedure, estimates, and agriculture. Nevertheless, he was not a popular figure within the party. His views on capital punishment, the Rhodesian situation, and the American intervention in Vietnam, which he had witnessed at first hand as part of a parliamentary delegation in 1967, were decidedly illiberal. He was ridiculed for a television interview in 1965 during which he predicted that Jo Grimond would be elected speaker and that he would gladly accept the Liberal leadership. His majority was reduced in 1966, and two years later he announced that he would not contest the next general election, in order to concentrate on his business career.

When he moved to the United States in 1970 Bessell's financial position worsened, and by 1974 he was bankrupt. He divorced in 1978 and immediately married his intimate friend, Diane Miller, spending the last decade of his life living modestly in California. His notoriety was to be enhanced by one further episode, however. A friend and ally of Jeremy Thorpe, Bessell was closely involved in the events which culminated in Thorpe's trial for the attempted murder of Norman Scott. Bessell was chief witness for the prosecution, but his credibility was systematically destroyed by George Carman QC; he wrote his memoir of the trial, *Cover up*, in 1981. A chain-smoker, Bessell died of emphysema on 27 November 1985, in Oceanside, Los Angeles, California. ROBERT INGHAM

Sources S. Freeman and B. Penrose, *Rinkagate* (1996) · L. Chester, M. Linklater, and D. May, *Jeremy Thorpe: a secret life* (1979) · D. Brack and M. Baines, eds., *Dictionary of liberal biography* (1998) · *WWW* · *The Times* (28 Nov 1985), 14g · *Cornish Guardian* (5 Dec 1985), 7a · *Cornish Guardian* (22 Oct 1964) · *Bath and Wilts Chronicle* (25 Aug 1921)

Archives Liskeard Liberal Club, Liskeard, Bodmin Liberal Association MSS | FILM BFI NFTVA, *What the papers say*, *World in action* · Granada TV · ITN Archive, London, 1960s–1970s · Reuter's, London, on Rhodesia 1960s–1970s; Thorpe trial | SOUND BL NSA

Likenesses photograph, repro. in *The Times* · photographs, repro. in Freeman and Penrose, *Rinkagate*, pl. 17

Bessemer, Sir Henry (1813–1898), steel maker, was born on 19 January 1813 at Charlton, near Hitchin, Hertfordshire, the only son of Anthony and Elizabeth Bessemer (a surname said to have been of Huguenot origin). He had an elder sister. According to Henry Bessemer, his father had been born in London but had been taken by his parents to

Sir Henry Bessemer (1813–1898), by London Stereoscopic Co.

the Netherlands, where he had been trained as an engineer. Anthony Bessemer then spent several years in France, where he became a member of the Académie Royale des Sciences and occupied a leading position as a die-sinker and engraver in the Paris mint. However, the French Revolution forced his hasty return to England, where he bought a small landed estate at Charlton and began a successful typefounding business in association with Henry Caslon (after whom his son was named).

Early inventions After elementary schooling, Henry Bessemer acquired practical experience in his father's workshop. He experimented with his own slide-lathe, toyed with molten type metal, and spent hours watching the workings of the village flour mill. However, when his father moved his business to London in March 1830, seventeen-year-old Henry arrived in the capital with no regular trade or profession. He never lacked self-confidence, though, and even then 'felt a consciousness that nature had endowed [him] with an inventive turn of mind, and perhaps more than the usual amount of perseverance' (Bessemer, 9). He immediately settled into his future career as an inventor.

Bessemer's ideas were not always successful, but they demonstrate a remarkable range and precociousness. There was work on the practical application of electroplating; the embossing of metal cards and fabric; a perforated die stamp; the construction of a type-composing machine; the perfection of a process for making imitation Utrecht velvet; the manufacture of bronze powder for gilt decoration; the development of sugar-refining machinery; the production of glass plate; and the use of plumbago waste for making pencils.

Two of these early ideas, developed in London in the 1830s and 1840s, had particular significance. The first was Bessemer's invention in 1833 of perforated die stamps, designed for use at the government Stamp Office. At that time, the removal of stamps affixed to old deeds (allowing the stamps to be fraudulently reused) was said to be costing the government £100,000 a year. Bessemer's solution, which he personally presented to the president of the Stamp Office, was a die stamp which perforated the deed with hundreds of tiny holes, making it virtually impossible to counterfeit. Later he improved this idea by inserting a date stamp in the dies. This invention was universally adopted by the government, but the simplicity of the date stamp meant that the promise of a permanent official job for him was never kept; nor was he ever given any acknowledgement or financial reward. Wearied and disgusted by this experience—which he did not forget—he turned to other ways of earning a living.

Bessemer was more successful in his experiments with bronze powder, which was used as a 'gold' paint in various forms of decoration. Until he turned his attention to it about 1843, bronze powder had been imported from Germany and, being virtually handmade, was very costly. He eventually found that he could make a cheaper powder by automating its manufacture. He declined to patent his ideas but entrusted the secrets to close relatives (whose discretion lasted thirty-five years!). He then installed machines of his own design at Baxter House, his workshop and residence at St Pancras, London. The manufacture of bronze powder secured his fortune. 'The large profits derived from it', he later wrote:

> not only furnished me with the means of obtaining all reasonable pleasures and social enjoyments, but, what was even a greater boon in my particular case, they provided the funds demanded by the ceaseless activity of my inventive faculties, without my ever having to call in the assistance of the capitalist to help me through the numerous heavy costs of patenting and experimenting on my too numerous inventions.   (Bessemer, 81)

He later estimated that on 110 patents he had spent £10,000 on administrative costs alone.

Bessemer's wealth from bronze powder enabled him to buy a new residence in Highgate (which he named Charlton House) and allowed him to use Baxter House entirely as a factory and workshop. He bought a brougham and, partnered by Robert Longsdon (later his brother-in-law), opened offices in Queen Street Place in the City. He now had a family, having married, on 7 April 1834, Ann (d. 1897), the daughter of his friend Richard Allen of Amersham. Their first son was named Henry; he later became a carpenter. The elder Bessemer was also assisted at Baxter House by Richard Allen and William D. Allen (d. 1896), his wife's brothers. By 1850 the first phase in Bessemer's career—in which he became securely established in his

chosen career as a professional inventor—was drawing to a close.

The Bessemer converter   The next phase in Bessemer's life, in which he became an international figure, began when the Crimean War focused his attention indirectly upon the properties of iron and steel. His previous work upon artillery had led to the development of a rotating shot. When the War Office declined to take an interest in the work, he took his invention to France to Emperor Napoleon III. In trials there it soon became apparent that the materials available for gun construction—such as the various types of cast- and wrought iron—were far too weak; while the only steel available at that time was a costly metal made in crucibles in Sheffield. As an alternative, he began experimenting at Baxter House in 1855 with a cupola or reverberatory furnace as a way of producing a superior metal.

Using an egg-shaped furnace (a converter) open at one end, Bessemer's idea was simple, but unconventional—blowing air into molten pig iron. This was not entirely new (blowing air through molten pig iron was the basis of the charcoal-refinery process), but his idea of blowing through molten iron in a vessel was bold, to say the least. Perhaps only an 'amateur' such as Bessemer, who had no training as a metallurgist but nevertheless had the 'splendid audacity of ignorance' (*Engineer*, 256), could have devised it. Ignoring the obvious risks, that molten metal might be blown out of the converter or could run back into the holes through which the air was supposed to enter, he watched the mass ignite into an inferno of unimagined intensity. Despite the fact that his scheme was fuelless, the oxygen in the air-blast rapidly burnt out the carbon and other elements, so purifying the iron—all within about thirty minutes. The result was what became known as mild steel, which had a carbon content of from 0.10 per cent to 0.20 per cent and was a highly satisfactory engineering material, superior to wrought iron and yet far cheaper than tool steel. Bessemer's new product, alongside Siemens–Martin open-hearth steel, was to transform industry in the Victorian age after 1860, as the way was now open for the production of large tonnages of mild steel—precisely the material needed for the railways, ships, bridges, and other areas of heavy engineering.

Having melted 700 lb of iron in a stationary converter at Baxter House, Bessemer felt confident enough to deliver his famous paper, *On the Manufacture of Iron and Steel without Fuel*, before the British Association for the Advancement of Science meeting at Cheltenham on 11 August 1856. His paper was reprinted in *The Times* on 14 August. Several iron companies, including the Dowlais works and Galloway of Manchester, showed an immediate interest and advanced Bessemer some £27,000. Well covered by patents (his patent no. 2768 on the tilting converter concept was issued in 1855), he must have looked forward to great riches. Instead, the Bessemer process immediately ran into major technical snags. The first commercial production runs were far from satisfactory and even completely unsuccessful. Bessemer metal was found to be 'cold short' (brittle at low temperatures) and 'rotten' (over-oxidized), faults which were due to the presence of phosphorus in the wrought iron and the fact that often the metal in the converter became wholly decarburized. Neither Bessemer himself, nor his licensees, initially appreciated this. Here his lack of metallurgical knowledge almost proved his undoing. As one critic remarked: 'It is nearly certain that he never really mastered the chemistry of his process ... and he took far more interest in the machinery he used than he did in the details of the process it carried out' (*Engineer*, 256).

Someone who did take an interest in the chemistry of the Bessemer process, however, was the metallurgist Robert F. Mushet. Shortly after the meeting at Cheltenham, Mushet was apparently visited at his home in the Forest of Dean by the manager of the Ebbw Vale Iron Company, who brought with him samples of defective Bessemer metal. Mushet immediately recognized that it was 'burnt' and soon remelted it with additions of a 'triple compound' of iron-carbon-manganese (known as spiegeleisen), which increased the carbon content and corrected the over-oxidation. Apparently, Bessemer journeyed to Coleford to meet Mushet and seek his help; but Mushet's link with the Ebbw Vale Iron Company prevented this. Almost certainly, though, Mushet's ideas were vital to Bessemer's future success. Also significant was technical assistance from abroad. In particular, Göran Göransson, general manager of a Swedish ironworks, was convinced of the soundness of Bessemer's ideas. By 1858 Göransson's redesign of the air-flow system of the converter had resulted in the production of the first successful run of ingots, which were made by a direct method. (Previously, Bessemer had granulated his metal from the converter and then remelted it.) After Göransson had sent samples of his ingots to England, William D. Allen soon reported that Bessemer too had made steel 'direct'.

Bessemer's steelworks By now Bessemer had launched his own company in the world's steel capital—Sheffield. In 1858 he opened the Bessemer Steel Works in Carlisle Street, partnered by William Galloway, the Manchester engineer, Robert Longsdon, and William D. Allen. The resources of the firm were apparently as little as £12,000, of which Bessemer and Longsdon contributed about £6000, Galloway £5000, and Allen £500. Bessemer intended 'not to work [his] process as a monopoly, but simply to force the trade to adopt it by underselling them in their own market ... while still retaining a very high rate of profit on all that was produced' (Bessemer, 175–6). In both intentions he succeeded brilliantly, and Sheffield steel makers began taking out licences. He pointed out with satisfaction that John Brown, next door to his plant, was the first to be 'converted', in 1860; and he was followed by Charles Cammell in 1861 and Samuel Fox in 1862.

In the 1860s, its viability proven, the Bessemer process began to 'take off'. By 1870 some fifteen British iron and steel companies were already manufacturing over 200,000 tons of Bessemer steel. This came only fifteen years after Britain's total steel output from the crucible had reached a mere 50,000 tons. However, Bessemer steel

production had hardly begun. By 1880 it had surpassed 1 million tons; by 1890 2 million tons, and it accounted for about two-thirds of steel production in the United Kingdom. Output was greatly boosted after the 1880s by Sidney Gilchrist Thomas's solution of the 'dephosphorisation' problem, which allowed the use of pig iron containing phosphorus. This upward trend was mirrored in all the steel-making nations, but especially in the USA, where Bessemer production was phenomenal. It began in 1865 at Troy, New York, where the American engineer, Alexander Holley, erected a converter on the banks of the Hudson River. In its first full month the converter made only 65 tons of ingots; but from this small beginning American Bessemer steel output soared to over 6 million tons by 1900. As in Britain, Bessemer steel was crucial for the building of the railway system, and supplying steel rails became the basis for many fortunes, notably so in the case of Andrew Carnegie. When Bessemer died in 1898, world steel production by his converter had reached 11 million tons, and a product that had sold for over £50 a ton from the crucible in the 1850s could now be bought for less than £5.

A controversial domination This remarkable domination was not achieved without controversy. In particular, Bessemer declined to acknowledge Mushet's contribution to his success, an action made easier by the fact that Mushet's patents on spiegeleisen (such as they existed) had lapsed in 1859. A celebrated controversy ensued between Bessemer and Mushet and their respective supporters in the popular and technical press. The reclusive and prickly Mushet proved more than a match for Bessemer in print, but commercially the latter's position was impregnable and Bessemer emerged from the dispute with his reputation intact, if not enhanced among his supporters. Others, including many historians of the later twentieth century, have thought differently, and even Bessemer later softened his position. In 1867 he granted his fellow inventor a £300 annual pension, though this was hardly a generous sum and even this came only after personal pleas from Mushet's daughter and friends. Bessemer also supported the award of the Iron and Steel Institute's Bessemer gold medal to Mushet in 1876. In the USA there were claims from a different quarter. William Kelly, a Pittsburgh ironmaster, argued that his previous work with a converter similar to Bessemer's gave him priority over the Bessemer patents in the USA, controlled by the Holley group. Though Kelly's work has endured as a 'legend' of American inventiveness, no evidence was produced, either at the time or subsequently, to support his claims, and his attempt to interfere with the American development of Bessemer steel had no impact.

The Bessemer converter brought its inventor fame and wealth. Already a successful businessman from his bronze powder, Bessemer had apparently earned by 1870 at least £1 million in royalties from his steel patents (of which there were forty-three between 1854 and 1880). In addition, his Sheffield company also made money, though Bessemer and his partners seem to have deliberately kept the firm small. (In 1895 its paid-up capital was only

£96,000.) In 1873 Bessemer claimed that each of the partners in the Sheffield works had withdrawn in profits eighty-one times the amount of capital each had originally subscribed. In that year he retired from active business: he relinquished the royalties from his bronze powder business to Richard Allen about 1873; and he sold his Sheffield investment to William D. Allen in 1877. At about this time he bought a large house at 165 Denmark Hill in south London, where he continued to search for new inventions. His later interests included a ship's saloon, designed to combat seasickness; an observatory; and the construction of a telescope and the grinding of lenses.

Honours, personality, and death Bessemer's numerous honours included the Albert gold medal of the Society of Arts in 1872; the Telford gold medal and the Howard quinquennial prize of the Institution of Civil Engineers; and election as a fellow of the Royal Society in 1879. That year he was knighted, after he—no doubt encouraged by his newfound prominence—had waged a well-publicized campaign for recognition of his previous work for the government Stamp Office. He was an honorary member of many foreign technical societies, and in the USA six manufacturing towns were named after him. In 1868 he was one of the founders of the Iron and Steel Institute, of which he became its second president in 1871. He later presented the institute with an endowment for the award of a Bessemer gold medal.

Over 6 feet tall and with (at least in photographs) an unsmiling persona, Bessemer looked every inch the Victorian man of iron. Some found him 'unassuming in manner' (*Journal of the Iron and Steel Institute*, 300), but that view seems misleading. His *Autobiography*, published posthumously in 1905 with an additional chapter by his son Henry, reveals an egotistical and uncompromising man: he never mentions Göransson, and Robert Mushet hardly features at all. Nor was his inventive prowess beyond reproach. As one writer remarked: 'His ideas singularly lacked proportion. He failed to catalogue all the conditions affecting an invention, and determining its success or failure; and to those whose existence he did recognise he was wholly incapable of attaching a just value' (*Engineer*, 256). Many of Bessemer's later creations, such as the Bessemer steamship with its anti-sickness saloon (on which he apparently spent £25,000), were costly fiascos. Yet even his critics had to admit his genius: 'The curious way in which he got results, almost, as it were, by instinct, was very remarkable. … It was quite useless to tell Bessemer that any given device would not answer. He seemed to possess some special power of making things succeed which ought to have failed' (ibid.). In fact, Bessemer's reputation as one of the great Victorian engineers has never been questioned, and as to his converter—which remained remarkably unchanged and produced steel in Britain as late as 1974—few would argue with one contemporary assessment that: 'No other invention has had such remarkable results' (*Journal of the Iron and Steel Institute*, 298).

Sir Henry Bessemer died (less than a year after the death of his wife) on 15 March 1898 at his residence, 165 Denmark Hill, London, and was buried at Norwood cemetery, London, on 19 March. He was survived by his two sons, Henry Bessemer and Alfred George Bessemer, and a daughter. GEOFFREY TWEEDALE

Sources H. Bessemer, *Sir Henry Bessemer, FRS: an autobiography* (1905) · *The Engineer* (18 March 1898), 256 · *Engineering* (18 March 1898), 341–3 · *Journal of the Iron and Steel Institute*, 53 (1898), 298, 300 · R. F. Mushet, *The Bessemer–Mushet process, or, manufacture of cheap steel* (1883) · E. F. Lange, 'Bessemer, Göransson and Mushet: a contribution to technical history', *Memoirs of the Literary and Philosophical Society of Manchester*, 57/17 (1912–13), 1–44 · G. Tweedale, 'Bessemer, Sir Henry', *DBB* · C. J. Erickson, *British industrialists: steel and hosiery, 1850–1950* (1959) · K. C. Barraclough, *Steelmaking, 1850–1900* (1990) · A. Birch, *The economic history of the British iron and steel industry, 1784–1879* (1967) · U. Wengenroth, *Enterprise and technology: the German and British steel industries, 1865–1895* (1994) · J. McHugh, *Alexander Holley and the makers of steel* (1980) · d. cert. · *CGPLA Eng. & Wales* (1898) · parish register, 1813, Herts. ALS · *IGI* · *The Times* (16 March 1898)

Archives ICL, student papers and corresp. relating to Bessemer medal · Rotherham Metropolitan Borough Archives, John Baker and Bessemer Ltd, minute books and other records | Glamorgan RO, Cardiff, Dowlais Iron Co. collection, Bessemer and Longsdon corresp., D/DG C.2 - Glamorgan Scientific

Likenesses E. W. Wyon, bust, 1867, Inst. CE · R. Lehmann, oils, exh. RA 1870, Institute of Materials · group portrait, photograph, 1896 (with his family), repro. in R. A. Hadfield, *The work and position of the metallurgical chemist* (1921) · Lock & Whitfield, woodburytype photograph, NPG; repro. in *Men of mark: a gallery of contemporary portraits* (1881) · London Stereoscopic Co., carte-de-visite, NPG [see illus.] · Spy [L. Ward], chromolithograph caricature, NPG; repro. in *VF* (6 Nov 1880) · photograph, repro. in *Engineer* · photograph, repro. in *Engineering*

Wealth at death £92,538 6s. 5d.: probate, 18 May 1898, *CGPLA Eng. & Wales*

Besswick, Lavinia. *See* Fenton, Lavinia (1710–1760).

Best, Charles (*fl.* 1602–1611), poet, was a contributor to Francis Davison's *Poetical Rapsodie*. This popular anthology, which underwent four editions between 1602 and 1621, contains verse from some of the most celebrated poets of the English Renaissance, including Sidney, Spenser, and Donne. The first edition of the anthology contains two pieces by Best, 'A Sonnet of the Sun' (18 lines) and 'A Sonnet of the Moon'. To the third edition (1611) he contributed ten additional poems, including 'An Epitaph on Henry Fourth, the Last French King', 'An Epitaph on Queen Elizabeth', and 'A Panegyrick to my Sovereign Lord the King'. Best's name is known only in connection with the *Poetical Rapsodie*.

A. H. BULLEN, *rev.* ELIZABETH GOLDRING

Sources F. Davison and others, *The poetical rhapsody*, ed. N. H. Nicolas, 2 vols. (1826)

Best, George (*c.*1555–1584), explorer, was the son of Robert Best and Anne Bowman, married at Merstham in 1548. He learned much about geography from his father who worked as an interpreter for the Muscovy Company in London, having escorted the first Russian ambassador to England in 1557. He was probably educated at Eton between 1565 and 1567, and subsequently rose quickly within the entourage of Sir Christopher Hatton, through whose household he met his wife, Edith Chatterton. They married on 6 August 1582.

Surviving financial accounts show George Best did not,

as claimed by the *Dictionary of National Biography*, sail with Martin Frobisher in 1576, although he did write about the journey. None the less, his evident skills in celestial navigation brought him into Frobisher's wardroom *en route* for 'Meta Incognita' (Baffin Island), in the *Ayde* in 1577, and then, as privy council interest in a north-west passage grew in 1577–8, into Frobisher's council for the voyage of 1578 as the commander of *Anne Francis*. By 10 December 1578 Best had published *A True Discourse of the Late Voyages of Discoverie, for the Finding of a Passage to Cathaya, by the Northwest, under Martin Frobisher Generall* showing that Frobisher was ordered to concentrate on recovering ores to the exclusion of a search for the north-west passage. Hinting it was a metallurgical gamble relying mainly on a claim of possession in the queen's name, he adds that adventurers in it 'sought secretly to have a lease at hir Majestie's hands of those places, whereby to enjoy the Masse of so great a publicke profit, unto their owne private gaines'. But he concludes, 'I finde in all that Countrie [Meta Incognita] nothing, that maye be to delite in, either of pleasure or of accompte, only the shewe of Mine[s], both of gold, silver, steele, yron and black leade, with divers pretty stones' (Best, *A True Discourse*, 3.68).

Richard Hakluyt suppressed this and other passages of *A True Discourse* (plus two maps and a preface hinting at Best's limited financial means) from subsequent printed versions of the text. In consequence his printer, Henry Bynneman, had to print two differing texts dated 1578, explaining that:

> I have without making privy the Authour, procured this coppie out of the hands of a friend of mine, who had the writing and perusing thereof … and have sought to conceale upon good causes some secretes, not fit to be published or revealed to the world. (b.iii–iv)

Probably knowing that two proof maps had already been supplied at the behest of the privy council for transmission to Spain in July 1578 by William Bodenham, Bynneman flouted the privy council's policy of imposing secrecy about the north-west passage (as formulated on 2 November 1578) by dedicating the work to Sir Christopher Hatton as vice-chamberlain and a privy counsellor. By December Bynneman had printed Best's woodcut world map 'albeit roughly formed without degrees of longitude or latitude' showing 'Frobisher's straightes', and another showing the newly discovered islands of Meta Incognita.

A derivative account of the voyage of 1577, *La navigation du Cap. Martin Frobisher anglois*, was published in Paris in 1578. Latin and Italian editions, appearing in 1580 and 1582, included agricultural descriptions that betray the involvement of a scrivener who, unlike George Best, cannot have seen polar tundra. This scrivener was probably his brother, Henry Best of Fleet Street, who abandoned a successful London career to buy agricultural estates at Middleton Quernhow and Elmswell in Yorkshire in 1590.

George Best, who lived a risky, violent life, avidly recorded skirmishes in the Arctic and even the wrestling abilities of a Cornishman and an Inuit in 1577. Although paid as senior officer under Frobisher, his £25 share in the Cathay Adventurers proved worthless. To Hatton's obvious distress he died in March 1584 in a duel with Oliver St John, the future Viscount Grandison. Best's will, made on 18 February 1584 and witnessed by a fellow captain from 1578, Gilbert Yorke, illustrates both his approach to 'the casual chances that man is subject unto' and his concern for Edith, his childless wife, and for William Chatterton, his father-in-law; he was worried about the debts that encumbered their estates at Lydiard Millicent in Wiltshire. Proved on 8 October 1584 with Edith as its executor, the will expected any unsold lands to be passed after her death to Robert Hatton. R. C. D. BALDWIN

Sources G. Best, *A true discourse of the late voyages of discoverie, for the finding of a passage to Cathaya, by the northwest* (1578) • V. Stefánson, *The three voyages of Martin Frobisher*, 1–2 (1938) • R. Hakluyt, *The principall navigations, voiages and discoveries of the English nation*, 3 (1589), 47–96 [incl. heavily ed. version of Best's bk] • G. Best, *La navigation du Cap. Martin Frobisher* (Paris, 1578) • will, PRO, PROB 11/67, sig. 32 • BL, Add. MS 15891, fol. 121b • N. H. Nicolas, *Memoirs of the life and times of Sir Christopher Hatton* (1847), 366 • W. Sterry, ed., *The Eton College register, 1441–1698* (1943), 6 • T. H. B. Symons, ed., *Meta Incognita: a discourse of discovery, Martin Frobisher's Arctic expeditions, 1576–1578* (1999) • C. B. Robinson, ed., *Rural economy in Yorkshire in 1641: being the farming and account book of Henry Best*, SurtS, 33 (1857) • D. D. Hogarth, P. W. Boreham, and J. G. Mitchell, *Martin Frobisher's northwest venture, 1576–1581: mines, minerals and metallurgy* (1994), 3, 14, 28, 31, 35, 46, 61 • W. W. Fitzhugh and J. S. Olin, eds., *Archaeology of the Frobisher voyages* (1993) • PRO, E 164

Wealth at death negligible given debts attached to the estate: will, PRO, PROB 11/67

Best, Henry (*c*.1592–1645), landowner and farmer, was probably born in Hutton Cranswick, Yorkshire, the second of the five sons and one daughter of James Best (*d.* 1617), yeoman of Hutton Cranswick (later gentleman of Elmswell, Yorkshire), and his wife, Dorothy (*d.* 1605), whose background and maiden name are not known; James Best married for a second and third time, and had two daughters and a son with his second wife. Nothing is known of Henry Best's early years, though his collection of books and his literary ability indicate a good education. When his father died in April 1617 he was living in Braintree, Essex, probably working in the shop of John Lawrence, grocer and apothecary, and one of the leading townsmen, whose daughter Mary married Best at about this time.

In the summer of 1617 Best travelled back to Yorkshire to manage the family estate at Elmswell, near Driffield, which had been bought by his father in 1598, and to supervise the upbringing of his young siblings and half-siblings. The estate, of nearly 1300 acres, had been left to his elder brother, Paul *Best, a scholar at Cambridge, but it was bought by Henry in 1618. He spent the next twenty-seven years at Elmswell, overseeing his farms and estate; he built a new house in the 1630s, and only occasionally visited places out of the district.

In the early 1640s Best compiled an account of his farming methods and other country matters, such as 'the fashions att our Country weddings', for the benefit of his son, John (1620–1669), who succeeded him as lord of the manor. Unfortunately, parts of the original manuscript, especially those dealing with tillage and the management of stock other than sheep, have been lost, but what remains of this farming book comprises the most detailed contemporary account of seventeenth-century farming practice. Throughout his control of the Elmswell estate Best also kept a memorandum book, in which he recorded in a haphazard fashion the things he wished to remember: the wages agreed with servants; debts owed and owing; the number of sheep in the shepherd's care. Although not an agricultural innovator, he was an astute farmer and businessman: he took great care in selecting seed and breeding stock; he knew the best markets in the region for a wide variety of products; and he endeavoured never to miss an opportunity for profit. He was always an active manager, out in the fields, exhorting his workers, ever watchful for the tricks of 'theevish and ill-disposed servants' or the lackadaisical habits of maids 'of a sluggish and sleepy disposition'. He was a man to whom fair dealing came naturally and he was a just, if firm, master.

Best had five sons and two daughters. His wife died in 1639 and he was predeceased by a son and a daughter. He was buried in Little Driffield, Yorkshire, on 22 June 1645.

DONALD WOODWARD, rev.

Sources D. Woodward, *The farming and memorandum books of Henry Best of Elmswell, 1642*, British Academy, Records of Social and Economic History, new ser., 8 (1984) · J. Foster, ed., *Pedigrees of the county families of Yorkshire*, 3 (1874)

Best [Beste], **Henry Digby** (1768–1836), Roman Catholic convert and author, was born in Lincoln on 21 October 1768, the son of Henry Best (1730–1782), prebendary of Lincoln from 1762. His mother, Magdalen (d. 1797), the daughter of Kenelm Digby of North Luffenham in Rutland, was descended from a long-established Roman Catholic family. From 1776, he attended Lincoln grammar school; several of his mother's Catholic relatives lived opposite the school, and Best's father predicted that they would convert him. In 1784, two years after his father's death, Best was sent by his mother to Oxford, where he matriculated from University College on 17 March 1785. After three terms he was nominated a demy of Magdalen College. During a vacation, he found a Douai translation of the New Testament among his father's papers, which confirmed his early leanings towards Roman Catholicism. His former schoolmaster deterred him, but he continued to be much influenced by a high-church friend at Magdalen, Richard Paget. He took his BA in 1788 and his MA in 1791, and entered holy orders in the Church of England. He was made a deacon in September of that year, and in December became curate of St Martin's, Lincoln. He also obtained a fellowship at Magdalen six weeks after taking his MA, and probably resided mainly in Oxford for the next six years. He published his first works, a treatise entitled *The Christian Religion Briefly Defended Against the Philosophers and Republicans of France* (1793) and a sermon preached at St Mary's, Oxford, on 24 November 1793. This sermon, which anticipated Tractarian doctrines, was republished under the title *Priestly Absolution* (1874). About the same time, he read Richard Newton's *Pluralities Indefensible* (1743), a work which greatly influenced him.

On the death of his mother on 10 April 1797 Best succeeded to a freehold estate, and was obliged to resign his fellowship. He returned to Lincoln, where he met Abbé Beaumont, a French émigré priest. As he was led to consider the doctrine of transubstantiation and other Catholic tenets, his doubts about Anglicanism increased. In May 1798 he went to London to meet the vicar apostolic, John Douglass, who put him under the care of a priest called Hodgson. On 26 May he was received into the Roman Catholic church at the chapel of St George's Fields. His conversion can be attributed not only to the influence of Beaumont and to his own theological studies but also to the influence of the Digbys, particularly his mother, who in his own words still had the 'rags of popery' about her ('Account', 11). Best was by no means ostracized after his conversion. A close friend at Magdalen, Henry Phillpots, who, as bishop of Exeter, engaged in a controversy with the Roman Catholic lawyer and historian Charles Butler, lamented Best's conversion, but still regarded him as a 'sincerely valued and esteemed friend' (*Priestly Absolution*, 236). Best was frequently a guest at the table of the president of Magdalen, Martin Joseph Routh.

In 1801 Best married Sarah, the daughter of Edward Sealy of Bridgwater and Nether Stowey. He spent much time at Bath, where his eldest son, Kenelm, was born, but also resided on one of his estates in Lincolnshire. Here he appears to have encouraged the Catholic population, helping to establish a congregation in Boston, and funding the building of a chapel almost single-handedly. He also made occasional contributions to Catholic periodicals. In 1818 he, his wife, and their six children, aged between three and seventeen, moved to France. After visiting Paris they spent over three years in Avignon and four months at Nice. In May 1822 they moved to Italy, where they stayed in Florence, Rome, and Naples, before returning to England in 1827.

Best recorded his travels in *Four Years in France* (1826), which was prefaced with an account of his conversion, and *Italy as it is* (1827). Both are highly discursive and readable works in which practical advice on such matters as the employment of foreign servants mingles with reflections on art and society. Refreshingly free of the anti-Catholic bias which most travel writing of the period exhibits, they offer an entertaining perspective on post-Napoleonic Europe. While the family was living in Avignon in 1820 Best's elder son, Kenelm, who had left Stonyhurst to join the expedition, died; some of the most moving passages of both works show Best confronting his grief. Best's next publication was his anecdotal *Personal and Literary Memoirs* (1829). He appears to have lived in Torquay for a time, but he died in Brighton on 27 or 28 May 1836. He was buried at the parish church of St Nicholas, Brighton. In 1846 his last work, a novel entitled *Poverty and the Baronet's Family, a Catholic Story*, was published posthumously, a few months after some of his articles had appeared in *Dolman's Magazine*.

Best was an unusual, even an eccentric, character. Wiseman, who had seen him in Rome at the jubilee celebrations of 1825, described him as 'the first clergyman who in our own times had abandoned dignity and ease, as the price of his conversion' (*Recollections*, 271), a reflection not entirely justified but which highlights the unusual timing of his conversion. His works, most of which were published under the name of 'Beste', are still very readable; he was justly commended for the 'terseness and raciness of his style' ('Biographical Memoir').

ROSEMARY MITCHELL

Sources H. D. Beste, 'Some account of the conversion of the author to the Catholic faith in 1798', in H. D. Beste, *Four years in France* (1826), 71–75 · 'Biographical memoir', H. D. Beste, *Poverty and the baronet's family, a Catholic story* (1846) · H. D. Best, *A sermon on priestly absolution*, ed. J. R. D. Beste (1874) · *DNB* · Foster, *Alum. Oxon.* · N. Wiseman, *Recollections of the last four popes and of Rome in their times* (1858)

Best, John (d. 1570), bishop of Carlisle, was supposedly born in Yorkshire of unknown parentage. He was probably of Halifax, referred to in his widow's will, and home to another early protestant of the same surname. Nothing is known of his schooling. A man of his name was a monk of Selby who in 1535 displeased the archbishop of York by his preaching, 'railing and jesting' at the hypocrisy of fasting. His preaching licence was revoked until he were 'waxed sadder' (*LP Henry VIII*, 9, no. 742). Best was certainly at King Henry VIII College, Oxford, in 1538–9, when his preaching was again criticized, this time by a chaplain of the college, and he was found eating meat in Lent at the house of an Oxford bookseller, accompanied by three others of his college, including one of his own students. Little is known of his movements for the next twenty years, but he appears to have pursued his studies during this period. Bachelor of grammar at Oxford in 1534, he had apparently become MA of an unknown university by 1559, and a BTh by 1561. Oxford made him a DTh *in absentia* in 1566.

About 1550 Best married Elizabeth Somner (the date may be inferred from the fact of two of the four children in his widow's will of 1574 being then still under age). Her antecedents are as obscure as his own, but the fact that her poverty led to her being allowed to retain the episcopal residence of Rose Castle between her husband's death and his successor's appointment suggests that neither he nor she came from families with any private means. In 1553 Best was briefly canon of Wells and prebendary of Wedmore, but was deprived by Mary in 1554 for marriage. Not found among the Marian exiles, he may be identified with the Master Best who was one of four preachers occasionally smuggled into Lancashire to minister to a Manchester protestant conventicle, suggesting a likely membership of the protestant underground in Yorkshire.

Best at last emerged from obscurity after the accession of Elizabeth. A select preacher in the north in 1559, he was rector of Romaldkirk, usually held *in commendam* with the see of Carlisle, on 4 August 1559, and was restored to his Wells prebend with the rectory of Street with Walton, Somerset. He was not consecrated as bishop of Carlisle until 2 March 1561, the long vacancy after the deprivation of Bishop Oglethorpe in June 1559 being usually ascribed to the difficulty of finding anyone willing to accept the

see. Even Bernard Gilpin, the Apostle of the North, refused his cousin Edwin Sandys's encouragement.

Gilpin may have been wise. The problems Best faced at Carlisle were enough to make anyone wax sadder. His clergy were obstinately unreformed, the laity little better. Even in his initial cautious optimism he wrote to Cecil in July 1561 of the over-mightiness of Lord Dacre, describing the clergy under his influence as the 'wicked imps of Antichrist' (PRO, SP 12/18/21). Six months later he complained that the rulers and justices 'winked at all things', and, owing to the supremacy of Dacre and Clifford in his diocese, he could himself achieve nothing (PRO, SP 12/21/13). Rumours and expectations of a French invasion further impeded reform. Moreover, the bishop lacked the support from his dean and chapter, which made the reforming task of Pilkington at Durham so much easier. Sir Thomas Smith, restored in 1560 to the deanery of which he had been deprived by Mary, was an absentee government servant who was ambassador to France for much of the 1560s, and there was no love lost between him and his bishop. Writing to Cecil in 1565, Smith spoke caustically of 'that busy bishop of Carlisle', who had made turmoil among the prebendaries, and wished Best had as much goodwill as tongue (*CSP for., 1564–5*, no. 980 (7)). In fact Smith misjudged the situation. He was relying on his vice-dean to bring the house out of trouble, whereas Best's investigation showed that the near bankruptcy of the chapter was caused by illegal and simoniac leases in which the vice-dean was the ringleader. Best was aware by 1563 of the 'evil doings of the prebendaries' in Smith's absence (Lansdowne MS 6, fol. 125), and won the support of Edmund Grindal, bishop of London and a native of the diocese, in his attempts to control and reform his corrupt chapter, which he described as consisting of 'ignorant priests or old unlearned monks' (Lansdowne MS 6, fol. 86).

Grindal accordingly supported Best's efforts to replace the prebendaries who died with committed reformers, men willing to tackle the Augean stables of the chapter as well as to undertake wider preaching responsibilities in the diocese. Even so, the saga of the chapter leases occupied much of the decade of Best's episcopate. In August 1567 he asked for an extension of his commendam of Romaldkirk to finance the needs of the church in Carlisle.

Best's episcopal register reflects problems he faced in his efforts to reform his wider diocese. The first two pages deal with the deprivation of Hugh Hodgson, provost of Queen's, Oxford, of the rectory of Skelton; as Hodgson was then sheltered by Lord Dacre, and the living given to a Dacre scion who was a Marian ordinand, Best's intention was frustrated. If he was able to see a protestant of his choice preaching to the German miners at Crosthwaite, his register reveals all too clearly the general shortage of suitable ordinands, and the failure or refusal of too many to present candidates with truly protestant credentials.

Best had few illusions about the leanings of most of the gentry. The covering letter to his report of 1564 on the JPs complains about the dead hand laid by the Clifford family on its hereditary shrievalty of Westmorland, of papists passing unapprehended and preaching in remote chapels, of JPs making a pretence only of favouring reform, and of tenants at risk of losing their farms if they declared their protestantism. The death of the fourth Lord Dacre in 1566, leaving only an infant heir, was a turning point; within two years there was a protestant rector at the Dacre stronghold of Greystoke and protestant converts in the parish. In December 1569, moreover, Best himself successfully resisted a last threat from the Dacres. Left as JP in charge of Carlisle in the absence of the warden of the west march during the northern rising, he was advised of a plan being made by the younger Dacres to capture the castle and assassinate him. Best strongly reinforced the garrison and faced the Dacres down when they arrived with a retinue and demanded an audience; by his firm stand in a tense situation he ended the possibility that they would reverse the new order in church and state.

Best was also shrewd in his assessment of the shortcomings of the other leading families in his diocese. If in 1561 he had thought Lord Wharton 'very well loved' (PRO, SP 12/18/21), by 1564 he knew him to be 'evil of religion'. Others were 'verie unfytt' or 'to be admoneshedd'. It was the lesser gentry and new men whom he found 'good and meat to contynue … in Relligion good and wyttye men' (Bateson, 50–51). Here he was able to find some support for the reform of his diocese.

In this last decade of his life Best emerged from obscurity to show himself a dogged and determined protestant, tackling with some success the task of bringing a conservative and reluctant diocese into line with Elizabeth's religious settlement. He died at Carlisle on 22 May 1570, and was buried in Carlisle Cathedral. Though he may have undervalued his own achievement, the delight of his successor, Richard Barnes, at the state of Carlisle diocese provides Best with an appropriate epitaph.

> Praise be to the Lord, who even in this utmost corner … has mightily prospered his gospel … there is not one within this little diocese that openly repines against religion, refuses … to come to church, or that shuns sermons, or openly speaks against the established religion.   (PRO, SP 15/20/84)

And on another occasion Barnes wrote: 'I find these Cumberland and Westmorland commonality far more conformable pliable and tractable than ere I found the better sort in Yorkshire' (PRO, SP 12/74/22).

MARGARET CLARK

Sources Emden, *Oxf.*, 4.46 · state papers domestic, Elizabeth I, PRO, SP 12/100, 12/18/21, 12/21/13, 12/10/44, 12/43/58, 12/44/6, 12/48/4,5, 12/74/22 · state papers domestic, addenda, Edward VI–James I, PRO, SP 15/14/13, 15/20/84 · BL, Lansdowne MSS, 6, fols. 86, 125; 7, fol. 57 · Best's episcopal register, Cumbria AS, Carlisle, DRC/1/3 · M. Bateson, ed., 'A collection of original letters from the bishops to the privy council, 1564', *Camden miscellany, IX*, CS, new ser., 53 (1893), 48–51 · *CSP for.*, 1564–5, no. 980 · *LP Henry VIII*, 9, no. 742; 13/1, no. 845; 14/1, no. 684 · *CPR, 1558–60*, 40; *1560–63*, 2, 147 · *Fasti Angl.* (Hardy), 1.125, 3.241 · *The acts and monuments of John Foxe*, new edn, ed. G. Townsend, 7 (1847), 562 · high commission act book, Borth. Inst., vol. 1 · parish register, Greystoke, Cumbria AS, Carlisle · *CSP dom.*, addenda, 1566–79, 148–50 · F. Heal, *Of prelates and princes: a study of the economic and social position of the Tudor episcopate* (1980)

Archives BL, Lansdowne MSS · Cumbria AS, Carlisle, diocesan and dean and chapter records · PRO, state papers 12, 15

Best, Paul (1590–1657), scholar and religious writer, was born in 1590 (before 12 August) probably at Hutton Cranswick, in the East Riding of Yorkshire, the first of the six children of James Best (*d.* 1617), yeoman farmer, and his first wife, Dorothy (*d.* 1605), whose background cannot be traced. In 1598 James Best purchased the manor of Elmswell, thereby elevating the family's status to that of minor gentry. In 1606 Paul was sent to Cambridge, where he matriculated as a pensioner at Jesus College. Roger Ley, his chamber-mate, records that Best was a pupil of Sir William Boswell and speaks highly of his academic attainments. Ley mentions not only Best's wit and scholarly breadth, but also his 'quaint and curious searches in Philosophy, above the ordinary strain [which] made me and others much admire him', and that for 'a serious study he excelled in the Mathematics, and for a pleasant one in Poetry' (BL, Add. MS 24482). Ley's testimony is borne out by Best's placing eleventh in the university examinations when he graduated BA in 1609–10. He proceeded MA in 1613, and on 8 September 1617 he was elected a fellow of St Catharine's College.

At his father's death in April 1617 Best inherited the manor at Elmswell, along with messuages in Beverley. The life of a scholar apparently held more appeal for Best than that of gentleman farmer, however, for on 13 February 1618 he sold his interest in Elmswell to his brother Henry *Best in exchange for a life annuity, and remained on at Cambridge until the early 1620s. Best nevertheless reinvested in two portions of the family holdings in October 1622 and was in Yorkshire as late as May 1623. At some point thereafter he embarked on his first trip to the continent, where we find him in Germany in 1624. Ley has him going out to fight for Gustavus Adolphus, referring either to the Swedish king's final campaigns against Poland (1621–9) or his intervention in Germany (June 1630–November 1632). Family papers show that Best was back in Yorkshire between November 1627 and October 1628, and again from April 1632 to September 1634, after which he reappears in 1644 as a soldier in the parliamentarian army—suggesting further travels on the continent during either or both of these intervals. Whatever the precise chronology, Ley relates that Best, who was 'fit to hold discourse with any man', disputed 'with others when he had opportunity' at the University of Greifswald in Pomerania, and other places in northern Germany, Poland, and Transylvania. There Ley reports that Best 'disputed with some Antitrinitarians, and more adhering to carnal reason than the mystery of faith, was drawn to the dangerous opinion [of] the denial of our Saviour's divinity' (BL, Add. MS 24482). This evidence, combined with his surviving writings, confirms that during one or more extended stays on the continent, Best came under the influence of the theology of the Polish Brethren (Socinians).

Best wasted no time in preaching his new faith on his

return to England. Some time shortly before February 1645, he submitted some of his papers to a minister whom he considered a friend (possibly Ley). These writings were promptly brought to the attention of the clergy in York, and Best was imprisoned on 14 February 1645. On 10 June the Westminster assembly of divines received a letter from the ministers of York, complaining of Best's 'horrid blasphemies' (Mitchell and Struthers, 101). The assembly responded immediately, and the same day reported *en masse* to the House of Commons about Best's 'Blasphemies … against the Deity of our Saviour *Jesus Christ*, and of the Holy Ghost, contained in Books, Treatises, and Notes of his'. The assembly appealed to parliament to use its authority to execute 'condign Punishment upon an Offender of so high a Nature; that, in references to the Crime, he may be made exemplary'. The house thanked the divines for acquainting them with Best's case so speedily and ordered that the committee of plundered ministers be appointed to examine his writings and report back to parliament. The committee was also empowered to question Best, and the house commanded that he be committed immediately to the Gatehouse prison in Westminster (*JHC*, 4.170–71).

The committee examined the prisoner on 7 July 1645 and on several occasions thereafter, but Best held steadfast. It was not until 28 January 1646 that their report was read to the house. The same day parliament resolved that the committee prepare an ordinance for punishing Best with death for his heresies. This was duly prepared and read twice to parliament on 28 March. The parliament then asked a delegation of divines to attempt to persuade Best to recant. When this also failed, Best himself was brought before the Commons on 4 April, where, on questioning, he denied 'the Tripersonality of *Athanasius*', calling it '*Romish*, and Popish' and saying that he detested it 'till he be otherwise convinced' (*JHC*, 4.500). He also explicitly denied that Christ was co-equal, co-eternal, and co-existent with the Father. On 29 April, with Best's case still under review, parliament called for a general ordinance for suppressing blasphemy and heresy (passed 2 May 1648).

Meanwhile, Best was irrepressible in confinement. The Westminster assembly reported on 16 December 1645 that, notwithstanding his imposed restraint, Best was continuing to spread his views by writing and other means. By Best's own account, he sent out no less than 100 petitions appealing for his release; these include an appeal to the assembly on 2 January 1646 and a printed petition of August 1646, in which he entreated the House of Commons for a speedy hearing or release. Epistolary solicitations to Speaker William Lenthall on 5 September 1646 and 21 June 1647 also survive. In April 1646 Best managed to arrange the printing of *A Letter of Advice unto the Ministers Assembled at Westminster*, in which he argues that the denial of liberty of conscience to others was a departure from the gospel, and that repentance was possible only so long as a heretic lived. As his imprisonment dragged on into its third summer without definitive

result, Best was prompted to publish his *Mysteries Discovered*, a densely written sixteen-page theological manifesto contending for the unbiblical nature of the Trinitarian doctrine. Parliament responded swiftly to this bold move on 24 July, and charged that all copies be suppressed and burned by the hangman. Best may have propagated his beliefs in prison as well, and possibly was responsible for introducing fellow prisoner John Biddle to Socinianism.

While Thomas Edwards and others held Best up as an example of the dangers of tolerating extreme heresy, some were reluctant to see anti-tolerationist forces gain ascendancy. The agenda of the Presbyterian assembly and its supporters was countered by a reticence to prosecute among Erastians and Independents in the Commons, whose interests, it seems, prevailed. Best was freed in late 1647. After his release he retired to Yorkshire, where he continued his study and writing. Best died, unmarried, on 17 September 1657 in Great Driffield, and was buried two days later in the churchyard at neighbouring Little Driffield.

Best's *Mysteries Discovered* reveals great learning and ability combined with an acerbic and forthright delivery. His cited sources include Christian Hebraists, travel literature, historical accounts, prophetic works, and theological treatises. Above all, Best reveals himself as a thoroughgoing biblicist, citing scripture no less that 330 times in this short pamphlet. While ostensibly an appeal for his release, Best unambiguously states his intentions to expose the 'lawlesse mystery' of the Roman church and to clear up the 'misty mysteries' of the Trinitarian obfuscation of the Bible (Best, *Mysteries Discovered*, 2). Declaring the doctrine central to the Roman apostasy, Best answers Trinitarian proof-texts and is careful to show that the Trinity is a late accretion, 'a verball kinde of Divinity, introduced by the Semi-pagan Christians of the third Century in the Western Church' (ibid., 11). Best also appeals for a right hermeneutic, contending that biblical truth is obtained by interpreting scripture by scripture, having 'respect to the scope, coherence, analogy, and the originalls, in discerning figurative forms and phrases according to the sence and meaning' (ibid., 4). There is no holding back when Best musters up the strongest apocalyptic epithets possible, pronouncing the Trinitarian 'hypostaticall union and communion of properties' to be 'reall contradictions, and the froglike croaking of the Dragon, the beast and false Prophet, *Revel. 16.13.* by vertue of a *Hocus Pocus* and a Babylonian mouth, thus after the precipice of this Romish *Jezabel*' (ibid., 14). Finally, Best argues that no political harm would ensue if England adopted greater religious toleration, and concludes with an appeal for further reformation in doctrine.

Best's case marks a turning point in the history of toleration in Britain. While placarded as a dangerous heretic and blasphemer by opponents of religious freedom, his situation (if not his views) enjoyed sympathy among those not eager to set a precedent in suppressing religious dissent. Nevertheless, the cases of Best and John Biddle served as a backdrop to the passing of the 1648 ordinance, which made denial of the Trinity a capital offence. Best's *Mysteries Discovered* was the first Socinian work to be written and published in England by an Englishman, and thus provided an early link between continental and British anti-Trinitarian theological currents. The work's fusion of prophecy and anti-Trinitarianism is unusual for a Socinian of this period, but is seen in later English anti-Trinitarians such as Isaac Newton, William Whiston, and Joseph Priestley. Anti-Trinitarian annotations in the Bodleian copy and positive citations by a Quaker in the 1650s, as well as coverage given by defenders of orthodoxy, show that Best's main published work was not only read and taken seriously but that its biblicist anti-Trinitarian theology resonated with some who were dissatisfied with the religious mainstream.　　STEPHEN D. SNOBELEN

Sources J. Hunter, 'Virorum notabilium memoranda. Collections for the lives of eminent Englishmen', Memoranda of Best family, 1851, BL, Add. MS 24482, fols. 69–85 • East Riding of Yorkshire Archives Service, Beverley, Best family papers, Howard-Vyse deposit, DD/HV • H. J. McLachlan, *Socinianism in seventeenth-century England* (1951) • *JHC*, 4 (1644–6) • *JHC*, 5 (1646–8) • proceedings for the committee of plundered ministers, BL, Add. MS 15669, fols. 103, 109, 110, 114, 121, 125, 174, 238 • proceedings for the committee of plundered ministers, BL, Add. MS 15670, fols. 21, 22, 24, 31, 37 • A. F. Mitchell and J. Struthers, eds., *Minutes of the sessions of the Westminster assembly of divines* (1874) • P. Best, *Mysteries discovered* (1647) • P. Best, *A letter of advice unto the ministers assembled at Westminster* (1646) • P. Best, *To certaine honorable persons of the House of Commons assembled in parliament* (1646) • P. Best, letters to Speaker William Lenthall, Bodl. Oxf., MSS Tanner 58–59 • *DNB* • T. Edwards, *Gangraena, or, A catalogue and discovery of many of the errours, heresies, blasphemies and pernicious practices of the sectaries of this time*, 3 vols. in 1 (1646) • J. R. Tanner, *The historical record of the University of Cambridge* (1917) • W. Grigge, *The Quaker's Jesus* (1658) • D. Woodward, *The farming and memorandum books of Henry Best of Elmswell, 1642*, British Academy, Records of Social and Economic History, new ser., 8 (1984)
Archives BL, memoranda of Best family, Add. MS 24482 [transcript] | Bodl. Oxf., MS Tanner 58 • Bodl. Oxf., MS Tanner 59 • East Riding of Yorkshire Archives Service, Beverley, collection of Best family papers, Howard-Vyse deposit

Best, Samuel [nicknamed Poorhelp] (**1737/8–1825**), self-styled prophet, of whom details of parentage and early life are unknown, was probably employed as a servant to several London families, where he gained a reputation for dishonesty (*Imposture*, 42). Another account states that Best had once been a 'Spital-fields weaver, in good circumstances' but, having disowned his wife and three children, was by 1787 a reclusive resident in Shoreditch workhouse. Under the name Poorhelp, Best gained a reputation for predicting visitors' health and 'future condition' by examining and licking their hands. One report suggests that he was attended incognito by both the bishop of Durham and George III, whom Best encouraged to greater acts of piety. Prophecies took place in workhouse rooms decorated with celestial figures and a portrait of John Wesley which Best shared with his 'two companions', a small child named Lord Cadogan and a bantam cock (*GM*, 56.1106, 57.116). Here, apparently without prior knowledge, Best provided details of visitors' personal history and future prospects while reciting obscure biblical passages from memory. His popularity was such that he moved to new

premises in Kingsland Road, London, where he was visited by members of fashionable society. Surviving on substantial quantities of bread, cheese, and rhubarb-flavoured gin, Best was said to spend his nights in conversation with celestial powers, including the angel Gabriel. Having predicted that the world would end by 1950, he lived the final thirty years of his life convinced of his duty to lead the children of Israel in rebuilding Jerusalem. Opinions of Best's abilities were varied. 'Clio', while recalling how one intelligent visitor had been 'fully convinced of his superior knowledge', attributed his character either to a 'rigid fanaticism … prevalent in weak minds' or to his being 'to all appearance insane' (*GM*, 57.115, 310). Best died, aged eighty-seven, at Bridport on 7 March 1825.

　　T. F. HENDERSON, *rev.* PHILIP CARTER

Sources *Imposture detected, or, Thoughts on a pretended prophet* (1787) • *GM*, 1st ser., 56 (1786), 1106 • *GM*, 1st ser., 57 (1787), 115–16, 309–10
Likenesses Farn, stipple (after Lewis), BM, NPG; repro. in W. Granger and others, *The new wonderful museum and extraordinary magazine*, 2 (1804)

Best, Sigismund Payne (**1885–1978**), intelligence officer, was born on 14 April 1885 in Cheltenham, Gloucestershire, the son of Dr George Payne Best (*d.* 1908), then senior physician at Birmingham General Hospital, and his wife, Catherine Sophia Allinson (*d.* 1908). His maternal grandmother was said to have been the daughter of an Indian maharaja. He was privately educated in Britain and Germany, his father having been appointed *Dozent* to the medical faculties of various German universities and practising privately in Vienna, Leipzig, and Dresden. At fifteen, Sigismund was apprenticed to a firm of chartered accountants, but he did not qualify. His father, mother, and brother all died within three months of each other in 1908. As the sole heir he was left with a private income of about £800 a year, on the strength of which he married and moved back to Germany, enrolling himself at the University of Munich and at an academy of music in Munich. He returned to England in 1911, becoming a member of the Purley rural district council and otherwise leading the life of a country gentleman. On the outbreak of war with Germany in August 1914 he was recruited into the newly created intelligence corps of the army and sent to France with the rank of second lieutenant. There in 1915 he made the acquaintance of the legendary head of the Secret Intelligence Service, the mysterious 'C', Mansfield Cumming. Cumming's son was killed in the same motor accident in which Cumming lost his leg, and Payne Best won his confidence as the man who arranged his son's burial. Early in 1915 he was sent to the Netherlands to set up an intelligence network to report directly to C. His net recruited Flemish refugees from Belgium and ran agents into German-occupied Belgium, concentrating on the German order of battle in Flanders. He survived various 'turf wars' with rival agencies and networks, ending the war with the rank of captain, earning an OBE and the Belgian Croix de Guerre, and being made a chevalier of the

French Légion d'honneur; he also received two unsuccessful recommendations for the Military Cross and two mentions in dispatches.

On demobilization Payne Best went into business in the Netherlands, where he remarried (his first wife had died in obscure circumstances). His new wife, Bridget Allardyce, was the daughter of a Dutch general. With the advent of Hitler to power in Germany and the increasing prospects of a new European war, he was recruited in 1938 into the newly formed 'Z' organization, a new branch of the Secret Intelligence Service (SIS) founded by one of C's deputies, Colonel Claude Dansey, to take over from the increasingly compromised SIS organization in Europe.

In summer 1939 C's successor, Admiral Sinclair, was diagnosed as suffering from terminal cancer (he died on 4 November 1939). There were two candidates for the succession, Colonel Dansey and Colonel Stewart Menzies. At the same time, Dansey was approached through a Free German organization in London, whose activities had enjoyed some SIS funding, on behalf of a group allegedly of senior German commanders, anxious to thwart Hitler's plans for war and to overthrow him. In fact a number of clandestine contacts between individual members and sections of the conservative-military-bureaucratic opposition to Hitler in Germany were already current, but so far as is known these had not been with the SIS, nor had any of them, so far, mentioned a military coup against Hitler. Menzies took up the contacts with energy and enthusiasm, in which he was supported, against the initial scepticism of the Foreign Office and of Payne Best, by the newly appointed head of the SIS station in The Hague, a Major Stevens. Stevens's previous experience of intelligence work had been confined to India. The contacts were taken very seriously in London. Communications with the allegedly dissident German officers were handled by the foreign secretary, Lord Halifax, himself. British strategy at this time was predicated on the hope that Germany's economic weakness would precipitate internal discontent, which, it was hoped, would be followed by some kind of internal upheaval in which Hitler would be neutralized or removed from office.

Unfortunately for Stevens and Payne Best, the original contacts proved to have originated with the German SS. The two men, accompanied by a Dutch intelligence officer, were lured to the Dutch–German border at the small village of Venlo and kidnapped across it by an SS commando led by the young and ambitious Walter Schellenberg, who ended the war a full general in the SS and head of the SS external intelligence service (which in 1944 had swallowed the German army's military intelligence arm, the Abwehr). In the turmoil the Dutch officer received fatal wounds. Both Payne Best and Stevens were held for a show trial, together with a German workman who had carried out a one-man attempt to kill Hitler with a bomb in the Munich Bierkeller in which Hitler's attempted coup of 1923 had begun, at the height of the exchanges between the as yet unmasked Schellenberg and the British. Most of the German intelligence was incorporated into the German declaration of 9 May 1940, justifying the German invasion of the Netherlands.

Payne Best and Stevens were incarcerated initially in the concentration camp at Sachsenhausen. But in the last days of the war they were added to the group of prominent European political figures and relatives of the allied war leaders whom the Germans were keeping as hostages in their forced migration ahead of the allied forces, ending up in the depths of the south Tyrol. Here Payne Best emerged as the undoubted leader of the hostages, persuading their SS guards to disobey orders to execute their charges, overriding a somewhat melodramatic plan by the local Italian partisans to storm their prison and release whoever was fortunate enough to survive such an adventure, and arranging for the prisoners to be liberated by a detachment of American soldiers.

Payne Best's reward was to be silenced by the SIS authorities and to be suspected of having given everything away, whereas the facts argue that his main fault was to leave Stevens to have his version of events accepted before Payne Best could return to England. The Treasury treated his financial problems with the same lack of engagement that it was to show to most other clandestine claimants upon British generosity. Payne Best was allowed to publish a very much bowdlerized account of the incident, being refused permission to cite the wealth of evidence produced by the official Dutch inquiry in 1947. In retirement he reverted to his youthful passion for classical music and devoted himself to encouraging various young musicians of promise. He died on 21 September 1978 at his home, 18 Lickhill Road, Calne, Wiltshire; his wife survived him.   D. CAMERON WATT

Sources IWM, Sigismund Payne Best papers • Unterstaatssekretär Akten betreffend Belgien-Holland-Luxemburg I, September 1939–Oktober 1940, Politischen Archiv des Auswärtigen Amts, R29875 • private information (2004) [widow] • C. Andrew, *Secret service: the making of the British intelligence community* (1985) • C. A. MacDonald, 'The Venlo affair', *European Studies Review*, 8 (1978), 443–64 • d. cert.

Best, Thomas (1570–1639), sea captain and master of Trinity House, was baptized on 8 June 1570 at Merstham, Surrey, the youngest son of Robert Best, an interpreter for the Muscovy Company, and Anne, formerly Bowman. Later, in 1623, Best told Sir William Conway that he had first taken ship in 1583, aged thirteen, and, like his elder brother George *Best (d. 1584), rose to authority through his navigational skill. Best was married three times: first to Anne, of Orpington, in 1584, second to Mary (d. 1624), of Faversham, and third to Dennis Ruth Stock (b. 1584), of Totnes, who survived him. Between 1588 and 1602 six of his children were baptized at St Dunstan, Stepney.

Exchequer port books show that in 1599 Best returned to London as master of the *Mermaid* from the Barbary coast before taking the ship back to the Levant in 1602. After his return he took the *Pearl* to Russia in May 1606, captaining her again on a voyage to Algiers and the Levant in 1609. Such voyages commended him to Sir Thomas Smith, governor of the monopoly companies involved in those trades, who in turn appointed him chief commander of the East India Company's tenth fleet, on 3 December 1611.

Best's fleet comprised *Dragon*, 600 tons, and three smaller ships, *Hosiander* under Thomas Aldworth, *James*, and *Solomon*. Best's journal, describing *Dragon*'s voyage up to 15 June 1614, shows that his fleet left Gravesend on 1 February 1612 and arrived at Surat on 3 September. Four Portuguese galleons and twenty-six fragattas under da Cunha drove Best's ships from their anchorage before Surat on 29 November. Thereupon Best manoeuvred *Dragon* as if to divide the Portuguese fleet in two before exploiting the harbour bar, tides, and the Tapti's river currents to fire fifty-six broadsides, being hit only twice in return fire. The Portuguese retreated at dusk, only to lose three of their four galleons by stranding in trying to gain the wind gauge against *Dragon* and the shallow-draughted *Hosiander* next morning. On the third day the Portuguese unsuccessfully dispatched a fireship towards *Hosiander*. Another battle followed on 23 and 24 December after Best had sailed away to reconsider his strategy in Mahuwa. Engaging four Portuguese galleons off Mahuwa the English fleet's guns put them to flight with 380 saker shot and 1700 small shot. The Mughal emperor was moved to accord the English rights to trade and fortify Surat and to trade at Swally and Acheen, having that grant presented to Best at Swally on 7 January 1613.

From January to April 1613 Best patrolled India's coast down to Cape Comorin, before landing at Acheen on 12 April to exercise trading rights. Its Mughal prince allowed trade only after a Portuguese whom Best had captured was released to him. Leaving Aldworth to establish further trade from Surat and Acheen, Best sailed on to secure trading rights in Siam's ports, where he put *Hosiander* into the country trade between those new coastal factories, Bantam and Japan. At Bantam, Best secured a warehousing that would enable the company to operate at the heart of far eastern trade, before leaving for England, richly laden, in December 1613.

When *Dragon* reached the Downs during the first week of June 1614 the company's court asked Best for a personal account. They considered that he deserved well for establishing their trade in permanent bases until they discovered the scale of the private trade of himself and his crew. None the less the tenth voyage turned a profit for the adventurers of 148 per cent, later revised to 320 per cent.

Best's reappointment, first proposed on 16 September 1614, split the court of committees. Best's insistence on both his private trade and having his son Nathaniel (*bap.* 4 Oct 1590) appointed as a factor ensured that the conflict festered until, on 27 January 1618, he begged the committees to set aside their charges and accept his son's service and his own suspension, a formula the privy council also approved on 28 January 1618.

Meanwhile Best's concern to improve Thames pilotage had led to his signing a petition for new lighthouses at Winterton Ness and Orford Ness in 1617. He won the lord chancellor's support, only to be frustrated by a royal grant of light dues to Erskine and Meldrum after Trinity House had built the towers. In 1618–19 Best was busy about his

Levantine business and with Trinity House's administration, following his election as master for that year. Thereafter Trinity House's transactions mention him 137 times. On 7 October 1620 Best certified charitable payments by Trinity House to William Leske's family in compensation for his capture by Barbary pirates. On 21 November 1621 Best headed the Trinity House signatories in commenting on admiralty proposals of 16 November for an improved 'barricado to protect the naval anchorage at Chatham'. Then, as deputy master (1621–6), he used his authority to propose deepening the main channel and anchorage, specifying both the cables required and the unconventional form of the two armed ships that would be needed to support the barricado. He advocated excluding all strangers from the Medway, which 'at present is as well known to them as to us', and having piles driven into its other shallower passages so that not even a wherry could pass (GL, MS 30045(2), fol. 66).

Best's quasi-naval prowess and navigational skill brought him several important naval commands, including the 700 ton *Garland*. He sailed in her with the squadron assigned to bring Prince Charles home after his unsuccessful Spanish marriage suit of 1623, before assuming command of a fleet based in the Downs. From there he detached himself in the *Garland*, with Edward Christian accompanying him in the *Bonaventure* (674 tons), to deal with Dutch 'insolence' in destroying a Dunkirk privateer at Leith and blockading another at Aberdeen. He agreed with the Dutch commander to escort the privateer from Aberdeen to a Flemish port, but in the Downs on 29 July the Dutch fleet again forcibly stopped her. Best chose to regard their action in not dipping flags in response to his protest as an insult, and scattered them with gunfire after dark. The Dutch fleet regrouped and demanded to see his authority to attack. Admiralty officials, fearing that the confrontation would escalate, ordered him to Gravesend before dismissing him and sending the Dunkirker home with a Dutch promise of safe conduct on 23 August 1623. As many naval officers supported Best's action his authority rapidly increased, especially inside Trinity House. High court of admiralty decisions accorded him letters of marque with Richard Salmon and Captain Spencer, in respect of the capture of the East Indiaman *Susan*, before he gained another naval command, the *Vanguard* (651 tons). He embarked at Portsmouth on 27 January 1627 for the disastrous siege of Île de Ré, and his commander-in-chief, Lord Willoughby, quickly promoted him to his council of war, and made him captain of the *Repulse* (700 guns).

Best's campaign for naval action against Levantine pirates saw him successively re-elected as Trinity House's deputy master by 3 January 1628, senior warden in 1632–3, and master in 1633–4 and 1637–8. In September 1630 he was appointed to the admiralty commission of inquiry into the keeping of ships at Chatham and Portsmouth, forcing Charles Harbord to produce for the commissioners in 1633 a map of the Medway barrage and the new dockyard at Chatham. In April 1632 Best was appointed to the admiralty commission of inquiry into the better manning of his majesty's ships. Its recommendations provoked the removal of Trinity House from its historic role in the commissioning of warships in 1633. In April 1638 he was appointed to an admiralty commission inquiring into frauds in timber supply to the royal dockyards.

Best died in mid-August 1639 at Ratcliffe, in Stepney, and was buried at St Dunstan, Stepney, on 23 August. His son Nathaniel took East India Company service in 1607, rising to command of *Eagle* in 1624, *Scout* in 1627, and in 1628 *Exchange* until she was captured by Turkish pirates sailing from Mocca to Surat. In 1633 Charles I confiscated Nathaniel's estate because he had forsaken Christianity to live in Turkish domains. Consequently Thomas's will provided generously for Nathaniel's wife, Anne, married at Stepney on 25 July 1622, and for her daughter, Marie. Best's daughter Elizabeth, baptized on 12 December 1602, married, on 1 January 1619, William Dethick, Garter king of arms. She and her daughter, Elizabeth, received legacies of £100 each from Best's estate while their children shared a further £100. Abigail Best, baptized 25 September 1596, inherited £50 and 'my picture'. She married an ironmonger, John Wallis, on 15 June 1615, and afterwards Rowland Jordan, a mariner of Limehouse, on 4 May 1624. Her son, William Rowland, also benefited by the will. Josias, baptized on 6 December 1596, was a haberdasher in the parish of St Edmund, Lombard Street, London, where he married Martha Salmon, daughter of Best's closest associate in Trinity House. He inherited shares in five Levant ships, *Jonas*, *Swan*, *Robert*, *James*, and *Speedwell*, plus their spare masts, sails, and equipment. Josias's son, Thomas, inspired by the bequest of his grandfather's 'India sword', sailed for Persia as purser of the *Lanneret* in 1645 and was the company's silk factor at Gambroon until his death in 1651.   R. C. D. BALDWIN

Sources W. Foster, ed., *The voyage of Thomas Best to the East Indies, 1612–14*, Hakluyt Society, 2nd ser., 75 (1934) · *DNB* · G. C. Harris, ed., *Trinity House transactions, 1609–1635* (1986) · G. C. Harris, *The Trinity House of Deptford Strand, 1514–1660* (1974) · will, PRO, PROB 11/181, fols. 148–9 · *CSP dom.*, 1619–23 · *APC*, 1617–19 · Best's journal of *Dragon*'s voyage, BL OIOC, L/MAR/A15 · C. R. Markham, ed., *The voyages of Sir James Lancaster, kt, to the East Indies*, Hakluyt Society, 1st ser., 56 (1877) · W. Foster, ed., *The travels of John Sanderson in the Levant, 1584–1601*, Hakluyt Society, extra ser., 67 (1930) · GL, MSS 30045(2), fols. 52, 65–6, 68; 30045(3), fols. 81v, 100, 253, 257 · T. S. Wilson, *The Muscovy Company in 1555* (1953) · parish registers, Stepney, St Dunstan, LMA · IGI

Archives BL, journal of *Dragon*'s voyage, L/MAR/A15 | GL, transactions, MS 30045(1), (2), and (3) · PRO, HCA 50/412 · PRO, SP 13/148/n93

Wealth at death see will, PRO, PROB 11/181, fols. 148–9

Best, Wilhelm Philipp (1712–1785), diplomatist, was born in Hanover, but he spent most of his working life in London. After completing his studies at the University of Helmstedt, he entered the service of George II's electoral government as *Geheimer Kanzleisekretär extraordinarius* ('privy chancellery secretary') in 1737. In 1746 he was posted to the Hanoverian legation in London, where he remained until about 1782, serving under five successive heads of legation. From 1770 he was styled *Hofrat* or 'counsellor'. From the 1750s to the 1770s he lived at 6 St James's Place.

Probably Best's most significant contribution to Anglo-Hanoverian relations during his long residence in London was as the *de facto* intermediary or representative of the University of Göttingen, the Hanoverian 'national' university, founded by the electorate's leading minister, Gerlach Adolph, Freiherr von Münchhausen (1688–1770), in 1737. It was probably in December 1752 that Münchhausen charged Best with overseeing the London side of the acquisition of books for the university's rapidly growing library. Best's surviving correspondence is one of the most important sources for the history of the library in this important early phase. By 1800 it was to become almost certainly the largest single assembly of books in the western world and an unparalleled resource for study and research. Books acquired through the London book trade formed a significant proportion of the estimated 133,200 held by the library by this date. Their presence in Göttingen contributed in no small measure to the increasing awareness of English-language authors in central and eastern Europe.

Best was responsible for ensuring the smooth dispatch of Göttingen's quarterly deliveries of books from London. They were normally sent by diplomatic courier via Harwich and Hamburg or Bremen, typically reaching Göttingen about two months after the orders had originally been dispatched. He was able to build a firm and lasting relationship with such members of the book trade as Thomas Osborne, Davis and Reymer, or John Ridley and his successors. His close working relationship with Osborne enabled the library to build its collection retrospectively through antiquarian purchases. In a later phase, when the emphasis had shifted to current publications, Ridley proved a remarkably well-informed and reliable supplier. Best's correspondence provides important evidence for the working methods of these booksellers and for the practical arrangements for the international book trade. It also shows the energy and enthusiasm with which he carried out his tasks.

Apart from book orders, Best advised and assisted the University of Göttingen and members of its faculty in a wide range of matters relating to British affairs. For example, he negotiated with the typefounder William Caslon (1692–1766) over the purchase of Arabic types for the university printer and pressed the case of the astronomer Tobias Mayer (1723–1762), and later his widow, in the Admiralty's competition for a practical method of determining longitude. His correspondence also supplies interesting information about his dealings with British officials and tradesmen.

From about 1782, when Best appears to have retired to Hanover, where he died in 1785, his role at the legation was gradually taken over by his son Georg August Best (1755–1823), who had studied law at Göttingen and returned to London as *Kammersekretär* in September 1778. Like his father, Georg Best also appears to have become quite well known in London society. In 1780 he was elected a member of the Royal Society. He remained in London during the French Revolutionary and Napoleonic wars, and the occupation of the electorate, being raised to a Hanoverian peerage in 1815. A notice of his death appeared in the *Gentleman's Magazine* of April 1823: 'In Sloane-street, aged 67, Baron Best, one of his Majesty's Privy Councillors, K. C. H. and F. R. S. &c.'.

GRAHAM JEFCOATE

Sources G. P. Jefcoate, 'Wilhelm Best und der Londoner Buchhandel: ein deutscher Diplomat im Dienst der Universitäts-bibliothek Göttingen im 18. Jahrhundert', *Leipziger Jahrbuch zur Buchgeschichte* [ed. M. Lehmstedt and L. Poethe], 6 (1996), 199–210 · B. Fabian, 'An eighteenth-century research collection: English books at Göttingen University Library', *The Library*, 6th ser., 1 (1979), 209–24 · *European Magazine and London Review*, 9 (1786), 65 · *GM*, 1st ser., 93/1 (1823), 381
Archives Göttingen University, Library Archives · State Archive of Lower Saxony, Hanover, MSS | Göttingen University, Michaelis MSS

Best, William Draper, first Baron Wynford (1767–1845), judge and deputy speaker, was born at Haselbury Plucknett, Somerset, on 13 December 1767, the third son of Thomas Best and his wife, Elizabeth Draper. He attended the grammar school at Crewkerne, and, being intended for the Anglican church, was admitted to Wadham College, Oxford, at the age of fifteen. He left Oxford without taking a degree two years later, however, on inheriting a considerable fortune from a cousin. He entered the Middle Temple on 9 October 1784, was called to the bar on 6 November 1789, and joined the home circuit.

Best soon secured an extensive practice, both on the home circuit and at Westminster Hall, chiefly in the common pleas, but also in the king's bench and exchequer, appearing in some of the main criminal trials of the day. On 6 May 1794 he married Mary Anne, the second daughter of Jerome Knapp, clerk to the Haberdashers' Company; they had four daughters and six sons.

In 1799 Best became a serjeant-at-law and in July 1802 was elected whig member of parliament for Petersfield. He was active in the impeachment of Lord Melville. In March 1809 he was elected recorder of Guildford in place of Lord Grantley. In October 1812 he was returned as the tory member for Bridport. On 7 December 1813 he was appointed solicitor-general to the prince of Wales and on 14 February 1816 he became the prince's attorney-general. In 1818 he became chief justice of Chester, and MP for Guildford.

Best resigned these offices when he was appointed puisne judge in the king's bench (30 November 1818) on Abbott's elevation to chief justice. He was knighted on 3 June 1819, made chief justice of the common pleas on 15 April 1824, and a member of the privy council on 25 May in the same year. In June 1829 he gave up his post on the bench on grounds of ill health and in exchange for a pension and a peerage. He was called to the House of Lords by the title of Baron Wynford of Wynford Eagle in the county of Dorset on 5 June 1829. More controversially, he was appointed one of the deputy speakers and showed himself a vehement supporter of the tory party and a strenuous opponent of the Reform Bill at every stage.

Best had no great reputation as a lawyer. As an advocate he had a forcible and pointed, but not always fluent, speaking style, though his arguments were clear and he was quick to exploit any weakness in his opponent's case. As a leader he was not always safe, and was much less successful in parliament than in court. As a judge he was notorious for bias and political prejudice.

Best was described in an obituary as a 'man of pleasure' whose devotion to the opposite sex 'amounted to a controlling passion' (*Law Magazine*, 316). As to his politics, the same writer said: 'he seems to have been governed but by one rule of action in politics, to aid that side from which most might be expected' (ibid., 313). On 11 June 1834, the University of Oxford conferred on him the degree of DCL.

Best had long suffered from congenital gout: he had to be carried to the House of Lords in an armchair and was given permission to stay seated when making speeches. He eventually died at his country seat of Leasons in Kent on 3 March 1845.

G. F. R. BARKER, *rev.* HUGH MOONEY

Sources *Law Magazine*, 33 (1845), 308–17 · *Law Review*, 2, 168–75 · *Law Times* (8 March 1845), 447 · *Annual Register* (1845), 255 · *GM*, 2nd ser., 23 (1845), 431–2 · Foss, *Judges* · J. Campbell, *Lives of the lord chancellors*, 4th edn, 10 vols. (1856–7) · John, Lord Campbell, *The lives of the chief justices of England*, 3 (1857) · *EdinR*, 35 (1821), 123–34, 410–21 · private information (2004) [James Draper]
Archives BL, letters to Sir Robert Peel and others
Likenesses W. Say, mezzotint, pubd 1815 (after H. W. Pickersgill), BM, NPG · J. Partridge, portrait, *c.*1826, Middle Temple, London · J. Doyle, pen and pencil cartoon, 1832, BM · F. Halpin, line engraving (after T. Lawrence), BM · H. W. Pickersgill, oils, Bridport town hall, Dorset · oils, Wadham College, Oxford

Best, William Mawdesley (1809?–1869), legal writer, was probably born in December 1809 at Haddington, East Lothian, the elder of the two sons of Thomas Best (1784–1813), captain in the Cameronian regiment, and his wife, Anne Kearney, of Tuam, Ireland. After his father's death he was educated in Ireland under a Mr Coghlan, and was subsequently admitted as a pensioner at Trinity College, Dublin, on 16 October 1826, where he later graduated BA (1831), LLB (1832), and MA (1834). On 2 July 1829 he was admitted as a student of Gray's Inn and was called to the bar on 11 June 1834. He practised afterwards as a special pleader and as a member of the home circuit and Kent sessions.

Best also wrote pamphlets and books on legal subjects. In 1844 he published his first major work, a treatise on presumptions of law and fact, which he dedicated to Baron Parke. It was followed in 1849 by his most influential work, *A Treatise on the Principles of Evidence*. This work, said by Baron Alderson to have exhibited more real brains than any other law book published during his lifetime, showed a critical appreciation of Roman law, of the work of contemporary foreign writers, and of Jeremy Bentham's *Rationale of Judicial Evidence*. Four editions of the *Treatise* were published while Best was alive, the second (1855) incorporating much of his earlier work on presumptions. After his death various editors took over subsequent editions, the last of which appeared in 1922. Editions were also published in Germany, America, and India.

With G. J. P. Smith (1805–1886) of the Inner Temple, Best edited a series of reports of cases in the court of queen's bench (1861–70). In 1864 he opposed the proposals for law reporting that were being put forward in connection with the formation of the Council of Law Reporting, on the grounds that they would destroy the reporters' independence and damage existing safeguards against error. Both he and Smith were among the few existing authorized court reporters who refused an offer of appointment from the new body. Best was a member of the Juridical Society and served on its council. In 1866 he became a bencher of Gray's Inn. But, probably for want of self-confidence, his practice at the bar failed to match his intellectual ability. It was said in *The Times* after his death that he had possessed all the attributes to have made him a remarkable and distinguished man, save only a belief in his own knowledge and the courage to use it to his advantage.

In 1858 Best had married his cousin, Caroline Georgiana Best (1828?–1900). The marriage was childless. Best died of apoplexy on 16 November 1869, at 87 Westbourne Terrace, London, a house owned by his mother-in-law, with whom he and his wife had lived since their marriage. He was buried on 23 November 1869 at Kensal Green cemetery.

C. J. W. ALLEN

Sources *The Times* (18 Nov 1869), 10–11 · *Law Magazine*, new ser., 28 (1869–70), 381–2 · W. Twining, *Rethinking evidence: exploratory Essays* (1990), 48–9 · W. T. S. Daniel, *The history and origin of the law reports* (1884) · *Book of orders* (Gray's Inn), vols. 8, 10, 12–14 · E. C. C. F. Best, pedigree chart of the Best family of Kent, 1968, Society of Genealogists, London · records, General Cemetery Company, Harrow Road, London · registers of births, deaths, and marriages, St Catherine's House

Wealth at death under £5000: probate, 7 Jan 1870, *CGPLA Eng. & Wales*

Best, William Thomas (1826–1897), organist, born at Carlisle on 13 August 1826, was the son of William Best, a local solicitor. In childhood he displayed a talent for music, and had some lessons with the organist of Carlisle Cathedral, whose name was Young, but his father wanted him to be a civil engineer. He was sent to study in Liverpool in 1840 but soon became organist of a Baptist chapel in Pembroke Road, and began a career in music. Best was mainly self-taught but had some lessons in counterpoint from John Richardson, organist of St Nicholas's Roman Catholic Church, and also, it appears, from a blind organist.

In 1847 Best was appointed organist at the church for blind people, and in 1849 to the Liverpool Philharmonic Society. He paid a visit to Spain in the winter of 1852–3, and then spent some time in London, acting as organist at the Royal Panopticon (later the Alhambra). He was also for a few months organist at St Martin-in-the-Fields and at Lincoln's Inn. In 1855, on the completion of the great organ in St George's Hall, Liverpool, he was appointed corporation organist there and conducted a grand concert as the climax of the festivities at the opening of the hall. He remained organist of St George's Hall for nearly forty years, giving three recitals weekly. For some years he worked in Liverpool as a teacher, and also became church organist at Wallasey in 1860. After three years he left this post and acted for some time as organist at Trinity Church,

Walton Breck; and, finally, he was organist at West Derby parish church. In 1859 he occasionally played organ solos at the Monday Popular Concerts in St James's Hall, London.

No performer equalled Best at the organ and he was frequently invited to inaugurate newly built organs all over the country. At the Handel festival in June 1871 he played an organ concerto with orchestral accompaniment and the experiment was so successful that he was engaged to give similar performances at subsequent festivals. He also inaugurated the huge organ in the Albert Hall in July 1871. In 1880 he was offered a knighthood, but he preferred to take a civil-list pension of £100. He also refused to be made doctor of music. However, the strain of his continual work as a performer, composer, editor, and teacher eventually made him ill and forced him to take a prolonged rest in 1881–2. He visited Italy, where during his convalescence he gave a grand recital in Rome, at the request of Liszt, and on his return to England he gave up teaching, and resigned his appointment at West Derby church. As the greatest living organist he was still much in demand as a performer, and he accepted an invitation to go to Australia to inaugurate the organ in the town hall at Sydney; he gave the inaugural recital there on 9 August 1890. By now he suffered from gout, and he expected the journey would improve his health; but it had the opposite effect, and after his return his public appearances were less frequent. He retired in February 1894. After suffering badly from dropsy, he died at his residence at 4 Seymour Road, Broad Green, Liverpool, on 10 May 1897, and was buried on 13 May in Childwall parish graveyard. He was survived by his wife, Amalia Caterina Fortunata Maria Best.

As a performer, Best was considered the finest organist of his time. His repertory was believed to include 5000 pieces, and he was remarkably successful in using the organ as a substitute for the orchestra. In addition he was a very brilliant pianist. He also published some piano and vocal pieces, although these had little success; his works for the organ were of greater importance, however, and enjoyed much contemporary popularity. He was still better known as an editor, one of his most notable editions being *Cecilia* (1883), a collection in fifty-six parts of original organ pieces by modern composers from various countries. He also published various thorough and helpful instructional manuals for students, including *The Modern School for the Organ* (1853), *The Practical Organ School* (1864), and *The Art of Organ-Playing* (1869). At the bicentenary of Bach's birth, in 1885, Best began an edition of Bach's organ works, which he had almost completed at his death.

Best was somewhat eccentric and in some ways a recluse. He associated little with other musicians, would not join the Royal College of Organists, and for many years refused to let any other organist play on his own organ. He kept the tuner in attendance at his recitals in St George's Hall, and would leave his seat in the middle of a performance to expostulate with him; on one occasion he informed the audience that the tuner received a princely salary and neglected his work. As a church organist he would indulge his fancies to the full in brilliant extemporizations, but his recitals in St George's Hall were invariably restrained and classical.

HENRY DAVEY, *rev.* NILANJANA BANERJI

Sources *New Grove* · Grove, *Dict. mus.* · Brown & Stratton, *Brit. mus.* · *MT*, 38 (1897), 382–3 · *Era Almanack and Annual* (1898) · *Monthly Musical Record*, 1 (1871), 91 · D. Baptie, *A handbook of musical biography* (1883) · *Musical Herald* (Jan 1890) · *Musical Herald* (June 1897) · *CGPLA Eng. & Wales* (1897)
Archives Lpool RO
Likenesses Elliott & Fry, portrait, repro. in *MT* · C. J. Praetorius, bronze relief, NPG · process block print, BM · wood-engraving (after photograph by Freeman), NPG; repro. in *ILN* (22 May 1897)
Wealth at death £2,707 2s. 3d.: resworn probate, Nov 1897, *CGPLA Eng. & Wales*

Besterman, Theodore Deodatus Nathaniel (1904–1976), psychical researcher and bibliographer, was born on 22 November 1904 in Łódź, Poland, and named Nataniel. He was the second son (there were no daughters) of Benjamin J. N. Besterman, diamond merchant, and his wife, Golda Augusta Krengiel, and probably grew up in Britain.

The single-minded energy which was Besterman's main characteristic brought him, early on and despite his lack of education, the chairmanship of the British Federation of Youth Movements (1925). Besterman claimed that he was largely self-educated at the British Museum Library and it is typical that his first separate publication should have been a bibliography (1924) of the well-known theosophist Annie Besant. He was investigating officer to the Society for Psychical Research, 1927–35, and published widely on associated matters.

In the early 1930s Besterman turned his attention towards bibliography, becoming both special lecturer at the London School of Librarianship and joint editor of the important, if short-lived, series Oxford Books in Bibliography, as well as writing his classic *The Beginnings of Systematic Bibliography* (1935). An indefatigable, largely single-handed, compiler and one who aimed essentially at making bibliographical and other information available, he published privately the first edition of his *A World Bibliography of Bibliographies* in 1939; this work, constantly enlarged, was to make his a household name with librarians worldwide. He was also closely associated with the British union catalogues of both periodicals and music, as well as being the first editor of the *Journal of Documentation*.

In these years Besterman published on American history and established his own private press, the Guyon House Press, which, however, came to an end when destroyed in the air raids of December 1940. During the Second World War he served in the Royal Artillery and the Army Bureau of Current Affairs, the latter foreshadowing his immediately post-war position as head of the department for the exchange of information in UNESCO, where he worked towards universal bibliographical control. Besterman's advocacy of his causes was ardent rather than diplomatic, and around 1950 he turned to publishing

the correspondence and works of Voltaire, a liberal spirit with whom he identified. Living, by agreement with the city of Geneva, in Voltaire's former house Les Délices, he founded the Institut et Musée Voltaire there (1952), while editing that writer's correspondence (107 vols., 1953–65) as well as the equally multi-volume series Studies on Voltaire and the Eighteenth Century. He created the conferences which gave birth to the International Society for Eighteenth-Century Studies and was the leading figure in the post-war rise of those studies outside the Anglo-Saxon world. Despite his intensive activity on both bibliographical and scholarly fronts, he wrote numerous other works and started a series of facsimiles of the printed sources of Western art, for which he collected both books and watercolours.

On 6 April 1925 Besterman married Henrietta Birley (*b.* 1893/4) of Hampstead, a secretary, but the marriage only lasted some ten years. Besterman subsequently married Evelyn, younger daughter of Arthur Mack, of New York. She had one son of her previous marriage. The marriage was dissolved in 1958 and Besterman married Marie-Louise van Muyden of Geneva.

Following disagreements with the Genevan authorities he moved in the later 1960s, first to London and then to Banbury, where he died at the Horton General Hospital on 10 November 1976, having arranged with the University of Oxford for the bequest of his scholarly research interests (the Voltaire Foundation) to the Taylor Institution there.

GILES BARBER, *rev.*

Sources *The Times* (12 Nov 1976) · *WWW* · m. cert. [Henrietta Birley] · b. cert. · d. cert.
Archives BL, corresp. with Lord Rayleigh, Add. MS 57729 · BL, corresp. with Society of Authors, Add. MS 63213 · Bodl. Oxf., corresp. with Graham Pollard · Rice University, Houston, Texas, Woodson Research Center, corresp. with Sir Julian Huxley · U. Oxf., Taylor Institution, corresp. with Nancy Mitford
Likenesses R. V. Darwin, portrait, U. Oxf., Taylor Institution
Wealth at death £824,311: probate, 7 Sept 1977, *CGPLA Eng. & Wales*

Beston, John (*d.* 1428), Carmelite friar and theologian, joined that order at Bishop's Lynn in Norfolk. He studied at Cambridge and Paris and incepted as DTh in both universities. He was entitled *magister* by 1424 when he was elected by the English provincial chapter, with William Thorpe, to represent the provincial, Thomas Netter (*d.* 1430), at the Council of Pavia–Siena. He returned to Bishop's Lynn in later life, where he is said to have been prior, and died there in 1428. He was a celebrated preacher on the scriptures, and a contemporary Carmelite from the same community, Alan Lynn, commented that: 'he explained the four senses of scripture in his preaching to the great edification of the people' (Bodl. Oxf., MS Bodley 73, fol. 139). These 'senses' were the traditional medieval categories of scriptural interpretation—literal, moral, allegorical, and mystical. None of Beston's works survives, but John Bale records some titles: collections of sermons on the gospels and epistles for all the year, ordinary questions and questions on Robert Holcot's 'Universals', a book on logic, and lectures on scripture. Leland saw a work entitled 'On the virtues and contrary vices' in the Carmelite house in London, which probably formed part of Beston's compendium of moral theology.

RICHARD COPSEY

Sources J. Bale, Bodl. Oxf., MS Bodley 73 (SC 27635), fols. 20, 36, 52, 52v, 78, 139, 197v · J. Bale, Bodl. Oxf., MS Selden supra 41, fol. 175v · J. Bale, BL, Harley MS 3838, fols. 93–93v, 201 · J. Barret, Bodl. Oxf., MS Selden supra 41, fol. 373v [ed. text in B. Zimmerman, *Monumenta historica Carmelitana* (1907), 1.404] · Emden, *Oxf.* · Bale, *Cat.*, 1.560 · *Commentarii de scriptoribus Britannicis, auctore Joanne Lelando*, ed. A. Hall, 2 (1709), 433 · J. Bale, *Illustrium Maioris Britannie scriptorum ... summarium* (1548), fol. 188

Betagh, Thomas (1738–1811), Jesuit, was born on 8 May 1738 in Kells, co. Meath, Ireland, into a family of tanners which had lost its lands in the Cromwellian wars. When the family moved to Dublin he attended John Austin's Jesuit school at Saul's Court, where his academic abilities were recognized. He was sent, probably in 1752, to the Jesuit seminary at Pont-à-Mousson in Lorraine, France, where he later taught languages and theology, and he also studied at the Ducal University in Nancy. He was ordained in 1762 and returned to Ireland in 1769 or 1770, where he taught at Saul's Court. After the 1773 suppression of the Jesuits he became a secular priest. Appointed curate to the parish of St Michael and St John, he continued his educational activity. In 1781 he set up the first of a number of parochial free schools for poor boys. By 1784 he was in charge of Saul's Court, which then was operating as a secondary school for both secular and regular clergy. It played a pivotal role in the re-establishment of the Catholic church in Dublin and Leinster as the penal laws eased, functioning as a bridge between the province's local schools and the continental network of universities and Irish seminaries. It also facilitated good relations between secular and regular clergy. Saul's Court helped to produce a generation of ecclesiastics willing to seek an accommodation with the government. Among its many distinguished pupils were Daniel Murray, archbishop of Dublin, and Peter Kenney SJ, founder of Clongowes Wood College.

Betagh was an important link too between the old Jesuits who joined before the 1773 suppression and those of the restoration, after 1814. Following the death of John Fullam in 1793 he became responsible for funds destined to finance the society's restoration and was instrumental in sending a number of his students to Carlow and later to Palermo for that purpose. A temperate man, in October 1796 he was described in William Corbet's account of the priests of Dublin as a political moderate (National Archives of Ireland, Rebellion MSS). In 1799 he became priest of the parish of St Michael and St John. He was named vicar-general and was a noted preacher. He opposed the proposed government veto on the appointment of Irish bishops in 1808. In 1810 he laid the foundation stone for the new church of St Michael and St John. He died at his home, 80 Cook Street, Dublin, on 16 February 1811 and was interred in George's Hill Presentation Convent, Dublin,

on 19 February 1811. His remains were moved later to the church of St Michael and St John, and in 1990 to Glasnevin cemetery.

THOMAS O'CONNOR

Sources Archives of the Irish Province of the Society of Jesus, Dublin, Betagh MSS · 'Prosopography of Irish Jesuits', Archives of the Irish Province of the Society of Jesus, Dublin · Menologies, 1800–99, Archives of the Irish Province of the Society of Jesus, Dublin, 1.10–16 · G. A. Little, *Fr Thomas Betagh* [1960] · W. Reed, *Rambles in Ireland* (1815) · *Walker's Hibernian Magazine* (Feb 1811) · *Freeman's Journal* [Dublin] (19 Feb 1811) · M. Blake, *Sermon preached on the lamented death of V. Rev. Thomas Betagh, DD* (1821) · *Dublin Magazine* (March 1811) · NA Ire., Rebellion MSS, 620/25/170 · *DNB*
Archives Archives of the Irish Province of the Society of Jesus, Dublin · NA Ire., Rebellion MSS
Likenesses J. Martyn, stipple and line engraving, pubd *c.*1811 (after W. Brocas), NG Ire. · W. Brocas, pencil drawing, NG Ire. · P. Turnerelli, effigy on a monument (dismantled), St Michael and St John's parish church, Dublin · prints, NL Ire.

Betham, Edward (*bap.* 1709, *d.* 1783), Church of England clergyman, the son of Robert Betham (*d.* 1719), rector of Silchester, Hampshire, was born at Silchester and baptized there on 17 November 1709. His father was murdered when he was ten, but this does not appear to have affected Betham's education, for he attended Eton College, and in 1728 proceeded to King's College, Cambridge. Betham graduated BA in 1732 and MA in 1736. He became a fellow of King's College in 1731, and was also for some time bursar. He served as senior proctor in 1751–2. Betham also entered the debate on the marriage of Cambridge fellows. In 1766 he described a motion to petition parliament to permit fellows to marry as 'a most violent flame' (Cooper, 4.340). In 1751 he became vicar of Teversham, Cambridgeshire and in 1770 he was presented by the provost and fellows to the living of Greenford Magna in Middlesex.

Betham was appointed one of the preachers at Whitehall, and in 1771 the provost and fellows of Eton College elected him to a vacant fellowship. Betham appears to have impressed his contemporaries equally by his learning and his benevolence. 'His fortune was not extensive, yet his liberality kept more than equal pace with it, and pointed out objects to which it was impossible for his nature to resist lending his assistance' (*GM*, 1063).

In 1780 Betham founded and endowed a charity school in his own parish of Greenford, having previously erected a schoolhouse there. He also gave £2000 towards the better maintenance of the botanical garden at Cambridge. His affection for Eton College was strikingly manifested in his will. He paid £700 for a marble statue of Henry VI, the founder, to be erected in the college's chapel, bearing the inscription 'Posuit Edvardus Betham, collegii hujusce socius'. In the statue's hand is a model of the college. A bust of Henry was also given to the college library by Betham, and other benefactions are associated with his name. Betham died on 24 November 1783 at his rectory at Greenford.

G. B. SMITH, rev. WILLIAM GIBSON

Sources Venn, *Alum. Cant.* · T. Harwood, *Alumni Etonenses, or, A catalogue of the provosts and fellows of Eton College and King's College, Cambridge, from the foundation in 1443 to the year 1797* (1797) · J. R. Tanner, ed., *Historical register of the University of Cambridge ... to the year 1910* (1917) · C. H. Cooper, *Annals of Cambridge*, 4 (1852), 340 · J. Ecton, *Thesaurus rerum ecclesiasticarum*, 3rd edn (1763) · *GM*, 1st

ser., 53 (1783), 88, 982, 1063 • A. Chalmers, ed., *The general biographical dictionary*, new edn, 32 vols. (1812–17)
Wealth at death £2000 bequest to Cambridge botanical garden: *GM*

Betham, John

Betham, John (1642?–1709), Roman Catholic priest, was possibly descended from Walliston Betham of Rowington, Warwickshire, and his wife, Emma, daughter of Robert Middlemore of Edgbaston, Warwickshire. He studied in the English College at Douai from 1663 to 1667, and was ordained priest there. Despite being associated with the controversial Thomas White, alias Blacklow, he went to Paris in 1667 and with Bonaventure Giffard and Edward Paston refounded Arras College as St Gregory's College. This was a house of higher studies for the secular clergy attached to the Sorbonne founded by Bishop Richard Smith in the early seventeenth century. He became first superior of the new college and he took his doctorate from the Sorbonne in 1678. He came onto the English mission, and in 1685 he was appointed one of the chaplains and preachers-in-ordinary to James II, a post he held until the 1688 revolution. Two of his sermons were later published. His friendship with influential Anglicans such as Archbishop William Wake and his views about religious toleration might explain his continued residence in England for a few years after the revolution. In 1692 he returned to France and was appointed preceptor (or tutor) at St Germain to James Stuart, prince of Wales, for whom he drafted *A brief treatise, with a particular respect to the children of great personages, for the use of his royal highness, the prince* (1693), an edition, in fact, of the first part of the Jansenist Pierre Nicole's *De l'education d'un prince* (1671). The book shows Betham's affinity with Port Royalist pedagogy with its emphasis on moral direction. He was soon locked in a struggle with the Jesuits who, supported by Queen Mary Beatrice, wished a Jesuit to replace him as the prince's tutor. In February 1704 he was summoned by Cardinal de Noailles to answer charges which accused him of attempting to attract the prince, now Jacobite King James III, towards Jansenism. Conscious that his position at court was becoming untenable he retired to St Gregory's, Paris, in January 1705 and died there on 20 April 1709. Dodd described him as 'a person of strict morals, grave, and reserved in conversation. The court was his cell, and he seldom appear'd in publick, but when duty called him forth' (Dodd, 3.485).　　　　　　　　GEOFFREY SCOTT

Sources G. Scott, 'John Betham et l'education du prince de Galles', *Revue de la Bibliothèque Nationale*, 46 (winter 1992) • A. F. Allison, 'The origins of St Gregory's, Paris', *Recusant History*, 21 (1992–3), 11–25 • G. Anstruther, *The seminary priests*, 3 (1976) • *Catholic Gentleman's Magazine*, 1 (1818), ix • J. A. Williams, 'Bishops Giffard and Ellis and the western vicariate, 1688–1715', *Journal of Ecclesiastical History*, 15 (1964), 218–28 • Gillow, *Lit. biog. hist.* • T. H. Clancy, *English Catholic books, 1641–1700: a bibliography*, rev. edn (1996) • 'The register book of St Gregory's College, Paris, 1667–1786', *Miscellanea, XI*, Catholic RS, 19 (1917), 93–160 • E. Duffy, 'A rubb-up for old soares; Jesuits, Jansenists, and the English secular clergy, 1705–1715', *Journal of Ecclesiastical History*, 28 (1977), 291–317 • B. Hemphill, *The early vicars apostolic of England, 1685–1750* (1954) • *Calendar of the Stuart papers belonging to his majesty the king, preserved at Windsor Castle*, 7 vols., HMC, 56 (1902–23), vols. 1–2 • *CSP dom.*, 1685–8 • C. Dodd [H. Tootell], *The church history of England, from the year 1500, to the year 1688*, 3 (1742), 485
Archives Westm. DA, Ep. Var., vol. 1 • Westm. DA, Paris seminary, vol. 1
Likenesses oils, Douai Abbey, Woolhampton; repro. in Scott, 'John Betham'
Wealth at death 250 livres; also bequests of property: Anstruther, *Seminary priests*

Betham, (Mary) Matilda

Betham, (Mary) Matilda (1776–1852), writer and miniature painter, was born at Stradbroke, Suffolk, the eldest of the fifteen children of the Revd William *Betham (1749–1839) of Stonham Aspal, Suffolk, and rector of Stoke Lacy, Herefordshire, and his wife, Mary, née Damant (1752/3–1839), the former wife of Whittocke Planque. William Betham was a distinguished antiquary, and his fine library awakened in Matilda an ardent love of literature, especially of history. She was sent to school, but only, it was said, to learn sewing, and prevent a too strict application to books. On visits to Cambridge she studied Italian with Agostino Isola, who had also taught the younger Pitt and William Wordsworth. Matilda taught herself miniature painting, and her portraits have great delicacy. But she remained too much of an amateur, and her success was limited. Belonging to a large family she made strenuous efforts to turn her talents to practical account, and she exploited her large miscellaneous historical reading effectively in her *Biographical Dictionary of the Celebrated Women of every Age and Country* (1804). Though fragmentary and unsystematic it is an entertaining work, and a genuine contribution to contemporary efforts to enhance the status of women.

Betham had already settled in London, where she gave Shakespearian readings, exhibited her portraits at the Royal Academy, and had a brief but brilliant period of literary and artistic success. She came to be on friendly terms with Charles and Mary Lamb, with Coleridge, Southey, Mrs Barbauld, and others. How high she stood in their esteem and liking may be gathered from their letters to her, including a laudatory verse epistle from Coleridge. This, and other correspondence, is printed in *A House of Letters* (1905). Matilda had already published two small volumes of verse, *Elegies* (1797) and *Poems* (1808), which attracted little attention, but in 1816 her *Lay of Marie* was well received. The work of the thirteenth-century poet Marie de France was an encouraging precedent for a woman with literary ambitions, and Matilda's poem effectively challenges comparison with Walter Scott's *Lay of the Last Minstrel*. Charles Lamb, who saw the volume through the press, thought it 'very delicately pretty as to sentiment' (to Robert Southey, 6 May 1815, *Letters of Charles and Mary Lamb*, ed. E. V. Lucas, 1905, 2.165). Though patronizingly expressed, this remark does help to define the sensitivity of her portrayal of feelings. Southey and Allan Cunningham were still warmer in their praise, Southey advising her to insert at the end of her fictitious *Lay of Marie* the real *Lais de Marie*, so as to give her book an antiquarian value. Matilda partially followed this advice, adding two appendices, the first containing extracts from a 'Dissertation on the life and writings of Marie, by M. La Rue', in the *Archaeologia*, vol. 13; the second not, unfortunately, the actual *Lais* from the Harley manuscripts, but only some paraphrases from them.

Family circumstances and poverty affected Betham's mental health, and in 1819 she was confined as insane. Southey saw her in June 1820, and remarked that she was 'perfectly sane in her conversation and manner, tho she has written me the maddest letters I ever saw' (*New Letters of Robert Southey*, ed. K. Curry, 1965, 2.215). She complained that her unconventionality made her family wish to keep her out of the way, and she did eventually retire to the country and relinquish her literary pursuits. But her friendships remained, and when, as an elderly woman, she once more settled in London, her wit, her stores of apt quotation and anecdote, her sweetness and cheerfulness of disposition, made her still a favourite, not only with the literary people of her own date, but with the new generation. 'I would rather talk to Matilda Betham than to the most beautiful young woman in the world', said a young man of her in her old age. She died at her home in Burton Street, London, on 30 September 1852.

ANNE GILCHRIST, *rev.* GEOFFREY CARNALL

Sources E. Betham, ed., *A house of letters* (1905) · *GM*, 2nd ser., 38 (1852), 549 · D. H. Reiman, introduction, in M. Betham, *Poems and elegies* (1978) · N. Cross, ed., *Archives of the Royal Literary Fund, 1790–1918* (1982–3), file 361 [microfilm] · *IGI*
Likenesses miniature, *c*.1801, repro. in Betham, ed., *House of letters* · pencil sketch, *c*.1840, repro. in Betham, ed., *House of letters*

William Betham (1749–1839), by H. S. Turner (after Matilda Betham, 1830)

Betham, William (1749–1839), antiquary, the third son of William Betham (*b.* 1698), was born at Little Strickland, near Morland, Westmorland, on 17 May 1749. His family seems to have been settled in the county from the twelfth century, and to have derived its name from the little village of Betham, near Milnthorpe. From the sixteenth century Betham's immediate ancestors resided at Little Strickland. He was educated at the public school of Bampton, was ordained in 1773, apparently without graduating at a university, and became chaplain to the earl of Ancaster. From 1784 to 1833 he was headmaster of the endowed school at Stonham Aspal, Suffolk. By 1829, when the church commissioners reported, the school had 'of late declined' from its earlier 'considerable repute'. He resigned the post in 1833, on being presented to the rectory of Stoke Lacy, in the diocese of Hereford. In 1774 he married Mary Planque (1752/3–1839), daughter of William Damant, of Eye, Suffolk, and widow of Whittocke Planque. They had fifteen children. Their eldest surviving son was Sir William *Betham (1779–1853), Ulster king of arms, and (Mary) Matilda *Betham (1776–1852), the author and miniaturist, was their eldest daughter.

Betham was the author of two antiquarian works. In 1795 he published by subscription, in London, *Genealogical Tables of the Sovereigns of the World, from the Earliest to the Present Period*, a folio volume giving pedigrees of royal families, beginning with the 'Antediluvian Patriarchs,' and concluding with the 'House of Cromwell'. It was dedicated to George III. Although 'a useful work', Lowndes considered it 'much less valuable' than the 'elaborate compilation' by Anderson, one of Betham's principal sources (Lowndes, 1.166). In 1801 at Ipswich the first volume was published of Betham's *The baronetage of England, or, The history of the English baronets, and such baronets of Scotland as are of English families, with genealogical tables and engravings of their armorial bearings*. Four further volumes followed at yearly intervals from 1802 to 1805. Sir M. M. Sykes described it as 'a very incorrect and imperfect work' (ibid.). An unprinted collection of letters, addressed to the author by the subscribers and others interested in the work during its progress, is in the British Library. Betham also made collections with a view to a history of Suffolk, but his advanced age compelled him to relinquish the undertaking; however, in 1814 Thomas Harral published the first and only part of a *History of Suffolk*, based on Betham's collections. Betham's papers were advertised for sale in the *Suffolk Chronicle* on 3 February 1833, and were bought by W. S. Fitch, who incorporated them in his hundred collections now in the Suffolk Record Office, Ipswich. Other papers are in the Partridge bequest to the Suffolk Record Office, Ipswich (HA 126:8775). Betham's work may be identified from the 'paper of very poor quality' and his 'atrocious hand' (Blatchly, 6).

Betham died, aged ninety, on 27 October 1839 at Westerfield Hall, Suffolk, the home of Barbara, his youngest daughter, and her husband, Edward Edwards. His wife had predeceased him on 21 July 1839, aged eighty-six. They were both buried in Westerfield church, Betham on 4 November 1839.   J. T. GILBERT, *rev.* COLIN LEE

Sources *GM*, 2nd ser., 12 (1839), 655–6 · BL, Davy MSS, Suffolk Collection, Add. MS 19118, 189–98 · J. M. Blatchly, *The topographers of Suffolk* (1988), 6 · J. Nicolson and R. Burn, *The history and antiquities of the counties of Westmorland and Cumberland*, 1 (1777), 223–6 · *Report of church commissioners*, 20 (1829), 593–5 · *VCH Suffolk*, 2.348 · W. T. Lowndes, *The bibliographer's manual of English literature*, ed. H. G. Bohn, [new edn], 1 (1871), 166 · *IGI*

Archives Suffolk RO, Ipswich, Fitch MSS, ref. q59 · Suffolk RO, Ipswich, Partridge MSS, HA 126: 8775 · Warks. CRO, letters to Sir Roger Newdigate
Likenesses Graf & Soret, lithograph (after M. Betham, 1830), repro. in BL, Add. MS 21033, frontispiece · H. S. Turner, lithograph (after M. Betham, 1830), BM, NPG [*see illus.*]

Betham, Sir William (1779–1853), antiquary, eldest surviving son of William *Betham (1749–1839) and his wife, Mary Planque (1752/3–1839), daughter of William Damant of Eye, Suffolk, was born on 22 May 1779 at Stradbroke, Suffolk. In his early years he acquired a practical knowledge of typography, and undertook to revise a portion of William Camden's *Britannia* for the edition published by Stockdale in 1806. In 1805 he went to Dublin to search for documents in connection with a law case on which he was employed. He found them, unarranged and neglected, in 'the tower' at Dublin Castle, and in the office of the Ulster king of arms. The sinecure office of keeper of the records in 'the tower' at Dublin Castle was at that time held by Philip Henry Stanhope, Lord Mahon, who, on Betham's representations, appointed him as his deputy. Betham also obtained the appointment of deputy to Admiral Chichester Fortescue, then Ulster king of arms.

Betham was knighted in 1812, and was appointed Ulster king of arms in 1820. He devoted much time to the preparation of catalogues and indexes to collections of records. In 1827 he published a volume of *Irish Antiquarian Researches*, illustrated with plates. This publication was succeeded in 1830 by the first volume of a work by him, *Dignities, feudal and parliamentary, and the constitutional legislature of the United Kingdom; the nature and functions of the Aula Regis, the Magna Concilia, and the Communia Concilia of England; and the history of the parliaments of France, England, Scotland, and Ireland, investigated and considered with a view to ascertain the origin, progress, and final establishment of legislative parliaments and of the history of a peer or lord of parliament.* This volume was reissued in 1834 with a new title-page, as *The Origin and History of the Constitution of England, and of the Early Parliaments of Ireland.* The author, in a preliminary note, stated that the title by which the work was first published inadequately expressed its real character, and that it had been thought expedient to republish it with one more fully declaring its contents and objects.

Betham also published in 1834 *The Gael and Cymbri*, which inquired into the origins of the Celtic peoples. In 1837 he issued *Observations on evidence taken before a committee of the House of Commons on the record commission.* Betham took an active part in the proceedings of the Royal Irish Academy, Dublin, after his admission to it as a member in 1826. He became one of its governing body, acted as secretary, and made several contributions to its publications. In 1840 differences arose in relation to the distribution of prizes and the publication of essays by George Petrie, and he apparently withdrew from the academy for many years. His last publication appeared in two volumes in 1842, with the explanatory title of *Etruria Celtica: Etruscan literature and antiquities investigated, or, The language of that people compared and identified with the Iberno-Celtic, and both shown to be Phoenician.*

Betham's large collection of manuscripts in Irish was purchased from him in 1850 by the Royal Irish Academy. He died in Dublin on 26 October 1853, and was buried at Monkstown, co. Dublin. As Ulster king of arms he was succeeded by Sir John Bernard Burke. Betham's genealogical and heraldic manuscripts were sold at auction in London by Sotheby and Wilkinson in 1860, chiefly to private collectors. Portions, however, were bought for the British Museum, London, and for the office of Ulster king of arms, Dublin.   J. T. GILBERT, *rev.* MICHAEL ERBEN

Sources W. Stokes, *The life and labours in art and archaeology of G. Petrie* (1868) · priv. coll. · Records of Office of Ulster King of Arms, Dublin · Royal Irish Acad. · *Fourth report*, HMC, 3 (1874) · G. Petrie, *A letter to Sir William Rowan Hamilton in reply to certain charges made against the author by Sir William Betham* (1840) · A. J. Webb, *A compendium of Irish biography* (1878) · C. Knight, ed., *The English cyclopaedia: biography*, 6 vols. (1856–8) [suppl. (1872)] · J. F. Waller, ed., *The imperial dictionary of universal biography*, 3 vols. (1857–63) · *Men of the time* (1887)
Archives BL, genealogical and heraldic collections, Add. MSS 19828–19865, 19996–19997, 21032–21033, 23683–23711, 24331, 34766, 38019, 44933 · Bodl. Oxf., pedigrees; English translation with notes of Ossianic poems; *Syllabus Chartarum et Literarum Patentium* · Coll. Arms, Irish genealogical collections [copies] · Genealogical Office, Dublin, abstracts and pedigrees · NL Ire., corresp. and papers · NL Scot., London pedigrees · priv. coll. · PRO NIre., Irish pedigrees · Royal Irish Acad. · W. Yorks. AS, Leeds, Yorkshire Archaeological Society, Betham's copy of Robert Glover's *Visitation of Yorkshire* with further additions | Office of the Chief Herald of Ireland, Dublin, Records of Office of Ulster King of Arms · Yale U., Beinecke L., letters to T. J. Pettigrew
Likenesses W. Drummond, lithograph, pubd 1836 (after D. Maclise), BM, NPG; repro. in *Athenaeum Portraits*, 20 (1836) · J. E. Jones, bust, exh. RA 1846?, Dublin Castle, Ireland

Bethel, Slingsby (bap. 1617, d. 1697), merchant and political economist, was baptized in Alne, in the North Riding of Yorkshire, on 27 February 1617, a younger son of Sir Walter Bethel (d. 1622), gentleman, and Mary Slingsby (1582–1662), daughter of Sir Henry Slingsby of Scriven, Yorkshire. Bethel's parents were enmeshed in complex northern kinship networks that foreshadowed some of his own future political connections. Through his father he was related to the viscounts Fauconberg; and through his mother he shared Percy ancestry with Algernon Sidney. Family marriages tied Bethel to the dukes of Buckingham, a connection he shared with Anthony Ashley Cooper, earl of Shaftesbury. Bethel's economic and religious heritages were equally complicated, with coal mining joining land as a source of wealth, and with both puritanism and Catholicism attracting the allegiance of some relatives. After the early death of his father, his mother's brother Sir Henry *Slingsby emerged as a paternal surrogate. Slingsby arranged his nephew's apprenticeship to Henry Vincent, a member of the London Leathersellers' Company, in 1630.

The republican merchant After completing his apprenticeship, Bethel left England in 1637 for Hamburg, where he prospered in the cloth trade of the Company of Merchant Adventurers. In the meantime his uncle, who shared his mother's puritanism, represented Knaresborough in the Short and Long parliaments before becoming an active

Slingsby Bethel (*bap.* 1617, *d.* 1697), by William Sherwin, 1680

royalist. Bethel returned to England in December 1649, and acted as a trustee for his uncle in the repurchase of Slingsby's sequestered lands, which cost him £7000. He was involved in other sequestration purchases as well. He was a member of a syndicate including Colonel Thomas Pride and Henry Brandreth, with whom the navy contracted for victualling in November 1650. Bethel was elected to the London common council for 1651 and also served as a deputy alderman. He supported the Navigation Act of 1651 and a proposal to make London a free port, both measures favoured by the Hamburg Merchant Adventurers, who hoped to gain commercial advantages over their Dutch competitors. About this time he married Mary Burrell. She was the daughter of Abraham Burrell of Midloe, Huntingdonshire, a member of the Long Parliament for the borough of Huntingdon after 1645, and of the Commonwealth's council of state in 1651–2.

Bethel may have returned to Germany in 1653 after joining other Hamburg merchants in petitioning the council of state for a convoy, but he was back in England by 1656. He bore little love for Oliver Cromwell, who executed his uncle for royalist plotting, and whose foreign policy he blamed for destroying the commercial prospects the Commonwealth had seemed to foster. After the protector's

death, Bethel was elected to Richard Cromwell's parliament for Knaresborough, where the Slingsby lands gave him a strong interest. He was the apparent author of *A True and Impartial Narrative of the most Material Debates* (1659) of that parliament, which appeared in a revised form in his *Interest of the Princes and States of Europe* (1680). A strong critic of the protectoral regime, he repudiated the 'Humble petition and advice' as contrary to the 'old law' and 'the ancient way of *England*'. 'The Law was ... fallen to the ground', through Richard's irregular succession, he maintained, 'and all Government reverted to its original, the people, who ought by their Representatives assembled in Parliament to bestow it as they should think fit'. But if Richard was willing to accept election by parliament, Bethel was prepared to accept him. He also had strong reservations about the power of the Cromwellian 'other house': the Commons must have superiority, he argued, because 'their proportion of propriety' now amounted to 'nearly ninety parts of a hundred' (*The Interest of the Princes and States of Europe*, 337, 342, 347).

Bethel returned to London affairs in 1659–60 after the collapse of the protectorate. The restored Rump Parliament included him, in July 1659, in the London and Westminster militia commission, and he eventually served as a militia colonel. At this time he was also recommended for a national committee to implement a new 'commonwealth or democracy' in a proposal that may have come from the circle of James Harrington (*A Proposition*). But he did not support the New Model Army's substitution, in October 1659, of military rule for the Rump. When General George Monck, in Scotland, signalled his dissatisfaction with the new committee of safety, Bethel opposed a hostile letter to Monck that was drafted by the army's supporters on the militia commission. When the Rump returned to power in December, Bethel was rewarded, like Anthony Ashley Cooper and General Monck himself, with an appointment to the new council of state and with an appointment to the Admiralty commission. As the movement for a free parliament swamped the Rump and began to take a strongly royalist turn, Bethel was among those Londoners who were apparently in sympathy with John Lambert's April 1660 rising, the last gasp of intransigent republicanism. Yet he also promoted his elder brother Henry, who had advocated a free parliament, for the Knaresborough seat in the Convention.

Bethel's whereabouts for much of the following decade are uncertain, but this was clearly 'the time of his Travels', in which he observed the commercial and constitutional circumstances of different states and probably drafted the observations he published in 1680 (Bethel, *The Interest of the Princes and States of Europe*, 'Advertisement to the reader'). He visited Edmund Ludlow, the regicide, in Switzerland in 1662–3 and spent time with the circle of republican exiles there. He apparently remained in touch with Ludlow thereafter, describing Ludlow after his death as 'a very intimate friend' (PRO, C10/245/13). In 1665 he was in Rotterdam at the same time as Algernon Sidney, and some similarities between their subsequent writings suggest a sharing of ideas.

Back in London by the late 1660s, Bethel seems neither to have returned to trade nor to have established a household: his wife had apparently already died, and he had no immediate family. In 1669 he was nominated for alderman in two wards with magisterial vacancies. These nominations came at a time when London merchants were increasingly critical of the government's response to the disruption of their trade by fire, plague, and the Second Anglo-Dutch War. London nonconformists, including Bethel's clerical friend Robert Ferguson, were also challenging the Restoration policy of religious coercion. The loyalist court of aldermen refused to consider Bethel for the bench, rejecting him and other aldermanic nominees with Commonwealth pasts like William Kiffin and Bethel's one-time partner Henry Brandreth, now a protégé of the duke of Buckingham. Whether Bethel actually sought to return to civic affairs or was merely promoted for office by unhappy citizens is unclear. The records of the Leathersellers' Company, of which he was a member with Kiffin, record criticism of him in 1670–73 for his failure to assume leadership responsibilities, though he did become a company warden in 1678.

An advocate for the interest of England Bethel owed his prominence at this time to his publications of 1668–71, which articulated the aspirations of the city's dissenting trading community. He was among the first English authors to adopt continental interest theory, and he also developed the idea of balance in his discussions of international affairs, trade, and religion. Both his *World's Mistake in Oliver Cromwell* (1668) and his *Principal Interest of England Stated* (1671) advocated the advancement of overseas trade as 'the principal Interest of *England*', encouraged the government to adopt more supportive policies, and implicitly criticized Charles II for not already having done so (*The Principal Interest of England Stated*, 2). Bethel pointed to the expensive and inconclusive Spanish war of Oliver Cromwell as an example of what the Restoration regime ought to avoid. The protector, whom Bethel also portrayed as a classical tyrant, had missed the mark on every score. He attacked Spain, when he should have seen that the true threat to English commerce was France. He had broken the 'Balance of *Europe*', damaging English trade with Spain, saddling the country with debt, opening the commerce of Spain and its colonies to the Dutch, and removing Spain as a check to French territorial aggrandizement (*The World's Mistake in Oliver Cromwell*, 11).

Cromwell had also damaged the 'reformed Interest', for his destruction of the balance between France and Spain had enabled Louis XIV to subdue French protestants and to pit the Netherlands and England, who were of 'one and the same Religion', against each other (*The World's Mistake in Oliver Cromwell*, 4; *The Principal Interest of England Stated*, 28, 30). Charles, on the other hand, had an opportunity to become the 'General Protector of the whole Protestant Religion' by standing against Louis and by releasing English trade from all the impediments that restrained it (ibid., 33). The greatest of these was the 'imposing upon

Conscience in matters of Religion' (ibid., 13). Such coercion discouraged protestant dissenters, the most 'industrious sort of people', from enriching the nation through their trade (*The World's Mistake in Oliver Cromwell*, 19). But by providing liberty for conscience and also by restraining commercial monopoly, reducing taxes on trade, establishing banks, and otherwise following the Dutch example, the Restoration government might advance the true interest of the country. Bethel's criticisms of Cromwell and his admiration for commercial republics reflected his Commonwealth past; but his prescriptions for English trade made him a prophet of the approaching commercial and financial revolutions.

Bethel appeared in print again in 1679–80, as the Popish Plot allegations toppled the regime of the earl of Danby and produced a crisis for the Restoration regime. In his *Account of the French Usurpation upon the Trade of England* (1679), he gave voice to the capitalist spirit of the city's trading men and to the Francophobia that fuelled urban anti-Catholicism. 'Money is the *primum mobile* which moves the Spheres, which are the hearts and hands of men' he observed. But, given the astute commercial policies of Louis XIV, 'all the moneys of *Europe*' were likely to be drawn to France, leaving English traders as 'Higlers and petty Chapmen' (pp. 2–4). He advocated such immediate remedies as the limitation of French imports, the encouragement of immigration, the establishment of free ports, and the reduction of customs duties. He further promoted these recommendations in his *Interest of the Princes and States* (1680), a historical survey of European affairs, which included an expanded version of the *Principal Interest of England Stated*. He also demanded reformation of the church; and in an extensive chapter about the decline of the reformed church in France, he condemned the English bishops for following the 'Proud, Merciless, and Bloody Principles of the Papists' (*The Interest of the Princes and States of Europe*, 330). His anti-Catholicism was implicit in his advocacy of trade and industry. As he had written in 1671 and repeated in 1680, an 'unaptness to business' was bred among Roman Catholics 'by the slavery they are in to the Church, and the encouragement given by it to idleness' (*The Principal Interest of England Stated*, 21).

Bethel's writings and intentions were a cause of alarm to the government: the secretary of state Sir Joseph Williamson was informed in 1678 that Bethel had publicly denied the legitimacy of Charles II and the duke of York, citing letters he had seen in 1660. In 1680 Bethel was thrust into the midst of the political crisis by his unexpected election as one of the two sheriffs of London and Middlesex.

The sheriff of London and Middlesex Although the French ambassador attributed Bethel's election to the intrigues of the republican Algernon Sidney and to a political resurgence in the city of those who had supported the Commonwealth, most evidence tells against interpreting the election as a 'republican capture of London' (Scott, *Algernon Sidney and the Restoration Crisis*, 173). As a member of the Green Ribbon Club, Bethel had ties to leading opposition figures other than Sidney; and loyalists made much of his connection to Shaftesbury. He was not in London at the time of his election and only agreed to hold for office because of 'the importunity of his friends' (London Newsletters, 7.83, 5 Aug 1680). His republican past was less important than his advocacy of trade in prompting his election, and it actually raised questions for leaders of the civic opposition. The lord mayor, Sir Robert Clayton, for instance, promoted a different candidate; and Bethel's fellow sheriff Henry Cornish was distrustful of him. The government was actually more concerned about the election of Cornish, who was better connected among civic nonconformists, than it was about Bethel's republicanism; and it was especially alarmed by Shaftesbury's attempt to get a petition for an immediate parliamentary sitting adopted by the electors. (Bethel rejected the republican label himself, claiming after the revolution of 1688 that it was employed by Cromwell and by Charles II after him to malign any who stood firmly for 'Magna Charta and the Laws' (The Providences of God, 1697, 93).)

The true significance of the London shrieval election in 1680 is to be found in the petition for a session, in the nonconformity of the two sheriffs, and in the organization it reflected by the emerging whig and tory parties. Since neither Bethel nor Cornish had qualified for office through the sacramental test, their election represented a deliberate challenge to the coercive Anglican regime in church and state. It was accompanied by printed calls for protestant union and for further reformation of the church. The initial election was thrown out on the grounds of Bethel's and Cornish's ineligibility; but both men were re-elected in July, after qualifying, despite Charles's personal presence in the city to promote loyalist candidates.

As sheriff, Bethel named Titus Oates as his official chaplain and insisted upon the appointment of the lawyer Richard Goodenough as under-sheriff, despite Cornish's misgivings. He duelled politically with the corporation's loyalist recorder Sir George Jeffreys, whom he attempted to have removed from office, and who was eventually forced to resign after an investigation of his political behaviour by the Commons. After the rejection of exclusion by the Lords in the second Exclusion Parliament, Bethel named the duke of Buckingham to the city freedom, fuelling rumours that Buckingham intended to take magisterial office in the city to co-ordinate better the opposition to York's succession. Buckingham returned the favour by appearing with the duke of Monmouth on Bethel's behalf when the sheriff stood, unsuccessfully, as MP for Southwark for the third Exclusion Parliament in February 1681. (Bethel was involved in an altercation with the king's waterman during the poll, and he was eventually fined after a prosecution for assault.) About the same time Bethel and Edward Whitaker, Monmouth's solicitor, launched an accusation of idolatry against the rector of All Hallows Barking for maintaining an image of St Michael above the communion table. After the dissolution of the Oxford Parliament Bethel was among the promoters of a city petition for another parliament. He was twice nominated for aldermanic vacancies during his shrievalty, but he was not chosen on either occasion.

What most disturbed the government about Bethel's and Cornish's conduct as sheriffs, however, was their selection of urban jurors. No sooner were they elected than opposition leaders were assuring themselves that they would at last 'have such juries … as will not let those who shall come to their trial upon the account of the [Popish] Plot come off' (London Newsletters, 7.84, 7 Aug 1680). Titus Oates's brother, a government informer, subsequently claimed that jurors were vetted and that seditious conversations occurred at Bethel's political club at the Queen's Arms tavern. In March 1681 the two sheriffs arranged the deposition of the plot informer Edward Fitzharris; and when the crown indicted Fitzharris for treason, Bethel sought unsuccessfully to preserve him and his testimony by empanelling a sympathetic Middlesex grand jury. When the crown arrested Shaftesbury and such urban whig activists as Stephen College and John Rouse in the summer of 1681, Bethel, Cornish, and Goodenough empanelled jurors known for their support of a protestant succession and parliamentary resettlement of the church. Their efforts contributed to the famous ignoramus return to the case against Shaftesbury, which occurred after Bethel left office.

Bethel's shrievalty was also notable for his frugality. While Cornish provided the customary hospitality and largesse, Bethel launched a reformation of the shrievalty. At the outset he pledged to 'avoid all public feasts and entertainments' (London Newsletters, 7.83, 5 Aug 1680). Maintaining that the expenses of high civic office encouraged citizens to 'have an eye to Wealth, more than Parts or Virtue' in their electoral choices, he feared that some future despot might seize 'the Liberties of the City' from wealthy office-holders 'of Corrupt Principles' (Bethel, An Act of Common-Council of the City of London, 1680, 6, 8). Magistrates should be chosen, Bethel wrote, for their 'integrity' and not because of their wealth or because of 'any regard' for customary 'ranks and orders' (Bethel, The Vindication of Slingsby Bethel Esq., 1681, 6). Strong evidence of his republican cast of mind, Bethel's approach to the shrievalty was also part of a broader vision of a city cleansed of oligarchy and extravagance and of a commercial nation invigorated by the diffusion of wealth and trade from their undesirable concentration in a single entrepôt.

As a loyalist reaction began to develop after the Oxford Parliament, Bethel's republican past, his 'sullen' disposition, and his official conduct provided tory writers with ideal material for portraying the urban whigs as infused with the spirit of rebellion (Burnet's History, 2.254). At the time of his election loyalist rumour attributed to Bethel a statement made in 1649 that, 'rather than the old king should have wanted an executioner, he would have done it himself'; and another story actually placed him on Charles I's scaffold (Luttrell, 1.49). Even whigs believed that Bethel had caused 'great prejudice' through his 'sordid' elimination of hospitality (Burnet's History, 2.254). One tory satirist suggested that any guests at Bethel's table were more likely to be served paragraphs than dinner. An anonymous poet savaged him as 'Sneaksby' and 'Esquire Spare-Penny' (Iter Boreale, or, Esq. Spare-Penny's Departure).

John Dryden brought the case against him to its poetic apogee by casting him in *Absalom and Achitophel* (1681), as Shimei, a stingy saint and inveterate plotter:

> When two or three were gather'd to declaim
> Against the monarch of Jerusalem,
> Shimei was always in the midst of them. …
> His bus'ness was by writing to persuade
> That kings were useless, and a clog to trade.

Bethel remained politically active in London after his shrievalty. In December 1681 he was reportedly working with Cornish and with the former lord mayor Sir Patience Ward to gather depositions, in the event of another parliament, to impeach those ministers responsible for the political trials of the previous summer. In March 1682 he spoke at a whig strategy session in Shaftesbury's town house after the return to London of the duke of York, reportedly condemning the Catholic successor to the throne as a political tarantula who 'will give us such a bite that we shall never awake' (London Newsletters, 8.32, 21 March 1682). Overcoming his aversion to banquets, he was among the promoters of a whig feast for Monmouth organized to coincide with a loyalist feast for York in April 1682. He was involved in orchestrating whig electoral participation in the disputed shrieval election of that year; and he was indicted for riot, with other whigs, after the initial midsummer's common hall.

Bethel left London before the conclusion of the shrieval election in 1682, travelling north and visiting Durham, Newcastle, and Scotland. The trip may have had a political motive: it coincided with Monmouth's late summer tour of the west country, and it aroused the government's suspicion. He was reportedly back in London by the end of September 1682, but no evidence connects him to the whig plotting of 1682–3. Convicted and fined 1000 marks in June 1683 for his part in the city 'riot', Bethel was imprisoned and his goods were seized. Having secured his release in January 1685, he left for the Netherlands before Monmouth's rebellion, when a warrant was issued for his arrest.

An agent of historical memory The government carefully tracked Bethel's movements in the Netherlands in 1685–6. He seems at first to have lodged in Amsterdam with Abraham Kicke (or Keck), the merchant who had sheltered the exiled Shaftesbury before his death. But he was soon in Utrecht after a failed government attempt to capture him in Amsterdam with Robert Ferguson and Sir Samuel Barnardiston, another exiled whig merchant. In Utrecht he was understandably 'very timorous' and fearful of notice (BL, Add. MS 41818, fol. 17). He was particularly worried about the shrieval profits he had left in the hands of Cornish, who was now indicted and executed for treason, and who reflected on Bethel in his trial. He conveyed his lands (said to be worth £1500 p.a.) to a nephew, the Gray's Inn lawyer William Bethel. In 1686 he was heavily involved, with John Trenchard and other exiles, in setting up a cloth manufactory in Leeuwarden, Friesland. They hoped to derive sufficient profits from the enterprise to finance future actions against James II. When James's government sought to break up this concern by offering pardons to its backers, Bethel was excluded and complained to the chief English agent in Utrecht. He may also have discussed a pardon with William Penn, who was in the Netherlands in summer 1686, before he reportedly left for Germany with the lawyer Thomas Hunt and slipped again from sight. James pardoned him in December 1687.

Bethel returned to London after the revolution of 1688, taking up residence in Fetter Lane. His reputation as a defender of public economy gained him election, on 24 June 1689, as an auditor of the city's chamber and bridge house accounts. As the whigs gained power in the corporation of London, he was twice promoted for alderman in the ward of Portsoken in 1689–90, but was not elected. He also led those whigs convicted of the 1682 city 'riot' in petitioning for a reversal of the judgment and for punishment of those responsible. In 1694 he provided £1000 of the original share capital of the Bank of England and served on a committee that prepared its by-laws.

Now in his seventies, Bethel had survived an astonishing personal history. The revolution, which soon produced war-related results unwelcome to some old whigs, provided him with a final opportunity to shape historical memory of the events through which he had lived. A friend of radical printers since the late 1670s, he resumed his acquaintance with some of them, and perhaps also with younger commonwealth-minded intellectuals, as he returned to his authorship. He reprinted *The Interest of the Princes and States of Europe* in 1691 and 1694. In 1691 he also brought out *The providences of God … in introducing the true religion; and … preserving the people in their rights and liberties*, to which he appended documents that recorded Charles II's legal harassment of the whigs. Twice reprinted in an expanded form, the work recounted the history of English protestantism and the political history of the Restoration, attributing the nation's repeated escapes from popery and arbitrary government to divine intervention.

But the revolution of 1688 was not yet complete for Bethel; and although the nation was withstanding the might of the French colossus, it had yet to learn the full lesson of its recent historical deliverance. Too many collaborators with arbitrary rule had crept back into government under William III, while 'Church-Bigots' preferred to divide protestantism through the sacramental test rather than to undertake the reformation necessary 'to make us again a Terror to our Enemies' (*The Providences of God*, 1697, 98). Worse, according to the old puritan and republican, the corruption of virtue since the Restoration had not been addressed: the Caroline court had diffused its debauchery among the political élite, while the preachers of passive obedience and non-resistance had weakened regard for civil liberties. Only a 'general Reformation of Manners' could provide the moral force necessary to defeat the French and to further the historical purposes of an impatient Providence: 'He will not suffer his Cause totally to fall, yet the less our Reformation is, the slower will [be] his Mercies to us' (ibid., 103, 121).

Bethel's historical and political agenda was undoubtedly influenced by the memoirs of his old friend Edmund

Ludlow, who, Bethel claimed, had entrusted the manuscript of *A Voyce from the Watch Tower* to him for publication before Ludlow's death. Bethel shared the voluminous and unwieldy manuscript with the bookseller and printer Awnsham Churchill in the summer of 1695. But before the manuscript could be reduced to some order, Bethel brought a chancery suit against Churchill for its return, apparently because of his dissatisfaction with the work of Churchill's redactor. Churchill concealed the identity of this individual from Bethel, but his abbreviation of the text and his alteration of its meaning were far too drastic for Bethel, who insisted that 'the mind and intentions of the author … be fully … pursued' in the published version (PRO, C10/245/13). The matter was unresolved at the time of Bethel's death in 1697; but the *Memoirs of Edmund Ludlow, Esq.* (3 vols., 1698–9) appeared shortly thereafter. The memoirs were a complete rewriting of Ludlow's text, which, compared with the surviving portions of the manuscript, transformed the intensely protestant and providentialist language that Ludlow shared with Bethel into the more urbane discourse of country whigs and republicans after 1689. The work was apparently done by John Toland, and its publication was intended to embarrass court whigs (especially the governing ministry) as apostates from revolutionary principles who had followed in the footsteps of Oliver Cromwell.

Slingsby Bethel died in London on 4 February 1697. He left the bulk of his estate, including his Yorkshire lands and his Bank of England stock, to his lawyer nephew William Bethel, now of Swindon, after reserving a £6000 investment in land for another nephew and the husband of a niece. He also left £20 to two dissenting divines: the independent Matthew Meade and the Presbyterian John Howe, with whom he had shared exile, to be distributed to deserving nonconformist clergy.　　GARY S. DE KREY

Sources A. McGowan, 'The political writings and activities of Slingsby Bethel, 1617–1697', MLitt diss., U. Cam., 2000 · A. B. Worden, introduction, in E. Ludlow, *A voyce from the watch tower*, ed. A. B. Worden, CS, 4th ser., 21 (1978), 13–20, 25, 32–7, 67–78 · A. B. Worden, 'Whig history and Puritan politics: the *Memoirs of Edmund Ludlow revisited*', *Historical Research*, 75 (2002), 209–13, 223, 234–7 · E. Ludlow, *A voyce from the watch tower*, ed. A. B. Worden, CS, 4th ser., 21 (1978), 101 · HoP, *Commons, 1660–90* · J. Scott, *Algernon Sidney and the Restoration crisis, 1677–1683* (1991), 15, 59, 62–4, 81, 106, 124, 129–30, 163, 165–7, 169–71, 173, 181, 273, 303, 343 · J. Scott, *Algernon Sidney and the English republic, 1623–1677* (1988), 124–5, 179–80, 210, 214–16, 220–21 · Greaves & Zaller, *BDBR*, 1.61–2 · *CSP dom.*, 1650, 503; 1651–2, 43, 46; 1652–3, 230, 249–50; 1659–60, 307, 325; 1671, 330, 338; 1678, 256; 1679–80, 558–9, 569, 573–5, 578, 581, 620; 1680–81, 39, 170, 231–2, 256, 330, 332, 334, 337, 340, 365, 426, 440, 496, 499, 505, 543, 545, 624, 697; 1682, 236, 238, 382; *Jan–June 1683*, 344; *July–Sept 1683*, 50, 83, 145; 1683–4, 240, 396; 1684–5, 285; 1689–90, 155 · G. de F. Lord and others, eds., *Poems on affairs of state: Augustan satirical verse, 1660–1714*, 7 vols. (1963–75), vol. 2, pp. 477–9 · BL, Add. MSS 41812, 199–200, 210, 220, 222–5, 250; 41818, 17, 40, 106–8, 185, 234–5, 248; 41819, 59–61, 84–5, 95–6, 200, 272 (Middleton papers, 10, 16–17) · R. L. Greaves, *Secrets of the kingdom: British radicals from the Popish Plot to the revolution of 1688–89* (1992), 14, 27, 33, 36, 98, 170, 249, 296–301, 305–10, 335, 337, 350, 370, 391, 418, 420 · Newdigate newsletters, 26 June 1680, Folger, L.c.952; 10 July 1680, Folger, L.c.959; 15–20 July 1680, Folger, L.c.961–3; 5–7 Aug 1680, Folger, L.c.969–70; 30 Sept 1680, Folger, L.c.989; 16 Oct 1680, Folger, L.c.995; 8 June 1681, Folger, L.c.1085; 7 July 1681, Folger, L.c.1097; 6 Oct 1681, Folger, L.c.1133 · L. Cong., manuscript division, London newsletters collection, 7.72–80 (10–29 July 1680); 83–4, 93 (5, 7, 28 Aug 1680); 103 (21 Sept 1680); 111–12 (10, 12 Oct 1680); 154, 158 (3, 12 Feb 1681); 232 (27 Aug 1681); 8.32 (21 March 1682); 42–3 (13 April 1682); 81 (8 July 1682); 124 (5 Oct 1682) · PRO, C10/245/13 [summary provided by A. B. Worden] · will, PRO, PROB 11/437, fols. 329–31 · G. S. De Krey, 'Rethinking the Restoration: dissenting cases for conscience, 1667–1672', *HJ*, 38 (1995), 53–83, esp. 61–3, 75–6 · M. Knights, *Politics and opinion in crisis, 1678–81* (1994), 131, 138–9, 163, 164n., 270–72, 277, 289–90, 295n., 309n. · A. B. Beaven, ed., *The aldermen of the City of London, temp. Henry III–[1912]*, 2 vols. (1908–13), vol. 1, pp. 104, 119, 164, 185, 248 · R. Ashcraft, *Revolutionary politics and Locke's two treatises of government* (1986), 43n., 72n., 179n., 247–8, 354, 413n., 456, 517n., 528 · N. Luttrell, *A brief historical relation of state affairs from September 1678 to April 1714*, 6 vols. (1857), vol. 1, pp. 49–50, 52, 56, 96, 119, 120, 124, 129, 132, 140, 187, 209, 257, 503; vol. 2, p. 30; vol. 3, p. 357; vol. 4, p. 179 · J. Foster, *Pedigrees of the county families of Yorkshire*, 2 vols. (1874), vol. 2, no pagination, 'Pedigree of Bethell of Rise' · Burnet's *History of my own time*, ed. O. Airy, new edn, 2 (1900), 253–4 · J. Farnell, 'The politics of the city of London (1649–57)', PhD thesis, University of Chicago, 1963, 248, 290–92, 294, 373 · *Narrative of the proceedings of the committee of the militia of London* [1659] · *A proposition in order to the proposing of a commonwealth or democracy* [1659] · *A true list of the names of those persons appointed by the Rump Parliament to sit as a council of state* [1680] · *Iter boreale, or, Esq. Spare-Penny's departure to the north* (1682)

Likenesses W. Sherwin, line engraving, 1680, BM [see illus.] · octavo print, pubd 1800 (*Slingsby Bethel Esqr. one of the Sheriffs of London and Middx. in the yeare 1680*), repro. in G. de F. Lord, ed., *Poems on affairs of state* (1963–75), vol. 2, facing p. 478

Wealth at death lands' reputed value £1500 p.a. in 1685–6: BL, Add. MS 41812, fols. 222–5

Bethell, Christopher (1773–1859),

Bethell, Christopher (1773–1859), bishop of Bangor, was the second son of the Revd Richard Bethell (*d*. 12 Jan 1806), of Wadham College, Oxford (BA 1755, MA 1759), rector of St Peter's, Wallingford, and his wife, Ann, daughter of James Clitherow, of Boston House, Middlesex, whom he had married in 1771. Christopher was born at Isleworth, Middlesex, on 21 April 1773, and educated at King's College, Cambridge, where he matriculated in 1792, and proceeded BA in 1796, MA in 1799, and DD in 1817. He obtained a fellowship in 1794 and was second member's prizeman in 1797. He was a fellow until 1808, when he was appointed rector of Kirby Wiske, Yorkshire, a living he held until 1830. He was dean of Chichester from 5 April 1814 until he became a bishop, and prebendary of Exeter from 22 June 1830. Lord Liverpool nominated him bishop of Gloucester on 11 March 1824. The duke of Wellington transferred him to the more lucrative see of Exeter on 8 April 1830, and again on 28 October in the same year to the still more lucrative see of Bangor, which he held until his death. His net annual income by the 1840s was, £4289 as bishop, plus £550 as rector of Llangristiolus.

Bethell was always identified with the high-church party and signed the remonstrance against R. D. Hampden. He wrote several theological works, notably *A General View of the Doctrine of Regeneration in Baptism* (1821, 4th edn 1845). His other works are chiefly charges and sermons. His ignorance of the Welsh language was a very great hindrance to his usefulness in the diocese of Bangor, where 195,000 out of 200,000 people understood little more than their native tongue. He did not oppose the separation of the archdeaconries of Bangor and Anglesey in 1844. He disliked the proposal to merge his diocese with that of St Asaph, and had a 'prickly indifference to public opinion' (Best, 405). He publicly expressed his irritation with the ecclesiastical commissioners in his *Remarks* (1859). Bethell died, unmarried, at the episcopal palace, Bangor, on 19 April 1859, and was buried in Llandygái churchyard on 27 April. At the time of his death he was the oldest prelate on the episcopal bench.

G. C. BOASE, *rev.* H. C. G. MATTHEW

Sources *The Guardian* (27 April 1859), 375 · *The Record* (23 April 1859), 3 · Venn, *Alum. Cant.* · G. F. A. Best, *Temporal pillars: Queen Anne's bounty, the ecclesiastical commissioners, and the Church of England* (1964) · *CGPLA Eng. & Wales* (1859)

Archives NL Wales, corresp. with earl of Powis · Trinity Cam., letters to J. H. Monk

Likenesses T. Lupton, mezzotint (after J. W. Gordon), BM, NPG

Wealth at death under £20,000: administration, 25 May 1859, *CGPLA Eng. & Wales*

Bethell, Richard, first Baron Westbury (1800–1873), lord chancellor, was born at Bradford-on-Avon, Wiltshire, on 30 June 1800, the son of Richard Bethell MD (*d.* 1831) of Bristol, and Jane Baverstock (*d.* 1825). After an education at Bath and Bristol he was taken at the age of fourteen to Wadham College, Oxford. Within a few months he was given a scholarship and, at the age of nineteen, he graduated in classics and mathematics. He was proud of the fact that from a young age he supported himself by his own efforts, and that his good standing as a classicist enabled him to stay in Oxford and become a fellow of his college. But his heart lay elsewhere. He was called to the bar as a member of the Middle Temple in 1820 and in 1823 he began to practise in the equity courts. After a few years his practice grew rapidly. On 19 November 1825 he married Ellinor Mary Abraham; they had seven surviving children. Ellinor died in 1863, and, ten years later, on 25 January 1873, shortly before his own death, Bethell married Eleanor Margaret Tennant who died in 1894. In 1840 he was made queen's counsel by Lord Cottenham. By 1841 he was popularly regarded as the busiest leader at the chancery bar and, in the following decade, his income often exceeded £20,000 a year. By the mid-1840s his national reputation as an equity lawyer was secure.

Early career In 1847 Bethell tried, and failed, to enter parliament as a Liberal-Conservative. Soon after he became known for supporting controversial reforms such as the secret ballot and the abolition of church rates. The latter commitment was the start of a lifelong participation in debates about ecclesiastical reforms. Within the profession, too, he came to the fore in the discussions then taking place at the inns of court. As a Middle Templar he tried with some success to persuade his inn to improve the legal education of prospective barristers. More than anyone else he was responsible for ensuring that the inn supported a new readership in civil law and jurisprudence. It became clear to the profession that Bethell was no conventional lawyer. On the contrary, his ability as a classicist, and his interest in far-reaching reform, attracted him to Roman law and civilian systems with their emphasis on

Richard Bethell, first Baron Westbury (1800–1873), by Sir Francis Grant, 1862

codes rather than cases. A legal radical was in the making.

In 1851 Bethell was returned as the member of parliament for Aylesbury. On a number of issues he began to confine his political radicalism within distinct bounds. For example he defended primogeniture. But on a topic such as the abolition of religious tests for Oxford and Cambridge he was a forceful reformer. His talent was noted, and in 1851 he was appointed vice-chancellor of the duchy of Lancaster. In 1852 he became solicitor-general and received a knighthood, and in 1856 he was made attorney-general. His capacity to grasp points of detail was clear to all in the way he carried through committee the Succession Duty Bill. He used his legal knowledge to good effect in the Fraudulent Trustees Bill and the Bankruptcy and Insolvency Bill. In 1855 he fearlessly complained that judicial business was conducted before the supreme court of appeal in a manner which would disgrace the lowest court of justice in the kingdom. But he attracted most attention for his conduct in the protracted debates on the reform of the law of divorce. Here, he opposed Gladstone, taunting him for inconsistency, and thereby confirmed a growing reputation for acerbic observations and complete ruthlessness in verbal dispute. He respected neither persons nor the press.

Lord chancellor Bethell's ambition was as obvious as his bravery, and his increasingly numerous enemies took delight in the way he was passed over in 1859 when Lord Campbell was appointed lord chancellor. With manifest self-discipline he accepted the position of attorney-general once again and continued to work as hard as he had ever done. In the summer of 1861 Campbell died and Bethell, his standing now beyond dispute, succeeded Campbell, and took the title of Baron Westbury of Westbury in the county of Wiltshire.

High office did nothing to reduce Westbury's interest in reform. As early as February 1862 he introduced a Transfer of Land Bill which surprised contemporaries in its attention to detail and its revolutionary principles. After much debate it was only government influence which ensured that it reached the statute book. In practice it proved to be a failure but the concepts in the act continued to play a part in the evolution of ideas relating to registered title. Problems in changing the law of property did nothing to diminish Westbury's interest in other reforms. Whenever he could, he continued his assault on the statute book. Before he became lord chancellor he had attempted and failed to achieve a consolidation of statute law. He subsequently ensured that a statute law commission continued to work on problems of consolidation and, in respect of obsolete statutes, outright repeal. In 1861 the first of the Statute Law Revision Acts was passed and there was a second measure in 1863. Much was achieved, but no one could pretend that all the old problems frequently encountered in statute law had been resolved.

Westbury was not surprised at the difficulties he encountered. For him, the problems of statute law were grave enough but they were less serious than the uncertainty (as he put it) of English case law. Echoing seventeenth-century debates he told the House of Lords that under the common law's system of precedent:

> the unlearned age governs the more learned, because you take your rule as it is laid down in an early and undeveloped stage of society, and you are compelled to abide by that rule … until the Legislature intervenes to rescue the law from the necessity of following that which is often unreasonable and absurd. But the contradiction and anomaly do not end there … We have all heard the vulgar phrase, 'the glorious uncertainty of the law'. It is the common opprobrium of our system, which has passed into a proverb, and the saying has taken its rise in the fact that no man can tell with certainty whether a particular case which he finds recorded, and which is supposed to govern the particular case in which he is interested, will or will not be followed by the judges. (*Hansard 3*, 171, 12 June 1863, 779–80)

Westbury had an intense distrust for the system of precedent. He went on to speak of 'the evil consequence of men being left without rudder, without light, without compass or chart in traversing the immense sea of judicial precedent whenever a new combination of circumstances arises' (*Hansard 3*, 171, 12 June 1863, 783). For him the common law was irrational. Ultimately the only answer lay in a major attempt to produce a digest of the law as it stood and then to use this as a foundation for a code. Westbury also saw that such a programme would require a novel administrative context and, in this regard, he called openly for a department or ministry of justice. He gained considerable support for his ideas. Legal reform was a fashionable topic during the third quarter of the nineteenth century. There were general doubts about the fitness of the ancient common law for an 'age of progress'.

Many of Westbury's ideas were reflected in Henry Maine's book *Ancient Law* (1861). Westbury had been successful in having Maine appointed to the Middle Temple readership in jurisprudence and civil law in 1852 and it is noticeable that, like Westbury, Maine constantly related classical history to contemporary Victorian problems, and, again like Westbury, Maine frequently had harsh things to say about the common law as an instrument of social change. The legal radicals of these years spoke as if they had spent their youth in Greece or Rome. Nor was Westbury alone when he turned from the common law and criticized the court of chancery. Dickens finished *Bleak House* in 1854, and it fixed the public view of that branch of the law for a generation.

The most distinguished of the judges of these years supported reform. It was not only Westbury who saw a need for change in the process for reporting and publishing decided cases. At times, others were even ahead of him. Westbury ardently wished to see reforms enabling a judge in any court always to be able to apply both law and equity so that suitors no longer ran the risk of discovering that they had commenced their case in the wrong place. Yet his commitment here was out-distanced by lords Hatherley and Selborne, and it was they who took credit for the momentous change when, eventually, it was achieved in its full form in the Judicature Act of 1873.

The distinctiveness of Westbury's contribution to legal reform lay not so much in the strength of his commitment to changing particular areas of the law as in the radicalism of his approach. He respected the ardour of other men such as Selborne, but felt that it was always necessary to look beyond the need for the reform in hand to the process of law making. Only the reform of law making provided a guarantee that any change did not itself become a part of an inefficient system of law. It is noticeable that there are not a great many reforms in substantive law to Westbury's credit; it is true that he had successes with divorce and bankruptcy, but here it is apparent that his primary concerns were often with procedural change.

Given the strength of his views about case law it might be thought that Westbury had almost disqualified himself from the judicial role of lord chancellor. In practice he soon revealed that as a judge he could compromise in the sense that he was prepared to use and to develop case law but he would do so in his own distinctive way. He could happily ignore precedent, as he did in the case of *Gann* v. *Free Fishers of Whitstable*, and he liked generally to refer to a 'few elementary principles', not least when he was about to overrule previous lord chancellors (Nash, 26). He produced useful advances in a number of areas of law, and his analysis of 'domicile' was notable. He was capable of using precedent without praising it.

If there was one decision for which contemporaries knew Westbury best it was to be found in the proceedings arising out of the publication of *Essays and Reviews* by Frederick Temple and others in London in 1860. Two pieces in particular in this collection scandalized certain churchmen. The essay by the Revd Doctor Rowland Williams could be taken to suggest that the Bible was the composition of devout or pious men, and nothing more. The Revd Henry Bristow Wilson had commended a form of biblical interpretation which, he argued, would allow a Christian to express the hope that the punishment of the wicked might not endure for all eternity. According to the law reports they were cited in the consistory courts for heresy and their cases were removed to the court of arches. The formal charge was of setting forth doctrines contrary to those of the Church of England contained in the articles of religion, the Book of Common Prayer and the formularies. The case was heard by the distinguished ecclesiastical lawyer Dr Lushington, and he revealed a sympathy for the authors at certain points but ultimately found against them. For example, he regarded the hope expressed by the Revd Wilson as inconsistent with the mention of everlasting fire in the Athanasian creed. There was an appeal against the decision to the privy council, and, here, Westbury, expressing the view of the majority, found for the appellants (*Williams* v. *Bishop of Salisbury*). He never in his life had any respect for any form of literalism, whether in legal or other matters: for him the chief response to any text should consist in looking behind mere words to issues of principle. For clergymen to suggest that the Bible should be interpreted in the way suggested by the authors was, surely, entirely congenial to him. In response to the judgment, it was popularly suggested that an appropriate epitaph for Westbury would be that 'he took away from orthodox members of the Church of England their last hope of everlasting damnation' (Atlay, 2.264).

But certain of the bishops were not amused. Led by Bishop Wilberforce, they proposed a formal condemnation of the whole book as heretical by means of a synodical judgment in convocation. Such a course had only been taken once during the previous three centuries, but they succeeded and condemnation was pronounced. This in turn was criticized by numerous people, including churchmen. For Westbury it was an irresistible opportunity for ridicule. He spoke of bringing the bishops to the bar of justice for punishment because they had exceeded their powers. He pointed out how delighted his friend the chancellor of the exchequer would be at the prospect of wealthy bishops being fined. He was only saved from recommending such an extreme course because the words used by convocation had been badly expressed and were unenforceable:

> I am happy to tell your lordships that what is called a synodical judgement is a well-lubricated set of words—a sentence so oily and saponaceous that no one can grasp it. Like an eel, it slips through your fingers, it is simply nothing.

He handed out gratuitous advice to those who would take the powers of convocation beyond their proper limits:

> their best security after protesting will be to gather up their garments and flee, and, remembering the pillar of salt, not to cast a look behind. I am happy to say that in all these proceedings there is more smoke than fire. The words of condemnation are innocent and innocuous, though they do not, probably, proceed from a spirit that is equally harmless. (*Hansard 3*, 176, 15 July 1864, 1546 and 1549)

The last observation, made almost in passing, was unfortunately of a piece with Westbury's capacity for personal remarks. It was the sort of aside which embarrassed his supporters. Wilberforce took advantage of this and, in subsequent arguments, turned Westbury's style against him: the public became as interested in the personalities as the issues. Unfortunately for Westbury this, and a number of other contentious debates, drew attention away from many of his achievements in his everyday work as lord chancellor. For example, he introduced reforms in the exercise of ecclesiastical patronage by the lord chancellor and these changes received strong support from both bishops and clergy.

Resignation and subsequent career In 1865 Westbury was forced to resign. The manner of his fall from office was as remarkable as his capacity for engendering argument. He misled a committee of the House of Lords in connection with the provision of a pension for a clerk in the house who had been forced to leave his post after he had converted some £18,000 to his own use. The matter was made considerably worse when it was realized that Westbury had appointed one of his sons, Slingsby, to the vacant office. At this point Westbury wished to resign but Palmerston refused to accept the offer. A second problem then arose in connection with the Leeds registrarship in bankruptcy. The sitting registrar was told that unless he resigned he would be required to show cause as to why he should not be dismissed. He was allowed to retire with a pension on the ground of ill health. The office was then given to a barrister called Walsh. Unknown to Westbury, Walsh had lent large sums of money to another of Westbury's sons and this son, Richard, had gone so far as to tell others that he could influence his father's appointments. Richard had been a bankruptcy registrar, a spendthrift, and, ultimately, an undischarged bankrupt. A select committee of the House of Commons inquired into the matter and found that Westbury had not been corrupt but his officials had been. Westbury offered to resign, but, again, the offer was declined. Eventually resignation became inevitable when, in response to the committee's report, there was a vote of censure. It was typical of the man that in the midst of all this turmoil he continued to hear cases and, on the one day between the formal announcement of his resignation and his resignation speech, he gave an important judgment on the law of nuisance in *St Helen's Smelting Co.* v. *Tipping* (the significance of this case was such that it was reconsidered by the House of Lords in the late twentieth century). It was also typical of the man that the next day he turned his resignation to good account with a speech in the House of Lords which was cheered even by his old opponents. But it was a sad end to his very active years in office.

Westbury's subsequent career was enlivened by his participation in vigorous parliamentary debates and useful public work. As always he was unable to resist controversy. In the parliamentary session of 1870 the bill to legalize marriage with a deceased wife's sister was defeated by a tiny minority in the House of Lords. It is possible that opposition by the bishops had been consolidated by Westbury's admonishments in the preceding debates. He attacked their reliance upon Levitical law:

> Were they to take the responsibility of restraining marriage, which is a part of man's natural independence, upon a critical interpretation of a passage in the Old Testament? … When he looked to the condition of our great towns and the general condition of our pauper population, he felt they were not in a condition to regard themselves as the special favourites of providence or the chosen depositories of divine truth. (*Hansard 3*, 201, 19 May 1870, 930)

Predictably, his Victorian detractors remembered that at one time his elaborate manner of speech had earned him the nickname Miss Fanny (Atlay, 2.223). In a less contentious and wholly constructive way he made an effort as an arbitrator to wind up the complicated affairs of the European Assurance Society. This accelerated a decline in his health and he died at his home, 75 Lancaster Gate, Hyde Park, London, on 20 July 1873. He was buried on 24 July in the Great Northern London cemetery, Southgate.

Westbury's life hardly invites comparison with that of other lord chancellors. His achievements and failings were unique. He disparaged both the common law and the statute book more than any other modern holder of the post. His respect for theory was unrivalled in its intensity, and his political energy could eclipse that of Brougham. His capacity for sarcasm had no parallel in Victorian chancellors, and exceeded even that of Lord Birkenhead in the twentieth century. His occasional lack of judgement in debate, and in the exercise of administrative duties, has been rivalled by some lord chancellors but never exceeded in its dramatic effect. Looking back on his career, late Victorians were surely right in seeing him as someone afflicted with both an overwhelming belief in his own intellectual superiority and an emotional need to prove this ability at every possible point, often at the cost of others. What made him so striking was the extent to which the quality of his mind often justified his own view of his talents. R. C. J. COCKS

Sources T. A. Nash, *The life of Richard, Lord Westbury*, 2 vols. (1888) · J. B. Atlay, *The Victorian chancellors*, 1 (1906) · A. H. M. [A. H. Manchester], 'Bethell, Richard', *Biographical dictionary of the common law*, ed. A. W. B. Simpson (1984) · Holdsworth, *Eng. law*, 16.70–90 · J. S. Anderson, *Lawyers and the making of English land law, 1832–1940* (1992), 106–13 · J. H. Baker, *Monuments of endlesse labours: English canonists and their work, 1300–1900*, The Hambleden Press with the Ecclesiastical Law Society (1998), 141–3 · *DNB* · GEC, *Peerage* · *CGPLA Eng. & Wales* (1873)

Archives Bodl. Oxf., corresp. and papers · Duke U., Perkins L., corresp. · Institute for Advanced Legal Studies, Russell Square, London · Middle Temple, London | BL, corresp. with W. E. Gladstone, Add. MS 44337 · Bodl. Oxf., corresp. with Samuel Wilberforce · PRO, letters to Lord Granville, PRO 30/29 · PRO, corresp. with Lord John Russell · U. Southampton L., letters to Lord Palmerston · Wilts. & Swindon RO, corresp. with Sidney Herbert

Likenesses J. Bailey, bust, 1852, Wadham College, Oxford · photograph, c.1860, NPG · F. Grant, oils, 1862, Middle Temple, London [*see illus.*] · M. Gordigiani, oils, 1941, NPG · Ape [C. Pellegrini], caricature, chromolithograph, NPG; repro. in *VF* (15 May 1869) · M. Gordigiani, oils, Gov. Art Coll. · D. J. Pound, stipple and line engraving (after photograph by Mayall), BM, NPG · W. Walker &

Sons, carte-de-visite, NPG · J. Watkins, carte-de-visite, NPG · photographs, NPG

Wealth at death under £300,000: administration with will, 23 Aug 1873, *CGPLA Eng. & Wales*

Bethune, Alexander (1804–1843), poet, was born at Upper Rankeillor, in the parish of Monimail, Fife, in late July 1804, the eldest of the three sons of Alexander Bethune (*d.* 1838) and his wife, Alison Christie (*d.* 1840), daughter of Annie McDonald. Owing to the poverty of his parents—both were servants—and the family moving from place to place, he received an extremely scanty education. Up to his twenty-second year he had been at school only from four to five months in all. His mother was a woman of superior intellect and force of character, who supplemented the formal education of Alexander and his brother John *Bethune (1812–1839).

In his fourteenth year Bethune was hired as a labourer, and lived a life of extreme hardship. In 1813 his parents had moved to the village of Lochend, near the Loch of Lindores. Here, aged twenty, he seized the opportunity of attending a night school taught by the Revd John Adamson, afterwards of Dundee. It was also during this period that he started writing poetry. Bethune also put himself under the professional instruction of his brother John, who had just completed his apprenticeship at the loom. The two spent their hard-won and still harder-saved earnings as labourers on equipment; but 1825 proved a disastrous year for weavers all over Scotland. In 1826 the two brothers were forced to seek employment as outdoor labourers, with 1s. a day for wage. On 11 November 1829 and again on 14 November 1832 while working in a quarry, Bethune was grievously injured and permanently disfigured by sudden blasts of gunpowder. Despite their acute poverty both brothers continued writing poetry which was published in the 'Poet's corner' of several local newspapers. *Tales and Sketches of the Scottish Peasantry* was published in 1838. Though it contained some poems by John, it was published only under Alexander Bethune's name. They received very favourable reviews and brought fame at once. His printer, Mr Shortrede of Edinburgh, gave the author the sale price of the first fifty copies disposed of as copyright payment. This yielded him far more money than he had ever dreamed of possessing.

Bethune's brother John had been appointed overseer on the estate of Inchtyre; about 1836 Alexander became his assistant. But within a year the estate passed to another proprietor, and their employment ended. Their home at Lochend, which formed part of Inchtyre, had therefore to be vacated. The brothers resolved to farm a piece of ground named Mountpleasant near Newburgh, Fife, and to build a home for themselves. To raise funds for this purpose they published *Lectures on Practical Economy* in 1839; but this work was completely unsuccessful. The brothers also started writing for Wilson's *Tales of the Borders*.

John Bethune died in September 1839, a great and lasting sorrow to Alexander who revised and edited his poems, and prefixed a pathetic memoir (1840). This proved a success; 750 copies were sold immediately, and a second edition was called for, which was published in

1841. The little volume brought Bethune to the notice of the wife of Frederick Hill, inspector of prisons for Scotland, who procured him employment as a turnkey at the Glasgow Bridwell. He found this post utterly uncongenial, however, and in March 1841 he gave it up within a fortnight to return to farming and writing.

In 1842 Bethune visited Edinburgh, and arranged with Adam and Charles Black for the publication of his most successful book, the *Scottish Peasant's Fireside*, a presentation of Scottish character among the lower classes, of scenery, and of manners which was published in 1843.

In 1842 Bethune fell ill and showed signs of pulmonary consumption. He was offered the post of editor of the *Dumfries Standard*, a Liberal and Free-Church newspaper then being started, which he conditionally accepted, but was forced to refuse because of his health. He died at Newburgh on 13 June 1843, and was buried beside his brother at Abdie churchyard on 17 June.

A. B. GROSART, *rev.* SAYONI BASU

Sources *Memoirs of Alexander Bethune, embracing selections from his correspondence and literary remains*, ed. W. M'Combie (1845) • J. Ingram, 'Biography of John and Alexander Bethune', in A. Bethune and J. Bethune, *Tales of the Scottish peasantry* (1884) [preface] • Anderson, *Scot. nat.*

Bethune, Sir Henry, first baronet and *de jure* ninth earl of Lindsay (1787–1851), army officer, the eldest child of Major Martin Eccles Lindsay Bethune (*d.* 1813), commissary-general in Scotland, and his wife, Margaret Augusta (*née* Tovey), was born at Hilton, near Perth, on 12 April 1787. He was appointed to the Madras artillery in 1804. In 1810, when a subaltern in the horse artillery, he accompanied Sir John Malcolm to Persia as an officer of the escort. His height—6 feet 8 inches—is said to have excited the admiration and curiosity of the Persians. On the departure of the mission Lindsay and Captain Christie, another remarkable Indian officer, together with several others, were permitted to remain in Persia to train the Persian artillery. He was so employed for several years, and served with the Persian army in engagements with Russian troops, distinguishing himself by his military skill and bravery. He returned to England in 1821, retiring in the following year from the service of the East India Company and settling in Scotland on the estate of Kilconquhar, to which he had succeeded on the death of his grandfather in 1819. On 9 July 1822 he married Coutts (*d.* 1877), a daughter of John Trotter of Durham Park, Hertfordshire, and they had three sons and five daughters. In 1834 he was sent back to Persia by the British government, and commanded a part of the Persian army in the war of succession in the following year, leading his division from Tabriz to Tehran, and quelling the rebellion against Muhammad Shah, the successor of the late shah, Fath-i-Ali Khan. For this service he received from the shah the order of the Lion and Sun, and on his return to England was created a baronet on 7 March 1836, in accordance with a request of the shah that the king would confer on Bethune some hereditary rank.

In 1836 Bethune was again sent to Persia, with the local rank of major-general, to take command of the Persian army, but owing to a misunderstanding arising from the Persian advance upon Herat, the shah's government declined to allow him to take up this command. He returned to England in 1839, and retired from military life. In that year he succeeded his kinsman Sir Patrick Lindsay (1778–1839), also an army officer, in the earldom of Lindsay, but this was not established until the House of Lords acknowledged the claim of his son Sir John Trotter Bethune, second baronet, to the earldom in 1878. Some years after his retirement Sir Henry Bethune revisited Persia, and died at Tabriz on 19 February 1851. He was buried in the Armenian churchyard in Tehran.

A. J. ARBUTHNOT, *rev.* JAMES FALKNER

Sources *Army List* • *Annual Register* (1851), 263 • J. W. Kaye, *History of the war in Afghanistan*, 3rd edn, 3 vols. (1874) • Burke, *Peerage* • Boase, *Mod. Eng. biog.* • GEC, *Peerage*
Archives NL Scot., corresp. and papers | NA Scot., corresp. with Sir John McNeill

Bethune, John (1725–1774), Church of Scotland minister and philosopher, was born on 6 September 1725 and baptized John Beton six days later, the son of Ferchard or Farquhar Beton or Bethune (1694–1746), minister of Croy, Nairnshire, of the Bethunes of Skye, and Margaret Rose (*d.* 1762) of Newton. After studying from 1738 to 1742 with David Verner at Marischal College, Aberdeen, where he received an MA degree, he is believed to have continued his studies in divinity at the University of St Andrews and the University of Edinburgh. He was licensed to preach by the presbytery of Lochmaben on 6 March 1750, and served for a time as tutor in the family of Carruthers of Holmains in Dumfriesshire. On 18 September 1754 he was called to the parish of Rosskeen, on the Cromarty Firth, well north of Inverness, and was ordained there on 2 October. On 16 December 1755 he married his cousin Janet, the daughter of his father's elder brother Daniel Bethune (1679–1754), his predecessor as the minister of Rosskeen. The couple had three daughters, none of whom survived childhood.

During his two decades at Rosskeen, Bethune produced three anonymous books. The first was *Four Short Discourses on Funeral Occasions, by a Minister of the Church of Scotland* (1758), consisting of sermons preached at Rosskeen in September 1756 and April 1758. Another work, a small duodecimo entitled *A Short View of the Human Faculties and Passions*, is an outline of philosophical terms and concepts. According to the advertisement prefixed to the 'second edition' that was announced in Edinburgh in March 1771, bearing a 1770 imprint, it initially appeared in 1766 in Bath, where the author had gone to restore his health, but no copy of a 1766 edition has been found.

Bethune's major work, *Essays and Dissertations on Various Subjects, Relating to Human Life and Happiness*, consists of fifteen essays and nine dissertations in two duodecimo volumes. A surviving letter from James Beattie, whose wife was the first cousin of Bethune, and who sometimes corresponded with him, establishes that the Bethunes lived in Edinburgh for several months during the spring and summer of 1770, while *Essays and Dissertations* was in the press. The same letter reveals that the author received 500 copies 'for the use of his subscribers'; the remaining 500 copies in the impression went to the publisher to cover 'the expence of the publication' (Beattie to James Dun, 14 Aug 1770, Aberdeen University Library, MS 30/12/10). Beattie's reference to Bethune as 'the Doctor' demonstrates that he had received an honorary DD degree by this time, though the university that granted it has not been traced. *Essays and Dissertations* was printed in Edinburgh by Patrick Neill and charged to the account of the Edinburgh bookseller Alexander Kincaid in September 1770. One title-page is dated 1770 and bears the joint imprint of Kincaid and Bell of Edinburgh and Edward and Charles Dilly of London, but the same impression was also issued with two other title-pages dated 1771, bearing the separate imprints of these Edinburgh and London firms. On 9 March 1771 it was advertised as a new publication in the *Edinburgh Evening Courant*, along with *A Short View*, which suggests that the author was given several months to dispose of his subscription copies before the book was released for retail sale. A note at the beginning of the book states that the fifteen essays, which are individually dated from 2 January to 1 November 1766, originally appeared in that year in a Bath periodical called *The Remembrancer*, while the author was in residence there. Another note, in the fifteenth essay, 'A letter from Lord B[o]l[i]ng[br]oke, to Mess. V[ol]t[air]e, H[um]e, and R[ou]ss[e]au', praises 'a new treatise' (1.131) by James Beattie entitled *An Essay on the Nature and Immutability of Truth*. Since Beattie's book was not published until 1770, Bethune's essays must have been revised in that year for publication in book form. The same note contains the author's wry comment that, in light of recent philosophical writings against Hume's scepticism by Beattie and his fellow Aberdonians, Alexander Gerard, George Campbell, and Thomas Reid:

> instead of any further disputation, a tomb-stone may be laid for Mr Hume in one of the college halls of Aberdeen, with the following short inscription: 'Here lies that huge bundle of ideas, or successive unperceived perceptions, once known by the name of David Hume, Esq'. (*Essay and Dissertations*, 1.131)

This remark is followed, however, by an allusion to the pleasing nature of Hume's 'genius and character' (ibid.), and later in the work Bethune comments favourably on other Edinburgh men of letters in Hume's circle, calling Adam Ferguson's *Essay on the History of Civil Society* 'one of the most animated performances in the English language' (ibid., 2.299) and Adam Smith 'one of the most rational and acute philosophers of this *philosophical age*' (ibid., 2.348). Smith returned the compliment by joining three others to nominate Bethune for membership of the Royal Society of London, citing the *Essays and Dissertations* specifically, and he was duly elected a fellow on 18 February 1773.

Bethune has sometimes been credited with authorship of *A Discourse upon Religion* (1772), a lengthy theological work published in Edinburgh late in 1771 or early in 1772. However, a note at the end of that book states that it was written and revised in the period 1729–35, and an advertisement by the editor (who may possibly have been Bethune) asserts that the author of the *Discourse* 'is now

dead' (i–ii; *Scots Magazine*, 33.649). Bethune died on 15 April 1774 after an unspecified 'severe illness of many years continuance', which he is said to have endured with 'patience and equanimity' (Whyte, 13).   RICHARD B. SHER

Sources P. J. Anderson and J. F. K. Johnstone, eds., *Fasti academiae Mariscallanae Aberdonensis: selections from the records of the Marischal College and University, MDXCIII–MDCCCLX*, 3 vols., New Spalding Club, 4, 18–19 (1889–98) · W. Bulloch, 'Roll of the fellows of the Royal Society', RS · *Edinburgh Evening Courant* (9 March 1771) · *The new statistical account of Scotland*, 14 (1845), 277–8 · J. V. Price, 'Bethune, John', *The dictionary of eighteenth-century British philosophers*, ed. Y. Yolton, J. V. Price, and J. Stephens (1999) · *Scots Magazine*, 33 (1771), 648–51 · 'Scots origins', www.scotsorigins.com · *Fasti Scot.*, new edn, 6.441, 7.67–8 · *James Beattie's London diary, 1773*, ed. R. S. Walker (1946) · [T. Whyte], *An historical and genealogical account of the Bethunes of the island of Sky* (1778); [new edn], ed. [A. A. Bethune-Baker] (1893)

Archives NL Scot., Patrick Neill Ledgers, Dep 196, ledger 1767–1773, fol. 42

Bethune, John (1812–1839), poet, was born at Upper Rankeillor, in the parish of Monimail, Fife, the second son of Alexander Bethune (*d.* 1838), agricultural day labourer, and his wife, Alison Christie (*d.* 1840), daughter of Annie McDonald. His elder brother was Alexander *Bethune (1804–1843), also a working-class poet. In 1813 his parents moved to Lochend, near the Loch of Lindores. He received no formal education; he was taught to read by his mother, and writing and arithmetic by his brother. From their early teens the two brothers earned their living by breaking stones on the road between Lindores and Newburgh.

John was apprenticed to the weaving trade in the village of Collessie, and had achieved such expertise by 1825 that he set up looms for himself in a house immediately adjoining his father's, with his brother as apprentice. The collapse of the Scottish weaving trade in the same year wrecked the project, and they were forced to return to outdoor labouring. While he was working on the estate of Inchtyre John's dedication so impressed the owner that he was appointed overseer in 1835, but shortly afterwards the estate changed hands and the post was lost.

According to his brother, John Bethune would eagerly seize any scrap of paper to write out his poems, and by the early 1830s he had amassed a large and miscellaneous collection of manuscripts. He contributed several pieces to Alexander's *Tales and Sketches of the Scottish Peasantry* (1838); in 1839 the two brothers published *Lectures on Practical Economy*, which proved unsuccessful. Writing as A Fifeshire Forester, John Bethune contributed many poems to the *Scottish Christian Herald* and the *Christian Instructor*. When his health failed in 1838, he gave up manual labour and attempted to live by his pen. He died of consumption on 1 September 1839 and was buried in Abdie churchyard. John Bethune's poems were collected and published with a prefatory memoir by his brother in 1840, with a second edition appearing in 1841. The life attracted some interest for its depiction of the trials of the intellectually gifted working man, and formed the source for the hero's poetic aspirations in Charles Kingsley's *Alton Locke* (1850).

DOUGLAS BROWN

Sources Anderson, *Scot. nat.* • M. F. Conolly, *Biographical dictionary of eminent men of Fife* (1866) • J. F. Waller, ed., *The imperial dictionary of universal biography*, 3 vols. (1857–63) • *Poems by the late John Bethune: with a sketch of the author's life, by his brother*, 2nd edn (1841) • *Memoirs of Alexander Bethune, embracing selections from his correspondence and literary remains*, ed. W. M'Combie (1845) • B. Maidment, ed., *The poorhouse fugitives: self-taught poets and poetry in Victorian Britain* (1987)

Bethune, John Elliot Drinkwater (1801–1851), administrator in India and educationist, elder son of Lieutenant-Colonel John *Drinkwater, later Drinkwater Bethune (1762–1844), and his wife, Eleanor, daughter of Charles Congalton of Congalton, Edinburghshire, was born at Ealing, Middlesex. He was educated at Westminster School and Trinity College, Cambridge, and was called to the bar from the Middle Temple in 1827. A committed Liberal, Drinkwater was employed in the early days of Lord Grey's ministry on several of the royal commissions investigating political and social reform and subsequently served for fourteen years as counsel to the Home Office, in which capacity he drafted much of the momentous legislation of the 1830s and 1840s, including the Municipal Corporations Act of 1835, the Tithe Commutation Act of 1836, and the County Courts Act of 1846. In 1836 he changed his surname to Bethune.

In 1848 Bethune was appointed a member of the supreme council of India, a post he retained until his death. Almost immediately after his arrival in Calcutta he fell foul of the Anglo-Indian community over the so-called Black Acts, his attempt to place British-born subjects under the criminal jurisdiction of the ordinary courts—courts which were often presided over by Indian judges. The notion of being tried by Indians was anathema to most Anglo-Indians, who vilified Bethune in the Calcutta press as an outsider and a radical. The acts were passed in 1850, but in London the court of directors took fright and ordered the legislation to be suspended. In 1883, over thirty years later, the equally fierce opposition to a similar measure, the Ilbert Bill, showed how far Bethune had underestimated the conservativeness of Anglo-Indian society. Bethune's championing of the Black Acts won him respect among educated Indians in Calcutta, although in this constituency too he incurred some unpopularity when he pushed through the Lex Loci Act, which relieved Hindu converts to Christianity of forfeiture of their rights to inherited property. Missionaries had long clamoured for this act and Indian critics feared that its passing represented a new level of missionary pressure on the government.

As well as his council duties Bethune served as the unpaid president of the council of education and in this capacity met several Bengali philanthropists who shared his interest in public education, among them Ramgopal Ghose, a merchant, and Dakshinaranjan Mukherjee, a wealthy landholder. In May 1849, with the financial assistance and moral backing of these men, Bethune opened a free school for respectable Hindu girls. Even though his objectives were not particularly radical—he aimed only to train the girls to be better wives and mothers—early opposition from conservative Hindus could have doomed the venture were it not for the fact that Bethune was relatively untainted by the civil service's traditions of racial superiority and readily sought tactical and educational advice from sympathetic Hindus. In November 1850, largely with his own funds, Bethune began building a permanent home for the school. He died in the following year before the building was finished, but in his will he dedicated all of his Calcutta property to the school's completion and maintenance. The governor-general, Lord Dalhousie, personally maintained the school until his departure from India in 1856, whereupon the government assumed responsibility for it and handed over its management to a multiracial governing body committed to providing free education for girls. In addition to the school, which after his death became known as the Bethune Girls' School, Bethune is credited with having persuaded both the Indian and home authorities to promote the cause of women's education in India, as evidenced by the court of directors' education dispatch of July 1854.

In 1833 Bethune published biographies of Galileo and Keppler in the series Lives of Eminent Persons (Society for the Diffusion of Useful Knowledge), and in 1848 *Specimens of Swedish and German Poetry*, a selection of his own translations from the works of Tegner and Schiller.

Bethune died, unmarried, in Calcutta on 12 August 1851 and was buried in the lower circular road cemetery there.

KATHERINE PRIOR

Sources *GM*, 2nd ser., 37 (1852), 92–6, 434 • J. C. Bagal, *Women's education in eastern India: the first phase* (1956) • H. V. Hampton, *Biographical studies in modern Indian education* (1947) • S. R. Mehotra, *The emergence of the Indian National Congress* (1971) • Bengal wills, BL OIOC • *Old Westminsters*, vol. 1 • W. W. Rouse Ball and J. A. Venn, eds., *Admissions to Trinity College, Cambridge*, 4 (1911) • H. A. C. Sturgess, ed., *Register of admissions to the Honourable Society of the Middle Temple, from the fifteenth century to the year 1944*, 2 (1949) • C. R. Wilson, ed., *List of inscriptions on tombs or monuments in Bengal* (1896)
Archives BL, Babbage MSS • BL, Peel MSS • BL OIOC, Broughton MSS • priv. coll., Bethune of Balfour MSS • Trinity Cam., letters to William Whewell • UCL, SDUK MSS, letters to Society for the Diffusion of Useful Knowledge
Likenesses stipple, after 1851, BL OIOC • watercolour on ivory, 1851, BL OIOC • photograph (after painting, c.1848), BL OIOC
Wealth at death estates and effects in Scotland went to brother; property in Calcutta (at least Rs 30,000 in value) left to East India Company for maintenance of his girls' school: Bengal wills, BL OIOC; *GM*

Bethune [*née* Peebles], **Margaret** (1820–1887), midwife, was born in Largo, Fife, on 2 October 1820, the only child of Margaret Walker (d. 1874), a linen worker. Her father was Andrew Peebles, a weaver of Lundin Mill. The family was not wealthy, although in 1847 Margaret Walker inherited some property in the village from her father. On 15 January 1844 Margaret Peebles married William Bethune, a coalminer. Their marriage ended tragically in June 1852 when William was the sole victim of a mining accident. Margaret Bethune was left with two young children, aged five and seven years, and her ageing mother all looking to her for support.

Largo had connections with the Edinburgh medical world. Two generations of doctors of the Goodsir family had formerly practised in the area and a recent minister of

Margaret Bethune
(1820–1887), by
unknown
photographer

peak of her career 60 per cent of her work was repeat business, indicating both the confidence of her established clients and a reputation which attracted others. Her relationship with the local doctor is hinted at in several ways. 1859, the year in which she first undertook the majority of the midwifery work, was pivotal. On two occasions both midwife and doctor were present at the normal delivery of an affluent client. The doctor may have been hoping to arrange a partnership in which Mrs Bethune would act as an obstetric nurse. She rejected the role and after 1859 the only occasions on which the doctor's presence was recorded were these at which he was needed to assist with obstetric emergencies. The local doctor always responded to her summons and on each occasion the mother recovered. Mrs Bethune's professional judgement was respected.

Mrs Bethune's career was not interrupted by the death of her mother in 1874. Following the death of her daughter-in-law in 1876, however, she abandoned her successful career and left the village for several months to care for her grandchildren. After this interruption she resumed her work but did not complete her records so accurately. She was found dead at Lundin Mill, Largo, on 10 April 1887, and was buried at the new cemetery, Largo. The cause of death was given as '(supposed) disease of the heart'.

BARBARA E. MORTIMER

Sources B. Mortimer, 'Margaret Bethune of Largo: a professional woman's work in nineteenth-century Scotland', *Social History of Medicine* [forthcoming] · M. Bethune, casebook, 1853–87, NA Scot., GD1/812/1 · Royal Maternity Hospital, Edinburgh, outdoor casebook, LHB3/18/2, vol. 1 · family MSS, priv. coll. · *Fife Advertiser* (19 June 1852) · register (birth), 2 Oct 1820, Largo, Fife · register (marriage), 15 Jan 1844, Kennoway, Fife · d. cert.

Archives NA Scot., casebook, GD1/812/1 · NRA, priv. coll., family MSS | Royal College of Physicians of Edinburgh, indoor casebook of Maternity Hospital · U. Edin., Lothian health archive, records of Maternity Hospital

Likenesses photograph (in old age), priv. coll.; copyprint, Queen Margaret University College, Edinburgh [*see illus.*]

Largo was Joseph Goodsir, a grandson of the first 'Dr John'. His cousin John Goodsir was professor of anatomy in the Edinburgh medical school. When Mrs Bethune was reaching her decision to undertake midwifery training, the medical man in Largo was Dr Lumgair, who had qualified at Edinburgh University in 1836 under the new regulations which required him to take a midwifery course. There was no shortage of information locally about the range of medical education available in Edinburgh. By Christmas 1852 Mrs Bethune had moved to Edinburgh to undertake training as a midwife in the maternity hospital there. She purchased a copy of Alexander Hamilton's *Concise Rules for the Conduct of Midwives in the Exercise of their Profession* (1793) and according to the rules of the hospital was required to attend lectures before being issued with a 'ticket' granting her access to the wards for three months' practical experience. Her 'ticket' was signed by Mr Buchanan, secretary of the hospital, on 27 December. Mrs Bethune did not complete the period of training. Instead she returned to Largo and on 27 February 1853 began to record her casebook.

The records continue until 1887, the year of her death. In all, the book records 1296 labours, all within the parish boundaries. There were twenty-nine still births and two maternal deaths, neither of these attributed to obstetric causes. The doctor's presence was recorded for only ten of the deliveries and in three cases the reason for the doctor's presence was not indicated.

Mrs Bethune rapidly established her position as a respected and able midwife. Comparison with the registrar's data for Largo shows that 1859 was the first year in which she attended the majority of births in the parish. From that date until at least 1876 she undertook the majority of the midwifery work in the village. Her records reflect the quality and professionalism of her work. Her clients represented most social classes in the village. Alternative attendants were available, including a doctor, yet at the

Béthune, Robert de (d. 1148), bishop of Hereford, is described as a Fleming by Robert de Torigni; however, his biographer, William of Wycombe, says he and Robert came from nearby villages, and the likelihood is that Béthune was born in Buckinghamshire, perhaps at Wingrave, to parents of Flemish extraction who had settled there after 1066. Wycombe describes the family as of knightly status; since Robert's eldest brother was called Gunfrid, it is possible that their parents were subtenants of Gunfrid de Chocques, a Fleming from near Béthune whose honour included the manor of Wingrave in Buckinghamshire. Gunfrid, Robert's brother, became a schoolmaster, and Robert, the baby of the family, was trained for the same profession. Gunfrid died after Robert had begun to teach, leaving children for whose futures Robert had to provide. This accomplished, he departed for France to study *divina pagina* under Guillaume de Champeaux and Anselm of Laon.

At this point, probably in the first decade of the twelfth century, Béthune formed the resolution to enter a religious order, although he had first to provide for Gunfrid's grandchildren. He is described by Wycombe as talking over entry into the religious life with Richard, abbot of St Albans from 1097 to 1119, raising the possibility that Béthune had been a schoolmaster at St Albans. Béthune had formed a clear idea of what he wanted to do before he discussed his future with Richard: he wanted to become an Augustinian canon and join the community at Llanthony in the Black Mountains in Wales, then in the process of being enlarged from a hermitage into a fully fledged priory. His decision to become an Augustinian may have been influenced by the fact that Guillaume de Champeaux had become one in 1108. Much of Béthune's career was taken up with the furthering of the cause of regular canons.

Béthune made his vows at Llanthony to Prior Ernisius, and soon won the respect of his fellow canons, being given the task of supervising the building of a cell at Weobley, founded by Hugh de Lacy on his deathbed *c*.1115. When Ernisius resigned the office of prior, in or by the mid-1120s, Béthune was elected to succeed him. Soon after this, in 1127, the see of Hereford became vacant, and about three years later the two most prominent local land-owners, Payn fitz John (*d*. 1137) and Miles of Gloucester (*d*. 1143), petitioned Henry I to give it to Robert, who was, according to William, unwilling to accept the see. It was certainly the case that his diocesan, Urban of Llandaff (*d*. 1134), who had territorial claims against the diocese of Hereford, was very hostile to the idea, and intervention from Pope Innocent II (*r*. 1130–43) was necessary to make Béthune accept election. Consecrated on 28 June 1131 at Rochester, he attended court fairly frequently in the first two years of his pontificate, while also playing an active role in his diocese, where he held two synods before the first anniversary of his consecration. He also very probably travelled to Troyes in November 1131 to obtain one privilege for his see, warding off Urban of Llandaff, and another for Llanthony.

Soon after Stephen became king, Béthune joined his supporters, attending Stephen's Easter court at Westminster on 22 March 1136 and witnessing his charter of liberties at Oxford in early April. However, the Welsh warfare that had immediately followed Henry I's death had intensified Béthune's responsibilities at Hereford, where the canons of Llanthony, chased from their priory, had sought refuge. During 1136 Béthune, working together with Miles of Gloucester, refounded the priory on a new site just outside Gloucester, endowing it with property claimed by the canons of Hereford Cathedral. This aroused the hostility of Ralph, the newly appointed dean of Hereford, and in December 1136 Béthune had to travel to Pisa, where he obtained a letter from Innocent II enjoining obedience on the clergy of his church and also a privilege for the Augustinian abbey of Cirencester. Wycombe presents Robert as a strict disciplinarian of his clergy, and this is borne out by a charter depriving two priests of their benefice for having concubines.

Fighting intensified in the Welsh marches in the late 1130s. In May 1138 Stephen came to Hereford to besiege Geoffrey Talbot, and wore his crown on Whitsunday in the cathedral; he issued several charters for the cathedral at this time. Robert de Béthune accompanied Stephen to the siege of Shrewsbury in August 1138, and then went with the papal legate, Alberic of Ostia, on his visit to Northumberland and Cumberland to negotiate with David I, king of Scots. When the Empress Matilda arrived in England in September 1139, Miles of Gloucester abandoned Stephen, and in 1140 took control of Hereford. Béthune, still supporting Stephen, had been forced to leave Hereford in 1139, and had to spend much of the next two or three years in Shropshire. During this time requests for the consecration of graveyards to act as sanctuaries for local village communities were frequent, and Béthune dedicated churches and chapels, not necessarily only to provide sanctuary, but also to create new, smaller parishes, in a diocese where the old Anglo-Saxon minster system, with large parishes, was still strong.

Early in 1141, though probably not before the battle of Lincoln, Béthune changed sides and supported the empress. He could now return to Hereford, take the fortifications away from the cathedral, and once more be on friendly terms with Miles of Gloucester. However, in 1143 Miles tried to impose a levy on the churches in his lordship, and Béthune retaliated with excommunication, placing the city under an interdict and himself retiring to the Augustinian house at Shobdon. While the two parties were negotiating peace terms, Miles was killed out hunting on Christmas eve 1143. Béthune could once more support Stephen.

During the 1140s Robert de Béthune acted on several occasions as papal judge-delegate, and in 1145 wrote to Eugenius III on behalf of Archbishop Theobald (*d*. 1161) against the claim of Bernard of St David's (*d*. 1148) to metropolitan status (Hereford was one of the sees that Bernard wished to see form a province for St David's). He also gave assistance to the canons of Shobdon, whose lands had been confiscated by Hugh de Mortimer (*d*. 1181). Béthune provided for them, while also persuading Mortimer to find new quarters for them—early in 1148 Mortimer gave the canons the old minster church of Wigmore. Soon after this, in March 1148, Béthune set out to attend the Council of Rheims. He fell ill on the third day of the council and died on 16 April in Rheims, at the abbey of St Nicaise, from where his body was brought back to Hereford Cathedral for burial. In his lifetime he was praised by William of Malmesbury, while his corpse was said to have worked miracles as it was carried back from Rheims. The medieval library catalogue of Llanthony Priory lists a collection of excerpts from Robert's letters, now lost; the most important sources for his career are the life written by William of Wycombe and his charters, over fifty of which survive.

JULIA BARROW

Sources Wycombe, 'Bethun life', *Anglia sacra*, ed. [H. Wharton], 2 (1691), 295–322 · B. J. Parkinson, 'The life of Robert de Béthune by William de Wycombe: translation with introduction and notes', BLitt diss., U. Oxf., 1951 · J. Barrow, ed., *Hereford, 1079–1234*, English Episcopal Acta, 7 (1993), xxvi, xxviiin, xxxvii-xl, li-lii, lxvi-lxxxi, ci, cx, cxv, 14–53, 303, 312–13 · R. Howlett, ed., *Chronicles of the reigns of Stephen, Henry II, and Richard I*, 4, Rolls Series, 82 (1889), 121 · *Reg. RAN*, 2.1710, 1715, 1724–5, 1736, 1740, 1765, 1827, 1957; 3.46, 132, 271,

274, 288, 384, 396, 460, 497, 511–13, 640, 701, 760, 787–8, 949 · *Letters and charters of Gilbert Foliot*, ed. A. Morey and others (1967), nos. 1–2 · A. Morey and C. N. L. Brooke, *Gilbert Foliot and his letters* (1965), 79, 268 · W. Holtzmann, ed., *Papsturkunden in England*, 1 (Berlin), Abhandlung der Gesellschaft der Wissenschaften zu Göttingen, new ser., 25 (1930–31), 239–40, 251–3, 256, 273–4 · W. Holtzmann, ed., *Papsturkunden in England*, 2 (Berlin), Abhandlung der Gesellschaft der Wissenschaften zu Göttingen, 3rd ser., 14 15 (1935 6), 150–53, 208 · W. Holtzmann, ed., *Papsturkunden in England*, 3 (Berlin), Abhandlung der Gesellschaft der Wissenschaften zu Göttingen, 3rd ser., 33 (1952), 150–53, 160–61, 171–3, 204 · D. Cox, 'Two unpublished charters of King Stephen for Wenlock Priory', *Transactions of the Shropshire Archaeological Society*, 66 (1989), 56–9 · J. C. Dickinson and P. T. Ricketts, eds., 'The Anglo-Norman chronicle of Wigmore Abbey', *Transactions of the Woolhope Naturalists' Field Club*, 39 (1967–9), 413–46 · J. G. Evans and J. Rhys, eds., *The text of the Book of Llan Dâv reproduced from the Gwysaney manuscript* (1893), 57–8, 63–4 · J. C. Davies, ed., *Episcopal acts and cognate documents relating to Welsh dioceses, 1066–1272*, 2, Historical Society of the Church in Wales, 3 (1948), 630 · John of Worcester, *Chron.*, 58–60 · T. W. Williams, 'Gloucestershire medieval libraries', *Transactions of the Bristol and Gloucestershire Archaeological Society*, 31 (1908), 78–195, 155 · F. G. Cowley, *The monastic order in south Wales* (1977), 30–31, 150–51, 191 · K. R. Potter and R. H. C. Davis, eds., *Gesta Stephani*, OMT (1976), 108–10 · D. G. Walker, 'Miles of Gloucester, earl of Hereford', *Transactions of the Bristol and Gloucestershire Archaeological Society*, 77 (1958), 66–84 · *Willelmi Malmesbiriensis monachi de gestis pontificum Anglorum libri quinque*, ed. N. E. S. A. Hamilton, Rolls Series, 52 (1870), 304–5 · F. Barlow, *The English church, 1066–1154: a history of the Anglo-Norman church* (1979), 100 · *Fasti Angl., 1066–1300*, [Hereford], 3

Sir John Betjeman (1906–1984), by Sir Cecil Beaton, 1955

Betjeman, Sir John (1906–1984), poet, writer, and broadcaster, was born on 28 August 1906 at 52 Parliament Hill Mansions, north London, the only child of Ernest Edward Betjemann (1871/2–1934), a furniture manufacturer, and his wife, Mabel Bessie Dawson (*d.* 1952). The family name, of Dutch or German origin, can be traced back to an immigration in the late eighteenth century. The poet adopted his style of it about the age of twenty-one.

Betjeman attended Byron House Montessori School, Highgate, and Highgate junior school, where he was taught by T. S. Eliot. In 1917 Betjeman boarded at the Dragon School, Oxford, and then unhappily at Marlborough College, and was active at both in school theatricals and in various forms of writing. He later recalled with affection, however, the influence of two Marlborough school masters: George Gidney and Clifford Canning, who 'made us aware that being good at games was not all' (*Betjeman: Letters*, 2.333). Betjeman entered Magdalen College, Oxford, in 1925 but was rusticated three years later after failing in divinity. To his father's deep disappointment he declined to enter the family business, becoming successively a preparatory school master (at Thorpe House School, Gerrard's Cross, and at Heddon Court, Cockfosters, Hertfordshire), private secretary to Sir Horace Plunkett, assistant editor of the *Architectural Review* in 1930, and film critic of the London *Evening Standard* in 1933. On 29 July 1933 he married Penelope Valentine Hester Chetwode (1909/10–1986), daughter of Field-Marshal Sir Philip Walhouse *Chetwode, first Baron Chetwode (1869–1950), commander-in-chief in India at the time. They then moved to Garrard's Farm in Uffington, in the Vale of the White Horse, Berkshire, where his wife, who later trekked in the Himalayas, was able to keep horses. Their son Paul was born there in 1937.

Betjeman's first two collections of poems, *Mount Zion* (1931) and *Continual Dew* (1937), showed a poet already fully formed, with the impeccable ear, delight in skill, and assured mastery of a wide range of tones and themes that so distinguished all his subsequent work in verse. In these early volumes, as later, Betjeman moved with perfect assurance from light pieces, *vers de société*, satirical sketches of muscular padres or philistine businessmen (as in the famously ferocious tirade 'Slough') to sombre reflections on the impermanence of all human things. In a remarkable variety of metres and manners the poems make an equally clear-cut impression on the reader, never drifting into obscurity and never influenced by the modernists. Here too he gave glimpses of the world of gas-lit Victorian churches and railway stations, of grim provincial cities and leafy suburbs that he was to make his own, not forgetting the grimmer contemporary developments, shopping arcades, and bogus Tudor bars that he saw effacing it and strove to resist.

These concerns are reflected in Betjeman's *Ghastly Good Taste* (1933), subtitled 'a depressing story of the rise and fall of English architecture', which attracted more immediate attention than either of his first books of poems. In it he attacked not only modern or modernistic trends but also the other extreme of unthinking antiquarianism; nor had he any time for the safely conventional. While still at school he had become interested in Victorian architecture, thoroughly unmodish as it was at the time. His writings on the subject, by reviving appreciation of the buildings of that era, prepared the ground for the Victorian Society's successful foundation in 1988. Further afield, he showed among other things his fondness for provincial architecture in his contributions to the Shell series of English county guides, of which the most notable is that on Cornwall, another enthusiasm acquired in boyhood. He had joined the publicity department of Shell in the mid-1930s. In 1937 Betjeman became a devoted member of the Church of England, speaking of it as 'the only salvation against progress and Fascists on the one side and Marxists of Bloomsbury on the other' (*Betjeman: Letters*, 1.171). His devotion to the church lay not only in his open admiration for its buildings, its liturgy, and its worshippers, but for its faith.

In the Second World War Betjeman volunteered for the RAF but was rejected and joined the films division of the Ministry of Information. He then became Britain's press attaché to the high commission in Dublin (1941–3), where his daughter Candida was born. Betjeman's official job in neutral Ireland was to sway public opinion in favour of the British, and as part of this strategy he arranged for the battle scenes of Laurence Olivier's *Henry V* (1944) to be filmed in Ireland (this depicted a heroic England massively outnumbered by its European enemies). He wrote regular reports on Irish politics based on high-level contacts within the Irish government, and factions within the Irish Republican Army (IRA). One IRA battalion planned to assassinate Betjeman, but the operation was called off because the IRA's head of civilian intelligence liked his poetry. Betjeman subsequently worked in P branch (a secret department) in the Admiralty at Bath.

In 1945 Betjeman moved to Farnborough, and in 1951 to Wantage, where his wife opened a tea-shop, King Alfred's Kitchen. Betjeman's poetical career began to flourish with the appearance in 1940 of *Old Lights for New Chancels* and continued with *New Bats in Old Belfries* (1945) and *A Few Late Chrysanthemums* (1954). Many of the poems in these three volumes became classics of their time, including 'Pot Pourri from a Surrey Garden', 'A Subaltern's Love-Song', and 'How to get on in Society'. His *Collected Poems* came out in 1958 and went through many impressions. *Summoned by Bells* is dated 1960, a blank-verse poem of some 2000 lines that gives an account of his early life up to schoolmastering days with characteristic animation, humour, sadness, and abundance of detail.

Both these volumes were widely successful, the first edition of the *Collected Poems* selling over 100,000 copies. Betjeman's poetry enjoyed a popularity not seen since the days of Rudyard Kipling and A. E. Housman. No doubt it was poems like the three mentioned above and the more obviously quaint period pieces that made an immediate appeal. Nor should one underestimate the sheer relief and delight that was felt at the appearance of modern poetry that was easy to follow and yielded the seemingly almost forgotten pleasures of rhyme and metre expertly handled. Nevertheless it may not be instantly obvious how so strongly personal a poet, one given moreover to evoking unfamiliar characters and places, should have proved so welcome.

The answer must lie in the closeness of the concerns of Betjeman's poetry to the ordinary day-to-day experience of his readers, also something rarely found in the work of his contemporaries. For all the delight in the past, it is the past as seen from and against the present; for all the cherished eccentricities—hardly repugnant as such to British taste anyway—the subject is ourselves and our own world. The point was well made by Philip Larkin, the friend and admirer who best understood his work:

> He offers us something we cannot find in any other writer—a gaiety, a sense of the ridiculous, an affection for human beings and how and where they live, a vivid and vivacious portrait of mid-twentieth-century English social life.
> (P. Larkin, 'It could only happen in England', 1971, in *Required Writing*, 1983, 204–18)

From 1951 Betjeman's marriage was troubled: his wife's conversion to Roman Catholicism in June 1949 had upset him greatly, and although he eventually became reconciled to her decision, they reached a joint decision to separate amicably. As Betjeman put it quite simply later: 'I love her. *But I cannot live with her for long without quarrelling*' (*Betjeman: Letters*, 2.473). He met Lady Elizabeth Georgina Alice Cavendish (*b.* 1926), sister of the duke of Devonshire, and lady-in-waiting to Princess Margaret, at a dinner party in 1951, and they embarked on a friendship that soon became a love affair. The relationship lasted until his death.

By the mid-1950s Betjeman's main income came from book reviewing, broadcasting, and his poems. He pursued a highly successful career as a broadcaster, and—with the help of the image he projected through television, engaging, diffident, exuberant, often launched on some architectural or decorative enthusiasm—he became a celebrated and much-loved figure in national life. He used this position zealously to defend many buildings threatened with demolition. He was able to save many of these, from St Pancras Station to Sweeting's fish restaurant in the City of London, although the Euston Arch was lost despite his vigorous campaign. Appropriately, it was at St Pancras, naming a British Rail locomotive after himself, that he made his last public appearance on 24 June 1983.

In later years Betjeman continued his work in poetry, publishing *High and Low* in 1966 and *A Nip in the Air* in 1974. The contents of these two volumes reveal no loss of energy; indeed, poems like 'On Leaving Wantage, 1972' embody a melancholy, even a tragic, power he had never surpassed. All the same, apart from the ebulliently satirical 'Executive', almost none of them have achieved much individual popularity. They were incorporated entire in the fourth edition of the *Collected Poems* in 1979. Those in *Uncollected Poems* (1982) were such as the poet was content should remain in that state and are unlikely to gain him many new readers, though lovers of his work would not be without any of them. Expressions of doubt and the fear of old age and death are strong and memorable in his poetry, but 'Church of England thoughts' are pervasive too, and one of its chief attractions, seldom given proper weight, has been the sense of an undemonstrative but deep Christian belief of a kind that could contain the harsh, ugly, absurd realities of present-day existence.

John Betjeman was a sociable man, one who loved company and valued it the more for being also shy. Although renowned for his youthful gregariousness and endlessly affable with all manner of people, his was a life rich in intimacy. Latterly he was partial to small gatherings, old friends, and a sufficiency of wine. His expression in repose was timid, perhaps not altogether at ease, and even at the best of times it was possible to surprise on his face a look of great dejection. But all this was blown away in an instant by laughter of a totality that warmed all who knew him. His presence, like his work in verse and prose, was full of the enjoyment he felt and gave.

Betjeman was chosen as poet laureate to universal acclaim in 1972. He received many distinctions besides, being awarded the Duff Cooper memorial prize, the Foyle poetry prize, and in 1960 the queen's medal for poetry. In that year too he was appointed CBE. In 1968 he was elected a companion of literature by the Royal Society of Literature, and in 1969 he was knighted. He was an honorary fellow of his old college, Magdalen (1975), and also of Keble College, Oxford (1972). He had honorary degrees from Oxford, Reading, Birmingham, Exeter, City University, Liverpool, Hull, and Trinity College, Dublin. He was also honorary associate of the Royal Institute of British Architects.

From the mid-1970s Betjeman had suffered increasingly from the onset of Parkinson's disease and after a series of strokes he died at Treen, his home in Daymer Lane, Trebetherick, Cornwall, on 19 May 1984. He was buried on 22 May in nearby St Enodoc churchyard, and a memorial service was held at Westminster Abbey on 29 June 1984. To his daughter Candida Lycett-Green he bequeathed his impressive library of 5000 volumes, the product of a lifetime's intelligent and discerning book collecting.

KINGSLEY AMIS, rev. M. CLARE LOUGHLIN-CHOW

Sources *The Times* (21 May 1984) · *The Times* (30 June 1984) · B. Hillier, *John Betjeman: a life in pictures* (1984) · B. Hillier, *Young Betjeman* (1988) · personal knowledge (1990) · *The Observer* (20 May 1984) · P. Taylor-Martin, *John Betjeman: his life and work* (1983) · m. cert. · d. cert. · W. S. Peterson, 'Sir John Betjeman as collector and book-designer', *The Book Collector*, 41 (1992), 477–97 · *John Betjeman: letters*, ed. C. Lycett Green, 2 vols. (1994–5) · www.channel4.com/history/microsites/R/real_lives/betjeman.html

Archives BL, MSS, drafts of poems, and corresp., Deposit 9417 · Highgate Literary and Scientific Institution, London, papers · State University of New York, Buffalo, corresp. and literary papers · University of Exeter Library, letters and papers · University of Victoria, British Columbia, McPherson Library, corresp., literary MSS, and papers | BBC WAC, corresp. with BBC staff · Bodl. Oxf., letters to O. G. S. Crawford · Bodl. Oxf., corresp. with Lionel Curtis · Bodl. Oxf., letters to E. W. Gilbert · Bodl. Oxf., letters to G. R. Hamilton · Bodl. Oxf., corresp. with William Heinemann · Bodl. Oxf., letters to Sidgwick and Jackson · Bodl. Oxf., letters to J. M. Thompson · CAC Cam., letters to Cecil Roberts · Christ Church Oxf., letters to Tom Driberg · Georgetown University, Washington, DC, letters to Christopher Sykes · King's AC Cam., letters to Sir George Barnes and Lady Barnes · King's AC Cam., letters to J. E. H. Steegman · Royal Society of Literature, London, letters to Royal Society of Literature · Tate collection, corresp. with Lord Clark · U. Durham L., letters to William Plomer · U. Leeds, Brotherton L., letters to *London Magazine* · U. Reading, letters to Jonathan Cape · Welwyn Garden City Library, corresp. with Sir Frederic Osborn | SOUND BL NSA, recordings of readings from his own works

Likenesses C. Beaton, photograph, 1955, Sothebys, Cecil Beaton archive [*see illus.*] · oils, 1979, repro. in Hillier, *John Betjeman*

Wealth at death £211,434: probate, 16 Oct 1984, *CGPLA Eng. & Wales*

Betson, Thomas (d. 1516), librarian, religious author, and compiler, is first recorded at Cambridge University, where he had studied civil law for two and a half years, canon law for two years, and practised for four years, when he was granted a grace in 1466–7 to proceed to the degree of BCnL. He was rector of Wimbish, Essex, from June 1466 until May 1481, the probable date of his becoming a deacon of the Bridgettine abbey of Syon, Middlesex.

Betson was the author–compiler of *A Ryght Profytable Treatyse to Dyspose Men to be Vertuously Occupyed* (*STC*, no. 1978), a devotional miscellany printed by Wynkyn de Worde in 1500 and the first printed of several Syon works written mostly in English for the instruction of both lay and religious readers. Among the fundamental texts he translated into English are the Pater noster, Ave Maria, creed, 'Seven sacraments', and ten commandments. Also included are such tracts as 'The seven degrees of humility', 'Obedience and Patience', passages from Gerson, St Bernard, and St Jerome, and prayers, one of them by St Bridget. Some of the material came from the *Ars moriendi* printed by Caxton in 1491 (*STC*, no. 786), while the *Treatyse* itself was used by Richard Whitford, brother of Syon, for his improved translation of St Bernard's *Epistola de perfectione vitae*, and by John Colman, master of St Mark's Hospital, Bristol, for his collection of religious treatises (Oxford, St John's College, MS 173).

Among manuscript passages in Betson's large and skilful secretary hand are Latin and English copies of the rules of Sts Saviour and Augustine (BL, Add. MS 5208, fols. 3v–19v, and London, Guildhall Library, MS 25524, formerly St Paul's Cathedral Library, MS 5, fols. 75–88v) and the only copy of the Syon 'Boke of sygnes' (Guildhall, MS, fols. 69v–72; edited by Hogg). He was also the original scribe of the catalogue of the Syon brethren's library (Cambridge, Corpus Christi College, MS 141, edited by Bateson with facsimile), and of one of three surviving pressmarks (BL, Harley MS 42, facsimile in *The New Palaeographical Society: Facsimiles of Ancient Manuscripts*). He was probably therefore the librarian responsible for the classification and expansion of the library, among the largest in England. The breadth of his range is revealed by the historical, legal, medical, philosophical, and theological works which he donated to the library in five volumes, or with which he filled his notebook (Cambridge, St John's College, MS E.6). A broadsheet produced for Syon (discussed and reproduced by Erler, 'Pasted-in embellishments', 191–4) comprises illustrations and verses 'To all the Saints' (also in the *Treatyse* and probably by Betson), a kneeling figure (probably of Betson), and Betson's 'TB' monogram. According to the Syon *Martiloge* he died at Syon on 20 February 1516 and was buried there.

W. N. M. BECKETT

Sources A. I. Doyle, 'Thomas Betson of Syon Abbey', *The Library*, 5th ser., 11 (1956), 115–18 · Emden, *Cam.* · The Syon *Martiloge*, BL, Add. MS 22285 · M. C. Erler, 'Pasted-in embellishments in English manuscripts and printed books, c.1480–1533', *The Library*, 6th ser.,

14 (1992), 185–206 • M. C. Erler, 'Syon Abbey's care for books: its sacristan's account rolls, 1506/7–1535/6', *Scriptorium*, 39 (1985), 293–307 • M. Bateson, A. I. Doyle, and V. Gillespie, eds., *Catalogue of the library of Syon Monastery, Isleworth*, [new edn] [forthcoming] • A. I. Doyle and V. Gillespie, eds., *Catalogue of the library of Syon Monastery, Isleworth* [forthcoming] • J. Betson, 'Notebook', St John Cam., MS E. 6 • M. R. James, *A descriptive catalogue of the manuscripts in the library of St John's College, Cambridge* (1913) • J. Hogg, ed., *The rewyll of Seynt Savioure*, 3: *The Syon additions for the brethren and the 'Boke of sygnes' from the St Paul's Cathedral Library MS* (1980) • H. S. Bennett, 'Notes on two incunables: *The abbey of the Holy Ghost* and *A ryght profytable treatyse*', *The Library*, 5th ser., 10 (1955), 120–21 • T. Betson, *A ryght profytable treatyse to dyspose men to be vertuously occupied* (1500) • STC, 1475–1640

Archives BL, Add. MS 5208, fols. 3v–19v • BL, Harley MS 42 • CCC Cam., MS 141 • GL, MS 25524, fols. 75–88v [copy] • St John Cam., MS E.6

Likenesses engraving, 1481–1516, repro. in Erler, 'Pasted-in embellishments', 191–4, fig. 3

Betterton, Henry Bucknall, Baron Rushcliffe (1872–1949), politician, was born at Woodville, Blackfordby, Leicestershire, on 15 August 1872, first son in the family of three sons and two daughters of Henry Inman Betterton (1844–1895), JP and brewer, and his wife, Agnes, daughter of Samuel Bucknall. Educated at Rugby School (1886–90) and Christ Church, Oxford, he obtained a fourth class in modern history in 1893. He was called to the bar by the Inner Temple at the age of twenty-four and practised as a lawyer for twenty years. On 19 December 1912 he married Violet, widow of Captain Hervey Greathed of the 8th hussars, and daughter of John Saunders Gilliat, formerly governor of the Bank of England. They had two daughters. Betterton was appointed OBE in 1918 and CBE in 1920 for his services as a member of the advisory board of the war trade intelligence department during the war. He entered politics as the Conservative member for the Rushcliffe division of Nottinghamshire in December 1918. He was parliamentary secretary to the Ministry of Labour during the Conservative administrations of 1923 and 1924–9 and was created a baronet in July 1929. In August 1931 Betterton was appointed minister for labour in the National Government of Ramsay MacDonald. It was during his three years in this role that Betterton made his most significant contribution to the shape of British government.

After earlier being a determined opponent of the centralization of unemployment relief, Neville Chamberlain, the chancellor of the exchequer, in 1932 proposed the creation of a new statutory commission which would take national control of the assessment and payment of relief for the able-bodied unemployed, taking away the powers previously held by local government. Despite this proposal generally being enthusiastically received within government, Betterton stood out in opposition, and for over a year he 'fought a dogged rearguard action' through the cabinet committee structure to change Chamberlain's plans (Lowe, 159). His criticisms were both practical and philosophical, but his main objection was that unemployment was an industrial problem and should be treated as such, while the new scheme simply 'applied Poor Law methods, through a Poor Law Commission, in Poor Law language' (Marquand, 733). Betterton, it has been said,

was 'on excellent terms with labour's left wing' (Lowe, 35) and was 'sympathetic to the objections raised by the socialists regarding the "means test"' and its use in unemployment relief (*The Times*, 19 Nov 1949, 7). Betterton argued strongly for the principle, which was important in the development of later welfare structures, of distinguishing between the needs and treatment of those out of work for industrial reasons and those requiring support because of sickness, old age, or other factors. In this he received the support of MacDonald, and on a number of points in cabinet 'Betterton inflicted on Chamberlain a series of rare defeats' (Lowe, 155). Betterton took through parliament the amended proposal as the Unemployment Act of 1934, and in June 1934 resigned from parliament to become the first chairman of the Unemployment Assistance Board established by the act, where he remained until 1941.

Betterton's character and his response to the needs of the unemployed in the years of economic depression were suggested by the fulsome praise he later received from both Labour and Liberal opponents. Viscount Addison said the labour movement 'had known him as a most sympathetic Minister of Labour in an exceedingly trying period' (*The Times*, 25 Nov 1949, 6). The Liberal Viscount Samuel described him as 'a man of benevolent mind, boundless good will, and unremitting devotion to the public service' (ibid.). In January 1935 he was created Baron Rushcliffe of Blackfordby, and in 1941 he was appointed GBE. He had been sworn of the privy council in 1931. Rushcliffe served on many committees and was chairman of the one which in 1943 determined an improved wage scale for British nurses which became known as the Rushcliffe scale. Addison said the nurses of Britain owed Rushcliffe 'a great debt' (*The Times*, 25 Nov 1949, 11). He was also active as chairman, from 1944, of the special committee on legal aid and legal advice, whose recommendations were broadly enacted in the 1949 Legal Aid and Advice Act, which introduced the modern system of legal aid.

Rushcliffe's first wife died in 1947. In April 1948 he married Inez Alfreda, Lady Snagge (d. 1955), whose first marriage had been dissolved, and who was the daughter of Alfred Lubbock of Par, Cornwall. They had no children. Rushcliffe died on 18 November 1949 at his home, The Gables, Blatchington Hill, Seaford, Sussex.

R. C. DAVISON, rev. MARC BRODIE

Sources *The Times* (19 Nov 1949) • *The Times* (25 Nov 1949) • Burke, *Peerage* (1939) • private information (1971) • GEC, *Peerage* • R. Lowe, *Adjusting to democracy: the role of the ministry of labour in British politics, 1916–1939* (1986) • K. Feiling, *The life of Neville Chamberlain* (1946) • D. Marquand, *Ramsay MacDonald* (1977) • J. Ramsden, *The age of Balfour and Baldwin, 1902–1940* (1978)

Likenesses W. Stoneman, photograph, 1943, NPG

Wealth at death £31,867 0s. 6d.: probate, 12 Jan 1950, CGPLA Eng. & Wales

Betterton [*née* Saunderson], **Mary** (*c.*1637–1712), actress and acting teacher, was about twenty-five when she and Thomas *Betterton (*bap.* 1635, *d.* 1710) obtained a marriage licence on 24 December 1662. Nothing is known of her childhood. According to John Downes, Mary Saunderson was among the first actresses Sir William Davenant hired for the Duke's Company in 1661 and lived with the others under the care of his wife (Downes, 49–50). Some months before Mary and Thomas got married Samuel Pepys noted gossip that implies they were living together (Pepys, 22 Oct 1662). However, this irregularity is the only one reported of Mrs Betterton. Unlike many of her colleagues, she attracted no sexual lampoons, and the Bettertons' marriage lasted 'in the strictest amity' through the vicissitudes of nearly forty-eight years (Account).

Mrs Betterton immediately became a leading actress, later a teacher, eventually the 'housekeeper'. Wilson lists more than sixty roles for her (Wilson, 117–19). Mrs Betterton played in both comedy and tragedy, succeeding best in serious and pathetic roles. Samuel Pepys referred to her as 'poor Ianthe' from her earliest part, in William Davenant's Siege of Rhodes. Her gift was not for 'airy' roles in comedy but for comparatively sedate ones, such as the exemplary Porcia in Samuel Tuke's Adventures of Five Hours or Florinda in Aphra Behn's Rover. She often played the second female lead and seldom appeared in farce. She excelled at dramatic parts such as the duchess of Malfi and her most enduring role, Lady Macbeth. Colley Cibber considered her 'so great a Mistress of Nature' that she could 'throw out those quick and careless Strokes of Terror from the Disorder of a guilty Mind … with a Facility in her Manner that render'd them at once tremendous and delightful' (Cibber, 161–2). Plots often, but by no means automatically, paired Mrs Betterton with her husband.

Between 1666 and 1669 Mrs Betterton's activities are poorly recorded. Following Davenant's death in 1668 Thomas Betterton became co-manager and could promote his wife's career, adapting scripts for her such as The Amorous Widow and The Roman Virgin. When the new Dorset Garden Theatre opened in November 1671, the Bettertons took up residence there rent-free as building superintendents. They shared their home with two informally adopted daughters, Anne *Bracegirdle, who was with them from the late 1660s, and Elizabeth Watson, who came about 1686, both of whom they trained to act. They were highly respectable. In the autumn of 1681 Mrs Betterton coached Princess Anne for a private production of Nathaniel Lee's Mithridates (Boswell, 131). The anonymous Life of Thomas Betterton (1749) reported an unconfirmed oral tradition that in the winter of 1674–5 Mrs Betterton gave lessons to Princess Anne and her sister Mary for the court masque Calisto.

By 1676 Mrs Betterton found that her age was presenting difficulties. When Elizabeth Barry joined the company, playwrights such as Thomas Otway, Thomas D'Urfey, and Aphra Behn chose to feature the younger woman in their scripts. The change was gradual: Mrs Betterton continued to receive dramatic roles, such as Jocasta in the Dryden-Lee Oedipus or Andromache in John Banks's Destruction of Troy (both autumn 1678), and Andromache in John Dryden's Troilus and Cressida (spring 1679). Like her male colleagues, she presumably continued to appear in the parts she 'owned'. Yet her new roles in serious plays began to shrink in size. The extreme is Lucrece in Lee's Lucius Junius

Brutus (December 1680), who kills herself at the end of a single scene. A gap in records of Mrs Betterton's career occurs between January 1682 and November 1689, when many old plays were revived after the King's and Duke's companies merged.

The handful of new roles Mrs Betterton acquired after this are distinctly mature, though Cibber ranked her among the 'principal Actors … at the Head' of the company he joined in 1690. In Dryden's Cleomenes (April 1692) she played the mother of the title character (acted by her husband). Southerne emphasized her age in his dyspeptic comedy The Maid's Last Prayer (February 1693). Mrs Wishwell, 'a Woman turn'd of fifty', makes her living as a society bawd. Dryden, producing Love Triumphant in January 1694, entrusted to Mrs Betterton the sizeable role of Queen Ximena.

In late November 1694 Mrs Betterton was among the senior actors who signed the 'petition of the players' against the oppressive management of Christopher Rich and Sir Thomas Skipwith (Milhous and Hume, 1483). With regard to her, the patentees responded that her 50s. per week was paid 'in Complement to Mr Betterton she not appearing in any parts to the satisfaction of the Audience' (ibid., 1486). Rosters for the company the rebels set up at Lincoln's Inn Fields in April 1695 included Mrs Betterton but she seems not to have performed (ibid., 1496, 1513, 1552, 1647). In the spring of 1703 she was listed as 'Housekeeper & to teach to act' at £80 a year in the plan drawn up by Vanbrugh for a new United Company (ibid., 1713). Cibber mentions that 'When she quitted the Stage several good Actresses were the better for her Instruction' (Cibber, 161–2). After the move to Vanbrugh's new theatre in April 1705, Mrs Betterton presumably became a pensioner. The last trace of her on a roster is a draft for autumn 1709 at the token sum of £25, but she was dropped from the implemented version (Milhous and Hume, 2053, 2064). She took her husband's death in April 1710 very hard: Steele reported that she temporarily lost her reason. According to Cibber, Queen Anne 'order'd her a Pension for Life, but she liv'd not to receive more than the first half Year of it' (Cibber, 161–2). The traditional widow's benefit was played for her on 4 June 1711; she wrote her will on 10 March 1712; and she died in London, and was buried beside her husband in Westminster Abbey on 13 April 1712. JUDITH MILHOUS

Sources C. Cibber, An apology for the life of Mr. Colley Cibber, new edn, 1, ed. R. W. Lowe (1889), 161–2 · J. H. Wilson, All the king's ladies: actresses of the Restoration (1958), 117–19 · J. Milhous and R. D. Hume, eds., A register of English theatrical documents, 1660–1737, 2 vols. (1991) · J. Downes, Roscius Anglicanus, ed. J. Milhous and R. D. Hume, new edn (1987) · Highfill, Burnim & Langhans, BDA, 2.96–9 · An account of the life of that celebrated tragedian, Mr Thomas Betterton (1749) · E. Boswell, The Restoration court stage (1660–1702): with a particular account of the production of 'Calisto' (1932), esp. 131, 180 · The Tatler (2 May 1710) · L. Hotson, The Commonwealth and Restoration stage (1928), esp. 233–4 · W. Van Lennep and others, eds., The London stage, 1660–1800, pt 1: 1660–1700 (1965) · Pepys, Diary · B. Podewell, 'Elizabeth Watson's childhood: biographical notes on a Restoration actress', Theatre Survey, 19/2 (1978), 180–82

Wealth at death £40; also bequests to be paid out of untraced government pension: Highfill, Burnim & Langhans, BDA

Betterton, Thomas (*bap.* 1635, *d.* 1710), actor and theatre manager, was baptized on 11 or 12 August 1635 at St Margaret, Westminster, London. His father, Matthew (*d.* 1663), was an under-cook to Charles I, according to Betterton's first biographer, Gildon. His mother was Frances, daughter of Thomas Flowerdew; the family lived in Tothill Street, Westminster. Betterton had an elder brother or half-brother of whom nothing is known and two younger brothers, William (1644–1661), briefly an actor, until he drowned, and Charles (1647–1678), apprenticed in the king's kitchen. Betterton also had two sisters, Mary, later Mrs Martin Kelly, and Frances, later Mrs John (?) Williamson.

As the authors of the *Biographical Dictionary* have said, Betterton is generally recognized as 'the greatest English actor between Burbage and Garrick', considered by some scholars 'better than either' (Highfill, Burnim & Langhans, *BDA*, 2.73). He was also the pre-eminent manager of his time. How he came to adopt a theatrical career is not known. Charles Gildon claimed that Betterton had little 'Education in the learned Languages' but had 'read much in *French*' and English (Gildon, 17). The anonymous *Account of the Life* (1749) claims that because he showed a 'great propensity' for reading, 'some learned profession' was planned, but nothing definite is known of his education (p. 5). The spurious *History* by William Oldys and others, published by Edmund Curll under Betterton's name in 1741, puts the actor at the battle of Edgehill. Since he was only seven years old at the time, the obvious intent was to link him to the royalist cause. Along with the future actor Edward Kynaston, Betterton was apprenticed to a bookseller. Gildon names John Rhodes, but Pope reportedly contradicted him. The 1749 *Life* suggests that the boys were bound to Sir William Davenant's publisher, John Holden, but surviving records show no trace of their apprenticeship. If Betterton's ended at twenty-one, he should have been released in 1656. While he was old enough to participate in Davenant's earliest unlicensed performances, they were too intermittent to support him, and he might well have got a job with a printer. John Crouch's *A Mixt Poem … upon the Happy Return of His Sacred Majesty Charls the Second* was printed for 'Thomas Bettertun at his shop in Westminster-hall, 1660', and a reissue of Crouch's poem *The Muses Joy for the Recovery of that Weeping Vine, Henretta-Maria* (1661) was printed for 'Tho. Batterton'. Although the name may be a coincidence, a second occupation was not unusual for actors after 1660, and the status of theatre at this time was uncertain. Yet if Betterton was ever a printer or bookseller, he does not appear to have been one long, and his later reluctance to allow publication of his own plays seems the more remarkable.

The early years Although Betterton's first appearance remains untraceable, John Downes documents his participation in the company organized by Rhodes in 1659 at the Cockpit in Drury Lane. Downes lists thirteen classic plays they mounted and comments that Betterton was 'highly Applauded', 'his Voice being then as Audibly strong, full

Thomas Betterton (*bap.* 1635, *d.* 1710), studio of Sir Godfrey Kneller [original, 1690s]

and Articulate, as in the Prime of his Acting' (Downes, 44–5). The emphasis on voice is important, because it sustained him as an actor long after his body had grown infirm, as Downes, writing in 1708, was well aware. The stroller Anthony Aston, who saw Betterton only towards the end of his career, emphasizes the defects of age in his description, but suggests that the proportions of the actor's body were less than ideal. Betterton's stature resulted as much from hard work as from natural gifts.

By 6 October 1660 the patentee Thomas Killigrew had absorbed actors from various sources into the King's Company. Betterton's name appears on government lists of that troupe and, by bureaucratic error, continues there for more than a year. However, on 5 November 1660 Betterton and nine other actors signed a formal sharing agreement with Sir William Davenant, constituting the Duke's Company. Had Betterton stayed with the senior actors under Killigrew, he would have been quite overshadowed, whereas in Davenant's organization he immediately became one of the leading actors. By 1 March 1661 Samuel Pepys was already describing him in his diary with superlatives: 'but above all that ever I saw, Baterton doth the Bondman [in Massinger's play of that name] the best', and Betterton was always Pepys's favourite actor. Part of the excitement of belonging to the young enterprise, along with the benefit of Davenant as teacher, was the challenge of competing against a much more experienced troupe. Downes proudly reports that Davenant imparted an approach to such plays as *Hamlet* and *Henry VIII* preserved in a direct line back to Shakespeare (Downes, 51–2, 55–6). The details of this genealogy are inaccurate, but the idea of passing on a traditional, correct way to do older plays is a sign of how this theatre worked. That idea was built into the repertory system, in which a small roster of actors 'owned' the roles they played as long as they remained with a company. According to Gildon, Betterton and one of his leading ladies, Elizabeth Barry, made a 'Practice' of consulting 'e'en the most indifferent Poet in any Part [they] thought fit to accept of' (Gildon, 16). Thus whenever possible the playwright remained the source of explication. But once interpretations were set, innovations were frowned on. Since a season's repertory might consist of between twenty and forty plays or more, unnecessary changes made for inefficiency. Gildon also quotes Betterton as saying that under Davenant they 'were obliged to make [their] Study [their] Business', and they learned their parts before rehearsals, so as to be able 'to enter thoroughly into the Nature of the Part, or to consider the Variation of the Voice, Looks, and Gestures, which should give [characters] their true Beauty' (ibid., 15). Aston acknowledged that 'from the Time he was dress'd, to the End of the Play', Betterton 'kept his Mind in the same Temperament' as his character 'required' (Cibber, 2.301).

Betterton's roles show a wide range, at first necessitated by the small size of the company but continued by choice throughout his career. From the beginning he usually played leading roles in Shakespeare (Hamlet, Pericles) and in new serious plays (Solyman the Magnificent in both parts of Davenant's *Siege of Rhodes*), but he also occasionally undertook shorter character roles (Sir Toby Belch in *Twelfth Night*; Mercutio in *Romeo and Juliet*). He was not afraid to appear as a villain (Deflores in Middleton's and Rowley's *Changeling*). He also played leads in comedy, though they tended toward the sober rather than the uproarious (Colonel Jolly in Abraham Cowley's *Cutter of Coleman-Street*). The pattern continued through his prime. In the 1680s he was the obvious actor to play Lear in Nahum Tate's adaptation of Shakespeare and to create both the betrayed Castalio in Thomas Otway's *Orphan* and Jaffeir in his *Venice Preserv'd*. His role in Ben Jonson's *Silent Woman* was the impotent and crotchety Morose, while for Nathaniel Lee he created the evil Nemours in *The Princess of Cleve*. His comic roles included the exuberant Beaugard in Otway's *Atheist* as well as the staid Torrismond in Dryden's *Spanish Fryar*. What he did not play was farce. Reliable documentation credits him with over 180 roles, one in roughly two of every three new plays produced by his companies, and since no cast is known for 128 more, Betterton's total number of roles must have been well over 200. (For a list, see Milhous, 'Census').

Because Betterton succeeded as a leading actor, he continued to be cast in major roles and to carry a heavy workload in comparison with that of his colleagues. In the years before 1665, when the theatre was closed by plague, he most often played with Henry Harris and opposite Mary Saunderson (*c*.1637–1712) [*see* Betterton, Mary] or Hester Davenport. Pepys noted Betterton's reputation as 'a very sober, serious man, and studious and humble' (Pepys, 22 Oct 1662). His rather oblique entry implied that Betterton and Mrs Saunderson were already living together though not married, but shortly after 24 December they plighted their troth in Islington, with the consent of Mary's mother.

The characteristics Pepys listed for Betterton contrast with the behaviour of Harris, who refused to act while demanding higher pay (Pepys, 22 July, 24 Oct 1663). Unable to replace him, Davenant capitulated, and for some time Harris outranked everyone else in salary. The Bettertons, meanwhile, accumulated shares in the company by investing their money when part-shares became available. They were on their own: when Betterton's father died in June 1663, he left his son a gilded seal ring that had belonged to his grandfather, but not money. Thomas and Mary continued as key actors both before and after the theatres were closed on account of plague from 5 June 1665 until 29 November 1666.

However focused on his craft, Betterton could sometimes be jolted into a spontaneous reaction onstage. Pepys was disgusted that Betterton and Harris both lost their concentration and laughed at a 'ridiculous mistake' during a late summer performance of Roger Boyle's *Mustapha* (Pepys, 4 Sept 1667). About a month later Pepys noted that Betterton was ill of a fever, and he did not return to the stage for several months, to the diarist's great regret (Pepys, 16 Oct 1667, 6 July 1668). Not only did Betterton miss out on several important new plays, but, more important, he was not fully recovered when Davenant died on 7 April 1668. Harris acknowledged in a later deposition that at this crisis he and Betterton 'were chose by all Parties interested in the said Theatre to manage the same' (PRO, C24/1144, no. 11).

The responsibilities of co-management Betterton and Harris served as administrators for Davenant's heir, Charles, who did not officially become head of the company until his majority in 1677, though at least four years earlier he was being consulted. On his behalf they undertook to erect a modern, purpose-built theatre in Dorset Garden that cost £9000. For this project, and probably on several other occasions, Betterton travelled to Paris to observe French theatrical practice and consult experts, though his trips are impossible to document precisely. The theatre, which opened on 9 November 1671, greatly increased the capacity of the Duke's Company to present machine spectacles such as Charles Davenant's opera *Circe* (1677), and Aphra Behn's machine farce *The Emperor of the Moon* (1687). The emphasis on spectacle which the Dorset Garden theatre made realizable was popular with audiences but controversial among critics at the time, and its benefits remained a matter of dispute long after the building had been demolished in 1709. Eighteenth-century lives of Betterton debate the issue entirely in abstract terms, but it remained a point of contention.

The possibilities of modern technology that the new theatre employed had entranced Sir William Davenant, but did not directly further Betterton's acting career, since the roles he played in the more spectacular productions were not large. The genres that benefited from the machine capacity called for music, and Aston reports that

Betterton could neither sing nor dance. However, he was the chief consultant for the staging of plays that used the technology. Dorset Garden helped undermine the ability of the rival King's Company to attract audiences.

Both as a convenience and in return for watching the premises, the co-managers lived rent-free in the 'Front Houses adjoining to the Theatre' (Hotson, 233). The Bettertons, who were childless, raised, educated, and trained for the stage two informally adopted daughters, both of whose fathers reportedly suffered financial difficulties. Anne *Bracegirdle joined them in the late 1660s, and Elizabeth Watson about 1686. The whole family were highly respectable. Unconfirmed oral tradition in the next century reported that in the winter of 1674–5 Betterton 'instructed the noble Actors, and supplied the Part of Prompter' for the court masque *Calisto*, while his wife taught the women, including the princesses Anne and Mary (*Account of the Life*, 11).

Like his mentor Davenant, Betterton was at least as concerned to develop new playwrights as he was to exploit the display features of the new theatre. He wrote nothing original. Instead, he made use of other writers' work in two forms: production adaptations, which involved comparatively minor changes, and thorough revamping, which combined plots from two or more plays into a new whole. Both kinds were carefully crafted to fit the actors available. (For a list of works, see below.) Betterton also worked closely with men and women who were interested in supplying new scripts. Among those he recruited were Aphra Behn, Thomas Otway, and eventually John Dryden, who in 1677–8 gave up a contract to write for the rival theatre.

A number of changes were inevitable in the late 1670s, as the twenty-year mark neared for the 'restored' theatre. The King's Company's actors who had resumed careers interrupted by the civil war were feeling their age, but so strong was tradition that they baulked at relinquishing roles to younger performers. Performances there sometimes ceased for weeks on end. In the Duke's Company the first generation of actresses either retired or cut back on their roles about this time, though the men had yet to face the challenge of age. Still, distractions could intervene. Between 1677 and 1681 Henry Harris pursued his political interests so vigorously that he acquired a variety of minor government posts, so he gradually transferred his roles and eventually his managerial duties to William Smith. The word of Betterton, as the more experienced manager, presumably had more weight, but its rule was not absolute. Since 1668 the managers' decisions had routinely been reviewed by the board of sharing actors as well as by representatives of the Davenant family, and building shareholders might also see the books and question policy if dissatisfied with their profits. In any case, unlike the King's Company, the Duke's house accomplished its second managerial transition smoothly, and the business prospered. The Bettertons' incomes cannot be determined at this date, but were certainly among the highest in the theatre.

The union of 1682　Betterton's part in the dissolution of the King's Company has been a stumbling-block for various biographers. Their information was limited to the memorandum of 14 October 1681, published by Gildon, in which Edward Kynaston and Charles Hart agreed with Charles Davenant, Betterton, and Smith to promote the union of the two companies (Gildon, 8–9). Stripped of context, the document seems to imply that the Duke's Company's representatives were suborning members of the other company to plot its downfall, a move which some biographers have read as contradicting Betterton's reputation for probity. However, the King's Company had already ceased to be a viable operation, and according to Betterton's sworn deposition in a later lawsuit the lord chamberlain, Henry Bennet, earl of Arlington, had already informed him 'that it was the King's will and Pleasure that the two patentees should unite and make one Good Company' (PRO, C24/1197, no. 56). Thus the agreement with Kynaston and Hart should be seen as an attempt to secure the services of two of the most knowledgeable members of the rival troupe, which finally closed just six months later.

As managers of the new United Company, Betterton and Smith attempted to employ large numbers of their former rivals, but integrating the separate repertories was not easy, and most of the senior actors died off or retired in short order. That left the United Company without competition and with access to the extensive repertory of King's Company plays. They could stage new productions of proven classics with much less risk than new scripts. With the union, Betterton gained such roles as Othello, Manly in Wycherley's *Plain Dealer*, Antony in Dryden's *All for Love*, and Leontius in Beaumont's and Fletcher's *Humorous Lieutenant*, previously unavailable to him. He also created Dorax in Dryden's *Don Sebastian* and the title role in Dryden's and Lee's *Duke of Guise* at this time. However, an unanticipated consequence of the focus on classics was that playwriting became a less attractive occupation for many would-be authors.

The United Company also took over the Drury Lane Theatre, in which it staged many of its productions that did not depend heavily on machinery, since the house was more congenial to actors. Dorset Garden remained the home of spectacular productions, one of which proved notably deleterious. Betterton and other members of the company, at the command of Charles II, went to France in August 1683 to 'fetch the designe' that would allow them to 'perform an Opera in like manner of that of France' (Wilson, 82). They made a contract with Louis Grabu, who set a libretto by Dryden. The inordinately expensive production was almost ready to open in February 1685, when the king unexpectedly died. While the theatre was closed as part of national mourning, they revamped *Albion and Albanius* to feature praise of James II as well as his late brother. Unfortunately, the opening occurred just days before the duke of Monmouth invaded. His rebellion closed the opera after only six showings, and the prompter Downes reported that, 'not Answering half the

Charge', it 'Involv'd the Company very much in Debt' (Downes, 84). This disaster prevented elaborate productions for several years and led to more emphasis on farce and light-weight comedy among new plays.

Charles Davenant, having developed interests other than theatre, sold his shares in the United Company to his brother Alexander on 30 August 1687, and in November the new proprietor named his 23-year-old brother Thomas manager. Thereupon Betterton and Smith returned to acting and advised the inexperienced new administration. A year later, as supporters of James II began mustering to fight for him if necessary, Smith left the United Company and went into the army. The revolution of 1688 slowed the financial recovery of the theatre, as extant profit declarations show. Betterton's income between 1683 and 1692 ranged from £282 to £487 (Milhous, 'United Company finances'). However, once William and Mary were established on the throne, the company undertook several expensive operatic productions, in an attempt, as Colley Cibber said, to 'bring home the *Indies*' (Cibber, 1.187). The scale of these semi-operas or English operas was larger than that of any play in the regular repertory, involving more musicians, singers, and dancers, not to mention costumes and special effects, all of which required rehearsal time to co-ordinate. They include the operatic *Prophetess*, with music by Purcell to a book Downes says Betterton adapted from Beaumont's and Fletcher's *Dioclesian* (1690), the Dryden–Purcell *King Arthur* (1691), and *The Fairy Queen* (1692), with music by Purcell to a book sometimes attributed to Elkanah Settle but more probably by Betterton. They cost large sums and brought only diminishing returns, according to both Downes and Cibber. Betterton was closely associated with these productions.

The proprietor, Alexander Davenant, had agreed to these operas in hope of recouping his own fortunes. He had in fact borrowed the money with which he bought out his brother, and when a chancery audit exposed financial problems dating back several years, Davenant fled to the Canary Islands. The shareholders met in October 1693 to cope with this crisis, whereupon Sir Thomas Skipwith and Christopher Rich revealed that they had lent Davenant the money with which he had purchased his shares. Since he had defaulted on their loans, his shares and patent now belonged to them, which made them patentees equal in power to Charles Killigrew. The new fiscal policies this troika imposed on the company were aimed at recouping their investment by stringent cost-cutting measures. Skipwith was merely a dilettante speculator, but Rich was a lawyer who had some experience of business. With the uneasy co-operation of Killigrew, they abruptly changed traditional practices. They limited spending on productions and buildings. They cut salaries. They deprived senior actors of long-held roles and gave them to lower-paid junior actors. The business model they espoused penalized actresses for getting pregnant and reduced or stopped paying certain levies to the parish.

Some retrenchment was necessary, but these policies were implemented too drastically. The senior generation

of actors could have been allowed to give up their roles gradually. The Bettertons might have taken the opportunity to retire, had they been well enough off. Unfortunately, they had lost a large sum—reported by Gildon as close to £8000 (but £2000 in *Account of the Life*)—invested in the cargo of a ship that was captured by the French. (This undertaking was said to originate with Sir Francis Watson, the father of the Bettertons' ward, and Dr John Radcliffe was another of the contributors.) Betterton tried to negotiate with the new patentees, but when they proved intransigent, he and fourteen colleagues made a deeply felt, if sometimes incoherent, protest to the lord chamberlain. The 'petition of the players' outlined departures from 'the whole Course & Method' of the past, which were presented as 'tending to the ruine & destruction of the Company'. The actors objected to being treated 'not as … the Kings & Queenes servants but the Claimers slaves' (PRO, LC 7/3, fols. 2–4). Many particulars followed, including a statement that Betterton had briefly served as manager in the aftermath of the 1693 crisis. The 'Reply of the patentees' on 10 December 1694 showed no hint of compromise, arguing that the changes under way were all business necessities and were entirely legal. But the aggrieved actors had the advantage that Betterton had known the lord chamberlain, Charles, earl of Dorset, for decades. Dorset got them, or at least their cause, a hearing before William III, and the result was permission to issue a licence for the 'rebels' to set up a separate company.

Lincoln's Inn Fields, 1695–1705 A group of eight of the rebels joined together in a co-operative; three of the participants were women (Elizabeth Barry, Anne Bracegirdle, and Elinor Leigh). They rented the tiny, disused theatre in Lincoln's Inn Fields and opened their season with Congreve's *Love for Love* on 30 April 1695. For a time popular sentiment favoured the 'new' theatre. However, the company was plagued by deaths and desertions; the split in the theatres generated numerous lawsuits that continued for a decade; the Collier controversy in 1698 raised moral questions about many plays in the repertory; new playwrights tended to go to the 'patent' company, whose young actors learned quickly; and the Lincoln's Inn Fields company began to show its age. Betterton, who was sixty when the new enterprise got under way, found that several of his fellow sharers were unwilling to do the work of management, though quite willing to complain. On 11 November 1700 the lord chamberlain appointed him sole manager of the company. Thereafter complaints charged that the formidable Mrs Barry and the *ingénue* Bracegirdle influenced Betterton's decisions. One disgruntled anonymous author referred to them as the 'Three Ruling B—s' (*The Lunatick*, 1705). To counter the lack of machine capacity at Lincoln's Inn Fields, virtuoso dancers and singers were brought in for short engagements, but their cost was not repaid. Whoever made the decisions, the ageing actors did not recapture their audience. Twice Betterton initiated unsuccessful attempts to reunite with the rival company, which was also having difficulties holding the attention of the town. Had he been able to afford it, Betterton would surely have retired in the face of these difficulties.

The late career In the spring of 1703 the playwright John Vanbrugh lined up noble sponsorship and undertook to build a splendid new theatre for London in the Haymarket. When it opened in 1705, Betterton and his fellow actors at Lincoln's Inn Fields accepted Vanbrugh's invitation to move there. In preliminary documents Betterton is listed first, with a salary of £150 a year and a £50 bonus 'more to teach' (PRO, LC 7/3, fols. 161–3). However, with the move Betterton resigned the management to Vanbrugh and Congreve. He continued to play a surprisingly rigorous schedule, given his age and declining health, and he also taught elocution privately. The Revd Ralph Bridges, who took lessons when preparing for his ordination sermon, told Sir William Trumbull that he 'received more benefit from hearing [Betterton] read one half-hour than I should have done in my whole life by my own study' (*Downshire MSS*).

By this time Betterton was playing more character parts, and the new roles written for him were shorter, though still substantial. Nicholas Rowe provided him with Sir Timothy Tallapoy in his comedy *The Biter* (1705), and the title role in *Ulysses* (1706). Resigning leads, Betterton switched from Don Henrique to Don Antonio in Samuel Tuke's *Adventures of Five Hours* and took up Thersites in Dryden's *Troilus and Cressida*, but retained Montezuma in his *Indian Emperour*. Falstaff became a staple of Betterton's repertory. His Othello continued to please, but his Hamlet was problematic: *The Tatler* (71, 22 Sept 1709) was polite about someone nearly seventy who 'acted Youth', but Aston used the role as an example of what he regarded as Betterton's stiff style of playing. The treasurer Zachary Baggs estimated that for the 1708–9 season Betterton collected as much as £450 from gifts and £76 from his benefit, as well as £113 in salary (but only the second and third numbers are reliable).

Late in his life Betterton journeyed to Stratford upon Avon to do research on Shakespeare, the results of which modern scholars have questioned, but Rowe thanked the actor for his contribution to the 1709 edition of Shakespeare. The young Alexander Pope became acquainted with Betterton and copied the picture of him from the Kneller studio. In 1712 the poet substantially edited Betterton's versions of passages from Chaucer, which he published in Lintot's *Miscellaneous Poems and Translations*.

Betterton's final appearance was as Melantius in Beaumont's and Fletcher's *Maid's Tragedy*, a benefit performance held for him on 13 April 1710, the profit from which is unknown. In order to perform, Betterton underwent extreme treatments for his gout and died from complications on 28 April at his lodgings at the Indian Man in Russell Street, Covent Garden. He was buried in Westminster Abbey on 2 May. Richard Steele, who attended the funeral, published a eulogy in *The Tatler* (no. 167) two days later. Betterton died intestate, leaving his widow in reduced circumstances. On 24 August 1710 Jacob Hooke began to auction, from Betterton's lodgings, his extensive collection of books, prints, drawings, and paintings, many of which were related to theatre. The *Daily Courant* lists a further sale on 7–15 December. The catalogue, *Pinacotheca Bettertonæana*, includes lots that may have been renderings for costumes in his English operas (such as nos. 32, 33, and 55).

Works, genuine and spurious Betterton did not acknowledge publication of his plays—perhaps because they were only adaptations—and many more have been credited to him than now seem justified (Milhous, 'Betterton's playwriting'). His production adaptations include *The Roman Virgin* (1669), made from Webster's *Appius and Virginia*; *The Prophetess* (1690), from the Fletcher–Massinger *Dioclesian*; and *King Henry IV, with the Humours of Sir John Falstaff* (1700), in which he played Falstaff. Betterton's more thoroughgoing adaptations were *The Woman Made a Justice* (1670; lost), probably from Montfleury's *La femme juge et partie*, and *The Amorous Widow* (premièred about 1670; printed in 1706 and 1710), from Thomas Corneille's *Le baron d'Albikrac* and Molière's *George Dandin*. Plays that have been attributed to him include adaptations of Massinger's *Bondman* and *Roman Actor*; the version of Middleton's *No Wit, No Help Like a Woman's* called *The Counterfeit Bridegroom*; that of Marston's *Dutch Curtizan* called *The Revenge*; the 1703 *Hamlet*; and *The Sequel of Henry the Fourth* (about 1721), made of parts of 2 *Henry IV* and *Henry V*. The *Life* by Gildon purports to reproduce a manuscript by Betterton on the subject of acting but is really a pastiche of French elocution texts (Gildon, 17–18; Howell).

Reputation Contemporaneous assessments of Betterton's career were posthumous and focused on the last twenty years, rather than on its totality. The most extensive appreciation is that of Colley Cibber (Cibber, 1.99ff.), who stresses Betterton's professionalism and range. Cibber was hired by Betterton, observed him closely over many years, and wrote after the end of his own career. Therefore his account is regarded as more reliable than the partial demurrer of Anthony Aston, a low comedian with limited interest in serious plays who saw Betterton only in semi-retirement and whose account emphasizes his failings more than his accomplishments. Yet Aston acknowledged that as prologue Betterton 'enforc'd universal Attention, even from the *Fops* and *Orange-Girls*' (Cibber, 2.300). The most concise statement of Betterton's philosophy of acting is found in the preface to Charles Johnson's *The Force of Friendship* (1710), the prologue to which was 'design'd' for Betterton. Speaking of the qualities of the ideal actor, Johnson said, 'Nature had indeed been very bountiful to Mr. *Betterton*, and yet Art and Labour had improv'd him wonderfully, and he confessed but lately, He was yet learning to be an Actor.' Although productions did not change much once set, Betterton was always eager to try new things.

In his capacity as manager Betterton implemented in English theatre the development of spectacle already accomplished in Italy and France. He exploited the potential of the new stage machinery, combined with music and dance as well as words, to offer productions of a kind not seen before by London audiences. The expense of this change of direction proved difficult to absorb in unsubsidized public theatres, but the policy of reinvesting profits in the company served to balance 'the bad with the good' nights, until Skipwith and Rich took over (petition of the players, PRO, LC 7/3, fols. 2–4). In the breakaway troupe Betterton repeated the pattern of his early years, cultivating new playwrights and offering as much variety as possible. Ultimately, the age of that company was an insurmountable problem.

Betterton was easy to work with, and his help was acknowledged by diverse playwrights such as Dryden for *Albion and Albanius* and *Don Sebastian*, Mrs Manley for *Almyna*, David Craufurd for *Courtship a-la-mode*, and Settle for *Distress'd Innocence*. The devotion that runs through *Roscius Anglicanus* is significant, because John Downes had observed Betterton close up, having worked with him as prompter throughout their careers. The challenges to Betterton's reputation were few. He seldom figured in scurrilous lampoons. The assertion in *A Satyr on the Players* (*c*.1684) that his 'cheif Prerogative' was 'each playing Drab to swive' is not borne out by any other rumours. The only subject that could focus criticism of Betterton was money, a risk endemic to his position. In *Poems on Affairs of State* (1703), he was described as 'kind Banker Betterton', who supported the improvident Otway (vol. 2, p. 142). However, about the same time a group of complaints about profit skimming show that some of his colleagues were unhappy with internal accounting procedures. Those complaints ended with his semi-retirement in 1705, and his overall reputation certainly recovered in his lifetime. Considering the burdens of acting and management that he carried for nearly fifty years, his reputation could hardly be spotless, but the few smirches are minor.

Because no record of day-to-day reception survives, Betterton remains an obstinately shadowy titan. Such records and commentary as have come down to us show that he stands among the handful of eminent actor–managers in the history of the English theatre—a worthy successor to Richard Burbage and predecessor of David Garrick and John Philip Kemble. JUDITH MILHOUS

Sources J. Downes, *Roscius Anglicanus*, ed. J. Milhous and R. D. Hume, new edn (1987) • C. Cibber, *An apology for the life of Mr. Colley Cibber*, ed. R. W. Lowe, 2 vols. (1889); repr. (New York, 1966) • A. Aston, *A brief supplement to Colley Cibber, esq.: his 'Lives of the late famous actors and actresses'* [1747]; repr. in C. Cibber, *Apology for the life of Mr Colley Cibber*, new edn, ed. R. W. Lowe, 2 (1889), [297]–318 • C. Gildon, *The life of Mr. Thomas Betterton* (1710); repr. (New York, 1970) • W. S. Howell, 'Sources of the elocutionary movement in England: 1700–1748', *Quarterly Journal of Speech*, 45 (1959), 1–18 • J. Milhous, *Thomas Betterton and the management of Lincoln's Inn Fields, 1695–1708* (Carbondale, 1979) • J. Milhous, 'United Company finances, 1682–1692', *Theatre Research International*, 7 (1981–2), 37–53 • J. Milhous, 'An annotated census of Thomas Betterton's roles, 1659–1710', *Theatre Notebook*, 29 (1975), 33–43, 85–94 • J. Milhous, 'The multi-media spectacular on the Restoration stage', *British theatre and the other arts, 1660–1800*, ed. S. Strum Kenny (1984), 41–66 • J. Milhous, 'Thomas Betterton's playwriting', *Bulletin of the New York Public Library*, 77 (1974), 375–92 • L. Hotson, *The Commonwealth and Restoration stage* (1928); repr. (New York, 1962) • Highfill, Burnim & Langhans, *BDA* • T. Betterton, [W. Oldys and others], *The history of the English stage* (1741) • *An account of the life of that celebrated tragedian,*

Mr. Thomas Betterton (1749) • Pepys, *Diary* • J. H. Wilson, 'Theatre notes from the Newdigate newspapers', *Theatre Notebook*, 15 (1961), 79–84 • J. Freehafer, 'The formation of the London patent companies in 1660', *Theatre Notebook*, 20 (1965), 6–30 • Z. Baggs, *Advertisement concerning the poor actors* (1709) [repr. in Cibber, *Apology*, ed. Lowe, 2.78ff.] • B. Podewell, 'Elizabeth Watson's childhood: biographical notes on a Restoration actress', *Theatre Survey*, 19 (1978), 180–82 • B. Podewell, 'Thomas Betterton's roles', *Theatre Notebook*, 32 (1978), 89–90 • M. Mack, *Alexander Pope: a life* (1985) • *Report on the manuscripts of the marquis of Downshire*, 6 vols. in 7, HMC, 75 (1924–95), vol. 1, pt 2, p. 859 [Bridges to Trumbull, 25 June 1708] • *Pinacotheca Bettertonæana, or, A catalogue of the books … of Mr. Thomas Betterton* (1710) [BL S.C. 246 (9)] • *Daily Courant* (16 Dec 1710) • *The Tatler*, 167 (4 May 1710)

Likenesses Greenhill, pastel, *c*.1663 (as Bajazet?), Kingston Lacy, Bankes collection • G. Kneller, portrait, 1708, Knole, Kent • E. W. Alais, engraving (after R. Williams) • J. B. Allen, engraving (after R. Williams) • W. Evans, engraving (after R. Williams) • Geoffrey, engraving (after R. Williams) • Jervas?, portrait (after G. Kneller), priv. coll. • studio of G. Kneller, oils, other versions, Garr. Club, Knole, Kent • studio of G. Kneller, oils (after original, 1690–99), NPG [*see illus.*] • R. B. Parkes, engraving (after R. Williams) • M. Vandergucht, engraving (after R. Williams) • R. Williams, mezzotint (after G. Kneller) • J. Wooding, engraving (after R. Williams) • two portraits, repro. in Rove, *Shakespeare*; formerly Betterton Sale, 1710

Wealth at death widow left in reduced circumstances: *The Tatler*

Bettes, John, the elder (*d*. in or before **1570**), portrait painter and wood-engraver, of whose parents nothing is known, was first recorded as carrying out decorative work for Henry VIII at Whitehall Palace, London, in 1531–3. A portrait of an *Unknown Man in a Black Cap* (Tate collection), signed (twice) 'faict par Johan Bettes Anglois', is dated 1545; the portrait was cut down at some time and the signed area is now affixed to the back of the panel. It is a sophisticated work which suggests that Bettes may have trained, or worked, with Hans Holbein the younger. In the accounts of Queen Katherine Parr for 1546/7, Bettes was paid a total of £3 for 'lymmyng' portraits of the king and of the queen which were engraved by one 'Gyles', and for six other pictures; the word 'lymming' suggests that these were miniatures. John Foxe attested that Bettes engraved a pedigree and vignette in Edward Halle's *Chronicle* (1550), and the engraved title-border in William Cunningham's *Cosmographical Glasse* (1559), signed IBF, is assumed also to be by him. A court-case record indicated that he was living in Westminster in September 1556. Foxe noted that he was dead by 1570.

Portraits of Sir William Cavendish (*c*.1545, trustees of the Chatsworth settlement, on loan to Hardwick Hall, Derbyshire) and Sir William Butts the younger (*c*.154[3?], Museum of Fine Arts, Boston) are clearly by the same hand as the signed Tate collection portrait, and recent technical analysis has borne this out. Works more doubtfully attributed to Bettes include *Unknown Lady of the Fitzwilliam Family* (*c*.1540–45, trustees of the Rt Hon. Olive Countess Fitzwilliam's settlement, Milton Park, Cambridgeshire); *Thomas Wentworth, First Baron Wentworth of Nettlestead* (1559, National Portrait Gallery, London); and *Henry FitzAlan, Earl of Arundel* (1558) and *Henry FitzAlan, Lord Maltravers* (*c*.1555), both at Arundel Castle, Sussex. He may have been the 'skilful Briton' who designed the woodcut portrait of the

Saxon ambassador to England, Franz Burchard, published in 1560. No extant miniatures have been satisfactorily identified as by his hand. George Vertue recorded seeing one miniature, now lost, of Sir John Godsalve 'made by John Betts'; Godsalve, like members of the Butts family, had also been painted by Hans Holbein.

The most talented member of a dynasty of painters, Bettes the elder has in the past often been confused with his son **John Bettes the younger** (d. 1616), portrait painter, who was said by Vertue to have trained with the miniaturist Nicholas Hilliard. No works by the younger Bettes can be identified with certainty. In 1578–9 he was paid for decorative work associated with the revels or court pageants and masques. In 1598 Francis Meres described him as a painter (*Palladis tamia*, 287), as did Richard Haydock in his translation of Giovanni Paolo Lomazzo's *Trattato dell' arte della pittura* (1584) of the same year. It has been suggested that Bettes the younger may have painted the portrait *Unknown Girl* (St Olave's School, Bromley, Kent), dated 1587 and signed I. B.—and thus a group of similarly highly stylized decorative female portraits—but this remains conjectural. Other surviving portraits signed IB include *A Gentleman of the Woore Family* (1587) and an *Unknown Elderly Lady* (ex Sothebys, 10 April 1991, lot 58). Richard Madox, a fellow of All Souls College, Oxford, recorded in his diary on 28 February 1582 that while in London 'M. Betts of Moregate made my picture and had 12s for yt' (E. S. Donno, ed., *An Elizabethan in 1582*, 1976, 89). This portrait is not known to have survived. Bettes married, first, on 1 December 1571, Magdalen Browne, and second, on 8 September 1614, Ellianor Harman (d. 1618?). Both marriages took place at St Gregory by Paul, London.

By 1593, when his son Thomas was buried at St Giles Cripplegate, London, Bettes was living in Grub Street and was described as 'picturemaker' (Edmond, 97). He subsequently moved to the parish of St Gregory by Paul (that is, adjoining St Paul's Cathedral); he died in January 1616 and was buried in St Gregory by Paul on 18 January. In his will he was described as a citizen of London and a painter–stainer, and he left to his son, also named John Bettes, items of professional painting equipment and a portrait of John Bettes the elder (presumed lost). This son may have been the J. Betts who signed a portrait of an *Unknown Lady* (1660; reproduced in *Connoisseur*, July 1917, 127) and at least two other portraits of the 1660s. An Edward Betts [*sic*], painter–stainer, presumably another son, died at Deptford in 1661 (Edmond, 98). A Mr Betts was named as the source of a recipe for gilding size, in two mid-seventeenth-century manuscripts relating to Edward Norgate's *Miniatura, or, The Art of Limning* (ed. J. M. Muller and J. Murrell, 1997, 192, 244n.). In 1598 Francis Meres also listed a Thomas Bettes as a painter; although apparently a kinsman of the family of artists, he is now thought to have been a cutler (Edmond, 190).   KAREN HEARN

Sources E. Auerbach, *Tudor artists* (1954), 153–4 · M. Edmond, 'Limners and picturemakers', *Walpole Society*, 47 (1978–80), 60–242, esp. 67, 97–8, 190, 195 · K. Hearn, 'Edward VI, Mary I and continental art', *Dynasties: painting in Tudor and Jacobean England, 1530–1630*, ed. K. Hearn (1995), 45–62, esp. 46–7 [exhibition catalogue, Tate Gallery, London, 12 Oct 1995 – 7 Jan 1996] · R. Jones, 'The methods and materials of three Tudor artists', *Dynasties: painting in Tudor and Jacobean England, 1530–1630*, ed. K. Hearn (1995), 231–9, esp. 231–5 [exhibition catalogue, Tate Gallery, London, 12 Oct 1995 – 7 Jan 1996] · R. Strong, *The English icon: Elizabethan and Jacobean portraiture* (1969), 65–8 · E. K. Waterhouse, *The dictionary of British 16th and 17th century painters* (1988), 26 · J. Foxe, *The first volume of the ecclesiasticall history contayning the actes and monumentes of thynges passed*, new edn (1570), 557 · G. P. Lomazzo, *A tracte containing the artes of curious painting, carvinge and buildinge*, trans. R. H. [R. Haydocke] (1598), 126–7 · E. Waterhouse, *Painting in Britain, 1530–1790*, 5th edn (1994), 22–3 · C. Dodgson, 'The portrait of Franz Burchard', *Burlington Magazine*, 12 (1908), 39–40 · Vertue, *Note books*, 5.72 · M. Davies, *National Gallery catalogues: the British school* (1946), 9–11 · A. M. Hind, *Engraving in England in the sixteenth and seventeenth centuries*, 1 (1952), 7 · E. Croft-Murray, *Decorative painting in England, 1537–1837*, 1 (1962), 156, 163 · IGI

Likenesses portrait? (bequeathed in will of his son to his grandson, proved 1616)

Bettes, John, the younger (d. 1616). *See under* Bettes, John, the elder (d. in or before 1570).

Bettesworth, George Edmund Byron (1780–1808), naval officer, was the second son of John Bettesworth of Carhayes, Cornwall, and his wife, Frances Elinor, daughter of Francis Tomkyns of Pembrokeshire. At an early age he was sent to sea as midshipman under Captain Robert Barlow, commanding the frigate *Phoebe*. In this ship he remained for several years, but in January 1804 he was acting lieutenant of the *Centaur*, and took part in the action with the *Curieux*, when the latter was captured. Bettesworth had received a slight wound but his commanding officer suffered so severely that he died, and his lieutenant succeeded to the command of the *Curieux*. He was confirmed as lieutenant on 1 May 1804 and was subsequently promoted commander on 21 November 1804. While in this position he engaged in an action with the *Dame Ernouf* about 60 miles from Barbados. After a sharp fight the French vessel surrendered, but Bettesworth was again wounded. In the same year (1805) he brought home from Antigua Nelson's dispatches informing the government of Villeneuve's homeward flight from the West Indies and on his own initiative followed the enemy until he could ascertain their course, thereby facilitating their interception by Sir Robert Calder's squadron. He received from Lord Barham a post captain's commission on 9 July 1805. Lord Byron, in October 1807, wrote:

> Next January … I am going to sea for four or five months with my cousin, Captain Bettesworth, who commands the Tartar, the finest frigate in the navy. … We are going probably to the Mediterranean or to the West Indies, or to the devil; and if there is a possibility of taking me to the latter, Bettesworth will do it, for he has received four-and-twenty wounds in different places, and at this moment possesses a letter from the late Lord Nelson stating Bettesworth as the only officer in the navy who had more wounds than himself.   (*The Works of Lord Byron*, ed. T. Moore, 1, 1832, 174–5)

The promised voyage never took place. Bettesworth married at St George's Hanover Square, on 24 September 1807, Lady Hannah Althea Grey, second daughter of the first Earl Grey.

In May 1808 Bettesworth was watching some vessels off Bergen, when it was deemed possible to cut some of them off from the protecting gunboats. In this attempt the *Tartar* became becalmed amid the rocks, and was attacked by five Danish gunboats and a schooner. Bettesworth was killed by the first shot on 16 May 1808. At the request of Earl Grey, the body was buried in the vault of the Grey family, at Howick church, Northumberland, on 27 May. Major Trevanion, 'a brother of Captain Bettesworth', was a chief mourner. Byron's grandmother was a Miss Trevanion. Bettesworth's widow married in October 1809 Edward Ellice, a well-known whig politician. Captain Bettesworth was only twenty-eight years old at the time of his death, and was considered the beau idéal of an English officer.   W. P. COURTNEY, *rev.* ANDREW LAMBERT

Sources D. Syrett and R. L. DiNardo, *The commissioned sea officers of the Royal Navy, 1660–1815*, rev. edn, Occasional Publications of the Navy RS, 1 (1994) · J. S. Corbett, *The campaign of Trafalgar* (1910) · *GM*, 1st ser., 78 (1808) · W. James, *The naval history of Great Britain, from the declaration of war by France, in February 1793, to the accession of George IV, in January 1820*, [2nd edn], 6 vols. (1826) · E. P. Brenton, *The naval history of Great Britain, from the year 1783 to 1822*, 5 vols. (1823–5)

Likenesses Coade, statue, 1812, St Michael's church, St Michael Caerhays, Cornwall

Bettmann, Siegfried (1863–1951), cycle and motor vehicle manufacturer, was born on 18 April 1863 at Nuremberg, Bavaria, youngest of the eleven children of Mayer Bettmann and his third wife, Sophie Weil. Educated in Germany, he taught himself the linguistic skills which enabled him to take up clerical posts throughout Europe. In London he befriended Maurice Schulte, a fellow Nuremberger and trained engineer, later his business partner.

On the continent Bettmann noticed that bicycles were appearing, and determined to exploit the new market. He established a London office and arranged for two Coventry firms to supply bicycles which were to carry Bettmann's own logo, Triumph, a name chosen because it sounded sufficiently English and superior to attract continental buyers. His company, S. Bettmann & Co., struggled at first and did not start to prosper until Schulte joined in November 1886. Schulte found a manufacturing base at Much Park Street, Coventry. Shortage of capital almost killed the venture, but a coterie of wealthy directors was assembled and the firm soon moved into a modern factory in Priory Street, Coventry, the financing being arranged by Bettmann. He contributed nothing to the design and manufacturing side, which was Schulte's province. Bettmann's role lay in marketing, in which capacity he travelled widely.

The New Triumph Cycle Company was successfully floated in May 1895 and the following three boom years saw Triumph's profits rise into six figures, persuading Bettmann to refloat the company at a grossly inflated capital of £130,000 which involved heavy debenture liabilities. A stormy period followed as the cycle boom petered out, until the motor cycle provided a product with which to forge a recovery. Bettmann claimed the credit for this inspirational move, though the fact that Schulte test-rode a German motor cycle suggests his role was greater than his jealous partner would admit to. Whatever the provenance of the Triumph motor cycle, its appearance in 1902 was a turning point for the company. Until the Triumph Trusty of 1904, motor cycles were notoriously unreliable. The design was Schulte's, with Bettmann's role being to seek orders from dealers and public bodies. By 1909 annual production at the Priory Street works had reached 3000.

On the Thursday before Britain entered the First World War in August 1914, the War Office asked Bettmann to organize a meeting of motor cycle manufacturers. They were informed that an expeditionary force would be sent to Belgium, and that motor cycles were required for dispatch riders. Shortly afterwards Bettmann received a request for one hundred, the first of many orders. The Model H, introduced in 1915, proved so reliable that 30,000 were ordered by the army during the conflict, a greater quantity than that ordered from any other motor cycle manufacturer.

In 1919 Bettmann, incensed at Schulte's desire to end bicycle production, engineered his removal. Schulte's departure was soon felt; the Model P motor cycle, launched in 1924, was a commercial disaster and soured Triumph's trustworthy reputation. At Bettmann's behest, the company moved uncertainly into motor car manufacture under the guidance of Captain Claude Holbrook. The Super Seven, a more sophisticated rival to the Austin Seven was produced by the Triumph Motor Company in the premises of a failed marque in Clay Lane, Coventry. Healthy export sales underpinned its success until the depression of the 1930s, which also adversely affected motor cycle sales. This time, the sale of the bicycle division could not be averted. Nor did Bettmann get his way over staying with light cars rather than moving into sports car production, and he resigned as managing director on 18 April 1933. He remained bitter about the turn of events, but his attempts to wallow in nostalgia by buying the rights to manufacture Triumph bicycles in 1936 proved unsuccessful.

Although he became a British citizen in 1895, Bettmann remained an outsider. In September 1914, anti-German hysteria led to his resignation as mayor of Coventry. After dallying with the Labour Party, Bettmann returned to the Liberal fold, serving as president of the Coventry Liberal Association (1937–40). In 1895 Bettmann married Annie Mayrick, a tradesman's daughter. The marriage was childless, and his wife was seriously ill from 1916 until her death in 1941. In 1920 Bettmann established the Annie Bettmann Foundation, a school for young business people. He died at his home, Elm Bank, Stoke Park, near Coventry on 23 September 1951.   STEVEN MOREWOOD

Sources S. Morewood, *Pioneers and inheritors: top management in the Coventry motor industry, 1896–1972* (1990) · S. Bettmann, 'Struggles: a man of no importance', autobiography, Coventry City RO · S. Bettmann, 'Cycle finance', ed. C. Nowell, *The Reader's Bulletin*, 1/4 (1923), 74–7 · I. Davies, *It's a Triumph* (1980) · I. Davies, *Pictorial history of Triumph motor cycles* (1985) · G. Robson, *The story of Triumph sports cars* (1972) · d. cert. · *The Times* (26 Sept 1951)

Betts, Annie Dorothy (1884–1961), apiculturist and expert on bee diseases, was born on 22 November 1884 at Claverley, Adelaide Road, Surbiton, Surrey, the daughter of Edward Peto Betts (1844–1918), civil engineer and financier, and his wife, Frances Ashenhurst Maclean (1853–1934). She was from a distinguished family of railway constructors that included her grandfather Edward Ladd *Betts (1815–1872) and her great-uncle Sir (Samuel) Morton Peto (1809–1889). Little is known of her education, but she gained an external London BSc degree in 1906.

During the First World War, Annie Betts engaged in aeronautical research on variable pitch airscrews, and, although she did not pursue a paid career thereafter, she was a lifelong member of the Royal Aeronautical Society, and published a paper, 'The effect of variable gearing on aeroplane performance', in the society's *Journal* in November 1923. Suffering from a progressive loss of hearing, she became a very private person. Little is known of her domestic life except that she lived in the family home at Camberley, Surrey, until early 1935, after her mother's death, and later in Horsham, Sussex.

Annie Betts kept bees from her teens, when she and her father were both members of the Surrey Beekeepers Association. Her notebooks, written between 1908 and 1924, show her early interest in the pollen loads of the honey bee and in practical bee anatomy. Her primary interest was in the field of bee diseases; she published her first paper in this area in 1912 in the *Annals of Botany*. An extended version, 'The fungi of the beehive', subsequently appeared in the *Journal of Economic Biology*.

Annie Betts was a regular and esteemed contributor to journals on bee-keeping, and was appointed editor of *Bee World* in 1929. She established the journal's position as the leading international apicultural magazine, and made it a source of inspiration to both scientists and progressive bee-keepers. Her skills as a linguist allowed her to maintain a trans-European correspondence during the inter-war period; she mastered Russian in order to extend the scope of her coverage of apicultural literature. Under her editorship *Bee World* opened up European apicultural science to the English-speaking world. She was rigorous in her assessment of her own work, as well as that of others, and willingly acknowledged her own misunderstandings. If the management of a small voluntary journal's finances and production was difficult in the inter-war period, the Second World War brought material shortages and unimaginable problems to an editor dependent on overseas correspondents. She was, however, able to maintain links between nations.

Alongside *Bee World*, Annie Betts built up the Apis Club Library, and then oversaw this important collection's transfer, with the journal, to the Bee Research Association (subsequently based at Cardiff as the International Bee Research Association). Her self-effacement was typified by a firm decline of any form of testimonial: when relinquishing her editorship in 1949, she said in her concluding *Bee World* editorial that she looked forward to doing things of interest outside the world of apiculture, including motorcycling.

Annie Betts died on 8 September 1961 at 43 The Broadway, Knaphill, Woking, Surrey. A bibliography of her works which appeared in *Bee World* after her death revealed the full extent of her voluminous output. She wrote two books, *Practical Bee Anatomy* (1923) and *The Diseases of Bees* (1935; later edn, 1951), and published more than 145 articles on various aspects of apiculture.

KARL SHOWLER

Sources O. Morgenthaler, 'In memory of Miss Annie D. Betts', trans. M. D. Bindley, *Bee World*, 42 (1961), 307–10 · E. Crane, 'Miss A. D. Betts: a bibliography', *Bee World*, 42 (1961), 310–13 · H. Mace, *Bee matters and bee masters* (1930), 128 · R. Brown, *Great masters of bee-keeping* (1993), 75–9 · Inst. CE, Frank Smith deposit · CGPLA Eng. & Wales (1961) · b. cert. · d. cert.
Archives International Bee Research Association, Cardiff
Likenesses photograph, repro. in Mace, *Bee matters* · photograph, repro. in Brown, *Great masters of beekeeping*
Wealth at death £16,765 13s. 10d.: probate, 7 Nov 1961, CGPLA Eng. & Wales

Betts, Edward Ladd (1815–1872), railway contractor, was born on 5 June 1815 at Buckland, near Dover, the eldest son of William Betts (d. 1867), contractor's agent, of Sandown, Kent, and his first wife, Elizabeth Hayward, daughter of Edward Ladd of Buckland. Betts was apprenticed to Richardson, a builder, at Lincoln, but showed a bent for engineering, for which the emerging 'railway age' was to offer vast scope.

Under the superintendence of his father, as agent for the great contractor Hugh McIntosh, Betts worked on building the Black Rock lighthouse at Beaumaris, north Wales. Then, when he was only eighteen, he superintended building for McIntosh the Dutton Viaduct on the Grand Junction Railway (Liverpool–Birmingham) under the engineer George Stephenson, a £54,000 undertaking that introduced him to the world of railway construction in which thereafter he was continuously engaged. At first he was working in conjunction with his father and brother as agent for McIntosh, after whose death in 1840 William Betts & Sons operated for about four years, securing contracts on the South Eastern Railway (including the Saltwood Tunnel, 1843), which Betts took over on his own account in 1845. At that time he also won a number of contracts in the Chester area. His work on the South Eastern Railway (his tender for the Tunbridge Wells–Robertsbridge section alone amounting to £270,000 in 1847) adjoined that of Samuel Morton *Peto. On 6 July 1843 he married Peto's sister Ann (b. 1821), with whom he had six sons and three daughters. After the dissolution of Peto's partnership with Thomas Grissell in 1846, Betts joined Peto in constructing the Great Northern Railway loop line from Peterborough through Boston and Lincoln to Doncaster, as well as its associated East Lincolnshire line from Boston to Louth. A formal partnership was established in

1848, with which his affairs were thereafter inextricably entwined.

During the early 1850s, a period of railway company consolidation in England, Peto and Betts turned their efforts overseas, undertaking the Danish railway system from 1852. That same year they began working on the formidable enterprise of the Grand Trunk railroad of Canada, linking Quebec with Montreal, Toronto, and Detroit, in which they were stockholders; their contract provided for their being paid in a mixture of cash, shares, and bonds. Betts undertook the actual management of this 539 mile loss-making venture (rescued from collapse by the Canadian government), in which a primary element was the construction of the huge Victoria Bridge across the St Lawrence River. To manufacture the requisite metal parts and rolling-stock, the partners set up the Canada Works in Birkenhead, which subsequently supplied their other worldwide contracts, such as the Buenos Aires–Rosario line, and those from Dünaberg to Vitebsk in Russia (220 miles), and from Algiers to Blida. In Australia their pioneering efforts were performed in collaboration with Thomas Brassey. In the USA Betts was involved in the New York to Chicago and St Louis line.

In the Crimean War, Betts undertook the organization of a railway from the British base at Balaklava to the front, which Peto had offered to construct, dispatching twenty-three large steamers with engineers, workmen, horses, and stores. Here, as in the partners' other undertakings, Betts's role 'lay in the execution of contracts—no one had a greater practical knowledge … his eagle eye would fasten on a rivet missing' (Peto, 51).

At home the partners' close involvement in East Anglian lines led them to undertake the London, Tilbury, and Southend, opened in 1854–6, which they leased as operators for twenty-one years from 1854, a speculation said in 1863 to be losing £24,000 a year. The *Railway Times* reported (27 September 1856) that Betts 'wielded for a brief season the destinies of the Eastern Counties [railway]', in which he, like Peto and Brassey, had become a shareholder. As chairman in 1851–2 Betts suppressed an engine drivers' strike, but an accident affecting his eyesight forced him to resign. He was also contractor for the Strood and Maidstone line in Kent. This ran close to his 'palatial residence' near Aylesford, Preston Hall, rebuilt in 1850 by John Thomas (Peto's architect) in a dreary Jacobean style, where in 1861 he employed five gardeners, a groom and coachman, and an indoor staff of eight women and three men servants. In 1858 Betts, already a magistrate and deputy lieutenant, became high sheriff of Kent. In the 1865 general election he unsuccessfully contested Maidstone as a Conservative. At his London home, 29 Tavistock Square, in 1851, describing himself as 'engineer', he employed two men servants, five women, and a page; by 1860 he had moved on to Great George Street, Westminster.

During the 1860s Peto and Betts involved themselves in expensive undertakings in the south-east, where rival lines fought to secure the traffic between London and the ports. It was their involvement in the affairs of the London, Chatham, and Dover Railway Company, for which they were building a metropolitan extension from London Bridge to Victoria (in partnership with Thomas Russell Crampton), that brought disaster. Paid entirely in the company's shares and debentures, entangled in dubious finance-raising schemes, and with their overseas operations hindered by the Danish and Austrian wars, Peto and Betts were forced to stop payment in the banking crisis of 1866. Their partnerships were made insolvent the following year. Their only subsequent contract was for minor alterations on the Metropolitan Railway, to which Betts gave close attention. In 1869 he travelled to Budapest in connection with abortive proposals for improving the navigation of the Danube.

An obituary speaks of Betts's 'untiring application … and indomitable energy … clear judgment … and vigorous mind that grasped at once the main points of a question, and quickly decided on its merits' (*PICE*, 35, 1872, 285–8). A stern rectitude in his dealings was said to be allied to a general benevolence and a warmth of friendship. After his bankruptcy, which necessitated his selling Preston Hall, Betts moved to Bickley, near Bromley, Kent, where he could still maintain a carriage. In 1871 his doctors sent him to winter in Egypt, where he died at Aswan on 21 January 1872, survived by his wife. He was buried at Aylesford.   M. H. PORT

Sources *PICE*, 36 (1872–3), 285–8 · *ILN* (24 Feb 1872), 187 · H. Peto, *Sir Morton Peto: a memorial sketch* (1893) · M. M. Chrimes, 'Hugh McIntosh, 1768–1840', *Transactions* [Newcomen Society], 66 (1994–5), 175–92 · R. S. Joby, *The railway builders: lives and work of the Victorian railway contractors* (1983) · census returns, 1851, 1861 · *London Directory* · *Railway Times* (27 Sept 1856)
Wealth at death under £16,000: probate, 7 June 1872, *CGPLA Eng. & Wales*

Betts, John (*c*.1623–1695), physician, was born in Winchester, the son of Edward Betts (*b. c*.1578) and his wife, Dorothy, daughter of John Venables, of Rapley in Hampshire. He was educated at Winchester College, was elected a scholar of Corpus Christi College, Oxford, in February 1643, and took the degree of BA on 9 February 1647. After being ejected by the parliamentary visitors in 1648, he applied himself to the study of medicine, and gained the degrees of BM and DM at Oxford on 11 April 1654. He was admitted a candidate of the College of Physicians, London, on 30 September 1654 and became a fellow on 20 October 1664.

Betts practised with great success in London, chiefly among fellow Roman Catholics. Following the Restoration he was appointed physician-in-ordinary to Charles II. His position in the College of Physicians was subject to the varying toleration of his faith. Under Charles II and James II Betts was censor of the college in 1671, 1673, 1685, and 1686, and was named an elect on 25 June 1685. His fortunes declined under the rule of William and Mary; on 1 July 1689 he was denounced to the House of Lords as a papist, and on 25 October 1692 was threatened with the loss of his place as an elect if he did not take the oath of allegiance to the king (Kirby, i, 372). As the next meeting of the college council was not quorate, he did not take the oath, and was allowed to remain undisturbed in his position, probably on account of his age (Cook, 193).

Betts published several medical works, which were largely conservative in their content. His treatise on blood, *De ortu et natura sanguinis* (1669), was attacked by the Helmontian physician George Thomson for repeating 'such Antiquated Errours of the Peripateticks' (Thomson, 139).

Betts was dead by 15 May 1695, when Edward Hulse was named an elect in his place; he was buried at St Pancras. His son, Edward Betts, also became a doctor of medicine, acquired a high reputation as a physician, and died on 27 April 1695. THOMPSON COOPER, *rev.* PATRICK WALLIS

Sources T. F. Kirby, *Winchester scholars: a list of the wardens, fellows, and scholars of … Winchester College* (1888) · Foster, *Alum. Oxon.* · Munk, *Roll* · G. Thomson, *Aimatiasis, or, the true way of preserving blood* (1670), 139 · D. Lysons, *The environs of London*, 3 (1795), 354 · A. Kippis and others, eds., *Biographia Britannica, or, The lives of the most eminent persons who have flourished in Great Britain and Ireland*, 2nd edn, 2 (1780), 297 · H. J. Cook, *The decline of the old medical regime in Stuart London* (1986), 193 · Wood, *Ath. Oxon.* · Wood, *Ath. Oxon.*: *Fasti* (1820), 90, 183 · BL, Add. MS 22136, fol. 8

Archives BL, Add. MS 22136, fol. 8

Betty, Henry Thomas (1819–1897). *See under* Betty, William Henry West (1791–1874).

Betty, William Henry West (1791–1874), actor, was born on 13 September 1791 in the parish of St Chad, Shrewsbury, the son of William Henry Betty (*d.* 1811), a farmer, of Hopton Wafers, Shropshire, and later manager of a linen factory in Ballynahinch, co. Down, and his wife, a Miss Stanton of Worcestershire. Betty's first visit to a play was in 1801, when he saw Sarah Siddons perform the role of Elvira in *Pizarro* by Richard Sheridan at the Belfast theatre. He declared that 'he should die if he were not permitted to become a player' (*Georgian Era*, 455), and his father apprenticed him to William Hough, the Belfast prompter. The boy's first stage appearance was on 11 August 1803 at Belfast in the role of Osman in *Zara* by Aaron Hill; later in the season he attempted such roles as Young Norval (*Douglas* by John Home), Rolla (*Pizarro*), and Romeo. Tours to Dublin, Cork, Waterford, Glasgow, and Edinburgh followed. At the last city, box-office receipts for six nights amounted to £844. Betty went on to Liverpool, Sheffield, and Chester.

Having been invited to the Theatre Royal, Covent Garden, Betty made the first of twelve appearances at 50 guineas a night on 1 December 1804. Intervening nights were played at Drury Lane at a higher salary, until overwork took its toll. From 18 December until the new year Betty rested, then during 1805 and the first half of 1806 he acted at both theatres. His repertory was extended to include such roles as Achmet (*Barbarossa* by John Brown), his opening role in London, and Frederic (*Lovers' Vows* by Elizabeth Inchbald). Most of the parts he essayed were of mature and often tyrannical characters: Osmond (*The Castle Spectre* by Matthew Lewis), Zanga (*The Revenge* by Edward Young), Hamlet, Richard III, and Macbeth. He made an extensive tour during the summer of 1805 while

William Henry West Betty (1791–1874), by John Opie, 1804 [as Young Norval in *Douglas* by John Home]

the patent theatres were closed, when he took in his former haunts and, additionally, Berwick, Coventry, Durham, Newcastle upon Tyne, North and South Shields, Preston, Stourbridge, Sunderland, Whitehaven, Wolverhampton, Worcester, and York. 'Bettymania' was beginning to wear thin by 1807, but the youth continued his provincial tours until 11 July 1808. He then made a temporary farewell at Stratford upon Avon and became a commoner of Christ's College, Cambridge, until his premature withdrawal in June 1811 on the death of his father, at Pym's Farm, Wem, Shropshire. Betty returned to Covent Garden from 5 November 1812 until 12 June 1813 to muted acclaim and thereafter restricted his appearances to the provinces. On 9 August 1824, after playing Sir Edward Mortimer (*The Iron Chest* by George Colman the younger), Betty took his final leave of the stage at the Southampton theatre.

As a child performer Betty was an attractive, agile boy, tall for his age (4 feet 6 inches) and with curly flaxen hair. His small features made him appear flat faced. His presence attracted attention, and something of his charisma is captured by John Opie in his portrait of Betty as Young Norval (1804). By the 1812 season, when Betty was in his early twenties, the stoutness that beset him throughout the rest of his life was already in evidence.

At the time of Betty's stage début the 'baby-bubble' (Ann Mathews's term for the phenomenon of the juvenile performers) captivated audiences; Betty's father, together with Hough, used this in promoting the boy. Hough had schooled him to be a professional. After watching Betty's

Achmet, James Boaden wrote: 'He turned himself, like a veteran, to his work—his eye never wandered from the true mark, and though not dark, it was quick and meaning [*sic*]' (*Georgian Era*, 456). William Hazlitt was fascinated by his Norval: 'he seemed almost like some "gay creature of the element", moving about gracefully, with all the flexibility of youth' (W. Hazlitt, *Works*, cd. P. P. Howe, 8.294). Adult roles, however, presented difficulties: a miniature tyrant screaming at towering adults left spectators unmoved. His principal weakness was his lack of vocal power and range, causing him to shriek if strength were required. He found difficulty with blank verse, ignoring its rhythm, which gave all of his speeches a 'tea-table familiarity' (William Godwin's phrase). Some critics faulted the audiences: Leigh Hunt charged them with being 'unmanly' and Thomas Campbell's declaration that the actor was no more than 'a hallucination in the public mind' (Russell, 364) veers towards a charge of mass hysteria. During the 1812 season it was evident the faults of the teenager had become exacerbated in the adult. His vocal limitations induced him to rant, blank verse was beyond him, his features remained flat, and with corpulence grace had deserted him. Watching Betty play Alexander the Great (*The Rival Queens* by Nathaniel Lee), Henry Crabb Robinson described him as a 'fat, fair, ranting, screaming fellow who might much better represent a Persian eunuch than a Macedonian conqueror' (E. Brown, 49).

One of Betty's difficulties was his complacent arrogance. By 1805 Hough had been dismissed, in spite of the general praise for his achievement in creating a boy wonder, and 'Peter Pangloss' reported Betty speaking about help with technical matters: 'Oh, that's nothing … when I am on … I am sure to bring them down; I engross the whole attention of the audience' (Playfair, 130). John Bannister recognized in the actor a lack of application and consequently the impossibility of improvement. Those who early in his career had referred to Betty as the Young Roscius, an allusion to David Garrick, had done the child actor no service. Betty regretted his necessary departure from the London stage, and in 1825 *The Times* reported that he had attempted to commit suicide.

Before 1819 Betty had quietly married Susanna Crow, a Shropshire girl, and in September of that year their only child, Henry Thomas, was born. After his theatrical career had ended Betty lived in London, at Holborn, the Adelphi, and 37 Ampthill Square, Highgate, where he died on 24 August 1874. He was buried in a tomb of his own design in Highgate cemetery.

His son, **Henry Thomas Betty** (1819–1897), was born in London on 29 September 1819. He studied theology, but after two years abandoned this and, with his father's help, prepared to become an actor. He made his first stage appearance at the Hereford theatre on 28 August 1838, playing Achmet (his father's first London role) in *Barbarossa*. The theatre was managed by John Boles Watson III (possibly Watson IV), in whose company Betty continued to perform. He played in various provincial companies until 1843, when he appeared at Edinburgh and Glasgow and then London, making his début at Covent Garden on 28 December 1844. Other London theatres at which he performed were the Pavilion, Queen's, and Olympic, where in 1854 he made his farewell to the stage.

To some extent Betty traded on the family name, reviving the roles his father had played. Nevertheless he was a capable actor, wrote an obituarist in the *Illustrated London News* (27 February 1897), 'of the Old-world "legitimate" type'. During his retirement he continued his theatrical connections as president of the Dramatic and Musical Benevolent Fund, and after his death left £5000 to the General Theatrical Fund and a further sum of the same amount on the death of his widow; the bequest was to be known as Betty's Fund for Poor Actors and Actresses. Betty died at The Betony, Thurlow Park Road, West Dulwich, on 7 February 1897 and was buried at Highgate cemetery.

PAUL RANGER

Sources G. Playfair, *The prodigy* (1967) · [Clarke], 'William Henry West', *The Georgian era: memoirs of the most eminent persons*, 4 (1834), 455–6 · Genest, *Eng. stage* · D. E. Baker, *Biographia dramatica, or, A companion to the playhouse*, rev. I. Reed, new edn, rev. S. Jones, 3 vols. in 4 (1812) · A. Mathews, *Anecdotes of actors* (1844) · J. Doran, *'Their majesties' servants': annals of the English stage*, 2 vols. (1864) · W. C. Oulton, *A history of the theatres of London*, 3 vols. (1818) · *The thespian dictionary, or, Dramatic biography of the present age*, 2nd edn (1805) · J. Boaden, *Memoirs of the life of John Philip Kemble*, 2 vols. (1825) · J. Bisset, ed., *Critical essays on the dramatic excellencies of the young Roscius* (1804) · W. C. Russell, *Representative actors* (c.1875) · *The London theatre, 1811–66: selections from the diary of Henry Crabb Robinson*, ed. E. Brown (1966) · CGPLA Eng. & Wales (1875) · CGPLA Eng. & Wales (1897) [Henry Thomas Betty] · *Memoirs of Mr W. H. W. Betty, the English Roscius: to which is affixed a sketch of the theatrical career of his son, Mr Henry Betty* (1846) · Adams, *Drama* [Henry Thomas Betty] · Boase, *Mod. Eng. biog.* [Henry Thomas Betty] · *ILN* (27 Feb 1897), 277 [obit. of Henry Thomas Betty] · 'Memoir of Mr Henry Betty', *Theatrical Times* (14 Nov 1846), 194 [Henry Thomas Betty] · W. Trewin, *The royal general theatrical fund* (1989) [Henry Thomas Betty]

Likenesses J. Opie, oils, 1804, NPG [*see illus.*] · medal, 1804, Theatre Museum, London · S. De Wilde, pencil, chalk, and watercolour, 1805, BM · S. De Wilde, pencil and chalk, 1805, priv. coll. · J. Northcote, oils, exh. RA 1805?, Petworth House, West Sussex · J. Roach, engraving, 1805, Jerwood Library of the Performing Arts, Greenwich, Mander and Mitchenson collection · R. Cooper, engraving, 1806 (as Captain Flash; after S. De Wilde), BM · G. H. Harlow, chalk drawing, 1810, NPG · W. G. Mason, engraving, 1846 (Henry Thomas Betty as Hamlet), repro. in *Theatrical Times* (14 Nov 1846) · G. Hollis, engraving (Henry Thomas Betty as Faulconbridge), repro. in *Tallis drawing room table-book of theatrical portraits, memoirs and anecdotes*, Tallis John & Co. (1851) · J. Northcote, oils, Royal Shakespeare Memorial Theatre Museum, Stratford upon Avon · J. Opie, oils, second version, Garr. Club · H. Singleton, pencil drawing, BM · prints, BM, NPG

Wealth at death under £35,000: probate, 11 March 1875, CGPLA Eng. & Wales · £56,825 16s. 5d.—Henry Thomas Betty: probate, 11 March 1897, CGPLA Eng. & Wales

Beulan (*fl. c.*1000–*c.*1050), priest, was probably the master (*magister*) of the scriptorium or monastic school responsible for the creation of the recension of the early ninth-century Cambro-Latin *Historia Brittonum* which first attributes its authorship to Nennius and has been followed in this error by later scholars. Internal analysis of this recension suggests that the monastery in question was located in north Wales, possibly on Anglesey; though it was probably not at Llanbeulan (in Llifon commote, Anglesey), which rather was the church of a Peulan (Poulan), not a Beulan. Despite some computistical calculations which might be taken to imply that the recension was drawn up in the early tenth century, most evidence would suggest that this work, and therefore Beulan's *floruit*, should be placed in the first half of the eleventh century. The scribe who drew up the recension under the direction of Beulan was probably called Euben (for Old Welsh Euuen, now Owain). Euben was also the author of two short Latin verses in honour of a fellow cleric Samuel, described therein as the *infans* of Beulan. It is not certain, however, that Samuel was the biological son of Beulan (a fact not impossible for an early medieval Welsh cleric) or simply his spiritual disciple. DAVID E. THORNTON

Sources T. Mommsen, ed., *Chronica minora saec. IV. V. VI. VII.*, 3, MGH Auctores Antiquissimi, 13 (Berlin, 1898) · Nennius, *'British history' and 'The Welsh annals'*, ed. and trans. J. Morris (1980) · D. N. Dumville, *Histories and pseudo-histories of the insular middle ages* (1990)

Beuno [St Beuno] (*d.* **653/659**), holy man, was the most important saint of north Wales, comparable to David in the south. His feast on 21 April is first attested in the twelfth-century Irish martyrologies of Tallaght and of Gorman, which draw on an exemplar of *c*.830. His epithet Casul Sych (Dry Cloak) is first found *c*.1135 in the anonymous *Vita sanctae Wenefredae*, where it is explained by a miracle story. According to the Welsh genealogies his father Bywgi was a great-grandson (or great-great-grandson) of Cadell Ddyrnllug, founder of the royal line of Powys in the time of Vortigern; if reliable, this would imply that Beuno flourished about the late sixth century. His principal church of Clynnog Fawr, or Llanfeuno, Caernarvonshire, was prominent throughout the middle ages, though never a bishop's see. An ancient Book of St Beuno, allegedly written by St Twrog, a disciple of Beuno, was extant at Clynnog in 1594, and was probably the source of the seventh- to twelfth-century charters summarized in Edward IV's confirmation charter granted to Geoffrey Trefnant. According to this, Beuno received Clynnog from Gwyddaint, a cousin of Cadwallon (*d.* 634), king of Gwynedd, 'for the sake of his name being written in St Beuno's Book' (Sims-Williams, 235). This grant is the main criterion for dating Beuno. A Latin *Vita sancti Beunoi*, alluded to *c*.1140 by Robert of Shrewsbury, in his *Vita sanctae Wenefredae*, chapter 20, is not extant, but was probably used *c*.1135 in the anonymous *Vita sanctae Wenefredae*, and was the main source for the vernacular *Buchedd Beuno* in the Book of the Anchorite of Llanddewibrefi of 1346, although the latter also draws on Robert's *Vita* for its account of Beuno and St Gwenfrewi (Winifred). The geographical pattern of events in *Buchedd Beuno* corresponds to the pattern of churches, wells, and so on dedicated to St Beuno or saints associated with him; both patterns may reflect the territorial interests and spiritual ties of the early community of Clynnog rather than historical fact.

The saint was born in Powys at 'Banhenic' on the River Severn, where he later built a church and planted an oak (*derwen*); identifications of 'Banhenic' have included Llanymynech, which is on the Vyrnwy however, and Trederwen Feibion Gwnwas, both in Montgomeryshire. Beuno was educated in Caer-went by 'Tangusius' (probably St Tatheus), and the local king, Ynyr Gwent, gave him land in Ewias (Llanveynoe, Herefordshire). After founding a church on his patrimony at 'Banhenic', Beuno went to Mawn, son of Brochfael, who gave him Berri(e)w. Prophesying the Anglo-Saxon conquest of the area Beuno then retreated to Meifod, to stay briefly with Tysilio (St Tysilio), before approaching Tysilio's brother, King Cynan ap Brochfael, who gave him Gwyddelwern, 'the place which got its name from the Irishman [Lorcán] whom Beuno raised from the dead there' (*Vitae sanctorum Britanniae et genealogiae*, 17). Later, according to the anonymous *Vita sanctae Wenefredae* as well as *Buchedd Beuno*, Beuno was driven out by the sons of Selyf ap Cynan ap Brochfael (*d.* 616), and, cursing their dynasty, he transferred his allegiance to their cousin, Tyfid ab Eiludd ap Cynan, who granted him land at the place which was later named Ffynnon Wenfrewi (Holywell, Flintshire) after Gwenfrewi, the daughter of Tyfid whom Beuno revived after her decapitation by Caradog ab Alawg. Cadfan, the historical king of Gwynedd, is introduced as a witness to this miracle and a benefactor of St Beuno. After Cadfan's death his son Cadwallon (*d.* 634) gave Beuno stolen land, at Gwredog, Caernarvonshire, and was duly cursed. Cadwallon's cousin Gwyddaint compensated the saint with the gift of Clynnog, where Beuno performed many miracles, such as the resurrection of Digiwg daughter of Ynyr Gwent. (Her brother Iddon is the grantor of charters of about the early seventh century in the Book of Llandaff.) The *Buchedd* ends with Beuno's holy death at Clynnog on Low Sunday, omitting the posthumous miracles to which Robert of Shrewsbury alludes. In the Roman Calendar Low Sunday fell on 21 April only once in the period 597–670, in 659, but in the 'Celtic' eighty-four-year cycle it so fell in 653 as well, which is the slightly more likely year for Beuno's death.

The origins of Clynnog church may go back to a seventh-century church centred on his grave, under the present Eglwys y Bedd (Church of the Grave). Folklore about Beuno's two miraculous bodies—one for Clynnog and the other for south Wales—was recorded by John Ray in 1662. By the nineteenth century Eben Fardd (Ebenezer Thomas) recorded three bodies—one for Clynnog, one for Nefyn, and one for 'somewhere else' (Thomas, 44–5), sometimes identified as Bardsey. A mass of material on Beuno's cult survives, including a report printed by Hearne on 'Superstitious practises prevailing in Wales in the year 1589', by a local Protestant informer called 'Mr Price' (the name is given in state papers). Beuno is represented in stained glass at Penmorfa, Caernarvonshire, and in a fourteenth-century stone pulpit at Shrewsbury Abbey. PATRICK SIMS-WILLIAMS

Sources P. C. Bartrum, ed., *Early Welsh genealogical tracts* (1966) · P. Sims-Williams, 'Edward IV's confirmation charter for Clynnog Fawr', *Recognitions: essays presented to Edmund Fryde*, ed. C. Richmond and I. Harvey (1996), 229–41 · Robert of Shrewsbury and others,

'Vitae S. Wenefredae', *Acta sanctorum: November*, 1 (Paris, 1887), 691–759 · A. W. Wade-Evans, ed., 'Hystoria o uuched Beuno', *Vitae sanctorum Britanniae et genealogiae* (1944), 16–22 · S. Baring-Gould and J. Fisher, *The lives of the British saints*, Honourable Society of Cymmrodorion, Cymmrodorion Record Series, 1 (1907) · A. W. Wade-Evans, 'Beuno Sant', *Archaeologia Cambrensis*, 85 (1930), 315–41 · G. Scott, ed., *Select remains of the learned John Ray* (1760) · E. T. [E. Thomas], 'Clynnog Fawr yn Arfon', *Y Gwladgarwr*, 6 (1838), 40–45 · *CSP dom.*, 1581–90, 603 · 'Superstitious practices prevailing in Wales in the year 1589', *Joannis Lelandi antiquarii de rebus Britannicis collectanea*, ed. T. Hearne, [3rd edn], 2 (1774), 648–50 · P. Ó Riain, 'The Tallaght martyrologies redated', *Cambridge Medieval Celtic Studies*, 20 (1990), 21–38 · D. J. O'Connell, 'Easter cycles in the early Irish church', *Journal of the Royal Society of Antiquaries of Ireland*, 7th ser., 6 (1936), 67–106 · D. McCarthy and D. Ó Cróinín, 'The "lost" Irish 84-year Easter table rediscovered', *Peritia*, 6–7 (1987–8), 227–42 · E. G. Bowen, *The settlements of the Celtic saints in Wales*, 2nd edn (1956) · F. Jones, *The holy wells of Wales* (1954) · E. R. Henken, *Traditions of the Welsh saints* (1987)

Likenesses stone statue, 14th cent., Shrewsbury Abbey, Shropshire, pulpit · stained glass, Penmorfa church, Caernarvonshire

Bevan, Aneurin [Nye] (1897–1960), politician, was born on 15 November 1897 at 32 Charles Street, Tredegar, in the Sirhowy valley, Monmouthshire, the sixth of the ten children of David Bevan, collier, and his wife, Phoebe, daughter of John Prothero, colliery blacksmith. Two of Bevan's five brothers did not survive infancy; a third, the family's first-born, had died at the age of eight, and a much loved younger sister died in her teenage years. These were some of the hard and established facts of the industrial revolution, by which, Bevan later wrote, 'we were surrounded'. What also circumscribed the family was the economic and social power of the Tredegar Iron and Coal Company, for which all of the male members of his family (and two-thirds of the adult males of Tredegar, population 25,000 and a company town in every sense as he grew up there) worked underground. The key to Bevan's life and his political direction lies within this communal and collective framework rather than in any individual biographical differences between himself and the people of whom he sought to be truly representative.

Bevan in south Wales: the early years Bevan's generation, in particular, was formed both by the dynamic economic expansion of the south Wales coalfield, with all its attendant social possibilities, before the First World War and by the post-war decline of the steam coal export trade, which thwarted that potential for cultural change which some had sensed all around them. When David Bevan died from pneumoconiosis in his favourite son's arms in 1925, he was asking for the *Daily Herald* and news of John Wheatley, socialist minister responsible for housing in the first Labour government of 1923–4, but his own youthful world had been one of liberal politics, Baptist religion, and that Welsh-language culture which had permeated the respectable working class of late Victorian times. At the end he was following his son, whose secular socialism broke with all those things. At home the boy, quickly and everlastingly known as Nye, was in thrall, as were all the family, to his formidable and competent mother—homemaker and dressmaker supreme—whom, in his sturdy

Aneurin Bevan (1897–1960), by Sir Cecil Beaton, 1940

frame and practical manner, he resembled. At school (Sirhowy elementary), an intense stammer and an unsympathetic schoolmaster ensured that his latent intellectual gifts were stifled and, barely fourteen, he left in 1911 to join his father and brother in the local colliery.

Bevan found himself on a fast learning curve. In these years before 1914 south Wales was in turmoil. Serious rioting had broken out in the densely populated central coalfield in 1910 as strikes led to social disturbance, and in 1911 Tredegar itself had seen attacks, with some anti-Jewish overtones, on shopkeepers. Bevan began to listen to those around him who were trying to make sense of the connecting elements in the surrounding chaos. His early literary taste for romance and adventure led him to the Tredegar Workmen's Institute and the discovery of an author such as Jack London who combined the romantic with the political; but his formative education was undertaken by a local Independent Labour Party (ILP) enthusiast Walter Conway, who also worked with him to eradicate his stammer in public speaking, and by Sydney Jones, a slightly older man based further down the Sirhowy valley at Blackwood, who took weekly social science classes, based on the Central Labour College's teaching, which Bevan assiduously attended. The philosophy he imbibed was an eclectic mix of Marxist economic theory, German monism via Dietzgen, workers' control as 'syndicalism' (or 'industrial unionism' in its Welsh guise), and a materialist conception of history. In the circumstances of his one-industry time and place, it served as both illumination and a practical way forward, provided there was also a mass union membership educated for direct action. By

1916 Bevan, a skilled collier, had become chairman of his local lodge which, in turn, was combining with other lodges in wartime protests against inadequate provision of affordable housing and food, in which he proved prominent. A comb-out of the pits for conscripts saw Bevan ordered before a tribunal for refusing his military call-up: he produced a medical certificate for nystagmus (an eye disease suffered by miners) and the case was dismissed.

Bevan was by now active in anti-war campaigns across south Wales, and already a delegate to the conferences of the South Wales Miners' Federation (SWMF) in Cardiff. That body, along with the National Union of Railwaymen, financed the Central Labour College in London, to which selected men were dispatched. His own attendance there, from 1919 to 1921, was scarcely that of a model student, but neither the rigid orthodoxies of the lecturing nor the constraints on his time (better spent, he felt, on the sights, sounds, and experiences of the capital than on the drummed-in pages of *Kapital*) were in line with the impatient, confident personality which his experiences had formed. He could not wait to return to Tredegar and effective action.

Bevan reflected in his quasi-autobiographical credo, *In Place of Fear* (1952), that in the post-war crisis the industrial workers of Britain, and especially the miners whose national strike of 1919 was averted by a royal commission whose majority report subsequently advocated nationalization of the mines, had been duped and defeated by the government at the behest of a capitalist class. This defeat was complete before 1921 had ended. For Bevan the general strike and miners' lock-out of 1926 was a tragic replay of a fight already lost. In his own life at the time he had plenty of opportunity to reflect on how late, and so how ineffective, direct action had been. In effect, his own leadership attributes were now used to agitate on behalf of the unemployed in whose ranks he found himself: there was some intermittent work as a labourer for the council; briefly, until one and then another pit closed, as a checkweighman on the men's behalf; and, from early 1926, paid work as a disputes agent for the local miners. He learned, with some bitterness, of the loss of benefit attendant on a sister's meagre income entering the household and saw, with even more bitterness, the social haemorrhaging of coalfield communities through migration. His own reputation, as an effective organizer and distinctive platform speaker, grew, especially during the long dispute of 1926 when he attended and spoke as a delegate at national conferences of the Miners' Federation of Great Britain. Towards the end of that desperate year, with appalling conditions of life in south Wales and the imminent destruction of the SWMF, the collective organization to which he had devoted most of his time and hopes, he was one of those who urged a negotiated return to work. It was a stance which marked him out from his close ally and contemporary Arthur Horner, the communist leader from the Rhondda who became president of the SWMF in 1936 and general secretary of the National Union of Mineworkers (NUM) in 1946. It has led some to the view that it was from this point on that Bevan put direct-action tactics

behind his youthful self in favour of electoral politics. The reality is rather that he spurned pre-ordained defeat in 1926 while never rejecting a twin-track route to the empowerment of the working class.

Thus, as early as 1922 Bevan had stood for and won a seat as a Labour councillor on the 'independent'-run Tredegar urban district council. Although there was not a Labour majority on this council until 1928, the year in which he was returned as a county councillor from the town for Monmouthshire, his activities through the 1920s were vigorously directed to raising political consciousness, through all manner of non-political ancillary activities, in order to root and sustain the Labour Party in Tredegar's locality. His approach to this—ranging from arguments for superior municipal housing and open public spaces, parks, and leisure activities to defence of the miners' own pre-war Tredegar Medical Aid Society and denunciation of the bureaucratic grip of the poor-law commissioners ('a new race of robbers') who replaced the local, and too sympathetic, board of guardians—was wide-ranging and imaginative. Much of the generous, expansive vision of the later Labour minister in power is directly traceable to the powerless, frustrated Labour councillor of these years. Some of his frustration, early and late, was with what he consistently regarded as an insufficiently radical Labour Party. However, at no time, despite his close personal and even philosophical links, did he consider joining the Communist Party which, though strongly supported in parts of south Wales, was not a force on his own patch and which, besides, he considered a national political cul-de-sac. Other traditional openings for young aspirants to political influence were increasingly closed as the SWMF shed members and official positions in the deepening economic crisis that turned south Wales into a region of long-term, mass unemployment until the Second World War. In 1929 the opportunity came, not entirely fortuitously, to stand for parliament in the Ebbw Vale constituency, which also embraced Rhymni and Tredegar.

Evan Davies, a miner's agent of the old school, had held the seat since 1920. His increasingly dilatory behaviour, allied to a political stance so moderate as to be deferential, infuriated the young turks of Tredegar, marshalled as they had been by Bevan into a debating society-cum-cell, the Query Club. When one of the quizzers, the diminutive and mischievous Archie Lush, became Davies's agent in 1927, the criticism mounted from within. Lush persuaded the SWMF's executive council to take the unusual step of balloting the local miners' lodges in the district as to which candidate should be preferred in the forthcoming election. Bevan topped the list on all three ballots held as others fell out and, as the miners' nominee, was adopted by the divisional Labour Party. The general election was called a month later and he entered parliament, aged thirty-two, in May 1929 as the member for Ebbw Vale.

The people's tribune as MP From this point Archie Lush, Bevan's closest friend, acted as his eyes and ears in the constituency. Bevan was freed to make his impact on the wider stage. As an untried back-bencher in Ramsay MacDonald's second Labour government (1929–31) that would not be easy, but Bevan had physical presence—almost 6 feet, with open blue-grey eyes and a shock of black hair—to match a debater's keen wit and a passionate anger scarcely banked down by the proprieties of the House of Commons, whose master, within a decade, he would become. It proved to be the natural forum for his forensic style and the scathing logic he deployed against opponents. Here, more than anywhere, Bevan's crafted performances gave the lie to accusations of demagoguery. He was, on the contrary, noticed immediately by the hallmark of his speeches: thoughtfulness brought to the point of originality by sincerity. He was not only noticed but taken up by talent spotters such as Lord Beaverbrook, whose entourage was as wide as it was unlikely, and by intellectuals in the party such as John Strachey, who were as uneasy as he was with MacDonald's consensual drift. His reputation, in the house, was made by full-fronted attacks on figures as major as his fellow countryman Lloyd George and, throughout the decade, by reminding the Commons of the unresolved condition of the unemployed in the so-called 'special areas'. At Westminster he cut a rather too raffish figure in the eyes of staider MPs. He clearly delighted in mixing with writers, actors, and journalists amid a metropolitan whirl. Bevan's social tastes and, soon, relatively high living, raised eyebrows and elicited quips (a 'Bollinger Bolshevik', a 'ritzy Robespierre', opined a not unfriendly Brendan Bracken, Churchill's close adviser). Yet his own self-assurance, allied to an unshakeable set of political principles and firm practice, left him as immune to these barbs as to the later, angrier comparisons with Hitler (from Gaitskell) and references to the 'Tito from Tonypandy', Churchill's wartime 'squalid nuisance'. Indeed, it was Bevan's very ability to combine social self-confidence with an abiding contempt for existing social structures which made him so dangerous an opponent in the cut and thrust of parliamentary debate: he oozed triumphalism, and he was, whenever the circumstance threatened to translate it into reality, hated more deeply for this by his political opponents than any other figure in mainstream politics in the twentieth century.

For Bevan, relations with his own party were often equally fraught. As MacDonald's Labour government floundered by 1931 into a shape-shifting National Government (the politics of coalition leads to 'the knacker's yard', thought Bevan) he more than flirted with the dynamism of Oswald Mosley's New Party and, by 1933, though Mosley's extra-parliamentary route to the far right had been quickly detected and rejected, Bevan was, in a ravaged south Wales, advocating workers' freedom groups as a kind of militia. If in volatile times this activity was not divorced from a wider context of monster demonstrations, stay-down strikes, and direct clashes with a confrontational police force, it was none the less typical of his impatience with the form of intra-parliamentary politics. As the international crisis deepened Bevan, along with other Labour Party left-wingers, urged an interventionist stance, as in the Spanish Civil War which he visited at first hand in 1938, on both his own party leadership and Neville Chamberlain's government. He was prominent in 1937 in the unity campaign, pulling together allies to the left, including even the Communist Party, as the Socialist League under the leadership of Sir Stafford Cripps ventured to break the mould of party stultification. That ended, with the league's dissolution, when Labour's national executive committee (NEC) forbade platform-sharing with communists; then, in early 1939, as Europe lurched towards war, the groundswell for a popular front proved irresistible to the grass roots but not to the party leadership. Cripps, from within the NEC but intransigent on these issues, was formally expelled from the party along with others, including one of his chief acolytes, Nye Bevan.

In all of this Bevan, whose membership was restored after a formal undertaking by him in December 1939, was a reluctant, if distinctly unruly, rebel. His contention was twofold: that the Labour Party required the invigoration of extra-parliamentary agitation to give it the purpose and courage it so singularly lacked as an opposition, but that, by historical circumstance, it was the chosen instrument of the British working class and, as such, alone capable of delivering any lasting change in the distribution of power. He resolutely, in the 1930s as in the 1950s, defended the right to argue, on an organized basis, for constitutional change within the party, but never willingly left it. Hence, the scorn with which he treated the decision of Jennie Lee to cling to the ILP when that founding section of the Labour Party defected, in righteous purity, in 1932.

His life with Jennie Lee Jennie *Lee (1904–1988) had entered the House of Commons in the same year as Bevan, but through an earlier by-election, in 1929, as the ILP member for North Lanark. Her gender, handsome looks, and fiery oratory made her a much better known figure in the public eye than Bevan was in those early years. They became friends rather than close confidants, and with more wariness on her part than his. Besides, she was deeply in love and soon caught up in a passionate affair with a man twenty years her senior, the influential Labour MP Frank Wise, whose marriage just about accommodated their open relationship. When Frank Wise died suddenly in 1933, Jennie and Nye pulled together politically as well as emotionally, quickly grew closer, and began to live together. Both railed against social conventions and both, but especially Jennie, insisted on maintaining freedom, sexual and professional, outside any partnership. None the less, and with this agreed, they married in 1934. Jennie Lee did indeed pursue a full-hearted career: as a journalist after the loss of her seat in 1935, and again, after the Second World War, as Labour MP for Cannock from 1945 to 1970. There is no doubt, though, that in the 1940s she increasingly recognized the scale of Bevan's capabilities and that she worked, with a growing number of disciples, notably the young journalist and MP in the 1945 intake Michael Foot, to help realize through his genius the ambitions they all shared. Bevan, initially somewhat reluctantly, accepted that there would be no children born to the marriage. Theirs was, in all other respects, and in the various lively homes they made and shared in London and in the country, a love affair that deepened and a significant alliance.

The wartime critic For his conduct as an irrepressible and much maligned critic during the war, Bevan needed all the support he could find. It was now that his mark was truly made as a politician of national stature. It was Bevan's distinction to use the freedom of the back benches to uphold parliament's right to question the executive even when a wartime coalition cabinet enjoyed widespread popular support as a government of national unity. This, he argued, was the essence of democracy. The case was made weekly in *Tribune*, the paper to which he had contributed anonymously since 1937 and which, from 1941 to 1945, he edited. George Orwell, literary editor and columnist from 1943, affirmed the 'progressive and humane' stance of the paper as an unusual and principled one. Bevan personalized the principle by now pitting himself against both the rotundities of Churchill's rhetoric and the allegedly expert direction of the war. On the latter he urged greater energy in prosecuting any advantage that occurred and was an early advocate of a second front as soon as the Soviet Union entered the war in June 1941. He depicted Churchill as an orator trapped by the traditions and the interests of the past, incapable of envisaging or desiring a post-war settlement not carved up by the great powers. He put himself forward as a tribune representative of 'the hope and aspirations for the future' on both domestic and international fronts. Nor did he confine his critique to overt Conservatism; in 1944 when regulation 1AA, to be installed by Ernest Bevin as wartime minister of labour, sharply restricted the individual's right to strike, he launched a fierce polemic against both the impracticality of the measure and its sinister precedent for a society in which working-class liberties had so largely derived from such freedom of action.

The anger directed against Bevan came, in large measure, from those in his own party whose trade union affiliation was affronted by his defence of the 'robust, dignified' rank and file against the 'cynical, irresponsible trade union official'. His libertarian stance was never clearer—'I do not represent the big bosses at the top', he told the Commons on 28 April 1944, 'I represent the people at the bottom, the individual men and women … this Regulation is the enfranchisement of the corporate Society and the disfranchisement of the individual' (*Hansard 5C*, vol. 399, col. 1072). Bevan led the parliamentary revolt, substantial when dissidents and abstainers from within the Labour Party were added together, and again faced up to calls for his expulsion. Instead, with gritted teeth the NEC required a written promise to toe the party line in future. He gave it, and by the end of that climactic year he had for the first time been elected by the constituency section of the party to the NEC, Labour's governing body. When he had been elected in 1928 to the Monmouthshire county council the *Western Mail* had labelled him in its report as a 'Socialist critic of Socialists' (Foot, 1.83). The sentiment was just as applicable in 1944; in the sixteen years of travail and achievement which now lay before

him Bevan unrelentingly offered up the constructive critique he felt his party needed and the British working class demanded.

Bevan threw himself into the general election of July 1945 with an optimistic conviction of victory few senior members of his party shared. He was vindicated by the landslide return of Clement Attlee's administration and by the offer, surprising to many, of a cabinet post as minister of health and housing. He joined the cabinet as not only its youngest member but also its most intriguing appointment.

Government minister to resignation Bevan's tenure of this office—over five years as it turned out—would not be considered a failure even if his record was judged on housing alone. At a time of considerable shortage of building materials and burdened by unwieldy layers of administrative and procedural responsibilities, Bevan none the less oversaw the building of over 1 million permanent homes down to 1950. Crucially, they were homes built to high standards—inside lavatories, three bedrooms, gardens—which neither his successor nor the Conservative government, which built more and more quickly, chose to maintain. Yet for Bevan, 'a rabbit-warren accommodation leads to a rabbit-warren mind' (Foot, 1.53), as he said in 1925. It was axiomatic that the first Labour government with a public-housing policy to inaugurate since John Wheatley in the 1920s should fulfil it with regard 'to the artistic and aesthetic aspect' of workers' housing, which Bevan had stressed as a young councillor in the even more benighted 1920s.

Relative success as a housing minister was, of course, eclipsed by the central achievement of Bevan's career—an achievement on which his reputation, then and now, squarely rests—the creation of the National Health Service (NHS). As minister of health he inherited a ramshackle structure of health care—notably a mixed provision of voluntary and municipal or public hospitals administered by literally hundreds of separate local authorities—and a set of vague proposals emanating from his wartime predecessor, Henry Willink, which failed to address the role of the general practitioner in any unified service. Bevan gripped the problem from the outset. By a combination of intellectual audacity and cautious practice he drove his proposals through cabinet by the end of the year, published his National Health Service Bill with accompanying white paper in March 1946, and saw the NHS legislation become law on 6 November 1946. It would be another two years before the NHS was fully instituted, on 5 July 1948, and that intervening period revealed just how radical the minister was being and just how virulent was the opposition he would arouse.

In essence Bevan proposed to nationalize the entire hospital service under a system of regional hospital boards and to abolish the sale and purchase of medical practices, with GPs becoming, in part, salaried employees of the state. The administrative structure devised to implement it was certainly complex, since various local government and professional interests needed to be assuaged by the plan, but the concept of a national service underlined

Bevan's determination to ensure universal access to first-class care, free at the point of delivery, not a minimum subsistence level of care unevenly distributed. Costs would be met by general taxation. 'Bevan's model', wrote Charles Webster, the official historian of the NHS, 'was … the private wing of the voluntary hospital rather than the poor law infirmary' (*The National Health Service: a Political History*, 1998, 24).

The major stumbling block to full implementation of the plan was the medical profession itself. The British Medical Association fought a bitter rearguard action and, as late as February 1948, a plebiscite of their members showed an 8 to 1 majority in favour of boycotting the entire scheme. Bevan railed, privately and publicly, against their short-sighted self-interest. He also moved to disrupt any overall medical coalition by a sequence of concessions and compromises. Consultants, influential in their potential role as peacemakers within the profession, were allowed, on full- or part-time contracts, to engage in private practice and to use the old voluntary pay-bed system within the new NHS, so non-co-operation from that quarter was averted. Bevan's much quoted acerbic comment 'I stuffed their mouths with gold' was, however, made in 1955 or 1956 (C. Webster, ed., *Aneurin Bevan on the National Health Service*, 1991, 218–22). In so far as GPs were concerned Bevan refused to budge over ending the sale and purchase of practices but, along with a number of minor compromises over conditions of service, he yielded over the small element of salaried remuneration with the further promise of legislating to rule out the future introduction of a salaried service. Arguably these concessions, effectively ending any significant opposition to the proposals, killed off any hopes of a fully socialist NHS (health centres staffed by salaried doctors and run by locally elected authorities) as proposed by the Socialist Medical Association. Unarguably, the NHS was warmly welcomed by the British public—Bevan could announce on its launch day that almost 94 per cent of the population had already enrolled—for whom it rapidly became a touchstone of national identity. Bevan had demonstrated creative political skills as a minister and accomplished practice as an administrator. His star within the cabinet was clearly an ascendant one.

Bevan chose this very moment to make the most notorious, possibly most damaging, speech of his career. At a time when Attlee urged his ministers, in general, to present the foundations of the welfare state as an act of national reconciliation, Aneurin Bevan, on 4 July 1948, at Belle Vue, Manchester, claimed the reforms as the conscious rebuttal of a pre-war Britain and its condemnation of 'millions of first class people to semi-starvation'. It was 'the Tory Party that inflicted those bitter experiences … [and] … so far as I am concerned they are lower than vermin' (Foot, 2.238). From now on, the 'Minister for Disease', as Churchill labelled him (ibid., 1.242), subjected to physical and verbal abuse by tories, was also seen as uncontrollable by key elements within his own party. Notwithstanding the probable spontaneity of the phraseology, both factions were instinctively right in thinking that Bevan not

only meant to sound irreconcilable but also wished to serve notice that the Labour government, beyond the administration of things, should move to shift the 'social psychology' of British political culture once and for all. He had talked in 1945 of a quarter of a century of Labour government and 'the complete political extinction of the Tory Party'. The year 1948 was, in every sense, the high-water mark of his desire and his delivery.

Although Bevan never repudiated any of the work of the two Attlee governments in which he served, his acceptance of collective responsibility scarcely hid a growing unease with aspects of its foreign policy (too subservient to American global interest; insufficiently Zionist) and its nervous, increasingly orthodox, economic policy. This stiffened as the balance of payments crisis and the 'dollar gap' led to financial austerity and, in 1949, devaluation. The latter was particularly promoted by Hugh Gaitskell, minister of fuel and power and not yet in the cabinet. Bevan supported the policy as inevitable. Its unstated implications, public expenditure cuts, were to be the price to pay. Their extent and their focus were what required resolution. When Cripps as chancellor of the exchequer had raised in 1949 the prospect of prescription charges in the NHS Bevan had swallowed that principle, though the point was deferred. Now, after Labour's victory with a reduced majority in the general election of February 1950, issues of principle threatened to destroy Labour's unity. In this dispute, down to his resignation from the government in April 1951, Bevan has, too often, been painted as the sole instigator and perpetuator of such disunity.

Now that the cabinet minutes have been scrutinized by historians it is not a view which is sustainable, though it is indeed accurate to see Bevan, from early 1950, as being at odds with the way in which the domestic priorities of his government were being translated into the American language of global containment and military rearmament. His own translation, by Attlee in January 1951, to the Ministry of Labour (with health demoted to a non-cabinet office) scarcely calmed his misgivings. Now, on a regular basis, he had to confront the realignment of manpower attendant on quickening rearmament. Neither wage restraint nor threatening dock workers for illegal strikes sat easily with him, but he complied as a government minister; what stretched his loyalty to incredulity was the manner in which the outbreak of the Korean War (June 1950) led, by August, when his first open disavowal is recorded, to a rearmament programme whose scale menaced the social and welfare capacities of the administration. His erstwhile ally, Sir Stafford Cripps, had retired on grounds of ill health in October 1950 and Hugh Gaitskell, Bevan's nemesis in this as in much else, was catapulted into the cabinet as chancellor of the exchequer. Bevan may have harboured vague hopes for the job, though more so for the foreign secretaryship which went to Herbert Morrison in March 1951, and certainly, with the steady loss of the government's elder statesmen, was being urged by Jennie Lee and Michael Foot to 'lead the left' as a precursor to leading, one day soon, the entire movement. Steadily and loyally, however, his critique was neither petty nor personal: it was, in a nutshell, that Gaitskell, demanding defence expenditure of £4700 million over three years, was miscalculating both what was strictly possible and what was socially desirable. Besides, the policy had been impelled not by any impeccable economic logic but by Attlee's visit to President Truman in December 1950 when Britain, in Bevan's cutting phrase, allowed itself 'to be dragged … behind the wheels of American diplomacy' (Foot, 2.335).

Bevan's objections, then, were twofold—he did not believe that the ideological war against communism, whose totalitarian regimes he loathed, was best fought by military posturing under an American banner; and he, specifically, saw no logic in levering money out of the NHS by imposing charges on spectacles and dentures (both quite symbolic appliances to an inter-war working class deprived of both) when the finance to be raised was only £23 million in a full year. If necessary the NHS budget, rising way beyond initial expectations but, as the Conservative government's Guillebaud committee of 1955 demonstrated, actually remarkably efficient value for money, could be capped and 'efficiencies' found within it. Gaitskell, however, pressed relentlessly on. The budget he wished to present would impose those particular charges. He felt the cabinet's authority, and most certainly his own (for he too threatened resignation), was at stake. Attlee, not for the first time, let matters drift. After the budget had gone before the house, Bevan brooded for two weeks—so intense was his inner battle between not splitting the government and, as he saw it, saving its soul—and then, in April 1951, with two junior colleagues, Harold Wilson and John Freeman, he resigned.

Bevan and the Bevanites In the general election of October 1951 Labour increased its popular vote by over a million, but, with the Liberals fielding many fewer candidates in the second general election within eighteen months, the Conservatives won a majority of seats. Within the year Gaitskell's unrealistic budget—'a political and economic disaster' in the words of that Labour government's historian, Kenneth O. Morgan (Morgan, 456)—had been overturned by a Conservative Party whose calculations on actually deliverable defence expenditure matched Bevan's own. Bevan's support within the Labour Party now rested firmly in the country and in the constituency sections; to the official hierarchy and to the trade unions, whose finance and block votes at party conferences dictated that hierarchy's personnel and policies, he was anathema. Bevanism was born in the throes of a civil war. In 1951 he headed the list of NEC members voted on by the constituency section of the party.

Despite the affiliation of close associates to the 'Keep Left' group formed during his tenure of office and the sharp criticisms mounted of Attlee's governments in *Tribune*, Bevan had, necessarily, kept himself aloof from any alternative leadership (when Cripps had attempted a coup against Attlee in 1947 Bevan was distinctly not interested in any such move). Now, with five supporters voted onto the NEC in 1952 and the official opposition supine, as he

felt, in the growing crisis of the cold war, he had no compunction about allowing a semi-organized group (the Bevanites) to coalesce, via public pronouncements and parliamentary caucus, around his name. The Labour Party's standing orders had explicitly banned any unofficial groups inside the party after the bitter 1952 conference. By dint of personality, not just his own, and disinclination, more clearly his than others, this faction never properly became a 'party-within-a-party', but its constant refusal to toe a party line made it seem definitively so to those who now saw the expulsion of Bevan as the antidote to chronic party disunity. His own role, a permanent minority within the shadow cabinet to which he had been elected in 1952, was to serve as a barometer of these discontents: in 1954 his dissociation, in the house, from Attlee's support of the South East Asia Treaty Organisation led to rebuke and resignation. Dissent from the Labour Party's foreign policy line rumbled on: the Bevanites stood out against German rearmament, and in 1955 it was another international matter which came close to causing a final breach.

This time Bevan appeared to contradict and humiliate Attlee directly in a Commons debate. Labour had moved an official amendment to the Conservative government's endorsement of the manufacture of the H-bomb and its retaliatory use even against conventional attack. The tinkering amendment, however, challenged neither assumption directly. Bevan asked publicly for Attlee's clarification over weapons' use. He did not get it, and so abstained. Gaitskell and Morrison, though not Attlee, now urged his full expulsion as a party member on the Parliamentary Labour Party (PLP), the shadow cabinet, and the NEC. Bevan narrowly survived. More importantly he offered a personal apology to Attlee. His jousting within the party was coming to an end. Perhaps he was wearying of failure, since his lifelong philosophy that ideals without power was not politics was becoming self-fulfilling.

Thus, in 1954 Bevan had left the NEC to challenge for the vacant treasurership of the Labour Party, a largely symbolic but important party post. He knew he would not win against Gaitskell, behind whom the right-wing votes of the Transport and General Workers' Union and the Municipal and General Workers' Union were rallied (he actually won NUM support in 1956), but, decades ahead of his time, was repudiating the 'irresponsible group of trade union bureaucrats' who were deciding 'the policy of the Labour Party' (Foot, 2.439–40). He was adamant, too, that 'I cannot possibly allow it to be thought that Gaitskell, who is a product of the public school …, is the natural representative of the industrial workers of Great Britain' (Jones, 'Rift and Conflict', 34). Natural, or not, within the existing framework, Gaitskell not only won there, he scooped the leadership after Labour lost its second election in a row in 1955 and Attlee retired. Gaitskell won an absolute majority of the PLP on the first ballot (157 votes) with Bevan (70) and Morrison (40) left behind.

Recrimination and reconciliation Any effective challenge to Gaitskell was now doomed. Bevan continued to make the case for a greater, not lesser, socialist dimension within the party, alongside a perennial call for education and consciousness-raising. He seemed also to accept that this was, again, a minority position to take. His task was to use his stature to see that it was not marginalized. He did not contest the leadership in 1956 and, with Gaitskell, mounted a telling campaign inside and outside parliament against Eden's collusive Suez adventure. Inside the shadow cabinet he was first given responsibility for colonial affairs and then for foreign affairs. Observers claimed to notice a greater thoughtfulness, a mellowing tinge, in his words and deeds. In 1957, after defeating George Brown, he became, at last, party treasurer. Abroad, his presence and influence was eagerly sought by a galaxy of international statesmen including Mendes France, Nenni, and Nehru. Many of these visited him at his last, delightful home (Asheridge Farm, Buckinghamshire), where a slightly unexpectedly bucolic Bevan beamed and, as ever, waxed eloquent ('star-tapping', he called it) on the literary, musical, and artistic tastes he had somehow, as if by osmosis in his packed life, bred into his bone. Always there would be, via a Marx whose materialism he never rejected, passing reference to the romantic libertarian, the Uruguayan Jose Rodo, whose *Motives of Proteus* (1929) he had long made his own. Part of his immense charm was his ability, indeed eagerness, to slough off pursuit of political trivia in the cause of good food, wine, and conversation. For many close acquaintances he was, in these moods, a boon companion.

Geniality was soured by the worst kind of quarrel, a family affair. In hindsight it was long coming. Bevan had always been impatient with the left's reluctance to become complicit with power-broking. He had sat in a cabinet that had approved British manufacture of the atomic bomb; he did not disapprove of similar British involvement in the hydrogen bomb. His concern was with British influence at four-power talks to secure multilateral nuclear disarmament. So, despite overlapping ambiguities of expression and intent, he was never a unilateral disarmer and, therefore, was isolated from an increasingly significant trend within the party and the wider labour movement. It all came to a head at the Brighton conference of 1957 when, speaking on behalf of the executive, he famously insisted that those who wished unilaterally to renounce the bomb, without consultation with allies or others, would send a British foreign secretary 'naked into the Conference Chamber' (Foot, 2.574). He was taken to mean 'naked' as 'disarmed'. In fact, he clearly meant 'naked' as having no power to affect the dealings of others. That was 'statesmanship'. The rest was, and his words flayed the skin of those who adored him but disagreed with him on this, 'an emotional spasm' (ibid., 2.575).

Jennie Lee clung to the view that his decline and fatal illness had their terrible origins in the bitterness of the rift here made. Michael Foot, who succeeded Bevan as MP for Ebbw Vale, was not immune from her wrath. Bevan himself, as in the 1959 general election, seemed to go out of his way to act as healer and reconciler, still adamant to the end that only the Labour Party, defeated for a third time in a decade, could rescue Britain from the vulgarity of a 'meretricious society'. To this end, despite private misgivings which were never allayed, he unstintingly supported Gaitskell's leadership and official party policy in these last years. At the party's inquest, in Blackpool in October 1959, he made one of his last great speeches, still invoking 'the language of priorities' as 'the religion of socialism' and still hammering home the message that 'the argument is about power … because only by the possession of power can you get the priorities correct' (Foot, 2.645). He was elected, unopposed, as deputy leader and treasurer of the party.

The mind still flared, but even to the most casual eye Bevan's body was betraying him. An exploratory operation at the end of December 1959 revealed a malignant cancer in the stomach. He returned to Asheridge, ostensibly to recuperate. The full truth was kept from him. On several occasions he rallied and talked of a vigorous re-entry into public life, but on 6 July 1960, at Asheridge Farm, he finally succumbed and died; his ashes were scattered above Tredegar.

His reputation Bevan's death established, at once, that widespread affection and respect for his life had caused a real sense of public grief. Press obituaries and a well-attended service in Westminster Abbey appeared to give him the final accolades of respectability and responsibility. Yet in his life itself nothing could have seemed less likely or less welcome. Aneurin Bevan was that rare being, a practical politician with a philosophy for his actions beyond the minutiae of political activity, which was, in turn, only the means to achieve social and cultural ends. When Bevan's petulance and egotism are assessed, along with his misjudgments and errors, his real substance as the pre-eminent British proponent of democratic socialism in the twentieth century outweighs everything. The NHS still survives as the last great, decidedly socialist, monument of the 1945 Labour government. His own legacy has been invoked, sometimes bewilderingly given his class-driven politics, by successive generations of Labour and new Labour leaders. His coruscating phrases are still mint fresh in the mouths of others; his political testament, *In Place of Fear* (1952), as fragmented and filigree brilliant as the man himself, remains in use and in print. Some of the tales of past struggles were given new lustre by Michael Foot, whose two-volume life of Bevan (1962, 1974) is a literary masterpiece of filial piety and historical evocation. Jennie Lee, who survived him to become in 1965 minister for the arts in Harold Wilson's first government and went to the Lords as Baroness Lee of Asheridge in 1970, tended his flame in the very title of her autobiography, *My Life with Nye* (1980). In 1972, on the open moorland above his valleys constituency, she dedicated four massively hewn standing stones to his memory. The memory did not fade. There were to be numerous streets and council estates and hospital wards in his name across Britain, and an evocatively demonstrative statue in the main thoroughfare of Cardiff, Wales' capital city, was erected in 1987.

The centenary of Bevan's birth in 1997 was attended by

extensive memorial celebrations in Wales and London, by further books and broadcasts about him, and by a national press row over the network television screening of a provocative BBC Wales screenplay by Trevor Griffiths which eventually won a Royal Television Society award. He could always cause trouble. He was a believer in beginnings over endings and this may yet, when the dust of his moment has finally settled, prove to be the source of his lasting appeal.   DAI SMITH

Sources M. Foot, *Aneurin Bevan: a biography*, 2 vols. (1962–73) · D. Smith, *Aneurin Bevan and the world of south Wales* (1993) · P. Hollis, *Jennie Lee: a life* (1997) · J. Lee, *My life with Nye* (1980) · C. Webster, *The health services since the war*, 1 (1988) · J. Campbell, *Nye Bevan and the mirage of British socialism* (1987) · K. O. Morgan, *Labour in power, 1945–1951* (1984) · G. Goodman, ed., *The state of the nation: the political legacy of Aneurin Bevan* (1997) · *The Times* (7 July 1960) · J. G. Jones, 'Evan Davies and Ebbw Vale', *Llafur*, 3 (1982) · J. G. Jones, 'Rift and conflict within the labour party in the 1950s: letters from Aneurin Bevan', *Llafur*, 7 (1997)

Archives HLRO, corresp. with Lord Beaverbrook · NL Wales, letters to Ebbw Vale CLP, related MSS and corresp. · Wellcome L., corresp. with Sir Ernst Chain | FILM BFI NFTVA, 'Profile', 25 May 1959 · BFI NFTVA, 'Nye Bevan talking to Jill Cragie', 1960 · BFI NFTVA, 'Nye!', 7 July 1965 · BFI NFTVA, 'Nye', 2 May 1982 · BFI NFTVA, documentary footage · BFI NFTVA, news footage · BFI NFTVA, party political footage | SOUND BL NSA, 'Nye' · BL NSA, 'Nye I knew', M4676R C1 · BL NSA, 'Makers of modern politics: Aneurin Bevan, the politician as hero, H511612 · BL NSA, current affairs recordings · BL NSA, party political recordings · IWM SA, 'Great political speeches', BBC Radio 4, 4 Sept 1992, 12801 · IWM SA, oral history interview

Likenesses photographs, 1934–59, Hult. Arch. · D. Low, pencil caricature, 1935, NPG · C. Beaton, photograph, 1940, NPG [*see illus.*] · P. Lambda, bronze bust, 1945, NPG · W. Stoneman, photograph, 1945, NPG · F. Topolski, charcoal, *c*.1954, NPG · H. Coster, photographs, NPG · R. Thomas, statue, Queens Street, Cardiff · photographs, NPG

Wealth at death £23,481 0s. 2d.: probate, 22 Nov 1960, *CGPLA Eng. & Wales*

Bevan, Anthony Ashley (1859–1933), orientalist and biblical scholar, was born at Trent Park, Barnet, on 19 May 1859, the eldest of the three sons of Robert Cooper Lee *Bevan (1809–1890), of Fosbury House, Wiltshire, and Trent Park, head of the great banking-house later known as Barclay & Co., and his second wife, (Emma) Frances *Bevan (1827–1909), hymn writer and biographer, daughter of Philip Nicholas *Shuttleworth, bishop of Chichester. The youngest son was the archaeologist and Hellenist Edwyn Robert *Bevan. Anthony Ashley Bevan was educated at Cheam, Surrey, the Gymnase Littéraire, Lausanne, and the University of Strasbourg, where he studied under Theodor Noeldeke, one of the greatest scholars in the field of oriental studies. He entered Trinity College, Cambridge, in 1884, and obtained a first class in the Semitic languages tripos of 1887. In 1888 he gained a Tyrwhitt Hebrew scholarship and the Mason prize for biblical Hebrew, and two years later was elected a fellow of his college and appointed lecturer in oriental languages. In 1893 he became lord almoner's professor of Arabic at Cambridge, a post previously held by his brother-in-law I. G. N. Keith-Falconer and by R. L. Bensly. It had a stipend of only £50 p.a., but Bevan had ample private means and was soon dispensed from the one obligation of lecturing

formally once a year. The post was abolished after his death. He was elected a fellow of the British Academy in 1916, resigning in 1928.

Bevan was:

> one of the dozen most learned Arabists, not of England and Europe only, but of the whole world. He was almost equally distinguished for his knowledge of Hebrew and Old Testament literature. He knew Syriac thoroughly and other Semitic languages well, and he had an excellent acquaintance with Persian language and literature. (Burkitt)

He also had a knowledge of Sanskrit, and was fluent in French, Italian, and German. His published work was relatively small, but what there is of it is of the highest scholarship. His edition of the satirical poems the *Naḳā'iḍ of Jarīr and al-Farazdak* (3 vols., 1905–12), was a tribute to his teacher the famous orientalist William Wright, who had initiated the project and then passed it on to his successor, Professor Robertson Smith, upon whose early death Bevan accepted the task of completing and publishing it over the subsequent twenty years. He also compiled an exhaustive volume of indexes and addenda to the *Mufaḍḍalīyāt* (1924), and so completed the edition of the poems edited by Sir C. J. Lyall. He was drawn more to classical Arabic than to later literature, but he was also interested in Manichaeism, and wrote an article on the subject for J. Hastings's *Encyclopaedia of Religion and Ethics* (vol. 8, 1915). In these and in his short commentary on the book of Daniel (1892), as well as in his other Old Testament studies, he always showed keen critical faculty and incisive judgement. Classical Hebrew was his interest, and although he was an enthusiastic pupil of Solomon Marcus Schiller-Szinessy, the university reader in Talmudic and rabbinic literature and a remarkable figure in his day, Bevan's attitude to medieval New Hebrew literature was not sympathetic. Throughout he was fastidious and scrupulously careful: as he observed in the course of one of his typically uncompromising reviews, 'even slight inaccuracies are liable to become sources of confusion'. His friends and pupils could well believe the story that he was almost reduced to tears on discovering a misprint in one of his own works.

If Bevan's output was slight he spared himself no pains in assisting his colleagues, among other ways by reading their proofs: many, including his brother Edwyn, were indebted to his scholarship. Even the inner circle stood a little in awe of his immense erudition and the authority which it gave him. He did much teaching, and as a teacher surprised his pupils by his methods and by his readiness to confess his inability to translate some Hebrew passage which they thought that they had mastered from their knowledge of the Authorized Version. But he was hospitable and at his ease with undergraduates. A hater of tobacco, he freely provided excellent cigars; witty, with a characteristic laugh and with a tongue like a rapier, he was a man of unbounded kindness and sympathy. He was generous with his inherited wealth. He was a benefactor of the university library and Museum of Archaeology, gave all his books to the faculty of oriental languages, and left £10,000 to Trinity College for such purposes as professorial fellows might think fit. Unostentatious, he was determined to ensure that his benefactions were made without drawing attention to himself.

Bevan had had an extremely evangelical upbringing, which led to later reaction; he was liberal and outspoken in his opinions. Slightly built and of middle height, he was scrupulously neat and tidy in dress and demeanour, and his politeness was almost a byword. He was over-particular about his food and over-anxious as to his health. He died, unmarried, at Stapleford, near Cambridge, on 16 October 1933.

S. A. COOK, rev. JOHN GURNEY

Sources F. C. Burkitt, 'Professor A. A. Bevan', *Cambridge Review* (27 Oct 1933), 45–6 · *The Times* (17 Oct 1933) · *The Times* (20 Oct 1933) · Venn, *Alum. Cant.* · Boase, *Mod. Eng. biog.* · personal knowledge (1949) · private information (1949)
Likenesses W. Stoneman, photograph, 1920, NPG · L. Underwood, pencil drawing, 1929, Trinity Cam. · photographs, Trinity Cam.
Wealth at death £135,242 8s. 2d.: probate, 25 Nov 1933, CGPLA Eng. & Wales

Bevan [*née* Vaughan], **Bridget** [*known as* Madam Bevan] (*bap.* **1698**, *d.* **1779**), educational benefactor, baptized on 30 October 1698 at Merthyr church in Llannewydd, Carmarthenshire, was the youngest daughter of John Vaughan (1663–1722) and his wife, Elizabeth Thomas (*d.* 1721), of Derllys, Carmarthenshire. She married Arthur Bevan (1689–1743), of Laugharne, on 30 December 1721 at Merthyr church. Her husband served as recorder of the Carmarthen Boroughs (1722–41), and as member of parliament for Carmarthen Boroughs (1727–41), and was appointed judge of equity in north and south Wales in 1735. He died on 6 March 1743, and was buried at Laugharne church.

John Vaughan was a great patron of the Society for Promoting Christian Knowledge (SPCK) and was responsible for the organization of the society's schools in Carmarthenshire between 1700 and 1722. His daughter inherited his interest in education and philanthropy and displayed this chiefly through her patronage of Griffith *Jones and his system of circulating schools. Jones, rector of Llanddowror, was already renowned for his powerful preaching, and had served as schoolteacher for the SPCK school at Laugharne under John Vaughan's supervision. Building on this experience, and with the welfare of his parishioners foremost in his mind, he established his first school at Llanddowror in 1731; the schools multiplied greatly from then on and many thousands had received instruction by the time of Jones's death, in 1761. Madam Bevan provided him with financial support and acted as adviser and confidante. An attractive woman, she and her husband moved in fashionable circles in London and Bath, and were friends of Lord Chesterfield. These connections were to prove useful in enlisting support towards the upkeep of the schools.

Following the death of his wife in 1755, Griffith Jones moved to Madam Bevan's house at Laugharne, where his cantankerous nature led the servants to dub him 'Old

Peevish'. He remained there until his death, in 1761, after which Madam Bevan took sole responsibility for the management and upkeep of the circulating schools for the following eighteen years. During that time she displayed considerable business acumen and organizational skills. Although this period in the history of the circulating schools is usually afforded scant attention by historians, the number of schools increased under her direction, particularly in the more Anglicized areas of the country. By 1764 news of the success of this educational initiative had reached the ears of Catherine the Great of Russia, who ordered her ministers to make enquiries about the scheme.

This chapter in Welsh educational history effectively came to a close with the death of Bridget Bevan, at Laugharne, on 10 December 1779; she was buried at Llanddowror church on 17 December 1779. Her will, dated 27 October 1779, left the funds entrusted to her by Griffith Jones, along with her own personal estate, to ensure the continuance of the circulating schools. However, two of the trustees, her niece Lady Elizabeth Stepney, and nephew Rear-Admiral William Lloyd, disputed the will and took possession of the money. The remaining two trustees, George Bowen, of Llwyn-gwair, and Zachary Bevan, of Laugharne, took the case to chancery in an attempt to recover the funds for the benefit of the schools. The legal dispute lasted until 1804, when it was finally judged that Madam Bevan's will should stand, but by this time the circulating schools had already perished for lack of funds. The work undertaken by Griffith Jones and Bridget Bevan was, in a sense, continued by the new Sunday schools, established from the late eighteenth century onwards in Wales.

ERYN M. WHITE

Sources *Welch Piety* (1740), 77 · M. H. Jones, 'Letters of Rev. Griffith Jones to Madam Bevan', *Trans. Carm. Antiq. Soc.*, 15 (1921–2), 1–4 · G. J. Thomas, 'Madam Bevan's will', *Trans. Carm. Antiq. Soc.*, 29 (1939), 43–52 · G. H. Jenkins, '"An old and much honoured soldier": Griffith Jones, Llanddowror', *Welsh History Review / Cylchgrawn Hanes Cymru*, 11 (1982–3), 449–68 · E. M. White, 'Popular schooling and the Welsh language, 1650–1800', *The Welsh language before the industrial revolution*, ed. G. H. Jenkins (1997), 317–41 · T. Kelly, *Griffith Jones, Llanddowror: pioneer in adult education* (1950) · J. L. Williams and G. R. Hughes, eds., *The history of education in Wales*, 1 (1978) · M. Clement, *The S.P.C.K. and Wales, 1699–1740* (1954) · M. G. Jones, *The charity school movement: a study in eighteenth century puritanism in action* (1938) · M. Clement, 'John Vaughan Cwrt Derllys a'i Waith', *Transactions of the Honourable Society of Cymmrodorion* (1942), 73–107 · W. M. Williams, *The friends of Griffith Jones* (1939) · M. Clement, ed., *Correspondence and minutes of the SPCK relating to Wales, 1699–1740* (1952) · F. Jones, *Historic Carmarthenshire homes and their families* (1987), 54, 98–9 · DWB
Likenesses A. Ramsay, oils, NL Wales
Wealth at death over £10,000 bequeathed to circulating schools: Thomas, 'Madam Bevan's will'

Bevan, Edward (1770–1860), apiarist and physician, was born on 8 July 1770 in London. His parents died when he was an infant, and he was sent to Hereford to the care of his maternal grandparents and in particular his mother's younger sister, who subsequently had a deep influence on him. His grandfather was a Hereford apothecary. At the age of eight he was adopted by his maternal uncle, John

Powle, a surgeon at Wotton under Edge, where he attended the local grammar school. At the age of twelve he was again bereaved when both his uncle and aunt died, and he returned to Hereford to enter the collegiate school before serving an apprenticeship to a Hereford city surgeon.

Bevan completed his medical education by attending three sessions at St Bartholomew's Hospital, London, where one of his lecturers was the influential surgeon John Abernethy. He then went to Mortlake, Surrey, as assistant to Dr John Clarke. On setting up in his own practice he moved to Stoke-on-Trent. He then became a partner in a practice in Congleton, Cheshire, where he married Miss Cartwright, second daughter of a leading Shropshire apothecary. In 1818, in response to improving medical standards, he successfully applied to the University of St Andrews for a degree of MD. His active medical career concluded at Mortlake, and he retired in his late forties. He then moved to a small estate, Woodland Cottage, at Bridstow, a mile north of Ross-on-Wye, where he embarked on his most enduring work.

At Woodland Cottage there were several beehives, which became the centre of Bevan's attention. His work on bee-keeping was encouraged by his wife and by his friend Richard Walond (1760–1838), rector of Weston under Penyard, treasurer of Hereford Cathedral, and a noted innovative bee-keeper. Bevan initiated an extensive correspondence with the leading apiarists of his day. He was well read in the field, and he tested the suggestions put to him. The fruit of this study was a carefully thought out assessment of contemporary knowledge about the honey bee and its culture, published as *The Honey-Bee* in 1827. After exploring the investigative work of Robert Golding of Hunton, Kent, he revised *The Honey-Bee* so that its second edition (1838) included an assessment of Golding's findings. Golding subsequently summarized his own work in a 58 page booklet *The Shilling Bee Book* (1847).

Between the two editions of *The Honey-Bee* Bevan moved to Ferryside, near Carmarthen, in south-west Wales, but returned to Hereford in 1849. His enthusiasm in old age was unabated: he was a private apicultural exhibitor at the Great Exhibition of 1851 in London. He published a lecture he gave to the Hereford Literary, Philosophical and Antiquarian Institution as *Hints on the History and Management of the Honey-Bee*; otherwise his published work was limited to magazine articles. He assisted Samuel Parkes in editing the third edition of the latter's *Rudiments of Chemistry* (1822), and he was a founder member of the Royal Entomological Society of London (1833). A translation into German of the first edition of *The Honey-Bee* was published in Stuttgart in 1828 and a compact English edition in Philadelphia in 1843.

Bevan died on 31 January 1860 at St Owens Street, Hereford. His executor was his niece Marianne Thomas, whom he and his wife had adopted as a girl; she had served for many years as his amanuensis and assistant.

An assessment of the significance of Bevan's work on bee-keeping came from the pen of the American apiarist L. L. Langstroth, who wrote in his 'Reminiscences' in *Gleanings in Bee Culture* (1892–3) that it was on reading the second edition of *The Honey-Bee* that he saw bee-keeping as a subject worthy of serious study. This led him to the investigations that laid the foundations of modern bee-keeping.   KARL SHOWLER

Sources J. P. Harding and others, *British bee books: a bibliography, 1500–1976* (1979) · L. L. Langstroth, 'Reminiscences', in L. L. Langstroth, *Gleanings in bee culture* (1892–3) · N. Wood, *Naturalist*, 4 (*c*.1838), 142–6 · *Hereford Times* (4 Feb 1860) · *The Cottage Garden and Country Gentleman's Magazine*, 23 (14–28 Feb 1860) · DNB · CGPLA Eng. & Wales (1860)
Archives priv. coll.
Likenesses lithograph, NPG; repro. in Wood, *Naturalist*, 143
Wealth at death under £200: probate, 7 April 1860, CGPLA Eng. & Wales

Bevan, Edward Latham (1861–1934). *See under* Bevan, William Latham (1821–1908).

Bevan, Edwyn Robert (1870–1943), ancient historian and philosopher, was born in London on 15 February 1870, the seventh son of Robert Cooper Lee *Bevan (1809–1890), banker, of Fosbury House, Wiltshire, and Trent Park, and the third with his second wife, the translator and poet (Emma) Frances Shuttleworth (1827–1909) [*see* Bevan, (Emma) Frances]. His siblings included the banker Francis Augustus *Bevan, the biblical scholar Anthony Ashley *Bevan, and the conspiracy theorist Nesta Helen *Webster.

While being educated at Monkton Combe School, Bevan insisted on having tuition in Greek, and won an open scholarship at New College, Oxford, of which he was later elected an honorary fellow. After obtaining first classes in classical moderations (1890) and *literae humaniores* (1892) he travelled in India, a visit which led to a permanent interest in Indian problems and personal friendship with many Indians. He next spent a year partly at the British School of Archaeology in Athens, partly on excavations in Egypt. On 25 April 1896 he married Mary (*d.* 1935), youngest daughter of the philanthropist and evangelist Granville Augustus William *Waldegrave, third Baron Radstock. They had two daughters.

By inheritance Bevan was a wealthy man, but in 1921 a widespread failure on the stock exchange suddenly engulfed all his investments and made him hastily look for paid work. He took the blow with his usual serenity; even his children did not know that anything particular had happened. King's College, London, offered him a post as lecturer in Hellenistic history and literature which he held from 1922 to 1933, when increasing deafness made teaching difficult and a legacy enabled him to retire. After this he devoted himself chiefly to problems of religion and philosophy. His Gifford lectures (Edinburgh), delivered in 1933 and 1934 and published as *Symbolism and Belief* (1938), are particularly notable.

Brought up in evangelical traditions and as a convinced Christian whose religion inspired all his activities, and who as an undergraduate used to hold meetings for prayer in his college rooms, Bevan, without abandoning the regular practice of a devotional life as unconcealed as it was unobtrusive, early emancipated himself from a belief in the inerrancy of scripture which might have restricted the freedom of his historical investigations. But nothing about any subject interested him so nearly as its bearing upon the Christian religion. Of that religion he found the classical statement in Philippians 2: 5–11. Those nearest to him spoke of the serenity of his faith, which was not disturbed by his full appreciation of the difficulties which made many of his contemporaries find it impossible to reconcile such a faith with the outlook of a modern educated thinker. Without denying the possibility of miracles he did not consider Christianity committed to any which differed in principle from the 'familiar miracle' involved in every determination of motion by desire or will. Even in respect of Christ's resurrection the Christian faith was not 'vain', so long as Christians were convinced that his disciples experienced an inner relationship with their risen master.

Like many religiously minded scholars of his generation Bevan owed much to Baron Friedrich von Hügel. He was a member of the London Society for the Study of Religion, of which von Hügel was the founder, and, with him, enjoyed and valued the friendship of the Jewish scholar and theologian C. J. Goldsmid-Montefiore. Like the latter he was an active member of the Society of Jews and Christians founded for the frank discussion of their mutual agreements and disagreements. He was also involved in the Student Christian Movement and was close to one of its prominent figures, John Leslie Johnston, a young fellow of Magdalen College, Oxford, who fell in the First World War. Bevan published a memoir of Johnston in 1921 and dedicated his *Christians in a World at War* (1940) to Johnston's memory. It is in this latter book, in the concluding essays of *Hellenism and Christianity* (1921), and in his presidential address of 1927 to the Oxford Society of Historical Theology on 'Some aspects of the present situation in regard to the gospel record' that Bevan's religious position can best be studied. To these should be added the book addressed to a wider public, *Christianity*, published in 1932 in the Home University Library.

It was through this deep devotion to the Christian religion that Bevan was drawn to the study of the Hellenistic age. In 1902, after seven years of concentrated study, he published *The House of Seleucus* (2 vols.), a pioneer work in Hellenistic history. The period fascinated him as the marriage place of Greek and Hebrew thought and the background of primitive Christianity. This book established him as one of the chief authorities on the Hellenistic age, and was followed in 1904 by *Jerusalem under the High Priests*, the chapters on 'Syria and the Jews' and 'The Jews' in the *Cambridge Ancient History*, vols. 8 and 9, two chapters on the Greeks in the *Cambridge History of India*, vol. 1, and those in the eleventh edition of the *Encyclopaedia Britannica* on Alexander, Lysimachus, Perdiccas, and the Ptolemies. Turning more to the Greek side of the same age, he wrote on deification in Hastings's *Encyclopaedia of Religion and Ethics*, on mystery religions in *The History of Christianity in the Light of Modern Knowledge* (1929), and in 1913 a book, *Stoics and Sceptics*. In the same year he published a small but

enlightening volume, *Indian Nationalism*, returning to the theme in *Thoughts on Indian Discontents* (1929).

The First World War took Bevan, after a short time in the Artists' Rifles, to the departments of propaganda and information and finally to the political intelligence department of the Foreign Office. For his services he was appointed OBE in 1920. His war writings included *The Land of the Two Rivers* (1917) on Mesopotamia, and *The Method in the Madness* (1917) on the psychological aberration which seemed to be at work in the German mind. He never forgot the nobler and more liberal elements in Germany, however, and translated Rudolf Olden's book *Is Germany a Hopeless Case?* (1940).

Bevan was exact and scholarly in his treatment of evidence; he used the resources of a fine imagination to understand past ages and to see contemporary events as processes rooted in the past. He considered the process of history not as a series of different civilizations but as 'a single *élan spirituel* in two efforts'. Behind the modern world was the Hellenic civilization, which he saw as 'the unique beginning of something new in the history of mankind'. It failed and was swamped by primitive barbarians, to recover and get a fresh embodiment in the modern 'western world'. True civilization was now, in the first half of the twentieth century, making 'its second try'.

Bevan received the honorary degrees of LLD, St Andrews (1922), and DLitt, Oxford (1923), and was elected FBA in 1942. He died at his London home, 38 Winchester Court, Vicarage Gate, on 18 October 1943.

Half a century of retrospect suggests a number of reflections upon Bevan's work: first, his activity as a translator and popularizer goes back, like his scholarly publishing, to 1902, and continued throughout his life, foreshadowing the explosion of translations and books designed to bring a knowledge of the Greek and Roman worlds to those without Greek and Latin; one particular piece is of additional interest, his contribution to *The Hellenistic Age* (1923), in origin a series of lectures given in the context of 'the employment of the Lewis Collection [at Corpus Christi College, Cambridge] as a stimulus to graduate work'. Bevan's scholarly production has worn less well: *Seleucus* is essentially an attempt at narrative history on a grand scale, whereas work since the First World War has concentrated, given the nature of the evidence, rather on synchronic studies of institutions and cultures, in particular in the context of the history of earlier states in the same geographical area. A. D. Momigliano recalled in 1986 the impact made at the time by *Sibyls and Seers* (1928); but Bevan's scholarly works have either like *Stoics and Sceptics* disappeared from bibliographies or figure only at the margins.

GILBERT MURRAY and CLEMENT C. J. WEBB, *rev.*
MICHAEL H. CRAWFORD

Sources G. Murray, *PBA*, 29 (1943) · Burke, *Gen. GB* (1952) · personal knowledge (1959) · private information (1959) **Archives** Bodl. Oxf., corresp. with Gilbert Murray **Wealth at death** £64,437 11s. 2d.: probate, 13 April 1944, *CGPLA Eng. & Wales*

Bevan [*née* Shuttleworth], (**Emma**) **Frances** (1827–1909), translator and poet, was born in Oxford on 25 September 1827, the eldest of three children of Philip Nicholas *Shuttleworth (1782–1842), warden of New College, Oxford (1822–40), and bishop of Chichester (1840–42), and Emma Martha Welch. Her father was anti-Tractarian and her mother pious: according to Henry Fox (later fourth Lord Holland), 'prim, precise and very dull' (Webster, 23). Intellectual from childhood, when her father enquired if she wished to take a story-book with her on a journey, she replied, 'No thank you Papa, I have my book on pneumatics to take with me' (ibid., 25). A gifted artist—apparently as a child her drawing won the praise of John Ruskin—she painted the reredos at Fosbury church, Wiltshire.

Frances developed high-church views. But when living with her widowed mother at Wykenham Rise, Totteridge, Middlesex, she met the evangelical Anglican Robert Cooper Lee *Bevan (1809–1890), a banker and eventually chairman of Barclay, Bevan, Tritton & Co. She became his second wife on 30 April 1856, and they resided at Trent Park, East Barnet, Hertfordshire, and later at 25 Prince's Gate, London. Bevan had four sons and two daughters from his first marriage, and he and Frances had eight children who survived into adulthood: Anthony Ashley *Bevan (1859–1933), who became professor of Semitic languages at Trinity College, Cambridge; Edwyn Robert *Bevan (1870–1943), later a religious scholar; and Hubert, Millicent, Gladys, Gwendolen, Enid, and Nesta. Shortly after her marriage Frances joined the Plymouth Brethren in Barnet. Her husband, however, remained Church of England.

Frances withdrew from society. She was distant from family life, not giving her children toys but only 'useful' presents and not permitting them fiction—although she did take pleasure in the writings of Lewis Carroll. She dressed in black with no ornamentation (but paradoxically allowing cosmetics), and her 'tall, majestic figure' (ibid., 38) had an 'air of command' (ibid., 71). She spoke French and German well, and published her first book of verse translations from German in 1858. Two similar works followed in 1859 and 1884. *Hymns of Ter Steegen, Suso and Others* (2 vols., 1894–7) became her most widely known collection and works from it passed into various church hymnaries. 'Sinners Jesus will Receive', a translation of a hymn by the Lutheran Erdmann Neumeister, enjoyed considerable popularity. As a translator she was not exact, and compared with, for example, John Wesley, passion is restrained. Among her own compositions, 'Midst the darkness, storm and sorrow', a Brethren standard, gave quintessential expression to her individualistic, otherworldly mysticism, and 'Christ, the Son of God, hath sent me' was a missionary favourite. In addition she produced religious tracts and seven books, mainly sketches of individuals such as the medieval mystic Mechtild von Magdeburg, the pietist Gerhardt Tersteegen, and John Wesley. Writing with a strong animus against Roman Catholicism, she attempted to trace an evangelical succession— often represented by capable women—which stressed

divine grace and assurance of salvation. Tersteegen's piety she found particularly congenial.

Due to Robert Bevan's gout, in later years the family spent the winter in Cannes, where Frances engaged in philanthropic activities. Even at the age of seventy she rose to read Hebrew at 8.30 a.m. She died on 15 March 1909 at Châlet Passiflora, Cannes. NEIL DICKSON

Sources N. H. Webster, *Spacious days* (1950) · J. S. Andrews, 'Frances Bevan: translator of German hymns', *Evangelical Quarterly*, 34 (1962), 206–13 · J. S. Andrews, 'Frances Bevan: translator of German hymns', *Evangelical Quarterly*, 35 (1963), 30–38 · D. M. Lewis, ed., *The Blackwell dictionary of evangelical history, 1730–1860*, 2 vols. (1995) [see also 'Bevan, Robert Cooper Lee', and 'Shuttleworth, Philip Nicholas'] · J. S. Andrews, '"Sinners Jesus will receive" — the British reception of Neumeister's hymn', *Evangelical Quarterly*, 55 (1983), 223–7 · J. S. Andrews, 'The recent history of the Bevan family', *Evangelical Quarterly*, 33 (1961), 81–92 · m. cert. · d. cert. · *CGPLA Eng. & Wales* (1909)
Likenesses photograph, repro. in Webster, *Spacious days*
Wealth at death £17,001 16s. 4d.: probate, 26 May 1909, *CGPLA Eng. & Wales*

Bevan, Francis Augustus (1840–1919), banker, was born on 17 January 1840 at 42 Upper Harley Street, London, the second son among the fourteen children of Robert Cooper Lee *Bevan (1809–1890), banker; his mother, Robert Bevan's first wife, was Lady Agneta Elisabeth Yorke, who died in 1851 when Francis was aged ten. His widower father did not immediately remarry and was assisted in bringing up the children by his deceased wife's maid, Lydia Marsh, and a private tutor, the Revd R. S. Tabor. Francis was then educated at Harrow School, before undertaking two years of foreign travel for which his taste persisted, with regular visits to the continent, and trips further afield to America, the Middle East, and India.

Bevan was married three times. In 1862 he married Elizabeth Marianne (1840–1863), daughter of Lord Charles James Fox Russell. They had one son. Bevan's second wife, whom he married on 19 April 1866, was Constance (1841–1872), youngest daughter of Sir James Weir Hogg, baronet. They had five sons. In 1875 he married Maria (d. 1903), second daughter of John Trotter of Dyrham Park, Barnet.

Bevan became a partner in the leading Lombard Street bank of Barclay, Bevan & Co. in 1859, succeeding as senior partner on his father's death in 1890. He was less decisive and rigid than his father and did not show his father's determination to maintain the bank's profitable independent existence at the heart of a national network of private banks. In 1896 he became the first chairman of a new corporate entity, Barclay & Co., which merged his Lombard Street partnership with the dominant East Anglian bank of Gurney & Co. (then controlled by the Barclay family and others), the north-eastern Backhouse Bank, and several smaller private banks. The new corporate bank grew rapidly, both by building new branches and by acquiring many small private banks whose owners warmed to Bevan's relaxed acceptance of their continuing local independence. However, the corporate bank was not as profitable as the old partnership, and from 1902 (when its shares were first quoted) the founding families' ownership interest was gradually diluted, becoming a minority one by the time Francis Bevan retired.

An Anglican, Bevan gave generously to a large number of Christian charities and missions; at a personal level, too, he was often uncritically open-handed. This generosity, together with his somewhat lax business instincts, appears to have led to a decline in the Bevan family fortune in real terms: his wealth at death was substantially below his father's, even in money terms. This was unlikely to have been due only to tax avoidance strategies, though certainly such strategies were more critical in 1919 than in 1890. The family estate at Trent Park, New Barnet, Hertfordshire, was sold in 1909 to Sir Edward Sassoon and Bevan settled at an old Mayfair house, at 1 Tilney Street, Park Lane. Although his son Cosmo (1863–1935) was a local director in Lombard Street from 1896 to 1933 and a main board director from 1905 to 1933, he was overshadowed in the bank's senior management by the professional manager Frederick Goodenough from 1917: Bevan's descendants in the bank, including another son, Bertrand Yorke (1867–1948) who also became director, did not produce another chairman until 1981.

Bevan enjoyed travel abroad, cricket, classical concerts, and motoring, but his latter years were marred by intermittent illness, and he retired from the chairmanship at the beginning of 1917. He continued to attend the board and committee meetings until his death from heart disease on 31 August 1919, at Monk Sherbourne, Granville Road, Eastbourne, aged seventy-nine. He was buried in the family vault at Trent Park churchyard.

LESLIE HANNAH

Sources M. Ackrill and L. Hannah, *Barclays: the business of banking, 1690–1996* (2001) · A. N. Gamble, *A history of the Bevan family* [1924] · P. W. Matthews, *History of Barclays Bank Limited*, ed. A. W. Tuke (1926) · *The Times* (2 Sept 1919) · E. Smart, 'Bevan, Francis Augustus', *DBB* · biographical file, Barclays Archives, Wythenshawe · d. cert. · *CGPLA Eng. & Wales* (1919) · m. certs. (3)
Archives Barclays Archives, Wythenshawe, Manchester
Likenesses G. Fiddes Watt, portrait
Wealth at death £410,879 15s. 9d.: probate, 17 Dec 1919, *CGPLA Eng. & Wales*

Bevan [*née* Bennett], **Hannah Marishall** (1798–1874), philanthropist, was born on 1 February 1798 in London, one of three children and the only daughter of William Bennett (d. 1818), tea merchant, and his wife, Hannah Fossick. She was brought up as a member of the Society of Friends. After her mother had suffered a stroke, leaving her partly paralysed, Hannah Bennett was sent to a school in Croydon at the age of twelve. Even as a child her unselfishness, humility, and strong powers of sympathy were very marked. On leaving school she nursed her mother until her death. The death of her father shortly afterwards, in 1818, left her with only her two brothers, William (1804–1843) and Samuel, for companions. Hannah kept house for both of them and, with Samuel, carried on her father's tea business. After his death from consumption she continued to live with William.

In April 1824 Hannah Bennett joined the British Ladies Society for promoting the reform of female prisoners, founded by Elizabeth Fry in 1821. In May she was appointed to visit the convict ships with Elizabeth Pryor, and she also campaigned for the better treatment of the female convicts during transportation. On 15 August 1827 she married Thomas Bevan (1804–1847), a surgeon in Liverpool Street, London.

In 1828—the same year in which her first child was born—Hannah Bevan was acknowledged as a minister of the Society of Friends. Her son died at thirteen months old, but she gave birth to five more sons and two daughters between 1829 and 1842. Occupied by her family and entertaining her large circle of friends, Hannah Bevan continued her philanthropic work, establishing, with the assistance of some friends, the Foster Street ragged school. Still a member of the British Ladies Society (although she stopped visiting the ships after her marriage), she sat on the society's subcommittee to discuss the future management of convict ships in 1831. Her resignation is not noted; she seems simply to have stopped attending the meetings.

In her later years Hannah Bevan took an active interest in the total abstinence cause: the first Band of Hope in London was formed at her house by her friend Thomas B. Smithies and consisted of some of her own children with a few neighbours. During the potato famine of Ireland in 1846 she worked energetically with others for the relief of those who were starving. She also assisted in the establishment of the First Day School in Quaker Street, Spitalfields (later merged with the Bedford Institute), and was a teacher there. With John Pryor and her brother William Bennett she aided the establishment of the Friends' Institute, which had its headquarters at White Hart Court. She was also deeply interested in the care of young men separated from their homes.

In 1847 Thomas Bevan became ill and died at the age of forty-three; Hannah's two youngest sons also became severely ill and died that year. In 1852 she moved to Darlington, where two of her surviving sons lived. She visited the inmates of the local workhouse and would invite the children to tea as a treat. However, 1859 saw the start of a long illness, and in June 1864 Hannah Bevan suffered a stroke, from which she never fully recovered. She soon afterwards moved back to London, where she lingered on for ten more years. She died on 7 November 1874 at Linden House, Laurel Grove, Penge, near Sydenham, and was buried at Winchmore Hill with her late husband and children.

Hannah Bevan's philanthropic concern for the disadvantaged of early nineteenth-century society was not unusual among Quaker women, and she was but one of many who gained their first experience of philanthropic work in Elizabeth Fry's British Ladies Society; the range of her subsequent involvements, however, is perhaps more remarkable.

AMANDA PHILLIPS

Sources *Annual Monitor* (1876), 3–19 · Boase, *Mod. Eng. biog.* · British Ladies Society meeting minutes, April 1824, Hackney RO · British Ladies Society meeting minutes, Jan 1831, Hackney RO · d. cert. · *CGPLA Eng. & Wales* (1874)

Wealth at death under £7000: probate, 17 Dec 1874, *CGPLA Eng. & Wales*

Bevan, (Edward) John (1856–1921), analytical chemist, was born on 11 December 1856 at 8 Argyle Street, Birkenhead, Cheshire, the son of Edward Bevan, master watchmaker, and his wife, Margaret Matilda Prosser. After attending private schools he became a laboratory assistant at the Runcorn Soap and Alkali Company. He was advised to continue his education and went to Owens College, Manchester, between 1877 and 1879. He then worked for three years for Alexander Cowan & Co. at Musselburgh Paper Mills. At Owens College he had met Charles Frederick Cross and the two chemists joined forces at the Jodrell Laboratory, Kew Gardens, with the aim of exploring the chemistry of cellulose, the major constituent of wood, cotton, flax, and paper. They went into partnership as analytical chemists at Lincoln's Inn in 1885. Bevan was appointed public analyst for Middlesex county council in 1892. He was president of the Society of Public Analysts in 1905–6, and vice-president of the Institute of Chemistry in 1905–8 and 1914–17.

The interest of Cross and Bevan in the chemistry of cellulose led them to the study of the viscose solutions produced by treating cellulose with a strong solution of caustic soda and then carbon disulphide vapour. An aqueous solution of this 'xanthogenate' regenerated cellulose on standing or when heated. They filed the key patent in May 1892, with their colleague Clayton Beadle (1868–1917). The three partners set up the Viscose Syndicate in 1893, with the aim of producing adhesives, films, coatings for natural fibres, and mouldings, and British Viscoid Ltd followed in 1896. The manufacture of fibres from viscose was pioneered by Charles Henry Stearn (1844–1919), who established the Viscose Spinning Syndicate with Cross in 1898. The British rights to viscose rayon fibre were acquired in July 1904 by Samuel Courtauld & Co., which began production at Coventry a year later. In May 1894 Cross and Bevan patented the manufacture of cellulose acetate, which was later developed and sold as a fibre by the British Celanese Company, in competition with viscose rayon.

Bevan was described by Charles Cross as 'genial and generous' and was popular with his fellow chemists. He died, unmarried, at 18 Dorset Square, Marylebone, London, on 17 October 1921.   PETER J. T. MORRIS, *rev.*

Sources C. F. Cross, *JCS*, 119 (1921), 2121–3 · C. F. Cross, *Journal of the Society of Chemical Industry Review*, 40 (1921), 418 · D. C. Coleman, *Courtaulds: an economic and social history*, 2 (1969), 10–14, 18–19, 372 · b. cert. · d. cert.

Wealth at death £2764 3s. 3d.: probate, 20 Dec 1921, *CGPLA Eng. & Wales*

Bevan, John Henry (1894–1978), intelligence officer and stockbroker, was born on 5 April 1894, at 4 Lower Berkeley Street, London, the younger son of David Augustus Bevan (1856–1937), stockbroker, and his wife, the Hon. Dame Maude Elizabeth Bevan (1856–1944). Educated at Eton College and Christ Church, Oxford, Bevan was commissioned as a territorial in the Hertfordshire regiment in October 1913 and served on the western front during the First World War, being twice mentioned in dispatches and winning the MC as a captain in 1917. In January 1918 he joined the specially selected staff of Field Marshal Sir Henry Wilson at the supreme war council as a GSO2; his speciality was writing strategic appreciations from the enemy's point of view during the great German offensives in spring 1918. After the war he spent three years with Hambros bank in Copenhagen before returning to the City to join the stockbroking firm founded by his father. In 1927 he married Lady Barbara Bingham (1902–1963), daughter of the fifth earl of Lucan; they had a son and two daughters.

A Territorial Army reservist, Bevan was recalled in 1939, working first in MI5 before joining as a major the staff of *Mauriceforce* for the ill-starred campaign in Norway. His career in strategic deception did not begin until his appointment as controlling officer by the chiefs of staff on 21 May 1942. Systematic, organized deception, as practised on an unheard-of scale during the Second World War, had its origins in the Middle East in 1940 under the sponsorship of General Sir Archibald Wavell and Lieutenant-Colonel Dudley Clarke of A force. Yet it was only in the early 1970s that their achievements and those subsequently of Bevan's London controlling section began to receive the historiographical acknowledgement they deserved, thanks to the release of official sources following the Public Records Act of 1967 and the publication of Sir John Masterman's *The Double-Cross System in the War of 1939 to 1945* in 1972.

In appointing Johnny Bevan, the chiefs of staff found an officer with the necessary combination of imagination, initiative, resilience, and sound military instincts, to say nothing of personal charm and persuasiveness. 'His most remarkable feature was a very fine forehead, both broad and deep; and one of his greatest assets an extraordinarily attractive smile', according to the novelist Dennis Wheatley, a member of the London controlling section (Wheatley, 59). The new controlling officer had to start from scratch—almost singlehandedly planning the cover and deception for operation Torch (the invasion of north Africa), winning the confidence of the prime minister and the chiefs of staff, and developing as wide a range of contacts as possible so as to 'sell' deception. Ever present was the strain of playing with dynamite, intensified for Bevan by recurrent insomnia. The main UK-based deception in 1943 misfired but the system was preserved, a system based on an unprecedented combination of watertight security and superb intelligence. MI5 had decided in June 1942 that they did indeed control all *Abwehr* agents in the country and from then on the latter were used with growing confidence for deception purposes; moreover, ULTRA intelligence made it possible to monitor the credibility of the agents with their controllers and to identify those strategic presuppositions of Hitler's that could most profitably be played up to mystify and mislead him. For no operation was it more urgent to induce Hitler to make 'a calculated false move' (Wingate, 'Narrative', 1.4) than the cross-channel invasion in 1944.

Bevan and the London controlling section made a

decisive contribution to the success of operation Overlord. Their primary function was to co-ordinate deception between theatres of operation and to formulate overall deception policy. This they fulfilled for the invasion by drawing up plan Bodyguard, the grand strategic deception for 1944, as well as implementing a number of supporting schemes involving liaison with a wide range of authorities from the Foreign Office to the Ministry of Economic Warfare. Bevan himself flew to Moscow, barely surviving a defective oxygen mask, to arrange Soviet co-operation with Bodyguard. The tactical cover plan for the cross-channel assault was, as always, planned and executed by the operational headquarters concerned, in this case the Supreme Headquarters, Allied Expeditionary Force (SHAEF). By this stage of the war large-scale visual deception had been reduced to a form of insurance against chance sightings by sporadic German aerial reconnaissance. To an extent totally unforeseen in 1942, reliance was now put upon the XX (or double-cross) agents, in particular Garbo and Brutus, backed up by bogus wireless traffic to 'validate' an inflated order of battle in the UK. Bevan was one of a handful of officers representing SHAEF, MI5, and the London controlling section, who worked quickly and at times off the record to preserve surprise for the assault and to put across Major Roger Hesketh's brilliant 'story' that the D-day landings were mere preliminaries to a more powerful invasion of the Pas-de-Calais, thereby pinning German reserves north of the Seine while the battle for Normandy was decided.

Appointed CB in 1945, Bevan returned to stockbroking; he also became chairman of the Equitable Life Assurance Society. His recreations remained those of the countryman, particularly gardening and ornithology. Once a year he hosted a dinner at Brooks's Club for his wartime associates, mostly majors and colonels, whose conventional background and appearance concealed such a rich talent for ingenuity and guile. Bevan died at the age of eighty-four of lung cancer on 3 December 1978 at 232 Cranmer Court, Sloane Avenue, London, and his body was cremated. JOHN P. CAMPBELL

Sources M. Howard, *British intelligence in the Second World War*, 5: *Strategic deception* (1990) · Historical record of deception in the war against Germany and Italy, 2 vols., PRO, CAB 154/100, 101 [Sir Ronald Wingate's narrative] · J. C. Masterman, *The double-cross system in the war of 1939 to 1945* (1972) · C. Cruickshank, *Deception in World War II* (1979) · M. Young and R. Stamp, *Trojan horses: deception operations in the Second World War* (1991) · M. Handel, ed., *Strategic and operational deception in the Second World War* (1987) · D. Wheatley, *The deception planners* (1980) · R. Wingate, *Not in the limelight* (1959) · D. Hart-Davis, *Peter Fleming: a biography* (1974) · C. E. Callwell, *Field-Marshal Sir Henry Wilson … his life and diaries*, 2 vols. (1927) · *Daily Telegraph* (15 Dec 1978) · *WWW* · private information (2004) · *Daily Telegraph* (24 Feb 1979)

Archives PRO, J. Bevan, Captain GS, 'The great offensive in France: German plans for the future', SWC 204, 6 May 1918, CAB 25/121 | PRO, historical record of deception in the war against Germany and Italy, 2 vols., CAB 154/100, 101

Likenesses portrait, repro. in D. Wheatley, *The deception planners* (1980)

Wealth at death £252,740: *Daily Telegraph* (24 Feb 1979)

Bevan, Joseph Gurney (1753–1814), religious writer, was born on 18 February 1753 in London, the only child of Timothy Bevan (1704–1786), pharmacist, and his second wife, Hannah Springhall (1714–1784), daughter of Joseph and Hannah Gurney. Raised as a member of the Society of Friends, he was of a lively and affectionate disposition and very quick to learn. From an uncle who was an artist and naturalist he derived a good deal of knowledge; his literary studies he pursued for some years under a physician who was also a classical scholar with a taste for poetry. Bevan's own love of poetry later induced him to recommend the study of Latin under certain restrictions; at the age of fifty he himself diligently studied Greek in order to read the New Testament. In his desire for fashionable clothing he twice changed his mode of dress but returned to his traditional, plain clothing out of regard for his mother. At the age of seventeen he was 'under serious impressions of mind' and thought it his duty to desist from using the heathen names of the months.

In 1776 Bevan married Mary (1751–1813), daughter of Robert and Hannah Plumstead of London; there were no children from the marriage. Mary also was a Quaker minister. Bevan's father now gave him a share in his business in Plough Court, Lombard Street, London. Bevan pursued his trade with integrity, fairness, and honesty, and retired from it in 1794 with a considerable diminution of capital, largely resulting from his generosity to others and his scruples. From conscientious motives he had refused, for example, to supply goods to armed vessels; likewise, chosen to act as a constable in his ward, he faithfully fulfilled the duties of his office rather than hire a substitute. In his journal he regretted his spiritual pride and want of resignation, while watching his spiritual state closely. He also recorded his attempts to control what he described as his naturally hot temper.

In 1794 Bevan began writing for an almanac published by James Phillips, and continued to do so for four years, with the exception of 1797, when his poem, 'Patience', was not finished in time. He also wrote a few poems in imitation of the psalms, and other pieces of verse. In 1796 he moved to Stoke Newington. In 1800 he wrote his *Refutation of the Misrepresentations of the Quakers*, appended to which was his 'Summary of the history, doctrine and discipline of Friends', which was in effect a very concise, official statement. Later translated into French, German, and Italian it was among four works presented by the society to the emperor of Russia and the king of Prussia when they were in London in 1814. In 1802 Bevan published his examination of Thomas Foster's *Appeal to the Society of Friends on the primitive simplicity of their Christian principles and church discipline*, (1801); by an investigation of Foster's work and of the writings of early Friends, Bevan's intention was to show that the Friends were not Unitarians. His *Thoughts on Reason and Revelation* (1805), a short publication of twenty-three pages, is divided into sections dealing with reason, revelation in general, infidelity, scripture, faith, and experience. In 1807 he published *The Life of the Apostle Paul*, and in 1810 he edited the tenth part of *Piety Promoted*, with a new historical introduction. Some of his letters and verse were published in 1815, with a short memoir of his life, edited by Josiah Forster under the title, *Extracts from the Letters and other Writings of the Late Joseph Gurney Bevan*.

For many years Bevan fulfilled with zeal the station of an elder providing his friends with information derived from his daily family readings of scripture, 'my habit of nearly thirty years' standing', as he put it in 1806. In 1794 he was clerk to the yearly meeting of Friends, in whose proceedings he was active and influential for over twenty-five years. Towards the end of the eighteenth century he became anxious to encourage an orthodox Quaker position compatible with an evangelical viewpoint. He played a major part in the controversy with the visiting American minister Hannah Barnard. She questioned the historical accuracy of much of scripture, while claiming to have views in accord with those of earlier major Quaker writers; Bevan had a leading role in opposing her views. He was described by the Quaker diarist James Jenkins, who was something of a cynic about the contemporary Quaker establishment, as 'our chief disciplinarian' (*Journal of the Friends' Historical Society*, 20, 1923, 73). On 23 May 1813 Mary Bevan died, following a fit that had resulted in severe memory loss. Bevan himself, who was now afflicted with cataracts, asthma, and dropsy, bore all these troubles with exemplary humility and patience. In the last part of his life two female friends, daughters of a Mr Capper, would read to him selections from John Kendall's *Collection of Letters*, Thomas Ellwood's journal, and Mary Waring's diary. The elder of the sisters had been married to Paul Bevan, one of Bevan's cousins; another cousin was the philanthropist and prison reformer Elizabeth Fry. Bevan spent the greater part of the closing days of his life at his cousin Paul's house at Tottenham. He died on 12 September 1814 and was buried at the Quaker burial-ground, at Bunhill Fields. His Quaker books, incorporated with the collection of his cousin Paul, became the nucleus of the important Bevan–Naish collection in Birmingham.

DAVID J. HALL

Sources *Extracts from the letters and other writings of the late Joseph Gurney Bevan; preceded by a short memoir of his life* (1821) · DNB · 'Dictionary of Quaker biography', RS Friends, Lond. [card index] · J. Smith, ed., *A descriptive catalogue of Friends' books*, 2 vols. (1867); suppl. (1893) · N. Penney, ed., *Pen pictures of London Yearly Meeting, 1789–1833* (1930) · 'The Quaker family of Bevan', *Journal of the Friends' Historical Society*, 22 (1925), 15–17 · R. M. Jones, *The later periods of Quakerism*, 1 (1921), 308 · *Journal of the Friends' Historical Society*, 20 (1923)
Archives RS Friends, Lond., letters, memoirs, and verses
Likenesses silhouette, 1809 (after S. Zachary), RS Friends, Lond., Gibson MSS, Ms vol 334/30 · silhouette, Friends' House Library, Pict. box B60

Bevan, Nesta Helen. *See* Webster, Nesta Helen (1875–1960).

Bevan, Robert Cooper Lee (1809–1890), banker, was born on 8 February 1809 at Hale End, Walthamstow, the eldest son of David Bevan (1774–1846), banker, and his wife, Favell Bourke Lee (1780–1841), who came from a prominent Caribbean slave-owning family. His father was a partner in the Quaker private banking firm of Barclay, Bevan & Co. of Lombard Street in the City of London. The writer

Favell Lee *Mortimer was his sister. In 1826—the year Robert left Harrow School to matriculate at Trinity College, Oxford—David Bevan had to withdraw from the management of the bank after a paralytic seizure. A few years later, when his father's condition worsened, Robert ended his studies without a degree and took his father's place as a partner.

The Bevans, unlike the other partners and many of their provincial banking correspondents, were not Quakers, for Robert's grandfather, Silvanus, had been disowned by the Friends for marrying a non-Quaker in 1773. However, in the course of the nineteenth century, secular and religious forces led most other Quaker bankers, including many of Robert's Barclay and Tritton partners, also to desert their faith. Bevan acquired all the apparently un-Quakerly trappings of the establishment at an early age: he was not only educated at Harrow and Oxford, but his religion was Anglican, and in politics he was a Conservative. Married twice, Bevan's first marriage, on 24 February 1836, was to Lady Agneta Elisabeth Yorke (d. 1851), daughter of Admiral Sir Joseph Sydney *Yorke and sister of the fourth earl of Hardwicke; and then on 30 April 1856 he married (Emma) Frances Shuttleworth (1827–1909) [see Bevan, (Emma) Frances], daughter of Philip Nicholas *Shuttleworth, the bishop of Chichester. There were fourteen children from the marriages, including the banker Francis Augustus *Bevan (1840–1919), the conspiracy theorist Nesta Helen *Webster (1875–1960), and the scholars Anthony Ashley *Bevan (1859–1933) and Edwyn Robert *Bevan (1870–1943).

The owner of 3913 acres, Bevan had estates at Trent Park at New Barnet on the northern outskirts of London, and also in Wiltshire, as well as houses in London and at Brighton and, in later years, a villa in Cannes. Yet, after an evangelical conversion in his late twenties, Quakers could not wholeheartedly condemn him for 'conformity to the world', for he began to lead a far more religious life than others who had experienced this establishment conditioning. His wives shared his austere, uncompromising religiosity and his second wife became in middle life a member of the reclusive Plymouth Brethren sect. Robert Bevan arranged open prayer meetings daily at 12.30 at the bank's offices in Lombard Street; he gave up hunting (a favourite sport in his youth) on grounds of conscience; and he spent extensively on church building and other charities, including the foundation of the London City Mission.

Barclays (as his bank was increasingly known) was at the centre of a network of (mainly Quaker) country bankers. The network proved its value in the financial crisis of 1824–5, while his father was at the helm. The Lombard Street bank then co-ordinated assistance to those firms short of easily accessible funds, but otherwise strong; while numerous insolvent banks failed, Quaker bankers and others with Barclay, Bevan & Co. connections generally did well. After Robert became senior partner of the Lombard Street bank, he faced similar tests. Perhaps his most difficult decision was in the mid-1860s, when his partners' Norwich relations, the Gurneys, attempted to rescue the once exemplary (but by then badly managed) London billbroking firm of Overend Gurney & Co. The ultimate collapse of Overend Gurney in 1866 ruined the Gurneys, but Bevan firmly refused either to back the Gurneys with the Lombard Street bank's resources or to recommend a Bank of England rescue of the insolvent (rather than merely illiquid) firm. However, the partners of Barclays did help individually on a charitable basis after the Gurney bankruptcies.

Bevan became the doyen of conservative private bankers. By 1890 his firm was the second largest of the London private bankers (after Glyn Mills & Co.) by its balance-sheet size. Its profits had tripled during Bevan's fifty-year career as an active banker and ten as a sleeping partner (in later life he wintered in Cannes). His estate at the end of his life made him indisputably a millionaire. There were several richer nineteenth-century bankers, but the partners' rate of profit at Barclay, Bevan & Co. under his leadership was normally about 30 per cent, better than that achieved by leading merchant bankers. Bevan showed that conservative private banking could more than hold its own within the provincial correspondent banking and short-term business lending functions in which his firm excelled, against the (less profitable) joint-stock banks that grew to dominate English banking during his career.

Robert Bevan died on 22 July 1890 at Trent Park, New Barnet, from gout and other debilitating illnesses.

LESLIE HANNAH

Sources M. Ackrill and L. Hannah, *Barclays: the business of banking, 1690–1996* (2001) · A. N. Gamble, *A history of the Bevan family* [1924] · P. W. Matthews, *History of Barclays Bank Limited*, ed. A. W. Tuke (1926) · Boase, *Mod. Eng. biog.* · Foster, *Alum. Oxon.* · IGI
Archives Barclays Archives, Wythenshawe, business papers
Likenesses Herkomer, portrait (in later life); priv. coll.
Wealth at death £953,382 11s. 11d.: resworn probate, Nov 1890, CGPLA Eng. & Wales

Bevan, Robert Polhill (1865–1925), painter, was born at 17 Brunswick Square, Hove, Sussex, on 5 August 1865, the fourth of the six children of Richard Alexander Bevan (1834–1918), a banker of Brighton, and Laura Maria Polhill (d. 1906). After four terms at Winchester College (1880–81) he was educated at home in Horsgate, near Cuckfield, Sussex, by private tutors, one of whom, A. E. Pearce, a designer for Doulton from 1873 to 1930, taught him drawing. His artistic education continued in London at the Westminster School of Art in 1888, in Paris in 1889–90 at the Académie Julian, and from 1890 to 1891 in the village of Pont-Aven in Brittany, the centre of an artists' colony dominated since 1886 by Paul Gauguin. In 1891 he spent time in Madrid to study the works of Velázquez and Goya on his way to Tangier, where he stayed until 1892 or 1893. He then returned to Pont-Aven where, in 1894, he met Gauguin. During his years in France he also met Renoir and Cézanne.

Because he enjoyed a degree of financial independence, Bevan was able to discover and nurture his talent slowly and to integrate his art and his life. He loved the country; above all he loved horses. In Tangier he was master of foxhounds for a season. Horses are the subject of his earliest surviving paintings, all done in Brittany. On his return to England in 1894 he went to live at Hawkridge on Exmoor where he could combine painting and hunting. In 1897 he met the Polish painter Stanislawa de Karlowska (1876–1952) and on 9 December they married in Warsaw. Their first child, Edith Halena, was born in December 1898; their second, Robert Alexander, in March 1901. Over the next ten years, in England (from 1900 in London at 14 Adamson Road, Swiss Cottage) and on long summer visits to Poland, Bevan worked largely in isolation, sustained by his early acquaintance with many-faceted French post-impressionism. For the rest of his career as a painter and lithographer he sought nourishment in Van Gogh's rhythmic draughtsmanship and directional brushwork, Gauguin's expressionist use of pure colour, and the schematic simplifications of definition evolved within the Pont-Aven school.

The Polish village scenes included in Bevan's first one-man exhibition in 1905—probably the most radical paintings by a British artist then to be seen in London—were barely noticed by the critics. It was not until 1908, when he contributed to the first Allied Artists' Association non-jury exhibition, that he was discovered by Spencer Gore and Harold Gilman and introduced into the circle orchestrated by Walter Sickert at 19 Fitzroy Street. Bevan was a founder member of the Camden Town group established in 1911, of the London group set up in 1913, and in 1914 of the Cumberland Market group. The last group was named after Bevan's studio at no. 49 where, in 1914 and 1915, he painted the horse-drawn carts in the great cobbled Camden Town square which served as London's hay market.

By 1906–7 the brilliant colours and joyous freedom of Bevan's earlier painting had given way to a more traditional, light-toned, impressionist palette and a more considered, broken touch. His unique contributions to the urban vocabulary of Camden Town group painting were cab-horse scenes and, from 1912, horse sales at Tattersalls, Aldridges, the Barbican, and Wards. He also painted his own neighbourhood, but his sunny views of spacious avenues on the borders of St John's Wood have little in common with the mean back streets of Camden Town painted by Sickert, Gore, and Gilman.

During the summer Bevan painted in the country, most often in the Blackdown hills on the Devon–Somerset borders. In 1912, 1913, and 1915 he was at Applehayes as a guest of the retired rancher and amateur painter H. B. Harrison; from 1916 to 1919 in a cottage rented near by, in the Bolham valley; and in 1920 and 1923–5 on Luppitt Common, further south in Devon. He responded energetically to the west country scenery, with its strong patterning of fields, woods, and clustered cottages, producing a series of paintings expressive of both the angular structure and the poetry of its landscape.

In 1925 Bevan was diagnosed as having cancer; he died—still little known outside his own circle—on 8 July in St

Thomas's Home, Lambeth, London, following an operation. He was survived by his wife. *The Cab Yard, Night* (exh. 1910, purchased 1913 by Brighton Art Gallery) was the only painting to enter a public collection during his lifetime. Despite memorial shows in 1926 and an Arts Council exhibition in 1956, his unique contribution to British art was not widely recognized until 1965, the centenary of his birth. In that year the Ashmolean Museum in Oxford arranged a comprehensive retrospective and R. A. Bevan, the artist's son, published his informative and well-illustrated memoir.   WENDY BARON

Sources R. A. Bevan, *Robert Bevan, 1865–1925: a memoir by his son* (1965) · F. Stenlake, *From Cuckfield to Camden Town: the story of artist Robert Bevan (1865–1925)* (1999) · W. Baron, 'Robert Polhill Bevan', in W. Baron and M. Cormack, *The Camden Town Group* (1980), 2–11 [exhibition catalogue, Yale U. CBA, 16 April–29 June 1980] · W. Baron, *The Camden Town Group* (1979) · *CGPLA Eng. & Wales* (1925) **Archives** AM Oxf., sketchbooks · Tate collection, corresp. and papers **Likenesses** R. Bevan, self-portrait, oils, *c.*1914, NPG **Wealth at death** £16,392 4*s.* 7*d.*: administration with will, 14 Aug 1925, *CGPLA Eng. & Wales*

Bevan, Silvanus (1691–1765), apothecary, was born in Swansea on 28 October 1691, the second son of Silvanus Bevan (1661–1727) and his wife, Jane, *née* Phillips. The descendant of influential and prosperous Welsh Quakers (his grandfather had been a Swansea alderman and a merchant), Silvanus moved to London as a young man and was apprenticed as an apothecary to a Mr Mayleigh. In July 1715, after serving his seven years' apprenticeship, Bevan gained his freedom of the Society of Apothecaries, and in December of the same year set up his own apothecary's shop at Plough Court, a cul-de-sac off Lombard Street. Bevan made the most of the Quaker reputation for honest dealing, which was an important consideration for purchasers of medicines at that time. His Quaker linkages were strengthened when he married Elizabeth Quare, daughter of the royal clockmaker Daniel Quare, at a Friends' meeting-house in the City on 9 November 1715.

Bevan had a laboratory, with a still for preparing his medicines, which were usually compounded according to recipes in the various published pharmacopoeias. Bevan's catalogues listed such exotic remedies as *mumia* (or Egyptian mummy), human skull, and a Venice treacle, which contained vipers. The business was well situated and Bevan—joined in partnership by his younger brother, Timothy Bevan (1704–1786)—prospered. Bevan increasingly practised medicine as well as pharmacy and became known as Dr Bevan. His interest in medicine is shown by a letter he sent in 1743 to the Royal Society (of which he had been elected a fellow in 1725), entitled 'An account of the extraordinary case of the bones of a woman growing soft and flexible'. He also took a keen interest in smallpox inoculation, corresponding on the subject with James Jurin, a well-known physician, who supported the practice of inoculation.

Silvanus Bevan became a rich man and later lived in some style in Hackney. When he was seventy in 1761, a visitor described him in his retirement as 'living well on good food and drinks … [surrounded by a] … variety of curious paintings and rich old china, and a large library containing books on most subjects'. He was described as 'one of the principal leading men among the Quakers' (Davies, 2.336–7). By then Bevan had relinquished his Plough Court partnership to his brother, Timothy, who continued the business (which in the nineteenth century, under William Allen and the Hanburys, became one of the leading chemists and druggists in London).

Bevan's first marriage produced a son, but both mother and infant did not long survive. He later married Martha, daughter of Gilbert Heathcote of Derbyshire, but they had no children. Bevan died at Hackney on 8 June 1765 and was buried at the Bunhill Fields burial-ground.

GEOFFREY TWEEDALE

Sources G. Tweedale, *At the sign of the plough: 275 years of Allen & Hanburys and the British pharmaceutical industry, 1715–1990* (1990) · A. A. Locke and A. Esdaile, *Plough Court: the story of a notable pharmacy, 1715–1927*, rev. E. C. Cripps (1927) · D. Chapman-Huston and E. C. Cripps, *Through a City archway: the story of Allen and Hanburys, 1715–1954* (1954) · A. N. Gamble, *A history of the Bevan family* [1924] · *The letters of Lewis, Richard, William and John Morris of Anglesey*, ed. J. H. Davies, 2 vols. (1907–9) · J. Burnby, 'A study of the English apothecary from 1660 to 1760', *Medical History*, suppl. 3 (1983) [whole issue]

Bevan, William Latham (1821–1908), Church of England clergyman, born on 1 May 1821 at Beaufort, Brecknockshire, was eldest of three sons of William Hibbs Bevan (1788–1846), then of Beaufort, but later of Glannant, Crickhowell, high sheriff for Brecknockshire in 1841, and Margaret, daughter of Joseph Latham, also of Beaufort, but originally from Broughton in Furness. With a stepbrother, Edward Kendall, his father ran the Beaufort ironworks, trading as Kendall and Bevan, until 1833.

Educated at Rugby School under Thomas Arnold, Bevan matriculated from Balliol College, Oxford, on 14 December 1838; but he immediately moved to Magdalen Hall on being elected Lusby scholar there. He graduated BA in 1842, with a second class in the final classical school, and MA in 1845. In 1844 he was ordained deacon, and in 1845, after a short curacy at Stepney, he was ordained priest and presented to the living of Hay, Brecknockshire, by Sir Joseph Bailey, who was married to his aunt. This living, though a poor one without a parsonage, he held for fifty-six years. He lived in no little style at Hay Castle, leased from Sir Joseph Bailey, later Lord Glanusk, who had bought the property in 1844. Francis Kilvert, the diarist, was a frequent visitor there. His private means enabled him to contribute largely to the restoration of the church, in 1866, and the erection of a town clock and tower, besides building a parish hall at his own expense in 1890. He was also prebendary of Llanddewi Aber-arth in St David's Cathedral (1876–9); canon residentiary of St David's (1879–93); archdeacon of Brecon from 1895 until 1907; proctor for the diocese of St David's (1880–95); examining chaplain to the bishop (1881–97); and chaplain of Hay Union (1850–95). Bevan married on 19 June 1849, at Whitney church, Herefordshire, Louisa (1829–1909), fourth daughter of Tomkyns Dew of Whitney Court; they had three sons and four daughters.

Bevan was known in his day for a number of pamphlets

written in defence of the Church in Wales during the controversy over disestablishment. A contributor to William Smith's *Dictionary of the Bible*, he also wrote some manuals on ancient geography. A competent historian, he is now remembered for his brief history of the diocese of St David's in the SPCK series of diocesan histories (1888).

In November 1901 Bevan retired from Hay to Ely Tower, Brecon. The house was so named because, built on ground which once was the bailey of Brecon Castle, there is in the garden the ruin of a tower where a bishop of Ely, John Morton, was imprisoned in the fifteenth century. Bevan died there on 24 August 1908, and was buried on 1 September at Hay, where his widow, who died on 23 October 1909, was also buried. He is commemorated in Hay church by carved oak choir stalls and a marble chancel pavement, given by his family in August 1910. The St David's diocesan conference in 1908 resolved on founding a diocesan memorial to him. The Archdeacon Bevan Trust, now administered in the diocese of Swansea and Brecon, is designed to encourage historical research.

Edward Latham Bevan (1861–1934), Church in Wales clergyman, the youngest son, the Teddy Bevan of Kilvert's diary, was born at Weymouth, where the family had property, on 27 October 1861. Educated privately, he entered Hertford College, Oxford in 1881 and graduated BA in 1884. Ordained to a title to Holy Trinity, Weymouth, 1886–91, he then became chaplain of the Gordon Boys' Home, Worthing (1891–6); then vicar of Brecon from 1897. He succeeded his father as archdeacon of Brecon in 1907 and was appointed suffragan bishop of Swansea in 1915. He became the first bishop of the diocese of Swansea and Brecon, created in 1923. He was then the national chairman of the Church of England Men's Society. His benefactions to the new cathedral, formerly the priory church, were considerable and the family home, Ely Tower, became the residence of his successors. He died unmarried on 2 February 1934 at Ely Tower, Brecon, and was buried on 8 February in Brecon Cathedral grounds.

D. L. THOMAS, *rev.* O. W. JONES

Sources *Church Times* (28 Aug 1908) · Foster, *Alum. Oxon.* · T. Jones, *History of Breconshire* (1930), 3. 101–5 · *DWB* · *WWW*, 1929–40 · *Western Mail* [Cardiff] (25 Aug 1908) · *Western Mail* [Cardiff] (28 Aug 1908) · *Guardian* (26 Aug 1908) · parish register (baptism), Llangattock, Brecknockshire, 27 May 1821 · parish register (marriage), Whitney, Herefordshire, 19 June 1849 · parish register (burial), Hay, Brecknockshire, 1 Sept 1908 · burial register, Brecon Cathedral, 8 Feb 1934
Wealth at death £69,807 7s. 3d.: resworn probate, 1 Oct 1908, *CGPLA Eng. & Wales* · £48,227 3s. 4d.—Edward Latham Bevan: resworn probate, 26 March 1934, *CGPLA Eng. & Wales*

Bever, John [John of London] (*d.* 1311?), Benedictine monk and historical writer, may have been a Londoner—in 1310 the archdeacon of Westminster was ordered to publish the excommunication for contumacy of 'Brother John of London, called Le Bevere' (Gransden, 'Continuations', 480, n. 40). Little is known of his life, but he is recorded in the Westminster infirmarer's rolls in 1294, 1298, and 1310–11, and in lists of abbey monks imprisoned on suspicion of robbing the king's treasury in 1303. In 1307 he protested against the deprivation of Prior Hadham, and he opposed

the election of Abbot Kedyngton in 1308. He died at Westminster Abbey, probably shortly after his last appearance in the infirmarer's rolls in February 1311.

Four works have been attributed to Bever, on evidence of variable value. His name appears at the end of a version of the *Flores historiarum*, the St Albans chronicle of Matthew Paris with its continuation composed at Westminster and going up to 1306, found in BL, Harley MS 641. This version, which belonged to St Augustine's Abbey at Canterbury, is a text of the second, or 'Merton', recension of the Westminster continuation, a recension that was evidently made for circulation and was more favourable to Edward I than the original; in the Harley text it ends with a note, not clearly in the text hand but contemporary, 'de edicione domini Johannis Bevere'. He may therefore have compiled the Merton recension, originally, it has been suggested, in a de luxe edition for presentation to Edward II at his coronation. In the Harley text the portion of the *Flores* covering the period before 1066 has been replaced by an abridgement of Geoffrey of Monmouth's *Historia regum*, with numerous Latin verses. The abridgement also circulated separately under the title *Tractatus de Bruto abbreviato*. Whether Bever was the author of the abridgement and the verses, which indicate wide reading in classical literature, as their editor has assumed, or was merely the compiler of a text conflating it with the Merton *Flores*, is not now possible to determine.

Bever was also firmly credited with another rhetorical work, the *Commendatio lamentabilis in transitum magni regis Edwardi quarti* (that is, Edward I). The attribution appears in BL, Arundel MS 20 *secundum Johannem de London*. It is effectively an obituary notice of Edward I addressed to Queen Margaret, which adopts both a warmer tone and a broader perspective on him than the Westminster continuation of the *Flores*, but adds no new information. It appears most commonly as an appendix to the circulated or Merton version of the Westminster *Flores*. Finally, a fourth short work, a *passio* or rhetorical account of the sufferings of the monks of Westminster when accused unjustly of robbing the king's treasury, is referred to in the original Westminster continuation as a text *secundum Johannem* available for circulation; but it is not now extant. All that can confidently be said amid these uncertainties is that Bever was among the Westminster monks who compiled histories and recorded contemporary events in various versions, some of them for circulation, in the first decade of the fourteenth century. His rhetorical style was suited to presentation pieces, but his skills as a historian did not stand out from the other, mainly anonymous, chroniclers of his house.

JEREMY CATTO

Sources 'Merton' recension of the 'Flores historiarum' and 'Tractatus de Bruto abbreviato', BL, Harley MS 641 · 'Commendatio lamentabilis', College of Arms, Arundel MS 20 · infirmarer's rolls, Westminster Abbey, muniments 5460, 6047, 9499B · H. R. Luard, ed., *Flores historiarum*, 3 vols., Rolls Series, 95 (1890) · W. Stubbs, ed., 'Commendatio lamentabilis in transitu magni Regis Edwardi', *Chronicles of the reigns of Edward I and Edward II*, 2, Rolls Series, 76 (1883), 3–21 · J. Hammer, 'The poetry of Johannes Beverus with extracts from his *Tractatus de bruto abbreviato*', *Modern Philology*, 34 (1936–7), 119–32 · E. H. Pearce, *The monks of Westminster* (1916) ·

A. Gransden, 'The continuations of the *Flores historiarum* from 1265 to 1327', *Mediaeval Studies*, 36 (1974), 472–92 · A. Gransden, *Historical writing in England*, 1 (1974) · J. Taylor, *English historical literature in the fourteenth century* (1987)
Archives BL, Arundel MS 20 · BL, Harley MS 641

Bever, Thomas (*bap.* **1725**, *d.* **1791**), lawyer and legal writer, was baptized at Stratfield Mortimer, Berkshire, on 22 September 1725, one of at least two sons of Thomas Bever, whose family had owned land in the parish since the fifteenth century, and of Ann, his wife. He graduated BA from Oriel College, Oxford, in 1748 and in the following year he became a fellow of All Souls, from where he graduated BCL in 1753. He graduated DCL in 1758 and was admitted to Doctors' Commons in the same year. He was subsequently judge of the Cinque Ports and chancellor of the dioceses of Lincoln and Bangor.

In 1762 the success of Blackstone's lectures on English law induced Bever to obtain the permission of the vice-chancellor and the consent of the regius professor of civil law (whose health was alleged to prevent him from lecturing) to deliver a course upon civil law which was intended to provide his auditors with that knowledge of the nature and general principles of law which should form part of a general education, rather than to prepare them for practice as advocates. He continued for some years, though his auditory was sometimes small enough to be accommodated in his rooms at All Souls, and published his introductory lecture in 1766 as *A discourse on the study of jurisprudence and the civil law, being an introduction to a course of lectures.* He left his manuscript of the course to his friend Dr John Loveday, upon condition that he would promise not to permit any part of it to be printed. It is now All Souls MS 109.

In 1781 Bever published *The history of the legal polity of the Roman state and of the rise progress and extent of the Roman laws.* An anonymous contributor to the *Gentleman's Magazine* wrote: 'Had it been seasoned with the gross licentiousness and heterodoxy of Gibbon, instead of containing many specimens of a rooted regard for the cause of Religion and Virtue, it might perhaps have met with more readers' (*GM*, 1798, 753). He intended to devote a second volume to the history of the Roman law from the rediscovery of Justinian's compilations in the twelfth century to his own time, but it never appeared, and he directed his executors to burn all manuscripts in his own hand on the subject of law (other than his lectures) at the first convenient opportunity.

Bever died unmarried at his house at Doctors' Commons on 8 November 1791, 'of an asthma which probably would not then have been fatal to him, if he had suffered himself to be removed from London to a less turbid air; but in what concerned his health he was incompliant and perverse' (Coote, 125–6). He was buried at the parish church of Stratfield Mortimer, Berkshire. The same author's judgement that he was 'a better scholar than writer, and a better writer than pleader' is, perhaps unintentionally, an unkind one, for as a writer he was neither very original nor very profound. His attempt to revive civil law lectures at Oxford had no lasting results, though Jeremy Bentham's statement that he gave lectures on Roman law which were laughed at (*Works of Jeremy Bentham*, 10.45) cannot have been founded on personal knowledge, for Bentham imagined that Bever had succeeded Blackstone as Vinerian professor and lectured in that capacity. Bever left an important collection of musical manuscripts to his friend Mr Windle, whose administrator dispersed it. He was also a patron of William Sherwin the engraver, who made him a present of his only known original work, a painting of Leonidas taking leave of his wife and son. His younger brother Samuel was his residuary legatee.

J. L. BARTON

Sources *GM*, 1st ser., 53 (1783), 667–70 · *GM*, 1st ser., 61 (1791), 662–3, 1068 · *GM*, 1st ser., 68 (1798), 517, 753–4 · *VCH Berkshire*, 3.426 · [C. Coote], *Sketches of the lives and characters of eminent English civilians, with an historical introduction relative to the College of Advocates* (1804), 125–6 · will, PRO, PROB 11/1210 · *The works of Jeremy Bentham*, ed. J. Bowring, [new edn], 11 vols. (1843–59), vol. 10, p. 45 · Foster, *Alum. Oxon.* · *DNB* · private information (2004) [Society of Genealogists]
Archives All Souls Oxf., MS 109
Wealth at death comfortable: will, PRO, PROB 11/1210

Beveridge [*née* Akroyd], **Annette Susannah** (1842–1929), orientalist, was born in Mount Street, Stourbridge, Worcestershire, on 13 December 1842, the third child and daughter surviving to adulthood of William Akroyd (*d.* 1869), a currier, and his wife, Sarah, *née* Walford, a daughter of the local livery stable owner. After his wife's death in 1849, Akroyd married Mary Anne Perks; three children of this marriage survived to adulthood. Akroyd, who became a prosperous businessman, was a notably energetic leader in civic affairs, in the Presbyterian–Unitarian chapel and in radical Liberal politics. Annette was deeply attached to him, and he was her lifelong model for uncompromising independence, plain speaking, and doing one's duty.

Unitarianism was a determining influence in Annette Akroyd's life. In January 1861 it brought her to the Unitarian-led Bedford College in London, where she completed a three-year course of study. At the college her commitment to secular and to women's education was reinforced—ignorant middle-class girls were just as needy in this respect as the poor, she once argued, and thus were equally fit subjects for philanthropy. On her father's death in 1869 the Akroyds moved permanently to London, where they were members of James Martineau's Little Portland Street Chapel. Throughout her life she expressed a desire for firmer faith, but seems to have been thwarted in attempts to achieve it by a tough-minded rationalism inherited from her father.

In 1872 Akroyd went to India to start a school for Hindu girls, a mission inspired in part by Keshub Chunder Sen (1838–1884), leader of the Brahmo Samaj, a Hindu reformist sect with historic ties to the Unitarians. In a visit to England in 1870 Sen had urged well-trained Englishwomen to come to India to provide a secular education for Indian women; in October of 1872 Annette Akroyd sailed for Calcutta determined not to be a part of the Anglo-Indian set. Almost immediately, however, she fell out with Sen and his Brahmos, as they were referred to, about the control and curriculum of the school. Their conflict was entangled in internal Brahmo disputes and very quickly she was identified with one Brahmo wing and attacked by the press of the other. By May 1873 she had broken with the Brahmos, continuing to run the school alone until 1875. She was wounded by what she regarded as dishonourable behaviour on the part of the Brahmos, all the more so, perhaps, because the episode ended her social activism. Her perceptions about this experience coloured her sharp public opposition to the Ilbert Bill of 1883, legislation which would have expanded the jurisdiction of native Indian judges over Europeans.

On 6 April 1875 Akroyd married Henry Beveridge (1837–1929), a judge in the Indian Civil Service. Between 1877 and 1885 they had two daughters and two sons. Although she has been portrayed as domineering towards her son William *Beveridge, Baron Beveridge, this characterization might legitimately be softened. Certainly she was a dutiful mother: her letters are full of anxiety about arranging for her children's health and education. Given life in the Indian Civil Service, such arrangements were not easy and fell almost exclusively on her.

Her husband's scholarly interests and her own progressive deafness promoted Annette Beveridge's turn to scholarship. It is typical of her steely virtue that she never gave way to physical handicap, but her letters contain a few poignant hints of the social isolation she sometimes felt. Her first translation was made in 1890, from German, of F. A. de Noer's *Emperor Akbar*, the preface of which gives a rare glimpse into her idealism about the British empire. After resettling in England in 1890 she began to learn Persian, initially as a distraction from grief: between 1890 and 1893 two of her four children died. Her first oriental translation was of the *Humayun-nama* (1902), from Persian. Her best-known translation is of Babur's autobiography, the *Babur-nama*. Although this important sixteenth-century classic had previously been translated from Persian into English, she was the first to translate it from the language in which Babur wrote, Chagatai Turkish. The project consumed nearly twenty years of her life because of the research required on fundamental matters, such as establishing the authentic text and knowledge of a language then little known in the West. The *Babur-nama* was published in four instalments between 1912 and 1921. Her translation is not felicitous from a literary point of view, but the hallmarks of her work—the most complete of indices, and scrupulous footnotes and appendices on matters of fact—have made it invaluable for later scholars. She died on 29 March 1929 at 26 Porchester Square, Bayswater, London, and was cremated on 2 April. Her husband Henry survived her by seven months. Her surviving son achieved lasting fame as the architect of the welfare state, and her daughter, Jeannette, married the historian R. H. Tawney. A scholarship in her name was established by her husband and children at Bedford College in July 1929.

M. A. SCHERER

Sources BL OIOC, Annette and Henry Beveridge MSS · BLPES, Beveridge MSS · W. Beveridge, *India called them* (1947) · *The Times* (1 April 1929) · M. A. Scherer, 'Annette Akroyd Beveridge: Victorian reformer, oriental scholar', PhD diss., Ohio State University, 1995 [incl. detailed bibliography of her works] · A. G. E., 'Mrs Beveridge', *Journal of the Royal Asiatic Society of Great Britain and Ireland* (1929), 729 [incl. an abbreviated bibliography of her works] · E. D. Ross, 'Henry Beveridge', *Journal of the Royal Asiatic Society of Great Britain and Ireland* (1930), 224–8 [incl. a bibliography of her works], esp. 226–7 · D. Kopf, *The Brahmo Somaj and the shaping of the modern Indian mind* (1979) · M. Borthwick, *The changing role of women in Bengal, 1849–1905* (1984) · Herefs. RO, William Akroyd MSS · M. J. Tuke, *A history of Bedford College for Women, 1849–1937* (1939) · records, Royal Holloway College, Egham, Surrey · d. cert.

Archives BL OIOC, corresp., diaries, and papers, MS Eur. C 176 · BLPES, family corresp. | Worcs. RO, William Akroyd MSS

Likenesses cameo profile, repro. in Beveridge, *India called them* · photographs, BL OIOC, Beveridge MSS · photographs, repro. in Beveridge, *India called them*

Wealth at death £4560 14s. 4d.: resworn probate, 6 June 1929, CGPLA Eng. & Wales

Beveridge, Erskine (1851–1920), textile manufacturer and antiquary, was born on 27 December 1851 at Priory House, Dunfermline, Fife, the eldest of the four children of Erskine Beveridge (1803–1864) and his second wife, Maria Elizabeth Wilson (1816–1873). He was educated at the Free Abbey School, Dunfermline (1857–61), at the Edinburgh Institution (1862–9), and at Edinburgh University (1870–74). Although Erskine Beveridge senior had established Dunfermline's first successful power-loom factory in 1851, his son's success in transforming the family firm into one of the foremost producers of linen damask in the world was not based on straightforward inheritance. When his father died in 1864 Erskine junior was only twelve years old. For the next ten years the company was run, in trusteeship, by an uncle. In 1874 the firm passed to the control of a partnership of Erskine junior, his brother Henry, and his half-brother, John Adamson Beveridge. This partnership, in which John was both much older and more experienced than his two brothers, was neither equal nor, perhaps, very comfortable. In 1887 John died, and in the following year Henry withdrew, leaving Erskine junior in sole command. A similar course was followed with regard to family property. In 1876 Erskine junior purchased St Leonard's Hill, his father's mansion house. In 1891 he completed the acquisition of his father's business and property by purchasing the estate of Brucefield, which adjoined the Dunfermline works.

Erskine Beveridge's control of the company coincided with a period of phenomenal growth in the world market for high-quality linen. The expansion of shipping lines and railway companies, and the culmination of gracious living in grand hotels, embassies, and country houses, created a demand for Dunfermline's staple product. Beveridge's business achievement rested on his exploitation of the huge North American market. This was by no means without difficulty. Competition from Germany and Ireland, and the increasingly protectionist trade policies of the United States, formed considerable obstacles. However, by employing modern business methods and marketing finesse, Beveridge was able to maintain steady and substantial profitability throughout his career. In 1892 he converted the firm to a limited liability company with himself as majority shareholder, general manager, and chairman. His two fellow directors were employees of the firm and included the manager of the New York warehouse. By 1903 three branch factories had been opened in addition to substantial expansion of the main works at Dunfermline, and Erskine Beveridge & Co. Ltd was recognized as a world leader in the fine linen trade.

Like his father Beveridge married twice and had two families. On 1 May 1872 he married Mary Owst (*b.* 1853), with whom he had six sons and a daughter. She died on 21 February 1904. On 29 January 1908 he married Margaret Scott Inglis, with whom he had two sons.

While Beveridge gave close personal supervision to his business interests throughout his life, he nevertheless found the time and energy to make a significant contribution to Scottish antiquarian studies. His first published work, *The Churchyard Memorials of Crail* (1893), was a massive compilation which was generally well received. Although this was his only publication of this nature, his notebooks testify to a lifelong habit of visiting burial-grounds and painstakingly recording inscriptions. Other publications included *A Bibliography of Dunfermline and the West of Fife* (1901) and *The Burgh Records of Dunfermline, 1485–1584* (1917). His purchase of a summer home at Vallay in North Uist also inspired Beveridge to undertake archaeological projects in the Western Isles, and two works, *Coll and Tiree: their Prehistoric Forts and Ecclesiastical Antiquities* (1903) and *North Uist: its Archaeology and Topography* (1911) were the result. After his death, his notes formed the basis of two further works: *The 'Abers' and 'Invers' of Scotland* (1923), a study of place names, and an annotated edition of *Fergusson's Scottish Proverbs* (1924). Beveridge's interest in photography is represented by a two-volume collection of collotype reproductions, published as *Wanderings with a Camera, 1882–1898* (1922).

Beveridge was awarded an honorary doctorate from the University of St Andrews, made a fellow of the Royal Society of Edinburgh, and appointed honorary sheriff-substitute for Fife. His public posts included those of town councillor, briefly, justice of the peace, and chairman of the Dunfermline hospital committee.

Through his pre-eminence in trade and his diligent, scholarly work, Erskine Beveridge gained the respect of his contemporaries. Despite this, it is possible to see his commitment to public life as less than wholehearted. As Dunfermline's largest employer, his economic fortunes were intricately linked to the town and surrounding district, but, as a member of the Scottish Episcopal church and a supporter of the Conservative Party, he was a marginal figure in the lively ecclesiastical and political life of his own community. As Beveridge's business career and to some extent his private interests show, he was happiest operating in areas where his control was total.

Beveridge's family home was St Leonard's Hill, Dunfermline, which commanded views of his estate, his company's works, and the homes of many of his employees. He died there on 10 August 1920 after an operation to remove a cancer of the throat, and was buried three days later in the old abbey churchyard, Dunfermline, after a funeral service at Holy Trinity Episcopal Church.

CHRIS NEALE

Sources H. Walker, *The story of Erskine Beveridge and St Leonard's works, 1833–1989* (1991) · S. A. Beveridge, *The story of the Beveridge families of England and Scotland* (1923) · N. J. Morgan, 'Beveridge, Erskine', *DSBB* · Erskine Beveridge & Co. Ltd, *Weave trust with truth* (1928) · *Dunfermline Journal* (14 Aug 1920) · *Dunfermline Press* (14 Aug 1920) · A. W. C. Hallen, *An account of the Beveridge family of Dunfermline* (1890) · Erskine Beveridge & Co. Ltd records, NA Scot., SRO BT2/2449 · D. Steel, 'The linen industry of Fife in the later 18th and 19th centuries', PhD diss., U. St Andr., 1975 · P. K. Livingstone, *Flax and linen in Fife throughout the centuries* (1952) · A. J. Warden, *The linen trade: ancient and modern* (1864) · D. Bremner, *The industries of Scotland: their rise, progress, and present condition* (1869)

Archives Dunfermline Central Library, corresp., galleyproofs, notes on Fife chuchyards, etc.

Likenesses J. Norval, photograph, *c.*1910, Dunfermline Central Library · photograph, repro. in *Dunfermline Journal*

Wealth at death £105,787 16s. 0d.: confirmation, 23 Oct 1920, *CCI*

Beveridge, William (*bap.* **1637**, *d.* **1708**), bishop of St Asaph, was the son of William Beveridge (1608/9–1640/41) and was baptized on 21 February 1637 at Barrow upon Soar, Leicestershire, where his grandfather, father, and elder brother John were successively vicars. He spent two years at the new free school at Oakham, Rutland, before being admitted a sizar at St John's College, Cambridge, where his schoolfellow William Cave, the future historian of the early church, later joined him. Another contemporary, Isaac Milles, said that Beveridge was 'very rarely if ever' to be seen in 'places of diversion', but normally spent his leisure hours 'either at a bookseller's shop, in useful conversation, or in his chamber at his study' (Baker, 2.646; Mullinger, 35–6). The master of the college, the puritan divine Anthony Tuckney, particularly assisted the young Beveridge, but his religious outlook seems to have been influenced rather by his tutor, Nicholas Bullingham, the senior dean, who at the Restoration was prominent in securing Tuckney's removal for not accepting the Book of Common Prayer.

Scholarship Beveridge graduated BA in 1656 and proceeded MA in 1660. He early revealed his main interest by his publication of an ambitious Latin treatise, *The excellency and use of the oriental tongues, especially Hebrew, Chaldee, Syriac and Samaritan, together with a grammar of the Syriac language* (1658, 2nd edn. 1664). In 1661 two prelates, anxious to encourage the younger generation of churchmen who had grown up since the civil war, favoured him. Robert Sanderson, bishop of Lincoln, ordained him deacon on 3 January and, unusually speedily, priest on 31 January, which enabled Gilbert Sheldon, bishop of London, to collate him to the vicarage of Ealing (then commonly known as Yealing), Middlesex. In his *Private Thoughts* in that year Beveridge resolved 'by the grace of God to feed the flock over which God shall set him with wholesome food, neither starving them by idleness, poisoning them with error, nor puffing them up with impertinences' (resolution 5). The small parish, however, allowed him time to continue his reading and writing. As well as his

William Beveridge (*bap.* 1637, *d.* 1708), by Michael Vandergucht, pubd 1709 (after Benjamin Ferrers)

Institutiones chronologicae of 1669 he published in 1672 at Oxford (where he had been incorporated into the university on 11 May 1669) his great *Collection of Canons Received by the Greek Church*, two large folio volumes of Greek and Latin, containing learned reproductions of accurate texts, but also claiming apostolic origin and sanction for markedly post-apostolic documents. His *Vindication of his Collection of the Canons* (1679) responded to an anonymous Latin attack (now known to be by Matthieu de Larroque of Rouen). Beveridge took an important part in assisting the development of the high-church position with other antiquaries and liturgists, who traced from the early Christian model their notion of the ideal relations between church and state.

St Peter Cornhill, London In 1672 the lord mayor and aldermen of London presented Beveridge to St Peter Cornhill, then being rebuilt by Sir Christopher Wren. He resigned Ealing and established his reputation as an active and conscientious parish priest, an exemplar of that religious revival in the Church of England which began after the Restoration of 1660 and continued into the 'Indian summer of the high church movement' in Queen Anne's reign. He held daily services and a weekly communion, upheld confession, taught the young, and visited the sick. Even the critical Denis Grenville praised his devout practice, which edified the city and increased his congregation every week—'He hath seldom less than fourscore some time six or seven score communicants and a great many young apprentices who come every Lord's with great devotion' (*Miscellanea, Comprising the Works and Letters of Denis Grenville*, Surtees Society, 1861, 37, xxi); and Robert Nelson declared him 'a pattern of true primitive piety'

and that many 'owed their change of lives, under God, to his instructions'. Beveridge was made a canon of Chichester in 1673 and collated to the prebendary of Chiswick in St Paul's Cathedral on 22 December 1674; he was created DD in 1679. Robert Boyle, the natural philosopher and chemist, used to say that his ideal Christian leader was Henry Hammond, chaplain to Charles I, among the dead and Beveridge among the living (Higham, 332). To Gilbert Burnet, he was, however, 'a man of great learning, a very practical preacher and a devout man and in the monastic way too superstitious and singular' (Baker, 2.704).

Beveridge's most famous sermon was his *A Sermon Concerning the Excellency and Usefulness of the Common Prayer*, which he preached at the consecration of his parish church in 1681 and which became a religious bestseller, reaching its forty-fourth edition by 1824. He had insisted that a chancel screen should be erected in St Peter's, which Wren disliked in his churches. Beveridge asserted in his sermon that such a screen not only preserved the church's unity with universal practice and satisfied the desire to avoid undesirable novelty and singularity in worship, but also enclosed the chancel as a special place for the celebration of the communion service by both the priest and the communicants.

In November 1681 Beveridge was appointed archdeacon of Colchester. He took seriously his twofold duty of supervising the clergy in the archdeaconry and of care over the temporal administration of its ecclesiastical property. He sought to be the friend and adviser of the clergy; and he was not satisfied with the churchwardens' presentments made to him at his visitations, but personally went to every parish, inspecting the condition of the churches and churchyards and ordering any necessary repairs or restorations to be undertaken.

Beveridge's sermon of 1681 on the Book of Common Prayer, when published, rapidly achieved four editions. In 1683 he preached two more popular sermons—in April as a governor of the Sons of the Clergy at their annual festival and in September on the anniversary of the great fire of London in 1666. On 5 November 1684 he was made a prebendary of Canterbury and he became president of Sion College in 1689.

Beveridge was one of those clergy—alongside Anthony Horneck, preacher at the Savoy Chapel, and William Smythies, curate of St Giles Cripplegate—who were mainly responsible for the spread of Anglican voluntary religious societies in London in the 1680s, devotional associations of laymen under the aegis of orthodox Church of England clergy. Burnet recalled, postdating the beginnings of this development a little, how

> In King James's reign, the fear of popery was so strong …
> that many, in and about London, began to meet often
> together, both for devotion and for their further instruction:
> things of that kind had been formerly practised only among
> the puritans and the dissenters: but these were of the
> church, and came to their ministers, to be assisted with
> forms of prayer and other directions: they were chiefly
> conducted by Dr Beveridge and Dr Horneck. (*Bishop Burnet's
> History*, 5.18)

After the revolution of 1688: comprehension, Bath and Wells, and the SPCK Beveridge stood apart from the scheme for comprehension of 1668 first projected by Sir Orlando Bridgeman, lord keeper of the great seal, John Wilkins, bishop of Chester, and Sir Matthew Hale, lord chief baron of the exchequer, with the intention of 'relaxing the terms of conformity to the established church' (Abbey and Overton, 175). In 1675 Edward Stillingfleet and John Tillotson revived the project and secured the approval of the leading nonconformists, but this was again defeated and was unsupported by Beveridge. So also with William III's scheme for a synod of divines. Beveridge's attitude to these reforms led John Tillotson to say to him, 'Doctor, doctor, charity is better than rubrics' (T. Birch, *The Life of … John Tillotson*, 1752, lxxxxviii). At the opening of convocation on 20 November 1689, however, when Beveridge preached the Latin sermon, he declared comprehension might be secured by some modifications in national or provincial usages, but not in fundamental, divine laws; and he was a member of the unsuccessful commission of divines to revise the prayer book and again consider comprehension.

Beveridge took the oath of loyalty to King William and Queen Mary, but in 1691—when selected to fill the see of Bath and Wells vacated by Thomas Ken, who would not take that oath—he spent three weeks considering the offer. He at first accepted the preferment, but then declined it. He finally decided that he could not agree with the legality of appointing new bishops to sees that were not canonically vacant since their occupants had been guilty of no ecclesiastical crime. He declared that he 'would not eat Dr. Ken's bread'. He had been urged not to take the bishopric by William Sancroft, the deprived archbishop of Canterbury. His refusal of it made him popular with the nonjurors but disliked at court, and he was violently criticized in a pamphlet, *A vindication of their majesties' authority to fill the sees of the deprived bishops, in a letter out of the country, occasioned by Dr. B—'s refusal of the bishoprick of Bath and Wells* (1691). In 1698 Beveridge was a prominent figure co-operating in the founding of the Society for Promoting Christian Knowledge (SPCK), the most striking post-revolution fruition of the movement for voluntary associations within the Church of England. Its purpose was to supervise the establishment of charity schools in England and Wales, to supply bibles and religious tracts both at home and overseas, and generally to encourage the strengthening and spreading of the Christian religion through education and missionary work.

Bishop of St Asaph, death, and reputation Beveridge ultimately became a bishop in the following reign, and was enthroned bishop of St Asaph on 16 July 1704. He resigned from the archdeaconry of Colchester, but was allowed to retain his St Paul's prebendary *in commendam*. The parochial clergy in Wales during Queen Anne's reign were poor (through the widespread impropriation of tithes under the Tudor monarchs) and therefore badly educated, a situation the bishop sought to remedy. He encouraged the use of the Welsh prayer book published for the use of his clergy, *A Plain and Easy Exposition of the Church Catechism*,

and distributed a Welsh translation of Robert Nelson's tract on confirmation. Most important probably was his introduction of the SPCK in Wales, which received a large share of the society's funds, and Welshmen took a prominent part in its affairs.

As bishop, Beveridge secured the appointment of William *Stanley as dean of St Asaph. Stanley was the son of William Stanley of Hinckley, Leicestershire, and Beveridge's sister Lucy, while Beveridge had in turn married a sister of the elder William Stanley. Beveridge's wife predeceased him, and no children survived them.

On 5 November 1704 Beveridge preached before the House of Lords on the Gunpowder Plot, and on 30 January 1705 he preached there on the martyrdom of King Charles I. As a member of the House of Lords he strongly opposed the Act of Union between England and Scotland, insisting that Scottish presbyterianism would endanger the Church of England.

Beveridge's last public appearance was on 20 January 1708. He died in his apartments in the cloisters of Westminster Abbey on 5 March 1708 and was buried in St Paul's Cathedral. He had stated in his will that he wished to be 'decently interred, but without pomp or tumult' (will, fol. 62v). Among his bequests were an endowment to Barrow and £100 to the Society for the Propagation of the Gospel. He left his books to William Stanley ('whome I should have made my Executor but that he is a Clergyman') in trust for him to set up a public library in St Paul's for the City clergy, and gave the advowson of Barrow upon Soar to St John's College, Cambridge, his old college (will, fol. 63v).

As his executor, Beveridge's secretary published several of his writings posthumously including his principal theological work, *An Exposition of the Thirty-Nine Articles* (1710). Though in most respects a high-churchman, Beveridge also showed that he accepted much of John Calvin's doctrine of predestination, holding that the number of the saved would be very few (by no means an uncommon juxtaposition of beliefs in the period). Nevertheless, his outlook continued to attract those who favoured his churchmanship. Collected editions of his sermons and other writings, all three of which are incomplete, have been edited by T. Gregory (2 vols., 1720), T. H. Horne (9 vols., 1824), and J. Bliss (Library of Anglo-Catholic Theology, 12 vols., 1843–8). On the other hand, Daniel Whitby, a contemporary polemical divine and advocate of concessions to nonconformists, was not an admirer of Beveridge's writings. He stated, 'He delights in jingle and quibbling, affects a tune and rhyme in all he says and rests arguments upon nothing but words and sounds' (D. Whitby, *A Short View of Dr. Beveridge's Writings*, 1711, 26).

LEONARD W. COWIE

Sources T. H. Horne, *Life of Beveridge* (1824) [preface to works] · M. Clement, *Correspondence and minutes of the SPCK relating to Wales, 1699–1740*, University of Wales: History and Law Series, 10 (1952) · M. Clement, *The SPCK and Wales, 1699–1740* (1954) · D. R. Thomas, *St Asaph* (1888) · R. T. Jenkins, *Hanes Cymru yn y ddeunawfed ganrif* (1931) · D. A. Jones, *A history of the church in Wales* (1926) · C. J. Abbey and J. H. Overton, *The English church in the eighteenth century*, new edn (1896) · J. H. Overton, *Life in the English church, 1660–1714* (1885) ·

N. Sykes, *From Sheldon to Secker: aspects of English church history, 1660–1768* (1959) · L. M. Hawkins, *Allegiance in church and state* (1928) · F. Higham, *Catholic and Reformed* (1932) · G. Every, *The high church party, 1688–1718* (1956) · E. H. Pearce, *The Sons of the Clergy* (1928) · T. Baker, *History of the college of St John the Evangelist, Cambridge*, ed. J. E. B. Mayor, 2 (1869) · W. Kennett, *Compleat history of England*, 3 vols. (1706), vol. 3 · G. D'Oyly, *The life of William Sancroft*, 2 vols. (1821) · Venn, *Alum. Cant.* · Foster, *Alum. Oxon.* · will, PRO, PROB 11/500, sig. 52 · J. B. Mullinger, *St John's College* (1901) · J. Spurr, 'The church, the societies and the moral revolution of 1688', *The Church of England, c.1689–c.1833: from toleration to tractarianism*, ed. J. Walsh, C. Haydon, and S. Taylor (1993), 127–42 · *Fasti Angl., 1541–1857*, [St Paul's, London] · *Fasti Angl., 1541–1857*, [Canterbury] · I. Green, *The Christian's ABC: catechism and catechizing in England, c.1530–1740* (1996) · I. Green, *Print and protestantism in early modern England* (2000)

Archives BL, Add. MSS 4724, 11, 4275 · Bodl. Oxf., MSS Tanner, corresp. · Bodl. Oxf., MSS Rawl. MSS, fol. 9, ii, 176 · Northumbd RO, Newcastle upon Tyne, letters to Elizabeth Neale, ZRI

Likenesses B. Ferrers, oils, c.1708, Bodl. Oxf. · M. Vandergucht, line engraving (after B. Ferrers), BM, NPG; repro. in W. Beveridge, *The true nature of the Christian church in twelve sermons* (1709) [*see illus.*]

Wealth at death £850; plus estate in Barrow upon Soar: will, PRO, PROB 11/500, sig. 52

William Henry Beveridge, Baron Beveridge (1879–1963), by Helen Muspratt, 1938

Beveridge, William Henry, Baron Beveridge (1879–1963), social reformer and economist, was born at Rangpur in Bengal on 5 March 1879.

Family and upbringing Beveridge was the second child and elder son of Henry Beveridge (1837–1929), a district sessions judge in the Indian Civil Service, and his second wife, Annette Susannah Akroyd (1842–1929) [see Beveridge, Annette Susannah], daughter of a Worcestershire businessman. Henry Beveridge's father was David Beveridge of Dunfermline, a Scots Presbyterian bookseller and publisher who had written a radical history of British rule in India. The Beveridge parents were rather unusual figures in the Victorian raj, for Henry was a passionate advocate of Indian nationalism and home rule, and Annette had originally travelled to India before her marriage as a pioneer of secondary education for Hindu women. Both parents were deeply attached to Indian culture, and both became distinguished oriental scholars and translators of Hindi and Persian texts. Of their four children only one apart from William survived childhood—their second daughter, Annette Jeanie, or Jeannette, who married R. H. Tawney, Beveridge's Balliol contemporary.

Throughout his life Beveridge idealized family relationships and tended to portray his own childhood as uniquely happy. Yet he privately admitted that he had few adult recollections of childhood before his late teens; and evidence of family correspondence suggests that this ideal childhood was almost entirely imaginary. At the age of five he was sent to a Squeers-like Unitarian boarding-school in Worcestershire, and he saw nothing of his parents for the next two years. Although intellectually precocious he was a sickly and solitary child with few friends. His mother, perhaps the main influence on his early life, was by turns domineering, neglectful, and violently possessive. In 1892 he won a scholarship to Charterhouse, where he was bullied for being bad at games and discouraged from pursuing his passionate interest in natural science and astronomy. He excelled in both classics and mathematics, but neither of these subjects captured his imagination, and he afterwards complained that both intellectually and emotionally his life at Charterhouse had been almost entirely barren. Later in life he frequently felt himself to be a natural scientist *manqué* and blamed his early education for blocking the possibility of a scientific career. These childhood experiences may perhaps help to explain certain characteristics that many people found puzzling about the adult Beveridge—that he was a man of powerful and at times dazzling intellect, who yet never seemed to have fully developed his creative faculties nor to have discovered his true intellectual métier.

Commitment to social reform In 1897 Beveridge went as an exhibitioner to Balliol College, Oxford, where he gained a succession of first-class honours in mathematical moderations (1898), classical moderations (1899), and *literae humaniores* (1901). He then studied for several terms in the chambers of a London commercial barrister, and was awarded a prize fellowship at University College, Oxford, in 1902. The following year he took the bachelor of civil law degree. A brilliant career seemed to lie before him in academic life or at the bar. At this point, however, in the face of fierce parental opposition, he decided to abandon the law and to devote himself to the study and cure of social problems. He accepted an invitation from Samuel Barnett to become sub-warden of the well-known Oxford settlement in the East End of London, Toynbee Hall. This decision was denounced by his father as 'sentimental philanthropy', but in fact Beveridge's motives were the reverse of sentimental. After reading T. H. Huxley he had become convinced that social problems could be studied with the same rigour and exactitude as natural phenomena, and that social policies should be grounded not in spontaneous charity but in applied social science.

Beveridge's commitment to social reform came at a crucial moment in the history of social policy in Britain. The statistics of mass poverty published by Charles Booth and Benjamin Seebohm Rowntree, the physical deterioration scare at the end of the Second South African War, and the debate on tariff reform all conspired to thrust social problems into the forefront of high politics. At Toynbee Hall Beveridge soon found himself in contact with reformers of all persuasions—progressive Liberals, 'national efficiency' Conservatives, Fabian socialists, Comtean positivists, and disciples of John Ruskin—all of whom were pressing for more positive government action on the social question. In particular he fell under the spell of Sidney and Beatrice Webb, and while rejecting their socialist economic policies he was strongly influenced by their concept of a national minimum wage and their theories of administrative reform. He became active in the old age pensions movement, in the free school meals campaign, and in pressure for government action on behalf of the unemployed. In 1904 he began to collect material for what eventually became *Unemployment: a Problem of Industry* (1909)—a pioneering study which explored the structural complexity of the market for labour. During the depression of 1904–5 he helped to set up the London Unemployed Fund; and in 1905 he became a leading member of the Central (Unemployed) Body—a semi-official committee set up under the Unemployed Workmen Act to harmonize relief works provided by local authorities, boards of guardians, and private charities. It was as a member of this body that Beveridge first began to campaign for a national system of labour exchanges—bodies which he claimed would streamline the market for labour, eliminate casual unemployment, and enable social welfare agencies to distinguish between the 'loafer' and the genuinely unemployed.

Toynbee Hall soon became too narrow a base for Beveridge's ambitions, and at the end of 1905 he accepted a post as a leader writer on social problems with the Conservative daily newspaper, the *Morning Post*. He also became a member of the editorial board of the Ruskinian journal, *St. George's Papers* (a connection that lasted until 1911). During the next three years he produced nearly 1000 leading articles on such socio-economic questions as unemployment and casual labour, eugenics and the environment, progressive taxation and social insurance, local rating reform and 'back to the land'. He argued not merely for specific social policies but for the development of a strong, centralized, bureaucratic state and for a far-reaching programme of social organization—claiming, like the Benthamites eighty years earlier, that regulation of society through social administration would strengthen rather than weaken the free market economy. Beveridge's commitment to an interventionist state was reinforced by a visit to Germany, where he inspected the system of labour exchanges and contributory social insurance set up by the Prussian government. He returned to England convinced that a dual policy of labour exchanges and state insurance offered the best practical solution to the unemployment problem, and he argued strongly for

both these policies in evidence to the royal commission on the poor laws in the autumn of 1907. A few months later he was introduced by the Webbs to Winston Churchill, the newly appointed Liberal president of the Board of Trade. Churchill at this stage of his career was strongly influenced by the claim of the national efficiency school that social reform was an urgent strategic and imperial necessity; and as a result of this meeting he invited Beveridge to join the Board of Trade as his personal assistant in preparing legislation on unemployment.

Civil servant: Board of Trade, Ministry of Munitions, and Ministry of Food Beveridge entered Whitehall as a non-established civil servant in July 1908 at a time when the Liberal government was embarking upon the most active and ambitious phase of its social legislation programme. He spent the next three years working closely with the Board of Trade's permanent secretary, Sir Hubert Llewellyn Smith, in drawing up the Labour Exchanges Act of 1909 and part 2 of the National Insurance Act of 1911. Under these acts labour exchanges under Board of Trade control were established in all parts of the country, and unemployment insurance was provided for two and a quarter million workers in heavy industries. Beveridge himself became a permanent civil servant in 1909 with administrative responsibility for the labour exchanges system, and by 1913 he had reached the rank of assistant secretary. During this period he was convinced that he was within reach of a final solution for the unemployment problem and was anxious to extend unemployment insurance and compulsory decasualization to the whole of the nation's labour force.

These ambitions were frustrated, however, by the outbreak of the First World War. In 1915 Beveridge, together with Llewellyn Smith, was temporarily drafted to the new Ministry of Munitions, set up under Lloyd George to deal with the crisis in production of shells. Beveridge fully supported Lloyd George's view that fighting the war required a total commitment of national resources, even if this involved encroachment on civil liberties, and with Llewellyn Smith he drafted the Munitions of War Act, which severely limited wartime collective bargaining and imposed a system of quasi-military discipline upon civilian workers in munitions. This act, which met with fierce resistance from the engineering unions and from the militant shop stewards' movement, was largely responsible for the prolonged mutual hostility that prevailed between Beveridge and the trade union movement for the next twenty-five years. In the summer of 1916 he returned to the Board of Trade, where he drafted a new Unemployment Insurance Act, which extended insurance to all workers employed in war production. This act was designed to take advantage of wartime full employment to insure workers against the probable onset of depression at the end of the war. It was opposed, however, by both sides of industry and further soured Beveridge's relations with the trade unions. His unpopularity with the labour movement was largely responsible for Beveridge's exclusion from the new Ministry of Labour, set up to co-ordinate all labour and employment policies at the end of 1916. In after years Beveridge looked back on this exclusion as the death blow to his dream of solving the unemployment problem, and as the main cause of the futility of government unemployment policies during the inter-war years. He was moved instead to the new Ministry of Food, where as second secretary he was made responsible for rationing and control of prices. Throughout 1917 domestic food supplies were severely hit by the German submarine campaign and by diversion of the mercantile marine to the transport of American troops. There were severe food shortages and long queues in many parts of the country, and in spite of some opposition from food traders a general rationing scheme drawn up by Beveridge was introduced at the end of the year. When the war came to an end in 1918 Beveridge was sent as British representative on an inter-allied food mission to central and eastern Europe, where he pressed unsuccessfully for instant and unconditional famine relief to the defeated powers. He had been appointed CB in 1916, and early in 1919 he was appointed KCB and became permanent secretary to the Ministry of Food, at thirty-nine one of the youngest men ever to reach that rank in Whitehall.

Beveridge throughout the war had been involved in prolonged discussions with the Webbs, Llewellyn Smith, and other administrative experts about the advance planning of post-war social and economic reforms. Nevertheless, his wartime experiences—and particularly the resistance to state regulation that he had met from both trade unions and employers—had gradually undermined his pre-war faith in the potential of a strong paternalist administrative state. The failure of co-operation between allied governments in the relief of Germany and Austria convinced him that European prosperity could be restored only by a revival of business confidence and a return to the gold standard and international free trade. Thus Beveridge emerged from the war considerably more sympathetic to traditional views of *laissez-faire* and considerably less enthusiastic for state intervention than he had been in 1914. He was highly critical of the view that food controls should be retained in peacetime; and in June 1919 he resigned from the civil service to take up the directorship of the London School of Economics (LSE)—a post offered him by his old friend and mentor, Sidney Webb.

Director of the LSE The LSE had been founded by the Webbs in the 1890s as a college of London University, and had been closely involved in the Edwardian national efficiency movement. In 1919 it was still a small college, catering mainly for part-time students, but Sidney Webb was convinced that the time was ripe for expansion in all areas of the social sciences. He looked to Beveridge as an ambitious and imaginative administrator to be the dynamo for that expansion. Over the next eighteen years Beveridge devoted himself to raising massive funds from such bodies as the Rockefeller Foundation, to a large-scale building programme, and to attracting a range of distinguished scholars in all branches of the social sciences—Tawney, H. J. Laski, L. T. Hobhouse, L. C. Robbins, F. A. Hayek, and Bronislaw Malinowski, to name but a few. In the early 1930s he was personally responsible for bringing to the

school many distinguished academic refugees expelled from Hitler's Germany—and for founding the Society for the Protection of Science and Learning, which secured posts for many other refugee scholars in universities in both England and America. As vice-chancellor of London University from 1926 to 1928 he laid the foundations for a new centralized university, and was responsible for acquiring and raising funds for the university's Bloomsbury site. By the early 1930s the LSE was recognized as one of the world's leading centres of the social sciences, and Beveridge himself was seen as mainly responsible for its prodigious growth. Yet, as in the civil service, many of Beveridge's activities attracted controversy and conflict. His day-to-day administrative methods were seen as despotic and high-handed by many of his staff. On matters of politics he held the view that academics should abstain from open commitment to ideologies and parties—a standpoint that brought him into recurrent conflict with the LSE's controversial professor of political science, Harold Laski. Beveridge had, moreover, very fixed ideas about how the social sciences should be properly conducted. Since his days in Oxford he had been strongly attached to the empirically based scientific positivism expounded by T. H. Huxley, and he was highly critical of those of his colleagues—including a majority of the school's economists and sociologists—who preferred a more deductive or analytical approach. To counteract what he perceived as excessive detachment from practical problems Beveridge established in 1930 a social biology department under Professor Lancelot Hogben, to carry out empirical research into problems of the real world, but the department was never integrated with the rest of the school and folded up after Hogben's resignation at the end of 1936.

Beveridge's relations with his colleagues were further hampered by his increasing intimacy with the school's academic secretary, his second cousin by marriage, Mrs Janet (Jessy) Mair, wife of David Beveridge Mair and daughter of William Philip, businessman and philanthropist of Newport, Fife. David and Jessy Mair had a son and three daughters, one of whom, Lucy, became professor of applied anthropology at LSE. An overbearing and temperamental Scotswoman, Mrs Mair had come to the school with Beveridge in 1919 (having been his secretary and aide during the war) and was highly unpopular with many of the school's professors. Throughout the 1930s there were complaints about the 'Beveridge–Mair dictatorship' and a general sense of relief when Beveridge decided to leave the school to accept the mastership of University College, Oxford, in 1937.

Return to Oxford and war Beveridge returned to Oxford with the avowed intention of devoting himself to the study of unemployment and to a statistical study of the history of prices which he had started nearly twenty years before. In 1937 he was elected a fellow of the British Academy—an honour that he accepted with some hesitation, fearing that it would identify him as a student of the humanities rather than a practitioner of science. His studies of both unemployment and prices were intended to demonstrate the superiority of empirical methods over abstract speculation, and both were designed to support the academic position that Beveridge had adopted at the LSE—namely, that the problems of society would only be solved by inductive measurement and observation, rather than by deductive theory or by campaigning for social change. Yet it may be doubted how profound was Beveridge's inner commitment to detachment from public life. Throughout his time at LSE he had periodically engaged in various kinds of public or political activity—as a participant in the Liberal summer school movement in 1922–4, as a member of the royal commission on the coal industry of 1925–6, as a campaigner for the family allowances scheme of Eleanor Rathbone in the late 1920s, and as chairman of the Unemployment Insurance Statutory Committee from 1934. From the mid-1930s onwards it seems clear that Beveridge was increasingly anxious to return to some more central role in public administration. Since Hitler's invasion of the Rhineland in 1936 he had become convinced that another war with Germany was almost inevitable—and he was equally convinced that Whitehall was making no preparations whatsoever for such an emergency. At the same time his involvement in the running of unemployment insurance seems to have revived his earlier faith in the capacities of enlightened public administration; he increasingly abandoned the rather exaggerated belief in a self-regulating free market that he had adopted in the 1920s, and by 1939 he had once again become committed to far-reaching state planning in both social and economic affairs. At the outbreak of war his ambition was to be given the task which he thought should have been his during the First World War, that of controlling and directing both civilian manpower and military recruitment.

Not for the first time in his life, however, Beveridge's hopes were doomed to disappointment. No summons came from Whitehall. Throughout the winter of 1939–40 Beveridge kicked his heels in frustration—occasionally meeting other similarly neglected veterans of the First World War such as J. Arthur Salter and J. M. Keynes. During these months Beveridge published numerous articles and made several broadcasts, arguing that the times required a totally new kind of socio-economic policy, both to mobilize resources for fighting the war and to lay the foundations of a more just and equal society after the return of peace. Not until a year after the outbreak of war was he invited by Ernest Bevin to carry out a survey of the government's manpower requirements; and in December 1940 he was appointed under-secretary in the Ministry of Labour with the special task of drawing up a list of reserved occupations. Beveridge's new career in Whitehall ended, however, almost before it had begun. From the start he made it clear that he was determined to take control of the wartime manpower programme. Ernest Bevin, possibly remembering Beveridge's clashes with the unions in the First World War, was equally determined that he should not do so. The result was that Beveridge was hived off into the chairmanship of an obscure interdepartmental inquiry into the co-ordination of social services—an inquiry that was not expected to report until after the war was over. Beveridge, who was under no illusions about what was happening to him, accepted his new appointment with tears in his eyes. Yet it was to prove in many ways the most important commission and the major drama of his life.

The Beveridge report Beveridge started work on his social services inquiry in June 1941 and within a few days had convinced himself that it offered the opportunity he had been looking for to determine the shape of British society after the war. Over the next eighteen months he carried out a detailed survey of the deficiencies in Britain's social services—focusing particularly on the long-term unemployed, on inadequate provision for health care, and on the widespread problem of poverty in childhood and old age. With the help of a committee of civil service advisers he interviewed hundreds of witnesses and consulted with economic experts like Keynes, Robbins, and James Meade. His proposals were drawn up in close consultation with representatives of the Trades Union Congress, with whom Beveridge at last found himself in close harmony. For perhaps the first time in his life he became fired with a vision of social justice as an ethical ideal, and in numerous articles and broadcasts he argued passionately for the forging of an ideal new society out of the ashes of war. His conception of how such a society should be organized was spelt out in the report *Social Insurance and Allied Services* in December 1942. In it he outlined a Bunyanesque vision of society's battle against the five giants of idleness, ignorance, disease, squalor, and want; and he put forward a programme for overcoming them which consisted of a free national health service, family allowances, government policies to maintain full employment, and universal subsistence level social insurance to include all classes in society and to cover all social contingencies from the cradle to the grave. Such a programme, Beveridge maintained, could eliminate poverty without in any way impairing the civil and personal freedoms that were central to the British political tradition. The linchpin of his programme he believed to be the maintenance of full employment, and his views on how this might be attained were spelt out in a second report, *Full Employment in a Free Society*, published without official endorsement in 1944. In this second report Beveridge argued that full employment could be achieved in a variety of ways—either by Keynesian-style fiscal regulation, or by direct control and deployment of manpower, or by total state control of the means of production. Beveridge's private papers suggest that at this stage in his career he had little objection to this latter policy, nor did he think it incompatible with personal freedom: 'private ownership of the means of production', he wrote, was 'not one of the essential British liberties' and could not be allowed to stand in the way of rebuilding British society after the war.

Beveridge's report of 1942 met with a cool response in Whitehall and from the Churchill government, but it proved overwhelmingly popular with the British public, and more than 70,000 copies were sold in the space of a few days. Early in 1943 the only major parliamentary revolt of the war forced the government to commit itself in principle to the Beveridge proposals—with the result that Beveridge's plan eventually became the blueprint for the welfare state legislation of 1944 to 1948. Shortly after the publication of his report Beveridge married, on 15 December 1942, his recently widowed cousin, Jessy Mair, and with his new wife he travelled about the country canvassing his proposals and addressing large public audiences. His curiously prophetic figure, with its straight white hair, sharp, bird-like profile, and high-pitched, meticulous Oxford voice, was flashed by Pathé News into every cinema in the country. Dazzled by this success, and disappointed by the government's lack of enthusiasm, Beveridge was tempted by the suggestion that he should promote his plan by going into politics. He had previously had no formal connection with any political party, but in 1944 he resigned the mastership of University College and entered parliament as Liberal MP for Berwick upon Tweed, at the same time setting up home with Lady Beveridge in a Northumbrian country house, Tuggal Hall. Almost certainly he hoped that the first post-war election would bring about the long-awaited Liberal revival and that he would find himself in charge of post-war reconstruction. In 1945, however, he lost his seat to the Conservative candidate, and he went to the House of Lords in 1946 as a Liberal peer.

Later life Beveridge in old age was employed in a series of rather peripheral public roles—as leader of the Liberals in the Lords, chairman of the Newton Aycliffe New Town corporation from 1947 to 1952, and chairman of the committee that opposed commercial broadcasting in 1949–51. As a private individual much of his time was spent in writing his autobiography (*Power and Influence*, 1953), a memoir of his parents (*India called them*, 1947), and other semi-autobiographical works. He did not hesitate to attack the shortcomings of the social legislation that emerged after 1945. He was highly critical of the Labour government for excluding the voluntary friendly societies from state insurance and for rejecting the principle of subsistence level pensions. His book *Voluntary Action* (1948) was a passionate defence of the role of the voluntary sector in provision of social welfare—and it was also, perhaps, an admission of doubt about the increasing bureaucratization of welfare that his own ideas on social policy had done much to bring about. In the mid-1950s he was very concerned about the erosion of pension values by continuous inflation, and spoke frequently on this subject in the House of Lords. Increasingly, however, he devoted himself to his *Prices and Wages in England from the Twelfth to the Nineteenth Century*, only one volume of which was published before his death. To his dying day Beveridge believed that it was this history of prices, rather than his much acclaimed report on social insurance, that would prove to be his 'main contribution to the understanding of modern problems' (Harris, 468).

Character and assessment Beveridge's life and personality may be, and indeed have been, interpreted in a number of different ways. Some people regarded him as a mechanistic bureaucrat with little feeling for the infinite subtleties and complexities of human life. Others saw him as a tireless if sometimes tactless campaigner for a more efficient, just, and compassionate social order. Throughout his life he continually clashed with colleagues who resented his autocratic ways and his chronic inability to suffer fools gladly. Yet in private life he is remembered by people who knew him well as gentle, humorous, quixotic, and humane. He was perceived by many, and indeed described himself, as a 'self-centred' person, yet he could devote himself with utter selflessness to a cause which fired his moral imagination. In middle life he had a reputation for hardness and harshness, but this was belied by the loving and unflagging care that he bestowed on his aged parents, both of whom lived with him almost continuously from 1918 until their deaths in 1929. It was belied also by the fact that he secretly gave away more than a third of his income to charitable causes, needy relatives, and friends. The abrasiveness of Beveridge's character may be partly ascribed to the unsatisfactory nature of his personal life: as a young man he had fallen deeply in love with, and unsuccessfully proposed marriage to, Mary (Cottie) Sanders, later famous as the novelist Ann Bridge. In middle age he deeply regretted his failure to find a suitable wife, and one of the attractions of Mrs Mair was undoubtedly that she provided him with the kind of close-knit family circle that he always cherished as the highest social ideal. Yet Beveridge had certain unusual characteristics that cannot be explained away simply in terms of personal unhappiness. For a man of such keen intellect he showed little interest in general philosophical ideas, and he sometimes admitted rather regretfully that many of the main intellectual currents of his generation had largely passed him by. He was curiously unconscious of many of the latent paradoxes and contradictions contained in his own beliefs—such as the view implicit in his writings of the early 1940s that it was possible almost indefinitely to expand the powers of the state without thereby modifying any of the basic structures of political, associational, and family life. Beveridge's intellectual blind spots may perhaps have been linked with the fact that from early childhood he had been cut off from the kind of scientific studies that might have been his true vocation. A more speculative conclusion is that such blind spots may be a necessary part of the mental equipment of all effective social reformers. 'I really do think', he had written at the age of nineteen, 'that no man can do really progressive work who has not one idea carried to excess … The man must have one great ideal to aim at, to a certain extent excluding all else, and his convictions must be very strong' (Harris, 34). In this early statement of faith lies the clue to many aspects of Beveridge's inner personality and of his public career.

Honours and death Beveridge received many honours. In addition to his earlier honours of CB and KCB, in 1946 he was created Baron Beveridge. He was awarded the degree of honorary LLD at the universities of London, Aberdeen, Birmingham, Chicago, Columbia, Melbourne, Paris, and Oslo; honorary DLitt at New Zealand and McGill; honorary

DLittHum at Pennsylvania; honorary doctor of social sciences at Brussels; and honorary DrEcon at Rotterdam. He was made an honorary fellow of Balliol, Nuffield, and University colleges, Oxford.

Beveridge and his wife retired to Oxford in 1954. She died in 1959; he survived her for four years until he died at his home, Staverton House, 104 Woodstock Road, Oxford, on 16 March 1963. They were buried together in Throckington churchyard, high on the Northumbrian moors. Upon Beveridge's death the barony became extinct.

JOSE HARRIS

Sources BLPES, Beveridge MSS · Lord Beveridge, *Power and influence* (1953) · J. Harris, *William Beveridge: biography*, 2nd edn (1997) · J. Beveridge, *Beveridge and his plan* (1954) · Lord Salter, *PBA*, 49 (1963), 461–70 · H. Wilson, Institute of Statisticians Beveridge memorial lecture, Senate House, U. Lond., 18 Nov 1966 · private information (2004) · *CGPLA Eng. & Wales* (1963)
Archives BL OIOC, corresp. with his parents, MS Eur. C 176 · BLPES, corresp. and papers · BLPES, papers relating to price history · BLPES, papers relating to unemployment · Commonwealth War Graves Commission, Maidenhead, corresp. and papers relating to autobiography | BLPES, Coal Commission papers · BLPES, corresp. with E. M. H. Lloyd · BLPES, papers relating to Ministry of Reconstruction · BLPES, letters to Sidney Webb and Beatrice Webb · Bodl. Oxf., corresp. with Lionel Curtis · Bodl. Oxf., corresp. relating to Society for Protection of Science and Learning · CAC Cam., corresp. with A. V. Hill · HLRO, corresp. with David Lloyd George · Joseph Rowntree Foundation Library, York, corresp. with B. Seebohm Rowntree · JRL, letters to the *Manchester Guardian* · Keele University Library, LePlay Collection, corresp. with Victor Veracis Branford · NA Scot., letters to Lord Lothian · PRO, papers · U. Newcastle, Robinson L., corresp. with Walter Runciman · Welwyn Garden City Central Library, corresp. with Sir Frederic Osborn | FILM BFI NFTVA, documentary footage | SOUND BL NSA, recorded talk · BLPES, recordings of speeches
Likenesses G. C. Beresford, photograph, 1917, NPG · W. Stoneman, two photographs, 1919–53, NPG · W. Nicholson, oils, 1927, London School of Economics · H. Muspratt, photograph, 1938, NPG [*see illus.*] · F. Man, photograph, 1939, NPG · A. Gwynne-Jones, oils, 1959, University College, Oxford · C. Beaton, photograph, NPG · H. Coster, photograph, NPG · B. Elkan, bronze bust, Balliol Oxf. · B. Partridge, pen-and-ink caricature, NPG; repro. in *Punch* (22 Nov 1944) · Ramsey & Muspratt, photograph, NPG
Wealth at death £22,122 12s.: probate, 3 Sept 1963, *CGPLA Eng. & Wales*

Beverley, Alfred of (d. 1154×7?), chronicler, was sacrist and treasurer of Beverley Minster, witnessing charters in favour of the town of Beverley, the nearby religious houses at Bridlington, Warter, and Watton, and the more distant Rufford, between about 1135 and 1154. Little more is known about him outside his own writings, the late fourteenth-century Beverley cartulary merely characterizing him conventionally as 'a man of praiseworthy life and … a studious investigator of the scriptures' (BL, Add. MS 61901, fol. 60v). Alfred was probably dead by about 1157, when one Robert attests as sacrist of Beverley.

Alfred of Beverley speaks of himself as contemporary with the removal of the Flemings from the north of England to Rhos in Dyfed (c.1110), and writes that he compiled his chronicle 'when the church was silent, owing to the number of persons excommunicated under the decrees of the council of London', an apparent reference to the council held at mid-Lent in 1143. His attention, by his own account, was first drawn to history by the appearance (before 1139) of Geoffrey of Monmouth's *Historia regum Britanniae*, and his chronicle depends heavily on Geoffrey's work, often quoting it verbatim and without acknowledgement. Alfred of Beverley's chronicle bears a variety of titles, most commonly *Historia de gestis regalibus regum Britanniae*, or simply *Annales*. Five of its nine books are devoted to the legendary history of Britain from Brutus to Arthur, and the remainder deals with Anglo-Saxon and Anglo-Norman history to 1129. Bede, Henry of Huntingdon, and Symeon of Durham, as well as Geoffrey of Monmouth, are quarried extensively. Alfred also quotes occasionally from Suetonius, Orosius, Pompeius Trogus, Hegesippus and Eutropius. The chronicle is largely derivative, and adds little to the information to be found in earlier authorities. Alfred's *Annales* survives in five manuscripts (including extracts), the most complete being NL Wales, MS Peniarth 384C. Hearne printed the *Annales* in 1716 from a poor fourteenth-century copy (Bodl. Oxf., MS Rawl. B.200).

Alfred of Beverley is also alleged to have collected and translated into Latin the liberties of his church (BL, Add. MS 61901, fols. 60v–69r, printed by Raine). The doubts some have expressed concerning Alfred's connection with this work cannot be substantiated: the surviving text does not include, as the critics supposed, any material later than Alfred's lifetime, and ends with documents from Stephen's reign or even earlier.

SIDNEY LEE, rev. J. C. CRICK

Sources R. T. W. McDermid, *Beverley Minster fasti: being biographical notes on the provosts, prebendaries, officers and vicars in the church of Beverley prior to the dissolution*, Yorkshire Archaeological Society, 149 (1993), 113 · *Aluredi Beverlacensis annales, sive, Historia de gestis regum Britanniae, libris ix*, ed. T. Hearne (1716) · [J. Raine], ed., *Sanctuarium Dunelmense et sanctuarium Beverlacense*, SurtS, 5 (1837), 97–108 · J. E. Burton, ed., *York, 1070–1154*, English Episcopal Acta, 5 (1988), nos. 86, 128, 129 · C. J. Holdsworth, ed., *Rufford charters*, 2, Thoroton Society Record Series, 30 (1974), 167 [no. 303] · W. Farrer and others, eds., *Early Yorkshire charters*, 12 vols. (1914–65), vol. 1, p. 99 · T. D. Hardy, *Descriptive catalogue of materials relating to the history of Great Britain and Ireland*, 2, Rolls Series, 26 (1865), 169–74 · A. Gransden, *Legends, traditions, and history in medieval England* (1992), 19–20, 24, 130, 133–4 · J. S. P. Tatlock, *The legendary history of Britain: Geoffrey of Monmouth's Historia regum Britanniae and its early vernacular versions* (1950), 210–11 · N. Wright, 'Twelfth-century receptions of a text: Anglo-Norman historians and Hegesippus' [forthcoming] · BL, Add. MS 61901, fols. 60v–69r · R. Sharpe, *A handlist of the Latin writers of Great Britain and Ireland before 1540* (1997), 54
Archives Bodl. Oxf., MS Rawlinson B.200 [copy] · NL Wales, MS Peniarth 384C

Beverley, Charles James. *See* Beverly, Charles James (1788–1868).

Beverley, Henry Roxby (1796–1863), actor, was a son of the actor William Roxby Beverly or Beverley (1764/5–1842) and his wife, Mary (1775/6–1851). William Beverley was at one time of Covent Garden Theatre, and thereafter manager of the house in Tottenham Street known at various times as the King's Concert Rooms, the Regency, the West London, the Queen's, and the Prince of Wales's Theatre. Henry Roxby Beverley first appeared as an actor at this house, then called the Regency. Full opportunities of practice were afforded him by his father, and he acquired some reputation as a low comedian. His first real success came in October 1838, when he replaced John Reeve at the Adelphi, and the following month he played the role of Newman Noggs in *Nicholas Nickleby*. He subsequently appeared in *Oliver Twist*, *Jack Sheppard*, and other melodramas, and made a name for himself performing the principal characters in *The Dancing Barber* and other farces. In September 1839 he undertook the management of the Victoria Theatre. After relinquishing this post he played in the provincial theatres, and was for some time manager of the Sunderland theatre and other houses, principally in the north of England, where he was an established favourite. Harry Beverley, as he was generally called, had more unction than usually characterized a low comedian, and was a humorous and sound if not a brilliant actor. He died on Sunday 1 February 1863, at 26 Russell Square, London, the house of his brother William Roxby *Beverly, the eminent scene painter. Another brother appeared on the stage as Robert *Roxby.

JOSEPH KNIGHT, rev. NILANJANA BANERJI

Sources *The Era* (8 Feb 1863) · Adams, *Drama* · Hall, *Dramatic ports.* · d. cert.
Likenesses prints, Harvard TC · prints, BM, NPG

Beverley, John of. *See* John of Beverley (*d.* 721).

Beverley, John (*fl.* 1374–1392), Carmelite friar and theologian, came from Beverley in Yorkshire. He joined the Carmelites in York, probably in the 1360s, for he was ordained deacon on 23 December 1374. He continued his studies at Oxford and he was a BTh by 1392, when he was one of the Carmelite theologians present at the trial of Henry Crump, a Cistercian charged with heresy, at Stamford. John Bale claims that Beverley incepted as a doctor and was a noted lecturer at Oxford. He records two works by Beverley which he saw in the library of Queen's College, Oxford: questions on the *Sentences* and a set of disputations. Neither work is now known to exist. In the past Beverley has often been confused with other individuals of the same name. However, there is no good reason to identify him either with the John Beverley who was a canon of Beverley in the 1360s and 1370s or (especially in view of his participation in the trial of Henry Crump) with the Lollard priest John Beverley, who was executed in 1414 for his participation in Oldcastle's rising, and was subsequently regarded as a martyr by fellow Lollards.

RICHARD COPSEY

Sources J. Bale, Bodl. Oxf., MS Bodley 73 (SC 27635), fol. 57v [printed in *Fasc. ziz.*] · J. Bale, Bodl. Oxf., MS Selden supra 41, fol. 174v · Emden, *Oxf.* · Bale, *Cat.*, 2.84 · J. Bale, *Illustrium Maioris Britannie scriptorum … summarium* (1548), fol. 47

Beverley, John (1743–1827), university administrator, was born in Norwich, where his father, William Beverley, was in the wine trade. Having been educated at Norwich School he matriculated from Christ's College, Cambridge, at Michaelmas 1764; he graduated BA in 1767 and proceeded MA in 1770. He was elected an esquire bedell of the

university in 1770, through the influence of Lord Sandwich, and remained in office until his death. Henry Gunning, who was one of his junior colleagues from 1789, gives an account of Beverley's careless and perfunctory performance of his duties. He was always in financial difficulties and, following his marriage on 25 April 1767 to Susanna, daughter of Cooper Thornhill, the celebrated rider from Stilton, he lived in an extravagant fashion, due in part to his growing family. To avoid financial embarrassment he resorted to a variety of ingenious expedients, and even ran a lottery by selling tickets to members of the university with the lure of winning musical instruments from his own collection and choice flowers. He became extremely adept at borrowing money from friends and colleagues and not repaying them.

Beverley was a great favourite with the earl of Sandwich, first lord of the Admiralty, who appointed him commissioner and comptroller of the sixpenny office, which he held from 1776 to 1817; he later gained an office in the Admiralty that was worth £100 p.a. He was a skilful musician, especially on the double bass, and frequently played at Sandwich's parties at Hinchinbrooke Castle, in Huntingdonshire.

As part of his university duties Beverley published poll books of university elections. He also issued a guide to his office, entitled *An account of the different ceremonies observed in the Senate House of the University of Cambridge throughout the year, together with tables of fees, modes of electing officers, forms of proceeding to degrees, and other articles relating to the customs of the university* (1788), and a couple of accounts of the Unitarian William Frend's trial in the vice-chancellor's court in 1794. The university authorities finally succeeded in replacing Beverley when they allowed him a deputy in 1821 on condition that he no longer resided in Cambridge. He died in London on 25 March 1827.

THOMPSON COOPER, rev. S. J. SKEDD

Sources Venn, *Alum. Cant.* · H. Gunning, *Reminiscences of the university, town, and county of Cambridge, from the year 1780*, 2 vols. (1854) · *Cambridge Chronicle* (30 March 1827) · *GM*, 1st ser., 51 (1781), 532 · IGI
Likenesses R. Dighton, caricature, coloured etching, NPG

Beverley, Peter (*fl.* 1566–1568), poet, was a member of Staple Inn in 1566. He may be the person of that name who matriculated pensioner from St John's College, Cambridge, in Michaelmas term 1553, graduated BA from Clare College in 1556–7, and became a fellow of Clare on 16 December 1556. His *Historie of Ariodanto and Jenevra* was entered in the Stationers' register to Henry Wekes, 1565–6. Its dedication to the 'Worshipfull M. Peter Reade' is dated 'from my chamber at Staple Inne. The first day of August', presumably 1566. Reade, a Norwich man, left Beverley (his godson) an annuity of £6 on his death in December 1568. This Norwich connection makes it unlikely that Beverley was a Yorkshireman by birth, as Prouty suggested.

Ariodanto and Jenevra is the earliest English translation from Ariosto's *Orlando Furioso*, although it is so free with its original that to call it a translation is misleading. In competent but artless fourteeners Beverley elaborates the tale of Ariodante and Ginevra from *Orlando Furioso*, cantos 4.51–6.16, which relates how Polinesso, the wicked duke of Albany, tricks the Italian Ariodante into believing that his love, the Scottish princess Ginevra, is unfaithful. Polinesso disguises Ginevra's maid as the princess, and kisses her in view of Ariodante and his brother. This episode from Ariosto provides the chief source for the trick played by Don John on Claudio in *Much Ado about Nothing*, although it is unlikely that Shakespeare came to it through Beverley's version. Beverley transforms his original (which he nowhere mentions) from a fabliauesque novella chiefly related by Ginevra's maid Dalinda, into a tale of *fine amour* which owes much to Chaucer's *Knight's Tale*. The complex sequence in which the events of the tale are related in Ariosto is replaced by simple chronological order. Beverley's Polinesso first steals a diamond engagement ring from Jenevra in order to trick Ariodanto into believing that she is unfaithful (an episode with no counterpart in Ariosto), and then resorts to disguising Dalinda, as he does in the original. Beverley adds lengthy courtly complaints and set-piece descriptions of times of day to each stage of the narrative. The work was reprinted by Prouty in 1950. Beverley's only other known work is a commendatory poem for Geoffrey Fenton's *Tragical Discourses* (1567).

COLIN BURROW

Sources P. Beverley, *The historie of Ariodanto and Jenevra, daughter to the king of Scottes, in English verse* [n.d., c.1565] · C. T. Prouty, *The sources of 'Much ado about nothing'* (1950) · Venn, *Alum. Cant.* · *STC, 1475–1640* · Arber, *Regs. Stationers*, vol. 2 · C. T. Prouty, 'George Whetstone, Peter Beverly, and the sources of *Much ado about nothing*', *Studies in Philology*, 38 (1941), 211–20 · W. J. Harrison and A. H. Lloyd, *Notes on the masters, fellows, scholars and exhibitioners of Clare College, Cambridge* (1953)

Beverley [Ingelberd], **Philip** (*d.* 1323×5), benefactor, was the son of Robert and Alice Ingelberd, and is first recorded in January 1303, when he was nominated to the church of Keyingham near Hull in Holderness, close to Beverley, on the recommendation of Walter Langton (*d.* 1321), then royal treasurer and bishop of Coventry and Lichfield. He obtained possession of Keyingham in June 1306, when he surrendered the church of Broughton in Hampshire of which he had been rector in 1305; he retained Keyingham until his death. He appears as master of arts in 1305. Between 1305 and 1311 he was granted several licences for absence to study, and eventually obtained a doctorate of theology. His importance revolves around the bequest of property in Keyingham and Paull that he made to University College, Oxford, in January 1318. From an income amounting to about £9 p.a. the college was to support two scholars or masters born near Beverley; its statutes stipulated that University College should favour candidates from the diocese of Durham, but it was from Beverley that the college's northern connections were to be maintained in subsequent years. A later source, the Meaux chronicle, attributes to Philip Beverley a reputation for saintliness. He may have known the canonist William Pagula (*d.* 1332?)—from Paull, near Hull—at Oxford. He may also have been the author of works on logic that Bale once saw in the library of Glastonbury Abbey. In 1322 Beverley obtained licence to establish a chantry in honour of the Virgin for himself and his ancestors at Molescroft close to Beverley. He died between April 1323 and 10 June 1325.

M. C. BUCK

Sources Chancery records · Emden, *Oxf.*, 1.184 · *Hist. U. Oxf.* 1: *Early Oxf. schools*, 290–91 · *Chronica monasterii de Melsa, a fundatione usque ad annum 1396, auctore Thoma de Burton*, ed. E. A. Bond, 3, Rolls Series, 43/3 (1868) · W. Smith, *Annals of University College* (1728), 96–7

Beverley, Robert of (*d.* 1285), master mason and sculptor, is first recorded in 1253, when he received £1 12*s.* for carving four vault-bosses for Westminster Abbey. In 1259 he was paid 3*s.* per week while working at Westminster Palace under Master John of Gloucester whom, late in the following year, he succeeded as master mason of Westminster Abbey. Robert was not granted a general appointment as master mason of the king's works such as John of Gloucester held from 1257, presumably because, unlike the latter, he was employed only in London. This changed in 1271 when he became surveyor of the king's works at the Tower of London and six specified castles and manors in Berkshire, Essex, Kent, and Surrey. The smaller number and geographical spread of the residences in his care, compared to those for which John of Gloucester had been responsible, probably explains why he was paid only half the fee of 12*d.* per day taken by his predecessor. In 1273 he had charge of the making of the tomb of Edward I's infant son John, the earliest documented instance of the designing of royal tombs at Westminster by the king's chief mason—a pattern which persisted for a hundred years and more. Following Edward I's return to England in 1274, Beverley oversaw the erection at Westminster of a number of wooden halls and kitchens ancillary to the new king's coronation on 19 August. Thereafter the volume of work carried out at the Tower and other London sites greatly increased and, presumably in recognition of this, Robert's fee rose to 12*d.* per day and 16*d.* when working elsewhere. In 1276 he received £3 6*s.* 6*d.* for his work in turning 300 lb of wax into an image of Henry III, for purposes which are not recorded. From 1278 Robert audited works accounts, which suggests that his Latinity was better than that of most medieval master masons.

Early in 1278 Beverley sat on a commission *ad quod damnum* which considered how the south-west part of London's wall should be extended so as to take in the new precinct which was about to be established for the Dominicans. Although the new priory buildings were not king's works in the strictest sense, Edward I was heavily involved in this project, and it is highly likely that Robert was the architect. The nave of the church incorporated high arcades but lacked a clerestory or vault, and it was therefore a forerunner of the many structurally light and open 'preaching naves' built in late medieval England by mendicant orders and parishes alike. The least altered part of Robert's work at the Tower is St Thomas's Tower, which consists of a watergate and an upper floor housing the king's lodgings. The timber rear wall of the lodgings is borne on a segmental arch whose extraordinary width makes space for royal barges to turn. At Westminster

Abbey the most important changes to the design adopted at the start of work in 1245 are those by John of Gloucester, but Robert also made some less conspicuous revisions. Cordial relations with the abbey are suggested by its grant to Robert c.1270 of a lifetime's supply of wine. Beverley died on 11 April 1285. He had a wife named Cecily.

CHRISTOPHER WILSON

Sources J. Harvey and A. Oswald, *English mediaeval architects: a biographical dictionary down to 1550*, 2nd edn (1984), 23–5 · H. M. Colvin and others, eds., *The history of the king's works*, 6 vols. (1963–82), vol. 1, pp. 98n., 108–9; vol. 2 · C. Wilson and others, *Westminster Abbey* (1986), 66–7, 81–2 · P. Binski, *Westminster Abbey and the Plantagenets: kingship and the representation of power, 1200–1400* (1995), 74–8 · E. M. Thompson, ed., *Customary of the Benedictine monasteries of Saint Augustine, Canterbury, and Saint Peter, Westminster*, 2, HBS, 28 (1904), 79

Beverley, Robert (1667/8–1722), historian, was born in Middlesex county, Virginia, the son of Major Robert Beverley (1635–1687), planter, and his second wife, Mary, *née* Keeble (1637–1678). He was educated in England, probably at Beverley grammar school, Yorkshire. In 1696 he married Ursula Byrd (1680?–1698), the sister of the landowner and diarist, William Byrd. The couple had one son, William (1695/6–1760), before Ursula's early death. Both his father and his older half-brother, Peter Beverley (1687–1729), had served as clerk of the Virginia house of burgesses, a position Robert achieved in 1696. When, two years later, the statehouse was consumed by fire, Beverley saved many of its records, which he transcribed and arranged. He sailed to England in 1703 to appeal to the privy council against a legal decision. He lost the appeal, but spent his time writing *The History and Present State of Virginia* which was published anonymously 'by an Indian' in London in 1705. Though he claimed in the preface to the second edition that he was inspired to write the *History* to correct the numerous errors in the account of Virginia in John Oldmixon's *British Colonies in America*, Beverley may have planned to write a history and probably brought materials with him, perhaps spending some time writing on the voyage to England. In the same preface he also identified the ignorance of and prejudice against America that he encountered in England as a motive behind the *History*. In truth, his father probably prejudiced him against the English authorities after the privy council barred him from office in 1678; the elder Robert Beverley had none the less fulfilled various government roles until 1 August 1686, when James II commanded that he be barred from all civil offices.

Beverley's *History ... of Virginia*, one of the most outspoken books of Americanism before the War of Independence, satirized the 'Rapacious and Arbitrary' English governors and objected to the 'heavy Impositions' put upon the American colonies by the English. Throughout his study Beverley celebrated Virginia's history and laws, featuring stories of early Virginia—among them the Lost Colony, Pocahontas saving Captain John Smith, Virginia's settlement by cavaliers, and the laziness of the ordinary southerner—which became standard features of

American history. In his personal life, he eschewed English material culture. Visiting Beverley's plantation on 14 July 1715, the Revd John Fontaine marvelled that he had 'no curtains' on the windows and that 'instead of cane chairs he hath stools made of wood, and lives upon the product of his land', which included his own vineyards and wine.

In addition to criticizing English culture, Beverley also celebrated American nature. Virginian planters continuously have

> their Eyes ... ravished with the Beauties of naked Nature. Their Ears are Serenaded with the perpetual murmur of Brooks, and the thorow-base which the Wind plays, when it wantons through the Trees; the merry Birds too, join their pleasing Notes to this rural Consort, especially the Mockbirds. (Beverley, 298)

Despite the originality and sincerity of its sentiments, large parts of the *History* derived from existing sources. Much of Beverley's supposedly first-hand information concerning Native Americans actually comes from Captain John Smith, most of his technical detail on Virginia's natural history was taken from John Banister, while a good deal of material on the government and present state of the colony comes from a manuscript by three Virginians, published later also as *The History and Present State of Virginia* (1727); and some information probably came from a manuscript history of Virginia by his brother-in-law, William Byrd of Westover. Nevertheless, Beverley's prose made his *History* enjoyable and he often gave even the borrowed material his own interpretation. Thus, in a series of chapters devoted to the Virginia Indians, he obliquely advanced the merits of deism. Moreover, the *History* proved popular, with four French printings between 1707 and 1718 and a second English edition in 1722.

In 1716 Beverley accompanied the Virginian lieutenant-governor, Alexander Spotswood, on the fabled 63-man exploration over the Blue Ridge Mountains to the Shenandoah. He also served in the Virginia house of burgesses. In 1722 Beverley brought out *An Abridgement of the Public Laws of Virginia* (2nd edn, 1728), which celebrated Spotswood in the dedication. He died on 21 April 1722, aged fifty-four, at his plantation, Beverley Park, King and Queen county, Virginia, and was survived by his son, William.

J. A. LEO LEMAY

Sources R. Beverley, *The history and present state of Virginia* (1947) · B. Tarter, 'Major Robert Beverley (1635–1687) and his immediate family', *Magazine of Virginia genealogy*, 31 (1993), 163–77 · F. Harrison, 'Robert Beverley, the historian of Virginia', *Virginia Magazine of History and Biography*, 36 (1928), 333–44 · J. A. L. Lemay, 'Robert Beverley's *History and present state of Virginia* and the emerging American political ideology', *American letters and the historical consciousness: essays in honor of Lewis P. Simpson*, ed. J. G. Kennedy and D. M. Fogel (1987), 67–111 · J. Fontaine, *Journal*, ed. E. P. Alexander (1972) · J. Ewan and N. Ewan, *John Banister and his 'Natural history of Virginia'* (1970) · J. A. L. Lemay, 'The Amerindian in the early American Enlightenment: deistic satire in Robert Beverley's *History of Virginia*', *Deism, masonry, and the Enlightenment: essays honoring Alfred Owen Aldridge*, ed. J. A. L. Lemay (1987), 79–92 · R. Arner, 'The quest for freedom: style and meaning in Robert Beverley's *History and present state of Virginia*', *Southern Literary Journal*, 8 (spring 1976), 79–

98 • L. Marx, *The machine in the garden* (1964) • J. Kukla, *Speakers and clerks of the Virginia house of burgesses, 1643–1776* (1981)

Beverley, Thomas of (d. after **1225**), abbot of Froidment and hagiographer, presumably originated at Beverley in the East Riding of Yorkshire. Following the death of his father, Hulno (who may have had Hungarian connections), he became attached to the household of Thomas Becket, most likely during the years when Becket was provost of Beverley, between 1154 and 1162. He followed Becket into exile, but parted company with the archbishop during the latter's stay at Pontigny between 1164 and 1166, choosing to make his way to the Cistercian abbey of Froidment in Picardy, where he became a monk and was later elected abbot. At Froidment Thomas wrote a life in verse and prose of his own sister Margaret, who died in 1192. Margaret followed Thomas into the Cistercian order, but before doing so she went on pilgrimage with their mother, Sibyl, to Jerusalem. Sibyl died there, but Margaret made further pilgrimages to Montserrat in Catalonia and Le Puy in central France, before taking vows at Sauve Benite. Thomas of Beverley's life of St Margaret of Jerusalem, much of which was published by Angel Manrique in his *Annales Cisterciennes*, provides a readable, almost picaresque, account of Margaret's eventful career, particularly notable for its detailed descriptions of the Holy Land. Thomas is also believed to have written a life of St Thomas of Canterbury, though his authorship of this work is contested. He evidently lived to a great age, dying some time after 1225.   E. L. O'BRIEN

Sources A. Manrique, *Cisterciensium, seu, Verius ecclesiasticorum annalium a condito Cistercio*, 4 vols. (Lyons, 1642–59), vol. 1, pp. 198–9, 226–7, 262–3 • P. Leyser, *Historia poetarum et poematum medii aevi* (1721) • C. de Visch, *Bibliotheca scriptorum sacri ordinis Cisterciensis*, 2nd edn (1656) • C. Henriquez, *Phoenix reviviscens* (1626) • T. von Froidmont, *Die vita des heiligen Thomas Becket*, ed. P. G. Schmidt (1991) • R. Sharpe, *A handlist of the Latin writers of Great Britain and Ireland before 1540* (1997) • D. H. Farmer, *The Oxford dictionary of saints*, 3rd edn (1992), 319

Beverley, Thomas (d. **1702**), Independent minister and author, about whom very few biographical details are available, is first mentioned as the 'Rector of Lilley in Hertfordshire' on the title page of his book entitled *The Principles of Protestant Truth and Peace* (1683). He graduated MA from King's College, Aberdeen in 1643. He was imprisoned during the mid-1680s, and was in prison still in 1691 (T. Beverley, *To the High Court of Parliament*, 1691, broadside; T. Beverley, *The Scripture Line of Time*, 1692, sig. A1r). After his release, having apparently abandoned his conformity, he became pastor to a congregation at Cutlers' Hall in London, and he remained in that position until 1697. He was also a sometime Sunday lecturer to Stephen Lobb's congregation in Fetter Lane during this period. After publishing sporadically in the years between 1668 and 1680 Beverley published more than fifty works during the 1680s and 1690s. Many of these publications affirmed his conviction that Christ would return to inaugurate his kingdom on earth in 1697. This belief was based on interpretations of biblical prophetic chronology which Beverley first presented in *A Calendar of Prophetic Time* (1684) and later

expanded in *A Scripture-Line of Time* (1687). He also published numerous pamphlets detailing his exegesis of specific elements of apocalyptic prophecy. Beverley perceived the political circumstances of the late 1680s in the context of unfolding apocalyptic accomplishment, seeing the removal of James II and the accession of William and Mary to the throne as evidence of divine intervention (*The Command of God to his People to Come out of Babylon*, 1688; *The Late Great Revolution in this Nation*, 1689). For Beverley these events also confirmed the decisive role that England would play in the overthrow of Roman Catholic power in Europe, which he believed would culminate in the eventual downfall of the papacy and of Louis XIV of France. Interest in his predictions also extended outside of England, with several collections of his works being translated and published in German.

While in prison Beverley began a correspondence with the Presbyterian divine Richard Baxter, a fellow prisoner in 1685–6, discussing their disagreement over the meaning of the prophecies of the book of Revelation. In 1691 Baxter challenged Beverley's opinions on the advent of Christ's millennial kingdom with *The Glorious Kingdom of Christ* (1691) and *A Reply to Mr. Tho. Beverley's Answer* (1691), to which Beverley replied directly in *The Thousand Years Kingdom of Christ* (1691) and *The Universal Christian Doctrine of the Day of Judgment* (1691). When Beverley's predictions were not realized in 1697 he modified his chronological calculations, establishing a new terminal date of 1701 for the achievement of apocalyptic fulfilment (*The Good Hope through Grace*, 1700; *An Appendix to a Discourse of Indictions*, 1700). Although several of his works were reprinted after 1701, the cessation of his prophetic interpretations corresponded with the passing of this date.

In addition to his apocalyptic speculations Beverley entered into literary debates over several of the significant theological issues of his time. In *The Whole Duty of Nations* (1681) he described the pre-eminent role that national churches played in advancing true Christianity. He discussed a national church that encompassed the public worship of the community of all true believers within a nation, but that also allowed for the religious differences of separate congregations founded upon sincere decisions of conscience. Beverley's ideas informed Baxter's later views on national churches (Keeble and Nuttall, 2.300; R. Baxter, *Against the Revolt to a Foreign Jurisdiction*, 1691, 345). Beverley also supported a strict Calvinist belief in righteousness by grace alone, instigated by criticisms and accusations of antinomianism by Baxter and Daniel Williams against ideas presented in the sermons of Tobias Crisp, which had been republished in 1690. Attempting to act as a mediator between the opinions of Crisp and Baxter, Beverley denied the antinomian charge, arguing instead that Crisp had simply concentrated his expositions on the doctrines of election and imputed righteousness through Christ (*A conciliatoy [sic] judgment concerning Dr. Crisp's sermons, and Mr. Baxter's dissatisfaction in them*, 1690; *A conciliatory discourse upon Dr. Crisp's sermons, on the observation of Mr. Williams's dissatisfactions in them*, 1692; *The true state of gospel truth, established upon the free election of God in Christ … in the way of a conciliatory discourse upon Mr. Williams his concessions*, 1693). Beverley continued to elaborate these doctrines of justification in several other of his later works.

In 1694 Beverley entered into the debate over anti-trinitarian ideas, publishing *A Compendious Assertion and Vindication of the Eternal Godhead of our Lord Jesus Christ*, which defended the doctrine of the divinity of Christ against Socinian opinions. In *Christianity the Great Mystery: in Answer to a Late Treatise, Christianity not Mysterious* (1696) he presented his belief in the fundamental mysterious nature of elements of Christianity, opposing John Toland's assertions that nothing in Christianity was beyond human reason. In 1699 Beverley wrote in defence of Thomas Burnet's *Theory of the Earth* (1684, 1690); *Reflections upon the 'Theory of the Earth'* (1699) argued that Burnet had preserved the mysteriousness of Christianity by maintaining the miraculous nature of the creation of the earth, and of the flood, and had upheld God's role in the operations of the natural world. Beverley also commended Burnet's opinions on the creation of a new heaven and new earth at the inauguration of the millennium. Beverley was in Colchester in 1701 (*A Sermon of Mr. Benjamin Perkins … Enlarged into a Discourse* (1701), sig. A2r), and he died in 1702.   WARREN JOHNSTON

Sources W. Wilson, *The history and antiquities of the dissenting churches and meeting houses in London, Westminster and Southwark*, 4 vols. (1808–14), vol. 2, pp. 63–6 • W. M. Lamont, *Richard Baxter and the millennium: protestant imperialism and the English revolution* (1979) • *Calendar of the correspondence of Richard Baxter*, ed. N. H. Keeble and G. F. Nuttall, 2 (1991) • E. Arber, ed., *The term catalogues, 1668–1709*, 3 vols. (privately printed, London, 1903–6); repr. (1965) • J. F. Kellas Johnstone and A. W. Robertson, *Bibliographia Aberdonensis*, ed. W. D. Simpson, Third Spalding Club, 2 (1930), 424 • P. J. Anderson, ed., *Roll of alumni in arts of the University and King's College of Aberdeen, 1596–1860* (1900), 14

Beverley, William Roxby. *See* Beverly, William Roxby (1810?–1889).

Beverly, Charles James (1788–1868), surgeon and naturalist, was born in August 1788 at Fort Augustus in the Scottish highlands, the son of a soldier stationed at the fort. He was apprenticed to a surgeon and entered the navy as assistant surgeon in 1810. For four years he served in the Baltic and, especially, the Mediterranean, and was present at the capture of Porto d'Anzo in 1813. Though up for promotion, he was sent home from the fleet in charge of the sick and wounded, having fallen ill himself. After he recovered he became assistant surgeon on HMS *Tiber*.

Beverly served as unofficial naturalist on two expeditions to the Arctic. The first occurred after his stint on the *Tiber* ended in 1818, when he was selected to be assistant surgeon on *Isabella*, which was about to take part in Parry's first expedition in search of the north-west passage. He served on this expedition in 1819–20, spending the winter in Melville Island, where he formed a herbarium which assisted in the description of plants that was published with Parry's *Journal* (1821). On his return from the Arctic he was highly commended for his skill and care in attending

to the sick and was promoted to full surgeon. His service was, however, interrupted by a disease of the eyes. On his recovery he was nominated supernumerary surgeon to the flagship at the naval station in Barbados, but considered the change from an arctic to a tropical climate too risky for his still uncertain health, so declined the appointment and afterwards left the navy to enter private practice in London.

Beverly's second expedition was in 1827, when he joined Parry in his dangerous attempt to reach the north pole, serving as a volunteer in the capacity of surgeon and naturalist. During this journey he assisted in the collection and naming of many botanical specimens, and also in the preparation of many of the examples of Arctic zoology which were brought back to England.

Beverly was married; his wife, who survived him, was called Harriet. In 1831 he was elected a fellow of the Royal Society, in recognition of his services to natural history as 'naturalist and surgeon in the voyages of Sir Edward Parry' (election certificate, Royal Society Library). During his later years he appears to have lived in Freshford, Somerset. He died at his last home, 6 Dagmar Terrace, Great Yarmouth, on 16 September 1868.

ROBERT HUNT, *rev.* P. E. KELL

Sources *PRS*, 17 (1868–9), 87–8 • W. E. Parry, *Journal of a voyage for the discovery of a north-west passage* (1821) • election certificate, RS • *CGPLA Eng. & Wales* (1868)

Wealth at death under £5000: probate, 26 Nov 1868, *CGPLA Eng. & Wales*

Beverly, William Roxby (1810?–1889), scene-painter, was born at Richmond, Surrey, probably in 1810, the youngest son of William Beverly or Beverley (1764/5–1842) and his wife, Mary (1775/6–1851). The elder Beverly, a well-known actor–manager, had abandoned his own surname of Roxby on taking to the boards, to distinguish himself from his uncle Henry Roxby (a wealthy hop merchant and brother-in-law of Sir James Sanderson, lord mayor of London), from whom he received a legacy in 1820. He slightly adapted the name of his father's birthplace as his own. The family consisted of four sons and a daughter, all of whom were identified with the stage—some under the name of Beverly or Beverley and others under that of Roxby; of these Henry Roxby *Beverley and Robert *Roxby are noticed separately. At an early age Beverly developed a remarkable aptitude for drawing, and quickly turned his attention to scene painting. Under his father's management of the Theatre Royal, Manchester, in July 1831, he painted a striking scene 'Island of Mist' for the dramatic romance *The Frozen Hand*. When later that year his father and his brothers Samuel and Robert Roxby acquired the Durham circuit, comprising Scarborough, Stockton, Durham, Sunderland, and North and South Shields, Beverly joined them, and for some years played comedy besides painting scenery. His work in the north-east created a very favourable impression, although one of his predecessors on the circuit had been Clarkson Stanfield. In December 1838 he was specially engaged to paint the major portion of the scenery for the pantomime *Number Nip* at Edinburgh, his principal contribution being a moving diorama depicting scenes from William Falconer's *Shipwreck*. In September 1839 his brother, Henry Beverly, assumed control of the Victoria Theatre in London for a short period, and there he began his work for the London theatres with the scenery for the pantomime *Baron Munchausen*.

In December 1842 Beverly was engaged as principal artist by Knowles of the Theatre Royal, Manchester, and in 1845 executed a beautiful act drop for the new Theatre Royal, which remained in use until about 1863, when he painted its replacement. In June 1846 his magnificent scenery was seen there in the opera *Acis and Galatea*. Earlier that year he had been engaged by J. M. Maddox as principal artist at the Princess's Theatre, London, where he painted the scenery for the revival of Planché's *Sleeping Beauty* and vividly imaginative backgrounds in the Christmas pantomime *The Enchanted Beauties of the Golden Castle*. At Easter in 1847 he provided a beautiful setting, with some ingenious transformations, for the revival of *A Midsummer Night's Dream*. While still continuing his association with the Princess's, Beverly proceeded to the Lyceum under the Madame Vestris–C. J. Mathews régime (1847–55), where his scenery illustrated the extravaganzas of J. R. Planché. Combining the pictorial talent of Stanfield with the ingenuity of the mechanist William Bradwell, Beverly achieved his greatest success in *The Island of Jewels* in December 1849, when, working on a device already developed by Bradwell, he pioneered the Victorian transformation scene (see the account of the Marylebone pantomime in the *Theatrical Journal* of 28 Dec 1848).

In 1851 Beverly assisted in the painting of the great diorama of Jerusalem and the Holy Land, the largest exhibited up to that time. That autumn he accompanied Albert Smith to Chamonix, and drew sketches from which he executed his dioramic views for *The Ascent of Mont Blanc*, as given by Smith at the Egyptian Hall, Piccadilly, in March 1852. His scenery at the Lyceum for Planché's *Good Woman in a Wood* (1852), and for *Once Upon a Time there were Two Kings* (1853), was enthusiastically greeted by contemporary critics such as George Henry Lewes and Professor Henry Morley. In March 1853 his waterfall scene in *A Strange History* so delighted the audience that they stopped the show until he had acknowledged the applause. Such a reception led Planché to remark sourly that 'the *last* scene became the first in the estimation of the management … As to me, I was positively painted out. Nothing was considered *brilliant* but the last scene' (Planché 2.135).

While still engaged at the Lyceum Beverly was in 1853 appointed scenic director at the Italian opera, Covent Garden, and painted scenery for *Rigoletto* on 16 May, and for many years provided the scenery for the chief operas produced under Gye's rule. On 16 August 1854 he married Sophia Burbidge (1832/3–1904), a former member of the Princess Theatre's *corps de ballet*, at the Old Church, St Pancras. At least two children survived to maturity, of whom his daughter Sophia was mother of the actor–manager, Owen Nares.

Beverly's memorable association with Drury Lane began under E. T. Smith in 1854, and lasted, with a few intermissions, through the successive managements of Edmund Falconer, F. B. Chatterton, and Sir Augustus Harris, down to 1885. He specialized in pantomime scenery; at Christmas 1855 he provided almost all the scenery for the holiday entertainments both at Drury Lane and at Covent Garden, and in December 1862 he also painted scenery for the Princess's Theatre pantomime *Riquet with the Tuft*. At Drury Lane during the next few years he furnished the mounting for several important Shakespearian revivals, including *King John*, *1 Henry IV*, and *Macbeth*, as well as for an elaborate production of *Comus*. Meanwhile Beverly had developed his skills as a traditional easel artist in both oils and watercolour, though he preferred the latter. Between 1865 and 1880 he showed twenty-nine pictures at the Royal Academy, most of them seascapes, the last being *Fishing Boats Going before the Wind: Early Morning*, and twenty-eight at various other exhibitions.

On the death of his last surviving brother, Robert Roxby, in 1866, what remained of the old and now failing Durham circuit passed into Beverly's hands, but the old stock company had been disbanded and all the surviving theatres leased out so that it brought him no profit. In 1869 the Durham theatre burned down and he soon parted with the others, except for Sunderland which he retained until 1888.

From 1868 to 1879 Beverly's scene painting was exclusively for the Drury Lane Theatre including a spectacular revival of *Antony and Cleopatra* in 1873 and *Richard III* in 1876. In October 1880 he worked on *Mary Stuart* at the Court Theatre, and in March 1881 he provided the scenery for *Michael Strogoff* at the Adelphi. In this play still-life accessories were, for the first time on the British stage, arranged to harmonize with the background, as in the French cycloramas. In 1884 Beverly painted a panorama of the lakes of Killarney, which was an integral feature of G. R. Rowe's play *The Donagh* at the Grand Theatre, Islington. Besides working in the same year for the Savoy and the Princess's he furnished a portion of the scenery for *Whittington and his Cat* at Drury Lane at Christmas, and next year was one of the painters for *Aladdin* there.

Failing eyesight forced him in 1885 to retire and he lived on in reduced circumstances until he died at his home, 45 South Hill Park, Hampstead, London, on 15 May 1889. At the Haymarket on 30 July 1890 a morning performance was given for the benefit of his widow.

After Clarkson Stanfield, Beverly was the most distinguished scene painter of the nineteenth century. He excelled in the practice of his art and assisted materially in its development. He interpreted the charm and mystery of atmospheric effects with exceptional success by his original method of 'going over' the cloth upon which the previously applied distemper was still wet. The last of the old school of one-surface painters, he was proficient in all the mechanical resources of the stage, but was resolutely opposed to the scene 'builders'. His transformation scenes made a major contribution to the success of mid-Victorian pantomimes and extravaganzas. Scenic artists who benefited from working under his direction included Samuel Bough, Hawes Craven, and the future journalist George Augustus Sala.

W. J. LAWRENCE, rev. C. D. WATKINSON

Sources Newcastle Weekly Chronicle (25 May 1889) · Newcastle Weekly Chronicle (1 June 1889) · H. R. Roddam, letter, Newcastle Weekly Chronicle (8 June 1889) · J. R. Planché, The recollections and reflections of J. R. Planché, 2 vols. (1872) · The life and adventures of George Augustus Sala, 2 vols. (1895) · W. W. Appleton, Madame Vestris and the London stage (1974) · M. R. Booth, Victorian spectacular theatre, 1850–1910 (1981) · R. King, North Shields theatres (1948) · D. Towland, The Stockton Georgian theatre (1991) · Men of the time (1887) · ILN (1 June 1889), 682 · The Times (20 May 1889) · D. W. J. Cruickshank, 'Revering the manes of his Jennings ancestors', Family Tree Magazine, 10/12 (Oct 1994), 3 · D. W. J. Cruickshank, letter, Family Tree Magazine, 11/4 (Feb 1995), 39 · CGPLA Eng. & Wales (1889)

Likenesses engraving (after photograph by Elliott & Fry), NPG; repro. in ILN, 682

Wealth at death £1056 1s.: probate, 31 July 1889, CGPLA Eng. & Wales

Beverton, Raymond John Heaphy (1922–1995), biologist and scientific administrator, was born on 29 August 1922 at 5 Forest Glade, Leytonstone, east London, the only child of Edgar John Beverton (1882–1968), commercial artist, and his wife, Dorothy Sybil Mary Heaphy (1891–1982), secretary and cookery demonstrator. His ancestors included Thomas Heaphy, official artist in the Peninsular War, and Charles Heaphy, also an artist, awarded the VC in the New Zealand wars. As a boy Beverton developed enthusiasms for music, fishing, and football; later he was a keen sailor. He was educated at Forest School, Snaresbrook (1930–39), and Downing College, Cambridge (1940–42 and 1946–7), reading physics, chemistry, and mathematics for part one of the tripos and gaining a first-class degree in zoology in part two, as well as a blue for association football. Between 1942 and 1945 he worked with the Operational Research Group, developing insulation for radar cables. In 1945 he worked at the government fisheries laboratory at Lowestoft under Michael Graham, director of fisheries research, on the exploitation of cod in the North Sea, and was sent to the Arctic on a commercial trawler. Although susceptible to seasickness he returned to the laboratory at Lowestoft in 1947. In the same year, on 10 June, he married Kathleen Edith Marner (b. 1922), scientific laboratory assistant; they had three daughters.

Beverton soon made valuable contributions to understanding the factors determining the survival of young plaice and, in collaboration with Sydney Holt, to theoretical fish population dynamics. Their paper 'On the dynamics of exploited fish populations' (1957) was one of the most important ever published in this field, providing the basis for much subsequent research. Beverton became deputy director of the fisheries laboratory in 1959. He also chaired committees for the International Council for the Exploration of the Sea (ICES) and the International Commission for North West Atlantic Fisheries. In 1965 he became the first secretary (chief permanent officer) of the newly formed Natural Environment Research Council, which initially had the object of promoting the work of diverse, virtually self-governing, research organizations dealing with oceanography, geology, hydrology, marine and freshwater biology, nature conservation, and, in the course of time, the British Antarctic Survey. Together with the chairman, Sir Graham Sutton, Beverton produced at short notice a forward look which was a valuable summary of the state of, and prospects for, environmental science. The first years employed his administrative skills constructively but politics and finance soon became dominant.

Adoption of the Rothschild report of 1972 on government research and development disrupted the organization which Beverton had built up, leading to differences of view concerning his role, particularly as accounting officer, and eventually to his resignation in 1980. In his term of office he had set a high standard of scientific excellence and care for the welfare of the council's staff. Beverton had maintained his interest in fisheries science during this administrative period and after leaving the Natural Environment Research Council continued it in academic work. After a year as a senior research fellow in the University of Bristol he was invited in 1982 to join the department of applied biology of the University of Wales Institute of Science and Technology (UWIST), Cardiff, as honorary professorial fellow, and then in 1984 to become professor of fisheries ecology. He taught at both undergraduate and MSc levels and participated with zest in field courses, where his wife assisted with the commissariat.

In 1988 Beverton became head of the school of pure and applied biology, responsible for the integration of four separate departments on a single site, the organization of new degree courses, and the establishment of several research groups, following the merger of UWIST and the University College of Cardiff. He continued research, providing one of the first convincing demonstrations of density-dependent mortality in commercial fish species. He also continued with the ICES as editor of its journal, and served on the councils of the Fisheries Society of the British Isles (president, 1983–8), the Freshwater Biological Association (vice-president, 1980–95), and the World Wildlife Fund UK (trustee, 1983–5). He carried a heavy workload after his official retirement in 1989 but resolutely made time to be with his family. He played the piano until deafness intervened. He died in the Royal Gwent Hospital on 23 July 1995 after a stroke, and after cremation at Christchurch in south Wales on 31 July his ashes were scattered in the North Sea, near where his researches began; his wife survived him. His distinctions included being made CBE (1968) and a fellow of the Royal Society (1975), and an honorary DSc degree of the University of Wales. He also received the silver medal (later renamed the Beverton medal) of the Fisheries Society of the British Isles (1995), the award of excellence of the American Fisheries Society (1993), and the award for outstanding achievement of the American Institute of Fisheries Biologists (1995). A reading room at the headquarters of the ICES, a meeting room in the Southampton Oceanography Centre, and a lecture theatre in the University of Wales, Cardiff, are dedicated to his memory.

G. E. FOGG

Sources D. H. Cushing and R. W. Edwards, *Memoirs FRS*, 42 (1996), 25–38 · private information (2004) [Mrs Kathleen Edith Beverton] · J. Sheail, *Natural environment research council: a history* (1992) · D. Pauly, 'Ray Beverton, FRS, 1922–1995', *ICES CIEM Information News*, 27 (Feb 1996), 57 · *The Times* (3 Aug 1995), 12a–d · D. Le Cren, 'Obituary, Professor Raymond John Heaphy Beverton, CBE, FRS, 1922–1995', *Freshwater Forum*, 5 (1995), 128–31 · *WW* (1995), 159 · M. Ben-Yami, 'Dr Beverton and fisheries science', *World Fishing* (March 1996), 38–9 · *CGPLA Eng. & Wales* (1995)
Archives ICES Headquarters, Copenhagen, Denmark, MSS · North Atlantic Fisheries College, Scalloway, Shetland, MSS | U. Glas., Archives and Business Records Centre, corresp. with Sir E. Bullard
Likenesses M. P. Sissenwine, photograph, RS · photograph, repro. in *The Times*
Wealth at death under £145,000: probate, 20 Sept 1995, *CGPLA Eng. & Wales*

Beville, Robert (*d.* 1824), barrister, was called to the bar at the Inner Temple between 1795 and 1799, and practised on the Norfolk circuit and at the Ely assizes, as well as in London and Middlesex, until 1807. In 1812 he became registrar to the Bedford Level Corporation, a post which he held for the rest of his life. He was also the recorder of Lynn, and magistrate of Worship Street court. In 1816 his address was Fen Office, 3 Tanfield Court, Temple.

Beville was the author of a small treatise, *On the Law of Homicide and Larceny at Common Law*, published in 1799 and much criticized the same year in the *London Monthly Review*. In 1813 a new edition of Dugdale's *History of Imbanking and Drayning of Divers Fens and Marshes* was announced in the *Gentleman's Magazine* as in preparation by Beville, but it did not appear. On 14 February 1801 Beville married a Miss Santer of Chancery Lane; they had two sons, Robert and Charles. He died in 1824.

J. M. RIGG, *rev.* BETH F. WOOD

Sources G. A. Voigt, *Famous gentleman riders* (1925) · *GM*, 1st ser., 71 (1801), 181 · Allibone, *Dict.* · *GM*, 1st ser., 83/2 (1813), 448 · *GM*, 1st ser., 88/1 (1818), 323 · Venn, *Alum. Cant.* · T. Cooper, *A new biographical dictionary: containing concise notices of eminent persons of all ages and countries* (1873)

Bevin, Elway (*c.*1554–1638), composer and musician, was probably born in Wells, Somerset, though his family may have been Welsh; the claim for his Welsh origins is made by Anthony Wood (Bodl. Oxf., MS Wood D.19(4)). Nor is it known when or where Bevin married, but he had a number of children with his wife, Alice. The parish registers of St Augustine-the-Less, Bristol, record the baptisms of six of their children between 1590 and 1603.

It is thought that Bevin was a pupil of Thomas Tallis, though the first firm evidence about his life and career dates from his admittance as a vicar-choral at Wells Cathedral on 10 May 1579. He remained at Wells until *c.*1584–5, and became master of the choristers at Bristol Cathedral on Lady day 1585. The first reference to him as the cathedral organist appears in 1589. In addition to holding his position at Bristol, Bevin became a gentleman-extraordinary of the Chapel Royal on 3 June 1605. Wood claims that Bevin taught the Bristol-born composer and organist William Child, who was apprenticed to one of the petty canons of Bristol Cathedral choir and who may have been a chorister there.

Bevin established a reputation as a composer of canons and church music. His creative ability is difficult to assess on the basis of the small quantity of his work that survives, but his most important work of liturgical music, his Dorian or short service, was sufficiently highly regarded to be included by John Barnard in his *The First Book of Selected Church Musick* (1641), and in later collections by Thomas Tudway and William Boyce. Despite his interest in strict polyphonic forms, some works, such as his three-part Browning setting, are more than mere exercises in theory. The examples that illustrate Bevin's *Briefe and Short Instruction in the Art of Musicke*, a manual for novices published in 1631, show him to have been a master of the canon, and this may well explain why both Purcell and Christopher Simpson thought highly of the book.

Bevin dedicated *A Briefe and Short Instruction* to the bishop of Gloucester, Godfrey Goodman, and may have owed his place at the Chapel Royal to him. Bevin professed a strong sense of obligation to Goodman for favours he had received from him. This gives some substance to the suspicion that Bevin may have been a recusant, since Goodman himself eventually left the Anglican church for Rome. Furthermore, it is recorded that on 2 January 1580 Bevin was temporarily suspended from his post at Wells Cathedral for having neglected to take communion for four years. It has also been claimed that he lost his positions at the Chapel Royal and at Bristol Cathedral because he was discovered to be a Roman Catholic, but there is no evidence to support this.

However, Bevin was finally dismissed from his post at Bristol on 14 February in either 1637 or 1638. The reasons for this are not entirely clear, but his growing infirmity was a major factor. Archbishop Laud's visitation of cathedrals in 1634 brought him to Bristol just a few years before Bevin's expulsion and death. Laud's report of the visitation refers to Bevin's increasing incapacity and its detrimental consequences for the music of the cathedral. Bevin is described as 'a verie old man, who, having done good service in the church, is not now able to discharge the place, but that hee is holpen by some other of the quier' (Spink, 43).

Bevin died in Bristol in October 1638, not long after his dismissal, and was buried on 19 October at St Augustine-the-Less. The fact that he was not buried in the cathedral has been taken as evidence that he was dismissed for recusancy. However, owing to the destruction in the Bristol riots (1831) of the cathedral records relating to Bevin's period, it is impossible to clarify the details of his career there.

HELEN BARLOW

Sources J. G. Hooper, *Elway Bevin* (1971) · H. W. Shaw, *The succession of organists of the Chapel Royal and the cathedrals of England and Wales from c.1538* (1991) · 'Bevin, Elway', *New Grove*, 2nd edn · 'Child, William', *New Grove*, 2nd edn · I. Spink, 'Music and society', *The seventeenth century*, ed. I. Spink, The Blackwell History of Music in Britain (1992) · R. McGuinness, 'Writings about music', *The seventeenth century*, ed. I. Spink, Blackwell History of Music in Britain (1992) · T. Dart and W. Coates, eds., *Jacobean consort music*, 2nd edn, Musica Britannica, 9 (1966)
Archives BL, Add. MSS 17784, 29289, 29430, 29996, 30085, 31403 · BL, RM 23 1 4, RM 24c 14, RM 24d 2 (1–203), RM 15f 2, K 2 d 14 · Bodl.

Oxf., Bodley Mus. Sch. D212–16, nos. 6, 38 · Christ Church Oxf., MSS 1001, 1220–1234 · FM Cam., 116, 117 · Royal College of Music, London, RCM 1045–1051

Bevin, Ernest (1881–1951), trade unionist, was born at Winsford, Somerset, on 7 March 1881, the seventh child of Diana (known as Mercy) Bevin (1841–1889). His mother, the daughter of Thomas and Mary Tidbould, married William Bevin, an agricultural labourer, in 1864. In 1876 or 1877 William Bevin left his family and Diana Bevin thereafter called herself a widow. Hence the father of Ernest Bevin is unknown. His mother earned a frugal living for herself and the children as a midwife, a domestic servant, and an occasional help in a public house, the Royal Oak, until her death in 1889. Ernest Bevin then lived with his sister Mary Jane and her husband, George Pope, a railway worker, in Morchard Bishop and then Copplestone, Devon.

Unskilled work in Bristol: socialism and trade unionism Bevin had a fragmented education. When his mother was alive he attended the Winsford church school and the Wesleyan Sunday school. After her death he attended Colebrook board school (1889–90), then Hayward Boys' School, Crediton (1890–92). After leaving school on 25 March 1892 he worked on two farms—first Chaffcombe, then Beers—before moving into Bristol in spring 1894 to join his brothers Jack and Albert. There, as a new migrant from the countryside, he took on a series of unskilled jobs. Jack worked in a butcher's shop in Clifton, and Albert was training as a pastry-cook at the Priory Restaurant. Bevin shared accommodation in Bishopston until 1900 with Jack and through Albert was employed in the Priory Restaurant's city centre bakehouse. He left to work as a van boy for the mineral water firm Brookes and Prudencios. He moved on to work in Jackson's butter shop in High Street, as a waiter in the Priory Restaurant, and as a conductor on the horse trams from December 1897 to March 1900.

From May 1900 until March 1906 Bevin worked as a van driver for the mineral water firm G. C. King, of York Street, St Paul's, which employed his brother Fred. He left his van to run the firm's refreshment rooms for two years. His final job before becoming a paid trade union official was as a van driver for John Macey's, another mineral water firm, where by working long hours he earned nearly £2 per week. During this period of relative job security he began what his friend and biographer Francis Williams called his 'lifelong partnership' (*DNB*) with Florence Anne Townley (*d.* 1968), the daughter of a wine taster at a Bristol wine merchants. It is not known when or where they married. They had one daughter.

Bevin became strong in his nonconformist beliefs as a young man. His mother had sent him to the Wesleyan Sunday school from the age of three, and when living with his sister at Copplestone he had attended the Ebenezer Chapel. In Bristol he attended numerous chapels but came to favour the Manor Hall Baptist Mission in St Mark's Road, Easton. On 5 January 1902 he was baptized. For a few years up to 1905 he was active in the chapel as a Sunday school teacher and a sidesman, and as a Baptist preacher

Ernest Bevin (1881–1951), by Felix H. Man, 1939–40

in Bristol and the surrounding area. He eagerly participated in the large-scale discussion class run by the Revd James Moffat Logan in the Old King Street Baptist Church. Bevin also learned much from Sunday morning classes run by the Adult School Movement and weekday evening classes run by both the YMCA in St James's Square and the city education committee. These experiences typified the drive for self-improvement characteristic of a section of the Victorian and Edwardian working class, and like many contemporaries they assumed for Bevin a political dimension.

After the end of the Second South African War (1899–1902) Bevin began attending socialist meetings, including those of the Social Democratic Federation and the Independent Labour Party (ILP). Perhaps he drew an element of didactic intolerance and a distaste for self-consciously ethical stances from the federation. The ILP appears to have been less of an influence. When a right-to-work committee was set up in Bristol, Bevin was its first secretary, from 1908 to 1910. He effectively followed other areas' style of campaigning, with highly publicized delegations to Augustine Birrell, local MP and chief secretary for Ireland, and the mayor of Bristol. He organized some 400 unemployed to attend morning service in Bristol Cathedral on 9 November 1908. In 1909 he stood unsuccessfully as a socialist in the city council elections.

Bevin's involvement in trade unionism came relatively late, but it soon became his full-time occupation. His connection with the dockers began in 1910, when he was twenty-nine. During a dock strike at Avonmouth and Bristol in June–July 1910 he was invited to run a relief fund. The Dock, Wharf, Riverside, and General Workers' Union (known as the Dockers' Union) urged Bevin to unionize the carters. Bevin rebuffed the recruitment efforts of the rival Workers' Union and in August 1910 successfully set up a carmen's branch of the Dockers' Union, with himself as chairman. He began his union career at a highly favourable time, at an upturn in trade and in trade union activity, and in a favourable place, already a key area of support for the Dockers' Union. After a year his branch had 2050 members and he had secured collective bargaining with local employers.

Official of the Dockers' Union In spring 1911 Bevin gave up his job delivering mineral water and became a paid trade union official as a district investigator of the Dockers' Union. He was soon working for the union throughout the south-west of England and south Wales. In March 1914 he became one of his union's three national organizers. Before the outbreak of the First World War Bevin was involved in talks with the General Labourers' National Council for consolidating its constituent unions, with semi-autonomous sections operating within the resulting large union. Bevin favoured such a merger, not least because of his experience in Bristol of a union covering dockers, transport workers, and general labourers. It revealed his concern for broader unity, to construct solidarity out of fragmentation and diversity.

During the First World War, Bevin acquired a national standing within the trade union movement. He was critical both of those in the labour movement who were strongly against the war and those who were strongly for it. Like most trade union leaders he opposed conscription, arguing that it would 'enslave labour'. At the TUC in 1915 he called for the immediate creation of a Ministry of Labour. In 1917 he declined the offer of a paid post as a government labour adviser, but earlier he did join the Bristol subcommittee of the Port and Transit Executive. In autumn 1915 he had his first experience of overseas trade union meetings as a TUC fraternal delegate to the annual convention of the American Federation of Labor, held in San Francisco. In 1916 he was elected to the executive committee of the National Transport Workers' Federation (NTWF) when Ben Tillett, the secretary of the Dockers' Union, stood down. The large NTWF had much weight in the British labour movement, unlike the 40,000-strong Dockers' Union.

Bevin increasingly aligned himself with the centrist trade unionists' position, distancing himself from the anti-war left of the First World War. In August 1917, at the Labour Party special conference which debated whether to send delegates to the proposed socialist conference at Stockholm, Bevin and his union backed Arthur Henderson in supporting the conference. However, he seconded a motion moved by William Adamson, the leading moderate miner and soon to be Henderson's successor as chair of the Parliamentary Labour Party, which restricted ILP or other socialist representation in a British delegation to the conference. Earlier, Bevin had struck a discordant note at the Leeds convention of June 1917, held to welcome the Russian revolution of February 1917. Bevin criticized peace sentiments while there was no change of

regime in Germany and made derogatory references to 'our fatuous friends of the ILP' and 'the professional politicians of the Labour Party' (Bullock, *Life and Times*, 1.75).

Bevin worked too hard during the difficult war years, and suffered a nervous breakdown in July 1918 from which he took three months to recover. He showed himself again a trade union Labour loyalist at the first post-war general election late in 1918, when he was defeated as the Labour candidate for Central Bristol. He had contested the seat in place of his friend Alderman Frank Sheppard, who stood down after the Labour Party voted to withdraw from Lloyd George's coalition government. Within the Dockers' Union Bevin frequently acted as Tillett's deputy after the latter was elected to parliament in 1917, and this role was formally recognized in May 1920 when the post of assistant general secretary was created for him. Membership had expanded rapidly in the post-war boom, reaching 70,000 in 1920, its income more than doubling from £65,000 to £141,000 in the same year.

Although Bevin often expressed class bitterness, he was a pragmatic and very effective trade union negotiator. In November 1916 he was one of several trade unionists who discussed industrial relations with Arnold Rowntree and afterwards with employers. This led to the establishment in June 1917 of the Bristol Association for Industrial Reconstruction with Bevin as a vice-president. After the First World War Bevin took no part in the national industrial conference of 1919–20, but he did participate in several national committees and subcommittees, including the committee on trusts and the central committee set up under the Profiteering Act of 1919. Along with J. R. Clynes and Arthur Henderson, leaders of the Labour Party, and Harry Gosling, president of the NTWF, he played a part in resolving the national railway strike of September–October 1919. With his trade union role centring more on London than Bristol, Bevin and his wife moved their home to London in February 1920. After renting flats in Adam Street and Gloucester Place, they bought a house, 130 The Vale, Golders Green.

Bevin consolidated his national prominence with his role as 'the Dockers' KC' during the inquiry in February and March 1920, chaired by Lord Shaw of Dunfermline, into the dockers' claim for national improved wages and conditions, held under the Industrial Courts Act of 1919. Bevin skilfully turned the twenty public sittings of the court of inquiry into a national stage on which he could indict the employers for the dockers' dire working conditions and standards of life. Bevin argued, 'The docker who is distributing goods is contributing as much to the national well-being as the capitalist who is manipulating money or handling shares' (Weiler, *Ernest Bevin*, 28). He also argued vehemently against the assumption that new houses with only one living room were sufficient for dockers and their families, calling instead for housing which enabled the dockers to have space to read and to develop other leisure interests. The inquiry report vindicated the claims of Bevin and the NTWF.

Bevin underlined his radical credentials with his opposition to British government aid for military intervention against Soviet Russia. When, in May 1920, dockers in the East India dock sought union backing to stop loading cargo marked 'OHMS Munitions for Poland' onto the *Jolly George*, Bevin readily agreed. In August 1920 he took the lead in pressing for the formation of a council of action to stop British involvement in a war against Russia and made its case when a deputation saw Lloyd George, the prime minister. At a mass meeting in Westminster Hall on 13 August, Bevin argued that Labour's 'willingness to take action to win world peace transcends any claim in connection with wages or hours of labour' (Bullock, *Life and Times*, 1.139). Further action proved unnecessary as the British government did not intervene and the Polish army repelled the Red Army. In contrast, Bevin won few plaudits in the labour movement over 'black Friday', 15 April 1921, the day when the miners' triple alliance allies voted against taking strike action to support the locked-out miners who were resisting substantial pay cuts. Bevin had, in fact, been supportive of the miners, but he and the other union leaders would not support the miners' leaders in declining further negotiations. His stance was probably influenced by a sharp appreciation of his own union's brittleness in the face of trade depression.

General secretary of the Transport and General Workers' Union
With his energy and the support he carried among the dockers, Bevin played the major part in creating the Transport and General Workers' Union (TGWU), a merger of fourteen unions with a combined membership of 300,000 which came into being on 1 January 1922. With the Dockers' Union at its core, the new amalgamation replaced the loose alliance of autonomous unions which comprised the Transport Workers' Federation with a centralized structure. It has been described as 'a monolithic achievement ruthlessly secured' (*DNB*). The NTWF and Robert Williams, its full-time secretary since 1912, were sidelined, and Tillett, Bevin's senior in the Dockers' Union, was pensioned off. At the same time Bevin shrewdly offered the TGWU's constituent unions the prospect of a quasi-federal structure, with existing union officers and executive committee members fitting into the new organization as trade groups. Those amalgamated included groups with reputations for militancy, including some sections of the dockers and the London bus workers. Bevin was elected general secretary by 96,842 votes to a communist-endorsed rival's vote of 7672. From the outset he was in a powerful position, and this was strengthened following the death in 1930 of Harry Gosling, the union's president, after which Bevin became the one full-time officer elected by all members (the other TGWU officers were appointed either by the appropriate trade groups or by the executive).

Bevin was willing and able to exercise great authority in the TGWU, which he saw as his union. Overworked, he suffered nervous exhaustion in December 1922, requiring a seven-week rest. Later, in 1929, Bevin gave the TGWU renewed impetus and more members by amalgamation with the Workers' Union. Although the latter was in poor shape financially, it brought into the TGWU members in sectors such as engineering that proved subsequently to

be areas of economic and therefore union expansion. Having broadened out from its original base of road transport workers and dockers, the TGWU, with over 650,000 members, became in the late 1930s Britain's biggest trade union.

Bevin fully committed the TGWU to supporting the Labour Party. By late 1923 his union sponsored more Labour MPs than any union but the Miners' Federation of Great Britain. Nevertheless he was ready to clash with a Labour government on industrial questions that concerned the conditions of his members. The life of the first Labour government (January–October 1924) coincided with an upturn in trade. Bevin had accepted wage reductions during the downturn of 1921–2 and pressed mostly successfully for wage increases when better economic conditions arrived. There was a national dock strike, and there were stoppages among London busmen and tramway workers. Ramsay MacDonald, Labour's first prime minister, felt that Bevin's strikes represented 'disloyalty' to Labour in office. Bevin was highly critical of what he saw as MacDonald's mid-Victorian outlook, his lack of consultation with the TUC, his readiness to invoke the Emergency Powers Act of 1920, and his failure to rebut quickly allegations linked to the Zinoviev letter, and he unsuccessfully pressed Arthur Henderson to stand for the leadership of the Labour Party. What was at stake was a clash between Bevin's view of the Labour interest, and a fundamentally ethical socialist outlook, which in such circumstances viewed the conduct of unions as sectional and unconstructive.

At the Labour Party conference in 1925 Bevin moved that 'in view of the recent Labour government it is inadvisable that the Labour Party should again accept office whilst having a minority of Members in the House of Commons'. Bevin said that he and his TGWU executive felt that in the circumstances of January 1924 it had been right to take office but that it was not acceptable to return to office 'when the condition of getting any legislation passed was a continuous compromise with other people' (*Labour Party Conference Report*, 1925, 244). The debate ended in acrimony, and defeat for Bevin, who once again spoke of politicians with distaste.

Bevin, who was elected to the general council of the TUC in 1925, was a major figure in the general strike of 1926. He had suffered much abuse from communists and others for not backing the miners on 'black Friday' in 1921. In 1925 Bevin backed the miners because he realized that a general attack on wage levels was imminent. He secured the support of his union's biennial delegate conference for full co-operation with the TUC in support of the miners. On 'red Friday', 31 July 1925, Stanley Baldwin's Conservative government, faced with strong trade union pressure and a general public sympathetic to the miners, gave a nine-month subsidy to the coal industry. Bevin, like most trade union leaders, expected a negotiated settlement to be reached in these nine months. When it was not, he worked tirelessly to secure an agreement. Once the general strike took place, he was the driving force behind the TUC's organization. When it was called off, he was the sole TUC leader to press Baldwin to ensure there was no victimization of returning strikers.

The general strike confirmed Bevin in his predisposition towards pragmatic collective bargaining. He recognized that it was no longer plausible that capitalism might be replaced or radically changed by industrial action. Instead, modernization, rationalization, and a scientific approach to economic problems became his chief concerns. He worked with Walter Citrine, secretary of the TUC, to make the TUC influential in developing national industrial and economic policy. Bevin had expressed clear views about international economic developments during the post-war boom (1919–20) and the discussions before Britain's return to the gold standard in 1925. He developed his ideas further in the late 1920s and afterwards. Like David Lloyd George, he gained much knowledge from talking to others, rather than from reading. Bevin was notable for advocating unconventional ideas; as at the TUC in 1927, when he called for the creation of a 'spirit of a United States of Europe—at least on an economic basis, even if we cannot on a totally political basis' (Bullock, *Life and Times*, 1.387–8). He also saw the need for British industry to modernize to stay competitive, a view reinforced by his fact-finding trips to the USA. In 1928 he readily joined the Mond–Turner talks between some employers and the TUC. He also believed the British labour movement needed to think big, and this was epitomized in his building Transport House in 1928 as a centre not only for the TGWU but also for the TUC and the Labour Party.

Bevin's thinking on economic issues became very influential in the labour movement after the Wall Street stock market crash of 1929. He served on Lord Macmillan's committee on finance and industry, appointed in November 1929 in response to rising unemployment. There, serving alongside J. M. Keynes, he made it clear that he viewed the devaluation of the pound as a desirable option. He also served with Keynes, whose ideas he absorbed, on the Economic Advisory Council, set up in January 1930, to advise the government. As a member of the TUC's newly created economic committee he readily accepted the need for tariffs to protect British industry. These developments reflected the development of a distinctive TUC approach to politics in some senses distinct from the Labour Party, a position which suited Bevin. He was dismissive of Philip Snowden's arguments that failure to buttress sterling would lead to international economic chaos. During the crisis of August 1931 which led to the fall of MacDonald's Labour government, Bevin played a leading role in confronting ministers and articulating the TUC general council's opposition to reductions in unemployment benefit, and to a surrender to economic orthodoxy. In doing so he strengthened cabinet opponents of cuts.

Bevin provided the labour movement with a solid trade union power base after the Labour Party's parliamentary strength was severely reduced in the general election of 1931. He stood unsuccessfully for the usually safe Labour seat of Gateshead, campaigning on the theme 'Vote Bevin and public control of banking in the interest of trade, commerce and the people' (Potts). For Bevin the villains were always financiers, whom he regarded as a burden on industrialists and workers alike. A central figure in the party's subsequent recovery, he epitomized the heightened involvement of the TUC general council in party affairs, destroying any lingering links and sympathies with those who had joined the National Government. Even before the election he had become chairman of the Society for Socialist Inquiry and Propaganda, what later would have been described as a socialist think-tank. Margaret Cole recalled a preliminary conference when Bevin 'took full part in all discussion, formal or informal … displaying a grasp of economic and financial essentials which some of the younger intellectuals had scarcely thought to find in a trade union official' (Cole, 196). After the election débâcle of 1931 Bevin was convinced of the need for more socialist education. However, when the society was merged into the newly formed Socialist League in 1932 Bevin was excluded from a leading role, a move which reinforced his suspicion of the egotism of many intellectual socialists.

With Walter Citrine, Bevin played a major part in moving the British labour movement away from a pacifist or near-pacifist foreign policy between 1935 and 1937 to one which recognized that collective security was likely to lead to war, so requiring the Parliamentary Labour Party to vote for rearmament. At the Labour Party conference of 1935 he was the leading critic of George Lansbury, the Labour Party leader, and Sir Stafford Cripps, the leading figure of the left. His verbal destruction of Lansbury was especially brutal; characteristically Bevin did not distinguish clearly between the individual and the issue. He emphasized that trade unionists were being martyred in fascist countries and condemned Lansbury for not accepting collective responsibility for decisions on war and peace. Lansbury resigned as leader a week later. Bevin was able to further his campaign to commit Labour to rearmament as chairman of the general council of the TUC in 1936–7. In the case of the Spanish Civil War his sympathies for the elected republican government against the Franco rebellion were balanced by suspicions of communism and hostility to united front politics. Bevin had opposed communist critics within the TGWU and the trade union movement generally and moved from a policy of non-intervention on Spain only when the Labour Party and TUC leadership did so, in response to strong pressure from their members.

In the 1930s Bevin and Citrine remained a powerful combination at the heart of the TUC. Citrine later wrote of Bevin, 'He had great drive and a measure of ruthlessness that I did not possess' (Citrine, 238). Bevin took a determined stance against communist challenges to trade union leaderships, not least in the TGWU. He was faced with a strongly supported and capable rank-and-file movement among London bus workers, which was set off in 1932 by dissatisfaction with a productivity deal Bevin had negotiated with the London General Omnibus Company to avoid redundancies and wage cuts. Later, after a failed strike during the coronation period in May 1937, the

TGWU ended the rank-and-file movement and soon after the leaders were expelled or suspended. However, Bevin and his colleagues allowed those leaders who remained loyal to the union to be readmitted. Thus he defended the hierarchical structure he had established in the TGWU and also the strategy of regaining ground lost since 1926, by cautious negotiation and the steady build-up of union strength. During 1937–8 he represented the TUC on a committee chaired by Lord Amulree to review the right of workers to have paid holidays, a cause which Bevin had long advocated. The committee's recommendations led to the Holidays with Pay Act (1938) which extended to 11 million wage earners the right to one week's annual holiday. This was one of Bevin's few successes in extracting concessions from the National Government; his industrial strategy during the 1930s, like that of his TUC allies, produced only modest results.

In the late 1930s Bevin was seriously thinking of retiring at sixty. His health was poor again after his exertions for the TUC in 1936–7. He and his wife took the opportunity to travel to Commonwealth meetings from July to October 1938. On his return he was involved in preparing the war organization of the docks, road haulage, milling, and demolition industries. After the outbreak of war in September 1939 one of his major tasks was working on various issues relating to British fishing fleets with Winston Churchill, newly returned to office as first lord of the Admiralty.

Minister of labour during the Second World War When Churchill became prime minister in May 1940, Bevin was top of his list of the Labour figures whom he sought for office. Bevin agreed to become minister of labour and national service in the coalition cabinet and, in October 1940, joined Churchill's inner war cabinet. He also entered parliament for the first time after a by-election in June 1940, being elected unopposed as MP for Central Wandsworth when the sitting Labour MP was given a peerage. Bevin held the seat until 1950; he was then elected for the safer constituency of Woolwich East, which he retained until his death.

The need for the efficient use of labour needs of war made Bevin's ministry pivotal on the home front. He was used to taking responsibility, and he was quick to centralize much power in his own hands. At his suggestion there was an attempt to co-ordinate his work with other supply departments through the production council, but Lord Beaverbrook, who used his long friendship with Churchill to go his own way as minister of aircraft production, often frustrated such efforts.

Having seen Arthur Henderson's role in the First World War, Churchill recognized the benefit of having a major trade unionist involved in wartime labour policy. For his part, Bevin was an unequivocal supporter of the war effort, looking back to his early years in the socialist movement to justify military conscription:

> I am an old member of the Social Democratic Federation; I never apologise for my faith, I still believe in the Citizen Army, a democratic army. I still believe it is a social

obligation to defend your own homestead.   (TGWU, *Report of Biennial Delegate Conference*, August 1941)

In industrial matters, Bevin wished to operate on a basis of consent and to protect trade union freedoms wherever possible. He was given extensive powers, more than he wished for in the case of the Emergency Powers Act passed in May 1940, which allowed him to mobilize and direct labour into industries essential for the war effort. He preferred, however, to rely on voluntary co-operation and addressed a conference of 2000 executive members of trade unions in Central Hall, Westminster, on 25 May 1940, to explain his powers and his policies and to seek the trade union movement's support. He then arranged for the two sides of industry to set up a small advisory council, drawn from the existing bigger National Joint Advisory Council, to give advice on the Ministry of Labour's work.

Bevin was keen to work with joint committees of employers and employees throughout industry. He had been sympathetic to such co-operation during and after the First World War, as well as after the general strike. Following Hitler's attack on Russia, his drive for more joint production committees was supported by the Communist Party, which was not only eager to support the Soviet Union but also to lessen managerial prerogatives. As well as protecting trade union freedoms, he also wished to use the enhanced position of Labour to improve conditions, especially in sectors where trade union organization was historically weak. In July 1942 he expressed the hope that 'by the time that hostilities cease, there will be not a single industry of any kind in the country that has not wage-regulating machinery of some kind or other' (Bullock, *Life and Times*, 2.194). He ended casual labour in the docks by creating the National Dock Labour Corporation and, in the face of considerable hostility from Conservative MPs, pressed ahead in 1942–3 with the regulation of the catering industry, the sector least covered by collective agreements or labour regulation. The catering wages board, set up in 1943, set minimum wages and enforced agreed standards over the industry. Its principle was broadened by the Wage Councils Act of 1945, for which he was largely responsible, which extended the powers of existing trade boards to enforce minimum standards. By the end of the Second World War there was a very great extension of collective bargaining.

Bevin was also determined that wartime conditions would buttress, not undermine, the official trade union leadership. During the First World War trade union officials' co-operation with employers and the state had left space for rank-and-file movements; the danger of this happening in the Second World War was reduced when the Communist Party threw its support behind the war effort. He took firm action against unofficial strike organizers, as on Tyneside in 1943, and in April 1944 gave himself additional reserve powers under regulation 1AA of the Emergency Powers (Defence) regulations. More generally, strikes and lock-outs were illegal under order 1305 (issued on 18 July 1940), though there was substantial unrest in the coal industry (which accounted for 56 per cent of all working days lost through strikes from 1940 to 1944).

Bevin insisted that the British people should receive social welfare in return for their all-out efforts in 'a total war'. Whereas in Russia the peasant armies were fighting to defend their land, in Britain 'the substitute is the vested interest of social security … in which all shall participate' (TGWU, *Report of the Biennial Delegate Conference*, August 1941). Six days earlier Bevin and his colleagues had successfully pressed for the inclusion of improved social security in the allied aims listed in the Atlantic charter. He was willing, however, to set aside the Beveridge report for the duration of Churchill's coalition government, becoming very angry with the Parliamentary Labour Party when it took a different view: he was concerned to keep the coalition together (fearing that Labour would lose an election if it fell); he regarded some of Beveridge's proposals, such as family allowances, as undermining the unions' role in wage bargaining; and he had a personal dislike for Beveridge himself. He believed that controls on the economy would have to be retained after victory. Speaking at the TGWU biennial conference on 3 August 1943, he predicted a necessity for 'three, four or five years of national discipline' in order to avoid 'an orgy of speculation, bringing with it all the troubles that arose after the last war' (TGWU, *Report of the Biennial Delegate Conference*, August 1943).

Bevin was a notably successful wartime minister. Churchill soon came to admire his toughness and determination and within five months included him in his small war cabinet. He was the major force in domestic policy while Churchill concentrated on war policy. Churchill saw Bevin as a possible war leader should anything happen to him and, in a speech in the House of Commons on 29 July 1941, paid a fulsome public tribute to Bevin's role in securing high industrial production. Churchill's personal detective was probably right in thinking his employer admired Bevin for being a Labour man of 'the old school who had been brought up among the working class' and was 'as English as the oak' and not a socialist intellectual (W. H. Thompson, *I was Churchill's Shadow*, 1951, 154). Bevin, a big (in all senses), self-confident, and egotistic man, could stand up to Churchill, who shared these qualities. The two men symbolized the national unity of the established classes and labour in fighting fascism.

During Bevin's period at the Ministry of Labour, Britain achieved a higher level of civilian mobilization than any other of the nations at war, a feat which was carried out 'with a speed and efficiency completely unmatched in any of the dictatorships' (*DNB*). Women were conscripted from December 1941. Responsible for securing labour to work in the mines, Bevin resorted from December 1943 to recruiting 'Bevin boys' by lottery from among those called up for national service. About 8.5 million workers were subject to his emergency powers, which were accompanied by the protection of guaranteed pay and conditions. His initiative extended the powers of the Ministry of Labour to cover the welfare of war workers, ensuring, for example, that they were provided with canteens. Quite

apart from the contribution to the war effort, his five years at the ministry were an impressive realization of the corporatist agenda to which he had committed himself after the failure of the general strike. Business, trade unions, and the state were to co-operate in running industry, the trade unions being brought into partnership on an equal basis. The working class backed the war effort, trade union membership grew, and the status of the TUC was transformed, as in many respects were working conditions. He hoped to create a structure for industrial relations which would persist into the post-war world, and to a large extent he succeeded. In 1946 joint industrial councils and trade boards, both of which had been greatly extended by Bevin during the war years, regulated the pay and conditions of 15.5 million out of 17.5 million workers (Bullock, *Life and Times*, 3.93). 'They used to say Gladstone was at the Treasury from 1860 to 1930', Bevin remarked of the late nineteenth-century Liberal prime minister's influence upon public policy, and boasted, 'I'm going to be at the Ministry of Labour from 1940 to 1990' (*DNB*).

Foreign secretary in Attlee's government   Bevin, like most of his contemporaries, was surprised by the scale (if not the fact) of Labour's victory in the general election of 1945. Attlee initially considered making him chancellor of the exchequer and Hugh Dalton foreign secretary, but at the last minute changed his mind—partly in order to keep a distance between Bevin and his arch-enemy Herbert Morrison (whom Attlee had already earmarked as supremo for domestic questions), and partly because he considered Bevin the more likely to adopt a robust stance in foreign affairs, and to carry the Labour Party with him. Bevin took office on 27 July 1945 and held the post until 9 March 1951, longer than any predecessor since Sir Edward Grey. Unusually for a twentieth-century foreign secretary, he was able to manage British foreign policy with very little interference from the prime minister, though this was more the result of his very close working relationship with Attlee than of his own dominating personality. As Attlee later recalled, 'My relationship with Ernest Bevin was the deepest of my political life' (Harris, 294). Bevin was assured of the prime minister's unqualified support even in his most unpopular decisions; while he in turn was utterly loyal to Attlee, even at the expense (as in 1945 and 1947, when Sir Stafford Cripps and others touted him as a possible replacement for Attlee) of his own personal ambitions. Alan Bullock's view, that Attlee and Bevin formed 'one of the most successful political partnerships in English history' (Bullock, *Life and Times*, 3.56), was widely shared by contemporaries.

Bevin and his senior officials initially viewed each other with a considerable degree of mutual suspicion. Like many of his Labour colleagues, he at first regarded the Foreign Office as dominated by effete and amateurish aristocrats, and one of his earliest papers on joining the war cabinet in 1940 had called for radical reform of the office's recruitment and promotion procedures. His senior officials in turn were wary of this self-confident but poorly educated scion of the working classes. Nevertheless, within a matter of months suspicion had given way to respect and a good deal of affection, as Bevin came to appreciate his officials' ability and professionalism, while they in turn came to appreciate his intelligence, political skill, and integrity. His first permanent secretary, Sir Alexander Cadogan, noted:

> He knows a great deal, is prepared to read any amount, seems to take in what he does read, and is capable of making up his own mind and sticking up for his (or our) point of view against anyone. (*Diaries*, 778)

Bevin's loyalty to his staff became legendary; they in turn were happy to endure countless evenings listening to him reminisce about his life, or to arrange shopping trips and other diversions for his wife. Above all, his staff appreciated his robust defence of policies with which they were, with few exceptions, in complete agreement.

The popular image of Bevin as a 'working-class John Bull' (Bullock, *Life and Times*, 3.82) aptly summarized his almost visceral patriotism. He believed wholeheartedly in Britain's 'world role', and in the British empire as a force for good, regarding with suspicion the hostility of the United States towards other nations' empires. He was reluctant to see early independence for India. He was a major advocate of boosting colonial development to aid the British economy—'our crime is not exploitation; it's neglect', he said of the colonial empire (Pearce, 95). He saw Britain's economic difficulties as merely temporary, and regarded Britain as uniquely placed to provide international leadership. He thought Britain had earned its right to remain at the 'top table'. He supported Britain's independent nuclear programme on the grounds that 'we've got to have the bloody Union Jack flying on top of it' (Bullock, *Life and Times*, 3.352). He viewed his task as foreign secretary from first to last as that of defending and wherever possible furthering Britain's national interests, which he defined in traditional, if not to say conservative, terms. In the case of British military action in Greece, he had defended the Churchill coalition's policies before a hostile Labour Party conference in December 1944; he viewed the prospect of victory for the communists and their allies in the Greek civil war as a danger to British interests in the Middle East and the eastern Mediterranean and, as foreign secretary, left the royalist reactionaries to prevail.

Bevin came to office with a profound mistrust of communism and the Soviet Union, and believed that Churchill had been insufficiently firm with Stalin. He had fought communism in the British and international trade union movements, and he bitterly resented the communist denunciations of him which had followed 'black Friday' in 1921 and the general strike in 1926. However, he had greatly admired Russian courage in repelling the German invasion of Russia. In August 1943 he told the TGWU's conference,

> It must have been a terrific thing for Russia, over the last twenty-one years, to have built a new economy in a tremendous effort to catch up with the economic development of the rest of the world and then in a few months to see most of it destroyed. If ever a nation is entitled to complete restoration, it is Russia. (TGWU, *Report of the Biennial Delegate Conference*, August 1943)

After the war Bevin did not altogether give up on the possibility of improved Anglo-Soviet relations until 1946 or possibly early 1947, but his suspicions of the Soviet Union remained strong, and grew stronger in the face of Stalin's pressures to dominate Europe and his refusal to abide by the British interpretation of the Yalta and Potsdam agreements. In Bevin's view, the Soviet Union was motivated by ambition more than fear, and was likely to seize every opportunity for territorial expansion and the spread of communism. At the Labour Party conference in May 1945 he was widely quoted as having said that 'Left understands Left, but the Right does not'; nevertheless, significantly, he was speaking of France rather than the Soviet Union, and his remarks were taken out of context (Bullock, *Life and Times*, 3.69). In office, he gave little comfort to those in his own party who hoped for a close understanding with the Soviet Union as part of a distinctively 'socialist' foreign policy, and during the first few years of his foreign secretaryship he endured a great deal more criticism from his own party than from the opposition benches.

'Let us wait until our strength is restored and let us meanwhile, with US help as necessary, hold on to [our] essential positions', Bevin wrote to Attlee in January 1947 (Bullock, *Life and Times*, 3.353). His belief that American help was needed in order to contain the Soviet threat led him to play a very active role in persuading the United States to abandon hopes of returning to its pre-war isolationism. Indeed, it can fairly be claimed that Bevin was one of the key architects of the cold war. In February 1947 his initially unwelcome warning to the Americans that Britain could no longer shoulder the burden of supporting the anti-communist forces in Greece and Turkey led within weeks to the announcement of American military aid to those countries, and the enunciation of the 'Truman doctrine'. In June 1947 his nimble response to secretary of state George Marshall's speech at Harvard calling for European co-operation as a prerequisite for American aid for European recovery (an offer made, Marshall later admitted, without any firm plan in mind) led swiftly to the creation of the Committee of European Economic Co-operation (from 1948 the Organization for European Economic Co-operation, which in turn was replaced by the Organization for Economic Co-operation and Development in 1961) and the elaboration of the Marshall plan, under which America donated some $13 billion of aid to Europe, including $2.7 billion to Britain. Bevin's biographer described his role in these negotiations as 'his most decisive personal contribution as Foreign Secretary' (A. Bullock, *Ernest Bevin: Foreign Secretary*, 1983, 404). Finally, he played a key part in the negotiations leading to the treaty of Dunkirk in March 1947 and the Brussels treaty in March 1948, which (following the Berlin crisis of 1948–9) led directly to the North Atlantic treaty of April 1949, instituting the North Atlantic Treaty Organization the following year.

Bevin was by no means an uncritical admirer of the United States, nor a slavish adherent of its foreign policy. Although, for example, he quickly agreed to American air bases in Britain during the Berlin blockade of 1948, and was ready to support the USA in Korea in 1950–51, the criticism (heard more often after the event than at the time) that he reduced Britain to the position of a satellite of the United States is fairly wide of the mark. Indeed, for much of his foreign secretaryship it was he who attempted to drag a reluctant America into foreign entanglements, rather than vice versa. There were numerous areas in which he refused to bow to American pressure: the development of the British atomic bomb was one, his recognition of communist China in October 1949 (on the grounds that this would better protect Britain's interests in Hong Kong and south-east Asia) another, his refusal to countenance the dismantling of the sterling area yet another.

Perhaps the most marked disagreement came over Palestine, which Bevin viewed through the prism of Britain's wider strategic and economic interests in the Middle East. He resisted the Jewish and American demand that Britain permit a further 100,000 Jewish immigrants to enter Palestine after the war, and was angered when Truman endorsed that figure without consulting Britain. His comment that American policy towards Palestine was determined by the fact that Americans 'don't want too many Jews in New York' led to an extremely hostile response when he visited that city, with dockers refusing to handle his luggage and him being booed at a baseball match (Williams, 260). His views were undoubtedly coloured by antisemitic sentiments; but also by outrage at the assassinations of British people by Jewish terrorists, by the British need to secure oil from the Middle East, and by his sympathy for the plight of the Palestinians. He observed to one Zionist deputation, 'Under the Jews the Arabs would have no rights but would remain in a permanent minority in a land they had held for 2,000 years' (Weiler, *Ernest Bevin*, 171). His decision to hand the mandate for Palestine back to the United Nations, and effectively to wash his hands of the Palestinian problem, was perhaps the most striking failure of his foreign secretaryship; nevertheless it is difficult to see how Britain could have overseen partition (the USA's preferred solution) without incurring widespread hostility in the region.

Bevin's attitude to Europe also gave rise to much criticism from the USA, as well as from his Conservative opponents and from later commentators. In fact, his attitude was complex, if not ambiguous. At various times he lent his weight to calls for European integration—notably in January 1948, when he called for 'the closest possible collaboration' between Britain and its European neighbours, and asserted that the government would 'do all we can to foster both the spirit and the machinery of co-operation' (*Hansard 5C*, 22 Jan 1948, 446.395–8). Nevertheless he supported his cabinet colleagues' rejection of Robert Schuman's invitation to take part in talks on a coal and steel community in May 1950 (he was in hospital at the time), and viewed the Pleven plan for a European army, elaborated by the French prime minister in October 1950, as a dangerous attempt to undermine NATO. His response in both cases was conditioned first by a belief that European integration should be subordinated to trans-Atlantic co-operation, secondly by an absolute mistrust of supranational, as opposed to intergovernmental, forms of integration, and thirdly by the belief that (as he and Cripps had put it in October 1949) Britain 'must remain, as we have always been in the past, different in character from other European nations and fundamentally incapable of wholehearted integration with them' (Bullock, *Life and Times*, 3.734). In his view, Churchill's vociferous support for European integration was a somewhat hypocritical attempt to make political capital out of an issue on which there was little fundamental disagreement—a view supported by the record of the Conservative government which took power in 1951.

Bevin's foreign policy received much criticism from many directions. He was attacked by the left for being a cold war warrior, especially over relations with the Soviet Union and Greece. He was also denounced for his stance on Palestine. Hugh Gaitskell complained in his diaries (2 February 1949) of Bevin and his 'pro-Arab policy' (*Diary of Hugh Gaitskell*, 98). These criticisms have been subsequently echoed by historians. At the Labour Party conference of May 1947, when he accused his critics on the left of stabbing him in the back, he delivered a powerful defence of his foreign policy. He observed in his conclusion, 'I know things are going to be difficult, and that is why I have cultivated for the first time in my life … a quite remarkable patience' (Labour Party, *Report of the 46th Annual Conference*, May 1947, 182). Hugh Dalton noted in his diary, 'He scored a very great personal success and swept away all opposition. He has a most astonishing—and unique—conference personality' (*War Diary*, 393). 'No man alive is so skilful at handling a working-class audience, mixing the brutal hammer blow with sentimental appeals', Richard Crossman wrote of Bevin's conference speech. 'He did not merely smash his critics; he pulverised them into applauding him' (*Sunday Pictorial*, 1 June 1947; quoted in J. Schneer, *Labour's Conscience: the Labour Left, 1945–51*, 1988, p. 63).

Bevin's success in such confrontations rested not just on his abilities, but on the trade union block votes that he inevitably secured. He symbolized the trade union link which remained at the heart of the party's identity. In February 1946 he went straight from a meeting of the United Nations general assembly to take part in a parliamentary debate on the repeal of the Trade Disputes Act (1927), which he regarded as a measure of revenge by Baldwin's government towards the union movement after the general strike:

> They cast the trade unions for the role of enemies of the State … I have never been an enemy of the state. I have been as big a constitutionalist as any member on the other side of the House, and I am fighting to remove the stigma which the Tory party in 1927 put upon me as the leader of a trade union. (Bullock, *Life and Times*, 3.231)

Bevin proved to be one of the strongest figures in Attlee's governments (from 1945 to 1951). He exercised authority in the Foreign Office, much as he had exercised it in the TGWU. His robust defence of British interests and his pro-American and anti-Soviet policies commanded respect from the Foreign Office officials, much of the Labour Party, Sir Winston Churchill, and much of the opposition. He was a workaholic, unhappy when he was not working excessive hours on Foreign Office files, and, apart from the company of his wife, had very few outside interests.

Bevin was also a powerful force in the post-Second World War Labour Party. This was an uneasy relationship. Bevin, used to crushing rebels in the TGWU, was not emollient to dissent in the Parliamentary Labour Party or Labour Party generally. He made no effort to listen to backbench MPs or to conciliate those with different views. He was ill at ease in meetings other than trade union gatherings. His blunt, even brutal defences of his policies to parliamentary or other Labour Party meetings became a normal style for some of the 'old Labour' centre-right leaders, especially trade union leaders, until the 1980s. Yet, until 1948 or thereabouts, he had immense prestige in the party and Sir Stafford Cripps and others saw him as the best alternative to Clement Attlee as leader and prime minister.

Death, legacy, and assessment Like Churchill, Bevin ate, drank, and smoked too much and took little exercise. As a result his health crumbled after 1945, and he was an unfit man weighing some 250 pounds. He suffered from angina. He was in a notably poor state of health in early 1947 and was in pain at a meeting in Moscow that March. He had an attack of angina in a Washington theatre in September 1949 and further attacks in the subsequent eighteen months. By 1950 it was a matter of time before his health required him to move to a less stressful post or retire. In January 1951 Bevin went to hospital with pneumonia. He recovered for a while but on 9 March, two days after his seventieth birthday, Attlee told him he would be replaced. He was appointed lord privy seal but died of heart failure at his London home, 1 Carlton Gardens, Westminster, on 14 April 1951.

When Bevin was cremated at Golders Green on 18 April 1951, crowds packed the roads to the building. Later in April some 2000 people, including Attlee and Churchill, attended his memorial ceremony in Westminster Abbey, where his ashes were buried. Churchill recommended his widow for an honour, and she became Dame Florence Bevin in 1952. When Churchill College was founded, the Transport and General Workers' Union donated £50,000 to a memorial library to Bevin.

Bevin was one of Britain's greatest trade union figures. His ministerial career marked the arrival of organized labour at the centre of policy making and the advent of corporatist approaches to the economy. Churchill commented to Anthony Eden of Bevin in October 1944 that Bevin was by 'far the most distinguished man that the Labour Party have thrown up in my time' (J. Colville, *The Fringes of Power*, 1985, 522). Bevin was perhaps second only to Churchill in the wartime coalition government and was a dominant figure in the post-war Labour governments. He had a strong sense of class and of his own struggle upwards from an educationally deprived background of rural poverty followed by dead-end jobs in his early working life. An unpredictable compound of insights and prejudices, he was intellectually highly able but he distrusted socialist intellectuals, though he was ready to refer to his own socialist credentials. In a radio broadcast of 1934 he observed,

> I have no confidence in the superman; the limitations of supposedly great men are obvious. I have spent my life among ordinary working people; I am one of them. I have seen them faced with the most difficult problems; place the truth before them—the facts, whether they are good or bad—and they display an understanding, ability and courage that confound the wisdom of the so-called great. (Bevin, 136)

This was a major part of his outlook, even if he was often ready to lead and demand support in superman style. He was a tough and often unforgiving trade union leader and politician, but his word was his bond. Effective and even courageous in office, he attracted the loyalty of those who worked with him.

The major substantial study of Bevin remains Alan Bullock's impressive three-volume biography. Of this, Peter Weiler, a later biographer, has reasonably commented, 'Bullock's stance is that of a Labour loyalist from a generation for whom Bevin was a hero' (Weiler, *Ernest Bevin*, viii). Bullock describes Bevin's 'identification with ordinary men and women' as 'the most consistent principle in his career' and his foremost political aim as being 'to bring the working class within the national community on equal terms' (Bullock, *Life and Times*, 3.92, 857). On that account generally, and more particularly by his success after 1926 in moving the labour movement away from syndicalism and back to its traditional attachment to political participation and free collective bargaining, Bevin has been adjudged 'the most effective democratic politician' in twentieth-century Britain (Bullock, *Bevin: a Biography*, xiii). Weiler's able biography emphasizes Bevin's explicit acceptance of the limits of the capitalist economy. Within these limits he sought a partnership with capital and the state; the co-operation of labour would be complemented by recognition and influence. For some critics this strategy is a matter for concern; but it also suggests that Bevin had a good grasp of the realities of British society from 1921 to 1951.   CHRIS WRIGLEY

Sources A. Bullock, *The life and times of Ernest Bevin*, 3 vols. (1960–83) • A. Bullock, *Ernest Bevin: a biography*, ed. B. Brivati (2002) [one-volume abridgement] • T. Evans, *Bevin* (1946) • F. Williams, *Ernest Bevin: portrait of a great Englishman* (1952) • P. Weiler, *Ernest Bevin* (1993) • R. Barclay, *Ernest Bevin and the foreign office, 1932–69* (1975) [privately published] • M. Stephens, *Ernest Bevin: unskilled labourer and world statesman, 1881–1951* (1981) • R. Pearce, 'Ernest Bevin', *Labour forces: from Ernest Bevin to Gordon Brown*, ed. K. Jeffrys (2003) • E. Bevin, *The job to be done* (1942) • E. Taplin, *The dockers' union* (1986) • K. Coates and T. Topham, *The history of the Transport and General Workers' Union* (1991) • G. Phillips, *The general strike* (1976) • P. Williamson, *National crisis and national government: British politics, the economy and empire, 1926–1932* (1992) • R. Croucher, *Engineers at war* (1982) • P. F. Inman, *Labour in the munitions industries* (1957) • H. M. D. Parker, *Manpower: a study of war-time policy and administration* (1957) • *The Second World War diary of Hugh Dalton, 1940–1945*, ed. B. Pimlott (1986) • W. Citrine, *Men and work: an autobiography* (1964) •

P. Weiler, *British labour and the cold war* (Stanford, 1988) · T. B. Burridge, *British labour and Hitler's war* (1977) · S. Brooke, *Labour's war: the labour party during the Second World War* (1992) · *The diary of Hugh Gaitskell, 1945–1956*, ed. P. M. Williams (1983) · A. Potts, 'Bevin to beat the bankers: Ernest Bevin's Gateshead campaign of 1931', *Bulletin of the Northeast Group for the Study of Labour History*, 11 (1977), 28–38 · M. Cole, 'The Society for Socialist Inquiry and Propaganda', *Essays in labour history, 1918–1939*, ed. A. Briggs and J. Saville (1977) · J. Shepherd, 'Labour and the trade unions: Lansbury, Ernest Bevin and the leadership crisis of 1935', *On the move*, ed. C. Wrigley and J. Shepherd (1991) · C. Wrigley, 'The Second World War and state intervention in industrial relations, 1939–45', *A history of British industrial relations, 1939–79*, ed. C. Wrigley (1996) · L. V. Scott, *Conscription and the Attlee government* (1993) · A. Deighton, *The impossible peace: Britain, the division of Germany and the origins of the cold war* (1990) · R. Martin, *TUC: the growth of a pressure group* (1980) · J. Hinton, *Shop floor citizens: engineering democracy in 1940s Britain* (1994) · B. Supple, *The history of the British coal industry*, 4 (1987) · J. Baylis, *The diplomacy of pragmatism: Britain and the formation of NATO* (1993) · S. Croft, 'British policy towards western Europe, 1945–51', *Shaping postwar Europe: European unity and disunity, 1945–57*, ed. P. M. R. Stirk and D. Willis (1991) · A. Deighton, ed., *Britain and the first cold war* (1990) · *The diaries of Sir Alexander Cadogan*, ed. D. Dilks (1971) · R. Edmonds, *Setting the mould: the United States and Britain, 1945–50* (1986) · D. W. Ellwood, *Rebuilding Europe: western Europe, America and postwar reconstruction* (1992) · K. Harris, *Attlee* (1982) · M. J. Hogan, *The Marshall plan* (1989) · D. Keohane, *Labour party defence policy* (1993) · C. Lord, *Absent at the creation: Britain and the formation of the European community, 1950–52* (1996) · R. B. Manderson-Jones, *The special relationship: Anglo-American relations and western European unity, 1947–56* (1972) · A. Milward, *The reconstruction of western Europe, 1945–51* (1984) · K. Morgan, *Labour in power, 1945–51* (1985) · R. Ovendale, ed., *The foreign policy of the British labour governments, 1945–51* (1984) · R. D. Pearce, *The turning-point in Africa: British colonial policy, 1938–48* (1982) · H. Pelling, *The labour government, 1945–51* (1984) · V. Rothwell, *Britain and the cold war, 1941–47* (1982) · J. Saville, *The politics of continuity: British foreign policy and the labour government, 1945–46* (1993) · J. W. Young, *Britain, France and the unity of Europe, 1945–51* (1984) · J. Zametica, ed., *British officials and British foreign policy, 1945–50* (1990) · b. cert. · d. cert. · *CGPLA Eng. & Wales* (1951)

Archives CAC Cam., corresp. and papers · PRO, private office papers · U. Warwick Mod. RC, corresp. and papers | BL, letters to Albert Mansbridge, Add. MS 65253 · Bodl. Oxf., corresp. with Clement Attlee · Bodl. Oxf., corresp. with Lionel Curtis · Bodl. Oxf., corresp. with third earl of Selborne · Bodl. RH, corresp. with Arthur Creech Jones · Borth. Inst., corresp. with Lord Halifax · CAC Cam., corresp. with Duff Cooper · CAC Cam., corresp. with Lord Halifax [copies] · CAC Cam., corresp. with Lord Halifax [copies] · HLRO, corresp. with Lord Beaverbrook · Joseph Rowntree Foundation Library, York, corresp. with B. Seebohm Rowntree · NL Wales, corresp. with Thomas Jones · PRO, corresp. with Hugh Dalton, CAB 127/209 · U. Warwick Mod. RC, corresp. with A. P. Young · U. Warwick Mod. RC, Transport and General Workers' Union papers | SOUND BBC WAC

Likenesses E. Whitney-Smith, bronze bust, 1929, Transport and General Workers Union headquarters, Liverpool · D. Low, chalk caricature, 1933, NPG · F. H. Man, photograph, 1939–40, NPG [*see illus.*] · C. Beaton, photograph, 1940, NPG · W. Stoneman, two photographs, 1940–41, NPG · H. Coster, photographs, 1940–49, NPG · Y. Karsh, bromide print, 1943, NPG · T. C. Dugdale, oils, 1945, NPG · G. Davien, oil caricature, 1946, NPG · J. Epstein, bronze bust, Tate collection · L. Illingworth, pen, ink, and wash drawing, NPG · photographs, Hult. Arch.

Wealth at death £13,988 10*s.* 5*d.*: probate, 12 June 1951, *CGPLA Eng. & Wales*

Bevington [*married name* Guggenberger], **Louisa Sarah** (1845–1895), poet and anarchist, was born on 14 May 1845 in St John's Hill, Battersea, Surrey, to Louisa and Alexander Bevington. The eldest of eight children (seven of whom were girls), she was brought up a Quaker. An early enthusiasm for science was fostered by her father. Later, interested by evolutionism, she became a friend of Herbert Spencer. Both her philosophical essays and her poems, which question religion and its moral authority, betray the influence of his ideas.

Bevington's first volume of poetry, *Key Notes*, was published in 1876 under the pseudonym Arbor Leigh (recalling Elizabeth Barrett Browning's eponymous heroine, Aurora Leigh) and was reprinted under her own name in 1879. It has the unusual distinction of having captured the interest of the apparently poetry-weary Charles Darwin, who is said to have read it in 1879 'after not having opened a volume of verse for fifteen years' (Miles, 261).

In 1881 Spencer solicited an article from Bevington defending scientific philosophy against critics who harped on its 'moral shortcomings'. Her reply, 'The moral colour of rationalism', appeared in the *Fortnightly Review*. A second volume of poetry, *Poems, Lyrics and Sonnets*, was published in 1882, and in 1883 she went to Germany, where she met and married the Munich artist Ignatz Felix Guggenberger. By the early 1890s she had returned to London alone. Little is known about the circumstances surrounding the breakdown of her marriage. Obituaries tentatively report that the couple soon found themselves 'out of tune with one another' (*Liberty*, 188).

On her return to London, Bevington became an active member of the anarchist movement. By this time London had become the 'headquarters of continental communist activity' (Oliver, vii), and she belonged to the circle which included the exiled Russian Prince Peter Kropotkin and the communard Louise Michel, whose work *Commune de Paris* she translated. As well as contributing articles to anarchist journals (among them *Liberty*, *Commonweal*, and *Freedom*) she lectured regularly at the Autonomie Club and favoured the 'short hair' and 'sensible short skirts and boots' (ibid., 153) worn by its female members. The detail contained in a letter written by Bevington about the Greenwich observatory explosion of 1894, in which an anarchist, Martial Bourdin, was killed (the incident on which Joseph Conrad based his 1907 novel, *The Secret Agent*), reveals her close involvement with the movement.

Louisa Sarah Bevington died, aged fifty, at her home, 25 Lechmere Road, Willesden Green, London, on 28 November 1895, having suffered for some years from heart disease. *Liberty* recorded that among the mourners at her funeral were Kropotkin and his wife. She was buried on 3 December in St Pancras cemetery, Finchley, without 'any religious ceremony whatever' (*The Torch of Anarchy*, 104). Many of her poems, written in short rhyming stanzas, demonstrate the insignificance of human concerns in the face of the vast scheme of evolution. Others engage with current social issues, most notably 'One More Bruised Heart', which deals movingly with the subject of child abuse. KATHARINE MCGOWRAN

Sources A. H. Miles, 'Louisa S. Guggenberger', *The poets and poetry of the century*, ed. A. H. Miles, 8 (1892), 261–4 · *Liberty* (Dec 1895) · G. Bellesso, Louisa Sarah Bevington's life and works, diss., Univerkity of Cá Foscari, Venice, 1996 · A. L. [A. Leighton], 'L. S. Bevington', *Victorian women poets: an anthology*, ed. A. Leighton and M. Reynolds (1995), 477–81 · *The Torch of Anarchy* (18 Dec 1895), 104 · *Weekly Times and Echo* (8 Dec 1895) · H. Oliver, *The international anarchist movement in late Victorian London* (1983) · J. Quail, *The slow burning fuse* (1978) · J. Conrad, *The secret agent* (1907) · b. cert. · d. cert.

Likenesses sketch, repro. in *Weekly Times and Echo*

Bevis, John (1695–1771), physician and astronomer, was born on 31 October 1695, the son of George Bevis of West Harnham, near Salisbury, Wiltshire. His father was a prominent figure during the revolution, having in 1688 spent £2000 to raise and maintain a company of infantry in support of the future king, William III. Bevis entered Christ Church, Oxford, in 1712 to study medicine, and while there he developed a general interest in the sciences. Optics was his particular passion, Newton's *Optics* his inspiration, and he became skilled at polishing lenses. He graduated BA in 1715 and MA in 1718, then spent several years in France and Italy, perhaps on further medical studies. He settled in 1728 in London, where he soon built up a flourishing medical practice, without neglecting astronomy.

By 1738 Bevis had acquired a collection of astronomical apparatus and built himself an observatory at Stoke Newington, to the north of London, where, to judge from his voluminous records, he was a tireless observer and computer. His records provided important data for establishing the configuration and scale of the solar system and accounted for certain irregularities in the lunar and planetary orbits. His friendship for Edmond Halley, with whom in 1736 he had observed the transit of Mercury at Greenwich, led him to prepare and amplify for publication in 1749 Halley's *Tabulae astronomicae*, printed twenty years earlier; a version with English text was issued in 1752. Bevis later claimed priority in discovering the Crab Nebula in 1731. On 28 May 1737, low in the west 'in the evening twilight at Greenwich' and using a non-achromatic refracting telescope of 24-foot focal length, he observed Venus occult Mercury, a unique observation not repeatable until 3 December 2133 (Ashbrook, 210). In 1739 he confirmed that James Bradley's theory of aberration extended to stars in right ascension, but he was unaware that the Italian astronomer Eustacio Manfredi had made this observation nine years earlier.

By 1745 Bevis judged that he had sufficient material to compile his *Uranographia Britannica*, a grandly conceived atlas of fifty-two plates representing the constellations and planets, each plate with detailed exposition, as observed by earlier astronomers and with numerous stars discovered by himself, accompanied by a catalogue of star positions. The undertaking was promoted and published by John Neale, a Fleet Street watchmaker and inventor, who collected subscriptions and had the plates engraved. At this time Bevis received through Pierre Maupertuis a diploma dated 11 June 1750 constituting him a member of the Berlin Academy of Sciences. But Neale was declared bankrupt in 1750. The plates were sequestered by the court of chancery and never released, tainting Bevis with the suspicion of malpractice.

Bevis regularly observed at the houses of his London associates, including the instrument makers James Short of Surrey Street, Jonathan and Jeremiah Sisson of the Strand, and George Graham of Fleet Street, and also his friends James Stephens, who kept a fine large Short telescope at Marlborough House, and Joshua Kirby at Kew. On 23 December 1743 he sighted the great comet of 1744, and in May 1759 Halley's comet; with Short and Kirby he observed the transit of Venus of 6 June 1761 from Savile House, and that of 3 June 1769 from Kew.

By 1753 Bevis was living at Red Lion Street, near Clerkenwell Green, on the north flank of the City. By 1758 he had moved to Clerkenwell Close, where he was resident at the time of his election to the Royal Society on 21 November 1765. He served as its foreign secretary from December 1766 to February 1771, and he was nominated foreign correspondent of the Academy of Sciences in Paris on 12 July 1768. Around 1759 he undertook lengthy chemical investigations of the two kinds of mineral water available at the nearby Bagnigge Wells; his booklet on these findings was issued in 1760 and republished several times up to 1819. With some of his acquaintances he took part in electrical experiments, and suggested that the charge of a Leyden jar could be strengthened by coating it with tinfoil. He was also the first to translate from the French of Matthew Maty the term 'achromatic' for the double lens of crown and flint glass which for the first time gave an image free from chromatism—the coloured fringes normally present in single lenses. George III consulted Bevis on the building of Kew observatory, and he was drawn onto several committees dealing with scientific matters. In 1764 the board of longitude employed him to calculate the results of Nevil Maskelyne's trial of John Harrison's watch H4, and in 1765 he chaired the parliamentary committee adjudicating the financial value of Tobias Meyer's lunar tables.

Bevis was a prolific correspondent and author, but much of his writing was anonymous. Besides the works he edited or translated, he contributed twenty-seven papers in *Philosophical Transactions* and others in the short-lived *Mathematical Magazine*, and submitted numerous letters, usually signed J. B. or B. J., to the *Gentleman's Magazine*.

In old age Bevis, who never married, took rooms in Brick Court, Middle Temple, where, though his view of the sky was severely limited, he was always willing to make his instruments available. While observing the sun's meridian altitude one day, he turned too hastily from telescope to clock and suffered a fall, from the effects of which he died on 6 November 1771. He was buried in Temple Church on 12 November. Bevis's executor James Horsfall FRS, librarian at Middle Temple, tried unsuccessfully to retrieve the plates of the *Uranographia*. Bevis's library and instruments, together with similar items from other owners, were sold at auction in 1785. Bevis was denied lasting fame by the destruction of his atlas.

A. M. CLERKE, *rev.* ANITA MCCONNELL

Sources R. Wallis, 'John Bevis, MD, FRS (1695–1771), astronomer royal', *Notes and Records of the Royal Society*, 36 (1981–2), 211–25 · J. J. Bernoulli, 'Précis de la vie de M. John Bevis', *Recueil des astronomes*, 2 (1772), 331–6 · R. Wallis, *Bibliography of John Bevis* (1981) · W. Ashworth, 'John Bevis and his *Uranographia* (c. 1750)', *Proceedings of the American Philosophical Society*, 125 (1981), 52–73 · J. Bevis, *An experimental enquiry concerning the mineral waters lately discovered at Bagnigge Wells, near London; with directions for drinking them* (1760) · *Register of burials at the Temple Church, 1628–1853* (1905) [with introduction by H. G. Woods] · J. Ashbrook, *The astronomical scrapbook: skywatchers, pioneers, and seekers in astronomy*, ed. L. J. Robinson (1984), 210–12 · K. J. Kilburn, M. Oates, and A. W. Cross, 'The ghost book of Manchester', *Sky and Telescope*, 96/5 (1998), 83–6

Bewick family (*per. c.*1775–*c.*1875), engravers, came from Northumberland. Thomas *Bewick (1753–1828) and his brother John *Bewick (*bap.* 1760, *d.* 1795), wood engravers, were the first and fifth of nine children born to John Bewick (*bap.* 1715, *d.* 1785), farmer and collier, and his second wife, Jane Wilson (1727–1785), at Cherryburn, Eltringham, Northumberland. John Bewick died unmarried, at Ovingham, Northumberland, after a promising career in the London engraving trade had been cut short by consumption. Thomas Bewick, whose principal business in Newcastle upon Tyne was as a general engraver on metal and copperplate printer, at the same time became celebrated as the father of modern wood engraving, his reputation being widely established by the publication of his two natural histories: *A General History of Quadrupeds* (1790) and *A History of British Birds* (2 vols., 1797 and 1804) [*see also* Bewick, Thomas, apprentices]. Thomas Bewick and his wife, Isabella Elliot (1752–1826), had four children, all of whom died unmarried. The eldest, **Jane Bewick** (1787–1881) was born on 29 April 1787 at Newcastle upon Tyne. She became very active in supporting her father in his business activities, dealing particularly with publishers and booksellers during the last ten years of his life. In 1825 John F. M. Dovaston described her as:

> mistress of her father's house, which she conducts … without bustle or disturbance. She also corrects the press for his works, and looks after the getting of them up; writes his letters of business; keeping his house and shops in order. Her great delight is in his fame. (Dovaston)

She supervised the production and publication of the two posthumous editions of *British Birds* in 1832 and 1847, and in an uneasy collaboration with her cousin, the Newcastle printer Robert Ward, edited and published her father's autobiographical *Memoir* in 1862. At about this time she made valuable notes on her father's acquaintances and on the narrative content of many of his vignette tailpieces. Her forthright and lively character is fully displayed in her letters home when travelling to London, Edinburgh, and Buxton. Together with her sister, **Isabella Bewick** (1790–1883), who was also born at Newcastle upon Tyne, on 14 January 1790, she was a jealous guardian of their father's posthumous reputation, carefully preserving his correspondence, original drawings, proofs, and the complete series of original woodblocks for his three principal works. They planned the gift of large collections of drawings and prints to the British Museum and to the Natural

History Society of Northumberland, Durham, and Newcastle upon Tyne (now Natural History Society of Northumbria). Deeply suspicious of would-be biographers of their father and metropolitan collectors such as T. F. Dibdin and the Revd Thomas Hugo, they were nevertheless susceptible to the flattery of a few others, Ruskin among them, and their surviving correspondence and the records of their release of small groups of prints and drawings provide a useful view of the nineteenth-century enthusiasm for their father's work. Jane died on 7 April 1881, to be followed by her sister Isabella on 8 June 1883—both at their home, 19 West Street, Gateshead, co. Durham. They were buried at St Mary's, Ovingham, Northumberland, on 12 April 1881 and 11 June 1883 respectively.

Robert Elliot Bewick (1788–1849), engraver, Thomas Bewick's only son, was born at Newcastle upon Tyne on 26 August 1788. Always a diffident character and prone to ill health, he was brought up in the business, apprenticed between 1804 and 1810, and in 1812 made partner in T. Bewick & Son, engravers and copperplate printers, but he failed to realize his father's ambitions for him. He was a meticulous draughtsman, a skilful practical engraver more at home on copper than on wood, but he had none of his father's inventive genius, nor any head for promoting a vigorous trade for himself in later years. His work on copper is to be seen in bill-heads, book-plates, and book illustration; as a wood engraver he contributed to his father's *Fables of Aesop* (1818) and produced a small group of blocks for the unpublished *History of Fishes* which first appeared in his father's *Memoir*. He made a quantity of highly finished drawings of fish which are now in the British Museum and several of which were shown in the first exhibition of the Northumberland Institution for the Fine Arts in 1822. Despite his father's despairing letter to Jane—'what can my Robert mean by poring constantly & stupifying himself with Perspective—he ought never to have the pencil out of his hand' (28 June 1814, Natural History Society of Northumbria)—he pursued his interest, and many of his perspective drawings of buildings and domestic interiors survive. His few wood engravings occasionally show the initials R. E. B., his copper engravings the full signature R. E. Bewick, and his drawings if not signed can sometimes be identified by his own captions. In her old age Jane Bewick frequently put a signature to the unsigned drawings in her care, not always accurately.

A touching account of Robert Elliot Bewick and his 'two tall old fashioned maiden sisters' is given in William Bell Scott's *Autobiographical Notes*:

> a heavy, slouching, able bodied countryman, as I thought, about fifty-five or so, with an absent, bewildered expression of face, the snow lying white on his penthouse eyebrows … to this man I felt drawn in a singular degree, mainly by the almost reverent simplicity and diffidence of his manner, which evidently prevented him adequately expressing himself. (Scott, 2.194–6)

The account continues with a description of Robert's skilful playing of the delicate, sweet-sounding Northumberland smallpipes. Encouraged by his father, who kept a record of the costs of his lessons, music, and instruments, he was playing at an early age, and was taught by John Peacock, one of the last of the old Newcastle pipers. It is his legacy of five manuscript collections of the melodies of the time which now keeps Robert Bewick's memory alive and which has played an important part in the renewal of interest in the traditional music of north-east England. He died on 27 July 1849 at the family home, 19 West Street, Gateshead, co. Durham, as did his sisters. The burial place of the family is in the graveyard of St Mary's, Ovingham, Northumberland.

Watercolours, drawings, and prints by Thomas, John, and Robert Elliot Bewick were given to the department of prints and drawings at the British Museum in 1882 (1882-3-11-1243-5558), and in 1884 to the Natural History Society of Northumberland, Durham, and Newcastle upon Tyne (Hancock Museum, University of Newcastle upon Tyne).　　　　　　　　　　　　IAIN BAIN

Sources J. F. M. Dovaston, 'A few short, hasty, and discursive notes, each taken on the spot, in a tour to the Hebrides, highlands, & Scotland, in July and August 1825', MS, priv. coll. · W. B. Scott, *Autobiographical notes on the life of William Bell Scott*, ed. W. Minto, 2 vols. (1892), 2.194–6 · letter of Thomas Bewick to Jane Bewick, 28 June 1814, Natural History Society of Northumbria, Newcastle upon Tyne · Jane Bewick's corresp. with collectors Edward Jupp and Edward Ford, priv. coll. · Jane Bewick's letters, many drafted for her father, to publishers and booksellers, Laing Gallery, Newcastle upon Tyne · A. Wheeler, 'Thomas Bewick's projected "History of British fishes" with notes on another book on fishes attributed to Bewick', *Festschrift für Claus Nissen* (1973), 651–86 · R. E. Bewick, 'Bewick's pipe tunes', MS, c.1810–1840, Gateshead Public Library, 69/17 · *A memoir of Thomas Bewick written by himself*, ed. J. Bewick (1862) [three grangerized copies, with annotation; proof sheets of this edn with ed.'s comments (priv. coll.)] · *A memoir of Thomas Bewick written by himself*, ed. I. Bain, rev. edn (1979) [full transcript of orig. MS with chronology and bibliography] · R. Robinson, *Thomas Bewick: his life and times* (1887), 204–6 · *CGPLA Eng. & Wales* (1881) [Jane Bewick] · *CGPLA Eng. & Wales* (1883) [Isabella Bewick] · family bible, Natural History Society of Northumbria, Newcastle upon Tyne · memorials, St Mary's churchyard, Ovingham, Northumberland

Archives BL, family and business corresp., memoir, Add. MSS 34813, 50826, 41481, 31027; Hodgson papers 50242 [T. Bewick] · Central Library, Newcastle upon Tyne, original woodblocks · Cherryburn, Northumberland, corresp. · Harvard U., Houghton L., letters, fms.Typ.434 · Hornby Art Library, Liverpool · Hunt. L., letters, HM 17300–17354; 17524–17525; 19744–19752 · Laing Art Gallery, Newcastle upon Tyne · London Library, notes · Natural History Society of Northumbria, Newcastle upon Tyne · Newberry Library, Chicago, original woodblocks [R. H. Middleton, gift] · Newcastle Central Library, Pease bequest, corresp. · Tyne and Wear Archives Service, Newcastle upon Tyne, corresp. and papers, 1269 · Tyne and Wear Archives Service, Newcastle upon Tyne, further corresp. · V&A, L3250–3262 · V&A, notes [R. N. Bewick] | BL, corresp. with J. Dovaston, Egerton MSS 3147–3148 · BL, corresp. with John Dovaston, Egerton MSS 3147–3148 [R. E. Bewick] · BL, corresp. with Sara Hodgson, Add. MS 50241 · BL, corresp. with Sir John Trevelyan and W. C. Trevelyan, Add. MS 31207

Likenesses J. Bell, oils, c.1805 (Robert Elliot Bewick), Natural History Society of Northumbria · J. Gilbert, portrait, 1852 (Jane Bewick) · photograph, c.1870 (Jane Bewick), Natural History Society of Northumbria, Newcastle upon Tyne · photograph, c.1880 (Jane Bewick), repro. in Bewick, ed., *Memoir*; priv. coll. · photograph, c.1880 (Isabella Bewick), repro. in Bewick, ed., *Memoir*; priv. coll. · photograph (Jane Bewick; after J. Gilbert), priv. coll.

Wealth at death £4000—Jane Bewick: will with codicil · £12,960 1s. 0d.—Isabella Bewick: will, 1883

Bewick, Isabella (1790–1883). *See under* Bewick family (*per.* c.1775–c.1875).

Bewick, Jane (1787–1881). *See under* Bewick family (*per.* c.1775–c.1875).

Bewick, John (*bap.* 1760, *d.* 1795), wood-engraver, baptized on 30 March 1760, was the fifth of nine children born to John Bewick (*bap.* 1715, *d.* 1785), farmer and collier, and his wife, Jane Wilson (1727–1785) [*see* Bewick family], at Cherryburn, Eltringham, Northumberland. He was a lively, active boy, with an amiable, outgoing personality, given to pranks and practical jokes. There is no record of his schooling but it is likely to have followed that of his elder brother Thomas *Bewick (1753–1828), after which he joined his father on the farm.

In October 1777 Thomas, then an engraver in partnership with Ralph Beilby in Newcastle, persuaded John to become his apprentice. John was ingenious and good with his hands, and became an accomplished artist without any seeming effort, flourishing in the workshop, which at that time was the sole source for metal- and wood-engraving in Newcastle upon Tyne [*see also* Bewick, Thomas, apprentices]. In his *Memoir* Thomas wrote:

> with my brother I was extremely happy—we Lodged together, he arose early in the Morning, lighted our fire—blacked our shoes, dusted the Room, made everything clean for breakfast, as well as any servant Girl could have done & he sewed & mended his own clothes &c and to crown all he was constantly cheerfull, lively & very active, & my friends were his friends—Mr Beilby was also as pleased with him as I could possibly be, for besides his affable temper, he took every kind of work in hand so pleasantly & so very soon learned to execute it well that it could not miss giving satisfaction. (*Memoir*, 79)

After five years John had become restless under the discipline of his more austere brother and was given his freedom. He nevertheless continued his contact with the workshop for a further four years, and it was probably at this period that the half-length pastel portrait of him, now in the Natural History Society of Northumbria, was drawn by George Gray. John's work as a wood-engraver up to that time is not easy to identify, although he did contribute some cuts to the 1784 edition of the *Select Fables* printed by Thomas Saint, for which his brother was primarily responsible. But he had confidence enough in his skills to set off for London by sea from North Shields on 6 August 1786 to seek work from Thomas Hodgson, of Clerkenwell, a wood- and metal-engraver and former employer of his brother.

John was enchanted with the sights of the city; 'I like London exceedingly well', he wrote, 'I hardly dare go out into the streets for their is so much entertainment at the shop windows &c that I can never get Home in time to my Work' (J. Bewick to T. Bewick, 16 Aug 1786). Through Hodgson he attracted the attention of Hodgson's customer Elizabeth Newbery, and her manager Abraham Badcock, vigorous publishers of books for children. A circle of Newcastle men, William Bulmer, fine printer, and Robert Pollard, engraver and printseller, in particular, further encouraged his social connections with London's

John Bewick (*bap.* 1760, *d.* 1795), by George Gray, *c.*1780

artists. Robert Robinson recorded, on unspecified authority, that John had about him 'a refinement in manner and speech' not possessed by his brother—traits surely acquired from mixing in such company.

After a year of working exclusively for Hodgson, which time saw his engraving of cuts for the *Emblems of Mortality* (1788), and—for Mrs Newbery—*The History of a Little Boy* (1786), and an edition of the *Fables of the Late Mr Gay* (1788), John's patience with his master wore thin. He spoke of 'a good deal of bother' with everything having to be done at Hodgson's price and that 'the more of his own way he had the worse he grew' (J. Bewick to T. Bewick, 1 Nov 1787). His brother felt Hodgson should have been charged double the 6s. paid for the *Emblems* blocks—'you have been … grinding out your Eyes to little purpose indeed' (T. Bewick to J. Bewick, 9 Jan 1788). By October 1787 John was renting rooms nearby at 7 Clerkenwell Green in the house of George Percival, a house- and sign-painter. From this address began the connection with the eccentric Dr John Trusler, who lived nearby and printed his books in his own house. Trusler, author of *Hogarth Moralized*, commissioned illustrations for nine of the sixty-eight titles so far identified as containing John Bewick's work: one of them, *The Habitable World Described*, issued in parts from 1788 to 1791, besides some tailpiece vignettes on wood, required drawings for copper engravers to follow; of the others, *Proverbs Exemplified* (1790) and *The Progress of Man and Society* (1791), demanded 50 and 108 wood-engravings respectively. The *Proverbs* were written by Trusler after Bewick had exercised his imagination on such texts as 'To Forget a Wrong is the Best Revenge' and 'What's Got over the Devil's back

is Spent under his Belly'—a task, he remarked to his brother, that would have puzzled the Devil himself to devise a subject of any kind (J. Bewick to T. Bewick, 4 Jan 1789). In his preface Trusler, unusually, gave Bewick well merited credit for the excellence of his invention and design.

Additional work in some fourteen more books for Mrs Newbery and sixteen similar titles for John Stockdale between 1788 and 1794 firmly established John Bewick in the history of book illustration for children. Of the Newbery titles *The Blossoms of Morality* (1796) and *The Looking Glass for the Mind* (1792), and of Stockdale's *The New Robinson Crusoe* (1788), remain the best remembered. In his last years John contributed to Le Grand's *Fabliaux* by Gregory Way, for which the engraving had to be finished by Thomas Bewick and his former apprentices Luke Clennell and Charlton Nesbit, and two examples of fine printing, *Poems of Goldsmith and Parnell* (1795) and Somervile's *The Chase* (1796), his designs being engraved posthumously by his brother.

Besides his work for books John cut a considerable number of blocks for jobbing work—trade cards, newspaper masthead devices, images for children's games, bookplates, and billheads, many of which have recently been identified and recorded (Tattersfield).

Although as an engraver John Bewick cannot match his brother, in certain of his qualities he is his superior, particularly in the invention needed for the illustration of a narrative text. In the grace and charm of his drawing of children he had no equal. Produced swiftly for low prices, many of his engravings show signs of haste and, though often lacking his brother's subtlety, the simplicity of his cutting was helpful to the common run of printer; his handling of trees and foliage is often more obviously formulaic and mannered. In each of the long series of illustrations the occasional signature 'JBewick' or 'JBk' is to be found.

More than forty of John's letters to his brother have survived, and before the onset of the tuberculosis that was eventually to destroy him, they display a delightful vivacity and lively turn of phrase, and latterly, a calm fortitude. They are filled with news of friends in London, the work of rivals, art exhibitions visited, discussion of his brother's business affairs as he acted as link and agent with the booksellers, and reports of animals seen in menageries which might provide material for the *General History of Quadrupeds*.

John Bewick kept working to the end, although his consumption became ever more a burden. A break of four months at home in Northumberland in the summer of 1789 brought a temporary improvement, and a move from Clerkenwell to the rural heights of Hornsey's Mount Pleasant, and then to Crouch End, gave him fresher air, and additional income from the drawing lessons he gave at Nathaniel Norton's nearby Hornsey Academy. But by autumn 1795 he returned finally to Northumberland, first to the care of his brother William at Cherryburn, and at the last with his sister in Ovingham, whence he wrote to his brother, 'I can only say that it is with pain that I can now whisper out my wants, I think a few Days more will relieve me from all my Pains and Troubles here' (11 Nov 1795). John Bewick died on 5 December 1795, unmarried—although there were two unrequited attachments—and greatly missed by friends and family. His grave is in the churchyard of St Mary's, Ovingham. William Bulmer wrote to Thomas Bewick, 'The death of your Brother has hurt me much I assure you—He was a young man whose private virtues & professional talents I equally admired' (W. Bulmer to T. Bewick, 10 Dec 1795). Although as an engraver overshadowed by his brother, John Bewick's career was cruelly cut short: a longer life and the wider opportunity promised by the connection with Bulmer might well have widened a reputation already supreme in the children's literature of his time.   IAIN BAIN

Sources N. Tattersfield, *John Bewick: engraver on wood, 1760–95* (2001) · letters of John Bewick and Thomas Bewick, priv. coll. · papers, priv. coll. · *A memoir of Thomas Bewick, written by himself*, ed. I. Bain (1975) · R. Robinson, *Thomas Bewick: his life and times* (1887) · E. Mackenzie, *An historical, topographical, and descriptive view of the county of Northumberland*, 2nd edn, 2 vols. (1825) · R. Welford, *Men of mark 'twixt Tyne and Tweed*, 3 vols. (1895)
Archives priv. coll., letters | Cherryburn, Northumberland · Laing Art Gallery, Newcastle upon Tyne · Natural History Society of Northumbria, Newcastle upon Tyne · Newcastle Central Library, Pease collection · Tyne and Wear Archives Service, Beilby-Bewick Workshop account books, 1269
Likenesses G. Gray, pastel drawing, *c*.1780, Natural History Society of Northumbria [*see illus.*]
Wealth at death debtors and creditors no more than a few pounds: letters between Thomas Bewick and Nathaniel Norton of Hornsey, 5 and 19 Feb 1796, priv. coll.

Bewick, Robert Elliot (1788–1849). *See under* Bewick family (*per. c.*1775–*c.*1875).

Bewick, Thomas (1753–1828), wood-engraver, was born at Cherryburn, Eltringham, Northumberland, on 10 or 12 August 1753, the eldest of the four sons and five daughters of John Bewick (*bap.* 1715, *d.* 1785), a tenant farmer and collier, and his second wife, Jane Wilson (1727–1785), of Ainstable, Cumberland. His paternal grandfather, also Thomas Bewick (1685–1742), had held the same tenancy.

Early life, apprenticeship, and first years of freedom The principal source for Bewick's early life is his autobiographical *Memoir*, written between 1822 and 1828, prompted by his family and spurred on by the threatened attempts of several contemporaries whom he considered ill-suited to the task. It was published by his daughter Jane in 1862, and he would have been surprised, though gratified, to find it established as a minor classic, not only on account of his importance as an artist and engraver and as 'the father of modern wood engraving', but also for his unique record of a north-country childhood and life as a craftsman in late Georgian England.

In the account of his early youth on the banks of the Tyne Bewick's growing passion for natural history is vividly recorded in his recollection of rural Northumberland and its inhabitants through the changing seasons. His first schoolmaster was so hopeless and the delights of the countryside so strong that truancy was inevitable; in time his father begged the Revd Christopher Gregson, vicar of

Thomas Bewick (1753–1828), by James Ramsay, 1823

Ovingham, to take him on, and here his lively nature was somewhat tamed. An early impulse to draw constantly filled the margins of his schoolbooks; the hearthstone was a makeshift sketchpad for his chalks. He soon, in the opinion of his 'rustic neighbours, became an eminent painter, and the walls of their houses were ornamented with an abundance' of his 'rude productions'—chiefly hunting scenes—'at a very cheap rate' (*Memoir*, 5).

On 1 October 1767, through the influence of his godmother Mrs Simons, Bewick was apprenticed to Ralph Beilby (1743–1817) of Newcastle upon Tyne, the son of a Durham silversmith, and at that time the sole general engraver in the town. Leaving the countryside to lodge with Beilby was a severe wrench:

> to part from the country & to leave all its beauties behind me, with which all my life I had been charmed in an extreme degree, & in a way I cannot describe—I can only say my heart was like to break. (*Memoir*, 36)

Beilby's trade was all-embracing. Although he was almost wholly concerned with the engraving of metal, from copper printing plates and domestic silver to clock faces, bottle moulds, coffin plates, and dog collars, he was clearly a good master, and the seven-year apprenticeship served young Bewick well. In his *Memoir* he wrote:

> I think he was the best master in the World, for learning Boys, for he obliged them to put their hands to every variety of Work—every job, coarse or fine, either in cutting or engraving I did as well as I could, cheerfully, but the wearisome business of polishing copper plates and hardening and polishing steel seals, was always irksome to me—I had wrought at this a long time, & at the coarsest kind of engraving ... 'till my hands became as hard & enlarged as those of a blacksmith. (ibid., 40–41)

In 1768 the mathematician Charles Hutton commissioned

Beilby to cut the geometrical figures on wood for his *Treatise on Mensuration*, and later claimed to have introduced the necessary tools and materials to him from London. Despite this claim, the use of wood as an engraving material first appears in Beilby's records in 1766. As he apparently had little liking for the medium, Hutton's commission was left to Bewick, who took to the simple reproductive work with some facility. Although it was only a minor part of the workshop activity, further commissions for engraving on wood now began to come in from north-country printers and tradesmen—a figure of St George and the dragon for a Penrith innkeeper attracted attention, and a series of forty-eight small cuts for *A New Lottery Book of Birds and Beasts for Children to Learn their Letters by*, printed in 1771 by Thomas Saint for William Charnley of Newcastle, gave the first hint of Bewick's skill in the drawing of animals.

In the last few months of his time Bewick began engraving the cuts for *Fables by the Late Mr Gay* (1779), in which the sixty-six headpieces and thirteen tailpiece vignettes begin to foretell the successes of Bewick's prime. The engraving for the fable of the hound and the huntsman so impressed his master that it was sent off, displayed with the text of the fable in a bordered quarto sheet, to the Society for the Encouragement of Arts, Manufactures, and Commerce in London, and was awarded a premium of 7 guineas on 4 January 1776.

From October 1774 Bewick spent most of his time at home, continuing to engrave for Beilby's workshop and for various printers in Newcastle, but towards the end of this period, delighting in his freedom, he took off for a walking tour into Cumberland to visit relatives, and then north into Scotland, through the Trossachs—a journey of more than 300 miles—before sailing home from Leith to Shields. His experiences form a vivid section of his *Memoir*.

Almost immediately Bewick decided to sail for London, where he found Newcastle friends and had as many commissions as he could handle from the engravers Isaac Taylor and Thomas Hodgson. Otherwise there was little that he liked about London. He found the people uncongenial and his fellow tradesmen, while anxious to see what he was doing, unwilling to reciprocate. In November 1776, in a letter to his godmother's daughter, Elizabeth Hymers, he wrote:

> I must first begin by telling you that I like it (or like to live in it) very badly … and tho' I might always continue to meet with the greatest encouragement imajinable—yet wou'd I rather live in both poverty and insecurity in NCastle.

He felt that she had been dazzled by the city's outward show, whereas he had found it impossible to overlook the many scenes of misery and villainy. She was not surprised at his reaction: 'I thought London wou'd not sute your grave turn.'

Little has been identified of Bewick's work in London before he returned north after no more than nine months, although a hornbook with well-drawn figures of birds and animals demonstrates well why his skill was so valued by his employers, who tried in vain to get him to stay.

The years of Bewick's prime, 1777–1800 Bewick had been unwilling to set up as a rival to Beilby. However, as soon as he returned from London mutual friends persuaded them into a partnership, which lasted for twenty fruitful years and saw the publication of much of the work on which Bewick's wider reputation rests. While the general trade of the workshop continued in metal engraving, with space set aside for the rolling presses used for printing copperplates, the amount of wood-engraving increased, though it seldom amounted to more than 10 percent of any week's activity.

The first thirteen years of the partnership saw the publication of more than eighty small books for children, for which Bewick engraved the illustrations commissioned by some eighteen printers and booksellers—half from Newcastle upon Tyne and the remainder from London, Durham, Berwick upon Tweed, Sunderland, and Glasgow. Such titles as *The Tale of Tommy Trip*, *Cinderella*, *Goody Goosecap*, and *Jacky Dandy*, as well as many books of fables and riddles and manuals for spelling and reading, made up the bulk of the activity. Apart from the completion of *The Fables of the Late Mr Gay* (1779), the most notable series of cuts during this time was for the *Select Fables*, also printed and published by Saint of Newcastle in 1784; the engraving here began to show real accomplishment in design and the handling of texture, light, and shade.

On 20 April 1786 Bewick married Isabella Elliot (1752–1826), the daughter of an Ovingham farmer and a woman of much practical good sense. They lived in a house in Circus Lane, at the Forth, a district beyond the western side of the old city wall, which had once been the home of Charles Hutton. The workshop, in St Nicholas's churchyard, was about fifteen minutes' walk from the Forth. Four children were born and brought up here: Jane *Bewick, the eldest, was to become her father's business manager; Robert Elliot *Bewick [see under Bewick family], the second child, was apprenticed to his father and became his partner in 1812. Bewick's letters to his children, and their replies, written when they took their annual holiday by the sea at Tynemouth and when their father was occasionally away from home, show them united in their affection for one another. They were well educated, and the surviving lists of the books in the house show them to have been widely read.

Of all the images associated with Bewick's name, the large engraving of *The Chillingham Bull* (5⅖ x 7⁷⁄₁₀ in.), commissioned by Marmaduke Tunstall of Wycliffe, North Riding of Yorkshire, has attracted most attention. It was printed in 1789 with the intention that it should eventually accompany an account of the wild white cattle being prepared by Tunstall. Bewick used the opportunity to show that, when needed, wood-engraving could match engraving on copper in its richness of effect. He later wrote to Francis Douce to say that he had been convinced that wood-engraving was capable of greater things than generally imagined. In the masterly treatment of foliage can be seen the influence of the copper-engraver William Woollet, examples of whose work Bewick is known to have owned. The print has been much sought after by collectors on account of early damage suffered by the block, which made perfect impressions rare.

Bewick's national reputation was fully established by his *General History of Quadrupeds*, published in 1790, and his *History of British Birds*—land birds in 1797, and water birds in 1804. The inspiration sprang from his great dissatisfaction with the crudely illustrated books of his youth. Although the compilation of the descriptive text for the *Quadrupeds* began as early as 1781, when Bewick applied to Squire Fenwick of Bywell for the history of his celebrated racehorse Match'em, much of the work relating to the text fell to Beilby:

> who being of a bookish, or reading turn, proposed, in his evenings at home, to write or compile the descriptions, but not knowing much about natural history, we got Books on that subject to enable him to form a better notion of these matters; with this I had little more to do, than in furnishing him, in many conversations & written memorandums, of what I knew of Animals, and of blotting out, in his manuscript what was not truth.   (*Memoir*, 106)

The engravings were likewise the work of evenings when Bewick's workshop day was over. Naturally his most successful subjects were those with which he was best acquainted and which he could draw from the life; some of the more exotic he was able to see in the travelling 'wild beast shows' of men such as Gilbert Pidcock and Stephen Polito, who in turn commissioned him to engrave large cuts for their posters and handbills.

When published, the *Quadrupeds* met with much praise, typified by the reaction in a letter written before 23 December 1790 by Matthew Gregson, an upholsterer and member of a Liverpool Print Society, whose members gave it 'the highest Encomiums of Praise' and for whom Gregson ordered sets of fine impressions without text. Other commercial work stemmed from the success of the book, a success which took it to seven editions totalling some 14,000 copies.

By summer 1791 the partners had begun to embark on their next spare-time enterprise. Bewick took time to visit Tunstall's collection of birds to obtain drawings of rare foreign species for what had first been projected as a general history. Ultimately the scope of the book had to be confined to British species and much of the Wycliffe work was set aside. After six years, and with the help of numerous correspondents who contributed both observations and specimens, the first volume of the *History of British Birds* was published in 1797 to even greater acclaim. Apart from the excellence of the principal figures, the numerous tailpiece vignettes that enlivened every spare space in the book came in for special notice. Of these tailpieces Bewick was later to remark:

> When I first undertook my labours in Natural History, my strongest motive was to lead the minds of youth to the study of that delightful pursuit; ... I illustrated them with all the fidelity and animation I was able to impart to mere woodcuts without colour; and as instruction is of little avail without constant cheerfulness and occasional amusement, I interspersed the more serious studies with Tale-pieces of gaiety and humour, yet even in these seldom without an endeavour to illustrate some truth, or point some moral. (*Memoir*)

Apart from lovingly observed landscape settings, the narrative content of many of Bewick's tailpieces is often ironic and displays a mordant view of the world and human folly: in a decaying churchyard a crumbling inscription, 'to the perpetual memory', is washed by the eroding sea; boys who cannot read lead a blind fiddler past a sign warning of man-traps; and a man evading a toll bridge drives his cow through deep water in the river below—losing his hat at a cost far greater than the toll. The gritty reality of the lives of the crippled old soldiers, road menders, blind beggars, and rain-soaked packmen who inhabit Bewick's landscapes is at odds with the sentimental view of those who now reproduce his work on pots and tea towels.

More than 600 blocks had been engraved for the two volumes of the *Birds* when the last of the eight editions of Bewick's lifetime had been published. The success of the book stimulated a torrent of letters from amateurs of natural history. As there was still much that was inexact in the classification and description of the species, Bewick found himself running a clearing house for information when he had little enough time to run his flourishing business. Any comparison of Bewick's work with that of his predecessors makes clear how original it appeared at the time. Not only was there truth in outline and animated posture, but the habitat was beautifully realized. On 13 November 1797 George Allen the antiquary wrote: 'I am in more raptures than I can possibly express ... your ingenious Work ... will ever remain inimitable and the Standard of the Art.' In later years the Revd Charles Kingsley wrote, in a letter dated 16 April 1867, of his father's response when a young hunting squire in the New Forest: his neighbours had laughed at him for buying a book about 'dicky birds', but he carried it about with him until their curiosity persuaded them that 'it was the most clever book they had ever seen'.

Two other celebrated books to which Bewick contributed during this period were printed and published in London by William Bulmer, a friend and contemporary who had also served his apprenticeship in Newcastle. *The Poems of Goldsmith and Parnell* (1795) and *Somervile's Chase* (1796) were produced for the then flourishing market for 'fine printing', and their wood engravings were essential to their success.

The end of the partnership and later years   At the end of 1797, after a growing dissatisfaction on Bewick's part which had first become manifest in 1790, the partnership was brought to an end. Beilby retired to concentrate on his watch-glass manufactory, and so work on the second volume of the *Birds* became Bewick's responsibility. The text was again a compilation, with assistance from the Revd Henry Cotes and other correspondents and with much recourse to earlier books. There was also greater assistance from the workshop apprentices. When Bewick first joined his partner, who already had Abraham Hunter as an apprentice, he took on his own brother John *Bewick (*bap.* 1760, *d.* 1795), and during the next twenty years they trained, among others, John Laws (later highly regarded as a silver-engraver), Robert Johnson (a talented watercolourist), and Charlton Nesbit, John Anderson, Henry White, Henry Hole, and William Harvey, all of whom became prominent in the trade [see Bewick, Thomas, apprentices]. In the engraving for the water birds the hand of Luke Clennell is very evident, particularly in many of the tailpieces.

In 1811 work began on Bewick's last book, his *Fables of Aesop and Others* (1818, 2nd edn 1823). He planned the enterprise during convalescence from illness, writing some fables of his own and reworking or taking unacknowledged contributions from others. The engravings were designed on the wood by Bewick with his drawing finished in the greatest detail; the cutting was done by apprentices under his close supervision and where necessary later refined by their master. Though containing many superb engravings, the book never claimed the affection and popularity of the *Quadrupeds* and *Birds*.

Other books of this period, illustrated for the trade and frequently noticed, were Thomson's *The Seasons* (1805), *The Hermit of Warkworth* (1805), *The Hive of Ancient and Modern Literature* (1806), and *The Poetical Works of Robert Burns* (1808). The designs for many of these were made by artists such as W. M. Craig and John Thurston, with the engraving often given to the apprentices.

The final significant wood-engraving of Bewick's life was an ambitious attempt to combine the effects of multiple blocks, printed in register to give expression to added textures such as driving rain. Intended to revive the moralistic cottage prints of his youth, his work was never fully completed, though he saw first proofs just before he died. Entitled *Waiting for Death*, and not published until 1832, the large image (11⅖ x 8½ in.) portrays an aged horse reduced to skin and bone, standing bleakly and unsheltered in a rocky field; the wooded prosperity of a country house is clearly seen in the distance.

Bewick's name has often been falsely attached to other vignette images of his time, and not only to the work of his many apprentices; this has not been helped by the faulty list of attributions made by Chatto and Jackson's *Treatise on Wood Engraving* (1839) or by the omnivorous collecting of the Revd Thomas Hugo, whose 'optimistic' two-volume catalogue has been the bible of bookseller and collector since it was published in 1866–8. Bewick's signature is rare; 'TB' in monogram is the most usual form, with the occasional spelling out of 'T. Bewick'. After prolonged acquaintance with the finest work in the *Birds*, his controlled handling of foliage becomes particularly clear to the eye, as does the confident balance of light and shade in his designs. He was what came to be described as a white-line engraver, which is to say that the block surface was seen as a solid black before work began, and that every cut was made to create white light. This was a far more expressive technique and more suited to the artist-engraver, unlike the method of later nineteenth-century reproductive engravers, who would cut away the wood from either side of a previously drawn line. Some idiosyncrasies appear in Bewick's standing figures, which often appear

awkward. In his final years, when he was preparing further tailpieces for his books, much of the cutting appears one-directional and reveals a fading nimbleness in the handling of the block. Often incorrectly credited with the invention of engraving on the end-grain of boxwood, Bewick can certainly be described as the reviver and improver of the craft; his delicate use of the technique of lowering those surfaces of the block which were to carry distances or soft textures was unsurpassed. It was of the greatest benefit to him to have had the long discipline of a trade training of great variety: the expression of his genius was thus unhindered by any technical uncertainty or inadequacy. Bewick's success brought respectability to the woodcut as a means of illustration and thus its universal use throughout the nineteenth century; no longer was it confined to the cheap broadsheet. Its capacity for combination with type was crucial, though it has to be remembered that fine engraving required good paper and printing and their attendant costs. As a writing engraver on metal Bewick produced some of the finest provincial banknotes of his time, as well as many excellent trade cards and armorial bookplates. He was much concerned with preventing forgery and was greatly affronted when asked by a government agent to engrave false assignats for circulation in France.

The *Memoir* is disappointingly short on matters relating to Bewick's engraving methods and more particularly on the training of his pupils. But the survival of a very large part of the Beilby–Bewick business records, together with several hundred fine preliminary drawings and a correspondence of more than 2000 letters, reveals much of the workshop's operation. The material relating to the running of the copperplate printing house is unique for the period.

Bewick's sober nature in early manhood changed little in later life. While respecting the opinions of others, he had a hearty contempt for ranters and bigots and the 'chaos of religious works' with which his youthful mind had been confused. His views on education foreshadowed the Education Act by fifty years, and there was much good sense in his attitude to such matters as fish conservation and land enclosure. Described as being 'an interesting-looking old man, of portly size, and of a good-humoured and social temperament' (*Memoirs of Dr Robert Blakey*, 35–6), with very wide-set eyes, he was convivial, and the company he found in Newcastle's radical debating clubs such as the Brotherly Society, which met at Whitfield's Golden Lion 'to unbend the mind … with a set of staunch advocates for the liberties of Mankind' (*Memoir*, 132), was essential to him throughout his life.

More sophisticated than the simple artist-craftsman so often portrayed, the rural genius praised by Wordsworth referred in his *Memoir* to Bacon, Locke, and Hume; he had a good library and a fine collection of prints, and the success of his books made him a man of substance. He had probably been afflicted with consumption in his earlier days, but regular exercise, a sturdy frame, and a robust constitution saw him through both this and a later illness which appears to have been a dangerously severe pleurisy.

In 1812, forced by the end of his tenancy, and not helped by the onset of this illness, Bewick reluctantly moved his family south across the Tyne to a new house on the edge of Gateshead. Despite earlier rash loans and investments, he had accumulated savings enough before he died to buy a freehold and to make over his copyrights and substantial sums in government stocks to his four unmarried children. He continued to walk across to his workshop and remained involved with the later editions of his books. He encouraged his son to work on a *History of Fishes*, which, through Robert's diffidence, was never published. Journeys to Edinburgh in 1823 and to London in 1828 saw him reunited with old friends and fêted by the naturalists and artists of the day. Bewick died at his home on Mirk Lane, Gateshead, on 8 November 1828, with his place secure in the history of British art and his name destined to be prominent in every history of his craft. He was buried on 13 November at the church of St Mary in Ovingham.

IAIN BAIN

Sources *A memoir of Thomas Bewick written by himself*, ed. I. Bain (1975); rev. edn (1979) [incl. chronology and bibliography] · C. Hutton, 'Some account of Mr. Thomas Bewick and other artists, in Newcastle upon Tyne', *Newcastle Magazine* (June 1822) · J. J. Audubon, *Ornithological biography* (1831) · *Memoirs of Dr Robert Blakey*, ed. H. Miller (1879) · S. Roscoe, *Thomas Bewick: a bibliography raisonné* (1953) · MS corresp., priv. coll. · Beilby–Bewick workshop records, Tyne and Wear Archives Service, Newcastle upon Tyne, 1269 · J. Bewick, MS notes on her father's correspondents, Laing Art Gallery, Newcastle upon Tyne · stamp office schedule, priv. coll. · parish register, Ovingham, St Mary, 19 Aug 1753 [baptism] · monument, St Mary's Church, Ovingham

Archives BL, memoir, Add. MS 41481 · BL, notes and papers for history of British birds, Add. MS 50826 · Cherryburn, Northumberland, corresp. · Harvard U., Houghton L., letters, fms. Typ.434 · Hornby Art Library, Liverpool, corresp., L3250–3262 · Hunt. L., letters, HM 17300–17354, 17524–17525, 19744–19752 · Laing Art Gallery, Newcastle upon Tyne, corresp. · London Library, notes and cuttings · Natural History Society of Northumbria, Newcastle upon Tyne, corresp. · Newcastle Central Library, Pease bequest, corresp. · priv. coll., business and family corresp. · Tyne and Wear Archives Service, Newcastle upon Tyne, corresp. and papers · V&A NAL, corresp. and papers, L 3250–3262 | BL, corresp. with Sir J. Trevelyan and W. C. Trevelyan, Add. MS 31207 · BL, corresp. with S. Hodgson, Add. MSS 50241, 50242

Likenesses G. Gray, portrait, *c*.1780, Laing Art Gallery, Newcastle upon Tyne · T. A. Kidd, line engraving, pubd 1798 (after Miss Kirkley), BM, NPG · W. Nicholson, oils, 1816, Laing Art Gallery, Newcastle upon Tyne · J. Ramsay, oils, 1816, Natural History Society of Northumbria · T. Ranson, line engraving, pubd 1816 (after W. Nicholson), BM, NPG · J. Summerfield, stipple, pubd 1816 (after D. B. Murphy), BM · J. Burnet, engraving, 1817 (after Ramsay, 1816) · J. Ramsay, oils, 1823, NPG [*see illus.*] · E. H. Baily, bust, 1825 (after life mask), Literary and Philosophical Society of Newcastle upon Tyne · T. S. Good, oils, 1828, Natural History Society of Northumbria · F. Bacon, line engraving, 1852 (after Ramsay; after *The Last Child*), BM, NPG · attrib. R. E. Bewick, pen-and-ink sketch, BM · E. D. Crawhall, watercolour drawing, Laing Art Gallery, Newcastle upon Tyne · J. Ramsay, portrait (after *The Last Child*, Newcastle Central Library); now missing

Wealth at death £1046 15*s*. 3*d*. in cash; legacies deducted £600 plus funeral and other expenses of £327 16*s*. 6*d*.; stock in trade valued at £530 6*s*.; household goods and furniture £136 3*s*. 3*d*.; plate, linen, and china £64 18*s*. 6*d*.; books, prints, and pictures £30 10*s*.; wines and other liquors £7 10*s*.; book debts £79 13*s*. 11*d*.: will, 3 Dec 1828; stamp office schedule, priv. coll.

Bewick, Thomas, apprentices (*act.* 1777–1828), wood-engravers, were twenty-nine young men trained in the Beilby–Bewick workshop between 1777, when Thomas *Bewick (1753–1828) joined Ralph *Beilby (*bap.* 1743, d. 1817) [*see under* Beilby family], and the time of Bewick's death in 1828. Eight of them were indentured during the twenty years of the partnership up to 1797, and twenty-one thereafter. Most of the information on the apprentices is to be found randomly in the workshop records, with some important supplementary material in Bewick's *Memoir* and his surviving correspondence. Their wages, loans, deductions, and occasional treats are recorded in varying detail, and their initials appear with tantalizing sparseness and irregularity beside the entries for specific engravings on which they had worked. The terms of engagement were founded on the universally accepted seven years from the fourteenth birthday, though often adjusted by circumstance: some would come on trial before their fourteenth year, others whose promise was late in being recognized might be taken on as late as eighteen; two came from other masters to complete their time. Negotiations with parents or guardians were not always straightforward, because if a premium was required, it could be hard to find, and subscriptions had to be raised. The terms could vary a great deal. Those set for John Anderson in 1792 required his father to pay a 60 guinea fee and provide his board and lodging for the first three years, after which his son would be paid 5*s*. a week for the remaining four years. Those who stayed on in the workshop after their apprenticeship was over would be likely to be paid on piece-work and could earn a guinea to £1 18*s*. a week.

Lawyers prepared the indentures, and the official 'binding' of the apprentice to master was often recorded as an occasion for celebration at an inn, with drink and music on the small-pipes. The apprentices came from varied walks of life: the occupations of their parents and guardians ran the gamut from a 'poor cottager', and a keelman, to a city lawyer, and an officer in a militia regiment. Their training would have been rigorous, covering all the skills of a general metal-engraving workshop, following the pattern of Bewick's own training under Beilby so vividly described in his *Memoir* (pp. 39–41). No account has yet come to light that gives a precise idea of the daily training routines of the apprentices; but we do know from the survival of many wood blocks—most of them bought by Julia Boyd and printed in her *Bewick Gleanings* (1886)—that copying Bewick's own finished engravings was a regular exercise for his pupils.

Fourteen of them eventually specialized in wood-engraving and of these eleven came to prominence in the trade, all but two in London. Two others became distinguished engravers, of silver and of copper, and settled in their specialities on their own in the north. Eight of the group, Bewick's brother John *Bewick, his son Robert Elliot *Bewick [*see under* Bewick family], Charlton *Nesbit, Luke *Clennell, William *Harvey, John *Jackson (1801–

1848), Robert *Johnson, and his cousin John *Johnson [*see under* Johnson, Robert], are noticed elsewhere; eight others in chronological order—John Laws, John Anderson, Henry Hole, Mark Lambert, Edward Willis, Isaac Nicholson, Henry White, and William Temple—are treated separately in what follows.

John Laws (1765–1844), silver-engraver, was born at Heddon Laws near Heddon on the Wall, Northumberland, the son of a farming family. He was apprenticed to Beilby and Bewick between March 1782 and March 1789, beginning at about seventeen and leaving finally in June 1790 to work from his home at Heddon. In Bewick's *Memoir* (p. 195) he is noticed as being brought up as a silver-engraver, specializing in ornamental and 'bright' engraving (faceted work which reflects light, executed with a lozenge graver), at which he was unrivalled in his time. He was greatly respected and did much for the Newcastle silversmiths, and various other craftsmen such as saddlers, gunsmiths, and clock- and watchmakers. A keen amateur naturalist and taxidermist, he took a year's break in America as a relief from the workbench and to improve his birds' nest and egg collection (Angus, 9). An important pattern book survives with his descendants, along with a ledger recording his work which shows that while his farm had latterly become his major preoccupation, he was working on silver within weeks of his death on 14 August 1844, aged seventy-nine.

John Anderson (1775–1808?), wood-engraver, was born at Foveran, Aberdeenshire, the son of James *Anderson (1739–1808), farmer, and his wife, Margaret Seton (*d.* 1788). James Anderson had written a number of papers on agricultural and other topics, and took a degree of LLD at Aberdeen before moving to Edinburgh where in 1790 he began publishing a periodical, *The Bee*. Its need for illustration led him to apply to Bewick, and from this connection his son John was taken on as an apprentice on 10 September 1792. Three years later he proved an unruly pupil and the partners were preparing to sue him for neglecting his work, insolence, provocation, wilfully bad work, and for totally absenting himself from their service (Weekley, 144). In May 1795, after settling part of an arbitrator's fee, Anderson's name disappears from the books, and he may have moved south with his father in 1797. That he had talent there is no doubt, and he was taken up in particular by the printer Thomas Bensley and the booksellers Vernor and Hood. His first acknowledged work, sixteen large vignettes after George Samuel, appears in Maurice's *Grove-Hill* printed by Bensley in 1799, followed by the first edition of Bloomfield's *The Farmer's Boy* in 1800, a work often falsely credited to Bewick. Although no signature has been observed on his work, his handling of tree foliage is very distinctive in its repetitive groupings and horizontal bias; he made full use of 'white line' and rich contrast. In 1799 his hand can be seen in an edition of *The Letters of Junius*, in title cuts for Zimmerman's *Solitude*, and in a few vignettes and figures in his father's periodical *Recreations in Agriculture, Natural History, Arts &c*, first published in London in that year. His career was short-lived. Henry Hole

wrote tantalizingly to Bewick (5 July 1805) 'Mr John Anderson is certainly gone to Botany Bay, but more of this hereafter'. The obituary of his father, who died in 1808, notes that John had 'lately' predeceased him (*GM*, Dec 1808). A 'speculation' has been referred to (Redgrave, *Artists*), and it could be that he was involved in some enterprise which either led to or forced his departure overseas. He should not be confused with his contemporary in America, Alexander Anderson, who copied Bewick's *Quadrupeds* and several of the works of John Bewick.

Henry Fulke Plantagenet Woolocombe Hole (1782–1852), wood-engraver, was the son of a captain in the Lancashire militia who, for marrying a butcher's daughter, had been dispossessed of the family's Devon estate, Ebberley Hall, near Torrington. He was apprenticed to Bewick between October 1794 and 3 October 1801, when he was responsible for a few of the engravings in the second volume of the *British Birds*. He appears to have come to the workshop aged about twelve, having lost his father. Bewick was obviously fond of him, and when he left for Liverpool, he took with him a letter of introduction to Thomas Vernon (4 Dec 1801), in which Bewick hoped Vernon might be able to provide advice and introductions, saying that his 'late pupil … knows little of mankind … has read a good deal, is of a poetic and romantic turn of mind, is unsettled, and does not know where to cast Anchor'. Hole found his feet and eventually had enough work to seek the workshop's assistance with a long series of cuts for a Bible: his commissioning letter of 14 September 1804 was wildly optimistic in expecting to get fifteen finished within a week, despite saying 'something showy will be the most appropriate, for *fineness* or *labour* of execution is out of the question'. Other work that came from Liverpool connections were cuts for *The Nurse* translated by William Roscoe from the Italian (3rd edn, 1804), and for the printer John McCreery's poem *The Press*, part 1 (1803). His large engraving *Seed Sown*, for Ackermann's *Religious Emblems* (1809), shows him to have been a skilful interpreter of the work of John Thurston. As a member of the Liverpool Academy he exhibited in 1814 his engraving *An Attempt to Restore the Old Method of Crosslining on Wood* (Redgrave, *Artists*). Through the intervention of Roscoe, Hole went to see his uncle in Devon, who to his astonishment, after a tour of the house and grounds and a good dinner, immediately made over the estate to him (Meyer). Twenty years after the completion of the Bible cuts, Bewick had still not had final payment (letter, 11 Oct 1826). Although claiming that the debt was the responsibility of Troughton, the publisher, Hole was no doubt encouraged to settle by Bewick's passing reference to adding a full account of his apprentices in his *Memoir*. He died at Roborough, Bickington, Devon, on 19 August 1852.

Mark Lambert (1781–1855), copper-engraver, was born at Fourstones, Hexham, Northumberland. Nothing is known of his background, and Bewick fails to mention him in his *Memoir*, but he and his son Mark William were to establish the most successful copper-engraving and printing business in Newcastle, to which the diffident Robert Bewick would have lost much trade in his later years. Lambert was probably apprenticed to Bewick in July 1797, although the records of him are curiously shorter on detail than in other cases: there is a cryptic entry 'Letter from Mark' of 8 April 1797, and he first appears on the wages for 19 June 1802 with 'Mark out of his time' on 14 July 1804, and a final payment on 1 September of that year (Beilby–Bewick workshop record). When independent, Lambert was primarily a writing engraver of great accomplishment, providing bill heads, trade cards, and bookplates on copper for local custom, along with ciphers and armorial work on silver; pictorial work was taken on by other hands such as the artist J. W. Carmichael, William Collard, and George F. Robinson, who worked with the firm for many years from 1841. Nearly all Lambert's work is signed and some of his own early bookplate vignettes have frequently been attributed to Bewick. He died on 28 September 1855.

Edward Willis (*bap.* 1784, *d.* 1842), wood-engraver, was the son of James Willis and his wife, Margaret Carr, of Swalwell, co. Durham, and was baptized at Whickham on 14 March 1784. He was a cousin of George Stephenson the railway engineer. Willis was apprenticed in August 1798 and ended his time on 17 August 1805, with Bewick recording in the work book 'never a cross word passed between us the whole seven years'. Willis remained in Newcastle and continued to engrave for the workshop, contributing some tailpieces to *The Poetical Works of Robert Burns* (Alnwick, 1808), until his departure for a four-year stay in London in 1809. He returned to Newcastle in 1813, after the death of his wife, to continue working for Bewick over the next four years, contributing briefly to the *Fables of Aesop* before finally returning to London in May 1817, where he died on 10 February 1842. Willis was Jackson's and Chatto's principal source for their list of attributions in the *Treatise on Wood-Engraving* (1839). His work was not distinguished and tended to move away from the 'white line' of his master; Bewick remarked that while with him he was 'on a par with Charlton Nesbit, but did not equal the mechanical excellence Nesbit had attained to in London' (*Memoir*, 199). His signature 'Willis' appears occasionally in a running hand. He was a slow and deliberate workman, and was described by F. W. Fairholt as 'a Chinese engraver, without an idea of doing aught but mechanically cut out lines drawn out on wood for him' (*Art Journal*, 1866, 179–80). His exact work on Thomas Hood's pen-and-ink sketches for *Whims and Oddities* bears this out.

Isaac Nicholson (1789–1848), wood-engraver, was born at Melmerby, Cumberland, baptized at Melmerby on 8 March 1789, and bound on 18 August 1804, completing his time on 6 July 1811. He was the only wood-engraver apprentice to remain in Newcastle all his life, continuing in the workshop for some time before setting up on his own. He worked on the reproductive cuts for Thornton's *Herbal* (1810) and on some of the blocks for *Recreations in Natural History* (1815) which had been prepared by Luke Clennell: these display all the vigour and freedom of Clennell's draughtsmanship but the cutting moves towards black line reproduction, which is often seen in Nicholson's small vignettes, where backgrounds of rock predominate, and in his groups of bunched foliage. A few of the cuts in the *Fables of Aesop* (1818) were from his hand and merit Bewick's record in the *Memoir*: 'both a good Apprentice & a good Artist—his engravings on Wood, are clearly or honestly cut, as well as being accurately done from his patterns'. He also did much work for Emerson Charnley, the Newcastle bookseller, in particular the vignettes for his *Select Fables* of 1820, and for the titles of a long series of annual *Fisher's Garlands*, too often attributed to Bewick, although many were engraved after Bewick's death. One was a blatant copy of one of the finest tailpieces in the *Birds*, the angler in the river, and roused Bewick to turn to the law for redress (letter to Charnley, 22 May 1826). To compare the two provides a valuable means of observing Bewick's mastery. Nicholson died on 18 October 1848.

Henry White (1784–1851), wood-engraver, was the son of Jonathan White, hatter and sword cutler in London, who died not long after his bankruptcy. He came to the workshop on 15 September 1804 after serving the first four years of his time with James Lee in London. Lee's death prompted White's uncle and guardian, H. S. Speck, to seek another master for him, much to the natural irritation of Lee's widow to whom, after four years' experience, he had become very useful. He was of course immediately useful to Bewick. He was involved in some of the cuts for Thomson's *The Seasons* (1805), for which Thurston had provided the drawings, and he engraved all the principal subjects and some tailpieces for Catnach and Davison's edition of *The Poetical Works of Robert Burns* (Alnwick, 1808). He had a somewhat dry manner which compares poorly with the vigorous effects of Clennell, who also worked on *The Seasons*. He left the workshop for London a few months after his time, in January 1808. Bewick remarked that in London 'he chiefly turned his attention, to the imitation of sketchy *cross hatching* on Wood, from the inimitable pencil of Mr Cruickshanks, & perhaps some other artists in this same way' (*Memoir*, 199–200). The work for which White is now specially remembered is to be found in Major's edition of Walton's *Complete Angler* (1824), and in Yarrell's *History of British Fishes* (1836): all of it mechanically excellent, but reproductive and reflecting nothing of what he might have absorbed from the example of Bewick.

William Temple (*bap.* 1798, *d.* 1837), wood-engraver, was baptized at All Saints, Newcastle upon Tyne, on 6 May 1798, the son of William Temple and his wife, Mary Gill. He was bound on 15 August 1812 and took to wood-engraving as readily as his fellow apprentice William Harvey. They were singled out by Bewick as being his principal assistants, along with his son Robert, in getting out the *Fables of Aesop*, for which Bewick prepared the drawings in great detail on the wood. Robert appears to have contributed the least to the enterprise; after Harvey left for London in September 1817 there were still some twenty or so blocks to be cut and these were probably the work of Temple. The tailpieces of a man negotiating a snowdrift on stilts, and the funeral cortège at Ovingham which ends the book, are Temple's work and both show a particularly delicate handling of the fine tracery of the branches in the winter trees. At the end of his time his father's death took him away to support the running of the family drapery business and wood-engraving lost a promising talent.

Of the remaining lesser figures, David Martin (*fl.* 1758–1781) and Abraham Hunter (1759–1808) were the earliest to join. Although Martin had been a fellow apprentice towards the end of Bewick's time, and contributed to the *Select Fables* of 1784, he apparently had little aptitude for his work and moved to other things (letter, 11 May 1819). Hunter, who appears to have left the workshop by July 1780 after about three years, set up a rival business in Newcastle and there are indications that the later relationship with his masters was not an easy one (Bewick, letter, 30 Sept 1788). Others to follow Hunter were Johnson, another cousin of Robert Johnson and as a wood-engraver and draftsman a minor contributor to the *History of British Birds* and the *Poems of Goldsmith and Parnell*; Henry Barnes, indentured and in the workshop between 1791 and 1794; Charles Hickson, apprenticed in 1795, a ward of Sir John Lawson and an idle braggart who absconded in 1800; John Harrison (1785–1818), a nephew of Bewick, who after leaving the workshop in 1814 specialized as a writing engraver; George Armstrong, apprenticed for two years, 1804–6, before setting up as a partner in Armstrong and Walker, engravers in Newcastle who were later to train John Jackson; John Bewick (1790–1809), another Bewick nephew who died after four years as an apprentice wood-engraver; John Armstrong, apprenticed in 1813 and staying after his time until leaving for the London wood-engraving trade in 1825; Matthew Bewick (1801–1832), the third nephew in the workshop, who was apprenticed in 1817 and continued as a copperplate printer; Alexander Reid, son of a Leith bookseller, apprenticed in 1817–24, an irritation to his master with nothing known of his subsequent career; Thomas Young, apprenticed in 1818–25 and William Hardy, apprenticed in 1827–34, who remain obscure; and finally James Reevely, who joined the workshop in 1824, and as a competent wood-engraver became Robert Bewick's right-hand man. It should be noted that Ebeneezer Landells, who was later a prominent figure in the London trade, both as engraver and as first editor of *Punch*, had been intended for Bewick's workshop and is often incorrectly referred to as his pupil. Although payments for indenture papers and a sketchbook were recorded in 1822, it appears that, as Bewick and Landell's father could not agree terms, the boy went to Isaac Nicholson, who had by then established his own business in Newcastle.   IAIN BAIN

Sources *A memoir of Thomas Bewick written by himself*, ed. I. Bain, rev. edn (1979) • A. Angus, 'Thomas Bewick's apprentices', *History of the book trade in the north* (1993) • Tyne and Wear Archive Department, Newcastle upon Tyne, Beilby–Bewick workshop records, 1269 • I. Bain, *The watercolours and drawings of Thomas Bewick and his workshop apprentices* (1981) • BL, Hodgson papers, Add. MS 50247 • W. A. Chatto and J. A. Jackson, *A treatise on wood engraving* (1839) • notes on Robert Johnson, McGill University, Montreal, Crawhall MSS • J. Vinycombe, *Lambert of Newcastle as an engraver of book-plates* (1896) • W. J. Linton, *The masters of wood engraving* (1889) • Redgrave, *Artists*, 2nd edn • M. Weekley, *Thomas Bewick* (1973) • *GM*, 1st ser., 78 (1808), 1053 • *GM*, 2nd ser., 38 (1852), 435 • J. Meyer, notes on Liverpool artists, Lpool RO • G. Chandler, *William Roscoe of Liverpool, 1753–1831* (1953)

Archives Liverpool RO, letters and prints [Henry Fulke Plantagenet Woolocombe Hole]

Bewick, William (1795–1866), portrait and history painter, was born at Darlington, co. Durham, on 20 October 1795, the son of William Bewick (1759–1844), upholsterer, and Jane Roantree (*d.* 1843), a Quaker descended from a local family of linen manufacturers. After attending a local school he was apprenticed to his father and began experimenting with painting and drawing, receiving his first tuition from itinerant artists, later from the Darlington painter George Marks. By the age of twenty he had accumulated a portfolio of drawings, and with £20 raised by the sale of these works left for London in 1815. Here by chance he met the rising historical and genre painter Benjamin Robert Haydon, who immediately accepted Bewick as a pupil, and with whom he remained for about three years. At Haydon's studio he met many famous men of the day, including Wordsworth, Hazlitt, and Keats. He worked hard under Haydon's influence, and besides working in his master's studio attended the Royal Academy Schools, and the dissecting rooms of the physiologist and surgeon Sir Charles Bell. His health, which had always been delicate, suffered from overwork, however, and he returned briefly to Darlington to recuperate before resuming work in London by completing a series of drawings of the Elgin marbles for the poet Goethe. He first began exhibiting his work in 1820, at the Society of Painters in Water Colours, but his first exhibit of note was his *Jacob Meeting Rachel*, which he exhibited at the British Institution in 1822, and later sent to the first exhibition of the Newcastle Institution, in that year. For the next seventeen years he exhibited only at Newcastle, Carlisle, and Glasgow. During the early part of this period he returned briefly to Darlington to paint portraits, then in the autumn of 1823 he visited Edinburgh, where he was warmly received by the city's leading artists and citizens. He formed an anatomical class in the Scottish capital, and spent much time producing life-sized likenesses of the celebrities he met, including the painter Sir William Allan, the Indian administrator, soldier, and historian Sir John Malcolm, and the writer and judge Lord Jeffrey. He next went to Glasgow, where he held an exhibition of his works, and again attracted portrait commissions. The same success attended his subsequent visit to Dublin in 1824, where his sitters included leading politician Daniel O'Connell. He then returned to Scotland and stayed with Sir Walter Scott at Abbotsford, drawing Scott's portrait while the author sat for Wilkie. On leaving Scotland Bewick returned to Darlington, where about 1826 he married Elizabeth Quelch (*d.* 1870), and painted a number of landscapes to enable him to visit Italy to study the Italian schools. Sir Thomas Lawrence, president of the Royal Academy, became aware of his intentions and offered him 100 guineas to copy Michelangelo's *Prophets and Sybils* in the Sistine Chapel. He had almost completed this commission when Lawrence suddenly died. He was recompensed for his work by Lawrence's executors on his return to London in 1830, following his four-year stay in Rome, and there resumed painting before once again returning to Darlington. He remained at Darlington until 1839, when he returned to London and again exhibited at the British Institution, and sent his first work to the Royal Academy, and the Suffolk Street Gallery. He continued to exhibit in London throughout this his final stay in the capital, but on returning to Darlington in 1842 he exhibited there on only one further occasion, when he sent his *The Historian Platina in Prison*, to the British Institution in 1848. He spent the remaining twenty-four years of his life at his home at Haughton-le-Skerne, near Darlington, his artistic efforts in the early part of this period confined to the production of the *Triumph of David* as an (unsuccessful) competition entry for the decoration of Westminster Hall, and the painting of occasional portraits and 'fancy pictures'. He died on 8 June 1866, at Haughton-le-Skerne, a substantial property owner in the village, and was buried in the churchyard there. His portrait work is extensively represented in the National Portrait Gallery and the British Museum, London, and the Scottish National Portrait Gallery, Edinburgh. Bewick was not a member of the family of Thomas Bewick, the engraver, as is sometimes believed.   MARSHALL HALL

Sources W. H. D. Longstaffe, *The history and antiquities of the parish of Darlington* (1854) • T. Landseer, ed., *The life and letters of William Bewick (artist)* (1871) • *The autobiography and journals of Benjamin Robert Haydon (1786–1846)*, ed. M. Elwin (1950) • J. R. Kirkland and M. R. Wood, *William Bewick of Darlington* (1989) • M. Hall, *The artists of Northumbria*, 2nd edn (1982) • *DNB* • *CGPLA Eng. & Wales* (1866) • F. Russell, *Portraits of Sir Walter Scott* (privately printed, London, 1987), 30 • inscription on gravestone, Haughton-le-Skerne churchyard, Haughton-le-Skerne, near Darlington, co. Durham
Likenesses W. Bewick, self-portrait, chalk, 1818, Durham County Library • J. Gibson, marble bust, 1853 (after model, 1827), National Gallery, London • W. Bewick, self-portrait, oils, U. Durham • W. Bewick, self-portrait, oils, dean and chapter of Durham • W. Bewick, self-portrait, pencil, Darlington Art Gallery • J. Brown, stipple and line engraving (after L. Macarten), NPG • T. Smyth, engraving (after C. Landseer), repro. in Longstaffe, *History and antiquities of the parish of Darlington*, 342
Wealth at death under £1500: probate, 26 July 1866, *CGPLA Eng. & Wales*

Bewley, Sir Edmund Thomas (1837–1908), lawyer and genealogist, was born in Dublin on 11 January 1837, the son of Edward Bewley (1806–1876), licentiate of the Irish colleges both of surgeons and of physicians, and his wife, Mary, daughter of Thomas Mulock (1791–1857) of Kilnagarna, King's county. He entered Trinity College, Dublin, in 1855 and obtained his BA in 1860, having won a classical scholarship in 1857 and a first senior moderatorship and gold medal in science in 1859. In 1863 he obtained an MA and proceeded LLD in 1885. He also obtained a BA (*ad eundem*) and later an MA (again with honours and first gold medal) from the Queen's University of Ireland. He was called to the Irish bar in 1862 and after four years of practice married Anna Sophie Stewart Colles; they had two sons and one daughter. In 1882 he took silk and from

1884 to 1890 was regius professor of feudal and English law in the University of Dublin. In 1890 he became a judge of the Supreme Court of Judicature of Ireland, and judicial commissioner of the Irish land commission. He retired in 1898 owing to poor health, and was knighted. He was elected FSA in 1908, and died at Gowran, co. Kilkenny, on 27 June 1908.

Bewley was an avid amateur genealogist and contributed articles to the *Genealogist*, *Ancestor*, and other journals, as well as having some of his research printed privately. His three books, *The Bewleys of Cumberland* (1902), *The Family of Mulock* (1905), and *The Family of Poe* (1906), were all investigations into family history; in the monograph on the Poe family he suggested that Edgar Allan Poe was descended from a family named Powell, who for generations were tenant farmers in co. Cavan. Bewley was also author of *The Law and Practice of Taxation of Costs* (1867), *A Treatise on the Common Law Procedure Acts* (1871), and joint author of *A Treatise on the Chancery (Ireland) Act, 1867* (1868).

D. J. O'DONOGHUE, *rev.* SINÉAD AGNEW

Sources E. T. Bewley, *The Bewleys of Cumberland* (1902) • *The Times* (29 June 1908) • *Irish Times* (29 June 1908) • F. E. Ball, *The judges in Ireland, 1221–1921*, 2 vols. (1926) • *CGPLA Ire.* (1908)
Wealth at death £16,487 18s. 1d.: resworn probate, 10 Aug 1908, *CGPLA Ire.* • £9332 3s. 10d. in England: Irish probate sealed in England, 4 Sept 1908, *CGPLA Eng. & Wales*

Bewley, William (1726–1783), surgeon apothecary and writer, was a native of Massingham, in Norfolk, where he was born on 5 September 1726. He practised as a surgeon apothecary in Great Massingham, but is better known for his contribution, which spanned twenty years, of articles and reviews to the *Monthly Review*. Although he spent most of his life in Norfolk, he corresponded with many eminent thinkers of his day, including Joseph Priestley, Cesare Beccaria, John Hunter, and Thomas Reid. He was a particular friend of Charles Burney, who frequently sought Bewley's opinions and advice, admiring his knowledge of science and literature.

In August 1783 Bewley, accompanied by his wife, made a last journey. He visited Priestley and then stayed with Burney at his house in St Martin's Street, London. Bewley fell ill and went into a coma on 4 September; he died the next day and was buried in St Martin-in-the-Fields. Burney wrote an obituary notice of Bewley, in the *Gentleman's Magazine*, in which he gave him the name of the Philosopher of Massingham and praised his work for the *Monthly Review*, describing it as being, 'written with a force, spirit, candour, and—when the subject afforded opportunity—humour, not often found in critical discussions'.

KAYE BAGSHAW

Sources B. Hill, 'The Philosopher of Massingham: William Bewley, 1726–1783', *The Practitioner*, 196 (1966), 580–84 • Madame D'Arblay [F. Burney], *Memoirs of Doctor Burney*, 3 vols. (1832) • R. Lonsdale, *Dr Charles Burney: a literary biography* (1965) • *GM*, 1st ser., 53 (1783), 805

Bexfield, William Richard (1824–1853), composer, was born at Norwich on 27 April 1824, the third son of Thomas and Anna Bexfield. He entered the cathedral choir at the age of seven, and studied music under the organist, Zachariah Buck, to whom he was articled from 1838. He learned the violin, trumpet, trombone, and drums, but he excelled as an organist when still quite young. In 1845, on the expiration of his articles, he obtained the post of organist at the parish church of Boston, Lincolnshire, and on 16 November 1846 took the degree of BMus at Oxford, where his name was entered at New College. His degree exercise was a canon in five parts. On the death of William Crotch in 1847 he became a candidate for the Heather professorship of music at Oxford, but without success, probably on account of his youth. In February 1848 he left Boston to become organist at St Helen's, Bishopsgate, London, the competition for which brought forward thirty-six candidates. In the following year he proceeded to the degree of MusD at Cambridge, his name being entered at Trinity College. On 4 April 1850 he married Mary Ann Millington, of Boston, with whom he had two children. Soon after his marriage he wrote the oratorio by which his name is best remembered, *Israel Restored*. This work was produced by the Norwich Choral Society in October 1851, and was again performed at the Norwich festival on 22 September 1852, when solo parts were sung by Pauline Viardot, Louisa Pyne, Charlotte Dolby, John Sims Reeves, Italo Gardoni, Charles Lockey, Karl Formes, Giovanni Belletti, and Willoughby Weiss. The worth of much of the music was at once recognized; but the text was fatally dull, and the whole work suffered from being forced by a local clique into injudicious rivalry with H. H. Pierson's *Jerusalem*, which was produced on the following day. Although the merits of Bexfield's work were acknowledged, both local and national press gave precedence to Pierson's oratorio. Bexfield's other published works are a set of organ fugues, a set of six songs (words by the composer), and a collection of anthems. He died from ulceration of the bowels at 12 Monmouth Road, Bayswater, on 28 October 1853, too young to have fulfilled the expectation aroused by the talents he displayed.

W. B. SQUIRE, rev. CLIVE BROWN

Sources *New Grove* · *IGI* · *Annual Register* (1853), 267 · *GM*, 2nd ser., 41 (1854), 102–3 · 'The Norwich festival', *MT*, 5 (1852–4), 75–6 · Foster, *Alum. Oxon.* · Venn, *Alum. Cant.* · m. cert. · d. cert.

Bexley. For this title name *see* Vansittart, Nicholas, first Baron Bexley (1766–1851).

Beyfus, Gilbert Hugh (1885–1960), barrister, was born on 19 July 1885 at 77 Linden Gardens, Kensington, London, the only son of Alfred Beyfus, a solicitor of 69 Lincoln's Inn Fields, and his wife, Emmie Marguerite Ruth, daughter of Robert Plumsted. Of Germanic Jewish origin on his father's side, he was educated at Harrow School and Trinity College, Oxford, where he was admitted as a history exhibitioner in 1904. An aesthete and amorous adventurer in a college then noted for its rugby players, he was not popular among his contemporaries and was, in the words of his college contemporary Christopher Chavasse, a future bishop of Rochester, 'driven into digs'. He took a second in jurisprudence in 1907, but redeemed himself with the certificate of honour in his bar finals. He was

called to the bar in the Inner Temple on 27 January 1908, and was a pupil to Harry Kirsch. He was doubly fortunate in his family, who made him financially independent and also provided him (through the solicitor's firm of Beyfus and Beyfus in Lincoln's Inn Fields) with the means to earn a living.

On the outbreak of the First World War, Beyfus was commissioned into the 3rd battalion of the duke of Westminster's regiment in August 1914 as a second lieutenant. While serving in Flanders with the 2nd battalion in April 1915, he was wounded at Ypres. Taken captive the following month, he remained a prisoner of war until December 1918. In 1919 he retired as a captain, with a mention in dispatches.

Resuming civilian life, Beyfus picked up the threads of his career at the bar. He sought to ride the two horses of law and politics, but was unable even to mount the second. He was twice rejected by the electorate: in 1910 as Liberal candidate for Cirencester and in 1922 as coalition candidate for Kingswinford. In 1923 he rejected an approach from the Liberals of East Nottingham, a seat which in the event was won for them by the young Norman Birkett. Beyfus's political ambitions never died, but equally they were never fulfilled. He joined the Conservative Party in 1937, applied (unsuccessfully) in 1941 for a seat at Hampstead, and applied again in 1945 at Derby, when he was—to his chagrin—rejected on grounds of age.

The possible loss to the House of Commons was the bar's certain gain, for Beyfus was able from his chambers at 3 Brick Court (1912–41) to develop a healthy practice, particularly in jury trials, but one which, because of the inadequacies of his first clerk, Woodward, was not in the first rank of junior work. In 1933 he became a queen's counsel and in 1940 was made bencher of his inn.

The epitome of the fashionable silk, specializing in libel, breach of promise, fraud, and blackmail, Beyfus appeared thereafter in many of the *causes célèbres* of his times—for example, Aneurin Bevan's action (1957) against *The Spectator* which had accused him of inebriation, and Liberace's action (1959) against the *Daily Mirror* which had accused him of homosexuality. Horatio Bottomley was another of his notable clients. He migrated to various sets in the confines of the Temple, but spent his last (and greatest) years in 2 Mitre Court Building.

Beyfus had a special interest in the law of gaming and wagering. In the case of *Dey* v. *Mayo* (1920), when briefed at a couple of hours' notice, he established in the Court of Appeal the proposition that an action could lie to recover gambling losses paid by cheque. He successfully defended the same proposition at the House of Lords in the later case of *Briggs* v. *Sutters* (1922) against the formidable team of Sir John Simon QC and Sir Edward Marshall Hall QC. The decision prompted amending legislation. In 1958 Beyfus successfully defended John Aspinall, who was prosecuted under an act of 1845 for keeping a common gaming house in his home to which he invited his large circle of friends to play *chemin de fer*. Beyfus used to maintain that all games were a mixture of skill and chance, except snap which was a game of pure skill.

Beyfus had the gift of addressing a jury in everyday speech which, through his art, was as compelling in style as it was commonplace in substance—not for him the flamboyant rhetoric of a Marshall Hall. He was a merciless cross-examiner, though a fair one, and a coiner of *bons mots*, polished and repolished under the glow of midnight oil—a technique perfected half a century later by George Carman QC. His wink, the product of a kick sustained when he fell from his horse in the bar point-to-point in 1923, he turned from handicap to weapon.

If he was unsuccessful as an aspirant parliamentarian, Beyfus was also disappointed in his ambition to become a judge. Many great advocates have become lesser judges. The lord chancellor never tested the proposition in Beyfus's case. It was not until 1950 that he had the opportunity to sit in the relatively lowly position of deputy chairman of the west Sussex quarter sessions.

In the era in which Beyfus practised, silks of stature were public figures. This added to the pressures of a life which, in its upper echelons, is as demanding as that of any profession. In later years Beyfus was the victim of ill health (including tuberculosis and cancer of the bowels) and underwent two serious operations. In 1958 the fiftieth anniversary of his call was the occasion for congratulations of bench and bar. Lord Goddard, the lord chief justice and another old Trinity man, was the principal speaker at the dinner in his honour. In May 1960 Beyfus retired. His last case was Mrs MacPherson's slander action against the duchess of Argyll.

Beyfus, handsome and moustached, stood a little short of 6 feet. He was a lavish host (although he claimed to prefer bread, cheese, and beer) and an enthusiastic traveller. He was a member of the Savage Club, and his extracurricular interests included the theatre (a love of his father's), hunting, fishing, and tennis. He owned a Hampstead town house and a seaside cottage at Frinton.

As barristers often do, Beyfus came to marriage late, after romances at different stages of his life with stage stars Zena Dare, Nellie Taylor, and Evelyn Large, but he made up for time lost. On 2 August 1929 he married Margaret Malone, star of the musical *Kidboots*. Nineteen years his junior, she was the daughter of Sydney Robert Squires, of independent means, but had changed her name by deed poll. They had one son, John. This marriage was dissolved and Beyfus married second on 2 July 1949 Joan Hilda Grant, who had also changed her name by deed poll. Formerly the wife of John Hook, from whom she was divorced, and daughter of Stanley Croker, an officer in the merchant navy, she was nearly forty years Beyfus's junior. This marriage was also dissolved, on account of her adultery with a doctor closer to her age. Finally he married on 16 July 1953 Eileen Louisa Hill (again forty years his junior and a nightclub dancer), the daughter of Arthur Hill, of no occupation, who survived him. His marriages appear to have been the triumph of hope over experience. He was a lonely man without true friends. It was characteristic that he had to pay for his own fiftieth anniversary dinner.

Unlucky to the last, Beyfus had expectations of a knighthood in the 1961 new year honours list. They were never realized, since he died on 30 October 1960 at his home, Derreen, Mill Lane, Bell Vale, North Ambersham, near Haslemere, Surrey. MICHAEL BELOFF

Sources I. Adamson, *The old fox* (1963) · *The Times* (31 Oct 1960) · archives, Harrow School · archives, Trinity College, Oxford · Inner Temple, London · *WWW* · b. cert. · m. certs. · d. cert.
Archives NAM, diaries kept while prisoner of war
Wealth at death £27,887 19s. 9d.: probate, 6 Jan 1961, *CGPLA Eng. & Wales*

Beynon, Sir (William John) Granville (1914–1996), physicist, was born on 24 May 1914 at Pen-y-bryn, Dunvant, a suburb of Swansea, Glamorgan, the youngest of the four children of William Beynon, a colliery checkweighman, and his wife, Mary, *née* Thomas. His parents were both Welsh and his father was a tall, sandy-haired, good-humoured, courageous man of impressive personality, a pillar of the community, with his manipulative skills as an 'ambulance man' being in great demand. When nine-year-old Granville fell from the parapet of Oystermouth Castle during a Sunday school outing and broke both his arms, his father set the bones and made the splints that resulted in a complete healing.

On completing his primary education at the village school Beynon entered Gowerton Boys' Grammar School, and, in 1931, the University College of Swansea, a constituent of the federal University of Wales. There he graduated with first-class honours in physics in 1934, and proceeded to research under the supervision of Professor E. J. Evans. In his early teens he tinkered with clocks, bicycles, and radios, took a keen interest in rugby football, and was sent by his parents for violin lessons. Later in his teens he and his father built a crystal radio; using it, he heard a Saturday night broadcast on science by E. V. (Edward) Appleton, with whom he later worked. At twelve he became a member of a band of young musicians called Urdd y Pobl Bach (the guild of young people) organized by the wife of a local solicitor, Arthur Morgan James, whose daughter, Megan Medi James, was also a member. Megan James also graduated with first-class honours in physics at Swansea. She and Granville Beynon were married at Ebenezer Congregational Chapel, Swansea, on 31 July 1942. They had a daughter and two sons.

Although E. J. Evans was not himself a distinguished researcher, he knew how to inspire and encourage promising students, several of whom became fellows of the Royal Society. After Beynon's death his wife found among his papers a much folded letter written in 1938 by Evans shortly after Beynon had started working at the National Physical Laboratory (NPL): 'I believe you have the ability to go far if you persevere. Always look for the unexpected. E. J.' (private information). Following graduation Beynon's PhD studies at Swansea under Evans were concerned with the natural and magneto-optical dispersions of organic liquids, mainly alkanols. They demanded painstaking measurement and quantitative analytical treatment, which Beynon took in his stride. Three of the four publications to emerge from his thesis work appeared in his own name in the *Philosophical Magazine*.

This work was, however, far removed from, and quite

unrelated to, that which Beynon pursued upon his appointment in January 1938 to the radio division (based at Ditton Park, Slough) of the NPL. By the late 1930s measurements of the ionosphere had revealed much; but there was an exigent need to understand the manner in which radio waves (of various wavelengths) were transmitted through the ionosphere to varying distances over the earth. This was the investigation on which Beynon, in conjunction with Edward Appleton, was first engaged at the Slough laboratory of the NPL. Two definitive papers under their joint authorship were published in the 1940s, dealing with theoretical and practical investigations of the reflection of radio waves incident obliquely on the ionosphere. These papers formed the basis for the UK method of predicting the conditions for radio-wave propagation. Although his collaboration with Appleton continued to be strong Beynon also discovered (at Slough) in work that was exclusively his own the earliest indication of horizontal motions in the ionosphere: in the so-called F_2 layer of the ionosphere between 200 and 350 km above the earth there is an east–west flow with a velocity of 430 km per hour.

After his return to a lectureship post at Swansea in 1946 (the year before Appleton received the Nobel prize for work on the physics of the upper atmosphere) Beynon continued to collaborate with Appleton on radio-wave absorptions and lunar tidal oscillations in the ionosphere. Both at Swansea, where he was assisted from 1947 by a younger colleague, G. M. Brown, and at Aberystwyth (another constituent college of the University of Wales), where he became professor and head of department in 1958, Beynon studied the 'winter anomaly' in ionospheric absorption, a phenomenon first reported in the mid-1930s. Collaboration with Brown, who also joined the staff at Aberystwyth, flourished. Their joint editorial work—including the production of the forty-eight volumes of the *Annals of the International Geophysical Year* (1957–8), arising from a major geophysical study over the sunspot maximum period, and the single volume *Solar Eclipses and the Ionosphere* (1956)—made them key figures in the ionospheric literature.

One of Beynon's great strengths as an experimentalist was the speed with which he identified and applied the potential of new techniques. This was exemplified by his use in the period 1968 to 1974 of the available Skylark, Skua, and Petrel rockets, launched from Australia and the Hebrides, for the refined measurement of radio-wave transmissions. His extraordinary effectiveness in designing and orchestrating international collaborations using rocket experiments throughout the 1970s involved experiments undertaken by his own group at Aberystwyth with teams from the NPL at Slough, Queen's University, Belfast, the Swedish Meteorological Institute at Stockholm, the University of Saskatchewan, and the Max Planck Institute of Heidelberg.

Of even greater significance was Beynon's early appreciation of the versatility of the incoherent radar scatter technique and its future value to his research programme at Aberystwyth and other centres in the UK. When J. J.

Thomson (discoverer of the electron) showed in 1906 that electromagnetic waves were incoherently scattered by electrons he also showed that the extent of the scattering (its so-called cross-section) was minute. What Beynon was quick to appreciate nearly sixty years later was that, with the availability of powerful radar sources and ever more sensitive means of detecting scattered photons, a vital role could be played in ionospheric research by the incoherent scatter technique. A national incoherent scatter radar facility was established initially in 1970 by collaboration between the Royal Radar Establishment at Malvern, the University College of Wales at Aberystwyth, and the NPL at Slough. This trio was the first to measure three components of the plasma velocity in both E and F regions of the ionosphere. The emergence of the enlarged body (involving the research councils of six nations) that constituted the European Incoherent Scatter Radar Facility (EISCAT), of which Beynon was regarded as the father, culminated in its official inauguration in 1981 in the presence of King Karl Gustav of Sweden.

Beynon's persuasive qualities, sense of humour, clearheadedness, and sheer ability appealed to scientists from widely different cultures. It explains why he was *persona grata* as much in Moscow as in Washington, and why he was elected to so many key committees: he was president of the International Union of Radio Science, and of the Special Committee for the International Years of the Quiet Sun, and a member of the national committee for space research of the Science and Engineering Research Council; he was also a member of Antarctic Research, Geodesy and Geophysics, and the International Council of Scientific Union. His role in international co-operation in solar-terrestrial physics was further enhanced during his editorship from 1976 to 1989 of the *Journal of Atmospheric and Terrestrial Physics*. He was also vitally interested in secondary and tertiary education. For eleven years he chaired the schools council committee for Wales and he also served as president of the education section of the British Association for the Advancement of Science. From 1972 to 1974 he was vice-principal of the University College of Wales, Aberystwyth. He was appointed CBE in 1959, elected FRS in 1973, and knighted in 1976. He received many honours and awards, including the Goddard prize of the National Space Club of America, and the Chree medal of the Institute of Physics.

Beynon was a devoted family man who greatly enjoyed music-making with his wife Megan and three children: Margaret, Meurig, and James. He also had a strong sense of community. During the depression of the 1930s, while still a student, he founded a social club and helped organize summer camps for the unemployed in his village, Dunvant. While a lecturer at the university in Swansea he trained his village chapel choir, which for several years performed Bach's St Matthew passion on Palm Sunday. At Aberystwyth in the early 1970s he was co-founder of, and an accomplished first violinist in, the Philomusica Orchestra of Aberystwyth, made up of musicians from 'town and gown'. Among his enormous circle of friends he was admired for his open personality, story-telling gifts, sense of humour, and prodigiously energetic gardening. Countless thousands of undergraduates taught by him at Swansea and Aberystwyth remembered him as one of the best lecturers they ever heard. He died of heart failure at the Abermad Nursing Home, Llanilar, Aberystwyth, on 11 March 1996. He was survived by his wife and their three children.   JOHN MEURIG THOMAS

Sources L. Thomas, *Memoirs FRS*, 44 (1998), 53–62 · *Journal of Atmospheric and Terrestrial Physics*, 56/7 (1994) · *The Independent* (16 March 1996) · *The Times* (22 March 1996) · *WWW* · personal knowledge (2004) · private information (2004) [Lady Beynon, widow; G. M. Brown] · b. cert. · m. cert. · d. cert.
Archives U. Edin. L., corresp. with E. Appleton
Likenesses photograph, 1976, repro. in Thomas, *Memoirs FRS*, 52 · photograph, repro. in *The Times*
Wealth at death under £145,000: probate, 8 May 1996, *CGPLA Eng. & Wales*

Gonville Aubie ffrench-Beytagh (1912–1991), by unknown photographer

Beytagh, Gonville Aubie ffrench- (1912–1991), dean of Johannesburg, was born in Shanghai, China, on 26 January 1912, the son of Leo Michael ffrench-Beytagh, the managing director of a cotton company, and his wife, Edith, formerly McIlraith. His father was a lapsed Irish Catholic seminarian. His mother left home when he was still young. He had a somewhat anarchic upbringing in China, followed by the irksome discipline of an English evangelical public school, Monkton Combe (which he disliked), and a slightly more tolerable time at Bristol grammar school. In England he was placed, with his brother and sister, under the legal guardianship of Miss Esylt Newbury, the daughter of a vicar, who operated a benign but restrictive regime. Desperate to be free from such constraints, just before his seventeenth birthday in 1929, he went to New Zealand to enrol on an agricultural course at Waitaki high school. He was soon expelled and embarked on two years of roaming, taking casual jobs, getting into fights, and sleeping rough. As a result of a chance encounter with a distant relative he renewed contact with his mother, now remarried and living in South Africa, and was persuaded to go to that country in 1933. (At first he was classified as an 'Asiatic' by the immigration authorities, obsessed by racial categorization even in the period before apartheid.) He found work as a clerk for a mining company in Johannesburg.

Searching for some purpose and order for his life, ffrench-Beytagh came into contact with the Johannesburg branch of Toc H, whose membership included Alan Paton. He experienced a yearning for Christian faith and a dawning sense of vocation to the priesthood. Geoffrey Clayton, bishop of Johannesburg, encouraged this commitment, and sent him for ordination training to St Paul's College, Grahamstown, at that time an all-white college. 'The college turned out to be a rather mausoleum-like, dull, brick structure which to me had the psychological impact of a prison', commented ffrench-Beytagh in his autobiographical *Encountering Darkness* (1973). Clayton urged him to persevere, and they remained close friends.

Gonville ffrench-Beytagh was ordained in 1938. Strongly aware of the anarchic tendencies in his personality, and subject to intense bouts of depression, he found great spiritual support in a catholic Anglican spirituality which combined discipline and regularity (he rose daily at 4 a.m. to say the office, and, as a priest, celebrated mass daily), with a sense of freedom and an understanding for the moral waywardness and intractability of the human personality. His pastoral ministry during the war years was pursued with great energy and revealed his gifts as a counsellor and spiritual adviser. His political consciousness remained undeveloped at this stage. He had little contact with non-Europeans in his ministry until he was appointed as priest in charge of St Alban's mission for the coloured (mixed race) community of Johannesburg. Nevertheless, after 1948 he had little sympathy with the National Party's racial policies, and he resigned his South African passport in protest at the passing of the 1953 Bantu Education Act, to which his bishop, Ambrose Reeves, was vigorously objecting.

In 1954 ffrench-Beytagh was invited to become dean of Salisbury Cathedral in Southern Rhodesia. Again his work was primarily among white Anglicans. But his liberal opinions on race, and his disdain for the reactionary nature of settler politics in Southern Rhodesia, gave an increasingly political edge to his ministry.

In 1965 ffrench-Beytagh returned to South Africa as dean of Johannesburg. For the first time his work brought him into intimate contact with Africans, as the cathedral was beginning to explore ways of embracing all communities in order to become a multiracial congregation. He now became involved in activities which in South Africa were construed as political. In church councils he spoke out against moves to suspend membership of the World Council of Churches (WCC) in protest against the fund to combat racism and WCC support for liberation movements in southern Africa, a campaign which infuriated white South Africa. He led a campaign against the continued house arrest of Helen Joseph, a member of the cathedral's congregation. He strongly criticized apartheid for the damage it caused to family life for Africans, and its criminalization of even the most law-abiding. It was in line with this concern that, when Defence and Aid (the organization for the support of political prisoners and their relatives) was banned in 1967, ffrench-Beytagh determined to continue its work. He set up a personal fund, using money given for this purpose by Alison Norman, a friend from his time in Rhodesia who was now living in Britain. He was careful to steer clear of any hint of association with the leaders of Defence and Aid, including Canon Collins in London, and with those who had worked locally for the organization, such as Winnie Mandela. But as far as the government was concerned ffrench-Beytagh's operation was merely a subterfuge for the continuing activities of Defence and Aid. The security machinery increasingly kept track of the dean's activities, using informers and *agents provocateurs*.

In 1970 ffrench-Beytagh was arrested and charged under the Terrorism Act of 1967. He was accused of incitement to overthrow the government, for example by urging members of Black Sash, the liberal women's organization, 'to support and prepare for a violent revolution'. He was also indicted for pursuing links with banned organizations such as the African National Congress and the South African Communist Party, for possessing their literature, and for using the money supplied by Alison Norman (who was named as a co-conspirator) to further the aims of those organizations to subvert the regime. His accusers included a member of his congregation, Ken Jordaan—in fact an undercover security officer who had himself incited ffrench-Beytagh to make incautious statements—and a putative member of Black Sash who was actually a government plant. The judge, finding him guilty on three counts, sentenced ffrench-Beytagh to the mandatory five years' imprisonment. This was overturned on appeal in 1972, and ffrench-Beytagh immediately left the country—a decision the wisdom of which he always doubted, and for which he felt a continuing sense of guilt.

Gonville ffrench-Beytagh became a curate at St Matthew's, Great Peter Street, Westminster, and in 1974 rector of a City of London church, St Vedast's. He became honorary canon of Canterbury Cathedral in 1973. His ministry of spiritual counselling and his frank writings and discussion on clinical depression, including *Facing Depression* (1978), were combined with an abiding concern for the dehumanizing effect of apartheid ('the blasphemy of apartheid', as he called it), and with a concern for prisoners of conscience. He retired in 1987, to live in an informal community organized by Alison Norman, who continued to give him practical and emotional support. His collection of meditations, *A Glimpse of Glory* (1986), with its extended commentary on George Herbert's poem 'Prayer', well illustrate the style and sources of his spirituality. He never married. He died at the London Hospital, Mile End, London, on 11 May 1991.   KEVIN WARD

Sources G. ffrench-Beytagh, *Encountering darkness* (1973) · G. ffrench-Beytagh, *A glimpse of glory* (1986) · G. ffrench-Beytagh, *Facing depression* (1978) · C. Michelman, *The Black Sash of South Africa* (1975) · *The Times* (15 May 1991) · *The Independent* (17 May 1991) · *The Independent* (20 May 1991) · *WWW*, 1991–5 · d. cert.

Archives LPL, Ramsey papers | SOUND BL NSA, Bow dialogues, 6 Nov 1973, C812/38 C4

Likenesses photograph, repro. in ffrench-Beytagh, *Encountering darkness* · photograph, repro. in *The Times* [*see illus.*] · photograph, repro. in *The Independent* (17 May 1991)

Wealth at death £135,358: probate, 8 Oct 1991, *CGPLA Eng. & Wales*

Bhabha, Homi Jehangir (1909–1966), theoretical physicist, was born on 30 October 1909 at Bombay in an established Parsi family, the eldest son of Jehangir Hormusji Bhabha (1876–1942) and his wife, Meheran Pandey (*d.* 1973). Bhabha's father was educated at Oxford and had studied law at Lincoln's Inn. For some years he was presidency magistrate in Bombay; later he joined Tata Sons and was associated with their scheme of hydroelectric power. Bhabha's mother came from the business family of Petit and was a granddaughter of Sir Dinshaw Maneckji Petit (1823–1901), the first Indian baronet and a philanthropist. Homi Bhabha's aunt Meherbai was married to Sir Dorab Tata. Bhabha had his early education in Bombay, first at John Cannon High School and then at Elphinstone College and the Royal Institute of Science, before studying engineering in 1927 at Gonville and Caius College, Cambridge, where Sir Dorab Tata had earlier spent two years and to which he had donated £25,000 in 1920. Cambridge at that time was bursting with excitement over the quantum theory of elementary particles and radiation. Bhabha wrote to his father asking his permission to switch to physics from engineering, which was agreed to, subject to his obtaining a first class in the mechanical tripos, which he did in June 1930. He received the degree of PhD from Cambridge in 1934.

Bhabha's main research at Cambridge concerned quantum electrodynamics. The process of electron–positron scattering, now called Bhabha scattering, was investigated by him in 1935 using Dirac's equation. This calculation provided evidence that negative energy electrons can indeed be identified with positrons. Bhabha and Heitler's cascade theory in 1937 explained the cosmic ray showers in terms of conversion of electron energy into quanta of radiation and their reconversion into secondary electron–positron pairs. Before their work it was suspected that quantum electrodynamics might fail to account for them. It was further known that the cosmic rays also had a penetrating component. Bhabha, in a brilliant phenomenological analysis of this component, suggested the existence of heavier electrons in 1937. These particles, muons, were discovered by Anderson and Neddermyer in 1938. Yukawa had proposed in 1935 that the nuclear force can be understood as arising through an exchange of heavy particles, now called mesons, between the nucleons. Bhabha was among the earliest workers on meson theory outside Yukawa's group in Japan. The word 'meson' was coined by Bhabha, Kemmer, and Pryce. Initially, the muons, postulated to explain the penetrating component of the cosmic rays, were thought to be the same particle as mesons. Bhabha worked on vector meson theory, with mesons obeying Proca's equation, in order to provide a better account of nuclear forces using both quantum perturbation theory and classical field theory. Bhabha was first to suggest that studying the variation of meson lifetime with velocity would provide a beautiful test of Einstein's time dilation formula.

Bhabha was on vacation in India in 1939 when war began in Europe. The war conditions made a return to England impossible. He therefore joined the special cosmic ray research unit, created for him by the Sir Dorabji Tata Trust, at the Indian Institute of Science at Bangalore in 1940. He was elected fellow of the Royal Society in 1941. At Bangalore he worked on classical relativistic spinning point particle theory (Bhabha–Corben equations). He also initiated balloon based cosmic ray experiments. During this period he began to feel more and more committed to India and decided to dedicate himself to bringing modern science and technology to the country. Bhabha wrote to J. R. D. Tata on 19 August 1943 regarding his ideas on building strong research groups in India. On being encouraged by him, he addressed, on 12 March 1944, to Sir Sorab Saklatvala, chairman of the Sir Dorabji Tata Trust, a formal letter containing a proposal to set up a new research institute which would be comparable to the best anywhere in the world. The proposed institute, named Tata Institute of Fundamental Research, was founded by the Sir Dorabji Tata Trust and the government of Bombay. It started functioning in June 1945 at Bangalore with Bhabha as its founder director. The institute soon shifted to Bombay and was formally inaugurated on 19 December 1945. At Bombay he worked on his theory of relativistic wave equations (Bhabha wave equation) for elementary particles. Bhabha had already visualized the possibility of the Tata Institute playing a role in the development of nuclear energy. In his original proposal he wrote, 'Moreover, when nuclear energy has been successfully applied for power production in say a couple of decades from now, India will not have to look abroad for its experts but will find them ready at hand' (Lala, 87–8). Bhabha's note to the prime minister, Jawaharlal Nehru, on the organization of atomic research in India, resulted in the setting up of the atomic energy commission of India in August 1948, with Bhabha as its chairman. An atomic energy establishment, later renamed the Bhabha Atomic Research Centre, was created at Trombay in January 1954, its initial trained manpower drawn from the Tata Institute. A separate department of atomic energy was created in August 1954 with Bhabha as secretary. Asia's first nuclear reactor, Apsara, became critical on 4 August 1956; nuclear grade uranium was produced in 1959; a plutonium plant was commissioned in January 1965. A power projects engineering division was created for the production of nuclear power, later known as the Nuclear Power Corporation of India. Bhabha presided with distinction over the international conference on developing peaceful uses of atomic energy organized by the United Nations and held in Geneva in 1955. Bhabha died in an air crash on Mont Blanc on 24 January 1966 on his way to a meeting of the scientific advisory committee of the International Atomic Energy Agency in Vienna.

Bhabha was a renaissance man, equally at home in the world of science and of arts. Like his hero Leonardo da Vinci he never married. A number of his paintings were collected in a volume entitled *Homi Bhabha as Artist* (1968); some are quite remarkable, for example his surrealist painting inspired by Mozart's aria 'Dove sono'. His many pencil sketches show a fine command of drawing. His deep interest in architecture and landscaping is reflected in the design and surroundings of the buildings of the Tata Institute of Fundamental Research and those of the Bhabha Atomic Research Centre at Trombay.

VIRENDRA SINGH

Sources H. J. Bhabha, *Collected scientific papers*, ed. B. V. Sreekantan, V. Singh, and B. M. Udgaonkar (1985) • R. M. Lala, *The heartbeat of a trust* (1984) • R. S. Anderson, *Building scientific institutions in India: Saha and Bhabha* (1975) • J. Cockcroft and M. G. K. Menon, *Homi Jehangir Bhabha, 1909–1966* (1967) • W. G. Penney, *Memoirs FRS*, 13 (1967), 35–55 • *Science Reporter* [Bhabha number] (Oct 1966) • *Physics Today* (March 1966), 108 • *Electrotechnics* [Bangalore] (Aug 1943) • J. J. Bhabha, ed., *Homi Bhabha as artist: a selection of his paintings, drawings and sketches* (1968) • private information (2004) • *Current Biography* (Sept 1956)
Likenesses B. Vittal, bronze bust, 1967, Tata Institute of Fundamental Research Collection, Bombay, India

Bhave, Vinoba (1895–1982), spiritual leader in India, was born Vinayak Narhari Bhave on 11 September 1895, the eldest of the five children (four brothers, one sister) of a Maharashtrian Brahman family in the village of Gagoda, Kolaba district, Bombay. His father, Narhari Shambhurao Bhave, an industrial chemist in the Buckingham mills, Baroda, and later a civil servant in the state, inculcated in Vinoba (as he became known) a commitment to science. By far the greater influences were his pious mother, Rukmini Devi, and his grandfather Shambhurao, an inandar and ayurvedic physician who ran his own village temple. Possibly his mother's dominant influence explains why all three surviving sons chose celibacy. In 1909 Vinoba joined his father in Baroda, where he received his education in Baroda School. He admired contemporary and historical examples of patriotism, such as western India's B. G. Tilak and the Italian Mazzini, and fell under the spell above all of the Maharashtrian saints, and of Shankara. In March 1916, abandoning his intermediate examination in Bombay, he chose to go to the holy Hindu city of Benares to study Sanskrit and philosophy. Gandhi's notorious speech at the laying of the foundation stone of Benares Hindu University profoundly influenced him, and in June 1916, aged twenty, he joined Gandhi in his ashram (community) in Ahmadabad, Gujarat.

Until Gandhi's assassination in January 1948 Vinoba worked out of the limelight with total dedication in the fields of social reconstruction and education. He opened a new ashram in Wardha, central India, in July 1921. Khadi, the hand-spun cloth which was one hallmark of Gandhi's politics, became his obsession.

In December 1932 Vinoba opened another ashram in the village of Nalwadi, 2 miles from Wardha, and gave more of his time to the plight of the 'untouchables' at the base of Hindu society, travelling widely through the villages of the locality. In 1938, to recover from ill health, he moved to an empty bungalow belonging to Jamnalal Bajaj, a wealthy supporter of Gandhi, in the village of Paunar, set on a mound above the River Dham in central India. This, the Paramdham ashram, was to remain his home until his death. Vinoba did not see Gandhi as his guru (spiritual guide) and insisted that one should pursue one's own ideals. But Gandhi, recognizing Vinoba's application of his ideals, saw him as a son. He selected him as the first to initiate individual non-violent opposition to the war; the resulting prison sentence troubled Vinoba little as he was disciplined by the austerity of ashram life. He came to be seen as Gandhi's spiritual heir as Nehru inherited the role of political leadership.

After Gandhi's assassination in 1948 Vinoba began the second phase of his life as the charismatic leader of a Gandhian inspired non-violent revolution, the Sarvodaya movement. In 1951 he found his vocation as the apostle of *bhoodan*, the free gift of land, an answer to landlessness and an alternative to violent socio-economic change. So began an extraordinary personal pilgrimage in which Vinoba walked the length and breadth of India, some 44,000 miles, returning to Paunar only in April 1964. In time the more individualist character of *bhoodan* gave way to the more socialist *gramdan*, the gifting of a whole village. But the gap between this ideal and reality was always huge; for example, the land gifted was often uncultivable. As the movement lost momentum in the 1960s, Vinoba was forced to compromise. He agreed to a *sulabh* (simplified) *gram*, whereby the landowner granted all his land to the village, but retained one-twentieth and never surrendered rights of inheritance. When almost the whole of the state of Bihar was seemingly incorporated in the movement by 1969, Vinoba announced his retirement. However, Bihar's subsequent history, and the plight of the lowest in society, cast doubt on the long-term efficacy of such non-violent and voluntary strategies for radical change.

Vinoba's Achilles heel was politics. He claimed to stand for a decentralized self-governing society, and, like Gandhi, affirmed that, with restraint, there would be no need for government. He claimed to reject the politics of power and stand for a partyless democracy, though significantly one based on consensus rather than majority rule. Yet he was always close to Nehru and came to look on his daughter, Indira Gandhi, as his own niece. Vinoba believed that structural change was almost incidental to a change in ethical outlook, to a transformation of values. But the rank and file of the post-Gandhian Sarvodaya movement for the welfare of all were driven by a genuine wish for structural change on behalf of the landless, and under the alternative leadership of J. P. Narayan were ready to engage in active confrontation with what they saw as a corrupt social and political system.

So began the third and least happy phase of Vinoba's career. Narayan, among others, challenged Indira Gandhi's dictatorial politics, and she responded with the imposition of an emergency regime in July 1975, which lasted for two years. Vinoba may have staved off a split in the Sarvodaya movement, but it was cosmetic. He screened the rift by undertaking a year-long vow of silence on 25 December 1975. When he did pronounce on the emergency, in writing in July, he did so in terms of its being an era of discipline, *anushasan parva*, seemingly sanctioning its repressiveness and earning himself the sobriquet 'the Saint of the Emergency'. His 'fast unto death' against cow slaughter in September 1976 can only disingenuously be seen as a challenge to Mrs Gandhi to return to democracy. She courted his support throughout, bribing him with promises of a nationwide celebration of the silver jubilee of the Sarvodaya movement and promising to step up distribution of land to the landless.

Vinoba can all too easily be portrayed as the cerebral Brahman, given his pedantry with words and his obsessive fascination with mathematics. His best-known writing was a commentary on the *Bhagavad gita*, first delivered in Dhulia gaol in 1932. The concept of desireless action, so prominent in this sacred text, underpinned his life's work. He feared for India's security, setting up the *shanti sena*, a kind of non-violent police force, as an answer to internal threats from communalism and external challenges from Pakistan and China. Himself a brilliant linguist, he championed the use of the Devanagari script, in which Hindi is written, for all the vernacular languages as a further means of strengthening Indian unity, despite the passionate concern for regional vernacular evident in India after independence. He saw himself as driven by compassion, by a politics of love, but there was in his life, as in that of Gandhi, that other 'saint' in Indian politics, a seemingly contradictory combination of self-punitive austerity and a genuine, almost maternal, search for the moral well-being of others.

On 9 November 1982 Vinoba had a heart attack. With characteristic physical detachment, he went on a fast and, in a manner appropriate for a modern saint, calmly prepared for death; this came at the Paramdham ashram on 15 November. He was cremated the following day on the banks of the River Dham, close to the Gandhi memorial. His ashes were placed in his *babakuti* (hut) at the ashram.

ANTONY R. H. COPLEY

Sources Kalindi, *Moved by love: the memoirs of Vinoba Bhave*, trans. M. Sykes (1994) · V. Tandon, *Acharya Vinoba Bhave* (1992) · S. Kumar, ed., *Vinoba Bhave: the intimate and the ultimate* (1986) · S. R. Bakshi, ed., *Struggle for independence* (1992) · G. Ostergaard, *The gentle anarchists* (1971) · G. Ostergaard, *Nonviolent revolution in India* (1985) · V. Bhave, *Talks on the Gita* (1960) [introd. by Jayaprakash Narayan] · S. Kumar, ed., *School of non-violence* (1960) · www.mkgandhi-sarvodaya.org/vinoba/vinoba.htm [Vinoba Bhave website], Nov 2001 · www.vinoba-non-violence.org [Vinoba Bhave website], Feb 2002 · *New York Times* (19 Nov 1982) · *The Times* (16 Nov 1982)

Bhopal, Hamidullah. *See* Khan, Sir (Muhammad) Hamidullah (1894–1960).

Bhownaggree, Sir Mancherjee Merwanjee (1851–1933), lawyer and politician, was born at Bombay on 15 August 1851, the son of Merwanjee N. Bhownaggree (d. c.1872), a Parsi merchant in Bombay of Persian origin, and his wife Cooverbai (d. 1896). Bhownaggree's father had risen from obscurity as a small-town postmaster to become head of

Sir Mancherjee Merwanjee Bhownaggree (1851–1933), by Sir Benjamin Stone, 1897

the Bombay state agency for the princely state of Bhaunagar, one of the 187 states of Kathiawar peninsula. Bhownaggree was educated at Elphinstone College, Bombay, and at Bombay University. His first choice of career was journalism, and he translated Queen Victoria's *Leaves from the Journal of our Life in the Highlands* into his native Gujarati. He married in 1872 a daughter of A. E. Chinoy; they had two sons, and a daughter who married a distinguished Bombay physician, Dr J. N. Bahadurjee.

Bhownaggree's father died in straitened circumstances, leaving no provision for his son, and in 1872 the Brahman ministers of Bhaunagar appointed Bhownaggree to succeed his father as agent, but at a modest salary. The Hindu ministers, who knew no English, made use of him to entertain European visitors and to cultivate the Anglo-Indian political officers. In 1882 he began to study law in England and acted as informal agent for the native chief or *thakur* of Bhaunagar, whom he advised to give money for the founding of the Northbrook Club (which earned the chief the Star of India), and to send a representative— namely himself—to the 1886 Indian and Colonial Exhibition, thus earning a CIE. In 1885 he was called to the bar at Lincoln's Inn, his studies being paid for by the *thakur*, whose generosity had made him rich, enabling him to live in style in London. In Bombay he founded the Avabai Bhownaggree Home for Nurses (1889) in memory of his only sister. He became judicial councillor for Bhaunagar, where he introduced English law reforms.

In 1892 the Congress leader, Dadabhai Naoroji, the first Indian to sit in the House of Commons and a fierce critic of British rule, paid a visit to India. His enthusiastic reception alarmed loyalist groups, and they resolved to put up their own MP. This was Bhownaggree, who was knighted (KCIE) in 1892 and was elected Conservative MP for Bethnal Green in 1895, the second Indian to sit in the house. Naoroji was defeated in the same election. At Bethnal Green, Bhownaggree defeated the working-man member George Howell, who deplored the fact that he was 'kicked out by a black man, a stranger from India, one not known in the constituency or in public life' (Leventhal, 212).

Assisted by a generous state pension from Bhaunagar (35,000 rupees, £2000) Bhownaggree settled in London at 196 Cromwell Road, leaving his wife in Bombay as the English climate made her ill. In parliament he followed the Anglo-Indian line. He supported Indian interests only on issues where all parties, nationalist and Anglo-Indian, were agreed, such as the removal of Indian grievances in South Africa. His claim to represent Indian opinion provoked resentment in India, and he was widely criticized in the national press. Critics claimed that as the creature of a 'native chief' he knew nothing of British India and was unknown outside his own princely state. An anonymous pamphlet published in 1897 entitled *The Indian Political Estimate of Mr Bhavnagri* [*sic*] purported to expose the Bhownaggree 'boom' by demonstrating his manipulation of the press to create a false impression of support. In 1897, when the Congress leader Gopal Krishna Gokhale made allegations at Westminster before the Indian parliamentary committee about the violation of Indian women by British soldiers in Poona, which he later withdrew, Bhownaggree denounced him in the house as a 'despicable perjurer' who had 'defiled the threshold of this building'. 'The words burnt into my heart', wrote Gokhale, and 'I made up my mind to devote my life … to the furtherance of our political cause in England' (Nanda, 129).

Bhownaggree lost his seat in the election of 1906, but he remained in London. Together with Naoroji, he was one of Britain's leading Indian residents, meeting Gandhi, for example, on his visit to London in 1906. He was chairman of the Parsee Association of Europe, the Northbrook Society, and the Indian Social Club. In 1916 he published a pamphlet, *Verdict of India*, refuting German allegations about British rule in India and proclaiming the unanimous loyalty of Indians to the imperial war effort. Bhownaggree died at his London house, 177 Cromwell Road, on 14 November 1933.   JANE RIDLEY

Sources *The Times* (15 Nov 1933) · *The Indian political estimate of Mr Bhavnagri, MP, or, The Bhavnagri boom exposed* (1897) · W. Hunter, *Bombay, 1885–1890: a study in Indian administration* (1892) · M. M. Bhownaggree, *The verdict of India* (1916) · B. R. Nanda, *Gokhale: the Indian moderates and the British raj* (1977) · A. Seal, *The emergence of Indian nationalism: competition and collaboration in the later nineteenth century* (1968); repr. (1971) · F. M. Leventhal, *Respectable radical: George Howell and Victorian working class politics* (1971) · DNB · CGPLA Eng. & Wales (1933)

Archives BL, Balfour MSS · Hatfield House, Hertfordshire, Salisbury MSS

Likenesses cartoon, 13 Dec 1896 (*Hindi Punch*), repro. in *Indian political estimate* · B. Stone, photograph, 1897, NPG [*see illus.*] · B. Stone, photographs, 1897–1902, Birmingham Reference Library · R. Beresford, portrait, 1927 · W. Stoneman, photograph, 1931, NPG · Spy [L. Ward], watercolour study, NPG; repro. in *VF* (18 Nov 1897)

Wealth at death £13,319 19s. 9d.: probate, 27 Dec 1933, *CGPLA Eng. & Wales*

Bhutto, Zulfikar Ali (1928–1979), president and later prime minister of Pakistan, was born on 5 January 1928 at Larkana, a medium-sized town on the Indus River in Sind, then part of British India. His father, Sir Shahnawaz Bhutto (1888–1957), was one of Sind's largest landlords, holding extensive property in the Larkana district. Although not a close political associate of Mohamed Ali Jinnah, Pakistan's founder, Sir Shahnawaz was a politician of considerable standing and sympathized with the Muslim League's demand that a separate country should be established for the Muslims of British India if the subcontinent became independent. Kurshid Bhutto, Zulfikar Ali's mother, was a Hindu of low social status who had converted to Islam and changed her name from Lakhi Bai before becoming Sir Shahnawaz's second wife. Social acceptance came slowly and grudgingly to her, a fact that troubled her son during his childhood and adolescence, and may have helped to mould his personality as well as his political views. As the only surviving son, Zulfikar Ali inherited most of the Larkana estate on his father's death in 1957. He also married twice: first at the age of twelve, to his cousin Sheerin Bhutto, who took the name Amir Begam. She was considerably his senior, and the marriage was one of convenience for the transfer of property. His second wife, whom he married on 8 September 1951, was Begam Nusrat, *née* Nusrat Ispahani (b. 1929), a woman of Iranian origin whom he met in Karachi. He and Nusrat had four children; three of them, Benazir (b. 1953), Mir Murtaza (b. 1954), and Shahnawaz (b. 1958), were to play an active role in Pakistan's politics.

Education and early political career Zulfikar Ali Bhutto (Zulfi to friends and family) was sent to Bombay for schooling, and then to the University of Southern California, the University of California, Berkeley, and Christ Church, Oxford, to study law. He returned to Karachi in 1953 and started legal practice at the Sind high court. Still virtually unknown, he was included in President Mirza's twelve-man cabinet following the coup of 7 October 1958. General Ayub Khan retained Bhutto as commerce minister when Mirza was shunted into exile in London less than three weeks later. But Bhutto's sights were set considerably higher. Immediately on joining the Ayub cabinet he began to prepare himself for the ministry of foreign affairs. However, it was while managing the petroleum portfolio that he began to reach out to the socialist world. He was convinced that Pakistan had large but undiscovered sources of oil and gas which the Western oil companies, holders of large 'exploration concessions', were

Zulfikar Ali Bhutto (1928–1979), by unknown photographer, 1965

not interested in exploiting. Accordingly, in 1961 he negotiated an oil exploration agreement with the Soviet Union which included Soviet provision of technical and financial assistance to Pakistan's Oil and Gas Development Corporation (OGDC). This was the first of several occasions when Ayub Khan, against his better judgement, succumbed to his young protégé's powers of persuasion. The OGDC did not produce any spectacular results, but that did not matter to Bhutto: the agreement with the Soviet Union had demonstrated that, even at a very young age, he had influence over President Ayub Khan that far exceeded that of the general's older colleagues.

Foreign minister Bhutto's big opportunity came in 1963, with the sudden death of the foreign minister, Muhammad Ali Bogra. He persuaded Ayub Khan to reassign him to the foreign ministry, which was done with reluctance by the president. Once put in charge of Pakistan's external affairs, he began to reshape the country's foreign policy, moving away from the explicitly pro-Western orientation of Ayub Khan and M. A. Bogra towards a more neutral posture. Despite the openly expressed unhappiness of Lyndon B. Johnson's administration in the United States, Bhutto developed close ties with China. Pakistan and China negotiated a border agreement, established commercial airline operations between the two countries, and increased the flow of trade between them. The initial talks on a boundary agreement took place in October 1962, precisely when Chinese troops, attacking across India's disputed north-eastern border with China, routed their Indian opponents before voluntarily withdrawing two months later. China agreed to establish large military-industrial complexes near the city of Wah, which already supported a large arms and ammunition industry.

Under Bhutto's restless direction of foreign policy, Pakistan entered what were, for the country, the uncharted waters of non-alignment. In *The Myth of Independence*, a book published in 1969 after he left the Ayub Khan government, Bhutto provided the reasons for the change in course he had engineered while still in office. The book was a rejoinder to Ayub Khan's political biography *Friends not Masters* (1967). According to Bhutto, a relationship between Pakistan and a country of the size and influence of the United States could not be on the basis of equality: any attempt to make such friends would consign the small countries of the 'third-world' to subordination. The only way out for these nations was to work in unison and pursue their collective self-interest. It is ironic that it was against this theoretical backdrop that Bhutto persuaded Ayub Khan to launch operation Gibraltar, an ill-advised and poorly conceived armed penetration by the personnel of Pakistan's armed forces into the Indian state of Kashmir.

Kashmir, a princely state nestling in the mountains of the Himalayas, was sandwiched between Pakistan's eastern and China's western borders. India bordered it to the south. In 1947 the Hindu maharaja of the state, which had a vast Muslim majority in the population, decided to opt for India under partition. Pakistan refused to accept the state's accession to India, and fought a war with India over the issue in 1948. United Nations intervention produced a ceasefire and a possible referendum (to be supervised by the UN) of the Kashmiris over their membership of India or Pakistan was promised. But the referendum was not held, and Bhutto took advantage of Pakistani restiveness to incite Ayub Khan to provoke a war of liberation against the Indian occupation of the state. Operation Gibraltar sought to infiltrate Pakistani-trained and armed guerrillas into the parts of Kashmir under Indian occupation. This operation began in August 1965, and quickly escalated into a full-scale war between India and Pakistan. On 6 September India launched a massive air, armour, and infantry attack on the city of Lahore, and Pakistan responded in kind at several points along the long border between the two countries.

Bhutto's motives for this action remain unclear; if his wish was to weaken Ayub Khan, the operation against India achieved some success. But it took Bhutto half a dozen years to realize the full political benefits of Ayub Khan's failed Kashmir adventure. Ayub Khan quickly recognized the folly of his actions. On 23 September, barely seventeen days after the war had begun, he announced a ceasefire agreement with India, which he negotiated with the help of the United Nations. Four months later, along with Prime Minister Lal Bahadur Shastri of India, Ayub went to the Soviet city of Tashkent and negotiated what he believed would be a more durable peace agreement between the two countries. Bhutto accompanied him to Tashkent, but appears not to have endorsed the substance

of the agreement. A few months after their return to Pakistan, Ayub and Bhutto finally parted company, Ayub making much in public debate of Bhutto's opposition to the Tashkent declaration. The people of Pakistan listened with interest. Here was an issue that exposed the Ayub regime at its most vulnerable point: its inability to use what was widely believed to be the country's military superiority over India to settle once and for all the dispute over Kashmir. Ayub Khan, therefore, not only guaranteed Bhutto's national political career by appointing him to his martial-law cabinet in 1958; he also provided Bhutto with an exceptionally potent political issue to pursue after expelling him from the cabinet in 1966.

The Pakistan People's Party In 1967, a year after leaving the government, and after weighing the offers from several opposition parties, Bhutto decided to form his own political organization, the Pakistan People's Party (PPP). In doing so, he was not being particularly innovative. He was following what had become an established tradition in the politics of opposition in Pakistan: to form a party of one's own rather than play second fiddle in someone else's political organization. The PPP's foundation papers reflected Bhutto's genius for timing. The party's programme represented an amalgam of intense nationalism (born out of Bhutto's campaign against the Tashkent declaration), socialism (reflecting the belief of several of his new political associates that the people were smarting under the unequal distribution of incomes caused by a sharp increase in national income during the Ayub period), and Islamic revival (representing Bhutto's view that the secularism of the Ayub period had not been popular with the majority of the population). The PPP initially drew its support from students, lawyers, and trade unionists, and its populist programme proved to be a heady electoral brew. The PPP won eighty-one of the 138 seats allocated to West Pakistan under Yahya Khan's legal framework order of 30 March 1970 (which had abandoned the principle of parity of seats between East and West Pakistan in the national assembly). The PPP was by far the largest political group representing West Pakistan in the national legislature. This set the stage for Bhutto's return to power, but before that happened Pakistan went through the wrenching experience of a civil war.

Only time and access to more sources will explain Bhutto's intransigence following the electoral victory of 1970. He refused to participate in the discussions that should have begun in the national assembly immediately after the elections to frame another constitution. He may have intended to provoke East Pakistan and force it out of the Pakistani union; he may have feared that any compromise on Pakistan's unity would endanger his position in the western wing. The fact remains that the position taken by Bhutto led to a confrontation between the military and the political leadership of East Pakistan. The civil war lasted for nine months. It ended with the surrender in Dacca of the Pakistani troops to the Indian forces and the Bengali guerrilla force the Mukhti Bahini, which had been forged after the brutal military crackdown in West Pakistan of March 1971. Defeat led in December 1971 to the resignation of President Yahya Khan and the appointment of Zulfikar Ali Bhutto.

Bhutto as president In so far as the conduct of domestic economic policies is concerned, the Bhutto era (December 1971 to July 1977) can be divided into two periods, before and after 1974. In the first, the Bhutto government pursued a socialist programme, capturing for the government all the commanding heights of the economy. Thirty-one large-scale industries, private banks, and insurance companies were nationalized in the early part of 1972, and a number of state enterprises were established to look after these sectors of the economy. External trade in rice and cotton, Pakistan's two principal export earners, was also brought under government control, as were all private colleges and schools. This programme was carried out by Dr Mubashir Hasan, Bhutto's finance minister, and J. A. Rahim, a close Bhutto associate from the time Bhutto had served as Ayub Khan's foreign minister. Both Mubashir Hasan and Rahim were avowed Marxists. However, they left the government in 1974, and Bhutto took command of the economy. The result was a total loss of orientation and a whimsical decision making that caused Pakistan to live quite beyond its internal and external means.

In foreign affairs Bhutto proved to be a much more imaginative and flexible manager. He negotiated the Simla agreement with Indira Gandhi in 1972, hosted the second meeting of the Organization of Islamic States at Lahore in 1974, recognized Bangladesh as an independent state also in 1974, and made some tangible advances in healing Pakistan's relations with Afghanistan. In keeping with the approach he had advocated during Ayub Khan's government, he realigned Pakistan's foreign relations away from a close dependence on the United States.

The record on domestic political management was mixed. Having been sworn in in December 1971 not only as president but also as chief martial-law administrator (despite being a civilian), Bhutto decided to keep operating under the protection of the military. In March 1972 he consolidated his control over the military by putting the army and air force under the charge of officers he trusted. At the same time he used his authority as the chief martial law administrator to introduce an interim constitution for Pakistan. The interim constitution gave him enormous authority. After allowing the formation of non-PPP governments in the smaller provinces of the North-Western Frontier and Baluchistan, he dismissed both a few months later on a charge of their alleged involvement with Afghanistan, which was accused of fomenting rebellion. The National Awami Party (NAP), the main party of the opposition and one of the two that had formed the government in Baluchistan and the North-Western Frontier Province, was banned. These were all surprising moves on the part of a politician who had campaigned so vigorously to restore democracy in the country.

In 1973 Bhutto, with his political skills once again on display, persuaded and cajoled the opposition into accepting a new constitutional arrangement for Pakistan. The constitution was passed by the national assembly and became effective on 14 August 1973, which was Pakistan's twenty-sixth anniversary. Bhutto stepped down from the presidency and became prime minister. Pakistan seemed finally to be set on a democratic course. However, Bhutto kept up an unrelenting pressure on the opposition—using all the state apparatus at his disposal, including the federal security force, to browbeat the opposition into submission even on its minor differences with the government. He seemed to be working towards the establishment of a one-party state in Pakistan. When in January 1977 he suddenly called national elections—the first to be held under the new constitution—he expected to catch the opposition unprepared. The opposition surprised him by preparing itself quickly: the Pakistan National Alliance (PNA) was born and a disparate set of parties agreed to compete with the PPP under a single political umbrella. In the days leading up to the elections the PNA began to draw large crowds to its rallies and these may have pushed Bhutto to summon help from the bureaucracy to ensure a respectable victory for the PPP. The elections were held on 7 March, and when the results were announced the opposition was very surprised by the massive and unexpected victory recorded by the PPP. The PNA responded with the only tactic the opposition in Pakistan had ever been able to use with some success against established governments: it called out its supporters in mass protests against what it saw as the 'great electoral fraud'.

Deposition and execution Skirmishes between the followers of the PNA and government security forces turned exceptionally bloody in May and June. Bhutto called in the army to restore law and order in the major cities, which it did, but it exacted a price by proclaiming Pakistan's third martial-law regime. Bhutto was deposed by the military. In the conflict that followed between him and his party on the one hand and General Zia ul Haq and the military on the other, Bhutto was the eventual loser. A series of court cases were brought against him, including one for the murder of a political opponent. He was sentenced to death by the Lahore high court in March 1978, and his appeal was rejected by the supreme court in February 1979 in a split decision. Two months later, on 4 April 1979, Zulfikar Ali Bhutto was hanged in Rawalpindi's central gaol, and his body was flown in an army aeroplane for burial in the family graveyard at Larkana. Thus ended a remarkable political career; but his death did not end for a while what came to be known as 'Bhuttoism' or the 'Bhutto factor' in Pakistani politics. General Zia ul Haq died in a plane crash in 1988, which once again opened up the country's political system, and Ghulam Ishaq Khan, a long-serving bureaucrat-turned-politician, became acting president. He went on to hold general elections in November 1988. The electoral triumph on that occasion of the PPP—under the combined leadership of Bhutto's widow, Begam Nusrat, and his eldest child, Benazir Bhutto—showed that Bhuttoism survived its founder. Benazir Bhutto became prime minister for the first time on 2 December 1988.

Zulfikar Ali Bhutto remained a highly contentious figure long after his death. Admirers pointed to his populist concern for the poor and his foreign policy successes. Detractors emphasized his authoritarianism, his economic failure, and his responsibility for the division of Pakistan. Within the PPP there was division between the left and those who accepted that the domestic and international constraints of the 1990s dictated the more pragmatic policies espoused during Benazir Bhutto's two governments. Even within the Bhutto family Zulfikar Ali Bhutto's mantle was contested between Benazir and her younger brother Mir Murtaza, who died in a police encounter in Karachi in November 1996.

SHAHID JAVED BURKI

Sources S. J. Burki, *Pakistan under Bhutto, 1971–1977* (1988) · B. Bhutto, *Daughter of the east: an autobiography* (1988) · S. Wolpert, *Zulfi Bhutto of Pakistan: his life and times* (1993) · Burke, *Peerage* (1939) **Archives** FILM BFI NFTVA, documentary footage **Likenesses** photographs, 1964–79, Hult. Arch. [*see illus.*]

Bianchi, Jane (1776–1858). *See under* Lacy, William (1788–1871).

Bianconi, Charles [*formerly* Joachim Carlo Giuseppe Bianconi] (1786–1875), transport entrepreneur, was born Joachim Carlo Giuseppe Bianconi on 24 September 1786 at the village of Tregolo in Lombardy, not far from Como. He came from a landowning family, and was the second of five children of Pietro and Maria Bianconi. His father farmed his own property, owned a silk mill, and acted as agent for a large estate.

Educated privately in his grandmother's house, and then at Abbé Radicale's School, Asso, Lombardy, Bianconi was intended for the priesthood; but at the age of nearly sixteen he was dispatched to the United Kingdom with a group of compatriots, to break up an imprudent love affair. The group settled in Dublin, and he was sent out to sell cheap prints. When his eighteen months' apprenticeship was completed, he resolved to start on his own account as an itinerant vendor of prints with a capital of about £100 which his father had given him on leaving Italy. In 1806 he opened a shop as carver and gilder at Carrick-on-Suir. After moving to Waterford he finally settled at Clonmel, where he added to his existing business dealings in bullion, which was in great demand by the government for the payment of its continental subsidies. Every extension of business deepened his sense of the need for better communications. In July 1815 he started to carry passengers, goods, and mail, in a one-horse two-wheeled car between Clonmel and Cahir, a distance of 10 miles with no public conveyance.

Initially Bianconi had few customers, but when he ran a competing service with a car not known to be his, the excitement of competition soon attracted traffic. The experiment succeeded financially. Bianconi, an astute businessman, was able to seize the opportunities provided by the new carriage tax (which led many people to sell their jaunting-cars) and the ending of the Napoleonic Wars (which made good horses available cheaply), and he steadily expanded his services. By 1832 he was conveying passengers and goods over 1633 miles of road, and in 1833 he secured a major mail contract through personal contact with the postmaster-general, the duke of Richmond. In 1843 he was invited to deliver a paper on his coaching establishment to the meeting in Cork of the British Association for the Advancement of Science, an invitation repeated for the Dublin meeting in 1857.

Bianconi's carrying service was a boost to commercial life. He stated in 1856 that after the more remote parts of Ireland had been opened up by his cars, calico, which had previously cost 8*d.* or 9*d.* a yard, was sold for 3*d.* and 4*d.* As an employer he was strict, but kindly and just. Merit always insured promotion, and pensions were liberally given. He boasted late in his career that no injury had been done to his property, and that none of his cars had been stopped, even when conveying mails through disturbed districts. However, some cars were attacked during the Waterford by-election of 1826.

In 1826 Bianconi gave up his shop in Clonmel, and on 14 February 1827 he married Elizabeth (Eliza) Hayes, daughter of a neighbour, whom he had known since she was a child. In 1831 he became naturalized as a British subject. A zealous Roman Catholic and an ardent Liberal, he was a friend and adherent of Daniel O'Connell; he also had many contacts in government circles. He took an active part in the civic affairs of Clonmel, and was twice elected mayor, in 1844 and in 1845. The establishment of railways in Ireland had then begun, and Bianconi refused invitations to oppose any of them, taking shares in some of the companies. Between 1846 and 1865 their growth forced him to discontinue some services, but he was able to introduce new ones as feeders to the railways.

In 1846 Bianconi purchased the estate of Longfield, in co. Tipperary, near Cashel, where he lived until his death; and most of the fortune which he had amassed during his lifetime was invested in the purchase of Irish land. In 1854 he played an important part in the founding of the Catholic University, Dublin. In 1863 he was appointed deputy lieutenant of the county of Tipperary, and in 1865 he began to withdraw from the business which he had created, disposing of it on liberal terms to his agents and others employed in working it. The remainder of his life he passed in improving his estates and promoting patriotic schemes.

Bianconi died from a stroke on 22 September 1875 at Longfield House, and was buried in the mortuary chapel he had built there. He was survived by his wife, but by only one of his three children. Bianconi played an important role in the transport history of Ireland, and, as his friend Anthony Trollope had commented in 1857, 'perhaps … no living man has worked more than he has for the benefit of the sister Kingdom' (Hall, 95).

FRANCIS ESPINASSE, *rev.* PETER BUTTERFIELD

Sources M. O'C. Bianconi and S. J. Watson, *Bianconi, king of the Irish roads* (1962) · T. P. O'Neill, 'Bianconi and his cars', *Travel and transport in Ireland*, ed. K. B. Nowlan (1973), 82–96 · M. J. O'Connell, *Charles Bianconi, a biography* (1878) · V. Glendinning, *Trollope* (1992) · N. John Hall, *Trollope* (1991) · C. Maxwell, *The stranger in Ireland* (1954) **Archives** priv. coll.

Likenesses J. P. Haverty, group portrait, watercolour lithograph, pubd 1845 (after his portrait, *The Monster meeting of the 20th September 1843, at Clifden in the Irish Highlands*, exh. 1854), NG Ire. • photograph • portraits, probably Longfield House, co. Tipperary, Ireland

Bibbesworth, Walter of (*b.* in or before **1219**, *d.* in or after **1270**), Anglo-Norman poet, was an Essex knight associated with the manor of Bibbesworth in Hertfordshire, who later possessed three manors in Essex—Saling, Latton, and Waltham. It is in Little Dunmow, 6 miles from the last, that he is thought to have been buried (possibly at the end of the 1270s). He was born not later than 1219 and his name occurs in the patent and close rolls and other records, though references towards the end of the century are probably to his son of the same name.

Walter wrote poetry and a celebrated guide to learning French for the purposes of estate management. The guide, known as *Tretiz*, consists of approximately 1134 rhyming octosyllables and survives in sixteen manuscripts, six of which bear a dedicatory epistle to Dionysia, or Denise, de Munchensi (*d.* 1304), second wife (from 1235) and, after 1255, widow, of Warin de Munchensi, scion of one of the wealthiest families of the time. The guide was probably composed in the period 1240–50 and was designed for the sons of noblemen, particularly, it is thought, Denise's own son William (*b.* 1235) and the two children, John and Joan, of the first marriage of her husband Warin. The French vocabulary denoting the practices of rural life is equipped in many of the manuscripts with English glosses, the bulk of which stem from the author. There is such variety in the transmitted texts, however, that a strictly critical edition of the *Tretiz* seems scarcely possible. The *Tretiz* remains the first teaching vocabulary, or *nominale*, in French and was reworked and extended by the incorporation of other treatises, probably *c.*1415, in Cambridge, Trinity College, MS B.14.40 where it is given the title *Femina nova* (Bibbesworth's treatise being understood as *Femina* or *Femme*).

Bibbesworth also wrote a poetic exercise in grammatical rhymes which appears in BL, Add. MS 46919, fols. 92*r*–93*r* (the following poem, which begins 'De bone femme la bounté', folios 93*r*–95*v*, is now usually attributed to Nicholas Bozon) as 'Les dytees moun Syre Gauter de Bybeswurthe' (a good text of the *Tretiz* is found on folios 2ra–14vb). A further work is a debate poem or *tençon* of six stanzas of twelve lines, a dialogue with Henry de Lacy, earl of Lincoln (1249–1312), which refers to the crusade of 1270, in which Bibbesworth participated and during which Henry, having taken the cross, was reluctant to leave on account of a lady whom he loved (Bodl. Oxf., MS Fairfax 24, fols. 19*r*–20*v*, 'Ceo est la pleinte par entre mis sire Henry de Lacy, counte de Nychole, et sire Wauter de Bybelesworth pur la croiserie en la Terre Seinte').   TONY HUNT

Sources A. C. Baugh, 'The date of Walter of Bibbesworth's *Traité*', *Festschrift für Walther Fischer* (1959), 21–33 • W. Rothwell, 'A misjudged author and a mis-used text: Walter de Bibbesworth and his *Tretiz*', *Modern Language Review*, 77 (1982), 282–93 • A. Owen, *Le traité de Walter de Bibbesworth sur la langue française* (1929); repr. (1977) • Peter of Langtoft, *Le règne d'Édouard I*ᵉʳ, ed. J. C. Thiolier (Créteil, 1989), 69–75

Archives BL, Add. MS 46919, fols. 92*r*–93*r* • Bodl. Oxf., MS Fairfax 24, fols. 19*r*–20*v*

Bibby, Joseph (1851–1940), animal feed and soap manufacturer, was born on 12 January 1851 at Conder Mill, Vale of Conder, Lancashire, the second of the three sons of James Bibby, farmer and miller, and his wife, Amelia Barnett. He attended an elementary school until 1861 and the Abbeystead School, Over Wyresdale, until 1865; he then joined his father in the milling business. An avid reader, he studied privately in his spare time.

Bibby was at first employed in a newly acquired warehouse in Lancaster, distributing the produce of the family mill, but he hankered after less restrictive employment. Soon after his twenty-first birthday, in 1872, he travelled steerage to Canada. Then, after six months in the United States, he was encouraged to return home by his father, who promised him and his younger brother James greater responsibility in the running of the firm.

Having seen at first hand the dramatic increases taking place in North American grain production, which would inevitably affect the livelihoods of millers in Britain, Bibby planned to diversify into the production of animal feeds. In 1878 he and his brother James were made partners in what became J. Bibby & Sons, when their father went into semi-retirement from the business. This allowed Bibby to begin research into improving the specifications of cattle feed. Hitherto, most farmers had used whatever fodder the merchants had on offer, sometimes to the detriment of their livestock. Bibby therefore experimented, on a small farm, with the development of specially blended (or compound) feeds for different requirements, such as rapid fattening, higher milk yields, or calf rearing. In 1881 he married Ruth Pye (1858–1946), two of whose sisters successively married his brother James. Joseph and Ruth had six sons (one of whom died in infancy) and two daughters.

As demand for feedstuffs grew, in 1882 Bibby felt able to replace the Lancaster warehouse by a five-storey steam mill, with a milling capacity of 60 tons a week. This was burnt down in 1885, the year the brothers decided to transfer milling to Liverpool, the major port for the transatlantic grain trade. There, they leased two upper floors of a warehouse very close to the docks; they also installed Anglo-American hydraulic presses for crushing seeds and extracting the oil. After rapid growth in 1886–8, they transferred the firm's head office to Liverpool and closed the Lancaster operations.

James Bibby used his organizational skills and sound judgement to the full on the production side, with a cousin acting as manager. In 1892 the mill at Liverpool was also badly damaged by fire and immediately rebuilt on an ampler scale. That year the firm planned to make soap with its stocks of oil, Bibby's Pure Soap appearing in 1896. Meanwhile, the energetic and publicity-minded Joseph Bibby managed the marketing side. He set up a team of direct representatives, who gradually replaced the earlier non-exclusive mercantile agents.

Joseph Bibby often said that, if the accident of birth had not made him a miller, he would certainly have gone into journalism; as the opportunity arose, he spent more and more time on writing and editorship. From 1886 onwards, he produced several one-off magazines, and in 1896 he launched *Bibby's Quarterly*. Intended mainly for farmers, it contained material of agricultural interest (including photographs of livestock reared on Bibby's feeds), as well as general articles. Of good technical quality, from 1904 to 1905 (when it closed) it was printed by a subsidiary plant of the firm. By then it had become an almost exclusively literary and artistic magazine, with excellent colour reproductions of celebrated paintings. Agricultural matters were covered in *Bibby's Farm and Dairy Notes*, published quarterly between 1905 and 1928. From 1906 to 1922 Joseph Bibby also produced *Bibby's Annual*.

Although brought up in a devout Methodist family, in 1889 Joseph Bibby joined the Theosophical Society. A number of articles by Annie Besant, and by other theosophists, subsequently appeared in his publications. A lifelong teetotaller, as a member of the Theosophical Society he now became a vegetarian. Although he continued to attend Methodist services regularly, his mixture of beliefs embarrassed some fellow worshippers.

By 1900 J. Bibby & Sons was claiming to have the largest feeding-cake mill in the world. Despite intense competition from rivals, it succeeded in doubling the output of animal feeds from about 100,000 tons in 1902 to 200,000 tons in 1914. With assets valued at about £1 million and a workforce of 3000, it had reached a size where it needed to become a limited company. In August 1914 J. Bibby & Sons Ltd was registered, with issued capital of £500,000. James Bibby was elected chairman, while Joseph, at the age of sixty-three, became vice-chairman. During the 1920s the company introduced a number of measures designed to improve the working conditions of staff: these included non-contributory pensions, subsidized canteens, workers' councils, and a recreation centre. Three sons of Joseph and three sons of James became directors, and this allowed their fathers to pursue other interests.

Joseph Bibby served as a Liberal member of Liverpool city council between 1904 and 1911, and was also a JP. He continued to write on social questions, and his books on *Social Progress* (1926) and *Capitalism, Socialism and Unemployment* (1929) were published by the firm. On James's death in 1928, Joseph succeeded him as chairman, but concerned himself little with running the business. He died at his home, The Priory, Upton Road, Bidston, Birkenhead, Cheshire, on 11 March 1940. He was survived by his wife.

T. A. B. CORLEY

Sources J. B. Bibby and C. L. Bibby, *A miller's tale: a history of J. Bibby & Sons Ltd* (1978) · J. B. Bibby and C. L. Bibby, 'Bibby, Joseph', *DBB* · *WWW*, 1929–40 · *Chambers's encyclopaedia*, new edn, 1 (1959) · *The Times* (13 March 1940) · d. cert.
Archives J. Bibby & Sons Ltd, Liverpool, unpublished records
Likenesses J. Bacon & Sons, photograph, repro. in Bibby and Bibby, *Miller's tale* · photograph, repro. in Bibby and Bibby, 'Bibby, Joseph'
Wealth at death £289,474 12s. 1d.: probate, 19 April 1940, *CGPLA Eng. & Wales*

Bibby, Thomas (1799–1863), poet, born at Kilkenny, was educated first at the local grammar school, and then at Trinity College, Dublin, where he obtained a scholarship. At the age of thirteen, Bibby won the gold medal for science, and he subsequently became one of the best Greek students of his day. He graduated in 1816, and went on to lead a studious but secluded life in his native Kilkenny, developing eccentricities which suggested to many that he was insane. One source even claims that he was confined by his relations in a private lunatic asylum in Dublin, and later released by his literary friends (Boase, *Mod. Eng. biog.*). Bibby published two dramatic poems in blank verse, *Gerald of Kildare* (1854), and its sequel, *Silken Thomas, or, Saint Mary's Abbey*; (1859). Although some of the ideas expressed in these works were felt to be erratic, his writings were nevertheless admired for their pathos, spirit, varied allusions, and delicate feeling, particularly in the address to his son, which served as the preface to the latter work.

Following a painful illness, Bibby died, aged sixty-four, on 7 January 1863, at his home at St Canice's Steps, Kilkenny. His brother Samuel Hale Bibby, a surgeon in Green Street, Grosvenor Square, London, shared his literary taste, but was considered to be more conventional. Bibby's writing remained popular for a while after his death, but he is now generally forgotten.

JAMES MEW, *rev.* JASON EDWARDS

Sources *Kilkenny Moderator* (10 Jan 1863) · *Kilkenny Moderator* (14 Jan 1863) · *GM*, 3rd ser., 14 (1863), 248 · R. Hogan and others, eds., *The Macmillan dictionary of Irish literature* (1980), 149–50 · Boase, *Mod. Eng. biog.*
Wealth at death under £200: administration, 31 Jan 1863, *CGPLA Ire.*

Bibelesworth, Walter de. *See* Bibbesworth, Walter of (*b.* in or before 1219, *d.* in or after 1270).

Biber, George Edward (1801–1874), writer, was born on 4 September 1801, at Ludwigsburg, Württemberg. After studying at the lyceum there, where his father was professor, he entered the University of Tübingen, and proceeded PhD, afterwards graduating LLD from Göttingen. His participation in the movement for German unity made it prudent for him to leave Württemberg, first for Italy and then for the Grisons, from where he went to Yverdun, becoming a master in a Pestalozzi institution there. He later published *Beitrag zur Biographie Heinrich Pestalozzi's* (1827) and *Henry Pestalozzi and his Plan of Education* (1831).

In 1826 Biber accepted the offer of a tutorship in England, and in 1830 he published *The Christian Minister and Family Friend* and *Christian Education*, the substance of lectures delivered in 1828 and 1829. Biber became the head of a flourishing classical school at Hampstead, and afterwards at Coombe Wood. On his arrival in England, Biber had 'no settled religious convictions', but decided to join the Church of England. Naturalized by act of parliament he was ordained to the curacy of Ham in July 1839, and the next year published *The Standard of Catholicity* (1840). In 1842 he published his *Catholicity v. Sibthorp* (a second edition of 1844 was entitled *The catholicity of the Anglican church vindicated, and the alleged catholicity of the Roman church disproved*).

In 1842 Biber was appointed to the new vicarage of Holy

Trinity, Roehampton, and worked there for thirty years. He took part in the establishment of the National Club in 1845, of the Metropolitan Church Union in 1849, and in 1850 of the Society for the Revival of Convocation. He was elected a member of the council of the English Church Union in 1863, and in this capacity was active in the case against J. W. *Colenso. However, he resigned from the union in June 1864, hostile to what he saw as medievalist and rationalist sympathies among the councillors. He strongly opposed the disestablishment of the Irish church in 1869 and sympathized with the Old Catholic movement of Germany, with one of the leaders of which, Dr Michaelis, he carried on a Latin correspondence. This was published in Latin, and appeared in English as *On the Unity of the Church* (1871). Biber attended the Old Catholic congress at Cologne in 1872. He was a principal writer in the *English Review*, which took the place of the *British Critic* in 1840. He wrote for the *Churchman's Magazine* in 1856–7 and for the *Literary Churchman* in 1859–62. He was also editor of *John Bull* in 1848–56. Early in 1872 Biber was presented by Lord Chancellor Hatherley to the rectory of West Allington, near Grantham. There Biber died, probably unmarried, on 19 January 1874.

Biber was an indefatigable pamphleteer, with over sixty works to his name. He moved on the edge of the Tractarian movement, but not uncritically. Notable among his publications are *The Seven Voices of the Spirit* (1857); *Royalty of Christ and the Church and Kingdom of England* (1857); *The Supremacy Question, or, Justice to the Church of England* (1847) which was expanded into *The Royal Supremacy over the Church, Considered as to its Origin and its Constitutional Limits* (1848); and *The Veracity and Divine Authority of the Pentateuch Vindicated* (1863).

ARTHUR H. GRANT, *rev.* H. C. G. MATTHEW

Sources *John Bull* (24 Jan 1874) · *Grantham Journal* (24 Jan 1874) · *English Churchman and Clerical Journal* (22 Jan 1874) · *English Churchman and Clerical Journal* (24 Jan 1874) · Crockford (1874) [incl. bibliography] · probate (1874)
Wealth at death under £1500: resworn probate, Jan 1875, *CGPLA Eng. & Wales* (1874)

Bicarton, Thomas (*fl.* **1570–1590**), author and teacher of rhetoric, was probably born in St Andrews, where his father, John Bicarton, a saddler, was an early adherent of the protestant congregation—but an unruly member. In 1559 John had become trustee for the property of the expelled Dominican community. Five years later, by refusing to present one of Thomas's siblings for baptism, he precipitated a conflict with the ministers resulting eventually in his excommunication. The social and economic effects of this finally compelled his submission, not long before his death in 1568. The family was connected with the Bicartons of Cash in north-west Fife: Thomas regularly described himself as 'a Caschaea' as well as 'Andreapolitanus'. As an orphan, however, he became the ward of Patrick Auchinleck, the St Andrews schoolmaster whose pupil he was and whose 'pious memory' he later celebrated in affectionate terms. In 1570–71—

perhaps aged only ten, though the evidence is inconclusive—he matriculated at St Andrews (St Leonard's College), taking his BA in 1573–4 and his MA in 1575–6. A later dedication shows that Bicarton valued particularly the philosophical teaching of his college regent, Robert Wilkie.

Bicarton evidently remained in St Andrews until at least the summer of 1578. It was a time of troubles for the university. Nothing is known of his attitude to the religious and political conflicts of the 1570s; but it is probably significant that he dedicated one of his poems to John Hamilton, a vigorous anti-protestant polemicist after his departure from St Andrews in 1575. Bicarton, at all events, was to make his later career in France, under the patronage of Archbishop James Beaton, ambassador there for Mary, queen of Scots. He went first, it seems, to Tours, where in 1579 he published some verses dedicated to Scévole de Sainte-Marthe. He was perhaps still in Tours when his *Institutiones oratoriae carmine conscriptae*, together with other items, appeared there in 1583: he is described on the title-page as 'orator, poet, and philosopher'. By 1584, when his *Aurearum prolis educandae institutionum libri duo* was published in Poitiers, he had probably moved to that city, as professor of rhetoric in the College of Puygarreau.

Bicarton's surviving works are collected in the aptly titled *Miscellanea* (1588), abounding in references to his academic colleagues, notably Bonaventure Ireland and Adam Blackwood, as well as to his St Andrews college friends. The contents of the book are in Latin, French, and (one brief item) Scots. It is probably fair to say that he displays a talent 'spoilt by the defects of his time' (Michaud, 4.284), but his 'Latino-scottish' verses comparing their subject to Helen of Troy have a certain charm, while his Latin versions of Ronsard are at least a literary curiosity. Most interesting of all, perhaps, is his panegyric on Thomas Aquinas—a life of the saint in verse followed by a prose oration on his merits. Together with his father's association with the St Andrews black friars, this may suggest a family affinity with the order of preachers.

Nothing is known of Bicarton's life after 1590, when he published a Latin version of the *Quatrains moraux* of Guy du Faur, seigneur de Pibrac. Dempster says that Bicarton was still alive in 1614; but while this is entirely possible there is no corroboration. J. H. BURNS

Sources T. Bicarton, *Miscellanea* (1588) · J. Durkan, 'The Bickertons: a Dominican connection', *Innes Review*, 23 (1972), 79–81 · A. de la Boudalière, 'Bibliographie Poitevine', *Mémoires de la Société des Antiquaires de l'Ouest*, 3rd ser., 1 (1908), 53–4 · J. M. Anderson, ed., *Early records of the University of St Andrews*, Scottish History Society, 3rd ser., 8 (1926) · A. I. Dunlop, ed., *Acta facultatis artium universitatis Sanctiandree, 1413–1588*, 2 vols., Scottish History Society, 3rd ser., 54–5 (1964) · L. G. Michaud and E. E. Desplaces, eds., *Biographie universelle, ancienne et moderne*, new edn, 45 vols. (Paris, 1843–65)

Bicchieri, Guala. *See* Guala (*c*.1150–1227).

Bicester. For this title name *see* Smith, Vivian Hugh, first Baron Bicester (1867–1956).

Bicheno, James Ebenezer (1785–1851), author and colonial official, was born on 25 January 1785 at Newbury, Berkshire, the only surviving son of James Bicheno (d. 1831), a well-to-do Baptist minister and schoolmaster at Newbury, who wrote politico-theological works, and his wife, Ann. The son spent the first part of his life at Newbury, and there wrote *An Inquiry into the Nature of Benevolence* (1817; republished in an extended form as *An Inquiry into the Poor Laws*, 1824), attacking the system of poor-law administration then prevailing in England. In his *Philosophy of Criminal Jurisprudence* (1819), he criticized the severity of the criminal code and objected to burdening 'the colonies with the refuse of our prisons'.

Bicheno married in 1821 but his wife died in childbirth within a year. On 17 May 1822 he was called to the bar by the Middle Temple and joined the Oxford circuit, but continued his economic and scientific studies. He had been elected a fellow of the Linnean Society in 1812, was secretary from 1825 to 1832, and wrote many papers on botany, zoology, and ornithology. In May 1827 he was elected a fellow of the Royal Society. In 1829 he visited Ireland, recording his impressions in *Ireland and its Economy* (1830); from 1833 to 1836 he served on the commission, chaired by Archbishop Whately, investigating the condition of the Irish poor, but disagreed with its report which advocated extensive public works. For a time he engaged in vain mining speculations in Wales, while residing at Tymaen, near Pyle, in Glamorgan.

In September 1842 Bicheno was appointed colonial secretary in Van Diemen's Land. He assumed office on 20 April 1843 and proved an efficient, though conservative, administrator. With a homely manner and portly appearance, calm, punctilious, and urbane, he helped to quieten his opponents in the legislative council, though his refusal to accept their demand to control financial policy caused annoyance. Privately he criticized Governor Eardley-Wilmot's alleged social misbehaviour, but defended him in public. Wilmot's successor, Sir William Denison, regarded Bicheno highly.

In 1848, Bicheno presided over the first public exhibition of pictures in Australia; he was one of the founders, foundation fellow, vice-president, and councillor of the local Royal Society, and contributed to its papers; he was a vice-president of the Mechanics' Institute and showed his interest in gardening, art, music, and good living. He died at Hobart Town of heart failure on 25 February 1851, and was buried in St David's cemetery, Hobart, on 1 March. He left an estate of about £1500, bequeathing his herbarium to the public museum at Swansea in Tasmania and his 2500 books to the Tasmanian Public Library.

A. G. L. SHAW

Sources J. West, *The history of Tasmania*, ed. A. G. L. Shaw, [new edn] (1971) · K. Fitzpatrick, *Sir John Franklin in Tasmania, 1837–1843* (1949) · P. L. Brown, ed., *Clyde Company papers*, 3 (1958) · *Annual Register* (1851) · G. Nicholls, *History of the Irish Poor Law* (1856) · *Report of the Royal Society of Van Diemen's Land for 1851* (1852) · I. Brand, *The convict probation system: Van Diemen's Land, 1839–1854* (1990) · *Hobart Town Advertiser* (1 March 1851) · AusDB

Archives National Archives of Australia, Hobart | Mitchell L., NSW, A. Cunningham MSS · Mitchell L., NSW, Deas Thomson MSS
Likenesses E. U. Eddis, portrait, Linn. Soc.
Wealth at death under £1600—in Australia: *AusDB*, 1.98

Bickerstaff, Isaac John (b. 1733, d. after 1808), librettist, was born in Dublin on 26 September 1733, the son of John Bickerstaff (d. 1751), a public official, and his wife, Jane, née Brereton (d. 1744). At the abolition of his father's post the eleven-year-old Isaac was made a page to Lord Chesterfield, lord lieutenant of Ireland, and the following year he was commissioned as an ensign in the Northumberland Fusiliers. At twenty-one he resigned his commission and moved to London with the intention of becoming a writer, but his first attempt at a libretto, *Leucothoë*, was neither set nor produced, and after some two years of efforts Bickerstaff returned to the forces, joining the marines with the rank of a second lieutenant. He did not, however, renounce writing and two years later, while still in uniform, he found his first success as a theatre writer when his little comic opera *Thomas and Sally* (music by Thomas Arne), an ingenuous piece about an English tar and his true-blue girl, was produced by John Beard at Covent Garden. In 1762 he turned out the more substantial *Love in a Village*, a full-length comic opera set with a largely pasticcio score, but including five fresh songs by Arne. *Love in a Village* scored an even larger success, proving itself the most successful comic opera to have been produced in Britain since *The Devil to Pay* (1731) and establishing itself alongside that work and such burlesque pieces as *The Beggar's Opera* (1728), *The Dragon of Wantley* (1737), and *Midas* (1762) as one of the most popular and enduring examples of musical theatre to have come from the English-language stage. It also contributed to the songbooks of the nation what would be Bickerstaff's most enduring song, 'The Miller of Dee'.

In 1763 Bickerstaff was relieved of his marine commission, according to the tale as a result of his impenitent and extremely active homosexual lifestyle, but possibly also at least partly because of military retrenchments following the end of the Seven Years' War. It has been pointed out by his biographer that he retained his half pay and pension status throughout his life, so, whatever the reason for his departure, it appears not to have been a dishonourable dismissal.

With *Love in a Village* a considerable success, however, the spendthrift and ever borrowing Bickerstaff now had a sufficient income and was able to devote himself fully to the theatre. Over the next decade he contributed to the London stage a rich list of comedies—including a version of Wycherley's *The Plain-Dealer*, the farce *The Absent Man*, a remake of *Tartuffe* as *The Hypocrite*, and *'Tis Well it's No Worse*—and, most particularly, of comic operas.

Love in a Village (which Bickerstaff owned had been textually inspired by an earlier work, *The Village Opera*, an admission that had won him many learned critical columns of abuse for plagiarism) was followed by a piece that announced its origins even more clearly. *The Maid of the Mill* (1765, music composed and arranged by Samuel

Arnold) was advertised by Bickerstaff and Beard as a musical version of a very well-known novel: it was 'based on Richardson's *Pamela*'. This was also a major success, and like its predecessor it went on to be played throughout the English-speaking world for more than a century following its first production.

Bickerstaff's next piece, *Love in the City* (1767), was a more ambitious work. This time he traded the simple maid, the honest tar, the grasping squire, the lordly gent, and their like for a set of much spikier and more individual characters in a lively tale which was illustrated with thirty-two musical numbers. The Covent Garden audiences, however, preferred the simplicities of his earlier pieces, and *Love in the City* was a failure. It did not, however, go under completely, for several years later Bickerstaff revised and shortened it, centring the rewrite on the show's most popular personality, the West Indian Priscilla Tomboy, who became the title-character of the musical play now called *The Romp*. In its new, star-vehicle form—played most notably by Mrs Jordan—the piece ultimately became as big an international success as its fellows.

In the meanwhile, however, dismayed by this failure, Bickerstaff retracked, and in his next piece he returned to the light and cheerful comic romanticism of his earlier pieces. *Lionel and Clarissa* (1768, music by Charles Dibdin) had a difficult start thanks to squabbling among Beard's successors at the head of the Covent Garden theatre, but it proved to be a survivor and returned to the London stage two years later as *A School for Fathers*, and again as late as 1925, in between which times it was played with great success throughout the English-speaking world.

Bickerstaff's next play, however, was to make a mark even beyond that world. *The Padlock* (1768) was produced not at Covent Garden, from which a disenchanted Bickerstaff had finally managed to break away, but by Garrick at Drury Lane. In essence it was no more original in its plot than his other hits—young lover whisks young beloved away from the old man who had intended to marry her—but, like *Love in the City* or, rather, like *The Romp*, it held one joyous piece of character writing that helped to turn it into the success that it became. Charles Dibdin, the composer of the piece, appeared black-faced in the low-comic, dialect role of the West Indian servant Mungo, with his soon-to-be famous song 'Dear heart, what a terrible life am I led'. Much thanks to Mungo, *The Padlock* triumphed at the Lane before going on to a career which saw it played more widely than any other of its writers' works; it was, for example, produced as *Das Vorhängeschloss* in Germany and as *A Lakat* in Hungary.

Oddly enough, after this success Bickerstaff wrote no more pieces in the mode that he had made so successful during the time of his contract with Garrick. He adapted a variety of comedies for Drury Lane; made a two-act musical, *The Captive*, out of a bit of Dryden, without success; and put together several shorter musical pieces: *The Ephesian Matron*, a version of *La serva padrona* entitled *The Maid the Mistress*, and a version of Farquhar's *The Recruiting Serjeant*. After this, suddenly, came the end.

Once again Bickerstaff's sexual habits got him into trouble. An encounter with a blackmailing soldier that found its way into the papers ended with the playwright's being forced to flee the country to avoid prosecution for the capital crime of sodomy. He changed his name and in the following months and years moved from St Malo to Marseilles to Vienna to Italy and, according to rumour, to half-a-hundred other places as well. It was said that he was still writing, that he had had a comic opera produced on the French stage, but no proof came. The only new Bickerstaff pieces to be seen after his flight were a redaction of Favart's *Les trois sultanes*, played at Drury Lane in 1775, and a little comedy with songs called *The Spoil'd Child*, rumoured to have been 'sent to Mrs Jordan from Bickerstaff in Italy'. Whether it was or not, it was a piece that gave good opportunities to its leading actress, and it won ready performances around the world. What finally became of Isaac Bickerstaff is unknown. He was sighted in many a city, including London, and, over the years, he was rumoured to be ghosting the works of Charles Dibdin from abroad. More definitely the records show that he was still receiving his army half pay in 1808. It seems he may have died soon after this.

In the manner of his time, Bickerstaff took much of the material for his shows—plotlines, characters, situations, speeches—from earlier works, both foreign and native, but his brisk and bright writing, his sense of theatre and of character, and his ability to fabricate an effective song from a melody old or new made him into the outstanding musical-theatre writer of his era before he became lost to a British theatre tradition which could ill afford to part with a man of such skill. KURT GÄNZL

Sources P. Tasch, *The dramatic cobbler: the life and works of Isaac Bickerstaff* (1972) · K. Gänzl, *The encyclopedia of the musical theatre*, 2 vols. (1994) · *IGI*

Bickerstaff, William. See Bickerstaffe, William (*bap.* 1728, *d.* 1789).

Bickerstaffe, Henry (*bap.* **1606**, *d.* in or after **1661**), Digger, was baptized on 6 July 1606 at White Notley, Essex, a younger son of Robert Bickerstaffe (*d.* 1640), landowner of Walton-on-Thames and Croydon, Surrey, and Katherine (*fl.* 1597–1640), daughter of John Lambert and his wife, Alys, of Banstead in the same county. His uncle Anthony Bickerstaffe was vicar at White Notley, and the Bickerstaffe family had close connections with the church: at least two of Henry's paternal uncles were in holy orders, while an aunt was married to Archbishop Whitgift's secretary, Michael Murgatroyd. The family also had court connections, with Henry's paternal grandfather and great-grandfather both holding minor office under Queen Elizabeth, and his father's half-brother, Hayward Bickerstaffe, serving as a page of the bedchamber to Charles I.

Bickerstaffe was apprenticed for seven years on 20 February 1626 to his elder brother Anthony, a linen draper who was a liveryman in the Skinners' Company and a resident of the London parish of Christ Church, Newgate Street. He was made free of the company on 11 April 1633, and by 1636 was living in the parish of St Gregory by St Paul, where his daughters Sarah and Mary were baptized, although the name of his wife is unknown. It is not certain whether he succeeded in setting up in business on his own, since the Skinners' Company registers have no note of his taking any apprentices. He seems to have left London and to have returned to the family home at Painshill on the borders of Walton and Cobham by 1 January 1640, when his son Edward was baptized. The Skinners' Company had no record of his place of residence when in 1641 he was listed as a poll-tax defaulter. On the death in September 1640 of Robert Bickerstaffe, the crown lease of Painshill passed to his eldest son, Anthony, but it is evident that Henry continued to live at Painshill while his older brother remained in London. During the civil war it was Henry who paid taxes and contributed loans to parliament in Walton, while his brother Anthony pursued his business interests in the City and became heavily involved in the high presbyterian movement in the capital.

In January 1642 Bickerstaffe served as a member of the inquisition jury which found that the whole county of Surrey lay outside Windsor Forest and was not subject to forest law. Later that spring he contributed 10s. towards the relief of Irish protestants, and in the following autumn he lent parliament £5 14s. 8d. worth of silver plate on the propositions scheme. In May 1643 he was appointed an assessor for the parliamentary weekly assessments in Walton, and in the summer of 1644 he shared with his neighbour William Starr, later a vigorous opponent of the Diggers, the costs of sending a soldier to fight at the siege of Basing House.

Bickerstaffe's first recorded contact with the future Digger leader Gerrard Winstanley came in January 1649, when the two of them acted as arbitrators at the Surrey assizes on behalf of the Kingston separatist and future Quaker John Fielder. Fielder was in dispute with the Kingston authorities over his imprisonment in 1645 for holding conventicles and for breach of the sabbath. In April 1649 Bickerstaffe joined Winstanley in the digging venture on St George's Hill. He was one of the signatories to *The True Levellers Standard Advanced* of April 1649, and in the following month he put his name to the second Digger pamphlet, *A Declaration from the Poor Oppressed People of England*. In June he was prosecuted with Winstanley and eight other Diggers in the Kingston court of record for trespassing upon St George's Hill, and was fined £10 and imprisoned. According to Winstanley's account of this episode, Bickerstaffe was released after three days at the instigation of Francis Drake, farmer of the manor of Walton, on whose behalf the action had been brought. It is not certain whether Bickerstaffe returned to the Digger colony after his release. He signed no further Digger manifestos, and on 24 October 1649 he purchased a tenement with malthouse and outbuildings in Heathen Street, later Eden Street, Kingston, for £180. He was to sell this property to a Kingston maltster for £205 in August 1652.

Bickerstaffe remained a resident of Kingston until after the Restoration. During the 1650s he collected rents for his nephew, James Bickerstaffe, on the family's properties in Walton and Cobham, and in 1658 was named as a defendant in a chancery case relating to the disputed ownership of this estate. On 30 September 1661 Bickerstaffe's career took a curious turn when he entered a bond for £200 to become keeper of Kingston gaol, where he had been imprisoned twelve years earlier. His tenure did not however last long, for a successor was appointed the following March. Nothing is known of his life thereafter, and no record has been found of his date or place of burial.

JOHN GURNEY

Sources J. Gurney, 'Gerrard Winstanley and the Digger movement in Walton and Cobham', *HJ*, 37 (1994), 775–802 · J. Gurney, 'William King, Gerrard Winstanley and Cobham', *Prose Studies*, 22/2 (1999), 42–6 · J. Gurney, '"Furious divells?" The Diggers and their opponents', *Prose Studies*, 22/2 (1999), 73–86 · transcripts of White Notley, Essex, parish registers, 1538–1812, Society of Genealogists, London, Mf. 492 · W. H. Challen, ed., *Carshalton parish register, marriages: 1538–1837* (1928) · W. B. Bannerman, ed., *The visitations of the county of Surrey … 1530 … 1572 … 1623*, Harleian Society, 43 (1899) · Venn, *Alum. Cant.*

Bickerstaffe, Isaac. *See* Bickerstaff, Isaac John (b. 1733, d. after 1808).

Bickerstaffe, William (*bap.* **1728**, *d.* **1789**), schoolmaster and antiquary, was baptized at St Mary de Castro, Leicester, on 18 August 1728, the eldest child and only son of William Bickerstaffe (c.1697–1739), glazier, and Hannah How (1697–1769), daughter of Joseph and Mary How. He followed his father in becoming a freeman of Leicester on 29 December 1749, and on 30 January in the following year was appointed under-usher, or schoolmaster, of the free grammar school of the borough. He was ordained deacon, with the qualification in the bishop's register of 'literate person', on 23 December 1770 and priest on 22 December 1771, and was licensed to a curacy at Syston in 1770. He was able to supplement his schoolmaster's salary of £19 6s. by serving as curate for seven years at St Mary's and six years at St Martin's with All Saints in Leicester as well as at the nearby parishes of Aylestone and Wigston Magna.

Bickerstaffe was known for his charity—he supported Sunday schools in Leicester and Aylestone with both time and money—and for his sense of humour: both Throsby and Nichols reproduced satirical pieces. The bulk of his writings, however, is on antiquarian and historical subjects. He was a correspondent of Nichols's and supplied details of archaeological remains, parish churches, and boundaries in Leicester for Nichols's *History and Antiquities*, the *Gentleman's Magazine*, and *Bibliotheca Topographica Britannica*.

Bickerstaffe's limited means remained a constant concern to him and led to a series of appeals for preferment to local parishes as they became vacant, later printed for their quaintness by Nichols in his *History and Antiquities* and in the *Gentleman's Magazine* (1789). In 1786 he described himself as 'a poor curate, unsupported by private property' and 'more inclined to a church-living than a wife' (*GM*, 204–5). He died, without preferment, in his sleep on 26 January 1789 and was buried three days later beside his parents and two sisters in the churchyard of St Mary de Castro, Leicester.

ROBIN P. JENKINS

Sources J. Nichols, *The history and antiquities of the county of Leicester*, 4 vols. (1795–1815); facs. edn (1971) · *Antiquities in Leicestershire* (1790), vol. 8 of *Bibliotheca topographica Britannica*, ed. J. Nichols (1780–1800) · *GM*, 1st ser., 59 (1789), 181, 203–5 · parish register, Leicester, St Mary de Castro, 1600–1733, Leics. RO, 8D59/15 · parish register, Leicester, St Mary de Castro, 1764–95, Leics. RO, 8D59/17 · subscription book, archdeaconry of Leicester, 1749, Leics. RO, 1D41/34/5 · bishop's register, 1770–71, Lincs. Arch., Lincoln diocesan archives · *Records of the borough of Leicester, 5: Hall books and papers, 1689–1835*, ed. G. A. Chinnery (1965) · *Records of the borough of Leicester, 6: The chamberlain's accounts, 1688–1835*, ed. G. A. Chinnery (1967) · *Records of the borough of Leicester, 7: Judicial and allied records, 1689–1835*, ed. G. A. Chinnery (1974) · J. Throsby, *The history and antiquities of the ancient town of Leicester* (1791) · M. C. Cross, *The free grammar school of Leicester* (1953)

Bickersteth, (John) Burgon (1888–1979). *See under* Bickersteth, (Kenneth) Julian Faithfull (1885–1962).

Bickersteth, Edward (1786–1850), Church of England clergyman and evangelical leader, was born in Kirkby Lonsdale, Westmorland, on 19 March 1786, the fourth of the five sons and seven children of Henry Bickersteth, a doctor, and his wife, Elizabeth Batty. Henry *Bickersteth (1783–1851), later master of the rolls and Baron Langdale, was his next elder brother. Edward Bickersteth was educated at Kirkby Lonsdale grammar school, and then at the age of fourteen moved to London to take up an appointment in the dead letter department of the General Post Office. He subsequently decided to pursue a legal career, and in November 1806 was articled to the firm of Bleasdale and Alexander. During this period in London he came under strong evangelical influence, and the conventional piety of his family background began to deepen into an intense spiritual striving and self-discipline. He proved himself a conscientious and successful articled clerk, and, in his leisure time, devoted himself to devotional and philanthropic activities.

On 5 May 1812 Bickersteth married Sarah (*d.* 1859), daughter of Thomas Bignold, at St Peter's, Norwich, and in the same year set up as a solicitor in that city in partnership with his brother-in-law, another Thomas Bignold. During the ensuing three years while Bickersteth practised as a lawyer in Norwich his religious interests continued to develop. He published a popular pamphlet entitled *A Help to the Study of the Scriptures* (1815) and took a prominent role in local evangelical societies, most notably in the successful formation of a branch of the Church Missionary Society (CMS), at that time still a relatively untried organization liable to be viewed with suspicion. These activities drew him to the attention of Josiah Pratt (1768–1844), secretary of the CMS, who in 1815 proposed to Bickersteth that he should be ordained and move to London to serve as his own assistant. The offer was accepted and, although Bickersteth lacked a university degree, he was speedily ordained deacon by the sympathetic Bishop Henry Bathurst of Norwich on 10 December 1815 and priest by Bishop Henry Ryder of Gloucester a mere eleven days later.

Bickersteth's first assignment in the full-time employment of the CMS was to carry out an inspection of the mission in Sierra Leone and neighbouring regions, where

Edward Bickersteth (1786–1850), by Samuel William Reynolds senior, pubd 1826 (after Alexander Mosses)

irregularities had been alleged. He sailed in January 1816, spent three months in Africa, and arrived home in August. His fairness and firmness in carrying out a difficult task won him the respect of both the CMS committee and the civil authorities and did much to secure the future of the missionary enterprise in west Africa, although some of the settlements which he visited later had to be abandoned.

On his return from Africa, Bickersteth assumed responsibilities as principal of the society's training college for missionaries and as a travelling secretary visiting local associations throughout England and Ireland. He was on the road for much of the year, covering enormous distances, raising funds, inspiring missionary enthusiasm, and, indirectly, doing much to foster the growth and cohesion of the evangelical party in the Church of England. In 1820 the missionary college, which was also the Bickersteth family home, moved from central London to Barnsbury House, Islington. When at home, Bickersteth delivered evening lectures to the candidates on missionary duties and conscientiously supervised their training. In 1824, on Pratt's retirement, Bickersteth succeeded him as secretary of the CMS. Much of the routine administration, including from 1825 the superintendence of the missionary college, was delegated to his assistants, but he continued himself to be very active in deputation work. In matters of general policy he was a spiritually minded and forward-thinking strategist, and was effective and sensitive in his correspondence with individual missionaries.

He presided over a great expansion in the work of the CMS, which had thirty-two missionaries when he joined in 1815, and 151 in 1831 shortly after his retirement.

During this period Bickersteth also established a growing reputation as an author of devotional and theological works and, when in London, preached to the afternoon congregation at the Wheler Chapel, Spitalfields. His six children were born between 1820 and 1830: his eldest daughter, Elizabeth, married her father's curate and eventual biographer, the theologian Thomas Rawson Birks (1810–1883), and his third child and only son, Edward Henry *Bickersteth (1825–1906), became bishop of Exeter in 1885.

In the late 1820s the ties of his growing family combined with his yearning for sustained pastoral work to cause Bickersteth to seek a more settled routine. He expanded his commitments at Wheler Chapel, and asked the CMS committee to reduce his travelling obligations. When they refused he decided to resign the secretaryship, and accepted the rectory of Watton, Hertfordshire, offered to him by Abel Smith MP. He moved in November 1830, and was to remain there for the rest of his life.

Watton was the ideal living for Bickersteth, a medium-sized rural parish accessible to London, in which he could exercise and develop his pastoral gifts, while maintaining and expanding his national role. The same zeal for the salvation of souls which had fired his activity as CMS secretary made him energetic in preaching and lecturing and in the visitation of his flock. Meanwhile, he was a familiar figure throughout the country because of his continuing deputation work on behalf of the CMS and other societies. His numerous published writings were both penetrating and accessible, and were suffused with his deep and attractive spirituality. In addition to sermons and theological works, he wrote hymns and prayers, and produced popular compilations of both. He also edited the Christian's Family Library, a series of republications of popular theological texts. His works enjoyed a very extensive sale on both sides of the Atlantic.

Above all, Bickersteth was a guide and mediator in turbulent and divided times, a man who combined strong principles with a sense that unity was itself an imperative. Thus in the early 1830s he had adopted a middle position in the Trinitarian controversy which divided the Bible Society. After 1830 he moved away from the post-millennialism characteristic of the early missionary movement in favour of a conviction that the premillennial advent of Christ was to be imminently expected, but he eschewed both Irvingite enthusiasm and high Calvinist fatalism, while his missionary zeal remained undimmed.

In the 1830s Bickersteth's prophetic speculations combined with his alarm at the resurgence of Roman Catholicism in England and his perception of the ecclesiological and theological tendencies of the Oxford Movement to stimulate him to strong opposition to 'popery' in both its Anglican and Roman forms. His polemic was developed in *The Progress of Popery* (1836) and *The Divine Warning* (1844). He actively supported the Reformation Society and the Protestant Association, and was a key promoter of the Parker Society, founded in 1840, which republished the works of the English Reformers, and of the Irish Church Missions to Roman Catholics, established in 1848. Nevertheless, even here he did not wholly lose a sense of balance: he upheld the importance of the sacraments of baptism and the Lord's Supper, urged his fellow evangelicals not to neglect the study of the early fathers, and advocated a positive protestant spirituality.

For Bickersteth the corollary of strong anti-Catholicism was a strong commitment to evangelical unity and, while remaining deeply committed to the Church of England, he was notable for his sympathy with those outside it. He was a friend of Thomas Chalmers (1780–1847) and in 1843 admired the stand taken by the founders of the Free Church of Scotland. He enjoyed warm relations with English nonconformists, continental protestants, and American Congregationalists and Presbyterians, and was accordingly a central figure in the formation of the Evangelical Alliance in 1846, a significant precursor of later more broadly based ecumenical activity.

In later life Bickersteth's emaciated appearance and poor speaking voice belied his enormous energy and influence. He was among the most significant and respected leaders in his generation both of the evangelical party in the Church of England and of the wider evangelical movement. Although his views on prophecy and his sympathy with dissenters exposed him to criticism from his fellow Anglicans, he radiated a personal holiness and love which disarmed those who differed from him. During the 1840s his health declined: he suffered a stroke in 1841 and a serious accident in 1846. Nevertheless he remained very active until the onset of his last illness in late January 1850. He died at Watton rectory on 28 February 1850 and was buried in Watton churchyard on 7 March.

JOHN WOLFFE

Sources T. R. Birks, *Memoir of the Rev. Edward Bickersteth, late rector of Watton, Herts*, 2 vols. (1851) · E. Stock, *The history of the Church Missionary Society: its environment, its men and its work*, 1–3 (1899) · M. Hennell, *Sons of the prophets: evangelical leaders of the Victorian church* (1979) · *DNB* · J. Wolffe, *The protestant crusade in Great Britain, 1829–1860* (1991) · J. Wolffe, 'The Evangelical Alliance in the 1840s', *Voluntary religion*, ed. W. J. Shiels and D. Wood, SCH, 23 (1986), 333–46 · J. Wolffe, 'North Atlantic evangelical thought in the mid-19th century', *Unity and diversity in the church*, ed. R. N. Swanson, SCH, 32 (1996), 363–75 · P. Toon, *Evangelical theology, 1833–1856: a response to Tractarianism* (1979) · *Random recollections of Exeter Hall in 1834–1837, by one of the protestant party* (1838) · *Christian Observer* (1850), 282–7 · C. E. Eardley, 'The Rev. Edward Bickersteth', *Evangelical Christendom*, 4 (1850), 132–9 · C. E. Smith, *A brief notice of the life of the Rev. Edward Bickersteth* (1850)

Archives Bodl. Oxf., letter-books and papers | U. Birm. L., CMS MSS · U. Edin., New College, Chalmers MSS

Likenesses S. W. Reynolds senior, mezzotint, pubd 1826 (after A. Mosses), BM, NPG [*see illus.*] · H. Meyer, stipple, pubd 1827 (after A. Robertson), BM, NPG · R. Woodman, engraving, 1851, repro. in Birks, *Memoir of the Rev. Edward Bickersteth*, frontispiece · T. A. Dean, stipple (after H. Room), NPG · A. Mosses, portrait, probably Walker Art Gallery, Liverpool · mezzotint, NPG · oils, repro. in Hennell, *Sons of the prophets*; priv. coll.

Wealth at death £14,000: will

Bickersteth, Edward (1814–1892), dean of Lichfield, born on 23 October 1814 at Acton in Suffolk, was the second son of John Bickersteth (1781–1855), rector of Sapcote in Leicestershire, and his wife, Henrietta (d. 1830), daughter and coheir of George Lang of Leyland, Lancashire. Henry *Bickersteth, Baron Langdale, and Edward *Bickersteth were his uncles; Robert *Bickersteth was his brother. Edward entered Trinity College, Cambridge, in 1831, and migrated to Sidney Sussex College, Cambridge, in 1833, graduating BA in 1836, MA in 1839, and DD in 1864. He also studied at Durham University in 1837.

In 1837 Bickersteth was ordained deacon, and in 1838 was curate of Chetton in Shropshire. In 1839 he was ordained priest, and became curate at the abbey in Shrewsbury. From 1849 to 1853 he was perpetual curate of Penn Street in Buckinghamshire. He was rural dean of Amersham in 1849. In 1853 he was appointed vicar of Aylesbury and archdeacon of Buckinghamshire, thus becoming a colleague of Samuel Wilberforce, bishop of Oxford, whose views he in considerable measure shared. In 1866 he was nominated an honorary canon of Christ Church, Oxford. He was select preacher at Cambridge in 1861, 1864, 1873, and 1878, and at Oxford in 1875. In 1864, 1866, 1869, and 1874 he presided as prolocutor over the lower house of the convocation of Canterbury. As prolocutor he was *ex officio* member of the committee for the Revised Version of the Bible, and he attended most regularly the sittings of the New Testament section. During his tenure of office an address to the crown was presented by the lower house requesting that a mark of the royal favour should be conferred on him, but nine years elapsed before he was installed dean of Lichfield on 28 April 1875. His chief achievement as dean was the restoration of the west front of Lichfield Cathedral, which was begun in 1877 and completed and dedicated on 9 May 1884.

Bickersteth was twice married. On 13 October 1840 he married Martha Mary Anne, daughter of Valentine Vickers of Cransmere in Shropshire. She died on 2 February 1881, and on 12 October 1882 he married Mary Anne, daughter of Thomas Whitmore Wylde-Browne of The Woodlands, Bridgnorth, Shropshire. Bickersteth resigned the deanery on 1 October 1892, and died without issue at Newstead House, Upper Holly Walk, Leamington Priory, Warwickshire on 7 October, his second wife surviving him. He was buried at Leamington Spa on 11 October.

Bickersteth was seen as a high-churchman, but also had evangelical tendencies. He published numerous sermons, charges, and collections of prayers. He also published *Diocesan Synods in Relation to Convocation and Parliament* (1867, 2nd edn, 1883), and *My Hereafter* (1883). He edited the fifth edition of *The Bishopric of Souls* (1877), with a memoir of the author, Robert Wilson Evans, and in 1882 contributed an exposition of St Mark's gospel to the Pulpit Commentary.

E. I. Carlyle, rev. H. C. G. Matthew

Sources *Liverpool Courier* (10 Oct 1892) · *The Guardian* (12 Oct 1892) · *Church Times* (14 Oct 1892) · Venn, *Alum. Cant.* · A. R. Ashwell and R. G. Wilberforce, *Life of the right reverend Samuel Wilberforce … with selections from his diary and correspondence*, 3 vols. (1880–82) · CGPLA Eng. & Wales (1892)

Archives Bodl. Oxf., Disraeli MSS · LPL, Tait MSS
Wealth at death £18,290 17s. 3d.: probate, 28 Dec 1892, CGPLA Eng. & Wales

Bickersteth, Edward (1850–1897), bishop of South Tokyo, Japan, born at Banningham rectory, Norfolk, on 26 June 1850, was the eldest son of Edward Henry *Bickersteth (1825–1906), bishop of Exeter (from 1885 until his resignation in 1900), and his wife, Rosa (d. 2 Aug 1873), daughter of Sir Samuel Bignold. His grandfather was Edward *Bickersteth (1786–1850). Educated at Highgate School, he obtained in 1869 a scholarship at Pembroke College, Cambridge; he graduated BA in 1873 and MA in 1876, and in 1874 he won the Scholefield and Evans prizes. He was ordained deacon in 1873 and priest in 1874 by the bishop of London, and from 1873 to 1875 he was curate of Holy Trinity, Hampstead. In 1875 he was elected to a fellowship at his college.

It was mainly through Bickersteth's exertions that the Cambridge mission to Delhi was founded, and in 1877 Bickersteth left England as its first head. The work grew under his care, and the influence of his example was felt beyond the limits of his own mission. He returned home in impaired health in 1882, and was appointed to the rectory of Framlingham, Suffolk. He had, however, resigned the living and was preparing for a return to Delhi when he was offered the bishopric of South Tokyo, Japan. He was consecrated and sailed for his diocese in 1886. He was at once involved in establishing the Nippon Sei-Ko-Kwai (Holy Catholic Church of Japan), which involved Japanese, Britons, and Americans, in what became in effect the indigenous Anglican church in Japan; Bickersteth's attempts at ecumenical negotiations with other churches failed in 1887.

Under the incessant work of the diocese Bickersteth's health again gave way. He came home, and, after a long illness, died on 5 August 1897 at Chiselton House, Chiselton, Berkshire. In his family Bickersteth represented a third generation of missionary zeal, but his churchmanship was more distinctively Anglican than that of Edward Bickersteth, his grandfather. His position is well represented in his volume of lectures, *Our Heritage in the Church* (1898).   A. R. Buckland, rev. H. C. G. Matthew

Sources S. Bickersteth, *Life and letters of Edward Bickersteth, bishop of South Tokyo* (1899) · E. Stock, *The history of the Church Missionary Society: its environment, its men and its work*, 4 vols. (1899–1916) · O. Cary, *A history of Christianity in Japan*, 2 vols. (1909)
Archives Bodl. Oxf., family corresp. | LPL, Benson MSS
Likenesses photograph, NPG · portrait, repro. in Bickersteth, *Life and letters*
Wealth at death £5417 10s. 10d.: probate, 2 Dec 1897, CGPLA Eng. & Wales

Bickersteth, Edward Henry (1825–1906), bishop of Exeter, the third child and only son of the Revd Edward *Bickersteth (1786–1850) and his wife, Sarah (d. 1859), eldest daughter of Thomas Bignold of Norwich, was born at Barnsbury Park, Islington, London, on 25 January 1825, when his father was secretary of the Church Missionary Society (CMS). Edward Bickersteth (1814–1892), dean of Lichfield, and Robert Bickersteth (1816–1884), bishop of

Edward Henry Bickersteth (1825–1906), by Elliott & Fry

Ripon, were his cousins. Brought up at the rectory at Watton, Hertfordshire, which his father accepted in 1830, he was educated entirely at home, his tutor being Thomas Rawson Birks (1810–1883), his father's curate and subsequently son-in-law. In the autumn of 1843 he entered Trinity College, Cambridge, graduating BA four years later as a senior optime and third classman in classics, and proceeding MA in 1850. His comparatively low place in the class lists was atoned for by his unique success in winning the chancellor's medal for English verse in three successive years, 1844–6, and in 1854 he also obtained the Seatonian prize for a sacred poem, 'Ezekiel'.

Ordained deacon in February 1848 and priest in 1849, Bickersteth became curate-in-charge of Banningham, near Aylsham, in Norfolk. For a few months in 1851 he was curate at Christ Church, Tunbridge Wells, but the following year Lord Ashley, later the earl of Shaftesbury, appointed him to the rectory of Hinton Martell, near Wimborne, Dorset, and in 1855 he became vicar of Christ Church, Hampstead, where he remained for thirty years. His incumbency there furnishes a typical example of the pastoral ideals of Victorian evangelical piety. He exercised a winning and persuasive ministry among his well-to-do congregation and in 1879 established daily services in his church. He also did many things outside his parish, frequently conducting not only parochial missions but also retreats and quiet days, which he pioneered among evangelicals. He was appointed chaplain to his cousin Robert Bickersteth, bishop of Ripon (1857–84); he was also rural

dean of Highgate (1878–85). On 24 February 1848, in the same month as his ordination as a deacon, Bickersteth married his cousin Rosa (d. 1873), daughter of Sir Samuel Bignold of Norwich, with whom he had six sons and ten daughters, and in 1876 he married his cousin Ellen Susanna, daughter of Robert Bickersteth of Liverpool, who survived him. Bickersteth had a hereditary interest in the CMS and was himself a devoted supporter of that society, serving on its committee throughout his Hampstead incumbency. He made several public appeals at critical times for extra giving to the work of the society, and he himself and his congregation were liberal contributors to its funds. In 1880–81 he inspected CMS work in India and Palestine during a long visit to the east, and in 1883 he inaugurated a scheme whereby £18,000 was raised to finance an extension to CMS headquarters.

As a hymn writer and poet Bickersteth won widespread recognition and popularity. While still a deacon he composed the hymn 'O brothers, lift your voices' for the CMS jubilee meeting of 1848, and fifty years later another entitled 'For my sake and the gospel's, go' when, as bishop of Exeter, he presided over the society's centenary celebrations. His long poem in blank verse, *Yesterday, To-Day, and for Ever*, which appeared in 1866, achieved a considerable success, selling more than 75,000 copies during his lifetime. In its description of the death of a Christian and of his heavenly destination it supplied evangelicals with poetry which did not offend their piety and took for them the place held by John Keble's *The Christian Year* among other church-people. In 1858 he published *Psalms and Hymns*, based on and extending his father's collection of hymns, *Christian Psalmody* (1833; new edn, 1841). However, Bickersteth's *The Hymnal Companion to the Book of Common Prayer* (1870; new edn, 1877) was of greater significance, rapidly superseding in many evangelical parishes all other compilations and becoming the evangelical equivalent to the recently published *Hymns, Ancient and Modern* (1861). His addition in *The Hymnal Companion* of a fourth verse of his own composition to J. H. Newman's 'Lead, kindly light' produced a mild protest from Newman in 1874. *From Year to Year* (1883) brought together many of his finest hymns and shorter poems, including what is probably his best-known hymn, 'Peace, perfect peace', reputedly the favourite hymn of Queen Victoria. Of his religious prose works the most widely circulated were his *Practical and Explanatory Commentary on the New Testament* (1864), intended especially for family use, and *The Master's Home-Call* (1872), a memorial tribute to his daughter Alice Frances, which Gladstone distributed to many of his friends. His other writings consisted very largely of sermons, addresses, and episcopal charges.

In January 1885 Bickersteth was appointed dean of Gloucester, but immediately after his institution the prime minister, Gladstone, pressed upon him the bishopric of Exeter in succession to Frederick Temple, who was translated to London. Bickersteth's appointment was probably intended as a counterpoise to the nomination of the Tractarian Edward King to the see of Lincoln, and both bishops were consecrated in St Paul's Cathedral on 25

April 1885, when Canon H. P. Liddon preached a celebrated sermon on the episcopal office. As a bishop Bickersteth displayed goodness rather than greatness, deep spirituality rather than intellectual brilliance or organizational ability. His peaceable nature inclined him to exaggerate points of agreement, and in his judgements of others he was often too charitable and lenient. For the more extreme evangelicals in his diocese he was undoubtedly something of a disappointment. It is revealing that, having come from a London parish where only the black gown was worn in the pulpit, Bickersteth found the eastward position was taken at the eucharist in the cathedral and that he himself, unlike his predecessor, henceforth conformed to this practice. However, he carried forward many reforms in the diocese which Temple had initiated, notably the employment of the residentiary canons of the cathedral in particular aspects of diocesan work. In 1894 he presided over the church congress at Exeter, and in an opening address advocated the compulsory retirement of clergy at the age of seventy unless a medical certificate of efficiency could be produced. He continued to be a firm friend of the Church Missionary Society, but he also promoted the cause of the Society for the Propagation of the Gospel, with which his eldest son, Edward *Bickersteth (1850–1897), was connected both as founder of the Cambridge Delhi Mission and later as bishop of South Tokyo. In 1891, accompanied by his wife and a daughter, he spent five months in Japan, visiting his son and other missionaries. The death of Edward six years later was a heavy blow, and following a serious attack of influenza Bickersteth resigned his see in 1900 and retired to London. After several years of ill health he died on 16 May 1906 at his home, 95 Westbourne Terrace, Paddington, and was buried in Watton churchyard three days later.

STEPHEN GREGORY

Sources F. K. Aglionby, *The life of Edward Henry Bickersteth* (1907) · Crockford (1906) · *The Guardian* (23 May 1906) · S. C. Carpenter, *Church and people, 1789–1889* (1933) · E. Stock, *The history of the Church Missionary Society: its environment, its men and its work*, 4 vols. (1899–1916) · Venn, *Alum. Cant.*, 2/1 · J. Julian, ed., *A dictionary of hymnology* (1892) · I. Bradley, *Abide with me: the world of Victorian hymns* (1997) · T. R. Birks, *Memoir of the Rev. Edward Bickersteth, late rector of Watton, Herts*, 2 vols. (1851) · *The Times* (17 May 1906) · *Men and women of the time* (1899) · K. Hylson-Smith, *Evangelicals in the Church of England, 1734–1984* (1988) · L. C. Sanders, *Celebrities of the century: being a dictionary of men and women of the nineteenth century* (1887) · *The Record* (18 May 1906)

Archives Bodl. Oxf., corresp. and papers · LPL, corresp. and papers, MS 2961 | BL, corresp. with W. E. Gladstone, Add. MSS 44423–44521, *passim* · LPL, corresp. with Edward Benson · LPL, corresp. with William Temple

Likenesses group photograph, 1886 (with two grandchildren), repro. in Aglionby, *Life of Edward Henry Bickersteth* · A. S. Cope, oils, exh. RA 1899, bishop's palace, Exeter; repro. in Aglionby, *Life of Edward Henry Bickersteth* · Elliott & Fry, photograph, NPG [*see illus.*] · photograph, NPG

Bickersteth, Henry, **Baron Langdale** (1783–1851), law reformer and master of the rolls, was born at Kirkby Lonsdale on 18 June 1783, the third son of Henry Bickersteth, physician, and Elizabeth, daughter of John Batty. Edward *Bickersteth (1786–1850) was his younger brother. He was educated at the local grammar school before being apprenticed to his father in 1797. In the following year he was sent to London to obtain further medical qualifications with his maternal uncle, Dr Robert Batty, an obstetrician. On the advice of this uncle, in October 1801 he went to Edinburgh for more medical studies, but was called home in 1802 to take care of his father's practice in his temporary absence. Settling down in the country as a general practitioner did not appeal to Bickersteth who decided to become a London physician. In order to obtain a medical degree, on 22 June 1802 he entered Caius College, Cambridge, and, on 27 October 1802 he was elected a Hewitt scholar. His health broke down through overwork after his first term. Through his uncle he obtained the post of medical attendant to Edward, fifth earl of Oxford, who was then on a tour in Italy. He stayed with the earl of Oxford until 1805, when he returned to Cambridge.

After three years of hard study Bickersteth graduated BA as senior wrangler and senior Smith's mathematical prizeman (1808), outdoing Miles Bland, later an eminent mathematician, Charles Blomfield, later bishop of London, and Adam Sedgwick, later a famous geologist. He was immediately elected fellow of Caius and decided to enter the law. On 8 April 1808 he joined the Inner Temple as a student and in 1810 became a pupil of John Bell, an eminent chancery counsel. He was called to the bar on 22 November 1811, and in the same year took his MA.

Bickersteth's professional progress was slow, retarded by his friendship with such radicals as Sir Francis Burdett and Jeremy Bentham. Bickersteth was a lifelong liberal: in 1819 he was offered a seat in parliament by Douglas Kinnaird but declined and never sat in the House of Commons. His bar business and reputation so improved that in August 1824 he was examined by the commission inquiring into the procedure of the court of chancery. His examination lasted four days, during which he revealed a thorough grasp of the subject and clearly demonstrated the need for the reforms which he advocated.

In May 1827 Bickersteth was appointed a king's counsel, and practised wholly in the court of Sir John Leach, master of the rolls, where he shared the lead of the court with Pemberton Leigh for many years. He became a bencher of the Inner Temple on 22 June 1827. In 1831 he declined the newly created office of chief judge in bankruptcy, in February 1834 the post of baron of the exchequer, and in September 1834 the solicitor-generalship. On 17 August 1835 he married Lady Jane Elizabeth Harley, the eldest daughter of his friend and patron, the earl of Oxford; they had one child, Jane Frances, who later married Alexander, Count Teleki, and died on 3 May 1870.

On 16 January 1836 Bickersteth became a member of the privy council, and three days later was appointed master of the rolls, succeeding Pepys, who became lord chancellor. On 23 January 1836 he was created Baron Langdale of Langdale in the county of Westmorland. He was a reluctant peer, accepting the title on condition that he have complete political independence and be allowed to devote himself to law reform. During Bickersteth's fifteen years as master of the rolls his judicial reputation was high.

Appeals against his decisions were few and rarely successful and he was involved in some highly celebrated cases, including *Gorham v. Bishop of Exeter* (1850).

As keeper of the rolls, Bickersteth earned the name of 'father of record reform'. His perseverance led the government to consent to provide an adequate repository for the national records. In the House of Lords he took no part in party controversy which he considered inconsistent with his judicial office, and devoted his time to legal reforms. He conducted the act for the amendment of wills through the house, and was the principal author of the acts for abolishing the six clerks' office as well as amending the laws governing attorneys and solicitors. His speech on the second reading of the bill for the better administration of justice in the high court of chancery, delivered on 13 June 1836, was afterwards published as a pamphlet. His reforms of the court of chancery were less thorough than he had hoped, for he was kept busy by his judicial and other duties. Bickersteth was also a trustee of the British Museum and head of the registration and conveyancing commission set up on 18 February 1847. During the illness of Lord Cottenham in 1850 he acted as speaker of the House of Lords.

Overwork once again affected Bickersteth's health, so that in May 1850 he had to decline the post of lord chancellor offered by Lord John Russell. He did, however, consent to act as the head of a commission until a lord chancellor was appointed (19 June 1850), but the task was too much for his failing health, and on 28 March 1851 he resigned as master of the rolls. Three weeks later on 18 April 1851 he died at Tunbridge Wells, where he had been staying on doctors' orders. He was buried on 24 April 1851 in the Temple Church.

Since Langdale had no son, the barony became extinct on his death. His wife survived him, and on the death of her brother Alfred, the sixth and last earl of Oxford, resumed her maiden name as the heiress of the Oxford family. She died on 1 September 1872.

G. F. R. BARKER, rev. HUGH MOONEY

Sources T. D. Hardy, *Memoirs of … Henry Lord Langdale*, 2 vols. (1852) · Foss, *Judges* · *Annual Register* (1851), 280–81 · *GM*, 2nd ser., 35 (1851), 661–3 · *Law Magazine*, 45 (1851), 283–93 · *Law Review*, 14 (1851), 434–6 · 'Memoir of Lord Langdale, the late master of the rolls', *Legal Observer*, 42 (1851), 436–7 · *Law Times* (17 May 1851), 59–60 · J. Campbell, *Lives of the lord chancellors*, 8 vols. (1845–69), vol. 8 · *EdinR*, 85 (1847), 476–90 · review, *QR*, 91 (1852), 461–503 · J. C. S. Nias, *Gorham and the bishop of Exeter* (1951)
Archives BL, letters to John Cam Hobhouse, Add. MSS 36456–36461 · Bodl. Oxf., letters to Sir William Napier · Bodl. Oxf., corresp. with Sir Thomas Phillipps
Likenesses H. Collen, miniature, 1829, NPG · S. Freeman, stipple (after G. Richmond), BM, NPG; repro. in *Bentley's Miscellany* (1852) · R. J. Stothard, lithograph (at the bench), NPG

Bickersteth, (Kenneth) Julian Faithfull (1885–1962), headmaster and Church of England clergyman, was born on 5 July 1885 at Ripon, Yorkshire, the third of the six sons of Canon Samuel Bickersteth (1857–1937), canon of Canterbury and chaplain to the king, and his wife, Ella Chlora Faithfull (1858–1954), the daughter of Professor Sir Monier Monier-*Williams. Ella, with Alice Liddell, was one of the

five or six little girls in Oxford on whom Lewis Carroll modelled his *Alice in Wonderland*. Julian Bickersteth was educated at Rugby School, and Christ Church, Oxford, where he took a second class in history in 1906; after a year tutoring in India he went to Wells Theological College. Ordained to a title in St Andrew's, Rugby (from where he played rugby football for the midland counties), he remained as a curate (for the only parochial experience of his ministry) until 1911, when he was appointed senior history master and chaplain at Melbourne Church of England grammar school, in Australia. Released by the school in 1915 to return to England, he volunteered for chaplaincy duties with the British expeditionary force in France. Chaplain to The Rangers, whom he came to love deeply, he then became senior chaplain of 56th London Division and finally deputy assistant chaplain-general, 15th corps. Frequently in heavy fighting, caring for the wounded, ministering to men condemned to execution, and taking burials (seventy on the second day of the battle of the Somme), he also, in spells behind the line, took special trouble over the men's spiritual welfare, organizing makeshift chapels, preparing officers and men for confirmation, and training servers, only to find himself burying most of them soon afterwards. He was twice mentioned in dispatches, and won the Military Cross for bravery in the field.

Demobilized in 1919, and accepting (without interview) an invitation to be headmaster of St Peter's Collegiate School in Adelaide, South Australia, Bickersteth gradually became important in Australian education. At St Peter's he increased numbers from 550 to 720 and built a war memorial hall, science laboratories, and several boarding-houses; he began the Headmasters' Conference for Australian Independent Schools, and was partly responsible for the founding in 1925 of St Mark's, the first residential college of Adelaide University. From 1928 to 1933 he was also senior chaplain to the Australian military forces.

In 1933, again without interview, Bickersteth was appointed (out of fifty-six applicants) headmaster of Felsted School in Essex; plunging enthusiastically into his first experience of English schoolmastering, he introduced a tutorial system, brought (with the help of his brother Burgon [*see below*]) a Canadian schools cricket eleven to Felsted, and joined in what was then the pioneering practice of employing teaching staff from the British empire. In 1935 he founded an annual conference of public-school chaplains, initiated taking boys for a weekend retreat in preparation for their confirmation, raised the school's academic and athletic reputation, and built a science block, an art school, and a sanatorium. The outbreak of war meant the evacuation of the whole school; they went to several big houses in the Wye valley. But he was not to oversee their return.

In 1942 Bickersteth accepted the pressing invitation of his old schoolfriend William Temple, on the latter becoming archbishop of Canterbury, to join his new staff, as archdeacon of Maidstone and (as his father had been before him) residentiary canon of the cathedral. He soon made his mark in the life of the diocese, cathedral, and city. Keeping up his concern for Christian education, he was much in demand preaching round the public schools; a keen governor of the Woodard Foundation, he took retreats and quiet days in many parts of the country. Made a chaplain to the queen in the first appointments after the coronation in 1953, he undertook several tours of Australia and America to raise awareness of and money for the needs of the mother church of the worldwide Anglican communion. He encouraged the foundation in Canterbury of the Institute of Heraldic and Genealogical Studies, which before long was internationally recognized, and soon awarding annually a Bickersteth medal for notable work on family history.

After retiring in 1955, Bickersteth took on the chairmanship of the new Archbishops' School in Canterbury, and saw through its first five years as a successful comprehensive school. In 1960, with much help from Burgon, he rescued for the Church of England the thirteenth-century Greyfriars' Chapel when it came on the open market, thus opening the way for a renewed Franciscan presence in the heart of Canterbury. He was also closely involved with the siting and funding of the University of Kent. He kept up his teaching and preaching and his travel until he had a heart attack at his desk on 16 October 1962, dying on the same day in the Kent and Canterbury Hospital. He was buried in his parents' grave just outside the east end of St Martin's Church, Canterbury.

Julian Bickersteth's younger brother, **(John) Burgon Bickersteth** (1888–1979), academic administrator, the fourth son of Samuel and Ella Bickersteth, was born on 14 January 1888, in London. Educated at Charterhouse School and Christ Church, Oxford (where like Julian he took a second in history), he captained the Oxford University association football eleven to victory in the 1911 varsity match, having won his blue in both 1909 and 1910; he had captained Charterhouse in 1908.

On going down from Oxford, Bickersteth volunteered for two years' service as a lay missionary with the Anglican church in western Canada, beginning at once to record his adventurous pioneering experiences in the Rocky Mountains by means of vividly written letters home, which on his return to England he was persuaded to put into book form; the result was the publishing of *The Land of Open Doors* (1914; repr. 1976). He spent 1913–14 in the University of Paris at the Sorbonne.

On the outbreak of war Bickersteth joined the Royal Dragoons, and served with them in France until demobilization; during long periods of cavalry inactivity he wrote and completed *A History of the 6th Cavalry Brigade* (1919); but he was also frequently in heavy fighting, and twice won the Military Cross. Demobilized in 1919, he then had two years teaching in the University of Alberta, but he decided that the post was not right for him and resigned; he was actually on his way home when, in 1921, he was offered and accepted the wardenship of Hart House in the University of Toronto. Both the building and the concept were new. The place was to be the cultural, artistic, and leisure centre for the undergraduates. He set to, and began at once to start fashioning this unique hub to a university community.

Granted leave of absence from the university in the spring of 1940, Bickersteth hastened home to the scene of action, and joined the Canterbury Home Guard at the height of the invasion scare. That autumn his old friend General McNaughton, commanding the Canadian forces in Britain, asked him to create the post of director of education for them. In 1943 the British army invited him to switch his allegiance, and do a similar, larger task for British troops—both those who were part of home defence, and the fighting divisions preparing to invade the continent. He devised the Army Bureau of Current Affairs pamphlets, followed by the British Way and Purpose ones, resigning in 1944 to return to Canada in preparation for the thousands of servicemen who would be making for the universities. He stayed until 1947, judging himself by then to be beyond the right age to respond properly to undergraduates' aspirations; so he wound up his affairs, and retired to Canterbury.

For the next thirty years Bickersteth devoted himself to the life and work of the cathedral, initially in the welcome company of both his aged mother and his brother Julian. Painstaking palaeography research in the cathedral library, membership of the council of its Friends, imaginative guiding round the cathedral itself, particularly if as so often the visitors were Canadians, who had made looking up 'the Warden' an important part of their English tour, filled his days. He also gave much time to prison visiting, prisons and borstals having been a lifelong interest; in fact by his eighties the Home Office was calling him the doyen of the prison visitors of England, 'greatly loved from Dartmoor to the Scrubs' (private information). In a lifetime of deep concern for the young, his abiding passion remained Hart House, the 26-year assignment for love of which he refused many significant offers in Canada and the UK. His reason was always the same: he was 'not prepared to give up the excitement and opportunities of Hart House' (Montagnes, *Strange Elation*, 17). In old age he was made a doctor of laws of Toronto University, and a member of the Order of Canada. He died in a nursing home outside Canterbury on 1 February 1979, and was buried beside his parents and Julian in St Martin's churchyard.

Julian had died seventeen years before Burgon, but their countless friends tended always to talk of them in one breath. Without question the very close friendship between these lifelong bachelor brothers developed in their shared experiences on the western front. The widely acclaimed *The Bickersteth Diaries 1914–1918*, an edited version of the eleven typescript volumes their mother put together from start to finish of the war, consists largely of excerpts from what were sometimes almost daily letters home. The family ties were immensely strong anyway; the heroism and carnage and agony simply served to deepen them. In every kind of circumstance, sometimes riding on horseback or by bicycle 40 miles to do so, they contrived to meet; two days before Morris, the fifth brother, was killed in action the three of them had a 'merry lunch' together and wrote a joint letter home. Both Julian's and Burgon's letters penetratingly reveal how the prevailing jingoism of the early part of the war gave way to disgust at the pointlessness of it all; but their faith held. They write about politics, education, religion, and the beauties of nature, in among graphic accounts of 'battle and murder and sudden death'.

The war over, and after they had gone up to the king side by side, each to receive his Military Cross, they went off again to the opposite ends of the earth, but invariably organized leave to tour the continent together (Burgon particularly was very knowledgeable on Romanesque churches, and monasticism), and they would always include a pilgrimage to Morris's grave in the Serre cemetery near where he had fallen. Julian, the older by two and a half years, was tall and debonair, a disciplined Anglo-Catholic priest to his fingertips; Burgon, the younger, was wiry and stocky, a wonderful listener, and a devout Anglican layman. Both brimful of ideas and both having the drive to carry them out with unflagging energy and boundless enthusiasm, both deeply committed to the cause of Christian education, they were also invariably great fun to be with. Thousands of English-speaking people came under their influence for good in the five or six middle decades of the twentieth century.

JOHN BICKERSTETH

Sources J. Bickersteth, ed., *The Bickersteth diaries, 1914–1918* (1995) · N. Smart, ed., *The Bickersteth family war diary*, 2 vols. (1999–2000) · *AusDB* · J. B. Bickersteth, *The land of open doors* (1914); repr. (1976) · I. Montagnes, *An uncommon fellowship* (1969) · I. Montagnes, *A strange elation: Hart House, the first eighty years* (2000) · M. R. Craze, *A history of Felsted School, 1564–1947* (1955) · personal knowledge (2004) · private information (2004) · *CGPLA Eng. & Wales* (1979) [(John) Burgon Bickersteth]
Archives Bodl. Oxf., corresp., diaries, and papers · LPL, papers · University of New Brunswick, letters [copies] | BL, letters to Albert Mansbridge, Add. MS 65258 · CAC Cam., reports to Lord Hankey on Canadian affairs · NL Wales, corresp. with Thomas Jones
Likenesses Karsh, photograph (John Burgon Bickersteth), Hart House · oils, St Peter's, Adelaide, Australia · oils, Felsted School, Essex · photograph, Hart House · photograph (John Burgon Bickersteth), priv. coll. · portrait, oils (John Burgon Bickersteth), Diocesan Office, Canterbury
Wealth at death £10,911 14s. 0d.: probate, 28 Nov 1962, *CGPLA Eng. & Wales* · £57,999—(John) Burgon Bickersteth: probate, 1979, *CGPLA Eng. & Wales*

Bickersteth, Robert (1816–1884), bishop of Ripon, was born at the vicarage, Acton, Suffolk, on 24 August 1816, the fourth son of the Revd John Bickersteth (1781–1855), vicar of Acton and later rector of Sapcote, Leicestershire, and his wife, Henrietta, *née* Lang (d. 1830). He was a nephew of Edward *Bickersteth, rector of Watton, and of Henry *Bickersteth, Baron Langdale; he was also a younger brother of Edward *Bickersteth (1814–1892), dean of Lichfield, and a cousin of Edward Henry *Bickersteth, bishop of Exeter. Robert Bickersteth was educated at home by his father and imbibed the intense evangelicalism of both parents. Initially he envisaged a medical career, for which he undertook training in Norwich, London, and Paris

between 1834 and 1836. He subsequently decided, however, to seek ordination, and to that end matriculated at Queens' College, Cambridge, in October 1837. He took his BA in 1841, MA in 1848, and DD in 1857. He was ordained deacon by Bishop Davys of Peterborough in 1841, and priest in 1842, serving initially as his father's curate at Sapcote. From 1843 to 1845 he was curate at St Giles, Reading, and then, briefly, at Clapham parish church. In late 1845 he became incumbent of St John's, Clapham Rise, which provided him with the resources to marry, on 21 July 1846, Elizabeth, third daughter of Joseph Garde, of Cork. Their family circle, which eventually consisted of five sons and one daughter, appeared an ideal of evangelical domesticity.

Bickersteth quickly acquired a reputation as a powerful and effective preacher, and drew large congregations to St John's. He was reverent, if austere, in his conduct of worship, and cultivated the devotional life of his congregation through the introduction of regular early celebrations of holy communion. He was meticulous in his pastoral care of the parish, held special services for the poor, and supported educational work. Meanwhile his proximity to London enabled him to take an active part in evangelical societies, notably the Irish Church Missions to Roman Catholics, which provided a focus for his deeply felt anti-Catholicism. On the death of his uncle, Edward Bickersteth, in 1850, he succeeded him as honorary secretary of that organization.

In 1851 Bickersteth became rector of the enormous London slum parish of St Giles-in-the-Fields, where he set up an elaborate system of parish visitation, staffed by numerous curates, city missionaries, and Scripture Readers. He reformed the Sunday and day schools, and facilitated a range of charitable and administrative effort for the improvement of the area. In 1854 he was appointed a residentiary canon of Salisbury, while also remaining rector of St Giles. His rapid rise through the hierarchy culminated in November 1856, when he accepted Lord Palmerston's offer of the bishopric of Ripon. He was consecrated at Bishopthorpe on 18 January 1857.

Bickersteth's appointment was a controversial one, seen as evidence of undue favouritism towards the evangelical party on the part of the prime minister and his adviser Lord Shaftesbury. However, the outcome was to vindicate the choice. The ancient diocese of Ripon had been revived only in 1836, but incorporating, as it did, most of the industrial part of the West Riding as well as the remote and extensive countryside of the Yorkshire dales, it presented a formidable challenge. Accordingly there was much wisdom in the choice of a man of Bickersteth's energy, commitment, and relative youth. He was pre-eminently a preaching and pastoral bishop, ceaselessly on the road, possessed of a passionate zeal to proclaim the Christian gospel, and always ready to make himself available to those in need of his counsel and support. An able and sensitive administrator who gained the respect and loyalty of clergy and laity alike, he presided over a notable period of recovery for the Church of England in his diocese. During his episcopate he consecrated

157 new or rebuilt churches, and greatly stimulated educational provision. Other indices of pastoral provision and achievement also showed significant upward trends.

Despite his own strongly held convictions Bickersteth took little part in the theological controversies of the period. He was no academic, and his published output consisted of sermons, lectures, and charges, rather than of learned treatises. Moreover, he was genuinely concerned to promote harmony and cohesion within his diocese, even in relation to people of standpoints significantly different from his own, such as W. F. Hook, the high-church vicar of Leeds. In the early 1860s he strongly criticized *Essays and Reviews* (1860) but refused to be a party to the prosecution of its authors; he reasoned with ritualist clergy rather than persecuting them. His contributions to debate in the House of Lords were rare but notable, particularly in 1869 in his forceful opposition to the disestablishment of the Church of Ireland, and in 1870 when, at odds with many of his fellow bishops, he supported the legalization of marriage with a deceased wife's sister. As the latter incident illustrated, his pastoral sense could soften doctrinal rigour, and in political terms he had reformist and liberal instincts, except on matters relating to the security of the established church.

Bickersteth facilitated a number of significant innovations, especially the holding of clergy retreats, parish missions, and the development of church congresses. He took a leading role in the foundation of the teachers' training college at Ripon, which later became part of the College of Ripon and York St John. Failing health restricted his activities in his last years and forced him to delegate much of his work to assistant bishops; this led to him being criticized for an indolence quite at variance with his character in his prime. He died at the bishop's palace, Ripon, on 15 April 1884 and was buried on 19 April in Ripon Cathedral precincts.   JOHN WOLFFE

Sources M. C. Bickersteth, *A sketch of the life and episcopate of the Rt Rev. Robert Bickersteth, DD* (1887) · D. N. Hempton, 'Bickersteth, bishop of Ripon: The episcopate of a mid-Victorian evangelical', *Northern History*, 17 (1981), 183–202 · *The Times* (16 April 1884) · *The Times* (21 April 1884) · J. Wolffe, *The protestant crusade in Great Britain, 1829–1860* (1991)
Archives Glamorgan RO, Cardiff, letters | BL, letters to W. E. Gladstone, Add. MSS 44440–79, *passim* · LPL, letters to Baroness Burdett-Coutts · N. Yorks. CRO, archives of the see of Ripon · W. Yorks. AS, Leeds, Ripon diocesan archives, archives of the see of Ripon
Likenesses Skelton, lithograph, pubd 1852, NPG · G. F. Watts, oils, 1878, Bishop's Mount, Ripon · Maull & Polyblank, cartes-de-visite, NPG · D. J. Pound, stipple and line print (after photograph by Mayall), BM, NPG; repro. in D. J. Pound, *Drawing room portrait gallery of eminent personages* (1859) · W. Walker & Sons, carte-de-visite, NPG · W. A. Wragg, lithograph, BM · engraving, repro. in Bickersteth, *Sketch*, frontispiece
Wealth at death £25,081 2s.: probate, 22 May 1884, CGPLA Eng. & Wales

Bickerton, Sir Richard, first baronet (1727–1792), naval officer, was born on 23 June 1727 and baptized on 4 July at St Mary Magdalen, Bridgnorth, the third son of Lieutenant Henry Bickerton, 4th dragoon guards, and his wife, Mary, *née* Dowdall, from Carrickfergus. Bickerton was educated at Westminster School, and on 21 March 1739 he entered the navy as captain's servant in the *Suffolk*; he served in the West Indies operations, including the attempt on Cartagena, left her in May 1742 for the *Stirling Castle*, and was rated midshipman in October. After short spells in Channel Fleet flagships he joined the *Cornwall*, flagship of Thomas Davers, his former captain in the *Suffolk* appointed to command in the West Indies. Davers promoted Bickerton lieutenant in the *Worcester* on 8 February 1746, where he remained until the peace. After being in the *Fougueux* between 1753 and 1756 he served in the *Royal George* until January 1758, when he became second lieutenant of the *Namur*, Edward Boscawen's flagship in the Mediterranean. He was promoted commander in the fireship *Aetna* on 2 August 1758, and captain in the *Glasgow* on 21 August 1759, after the battle of Lagos. In her he went to the West Indies again, before moving to the *Lively* in May 1761. Bickerton had married on 2 January 1758, at St Margaret's Westminster, Mary Anne, eldest daughter of Thomas Hussey of Wrexham. They had two sons and two daughters, among them the naval officer Sir Richard Hussey *Bickerton, second baronet.

After a brief spell at home Bickerton was appointed to the *Devonshire* in April 1762 with Sir George Pocock's fleet at Havana, but when he arrived there previous changes on the station led to his exchanging into the *Temeraire* before returning home when the British forces withdrew from Cuba. In 1767 he commanded the *Renown* in the West Indies. For the armament for the Falkland Islands dispute in 1770 he was appointed to the *Marlborough*; he remained in her for three years, and steered the king's barge at the naval review of June 1773, being knighted as a result. He then commanded the yacht *Augusta* until appointed to the *Terrible* when war with France was imminent. He was created a baronet on 29 May 1778, when the king visited Portsmouth. In the *Terrible* he was in the fleet at the battle off Ushant on 27 July; he continued with the Channel Fleet in 1779, and was with it again (after moving to the *Fortitude*) in 1780 and 1781, taking part in the second relief of Gibraltar in April 1781.

Late in 1781 Bickerton was appointed commodore (first class) to command a squadron of reinforcements for the East Indies; with his broad pennant in the *Gibraltar* he sailed on 6 February 1782 with six other ships of the line, two frigates, and a convoy conveying troops. The passage was slow; time had to be spent at Rio owing to sickness, and he arrived at Bombay in September. On receiving news of the actions between Sir Edward Hughes and the French commander Suffren, he hastened on to Madras but, giving a wide berth to Ceylon to avoid Suffren, missed Hughes, who was withdrawing to Bombay for the monsoon season, and so returned to Bombay himself; the two forces were united there only in December. For the following campaign Bickerton's ships gave Hughes a numerical superiority, but though they took a full part in the action off Cuddalore on 20 June 1783, the engagement was indecisive. Bickerton left Bombay on his return in December 1783, and reached England in June 1784. He was appointed, again a commodore, to command the Leeward

Islands station in September 1786. However as a result of a dispute over an imprest against him concerning expenses incurred for the sick at the Cape of Good Hope on the return from India, he resigned the command. Nevertheless after reaching flag rank on 24 September 1787 he held a command in the Spanish armament of 1790, in the *Impregnable*, and then continued by taking the command at Plymouth, in the *St George*, becoming rear admiral of the white on 21 September 1790. From 1790 until his death he was MP for Rochester, but took little part in parliamentary proceedings. Bickerton's wife, Mary Anne, was the heir of Lieutenant-General Vere Warner Hussey, of Woodwalton, Huntingdonshire, and this led to Sir Richard's purchasing Upwood House nearby, which he made his seat. Bickerton's elder son, who entered the navy, inherited the baronetcy and later took the additional name of Hussey.

Richard Bickerton died of an apoplectic fit in London on 25 February 1792 while on leave from the command at Plymouth, and was buried in the family vault at Upwood House. He left his property and money to his wife and children. Little emerges of his character; clearly he was quite well regarded as he was more or less continuously employed, but not so exceptionally as to relieve Hughes, who had served five years in the East Indies in 1783.

A. W. H. PEARSALL

Sources H. W. Richmond, *The navy in India, 1763–1783* (1931) · D. Syrett, ed., *The siege and capture of Havana, 1762*, Navy RS, 114 (1970) · *The private papers of John, earl of Sandwich*, ed. G. R. Barnes and J. H. Owen, 4 vols., Navy RS, 69, 71, 75, 78 (1932–8) · GEC, *Peerage* · *GM*, 1st ser., 62 (1792), 280 · R. Beatson, *Naval and military memoirs of Great Britain*, 3 vols. (1790) · J. Charnock, ed., *Biographia navalis*, 6 (1798), 349 · muster books, PRO, ADM 36/633; 3637; 4010; 4667; 6253; 11567 · logs, PRO, ADM 51/397 · R. G. Thorne, 'Bickerton, Richard', HoP, *Commons, 1790–1820*

Wealth at death Upwood House; designated £12,000 for family trusts

Bickerton, Sir Richard Hussey, second baronet (1759–1832), naval officer, was born on 11 October 1759, the only surviving son of Sir Richard *Bickerton, first baronet (1727–1792), rear-admiral and politician, and Mary Anne, daughter of Thomas Hussey of Wrexham. He entered the navy in December 1771, on the *Marlborough*, then commanded by his father. In that ship, and afterwards in the yacht *Augusta*, he continued with his father until 1774, when he was appointed to the *Medway* (60 guns), flagship in the Mediterranean. Two years later he was transferred to the frigate *Enterprise*, and afterwards to the *Invincible* with Captain Hyde Parker. On 16 December 1777 he was made lieutenant in the *Prince George*, commanded by Captain Charles Middleton (afterwards Lord Barham). He followed Middleton to the *Jupiter* (50 guns), and when the latter was appointed comptroller of the navy he recommended Bickerton to Captain Francis Reynolds, his successor in command of the *Jupiter*, who appointed Bickerton first lieutenant.

On 20 October 1778 the *Jupiter*, in company with the frigate *Medea*, fell in with the French ship *Triton* (64 guns) on the coast of Portugal. A brisk action followed in which both ships suffered severely. Although no particular advantage was gained on either side, the odds against the *Jupiter* were considered so great as to render her equal engagement equivalent to a victory. Bickerton was accordingly promoted on 20 March 1779, and appointed to command the sloop *Swallow*. After nearly two years' service in the channel, during which, on 2 January 1780, she took part in the interception of a Dutch convoy carrying naval stores to France, the *Swallow* was sent to join Sir George Rodney in the West Indies, where Bickerton participated in the capture of St Eustatius, which proved valuable in the extreme to its captors. On 8 February 1781 Rodney promoted Bickerton to post rank with command of the *Gibraltar*.

Bickerton commanded the *Invincible* in the action between Sir Samuel Hood and De Grasse off Martinique. After briefly commanding the *Russel* and then the *Terrible*, he was sent home in command of the frigate *Amazon*. In September 1783 he was given command of another frigate, the *Brune*, decommissioned at the conclusion of peace, and in 1787 he was appointed to the frigate *Sibylle*, in the West Indies. On 25 September 1788 he married Anne, daughter of James Athill of Antigua. The couple had no children. Bickerton returned home in 1790, and succeeded to the baronetcy upon the death of his father in February 1792. At the outbreak of war in 1793 he was given orders to commission the *Ruby* (64 guns) for service in the channel. Towards the end of 1794 he was transferred to the *Ramillies*, in which he transported General Sir John Vaughan to the West Indies and then proceeded to Newfoundland; he returned at the end of 1795 in order to form part of the North Sea Fleet under Admiral Adam Duncan (1796), and the Channel Fleet in 1797 under Lord Bridport. In 1798 he commanded the *Terrible*, still in the Channel Fleet, and on 14 February 1799 he attained the rank of rear-admiral. In the autumn of the same year he hoisted his flag at Portsmouth as assistant to the port-admiral. In May 1800 he was sent to the Mediterranean with his flag on the *Swiftsure*, in which he transported generals Abercromby, Moore, and Hutchinson to Egypt. He then took immediate command of the blockade of Cadiz, a position he held until joined by Lord Keith in October. During 1801, with his flag in the *Kent*, he was employed on the coast of Egypt, conducting the blockade of Alexandria in the absence of the commander-in-chief, and providing close support for the besieging army commanded by Lieutenant General Hutchinson. Afterwards he superintended the embarkation of the defeated French army. For his services at this time he was created knight of the Crescent by the sultan on 8 October 1801. During the short peace he remained in the Mediterranean as commander-in-chief, and, on the renewal of the war, as second in command under Lord Nelson, with whom he served at the blockade of Toulon. Nelson refused to receive the thanks of the corporation of London for his command of the blockade unless Bickerton were included in the commendation.

In May, when Nelson sailed for the West Indies, Bickerton, with his flag in the *Royal Sovereign*, was left in command. He returned home because of a liver ailment, and soon afterwards took office at the Admiralty board, where he continued until 1812, when he was appointed commander-in-chief at Portsmouth. He was elected MP for Poole in February 1808 and served as a supporter of the tory government; he did not seek re-election at the dissolution in 1812. His active service ended after the grand review in 1814, organized to honour the visiting foreign monarchs, at which he commanded in the second post under the duke of Clarence. He attained the rank of vice-admiral on 9 November 1805, and admiral on 31 July 1810; was made KCB on 2 January 1815; and became lieutenant-general of marines on 5 January 1818, before succeeding William IV as general of marines in June 1830. In 1823 he assumed, by royal permission, his mother's maiden name of Hussey before that of Bickerton. On his death, on 9 February 1832, the baronetcy became extinct.

J. K. LAUGHTON, *rev.* NICHOLAS TRACY

Sources J. Marshall, *Royal naval biography*, 1/1 (1823), 125 · J. Ralfe, *The naval biography of Great Britain*, 2 (1828), 277 · *Naval Chronicle*, 13 (1805), 337 · R. G. Thorne, 'Bickerton, Sir Richard', HoP, *Commons* **Archives** Archives Nationales du Québec, instructions concerning effectiveness of 'Shorter' propeller | BL, letters to Lord Nelson, Add. MSS 34917–34930, *passim* · BL, letters to Lord Spencer · NMM, corresp. with Lord Keith · NMM, letters to Sir Thomas Foley **Likenesses** W. Ridley, stipple, pubd 1803 (after T. Maynard), NPG · F. Chantrey, medallion on marble monument, Bath Abbey

Bickford, William (*bap.* 1774, *d.* 1834), currier and inventor of the safety fuse, was baptized in Ashburton, Devon, on 23 January 1774, the son of William and Mary Beckford. He was in business as a currier, dressing and colouring tanned leather, first rather unsuccessfully in Truro and later in Tuckingmill near Camborne in Cornwall. He was not involved in any way with the mining that was carried on in the surrounding area, but he was greatly affected by the frequent serious, and often fatal, accidents suffered by the miners through premature blasting explosions.

Gunpowder had been in widespread use in Europe in mining and quarrying since the early seventeenth century, but 200 years later the techniques available for detonating the charges were still very primitive. One method was simply to set fire to a 'train' of gunpowder leading to the charge itself, the length of the train corresponding roughly to the time delay before the charge exploded; a later method involved a kind of fuse of goose quills filled with gunpowder. Both methods were dangerously unreliable, even when (and it was not always the case) the greatest care was exercised by the shot-firers.

Bickford was determined to make a safer type of fuse, and although he was no scientist he carried out a series of experiments with many different combinations of materials until, having nearly despaired of ever achieving his goal, he visited a friend in his rope-walk and suddenly hit on the idea of spinning a light rope or cord round a tightly packed central core of gunpowder. The idea was simple, but devising a machine for the manufacture of his 'safety fuse' was beyond Bickford himself, so he took into partnership Thomas Davey, a working miner with a talent for solving mechanical problems. The Bickford safety fuse, as patented on 6 September 1831 (no. 6159), consisted of two layers of flax yarn enclosing a central core of gunpowder, the whole being made watertight with varnish or tar. The resulting fuse was much more accurate and consistent in its timing, and had a much better resistance to water and the various kinds of treatment to which it was inevitably subjected in the mines. It raised the level of both safety and productivity and was therefore popular with both miners and management.

Bickford himself fell seriously ill before his fuse could be manufactured in any quantity, and it was only after his death in 1834 that a factory was established at Tuckingmill which continued to make various types of fuse, seldom departing very far from the original specifications, for almost 130 years. Bickford's family, along with those of his partner, Davey, and Davey's son-in-law George Smith, were involved in the management of Bickford, Smith & Co. up to the time of its final closure in 1961.

William Bickford married Susanna Burall in April 1802 at Illogan, Cornwall. They had two sons, baptized in Truro in 1808 and 1809, both called William (presumably the first died). Bickford died in Tuckingmill and was buried there on 7 October 1834.

RONALD M. BIRSE, *rev.*

Sources T. G. Tullock, ed., *The rise and progress of the British explosives industry* (1909) · *ICI Magazine*, 34 (1956), 239 · register, Cornwall RO, P88/1/26 [burial], p.43 no.341

Bickham, George (1683/4–1758), engraver and writing-master, was born in London; he was said to have been seventy-four when he died in 1758. The son of John Bickham, whose wife was probably named Bridget, he occasionally used the initials G. J. and G. J. B. and the pen-name George Johns'son in his publications. The dates of his marriage to Elizabeth and the birth of his eldest son, George *Bickham the younger (*c.*1704–1771), are unknown, but the births of two younger children, Elizabeth (*b.* 1705) and John (*b.* 1706), are recorded in the registers of St Giles Cripplegate. Bickham was apprenticed to the writing-master and engraver John Sturt and quickly gained a good reputation among writing-masters as an engraver of calligraphy. Joseph Champion claimed Bickham surpassed his master by being the first to cut through wax on copper without tracing the design first, thus transmitting the master's original more faithfully. He also engraved portraits, the most important being a series of famous writing-masters which appeared as frontispieces in their writing copybooks; some examples may be found in the British Museum, London.

In his first surviving trade card, of 1705, Bickham advertised himself as a copperplate-engraver and teacher of drawing at Hoop Alley in Old Street, London. Later trade cards and advertisements in his writing copybooks indicate that he moved premises frequently: an undated trade card advertised drawing lessons at his house in Hatton Garden, and in 1712 he advertised that youths were boarded and taught writing, drawing, and engraving at his house in Brentford End, Middlesex. In 1723, while living in the parish of St Leonard, Shoreditch, in London, he was declared insolvent and imprisoned. Three years later he designed and engraved several plates in Thomas Weston's *Writing, drawing and ancient arithmetick for the use of the*

George Bickham (1683/4–1758), by George Bickham, pubd 1741

young gentlemen at the academy at Greenwich, a school at which his son George later taught drawing. Several combination drawing and writing copybooks were published by George Bickham in the 1720s and early 1730s, and it is impossible to say for certain whether father, son, or both were responsible for them, since by this date both taught drawing and both were skilled engravers. Often—as in the case of *The Drawing and Writing Tutor*—the first edition is undated and later editions contain additional plates clearly engraved by the son. However, the invention of plates which cleverly combined simple drawing examples with calligraphic text can undoubtedly be attributed to the father.

In the 1730s the elder Bickham seems to have settled fairly permanently in the Clerkenwell district of London, where his *Penmanship in its Utmost Beauty and Extent* (1731) was sold from his premises in Warner Street. Two years later he embarked on his most important contribution to British engraving, *The Universal Penman*, a joint work with his son and John Bickham (*fl.* 1730–1750), his son or brother, which was sold from his house in James Street, Bunhill Fields. Issued in fifty-two parts from 1733 to 1741, it was the culmination of his work as an engraver of calligraphy: it contained examples by twenty-five contemporary writing-masters on 212 folio copperplates, many embellished with decorations engraved by his son, as the elder Bickham firmly believed that drawing was a necessary qualification for the man of business.

The British Monarchy, advertised by Bickham in its preface as the 'Last Performance that I propose to publish of this

Nature', was issued to subscribers from 1743 to 1748. It was also a combination of letterpress and images, but the purpose of this publication was to promote the study of geography by providing maps and a text which described the history, goods, commerce, and agriculture of the different counties of Britain and her colonies. At about the same time Bickham began experimenting with colour printing by superimposing trimmed and sometimes coloured counterproofs of engravings after old masters, flowers, animals, and other images over his old engraved plates of penmanship: *The Museum of the Arts, or, The Curious Repository* (*c.*1745) contained nearly eighty examples. Work which can be definitely assigned to the elder Bickham ceased shortly after this date, by which time his son had a thriving business in May's Buildings, Covent Garden, and was no longer signing himself 'Junior'. According to William Massey, the elder Bickham moved to Red Lion Street, Clerkenwell, and shortly afterwards died there, of palsy on 4 May 1758. He was buried in an unmarked grave by the vestry door of St Luke's, Old Street. His portrait was drawn, engraved, and published by his son in 1741.

KIM SLOAN

Sources W. Massey, *The origin and progress of letters: an essay in two parts* (1763) · A. Heal, *The English writing-masters and their copy-books, 1570–1800* (1931) · N. R. Davison, 'Bickham's "Musical entertainer" and other curiosities', *Eighteenth-century prints in colonial America: to educate and decorate*, ed. J. D. Dolmetsch (1979), 98–122 · K. Sloan, 'Bickham, George, the elder', *The dictionary of art*, ed. J. Turner (1996) · D. P. Becker, *The practice of letters: the Hofer collection of writing manuals 1514–1800* (1997) · *Engraved Brit. ports.* · J. M. Friedman, *Color printing in England, 1486–1870* (1978), 8–9 [exhibition catalogue, Yale U. CBA, 20 April – 25 June 1978]

Archives BM, department of prints and drawings, trade cards | V&A NAL, Ambrose Heal collection

Likenesses G. Bickham, etching, 1741, AM Oxf., BM; repro. in Heal, *English writing masters*, pl. 2 [*see illus.*] · G. Bickham, line engraving, BM; repro. in G. Bickham, *The universal penman, or, The art of writing* (1741)

Bickham, George (*c.*1704–1771), engraver and printseller, the son of the engraver George *Bickham (1683/4–1758) and his wife, Elizabeth, was probably born about 1704 in London. He trained as an engraver and became one of the most vibrant, energetic, and enigmatic figures in the London print trade. He often sailed close to the wind in matters of piracy, obscenity, and political acceptability, but he was easily the most talented political satirist of his period and drove forward innovations in many other fields. In the late 1720s he worked as a journeyman for other printsellers, engraving for the Bowles and Overton families. This early work included copies of John Wootton's *Hunting* (1726) and William Hogarth's *Harlot's Progress* (1732). He also worked for his father on his publishing projects.

In the early 1730s Bickham designed and engraved for fansellers many of the 'speaking fans' then in vogue. These were engraved expressively with words and images, sometimes of a political or satirical nature. Bickham began to publish on his own account towards the end of the decade. One of his first ventures, launched in 1737, was *The Musical Entertainer*, a series of engraved song sheets. He first advertised political satires and sporting prints in 1740, and after that date he became a prolific publisher of a wide variety of prints. About 1750 he was busily promoting the landscape gardens at Stowe and other tourist sites, including Hampton Court and Windsor, with sets of prints and printed guides and simultaneously publishing pattern books for Gothic and Chinese garden architecture. He developed a big stake in printed chinoiserie, publishing printed wallpaper as well as books of ornament.

Bickham's political prints include some of the most imaginative designs of the mid-century, such as *Great Britain and Ireland's Yawn* (1743), which celebrated the fall of Walpole. Several times he attracted the attention of the government. Their agents provided the information that 'Geo Bickham keeps a rolling press in his own house' (PRO, SP dom Geo II, gen. vol. 146, fols. 359–60) on the occasion that they recovered 'about 150 Obscene books with all sorts of Obscene Postures Seized out of Mr Bickhams Escrutore'—perhaps the 'cuts to the School of Venus' which he advertised in 1745. Similarly, Bickham's defence, that 'the Business of his Shop is carried on by his Wife & that he never concerns himself therein', provides evidence that by that date he was married, probably to the Elizabeth Bickham who was his executor.

Bickham's output was enormously varied and controversial; he competed with rivals in many fields. Where he was unsuccessful it was possibly because he was undercapitalized rather than for want of invention or determination. In addition to his activity as an engraver and publisher he taught etching, undertook engraving, seal engraving, and framing, and sold drawing materials. Only two apprentices are recorded: William Austin, who was accepted in 1747, and Thomas Butcher, in 1759. His undated *List of Books, Prints, Metzotintos &c* (c.1760) reveals a wide assortment of cheap prints, including garden views, satires, sporting prints, naval subjects, theatrical prints, Rembrandt copies, borders, and drawing books. He exhibited with the Free Society of Artists between 1761 and 1765, showing ambitious reproductive etchings after Rubens and in imitation of Rembrandt.

On 25 April 1767 it was announced in the *Public Advertiser* that Bickham had 'retired into the Country', and that his business would be continued by his nephew and former apprentice Thomas Butcher, who gave his previous address as the White Horse in Newgate Street (Overton's shop). Bickham died at his home in Kew Lane, Richmond, Surrey, on 21 June 1771, leaving his property to his widow, Elizabeth. A sale for her benefit of his copper plates and rolling press was advertised in the *Public Advertiser* on 9 January 1772. Some of his prints are held in the British Museum, London.   TIMOTHY CLAYTON

Sources T. Clayton, *The English print, 1688–1802* (1997) · M. Harris, 'Scratching the surface: engravers, printsellers and the London book trade in the mid-eighteenth century', *The book trade and its customers, 1450–1900: historical essays for Robin Myers*, ed. A. Hunt, G. Mandelbrote, and A. Shell (1997) · H. Atherton, *Political prints in the age of Hogarth* (1974) · N. Valpy, 'Plagiarism in prints: the *Musical*

entertainer affair', *Print Quarterly*, 6 (1989), 54–9 · private information (2004) [Kim Sloan, Surrey RO] · D. Hunter, '*Pope v. Bickham*: an infringement of *An essay on man* alleged', *The Library*, 6th ser., 9 (1987), 268–73 · P. H. Muir, 'The Bickhams and their *Universal Penman*', *The Library*, 4th ser., 25 (1944–5), 162–84 · M. Snodin, 'George Bickham Junior', *V&A Museum Album* (1983), 354–60 · PRO, SP dom Geo II, gen. vol. 146, fols. 359–60 · *London Evening-Post* (16–19 Feb 1740) · *Public Advertiser* (9 Jan 1772) · J. Döring, *Eine Kunstgeschichte der frühen englischen Karikatur* (Hildesheim, 1991)

Likenesses G. Bickham, line drawing, BM; repro. in G. Bickham, *The universal penman, or, The art of writing*, 52 pts (1733–41)

Wealth at death see will, Surrey HC

Bickley, Thomas (c.1518–1596), bishop of Chichester, was born at Stowe, Buckinghamshire. He became a chorister of Magdalen College, Oxford, in 1531, a demy in 1534, and a probationary fellow on 25 July 1540; he was confirmed in his fellowship a year later, on 26 July 1541. He was admitted BA in 1540 and incepted MA in 1546. Apparently an enthusiastic supporter of the reformed cause, he was involved in an incident in Magdalen College chapel on Whit Sunday 1548, when a priest was attacked as he celebrated mass. The celebrant was manhandled, various service books were damaged, and Bickley was said to have taken away the consecrated host and broken it in an irreverent manner. The whole incident may well be related to the introduction from Easter that year by royal proclamation of the order of the communion, an English rite for communion in both kinds (bread and wine), to be inserted into the Latin of the Sarum mass. An interim measure before the full introduction of a liturgy in English in the Book of Common Prayer of 1549, it contained much that would become familiar from the 1549 service, including breaking the consecrated hosts by the celebrant. Thus Bickley's action in breaking the hosts was doubtless that of a zealous reformer.

Bickley's career does not appear to have suffered as a result of this incident. He was ordained deacon at Oxford in April 1551, and was subsequently appointed as chaplain of the Edward IV chantry at St George's Chapel, Windsor Castle, from which he resigned on 31 October the following year; in July he was admitted BTh and became a royal chaplain. In that year the radical party in the college won a notable victory when, after the intervention of the privy council, Walter Haddon was elected president. Bickley was chosen vice-president and Thomas Bentham, future bishop of Coventry and Lichfield, one of the two deans of arts. Both were expelled following Queen Mary's accession in 1553, during a visitation of the college by Stephen Gardiner, bishop of Winchester. Bickley went into exile in France, studying at Paris and Orléans.

Upon his return to England at Elizabeth's accession Bickley was rapidly promoted, soon becoming chaplain to Matthew Parker, archbishop of Canterbury, and in 1560 chancellor of Lichfield Cathedral, where Thomas Bentham now presided as bishop. In November 1561 Bickley was an unsuccessful candidate for the presidency of Magdalen, which went to another former fellow and exile, Laurence Humphrey. In 1563, as a proctor for the clergy of Coventry and Lichfield diocese, he voted in convocation in

Thomas Bickley (c.1518–1596), by unknown artist, 1585–96

favour of liturgical reforms—effectively for a radical revision of the Book of Common Prayer of 1559; after the counting of proxy votes the proposals were defeated by a majority of one. Thereafter, however, Bickley appears to have toed Parker's increasingly authoritarian line. At Easter 1566, just after the archbishop had suspended thirty-seven city of London ministers for refusing canonical vestments, he was dispatched by Parker to preach in the parish of St Giles Cripplegate, where yet another former fellow of Magdalen, Robert Crowley, had been orchestrating opposition to Parker's drive for conformity. Parker reported that Bickley had been heard 'quietly', though from the context it must be doubted whether he had gone so far as to wear the surplice. On 26 September Parker described Bickley, now a candidate for one of the Canterbury prebends in the crown's gift, as one 'who hath done service and is ready to continue, and is both honest and well-learned' (*Correspondence*, 290).

Although Bickley never became a prebendary of Canterbury other preferments followed, most notably the archdeaconry of Stafford in 1567; in 1569, moreover, he was admitted warden of Merton College, Oxford, at the behest of Parker as the college's visitor. Parker expressed the hope that Bickley would prove a trustworthy head of a foundation that had yet to prove its loyalty to Elizabeth's settlement. His confidence does not seem to have been misplaced, since in 1570, casting about for a possible bishop of Oxford, Parker informed Sir William Cecil that Bickley was 'disciplinable, and will be ruled by counsel, and is of his nature both sincere and stout enough, and apt to govern' (*Correspondence*, 360). Bickley incepted as DTh in July 1570. No bishop of Oxford was appointed until 1589,

and Bickley continued into the 1580s (and his seventh decade) as warden of Merton. During his tenure the college welcomed a succession of protestant refugees while its library was expanded through a levy on newly elected fellows, the money raised being spent on books. Bickley's diligence in pastoral care was graphically demonstrated in 1577, when during a severe outbreak of plague he was the only Oxford head to remain in the city, where he dutifully attended the sick.

In 1581 Bickley fell foul of Parker's successor Edmund Grindal, over an illegal election to a Merton fellowship, finally making humble submission that he and the fellows had acted in contempt of Grindal's rights as college visitor. But at the beginning of his primacy in 1583 John Whitgift suggested him for promotion, either as dean of Westminster or as bishop of Chichester or else Bath and Wells. He pressed Lord Burghley for Bickley's elevation on at least one further occasion, and on 30 January 1586, despite the fact that as archdeacon of Stafford he had recently earned the earl of Leicester's hostility by suspending one of his chaplains, Bickley was consecrated to Chichester by Whitgift and bishops John Aylmer of London and John Piers of Salisbury. Opinions have differed as to his effectiveness as diocesan. At sixty-eight possibly the oldest man consecrated under Elizabeth, he has been seen as 'a tired old man slumbering away in his diocese … the most procrastinatory bishop in England' (Manning, 204). The balance of probabilities, however, is that he continued into old age as a conscientious administrator who monitored nonconformist activity, at least within the immediate vicinity of Chichester itself, and attempted to provide for regular sermons and other measures of control in a diocese where Catholicism remained more strongly entrenched among the ruling élite than anywhere else in the home counties.

Bickley died on 30 April 1596 at his palace of Aldingbourne and was buried in his cathedral on 26 May. In his will he left £40 to Magdalen College for the ceiling and paving of the school, and £100 to Merton College to endow a university sermon, which was to be preached by one of the fellows in the college chapel on 1 May. A memorial tablet, with an effigy of the bishop kneeling at prayer and a text praising his diligence in administering his diocese, was placed on the north side of the cathedral presbytery, near the high altar. Some time after 1658 it was removed to its present position, on the north wall of the lady chapel. KENNETH CARLETON

Sources Emden, *Oxf.*, 4.91 · W. Stubbs, *Registrum sacrum Anglicanum*, 2nd edn (1897) · *Fasti Angl.*, 1541–1857, [Chichester] · *VCH Sussex*, vol. 3 · *Hist. U. Oxf.* 3: *Colleg. univ.* · *Correspondence of Matthew Parker*, ed. J. Bruce and T. T. Perowne, Parker Society, 42 (1853) · K. Fincham, *Prelate as pastor: the episcopate of James I* (1990) · P. Collinson, *Archbishop Grindal, 1519–1583: the struggle for a reformed church* (1979) · R. B. Manning, *Religion and society in Elizabethan Sussex* (1969) · 'Letters of Thomas Wood, puritan, 1566–1577', ed. P. Collinson, *BIHR*, special suppl., 5 (1960) [whole issue] · C. M. Dent, *Protestant reformers in Elizabethan Oxford* (1983) · F. O. White, *Lives of the Elizabethan bishops of the Anglican church* (1898) · Lansdowne MSS, BL, MSS 42, 109/29 · *DNB*

Archives W. Sussex RO, Episcopal register, Ep.I/1/7

Likenesses oils, 1585–96, Magd. Oxf. [*see illus.*] · memorial tablet with effigy, lady chapel, Chichester Cathedral; repro. in *VCH Sussex*, vol. 3, p. 135 · oils, second version, Merton Oxf.
Wealth at death see will, W. Sussex RO, STC 1/14/4176–2

Bicknell, Alexander (*d.* 1796), writer, is of obscure origins. Of his life little is known except that his books appeared between 1775 and 1794, his first four titles being anonymous. *The Benevolent Man* (1775), a travel story, is a 'vehicle' for bourgeois domesticity. Promoting rank-conscious education for tradesmen's daughters along with the reforms of Hanway, Howard, and Whitworth, Bicknell writes as a loyal Hanoverian and protestant. This was followed by *The History of Edward Prince of Wales, Commonly Termed the Black Prince* (1776). The index in the *Monthly Review* for 1777 names Bicknell as the author, but the review finds the style and content of the 'historic tale' inauthentic. Dedicated to the prince of Wales, this work heralds the prince as descendant of Edward to affirm its Hanoverianism. A compilation otherwise without named sources, it acknowledges Froissart. *The History of Lady Anne Neville* (1776) was scorned by the *Monthly Review* (vol. 55) which claimed that the book's 'vicious' style would ensure that it would not 'survive its first winter'. Bicknell heightens his subject's erotic susceptibility to court intrigue, following Prévôst. Also noticed in volume 55 of the *Monthly Review* was *Isabella, or, The Rewards of Good Nature*: a 'very amiable picture of conjugal tenderness and prudence'. Its anonymous title-page says that its author wrote *The Benevolent Man* and *The History of Lady Anne Neville*.

Bicknell's name finally appeared on the title-page of *The Life of Alfred the Great, King of the Anglo-Saxons* (1777). It was belittled in the *Monthly Review* (58, 1778, 402). A sixth title, *Philosophical disquisitions on the Christian religion, addressed to Soame Jenyns, esq., and Dr. Kenrick*, appeared in 1777. The *Monthly Review* (57, 1777, 331) reports this anonymous work as upholding George Cheyne's eccentric theory of spirits lapsed from a pre-existent state and faults it for applying poetic licence in Plato, Shakespeare, Milton, and Pope to Christian doctrine. In *Prince Arthur: an Allegorical Romance* (1779) Bicknell's prose paraphrase of Spenser's *Faerie Queene* purports to extract the beauties from the allegory and to teach love of glory to all ranks. The first volume has an essay on allegory, the second one on romance. The title-page of *The putrid soul: a poetical epistle to Joseph Priestley. LL.D. F.R.S. on his disquisitions relating to matter and spirit* (1780) names Bicknell as the compiler of Carver's *Travels through the Interior Parts of North America*. In attacking Priestley, Bicknell cites his own *Disquisitions on the Christian Religion* (pp. 32–3). The *Monthly Review* (63, 1780, 467–8) found him deficient as 'poet, philosophe and theologist'; to Priestley's 'highly rectified spirit of matter' he opposes 'the last runnings of modern mysticism' taken from 'the dregs of Platonism'.

Eight years lapsed before Bicknell's name reappeared on a title-page. According to the *Monthly Review* (78, 1788, 522–3) *The Patriot King, or, Alfred and Elvida* (1788) sinks to the level of John Home's *Alfred* rather than rises to the sublimity of Thomson's hero: his imitation of Shakespearian magic is poor and his diction lacks dignity. The *Gentleman's Magazine* (58/1, 1788, 427) is positive: it is his first 'effort of genius'. Among the 162 subscribers were Joseph Banks, Charles Burney, William Chambers, John Coakley Lettsom, Richard Price, and Thomas Warton. Subscribers included 13 fellows of the Royal Society, 5 MPs, 5 MDs, 9 titled persons, and 11 clergymen.

A leaf of advertisements in the first edition of *The Patriot King* adds two titles to Bicknell's output: *A Monody (after the Manner of Milton's 'Lycidas')* on the Death of Mr. Linley, junior and *More Odes upon Odes, or, A Peep at Peter Pindar, or, Falsehood Detected, or, What you will*. His poem 'Vauxhall' was printed in the *General Magazine and Impartial Review* (July 1787, 105–6). Next he published an essay on the vulnerability of tradesmen's daughters to fortune hunters, a topic broached in *The Benevolent Man* (*General Magazine and Impartial Review*, August 1787, 145). 'Observations on the mottos annexed to the arms of the nobility', a satirical essay on aristocracy, appeared next (*General Magazine and Impartial Review*, September 1787, 180–84). Such journalism led to book projects, as with 'Caricatures explained' (*General Magazine and Impartial Review*, February 1789, 53–61). Here Bicknell treats paintings by Bunbury and Rowlandson as documents of social history, narrating the pretensions of the Griskins as they consider sitting for a family portrait. This piece is the basis of *Painting personified, or, The caricature and sentimental pictures, of the principal artists of the present times, fancifully explained* (1790). The *Monthly Review* (4, 1791, new ser., 109) derides it, but the *General Magazine and Impartial Review* (March 1790, 117–20) finds it amusing. Bicknell's *Doncaster Races, or, The History of Miss Maitland* appeared before *Painting Personified*, with no year on the title-page.

Bicknell's name was not seen on title-pages from 1780 to 1788 on account of his editorial work. Jonathan *Carver's *Travels through the Interior Parts of North America* appeared in 1778. He turned Carver's journals into a stylized account of a search for the north-west passage, adding materials from French missionaries. Bicknell's closeness to Carver is shown by his 'Anecdote of the late Captain Carver' in the *European Magazine* (4, November 1783, 346–7).

One other project of Bicknell's was *An apology for the life of George Ann Bellamy, late of Covent Garden Theatre, written by herself* (5 vols., 1785). He was widely thought to have written *The Memoirs of Mrs. Sophia Baddeley, Late of Drury Lane Theatre, by Mrs. Elizabeth Steele* (6 vols., 1787). The *European Magazine* (July 1787, 41) described Bicknell as 'one of the most *industrious* and *universal* book-makers in England' and said that Mrs Steele exposed him 'in the public prints for his *inability* or *misconduct* in the task of correcting and arranging the disgraceful materials necessary to compose the wretched history of an unhappy Courtesan'. The *General Magazine and Impartial Review* (June 1787, 20) held that Baddeley's story emulates the '*pious* and *sentimental* labours' of Mrs Bellamy and 'her amanuensis' from 'pecuniary gratification'. Mrs Steele and 'her *goose-quill* friend' are ironically praised.

Bicknell's final works indicate perhaps a desire for respectability. *The Grammatical Wreath, or, A Complete System of English Grammar* appeared in 1790. The *General Magazine and Impartial Review* (February 1790, 67) lauds the book for regulating philological disorder and for employing genius and keen taste in investigation. The *Monthly Review* (5, 1791, new ser., 100–01) grants it has a greater variety of matter than most digests but thinks its overelaborateness will be more useful to teachers than scholars. His *A History of England and the British Empire Designed for the Instruction of Youth* was published in 1791. The *Monthly Review* (5, 1791, new ser., 100), while disparaging the market impulses behind such compendiums, finds his among the best; it is well compiled and accurate, and its maps seem unique. *Instances of the Mutability of Fortune, Selected from Ancient and Modern History* appeared in the same year. Bicknell worked on this text over a long period, its early sections having appeared in the *European Magazine* (November 1783, 328–30; December 1783, 417–21; 5 February 1784, 105f.). The *Monthly Review* notices the 1792 edition (9, 1792, 116), the reviewer finding the eighteen accounts concisely and pleasantly told and endorsing the author's moral purposes. Bicknell offers verse captions throughout. He acknowledges his historical sources, citing himself in his instance of 'Alfred'.

Bicknell must have worked on other compilations, such as the abridgement of Peter Longueville's *The Hermit* (1727) that, according to *ESTC*, was published in Hartford by John Babcock in 1799. Bicknell aspired to genteel authorship, but his works were largely derivative and often won him dispraise. Editing brought him near to commercial success. His title-pages imply ongoing relations with publishers and booksellers. His work for journals was more extensive and his books reviewed more widely and positively than has been supposed. Gaps between dates of composition and publication imply that his writerly trajectory followed the typical career of a hack. Bicknell died in St Thomas's Hospital, London, on 22 August 1796.

ROBERT JAMES MERRETT

Sources *ESTC* · *The eighteenth century* [microfilm: Research Publications, Inc, Woodbridge, Connecticut] · *Monthly Review* · *European Magazine and London Review* · *General Magazine and Impartial Review* · *GM* · *The journals of Jonathan Carver and related documents, 1766–1770*, ed. J. Parker (1976) · L. Melville, *Stage favourites of the eighteenth century* [n.d.] · *DNB* · A. Bicknell, *The benevolent man* (1775)
Archives BL, letters concerning application for a grant from the Royal Literary Fund

Bicknell, Clarence (1842–1918), archaeologist and botanist, the youngest son of Elhanan *Bicknell (1788–1861), financier and art patron, and his third wife, Lucinda Sarah (1801–1850), sister of Hablot Knight Browne, was born at Herne Hill, Surrey, on 27 October 1842. Herman *Bicknell, orientalist and traveller, was his brother. Clarence was admitted to Trinity College, Cambridge, in January 1861, graduated BA in 1865, and proceeded MA in 1873. Despite the Wesleyan and Unitarian influences in his family background and its liberal and reformist independence of thought, which characterized his own attitudes later, he chose a conventional career in the Church of England: he was ordained deacon in 1866, priest in 1868, and held curacies at St Paul's, Newington, Surrey (1866–72), and Stoke upon Tern, Shropshire (1875–81).

For health reasons Bicknell adopted the practice of wintering abroad. In 1878 he visited Bordighera on the Italian 'coast of flowers', a congenial setting for a man with wide natural history interests and a particular expertise in botany. Here in the following years he ministered to the religious needs of the large British community, made the Villa Rosa his home, and created the Bicknell Museum. The museum had a dual purpose: to house his books and naturalist collections, but also to provide a meeting-place in which the local community could pursue their cultural and intellectual interests. He included a stage for concerts, and the two large pots designed to receive umbrellas bear inscriptions in Esperanto, testifying to his enthusiasm for an international language. Esperanto appears again on a plaque in Bordighera's English library, built by Bicknell largely at his own expense. A typically Victorian innovator, he was also a vegetarian, an enemy of the water-closet in the cause of organic husbandry, and a spartan devotee of personal ablutions in icy mountain torrents.

In 1885 Bicknell published *Flowering Plants and Ferns of the Riviera and Adjoining Mountains*, illustrated with eighty-two of his own paintings, and in September of that year he made what was to be a momentous journey to the Val des Merveilles, a series of glacial lakes in the maritime Alps at about 2200 yards along the western flank of Mount Bego. Six years earlier he had made an abortive attempt to inspect the rock engravings there, on which there was little reliable information, but unseasonably late snow had thwarted him. At this second attempt he sketched about fifty of the mysterious prehistoric designs. His curiosity was aroused, but his principal occupation continued to be his botanical work, culminating in 1896 with the publication of his *Flora of Bordighera and San Remo*.

In the following summer Bicknell rented a house at Casterino on the gentler slopes of Mount Bego, where he could combine his studies of alpine plants and the rock engravings. In September he sent a piece of incised rock to the British Museum with a report of his discoveries. Increasingly his summers were spent in amassing his collection of drawings, rubbings, and photographs, on which he based his first papers in Italian scientific journals. In 1902 he published in Bordighera *The Prehistoric Rock Engravings in the Italian Maritime Alps*, and a further account of his explorations followed in 1903. The unwelcome news that year that his rented base in Casterino had been sold, and that no other was available, was met with his decision to build a place of his own. All materials had to be transported by mules from Tende. Work began in 1905 and a year later Casa Fontanalba was ready for Bicknell's annual visit in June to 'my beloved mountain cottage and the free life I so enjoy' (Bicknell to Baroness Helene von Taube, 29 Sept 1913, NHM, 92 BIC).

The pattern of Bicknell's life was now set. Although he visited Ceylon in 1907 to see the island's plants and butterflies, and Britain in 1910 and 1913, his increasing preoccupation was with the innumerable representations of a horned creature or stag-headed god and of typical Bronze

Age daggers, and with the strange patterns defying interpretation, which cover so many rock surfaces at 2000–2500 metres surrounding the great peak of Bego. With his assistant Luigi Pollini, Bicknell gradually built up his astonishing documentation of over 11,000 petroglyphs which form the basis of his *Guide to the Prehistoric Rock-Engravings in the Maritime Alps*, published in 1913. By his labours over twelve summers he had focused international attention on one of the major monuments of European archaeology, and he continued to add to the record. On 18 August 1913 he wrote to Baroness von Taube:

> Luigi and I have been camping out for 2 nights, 4 hours away, and again exploring the rock figures … I cannot do quite as much as ten years ago … but I intend to fight on as long as possible, and so help those that come after. (Bicknell to Baroness Helene von Taube, NHM, 92 BIC)

Bicknell died unmarried at Casa Fontanalba on 17 July 1918 and was buried in the cemetery at Tende. Fifty years later the publication of French and Italian translations of his *Guide* was undertaken by the International Institute of Ligurian Studies, which had inherited Bicknell's museum and its traditions, in this area of historically alternating national sovereignty. To mark the occasion France and Italy combined to honour Bicknell's memory with laudatory plaques on his chalet at Fontanalba and on the rock face at Les Mesches, the gateway to Mount Bego. Nor has his distinction as a botanist been forgotten: a subspecies of the giant knapweed, which is a speciality of the alpine area, was officially named in 1973 *Leuzea rhapontica bicknellii*.

DESMOND HAWKINS

Sources E. Bernadini, *Le alpi marittime* (1979), 142–8 · A. N. Branghain, *The naturalist's Riviera* (1962) · NHM, 92 BIC · BM, Bicknell corresp. · D. Hawkins, 'Labour of twelve summers', *Country Life*, 173 (1983), 1112–16 · H. Lumley and others, *Les gravures rupestres de l'âge de bronze dans le région de Mt. Bégo* (1976) · *South European letters, 1901–1914*, RBG Kew, 148 · Desmond, *Botanists*, rev. edn · *DNB* · private information (2004) · personal knowledge (2004)
Archives BM · Museo Bicknell, Bordighera, Italy · NHM
Likenesses photograph (in later years), Istituto Di Studi Liguri, Via Romana 39, Bordighera, Italy · photograph (in later years), Carnegie Mellon University, Pittsburgh, Pennsylvania
Wealth at death £1172 18s.: administration with will, 7 Nov 1918, *CGPLA Eng. & Wales*

Bicknell, Elhanan (1788–1861), art patron and businessman, was born on 21 December 1788, at 8 Blackman Street, Southwark, London, the second son of William Bicknell (1749–1825) and his wife, Elizabeth, *née* Randall (1756–1821), of Sevenoaks, Kent. William was a friend of John Wesley and the Unitarian minister Elhanan Winchester, after whom he named his son. In 1789 William sold the serge manufacturing business which his grandfather had established at Taunton and Newington, and set up a school at Ponders End, moving it to Tooting Common in 1804; there Elhanan was educated, with Thomas Wilde, afterwards Lord Chancellor Truro. In 1808 he was sent to Caus, near Shrewsbury, to learn farming, but at the end of a year he abandoned that project; he returned to London and joined his uncle's firm at Newington Butts. John Walter Langton (1746–1822) had invented a process of using

spermaceti, derived from whale oil, for the manufacture of candles; the company established to exploit his discovery—which became Langton and Bicknell—thrived. About 1835 Bicknell foresaw how the repeal of the navigation laws, then in debate, would injure his trade, yet he disinterestedly supported the abolition of all protection.

From about 1838 Bicknell was a close friend of the painter David Roberts, and started to make a collection of modern British art. In 1845–6, probably inspired by Bicknell's business, J. M. W. Turner painted four whaling pictures. Paintings and sculptures, such as Edward Hodges Baily's *Eve*, adorned the principal rooms of Bicknell's house, which were always hospitably open to artists and art connoisseurs; visitors included John Ruskin, who from 1823 to 1842 lived opposite Carlton House, Herne Hill, to which Bicknell had moved about 1819. Apart from Thomas Gainsborough and Richard Wilson, the artists represented in his collection were those active in London about 1840, such as David Roberts, Clarkson Stanfield, William Collins, Augustus Callcott, William Hilton, Edwin Landseer, Charles Eastlake, and Turner, by whom Bicknell had choice works ranging from two small landscapes first exhibited in 1810–12 to some of his best paintings of Venice and watercolours of Switzerland of the early 1840s. Bicknell wanted to leave his collection to the nation, but for family reasons his pictures were sold after his death at Christies auction rooms in April 1863, realizing over £75,000.

In politics and in theology Bicknell was an enthusiastic and progressive liberal. He was a principal contributor to the building of the Unitarian chapel at Brixton, and gave £1000 to the British and Foreign Unitarian Association. He married four times: first, on 16 October 1810, to his first cousin and sister of his partner, Hannah Wootton Langton (1787/8–1815), with whom he had a son, Elhanan (1813–1860). He married second, on 13 February 1817, Mary Jones (d. 1827); their son, Henry Sanford Bicknell (1818–1880), married David Roberts's daughter and had his own art collection. His third marriage, to Lucinda Sarah (1801–1850), sister of the illustrator Hablot K. Browne, took place on 5 May 1829, and among their children were Herman *Bicknell (1830–1875), the orientalist, Algernon Sidney Bicknell (1832–1911), author, and Clarence *Bicknell (1842–1918), botanist. Finally, on 14 August 1851, Elhanan married Louisa Holland (1803/4–1884), widow of Henry Jones. Bicknell's health failed in 1861, and in the summer of that year he retired from business. He died at Carlton House on 27 November 1861, and was buried at Norwood cemetery on 3 December.

SELBY WHITTINGHAM

Sources P. Bicknell and H. Guiterman, 'The Turner collector: Elhanan Bicknell', *Turner Studies*, 7/1 (1987), 34–44 · A. S. Bicknell, *Five pedigrees* (1912) · J. J. Howard and F. A. Crisp, eds., *Visitation of England and Wales*, 21 vols. (privately printed, London, 1893–1921), vol. 17, pp. 33–46; vol. 21, p. 77 · D. S. Macleod, *Art and the Victorian middle class: money and the making of cultural identity* (1996), 393–5 · E. Browne, *Phiz and Dickens as they appeared to Edgar Browne* (1913), chap. 4 · G. F. Waagen, *Treasures of art in Great Britain*, 2 (1854), 349–54 · 'The collection of Elkanah [sic] Bicknell, esq., at Herne Hill', *Art Journal*, 19 (1857), 8–10 · *The Athenaeum* (7 Dec 1861), 769 · *Christian Reformer, or, Unitarian Magazine and Review*, new ser., 18 (1862),

55–9 · P. Bicknell, 'Turner's *The whale ship*: a missing link?', *Turner Studies*, 5/2 (1985), 20–23 · K. Sim, *David Roberts R.A., 1796–1864: a biography* (1984) · 'Clarence Bicknell', *On Beacon Hill*, 2 (1996–7), 1–4 [an occasional newsletter about the Bicknell family] · *The Times* (30 Nov 1861), 1a · cemetery records, West Norwood cemetery, London

Archives NL Scot. · NRA, priv. coll., Bicknell sales of 1863, Christies catalogues annotated and interleaved [microfilm copy at FM Cam.] | NL Scot., Roberts MSS

Likenesses S. Drummond, oils, 1789, priv. coll. · S. Drummond, oils, c.1796, priv. coll. · T. Phillips, oils, c.1830, Vintners Hall, London · T. Phillips, oils, in or before 1842 · C. Baugniet, lithograph, 1864, priv. coll. · S. Drummond, group portrait, oils, priv. coll.

Wealth at death £400,000: resworn probate, Nov 1866, *CGPLA Eng. & Wales* (1861)

Bicknell, Herman (1830–1875), orientalist and traveller, was born at Herne Hill, Surrey, on 2 April 1830, the third son of Elhanan *Bicknell (1788–1861) and his third wife, Lucinda Sarah (1801–1850), who was the sister of Hablot Knight Browne ('Phiz'). Clarence *Bicknell (1842–1918), archaeologist and botanist, was his brother. He was educated at Paris, Hanover, and London (University College and St Bartholomew's Hospital). After becoming a member of the Royal College of Surgeons in 1854 and passing the military medical examination, he joined the 59th regiment at Hong Kong in 1855 as assistant surgeon, whence he was transferred, in 1856, to the 81st regiment at Mian Mir, Lahore. While in India, where he served for four years, throughout the period of the mutiny, he studied oriental dialects, and managed to explore parts of Java, Tibet, and the Himalayas. On returning to England, by the Indus and Palestine, he exchanged into the 84th regiment, and was placed on the staff at Aldershot, but soon resigned his commission to devote himself entirely to travel and languages.

From this period Bicknell undertook many journeys from the Arctic regions to the Andes of Ecuador, and from America to the Far East, especially to undertake research in ethnology, botany, and general science. He was a keen alpinist and had climbed most of the main Swiss mountains, sustaining an injury when attempting the Matterhorn. In 1862 he started from London disguised as an English Muslim and went to Cairo, where he lived for a considerable period in the native quarter of the city. By this time intimately acquainted with the habits and manners of Islam, in the spring of the same year he joined the annual pilgrimage to Mecca, a dangerous exploit which he accomplished successfully. In 1868 he passed by Aleppo and the Euphrates to Shiraz, where he lived for some months in 1869, familiarizing himself with life in Persia, to aid his translation of the chief poems of Háfiz, the fourteenth-century poet of Shiraz, which he had been revising for fifteen years. But on 14 March 1875, before the manuscripts had received their final corrections, he died suddenly, at 48 Seymour Street, Portman Square, London, and was buried at Ramsgate, where he lived at 20 Royal Crescent with his wife, Elizabeth Anne, who survived him. After his death his brother, Algernon Sidney Bicknell, completed his volume on Háfiz which was published in 1875. It was essentially a prosodic exercise by a man

who had little real appreciation of Hafiz, and it was never influential.

Bicknell had great powers of endurance, and was a fair draughtsman, and a fine linguist. Besides his translation of Háfiz he published a few pamphlets. Despite the considerable wealth of his father, his own estate was valued at less than £1500.

A. S. BICKNELL, *rev.* ELIZABETH BAIGENT

Sources *The Times* (25 Aug 1862) · *CGPLA Eng. & Wales* (1875) · Boase, *Mod. Eng. biog.* · private information (1885) · private information (2004)

Wealth at death under £1500: probate, 23 April 1875, *CGPLA Eng. & Wales*

Bicknell, James David (1906–1988), record producer, was born on 1 September 1906 at 42 St John's Wood Road, London, the son of Gilbert Elhannan Bicknell, stockbroker, and his wife, Florence Ferrier Ross. He was educated in the high Anglican tradition of Marlborough College between 1919 and 1924, and gained a musical training in London and Paris. Bicknell intended to follow his father into the City, but at the age of twenty-one met Trevor Williams, chairman of the Gramophone Company (popularly known as HMV) and a friend of the Bicknell family, who offered him a job in the company's international artistes department. Bicknell later recalled that joining the business, for which his mother had worked before her marriage, made him feel as if he were coming home.

In 1927, the year Bicknell joined the international artistes department, the record industry was still undergoing a period of technological transition from mechanical to electrical recording. The new process made records sound more realistic and permitted large-scale recordings of orchestral and other works. As the existing catalogue of records had been rendered obsolete by these changes, the company was engaged in a major re-recording programme. At the time Fred Gaisberg, the British record industry's founding father, was the artistic director of the international artistes department. He took the young Bicknell under his wing and taught him the basics of artist and repertoire management. As Gaisberg's assistant Bicknell was involved in recording important performers such as Alfred Cortot, Jacques Thibaud, Pablo Casals, and Fritz Kreisler. In 1931, in the midst of the great depression, the Gramophone Company merged with its competitor, the Columbia Graphophone Company, to form Electric and Musical Industries Ltd (EMI). Despite the difficulties caused by the depression, the 1930s were a highly creative time for Bicknell. Among the many important recordings he made during the 1930s was a series of Mozart operas by the newly formed Glyndebourne Company, including first ever complete recordings of *La nozze di Figaro*, *Don Giovanni*, and *Così fan tutte*, which remained touchstones of performance on record into the late twentieth century.

Bicknell's career was interrupted by war service, when he was commissioned into the Oxford and Buckinghamshire light infantry, serving in Britain, France, and Germany. He was appointed MBE for bravery under fire. In 1946 he returned to EMI where he immediately began to rebuild the classical catalogue. He visited Italy and made contracts with rising young artists, such as the conductors Victor de Sabata and Guido Cantelli. They included the Italian violinist Giaconda de Vito (1907–*c*.1994), daughter of Giacomo de Vito, a doctor of agriculture, whom Bicknell married on 16 November 1949. They had no children. The decade following his return was one of great upheaval for EMI. The company lost much of its classical repertoire when its two American licensees, RCA Victor and American Columbia, terminated their agreements. In addition, EMI's late entry into the LP market meant that in order to compete it had to create a fresh catalogue in a short time. It was during this period that Bicknell and his colleague Walter Legge made the transition from artist and repertoire managers to record producers, responsible for creating a unique artistic form of performance on records. Bicknell was responsible for many of Cantelli's great recordings and those of another major post-war signing, the Spanish soprano Victoria de los Angeles.

In 1957 Bicknell became manager of EMI's international artistes department and gave up record making altogether. However, he supervised the modernization and expansion of the company's classical recording programmes, introducing stereo recording in 1957—a move which required the complete remaking of the existing classical catalogue. His period as manager was clouded by the difficulties he encountered trying to manage Walter Legge, whose costs were seen as increasingly extravagant by EMI's dynamic new chairman Sir Joseph Lockwood. However, by the time he retired in 1971, ending a supremely successful career spanning forty-four years and encompassing some of the most dramatic changes in the history of the record industry, he had created a major catalogue of classical music, expanded the range of music available to consumers, and dramatically increased sales of such records.

On his retirement Bicknell became EMI's honorary archivist, and continued to sit on several important committees such as the advisory panel to the Arts Council, and the governing committee of the British Institute of Recorded Sound. A tall distinguished man and a refined gentleman of the old school, Bicknell lived out his retirement with his wife in their Hertfordshire home, with occasional visits to their apartment in Rome and other travels. Curiously, he never wrote his memoirs, but, courteous to the end, he remained a major source of knowledge for broadcasters and historians of the recording industry.

Bicknell died, aged eighty-two, of bronchopneumonia and cancer of the pharynx at his home, Flint Cottage, Troutstream Way, Loudwater, Hertfordshire, on 5 September 1988. Throughout his career, Bicknell combined extraordinary ability in the field of recording with a diplomatic, easy-going personality—an essential feature in the often difficult atmosphere of the recording studio—which earned him the respect of colleagues and artists alike. At his retirement lunch in 1971, the veteran pianist Gerald Moore described Bicknell as 'a loveable character … who did his work with such enormous dignity and extraordinary modesty'.   PETER MARTLAND

Sources staff files, Central Research Laboratories, Hayes, Middlesex, EMI Music Archives · *The Guardian* (9 Sept 1988) · *The Independent* (16 Sept 1988) · *The Times* (8 Sept 1988) · b. cert. · m. cert. · d. cert. · M. Kennedy, *The Oxford dictionary of music*, rev. edn (1985) · P. Martland, *Since records began: EMI, the first 100 years* (1997)
Archives Central Research Laboratories, Hayes, Middlesex, EMI Music Archives | FILM BBC Television, 'Memories of a musical dog', *Omnibus*, 1988 | SOUND BL NSA, London · Central Research Laboratories, Hayes, Middlesex, EMI Music Archives
Likenesses portrait, Central Research Laboratories, Hayes, Middlesex, EMI Music Archives, staff file

Bicknell [*née* Younger], **Margaret** (1681–1723), actress and dancer, was born on 11 November 1681 in Edinburgh, the daughter of James Younger, a soldier, and his wife, Margaret Keith. Both of her parents were born in Scotland. She was the elder sister of the actress and dancer Elizabeth *Younger. By 1700 she had moved to London, where she married Peter Bicknell in the church of St Mary Magdalen, Knightrider Street, on 2 February 1700. Nothing is known of her husband except that he predeceased her. Her mother was buried at St Paul's, Covent Garden, on 11 February 1713.

Mrs Bicknell's first recorded appearance on the stage was in a *Scotch Dance* at Drury Lane on 20 August 1702, although she must have begun her career earlier. On 1 July 1703 at Drury Lane she was billed as Hoyden in John Vanbrugh's *The Relapse*. During the 1706–7 season she appeared at the Queen's Theatre, Haymarket, as the Lass in Richard Brome's *The Northern Lass*, Pert in George Etherege's *The Man of Mode*, and Cherry in George Farquhar's *The Stratagem* (a part she created). In January 1708 she returned to Drury Lane, where her début in the title role of William Wycherley's *The Country Wife* attracted the attention of Sir Richard Steele, as he later recalled: 'Mrs Bignell did her part very happily and had a certain grace in her rusticity, which gave us hopes of seeing her a very skilful player and in some parts supply our loss of Mrs Verbruggen' (*The Tatler*, 16 April 1709).

After another season at the Queen's Theatre, Mrs Bicknell returned to Drury Lane, where she remained for the rest of her career. She was a comic actress, and among her most notable roles was Silvia in Farquhar's *The Recruiting Officer*; for John Gay she created the parts of Alison (the title role) in his first play *The Wife of Bath* (1713) and Kitty Carrot in *The What d'ye Call it* (1715). She was also a comic dancer and drew the admiration of Sir Richard Steele in *The Spectator* for 5 May 1712:

> It would be a great Improvement, as well as Embellishment to the Theatre, if Dancing were more regarded, and taught to all the Actors. One who has the Advantage of such an agreeable girlish Person as Mrs. *Bicknell*, joyned with her Capacity of Imitation, could in proper Gesture and Motion represent all the decent Characters of Female Life.

Her most popular dance was *Tollet's Ground*, performed with her sister. In 1717 she danced Aglaia in John Weaver's innovative *The Loves of Mars and Venus* and Andromeda (Colombine) in his pantomime *The Shipwreck, or, Perseus and Andromeda*. For John Thurmond she danced Colombine in his pantomimes *The Dumb Farce* (1719) and *The Escapes of Harlequin* (1722).

Mrs Bicknell died at her home in Poland Street, London,

on 24 May 1723, 'of a Consumption', according to the *Daily Journal* of 25 May. She was buried at St Paul's, Covent Garden, on 27 May. In her will she described herself as a widow, and left the bulk of her estate including her house in Poland Street to Charlotte, the illegitimate daughter of her sister Elizabeth.					MOIRA GOFF

Sources E. L. Avery, ed., *The London stage, 1660–1800*, pt 2: *1700–1729* (1960) · *The Tatler* (16 April 1709) · *The Spectator* (5 May 1712) · T. Betterton, [W. Oldys and others], *The history of the English stage* (1741), 162–3 · *IGI* · *Daily Journal* (25 May 1723)
Wealth at death cash bequests of £155; possessions incl. house in Poland Street, London: will, PRO, PROB 11/591, sig. 115

Bicknor [Bykenore], **Alexander** (*d.* 1349), archbishop of Dublin, took his name from Bicknor in Gloucestershire. He was probably born in the 1260s. It is assumed that he obtained his title of master following study at Oxford, although there is nothing to prove this. It is possible (although there is no direct evidence) that Bicknor owed his initial career in England and later in Ireland to the patronage of Joan de Valence, countess of Pembroke and lady of Wexford, whose castle at Goodrich, Herefordshire, very close to Bicknor's presumed birthplace, was one of her favourite residences.

Bicknor's first recorded official duty was an inquiry into weirs on the River Severn in 1291. In 1301 and 1302 he was a collector of the fifteenth in Gloucestershire. In 1305 he accompanied the justiciar John Wogan to Ireland, but probably returned to England since in 1306 he was again appointed as a tax collector in Gloucestershire. In June 1307 he was appointed as escheator of Ireland and in October treasurer of the Dublin exchequer. In early 1311 Bicknor was unanimously elected as archbishop of Dublin by the chapters of both Dublin cathedrals, St Patrick's and Holy Trinity (commonly called Christ Church). His election was however quashed by the pope in favour of another royal servant, John Lech. In June 1311 Bicknor was appointed to represent the king at the forthcoming general council at Vienne, but did not in fact go. Following Lech's death in August 1313 Bicknor was again elected as archbishop, but this time only by the chapter of St Patrick's, the rival chapter choosing the chancellor of Ireland, Walter Thornbury. Bicknor gave up office as treasurer on 15 April 1314 to go to Avignon to pursue his claims, which were supported by Edward II, but by the time he arrived there about June 1314 the pope was dead. Bicknor appears to have remained at Avignon, with the approval of Edward II, until on 20 August 1317 he was at last provided to Dublin by the new pope, John XXII, and was consecrated at Avignon on 25 August. By the early autumn of 1317 Bicknor had returned to England where for the time being he remained, making an important contribution to the negotiations between Edward II and the earl of Lancaster which led to the treaty of Leake in August 1318. He was also present at St Paul's in November 1317, when the papal legates published bulls excommunicating Robert I of Scots.

On 11 August 1318 Bicknor was appointed as *custos* and justiciar of Ireland, holding office until March 1319. On 9 October 1318 he arrived in Dublin for the first time since his election as archbishop nearly six years earlier. Early in 1320 he held a provincial synod, whose twenty-three statutes ranged from the duty of paying tithes to the observance of the feasts of St Patrick and other Irish saints. Bicknor's sermon against sloth and idleness, which he preached in Holy Trinity Cathedral, may also belong to this time. In February 1321 at St Patrick's Cathedral he instituted the new university, with faculties of theology and law and with statutes modelled on Oxford, which had originally been authorized by Clement V in 1312. The university however had a very brief existence, becoming swallowed up almost at once by Bicknor's many other preoccupations.

As early as November 1319 Bicknor had been ordered to present his accounts as treasurer of Ireland for audit at the English exchequer. The audit finally began in October 1323 and continued until June 1325. In March 1324 Bicknor was sent to Gascony to inquire into the St Sardos dispute, and in October 1324 was appointed to negotiate a marriage between Prince Edward and the king of Aragon's daughter. However, in May 1325 Edward II asked the pope to remove Bicknor from office on the grounds that he was responsible for the loss of La Réole in September 1324, for allegedly accusing Hugh Despenser the younger of treachery, and for wasting the revenues of Ireland. Although the attack on Bicknor was politically motivated and there was some genuine confusion in his accounts, there was also ample evidence that he had committed acts of fraud and forgery. In October 1325 he appeared before the exchequer at Westminster and admitted his guilt, and in December following Bicknor's goods, chattels, and lands in England and Ireland were confiscated (including those of his archbishopric). Bicknor joined Isabella after her landing in England in September 1326 and was present at Bristol on 26 October when the future Edward III was proclaimed *custos* of the realm. Despite his support for the new regime Bicknor was not pardoned for his financial misdeeds as treasurer, while he was also pursued for alleged irregularities as justiciar in 1318–19. After much harassment by the exchequer he was finally pardoned by Edward III in June 1344, without ever formally closing his accounts.

Meanwhile he experienced other serious problems. Bicknor had been excommunicated in 1325 for nonpayment of debts owed to the pope and was still resisting papal demands as late as 1335. He was also involved in a long-running dispute with one of his bishops, Richard Ledred of Ossory, who in 1324 had accused members of the Outlaw family of witchcraft, heresy, and usury. The dispute was still unsettled when Clement VI became pope in 1342. On Bicknor's refusal to go to Avignon, Archbishop Fitzralph of Armagh was commissioned in 1347 to hold an inquiry into the state of the archdiocese of Dublin. This led in April or May 1349 to Fitzralph's expulsion from the city of Dublin by royal officials at Bicknor's instigation. The episode was also part of the continuing dispute over the primacy, which had long been an issue but had returned to prominence with Bicknor's claims to the title of 'primas Hiberniae' traditionally accorded to Armagh.

Bicknor died in Dublin on 14 July 1349, possibly of the plague which was then raging in Ireland.

Although Bicknor played a useful role both in Ireland and in England during the reign of Edward II, he seems to have been naïve and, unlike some other prelates, did not have the ability (or the lack of scruple) needed for survival during the troubled times in which he lived. In many respects his career from 1327 on was little more than an extended postscript.

J. R. S. PHILLIPS

Sources Emden, *Oxf.* · T. W. Moody and others, eds., *A new history of Ireland*, 2: *Medieval Ireland, 1169–1534* (1987); repr. with corrections (1993); 9: *Maps, genealogies, lists: a companion to Irish history, part 2* (1984) · J. A. Watt, *The church and the two nations in medieval Ireland* (1970) · A. Gwynn, *Anglo-Irish church life fourteenth and fifteenth centuries* (1968), vol. 2/4 of *A history of Irish Catholicism* · J. R. S. Phillips, *Aymer de Valence, earl of Pembroke, 1307–1324: baronial politics in the reign of Edward II* (1972) · K. Walsh, *A fourteenth-century scholar and primate: Richard FitzRalph in Oxford, Avignon and Armagh* (1981) · R. M. Haines, *The church and politics in fourteenth-century England: the career of Adam Orleton, c. 1275–1345*, Cambridge Studies in Medieval Life and Thought, 3rd ser., 10 (1978) · R. M. Haines, *Archbishop John Stratford: political revolutionary and champion of the liberties of the English church*, Pontifical Institute of Medieval Studies: Texts and Studies, 76 (1986) · P. Chaplais, ed., *The War of Saint-Sardos (1323–1325): Gascon correspondence and diplomatic documents*, CS, 3rd ser., 87 (1954) · J. F. Lydon, ed., 'The enrolled account of Alexander Bicknor, treasurer of Ireland, 1308–14', *Analecta Hibernica*, 30 (1982), 7–46 · J. F. Lydon, 'Alexander Bicknor—archbishop and peculator', *History Ireland*, 1/2 (1993) · B. Williams, 'The sorcery trial of Alice Kyteler, 1324', *History Ireland*, 2/4 (1994), 20–24 · A. Gwynn, 'The medieval university of St Patrick's, Dublin', *Studies: an Irish Quarterly Review*, 27 (1938), 199–212, 437–54 · J. T. Gilbert, ed., *Chartularies of St Mary's Abbey, Dublin: with the register of its house at Dunbrody and annals of Ireland*, 2 vols., Rolls Series, 80 (1884) · H. J. Lawlor, 'Calendar of the *Liber ruber* of the diocese of Ossory', *Proceedings of the Royal Irish Academy*, 27C (1908–9), 159–208 · A. Gwynn, ed., 'Some unpublished texts from the Black Book of Christ Church, Dublin', *Analecta Hibernica*, 16 (1946), 281–337 · J. T. Gilbert, ed., *'Crede Mihi': the most ancient register book of the archbishops of Dublin before the Reformation* (1897) · J. Mills, ed., *Account roll of the priory of the Holy Trinity, Dublin, 1337–1346* (1996) · C. McNeill, ed., *Calendar of Archbishop Alen's register, c.1172–1534* (1950), 169–98 · D. Renn, *Goodrich Castle, Herefordshire* (1998)
Archives Bibliothèque Nationale, Paris, MS Latin 5954
Wealth at death inventory, 1349, Lydon, 'Alexander Bicknor' · property, confiscated by crown in 1325, valued at £553 1s. 3¾d.: McNeill, ed., *Calendar*

Bidder, George Parker (1806–1878), civil engineer, was born on 13 June 1806 in Moretonhampstead, Devon, the third son and sixth of nine children of William Bidder (1768–1844), a stonemason, and his wife, Elizabeth, *née* Parker (1769–1844). He and two of his brothers reportedly had remarkable memories. Unlike most children born with similar gifts, Bidder was able in later life not only to delve into his mental processes and explain them, but also to use them throughout a successful engineering career. He received little formal schooling and was taught no more arithmetic than counting to 100 by his brother, yet it was soon noticed that young Bidder had an extraordinary ability to handle numbers without writing them down. This led to his powers being exhibited, first at local fairs before he was six and then at an increasingly wide range of venues in many parts of Britain, his feats being recorded in a succession of pamphlets. In October 1816 a group of benefactors at St John's College, Cambridge, sent

George Parker Bidder (1806–1878), by unknown artist

him to Wilson's Grammar School, Camberwell, Surrey, but public exhibitions clearly proved too lucrative to allow him to stay longer than about six months. During 1817 Bidder appeared before Queen Caroline, wife of George III. The questions which she and the royal princes asked were widely reported. Despite this gruelling upbringing, the boy remained balanced, modest, and cheerful.

Sir Henry Jardine, king's remembrancer for Scotland, noticed Bidder while he was being exhibited in Edinburgh in 1819 and arranged for a year's private coaching before sending him to Edinburgh University in 1820 to study mathematics and natural philosophy. In 1822 he was awarded the magistrates' prize for higher mathematics, but he left in May 1824 without taking a degree. In 1846 his growing prosperity allowed him to commemorate his benefactor by founding the Jardine bursary at the university. Addressing the Institution of Civil Engineers on mental calculation in 1856, he explained how his apparently unconventional methods had occurred to him simply as convenient for mental operations. His original ignorance of concepts such as squares and cube roots was such that he learned them only from his questioners. Ultimately he developed methods to calculate compound interest and logarithms mentally. He retained his powers to the end of his life.

Bidder's first employment was with the Ordnance Survey, first in south Wales and subsequently in London, but within a year he joined Henry Robinson Palmer, founder of the Institution of Civil Engineers, who had himself only recently ceased to be Thomas Telford's pupil. Bidder did a little work with Telford, and on his own account, during the next few years, but mostly he was employed by either Palmer or James Walker and his partner, Alfred Burges, on various surveys and works at increasing levels of responsibility until he was resident engineer at the reconstruction of Brunswick wharf, Blackwall, with its pioneering use of cast-iron sheet piling, completed in 1834. For about a year early in this period he supplemented his income by taking part-time work at the Royal Exchange Assurance Corporation. In 1826 he first appeared before a parliamentary committee helping Palmer to oppose the second Liverpool and Manchester Railway Bill. On that occasion, as he later remarked, his opposition was 'fortunately … utterly unsuccessful' (Bidder, 275). Such work thereafter took up a great deal of his time. His memory and powers of mental calculation made him a formidable witness. When Brunswick wharf was finished, Bidder was reintroduced to Robert Stephenson whom he had met in Edinburgh. Stephenson hired Bidder to work on several aspects of the London and Birmingham Railway, including a survey and plan of the incline down to Euston Station and the station itself, all within six weeks, to meet a parliamentary deadline. He left the railway in mid-1835 to become effectively Stephenson's partner, and in the same year he married Georgina Warren Harby (1808–1884), daughter of Thomas Harby, retired sea captain, of Pekin Place, Poplar, and his wife, Sarah.

Bidder demonstrated a clear grasp of technical and financial aspects of a problem, and his works were characterized by simplicity and economy. He was perforce largely preoccupied with railways during and after the railway mania of 1845 and was actively involved in the 'battle of the gauges'. Although Bidder was less well known than his contemporaries Robert Stephenson, Isambard Kingdom Brunel, and Joseph Locke, Charles Manby prefaced his memoir of Bidder (1878) with the observation that 'a more justifiable association would probably be that of Stephenson, Brunel and Bidder' (Manby, 279). Manby was well qualified to judge, having been secretary of the Institution of Civil Engineers from 1839 to 1856, when all four were most active.

Bidder's fascination with the dynamics of moving water led him to problems of tidal scour on coasts and estuaries; the heated debates about the parallel problems of water supply and sewerage, especially in London where he played an important part; the committee for warship design; his experiments with steam trawling; the rebuilding of his own yacht, Mayfly; his help to Froude during his early model tests; but above all, work on docks with which he was involved throughout his career—the original Victoria docks, London, being probably his greatest technical achievement.

The successful trials at Euston in 1837 convinced Bidder of the immense significance of the electric telegraph. He was responsible for the London and Blackwall's becoming the first railway to be equipped throughout with telegraph facilities from the time it was opened in 1840. In 1845–6 he joined William Fothergill-Cooke in establishing the Electric Telegraph Company, with which he remained closely associated until it was nationalized in 1870. He was also involved in the development of submarine telegraph facilities; as early as 1850 he foresaw the global possibilities of telecommunication.

In his prime, Bidder stood 5 feet 9 inches, a commanding figure for the time. His hair went white at an early age and for much of his life he wore a large beard. He was an active member of the Institution of Civil Engineers for nearly fifty years and president in 1860–61. The only papers he presented were 'On mental calculation' (1856), his presidential address (1860), and, jointly with his son, 'The national defences' (1861). He presided over the mechanics section of the British Association for the Advancement of Science (1868). He was an enthusiastic contributor to discussions, and revelled in debate and controversy. His robustness led a few who did not know him well to label him as brusque and rude, but his wide circle of devoted friends, many of long standing, showed they were mistaken. Although baptized in the Presbyterian chapel where his mother was an active member, and having been coached for a year by a minister of the Church of Scotland, Bidder was a practising member of the Church of England. The concluding paragraphs of his Devonshire Association presidential address (1869) set out his firmly held beliefs.

Bidder's letters to his wife while he was away give a vivid picture of his activities. The Bidders raised eight children; the eldest, a son also called George Parker Bidder (1836–1896), became a QC, specializing in parliamentary work. Their other son was ordained and, as bursar of St John's College, Oxford, successfully retrieved the college's finances. The Bidders mostly lived in Surrey, first in Walworth, then for eighteen years at Mitcham Hall. In 1864 they built Ravensbury Park House on land they owned west of the River Wandle. In 1862 they had bought a house on Paradise Point, Dartmouth, which they renamed Ravensbury. They used it as a holiday home and base for their yacht but were about to move to a larger house in nearby Stoke Fleming when Bidder died unexpectedly of heart problems at Ravensbury on 20 September 1878. He was buried in Stoke Fleming churchyard.

H. T. WOOD, rev. E. F. CLARK

Sources G. P. Bidder, 'On mental calculation', PICE, 15 (1855–6), 251–80, esp. 275 · C. Manby, 'Memoir of George Parker Bidder', PICE, 57 (1878–9), 279, 294–309 · E. F. Clark, George Parker Bidder: the Calculating Boy (1983) · CGPLA Eng. & Wales (1878) · d. cert. · Devon RO

Archives Sci. Mus., business corresp. and papers; corresp. and papers

Likenesses H. Meyer, stipple and aquatint, pubd 1817 (after W. Waite), BM, NPG · R. Cooper, stipple, pubd 1819 (after W. S. Lethbridge), BM · J. S. Cotman, pencil drawing, 1819, V&A · J. H. Robinson, line engraving, pubd 1819 (after Hayter), BM, NPG · W. Brockedon, chalk drawing, c.1825, NPG · J. Lucas, mezzotint, pubd 1848, BM · Dever, oils, c.1864, U. Edin. · oils, c.1870, Inst. CE · H. C. Fehr, marble bust, 1899, Inst. CE · S. Freeman, stipple (aged nine; after J. King), BM, NPG · D. Turner, etching (after J. S. Cotman), BM, NPG · marble bust, NPG · miniature [see illus.] · oils, Inst. CE

Wealth at death under £90,000: probate, 31 Oct 1878, CGPLA Eng. & Wales

Bidder, George Parker (1863–1953), marine biologist, was born on 21 May 1863 in Kensington, London, the elder son of George Parker Bidder QC (1836–1896), of Lincoln's Inn, amateur astronomer and cryptographer, and his wife, Anna, second daughter of John Robinson McClean, civil engineer and MP. Bidder was educated at King's preparatory school, Brighton, and at Harrow School from 1876 to 1881. He went to University College, London, 1881–2, and attended E. Ray Lankester's lectures. From there he went as an exhibitioner in mathematics and science to Trinity College, Cambridge, and took the natural sciences tripos in 1884 and 1886. He occupied the Cambridge University table at the zoological station in Naples in 1886, 1887, and 1888, investigating the biology of sponges. His application for a fellowship at Trinity College in 1888 was unsuccessful, so he continued with his research at Naples at the invitation of the director, making visits in 1890, 1891, and 1893. A night owl, he started his research day in the early evening and went to bed in the early morning. This habit led to his purchase of the Tramontano Hotel in Naples in 1889. Apparently he had been woken up one afternoon exceptionally early. He was told this was essential as the hotel was being sold. When he was told the selling price he wrote out a cheque for more than this, and bought the hotel. He renamed it Parker's Hotel and sold it in 1922.

Bidder inherited the gift of visualizing numbers from his grandfather, George Parker *Bidder (1806–1878), who was known as the Calculating Boy. Bidder enjoyed using mathematics in his research and was noted for his accurate observations and experiments. He published eighteen papers on various aspects of sponges. In 1928, with Mrs Vosmaer-Roell, he published a revised version of Gualth Vosmaer's *Bibliography of Sponges, 1551–1913*, which has 3800 references in chronological order. Besides being a gifted scientist Bidder was imaginative and an able linguist. He published two books of poetry in 1899, *By Southern Shore* and *Merlin's Youth*. He questioned the translation of the word 'arcus', as used in Horace's *Carminum*, 3.26, and showed with thorough research that 'arcus', as used in the original manuscript, must have meant a bow drill, though not usually translated as this.

In 1890 Bidder made his first visit to the Plymouth marine laboratory; he began to work there in 1893. He continued his research on sponges at Plymouth until his father died in 1896. His father died following a street accident in Manchester and Bidder had to devote much of his time to sorting out his many business interests (besides being a barrister he had been chairman of several companies, including the Cannock Chase colliery). Bidder inherited much of his father's wealth. He was managing director of Cannock Chase colliery from 1897 to 1908 and chairman from 1915 to 1919. In 1899 he married Marion Greenwood (1862–1932) [see Bidder, Marion Greenwood], a physiologist from Newnham College, Cambridge. They started married life in Plymouth and moved to Cavendish Corner, 221 Hills Road, Cambridge, in 1902. They had two daughters.

In 1905 Bidder had tuberculosis confirmed. After leaving Papworth Hospital, he lived the life of a semi-invalid for

the next decade, but ultimately made a complete recovery. During this rest he read widely, and experimented with bottom trailers which could be used to research the movements of submarine currents. As a result of this he worked at HMS *Vernon* during the First World War. He was made ScD by Cambridge University in 1916 (he lectured at the university on sponges in 1894 and 1920–27).

In 1902, as government funds were not forthcoming, Bidder purchased a steam trawler, renamed the *Huxley*, for North Sea exploration, under the auspices of the International Council for the Exploration of the Sea, and let the ship to the Marine Biological Association. In 1910, with the proceeds of the sale of the ship, the Ray Lankester Fund was formed to finance one-year research tenures at Plymouth. In 1920, when the association needed to expand, Bidder gave half of the projected cost of the buildings.

Bidder was president of the Marine Biological Association from 1939 to 1945 and of the zoology section of the British Association in Leeds in 1927. He bought the *Quarterly Journal of Microscopical Science* to ensure its continued publication, and did the same for the *Journal of Experimental Biology*, forming the Company of Biologists to run it. He was a vice-president of the Linnean Society in 1924 and 1931, and zoological secretary in 1928–31. He died on 31 December 1953 at the Evelyn Nursing Home, Cambridge. A memorial service was held in Trinity College chapel in Cambridge on 23 January 1954.

CATHARINE M. C. HAINES

Sources F. S. Russell, 'George Parker Bidder (1863–1953)', *Journal of the Marine Biological Association of the United Kingdom*, 34 (1955), 1–13 · CUL, Bidder MS Add. 9227 · Venn, *Alum. Cant.* · *The Times* (1 Jan 1954) · *The Times* (25 Jan 1954) · *The Times* (3 Feb 1896) · G. P. Bidder, 'Arcus', *Journal of Philology*, 35 (1919), 113–27 · *Horace: the odes and epodes*, trans. C. E. Bennett, rev. edn (1927); repr. (1952) · Horace, *Carminum*, 3.26 · private information (2004) · *WWW*, 1951–60 · *CGPLA Eng. & Wales* (1954) · C. F. A. Pantin, 'Dr G. P. Bidder', *Nature*, 173 (1954), 802–3 · G. S. Carter, *Proceedings of the Linnean Society of London*, 166th session (1953–4), 34–7
Archives CUL, papers; scientific and personal papers · Harrow School, Middlesex, chemistry notes, letters, telegrams · Marine Biological Association of the United Kingdom, Plymouth, corresp. and papers | Rice University, Houston, Texas, Woodson Research Center, corresp. with Sir Julian Huxley · U. Cam., Cavendish Laboratory, corresp. with his daughter, Anna McClean Bidder
Likenesses R. S. Eves, oils, 1934, Marine Biological Association, Plymouth · Ramsey and Muspratt, photograph, 1934, repro. in Russell, 'George Parker Bidder', frontispiece · M. Spooner, caricature, Marine Biological Association, Plymouth · photograph, Marine Biological Association, Plymouth
Wealth at death £77,179 11s. 11d.: probate, 6 May 1954, *CGPLA Eng. & Wales*

Bidder, Marion Greenwood [née Marion Greenwood] (1862–1932), physiologist, was born on 24 August 1862 at 181 Coltman Street, Anlaby Road, Myton, Hull, the sixth child and younger daughter of George Greenwood (1818–1888), shipping agent and Baptist lay preacher, and his wife, Agnes Hamilton (1825–1902). They moved to Oxenhope, Yorkshire, when she was seven.

Marion Greenwood went to the Bradford Girls' Grammar School as one of its first pupils; when just seventeen, she went with a school scholarship to Girton College,

Cambridge. There she took the Previous examination, then a double first in the natural sciences tripos, newly available to women: part one in botany, physiology, and zoology in 1882, part two in physiology in 1883. Inspired by the physiologist Michael Foster, she began her research on digestive processes in the university physiological laboratory, sharing a bench with William Hardy. With a Bathurst research studentship from Newnham College, she was one of the first women to do independent research in Cambridge, and first holder of Girton's Gamble prize, in 1888.

In 1884 Newnham appointed Greenwood demonstrator and lecturer in physiology and botany at the Balfour Laboratory, in Downing Place, newly opened for the women students' practical work in biology, the university laboratories being closed to them. J. N. Langley, Foster's demonstrator and his successor in 1903, advised against her accepting the demonstratorship, but she 'trusted it would mean no lessening of research, only a better arranging of the day's work'. E. Rebecca Saunders, one of her first pupils, took over the botany in 1888.

Marion Greenwood was head of the Balfour Laboratory from 1890 to 1899, organizing the courses, assembling equipment and reagents, and preparing microscopic sections, 'with only a young untrained boy as general laboratory attendant'; as Rebecca Saunders wrote in 1932: 'had Miss Greenwood not been endowed with a splendid constitution she could hardly have accomplished all that was required, and carried out research work at the same time' (Saunders). Her work included advanced demonstrations in the university laboratory. She lived in Newnham from 1888, as lecturer and director of studies in biology, supervising (tutoring) the women physiology students, walking the 3 miles between Newnham and Girton. Newnham and Girton set up natural sciences clubs in 1883 and 1884, the men's societies being closed to them, and she gave a paper on diphtheria to a joint meeting in 1894.

Despite a heavy teaching load Greenwood pursued her research. Following histological examination of gastric glands, of interest to Langley, she developed her classic studies of digestion in protozoa, publishing eight papers in the *Journal of Physiology* (1884–96), one of them with Rebecca Saunders. In 1895 she became the first woman to give a paper (on food vacuoles in infusoria, published in *Philosophical Transactions of the Royal Society*, series B) in person to the Royal Society. When the microbiologist Ilya Mechnikov (a Nobelist, with Ehrlich, in 1908) visited Cambridge in 1898 he told Sir Michael Foster he admired the papers of a young man called Greenwood, and Foster was happy to introduce an attractive young woman.

Marion Greenwood 'possessed in high degree the gift of literary appreciation' (Saunders), which she shared with the students; she loved Browning, Jane Austen, Peacock, Meredith, and Tennyson. Trained by her mother in housewifely duties, she enjoyed cooking, and examined in cookery for the Gloucestershire School of Cookery and Domestic Economy. With Florence Baddeley, she published *Domestic Economy in Theory and Practice: a Textbook for Teachers*

and Students in Training (1901; 2nd edn, 1916), with information on nutrition, bacterial contamination of foods, and general hygiene.

Marion Greenwood gave up teaching and research in 1899 soon after her marriage to George Parker *Bidder (1863–1953), a marine biologist of independent means. They lived first in Plymouth, where he worked on sponges at the Marine Station, but she was unable to do research. They returned to Cambridge in 1902. George Parker Bidder was found to have tuberculosis in 1905, and his health was a major preoccupation for a few years. Their daughters, Caroline Greenwood Bidder (Mrs Barclay Russell) and Anna McClean Bidder, born in 1900 and 1903, went to Girton and Newnham respectively. Anna, who became a marine zoologist, was a founder, then first president of Lucy Cavendish College, Cambridge.

The Bidder home at Cavendish Corner was a centre of hospitality to a wide range of people. Marion Bidder was president of the Cambridge Women's Liberal Association and a warm suffragist, promoting the election of women to town and county councils. She had a strong sense of public duty: while at Newnham she organized a Sunday class for working men in Barnwell. She was an associate of Newnham College, 1893–1904, member of council, 1894–6, for many years a poor-law guardian, and vice-chairman of the Cambridgeshire Voluntary Association for Mental Welfare, the first of its kind in the country. She sat on the Women's War Agricultural Committee, 1916–17, was a governor of Homerton Teacher Training College for eighteen years, chairman of trustees from 1925, and governor of Girton College, 1924–32. Hardy wrote in his obituary of her in *Nature* that she combined unusual intellectual distinction with great personal charm, and the gift of comradeship. She died at the Evelyn Nursing Home, Cambridge, on 25 September 1932. She was buried in Cambridge.   JOAN MASON

Sources [A. B. White and others], eds., *Newnham College register, 1871–1971*, 2nd edn, 1 (1979), 177 · K. T. Butler and H. I. McMorran, eds., *Girton College register, 1869–1946* (1948), 636 · M. L. Richmond, '"A lab of one's own": the Balfour biological laboratory for women at Cambridge University', *Isis*, 88 (1997), 422–55 · W. B. Hardy, *Nature*, 130 (1932), 689–90 · E. R. Saunders, *Newnham College Roll Letter* (1933), 61–6 · M. B. Thomas, *Girton Review*, Lent term (1933), 3–5 · *The Times* (27 Sept 1932) · *Keighley News* (1 Oct 1932) · private information (2004) [Anna Bidder]

Likenesses portrait, Newnham College, Cambridge · portrait, Girton Cam.

Wealth at death £26,591 17s. 9d.: probate, 28 Feb 1932, CGPLA Eng. & Wales

Biddle, Hester (1629/30–1697), Quaker minister and writer, spent her childhood in Oxford. She twice refers to having been born an Anglican, but nothing else is known of her family origin. She wrote only under her married name, so her marriage to Thomas Biddle (d. 1682), a cordwainer, occurred before 1655. Until 1666 they lived in the Old Exchange (Royal Exchange), City of London, but after the great fire they moved south of the river to Bermondsey Street. They had four children, all sons: Quaker records identify Daniel (1660–1685), Benjamin (b. 1663), and two sons named Thomas (one dying in 1666, his brother living 1668–70). Hester was widowed in 1682, when Thomas died of unknown causes, and she subsequently lived in relative poverty, receiving 5s. weekly as a 'poor Friend' from the Peel monthly meeting (Rickman, 39–41).

Most of what is known about Hester Biddle relates to her religious experiences as a Quaker. She received a traditional religious upbringing from her parents, and disapproved of the abolition of the Book of Common Prayer. She became a Friend in response to the preaching of Edward Burrough and Francis Howgill in 1654, and thereafter she became an active Quaker minister and writer. She is sometimes believed to be the woman known to Quaker leader George Fox for predicting the return of Charles II, but the evidence for this well-known story is an unsubstantiated reference in an eighteenth-century text and so must be treated with caution.

Hester Biddle travelled extensively, both at home and abroad. Within the 'four kingdoms' of the British Isles, her ministry included Oxford (1655), Cornwall (1656), Ireland (1659), and Scotland (1672). Her journeys abroad were also numerous, and accounts exist of ministry and travels in Newfoundland (1656, with Mary Fisher), the Netherlands (1656, 1661), Barbados (1657), Alexandria (now Egypt, 1658; on her way she met Katherine Evans, Sarah Cheevers, and Mary Fisher), and France (1694–5). The last-named journey is the most oft-cited; having visited Mary II, Biddle gained a pass to address Louis XIV, whom she urged to pursue politics of peace.

Biddle's ministering brought her into conflict with local authorities and the state church, resulting in fourteen cases of detention. During the 1650s, when Quakers were encouraged to preach in public to spread their faith, Biddle criticized the clergy, mayors, and magistrates. She was in Oxford and Cambridge in 1655, producing a broadside that reminded 'corrupt' university-educated churchmen that 'God exalteth the poor in spirit, but the rich he sendeth empty away' (Wo to the City of Oxford, 1655). This radical rejection of social hierarchy and authority is reflected, too, in her imprisonment at Banbury for 'some zealous reprehension uttered against the Mayor and the Magistrates' (Besse, 1.564). Other arrests included Launceston (1656) and Godalming (1659), where she was 'much beaten and abused' (ibid., 1.689). The report of her trial for preaching in 1662 included a defence of women's speaking in response to the jury's astonished remark that 'they never heard of a woman to speak before', and a refusal to allow alderman Richard Browne to reprimand her for travelling without her husband (A Brief Relation, 35). Letters referring to her consequent confinement in Bridewell and to later imprisonments, one of them for 'writing a book', are in the Public Record Office and in Friends' Library, London.

Between 1655 and 1662 Biddle was the author of fiery pamphlets that show an acute awareness of social and economic inequality. Typical of her stance is a challenge issued in The Trumpet of the Lord (1662):

did not the Lord make all men and women upon the earth of one mould, why then should there be so much honour and

respect unto some men and women, and not unto others, but they are almost naked for want of Cloathing, and almost starved for want of Bread? (p. 12)

Biddle died in St Sepulchre's parish, Clerkenwell, London, on 5 February 1697, aged sixty-seven, suffering from a 'stoppage' (Quaker register of burials). The administration of her estate was granted to her son Benjamin on 19 February. She was a radical writer and activist who advocated social equality, arguing from a direct sense of empathy: 'the poor … are ready to famish, for whose estate and condition my heart is pained within me' (A Warning from the Lord God … unto … London, 1660, 11).

ELAINE HOBBY and CATIE GILL

Sources Quaker register of births, marriages, and burials, RS Friends, Lond. • A brief relation of the persecutions … London (1662) • J. Besse, A collection of the sufferings of the people called Quakers, 2 vols. (1753) • H. J. Cadbury, 'Friends and the inquisition at Malta', Journal of the Friends' Historical Society, 53 (1972–5), 219–25 • CSP dom., 1662–4 • G. Croese, The general history of the Quakers (1696) • R. Foxton, 'Hear the Word of the Lord': a critical and bibliographical study of Quaker women's writing, 1650–1700 (Melbourne, 1994) • E. Hobby, '"O Oxford thou art full of Filth": the prophetical writings of Hester Biddle', Feminist criticism: theory and practice, ed. S. Sellers (1991), 157–69 • N. Penney, ed., Extracts from the state papers (1913) • The journal of George Fox, ed. N. Penney, 2 vols. (1911) • L. L. Rickman, 'Esther Biddle and her mission to Louis XIV', Journal of the Friends' Historical Society, 53 (1972–5), 38–45 • J. Smith, A descriptive catalogue of Friends' books, 2 vols. (1867) • A. P. Vella, The tribunal of the inquisition in Malta (Royal University of Malta, 1964) • administration, GL, MS 9/68/28, fol. 54v

Archives RS Friends, Lond.

Biddle, John (1615/16–1662), schoolmaster and religious controversialist, was baptized on 14 January 1616 at Wotton under Edge, Gloucestershire, the first of two sons of Edward Biddle (d. 1625), tailor, and his wife, Jane Hopkins.

Early years and education Biddle's scholarly prowess was recognized from an early age, and his education at the free grammar school of Wotton was provided for by a £10 annual exhibition from George, Lord Berkeley. Further support for his 'better education … in learning' was left for him in his father's will (H. Y. J. T., 81). Several testimonies to his academic abilities survive. One seventeenth-century biographer records that the young Biddle 'did not only with ease surpass those his Schoolfellows of the same Rank, but, in Time, even out-run his Instructions, and became Tutor to himself'. Excelling particularly in the classics, Biddle produced at school translations of Virgil's Bucolics and the first two satires of Juvenal; these were published at London in 1634. He is also credited with the composition and delivery of 'an elaborate Oration in Latin' on the occasion of a schoolmate's funeral (A Short Account, 4).

On 27 June 1634, at the age of eighteen, Biddle matriculated at Magdalen Hall, Oxford—then a bastion of puritanism. His first biographer reported that as an undergraduate 'he did so Philosophize [that] he was determined more by Reason than Authority'; and an austere moral tone is evinced from a tract he penned at this time against dancing (A Short Account, 4). Biddle graduated BA on 23 June

1638 and then established himself as a tutor at his college.

Schoolmaster and anti-trinitarian exegete Biddle obtained a solid reputation as a teacher, and before he took his second degree he was offered the mastership of his old school in Wotton. Although he declined this, about the time his MA was conferred on 20 May 1641 Biddle was invited to take up the mastership of the Crypt School in Gloucester. This invitation was accepted, and Biddle arrived in Gloucester with the recommendation of the Magdalen teaching fellows. On 26 May the city council tripled the master's stipend to £30 and formally appointed Biddle to the post. His earliest biographer testifies that he discharged his duties to the great satisfaction of both his sponsors and the parents of his pupils, and Anthony Wood affirms that he was there 'for a time ... much esteemed for his diligence in his profession, severity of manners, and sanctity of life' (Wood, *Ath. Oxon.*, 2.197).

Biddle at that time showed diligence in the free study of scripture, and it was now that he came to argue that the received doctrine of the Trinity formed no part of the inspired word of God. Biddle was evidently not content to keep this discovery to himself for word of his heresy began to circulate in Gloucester (in parliamentarian hands since 1643), prompting a group of alarmed presbyterians to raise the matter with the magistrates. As a consequence, Biddle was arrested and imprisoned a few days after Easter 1644. Compelled by the authorities to vindicate his beliefs through a written subscription, he did so on 2 May 1644. As his statement lacked orthodoxy (he admitted only one person in the divine essence, and his affirmation of the unity of Christ with God was ambiguous on the point of essence), he was constrained to give assent to the tri-personality of the 'Divine Essence'. This he did about two weeks afterwards, yet, although his second statement conformed more closely to the teachings of Athanasius, an element of equivocation may be evident in his use of the term 'person'. The precise form of his departure from orthodox trinitarianism at this point is impossible to gauge; it is probable that the schoolmaster's views were still inchoate.

After his release Biddle returned to his mastership and, it is clear, his heretical theological enquiries. By the latter half of 1645 his views on the Holy Spirit had congealed sufficiently for him to commit to writing a series of arguments against the orthodox view that the Holy Spirit is a co-equal person in the Godhead. Once more his heretical escapades were betrayed to the magistrates. After being relieved of his duties at the Crypt School in October, he was examined on 2 December by parliamentary commissioners in Gloucester. It was determined that he should appear before parliament and, although then suffering from a raging fever, that he should be held in gaol until his case could be heard. However, on 8 December the mayor of Gloucester, Lawrence Singleton, secured Biddle's release on bail after guarantees had been made that the prisoner would appear in Westminster when demanded. For about half a year Biddle waited in Gloucester. About

June 1646 Archbishop James Ussher, already aware of Biddle's heresy and in transit from Wales to London, met with Biddle and unsuccessfully tried to convince him of the waywardness of his chosen path. Ussher tried to impress on Biddle that he was either 'in a damnable Errour, or else the whole Church of Christ, who had in all ages worshipped the Holy Ghost had been guilty of Idolatry' (Edwards, 88). Biddle, however, was unmoved.

London heresy trials Some time in the summer of 1646 Biddle was finally called to Westminster. There, before a committee specially convened by parliament, he made an open confession of his unorthodox views on the Holy Spirit. When pressed on the deity of Christ, however, he refused to commit himself, claiming that he had not yet sufficiently studied the matter. Biddle suggested his willingness to be persuaded of his error and called for the appointment of a theologian to dispute with him. The committee apparently ignored this request, and Biddle was remanded to custody in Westminster's Gatehouse prison, whose walls then contained Paul Best, another notorious anti-trinitarian. Meanwhile, word of Biddle's heresy began to spread. In the third part of his infamous *Gangraena* (December 1646) the heresy-hunting presbyterian Thomas Edwards reported on Biddle's denial of the deity of the Holy Spirit and complained that his scandalous case remained unheard. After nine months of incarceration Biddle made a direct epistolary appeal on 1 April 1647 to Sir Henry Vane the younger, asking that he be granted either a hearing or his freedom. Vane was a prominent Independent MP who had studied at Magdalen Hall shortly before Biddle; crucially, he was also a proponent of toleration who had been a member of the parliamentary committee originally assigned to Biddle's case. When Vane duly intervened on Biddle's behalf, however, the committee responded by placing Biddle under closer guard and referring his case to the Westminster assembly of divines 'for his Conviction' (*A Short Account*, 5). This turn of events elicited from a now exasperated Biddle the publication in early September 1647 of his *Twelve Arguments* against the deity of the Holy Spirit.

The *Twelve Arguments* In this thin 24-page tract, published in his own name, Biddle confidently set out his doctrinal case and requested an impartial examination, rather than mere 'invectives, railings, or reproachful terms, [which] are no convincing Arguments' (Biddle, *Twelve Arguments*, sig. A4r). In a series of twelve syllogisms Biddle contends that the Holy Spirit cannot be very God. Among these, he shows that: (1) he is distinguished from God; (3) he does not speak for himself; (6) he was sent by another; (7) he is described as the gift of God; and (8) he changes place and (12) has a will distinct from God. As the full title of the tract promises, these claims are backed up by scriptural testimony. The twelve arguments themselves are primarily a negative exercise and offer little by way of explanation of Biddle's positive views on the Holy Spirit. This comes in the April 1647 letter to Vane, prefixed to the twelve arguments, in which Biddle confesses his belief that the Holy

Spirit is none other than 'the chiefe of all Ministring Spirits, peculiarly sent out from Heaven to minister on their behalfe that shall inherit salvation'. Biddle placed him 'both according to the Scripture, and the Primitive Christians … in the third ranke after God and Christ, giving him a preheminence above all the rest of the Heavenly Host' (ibid., 1). As God's principal angelic minister, the Holy Spirit also stands as the righteous corollary to the chief wicked spirit and adversary, Satan.

In the same letter Biddle also boldly compared the solid scriptural foundation of his own position with that of his adversaries, who

> endeavour to delude both themselves and others with Personalities, Moods, Subsistences, and such like brainsick Notions, that have neither sap nor sence in them, and were first hatched by the subtilty of Satan in the heads of Platonists, to pervert the Worship of the true God.   (Biddle, *Twelve Arguments*, 4)

Such caustic language could not have helped his cause, but it is characteristic of Biddle's style and confidence. In his preface Biddle complained that he had 'a long time waited upon learned men for a satisfactory Answer to these Arguments, but hath received none'. He thus hoped that

> the publishing of them will be a meanes to produce it, that he may receive satisfaction, and others may be held no longer in suspence, who are in travell with an earnest expectation of a speedy resolution, as well as he.   (ibid., sig. A3r)

Although Biddle was to be disappointed in his desire for a speedy resolution, the response to his first request was almost immediate. On 6 September parliament ordered the burning of the *Twelve Arguments* and directed the committee for plundered ministers to interrogate the author. The tract was burned on 8 September, and the printer, Elizabeth Gosling, commanded to appear before the committee. The sensation caused by the burning, however, also served to fan the flames of curiosity and stir up sales. A second printing was reportedly run off in October, while the first refutation, the anonymous twelve-page *God's Glory Vindicated and Blasphemy Confuted*, appeared in the middle of September. Concern over the growth of heresy as exemplified by anti-trinitarians such as Paul Best and Biddle led to parliament publishing an ordinance for the punishment of blasphemy and heresy on 2 May 1648: denial of the Trinity was made a capital offence.

The *Confession of Faith* Despite the very real legal dangers, Biddle continued another work that the orthodox viewed as extremely heretical and provocative. In November 1648, still within the walls of the Gatehouse prison, he published anonymously *A Confession of Faith Touching the Holy Trinity, According to the Scripture*. In this twenty-page pamphlet Biddle broadens his consideration of trinitarian issues through six articles of faith, and for the first time turns his attention to the person of Christ and his relationship with the Father: (I) only the Father, Biddle maintained, is the 'one most high God, Creator of heaven and earth'; (II) Christ is the 'one chief Son of the most High God' and 'perpetual Lord and King, set over the Church by

God', thus making him 'second cause of all things pertaining to our salvation'; and Biddle's already established position on the Holy Spirit is reiterated in article VI (Biddle, *Confession*, 1, 9). As with the *Twelve Arguments*, each article is backed up with a series of biblical proof texts. This may not have been the only work Biddle released this year. An anonymous work entitled *To the Law, and to the Testimony*, which appeared in March, has been attributed to Biddle on highly plausible grounds, including the general tenor of its argumentation.

Some time during this period of imprisonment, a Staffordshire justice of peace offered security and temporarily gained Biddle's freedom, bringing him, according to Wood, to Staffordshire as his chaplain and preacher of a local congregation. This respite from gaol was short-lived. When John Bradshaw, president of the council of state, heard of his release, Biddle was returned to prison and placed under a stricter regime than before. There Biddle remained until February 1652, when an Act of Oblivion set him at liberty. Towards the end of this period of imprisonment, some alleviation of his financial condition came when the printer Roger Daniel employed him to correct the proofs of his edition of the Greek Septuagint, which was published in 1653. Biddle's release initiated a flurry of activity. Not only did he network with supporters in London and apparently assemble around him the nucleus of a unitarian congregation, but the early 1650s also marks Biddle's most productive period of publication.

Renewed publication In April 1653 Biddle republished amended and enlarged editions of his *Twelve Arguments* and *Confession of Faith* with the collective title *The Apostolical and True Opinion Concerning the Holy Trinity, Revived and Asserted*. His undated *Testimonies of Irenaeus* and other early church writers was released about the same time and sold bound with the above. A previous edition of this work was possibly published as early as 1648. Putting his classical training to use, Biddle also produced translations of three Socinian works, including Joachim Stegmann senior's eirenicist *Brevis disquisitio* (March 1653), Samuel Przypkowski's *Vita* of Fausto Sozzini (June 1653), and the same author's *Dissertatio de pace* (October 1653). An English translation of the Socinian Racovian catechism that had appeared in July 1652 was almost certainly produced by him as well, containing as it does a Biddle-like digression on the Holy Spirit. The Socinian Benedykt Wiszowaty attributed this translation to Biddle in the late seventeenth century and, like *To the Law, and to the Testimony*, it can be found bound with collections of Biddle's 1653 and 1654 works in several extant examples. These translations testify to Biddle's discovery of the Polish Brethren, in whom he found spiritual communion, despite the Socinian rejection of the personality of the Holy Spirit.

February 1654 saw the publication of an original bipartite work entitled *A Twofold Catechism*, which comprised *A Scripture-Catechism* and *A Brief Scripture-Catechism for Children*. These catechisms reveal a growing consciousness on Biddle's part of the needs of an incipient unitarian church. His doctrine is set out through a series of leading questions that are answered with confirming scriptural quotations. The catechisms clarify further his views on the Son and the Spirit, and also highlight other elements of his theology not previously articulated, such as mortalism. This round of publication provoked a sharp outcry from the orthodox and was met with a torrent of written replies, not the least of which was John Owen's monumental 700-page attack on the *Scripture-Catechism*, the *Vindiciae evangelicae* (1655). Biddle's unitarian crusade had not gone unnoticed among continental anti-trinitarians, as evidenced by the supportive letter Jeremias Felbinger sent to Biddle in August 1654.

Parliament acted on 12 December. Biddle was summoned, the printers and publishers of his books sent for, and the *Apostolical and True Opinion Concerning the Holy Trinity* and the *Twofold Catechism* ordered burnt by the hangman. The members of parliament were particularly worried that the *Twofold Catechism* was intended for the dissemination of 'many blasphemous and heretical Opinions' (*JHC*, 7.405–6). Biddle found himself back in the Gatehouse, and at this point was in danger of suffering capital punishment for his theological misdemeanours, but Oliver Cromwell's dissolution of Barebone's Parliament on 22 January 1655 put a halt to proceedings. On 10 February Biddle, his publisher Moone, and the printer were released on bail on condition that they appear at the beginning of the next law term in May. Their case was postponed until 28 May and, after appearing on that day, they were set free.

Further controversies and exile Upon his release, the irrepressible Biddle returned immediately to preaching in London. This preaching does not appear to have been without success, and among those attracted to Biddle's views were members of the congregation of John Griffiths, a General Baptist. Griffiths's response was to challenge Biddle to a public disputation on the question 'Whether Jesus Christ be the most High or Almighty God?' (Wood, *Ath. Oxon.*, 2.200). After some hesitation Biddle consented, and the debate was held in Griffiths's London church on 28 June with a follow-up meeting planned for 5 July. Before this second meeting could take place, however, word reached the council of state on 3 July that Biddle had denied the deity of Christ 'in presence of about 500 persons … some hours together' (*CSP dom.*, 1655, 224). Biddle found himself in prison yet again. A group of anti-tolerationist presbyterians appealed for Biddle to be tried under the 1648 ordinance, and on 10 July he was charged with 'publickly denying that Jesus Christ was the Almighty or most High God' and transferred from the Poultry Compter to Newgate. Despite the hostile forces arrayed against him, Biddle was not without support from both his personal friends and the ranks of Baptists and Independents concerned at the precedent set by his persecution. Two pamphlets attacking Biddle's prosecution and appealing for liberty of conscience were published by Richard Moone. To these were added Biddle's own appeals, first to Cromwell and then to Henry Lawrence, president of the council of state (printed in October as *Two Letters of Mr. Biddle*). Cromwell intervened on 5 October. By his order Biddle was banished to St Mary's Castle on the

Isles of Scilly, where he was beyond the reach both of the courts and the writ of habeas corpus. Thus Biddle's life was spared. At the same time, the troublesome anti-trinitarian was conveniently removed far from the impressionable ears of the London laity.

Biddle spent almost three years in exile. Although physically confined to Scilly, Biddle continued his free-spirited excursions into scripture. In particular, he turned his attention to the interpretation of the Apocalypse—the prophecy the Apostle John had received during his banishment on the isle of Patmos. According to three late seventeenth-century sources, the results of these hermeneutical labours were published as *An Essay to the Explaining of Revelation* (1661). If this commentary on Revelation 13–22 was in fact penned by Biddle, however, it represents not only a new departure (the author espouses a pre-millenarian eschatology and belief in a future kingdom of God on earth) but also a retreat from his mortalism of 1654 (the author actively contends for the literal eternity of hell torments). Nevertheless, the author does avoid explicit references to the Trinity and the deity of Christ, and the oblique discussions of Christology are certainly compatible with a non-trinitarian stance. The writer also appeals to reason and makes his opposition to abstruse and allegorical hermeneutics plain.

Final imprisonment and death In late spring 1658 Biddle was called to the king's bench in Westminster, and on 5 June, after no grounds for further detention could be found, was released by Lord Chief Justice Sir John Glynn. Again at liberty in London, Biddle once more returned to his anti-trinitarian networking and preaching. Among Biddle's London theological sympathizers was the girdler and mercer Thomas Firmin, with whom the former had stayed before his exile to the Isles of Scilly. On the advice of Firmin and his other friends, Biddle retired to the country during Richard Cromwell's first parliament, but afterwards returned to London, where he continued to preside over a small dissenting conventicle into the early years of the Restoration. This state of affairs lasted until 1 June 1662, when the authorities acted and Biddle again found himself inside prison walls, along with some of his friends. He was charged after a hearing with a £100 fine and ordered 'to lie in Prison till paid' (*A Short Account*, 9). This time Biddle's only release came in death. On 22 September 1662 he succumbed to a disease brought on by the foul and confined state of his quarters in Newgate; almost a decade of his short life had passed in prison. Biddle was interred by his disciples in a burial-ground adjoining the old Bethlem Hospital in Moorfields. He may have been the John Biddle of St Stephens, Coleman Street, London, whose estate was administered the same year.

Legacy of 'the Father of English Unitarianism' Long after his death John Biddle continued to exert an influence on non-trinitarian theology through his original works and translations of Socinian titles. Biddle's catechisms were in turn translated into Latin in 1664 by the young Nathaniel Stuckey, apparently a member of the congregation Biddle left behind. Testimony to the value of this translation on the continent is found in a transcription of the Latin *Scripture-Catechism for Children* made by the late seventeenth-century Transylvanian unitarian Máté Dersi. In addition to the works noted above, Benedykt Wiszowaty also attributed to Biddle *The Morality of the Seventh-Day-Sabbath Disproved* (1683) and two-thirds of the translation of the Socinian Johann Crell's *Two Books … Touching one God the Father* (1665). His *Twelve Arguments*, *Confession of Faith*, and *Testimonies* were republished in 1691 as part of the first collection of unitarian tracts, *The Faith of one God*, thus granting them new life in the trinitarian controversies of the 1690s.

Apparently unaware of the Socinians when he began his theological excursions, Biddle came to share with them marked biblicist, primitivist, and anti-creedalist tendencies, along with a disdain for unscriptural neologisms, post-apostolic doctrinal novelty, and the use of Platonism in theology. Also similar to the Polish Brethren is his ethical drive and emphasis on the need for a life of holiness. Biddle's Christology is difficult to pin down. It is clear, however, that he was no Christological humanitarian in the sense of later unitarians, and in his schema of one God the Father, with a subordinate, non-eternally generated Son, and angelic Holy Spirit, there is a similarity to the Arian system.

Although he was viewed by the orthodox as a contumacious heretic, Biddle was widely viewed as a pious, upright man with a powerful grasp of scripture; he is said to have memorized the New Testament in English and Greek up to the fourth chapter of Revelation. Even if few accepted his notion of the Holy Spirit, the influence of his writings, translations, private preaching, and networking, along with the direct impact he had on radical dissenters such as Firmin, there is enough to justify his epithet 'the father of English Unitarianism'. STEPHEN D. SNOBELEN

Sources H. J. McLachlan, *Socinianism in seventeenth-century England* (1951) · *A short account of the life of John Bidle* (1691) · Wood, *Ath. Oxon.*, 1st edn, vol. 2 · J. Toulmin, *A review of the life, character and writings of the Rev. John Biddle* (1791) · *CSP dom.*, 1651; 1655 · H. Y. J. T., 'A "Crypt" schoolmaster', *Gloucestershire N&Q*, 8th ser., 6 (1894–5), 79–82 · *JHC*, 7 (1651–9) · E. Wilbur, *A history of Unitarianism in Transylvania, England, and America* (1952) · L. Szczucki, 'Bibliographia antitrinitaria', *Archiwum Historii Filozofii i Myśli Społecznej*, 38 (1993), 165–73 · T. Edwards, *The third part of Gangraena* (1646) · administration, GL, MS 9168/20, fol. 69r

Biddlecombe, Sir George (1807–1878), naval officer and hydrographer, born at Portsea, Hampshire, on 5 November 1807, was the son of Thomas Biddlecombe of Sheerness Dockyard, who died on 12 September 1844. He was educated at Dr Neave's school, Portsea, and joined the merchant navy, in the ship *Ocean of Whitby*, as a midshipman in 1823. He was an officer in the East India Company's navy in 1825–8. Passing as a second master in the Royal Navy in May 1828, he was soon after employed in surveying in the *Aetna* and the *Blonde* until 1833. He was on active service in various ships from 1833 until 1854, and was known for his skill in naval surveys in many parts of the world. While in the *Actaeon*, in 1836, he surveyed a group of islands discovered by her in the Pacific. When attached to the *Talbot*, 1838–42, he surveyed numerous anchorages

on the Ionian station, in the Greek archipelago, and up the Dardanelles and Bosphorus; he examined the south shore of the Black Sea as far as Trebizond, as well as the port of Varna in eastern Bulgaria, and prepared a survey, published by the Admiralty, of the bays and banks of Acre. He also displayed much skill and perseverance in surveying the Skerki shoals in the Mediterranean where he discovered many unknown patches. A plan which he proposed for a 'hauling-up slip' was approved by the authorities, and money was voted for its construction. In 1842 he married Emma Louisa, third daughter of Thomas Kent; she died on 13 August 1865. For his survey of Port Royal and Kingston, Jamaica, he received the thanks of the common council of Kingston, and in August 1843 he rendered notable and dangerous service during a fire in the town.

Few officers saw more active service. Biddlecombe served as master of the *St Vincent* bearing Admiral Sir Charles Napier's flag from 1847 to 1849. As master of the Baltic fleet, 14 March 1854, he reconnoitered the southern parts of the Aland Islands, Hango Bay, Baro Sound, and the anchorage of Sveaborg, preparatory to taking the fleet to those places. He conducted the allied fleets to Kronstadt, and taking charge in Led Sound of the steamer *Prince*, with upwards of 2000 French troops on board, he carried that ship to Bomarsund, and was afterwards present at the fall of that fortress. His services in the Baltic led many officers, notably the fleet surveyor Captain Bartholomew Sulivan, to consider that he had influenced Napier to follow an unnecessarily cautious policy. He was employed as assistant master attendant at Keyham yard, Devonport, 1855–64, and from 1864 to January 1868 as master attendant of Woolwich yard. In 1866 he married Emma Sarah, daughter of William Middleton; she died on 6 May 1878, aged forty-nine. He was made a CB on 13 March 1867, but the highest rank he obtained in the navy was that of staff captain on 1 July in the same year. He was knighted by the queen at Windsor on 26 June 1873 and received a Greenwich Hospital pension soon afterwards.

Biddlecombe's publications included *Naval Tactics and Trials of Sailing* (1850), *Steam Fleet Tactics* (1857), and *The Autobiography of Sir George Biddlecombe* (1878). His died at his home, 68 Granville Park, Lewisham, London, on 22 July 1878. Biddlecombe's tactical ideas were simple and overly mechanistic. They had no influence on British practice.

G. C. BOASE, *rev.* ANDREW LAMBERT

Sources A. D. Lambert, *The Crimean War: British grand strategy, 1853–56* (1990) · NMM, Napier MSS · BL, Napier MSS · PRO, Napier MSS · O'Byrne, *Naval biog. dict.*, [2nd edn] · *The autobiography of Sir George Biddlecombe* (1878) · Boase, *Mod. Eng. biog.*
Archives Duke U., Perkins L., memoirs | BL, Napier MSS · NMM, Napier MSS · PRO, Napier MSS
Wealth at death under £7000: probate, 5 Sept 1878, *CGPLA Eng. & Wales*

Biddles, James (1815–1871?), actor and theatre manager, was born at Mountsorrel, near Loughborough, the eldest of the seven sons of James Biddles, a Leicestershire farmer, and his wife, Elizabeth. James Biddles the younger married Ann Maria Phillips (d. 1843) at St Margaret's Church, Leicester, on 11 December 1831. The couple's first two children died in infancy, but four daughters survived, of whom the older two, Adelaide Helen *Calvert [see under Calvert, Charles Alexander] and Clara, became actresses of distinction. Marriage and baptismal records show that during early manhood Biddles engaged in a variety of occupations, including innkeeper, tobacconist, and stage performer.

By the mid-1830s Biddles featured regularly in the play-bills and newspaper announcements for the Leicester Theatre: as Guildenstern to W. C. Macready's Hamlet and as Faldo in the afterpiece *The Happiest Days of my Life* (26 September 1834); as Petro in Pocock's *The Miller and his Men* (6 October 1834); and as Robin Roughead in the farce *Fortune's Frolics* (24 February 1835), which was part of a bill which included 'The Celebrated Infant [Charles] Kean' in *Richard III*.

Typically, for the time, Biddles joined a stock company, that of Mr Harvey, who ran the Plymouth, Weymouth, Exeter, Jersey, and Guernsey circuit. In the summer of 1842 both Biddles and his wife appeared in Weymouth, then travelled to Guernsey, and returned to the mainland in January 1843 for a season in Exeter. In Exeter, Adelaide, aged seven, appeared with Henry Betty, son of the 'Infant Roscius', and with Charles and Ellen Kean. In her memoirs Adelaide recalled that her father was 'the low comedian, and very popular' with audiences (Calvert, 5).

On 1 October 1843 Ann Maria Biddles died from consumption at the age of thirty. With four young daughters to support, Biddles and his brother Tom devised a comic lecture, 'Pickings from Punch', which they toured around the country. At the end of 1844 Biddles had a very different sort of engagement at a leading metropolitan theatre, Covent Garden, where he was a member of the chorus in the elaborate production of Sophocles's *Antigone*. From the anonymity of the chorus he progressed, early in 1845, to First Gravedigger, then Third Witch, and finally Glavis in Bulwer-Lytton's *The Lady of Lyons*—all part of the aforementioned Henry Betty's none too successful London début.

Although Covent Garden conferred status, it offered limited scope for a low comedian and Biddles left to pursue his career elsewhere. During an engagement at Astley's equestrian theatre he met and married his second wife, Malvina Bridges, the daughter of the ringmaster. He then took over the management of the Bower Saloon, a minor theatre near to Westminster Bridge, where he presided from 1845 to 1854, presenting plays suited to the local clientele by, among others, T. E. Wilks, J. T. Blake, J. H. Haines, and S. T. Atkyns. Nautical melodramas, so-called dog dramas, and pantomimes were the specialities of the house, but Biddles also infiltrated more serious fare, such as *Macbeth* and Sheridan Knowles's *William Tell*.

Biddles encouraged the careers of his daughters Adelaide and Clara, and when they reached their teens it must have been apparent to him that his family possessed greater talents than he did himself. In 1854 he 'fee'd' a theatrical agent to induce Thomas Barry, who was in Europe engaging actors for the forthcoming opening of the new Boston Theatre, to attend a performance at the Bower, as a result of which the whole Biddles family was contracted. Following a protracted voyage aboard a small but cheap vessel, the family arrived in Boston. Adelaide and Clara quickly established themselves as leading attractions, but Biddles and his wife were little used. In 1855 he prevailed upon a willing Barry to release himself and his wife from their contracts. Ever resourceful, he then set up a small company with an American actor in order to tour farces. To facilitate this venture he took American citizenship.

Like her father, Clara Biddles (1840–1905) remained in America; she married first Thomas Barry, who had brought her to the United States and who was her senior by some forty years, and second the English actor William Redmund. Biddles returned to England for Adelaide's marriage to Charles *Calvert in 1856, but he spent the rest of his life in his adopted country, where, according to Adelaide's memoirs, he died, in Iowa, in 1871.

James Biddles's career encompassed a tremendous range of theatrical activity: an important provincial theatre (Leicester); a stock company circuit; one of the major metropolitan houses (Covent Garden); the home of equestrian drama (Astley's); a minor theatre (the Bower Saloon); and, in the New World, initially in Boston and then, as the frontiers rolled back, west as far as Iowa. Personally, Biddles was a man of considerable and diverse talents, great resourcefulness, and profound resilience. Over and above such importance as may be ascribed to him individually, he represents strata of theatrical activity to which the majority of his profession devoted their careers which, for the most part, are unrecorded by posterity.

RICHARD FOULKES

Sources C. Calvert, *Sixty-eight years on the stage* (1911) · R. G. Foulkes, *The Calverts—actors of some importance* (1992) · *The Era* [various dates] · *Leicester Journal* · R. Leacroft and H. Leacroft, *The theatre in Leicester* (1986) · d. cert. [Ann Maria Biddles] · Leics. RO, Biddles papers
Archives Lambeth Archives, London · Leics. RO · Theatre Museum, London

Biddulph, Francis (*bap.* 1734, *d.* 1800), banker, was baptized at Ledbury, Herefordshire, on 3 March 1734, the last of eight children of Robert Biddulph (1682–1772) and his wife, Anne, daughter of Benjamin Joliffe of Cofton Hall, Worcester. He had five brothers and two sisters, though two brothers and both sisters had died before Biddulph was born. Biddulph never married and had no children. His eldest brother, Michael Biddulph (1724–1800), became his next of kin following the death of his father in 1772; his mother died in 1760.

Biddulph's involvement in metropolitan financial circles dates from the early 1750s when he was active in the City of London, probably as a goldsmith. Like many others of this trade before him, Biddulph soon made the transition to bona fide banker and by about 1755 was in business in St Paul's Churchyard. In 1757 he decided to establish a new and independent banking house and asked an old Herefordshire neighbour, Sir Charles Cocks of Eastnor, near Ledbury, to send someone to London to assist the new enterprise. Thus it was that James and

Thomas Somers Cocks, sons of Sir Charles, joined Biddulph to form the house of Cocks, Biddulph & Co., in St Paul's Churchyard. In 1759 the firm moved to 43 Charing Cross, in the City of Westminster.

The nature and conduct of the banking business at Charing Cross were shaped in part by Biddulph's character and provincial origins. Cocks, Biddulph & Co. were considered exceptionally discreet, even among the somewhat closed world of the aristocratic West End banks. Such discretion attracted some notable customers, including the dukes of Gloucester and Northumberland, the bishop of London, the Oxford colleges of Exeter and Brasenose, and the dean and chapter of Lincoln Cathedral. The bank also acted as agent in the capital for a number of country banks in Wales and the west, and for Hereford and St David's cathedrals. Thus Biddulph combined the provision of personal banking services to the aristocracy and gentry with interests in the church and provincial trade and industry. He moved not only between London and the provinces, but also among the many distinct social worlds of the eighteenth century.

Biddulph lived for much of his life in the banking house in Charing Cross, within the parish of St Martin-in-the-Fields. He died, intestate, in Brighton on 25 October 1800. On the death of his brother Michael in December 1800, a large part of his considerable fortune went to Michael's son Robert Biddulph, MP for Hereford.   IAIN S. BLACK

Sources G. Chandler, *Four centuries of banking*, 1 (1964) • *Cocks, Biddulph & Company, 1759–1920* (1978) • F. G. Hilton Price, *A handbook of London bankers* (1876) • *The Times* (29 Oct 1800) • bishop's transcripts, Ledbury, 1733–4, Herefs. RO

Archives Herefs. RO | Barclays Bank Group Archives, Records of Cocks, Biddulph & Co. of Charing Cross, MSS

Wealth at death £57,605: PRO, death duty registers, IR 26/183

Biddulph, Sir **Michael Anthony Shrapnel** (1823–1904), army officer, born on 30 July 1823 at Cleeve Court, Somerset, was the eldest surviving son of Thomas Shrapnel Biddulph of Amroth Castle, Pembrokeshire, prebendary of Brecon, and his wife, Charlotte, daughter of James Stillingfleet, prebendary of Worcester and great-grandson of Edward Stillingfleet, bishop of Worcester. In 1843 he added to his forenames the surname of Lieutenant-General Henry Shrapnel, brother of his paternal grandmother, Rachel.

Biddulph was initially educated by a private tutor in expectation of entering the church and inheriting a large personal fortune. However, after his family suffered heavy financial losses speculating on coal mining in Wales and was forced to sell the family seat, he changed the direction of his career, and on 19 November 1840 entered the Royal Military Academy at Woolwich. While a gentleman cadet at Woolwich, he was awarded the Royal Humane Society's silver medal for saving a comrade from drowning in the canal at the Royal Arsenal on 25 August 1842. Biddulph was commissioned second lieutenant Royal Artillery on 17 June 1843, and was promoted lieutenant on 26 April 1844. He served three years in Bermuda and then at various British stations until 1853, being promoted second captain on 4 October 1850. When the Crimean War broke out

in the spring of 1854 Biddulph was ordered to Turkey with the British army as adjutant of the Royal Artillery.

Biddulph accompanied the army from Varna to the Crimea in September, and took part in the battles of the Alma, Balaklava, Inkerman, and the Chernaya. During the siege of Sevastopol he served as assistant engineer in the trenches outside the city, helped repulse a Russian sortie on 26 October 1854, and assisted in the three bombardments of the fortress. Following the successful French assault on the Malakhov redoubt, on 8 September Biddulph was sent by Lord Raglan to the French commander to ascertain whether his troops could hold the position. He received the laconic and well-known answer 'J'y suis, j'y reste'. Biddulph was later attached to the quartermaster-general's staff during the remainder of the conflict, and was appointed director of submarine telegraph cables in the Black Sea. He demonstrated his prowess as a horseman when he won a grand point-to-point race held by the allied army in front of Sevastopol. For his services during the war Biddulph was mentioned in dispatches, given a brevet majority (12 December 1854) and a brevet lieutenant-colonelcy (6 June 1856), was made a member of the Légion d'honneur, and received the Turkish Mejidiye (fifth class). In 1857 Biddulph married Katherine Stepan (d. 27 Sept 1908), daughter of Captain Stepan Stamati of Karani, Balaklava; the couple had five sons and five daughters.

When the war ended Biddulph was employed on special telegraph construction work in Asia Minor until 1859, and on his return to England was on the first Atlantic cable committee. He then served in Corfu until 1861, when he went to India following the amalgamation of the royal and the East India Company's armies. He rose steadily through the ranks, being promoted brevet colonel on 14 August 1863 and regimental lieutenant-colonel on 10 August 1864. On 20 February 1868 he was appointed deputy adjutant-general for Royal Artillery in India, and on 30 March 1869 was promoted major-general. When he relinquished his staff appointment at the end of five years he was made a CB (24 May 1873).

Following a furlough in England, Biddulph returned to India in September 1875 and took up command of the Rohilkhand district. When hostilities with Afghanistan appeared likely, two years later, he was given command of a large reinforcement sent to bolster the isolated garrison at Quetta; there he was also made responsible for creating a base for operations in southern Afghanistan and for reconnoitring and preparing the route towards Kandahar. Subsequently he commanded the 2nd division of the southern Afghanistan field force, under the command of Sir Donald Stewart, when the Second Anglo-Afghan War broke out. His division advanced into Afghanistan by way of the Khojak Pass through the Khwaja-Amran range of mountains and was present on 8 January 1879 when Kandahar was occupied. Biddulph led a reconnaissance to Girishk on the banks of the Helmand River, looking for supplies, before returning on 1 March to Kandahar. As it proved difficult to support a large force at Kandahar, later that month he returned to India in command of the Thal-

Chotiali field force, along a rugged route never before used by European travellers or a body of armed troops. Despite preliminary negotiations with the local inhabitants by Sir Robert Sandeman, the agent to the governor-general in Baluchistan, and other endeavours not to alarm them, the first column encountered growing signs of hostility and was attacked at Baghao by 2000 Bori Kakars led by Shah Jahan of Zhob. Heavy losses were inflicted on the opposing tribesmen and Biddulph's advance continued without further incident. He finally surrendered the command of his troops on 1 May 1879, at Multan. For his services during the Second Anglo-Afghan War he was mentioned in dispatches, received the thanks of both houses of parliament, was awarded the campaign medal, and was appointed KCB on 25 July 1879.

In 1880 Biddulph was given the prestigious command of the Rawalpindi district in India, where he entertained the amir of Afghanistan at the grand durbar of 1884 and the duke of Connaught on his tour of inspection in 1885. He was promoted lieutenant-general on 13 February 1881, colonel commandant of Royal Artillery on 14 July 1885, and general on 1 November 1886, when he finally left India. Following his return to England he served as president of the ordnance committee (1887–90).

Biddulph retired from the army on 30 July 1890 and was offered a colonial governorship, which he refused. Between 1879 and 1895 he served as groom-in-waiting to Queen Victoria and from 1895 as an extra groom-in-waiting successively to Queen Victoria and Edward VII. From 1891 to 1896 he was keeper of the regalia at the Tower of London. On 25 May 1895 he was made GCB, and in 1896 was appointed gentleman usher of the black rod, holding that office until his death. An all-round and enthusiastic sportsman, he was also an accomplished painter of landscape in watercolour. Biddulph died at his home, 2 Whitehall Court, London, on 23 July 1904, and was buried at Kensal Green cemetery.

T. R. MOREMAN

Sources DNB · *The Times* (25 July 1904) · H. B. Hanna, *The Second Afghan War*, 3 vols. (1899–1910), vols. 1, 2 · B. Robson, *The road to Kabul: the Second Afghan War, 1878–1881* (1986) · M. A. Biddulph, 'The march from the Indus to the Helmund and back', *Journal of the Royal United Service Institution*, 24 (1880), 613–65 · M. A. S. Biddulph, *Assault of Sevastopol* [1855] · *Men and women of the time* (1891) · private information (1912) · *CGPLA Eng. & Wales* (1904)
Archives Balliol Oxf., corresp. with Sir Robert Morier
Likenesses Spy [L. Ward], watercolour caricature, NPG; repro. in VF (21 Nov 1891) · wood-engraving (after photograph by Maull & Fox), NPG; repro. in ILN (21 Dec 1895)
Wealth at death £3769 8s.: probate, 6 Aug 1904, *CGPLA Eng. & Wales*

Biddulph [*alias* Fitton], **Peter** (1602–1657), Roman Catholic priest, was born in the county town of Stafford, the fourth son of Richard Biddulph of Biddulph Hall and his wife, Anne, daughter of John Draycott of Painsley, a recusant couple who had two other sons as priests, each of whom also used the alias Fitton. After some schooling in England, where he learned Latin and Greek, Peter studied at the English College at St Omer from 1613 until 1619, when he went to join the English College at Rome, which he

entered on 28 October. He received minor orders on 11 July 1621, but two years later, on 23 October 1623, he was expelled for insubordination with five others. He was considered the ringleader of the affair, which became known as the Fitton rebellion, but the Vatican authorities took a more tolerant view, ordering the college on 21 November 1624 to send Biddulph and most of his fellow rebels to Douai, where they were to continue their studies at the expense of the English College.

Biddulph was ordained priest at Cambrai on 24 September 1625 and remained at Douai until May 1627, save for a brief visit to Paris in 1625. On 14 May 1627 he left for England but returned to Douai on 13 November, moving to Paris a week later, where he continued his studies at Arras College. In July 1631 he was sent to Rome as clergy agent for Bishop Richard Smith, who had taken up residence at Paris that year. Smith's attempts to exercise episcopal authority did not get a sympathetic hearing in Rome and Biddulph's position was an unenviable one, especially given his previous relations with the English College. He asked to be allowed to return home in 1636, and this was granted in March 1638, when he was admitted to court. He gained some credit there and in 1640 was again sent to Rome as clergy agent, this time with the additional responsibility of representing Queen Henrietta Maria until the arrival there of Kenelm Digby. He left Rome in 1643 and was made dean of the English chapter in 1644, though he does not seem to have resided in England but operated through his subdean, Mark Harrington. He was probably living in the exile Catholic community at Paris during these years and was named, along with William Clifford, as superior of the Collège de Tournai on 20 April 1645. He apparently returned to London to preside at the general assembly of the chapter held in August 1649, and was sent once more to Rome as clergy agent in May 1650, remaining there until 1654, and resigning the agency in January 1655, when he was living in Florence. On the death of Bishop Smith his name was one of those presented to the papal nuncio as episcopabilis. The following year the London chapter wanted him to resume his work as agent in Rome, but his health was poor, and he was given the post of librarian to Prince Leopold, the brother of the grand duke of Tuscany. He died at Florence in the middle of 1657, his death being noted by the chapter at London on 29 July.

WILLIAM JOSEPH SHEILS

Sources G. Anstruther, *The seminary priests*, 2 (1975) · G. Holt, *St Omers and Bruges colleges, 1593–1773: a biographical dictionary*, Catholic RS, 69 (1979) · A. Kenny, ed., *The responsa scholarum of the English College, Rome*, 1, Catholic RS, 54 (1962) · T. A. Birrell, 'English Catholics without a bishop, 1655–1672', *Recusant History*, 4 (1957–8), 142–78 · C. M. Hibbard, *Charles I and the Popish Plot* (1983)
Archives Westm. DA, letters as agent in Rome

Biddulph, Sir Robert (1835–1918), army officer, was born on 26 August 1835 in London, the second son of Robert Biddulph MP JP, of Ledbury, Herefordshire, and his wife, Elizabeth, daughter of the philanthropist George *Palmer MP, of Nazeing Park, Essex. He entered the Royal Military Academy, Woolwich, in 1850, and passed into the Royal

Artillery in 1853. In the following year he went to the Crimea, and served at the Alma, Balaklava, and the siege of Sevastopol.

In the Indian mutiny Biddulph was on the staff of Sir Colin Campbell as brigade major during the siege and capture of Lucknow. At this period he met Garnet Wolseley, with whom he formed a lifelong friendship. After Lucknow he joined the staff of Sir James Hope Grant as deputy assistant adjutant-general, Oudh field force, and, with the rank of captain, accompanied Hope Grant to China in 1860. He served in all the actions of the campaign which terminated in the fall of Peking (Beijing). He returned to India, and was promoted major in 1861 and lieutenant-colonel in 1863. Biddulph married in 1864 Sophia (d. 1905), daughter of the Revd Anthony Lewis Lambert, rector of Chilbolton, Hampshire, and widow of Richard Stuart Palmer of Calcutta. They had four sons and six daughters.

Biddulph returned to England in 1865 and served as assistant boundary commissioner for the Reform Act (1867). In 1871 he was called from the staff at Woolwich to be private secretary to Edward Cardwell, secretary of state for war, and contributed to Cardwell's reforms. He had previously thought much on army reform, and Cardwell, recognizing his qualities, appointed him assistant adjutant-general at the War Office, where he remained until 1878, having been promoted colonel in 1872.

In 1878 Biddulph was selected for special service in Cyprus under Sir Garnet Wolseley, and in the following year he went to Constantinople as commissioner to arrange the financial details under the Anglo-Turkish convention of 1878. On Wolseley's departure for South Africa a few months later, Biddulph succeeded him as high commissioner and commander-in-chief in Cyprus, where his activities included reform of the currency, administration of justice and taxation, anti-locust measures, and public works. In 1883 he was promoted major-general. He was popular in Cyprus, and the imperial government offered him a higher appointment in Natal which, for family reasons, he declined. He went home in 1886 to take up the post of inspector-general of recruiting. He was made lieutenant-general in 1887 and general in 1892.

Biddulph was director-general of military education from 1888 to 1893, and in 1893 briefly quartermaster-general. From 1893 to 1900 he was governor and commander-in-chief at Gibraltar, where he was concerned with currency reform, and also responsible for rearmament and the construction of new harbour and dockyard works.

Biddulph returned to England in 1900, and later was president of the court of inquiry on the administration of the army remount department, investigating alleged corruption during the Second South African War. In 1904 he published *Lord Cardwell at the War Office*, an adulatory, but useful, account. Also in 1904 he was appointed army purchase commissioner, the last person to hold that office, and as such he completed one of Cardwell's great reforms, the abolition of the purchase of commissions. In 1914 he succeeded Lord Roberts as master gunner of St James's Park.

Biddulph's forte was administration, but his military qualities were also considerable. Throughout his life he was guided by strong religious principles. He was created KCMG (1880), GCMG (1886), and GCB (1899). He died at his residence, 83 Cornwall Gardens, Kensington, London, on 18 November 1918, and was buried in Charlton cemetery, Woolwich.   C. V. OWEN, *rev.* JAMES LUNT

Sources *The Times* (20 Nov 1918) · *The Times* (26 Nov 1918) · *Hart's Army List* · R. Biddulph, *Lord Cardwell at the war office: a history of his administration, 1868–1874* (1904) · O. Wheeler, *The war office past and present* (1914) · *WWW, 1916–28* · *CGPLA Eng. & Wales* (1918)
Archives Royal Artillery Institution, Woolwich, London, corresp. and papers | BL, corresp. with Sir Austen Layard, Add. MSS 39026–39034, 39133–39134 *passim* · BL OIOC, letters to Mrs Charles Berkeley, MSS Eur. · Bodl. Oxf., letters to Lord Kimberley
Likenesses photograph, governor's residence, The Convent, Gibraltar
Wealth at death £34,192 6s. 5d.: probate, 28 Dec 1918, *CGPLA Eng. & Wales*

Biddulph, Sir Thomas Myddleton (1809–1878), courtier and army officer, born on 29 July 1809, was the second son of Robert Biddulph of Ledbury and Charlotte, the daughter and coheir of Richard Myddleton MP, of Chirk Castle, of the old Welsh family of Myddleton of Gwaenynog. He was educated at Eton, and became a cornet in the 1st Life Guards in 1826, rising to the brevet rank of general in 1877. He was gazetted on 16 July 1851 as master of Queen Victoria's household, for which office he had been selected by Baron Stockmar, and in 1854 he was appointed an extra equerry to the queen.

On 16 February 1857 Biddulph married one of the queen's maids of honour, Mary Frederica (1824–1902), only daughter of Frederick Charles William Seymour and his first wife, Lady Mary Gordon. They had a son and a daughter. He was created KCB on 27 March 1863, and was appointed one of the joint keepers of her majesty's privy purse in 1866, in succession to Sir Charles Beaumont Phipps, and in conjunction with General Charles Grey. On Grey's appointment as private secretary to Queen Victoria on 30 April 1867, Sir Thomas Biddulph became sole keeper of the privy purse. In this office, he supervised the queen's financial affairs, with particular responsibility for the royal household, and played an important part in the negotiation of royal grants. In 1877 he was sworn of the privy council. From 1866 until his death he was receiver-general of the duchy of Cornwall, and from 1873 of the duchy of Lancaster.

Sir Thomas Biddulph's official duties involved close attendance on the queen, although she relaxed her usual residence requirements in his case, in order to retain his services. He died at Abergeldie Mains, near Balmoral, on 28 September 1878, after a short illness, during which he was daily visited by the queen; he was buried at Clewer.

Sir Thomas Biddulph's relationship with the queen was not entirely harmonious, and he increasingly resented her habit of sending him instructions through her ladies-in-waiting, and her lack of consideration for the families of her household. He was regarded by other members of the royal family as a bulwark against the supposed radicalism of her private secretary, Henry Ponsonby. Both the

Sir Thomas Myddleton Biddulph (1809–1878), by Heinrich von Angeli, 1878

queen and her family respected his advice, and after his death Victoria described him as 'one of the best of men, and so straightforward, sensible and true' (Ponsonby, 53).

ARTHUR H. GRANT, rev. K. D. REYNOLDS

Sources Burke, *Gen. GB* · A. Ponsonby, *Henry Ponsonby, Queen Victoria's private secretary: his life from his letters* (1942) · *The letters of Queen Victoria*, ed. G. E. Buckle, 3 vols., 2nd ser. (1926–8), vol. 1, pp. 302–4 · Queen Victoria, *More leaves from the journal of a life in the highlands, from 1862 to 1882* (1884) · T. Martin, *The life of … the prince consort*, 5 vols. (1875–80) · W. A. Lindsay, *The royal household* (1898) · Boase, *Mod. Eng. biog.* · *The Times* (30 Sept 1878) · *The Times* (8 Oct 1878)

Archives Royal Arch. | BL, corresp. with Sir H. Layard, Add. MSS 38933–38936, 39131 · Bodl. Oxf., corresp. with H. W. Acland · Bodl. Oxf., corresp. with Disraeli · Bodl. Oxf., corresp. with Lord Kimberley · Bodl. Oxf., corresp. with Sir J. G. Wilkinson · LPL, corresp. with A. C. Tait · Lpool RO, letters to fourteenth earl of Derby · Suffolk RO, Ipswich, corresp. with Cranbrook · U. Southampton L., corresp. with W. F. Cowper, 25760

Likenesses H. von Angeli, oils, 1878, Royal Collection [*see illus.*] · H. von Angeli, oils, second version, Chirk Castle and Garden, Wrexham · photograph, repro. in Ponsonby, *Henry Ponsonby*, facing p. 52

Wealth at death under £25,000: probate, 7 Nov 1878, *CGPLA Eng. & Wales*

Biddulph, Thomas Tregenna (1763–1838), Church of England clergyman, was the only son of the Revd Thomas Biddulph and his first wife, Martha, daughter and coheir of the Revd John Tregenna, rector of Mawgan, Cornwall. He was born at Claines, Worcestershire, on 5 July 1763, moving in 1770 to Cornwall when his father became vicar of Padstow. Biddulph was educated at the grammar school, Truro, and at the Queen's College, Oxford, where he matriculated in 1780, graduating BA in 1784 and MA in 1787. He married, on 19 February 1789 at Bradford-on-Avon, Wiltshire, Rachel (*d.* 10 Aug 1828), daughter of Zachariah Shrapnel and sister of his Oxford friend Joseph Shrapnel.

Biddulph was ordained by Bishop John Ross of Exeter, 26 September 1785, to serve as curate to his father at Padstow. He subsequently served as curate at Ditcheat, Somerset (1786); St Mary-le-Port, Bristol (1787); Wansborough, Wiltshire (1788); Congresbury and Wick St Lawrence, Somerset (1789); and again at St Mary-le-Port (1789) before being appointed vicar of his father's former parish of Bengeworth, near Evesham, Worcestershire, in 1793. Though remaining incumbent at Bengeworth until 1803 he resided elsewhere, for between 1799 and 1838 he also served as perpetual curate of St James's, Bristol, and St John the Baptist, Durston, Somerset. At Bristol, his reputation as a preacher and parish priest was acquired; his evangelical doctrines at first being unpopular with his parishioners, in the course of time his services were rewarded by their respect and affection.

Biddulph was a prodigious author of religious works. He was also active in a number of evangelical societies, including the Church Missionary Society, the British and Foreign Bible Society, the Protestant Reformation Society, and the Church Pastoral Aid Society. Moreover, he served as first secretary and treasurer of the Bristol Clerical Education Society which, like the Elland Society, provided financial support for evangelicals studying at university prior to ordination. On his initiative, in 1789 the society commenced publication of the *Christian Guardian* (initially *Zion's Trumpet*), which became the mouthpiece of provincial, conservative evangelicalism.

Biddulph was a determined Calvinist who held a high doctrine of providence. Together with William Romaine, he imbibed the biblical philosophy of John Hutchinson as advanced in the celebrated work *Moses's Principia* (1724). In 1816 Biddulph published a heated attack on Richard Mant's high-church views on baptismal regeneration. This was an attempt by Biddulph to counter the growing influence of the Western Schism, especially in and around Durston where George Baring—his former curate but now leader of the Schism, which comprised Calvinists who seceded from the Church of England—held court. In 1837, as the influence of the Oxford tract writers increased, Biddulph republished the work in a revised form; this foreshadowed the Gorham controversy which would soon embroil the evangelical party in a national debate over the doctrine of baptismal regeneration.

Biddulph was the recognized leader of the evangelical movement in Bristol (regarded as 'virtually Bishop of Bristol' by some) and throughout much of the west country, a mainstay of English provincial evangelicalism. In 1835 he built St Matthew's, Kingsdown, Bristol, of which his son Theophilus became first vicar. Biddulph died at his home in St James's Square, Bristol, on 19 May 1838, and was buried at St James's on 29 May. GRAYSON CARTER

Sources L. P. Fox, 'The work of the Reverend Thomas Tregenna Biddulph', PhD diss., U. Cam., 1953 · D. M. Lewis, ed., *The Blackwell dictionary of evangelical biography, 1730–1860*, 2 vols. (1995) · Foster, *Alum. Oxon.* · Boase & Courtney, *Bibl. Corn.* · *GM*, 2nd ser., 10 (1838),

331–4 • *Christian Guardian* (1838), 257–63 • D. W. Bebbington, *Evangelicalism in modern Britain: a history from the 1730s to the 1980s* (1989), 57, 58, 61 • P. Toon, *Evangelical theology, 1833–1856: a response to Tractarianism* (1979) • *DNB*

Likenesses E. H. Baily, bust, St James's Church, Bristol • Opie, portrait • W. Ridley, stipple, BM, NPG; repro. in *Evangelical Magazine* (1805) • miniature, priv. coll.

Bidgood, John (1624–1691), physician, the son of Humphrey Bidgood, an apothecary of Exeter, was born in that city on 13 March 1624. His father was poisoned in 1641 by his servant, Peter Moore, a crime for which the offender was tried at the Exeter assizes, and executed on 'the Magdalen gibbet belonging to the city', his dying confession being printed and preserved in the British Library. The son was sent to Exeter College, Oxford, about 1640, and admitted a Petreian fellow on 1 July 1642. On 24 January 1648 he graduated BM, but in the following June was ejected from his fellowship by the parliamentarian visitors. After this he studied at Padua and became MD of that university. With this diploma he returned to England, and, after a few years' practice at Chard in Somerset, he settled in his native city, where he remained until his death.

On the Restoration, in 1660, Bidgood resumed his fellowship, and in the same year (20 September 1660) was incorporated DM at Oxford. Two years later he resigned his fellowship, possibly because a kinsman, who had matriculated in 1661, was then qualified to hold it. In December 1664 he was admitted to the College of Physicians as honorary fellow—an honour which he acknowledged by the gift of £100 towards the erection of their new college in Warwick Lane—and in 1686 was elected as an ordinary fellow. Some years before his death he retired to his country house of Rockbeare, near Exeter, but he died in the cathedral close, Exeter, on 13 January 1691, and was buried in the lady chapel in the cathedral. A flat stone in the pavement, with an English inscription, indicated the place of his burial, and a marble monument with a Latin inscription to his memory was fixed in the wall of the same chapel by his nephew and heir. An extensive practice brought Bidgood a large fortune, but his good qualities were marred by a morose disposition and by a satirical vein of humour. He left the sum of £600 to St John's Hospital at Exeter. Bidgood, who never married, disinherited his son, John Sommers (BA, Trinity College, Oxford, 1678). W. P. COURTNEY, *rev.* MICHAEL BEVAN

Sources Munk, *Roll* • *A catalogue of all graduates … in the University of Oxford, between … 1659 and … 1850* (1851) • C. W. Boase, ed., *Registrum Collegii Exoniensis*, new edn, OHS, 27 (1894) • J. Prince, *Danmonii orientales illustres, or, The worthies of Devon* (1701) • R. Izacke and S. Izacke, *Remarkable antiquities of the city of Exeter*, 3rd edn (1731)

Wealth at death £25,000–£30,000: Munk, *Roll*

Bidlake, John (1755–1814), schoolmaster and Church of England clergyman, was born in Plymouth, the son of Richard Bidlake, a jeweller of that city who came from a family with Totnes connections. His home life appears to have been a source of happiness to him, judging by some of the references in his semi-autobiographical 'Youth: a Poem'.

And I, can I forget the parent's dome;
The dear attachments, and the native home!

How pin'd my restless thought each irksome day,
Torn from the centre of delight away!
(Bidlake, *Poetical Works*, 9)

He was educated at Plymouth grammar school; he was a gifted schoolboy and he proceeded to Christ Church, Oxford, which he entered as a servitor on 10 March 1774. He matriculated at the university on 16 March; he took his BA degree in 1778, and those of MA, BD, and DD in 1808.

Bidlake was ordained as an Anglican priest but made teaching his principal career, acting from 1779 until his retirement in 1810 as headmaster of Plymouth corporation grammar school. He was also curate from 1789 of the Anglican chapel of ease in Stonehouse (later St George's Church); neither post brought Bidlake much remuneration. Before appointment as chaplain to the duke of Clarence (subsequently William IV) and, towards the end of his life, to the prince regent, Bidlake supplemented his stipends by publishing occasional verse and some seven sermons as well as three volumes of collected discourses on mainly religious subjects (1795, 1799, and 1808). In all his writings he sought to be accessible to a non-intellectual readership; as the preface to his lectures of 1811 put it, 'He has not laboured to be abstruse, nor does he profess to claim the praise of originality'. His earliest poem was the anonymous *Elegy Supposed to be Written on Revisiting the Place of a Former Residence* (1788); it was followed by *The Sea* (1796), *The Country Parson* (1797), *Summer's Eve* (1800), *Youth* (1802), and *The Year* (1813). Three volumes of his poetical works appeared, in 1794, 1804, and 1814. At their best his poetical effusions had a lyrical intensity but they seldom rose above the imitative. (The manuscripts of his poems are held by Plymouth Central Library.) His ambitious verse play *Virginia, or, The Fall of the Decemvirs; a Tragedy* (1800) was acted out by his own pupils. With younger audiences in mind he brought out *Eugenio, or, The Precepts of Prudentius* and an *Introduction to the Study of Geography* in 1808. Bidlake also tried his hand at journalism; he produced three numbers of a periodical called *The Selector* at Plymouth in 1809 but there were no more.

Bidlake was a patient, unassuming man of many talents, including painting. As a writer he excessively diversified his output and, in the words of one obituarist, failed to concentrate 'the brilliant rays of his powerful intellect' (*GM*, 84/1). It was as an idiosyncratic schoolmaster that Bidlake made the most impression on contemporaries. Sir Charles Eastlake and Benjamin Haydon were both among his pupils. While Haydon appreciated his teacher's pronounced sense of the beauties of nature he rather harshly judged Bidlake a 'smatterer' and opined that no one could leave school 'without lamenting the time lost in getting a little of everything, without knowing correctly the principles of anything' (*Diary*, ed. Pope, 5). Whatever his shortcomings Bidlake was undoubtedly devoted to the welfare of his pupils. He articulated his pedagogic values before the boys in his 1802 oration and there insisted that, in his sight, 'The sole end of life, and of all human pursuits, is to find happiness in giving it to others' (Bidlake, *A Sermon*, 52).

Academic recognition finally arrived in 1811 in the form

of election to the Bampton lectureship. Sadly it came too late for Bidlake. Taking 'the truth and consistency of divine revelation' as his subject and emphasizing the consistency of the Mosaic and Christian revelations, he suffered a cerebral stroke while delivering his third discourse, from which blindness resulted. He had already given up his teaching post. He published his Bampton lectures in spite of the blindness that prevented him from checking his own pages but his affliction forced him to resign his Stonehouse curacy. Deprived as he thus was of any means of material support, a charitable appeal to the public was made on his behalf in June 1813. He died shortly afterwards, at Plymouth on 17 February 1814, and was buried in St Andrew's Church on 5 March. He never married.

NIGEL ASTON

Sources J. Bidlake, *Sermons on various subjects*, 2 vols. (1795–9) • J. Bidlake, *Poetical works* (1804) • J. Bidlake, *A sermon preached at St Andrew's Church, Plymouth, October 12, 1802, before the gentlemen educated at the Plymouth grammar school together with an oration delivered in the Guildhall on the same day* (1802) • *GM*, 1st ser., 83/1 (1813), 560 • *GM*, 1st ser., 84/1 (1814), 410 • Foster, *Alum. Oxon.* • *The historical register of the University of Oxford … to the end of Trinity term 1900* (1900), 116–18 • R. N. Worth, *History of Plymouth from the earliest period to the present time* (1890), 462 • C. W. Bracken, *A history of Plymouth and her neighbours* (1931) • *The autobiography and memoirs of Benjamin Robert Haydon, 1786–1846*, ed. A. P. D. Penrose (1927) • Christ Church Oxf.
Likenesses etching, NPG

Bidstrup, Jesper (1763–1802). *See under* Industrial spies (act. c.1700–c.1800).

Bidwell, Shelford (1848–1909), physicist and developer of telephotography, was born on 6 March 1848 at Thetford, Norfolk, the eldest son of Shelford Clarke Bidwell, brewer, of Thetford, who was married to his cousin Georgina, daughter of George Bidwell, rector of Stanton, Norfolk. Educated under the Revd J. J. Tuck, of Stevenage, Hertfordshire, and at Hyde Abbey School, Winchester, Bidwell entered Gonville and Caius College, Cambridge, on 3 March 1866, as a pensioner, graduating BA (as a junior optime in the mathematical tripos) in 1870, and LLB (with a second-class honours in the law and history tripos) in 1871; he proceeded MA in 1873. Called to the bar at Lincoln's Inn on 27 January 1873, he joined the south-eastern circuit, and practised for some years, but finally devoted himself to scientific study, specializing with success in electricity and magnetism and in subjective phenomena of vision. He married, on 8 April 1874, Annie Wilhelmina Evelyn, daughter of Edward Firmstone, rector of Wye, near Winchester; they had one son and two daughters.

Bidwell traced the beginning of his scientific interests to friendships formed among members of the Physical Society of London, which he joined, soon after its foundation, in 1877. Obscure and apparently paradoxical phenomena fascinated him, and he showed exceptional subtlety and ingenuity in endeavours to account for them. He was an excellent mechanic and equipped a workshop in his house, where he personally constructed the many instruments which he devised. His first communication to the Physical Society, 'On the influence of friction upon the generation of a voltaic current', was read on 13 March 1880. About 1880, he began an investigation of the photo-conductive property of selenium, which had been discovered in 1873 by Smith and May. This work led to an important practical application. On 11 March 1881 he lectured at the Royal Institution on 'Selenium and its applications to the photophone and telephotography', and described an instrument which he had devised for electrically transmitting to a distant place, via a conducting path, still pictures of natural objects. As he reported in the article 'Telephotography' (in *Nature*, 23, 1881, 344–6):

> In order to ascertain whether my ideas could be carried out in practice, I undertook a series of experiments, and these were attended with so much success that although the pictures hitherto actually transmitted are of a very rudimentary character, I think there can be little doubt that if it were worth while to go to further expense and trouble in elaborating the apparatus excellent results might be obtained.

A paper 'On telegraphic photography', read at the York meeting of the British Association in 1881, further described the invention. His endeavours in this field were among the earliest to be published.

Bidwell's interests extended to meteorology, and in 1893 he lectured at the Royal Institution on 'Fogs, clouds, and lightning', and before the Royal Meteorological Society, of which he was a fellow, on 'Some meteorological problems'. Another of his Royal Institution discourses, 'Some curiosities of vision' (1897), appeared in enlarged form as *Curiosities of Light and Sight* (1899). Bidwell, who was a skilful lecturer, was also a clear and sound writer. Many papers on physics appeared in *Nature* and the chief scientific periodicals, and for the *Encyclopaedia Britannica* (tenth and eleventh editions) he wrote the article 'Magnetism'.

Elected FRS on 4 June 1886, Bidwell served on the society's council in 1904–6. He was president of the Physical Society in 1897–9, and an associate member of the Institution of Electrical Engineers in 1881. He served on the council of the institution in 1883–4, and became a full member in 1884. In 1900 he obtained the degree of ScD from the University of Cambridge.

In 1908 Bidwell wrote a letter on 'Telegraphic photography and electric vision [television]' (*Nature*, 4 June 1908), which was a comment on an optimistic report, in *The Times*, that within a year 'we shall be watching one another across hundreds of miles apart'. Bidwell emphasized the impracticability of such proposals because of the formidable nature of synchronizing, by mechanical means, the receiver to the transmitter of a high-definition television system. A. A. Campbell Swinton responded (*Nature*, 18 June 1908) to Bidwell's letter and proposed an all-electronic solution based on the use of cathode-ray tubes. His scheme was fully described in his 1911 presidential address to the Röntgen Society. It was the first all-electronic television scheme to be delineated and directly influenced the research and development team which evolved the world's first, public, all-electronic, high-definition television system.

Bidwell died at his house, Beechmead, Oatlands Chase, near Weybridge, Surrey, on 18 December 1909, and was buried at Walton cemetery, near Weybridge.

T. E. JAMES, *rev.* R. W. BURNS

Sources 'Dr. Shelford Bidwell', *Nature*, 82 (1909–10), 252–3 • *Engineering* (24 Dec 1909), 864 • 'Dr Shelford Bidwell', *Proc. Phys. Soc.*, 22 (Dec 1909), 11 • *The Times* (25 Dec 1909), 9d • *Journal of the Institution of Electrical Engineers*, 45 (1910), 769 • Inst. EE • J. Venn and others, eds., *Biographical history of Gonville and Caius College*, 2: 1713–1897 (1898) • m. cert. • d. cert.

Wealth at death £38,997 3s.: resworn probate, 31 Jan 1910, CGPLA Eng. & Wales

Bidwell, (Reginald George) Shelford (1913–1996), army officer and military historian, was born on 12 August 1913 at Brooklyn, Sydenham Avenue, Beckenham, Kent, the son of an Indian army officer, Lieutenant-Colonel Reginald Frank Bidwell (1868–1936), and his wife, Mabel Alice Graves, *née* Petley (1878–1948). He had a younger brother who died in infancy, and a half-sister from his mother's first marriage, the poet and novelist Ida Affleck Graves (1902–1999). The Bidwell family had roots in Norfolk and Devon, and had produced an array of churchmen, imperial administrators, and warriors. Bidwell's maternal grandfather, Eaton Wallace Petley, had served in the Royal Navy, in the Royal Indian Marines, and was created CIE for a marine survey of India. Shelford's early childhood was spent in India: his father had been commissioned into the 101 (Bombay) grenadiers, with whom he served in the First World War. In 1919 Colonel Bidwell was invalided out of the Indian army, and he returned to England, taking a house in Looe, Cornwall. Shelford attended a preparatory school, Abbotsford, in Burgess Hill, Sussex, and then Wellington School in Somerset (1923–1931). From 1931 to 1933 he was a cadet at the Royal Military Academy, Woolwich, where he passed out near the top of his class. In September 1933 he was commissioned into the Royal Artillery.

For the first five years of his military career Bidwell was again in India, and served with 18 Talavera battery, 3rd field brigade. With the outbreak of war in 1939 he was posted back to England, where he met and then married Pauline Mary Le Couteur (1913–1993), who was always known as Peggy. A secretary, she was the daughter of Frank Le Couteur, editor of *The Bystander* (before it amalgamated with *The Tatler*). The Le Couteurs were a French-speaking family from Jersey. The Bidwells had two daughters, Penelope Jane (*b.* 1941) and Georgina May (*b.* 1948).

In 1940–41 Bidwell was promoted captain and served as adjutant, 141 field regiment (Dorsetshire yeomanry), before in 1943 commanding a battery of 74 medium regiment (Surrey and Sussex yeomanry) in Tunisia, where he was mentioned in dispatches. In June 1943 he was promoted major, and he served as brigade major (Royal Artillery) in 2nd army group Royal Artillery, taking part in the Salerno landings. From June 1944 he served in Italy for the remainder of the war at HQRA on the staff of 6th armoured division, except for a tour as a member of the directing staff of Staff College, Haifa, in Palestine in October 1944. He had previously been a student there (March–May 1944). In 1945 Bidwell was appointed second in command of the 1st Royal Horse Artillery. He thereafter transferred to the Royal Horse Artillery.

In the post-war years Bidwell served mainly in the British army of the Rhine (BAOR), commanding a battery of 5 Royal Horse Artillery (1946), and as second-in-command of 2 Royal Horse Artillery (1950–52). The intervening years were spent as a general staff officer grade 2 in the War Office in military intelligence 3. In 1952 he was promoted lieutenant-colonel and served at west African command headquarters in Accra, Gold Coast, where he helped plan the defence structure of a future independent Ghana. He returned to Germany to command not a Royal Horse Artillery regiment, but 58 medium regiment (1953–6). By this date Bidwell had developed into a tough and experienced soldier: an imposing, rather florid, thick-set man. His red hair provoked the inevitable familiar name 'Ginger' (which he adopted himself, to such an extent that unwary subalterns assumed that was what his second initial stood for). He had a quick, explosive temper, and demanded the highest standards. His passionate intellectual curiosity and drive for professional excellence had been stimulated by command of citizen soldiers during 1939–45 for whom he had developed an abiding admiration and respect. His forbidding exterior concealed a much more thoughtful, contemplative man who encouraged young officers to think things out for themselves. He was an imaginative teacher, and a kind and considerate mentor.

After laying down command Bidwell was decorated with the OBE and promoted colonel. He spent two years as chief instructor (tactical employment wing) at the Royal School of Artillery. Having trained with horse-drawn guns in the 1930s, he now found himself devising a handbook for the use of tactical nuclear weapons. In 1958 he was promoted brigadier, and served as commander Royal Artillery of the 2nd division of the BAOR. In 1961 his military career reached its climax when, after a tour commanding the north Malaya sub-district, he was posted as brigadier Royal Artillery to Far East land forces headquarters, Singapore, to command the artillery during the 'confrontation' with Indonesia in Borneo. In 1964 he returned to England to command the south-west district, with its headquarters at Taunton.

Bidwell's military career was distinguished, but within limits, for despite his real abilities he did not reach the very top jobs in the army. Of his thirty-one years' service, twenty-six were spent abroad. His last appointment was probably considered a reward for meritorious service, allowing him an easy and quiet transition to retirement, returning to his roots in the west country, following the sleepy rural pursuits of most retired brigadiers. Bidwell's 'retirement' after August 1968 was, however, the most important part of his career.

Bidwell had always been an omnivorous reader; as soon as he retired (based in Suffolk, which was rather nearer to London), he began serious research for his own books. In 1970 he produced *Gunners at War*, one of his most important works. Although it draws upon his personal experience, it is an authoritative, wide-ranging, trenchantly argued book of high intellectual quality. It demonstrates the importance of concentration in artillery tactics, and denounces the falsity of a doctrine, popularized by Captain Sir Basil Liddell Hart, that underestimated the importance of artillery, dispersing its power and decentralizing its command system. He later returned to this theme (with Dominick Graham as co-author) in *Firepower: British Army Weapons and Theories of War, 1904–45* (1982). Bidwell developed another theme that was implicitly critical of Liddell Hart: that British security required a continental commitment. He championed the British military record on the western front in 1914–18, and described Field Marshal Sir Douglas Haig as a 'first rate general'—a judgment that went strongly against the grain at this date. Bidwell had exchanged a vigorous correspondence with Liddell Hart before his death in 1970, and befriended another of the latter's critics, John Terraine.

In 1971 Bidwell was appointed editor of the *Journal of the Royal United Services Institute*, which had embarked on a programme of modernization. He transformed the journal's appearance, a move designed to widen its appeal, and he also promoted the study of military history. It was such a blend of contemporary perspectives informed by the study of history that shaped his most important book, *Modern Warfare: a Study of Men, Weapons and Theories* (1973). This pioneering and under-praised book concentrated on what was then termed 'conventional' war. Bidwell was not hypnotized by nuclear weapons and he certainly could not ignore them, but he developed ideas about the operational level of war long before theorists gave it such a label. *Modern Warfare* provides the most penetrating critique of Liddell Hart's strategy of the indirect approach. Bidwell condemns the idea that 'cheap, tiny armies' could win wars without bloodshed. 'Wars are not decided by "great captains" riding the storm of battle and taking decisions based on intuition' (pp. 213–14). He contends that modern warfare was governed by the deployment of resources, that is, by scale: numbers, weapon-power, extensive communication networks, and commanders who depended on the labour of large staffs; Bidwell was especially strong on morale, man-management, and public opinion. It followed from Bidwell's analysis that the Soviet build-up on the NATO central region should be met with an increase in the size of British forces deployed in Germany. In *World War 3* (1978), Bidwell assembled a team of authors who predicted how such a conflict might develop.

During the 1970s Bidwell produced a series of diverse and important works. *Swords for Hire: European Mercenaries in Eighteenth Century India* (1971) reflects his lifelong interest in the subcontinent; Bidwell himself believed that he owed his election as a fellow of the Royal Historical Society to it. Artillery themes remained important, and he produced *The Royal Horse Artillery* (1973), *Artillery Tactics, 1939–1945* (1976), and as editor, *Brassey's Artillery of the World* (1977). *The Women's Royal Army Corps* (1977) was testimony to his lifelong support of the professional advancement of women. In 1976 Bidwell retired from the Royal United Services Institute, where he had risen to deputy director and editor-in-chief, so that he could concentrate on his writing. Largely at his instigation, his successor as editor of the institute's journal was a woman: Jennifer Shaw. Bidwell remained a vice president of the institute until his death.

In 1979 Bidwell's writings changed direction with *The Chindit War: the Campaign in Burma, 1944*. This book is probably his central contribution to historical scholarship. It presents a balanced analysis of the Chindits and their mercurial founder, Orde Wingate. Thereafter Bidwell collaborated with Professor Dominick Graham on two important works on the campaigns of the Second World War: *Tug of War: the Battle for Italy, 1943–1945* (1986) and *Coalitions, Politicians and Generals: some Aspects of Command in Two World Wars* (1993). The latter is somewhat diffuse, but makes perceptive observations on the constraints imposed by coalition warfare, especially in the Anglo-American alliance of 1944–5.

From about 1993 onwards, Bidwell's powers began to fail. He died from cancer at the Whittington Hospital, Islington, London, on 23 August 1996, and was later cremated. Shelford Bidwell was a much more complex personality than he appeared. At first glance, he resembled a typical retired brigadier, fond of claret with lunch at his club, peering at a menu through his monocle, barking derisively across the table, saying of one of whose views he thoroughly disapproved that 'he's so wet you can shoot snipe off him'. He was certainly a colourful figure, with strong opinions, and full of fun. But he was so much more than a highly competent, professional soldier. He was an inspired teacher with a gift for befriending the young; his interest was genuine and he took great pains to advance the careers of those who aroused his interest. Bidwell was intellectually a late developer, but had a very sharp brain, equipped with a penetrating intellect; he was a formidable advocate, especially on paper. He was not conventional, despite his appearance. Both the military policies he advocated and the general attitudes he evinced were more radical than he was given credit for. He was a major historian, one of the most gifted soldier–historians writing in the late twentieth century. But his major achievement, which went largely unsung, was to elevate British military thought to levels that it had not enjoyed since before 1939. At a time when interest in military affairs had been submerged by a tide of theorizing absorbed by nuclear strategy, Bidwell was a perspicacious forerunner of those who transformed British military thought and doctrine in the 1990s.   BRIAN HOLDEN REID

Sources S. Bidwell, 'Personal record', priv. coll. [compiled for Royal Artillery] · b. cert. · d. cert. · *RUSI Journal* (Oct 1996) [Royal United Services Institute] · *Gunner* (1996), 16 · *The Times* (3 Sept 1996) · personal knowledge (2004) · private information (2004) [daughters]
Archives IWM, working paper on Chindits · priv. coll., working papers | King's Lond., Liddell Hart C., corresp. with Sir Basil Liddell Hart
Likenesses photographs, priv. coll.

Bidwill, John Carne (1815–1853), botanist and traveller, was born on 5 February 1815 at Exeter, the son of Joseph Green Bidwill and his wife, Charlotte, *née* Carne. At the age of seventeen he travelled to Canada, and then in 1838 to New South Wales, and entered into business as a merchant at Sydney. In February 1839 he embarked on an expedition to New Zealand. From Tauranga he made his way into the mountains of the interior, and at Rotorua he met the first European to visit Taupo, Revd Thomas Chapman. Bidwill himself explored the shores of Lake Taupo and climbed Mount Ngauruhoe, thereby incurring the wrath of the local chief, Te Heuheu, for violating the mountain's tapu (sacred) status. He visited New Zealand again in 1840 when he travelled to Port Nicholson and Wanganui, and in 1848, to Nelson, to observe and collect botanical specimens. His *Rambles in New Zealand* was published in 1841. An inveterate traveller, he journeyed to Tahiti in 1845 and spent a year there.

From September 1847 Bidwill briefly held the post of government botanist and director of the Sydney Botanic Gardens. In 1849 he was appointed commissioner of crown lands for Maryborough, Queensland, in which capacity he is credited with the discovery of gold at Gympie. He was also chairman of the bench of magistrates for Wide Bay district, New South Wales. In 1853, while engaged in marking out a new road in bush, he became lost for eight days without food, and his health never recovered from the effects of starvation and privation. He died at Tinana, Maryborough, in March 1853.

Bidwill was a keen botanist and an assiduous collector, both in New Zealand (especially of alpine plants) and Australia. He contributed papers on horticultural subjects to the *Gardener's Chronicle*, corresponded with Sir William Hooker, and sent many specimens to Kew for classification. A number of plants have been named after him, including the *Araucaria bidwilli*, *Veronica bidwilli*, and *Forstera bidwilli*.   JANE TUCKER

Sources A. H. McLintock, ed., *An encyclopaedia of New Zealand*, 3 vols. (1966) · R. Glenn, *Botanical explorers of New Zealand* (1950) · J. C. Bidwill, *Rambles in New Zealand* (1841)
Archives RBG Kew, corresp. with Sir W. J. Hooker

Biffen, Sir **Rowland Harry** (1874–1949), geneticist and agricultural botanist, was born on 28 May 1874 at Cheltenham, the eldest of the family of two boys and three girls of Henry John Biffen, headmaster of the Christ Church higher grade school at Cheltenham, and his wife, Mary. He was educated at Cheltenham grammar school and entered Emmanuel College, Cambridge, in 1893 as an exhibitioner. He was placed in the first class of both parts of the natural sciences tripos and in 1896 he became Frank Smart student in botany at Gonville and Caius College, studying under H. Marshall Ward. Here he was introduced to the 'new botany', an experimentalist school of botany which sought to gain greater visibility and financial support for its programme by undertaking ostensibly economic work. Thus, shortly after graduating, Biffen accompanied a small expedition to Brazil, Mexico, and the West Indies to study rubber production. On returning to Cambridge he served as university demonstrator in botany under Ward, investigating fungi and developing a new method of handling rubber latex (patent no. 3909 of 1898). In 1899 he married Mary (d. 1948), eldest daughter of Edmund Hemus of Holdfast Hall, Upton-on-Severn. That same year Biffen took up a lectureship in agricultural botany in the newly established school of agriculture in the

University of Cambridge. The position was eventually elevated to a professorship, which he held from 1908 until his retirement in 1931.

Biffen was a reluctant teacher but an imaginative experimenter, and he enthusiastically embraced the Mendelian theory of inheritance espoused in Cambridge, and in England more generally, by William Bateson. Biffen's earliest investigations in this field established the applicability of Mendelian principles to the mode of inheritance of physiological as well as morphological characters in plants. In 1903, for example, he published evidence that the inheritance of the length-of-life cycle in wheat conformed with Mendelian principles, and predicted that this would prove to be the case even with a physiological character such as resistance to specific plant diseases. Two years later he furnished proof of this in his paper on the yellow rust disease of wheat, 'Mendel's laws of inheritance and wheat breeding', which appeared in the first issue of the journal he himself had helped to establish, the *Journal of Agricultural Science*. This discovery quickly expanded into the realization that all hereditary characteristics of plants and animals were transmitted in Mendelian fashion. Although his subsequent genetic researches helped to enlarge and develop knowledge of heredity without fundamentally influencing it, he played an important role, in 1918, in establishing the Genetical Society and thus in helping to bolster the new discipline of genetics.

Biffen's principal interest was in applying the Mendelian theory of heredity to improve English wheat. Little Joss (1910) and Yeoman (1916) were two of his best known productions, developed to meet the needs of his close supporters in the Home Grown Wheat Association, and have since been used as parents by several successful breeders. Indeed, a plant breeding institute was founded by government grant for the expansion of Biffen's work in improving wheat, and he was its director from 1912 to 1936. He was also closely involved with the founding of the National Institute of Agricultural Botany, which aimed to market varieties produced by the Plant Breeding Institute and control the quality of corn and other crop varieties sold to English farmers.

Biffen was knighted in 1925. Academic honours included his election as FRS (1914), the Royal Society's Darwin medal (1920), a professorial fellowship at St Catharine's College (1909), and an honorary fellowship at Emmanuel College (1911). He received the honorary degree of DSc from the University of Reading in 1935.

Biffen was a keen gardener. His beautiful garden included many fine specimens, especially of auriculas, which he himself bred. He was an expert in the identification of British wild flora in photography and in archaeology, a hobby shared with his sometimes rival in botanical matters, John Percival, professor of agricultural botany in Reading. Although he was entirely untaught, his sketches and watercolours, most of them landscapes, were of high quality. Although a vigorous walker, Biffen was slight in build and delicate in constitution. He was a confirmed pipe smoker and voracious reader. The quiet of garden, countryside, and laboratory suited him best and he shunned routine administration and any but intimate society. Unfailingly calm in mind, in judgement discerning and charitable, he was a high exemplar to his pupils and his friends. He died in Cambridge on 12 July 1949. His wife had died the previous year. They had no children.

F. L. ENGLEDOW, *rev.* PAOLO PALLADINO

Sources F. L. Engledow, *Obits. FRS*, 7 (1950–51), 9–25 · P. Palladino, 'Between craft and science: plant breeding, Mendelian genetics, and British universities, 1900–1920', *Technology and Culture*, 34 (1993), 300–23 · *The Times* (15 July 1949) · *CGPLA Eng. & Wales* (1949) **Archives** CUL, C. C. Hurst MSS · John Innes Centre, Norwich, W. Bateson MSS · U. Reading, J. Percival MSS **Likenesses** K. Green, oils, 1926, U. Cam., school of agriculture **Wealth at death** £24,655 6s. 4d.: probate, 15 Sept 1949, *CGPLA Eng. & Wales*

Biffin [Beffin; *married name* Wright], **Sarah** (1784–1850), miniature painter, was born on 25 October 1784 at East Quantoxhead, Somerset, and baptized there, at the church of St Mary the Virgin, on 31 October. She was the third of five children of Henry John Beffin (1747/8–1835), shoemaker, and his wife, Sarah, *née* Perkins (1746/7–1840), who were married in that church on 11 June 1772. The baptismal register records that Sarah was 'born without arms or legs', a condition now known as phocomelia. She grew to be 37 inches tall. The family lived in a seventeenth-century farmworker's cottage which in the nineteenth century was joined to a neighbouring cottage, to become Townsend House.

Aged about thirteen Sarah Biffin bound herself by contract to the service of Emmanuel Dukes, a travelling showman. He described her as 'The Eighth Wonder!' and in one of his handbills stated that she would demonstrate:

> before the Nobility, Gentry and the Public in general her skills in the use of the needle, scissars, pen and pencil etc. wherein she is extremely adroit; she can cut out and make any part of her own clothing [and] sews extremely neat

and how 'she writes well and has practised in the polite art of drawing 16 months and in miniature paintings only 3 months, all of which she performs principally with her mouth'. It is also there stated that she charged 3 guineas for a miniature on ivory. Examples of Dukes's handbills are preserved in the British Museum and in the Hornby Library collection, Liverpool City Library. Henry Morley's *Memoirs of Bartholomew Fair* (1859) includes illustrations after Thomas Rowlandson's caricatures of scenes at Bartholomew fair in 1799; one of these details a drawing on the side of a showman's van of a limbless woman who resembles a mermaid, above whose head is inscribed the name Miss Biffin. Morley disapproved of this 'libel on Miss Biffin' and recorded biographical information about her 'life among caravans' and her meeting the Irish peer the earl of Morton in 1808 (Morley, 468). Morton obtained for her the favour of George III and arranged for her further instruction in the art of miniature painting with William Craig, painter in watercolours to Queen Charlotte and the duchess of Kent. George IV, William IV, Queen Victoria, and Prince Albert also patronized her. In *British Miniaturists* Basil Long recorded:

Sarah Biffin [Wright] (1784–1850), by Henri Grevedon, 1823

my grandfather George Long describes in his memoirs how he saw Miss Biffin at work in Birmingham in 1808—'Her appearance was handsome, as seemingly seated on a cushion she deftly plied her needle with her mouth, with which too she threaded it, her work resting on her shoulder stump. She worked both in plain sewing and embroidery, but she also painted miniature portraits, handed round for inspection, and she wrote her name, in an excellent lady's handwriting as we should call it, but executed, as all else, by her mouth alone.' (Long, 30)

Long noted, of a miniature of the Hon. Eliza Maria Sydney Smythe by Sarah Biffin, that it was 'painted with a sure touch' (ibid.).

After sixteen years of service to Dukes, during which time she shared the domestic life and kindness of his family, Sarah Biffin agreed to be released from her contract, and, assisted by the earl of Morton, became an independent painter of miniature portraits with a studio in the Strand, London. In 1821 she was awarded the silver medal of the Society of Arts for a historical miniature. She was introduced by the earl of Morton (who died in 1827) to the royal court in Brussels, where she received commissions for miniatures. On 6 September 1824 she married William Stephen Wright (*d.* in or before 1850), a banker's clerk, at Kilton church, Somerset, but the couple appear to have separated soon afterwards. In later years she noted that 'he allowed her out of a very moderate salary, forty pounds per annum' (amended edition of Richard Rathbone's appeal, 1847, Hornby Library collection, Liverpool). She also received, until her death, a civil-list pension of £12 per annum, although the date that this award was first made remains unconfirmed. As Mrs E. M. Wright, Sarah exhibited two miniatures at the Royal Academy in 1831 and 1832. An advertisement of 1840 in the Hornby Library collection, Liverpool, gives notice of an exhibition of the work of Mrs Wright, late Miss Biffin, at 18 New Street, Birmingham. A self-portrait of Sarah, of 1837, was lent to the miniatures exhibition held at the South Kensington Museum in 1865, when it was stated in the catalogue to have been painted in Brighton, 'where Miss Biffin lived and worked for many years' (p. 130). Notable among her surviving works is the full-size portrait in oils of Fanny Maria Cox (1833; Walker Art Gallery, Liverpool) and a miniature of Edward, duke of Kent (1839; Royal Collection), after a portrait by George Dawe.

In April 1841 Sarah Wright was living at 116 High Street, Cheltenham; in a letter of September of that year, sent from London to an unnamed correspondent, she mentioned her 'intended project' to visit America, and may have travelled to Liverpool with this plan in mind (MS letter, Harvard University). Instead she established a studio in Liverpool and developed a clientele among wealthy families there. From 1842 the signature on her paintings reverts to the name Miss Biffin. Exhibitions of her work were held at the Liverpool Collegiate School in Shaw Street (1843) and at the Mechanics' Institution, Liverpool (1844). In *Gore's Directory of Liverpool* for 1847 she is recorded as Elizabeth Biffin and living at 44 Duke Street; in 1849, under the same name, she is listed as living at 8 Duke Street. She was befriended by the collector Joseph Mayer, who bought some of her pictures. Her letters to him record her several changes of address that indicate a gradual decline from her initial success, and the deterioration of her health. Mayer preserved her letters and the works that he acquired from her and later gave these, with other collections, to the founding collection of the Liverpool Museum. They now form part of the Hornby Library collection, Liverpool Central Library. In 1847 the Liverpool philanthropist Richard Rathbone launched an appeal to secure an annuity for Sarah Biffin. Subscribers included royal patrons and the singer Jenny Lind. She died in her sixty-sixth year at her lodging, 8 Duke Street, Liverpool, on 2 October 1850, when her name was recorded on her death certificate as Sarah Wright; she was buried in St James's cemetery on 5 October. Her gravestone no longer survives but her epitaph is recorded in James Gibson's manuscript collection 'Epitaphs and inscriptions in St. James's cemetery' (vol. 7, p. 229, MS, Lpool RO, H929.5GIB).

Sarah Biffin's remarkable life became the subject of many literary references, both during her lifetime and afterwards. These include 'An author's visit to Croydon fair', in *Sporting Magazine* (October 1810); Thomas Hood's poem *The Mermaid of Margate* (c.1820); R. S. Surtees' *Handley Cross* (1843); and a contribution from W. M. Thackeray in *Frazer's Magazine* (February 1847). A number of references to her in works by Charles Dickens include those in *Nicholas Nickleby* (1838), chapter 37; *The Old Curiosity Shop* (1840), chapter 19; *Martin Chuzzlewit* (1843), chapter 28; *Little Dorrit* (1855), book 2, chapter 18; and 'A Plated Article', in *Reprinted Pieces* (1858).

Two miniatures by Sarah Biffin are in the Victoria and Albert Museum, London; her miniatures of Robert and Hannah Farlam (1845) are in the Williamson Art Gallery, Birkenhead; her portrait of an unknown lady (1845) is in

the Admiral Blake Museum, Bridgwater, and her portrait of Céline Celeste (or Madame Taglioni; 1844), in *The Maid of Kashmir*, was sold at Sothebys in May 1985.

Winifred Leybourne

Sources S. Biffin, 'Collection of documents, drawings, &c.', Liverpool Central Library, Hornby Library collection [a collection of engraved portraits, watercolours, handbills, and letters written by S. Biffin; Rathbone appeal and subscription list] • W. Leybourne, 'Sarah Biffin, miniaturist', *The Dickensian*, 93 (1997), 165–84 • Lpool RO, G. Hardy papers, Acc. no. 5679 • *DNB* • B. S. Long, *British miniaturists* (1929) • 'Sarah Biffin, the armless artist of Quantoxhead', *Somerset Year Book* (1925), 65–8 • H. Morley, *Memoirs of Bartholomew fair* (1859) • C. Mackie, *Norfolk annals: a chronological record of remarkable events in the nineteenth century*, 1: *1801–1850* (1901) • H. Wilson and J. Caulfield, *Wonderful and eccentric characters* (1869) • Redgrave, *Artists* • T. Frost, *The old showmen and old London fairs* (1874) • *Liverpool Athenaeum* (12 Oct 1850) • *GM*, 2nd ser., 34 (1850), 668 • *Liverpool Mercury* (11 Oct 1850) • *Liverpool Mail* (12 Oct 1850), 339–40 • *Art Journal*, 12 (1850) • 'Notes and queries', *Manchester City News* (1880) • *N&Q*, 7th ser., 6 (1888), 229 • 'Miss Biffin (Mrs Wright)', Walker Art Gallery, Liverpool [typed list of paintings by Miss Biffin, loaned for exhibition in Liverpool Museum, 1925] • P. Joyner, *Artists in Wales* (1994) • *An interesting narrative and proposals for a print of Miss Beffin, to be dedicated, by permission to H.R.H. the Princess Augusta* [copy of this rare leaflet slipped into D. Lysons, 'Collecteana: a collection of paragraphs from newspapers relating to giants, monstrosities, etc.', BM, BM.1889 e5.; another in Shrewsbury Museum]
Archives Harvard U., letter | Liverpool Central Library, Hornby Library collection, letters, documents
Likenesses S. Biffin, self-portrait, miniature on ivory, *c.*1810, Wellcome L. • S. Biffin, self-portrait, 1821 • R. W. Sievier, stipple, pubd 1821 (after self-portrait, 1821); impression, BM • H. Grevedon, lithograph, 1823, BM, NPG [*see illus.*] • R. J. Stothard, lithograph (after self-portrait, 1847); impression, BM

Big Bear [Mistahimaskwa] (*c.*1825–1888), leader of the Plains Cree, was born north of Fort Carlton in Ruperts Land, Northwest Territories, the son of Black Powder (*d. c.*1864), a minor chief. His parents were of Plains Cree and Saulteaux background. Big Bear had three wives: the Wallowing One, whom he married about 1850 and who died about 1860; Root Grubbing Woman, whom he married in the 1860s and who died about 1885; and Running Second, who married him in the mid-1870s but deserted him in 1887. He had at least five children. In his youth he was a noted warrior and gained renown as a spiritual leader, and when Black Powder died about 1864, Big Bear became chief of his father's band. By 1870 he had become one of the principal leaders of the Plains Cree. He gained notoriety among non-native people in 1876, when he refused to make a treaty with the government of Canada.

Big Bear and the Cree wanted the economic assistance that the Canadian government offered in the Fort Pitt treaty. However, Big Bear rejected the treaty because it made the Cree subject to Canadian laws and institutions over which they had no influence. He believed that the resources promised therein were only bait in a trap which, if taken, would give the Canadian government control of the Cree. He attempted to have the treaty modified to remove the offensive clauses, but to no avail, and he and more than half the Cree nation did not sign it. In the period from 1877 to 1883 the Cree moved to the

Cypress Hills, the site of the last remaining buffalo ranges in Canada. There they were free from external control while Big Bear tried to negotiate changes to the treaty which would give the Cree autonomy in a Cree territory.

The extinction of the buffalo and the resultant widespread starvation forced the Cree to leave the Cypress Hills and submit to the treaty, since the Canadian government refused to assist any Cree who did not. By 1883 Big Bear's huge following was briefly dispersed. However, he did not abandon his goal of attaining Cree autonomy in a Cree territory, but simply changed the site, from the Cypress Hills to the Battleford region. By 1884 support for this goal was widespread among the Cree, even among those leaders who had not been with him in the Cypress Hills. An important new participant was **Poundmaker** [Pitikwahanapiwiyin] (1842–1886), a Plains Cree chief, the son of Skunk Skin (Sikawayan; d. c.1843). Fearful of Big Bear's growing influence, Canadian authorities in 1884 tried unsuccessfully to use the tiny North-West Mounted Police force to break up the meetings he and his associates were holding throughout the Northwest Territories. It was the extremely harsh winter of 1885 and the following métis uprising on the South Saskatchewan River that ultimately destroyed Big Bear's enterprise.

The Canadian government again used starvation as an instrument to control the Cree. Objecting to such treatment and having lost patience with Big Bear's refusal to use violence to accomplish his goals, the young men of his band picked Big Bear's eldest son Imasees (Little Bad Man) and the war chief Wandering Spirit as their new leaders. In March 1885, when officials at Frog Lake refused to provide rations to Big Bear's band, they were murdered by its new leaders. This action provided the Canadian authorities with the opportunity to destroy Big Bear and his movement. Although he was aware that the Cree movement was not related to the métis uprising that also began in 1885, the lieutenant-governor, Edgar Dewdney, treated both as part of one rebellion. Big Bear was labelled a rebel to justify the use of military forces to suppress the movement for Cree autonomy. These troops were also used against Poundmaker and the Battleford Cree, who were considered rebels because the starving Cree looted the abandoned town of Battleford to get food.

Big Bear and Poundmaker were arrested and charged with treason-felony. Both were convicted in the autumn of 1885, but, because of their deteriorating health, Poundmaker was released after serving only a few months of his sentence, and Big Bear after serving two years. Both died within months of their release: Poundmaker of a burst blood vessel in his throat, on 4 July 1886 at Blackfoot Crossing; Big Bear of tuberculosis, on 17 January 1888 on the Poundmaker Reserve, Northwest Territories. Both men were great leaders who realized that they could not defeat white men by fighting, and who hoped instead to negotiate reasonable treaties as a basis for co-existence.

JOHN L. TOBIAS

Sources J. L. Tobias, 'Canada's subjugation of the Plains Cree, 1879–1885', *Canadian Historical Review*, 64 (1983), 519–48 · H. A. Dempsey, *Big Bear: the end of freedom* (1984) · R. Weibe, 'Mistahimaskwa', *DCB*, vol. 11 · R. Allen, 'Big Bear', *Saskatchewan History*, 25 (1972) · N. Sluman, *Poundmaker* (1967) · W. B. Fraser, 'Big Bear, Indian patriot', *Alberta Historical Review*, 14 (1966), 1–13 · A. Morris, *Treaties of Canada with the Indians of the Manitoba and the North-West territories* (1880) · B. Beal and R. MacLeod, *Prairie fire, the 1885 northwest rebellions* (1984) · G. F. G. Stanley, *The birth of western Canada: a history of the Riel rebellions*, 2nd edn (1961); repr. [1970] · R. Jefferson, *Fifty years on the Saskatchewan* (1929) · C. Innes, *The Cree rebellion of 1884; sidelights of Indian conditions subsequent to 1876* (1926) · J. R. Miller, *Big Bear (Mistahimusqua): a biography* (1996)

Archives Glenbow Archives, Calgary, Alberta, Dewdney MSS · NA Canada, Department of Indian Affairs files, Black series, record group 10 · NA Canada, Macdonald MSS

Likenesses photograph, 1886, NA Canada · photograph, 1886, Glenbow Alberta Institute, Calgary · photograph, 1886 (Poundmaker), Glenbow Alberta Institute, Calgary · photograph, 1886 (Poundmaker), NA Canada

Big Daddy. *See* Crabtree, Shirley (1930–1997).

Bigg, Charles (1840–1908), schoolmaster and ecclesiastical historian, was born on 12 September 1840 at Higher Broughton, near Manchester, the second son of Thomas Bigg, a Manchester merchant, and Sarah Elden. Educated at Manchester grammar school, his election to an open scholarship at Corpus Christi College, Oxford, in 1858 was a prelude to repeated university distinction: he was awarded first-class honours in classics in the final schools (1862), the Hertford scholarship for Latin (1860), the Ireland scholarship and the Gaisford prize for Greek prose (1861), and the Ellerton theological essay (1864); a DD degree followed in 1876. Frederick Walker judged him 'to stand at the head of all scholars proceeding from Oxford' during the 1860s ('Testimonials in favour of the Rev. Charles Bigg', 12).

The teaching of classics Bigg found such an unexpected delight that in 1865, the year after his ordination, he left Oxford for the life of a schoolmaster and became second classical master at Cheltenham College. He did not look back, relishing the classroom and publishing school editions of Thucydides and Xenophon. On 2 January 1867 he married Millicent Sale; they had three sons and a daughter. According to Alfred Barry, 'none could better unite the old and the new in education' ('Testimonials', 10), and in 1871 Bigg was elected principal of Brighton College. Here his reform of the scholarships, his introduction of national advertising, and his renewal of drains indicate practical vigour, while his promotion of science and rejection of athleticism suggest a discernment then unique among public school headmasters. Cyril Starkey, one of his pupils and later headmaster of Edinburgh collegiate school, claimed 'there was never a keener or more stimulating teacher, nor a kinder and wiser friend to his staff and boys' (Starkey, 425–6).

In 1881 Bigg resigned after a brief but bitter dispute with obtuse governors and returned to Oxford as chaplain to his old college, Corpus Christi. There his warm humanity and absence of self-importance won him a signal following among undergraduates. There too began his enduring study of the early church, the first fruits of which appeared in his Bampton lectures on 'The Christian Platonists of Alexandria' (1886). These re-established the centrality of Origen and revived interest in Christian mysticism, and they at once won Bigg recognition as a careful scholar and an acute philosopher and theologian.

In 1887 Bigg became rector of Fenny Compton, Warwickshire, and from 1889 he was also bishop's examining chaplain and honorary canon of Worcester. Mandell Creighton similarly appointed him his examining chaplain for Peterborough and then London; in October 1900 he assigned Bigg a leading part in the Fulham Palace conference. Pastoral commitments did not obstruct scholarship. In 1898 Bigg published *The Doctrine of the Twelve Apostles* and in 1901 the strongly conservative *Epistles of St Peter and St Jude* for the International Critical Commentary. More important were editions of devotional works such as *The Confessions of St Augustine* (1897), *The Imitation of Christ* (1898), and William Law's *Serious Call* (1899). Deceptively little, these offered archaeologically accurate texts rendered in accessible English, with crisp introductions proffering instruction in contemplative spirituality.

Bigg returned again to Oxford in 1901 as regius professor of ecclesiastical history. His earnest small voice was soon in demand to preach and to lead retreats, for Bigg possessed the capacity to speak directly to each individual in a congregation (some of his addresses were published posthumously in 1909 under the apposite title *The Spirit of Christ in Common Life*).

Proctor for the chapter of Christ Church in convocation from 1903, Bigg held a firmly eirenic position in church politics: he regarded ritual questions as 'in themselves absolutely indifferent' (C. Bigg, *Wayside Sketches in Ecclesiastical History*, 1906, 229) and reminded hotheads of 'the low hills by which all our controversies are bounded' (C. Bigg, ed., *The Imitation of Christ*, 1910, 40). A key supporter of the 1903–4 abortive proposal to admit non-Anglicans as examiners for the Oxford theological school, he was shouted down in the university's convocation as 'Judas' and 'Antichrist'.

In 1905 Bigg published *The Church's Task under the Roman Empire*, followed in 1906 by various lectures entitled *Wayside Sketches in Ecclesiastical History*. Both illustrate his hope that study of church history 'would materially change our attitude towards divisions of opinion by enlarging charity' (*The Church's Task under the Roman Empire*, ix). He was seized with paralysis at Christ Church on 13 July 1908, having just sent to press the most important of his works, *The Origins of Christianity* (1909). He never regained consciousness and died two days later. He was buried in Osney cemetery, Oxford, on 19 July. Brighton College erected a memorial window. Dean W. R. Inge estimated that 'his influence was deep, rather than wide; he was content to be a teacher of teachers' (Inge, 1).

MARTIN D. W. JONES

Sources C. Starkey, 'Charles Bigg: in memoriam', *Brighton College Magazine*, 12/8 (July 1908), 425–7 · M. D. W. Jones, *Brighton College, 1845–1995* (1995) · *The Times* (16 July 1908) · W. R. Inge, 'Charles Bigg', *Journal of Theological studies*, 10 (1908–9), 1–2 · C. Bigg, *The spirit of Christ in common life* (1909), v–viii · V. H. H. Green, *Religion at Oxford*
and Cambridge (1964) · *The Times* (20 July 1908) · 'Testimonials in favour of the Rev. Charles Bigg … elected to the principalship of Brighton College', 1871, Brighton College, Brighton
Archives Brighton College, Brighton, archives
Likenesses photographs, *c.*1875–1901, Brighton College · W. & A. H. Fry, photograph, *c.*1880, Brighton College · photograph, *c.*1905, Christ Church Oxf. · print, NPG

Bigg, John Stanyan (1828–1865), poet and journalist, was born at Ulverston, Lancashire, on 14 July 1828. He was educated at the old Town Bank School in Ulverston and at thirteen was sent to a boarding-school in Warwickshire. On his return to his home town three years later, he worked with his father in the family business.

In 1848 Bigg began work as editor of the *Ulverston Advertiser*, and during this year published his first work, *The Sea King: a Metrical Romance in Six Cantos*, with copious notes. The romance was inspired by his study of Sharon Turner's *History of the Anglo-Saxons*. The poem attracted the attention of several literary figures, including Edward Bulwer-Lytton and James Montgomery.

In 1854 Bigg went to Ireland, where he edited the *Downshire Protestant*. At Downpatrick, co. Down, he married Rose Anne Hart Pridham; the couple had three children. While in Ireland he contributed to several London journals. In 1854 he wrote his best-known poem, *Night and the Soul*, which first appeared in *The Critic* in 1854 and was subsequently republished in England and the United States, running to several editions. With its publication he was swiftly classed with the emergent Spasmodic school of poets, and George Gilfillan, the inspirer and defender of the Spasmodics, compared him to William Wordsworth. However, even Gilfillan dampened down this praise by suggesting that 'many of his passages would be greatly improved by leaving out every third line' (Gilfillan, 267). But Bigg's reputation as a promising young poet was dealt its death blow by the publication of William Aytoun's spoof Spasmodic tragedy, *Firmilian* (1854), several months after the brief success of *Night and the Soul*. Gilfillan and his protégés were the butts of Aytoun's vituperative parody, and Aytoun not only destroyed Gilfillan's influence as a literary critic but also attacked Bigg as one of the poets who 'tear their hair, proclaim their inward wretchedness, and spout sorry metaphysics in still sorrier verse for no imaginable reason whatsoever' (Weinstein, 189). Turning away from poetry, Bigg produced a novel, *Alfred Staunton* (1859), which was moderately successful.

In 1860 Bigg left Ireland and returned to Ulverston, where he resumed the editorship of the *Ulverston Advertiser*. In 1862 he attempted to follow up *Night and the Soul* with *Shifting Scenes, and other Poems*, but the collection failed to inspire critical interest, and by 1866 James Hannay was able to comment in the *North British Review* that 'the Spasmodic school no longer exists as a school'. Bigg died at 7 Hoad Terrace, Ulverston, on 19 May 1865, aged thirty-six. He was survived by his wife.

KATHERINE MULLIN

Sources Boase, *Mod. Eng. biog.* · Allibone, *Dict.* · G. Gilfillan, *A gallery of literary portraits* (1845), 255–68 · M. A. Weinstein, *William Aytoun and the Spasmodic controversy* (1968) · J. Hannay, 'Some recent humorists: Aytoun, Peacock, Prout', *North British Review*, 45 (1866),

75–104 • *GM*, 3rd ser., 18 (1865) • review of *Night and the soul: a dramatic poem* by J. Stanyan Bigg, *The Athenaeum* (28 Oct 1854), 1296–7 • review of *Shifting scenes, and other poems* by J. Stanyan Bigg, *The Athenaeum* (21 June 1862), 821–2 • *Ulverston Advertiser* (25 May 1865) • *DNB* • d. cert.

Archives BL, loan 96

Wealth at death under £1500: probate, 12 July 1865, *CGPLA Eng. & Wales*

Bigg, William Redmore (1755–1828), painter, was born in Felsted, Essex, in January 1755, the son of William Bigg and Grace Redmore, who were married in Bulmer, Essex, in 1749. According to Joseph Farington, he received a good classical education (Farington, *Diary*, 9.3211). Bigg lived and worked in London and on 10 January 1784 at St Mary's, Colchester, married Martha Frost (*d.* 1828); they had a son and a daughter. He entered the Royal Academy Schools in December 1778, studying under Edward Penny RA (1714–1791), whose influence is apparent in his choice of conversation pieces and popular themes of charity and virtue. His prolific exhibiting career lasted between 1780 and 1827, and included 129 works at the Royal Academy, and others at the Free Society and the British Institution, among which were landscapes, portraits, and conversation pieces. Several were engraved as mezzotints and some were conceived as decorative moralizing pendants, which had a popular appeal in the 1780s. He produced small-scale pictures, competently painted with freshly observed detail and decoration in the costumes and good effects of light and shade. His cottagers are always dignified and 'obviously virtuous' (Waterhouse, *18c painters*, 52), his chief characters elevated. Engravers who produced prints after his works include John Raphael Smith and William Ward (1766–1826). A mezzotint by Ward after Bigg's painting of 1799, *The Sailor's Orphans, or, The Young Ladies' Subscription*, is in the Fitzwilliam Museum, Cambridge. Typical compositions are *The Rapacious Steward or Unfortunate Tenant* (exh. RA, 1801) and *The Benevolent Heir, or, The Tenant Restored to his Family* (exh. RA, 1797; Yale U. CBA; repr. Johnson, 97). Bigg's conversation pieces, for example his composition of an aristocratic woman engaged in an act of charity accompanied by her children and her African servant, *A Lady and her Children Relieving a Cottager* (exh. RA, 1781; Philadelphia Museum of Art; repr. Dorment, fig. 7), demonstrate an interest in contemporary social concerns. Taste for this kind of art declined after the 1780s and Bigg struggled to earn a living. Farington records his poverty and efforts to advance his career (Farington, *Diary*, 9.3211). He augmented his income by picture dealing and restoring works of art, including those belonging to Lord Lyttleton and Lord Guilford. He restored Sir Joshua Reynolds's portrait of Lord Rodney, bought by Lord Egremont and now at Petworth House, Sussex. Bigg was elected an associate of the Royal Academy, but it was not until 1814 that he became a Royal Academician. He served on the hanging committee in 1815 with Thomas Stothard and William Theed, although persistent ill health limited his activity. Bigg was a frequent visitor to Farington, knew Sir John Soane, was a friend of Sir Joshua Reynolds and John Constable, and was much appreciated for his gentle and gentlemanly nature by the latter, with whom he shared a common interest in the Essex and Suffolk countryside. Constable replaced Bigg as Royal Academician in 1828. Bigg also knew C. R. Leslie and sat for the figure of the knight in *Sir Roger de Coverley Going to Church*. Bigg died at his home, 116 Great Russell Street, London, on 6 February 1828. His *Girl at a Cottage Door, Shelling Peas* and *Girl Gathering Filberts* (both 1782) are in Plymouth City Museum and Art Gallery.

Ernest Radford, *rev.* Heather M. MacLennan

Sources R. Dorment, *British painting in the Philadelphia Museum of Art from the 17th century through the 19th century* (1986) [incl. bibliography] • Farington, *Diary* • C. R. Leslie, *Memoirs of the life of John Constable*, ed. J. Mayne (1951); repr. (1980) • Waterhouse, *18c painters* • Graves, *RA exhibitors* • B. Stewart and M. Cutten, *The dictionary of portrait painters in Britain up to 1920* (1997) • W. T. Whitley, *Art in England, 1821–1837* (1930) • R. Walker, *National Portrait Gallery: Regency portraits*, 2 vols. (1985) • E. D. H. Johnson, *Paintings of the British social scene from Hogarth to Sickert* (1986) • *GM*, 1st ser., 98/1 (1828), 376 • J. Barrell, *The dark side of the landscape: the rural poor in English painting, 1730–1840*, [another edn] (1980) • J. Turner, ed., *The dictionary of art*, 34 vols. (1996) • S. C. Hutchison, 'The Royal Academy Schools, 1768–1830', *Walpole Society*, 38 (1960–62), 123–91, esp. 143 • *IGI* • Graves, *Brit. Inst.* • Graves, *Soc. Artists* • *John Constable's correspondence*, ed. R. B. Beckett, 4, Suffolk RS, 10 (1966), 244–6 • *John Constable: further documents and correspondence*, ed. L. Parris, C. Shields, and I. Fleming-Williams, Suffolk RS, 18 (1975)

Likenesses W. Barnard, mezzotint, pubd 1831 (after W. Fisk), BM, NPG • C. R. Leslie, oils, repro. in Beckett, ed., *John Constable's correspondence*, pl. 19 • H. Meyer (after C. R. Leslie)

Biggar [*married name* Montlake], **Helen Manson** (1909–1953), sculptor, film-maker, theatre designer, and political activist, was born on 25 May 1909 at Dudley Drive, Hyndland, Glasgow, the eldest of three daughters of Hugh and Florence Biggar. She grew up in a socialist household, her father being a Christian socialist and founder member of the Independent Labour Party, and her uncle, John Biggar, a Labour councillor and future lord provost of Glasgow.

Helen's childhood was blighted by illness and accidents: an operation to remove a tubercular gland from her neck, and two major injuries to her spine, left her permanently short in size. From 1918 she attended a school for handicapped children and there her artistic flair was nurtured. In 1925, at the age of sixteen, she gained admission to Glasgow School of Art (GSA), and was awarded a diploma in textile design in 1929. From 1929 to 1931 she did postgraduate work in sculpture, winning a travel scholarship to London in 1930. She divided her energies in Glasgow over the next fifteen years between sculpting, filmmaking, and theatre design, and from 1934 a growing communist activism. Helen Biggar's artistic activities were based in a variety of studios where she produced sculptures for Glasgow patrons. On return visits to GSA, she worked with contemporaries like Emilio Coia and Benno Schotz, and in her most fruitful collaboration from 1934, Norman McLaren, a young GSA film-maker whose political and artistic temperament matched her own exactly. The two produced numerous political film treatments and scripts, ranging in subject from local health issues to world peace, but their major achievement was the short agitprop film *Hell Unlimited* (1936). This ground-

Helen Manson Biggar (1909–1953), by Benno Schotz, 1932

breaking combination of live action and animation attacking the international arms trade won festival awards, toured the country's political meetings when bought by Kino Films, and is today recognized as the most innovative and powerful political film produced in Britain.

By this time Helen Biggar was involved with Glasgow Kino, touring films to raise funds for Spanish republican causes and filming subjects such as Glasgow's 1936 hunger marchers, unemployed textile workers who occupied a Hawick mill to make goods for Spain, and Glasgow's 1938 May day march (*Challenge to Fascism*, 1938).

In 1938 Helen Biggar joined the Glasgow Workers' Theatre Group, designing their agitprop stage shows such as *On Guard for Spain* (1938), *Spanish Pageant* (1939), *We Need Russia* (1939), and their Living Newspapers. Her workers' theatre collaborations with director Robert Mitchell and artist Tom MacDonald continued when Glasgow Unity Theatre was founded in 1940. Over the next five wartime years, she designed some of their major productions—*Distant Point* (1941), *Major Operation* (1941), *Song of Tomorrow* (1943), *The Night of the Big Blitz* (1944), *Starched Aprons* (1945), *Remembered Forever* (1945), *Awake and Sing* (1945), the Co-op centenary pageant of 1944, and the legendary *Lower Depths* (1945), which transferred triumphantly to London in 1945 and the first Edinburgh Festival in 1947.

Helen Biggar's wartime Glasgow art circle included refugee artists like Josef Herman and Jankel Adler, and talented locals like Robert Frame and Eli Montlake, some of whom joined her in London when she moved there permanently in 1945. They exhibited as the New Scottish Group at the Edinburgh Festival in 1947; and as the Gorbals Artists when Glasgow Unity brought their famous production of *The Gorbals Story* (1946) to London in 1948. On 11 October 1948 Helen Biggar married Eli Montlake at Wandsworth register office.

In London Helen Biggar (as she remained known) resumed her film activity with a contribution to the independent *Ta-ra-ra-boom-de-ay* (*A Century of Song*) in 1946; and

she continued her theatre work freelance for companies like Glasgow and London Unity. In 1950 she began her most permanent employment, as wardrobe mistress and costume designer for Ballet Rambert, with which she toured the country.

Helen Biggar died of a brain haemorrhage at St Mary Abbot's Hospital, London, on 28 March 1953. Her cremation at Golders Green was attended by luminaries from the artistic, theatrical, and ballet worlds of London and Glasgow. She was survived by her husband.

Helen Biggar's pioneering merging of politics and the arts, and her courage and energy in overcoming her physical handicaps to become an independent artistic spirit, made her a model for the political art and feminist movements which emerged a generation later.

DOUGLAS J. ALLEN

Sources A. Shepherd, 'Helen Unlimited', c/o Billie Love Historical Collection, 3 Winton Street, Ryde, Isle of Wight · A. Shepherd, 'Helen Biggar and Norman McLaren', *New Edinburgh Review*, 40 (1978), 25–6 · A. Shepherd, 'Art in wartime Glasgow', *Jewish Quarterly* (Oct 1976) · D. Allen, 'Workers' films: Scotland's hidden culture', *Scotch reels*, ed. C. McArthur (1982), 93–9 · B. Hogenkamp, *Deadly parallels: film and the left in Britain, 1929–39* (1986) · J. Hill, 'Towards a Scottish peoples's theatre: the rise and fall of Glasgow Unity', *Theatre Quarterly*, 7 (Sept–Dec 1977), 24 · private information (2004) · Birmingham Film Workshop, *Traces left*, video documentary, 1983 · National Film Board of Canada, *Creative process: Norman McLaren*, video documentary, 1991
Archives FILM BFI NFTVA · Scottish Film Archive, Glasgow
Likenesses photographs, *c.*1930–1949, Billie Love Historical Coll., 3 Winton Street, Ryde, Isle of Wight · B. Schotz, sculpture, 1932; Christies Scotland, 24 Sept 1997, lot 1 [*see illus.*]

Biggar, Joseph Gillis (1828–1890), politician, born in Belfast on 1 August 1828, was the eldest son of Joseph Biggar, merchant and chairman of the Ulster Bank, and Isabella, daughter of William Houston of Ballyearl, co. Antrim. He was educated at Belfast Royal Academy, and, having entered his father's business of a provision merchant, became head of the firm in 1861, and carried it on until 1880. His parents were Presbyterians, but Biggar was in 1877 received into the Roman Catholic church, which he described as the national religion. His first political activity was his intervention in the Belfast constituency in 1868, when he supported the successful Liberal and independent Conservative candidates, Thomas McClure and William Johnston, against the Conservatives. In 1871 he was elected a town councillor, and he acted as chairman of the Belfast water commission until March 1872. After adopting strong nationalist views, he fomented dissensions among the Orangemen of his native town, and joined Isaac Butt's Home Rule Association in 1870. Two years later he contested Londonderry as a nationalist, and was last on the poll of the three candidates, gaining only eighty-nine votes. But at the general election of 1874 he was returned as one of the home-rule members for the county of Cavan; he subsequently continued to sit for the constituency until his death. At the close of 1875 he joined the Irish Republican Brotherhood (the Fenians), and was soon afterwards elected to the supreme council. But in August 1877, having refused to be bound by a resolution of

Joseph Gillis Biggar (1828–1890), by unknown photographer

the executive to break off all connection with the parliamentary movement, he was expelled from the body, which he declared he had only joined 'to checkmate the physical force theory'. He had no further relations with the Fenians.

Elected to parliament as a supporter of Butt, Biggar was from the very first no more than Butt's nominal follower. At the end of his first session (30–31 July 1874), Biggar made two motions to report progress, a procedural device which would have delayed the committee stage of a bill retaining coercion legislation in Ireland; these were disavowed by his leader. During the next year, 1875, he came to prominence by his persistent practice of a scheme of parliamentary 'obstruction', which consisted in delaying the progress of government measures (especially those relating to Ireland) by long speeches, numerous questions, motions for adjournment or for reporting progress, and the like. On the night that C. S. Parnell, who soon gave Biggar's tactics active support, took his seat in parliament (22 April 1875), Biggar made his first great effort when the house was going into committee on the renewal of the Irish Peace Preservation Bill by speaking continuously for nearly four hours. Five nights later, when the prince of Wales and the German ambassador were listening to the debate, Biggar 'espied strangers', and compelled the speaker to order the galleries to be cleared. Disraeli, severely reproving Biggar, obtained the unanimous suspension of the standing order which he had invoked. On 12 April 1877 Biggar and Parnell were openly denounced by Butt for their obstruction to the Mutiny Bill. They kept the house sitting for twenty-six hours before the Transvaal

Annexation Bill could be got out of committee at 2 p.m. on 1 August. A meeting at the Rotunda, Dublin, afterwards approved Biggar's and Parnell's action, and Butt thereupon retired from the leadership of the home rulers.

On 21 October 1879 Biggar was elected one of the treasurers of the newly founded Land League. For his conduct during the land agitation he was indicted with Parnell in the autumn of 1880, when the prosecution failed owing to the disagreement of the jury. On returning to Westminster he took a prominent part in the opposition to Gladstone's Irish policy. In the course of the all-night sitting of 25–6 January 1881, after having been called to order five times, he was named by the speaker and temporarily suspended. Nothing daunted, he took an active part in the forty-one hours' sitting which was necessary before the government could obtain the first reading of the Protection of Persons and Property Bill on 2 February. He was one of the thirty-seven Irish members who were suspended the following day for disorderly conduct. In the same session he denounced the Irish Land Bill as 'thoroughly bad' before he even knew its provisions. After a short visit to Paris in 1881–2, caused by the suppression of the Land League and the transference of its headquarters to France, Biggar resumed his parliamentary activity. At the end of 1881 warrants were issued for his arrest, but he was one of the few Irish leaders who were never imprisoned. Early in 1883 proceedings were instituted against him in Ireland for styling Lord Spencer a 'bloodthirsty English peer' but were suddenly dropped. Biggar's powers of parliamentary obstruction were considerably crippled by the new rules of procedure which were introduced in 1888 by W. H. Smith. Thenceforth he treated the house with greater respect, and eventually became quite a favourite with it.

Biggar was one of those Irish politicians whose conduct was investigated by the special commission of judges appointed to inquire into the accusations made by *The Times* in 1887 against Parnell and his allies. Biggar conducted his own case. In giving his evidence on 29 May 1889 he was severely pressed by the counsel for *The Times* as to his relations with the Fenians, and as to his connection with the land agitation. He would admit no cognizance of the management or disposal of the league accounts, although he was admittedly one of the treasurers, always taking shelter under the plea of defective memory. His advocacy of boycotting formed an important feature in the whole case. Biggar advocated the extreme doctrine that any boycotting short of physical force was justifiable, and extensive extracts from his speeches are cited in the report of the judges to support their findings on that count. His address to the court, delivered on 24 October, occupied only about a quarter of an hour. The special commission did not exonerate the Parnellites completely, and the report's 'guilty' category found the respondents culpable of conspiracy to promote agrarian agitation for the non-payment of rents; and that they were implicated in activities tending to defend crime and outrage.

Parnell considered Biggar a valuable auxiliary, despite Biggar's determined but unsuccessful attempt to prevent Parnell foisting Captain O'Shea on the Galway electors in

1886, and he enjoyed unbounded popularity among the Irish members; even his opponents came in time to recognize his honesty and good nature. He died of heart disease at his home, 124 Sugden Road, Clapham Common, London, on 19 February 1890. A requiem mass, said for him the next day at the Redemptorist church, Clapham, was attended by the Irish members, and the body was then taken to Ireland. His funeral service was held in St Patrick's Church, Donegal Street, Belfast, on 24 February, and his funeral procession to Carnmoney cemetery was reputedly the largest ever seen in the town. He was, after his conversion, a devout Roman Catholic. During the later years of his life Biggar was in very comfortable financial circumstances. One result of his residence in Paris in 1882 was a suit for breach of promise of marriage by one Fanny Hyland, who in March 1883 recovered £400 damages. He remained unmarried, and the bulk of his fortune, some £40,000, was left to a natural son.

Probably no member with fewer qualifications for public speaking ever occupied so much of the time of the House of Commons. None practised parliamentary obstruction more successfully. His short, stout appearance and strong northern Irish accent did not endear him to his contemporaries; Disraeli remarked 'What is that?' on first hearing Biggar speak in the house (Lucy, *Salisbury Parliament*, 244). But he had great shrewdness, unbounded courage, and a certain rough humour.

G. Le G. Norgate, *rev.* D. George Boyce

Sources F. Healey, 'Joseph Gillis Biggar: home ruler and parliamentarian', *Clio* (autumn 1969), 9–13 • T. MacKnight, *Ulster as it is, or, Twenty-eight years' experience as an Irish editor*, 1 (1896), 167–8, 266–72, 274 • F. S. L. Lyons, *Charles Stewart Parnell* (1977), 50–52, 59–60, 322–9, 331–2 • R. B. O'Brien, *Life of Parnell*, 2 vols. (1898) • H. W. Lucy, *A diary of two parliaments*, 2 (1886) • H. W. Lucy, *A diary of the Salisbury parliament, 1886–1892* (1892) • *ILN* (20 Nov 1880) • J. Macdonald, *Diary of the Parnell commission* (1890) • Gladstone, *Diaries*

Archives NL Ire., corresp. and papers relating to Irish parliamentary party • PRO NIre., corresp.

Likenesses F. Pegram, pencil sketches, 1888, V&A • S. P. Hall, pencil drawing, 1889, NPG • H. Furniss, caricature, *c.*1892, repro. in Lucy, *Diary of the Salisbury parliament*, 246 • Spy [L. Ward], chromolithograph, NPG; repro. in *VF* (21 July 1877) • photograph, NPG [*see illus.*]

Wealth at death £3170 in England: Irish probate sealed in England, 29 May 1890, *CGPLA Eng. & Wales* • £37,341 7*s.* 7*d.*: probate, 9 May 1890, *CGPLA Ire.*

Biggar, Walter (*d.* 1376/7), administrator, is of unknown origins, and his early career is very obscure. When David II was released from English captivity in October 1357, he immediately appointed Biggar clerk of the wardrobe. Biggar's introduction to David's court may have been through an association with the family of one of the king's most loyal and trusted retainers, Malcolm Fleming, earl of Wigtown—in June 1358 Biggar appears in papal records as rector of Biggar, a benefice in the gift of the Fleming lords of Biggar (although this is the only example of his using this designation). A predecessor as rector of Biggar, Henry, had been described in the 1320s and 1330s as Fleming's clerk and had served as clerk of liverance, the officer responsible for the purchase of provisions for the royal household, in the court of David II's father, Robert I.

Biggar was clerk of the wardrobe until autumn 1358, when he became deputy chamberlain to Thomas, earl of Mar. In April 1359 Biggar replaced Earl Thomas as chamberlain, and at about the same time was made rector of Errol, a benefice in the gift of the monastery of Coupar Angus. His term as chamberlain, the chief financial officer of the Scottish crown in the fourteenth century, was dominated by the need to produce ransom payments of 10,000 merks per annum to the English crown under the terms of the treaty of Berwick of October 1357. The treaty had secured David II's release from an imprisonment in England which began with the king's defeat and capture at the battle of Nevilles Cross in October 1346. Biggar exercised the chamberlainship without interruption until April 1363, when he was removed from the post in favour of Sir Robert Erskine. Biggar's demission of office may have been connected to the baronial rebellion against David II which broke out in March 1363. One of the complaints of the rebels concentrated on the misuse of money levied for the king's ransom, and Biggar, as David's chief financial officer, may have been the target of particular resentment. Alternatively, the king may have felt that at a time of political confrontation royal financial resources were best supervised by one of his close political allies, Erskine, rather than a career civil servant. Certainly there was no noticeable opposition to Biggar's reappointment to the office on 14 December 1364; he continued to serve as David II's chamberlain until the king's death in February 1371, his tenure being marked, then as earlier, by the regularity of exchequer audits and the general efficiency of the crown's financial administration. Biggar was retained as chamberlain by the new king, Robert II, until his own death on a date between 14 March 1376 and 28 January 1377.

S. I. Boardman

Sources G. Burnett and others, eds., *The exchequer rolls of Scotland*, 1–2 (1878) • *CEPR letters*, vol. 3 • *Scalacronica, by Sir Thomas Gray of Heton, knight: a chronical of England and Scotland from AD MLXVI to AD MCCCLXII*, ed. J. Stevenson, Maitland Club, 40 (1836)

Bigge, Arthur John, Baron Stamfordham (1849–1931), courtier, was born on 18 June 1849 at Linden Hall, near Morpeth, Northumberland, the son of John Frederick Bigge (1814–1885), vicar of Stamfordham, Northumberland, and his wife, Caroline Mary (*d.* 1901), only daughter of Nathaniel Ellison, a barrister and bankruptcy commissioner in Newcastle upon Tyne.

Bigge attended Rossall School in the 1860s, and was commissioned into the Royal Artillery in 1869 after training at the Royal Military Academy, Woolwich. He became friends with the prince imperial, a fellow officer in the artillery, the son and heir of Napoleon III and Empress Eugénie of France, who were then living in exile in England. The prince wanted to see military action and, against the wishes of Disraeli, the prime minister, the queen secured him an attachment to a unit sent to South Africa during the Anglo-Zulu War of 1879. He was killed by Zulus in a surprise attack; Bigge, who served both in the Zulu and Cape Frontier wars, and was mentioned in dispatches

Arthur John Bigge, Baron Stamfordham (1849–1931), by Rudolph Swoboda, 1889

after the battle of Kambala (29 March), was asked to Scotland by Eugénie and the queen to give his account of the ambush (though he had not actually witnessed it).

Bigge impressed the queen, who found him 'clever, amiable and agreeable' (*DNB*), at a time when her private office was in transition. Her private secretary, Sir Henry Ponsonby, was carrying an extra burden owing to the death of the keeper of the privy purse, Sir Thomas Biddulph. Ponsonby accepted the queen's insistence that young Bigge, who had no administrative experience or knowledge of the court, should be hired as his assistant; as a Liberal, Ponsonby was suspicious of Bigge's toryism, but was surprised to find him a congenial companion. Bigge was not as quick-witted as his chief: one later observer described him as 'sound and painstaking; simplicity and honesty, good sense, loyalty and keenness were all his life the chief features of his character' (Gore, 39). His political imagination was limited, but he was a conscientious assistant to Ponsonby, and when the latter died in 1895 he was the obvious replacement. Queen Victoria expressed complete confidence in him, and he was made a KCB, which he had declined two years earlier (Emden, 204); he had been made CB in 1885 and CMG in 1887. He had married, on 10 February 1881, Constance Neville (d. 1922), the

daughter of the Revd William Frederick Neville and his wife, Fanny Grace, *née* Blackwood. They had a son and two daughters.

Bigge's first spell as private secretary to the sovereign lasted from May 1895 until the death of Queen Victoria in January 1901. They were trying years, as the queen was growing old and she was seeing fewer people. What work she accomplished was often channelled through her ladies-in-waiting or Indian servants, and Bigge saw her more rarely than had Ponsonby. It fell to him early in his tenure of the post to smooth the resignation of the queen's cousin, the elderly duke of Cambridge, as commander-in-chief of the army, and he helped to manage the diamond jubilee celebrations in 1897. Edward VII, on his accession in 1901, kept his existing private secretary, Sir Francis Knollys, and Bigge spent his reign filling the same role for George, duke of York, who shortly became prince of Wales. Once the pupil of Ponsonby, he now became the teacher of a young sailor of somewhat limited education as he travelled around the British empire. Bigge wrote his speeches, becoming 'accepted as one of the first of his age in the composition of speeches and memoranda' (Gore, 41), and gave the young man lessons in deportment. He was not successful, however, in persuading Prince George and Princess May (later Queen Mary) to move from York House on the Sandringham estate to a place where they might more easily cultivate a wider range of contacts. Bigge once told the prince to smile more during public appearances, to which he received the reply that sailors never smiled on duty: Bigge's rejoinder—that 'the duties of a sailor and those of the heir to the throne were not identical'—earned the young man's respect (Nicolson, 64–5). Several heartfelt letters from the prince to Bigge, thanking him for his guidance and friendship, have survived; after Bigge died, George V, as he became, said of him: 'he taught me how to be a King' (ibid., 452).

The constant crowds of cheering colonials on his travels with the prince entrenched Bigge's enthusiasm for empire. On the former's accession as George V in May 1910 Bigge became a privy councillor and, for the second time, private secretary to the sovereign, a position he held jointly with Knollys. A clash between them was not long in coming. Bigge advised the king against giving the Liberal government pre-election 'contingent guarantees' as to his future conduct in enabling the passage of legislation to restrict the power of the House of Lords (the Parliament Act); Knollys, a Liberal, took the opposite view, to which the king eventually acceded. Subsequent events led the monarch to lose confidence in Knollys, who resigned in March 1913, leaving Bigge—ennobled as Baron Stamfordham (23 June 1911), though the king continued to address him by his surname—as principal private secretary. Bigge travelled with George V and Queen Mary to India in 1911, where he advised against the monarch's going on a tiger shoot lest it appear frivolous; he was appointed GCIE that year, and GCB in 1916. He had, however, earned the enduring mistrust of the Liberal government by his earlier actions; the marquess of Lincolnshire observed that he was a 'very strong Tory and does not hesitate to show his colours' (Rose, *King George V*, 141), while Asquith, the prime minister, complained of the tone and content of some of his communications (ibid.). On this rock foundered his attempt to help the king broker a compromise over Irish home rule; both men feared a civil war if this measure were pushed through. A subsequent indicator of ministerial alienation came when Lloyd George's secretaries made Stamfordham wait on a hard wooden chair when he came to call. Following the controversy over the Parliament Act he behaved with greater caution—to the degree that he earned the sobriquet of 'Better-not' (ibid., 122).

During the First World War Stamfordham lost his only son, John Neville (1887–1915). He demonstrated the political acumen he had acquired in his service under Victoria and Ponsonby when, in response to widespread anti-German sentiment, he suggested that Windsor should replace Saxe-Coburg-Gotha as the royal family name. He also advised that the king's civil list be cut down and money refunded to the exchequer so that the royal family might share some of the wartime hardships of ordinary people. At the time of the Russian Revolution Stamfordham wrote:

> We must endeavour to induce the thinking working classes, Socialist and others, to regard the crown, not as a mere figure-head … but as a living power for good, with receptive faculties welcoming information affecting the interests and social well-being of all classes.   (Nicolson, 308)

He helped the king to face down the levelling temper of demobilized troops by stepping up the royal family's charitable works, and kept him informed about the growth of republicanism; George V had previously written to him, in gratitude 'I know you always tell me the truth however unpleasant it may be' (29 Dec 1913; Gore, 148). Stamfordham supported G. E. Buckle, the former editor of *The Times*, in continuing the publication, begun by Lord Esher, of Queen Victoria's papers. Such activities undoubtedly helped to bolster the monarchy's standing as a cultural icon, if they did little to recover direct political influence over ministers of the crown.

After his wife died in 1922 Stamfordham lived with his unmarried daughter Margaret at St James's Palace and at Windsor. It was his duty, in 1923, to tell Lord Curzon that his membership of the House of Lords effectively precluded him from becoming prime minister. His kindness when the first Labour government took office the following year was later recalled by Ramsay MacDonald. Stamfordham died in post at St James's Palace on 31 March 1931, following an operation two weeks earlier from which he never recovered, and was buried at Brompton cemetery on 4 April. His title became extinct with his death. The king wrote in his diary 'I shall miss him terribly. His loss is irreparable' (Pope-Hennessy, 549). Owen Morshead, a royal librarian who knew both men, wrote of Stamfordham's 'absence of self-esteem which responded to a like quality in his master, establishing between them more than a merely professional relationship throughout the thirty years of their association' (*DNB*).

Stamfordham was 'slight of build and unassuming in manner' (Rose, *King George V*, 49). His memoranda were invariably delivered hand-written in a large script—a habit originating in Queen Victoria's poor sight and prejudice against typewriters. His period of service covered a time of enormous change and upheaval; his awareness of public opinion and the innovations he fostered helped to ensure the survival of the monarchy into a new era. Unusual among courtiers in coming from a non-aristocratic background, he might be said to have founded a dynasty himself—his grandson Michael Adeane served as private secretary to Elizabeth II from 1954 to 1972.

WILLIAM M. KUHN

Sources *DNB* · V. Bogdanor, *The monarchy and the constitution* (1995) · H. Nicolson, *King George the fifth* (1952) · K. Rose, *King George V* (1984) · K. Rose, *Kings, queens and courtiers* (1985) · F. Prochaska, *Royal bounty: the making of a welfare monarchy* (1995) · W. M. Kuhn, *Henry and Mary Ponsonby* (2002) · *The Times* (1 April 1931) · *The Times* (19 May 1931) · *The Times* (12–31 March 1931) · *The Times* (6 April 1931) · L. G. Pine, *The new extinct peerage* (1973) · J. Gore, *George V: a personal memoir* (1949) · P. H. Emden, *Behind the throne* (1934) · J. Pope-Hennessy, *Queen Mary* (1959) · *CGPLA Eng. & Wales* (1931)
Archives BL, corresp., Add. MSS 48599, 48371, 48378, 48922, 48931 | BL, corresp. with Lord Bertie, Add. MS 63012 · BL, corresp. with John Burns, Add. MS 46281 · BL, corresp. with Sir Henry Campbell-Bannerman, Add. MSS 41206, 41208 · BL, letters to Sir Edward Walter Hamilton, Add. MS 48599 · BL, corresp. with Viscount Long, Add. MS 62405 · BL, corresp. with Lord Northcliffe, Add. MS 62155 · BL, corresp. with Lord Selborne, Add. MS 46003 · BL OIOC, letters to Sir Harcourt Butler, MSS Eur. F 116 · BL OIOC, letters to Lord Reading, MSS Eur. E 238, F 118 · Bodl. Oxf., corresp. with Viscount Addison · Bodl. Oxf., corresp. with Herbert Asquith · Bodl. Oxf., corresp. with Robert Bridges · Bodl. Oxf., corresp. with Sir Henry Burdett · Bodl. Oxf., corresp. with Geoffrey Dawson · Bodl. Oxf., corresp. with Sir William Harcourt and Lewis Harcourt · Bodl. Oxf., corresp. with Lord Kimberley · Bodl. Oxf., letters to Arthur Ponsonby · Bodl. Oxf., corresp. with Sir Horace Rumbold · Bodl. Oxf., corresp. with Lord Selborne · Bodl. Oxf., corresp. with Sir W. L. Worthington-Evans · CKS, letters to Akers-Douglas · CUL, corresp. with Lord Hardinge · CUL, corresp. with Sir Samuel Hoare · HLRO, corresp. with Andrew Bonar Law · HLRO, corresp. with John St Loe Strachey · HLRO, corresp. with Herbert Samuel · Lambton Park, Chester-le-Street, co. Durham, corresp. with third earl of Durham · NA Scot., corresp. with A. J. Balfour · NL Aus., corresp. with Viscount Novar · NL Aus., corresp. with first Viscount Stonehaven · NL Scot., corresp. with Lord Haldane · NL Scot., corresp. with fourth earl of Minto · NL Scot., corresp. mainly with Lord Rosebery · Nuffield Oxf., corresp. with Lord Mottistone · PRO, letters to Lord Midleton, PRO 30/67 · PRO NIre., corresp. with Edward Carson · Royal Arch. · U. Birm. L., corresp. with Austen Chamberlain · U. Durham L., corresp. with Sir Reginald Wingate · U. Newcastle, Robinson L., corresp. with Walter Runciman
Likenesses R. Swoboda, portrait, 1889, Royal Collection [*see illus.*] · W. Stoneman, photograph, 1917, NPG · F. Dicksee, print, 1919, NPG · H. A. Oliver, oils, 1927, priv. coll. · F. Dodd, charcoal drawing, 1931, Royal Collection · Spy [L. Ward], caricature, NPG; repro. in *VF* (6 Sept 1900) · black and white photograph, repro. in *The Times* (1 April 1931)
Wealth at death £143,767 17*s.* 3*d.*—unsettled property of gross value: probate, 14 May 1931, *CGPLA Eng. & Wales* · net personalty £140,947: *Times* (19 May 1931)

Bigge, John Thomas (1780–1843), judicial commissioner, was born on 8 March 1780 at Benton House, Northumberland, the fourth of ten children of Thomas Charles Bigge (1739–1794), landowner, banker, and sheriff of Northumberland, and his wife, Jemima (1748–1806), daughter of

William Ord and his wife, Anne. The Bigges supposed their ancestry, in Kent and Essex, to predate the Norman conquest. John Thomas was educated at Newcastle Free School and Westminster School (1795). In 1797 he entered Christ Church, Oxford (BA 1801, MA 1804). Although financially independent through a legacy, he chose a bar career, being called at the Inner Temple (1806), and practised on the northern circuit and in London.

In 1810, while accompanying his unwell sister, Eliza, to Madeira, Bigge met and befriended Sir Ralph Woodward, also escorting an ailing sister. Woodford, by 1812, became governor of Trinidad and recommended Bigge to the vacant chief justiceship there. Commissioned on 5 July 1813, Bigge made a concentrated study of Spanish laws and language as used in Trinidad courts, and reformed court business which he found in confused arrears. He recommended the displacement of Spanish by English institutions, particularly jury trial.

Bigge undertook many extra-judicial duties, auditing the colony's accounts, and inquiring into financial mismanagement and corruption. His recommendations concerning slave emancipation were commended by the Colonial Office, which, on his seeking leave in 1818, invited him to become commissioner of inquiry into the New South Wales convict settlement. He accepted and resigned from the bench. New South Wales, appointed a place to which convicts might be transported, had changed much since 1788. The rebellion that dislodged Governor William Bligh in 1808 might have stimulated a wider revolution, but order was restored under Governor Lachlan Macquarie. Autocratic, like his predecessors, Macquarie had new policies. He saw New South Wales as a future free colony, not as a perpetual gaol, and he believed in readmitting to society convicts who had served their sentences (emancipists). Because members of the armed forces and emancipists alike stayed on to take land grants, and capitalists invested in the pastoral promise of the country, the settlement's future had to change.

Bigge's inquiries, politically motivated to delay change, looked to making transportation more cost-efficient while restoring its terror to discourage crime in England. An inquiry into New South Wales in 1812, along with copious recommendations from officials and individuals, made a further inquiry superfluous. But it was expedient. Macquarie, who had sought leave to retire, but had not received a reply dissuading him, was shocked at Bigge's arrival in Sydney in September 1819, bearing a dormant commission as governor should Macquarie resign. At first reassured by Bigge's credentials and demeanour, Macquarie believed that the inquiry would vindicate him. But there was soon friction, particularly over Bigge's insistence on economies, especially the deployment of convict labour from town developments to rural work.

Bigge, while recording minute evidence of continuing historical interest—a 'book of petty details', remarked the Sydney *Monitor* (3 February 1827)—used inquisitorial methods owing more to Trinidad than to Westminster. Natural justice and procedural fairness were denied, to Macquarie's prejudice. Three reports followed: 'State of

the colony' (1822); 'Judicial establishments' (1823); and 'State of agriculture and trade' (1823). Conceived in controversy, they retain that character, still stimulating disagreement as to their worth. They collectively strengthened the future of New South Wales as a free colony, while denying such concessions to democracy as a franchise and jury trial. The ensuing New South Wales Act (4 Geo. IV c.96) conceded only a nominated legislature and embryonic court structure.

Rejecting a judicial post at Gibraltar, Bigge agreed in 1823 to be a joint commissioner inquiring into the Cape and other colonies. The inquiries were prolix. Reports, not completed until 1830, stimulated some government and court reforms. Declining, because of illness, to inquire into clerical establishments in 1832, Bigge, still unmarried, led a secluded life until his accidental death at the Grosvenor Hotel in London on 20 December 1843. He was interred in All Saints' cemetery, Fulham, his considerable estate being distributed among nephews and nieces.

J. M. BENNETT

Sources J. Ritchie, *Punishment and profit: the reports of Commissioner John Bigge* (1970) • J. Ritchie, *The evidence to the Bigge reports*, 2 vols. (1971) • J. M. Bennett, 'The day of retribution', *American Journal of Legal History*, 15 (1971), 85–106 • M. H. Ellis, *Lachlan Macquarie* (1947) • J. Ritchie, *Lachlan Macquarie* (1986) • C. H. Currey, *Sir Francis Forbes* (1986) • J. M. Bennett, *Some papers of Sir Francis Forbes* (1998) • I. E. Edwards, *The 1820 settlers in South Africa* (1934)
Archives Mitchell L., NSW, Bonwick transcripts | Derby Central Library, letters to R. J. Wilmot Horton
Likenesses portrait, priv. coll.
Wealth at death over £45,000: Ritchie, *Punishment and profit*, 256; administration, PRO, PROB 6/220, fol. 274

Bigge, Sir Lewis Amherst Selby-, first baronet (1860–1951), civil servant and author, was born on 3 April 1860 at Oakwood, Kent, the second son of Charles Selby Bigge (1834–1889), landowner and JP, and his wife, Katharina (d. 1918), daughter of John Scott Ogle. He had two brothers. Educated at Winchester College until 1879, where his contemporaries included R. L. Morant and H. A. L. Fisher, he went on to hold a scholarship at Christ Church, Oxford, gaining firsts in classical moderations (1881) and in *literae humaniores* (1883). He was elected to a fellowship of University College, Oxford, in 1883 and tutored in philosophy, developing a particular interest in the work of the eighteenth-century British moralists. He considered Hume's *Treatise* as possibly the most important philosophical work in the English language and published indexed editions of Hume's works, as well as an anthology of the writings of the moralists, which are still highly regarded by philosophers.

On 15 September 1885 Selby-Bigge married Edith Lindsay (1864–1939), daughter of John Robert Davison QC MP; they had a son and two daughters. After his marriage Selby-Bigge commenced studying law, and was called to the bar in 1891 by the Inner Temple. In 1894 he was appointed to the Charity Commission as an assistant commissioner where his somewhat cautious and conservative approach melded admirably with both the work and his colleagues. The transfer of the commission's educational work to the newly created Board of Education after 1900

Sir Lewis Amherst Selby-Bigge, first baronet (1860–1951), by Walter Stoneman, 1927

led to his joining the board as a senior examiner and acting assistant secretary in the charitable trusts division in 1903.

Selby-Bigge's work prior to 1907 was devoted chiefly to resolution of the complicated legal and administrative problems affecting the nation's voluntary schools arising from the implementation of the 1902 Education Act. This entailed sensitive and delicate negotiations with a variety of denominational bodies and in them he was highly successful, an accomplishment which reflected both his professionalism and his constant delight in creating order out of chaos. His promotion to a principal assistant secretaryship in 1907 was recognition of his considerable administrative skills and he worked more closely with Sir Robert Morant, the permanent secretary, whom he found a challenging but inspirational mentor. Morant's transfer to the National Health Insurance Commission in 1911, because of the damaging affair of the Holmes circular and his conflicts with the elementary school teachers and local education authorities, resulted in Selby-Bigge's succeeding him at the board.

Faced with a muted response to his appointment, a generally hostile teaching world, and a new and untried president in J. A. Pease, as well a poor performance as a witness before the royal commission on the civil service, Selby-Bigge found his initial period as secretary both challenging and formative. His subsequent adoption of a more consultative and conciliatory approach enabled him both to heal existent schisms and to create the beneficial model

of dual authority and partnership which came to characterize the relationship of the board, and its successors, with the local education authorities for much of the century. Essentially pragmatic rather than visionary in his approach to education administration and reform, he shared some of his predecessor's élitist views about the development of the nation's education system and tended to be sceptical about ill-planned or idealistic enthusiasms related to it. Although the events of the First World War reinforced the case for education reform, Selby-Bigge ensured that the board's pre-war views remained paramount through both his membership of Lord Haldane's education committee of 1916—Haldane thought him 'a black-browed man, very jealous, and full of red tape and sealing wax' (Sherington, 179)—and his close working relationship with H. A. L. Fisher (as president). If the passage of the 1918 Education Act was a triumph for Fisher its contents could also be considered a success for Selby-Bigge.

The creation of both a superannuation scheme and new (Burnham) salary scales for teachers, in 1918 and 1921 respectively, were other signal developments in which Selby-Bigge played a major role. Post-war economic exigencies, however, prevented or impeded the implementation of many of the reforms he valued and also coloured much of his remaining period in the board. None the less, his effective partnership with Fisher ensured that the board deflected or reduced many of the stringent economic cuts to the education system desired by an austere Treasury and the Geddes committee.

Selby-Bigge's seminal role in education developments between 1911 and 1925 has been seen by some as one which either hindered or endangered education reform. Christopher Addison felt he was too much the finicky don, inclined to split hairs and miss key opportunities, while J. Dover Wilson believed his conservative approach effectively betrayed the nation's future. Some historians, notably G. Sherington and B. Simon, have criticized him for continually attempting to reinforce the board's powers, whereas others have indicted him for the lack of development of technical education. One of his colleagues, however, claimed that he had made the Board of Education the headquarters of civilization (*Times Educational Supplement*, 29 June 1951).

In his retirement Selby-Bigge maintained a keen interest in education, publishing several articles about English and Indian education as well as a seminal text on the Board of Education. He served on national and Indian advisory committees, was a co-opted member of East Sussex local education authority until 1946, a governor of Lewes County Boys' School for seventeen years, and a JP. He was appointed CB in 1905 and KCB in 1913; in 1919 he was created baronet; in 1946 he was appointed OBE. He died at his home, Kingston Manor, near Lewes, Sussex, on 24 May 1951, and was buried on 26 May at Kingston church. His son, John Amherst Selby-Bigge (1892–1973), an artist, succeeded to the baronetcy.   N. D. DAGLISH

Sources S. Petriburg, 'Sir Amherst Selby-Bigge', *Times Educational Supplement* (29 June 1951) · G. Sherington, *English education, social*

change and war, 1911–1920 (1981) · Nuffield Oxf., Gainford MSS · *The Times* (25 May 1951) · *Sussex Daily News* (26 May 1951) · *Sussex Express* (1 June 1951) · M. G. Holmes, *The Times* (30 May 1951) · L. A. Selby-Bigge, *The board of education* (1927) · B. Simon, *The politics of educational reform, 1920–1940* (1974) · H. A. L. Fisher, *An unfinished autobiography* (1940) · J. D. Wilson, *Milestones on the Dover road* (1969) · Burke, *Peerage* · private information (2004)

Archives BL, corresp. with Albert Mansbridge, Add. MSS 65196, 65253 · Bodl. Oxf., corresp. with Viscount Addison relating to YWCA women's day · NL Wales, corresp. with Sir J. H. Lewis · Nuffield Oxf., Gainford MSS · PRO, board of education papers **Likenesses** photograph, 1914, Nuffield Oxf., Gainford MSS; repro. in *Berlin Tageblatt* · W. Stoneman, photograph, 1927, NPG [*see illus.*] · photograph, 1929, repro. in M. Hartog, *Philip Hartog: a memoir* (1949), 90 **Wealth at death** £26,479 6*s.* 6*d.*: probate, 10 Aug 1951, *CGPLA Eng. & Wales*

Biggs, Caroline Ashurst (1840–1889), novelist and campaigner for women's suffrage, was born in St Margaret's, Leicester, on 23 August 1840, the second daughter of Matilda Ashurst *Biggs (1816/17–1866) and Joseph *Biggs (1809–1895) [*see under* Biggs, John (1801–1871)], hosiery manufacturer, of Leicester. Under her mother's influence she developed at an early age a strong belief in the political and social emancipation of women. In August 1858 she wrote to Joseph Cowen, secretary of the Northern Reform Union:

> I deeply regret that it [the union] limits its desires of obtaining political rights … to men alone, in defiance of its motto 'Taxation without Representation is Tyranny' … I do not feel inclined to become a member of any society which … is purely selfish in its object, and does not recognise the principle of justice and rights for all mankind. (Joseph Cowen Collection, Tyne and Wear Archives, C137, C146)

Another of the causes that Biggs shared with her mother was anti-slavery. In 1862 she published a three-volume novel, *White and Black: a Story of the Southern States*, which was praised by the Italian republican exile Giuseppe Mazzini, a close friend of the Biggs family.

During the 1860s, probably after her mother's death in 1866, Biggs moved to London, where she joined the small group of middle-class feminists, including Henrietta Taylor and Millicent Garrett Fawcett, that set up the first organized women's suffrage movement. There was a strong family involvement—her aunts Caroline *Stansfeld and Emilie *Venturi were both active supporters of women's suffrage. She was made assistant secretary of the London National Society for Women's Suffrage (NSWS), alongside Clementia Taylor, in 1867, a post which she held until 1871. In this role 'Her ready pen, methodical work and untiring industry soon proved her an invaluable ally' (Blackburn, 63–4). When the NSWS split into two groups in 1872 she became honorary secretary of its central committee, and she remained a committee member until her death. Following the passage of the 1867 Reform Act she was involved in the campaign in London to place women with property qualifications on the electoral register. After the negative decision of the court of common pleas in 1868 (*Chorlton* v. *Lings*) her attention focused on public campaigns and petitions in support of the annual parliamentary bill sponsored by Jacob Bright. Each year she was

Caroline Ashurst Biggs (1840–1889), by Elizabeth S. Guinness, 1897 (after unknown photographer, *c.*1875)

heavily engaged in public speaking tours, speaking on twenty-three occasions in south Wales during 1873.

The mid-Victorian campaign for women's suffrage was overtly constitutional and non-militant. The exclusion of married women from the initial campaign aims became a perennial source of contention within the movement, not least for Biggs's married aunts. The related question of the legal status of women in marriage was the background to her second novel, *Waiting for Tidings* (1874). In 1879 she published a short pamphlet, *Ought Women to have the Right to Vote for Members of Parliament*. This was followed in 1889 with *A Letter from an Englishwoman to Englishwomen* (published by the central committee of the NSWS) in which she emphasized the fact that the role of women was expanding within political parties, yet 'while competent to instruct voters in their duties, they are pronounced incompetent to give a vote themselves'.

Biggs opposed allowing the new women's sections of the political parties to affiliate to the NSWS, as was debated in 1888. She was one of a small group, mainly from the older generation of feminists—including Millicent Fawcett, Lydia Becker, and Helen Blackburn—that broke away to form a new central committee of the NSWS. Biggs's views on political affiliation prevailed after her death, when the various wings of the movement were consolidated under the National Union of Women's Suffrage Societies in 1897.

Biggs was also keen to promote the work of women in local government (opened up to women by the Municipal Franchise Act of 1869), both in her position as editor (1870–89) of the *Englishwoman's Review* and as committee member of the Society for Promoting the Return of Women as Poor Law Guardians. In 1887 the society reprinted one of her editorial articles, 'Women as poor law guardians', in which she called on women of property in London to stand for election. That year also saw the publication of the third volume of the monumental *History of Woman Suffrage*, edited by the American feminist Elizabeth Cady Stanton. Biggs was author of the chapter on Great Britain, and took the opportunity to pay homage to the earlier generation of English feminists, including her mother. Early in 1889 she added her signature to a statement of protest against the candidacy, as alderman on the London county council, of Sir Charles Dilke, who had been involved in a celebrated divorce case. As with many Liberal suffragists there was a strong moral basis to her feminism.

Biggs died, unmarried, at her home, 19 Notting Hill Square, London, on 4 September 1889. In 1893 her friend and colleague Helen Blackburn included her portrait in an exhibition of eminent British women in Chicago.

JONATHAN SPAIN

Sources H. Blackburn, *Women's suffrage: a record of the women's suffrage movement in the British Isles* (1902) · P. Levine, *Victorian feminism, 1850–1900* (1987) · J. Rendall, ed., *Equal or different: women's politics, 1800–1914* (1987) · S. Oldfield, *Collective biography of women in Britain, 1550–1900: a select annotated bibliography* (1999) · *Mazzini's letters to an English family*, ed. E. F. Richards, 3 vols. (1920–22) · b. cert. · d. cert.
Archives Tyne and Wear Archives Service, Newcastle upon Tyne, letters to Joseph Cowen, C137, C146
Likenesses portrait, exh. 1893; women's hall, University of Bristol, 1894; now lost · E. S. Guinness, portrait, 1897 (after unknown photographer, *c*.1875), Girton Cam. [*see illus.*]
Wealth at death £1642: administration, 7 Oct 1889, *CGPLA Eng. & Wales*

Biggs, Charles Henry Walker (1845–1923), technical journalist and journal editor, was born Charles Henry Biggs on 23 May 1845 in Haddenham, Buckinghamshire, the son of Elizabeth Walker Biggs and an unknown father. He was probably educated in Reading. According to one obituary he soon showed a technical bent for 'in the school laboratory he made the first self-contained matches, but he did not develop them commercially' (Collins, 2617); this statement cannot be corroborated. In his early working life Biggs was a schoolmaster and tutor in Reading. On 16 December 1869 at St Mary's parish church, Reading, he married Susan Wiltshire, born 1848 in Hanbury, Warwickshire, the daughter of Josiah Wiltshire, carman. There were four children, two boys and two girls.

In 1870 Biggs communicated a paper to the British Association for the Advancement of Science (BAAS), 'Middle-class schools as they are, and as they ought to be', and the following year wrote *The Class and Home Lesson Book of English Grammar*. Having a bias towards education on scientific subjects Biggs is said to have 'proceeded to a science lectureship at King's College, London' (Collins, 2617), an appointment unsubstantiated by the college's archival records. In 1876 he communicated another paper to the BAAS, 'On a new voltaic battery'. He had taken up journalism and, according to Collins, 'started the *Journal of Education*, published from Reading', but his exact role with regard to this periodical, and when, is not clear. However, it came to deal so much with applied electricity, then in its infancy, that he became known as a specialist in this area. As such he was offered, in 1878, the position of editor of

the newly revived periodical *The Electrician*, subtitled 'A weekly journal of theoretical and applied electricity and chemical physics'. Nahin, though, feels 'he probably was hired mostly for writing skills and an administrative ability to get the journal produced each week on time' (Nahin, 104). It did, however, begin to publish 'extensive reports of scientific meetings, accounts of inventions and discoveries, articles instructing readers in electrical principles, and even discussions of quite arcane theoretical points' (Hunt, 70).

As early as November 1878, for editorial purposes, Biggs was asking the Institution of Electrical Engineers for access to papers which were to be read before it. In late 1882 he first accepted regular articles by Oliver Heaviside for *The Electrician*. He was subsequently to be not only Heaviside's editor but also his champion. He failed, as did everyone, in his attempts to get Heaviside to be more sociable, but succeeded not only in keeping him from libelling William Preece, with whom Heaviside was having a running battle over certain aspects of electrical theory, but also in helping his 'crusade against contemporary "scienticulists", as Heaviside called his bogies' (Appleyard, *History*, 49). He 'exhibited tolerance towards his obscurities and tact towards his idiosyncrasies' (R. Appleyard, *Pioneers of Electrical Communication*, 1930, 227).

Biggs was elected a fellow of the Royal Geographical Society in 1868 and a fellow of the Chemical Society in 1872. He was also an active member of a social group of electricians called the Dynamicables which had been founded in 1883 under the name the Electric-Arc Angels. He was elected to membership of the Institution of Electrical Engineers in 1878, his proposers being Josiah Latimer Clark, Alexander Muirhead, and Andrew Jamieson, and he remained an active member for over thirty years. He became a member of the Physical Society in 1889.

As a member of the BAAS from 1882 Biggs communicated further papers to its meetings, 'Secondary batteries and the economical generation of steam for electrical purposes' (1883, with W. W. Beaumont) and 'Distribution by transformers and alternate current machines' (1887, with W. H. Snell). He had three papers appear in the *Engineers' Society Transactions*, on electric light engineering (1882, again with Beaumont), on the depreciation of plant and works under municipal and county management (1902), and on the mechanics of dust (1909). He also presented two papers to annual meetings of the Incorporated Association of Municipal and County Engineers: 'Electric mains and methods of laying' (1893, in West Bromwich) and 'Analysis of Macadam road construction' (1902, in Bristol). In the 1890s Biggs wrote several books on electrical engineering, including two editions of *Practical Electrical Engineering* with Beaumont and others, and one on mechanical engineering, but they met with no great acclaim.

Biggs also took out numerous patents, including four on secondary batteries (1881–2, with Beaumont and D. G. Fitzgerald) and three on sanitary pipe joints (1901–3). Other patent applications for visiting cards (1893) and treating sewage (1913) were not pursued. Biggs's friendship with

Beaumont, himself a technical writer (particularly regarding motoring and electric vehicles) and a sometime joint editor of *The Engineer*, may have begun in Reading where Beaumont (*b*. 1848) was educated.

Biggs relinquished editorship of *The Electrician* in October 1887, although probably not voluntarily. In 1888 he became editor and co-owner of a new periodical, the *Electrical Engineer*. In one editorial he referred to his defence of Heaviside's articles in the face of opposition from both the owners and the other staff as a reason for leaving *The Electrician*, but it has been suggested that there may have been pressure brought to bear by Preece (Nahin, 162), although in late 1889 Biggs wrote defending Preece, who was misquoted by the popular press when commenting critically on the use of electricity for criminal executions (Nahin, 183, n. 76). Certainly the owners of *The Electrician* were in fear of a libel suit possibly being brought against them if Biggs continued to publish Heaviside's decrying of Preece's 'quackery' (Hunt, 142–3). Now, though, Biggs converted the *Electrical Engineer* from a monthly to a weekly journal. It subsequently amalgamated with *Electrical Engineering*.

As an editor Biggs started the *Contract Journal and Specification Record* which was successful and of great benefit both to the municipal engineering profession and to contractors. He relinquished editorship upon the death of his long-time partner in the venture, subsequently establishing *Contractors' Record and Municipal Engineering* which he edited until his death in 1923. It began life as *Biggs and Sons' Contractors Journal*. Biggs was also a printer and publisher of technical works, Biggs & Co. having offices at 139–40 Salisbury Court, Fleet Street, from 1890 to 1909.

Of cheerful disposition and an informed conversationalist, Biggs was interested in history and archaeology, and in walking, particularly in areas to the south of London. He often prepared interesting illustrated descriptions of places to visit which he printed and would present to friends and colleagues, especially members of the Institution of Municipal and County Engineers. Biggs died of a stroke and heart disease at his home, 42 Therapia Road, Honor Oak, Southwark, London, on 13 December 1923. He was buried in Honor Oak on 18 December. His wife survived him; one son, Charles H. Biggs, continued to edit *Contractors' Record*. ROBERT SHARP

Sources P. J. Nahin, *Oliver Heaviside: sage in solitude* (1988) · *The Electrician* (21 Dec 1923), 705 · R. Appleyard, *The history of the Institution of Electrical Engineers, 1871–1931* (1939) · A. E. Collins, *Biggs and Sons' Contractors' Record and Municipal Engineering* (19 Dec 1923), 2617 · *Electrical Review*, 93 (1923), 946 · B. J. Hunt, *The Maxwellians* (1991) · b. cert. · m. cert. · d. cert.
Likenesses photograph, repro. in *The Electrician*
Wealth at death £56 17s. 9d.: administration, 16 May 1924, CGPLA Eng. & Wales

Biggs, (Rosa) Frances Emily. *See* Swiney, (Rosa) Frances Emily (1847–1922).

Biggs, (Felicity) Jane Ewart- [*née* Felicity Jane Randall], **Baroness Ewart-Biggs** (1929–1992), politician, was born in India on 22 August 1929, the second child and only daughter of Basil FitzHerbert Randall, a major in the

Indian army, and his wife, Rena. After her father died when she was only a few months old, her mother returned to England with her two children. Jane was sent as a border to Downe House School near Newbury and later attended secretarial college. She worked as a secretary at the Foreign Office before joining the Savoy Hotel. On 5 May 1960 she married Christopher Thomas Ewart Ewart-Biggs (1921–1976), a diplomatist; they had one son and two daughters. Marriage opened a new life to Jane Ewart-Biggs, and at successive postings in Algiers, London, Brussels, and Paris she happily combined the responsibilities of a mother with the duties of a diplomatist's wife—a life that she described in her memoir *Pay, Pack and Follow* (1984).

This existence came to an abrupt end on 21 July 1976 when Christopher Ewart-Biggs, the newly appointed British ambassador to Ireland, was assassinated by the Provisional IRA, his car blown up by a landmine outside Dublin. Jane Ewart-Biggs learned of his death over her car radio while she was driving in London. After the memorial service in St Patrick's Cathedral, Dublin, she found sufficient self-control to deliver a special broadcast on Irish television, in which she declared: 'I feel no bitterness, there is no hatred in my heart' (*The Times*, 10 Oct 1992). Her message was 'a beacon at a dark time for Ireland' (*The Times*, 15 Oct 1992), and she subsequently became involved in the non-sectarian peace movement founded by Mairead Corrigan and Betty Williams. She also launched a memorial fund in her husband's name which established the Christopher Ewart-Biggs literary prize, to recognize work that encouraged a greater understanding between the British and Irish peoples.

Involvement in causes that her husband held dear, and in particular that of European integration, was one of the ways in which Jane Ewart-Biggs outwardly came to terms with his death. At a deeper level she struggled with a sense of 'desperate injustice, despair, loss and waste' (*The Guardian*, 14 Sept 1988). She found an antidote in work and joined the Labour Party, a step that surprised some friends but which reflected a long-held commitment to socialism. Her hopes of selection as a candidate first for the European parliament and then the Greater London council were frustrated by selection committees wary of her background. But her energy, determination, and charisma made her an undoubted asset to the party, and in 1981 she was created a life peer. Tall and elegant, with striking good looks, Jane Ewart-Biggs was for some the epitome of 'radical chic'. In the House of Lords she impressed fellow peers as 'the only person here with a waist' (*Daily Telegraph*, 9 Oct 1992). But media attention on her image obscured the seriousness with which she approached her new role. She was always meticulously prepared, and she became an effective speaker without ever being a natural orator. Her ability and industry were recognized when in 1983 she was appointed Labour front-bench spokesman on home affairs. In 1987 she was given responsibility for consumer affairs and overseas development as well, and in 1988 she became an opposition whip.

Jane Ewart-Biggs was strongly critical of the social policies of the Thatcher governments and defended the 'new poor'—single parents, the unemployed, and the elderly. She identified with 'alternative Britain' and was involved in prison reform, the Charter 88 movement, and the National Council for One-Parent Families. As a feminist she advocated the creation of a ministry for women. Her concern about world poverty and its effect on children led to her appointment in 1984 as the president of the British committee of UNICEF. She was especially proud of this connection and travelled widely to further UNICEF's work, making two visits to the drought-stricken regions of Sudan. With all of these competing claims she never lost sight of the cause that was her introduction to public life. She was a member of Lord Kilbrandon's all-party commission of inquiry on Northern Ireland in 1984 and supported its recommendation of an increased role for the Dublin government in the province. She also favoured the Anglo-Irish agreement of 1985 and opposed the reintroduction of internment. But she felt a lasting repugnance towards some of those involved in politics in Northern Ireland, and on one occasion she declined to share the platform at an Oxford Union debate with Gerry Adams, leader of Sinn Féin.

In 1991 Jane Ewart-Biggs was diagnosed with cancer, and her last appearances in the House of Lords, in 1992, were in a wheelchair. On 18 September 1992, three weeks before her death, she married her partner of fourteen years, Kevin Patrick O'Sullivan, a consulting engineer. The ceremony took place in the Charing Cross Hospital, Fulham, where she died on 8 October 1992.

MARK POTTLE

Sources *The Independent* (9 Oct 1992) · *The Independent* (20 Oct 1992) · *Daily Telegraph* (9 Oct 1992) · *The Times* (10 Oct 1992) · *The Times* (15 Oct 1992) · *The Guardian* (14 Sept 1988) · *Press Association* (9 Oct 1992) · *Evening Standard* (11 March 1993) · J. Ewart-Biggs, *Pay, pack and follow* (1984) · J. Ewart-Biggs, *Lady in the Lords* (1988) · J. Ewart-Biggs, 'Recognizing the dual role of women', *Women: neglected majority or monstrous regiment?*, ed. J. Neuberger (1987) · m. certs. · d. cert.

Likenesses photograph, repro. in *The Independent* (9 Oct 1992)

Wealth at death £570,812: probate, 19 Feb 1993, *CGPLA Eng. & Wales*

Biggs, John (1801–1871), hosier and political reformer, was born at Leicester, first of the seven children of John Biggs (1774–1827), hosier, and his wife, Elizabeth, *née* Heggs (1780–1862), of Arnesby, Leicestershire. By the time his father died in 1827 the firm of John Biggs & Sons was firmly established and his family were worshipping among the dissenting élite at the Unitarian Great Meeting.

John made his father's firm one of the largest in Leicester, noted for its export trade to North America and Australia, and its innovations in fancy hosiery and glovemaking. In 1859, when he invested heavily in equipping a steam-powered factory, it became one of the most modern. Respected even by Chartists as a model employer, he exposed the malpractices to which the framework-knitters were commonly subjected, welcomed a bill to abolish frame-rent, the source of most abuses, and demanded greater regulation of children's employment.

From 1826 Biggs participated vigorously in the local reform agitation, helped found the Political Union and Reform Society, and liberally supported the anti-cornlaw campaign. In 1846, he and a fellow hosier were publicly acclaimed as 'the Cobden and Bright of the Midland Counties'.

Meanwhile Biggs was among the leaders of the reformed corporation of Leicester, mayor in 1840, 1847, and 1856, and borough magistrate from 1840. His hopes that reform would initiate a municipal renaissance were soon frustrated when his modest proposals for street-widening and a new town hall were rejected in 1845 by the Improvement committee in an ill-tempered squabble between 'expenders' and 'economists'.

Disillusioned with the Reform Society and having quarrelled with the MPs it supported, Biggs began in 1847 an ultra-radical crusade, aiming to win control of its electoral machine, to obtain the election of genuinely radical MPs, and to agitate for a truly popular franchise. The success of his initial coup, which secured control of the Reform Society, ejected the sitting MPs, and won the election of his two radical candidates, provoked a fifteen-year-long battle between the factions. Biggs was himself elected MP for Leicester in 1856. At this point he dominated the scene like a political boss, the electoral machine at his command, the radical newspaper at his disposal. To his opponents he was the 'Dictator', leader of a 'Chartist clique'. It was a precarious dictatorship, however, maintained by his uncompromising commitment to total victory, and his audacity in facing one setback after another. Finally a by-election in 1861 produced the setback from which he could not recover—a Conservative victory. The only answer was Liberal reunion; the only way was by compromise. Biggs would not oppose it; but he would not take part in it. In 1862 he gave up his parliamentary seat, resigned from the municipality, and withdrew completely and finally from politics. Political failure coincided with financial failure, possibly the result of slack trade, costly new machinery, and political expenses. In 1862 his house, used as security for a debt of £10,086, had to be sold, including his collection of allegedly 'old master' paintings. The business was sold to another firm as a going concern. At the same time Biggs suffered severe personal loss within his household. In the space of a few months his mother, his sister, and her husband, J. F. Hollings, editor of the radical *Leicestershire Mercury*, historian and luminary of the Literary and Philosophical Society, all died; the last by his own hand.

For the rest of his life Biggs lived in a terrace house, 46 West Street, near the prison. After he died there, unmarried, on 4 June 1871, his estate was valued at 'under £1000'. He was buried on 8 June at Welford Road cemetery. The service was conducted by the Revd C. C. Coe, minister of the Great Meeting, whose sermon was afterwards published. Biggs was not forgotten by the public. A subscription, intended to provide a memorial over his tomb, received such support that a public statue was decided upon. Among the donations was a sum contributed by Leicester men who had emigrated to Philadelphia, USA. The statue, created by G. F. Lawson, was of Shap granite, 7 feet tall and mounted on a plinth. It presented Biggs in dignified maturity, upright, sturdy, and benign. Erected in Welford Place, it was later replaced by a bronze cast and set up facing in a different direction.

Unpretentious and generous in prosperity, dignified in adversity, John Biggs won a unique place in the affections of the Leicester public. He was less successful in the House of Commons. He addressed it seven times in his first year as MP, but his 'homely style' (*Leicester Journal*, 28 Feb 1862) seems to have failed to earn more than patronizing respect for his integrity. After that he was a silent member.

A judgement on Biggs must include events after his death. Within five years Leicester was at last dignified by a new town hall. Frame-rent was abolished in 1875. The Education Acts helped to end the evils of children's employment. His radical campaign rescued the local Liberals from their inertia, and after 1867 the reunited party profited from his cultivation of the popular forces when the non-electors he had rallied became the electors of the new order.

William Biggs (1805–1881), hosier and political reformer, was born in Leicester on 18 January 1805, the third child of John Biggs and Elizabeth Heggs. On 26 May 1837 he married Mary Deborah, daughter of John Worthington, yarn merchant, of Leicester. This allied him with a family of distinguished Unitarian ministers; and in her he found a wife who, the few surviving letters suggest, shared the excitement of his political career, and communicated it to their children.

An active partner in the family firm, William, like his brother John, also pursued a political career. Elected to Leicester town council in 1836, he served it continuously for thirty years, was elected mayor in 1842, 1848, and 1859, and appointed JP in 1850. In July 1852 he was elected MP for Newport, Isle of Wight, and represented it until his resignation in December 1856.

As a councillor, Biggs got rid of the old corporation's historic regalia, organized the police force, and supported John's proposals for extensive improvements. As mayor in 1859 he welcomed the volunteer movement, and secured the formation of a company of the rifle corps in Leicester.

William Biggs's speech to the 1841 Derby commercial convention won him a regional reputation; and although his midland counties charter of 1842 failed to rally Chartists to his middle-class leadership, his initiative helped secure the invitation to stand for Newport. He spoke twenty times in the house, mostly in support of progressive or charitable causes, notably the Homes for Penitent Females, the Leicester branch of which he had helped to found; but his didactic style did not please.

The sale of the family firm forced William Biggs's sons to seek careers elsewhere. After 1866 he followed three of them to Liverpool. He died there on 8 October 1881 at his house in Upper Parliament Street. He was buried in Welford Road cemetery, Leicester, beside his brother John.

Biggs was survived by his wife, daughter, and four sons, of whom the third, Arthur Worthington Biggs, was knighted in 1906.

Joseph Biggs (1809–1895), hosier and supporter of Italian independence, was born in Leicester, the fourth son of John Biggs and Elizabeth Heggs. Co-partner in the family firm, he managed the glove department and gave evidence to Muggeridge's inquiry for the royal commission on framework-knitters. In 1837 he married Matilda, daughter of W. H. Ashurst, solicitor, of London [see Biggs, Matilda Ashurst], and, by 1852, had moved to Barden Park, Tonbridge. Through the Ashursts, Biggs was introduced to an extensive circle of progressive friends, including the Italian patriot Giuseppe Mazzini, with whom Matilda maintained an intimate correspondence until her death on 15 October 1866. Mazzini visited Matilda, possibly at Leicester, certainly at Barden Park. Although Biggs at first showed an understandable reserve, he, with his children, became warmly attached to him, and subscribed to his cause. In 1852, after a prolonged visit to Italy, he wrote an indignant letter about its rulers, and in 1854 drew up a paper on British policy, which Mazzini highly commended. Although privately complaining of a lack of spontaneity in Biggs, Mazzini continued to give him warm greetings and send Christmas presents to his daughters. After Matilda's death, Biggs moved to Notting Hill Square, London. By 1893 he was living in St John's Wood. He died there in 1895 at his home, 3 Alexandra Road. He was survived by three of his four daughters one of whom, Maude Ashurst Biggs, posthumously published extracts from her father's American diary, *To America in Thirty-Nine Days: before Steamships Crossed the Atlantic* (1927).

R. H. EVANS

Sources R. H. Evans, 'The Biggs family of Leicester', *Leicestershire Archaeological and Historical Society Transactions*, 48 (1972–3), 29–58 · R. H. Evans, 'John Biggs of Leicester, 1801–1871', *Clio*, 3 (1971) [University of Leicester History Society] · C. Ashworth, 'Hosiery manufacture', *VCH Leicestershire*, 4.303–13 · R. A. McKinley and C. T. Smith, 'Social and administrative history since 1815', *VCH Leicestershire*, 4.251–302 · R. H. Evans, 'Parliamentary representation since 1835', *VCH Leicestershire*, 4.201–50 · A. Temple Patterson, *Radical Leicester: a history of Leicester, 1780–1850* (1954) · C. C. Coe, *Sermon preached in memory of John Biggs* (1871) · *Mazzini's letters to an English family*, ed. E. F. Richards, 3 vols. (1920–22) · CGPLA Eng. & Wales (1871) · d. cert. [John Biggs] · *Leicester Chronicle and Leicestershire Mercury* (10 June 1871) · private information (2004) [William Biggs memorandum book in possession of Mrs Wendy Fraser (née Biggs)] · *Leicestershire Trade Protection Society Directory of Leicester* (Dec 1870) · *Leicester Journal* (16 June 1871)
Archives Leics. RO, William Biggs, 'Scrapbook', LM 5D61
Likenesses oils, c.1840, Leicester town hall · G. F. Lawson, bronze statue, 1873, Welford Place, Leicester
Wealth at death under £1000: probate, 26 June 1871, CGPLA Eng. & Wales

Biggs, Joseph (1809–1895). *See under* Biggs, John (1801–1871).

Biggs, Matilda Ashurst (1816/17–1866), campaigner for women's rights and supporter of Italian independence, was born in Muswell Hill, Middlesex, the second daughter of William Henry *Ashurst (d. 1855) and his wife, Elizabeth Ann Brown (d. 1854), of Muswell Hill, Middlesex.

Elizabeth Ann *Ashurst (known as Eliza), Caroline *Stansfeld, and Emilie *Venturi were her sisters. Her father, a successful radical solicitor, held advanced views on the rights of women, and the household in which she and her sisters grew up was a centre of political discussion and activity on the radical causes of the day. On 11 October 1837 she married Joseph *Biggs (1809–1895) [see under Biggs, John (1801–1871)], the youngest brother and partner in the family hosiery firm in Leicester. The Biggs family had a reputation as progressive employers; Joseph's two elder brothers, John (1801–1871) and William (1805–1881), were prominent radical leaders in municipal politics, who became MPs, respectively, for Leicester (1856–62) and for Newport, Isle of Wight (1852–7).

Matilda and Joseph Biggs settled in Leicester. Although the marriage was to produce four daughters Matilda's was not to be a life of quiet domesticity. She continued to share her family's interest in the anti-slavery question and attended the world anti-slavery convention in London in June 1844 with her father and sister Eliza. The exclusion of the American female delegation from participation in the proceedings led her to a lifelong interest in the political emancipation of her sex. During 1847 she circulated in Leicester one of the earliest printed leaflets in favour of female suffrage, sent to her by a fellow anti-slavery campaigner, Anne Knight (1786–1862). Later in 1859 Biggs openly criticized the Northern Reform Union's refusal to campaign on universal suffrage, writing to the *Newcastle Chronicle*:

> I feel it an injustice that I, who am equally taxed with men, should be denied a voice in making the laws which affect and dispose of my property, and made to support a State, where I am not recognised as a citizen … The Northern Reform Society, which takes its stand upon 'justice', should claim for us at least that we be exempted from the duties, if we are to be denied the rights belonging to citizens. (19 Feb 1859; Biggs, 839)

Biggs also sought to improve the condition of women through local philanthropy; together with her sister Emilie she established a rescue home for prostitutes in Leicester.

The other great cause of Biggs's life, which she shared with her sisters, was that of an independent and unified Italian republic. Following Giuseppe Mazzini's introduction to the Ashurst family in 1844 she developed a long and close, if somewhat stormy, friendship with the Italian revolutionary, though she did not succumb to his religious ideals. Through her marriage she brought Mazzini into contact with the world of English provincial radicalism; his letters to her reveal her long-standing commitment to the cause of Italy through local fund-raising and propaganda activities. For a period in 1850 she was also actively involved in clandestine activity in the south of France. In order to finance republican ventures Mazzini started a scheme of selling bonds, redeemable by the future government of a liberated Italy. His fellow conspirator, Felice Orsini, was given the concession for Piedmont, and Biggs journeyed from England to help distribute the bonds among French and Italian sympathizers. She also accompanied Orsini with letters of introduction from

Mazzini to encourage a common front among the leaders of the various national independence movements of Europe. After Orsini's arrest she raised funds on his behalf.

In 1851, following a winter sojourn in Genoa with her sister Emilie, Biggs returned to England, where she and her sister were among the original seventy-five women who joined the council of the Society of the Friends of Italy. Thereafter her activities appear to have been confined to subscription campaigns and letter writing. In April 1854 Mazzini wrote to her: 'Go on you, and your pretty aides-de-camp, writing for Italy, and creating sympathies for a possible movement' (*Scritti*, 52.116–17, 18 April 1854). During the Polish uprising of 1863 she pressed Mazzini to use his influence to bring aid to the insurgents but none was to be forthcoming.

By 1852 Joseph Biggs had retired from business, probably owing to poor health, and the family moved to Barden Farm, near Tunbridge Wells. In the early 1860s Biggs & Sons Ltd came close to bankruptcy and the scale of business was drastically curtailed, with a consequent diminution in the family's income. Moreover, Matilda's health also was now failing. In July 1865 Mazzini wrote to Emilie, confirming that she was in the last stages of consumption: 'The first impression had been favourable; but long attentive watching makes me despair. I think she is glad of my visits' (*Letters to an English Family*, 3.109). She died at Barden Farm on 15 October 1866 and was survived by her husband and four daughters. Little is known of the eldest, Elizabeth Ashurst Biggs, or of Ada, the youngest. The second child, Caroline Ashurst *Biggs (1840–1889), became a prominent suffragist in her own right.

The third daughter, **Maud Ashurst Biggs** (1857–1933), took up her mother's interest in the subjugated nations of Europe, in particular the cause of Poland. During the 1880s she sought to revive interest in the struggle for Polish independence by bringing the epic poems of Adam Mickiewicz to a wider English audience. In 1882 she published *Konrad Wallenrode*, a translation of his historical poem, which took as its theme the suppression of Lithuania by the Teutonic order—a political allegory whose contemporary significance had escaped the Russian censors. In 1885 she followed this with *Master Thaddeus, or, The Last Foray in Lithuania*, a translation of a historical poem descriptive of the struggle for independence during the Napoleonic era.

Maud Ashurst Biggs was a longstanding member of the council of the Literary Association of the Friends of Poland, which had been established under mainly aristocratic patronage in 1832 to provide material support to Polish émigrés. Under the aegis of the association she published a pamphlet in 1886 entitled *The Forgotten Nation*; in this she expressed support for the constitutional rather than revolutionary claims for a Polish nation, drawing attention to the continued religious persecution of Poles in the Russian territories and the Bismarckian programme of 'Germanization' in the Prussian provinces. This had resulted in the forced expatriation of many thousands of Poles with subject status in the Russian and Austrian territories. Some of these Poles had emigrated to

London, where they received material help from the Literary Association alongside the dwindling number of émigrés who had gone to England after the events of 1830 and 1863.

During the late 1890s Biggs lived in Paris, where she was in contact with the close circle of Polish émigrés, including Ladislas Mickiewicz, son of the famous poet. In 1898 they corresponded about the possibility of publishing the letters of Mazzini to her mother on the Polish cause. These were finally published in the 1920s by E. F. Richards in *Mazzini's Letters to an English Family*. Biggs lived to witness the creation of a new Poland following the First World War. In 1920 she published a translation of a collection of Polish fairy tales and in 1924 she wrote a history of the Literary Association of the Friends of Poland from 1832 to the present day. She maintained a watchful and maternal eye on developments in Poland during the last years of her life. Fearing the destruction of its primeval forests from economic development she wrote:

> as one to whom the national, romantic and poetic memories of Poland are hardly less dear than to the Poles themselves, I trust that they will not for the mere sake of material gain, suffer to perish all that natural beauty so deeply associated with the historic past and with the immortal memory of Mickiewicz, poet and patriot alike. (*The Times*, 28 July 1924)

Following her residence in Paris Biggs later settled at Idbury Manor, Kingham, Oxfordshire. There she set up the Village Press, a small publishing house under whose imprint she published extracts of her father's diary of his journey to America in 1837, *To America in Thirty-Nine Days: before Steamships Crossed the Atlantic*, which remains a well written and interesting account of social and economic life in New York during the early mid-nineteenth century. Other titles that she published included a history of the Women's Institute by J. W. Robertson Scott and a volume of poems by Theo Varlet, translated by Malcolm McLaren.

Biggs died, unmarried, at Idbury on 14 July 1933. In keeping with her feminist heritage she made small bequests to the Society for the Employment of Women and to the Elizabeth Garrett Anderson Hospital for Women, as well as a legacy to the Home for Lost and Stray Cats, London.

JONATHAN SPAIN

Sources *Mazzini's letters to an English family*, ed. E. F. Richards, 3 vols. (1920–22) • *Scritti editi ed inediti di Giuseppe Mazzini*, 94 vols. (Imola, 1906–43) • C. Midgley, *Women against slavery: the British campaigns, 1780–1870* (1992) • C. A. Biggs, 'Great Britain', *History of woman suffrage*, ed. E. C. Stanton, S. B. Anthony, and M. J. Gage, 3 (1886), 833–94, esp. 837–9 • R. H. Evans, 'The Biggs family of Leicester', *Leicestershire Archaeological and Historical Society Transactions*, 48 (1972–3), 29–58 • A. Temple Patterson, *Radical Leicester: a history of Leicester, 1780–1850* (1954) • H. Hartoff, *Roll of the mayors and lord mayors of Leicester, 1209–1935* (1936), 197 • Boase, *Mod. Eng. biog.*, 1.275 • *The Times* (28 July 1924), 8c • *The Times* (8 Sept 1933), 18f • *DNB* • m. cert.
Likenesses portrait, *c*.1848 (with her daughter, Elizabeth; after daguerreotype), repro. in Richards, ed., *Mazzini's letters to an English family*, vol. 3
Wealth at death under £10,000: administration with will, 14 Feb 1867, CGPLA Eng. & Wales

Biggs, Maud Ashurst (1857–1933). *See under* Biggs, Matilda Ashurst (1816/17–1866).

Biggs, Noah (*fl.* 1651), medical practitioner and social reformer, was active in the 1650s, though his identity and background remain obscure. It is possible that he was Henry Biggs, a surgeon employed at the dockyards of Deptford and Woolwich in 1649–53 to work with his father, Thomas Biggs, who had fallen ill and that 'Noah' is a pseudonym stemming from their work environment. The one publication of Noah Biggs, *Mataeotechnia medicinae praxeos: the Vanity of the Craft of Physick* (1651), was addressed to the 'new commonwealth parliament' which, Biggs underlined, had been ordered by Cromwell to reform the professions. Although one of the introductory poems in the work is signed 'R. B. iatrophilos', the style bears little similarity with the one extant poem of the chemist Robert Boyle, even if Boyle's personal commitment in the period to such causes as open communication of medical receipts cannot be in doubt. On the other hand another introductory poem bears the signature 'W. R.', which may indeed refer to the unlicensed medical doctor William Rand, later the projector of a 'College of Graduate Physicians' to rival the established College of Physicians, though no conclusive evidence is available.

Though Biggs has been frequently characterized as a follower of Paracelsus, his work seems more strongly to reflect the teaching of the Flemish chemical physician, J. B. van Helmont, who had modified Paracelsian teachings in significant ways. The spiritually corrupt academicians, argued Biggs, relied on ancient pagan sources for herbal medicines, sterile anatomical investigations, and the dangerous practices of purging and bloodletting. Instead, Biggs advanced the spiritual philosopher's alchemical operations, which focused on the purification of substances by fire, known as the art of pyrotechny.

Biggs's work can be viewed as part of the puritan effort to reform natural philosophy, medicine, and education. It is not known for how long he continued to be involved with the movement for the radical reform of knowledge. If the identification with Henry Biggs is correct, then he seems to have died as early as 1653 (according to the public records, Thomas Biggs was restored as master surgeon to the shipyards in 1653 when his son died). However, this identification has not been definitely confirmed.

MALCOLM OSTER

Sources C. Webster, *The great instauration: science, medicine and reform, 1626–1660* (1975) • H. J. Cook, *The decline of the old medical regime in Stuart London* (1986) • A. G. Debus, 'Paracelsian medicine: Noah Biggs and the problem of medical reform', *Medicine in seventeenth century England: a symposium held … in honor of C. D. O'Malley* [Berkeley 1974], ed. A. Debus (1974), 33–48 • *CSP dom.*, 1649–50, 532; 1652–3, 551–2 • R. Boyle, 'A miscellaneous collection, begun March the 25th 1648–9', RS, Boyle MS 3, fol. 146

Biggs, William (1805–1881). *See under* Biggs, John (1801–1871).

Bigham, John Charles, first Viscount Mersey (1840–1929), judge, was born on 3 August 1840, the second son of John Bigham, a Liverpool merchant, and his wife, Helen, daughter of John East, also of Liverpool. After being educated at the Liverpool Institute, Bigham went to London University where he matriculated but did not graduate, continuing his education in Paris and Berlin. In 1870 he was called to the bar by the Middle Temple and joined the northern circuit.

Times were prosperous and there was plenty of work for barristers both in the north of England and in London. Bigham, learned, industrious, and self-confident, obtained a large share of the commercial business in Liverpool, where his local connections helped, and also at Westminster. On 17 August 1871 he married Georgina Sarah Rogers (d. 1925), the daughter of a Liverpool man named John Rogers. They had three sons, the first being born in 1872.

Having private means and ambition, Bigham became queen's counsel (1883) after only twelve years as a junior. His practice prospered: although he did not have great physical presence, being short and soft-spoken, he nevertheless developed great powers of advocacy. Slow and concise in speech, he was a skilful cross-examiner and his statements were lucid. Unlike many learned lawyers, he was as successful in addressing a jury as he was in arguing a point of law before a judge. He became pre-eminent as a commercial lawyer because of the familiarity with business methods implied by his family background. When the commercial court was established in 1895, he and the king's bencher Joseph Walton (1845–1910) divided virtually all of the important commercial cases between them for the next two years. Bigham's concision made him a particularly congenial advocate from the point of view of James Charles Mathew (1830–1908), the first judge to preside over the court, who was renowned for the speed of his judgments. During his last decade at the bar Bigham's practice was enormous, and he was one of the richest lawyers in his circle.

In November 1885 Bigham stood unsuccessfully for parliament as Liberal candidate for the Toxteth division of Liverpool, and he was again defeated in July 1892 when he stood for the Exchange division of Liverpool. In 1895 he was elected for Exchange as a Liberal Unionist. He made little impact in the House of Commons. One of his few interventions in debate was in support of a bill which became the Liverpool Court of Passage Act (1896), and he was also a member of the committee of inquiry into the Jameson raid of 29 December 1895 in South Africa.

In 1897 five judgeships of the Queen's Bench Division became vacant either by death or retirement, and Bigham was appointed by the lord chancellor, Lord Halsbury, to succeed Sir Lewis William Cave, a choice of which the bar approved. Bigham was immediately put on the rota of judges in charge of the commercial list, and often presided in the court where he had made a name for himself as an advocate.

As a judge Bigham disliked tedious arguments and was full of robust common sense, which often led him to take short cuts or to force the parties into a settlement. But his judicial worth was recognized by appointments to preside over the court of the railway and canal commission (1904), to act as bankruptcy judge and to assist the Court of Appeal and the Chancery Division. In 1902, after the Second South African War, he was also made a member, along with Lord Alverstone, the lord chief justice, and Major-General Sir John Ardagh, of a royal commission for the revision of martial law sentences.

Bigham's judgments, particularly of criminal cases, were not immune from criticism. In 1902 a Wiltshire woman, charged with the ill treatment of a child, appeared before him at the Old Bailey. The jury acquitted her on the more serious charges, so Bigham imposed a fine of £50, which was criticized as unduly lenient. In January 1904 Bigham tried Whitaker Wright (1845–1904) for company fraud. The law officers had declined to prosecute, but Bigham's handling of the private prosecution was said to have helped to secure conviction. The counsel for the defence complained of Bigham's unjudicial hostility to the defendant.

In 1909 Bigham was appointed to succeed Sir Gorell Barnes (afterwards Lord Gorell) as president of the Probate, Divorce, and Admiralty Division, which still preserved a tradition of dignity and austerity, but Bigham brought the spirit of the commercial court to the trial of matrimonial cases. Giving evidence before the divorce commissioners in 1910, he said he did not regard divorce from a religious point of view at all. He found divorce work uncongenial, but was completely at home with the Admiralty business. His tenure as president was short: in March 1910 he retired for health reasons. He had been a judge for less than fifteen years, but was given a pension because of his 'permanent infirmity', and was raised to the peerage as Baron Mersey of Toxteth in the county of Lancaster.

Over the next twenty years Mersey did much voluntary public and judicial work. As a peer who had held high judicial office he heard appeals in the House of Lords, and he sat regularly on the judicial committee of the privy council. In 1912 he was appointed commissioner to inquire into the sinking of the SS *Titanic*. In this connection, a recent work (1998) characterized his court persona as 'autocratic, impatient and not a little testy', but noted the 'surprising objectivity' of the inquiry's findings (D. A. Butler, 193). In 1913 he presided over the international conference on safety of life at sea; and in 1914 he held the court of inquiry in Canada on the loss of the SS *Empress of Ireland*. After the outbreak of war in 1914 the prize court was established, and he was invited to preside over the board of the judicial committee which heard prize court appeals and he continued to do so during the first two years of the war. The cases of the *Roumanian* (1916, as to the right to seize enemy property on land) and the *Odessa* (1916, as to the claims of pledgees of cargo seized as prize) were among those dealt with by him. In 1915, as wreck commissioner, he inquired into the destruction of the SS *Falaba* and the SS *Lusitania*. He has been implicated in conspiracy theorists' claims of a cover-up over the sinking of the latter: this remains highly conjectural, though the conclusion of the inquiry (which blamed Germany for the tragedy without reservation) was without doubt politically convenient.

Mersey was created a viscount in 1916. Increasing deafness hampered his ability to discharge his judicial duties, but in 1921, when there were heavy arrears in the divorce court, he helped to clear the lists with all his old efficiency.

Mersey was said to have been good company and enjoyed entertaining and being entertained. He was devoted to the Middle Temple, and in his extreme old age continued to dine with the benchers despite physical infirmities, perhaps through loneliness after his wife's death in 1925. He died at the Beach Hotel, Littlehampton, Sussex, on 3 September 1929 and was succeeded in the viscountcy by his eldest son, Charles Clive Bigham.

HUGH MOONEY

Sources DNB · *The Times* (4 Sept 1929) · *Law Journal* (7 Sept 1929) · D. A. Butler, '*Unsinkable': the full story of RMS Titanic* (1998) · R. D. Ballard, *Exploring the Lusitania* (1995) · J. Butler, *The liberal party and the Jameson raid* (1968) · *CGPLA Eng. & Wales* (1929)
Likenesses H. T. Glazebrook, portrait, exh. RA 1904 · Spy [L. Ward], chromolithograph, NPG; repro. in *VF* (3 Feb 1898) · W. Stoneman, photograph, NPG · portrait, repro. in *ILN*, 110 (1897), 174 · portrait, repro. in *ILN*, 111 (1897), 561
Wealth at death £80,603 6s. 2d.: resworn probate, 19 Oct 1929, *CGPLA Eng. & Wales*

Bigland, John (1750–1832), schoolmaster and educational writer, was born at Skirlaugh in Holderness, Yorkshire, of poor parents. At the age of one he went to live with his grandparents. He quickly learned to read under his grandmother's tuition and reputedly was able to read the entire Bible before he was five. He spent four or five years at a local school where he learned writing and arithmetic, and was encouraged to read widely in geography and history by two neighbours. Following his grandmother's death and his grandfather's remarriage, to a seventeen-year-old girl, he returned to his father's home and started working as a gardener. Ill treated by his father, he escaped when about sixteen and travelled south across the Ouse. After various jobs he found work with a gang of navvies in the fens in the summer months, and in the winter opened a school for reading and writing in a barn near March, in the fens, which allowed him to study Latin in the evenings. After nearly two years he left for London, where he briefly worked as a schoolteacher, and then spent six years as private tutor to an American merchant. He travelled to France, Belgium, and Spain with his employer, whom he discovered was a smuggler, and fortuitously declined to sail with his employer and his family to Philadelphia, as their ship was wrecked off the Spanish coast.

Bigland arrived in Dover nine years after he had left England, and travelled to Yorkshire, where he planned to open a school but instead worked as a private tutor for the next four years. He successfully ran a school in Harpham, Yorkshire, until the number of pupils fell below an average of fifty whereupon he gave up the school for an assistant mastership in a London boarding-school. Although he returned to Harpham for a while to reopen the school he soon moved on, and spent the next eleven years at three successive schools: at Bole or Gainsborough; at Finningley, in Nottinghamshire; and finally at Rossington, near Doncaster. It was at this point, when entering his fifties, that Bigland started writing. He published his first work, *Reflections on the Resurrection and Ascension of Christ*, in 1803; this was an account of the arguments and evidence that

he had found convincing in countering his religious scepticism. It was well received, and this encouraged him to continue writing for a living; his second work, *Letters on the Study and Use of Ancient and Modern History* (1804), earned him 25 guineas. As he explained in his memoirs:

> I soon discovered, that by persevering in some sort of composition, there was a prospect of acquiring, in time, both reputation and emolument—and the pursuit would then be more beneficial, as well as more pleasant, than the irksome and embarrassing business of keeping a school. (*Memoir*, 149)

The majority of Bigland's twenty or so published titles were popular historical and geographical works aimed at the school market. His travels and linguistic abilities naturally dictated the subjects that he chose; thus he wrote on English, French, and Spanish history and on the political situation in Europe following the French Revolution. He wrote a history of the Jews, 'peculiarly calculated for the use of schools and of young persons', published in 1820, and *Letters on Natural History: Exhibiting a View of the Power, Wisdom, and Goodness of the Deity* (1806). He contributed magazine articles and brought both Lord Lyttelton's and Oliver Goldsmith's histories of England up to date.

Towards the end of his life Bigland lived at Finningley, where he tended the vegetables and flowers in his garden. He made one last trip to satisfy his wanderlust, and travelled to Paris, via Dieppe, in the summer of 1818. He died, unmarried, at the age of eighty-two, at Finningley on 22 February 1832, having written a lively account of his life in his final years.

JAMES MEW, rev. S. J. SKEDD

Sources *Memoir of the life of John Bigland, written by himself* (1830) · *GM*, 1st ser., 102/1 (1832), 645 · E. Rhodes, *Yorkshire scenery, or, Excursions in Yorkshire* (1826) · G. Poulson, *The history and antiquities of the seigniory of Holderness*, 2 vols. (1840–41), 2.19
Likenesses H. Meyer, stipple, pubd 1806 (after T. Uwins), NPG · W. Ward, mezzotint, pubd 1811 (after J. R. Smith), BM, NPG

Bigland, Ralph (1712–1784), herald and cheesemonger, was born on 29 January 1712 at Stepney, Middlesex, the only son of Richard Bigland (1658–1725) of Wapping, tallow chandler, and his second wife, Mary (1676–1736), daughter of George Errington of Benwell, Northumberland. His father was a native of Westmorland, descended from the Bigland family of Bigland, Lancashire.

In 1728 Bigland was apprenticed within the Tallow Chandlers' Company to Edward Olive, a Wapping cheesemonger. Made free of the company in 1737, he served as its master in 1772, but it was as a cheesemonger that he carried on trade for upwards of twenty years. He was based at Fetter Lane, London, from at least 1738, but during the 1740s his occupation took him to the Low Countries and also for a while to Leith in Scotland. The War of the Austrian Succession found him in Flanders, where he supplied cheese to the allied armies and was able to record his impressions of the battle of Fontenoy.

Bigland's antiquarian interests were already in evidence: he made notes of monumental inscriptions in the Low Countries and in Scotland. About 1750 he embarked

Ralph Bigland (1712–1784), by Charles Townley, 1771 (after Richard Brompton)

on a similar exercise in Gloucestershire. His connection with that county seems to have arisen from his marriage in 1737 to Anne Wilkins (*c*.1715–1738), the daughter of a farmer and cheese supplier resident in Frocester. She died soon after the birth of their only child, Richard, who was thereafter brought up in Frocester by the Wilkins family.

In subsequent years, though never fully resident in Gloucestershire, Bigland made frequent visits. In the course of time he traversed the whole county, accumulating a variety of historical information and making it his particular business to record the inscriptions on everything from the grandest church monuments to the humblest gravestones. Although he clearly had helpers, he did much of the work himself. These antiquarian concerns, for long subsidiary to cheesemongering, brought about a change of career in 1757, when he was appointed Bluemantle pursuivant at the College of Arms. The following year he remarried; his second wife, Anna Weir (1729–1766), was Scottish. The union produced two children, both of whom died in infancy.

Promoted to the office of Somerset herald in 1759, Bigland possessed skills ideally suited to his new profession. His sketches of coats of arms and churches show that he was no mean draughtsman, and he was a methodical genealogist. In 1764 he published *Observations on Marriages, Baptisms, and Burials, as Preserved in Parochial Registers*, in which he advocated the inclusion of much greater detail in church registers. He also called for the better safekeeping and detailed indexing of such records. All his ideas were remarkably in advance of their time. Together with his friend and colleague Sir Isaac Heard, he deserves

much of the credit for re-establishing the College of Arms as a natural centre for genealogical enquiry. In 1772 they were reckoned to be the most active practising heralds, each of them earning between £500 and £600 per annum. Bigland climbed steadily in the heraldic hierarchy and was a king of arms for the last eleven years of his life, becoming Norroy in 1773, Clarenceux in 1774, and finally Garter in 1780. For a late starter it was an impressive ascent.

Bigland remained busy to the end, and died in his rooms in the College of Arms on 27 March 1784. He was buried on 8 April in Gloucester Cathedral, where a handsome monument bearing his coat of arms was erected, thereby fulfilling a request made in his will. Practising what he preached, he had himself drafted the inscription, which contains a quantity of genealogical information.

Bigland's fame rests on the posthumous publication of his *Historical, Monumental and Genealogical Collections, Relative to the County of Gloucester*. Richard Bigland, keen to get his father's *magnum opus* into print, employed James Dallaway to edit the work, and between 1786 and 1794 the first and second volumes, covering 180 parishes, were issued in instalments. Thereafter, the project had a chequered history, and the remaining sections appeared in fits and starts between 1819 and 1889. Material relating to two Bristol parishes remained unpublished until the whole work was reprinted in the 1990s.

Gloucestershire is probably unique in possessing such a comprehensive record of the epitaphs that could be seen in churchyards in the eighteenth century. Inevitably, given the scale of the work, there are errors of transcription, but on the whole it is a supremely useful source, and its significance has increased with the years. Many of the inscriptions that Bigland noted down have long ago disappeared through the natural erosion of stone and the deliberate clearance of churchyards. Moreover, the immense growth of interest in genealogy has meant that his *Collections* are consulted by an ever-increasing number of family historians. Bigland's legacy is, in every sense of the word, monumental.

P. L. DICKINSON

Sources B. Frith, introduction, in R. Bigland, *Historical, monumental and genealogical collections, relative to the county of Gloucester*, ed. B. Frith, 4 (1995), xi–xxvii · E. Prince, 'Ralph Bigland and his kin', typescript, 1989, Coll. Arms [another copy in Glos. RO] · I. Gray, 'Ralph Bigland and his family', *Transactions of the Bristol and Gloucestershire Archaeological Society*, 75 (1956), 116–33 · A. Wagner, *Heralds of England: a history of the office and College of Arms* (1967) · E. Prince, 'A monumental irony', *Coat of Arms*, new ser., 9 (1991–2), 110–15 · J. Goodall, 'Garter Bigland's funeral, 1784', *Coat of Arms*, new ser., 9 (1991–2), 40–42 · A. R. Wagner, *The records and collections of the College of Arms* (1952) · W. H. Godfrey, A. Wagner, and H. Stanford London, *The College of Arms, Queen Victoria Street* (1963) · Coll. Arms, MS Howard, 131–4 · parish registers, St Dunstan's, Stepney, LMA · GL, Tallow Chandlers' Company MSS · F. A. Hyett and W. Bazeley, *The bibliographer's manual of Gloucestershire literature*, 1 (1895) · *GM*, 1st ser., 54 (1784), 239 · will, PRO, PROB 11/1115, sig. 187

Archives Bodl. Oxf., Gloucestershire collections and transcripts · Coll. Arms, heraldic and genealogical collections · Glos. RO, family corresp. and papers · Gloucester Public Library | Glos. RO, E. F. M. Prince MSS · Glos. RO, pedigree with later additions of

Veel family · priv. coll., pedigree of Dolyns and Dolyns-Yate families · Wakefield Reference and Information Library, notes relating to Lowther and Bigland families

Likenesses R. Brompton, oils, 1759–71, Coll. Arms · C. Townley, mezzotint, 1771 (after R. Brompton), BM, NPG [*see illus.*] · engraving, 1771 (after R. Brompton) · engraving, 1803, repro. in M. Noble, *A history of the College of Arms* (1805)

Wealth at death several personal bequests of £50; charitable bequest of £100: will, PRO, PROB 11/1115, sig. 187

Bignell, Henry (*b.* **1611**, *d.* in or after **1653**), Church of England clergyman, was born in the parish of St Mary, Oxford, in July 1611, and baptized on 17 July, the son of Foulke Bignell of Souldern, Oxfordshire. His mother was probably Avis Fishe, who had married Foulke Bignill at St Giles', Oxford, on 2 October 1610. Admitted to Brasenose College on 3 June 1629, he matriculated on 18 November 1631 and graduated BA from St Mary Hall on 20 October 1632. Having subscribed on 23 December 1632, he was ordained, and became a schoolmaster and preacher. In 1642 he published *The Son's Portion: Containing Morall Instructions for the Education of Youth in Knowledge*. In 1645 he was made rector of St Peter le Bayly, Oxford, and in 1647 he was referred to the Westminster assembly as a possible replacement for Jasper Mayne at Cassington in the same county, but he was afterwards ejected from St Peter's for 'scandal and drunkenness' (Wood, *Ath. Oxon.*, 3.406). According to Anthony Wood, in '1653 he was perpetually silenced, and commanded to leave Oxon ... because he was drunk and could not for stammering and faultering ... speak out his funeral harangue from the reader's pew in St Mary's church'.

Wood's assertion that, shortly before the Restoration, Bignell went with Sir John Danvers to the West Indies and died there, seems doubtful. He may have been the Henry Bignill who was curate of Crowhurst, Surrey, between 1652 and about 1658 and who seems to have officiated at Petersham in the same county between 1656 and 1659. This man certified on 30 July 1664 that he had performed a marriage ceremony at Petersham for Prince Rupert and Lady Frances Bard. Details of Bignell's later career and the date of his death are unknown.

A. R. BUCKLAND, rev. VIVIENNE LARMINIE

Sources Foster, *Alum. Oxon.* · Wood, *Ath. Oxon.*, new edn, 3.406 · *Walker rev.*, 298 · W. J. Oldfield, 'Index to the clergy whose ordination, institution, resignation, licence or death is recorded in the diocesan registers of the diocese of Oxford ... 1542–1908', 1915, Bodl. Oxf., MS Top. Oxon. c. 250 · [C. B. Heberden], ed., *Brasenose College register, 1509–1909*, 1, OHS, 55 (1909), 157 · BL, Add. MS 4346, fol. 208 · *IGI* [from St Giles parish register] · E. Scott, 'The marriage of Prince Rupert', *EngHR*, 15 (1900), 760–61 · *VCH Surrey*, 3.532 · O. Manning and W. Bray, *The history and antiquities of the county of Surrey*, 2 (1809), 371; repr. (1974)

Bignold, Sir Samuel (1791–1875), businessman and politician, was born on 13 October 1791, the third son in the family of three sons and three daughters of Thomas *Bignold (1761–1835), businessman, and his wife, Sarah (1752–1821), widow of Julius Long and daughter of Samuel Cocksedge of Hopton, Suffolk. Thomas Bignold, a banker and wine merchant, was the founder in 1797 of the Norwich Union Fire Insurance Society and eleven years later of the Norwich Union Life Insurance Society. The two institutions were legally separate. Both were based on the mutual principle and owned by their policy holders, with no shareholders. Thomas was secretary of both, as Samuel also was destined to become. Thomas, though an able man of business, was eccentric and cantankerous. A potential client, who had heard that he would insure any risk at a price, asked whether Bignold would insure him against being bitten by a mad dog. 'No', was the reply, 'because if you were to be bitten by a dog, I should not consider that the dog was mad' (Blake, 21). There was a rebellion by the policy holders in 1818. Thomas was ousted and Samuel elected in his place, and he held the position for nearly sixty years, enduring a series of furious self-exonerating pamphlets from his displaced father.

Samuel was educated partly in Norwich and partly in Bury St Edmunds. He was a fair-haired youth with strikingly bright steel-blue eyes. On leaving school he went into the insurance business. On 12 October 1815, after an engagement of nearly three years, he married Elizabeth Jex Atkins (*d.* 1860), only daughter and heir of William Atkins of Walcott Hall and Ridlington, Norfolk, a substantial landowner. They had six sons and seven daughters.

Bignold's primary interest was the Fire Insurance Society. The trouble with fire brigades in Norwich and the other cities where the society operated was all too often shortage of water and excess of alcohol. Bignold laid down strict rules on drink and good conduct. He also had firm criteria for any applicant to join the society's head office. He had to be a good writer, clean shaven, a tory, and a Christian. Bignold throughout his life was an emphatic adherent to what was in those days the minority party in Norfolk. He took a keen interest in public affairs. He was mayor of Norwich four times (in 1833, 1848, 1853, and 1872). He had much correspondence with Lord Douro, eldest son of the duke of Wellington and tory MP for Norwich. Bignold himself, just after receiving a knighthood, became member for Norwich in a by-election in 1854 but lost his seat at the general election of 1857. He tried but failed to get it back. He was a great admirer of Disraeli but rejected his request to the Life Insurance Society for a loan on rather dubious security. However, he met the great man and was seduced into making a personal loan. As he wrote to Lord Douro, 'really D. was so persuasive' (Blake, 46).

The great expansion of the Norwich Union occurred after Bignold's time. But there would have been nothing to expand if he had not coped with its many vicissitudes. One of these was a major challenge in 1837 by the policy holders, who objected to the septennial valuation and the low level of bonuses. His own remuneration was said to be too high; and why keep the headquarters in Norwich rather than London? Bignold won the day. A notable accession to the union in 1866 was the takeover of the Amicable Society, the oldest mutual life insurance institution in Britain, negotiated by Bignold's nephew, C. J. Bunyon, the union's actuary.

Bignold moved in 1820 from his country house to a mansion in Surrey Street, Norwich (Bignold House), which became not only his private home but the headquarters of the Norwich Union. By the end of his life he had numerous directorships, but he combined these and his public duties without neglect of the Norwich Union. Described as father of the city, he died in Bignold House on 2 January 1875, a 'Norwich Notable'. He was buried at St Margaret's, Old Catton, Norwich.   ROBERT BLAKE

Sources R. Bignold, *Five generations of the Bignold family, 1761–1947, and their connection with the Norwich Union* (1948) · E. Price, *Norwich Union, an historical sketch* (privately printed, [n.d.]) · R. Blake, *Esto perpetua: the Norwich Union Life Insurance Society* (1958) · J. Mantle, *Norwich Union: the first 200 years* (1997) · R. Ryan, 'A history of the Norwich Union Fire and Life Insurance Societies from 1797 to 1914', PhD diss., University of East Anglia, 1984 · R. Ryan, 'The early expansion of the Norwich Union Life Insurance Society, 1808–37', *Business History*, 27 (1985), 166–96 · Burke, *Gen. GB*
Likenesses J. P. Knight, oils, repro. in Blake, *Esto perpetua*, 52
Wealth at death under £120,000: probate, 15 Feb 1875, *CGPLA Eng. & Wales*

Bignold, Thomas (1761–1835), founder of the Norwich Union insurance company, was born in Westerham in Kent, the second of the eight surviving children of John Bignold (*c.*1734–1795), a prosperous tenant farmer, and his wife, Elizabeth, *née* Outram, also of Westerham. It is not known where he attended school, but he was sufficiently well educated to become an exciseman before moving to Norwich in the early 1780s. By 1785 he had married Sarah Long, *née* Cocksedge (1752–1821), and taken over the shop premises which Sarah's first husband had rented until his death in 1783 and which she had since managed as a widow. Between 1786 and 1793 they had three sons and three daughters. Bignold became a churchwarden and a freeman grocer, with an increasingly prosperous small business as a wine and hop dealer.

In 1792 Bignold also became the first secretary of Norwich General Assurance, a joint-stock fire insurance company backed by wealthy local merchants and manufacturers. Apart from his bookkeeping skills, he was probably chosen because he had avoided the bitter partisanship of Norwich politics and never became actively involved with either the local whigs and radicals or the tories. Indeed, he switched political allegiance to exploit business opportunities, having voted for the whigs until 1806, then converting to the tories in line with changes on the Norwich Union board. Meanwhile, in 1797 he had parted with a Norwich General board intent on controlling the scale of their risks, and had founded the Norwich Union Fire Insurance Society with support from the city's extreme radicals, who were chiefly local shopkeepers. Norwich Union was a mutual institution, in which its policyholders shared in all profits. In return they also funded the society's risks with their premiums, which were retained for seven years to pay any losses before profits were redistributed as a septennial bonus.

Freed from influential local restraint and any need to raise capital, Bignold launched Norwich Union on a remarkable course of expansion. When his early directors objected in 1806, he ousted them by persuading local tory policyholders to back his ambitious attack on an insurance market dominated by London joint-stock companies which viewed provincial rivals as upstarts worthy only of a takeover. Bignold defied them by appointing some 500 agents across Britain over the next decade and introducing profit sharing to fire insurance on a far larger scale than any previous firm. The same agency network offered life insurance after he founded a mutual Norwich Union Life Insurance Society in 1808, threatening other rivals in a traditionally conservative business with tireless canvassing and press advertising to emphasize that fire insurance was cheaper with Norwich Union and that life policies were not only for the wealthy. Control remained within Bignold's family, with key posts for his three sons and two sons-in-law. He also persuaded prominent individuals throughout Britain to become trustees, which gave the largely unknown Norwich Union vital respectability.

By then, however, Bignold was well known for his eccentric behaviour when challenged. He had forced those Norwich Union directors who disagreed with him out of head office in 1806 by threatening them with a pair of pistols, which he later alleged were not loaded. On a later occasion, his truculent answers to the 1817 parliamentary select committee investigating misuse of extents in aid (crown writs to recover land) verged on open contempt. This trait continued with claimants. By 1818 Norwich Union had recruited 70,000 fire policyholders by applying the mutual principle on a massive and unprecedented scale. But claims had also increased after 1815 and were threatening bonuses during the post-war recession. Bignold could have retrenched, because Norwich Union still held sufficient reserves and agencies to sustain business after discontinuing bad risks. Most agents also took Norwich Union Life Society premium commissions and wanted to continue. But he had already overreacted, having moved to London in 1816 and resisted claims which he believed fraudulent with costly lawsuits. The 'moral risk' of insurance was widely appreciated, and he justifiably doubted many claims made in difficult years. However, rivals were paying up quietly, while tightening up on underwriting. Bignold did neither, and legal costs rose while new business slumped. Rather than sink with their intransigent father, his sons backed Norwich Union's directors and took over. Norwich Union continued growing, itself a tribute to Bignold, who was informally offered reconciliation with a generous retirement income by his sons. Instead, he began further lawsuits to overturn his dismissal and also embarked on a bizarre range of businesses, including the manufacture and retail of shoes with revolving heels, which led in 1823 to his bankruptcy. He spent sixteen stubborn months in the king's bench prison before compromising with his third son, Sir Samuel *Bignold, who secured his release and retirement in comfort to Westerham. Bignold died there on 11 August 1835 after prolonged ill health, which began six years earlier when he fell from a horse and broke his leg. He was buried at Old Catton church near Norwich, beside his wife, who had died in 1821.   ROGER RYAN

Sources R. Ryan, 'A history of the Norwich Union Fire and Life Insurance societies from 1797 to 1914', PhD diss., University of East Anglia, 1984 · R. Ryan, 'The Norwich Union and the British fire insurance market in the early nineteenth century', *The historian and the business of insurance*, ed. O. M. Westall (1984), 39–73 · R. Ryan, 'The early expansion of the Norwich Union Life Insurance Society, 1808–37', *Business History*, 27 (1985), 166–96 · R. Bignold, *Five generations of the Bignold family, 1761–1947, and their connection with the Norwich Union* (1948) · R. Blake, *Esto perpetua: the Norwich Union Life Insurance Society* (1958) · 'A few plain facts for the consideration of insurers with the Norwich Union Fire Office', Norwich Central Library, File 12F, Norwich Union Societies, 1805–1889 · Records of the court of bankruptcy, 1823–34, PRO, B1, B3 · Orders and examinations, depositions and proceedings, PRO · transcripts, Westerham parish, CKS, DRb (Rti/389, 1754, 1756–1769)

Archives Colman and Rye Library, Norwich · Norwich Union Museum

Likenesses J. Clover, portrait, *c*.1816, Norwich Union Museum

Bigod, Sir Francis (1507–1537), rebel, was born at Seaton in Hinderwell, Yorkshire, on 4 October 1507, the eldest son of Sir John Bigod and Joan, the daughter of Sir James Strangways, who acted as godfather, with the prior of Guisborough as the other godfather and Agnes Baynton as godmother. By 1514 Sir John had been killed by the Scots, perhaps at Flodden in 1513, and Francis's grandfather Sir Ralph died in 1515 leaving the seven-year-old Francis as heir. As such, he was descended both from the Bigods (who were earls of Norfolk until 1306) and from the lords Maulay of Mulgrave Castle near Scarborough. On 9 May 1515 his wardship was secured by Cardinal Wolsey, who reassured Strangways of his good intentions for the boy. Francis's long minority may have been spent principally in Wolsey's household and at Oxford University, where he did not take a degree. He became a committed protestant with scholarly theological interests, and met the future minister Thomas Cromwell and the reformer Thomas Garrett. Since his proof of age was delayed until 23 September 1529, it was presumably Wolsey who selected Katherine Neville (*d.* 1566), daughter of William, Lord Conyers, as his bride and received her marriage portion. Wolsey himself dispensed them from impediments on 4 November 1528.

Even allowing for the jointures of his grandmother Agnes and his mother, Joan, respectively now married to Sir Ralph Eure and Sir William Malliverer, and the former's dower, Bigod entered a substantial estate free of debt that included two residences, Settrington and Mulgrave, where he regularly stayed. His financial position was sound. Yet by 1533 he was in difficulties and already complaining about his 'bare entering' of his estates and the lack of a suitable house: references to be understood perhaps by an absence of cash and by unfashionable architecture. More satisfactory accommodation was secured by frequent stays at Hornby, the residence of his father-in-law, Lord Conyers, and reputedly by new construction at Mulgrave Castle. His shortfall in cash was corrected by borrowing. One debt due at Michaelmas 1533 was put off a year. His distress was not apparently alleviated by 700 marks paid to him by Lord Latimer for the marriage of his daughter Margaret to Bigod's infant son Ralph, on whom Francis settled lands worth £50 a year and for whom he contracted not to alienate the rest. That was on 12 October 1534; by 31 January 1535, Francis had persuaded Latimer to buy lands worth £40 a year for £700 payable in instalments. Lands were also sold to Sir William Sidney. Others, on 4 November 1535, were settled on Francis's brother Ralph. In desperation for a loan, he once offered Cromwell £100 a year secured on Settrington itself, already dismembered by sales. Although there is no concrete evidence, he was allegedly building both at his principal residences and at local churches, including a chapel at Healaugh Park. He certainly had other expensive habits: attendance at court, constant travel, and supporting protestant preachers and a large household. It was Bigod's financial incompetence that was destroying his inheritance even if, as alleged, his creditors showed no mercy to a reputed heretic.

Idealistic and puritanical ahead of his time, 'a lover of evangelical truth' (Bale, *Index*, 72), Bigod corresponded with reformers everywhere, heard several sermons a day, and even aspired to a clerical career. He was a natural agent for Cromwell in the north, where few shared his enthusiasm for protestantism and the Henrician reformation, and where his knighthood, landholding, and offices (he served as a JP from 1532) conferred standing. Bigod was returned to the 1529 and 1536 parliaments for an unknown constituency. He helped compile the *valor ecclesiasticus*, and enforced the royal supremacy even on bishops and monks whom he corrected and punished: the monk George Lazenby of Jervaulx, the most blatant offender he detected, was executed. He considered monasteries to be corrupt and wealthy in defiance of their professions of poverty. Their tithes should be used to support well-paid preachers, he argued in 1533–6 in his *Treatise Concernyng Impropriations of Benefices*. Unlike Cromwell, Bigod wanted monasteries reformed rather than dissolved. In several cases he undertook the task of reform himself. His support for sanctuaries also flouted government policy. Such contradictions were highlighted by his quarrel as under-steward with Whitby Abbey, which brought him into conflict with his Eure step-grandfather. Bigod provoked a riot in 1535, was indicted at York assizes (falsely, so he claimed), probably in January 1536, and sought to depose the abbot. On 4 March 1536, at Malton, Bigod's servants murdered Davy Seignoiry, a servant of Sir Ralph Eure the younger. Although they had acted without the sanction of their master, who condemned them and refused them any protection, he was nevertheless seriously embarrassed.

The protestant Bigod naturally initially opposed the Catholic Pilgrimage of Grace later in 1536 and fled from Mulgrave Castle by sea. Driven into Hartlepool, where the commons tried to lynch him, he went home and was captured, participating henceforth in the pilgrimage at the siege of his step-grandfather Eure at Scarborough and at the Pontefract council, where his paper on the proper relationship of church and state attracted little support. However, Bigod unexpectedly found his promotion of the church and opposition to royal intervention in religion was shared by the pilgrims. Following their disbandment in December 1536, he doubted the king's good faith, fearing that Henry would garrison Hull and Scarborough as a basis for repression. It was to fulfil the king's promises that on 16 January 1537 Bigod launched another revolt: a loyal uprising. His plan was that of his tenant and ally, the yeoman John Hallam of Yorkswolds. Bigod dispatched the pilgrim articles unavailingly to Richmondshire, Durham, York, and the Percies, tendered the pilgrim oath, and himself spoke inspiringly from a hilltop. Former pilgrims, whether aristocrats or the commons of Hull, remained unconvinced. Lord Lumley's son George was to seize Scarborough, and Hallam Hull, on 16 January; both failed ignominiously. Bigod's subsequent assault on Hull on 19 January was pre-empted by a dawn raid on Beverley that captured almost all his men; sixty-two captives were identified. Bigod escaped, first to Mulgrave and then to Cumberland, where he was captured (10 February) and imprisoned in Carlisle Castle. Examination, trial, and hanging at Tyburn (on 2 June 1537) followed. He was buried the same day at London's Greyfriars. His uprising enabled Henry VIII to wreak revenge on those implicated in the 1536 revolt, very few of whom rose in 1537. Bigod's widow, son, and daughter Dorothy Radcliffe (his ultimate heir) benefited from the reversal of his attainder in 1549–50. His widow, Katherine, died in 1566.

MICHAEL HICKS

Sources A. G. Dickens, *Lollards and protestants in the diocese of York, 1509–1558* (1959) · F. Bigod, 'A treatise against impropriations of benefices', ed. A. G. Dickens, *Tudor tracts*, Yorkshire Archaeological Society, record ser., 125 (1959) · M. H. Dodds and R. Dodds, *The Pilgrimage of Grace, 1536–1537, and the Exeter conspiracy, 1538*, 2 vols. (1915) · M. L. Bush and D. Bowes, *A study of the post-pardon revolts of December 1536 to March 1537 and their effects* (1999) · C. Moor, 'The Bygods, earls of Norfolk, Bygod of Settrington, etc.', *Yorkshire Archaeological Journal*, 32 (1934–6), 172–213 · Emden, *Oxf.* · HoP, *Commons, 1509–58* · PRO, SC 6/Hen VIII/3444; E 150/1227/11 · *Hall's chronicle*, ed. H. Ellis (1809) · *LP Henry VIII*, vols. 2–13 · [J. Raine], ed., *Testamenta Eboracensia*, 3, SurtS, 45 (1865) · J. G. Nichols, ed., *The chronicle of the grey friars of London*, CS, 53 (1852) · *Heraldic visitation of the northern counties in 1530, by Thomas Tonge*, ed. W. H. D. Longstaffe, SurtS, 41 (1863) · PRO, C142/50/115 · Bale, *Index*

Wealth at death £385 p.a.: PRO, SC 6/Hen VIII/3444, 1536–7

Bigod, Hugh (I), first earl of Norfolk (*d.* 1176/7), magnate, was the second son of Roger (I) *Bigod (*d.* 1107), sheriff of Norfolk and Suffolk, and his second wife, Alice de Tosny. On the death of his half-brother William in the wreck of the *White Ship* in 1120, Hugh succeeded to the family's enormous estates in East Anglia, and he also inherited *c.*1130 estates in Yorkshire from his aunt, Albreda de Tosny. By 1135 there were 125 knights enfeoffed on his lands. He was married twice, first to Juliana de Vere (*d.* 1199/1200), with whom he had one son; the marriage was annulled, and Bigod married, secondly, Gundreda (*d.* 1206×8), daughter of Earl Roger of Warwick, with whom he had two sons.

Bigod's political career spanned five decades and service under four monarchs, beginning in 1120, with his appointment as a royal steward. He was frequently in attendance on Henry I, attesting forty-seven charters between 1121 and 1135. In 1135 he played a leading role in determining the disputed royal succession, taking an oath that Henry I on his deathbed had bequeathed the crown to his nephew Stephen, count of Blois. It would later be claimed that

Hugh had not in fact been present at Henry's death, but at the time Bigod's declaration persuaded the archbishop of Canterbury to crown Stephen, and helped to induce the Anglo-Norman aristocracy to abandon the claim of King Henry's daughter, the Empress Matilda. Although Stephen confirmed Bigod as royal steward, an uneasy relationship soon developed between the two men. Bigod's lands were predominantly in Suffolk, based upon his castles at Framlingham, Bungay, and Walton. It seems clear that he aspired to extend his power into Norfolk as well, and when in 1136 there were rumours of Stephen's death, he occupied Norwich Castle. In 1140 Bigod rebelled twice, but in August 1140 an agreement was reached between him and King Stephen. Bigod was made earl of Norfolk, and in January 1141 he supported Stephen at the battle of Lincoln, though he fled as soon as fighting began. At the Council of Oxford in April 1141, however, he defected to Matilda, who did not recognize Stephen's creations. Bigod again received the earldom of Norfolk, but was unable to enforce his authority in that county. The sheriff of Norfolk ruled over Norwich and eastern Norfolk, while the Warenne and d'Aubigny families, who dominated western Norfolk, remained loyal to Stephen.

Eastern Suffolk, however, was described as *terra Hugonis Bigod*: royal manors were depleted of their stock, and Bigod seized five knights' fees. In 1144 he supported Geoffrey de Mandeville in the latter's rebellion against Stephen, and in 1147 he received Archbishop Theobald, who had been excluded from the country by the king, at Framlingham Castle. The bishops of London, Norwich, and Chichester visited the primate there, and Theobald judged ecclesiastical cases under Earl Hugh's protection. Although the earl's men attended the joint shire court of Norfolk and Suffolk at Norwich, *c.*1147–50, royal sheriffs were unable to exercise authority in eastern Suffolk in the late 1140s, and Bigod remained actively opposed to Stephen, being described in 1149 as 'an inveterate enemy of the king's cause' (*Gesta Stephani*, 223). In 1153, however, the civil war in East Anglia ended, after Earl Hugh surrendered Ipswich Castle to King Stephen. Stephen had earlier given the county of Norfolk to his second son, William. Late in 1153 the treaty of Winchester confirmed this grant, but in an apparent attempt at compromise, probably made at the insistence of Henry Plantagenet, Stephen bestowed on Bigod the title of earl, without a territorial designation, but with the earl's third penny from Norfolk, and also four royal manors in East Anglia with an annual value of £114. Between 1154 and 1156 Bigod or his subtenants accounted for the county farm of Norfolk and Suffolk.

Although Henry II suppressed many of the earldoms created in the reign of Stephen, in 1154 he regranted to Bigod the earldom (specifically) of Norfolk, along with the other rights delegated in 1153. In 1157, however, as part of a general programme of pacification in East Anglia, the king took control of all the castles of William de Blois and Hugh Bigod. The latter did not recover Framlingham, which for a time, at least, was manned by royal mercenaries, until 1165. Nevertheless, during the war of 1157–8 between Henry II and Prince Owain of Gwynedd, Earl Hugh took over responsibility for the administration of East Anglia from the sheriffs of Norfolk and Suffolk.

Throughout the late 1150s and the early 1160s Hugh Bigod was regularly at the royal court. In 1163 he was one of the twelve hostages whom the king offered to the count of Flanders as part of that year's treaty. In 1164–5 he supported Henry II's campaigns in Wales, paying for a retinue. In 1166 he was excommunicated by Archbishop Thomas Becket, following a dispute with Pentney Priory in Norfolk in the previous year. But the most important development in which Bigod was involved in the late 1160s was the construction of two new East Anglian castles, at Orford and Bungay. Bungay stood at the junction of the major roads running north-west and north-east towards Norwich where they crossed the River Waveney. Earl Hugh was charged £1000 by Henry II in 1165, presumably for licence to build at Bungay: 500 marks were paid in the first year, followed by smaller instalments for the next third over the following two years. In 1168–9, however, the barons of the exchequer ordered that he was not to be summoned for the remaining 500 marks unless the king demanded it, effectively exempting Bigod from further payment. Earl Hugh's fine may have paid for building the king's own splendid castle at Orford. Both castles were probably built principally in order to defend the coastal region of East Anglia from invasions from the continent, though the king may also have intended Orford to act as a control upon the earl.

Hugh Bigod's excommunication was quashed by a royal council in 1169. According to Matthew Paris, the earl's health deteriorated in the 1170s. Nevertheless, in 1172 he supported the rebellion of Henry, the Young King, the eldest son of Henry II. In return for his backing, Earl Hugh was offered the constableship of Norwich Castle, and the honour of Eye, which he may have intended to leave to his two sons from his second marriage. Be that as it may, when the earl of Leicester landed at Walton in Suffolk on 29 September 1173 with a force of Flemish mercenaries, he was joined by Bigod, and together the two earls captured Haughley Castle on 13 October. However, their attack on Walton Castle and the town of Dunwich failed, and after their return to Framlingham the earl of Leicester was forced to return to his own estates. But on 15 May 1174 more Flemish mercenaries, dispatched by the count of Flanders, landed at Orwell in Suffolk, and on 1 July 1174 they joined 500 of Bigod's soldiers. They captured Norwich Castle, but on all other fronts the rebels were defeated, and Bigod was forced into submission. On 25 July 1174 he swore an oath of homage to Henry II, and was fined £466. Arrangement was made for the safe conduct of the Flemish mercenaries out of the country, and Bigod's castle at Framlingham was demolished. The damage to his own estates was assessed at £94.

Hugh Bigod retained his earldom and Bungay Castle, as well as the four royal manors first granted to him in 1153, but he may have lost the right to collect the earl's third penny. In 1176 he went on pilgrimage to Jerusalem, but died on the journey, some time before 9 March 1177. His body was brought back to England, for burial near to other members of his family at Thetford Priory, to which he had granted numerous estates during his lifetime. The earldom of Norfolk passed to his eldest son, Roger (II) *Bigod, but there was a dispute between his wives and sons over the estates that he had acquired, which was finally resolved only in 1199.   A. F. WAREHAM

Sources R. Howlett, ed., *Chronicles of the reigns of Stephen, Henry II, and Richard I*, 4, Rolls Series, 82 (1889), 193 · *Materials for the history of Thomas Becket, archbishop of Canterbury*, 1, ed. J. C. Robertson, Rolls Series, 67 (1875), 491 · John of Salisbury, *Historia pontificalis: John of Salisbury's memoirs of the papal court*, ed. and trans. M. Chibnall (1956), 84 · W. Stubbs, ed., *Gesta regis Henrici secundi Benedicti abbatis: the chronicle of the reigns of Henry II and Richard I, AD 1169–1192*, 2 vols., Rolls Series, 49 (1867), 1.60–61 · *The historical works of Gervase of Canterbury*, ed. W. Stubbs, 1: *The chronicle of the reigns of Stephen, Henry II, and Richard I*, Rolls Series, 73 (1879), 136, 203 · Henry, archdeacon of Huntingdon, *Historia Anglorum*, ed. D. E. Greenway, OMT (1996), 706–7, 728–31 · *Radulfi de Diceto … opera historica*, ed. W. Stubbs, 1: 1148–79, Rolls Series, 68 (1876), 377–8, 381 · Great Britain Exchequer, *The great rolls of the pipe for the second, third, and fourth years of the reign of King Henry the second, AD 1155, 1156, 1157, 1158*, ed. J. Hunter, RC, 31 (1844), 8–10 · R. Foreville, *L'église et la royauté en Angleterre sous Henri II Plantagenet, 1154–1189* (Paris, 1943), 206–9 · *Paris, Chron.*, 2.291 · A. Wareham, 'The motives and politics of the Bigod family, c.1066–1177', *Anglo-Norman Studies*, 17 (1994), 223–42 · R. A. Brown, 'Framlingham Castle and Bigod', *Castles, conquest, and charters: collected papers* (1989), 187–208 · S. J. Bailey, 'The Countess Gundred's lands', *Cambridge Law Journal*, 10 (1948–50), 84–103 · K. R. Potter and R. H. C. Davis, eds., *Gesta Stephani*, OMT (1976) · W. L. Warren, *Henry II* (1973) · GEC, *Peerage*, new edn, 9.579–86 · M. Chibnall, *The Empress Matilda* (1991)

Bigod, Hugh (III) (*b.* in or before **1220**, *d.* **1266**), baron and justiciar, was a younger son of Hugh (II) Bigod, earl of Norfolk, who died in 1225. His mother was Matilda (or Maud; *d.* 1248), the eldest daughter and eventual coheir of William Marshal, earl of Pembroke, who later in 1225 took as her second husband William (IV) de Warenne, earl of Surrey. By the early 1240s his mother had given him a substantial holding in Sussex centred on Bosham, which was part of the Marshal inheritance, and by the early 1250s (and perhaps earlier) he held the manor of Settrington close to Malton in the East Riding of Yorkshire, part of the Bigod family inheritance. By February 1244 he had married Joan, the widow of Hugh Wake: by this marriage he gained possession of her dower lands, of the Wake family lands during the long minority of the heir, Baldwin, who came of age only in 1259, and of Joan's inheritance (she was daughter and sole heir of Nicholas de Stuteville, lord of the northern baronies of Cottingham and Liddel Strength). During the 1240s he played some part in the management of the estates of his elder brother, Roger (III) *Bigod, earl of Norfolk, assisting Roger's bailiff in preventing John Mansel from taking possession of the manor of Wilton in Pickeringlithe unless Mansel agreed to hold it directly of the earl.

In 1252 Bigod was one of a group of magnates who stood surety for Henry III for the payment of various sums to Simon de Montfort for the government of Gascony. Shortly afterwards he began to receive marks of royal favour: a grant of the forestership of Farndale in fee, temporary custody of the manor and castle of Pickering, and the right to hold markets and fairs at two of his wife's Yorkshire manors. In 1257 he was sent to Galicia as a royal envoy, and in 1257–8 was involved in the negotiations leading up to the treaty of Paris and the making of peace between Henry III and Louis IX of France. By 1257 at the latest he had become a member of the king's council, and in May or June 1258 was one of the twelve chosen by the barons and earls as part of the reforming council of twenty-four (the other twelve being chosen by the king). That he was also acceptable to the king's side is shown by the fact that it was the king's party who then chose him as one of the four men with power to nominate the king's new council.

It was shortly after this, during the course of the Oxford reforming parliament (on about 16 June 1258), that Bigod was appointed to the newly revived post of chief justiciar of England. Although Matthew Paris describes him as experienced in the law of the land there is little in what is known of his life and career up to this time to confirm such a characterization, and no reason to suppose that he had received any kind of legal training. The provisions of Oxford indicate that the reformers saw as his principal role the remedying of official misconduct, on the part of both royal justices and royal and seignorial officials, and originally intended that he should hold office only for a single year. In practice he remained in office for well over two years, until mid-October 1260, and a great deal of his time was spent on business other than the remedying of grievances; much of this was of a legal nature. During law terms Bigod sat regularly in the court *coram rege*. During vacations he and his associates heard petty assizes and delivered gaols. But he was also a member of the king's council, and during Henry III's absence from England between mid-November 1259 and late April 1260 acted as regent. So slow was the progress Bigod made in dealing with the grievances which the reformers had solicited from each county in the summer of 1258 that alternative arrangements had to be made at the Westminster parliament of October 1259. His efforts were now to be supplemented by the work of five other panels of special justices. In the end he seems to have dealt only with the grievances of Surrey, Kent, Hampshire, Essex, and London.

It may have been the irresistible combination of personal interest and commitment to the arrangements made at the Oxford parliament which led Bigod to refuse to surrender the castles of Scarborough and Pickering to Henry III in May 1261 without a majority decision of the council. But by October of the same year he had clearly been won over to the king's side, and he remained loyal to Henry thereafter. He fought for him at the battle of Lewes in 1264, and afterwards escaped to France by way of Pevensey with his half-brother, John de *Warenne, earl of Surrey. After the royalist victory at the battle of Evesham in the following year he returned to the ranks of the king's close advisers. He had died by 7 November 1266.

Hugh Bigod and his wife had a daughter, Joan, who married Philip *Kyme (d. 1323) [see under Kyme family], lord of the barony of Sotby, who came of age in 1277. Bigod had

purchased his wardship and marriage from Henry III in November 1259, probably with Joan specifically in mind. But his heir was his son Roger (IV) *Bigod. Only four years after his father's death Roger also succeeded his uncle as earl of Norfolk.   PAUL BRAND

Sources GEC, *Peerage* · *Chancery records* · PRO, KB 26 · PRO, JUST 1 · C. Roberts, ed., *Excerpta è rotulis finium in Turri Londinensi asservatis, Henrico Tertio rege, AD 1216–1272*, 2, RC, 32 (1836), 448 · J. Parker, ed., *Feet of fines for the county of York*, 4: *from 1232 to 1246* (1925), Yorkshire Archaeological Society, 67 (1925), 108 · Paris, *Chron.*, 5.698

Bigod, Roger (**I**) (*d.* **1107**), administrator, was probably the son of Robert Bigod, who in 1055 betrayed the rebellious plans of his lord, the count of Mortain, to Duke William and received as his reward a minor subtenancy held from the bishop of Bayeux in the Calvados region. Although Wace claimed that the Bigods' ancestor had fought at Hastings, no contemporary source supports this view, and the chronology of Roger Bigod's own life makes it very unlikely that he himself took part in the 1066 campaign. The family's later distinction probably led to this invention.

Roger Bigod first appears in 1075 when the bishop of Bayeux, perhaps seeking to enhance his power in East Anglia, granted to his subtenant Bigod a substantial share of the forfeited estates of the rebellious Earl Ralph de Gael, who had been expelled from the kingdom. From 1081 until 1086 Bigod served as sheriff of Norfolk, and the tenure of this office may have allowed him to assemble a great honour from the landholdings of Anglo-Saxon royal agents. In 1086 his East Anglian honour was valued at £430, which is the fifteenth highest valuation in Domesday, a remarkable rise from his father's state of penury in 1055. In 1087 William II removed Bigod as sheriff of Norfolk. Reacting swiftly, Bigod either seized or fortified Norwich Castle, and ordered one of his subtenants to seize the manor of Southwold from the abbey of Bury St Edmunds. These actions forced William II to recognize that he had made a mistake, and in 1091 Bigod was reappointed as sheriff of Norfolk and became a steward of the royal household. Rebellion enhanced Bigod's status, and he held both of these offices until his death.

Bigod was married twice, first to Adelaide and second to Alice de Tosny; Hugh (I) *Bigod was the son of the second marriage. He founded Thetford Priory *c.*1104 and was a patron of Norwich Cathedral priory. On his death at Earsham in 1107 the cathedral monks of Norwich claimed that Bigod had promised his body to them before the foundation of Thetford Priory, while the monks of Thetford claimed on dubious evidence that Bigod had bequeathed his body to them. A fourteenth-century account records that the bishop resolved the dispute by taking Bigod's body from Earsham back to Norwich on a cart in the middle of the night against the pleas of the sheriff's widow and men. Whether this account can be accepted is a moot point, but a writ of 1106 confirms that the king recognized the justice of the cathedral monks' claim. At issue was probably the right to retain estates which Bigod had donated to these houses, as well as the prestige to be gained from having the tomb of such a great local ruler.

A. F. WAREHAM

Sources A. Farley, ed., *Domesday Book*, 2 vols. (1783), vol. 2 · *Reg. RAN*, vols. 1–2 · *Le 'Roman de Rou' de Wace*, ed. A. J. Holden, 3 vols. (Paris, 1970–73) · A. Wareham, 'The motives and politics of the Bigod family, c.1066–1177', *Anglo-Norman Studies*, 17 (1994), 223–42 · CCC Cam., MS 329 fol. 106b
Wealth at death £430—renders: Farley, ed., *Domesday book*, vol. 2

Bigod, Roger (II), second earl of Norfolk (c.1143–1221), magnate, was the only son of Hugh (I) *Bigod, earl of Norfolk (d. 1176/7), and his first wife, Juliana (d. 1199/1200), sister of Aubrey (III) de *Vere, earl of Oxford. After repudiating his first wife, Hugh married Gundreda (d. 1206x8), daughter of Earl Roger of Warwick, and with her had two further sons, Hugh (d. c.1203) and William. Roger (II) Bigod married Ida, of unknown parentage, with whom he had four sons, Hugh (II) (d. 1225), William, Ralph, and Roger, and two daughters, Mary, who married Ralph fitz Robert, and Margery, who married William of Hastings.

The accession of Roger (II) Bigod to his father's estates provides a stunning example of how a medieval king could profit from family squabbles among his higher aristocracy. When Hugh Bigod repudiated his first wife in favour of Gundreda and then produced two more sons with his name, he brought upon his first son a dispute over the inheritance which would muddy the waters for over twenty years after his death. No sooner had Hugh been placed in the ground at Thetford Priory, than Gundreda, like the wicked stepmother of legend, asserted the claim of her first son by Hugh, confusingly also named Hugh, to certain of her late husband's estates which, she claimed, had been acquired during his lifetime and which he had bequeathed to Hugh as was his right. Never a man to miss an opportunity to keep his barons in check, Henry II took possession of large parts of Bigod land in Norfolk and refused to recognize Roger's claim to the earldom, which his father seems to have lost in 1174.

The roots of this antipathy towards the Bigod family go back to Hugh's participation in the revolt of 1173–4 against Henry II, which resulted in the destruction of Framlingham Castle, seemingly the Bigod *caput*, and the lasting enmity of the king. When Hugh died in 1176 or 1177 and Gundreda pushed her son's claims to part of the Bigod inheritance, Henry II felt no compunction in making Roger (who was by this time already of age) feel extremely uncomfortable by allowing the case to continue unresolved, refusing to allow him the earldom of Norfolk, and confiscating these disputed lands. It is a true testament to the fear that a powerful magnate like the earl of Norfolk could engender in a twelfth-century king that, despite the fact that Roger himself had remained faithful during the rebellion of 1173–4 and can be found in the king's service before 1176, Henry II still felt the need to take advantage of Roger's little local difficulty to hold him in check.

The saga of the claims of Gundreda and Hugh to a part of Roger's inheritance was to dog the earl until 1199. There was one light on the horizon, however. The accession of Richard I in 1189 brought Roger (II) back into royal favour. The new king bestowed upon Roger the long-awaited earldom of Norfolk for the relatively paltry sum of 1000 marks. From that moment on circumstances improved for the newly belted earl. He can be found with the king on a regular basis before Richard embarked on crusade, and he supported the interim government throughout the difficult years of the king's absence. It seems that Roger (II) also had a part to play in Richard's release from captivity and was in Germany when Richard's freedom was secured. At Richard's second coronation in 1194 Bigod was one of four earls given the privilege of carrying the silken canopy that covered the king. He was a baron of the exchequer between 1194 and 1196, and also served as a justice on eyre and *coram rege* during Richard's reign. And he had the hereditary stewardship of the royal household returned to him. Roger (II) also found time to serve in Richard's armies on the continent. The conclusion of more than twenty years' squabbling with his half-brother, Hugh, in 1199 for a settlement of an estate held of the earl, worth a scant £30, merely served to set the seal on a thoroughly successful reign for Bigod. It was at this point, also, that Bigod set about rebuilding Framlingham Castle, much improved from the structure destroyed in 1176, in stone and in the 'new fashion'. The castle as it stands today is mostly from this date.

The story of a successful and loyal king's earl continued well into the next reign. Bigod was present at John's coronation on 27 May 1199, and was dispatched thence to the king of Scots, to bring him to John for the performance of homage. He seems to have executed his military duties to John in Normandy and was one of the earls who was in constant attendance upon the king. He went to Poitou in 1206 and can be found on the royal campaigns in Scotland (1209), Ireland (1210), and Wales (1211). Despite this record of service Earl Roger joined the rebel side in the civil war that marked the end of King John's reign. Financial pressure may have been a reason. The scutage due on some 160 knights' fees, which the earl came to hold by the end of his life, was liable to be heavy, so much so that in 1211 Bigod struck a bargain with the king to pay 2000 marks (£1333 6s. 8d.) for respite during his lifetime from demands for arrears, and for being allowed to pay scutage on only 60 fees in future. He was pardoned 360 marks of this debt, but paid the substantial sum of 1340 marks in 1211 and 1212. Nor was this the only way in which John showed himself less than favourable towards the earl. In 1207 one William the Falconer brought an action against Bigod at Westminster, but when the earl objected to the chosen jurors on the grounds of their likely bias, his arguments were ignored by the king, who ordered that the case proceed. Both Earl Roger (now probably over seventy) and his son, Hugh Bigod (d. 1225), were later named as being among the committee of twenty-five set up by Magna Carta to control the king, for which they were both declared excommunicate by Pope Innocent III (r. 1198–1216) in December of that year.

John's irritation at Bigod's defection and the subsequent

events illustrate clearly how the king intended to bring his magnates to heel. After a lightning campaign in the north, during which he effectively reduced his opponents there to submission, John returned to East Anglia, also a centre of resistance. Judging from John's actions in March 1216, Earl Roger was the linchpin in this resistance to the king. Framlingham Castle was quickly invested, and equally quickly taken. The king then sent letters of safe conduct to Bigod in an attempt to bring him into line. Meanwhile John systematically stripped the earl of his followers in the area by pardoning those captured and returning to them seisin of their properties, while declaring those who refused to submit disseised of their lands. But, despite these tactics, Roger and Hugh Bigod remained in rebellion, and indeed did not return to the loyalist fold until after the peace of Kingston (though before the peace of Lambeth) in September 1217. By April 1218 Bigod had received back all his lands and titles and withdrawn into semi-retirement, rarely appearing in the royal records before his death some time before 2 August 1221. He was succeeded as earl by his son Hugh (II) Bigod, who was of age at the time of his father's death, and who in 1206 or 1207 married Matilda, daughter of William (I) *Marshal (d. 1219). Their children included Roger (III) *Bigod, earl of Norfolk, and Hugh (III) *Bigod, the baronial justiciar.

Earl Roger (II) Bigod made a number of religious benefactions during his long life. He continued the family tradition of patronizing Earls Colne Priory, Essex, and the abbeys of Wymondham, Norfolk, and Rochester, Kent. He made grants to monasteries at Bungay, Suffolk, Carrow, Norfolk, Hickling, Norfolk, Leiston, Suffolk, and Sibton, Suffolk, as well as to the two cells of Rochester at Felixstowe, Suffolk, and at Harwich, Essex. All these grants mark him as a conventionally pious man of his age. Roger (II)'s period as earl of Norfolk was clearly a success, notwithstanding his being on the wrong side in the civil war against King John. His father, Hugh (I), had ended his life in disgrace and bequeathed a legacy to Earl Roger of Henry II's enmity and an inheritance dispute. By the time that Earl Roger himself died, the Bigod lands were secured and indeed probably expanded. Framlingham Castle was rebuilt, and, despite falling to the king's forces in March 1216, it did not suffer the same fate as its predecessor but remained the family *caput* until the eventual demise of the family in 1306. Moreover, Earl Roger left his son an undisputed inheritance.   S. D. CHURCH

Sources S. A. J. Atkin, 'The Bigod family: an investigation into their lands and activities, 1066–1306', PhD diss., U. Reading, 1979 · R. A. Brown, 'Framlingham Castle and Bigod, 1154–1216', *Proceedings of the Suffolk Institute of Archaeology*, 25 (1951), 127–48; repr. in R. A. Brown, *Castles, conquest and charters: collected papers* (1889), 187–208 · *Pipe rolls*, 13–14, 16 John; 2 Henry III · R. V. Turner, *The king and his courts* (1968), 108 · W. Stubbs, ed., *Select charters and other illustrations of English constitutional history*, 9th edn (1913), 164 [repr. with corrections, ed. H. W. C. Davis (1921)]

Wealth at death £162 3s. 4d.—knights' fees in Norfolk and Suffolk: Atkin, 'The Bigod family', 178; *Pipe rolls*, 13–14, 16 John, 177

Bigod, Roger (III), fourth earl of Norfolk (c.1212–1270), magnate and courtier, was the eldest son of Hugh (II) Bigod, earl of Norfolk, and his wife, Matilda Marshal (d.

1248). Hugh (III) *Bigod was his brother. Roger was a minor when his father died in 1225; his wardship went first to William (I) *Longespée, earl of Salisbury, but was transferred to *Alexander II, king of Scots, in 1226, when Salisbury died. Bigod had married Alexander's sister Isabella at Alnwick in May 1225. On 22 May 1233 Bigod was knighted at Gloucester by Henry III and invested with his earldom. In late July he appeared at High Wycombe, Buckinghamshire, among the supporters of his rebellious uncle Richard Marshal, earl of Pembroke, but by 8 September Bigod had submitted to the king and recovered all his property save Framlingham Castle, Suffolk, which the king held until February 1234. In January 1236, at the wedding of King Henry and Queen Eleanor, Bigod laid unsuccessful claim to the stewardship of England.

A noted tourneyer, Bigod distinguished himself in February 1237 at a politically charged tournament at Blythe, Nottinghamshire. As late as 1257 a serious illness was attributed to his exertions on that occasion. Having been one of the king's proctors in truce negotiations with France, Bigod urged that the truce be upheld in 1242. Nevertheless, he accompanied the king's expedition to Gascony, took a notable part in the skirmish at Saintes on 22 July, and returned to England in late autumn. In 1244 Bigod was among those chosen to negotiate with the king over the so-called 'paper constitution'. In 1245 he led an English delegation to the papal court at Lyons to protest against papal exactions from the English church. He also began annulment proceedings against his wife, Isabella, alleging consanguinity. Bigod was involved in further protests against papal exactions in March 1246, and in October 1249 went again on an embassy to Lyons. He did not formally take back his wife, however, until 1253, when a final verdict in favour of the marriage was declared by the church.

In 1246 Bigod became marshal of England in right of his mother, Matilda, eldest daughter of William (I) *Marshal, earl of Pembroke (d. 1219), and so heir to the office when her brothers all died childless. Upon his mother's death in 1248 Bigod also inherited substantial Marshal properties, especially in Ireland. Attached to this inheritance, however, was an obligation to make dower payments to the king's sister Eleanor, widow of William (II) Marshal (d. 1231) and wife of Simon de Montfort, earl of Leicester. The failure of Bigod and the other Marshal heirs to make good on these dower payments complicated relations between the king and his earls for years to come.

Throughout the 1240s and 1250s Bigod remained closely attached to the royal court. His extensive landholdings made him one of the half-dozen wealthiest earls in England, while his military prowess, diplomatic experience, and position as earl marshal made him a valued witness to royal charters and a central figure in negotiations between the king and his parliaments. By the mid-1250s, however, tensions between the king and Bigod were growing. As marshal, Bigod accompanied the military expedition of 1253 to Gascony, and argued unsuccessfully for an aid to support it in the parliament of January 1254, but he left the army in May 1254 in what Matthew Paris suggests were rancorous circumstances. In 1255 a violent quarrel erupted in parliament between Bigod and the king, resulting in a brief attempt by the king to summon all Bigod's outstanding debts for immediate repayment. Some of these debts derived from the Marshal inheritance, others from a long-standing dispute over the military service assessments of the earldom of Norfolk. The king's summons was quickly revoked, however, and Bigod's large debts remained unpaid.

More enduring were the hostilities generated by the king's Lusignan relatives. In 1256 Bigod came into open conflict with Aymer de Lusignan (d. 1260). In April 1258 he supported his brother-in-law, John Fitzgeoffrey (d. 1258), in yet another dispute with Aymer, joining in a sworn compact with several other great men to demand the expulsion of the king's Poitevin relatives and the reform of the realm. When the confederates appeared in arms at parliament at the end of that month, Bigod acted as their spokesman, and in the provisions of Oxford, drawn up in June and July, he was named to both the committee of twenty-four and the council of fifteen.

Bigod was active on the reform council until early 1260, when he supported King Henry's refusal to allow the Candlemas parliament of 1260 to meet in the king's absence. Bigod continued to regard the provisions as binding, however, and in 1261 took up arms again when the king appointed sheriffs in violation of them. In November 1261 he was one of three baronial representatives who negotiated the treaty of Kingston; and in January 1263, when the king reissued the provisions, he was one of four men whose advice the king promised to observe in future. In October 1263, however, when Simon de Montfort and his supporters broke decisively with the king, Bigod joined the king's side, and was listed among the king's supporters in the mise of Amiens of 23 January 1264. Bigod took no known part in the battle of Lewes on 14 May 1264, but afterwards co-operated with Montfort's government in East Anglia until Montfort's death at Evesham on 4 August 1265. Bigod died childless on 3 or 4 July 1270 and was buried at Thetford, Norfolk, two months after resigning as marshal of England in favour of his nephew Roger (IV) *Bigod, who became his heir. Isabella, his wife, was buried at Blackfriars, London, but the date of her death is unknown. ROBERT C. STACEY

Sources Chancery records · Paris, Chron., vols. 3–5 · GEC, Peerage · J. R. Maddicott, Simon de Montfort (1994) · D. A. Carpenter, 'Kings, magnates and society: the personal rule of King Henry III, 1234–1258', Speculum, 60 (1985), 39–70 · D. A. Carpenter, 'What happened in 1258?', War and government in the middle ages, ed. J. Gillingham and J. C. Holt (1984), 106–19 · R. F. Walker, 'The supporters of Richard Marshal, earl of Pembroke, in the rebellion of 1233–1234', Welsh History Review / Cylchgrawn Hanes Cymru, 17 (1994–5), 41–65 · Ann. mon., vol. 4 · CIPM, 2, no. 744

Bigod, Roger (IV), fifth earl of Norfolk (c.1245–1306), magnate and soldier, was the son of Hugh (III) *Bigod (b. in or before 1220, d. 1266), justiciar of England. He succeeded to his father's lands in 1266, and to the earldom of Norfolk when his uncle, Roger (III) *Bigod, died in 1270. He was twice married, first in 1271 to Aline Basset, widow of Hugh

Despenser, who died in 1281, and second in 1290 to Alice, daughter of the count of Hainault.

The hereditary office of marshal of England was entrusted to Bigod shortly before his uncle's death, and he performed the ceremonial duties associated with the office at Edward I's coronation. He served in all the major campaigns of Edward's Welsh wars (1277, 1282–3, 1287, and 1294–5). In the first war Bigod campaigned in north Wales, with the main royal army; in the later stages he commanded a force at Flint. In 1282, as was proper for the earl marshal, he again served in the main royal army in north Wales, performing his duty of registering the troops who were performing feudal service. In 1287 there was some dispute about his role as marshal, and he obtained royal letters testifying that nothing he had done on the orders of Edmund, earl of Cornwall, the regent, should prejudice his position in future. When the Welsh rebelled in 1294, he was ordered to go to fight in south Wales, and the king appointed Roger de Moels as marshal there. Bigod protested; once again the king promised that no precedent would be made of what had happened.

Bigod appears to have been in some financial difficulties by the 1290s. He owed money to Italian bankers, and in 1291 handed over some of his manors to the king. Relations between Bigod and Edward I deteriorated, with demands from the exchequer that the earl should pay off long-standing debts to the crown. In 1293 he owed £2232, and he petitioned in parliament that he should be excused payment. It was agreed that £1432 should be paid off in annual instalments of £100. The combination of grievances over his debts, and anger at the way that his rights as hereditary marshal had been disregarded, led to the earl's playing a leading role in the opposition to the king in 1297. At the Salisbury parliament in February a celebrated row occurred between them. The earl objected to the king's plan that he should be sent to fight in Gascony, while Edward himself campaigned in Flanders. 'By God, Sir Earl, either go or hang', declared Edward (Prestwich, 416); the earl did neither. When a muster took place at London on 7 July, Bigod and his colleague Humphrey (VI) de Bohun, earl of Hereford, the hereditary constable, were ordered to register those who had come to serve, as was customary when a feudal summons had been issued. This summons, however, did not take the normal form, and the earls refused the king's demand. They were promptly deprived of their offices. The opposition of the earls was not confined to the issue of military service; on the day that the king sailed for Flanders (22 August) they appeared with armed force at the exchequer to protest at the arbitrary imposition of a tax of an eighth. The crisis was eventually settled on 10 October, when the regency council agreed to confirm Magna Carta and the charter of the forest, and in the Confirmatio cartarum accepted additional concessions demanded by the opposition. The king, in Flanders, confirmed the concessions on 5 November, and pardoned Bigod and his colleagues. Details of the backing Bigod received in this period are revealed in two lists of his household, one from 1294–5, the other from 1297. The latter reveals a following that included five bannerets, nine knights, and some twenty men-at-arms and serjeants. An indenture Bigod drew up with John of Seagrave in 1297 shows how he recruited men by offering fees, robes, and wages.

Bigod was involved in the hearings of the Great Cause of 1291–2 over who should succeed to the Scottish throne: he was one of the magnates asked in 1292 to examine the pleadings. He campaigned with the king in Scotland in 1296, and was almost certainly of the opinion that Edward should not have departed for Flanders in 1297, when the Scottish situation was at a critical point as a result of William Wallace's rising. In the autumn of 1297 he entered into a contract to serve in Scotland with 130 cavalry for the winter campaign. He took part in the expedition of 1298, which culminated in the English triumph at Falkirk, but only after exacting promises that the king would observe the charters. After the battle of Falkirk he was angry at the way in which the king made grants of land in Scotland; once again he felt that his rights were being overridden. In 1299 he demanded a further confirmation of the charters from the king, and was clearly aggrieved at what he regarded as the king's evasiveness. He took no further part in Edward's Scottish campaigns, and entrusted his role as marshal to John of Seagrave.

Bigod held important lands in the Welsh marches, notably the lordship of Chepstow, as well as substantial estates in Norfolk, and highly profitable lands in Ireland. Many of his manorial accounts survive. He was responsible for major works at Chepstow Castle, where he built the present gatehouse and front, as well as luxurious domestic accommodation. He also built at Bungay in Suffolk, receiving a licence to crenellate in 1294.

In 1302 Bigod surrendered to the king his office of marshal and his lands, on condition that they should be regranted to him for life, and that he should receive an additional £1000 a year in land. By one account this was to spite his brother John, a cleric. John had lent Roger appreciable sums of money in the past, and demanded prompt repayment. It was in order to disinherit him that Roger struck the deal with the king. In 1305 a further arrangement was made: the earl was pardoned all his debts to the crown, on condition that his heir should pay £20,000 on his coming of age. As he had no heirs, there was little danger in this agreement, and although one chronicler explains these dealings as royal revenge for the earl's opposition, this seems unlikely. Bigod died in 1306, at a date before 6 December; his lands and office duly reverted to the crown, as had been agreed in 1302.

MICHAEL PRESTWICH

Sources Ann. mon. • Bartholomaei de Cotton … Historia Anglicana, ed. H. R. Luard, Rolls Series, 16 (1859) • Chancery records • Chronica Johannis de Oxenede, ed. H. Ellis, Rolls Series, 13 (1859) • W. Stubbs, ed., Chronicles of the reigns of Edward I and Edward II, 2 vols., Rolls Series, 76 (1882–3) • The chronicle of Walter of Guisborough, ed. H. Rothwell, CS, 3rd ser., 89 (1957) • M. Prestwich, ed., Documents illustrating the crisis of 1297–98 in England, CS, 4th ser., 24 (1980) • H. R. Luard, ed., Flores historiarum, 3 vols., Rolls Series, 95 (1890) • J. Ridgard, ed., Medieval Framlingham: select documents, 1270–1524 (1985) • N. Denholm-Young, Seigneurial administration in England (1937) • M. Prestwich, Edward I (1988) • CIPM, 4, no. 434

Archives Arundel Castle, family papers
Wealth at death financially embarrassed: CIPM

Bigsby, John Jeremiah (1792–1881), surgeon and geologist, was born on 4 August 1792 in Nottingham, the son of Dr Jacob Bigsby and his wife, Mary. Like his father, he pursued a career in medicine. He was first sent to school at St Andrews and then to Edinburgh University, where he graduated as doctor of medicine in 1814, joining the Edinburgh Infirmary as a resident shortly thereafter.

On 14 March 1816 Bigsby joined the army as an assistant surgeon, and served briefly at the Cape of Good Hope. In 1818 he moved to British North America, where he served as an assistant staff surgeon at Quebec. On a journey westward in 1818 his interest in the geological structures of the St Lawrence region was awakened, and he soon received instructions from the army's medical department to undertake a study of the geology of Upper Canada. During the summer of 1819 he travelled widely in the region collecting geological specimens, then returned to Quebec in the autumn and collected additional specimens on the north shore of the St Lawrence River.

Bigsby received his second commission in the winter of 1820–21, as assistant secretary and medical officer to the British party of the international boundary commission which arose out of the treaty of Ghent (1814). His explorations with the British and American survey in the summer of 1820 took him through northern Lake Huron, and in 1821 through the Lake St Clair and Lake Erie region. During the summer of 1822 the commission was idle, but Bigsby continued his own geological explorations of the Niagara Falls region. Then, in 1823, the boundary survey party resumed its work in the region to the west of Lake Superior to the Lake of the Woods along the forty-ninth parallel.

In 1820–25 Bigsby submitted reports of his field experiences and findings to various scientific journals, notably Benjamin Silliman's American Journal of Science, and to the Geological Society of London. He also submitted more theoretical papers, one of them, 'On the utility and design of the science of geology', in 1824. As a result of his efforts he was elected a fellow of the Geological Society of London in 1823 and became an honorary member of the American Geological Society in 1824, and a foreign member of the American Philosophical Society in 1825.

In 1827 Bigsby returned to England, and took up medical practice in Newark-on-Trent. Probably in the same year, he married Sarah Beevor of Newark. They later had two children. Bigsby became senior physician at the Newark hospital in 1840, after having served as local alderman and mayor. He continued in his scientific studies, writing local medical matters, and reading several papers to the London Geological Society.

With a modest income derived from his practice and his marriage Bigsby was able to move to London in 1847, and thereafter devoted greater effort to his writing and scientific papers. In 1850 he published a fine two-volume memoir of his earlier field experiences with the boundary commission, entitled The Shoe and Canoe. He also continued, from 1850 until 1864, to read and publish various geological papers on North America. With the support of the Royal Society he prepared in 1868 an extensive glossary of North American fossils entitled *Thesaurus Siluricus*. In the following year he was elected a fellow of the Royal Society, and received the Murchison medal of the society for his contributions. In his eighty-fifth year he published a second thesaurus, *Thesaurus Devonico-Carboniferous* (1878), and he was working on a third, relating to the Permian, when he died in 1881.

Before he died Bigsby founded a gold medal in his name for the Geological Society, to be awarded biennially to a student of American geology under the age of forty-five. His will bequeathed his library and geological works to the borough of Nottingham, for the use of students at the new University College at Nottingham. Bigsby was widely respected for his papers based on pioneering field work in North America. *The Geological Survey of Canada Report* of 1863 acknowledges his contributions to determining the mineralogy of the Lake Superior region, and notes that 'among the pioneers in Canadian geology, no observer was more accurate than Dr. J. J. Bigsby'. One of the Canadian recipients of the Bigsby medal, George Mercer Dawson, honoured the donor by naming a beautiful location he discovered on the Pacific coast, Bigsby Inlet, in the Queen Charlotte Islands. Bigsby died at home at 89 Gloucester Place, Portman Square, London, on 10 February 1881.   A. W. RASPORICH

Sources J. J. Bigsby, *The shoe and canoe, or, Pictures of travel in the Canadas*, 2 vols. (1850) · R. Etheridge, *Quarterly Journal of the Geological Society*, 37 (1881), 39–41 · *PRS*, 33 (1882), xvi–xvii · J. J. Bigsby, 'Localities of Canadian minerals with notes and extracts', *Literary and Historical Society of Quebec* (1827), 1–73 · J. Delafield, *The unfortified boundary: a diary of the first survey of the Canadian boundary line*, ed. R. McElroy and T. Riggs (1943) · M. Zaslow, *Reading the rocks: the story of the geological survey of Canada* (1975) · S. Zeller, *Inventing Canada: early Victorian science and the idea of a transcontinental nation* (1987) · d. cert. · *DCB*, vol. 11 · Boase, *Mod. Eng. biog.* · *The Times* (15 Feb 1881) · *The Times* (13 April 1881) · U. Nott. L., department of manuscripts and special collections · Newark library

Archives BGS, maps of Canada

Wealth at death under £9000: probate, 17 March 1881, *CGPLA Eng. & Wales*

Bigsby, Robert [Robert Grymbald Bigsby] (*bap.* 1806, *d.* 1873), antiquary, was born at Castle Gate, Nottingham, and baptized in Nottingham on 12 April 1806, the eldest child and only son of Robert Bigsby (1764–1825) and his wife, Sophia (*b.* 1781), daughter of John and Elizabeth Bray of Southwell. He had two sisters, Sophia Maria (*b.* 1809), who married Samuel Smith in 1839, and Dorothy. His first cousin was the distinguished geologist John Jeremiah Bigsby (1792–1881), elder son of Jacob Bigsby MD (1760–1844) of Nottingham. Other paternal uncles were the Revd Jeremiah Bigsby, rector of St Peter's, Nottingham, and the Revd Thomas Bigsby (*b.* 1757), of Stanton by Dale, Derbyshire, who married into the Stanhope family and is said to have acquired Drake memorabilia formerly owned by Philip Dormer Stanhope, fourth earl of Chesterfield (1694–1773).

The Bigsby family seems to have come from Stowmarket in Suffolk, but Robert Bigsby's early life was spent at Castle Gate, Nottingham, where his father, an attorney, held the post of registrar of the archdeaconry of Nottingham from about 1790 until his death. The younger Robert was educated at Repton School from 1818 and later lived in the area for eleven years while researching its history. On 2 December 1827 he married, in Repton, Elizabeth Swift (1808–1847), the daughter of William Swift and Mary, his wife, of Southwell. Their first child, Robert Henry, was baptized at Prestwold in Leicestershire on 6 October 1828 and another son, Bernard Edward Sulyard Drake, was baptized on 12 September 1835 at St Peter's, Derby.

Robert Bigsby was intended for a legal career, but never qualified, and instead devoted himself to literary and antiquarian pursuits. On 16 February 1837 he was elected fellow of the Society of Antiquaries and presented to the society a portrait, which it still has, of the antiquary William Burton, brother of Robert Burton. Four months later, on 8 June 1837, described as 'of Derby', and 'a gentleman much attached to science' (Royal Society election certificate, Royal Society Archives), Bigsby was elected a fellow of the Royal Society. His association with these learned bodies was brief and inglorious; he was removed from both in 1845 because of non-payment of subscriptions.

Bigsby was an ardent and eloquent advocate of public recognition and state financial support for men of letters. In 'Poetry and Poets' in *Miscellaneous Poems and Essays* (1842), he advanced 'the Claim of Literary Genius to Encouragement and Reward from the State' (*Miscellaneous Poems and Essays*, 323–40); elsewhere in this work he proposed a 'Temple of British Fame' (ibid., 201–14). Later publications commented on *The Expediency of Founding a National Institution in Honour of Literature* (n.d.) and described *National Honours and their Noblest Claimants* (1867). In 1858 he applied to Sir Thomas Phillipps for a recommendation for a state pension 'in consideration of long and meritorious literary services' (Bodl. Oxf., MS Phillipps-Robinson c.546, fols. 101r–105r) and, on 16 January 1860, was awarded a civil-list pension of £100.

Bigsby's first published work was a poem, 'The Triumph of Drake, or, The Dawn of England's Naval Power' (1839), and he collected a number of curios supposedly associated with Sir Francis Drake, including, from his uncle the Revd Thomas Bigsby, an astronomical compendium which he wrongly identified as an astrolabe. In 1831 he presented this instrument to King William IV, who in turn gave it to Greenwich Hospital, whence it passed into the collections of the National Maritime Museum. In 1861 Bigsby donated to the British Museum an eighteenth-century horn box bearing Drake's coat of arms.

When Bigsby published *An Historical and Topographical Description of Repton* (1854), with seventy valuable illustrations, including some by his son Robert Henry, it was the first substantive account of this ancient Derbyshire settlement, but his failure to gain access to local archives, such as those of Repton School, limited its historical value. In addition to the author's portrait, the volume included a sketch of his then home, Wilfred Cottage, in Church

Street, Ashby-de-la-Zouch, Leicestershire. By 1855 Bigsby had apparently moved away. His relations with local tradespeople in Ashby were acrimonious; a contemporary verse squib survives in the Leicestershire Record Office, satirizing his pomposity and snobbishness and, in particular, his insistence on the title of honorary LLD.

Bigsby was a portly, strong-featured man, with a contemporary reputation as a 'virtuoso' and collector of curiosities. A member of the order of St John of Jerusalem and a freemason, he was a prolific contributor to reviews and magazines for over thirty years. Literary works included poems, essays, historical tales and dramas, genealogical and mythological surveys. His topographical studies, the last of which was his edition of *The History and Antiquities of the Parish Church of St Matthew, Morley, by the late Rev. Samuel Fox* (1872), testify to the development of mid-Victorian interest in the local history of Derbyshire, an enthusiasm shared by antiquaries such as Llewellynn Jewitt and John Joseph Briggs of King's Newton. Robert Bigsby died at his home, 4 Beaufort Terrace, Peckham Rye, London, on 27 September 1873. MARGARET O'SULLIVAN

Sir John Harvard Biles (1854–1933), by Bassano, 1921

Sources R. Bigsby, *Miscellaneous poems and essays* (1842) · R. Bigsby, *An historical and topographical description of Repton* (1854) · Bodl. Oxf., MSS Phillipps-Robinson · election certificate, RS · Bigsby-Ison, correspondence and poem, Leics. RO, Misc. 264A and 264B · parish register, Repton, Derbyshire, 2 Dec 1827, Derbys. RO [marriage] · parish register, Repton, Derbyshire, Derbys. RO [burial] · parish register, Nottingham, St Peter, 12 April 1806, Notts. Arch. [baptism] · parish register, Nottingham, St Peter, 17 Jan 1803, Notts. Arch. [marriage] · *Repton School Register, 1620–1894*, ed. F. C. Hipkins (1895), 72, 104 · *CGPLA Eng. & Wales* (1873) · RS, Bigsby letters, 1839–1847 · parish register, Southwell [baptism]
Archives Bodl. Oxf., Phillipps-Robinson MSS · Leics. RO, Bigsby-Ison MSS · RS
Likenesses engraving (after daguerreotype by T. C. Browne), repro. in Bigsby, *Historical and topographical description*, frontispiece
Wealth at death under £200: administration, 5 Nov 1873, *CGPLA Eng. & Wales*

Bikaner, Sir **Ganga Singh Bahadur**. *See* Singh, Ganga (1880–1943).

Biles, Sir **John Harvard** (1854–1933), naval architect, was born at Portsmouth on 6 January 1854, the third son of John Biles, an official at Portsmouth Dockyard, and his wife, Margaret, second daughter of William Groombridge, of Ernehill, Kent. His childhood was spent at Portsmouth, where his interest in ships was quickened and his natural bent for mechanics was encouraged by his surroundings. He was educated at G. L. Oliver's school (subsequently the Mile End House School), Portsmouth; he then served his apprenticeship at Portsmouth Dockyard, when wood was being largely superseded by iron, and sails by steam power. The *Devastation*, on which he was chiefly engaged, was the first of the modern ships built entirely by the new methods.

In 1872 Biles came first on the list of candidates for a scholarship at the Royal School of Naval Architecture and Marine Engineering, moving in 1873 to the Royal Naval College, Greenwich, where he finished his three-year course in 1875. As was customary, he returned to the dockyards for practical experience, mainly at Pembroke, until in 1876 he was appointed Admiralty overseer at the Landore ironworks in south Wales, where he gained intimate knowledge of steel manufacture. Also in 1876 he married Emma Jane (*d*. June 1933), only child of Richard Hoskyn Lloyd of Pembroke. They had one son and two daughters.

Biles's ability was soon recognized, and on joining the Admiralty in 1877, he was given full opportunity to use his growing skill and knowledge. At this time no great importance was attached to the investigations of William Froude in estimating resistance of ships' models, but Biles, with his quick perception and vision, rightly judged the value of Froude's work, and studied its possibilities while he was still at the Admiralty.

In 1880 Biles was offered the post of chief designer to Messrs J. and G. Thomson, of Clydebank (later Messrs John Brown & Co.), where his reputation as a naval architect was soon established. Under his guidance the firm became famous for both naval and merchant ships, and his study of Froude's work led to improvements in hull form which resulted in faster passenger vessels. The *City of Paris* and *City of New York*, built in 1887, were revolutionary in design and construction, demonstrating the advantages of lighter construction coupled with adequate strength, made possible by scientific design.

In 1891 Biles was appointed to the chair of naval architecture in Glasgow University, a post he held until 1921. There he was popular for his teaching and his sympathetic understanding of his students, many of whom later became distinguished naval architects. He combined university lecturing with practical work on designs for various firms, and gave his students practical experience by allowing them to help with the plans. In 1907 he opened offices in Broadway, Westminster, as a consulting naval architect and engineer. His reputation was almost worldwide: he travelled widely, particularly in North and South America and in India, where his work was so highly regarded that on the death of Sir E. J. Reed, in 1906, he was appointed consulting naval architect to the India Office. The British Admiralty called him in as a consultant on many occasions, and he was associated with the development of river and shallow-draft vessels for use in Mesopotamia during the First World War.

Among the many government committees on which Biles served were the dry-dock experiments on the *Wolf* (1901–3) to test for the first time by actual measurements the stresses on the hull of a destroyer, a successful piece of experimental work which proved that the structure of a ship behaved as a beam; the Board of Trade departmental committee on boats and davits (1912) after the *Titanic* disaster; the ship designs committee (1904–5) appointed by Lord Fisher, from which emerged the design of the *Dreadnought*, completed under Sir Philip Watts, director of naval construction at the Admiralty. For his services on these and other committees he was knighted in 1913 and appointed KCIE in 1922. In 1926 he chaired a committee to examine the management of the royal dockyards. He was elected a member of council of the Institution of Naval Architects in 1889, vice-president in 1905, and honorary vice-president in 1919. His first paper, 'Some results of curves of resistance and progressive measured mile speed curves', was read to the institution in 1881, and his last, 'Draught and dimensions of the most economical ship', in 1931. For many years he served on the court of the Worshipful Company of Shipwrights and was master of the company in 1904. He published *The Marine Steam Turbine* in 1906 and *The Design and Construction of Ships* in 1908. The honorary degree of LLD was conferred upon him by the universities of Yale (1901) and Glasgow (1922), and of DSc by Harvard (1908). He was an honorary member of the Japanese Society of Naval Architects, and was decorated with the Egyptian order of Osmanieh in 1906.

Biles was a man of remarkable vitality, genial disposition, and physical stamina. That his work did not absorb all his energy is shown by his filling in his spare time, when working on the *Devastation*, reading the whole of Alison's *History of Europe* seated in the double bottom of the ship. A keen yachtsman, he won many prizes at Cowes, Dublin, and the Clyde regattas with his yawls *Caress* and *Lais*. He lived at Highfield, Wentworth estate, Virginia Water, Surrey, where he died on 27 October 1933, his wife having predeceased him by only four months.

EUSTACE HENRY WILLIAM TENNYSON-D'EYNCOURT, *rev.*
ANDREW LAMBERT

Sources D. K. Brown, *A century of naval construction: the history of the Royal Corps of Naval Constructors, 1883–1983* (1983) · *The Times* (28 Oct 1933) · *Nature*, 132 (1933), 702 · private information (1949) · *WWW*, 1929–40 · *CGPLA Eng. & Wales* (1934)

Likenesses Bassano, photograph, 1921, NPG [*see illus.*] · M. Greiffenhagen, portrait, priv. coll.

Wealth at death £14,515 19s. 5d.: probate, 10 Jan 1934, *CGPLA Eng. & Wales*

Bill, Robert (1754–1827), mechanic and inventor, was the son of William Bill and Mary, *née* Walton. Robert's father and uncle (Francis) had married coheirs Mary and Dorothy, daughters of William Hall Walton. The Bills of Farley Hall near Cheadle were an old Staffordshire family and from William's marriage the Bills inherited a large, freehold estate at Stanshope, Staffordshire.

Bill was intended for the army and thus did not progress beyond a school education. However, having a small, independent fortune, he did not enter a military profession but instead busied himself with literary pursuits and experiments for the public good. The walls of his garden at Stone, Staffordshire, were built so as longer to retain the sun's heat; his hothouse and grapery were warmed by iron cylinders; and his house was heated by a novel method of circulated hot air.

In 1795 Bill wrote and privately published a treatise on the danger of a paper currency in which he incidentally proposed the use of iron tanks for keeping and preserving water on board ship. These were later introduced with great efficacy into the navy although Bill received no reward or credit.

Upon moving to London Bill invested a large sum of money in a company formed to supply gas lighting for streets and houses. His chemical and mechanical knowledge was of great use in the planning, erecting, and regulation of apparatus but he left the company after falling out with the proprietors. Bill's enthusiasm and energy quickly turned from one project to another. He invested much effort and expense in the promotion of Edward Massey's logs for measuring a ship's way at sea. In 1806 he had printed and published *A short account of Massey's patent log and sounding machine, with the opinions of several captains in the navy … who have made trials with them*. Again, though, he received no reward from his investment. In 1811 he patented a machine for washing clothes and in 1813 the Navy Board tested his steam cooking apparatus. He pursued a system of elastic springs for keeping pianofortes in tune for an indefinite time. In 1820 he took out a patent for making ships' masts of iron; their subsequent failure at government trial he blamed on his instructions being incorrectly carried out when the masts were supported by elastic ropes instead of iron shrouds.

Bill's later years were chiefly concerned with experiments to render inferior species of timber more durable than any wood known but at small expense. After eight years of severe government testing the Navy Board was so convinced of the merits of the invention that he was authorized to build a ship at Deptford Dockyard using such timber. He did not live to carry this to fruition dying, after several weeks of illness, of angina pectoris at Great Bridge Cottage, Great Bridge, near Tipton, Staffordshire, on 23 September 1827. For several years prior to his death he had been living at Wednesbury.

Bill had married Sarah Perks, the daughter of an eminent solicitor; he was survived by her and their three daughters, Mary, Sarah, and Constantia. He was large in stature and, when not pursuing interests in natural philosophy, metaphysics, and experimental chemistry (he had a valuable library and expensive apparatus connected with the subject), he had a relish for painting, music, and poetry.   ROBERT SHARP

Sources *GM*, 1st ser., 97/2 (1827), 466–8 · will of Robert Bill, PRO, PROB 11/1755 · *DNB*
Archives Staffs. RO

Bill, William (*d.* **1561**), dean of Westminster, son of John Bill, was born at Ashwell, Hertfordshire, at the time a manor of Westminster Abbey. He was educated at St John's College, Cambridge, graduating BA in 1532–3, MA 1536, BTh 1544, and DTh 1547. As an undergraduate he was taught by John Cheke and Thomas Smith, and he adopted their new fashion of Greek pronunciation, an issue then much debated in Cambridge. Bill could not afford the modest sum payable to the college before he could be admitted to a fellowship; on his behalf Cheke petitioned Queen Anne, by way of her chaplain, Matthew Parker. Bill was duly elected on 7 November 1535. Among his contemporaries was Roger Ascham, and William Cecil was an undergraduate of the college (probably Bill's pupil). Between 1541 and 1543 Bill was Greek reader in the university, supported from the revenues of the new cathedral of Westminster. He was subsequently Linacre lecturer in physic, and on 10 March 1547 was elected master of St John's. In May that year he was appointed JP for Cambridgeshire, and on 9 June was admitted to the rectory of Sutton, Bedfordshire. In 1549 he served as vice-chancellor of Cambridge, hosting the royal visitation of the university which began in May. He became a familiar preacher at court and at Paul's Cross. In December 1550 he was named a tax collector for Cambridgeshire. On 19 March 1551 he was admitted to the rectory of Sandy, which, with Sutton, he retained for life. On 19 November following, having resigned the mastership of St John's, he was granted that of Trinity by Edward VI.

Bill had been licensed to preach early in Edward's reign, and on 18 December 1551 he was named one of six chaplains extraordinary to the king, who were supposed to alternate between attendance and itinerant preaching. On 6 March 1552 Bill received an annuity of £40 for this post. In October 1552 he and other royal chaplains examined and signed the (then) forty-five articles of religion. In June 1553 he was designated bishop of a new see of Newcastle upon Tyne; this had more to do with the duke of Northumberland's wish to profit from dismemberment of the bishopric of Durham than any pastoral mission envisaged for Bill. The plan collapsed with the king's death and Northumberland's failed coup. Bill was among those who hosted Northumberland when he visited Cambridge on 15 July in his last attempt to prevent Mary's accession. When this nevertheless occurred Bill was deprived of his mastership; it is said that he was actually manhandled from his stall by two fellows, George Boyse and Robert Gray. Bill received a royal pardon on 18 October 1553 and spent the rest of Mary's reign in quiet conformity at Sandy. It is not improbable that Bill's brother Thomas (*d.* 1552), who had been physician to Henry VIII and Edward VI, knew or suspected something of the illness which would shorten the queen's life (and therefore his brother's retirement).

Very likely Bill was in touch with Elizabeth's household at nearby Hatfield, and a role was designed for him in shaping the Elizabethan church. Indeed, he may well have been at Hatfield at the time of the queen's accession, since by next day he had been designated almoner and chosen to preach at Paul's Cross on the following Sunday, 20 November. According to Sandys, this key sermon was delivered 'to the great delight of the people' (Robinson, 4), being intended to promise reform while maintaining public order. A week later it was denounced as heresy by John Christopherson, Bill's successor at Trinity. Bill attended Mary's funeral as the new queen's almoner on 14 December, and on 1 January 1559 had the customary warrant for distributing alms. On 11 January he was restored to his Cambridge headship. On 9 April he again occupied the pulpit at Paul's, explaining why the Westminster Abbey conference had ended in the imprisonment of the Catholic leaders. On 5 July, having first (25 June) been made a fellow, he was elected provost of Eton. On 19 July he was appointed to the first ecclesiastical commission, and on 20 September he was instituted to the prebend of Milton Ecclesia in Lincoln Cathedral (having acquired the nomination from a grant to his brother).

Cecil listed Bill second only to Parker among clergy suitable for advancement, but although he was subsequently considered for the see of Salisbury he appears to have refused promotion. Nevertheless he was chosen to preside over the refoundation of Westminster Abbey as a collegiate church following the dissolution of the Marian monastery in June 1559. Bill is referred to as dean by March 1560, but was not formally appointed until the foundation (21 May); he and his chapter were installed on 30 June. Bill was now head of three major collegiate establishments. He spent about fifteen weeks a year at Eton, despite licence for permanent non-residence, and received the queen on a visit. At Cambridge, where he was also one of the royal visitors of July 1559, he helped to devise the proctors' cycle. At Westminster he made the first draft of the statutes for the second (or Elizabethan) collegiate church, which are the basis of the constitution by which Westminster Abbey still operates. His scheme follows the 1544 model common to the Henrician cathedrals, but with a more detailed curriculum for the school.

Bill died at Westminster on 15 July 1561 and was buried five days later in St Benedict's chapel, Westminster Abbey, where a monumental brass (a rare late example) remains. To the abbey he left a set of tapestries depicting Old Testament subjects (thought to be those still in the Jerusalem Chamber) and half his theological books; the other half was divided between Eton and Trinity. He gave 100 marks for the building of the new chapel at Trinity, and made provisions for the scholars of all his colleges. His personal property (in Hertfordshire, Cambridgeshire, and Essex) went to the children of his brothers John and Thomas, and to his sisters Elizabeth Gosnall and Mary Samwell. Cecil was one of his overseers.

C. S. KNIGHTON

Sources CPR, 1547–8, 81; 1550–53, 111, 382; 1553, 352; 1553–4, 467; 1558–60, 28, 63, 118 · CSP dom., 1547–53, nos. 74, 222, 739, 829; 1553–8, no. 961 · APC, 1552–4, 148 · CSP Scot., 1547–63, 345 · The chronicle and political papers of King Edward VI, ed. W. K. Jordan (1966), 101 · H. Robinson, ed. and trans., The Zurich letters, comprising the correspondence of several English bishops and others with some of the Helvetian reformers, during the early part of the reign of Queen Elizabeth, 1, Parker Society, 7 (1842), 4 · The diary of Henry Machyn, citizen and merchant-taylor of London, from AD 1550 to AD 1563, ed. J. G. Nichols, CS, 42 (1848), 149, 178, 201, 226 · H. C. Maxwell Lyte, A history of Eton College, 1440–1898, 3rd edn (1899), 165–6, 169–70 · T. Baker, History of the college of St John the Evangelist, Cambridge, ed. J. E. B. Mayor, 1 (1869), 124–9 · C. S. Knighton, ed., Acts of the dean and chapter of Westminster, 2 (1999), 22 · Westminster Abbey Muniments, 6478, fol. 2; 37939 · PRO, SP 12/4, nos. 38–9 · Correspondence of Matthew Parker, ed. J. Bruce and T. T. Perowne, Parker Society, 42 (1853), no. 3 · W. S. Hudson, The Cambridge connection and the Elizabethan settlement of 1559 (1980), 12, 54–6, 103, 108, 122, 137n. · D. M. Owen, Cambridge University Archives: a classified list (1988), 67 · Venn, Alum. Cant., 1/1.151 · J. Venn, ed., Grace book Δ (1910), 55, 452 · M. Dewar, Sir Thomas Smith: a Tudor intellectual in office (1964), 17 · Calendar of the manuscripts of the most hon. the marquis of Salisbury, 7, HMC, 9 (1899), 169 · will, PRO, PROB 11/44, fols. 296v–297 · J. S. N. Wright, The brasses of Westminster Abbey (1969) · [W. Camden], Reges, reginae, nobiles (1600)

Likenesses brass effigy on monument, in or after 1561, Westminster Abbey, London; repro. in Wright, Brasses of Westminster Abbey, 35

Wealth at death lands in Essex, Hertfordshire, Cambridgeshire, and London; particular cash bequests of more than £360: will, PRO, PROB 11/44, fols. 296v–297

Billfrith [St Billfrith] (d. 750×800?), anchorite, is mentioned in the Old English colophon which the scribe Aldred added to the Lindisfarne gospels (BL, Cotton MS Nero D.iv) at some time between 950 and about 970, when they were at Chester-le-Street. After naming Eadfrith, who wrote the gospels, and Æthelwald, who bound them, the colophon continues: 'And Billfrith, the anchorite, forged the ornaments which are on the outside, and adorned it with gold and gems and gilt-silver, pure metal' (Kendrick and others, 2.10). Billfrith's work does not survive and the gospels are now in a modern binding. It is likely, however, that it was in existence when Symeon of Durham was familiar with the book in the late eleventh and early twelfth centuries, when it was at Durham, for in describing the miraculous preservation of the book from sea water, he refers to its 'enrichment of gems and gold on the outside'. He evidently knew some traditions about the book, but it is unlikely that he knew any more about Billfrith's part in it than is mentioned in the colophon, for he goes on to state that 'Æthelwald ... ordered it to be adorned with gold and gems; and ... St Billfrith the Anchorite ... executed Æthelwald's wishes and commands with a craftsman's hand, producing an outstanding piece of work. For he was distinguished in the goldsmith's art' (Sym. Dur., Opera, 1.67–8). This appears to be a paraphrase of the colophon, but with a misunderstanding of the Old English so that Symeon has wrongly attributed to Æthelwald only the role of commissioning Billfrith, rather than that of binding the book. In fact, it is possible

that Billfrith's work was done rather later than Æthelwald's, which was probably carried out c.700. The reason for this is that Billfrith's name appears in the list of anchorites in the Liber vitae of Durham as it was compiled in the early ninth century (BL, Cotton MS Domitian vii, fol. 18). It there appears in a group of names which include the anchorite Echa, who died in 767, so that it is plausible to suggest that Billfrith too may have died in the second half of the eighth century. If that was the case, his work on the gospels would have been a generation later than Æthelwald's. The only other information about Billfrith is provided by Symeon of Durham, who records that a portion of his relics was taken to Durham by the sacrist Alfred, son of Westou, in the middle years of the eleventh century, and enshrined with the body of St Cuthbert. It is not possible to verify this statement, nor to determine from where the relics were brought, but they are indeed listed in an early twelfth-century Durham relic list.

DAVID ROLLASON

Sources T. D. Kendrick, T. J. Brown, R. L. S. Bruce-Mitford, and others, eds., Evangeliorum quattuor Codex Lindisfarnensis, 2 vols. (1960) · Symeon of Durham, Opera · [A. H. Thompson], ed., Liber vitae ecclesiae Dunelmensis, SurtS, 136 (1923) · C. F. Battiscombe, ed., The relics of St Cuthbert (1956)

Billing, Archibald (1791–1881), physician, was the son of Theodore Billing of Cromlyn, Ireland, and was born there on 10 January 1791. He entered Trinity College, Dublin, in 1807, graduated BA (1811), MB (1814), MD (1818), and was incorporated MD at Oxford on his Dublin degree on 22 October 1818. He spent some time in clinical study at Irish, British, and continental hospitals before settling in London about 1815. Billing was admitted a member of the Royal College of Physicians on 22 December 1818, and a fellow on 22 December 1819. He was censor of the college in 1823, and councillor from 1852 to 1855. Billing taught at the London Hospital from 1817, and was elected physician on 2 July 1822. In 1823 he began a course of clinical lectures, the first course of that kind given in London, combined with regular bedside teaching.

Billing's The First Principles of Medicine, which in its first issue in 1831 was hardly more than a pamphlet, grew to a bulky textbook. It became very popular, and ran to six editions. Billing gave special attention to diseases of the chest and was among the first medical teachers in London to make auscultation, as introduced by Laennec, a part of regular teaching. Billing's views on the cause of the sounds of the heart, first put forward in 1832, were only partially accepted. He restated them in the London Medical Gazette (26, 1840, 64), and also in his Practical Observations on Diseases of the Lungs and Heart (1852), a work much less successful than First Principles. Billing's aim in all his writings was to base medicine on pathology; their most striking feature is clearness of thought, and a striving after logical accuracy which sometimes appears overstrained. Beginning as an innovator, he came in the end to be conservative, and was opposed to what he regarded as the teachings of the German school.

Billing gave up lecturing at the London Hospital in 1836 and resigned as physician in 1845. He was invited to become a member of the senate of the University of London in 1836, and served on that body for a number of years. He became a fellow of the Royal Society in 1844. Billing took a great interest in art, and was himself a fair amateur artist and a connoisseur of engraved gems, coins, and similar objects. He published *The Science of Gems, Jewels, Coins and Medals, Ancient and Modern* (1867), an elaborate textbook, illustrated with photographs, which reached a second edition; a Mrs Billing is named as the translator of the book's appendix. Billing was a man of great physical as well as mental activity, and was perhaps the last London physician who occasionally visited his patients on horseback. He had been retired for many years before his death, which occurred at his house at 34 Park Lane, London, on 2 September 1881.   J. F. PAYNE, *rev.* MICHAEL BEVAN

Noel Pemberton Billing (1881–1948), by Elliott & Fry, 1920s

Sources *Medical Circular*, 1 (1852), 243 · *Medical Times and Gazette* (17 Sept 1881), 373 · *Proceedings of the Royal Medical and Chirurgical Society*, 9 (1880–82), 129 · *Medical Directory* (1881), 76–7 · Munk, *Roll* · BL cat.
Likenesses C. Baugniet, lithograph, 1846, BM, NPG · woodcut, repro. in *Medical Circular*
Wealth at death £45,546 12s.: probate, 26 Nov 1881, CGPLA Eng. & Wales

Billing, Noel Pemberton (1881–1948), aviator and self-publicist, was born on 31 January 1881 in Hampstead, the youngest child of Charles Eardley Billing, a Birmingham iron-founder, and his wife, Annie Emilia Claridge. He was educated at the high school, Hampstead; Cumming's College, outside Boulogne; Westcliff College, Ramsgate; and Craven College, Highgate. At the age of thirteen Billing stowed away on a ship bound for Delagoa Bay. In Durban he drifted into a succession of menial jobs before joining the Natal mounted police. From 1899 to 1901 he fought in the Second South African War. In 1903 he finally returned to England, and in the same year he married Lilian Maud (d. 1923), daughter of Theodore Henry Schweitzer, of Bristol. There were no children.

Billing was quick to see the military significance of air power, and this gave purpose to an otherwise chaotic life. He edited the new journal *Aerocraft* (1908–10), and in 1908 designed and tested, on his own airstrip in Fambridge, Essex, three light monoplanes, two of which left the ground. Billing then threw himself into land speculation, writing, yacht broking, and ship-running. By 1913 he had amassed enough capital to found a yard on Southampton Water, where he pioneered the construction of flying boats (supermarines). With characteristic bravado he had meantime obtained a pilot's certificate after only four hours two minutes in the air.

In 1914 Billing joined the Royal Naval Air Service. He organized the raid on the Zeppelin sheds in Friedrichshafen in November 1914. But in early 1916, then a squadron commander, he retired in frustration in order to publicize his complaints about the way the war in the air was being conducted. The tall, monocled, and debonair Billing drew large enthusiastic crowds to his meetings. Although

defeated as an independent candidate at Mile End in January 1916, he succeeded two months later at another parliamentary by-election at East Hertfordshire. Revelling in his role of 'first air member', Billing campaigned for a unified air service, helped force the government to establish an air inquiry, and advocated reprisal raids against German cities. He also became adept at exploiting a variety of popular discontents. In spring 1918 his increasingly outrageous language led to his being sued for criminal libel by the dancer Maud Allan. With his usual flair for publicity, Billing conducted his own defence, amusing and scandalizing the nation with his claim that the German government was in a position to blackmail 47,000 prominent British 'perverts', among them Herbert Asquith and his wife, whose names, he alleged, figured in a 'black book'. On being acquitted, Billing further annoyed the main parties by running his own 'purity' candidates at by-elections, under cover of an organization called the Vigilantes, of which he was president.

Although Billing retained his seat at the general election of 1918, ill health forced his retirement in 1921. In 1928 he had a play, *High Treason*, performed at the Strand Theatre. But most of his time was now absorbed by his various inventions, which included a miniature camera, a two-sided stove, and a gramophone; he claimed to have taken out 500 patents.

At the start of the Second World War Billing produced a design for a pilotless flying bomb; the British authorities turned it down. In 1941 he stood as an independent candidate in four by-elections, but although he retained his deposit on each occasion, there was to be no political comeback for this highly cantankerous patriot. Billing died on 11 November 1948 on his motor yacht *Commodore*, The Quay, Burnham-on-Crouch, Essex.

G. R. SEARLE, *rev.*

Sources N. Pemberton Billing, *P.-B.: the story of his life* (1917) · G. R. Searle, *Corruption in British politics, 1895–1930* (1987) · P. Hoare,

Wilde's last stand: decadence, conspiracy and the First World War (1997) · *CGPLA Eng. & Wales* (1949)
Archives FILM BFI NFTVA, news footage · BFI NFTVA, propaganda film footage (Vigilantes: morality pressure group)
Likenesses Elliott & Fry, photograph, 1920–29, NPG [*see illus.*]
Wealth at death £13,813 13s. 0d.: probate, 10 May 1949, *CGPLA Eng. & Wales*

Billing, Sir Thomas (*d.* 1481), justice, was perhaps born in Northamptonshire, the county with which he was most closely associated in later life. His parentage is unknown, and so his origins were doubtless modest. His coat of arms included an annulet in fesse point, apparently for difference, which would suggest that he was a fifth son. He was trained as a lawyer and was a member of Gray's Inn, where he was twice reader, conjecturally first in 1437 and again in 1445. In his professional career he appears to have been most closely associated with the city of London: without break, he served successively as its common serjeant (elected October 1443), under-sheriff (elected July 1449), and finally recorder (elected September 1450; resigned October 1454). In the last office he so pleased the mayor and aldermen that after his resignation he was granted both a fee of 20s. yearly and an annual present of 5 yards of good woollen cloth, for his diligent and fruitful service at the time of the 'great disturbance' (Cade's uprising of 1450) and afterwards. He was MP for Northamptonshire in the parliament of 1445–6, and for London in the first parliament of 1449.

Billing was created serjeant-at-law on 2 July 1453, and on 21 April 1458 was appointed a king's serjeant; as the latter he was again summoned to parliament, from 1459 onwards. In the early 1450s he was one of the lawyers retained by Queen Margaret of Anjou, and he was doubtless regarded as a supporter of the Lancastrians; at the Coventry parliament of November–December 1459 he was apparently one of the crown's legal advisers who drafted the bill attainting the duke of York and his leading followers. Nevertheless he must have changed his allegiance—perhaps after the battle of Northampton (10 July 1460)—for he was reappointed king's serjeant on 8 April 1461. On 9 August 1464 he was made a justice of the court of king's bench, and on 23 January 1469 he succeeded Sir John Markham as chief justice of that court; he retained the office through the Lancastrian readeption and after the restoration of Edward IV (being reappointed on 9 October 1470 and 17 June 1471), until his death. He appears to have been knighted only in 1475.

Billing was twice married: first to Katharine, daughter of Roger Gifford of Twyford, Buckinghamshire, who died on 8 March 1480; and then, late in his life, to Mary, daughter of John Folville and heir of Robert Wesenham of Conington, Huntingdonshire. She had previously been the wife of William Cotton of London (*d.* 1459), who was perhaps a lawyer, and then of Thomas Lacy (possibly another lawyer; he had been an executor of William Cotton's will). She died on 14 March 1500, according to her funerary monument, which formerly stood in St Margaret's Church, Westminster, the south aisle of which she had paid to be rebuilt. Billing died on 5 May 1481, and was buried in Biddlesden Abbey, Buckinghamshire; a memorial brass to him was later removed to the nearby church of Wappenham, Northamptonshire. The Billing male line ended with the death of his son Thomas in 1509, but his granddaughter Joan Billing (*d.* 1517) married John Haugh who became a justice of the king's bench.

NIGEL RAMSAY

Sources J. C. Wedgwood and A. D. Holt, *History of parliament*, 1: *Biographies of the members of the Commons house, 1439–1509* (1936), 76 · B. R. Masters, 'The common serjeant', *Guildhall Miscellany*, 2 (1960–68), 379–89, esp. 384–5 · E. W. Ives, *The common lawyers of pre-Reformation England* (1983), 27, 383 · Baker, *Serjeants*, 163 · Sainty, *King's counsel*, 11 · S. E. Thorne and J. H. Baker, eds., *Readings and moots at the inns of court in the fifteenth century*, 1, SeldS, 71 (1954), xxxii, lv · G. Baker, *The history and antiquities of the county of Northampton*, 1 (1822–30), 730 · B. Willis, *The history and antiquities of the town, hundred, and deanry of Buckingham* (1755), 152–3 · H. Ellis, ed., *The visitation of the county of Huntingdon ... 1613*, CS, 43 (1849), 27 · testament of William Cotton, PRO, PROB 11/4, sig. 15 · *VCH Huntingdonshire*, 3.147–8 · J. Weever, *Antient funeral monuments*, ed. W. Tooke (1767), frontispiece · N. L. Ramsay, 'The English legal profession, c.1340–1450', PhD diss., U. Cam., 1985, appx, xlix–l · *Chancery records* · J. G. Bellamy, *The law of treason in England in the later middle ages* (1970), 197
Likenesses memorial brass, Wappenham church, Northamptonshire

Billingham [Bullingham], **Richard** (*fl. c.*1344–*c.*1361), logician and theologian, was associated with Merton College, Oxford, as a fellow from *c.*1344 until *c.*1361. He held many offices at the college, was sub-warden for several years and is said to have presented to the college library tables on logic and philosophy that he had probably compiled himself; this material does not appear to have survived. He obtained from the university the degrees of MA and BTh. In March 1349, following the election of Dr William Hawkesworth as chancellor of the university, Billingham, with other fellows of Merton, was involved in disturbances in support of John Wylyot, also of Merton, who in fact became chancellor following Hawkesworth's death in April that year. The disputes concerning these elections produced rowdy disturbances in the university church of St Mary. Billingham wrote several important textbooks for use in the teaching of logic of which the most influential was his *Speculum puerorum* or *Terminus est in quem*. Here he discusses how propositions might be proved and suggests three modes of proof later adopted and expanded by John Wyclif. His works were widely studied in universities in England and on the continent, especially in those of the Holy Roman empire. Later English logicians relied heavily on his writings and, after study at Oxford, distinguished Italian scholars such as Paulo da Venezia spread an awareness of his arguments in their native country. It has been suggested that Billingham also wrote a commentary on the *Sentences* of Peter Lombard of which extracts only survive, and that these show a sceptical attitude to theological arguments associated with the followers of William Ockham. Others have challenged the opinion that Billingham's writings give evidence of any strong affinities with nominalist views.

JOHN M. FLETCHER

Sources Emden, *Oxf.*, 1.188–9 · A. Wood, *Historia et antiquitates universitatis Oxoniensis*, trans. R. Peers and R. Reeve, 2 vols. (1674), vol. 1, p. 171 · J. A. Weisheipl, 'Repertorium Mertonense', *Mediaeval Studies*, 31 (1969), 174–224, esp. 176–7 · P. V. Spade and E. J. Ashworth, 'Logic in late medieval Oxford', *Hist. U. Oxf. 2: Late med. Oxf.*, 35–64 · W. J. Courtenay, *Schools and scholars in fourteenth-century England* (1987)

Billinghurst, (Rosa) May (1875–1953), suffragette, was born on 31 May 1875 at 35 Granville Park, Lewisham, London, the second of nine children of Henry Francombe Billinghurst (*c.*1832–1912), bank manager, and his wife, Rosa Ann Billinghurst, *née* Brimsmead. At the age of five months she suffered an illness which resulted in paralysis from the waist down. For the rest of her life her legs were strapped in irons and she relied on the use of an invalid tricycle for mobility.

As a young woman May Billinghurst worked among Greenwich workhouse inmates, and with poor children in the Deptford slums. She also joined one of her sisters in the work of rescuing young girls from prostitution in Greater London. It was the injustices she encountered while engaged in this work that shaped her political beliefs and led her to join the fight for women's suffrage. She had been a member of the Women's Liberal Association, but resigned in early 1907 to join the newly formed Lewisham branch of the militant Women's Social and Political Union (WSPU). She became heavily involved in organizing campaign events and public meetings, and in June 1910 she helped form the Greenwich branch of the WSPU, becoming its honorary secretary. A familiar face now at WSPU events and demonstrations she became widely known as 'the cripple suffragette'. Her disability was certainly no bar to her participation in the physically demanding activities undertaken by suffragettes.

May Billinghurst joined her comrades at the WSPU demonstration in London on 18 November 1910, which was to become known as 'black Friday'. She was badly assaulted by the police, who, having pushed her down a side road by twisting her arms behind her back, pocketed the wheel valves of her tricycle leaving her unable to escape from the angry crowd. These harrowing events only made her more determined to participate in militancy. Four days later she was arrested at another demonstration and subsequently imprisoned for five days, for attempting to push her tricycle through a cordon of police. In March 1912 she was once again imprisoned for militant activity, sentenced to one month in Holloway prison for window-smashing.

A final term in prison in January 1913 for destroying the contents of a post-box was to test to the limits her political convictions. On starting her eight-month sentence in Holloway prison on 9 January 1913, she immediately went on hunger strike. Against the medical opinion of her own doctor, despite her infirmities, and against her will, the prison authorities attempted forcibly to feed her several times. One attempt to gag open her mouth was so violent that her teeth were damaged and her cheek gashed open. After serving only ten days, she was released from Holloway by the order of the home secretary. After her release she campaigned to stop the forcible feeding of suffragette prisoners and continued to battle for the vote.

With the onset of war May Billinghurst left Lewisham and went to live with her artist brother Henry Billinghurst in Regent's Park village. Her commitment to feminist societies continued throughout her life: she was a member of the Suffrage Fellowship and the Women's Freedom League, donating £100 in 1953 to Jill Craigie's Equal Pay Film Fund. The last few years of her life were spent living at 2 Fordbridge Road, Sunbury-on-Thames. She died on 29 July 1953 in St Mary's Hospital, Twickenham, from heart failure while recovering from pneumonia. Her unrelenting commitment to the welfare of women and her belief in reincarnation led her to leave her body to the London School of Medicine for Women.

May Billinghurst's obituary in the *Women's Freedom*

(Rosa) May Billinghurst (1875–1953), by unknown photographer, 1908 [centre, on her invalid tricycle]

League Bulletin on 4 September 1953 described her as having 'a strong sense of humour, even perhaps, a mischievous one … full of life and courage and not to mention jollity … [thinking] of this life as but one of many'.

HAYLEY TRUEMAN

Sources Women's Library, London, Billinghurst MSS, Autograph letter collection • H. Trueman, 'Going down in history—a portrait of Rosa May Billinghurst, militant suffragette', MA diss., University of Westminster, 1997 • *Women's Freedom League Bulletin* (4 Sept 1953) • I. Dove, *Yours in the cause: suffragettes in Lewisham and Greenwich* (1988) • C. Morrell, *'Black Friday' and the violence against women in the suffragette movement* (1981) • J. Purvis, 'The prison experiences of the suffragettes in Edwardian Britain', *Women's History Review*, 4 (1995), 103–33 • census returns for district of Lee, Lewisham, Kent, 1881, 1891 • b. cert. • d. cert. • will • *CGPLA Eng. & Wales* (1953)
Archives Women's Library, London, corresp. and papers relating to suffragette activities
Likenesses photographs, *c.*1908–1914, Women's Library, London [*see illus.*]
Wealth at death £24,343 11*s.* 2*d.*: probate, 24 Sept 1953, *CGPLA Eng. & Wales*

Billings, Joseph (*c.*1758–1806), explorer and hydrographer in Russia, was born about 1758 probably into the family of Joseph Billing, a fisherman, at Yarmouth. Other sources suggest that his parents were Thomas and Mary Billing, members of the gentry, and that he had a birth date of 6 September 1761 at Turnham Green, Chiswick, but this is less probable. After seven years with the coal fleet, he studied watch making. In April 1776 he joined the *Discovery* from Turnham Green as an able seaman on Cook's last voyage, acting as an assistant astronomer, and transferred to the *Resolution* in September 1779. Following service on the *Conquestador* and from May 1781 on the *Crocodile*, he became in July 1782 master's mate on the *Resistance* to Captain James King, often accompanying him on visits to Sir Joseph Banks, president of the Royal Society, with charts. He was imprisoned in December 1782 for a debt and the *Resistance* sailed to the West Indies without him, but a letter to Banks secured his release from the king's bench prison on 14 January 1783. After nearly commanding an Eastindiaman to Kamchatka, he transferred to the Russian navy as a midshipman in October 1783 and was promoted lieutenant in January 1794. According to a letter from Billings in the naval archives, he entered Russian service with the aim of participating in an expedition on the strength of his own experience during 1778 and 1780 with the *Discovery* and the *Resolution*, which sailed through the Bering Strait probing the pack ice north of Chukotka to assess the practicability of a northern passage to Europe. British claims to free trade by right of discovery and by opening the sea route to Kamchatka, together with the departure of the comte de la Pérouse's voyage of discovery to Kamchatka, accelerated the Russian north-eastern geographical and astronomical expedition of 1785–94, which Catherine II confirmed by an *ukaz* to the Russian admiralty in August 1785, appointing Billings its leader with the rank of lieutenant-captain.

The expedition's main tasks were to map the area from the mouth of the River Kolyma in north-east Siberia along the east Siberian sea shoreline to the Bering Strait; to chart the Chukotka peninsula inland from the Bering Strait as far as Cape Shelagsky; and to provide accurate maps of the chain of Aleutian Islands and others lying between Kamchatka and the American coast. Billings's instructions, drawn up by Professor P. S. Pallas, the eminent natural historian and scientist at the St Petersburg Academy of Sciences, covered all aspects of the expedition, including ethnography, and its 141 members were fully equipped with scientific instruments. In June 1787 the *Pallas* and *Yasashna*, ships commanded respectively by Billings and his Russian aide Gavriil Sarychev (subsequently hydrographer-general to the Russian navy), put to sea from Nizhnekolymsk on the River Kolyma, but their repeated attempts to reach the north Pacific were thwarted by icebergs, forcing them to return to the port of Okhotsk, where Lieutenant Robert Hall (later an admiral and governor of Archangel) and Vitus Bering's grandson had built two ships for the next stage of the expedition which lasted from September 1789 to 1791. Billings, by now a captain of the second rank, took over command of the *Slava Rossii*, with Sarychev as his second officer, the other ship having been scuttled in Okhotsk harbour. From Kamchatka, and later joined by Hall in the *Chorny Oryol*, they surveyed large areas of the Pacific, making detailed descriptions of the peoples and places they visited. During 1791 Billings, promoted to captain of the first rank, again attempted in vain to reach the River Kolyma, this time by the sea route through the Bering Strait. Following instructions he then handed over command of the *Slava Rossii* to Sarychev while he travelled overland across northern Chukotka to its most north-western point at Cape Shelagsky, a journey lasting six months. This final phase of the expedition, begun in the autumn of 1791 and completed in February 1792 under extremely difficult conditions, made an outstanding contribution to the geographical knowledge of Chukotka by providing the first detailed and reliable maps and accounts of it, compiled by Billings and others. The expedition accomplished most of its tasks and returned to St Petersburg in March 1794 with a rich crop of material—many new species of birds and animals and numerous ethnographic items associated with the Aleuts and the north-east Asian peoples. The Russian naval archives at St Petersburg hold Billings's reports and letters written during the expedition, his productive journals from 1785 to 1792 and F. V. Karzhavin's contemporary Russian translation of them, as well as seventeen maps by Billings. Cape Billings, at the west entrance to Gulf Long in the east Siberian sea, and three other geographical locations have been named after him. William Eton, who wrote on trade, recorded details of several conversations with Billings which shed more light on the expedition, in particular Russian claims to all the American coast as far as lat. 56½° N by prior discovery, and the abuses of Russian merchants in plundering and depopulating islands. Billings also described his involvement in Russian expansionist plans for territory on the River Amur.

In August 1795, awarded the order of St Vladimir and financially rewarded for leading the expedition, Billings transferred from the Baltic to the Black Sea Fleet at his own request. On his arrival at Sevastopol, he was appointed commander of the frigate *Svyatoy Andrey*, returning to St Petersburg on an official visit from 30 September 1796 to 24 February 1797. Between June and August 1797 he conducted an extensive hydrographic survey of the Black Sea area on the gunboat *Rozhdestvo Bogoroditsy* before resuming command of the *Svyatoy Andrey* and then, in March 1798, captaining the *Svyatoy Mikhail*, a new ship built at Kherson. However, in May of that year he continued his very comprehensive survey of the Black Sea coastline from Sevastopol, refusing to return to his former ship on the grounds that he had been commissioned to map the Black Sea by the chief naval authorities. On 9 May 1799 Billings was promoted captain-commodore. Utilizing his own very accurate findings and the data of previous surveys, he drew up an atlas, highly valued by hydrographers as a navigation guide to the Crimean coast, under the title of *Maps and views of the Black Sea area belonging to the Russian empire, compiled by Fleet Captain-Commodore Billings* (1799). Although nominated to command a recently proposed 100 gun ship on 21 May 1799, he never took up the post but was discharged from the navy on 28 November with a full pension. Joseph Billings served his adopted country conscientiously and patriotically, combining great powers of endurance with humanity for oppressed peoples. After living for a short while in the Crimea he retired to Moscow, where he died in 1806 and was buried. His wife, Yekaterina, *née* von Pestel (*b.* 14 June 1772), died at Moscow on 18 June 1827.   JOHN H. APPLEBY

Sources A. I. Alekseev, 'Joseph Billings', *GJ*, 132 (1966), 233–8 · M. Sauer, *An account of a geographical and astronomical expedition to the northern parts of Russia* (1802) · expedition of Eton and Billings, NL Scot., MS 1075, fols. 212–17 · admiralty muster books, PRO, ADM 36/7347, 8049, 9730, 9742 · commitment book, PRO, PRIS 4/9, fol. 35 · J. Billings, letter to Sir Joseph Banks, 8 Jan 1783, RBG Kew, Banks MSS, vol. 1, doc. 122 [copy at NHM, Botany Library, Dawson Turner Collection, 3.2–3] · *Katalog atlasor kart i planor arkhiva Gidrograficheskago Departamenta Morskago Ministerstva* [Catalogue of atlases, maps, and plans of the hydrographic department's archives of the naval ministry], 2 vols. (1849–52) · B. Maslennikov, *Morskaia karta rasskazyvayet istoriyu* [The naval map tells a story], ed. N. I. Smirnov, 2nd edn (Moscow, 1986) · Z. D. Titova, *Etnograficheskie materialy Severo-Vostochnoi geograficheskoi ekspeditsii, 1785–1795* (Magadan, 1978) · A. G. Cross, *By the banks of the Neva: chapters from the lives and careers of the British in eighteenth-century Russia* (1997) · *Nova Acta Academiae Scientiarum Imperialis Petropolitanae*, 12 (1801), 21–5, 29–32; 13 (1802), 346–51 · T. V. Stanyukovich, *Etnograficheskaya nauka i muzei* (Leningrad, 1978) · *The correspondence of Jeremy Bentham*, 3, ed. I. R. Christie (1971), 281 · M. I. Belov, *Arkticheskoe moreplavanie s drevneisheikh vremen do serediny XIX veka* [Arctic navigation] (Moscow, 1956) · *John Ledyard's journey through Russia and Siberia, 1787–1788: the journal and selected letters*, ed. S. D. Watrous (1966)
Archives Russian naval archives, St Petersburg, expedition journals, fond 913, op. 1, d. 160, 243 and 258 · Russian naval archives, St Petersburg, service record, fond 406, op. 7, d. 55, fols. 184v–185 | NL Scot., Eton and Billings expedition, MS 1075, fols. 212–17 · Russian naval archives, St Petersburg, Billings expedition reports, letters, maps, etc., fonds 172, 179, 198, 212, 214, 913, and 1331

Billings, Robert William (1813–1874), architect and author, was born in London. Of his parents, nothing is known. At the age of thirteen, he was apprenticed to John Britton, the eminent topographical draughtsman for

seven years, during which time he acquired excellent skills in drawing, which he afterwards exemplified in a series of works, published at brief intervals over the next fifteen years. He illustrated George Godwin's *History and Description of St Paul's Cathedral* (1837) and Frederick Mackenzie's *Churches of London* (2 vols., 1839), of which the plates were chiefly engraved by John Le Keux. He also assisted Sir Jeffry Wyatville on drawings of Windsor Castle, and prepared numerous views of the ruins of the old houses of parliament after the disastrous fire.

Billings's own publications included: *Illustrations of the Temple Church, London* (1838); *Gothic Panelling in Brancepeth Church, Durham* (1841); *Kettering Church, Northamptonshire* (1843); and the more important *Architectural Illustrations and Description of the Cathedral of Carlisle* (1840) and *Architectural Illustrations and Description of the Cathedral Church at Durham* (1843). His highly regarded *Illustrations of the Architectural Antiquities of the County of Durham* (1846; repr. 1974) preceded his greatest work, for which he is chiefly remembered, *The Baronial and Ecclesiastical Antiquities of Scotland* (4 vols., 1845–52), a magnificent collection of 240 illustrations, with an explanatory text. His other works, dealing almost exclusively with the technicalities of his art, are: *An attempt to define the geometric proportions of Gothic architecture, as illustrated by the cathedrals of Carlisle and Worcester* (1840); *Illustrations of Geometric Tracery, from the Panelling Belonging to Carlisle Cathedral* (1842); *The Infinity of Geometric Design Exemplified* (1849); and *The Power of Form Applied to Geometric Tracery* (1851). From 1834 to 1837 Billings lived in Bath, where he executed watercolour drawings of churches. Examples of his watercolours are in the Victoria Art Gallery, Bath, and the National Gallery of Scotland, Edinburgh.

After 1852, Billings turned his attention to his professional practice, which expanded rapidly. His designs were exhibited regularly at the Royal Academy between 1845 and 1872, and record his work on: the restoration of the chapel of Edinburgh Castle (a government commission); the Douglas Room in Stirling Castle; Gosford House, East Lothian, for the earl of Wemyss; the restoration of Hanbury Hall, Worcestershire; Crosby upon Eden Church, Cumberland; Kemble House, Wiltshire; and additions to Castle Wemyss, Renfrewshire, for John Burns. He was engaged on the last of these at the time of his death, having built the castle itself many years before. Of his built works, recent architectural historians have commented: 'it is curious that so sensitive and so exquisite a draughtsman should have designed such brutally detailed buildings' (Gomme and Walker, 20).

Billings was elected an associate of the Institute of British Architects in 1835, and later became director of the Crystal Palace board. On 21 April 1836 he married Antoinette, *née* Clarkson (*d.* 1884). After 1865 he lived at Putney, where he purchased an old English residence, The Moulinère, which had once been occupied by the famous duchess of Marlborough. He died there on 14 November 1874 and was survived by his wife.

During the latter years of his life Billings began to execute a panoramic view from the dome of the interior of St

Paul's Cathedral. The unfinished drawing, which is on a very large scale, was deposited in the library of the dean and chapter in 1884. Many of the drawings he prepared for publication are now in the RIBA drawings collection.

ANNETTE PEACH

Sources Dir. Brit. archs. • The Builder, 32 (1874), 982 • Catalogue of the drawings collection of the Royal Institute of British Architects, Royal Institute of British Architects, 20 vols. (1969–89) • Mallalieu, Watercolour artists • Graves, RA exhibitors • A. Gomme and D. Walker, Architecture of Glasgow, rev. edn (1987) • R. W. Billings, Illustrations of the architectural antiquities of the county of Durham (1846); repr. (1974) • Sessional Papers of the Royal Institute of British Architects (1876–7), 5 • CGPLA Eng. & Wales (1874)
Archives NG Scot. • RIBA, Nomination MSS, Av 1 p. 28 • RIBA BAL, MSS Collection • Victoria Art Gallery, Bath | NL Scot., letters to Blackwoods
Wealth at death under £2000: probate, 12 Dec 1874, CGPLA Eng. & Wales

Billingsley, Sir Henry (d. 1606), merchant and translator, was the third son of William Billingsley (d. 1553), haberdasher, and his wife, Elizabeth Hardy (or Harlow). The Roger Billingsley named by Wood as his father was in fact his grandfather. He matriculated pensioner at St John's College, Cambridge, in 1550 and was a scholar there in 1551. Wood says 'he spent some time among the muses in this [Oxford] university' (Wood, Ath. Oxon., 1.761), where he developed a taste for mathematics, allegedly from David Whitehead (1492–1571), a former Augustinian friar turned protestant priest. Billingsley took no degree in either place; he was apprenticed to a London haberdasher, was made free of the Haberdashers' Company by patrimony on 6 November 1560, and prospered in that trade. He rose to be master of the Haberdashers' Company in 1584–5, 1590–1, 1595–6, and 1605–6.

Billingsley's first translation, and one which he noted at the end of the text as having been 'most faithfully perused by M. David Whitehead', was Most learned and fruitfull commentaries of D. Peter Martir Vermilius, … upon the epistle of S. Paul to the Romanes … lately translated out of Latine unto Englishe, by H. B. (1568). The work for which he was best known was the translation of Euclid's Elements of Geometry (1570). Billingsley's own volume of Euclid, now in Princeton College Library, comprised a Greek text and a copy of Proclus on book 1, both published in 1533, bound with a Latin text which had come through the Arabic, translated by Adelard of Bath, then by Campanus, 1558, and the first Greek to Latin translation by Zamberti, published in Venice in 1505. Campanus was responsible for confusing the mathematician Euclid of Alexandria with a later Euclid, a philosopher of Megara, an error which Billingsley perpetuated. Billingsley's manuscript notes in his volume show that he worked mainly from the Greek, corrected by Zamberti's Latin version, supplementing it with extensive additions and commentaries taken from the earlier editions. In a preliminary note 'from the Translator to the Reader' he explained why he had undertaken this monumental task: 'without the diligent studies of Euclides Elementes it is impossible to attaine unto the perfect knowledge of Geometrie, and consequently of any other

of the Mathematicall sciences'. Its usefulness was considerably increased by a 'Mathematical preface' contributed by John Dee, in which he classified and described the mathematical arts. He also corrected the translation of passages which Billingsley had failed to understand. Dee too saw the value of a translation into English, which, when mathematical accuracy was becoming necessary for technical development, brought Euclid within reach of those who came to mathematics from the craft side. He was very proud of his preface, which became better known than Billingsley's translation.

Billingsley undertook various royal and civic duties: he was alderman of Tower ward (1585–92) and thereafter of Candlewick ward until his death. In 1594 he became president of St Thomas's Hospital, and from 1598 was farmer of the customs at the Port of London. He was senior alderman in 1596, when Queen Elizabeth made it known that she did not want Billingsley as lord mayor. Under protest the aldermen elected Thomas Skinner, but he died in December, two months after entering office, and Billingsley was then elected. He was knighted in 1597 at a date between 19 January and 21 February.

From his first marriage, to Elizabeth Bourne (1541/2–1577), Billingsley was left with at least five children, including his heir, Henry (b. 1564), who entered Gray's Inn in 1591, was knighted by James I in 1603, and who inherited Liston, Gloucestershire, where in 1613 he entertained Queen Anne. Billingsley's second marriage, to a widow, Bridget (d. 1588), daughter of Sir Christopher Draper, was childless; the third, to Kathleen Killigrew, widow Trappe, may have brought more children, but the fourth, in 1598, to Elizabeth (d. 1605/6), daughter of Richard Peacocke of Finchley, and widow of Rowland Martyn, and fifth, to Susan Tracey (d. 1633), widow Barger, were also childless. Billingsley's will demonstrates his considerable wealth; he had already given, or now bequeathed, property and money in excess of £1000 to his surviving children, Henry, Thomas, John, Elizabeth (and her husband John Quarles), and Katharine. He founded two scholarships at St John's College, Cambridge, and gave money to Emmanuel College, Cambridge, for the purchase of land, and to his nephew Martin Billingsley (1591–1622), writing-master. A joint bequest with Elizabeth Martyn, consisting of 1s. a week to the poor of St Katharine's parish, and £200, was annotated on the parish benefactions board, 'which their heirs have not paid' ('Jewers' monumental inscriptions', fol. 592). Billingsley's first wife was buried at St Katharine Coleman; his second was buried at St Dunstan-in-the-East; his fourth asked in her will to be buried alongside her first husband, Rowland Martyn, at St Gregory by Paul, and desired that her monument should record both spouses 'because they dealt so lovingly with me both in their lives' (ibid., fol. 593). Billingsley died in November 1606 in London and was buried at St Katharine Coleman, London, on 18 November.

ANITA McCONNELL

Sources 'Jewers' monumental inscriptions', GL, MS 2480/2, fols. 584, 588–9, 592–4 • A. B. Beaven, ed., The aldermen of the City of London, temp. Henry III–[1912], 2 vols. (1908–13) • Venn, Alum. Cant. • A. G.

Debus, 'Introduction', in J. Dee, *The mathematicall praeface to the elements of geometrie of Euclid of Megara* (1570) (New York, 1975), 1–30 • will, PRO, PROB 11/108, sig. 91 • parish register, London, St Katharine Coleman, GL • R. Cooke, *Visitation of London, 1568*, ed. H. Stanford London and S. W. Rawlins, [new edn], 2 vols. in one, Harleian Society, 109–10 (1963), 69–70 • R. Tresswell and A. Vincent, *The visitation of Shropshire, taken in the year 1623*, ed. G. Grazebrook and J. P. Rylands, 1, Harleian Society, 28 (1889), 46–7 • *The visitation of London, anno Domini 1633, 1634, and 1635, made by Sir Henry St George*, 1, ed. J. J. Howard and J. L. Chester, Harleian Society, 15 (1880), 71 • Haberdashers' Company, freedom admissions, GL, MS 15857/1, fol. 98v • Wood, *Ath. Oxon.*, new edn, 1.761–2 • repertories of the court of aldermen, CLRO, vol. 41, 204 • private information (2004) [Society of Genealogists] • D. M. Simpkins, 'Early editions of Euclid in England', *Annals of Science*, 22 (1966), 225–49 • W. Jaggard and T. Pavyer, *A view of all the right honourable the lord mayors of this honorable citty of London* (1601)

Likenesses woodcut, repro. in Jaggard, *View of all the lord mayors*
Wealth at death over £1000: will, PRO, PROB 11/108, sig. 91

Billingsley, John (1625–1683), clergyman and ejected minister, was born on 14 September 1625 at Chatham, Kent, the son of Thomas Billingsley. He attended Rochester School before matriculating on 8 July 1642 at Exeter College, Oxford. He was admitted to St John's College, Cambridge, in 1644 and graduated BA in 1648, but the same year he returned to Oxford on his election to a Kentish fellowship at Corpus Christi College. He proceeded MA in 1649, and on 26 September that year received presbyterian ordination at St Andrew Undershaft, London. In July 1650 he became vicar of Faringdon, Berkshire. In 1652 he was appointed vicar of Addingham, Cumberland, as part of the initiative to send godly preachers to the remoter parts of England. Active in the local association of ministers, he was a strong advocate of presbyterian discipline in church government and a penetrative preacher whose 'style was plain … [and] voice, sweet and audible, tho' not very strong' (Calamy, *Abridgement*, 2.169). Also in 1652 he married Mary, daughter of Immanuel *Bourne, presbyterian rector of Ashover, Derbyshire. They had two children who survived into adulthood, a daughter, Joyce, and a son, John *Billingsley (1657–1722).

On 18 March 1654 Billingsley was presented to the living at Chesterfield, Derbyshire, under authority of the great seal. Along with several other local ministers he held a dispute there with the Quaker James Nayler on 3 January 1655, which his father-in-law, Immanuel Bourne, recounted in his *A Defence of the Scriptures* (1656). The dispute became more contentious as Billingsley subsequently published *Strong Comforts for Weak Christians* (1656) and later *The Grand Quaker Prov'd a Gross Liar*, the latter provoking George Fox to publish a reply. Appointed to the Derbyshire commission on 24 October 1657, Billingsley became a prominent figure in local affairs and did not hide his royalist sympathies. He 'prayed publickly for the king when it was hazardous to do it' (Calamy, *Abridgement*, 2.170) and was summoned before the council on 17 September 1659 to answer charges of misdemeanour. The Restoration spared him further prosecution but not Anglican reprisals. On 16 July 1661 he was presented at the Derbyshire sessions for neglecting to read common prayer and in 1662 he was ejected from his living. At his farewell sermon he complained 'that the prelatical ministers, at least some, were put out for murder, drunkenness, whoredom & c—but such as himself, for being too holy and too carefull of religion' (Calamy rev., 54). Billingsley was severely reprimanded by the bishop of Lichfield for this outburst and he subsequently made profuse apologies. Some time in or before 1665, his first wife having died, he married Alice, whose other name is unknown.

Billingsley remained in the Chesterfield area until the passing of the Five Mile Act when he moved to Mansfield. Here he enjoyed the friendship of the vicar, John Firth, and the fellowship of other ejected presbyterian ministers. He went once a fortnight to preach at Chesterfield, often travelling late at night to avoid detection. In 1669 he was identified as preaching in Mansfield and in 1672 licensed to preach at both Nottingham and Mansfield. His frail health was considerably weakened by these many exertions and towards the end of his life, as his itinerant activities were curtailed, he established a dissenting academy at Mansfield as an alternative means of livelihood. Surviving records suggest that his son, John, had responsibility for running it. Not long afterwards, on 30 May 1683, Billingsley died at Mansfield; he was buried there on 1 June. According to Baxter, 'he made actual preparation for death' (Carpenter, 84). No funeral sermon was to be given, by his order, possibly to avoid confrontation with the authorities, but a 'suitable consolatory Discourse was preached to his family on the Lord's day following by Mr Sylvestor' (Calamy, *Abridgement*, 2.170). His will, proved at York on 21 June 1683, bequeathed £202 in cash alone. His inventory is severely damaged but valued his goods in excess of £100, of which his library of 47 folios, 122 quartos, and 217 lesser books was valued at £44. The majority of these appear to have been incorporated into the academy's library. His widow died on 18 September 1690.

STUART B. JENNINGS

Sources Calamy rev. • J. Nayler, *A dispute between James Nayler and the parish teachers of Chesterfield* (1655) • will and inventory, 21 June 1683, Notts. Arch., PRNW • E. Calamy, ed., *An abridgement of Mr. Baxter's history of his life and times, with an account of the ministers, &c., who were ejected after the Restauration of King Charles II*, 2nd edn, 2 vols. (1713) • I. Bourne, *A defence of the scriptures* (1656) • J. H. White, *The story of the old meeting house, Mansfield* (1959) • Venn, *Alum. Cant.* • Wood, *Ath. Oxon.*, new edn • C. G. Bolam and others, *The English presbyterians: from Elizabethan puritanism to modern Unitarianism* (1968) • B. Carpenter, *Some account of the original introduction of Presbyterianism into Nottingham and the neighbourhood* (1862)

Wealth at death £202 in cash; more than £100 in goods; land in Derbyshire: will and inventory, Notts. Arch., PRNW 21 June 1683

Billingsley, John (1657–1722), Presbyterian minister, was born at the vicarage at Chesterfield in Derbyshire, the only son of John *Billingsley (1625–1683), vicar of Chesterfield, and his wife, Mary (d. in or before 1665), daughter of the puritan minister Immanuel Bourne. Educated at Nottingham by John Reyner (son of Edward Reyner, the presbyterian minister of Lincoln), Billingsley briefly attended Trinity College, Cambridge, but did not matriculate. Instead he continued his studies under his father, who kept a school in Mansfield, Nottinghamshire, and his uncle, John Whitlock the elder. In a remarkable instance of hereditary succession Billingsley, John Oldfield, and Samuel Coates were ordained together by their fathers at Mansfield in September 1681. On 22 August 1682 Billingsley married Dorcas Jordan (*d.* 1717) at Oliver Heywood's chapel at Coley, Northowram, Yorkshire. After preaching for a time to his father's former flock at Chesterfield, he moved to Sheffield to assist the Presbyterian Edward Prime. He ministered in and around Selston, Nottinghamshire, from about 1687 to 1694, when he accepted a call to succeed Samuel Charles as pastor to a joint congregation of Presbyterians and Independents at Kingston upon Hull. There he remained until 1706 when he was elected to replace Samuel Rosewell as assistant to William Harris at the Presbyterian meeting of Crutched Friars, London. He also preached a Sunday evening lecture to a society of young men at the Old Jewry, in which he expounded the Westminster assembly's shorter and larger catechisms. Despite his own orthodoxy, when the Exeter Trinitarian controversy divided London dissenters at the Salters' Hall synod in 1719 Billingsley sided with the non-subscribers, who thought the imposition of religious tests of any sort violated the fundamental principle of dissent. It is not clear whether his decision was at all affected by the prominent role taken by his cousin Nicholas Billingsley, of Ashwick, Somerset, in sheltering the Arians Hubert Stogdon and James Foster.

With its uncompromising insistence that 'strictness is not fanaticism', Billingsley's first work, *The Believer's Daily Exercise* (1690), placed him squarely within the godly tradition. Dedicated to his Selston congregation, it offered a wealth of practical guidance to help serious Christians distinguish themselves from hypocrites and formalists. This included warning readers against wasting their mornings 'between the comb and the glass', like 'the gaudy butterflies and gay peacocks of our days', and advising them, quite specifically, on what and how to read (pp. 71, 9). Personal reformation alone, however, was not sufficient, as Billingsley made clear in his two sermons preached before the societies for reformation of manners in Hull and London (1700, 1706). Christians must be reformers, first of themselves, 'but next of others also' (Billingsley, *A Sermon Preached to the Societies for the Reformation of Manners*, 1706, 20). After defending the societies from the usual charges of canting and meddling, Billingsley employed the language of patriotic whiggery in contrasting the slavishness sown in their debauched subjects by absolute monarchs with the sobriety which sustained England's freedom: 'sobriety and the love of liberty are twins that laugh and live, mourn and die together' (ibid., 18). Besides a number of separate sermons he also published *Brief Discourse of Schism* (2nd edn, 1714), and the exposition of the epistle to Jude in the continuation of Matthew Henry's commentary. William Harris edited his posthumous *Sermons Against Popery* (1723).

Billingsley and his wife had five children, including one son, John, a dissenting minister in Dover, Kent, who dedicated a sermon to his father in 1717. John subsequently married a sister of Sir Philip Yorke, later Chancellor Hardwicke, conformed to the Church of England, and became a prebendary of Bristol. In addition to suffering all his life under a 'crazy constitution', Billingsley was naturally melancholy. During his last sickness, he confessed, '[I] pretend not to transports of affection, and rapturous joys; for … you know my temper and make' (Harris, 256–7). He died, probably in London, on 2 May 1722, and was buried on 13 May in Bunhill Fields. Harris published funeral sermons for both Billingsley and his wife in his *Funeral Discourses* (1736). JIM BENEDICT

Sources W. Harris, *Funeral discourses* (1736), 223–57 • W. Wilson, *The history and antiquities of the dissenting churches and meeting houses in London, Westminster and Southwark*, 4 vols. (1808–14), vol. 1, pp. 76–82 • A. Gordon, ed., *Freedom after ejection: a review (1690–1692) of presbyterian and congregational nonconformity in England and Wales* (1917), 82–3, 215 • *Calamy rev.*, 53–4, 399, 418, 408 • *The nonconformist's memorial … originally written by … Edmund Calamy*, ed. S. Palmer, [3rd edn], 1 (1802), 402 • J. H. Turner, T. Dickenson, and O. Heywood, eds., *The nonconformist register of baptisms, marriages, and deaths* (1881) • *The Rev. Oliver Heywood … his autobiography, diaries, anecdote and event books*, ed. J. H. Turner, 4 (1885), 130 • [J. Hunter], ed., *Letters of eminent men, addressed to Ralph Thoresby*, 1 (1832), 162 • N. Billingsley, *A sermon occasioned by the death of… Hubert Stogdon* (1728) • M. Henry, diary, 1705–13, Bodl. Oxf., MS Eng. misc. e. 330, fol. 110

Billingsley, Martin (1591–1622), writing master, was born in London, the eldest son of Martin Billingsley, a freeman of the Company of Haberdashers, and his wife, Elizabeth. He was baptized on 18 July 1591 at St Antholin's, Budge Row, in the parish where his parents lived. Nothing is known of his youth or education, although one biographer declares he was entirely self-taught. We can also assume that he came from an educated and perhaps comfortable family, as his great-uncle Sir Henry Billingsley was the first person to translate Euclid into English and also served as lord mayor of London in 1597.

Despite his short life, Billingsley published one important engraved copybook and also taught penmanship to one notable student. His first publication, *The Pen's Excellencie, or, The Secretaries Delighte* (1618), introduced by an armigerous portrait engraved by William Hole, reveals all the confidence, even arrogance, that was typical of later penmen such as George Shelley and Joseph Champion. Promoting himself as a 'master in the art of writing', Billingsley dedicated *The Pen's Excellencie* to Prince Charles, 'whose *servant* he calls himself' (Massey, 2.24). Although no documentation regarding his position as writing-master to the young Charles I survives, it is corroborated in John Bagford's 'MS catalogue of Copy-Books', where Billingsley is described as 'writing master to King Charles ye First when he was Prince' (Heal, 18). If this was indeed the case, then Billingsley was evidently an able teacher: according to William Massey's *The Origin and Progress of Letters* (1763), Charles's manuscripts display a surprisingly good 'Italian hand'—the writing style favoured by Billingsley.

The Pen's Excellencie further suggests the nature of Billingsley's character. Although a modest work of only twenty-eight small quarto plates, it has justly been described as the first English copybook of any pretensions. It was also prefaced with a sizeable discursive introduction where Billingsley sought to promote the status of penmanship and, at the same time, to deter critics by making a distinction between his own performances and those of 'Botchers', that 'number of lame Pen-men who … intrude themselves into the society of Artists' (Heal, 18). He then went on to provide directions for cutting quills and making ink and, importantly, to define the six different hands ('Secretary', 'Bastard-Secretary', 'Roman', 'Italian', 'Chancery', and 'Court-hand'), explaining the derivation, benefits, and uses of each. The plates, however, were executed primarily in 'neat Italian hand and small secretary' (Massey, 2.24). The success of *The Pen's Excellencie* can be judged from the appearance of a second edition in 1637, which was published by Thomas Dainty fifteen years after Billingsley's death.

There seems to have been some confusion over the other copybooks produced by Billingsley during his career. Ambrose Heal, whose *The English Writing-Masters and their Copy-Books, 1570–1800* (1931) is the most authoritative existing source, discounts four titles that have previously been ascribed to Billingsley's hand. Following Heal's reappraisal it now appears that during his lifetime Billingsley published only one other copybook, entitled *The Pen's Paradise* (n.d.), but in the 1660s the publisher Peter Stent recycled some of the copperplates reproducing his penmanship under a variety of titles. Billingsley died in 1622 and was buried in St Swithin's Church on 26 August.

LUCY PELTZ

Sources A. Heal, *The English writing-masters and their copy-books, 1570–1800* (1931) · A. M. Hind, *Engraving in England in the sixteenth and seventeenth centuries*, ed. M. Corbett and M. Norton, 3 vols. (1952–64) · W. Massey, *The origin and progress of letters: an essay in two parts* (1763) · *Engraved Brit. ports.* · G. Meissner, ed., *Allgemeines Künstlerlexikon: die bildenden Künstler aller Zeiten und Völker*, [new edn, 34 vols.] (Leipzig and Munich, 1983–) · J. I. Whalley, *The pen's excellencie: calligraphy of western Europe and America* (1980)
Likenesses T. Dainty, engraving, repro. in M. Billingsley, *The pen's excellencie* (1637), frontispiece · J. Goddard, engraving, repro. in M. Billingsley, *The pen's excellencie* (1651), frontispiece · W. Hole, engraving, repro. in M. Billingsley, *The pen's excellencie* (1618), frontispiece

Billingsley, Nicholas (*bap.* **1633**, *d.* **1709**), religious poet and Presbyterian minister, was baptized at Faversham, Kent, on 1 November 1633, the son of Nicholas Billingsley (*b. c.*1599) and his wife, Letitia Besbeche. The elder Nicholas, master of Faversham School, became rector of Betteshanger and vicar of Tilmanstone (both also in Kent) in 1644. The younger Nicholas attended Eton College from about 1648 to 1654. His education appears, however, to have been dogged by ill health. He had hoped to go to King's College, Cambridge, but instead went to Merton College, Oxford. There, according to Anthony Wood, 'having had a long sickness hanging upon him, [Billingsley] was dispenced with by the venerable congregation of eight terms' (Wood, *Ath. Oxon.: Fasti*, pt 2)—a statement which would explain the short period between his matriculation on 10 March 1657 and his graduation as BA the following year. Billingsley dedicated his first published work to the Bristol physician whom he believed had saved his life.

Billingsley's first two collections of poetry were the product of these chequered years. *Brachy-martyrologia, or, A breviary of all the greatest persecutions which have befallen the saints and people of God from the creation to our present times*, published in May 1657 with dedications dated 11 March and 6 April 1656, told selections from Foxe's book of martyrs in rhyming couplets. *The Infancy of the World*, published in August 1658, was dedicated to the provost of Eton, Francis Rous. Billingsley seems to have been working on this fine collection, completed at Canterbury in December 1656, since the age of fifteen. The work included a ten-part poem in rhyming couplets, which celebrated the creation of the world and dramatized the fall of mankind, along with other religious poetry in a classical style imitative of Robert Herrick yet with thematic concerns close to those of John Milton. His poetry throughout his career reflected Billingsley's presbyterian admiration of the beauty of the world, the moral capabilities of humans, and the shape of the church.

Billingsley dedicated one part of *Brachy-Martyrologia* to the sheriff and to four ministers of Herefordshire; in the month the book was published he was admitted—on 28 May 1657—as vicar of Weobley in the same county, a living for which he was assessed for the clerical subsidy of 1661 at £80 per annum. Billingsley married Grace Hawes (1634?–1701), the only daughter of Richard *Hawes, minister of Leintwardine in the same county from 1659. After the Restoration, Billingsley was indicted at Hereford assizes on 1 August 1662 for seditious words; he pleaded not guilty. He was ejected from his living under the Act of Uniformity and settled with his family and his father-in-law at Abergavenny, Monmouthshire, where he kept a school. Although Calamy described him as a nonconformist, he is perhaps as well characterized at this time as a 'dubious conformist' (*Calamy rev.*, 54): he subscribed to the Thirty-Nine Articles in order to become master of Abergavenny School on 15 February 1664 and was ordained deacon in the Church of England three weeks later on 6 March 1664. Three years later, with the aid of the conforming presbyterian Sir Edward Harley, patron of the Herefordshire godly, he became curate of Blakeney, Gloucestershire. Blakeney was a chapelry in the parish of Awre in the Forest of Dean, a living in the gift of the Haberdashers' Company. Billingsley was also offered, but scrupled against accepting, the vicarage itself. He subscribed to take up the living on 25 February 1667. Soon after he explained his reconciliation in a poem dated 15 March 1667:

> True, I was one of Levi's turn'd out Tribe,
> Who never durst against my conscience sin,
> Nor claw Church-livings with an unjust bribe,
> And stoutly swear I honestly came in.
> (Billingsley, *Treasury*, sig. A4v)

These lines appeared in his volume of poetry published in 1667 by the presbyterian publisher Thomas Parkhurst, the moralistic, epigrammatic *Thesauro-phylakion, or, A treasury of divine raptures, consisting of serious observations, pious ejaculations, select epigrams*, which he dedicated to Harley and the Haberdashers' Company as well as to the old parliamentarian officer John Birch and to Mary, Lady Vaughan and Sir Henry Vaughan.

Billingsley is an interesting example of the precariously conforming. He made interpolations in the prayer-book service and often wore his surplice across his shoulders in minimal compliance with the canons of the church. According to one hostile observer, he 'would sometimes impose on his Auditors a hymn of his own making' (*Calamy rev.*, 54). The accusation enabled the writer to abuse Billingsley's literary talents as 'a wretched pretender to poetry' and to point up that such presumption was taking place in the parish (allegedly) of Sternhold and Hopkins, whose sixteenth-century metrical translations of the psalms still dominated the music of church and meeting-house. If Billingsley was indeed writing hymns for his congregation it puts him in tune with a development within nonconformity rather than with the practice of the established church. Billingsley's father-in-law, Hawes, who continued to live with Billingsley until his death in 1668, was tolerated by the bishop to preach occasionally in Awre despite his failure to subscribe.

While William Nicholson was bishop of Gloucester and Mr Jordan was vicar, Billingsley was left in peace. But with the vicar's death in 1668, two successive high-church vicars sought his ruin. The succeeding bishop, Robert Frampton, and his chancellor, Richard Parsons, were bitter opponents. According to Calamy the chancellor, after hearing Billingsley preach a visitation sermon in which he reproved the lives of the clergy, so far forgot himself as to pluck the preacher by the hair in the open street, saying, 'Sirrah, you are a rogue, and I'll bind you to your good behaviour' (Calamy, *Abridgement*, 2.358). After this incident, Billingsley faced suspensions and other penalties for 'want of that conformity to which his place did not oblige him' (ibid.). He complied so far as 'to read more or less of the Common-Prayer, and to wear the Surplice, after the bishop had given it under his Hand that 'twas not requir'd to be worn upon the account of any suppos'd Holiness in the Garment, but only for Decency and Comliness' (ibid., 359).

Despite suspensions Billingsley weathered the persecution of Frampton and Parsons. He finally resigned in 1689, a date suggesting that the trigger was the failure of comprehension. Frampton's more moderate successor, Edward Fowler, was unable to persuade him to return to the Anglican fold. In 1691 the Common Fund survey noted that Billingsley was 'quite comme off from the Church of England, with about 200 of his parish, who have Sett up a meeting for him in the parish, they have subscribed 16*l.* or 17*l.* per annum, desire Some assistance' (Gordon, 45). He was also acting as an itinerant preacher elsewhere in Gloucestershire. The fund accordingly granted him £10 a year from 1692 to 1702, and again in 1704–5 when he was recorded as living in Bristol.

It was at St James's, Bristol, that Billingsley's wife, Grace, was buried on 16 April 1701. She is limned in 'Carmen lugubre', an elegy written by Nicholas on her death, which describes her piety, noting the time she spent in her 'shut closet' where she read prodigiously, and praising her devotion to godliness within a companionate marriage:

> Look what remarks she in the day had read,
> She likely told us e'er we went to bed.
> (Billingsley, 'Carmen lugubre')

Their son Nicholas described his mother as a devout Calvinist who 'took more than ordinary care in our Education, and instil into us a lively sense of Divine Goodness' (Billingsley, *Rational and Christian Principles*, 75).

Billingsley died at Bristol in December 1709 and was buried on 28 December at St James's. Calamy does not mention his poems in his *Account*, but Richard Baxter had in his possession a manuscript of Billingsley's entitled, 'Theological reflections on God's Admirable master-piece' (now lost), on which he wrote on the fly-leaf:

> The poetry of this book I leave to the judgment and relish of the reader; the philosophical and theological matter, as far I had leisure to peruse it, is such as is agreeable to the authors that are most commonly esteemed. (*DNB*)

Grace and Nicholas had seven children, of whom four were alive in 1702. Both their sons became Presbyterian ministers. Richard (1660–*c*.1713), became minister of Whitchurch, Hampshire, and was in turn the father of another minister, Samuel, whose ordination sermon was preached by John Bowden in 1725; Nicholas, minister of Ashwick in Somerset, published in the Arian controversy in the 1720s, was commended by John Dunton in his *The Dissenting Doctors*. SHARON ACHINSTEIN

Sources *Calamy rev.* · A. Gordon, ed., *Freedom after ejection: a review (1690–1692) of presbyterian and congregational nonconformity in England and Wales* (1917) · *DNB* · S. Rudder, *A new history of Gloucestershire* (1779) · E. Calamy, ed., *An abridgement of Mr. Baxter's history of his life and times, with an account of the ministers, &c., who were ejected after the Restoration of King Charles II*, 2nd edn, 2 vols. (1713) · W. Sterry, ed., *The Eton College register, 1441–1698* (1943) · Foster, *Alum. Oxon.* · N. Billingsley, *Brachy-martyrologia* (1657) · N. Billingsley, *The infancy of the world* (1658) · N. Billingsley, *Thesauro-phylakion, or, A treasury of divine raptures* (1667) · N. Billingsley, 'Carmen lugubre', 1702?, DWL · N. Billingsley, *Rational and Christian principles* (1721) · *The life and errors of John Dunton*, [rev. edn], ed. J. B. Nichols, 2 vols. (1818) · *CSP dom., 1671–2* · Wood, *Ath. Oxon.: Fasti* (1820), 213

Billington [*née* Weichsel], **Elizabeth** (1765–1818), singer, was born in Litchfield Street, Soho, London, on 27 December 1765, the first of the three children of Carl Friedrich Weichsel (1728–1811) and his wife, Fredericka Weirman (*d.* 1786). Weichsel, a native of Freiburg, Saxony, was principal oboist at the King's Theatre and Vauxhall Gardens; Fredericka sang at Vauxhall for twenty-two seasons and also at the Lenten oratorios. Elizabeth's eldest brother, Charles (1767–1850), became an accomplished violinist, and led the King's Theatre band and Philharmonic Society during the early nineteenth century.

Trained from early childhood by their father, Elizabeth and Charles were brought out as prodigies and performed concertos on piano and violin respectively during their mother's benefit concert at the Haymarket on 10 March 1774. With further tuition from J. S. Schroeter and J. C.

Elizabeth Billington (1765–1818), by Sir Joshua Reynolds, 1789

Bach (who had taught her mother), Elizabeth developed into a fine pianist and played in public even after her singing career had taken off. She first appeared as a vocalist at her mother's benefit concert on 20 March 1775. She also composed, and published, two sets of keyboard sonatas before her twelfth birthday, as well as three sonatas for violin and piano in 1792.

Despite this early celebrity, Elizabeth's childhood was far from tranquil. Her parents' marriage was a stormy one, causing some to doubt Elizabeth's legitimacy: Lady Morgan, for example, named her own parent, the Irish actor Robert Owenson (1744–1812), as the true father of Mrs Billington (*Lady Morgan's Memoirs*, 1.82–3). Weichsel's regime was harsh even by the standards of the day, and the scurrilous *Memoirs of Mrs Billington* published by James Ridgway in 1792 also hint at incest. In August 1777, aged twelve, Elizabeth accused her godfather, the violinist Joseph Agus (1749–1798), of attempting to rape her: he was convicted on evidence she gave in court at the Kingston assizes on 19 March 1778, as the *Gazetteer and New Daily Advertiser* reported two days later. Though this must have proved traumatic, she still honoured her engagement to perform a piano concerto at the Covent Garden oratorios the following evening.

Among Elizabeth's early voice teachers was James Billington (1756–1794), who also played double bass at Drury Lane and Vauxhall: according to R. J. S. Stevens, he 'had but shallow knowledge of singing' (Stevens, fol. 66), but knew enough to recognize his pupil's potential. He and Elizabeth were married on 13 October 1783 at St Mary's, Lambeth, with her mother as a witness—the ceremony apparently going ahead without Carl Weichsel's consent.

In November Elizabeth travelled to Dublin with her new husband, her father, and her brother, and commenced her theatrical career at Smock Alley opposite Giusto Ferdinando Tenducci in a version of Gluck's *Orfeo ed Euridice* (5 January 1784). Though she suffered at first from comparison with Eliza Wheeler, she gradually won over her Irish audiences. Her private life, however, soon degenerated into turmoil: a daughter was born in the summer of 1784, but died shortly afterwards in Dublin, while the Billingtons were touring the provinces (Cork, Nenagh, and Waterford); Elizabeth deserted her husband briefly for a Mr Kray, and then for Richard Daly, a theatre manager and an infamous seducer of actresses, who apparently paid Billington for his wife's favours. Following a serious illness which prevented her from working, she and her husband left Ireland for London.

At Covent Garden, on 13 February 1786, Elizabeth appeared as Rosetta in Thomas Arne's *Love in a Village*—a trial night 'by royal command' which brought further prestigious engagements. By consensus, she was considered extremely beautiful, but her acting lacked emotion and refinement, and her singing as yet was unremarkable. From 1786, however, she worked to improve her voice with a succession of prominent singing-masters, even visiting the elderly Antonio Sacchini in Paris for lessons in July, after the close of the season. Her diligence soon reaped dividends: within two years Burney could declare that 'no song seems too high or too rapid for her execution', praising in particular her 'exquisitely sweet' tone and 'considerable' knowledge of music (Burney, 2.1021).

Elizabeth appeared at the Handel commemorations (1786), the Professional Concerts (1786–8, 1791–2), Vauxhall Gardens, the Lenten oratorios, the Oxford musical meetings, Rauzzini's concerts in Bath, and the provincial festivals during the summer months, and revisited Ireland in the early 1790s. On these occasions she excelled in bravura numbers such as 'The soldier tir'd' (Arne's *Artaxerxes*), but a particular favourite was 'Sweet bird' (Handel's *L'allegro ed il penseroso*), in which she was usually accompanied by her brother Charles on the violin. The extent to which she improvised ornamentation during performance invariably caused disagreement among critics: for Burney and others, she never exceeded the bounds of taste, but when George III approved her engagement at the Concerts of Ancient Music (1786–7) he stipulated she was to 'sing pathetick songs and not to over grace them' (letter, 23 March 1786, BL, Egerton MS 2159, fol. 57).

Elizabeth's personal life was ruthlessly exposed to public scrutiny by Ridgway's publication of her *Memoirs* on 14 January 1792. Fact was larded with innuendo and salacious gossip, and letters written to her mother from Ireland were reproduced, which she had tried unsuccessfully to recover: 'you couldn't get a single copy after 3 o'clock in the afternoon', noted Joseph Haydn with amazement in his journal (*Collected Correspondence*, 255). The scandal surrounding the *Memoirs* and subsequent libel proceedings created a propitious moment for her to withdraw from public life, and in 1793 she embarked on a tour of Italy with her husband and brother, initially for pleasure.

At Naples Elizabeth met Sir William and Emma Hamilton, who prevailed on her to sing at one of their musical parties. The king and queen of Naples were among the company, and at their invitation she made a triumphant début at the Teatro San Carlo on 30 May 1794, in Bianchi's *Inez de Castro*, written specially for her. The occasion was marred, however, by the sudden death of her husband from a stroke, and by the eruption of Vesuvius, which the Neapolitans attributed to the performance of an English 'heretic' (protestant) at San Carlo.

Mrs Billington cultivated the finest reputation ever achieved in Italy by an English singer. Between 1796 and 1799 she sang at Venice, Bergamo, Bologna, Milan, Florence, Leghorn, Padua, and Trieste in roles created for her by Paisiello, Paer, Nasolini, Himmel, and other leading composers. While in Milan (1798-9), where she was a frequent guest of Madame Bonaparte, she married a French commissary named Felican (or Felissent), and moved with him to an estate she had purchased at St Artien, near Venice. She probably intended to settle there, but Felican grew increasingly violent towards her, and in 1801 she fled to England.

Rumours of her continental success having preceded her, Mrs Billington was fêted on her reappearance as Mandane in Arne's *Artaxerxes* (Covent Garden, 3 October 1801). Drury Lane and Covent Garden took the unusual step of engaging her to sing on alternate nights. Following Brigida Banti's retirement, she was also courted by the Italian Opera Company at the King's Theatre, where she sang serious roles from December 1802 until she too withdrew from the stage, in August 1806 (having received an unprecedented £2600 for her final season). She was, it seems, the first native soprano to enjoy such prolonged supremacy at London's Italian opera house. Peter von Winter, the house composer, wrote new operas to display her talents, including *Il trionfo dell'amore fraterno* (22 March 1804), and for some this was a 'short summer of good music' (*Harmonicon*, 8, 1830, p. 71), culminating in her benefit performance as Vitellia in *La clemenza di Tito* (27 March 1806). This was the first time a Mozart opera had been produced in London, and the score was loaned by the prince of Wales, rumoured, along with the dukes of Sussex and Rutland, to have been among her lovers.

From 1806 Mrs Billington continued as a concert singer, and, together with John Braham and Giuseppe Naldi, promoted an annual subscription series of vocal and instrumental music between 1808 and 1810. On 3 May 1811 she gave a farewell performance at her brother's benefit concert and retired to her riverside villa in Fulham for health reasons, perhaps related to her increasing obesity. She

refused all later offers of engagements, but reappeared briefly at a 'Grand Concert for the benefit of the German sufferers in the late campaign' at Whitehall Chapel on 28 June 1814 (*The Times*, 29 June 1814). Felican arrived in London in 1817 and begged her to return with him to St Artien; she dutifully complied, but was taken ill on 18 August 1818 and died a week later, on 25 August, the result, according to London rumour, of a beating from her worthless husband. RACHEL E. COWGILL

Sources [J. Ridgway], *Memoirs of Mrs Billington, from her birth* (1792) · *An answer to the memoirs of Mrs Billington* (1792) · parish register (baptism), St Anne's, Soho, Westminster, 24 Jan 1766 · parish register (marriage), St Mary's, Lambeth, 13 Oct 1783 · S. D. [J. Sterland ?], 'Chronicles of the Italian opera in England', *The Harmonicon*, 8 (1830), 10-13, 70-73 · *The Wynne diaries*, ed. A. Fremantle, 2 (1937), 210; 3 (1940), 77, 135, 281 · 'Mara, Billington, and Catalani', *Quarterly Musical Magazine and Review*, 1 (1818), 164-70 · 'Mrs Billington', *Quarterly Musical Magazine and Review*, 1 (1818), 175-80 · 'Letter to editor: on Mara, Catalani, and Billington', *Monthly Magazine*, 24 (1807), 5 · 'Memoir of Mrs Billington', *Monthly Magazine*, 46 (1818), 469-71 · 'Memoir of Mrs Billington', *The Harmonicon*, 8 (1830), 93-7 · T. Billington, preface, *Love canzonets* (1784) · *The Times* (29 June 1814) · W. Gardiner, *The music of nature* (1832), 107-8 · R. J. S. Stevens, 'Lectures', GL, GMus 472 · M. Kelly, *Reminiscences*, 2nd edn, 2 vols. (1826); repr., R. Fiske, ed. (1975) · R. Edgcumbe, *Musical reminiscences of an old amateur: chiefly respecting the Italian opera in England for fifty years, from 1773 to 1823*, 2nd edn (1827), 87-99, 114-16 · *Lady Morgan's memoirs: autobiography, diaries, and correspondence*, ed. W. H. Dixon, 1 (1862), 82-3 · *The John Marsh journals: the life and times of a gentleman composer*, ed. B. Robins (1998) · W. T. Parke, *Musical memoirs*, 2 (1830), 142-6 · Burney, *Hist. mus.*, new edn, 2.1021 · G. Hogarth, *Memoirs of the opera*, 2nd edn, 2 (1851), 277-83 · T. Busby, *Concert room and orchestra anecdotes of music and musicians, ancient and modern*, 3 vols. (1825), vol. 1, pp. 151-4, 212-14, 217-18; vol. 2, pp. 4-5 · H. Angelo, *Reminiscences*, 1 (1828) · BL, Egerton MS 2159, fols. 57, 66 · *Oxberry's Dramatic Biography*, 3/36 (1825), 55-65 · J. Doane, ed., *A musical directory for the year 1794* [1794] · *The Examiner* (28 Sept 1818), 616 · E. Waters, *Opera glass* (1808) · L. Hunt, *The autobiography of Leigh Hunt*, ed. J. E. Morpurgo (1949), 125 · *The collected correspondence and London notebooks of Joseph Haydn*, ed. H. C. Robbins Landon (1959), 255, 262, 273 · F.-J. Fétis, *Biographie universelle des musiciens, et bibliographie générale de la musique*, 2nd edn, 1 (Paris, 1860), 415-17 · *Captain Gronow: his reminiscences of Regency and Victorian life*, ed. C. Hibbert (1991), 86 · *Leaves from the journals of Sir George Smart*, ed. H. B. Cox and C. L. E. Cox (1907), 47-8 · S. McVeigh, *Calendar of London concerts, 1750-1800* [unpublished computer database, Goldsmiths' College, London] · N. Salwey and S. McVeigh, 'The piano and harpsichord in London's concert life, 1750-1800: a calendar of advertised performances', *A handbook for studies in 18th-century English music*, ed. M. Burden and I. Cholij, 8 (1997), 27-72 · R. Cowgill, 'Calendar of Mozart performances in London, 1801-29', 1996, University of Huddersfield [database] · M. Sands, 'Billington, Elizabeth', Grove, *Dict. mus.* (1954) · DNB

Archives SOUND Barbara Harbach (harpsichord), Sonatas Op. 1 and 2 (1995), Hester Park CD 7703

Likenesses F. Bartolozzi, stipple, pubd 1786 (after R. Cosway), BM · J. Reynolds, portrait, 1789, Beaverbrook Art Gallery, Fredericton, New Brunswick [*see illus.*] · J. Gillray, etching, pubd 1801 (after his portrait), NPG · T. Burke, stipple, pubd *c.*1802 (after S. de Koster), BM, NPG · J. Ward, stipple, pubd 1808 (after J. Reynolds), BM · F. Bartolozzi, chalk drawing, Royal Collection · possibly by F. Buck, miniature, V&A · J. J. Masquerier, oils, Garr. Club · G. Romney, oils (as St Cecilia), Boston Museum of Fine Arts · W. Wellings, watercolour drawing (in *Artaxerxes*), BM · prints, BM, NPG

Billington, Mary Frances (1862-1925), journalist, was born at Chalbury rectory, Wimborne, Dorset, on 6 September 1862, the only daughter (she had three brothers) of the Revd George Henry Billington (*d.* 12 Dec 1904), rector of Chalbury, and his wife, Frances Anne (daughter of the Revd T. Barber). Billington was educated at home and, once she could read at the age of eight, was encouraged to read *The Times* and other leading newspapers. In this way she absorbed some of the elements of her future profession, so much so that she was earning enough to support herself from her late teens. She began her career in journalism by writing about something she knew well—Dorset ghosts—and earned her first guinea by contributing to the 'turn-over' column in Sir George Armstrong's *Globe* which, in its time, was the launch pad for many an aspiring journalist.

In August 1888 Billington went to Southampton to assist in the establishment of the *Southern Echo*. While there she attracted the attention of John Passmore Edwards, the proprietor/editor of the London *Echo*. A country girl born and bred, she was just the person to write a series on the recent enfranchisement of the agricultural labourer. For just over two years, she worked full-time on the *Echo*, then regarded as the most successful London evening newspaper. This gave her a thorough training in journalism in which, as she later recalled, she recorded little of public importance but widened her expertise by reporting anything from East End parties to ragged school prize days. Edwards also encouraged her to write 'descriptive' articles, ranging from articles on penny waxwork shows to those which she described as 'mostly related to the seamy side of female life'. Billington made good use of the advice, and introductions to other newspapers, offered by her fellow male journalists, and obtained a staff position on the *Daily Graphic*, prior to its establishment in 1890. She was the first woman to be appointed as a special correspondent on feminine interests. So, in 1890, she reported the funeral of Mrs Catherine Booth, the founding 'Mother of the Salvation Army', and, in 1891, became one of the first women to don heavy diving equipment and dive underwater at the Royal Naval Exhibition. During 1892 she branched out into reporting on the preparations in Westminster Abbey for Tennyson's funeral and, two years later, on the opening of Tower Bridge. She also played an important role in the formation of the Society for Women Journalists (SWJ) and, in May 1894, was appointed its first vice-president.

Then, becoming even more adventurous, Billington persuaded the editor of the *Daily Graphic* that too little attention had been devoted to the role of women in India and secured the commission to visit there. This yielded a series of twenty-eight articles and she published these, in 1895, as *Women in India*. When sending Gladstone a copy of the book to thank him for his help with the expedition, she thought it politic in her letter to belittle 'that silliest of crazes, woman's suffrage'. In 1897 she was recruited to run the women's department of the *Daily Telegraph*, and worked on the paper until her death in 1925.

Throughout the First World War Billington served as president of the SWJ and also arranged some of her articles into books on how women contributed to the war effort, highlighting the bad management of some army camps. She also furthered the cause of women journalists by lecturing on journalism to SWJ members and to the London School of Journalism. She once wrote that for women to succeed in the male-dominated world of British journalism they needed 'true grit'—something she exhibited in her own pioneering career.

Throughout most of her working life in London, Billington lived at 23 Warwick Square, Belgrave Road, London, and she died there on 27 August 1925. She was buried in the Chalbury church where her father had served as rector from 1861 to 1904.   FRED HUNTER

Sources M. F. Billington, 'Experiences of a presswoman', *Our Own Magazine*, 12 (1895), 10–11 · M. F. Billington, 'With my camera in India', *Our Own Magazine*, 12 (1895), 54–6 · M. F. Billington, 'Women in journalism', *Sell's dictionary of the world's press* (1891), 58–62 · M. F. Billington, 'How can I earn my living, 4: in journalism, art, or photography', *Young Woman*, 2 (1893–4), 307–10 · M. F. Billington, 'The adventures of a lady journalist', *Young Woman*, 7 (1898–9), 135–7; 218–20; 371–5; 422–4 · M. F. Billington, *Women in India* (1895) · M. F. Billington, *The Red Cross in war* (1914) · M. F. Billington, *The roll-call of serving women* (1915) · *The Times* (28 Aug 1925) · Venn, *Alum. Cant.* · d. cert. · *CGPLA Eng. & Wales* (1925)
Wealth at death £2632 18*s.* 3*d.*: probate, 23 Dec 1925, *CGPLA Eng. & Wales*

Billington, Thomas (*b.* 1754, *d.* in or before 1832), composer, was born in Exeter, and described himself as a 'harpsichord and singing master'. He was a chorister in St Peter's Cathedral, Exeter. On 6 April 1777 he was elected a member of the Royal Society of Musicians. His brother James, a double bass player and singing teacher, and the first husband of the famous singer Elizabeth Billington (*née* Weichsel), was elected a member of the same society on 6 January 1782. A third brother, Horace, was a well-known painter and died at Glasshouse Street, London, on 17 November 1812. Billington sang glees and catches, with Rheinhold, Champness, and others, at the end of a performance at Covent Garden Theatre on 6 May 1783, and appeared as a tenor at Westminster Abbey and the Pantheon in the first Handel memorial concerts in May and June of 1784. The RSM detailed him to sing at the annual charity concerts for the clergy at St Paul's Cathedral in 1790, 1791, and 1792. He was an industrious composer and compiler, and was noted for his secular cantatas for soloists, chorus, and orchestra, and for setting serious and solemn examples of verse. His most remarkable productions are settings of poems such as Gray's *Elegy* (op. 8, 1784), Pope's *Eloisa to Abelard* (1786), and Young's *Night Thoughts* (1788), the last in essence a secular oratorio in three acts, each with its own overture. This piece includes music by Handel and Arne as well as by Billington himself, and is typical of how he usually constructed works using his own and other composers' music. In addition Billington published, mostly at his own expense, several sets of instrumental duos, trios, and quartets, sonatas, short solo cantatas, *Love Canzonets*, 'pastoral ballads', and a setting of Pope's *Messiah* (1786). He also arranged works by Corelli, Geminiani, and Boccherini, and produced *Some Observations on Singing* (1784). During the greater part of his professional career he lived and taught at 24 Charlotte Street,

Rathbone Place, London, but in 1824 he moved to Sunbury, Middlesex. He died, possibly in Tunis (see *GM*, 1812) or Tours (according to Highfill, Burnim & Langhans, *BDA*), in 1832 or earlier, leaving a widow and a daughter, the wife of Nehemiah Southwell Price of Pond Street, Hampstead.

W. B. SQUIRE, *rev.* DAVID J. GOLBY

Sources Highfill, Burnim & Langhans, *BDA* · R. Fiske, 'Billingham, Thomas', *New Grove* · *GM*, 1st ser., 82/2 (1812), 501 · *GM*, 1st ser., 102/1 (1832), 382
Wealth at death see details of will, Highfill, Burnim & Langhans, *BDA*

Billington, William (1825–1884), poet, was born at Samlesbury in the Ribble valley, Lancashire, on 3 April 1825, when his unemployed hand-loom weaver parents, Benedict and Ann, *née* Bolton, were working as road navvies. He was baptized at St Mary's Roman Catholic Church in Samlesbury on 10 April 1825. Previous confusion over his date of birth was due to an error on his tombstone, which gave it as 1827. Billington's father died aged thirty-eight in 1832, and three of the children died from tuberculosis before 1837. Ann supported the four survivors, two of whom were invalids, by hand-loom weaving, going without sleep, helped by William, during one night per week. Billington learned to read and write at Catholic Sunday schools, and although his mother was illiterate, she knew many songs, sung to William during their night-time work. The songs and satires composed for oral performance by her brother, Robert Bolton, and the example of Richard Dugdale, the Bard of Ribblesdale, with whom Billington began a lifelong friendship in his teens, also inspired him to write poetry.

Billington loathed the factory work through which he supported his family in Blackburn after marrying Elizabeth Walmsley (*c.*1828–1857) on 24 June 1846. Because of ill health he became a publican (subsequently taking to drink) after his second marriage, to Maria Fairbottom (*b.* 1844/5) on 13 July 1867. Although both wives were illiterate, and Maria abandoned him and their young child in contempt for his intellectual interests, Billington was an insatiable autodidact. He committed to memory many lines from the major English poets, from Chaucer to Wordsworth, was a founder member of the Blackburn Mechanics' Institute, taught grammar in a school in exchange for lessons in mathematics, advised trade unions, lectured on and debated religion and politics at any opportunity, and formed a mutual improvement society, which met in a hayloft. He travelled around the north and midlands to read and sell his poems. The beershop he ran in Bradshaw Street from 1875 became the forum for Billington's debating skills; known as Poet's Corner, it was where Blackburn's large coterie of dialect poets met, despite its owner's penchant for devastating criticism.

The subjects of Billington's writings in newspapers, broadsheets, and pamphlets ranged widely. His first reputation was as a 'public denier and assailant of … religious belief' (Abram), but he was known as the Blackburn Poet before he died from tuberculosis on 3 January 1884, at Bradshaw Street, Blackburn, and has since been mainly remembered for his dialect ballads about the impact on workers of the cotton famine of 1861–4. Published as a broadsheet at the height of the panic, 'Th'shurat weyvur' sold 14,000 copies and, like 'Aw Wod this War Wur Ended' of 1863, it has been frequently anthologized. Selections of Billington's prose and poems, many first published in the *Blackburn Standard* and the *Blackburn Times*, appeared as *Sheen and Shade* (1861) and *Lancashire Songs with other Sketches* (1883).

JOHN LANGTON

Sources M. I. Watson, *William Billington: cotton operative, teacher and poet* (1984) · G. C. Miller, 'Focus on yesterday: William Billington', *Blackburn Times* (31 March 1900) · 'Billington, William, dialect poet', G. C. Miller, *Blackburn worthies of yesterday: a biographical galaxy* (1959), 38–42 · A. W. Abram, *Blackburn characters of a past generation* (1894), 221 · B. Hollingsworth, ed., *Songs of the people: Lancashire dialect poetry of the industrial revolution* (1982), 98–9, 112–3, 145, 147–8, 151–2 · m. certs. · IGI
Likenesses photograph, repro. in W. Billington, *Lancashire poems with other sketches* (1853) · photograph, repro. in Watson, *William Billington*, cover · photograph, repro. in Miller, 'Focus on yesterday'

Bilney, Thomas (*c.*1495–1531), evangelical reformer and martyr, known as Little Bilney on account of his short stature, was born in Norfolk, most likely at Norwich. Of his parents nothing is known, except that they survived him. Sent up to Cambridge at an early age (*c.*1510), he read law at Trinity Hall and in September 1519 was ordained a priest at Ely. Admitted to the degree of BCnL in 1521, Bilney was elected to a fellowship at Trinity Hall three years later, and also served as a proctor of the university.

Convert and preacher Bilney might have settled quietly into life as a Cambridge don, had he not undergone a personal religious conversion. In 1516 he had purchased a copy of Erasmus's recent Latin translation of the New Testament, initially attracted chiefly by its fine prose style. He later related how a casual reading of the scriptures produced dramatic spiritual consequences:

> I chanced upon this sentence of St Paul in I Tim. 1 'It is a true saying, and worthy of all men to be embraced, that Christ Jesus came into the world to save sinners, of whom I am the chief and principal'. This one sentence, through God's instruction and inward working, which I did not then perceive, did so exhilarate my heart, being before wounded with the guilt of my sins, and being almost in despair, that immediately I felt a marvellous comfort and quietness. (*Acts and Monuments*, 4.635)

Following this experience Bilney rapidly became a leading figure in the circle of early reformers at Cambridge, and was credited with a number of conversions, most notably that of Hugh Latimer (whom he first approached under guise of making his confession). Active in public with preaching and pastoral work, in private Bilney led a life of stern asceticism; he slept little, ate simply, and displayed a strong aversion to music, whether it was the 'dainty singing' of Cambridge choirs or the recorder playing of his college neighbour Thomas Thirlby (later bishop of Ely).

In July 1525 Bishop West of Ely licensed Bilney to preach throughout his diocese, and he began to carry his evangelical message beyond the confines of the university to pulpits throughout East Anglia. His activities attracted the attention of the ecclesiastical authorities, but Cardinal Wolsey treated him leniently, simply demanding that he swear an oath not to preach Lutheran heresy. Undaunted, in mid-1527 Bilney embarked upon his most ambitious preaching tour, accompanied by his Cambridge colleague (and earlier convert) Thomas Arthur. At Ipswich, Bilney denounced pilgrimages to popular shrines like Walsingham and warned of the worthlessness of prayers to the saints, while at Willesden he attacked the custom of leaving offerings before images, declaring that 'Jews and Saracens would have become Christian men long ago, had it not been for the idolatry of Christian men, in offering of candles, wax and money, to stocks and stones' (*Acts and Monuments*, 4.626). His campaign against idolatry culminated in a Whitsuntide sermon at St Magnus the Martyr in London, in which he urged the king to smash images in imitation of the royal iconoclasts of ancient Israel. Bilney's powerful preaching elicited contrasting responses from his listeners: at least twice he was plucked from the pulpit by incensed opponents, while his words inspired others to individual acts of iconoclasm.

Trial for heresy Given their provocative message, it was scarcely surprising that Bilney and Arthur soon found themselves in trouble with church authorities fearful of heresy spreading from the continent. Arrested, the two men appeared before Wolsey and a panel of bishops at Westminster on 27 November 1527. Wolsey's sole interest was in hunting Lutherans, however; when Bilney denied any sympathy for the German reformer and his doctrines, the cardinal lost interest in the case and left Bishop Tunstal of London to preside over the trial in his place. In answer to the articles put to him by the bishops, Bilney affirmed that Luther was 'a wicked and detestable heretic', and acknowledged the authority of the church and her laws. He even offered an orthodox (albeit ambiguous) reply on the question of images: 'cum sint libri laicorum, adorare oportet' ('when they are the books of laymen, it is proper to revere them'; *Acts and Monuments*, 4.625–6). The bishops then took evidence from witnesses who had heard the accused preach against images and pilgrimages and denounce prayers to the saints. Confronted by these damning depositions and appreciating his predicament, Bilney pursued a shrewd legal strategy, seeking to frustrate the trial by claiming that he could no longer remember the substance of his sermons, and so could make no further answer. Bilney also wrote to Tunstal seeking a private interview to explain his views in detail (perhaps even hoping to convert his judge as he had Latimer and others), but the bishop prudently declined the request. On 4 December the trial reconvened, but each time that Bilney was invited to recant he instead challenged his judges to condemn him, convinced perhaps that they would not dare to do so. At last the frustrated Tunstal began to pronounce sentence, but then unexpectedly adjourned the court before finishing, apparently to furnish Bilney a final opportunity to reconsider his perilous position. The following morning the accused remained obdurate, and sought a further delay by asking to produce witnesses of his own to clear himself through compurgation. After lengthy consultation his judges refused this irregular request, but nevertheless granted Bilney two further days to consult his friends before giving a final answer.

Having exhausted his legal options and facing the flames, Bilney at last submitted on 7 December 1527. After abjuring he was ordered to do penance and then imprisoned. Yet Bilney's legal gambits had not been in vain; he succeeded in saving his tender conscience, for the abjuration which he read aloud had been carefully crafted and was probably unique. In it Bilney renounced 'all maner of heresies and articles folowynge whereuppon I am now diffamyd noted vehemently suspected and convicted' (Guildhall Library, MS 9531/10 fol. 120r), thereby avoiding any clear admission that he himself had preached heresy. Thomas More, who attended the trial, criticized this extraordinary formula 'wherof I never sawe the lyke, nor in so playne a case never wolde were I the judge suffer the lyke hereafter' (More, 271). Throughout his trial Bilney had skilfully exploited Bishop Tunstal's evident reluctance to condemn him. For his part More denounced Bilney as a perjurer who cleverly feigned penitence. Likewise the poet John Skelton rebuked him:

> Men have you in suspicion
> how ye have small contrycion
> of that ye have myswrought.

Prophetically Skelton warned Bilney to amend his preaching

> or els doutlesse ye shalbe blased,
> and be brent at a stake,
> if further busynesse that ye make.
> (*John Skelton: the Complete English Poems*, 379, 382)

Such attacks were judged necessary by the authorities, for it was widely believed that Bilney was no heretic and had simply fallen victim to the vindictiveness of the friars, whose greed he had harshly criticized in his sermons. Six months after the trial, for example, a London priest was in trouble for declaring: 'they that say trouth er [are] ponyshed as bylney and Arthure was' (Davis, 'The trials of Thomas Bylney', 784).

Relapse and condemnation Bilney remained in prison from December 1527 until his release early in 1529, now broken in spirit. Once back in Cambridge he was overwhelmed with guilt and shame for having abjured, and his friends feared for his health. This inner turmoil reached a crisis one evening in early 1531 when Bilney announced to his friends that he was 'going up to Jerusalem' and set off for Norwich to court martyrdom. He began to preach in the open air, renounced his earlier recantation, and distributed copies of Tyndale's forbidden works. He then travelled up to London, where he was arrested in early March and returned a prisoner to Norwich. As a relapsed heretic, Bilney had little hope of escaping the flames.

At his trial, conducted before the chancellor of Norwich diocese, Thomas Pelles, Bilney shrewdly appealed to the king as supreme head of the church, in an effort to postpone his certain condemnation. Pelles, however, was anxious to conclude the proceedings quickly and refused the request (a ruling which would have serious repercussions). Bilney was swiftly condemned, degraded from his orders, and delivered to the sheriffs of Norwich, who ironically included his friend Thomas Necton. While awaiting execution of the sentence he was imprisoned for some weeks in the Norwich Guildhall, where he composed several homilies and drafted a final letter to his elderly parents. He regularly heard mass while in prison.

On 19 August 1531 Bilney was taken under guard, accompanied by a number of his clerical friends, to a spot outside Bishopsgate known as the Lollards' Pit, where a large and sympathetic crowd had gathered, which included the future archbishop of Canterbury Matthew Parker. At the place of execution he was shown a written recantation by Pelles, which he read over silently. After reciting the creed Bilney addressed the assembled crowd, expressing regret for having preached without licence (but not for the content of those sermons) and absolving the friars of any responsibility for procuring his death. Bilney concluded by denying that he had ever taught heresy, and affirming his Catholic faith. The fire was then lit and, its flames fanned by a strong wind, Bilney soon perished.

Ambiguous legacy In the wake of Thomas Bilney's death a wave of iconoclasm swept across East Anglia, while in Norwich itself there was considerable unease at Pelles's summary proceedings in the case, and particularly his dismissal of Bilney's appeal to the king. In response to these concerns, and fearing that he had erred in not acting upon Bilney's appeal himself, the mayor of Norwich, Edward Reed (one of the city's MPs), determined to raise the matter in the parliament which was to reassemble in January 1532. In preparation for this, six weeks after the execution Reed summoned those of his colleagues present at the Lollards' Pit to sign an agreed statement of events. John Curatt, an alderman and rival of Reed, refused to sign, maintaining that Bilney had read aloud a recantation. Curiously, however, he had not heard it himself, for he had stooped to lace his shoe at the crucial moment! Fearful of a parliamentary inquiry into the Bilney affair, the diocesan chancellor Pelles persuaded a sympathetic Lord Chancellor More to conduct his own investigation. In late November 1531 More examined both Reed and Curatt. The mayor maintained that the record of Bilney's final words submitted by Pelles did not accord with his own recollection, and that Bilney had never confessed himself a heretic. For his part Curatt repeated his improbable story about his loose shoelace. Frustrated by political rivalries within the Norwich civic government, More's inquiry soon ground to a halt. Fears of the wider repercussions of Bilney's treatment were well-founded, however, for anger with Pelles's behaviour and a sentiment that Bilney had suffered unjustly contributed to anti-clerical animus which produced the supplication against the ordinaries presented to the king by the Commons in March 1532.

Despite his martyrdom Bilney's life and death presented considerable problems for protestant reformers and historians. While a vigorous opponent of idolatry and critic of the mendicants, he also condemned Luther as a heretic, recanted at his first trial, and apparently died reconciled with the church. While he was praised by his friend (and convert) Hugh Latimer for his purity and simplicity of character, other reformers were less charitable.

Writing in 1533 to the imprisoned John Frith, William Tyndale urged his friend to stand firm in the faith, for the martyrdom of those who previously abjured was 'not glorious': 'Let Bilney be a warning to you' (*LP Henry VIII*, 6, no. 458). The martyrologist John Foxe struggled to portray Bilney as a protestant proto-martyr, but did credit him as 'the first framer of the university [of Cambridge] in the knowledge of Christ' (Porter, 44). Bilney is best seen, perhaps, as an early evangelical, stressing the importance of personal faith and criticizing the abuses of the medieval penitential system. His attacks upon pilgrimages and images place him closer to the native tradition of Lollardy than to the 'new learning' from the continent. Although small in stature, Thomas Bilney was a bold and impatient preacher of the gospel who, having previously escaped punishment through the leniency of Cardinal Wolsey and Bishop Tunstal, in the end fell victim to the fresh prosecution of heretics which followed Thomas More's appointment as lord chancellor in October 1529. Despite the ambiguity of Bilney's status as a protestant *avant la lettre*, his place of honour among early reformers in Cambridge was confirmed in 1955, with the unveiling of a tablet commemorating Thomas Bilney (together with Hugh Latimer and Robert Barnes) in the city church of St Edward, whose pulpit he had often occupied. P. R. N. CARTER

Sources *The acts and monuments of John Foxe*, new edn, ed. G. Townsend, 8 vols. (1843–9) · G. Walker, 'Saint or schemer?: the 1527 heresy trial of Thomas Bilney reconsidered', *Journal of Ecclesiastical History*, 40 (1989), 219–38 · J. F. Davis, *Heresy and reformation in the south-east of England, 1520–1559*, Royal Historical Society Studies in History, 34 (1983) · J. Y. Battey, *On a reformer's Latin Bible: being an essay on the Adversaria in the Vulgate of Thomas Bilney* (1940) · E. Gow, 'Thomas Bilney and his relations with Sir Thomas More', *Norfolk Archaeology*, 32 (1958–61), 292–310 · W. A. Clebsch, *England's earliest protestants, 1520–1535* (1964) · M. Aston, *England's iconoclasts* (1988) · G. Rupp, 'The "recantation" of Thomas Bilney', *London Quarterly and Holborn Review*, 167 (1942), 180–86 · St Thomas More, *A dialogue concerning heresies*, ed. T. M. C. Lawler and others, 2 vols. (1981), vol. 6 of *The Yale edition of the complete works of St Thomas More* · C. Crawley, *Trinity Hall: the history of a Cambridge college, 1350–1975* (1976) · H. C. Porter, *Reformation and reaction in Tudor Cambridge* (1958) · register of Cuthbert Tunstal, bishop of London, GL, MS 9531/10, fol. 120r · J. Guy, *The public career of Sir Thomas More* (1980) · *John Skelton: the complete English poems*, ed. J. Scattergood (1983) · *LP Henry VIII*, 6, no. 458 · J. F. Davis, 'The trials of Thomas Bylney and the English Reformation', *HJ*, 24 (1981), 775–90
Likenesses engraving (*Thomas Bilney plucked from the pulpit*), repro. in *Acts and monuments of John Foxe*, 474

Bilsland, (Alexander) Steven, Baron Bilsland (1892–1970), banker and Scottish business leader, was born on 13 September 1892, at 28 Park Circus, Glasgow, second but only surviving son of Sir William *Bilsland, first baronet (1847–1921), and his wife, Agnes Ann Steven (d. 1935). His father was a rich baker, who received a baronetcy (1907) during his lord provostship of Glasgow.

Steven Bilsland was educated in Glasgow, and at St John's College, Cambridge, of which he became an honorary fellow (1956). During the First World War he was a captain in the Cameronians (8th battalion the Scottish Rifles), served on the staff, and was awarded the MC. In the immediate post-war period he was a director of Gray, Dunn & Co., biscuit manufacturers, and of the private banking firm of Bilsland Brothers. In 1921 he succeeded to the baronetcy, and afterwards became chairman of the family bank.

During the early 1920s Bilsland joined the boards of the Union Bank, the Glasgow Stockholders Trust, and the Scottish Amicable Life Insurance Society. He was a caring capitalist, who felt responsible for promoting the good of others, and constantly supported projects to further Scottish economic progress. He served on the advisory board of Credit for Industry, formed in 1934 as a subsidiary of the Union Dominion Trust to provide finance of up to £50,000. In 1938 he advocated the establishment of a Scottish Development Finance Corporation to provide, in conjunction with Scottish banks, funding and constructive ideas for businesses, but this idea was resisted by other bankers. Bilsland was, however, involved in founding the Industrial and Commercial Finance Corporation set up to invest in smaller companies, and remedy the Macmillan gap (1945). As chairman of the Union Bank he negotiated its merger (1950–52) with the Bank of Scotland, of which he became deputy governor (1955) and governor (1957–66). He also rose to be chairman of the Glasgow Stockholders' Trust and president of Scottish Amicable.

In 1922 Bilsland married Amy Janet (d. 1979), only daughter of David Colville, iron and steel master; the marriage was childless, and Bilsland was ebullient, kind, and attentive with children. His sister Agnes (1890–1970) had previously married Amy's cousin David John Colville, afterwards first Baron Clydesmuir. As a result of these connections he was a director of Colvilles Ltd, steel makers (1937–65), with a special interest in finance. He joined the boards of John Brown & Co., Clydebank shipbuilders, and in 1947 of Burmah Oil, where the chairman relied on his common-sense assessment of new proposals and strategic policy.

Intent on reducing Scottish unemployment Bilsland, together with Sir James Lithgow and Lord Elgin, promoted the Scottish Development Council in 1931. He was also an influential member of the Scottish Council on Industry. When these two bodies were combined as the Scottish Council (Development and Industry), Bilsland was first chairman of the executive committee (1946–55) and president from 1946. He often represented the council in the USA, where he received the medal of freedom and honorary foreign membership of the American Academy of Arts and Sciences. His mantle at the Scottish Council was assumed by his nephew Ronald John Bilsland Colville, second Baron Clydesmuir, who admired him deeply.

In the early 1920s Bilsland became a director of Workmen's Dwelling Company Ltd; later, as first chairman of Scottish Industrial Estates Ltd (1937–55), and of Lanarkshire Industrial Estates (1938–55), he pioneered industrial estates as a way of stimulating new industries in Scotland. Bilsland's association with this work led to his honorary associateship of the Royal Institute of British Architects.

Bilsland was president of Glasgow chamber of commerce (1933–5), honorary colonel of 57th Searchlight regiment of the Royal Artillery, and district commissioner for civil defence in western Scotland, responsible for organizing 60 per cent of the Scottish population (1940–44). He was a Glasgow magistrate (1927), deputy lieutenant for Inverness-shire (1942), a member of the queen's bodyguard for Scotland, received honorary degrees from the universities of Glasgow (1948) and Aberdeen (1956), and the freedom of Aberdeen (1956). He was created Baron Bilsland, of Kinrara, Inverness-shire (31 January 1950) and became a knight of the Order of the Thistle in 1955. He died after a stroke, at his home, 69 Kelvin Court, Glasgow, on 10 December 1970. His hereditary titles became extinct.   RICHARD DAVENPORT-HINES

Sources *The Scotsman* (11 Dec 1970) · *Glasgow Herald* (11 Dec 1970) · *Glasgow Herald* (14 Dec 1970) · *The Times* (15 Dec 1970) · private information (1996) [from Tam Dalyell, MP, 11/1996] · P. L. Payne, *Colvilles and the Scottish steel industry* (1979) · T. A. B. Corley, *A history of the Burmah Oil Company*, 2: 1924–1966 (1988) · A. Slaven, *The development of the west of Scotland, 1750–1960* (1975) · S. G. Checkland, *Scottish banking: a history, 1695–1973* (1975) · R. Coopey and D. Clarke, *3i: fifty years investing in industry* (1995) · b. cert. · d. cert. · Burke, *Peerage* (1970) · *The Times* (Aug 1921) · *DSBB* · *WW*
Likenesses oils, probably Bank of Scotland
Wealth at death £397.730 18s.: confirmation, 31 Dec 1970, *CCI*

Bilsland, Sir William, first baronet (1847–1921), bread and biscuit manufacturer, was born on 17 March 1847 at Ballat, Stirlingshire, the eldest of four surviving sons of James Bilsland, a farmer, and his wife, Anne, daughter of William Blair. Educated at Dalmonach School, Bonhill, north of Dumbarton, at the age of fourteen he was apprenticed to, and then worked for, a grocer and provision merchant in Glasgow. By 1872 he had saved up enough money to set up his younger brothers, John, James, and Alexander, in bakeries, of which they had six in 1875. To help build up capital, they paid themselves very modest wages. As demand for their bread grew, in 1880 Bilsland Brothers—a partnership since 1877—erected a brand new bakery in Hyde Park Street. Unusually for their trade, they installed the latest machinery from Baker Perkins of Peterborough, whose links with developers of baking technology in the United States led to the purchase of an American revolving oven a few years later.

In 1885 Bilsland married Agnes Anne (d. 1935), third daughter of Alexander Steven, a Glasgow engineer. They had two sons and two daughters. The company's main product was the 2 lb white loaf, and in 1900 the factory was turning out 23,000 dozen of these loaves a week and had 200 employees. The technically trained youngest brother, John, ran the production side, which left William free to concentrate on marketing. He built up a fleet of motorized and horse-drawn vans to deliver the bread to 1600 retailers in the Glasgow district, and he created markets in nearby towns and in the western highlands and islands, sending consignments by rail. His success was due partly to his deep understanding of the grocery trade; he took a special interest in the local grocers' and provision merchants' association.

As the market for bread was limited, in 1890 Bilsland began to diversify by acquiring a partnership in Gray, Dunn & Co. of Glasgow, biscuit makers to the queen, a firm then in a stagnant condition. He steadily built it up into one of the leading biscuit firms in Scotland. However, he did not introduce more profitable 'fancy lines', such as scones and cakes, into the bread factory, and he gradually lost his technical lead under intense competition. As senior partner and, from 1915 onwards, chairman of Bilsland Brothers Ltd, he was an autocrat, and the firm marked time while he became ever more immersed in outside interests.

A member of the city council from 1886, Bilsland was lord provost of Glasgow from 1905 to 1908. He was created a baronet in 1907, awarded an honorary LLD from Glasgow University, and made a member of several foreign orders. He was also deputy lieutenant and a JP. His ambitious plan for extending the city boundaries was achieved in 1912, and he took particular interest in promoting leisure facilities, most notably the art gallery at Kelvingrove for the middle classes and the People's Palace and Winter Gardens in the east end for the 'plebs'. Being a lifelong abstainer, he was chairman of the Scottish departmental committee on inebriates, which reported in 1909. His directorships included that of the Royal Bank of Scotland from 1915 onwards. He set up the District Visitors' Association, actively involved himself in relief schemes during the unemployment crisis of 1908, and was chairman of the Glasgow Workmen's Dwellings Company.

Bilsland was a committed Liberal, and as a member of the United Free Church he sat on a committee planning reunion with the Church of Scotland, achieved in 1929. He began weekly meetings for the partners, and later for the board, with a prayer of thanks for the Lord's continuing blessing on the business, and he made regular charitable donations of £1000–2000 a year. Employees were considerately treated in the clean and well-ventilated factory, and relatively high wages were supplemented by cash bonuses and free bread; however, he excluded all trade unions. Bilsland remained chairman until his death, on 27 August 1921, at Gartur, Cambusbarron, Stirlingshire. The baronetcy was inherited by his second son, (Alexander) Steven *Bilsland, later Baron Bilsland.

T. A. B. Corley

Sources N. J. Morgan, 'Bilsland, Sir William', *DSBB* · P. Mathias, *Retailing revolution: a history of multiple retailing in the food trades based upon the Allied Suppliers group of companies* [1967], 312–22 · A. Muir, *The history of Baker Perkins* (1968), 36–40 · *WWW*, 1929–40 · *Glasgow Herald* (29 Aug 1921) · *The Times* (29 Aug 1921) · Burke, *Peerage*
Likenesses photograph, Mitchell L., Glas.
Wealth at death £50,000: Morgan, 'Bilsland, Sir William' · £5005 5s. 5d.: 1922 · £753 14s. 5d.—eik additional estate: 1923 · £131 5s. 0d.—second eik: 1923

Bilson, Thomas (1546/7–1616), bishop of Winchester, was one of the five children of Harmon Bilson (d. 1592) and his wife, Jone (d. 1557). Of German descent but settled in Winchester for two generations, the Bilsons displayed a commitment to the city and to learning that would be reflected in Thomas's career. His grandfather was a brewer in Winchester and his father was an alderman as well as a graduate and former fellow of Merton College, Oxford.

Thomas Bilson (1546/7–1616), by unknown artist, 1611

During Thomas's childhood his uncle Leonard, also formerly of Merton, was the 'learned' master of the free school at Reading, while his stepmother Agnes was the sister of the scholar and musicologist Thomas Stemp, warden of Winchester College.

Early career and writings Bilson entered Winchester College as a scholar in 1559 and from there he proceeded to New College, Oxford, becoming a fellow in 1563, graduating BA in 1566, and proceeding MA in 1570. While at Oxford he was supported by a trust fund for poor scholars established by Robert Nowell. Bilson resigned his fellowship in 1572 but had already ventured on a career as a teacher at Winchester College, where his apprenticeship coincided with the visitation in 1570–71 of Bishop Robert Horne, designed to eradicate lingering Catholicism. Henry Garnet, then a pupil, later recalled that Bilson 'was not at that time malicious' towards the old religion, whereas the headmaster, Christopher Johnson, and Stemp were 'Catholics at heart', and Johnson resigned (Caraman, 6). No less a patron than Matthew Parker, archbishop of Canterbury, then wrote to the college fellows along with four other bishops commending Bilson to the vacancy: only his appointment, they said, would 'satisfie our expectation' (Winchester College muniments, no. 23441). When it came, in 1572, there was an exodus of scholars as the college conformed to Horne's injunctions.

Bilson resigned the headmastership in 1579 in order to concentrate on theological study, proceeding BTh that June and DTh in January 1581, the year he was elected warden of the college in succession to Stemp. Having acquired the canonry of the second prebend at the cathedral along with four Hampshire livings, Bilson now became 'infinitely studious and industrious in Poetry, in

Philosophy, in Physick, and lastly (which his genius chiefly call'd him to) in Divinity' (Harington, 72–3). During these years he produced two substantial and significant works, *The True Difference betweene Christian Subjection and Unchristian Rebellion* (1585) and *The Perpetual Governement of Christes Church* (1593). In the course of well over half a million words the two books established Bilson, alongside Richard Hooker, as the most scholarly and learned of a group of contemporary writers who used the joint challenge of papal supremacy and presbyterian democracy both to carve out a defence of the Church of England and elucidate an English theory of secular governance. Bilson's conclusions were that religion could provide no ground for rebellion and that the secular power of princes was immune from the spiritual jurisdiction wielded by the church; nevertheless, political resistance was legitimate if grounded in the legal and constitutional structure of a particular society. Moreover, hereditary monarchy was by 'the manifest subscription of God' the best form of government (Lake, 133). However, this had to be willed by the people at its outset and there were certain circumstances in which subsequent resistance against tyranny was permissible. In such manner Bilson rejected both the pope's deposing power and the election of church ministers while supporting the political resistance of protestants on the continent.

Bilson pursued his work with a passion. When he first came across William Allen's *Apology and True Declaration* (1581) he felt 'forced for two yeares to lay all studies aside, and addict my selfe wholy' to understanding and attacking its papal claims (Bilson, *True Difference*, 1586, sig. A1). Similarly, when the presbyterian challenge was mounted against the established church he felt obliged by 'causes of such great and good regard ∴ to examine the chiefe groundes of both Disciplines' (Bilson, *Perpetual Governement*, sig. ¶4r). At Winchester, Bilson was the first married warden of the college, breaking with tradition by dining with his family rather than with the fellows and scholars in hall. Privacy and the call of his study were personal priorities and Bilson built himself a substantial house in the college, apparently at his own expense. Nevertheless, the obligations of his office made calls on his time. Not only was there a steady flow of college business requiring his attention, but Bilson also estimated that in his fifteen years as warden he spent £1000 in legal fees defending college interests from unavoidable lawsuits, at a time when the inflationary pressures of successive harvest failures between 1594 and 1597 made recurrent budgeting difficult. Beyond the college precincts he was also active in the drive against Catholic recusancy in the diocese. In March 1585 he complained to Sir Francis Walsingham that sanctions against Catholics were too lax and he sat on the diocesan commission that had been established in the mid-1570s to tackle the problem.

Worcester and Winchester His writing had brought Bilson to prominence, marking him out as a theologian of national political significance and cementing in his own mind the desire to exercise episcopal authority. In autumn 1594 he was offered the deanery of Windsor by William Cecil, Lord Burghley, but made it clear that he had no wish to go there, advising Archbishop John Whitgift 'from his owne mouthe' that Windsor was 'no place for him' (BL, Lansdowne MS 80, fol. 24). Bilson had resolved that only a bishopric would lure him from Winchester. Moreover, as he explained to his colleagues, a bar to becoming dean of Windsor in addition to his existing duties was that the Winchester College statutes permitted only six weeks non-residency in any year. One vacant see was Worcester and Bilson expressed interest in it even though, during the vacancy, the diocese had lost land to the crown without having its valuation for tax revised downwards. After much bartering at court during autumn and winter 1595–6 among at least five privy councillors, Bilson emerged successful through the decisive intervention with the queen on his behalf by Robert Devereux, second earl of Essex. Formally elected on 20 April 1596, his nomination received royal assent on 10 May and he was consecrated on 13 June.

Bilson's career was at a turning point. Having laid theological foundations he now sought to put into practice his model of strong episcopal government closely linked to secular authority. In his first few weeks at Worcester he made a favourable impression. He assisted Sir Robert Cecil in resolving the delicate problem of his successor at Winchester College, where the queen had attempted to impose an ineligible candidate. In doing so he persuaded Cecil that despite reports to the contrary he had improved rather than impoverished the finances of the college during his time as warden. Most significantly from a political point of view, within five weeks of his consecration at Worcester he had compiled a detailed 'view' of the state of his new see expressed in terms designed to appeal to his patrons. It contained an inventory of leading Catholic recusants along with proposed measures for their control, which closely mirrored Burghley's ideal for local action against Catholics. Moreover, by including in his account those protestant recusants 'precisely conceited' against the authorities who 'trouble the people as much with their curiosity as the other with their obstinacy' (*Salisbury MSS*, 6.265–7), Bilson was attuned to a political situation in which Whitgift was wresting from Burghley control of the definition and reach of recusant policy. However, Bilson never put these plans into effect, for in September 1596 the bishopric of Winchester became vacant. Bilson had been at Worcester a mere fifteen weeks but the way was opening for him to return to his native city as its bishop.

It seems that Cecil began to favour Bilson's candidacy for Winchester early in 1597, and the confirmation of this move coincided with the elevation of Richard Bancroft, Whitgift's chaplain, to the bishopric of London. Their joint emergence in senior positions signalled the arrival on the national stage of two men who, over the previous decade, had led the theological argument in print for stronger and more assertive episcopal government. But in Bilson's case there was an added dimension. His accommodating manner suggested that he might be just the man to confront the most notorious of Elizabeth I's demands for alienations from the church for the benefit of the laity—that Sir Francis Carew be granted revenues 'clear to his purse' of 2000 marks per annum, or approximately one-third of the rental value of the diocese (*Salisbury MSS*, 6.139). At first Bilson declared himself 'very willing' to pay Carew an amount to be set by Cecil (ibid., 7.220). In this way he avoided the mistake of his predecessor but one, William Wickham, of raising objections before ensuring that his translation to the see had received royal assent. However, once confirmed as bishop on 13 May 1597 Bilson began to bargain hard in an attempt to minimize the loss to the diocese and defend himself from accusations of simony. A compromise deal was struck. Cecil told Carew to be satisfied with an annual income of £1200 from five major manors of the see for sixty years and Bilson, while not granted the postponement he sought, persuaded Cecil to accept a further proposal—four years in which to pay his first fruits and the award to himself of those summer rents from the now vacant diocese of Worcester that otherwise would have reverted to the crown.

As bishop of Winchester from 1597 Bilson combined the role of national churchman with that of businesslike diocesan. He preached in London, was active in the House of Lords, and also attended every recorded meeting of his diocesan commission (held at his residence at Bishops Waltham), supervising the 'exercises' of would-be preachers. If, unusually among his contemporaries, Bilson delegated the work of his consistory court at Winchester to his chancellor and seldom participated in his diocesan visitations, he presided over a commission that went to unusual lengths to impose fines on moral offenders and censure nonconformist ministers. However, its main business was to encourage recusants to conform, consult with their local minister and take bonds for their future appearance—Bilson believed that excommunication was a meaningless sanction. Inevitably, financial management also occupied his attention. To stabilize revenues in the aftermath of the alienation to Carew, he extended the practice of his predecessor, Thomas Cooper, in converting fixed-term leases to life interest. An additional attraction was that when such conversions arose Bilson was able to exercise patronage for the benefit of relatives.

Theological controversy Between 1597 and 1604 Bilson was engaged on his last major theological enterprise. In Lent 1597 he had preached before the queen, and he amplified his ideas in a sermon at Paul's Cross in London soon after. His chosen theme was highly sensitive. The execution of the separatists Henry Barrow and John Greenwood in 1593 had arisen, in part, from their rejection of a literal understanding of the statement in the apostles' creed that Christ descended into hell. This dogma had been qualified in the forty-two articles of 1553 but was restated literally in the Thirty-Nine Articles of 1563, an interpretation now upheld by Bilson from the pulpit. Uproar ensued. On the prompting of a heckler 'a sudden and causeless fear' took hold of some in the congregation, moved to believe by Bilson's words that the cathedral was about to collapse. In the panic that followed an eyewitness recounted how the tumult 'put some of the gravest, wisest, and noblest of

that assembly into evident hazard of their lives' (Cassan, 68–9). Although calm was restored Bilson was shaken by the 'vehemencie' of his opponents but pressed by others 'to knowe what they might safelie beleeve' (Bilson, *Certain Sermons*, sig. A2). At Whitgift's urging Bilson prepared a text of both sermons for the press, but after consulting with Burghley in May it was decided that, with a new parliament imminent and the controversy still raging, publication should be delayed so as neither to 'effect novelties' nor 'breed gyddynes in the peoples heades' (BL, Lansdowne MS 84, fol. 172). Indeed, the controversy refused to die down. Bilson's teaching was attacked in print on two fronts: by Henry Jacob for maintaining that Christ descended bodily into hell, and by the Hebraist Hugh Broughton for mistaking Hades, the place of departed souls awaiting judgment, for hell itself, the place of torment for the damned. In September 1602, during Elizabeth's last visit to the bishop's residence at Farnham Castle, Bilson reported that she urged him to reply to his critics at greater length so as 'neither to desert the doctrine, nor to let the calling, which I beare in the Church of God, to be trampled under foot by such unquiet Refusers of trueth and authoritie' (Bilson, *Survey of Christs Sufferings*, sig. A). The result, in 1604, was his last recorded publication, a treatise of a further half-million words entitled *The Survey of Christs Sufferings*.

The appearance of *The Survey* was delayed by sickness which, Bilson complained, 'detained me two yeeres from studie'. Nevertheless, he preached at James I's coronation in July 1603 and was one of the main disputants at the Hampton Court conference in January 1604, called by the king to examine the complaints of the puritans. Bilson was opposed to the conference, and according to Stephen Egerton had suggested to James that:

> the Bishops (being esteemed the father and pillars of the Church, for gravitie, learning & government, &c both at home and in forraine parts) might not be so disparaged as to conferre with men of so meane place and quality. (Shriver, 56)

Bilson's poor health ensured that he was overshadowed by the more assertive figure of Bancroft, and all reports of the conference agreed that Bancroft had been highly combative whereas Bilson's critics thought it notable that he 'stoode mute: and said little or nothing' (Usher, 340).

Political involvements When Whitgift died on 29 February 1604 Bancroft, Bilson, and Tobie Matthew emerged as front runners for the primacy. Bancroft prevailed because, it was believed, he was 'more exercised in affaires of the State' (Harington, 71). Ill health may also have played a part, for Bilson was now suffering from sciatica, arthritis, vertigo, 'a continual singing in my head ... many obstructions and extreme windiness' (*Salisbury MSS*, 17.6). In response to these reverses Bilson reassessed his priorities. For over twenty years he had been preoccupied with theological exposition; indeed it was John Harington's view that 'his rising was meerly by his learning' (Harington, 71). In 1605 he helped to co-ordinate those translating the King James Bible, but he no longer felt able to write for the press himself. In the same year he had to abandon plans to answer a new treatise by Henry Jacob on account of 'extreme weakness' resulting from his ailments (*Salisbury MSS*, 17.141). Instead his attention was directed increasingly toward national politics. He involved himself in private hearings and in parliament with the cases of those ministers deprived under Bancroft's drive for subscription of 1604–5, and after 1607, unlike most of his episcopal peers, he ceased attending the local quarter sessions in his diocese, instead becoming one of the two or three bishops who sat regularly in Star Chamber. Although he participated in his diocesan visitation in 1606, he was absent in 1609 and 1612.

On Bancroft's death in 1611 Bilson was again a candidate for the archbishopric of Canterbury. That it should have gone to George Abbot was galling to him: his record of service was much the more conspicuous and the two men had quarrelled during 1606–7 over their respective jurisdictions as bishop and dean of Winchester. More than ever this set Bilson on a course aiming at secular power and patronage, a cause that James assisted by calling on him in 1613 to adjudicate in the sensational divorce case between Robert Devereux, third earl of Essex, and his wife, Lady Frances Howard. When Bilson ruled for Essex this brought him into direct conflict with Abbot, who wrote an account of the affair designed, in part, to discredit his rival. The primate maintained that Bilson's conduct had been reprehensible—'with scoffs, and imperious behaviour, he played the advocate all … day'—while his judgment was distorted by the 'old grudge' he bore towards Abbot who now held the archbishopric that Bilson had 'so desired'. Moreover, recounted Abbot, Bilson had been 'put in hope' that his involvement in the case would secure him membership of the privy council and a knighthood for his son (*State trials*, 823, 817). A separate report sympathetic to Abbot recounted how, after the judgment was given, public opinion turned against Bilson so strongly that his son-in-law complained of the 'perpetual scorn' in which his family would be held and how he was lampooned, men cautioning him that he might find his own marriage dissolved without warning. Bilson's son Thomas, now duly knighted, was also the butt of jokes, a 'merry fellow' having renamed him Sir Nullity. Bilson was depressed and it was said that in particular 'the nick-naming of his son much affected him' (ibid., 833, 829). In a further slur, the archbishop's elder brother Robert Abbot chose this moment to publish the libellous story that, when headmaster at Winchester, Bilson had been so harsh in the use of corporal punishment that his pupils, led by Garnet, had formed a conspiracy to cut off his right hand. Despite these set-backs Bilson retained his appetite for politics. James so appreciated his regular visits to Farnham Castle that in 1608 he obliged Bilson to lease it to Viscount Haddington. Although the king demanded similar alienations elsewhere, Bilson was nevertheless prominent in parliament in 1614 in advocating a new subsidy, arguing that the relief of the king was the religious duty of the people.

Bilson's last assault on secular office occurred in the summer of 1615 when, energetically supported by Robert Carr, earl of Somerset, and despite worsening health, he pressed for the position of lord privy seal. In mid-June Bilson went to London and 'lay hid a great while' before appearing at the court to press a case which, in John Chamberlain's view, made him look absurd. It was, he thought, 'a straunge ambition for a man of his wisdome, yeares and infirmities to aspire to a place with so many difficulties which he cannot long enjoy'. Why, wondered Chamberlain, should Bilson 'suffer himself to be led along after other mens humours and uncertain promises', especially when his actions were satirized in 'a bill clapt up upon the New Exchange'? This offered a reward for information about the missing bishop who, it said, had 'privilie run out of his dioces'. Three weeks later, irritated by the strength of the canvassing on Bilson's behalf, James sent him home 'with goode wordes' but no promises (*Letters of John Chamberlain*, 1.603, 609). In the event, Bilson received instead the reward dangled before him in 1613—membership of the privy council, to which he was sworn at Farnham late in August.

Death and assessment In the remaining months of his life Bilson attended the council regularly and in his last interview with James argued for the release of Sir Walter Ralegh from custody, a case in which he had been involved since 1603. On 17 June 1616 he was taken ill at Greenwich, died the following day 'of apoplexy' at Sir Francis Godwin's house in Westminster, and was buried the same day in Westminster Abbey (*CSP dom., 1611–18*, 375). He was survived by his wife, Anne, and several children. He appears to have died wealthy. By 1613 he had promised to keep the family of his daughter and son-in-law Sir Richard Norton during his lifetime, and he was able to purchase estates in Sussex and Hampshire for his dependants which may have passed to them before his death. James Montagu, his successor as bishop, obtained £1000 from Anne in respect of dilapidations to the diocese and set about repairing its buildings and manors, the majority of which were said to be out of repair.

If Bilson's reputation as a career prelate was tarnished from 1613, his stock as a theologian rose in the thirty years after his death. He was clearly within the Calvinist mainstream of his time yet also a patron of those who would become Arminians through a network centred on New College, Winchester, and Wells. Moreover, the defence that Bilson mounted in his printed works of the ambiguity within the Henrican vision of royal supremacy enabled both Laudians and puritans of the 1630s and 1640s to find arguments in his books to support their positions. In Bilson's lifetime Harington reported that Prince Henry regarded him as 'one of the most eminent of his ranck' (Harington, 71), while Thomas James, Bodley's first librarian and a pupil of Bilson at Winchester, described him in 1625 as 'one of the profoundest Scholars' England had produced (BL, Lansdowne MS 983, fol. 156). For Fuller (1662) he was 'as reverend and learned a prelate as England ever afforded' (Fuller, *Worthies*, 211). As late as 1827 Bilson was still accounted among the most eminent of Elizabethan prelates and one who wrote in a 'more clear and elegant style than any of the divines, his contemporaries' (Cassan,

75). By 1885, however, Bilson's entry in the *Dictionary of National Biography* described his published theology as 'superfluously learned and unattractive … halting in its logic and commonplace in its proofs', and in 1898 F. O. White argued that his career was in many respects 'discreditable' and nepotistic (White, 359). More recent assessments of Bilson have had a dual emphasis: consideration of his financial affairs and systematic appraisal of his theology.   WILLIAM RICHARDSON

Sources P. Lake, *Anglicans and puritans? Presbyterianism and English conformist thought from Whitgift to Hooker* (1988) · K. Fincham, *Prelate as pastor: the episcopate of James I* (1990) · F. Heal, 'Archbishop Laud revisited: leases and estate management at Canterbury and Winchester before the civil war', *Princes and paupers in the English church, 1500–1800*, ed. R. O'Day and F. Heal (1981), 129–51 · T. Bilson, *The true difference betweene Christian subjection and unchristian rebellion* (1585–6) · T. Bilson, *The perpetual governement of Christes church* (1593) · T. Bilson, *The effect of certain sermons touching the full redemption of mankind* (1599) · T. Bilson, *The survey of Christs sufferings for mans redemption* (1604) · J. Harington, *A briefe view* (1653) · F. O. White, *Lives of the Elizabethan bishops* (1898) · P. Collinson, *The religion of protestants* (1982) · *State trials*, vol. 2 · *The letters of John Chamberlain*, ed. N. E. McClure, 1 (1939) · BL, Lansdowne MSS 80, fol. 24; 84, fol. 172; 983, fol. 156 · W. H. Challen, 'Thomas Bilson, bishop of Winchester, his family and their Hampshire, Sussex and other connections', *Papers and Proceedings of the Hampshire Field Club*, 19 (1955), 35–46 · P. Caraman, *Henry Garnet, 1555–1606, and the Gunpowder Plot* (1964) · F. Shriver, 'Hampton Court revisited: James I and the puritans', *Journal of Ecclesiastical History*, 33/1, 48–71 · R. G. Usher, *The reconstruction of the English church*, 2 (1910) · T. Fuller, *The worthies of England*, ed. J. Freeman, abridged edn (1952) · S. H. Cassan, *The lives of the bishops of Winchester*, 2 (1827) · *Calendar of the manuscripts of the most hon. the marquis of Salisbury*, 24 vols., HMC, 9 (1883–1976), vols. 6–7, 17 · *CSP dom.*, 1611–18 · T. F. Kirby, *Winchester scholars: a list of the wardens, fellows, and scholars of … Winchester College* (1888) · Winchester College, muniments, 23441 · J. Nichols, *The progresses … of King James the First*, 1–3 (1828) · N. Tyacke, *Anti-Calvinists: the rise of English Arminianism, c.1590–1640* (1987) · R. Custance, ed., *Winchester College: sixth-centenary essays* (1982) · W. Lamont, 'The rise and fall of Bishop Bilson', *Journal of British History*, 5/2 (1966), 22–32 · *Letters of King James VI and I*, ed. G. P. V. Askrigg (1984) · W. B. Richardson, 'The religious policy of the Cecils, 1588–1598', DPhil diss., U. Oxf., 1994 · Foster, *Alum. Oxon., 1500–1714*, 1.124 · *DNB*

Archives LUL, 'Mirrour of virtues and vices', MS 296 | BL, Lansdowne MSS, 77, 79, 80, 84, 145 · BL, Add. MS 6177 · BL, Burney MS, 366 · Bodl. Oxf., Rawl. MSS D47, D1175 · Bodl. Oxf., Western MSS, 28, 184 · LPL, MS 943 · New College, Oxford, muniments · Winchester College, muniments

Likenesses portrait, 1611, Winchester College [see illus.] · oils, LPL

Wealth at death wealthy: F. Heal, *Of princes and prelates* (1980), 313

Binckes, William (*bap.* 1653, *d.* 1712), dean of Lichfield, was baptized on 25 June 1653, at St Mildred Poultry, London, the son of Richard Binckes of Cheapside. His parents had had several sons and daughters before William and he was to be survived by at least two sisters. He was educated at Westminster School and St John's, Cambridge, where he was admitted pensioner on 1 April 1671, aged eighteen. His education seems to have been made possible by the family of Admiral Sir Francis Wheeler who was his cousin. He graduated BA in 1675 and MA in 1678, and was a fellow of Peterhouse in 1677–83. He was rector of Kelshall in Hertfordshire in 1681–2, and in 1683 was appointed by the

Wheelers as vicar of Leamington Hastings in Warwickshire. In 1683 he also gained the prebendary of Nassington, Lincoln. In 1697 he became prebendary of Dasset Parva, Lichfield. He proceeded DD in 1699, and was installed as dean of Lichfield on 19 June 1703.

Binckes first achieved notoriety for a sermon preached to convocation on 30 January 1702. This occasion, the anniversary of the execution of Charles I, often produced wild panegyrics of the martyred king from tory-leaning clerics, but Binckes exceeded even the traditions of the day with passages comparing Charles, rather favourably, to Christ. By 16 May, the sermon had come to the attention of the House of Lords, which resolved that the parts of it suggesting the English had committed a greater crime in 1649 than the Jews had perpetrated at Calvary gave 'just Scandal and Offence to all Christian People' (*JHL*, 17.132). The Lords stopped short of having the sermon declared blasphemous, or ordering it to be burnt, but they did ask John Hough—Binckes's ordinary as bishop of Lichfield and Coventry—to discipline its author. Two things may be said in mitigation of Binckes here. First, he was unlucky to get caught in the crossfire of party pamphleteering. His sermon only came to public attention when attacked by the vehemently whig *Animadversions upon the Two Last 30th of January Sermons*, an incendiary publication denigrating Charles I's memory which had been condemned to be burnt by the Lords just before they turned to deal with Binckes. Second, some of the preacher's arguments were embarrassingly cogent. A supporter was able to write a solid *Explanation of some Passages* in the sermon (1702), and Binckes's point that Charles's virtue was more impressive than that of Christ, since Christ's divine nature meant he had no choice but to be virtuous, had a certain logic.

While struggling to limit the damage done by his sermon, Binckes began his career as a champion of the lower house of convocation. A member of this body during its 1701–2 session, he joined its 'high-church' majority in demanding that it be allowed to conduct business without permission from the house of bishops. His *Expedient Proposed* (1701) put this argument, and his *Prefatory Discourse* (1702) revealed the underlying reason for it. The *Discourse* attacked Bishop Gilbert Burnet's *Exposition of the Thirty Nine Articles* (1699) for introducing anti-episcopal, anti-Trinitarian, and pro-dissenting interpretations of Anglican doctrine, and stated that the lower house of convocation must be able to act against such heterodoxy without hindrance from bishops contaminated by it.

Fired by these fears for the future of the Church of England, Binckes was active in the 1702–3 convocation and preached an anti-dissenting sermon before the House of Commons on 5 November 1704. In that year he was rewarded for his zeal by election as prolocutor (chair) of the lower house of convocation. Binckes was re-elected to this post for the next session, and consequently played a central role in the 'church in danger' crisis of 1705–6. In particular, Binckes led his house in rejecting the bishops' address to the queen, a document which had denounced those (like Binckes) who had been warning that the established church was under threat from dissent and heresy.

The prolocutor also submitted an alternative draft of the address, he helped draw up a justification of the lower house's conduct, and was accused by the bishops' side of hiding the lower house's minutes to obscure his disloyal extremism. By 1707 the prolocutor was again involved in procedural disputes, when he led the lower house in protesting that the queen could not prorogue them while parliament was still sitting. When the bishops summoned the lower clergy to hear the queen's dismissive response to this on 10 April, Binckes failed to go, and Archbishop Thomas Tenison took the opportunity to censure his adversary with a writ of contumacy. Binckes was forced to submit to this, and apologized for his earlier absence.

Although this record reveals a clear enthusiast for the high-church cause, there is evidence that Binckes actually took a more moderate line than many on his side of the argument. He constantly appealed for church unity; he suggested conciliatory resolutions of procedural disputes in convocation; he was unusually courteous in his dealings with the bishops; his absence on 10 April 1707 seems to have been the result of misunderstanding rather than contempt; and he rejected suggestions that he should refuse to submit to Tenison over the writ of contumacy. Such moderation earned Binckes grudging respect from enemies, but appears to have cooled the ardour of allies. His behaviour in 1707 was criticized from high-church positions and he was not re-elected prolocutor after that year.

Outside the bearpit of convocation Binckes showed a concern for pastoral provision in the Lichfield diocese, which again led him away from high-church stereotypes. In 1705 he preached before the commissioners building the new parish church of St Philip's in Birmingham, welcoming the benefit a new church would bring and, remarkably, thanking local dissenters for their financial support. Binckes also left church plate to his parish of Leamington Hastings (1699); gave gifts to the poor of Lichfield and Leamington on his death; and built the existing deanery in the cathedral close at Lichfield (1704–7), a two-storey, seven bay edifice, praised by Pevsner.

Binckes died on 19 June 1712 and was buried at Leamington Hastings. His will mentioned no wife or children, and thanked his younger sister Dorothy for her care of his domestic affairs. By this will Binckes made provision for his siblings and for a nephew by his eldest sister (mostly out of the proceeds of £200 worth of South Sea stock), and left the residue of his estate to members of the Wheeler family. While the will's preamble, stressing his membership of a 'Catholick' established church, might confirm him as a high-churchman, Binckes's career also illustrated the complexity and ambiguity of any such description.   TONY CLAYDON

Sources Venn, *Alum. Cant.* · *Fasti Angl.* (Hardy), 1.193; 2.564, 600 · *The resolutions and proceedings of the right honourable the lords spiritual and temporal in parliament assembled on Saturday the 16th May 1702* (1702) · *JHL*, 17 (1701–4), 132 · *Animadversions upon the two last 30th of January sermons, the one preached to the Honourable House of Commons, the other to the Lower House of Convocation* (1702) · *An explanation of some passages in Dr Binckes' sermon preached before the lower house of convocation* (1702) · *An account of the proceedings in the convocation which began Oct 25 1705* (1706) · [E. Gibson], *An account of the proceeding in convocation, in a cause of contumacy* [1707] · *Staffordshire*, Pevsner (1974) · *VCH Warwickshire*, vol. 6 · T. Lathbury, *A history of the convocations of the Church of England* (1853) · G. Every, *The high church party, 1688–1718* (1956) · J. P. Kenyon, *Revolution principles: the politics of party, 1689–1720* (1977) · PRO, PROB 11/528, fols. 80v–81v · Cobbett, *Parl. hist.*, 6.22–3 · *CSP dom.*, 1703–04, 263, 265 · IGI

Bindley, Charles [*pseud.* Harry Hieover] (**1795/6–1859**), writer on field sports, concentrated upon hunting and stable management. His first work of any importance was *Stable Talk and Table Talk, or, Spectacles for Young Sportsmen* (2 vols., 1845–6). It provides only passing hints about Bindley himself—that around 1825–30 he had been 'on duty' near Dublin, that he spent most time in Leicestershire and Lincolnshire, that he had travelled in Spain and France (tending to get into fights over French road manners), and that his father had been 'for fifty consecutive years an enthusiastic fox-hunter' (Hieover, 1.421). In writing he admitted to not being one of those for whom 'pecuniary advantage was quite beneath their consideration' (ibid., 1.iii), despite having been careful, since losing £50 at his first race meeting (Newmarket, aged fifteen), never to venture more than £5 on any one bet.

In *Stable Talk*, a rollicking 'Hunting Song' and 'The Doctor, a True Tale', comically rhymed, helped to enliven Bindley's animated prose. *The Stud for Practical Purposes and Practical Men* (1849) included two illustrations, each engraved 'from a painting by the author', representing a well-shaped roadster, 'A Pretty Good Sort for most Purposes' and a wicked-looking, unsightly hack, 'Rayther a Bad Sort for any Purpose'. Other books from the same hand were *Practical Horsemanship* (1850), with illustrations portraying the one 'Going like Workmen' and the other 'Going like Muffs', and *The Hunting Field* of the same year, with pictures of 'The Right Sort' and 'The Wrong Sort'. In 1852 under the pseudonym Harry Hieover he produced a new edition, carefully revised and corrected by him, of Delabere Blaine's *Encyclopaedia of rural sports, or, Complete account, historical, practical, and descriptive, of hunting, shooting, fishing, racing, &c.* Perhaps actuated by the financial pressures at which he had hinted, Bindley continued to produce sporting books and essays at a considerable rate for the rest of the decade.

Bindley's health had been seriously declining, and in November 1858, in hopes of improving it, he left London for Brighton, where he became the guest of his friend, Sir Thomas Barrett-Lennard bt, and died in his friend's house, 7 Lewes Crescent, Kemp Town, Brighton, on 10 February 1859, aged sixty-three. In the number for that very month of the *Sporting Review* appeared his last contribution to the magazine, 'Riding to Hounds, by Harry Hieover'. He was a sporting writer of the old school, and seemed to write under the same exhilaration of spirits as he might have felt when going across country.

CHARLES KENT, *rev.* JULIAN LOCK

Sources *Sporting Review*, 41 (1859), 155 · *GM*, 3rd ser., 6 (1859), 344 · H. Hieover [C. Bindley], *Stable talk and table talk, or, Spectacles for young sportsmen*, 2 vols. (1845–6) · Boase, *Mod. Eng. biog.*

Likenesses H. Adlard, stipple, pubd 1846 (after J. W. Childe), BM, NPG · portrait, repro. in Hieover, *Stable talk and table talk* · portrait, repro. in H. Hieover [C. Bindley], *The pocket and the stud* (1848)

Bindley, James (1739–1818), book collector, was born in London on 5 January 1739, the second son of John Bindley (d. 1761), a prosperous distiller, and his wife, Alice, *née* Odell (*fl.* 1727–1760), of Finchley. The family residence was in St John Street, Smithfield, and Bindley was educated under Dr Lewis Crusius at the nearby Charterhouse. Here, while acting in Terence's *Electra*, he was noticed by Bishop Edmund Keene, who persuaded his father, who had intended him for the law, to send him instead to Peterhouse, Cambridge, where Keene was master. Bindley matriculated in 1756, graduated BA in 1759, and proceeded MA in 1762. He was a fellow of Peterhouse from 1762 to 1778. He studied for the church, but on the appointment of his brother John to the board of excise in 1763, he replaced him as a partner in the family business. John Bindley (1728–1786), an adherent of Charles Jenkinson, and MP for Dover (1766–8), was also responsible for his brother's appointment as a commissioner of the stamp office on 5 January 1765. Bindley held this position until his death, performing his duties with remarkable diligence. In 1775 he compiled an anonymous *Collection of the Statutes now in Force, Relating to the Stamp-Duties*, his only publication. In 1781 he became senior commissioner.

A self-avowed 'incurable Bibliomaniac' (BL, Add. MS 34568, fol. 188b), Bindley lavished almost his entire income on his collections of medals, engravings, and books. His library was rich in English rarities of the Elizabethan and Stuart periods. Generous in his assistance to two generations of scholars, he counted among his friends Thomas Park, James Boswell the younger, Francis Douce, the Revd James Granger, and Edmond Malone, the last of whom considered him 'indefatigable in the pursuit of truth' (*The Correspondence of Thomas Percy & Edmond Malone*, ed. A. Tillotson, 1944, 171). In 1814 Isaac D'Israeli declared that Bindley 'preserves among us the spirit of the BODLEYS and the SLOANES' (I. D'Israeli, *Quarrels of Authors*, 1814, 1.xiii). Dedicatee of the pseudonymous *Chalcographimania* (1814), in which he features, and of Joseph Haslewood's edition of *The Dialogues of Creatures Moralised* (1816), Bindley was amused and flattered by Dibdin's depiction of him as Leontes in *Bibliomania* (2nd edn, 1811) and *The Bibliographical Decameron* (1817). He contributed many notes to William Bray's edition of John Evelyn's diary (1818), on reading the proofs of which he recalled with pleasure his own continental tour of 1763–4, undertaken with Louis Dutens. He similarly assisted his friend John Nichols, reading every sheet of the *Literary Anecdotes* (8 vols., 1812–15). This is also dedicated to him, as is the fourth volume of Nichols's *Illustrations* (1822), in which he is described as a 'kind-hearted and intelligent Bibliographer' (p. vii).

While still an undergraduate, on 25 July 1757, at Wigston in Leicestershire, Bindley married Frances Buzard (c.1736–1779). The couple had no children. A lifelong invalid, Bindley died at his apartments in Somerset House on 11 September 1818. At his death he was father of the Society of Antiquaries, having been elected a fellow on 13 June 1765. Bindley's executrix, Mrs Mary Lines (c.1734–1825), had lived with him platonically for some years prior to his death, unknown even to his closest friends. His collections were auctioned, and the proceeds divided among four nephews and nieces. The prints (including many fine British portraits) and medals were sold by Samuel Sotheby in four sales between January and July 1819, for approximately £7700. The bulk of the library was sold by Robert Harding Evans in four sales between December 1818 and August 1820, fetching approximately £13,500. Evans, who had won the right to auction the books by improving on Sotheby's terms while the latter was in Paris, catalogued them negligently, burying valuable items in general lots. Nevertheless, tremendous prices were achieved, with Richard Heber, James Perry, and Robert Triphook prominent purchasers. Some of the rarest books, from Narcissus Luttrell's library, and acquired by Bindley at the Wynne sale of 1786, had been used by Scott in preparing his edition of Dryden. Many items were subsequently acquired by public collections, but often still bear Bindley's distinctive armorial bookplate. Old-fashioned in appearance, and with a remarkably retentive memory, Bindley was, according to Philip Bliss, 'a most worthy man; polite & friendly in his manners, pleasant in his conversation, and endowed with good taste refined by great classical attainments' (BL, Add. MS 34568, fol. 188b). He was buried on 17 September 1818 in the church of St Mary-le-Strand, where a fine memorial tablet, executed by Josephus Kendrick at Mrs Lines's expense, and the first to be erected in the church, is now placed in the gallery.

MARC VAULBERT DE CHANTILLY

Sources parish register, Holborn, St Sepulchre, 24 Jan 1739 [baptism] · parish register, London, St Benet Paul's Wharf, 2 May 1727 [marriage: John Bindley and Alice Odell, parents] · parish register, London, St Mary-le-Strand, 17 Sept 1818 [burial] · PRO, E 112/1614, no. 1287; IR 27/164, fol. 28 · will, PRO, PROB 11/862, fols. 48a–49a [John Bindley] · will, PRO, PROB 11/1609, fols. 39b–40a · LondG (12–15 Feb 1763) · LondG (1–5 Jan 1765) · GM, 1st ser., 49 (1779), 472 · GM, 1st ser., 56 (1786), 183 · GM, 1st ser., 88/2 (1818), 280, 631–2 · GM, 1st ser., 89/1 (1819), 579 · BL, Add. MS 15951, fols. 3–4; Add. MS 25102, fols. 238–9; Add. MS 34568, fols. 188–9; Althorp.G.334, Dibdin to Spencer, 11 Dec 1818 · L. B. Namier, 'Bindley, John', HoP, Commons, 1754–90, 2.90–93 · BL, S. C. Evans 9 (1–5); S. C. Sotheby 110 (1–4), Lugt 9502, 9526, 9587, 9636 · Venn, Alum. Cant., 2/1.263 · T. F. Dibdin, Reminiscences (1836), 294, 620–22 · S. Sculptor [W. H. Ireland], Chalcographimania, or, The portrait-collector and printseller's chronicle (1814), dedication and 134–5 · S. De Ricci, English collectors of books and manuscripts (1930), 30, 94, 104 · W. Y. Fletcher, English book collectors (1902), 244–8 · R. Gunnis, Dictionary of British sculptors, 1660–1851, new edn (1968), 226 · private information (2004) [R. W. Lovatt, Peterhouse, Cambridge; A. James, Society of Antiquaries] · Letters between Rev. James Granger … and many of the most eminent literary men of his time, ed. J. P. Malcolm (1805), 116–17, 384–9
Archives Bodl. Oxf., Douce papers; Hughenden papers deposit; Malone papers
Likenesses J. Parry, etching, pubd 1813, BM, NPG · J. Basire, engraving, 1818 (after drawing, aged forty-eight), repro. in Nichols, Illustrations, 4 (1882), frontispiece · W. Holl, stipple, pubd 1819 (after drawing by W. Behnes), BM, NPG · W. Say, mezzotint, 1819 (after drawing, aged forty-eight), BM; repro. in J. Ames, Typographical antiquities, ed. Dibdin (1819)
Wealth at death books, prints, and medals sold after death for £21,255 19s. 6d.; death duty paid on £21,128 10s. 3d.: PRO, death duty

registers, IR 26/734, fols. 72*b*–73*a*; BL, S. C. Evans 9 (1–5); BL, S. C. Sotheby 110 (1–4)

Bindoff, Stanley Thomas [Tim] (1908–1980), historian, was born at 13 Stirling Place, Hove, Sussex, on 8 April 1908, the son of Thomas Henry Bindoff, a barman, later described as a licensed victualler's manager, and his wife, Mary Jane Emma Ball. Educated at Brighton grammar school under a great history master, A. E. Wilson, he went on to University College, London (UCL) in 1926, when J. E. Neale was about to succeed A. F. Pollard. After graduation, he kept the wolf from the door as a research assistant, a professional indexer, and as history tutor to the future King Farouk of Egypt. In 1935 Bindoff joined the staff of University College, and with the outbreak of war followed the department to north Wales, where he lived among the slate quarries and Bible-black chapels of Bethesda, later acknowledging the hospitality of its 'kindly folk'. There followed three years with the naval intelligence division of the Admiralty. On 18 April 1938 he married Marjorie Blatcher (*b.* 1906/7), Pollard's research assistant, an authority on the technicalities of legal history. At the age of forty-two, Bindoff confessed that he had enjoyed 'a career remarkable chiefly for its uneventfulness'. The thirty years of life which remained were not so much eventful as filled with selfless service. In 1951 Bindoff was appointed the first professor of history at Queen Mary College in the Mile End Road, London, where his impact was great. He became a statesman in the complex affairs of the University of London. Bindoff remained at Queen Mary College until retirement, after which he continued to live in Surbiton, which makes a suitably undramatic terminal point.

In 1950 Bindoff published his *Tudor England* in the Pelican History of England series. Since he is remembered as a Tudor historian, it might be thought that, Elisha-like, he had simply taken on the Pollard–Neale mantle. But the truth was more interesting. University College had engaged the services of the greatest Dutch historian of his generation, Pieter Geyl. Under Geyl's supervision Bindoff wrote an MA thesis, 'Great Britain and the Scheldt, 1814–1839', based on research in Dutch and Belgian archives, as well as in the papers of Lord Palmerston. Harold Temperley was another influence. In 1945 the Dutch government sponsored the publication of *The Scheldt Question to 1839*, which traced this long-running diplomatic issue from its beginnings in the fourteenth century. The book was dedicated to Geyl, with whom Bindoff had co-operated in translating *The Netherlands Divided* (1936), part of his *Geschiedenis van de Nederlandsche stam* (1934). *The Scheldt Question* is spoken of with respect, so that it is distressing to report that it was first borrowed from the Cambridge University Library in February 1998.

The fate of *Tudor England* was different. It was a runaway success. And here we detect the influence of R. H. Tawney, for Bindoff had used his Tudor special subject teaching (reflected in Tawney and Power, *Tudor Economic Documents*) to strengthen his credentials as an economic and social historian, at a time when social history was still a literary,

and humane, pursuit. So *Tudor England* was more a history of the English people than of the English state, and its epicentre was a chapter which analysed the interactive economic and social crises of the 1540s, a time as pregnant with change for the Englishman's getting and spending as the 1530s were for his governance and creed. Elsewhere he put into the mouths of the Norfolk farmers who made the so-called Ket's rebellion of 1549, and who lay in their mass grave at Dussindale, this *prosopopeia*: 'What sort of people do they think we were? We who lie here were honest, sober, sturdy folk, having God and the commonwealth before our eyes.' Bindoff was a man of conservative inclinations, but this was a book redolent with the values of Clement Attlee's England. It was also saturated in the language of the Bible (and of Shakespeare), although the Bindoffs had married in a register office.

Bindoff never wrote another book. In 1978, at seventy, the editors of his Festschrift (*Wealth and Power in Tudor England*) counted twenty-nine published items, not including a modest batch of reviews. The books which Bindoff never wrote were his postgraduate students, with whom he spent countless hours, in seminars (in 1952 Bindoff detached himself from the Neale seminar and began to preside over his own), in the tea-room of the Institute of Historical Research, and often in the pubs of Store Street. The pipe, the gruff and slow-moving voice: these were what laboriously animated the most important experience of their lives for many of these pupils.

Bindoff's later years were dominated by the History of Parliament, a gazetteer of members and constituencies of the House of Commons. Bindoff was the editor of the section covering the parliaments of 1509–58, and the three stout volumes which appeared in 1982 were published in his name. Once again, Bindoff's massive learning was modestly concealed rather than displayed. He wrote no general introduction, and while his personal input to all of the biographical essays was considerable (and one of the last things he did was to read the proofs), he appended his initials to only nine of the 2263. One of these subjects was Thomas Cromwell, but the remaining eight were MPs so obscure that even their very names are in doubt. Either no other member of the team wanted, or was trusted, to handle these hard cases; or, more plausibly, Bindoff took characteristic pleasure in the sublimely pointless task of establishing the real identity of Edward Lloyd, or Floyd, or Powell, or Sooll, the MP for Buckingham in 1529. Students were told that that was what history was all about. However, Bindoff called the 'H. of P.' 'the monkey on my back' and regretted that he never wrote the ambitious books projected, on Antwerp and on the international economics of early modern northern Europe.

Bindoff fell ill with bronchopneumonia in the winter of 1980 and died on 23 December at 24 Langley Avenue, Surbiton, Surrey, survived by his wife Marjorie, a son, and a daughter.　　　　　　　　　　　　　　　PATRICK COLLINSON

Sources personal knowledge (2004) · P. Collinson, *Tudor England revisited* (1995) · R. F. Leslie and A. G. Dickens, 'S. T. Bindoff: an appreciation', *Wealth and power in Tudor England: essays presented to*

S. T. Bindoff, ed. E. W. Ives, R. J. Knecht, and J. J. Scarisbrick (1978), xv–xxi · W. Lamont, *History Workshop Journal*, 12 (1981) · S. T. Bindoff, *Tudor England* (1950) · S. T. Bindoff, *Ket's rebellion 1549* (1949) · b. cert. · m. cert. · d. cert. · *CGPLA Eng. & Wales* (1981)

Archives JRL, *Manchester Guardian* archives, letters to the *Manchester Guardian*

Likenesses photograph, repro. in Ives, Knecht, and Scarisbrick, eds., *Wealth and power in Tudor England* (1978), frontispiece

Wealth at death £107,188: probate, 14 Aug 1981, *CGPLA Eng. & Wales*

Bindon, David (*c*.1690–1761). *See under* Bindon, Francis (*c*.1690–1765).

Bindon, Francis (*c*.1690–1765), portrait painter and architect, was the fourth son of David Bindon (*d.* 1733) of Cloony, co. Clare, and his wife, Dorothy Burton, the daughter of Samuel Burton of Buncraggy, co. Clare, Ireland. Bindon's father had been member of the Irish parliament for Ennis, co. Clare, a seat the family partially controlled, and he was a substantial land owner in co. Clare. In 1713 Bindon is recorded as studying at the academy in Great Queen Street, London, where Sir Godfrey Kneller was governor. He studied painting and architecture in Italy and on his return to Ireland worked as a portrait painter and architect. Bindon was a scholar, he owned a notable library, and counted among his friends Jonathan Swift, whose portrait he painted several times between 1735 and 1740 (National Gallery of Ireland and St Patrick's Cathedral, Dublin, and Howth Castle, co. Dublin). In connection with this portrait an epistle, in Latin verse, was addressed to Bindon by William Dunkin: 'Epistola ad Franciscum Bindonum'. Of this an English poetical version was published in 1740, *An epistle to Mr. Bindon, occasioned by his painting a picture of the Rev. Dr. Swift, dean of St. Patrick's.* Through his social and scholarly connections he received commissions to paint Lionel, first duke of Dorset, lord lieutenant of Ireland (1734); Lord Clare (1740); Hugh Boulter, archbishop of Armagh (1742; TCD); Richard Baldwin, provost of Trinity College, Dublin (1747; TCD); Eaton Stannard, recorder of Dublin (1747); Dr Patrick Delany, dean of Down; and Charles Cobbe, archbishop of Dublin. Work by Bindon was frequently engraved by James McArdell (1728/9–1765), Andrew Miller (*fl.* 1737–1763), and John Brooks (*fl.* 1730–1756), and his portraits of Swift, Archbishop Boulter, Charles Cobbe, Brigadier-General Richard St George, Henry Singleton, chief justice of Ireland, and Hercules Rowley MP were all published in Dublin. Bindon executed small-scale portraits in oils on copper such as his portrait of Turlough O'Carolan, the composer and harpist (National Gallery of Ireland), and enamel miniature portraits.

Bindon's portraits are stiff and awkwardly posed: his reputation as a painter was based on the lack of competition rather than on his skill. However he enjoyed the esteem of his fellow painters and in 1733 he was presented with the freedom of the Guild of St Luke the Evangelist, the Cutlers, Painter–Stainers and Stationery Company of Dublin. Bindon taught painting and he is known to have had the portrait painter Charles Exshaw (*fl.* 1749–1771) as a pupil.

The attribution of much of Bindon's architectural work is problematical. His name has been linked with many buildings in Ireland, but the buildings firmly attributed to him are his country houses in co. Kilkenny. Bindon designed Bessborough (*c*.1744) for Brabazon Ponsonby, first earl of Bessborough; Woodstock (*c*.1745) for Sir Edward Fownes (now a ruin); and Castle Morres (dem.). Bindon's architectural style is related to the work of the German architect Richard Castle, who was the leading architect of his day in Ireland. Bindon collaborated with Castle during the 1740s and he probably completed Russborough, co. Wicklow, after Castle's death in 1751. As with his portrait painting, his buildings confirm Bindon's status as a gentleman-amateur rather than an innovative professional. He was listed as a subscriber to John Aheron's *General Treatise on Architecture* published in Dublin in 1754.

In 1750 Bindon had been granted an annual government pension of £100 which was a rare honour for a painter. By 1758 he had become slightly blind and he gave up painting. On the death of his elder brother **David Bindon** (*c*.1690–1761), writer on trade and commerce and author of two tracts on Wood's coinage, Bindon became member of parliament for Ennis, co. Clare, and inherited more of his family estates in co. Clare. In 1762 he was made a freeman of Limerick. Bindon died, unmarried, in Dublin, on 23 May 1765 'in his chariot, on his way to the country' (*Faulkner's Dublin Journal*, 4–8 June 1765). He left most of his possessions to Francis Ryan (*fl.* 1756–1788), a Dublin portrait painter. J. T. GILBERT, *rev.* PAUL CAFFREY

Sources *Faulkner's Dublin Journal* (4–8 June 1765) · W. G. Strickland, *A dictionary of Irish artists*, 1 (1913), 63–7 · the Knight of Glin, 'Francis Bindon, *c*.1690–1765: his life and works', *Quarterly Bulletin of the Irish Georgian Society*, 10/2–3 (1967), 1–36 · I. Bignamini, 'George Vertue, art historian, and art institutions in London, 1689–1768', *Walpole Society*, 54 (1988), 1–148 · A. Crookshank and the Knight of Glin [D. Fitzgerald], *The painters of Ireland, c.1660–1920* (1978) · H. Potterton, '"A commonplace practitioner in painting and etching": Charles Exshaw', *The Connoisseur*, 187 (1974), 269–73 · P. Caffrey, *John Comerford and the portrait miniature in Ireland, c.1620–1850* (1999), 19–20 · P. Caffrey, 'Irish portrait miniatures, c.1700–1830', PhD diss., Southampton Institute, 1995 · E. McParland, 'Bindon, Francis', *The dictionary of art*, ed. J. Turner (1996) · *Illustrated summary catalogue of paintings*, National Gallery of Ireland (1981) · H. F. Berry, *A history of the Royal Dublin Society* (1915), 24 · 'Index of freemen of Limerick, 1746–1836', *North Munster Archaeological Journal*, 3 (1942–3), 105 · J. Ingamells, ed., *A dictionary of British and Irish travellers in Italy, 1701–1800* (1997), 91 · J. Kerslake, *National Portrait Gallery: early Georgian portraits*, 1 (1977), 20, 24

Bing, Geoffrey Henry Cecil (1909–1977), barrister and politician, was born on 24 July 1909 at Craigavad near Belfast, the only son and elder child of Geoffrey Bing, headmaster of Rockport School and Orange lodge supporter, of Rockport, Craigavad, co. Down, and his wife, Irene Hare Duke. He was educated at Tonbridge School and Lincoln College, Oxford, where he obtained a second class in modern history in 1931. He was Jane Eliza Procter visiting fellow at Princeton University in 1932–3. He was called to the

Geoffrey Henry Cecil Bing (1909–1977), by Bassano, 1946

bar at the Inner Temple (1934), at Gibraltar (1937), the Gold Coast (1950), and Nigeria (1954).

Bing's early experience in Ulster gave him a hatred of discrimination and a willingness to defend human rights wherever they were threatened. He became a sort of joyful revolutionary, hurled himself into every scene where his interests were engaged, and always emerged with a good story, however sombre his report. In the mid-1930s he helped to give early strength to the Haldane Society and the National Council for Civil Liberties, founded by Ronald Kidd in 1934. He entered several prisons in fascist countries in search of the 'disappeared', and joined the International Brigades in Spain as a journalist, barely escaping at Bilbao.

Bing was himself very much at home in these left-wing and radical surroundings, and some of his own foreign exploits were aimed at investigating or enlarging an embryo story. He became one of the first anti-Nazis of the 1930s. Nevertheless, when he was called up in the Royal Signals in 1941, Bing's left-wing reputation was still such that he had no prospect save the most menial in a large home establishment. A serious political battle had to be fought in his favour before he was given any chance of worthwhile employment. He then entered an officer cadet training unit, from which he passed out top.

In 1943 Bing did experimental work with parachutes in the GSO2 airborne forces development centre. One of the experiments undertaken disfigured his face for many years. In 1943 he was a signals officer in north Africa and in 1944 accompanied the British liberation forces in western Europe with the rank of major. He was wounded and mentioned in dispatches. In 1940 Bing married Christian Frances, the former wife of Edward Archibald Fraser Harding, and daughter of Sir Ralph Barrett Macnaghten Blois, ninth baronet, of Cockfield Hall, Yoxford, Suffolk; they had two sons. His wife for a time helped Claud Cockburn with his left-wing newspaper *The Week*.

In 1945 Bing was elected Labour MP for Hornchurch, a seat he held until 1955. He was at once appointed as an unpaid junior whip. It was generally thought that this was a mistake for another man of a similar name, who was as much to the right of the party, and so acceptable to Ernest Bevin, as Bing was to the left. The appointment lasted for nine months and then was ended without comment. Bing's first marriage was dissolved in 1955 and in 1956 he married Eileen Mary, daughter of Frederick Cullen, alderman and parliamentary agent for Hornchurch; they had one adopted son.

Bing returned to the back benches where he became 'the unrestrained leader of a small group of radicals, never fully trusted by their colleagues and known as "Bing Boys"' (*The Times*, 25 April 1977). A committed supporter of communist China, he was nicknamed the Mandarin. He also specialized in Northern Ireland, the brewers' monopoly, and parliamentary procedure. In the years after the war his was almost the sole voice calling for help for the Ulster minority. He became adept at the parliamentary devices whereby any issue can be raised, perhaps late at night, which no deputy speaker can reject. Indeed, when Labour was in opposition he was called on by colleagues to guide them through the intricacies of this procedure.

At the bar (he took silk in 1950) Bing built up a small practice in west Africa where he met Dr Kwame Nkrumah, leader of the main party in the Gold Coast. In 1955 the programme for independence was already arranged and Nkrumah urgently needed a legal and constitutional adviser. Bing, having lost his parliamentary seat, got the job in 1956. In 1957 he was appointed attorney-general in Ghana (previously the Gold Coast) and was thus involved in many of the territory's problems. The British government seemed obsessed with the idea that all colonial civil servants would withdraw; Bing had to dissuade them. He also had to order Emil Savundra out of the country for fraud at a time when his true character was not known.

As Nkrumah's right-hand and trusted adviser, Bing played a controversial role 'whether it was to increase press restrictions, a new presidential constitution, or removing the Chief Justice, the elaborate legalism of Bing's mind would find a way to do it.' (*The Times*, 25 April 1977). When a *Daily Telegraph* journalist was arrested Bing announced, on behalf of the Ghanaian government, that he could have any counsel he chose; when Christopher Shawcross QC arrived, Bing, on the orders of Krobo Edusie, the minister of the interior, announced that he was excluded—an act which made it impossible for Bing ever again to work at the English bar. It is arguable that he should have resigned as attorney-general rather than act on Edusie's order.

Bing ceased to be attorney-general in 1961, whereupon he became Nkrumah's adviser. Emancipation of the African colonies was new and the one-party African state was unforeseen. Bing and Nkrumah thought that a liberated colony must try to establish an independent economy, an effort which seemed to require one-party dictatorship whether benign or evil. When Nkrumah was ousted by a *coup d'état* in February 1966 Bing was arrested and illtreated. He had done no wrong and after some months was sent home. He had been appointed CMG in 1960. His aptly named memoir of Nkrumah's Ghana, *Reap the Whirl-wind*, appeared in 1968. Bing died in London on 24 April 1977.   JOHN PLATTS-MILLS, *rev.*

Sources G. Bing, *Reap the whirlwind* (1968) · G. Bing, *John Bull's other Ireland* (1950) · personal knowledge (1986) · private information (1986) [family] · *WWW* · *CGPLA Eng. & Wales* (1977) · *The Times* (25 April 1977)
Likenesses Bassano, photograph, 1946, NPG [*see illus.*]
Wealth at death £11,372: probate, 24 June 1977, *CGPLA Eng. & Wales*

Bing, Gertrud (1892–1964), scholar, was born in Hamburg, Germany, on 7 June 1892, the third child of Moritz Bing, merchant, and his wife, Emma Jonas. She was educated in Hamburg, where she qualified as a schoolteacher and taught for eighteen months. In 1916 she entered the University of Munich to read philosophy, German literature, and psychology. After returning to teaching for a year in 1918, she resumed her studies at the newly founded University of Hamburg under Ernst Cassirer, whose philosophy of symbolic forms preoccupied her throughout her life. She took her PhD degree in 1921 and in 1922 joined the Kulturwissenschaftliche Bibliothek Warburg, a private foundation in Hamburg, in which she was successively librarian and personal assistant to Aby Warburg. After Warburg's death in 1929 she took a major part, as assistant to Fritz Saxl, in the activities of the Bibliothek Warburg and in its removal to Britain in 1933. After 1944, when the Warburg Institute was incorporated in the University of London, Gertrud Bing, as assistant director, took on the work of administrator, first for Saxl, then for Henri Frankfort, whom she had herself proposed should succeed him. In 1955 she in her turn was appointed director of the institute and professor of the history of the classical tradition in the University of London. By 1959, when she retired and was elected honorary fellow of the institute, it had been lodged in its new premises in the Bloomsbury precinct of the university. In the same year she received an honorary DLitt from the University of Reading.

Gertrud Bing's career was one of devotion to scholarship and to the principles on which Warburg had founded his library. She came to accept wholeheartedly Warburg's approach to history, especially the history of the classical tradition and its influence on European civilization. As Warburg's literary executor she edited his *Gesammelte Schriften* (1932), in which her own learning and her gift of understanding and interpreting the ideas of others were fully evident. These talents she was to develop still further in the criticism and editing of scholarly books and articles during her whole life. Saxl's *Lectures*, which she brought out in 1957, was one example among many. One of her last acts was to arrange for the publication of a selection of Warburg's writings in Italian translation (*La rinascita del paganesimo antico*, 1966) and to contribute to it a study of Warburg.

Short, dark, and spectacled, with a serious expression which easily changed to a friendly smile, Gertrud Bing impressed all by her strength of purpose, courage, and humanity. The scholarly concerns of others rapidly became her own. Discussion of them, by telephone or letter, was as much a pleasure to her as it was a benefit to those whose work was being discussed. Her standards were high, her range of competence large. As a critic she was often formidable, never solemn or unfair, always firm and patient, sympathetic and tactful, willing to bring her retentive, scrupulous, and orderly mind to bear on the drafts of friends and colleagues all over the world. She knew how established scholars and beginners alike needed encouragement, but she was never over-indulgent: in the end, she believed, she could only help so far and the final responsibility was the author's.

Gertrud Bing's willingness to devote her time to others was only one reason why she published so little herself. Her masterly memoir of Saxl, in the volume of memorial essays edited by D. J. Gordon in 1957, made no mention of the part she played in the evacuation of the Warburg Institute, its staff, and library, from Nazi Germany to Britain. British and continental scholars were attracted to the 'new' institute in London as much by the personal interest and stimulus offered by Bing (neither she nor her friends used her forename), Saxl, and their colleagues as they were by the novel approaches to historical studies which the library invited. To refugee scholars, among many others who came for practical help and counsel as well as for their own research, Bing was as remarkable for her understanding of human problems and help in resolving them as for her intellectual guidance. Throughout her career and in retirement, she made the institute the centre of her interest and of her studies.

Like Warburg, whom she accompanied on his last visits between 1927 and 1928, and like Saxl, Bing had a lifelong attachment to Italy, especially to Florence. Her knowledge of the country, in the Renaissance and the present, was deep and instinctive. Nothing pleased her more about the Warburg Institute than its traditional associations, continually renewed and fostered, with Italian scholars and scholarship. But Britain had become her home; she was naturalized in 1946; and her house in Dulwich, where she lived for nearly thirty years, with a garden which she herself planted and cultivated, was a meeting-place for friends and scholars from all over the world. She died, unmarried, in University College Hospital, London, on 3 July 1964.   ENRIQUETA FRANKFORT, *rev.*

Sources *Annual Report* [Warburg Institute] (1963–4) · *Gertrud Bing, 1892–1964* (privately printed by Warburg Institute, 1965) [with bibliography] · private information (1981) [friends, colleagues at Warburg Institute] · personal knowledge (1981) · *The Times* (6 July 1964) · *CGPLA Eng. & Wales* (1964)
Archives Warburg Institute Archives, London
Likenesses photographs, repro. in *Gertrud Bing* · photographs, Warburg Institute Archives
Wealth at death £5213: probate, 24 Nov 1964, *CGPLA Eng. & Wales*

Bing, Sir Rudolf Franz Joseph (1902–1997), opera manager, was born in Vienna on 9 January 1902, the son of Ernst Hoenigsvald Bing, head of the Austro-Hungarian Steel and Iron Trust, and his wife, Stefanie. The youngest

Sir Rudolf Franz Joseph Bing (1902–1997), by Lotte Meitner-Graf

open his first season, Ebert directed Verdi's *Macbeth*, scoring a huge success; the following season Fritz Busch conducted Verdi's *Un ballo in maschera*.

In 1933 both Ebert and Bing (who, though a Roman Catholic, was of Jewish descent) were dismissed by order of the Nazi party, which had gained power in Berlin. Bing was unemployed in Vienna when he heard from Busch in England: he and Ebert were working at Glyndebourne in Sussex, where a bold Englishman, John Christie, had built an opera house for his singer wife. The first season took place in the summer of 1934, presenting two operas by Mozart. Bing was engaged as talent scout and general dogsbody; in 1935 he became general manager of the Glyndebourne festival, with year-round employment and a London office.

Bing's skills as an organizer were extremely useful to Glyndebourne in its early years, and the festival grew from the original twelve performances of two operas to thirty-eight performances of five operas in 1939. With the outbreak of the Second World War, future plans were shelved. Evacuees descended on Glyndebourne, but the company ran a tour of John Gay's *The Beggar's Opera* in the spring of 1940, which ended at the Theatre Royal, Haymarket. Though Bing and his wife were technically enemy aliens—their British citizenship came through in 1946—they were not interned. Bing worked as divisional manager at the department store Peter Jones.

Bing conceived the idea of an Edinburgh international festival in 1945. He realized that Glyndebourne was not sustainable in its pre-war format, but that as part of a larger festival devoted to opera, concerts, ballet, and theatre it would be viable. After two years' hard work, Bing presented the first Edinburgh festival in August 1947. Glyndebourne offered *Le nozze di Figaro* and *Macbeth* while there were concerts by the Vienna Philharmonic Orchestra conducted by Bruno Walter, in one of which Kathleen Ferrier sang in *Das Lied von der Erde* by Gustav Mahler. The Glyndebourne company continued to appear at Edinburgh in 1948 and 1949.

In March 1949 Bing, visiting New York to raise funds for Glyndebourne, met Edward Johnson, the Canadian tenor who had been general manager of the Metropolitan Opera since 1935 and now wished to retire. With the Edinburgh festival successfully launched, Bing could not resist the challenge, and Johnson promised to support him as his successor. The Metropolitan secured Bing's release from his Edinburgh contract, and in November 1949 he and his wife arrived in New York for an 'observation year'.

The Metropolitan Opera at that time was on the verge of collapse. There were many good singers, mostly American, on the roster, but a serious shortage of good conductors, while production values were non-existent; operas were thrown on stage with little or no rehearsal. The board, which held the purse strings, considered money spent on designers and new scenery a complete waste. Some of the ancient sets were extremely shaky. According to Bing, 'when the soprano took a deep breath on the Met stage [in *Il trovatore*] the whole castle behind her would be seen to tremble' (Bing, 106).

of four children, he left school at the age of sixteen. He trained his attractive light baritone voice, but did not consider becoming a professional. In 1919 he obtained a job with the Viennese booksellers Gilhofer and Ranschburg. A year later he moved to Hugo Heller's bookshop, which also ran a concert agency, and Bing was soon working on that side of the business. In 1923 the Heller agency moved to larger premises and began dealing with operatic as well as concert artists. Bing managed two concerts given by the British tenor Alfred Piccaver at the Albert Hall, London. He left Vienna in 1927 for Berlin, where he married the Russian dancer Nina Schelemskaya-Schelesnaya in the same year and met the great German actor Carl Ebert, who was retiring from the stage to take up direction.

In 1928 Ebert became general manager of the Hessisches Staatstheater, Darmstadt, and Bing was appointed his assistant. 'The techniques of organising I acquired in Darmstadt stood me in good stead all my life', he wrote later (Bing, 23). Bing spent two fruitful years in Darmstadt, where Karl Böhm was musical director and Max Rudolf the second conductor, but he found the small town frustrating, so in 1930 he moved back to Berlin, where he worked for six months for a film company. Then in 1931 he became assistant administrator of the Charlottenburg opera (Städtische Oper), with Ebert as general manager. To

Bing appointed Max Rudolf, an excellent administrator and conductor, as his assistant, and started planning his first season immediately. He intended to open with Verdi's *Don Carlos*, directed by Margaret Webster and designed by Rolf Gérard. The board jibbed at the cost of the production and of a three-week rehearsal period, but one of the sponsors, a supporter of Bing, sold a Rembrandt to cover the cost. This *Don Carlos* was still in good shape eighty performances and twenty-two years later when Bing retired.

Among Bing's most consequential innovations at the Metropolitan was to introduce black singers. Marian Anderson, the great contralto, sang Ulrica in *Un ballo in maschera* in 1955. She was no longer in her prime vocally, but her symbolic appearance paved the way for many fine American artists to sing there. The Italian soprano Renata Tebaldi, who sang with the company for twenty years, also made her début that year, and in the following season Bing engaged Maria Callas.

Perhaps the most important event during Bing's years at the Metropolitan was the move to the Lincoln Center, New York. The old house closed on 16 April 1966, and the new 'Met' opened on 16 September 1966 with the première of *Antony and Cleopatra* by Samuel Barber. In 1958 Barber's *Vanessa* had been successful, but the new opera was a disaster, despite Leontyne Price's fine Cleopatra. Bing had planned nine new productions for the opening season—several too many, as he later admitted. The New York première of Richard Strauss's *Die Frau ohne Schatten*, conducted by Karl Böhm, was a triumph, but another new opera, *Mourning Becomes Electra* by Marvin Davy Levy, was less popular. In 1968 Bing inaugurated a cycle of Wagner's *Ring*, conducted and directed by Herbert von Karajan, but only the first two operas were given, and the cycle was not completed until after Bing had left the Metropolitan in 1972. He had achieved most of his aims, dragging the company into the twentieth century; in his book *5000 Nights at the Opera* (1972), Bing graphically describes the many battles he fought and the difficulties he overcame.

Bing was appointed CBE in 1956 and promoted KBE in 1971. After his retirement he remained in New York, teaching and lecturing at Brooklyn College, the City University of New York, and elsewhere. His wife, Nina, died in 1983, and soon afterwards he became ill with Alzheimer's disease. In January 1987 he married Carroll Lee Douglas (*b.* 1939/40), who had nursed him in hospital. She spent nearly all his money before he was declared incompetent by the court; the marriage was annulled in 1989. He died on 2 September 1997 at the Hebrew Home for the Aged in the Bronx, New York. He had no children.

ELIZABETH FORBES

Sources R. Bing, *5000 nights at the opera* (1972) · D. Hamilton, ed., *The Metropolitan Opera encyclopedia* (1987) · S. Hughes, *Glyndebourne* (1965) · F. Busch, *Pages from a musician's life* (1953) · *Daily Telegraph* (4 Sept 1997) · *The Times* (4 Sept 1997) · *The Guardian* (4 Sept 1997) · *The Scotsman* (4 Sept 1997) · *The Independent* (4 Sept 1997) · *WWW*
Likenesses group portrait, photograph, 1949, repro. in *Daily Telegraph* · photograph, 1950, repro. in *The Independent* · photograph, 1987 (with Carroll Douglas), repro. in *The Scotsman* · P. Johns, photograph, repro. in *The Guardian* · L. Meitner-Graf, photograph, repro. in Bing, *5000 nights at the opera* [*see illus.*] · photograph (with Maria Callas), repro. in *The Times* · photographs (Hult. Arch.)

Bing, Stephen (*bap.* 1610, *d.* 1681), singer and music copyist, was born in Canterbury and baptized on 20 September 1610 in the parish of St George the Martyr, the only son and second of five children of Stephen Bing (*d.* 1632?), probably a beer-brewer, and his wife, probably Mary (*d.* 1638?). He gained his early musical training from 1617 or 1618 to 1624 as a chorister at Canterbury Cathedral but probably left Canterbury soon after his voice changed, and, although little is known of his activities between 1625 and 1640, it seems likely that he moved to Cambridge some time during the 1630s. There he became acquainted with Sir Christopher Hatton (1605–1670), who was active as a patron of musicians, poets, and Laudian clergymen, and with Hatton's musicians and copyists, in particular George Jeffreys and John Lilly.

In 1641 Bing was appointed a minor canon at St Paul's Cathedral, London, a position which required that the holder be ordained as well as possess a good voice. It is from this period that we have the first evidence of Bing's copying activity, his handwriting appearing in manuscripts of consort music by Coprario, Orlando Gibbons, Lupo, Jenkins, and others. With the outbreak of hostilities in 1642, Bing left St Paul's some time after midsummer and probably joined the king's supporters in Oxford. There he was apparently reunited with Jeffreys, and with Sir Christopher Hatton, now comptroller of the king's household and thus responsible for the music at the Oxford court. Surviving manuscripts suggest that Bing was closely involved, for example as one of the copyists of the 'Great set', a royalist compendium of consort music which represents one of the most comprehensive and valuable sources of English instrumental music in existence (Christ Church, Oxford, MSS). When Oxford yielded to parliamentarian forces on 20 June 1646, Bing probably took advantage of the surrender terms to return to his former employment at St Paul's Cathedral. In April 1649, however, an act of parliament abolishing 'Deans, Deans and Chapters, Canons, Prebends, and other Offices' and requiring the sale of ecclesiastical land and property deprived Bing of both his job and his home. Thereafter, like many redundant church and court musicians during the Commonwealth, Bing supported himself by teaching. He lived, as John Batchiler's *The Virgin's Pattern* (1661) reveals, in Hackney.

Following the Restoration, Bing was appointed senior cardinal (most senior of the minor canons) at St Paul's Cathedral and also served as warden of the college of minor canons between midsummer 1660 and 1662. During the great plague year of 1665 he stayed at the cathedral, acting as almoner to the new dean, William Sancroft, absent in Tunbridge Wells, and ensuring, with a handful of others, that prayers and services continued. He reported to Sancroft his officiating in place of a dying clergyman 'for none else would do it except they are paid for it' and distributing the dean's charity in surrounding parishes until he had 'outrun the bank' (Matthews and Atkins, 177–8). After the destruction of St Paul's Cathedral in the great fire of 1666, Bing was appointed in 1667 senior vicar-choral at Lincoln Cathedral. During this time he was engaged on his Restoration liturgical copying activities, as evidenced in the set of eight books known as the Bing–Gostling partbooks (York Minster, MSS M 1 S), although the majority of pieces appear to have been added following his appointment on 1 April 1672 as lay vicar at Westminster Abbey. Bing also renewed his connections with St Paul's and by midsummer his signatures resume in the minor canons' accounts. At Westminster Abbey in the late 1670s Bing was a colleague of Henry Purcell and copied a number of the composer's early anthems. Bing, who had at a date unknown married Katharine (of whom no details survive), died in London on 26 November 1681 and was buried on 1 December at St George the Martyr, Canterbury. The impressive range of his activities and his long-term and close associations with the country's leading musicians and most influential musical patrons testify to his important status among seventeenth-century English music copyists.   JONATHAN P. WAINWRIGHT

Sources J. P. Wainwright, *Musical patronage in seventeenth-century England: Christopher, first Baron Hatton (1605–70)* (1997) · P. Willetts, 'Stephen Bing: a forgotten violist', *Chelys*, 18 (1989), 3–17 · S. Boyer and J. P. Wainwright, 'From Barnard to Purcell: the copying activities of Stephen Bing', *Early Music*, 22 (1995), 620–48 · J. P. Wainwright, 'The Christ Church viol-consort manuscripts reconsidered: Christ Church, Oxford music manuscripts 2, 397–408 and 436; 417–418 and 1080; and 432 and 612–613', *John Jenkins and his time: studies in English consort music*, ed. A. Ashbee and P. Holman (1996), 198–241 · W. Shaw, *The Bing–Gostling part-books at York Minster* (1986) · D. Pinto, 'The music of the Hattons', *Royal Musical Association Research Chronicle*, 23 (1990), 79–108 · R. F. Ford, 'Minor canons at Canterbury Cathedral: the Gostlings and their colleagues', PhD diss., U. Cal., Berkeley, 1984 · W. R. Matthews and W. M. Atkins, eds., *A history of St Paul's Cathedral and the men associated with it*, 2nd edn (1964), 176–9 · J. M. Cowper, ed., *The register booke of the parish of St George the Martyr* (1891) · Walker rev. · J. Batchiler, *The virgin's pattern: in the exemplary life, and lamented death of Mrs Susanna Perwich* (1661) · W. S. Simpson, *The chapter and statutes of the college of the minor canons in Saint Paul's Cathedral, London* (1871) · J. L. Chester, ed., *The marriage, baptismal, and burial registers of the collegiate church or abbey of St Peter, Westminster*, Harleian Society, 10 (1876) · will, PRO, PROB 11/368/179 · *New Grove*
Wealth at death many bequests to family incl. land in Grantchester, Cambridge: will, PRO, PROB 11/368/179

Binge, Ronald (1910–1979), composer, was born at Derby on 15 July 1910, the eldest of three children of Lawrence Binge, iron moulder, and his wife, Florence Gertrude Davies. His father served as a soldier in the First World War, dying of his wounds in 1920. As a boy Ronnie, as he was known, sang in St Andrew's Church, Derby, soon learning the piano and organ. Private lessons in harmony and counterpoint followed. Straitened circumstances precluded a college education, and at the age of seventeen he took employment as organist at a local cinema, arranging and composing for its small orchestra for silent films.

In 1931 Binge became pianist to a light orchestra at Great Yarmouth, also playing the piano accordion, upon which he eventually became a virtuoso. After moving to London he played in theatre, dance, and café ensembles. In 1935 he began his long association with Mantovani as arranger for his new Tipica orchestra, also playing the accordion.

Among his compositions was music for the film *Thirteen Men and a Gun*.

Binge served in the Royal Air Force from 1940 to 1945; but it was not long before he began directing musical activities in association with Sidney Torch. He composed his first orchestral success, *Spitfire*, at that time. In 1942 he became a link trainer (flight simulator) operator, and in 1944 he met Vera (b. 1922/3), daughter of James Simmons, an electrician. They were married on 2 June the following year. After demobilization, Binge reactivated his association with Mantovani. Much in demand as arranger, he scored Noël Coward's musical *Pacific 1860* for the Drury Lane Theatre in 1946.

Binge's successful compositions included *Madrugado*, *Las Castañuelas*, *The Red Sombrero*, and *Trade Winds*. A composition entitled *Prelude: the Whispering Valley* featured solo piano with strings. In 1951 he was given a free hand for a new recording while Mantovani was away on tour: in this he created the striking 'cascading strings' effect, which brought international acclaim to the new-style Mantovani orchestra. In his BBC radio programme *Sunday Rhapsody* Mantovani also performed Binge's compositions. The most notable work by Binge was *Elizabethan Serenade*, which became an outstanding international success, winning an Ivor Novello award in 1957. Its vocal version, *Where the Gentle Avon Flows*, with words by Christopher Hassall, was issued in several forms.

After these broadcasts Ronald Binge brought to an amicable end his association with Mantovani to concentrate on composition. His subsequent works included music for the films *Desperate Moment* (1953), *The Runaway Bus* (1954), *Dance Little Lady* (1954), *Our Girl Friday* (1953), and many for American television. He received commissions for BBC light music festivals in 1952 (*Thames Rhapsody*) and 1956 (saxophone concerto). He hoped (without success) that colleagues would forget his 'Mantovani sound' achievement, though variants of it came with 'Dance of the Snowflakes' (which can be characterized as 'cascading strings' with trills on) and 'Cornet Carillon', an immediate hit with brass bands.

Binge produced many miniatures for the recorded background music libraries of publishers. The best-known were 'The Watermill', used as the signature tune for BBC television's *The Secret Garden*, and the deceptively simple 'Sailing By', long cherished as late-night signing-off music for BBC Radio 4. Later compositions include the *Saturday Symphony* (1966–8), *Te Deum* (1970), and two albums for solo guitar. From 1952 Binge devised and conducted his own BBC radio programme called *String Song*, creating a new spaciousness in monaural sound. From that time on he regularly conducted his own works at home and abroad.

On a basis of impeccable technique, Binge's originality is evident in his turn of melody (often of an engaging, quirky nature), his intimate understanding of players and their instruments, and a novel use of texture. *The Tales of Three Blind Mice* demonstrated his mastery of counterpoint. He composed two ingenious 'palindromes', a toccata for piano entitled *Vice Versa* and *Upside, Downside* for a school trio, which reads exactly the same whichever way up the performer places the music. Binge was elected a member of the Royal Philharmonic Society in 1951. He believed firmly in the encouragement of 'light music', however inadequate the term, as its own genre. For some years he served on the BBC music advisory committee and the council of the Songwriters' Guild of Great Britain, and also as a director of the Performing Right Society. Ronald Binge died of cancer on 6 September 1979 at Ringwood, Hampshire; he was survived by his wife, son, and daughter. ERNEST TOMLINSON

Sources A. Lamb, 'Binge, Ronald', *New Grove* · personal knowledge (2004) · private information (2004) [Vera Parton; George Elrick; Mike Carey] · transcript of BBC interview with Ronald Binge, 24 Sept 1969, priv. coll. [programme: *Home this afternoon*; interviewer: Ken Sykora] · m. cert. · *CGPLA Eng. & Wales* (1979) · M. Carey, *Sailing by: the Ronald Binge story* (2000)

Archives SOUND BL NSA, documentary recording · BL NSA, performance recordings

Wealth at death £12,656: probate, 24 Oct 1979, *CGPLA Eng. & Wales*

Bingham. For this title name *see* Willoughby, Margaret, Lady Willoughby [Margaret Bingham, Lady Bingham] (*c*.1401–1493) [*see under* Willoughby family (*per*. 1362–1528)].

Bingham, George (1715–1800), Church of England clergyman and antiquary, was born on 7 November 1715 at Melcombe, Dorset, where his family had lived for several centuries. He was the sixth son of Richard Bingham, MP at various times for Bridport and for Dorset, and his wife, Philadelphia, daughter and heir of John Potinger and his wife, Philadelphia Ernle. Encouraged as a boy by his maternal grandfather, he entered Westminster School in June 1726 and was elected as a scholar to Trinity College, Cambridge, in 1732 but chose instead to go up to Christ Church, Oxford, on 25 May 1732. He took his BA on 28 January 1736 and was elected a fellow of All Souls in 1738; he graduated MA in 1739 and BD in 1748.

According to Bingham's son Peregrine 'no man was ever more zealous … for the credit of the university of Oxford, and that of the College of All Souls' (Bingham, *Dissertations*, xxxi), and in 1747 he served as proctor to the university and bursar to his college. At All Souls he formed close friendships with both his fellow bursar, William Blackstone, and Benjamin Buckler, with whose *Stemmata Chicheleana* (1765) he assisted. On 23 May 1748 he was instituted to the rectory of Pimperne, Dorset, and in the same year he resigned his fellowship and married Sarah Beale. They had three children: John, Peregrine *Bingham (1754–1826), and Sarah. However, on 22 May 1756, shortly after the birth of their daughter, Bingham's wife died, in her thirty-sixth year. Bingham then moved briefly to More Critchell, to which living he had been presented by Sir Gerard Napier in 1755, but finding that the village was damp and unhealthy he soon returned to Pimperne. He preached regularly in both places, often repeating sermons that he had composed while at All Souls. He was elected proctor for convocation to the diocese of Salisbury in 1761, 1768, 1774, and 1780, and from 1774 the living of

Long Critchell was annexed to him. In 1768 his eldest son, then captain of the school at Winchester, was accidentally drowned before the eyes of his younger brother while they were swimming in the River Itchen. This event rendered Bingham 'inconsolable' and 'cast a gloom over his countenance during the remainder of his life' (ibid., li).

In 1772 Bingham published anonymously a dissertation on the millennium, *Ta chilia etē*. This was prompted by the work of Joseph Greenhill and attacked those who argued that the millennium had passed. Bingham developed his ideas more fully in *Dissertationes apocalypticae* and suggested that the number of the beast mentioned in the book of Revelation referred to Muhammad rather than to the papacy. In December 1799 he remarked to Richard Gough that 'the grand scene is opening in which Mahometanism is to be destroy'd, & Popery reformed. The enterprizing Buonaparte, whatever his fate, is a sword in the hand of Providence' (Bodl. Oxf., MS top. Dorset d. 3, fol. 176). Bingham's apocalyptic speculations won approval from Bishop Thomas Newton, to whom he dedicated *A Vindication of the Doctrine and Liturgy of the Church of England* (1774), which he published in response to the resignation of Theophilus Lindsey from his living at Catterick, following parliament's rejection of the Feathers tavern petition against clerical subscription to the Thirty-Nine Articles, and in which he criticized Socinian interpretations of the history of the early church. He was nevertheless surprised to be asked to act as Warburtonian lecturer in 1781. He declined the honour since he did not believe, as the lectures were supposed to prove, that the Roman Catholic church was guilty of apostasy. In 1782 he suffered a stroke and, while recuperating at Bath, composed a short essay about Paul at Athens.

For many years Bingham conducted an antiquarian correspondence with Gough and others, and in the 1790s he provided considerable material for the second edition of *The History and Antiquities of the County of Dorset* (4 vols., 1796–1815), including biographical anecdotes of the compiler, John Hutchins. He bore his old age with resignation, writing in 1792 that 'whatever befalls us is best, and that want of success has always a blessing in reserve' (Bingham, *Dissertations*, lx), and died at Pimperne on 11 October 1800; he was buried in the chancel of the parish church. In 1804 his son Peregrine printed *Dissertations, Essays, and Sermons*, a collection of several of his unpublished writings, with which were included a commentary on the Song of Songs and an edition of his attack on Lindsey.

SCOTT MANDELBROTE

Sources *GM*, 1st ser., 73 (1803), 1017–20; 74 (1804), 117–20 · G. Bingham, *Dissertations, essays, and sermons*, ed. P. Bingham, 2 vols. (1804) · [G. Bingham], *Ta chilia etē: a dissertation on the millennium* (1772) · Bodl. Oxf., MS Top. Dorset d. 3, fols. 161–85 · Bodl. Oxf., MS Top. Gen. d. 2, fols. 16–22 · G. Bingham, *A vindication of the doctrine and liturgy of the Church of England* (1774) · Bodl. Oxf., MS Gough Gen. Top. 42, fols. 12, 338 · J. Hutchins, *The history and antiquities of the county of Dorset*, 2nd edn, ed. R. Gough and J. B. Nichols, 4 vols. (1796–1815) · *Old Westminsters*, 1.88–9 · *DNB*

Archives Bodl. Oxf., sermons, MSS Dep. e. 299, Dep. c. 647, Dep. d. 688 | Bodl. Oxf., MS Top. Dorset d. 3, fols. 161–85

Bingham, George Charles, third earl of Lucan (1800–1888), army officer, eldest son of Richard Bingham, second earl of Lucan (1764–1839), and Lady Elizabeth (1770–1819), divorced wife of Bernard Edward Howard (later duke of Norfolk) and daughter and coheir of Henry Belasyse, third earl of Fauconberg of Newborough, was born in the parish of St George, Hanover Square, London, on 16 April 1800. His only brother, Richard Camden (1801–1872), joined the diplomatic service, and he had four sisters: Elizabeth (d. 1838), Anne (d. 1850), Louisa (d. 1882), and Georgiana (d. 1849).

Early years Bingham attended Westminster School, entering in 1814, and became an ensign in the 6th foot on 29 August 1816. On exchanging into the 3rd foot guards as ensign and lieutenant on 24 December 1818, he went on half pay the next day, before purchasing a lieutenancy in the 8th foot on 20 January 1820. Bingham obtained a company in the 74th foot on 16 May 1822 and immediately went on half pay before securing a captaincy in the 1st Life Guards on 20 June. He became a brevet major on 23 June 1825 and on 1 December purchased a majority in the 17th lancers. Bingham further purchased promotion to lieutenant-colonel, allegedly for £25,000 (£5000 above the regulation price), on 9 November 1826 and held command of the regiment in Ireland and England until 14 April 1837, when yet once more he went on half pay. During Bingham's time in command he 'brought the regiment up to a very high pitch of efficiency' and proved 'a keen soldier, who had taken pains to study his profession' (Fortescue, 123). After reviewing the 17th lancers (nicknamed Bingham's Dandies on account of the splendid uniforms financed by their commanding officer) at Windsor, William IV pronounced them 'perfect' (Parry, 198). For some months in 1828–9 Bingham was away from the regiment, serving on the staff of Prince Vorontsov in Bulgaria during Russia's campaign against Turkey, after which he received the Russian war medal and became a knight of the order of St Anne (second class). In some accounts he is credited with commanding a cavalry division before Adrianople.

At this time Bingham's intellectual powers were deemed 'of a very high order', the duke of Wellington 'thought well of him' and Sir Robert Peel believed him 'a fine, high-spirited young fellow' (Woodham-Smith, 107). On 21 February 1829 Bingham married Lady Anne (1809–1877), seventh daughter of Robert Brudenell, sixth earl of Cardigan, and sister of the commander of the light brigade in the Crimea. They had two sons and four daughters: George (8 May 1830–1914), captain and lieutenant-colonel in the Coldstream Guards and his father's aide-de-camp in the Crimea; Richard (b. 8 Jan 1847), a Royal Navy officer; Augusta; Elizabeth (d. 1857); Lavinia (d. 1864); and Anne-Sarah (d. 1855). The explosive relationship of the parents, however, led to their permanent separation about 1850. The Bingham family owned estates at Castlebar in Ireland, and during 1826–30 Bingham was a tory MP for co. Mayo. He succeeded to the earldom on the death of his father on 30 June 1839, and in 1840 was elected a representative Irish peer in the House of Lords. In 1845 he was appointed lord lieutenant of Mayo. Meanwhile, still on

George Charles Bingham, third earl of Lucan (1800–1888), by Sir Francis Grant, 1855

half pay, he set out to modernize the family holdings by creating large farms using new agricultural techniques and machinery. Many tenants were evicted from their dilapidated homes and lost their livelihood with the abolition of small plots and strips. Lucan clashed, too, with his land agent, accusing him of corruption and taking him to court for alleged poaching. Lucan's uncontrolled outbursts during the trial led to his being removed from the bench of magistrates. On 16 November 1849, in *The Times*, Sidney Godolphin Osborne defended Lucan as 'a practical man: that which he determines to do he sets about at once not suffering the expense of pocket or popularity to interrupt him'. To the people of Mayo, however, he 'exhibited all the inherited ferocity of the Binghams' (Woodham-Smith, 119).

Lucan's asperity was not limited to Castlebar. His father had built another house at Laleham, near Staines, Middlesex, and there he clashed with the rector over his plans to demolish and rebuild the church, farm hands for their unpunctuality, and even with the lord chamberlain, to whom he wrote sharply on 8 December 1853. Lucan declared that he would 'submit no longer to so intolerable a nuisance' (Woodham-Smith, 138) as royal swans regularly invading his land, and he threatened to shoot them at regular intervals until all were dead or removed from the nearby River Thames. In the army he advanced to colonel on 23 November 1841 and major-general on 11 November 1851. When Britain was on the brink of war with Russia, Lucan volunteered to command an infantry brigade. Instead on 21 February 1854 he was put in charge of the cavalry division on the recommendation of the commander-in-chief at Horse Guards, Lord Hardinge, without reference to the commander of the expeditionary force, Lord Raglan. Neither of Lucan's brigade commanders (the earl of Cardigan and Sir James Scarlett, appointed respectively to lead the light and heavy brigades) had any experience of war, and to make matters worse Cardigan and his brother-in-law heartily detested one another.

The Crimean War Friction occurred once the troops reached Turkey, where Raglan enigmatically wrote to his wife, on 5 May, that Lucan had arrived. In command, Lucan insisted on attention to minute matters of discipline and administration, which irked Cardigan. When the light brigade went to Bulgaria in June, Lucan remained at divisional headquarters at Kulali, near Scutari, in Asiatic Turkey. Cardigan thus argued that his was an independent command, which Raglan unwittingly encouraged by dealing directly with him. When Lucan did reach Varna, where he was promoted local lieutenant-general on 18 August, relations between the two men scarcely improved. Perhaps sensing disaster, Raglan tried to keep Lucan at Varna to await completion of the heavy brigade. However, as divisional commander, Lucan cited Wellington's practice in the peninsula to support his right to land with the force which invaded the Crimean peninsula on 14 September 1854, even though only the light brigade was present. Shortly after the British, French, and Turkish troops began a 30 mile march southwards towards Sevastopol, during the afternoon of 19 September two regiments of the light brigade under Cardigan crossed the narrow Bulganek Stream to confront enemy cavalry. Lucan in person reinforced them with two more regiments, but Raglan then noticed massed infantry concealed ahead and ordered Lucan to withdraw, to Cardigan's chagrin. Unfairly, Lucan was blamed for lack of initiative. Next day, when the infantry and artillery swept aside a formidable enemy defensive position on the south bank of the Alma River, the cavalry passively guarded against a surprise flank attack. With the enemy in flight, the light cavalry set off in pursuit, but were recalled by Raglan. Yet again, Lucan was unjustly blamed.

The allies soon resumed their advance on Sevastopol, electing to march round it to the east and mount a siege from upland to the south. During the flanking movement, Lucan led the cavalry in the van of Raglan and his staff. Misled by his guides, Lucan took his squadrons down the wrong path in a wood, and Raglan very nearly rode into Russian troops moving westwards out of the naval port. Hastily redirected, as he galloped past the commander-in-chief Raglan loudly reproved him: 'Lord Lucan, you are late!' (Sweetman, 231). The fault was hardly Lucan's. As the troops settled down to besiege Sevastopol, Cardigan and Lucan continued to quarrel, with the former complaining about undue interference in the running of his brigade and Lucan insisting on rigid adherence to administrative procedures and orders. When his senior staff officers failed to quell the acid exchanges, Raglan wrote personally to them both as 'gentlemen of high honour and of elevated position in the country independently of their military rank … earnestly to recommend to them to communicate frankly with each other' (ibid., 235). It was a forlorn hope. The battle of Balaklava, on 25 October, provided the high point of acrimony. The previous night Lucan had sent his son, his aide-de-camp, to warn Raglan that the enemy was planning an attack on the vital British supply port, at the southern extremity of a plain, which lay beneath the siege lines. Effectively, it was divided into two valleys, north and south, with four redoubts manned by Turkish militia on the ridge between them acting as the outer defences of Balaklava. However, aware of other false reports of this nature, Raglan ordered no extra precautions. At dawn on 25 October, accompanying a cavalry patrol in the south valley, Lucan saw that the redoubts were under attack. He warned Raglan, took the heavy brigade forward, and sent a troop of horse artillery onto the western end of the ridge, seeking to deter the enemy. In vain. The redoubts fell, and Lucan withdrew both his brigades out of range. On the upland, Raglan had a bird's eye view of the plain denied to Lucan. He saw some 2000 enemy cavalry moving along the north valley, in dead ground to Lucan, part of which wheeled south towards Balaklava. He sent an order to Lucan to assist the small force commanded by Major-General Sir Colin Campbell near the village of Kadikoi, midway between the ridge and the port. Before doing so Lucan instructed Cardigan to stand fast, and the precise nature of his order would cause future heated dispute. The Russians advancing on Kadikoi were driven off by the 'thin red line', but as Scarlett led his regiments across the south valley the main body of Russian cavalry crested the ridge. Lucan ordered Scarlett to attack them, and the successful charge of the heavy brigade followed. As the Russians scattered, the light brigade did not move. Lucan blamed Cardigan for wilful inactivity, the brigade commander insisted that he was obeying orders to act defensively. Lucan could justifiably claim that the situation had changed drastically since the light brigade had been left in a detached position with the bulk of the heavy brigade expected to be 4 miles away at Kadikoi. Cardigan's 700 sabres were on the flank of the heavies as they charged.

Realizing that enemy troops were preparing to tow away guns captured in the Turkish-manned redoubts, Raglan ordered Lucan to prepare to prevent this, adding that two infantry divisions were on their way down from the upland to assist. Lucan therefore retained the heavy brigade in the south valley, moved the light into the north valley, and took post himself between the two at the western end of the ridge from which he could see no enemy troops. There he awaited arrival of the promised infantry.

At about 10.40 a.m. Raglan dispatched another order: 'Lord Raglan wishes the cavalry to advance rapidly to the front, and try to prevent the enemy carrying away the guns. Troop of horse artillery may accompany. French cavalry is on your left. Immediate', which was carried to Lucan by a volatile aide-de-camp, Captain Edward Nolan. What verbally passed between him and Lucan became a matter of intense dispute when Nolan could not defend himself. Riding with the light brigade, he was killed shortly after it started down the north valley. For, whatever Nolan said, it convinced Lucan that he must send the brigade along the north valley to attack a battery of field guns drawn up at its end. To compound Cardigan's problems, enemy infantry and artillery were also holding the high ground north and south of the valley. The roll-call after the resultant debacle totalled 195 out of 673, and the bitter recriminations started. Lucan had initially led two regiments of the heavy brigade in support, but halted and withdrew them after they incurred severe casualties and he had been wounded in the leg (which would immobilize him for two to three days and make him limp for some time after).

Recriminations and defence   Immediately after the action, Raglan blamed Cardigan, who replied that he had received a direct order from a senior officer (Lucan). That evening, Raglan accused Lucan of losing the light brigade. Lucan protested that he was only following orders, but Raglan told him that, as a lieutenant-general, he should have exercised his discretion. Next day, to help him prepare his dispatch for the government, Raglan asked Lucan for a copy of the order, as he had not retained one, and this began a series of different versions which circulated in years to come. Lucan was assured that he would not be censured, Cardigan was invalided back to England, and the war went on, with the cavalry deployed in support during the battle of Inkerman on 5 November 1854—that is, until Raglan's dispatch, which Lucan had not hitherto seen, became public. In it Raglan criticized Lucan for misinterpreting the order: 'from some misconception of the instruction to advance, the Lieutenant-General considered that he was bound to attack at all hazards' (Sweetman, 264). Lucan reacted swiftly, penning a vigorous defence to Raglan on 30 November 1854 and insisting that this be given the same prominence as the dispatch: 'Surely, my lord, this is a grave charge and imputation reflecting seriously on my professional character' (ibid.). He refused to withdraw the letter, and Raglan duly forwarded it to the duke of Newcastle, secretary of state for war and the colonies, with attached observations of his own. Raglan pointed out that 'attack' did not appear in the order, Lucan had sought the assistance of neither the horse artillery nor French cavalry, and had taken no steps to reconnoitre the enemy dispositions despite being warned of an impending action. Such antipathy between the commander-in-chief in the field and one of his divisional commanders could not be tolerated. Lucan was recalled and left the Crimea on 14 February 1855. Before he did so, on 20 January he had drawn up a plan for a military

muleteer corps to provide land transport, rather than the civilian commissariat.

Back in England, Lucan strove to clear his name. Twice demands for a court martial were refused on the grounds that his recall rested on his relations with his superior officer not professional misconduct. He took his case to the floor of the House of Lords on 19 March 1855, without noticeable success. Lucan then defended himself strongly before the House of Commons select committee, chaired by J. A. Roebuck, inquiring into the state of the army before Sevastopol, prompting the *United Service Gazette* on 9 June 1855 to observe: 'Lord Lucan's errors are bad, his defence worse'. In April 1856 he appeared in front of the board of general officers convened at Chelsea Hospital to investigate claims that he and others had been maligned in a report about conditions in the Crimea by Sir John Mc Neill and Colonel Alexander Tulloch. Lucan published separately his evidence to the Chelsea board, which ranged beyond 'the unwavering incorrectness of the figures and facts contained in the Report' and its 'unpardonable' bias (Lucan, 4). He had always complied with 'the rules of the service' (ibid., 64). Furthermore, 'I lived in a common bell-tent, close to and amongst the regiments, and only restricted my visits to the lines from scruples of creating the jealousy of my brigadiers' (ibid., 62). Lucan also contrived once more to shift blame onto Raglan: 'I was responsible to, and not responsible for, the commander-in-chief' (ibid., 65), neither sensible nor tactful given Raglan's death in post. In fact, although the board exonerated Lucan, his own words underlined his overbearing nature, insensitivity to others, and inflexibility. Further to support his overall case, in 1856 he published his divisional orders and correspondence as *English Cavalry in the Army of the East*. Meanwhile, the mutual antagonism between him and Cardigan continued to fester. Both wrote letters to *The Times* in April 1855 about the other's actions over the heavy brigade charge, and Lucan was widely thought to have sponsored George Ryan's critical pamphlet in that year, *Was Lord Cardigan a hero at Balaclava?* Eight years afterwards, Lucan offered to support Raglan's nephew and aide-de-camp in the Crimea, Somerset Calthorpe, after Cardigan brought a libel action against him for unflattering references to the light brigade commander's conduct during the charge in his book *Letters from Headquarters*. His brother-in-law promptly challenged Lucan to a duel, and pure farce ensued. Lucan travelled to Paris for the confrontation, Cardigan was delayed in England and landed in Calais as Lucan left the French capital for London again. On 25 October 1863 Lucan was invited to chair the Balaklava day dinner in London, and predictably Cardigan refused to attend.

Later life   Lucan's active military career ended in February 1855. He became a commander (third class) of the Légion d'honneur and knight (first class) of the Turkish order of the Mejidiye. On 5 July 1855 he was appointed KCB, and from November 1855 to 1865 was colonel of the 8th hussars. He was promoted lieutenant-general on 24 December 1858, general on 28 August 1865, and field marshal on 21 June 1887, and was made GCB on 2 June 1869. He was colonel of the 1st Life Guards from February 1865 until his death. He regularly attended the Lords and proposed a useful amendment in 1858 to settle a confrontation of the two houses on the oath of allegiance for non-Christians: each house could vary the wording. He died at his home, 12 South Street, Park Lane, London, on 10 November 1888 and was buried at Laleham, Middlesex. The coffin, escorted by 100 NCOs and men of the Life Guards, lay on a gun carriage drawn by horses of chestnut troop, Royal Horse Artillery. His wife having predeceased him on 2 April 1877, he was survived by his two sons and one daughter, Lady Augusta Alington.

William Howard Russell thought Lucan 'a hard man to get on with' (Russell, 118), and many soldiers and civilians undoubtedly agreed. However, Lord George Paget, commanding the 4th light dragoons, referring to Lucan's 'consideration and forebearance' when 'with much trepidation' he was deputed to reason with his divisional commander about out-of-date drill manoeuvres, wrote that 'he evinced qualities which certainly … set my mind at rest as regards the character of the man under whom I was to serve before the enemy' (Paget, 217). Lieutenant-Colonel G. W. Mayow, a cavalry division staff officer, similarly held: 'Lord Lucan—all I can say of him is that he not only thought of his cavalry by day, but dreamt of them by night' (ibid., 221). Lucan was not utterly insensitive. Paget recorded that he had tears in his eyes after Raglan blamed him for the light brigade's losses, and Captain Robert Portal of the 4th light dragoons independently noted that Lucan was 'dreadfully cut up' (Moyse-Bartlett, 232). Nor did he lack courage, at sixty-six being prepared to duel with Cardigan. Those who pointed to his unfitness to command the cavalry division ignored the fact that he was the only senior officer previously to have fought in the area and to have firsthand experience of the Russian army in the field. Of his time in the Crimea, which has largely shaped posterity's view of Lucan, Lieutenant Walker Heneage of the 8th hussars referred to 'unlucky Lucan … for heaven's sake let a man have fair play' (ibid., 244)—difficult to achieve for a man whose stubbornness and hectoring manner caused widespread offence.

JOHN SWEETMAN

Sources Army List · GEC, Peerage · Burke, Peerage (1887) · J. W. Fortescue, A history of the 17th Lancers, 1: 1759–1982 (1895) · C. Woodham-Smith, The reason why (1957) · J. Sweetman, Raglan: from the Peninsula to the Crimea (1993) · D. Thomas, Cardigan: the hero of Balaclava (1987) · M. Adkin, The charge: why the Light Brigade was lost (1996) · D. H. Parry, The death or glory boys: the story of the 17th lancers (1899) · R. H. Murray, The history of the VIII king's royal Irish hussars, 1693–1927, 2 (1928) · earl of Lucan, Reply of Major-General the earl of Lucan KCB to the Chelsea inquiry (1856) · A. Lambert and S. Badsey, The war correspondents of the Crimean War (1997) · W. H. Russell, The great war with Russia (1895) · G. Paget, The light cavalry brigade in the Crimea (1881) · Annual Register (1888) · The Times · United Service Gazette · H. Moyse-Bartlett, Louis Edward Nolan (1971)

Archives NRA Scotland, priv. coll., Charteris MSS, letters to Lord Wemyss from the Crimea

Likenesses portrait, 1832, repro. in Fortescue, History of the 17th lancers, facing p. 120 · F. Grant, oils, 1855, Gov. Art Coll. [see illus.] · stipple and line engraving, 1878 (after photograph), BM; repro. in E. H. Nolan, The illustrated history of the war against Russia (1855–7) · Ape [C. Pellegrini], chromolithograph cartoon, pubd 1881, NPG;

repro. in VF (23 April 1881) · M. Hanhart and N. Hanhart, lithograph, NPG · T. W. Hunt, stipple and line engraving (after a daguerreotype), NPG · D. J. Pound, stipple and line engraving (after photograph by J. Watkins), NPG; repro. in D. J. Pound, The drawing room portrait gallery of eminent personages … engraved on steel by D. J. Pound (1859) · carte-de-visite, NPG · watercolour drawing, NG Ire.

Wealth at death £59,918 5s. 11d.: resworn probate, Nov 1890, CGPLA Eng. & Wales (1889)

Bingham, Sir George Ridout (1777–1833), army officer, descended from an old Dorset family, was born on 21 July 1777, the fourth son of Richard Bingham, colonel of the Dorset militia, and the elder son of his second wife, Elizabeth, daughter of John Ridout of Dean's Leaze, Dorset. He entered the army in June 1793 as ensign in the 69th foot, serving with the regiment in Corsica and with one of the detachments which embarked as marines under Admiral Hotham, in the Gulf of Genoa. Promoted captain in the 81st foot in 1796, he served with it at the Cape, and took part in the Cape Frontier War of 1800 on the Sundays River. In 1801 he became major in the 82nd foot, and was with the regiment in Minorca until the island was restored to Spain at the peace of Amiens. In 1805 he was appointed lieutenant-colonel of the newly raised 2nd battalion 53rd foot in Ireland, and, going with it to Portugal four years later, fought at its head throughout its distinguished Peninsular career, beginning with the expulsion of the French from Oporto in 1809, and ending with the close of the Burgos retreat in 1812. The battalion was then reduced to a remnant, and having no home battalion to relieve or reinforce it (the 1st battalion being in India), was sent home; but four companies were left in Portugal, and these, with four companies of the 2nd Queen's regiment, were formed into a provisional battalion which, under Bingham's command, served in the subsequent campaigns in Spain and the south of France, including the victories at Vitoria, in the Pyrenees, and on the Nivelle. Bingham was awarded the Portuguese order of the Tower and Sword, and was made a KCB (January 1815). In September 1814 he married Emma Septima, youngest daughter of Edmund Morton Pleydell; they had no children.

When it was decided to send Bonaparte to St Helena, Bingham was appointed senior officer of the garrison, accompanied him to St Helena, and continued to serve there with the rank of brigadier-general, as second in command under Sir Hudson Lowe, until 1819, when he returned home on his promotion to major-general. Sir George was subsequently on the Irish staff, and commanded the Cork district from 1827 to 1832, a most difficult period in which the unrest aroused by the Catholic emancipation controversy was aggravated by agrarian crime, famine, and disease. In June 1831 he was appointed colonel of the 2nd battalion, the rifle brigade. In Ireland, as at St Helena, Sir George Bingham's tact and kindliness appear to have won general esteem. He was regarded as a thorough gentleman as well as a brilliant soldier. He died at Cumberland Terrace, Regent's Park, London, on 3 January 1833.

H. M. CHICHESTER, rev. DAVID GATES

Sources GM, 1st ser., 103/1 (1833), 274 · R. Cannon, ed., Historical record of the fifty-third, or the Shropshire regiment of foot (1849), 69 ·

J. Hutchins, *The history and antiquities of the county of Dorset*, 2nd edn, ed. R. Gough and J. B. Nichols, 4 (1815) **Archives** BL, diary of voyage to St Helena, RP 1718 [copy] · Dorset RO, diary and letters from St Helena | BL, corresp. with Sir Hudson Lowe, Add. MSS 20115–20233 *passim* **Likenesses** W. J. Ward, mezzotint, pubd 1835 (after H. W. Pickersgill), BM

Bingham, John (1612/13–1689), ejected minister and classical and oriental scholar, was born at Derby, the son of Henry Bingham. After attending Repton School from 1628, he was admitted sizar at Gonville and Caius College, Cambridge, on 10 June 1631, aged eighteen. Having moved to Magdalene College he graduated BA in 1636. When he was twenty-six a foot he had injured as a child had to be amputated and the trauma of this prematurely turned his hair white.

From 1640 to 1652 Bingham was master at the free school in Derby. He was an excellent classical and oriental scholar, fluent in Latin, Greek, Hebrew, Syriac, and Arabic. He published nothing under his own name, but assisted Brian Walton in the composition of the polyglot Bible (1657). For many years Bingham resisted pressure to take up pastoral responsibilities within the church, finally taking on a living only after considerable persuasion. Presented by William Cavendish, earl of Devonshire, to Marston upon Dove, Derbyshire, he was formally admitted on 28 October 1656. Over the next four years he 'constantly attended on the Classis of ministers that met at Derby' (Calamy, *Abridgement*, 2.188). On 16 May 1661 he was married at Spondon to Elizabeth Bomford of Chaddesdon. They had one son who survived them, Thomas, a mercer at Derby.

Despite considerable enticement by Archbishop Gilbert Sheldon, a long-time acquaintance, Bingham felt unable to conform in 1662 and so was ejected from his living. The loss of such a scholar weighed heavily upon the church authorities. After the passing of the Five Mile Act he moved to Bradley Hall, where for three years he 'taught several Gentlemen's sons, who Boarded with him' (Calamy, *Abridgement*, 2.188), again a reflection of his considerable academic repute. He subsequently moved to Brailsford, where he was to remain for seven years. Here he and his family attended the parish church every Sunday morning but in the afternoon he preached at his own house 'to the numbers that was not prohibited by the Act [of Uniformity]'. He subsequently incurred the wrath of the local incumbent, who proceeded to have him excommunicated. This sentence outraged parishioners and supporters and Bingham sought to defuse the situation by moving his household to Upper Thurvaston in the parish of Sutton, where he remained until his death. Edmund Calamy claimed he was licensed in 1672 to preach at Hollington, though his name is not included in the list of licences issued. When he was seventy Bingham broke his arm in a fall from his horse. His latter years were marked by frail and declining health, though he maintained his scholarly pursuits. He died on 3 February 1689, aged eighty-two according to Calamy, although his university record suggests this was an exaggeration. He was buried at Upper Thurvaston, with Mr Crompton preaching his funeral sermon. STUART B. JENNINGS

Sources *Calamy rev.*, 55–6 · administration of estate, proved at Birmingham, 13 Feb 1688/1689, Lichfield RO, Staffordshire · E. Calamy, ed., *An abridgement of Mr. Baxter's history of his life and times, with an account of the ministers, &c., who were ejected after the Restauration of King Charles II*, 2nd edn, 2 vols. (1713) · *DNB* · A. Macdonald, *A short history of Repton* (1929) · Venn, *Alum. Cant.* · J. Pendleton, *History of Derbyshire* (1966) **Wealth at death** £66 13s. 6d.—personal estate: administration, Lichfield RO, proved at Birmingham, 13 Feb 1689

Bingham, (Richard) John, seventh earl of Lucan (*b.* 1934, *d.* in or after 1974), suspected murderer, was born on 18 December 1934 at 19 Bentinck Street, Marylebone, elder son of (George Charles) Patrick Bingham, sixth earl of Lucan (1898–1964), and of Kaitilin Elizabeth Anne Dawson (1900–1985), niece of the last earl of Dartrey. In 1940 he and his siblings were evacuated to the United States, and they spent five years living on the sumptuous estate of an American millionairess, Marcia Brady Tucker, in upstate New York. After returning to England in 1945 the contrast between the luxuries of his war years and the meagreness of post-war Britain vexed him. He was a troubled, silent child prone to food fads and rages. In adolescence he was irked by the austere habits and progressive values of his parents, who were active, selfless members of the Labour Party. His father, who had been a battalion commander in the Coldstream Guards, became Labour's unassuming but effective chief whip in the House of Lords (1954). By contrast John Bingham held reactionary views, was deeply interested in money, and craved all the accoutrements and veneer of wealth. He seemed to make a study of being anachronistic.

At Eton College, Bingham took to gambling and persistently broke bounds to attend the races. During his national service (1953–5) he was a second lieutenant in his father's regiment, stationed mainly in the north Rhine town of Krefeld, where he became a keen poker player. In 1955 he joined a small merchant bank, William Brandts, at a salary of £500 a year. His plan was to accumulate £2 million: 'motor-cars, yachts, expensive holidays and security for the future would give myself and a lot of other people a lot of pleasure', he wrote (Moore, 53). He began attending John Aspinall's illicit gambling parties, where backgammon and chemin de fer were played. After a coup at 'chemmy', in which he is said to have won £26,000 in two nights, he retired from Brandts about 1960 and thereafter lived as a professional gambler.

Bingham was a shy, taciturn young man, with a clipped voice, who was popular in masculine society for his dry humour and dashing exploits. Tall, straight-backed, spruce, and debonair, with a luxuriant guardsman's moustache, he was a perfectionist who, if he could not excel at an activity, would not undertake it. During the 1950s he raced a greyhound named Sambo's Hangover and joined the British bobsleigh team at St Moritz. Later, seeking further thrills, he commissioned an expensive

(Richard) John Bingham, seventh earl of Lucan (b. 1934, d. in or after 1974), by Bassano

powerboat, *White Migrant*. It sank while he was in the lead at the Cowes offshore powerboat race of 1963.

On 28 November 1963 (two months before he inherited the earldom) Bingham married Veronica Duncan (b. 1937). They had one son and two daughters. Veronica Lucan was the daughter of Charles Ronald Moorhouse Duncan, a half-pay artillery officer who had divorced Lord Castlemaine's daughter so as to be free to marry, on 21 October 1936, Thelma Winifred Watts, a nineteen-year-old Bournemouth hotel bookkeeper. Duncan was killed in a motoring accident on 21 January 1939, the eve of his forty-third birthday; his widow subsequently married a publican who ran a country hotel.

Lucan combined the high tension of gambling, powerboats, and perilous winter sports with outward self-control and a narrow, joyless domestic routine. In London he went daily to Aspinall's resplendent gaming club in Berkeley Square, the Clermont, where he was on the 'free list' for food and drink. He ate a similar lunch every day, played backgammon in the afternoon, returned to his house in Lower Belgrave Street to change, and then reappeared at the Clermont, where he dined and gambled until the early morning. At night Veronica Lucan accompanied him, but this life became grim and distressing for her. By 1968 her emotional fragility was palpable; Lucan's obsession with her difficulties intensified. The marriage grew increasingly disturbed, especially after the birth of

the Lucans' third child in 1970, and in 1973 they separated.

Lucan strove to win custody of his children, who were wards of court, but in June 1973, after expensive litigation, they were returned to their mother. He was desolated by this decision and became fanatical about protecting them. His domestic misfortunes took him into debt, and under the stress of his circumstances he began losing heavily at the Clermont and chasing his losses. 'Aspers' had sold the Clermont to Hugh Hefner's Playboy organization in 1972, and without his protection Lucan's debts became pressing. He started drinking heavily and spying on the Lower Belgrave Street house. In the darkened basement there, on 7 November 1974, the Lucan nanny, Sandra Rivett, was bludgeoned to death with a piece of lead piping. Lady Lucan escaped from the murder scene and her account of events led police to issue a warrant (12 November) for Lucan's arrest for the Rivett murder and the attempted murder of his wife. Subsequently, in June 1975, the jury at the inquest on the dead nanny named Lucan as her murderer, whereupon the Westminster coroner committed him for trial at the central criminal court.

These moves had little practical effect, for after the night of 7–8 November Lucan was never seen again, although his car was found abandoned at Newhaven on 11 November. Most of his friends, including Sir James Goldsmith and Aspinall, believed that he had murdered the nanny in mistake for his wife and had then honourably 'fallen on his sword' (*The Spectator*, 18 June 1994, 9). They surmised that he threw himself overboard from a cross-channel ferry or scuttled his boat in the channel. However, members of Lucan's family believed that Rivett was the intended victim and had been murdered by an associate. Suspicions that Lucan was spirited to safety overseas by rich, unscrupulous members of Aspinall's set appealed to some journalists and police officers. His disappearance fascinated newspaper readers and conspiracy theorists: the Lucan mystery provided more figures of speech than the crew of the *Marie Celeste*. The Chancery Division of the High Court ruled in 1992 that Lucan was presumed to have died on or after 8 November 1974, and granted full probate on his estate in 1999. Nevertheless the same year the lord chancellor refused an application by Lucan's son, George Charles Bingham, Lord Bingham (b. 1967), to take his seat in the House of Lords as the eighth earl of Lucan.

RICHARD DAVENPORT-HINES

Sources S. Moore, *Lucan, not guilty* (1987) · P. Marnham, *Trail of havoc: in the steps of Lord Lucan* (1988) · N. Lucas, *The Lucan mystery* (1976) · J. Ruddick, *Lord Lucan: what really happened* (1994) · R. Sansom and R. Strange, *Looking for Lucan* (1994) · D. Gerring and R. Brimmell, *Lucan lives* (1995) · J. Fox, 'A bad day for Eton', *New Review*, 3 (May 1976), 11–26 · *Sunday Times* (8 June 1975) · K. Tynan, *Letters*, ed. K. Tynan (1994), 556 · M. Spark, *Aiding and abetting* (2000) · *The Times* (19 Dec 1934), 17b; (22 Jan 1964), 15a; (20 Nov 1985), 16g · b. cert. [Veronica Duncan]

Archives priv. coll. | FILM BFI NFTVA, *True stories*, Channel 4, 28 May 1996

Likenesses Bassano, photograph, NPG [*see illus.*]

Wealth at death £14,709: probate, 1999, *CGPLA Eng. & Wales* · inherited £250,000 in 1963; but debts and overdraft totalled £85,000 by 1974

Bingham, Joseph (*bap.* **1668**, *d.* **1723**), ecclesiastical historian, was baptized on 28 September 1668 at All Saints', Wakefield, Yorkshire, the son of Francis Bingham (*b.* 1625, *d.* in or after 1680), of Wakefield, a nonconformist, who had originally been apprenticed as a cutler. He was educated at Wakefield grammar school and matriculated from University College, Oxford, on 26 May 1684 and graduated BA in 1688. He was elected a fellow on 1 July 1689 and proceeded MA in 1691. By June 1691 he was a tutor, one of his first pupils being another native of Wakefield, John Potter, the future archbishop of Canterbury. Bingham was ordained deacon on 20 December 1691 by the bishop of Oxford, and ordained a priest on 12 March 1693.

Bingham's promising university career was cut short following a topical sermon preached at St Peter-in-the-East on 28 October 1695 on the Trinity, in which he expounded on the patristic notions of *ousia*, *persona*, and *substantia*. It was denounced as heretical to the vice-chancellor by John Beauchamp, a fellow of Trinity, and the hebdomadal board condemned part of it as 'false, impious and heretical' (Barnard, 'Bingham and asceticism', 300). Other charges were also levelled including accusations of Arianism, tritheism, and the heresy of Valentinus Gentilis, and Bingham was denounced by Robert South as a follower of Dr William Sherlock. To avoid deprivation Bingham resigned his fellowship on 23 November 1695 and was then presented to the rectory of Headbourne Worthy, near Winchester, by Dr John Radcliffe, another native of Wakefield, who had recently purchased the advowson. From this preferment, valued at about £100 per annum, and conveniently situated near to the cathedral library, Bingham undertook his scholarly research into the antiquities of the church. Nor did his exile from Oxford curtail his appetite for controversy, for soon after his appointment to Headbourne Worthy he preached a visitation sermon on 12 May 1696 on the same subject, and returned to the subject in the following year in a visitation sermon preached on 16 September 1697. All three sermons were published as *Three Sermons on the Trinity*.

On 26 November 1702 Bingham married Dorothy (1672–1755), daughter of Richard and Constance Pocock of Colemore, Hampshire. They had ten children, two sons and four daughters surviving their father. In 1706 Bingham published *The French Church's Apology for the Church of England*, which 'contains a modest vindication of the doctrine, worship, government, and discipline of our church from the chief objections of dissenters, and returns answer to them upon the principles of the reformed church of France' (*DNB*). It was dedicated to Thomas Tenison, archbishop of Canterbury, who Thomas Hearne felt would 'grumble at his writings against dissenters' (*Remarks*, 1.221). In 1708 the first volume of Bingham's *Origines ecclesiasticae, or, Antiquities of the Christian Church* was published. By 1711 three volumes had been published. Bingham was then diverted into a controversy concerning lay baptism, responding to Roger Lawrence's *Lay Baptism Invalid* (1708) with his *Scholastical History of Lay Baptism*

(1712). This was originally intended as a chapter in the *Origines*, but Bingham decided to publish it separately to refute the view that those who had not been baptized by an episcopally ordained minister lacked true Christian initiation. Bingham contended that the ancient church when she received members of other sects 'did not recognize their ordinations, but by her determination gave them the authority which they had not previously possessed' (Every, 129–30).

In 1712 Bishop Jonathan Trelawny of Winchester collated Bingham to the rectory of Havant, near Portsmouth, which he was allowed to hold with Headbourne Worthy. In May 1713 Bingham approached the lord treasurer, Robert Harley, earl of Oxford, after hearing that Oxford, a noted patron of scholarly research, approved of his historical endeavours. After detailing his 'labouring hard at this work' almost twenty years and his financial commitment to six children and 'some poor relations that depend also entirely upon my charity', he requested from Oxford some further preferment to continue 'the work of the antiquities of the church'. His ideal was a prebend of Winchester, 'where my business chiefly lies among the books of the library' (*Portland MSS*, 5.289), but realizing that this would not be possible he asked for any place that would answer his designs. However, he did not receive another living, and yet he continued to ask Oxford for patronage, including a place at Charterhouse for his son Joseph. Moreover, Bingham seems to have lost money in government lottery schemes and also in the South Sea Bubble.

Work continued on the *Origines*, the tenth and final volume being published in 1722, Bingham telling Hearne 'he hath been twenty years about it' (*Remarks*, 8.19). Bingham's aim as outlined in the work was:

> to give such a methodical account of the antiquities of the christian church as others have done of the Greek and Roman and Jewish antiquities, by reducing the ancient customs, usages, and practices of the church under certain proper heads, whereby the reader may take a view at once of any particular usage or custom of christians for four or five centuries. (*DNB*)

It covered 'the hierarchy, ecclesiology, territorial organization, rites, discipline, and calendar of the primitive church' (Barnard, 'Bingham and the early church', 197), based on primary sources.

Bingham was working on a second edition of the *Origines*, together with an abridgement, when he died on 17 August 1723. He was buried at St Swithen's, Headbourne Worthy. His undated will left £50 and half his books to each of his two sons, Richard and Joseph, £100 each to his four daughters, and £50 to his sister, Welcom. To his wife he left 'my house and yard' in Headbourne Worthy and the 'right and title' (PRO, PROB 11/594, Fol. 8*r*) to the *Origines*. However, his wife appears to have ended her life in relative poverty, dying in 1755 in Bishop Warner's College for Clergymen's Widows at Bromley. The *Origines* was translated into Latin and published by J. H. Grischovius of Halle between 1724 and 1729; a German abridgement was published in Augsburg between 1788 and 1796. *The Works of the Rev. Joseph Bingham*, edited by R. Bingham, was published in nine volumes in 1840, with a new edition in ten volumes in 1855.

STUART HANDLEY

Sources Foster, *Alum. Oxon.* · L. W. Barnard, 'Joseph Bingham and asceticism', *Monks, hermits, and the ascetic tradition*, ed. W. J. Sheils, SCH, 22 (1985), 299–306 · L. W. Barnard, 'Joseph Bingham and the early church', *Church Quarterly Review*, 169 (1968), 192–205 · *Hist. U. Oxf.* 5: *18th-cent. Oxf.*, 397–9 · *The manuscripts of his grace the duke of Portland*, 10 vols., HMC, 29 (1891–1931), vol. 5, p. 289 · *N&Q*, 13th ser., 4 (1927), 273 · *Remarks and collections of Thomas Hearne*, ed. C. E. Doble and others, 11 vols., OHS, 2, 7, 13, 34, 42–3, 48, 50, 65, 67, 72 (1885–1921) · IGI · will, PRO, PROB 11/594, fol. 8r · G. V. Bennett, *The tory crisis in church and state, 1688–1730: the career of Francis Atterbury, bishop of Rochester* (1975), 151–2 · G. Every, *The high church party, 1688–1718* (1956), 129–30 · BL, Add. MS 4253, fol. 71–71b · I. Guest, *Dr. John Radcliffe and his trust* (1991), 25
Archives Bodl. Oxf., sermons

Bingham, Margaret. *See* Willoughby, Margaret, Lady Willoughby (*c*.1401–1493), *under* Willoughby family (*per.* 1362–1528).

Bingham [*née* Smith], **Margaret, countess of Lucan** (*c*.1740–1814), miniature painter, was the daughter of James Smith MP, of Canons-Leigh, Devon, and St Audries, Somerset, and his wife, Grace. She married, on 25 August 1760, Sir Charles Bingham (1735–1799), later Baron Lucan (1776) and first earl of Lucan (1795). She started to paint miniatures about 1771, usually in watercolour on ivory and frequently signed with the monogram M. B., M. L., or M. B. L. She became an expert copyist and reproduced many miniatures by Isaac and Peter Oliver, John Hoskins, and Samuel Cooper. Horace Walpole, with whom she was acquainted, claimed that she was gifted 'with a genius that almost depreciates those masters when we consider that they spent their lives in attaining perfection; and [she], soaring above their modest timidity, has transferred the vigour of Raphael to her copies in watercolours' (Walpole, *Anecdotes*, 4.xviii, xix). There are frequent allusions to her in Walpole's letters and his praise becomes somewhat exaggerated. He writes, for example, 'Lady Bingham is, I assure you, another miracle' (Walpole, *Corr.*, 32.155) and 'They are so amazed and charmed at Paris with Lady Bingham's miniatures, that the Duke of Orleans has given her a room at the Palais Royal to copy which of his pictures she pleases' (ibid., 32.298). However, Mrs Delany, the commentator on late eighteenth-century society and court life and herself an amateur artist, was more circumspect in her assessment and in particular criticized Lady Lucan for her poor draughtsmanship: '[she] would often totally mistake the distance between one feature and another (till it was pointed out to her) and yet imitate colouring and finishing to perfection' (*Autobiography … Mrs Delany*, 1861, 6.420n.).

The consensus among recent critics is that Lady Lucan 'was not a first-rate miniaturist; her work usually betrays the amateur's hand' (Long, 280). However, many of her copies are of historic, if not aesthetic, value in providing records of original miniatures which, in some cases, no longer exist. Her miniature of John Maitland, first duke of Lauderdale, after Samuel Cooper (1774) is an example of this (Dutch royal collection). Her most significant work

was the embellishment with miniatures and illuminations of a five-folio-volume edition of Shakespeare's historical plays in the library at Althorp, Northamptonshire. This monumental task took sixteen years to complete.

Lady Lucan died on 27 February 1814 in St James's Place, London, leaving five children: Lavinia, who married George John *Spencer, second Earl Spencer in 1781; Eleanor Margaret, who married Thomas Lindsay; Louisa and Anne, who both died unmarried; and Richard, second earl of Lucan, the only son and heir. A collection of fourteen miniatures by her remains at Althorp, but a large number of miniature copies by her were sold by the order of the earl of Lucan in 1922 (Knight, Frank, and Rutley, Laleham House, Surrey, 28 November 1922, lots 230–313). A collection of miniatures by Lady Lucan was sold at Christies, South Kensington, on 10 October 2000 (lots 77–101).

ERNEST RADFORD, *rev.* V. REMINGTON

Sources *GM*, 1st ser., 84/1 (1814), 301 · *GM*, 1st ser., 85/1 (1815), 280 · Walpole, *Corr.*, 32.155, 298 · H. Walpole, *Anecdotes of painting in England: with some account of the principal artists*, ed. J. Dallaway, [rev. and enl. edn], 4 (1827), xviii, xix · *The autobiography and correspondence of Mary Granville, Mrs Delany*, ed. Lady Llanover, 1st ser., 3 vols. (1861) · *The autobiography and correspondence of Mary Granville, Mrs Delany*, ed. Lady Llanover, 1st ser., 3 vols. (1861); 2nd ser., 3 vols. (1862) · R. E. MacCalmont, *Memoirs of the Binghams* (1915) · B. S. Long, *British miniaturists* (1929), 280–1 · D. Foskett, *Miniatures: dictionary and guide* (1987), 114, 354, 592 · L. R. Schidlof, *The miniature in Europe in the 16th, 17th, 18th, and 19th centuries*, 1 (1964), 85 · G. C. Williamson, *The history of portrait miniatures*, 1 (1904), 201 · K. Schaeffers-Bodenhausen and M. Tiethhoff-Spliethoff, *The portrait miniatures in the collection of the house of Orange-Nassau* (1993), 386 · Burke, *Peerage* · *Debrett's Peerage* (1979) · sale catalogue (2000), lots 77–101 [Christies, 10 Oct 2000]
Archives BL, letters to Lord Spencer
Likenesses H. D. Hamilton, pastel, 1774, Walpole Library, Farmington, Connecticut; repro. in Walpole, *Corr.*, 32, facing p. 418 · A. Kauffmann, oils, Althorp, Northamptonshire · L. Spencer, drawing, repro. in the Althorp volumes of *Shakespeare's historical plays, illuminated by Lady Bingham*, vol. 5, colophon · engraving (after A. Kauffmann), repro. in MacCalmont, *Memoirs of the Binghams*, facing p. 114
Wealth at death see will and administration; March 1814, *Complete peerage*

Bingham, Peregrine (1754–1826), biographer and poet, was the second son of George *Bingham (1715–1800), rector for fifty-two years of Pimperne, Dorset, and Sarah Beale (*d.* 1756). He was educated at Winchester College, before matriculating at New College, Oxford on 15 March 1771. He was admitted as a scholar there on 31 August 1772, and he proceeded BCL on 7 July 1780. He was a fellow of New College from 1774 to 1787. He became rector of Edmondsham, Dorset, on 8 January 1782, and of Berwick St John, Wiltshire, in 1817. At one time he was chaplain of HMS *Agincourt*.

Bingham wrote memoirs of his father, prefixed to *Dissertations, Essays, and Sermons, by the Late George Bingham, B.D.* (2 vols., 1804). These memoirs, which are abridged in John Hutchins's *The Histories and Antiquities of … Dorset*, gave rise to a controversy between the author and the rector of Critchill which is evident in his *Sequel or Continuation of the*

Memoirs (1805) and *An Answer to the Reply or Defence of the Rector of Critchill* (1805). Bingham also wrote *The Pains of Memory, a Poem, in Two Books* (1811; 2nd edn, 1812) and *Law of Infancy and Coverture* (1816). He married Amy, daughter of William Bowles; they had two sons, one of whom was Peregrine *Bingham the younger (*bap.* 1788, *d.* 1864), a legal reporter and writer. Bingham died on 28 May 1826, aged seventy-two.

THOMPSON COOPER, *rev.* REBECCA MILLS

Sources Allibone, *Dict.* · Foster, *Alum. Oxon.* · Watt, *Bibl. Brit.*, 1.114f. · Burke, *Gen. GB* (1858) · *GM*, 1st ser., 74 (1804), 445, 1041–2 · *GM*, 1st ser., 96/2 (1826), 91–2 · [J. Watkins and F. Shoberl], *A biographical dictionary of the living authors of Great Britain and Ireland* (1816) · L. Baillie and P. Sieveking, eds., *British biographical archive* (1984), fiche 107, frames 296–8 [microfiche]

Bingham, Peregrine (*bap.* 1788, *d.* 1864), legal writer and reformer, was baptized at Radclive, Buckinghamshire, on 19 April 1788, the eldest son of the Revd Peregrine *Bingham (1754–1826) and his wife, Amy, *née* Bowles. He was educated at Winchester College and at Magdalen College, Oxford (BA, 1810), admitted to the Middle Temple in London in 1811, called to the bar on 27 November 1818, and practised on the western circuit before becoming a police magistrate in London. He married in 1816 Eliza, daughter of James Bolton, a London attorney. There were two children by the marriage, a daughter and a son, named—somewhat unimaginatively—Eliza and Peregrine.

For many years Bingham compiled law reports. Between 1821 and 1840 he was solely or jointly responsible for nineteen volumes of cases. He was the author of *The Law and Practice of Judgments and Executions* (1815), *The Law of Infancy and Coverture* (1816), and *A Digest of the Law of Landlord and Tenant* (1820). His *System of Shorthand on the Principle of the Association of Ideas* (1821) failed to win adherents.

As a young lawyer Bingham was friendly with John Austin and Nassau Senior, both of whom had chambers at Lincoln's Inn. But the most notable and influential of his associates was the elderly Jeremy Bentham, the utilitarian philosopher and reformer. In September 1818 Bentham described Bingham as 'a newly acquired and most valuable disciple', who 'is already in possession of most of my ideas respecting morals politics and legislation', and who 'without effort becomes master of every thing as soon as he looks at it, and in a condition to preach it, and defend it, and apply it every where' (*Correspondence of Jeremy Bentham*, 9.261). Bingham, for his part, wrote that Bentham's work had opened his eyes. He edited Bentham's *Book of Fallacies*, which was published in 1824, and in the same year he contributed a series of articles to the *Westminster Review*, the periodical established to propagate the utilitarian message. In these pieces he emerges as a stern critic of sentimentality, a rather tiresome advocate of precise definitions, and an enthusiast for the democratic institutions of the United States. It was small wonder that John Stuart Mill, who worked with him on the *Westminster Review*, regarded Bingham as having 'adopted with great ardour Mr Bentham's philosophical opinions' (*Autobiography and Literary Essays*, 97).

Bingham went on to be co-editor of the ill-fated *Parliamentary History and Review*, which for the three years of its life (1826–8) printed parliamentary debates with commentary from a radical perspective. As a member of the municipal corporations commission, which paved the way for the 1835 Municipal Corporations Act, he was seen as a doctrinaire Benthamite, committed to the idea of 'scientific legislation'. There is little evidence, however, that he was influential; to the contrary, Bingham and Charles Austin, the other identifiably utilitarian commissioner, seem to have had little impact on a process that appears to have been driven primarily by party considerations. From 1840 until about 1860, Bingham was the presiding magistrate at Great Marlborough Street court, and he also held the office of recorder of Southampton. Bingham died at his home in Gordon Square, London, on 2 November 1864.

STEPHEN CONWAY

Sources DNB · *The collected works of John Stuart Mill*, 1: *Autobiography and literary essays*, ed. J. M. Robson and J. Stillinger (1981) · *The correspondence of Jeremy Bentham*, 9, ed. S. Conway (1989) · *The correspondence of Jeremy Bentham*, 10, ed. S. Conway (1994) · W. Thomas, *The philosophic radicals: nine studies in theory and practice, 1817–1841* (1979) · *Law Times* (5 Nov 1864), 6 · Foster, *Alum. Oxon.* · IGI
Archives UCL, Bentham MSS, letters
Wealth at death under £25,000: probate, 22 Dec 1864, CGPLA Eng. & Wales

Bingham, Sir Richard (1527/8–1599), soldier and president of Connacht, was the third son of Robert Bingham of Melcombe-Bingham, Dorset, and his wife, Alice, daughter of Thomas Coker of Mappowder in the same county. His elder brothers were Robert and Christopher; he also had two sisters and five younger brothers, Sir George, Roger, Sir John, Thomas, and Charles, two of whom, like him, served in Ireland. Richard Bingham pursued a military and naval career that took him to many parts of Europe. His earliest military adventure was apparently with Protector Somerset's expedition to Scotland in 1547. He served with the Spaniards against the French at the battle of St Quentin in 1557 and in October 1558 participated in a naval expedition against the 'out-isles' of Scotland in which William Fitzwilliam was also involved. In the early years of Elizabeth's reign he fought against the Turks with the Spaniards and Venetians under Don John of Austria. He may have taken part in the conquest of Cyprus and the battle of Lepanto (7 October 1572). In 1573 and 1574 he was in the Low Countries reporting to Sir William Cecil from Delft and Dortrecht on the conflict with Spain. Late in 1576 he accompanied Sir Edward Horsey on an abortive mission to Don John to negotiate a peace between Spain and the states general of the United Provinces. In March 1578 Queen Elizabeth granted Bingham an annuity of 50 marks in recognition of his military and diplomatic services. Later in 1578 he fought as a volunteer under the Dutch flag against Spain. He was described by Sir Nicholas Le Strange as 'a man eminent both for spiritt and martiall knowledge, but of very small stature' (Thoms, 18).

In 1579 Bingham was sent to Ireland to assist in the suppression of the Desmond rebellion. He was captain of the

Sir Richard Bingham (1527/8–1599), by unknown artist, 1564

Swiftsure in autumn 1580 which helped in the Munster offensive under Admiral Winter against the Spaniards and Italians who had landed at Smerwick harbour to support James Fitzmaurice. Bingham took part in the massacre of the garrison at Dún an Óir on 10 November 1580 when a large number of Italians who had been offered protection were killed. After spending the winter off the Kerry coast, the *Swiftsure* reached Bristol on 9 January 1581. In August Bingham was among those put from the Portuguese voyage by Sir Francis Drake. Bingham was still serving with the *Swiftsure* late in 1583, being then an admiral. In September 1583 he was instructed by the queen to seize Dutch ships for debts due to her, while ostensibly working to apprehend pirates on the narrow seas.

Following the death of Sir Nicholas Malby in March 1584 Bingham was appointed as president of Connacht to succeed him. He was knighted by Sir John Perrot in St Patrick's Cathedral, Dublin, on 21 June 1584. A commission for martial law was issued to him on 8 July, and a commission for military government of the province was issued at the same time, Bingham being appointed commander of the forces in the field in the absence of the lord deputy. During his first year he regularly complained of his inadequate fee, which did not meet the expenses of his household. He initially regarded the Connacht presidency as the 'most painful and troublesome government in the country and the least commodious' (PRO, SP 63/111, no. 54), and thought of returning to life as captain of a small band. He sought unsuccessfully to establish himself at Roscommon Castle at the expense of Malby's heirs. But by the beginning of 1585, though still in dispute with Henry Malby, he had come to terms with his new surroundings. Having made plans to reduce the expenditure on his household,

Bingham evidently realized that the provincial government could be made profitable. Still maintaining an interest in overseas military ventures, he contacted Leicester in July 1585 concerning an expedition to Flanders, but noted in the same month that he wished to continue in his office in Connacht. His initial encounters with the earl of Clanricarde were positive, and Bingham believed that the Irish of Connacht were willing to conform peacefully to English ways. Following the successful negotiation of the composition of Connacht in the summer of 1585, whereby the finances of the provincial administration were put on a sure footing and the prospects for a peaceful and increasingly Anglicized province were greatly enhanced, Bingham asserted that he planned never to leave Connacht without assurance of something better. He had leases of Boyle and Ballymote, but resented the loss of Roscommon to Henry Malby and challenged the claim of the treasurer, Wallop, to have a lease of Athlone, previously reserved for the use of the president of Connacht. In his later years in Connacht, Bingham had yearly leases of Athlone and Ballymote at rents of £54 and £16, but still complained that his predecessor had fared better.

Bingham's reputation as one whose harsh administration goaded the Irish of Connacht into rebellion owed much to the influence enjoyed by his enemies in the Dublin government. That reputation continues despite a spirited effort by H. T. Knox to demonstrate the extent to which Bingham was the victim of personal animosities. In particular, the hostility of the lord deputy, Sir John Perrot, and within Connacht the activities of Theobald Dillon and Francis Barkeley created serious difficulties for Bingham. Although the executions which followed the Galway assizes early in 1586, and Bingham's actions against the Mayo Burkes who went into rebellion in the summer of that year, were both within the remit of his commissions, his work was censured. The massacre at Ardnaree on the River Moy on 22 August 1586 of a large number of Scots, who were on their way to assist the Burkes, earned him a reputation as a merciless governor. However, it appears to have been his military success rather than his harshness that aroused the hostility of Lord Deputy Perrot. Bingham complained to the privy council that he never thought his service against the Scots in Mayo would have earned him such hatred and disgrace with the lord deputy that he was forced to leave his charge. He claimed that Perrot's undermining of his authority had undone the good of the military successes he had achieved.

By February 1587 the privy council had cleared Bingham of charges brought against him, finding they were maliciously brought by Theobald Dillon. In May of that year Bingham was withdrawn from Connacht temporarily for service in Flanders. He left in July, being replaced initially by Sir Thomas Le Strange and in September by his own brother George Bingham. On 11 January 1588 he married Sarah (1564/5–1634), daughter of John Heigham of Gifford's Hall, Wickhambrook, Suffolk. Bingham was restored to the government of Connacht in spring 1588, reaching Athlone in May. He involved himself in a controversy over the legitimate succession to Sir Donnell O'Connor Sligo, and in September he actively implemented the government proclamation to execute any survivors of the Spanish Armada found in Connacht.

A new outbreak of rebellion among the Mayo Burkes in spring 1589 created renewed tension between the lord deputy and Bingham. New accusations of misgovernment were brought against him and controversy ensued when Sir Francis Walsingham, a lifelong supporter of Bingham, pointed out to the lord deputy that the men appointed as commissioners to examine Bingham's actions were his arch-enemies within the Dublin administration. By December 1589 Bingham had again been cleared of any charges of misgovernment, and for the following four and a half years governed the province in relative peace. He could not comprehend why 'I am tearmed crewell for doing her Majestie trewe service' (PRO, SP 63/170 no. 45).

The outbreak of the Nine Years' War in Ulster created a renewed atmosphere of unrest in Connacht by the mid-1590s. When O'Donnell came to mid-Roscommon in March 1595 Bingham did not have sufficient military strength to repel him. He was eventually assigned two untrained companies and given instructions to defend Connacht. The supporters of O'Donnell considered him 'the greatest monster of all the English that were then in Ireland' (Ó Cléirigh, 1.101). Tension with the Dublin government continued, and Bingham was summoned before the lord deputy and council in July 1596 to answer further complaints. On 23 September he departed for England, believing there was a plot by Sir John Norris to murder him. On arrival in London he was suspended from his office and imprisoned for leaving Ireland without permission, but was released in November because of ill health. On his return journey to Ireland he was accompanied by Sir Conyers Clifford, who had been appointed to replace him in Connacht, and who left him behind at Chester owing to illness. The government, realizing the depth of animosity shown by Sir John Norris and Sir Geoffrey Fenton towards Bingham, decided the trial should be before the whole council in Dublin, but in the event it seems never to have taken place. Bingham continued to enjoy favour in London, and when plans were being drawn up for the earl of Essex's expedition to Ireland, Sir Francis Bacon advised Essex to be wary of Sir William Fitzwilliam and Sir John Norris but to have special regard for Bingham's advice. His considerable expertise as a military commander was clearly valued by his supporters despite his persistent lack of subtlety in his dealings with his political opponents. Together with the elderly Richard Burke, third earl of Clanricarde, Bingham was admitted to Gray's Inn, London, on 17 March 1598, probably as a result of the ongoing patronage of Sir Francis Walsingham.

In September 1598 Bingham left England with five thousand men to assume the office of marshall of Ireland, but he died in Dublin on 19 January 1599. His body was returned to London for burial in Westminster Abbey. A memorial to him was erected there by his former servant Sir John Bingley and a portrait painted in 1564 is in the National Portrait Gallery, London. Lady Bingham survived her husband and subsequently married Edward Waldegrave, of Lawford, Essex. She died at Lawford on 9 September 1634, aged sixty-nine, and was buried in the church there. Sir Richard evidently had no title to property in Ireland and the family's Dorset estates were inherited by Henry, eldest son of his younger brother George.

BERNADETTE CUNNINGHAM

Sources CSP Ire., 1574–1600 · CSP dom., 1581–97 · H. T. Knox, 'Sir Richard Bingham's government of Connaught', *Journal of Galway Archaeological and Historical Society*, 4 (1906), 161–76; 181–97; 5 (1907), 1–27 · L. Ó Cléirigh, *The life of Aodh Ruadh Ó Domhnaill*, ed. P. Walsh and C. Ó Lochlainn, 2 vols., ITS, 42, 45 (1948–57) · *The Irish fiants of the Tudor sovereigns*, 4 vols. (1994) · R. Lascelles, ed., *Liber munerum publicorum Hiberniae … or, The establishments of Ireland*, 2 vols. [1824–30] · *The letters and life of Francis Bacon*, ed. J. Spedding, 7 vols. (1861–74), vol. 2 · CSP for., 1572–7 · W. J. Thoms, ed., *Anecdotes and traditions, illustrative of early English history and literature*, CS, 5 (1839), 18 · J. Foster, *The register of admissions to Gray's Inn, 1521–1889, together with the register of marriages in Gray's Inn chapel, 1695–1754* (privately printed, London, 1889), 93 · W. A. Shaw, *The knights of England*, 2 (1906) · AFM, vols. 5–6 · R. O'Flaherty, *Chorographical description of West or Iar Connacht*, ed. J. O'Donovan (1849), 187–229 · Burke, *Gen. Ire.* (1858), 88 · B. Cunningham, 'Political and social change in the lordships of Clanricard and Thomond, 1569–1641', MA diss., University College Galway, 1979

Archives PRO, SP 63 | BL, Irish papers, Cotton MSS, Titus b xii–xiii

Likenesses oils, 1564, NPG [*see illus.*]

Bingham, Richard, the elder (1765–1858), Church of England clergyman, was born on 1 April 1765. He was son of the Revd Isaac Moody Bingham, rector of Birchanger and Runwell, Essex, and great-grandson of Joseph *Bingham (*bap.* 1668, *d.* 1723), author of *Origines ecclesiasticae*. He was educated at Winchester College, where he was on the foundation, and at New College, Oxford, where he graduated BA on 19 October 1787 and BCL on 18 July 1801. He was married at Bristol to Lydia Mary Anne, eldest daughter of Rear-Admiral Sir Charles *Douglas, baronet, and his second wife, Sarah, daughter of John Wood, on 10 November 1788, by which time he was a fellow of his college and in holy orders. Richard *Bingham (1798–1872) was their son.

In 1790 Bingham was appointed to the perpetual curacy of Holy Trinity Church, Gosport; in 1796 he became vicar of Great Hale, near Sleaford, Lincolnshire, and was appointed, on 22 July 1807, in succession to his father, to the prebendal stall of Bargham in Chichester Cathedral, which position he held until his death. In 1813, being then a magistrate for Hampshire of twelve years' standing, he was convicted at the Winchester summer assizes of having illegally obtained a licence for a public house, when no such public house was in existence, and of having stated a false consideration in the conveyance of the house with intent to defraud the revenue by evading an additional stamp duty of £10. On 10 November 1813 a motion was made in the king's bench for a new trial. In spite of many affidavits to his character he was sentenced on 26 November 1813 to six months' imprisonment in the county gaol at Winchester. In an appeal to public opinion dated 23

December 1813 Bingham vehemently asserted his innocence.

In 1829 Bingham published, by subscription, the third edition of the *Origines ecclesiasticae* of his ancestor, adding references from the author's manuscript annotations in a private copy of his own book, and Joseph Bingham's three *Trinity Sermons*; he prefixed the edition with a life of Joseph Bingham. The bankruptcy of the printer while the work was passing through the press caused much delay in its distribution. Bingham died at his home at Newhouse, Gosport, on Sunday 18 July 1858, and was buried on Tuesday 27 July in the vaults of Trinity Church in the presence of a very large number of his friends and parishioners.

ARTHUR H. GRANT, *rev.* H. C. G. MATTHEW

Sources Foster, *Alum. Oxon.* · Boase, *Mod. Eng. biog.* · *Hampshire Telegraph* (24 July 1858) · *Hampshire Telegraph* (31 July 1858) · *Annual Register* (1813) · *GM*, 1st ser., 77 (1807) · *GM*, 2nd ser., 27 (1847) · *GM*, 3rd ser., 5 (1858)
Wealth at death under £200: probate, 22 Oct 1858, *CGPLA Eng. & Wales*

Bingham, Richard, the younger (1798–1872), Church of England clergyman and author, was the eldest son of Richard *Bingham, the elder (1765–1858), and his wife, Lydia Mary Anne, *née* Douglas. He was educated at Magdalen Hall, Oxford, where he graduated BA in 1821 and MA in 1827. He was ordained deacon in 1821, and priest in 1822, and became curate to his father in his incumbency of Holy Trinity Church, Gosport. Here he remained for over twenty-two years. He married, on 4 May 1824, Frances Campbell, daughter of J. Barton, of Mount Pleasant, Jamaica, and took pupils.

Bingham published by subscription two small volumes of sermons in 1826 and 1827, and in 1829 *The warning voice, or, An awakening question for all British protestants in general, and members of the Church of England in particular, at the present juncture*. He seceded from the British and Foreign Bible Society in 1831, on account of its readiness to co-operate with Socinians, and soon after published an account of the circumstances. He issued by subscription a volume entitled *Sermons* (1835), and in 1843 *Immanuel, or, God with Us*. Twelve years later he produced the standard edition of his ancestor, Joseph *Bingham, *The Works of the Rev. Joseph Bingham, MA* (10 vols., 1855).

In 1844 Bingham was presented by the trustees to the perpetual curacy of Christ Church, Harwood, Bolton-le-Moors; during his incumbency he lost (28 February 1847) his eldest daughter, Frances Lydia, aged twenty-one, and his youngest son. Frances Bingham had published *Hubert, or, The Orphans of St Madelaine; a Legend of the Persecuted Vaudois* (1845), and at the time of her death left remnants which were published by her father in 1848 as *Short Poems, Religious and Sentimental* and passed through two editions. Bingham became in 1853 curate at St Mary's, Marylebone, the rector of which was John Hampden Gurney, to whom he afterwards dedicated *Sermons* (1858). In 1856 he became vicar of Queenborough in the Isle of Sheppey. In 1870 he retired from this living to reside at Sutton, Surrey, where he died on Monday 22 January 1872.

Bingham was an energetic advocate of liturgical revision, and a member of the council of the Prayer Book Revision Society. In 1860 he published *Liturgia recusa, or, Suggestions for revising and reconstructing the daily and occasional services of the United Church of England and Ireland*. He supplemented this volume by an elaborate model of a liturgy, *Liturgiæ recusæ exemplar: the prayer book as it might be* (1863), with a dedication to Lord Ebury, which reflected Bingham's evangelical inclinations. Bingham also published *The Gospel According to Isaiah* (1870) and *Hymnologia Christiana Latina, or, A Century of Psalms and Hymns and Spiritual Songs* (1871).

ARTHUR H. GRANT, *rev.* H. C. G. MATTHEW

Sources Crockford (1872) · *Clergy List* (1841–72) · *The Guardian* (31 Jan 1872) · Foster, *Alum. Oxon.*

Bingham [Byngham], **William** (d. 1451), ecclesiastic and founder of Christ's College, Cambridge, may have been the William Byngham who was presented to the vicarages of Hutton, near Beverley, Yorkshire, and Alverstoke, Hampshire, by Henry IV in 1401–2. More probably, the future founder of Godshouse may be identified with a William Byngham who between 1408 and 1420 regularly served as a proctor of Master Henry Rumworth, one of Henry V's chaplains. There can in any case be no doubt that the William Bingham who exchanged the rectory of Carlton Curlieu in Leicestershire (to which he had been instituted the previous year) for that of St John Zachary, London, on 25 May 1424, was the London parish priest who before long began to seek a novel and ambitious remedy for the country's 'grete scarstee of maistres of Gramer' (Lloyd, 356–7).

Bingham's alarm at the alleged decline in the number of grammar teachers within the kingdom was based on some personal experience: in his first extant petition (1438–9) to Henry VI he lamented the closure of no less than seventy schools between Southampton and Ripon during the previous fifty years. However, there can be equally no doubt that Bingham, not a university graduate himself, was encouraged to found a university-based college specifically devoted to the training of grammar masters by a wide circle of London acquaintances, notably by John Brokley, mayor of the city in 1433–4. Brokley was associated with Bingham in the purchase of part of the original site of this new college of Godshouse (on the east side of Milne Street, Cambridge) as early as 1437. Very early in the history of its foundation, however, Bingham began to encounter formidable opposition, above all on the part of Henry VI himself, who by the summer of 1442 had decided to incorporate the site of Godshouse within his own new college, now known as King's. Only Bingham's personal energy and tenacity prevented Godshouse from disappearing into early oblivion. By the summer of 1446 he had acquired a large alternative site on St Andrew's Street near Barnwell Gate, and it was there that Godshouse (refounded and renamed Christ's College by Lady Margaret Beaufort in 1505–6) at last began its continuous history. By the terms of Henry VI's long-delayed foundation charter to Godshouse (16 April 1448) Bingham was at last appointed head or proctor of his new college, then intended to comprise as many as sixty other scholars. By no means all of Bingham's educational ideals and innovative plans of the 1430s and 1440s were to be fulfilled: but when he died on 17 November 1451 (to be buried before the rood cross of St John Zachary), there could be no doubt that Godshouse itself would survive, and that this London parish priest had helped to stimulate a highly significant new wave of collegiate foundations at Cambridge.   R. B. DOBSON

Sources A. H. Lloyd, *The early history of Christ's College, Cambridge* (1934) · H. Rackham, *Early Statutes of Christ's College* (1927) · A. L. Peck, *The Lord King's College of God's-House, 1448–1948* (1948) · D. R. Leader, *A history of the University of Cambridge*, 1: *The university to 1546*, ed. C. N. L. Brooke and others (1988), 40–41, 225–6, 259–60, 262 · A. B. Cobban, *The medieval English universities: Oxford and Cambridge to c.1500* (1988), 196, 249 · J. Peile, *Christ's College* (1900), 1–8 · A. B. Cobban, *The King's Hall within the University of Cambridge in the later middle ages*, Cambridge Studies in Medieval Life and Thought, 3rd ser., 1 (1969), 79–80 · Emden, *Cam.* · Emden, *Oxf.* · CPR, 1399–1401, 442; 1401–5, 182
Archives Christ's College, Cambridge, muniments

Bingley. For this title name *see* Benson, Robert, Baron Bingley (*bap.* 1676, *d.* 1731).

Bingley, Blanche. *See* Hillyard, Blanche (1863–1946).

Bingley, William (1774–1823), naturalist and priest, was born at Doncaster, Yorkshire, early in January 1774 and baptized there on the 7th. He was orphaned while still very young. He was educated at a school in Doncaster, where his friends urged him to pursue a career in law, but his own inclinations were for a more tranquil life in the church. With this end in mind he matriculated at Peterhouse, Cambridge, in 1795, graduating BA in 1799 and MA in 1803. He was ordained deacon at York in 1799 and became curate at Mirfield in the West Riding of Yorkshire in the same year.

Bingley was a noted writer on botany, topography, and popular zoology. His travels in Wales while still an undergraduate formed the basis of his two-volume, illustrated, *Tour of North Wales* (1800; 2nd edn, 1814), which includes a catalogue of Welsh plants. He returned to Wales in 1801 and afterwards issued a topographical account, *North Wales* (2 vols., 1804). During the same period he published one of his most popular zoological works, *Animal Biography* (1802), which went through multiple editions and was translated into a number of European languages. In a similar vein he published *Memoirs of British Quadrupeds* (1809), and *Animated Nature* (1814). These works gave an entertaining and palatable introduction to the basic zoological facts: *Animated Nature*, a contemporary noted, contained nothing which might 'prove offensive to the most delicate female mind' (Bingley, vii).

Bingley served as curate of the priory in Christchurch, Hampshire, from 1802 to 1816. From 1816 to 1823 he was minister of Fitzroy Chapel (St Saviour's) in Charlotte Street, London. He was married but his wife's name is not known. His son, William Richard Bingley, published (and amended) the third edition of *North Wales* (1839). Though

Bingley continued to publish on natural history, producing, among other works, *A Practical Introduction to Botany* (1817), he also indulged a strong taste for compilation. Among his compilative (and none too critical) works were *Musical Biography* (1814), a series of popular biographical compilations on British characters, eminent voyagers, celebrated travellers, and Roman characters, and six volumes of travel writings designed as abridged popular versions of the accounts given by those who actually did the travelling.

Bingley's major projected work was his county history of Hampshire. Though much material was collected he did not live to complete this, and only a small portion of it was ever published (*The Topographical Account of the Hundred of Bosmere*, privately published in 1817). He died at his home in Charlotte Street, London, on 11 March 1823 and was buried at St George's Church, Bloomsbury.

W. P. COURTNEY, *rev.* P. E. KELL

Sources W. Bingley, *Biography of celebrated Roman characters* (1824) · [J. Watkins and F. Shoberl], *A biographical dictionary of the living authors of Great Britain and Ireland* (1816) · B. D. Jackson, *Guide to the literature of botany* (1881), 37, 41 · G. A. Pritzel, ed., *Thesaurus literaturae botanicae omnium gentium* (Leipzig, 1851), 22 · GM, 1st ser., 93/1 (1823), 472 · Venn, *Alum. Cant.* · Desmond, *Botanists*, rev. edn
Archives Hants. RO | Bodl. Oxf., Phillipps-Robinson MSS · Hants. RO, letters to James Harris · Linn. Soc., Smith MSS
Likenesses W. Ward, mezzotint, BM

Binham, Simon (*fl. c.*1350), Benedictine monk and chronicler, was probably born in East Anglia and became a member of the priory of Binham, Norfolk, one of the cells of the abbey of St Albans. He is first recorded as supporting his prior in resisting the unjust exactions of Hugh, abbot of St Albans (1309–27). After Hugh appealed to Edward II for assistance, Binham and the other rebellious monks were brought to St Albans and imprisoned, but he was later released and lived to become an influential member of the house, for in the time of Abbot Michael (1335–49) he was chosen by the chapter as one of the three receivers or treasurers of the collections made for the support of scholars and needy brethren.

Binham's real claim to fame, however, rests on his apparent role as one in a long line of St Albans chroniclers. As V. H. Galbraith has demonstrated, St Albans was an active centre of historical writing in the later middle ages. The *Flores historiarum* of Roger of Wendover (*d.* 1236) and Matthew Paris's *Chronica majora*, both compiled in the thirteenth century, began the tradition of historical writing at St Albans. This tradition was not a continuous one; after the death of Paris in 1259 the scriptorium fell silent for almost a generation. Under the abbacy of John Maryns (1302–8), however, the writing of history was revised. According to Thomas Walsingham, writing about 1400, after Paris 'William Risangre, Henry Blankfrount, Simon Bynham and Richard Savage successively wrote chronicles' (*Annales … Amundesham*, 2.303). Beginning in the early fourteenth century, then, several smaller texts were compiled in an effort to pick up the *Chronica majora* where Paris had left off in 1259. William of Rishanger was apparently the author of the *Opus chronicorum*, covering the years 1259–97 (with a preface explaining events down to 1307). A continuation of Rishanger's chronicle, the *Annals of John Trokelowe*, covers events in the period 1307–23, and Henry Blaneford wrote a brief continuation for the years 1323–4. Whether or not even these brief texts were really the work of Rishanger, he has also been credited with a history—the so-called *Chronica Willelmi Rishanger*—dealing with events in the period 1259–1307. Galbraith, however, has called this attribution into question, pointing out among other things that its earliest manuscript (BL, Royal MS 14 C.vii) was written soon after 1350, by which date Rishanger was surely dead (he would have been eighty years of age in 1330). This chronicle is not without importance, as it may have been used by Walsingham in the compilation of his *Chronica majora*. For Galbraith, therefore, this text represents 'a unique survival of historical writing at St Albans in the period between Rishanger and Walsingham' (*St Albans Chronicle*, xxxv). Owing to the apparent date of its composition, this chronicle was probably written by either Simon Binham or Richard Savage, whose works have otherwise become lost.

GEORGE B. STOW

Sources *Annales monasterii S. Albani a Johanne Amundesham*, ed. H. T. Riley, 2 vols., pt 5 of *Chronica monasterii S. Albani*, Rolls Series, 28 (1870–71), vol. 1, p. lxvi; vol. 2, p. 303 · *Gesta abbatum monasterii Sancti Albani, a Thoma Walsingham*, ed. H. T. Riley, 3 vols., pt 4 of *Chronica monasterii S. Albani*, Rolls Series, 28 (1867–9), vol. 2, pp. 131, 305 · T. Walsingham, *The St Albans chronicle, 1406–1420*, ed. V. H. Galbraith (1937), xxvii, xxxv · A. Gransden, *Historical writing in England*, 2 (1982), 5
Archives BL, Royal MS 14 C.vii

Binham [Bynham, Vynham, Rynnan], **William** (*fl. c.*1374–1396), prior of Wallingford and theologian, probably came from Binham in Norfolk. There was a Benedictine priory there dependent on St Albans Abbey, and Binham became a monk in the latter house. If he was the opponent mentioned in a text by John Wyclif (discussed below), he must by the time of the composition of that tract have been a doctor of theology, presumably of Oxford University. By 1379 he was prior of Wallingford, Berkshire, another dependency of St Albans; he still held that position in 1396 when he was too sick to attend the election of a new abbot of St Albans. Nothing further is known of his career.

John Bale states that Binham wrote a book *Contra Vuiclevi propositiones*, and for Wyclif records a *Contra Bynhamum monachum*, neither with an incipit. Binham's work does not survive; Wyclif's text is probably that which survives in a single manuscript, probably of French origin, where the adversary's name is given as William Vynham or Vymham; a second determination, there linked to the first, is found in a further three medieval copies, but, though it has been assumed that the opponent is the same, no name is given. An early Hussite catalogue gives Wyclif's opponent in the first the name of William Rynnan. From Wyclif's citations it appears that Binham had argued for the right of the clergy to civil dominion, had defended the exemption of the clergy from aspects of civil law, and had maintained the inalienability of ecclesiastical temporalities. The date of Binham's exchanges with Wyclif was probably between 1374 and the reception in England of Gregory XI's condemnation of the latter in October 1377.

ANNE HUDSON

Sources W. H. Turner and H. O. Coxe, eds., *Calendar of charters and rolls preserved in the Bodleian Library* (1878), 4 · *Gesta abbatum monasterii Sancti Albani, a Thoma Walsingham*, ed. H. T. Riley, 3 vols., pt 4 of *Chronica monasterii S. Albani*, Rolls Series, 28 (1867–9), vol. 3, p. 426 · J. Wyclif, *Opera minora*, ed. J. Loserth (1913), 415–35 · Bale, *Cat.*, 1.458 · *John Wiclif's Polemical works in Latin*, ed. R. Buddensieg, 1 (1883), lxiv

Binney, Edward William (1812–1881), geologist and philanthropist, was born on 7 December 1812 at Morton Hall, near Gainsborough, Lincolnshire, the youngest of the seven sons and two daughters of Thomas Binney (1762–1835), landowner and maltster, and his second wife, Elizabeth Cross (*d.* 1843) of Gringley, Nottinghamshire. He attended four schools before being sent to Gainsborough grammar school at the age of seven. He was a good scholar, excelled at sports, and delighted in observing and collecting minerals and animals during long walks in the country. Although inclined to study chemistry which, like natural history, had attracted his attention since childhood, on his brother Mordecai's advice he left school at sixteen and began to study law.

In 1828 Binney was articled to a solicitor in Chesterfield, Derbyshire, where he continued to collect fossils, particularly from the coal measures. Here he came into contact with miners and began his lifelong appreciation of practical geology. In 1833 Binney moved to London after his refusal to abandon his whig sympathies with reform resulted in a clash with his employer. Often forced to work without remuneration, only with the help of Mordecai did he complete his legal training in London, qualify as a solicitor, and take chambers in Manchester in 1835.

On arrival Binney joined the Manchester Mechanics' Institution, and quickly made friends with John Leigh, with whom he read his first geological paper at the Literary and Philosophical Society in 1835. In 1838 he was active in founding the Manchester Geological Society, paying particular attention to the museum which he insisted should be free to the public, especially to working men. His numerous geological works were devoted primarily to the study of the coal measures, and he contributed to the controversial debate on the origin of coal, arguing for its marine formation from vegetation growing in shallow seas. He was elected fellow of the London Geological Society in 1853 and, through his work with Joseph Dalton Hooker on coal plants, of the Royal Society in 1856.

Although Binney's research interests were specific, his wider views on science shaped his political, philanthropic, and business concerns. Like Leigh he worked to improve the sanitary condition of Manchester, contributing to Lyon Playfair's *Second Report … into the State of Large Towns* (1845). His geologizing in mining areas led to his proposal to Joseph Brotherton MP that women be prohibited from working in pits. Disappointed by the failure of mechanics' institutes to inspire working-class interest in science, when Binney encountered the network of pub meetings held by Lancashire working men interested in natural history he did his utmost to promote this activity. Soon after his 1842 election to the Manchester Literary and Philosophical Society, learning of the destitution of some artisan mathematicians and botanists, he attempted to establish a public society for 'the relief and encouragement of scientific men in humble life' (*Manchester Guardian*, 13 Dec 1843). Believing that conditions imposed by the Revd Richard Parkinson concerning the morality of the recipients scuppered the aims of this proposed society, Binney administered a private subscription fund from 1844, presenting donations at an annual dinner he gave for scientific artisans. In particular, he encouraged the shoemaker Richard *Buxton (1786–1865) to publish a Manchester flora in 1849 to which Binney anonymously contributed a geological preface, and defended him vigorously against competition from the botanist Leo Hartley Grindon, with whom Binney had several unpleasant skirmishes. Binney also helped the blacksmith Samuel Gibson, the radical reformer Samuel Bamford, and the electrician William Sturgeon, for whom he campaigned for a £50 government pension.

Throughout his life Binney argued for the opening of museums on Sundays and stressed the social benefits of the practical pursuit of science by a wide range of participants. He thus opposed Owens College, founded in 1851, not for its educational aims but for the consequent exclusion of practical men and amateurs from science. He sometimes shocked others by the candid expression of his views, gaining a reputation for being a 'storm centre in Manchester scientific circles' as Francis Nicholson recalled in *Memoirs and Proceedings of the Manchester Literary and Philosophical Society* (58, 1913, 9).

Binney's career exemplified his belief in the essential connections between practical knowledge and science. He achieved enormous commercial success in collaboration with James Young and Edward Meldrum in their manufacture of paraffin from bituminous coals at Bathgate, Linlithgowshire, despite fighting several expensive legal challenges over patents. The partnership lasted from 1851 to 1864 and made a vast profit from three companies, as well as establishing the industrial foundation of the paraffin or shale oil industry in Europe, America, and Australia.

As his wealth accrued, Binney abandoned his legal profession. On 28 August 1856 he married Mary Christiana Jones (*d*. 1882), daughter and coheir of the Revd David Jones; they had six children. In the 1860s, in addition to his home near Manchester, he purchased an estate, Ravenscliff, on the Isle of Man, and increased his investments through mining concerns in Scotland. He suffered a stroke when travelling between Douglas and Liverpool, and died eleven days later, on 19 December 1881, at his home at 11 Spring Bank, Crumpsall, near Manchester. He was buried in the Binney family vault at the abbey church, Worksop, Nottinghamshire, on 23 December.

Binney disliked clergy who opposed science but he claimed to enjoy a good sermon. He shunned the ostentation of polite society and was considered peculiar for enjoying the company of scientific working men. He devoted himself to institutional science in Manchester, serving as president of the Geological Society in 1857–9 and 1866–7 and of the Literary and Philosophical Society regularly between 1862 and 1881; James Prescott Joule presented a portrait of Binney painted by W. H. Johnson to the latter society. Binney was a large and imposing man, whose remarkable outspokenness was considered 'ungentlemanly & disgusting' by his enemies, but an indicator of honour, affection, and 'sterling nature' by his friends, among whom the closest were Leigh, Joule, and John Harland. As his obituarist in the *Manchester Examiner and Times* (21 December 1881) remarked, 'he was a strong friend although a good hater'.   ANNE SECORD

Sources J. Binney, *The centenary of a nineteenth century geologist: Edward William Binney* (1912) · R. A. Smith, 'A centenary of science at Manchester', *Memoirs of the Literary and Philosophical Society of Manchester*, 3rd ser., 9 (1883) [whole issue] · J. P. Joule, 'Edward William Binney', *Nature*, 25 (1881–2), 293–4 · *Manchester Examiner and Times* (21 Dec 1881) · *Manchester Guardian* (22 Dec 1881) · K. Wood, *Rich seams: Manchester Geological and Mining Society 1838–1988* (1987), 5–34 · R. H. Kargon, *Science in Victorian Manchester* (1977) · E. W. Binney, *A few remarks respecting Mr. R. Buxton, the author of 'The Manchester Botanical Guide'* (1863) · 'Botanists: annual meeting', *Manchester City News* (20 April 1878) · P. Lucier, 'Court and controversy: patenting science in the nineteenth century', *British Journal for the History of Science*, 29 (1996), 139–54 · J. Butt, 'The Scottish oil mania of 1864–6', *Scottish Journal of Political Economy*, 12 (1965), 195–209 · 'Notes on the Society for the Promotion of Natural History contained in minutes of the meetings of the trustees of Owens College', Man. CL, MS 378.42.M.60, vol. 9, fol. 6 · *CGPLA Eng. & Wales* (1882) · Burke, *Gen. GB* (1972)

Archives BGS · Manchester Museum · NHM · U. Cam., Sedgwick Museum of Earth Sciences, geological specimens | University of Strathclyde, Glasgow, corresp. with James Young

Likenesses W. H. Johnson, oils, Manchester Literary and Philosophical Society, Manchester · oils, priv. coll. · photograph, repro. in Binney, *The centenary of a nineteenth century geologist*

Wealth at death £109,278 4s. 2d.: probate, 31 March 1882, *CGPLA Eng. & Wales*

Binney, Sir (Frederick) George (1900–1972), explorer and blockade runner, was born on 23 September 1900 at Great Bookham, Surrey, the second of two sons of Maximilian Frederick Breffit Binney (1859–1936), vicar of Richmond, Surrey, and his first wife, Emily Blinkhorn, who died when Binney was born. There were two more sons of a second marriage. He won a scholarship from Summer Fields, Oxford, to Eton College and later to Merton College, Oxford. He obtained a third class in English in 1923. At Oxford, at a chance meeting with Julian Huxley in Blackwells, he was asked as editor of *Isis* to back an expedition to Spitsbergen and to become its organizer and secretary. This was the Oxford University Spitsbergen expedition of 1921. In 1923 he organized and led the Merton College Arctic expedition and in 1924 the Oxford University Arctic expedition. The first to use a seaplane for Arctic surveys, he recorded his experiences in his book *With Seaplane and*

Sledge in the Arctic (1925). His achievements were recognized by the Back award of the Royal Geographical Society, the gold medal *de la roquette* of the Geographical Society of Paris, and in 1957 by the founder's gold medal of the Royal Geographical Society.

Binney joined the Hudson's Bay Company in 1926, and spent the winters in England recruiting young apprentices and the summers planting them on trading stations in the Canadian Arctic. A *Times* leader on his *The Eskimo Book of Knowledge* (1931), the first book other than the Bible to be made available to the Inuit in their own language, led his chairman to offer him promotion to the company's headquarters in Winnipeg, but he refused and joined the United Steel Companies Ltd the next day. He was appointed to build up a central export department and became the company's export director, distinguishing himself by his remarkable success as an unconventional negotiator. He remained with United Steel until it was nationalized, travelling the world on its behalf, from Europe to North and South America, Russia, Iran, India, and the Far East.

Having narrowly missed service in the First World War, Binney was determined to play a part in the second. In December 1939 he was sent by iron and steel control (Ministry of Supply) as their Scandinavian representative to Sweden to negotiate the purchase and shipment of special steels, machine tools, and ball-bearings which were vital for the British armament industries. The German invasion of Denmark and Norway on 9 April 1940 cut Sweden off from the West, whereupon Binney decided to run the gauntlet of the Skagerrak blockade. He defeated opposition to his plan at home and in Sweden and was given diplomatic status as assistant commercial attaché at the British legation; he recruited British, Norwegian, and Swedish crews for five Norwegian merchantmen. Operation Rubble, as it was called, sailed from Bro Fjord north of Göteborg on 23 January 1941 with Binney as commodore. It got through to Kirkwall in the Orkneys with 25,000 tons of vital war supplies and five ships for the allied merchant fleets. Binney refused an important appointment in Washington, and returned to Sweden to run operation Performance in March 1942 with ten ships. Only two got through, with 5000 tons of cargo, two returned to Sweden, and the rest were sunk or scuttled.

Binney was expelled from Sweden as *persona non grata* for smuggling scuttling charges and arms on board his ships but reappeared as commander, Royal Naval Volunteer Reserve, in 1943 in charge of operation Bridford. This consisted of a flotilla of five motor coasters (of which two were lost) which delivered 347½ tons of valuable cargo while another 88 tons were airlifted. Having been invalided out after a heart attack, Binney still involved himself in yet another operation—Moonshine—which delivered arms to the Danish resistance. He was knighted in 1941 and appointed to the DSO in 1944 for these remarkable exploits. His unique contribution to the war effort was to help meet the shortfall of ball-bearings when there were too few coming from British factories and insufficient imports from the USA and Canada. After demobilization in 1945 Binney returned to United Steel, and left it

once only—for a brief foray for the government as leader of the UK trade and industrial mission to Ghana in 1959.

This jovial buccaneer with his puckish sense of humour, his stocky physique, ruddy complexion, and keen blue eyes was a man of discriminating taste in books, antiques, and the good things of life. Binney's homes were perfect settings for his treasures, and his restoration of his home, Horham Hall, Thaxted, Essex, was typical of his taste. He was an obstinate individualist with scant respect for authority, a man of impeccable integrity, and meticulous in his attention to detail. Cyril Alington, his headmaster at Eton, called him 'the ingenious and ingenuous Binney': this he always remained.

Binney was married first, on 7 May 1946, to Evelyn Mary, widow of Flight-Lieutenant A. P. F. Fane RAFVR, and elder daughter of Thomas G. Marriott, of Putney Hill, London. This marriage was dissolved in 1954 and the following year Binney married Sonia, widow of Lieutenant-Colonel Francis Crofton Simms MC, and daughter of Paymaster Rear-Admiral Sir William Marcus Charles Beresford Whyte. He adopted her son Marcus. He died on 27 September 1972 at his home, Domaine des Vaux, Haut de la Vallée, St Lawrence, Jersey, Channel Islands.

PETER TENNANT, *rev.*

Sources CAC Cam., Binney MSS · R. Barker, *The blockade busters* (1976) · private information (1986) [Binney family] · personal knowledge (1986) · Burke, *Peerage* (1967)
Archives CAC Cam., corresp. and naval papers
Wealth at death £1500 in England and Wales: probate, 27 Nov 1973, *CGPLA Eng. & Wales*

Binney [Benny], **Thomas** (1798–1874), Congregational minister, was born on 30 April 1798 at Newcastle upon Tyne, presumably the Thomas Benny who was baptized on 3 June 1798 at Wall Knoll Presbyterian Chapel. If so, he was the son of John Benny, who was baptized on 5 September 1759 at Wooler West Presbyterian Chapel in north Northumberland, the son of Edward and Anne Binney. John Benny was an elder in the congregation at Wall Knoll. After attending a local school Thomas Binney spent the years from 1811 to 1818 as an apprentice to a bookseller. Despite working long hours he was able to study Latin and Greek under the tuition of a Presbyterian minister, as well as exercising himself in English composition by writing in imitation of Samuel Johnson and composing poetry in imitation of *Paradise Lost*. He left the Presbyterian church, became a Congregationalist, and in 1819 entered the Wymondley Academy, Hertfordshire. In 1823 he became minister of the New Meeting, Bedford, but left after twelve months. He received a call from St James's Street Chapel, Newport, Isle of Wight, in August 1824 and was inducted into the pastorate on 29 December 1824. At a church meeting at King's Weigh House, Eastcheap, London, on 14 May 1829 it was resolved to invite him to become minister there at a salary of £600 a year. He accepted and remained there until his retirement.

In 1832 plans to widen the approach to London Bridge made it necessary to demolish the chapel, and a new one to accommodate 1000 people was built in Fish Street Hill

Thomas Binney (1798–1874), by London Stereoscopic Co.

at a cost of £16,000. Binney spoke at the stone-laying ceremony, and when the speech was published he added an appendix in which he included the declaration that the established church 'is an obstacle to the progress of truth and godliness in the land; that it destroys more souls than it saves; and that, therefore, its end is most devoutly to be wished by every lover of God and man' (Kaye, 67). It sparked off an animated controversy and brought instant public attention to its author. In later years he admitted that he began life as a high-Independent, but he was soon to prove himself a moderate dissenter. He certainly objected to the state establishment of religion, but he also pleaded for closer co-operation between dissenters and Anglicans, with joint communion services and exchange of pulpits, in *The Ultimate Object of the Evangelical Dissenters* (1834), and argued in *Dissent not Schism* (1834) that disagreement about church government was a secondary matter and nonconformity should not be construed to mean the renunciation of Christianity. Desire for closer fellowship between churches of his own denomination also led him to support the inauguration in 1832 of the Congregational Union of England and Wales, of which he was chairman in 1848.

King's Weigh House was a church consisting of young city businessmen, members of the middle class, and a few rich people, none perhaps quite as rich as the philanthropist Samuel Morley (1809–1886). People of this kind found Binney's new style of preaching very much to their taste. In dress and demeanour he symbolized the passing of the age of the silver shoe-buckle, the knee-breeches, and the gold-headed cane. He discarded the black preaching gown. His sermons were in the main expository, although he occasionally exploited some topical item of news. They were never more than thirty minutes in his earlier years, but twice that length later. Since his voice was comparatively weak, he adopted a conversational style, eschewing rhetorical flourishes and flights of imagination, preferring to construct a clear, logical argument. He was at his best when demonstrating the relevance of the gospel to everyday life. During his last years, his preaching declined in quality and lost its early intensity. But even that did not diminish his popularity as preacher and lecturer. The founder of the Young Men's Christian Association, Sir George Williams (1821–1905), was a member of the church, and Binney was in regular demand as a lecturer in meetings of the association. His best-known lecture was *Is it Possible to Make the Best of both Worlds?* (1853). It sold 31,000 copies in its first year and by 1856 was in its tenth edition. He pioneered the introduction of more formal liturgical elements into dissenting worship. He had bewailed the low standard of congregational singing in his introduction to the *Weigh House Tune Book* (1843) and one of his best sermons was *The Service of Song in the House of the Lord* (1848). He promoted the interest in liturgy by editing the American C. W. Baird's *Chapter on Liturgies* (1856) and adding an appendix, 'Are dissenters to have a liturgy?' With these convictions he introduced at his church anthem singing, the chanting of psalms, public confession, and responsive prayers. But surprisingly he consistently opposed the introduction of an organ in his church. Among the numerous hymns that he composed, only 'Eternal light, eternal light' is still in use.

Binney was not a learned theologian and objected to the use of technical theological jargon. He rejected the idea that Christ's death was the price paid for human sin as well as the concept of a substitutionary atonement. In fact, his thinking exemplifies the gradual disintegration of the traditional Calvinism of Congregationalists. Yet he was described by his contemporaries as an evangelical and was one of the trustees of the *Evangelical Magazine*. He was not a political activist. Although he had strong private political convictions, he stood apart from the various campaigns that characterized dissenting activities in the Victorian era. Apart from the Congregational Union, the one organization that had his enthusiastic support was the Colonial Missionary Society, which was brought into being on 13 May 1836, and of which he was the main founder. This was inspired by the fact that many of the young men in his church were emigrating to Australia.

Binney was twice married. His first wife was Isabella Barbara Nixon, who died in 1843. They had four sons who emigrated to Australia and died there. His second wife was Elizabeth Piper, the daughter of Thomas Piper, one of his deacons. She survived him.

In November 1855 Thomas Toke Lynch (1818–1871) published *Hymns for Heart and Voice: the Rivulet*. James Grant (1802–1879), the editor of the *Morning Advertiser*, attacked it as a volume containing 'not one particle of vital religion or evangelical piety' (Jones, 250). A furious controversy erupted which all but destroyed the Congregational Union. Binney was appalled and sought to restore peace by suggesting that the union should cease to transact public business and confine itself to spiritual and devotional fellowship. The controversy brought about an attack of the debility that occasionally affected him, and he visited Australia to seek better health. Again he was engaged in controversy when the bishop of Adelaide wrote to him to explain why he could not accede to the request of many prominent Australians, including the governor, to allow him to preach from Anglican pulpits. He also visited Tasmania and addressed its Congregational Union on 'The church of the future'.

In his latter years, Binney's health deteriorated. In 1865 he was assisted in the ministry by Llewelyn David Bevan (1842–1918) of New College, London, and in June 1869 he resigned. In the following December he was presented with a cheque for £1333 as a token of appreciation for his services. He continued to preach until 1873 and lectured on homiletics at New College. By the end of 1873 he was suffering acutely from ill health. He died at his home, Doric Lodge, in Upper Clapton, on Tuesday 24 February 1874. His funeral was attended by a huge crowd. The service was held at Stamford Hill Congregational Church and the interment was on 2 March at Abney Park.

Of Binney's eighty-two publications, most were individual sermons and lectures, of which the most significant have been mentioned. Binney was a towering figure in his time and was considered one of the leading representatives of nonconformity, as his honorary doctorates from Aberdeen in 1852 and an American university in 1861 testify, but he can hardly be considered a typical one.

R. TUDUR JONES

Sources *The Times* (25 Feb 1874), 6 • J. Stoughton, ed., *A memorial of the late Rev. Thomas Binney, LL.D* (1874) • H. Allon, ed., *Sermons preached in the King's Weigh House Chapel, London, 1829–69* (1869) • E. P. Hood, *Thomas Binney: his mind life and opinions* (1874) • E. Kaye, *The history of King's Weigh House Church* (1968) • B. Dickey, 'Marginalising evangelicals: Thomas Binney in South Australia, 1858–1859', *Journal of the United Reformed Church History Society*, 4 (1987–92), 540–65 • G. Walker, *Our sons far away: a century of colonial missions* (1936) • A. Peel, *These hundred years: a history of the Congregational Union of England and Wales, 1831–1931* (1931) • A. Peel, *The Congregational two hundred, 1530–1948* (1948), 154–5 • 'Thomas Binney', *Evangelical Magazine and Missionary Chronicle*, [4th ser.], 6/[1] (1874), 187–92 • *Baptist Magazine*, 66 (1874), 162–5 • M. D. Johnson, *The dissolution of dissent, 1850–1918* (1987) • IGI • parish registers and church books, Northumbd RO • R. Tudur Jones, *Congregationalism in England, 1662–1962* (1962) • R. W. Dale, *History of English congregationalism*, ed. A. W. W. Dale (1907) • correspondence and papers, DWL, Binney MSS • *CGPLA Eng. & Wales* (1874) • *The Times* (25 Feb 1874) • C. Binfield, *George Williams and the YMCA: a study in Victorian social attitudes* (1973), 24–34

Archives DWL, corresp. and MSS | BL, corresp. with W. Hone, Add. MS 40120

Likenesses W. Holl, stipple, pubd 1830 (after J. R. Wildman), NPG • C. Baugniet, lithograph, pubd 1846, BM, NPG • L. Dickenson, oils, 1870, Congregational Centre, Castle Gate, Nottingham • J. Cochran, stipple and line engraving (after W. Gush), NPG • F. Croll, line engraving, BM, NPG • London Stereoscopic Co., photograph, NPG [*see illus.*] • M. D. [G. Montbard], watercolour drawing, NPG; repro. in *VF* (1872) • oils, DWL; later version, oils, Memorial Hall Trust, London • photographs, NPG

Wealth at death £2000: probate, 2 April 1874, *CGPLA Eng. & Wales*

Binnie, Sir Alexander Richardson (1839–1917), civil engineer, was born at 77 Ladbroke Grove, London on 26 March 1839, the eldest son of Alexander Binnie, a Bond Street wholesale clothier, and his wife, Hannah, daughter of Isaac Carr of Johnby, Cumberland. He was educated privately and articled in 1858 to Terence Woulfe Flanagan, after whose death in 1860 he transferred his pupillage to John Frederic Bateman (later La Trobe Bateman).

From 1862 to 1866 Binnie worked on railway construction in mid-Wales. He married in 1865 Mary (*d.* 1901), daughter of Dr William Eames, a physician, of Londonderry. They had two sons and three daughters. In 1867, after examination, he was appointed an executive engineer in the public works department of India. He was stationed at Nagpur in Central Provinces where in 1873 he constructed the waterworks and supply from Ambajiri, 4 miles away. Binnie and Major Lucey Smith discovered coal at Warora (Chanda district); this led to the construction of the Wardha–Warora branch of the Great Indian Peninsula Railway and the opening up of the coalfield (worked from 1871 to 1906), for which Binnie received a commendation from the government of India. He returned from India for reasons of health in 1873. Subsequent to his return he was influential, through approaches to the secretary of state for India, the marquess of Hartington, and the prime minister, for improvements in the terms of service for the public works department. As a mark of appreciation the PWD engineers presented him with a portrait of himself in 1886.

In 1875 Binnie was appointed waterworks engineer to the city of Bradford, a post of great responsibility following the catastrophic failure of Sheffield's Dale Dyke Dam in 1864. His first concern was to safeguard the security of existing reservoir dams at Stubden, Leeshaw, and Leeming reservoirs by the provision of adequate spillways and for the design and construction of reservoirs at Barden and Thornton Moor. He prepared the scheme for water supply from the Nidd valley which was undertaken under his successor. Binnie understood the fundamental need for reliable hydrological data on which to base the design of reservoirs, leading to a significant publication 'On mean or average rainfall and the fluctuation to which it is subject' (*Proceedings of the Institution of Civil Engineers*, 109, 1891–2, 3–92).

In 1890 Binnie was appointed chief engineer to the London county council. He was responsible for the construction of the Blackwall road tunnel beneath the Thames in consultation with Sir Benjamin Baker and James Greathead (1889–97) and for the construction of the Greenwich foot tunnel (1899–1902) and the Barking road bridge over the River Lea. In 1891, with Baker, he prepared a report to the London county council on the reconstruction and extension of the main drainage of London and started upon the treatment works at Barking and Crossness which it recommended. He also designed the works for Highgate Archway, for widening the Strand, and for the construction of the Aldwych and Kingsway, connecting the Strand to Holborn. Binnie was appointed knight bachelor in 1897. At that time he was working towards the acquisition by the London county council of the private water companies supplying the capital, with a plan for augmenting supplies from the River Wye in Wales. A royal commission, however, recommended the setting up of the separate Metropolitan Water Board. Binnie resigned from the county council in 1901 and on the last day of the year set up his own consultancy at 9 Great George Street, Westminster. He was in partnership with his son William James Eames *Binnie (who had been working with him since 1902) from 1904, and for a short time from 1903 his other son, A. T. Binnie, also assisted him; he left the firm to study medicine.

Binnie acted as principal engineering adviser to the Metropolitan Water Board during arbitration relating to the purchase of the water companies in 1903–4. In 1906 he reported to the government of Ireland on the Bann and Lough Neagh drainage scheme. From 1905 to 1907 he served as chairman of the vice-regal commission on the arterial drainage of Ireland. He visited Malta in 1909 to report on water supply. In 1909, on the death of George Frederick Deacon, the practices of Binnie and Deacon were combined as Sir Alexander Binnie, Son, and Deacon. In 1910–11, Binnie reported on the water supply and drainage for St Petersburg and in 1913 on the water supply for Ottawa. He was concerned with many other water and, later, water-power, schemes throughout the world. He published *Rainfall, Reservoirs, and Water Supply* in 1913, based on a series of lectures commissioned by the Chadwick trustees.

Binnie was admitted as an associate of the Institution of Civil Engineers in 1865 and as a member in 1878. He was elected president in 1905. An arterial aneurysm a few years before his death necessitated the amputation of one leg. From 1892 he again lived at 77 Ladbroke Grove, London, but he died at Beer, Devon, on 18 May 1917 while on holiday. He was buried at Brookwood cemetery, near London.   E. I. CARLYLE, *rev.* ALAN MUIR WOOD

Sources *The Engineer* (25 May 1917), 470 · *PICE*, 203 (1916–17), 413–15 · priv. coll., family archives · *The Times* (19 May 1917) · private information (2004)
Archives priv. coll., family papers
Likenesses F. Holl, oils, 1886, priv. coll. · G. Reid, oils, 1906, Binnie Black and Veatch (?)
Wealth at death £10,335 2s. 6d.: probate, 27 June 1917, CGPLA Eng. & Wales

Binnie, Geoffrey Morse (1908–1989), civil engineer, was born in Kensington on 13 November 1908, the youngest of three brothers. His mother was Ethel Morse (1871–1947). His father, William James Eames *Binnie (1867–1949), and grandfather, Sir Alexander Richardson *Binnie, were both distinguished engineers who together, in 1902, founded

the firm of consulting engineers which evolved into Binnie & Partners. He was educated at Charterhouse and read for the mechanical sciences tripos at Trinity Hall, Cambridge. Binnie then served as pupil to a distinguished Swiss engineer, H. E. Gruner, working on hydro-electric projects, and in the testing laboratory of R. Haefeli, attending selected lectures at the Eidgenossische Technische Hochschule, Zürich.

Binnie joined the family firm in 1932, working for four years on the Gorge Dam (Jubilee Dam) project for water supply in Hong Kong. He was taken into partnership on 1 January 1939. On the outbreak of war that year he volunteered for the Royal Engineers, seeing service in Abyssinia, Iran, and Iraq. At the end of the war in 1945 he returned to his firm which, after reduction to a small core, returned to the undertaking of major projects. The two principal projects associated with Binnie are Dokan Dam in Iraq and Mangla Dam in Pakistan. With the concrete arch design of the Dokan Dam, which was begun in 1948, Binnie introduced a technology unfamiliar to Britain and stimulated numerical methods of analysis not previously applied to such a structure. When Binnie was commissioned in 1957 to direct the planning, design, and construction of the Mangla Dam, this was the largest single project undertaken by a consulting engineer. Despite several serious problems the dam was completed in 1967, a year ahead of schedule.

Binnie retired in 1972 but continued to work as a consultant until 1981. He was a vice-president of the Institution of Civil Engineers in 1970–72 (his father and grandfather had been president in 1938 and 1905 respectively), and was elected a fellow of the Royal Society in 1975 and a founder fellow of the Fellowship of Engineering in 1976.

Binnie suffered partial deafness from birth, a disability which intensified with age. He recalled with gratitude those who, particularly in his early years, helped him to surmount this handicap. He was married first in 1932 to Yanina Parycko, a refugee from Poland, who travelled widely with Binnie and contributed to his outstanding concern for the welfare of staff and their families on major projects in remote areas. She died following a long illness in 1964, leaving a son and a daughter. During retirement, Binnie developed an interest in the history of dams, encouraged by his second wife, Elspeth Maud Cicely Thompson (d. 1987), a historian whom he married in 1964. He is remembered as a sociable, considerate, thoughtful man who never lost his sense of fun. He lived at St Michael's Lodge, Benenden, Kent, and died after a heart attack at Benenden, on 5 April 1989.

ALAN MUIR WOOD

Sources A. M. Wood, *Memoirs FRS*, 36 (1990), 45–57 · private information (2004)
Archives Inst. CE
Likenesses portrait, Binnie and Partners
Wealth at death £597,954: probate, 15 June 1989, CGPLA Eng. & Wales

Binnie, William James Eames (1867–1949), civil engineer, was born at Londonderry on 10 October 1867, the eldest son of Alexander Richardson *Binnie (1839–1917) and his wife, Mary Eames (d. 1901). He was educated at Bradford grammar school, Rugby School (in his own words 'a worse school for a boy who ultimately hoped to follow in his father's footsteps as a civil engineer could hardly have been chosen'), and Trinity College, Cambridge (1885-8), where he was awarded a degree in the natural sciences tripos. He then spent a year at Karlsruhe, studying chemistry in preference to civil engineering.

Binnie was articled to his father, then waterworks engineer at Bradford, with periods working with S. Pearson & Son (1892), first on the Lancashire, Derby, and East Coast Railway, then as assistant engineer on the headworks of the Elan valley water scheme for Birmingham. In 1896 he joined Sir Benjamin Baker to work on the section of the Central London Railway between Shepherd's Bush and Marble Arch as designer and subsequently resident engineer. He also worked on the Khedival graving Dock, Alexandria, from 1900 to 1902 as resident engineer. Binnie married in 1900 Ethel (1871-1947), eleventh child of Joseph Ramey Morse of Lound Hall, Suffolk. They had three sons, including Geoffrey Morse *Binnie, who followed his father in profession and in the same practice.

In September 1902 Binnie joined his father in private practice (from 1904 as partner, as senior partner from 1917), undertaking work predominantly concerning water supply and, later, hydroelectric generation, including projects for Birkenhead, Taf Fechan Water Board, Belfast, Durham County Water Board, Oxford, Kano (Nigeria), Singapore, and Rangoon. The firm was known as Sir Alexander Binnie & Son, becoming Sir Alexander Binnie, Son, and Deacon in 1909 on the death of George Deacon. From 1934 the partnership became Binnie, Deacon, and Gourley. Binnie was one of the promoting engineers for the Lochaber Water Power Bill of 1921 (with C. S. Meik) and for the Grampian Water Power Bill (with W. T. Halcrow) in 1929. He was a member of the Ouse drainage commission (1925), and engineering adviser to the Doncaster area drainage commission (1926). He also served as technical adviser to the British representative on the Central Rhine commission (1922) and as one of the three commissioners for heightening the Aswan Dam (1928) and for the development of hydro-power from the Nile (1937).

Binnie was elected president of the Institution of Sanitary Engineers in 1917 and of the Institution of Water Engineers in 1921. He followed in his father's footsteps by being admitted as associate member of the Institution of Civil Engineers in 1892, member in 1900, and elected as president in 1938. He was a recognized authority on flooding and water conservation. His publications included 'Reservoir storage in relation to stream flow' with Herbert Lapworth (Proceedings of the Institution of Water Engineers 1913) and 'Floods, with special reference to waste-weir capacity' (Institution of Civil Engineers' Conference Report, pt 1, 1928, 148-52). He was chairman of the Institution of Civil Engineers' committee on floods which issued a much respected interim report on floods in relation to reservoir practice in 1933. He was chairman of the British committee of the international committee on large dams from 1933 to 1946. His most notable project was the Gorge Dam in Hong Kong ('The Gorge Dam', with H. J. F. Gourley, Journal of the Institution of Civil Engineers, 11, 1938-9, 179-206).

Binnie became an honorary member of the American Society of Civil Engineers and of the New England Waterworks Association. He was made a chevalier of the French Légion d'honneur in 1948, yet received no public recognition in Britain. He travelled extensively. While he was returning from Hong Kong in June 1940, Italy declared war and France capitulated: his French airliner deposited him at Algiers whence he reached Gibraltar by signing on as pantryman to assist the Chinese cook of a small collier whose Turkish crew had mutinied. He completed the journey safely.

While Binnie gained much advantage from having a distinguished civil engineer as his father, he displayed his personal merit and innovative thinking from an early age. At the 1890 Leeds meeting of the British Association, for example, he described experiments in measuring the size and frequency of drops of water as part of a project for making his own electric self-recording rain-gauge (Royal Meteorological Society Quarterly Journal, 18, 1892, 6-11). He was a prudent innovator, tempering enthusiasm with experience, eminent but modest. Binnie retired to Appletree Cottage, Church End Lane, Tilehurst, near Reading, where he died on 4 October 1949.

CECIL CARR, rev. ALAN MUIR WOOD

Sources The Engineer (14 Oct 1949), 437 · Journal of the Institution of Civil Engineers, 33 (1949-50), 153-4 · The Times (5 Oct 1949) · priv. coll., family archives · private information (1959) · N. Douglas, Looking back (1933) · CGPLA Eng. & Wales (1950)
Archives priv. coll.
Likenesses J. St H. Lander, oils, 1939, Inst. CE
Wealth at death £30,539 9s. 8d.: probate, 20 Feb 1950, CGPLA Eng. & Wales

Binning. For this title name see Hamilton, Charles, Lord Binning (1697-1732).

Binning, Hugh (1627-1653), philosopher and Church of Scotland minister, was born at Dalvenan, Ayrshire, the son of John Binning, the proprietor of Dalvenan, and Margaret M'Kell, daughter of Matthew M'Kell (or M'Kail), the parish clergyman of Bothwell, Lanarkshire. Margaret M'Kell's brother Hugh M'Kail, a minister in Edinburgh, was the uncle of Hugh M'Kail, a presbyterian minister, who was imprisoned, tortured, and finally hanged at Edinburgh on 22 December 1666 for his participation in the Pentland rising. Binning's father had inherited the considerable landed estate of Dalvenan and Hugh was given a liberal education. At thirteen he entered the University of Glasgow, to study philosophy. His professors there (who included James Dalrymple, later Viscount Stair) were quickly impressed by Binning's extensive knowledge and philosophical acumen and he took his degree of MA 'with much applause' on 27 July 1646 (Works, ed. Leishman, 2nd edn, xxxvi). He then began to study divinity, 'with a view to serve God in the holy ministry' (Howie, 202). However, when James Dalrymple subsequently resigned his post as regent at Glasgow, Binning was strongly encouraged by the Glasgow presbytery to apply for the chair. As was customary at the time, all the members of the universities in the kingdom who had 'a mind to the profession of philosophy' were invited to 'sist' themselves before the senatus to 'compete for the preferment' (ibid.). Binning and two other candidates were selected for 'trials', in the light of which the college masters favoured Binning. However, the university principal, Dr John Strang, preferred one of the other candidates—'a citizen's son' of competent learning and a person of 'more years' than Binning (ibid., 203). But when a member of faculty suggested an extempore public debate between the two candidates—'upon any subject [the masters] should be pleased to prescribe'—Binning's opponent immediately withdrew, he and his supporters being unwilling to face 'such an able antagonist' (ibid.). Thus, in November 1646, aged only eighteen, Binning was elected regent in philosophy at the University of Glasgow.

Despite his having very little time for preparation, Binning's lectures were by all accounts extremely well received. Famously, he is described as being among the first to try to rescue philosophy in Scotland from the 'barbarous terms and unintelligible jargon of the schoolmen' (Howie, 203). As a preacher he followed Luther's maxim 'they are the best preachers to the people, who teach them in a plain, familiar and perfectly simple way' (*Works*, ed. Leishman, 2nd edn, xxx). Moreover, Binning's justification for his pedagogy was not merely pragmatic: 'Ye should remember that the Lord speaks in our terms, and, like nurses with their children, uses our own dialect' (*Works*, ed. Leishman, 3rd edn, 74).

For Binning, philosophy was the servant of theology. Hence it is reasonable to anticipate a parallel pedagogy at work in his philosophical teaching. This places Binning at the forefront of a distinctive tradition at Glasgow subsequently extended in the teaching of Francis Hutcheson and culminating in Adam Smith's lectures on rhetoric and *belles-lettres*. He held his post with increasing influence for about three years. At the same time he continued to pursue his theological studies, and having obtained a licence as a minister he received a call to the parish of Govan near Glasgow on 25 October 1649. On 8 January following he was ordained at Govan; he resigned his professorship the following year. In 1650 he married Mary or Maria Simpson (*d.* 1694) (sometimes erroneously given as Barbara), daughter of the Revd James Simpson, the parish minister of Airth in Stirlingshire (who has been wrongly described as an Irish minister). They had one son. Binning continued his philosophical and theological studies, but also devoted himself to his sermons and pastoral duties, with considerable success. As a preacher he regularly attracted vast crowds. When (in 1651) the church found itself split into resolutioners (who supported the king) and protesters (who opposed him), Binning sided with the latter. He then wrote and published his *Treatise on Christian Love*—a moving and compelling plea to Christians to overcome their differences and unite in the love of God and fellowship with one another. The *Treatise* was highly regarded by his contemporaries and continues to be so. Binning is said to have played a prominent part in the open debate before Cromwell at Glasgow in April 1651 between the independents and presbyterians. His intellect, eloquence, and extensive knowledge of theology made him a formidable opponent in debate. A contemporary, James Durham, professor of divinity at Glasgow, famously observed 'that there was no speaking after Mr Binning' (Howie, 206). On this occasion his success in debate is said to have so embarrassed Cromwell's party of independents that Cromwell himself asked the name 'of that learned and bold young man', and when told it was Binning, Cromwell replied, 'He hath bound well indeed, but' (putting his hand on his sword) 'this will loose all again' (ibid., 205).

That a debate before Cromwell took place at Glasgow is certain, but the precise nature of that debate cannot be conclusively established. While there is no record of the specific content of Binning's arguments on this occasion, his stance on matters political and theological was invariably pacifying and conciliatory. Indeed the use of theological and philosophical arguments to transcend the disputes and divisions of his time is definitive of Binning's work and is well exemplified both in the *Treatise* and the later *Heart-Humiliation*. Despite being plagued by ill health throughout his short life he was a prolific author. In addition to the texts cited above he composed several other works, including collections of lectures, sermons, and essays on the theological controversies definitive of his time. His writing is informed by his knowledge of philosophy and theology but also shows a genuine concern to communicate effectively with a non-academic audience. Though none of his works were published in his lifetime the majority were published posthumously. His *Collected Works* exists in three editions in English and his writings were also translated into Dutch by James Coleman—a minister at Sluys in Flanders—and subsequently published at Amsterdam in at least four editions.

Binning died of consumption at Govan in September 1653 and was buried in his churchyard there. His son, John, inherited the estate of Dalvenan on his grandfather's death. His part in the insurrection at Bothwell Bridge in 1679 resulted in the forfeiture of the estate and, ultimately, insolvency. In 1690 parliament rescinded forfeitures and fines for the period 1665–88, but Dalvenan was not restored to John Binning. In 1704, having obtained a patent, John Binning successfully applied to the general assembly of the Church of Scotland for approval of a single-volume edition of his father's writings.

PAUL TOMASSI

Sources DNB · *The works of the Rev Hugh Binning*, ed. M. Leishman, 3rd edn (1851) · *The works of the Rev Hugh Binning*, ed. M. Leishman and E. J. Alexander (1842) [incl. preface and 'Life' by the ed.] · *The works of the pious, reverend and learn'd Mr Hugh Binning* (1735) [incl. Patrick Gillespie's 'Note to the reader' in its orig. form] · *The works of the Rev Hugh Binning with a life of the author*, ed. J. Cochrane, 3 vols. (1839–40) · J. Howie, *The Scots worthies*, ed. W. McGavin, [new edn] (1846) · T. F. Torrance, *Scottish theology: from John Knox to John McLeod Campbell* (1996)

Binning [Benyng], **William of** (*d.* in or after **1258**), abbot of Coupar Angus, was prior of Newbattle Abbey when elected abbot of Coupar Angus on 29 November 1243. His name probably originated from the barony of Binning in the parish of Uphill, Linlithgowshire. A witness to one royal and one private charter, he resigned office in the chapter house of Melrose Abbey on 29 September 1258. His claim to significance is that Alexander Myln, in his sixteenth-century lives of the bishops of Dunkeld, attributed to Binning, when he was prior, the writing of a life of John the Scot (d. 1203), bishop of Dunkeld and claimant to St Andrews. This life has not survived.

A. A. M. DUNCAN

Sources D. E. Easson, ed., *Charters of the abbey of Coupar-Angus*, 2, Scottish History Society, 3rd ser., 41 (1947), 269 · A. Myln, *Vitae Dunkeldensis ecclesiae episcoporum*, ed. T. Thomson, Bannatyne Club, 1 (1823), 8 · A. O. Anderson and M. O. Anderson, eds., *The chronicle of Melrose* (1936), 91, 116

Binns family (*per. c.*1810–1897), drapers, originated with **George Binns** (1781–1836), born at Crawshawbooth, Lancashire, on 8 March 1781, the fourth son of David Binns, a clogger, and his wife, Ann Robinson. The Binns family were Quakers who had extensive links with other Quaker families throughout the north of England. David and Ann, along with their eldest children, began a drapery and later grocery shop in which George learned his craft. The family soon entered the expanding cotton trade, putting out work to local hand-loom weavers and selling finished calicoes in Manchester. After George's marriage on 30 January 1807 to Margaret, the daughter of Joshua and Rachel Watson of Staindrop, co. Durham, he began to look for an opening near by. In 1811 he purchased the woollen drapery and linen shop of Thomas Ellerbury at 176 High Street, Bishopwearmouth, a part of Sunderland, co. Durham, which employed a journeyman and three apprentices. His nephew David Binns, the son of his elder brother Richard, came as apprentice in 1814 and was quickly entrusted with buying for the shop in the Manchester market and travelling around the local mining villages to sell goods. David left in 1822 to manage another drapery business for his uncle at Staindrop and was replaced by George's eldest son, Henry Binns [*see below*]. In addition to Henry, there were seven other children, including George Binns (1815–1847), a prominent Wearside Chartist. The whole family were radicals and maintained close associations with local Quaker families such as the Grimshaws, the Richardsons, and the Robsons. The elder George Binns died in Sunderland on 19 February 1836, and the shop was left to Henry.

Henry Binns (1810–1880), born in Sunderland on 19 June 1810, was a deeply committed Quaker and an active member of the British and Foreign Anti-Slavery Society, and he advertised his refusal to sell 'any goods manufactured from cotton not warranted to be free labour grown', giving his customers the opportunity to strike an 'effectual blow to the traffic so opposed to the services of religion and humanity' (advertisement, Binns MSS). Nevertheless, the business prospered and moved to larger premises on the other side of Bishopwearmouth's high street in 1844. Binns's opposition to slavery was a reflection not just of his religious principles but also of his political

views, which embraced further constitutional reform and the repeal of the corn laws. Through Quaker circles in Newcastle upon Tyne he knew John Bright before the Anti-Corn Law Association was founded in 1839, and he and his brother George were involved in the growing protest movement, helping to form the Durham branch of the National Charter Association in 1838. George and James Taylor, his partner in a local bookshop, were the most active, printing tracts, handbills, and posters and speaking throughout the north-east. Both were arrested in 1839 along with other Chartist leaders, but they continued their activities until their trial in summer 1840. George Binns was imprisoned for six months, and Henry himself was briefly detained with Bright but was not put on trial. After his release George was elected to the executive of the National Charter Association in June 1841, coming fifth in the poll.

George Binns's health had suffered during his time in prison and he left Sunderland for Port Nelson, New Zealand, in August 1842; he died there of tuberculosis on 5 April 1847. His obituary in the *Northern Star* on 5 February 1848 described him as 'a handsome, high spirited talented true-hearted man—every inch a democrat'. Henry Binns was involved in Bright's attempt to stand against Lord Dungannon for the Durham parliamentary seat in March 1843, his bid to be nominated for the Sunderland seat, and his eventual election for Durham in July. Unlike some Quakers, Binns did not break with Bright over his opposition to the Anti-Slavery Society's call for tariffs on goods produced by slave labour.

Henry Binns married Elizabeth Bowron, probably in 1836. They had ten children, the eldest of whom, Sir Henry *Binns (1837–1899), emigrated to Natal in 1858. Elizabeth died in childbirth in 1855 and Henry retired in 1865 to Croydon, Surrey, where the following year he married Emma Andrews, the widow of John Grimshaw. She died in 1868; Henry died at his home, 62 Lansdowne Road, Croydon, on 17 January 1880.

The shop was left to Henry's second son, **Joseph John Binns** (1839–1922), born in High Street, Bishopwearmouth, on 14 October 1839, who married, probably in 1874, Rosa Robinson of Nottingham. The growing prosperity of the north-east allowed him to expand the business, and in 1878 he achieved a turnover of £17,500 and a profit of £3500. In October 1884 the shop moved to larger premises nearer the centre of Sunderland, and it became a proper department store with three floors. In 1897 the business was floated as a limited liability company, whereupon effective control passed out of the family, though Joseph Binns remained as chairman until his death. He died at his home, Bainbridge Holme, Sunderland, on 21 March 1922; he was survived by his wife.

MICHAEL S. MOSS

Sources M. Moss and A. Turton, *A legend of retailing: House of Fraser* (1989) · Binns papers, U. Glas., Archives and Business Records Centre, House of Fraser archives · J. Epstein and D. Thompson, eds., *The Chartist experience: studies in working-class radicalism and culture, 1830–60* (1982) · J. West, *A history of the Chartist movement* (1920) · R. G. Gammage, *History of the Chartist movement, 1837–1854*, new edn (1894); repr. with introduction by J. Saville (1969) · *Northern Star* (5

Feb 1848) [G. Binns, jun.] · d. cert. [H. Binns, sen.] · d. cert. [J. J. Binns] · *CGPLA Eng. & Wales* (1922) [Joseph John Binns]
Archives U. Glas., Archives and Business Records Centre, House of Fraser archives, Binns MSS
Wealth at death under £4000—Henry Binns: probate, 8 March 1880, *CGPLA Eng. & Wales* · £45,083 11*s*. 1*d*.—Joseph Binns: probate, 21 July 1922, *CGPLA Eng. & Wales*

Binns, George (1781–1836). *See under* Binns family (*per. c.*1810–1897).

Binns, Henry (1810–1880). *See under* Binns family (*per. c.*1810–1897).

Binns, Sir Henry (1837–1899), politician in Natal, son of Henry *Binns (1810–1880) [*see under* Binns family] of Sunderland and Croydon, and Elizabeth Bowron (*d*. 1855), was born at Sunderland, co. Durham, on 27 June 1837, and educated at Ackworth and York. In 1858 Binns emigrated, arriving on 14 September in Natal, in its early days as a separate colony. He took up agriculture, and bought a property called Umhlanga (turned into a sugar estate in 1860) at Riet River, near Phoenix, Victoria county. In 1861 he married his cousin Clara, daughter of John Acutt of Riverton; they had one son. Subsequently Binns, a relative, Robert Acutt, and a friend amalgamated their estates. In 1868 Binns floated the Umhlanga Valley Sugar Estate Company in England and became its general manager; he retired in 1892.

Binns entered public life in 1879, selected by Sir Garnet (later Viscount) Wolseley as a nominee member of the legislative council under the crown colony system. After the first elections, in 1883, he represented Victoria county until his death. In 1888 he was a delegate from Natal to the conference at Bloemfontein on a South African customs union. The inaugural union was only partial and Natal did not join. In 1890 Binns was a delegate for the extension of the Natal Government Railway to Harrismith in the Orange Free State. In December 1893 he was sent to India to negotiate Indian labour for the sugar estates, and the return of previously indentured labourers to India.

Originally opposed to self-government for Natal, by 1893 Binns supported Sir John Robinson's policy introducing the reform; but he declined to join the first ministry under the new constitution, and so became a sort of leader of the opposition, whose duty it was, as far as possible, to support the ministry. In 1897, after the retirement of Sir John Robinson and Henry Escombe, Binns was appointed prime minister. On 5 October 1897 he became colonial secretary and minister of agriculture, but soon resigned the latter portfolio. He resolved the discontent of the Natal civil service and concluded an extradition treaty with the South African Republic. He marked the queen's jubilee by offering a monthly supply of coal from Natal for the use of the British navy. His first session of parliament began on 24 November 1897 and dealt mainly with the incorporation of Zululand and then with Binns's particular interest—the entrance of Natal into the South African customs union, on which a conference was held in May 1898 at Cape Town. Binns was the chief delegate from Natal, a convention was settled and in compliance, on 20

May, he introduced a resolution in favour of the union into the Natal parliament. The policy was bitterly opposed, but Binns carried the enabling bill, read a third time on 30 June, through the assembly. However, his health failed on 6 July and he was unable to enter the house for the remainder of the session. He went to the Berea, returning to Pietermaritzburg in December 1898. In January 1899 he attended the postal conference at Cape Town and on 11 May was present at the opening of the Natal parliament, but he soon became ill again, and died at Pietermaritzburg on 6 June 1899. His body lay in state at the vestibule of the house of assembly and was buried on 7 June at the military cemetery, Pietermaritzburg. He was survived by his wife.

Binns's political life was marked by his courage and persistence. He was a pungent and succinct speaker, a good critic of finance, and a sound businessman, and was instrumental in developing the sugar industry in Natal; he was also a director of the Natal Bank and of the Durban Telephone and Tramways companies. He was made KCMG in 1898.   C. A. HARRIS, *rev.* LYNN MILNE

Sources *Times of Natal* (6 June 1899) · *Natal Mercury* (7 June 1899) · *African Review* (10 June 1899) · A. F. Hattersley, 'Binns, Sir Henry', *DSAB* · Binns papers, U. Glas., Archives and Business Records Centre, House of Fraser archives
Likenesses bust, provincial council building, Pietermaritzburg, Natal · photograph, repro. in *Natal Witness* (24 June 1963)

Binns, John (1772–1860), radical and journalist, was born in Dublin on 22 December 1772, the second son of John Binns (*d*. 1774), a well-to-do ironmonger active in local politics, and Mary Pemberton. In 1774 his father was lost at sea returning from a trip to England. John was educated at a common school and then at a classical academy, but when he was about ten he and his elder brother, Benjamin, left the house of their mother's second husband, George McEntegart, in Drogheda and walked to Dublin, where they were taken in by their grandfather. In 1786 John was apprenticed to a soap-boiler.

In April 1794 the Binns brothers moved to London. For a while they lived off funds from their father's estate, then Benjamin set up in business as a plumber with John as his assistant. John made the acquaintance of Francis Place, and towards the end of 1794 he joined the *London Corresponding Society (LCS). He rapidly became an influential member of the society, chairing the general committee, and on 26 October 1795 he chaired the open-air public meeting held at Copenhagen House to protest against the two new 'treason and sedition bills'. His radical activities led to involvement in debating clubs and, probably some time in 1796, he entered into a partnership with two notable radical speakers, John Gale Jones and William Wright, to manage debating rooms of their own in the Strand. Early in 1796, in an attempt to revitalize the radical movement, the LCS resolved to send delegates into the provinces to encourage similar, but struggling, societies. Binns travelled to Portsmouth to assist the local radicals, but was recalled to London when the LCS heard of a plot to press him into the navy. Shortly afterwards, in company with Gale Jones, he journeyed to Birmingham.

Here, while addressing separate meetings, both men were arrested and charged with uttering seditious words. Released on bail, it was over a year before they were brought to trial. Gale Jones was found guilty at the Warwick spring assize in 1797, but never sentenced; Binns was acquitted at the following summer assize.

In the period between his arrest and trial Binns returned briefly to Dublin. Back in London, following his acquittal, both he and his brother became involved in the shadowy organization of United Englishmen or United Britons, which linked extremist English radicals and Irish revolutionaries. Binns's own *Recollections* is rather coy about these links and the intentions of the radicals, but information surviving in government papers, while fragmentary, suggests that John and his brother were much more deeply implicated in conspiracy and the attempts of the United Irishmen to enlist French military assistance than his own account implies. The Binns brothers were closely involved with both Arthur O'Connor, editor of *The Press*, the semi-official paper of the United Irishmen, and Father James Coigley, a Catholic priest who acted as an emissary from the United Irishmen to both France and the United Englishmen. Early in 1798 John travelled to Kent seeking to arrange passage to France for O'Connor and Coigley. On 28 February he was arrested in Margate, together with O'Connor, Coigley, and their two servants. Charged with high treason, the five were imprisoned in the Tower of London before being tried at the assizes held in Maidstone in May. Leading members of the parliamentary opposition testified on O'Connor's behalf and the government was reluctant to reveal the origins of its secret information on the United Irishmen. As a result all were acquitted, except Coigley, who had been arrested with incriminating correspondence in his pocket, and who was executed on 7 June. Although acquitted, Binns decided to lie low for a while with friends in Derbyshire and Nottinghamshire; during this period he used his mother's maiden name of Pemberton. Towards the end of 1798 he returned to London and went to work in a blacksmith's shop at St Pancras. When the government launched another attack on the popular radicals in March 1799, Binns was arrested under the suspension of the Habeas Corpus Act. From May 1799 until February 1801 he was incarcerated, without charge, in Gloucester gaol.

In the summer of 1801 Binns left England for the United States, never to return. He settled initially in Northumberland, Pennsylvania, where he began a new career as a political journalist, first with the *Northumberland Gazette* and then with his own successful newspaper, the *Republican Argus*. He opened a large printing house and book shop, and in 1806 he married another British emigrant, Mary Ann Bagster (*c.*1783–1852?). The marriage ceremony was conducted by Joseph Priestley, who was also resident in Northumberland. Early in 1807 Binns moved to Philadelphia, where he established another successful newspaper, the *Democratic Press*, on which he continued to work until 1829. He became an alderman of Philadelphia in 1822, and, in spite of a decline in his fortunes and the popularity of his paper, he continued to hold this position

until 1844. He published his *Recollections of the life of John Binns: twenty-nine years in Europe and fifty-three in the United States* in Philadelphia in 1854. He died there, in relative obscurity, on 16 June 1860. CLIVE EMSLEY

Sources J. Binns, *Recollections of the life of John Binns* (1854) · M. Thale, ed., *Selections from the papers of the London Corresponding Society, 1792–1799* (1983) · M. Elliott, *Partners in revolution: the United Irishmen and France* (1982) · A. Goodwin, *The friends of liberty: the English democratic movement in the age of the French Revolution* (1979) · R. Wells, *Insurrection: the British experience, 1795–1803* (1983) · *State trials* · M. Durey, *Transatlantic radicals and the early American republic* (1997)
Archives PRO, H.O. 42.42 · PRO, T.S.11.959.3505
Likenesses M. Haughton, stipple, pubd 1797 (after M. Haughton), NPG

Binns, Joseph John (1839–1922). *See under* Binns family (*per. c.*1810–1897).

Binstead, Arthur Morris [*nicknamed* Pitcher] (1861–1914), journalist and author, was born on 6 January 1861 at 106 Great Titchfield Street, Marylebone, London, the son of Arthur William Binstead, manager of the Continental Gallery in Bond Street, and his wife, Mary Ann Morriss. Educated at various private schools in London, but primarily at Dr Templeman's school in Mount Street, Grosvenor Square, Binstead's first job was in a counting-house, which he left to join Joe Capp, a 'rough diamond' who ran a sporting press agency. During his time there he was introduced to the seamier side of racing, as he mixed with bookies' runners, tipsters, and 'the boys' who made their living from fleecing those innocents foolish enough to cross their path.

In 1884 Binstead joined the *Pink 'Un* (the *Sporting Times*), whose eccentric staff included the Dwarf of Blood (Colonel Newnham-Davis), the Stalled Ox (Jimmy Davis), and the irrepressible Shifter (Willie Goldberg). The *Pink 'Un* was famous for its uninhibited comment on racehorse owners, welshing bookmakers, theatrical productions, and any other topic of the moment. Binstead, whose nickname Pitcher came from his skill at 'pitching the tale', made his mark by drawing on a wider field. Accounts of fights in the Pelican Club or the measures taken by his *Pink 'Un* colleagues to evade bailiffs were interspersed with the adventures of costermongers in the East End.

A tall, well-built man with a grave and courteous manner, Binstead had the gift of making friends at every level of society and took a pride in drawing his stories from life. The characters on the disreputable fringes of racing furnished him with inexhaustible material. His readers learned how to enter a racecourse without paying and the need for caution in casual acquaintanceships made in West End bars. The anecdotes of his barber in Covent Garden (Funny Fred) appeared regularly in the *Pink 'Un*, as did the experiences of Captain Flash, the leader of a racegang. The word 'prison' in one of Binstead's articles nearly led to an action for slander by the gallant captain, but this was settled out of court with damages of two whiskies, a ham sandwich, a cigar, and 5*s*. in cash. And the slanderer would have kept his 5*s*. had he won the toss!

Binstead married Laura (*b.* 1864/5), daughter of Henry

Hirschfield, at the Central United Synagogue in Great Portland Street, London, on 22 December 1886; they had a daughter, Dora, and a son. Binstead wrote for the *Pink 'Un* for some twenty-eight years and it became understood that he would succeed the proprietor, John Corlett, when the latter retired. He never forgave Corlett for selling the paper to West de Wend Fenton in 1912 and left immediately with several others to start a rival paper, *Town Topics*.

Binstead's two books of reminiscences, *A Pink 'Un and a Pelican* (1898; written with Ernest Wells) and *Pitcher in Paradise* (1903), were admired by such stylists as E. V. Lucas and P. G. Wodehouse and remain among the best and most amusing records of bohemian London at the end of the nineteenth century. He died of Bright's disease and bronchitis at his home, 291b Camden Road, Holloway, London, on 13 November 1914 and was cremated at Golders Green crematorium. His wife survived him.

N. T. P. MURPHY

Sources A. M. Binstead, *Pitcher in paradise* (1903) · A. M. Binstead and E. Wells, *A Pink 'Un and a Pelican* (1898) · G. Deghy, *Paradise in the Strand* (1958) · J. B. Booth, *Old Pink 'Un days* (1924) · J. B. Booth, *Sporting times* (1938) · J. B. Booth, *Master and men: Pink 'Un yesterdays* (1927) · private information (2004) · b. cert. · m. cert. · d. cert. · *WWW* · *The Post Office London directory* (1900); (1907–14)
Likenesses Bassano, photograph, repro. in Booth, *Old Pink 'Un days*
Wealth at death £336 3s. 10d.: probate, 9 Dec 1914, *CGPLA Eng. & Wales*

Binyon, Basil (1885–1977), electrical engineer, was born on 23 April 1885, at 5 Henley Road, Ipswich, Suffolk, the third of four children of Brightwen Binyon (1852–1905) and his wife, Rachel Mary (1853–1949), daughter of William Cudworth and his wife, Mary. His father, an architect and an accomplished painter in watercolours, had a number of important commissions, including the design of Ipswich corn exchange, Aldermaston Manor, and Sunderland town hall. Basil's childhood was spent between Ipswich and Yorkshire where he had a number of relatives. After education at Leighton Park School, Reading, from *c*.1898 to 1903, he went up to Trinity College, Cambridge, where he read natural sciences and obtained a good degree.

For his practical training Binyon went to the Cambridge Scientific Instrument Company where he was introduced to commercial engineering manufacture. In 1909 he worked with Marconi on the first transatlantic Morse code radio transmissions from Poldhu, Cornwall, to Newfoundland. He continued to work with Marconi until the First World War, when he joined the Royal Naval Air Service, then in its infancy. Working with Royal Flying Corps personnel at Cranwell, in Lincolnshire, he produced some of the first airborne radio equipment for Morse telegraphy. Later the equipment was improved to make radio telephony possible between aircraft in flight and a ground station. Binyon's work was recognized with his appointment as OBE. He married, on 20 September 1913, Gladys Elise Rosa (1885–1960), daughter of John Howard Keep. They had three children, Roger Basil, who was killed in the Arnhem landing in 1944, Margaret Howard, and Hugh Douglas, who both survived them.

Binyon used his wartime experience to set up the Radio

Communication Co. Ltd which developed into a worldwide long wave communications network in the 1920s and early 1930s. The company produced equipment and operators for many merchant and naval ships of the period. He also founded a company to make domestic radio sets and components under the trade mark Polar and his interest in this field led to his appointment in 1922 as one of the directors of the original British Broadcasting Company, the remaining directors under Lord Gainforth's chairmanship being representatives of other firms manufacturing home radio receivers. Binyon played his part in establishing the technical standards which, developed over the years, established the BBC's high reputation.

Binyon's strong position in the radio field led to his being appointed chairman of the Institution of Electrical Engineers' wireless section for 1925–6. His chairman's address, presented to the institution in November 1925, was a comprehensive review of marine wireless equipment at the time. Towards the end of the 1920s a rationalization took place in the commercial radio industry, one of the results of which was that Binyon's Radio Communication Company merged with Marconi to form a strong international marine radio communication organization which supplied equipment and personnel to the merchant navies of several countries. Initially Binyon thought that this merger would mark the end of his association with the company he had built up, but he was invited to join the Marconi board and until 1935 he contributed actively to its work. In 1936 he accepted an invitation to become a director of the Buenos Aires Water Company, which position he held until 1938. This involved regular trips to supervise the company's operations on site.

During the Second World War Binyon had a distinguished career with the Royal Observer Corps, for which he devised ingenious predictors based upon alarm clock mechanisms. These played an important part in the air defences of London in 1940–41 before radar was widely available. The south-eastern sector of the Royal Observer Corps, of which Binyon was commandant, was in the front line of these defences.

Throughout his adult life Binyon had a great interest in making things, and had a well-equipped workshop with a lathe in the basement of his house. There he made a number of ingenious devices for time-lapse photography which he used to produce accelerated motion cine films of clouds and of flowers opening, which were a novelty at the time. After the war he built working model steam locomotives with which he entertained his grandchildren and many others. His first wife died in 1960, and on 28 April 1962 Binyon married Violet Mary (1900–1989), daughter of John Walter Hibbert.

In retirement he divided his time between his large house, Hawthornedene in Hayes, Kent, and his seaside home at Thatchways, West Wittering, Sussex, where he regularly played host to large parties of family and friends who enjoyed sea bathing and sailing at the nearby Itchenor sailing club. After his second marriage he moved from Hayes to 14 The Glen, Farnborough Park, Kent. Throughout his life Binyon was keen on winter sports and served a term as president of the Ski Club of Great Britain. Binyon died on 4 April 1977 at Farnborough Hospital, Kent, of heart failure. He was buried at Hayes parish church.

G. B. R. FEILDEN

Sources *WWW, 1971–80* · B. Binyon, chairman's address to wireless section, 4 Nov 1925, Inst. EE · *Important Personalities* (1926), 51 · *Institution of Electrical Engineers News* (June 1977) · private information (2004) · personal knowledge (2004) · b. cert. · m. certs. · d. cert.

Archives Inst. EE

Likenesses Lafayette Ltd, photograph, c.1925 · Elliott & Fry, photograph, repro. in *Important Personalities*

Wealth at death £8883: probate, 4 July 1977, *CGPLA Eng. & Wales*

Binyon, Edward (1828–1876), landscape painter, was born in Manchester. He painted in oils and watercolours and exhibited nine paintings, mainly of Capri and Naples, at the Royal Academy between 1857 and 1876, including *The Arch of Titus* (exh. 1859), *Coral Boat at Dawn, Bay of Naples* (exh. 1875), and *Hidden Fires: Vesuvius from Capodimonte* (exh. 1876). He also exhibited at the Society of British Artists and the Dudley Gallery in London. His *The Bay of Mentone* was frequently reproduced. Binyon died on 18 July 1876 at via Piazza 5, Capri, where he had lived for many years. He was survived by his wife, Mary.

R. E. GRAVES, *rev.* ANNE PIMLOTT BAKER

Sources J. Johnson, ed., *Works exhibited at the Royal Society of British Artists, 1824–1893, and the New English Art Club, 1888–1917*, 2 vols. (1975) · Graves, *RA exhibitors* · Boase, *Mod. Eng. biog.* · *CGPLA Eng. & Wales* (1877)

Wealth at death under £600: administration, 1 June 1877, *CGPLA Eng. & Wales*

Binyon, (Robert) Laurence (1869–1943), poet and art historian, was born on 10 August 1869 at 1 High Street, Lancaster, the second of the nine children of Frederick Binyon (1838–1900), vicar of Burton in Lonsdale, Yorkshire, and his wife, Mary (1839–1919), daughter of Robert Benson Dockray (1811–1871), resident engineer of the London and Birmingham Railway and designer of the Camden Town Roundhouse, London, and his wife, Mary (1816–1883). Both his father's and his mother's families were of Quaker ancestry. Binyon won a scholarship to St Paul's School, London, in 1881 and later to Trinity College, Oxford, where he took a first in classical moderations in 1890 and a second in *literae humaniores* in 1892. A published poet at sixteen, he won the Newdigate prize for poetry with *Persephone* in 1890 and the same year published *Primavera: Poems by Four Authors* with his cousin Stephen Phillips, Manmohan Ghose, and Arthur Cripps.

In September 1893 Binyon joined the staff of the British Museum, where he would spend his entire career. He began in the department of printed books, but in April 1895 transferred to his first choice, the department of prints and drawings, then under the keepership of Sidney Colvin. A keen artist as well as poet at school, during the 1890s he studied wood-engraving with William Strang and produced woodcuts for several of his own books. His first book of art history was *Dutch Etchers of the Seventeenth Century* (1895), but it was in the field of British art that he first established his scholarly reputation with his four-volume catalogue of the museum's British drawings

(Robert) Laurence Binyon (1869–1943), by William Strang, 1898

(1898–1907). His writings on the British watercolourists, from *John Crome and John Sell Cotman* (1897) to *English Watercolours* (1933), and on William Blake helped lay the foundation for their modern critical reputations. As art critic of the *Saturday Review* (1906–11) he championed the work of young British artists such as Augustus John. At about this time he was also part of a circle of intellectuals and artists, including Charles Ricketts, Lucien Pissarro, and Edmund Dulac, who regularly met at the Wiener Café in New Oxford Street.

In the mid-1890s Binyon had become interested in Asian art. With Colvin's support he built up the museum's collections of Chinese, Japanese, and later Indian art. His exhibitions, lectures, essays, and pioneering books such as *Painting in the Far East* (1908; rev. edns, 1913, 1923, 1934) and *The Flight of the Dragon* (1911) helped make Asian art accessible to a wider audience, influenced young writers and artists, and earned him an international reputation in this emerging field. He made an important contribution to East–West understanding through his insistence that the philosophies which lay behind Asian art had much to teach the twentieth-century West. Promoted to assistant keeper in August 1909, he instigated the establishment of the semi-autonomous sub-department of oriental prints and drawings in 1913 and became its first head, with Arthur Waley as his assistant.

Binyon's first love and ambition remained, however, poetry. In the decade following *Lyric Poems* (1894) he wrote prolifically, most notably the impressionist urban poems in his two *London Visions* books (1896, 1899). With his friends W. B. Yeats and Thomas Sturge Moore he worked towards the revival of poetic drama on the London stage and had some success with his verse-drama *Attila*, produced by Oscar Asche in 1909 with costumes by Charles Ricketts and music by Sir Charles Stanford. Binyon's long, grave face, captured in Edmund Dulac's splendid 1912 caricature in the style of the Japanese artist Sharaku, belied a warmth, generosity, and quiet humour which endeared him to a wide circle of friends. The American poet Ezra Pound met him in 1909 and found him 'one of the best loved men in London', with 'a sort of pervading slow charm in him & in his work' (Qian, 182).

On 12 April 1904 Binyon married Cicely Margaret Pryor Powell (1876–1962), daughter of Henry Pryor Powell, merchant, and in December they had twin daughters, Helen and Margaret. When their third daughter, Nicolete, was born in 1911, they moved from 8 Tite Street, Chelsea, to 118 Belgrave Road, Pimlico, where they lived until moving into a house within the British Museum in 1919. In the early years the family struggled financially, obliging Binyon to take on more reviewing and other work which taxed his health and kept him from devoting his full energies to his creative work, but the marriage was a profoundly happy one, which he celebrated in numerous love poems throughout his life. They were a talented family. Cicely Binyon wrote children's history books, edited anthologies, and made translations, while Helen Binyon (1904–1979) became an engraver, Margaret a writer of children's books illustrated by Helen, and Nicolete Binyon (1911–1997) [see Gray, Nicolete] a distinguished calligrapher and art scholar.

On 21 September 1914, less than seven weeks into the First World War, *The Times* carried what would become Binyon's most famous poem, the remarkably prescient elegy 'For the Fallen'. As the casualty lists grew, the poem became the focal expression of national grief, both alone and in Sir Edward Elgar's choral work *The Spirit of England* (1916–17). Its central quatrain was carved on cenotaphs and tombstones worldwide and is still recited at annual Remembrance day commemorations:

> They shall grow not old, as we that are left grow old:
> Age shall not weary them, nor the years condemn.
> At the going down of the sun and in the morning
> We will remember them.

Over age for active service, Binyon worked as an orderly in a military hospital in France for periods in 1915 and 1916, the subject of his finest war poem, 'Fetching the Wounded'. In 1917 he was dispatched by the Red Cross to report on work being done by British volunteers for the French wounded, refugees, and other victims of the war, published as *For Dauntless France* (1918).

During the 1920s Binyon wrote prolifically. *The Secret* (1920) was followed by the long visionary odes *The Sirens* (1924–5) and *The Idols* (1928), expressions of a spirituality founded on personal mystical experience rather than religious dogma. The high point in his career as a dramatist came in 1923 when his verse-tragedy *Arthur* was staged at the Old Vic, in London, for which Elgar wrote the music

and conducted the orchestra on the first night. Later plays included *Boadicea* (1927) and *The Young King* (1934). His writings on art ranged from *Japanese Colour Prints* (1923), written in collaboration with J. J. O'Brien Sexton, to *The Followers of William Blake* (1925). He also turned his attention to Persian art with books such as *The Poems of Nizami* (1928) and helped organize the landmark International Exhibition of Persian Art in London in 1931.

Since the 1890s Binyon had longed to travel to Asia but, after several attempts to organize an official British Museum mission were thwarted by the war and lack of funds, it was not until 1929 that he made his only trip to the Far East at the invitation of a group of Japanese admirers. Although he also took the chance to travel in China, Korea, Indo-China, and Ceylon, his main destination was Japan, where he mounted an exhibition of British watercolours and gave a lecture series at Tokyo Imperial University, published as *Landscape in English Art and Poetry* (1930). He later explored aspects of his Asian experience in two of his finest poems, 'Koya san' and 'Angkor'.

By the time his two-volume *Collected Poems* appeared in late 1931, Binyon was an elder statesman in the world of letters, prominent on the prize-awarding committee of the Royal Society of Literature and, with his friend John Masefield, a leading proponent in the revival of verse-speaking. He continued to extend his range with books such as *Akbar* (1932), a biography of the Mughal emperor. In July 1932 he became keeper of the department of prints and drawings at the British Museum, and was appointed to the Order of the Companions of Honour. He retired in September 1933, having, in Harold Laski's words, served the museum for forty years 'in a spirit worthy of its own life' as 'one of the great temples of the human spirit' (Laski, 8). In the same year he was awarded the honorary degree of DLitt at Oxford University and became an honorary fellow of Trinity College. Having lectured in the United States in 1912, 1914, and 1926, he spent the 1933–4 academic year at Harvard University as Charles Eliot Norton professor of poetry, where his lectures on *The Spirit of Man in Asian Art* (1935) eloquently summed up his life's work on Asian art.

Binyon returned to England in June 1934 and he and his wife settled in a farmhouse in Streatley on the Berkshire downs. He continued to lecture and help organize exhibitions such as the International Exhibition of Chinese Art at the Royal Academy in London in 1935–6, and to travel, including a term as Byron professor of English literature in war-threatened Athens in early 1940. During this last decade, however, he was at last able to devote himself to poetry. The result was the finest poetry of his life, greater perhaps than that of any of his generation except Yeats, published in *The North Star and other Poems* (1941) and posthumously in *The Burning of the Leaves* (1944) and the unfinished *The Madness of Merlin* (1947). He also completed a *terza rima* translation of Dante's *Divina commedia* (*Inferno*, 1933; *Purgatorio*, 1938; *Paradiso*, 1943) which was admired by Pound, T. S. Eliot, and other younger poets.

On 10 March 1943, days after making final revisions to the *Paradiso* proofs and in the middle of writing the lyric 'Winter Sunrise', Laurence Binyon died of bronchopneumonia at Dunedin Nursing Home, Bath Road, Reading, and was buried on 13 March in the churchyard of St Mary's, Aldworth, Berkshire. He was survived by his wife. Among many other tributes, Cyril Connolly mourned the passing of 'a wise, poor, happy and incorruptible lover of truth and beauty', a man who knew 'how to be both warm and detached, in fact, a sage' (Connolly, 201).

JOHN HATCHER

Sources J. Hatcher, *Laurence Binyon: poet, scholar of East and West* (1995) · D. Steel, 'Introduction', *Laurence Binyon and Lancaster: an exhibition held at Lancaster Museum 28th April–26th May 1979* (1979), 3–19 · Z. Qian, *Orientalism and modernism* (1995) · H. Laski, 'Scholarpoet', *Daily Herald* (11 Sept 1933), 8 · C. Connolly, 'A London diary', *New Statesman and Nation* (27 March 1943), 201 · N. Gray, 'Friends of my father, Laurence Binyon', *Private Library*, 3rd ser., 8 (1985), 79–91 · private information (2004) · b. cert. · m. cert. · d. cert.
Archives BL · Hunt. L. | BL, corresp. with Sir Sydney Cockerell, Add. MS 52705 · BL, corresp. with League of Dramatists, Add. MS 63360 · BL, corresp. with Macmillans, Add. MS 54998 · BL, letters to Sir Michael Sadler, Add. MS 49997 · BL, letters to Charles Ricketts, Add. MSS 58090–58091 [1903–1917] · BL OIOC, letters to William Rothenstein, MS Eur. B 213 · Bodl. Oxf., letters to the *Atlantic Monthly* · Bodl. Oxf., corresp. with Robert Bridges · Bodl. Oxf., letters to H. A. L. Fisher · Bodl. Oxf., corresp. with Gilbert Murray · Bodl. Oxf., corresp. with Sir Aurel Stein · Harvard U., letters to William Rothenstein · Harvard University, near Florence, Center for Italian Renaissance Studies, letters to Bernard Berenson · LUL, letters to T. Sturge Moore and family · NRA, priv. coll., letters to Sir Edward Elgar · Royal Society of Literature, London, letters to the Royal Society of Literature · U. Birm., letters to Oliver Lodge · U. Glas., letters to D. S. MacColl · U. Leeds, letters to Charles Wilson · U. Leeds, Brotherton L., letters to Edmund Gosse · U. Reading, letters to Charles Elkin Matthews · U. Texas, letters to John Masefield, Grant Richards, Richard Church, Edmund Gosse, Charles Elkin Mathews, Harley Granville-Barker, Lillah McCarthy, Edmund Blunden, and others · Worcester College, Oxford, letters to C. H. O. Daniel
Likenesses W. Rothenstein, lithograph, 1898, BM, NPG · W. Strang, two etchings, 1898–1918, BM, NPG [*see illus.*] · W. Strang, pencil drawing, 1901, BM, NPG · E. Dulac, watercolour, 1912 · H. Murchison, photograph, *c*.1913, NPG · W. Rothenstein, pencil drawing, 1916, Man. City Gall. · F. Dodd, charcoal drawing, 1920, Athenaeum Club, London · E. Kapp, charcoal or wash drawing, 1921, Barber Institute of Fine Arts, Birmingham · H. Coster, photographs, *c*.1934, NPG · G. C. Beresford, photograph, before 1938, NPG · B. Thomas, caricature, BM; repro. in *Punch* (14 Nov 1923), 464
Wealth at death £6148 7s. 8d.: probate, 6 July 1943, CGPLA Eng. & Wales

Bion, Wilfred Ruprecht (1897–1979), psychoanalyst, was born on 8 September 1897 at Mathura, Uttar Pradesh, India, the elder son (there was one daughter) of Frederick Fleetwood Bion (1870?–1949), civil engineer, and Rhoda Salter Kemp (1869?–1939). Bion spent his first eight years in India, described vividly in his autobiography, *The Long Weekend* (1982), in which he recaptured both the vividness of India and some of his early psychological difficulties: his fear of his father's anger, his deeply felt hatred of both parents, the dreams in which 'Arf Arfer' (his father) made a terrifying appearance. These were compounded when,

aged eight, he returned with his mother and sister to England for schooling at Bishop's Stortford College, a nonconformist public school, which he attended from 1905 to 1915. The period between the ages of eight and twelve he looked back on as appalling, subject to cataclysmic storms of confusion and religious guilt; only sex, 'wiggling' (Bion, *Long Weekend*), redeemed him. From the age of twelve he spent holidays with the families of schoolfriends, where he found hospitable warmth, and began to appreciate the good qualities of school, its intellectual and emotional liveliness. Bion's youth was overshadowed by the First World War. He was of the generation who felt doomed, and who did not expect to survive military service, which he scarcely did, being one of the few survivors of the tank regiment at the battle of Cambrai. Bion's DSO celebrated his bravery in saving the crew of his disabled tank. He was also a chevalier of the Légion d'honneur and was mentioned in dispatches. In his *War Memoirs* (1997) Bion recounts his prolonged, dangerous experiences over two years in the front line. His distinguished military career held him in good stead in military psychiatry during the Second World War.

In 1919 Bion entered Queen's College, Oxford, to read modern history, graduating in 1921. The philosophical bent which marked his future writings was stimulated by his tutor, H. J. Paton, a Kantian moral philosopher. A good athlete, Bion was a rugby blue and a swimming half-blue. After graduating Bion returned to Bishop's Stortford College, where he taught history and French and stimulated enthusiasm for both rugby and swimming. His interest in psychoanalysis already aroused, he studied medicine at University College Hospital, London, in 1924, graduating MRCS LRCP in 1930, and was awarded the gold medal for clinical surgery. Bion worked for the great neurosurgeon and psychologist Wilfred Trotter, who was brother-in-law to Ernest Jones, the leading British psychoanalyst.

From 1933 until 1948 Bion worked at the Tavistock Clinic where, in 1936, the writer Samuel Beckett was his patient. Bion did not train as a psychoanalyst until after the Second World War, though he had personal psychotherapy in the 1930s with J. Hadfield and one year of psychoanalysis with his future mentor and colleague, John Rickman, with whom he later had a productive working collaboration at Northfield Military Hospital. In 1939 Bion joined the Royal Army Medical Corps and was one of the psychiatrists appointed to a senior position by J. R. Rees, director of the pre-war Tavistock Clinic. He held the rank of major. His brief appointment to the training wing at Northfield Military Hospital led to a significant publication with Rickman on what was later known as the 'first Northfield experiment'. Bion introduced the leaderless group method of officer selection which significantly improved both the quality and the quantity of officers for the greatly enlarged post-Dunkirk British army. This period of his life was darkened by the death in childbirth, in 1945, of his beautiful actress wife Elizabeth (Betty) McKittrick Jardine (*b.* 1904), daughter of William James Jardine, cotton manufacturer, whom he had married on 17 April 1940. Their daughter, Parthenope (*d.* 1998), became a psychoanalyst. On his return to the Tavistock Clinic, Bion was appointed chairman of the medical committee. Accorded great respect and authority by his colleagues, he was responsible for the radical reshaping of the clinic, which had followed an eclectic approach, to one strictly psychoanalytic.

Bion had developed a theory of unconscious group processes as a result of his wartime experiences. He observed that individuals in a group unconsciously disown parts of their mentalities and contribute to a group mentality, then behaving as if in the grip of powerful unconscious forces. These he named as the basic assumptions of dependence, fight–flight, and pairing. These forces interfere with the work mentality of the group unless and until they have been made conscious. Bion's basic assumptions theory was adopted by his colleagues at the Tavistock Clinic and the Tavistock Institute of Human Relations, which was formed for psychological work in industry and organizations. Bion himself soon ceased to work with groups and for the rest of his professional life concerned himself with psychoanalytic training and the treatment of severely disturbed persons, schizoid, borderline, and psychotic. His experiences formed the basis of many influential papers and books in which he developed original ideas on the birth of the capacity for thought in earliest infancy and how this is lost in the psychoses. His insight into psychotic states of confusion, persecution, and appalling guilt arose from his recall of his own disturbed childhood where he was himself close to madness. His *Experiences in Groups and other Papers* was published in 1968.

Bion's analysis with Melanie Klein was a powerful influence on his personality and mind but he went on to develop his original ideas about thinking and its disturbances. Bion's concept of 'containment' advanced Klein's concept of projective identification (that an infant attempts to rid itself of unacceptable and unbearable parts of the self by projection into the outer world) into an interpersonal process. When the infant's unbearable experience is understood as communication and appropriately responded to by the mother, then the infant can regain the disowned part, now made bearable, transformed through the interpersonal relation. His work had great influence on psychoanalytic studies of schizophrenia. Though his writing style is often condensed, combining psychoanalytical thought and philosophical argument, which can make for difficult reading, his legacy, as in *Cogitations* (1994), is a considerable addition to the study of mental processes of infancy and in severe mental illness.

Bion was director of the clinic of the British Psychoanalytical Society in 1955–62, and its president in 1962–5. In 1968 he left Britain to live for eleven years in Los Angeles, which he left to return to England in his dying year. His period in North America allowed him the freedom of thought and action which he would not have had staying in London. His ideas were also influential in Latin America through his visits there. He considered that in London he would have either become a mystic in conflict with the establishment or 'loaded with honours and sunk without trace'.

Bion was a large bulky man, round faced, red cheeked; his voice was deep and his manner shy. An encounter with him was a memorable experience; he possessed an original mind and focused his concerns and attention on deep and difficult psychic issues. His spontaneous humour was reserved for his family and can be seen in his letters to them published in his autobiography. He began a happy second marriage on 9 June 1951 to Francesca (Patricia Ivy) McCallum (*b*. 1922), a widow, daughter of Archibald John Purnell, schoolmaster. She was a researcher at the Tavistock Clinic, and together they had two further children, Julian (*b*. 1952) and Nicola (*b*. 1955).

Bion died in the John Radcliffe Hospital, Oxford, of myeloid leukaemia on 8 November 1979 and was cremated in Oxford on 12 November. His ashes were buried two days later at Happisburgh church, Norfolk, a county which he loved and in which he spent many holidays. He was survived by his second wife.   MALCOLM PINES

Sources W. R. Bion, *The long weekend: part of a life* (1982) · W. R. Bion, *All my sins remembered: another part of a life* (1985) · J. Symington and N. Symington, *The clinical thinking of Wilfred Bion* (1966) · m. certs. · d. cert. · W. R. Bion, *War memoirs, 1917–19*, ed. F. Bion (1997) · private information (2004)
Wealth at death £44,275: probate, 27 Feb 1980, *CGPLA Eng. & Wales*

Biondi, Sir Giovanni Francesco (1572–1644), diplomat and romance writer, was born at Lesina (now Hvar), Croatia. His family, whose surname was Biundović until the 1600s, was noble but of modest means. Giovanni took a law degree at Padua and, after a period in Venice, departed for Paris as secretary to the Venetian ambassador, Pietro Piruli. Here (in 1606–8) he adhered to the reformed doctrines and assembled a good number of protestant books, which the Italian historian Paolo Sarpi (with whom Biondi shared significant acquaintances such as Giacomo Castelvetro and Isaac Casaubon) was later to consult. Biondi returned to Venice and got in touch with Sir Henry Wotton, then ambassador to the Republic. Through Wotton, Biondi managed to be invited to England in 1609, where he illustrated to James I his plan 'to introduce Religion into Italy' (*CSP dom.*, *1629–31*, 347; Benzoni, 22). Biondi was then sent back with money to purchase and spread 'heretic' publications. His ties with England, however, were deepening: Biondi corresponded with Robert Cecil, earl of Salisbury (1609–12), and when he was sent by the Venetians on a mission to the Dauphiné and Provence in 1610 he dispatched relations to England.

Biondi went to Savoy with Wotton in March 1612, but when Prince Henry's death 'ended all hope of a Savoyan match' the Dalmatian found himself back in London without a precise occupation (cf. PRO, SP 99/10/239). Biondi had been corresponding with Dudley Carleton, ambassador in Venice after Wotton, since September 1611, and in 1613 Carleton convinced Biondi to remain in England. Wotton provided employment, taking Biondi to The Hague in 1614 and later recommending him to Sir Ralph Winwood. Probably through the latter's influence (cf. *CSP Venice*, *1615–17*,

380) Biondi was appointed the king's representative at the general Calvinist assembly at Grenoble in 1615, where he worked to secure the Huguenots to the side of the prince of Condé. From about this date, Biondi seems to have been a double agent: before leaving London he had shown all 'his instructions in the original' to the Venetian ambassador Antonio Foscarini (*CSP Venice, 1613–15*, 542). As late as 1633 he was described by Vincenzo Gussoni, then ambassador of the Republic, as 'an individual who continues in the confidential relations at this Court which he has always had with all my predecessors' (*CSP Venice, 1632–6*, 148; also *CSP Venice, 1615–17*, 359–60).

Whatever his ties with the Venetians, Biondi (a lifelong member of the Venetian Accademia degli Incogniti) received an English pension of 400 crowns a year from 1615, and was an envoy to northern Italy, where James hoped to create an anti-Spanish league. Being sent again to Piedmont in December 1616, he later became the duke of Savoy's sole agent in England (1617–20). Commenting on his situation, Biondi declared that he was serving 'two Masters, against the Gospel's precepts' (Benzoni, 27), although no particular recognition ever came from Savoy (as none came from Venice). He was, however, knighted by James I in 1622 and made a gentleman of the privy chamber shortly after. About 1622 he married Mary Mayerne, sister of Sir Theodore, the king's physician.

In 1624 Biondi published the first of his baroque novels, *L'Eromena*, to be followed by two others, *La Donzella Desterrada* (1627; the preface mentions an unsuccessful attempt to translate Sir Philip Sidney's *Arcadia*) and *Il Coralbo* (1632). These books, which inaugurated a new phase of chivalric romance, were translated into English (1632, 1635, and 1655), French, and German. In 1626 Biondi obtained a lifelong yearly concession of £200 for himself and his wife. In 1628 he was granted exemption from all taxation. His situation in the 1630s, however, does not appear flourishing, his pension not being paid regularly. To Charles I he dedicated his historical compilation on the War of the Roses, *L'istoria delle guerre civili d'Inghilterra* (3 vols., 1637–44), which was almost immediately translated into English by Henry Cary, earl of Monmouth (1641–4). In 1640 Biondi left England for Aubonne, near Lausanne, Switzerland, where he died in 1644 and was buried in the local church. CARLO M. BAJETTA

Sources PRO, SP 85/3/141, 99/6/73, 99/7/366, 92/1/221, 92/1/223; 78/64/63 · PRO, SP 99/8/112, 124, 149, 153, 165, 169, 175, 221, 223, 247; SP 99/10/12; SP 99/11/16; SP 99/12/12, 100; SP 99/15/152, 99/17/70 · *CSP Venice, 1613–17*; *1632–6* · *CSP dom., 1611–38* · G. Benzoni, 'Giovanni Francesco Biondi: un avventuroso dalmata del '600', *Archivio Veneto*, 5th ser., 80 (1967), 19–37 · D. Savoia, 'Sir Giovanni Francesco Biondi and the court of James I', *Cultural exchange between European nations during the Renaissance*, ed. G. Sorelius and M. Srigley (1994), 153–9 · A. M. Ghisalberti and others, eds., *Dizionario biografico degli Italiani*, 56 vols. (Rome, 1960–) · *DNB* · D. Savoia, 'Sir Giovanni Francesco Biondi: an Italian historian of the War of the Roses', *Journal of Anglo-Italian Studies*, 1 (1991), 51–3 · *STC, 1475–1640*

Archives PRO

Likenesses Harding, pen and ink wash, NPG · engraving, repro. in *Le glorie de gli incogniti, o vero, Gli huomini illustri dell'accademia de' signori di Venetia* (1647), facing p. 241

Birch, Charles Bell (1832–1893), sculptor, was born in Brixton, Surrey, on 28 September 1832, the son of the author Jonathan *Birch (1783–1847) and his wife, Esther, *née* Brooke. At the age of twelve he became a pupil at the School of Design at Somerset House, London, where he remained for two years before accompanying his father to Berlin, where he studied at the Kurfürstliche Akademie der Künste and as an apprentice in the studios of the renowned German sculptors Ludwig Wilhelm Wichmann and Christian Daniel Rauch. While in Germany he produced his first important work: a bust of the then English ambassador, the eleventh earl of Westmorland, which was executed in marble for Friedrich Wilhelm IV, the king of Prussia.

On his return to Britain in 1852, Birch entered the Royal Academy Schools, where he gained two medals. In 1859 he entered the studio of John Henry Foley, whose principal assistant he was for the next ten years; while there he modelled the Arab horse in Foley's statue of General Outram, and after Foley's death in 1874 he succeeded to his studio. Birch's German education and his sympathies in art, along with his father's friendship with the Prussian royal family, initially commended him to the notice of the English court, resulting in crown prince Friedrich Wilhelm of Prussia sitting to him for a portrait bust at Buckingham Palace shortly before his marriage to the princess royal in 1858.

Despite inspiring the admiration of the royal family, Birch's artistic progress was relatively slow until 1864, when the Art Union of London awarded him a premium of £600 for his group *A Wood Nymph*, his first really popular work, which was later exhibited in Vienna, Philadelphia, and Paris. In 1880 he acknowledged his gratitude for this premium, giving the Art Union twenty original designs illustrating Byron's poem 'Lara' which were published in 1880.

Birch was, however, an increasingly successful sculptor in his later life, receiving many civic, political, aristocratic, and imperial commissions. He was also a frequent exhibitor at the Royal Academy in Burlington House, where his realistic and vigorous military groups were much admired, particularly *The Last Call* (1879) and *Lieutenant Walter Hamilton* (1880); the latter work was sent to Dublin and its popularity led to Birch being elected an ARA in April 1880. In that year, however, he also produced the work by which he is most likely to be remembered: the unfortunate bronze griffin on the Temple Bar memorial (designed by Sir Horace Jones) at the beginning of Fleet Street, London.

Birch's portraiture was much more popular, and it included many imperial heroes; distinguished members of parliament, including Lord Beaconsfield, W. E. Gladstone, and Lord John Russell; various members of the British aristocracy; leading lights of the theatre world; and, on two occasions, Queen Victoria herself, the first statue destined for Aberdeen, the second for Udaipur in India. His work was particularly popular in Liverpool and in Sydney, Australia, where many of his statues were displayed. Alongside his successful work in marble and bronze portraiture he also worked in various other genres and with many other materials. He was commissioned to design and make a variety of silver statuettes for race cups, including an equestrian statuette of William III, ordered by the king of the Netherlands as a prize for the Orange Cup at Goodwood. Birch was also a creditable medallion portraitist, exhibited watercolours at the Royal Academy, and contributed as a draughtsman on stone and wood to the *Illustrated London News* and other Victorian periodicals. In 1858 *CVIII Bible Pictures* was published from his designs, the first of several biblical works he illustrated for the publisher Bagster. In the early 1870s he joined in the 'New Sculptural' vogue for works in terracotta and bronze.

Birch was considered by the majority of his contemporaries to possess good, if not outstanding, chiselling skills, and to be one of the most reliable portraitists of his generation, who was faithful to likeness and accurate in anatomy—the prestige of whose work contributed much to the increasing reputation of the British school. His eighty-two Royal Academy sculptures ensured that his artistic reputation survived well beyond his death (at King's College Hospital, London, on 16 October 1893), though it has diminished considerably since then.

CAMPBELL DODGSON, *rev.* JASON EDWARDS

Sources Boase, *Mod. Eng. biog.* • Graves, *RA exhibitors* • *The Times* (18 Oct 1893) • *Building News*, 65 (1893), 526 • *The Athenaeum* (21 Oct 1893), 560 • *The Athenaeum* (28 Oct 1893), 597 • *ILN* (21 Oct 1893) • *Magazine of Art*, 17 (1893–4), 80–82 • reports, Art Union of London, 1863–4 • *CGPLA Eng. & Wales* (1893)
Likenesses S. Lucas, portrait, repro. in *Magazine of Art*, 80 (1894) • R. W. Robinson, photograph, NPG; repro. in R. W. Robinson, *Members and associates of the Royal Academy of arts, 1891* (1892)
Wealth at death £591 10s.: probate, 25 Oct 1893, *CGPLA Eng. & Wales*

Birch, Eugenius (1818–1884), civil engineer, was born at Gloucester Terrace (later Pitfield Street), Shoreditch, on 20 June 1818, the son of John Birch, corn dealer, and his wife, Susanna. An elder brother, John Brannis Birch, was born in 1813. Birch showed considerable mechanical and artistic talent at an early age. Educated in Brighton, and then at Euston Square, London, he was enthralled by the works on the London–Birmingham railway. He was trained in a succession of London's engineering works—Samuel Wright, J. and G. B. Blyth, and R. A. and O. Robinson—as well as attending a mechanics' institute. In November 1835 the London and Birmingham and Great Western railways offered a prize for first-class carriage design. Although he was unsuccessful in the competition, his method of putting the wheels under the carriages was adopted by the London and Greenwich Railway. In 1837 he received a silver Isis medal from the Society of Arts for his drawing of a marine steam engine, and in 1838 the Institution of Civil Engineers' Telford medal for his drawings and description of Huddart's rope machinery. In 1839 Birch was elected a graduate of the Institution of Civil Engineers. At that time he and his brother were working for Rowland Macdonald Stephenson (1808–1895). On 10 February 1842 Birch married Margaret, daughter of Charles

Gent, of Moss Side, Manchester, a manufacturer. There were no children.

In 1843 Stephenson left for Calcutta in connection with the East India Railway which he had been promoting, and meanwhile Birch entered into partnership with his elder brother. They were engaged in various unsuccessful railway schemes in the years of the 'railway mania' including the Leek and Mansfield, Manchester and Rugby orient and Salisbury and Swindon railways. Birch designed the Kelham and Stockwith bridges in Nottinghamshire and many of the bridges on the East India Railway between Calcutta and Delhi. The Birch brothers had an office at 3 Cannon Row, Westminster, from 1841 to 1856, and at 43 Parliament Street from 1858 to 1864. From 1864, after the death of his brother, Birch occupied offices at 7 Westminster Chambers, Victoria Street, London SW1.

Birch's fame rested mainly on the fourteen seaside piers he built around the coasts of England and Wales. The longest surviving were Aberystwyth (shortened), Birnbeck (Weston-super-Mare), Blackpool's North Pier, Bournemouth, Eastbourne, Hastings, and the West Pier, Brighton. Experts consider his finest achievement to be the West Pier, with its elegant cast-iron kiosks, railings, and windscreens. Birch's piers were noteworthy for their screw-pile method of construction, which he pioneered at Margate. This method, based on Alexander Mitchell's patent, involved screwing the cast-iron columns into the sea-bed, sometimes by means of a winch mounted on a barge. Birch was also a great believer in the corrosion-resistant qualities of cast-iron columns, and this confidence was fully vindicated by time. Apart from his piers, he carried out the Devon and Somerset Railway, Exmouth docks, Ilfracombe harbour, and Eastbourne, Margate, and west Surrey waterworks.

Birch was also a talented artist. Apart from his early technical drawings, he painted over a hundred watercolours during a visit to Italy, Egypt, and Nubia in the winter of 1874–5. He died at his home, Laurieston Lodge, West End, Hampstead, on 8 January 1884.

JOHN R. LLOYD, *rev.* MIKE CHRIMES

Sources *PICE*, 78 (1883–4), 414–16 • S. Adamson, *Seaside piers* (1977) • m. cert. • d. cert.
Archives Inst. CE, communications, membership records
Wealth at death £3970 7s. 2d.: probate, 15 March 1884, *CGPLA Eng. & Wales*

Birch, Francis Lyall [Frank] (1889–1956), intelligence officer, was born on 5 December 1889 at 15 Ennismore Gardens, Knightsbridge, London, the third son of John Arden Birch, banker, and his wife, Charlotte Mary Leycester Stopford (*d.* 22 Oct 1935) (who later married the ninth Viscount Barrington, and was a philanthropist and traveller in South Africa). Frank Birch was educated at Eton College and at King's College, Cambridge, where he was an exhibitioner in modern languages in 1909 and a foundation scholar in history in 1911. He obtained a double first in the history tripos and was awarded the Winchester reading prize in 1912.

During the First World War Birch served as an able seaman in the channel, the Atlantic, and the Dardanelles until he was recruited in 1916 for Room 40, the Royal Navy's code-breaking unit, where he worked on the decrypted messages as an intelligence analyst. In 1920 he completed a massive internal history, 'A contribution to the history of German naval warfare 1914–1918', with W. E. F. Clarke, a co-worker from Room 40.

Birch was a fellow of King's College, Cambridge, from 1916 to 1934, and a history lecturer at Cambridge from 1921 to 1928, when he resigned to become a theatre producer and actor. Little is now remembered about his theatrical career, except that he excelled as the Widow Twankey in the pantomime *Aladdin*. On 10 October 1919 Birch married the Hon. Vera Benedicta Gage (*b.* 1898/9), daughter of Henry Charles, fifth Viscount Gage. There were no children.

From 1937 onwards, with a number of dons, Birch advised Alastair Denniston, the operational head of the Government Code and Cypher School (GCCS), on recruiting 'men of the professor type' (as Denniston quaintly described them) for GCCS's initial wartime establishment. The newcomers were to prove vital to GCCS's later successes against the Wehrmacht's complex Enigma cipher machine.

Birch joined GCCS at Bletchley Park in September 1939, as head of the German subsection of the naval section. Initially he had only two members of staff, since the others had been moved to the Admiralty's naval intelligence division to be a liaison unit (ID8G) with GCCS. However, GCCS had broken no Kriegsmarine codes, so there was little to liaise on. ID8G therefore started traffic analysis (studying radio networks, call signs, and so on), and attacked minor German naval codes, as did Birch's subsection. There was not room for two competing units: his flourished, while ID8G's role dwindled.

By August 1940 Birch had been worried for a long time about naval Enigma. He thought that if Hut 8, which was responsible for attacking it, systematically tried his 'cribs' (probable plain text) with GCCS's sole 'bombe' (a high-speed solving aid for Enigma) they would work. But he had not fully understood the problem, largely because of the inability of Alan Turing, then head of Hut 8, to explain himself clearly. Birch's approach would have taken years—and was beyond the capacity of a single bombe. Birch complained bitterly that Hut 8 was not getting its fair share of bombe time, and about the shortage of bombes. He became increasingly dissatisfied with Denniston, who lacked the drive to press for enough bombes. Birch's views were a major factor in Denniston's replacement by Edward Travis in February 1942. In June 1941 Birch succeeded Clarke as head of the naval section (Hut 4), which was responsible for all naval crypt analysis (except Enigma) and for translating and analysing the decrypted signals of the German, Italian, Japanese, French, and Spanish navies.

Hut 8 broke Dolphin, the principal naval Enigma cipher, from mid-1941 onwards with the aid of captured material, the need for which Birch had urged on the Admiralty. However, the Atlantic U-boats started to use a new, four-rotor Enigma machine on 1 February 1942. GCCS was blind against their cipher, Shark, for many months. Despite GCCS's strong initial objections, the United States Navy was determined to attack Shark. In September 1942 it accordingly decided to embark on a massive building programme for four-rotor bombes. This required GCCS's assistance, while GCCS badly needed help with Japanese naval codes. Birch therefore travelled to Washington, DC, with Travis to negotiate the first major wartime signals intelligence accord with the United States—the Holden agreement of October 1942. The agreement provided for 'full collaboration' between GCCS and its United States Navy counterpart, OP-20-G, on Kriegsmarine ciphers, but for GCCS to abandon Japanese naval cryptanalysis, except for a research unit.

The Holden agreement proved invaluable for both sides, but GCCS probably gained the most. OP-20-G's superb four-rotor bombes performed a vast amount of work for Hut 8 from autumn 1943 onwards, and for Hut 6 (army and air force Enigma) in 1944 and 1945. However, the agreement assigned a very minor role on Japanese naval codes to GCCS's outpost, the Far East Combined Bureau (later HMS *Anderson*), which led to a long-running dispute. *Anderson* and Admiral Sir James Somerville, the commander-in-chief of the Royal Navy's Eastern Fleet, wanted the agreement's Japanese provisions to be abrogated, which was completely unrealistic. *Anderson* also constantly bombarded Birch with demands for staff and equipment, but they could not be supplied until towards the end of the war in Europe, which had priority. Birch was a moving force behind the naval BRUSA (Britain–United States of America) agreement of January 1944, which helped to solve *Anderson*'s problems by providing for greatly improved communication links between *Anderson* and OP-20-G and its outstations.

Birch was 'a many-sided human being—a rather dull historian, an acceptable drinking companion, a mysterious private personality, a brilliant talker and a born actor' (Fitzgerald, 93). His only significant publication for public consumption was an account of the pedigree of leading racehorses (1926). Although he was not a born leader, and at times had a heavy-handed managerial style, which was an unwise approach to GCCS's free spirits, he cared deeply about his staff and was highly popular with the junior members of his section in consequence. He was appointed OBE in 1919 and CMG in 1946.

In 1945 Birch became head of the historical section of the post-war Government Communications Headquarters, as GCCS became. He wrote a hard-hitting internal 'History of naval sigint', and supervised numerous other histories of GCCS's outstanding wartime work. Birch died on 14 February 1956 at his home, 11 Montpelier Walk, Knightsbridge, London; his wife survived him.

RALPH ERSKINE

Sources *WWW*, 1951–60 · R. L. Benson, *A history of U.S. communications intelligence during World War II: policy and administration* (1997) · W. F. Clarke, 'Bletchley Park, 1941–1945', *Cryptologia*, 12/2 (1988), 90 · R. Erskine, 'The Holden agreement on naval sigint: the first BRUSA?', *Intelligence and National Security*, 14/2 (1999), 187–97 · P. Fitzgerald, *The Knox brothers* (1977) · F. H. Hinsley and others, *British intelligence in the Second World War*, 1 (1979) · D. Kahn, *Seizing* *the Enigma: the race to break the German U-boat codes, 1939–1943* (1991) • A. Dakin, 'The Z watch in Hut 4, part I', *Codebreakers: the inside story of Bletchley Park*, ed. F. H. Hinsley and A. Stripp (1993), 50–56 • *CGPLA Eng. & Wales* (1956) • Burke, *Peerage* (1939) • b. cert. • m. cert. • d. cert. • B. P. Kanner, *Women in context: two hundred years of British women autobiographers* (1997) • A. P. Mahon, 'The history of Hut Eight', PRO, HW 25/2 • 'History of I. D. 8. G.', PRO, HW 3/164 • Papers by Birch, PRO, ADM 223/479, HW 3/132

Archives BL, corresp. with Society of Authors, Add. MS 63214 | SOUND BL NSA, documentary recordings

Wealth at death £11,428 18s. 9d.: probate, 21 April 1956, *CGPLA Eng. & Wales*

Birch, George Henry (1842–1904), architect and museum curator, was born on 2 January 1842 in Canonbury, London, the fourth son of Charles Birch and his wife, Emma Eliza Cope. He was educated at Darnell's private academy in Theberton Street, Islington, and was articled in 1858 to the architect Charles Gray, before transferring to George Truefitt on Gray's retirement. He also worked as an improver in the office of Sir Matthew Digby Wyatt for two years, and then with William White and Ewan Christian.

As a practising architect Birch designed, among other works, the interior of Acton Reynald Hall, Shrewsbury; the restoration of St Mary's, Edstaston, Shropshire (1882–3); and the redecoration of St Nicholas Cole Abbey, London (1884). He was better-known, however, as an antiquarian, and was a leading authority on all matters relating to the history, both domestic and architectural, of London. In 1884 he produced his most successful work for the health exhibition held at South Kensington in that year—a scholarly and costly re-creation of the 'Old London Street', a picturesque but insanitary thoroughfare lined with medieval and Tudor buildings, the first attempt ever made to reproduce old London on such a scale.

Birch was elected an associate of the Royal Institute of British Architects in 1876; he served twice, in 1871–2 and 1872–3, as vice-president of the Architectural Association and in 1874–5 was its president. Some of his drawings collection is held in the British Architectural Library at the Royal Institute of British Architects; other items remain in a private collection. He became a fellow of the Society of Antiquaries in 1885 and honorary secretary of the London and Middlesex Archaeological Society from 1877 to 1883. For many years he also took a leading part in the affairs of the St Paul's Ecclesiological Society: many papers by him being published in the society's *Transactions*.

On 19 November 1894 Birch succeeded Wyatt Papworth as curator of Sir John Soane's Museum. As a practising architect with proven historical and archaeological interests, he was—as *The Builder* (vol. 86, 21 May 1904, 555) stated—'emphatically the right man in the right place'. Under his curatorship the museum became far more accessible to a wider range of people: he doubled the number of visitors in ten years, partly by opening on Saturday afternoons to the increasing number of rambling clubs and societies exploring historic buildings at the time. He installed electricity in 1897, although its cost was a great worry to him. Among his publications, which are chiefly on subjects relating to the topography of London, he is principally remembered for *London Churches of the XVIIth and XVIIIth Centuries* (1896), a monumental study with superb photographs by Charles Latham, reproduced in collotype.

Birch had a strong interest in architectural and topographical drawing and was a member of the drinking and sketching club known as the 'Picts' or 'Goths'; his surviving collection of drawings, in the possession of his great-niece Mrs Margaret Christie, contains a number relating to the club. Birch was popular with his friends and colleagues: he spared no pains in assisting and guiding his visitors to his museum or in making models and toy houses for children, with whom he was a great favourite. He died, unmarried, from bronchitis on 10 May 1904 at his home in Sir John Soane's Museum, two days after returning from a visit to Italy, and was buried in Islington cemetery, Finchley. A photograph of Birch is retained at the museum, a stout figure wearing a smoking cap seated in the dining-room at the Soane.

MARGARET RICHARDSON

Sources *The Builder*, 86 (1904), 528, 555 • *RIBA Journal*, 11 (1903–4), 396, 445 • *DNB* • L. W. Ridge, *AA Notes*, 18 (1904), 89 • nomination papers, RIBA BAL, A, V, 97 • trustees' minutes and curator's diaries, 1894–1904, Sir John Soane's Museum • M. Pinney, 'Picts and Goths: architectural drawings and books from the collection of George H. Birch (1842–1904)', typescript catalogue of an exhibition held at the Church Farm House Museum, Hendon, 1988 [copy in Sir John Soane's Museum] • 'Old London Street', *The Builder*, 47/1, 2 (1884), 188, 550 • *CGPLA Eng. & Wales* (1904)

Archives RIBA BAL, RIBA nomination papers • Sir John Soane's Museum, London, trustees' minutes and curator's diaries

Likenesses photograph, c.1900, Sir John Soane's Museum

Wealth at death £247 8s.: administration, 17 June 1904, *CGPLA Eng. & Wales*

Birch, James (d. 1800?), sectary and prophet, was born in Wales, but nothing more is known about his early life. As a young man he moved to London, where he worked as a watch-motion maker, living in Brewer's Yard, Golden Lane, Old Street, and later in Little Moorfields. He had converted to the Muggletonians before 1 July 1759, when his name first appears in their records; his wife is mentioned on 22 July 1759. In December 1771 he wrote a verse account of his conversion and in the same year his name appears on the subscription list of *The Saint's Triumph, and the Devil's Downfall*, written by the Norwich Muggletonian John Brown.

About 1772 Birch was responsible for a serious secession in the Muggletonian ranks. Believing that the Muggletonians had lost their sense of urgency and immediacy he sought to revive the original doctrines of John Reeve who, together with his cousin Lodowicke Muggleton, had founded the sect in 1652. To Birch the issue of 'immediate notice', which Muggleton had rejected, was fundamental, for he shared Reeve's belief that God was an interventionist who took immediate notice of human actions, and thus upheld the efficacy of prayer. In endorsing the doctrine of immediate notice Birch attracted a certain following and led a party within the sect, which had experienced previous eruptions of Reevite heresy. Only when in 1778 Birch claimed to be the new prophet of the movement after God had spoken directly to him did separation become inevitable. Birch and his 'high priest', William Matthews of Bristol, were denounced as false prophets, and their followers, the Birchites, were known as the antichurch. Ten of his own followers, led by Martha Collier, withdrew from the Birchites but, still believing in immediate notice, were rejected by the orthodox Muggletonians.

At the height of his influence Birch led a group of between fifty and sixty followers, about thirty of whom were based in London. Most of the others lived in south Wales, particularly in Pembrokeshire. Numbers dwindled in the early nineteenth century and the Birchites had practically disappeared by mid-century; two followers were still alive in 1871. The last occurrence of Birch's name in the Muggletonian archives is in 1795, but about 1800 he published 'two strange and incoherent books', *The book of cherubical reason, with its law and nature, or, Of the law and priesthood of religion* and *The Book upon the Gospel and Regeneration*, which, according to Alexander Gordon, 'read like the productions of a madman' (Gordon, 'Ancient and Modern Muggletonians', 52). Birch is believed to have died in October 1800, probably in London.

ALEXANDER GORDON, *rev.* M. J. MERCER

Sources A. Gordon, 'Ancient and modern Muggletonians', *Proceedings of the Liverpool Literary and Philosophical Society*, 24 (1869–70), 51–2 · C. Hill, B. Reay, and W. Lamont, *The world of the Muggletonians* (1983), 127, 138–41 · T. L. Underwood, *The acts of the witnesses* (1999), 14–15 · E. P. Thompson, *Witness against the beast* (1993), 82, 85, 118 · W. Lamont, 'The Muggletonians, 1652–1979: a "vertical" approach', *Past and Present*, 99 (1983), 22–40 · Alexander Gordon's notes, JRL

Archives BL, Muggletonian archive, Add. MSS 60168–60256

Birch, John (1615–1691), parliamentarian army officer and politician, was born on 7 September 1615, the second, but first surviving, son and heir of Samuel Birch (*d.* in or after 1648) of Ardwick Manor, near Manchester, and Mary (*d.* 1659/60), daughter of Ralph Smith of Doblane House, Lancashire. The Birches of Ardwick were probably a cadet branch of the Birches of Birch Hall, one of the 'Genevas of Lancashire' (Heath-Agnew, ix). John Birch's father became a presbyterian elder and county committeeman after the civil war, and the eminent Lancashire nonconformist divine Henry Newcome preached at his mother's funeral on 16 January 1660. His brother Samuel *Birch (1620/21–1680) was a parliamentarian captain and later a vicar at Bampton, Oxfordshire, until being ejected in 1662. Another brother, Thomas, corresponded with Richard Baxter, held Hampton Bishop rectory near Hereford (1654–83), and became a fellow of Manchester collegiate church.

Military career Birch's activities before the civil war are obscure, although he would later admit to a lack of formal education. In 1633 he moved to Bristol, where he developed an extensive trade as a wine merchant. There he met his first wife, Alice (*d.* 1675), daughter of Thomas Deane of Bristol and widow of Bristol grocer Thomas Selfe, and they had five children—Mary, John, Samuel, Elizabeth, and Sarah. By the summer of 1642 Birch commanded a Bristol company of puritan volunteers who in March 1643 foiled a

royalist conspiracy. In July a royalist assault on the city succeeded and he lost his fortune. He sold his remaining merchandise, found a commission in the regular parliamentarian army under Sir Arthur Hesilrige, and brazenly demanded that the committee of safety repay his losses. His first actions as regimental commander in December were successful at Alton and Arundel Castle and at the latter he was seriously injured and given up for dead. But he returned to lead his regiment at Alresford, the siege of Winchester, and Cropredy Bridge, and his actions were among the few bright spots in the earl of Essex's western campaign in mid-1644. Hesilrige took over his regiment and converted them to dragoons; Birch, now colonel, was given command of a regiment from Kent and was back in action by September. His regiment helped the New Model Army capture Bridgwater and Bristol, and parliament appointed him governor of Bath and then Bristol.

Although Birch had considered resigning from the army in November 1645, the capture of Hereford on 18 December following capped his military career. Malcontents from the Hereford royalist garrison revealed to him that the walled city, which had resisted the Scots' siege, could be infiltrated. After a subterfuge of marching his troops away from the area Birch made a hard march back in the evening (several soldiers died in the snow) and hid his men. He then disguised several soldiers as a repair crew who were admitted, opened the gates, and allowed Birch's troops to pour into the city. Some 120 royalist lords, knights, and gentlemen were captured. Parliament was ecstatic and Birch was appointed governor of Hereford Castle. He earned the enmity of the dean, Herbert Croft, by opening the Hereford vicars' choral cloisters to those made homeless by his men's attack, the memory of which long rankled in the county.

Birch continued to assist the mopping up campaign in the southern Welsh marches by besieging Goodrich and Raglan castles in June and August 1646, and he increasingly focused on Herefordshire politics. After attempting to replace Edward Harley as junior knight for the shire he retreated to Leominster to be returned to parliament in September 1646 (and was appointed high steward there in 1648). By late 1646 local feeling ran against Birch's troops, and, when he tried to quarter his cavalry on former royalists and neutrals, Edward Harley and others complained. As a result Birch planned to send his regiment to Ireland. In the tumultuous summer of 1647 his troops mutinied and briefly seized the colonel and his brother Major Samuel Birch. Soon afterwards he divested his remaining military ties and purchased the Homme near Leominster, where his family lived until 1661.

Interregnum, intrigue, and politics Birch was briefly active as a presbyterian member in the Long Parliament. He was sent to Edinburgh in June 1648 to protest against the Scots' engagement with Charles I, and he let it be known that he would resist 'an evil-grounded peace' (Underdown, 89). He was purged, nevertheless, by Colonel Pride in December 1648, and was indeed among the forty-three arrested MPs and one of the last to be released in January. Edmund Ludlow later complained that Birch 'used to neglect no opportunity of providing for himself' (Underdown, 240), and certainly, after parliament's finance committee agreed to pay him £1050 with interest for money lent to Lord Essex in 1642, he bought church lands in his adopted shire, particularly the bishop's palace at Whitborne. But his outspokenness during the 1650s was not based on self-interest. He refused the engagement and he and his brother attended upon Charles II at Worcester in 1651 (although he left before the battle began). Later he baited the Cavalier Parliament by noting that '[w]hen I waited on the King at *Worcester*, I saw very few there besides myself' (Grey, 6.366). During the interregnum he baited local radicals and as a result was imprisoned, by his own count, twenty-one times. A letter from the radical governor of Hereford to Oliver Cromwell in 1655, after Penruddock's rising, reveals Birch relishing his role as gadfly:

> Col. Birch … in the middle of the Assizes … gave out before the judges, that the present insurrections …, did not consist of cavaliers, but a company of silly Quakers. … He also told me … that the great matter was our own jealousies, and fears. Considering this, and what we know of his carriage when the Scots were in Worcester …, I thought it my duty … to secure him, which I have done, and as his sword was taking from him, (he refusing to deliver it), said, though my sword is short now, it may be long enough within a while, (the sword hanging by his side, being a little short sword), and very angrily asked me, whether I had orders to secure him. I answered, if I have not, you will question me. He replied, yes, that I will.   (*Diary of the Rev. Henry Newcome*, 205n.)

James Berry, major-general of Herefordshire and Worcestershire, who secured Birch's release, noted that 'the man is popular in these parts, and he loves to be so. He is taken for a great wit, and guilty of some honesty …, but he professeth desire of peace, and settlement' (ibid.).

Returned to parliament for Leominster in 1656 Birch was among those denied the right to take their seats. He also supported Herefordshire presbyterians in their unsuccessful election bids against more radical individuals. One memoir claims that after Cromwell's death he 'harangued' the spectators at a local horse race on 'the distractions of the state' and the need for a restoration (Bodl. Oxf., MS top. Cheshire.e.7, fol. 38). Yet the government needed his organizational skill and employed him as a commissioner of excise in 1657. He was again returned for Leominster in Richard Cromwell's parliament in January 1659. Although initially not allowed to sit he went on to become one of the most active members. He spoke forcefully for settling Richard's title and for a settlement under a single person and parliament, and against a republic and the 'Instrument of government'. His enemies claimed with little evidence both that he supported Booth's rising and that he stayed in touch with his former and anti-monarchical soldiers in London long after they were disbanded in 1660.

Readmitted to the Long Parliament with his fellow secluded members in February 1660 Birch was appointed to the new council of state. Alongside two other individuals he was authorized by Monck to take charge of the Hereford garrison, to slight the castle and city walls, and to take the arms to Ludlow. However, local royalists resented Birch and during April, when he was returned for Leominster to the Convention (despite Edward Massey deploying his interest in the borough against him), rumours circulated that the garrison 'had not nowe beene demolished but for Coll. Birch …, from whom noe good can be expected' (BL, Add. MS 70007, fols. 76–7). But the government valued him more than they feared him, as witnessed by his appointment as a Herefordshire militia officer in May. Thereafter he briefly oversaw both the Admiralty and the disbandment of the army, and it was not the last time he bothered Samuel Pepys with 'scrupulous inquiries' into navy accounts (Ferris, 1.654). Moreover, in February 1661 he became auditor of the excise for life with a salary of £500 p.a. and worth perhaps double that.

The Cavalier and Exclusion parliaments Birch had inserted himself uneasily into the rather insular Herefordshire squirearchy. He had spent nearly £2500 on church lands in the county, and in 1660 Richard Baxter interpreted his desire for Baxter to accept the offer of the bishopric of Hereford as a means of insuring his purchases, trusting that such a moderate figure was less inclined to demand their return. By 1670 the eventual incumbent, Bishop Croft, calculated that he had paid £2000 to 'the greedy harpy' Birch (Heath-Agnew, 117) 'to cleer ye B[isho]prick. of all incumbrances' (Bodl. Oxf., MS Tanner 147, fol. 79), and the two did not agree terms until 12 April 1672. However, his interest in Leominster had all but evaporated by the Restoration, and in 1661 he purchased Garnstone estate, just outside Weobley, and cultivated an interest in that tiny borough. At the level of local politics he was listed on the Herefordshire *Libri Pacis* from 1660, but did not attend quarter sessions before 1666, and was to be most active from 1675 to 1680. On the national level he retreated to a safe government seat for Penryn borough in the 1661 elections.

In the Cavalier Parliament, Birch advanced several forward-looking if unsuccessful schemes, ranging from a plan to rebuild London after the fire to bills to force landlords to sow flax and hemp to employ the poor. He also oversaw attempts to implement the act for River Wye navigation after it was passed in 1662 until well into the 1670s. However, his greatest contribution was on the subject of religion. During debate on the Conventicle Act in 1663 he acted as teller for the rejected proviso on behalf of those who received the sacrament at least once every three years. He conformed, at least outwardly, to the Church of England, although he occasionally met the presbyterian Newcome, and gave one ejected minister £5 each year. Birch also supported religious comprehension. When he was called on to introduce a loosely worded bill in 1667 he prevaricated, but in early 1668 he did indeed introduce a more carefully drafted version for including moderate nonconformists within the established church. He repeatedly defended dissenters as the trading part of the nation and sought comprehension rather than toleration of separate sects and Catholics. But the Commons responded by introducing the second Conventicle Act instead, and, despite his last-ditch fight against it, it passed the house. He repeatedly antagonized the Commons by his 'shameful' attack on the Act of Uniformity and his comment that he 'knows not what churches are for, if they are not to be preached in' (Heath-Agnew, 140, 151). Perhaps in response to such puritan sentiments the Lords slighted him by referring to 'John Birch, Esq.' rather than his cherished army rank (ibid., 177), and he also seems to have carried on a low-key war with local Herefordshire churchmen. In 1676 rumours spread to London that he had asked his parish priest to marry him to his common-law wife of the past fifteen years, although his lawful wife still lived. In fact, Alice had died on 3 September 1675 and he did then marry Winifred (d. 1717), daughter of Matthew Norris of Weobley.

During the second half of the 1670s Birch increasingly warned about the French threat abroad and the popish threat at home. In 1674 he spoke against the Third Dutch War and in 1677 he demanded an anti-French alliance. As late as May 1679 he supposedly advised the imprisoned earl of Danby to give the Commons 'a deduction of the affairs of state from the time the Triple Alliance was broke' in 1668 (Buckinghamshire MSS, 409). Even while he criticized court policy he worked hard building the crown's revenue; Andrew Marvell labelled him 'Black Birch' for his work on the hated excise (Heath-Agnew, 131), and anti-court pamphlets labelled him a pensioner. The Treasury commissioners were also so reliant on him to examine various accounts that Danby could not afford to dismiss him despite his anti-court sentiments.

Birch was well primed to believe in a popish plot when the scare broke in the autumn of 1678. In early 1674 he had reminded the Commons that a Catholic priest seized in Herefordshire in 1671 had been freed, presumably, by powerful friends. He also warned against the division of 'Religion into any other rivulets than Papist and Protestant' (Grey, 2.228). On 15 April 1678 he reported to the Commons upon the mood of Herefordshire where 'they are in fear of Popery and worse' (ibid., 5.273-4). Upon discovery of the Popish Plot parliament ordered Birch to search the cellars and he complained when prayers contained 'not one word in them of the Papists, nor the Plot named' (ibid., 6.170). Yet he spoke against motions to detect Catholics because he claimed that such tests 'may turn against us another time' (ibid., 6.87-8). In April 1679 the old trooper, now returned for Weobley, feared that '[i]f the Plot had taken effect, the Army must have fallen to the next person upon the Throne' (ibid., 7.68).

Historians have labelled Birch an exclusionist whig, but he followed a tortuous route towards supporting the Exclusion Bill, often wavering and toying with expedients. Although, in May 1679, Birch spoke for exclusion and urged withholding supply until the king assented, he also spoke against those attacking Lord Halifax for opposing exclusion in the Lords. By 1680, although he was heartened by the king's willingness to search for expedients, he continued to fear 'the power and strength of the Duke's party' (An Exact Collection, 113). Finally, in the third Exclusion Parliament he at first urged a day be devoted to considering expedients and spoke in favour of 'limitations' (Heath-Agnew, 189), but two days later noted that 'where 10 were of the mind for this [exclusion] Bill a twelvemonth ago, there are an 100 now that will bleed for it' (Cobbett, Parl. hist., 4.1330-31).

Birch, in his rationale for agreeing to the extra-parliamentary and extra-constitutional association, significantly shifted from attacking popery to attacking the high Anglican defence of absolute monarchy. He believed that the clergy's 'Laudean principles' had made them defend 'the King's absolute authority' in 1641 and again in 1680 (Cobbett, Parl. hist., 4.1240-41). 'Popery never can nor will grow but by absolute Government' (Grey, 8.34), he exclaimed in November 1680; and he found such a link in the southern marches in the power and crypto-Catholic clientele of the marquess of Worcester. In December 1680 and January 1681 Birch joined a chorus of local MPs who denounced the evil influence of Worcester. He drove home the point about papists in masquerade: 'Queen Mary came in by Protestants' (ibid., 8.194-5). After the Oxford parliament he met the earl of Shaftesbury when the latter sought the Herefordshire members' commitment to arms. But although he organized a cabal in the county he failed to appear and backed away from commitment to radical action (CSP dom., 1682, 290-92).

However, Birch's opponents at Westminster and in Herefordshire were not quick to forget his criticisms of the regime. In 1680 he was removed from the commission of peace and libels circulated against him. In early 1683 a local informant considered him to be among 'other ill-affected persons' (CSP dom., Jan-June 1683, 93-4) and he eventually lost his Weobley seat in 1685. By then Birch had retreated to the role of country squire, improving his estate and repairing Weobley church.

Final years In 1688 the ageing colonel roused himself to action. Although James II, in February 1687, had considered making Birch a deputy lieutenant, Birch firmly supported William of Orange. He slipped out of London and contacted Robert Harley and both joined William at Salisbury, where Birch helped convince the prince to descend upon London without first securing Oxford and presented him with a £40 subscription from the Herefordshire gentry.

Re-elected for Weobley to the convention of 1689, Birch was amazingly active in parliament during the last two years of his life. His speeches often referred to events from the 1640s, 1650s, and 1660s—in effect, framing his life. He prefaced his opposition to fasting on 30 January 1689 with a reference to the fight against tyranny and popery during the past forty years. He compared the Restoration Convention to that of 1689 in order to argue that drastic actions, such as excluding some members, were sometimes necessary in 'great revolutions' (Cobbett, Parl. hist., 5.131). In March, during a debate on whether to insist that the monarch uphold the church as by law established, he reminded parliament of how the Scots had rebelled 'when abp. Laud would not have a hair bated of the Discipline of the Church; and what followed upon it? That brought on the war in England' (ibid., 5.203). And in June he claimed to be one of the few surviving MPs who had been in parliament when the Popish Plot 'was so clearly proved, that all England was satisfied' (ibid., 5.294–5). In December he compared the Jacobite rising in Ireland with the Irish rising in 1641.

By April 1690 Birch admitted that he was 'an ancient man' (Cobbett, *Parl. hist.*, col. 609, 28 April 1690), and he disappears from parliamentary debates. He returned to Garnstone, which had roughly doubled in size since he had purchased it. His eldest son predeceased him and he used his Lancashire manors to benefit his son's daughters. He himself died at Garnstone on 10 May 1691 and he was buried at Weobley church. Yet even in death the old parliamentarian trooper stirred up controversy. He had arranged for a monument to himself to be constructed in Weobley church in full military gear which not only trumpeted his parliamentarian military service but also was built so that its railings extended into the raised altarway. In 1694 Bishop Gilbert Ironside went personally to Weobley to deface the monument. The monument and inscription remain visible today (although the reinscription altered his birth date to 1626), and so do the holes where the railings were ripped out. Birch's youngest daughter, Sarah, inherited Garnstone on the condition that she marry the second son, John, of his brother Thomas. This John Birch, a successful barrister, also inherited Birch's Weobley seat, which he held almost continuously from 1701 until his death in 1735.

Assessment Historians have long been drawn to the colourful character of Birch. His contemporaries painted him as 'immoral' (Herbert Aubrey, in Ferris, 1.660), vile (Massey), or opportunistic (Ludlow and Baxter), although Harley recalled him as his 'ancient friend and companion in arms for religion and liberty' (BL, Add. MS 70234). Bishop Burnet gave a balanced if critical judgement: 'He was the roughest and boldest speaker in the House …, [who] spoke always with much life and heat: but judgment was not his talent' (Ferris, 1.660). The next generation forgot the great Commons man, but in the Victorian era Thomas Babington Macaulay lauded 'Honest Birch' (Heath-Agnew, xi), Thomas Heywood produced a somewhat unreliable encomium of him in his edition of Newcome's diary, and in 1864 John Webb edited John Roe's military memoir of Colonel Birch.   NEWTON E. KEY

Sources E. Heath-Agnew, *Roundhead to royalist: a biography of Colonel John Birch, 1615–1691* (1977) • J. P. Ferris, 'Birch, John', HoP, *Commons, 1660–90*, 1.653–60 • A. Grey, ed., *Debates of the House of Commons, from the year 1667 to the year 1694*, 10 vols. (1763), vols. 2–8 • *The diary of the Rev. Henry Newcome, from September 30, 1661, to September 29, 1663*, ed. T. Heywood, Chetham Society, 18 (1849) • 'Biographical essays by the Revd John Watson', 1778, Bodl. Oxf., MS Top. Cheshire e.7 • Cobbett, *Parl. hist.*, vols. 4–5 • *The diary of John Milward, esq., member of parliament for Derbyshire, September, 1666 to May, 1668*, ed. C. Robbins (1938) • D. Underdown, *Pride's Purge: politics in the puritan revolution* (1971) • T. Rowlands, '"As black as Hell to my own people": James II's reputation in Herefordshire', *Midland History*, 14 (1989), 43–52 • I. Atherton, ed., *Sir Barnabas Scudamore's defence against the imputations of treachery and negligence in the loss of the city of Hereford in 1645* (privately printed, Akron, Ohio, 1992) • *The life and times of Anthony Wood*, ed. A. Clark, 3, OHS, 26 (1894) • *The debates in the honourable House of Commons* (1681) • *An exact collection of the most considerable debates in the honourable House of Commons* (1681) • *The letter books of Sir William Brereton*, ed. R. N. Dore, 2, Lancashire and Cheshire RS, 128 (1990) • *The manuscripts of his grace the duke of Portland*, 10 vols., HMC, 29 (1891–1931), vols. 1, 3 • BL, Add. MS 70007, fols. 76–7 • Bodl. Oxf., MS Tanner 147 • *The manuscripts of the earl of Buckinghamshire, the earl of Lindsey … and James Round*, HMC, 38 (1895) • CSP dom., 1682; Jan–June 1683
Archives Herefs. RO, bond, 057/11 • Herefs. RO, papers, AK 10/1–8 | BL, list of Herefordshire delinquents, Add. MS 70061 • Bodl. Oxf., corresp. with William Lenthall
Likenesses marble statue, c.1691, Weobley church

Birch, John (1745x9–1815), surgeon, was the second child and only son of the three children of Thomas Birch, merchant. The family was clearly wealthy as in February 1763 Birch was apprenticed to the surgeon Thomas Smith for the substantial fee of £400. He was admitted to the Surgeons' Company in 1770 and set up practice in London, first in Essex Street, later in Spring Gardens. Birch held a number of prestigious posts: he purchased a commission as surgeon to the Horse Grenadier Guards in 1770, from which he retired on 25 April 1779; from 1784 he served as surgeon at St Thomas's Hospital; he later became surgeon-extraordinary to the prince regent. Birch was conservative in his medical opinions, and at St Thomas's he opposed the new emphasis on anatomy and dissection in its medical teaching, championed by Henry Cline jun. Astley Cooper, another advocate of the new form of training, described Birch as 'a sensual man; clever, but a bad surgeon. He had neglected anatomy, and was therefore afraid of all operations which required a knowledge of it' (Parsons, 3.37–8). Birch certainly resigned his post as lithotomist at the hospital in 1812, but this was probably due to advancing years rather than lack of dexterity.

Birch was an avid supporter of the medical use of electricity, which he believed in many cases offered an alternative to surgery. This form of therapy enjoyed a considerable vogue in the late eighteenth century following the discovery of the electrical nature of the nerve impulse, although it never became a fully accepted part of the therapeutic armamentarium. Treatment involved transmitting electric shocks from a Leyden jar to patients seated in an insulated chair. Single shocks were applied locally to the affected part through a wooden or metal 'director', or, alternatively, multiple shocks, making up an 'electrical fluid', were drawn through the body. The idea was to stimulate weak nerves, muscles, and vessels in the body, encouraging the circulation and the flow of secretions. Birch's four publications on the topic offered no new insights but simply described cases from his private practice and his clinic at St Thomas's. He claimed to have successfully treated a wide variety of acute and chronic disorders—weak and stiff joints, localized paralysis, fevers, skin diseases, impotence, melancholy, kidney and bladder complaints, and particularly amenorrhoea.

Birch also revealed his conservative views in opposing the substitution of vaccination for the older practice of inoculation—deliberate infection with smallpox. He was the most prestigious of the handful of practitioners who stood against Edward Jenner's discovery and offered some of the more moderate and reasoned arguments in a heated debate which lasted throughout the 1800s. In his *Letter Occasioned by the many Failures of the Cow-Pox* (1805) and *Serious Reasons for Objecting to the Practice of Vaccination* (1806) Birch argued that inoculation offered complete security, while the growing number of reported cases of smallpox after vaccination proved that the procedure was not, as Jenner and his supporters claimed, a certain preventative. Birch ridiculed the pro-vaccinators' attempts to explain away these failures as a result of vaccination with spurious cowpox. Birch also argued that the new practice was dangerous: the operation provoked acute and fatal inflammation or chronic skin complaints. The latter, Birch claimed, were unique to vaccinated children and not, as Jenner's supporters countered, pre-existing cases of scrofula. Birch was one of the few writers to point to the most serious flaw in Jenner's writings—his failure to explain the relationship between cowpox and smallpox, and thus the mechanism by which vaccination could induce immunity.

Birch died on 3 February 1815 at his home in New Street, Spring Gardens, London. He was buried the next day alongside members of his family in the church of St Margaret Pattens, Rood Lane, Eastcheap, where a memorial tablet was placed extolling his professional virtues and enthusiasms. DEBORAH BRUNTON

Sources R. B. Fisher, *Edward Jenner* (1991) · Watt, *Bibl. Brit.* · A. Peterkin and W. Johnston, *Commissioned officers in the medical services of the British army, 1660–1960*, 1 (1968) · private information (2004) · F. G. Parsons, *The history of St Thomas's Hospital*, 2, 3 (1934–6) · P. J. Wallis and R. V. Wallis, *Eighteenth century medics*, 2nd edn (1988) · examinations book, Company of Surgeons, RCS Eng. · *GM*, 1st ser., 88/1 (1818), 188 · War Office succession book, PRO, 25/210, 27, 25/211, 71

Likenesses C. Williams, etching, 1802?, Wellcome L. · J. Lewis, stipple and line engraving (after T. Phillips), RCS Eng., Wellcome L.

Birch, Jonathan (1783–1847), translator, was born in Holborn, London, on 4 July 1783. When young he wanted to become a sculptor, but in October 1798 he was apprenticed to an uncle in the City. In 1803 he entered the house of Johann Argelander, a wealthy timber merchant at Memel, East Prussia; the site of the house has been marked since 1993 by a memorial plaque. He remained there until Argelander's death in 1812, much of his time being employed in travelling in Russia, Finland, Sweden, and Denmark. In 1807 the three eldest sons of Friedrich Wilhelm III of Prussia took refuge with Argelander for eighteen months. They became enduring friends of both Birch and Friedrich Wilhelm Argelander, son of the merchant, who became a distinguished astronomer.

In 1812 Birch returned to England and turned to literary pursuits. In 1823 he married Esther Brooke, of Lancaster. They had five children, of whom a boy and a girl survived. His son, Charles Bell *Birch (1832–1893), became a sculptor. His father's friendship with Friedrich Wilhelm IV secured him several commissions.

After many minor essays in literature Birch published

Fifty-one Original Fables, with Morals and Ethical Index, illustrated by Robert Cruickshank (1833). The preface is signed 'Job Crithannah', an anagram of the author's name. Crown Prince Friedrich Wilhelm accepted a copy, and renewed the friendship formed at Memel. Birch then produced *Divine Emblems* (1838), again illustrated by Robert Cruickshank, under the pseudonym Johann Albricht, A.M. (another anagram of Jonathan Birch). He sent Crown Prince Friedrich Wilhelm a copy and received in return a gold medal, of which only thirty were struck and which the prince gave to his particular friends.

Birch then undertook a complete verse translation of Goethe's *Faust*. The first English translation had appeared in 1823, but Birch was the first to attempt part one and part of part two. Part one (1839) was dedicated to the crown prince, who, on coming to the throne in 1840 as Friedrich Wilhelm IV, sent him the 'great gold medal of homage'. Others, however, were less favourably impressed. The *Dublin Review* (1840) declared that 'As a translation it is bad, as a poetic translation it is worse, but as a translation of *Faust* it is worst of all.' In 1841 Birch was elected 'foreign honorary member of the Literary Society of Berlin', the only other Englishman thus honoured being Thomas Carlyle. His translation of part of the second part of *Faust* was published in 1843 and was dedicated to Friedrich Wilhelm of Prussia. Together the two parts of the translation have met near universal condemnation, and are now chiefly remembered for a reissue of 1886 (now very rare: a copy exists in the Beinecke Library, Yale), each page of which carried the boldly printed slogan 'Beecham's Pills'. Birch kept alive his attachment to the Prussian royal house with his two translations of Rulemann Friedrich Eylert's works on the domestic and religious life of Friedrich Wilhelm III (1844 and 1845). In 1846 Friedrich Wilhelm IV offered him a choice of apartments in three of his palaces. He chose Bellevue, near Berlin, mainly for the sake of his son's artistic studies. At the end of 1846 Birch settled in Prussia and completed his last work, a verse translation after Carl Lachmann's text of the *Nibelungen Lied* (Berlin, 1848). While his work was still in the press he was taken ill, and he died at Bellevue on 8 September 1847.

THOMPSON COOPER, *rev.* ELIZABETH BAIGENT

Sources private information (1885) · 'Gedenkstaetten', www.astro.uni-bonn.de/~pbrosche/aa/ema/ema07.txt, 1 June 2003 · C. Sammons, 'The collection of German literature', www.library.yale.edu/beinecke/blgycgl.htm, 1 June 2003 · L. Baumann, *Die englischen Übersetzungen von Goethes Faust* (Halle, 1907) · W. Heinemann, *Goethes Faust in England und Amerika* (Berlin, 1886) · C. F. Schreiber, *A note on Faust translations* [n.d., c.1930]

Birch, Sir Joseph, first baronet (1755–1833), politician, was born on 18 June 1755, the first son of Thomas Birch (d. 1782), a merchant at Liverpool. Like his father Birch was a merchant and had diverse commercial interests, ranging from shipowning and brewing to landholding in Jamaica and stock in the East India Company. It was this personal wealth that allowed him to pursue his political interests, especially in such notoriously expensive boroughs as Liverpool and Nottingham. On 6 March 1786 he married

Elizabeth Mary, the daughter of Benjamin Heywood, a prominent Liverpool merchant banker, with whom he had one surviving son and three daughters.

Birch's first foray into politics came in 1802, when he unsuccessfully contested his home town of Liverpool; he was returned as a whig, however, for the borough of Nottingham, not only because of his political sentiments but also because he was willing to use his own money to finance the campaign and possibly because of his nonconformity (he was a Unitarian). His success was short-lived: the defeated tory candidate Daniel Parker Coke successfully petitioned against Birch's return on the grounds that the returning officer, magistrates, and corporation of Nottingham had been biased against Coke in favour of Birch. Birch's election was declared void and at the subsequent by-election in 1803 Coke defeated him. In 1803 Birch made an explicit appeal to the 'working class' of Nottingham and portrayed the election of that year as a struggle between rich and poor, but such early radicalism was not much manifested in his later political career, which was one of 'an orthodox, well behaved, reforming Whig' (Thomis, 156–7).

Birch stood at Nottingham again in 1806 but was defeated, and in 1812 he was nominated against his wishes only to be withdrawn when it became clear that he was contesting St Ives, as it turned out, unsuccessfully. He eventually succeeded in becoming an MP again when shortly after the 1812 election he was returned on the influence of Joseph Hague Everett for the constituency of Ludgershall, Wiltshire. He served throughout the remainder of the parliament of 1812 for Ludgershall, his whig credentials being confirmed by his joining Brooks's Club in April 1815. At the election of 1818 his attention returned to Nottingham. By 1818 the corporation of Nottingham had 'abandoned any last remaining pretence to neutrality in Parliamentary contests' (Thomis, 146) but Birch's successful return at the head of the poll for Nottingham in 1818 was also seen at the time as stemming in part from his support among moderate tories who put aside politics and recorded a personal vote in his favour. Birch served as MP for Nottingham until he retired in 1830. He was created a baronet in September 1831 and died on 22 August 1833.

STEPHEN M. LEE

Sources M. I. Thomis, *Politics and society in Nottingham, 1785–1835* (1969) • P. A. Symonds and R. G. Thorne, 'Birch, Joseph', HoP, *Commons, 1790–1820* • P. A. Symonds and R. G. Thorne, 'Nottingham', HoP, *Commons, 1790–1820*, 2.317–20

Birch, Lamorna. *See* Birch, Samuel John (1869–1955).

Birch, (Evelyn) Nigel Chetwode, Baron Rhyl (1906–1981), economist and politician, was born in London on 18 November 1906, one of two sons (there were no daughters) of General Sir (James Frederick) Noel *Birch (1865–1939) GBE KCB KCMG and his wife, Florence Hyacinthe (1876–1938), the daughter of Sir George Chetwode, sixth baronet, and sister of Field Marshal Lord Chetwode. Educated at Eton College, he became a partner in the stock-broking firm of Cohen Laming Hoare. A skilful operator, especially in the gilt-edged market, he acquired at an early age a sufficient fortune to assure him independence. He joined the Territorial Army (King's Royal Rifle Corps) before 1939 and served in the Second World War on the general staff in Britain and the Mediterranean theatre, attaining the rank of lieutenant-colonel in 1944.

Birch was elected to parliament for Flintshire in 1945 and quickly made a formidable reputation on the Conservative opposition benches for his mordantly witty interventions and speeches, and for his advocacy of strictly honest public finance and his critique of the prevalent Keynesian trend. He married on 1 August 1950 Esmé Consuelo Helen (*b*. 1908) OBE, daughter of Frederic Glyn, fourth Baron Wolverton. There were no children. On forming his government, in November 1951 Winston Churchill appointed Birch—some believed as a result of mistaken identity—not, as was expected, to a financial post but as parliamentary under-secretary at the Air Ministry and subsequently at the Ministry of Defence (from the end of February 1952).

Birch attained ministerial rank in October 1954 as minister of works where he enjoyed, as he said, 'gardening with a staff of three thousand' and deserved to be remembered for his insistence upon retaining the trees in Park Lane when it was widened. He served in the government of Sir Anthony Eden as secretary of state for air from December 1955; but the first appointment in his special field came only when Harold Macmillan made him economic secretary to the Treasury—technically a demotion—in January 1957.

Birch supported and encouraged the chancellor of the exchequer, Peter Thorneycroft, in evolving a theory of inflation which was the recognizable forerunner of the monetarism of later decades, and when Thorneycroft failed to obtain from his cabinet colleagues the restraint in public expenditure he considered essential, Birch joined him and the financial secretary (J. Enoch Powell) in the triple resignation on 6 January 1958 which Macmillan, in a jaunty phrase which became famous, dismissed as 'a little local difficulty'.

Though he never held office again, Birch exercised great influence on economic and financial questions and continued to castigate what he regarded as the lax and inflationary proclivities of Macmillan's government. When Macmillan was about to be toppled by the scandal of the 'Profumo affair', Birch demanded his resignation in a philippic long famous for its closing phrase from Robert Browning's 'The Lost Leader', 'Never glad confident morning again', which went down in parliamentary memory along with his exclamation to a full house on the announcement of Hugh Dalton's resignation: 'They've shot our fox!' The failing eyesight which increasingly inhibited Birch's other activities did not interfere with his stream of contributions to economic debate, which, though meticulously prepared, were invariably delivered without a note.

Birch, who once accused the Treasury of 'the reckless courage of a mouse at bay', was representative of a distinctive element in the House of Commons after the Second World War. He combined with personal courage, independence, and integrity an understanding of public finance and economic affairs acquired and perfected in the practical life of the City. He was appointed OBE in 1945 and sworn of the privy council in 1955.

Having continued from 1950 to represent West Flint, where he resided at Saithailwyd ('Seven Hearths'), near Holywell, Birch went to the House of Lords in 1970 as a life peer, Baron Rhyl. He died on 8 March 1981 at Holywell House, Swanmore, Hampshire.

J. ENOCH POWELL, *rev.*

Sources personal knowledge (1990, 2004) · *The Times* (10 March 1981) · *WWW*
Archives IWM, interview
Wealth at death £335,951: probate, 29 April 1981, *CGPLA Eng. & Wales*

Birch, Sir (James Frederick) Noel (1865–1939), army officer, was born at Llanrhaeadr, near Denbigh, Denbighshire, on 29 December 1865, the second son of Major Richard Frederick Birch (*d.* 1915), of Maes Elwy, St Asaph, and his wife, Euphemia Mercer, eldest daughter of James Somerville, of Edinburgh. Having been educated at Giggleswick, Marlborough College, and the Royal Military Academy, Woolwich, he was commissioned into the Royal Artillery on 29 April 1885, and five years later won appointment to the Royal Horse Artillery (RHA). In 1894–5 he was aide-de-camp to the general officer commanding, Woolwich district, and in the latter year he went to the Asante kingdom. He served in South Africa in the cavalry division, under Sir John French, and then commanded a battalion of imperial yeomanry in 1902. On 21 October 1903 he married Florence Hyacinthe (1876–1938), youngest daughter of Sir George Chetwode and sister of the future Field Marshal Lord Chetwode. They had two sons, the elder being (Evelyn) Nigel Chetwode *Birch (later Baron Rhyl). From 1905 to 1907 Birch, who was known as an outstanding horseman and whip, commanded the riding establishment at Woolwich. His approach was probably the forerunner of the Weedon system for training instructors in equitation. He published *Modern Riding* in 1909 and *Modern Riding and Horse Education* (1912).

Having become a lieutenant-colonel in 1912, Birch took the 7th brigade of the RHA to France in 1914 with the cavalry division, under Edmund Allenby. He became brigadier-general, general staff of the cavalry corps, in January 1915 and, in March, commander Royal Artillery of 7th division. At Givenchy he commanded the artillery of the 4th corps, under Sir Henry Rawlinson, and at Loos, the artillery of the 1st corps, under Hubert Gough, in early attempts at placing the command and control of artillery at the highest practical level, though lacking the means to make this effective. He was briefly general officer commanding, Royal Artillery Fourth Army, until Sir Douglas Haig advanced him to artillery adviser at general headquarters (GHQ) on 28 May 1916, thus making him the leading gunner in France, which he remained until April 1919. His rapid progress in fact owed very much to Haig's influence; they had known each other for many years.

Known widely as 'Curly' (none knew why), Birch was noted for having tremendous presence. Those who

Sir (James Frederick) Noel Birch (1865–1939), by Walter Stoneman, 1919

worked with him admired his charm, understanding, and sense of humour and equally his patience and determination. Opinions vary about his exact relationship with Haig, Birch being only an adviser though he exercised command later. It is certain that his time at GHQ saw tremendous improvements in the equipment and control of artillery; Haig had chosen well. Birch exercised control through the staff he had selected whom he worked as hard as he did himself. He was responsible for everything to do with artillery. His letter, of 24 June 1916, on the provision and organization of heavy artillery (Farndale, 358–63), exemplifies a major aspect of his work and also the way in which he started, immediately upon his appointment, to deal with a matter of the utmost importance. Birch played a prominent role in the development of the artillery: gun and ammunition production programmes were formalized, the supply of units regularized, and a chain of command established. Those, including Sir William Robertson, the chief of the Imperial General Staff, who thought that Birch was neither practically nor theoretically up to date, missed the point; his large and talented staff performed outstandingly under his leadership. With other senior gunners, he formed that extremely effective artillery which played a vital part in eventual victory.

Birch was promoted major-general in 1916 and lieutenant-general in 1919. On 1 February 1920 he became director of remounts after which he continued the slow move towards mechanization. He became director-general territorial and volunteer forces on 13 February 1921. On 1 October 1923 he was made master-general of the ordnance (MGO) and a member of the Army Council. His time as MGO, in a period of severe retrenchment, where up to 90 per cent of the limited money available was spent on the other two services anyway, nevertheless saw early experiments in the mechanization of the field artillery. He was rejoined by his talented staff officer of 7th division, 1st corps, and GHQ days, S. W. H. Rawlins, as a director of artillery. It was probably Rawlins who introduced proposals for a tracked, self-propelled gun which appeared in two forms, both becoming known as 'Birch' guns, but Birch gave strong support to the proposals. The process of selecting artillery from the thousands of pieces available after the war, for continued service or for disposal, continued. There were few resources available for anything new, though design work continued during this period of economic depression and some advances were made in tank design, a subject of much interest to Birch. The developments in mechanical draught for field artillery were also important and began during his time as MGO.

Birch became a colonel commandant Royal Artillery (1919) and Royal Horse Artillery (1928), having been an aide-de-camp to George V (1915–16). Frequently mentioned in dispatches, Birch was appointed CB in 1916, KCMG in 1918, KCB in 1922, and GBE in 1927. He also received a number of foreign awards. He became a general on 1 October 1926 and retired the following year, when his appointment ended, to become a director of Vickers Armstrong. His value now lay in his experience and in his powerful support for mechanization dating from his time as MGO. Birch died in King's College Hospital, London, on 3 February 1939, and a memorial service was held in the chapel of the Royal Hospital, Chelsea, on 7 February; Lady Birch had predeceased him on 4 October 1938.

P. G. W. ANNIS

Sources M. Farndale, *History of the royal regiment of artillery*, 1: *Western front, 1914–18* (1986) · B. P. Hughes, ed., *History of the royal regiment of artillery* (1992) · S. Bidwell and D. Graham, *Fire-power, British army weapons and theories of war, 1904–45* (1982) · J. D. Scott, *Vickers: a history* (1962) · H. C. C. Uniacke, ed., *Royal artillery war commemoration book* (1920), 393 · WWW · *Army List* · *Royal artillery (blue) list* · Walford, *County families* · Burke, *Peerage* (1939) · J. E. Edmonds, ed., *Military operations in France and Belgium, 1914*, 2nd edn, 2 vols., History of the Great War (1925) · *The Gunner*, 20/12 (March 1939), 357–9 · *The Gunner*, 21/1 (April 1939), 5 · *RA Regimental News* (March 1939), 646–8 [appreciation by Major-General G. H. A. White] · *CGPLA Eng. & Wales* (1939)

Archives CUL, Vickers archives, letters · Royal Artillery Institution, Woolwich, London, S. W. H. Rawlins, 'A history of the development of the British artillery in France, 1914–1918', MD 1162 | FILM IWM FVA, news footage

Likenesses F. Dodd, charcoal and watercolour, 1917, IWM · two photographs, 1918–19 (with D. Haig), IWM · W. Stoneman, two photographs, 1919–31, NPG [*see illus.*] · photograph, in or after 1928, Royal Artillery Institution, Woolwich, London · O. Birley, portrait, probably priv. coll.

Wealth at death £13,383 0s. 3d.: probate, 29 March 1939, *CGPLA Eng. & Wales*

Birch, Peter (1651/2–1710), Church of England clergyman, was born at Birch, Lancashire, the eighth child of Thomas

*Birch (*bap.* 1608, *d.* 1678), of Birch Hall in the parish of Manchester, a colonel in the parliamentarian army and MP for Liverpool, and his wife, Alice (*d.* 1697), daughter of Thomas Brooke of Norton, Cheshire, and his third wife, Ellen Gerrard. Thomas Birch was a loyal servant of the republic in the 1650s, and to the end was a committed puritan who ensured that Birch chapel was a haven for nonconformist ministers in the 1660s and 1670s.

Raised as a presbyterian by his father, Peter Birch was still committed to nonconformity when he began his education at Emmanuel College, Cambridge, in 1667. Some time afterwards he left Cambridge and in 1670 moved with his twin brother, Andrew Birch, to the city of Oxford, where they lived with John Foulks, an apothecary, and studied in the Bodleian Library with a private tutor, William Assheton of Brasenose College. At Oxford, Birch declared his conformity to the established church by publicly taking the sacrament of holy communion. Dr John Fell, then dean of Christ Church, Oxford, facilitated his admission to Christ Church and the passage of his degree, urging a convocation of the university, 'That when so many run away from the church, you would think fit to encourage one who addresseth himself as free and thorough convert' (Wood, *Ath. Oxon.*, 4.660). Matriculating at twenty-one, on 12 May 1673, Birch was able to apply his terms of study at Cambridge to his present course of study, making it possible for him to graduate BA on 23 March 1674 and proceed MA three months later (on 23 June), soon after his move to Christ Church. He would later proceed BD (on 4 February 1684) and DD (7 July 1688).

After graduating BA Birch remained in Oxford, serving first as a chaplain of Christ Church and preaching occasionally in the Oxford area. To Anthony Wood in December 1675 Birch was an example of how Fell had preferred 'Fanaticks and rogues … sooner than try sons of the Church of England'. Five years on, however, he recorded with satisfaction how Birch, 'a zealous man for the Church of England', 'swinged the phanaticques and presbyterians away' in the sermon that he delivered at the university church on 30 January 1681 on the fast day appointed to commemorate the execution of Charles I (*Life and Times of Anthony Wood*, 2.332; 2.514). In June 1685, as chaplain to the militia regiment, he delivered an exhortatory sermon as news came through to Oxford of Monmouth's rebellion. He also served as curate of St Thomas's parish before being appointed rector of St Ebbe's Church (1685–6) and lecturer at Carfax. While at St Ebbe's, on 19 November 1686, Birch married his first wife, Mary (*d.* 1688), the daughter of the poet Edmund *Waller, at St Peter-le-Poer, London. Some time after this Birch was made chaplain to James, duke of Ormond.

In 1689 Birch was appointed as chaplain to the House of Commons and as a prebendary of Westminster Abbey, being installed on 17 October of that year. He appears to have served as subdeacon and archdeacon of Westminster. Following the elevation of Thomas Tenison to the see of Lincoln, Bishop Compton of London named Birch to the rectory of St James's, Westminster, on 11 July

1692. However, Queen Mary almost immediately claimed the crown's right to appointment to the living and chose William Wake instead. Defeated in the court of king's bench in November 1694 Birch appealed to the House of Lords, who likewise decided against him in January 1695 by forty votes to thirty; the teller on behalf of Birch was the high-church earl of Rochester. Two months later, on 19 March 1695, the dean and chapter of Westminster named him to the living of St Bride's, Fleet Street, London, which he held until his death.

Birch's published works consist of several sermons, some of which were preached before the House of Commons. The most prominent of these was preached on 30 January 1694, the sermon for the fast day appointed to commemorate the execution of Charles I. The sermon applied David's lament over the fall of God's anointed, Saul, to the death of Charles (2 Samuel 1: 21). The sermon, which affirmed the divine right of kings, seemed to bring into question the legitimacy of William III and Mary II. The sermon caused considerable controversy and elicited an anonymously published response entitled *A Birchen Rod for Dr Birch*, which accused Birch of impugning the honour and title of the reigning monarchs by maligning the 'defensive arms by which they made a conquest of England's affections' (*Birchen Rod*, 24). The tory sentiments of the sermon and its apparent offence to the monarchs helped spark off the campaign by some whigs to abolish 30 January as a fast day, and may have contributed to the loss of St James's.

Birch, having lost his first wife in 1688, married Martha (*c.*1653–1703), daughter of Samuel Vyner and widow of a wealthy London merchant, Francis Millington, on 24 November 1697. She died on 28 May 1703, after which the widower married Sybil Wyrley (*d.* 1708), the daughter and coheir of Humphrey Wyrley of Handsworth, Staffordshire. She died on 12 August 1708, but this last marriage produced two children, Humphrey Wyrley Birch (1706–1747) and John Wyrley Birch (1707–1775).

Birch's prospects for promotion improved after the accession of Queen Anne, and in 1702 Narcissus Luttrell reported the rumour that Birch was going to be appointed dean of Westminster. The following year he noted that Birch 'stands fair for the bishoprick of St Asaph, vacant by the death of Dr. Jones' (Luttrell, 5.298). Neither of these possibilities came to fruition and Birch died on 2 July 1710 and was buried in Westminster Abbey two days later. At the time of his death his two sons were left in the guardianship of his sister Deborah Birch, who was named executor in his will, dated 27 June 1710. He bequeathed his estate to his elder son, Humphrey, providing from that estate an annual allowance of £200 for his younger son, John. ROBERT D. CORNWALL

Sources J. Booker, *The history of the ancient chapel of Birch, in Manchester parish*, Chetham Society, 47 (1859) · Wood, *Ath. Oxon.*, new edn · J. L. Chester, ed., *The marriage, baptismal, and burial registers of the collegiate church or abbey of St Peter, Westminster*, Harleian Society, 10 (1876) · Foster, *Alum. Oxon.* · Venn, *Alum. Cant.* · N. Luttrell, *A brief historical relation of state affairs from September 1678 to April 1714*, 6 vols. (1857) · R. Newcourt, *Repertorium ecclesiasticum parochiale Londinense*, 1 (1708) · J. Le Neve, *Fasti ecclesiae anglicanae* (1716) · Nichols,

Lit. anecdotes, vol. 9 · Allibone, *Dict.* · *IGI* · *A birchen rod for Dr. Birch* (1695) · *The manuscripts of the House of Lords*, new ser., 12 vols. (1900–77), vol. 1, pp. 399–400 · *The life and times of Anthony Wood*, ed. A. Clark, 2, OHS, 21 (1892), 250, 308; 3, OHS, 26 (1894)
Wealth at death estate to eldest son, Humphrey, and provided £200 per year to younger son, John: will, repro. in Booker, *History*

Birch [*formerly* Catlin-Birch], **Reginald** (1914–1994), trade unionist and political activist, was born Reginald Catlin-Birch on 7 June 1914 at 4 Chichester Terrace, Kilburn, London, one of the five children of Charles Catlin-Birch (*d.* 1928/9), house painter and builder, and his wife, Annie Rolfe. A skilled worker, his father was a craftsman who according to his son 'did all the posh work for artists up in St. John's Wood'; when, periodically, he was out of work, he refused to take dole money 'because', Birch explained, 'that would demean him' (*The Guardian*). His father died when Birch was fourteen, but not before he had nurtured his son's interest in books and literature. Birch attended St Augustine's elementary school, Kilburn, and left at fourteen to become an apprentice toolmaker. After completing his apprenticeship he became politically more and more aware, and developed a reputation as an agitator—a serious handicap to any young man seeking regular employment during the depression. In 1938 he joined the Communist Party, drawn in by the Spanish Civil War; he had already helped to organize nightly demonstrations and meetings as well as collections of food and money in support of the republican forces fighting Franco. He later observed that the Spanish Civil War 'was the only political issue in my life which roused the British working class' (*The Times*). As a skilled toolmaker he had already become a member of the Amalgamated Engineering Union, whose north London district committee was dominated by Communist Party members.

Birch's great mentor at that time was Wal Hannington, who had organized and led the National Unemployed Workers' Movement as well as some of the big hunger marches of the 1930s. They met at Swift's Scales, a small engineering firm in Stonebridge, north-west London, where Hannington was convenor. It was there that Birch, under Hannington's tutelage, led his first strike—flying in the face of wartime regulations, which prohibited unofficial strikes. The strike, which began over the sacking of a worker, quickly led to legal action against Birch and six other shop stewards. The legal wrangle dragged on for weeks while the shop stewards remained in custody, but by the time the case was heard in July 1941 the Soviet Union was at war—an event which transformed the war in Birch's eyes from a 'capitalist conflict' to a 'war against fascism'. In the end the recorder, announcing judgment, bound the defendants over to keep the peace for two years. On 28 February 1942 Birch married Dorothy Lawson (*b.* 1911/12), schoolteacher, of Acton, west London, and daughter of George Lawson, tram driver. They had three sons, one of whom became a distinguished surgeon, another an engineering technician, and the third a photographer.

The war over, Birch concentrated on his activity within the Amalgamated Engineering Union and the Communist

Reginald Birch (1914–1994), by Harrison

Party, and in 1956 he was elected a member of the party's national executive. Four years later he became a full-time official of the Amalgamated Engineering Union, elected to the then powerful position of north London divisional organizer. The north London district then contained some 8 per cent of the union's membership and was effectively controlled by the Communist Party. This made Birch very much a local trade union 'emperor'. In 1966 he was elected to the national executive of what by then had become the Amalgamated Union of Engineering Workers, one of the most influential executive bodies in the British trade union movement. The appointment came during a period of considerable industrial unrest, much of it unofficial, and focused on the motor industry, printing, docks, and transport. Birch had great influence among the communist shop stewards in the car industry, notably at Ford, and inevitably he became involved in a series of disputes which frequently brought him into conflict with his own union's top leadership and with other unions. He was especially involved in the prolonged Ford strike of 1971, as well as with strikes among airport maintenance engineers, and the Fleet Street machinists who were members of the Amalgamated Union of Engineering Workers. His great adversary in the union was its Roman Catholic, right-wing president, Sir William Carron, whom Birch twice challenged for the presidency. The second attempt in 1967 led Birch to break with the official Communist Party and form his own far-left Communist Party of Great Britain (Marxist-Leninist), which pursued an active Maoist

line. Birch was frequently invited to China and was the only British trade union leader to have an audience with Mao Zedong. His defection from the Communist Party was triggered when the party chiefs decided to back Hugh Scanlon (an ex-communist) rather than Birch to challenge Carron, on the ground that Scanlon stood a better chance of success. This proved correct, but Birch never forgave the Communist Party—nor Hugh Scanlon.

Birch's election in 1975 to the general council of the Trades Union Congress (TUC) meant that its leadership for the first time included a Maoist campaigner, someone who publicly declared himself indifferent to democracy and who argued the need for a workers' revolution which, he recognized, might well be 'ugly, protracted and bloody' (*The Independent*, 17 June 1994). Birch's TUC colleagues were mostly bemused by him, regarding him as a 'one-off' character whose enigmatic performances at their meetings evoked a mixed response of irritation and mock-amusement, coupled with remarks about his being 'the delegate for Albania'—a reference to Birch's frequent visits to that country, when it was China's lone European ally. Birch remained studiously unaffected by the attitude of his TUC colleagues, whom he frequently described as 'an effing bore' (ibid.). He was a member of the Energy Commission from 1977 to 1979.

The most memorable vignette of Birch's negotiating prowess came from one of his innumerable sessions with Ford management. Discussions on pay, working hours, and conditions were stalling when Ford management offered an unexpected concession on death benefits. At this point Birch started tapping the underside of the table and moaning. The company's chief negotiator looked across the table with astonishment and asked, 'Mr Birch, whatever is the matter? Are you all right?' Birch grinned and replied, 'I am in touch with my dead members on the other side. They want to know if your kind offer is retrospective' (*The Independent*, 17 June 1994). The meeting convulsed in laughter—but Birch had made his point.

Birch retired in 1979. His final days were spent trying to sustain his Maoist Communist Party and developing party bookshops in London and Brighton. He died of heart failure at Edgware General Hospital, Edgware, London, on 2 June 1994, survived by his three sons. The Communist Party of Great Britain (Marxist-Leninist) collapsed soon after his death.

Birch was a modern embodiment of the classic, rebellious, working-class figure who might have stepped out of a Dickens novel (for his cockney wit) or a Jack London epic (for his heroically eccentric political activities). This small, almost diminutive, figure with a mischievously wistful smile and a slow, strolling, languid gait which, along with his hunched shoulders, always appeared to make him look older than he was, became one of the most extraordinary mavericks on the trade union scene during the 1960s and 1970s. A revolutionary communist, a formidable trade union negotiator, a gentle, kind man, even if given to occasional volcanic outbursts of righteous anger at the follies of ordinary capitalist mortals, and a man of outstanding literary knowledge—he was an expert on

Henry James, Voltaire, Victor Hugo, Smollett, Fielding, and Upton Sinclair, as well as Marx—and a music buff who could converse on the qualities of Beethoven and Mozart as well as on most of the great jazz composers, he represented a special category of Englishness: he was, in Arnold Bennett's term, 'a card'. He was full of the paradoxes of his age, as intellectually agile as a professor and as sharp as a hunted fox, as warm to friends as he was icy to the class enemies, full of wit, humour, and self-parody as he sparred with friend and foe. Inevitably his personality was touched with a deep sadness as, towards the end of his life, he recognized the corrosiveness of much that he had once held supreme. Shortly before his death he confessed that, as he looked across the global political scene, he possessed one unshaken personal satisfaction and consolation: 'I am a skilled craftsman, a tool-maker, and I am proud to be classed as a skilled worker. It is very important to me that I know I can make things with these hands while the world is going mad' (personal knowledge). It was a penetrating confession.   GEOFFREY GOODMAN

Sources Trade Union Congress annual conference reports · minutes of the Trade Union Congress general council, 1975–9 · J. L. Jones, *Union man: an autobiography* (1986) · N. Fishman, *The British communist party and the trade unions, 1933–45* (1995) · W. Hannington, *Unemployed struggles, 1919–1936* (1937) · *The Times* (9 June 1994) · *The Guardian* (8 June 1994) · *The Independent* (17 June 1994) · *The Independent* (22 June 1994) · *WWW, 1991–5* · private information (2004) · personal knowledge (2004) · b. cert. · m. cert. · d. cert.
Likenesses D. McPhee, photograph, 1977, repro. in *The Guardian* · Harrison, photograph, News International Syndication, London [*see illus.*] · photograph, repro. in *The Times* · photograph, repro. in *The Independent* (17 June 1994)
Wealth at death under £125,000: administration with will, 23 June 1995, *CGPLA Eng. & Wales*

Birch, Sir Richard James Holwell (1803–1875), army officer in the East India Company, came of a well-known Anglo-Indian family, and was the son of Richard Comyns Birch, Bengal civil service, and his wife, Frances Jane, daughter of William Rider, sheriff of Calcutta; he was a grandson of John Zephaniah Holwell, Bengal civil service (author of the famous account of his sufferings in the Black Hole of Calcutta). Birch was born in Calcutta on 26 January 1803 and educated at Cheam School, Surrey (under the Revd James Wilding). He received a commission as an ensign in the 26th Bengal native infantry in January 1821, and studied at Trinity College, Cambridge, in 1823–4 before resuming his army career. His numerous relations in India ensured his rapid promotion and almost continuous service on the staff. He married at Delhi on 2 November 1831 Elizabeth Cuninghame, daughter of Sir Jeremiah Bryant (1783–1845).

After acting as deputy judge-advocate-general at Meerut, and as assistant secretary in the military department at Calcutta, Birch was appointed judge-advocate-general to the forces in Bengal in 1841. In this capacity he accompanied the army in the First Anglo-Sikh War (1845–6), was mentioned in dispatches, and was promoted lieutenant-colonel. In the Second Anglo-Sikh War (1849) he was appointed to the temporary command of a brigade after the battle of Chilianwala. He distinguished himself at the

battle of Gujrat and was made a CB in 1849; he continued to serve as brigadier-general in Sir Colin Campbell's campaign in the Kohat Pass in 1850. He then reverted to his appointment at headquarters, and in 1852 received the important post of secretary to the Indian government in the military department. He was promoted colonel in 1854, major-general in May 1858, and still held the secretaryship when the Indian mutiny broke out in 1857. His services at this time were most valuable, though he never left Calcutta, for his thorough knowledge of the duties of his office and his long official experience enabled him to give valuable advice to Lord Canning, the governor-general, and to Sir Colin Campbell when he arrived to become commander-in-chief. These services were recognized by a KCB in 1860, and in 1861 he left India. In the following year Birch was promoted lieutenant-general and retired on full pay. In 1868 he married Mary, daughter of Captain George P. Burden. On 25 February 1875 he died at Venice, aged seventy-two, his wife surviving him.

H. M. STEPHENS, *rev.* JAMES FALKNER

Sources *Army List* · *The Times* (10 March 1875) · *Hart's Army List* · *East-India Register* · V. C. P. Hodson, *List of officers of the Bengal army, 1758–1834*, 1 (1927) · Venn, *Alum. Cant.* · Boase, *Mod. Eng. biog.*
Likenesses photograph, *c*.1865, priv. coll.
Wealth at death under £200: administration with will, 21 April 1875, *CGPLA Eng. & Wales*

Birch, Samuel (1620/21–1680), ejected minister and schoolmaster, was baptized in Manchester on 18 February 1621, a younger son of Samuel Birch (*d.* in or after 1648) of Ardwick Manor, Manchester, and Mary (*d.* 1659/60), daughter of Ralph Smith of Doblane House, Lancashire; his elder brother was John *Birch (1615–1691). He matriculated from Brasenose College, Oxford, on 3 March 1637, aged sixteen. During the civil war he held a commission as a captain in the parliamentarian army 'but when he found Things were run to extremity, he quitted it and returned to Oxford' (*Calamy rev.*, 356) where on 18 July 1655 he was created MA from St Mary Hall and on 11 October became chaplain to Corpus Christi College. Some time during this period he married Mary, with whom he had a son and five daughters. On 22 September 1658 the board of triers, which examined candidates for the ministry during the interregnum, appointed him to the second portion of the vicarage of Bampton, Oxfordshire. He was ejected in 1662, but stayed in the parish, renting the vicarage and preaching on Sunday nights. The Five-Mile Act, which forbade ejected nonconformist ministers from preaching within 5 miles of their former parishes, forced him to move in May 1664 to a house in Shilton, Berkshire, just over 5 miles away.

By 1665 Birch had opened a 'conventicling school' for the sons of dissenter parents who feared to send them to the university. It was held in a house provided by local gentlemen and belonging to one of them, and was so popular that by 1679 'no chamber was to be had without three beds in a room' and many of the scholars 'lay together' in the same bed (*Portland MSS*, 364). Among his students were several future government ministers, sons of 'socially eminent and politically active puritan families' (Beddard,

354). They included Robert Harley, later earl of Oxford, Thomas, later marquess of Wharton and Simon, first Viscount Harcourt. It was said that fourteen MPs in one session of Queen Anne's parliaments had been his pupils.

Despite presentments to the bishop of Oxford for unlicensed teaching and absence from communion, and constant harassment by some magistrates, Birch continued to teach until a few weeks before his death. He owed his survival partly to his appointment as chaplain to Philip, fourth Baron Wharton, a nonconformist sympathizer, and partly to support from the local gentry. Following the declaration of indulgence of 1672 he was granted a licence to preach in his own house. Birch died at Shilton on 22 January 1680 leaving land and property in Openshaw, Manchester, and Lefield, Oxfordshire, to his widow, Mary, and his son, Samuel, and substantial sums to his unmarried daughters; he was buried at Shilton. His son, born soon before his ejection from Bampton, had matriculated at St Edmund Hall, Oxford, in June 1679.

JOAN A. DILS

Sources Calamy rev., 356–7 · W. A. L. Vincent, The grammar schools: their continuing tradition, 1660–1714 (1969), 206–7 · will, 1680, PRO, PROB 11/362/14 · R. A. Beddard, 'Restoration Oxford and the making of the protestant establishment', Hist. U. Oxf. 4: 17th-cent. Oxf., 803–62 · The manuscripts of his grace the duke of Portland, 10 vols., HMC, 29 (1891–1931), vol. 3, pp. 324, 364 · G. L. Turner, ed., Original records of early nonconformity under persecution and indulgence, 2 (1912), 416, 944 · parish registers, Bampton, Oxfordshire, 1538–1695, Oxfordshire Archives, PAR/16/R1 · parish registers, Bampton, Oxfordshire, 1653–97, Oxfordshire Archives, PAR/16/R2 · parish register of Shilton, Oxfordshire, 1662–81, Oxfordshire Archives, Par Shilton d1 · private information (2004) [Berkshire Family History Society] · J. P. Ferris, 'Birch, John', HoP, Commons, 1660–90, 1.653–60

Archives Mansfield College, Oxford, MSS 'Book of Prayers' | Bodl. Oxf., letters to Lord Wharton

Wealth at death messuage, tenement, and lands in Openshaw, Manchester; cash bequests £350 but in future at 'staggered' dates, from Openshaw lands profits: will, 1680, PRO, PROB 11/362/14

Birch, Samuel (1757–1841), politician, playwright, and pastrycook, was born in London on 8 November 1757. He was the son of Lucas Birch, who carried on the business of a pastrycook and confectioner at 15 Cornhill, an area of the City of London long associated with food production, the street name deriving from a corn market that once stood on the site. The business was established in the reign of George I by a Mr Horton, the immediate predecessor of Lucas Birch. Samuel Birch was educated at a private school kept by Mr Crawford at Newington Butts, and on leaving school was apprenticed to his father. Early in life, in 1778, he married the daughter of Dr John Fordyce, with whom he had a family of thirteen children.

Samuel Birch was elected one of the common council on 21 December 1781, and in 1789 became deputy of the Cornhill ward. In May 1807 he was elected alderman of the Candlewick ward in the place of Alderman Hankey. When young he devoted much of his leisure time to study and the improvement of his literary taste; he was a frequent attendant of a debating society which met in one of the large rooms formerly belonging to the King's Arms tavern, Cornhill. In politics he was a strenuous supporter of Pitt's administration, though he vigorously opposed the repeal of the Test and Corporation Acts. He became a frequent speaker at the common council meetings. When he first proposed the formation of volunteer regiments at the outbreak of the French Revolution, not a single common councilman supported him. Subsequently, when the measure was adopted, he became the lieutenant-colonel commandant of the 1st regiment of Loyal London volunteers. The speech which he delivered in the Guildhall on 5 March 1805 against the Roman Catholic petition was published in that year and was severely criticized in an article entitled 'Deputy Birch and others on the Catholic claims', which appeared in the Edinburgh Review (10.124–36). It was, however, highly commended by the king, and the freedom of the city of Dublin was twice voted him at the midsummer quarter assembly of the corporation of that city on 19 July 1805 and 18 July 1806, for his advocacy of the protestant ascendancy in Ireland. In 1807 he published the related Speech in the Common Council on the Admission of Papists to Hold Commissions in the Army.

In 1811 Birch was appointed one of the sheriffs of London, and on 9 November 1814 he entered on his duties as lord mayor. Tory though he was, he opposed the Corn Bill of 1815, and presided at a meeting of the livery in common hall on 23 February 1815, when he made a vigorous attack on the intended prohibition of the free importation of foreign corn. The course he took on this occasion was commemorated by a medal struck in his honour, on the obverse side of which is the bust of the lord mayor, and on the reverse a representation of a wheatsheaf, with the legend 'Free Importation, Peace and Plenty'. During his mayoralty the marble statue of George III by Chantrey, the inscription on which was written by Birch, was placed in the council chamber of Guildhall. Almost his last act as lord mayor was to lay the foundation-stone of the London Institution in Finsbury Circus (then called the Amphitheatre, Moorfields) on 4 November 1815. In addition to his political and literary careers, Birch ran the family catering business aided by his nephew George Ring. The firm provided the catering for the lavish Waterloo Feast held during Birch's mayoralty. In 1836 Birch sold the business to the firm of Ring and Brymer who continued the catering connection as specialist caterers to Trusthouse Forte.

Birch was a man of considerable literary attainments, and he wrote a number of poems and musical dramas, of which the Adopted Child was by far the most successful. A musical farce containing in Act IV a song that became an immediate popular favourite, the play was published in 1795, the year of its first performance. It was also performed in 1796, 1797, and 1799. Birch's plays were frequently produced at Drury Lane, Covent Garden, and Haymarket theatres in the 1790s. Among his other published dramas was The Smugglers (1796), a melodrama first produced at Drury Lane on 13 April 1796, and thereafter at Drury Lane in 1797, 1798, and 1799. The play was Birch's most popular melodrama and a box-office success. Birch also wrote the following dramatic pieces, which were never published: The Mariners (1793), a musical farce first produced at the opera house in the Haymarket on 10 May 1793; *The Packet Boat, or, A Peep behind the Veil* (1794), a farce first produced at Covent Garden on 13 May 1794; *Fast Asleep* (1797), a musical farce based on James Powell's *The Narcotic* and produced at Drury Lane on 28 October 1795; and *Albert and Adelaide, or, The Victim of Constancy* (1798), a melodrama first produced at Covent Garden on 11 December 1798. *Albert and Adelaide* was unfavourably reviewed as a species of pantomime and dumb show in the *Monthly Mirror* of December 1798. C. Beeches Hogan, editor of *The London Stage*, has disputed the claim made in the playbill that the play was 'Taken from the German' and credits the source to *The Captive of Spilburg*. In his dramatic works Birch collaborated closely with the composer Thomas Attwood who provided much of the music for his plays.

In addition to his literary career as a playwright, Birch was also a sometime actor and writer of sermons. His varied activity was the subject of a clever skit, in which a French visitor to London meeting with 'Birch the pastry-cook' in such different capacities as Guildhall-orator, militia-colonel, poet, and so on returned to France, believing him to be the emperor of London.

Birch retired from the court of aldermen in December 1839, and died at his house, 107 Guilford Street, London, on 10 December 1841, aged eighty-four.

G. F. R. Barker, *rev.* Gail Baylis

Sources C. B. Hogan, ed., *The London stage, 1660–1800*, pt 5: *1776–1800* (1968) · *The Times* (13 Dec 1841) · *BL cat.* · A. Milford, *Lord mayors of London: 800 years* (1989) · J. Stow, *A survey of London*, rev. edn (1603); repr. with introduction by C. L. Kingsford as *A survey of London*, 2 vols. (1908); repr. with addns (1971), bk 1, p.187 · D. E. Baker, *Biographia dramatica, or, A companion to the playhouse*, rev. I. Reed, new edn, rev. S. Jones, 3 vols. in 4 (1812) · d. cert.
Archives Hunt. L., Larpent MS
Likenesses W. Ridley, stipple, pubd 1805 (after S. Drummond), BM, NPG · oils, 1877, GL

Birch, Samuel (1813–1885), Egyptologist, was born on 2 or 3 November 1813 in London, eldest son of the Revd Samuel Birch (1780?–1848), rector of St Mary Woolnoth, later a prebendary of St Paul's Cathedral and vicar of Little Marlow, Buckinghamshire, and his wife, Margaret, daughter of William Browning, of Woburn Place, London. His grandfather, Samuel *Birch (1757–1841), was a dramatist and pastry-cook, and had been lord mayor of London in 1814–15. His father had a distinguished academic record, having been for many years professor of geometry at Gresham College, London. Surprisingly, therefore, young Samuel, after an early education at preparatory schools in Greenwich and Blackheath, followed by five years at Merchant Taylors' School (1826–31), did not proceed to university.

At school Birch began his studies of Chinese, and the promise of a position in China may have led him to forgo university. He did not, however, go to China, but briefly held an appointment in the Public Record Office before becoming an assistant in the department of antiquities in the British Museum in January 1836. His initial task, to catalogue the Chinese coins in the museum, led his grandfather to comment: 'Good God, Sammy! has the family come to that?' (*DNB*). On 22 July 1839 he married Charlotte Francis, daughter of Samuel Frederick *Gray, a botanist and pharmacologist.

Chinese studies remained important throughout Birch's life, but Egyptology captured his main attention. He is best remembered as one of the first British Egyptologists. He began his Egyptological studies before he entered the British Museum, when Egyptology was in its infancy. Of British scholars, only John Gardner Wilkinson had as yet shown a proper comprehension of the ancient Egyptian language. His great work, *The Manners and Customs of the Ancient Egyptians*, was published the year after Birch entered the museum, and it was appropriate that Birch should produce a revised edition in 1878, adding much new material.

When Birch joined the department of antiquities it covered the whole of the ancient world, coins, the Orient, and medieval material. Birch ranged widely in all fields, as required, and his early non-Egyptological publications included: *Catalogue of the Greek and Etruscan Vases* (1851), with C. T. Newton; *History of Ancient Pottery and Porcelain* (1858); *Inscriptions in the Cuneiform Character* (1851), revised by S. Birch and Sir H. C. Rawlinson; and *Inscriptions in the Himyaritic Character* (1863). A large number of shorter articles on coins and classical and British antiquities appeared in the appropriate learned journals.

Edward Hawkins, the benign keeper of antiquities, generously nurtured young talent, and he especially encouraged Birch's numismatic interests. In Egyptological matters Hawkins's support was crucial. From the outset of his museum career Birch's interest lay primarily in the Egyptian language, in the translation of and commentary on texts, and especially in the reading of Egyptian texts on papyri, many of which were written in the little-understood hieratic and demotic scripts. When Birch entered the museum the holdings of papyri were preserved in the department of manuscripts. Birch sought them out and in 1838 initiated their publication. Between 1841 and 1844 three large fascicles of *Select Papyri in the Hieratic Character* appeared, with introductory remarks by Birch. This pioneering work was the first of many issued under Birch's editorship. Meanwhile, undoubtedly at his instigation, all the ancient Egyptian papyri were transferred to the department of antiquities, where they could more easily be studied by Birch, who alone had the competence to do so. He did not neglect the main collections of Egyptian antiquities in the museum, and in 1842–3 he co-operated with Joseph Bonomi and Francis Arundale in producing *The Gallery of Antiquities Selected from the British Museum*.

In 1844 Birch became an assistant keeper in the department of antiquities. When Hawkins retired in 1860 the department was subdivided, and in 1861 Birch became keeper of oriental, British, and medieval antiquities. In 1866, after further departmental division, he became keeper of oriental antiquities, and from then until his death he was able to concentrate his scholarly efforts on Egyptian antiquities. He continued the publication of important texts in *Inscriptions in the Hieratic and Demotic Character* (1868) and *Facsimile of an Egyptian Hieratic Papyrus of the Reign of Ramesses III* (1876), the latter concerning the longest known ancient papyrus. He contributed translations of many important historical texts to the series *Records of the Past* (1874–81). In 1883 he produced an influential commentary on the important Northumberland collection, *Catalogue of the Collections of Egyptian Antiquities at Alnwick Castle*. His articles in learned journals continued unabated, and he made important contributions to many works of others, not least the English translation of C. C. J. Bunsen's *Egypt's Place in Universal History*. He revised the 1867 edition, including in the last volume his own translation of the 'Book of the dead', an Egyptian grammar, and an Egyptian dictionary. In these he provided the first useful working tools for English-speaking students of ancient Egypt.

The founding in 1870 of the Society of Biblical Archaeology was largely Birch's achievement, and for the rest of his life he supported it by public lectures and by contributing regularly to its *Transactions* and *Proceedings*. He did not welcome the establishment of the Egypt Exploration Fund in 1882, objecting to what he called sentimental archaeology directed at a gullible public. Undoubtedly he feared the competition to his society offered by a popularly based organization mounting glamorous excavations in Egypt. His fears, if they were such, were in the end justified, and his society was wound up after the First World War. The Egypt Exploration Society (as the fund had become) continued to flourish throughout the twentieth century.

All sources agree that Birch, in addition to being a scholar of the first importance, was a public servant devoted to his duties, and a man of extraordinary kindliness and generosity. He was free from malice and worldly ambition. He was a desk scholar who was content to work on the material in the museum, or sent to him for study. He never went to Egypt. Sir Ernest Budge, himself a young recruit into Birch's department, wrote with great affection in *By Nile and Tigris* (1920):

> His greyish-green eyes were deep-set, and nothing escaped them, and when he was moved to mirth they laughed before the muscles of his mouth relaxed. … His gait was that of a man whose thoughts travel faster than his feet, and the length and quickness of his strides indicated with more than ordinary clearness the working of his mind at the moment. (1.20)

The epigraph on Birch's gravestone in Highgate cemetery encapsulates his modesty and fame: 'Samuel Birch D.C.L., LL.D, F.S.A., Etc., Etc., The Egyptologist'. He was much honoured for his services to scholarship. He was a corresponding member of the Archaeological Institute of Rome (1839), the Berlin Academy (1851), the Academy of Herculaneum (1852), and the Académie des Inscriptions et Belles-Lettres (1861). He was an honorary LLD of the universities of Aberdeen (1862) and Cambridge (1875), DCL of Oxford University (1876), and honorary fellow of the Queen's College, Oxford (1877). Among numerous foreign awards, he received from the emperor of Germany the cross second class of the order of the Crown (1874), and from the emperor of Brazil the order of the Knight of the Rose (1875).

Samuel Birch died at his home, 64 Caversham Road, Camden Town, London, on 27 December 1885, and was buried at Highgate new (east) cemetery. He was survived by his second wife, Sarah (1839–1908), several daughters, and three sons, one of whom, Walter de Gray Birch, was an assistant in the department of manuscripts at the British Museum. His first wife, Charlotte, predeceased him by many years.   T. G. H. JAMES

Sources E. A. W. Budge, 'Memoir of Samuel Birch, LL.D., D.C.L., F.S.A., &c., President', *Transactions of the Society of Biblical Archaeology*, 9 (1886), 1–41 [incl. bibliography] · *Biographical notices of Dr. Samuel Birch from the British and foreign press* (1886) [with an introduction by Walter de Gray Birch, F.S.A., incl. bibliography] · E. A. W. Budge, *By Nile and Tigris* (1920), 1.6–37 · *DNB* · *Brighton Guardian* (6 Jan 1886)
Archives AM Oxf., notebooks · BM | BL, corresp. with Sir Austen Layard, Add. MSS 38942–39038 · Bodl. Oxf., corresp. with Sir J. G. Wilkinson · CUL, corresp. with Joseph Bonomi
Likenesses bas-relief medallion head, 1846, repro. in *Biographical notices of Dr. Samuel Birch*, frontispiece · bas-relief head on gravestone, Highgate cemetery, London · oils, BM · wood-engraving, NPG; repro. in *ILN* (16 Jan 1886)
Wealth at death £4461 7s. 5d.: resworn probate, May 1887, *CGPLA Eng. & Wales* (1886)

Birch, Samuel John [*known as* Lamorna Birch] (1869–1955), painter, was born on 7 June 1869 at The Cottage, Rudgrave Square, Egremont, Cheshire, the eldest of the nine children of John Birch (1839–1900), house painter and decorator, and Elizabeth Glover (1845–*c*.1930). His early years were spent mostly in Manchester, where his family lived in acute poverty. He left board school at the age of twelve to work for an oilcloth manufacturer in the city. An eleven-hour working day left little time for art, but his mother encouraged him and at the age of fifteen he exhibited at the Manchester City Art Gallery. When he was nineteen he moved to Halton, beside the River Lune, near Lancaster, where he worked in a mill and lodged with a former river bailiff who taught him all he knew about fishing and the countryside. Encouraged by the philanthropic Storey family at Lancaster, he painted steadily at weekends and in 1892 settled in Cornwall as a full-time painter. The following year, while still only self-taught, he exhibited the first of 237 pictures at the Royal Academy, in London.

Birch set up on his own in the countryside a few miles west of Newlyn, lodging with a farmer at the head of the Lamorna valley. The valley, where he lived for sixty-three years and where he founded his own colony of artists and writers, provided him with his working name, Lamorna Birch, which he adopted to avoid confusion with the painter Lionel Birch, and from 1896 he signed his work 'S. J. Lamorna Birch'. He became one of a second generation of Newlyn painters attracted to Cornwall in the 1890s by *plein-air* artists working in the circle of Stanhope Alexander Forbes, founder of the Newlyn art colony. Urged by Forbes to study in France, Birch spent the first

Samuel John Birch [Lamorna Birch] **(1869–1955)**, by James
Ardern Grant, 1946

seven months of 1896 at the Académie Colarossi in Paris.
In January 1902 he married his pupil, Emily Houghton Vivian (1869–1944), and moved to Flagstaff Cottage, overlooking Lamorna Cove. Two daughters, Elizabeth Lamorna
Birch (1904–1990) and Joan Birch (1909–1996) were born
there.

Birch painted in oils and watercolours, working with
plein-air realism in the Barbizon tradition. He liked to
begin work soon after day-break, cycling into the countryside where he stored his canvases in the barns of farmer
friends. He had a strong eye for colour and atmospheric
detail and was adept in observing the fleeting effects of
light and shade. Estate owners who invited him as their
house guest to give painting lessons introduced him to
their friends and thus opened up lucrative outlets for his
art. He went on to enjoy the attention of wealthy patrons
such as Sir John Roberts, the Scottish tweed manufacturer, and Ranald Valentine, of the Dundee art-publishing
house, both of whom acquired large collections of his
work. Birch worked with terrier-like energy, producing
about 20,000 pictures of all kinds, including etchings,
over a period of seventy years. His pictures are represented in collections throughout Britain and overseas, notably in the former dominions where his work was
admired for its quintessential Englishness. *Cornwall*,
painted near Lamorna, was purchased in 1911 for the
Brown memorial collection in Providence, Rhode Island,

and in 1913 *Wengen Heights* was acquired for the Canadian
national collection.

Birch painted water with the understanding of both artist and fisherman and was fascinated by the force and
thrust of swollen rivers, with water creaming around
rocks and boulders or touching river-banks lined with
snow. Sometimes he painted himself in an angling pose or
used artist friends such as Robert Morson Hughes and
Peter Moffat Lindner as models. About 1918 he produced a
great number of pencil drawings touched in lightly with
colour, and they included some outstanding sculptural
compositions of hill and rock formations. His obituarist in
The Times thought that these pictures were technically his
most successful, saying that 'in them his charm of line
found unhindered expression' (8 Jan 1955). At the peak of
his powers in the 1920s Birch's enthusiasm for bold juxtapositions of colour was given full rein. His river pictures
and a love of landscapes with deep, dramatic skies and
gilded clouds made him hugely popular, and tens of thousands of greetings cards and fine-art prints were produced
from his work. In 1938 his *St Ives, Cornwall* (Tate collection)
was bought for the nation under the Chantrey bequest. He
was a clever businessman, but his exploitation of popular
themes such as snow and sunsets suggested that he was
more aware of his customers than of what made good art.
Moreover, his large output meant inevitably that inferior
work reached the market under his signature.

Birch travelled widely. His visit to New Zealand in 1936–
7, the first by a Royal Academician, brought him up
against nationalist sentiment among artists strongly
opposed to his presence in their country, but he stoically
survived their attacks. He was elected a member of the
Royal British Colonial Society of Artists in 1905, and the
Royal Society of Painters in Water Colours and the Royal
West of England Academy in 1914, and became an ARA in
1926 and an RA in 1934. He had a neat pointed beard and
wore small round spectacles and heavy tweed suits with
knickerbocker-style breeches, which gave him the bearing less of an artist than of a well-to-do country doctor. In
keeping with his love of angling he often wore an old felt
hat covered in fishing-flies and he readily acknowledged
his idyllic life at Lamorna where he worked from a studio
beside a trout stream. In his autobiography, *An Artist's Life*,
Sir Alfred Munnings said of Birch: 'When he was not painting he was fishing; when he was not fishing he was painting' (1950, 295). He was boyish and fun-loving, and
enjoyed tap-dancing and entertaining friends with his
pranks and jokes, but underneath was a serious painter
determined to succeed through hard work. After suffering
a mild stroke Lamorna Birch died at his home on 7 January
1955. He was buried on 10 January in the old cemetery at
Paul, near Newlyn.   AUSTIN WORMLEIGHTON

Sources A. Wormleighton, *A painter laureate: Lamorna Birch and his
circle* (1995) · Lamorna, Cornwall, Lamorna Birch estate and family
archives · RA · *The Times* (8 Jan 1955) · L. Knight, *Lamorna Birch as I
knew him* (1956) · CGPLA Eng. & Wales (1955) · street directories,
Egremont, Cheshire · private information (2004)
Archives FILM BBC television interview Easter 1953
Likenesses L. Knight, group portrait, oils, 1913, U. Nott. · J. A.
Grant, pastel drawing, 1946, NPG [*see illus.*] · portraits, priv. coll.

Wealth at death £26,672 2s. od.: probate, 30 March 1955, *CGPLA Eng. & Wales*

Birch, Thomas (*bap.* 1608, *d.* 1678), parliamentarian army officer, was baptized on 5 June 1608 at Eccles, Lancashire, the only son of George Birch (*d.* 1611) of Birch, near Manchester, and his wife, Anne, daughter of Ellis Hey of Monkshall in the parish of Eccles. On 21 October 1623 at Warrington he married Alice (*d.* 1697), eldest daughter of Thomas Brooke of Norton, Cheshire. They had five sons and five daughters.

Although the Birches owned a substantial house and property assessed at £250 a year in 1641 the influential position which Thomas Birch acquired in Lancashire during the civil war and the Commonwealth was based first and foremost upon his success as a military commander. In March 1642 he was appointed by parliament a deputy lieutenant in Lancashire under the lord lieutenant, Lord Wharton. In June he received a commission from Wharton to raise a regiment of foot. Regarded as one of the 'captains of best rank and quality' (Beamont, 9), Birch was present in Manchester on 15 July when Lord Strange (later the earl of Derby) tried to secure the town for the king. Prompt action by Birch, who assembled his men in the market place, maintained parliamentarian control. During the action Birch took refuge under a 'cart of gorsses' (ibid., 6) and was thereafter known as 'Lord Derby's carter'—a sobriquet which, according to nineteenth-century writers, explained Birch's malice towards Lord Derby and his family. In October he was present at the siege of Manchester, and afterwards he led his company to take possession of Townley Hall, near Burnley. He was promoted major in Colonel Ashton's regiment in December and was involved in the capture of Preston for parliament in February 1643. From here he was sent to occupy Lancaster, which he took without bloodshed, establishing a garrison in the castle. On 15 March Ferdinando, Lord Fairfax made him colonel of a foot regiment, and following Prince Rupert's unsuccessful attempt upon Liverpool in June 1644 he was appointed governor of this important port.

Four years later Birch was instructed to keep a close eye on the daughters of the earl of Derby. According to one source he subsequently imprisoned them in Liverpool Castle in order to bring pressure to bear upon their father to release certain parliamentarian prisoners. He also persuaded parliament in February 1650 to provide £100 from Derby's sequestered estates to 'repair the garrison of Liverpool' (*JHC*, 2 Feb 1650). In April 1651, faced with the possibility that Charles II might invade England from Scotland by the western route, Birch and the other deputy lieutenants of Lancashire raised a militia force, which joined forces with the regular troops of Colonel Robert Lilburne. On 25 August 1651 they routed Derby's royalist army at Wigan. Birch wrote in jubilation to parliament that there were 'none left in the county competent to make opposition' (Ormerod, 296). In September Derby was put on trial for his life, a possible opportunity for Birch to revenge the insults at Manchester in 1642. However, it seems that though Birch was on the commission to try Derby he did not attend any of the sittings. In November, after the earl's execution, Birch was in joint command of an expedition to secure the Isle of Man, still held by the countess of Derby. The stronghold of Rushen was stormed and the island surrendered, the countess being conveyed to Liverpool Castle and subsequently to Chester for greater security. Early antiquaries, imbued with romantic sensibilities for the ill-fated cavaliers, disapproved of Birch's role in the fall of the house of Stanley and thus he became stigmatized as a 'Parliamentarian of a somewhat brutal type' (*VCH Lancashire*, 4.306).

With the collapse of the traditional leadership within the county community of Lancashire Birch established a remarkable ascendancy, underpinned by parliamentary, administrative, and military office. As a sequestration officer from 1643, he appears to have been very diligent, if a little inflexible. In 1646 he accused the sequestration committee of having made 'divers undue and unwarrantable allowances to wives and children of notorious papists and delinqts' (Blackwood, 114). A similar lack of sympathy for the easy-going habits of his colleagues accounts for his brusque action in removing the clergy of the collegiate church of Manchester who, albeit dissolved in 1643, were still enjoying the perquisites of their estates in 1649. Similarly his infamous intervention in the charitable endeavours of Humphry Chetham—he insisted upon written guarantees for Chetham's proposed charitable use of certain lands sequestered from Derby—was clearly justified.

A member of the county committee from 1645, Birch was an implacable enemy of the king and totally loyal to the republic. In 1649 he was elected MP for Liverpool; one of only four 'recruiters' to the Rump, he was also unique as an army officer. But he was among the sixty men of military rank who sat in Barebone's Parliament, and was called to all three protectorate parliaments, including Richard Cromwell's parliament of 1659. He was among signatories to the remonstrance on being secluded in September 1656. He stood up for the interests of his fellow countrymen, especially on matters of religion and taxation. When Sir William Brereton, the military supremo of the north-west, cast an eye towards Lancashire, to enforce monthly taxation, Colonel Birch spoke out claiming that 'the said order [for monthly assessment] was illegal and the earle of Strafford lost his life for such a like act and that, yor proceedings therein were arbitrary' (Morrill, 147). Such candid perspectives ensured that Birch was briefly imprisoned.

It has been suggested that Birch used his position to enrich himself at the expense of the unfortunate royalists. He was one of six individuals known to have spent over £2000 in purchasing royalist land. But this can be explained by the award made to him by parliament in December 1650 of arrears in pay. This sum—£1805 13s. 8d.—was still owing to him in January 1652 when he was allowed to purchase confiscated lands in lieu. Some of these were crown lands and lands of the earl of Derby, which in the long run were poor investments and were lost to Birch after the Restoration. Later accusations that he purchased property with forged debentures and pocketed parliamentary bonds remain unproven. One of his projects in July 1659 was to secure the materials and site of Liverpool Castle, which the council of state regarded as superfluous, but nothing came of his scheme as Booth's supporters seized the castle in August. The subsequent history of his family provides little evidence to suggest that Birch made their fortune.

Birch's commitment to parliament and the Commonwealth was enhanced by his radical puritanism. He was devoted to the cause of establishing a preaching ministry in Lancashire. Initially he appears to have supported congregationalism, but from the late 1650s he is found promoting ministers of the presbyterian persuasion. During the parliament of 1657–8 he criticized a bill to augment the livings of needy ministers, pointing out that such provision would not help the large parishes of Lancashire, which needed subdivision. In 1640 Thomas Birch had organized a subscription to create an endowment fund for an 'orthodox preaching minister of the gospel' to serve the chapel established at Birch by his grandfather and throughout his life it attracted a number of eminent divines, among them John Wigan, an Independent and a 'painfully godly preaching minister' (Booker, 146) who was at Birch between 1646 and about 1650. The Revd Robert Birch—a member of the family—is referred to in 1659.

Birch was once again active in securing Lancashire during the rising of Sir George Booth in 1659, gathering his forces in the north of the county and, as in 1651, combining with Lilburne. On 22 August he reported to parliament the news of Booth's defeat at Winnington Bridge by Major-General John Lambert. Following Lambert's removal from command of his regiment by the restored Long Parliament in January 1660 the new commander-in-chief, General George Monck, made Birch its colonel in a gesture of gratitude for his loyalty. In the meantime, having secured Manchester, Birch protected the presbyterian minister of its collegiate church, Henry Newcome, whom he had helped choose in 1656 and who had been a supporter of the rising.

Birch's reputation as a supporter of republicanism was such that in 1663 his name was linked with John Wildman and John Hutchinson as one of the leaders of a radical rising in the north. This was apparently untrue, and after the Restoration he passed his life peacefully in Liverpool, where he was joint bailiff in 1664. He lived in a 'very pretty house' (Heywood, *The Moore Rental*, 89) in More Street, which apparently he built himself. Congregationalism at Birch apparently collapsed in 1662, but a family trust had been established to maintain the ministry in the name of Colonel Birch's eldest son, Thomas, and though the colonel took the oath demanded by the Act of Uniformity he continued to support radical preachers at Birch Chapel. In November 1666 Birch was accused of breaking the Conventicles Act by allowing preaching there by a group of wandering ministers from Germany, who denounced all manner of woe in England and urged the congregation to flee to Germany. In 1669 it was said that nonconformists preached there every Sunday. In 1672, following the declaration of indulgence, the celebrated presbyterian preacher Henry Finch (1633–1704) became minister there and, notwithstanding local opposition, he remained, supported by the colonel's widow, Alice, until her death in 1697. Birch died in More Street, 'deaf and in his dotage' (Heywood, *Norris Papers*, 60), on 6 August 1678, when he was said to be aged seventy-one. His heir was his eldest son, Thomas (1629–*c*.1700), known as 'the antiquary'. A younger son, Peter *Birch (1651/2–1710), conformed and became an Anglican clergyman and a tory.

DAVID WHITEHEAD

Sources J. Booker, *The history of the ancient chapel of Birch, in Manchester parish*, Chetham Society, 47 (1859) · *VCH Lancashire*, vol. 4 · E. Bloxap, *The great civil war in Lancashire* (1910) · G. Ormerod, ed., *Tracts relating to military proceedings in Lancashire during the great civil war*, Chetham Society, 2 (1844) · E. Robinson, *A discourse of the warr in Lancashire … betweene King Charles and the parliament*, ed. W. Beamont, Chetham Society, 62 (1864) · *JHC*, 6–7 (1648–59) · R. Halley, *Lancashire, its puritanism and nonconformity*, 2 (1869) · G. E. Aylmer, *The state's servants: the civil service of the English republic, 1649–1660* (1973) · D. Underdown, *Pride's Purge: politics in the puritan revolution* (1971) · J. S. Morrill, *Cheshire, 1630–1660* (1974) · T. Heywood, ed., *The Moore rental*, Chetham Society, 12 (1847) · [H. Newcome], *The autobiography of Henry Newcome*, ed. R. Parkinson, 1, Chetham Society, 26 (1852) · T. Heywood, ed., *The Norris papers*, Chetham Society, 9 (1846) · B. G. Blackwood, *The Lancashire gentry and the great rebellion, 1640–60*, Chetham Society, 3rd ser., 25 (1978)

Wealth at death £184 13s. 11d.: inventory, 14 Aug 1678, Booker, *History of the ancient chapel of Birch*, 97

Birch, Sir Thomas (*c*.1690–1757), judge, was born at Harborne, in Staffordshire, the eldest son of George Birch and his wife, Mary, daughter of Thomas Foster. He was admitted to the Inner Temple in 1709, and called to the bar in 1715, but did not become a bencher until he was a serjeant-elect. He took the coif in company with Chief Justice Lee in 1730, and was one of the last serjeants admitted to Serjeants' Inn, Fleet Street, which the serjeants vacated that year. In 1740 he was appointed one of the king's serjeants, and was knighted for his services in that office after the 1745 uprising. Although he retained a connection with Staffordshire, serving as sheriff in 1745–6, he resided at Southgate, near London. In June 1746 he succeeded Mr Justice Fortescue-Aland as one of the puisne justices of the common pleas, and retained that office until his death. Birch and his wife, Sarah (*d*. 1754), daughter and coheir of John Teshmaker, had three sons and two daughters. On 16 February 1757 Lord Hardwicke wrote to George II that: 'Mr Justice Birch … is dangerously ill, and it is thought cannot recover' (Harris, 3.3); his death followed on 15 March 1757. On 22 March he was buried at Edmonton, Middlesex.

J. H. BAKER

Sources Baker, *Serjeants* · Sainty, *King's counsel* · Sainty, *Judges* · Inner Temple, London · W. Musgrave, *Obituary prior to 1800*, ed. G. J. Armytage, 1, Harleian Society, 44 (1899) · *GM*, 1st ser., 27 (1757), 142 · G. Harris, *The life of Lord Chancellor Hardwicke*, 3 vols. (1847) · F. A. Inderwick and R. A. Roberts, eds., *A calendar of the Inner Temple records*, 5 vols. (1896–1936), vols. 1–3 · D. Lysons, *The environs of London*, 4 vols. (1792–6) · *DNB*

Birch, Thomas (1705–1766), compiler of histories and biographer, was born on 23 November 1705 at Clerkenwell, the eighth of ten children of Joseph Birch (*c*.1667–1730) and his wife, Rebecca (*d*. 1746). In 1700 his parents had moved from Birmingham to London, where Joseph was a coffee mill maker in St George's Court, Clerkenwell. Both Birch's parents were Quakers and he was educated at the school of fellow Friend John Owen in Hemel Hempstead from 1717, and, from 1719, at that of Josiah Welby at Turnbull Street, Clerkenwell. Having sought permission not to enter the family business Birch worked from 1722 as an usher in various schools including Owen's, where he entered a three-year agreement in 1723.

From about 1726 Birch appeared bent upon a career in the established church, abandoning his Quaker roots. He married Hannah, daughter of the Revd Cox, curate of St Botolph without Bishopsgate, in 1728. A son, Joseph, was born on 17 July 1729 but mother and son both died shortly thereafter and were buried in the cemetery of St James's, Clerkenwell. This occasioned Birch's first public literary production, a poem 'On the Death of a Beloved Wife', which appeared in the *Whitehall Evening Post* of 15 November 1729.

At St James's Birch was baptized on 15 December 1730, ordained deacon on 17 January 1731 and priest on 21 December 1731. In 1732 he was presented to the vicarage of Ulting in Essex through the patronage of Sir Philip Yorke, later Lord Chancellor Hardwicke. He also acted as tutor to one of the Yorke sons. (Birch's subsequent career was to depend crucially on Hardwicke family patronage.)

In 1732 Birch was appointed to the *General Dictionary, Historical and Critical*, an expanded version of the earlier English translation of Pierre Bayle's *Dictionnaire historique et critique*. Although he was one of three chief editors Birch undertook the vast majority of the new biographical entries in the ten-volume edition issued from 1734 to 1741. This work was not only a major achievement but also provided numerous contacts in the learned and scientific worlds from whom Birch gained help in his historical work. His election to the Royal Society on 20 February 1735 and to the Society of Antiquaries on 11 December 1735 owed much to these contacts. Separate historical works also grew out of the *General Dictionary*. First came *The Works of Mr John Greaves* (1737) followed by the complete collection of the works of John Milton (1738) and the massive seven-volume compilation of the state papers of John Thurloe (1742).

Under Hardwicke family patronage Birch gained a number of church appointments: the living of Llandewi Felffre in Pembrokeshire in 1743, the rectory of St Michael Woodstrett at Epsom in 1744, and the living of St Margaret Pattens and St Gabriel Fenchurch in 1746. Birch also took up *in absentia* the living of Debden, near Newport, Essex, in February 1761. He was elected president of Sion College in 1759. Birch neither performed onerous clerical duties nor pursued progressive preferment. As an absentee pluralist his literary employments were regarded as a fulfilment of his duties.

From 1735 Birch was the eyes and ears of first Lord Chancellor Hardwicke and then his eldest son, Philip Yorke (later Lord Royston and second earl of Hardwicke), reporting on court proceedings and debates in the houses of parliament for his patrons as well as attending to numerous miscellaneous duties. In 1741 Philip Yorke commissioned Birch to write him a weekly letter providing news of the London scene during Philip's absences. These letters, written to within a few days of Birch's death, give a sustained account of the literary, scientific, political, and military events of the time. Birch also worked on Philip Yorke's project *The Athenian Letters* (privately printed, 1741–3). His own historical work continued, including *The Works of the Honourable Robert Boyle* (1744), on which much of the work was done by the Revd Henry Miles, *Memoirs of the Reign of Queen Elizabeth* (1754), *Lives and Characters of Illustrious Persons* (1747–52), and *The History of the Royal Society of London* (1756–7).

Birch served as secretary of the Royal Society from 25 January 1752 until November 1765. As part of the Hardwicke circle which exercised considerable influence in the society, Birch was placed at the hub of the London learned world. A major figure in the Society of Antiquaries, of which he had been director (1737–47), he was also an elected trustee on the newly established British Museum. Much scientific business of the day passed across his desk for the *Philosophical Transactions of the Royal Society* but Birch himself contributed only five short communications. Their topics, including a Roman inscription and an account of earth tremors, constitute a typical contribution from a scholar keenly interested in, but not primarily devoted to, natural philosophical inquiry.

When not transcribing, collating, or compiling, Birch enjoyed convivial company. He had pursued the writer Elizabeth Carter in 1738–9 without success and so continued the life of the widower. His gift for conversation and fund of information were widely appreciated. Samuel Johnson, according to Boswell, said: 'Tom Birch is as brisk as a bee in conversation; but no sooner does he take a pen in his hand, than it becomes a torpedo to him, and benumbs all his faculties' (Hill, 1.159). There were kinder estimates of Birch as a writer, but he was undoubtedly a compiler rather than a historian. His strength was the hard graft of collection and compilation, not interpretation or stylish exposition.

Birch died on 19 January 1766 after falling from his horse on the Hampstead Road. His friend Dr William Watson, who was called to him, diagnosed a stroke of apoplexy. Birch was buried in the chancel of St Margaret Pattens, Rood Lane, London, on 23 January 1766. He left his library and manuscripts to the British Museum and stipulated that the income from the residue of his estate be used to supplement the stipends of three under-librarians at the museum.

DAVID PHILIP MILLER

Sources A. E. Gunther, *An introduction to the life of the Rev. Thomas Birch D.D. F.R.S., 1705–1766* (1984) • J. M. Osborn, 'Thomas Birch and the *General dictionary*, 1734–1741', *Modern Philology*, 36 (1938–9), 25–46 • *DNB* • E. Ruhe, 'Birch, Johnson, and Elizabeth Carter: an episode of 1738–39', *Publications of the Modern Language Association of America*, 73 (1958), 491–500 • D. P. Miller, 'The "Hardwicke circle": the whig supremacy and its demise in the 18th-century Royal Society', *Notes and Records of the Royal Society*, 52 (1998), 73–91 • M. B. Hall, 'Henry Miles, FRS (1698–1763) and Thomas Birch, FRS (1705–66)', *Notes and Records of the Royal Society*, 18 (1963), 39–44 • L. M. Knapp, 'Comments on Smollett by the Rev. Dr Thomas Birch', *N&Q*, 210

(1965), 218–21 · T. Birch, *The history of the Royal Society of London*, 4 vols. (1756–7); repr. with introduction by A. R. Hall (1968), vol. 1, pp. xi–xxiv · *Boswell's Life of Johnson*, ed. G. B. Hill, 6 vols. (1887) · J. Almagor, 'The correspondence between Thomas Birch and Philip Yorke as a chronicle of its age: the case of the War of the Austrian Succession (1740–1748)', *Lias*, 21 (1994), 135–79 **Archives** BL, Add. MSS 4101–4478, 6192, 6209, 6226, 6269, 6399, 39826 | BL, corresp. with Lord Hardwicke, Add. MSS 35396–35400 · Yale U., letters to Lord Hailes **Likenesses** oils, 1735, BM · oils, *c.*1735, NPG · J. Wills, oils, 1737, RS · J. Faber, mezzotint, 1741 (after J. Wills, 1737), BL **Wealth at death** see wills, Gunther, *Introduction to the life*, 89

Birch, Thomas Ledlie (1754–1828), minister of the Presbyterian General Synod of Ulster, was born at Birch Grove, Gilford, co. Down, the youngest child of John Birch, linen merchant and farmer, and Jane Ledlie (1716–1791). He graduated MA from Glasgow University in 1772. He was licensed by Dromore presbytery in 1775 and ordained in Saintfield by Belfast presbytery on 21 May 1776. He married a relative, Isabella Ledlie (1760–1836), in December 1783. He was one of the most active ministers in the General Synod of Ulster with a congregation of over 900 families. Many Ulster Presbyterians had ties of kinship with the Americans. During the American War of Independence Birch considered that Great Britain had levied an unnatural war upon colonists, many of whom were his brethren. In 1784 he assisted in the preparation of an address to George Washington by the Yankee Club of Stewartstown, co. Tyrone, expressing satisfaction that the colonists had overthrown the yoke of slavery. Washington sent a favourable reply.

A supporter of the Irish Volunteers, Birch served as chaplain to the local corps, the Saintfield light infantry. When the volunteers were disbanded, and the more radical Society of United Irishmen was founded in Belfast in 1791, he approved its aims of full parliamentary reform and Catholic emancipation, and formed the first United Irish society in co. Down in January 1792. Soon afterwards he reported to Wolfe Tone that he 'had no doubt but that the cause was spreading most rapidly' (*Autobiography of Theobald Wolfe Tone*, 1.116). On Christmas day 1792 his congregation approved resolutions similar to those earlier passed by the Saintfield United Irishmen. A regular attender at synod, in 1793 Birch gave the synodical address *The Obligation upon Christians and Especially Ministers to be Exemplary in their Lives*, which was published in 1794. This was 'a commonplace address, remarkable for nothing, except for fixing on 1848 as the time for the fall of the Papacy' (Witherow, 285). The Society of United Irishmen had been a perfectly legal movement at its inception, but by 1796 it had come under suspicion from the Irish authorities as a subversive military force planning to rebel against the state. The government resorted to draconian military tactics, including flogging of suspects and burning of dwellings. Many United Irish supporters left the movement but Birch remained true to the cause.

In 1796 some dissident members of his congregation, assisted by the Seceders, a rival Presbyterian denomination, established a second Presbyterian congregation in Saintfield. Incensed at their actions Birch penned a scathing pamphlet, *Physicians Languishing under Disease*, in which he denounced all Seceders as cheats, hypocrites, defamers, revilers, and disturbers of the peace of the church. In 1797 eleven members of his congregation were charged with attacking the dwelling of a local yeoman. While attending their trial Birch himself was arrested and charged with high treason. Released on bail to appear before the next assizes, he was acquitted after a lengthy trial. In April 1798 he was again before the courts, this time charged with having offered a bribe to a witness not to prosecute a United Irishman. At trial the person concerned withdrew his evidence and Birch was again discharged.

The first eruption of the United Irish rising in co. Down was at Saintfield on 9 June. Birch was present in the insurgent camp at Creevy Rocks, a hill on the outskirts of the village, on 10 June, which has become known as Pike Sunday. He has been credited with preaching to the rebels, using as his text Ezekiel 9: 1, 'draw near, even every man with his destroying weapon in his hand'. He was arrested three days after the defeat of the rebels at Ballynahinch, and charged with rebellion and treason. At the court martial in Lisburn his enemies confidently expected him to be condemned and executed. However his brother Dr George Birch was captain of the Newtownards yeomen and had fought on the king's side at Saintfield. Dr Birch exerted his influence with the military authorities and it was arranged that if his suspect brother agreed to exile his life would be spared. Birch assented. However he was not released immediately. He was taken to Belfast and put on board a prison ship on Belfast Lough, in company with a number of other arrested United Irishmen. He was released on 16 August 1798 and he sailed from Belfast to New York, arriving in September. Soon afterwards he published a firsthand account of the conditions prevailing in Ireland, and in the Saintfield district in particular, before and during the days of the rebellion, entitled *Letter from an Irish Emigrant*.

In 1799 Birch moved with his family to Philadelphia, having received a call from former members of Saintfield congregation. He failed to persuade the Ohio presbytery to admit him as a member. After further attempts in 1800 and 1801 he appealed to the general assembly, but in vain. Combative as ever, in 1804 he successfully sued the clerk of the Ohio presbytery for slander, a verdict overturned on appeal. He was eventually received by the Baltimore presbytery. He purchased a farm in the vicinity of Washington in 1804, and died at Freeport, Armstrong county, on 12 April 1828. His widow died in Cadiz, Ohio, on 25 November 1836.   W. D. BAILIE

Sources A. McClelland, 'Thomas Ledlie Birch, United Irishman', *Proceedings and Reports of the Belfast Natural History and Philosophical Society*, 2nd ser., 7 (1965), 24–35 · *Belfast News-Letter* (22 June 1798) · court martial of Revd Thomas Ledlie Birch, 18 June 1798, NA Ire., Rebellion MSS, 620/29/5 · R. M. Young, *Ulster in '98: episodes and anecdotes* (1893) · *The autobiography of Theobald Wolfe Tone, 1763–1798*, ed. R. B. O'Brien, 2 vols. (1893) · T. Witherow, *Historical and literary* *memorials of presbyterianism in Ireland, 1731–1800* (1880) · D. A. Wilson, *United Irishmen, United States: immigrant radicals in the early republic* (1998) · J. McConnell and others, eds., *Fasti of the Irish Presbyterian church, 1613–1840*, rev. S. G. McConnell, 2 vols. in 12 pts (1935–51) · *DNB*

Likenesses photograph (after unknown artist), repro. in McClelland, 'Thomas Ledlie Birch', 25

Birch, William Russell (1755–1834), enamel painter and printmaker, was born in Warwickshire on 9 April 1755, the son of Thomas Birch, a noted surgeon, and his wife, Mary Russell. After an unsuccessful start at a Latin school he was taken in by a wealthy cousin, William Russell of Birmingham, who soon apprenticed him to the London jeweller and goldsmith Thomas Jeffreys. Six years later he left to study the painstaking art of enamel painting with Henry Spicer.

Specializing in miniature copies after many of the leading artists of the day, including Sir Joshua Reynolds, Birch made his London début at the Society of Artists exhibition of 1775 with two enamels of classical subjects—one a *Head of Psyche*, the other *Jupiter and Juno*. These were submitted from 'Mr Speaker's 11, Henrietta Street, Covent Garden' (Graves, *Soc. Artists*). By 1787 Birch had moved to the more genteel area of Hampstead Heath. Despite having won Society of Artists' awards in both 1784 and 1785 for technical improvements in enamel painting, he evidently preferred to exhibit at the Royal Academy: between 1781 and 1794 he sent forty-one pieces to its annual exhibitions.

About the same time Birch turned his attention to reproductive printmaking, where he was particularly successful in adapting his skills for translating larger works to a smaller scale. This can be seen in a series of thirty-six stipple engravings of landscapes which—despite its very English subject matter—was given the French title *Délices de la Grande Bretagne* (1788–90). The picturesque quality of these engravings reveals Birch's own particular love of sketching tours in the countryside. Published by Dilly, Edwards, and Manson, *Délices de la Grande Bretagne* sold for 3 guineas in boards and at 5 guineas for proof impressions. These detailed and delicate plates were successful enough to win 250 subscribers, including royal and literary figures as well as other artists.

The turmoil of the French Revolution and the encouragement of some relatives in Maryland induced William Birch and his son Thomas (1779–1851), who later became a noted marine painter, to emigrate to America in 1794. They immediately settled in Philadelphia, where there was a thriving art market: consequently Birch began to send work to various local exhibitions, among them the Columbianum, the Society of Artists, the Pennsylvania Academy, and the Artists' Fund Society. Together with his son, he worked on an engraved series of *Views in Philadelphia* (1800), which remains important as a unique early record of an American city. He also published two views of New York city in 1802 and a subscription series of views of country seats around Philadelphia entitled *The Country Seats of the United States of America* (1808). Although he continued to work as a publisher and printmaker, his reputation, in America, was boosted by the nearly sixty enamels

and miniatures he produced. Commissioned by a Mr Van Stapborst of the Netherlands in 1796, the most celebrated of these was of George Washington, which was thought to be a good though flattering likeness. Birch was also noted among Philadelphia connoisseurs for his large collection of European prints and paintings, which 'enriched Philadelphia's artistic resources' (*ANB*, 803). Such was Birch's success that in 1812 he moved out of town to the country estate of Springland, near Bristol in Philadelphia. He died on 7 August 1834 in Philadelphia.   LUCY PELTZ

Sources C. E. Soltis, 'Birch, William Russell', *ANB* · B. Adams, *London illustrated, 1604–1851* (1983) · G. Meissner, ed., *Allgemeines Künstlerlexikon: die bildenden Künstler aller Zeiten und Völker*, [new edn, 34 vols.] (Leipzig and Munich, 1983–) · Graves, *Artists* · Graves, *RA exhibitors* · Graves, *Soc. Artists* · W. S. Baker, *American engravers and their works* (1875) · G. C. Groce and D. H. Wallace, *The New York Historical Society's dictionary of artists in America, 1564–1860* (1957) · G. C. Williamson, *The history of portrait miniatures*, 2 vols. (1904) · W. Birch, *The life of William Russel Birch 'enamel painter'* written by himself, Historical Society of Philadelphia, Brok MSS, 2 vols.

Birchall, Edward Vivian Dearman (1884–1916), philanthropist, was born on 10 August 1884 at Bowden Hall, Upton St Leonards, Gloucestershire, the son of John Dearman Birchall esquire, and his wife, Emily Jowitt. His mother died at or soon after the birth. Nothing is known about his early life or education, but he became one of the foremost figures in the new philanthropy movement that emerged in Edwardian Britain. He was committed to a new form of philanthropy which provided advice, rather than money, for the poor. This new movement was based upon three principles. First, it wished to organize 'helpers' who would exercise personal responsibility for the poor by visiting and keeping a social casebook on each family. Second, it aimed to act as a clearing-house for cases of need, thus reducing the overlapping charitable effort and rooting out scroungers and beggars. Third, it aimed to form a partnership between private and public bodies through which social work could flow. Collectively, these were the basis of the new philanthropy, the scientific approach to dealing with the poor. Birchall was deeply associated with such principles through the Birmingham Civic Aid Society, the Guild of Help, and the Agenda Club.

The Birmingham Civic Aid Society was formed by Birchall and his associates in 1906. Birchall remained attached to it until drawn away from active participation by the First World War. It was through this organization that he was involved in the burgeoning Guild of Help movement which saw itself as the embodiment of the new philanthropy. Birchall represented the Birmingham Civic Aid Society at most of the annual conferences that it organized between 1908 and 1914, and was particularly prominent at the Sheffield conference held on 4 May 1910. It was at this conference that the decision was taken to form the National Association of the Guild of Help (NAGH), and Birchall was part of the provisional committee which presented the constitution of the new body for acceptance at the annual conference of the Guild of Help at Birmingham in May 1911. At this point forty guilds joined the NAGH and eighteen others considered their position. Birchall became part-time honorary secretary of the

NAGH, a post which he retained until the First World War, combining it occasionally with the post of honorary treasurer, as he did from 1914 to 1915. Having volunteered for the army in 1915 he relinquished this post, becoming president of the NAGH. However, when he gained a commission as captain in the army he gave up his post as honorary treasurer to F. B. Bourdillon and his post as president to H. B. Saint.

Birchall was deeply concerned at the health and social well-being of Britain and, in February 1911, helped form the Agenda Club, of which he became honorary secretary. The Agenda Club was an organization of men in all parts of the country who realized that 'all is not well with England' (Laybourn, 90). Its members saw themselves as the English samurai, inviting a Japanese official to their first annual meeting, and proclaiming respect for 'these Samurai, careless of material gain' (ibid.). They further reflected that 'This civic heroism, so much less common then, as experience proves, than the high ardours of military heroism is, we take it, the point which the Agenda Club wished to symbolise' (ibid.). It was the Agenda Club which appealed for guilds and other charitable organizations to focus upon health by holding one week in the year—28 April to 4 May 1912 being the first—as a week when public health measures would be discussed in towns throughout the country. In 1912 the idea was taken up by ten London boroughs and thirty provincial towns.

Birchall was given the commission of captain in the summer of 1915 in the Oxfordshire and Buckinghamshire light infantry. He died of wounds received in action, in France, on 10 August 1916, and was buried in a war grave near Le Touquet. For having entered the enemy's trenches and refused help, although dangerously wounded, until the position was firmly held, he was appointed DSO. In his will he left £1000 to introduce new schemes for the Guild of Help: part of the proceeds were to be used to endow an annual lecture, the first series of which was to be delivered at the universities of Oxford, London, and Birmingham, with which Birchall had been connected. It was partly out of Birchall's efforts and legacy that the National Council of Social Service was formed in 1919, the main objective of which was the formulation of national policies of voluntary work and co-operation with the state.

KEITH LAYBOURN

Sources K. Laybourn, *The Guild of Help and the changing face of Edwardian philanthropy* (1994) • M. Brasnett, *Voluntary social action: a history of the National Council of Social Service, 1919–1969* (1969) • O'M. Creagh and E. M. Humphris, *The V.C. and D.S.O.: a complete record*, 3 vols. [1920–24] • b. cert. • d. cert. • *CGPLA Eng. & Wales* (1917) • E. Macadam, *The new philanthropy* (1934) • private information (2004)
Wealth at death £45,815 2s. 10d.: probate, 12 Feb 1917, *CGPLA Eng. & Wales*

Birchensha, John (*c.*1605–1681?), musical theorist and teacher, was (according to Flood, 214) a son of Sir Ralph Birchensha (*c.*1565?–1622?) and his wife, Elizabeth (*d.* after 1618). They were possibly the Raphe Byrkenshaw and Elizabeth Morall who were married at Barnsley, Yorkshire, on 15 September 1586. Ralph Birchensha was sent to

Ireland by the government in 1598 as controller of musters. After his death John, whom Anthony Wood described as 'a gentile man', remained in Ireland in the household of George FitzGerald, sixteenth earl of Kildare, until the rising of 1641 (Wood, fol. 19). In Playford's *A Musicall Banquet* (1651, sig. A4) he was listed as a viol teacher in London, though it was as an instructor of the fundamentals of composition that he won renown. Birchensha claimed in a letter to the Royal Society of London that by following his rules 'not only those, who skilfully can sing or play on some Instrument, may learn to compose but also those, who can neither sing nor play' (26 April 1664, Royal Society, letter book copy, 1.166–73). The clearest exposition of these rules is to be found in an autograph manuscript, Brussels, Bibliothèque Royale Albert Ier, MS II 4168 (*olim* 6689). To Evelyn they represented 'a mathematical way of composure very extraordinary: True as to the exact rules of art, but without much harmonie' (Evelyn, 3 Aug 1664). Pepys took a course of lessons from him which ended 'in a pet' when Pepys dared to criticize the rules (Pepys, 27 Feb 1662). Captain Silas Taylor, who brought Birchensha's ideas to the attention of the Royal Society, was a more enthusiastic follower. Thomas Salmon studied with him, on Matthew Locke's recommendation; Birchensha later wrote a preface to Salmon's *Essay to the Advancement of Musick* (1672). A jesting allusion to his method occurs in Thomas Shadwell's *The Humorists* (1671): 'Berkenshaw is a rare fellow, give him his due, fa la la, for he can teach men to compose that are deaf, dumb, and blind' (*Complete Works of Thomas Shadwell*, 1.221).

Birchensha gained a reputation as a savant in matters pertaining to harmonic proportion and tuning. Henry Oldenburg, the secretary of the Royal Society, described him as 'in Musica tum theoretica tum practica apprime versatus' ('very experienced both in theoretical and in practical music'; *Correspondence*, 7 June 1673). William Brouncker, Nicolaus Mercator, John Pell, and John Wallis were among the mathematicians who examined his propositions (Gouk, 61, 188). In 1662 the first of several papers from him was presented to the Royal Society, and meetings of the society on 3 and 10 August 1664 were followed by concerts of instrumental music by him, one of which was attended by Evelyn and the other by Pepys. In 1664 he published his *Templum musicum*, a translation of part of J. H. Alsted's *Encyclopaedia*. Though never elected a fellow, he was invited on 10 February 1676 to demonstrate to the Royal Society his 'compleat Scale of Musick', a chart displaying 'all consonant and dissonant intervals suitable to musical Harmony' with their ratios in Pythagorean intonation; this was likely another version of 'his great Card of the body of Musique' which Pepys had been shown on 24 February 1662 at Birchensha's house in Southwark. His most substantial surviving theoretical work is an unpublished 'Compendious discourse of the principles of the practicall & mathematicall partes of musick' which he wrote for Robert Boyle, the brother-in-law of his former patron the earl of Kildare (autograph manuscript, Royal Society, Boyle papers, 41.1). He worked for years on a treatise, 'Syntagma musicae', which was to have summed up his ideas about the philosophical, mathematical, and practical aspects of music; subscriptions were invited in 1672, and a detailed synopsis was read to the Royal Society on 10 February 1676 (Royal Society, classified papers, XXII.(1).7), but the book itself never appeared.

Birchensha's importance rests on his certainty, extraordinary among professional musicians, that nearly every aspect of music could be rationalized. He has been described, unjustly, as a quack; but his failure to publish 'Syntagma musicae' restricted his influence as a theorist, and his compositions, which include psalm settings and instrumental suites, seem clumsy and charmless when set beside the best English work of the period. He was almost certainly the John Birchenshaw buried in Westminster Abbey cloisters on 14 May 1681.

CHRISTOPHER D. S. FIELD

Sources C. D. S. Field, 'Birchensha, John', *New Grove*, 2nd edn · L. E. Miller and A. Cohen, *Music in the Royal Society of London, 1660–1806* (1987) · W. H. G. Flood, *A history of Irish music*, 3rd edn (1913) · P. Gouk, *Music, science and natural magic in seventeenth-century England* (1999) · *The correspondence of Henry Oldenburg*, ed. and trans. A. R. Hall and M. B. Hall, 1–11 (1965–77) · Pepys, *Diary* · Anthony Wood's notes on musicians, Bodl. Oxf., MS Wood D.19.4 · Evelyn, *Diary* · T. Birch, *The history of the Royal Society of London*, 4 vols. (1756–7) · L. E. Miller, 'John Birchensha and the early Royal Society: grand scales and scientific composition', *Journal of the Royal Musical Association*, 115 (1990), 63–79 · J. L. Chester, ed., *The marriage, baptismal, and burial registers of the collegiate church or abbey of St Peter, Westminster*, Harleian Society, 10 (1876) · *CSP Ire.*, 1598–1632 · *The complete works of Thomas Shadwell*, ed. M. Summers, 5 vols. (1927)
Archives RS

Birchington, Stephen (*d.* 1407), Benedictine monk and historical writer, doubtless took his name from Birchington on the Isle of Thanet, Kent. He became a monk of the cathedral priory of Christ Church, Canterbury, in 1382. In the late 1390s he was one of the priory's two treasurers; in the opening years of the fifteenth century he held the senior post of warden of the priory's manors; and in 1404–5 he served as the prior's chaplain. He died on 21 August 1407, presumably at Christ Church, where he was probably buried.

In the account of the Christ Church monks by the late fifteenth-century Canterbury monk Thomas Cawston, Birchington is stated to have written about the lives of the archbishops of Canterbury. From this, and from John Joscelyn's references to Birchington in his mid-sixteenth-century biographical notices of archbishops of Canterbury, Henry Wharton inferred in his *Anglia sacra* (1691) that Birchington wrote the series of archiepiscopal lives in Lambeth Palace Library, MS 99. On the strength of similarities of style and method, Wharton thought that a chronicle of England and sets of lives of the popes and emperors in the same manuscript were also Birchington's work.

The lives of the popes and emperors are now known to be by the French ecclesiastic Bernard Gui (1260–1331), however, and Wharton's other suggestions are countered by the fact that the chronicle ends in 1367 and the lives of the archbishops end with the accession of William Wittleseye in 1369; the life of Archbishop Simon Islep, who died

in 1366, seems to have been written from personal knowledge, while the chronicle has various details about the 1350s and 1360s that only a contemporary is likely to have known. Most probably, therefore, both these latter works were written by a monk of Christ Church who was at least a generation senior to Birchington; Birchington's role was that of a continuator, and his own composition, which would have covered the late fourteenth century, does not appear to have survived.

NIGEL RAMSAY

Sources [H. Wharton], ed., *Anglia sacra*, 1 (1691), xix–xx · 'Stephani Birchingtoni historia de vitis archiepiscoporum Cantuarensium', *Anglia sacra*, ed. [H. Wharton], 1 (1691), 1–48 · W. G. Searle, ed., *Christ Church, Canterbury*, 2: *List of the deans, priors, and monks of Christ Church Monastery*, Cambridge Antiquarian RS, 34 (1902), 183 · *Chronica Johannis de Reading et anonymi Cantuariensis, 1346–1367*, ed. J. Tait (1914), esp. 63–75 · J. Greatrex, *Biographical register of the English cathedral priories of the province of Canterbury* (1997), 107 · Canterbury Cathedral Archives, MS Lit. D. 12, fol. 18*v* · Canterbury Cathedral Archives, DCC Ebony 72

Birchley, William. *See* Austin, John (1613–1669).

Birckbek, Simon (1583/4–1656), Church of England clergyman and religious controversialist, was born at Hornby in Lancashire, the son of Thomas Birckbek. He became a student at Queen's College, Oxford, in 1600, acted as a 'serving child' and as tabardar, and graduated BA in 1604, proceeding MA in 1607. After entering holy orders about 1607 he became noted as a preacher and disputant, as well as for his extensive knowledge of the fathers and scholastics. He remained at Queen's College as a fellow and proceeded BD in 1616. The following year he was made vicar of the church of Gilling in Yorkshire, and also of the chapel of Forcet, near Richmond in the same county, by the patronage of his kinsman Humphrey Wharton. His most important work, *The Protestant's Evidence* (1634), argued the historical continuity of contemporary Church of England doctrine, juxtaposing selections from theological writers from the first to the sixteenth centuries with extracts from Catholic teaching since the Council of Trent. Apparently valued by Selden (Wood, *Ath. Oxon.*, 3.421), the work was reissued in 1657 in a revised edition with an appended 'Answer to the antidotist', responding to a critic. The 1657 edition was republished in 1849 under the editorship of John Cumming. Birckbeck published at least two other works, and retained his living until his death. He was buried in Forcet Chapel on 14 September 1656, his wife, Bridget, having predeceased him.

RONALD BAYNE, *rev.* R. M. ARMSTRONG

Sources Wood, *Ath. Oxon.* · S. Birckbek, *The protestant's evidence*, rev. edn (1657) · will, PRO, PROB 11/263, sig. 152

Bird, Alfred (*bap.* 1811, *d.* 1878), chemist and food manufacturer, the fourth son of John Bird (1780–1846), astronomer and lecturer, and his wife, Mary, *née* Bland, was baptized at Nympsfield, Gloucestershire, on 25 August 1811. According to family tradition, he was the great-grandson of John Bird (1709–1776), instrument maker, but there is no evidence to substantiate this. Of Alfred's four brothers, the eldest, John (1805–1848), became an astronomer, schoolteacher, and Baptist minister. Two others, Henry and William, served in the 4th light dragoons in Afghanistan and

Alfred Bird (*bap.* 1811, *d.* 1878), by Henry John Whitlock

Ireland, and the youngest, Frederick Bird FRAS (1816–1876), developed unique new processes for polishing telescope mirrors, and became chaplain of Birmingham general cemetery.

Little is known of Alfred Bird's early education, but he was apprenticed to Philip Harris & Co., the well-known Birmingham druggists and chemists. In 1837 he set up his own shop in Bell Street, Birmingham, under the title 'Alfred Bird, experimental chemist'. On 23 October 1835 he had married Elizabeth Lavinia Ragg (1810–1888) in Nottingham; because of her digestive problems, her intolerance of live-yeast products, and her allergy to eggs, he embarked upon extensive research into alternatives. In 1843 he succeeded by producing 'Bird's Fermenting Powder' which later became better known as baking powder. This could be used as a live-yeast substitute in baking bread, buns, and cakes, and instantly overcame his wife's problems, and those of many other similar sufferers. There was an immediate demand for the product, and he went on to produce another innovation, custard powder, which contained no eggs, was simple to use, tasted very good, and yet was both nutritious and inexpensive.

Bird's friends persuaded him to develop these products commercially, and there was a rapidly increasing demand for them; this necessitated a move to larger premises at 69 Worcester Street, Birmingham. Production greatly increased, and distribution became nationwide. In 1855

the duke of Newcastle, the war minister, was persuaded, after carefully regulated trials, that the baking powder would facilitate the production of fresh bread for the British army in the Crimean War. Large quantities were shipped out, and in later years Bird claimed that his product had been useful not only to front line troops, but also to Florence Nightingale at Scutari. It was also claimed to have been used in the Franklin Arctic expedition. An early pioneer of advertising, Bird advertised his baking powder in 1855, and in the press from 1860. In the shop in Worcester Street, the company motto was prominently displayed:

> Early to bed, Early to rise,
> Stick to your work, and Advertise.

While development of the business, together with increased production, efficient marketing, and good distribution, always remained his top priority, Bird also carried out investigations in the fields of physics, meteorology, electricity, and magnetism. He constructed a water barometer described in the *Philosophical Magazine* (1865). He also devised a plan for demonstrating wind direction and air movements. He lectured extensively on electricity, on electric storage batteries, and electromagnetism. On a lighter note he invented a night-light which could be refuelled while still alight, and he perfected a device to keep a ball suspended on a jet of water, which he placed in his shop window as a deliberate ploy to attract passers-by to his business. It was later modified for fairground shooting booths.

In the course of investigations into the laws of sound, Bird, a competent musician, constructed a set of harmonized glass bowls which, encouraged by his friend, Sir Michael Costa, the eminent conductor, he demonstrated before the Royal Institution, and later, by royal command, played before Queen Victoria at Buckingham Palace. Family records note his playing 'Isle of Beauty Fare thee Well' on the glasses when his eldest daughter, Jessie Martha Lowcock, departed on her honeymoon in 1870. Always devoted to his family, he raised two daughters and two sons. Five other children did not survive beyond infancy.

Bird was a practising Christian and an earnest student of the Bible. He was elected a fellow of the Chemical Society on 20 January 1870, and was a founding member of the Philosophical Society. Following a long illness arising from congestion of the lung, he died on 15 December 1878 at his home at 366 Bristol Road, Birmingham. He was buried on the 21st at Key Hill cemetery, Birmingham. Pioneering work in developing convenience foods by the firm of Alfred Bird & Sons was continued by his eldest son, Sir Alfred Frederick *Bird, first baronet, of Tudor Grange, Solihull. Three later generations of the family served with the firm, which was bought in 1947 by the General Food Corporation, which in turn merged with the Philip Morris Company in 1985. Bird's custard, first of the convenience foods, remains a household name throughout the world.

J. R. TURNER

Sources private information (2004) • J. Foley, *The food makers: a history of General Foods Ltd* (1972) • *Daily Sketch* (25 June 1937), 19, 26 • *Birmingham Sketch* (Nov 1959), 46–7 • *JCS*, 35 (1879), 266 • fellowship records, Chemical Society · A. Bird, 'An account of the water-barometer constructed and erected by Alfred Bird, experimental chemist, Birmingham', *London, Edinburgh, and Dublin Philosophical Magazine*, 4th ser., 30 (1865), 349–55 · parish register, Nympsfield, 25 Aug 1811, Glos. RO [birth] · census returns · *Sunday Telegraph* (27 Feb 1994) · burial records, Handsworth cemetery, Birmingham · *Birmingham Daily Post* (16 Dec 1878) · *Daily Gazette* (16 Dec 1878) · *Windsor Gazette* (21 Dec 1878) · d. cert. · family bible, Solihull library [copy]

Likenesses H. J. Whitlock, photograph, priv. coll. [*see illus.*]

Wealth at death under £9000: probate, 10 Jan 1879, *CGPLA Eng. & Wales*

Bird, Sir Alfred Frederick, first baronet (1849–1922), food manufacturer, was born in Birmingham, on 27 July 1849, the elder son of Alfred *Bird, FCS (*bap.* 1811, *d.* 1878), and his wife, Elizabeth Lavinia Ragg, a martyr to dyspepsia. To overcome his wife's allergies to yeast products and to eggs, Alfred senior, an experimental chemist and analyst, had invented a baking powder and a cornflour-based custard powder, and had begun making these.

While at King Edward's School, Birmingham, Bird planned to read for the bar, but on leaving school in 1867 he entered his father's business, and helped to launch Bird's blancmange powder, in fourteen flavours. In 1875 he married Eleanor Frances, eldest daughter of Robert Lloyd Evans, a tobacconist, of Handsworth. They had four sons and two daughters. Three years later Alfred senior died, and Bird ran the firm jointly with his father's younger brother, who not long afterwards retired and died.

As sole owner, Bird at once planned a modern factory, with up-to-date machinery, to replace the outdated premises. After demand began to soar he opened an even larger factory on a new site in 1886; this burnt down a year later, and he had a specially designed works erected. He then diversified into other convenience foods, such as an egg substitute in 1890, jelly crystals in 1895, and tablet jellies a few years later. Although he continued to make some toiletries and chemist's products, they were not compatible with foodstuffs, and were discontinued after 1905.

To market his rapidly increasing output, as early as 1880 Bird was using pictorial advertisements, the speciality of his London agent, T. B. Browne, who gave Bird's products an equally colourful image to those of his other clients, Cadburys and Pears. Instead of the previous costly system of direct contact with retailers, Bird appointed a network of wholesale agents throughout Britain, who worked with the salesmen he hired. The sales force developed into one of the most effective in the field of groceries.

In 1900 Bird and two of his four sons, Robert and Geoffrey, registered Alfred Bird & Sons Ltd, with authorized capital of £300,000, their prospectus being dismissed by *The Statist* (23 June 1900) as 'slipshod'. They set up a London office and warehouse for the metropolitan trade. Bird remained chairman and managing director until his retirement in 1905. He then stood as a Conservative for Wednesbury in the 1906 general election, but lost rather badly. Two years later he became JP for the county of Warwickshire. Elected to Wolverhampton West in January

Sir Alfred Frederick Bird, first baronet (1849–1922), by Bassano, 1918

1910, he held the seat until he died. He was not regarded as a great debater, and never rose higher than parliamentary private secretary to the under-secretary of state for the colonies in the First World War.

While appearing genial to outsiders, Bird was a strict father and employer, requiring a high level of dedication in exchange for better wages and working conditions than elsewhere in Birmingham. He was exceptionally keen on physical fitness. As a youth he had been a good athlete, and was given a penny-farthing bicycle on his nineteenth birthday; later, he broke the record for tricycling from Land's End to John o' Groats. A pioneer motorist, he became a founder member of the Royal Automobile Club in 1897. Bird was also an ardent mountaineer and member of the Alpine Club. He was a connoisseur of fine art, and his home, Tudor Grange, Solihull, contained a number of important paintings, some of which he gave to the houses of parliament.

Bird was made a deputy lieutenant of Warwickshire in 1916, at a time when he was generously helping discharged former servicemen. Knighted in 1920, he was raised to a baronetcy in the new year honours list of 1922. A month later, he was knocked down by a car, while crossing Piccadilly, and died shortly afterwards, on 7 February 1922, in St George's Hospital, Knightsbridge, London. He was buried on 12 February.   T. A. B. CORLEY

Sources N. Mutton, 'Bird, Sir Alfred Frederick', *DBB* · J. Foley, *The food makers: a history of General Foods Ltd* (1972), 1–14 · *The Times* (8 Feb

1922) · *The Times* (10 Feb 1922) · *The Statist* (23 June 1900) · *WW* · d. cert.
Likenesses Bassano, photograph, 1918, NPG [*see illus.*] · portrait, repro. in Foley, *Food makers*, 3
Wealth at death £653,656 12s. 9d.: probate, 23 March 1922, *CGPLA Eng. & Wales*

Bird, Charles Smith (1795–1862), theological writer, was the last but one of six children, born in Union Street, Liverpool, on 28 May 1795, the son of Charles Smith Bird, a West Indian merchant. His father was strongly evangelical to the point of forbidding his children to read Shakespeare. After attending several private schools, Bird was articled to a firm of conveyancing solicitors at Liverpool in 1812. His leisure time was spent at the Athenaeum reading-room in the study of theology. He returned to school at Dr Davies's, of Macclesfield, in 1815, and from there went to Trinity College, Cambridge, matriculating in 1816. As an undergraduate, he chose only fellow Christians as companions, and he was, throughout his adult life, a strong protestant. He became a scholar of Trinity in 1818, was third wrangler in 1820, and elected a fellow of his college.

Bird was then ordained and became curate of Burghfield, 6 miles from Reading. He took a house at Culverlands, near Burghfield, in 1823. He added to his income by taking pupils, a practice he continued for twenty years. One of them was T. B. Macaulay. On 24 June 1823 he married Margaret Wrangham, of Bowdon, Cheshire. He now frequently sent contributions to the *Christian Observer*. It was against the Irish educational measures that he wrote his 'Call to the protestants of England', later published with his poems. In 1839 Bird edited a strongly protestant monthly periodical, the *Reading Church Guardian*; the publication languished for a year and then died. In 1840 Bird became a sort of Sunday curate to a Mr Briscoe at Sulhamstead. Having given up his house at Burghfield, he was glad to accept the curacy of Fawley, some 3 miles from Henley-on-Thames.

In 1843 Bird became vicar of Gainsborough, to which was attached a prebendal stall of Lincoln. In this old-fashioned market town Bird passed many happy years. His course of life was regular and tranquil. Occasionally he lectured at the Gainsborough Literary and Mechanics' Institute on natural history, English literature, and other subjects of interest. In the summer of 1844 he went to Scotland, and in the next year preached before Cambridge University four sermons on the parable of the sower. About this time the proposal for the admission of Jews into parliament aroused Bird's indignation. His 'Call to Britain to remember the fate of Jerusalem', one of his longer poems, may be read with interest. In 1849 cholera ravaged Gainsborough, and Bird assiduously and bravely administered to the wants of the sufferers.

In 1852 Bird himself suffered a severe illness. In 1859 he was appointed chancellor of the cathedral of Lincoln, and left Gainsborough. He died at the chancery, aged sixty-seven, on 9 November 1862, his wife surviving him. Friends at Gainsborough decorated the church with a painted window in his memory. He was buried in the country churchyard of Riseholme.

Bird was an ardent entomologist, and had managed to satisfy himself that insects were almost, if not entirely, devoid of feeling; yet he would not allow any to be killed by his children until he was convinced of their rarity. He became a fellow of the Linnean Society in 1828. There is an article of his in the *Entomological Magazine* for August 1833, and the Liverpool feather-horned *Tinea*, or *Lepidocera Birdella*, was honoured by John Curtis with his name.

Bird published many theological pamphlets, often attacking Tractarianism and defending the Reformation. He was cautious about the revival of convocation. He also published poems and left an autobiography, edited by his son, the Revd Claude Smith Bird.

JAMES MEW, rev. H. C. G. MATTHEW

Sources Venn, *Alum. Cant.* · C. S. Bird, *Sketches from the life of the Rev. Charles Smith Bird* (1864) · *GM*, 3rd ser., 13 (1862), 786
Archives LPL, letters to Charles Golightly
Likenesses portrait, repro. in Bird, ed., *Sketches … of the Rev. Charles Smith Bird*
Wealth at death under £30,000: probate, 13 Dec 1862, *CGPLA Eng. & Wales*

Bird, Edward (1772–1819), genre and history painter, was born in Cat Yard, Berry Street, Wolverhampton, on 12 April 1772 and baptized there the same day, one of the many children of a local carpenter (*d. c.*1810). After attending the free grammar school he was apprenticed at the age of thirteen as a japanning artist to the firm of Jones and Taylor at the Old Hall Works, Wolverhampton. On completion of his term he first set up as an independent artist in the town, before moving to Bristol about 1794. He later married Martha (1779/80–1846), youngest daughter of John Dodrell, a Bristol engraver. In 1797 he advertised his services, offering drawing lessons as a historical and landscape painter, but there is strong evidence that he had first been obliged to continue his trade as a painter of tea trays at the Japan and Pontypool manufactory at Temple Back, Bristol.

A painted cartouche within a self-portrait of about 1805 (City Museum and Art Gallery, Bristol) proclaims Bird to be a portrait painter. He also undertook book illustrations which included topographical views of Bristol and, together with the Bristol marine artist Nicholas Pocock, the illustrations for William Williams's *The Journal of Penrose, Seaman* (drawings, Lilly Library, Indiana University, Bloomington, Indiana). One of his earliest securely dated oil paintings, *Falstaff* (1807; City Museum and Art Gallery, Bristol), reflects a long-standing interest in the theatre which had begun in Wolverhampton. At Wolverhampton also, Bird's first commission is said to have been a painting for a Roman Catholic chapel, and in Bristol he undertook the large altarpiece for St Paul's, Portman Square, the building of which was completed in 1794. This variety reflects both his versatility and the difficulties of working in a provincial city in the first decade of the nineteenth century. His coming success was to be of crucial encouragement to the artists, amateurs, and patrons of Bristol and to lay the foundations for the emergence of the Bristol school about 1820.

Bird himself also benefited greatly from the connections and contacts of his Bristol friends such as George Cumberland, with whom he was certainly well acquainted by 1806. Cumberland wrote of Bird that 'for some years he was the centre of a society assembled to make drawings in the evening before supper, where the greater number of members were amateurs' (*Catalogue*, 16). In 1809 Bird first exhibited at the Royal Academy, showing an interior scene with an old soldier entitled *Good News*. Hung next to David Wilkie's *The Cut Finger* (priv. coll.), it immediately attracted attention and Bird found himself championed as the reluctant rival of an artist whom he admired. The following year the prince regent bought Bird's *The Country Choristers* (Royal Collection) at the Royal Academy and then, with the advice of Benjamin West, commissioned Wilkie to paint a pendant which was to be *Blind Man's Buff* (1813; Royal Collection). In 1811 Bird showed *The Reading of the Will Concluded* (City Museum and Art Gallery, Bristol), which has much sensitive observation of human nature. He was elected an associate of the academy the following year and a full member in 1815 only six years after his first appearance. It was in 1815 that he exhibited *The Departure to London* (ex Christies, South Kensington, 9 March 2000, lot 259), a moving and charming account of a young man's farewell to his family which is full of the incidental detail of a modest country home. More strongly coloured and subtly, if self-consciously, composed than many of his paintings, it shows that Bird's earlier debt to seventeenth-century Dutch interior scenes had been succeeded by a quotation from Jean-Baptiste Greuze (1725–1805).

Bird's own ambitions and the circle of sophisticated amateurs that gathered around him encouraged him to attempt more elevated scenes, higher in the hierarchy of genres. The Revd John Eagles was to admit his part:

> his best scenes were those of the simple, honest dealings and ways of more humble and common life, where there was some sentiment, some moral good, … never man loved innocence for its own sake more than he. That he left this style, and attempted the grand and scriptural, was much to be regretted … And I will not refuse to take myself my portion of the blame; for I did constantly instigate him to the attempts. (Eagles, 138)

Both Eagles and his father, who corresponded with Sir Walter Scott concerning appropriate costume for the scene, were involved with *Chevy Chase*, shown at the British Institution in 1812 and purchased by the marquess of Stafford for 300 guineas. Bird was appointed historical painter to Princess Charlotte in 1813 when he also won the annual premium of 300 guineas at the British Institution for *The Death of Eli*. Other substantial historical and religious scenes followed, culminating in an ambitious project, initiated in 1814, to paint the restoration of the Bourbon monarchy. Both *The Embarkation of Louis XVIII at Dover* (City Museum and Art Gallery, Bristol) and *The Landing of Louis XVIII at Calais* (Wolverhampton Art Gallery) were over-crowded with portraits, which demanded frequent and often unrewarding journeys to London.

Bird was already plagued with ill health and in 1818 he was unable to believe in the prince regent's endlessly delayed decision not to acquire *The Embarkation*. The earl of Bridgewater, who had already purchased *The Landing* for 1000 guineas, could only acquire it after Bird's death on 2 November 1819. Bird had been too ill to paint throughout the year and left his wife and three surviving children heavily in debt. His friends and patrons and the Royal Academy responded promptly, contrary to the inaccurate account in *Lives of the British Artists* by Allan Cunningham, whom Eagles justly called a 'careless slanderer' (Revd J. Eagles to Richard Smith, 6 March 1830, Bristol Reference Library, SR50 B28436). A grand funeral was held and 300 persons are said to have followed the hearse from Bird's home at 8 Kings Parade to Bristol Cathedral, where he was buried in the cloister at the foot of the steps into the transept.

The following year a large and financially successful exhibition of Bird's work was held at the Bristol Fire Office, the first substantial retrospective exhibition to be devoted to a single artist outside London. Within Bristol Edward Villiers Rippingille (1798–1859), Rolinda Sharples (1793–1838), Samuel Colman (1780–1845), and William West (1801–1861) were all to be directly influenced by Bird's genre paintings. His importance to Bristol was broader still. His friend Dr John King (1766–1846), whose portrait Bird painted (City Museum and Art Gallery, Bristol), recalled in 1839:

> about 40 years ago the late Edw. Bird was the only artist of talent in this city. It was here that his genius developed with rapid strides; his society soon became the centre of attraction to all those who had enough of good taste … Thus was spontaneously framed a small society of art-loving friends, from which all that Bristol can now boast of artists and amateurs has descended. (scrapbook of reviews, 14)

FRANCIS GREENACRE

Sources S. Richardson, *Edward Bird, 1772–1819* (1982) [exhibition catalogue, Wolverhampton Art Gallery and Geffrye Museum, London] · *Arnold's Library of the Fine Arts*, 4 (Feb 1833), 257–65 · *Catalogue of pictures painted by the late Edward Bird exhibited at Bristol, 1820, with some account of the late Mr Bird by G. Cumberland* (1820) [exhibition catalogue] · J. Eagles, *The sketcher* (1856), 133–40 [essays reprinted from *Blackwood's Edinburgh Magazine* (1833–5)] · F. Greenacre, *The Bristol school of artists: Francis Danby and painting in Bristol, 1810–1840* [1973] [exhibition catalogue, City Museum and Art Gallery, Bristol, 4 Sept – 10 Nov 1973] · A. Cunningham, *The lives of the most eminent British painters, sculptors, and architects*, 2 (1830), 242–59 · Graves, *RA exhibitors* · Graves, *Brit. Inst.* · volume of autograph letters, Bristol Reference Library, SR50 B28436 · S. Hutton, *Bristol and its famous associations* (1907) · D. H. Dickenson, *William Williams: novelist and painter of colonial America* (Bloomington, 1970) · scrapbook of reviews by John King for *Bristol Times and Mirror*, City Museum and Art Gallery, Bristol, Mt 3742 · memorial, Bristol Cathedral

Likenesses E. Bird, self-portrait, oils, *c*.1805, City Museum and Art Gallery, Bristol · J. Eagles, watercolour, 1812, City Museum and Art Gallery, Bristol · F. Chantrey, pencil drawing, 1816, NPG · F. Chantrey, plaster bust, City Museum and Art Gallery, Bristol · J. Eagles, pencil, City Museum and Art Gallery, Bristol · H. Jackson, lithograph (after B. Murphy), BM · E. V. Rippingille, oils, priv. coll.

Bird, Francis (1667–1731), sculptor, was born in the parish of St Martin-in-the-Fields, London. Nothing is known of his parentage. He enjoyed an exceptionally cosmopolitan sculptural education: at the age of eleven he was sent to Flanders to train, where, according to Vertue, he worked under a statuary named Cozins; he later travelled to Rome, but his movements there are unclear. When he returned to London, aged about twenty-two, he was employed in the workshops of Grinling Gibbons and Caius Gabriel Cibber. In this period he probably took a number of independent monumental commissions, most notably the monument to Dr Richard Busby in Westminster Abbey (1695). Despite his youthful successes, Bird does not appear to have regarded his continental training as complete: about 1695 he returned to Rome and spent nine months in the workshop of Pierre Legros. He made a number of other visits to Rome in his lifetime.

Bird was back in London by 1700, and some time in 1707 he married Hester (c.1680–c.1767), the daughter of Edward Chapman, a stone mason and contractor with a yard at Red Lion Square, and his wife, Margaret Wilcock (or Wilcox). They had five daughters and a son: Margaret (1713–1795), Clare, a Mrs Dickinson, Hester (1722–1809), Anne, and Edward Chapman (c.1715–1792). After his return Bird built a more sustained independent career. A sign of his rise to prominence was the award of the commission to design and carve most, if not all, of the figurative embellishments over the west portal of Wren's St Paul's Cathedral. In December 1706 his shop completed work on the great pediment, providing a scene of the conversion of St Paul of 64 feet in length. This work accorded with a fine model by the sculptor which is now preserved among the cathedral's collection of antiquities. Bird's shop continued to work on figures for the exterior of the cathedral until 1721, its master receiving a total payment for the work of £2040.

Between 1711 and 1712 Bird's workshop produced its most publicly conspicuous work, the marble statue of Queen Anne, towering over four feminine figures symbolic of the extent of her dominion, which stood before the great western staircase to the cathedral. A Victorian copy of this monument, by Richard Belt, now stands in place of Bird's original, which has survived, much damaged, in what was once the garden of Augustus Hare at Holmehurst, near Hastings. While his shop was carving the monument to Queen Anne, Bird received his greatest funerary commission, the tomb of John Holles, duke of Newcastle (d. 1711), for Westminster Abbey. This towering pile, commissioned by Henrietta, countess of Oxford, was designed by James Gibbs and featured as an engraved illustration in the latter's *Book of Architecture* of 1728. After completing this great commission Bird took on a series of monuments in the abbey: those to the memory of Admiral Henry Priestman (d. 1712), Sidney, first earl of Godolphin (d. 1712), Thomas Sprat, dean of Westminster (d. 1713), and Admiral John Baker (d. 1716). Bird's dominance over the figurative sculpture market was even more clear in Oxford than in London. For a period between 1717 and 1721 he sustained a virtual monopoly over sculptural commissions within the patronage of that city's university and colleges. The fine figures of Dr Radcliffe (1717; University College) and Lord Clarendon (1721; Clarendon Buildings) remain among the most conspicuous evidence of the quality of his productions.

Despite his extensive experience of continental sculpture, Bird was unable to sustain the attention of fashionable cosmopolitan society in London. Always a designer of baroque verve, he fell behind the pace of fashion in the 1720s when noted aristocratic connoisseurs demanded a more rigorous pursuit of ancient classical precedent. The end of Bird's dominance was spelt in 1720, when a wave of newly arrived Flemish sculptors, schooled in strict adherence to the antique, began to win the most prestigious contracts. He was passed over for an important Westminster Abbey funerary commission, that to John Sheffield, first duke of Buckingham: two sculptors who had recently been employed in Bird's shop, Peter Scheemakers and Laurent Delveaux, executed this work, and their ascending stars were to eclipse that of their former master. By 1722 the architect James Gibbs had transferred his favours to another recently arrived Fleming, Michael Rysbrack. Hence Bird proved capable of acquiring only the occasional grand monumental commissions, such as that to the memory of the Cavendish family at Bolsover in Derbyshire (1728). However, his monument to Dr Grabe (erected after 1727) shows that there were still opportunities for him to make use of a figure composition based on late baroque Roman formats in the context of Westminster Abbey.

Bird was also a dealer in Italian marbles. He was appointed one of the directors of Kneller's art academy in 1711. Bird and his father-in-law, both Catholics, were forced to register their estates following the Jacobite rising of 1715. Edward Chapman died in 1729, leaving most of his estate to his daughter and son-in-law; this was of considerable value and included an estate in Windsor. At Christmas 1729 Bird suffered a serious accident: he slipped while leaving a tavern and broke his leg, which was badly set. A long illness followed, ending his career. He died of dropsy on 27 February 1731, aged sixty-four, and was buried in a vault in the church of St Andrew's, Holborn. His wife survived him and lived to the age of eighty-seven. The sale of Bird's possessions took place twenty years after his death, on 30 April 1751 at Langfords, Covent Garden, and included a considerable collection of prints, drawings, and models. His son, Edward, followed his father into the marble and stone-carving business and became one of the most notable marble dealers of mid-eighteenth-century London. E. C. Bird was, however, not able to sustain the fortunes of his family and became bankrupt in 1770, there being a sale of the entire stock of his Westminster yard on 4 April 1771.

Bird was for about a decade between 1710 and 1720 the most prestigious figurative sculptor working in London. His obituary in the *Gentleman's Magazine* of 1731 celebrated him as the sculptor of 'many lofty tombs and magnificent monuments in Westminster Abbey and other places' (*GM*, 1st ser., 1, 1731, 83). He may be counted one of a line of

English-born sculptors who, through training abroad, succeeded in competing with the technically accomplished immigrants from Europe. MATTHEW CRASKE

Sources M. Whinney, *Sculpture in Britain, 1530 to 1830*, rev. J. Physick, 2nd edn (1988) · Vertue, *Note books*, vols. 2–3 · R. Rendel, 'Francis Bird, sculptor, 1667–1731', *Recusant History*, 11 (1971–2), 206–9 · J. Le Neve, *Monumenta Anglicana*, 5 vols. (1717–19) · *GM*, 1st ser., 1 (1731), 83 · R. Gunnis, *Dictionary of British sculptors, 1660–1851*, new edn (1968) · faculty office allegations, LPL · admon, PRO, PROB 6/107, fol. 55; PROB 6/127, fol. 229*r* · will, PRO, PROB 11/787, sig. 102 [Hester Bird]

Bird, Golding (1814–1854), physician, was born at Downham, Norfolk, on 9 December 1814, the eldest of three sons and two daughters born to Golding Bird, a former official in the Inland Revenue who had worked for many years in Ireland, where he had married Marianne. As a child, Bird had suffered an attack of rheumatic fever and endocarditis which left him with a stooping posture and a limp. Bird and his younger brother Frederic, who followed him into the medical profession, received their early education from a clergyman at Wallingford, Berkshire. By the time they moved to a school in London, Bird was well versed in the classics and had acquired a taste for chemistry and botany, which he demonstrated by tutoring his classmates, a practice which was frowned on by his teachers. In December 1829 Bird's father apprenticed him to William Pretty, apothecary, of Burton Crescent, London, where he remained to the end of his term in 1833, meanwhile in 1832 entering himself as a student at Guy's Hospital. Bird was always an eager participant in societies and at Guy's he joined the Pupil's Physical Society where his first publication dealt with the analysis of urine. His industry and chemical knowledge caught the attention of his teachers, especially Thomas Addison and Sir Astley Cooper; the latter invited Bird to write a section on breast milk for his book on diseases of the breast. He then submitted a dissertation on pathological chemistry applied to the diagnosis of disease, which admitted him to fellowship of the Senior Physical Society. He was an outstanding student, gaining prizes for medicine, obstetrics, and ophthalmic surgery. The Society of Apothecaries awarded him a botany prize and on 21 January 1836 awarded him a licence without examination.

Bird set up in general practice at 44 Seymour Street, Euston Square, but, possibly because of his youth, attracted few patients. He therefore took the MD at St Andrews, where residence was not required, on 24 April 1838, followed two years later by the MA. He became licentiate of the College of Physicians of London on 30 September 1840 and was elected a fellow on 9 July 1845. By 1841 he was in practice as a physician, holding appointments as physician to the Finsbury Dispensary, lecturing at the Aldersgate school of medicine, and living in the family home at Wilmington Square, Clerkenwell. He moved to a larger house at 19 Myddleton Square in preparation for his marriage on 3 March 1842 to Mary Ann Brett, sister of his friend R. Hargrave Brett. They raised a family of two daughters and three sons, moving to a larger house in Russell Square in 1850.

From 1836 Bird had been lecturer on natural philosophy at Guy's and in this capacity he delivered the lectures which formed the basis of his *Elements of Natural Philosophy* (1838). This popular book was acclaimed for its clear and direct style but criticized for its lack of mathematical rigour. Bird saw it through three editions; the fourth and fifth were improved by Charles Brooke, who rewrote the sixth edition in 1867. From his study of the large collection of urinary calculi at Guy's, Bird wrote *Urinary Deposits, their Diagnosis, Pathology and Therapeutical Indications* (1844). It ran through five editions, the last edited by L. Birkett in 1857. About 1843 he was put in charge of the children's ward, leading to a series of reports on children's diseases.

Bird also lectured on the contributions of electricity to medical treatment, using and devising a range of apparatus. Treatments generally employed either static electricity, derived from a friction machine, to electrify the skin—the 'electric bath'—or galvanic, where power supplied from a battery delivered a shock. Bird, a member of the London Electrical Society, sought to dissociate hospital specialized treatments from the quacks' claims for electricity as a universal panacea. He was put in charge of the new electrical treatment room at Guy's, where he investigated the value of shock treatment to relieve paralysed limbs and the action of electricity on the nervous system. His series of lectures to the Royal College of Physicians in March 1847 discussed electricity in its physiological and therapeutical relationships, showing its rational applications and linking these to the work of other reputable scientists. The lectures were published in the *London Medical Gazette* during the year, and were well received beyond the medical world.

Bird joined the freemasons in 1841 but left in 1853; he was also a member of the Linnean and Geological societies, and was elected fellow of the Royal Society in January 1846. He was also a corresponding member of several learned societies in Europe. Bird was an active Christian and thought of himself as both a physical and a spiritual healer. His ambition was to form a Christian Medical Association, and a resolution to this end was passed by a group of like-minded friends at his London home on 17 December 1853; he did not live to take part in the first public meeting, held in November 1854. By the late 1840s he was beginning to suffer the recurrent attacks of illness diagnosed by his brother and other colleagues as heart disease. A long holiday with his wife at Tenby, in Pembrokeshire, while it afforded him the leisure to take up his earlier interest in botany, did not effect a cure. He resigned his hospital appointments on 4 August 1853 and the following year retired from practice. He purchased an estate, St Cuthbert, at Tunbridge Wells, Kent, and stayed at Hastings while the house was being renovated, but his enjoyment of his new property was brief, for he died at St Cuthbert on 27 October 1854. He was buried at Tunbridge Wells cemetery. Bird's widow founded at Guy's Hospital the Golding Bird gold medal and scholarship for bacteriology, and one of his sons, Cuthbert H. Golding Bird, followed his father as lecturer in physiology and assistant surgeon at Guy's.

J. F. PAYNE, *rev.* ANITA McCONNELL

Sources F. Bird, *Association Medical Journal*, 3 (5 Jan 1855) • J. H. Balfour, *Biographical sketch of the late Dr Golding Bird* (1855) • N. G. Coley, 'The collateral sciences in the work of Golding Bird (1814–1854)', *Medical History*, 13 (1969), 363–76 • W. Hale-White, 'Golding Bird, assistant physician to Guy's Hospital, 1843–1854', *Guy's Hospital Reports*, 4th ser., 6 (1926), 1–20 • I. R. Morus, 'Marketing the machine: the construction of electrotherapeutics as viable medicine in early Victorian England', *Medical History*, 36 (1992), 34–52 • S. Wilks and G. T. Bettany, *A biographical history of Guy's Hospital* (1892), 245–50 • census returns, 1841 • m. cert. • d. cert.
Archives RCS Eng., corresp.
Likenesses photograph, repro. in *Guy's Hospital Reports*

Bird, Henry Edward (1829–1908), chess player, born at Portsea, Hampshire, on 14 July 1829, was the son of Henry Bird, of a Somerset family, and his wife, Mary Ellen, and was baptized at St Thomas's, Portsmouth, on 7 August. His father afterwards kept a shop in south London. Bird had only fifteen months' schooling, but he educated himself and as a boy developed notable powers of memory. From 1846 to 1857 he was clerk to an accountant in London, and was afterwards partner in the firm of Coleman, Turquand, Young & Co. During the financial crises of 1847, 1857, and 1867 Bird was greatly occupied in professional business, and between 1860 and 1866 he paid four visits to Canada and America. He was especially interested in railway finance and management: he wrote on the subject (including *Analysis of Railways*, 1868), gave evidence before the parliamentary committee on amalgamations of home railways in 1868, and framed statistical tables for the Great Eastern Railway.

However, Bird's serious interest through life lay in chess. He learned the moves by watching the games at Raymond's Coffee House near the City Road gate in 1844, moved from there to Goode's, Ludgate Hill, and so to Simpson's, in the Strand, where the professionals at first gave him the odds of queen. H. T. Buckle, the historian, who was considered the leading amateur in England, soon found Bird too much for him at the odds of pawn and move.

In 1851 in the great international tournament Bird was beaten by Bernard Horwitz, but afterwards he played eighteen games with the great Anderssen with an even result. With Howard Staunton he played only two games on even terms and won both, but this at a date when Staunton's best days were over. In 1866 he played (after work) a match of eighteen games against Steinitz and was only beaten by seven to five (with six games drawn) up to the point when he had to leave for America. Bird was a friend of Steinitz's rival John Hermann Zukertort, who lived in the Walworth Road, near Bird's own house in Heygate Street. In 1889 he won nine and a half out of ten games and first prize in the British Chess Association tournament without losing a single game. In tournaments his eccentric play might defeat players such as Chigorin (1883) or Lasker (1892); in matches, however, the result was different.

After his retirement from professional work, Bird fell on hard times. Members of the St George's chess club purchased an annuity for him, however, which enabled him to spend his last days in comfort. He died at his home, 16 Chetwode Road, Upper Tooting, on 11 April 1908 and was buried in Streatham cemetery on the 16th. He married young and was left a widower in 1869.

Bird was well known for his rapidity—he described Steinitz as world champion 'at the usual slow time limit' (Bird, 74)—for his dash, and for his eccentric openings (Bird's opening being that of the king's bishop's pawn). He was the most popular referee of his time and answered more questions about chess than any of his contemporaries. He never took his game too seriously: 'a player of dashing originality, his success was limited by a predilection for risky and unusual openings' (Coles, 23). He was content 'making the most extraordinary moves ... Amidst it all he laughed, and joked, and was happy' (*British Chess Magazine*, 28, 1908, 251). Though a fairly prolific author, his talents were perhaps not best suited to the system and precision of chess analysis, as Steinitz opined, reviewing Bird's *Chess Openings* (1878). His *Chess History and Reminiscences* (1893) and *Chess Novelties* (1895) were dedicated to his favourite opponent and patron, W. J. Evelyn of Wotton. Among his opponents at the chess clubs and divans were Buckle, Bradlaugh, Isaac Butt, Lord Randolph Churchill, Ruskin, and Prince Leopold. For a time he was chess correspondent of *The Times*.

THOMAS SECCOMBE, *rev.* JULIAN LOCK

Sources D. Hooper and K. Whyld, *The Oxford companion to chess*, 2nd edn (1992), 40 • *British Chess Magazine*, 28 (1908), 211, 248–51 • *The Times* (16 April 1908), 8 • *Annual Register* (1908) • *WWW*, 1897–1915 • H. E. Bird, *Chess history and reminiscences* (1893) • P. W. Sergeant, *A century of British chess* (1934) • R. N. Coles, *Battles-royal of the chessboard* (1948) • F. Reinfeld, *Treasury of British chess masterpieces* (1950) • J. du Mont, *Two hundred miniature games of chess* (1941) • L. Hoffer, 'The chess masters of today', *Fortnightly Review*, 46 (1886), 753–65 • *CGPLA Eng. & Wales* (1908) • d. cert. • www.familysearch.org, Jan 2003
Likenesses J. Rosenbaum, group portrait, oils, 1880 (*Chess players*), NPG; repro. in K. Matthews, *British chess* (1948), 30 • engraving (after photograph), repro. in Bird, *Chess history and reminiscences*, frontispiece • portrait, repro. in *Chess Monthly* (March 1889)
Wealth at death £35 0s. 10d.: administration, 1 May 1908, *CGPLA Eng. & Wales*

Bird, Isabella Lucy. *See* Bishop, Isabella Lucy (1831–1904).

Bird, James (1788–1839), poet and playwright, was born on 10 November 1788 at Deerbolt's Hall, Earl Stonham, Suffolk, the eighth of the nine children of Samuel Bird (1749–1826), farmer, and his wife, Anne, *née* Wink (1748–1837). He was educated at the local village day school, and briefly at Needham Market grammar school, after which he was apprenticed to a miller for three years. A romantic story is told from his youth, that when the fame of John Kemble, the actor, reached Earl Stonham, Bird journeyed to London to witness his performance, returning on foot and penniless. About 1814 he was in a position to hire two windmills at Yoxford, but after five years of little success as a miller he abandoned the trade and began work early in 1820 as a bookseller, stationer, and druggist. He was married in 1816 to Emma (1792–1872), daughter of George Hardacre, a bookseller from Hadleigh. They had sixteen children, of whom thirteen survived infancy.

Before Bird was sixteen years old he had written poetry,

and later he contributed some of his early poems to the *Suffolk Chronicle*, whose editor, Thomas Harral, became a close friend. In 1819 he published his first long poem, *The Vale of Slaughden*, a story of the invasion of East Anglia by the Danes. It was first issued by subscription, but its success induced a London publisher, three months after its appearance, to undertake an edition for the public. In 1820 Nathan Drake in his *Winter Nights* (2.184–244) reviewed it at length, and claimed for Bird the same rank in literature as that attained by Robert Bloomfield. Bird's second publication was a mock-heroic poem entitled *The White Hats* (1819), in which he humorously attacked the radical reformers. This was shortly followed by *Machin, or, The Discovery of Madeira* (1821). In 1823 he published *Poetical Memoirs: the Exile*, set in Scandinavia, the first part of which formed a spirited imitation of Byron's *Don Juan*; a second edition appeared in 1824. His edition of D. E. Davy's *A Short Account of Leiston Abbey* was printed in 1823, and next appeared *Dunwich: a Tale of the Splendid City* (1828) and *Framlingham: a Narrative of the Castle* (1831). *The Emigrant's Tale* (1833) was published in a volume with some 'metropolitan sketches', and other shorter miscellaneous poems. His last volume was *Francis Abbott, the Recluse of Niagara* (1837), founded on Sir James Alexander's *Transatlantic Sketches*. This final work also contained a second series of urban sketches. Much of Bird's early poetry indicates an intimate acquaintance with Dryden and Pope, and demonstrates the influence of Byron and Campbell, but his later work is in a more original style.

Bird also wrote two dramas, entitled *Cosmo, Duke of Tuscany: a Tragedy*, published in 1822, and *The Smuggler's Daughter*, published in 1836. The first was performed several times at small London theatres, but the managers of the chief playhouses refused to examine it. The second was successfully produced at Sadler's Wells in October 1835.

Bird died of consumption at Yoxford on 26 March 1839 and was buried in the village churchyard. The following year Harral published selections from his poems, which Bird himself had begun, with a memoir. His eldest child, Dr George Hardacre Bird, was married in 1842 to Mary Ann, youngest daughter of the poet Edwin Atherstone.

SIDNEY LEE, *rev.* ANDREW ATHERSTONE

Sources T. Harral, *Aldine Magazine* (1839), 297 · BL, Davy's Suffolk collections, Add. MS 19118, fols. 280, 287 · letters to Charles Sloman, printer, Suffolk RO, Ipswich · *GM*, 2nd ser., 11 (1839), 551 · d. cert.
Archives Suffolk RO, Ipswich, letters, literary MSS, memoir of his life
Likenesses Harvey, drawing (after a portrait by Pardon, 1826), repro. in Harral, *Aldine Magazine* · engraving, Suffolk RO, Ipswich, letters to Charles Sloman
Wealth at death under £1000: will, 3 Aug 1839, proved

Bird, Sir James (1883–1946), naval architect and aircraft manufacturer, was born on 19 March 1883 in London, the second son of Samuel Bird, merchant, of East Cowes, Isle of Wight, and his wife, Freda. He was educated at Marlborough School, where he was a prefect, played in the hockey eleven, and captained the football fifteen. He next served an apprenticeship with Armstrong Whitworth & Co. Ltd,

Sir James Bird (1883–1946), by Walter Stoneman, 1946

and then practised as a consulting naval architect from 1902 until the outbreak of war in 1914 when he joined the Royal Naval Air Service. He took an early interest in flying and built his first aircraft in 1909 at Wivenhoe, Essex, where he became managing director of the Rennie Forrestt shipbuilding, engineering, and dry dock company. He obtained his aviator's certificate in 1915 and rose to the rank of squadron commander. Bird was appointed OBE in 1916 when he left the Royal Naval Air Service to manage the Supermarine Aviation works, Southampton.

In 1919 Bird became a director of Supermarine and in 1923 bought control of the firm from Hubert Scott-Paine and became its managing director. With R. J. Mitchell as chief engineer and designer the firm went from strength to strength in the production of seaplanes, and in 1927 gained first and second place in the Schneider Trophy race at Venice. In the same year the company provided the flying boats for the Royal Air Force's Far East formation flight from Plymouth to Singapore, round Australia, and back to Singapore. In 1928 Bird sold out to Vickers, becoming a director of Vickers (Aviation) Ltd though still managing Supermarine. On the outbreak of war in 1939 Bird reluctantly agreed with Vickers and the Air Ministry that it was his patriotic duty to emerge from semi-retirement and return to the works to supervise the production of Mitchell's famous Spitfire. Bird was the right man for a task upon which so much depended. He had great technical and practical knowledge, a gift for organization, and a personal charm and kindliness which made it easy for others to work as his colleagues or subordinates. He faced the subsequent destruction of the works by enemy action with his usual cheerful fortitude and at once set about the immense task of organizing dispersal factories in the south of England. Nearly 19,000 Spitfires had been built before he retired at the end of the war. In 1945 he was knighted for his services.

Bird was for many years a member of the council of the Society of British Aircraft Constructors, served as chairman of the Royal Aero Club Schneider Trophy committee, and was on the aviation committee of Lloyd's. He was prominent in the business life of Southampton and was for long a member of the Southampton Harbour Board. He was always fond of the sea and spent most of his spare time in the summer racing his yacht. He looked more like a naval officer than a businessman, with a strong face, always very bronzed, clear blue eyes, and dark hair. Bird married three times. With his second wife he had one son, John Samuel Bird, who became a test pilot. His third wife, whom he married in 1937, was Pamela, the younger daughter of Arthur Ramsden. The strain of the war, however, impaired his health and he died at his home, Park Place, Wickham, Hampshire, on 13 August 1946, after a shooting accident caused by a heart attack. He was cremated in Southampton on 17 August.

C. R. GRAY, rev. PETER FEARON

Sources R. Higham, 'Bird, Sir James', DBB · *The Times* (16 Aug 1946), 2c [inquest] · *The Times* (15 Aug 1946)
Likenesses W. Stoneman, photographs, 1946, NPG [*see illus.*]
Wealth at death £381,024 10s. 1d.: probate, 2 Dec 1946, CGPLA Eng. & Wales

Bird, John (d. 1558), bishop of Chester, is said by John Bale to have come from an old Chester family, and to have been born in Coventry, where he joined the Carmelite friars. He incepted as doctor of theology at Oxford on 20 February 1514 and preached the university sermon on the feast of the Ascension following. In August 1516 he was elected provincial at the Carmelite chapter held in Bishop's Lynn. Afterwards, as vicar-general, he made a visitation of the province; letters of confraternity that he issued survive (Bodl. Oxf., MS Rawl. D.366). In May 1517 he attended the order's general chapter in Siena. He left office in 1519 owing to a new statute limiting provincials to a three-year term, but was re-elected in 1522 and held office until the dissolution. In 1531 he attended the trial for heresy of Thomas Bilney in Norwich. A supporter of Henry VIII's divorce, he wrote a treatise in its favour which survives. In 1535 he accompanied Bishop Edward Fox and Thomas Bedyll on their mission to Katherine of Aragon to persuade her to relinquish the title of queen. At Easter 1537 he preached before the king.

On 11 June 1537 Bird was named as suffragan to the bishop of Llandaff, with the new title of bishop of 'Penreth' (not Penrith in Cumberland but more likely Pen-

tyrch near Llandaff), and was consecrated at Lambeth Palace on 24 June. He was translated to the diocese of Bangor on 24 July 1539. Bird was involved in the negotiations for Henry VIII's marriage to Anne of Cleves, and in 1539 he accompanied Nicholas Wotton to Germany, with instructions from Thomas Cromwell to obtain her picture for the king. The following year, on 9 July 1540, he was a member of the royal commission which met in the chapter house in Westminster and declared the marriage between the king and Anne null and void.

On 4 August 1541 Bird was translated to the newly formed diocese of Chester. In addition to facing the problem of creating a new diocesan administration, he received less from his see than any other English bishop except that of Rochester. To save money, he appointed no archdeacon but devolved some of his authority to the rural deans. He appointed a chancellor to reside at Chester and a commissary for Richmond; the men he chose had local connections, which may have helped make the new episcopal administration more acceptable to the gentry of the diocese, but they were also apt to be inefficient and unreliable. To augment his income Bird negotiated an exchange of property with the crown, but the scheme misfired, and the diocese lost the valuable Derbyshire manor of Weston while receiving in return five rectories and eight advowsons whose real value was considerably less than their nominal one. Unwisely he granted annuities to influential local people and favoured others with generous long leases of episcopal property, thereby worsening his financial position. In 1552 he was admitted to Wistaston church, Chester, doubtless to augment his income, but in the following year he still owed the crown nearly £1100 for tenths and subsidies.

Bird had married while a bishop and so, following the accession of Mary, he was deprived of his see on 16 March 1554. He put aside his wife, and on 6 November 1554 was collated as vicar of Great Dunmow, Essex. Burnet describes an occasion in July 1555 when:

> Bird, that had been bishop of Chester, and was deprived for his marriage, did now think fit to repent, and engaged so far that Bonner made him his suffragan. He was blind of an eye; and being appointed to preach before the bishop, he chose those words for his text, 'Thou art Peter'; but whether his conscience smote him, or his memory failed, he could go no further. So, instead of matter of triumph upon the apostacy of such a man, the shame of such a dumb action turned the triumph to the other side. (Burnet, 2.789)

Bird's partial blindness seems to have been an affliction acquired in old age. In the autumn of 1555 he visited Bishop Bonner in Fulham bearing some apples and a bottle of wine as gifts. Thomas Haukes, imprisoned for refusing to have his child baptized, remembered being called into the orchard to face the two bishops, where Bird exhorted him: 'Alas, good young man! you must be taught by the church, and by your ancients; and do as your forefathers have done before you' (Foxe, 7.104). Bird died at Great Dunmow on 25 October 1558 and was buried in his parish church.

Apart from his treatise in favour of the king's divorce, Bird's other compositions are lost: they included a homily preached at the funeral of Edmund Bury, prior of Calais, in 1523, a collection of sermons, lectures on St Paul, and a tract on justification by faith. Bale, who knew him well, commented that Bird was: 'a man of modest abilities, with a honeyed tongue, a keen disputant and not ineffective preacher' and 'a particularly handsome man, … but (to be deplored in such a man) he was rather remiss in correcting the faults of others, being swayed by his own good nature' (BL, Harley MS 3838, fols. 110v, 41). Bird's ability to charm served him well and he was willing to adapt his views to suit successive regimes before apparently returning to Catholic belief on the accession of Mary.

RICHARD COPSEY

Sources Bale, *Cat.*, 1.724 • Emden, *Oxf.*, 1.191 • Cooper, *Ath. Cantab.*, 1.190–91 • J. Foxe, *The acts and monuments of John Foxe*, ed. J. Pratt, [new edn], 8 vols. (1877); repr. (1903), vol. 4, pp. 642–3; vol. 7, p. 104 • *LP Henry VIII*, 4/2, no. 3380(8); 6, no. 1057; 12/1, no. 726; 12/2, nos. 96, 191(19); 14/2, nos. 113(25), 264(2, 9); 15, nos. 500, 613(21), 860–61, 921; 16, nos. 1135(4, 6), 1369, 1377; 19/1, nos. 273, 1032(5); 20/2, no. 1029; 21/1, nos. 302(30), 967, 970, 1280(1, 2, 3); 21/2, nos. 183, 199(135, 137), 574, 759, 770(7, 8, 80), 771(10) • G. Bedouelle and P. Le Gal, *Le 'divorce' du roi Henry VIII: études et documents* (Genève, 1987), 322 • G. Burnet, *The history of the Reformation of the Church of England*, new edn, 2 vols. (1841) • G. Watson, 'A misappropriated bishop', *Transactions of the Cumberland and Westmorland Antiquarian and Archaeological Society*, 15 (1897–9), 303–8 • BL, Harley MS 3838

Archives PRO, treatise in favour of Henry VIII's divorce, SP 1/62/53–58

Bird, John (1709–1776), maker of scientific instruments, was born in December 1709 in Bishop Auckland, co. Durham, and baptized at St Andrew's Church there on the 27th, the son of John Bird (b. 1687) and his wife, Dorothy, née Nelson. She died at or soon after his birth and was buried in the same church on the day of his baptism. A commonly cited account of Bird's early years is that published by William Ludlam in his *Introduction and Notes on Mr Bird's Method of Dividing Astronomical Instruments* (1786), where it is said that he was a weaver who, finding himself one day in a clockmaker's shop, was struck by the irregular dividing on a brass clock dial and devised a method to improve on this, becoming so skilled that it came to occupy much of his time. This story was challenged by Bird's friend of later years, the clockmaker Alexander Cumming, who annotated his copy of Ludlam's book as follows:

> Mr Bird told me himself that he was apprentice to his uncle a clothier, that a watch maker's apprentice who was a companion of his having received from his master a watch to engrave in his absence, … the apprentice after his master was gone expressing to Jack Bird that he could not engrave it … Bird told him, anyone could do it; and took the engraver and did it.

On the watchmaker's return, Bird's part was soon discovered, the outcome being that the watchmaker recommended Bird's uncle to put him to some business where his natural faculty could be applied. The years following this episode are obscure; it was 1740 before Bird emerged into the light of history.

On his arrival in London, Bird was employed in the workshop of Jonathan Sisson, on the corner of Beaufort Buildings in the Strand, where he assisted in dividing the standard yards commissioned by the Royal Society for the

John Bird (1709–1776), by Valentine Green, pubd 1776 (after Lewis)

comparison of English and French measures. Through Sisson, he met and worked for George Graham, and it is likely that Bird's hand was set to several instruments signed by these two famous craftsmen. By 1745 he was established in his own workshop in York Buildings, on the Strand, making machine tools and small mathematical instruments. He soon received orders to design and make large astronomical instruments for major observatories at home and abroad. He took an apprentice, William Ralph Cole, in 1746, but it is not known whether this man continued to work for him. In 1749–50 Bird constructed a transit instrument and a mural quadrant of 8 foot radius for the Greenwich Royal Observatory. This was the first such quadrant to be made entirely of brass, replacing the earlier type where a brass arc was fixed to an iron frame. Such bimetallic quadrants were cheaper and easier to construct, but had the disadvantage that the two metals expanded unequally when the temperature changed, thus distorting the frame. Bird's quadrant weighed about 8 cwt and had a double arc, one with ninety and the other with ninety-six divisions, accurately cut by Graham's method of continual bisection. It cost £300 and gave sixty-two years of valuable service. The quadrant was much admired and orders for others of the same kind arrived, from the observatories of St Petersburg (for a quadrant of 8 foot radius, delivered in 1752), Cadiz, Stockholm (delivered 1753), and Göttingen (for a quadrant of 6 foot radius, costing £260, with a 12 foot telescope, paid for by the Hanoverian king George II and completed in 1755). Many smaller moveable quadrants, telescopes, and other fine instruments left Bird's workshop destined for the private observatories of wealthy amateurs who could afford the best instruments available.

The astronomer at Göttingen, Tobias Meyer, devised a repeating circle by which seamen could observe the stars in order to calculate their positions from Meyer's star tables. A wooden model of this circle was sent to the Admiralty and passed to Bird to make up in brass. It was tested at sea by Captain John Campbell, who found it far too cumbersome for effective use. He came back to Bird and together they devised a new instrument, based on the Hadley octant, with its scale extended to 120 degrees and made to astronomical standards. This was the first marine sextant: used in conjunction with Meyer's tables, it revolutionized navigation.

During 1758 Bird was so unwell that he was obliged to leave London for the sake of his health. He recovered, however, and returned to his business, preparing yet another mural quadrant for the Spanish naval observatory at Cadiz, and a new standard yard for the government. In 1766 he sent in a proposal to the commissioners of the board of longitude, offering for the sum of £500 to instruct an apprentice, and occasionally other persons, in his method of making astronomical instruments, and to write an account of this method. He added that the house in which he lived was damp and out of repair, and asked if the board would build more commodious premises for him on the Surrey side of Westminster Bridge. The board debated the matter with Bird, and gave its approval. Two books were duly written and published, *The Method of Dividing Astronomical Instruments* in 1767 and *The method of constructing mural quadrants exemplified by a description of the brass mural quadrant in the Royal Observatory at Greenwich* in 1768, reissued as a single volume in 1785. By further order of the board a half-size wooden model of the Greenwich quadrant was prepared and lodged in the British Museum, but it is now lost. There is no record of any apprentices being bound to Bird, and he never took up the order to build himself a house on the Surrey side of the river. In November 1770 he was again ill and unable to work—he suffered from the painful complaint of gravel—and continued to occupy his quarters on the Strand, where from the roof he had a clear view to the south and could test his telescopes and other instruments before delivery.

Most foreign astronomers visiting London called on Bird, to place orders or simply to discuss matters of common interest. In 1763 the astronomers Jerome de Lalande and Thomas Hornsby lunched with him after their visit to Greenwich; Benjamin Franklin, writing from London in 1768 about two instruments ordered by John Winthrop for Philadelphia, remarked that Bird did all his work with his own hands (rather than subcontract it) for the sake of greater truth and exactness, and that he was being delayed by demands from France and Russia, as well as those from Philadelphia, stimulated by the forthcoming transit of Venus. In 1771 Jean Bernoulli noted that Bird's instruments were the most esteemed, and also the most expensive, and that Bird polished his own lenses, usually a chore put out to working opticians. Also in 1771 Bird began work on his last major commission, two mural quadrants

and a transit for the new Radcliffe Observatory, Oxford. Although he agreed to decline all other work, the size of the Radcliffe instruments obliged him to move to larger premises and in 1772 he took a new house in Little Marylebone Street, on the northern margin of Westminster, where he built a wooden workshop at the rear in which to divide the quadrants. It was a move for the better; Bird wrote to Hornsby, then the Radcliffe observer:

> For my own part, I wish that I had made my escape from fog and smoak some years sooner, for I find myself in much better health since I have breathed good air. I still have some remains of my old disorder but it is very moderate—I hope it will go quite off.   (Royal Astronomical Society, Radcliffe MS A1.18)

The work proceeded smoothly and on schedule, the various items being delivered as they were ready.

Bird died on 31 March 1776 and was buried at St Marylebone on 6 April. He was unmarried. In his will he instructed his executors, Captain Campbell, for whom he had made the sextant, and Alexander Aubert, astronomer, to invest money for an annuity for his servant Mary Cable (*d.* 1788), and after her death for the income to be paid to the assistant at the observatory in Oxford in perpetuity. Bird's instruments are characterized by a delicacy of figure, the result of his skill in shaping and connecting the various parts so as to achieve strength with lightness. They were much in demand in their day and are now highly valued by collectors.   ANITA MCCONNELL

Sources A. McConnell, 'From craft workshop to big business', *London Journal*, 19 (1994), 36–53 · minutes of the Board of Longitude, CUL, RGO 14 · letters, RAS · *Miscellaneous works and correspondence of the Rev. James Bradley*, ed. [S. P. Rigaud] (1832); repr. (1972) · E. Forbes, *Tobias Mayer, 1723–62: pioneer of enlightened science in Germany* (1980) · MHS Oxf., MSS Museum 220–1 · Bodl. Oxf., MS DD Radcliffe e. 2 · Jerome Lalande. *Journal d'un voyage en Angleterre, 1763*, ed. H. Monod-Cassidy (1980) · J. Bernoulli, *Lettres astronomiques* (1771) · *The papers of Benjamin Franklin*, 15, ed. W. B. Willcox (1972), 166–7; 16, ed. W. B. Willcox (1972), 65–7 · parish records · *GM* · will, PRO, PROB 11/1018
Archives Bodl. Oxf. · CUL, Board of Longitude · RAS
Likenesses V. Green, mezzotint, pubd 1776 (after Lewis), BM, NPG [*see illus.*]
Wealth at death £1000 for servant's annuity; residue to executors: will, PRO, PROB 11/1018

Bird, (Cyril) Kenneth [*pseud.* Fougasse] (1887–1965), cartoonist and journal editor, was born on 17 December 1887 at 26 Westbourne Terrace Road, London, the younger son of Arthur Bird, a London merchant and a prominent cricketer and first-class shot, and his wife, Mary Wheen. He began his formal education in 1893 at Warwick House, a day school in London, and from 1898 he boarded at Farnborough Park School, Hampshire. In 1902 he entered Cheltenham College, where he had an outstanding record, becoming head boy at the age of sixteen. Bird aspired to be an artist but his father told him he would never be rich enough to 'keep him'. Instead, in 1904 he began to study civil engineering at King's College, London. He was president of the university union and the engineering society, boxed, and played rugby, a lifelong interest. Meanwhile he attended art classes at the Regent Street Polytechnic

(Cyril) **Kenneth Bird** [Fougasse] (1887–1965), by Howard Coster, 1934

and at the London School of Photo-Engraving and Lithography in Bolt Court. He also became a machine-gun instructor in the Artists' Rifles.

Bird graduated with a BSc in civil engineering in 1908 and became an associate member of the Institution of Civil Engineers. The Steel Company of Scotland sent him to Spain to survey iron mines, and in 1909 he joined Easton, Gibb & Son at Rosyth at the naval base outside Edinburgh. He continued to play rugby, and in 1913 he played in the final international trials and scored the only try. Had he not been knocked unconscious, he would have been certain of his cap for Scotland. In August 1914 he applied for urgent release from the dockyard, a reserved occupation, and in September joined the army as a second lieutenant in the Royal Engineers. On 16 September 1914 he married Mary Holden (Mollie) Caldwell, an oil painter, watercolourist, and etcher who worked under the name of Mary Holden Bird. The couple had no children.

Bird's military career was brief. At Gallipoli in 1915 a shell shattered his back and he was sent home apparently permanently disabled. For three years he was unable to walk, so with the encouragement of his wife he turned to cartooning. While he was confined to his bed he took a correspondence course from Percy V. Bradshaw. In 1916 *Punch* accepted *War's Brutalizing Influence*, signed Fougasse (the name given to a First World War French mine which might or might not explode), and he became a regular contributor to the magazine. Kenneth Bird adopted the pseudonym Fougasse to avoid confusion with the *Punch* contributor W. Bird, the pseudonym of Jack B. Yeats.

Bird refined and simplified his cartooning style into a modernist shorthand. He had a gift for capturing movement in line and facial expression. Collections of his drawings soon appeared, including *A Gallery of Games* (1921) and *Drawn at a Venture* (1922), the latter with a preface by his close friend A. A. Milne. In 1924 he designed, by invitation, a miniature book for Queen Mary's doll's house. By the late 1920s his drawings became linear and abstract, using only a few lines to lure and involve the viewer, and his idiosyncratic style became established. Meanwhile he did some striking humorous advertisements for Austin Reed, Pyramid handkerchiefs, and the London Underground, among others. Alongside H. M. Bateman he developed the strip cartoon in *Punch* and in advertisements. The critic Bevis Hillier observed that: 'As his cartoons relied more on telling observation rather than on exaggeration, his drawings are a vivid pictorial chronicle of "U" Britain between the Great War and the mid-1950s' (Hillier, 12). His drawings for *Punch*, especially in its annual *Almanacks*, and his jaunty, humorous linear advertising work made him a rapid success. Among his collections were *PTO* (1926), *E. & O. E.* (1928), and *Fun Fair* (1934). He and his wife exhibited together. In 1933 he followed her into Christian Science, telling her before his conversion, 'It must be a marvellous religion, if it teaches old women to mind their own business' (ibid., 15). He neither drank nor smoked. In 1936 he became a fellow of King's College, London.

In 1937 Bird succeeded George Morrow as *Punch*'s art editor. Working with the editor E. V. Knox (Evoe), he sought to remake *Punch* into a truly humorous comic weekly. He improved and modernized *Punch*'s look, injecting a strong American advertising influence. To develop active rather than passive readers, its captions were shortened and its jokes were sped up. His ideal was a cartoon which did not need a caption. A skilful humorist, he gently teased the English with his terse one-line captions. These reflected his awareness of a shortening in the audience's attention span which resulted from the talking film and radio broadcasting. He gave detailed direction to the drawings in *Punch* and established a tradition of encouragement, accessibility, and technical expertise for its artists. A number of its cartoonists, such as Thomas Derrick, David Langdon, Paul Crum (Roger Pettiward), J. H. Dowd, and Anton (Antonia Yeoman and H. Underwood Thompson), gravitated to his simplified line and compressed jokes. He nurtured such unique talents as Pont (Graham Laidler).

Bird had a very productive war. In their spare time he and his wife were air raid wardens in Kensington. While continuing as *Punch*'s art editor and as a cartoonist, he volunteered his artistic services to the government. His distinctive style and sensibility—a blend of crisp linear images and gentle if pointed humour—produced memorably effective propaganda and information. What the critic Bevis Hillier called 'his hieroglyphic almost notional style' was stimulated by the need to get wartime messages across unambiguously (Hillier, 21). His anti-gossip series, Careless Talk Costs Lives (which became and remained a national catch-phrase), incorporating Hitler, Goebbels, and Goering listening to indiscreet conversations, was widely appreciated, as was his work for several government ministries. In 1950 Princess Elizabeth observed: 'How carelessly we should have talked during the war but for Fougasse' (Houser, *Saturday Evening Post*, 28 Jan 1950, 27). A sample of his voluminous wartime work may be found in his *A School of Purposes: a Selection of Fougasse Posters, 1939–1945* (1946). He was appointed CBE in 1946, and was a member of the BBC's *The Brains Trust*.

In 1949 Bird became *Punch*'s seventh editor, the first to have drawn his way to the editorial chair. Design, layout, and typography remained his major concern. He restyled the magazine, removing the advertisements from the front cover, and dropped the second cartoon. He supervised two special issues to celebrate the Festival of Britain (1951) and the coronation (1953), for which he designed delightful covers. His patronage of a number of comic artists, especially Ronald Searle, Rowland Emett, Giovannetti, R. C. Sheriffs, and André François brightened those years of austerity. The choice of writers, who were now given bylines, he left to H. F. Ellis, his literary editor. A genial mild man, Bird did not direct *Punch* to take an editorial point of view. 'So we had a paper that was mostly very elegantly done about nothing much' (Praeger, 238), or 'a Conservative organ without the courage of its Conservative convictions' (Price, 302).

Bird retired as editor unreluctantly in 1952 but continued to contribute to *Punch*. His genteel professionalism and the clarity of his notions about comic art are most effectively laid out in *The Good-Tempered Pencil* (1956), where he wrote: 'pictorial humour is simply a short hand by which humorous ideas may be absorbed by the reader with the minimum effort' (Fougasse, 14–15). To illustrate his ideas about twentieth-century comic art he cited Max Beerbohm, Phil May, and Paul Crum, but characteristically none of his own work. Comedy, he wrote, is more effective than tragedy, 'and I remain confident that *The Taming of the Shrew* must have saved more wives from being smacked by their husbands than even *Othello* has' (ibid.). During his career he illustrated more than thirty books and pamphlets and designed hundreds of posters. He died in London at his home, 115 Swan Court, on 11 June 1965. He was survived by his wife. A memorial exhibition of his work was held the following year at the Fine Art Society, London.   PETER MELLINI

Sources B. Hillier, ed., *Fougasse* (1977) · *DNB* · Fougasse [K. Bird], *The good-tempered pencil* (1956) [incl. bibliography] · R. G. G. Price, *A history of Punch* (1957) · K. Bird, 'Drawing and reproduction', in R. G. G. Price, *A history of Punch* (1957), appx 4, pp. 356–69 · Fougasse file, *Punch* Library and Archive, London · Evoe file, *Punch* Library and Archive, London · M. Girard, 'World War II poster artists: Abram Games and Fougasse', honours diss., Stanford University, 1993 · A. Prager, *The mahogany tree: an informal history of 'Punch'* (1979) · *Punch*, 150–225 (1916–53) · J. Jensen, 'Sorry! Not quite!', unpubd MS, 1998 · *CGPLA Eng. & Wales* (1965) · b. cert. · *The Times* (14 June 1965)

Archives *Punch* Library and Archive, London · IWM | SOUND BBC Archives

Likenesses H. Coster, photographs, 1934, NPG [*see illus.*] · D. Low, pencil cartoons, NPG · photograph, repro. in Hillier, ed., *Fougasse* · photographs, *Punch* Library and Archive, London

Wealth at death £4974: probate, 7 Sept 1965, *CGPLA Eng. & Wales*

Bird, Mary Rebecca Stewart (1859–1914), missionary, was born on 23 June 1859 at Castle Eden rectory, co. Durham, the fifth of the six children of Charles Robinson Bird (*d.* 1886), rector of Castle Eden, and Harriet Oliver (*d.* 1911), *née* Watson, daughter of a Bath physician. Her paternal grandfather was Robert Merttins *Bird of the Bengal civil service and she was closely related to Isabella Lucy *Bishop (*née* Bird) and the families of Archbishop J. B. Sumner and William Wilberforce. Physically small and delicate in health she was educated at home where she was called Tiny by her brothers and sisters.

Mary's interest in missionary work is said to have been stimulated by a Church Missionary Society (CMS) meeting she attended at the age of sixteen, but it was not until 1890 that she offered herself to the CMS. She had been the constant companion of her father until his death in 1886, helping him in his pastoral work among school children and factory girls. She then undertook training at The Willows (since named Kennaway Hall), the CMS training school at Stoke Newington, London, where she received both theological and basic medical instruction, and in April 1891 she joined the CMS mission in Jolfa, the Christian Armenian suburb of Esfahan, in Persia. There she learned Persian, studied medical books, and taught English in the Armenian Girls' School. She also opened a dispensary for women and children, dispensing medicines and performing minor operations and often attracting a hundred or more patients daily. Her afternoons were usually spent visiting surrounding villages. Twice in 1895 she attempted to establish dispensaries in Muslim Esfahan, braving the hoots and missiles of young boys and students as she rode there on her donkey, but she was forced to stop after a few months by the intense hostility of the mullahs.

While on home leave in 1897–8 Mary went briefly to Canada on behalf of the CMS and also wrote for them a short book, *Persian Women and their Creed* (1899), describing the Muslim religion and customs and the work of the CMS and herself. On her return to Persia in April 1899 she joined the newly opened CMS mission in Yazd. After a few months there she proceeded to the even more remote desert town of Kerman, where in addition to teaching and evangelizing she opened a dispensary for women and children. At the end of 1903 she felt obliged to return home to look after her ageing mother and only returned to Persia in September 1911 after her mother's death. She again worked in Yazd, this time for two years, before moving to Kerman at the end of 1913. She contracted typhoid there while nursing Swedish gendarmerie officers in the mission hospital and died in camp at Deh Saheb outside the town on 16 August 1914. She was buried the following day in Kerman's small Christian cemetery.

Mary Bird was, with Laura Stubbs, with whom she travelled to Jolfa in 1891, the first single woman sent to Persia by the CMS. She showed considerable courage in her attempts to open dispensaries in the then fanatical Muslim quarters of Esfahan. Best-known for her medical work she regarded this as an adjunct to her evangelical mission. Although her work in Esfahan caused difficulties with the authorities she was a popular figure both there and in Kerman where, in the words of the British consul P. M. Sykes, she was an 'immense power for good'. She was known to the Persians as Maryam *khanum* (lady) and Maryam *hakim* (doctor).   DENIS WRIGHT

Sources C. C. Rice, *Mary Bird in Persia* (1916) · *Church Missionary Review*, 65 (1914), 586, 632 · E. Stock, 'Mary Bird of Persia', *Church Missionary Gleaner*, 41 (1914), 157 · U. Birm. L., special collections department, Church Missionary Society archive · R. E. Waterfield, *Christians in Persia* (1973) · M. R. S. Bird, *Persian women and their creed* (1899) · J. Chappell, *Three brave women* (1920) · J. Powell, *Riding to danger: the story of Mary Bird of Persia* (1949)
Archives U. Birm. L., Church Missionary Society archive
Wealth at death £8405 9s. 2d.: probate, 28 Jan 1915, *CGPLA Eng. & Wales*

Bird, Richard (*d.* 1609), Church of England clergyman and private tutor, matriculated as a sizar from Trinity College, Cambridge, in February 1565, and was elected a scholar in the same year. He graduated BA early in 1569, became a fellow in 1570, and proceeded MA in 1572.

Bird appears later to have served as curate in or around Saffron Walden, Essex. Here, in 1576, he encountered a group of dissenters who suggested that the moral law embodied in the commandments was no longer binding. Bird sought and received the advice of John Whitgift, then the master of his college, as to the best way of replying. Despite his marriage in the same year to Elizabeth, of whom no more details are known, he maintained his connection with Trinity, proceeding BD in 1580 and serving the college as junior bursar in 1579–80 and junior dean in 1581–2. Also in 1582 he acquired the rectory of Woodchurch, Kent.

Subsequently Bird was appointed tutor to William Cecil, eldest son of Sir Thomas Cecil, heir of the lord treasurer, Lord Burghley. On 3 November 1585, while travelling with Bird in France, the young man was reported to be attending exercises with the Jesuits, and he embraced the Roman Catholic faith soon afterwards. The conversion of the future head of a leading family was a source of grave concern, and Bird was blamed, at least by Sir Edward Stafford, the English ambassador in Paris. In January 1586 Bird wrote to Burghley that Stafford had publicly denounced him as a traitor, threatened him with a whipping, and subjected him to other indignities. Bird protested that he had endeavoured to fulfil his duties as tutor conscientiously, but had been 'robbed of the sowle of that young gentleman by wicked and treacherous men' (BL, Lansdowne MS 46, fol. 18).

The episode was not fatal to Bird's prospects. On 21 March 1589 he was collated to the archdeaconry of Cleveland, in the diocese of York, and on 29 September 1590, on the presentation of William Woodhall of Walden, Essex, he was instituted as canon of the tenth prebend of Canterbury Cathedral. He resigned his archdeaconry on 19 April 1601. By December 1597 Bird was also vicar of Brooklands in Kent, and he held the living until his death. He was created DD in 1608. Bird died in June 1609 and was buried in Canterbury Cathedral on 19 June.

THOMPSON COOPER, *rev.* STEPHEN WRIGHT

Sources BL, Lansdowne MS 46, no. 9, fols. 18–19 · W. W. Rouse Ball and J. A. Venn, eds., *Admissions to Trinity College, Cambridge*, 2 (1913) · Venn, *Alum. Cant.* · *Fasti Angl., 1541–1857*, [York] · J. Strype, *The life and acts of John Whitgift*, new edn, 3 vols. (1822), vol. 1 · J. Strype, *Annals of the Reformation and establishment of religion … during Queen Elizabeth's happy reign*, new edn, 2/2 (1824) · E. Hasted, *The history and topographical survey of the county of Kent*, 3 (1790) · *CSP for.*, 1585–6

Bird, Robert Merttins (1788–1853), East India Company servant, was the son of Robert and Lucy Bird of Taplow, Buckinghamshire. He arrived in Bengal in 1808 as a writer and began his career as an assistant to the registrar of the court of appeal (*sadr diwani adalat*) in Calcutta. He was subsequently employed in various judicial capacities in Calcutta, Benares, and Jaunpur. In 1810 he married Jane Grant Brown, daughter of the chaplain David *Brown of the college of Fort William. Bird's first independent charge came in 1820, when he was appointed as judge and magistrate in Gorakhpur in the North-Western Provinces. Following the death of his wife, Bird remarried at Cape Town in 1824; his new wife was also called Jane.

In 1829, with his appointment as commissioner of revenue and circuit in Gorakhpur, Bird's career shifted from the judicial to the land revenue sphere and this was to be of immense importance to the history of the North-Western Provinces and British India more generally. In 1831 he was promoted to the *sadr* board of revenue on deputation, then spent a period as commissioner of the Farrukhabad division, and then rejoined the board in 1834. Bird gradually developed a remarkable knowledge of the land tenures of the country, and a formidable administrative capacity, and was soon regarded as one of the ablest revenue officers in the company's service. He was struck by the extent to which the legal framework of the existing settlement was often 'wholly distinct' from the actual situation on the ground (Mason, 1.296).

It was Holt Mackenzie who had carefully devised a land revenue system for the North-Western Provinces, designed to preserve ancient rights (especially of village communities) with a moderate squeeze on superior landholders, but his regulation 7 of 1822 had, in practice, proved laborious and too detailed. Bird was uneasy about the difficulties that had emerged in its workings and wished 'to have each fact fixed before I found a principle upon it' (Husain, 199); he wanted to adopt a more empirical approach based on the revenue history of the villages in place of the deductive and theoretical methods hitherto used.

In 1832 Lord William Bentinck (governor-general, 1828–35) undertook a review of the land revenue policy of the North-Western Provinces. Bird put forward a strong case for the protection of the rights of peasant cultivators linked with a fixed, but not permanent, settlement of the revenue demand. Fixed rents should not be arbitrary but should be calculated from the money rents then prevailing in the North-Western Provinces, although, in practice, rough and ready reckoning was still required; this was in place of the previous, more theoretically based method of calculating rent in the form of net produce, which involved an estimate of the average gross produce of different soils and the subtraction from it of nominal values for profits and wages.

Bird firmly believed that the cultivators, except tenants at will, had the right to a fixed rent and that this would not infringe the rights of the superior land revenue holders (the *zamindars*, rajas, and *talukdars*) whose interests did not arise directly from the land (Husain, 199). He was equally convinced that no right of property existed between the cultivator and the monarch; he found the ideal principles (though not necessarily implementation) of land revenue settlement in Sir Thomas Munro's ryotwari system in Madras, which alone preserved, in his view, the 'pure original system of Indian revenue administration' (Metcalf, 61).

This inevitably led Bird to favour the resident cultivators over the traditional intermediaries; he considered, for instance, the *zamindars* as 'a host of unproductives' wasting their resources on expensive marriages and other extravagant habits (Husain, 199–200). Such criticism of the superior land revenue holders was not new in 1832, but Bird's practical zeal in pursuit of a fixed settlement with resident cultivators was. Despite his considerable awareness of the historical background of land revenue in the North-Western Provinces, he was still capable of 'passionate dogmatic assertion' when it suited (Rosselli, 259).

When, in 1833, Bentinck revised the revenue system of the North-Western Provinces through regulation 9, Bird was chosen to oversee the task. Its implementation, therefore, bore his imprint aided by subordinates of his own choice with whom he worked closely. He also recognized the important contribution of able Indian personnel. The new settlement was intended to be simpler than that of regulation 7, setting provisional revenue demands for similar tracts and then working from the aggregate to the detail. It involved the survey of each village and the preparation of a map showing individual fields, land held in severalty and that held collectively, and a village register to record the boundaries and the rights, privileges, and liabilities that went with them; a thirty-year settlement was to be made either with individual cultivators, a landholder, or the village brotherhood (which did not necessarily include all the inhabitants), but only where such rights already existed. Bird was also careful to involve village accountants in the new method, an element of popular scrutiny was provided for, and he established a system of local self-government. While his survey was not perfect, it was much superior to anything that had gone before and was the most complete that had yet been made in India.

Bird's energy and determination meant that the revision was completed within ten years. In that time an area of 23,000 square miles with a population of about 23 million was surveyed; in 1867 Marshman described this as 'the greatest fiscal achievement of the Company's Government' (Marshman, 3.48). By the time that Bird retired from India in 1842, the land system of the North-Western Provinces had taken on the basic shape that it was to retain until the end of British rule. The new settlement, in the event, did not just record existing land revenue practice but initiated significant social and economic changes. Through the fixing of rights and obligations land took on a market value as never before. Bird did not share Bentinck's desire to sustain a superior land revenue holding class. He wanted instead to create a more egalitarian society justified through 'a desire for the welfare of the people' and 'the greatest happiness principle' (Husain, 200).

Bird's own view of his achievement was not straightforward. He could simultaneously argue that ryots varied from settled tenants to 'mere labourers' and yet that all shared certain rights; he could also view the result of regulation 9 as being in favour of the collective village brotherhoods and yet facilitating 'the sale of land to a degree which never existed before' (Rosselli, 259). In the aftermath of the Indian mutiny land sales were often identified as a major factor in breaking up the village community and the stability it gave; this debate of cause and effect still continues. Bird also helped form a school of administration in the North-Western Provinces which, after further moulding by James Thomason (lieutenant-governor 1843–53), played an important role in consolidating British rule in the Punjab after 1849.

Bird retired from India in 1842 and spent the rest of his life in Britain in relative obscurity. His life and career were characterized by a strong evangelical commitment and, on returning to England, he became an active member of the Church Missionary Society and undertook much work on its behalf. He was widowed once more, and married, on 1 March 1848, Henrietta Maria Jane Grenfell, daughter of Pascoe Grenfell of Taplow. In 1853 he was called upon to give evidence before the committee of the House of Commons considering the renewal of the East India Company's charter. He died soon afterwards, at Taplow Hill Lodge, Termoham, Torquay, on 22 August 1853, making provision in his will for five sons and three daughters.

A. J. ARBUTHNOT, *rev.* DAVID J. HOWLETT

Sources P. Mason [P. Woodruffe], *The men who ruled India* (1954) · J. Rosselli, *Lord William Bentinck: the making of a liberal imperialist, 1774–1839* (1974) · I. Husain, *Land revenue policy in northern India* (1967) · T. R. Metcalf, *Land, landlords, and the British raj: northern India in the nineteenth century* (1979) · E. Stokes, *The English utilitarians and India* (1959) · J. Marshman, *The history of India* (1867) · *DNB* · will · m. cert. · d. cert. · private information (1997)

Archives BL OIOC, Bengal revenue consultations and dispatches, company personal records

Bird, Ruth (1899–1987), historian and schoolteacher, was born on 26 May 1899 at 62 St Quintin Avenue, Kensington, London, the second of the two children of George Bird (1863–1912), entrepreneur and engineer, and his wife, Theresa Mary (1867–1953), daughter of Thomas Edwards, chemist, and his wife, Hannah. The Bird family had been wealthy London merchants during the nineteenth century, but the early death of Ruth's father in 1912 proved detrimental to his family's finances. Ruth's brother, Harold (1896–1962), was educated at Charterhouse School and from 1909 until 1917 Ruth boarded at Elstree Grange in

Eastbourne, where her academic ability was recognized in her outstanding success in public examinations.

Ruth Bird studied at Bedford College, London, from 1917 to 1922. In 1920 she was the only historian awarded first-class honours in the BA examinations. In May 1921 she received the inaugural grant of the Amy Lady Tate scholarship, which covered tuition fees and use of the newly opened Institute of Historical Research, while she studied at Bedford College under the direction of J. W. Allen and Miss Jeffries Davis. Her master's degree, awarded in December 1922, was the ninth history MA in the college's history, but the first distinction.

Ruth Bird started teaching at Truro Girls' High School in 1923. In 1926 she moved to the Wyggeston Grammar School for Girls in Leicester where she remained until she retired in 1959, having been senior mistress. She obtained no specific teaching qualifications, but loved her chosen career, and was an inspirational and enthusiastic classroom teacher. Her former pupil Professor Claire Cross described her as 'perhaps the greatest (teacher) I ever met' (private information).

A small, slight figure, with a short severe hair cut, Ruth Bird possessed great natural authority and a remarkably warm smile. She dressed simply, lived humbly, and owned little. Ruth's membership of the Anglican third order of Franciscans and her commitment to its principles of humility and simplicity explain her exceptionally austere and frugal lifestyle, rather than lack of funds. She was initially linked with the order at Burnham Priory at Taplow and later with the convent at Lingfield. Her vicar at Horsted Keynes knew Ruth as a dedicated 'practising Christian, devout and faithful in her prayer life, in worship and private study' (private information) and although her beliefs were private and she was no evangelist she saw no separation between secular and spiritual worlds. Her faith was evident.

Although she was a keen traveller and a teacher who emphasized the international perspective to history as a means of furthering peace among nations, Ruth Bird's own scholarly studies were consistently local. Her main publication, *The Turbulent London of Richard II* (1949), was a revision of her master's thesis, 'Civic factions in London and their relation to political parties, 1376–1399', which she prepared for publication during a year's refresher in 1935–6 at the London School of Economics. Her thorough research enabled her to analyse the intricacies of the shifting alliances between the city's guilds, thus revealing deep political and personal complexities, which have precluded any subsequent simplistic assessment of the situation.

While in Leicester Bird co-wrote entries on the villages of Humberstone and Knighton for the Leicestershire Victoria county history (1958). On her retirement to Sussex in 1963 she immersed herself in the local history of Horsted Keynes, where she co-wrote a history of the village, and edited two volumes of 'day books' kept by Giles More, a seventeenth-century incumbent of the parish church of St Giles. The second part of *The Journal of Giles More* appeared as volume 68 of the Sussex Record Society in 1971. At the time of her death Ruth Bird was co-writing a history of the local Horsted Keynes school, a seventeenth-century charitable foundation by Archbishop Robert Leighton.

Ruth Bird's health was undermined in her later years by a weak chest, though she remained mentally alert. She died in hospital in Haywards Heath on 24 January 1987 aged eighty-seven, and her ashes were buried in Horsted Keynes churchyard on 31 January 1987.

D. ANNE WELCH

Sources Royal Holloway College, Egham, Surrey, archives · private information (2004) [Pauline Bird, S. Pleydell, H. Rawlings, J. Rawlings, M. Hobbs, C. Cross, S. Badham, P. Nightingale, M. Hill-Tout] · copies of Bird wills, Principal Registry of the Family Division, London · b. cert. · m. cert.
Archives Royal Holloway College, Egham, Surrey
Likenesses photograph, 1945–9, priv. coll.
Wealth at death £126,919: probate, 15 May 1987, *CGPLA Eng. & Wales*

Bird, Samuel (*d.* 1603), Church of England clergyman, was the son of Samuel Bird of Walden, Essex. He matriculated as a pensioner of Queens' College, Cambridge, at Easter 1566, graduated BA in 1569–70, and commenced MA from Corpus Christi College in 1573. In November 1573 he was elected a fellow of Corpus Christi and was admitted on 30 April following. He vacated his fellowship in 1576 and disappears from the historical record until May 1592 when he became minister of St Peter's, Ipswich, where he remained until his death in 1603. Suggestions that in the sixteen-year interim Bird was employed as a schoolmaster, in either London or Suffolk, probably result from confusion with namesakes.

What is clear is that, not later than 1580, Bird had experienced a conversion to a godly way of life. The evidence for this appears in his first published work, *A friendlie communication or dialogue betweene Paule and Demas wherein is disputed how we are to use the pleasures of this life* (1580), which contains a particularly strong attack upon the perils of playing cards and dice. In the preliminary 'Epistle to the Christian Reader' Bird confesses that he had 'grieved good hearts in following foolish games' and that 'it shall make more for the glorie of God, and more against this sinne, when it is cried out uppon, of him that hath had his delight therein'. The work is notable for a number of references to his time in Cambridge but gives little information as to Bird's circumstances in 1580, describing him simply on the title-page as 'Master of Art and fellow not long since of Benet Colledge', the name by which Corpus Christi was familiarly known. He speaks of having been granted 'so great leasure', and incidental references make it clear that he resided in a town either in Essex or Suffolk. Little is known of his ministry at St Peter's, Ipswich. When Bishop William Redman went on visitation in 1597, the churchwardens disclosed a catalogue of nonconformist offences: Bird did not wear the surplice, omitted the sign of the cross in baptism, permitted fathers to answer for the child in baptism, did not bid holy days and fast days, and did not perambulate. He preached on Tuesdays and Sundays but 'whether licensed or noe they knowe not'

(Williams, 157–8). His punishment was reserved but his practice was matched by that of his colleagues in other Ipswich parishes at this time.

Both *The lectures of Samuel Bird of Ipswidge upon the 8 and 9 chapters of the second epistle to the Corinthians* and *The lectures of Samuel Bird of Ipswidge upon the 11 chapter of the epistle unto the Hebrewes and upon the 38 Psalme* were published in Cambridge by John Legate in 1598, having been prepared for the press in the autumn of 1597. The first work, a treatise on generosity, provides evidence of Bird's close association with John Moore of Ipswich, an influential and godly alderman. The second was dedicated with praise to Edward Bacon of Shrubland Hall, describing him in the dedicatory epistle as one who had learned 'not to spende your witte and your studies and your revenewes upon haukes and dogges and gawdish apparell', accounting 'the rebuke of Christ greater riches then to enjoy the delights of sinne for a season'. Both are works of scriptural exposition in a plain style laced with pungent sayings and illustrations, and may have begun life as parish sermons or in the context of a combination lecture.

Bird married at least twice and had five sons, Samuel, Josias, Joseph, Nathaniell, and Jonathan, and four daughters, Dorothie, Elizabeth, Sara, and Marie. His will makes mention of four stepdaughters from a later marriage. His son Samuel received an exhibition scholarship from the corporation of Ipswich to pursue his studies at Cambridge. Bird's stipend at St Peter's was a respectable £30 per annum and at his death he possessed land and a butcher's shop in Ipswich as well as a house in Haddenham. When he came to write his will on 26 July 1603, in the context of an outbreak of 'generall plauge and mortallitie' in and near Ipswich, his sole bequest was both personal and warmly evangelical. He had died by 30 November, when his will was granted probate. JOHN CRAIG

Sources S. Bird, *A friendlie communication or dialogue betweene Paule and Demas wherein is diputed how we are to use the pleasures of this life* (1580) · S. Bird, *The lectures of Samuel Bird of Ipswidge upon the 8 and 9 chapters of the second epistle to the Corinthians* (1598) · S. Bird, *The lectures of Samuel Bird of Ipswidge upon the 11 chapter of the epistle unto the Hebrewes and upon the 38 Psalme* (1598) · will, 1603, PRO, PROB 11/102, sig. 94 · BL, Add. MS 25344 · D. MacCulloch and J. Blatchly, 'Pastoral provision in the parishes of Tudor Ipswich', *Sixteenth Century Journal*, 22 (1991), 457–74 · R. Masters, *The history of the College of Corpus Christi and the B. Virgin Mary ... in the University of Cambridge* (1753) · R. G. Usher, ed., *The presbyterian movement in the reign of Queen Elizabeth, as illustrated by the minute book of the Dedham classis, 1582–1589*, CS, 3rd ser., 8 (1905) · Venn, *Alum. Cant.*, 1/1.156 · J. Webb, 'Peter Moone of Ipswich (d.1601): a Tudor tailor, poet and gospeller and his circle', *Proceedings of the Suffolk Institute of Archaeology and History*, 38 (1993–6), 35–55 · J. F. Williams, ed., *Diocese of Norwich, Bishop Redman's visitation, 1597*, Norfolk RS, 18 (1946)
Wealth at death see will, 1603, PRO, PROB 11/102, sig. 94

Bird, Theophilus (*bap.* 1608, *d.* 1663), actor, was born into a theatrical family, if indeed he was the child baptized at St Leonard, Shoreditch, on 7 December 1608, the son of William Bird or Borne (*d.* 1624), an actor with Prince Henry's Men, later Palsgrave's Men, at the Fortune playhouse, in the immediate vicinity of which the elder Bird was living by 1622. The first record of Theophilus Bird's acting comes

in 1625, when he played Paulina in Massinger's *The Renegado*, performed by Queen Henrietta's Men at the Cockpit playhouse in Drury Lane. He remained a member of that company until 1636–7, and continued to play female roles into his twenties, including Toota in Heywood's *The Fair Maid of the West*; by 1635 he had begun to take male roles: in that year he played Massanissa in Nabbes's *Hannibal and Scipio*. During the prolonged plague of 1636–7 the manager of the Cockpit, Christopher *Beeston, installed a new resident troupe, the King and Queen's Young Company (or Beeston's Boys), which Bird joined. About the same time he allied himself to the theatrical clan of the Beestons by marrying Christopher's daughter Anne, with whom he was to have seven children. The two eldest died young and were buried at St Giles-in-the-Fields, in which parish Bird seems to have lived for all his adult life in London; he was in turn buried at the church.

Bird changed companies again in or after 1638, no doubt following his father-in-law's death in October of that year, becoming a member of the King's Men, with which group he retained associations until the foundation of the new King's Company in 1660. His position in the pre-war company later became a matter of some dispute with his fellows; in 1655 he sued them for not having received his share of money and goods when they disbanded, after the prohibition of playing in September 1642. Their reply was that he had not fully paid the £200 agreed upon when he first joined them. Notwithstanding this disagreement he was a sharer in the company organized in January 1648, with John Lowin, Richard Robinson, Robert Benfield, Thomas Pollard, Hugh Clarke, and Stephen Hammerton. It appears that the actors intended to reopen the Blackfriars playhouse, although there is no evidence that they succeeded. They probably performed *ad hoc* in other places, but by July the company had reconstituted itself, and Bird apparently left it, perhaps because of the money quarrel he subsequently took to law. He then became involved in theatrical investment with his brother-in-law William *Beeston: in 1652 he bought a share of the lease of the Salisbury Court playhouse, where a number of surreptitious performances were given in the interregnum period, and he may have acted in Killigrew's *Claricilla*, performed in March 1653 and interrupted by a raid by government soldiers.

By 1659–60 public playing was resumed at three surviving playhouses: Salisbury Court, the Cockpit in Drury Lane, and the Red Bull. Bird perhaps performed at the theatre in which he held a stake, but by this date he was also related to a second leading actor, Michael *Mohun, who had married his daughter Anne. The two men had known each other since the 1630s, when Mohun had been a member of Beeston's Boys at the Cockpit. In 1660 Mohun led the troupe at the Red Bull, and Bird may have performed with him there; he may also have followed Mohun in joining the King's Company in mid-1660, though Bird's presence was not officially registered until late in 1661.

Bird's career with the King's Company accordingly lasted only two or three seasons, during which time he may have played the Duke of Missena in Flecknoe's

Erminia and Woolfort in Fletcher's *Beggars' Bush*; he played Lord Audley in Heywood's *The Royal King and the Loyal Subject*, possibly the Second Lord in Shirley's *The Cardinal*, and he was injured in a stage accident during a performance of Suckling's *Aglaura* in September 1662: Pepys noted that 'Bird hath lately broke his leg, while he was fencing' in the play (Pepys, 3.204). Bird held a full acting share in the company, but perhaps only during his active membership, since it is not mentioned in his will; yet he did leave jointly to his sons Theophilus (also an actor) and George 'all my right and title in all the playes and play books that are mine' (Guildhall Library, MS 9172/55). Bird also wrote occasional prologues: two survive in the 1639 edition of Ford's *The Lady's Trial* and the 1658 edition of *The Witch of Edmonton*. He signed the dedications to the Beaumont and Fletcher folio of 1647, and to Ford and Dekker's *The Sun's Darling* (1656).

Bird died in London. He made his will on 20 March 1663, and was buried at St Giles-in-the-Fields on 31 March. In the lengthy religious preamble to the will he beseeched God 'to receive mee into the number of his Elect and chosen company and according to the Full trust and beleife which I have reposed onely in his Ineffable mercy through the Shedding of his most precious Blood, and through the same Faith I have full hope I shall live againe and See my Lord and Redeemer' (Guildhall Library, MS 9172/55). He named his wife, Anne, as his executor and chief beneficiary; to each of his surviving children, Anne Mohun, Mary, Theophilus, George, and Elizabeth, he left 20 shillings, and a similar amount to the poor, in addition to the professional bequest to his sons noted above. The will says little of his entire worth, but the Bird family is likely to have been comfortably off; Anne Bird had inherited £300 from her father at his death in 1638.

JOHN H. ASTINGTON

Sources Highfill, Burnim & Langhans, *BDA* · J. Milhous and R. D. Hume, 'New light on English acting companies in 1646, 1648, and 1660', *Review of English Studies*, new ser., 42 (1991), 487–509 · J. Milhous and R. D. Hume, 'Manuscript casts for three plays by Shirley in the 1660s', *Theatre Notebook*, 39 (1985), 32–6 · E. A. J. Honigmann and S. Brock, eds., *Playhouse wills, 1558–1642: an edition of wills by Shakespeare and his contemporaries in the London theatre* (1993) · G. E. Bentley, *The Jacobean and Caroline stage*, 7 vols. (1941–68) · will, 20 March 1663, GL, MS 9172/55 · Pepys, *Diary*, 3.204
Wealth at death likely to have been comfortably off; £6 in bequests; personal property to widow: will, 20 March 1663, GL, MS 9172/55; microfilm copy MS 9171/31, fols. 242v–243v

Bird, Sir William (1560/61–1624), civil lawyer, was the second son of William Bird, gentleman, of Saffron Walden, Essex, and Maria, daughter of John Woodhall, also of Walden; Bird was born in Walden. He matriculated at All Souls College, Oxford, on 28 November 1581, aged twenty, having become a fellow in 1578. He devoted himself to the study of the civil law, receiving the degrees of BCL in 1583 and DCL in 1588. He was admitted as an advocate of the arches on 27 April 1589 and became a member of Doctors' Commons on 14 October 1590. His early career was spent mainly at Oxford, where he became acting vice-chancellor of the university in 1591 and dean of All Souls in 1593. In

1597 he became more active in the London courts, especially the court of admiralty, where he practised until 1615, and the court of delegates, where he served frequently until 1622. In 1604 he resigned his fellowship at All Souls and took up residence at Doctors' Commons. In 1608 he succeeded Thomas Crompton DCL as MP for the University of Oxford. Bird represented the civil lawyers at the conference with the common law judges concerning prohibitions in 1611, and in the same year he was appointed judge of the prerogative court of Canterbury, together with Sir John Bennet. Bird succeeded to that post by himself in 1622, after Bennet was prosecuted for corruption. In 1615 Bird defended Samuel Pallachia against a £3000 suit brought by the count of Gondomar, the Spanish ambassador. Bird claimed that his client, who had been accused of being an impostor, was a public minister of the king of Barbary and deserved the same respect as the Spanish ambassador. In 1617 he and Sir Edward Conway were sent to survey Jersey, hold a general muster, and inquire into the abuses and defects of its martial and civil government. They also reported on ecclesiastical government, indicating that the ministers of the twelve parishes on the island, which followed the form and discipline of the Reformed churches of France, were ready for conformity with England. The laity, however, according to Bird and Conway, feared the assertion of ecclesiastical authority and the formalities of a law unknown to them.

Bird was knighted on 22 March 1617. He reached the high point of his career with his appointment as dean of the court of arches on 23 June 1618. Like many civil lawyers, Bird also served as a master in chancery and in that capacity he and three others were accused in the parliament of 1621 of taking improper fees against the terms of the statute of 1 Jac. c. 10. Bird and his colleagues argued that the intent of the statute was not to deprive the masters of their fees. Bird's last judicial appointment was as a member of the high commission in 1620.

Bird held a house in Walthamstow, Essex, in the right of his wife, Jane, as well as the rectory of Ickleton, Cambridgeshire. Although he had been appointed JP for Essex in 1603, his service as master in chancery and judge of two of the courts of the archbishop of Canterbury allowed him to spend only a few weeks in the year in his home county. In 1623 he petitioned Conway, now secretary of state, for exemption from his duty to show his horse and armour at the county muster. Bird was buried on 5 September 1624 in Christ Church, Newgate, London. By the terms of a signed testament he bequeathed the lease of his house to his wife, who received a renewal of his grant to the rectory of Ickleton in November. He and his wife did not have any children.

BRIAN P. LEVACK

Sources *Reg. Oxf.*, 2/1, 2/2, 2/3 · B. P. Levack, *The civil lawyers in England, 1603–1641* (1973) · BL, Lansdowne MS 152, fols. 352–3 · PRO, SP14/152, fol. 71 · C. T. Martin, *Catalogue of the archives in the muniment room of All Souls' College* (1877) · BL, Lansdowne MS 664, fols. 7r–9r · S. Bond, *The chapter acts of the dean and canons of Windsor* (1966) · M. B. Rex, *University representation in England, 1604–1690* (1954) · will, 9 Sept 1568, Essex RO, CR6 [William Bird senior] · G. D. Squibb, *Doctors' Commons: a history of the College of Advocates and Doctors of Law* (1977) · R. Griffin, *The history of Audley End* (1836) · W. Notestein, F. H.

Relf, and H. Simpson, eds., *Commons debates, 1621*, 7 vols. (1935) · Wood, *Ath. Oxon.: Fasti* (1815), 240

Birdsall, John [*name in religion* John Augustine] (1775–1837), Benedictine monk, was born on 27 June 1775 at Liverpool, the son of Cottam Birdsall (1743–1829), a grocer, and his wife, Elizabeth (1744–1818). His childhood was spent in Liverpool but his parents eventually settled in Richmond, Yorkshire, where they stayed for the rest of their lives. Birdsall was educated at the English Dominican school at Bornhem, in Flanders, which was closed by the incursion of the French Revolution in 1794. In 1795 he entered the novitiate of the English Benedictine abbey of Lamspringe in the bishopric of Hildesheim. He made his solemn profession there on 6 November 1796 and was ordained priest on 30 May 1801. In September 1802 he became prefect (as the headmaster was known) of the small school at Lamspringe, where his pupils included Peter Augustine Baines (1787–1843), who was later to play a crucial part in his life. He returned to England after the seizure of Hildesheim by Prussia and the suppression of his monastery on 3 January 1803. After some time at Ampleforth College, Yorkshire, where most of the Lamspringe students were relocated, he was appointed assistant priest to the Benedictine mission at Bath, where he resided from 1806 to 1809. Birdsall pursued two careers simultaneously: he was on the one hand an active missioner and builder of chapels, while on the other he acted as head of a religious congregation struggling for survival after the seemingly disastrous closure of its continental houses during the French Revolution.

Cheltenham, a town in which population increased from 3000 to 20,000 in the first quarter of the nineteenth century, was to be the centre of Birdsall's activities for most of his active life. An attempt to establish a Benedictine mission in 1805 under Dom James Calderbank (1770–1821) had failed, and the Cheltenham Catholics had to rely on visits from the resident priest at Gloucester and, from 1807, on the ministrations of Abbé Nicolas Alexandre César Robin (*d.* 1811), an exiled priest from the French diocese of Laon, who celebrated mass in hired rooms. Birdsall was appointed to the town in 1809 and through the use of his *peculium*, the personal pension allowed to monks on the mission, and donations from family and friends, was able to open a chapel in Somerset Place on 3 June 1810. With various later extensions it had a seating capacity of some 500. Attached to it was a clergy house and, from 1827, a charity school. Birdsall's early years at Cheltenham were marked by quick and solid progress but, after 1824 with the appointment of the evangelical Francis Close (1797–1882) as curate (and from 1826 incumbent) of Cheltenham, he became increasingly involved in controversy with the established church. 'We Catholics are said to be idolaters of images,' he once remarked characteristically, adding, as he pointed to the two carved angels that flanked the altar-steps of his chapel, 'Now I gave £4.16s for those two statues, and if anybody will send me a five-pound note for the pair I'll let him have them with pleasure. *That's* how I worship them' (*DNB*).

Lamspringe's buildings, which Birdsall revisited in 1828

and 1830, suffered very little as a result of its closure, but its community was dwindling and scattered. Birdsall sought to revive it at Broadway, Worcestershire, where he established a mass centre in 1826. A property was acquired in 1828, the foundation-stone for a monastic house laid in 1830, and the first mass in the newly completed chapel celebrated in 1831. In his last years he spent an increasing proportion of his time at Broadway in his 'German College', conducted, as *The Laity's Directory* (1836) put it, 'by the Gentlemen formerly of Lamspringe'.

Cheltenham and Broadway formed the relatively stable base for Birdsall's national work. From 1814, when he was elected a definitor of the southern Benedictine province, until his death he was at the centre of the struggle for survival and identity within the English Benedictine congregation. In 1822 he was elected provincial of Canterbury by general chapter and was re-elected in 1826. In the same year he became president-general, which he was to remain until 1837. In 1829 he was pro-vicar apostolic of the western district for the ailing Bishop Peter Bernadine Collingridge (1757–1829). He received the titular dignities of cathedral prior of Winchester in 1826 and abbot of Westminster in 1830.

The period of Birdsall's office was a difficult one. The Catholic community was coming to terms with the institutional and financial implications of emancipation. The Benedictines in their two principal centres at Ampleforth and Downside were fighting for survival, faced with dwindling numbers and the loss of many continental houses during the French Revolution. One of the most well-known Benedictines, Bishop Baines, vicar apostolic of the western district 1829–43, wanted to use the manpower and finance of his monastic congregation to create what he thought would be an effective church structure adapted to the needs of the time. He aimed to depopulate his own monastery at Ampleforth, close Downside, and transfer the rich mission of Bath to his own jurisdiction. Prior Park in Bath was to be developed as the magnificent setting for his episcopate. Birdsall's severe, headstrong, and determined personality led him to resist Baines on all levels. Baines conceded that Birdsall's election as president-general was because of his ability 'to wage war with a bishop' (O'Donoghue, 19). Birdsall 'continued throughout life', as his unsympathetic biographer Dom Athanasius Allanson put it, 'to be much opposed to the arbitrary dealings of others' (Allanson, 2.248). His ultimately successful confrontation with Baines probably saved the English Benedictines from extinction. His influence on his fellow monks was not merely defensive.

Like Baines, Birdsall was a man of vision who gave great encouragement to those such as Dom Bede Polding (1794–1877) who were establishing the Australian mission, the great enterprise of the nineteenth-century English Benedictines. Birdsall saw the Australian mission as part of the Catholic contribution to the British empire. 'For our Island', he wrote in 1820 to Nicholas Wiseman, then in Rome, 'is in constant intercourse with all the countries of the East by means of their commercial relations, and might be made a sort of Head Quarters from which the

Church would be able to exercise its authority and disperse its blessings to all around us' (Birdsall to Wiseman, 15 Aug 1829, Wiseman MSS).

Birdsall's activities left him little time for writing, although he published *Christian Reflections for every Day in the Month* in 1822, a translation from an eighteenth-century French original. A portrait of him, showing a solid figure in middle age, is housed at Downside. Birdsall died at the college in Broadway on 2 August 1837. A memorial tablet at Cheltenham did not survive the rebuilding of his chapel, while the inscription on his tomb in the Catholic graveyard at Broadway, or Vialta (the Roman form he used in his diary), is now difficult to decipher.

DOMINIC AIDAN BELLENGER

Sources J. A. Birdsall, MS diary, 1779–1832, Downside Abbey, near Bath · A. Allanson, 'Biography of the English Benedictines', 2 vols., 1850, Downside Abbey, near Bath [life of Augustine Birdsall], 2.247–91 · English College, Rome, Wiseman MSS · *DNB* · T. B. Snow, *Obit book of the English Benedictines from 1600 to 1912*, rev. H. N. Birt (privately printed, Edinburgh, 1913) · *Laity's Directory* (1836) · *Catholic Record Society* [obituaries], 12 (1913) · F. O'Donoghue, *The bishop of Botany Bay: the life of John Bede Polding, Australia's first Catholic archbishop* (1982)
Archives Downside Abbey Archives, Downside Abbey, near Bath · Broadway, registers, 1828 | Roman Catholic church, Broadway, Worcestershire
Likenesses oils, Downside Abbey, near Bath · silhouette, Downside Abbey, near Bath

Birdwood, Sir George Christopher Molesworth (1832–1917), administrator in India, was born at Belgaum in the Bombay presidency on 8 December 1832, the eldest son of General Christopher Birdwood (1807–1882) of the Bombay infantry and his wife, Lydia Juliana, daughter of the Revd Joseph Taylor of the London Missionary Society. His younger brother was Herbert Mills *Birdwood, a judge in India. George was educated at the new grammar school, Plymouth, the Dollar Academy, Clackmannanshire, and the University of Edinburgh. In 1854 he obtained the degree of MD and was admitted to the Royal College of Surgeons, whereupon he joined the Bombay medical service as an assistant surgeon.

On 19 February 1856, shortly after his return to Bombay, Birdwood married the 24-year-old Frances Anne, eldest daughter of Edward Tolcher RN of Harewood, Plymouth, with whom he had three sons and two daughters. After his marriage he took part as a naval surgeon in the Persian expedition of 1856–7. Upon his return and in addition to his professional duties Birdwood devoted himself to a variety of social and cultural institutions that helped to shape the new, post-1857, city of Bombay. While holding the chairs first of anatomy and physiology and then of botany and materia medica at Grant Medical College, he was registrar to the newly founded University of Bombay, curator of the government museum, secretary to the Bombay branch of the Royal Asiatic Society, a founder of the Victoria Botanical Gardens, and a member of the municipality. These activities culminated in his election in 1864 as sheriff of Bombay. Within a few months, however, his health collapsed and he resigned from the medical service. In 1868 he returned to England, not, as he initially

thought, to retire but to begin a new career promoting opportunities for cultural and intellectual exchange between Indians and Britons.

Birdwood followed keenly the arts and crafts movement and while still in Bombay had been put in charge of the Indian exhibits at the Paris Exhibition of 1867. In 1871 the India Office charged him with supervision of the Indian collections in a series of special exhibitions to be held at South Kensington; in 1875 he was appointed keeper of the Indian Museum and assistant reporter on the products of India. He helped organize the Indian exhibits at all the principal international exhibitions of the period and used his contacts with British designers and textile manufacturers to promote the use of Indian raw materials. In 1880 he published *The Industrial Arts of India*, which along with his various exhibition catalogues established him as one of Europe's leading authorities on Indian handicrafts.

In 1879 Birdwood was appointed special assistant in the revenue and statistical department of the India Office, a post created specifically for him. In 1890 he published the *Report on the Miscellaneous Old Records of the India Office*, and in 1893 *The Register of Letters of the Governour and Company of Merchants of London Trading into the East Indies, 1600–1610*, edited with the assistance of William Foster. The unexpected interest generated by these volumes pushed the India Office towards more active preservation of its oldest records.

Birdwood retired from the India Office in 1905 but continued to write on all manner of Indian topics. Most of his prodigious output was in the scattered form of reports, articles in learned journals (especially so in the case of his botanical writings), contributions to newspapers, and introductions or appendices in the books of others. It was a letter of his to *The Times* in 1882 which inspired the commemoration of the anniversary of Disraeli's death (19 April) as primrose day. *Sva*, a collection of his essays published in 1915, amply illustrates both his enthusiasm for all kinds of knowledge about India and the occasionally fanciful and romantic interpretations that he fashioned with it. He was renowned for his kindness to anyone who showed an interest in India and also for his hospitality to Indian students newly arrived in England.

Birdwood was knighted in 1881 and made KCIE in 1887. He died at his home at 5 Windsor Road, Ealing, London, on 28 June 1917 and was buried in Acton cemetery.

VALENTINE CHIROL, *rev.* KATHERINE PRIOR

Sources introduction to George Birdwood MSS, BL OIOC · *The Times* (29 June 1917), 1, 9 · *The Times* (3 July 1917), 11 · D. G. Crawford, *A history of the Indian medical service, 1600–1913*, 2 (1914) · *DNB* · ecclesiastical records, BL OIOC · surgeons' entrance papers, BL OIOC
Archives BL OIOC, corresp. and papers, MS Eur. F 216 · V&A NAL, notes for his 'Anya Silpa Darpana' | Bodl. Oxf., corresp. with Lord Kimberley · CUL, corresp. with Lord Hardinge
Likenesses A. Gilbert, bronze bust, exh. RA 1892, RSA · Elliott & Fry, photograph, *c*.1895, BL OIOC · photograph, *c*.1900, BL OIOC
Wealth at death £389 4s. 6d.: probate, 31 Aug 1917, *CGPLA Eng. & Wales*

Birdwood, Herbert Mills (1837–1907), judge in India, was born at Belgaum, Bombay presidency, on 29 May 1837, the third son in the family of fourteen children of General

Herbert Mills Birdwood (1837–1907), by Lock & Whitfield, pubd 1889

Christopher Birdwood (1807–1882), of Pucklechurch, Gloucestershire, from an old Devon family, deputy commissary-general of the Bombay army, and his wife, Lydia Juliana, eldest daughter of the Revd Joseph Taylor, agent of the London Missionary Society in the southern Maratha country. His great-grandfather Richard Birdwood (1745–1810), mayor of Plymouth in 1796, and his grandfather Peter Birdwood (1773–1839), major in the Plymouth volunteers, were both agents at Plymouth of the East India Company. His eldest brother was Sir George Christopher Molesworth *Birdwood (1832–1917).

Educated at the Plymouth new grammar school and Mount Radford School, Exeter, Birdwood matriculated at Edinburgh University in 1851, was gold medallist in mathematics in 1853 and 1854, but did not graduate. In October 1854 he entered Peterhouse, Cambridge, and graduated BA in 1858 as twenty-third wrangler in the mathematical tripos and with a second class in the natural science tripos (MA 1863, LLM 1879, LLD 1890). At once elected a fellow of his college, he took eighteenth place in the Indian Civil Service examination. He was admitted to Lincoln's Inn on 9 June 1877 and called to the bar in 1889. In October 1901 he was elected an honorary fellow of Peterhouse.

Birdwood arrived in Bombay on 26 January 1859, and served as assistant collector successively in Thana, Broach, Surat, and Ahmadabad. On 29 January 1861 he married Edith Marion Sidonie (d. 1912), eldest daughter of Surgeon-Major Elijah George Halhed Impey FRCS, of the Bombay horse artillery and postmaster-general of the Bombay presidency; they had a daughter and five sons. In

1863 Birdwood became under-secretary in the judicial, political, and educational departments and secretary to the Bombay legislative council. In June 1866 he went to Kathiawar as first political assistant, and in 1867 returned to Bombay as acting registrar of the high court. In December 1871 he was appointed judge of the Ratnagiri district, and was subsequently transferred to Thana and then to Surat. In Ratnagiri he won a reputation for independence by deciding against the government in cases which challenged the legality of the operations of the revenue survey department.

In February 1881 Birdwood went to Karachi as judicial commissioner and judge of the Sadr court in Sind. He steadily improved the work of the subordinate courts in the province. He laid out to a new design the Karachi public gardens, which extended to some forty acres, establishing there a fine zoological collection. He stimulated the volunteer movement by serving in the local corps. From January 1885 to April 1892 he was judge of the Bombay high court, and from April 1892 to April 1897 was judicial and political member of the executive council of the governor of Bombay. His term of office coincided with the plague epidemic, the great famine of 1897, and the political unrest leading to the murder at Poona in June 1897 of W. C. Rand, chairman of the plague committee, and of Lieutenant O. E. Ayerst. In June 1893 he was created a CSI. He was acting governor of the presidency in the brief interval between Lord Harris's departure and Lord Sandhurst's arrival (16 to 18 February 1895). While efficiently performing his judicial and political duties, he actively interested himself in educational and scientific movements. He had been a fellow of Bombay University since 1863 and dean of arts in 1868, 1881, 1888, and 1890. He was vice-chancellor in 1891–2. He was president of the botanical section of the Bombay Natural History Society, and compiled for its *Journal* (vols. 1 and 2, 1886) a comprehensive catalogue of the flora of the Matheran and Mahabaleshwar hill stations (reprinted separately, 1897). He was for many years president of the Agri-Horticultural Society of Western India. Between 1871 and 1890 he edited, solely or with Mr Justice Henry J. Parsons, volumes 4 to 11 of the acts and regulations in force in the Bombay presidency, commonly known as West's code.

After his return to England in April 1897 Birdwood collaborated with Mr Justice Wood Renton and E. G. Phillimore in a revised edition of Burge's *Commentaries on Colonial and Foreign Laws* (vol. 1, 1907), editing the Indian portion. He practised before the privy council on Indian appeals, and in the important case of the *Taluka of Kota Sangani* v. *State of Gondal* (1904) he, with Sir Edward Clarke as his leader, obtained a judgment upholding the sovereignty of the Kathiawar chiefs, and sustained the contention that their courts were outside the appellate jurisdiction of the British courts. To the *Journal of the Royal Society of Arts* he contributed in 1898 papers on the history of plague in western India which were awarded the society's silver medal. He also published articles in the *National Review* and elsewhere. At Twickenham, where he finally settled, he was active in local affairs and did much philanthropic work. He was a JP for Middlesex and a commissioner of Richmond Bridge. He also enjoyed gardening.

Birdwood died of pneumonia at his residence, Dalkeith House, Cambridge Park, Twickenham, Middlesex, on 21 February 1907, and was buried at Twickenham cemetery.

Birdwood's daughter, Edith Jane, married General Sir Robert Charles Ochiltree Stuart, inspector-general of ordnance in India. Birdwood's five sons all served in the army in India. The eldest son, Captain Herbert Christopher Impey Birdwood RE, died at Ambala in 1894. The second son was William Riddell *Birdwood, first Baron Birdwood (1865–1951).   F. H. BROWN, *rev.* ROGER T. STEARN

Sources *Representative men of India* (1889) · *The Times* (23 Feb 1907) · personal knowledge (1912) · private information (1912) [G. Birdwood] · Venn, *Alum. Cant.* · *WWW, 1897–1915* · Burke, *Peerage* (1999) · Boase, *Mod. Eng. biog.* · W. P. Baildon, ed., *The records of the Honorable Society of Lincoln's Inn: admissions*, 2 (1896) · D. Laing, ed., *A catalogue of the graduates … of the University of Edinburgh*, Bannatyne Club, 106 (1858) · W. W. Hunter, *Bombay 1885 to 1890: a study in Indian administration* (1892) · B. R. Nanda, *Gokhale: the Indian moderates and the British raj* (1977) · J. C. Masselos, *Towards nationalism: group affiliations and the politics of public associations in nineteenth century western India* (1974) · P. Spear, *The Oxford history of modern India, 1740–1947* (1965)

Likenesses Lock & Whitfield, photograph, pubd 1889, NPG [*see illus.*]

Wealth at death £5620 8s. 1d.: probate, 10 April 1907, *CGPLA Eng. & Wales*

William Riddell Birdwood, first Baron Birdwood (1865–1951), by John Singer Sargent, 1916

Birdwood, William Riddell, first Baron Birdwood (1865–1951), army officer, was born at Kirkee, India, on 13 September 1865, the second son of Herbert Mills *Birdwood (1837–1907), under-secretary to the government of Bombay, later a High Court judge, and his wife, Edith Marion Sidonie (*d.* 1912), daughter of Surgeon-Major Elijah George Halhed Impey, of the Bombay horse artillery. All five sons were to serve the army in India.

Career up to 1912 Educated at Clifton College, Birdwood obtained a commission in the 4th battalion, Royal Scots Fusiliers, in 1883. He entered the Royal Military College, Sandhurst, but as a result of the Panjdeh incident of 1885 he was gazetted earlier than he expected to the 12th lancers and embarked for India in that year; he transferred to the 11th Bengal lancers at the end of 1886. He first saw active service in the Black Mountain expedition in 1891; and acquitted himself well in the Tirah expedition in 1897, having been promoted captain in 1896. In 1893–8 he was adjutant of the viceroy's body guard. Birdwood married in 1894 Janetta Hope Gonville (*d.* 1947), daughter of Sir Benjamin Parnell Bromhead, fourth baronet. It was a very happy marriage. They had two daughters and a son.

Birdwood went in November 1899 to South Africa as a special service officer and was appointed to the staff of the Natal mounted brigade commanded by Lord Dundonald. He took part in the battle of Colenso and in the further campaigns to relieve Ladysmith; he was later wounded and five times mentioned in dispatches. When the Natal force was broken up towards the end of 1900 Birdwood

became deputy assistant adjutant-general to Lord Kitchener, and on the conclusion of the Second South African War he accompanied Kitchener to India as his assistant military secretary (1902–4) and military secretary (1905–9). Birdwood's relationship with Kitchener was one of the decisive elements in his career: 'we seemed to take to each other at once, and for the next nine years [1900–09] I was scarcely ever away from him' (Birdwood, *Khaki and Gown*, 117).

Birdwood was promoted colonel in 1905 and in 1908 was chief staff officer to Sir James Willcocks in the Mohmand field force. He was appointed to the DSO, mentioned in dispatches, and appointed CIE. He became brigadier-general in 1909 and major-general in 1911. From 1909 to 1912 he was in command of the Kohat independent brigade.

First World War to 1915 In 1912, after a short period as quartermaster-general, Birdwood became secretary to the government of India in the army department and a member of the governor-general's legislative council. He was thus called upon to play an important part in the dispatch of the Indian army units to France, Egypt, and Mesopotamia after the outbreak of war in 1914. In December he was given command of the new Australian and New Zealand contingents being sent to Egypt, with corps commander status and the rank of lieutenant-general.

Birdwood at once discerned the outstanding quality of the independent and ardent young Anzacs. He built up an excellent staff and training was put in hand. The original intention was to send the troops to France after training but they were destined for an earlier and more spectacular initiation. A few days after Admiral Carden opened the naval assault on the Dardanelles on 19 February 1915, Birdwood was instructed by Kitchener, now secretary of state for war, to proceed to the Dardanelles and to report back. Birdwood was at once impressed by the difficulties of a purely naval attack, and he reported to this effect at a time when Winston Churchill was urging Kitchener to send the 29th division to the eastern Mediterranean theatre 'to support our diplomacy'. Kitchener at this stage was vacillating, but some Anzac units and others of the Royal Naval division were sent to the island of Lemnos where Admiral Wemyss was endeavouring to create an advanced supply base with no staff and hardly any facilities. It was Kitchener's intention that Birdwood should command any military force that might be needed; but his decision on 10 March to send the 29th division was one of the factors which resulted in the appointment of Sir Ian Hamilton to take command of what was to be called the Mediterranean expeditionary force. One consequence of this decision was that the preparatory work done by Birdwood's staff was largely negatived. Hamilton's failure to bring Birdwood's staff into his planning and the extent to which he ignored his administrative staff were factors which caused friction.

Gallipoli, 1915–1916 After the failure of the naval attack of 18 March and the decision taken jointly on 22 March and without reference to London by Hamilton and Carden's successor Admiral De Robeck to deliver a combined naval and military attack as soon as Hamilton's force had been reorganized, Birdwood was strongly opposed to any landings on the Helles beaches of the Gallipoli peninsula (which he had previously favoured) as the vital element of surprise had been lost. In this he was strongly supported by Aylmer Hunter-Weston (29th division), Archibald Paris (Royal Naval division), and Sir John Maxwell (general officer commanding, Egypt). Hamilton stuck firmly to the plan to land the 29th division at Helles and rejected Birdwood's arguments for a landing on the Asiatic shore of the Dardanelles.

The role of the Anzac corps was to land on the Peninsula at a point just north of the conspicuous promontory of Gaba Tepe on the western shore of the Gallipoli peninsula and advance eastwards to the eminence of Mal Tepe, thus cutting off the Turkish forces opposed to the 29th division at Helles. Birdwood determined to land his covering force at first light, with no preliminary naval bombardment, in order to achieve the maximum of surprise. The combined assault took place on Sunday 25 April. The Anzac covering force, for reasons which have never been satisfactorily explained, landed in some confusion well to the north of Gaba Tepe in a small bay subsequently known as Anzac Cove. In spite of this initial error the surprise was almost complete, and some units penetrated deep inland against hastily gathered Turkish resistance. The momentum of the advance was not maintained. Colonel Mustafa Kemal, commanding the Turkish 19th division at Boghali,

engaged all available forces. The steep cliff and precipitous gullies above Anzac Cove became the scenes of fierce and unco-ordinated fighting throughout the day. By evening a thin drizzle was falling on the exhausted dominion troops, Anzac Cove was the scene of serious congestion and confusion, and the ground secured was in fact a small perimeter which penetrated inland barely a thousand yards in places. In these depressing circumstances, Birdwood's divisional commanders urged him to recommend evacuation. Against his own inclinations Birdwood did so. In the general confusion the message was not addressed to anyone and it was only by chance that Hamilton received it. His reply was a firm order to hold on.

For six months the Anzacs defended their wretched, tiny, and arid fragment of coast, overlooked by the enemy and constantly exposed to their fire. Intense heat and disease subsequently added to the already severe burdens of the resolute dominion troops. Birdwood may be faulted for certain aspects of his handling of Anzac operations, and particularly for the failures of the night attacks of 2–3 May and for the heroic but poorly commanded attempt to seize the Sari Bair heights on 6–9 August. He may also be criticized for failing to appreciate until too late the debilitating effects of sickness on the Anzac troops which played a significant part in the failure of the August attacks. But in defence his confident and determined example and bearing fully merited the tribute of Hamilton that he was 'the soul of Anzac'.

Birdwood was one of the very few British commanders to leave Gallipoli with an increased reputation. In one respect he was fortunate. The failure of the 9th corps under Sir Frederick Stopford at Suvla on 6–9 August obscured the errors of Birdwood and Alexander Godley at Anzac, both then and later. When, following Hamilton's recall in October, Sir Charles Monro recommended evacuation, Kitchener wanted to appoint Birdwood in his stead. Birdwood, greatly to his credit, protested and the proposal was shelved. It was ironic that Birdwood, the only senior commander initially opposed to evacuation (he subsequently agreed that the decision was right), should eventually be in executive command of the evacuation, as commander of the Dardanelles army under Monro, when the cabinet decided upon it. This brilliantly successful operation in December 1915 and January 1916 rightly increased his already high reputation.

France, 1916–1918 After the death of Sir William Bridges at Anzac in May 1915 Birdwood had been made responsible to the Australian minister of defence for administration in addition to his responsibility to the War Office for the conduct of military operations. It was largely due to Birdwood that this arrangement worked so well.

At the end of March 1916 the two Anzac corps embarked for France, the first under Birdwood's command. In November 1917 it was renamed the Australian corps and comprised the five Australian divisions in France. In May 1918 Birdwood took command of the Fifth Army. He was promoted general in 1917 and after the war awarded £10,000 and created a baronet (1919).

Birdwood had proved himself a brave and resolute soldier and keenly alive to the importance of personal relations. But the failings demonstrated in the attack on Gallipoli were also evident in France. As was written after his death, he remained a character, a virile personality rather than a master of war. His unconcealed eagerness for personal recognition was one facet of his character which some found unattractive. If not in the first, he was high in the second rank of British commanders in the First World War.

India and retirement After the war Birdwood commanded the northern army in India (1920–24) and in 1925 was preferred to Sir Claud Jacob as commander-in-chief. He was promoted field marshal at the same time. He was a good commander-in-chief with a deep and sympathetic knowledge of the country and its peoples.

The one position Birdwood coveted but did not attain was the governor-generalship of Australia. On his retirement from India in 1930 he was elected, somewhat unexpectedly, to the mastership of Peterhouse, Cambridge, an office which he exercised with manifest enjoyment until 1938. In 1935 he was appointed captain of Deal Castle and in 1938 was created Baron Birdwood of Anzac and Totnes. He had been appointed CB (1911), KCB (1917), and GCB (1923); KCSI (1915) and GCSI (1930); KCMG (1914) and GCMG (1919); and GCVO (1937). His long and distinguished life, darkened in later years by failing eyesight, ended on 17 May 1951 when he died in his apartments at Hampton Court Palace. His son, Christopher Bromhead (1899–1962), succeeded to the title. R. R. JAMES, *rev.*

Sources Australian War Memorial, Canberra, Birdwood MSS · W. Birdwood, *Khaki and gown: an autobiography* (1941) · Lord Birdwood, *In my time: recollections and anecdotes* [1946] · C. F. Aspinall-Oglander, *Military operations: Gallipoli*, 2 vols., History of the Great War (1929–32) · C. E. W. Bean and others, *The official history of Australia in the war of 1914–1918*, 12 vols. (1921–43) · R. R. James, *Gallipoli* (1965) · *The Times* (18 May 1951) · *The Times* (22 May 1951) · *The Times* (25 May 1951) · *The Times* (30 May 1951) · private information (1971) · *CGPLA Eng. & Wales* (1951) · E. M. Andrews, *The Anzac illusion* (1993) · P. Dennis and others, *The Oxford companion to Australian military history* (1995) · J. Robertson, *Anzac and empire* (1990)
Archives BL OIOC, corresp. and papers, MS Eur. D 686 · IWM, letters and reports · NAM, diaries, letters, and papers · St Ant. Oxf., Middle East Centre, comments and notes relating to Egypt · U. Leeds, Brotherton L., letters and papers | BL, corresp. with E. T. H. Hutton, Add. MS 50089, *passim* · BL, corresp. with Sir A. J. Murray, Add. MS 52461, *passim* · BL, corresp. with Lord Northcliffe, Add. MS 62159 · BL OIOC, letters to Sir Harcourt Butler, MS Eur. F 116 · BL OIOC, letters to Sir Alfred Lyall, MS Eur. F 132 · BL OIOC, letters to Lord Reading, MSS Eur. E 238, F 118 · BL OIOC, corresp. with E. F. Younghusband, MS Eur. F 197 · Bodl. RH, corresp. with C. W. G. Walker · CAC Cam., corresp. with Sir John De Robeck · CUL, corresp. with Lord Hardinge · Lpool RO, corresp. with earl of Derby · NL Aus., corresp. with Viscount Novar · NMM, letters to Sir Cecil Thursby · NRA Scotland, priv. coll., corresp. with Sir John Ewart · PRO, corresp. with Sir George Arthur, PRO 30/12; WO159 · PRO, corresp. with Lord Kitchener, PRO 30/57; WO159 · Wilts. & Swindon RO, corresp. with Viscount Long | FILM IWM FVA, actuality footage · IWM FVA, news footage
Likenesses J. S. Sargent, chalk drawing, 1916, NPG [*see illus.*] · F. Dodd, charcoal and watercolour drawing, 1917, IWM · W. Orpen, pencil and watercolour drawing, 1917, IWM · A. Hayward, oils, 1919, IWM · W. Stoneman, two photographs, 1919–31, NPG · W. Urwick, oils, 1920, Cavalry and Guards Club, London · J. S. Sargent, group portrait, oils, 1922 (*General officers of World War I*), NPG · S. de Strobl, terracotta bust, 1936, IWM · W. Stoneman, photograph, NPG · oils, Peterhouse, Cambridge
Wealth at death £2085 5s. 6d.: probate, 8 Dec 1951, *CGPLA Eng. & Wales*

Birinus [St Birinus] (*d. c.*650), bishop of Dorchester, was the first bishop of the see of the Gewisse, whose rulers subsequently became kings of the West Saxons. He was consecrated bishop in 634 by Bishop Asterius of Milan in Genoa on the orders of Pope Honorius and given a general brief to convert pagan Anglo-Saxons. Birinus's own ethnic identity is never stated, but the form of his name suggests that he could, like other early missionaries to the Anglo-Saxons, have been a Frank. Bede relates that when Birinus arrived in Britain he visited the Gewisse first and, finding them all pagan, decided to stay among them rather than to go further seeking others to evangelize. King Cynegils was baptized by Birinus in 635, with his overlord King Oswald of Northumbria as godfather. Subsequently Birinus baptized Cynegils's son Cwichelm in 636 and in 639 his grandson Cuthred to whom he became godfather. Another son of Cynegils, Cenwalh, who succeeded him *c.*642, remained unconverted until after the bishop's death, which had occurred by *c.*650. Birinus is said by Bede to have built churches and converted many people, but no detailed traditions seem to have survived to be included in his eleventh-century life, which was probably written in Winchester. The only recorded miracles are his miraculous preservation from a shipwreck on the way to Britain, when he walked on water, and the healing of a blind and deaf woman; neither contains any convincing circumstantial details. Birinus was buried at Dorchester, but was subsequently translated to Old Minster, Winchester, in the episcopate of Hædde, by which time the West Saxons had lost control of the Dorchester-on-Thames area. Birinus appears regularly in late Saxon calendars with the feast day of 3 December. His cult was revived by Bishop Æthelwold of Winchester who translated his body on 4 September 980 and he figures prominently in Winchester liturgies. In the thirteenth century the canons of Dorchester claimed that they possessed the saint's body and part of his supposed shrine survives there.

BARBARA YORKE

Sources Bede, *Hist. eccl.*, 3.7 · *ASC*, s.a. 634, 635, 639, 650 [texts A, E] · D. Townsend, ed., 'An eleventh-century life of Birinus of Wessex', *Analecta Bollandiana*, 107 (1989), 129–59 · R. C. Love, ed. and trans., *Three eleventh-century Anglo-Latin saints' lives: Vita s. Birini, Vita et miracula s. Kenelmi, and Vita s. Rumwoldi*, OMT (1996)
Likenesses portraits, late medieval

Birk [*née* Wilson], **Alma Lillian**, Baroness Birk (1917–1996), politician and journalist, was born on 22 September 1917 at 10 Belgrave Place, Brighton, the daughter of Barnett Wilson (formerly Woolfson) of Stamford Hill, London, and his wife, Alice, *née* Tosh. Her father ran a successful greeting-card company, and she enjoyed a comfortable upbringing. She was educated at South Hampstead high school and the London School of Economics (LSE). Her youthful socialism became more deeply rooted at the LSE, and after graduating she was involved in Labour politics in Finchley. She married, on 24 December 1939, at Hampstead Garden Suburb synagogue, Ellis Samuel Birk (*b.* 1914/15), then a solicitor's clerk, of East Finchley. They had one son and one daughter. Alma and Ellis Birk shared a commitment to socialism and both supported the Fabian Society. While he was stationed in Wiltshire with the army during the war she unsuccessfully contested a seat on Salisbury city council. She later won a seat on Finchley borough council and served as leader of the small Labour group from 1950 to 1953. A woman of great energy, and matching ambition, she was involved with the Howard League for penal reform, the Hendon hospital group, and numerous organizations concerned with child welfare and the Jewish community. At the general election of 1950 she contested Ruislip-Northwood, a Conservative stronghold, for the Labour Party: she was a distant second. Her chances were better at Portsmouth West in 1951, where she lost narrowly. She was encouraged to stand again, only to lose by a greater margin in 1955. It was her last parliamentary candidacy.

Besides politics, Alma Birk's other great interest lay in journalism. She began with a column in *Forward*, a Labour weekly of Gaitskellite leanings, and from there she moved to the *Daily Herald*, which was acquired by the Mirror Group, to which her husband was legal adviser. Her journalistic career entered an exciting new phase when she became associate editor of *Nova*, a post she held from 1965 to 1969. *Nova* proclaimed itself as: 'The new kind of magazine for the new kind of woman'. With Dennis Hackett, the editor, Birk assembled a team of writers who dealt frankly with social and sex problems. It was a radical departure from the 'standard diet of knitting patterns and home hints' (*Glasgow Herald*, 2 Jan 1997). Birk contributed her own articles and made sure that *Nova* stood out on the news-stands with arresting covers. The magazine had a lasting influence, although within a few years of the arrival of *Cosmopolitan* it had folded, outpaced by a racier rival. By then Birk had moved on, her career firmly directed towards politics.

In 1967 Harold Wilson recognized Birk's political and public activities with a life peerage. She was to be a working peer, intended to strengthen the Labour element in the upper chamber. To some observers, though, it was a blatantly political appointment, since Ellis Birk was by now powerful in the Mirror Group, upon which the prime minister relied for press support. Alma Birk nevertheless proved a highly conscientious and effective member of the upper house, where her elegant dress, slim figure, and gold-auburn hair attracted special attention. She would remark self-deprecatingly, 'they call me the poor man's Barbara Castle', but to the friends who knew the extent of her husband's directorships 'she was more the rich man's Barbara Castle' (*The Times*, 31 Dec 1996). As chairman of the Health Education Council from 1969 to 1972 she impressed her chief, Richard Crossman, with her dynamism and executive ability, and she used to good effect the talents as a publicist that she had developed at *Nova*. In March 1974 she was made a government whip, and in

October she became parliamentary under-secretary of state at the Department of the Environment, with responsibility also for transport and Treasury affairs. Shortly before the general election of 1979 she became minister of state in the privy council office.

Birk continued to give devoted service when Labour were in opposition. She was front-bench spokesman on the environment from 1979 to 1986 and on the arts, libraries, heritage, and broadcasting from 1986 to 1993, the role in which she was probably happiest. She and her husband were notable patrons of the performing arts and in particular of the open-air theatre at Regent's Park, from which she took her title. She was a member of the Theatres' Trust, a director of the British Film Institute, and president of the Association of Art Institutions (1984–96). Her long list of public commitments included being a prison visitor at Holloway from 1967 to 1971, vice-president of the Council of Children's Welfare from 1968 to 1975, vice-president of Redbridge Jewish Youth Centre from 1970, and a member of the Holocaust Memorial Committee. Although frail from illness in her last days, Alma Birk would still respond to a three-line whip in the House of Lords, where she could be found 'walking with a stick ... chatting her lively way through the division lobby' (*The Independent*, 3 Jan 1997). She died of breast cancer on 29 December 1996 at her home, Flat 1, 34 Bryanston Square, Westminster, survived by her husband, son, and daughter.   MARK POTTLE

Sources *The Independent* (16 Feb 1992?) · *The Independent* (3 Jan 1997) · *The Guardian* (31 Dec 1996) · *The Times* (31 Dec 1996) · *The Herald* [Glasgow] (2 Jan 1997) · WWW · R. H. S. Crossman, *The diaries of a cabinet minister*, 3 vols. (1975–7) · B. Pimlott, *Harold Wilson* (1992) · *Nova* (Jan–Dec 1965) · D. Gibbs, ed., *Nova, 1965–1975* (1993) · F. W. S. Craig, *British parliamentary election results, 1950–1970* (1971) · b. cert. · m. cert. · d. cert.

Likenesses photograph, repro. in *The Independent* (3 Jan 1997)

Wealth at death £710,715: probate, 12 Feb 1997, *CGPLA Eng. & Wales*

Birkbeck, George (1776–1841), physician and educationist, was born in Settle, Yorkshire, on 10 January 1776, the son of William Birkbeck (*b.* 1745), a Quaker merchant, manufacturer, and banker, and his wife, Sarah (1750–1790), daughter of George Braithwaite of Kendal. He briefly attended Giggleswick School; then, aged eight, he went to board for six years at a Quaker school in Newton in Slaidburn, Lancashire. Following his mother's death in 1790 he lived at Hebblethwaite Hall, near Sedbergh, with a relative, Robert Foster. There he learned mathematics under John Dawson and developed a desire to study medicine.

Birkbeck became a pupil of Dr Garnett of Knaresborough in 1792–3, from where he moved to Leeds to study pharmacy, medicine, and surgery. With this grounding he enrolled as a medical student at Edinburgh University in 1794 and joined the Royal Medical Society. He left his course in 1795–6 to study at several private medical schools in London, but returned to Edinburgh in 1796 and took his MD in 1799. With the support of Dugald Stewart, Birkbeck was appointed professor of natural philosophy at the Anderson's Institution, Glasgow, in December 1799 and began his long and distinguished career in medicine and popular education.

A desire to provide education for the working classes led to Birkbeck offering free extra-curricular lectures on popular science, and this 'mechanics' class' became very popular. Manoeuvred into introducing a fee, Birkbeck resigned his chair in August 1804, though he revived the class in Birmingham in 1805–6, and delivered courses in Liverpool and Hull. Birkbeck had moved to Birmingham infatuated with Catherine, daughter of Sampson Lloyd of the city's Quaker banking family. They married on 15 May 1806 at Berkswell, Warwickshire, and moved to Finsbury Square, London, where Birkbeck set up a medical practice. A son, William Lloyd, was born on 3 March 1807; nine days later Catherine died. Devastated, Birkbeck immersed himself in his work. He became physician to the General Dispensary, Aldersgate Street (a novel body which treated out-patients and undertook home visits); he was admitted as licentiate of the Royal College of Physicians in 1808; and he wrote for the *London Medical Review* between 1808 and 1812. He also moved to 25 Cateaton Street, to be closer to the dispensary.

As befitted a busy and successful medical professional, Birkbeck received many honours and appointments. He became fellow of the Medical Society of London in 1807, and delivered its anniversary oration in 1810. He was admitted as a member of the Medical and Chirurgical Society in 1807 and elected an honorary member of Guy's Hospital Physical Society. He joined the Edinburgh Club and the Geological Society, was elected fellow of the Astronomical Society in 1820 and, in 1823, the first president of the Meteorological Society of London. He also became closely involved with the London Institution, a body established in 1805 to diffuse science and the arts through lectures and public demonstrations of experiments. From 1820 he offered free lectures to all comers, as he had done earlier in Glasgow; and from 1822 to his death he served as manager.

On 9 July 1817 Birkbeck married Anna Margaret Gardner (*b. c.*1794, *d.* in or after 1851), youngest daughter of Henry Gardner, Liverpool merchant. They had five children: Anna Margaret (*b.* 1818), George Henry (*b.* 1820), Charles (*b.* 1822–4), Frances Georgina (*b.* 1824), and Thomas Brougham (*b.* 1826). The expanding family caused the Birkbecks to move to 50 Broad Street in 1822–3.

In December 1823 Birkbeck, supported by Lord Brougham, inaugurated the London Mechanics' Institution, a metropolitan imitator of the recently formed Glasgow Mechanics' Institute, which in turn had grown out of Birkbeck's early mechanics' class. Birkbeck was invited to become the first president and in 1824–5 lent £3700 towards the cost of constructing a lecture theatre. Such middle-class patronage, encouraged by Francis Place, angered the institution's founders, the working-class radicals J. C. Robertson and Thomas Hodgskin, who wanted the institution to be an organization entirely independent of the middle class. Despite the subsequent withdrawal of Hodgskin and Robertson, the institution flourished during Birkbeck's life and, though suffering a decline in its fortunes after his death, it enjoyed a revival after 1867 as the Birkbeck Literary and Scientific Institution, and was renamed Birkbeck College in 1907, becoming a constituent school of London University in 1920.

Birkbeck was one of the original promoters of the foundation of London University in the 1820s and worked for the Society for the Diffusion of Useful Knowledge. He opposed the libel laws, campaigned against the newspaper taxes in the 1830s (joining 'the friends of liberty'), and promoted a reform of the patent laws (1827). His only party political act was to second George Grote as MP for the City of London in 1832, but he was a lifelong friend and supporter of Lord Brougham, expressing a whig-radicalism that emphasized the need for free institutions, enterprise, and expression of opinion, and delighting in particular in the introduction of the penny post. He supported moves to end colonial apprenticeship; he was a supporter of Polish independence in 1832, joining the Literary Association of the Friends of Poland; and in 1840 he helped with William Linton's petition to save the Chartists Frost, Williams, and Jones from execution.

Birkbeck's health had been deteriorating for three years before the attack of prostatitis from which he died at his London house, 38 Finsbury Square, on 1 December 1841. His funeral took place in Kensal Green cemetery on 13 December after a thousand-strong procession from his home, headed by members of the Mechanics' Institution. He was a man of intense energy and religious conviction, given to personal abstemiousness but public generosity. A teacher rather than an originator, he was a gifted public speaker and chairman. His eldest son, William Lloyd Birkbeck (1806–1888), became Downing professor of the laws of England at Cambridge.   MATTHEW LEE

Sources T. Kelly, *George Birkbeck* (1957) · C. D. Burns, *Short history of Birkbeck College* (1924) · J. Godard, *George Birkbeck* (1884) · J. R. Sutherland, 'George Birkbeck, 1776–1841', *Birkbeck College report on the session, 1941–1942* (1942) [suppl.] · H. Clutterbuck, *A brief memoir of George Birkbeck, M. D., read before the Medical Society of London* (1842) · T. Kelly, 'George Birkbeck, 1776–1841', *International biography of adult education*, ed. J. E. Thomas and B. Elsey (1985), 41–3 · W. A. C. Stewart and W. P. McCann, *The educational innovators*, 2 vols. (1967–8) · *GM*, 2nd ser., 17 (1842), 216–17

Archives BL, Add. MSS · Glasgow Royal Technical College, corresp. · University of Strathclyde, Glasgow, MSS · Wellcome L. | BL, Place MSS · Co-operative Union, Holyoake House, Manchester, Robert Owen MSS · priv. coll., Settle MSS · UCL, corresp. with Lord Brougham · UCL, letters to the Society for the Diffusion of Useful Knowledge · Yale U., Beinecke L., letters to T. J. Pettigrew

Likenesses W. Bewick, oils, 1823, Glasgow Royal Technical College · S. Lane, oils, 1825, Birkbeck College, London · H. Dawe, mezzotint, 1827 (after S. Lane), BM, NPG; repro. in Burns, *Short history of Birkbeck College* · G. Adcock, stipple, BM · T. Woolnoth, stipple (after Wageman), NPG

Wealth at death under £9000 in cash, plus interest in a worsted concern in Yorkshire; excl. bad debts of Mechanics' Institution: Kelly, 'George Birkbeck'

Birkbeck, Morris (1764–1825), farmer and writer, was born on 23 January 1764 in Settle, Yorkshire, the only child of Morris Birkbeck (1734–1816), Quaker minister, and his wife, Hannah, *née* Bradford, of Lancaster, who died a few days after his birth. On 23 April in 1794 he married Prudence Bush, daughter of Richard Bush, a prominent

Morris Birkbeck (1764–1825), by unknown engraver, pubd 1825

Quaker of Wandsworth, Surrey, and his wife, Prudence. Seven children were born before Birkbeck was left a widower in 1804. He never remarried.

Educated at the Friends' school in Tottenham from 1772 until 1776, when his father apprenticed him to a sheep farmer in Yorkshire, Birkbeck afterwards spent two years observing advanced agricultural techniques on large farms in Norfolk. With money borrowed from an uncle, a banker, he leased a farm in Hanford, Dorset, in 1785. By 1792 he was able to lease a farm of 1500 acres near Wanborough, Surrey. There he established his position as a successful commercial farmer with a reputation for importing and breeding merino sheep.

About 1802 Birkbeck withdrew from the Society of Friends and thereafter professed no religion. A decisive meeting with Richard Flower in 1811 enhanced his radical leanings. Flower had ties with major figures of Unitarian radicalism and early Romantic literature. With Flower's son George, Birkbeck toured France during the summer of 1814 and published his impressions in Notes on a Journey through France (1814). His praise of the beneficial effects of the French Revolution on the land, agriculture, education, and standard of living aroused considerable controversy.

A man who chafed at his inability to vote or hold public office, and at paying tithes, Birkbeck had a vision of founding a colony in republican America. Following his father's death in 1816, he emigrated at the age of fifty-three with four of his children to Virginia, where George Flower had bought land. Birkbeck had other ideas, and announced that he intended to settle north of the Ohio River because of his profound hatred of slavery.

After arriving in Boltonhouse Prairie in Edwards county, Illinois Territory, in the summer of 1817, and immediately purchasing about 1500 acres, Birkbeck published in 1818 both an account of the journey in Notes of a Journey from the Coast of Virginia to the Territory of Illinois and an enthusiastic invitation to others to emigrate to his projected colony in Letters from Illinois. Written in plain but lively prose that masked the underlying Romanticism of his message, the second book in particular praised the natural beauty of the prairies and the ease with which they might be cultivated. The two books received an astonishing reception not only in Britain but also on the continent of Europe. The fierce controversy they aroused in the press, journals, and pamphlets on both sides of the Atlantic magnified their impact. During the next few years, the 'English Prairie' became a required stop for British travellers in the west, who in turn published differing assessments. The fame of Birkbeck's pioneering venture undoubtedly contributed to the rise in emigration during the hard times and political repression of the post-war period.

At one time scholars gave Birkbeck credit for recognizing the agricultural potential of prairie land, but there is no evidence that he cultivated the grassland. Although he presented ideas on ditching and fencing in his presidential address in 1823 to the first agricultural society in Illinois, his methods were not adopted. Above all, the projected colony failed to prosper. His hopes of founding a morally upright community were shattered when he learned of George Flower's adultery. He severed completely all communication with his wealthier partners. Even his most severe critics conceded his integrity and the persuasiveness of his pen. Because of his sanguine temperament, he misled himself as he misled others. He did none the less secure an honoured place in the history of Illinois. His newspaper articles and a pamphlet under the pseudonym Jonathan Freeman helped turn the vote against calling a special convention to amend its constitution of 1818 to legalize slavery.

Returning from a visit to Robert Owen in New Harmony, Indiana, on 4 June 1825, Birkbeck was drowned while attempting to swim his horse across the Fox River and was later buried at New Harmony. The small fortune that he had brought to America had disappeared. On his death he left 600 acres and a large house.

CHARLOTTE ERICKSON

Sources G. S. Thomson, A pioneer family: the Birkbecks in Illinois, 1818–1827 (1953) • G. Flower, History of the English settlement (1882) • G. Boewe, Prairie Albion (1962) • R. Birkbeck, The Birkbecks of Westmorland (1900) • R. Birkbeck, 'Morris Birkbeck', Indiana Magazine of History, 31 (1935), 232–5 • M. A. Salter, 'George Flower comes to the Illinois country', Journal of the Illinois State Historical Society, 69 (1976), 214–23 • B. P. Birch, 'Initial perception of prairie', Frontier settlement: papers from an International Geographical Union Symposium [Edmonton and Saskatoon 1972], ed. R. G. Ironside (1974), 178–94 • M. A. Salter, 'Bankrupts and scoundrels', Transactions of the Illinois State Historical Society (1989), 11–19 • T. C. Pease, The frontier state, 1818–1848, repr. (1987) • M. A. Salter, 'Morris Birkbeck's empire on the prairies', Selected papers on Illinois history, ed. B. D. Cadman (1981) • P. Angle, 'Morris Birkbeck', Chicago History, 8 (1967) • J. R. Walker and R. W. Burkhardt, eds., Eliza Julia Flower (1990) • digest registers (births), RS Friends, Lond. [23 Jan 1764] • digest registers (marriages), RS Friends, Lond., 23 April 1794

Archives Illinois Historical Survey, Urbana, Illinois • Knox College, Galesburg, Illinois • U. Leeds, Brotherton L. • University of Sydney, Fisher Library | Chicago Historical Society, Chicago, Flower MSS • Illinois State Historical Society Library, Springfield,

Illinois, Flower MSS · Indiana Historical Society Library, Indian-
apolis, John Ingle letters
Likenesses engraving, pubd 1825, Knox College, Galesburg, Illinois [*see illus.*] · sketch, Knox College, Galesburg, Illinois
Wealth at death fortune had disappeared: Salter, 'Bankrupts
and scoundrels'

Birkenhead. For this title name *see* Smith, Frederick
Edwin, first earl of Birkenhead (1872–1930); Smith, Frederick Winston Furneaux, second earl of Birkenhead
(1907–1975).

Birkenhead [Berkenhead], **Sir John** (1617–1679), journalist and poet, was born on 24 March 1617 in Northwich,
Cheshire, the sixth child of Randall Birkenhead (1581–
1633), a saddler, alehouse-keeper, and chapel clerk, and
his wife, Margaret, of whom little is known. John attended
the free Witton grammar school.

In 1632 Birkenhead entered Oriel College, Oxford, as a
servitor. His tutor was Humphrey Lloyd; otherwise, his
early university career is scantly documented. Evidently,
he flourished; years later an anonymous enemy, calling
him 'a Student in the Law', would backhandedly acknowledge that Birkenhead 'hath learned very well, and is
become as good a Scholler as his Tutors, & Professours'
(*True Character of Mercurius Aulicus*, 1645, 2–3).

In August 1636 Archbishop Laud, visiting the university,
'had occasion to have some things well transcribed, and
this Birkenhead was recommended to him, who performed his businesse so well, that the archbishop recommended him to All Soules' College to be a fellow' (*Brief
Lives*, 1.104). In January 1637 he was admitted for his BA
degree, awarded *in absentia* the following month, when he
was at Lambeth performing scribal and probably more
substantive duties for Laud.

The patronage of the archbishop—and the circumstances and events of the looming civil war—were to
determine Birkenhead's career and forever fix his identity
as an arch-royalist, as the quasi-official spokesman for
king and court Mercurius Aulicus. He was granted the MA
degree in 1639, by Laud's petition, and concurrently
became a full fellow of All Souls.

In 1641, parliament having committed the archbishop
to the Tower, Birkenhead again took up residence at
Oxford, associating with other Laudians, whose patron
was Dr Brian Duppa. The most notable member of that
'knot of the choicest Oxford Wits always together'
(D. Lloyd, *Memoires*, 1668, 425) was the poet and playwright
William Cartwright. Those young royalists contributed
prolifically to the several university miscellanies commemorating royal births, weddings, and other occasions.
Birkenhead wrote poems for two such collections in
1643.

By then, the embattled king and his court had sought
refuge at Oxford, from where the doomed military
effort—and whatever else of the king's state functions
remained—were conducted. One crucial, ongoing
engagement of the civil war was the struggle to win the
hearts and minds of the public. At Oxford the royalist
propaganda machine discovered John Birkenhead, not

only a fierce loyalist but also an emerging genius at satire
and polemic.

Mercurius Aulicus, the weekly 'intelligencer' of the king's
party, and England's first official newsbook, ran from
January 1643 to September 1645, with only a few interrup-
tions—118 numbers in all, some 1700 closely printed
pages. For the first few issues Birkenhead assisted the
principal author, Peter Heylin, whose style was comparatively tame. However, from mid-1643 onward rival newsbooks recognized Birkenhead as the person responsible
for the lively amalgam of factual information, witty invective, brilliant satire, and all the modern weapons in a
relentless war of words: the 'inside' story, the embarrassing quotation, the 'planted' idea, the not-quite denied
rumour. The various rebel factions were forced to respond
with newsbooks of their own, two dozen of them, the
most important being *Mercurius Britanicus* (1643–6), whose
misspelt title *Aulicus* did not fail to deride. None, however,
was able to rival Birkenhead in facile style, wit, vitriol, or
even the presentation of accurate news; after all, he had
the best 'sources', the king's entire bureaucracy and spy
network.

Besides the newsbooks, on which his reputation principally rests, Birkenhead also published a number of
polemic and satiric pamphlets. His contemporaneous
fame is attested not only by the frequency with which
adversaries singled him out for denunciation or grudging
praise but also by his contributions to others' publications, including prefaces to Richard Whitlock's *Zoötomia*
(1654) and the 1655 edition of John Denham's *Cooper's Hill*.

Birkenhead's talent as a poet has perhaps been unfairly
minimized, even by his modern biographer, P. W.
Thomas, who did so much to elucidate the facts of his life
and to define the nature of his satiric genius. Only twenty-
three poems survive. Some are sophisticated creations,
especially his commendatory poems, including ones for
the first folio of Beaumont and Fletcher's *Comedies and Tragedies* (1647), for his friend Cartwright's posthumous *Comedies, Tragi-Comedies, with other Poems* (1651), and for Henry
Lawes's *Second Book of Ayres* (1655). At their best moments,
those poems compare favourably with the most famous
examples of their minor genre, such as Ben Jonson's on
Shakespeare and Thomas Carew's on Donne. Birkenhead's tribute to Cartwright is not only his best poem, it is
also the longest commendatory poem in existence, at 240
lines. Henry Lawes set several of Birkenhead's lyric poems
to music. Three of those, translations from the Greek
Anacreontea, are arguably superior to better-known translations by Birkenhead's contemporaries Robert Herrick,
Thomas Stanley, and Abraham Cowley. A 240-line monody
on the beheading of King Charles, *Loyalties Tears Flowing*,
published twice as a booklet in the regicide year (1649),
exhibits less of the satirical stridency that characterizes
much of Birkenhead's writing and more a sense of controlled indignation and genuine sorrow.

At the Restoration, Birkenhead's loyalty and diligence
in the cause of the martyred king were rewarded. He
regained his Oxford fellowship, and in April 1661, on the

recommendation of Charles II, he was awarded a doctorate of civil law. From 1660 to 1663 he held the office of licenser of the press, a function that coincided with his editorship of the new official newsbook, *Mercurius Publicus*.

Birkenhead was elected to parliament from Wilton, Wiltshire, in June 1661. In November 1662 the king knighted him. The following June he became one of the founding members of the Royal Society, sitting on the committee to improve the use of the English language. His acquaintances were prominent literary figures of the age: James Shirley, Edmund Waller, Henry Vaughan, Jeremy Taylor, Henry More, John Evelyn, Thomas Sprat. In the famous coterie of Katherine Phillips, 'The Matchless Orinda', Birkenhead was nicknamed Cratander, after the title character in Cartwright's play *The Royal Slave*. In 1668 John Dryden referred to him as 'my worthy friend' (J. Dryden, *Essays*, ed. W. Ker, 1926, 1.122).

Never married, and childless, Birkenhead died on 4 December 1679, at his lodgings in Whitehall, after a humiliating rebuff in his attempt to hold his parliamentary seat. He was buried 'near to the School door' in the churchyard of St Martin-in-the-Fields, Westminster (Wood, *Ath. Oxon.*, new edn, 1813–20, 3.1205). No marker or memorial remains. CHARLES CLAY DOYLE

Sources P. W. Thomas, *Sir John Berkenhead, 1617–1679: a royalist career in politics and polemics* (1969) · Wood, *Ath. Oxon.*, new edn · *Brief lives, chiefly of contemporaries, set down by John Aubrey, between the years 1669 and 1696*, ed. A. Clark, 2 vols. (1898) · C. C. Doyle, '"To my ingenious freind Captaine LL": an attribution', *N&Q*, 217 (1972), 173–4 · C. C. Doyle, 'An unhonored English Anacreon: John Birkenhead', *Studies in Philology*, 71 (1974), 192–205 · C. C. Doyle, 'The poetry of John Birkenhead', PhD diss., U. Texas, 1969
Archives BL, notes for a Commons speech in March 1663, MS Lansdowne 958, fols. 17–25
Wealth at death moderately prosperous: Thomas, *Sir John*, 1–2 · bequests: will

Birket [Birkhead], **George** (1549–1614), Roman Catholic archpriest, was the son of Robert Birket and Isabel Salvin of West Brandon, co. Durham. He matriculated at Douai University in 1576 or 1577 and was ordained priest at Cambrai on 6 April 1577. On 3 February 1578 he was one of the first group of students to start the English College in Rome. He left Rome in September 1580 and arrived at Rheims on 16 October, proceeding to England on the 29th. He was staying with the Bellamy family at Harrow, Middlesex, in October 1581 but wrote to William Allen from London on 24 April 1583. He returned to Rheims before 8 August 1583 taking relics of Edmund Campion to Allen. He was still there in December 1584.

It is not known when Birket returned to England, but when George Blackwell was appointed to govern the clergy as the first archpriest of England in 1598 Birket was appointed as one of his assistants. He took up residence with Lord Montague some time before 1605. In 1607 Blackwell took the oath of allegiance to the crown. It had been skilfully devised, it seems, by the ex-Jesuit, Sir Christopher Perkins, to trip the conscience of the Catholics. As a consequence Blackwell was removed from office and in 1608 Birket succeeded him as archpriest until his death.

During his period of office a very articulate minority of the secular clergy, who resented what they took to be the excessive influence of the Jesuits, continued to agitate for bishops. They believed that it was Jesuit influence, especially Robert Parsons's, which was holding up a Roman decision favourable to themselves. Birket sent Richard Smith to Rome in 1609 as his agent to try once again for bishops. It was Parsons who told him how to go about it since Rome was tired of formal appeals which ignored previous directives, lacked courtesy, and viewed the Jesuits as enemies. Acting against Parsons's advice, and too little observant of protocol, Smith made no progress. Parsons and his ally Thomas Fitzherbert informed Birket frankly of Smith's errors. But Birket felt that he owed it to his agent to support him, and he told Parsons to desist from what he regarded as carping criticism and from the continuation of a correspondence which could only reflect on his own loyalty to his chosen representative. Doubtless Birket's was a difficult task trying to keep spirited and sometimes wayward steeds roughly united in drawing his coach in one direction. Smith brought the appointment of a Catholic bishop for England no nearer. It was in fact delayed until 1623; Smith followed as bishop of Chalcedon in 1624. Meanwhile in September 1610 Birket was apparently obliged to leave Lord Montague's establishment, no doubt for security reasons, but probably stayed within his orbit.

Birket used the aliases of Hall and Lambton: his uncle was named Joseph Lambton. He enjoyed the reputation of a man discreet, hard-working, and with a considerable ability for getting along with all parties. Not until the episode of Smith's agency was there any misunderstanding with Parsons. Even then it seems to have left no grudges on either side. The report of a spy in 1580 described Birket as 'about forty years of age, short of stature, slender and lean, his face full of wrinkles, pale of colour, his beard black and thick, and cut short' (Talbot and Aveling, 209). He died on 6 April 1614. FRANCIS EDWARDS

Sources G. Anstruther, *The seminary priests*, 1 (1969) · F. Edwards, *Robert Persons: the biography of an Elizabethan Jesuit, 1546–1610* (1995) · Berks. RO, Milton House collection, Q9 · H. Foley, ed., *Records of the English province of the Society of Jesus*, 6 (1880), 69 · J. Morris, ed., *The troubles of our Catholic forefathers related by themselves*, 2 (1875), 53 · *Letters of Thomas Fitzherbert, 1608–1610*, ed. L. Hicks, Catholic RS, 41 (1948) · Westm. DA, XI, no. 67; X, no. 85 · W. Kelly, ed., *Liber ruber venerabilis collegii Anglorum de urbe*, 1, Catholic RS, 37 (1940) · T. F. Knox and others, eds., *The first and second diaries of the English College, Douay* (1878) · *The letters and memorials of William, Cardinal Allen (1532–1594)*, ed. T. F. Knox (1882), vol. 2 of *Records of the English Catholics under the penal laws* (1878–82) · *Calendar of the manuscripts of the most hon. the marquess of Salisbury*, 17, HMC, 9 (1938), 500 · *Dodd's Church history of England*, ed. M. A. Tierney, 5 vols. (1839–43), vols. 4–5 · C. Talbot, ed., *Miscellanea: recusant records*, Catholic RS, 53 (1961)
Archives Georgetown University, Washington, DC, corresp. | Archivum Romanum Societatis Iesu, Rome, Fonds Gesuitico 651

Birkett, (William) Norman, first Baron Birkett (1883–1962), barrister and judge, was born at Ulverston, Lancashire, on 6 September 1883, the fourth of the five children of Thomas Birkett (d. 1913) and his first wife, Agnes (d. 1886), daughter of Moses Tyson, butcher. His mother died

(William) Norman Birkett, first Baron Birkett (1883–1962), by Claude Rogers, 1958

when he was three. His father was a draper with a substantial business at Ulverston, a prominent Wesleyan, active in the urban district council and the Liberal Club. Norman Birkett was educated at the Wesleyan day school at Ulverston until he was eleven, and then at the higher-grade school at Barrow. He left school at fifteen and started in one of his father's shops as an apprentice. It was not long before he became a local preacher on the Ulverston Methodist circuit. His success was such that his father, who had decided that his son would never make a good draper, allowed him to leave the business when he was twenty-one and to study at home for the Wesleyan ministry. After about a year, the Methodist minister who was coaching him suggested he should go to Cambridge and read for a degree in history and theology.

So in 1907 at the age of twenty-four Birkett went up to Emmanuel College where he spent four years. He became president of the union in 1910 and obtained a second class in history in part one of his tripos (1909) and a second in law in part two (1911). He also obtained a first class in the theological special examination in 1910. Birkett did not find the change from theology to law an easy one to make, since he knew that it would disappoint his father. But he had blossomed in Cambridge and felt, as he told his father, that he would 'find the ministry rather cramping'. His confidence that he could get to the bar without being a further burden on his father was justified. He was lucky enough to get a job as private secretary to one of the Cadburys at Birmingham; this paid him £200 a year with time to work for his bar examinations. He was called to the bar

by the Inner Temple in June 1913 and in the following September started practice as a local at Birmingham where obviously his prospects were best.

Birkett was thirty when he went to the bar but, like many who start practising at that age, he soon made up for lost time. His progress was naturally hastened by the fact that when war broke out in 1914 most of his competitors went into the services, whereas Birkett himself was twice rejected as medically unfit. It was unusual, but not unheard of, for a junior barrister who had succeeded at a local bar to move to London to spread his wings. In 1920 Birkett made the move and entered the chambers of Sir Edward Marshall Hall, then at the height of his fame and fashion; Birkett acquired also the services of Edgar Bowker, Hall's clerk and one of the most successful of his time. On 25 August the same year (1920) Birkett married Ruth (d. 1969), daughter of Emil Nilsson, of Sweden; the marriage brought him lifelong happiness and a son and a daughter. The move to London was of course intended to lead to a silk gown; and after four years, when his earnings were over £4000, Birkett felt justified in taking the step; he was made KC in 1924.

From then until the outbreak of war in 1939 Birkett led a glorious life. The speed of his success was due in some measure to the talent of his clerk and to the ill health of Marshall Hall which gave Birkett unexpected chances. But these aids did no more than hasten his recognition as one of the foremost advocates of his time. In his first year as a silk he doubled the earnings of his last as a junior; and thereafter, although some of the sensational murderers he defended cannot have been sensational payers, his earnings averaged around £25,000 a year. Speaking thirty-five years later of Marshall Hall, Birkett said:

> The age that produced and gloried in his spectacular triumphs in the courts, has passed away for ever. The advocate no longer plays the part in our public life that he once did. The fashionable divorce suit, the sensational libel action, the great murder trial—they are no longer the dramatic events that once occupied public attention to the exclusion of almost everything else.

Hall died in 1927, but the great age continued until the Second World War; when that was over the special jury list perished and advocacy changed its bright apparel for a sober suit. Birkett had not the grandiose appearance of Hall—he was lanky, had untidy red hair, angular features, and spectacles—but he had the golden voice. In all the forensic gifts he was highly skilled but in chief he was an orator. Oratory itself was changing: tawdriness was more easily detected and men were beginning to look for earnestness and sincerity; these were Birkett's qualities, founded on his great integrity. He gave all he had to all his cases, often to the point of nervous exhaustion. At the bar he was universally liked; there can hardly have been anyone who knew him who did not receive from him some piece, great or small, of kindness or of courtesy. Of the many famous cases with which he was connected may be mentioned his defence in the Gladstone libel case (1927), of Clarence Hatry (1930), of Maundy Gregory in the 'honours case' (1933), of the murderers Mancini (1934) and Dr

Ruxton (1936), as well as his prosecution of another murderer, A. A. Rouse, in the 'blazing car case' (1931).

During this time Birkett was also in politics. He first stood for parliament in the post-war election of 1918 when, like many other Liberals without the 'coupon', he was at the bottom of the poll. Thereafter he shared the vicissitudes of the Liberal Party, with the result that he was in the house only briefly, in the parliaments of 1923–4 and 1929–31, representing Nottingham (East). He wanted very much to hold one of the law offices; but while many of his contemporaries, despairing otherwise of a political future, moved either to the left or to the right, he would not swerve.

Birkett held his last brief on the first day of the Michaelmas term in 1939 after the war broke out. Then he accepted the chairmanship of a committee to advise the home secretary on cases of detention under the emergency powers. The work was unpaid, and in June 1941 he was knighted in recognition of his services. In 1928 Birkett had refused a seat on the High Court bench: 'I wasn't really drawn to the judicial office', he said later, 'I loved the Bar so much'. When the offer was made again in November 1941, he was fifty-eight and must have sensed that, if ever he went back to the bar, things would be very different. He accepted, and went to the King's Bench.

It is rare for an impassioned advocate to be made a judge, for fear that he will be lacking in judicial restraint and unable not to take sides. Birkett proved the contrary. Greatly helped by an innate diffidence, he made himself an excellent judge of first instance. But he had to school himself rigorously as his diary shows. 'The truth is I like the limelight, and cannot bear now to be in obscurity', he recorded after three months on the bench. Ill health troubled him and he was often depressed. He was at the bottom of the judicial ladder, junior to many whom he had led to the bar. A great chance came and went in 1945 when the prime minister and the lord chancellor selected him to be the British judge at the projected trial of German war criminals with the likelihood of presiding over the international tribunal. But the men of protocol thought that someone higher in the judicial hierarchy was required. So in the end Birkett went to Nuremberg only as the alternate to Lord Justice Lawrence. When at the end of the proceedings Lawrence was made a baron, as Lord Oaksey, and Birkett's work went unrecognized, he was dreadfully upset; he was consoled in 1947 by a privy councillorship. He yearned for promotion to the Court of Appeal for which he was unsuited, since he was neither an especially acute lawyer nor a profound one. When eventually it came in 1950, he found the work dull and it became duller. At the end of 1956, as soon as he had served the fifteen years on the bench which entitled him to a pension, he retired.

Thereafter he lived for five reviving years. In January 1958 he went to the House of Lords. In the same year Cambridge gave him an honorary LLD; he had been an honorary fellow of his college since 1946 and already had honorary degrees from London (where he was chairman of the university court), Birmingham, and Hull. His interests had always been wide—cricket, literature, especially Dickens, the City of London (he was four times master of the Curriers' Company), the preservation of the English countryside, especially the Lakes from which he came. He revelled in speech and excelled in every form of speech making and on the radio and television. He was asked everywhere, from prize-givings to the great Bar Association meetings of America where he was as popular as in Britain; he became president of the Pilgrims in 1958 in succession to Lord Halifax. He did not speak much in the House of Lords, but in 1962 he was stirred by a private bill (but one which had the blessing of the government) to secure Manchester's water supply by, its opponents said, the despoiling of Ullswater. On 8 February he moved the rejection of the bill and with a speech which once again plucked the strings of advocacy he carried the house by 70 votes against 36. His life thus rounded, two days later he died, at 20 Devonshire Place, St Marylebone, London, on 10 February 1962, and was succeeded by his son, Michael (b. 1929).

DEVLIN, rev.

Sources H. M. Hyde, *Norman Birkett* (1964) • personal knowledge (1981) • Burke, *Peerage* (1999)
Archives NRA, papers • U. Lond., Institute of Advanced Legal Studies, papers relating to Nuremberg war trials | BLPES, letters to Violet Markham • Bodl. Oxf., corresp. with Lord Monckton | FILM BFI NFTVA, news footage
Likenesses C. Rogers, portrait, 1958, U. Lond., Senate House [*see illus.*] • M. Codner, portrait, priv. coll. • L. Knight, portrait, IWM • D. Low, pencil caricature, NPG • F. Topolski, portrait, NPG • photographs, repro. in Hyde, *Norman Birkett*
Wealth at death £43,294 13s. 0d.: probate, 11 May 1962, CGPLA Eng. & Wales

Birkhead, George. *See* Birket, George (1549–1614).

Birkhead, Henry (1617–1696), Latin poet, was born in the St Paul's Head tavern, in St Paul's Churchyard, London, and was baptized on 25 September 1617, the son of John Birkhead (d. in or before 1627), the tavern-keeper, and his wife, Margaret, *née* Faldoe (1596/7–1677). He was educated at Thomas Farnaby's celebrated school in Cripplegate, and became a gentleman commoner of Trinity College, Oxford, in 1633, and a scholar on 28 May 1635. He graduated BA on 13 February 1637. Shortly afterwards he contemplated moving to St Omer. His conversion, however, was brief; Archbishop Laud personally exerted his influence to bring him back, and he was elected a fellow of All Souls, Oxford, 'being … esteemed a good philologist', in 1637. Laud, on trial for his life, was to use Birkhead as an example of his own anti-popery: 'Birkhead … was seduced by a Jesuit, and brought up to London to be conveyed beyond the seas. His Friends complained to me: I had the happiness to find him out, and the blessing from God to settle his Conscience' (Pittock, 14, 38). Laud's patronage led in 1640 to an appointment in the Norwich diocesan registry. Birkhead became MA on 5 June 1641, and turned to studying law. He was a regular contributor of Latin, Greek, and English verse to Oxford commemorative collections (for example, sixty-seven iambics in *Horti Carolini rosa altera*, 1640).

During the civil war Birkhead remained in Oxford, contributing to the English verse commemorative volume for Sir Bevill Grenvill (1643), providing an English ode for *Musarum Oxoniensium epibateria* (1643), and writing Latin poetry on contemporary events. The execution of his patron, Laud, in January 1645 led to a heartfelt Latin ode, in irregular metre: this and other poems he published privately and anonymously under the title *Poematia* (1645). Birkhead submitted to the parliamentary visitors in 1648, was appointed dean of arts at All Souls in 1649, and in 1654 contributed verses celebrating the peace. Having also, in 1653, begun to study medicine, he returned to law a few years later. By 1656 he felt able to acknowledge authorship of an expanded collection of his poems, titled *Poematia*; Laud, though, could not be praised in safety, and the ode on his martyrdom was transferred to Cranmer. The volume was reissued as part of a collaboration with Henry Stubbe of Christ Church, *Otium literatum* (c.1658). Birkhead displays some ingenious epigrammatic variety on a range of frivolous and serious topics, such as his limping iambics 'In ventricosum gulonem':

Gulo, videtur ire cum Assecla, Solus;
Ipse ut Minister, praevium sequens Ventrem:
Dupliciter hinc Abdomini est gravi servus.

He translates this as 'on Dr Glut' (pp. 126–7):

He, though Alone, seemes with his Man to strut;
His Paunch before; as large, Behind goes Glut:
Thus he is doubly Slave to his cram'd Gut.

Birkhead resigned his fellowship at All Souls in 1657, taking pains to reject any suggestion of involvement in the corruption of which the college was being accused. He practised law in London, with chambers in the Inner Temple, and in Norwich, where he prospered as registrar. He wrote an English play, 'The Female Rebellion', a tragicomedy concerned with divine right, and in 1684 arranged a reprinting (most unusually for such volumes) of the 1643 *Verses on the Death of … Sir Bevill Grenvill*, dedicated to Grenvill's son, the earl of Bath.

Birkhead appears to have married, on 6 May 1677, Jane Stevenson, housekeeper to the duke of Buckingham. Although his relations with her, like his financial affairs, were to prove complicated, his letters continue to indicate his affection, albeit from a distance—'Dear Soul' (1689) and 'Dear Heart' (1692), in which he mentioned 'a long impertinent story of Elizabeth of Sunderland' (Pittock, 112–13). Birkhead died on 8 September 1696 and was buried at St Margaret's, Westminster. His will offers 5s. to sister and niece; as for Jane Stevenson:

whom I have formerly called and written to as my wife to save her credit in the world though I was never married to her … She is of Monkwearmouth in the County of Durham. I write this in the presence of God who knowes she has been extream false and many wayes exceeding injurious to me. And therefore I bequeath her but one shilling.

Birkhead is chiefly remembered for leaving his lands 'in trust to maintain … for ever a Publick Professor of Poetry in the University of Oxford' (Pittock, 121–30). The establishment of the poetry professorship did not run smoothly: problems were caused by the confusion of Birkhead's estate, and the low salary offered (£25 was quoted, later £30) made the position little sought after. Hearne noted that 'Mr [Anthony] Alsop of Christ Church formerly made interest for the Place … but he did not stir for it now upon Account of the smallness of the Sallary, and that's the Reason too that none else mov'd for it' (31 July 1708; Pittock, 127). Alsop was probably the finest Latin poet in Oxford at the time. Joseph Trapp became the first professor: he lectured in Latin about Latin poetry, as his successors did for many years. D. K. MONEY

Sources J. H. Pittock, *Henry Birkhead, founder of the Oxford chair of poetry* (1999) · J. W. Mackail, *Henry Birkhead and the foundation of the Oxford chair of poetry* (1908) · *Hist. U. Oxf.*, vols 4–5 · D. K. Money, 'A diff'rent sounding lyre: Oxford commemorative verse in English, 1613–1834', *Bodleian Library Record*, 16 (1997–9), 42–92 · D. K. Money, *The English Horace: Anthony Alsop and the tradition of British Latin verse* (1998) · will, PRO, PROB 11/435, sig. 242

Birks, Thomas Rawson (1810–1883), Church of England clergyman and theologian, was born on 28 September 1810 at Staveley, Derbyshire, the younger son of Thomas Birks, a tenant farmer of the duke of Devonshire. The family were Baptists, and after first attending the village school and then a boarding-school in Chesterfield, Birks was sent at the age of sixteen to the dissenting academy at Mill Hill, near London, where he later became an assistant master. Funds were provided to send him to Cambridge, and in 1830 he matriculated at Trinity College, having in the same year joined the Church of England. Three years later he won a scholarship and gained the chief English declamation prize for his oration 'Mathematical and moral certainty', earning high praise from William Whewell, the master of Trinity. In 1834 he took his BA as second wrangler and second Smith's prizeman and became a fellow of Trinity. In 1843 and again in 1844 he won the Seatonian prize for religious poetry.

Birks was ordained deacon in 1837 and priest in 1841, and for some years was tutor and then curate to Edward Bickersteth, the rector of Watton, Hertfordshire, and former secretary of the Church Missionary Society, whose memoir he compiled in 1851. In 1844 Birks resigned his Trinity fellowship to marry Bickersteth's eldest daughter, Elizabeth (b. 1820), and moved to Kelshall, Hertfordshire, as rector. There were eight children, of whom the eldest son, Edward Bickersteth Birks, also became a fellow of Trinity. Birks's first wife died in 1856, and on 17 May 1866 he married Georgina Agnes, daughter of Colonel Beresford and widow of Major James Douglas. He had just returned to Cambridge as incumbent of Holy Trinity Church, and soon became active in university affairs, giving Bible readings for both undergraduates and more senior members and preaching before the university on a number of occasions. He was a member of the board of theological studies and in 1867–8 an examiner for the theological tripos. In 1871 he was appointed an honorary canon of Ely Cathedral.

Throughout his ministry Birks was a scholarly and wide-ranging apologist for evangelicalism, being the author of more than fifty books and pamphlets, many of them originally delivered as lectures. He was increasingly concerned to respond thoughtfully but critically to the theological, philosophical, and scientific challenges of his day, and this sometimes led him to adopt positions at variance with contemporary evangelical orthodoxy. At Watton he engaged in a close study of biblical prophecy and, like his rector and future father-in-law, became a convinced champion of the premillennial position. He expounded his views in a series of lengthy treatises, commencing with *First Elements of Sacred Prophecy* (1843) and *The Four Prophetic Empires* (1844), and he edited a volume of lectures by twelve Anglican clergy entitled *The Hope of the Apostolic Church* (1845).

Birks was a pioneer among evangelicals in seeking to provide answers to the doubts raised by biblical critics and scientists over the authority of the Bible. In 1850 he published an edition of William Paley's *Horae Paulinae*; two years later his own *Horae evangelicae* defended the historicity and consistency of the gospel narratives, and this was followed by *Modern Rationalism and the Inspiration of the Scriptures* (1853), which rejected the dogma of absolute inerrancy. Even before Darwin's *Origin of Species* had appeared in 1859 Birks was tackling some of the issues highlighted by modern science in *The Treasures of Wisdom, or, Thoughts on the Connection between Natural Science and Revealed Truth* and *The Difficulties of Belief in Connexion with the Creation and the Fall*, both of which were published in 1855. As a riposte to *Essays and Reviews* (1859) he wrote *The Bible and Modern Thought* (1861), one of his most important contributions to theological debate, while in reply to J. W. Colenso and other Old Testament scholars he published *The Exodus of Israel* (1863) and *The Pentateuch and its Anatomists* (1869).

In common with most other Anglican evangelicals of the Victorian age Birks sought to maintain the protestant character of both the institutions of government and the established church and to warn against the inroads of Roman Catholicism and secular thought. Many of his lectures and articles in religious periodicals focused on these concerns, as did more substantial studies such as *The Christian State* (1847) and *Church and State* (1869), the second dealing in particular with the question of the disestablishment of the Irish church.

During the 1860s Birks developed his thinking on the nature of redemption and eternal punishment, first in *The Ways of God* (1863) and more especially in *The Victory of Divine Goodness* (1867). The latter book, while rejecting both universalism and annihilationism, denied that the wicked would suffer everlasting misery, but instead asserted that God's grace and mercy would compel them to acknowledge the divine goodness as displayed in a redeemed world. In the ensuing controversy Birks was widely criticized by other evangelicals for his novel views, notably by the Free Church of Scotland theologian R. S. Candlish, to whom he replied in *The Atonement and the Judgment* (1870). However, in November 1869 he considered it expedient to resign his position as an honorary secretary

of the Evangelical Alliance, having held that office since 1850.

In 1872, following the death of F. D. Maurice, Birks was appointed Knightbridge professor of moral philosophy at Cambridge, a position he held until his death. Followers of Maurice protested that the selection of a pronounced evangelical for this post was a retrograde step, though ironically Maurice was dismissed from his chair at King's College, London, in 1853 for teaching a doctrine of eternal punishment not unlike that espoused in Birks's *The Victory of Divine Goodness*. His first course of lectures to undergraduates was published as *First Principles of Moral Science* (1873), and the following year his *Modern Utilitarianism* compared the systems of Paley, Bentham, and J. S. Mill. The evolutionary theories of Darwin and Herbert Spencer were assailed in three works: *The Scripture Doctrine of Creation* (1872), *Modern Physical Fatalism and the Doctrine of Evolution* (1876), and *Supernatural Revelation* (1879). Meanwhile his literary output in other fields continued unabated. In 1874, for example, his *Companion Psalter* appeared, containing 450 versions of the psalms (a quarter of them composed by Birks himself) and intended to supplement the hymnbooks of the day.

A succession of strokes from 1875 onwards compelled Birks to resign from Holy Trinity in 1877, but he did not significantly curtail his intellectual endeavours until a fourth stroke in 1880 caused lasting paralysis. Birks died at his Cambridge home, 6 Salisbury Villas, on 19 July 1883, and was survived by his second wife and several children from his first marriage. He was buried in Cambridge cemetery five days later.   STEPHEN GREGORY

Sources Venn, *Alum. Cant.* • *The Record* (27 July 1883) • D. M. Lewis, ed., *The Blackwell dictionary of evangelical biography, 1730–1860*, 2 vols. (1995) • Crockford (1882) • I. Randall and D. Hilborn, *One body in Christ: the history and significance of the Evangelical Alliance* (2001) • Boase, *Mod. Eng. biog.*, vol. 1 • *The Times* (23 July 1883) • *Men of the time* (1879) • G. Rowell, *Hell and the Victorians* (1974) • D. W. Bebbington, *Evangelicalism in modern Britain: a history from the 1730s to the 1980s* (1989) • J. R. Moore, *The post-Darwinian controversies* (1979) • *Evangelical Christendom*, 24/2 (1870); 24/3 (1870) • T. R. Birks, *The atonement and the judgment* (1870) • L. C. Sanders, *Celebrities of the century: being a dictionary of men and women of the nineteenth century* (1887) • *Clergy List* (1841) • *Clergy List* (1844) • T. R. Birks, *Memoir of the Rev. Edward Bickersteth, late rector of Watton, Herts*, 2 vols. (1851) • *GM*, 4th ser., 2 (1866), 103 • *DNB*

Likenesses T. C. Wageman, watercolour, Trinity Cam.

Wealth at death £8175 16s. 11d.: probate, 9 Aug 1883, *CGPLA Eng. & Wales*

Birla, Ghanshyamdas (1894–1983), businessman and politician in India, was born in the small village of Pilani in Rajputana, India, on 10 April 1894, the son of Raja Baldeodas Birla (*c*.1862–1957) and his wife, Yogeshwari Singhi (*c*.1863–1963). The Birlas were of the mercantile caste known as the Marwaris, whose roots can be traced back to seventeenth-century Rajputana. His family migrated from Rajputana in the mid-nineteenth century to Bombay in order to exploit the commercial opportunities developing there. In 1872 they were driven from Bombay by the plague and moved to Calcutta, where the family quickly

Ghanshyamdas
Birla (1894–1983),
by unknown
photographer

established itself as a leading commercial *gaddi* (trading house) in Bara bazaar, the commercial heart of the city.

Birla's origins in such a very traditional trading caste were to influence his personality and values for the rest of his life. While not formally educated, he received the customary mercantile grounding in arithmetic and basic literacy. In his later life he assiduously pursued a regime of self-education and wrote widely and well, particularly on economic matters. At the age of twelve he joined the family firm and at sixteen had established himself as an independent jute broker. He was married twice: first, in 1908, to Durgadevi Somani (*c.*1896–1909), with whom he had one son, and then, in 1912, to Mahadevi Karva (*c.*1900–1926) with whom he had two more sons and three daughters. He was widowed for a second time in 1926 and never remarried.

Birla swiftly demonstrated outstanding entrepreneurial and business acumen, qualities that were shown to extraordinary effect during the First World War. The opportunities of the war and immediate post-war period for speculation on the Calcutta stock exchange and in the jute, silver, and opium futures market were considerable, and brought the family an enormous fortune. In 1919 Birla used these profits to invest in and run jute mills—hitherto a sector dominated by the British merchant community in Calcutta. He was, therefore, a pioneer of the Indian-owned modern industrial sector, moving later into cotton textiles in the 1920s and into automobile manufacture and insurance in the 1930s and 1940s. He never, however, wholly eschewed the trading and speculative businesses where his fortune had originally been made. By the outbreak of the Second World War the assets of the Birla group far exceeded those of any of the British managing agency houses, and were second only to those of the great Tata group of Bombay.

Birla was not only an innovator in the practical sphere of business; he was also an important pioneer of business organizational activity. He was the prime mover in setting up the Indian Merchants' Chamber in Calcutta in 1926 and a founder member of the Federation of Indian Commerce

and Industry in 1927. The latter body rose swiftly to compete effectively for influence over officials and government economic policy in the last decades of the raj. Birla's role was enhanced by his ownership of the business periodical the *Eastern Economist*, and of the influential *Hindusthan Times*, which he bought in the late 1920s. His standing within the emerging Indian industrial class was fully recognized by the British imperial government, which went to some lengths to woo him from his affiliation with the nationalist movement. He was a member of several official commissions into financial and economic matters and he was befriended by both Churchill and Wavell, the viceroy, during the Second World War. However, in 1932 he declined the offer of a knighthood.

Birla's talents were never narrowly confined to business matters. From an early age he showed an absorbing interest in and aptitude for politics. Ironically, for a man who was to become one of the founding fathers of Indian industrial capitalism, Birla had a brief involvement with the revolutionary terrorist movement endemic in early twentieth-century Bengal. In 1914 he was forced underground for several months to evade imprisonment after being accused of hiding consignments of ammunition during the famous Rodda & Co. conspiracy case. His influential family was eventually able to have the arrest warrant rescinded. He is, however, better known for his involvement in the more conventional political activity of the Indian National Congress. His interest in nationalism was, in part, the consequence of his family's struggle, as relative newcomers to Calcutta, to establish their social and commercial standing among both the chauvinistic British and orthodox Hindu Marwari commercial communities. The excommunication of the Birla family by the powerful and ultra-traditional Marwari Association after his brother's marriage to a woman deemed to be of inferior status led Birla to embark upon a bitter and polarizing battle within the community, during which he sought to represent his approach to business and politics as a challenge to tradition and conservatism. This was symbolized by his personal enthusiasm for the Indian nationalist movement. His example influenced more progressive Marwaris to become loyal and generous supporters of the nationalist movement.

Though a reformist within his own community, Birla remained in many ways an orthodox Hindu and was attracted by the more culturally conservative wing of the nationalist movement, represented by such champions of Hindu cultural assertion as Lala Lajpat Rai and Madan Mohan Malaviya. He was a strong supporter and benefactor of Malaviya's great project the Benares Hindu University. In 1924 he helped him to form the Independent Congress Party (ICP), a faction within Congress which espoused the more exclusivist rhetoric of a resurgent Hindu India. In 1926 Birla was elected to the central legislative assembly as a representative of the ICP, and many saw him as a potential leader of the Hindu wing of the Indian nationalist movement. However, by the end of the 1920s Birla's sympathies had shifted towards the Gandhian wing of the movement.

Birla is perhaps best known for his close friendship with Gandhi, whom he first met in 1916; indeed it was at Birla's residence in New Delhi that Gandhi was assassinated in 1947. Though never formally a member of Congress and always willing to parley with the British, Birla became a convinced and passionate devotee of Gandhian nationalism. He is known to have financed Gandhi's ashrams and other philanthropic ventures, once commenting wryly on the enormous cost to himself of keeping the mahatma in poverty. The degree of his financial support for and influence over the political activities of Gandhi, particularly during the civil disobedience campaign, is a matter of some controversy. It is clear, however, that Birla was a trusted adviser of the mahatma. There is some evidence that he was instrumental in the decision to suspend the civil disobedience movement when it was felt to be harming Indian commercial interests. He was certainly associated with Gandhi's negotiations of the Gandhi–Irwin pact in March 1931, by which the mahatma agreed to attend the second session of the round-table conference talks on Indian constitutional development in London. Birla accompanied Gandhi to London for these talks, held in autumn 1931, as his personal adviser and also as an official delegate representing Indian big business. While there he engaged in private discussions with representatives of the Treasury and British business in India to try to reach agreement on a number of commercial and financial matters.

Birla's links with Congress were not limited to the mahatma. With Gandhi's withdrawal from active politics after 1934, he developed close relations with those Congress politicians most sympathetic to business interests and to constitutional methods, such as C. Rajgopalachari and Rajendra Prasad. He was particularly associated with Vallabhbhai Patel, Gandhi's shrewd political lieutenant in Gujarat and the unofficial leader of the so-called Congress right. By the late 1930s Birla's personal contributions to the movement, his ability to mobilize funds from Indian business, and his expertise on financial and commercial matters had made him indispensable to the Congress leadership, and he came to exert unrivalled influence over its economic policy. His role as chief strategist for Indian big business was confirmed when he co-authored the important wartime Bombay plan, the Indian industrialists' vision of development after independence. This called for an essentially capitalist economy in which dynamic business groups would promote rapid industrialization assisted by a strong central state. The pragmatism implicit in this approach to the economy also infused his attitude to India's communal problems. Having conducted an early study on the economic feasibility of an independent Pakistan, he concluded that a separate Hindu India would reap most of the economic benefits of secession. He became a discreet lobbyist for the partition solution, and was to play an important role in organizing the division of economic assets after the creation of Pakistan.

The years immediately after independence dealt serious blows to Birla's influence and he began to withdraw from political life. The assassination of Gandhi in 1947 and the death of Vallabhbhai Patel in 1950 removed his closest allies within Congress and any potentially effective curbs on Nehru's ascendancy. He enjoyed somewhat cool relations with Nehru, whose socialism he had always regarded with suspicion and hostility. But although he was opposed to nationalization and other restrictions on the private sector, Birla remained aloof from the right-wing business-backed Swatantra Party, founded in 1952 to oppose Congress. He continued to behave pragmatically in political and business matters and was the first to invest in Kerala after its election of a communist government in 1957; on meeting Khrushchov in Moscow 1961, he offered to establish factories in the Soviet Union. His loyalty was recognized in 1957 when he was awarded one of the Indian state's highest honours, the *padma vibhushan*.

After independence, therefore, Birla concentrated on his business, philanthropy, and writing. He wrote widely on economic and industrial issues, but is best-known for his memoir *In the Shadow of the Mahatma*, published in 1953, which includes extracts from his thirty-year-long correspondence with Gandhi. Of his many philanthropic activities perhaps the most important to him was a project to develop a technical university, the Birla Institute of Science and Technology, in his native village of Pilani. He was also co-founder and president of the Harijan Sevak Sangh, an organization devoted to liberating untouchables from the injustices of the caste system. In the 1950s and 1960s he oversaw his empire's expansion from cotton and jute textiles, aviation, automobiles, banking, and insurance into synthetic fibres, shipping, tea, cement, fertilizers, chemicals, and aluminium. The Birla corporate group achieved extraordinary growth, from twenty companies and assets of Rs 25 crores in 1946 to 150 companies and assets of over Rs 292 crores in 1965. During the populist phase of Mrs Gandhi's premiership in the 1970s, when private enterprise was discouraged, the Birla group became the first Indian multinational, establishing factories in Ethiopia, Thailand, Malaysia, and the Philippines. During the 1970s Birla began to execute a complex succession plan for the increasingly labyrinthine Birla empire, and the division of his assets among his sons and nephews was managed smoothly and amicably. At his death in London, at the Middlesex Hospital, on 11 June 1983, the total assets of the Birla group were estimated to be worth about Rs 2000 crores—the second biggest corporation in India.

Birla's life demonstrates several aspects of twentieth-century Indian history. His participation in the nationalist struggle exemplifies the centrality of business and mercantile interests to Congress and the ambiguous and ambivalent balance of ambition for modernity and respect for tradition that India's nationalist movement peculiarly embodied. His own family firm's transformation from traditional trading house to multinational corporation was a common Indian twentieth-century experience writ large. In many ways his vision of a modern industrial India, achieved by private and public collaboration, has been closer to the reality of independent India than Gandhi's rural arcadia or Nehru's socialist utopia.

A.-M. MISRA

Sources A. Ross, *The emissary: G. D. Birla, Gandhi and independence* (1986) · *Hindusthan Times*, 60/161 (12 June 1983) · *Times of India* (12 June 1983) · G. D. Birla, *In the shadow of the mahatma: a personal memoir* (Calcutta, 1953) · D. K. Taknet, *B. M. Birla: a great visionary* (1996) · R. N. Jajni, *G. D. Birla* (New Delhi, 1985)
Archives priv. coll., papers | SOUND BL NSA, documentary recording
Likenesses photograph, repro. in G. D. Birla, *Path to prosperity: a collection of speeches and writings of G. D. Birla* (1950) · photograph, Harvill Press, London [*see illus.*]
Wealth at death Rs 2000 crores: A. Ross, *The emissary: G. D. Birla, Gandhi and independence* (1986)

Birley, Eric Barff (1906–1995), historian and archaeologist, was born on 12 January 1906 at his parents' home, The Poplars, Worsley Road, Swinton, Manchester, Lancashire, the youngest of four sons (there were also two daughters) of Joseph Harold Birley (*b.* 1870), a Manchester businessman, and his wife, Edith Gladys Fernandes Lewis. He was educated at Clifton College and at Brasenose College, Oxford, where he read *literae humaniores* (Greats). After graduating in 1928 he was appointed to a teaching post at Armstrong College, Newcastle upon Tyne, from which he transferred to a lectureship at Durham University in 1931. He held a readership from 1943 to 1956 (during which period he was also vice-master and master of Hatfield College) and professor of Romano-British history and archaeology in 1956, a chair that he held until his retirement in 1971. Honours included election as FSA in 1931 and FBA in 1969, the appointment as MBE in 1943, honorary doctorates at the universities of Heidelberg, Freiburg im Breisgau, and Leicester, an honorary fellowship of Brasenose College, and presidency of the Dumfriesshire and Galloway Society and of the Society of Antiquaries of Newcastle upon Tyne.

The early intellectual and academic influences on Birley were his Brasenose tutor in ancient history, Michael Holroyd, and R. G. Collingwood, who leavened his philosophical activities with an interest in the history and particularly the epigraphy of Roman Britain. Birley's academic career was founded on a central preoccupation with matters archaeological. His interest in the area of Hadrian's Wall had been aroused by Collingwood, who was to inaugurate the standard corpus of Romano-British inscriptions. Birley's early work included studies of imported Roman Samian pottery and excavations at Housesteads, Birdoswald, and Vindolanda. It was at the last site that he purchased the house at Chesterholm which had once belonged to the nineteenth-century antiquary Anthony Hedley. These interests remained constant and central throughout his career; his influential views on the date of the Roman withdrawal from Scotland in the early years of the second century AD, before the building of Hadrian's Wall, were founded on his study of the Samian pottery.

The advent of the war, which took some toll of Birley's health and stamina, brought a position in which he worked in military intelligence, with a particular interest in the structure of the German military command. His experience here was to be influential in steering his interests in a slightly different direction, although in an area in which he had long shared an interest with his friend and

distinguished contemporary Ronald Syme, later Camden professor of ancient (Roman) history at Oxford. The two main areas of Birley's contribution to ancient history in the mature years of his career are perhaps best illustrated by two activities of the year 1949. He took a leading role in organizing the first International Congress of Roman Frontier Studies, which took place in Durham and initiated a regular series of such conferences; his formative role was recognized in 1974, when he was elected honorary life president of the Congress of Roman Frontier Studies. In 1949 he also wrote an influential paper on career patterns of the equestrian officers of the Roman army, in which he examined the principles of selection and advancement using, above all, the evidence of inscriptions and prosopographical methods (*Durham University Journal*, December 1949, 8–19). This was to be followed in 1954 by a comparable treatment of the careers of senators in the emperor's service, in which he suggested that evidence for posts early in the career indicated some degree of preselection of those destined for important military commands and the consulship (*PBA*, 39, 1954, 197–214).

For more than half a century and well into his retirement years Birley was a leading figure in Romano-British history, archaeology, and epigraphy, though his interests were by no means confined to Roman Britain. He produced academic work of high standards and lasting value, including *Research on Hadrian's Wall* (1961) and articles which were collected in two major anthologies, *Roman Britain and the Roman Army* (1953) and *The Roman Army: Papers, 1929–86* (1988). That he never wrote a single magisterial work of historical synthesis, of which many thought him capable, should not indicate lack of influence or historical vision. These qualities are emphasized by the fact that he was widely thought of, both in Britain and northern Europe, particularly Germany and the Danube lands, where many of his closest academic friends and kindred spirits worked, as the founding figure of a 'school' of pupils engaged at Durham and Newcastle in the study of Romano-British archaeology, military history, and applied epigraphy. Many of these went on to enjoy distinguished academic careers. If he inspired loyalty in his pupils, which he certainly did, he was not the man to shy away from expressing his views forthrightly. His avowedly severe review (*Journal of Roman Studies*, 56, 1966) of the first volume of *Roman Inscriptions of Britain* (1966), published under the joint editorship of R. G. Collingwood and R. P. Wright, took the study to task on a host of details and for failure to exploit and apply the results of epigraphical research by treating inscriptions as historical documents. It indicated, as many of his colleagues well knew, that Birley commanded a mine of detailed information and historical insight, much of which was to remain unpublished.

Birley married Margaret Isabel (Peggy) Goodlet, daughter of the Revd James Goodlet, minister of Forest Hall Presbyterian Church, Northumberland, on 5 April 1934. They had two sons, both of whom followed their father's professional interests. The elder, Robin, excavated at Vindolanda, as his father had done, and was responsible for the important discovery of the Vindolanda writing tablets; the younger, Anthony, held chairs of ancient history at the universities of Manchester and Düsseldorf and wrote, among other things, biographies of three Roman emperors, Hadrian, Marcus Aurelius, and Septimius Severus. Eric Birley spent his final years living with his wife in close proximity to their elder son, Robin, at Carvoran, where the latter had established a 'museum of the Roman army'. He died at home at Carvoran House, Carvoran, Greenhead, Northumberland, on 20 October 1995.

ALAN K. BOWMAN

Sources *The Times* (15 Nov 1995) · J. Wilkes, *The Independent* (26 Oct 1995) · personal knowledge (2004) · *WW* (1995) · Burke, *Gen. GB* (1937) · Oxf. UA · b. cert. · *CGPLA Eng. & Wales* (1996)
Archives Bodl. Oxf., corresp. with O. G. S. Crawford
Likenesses photograph, repro. in *The Times* · photograph, repro. in *The Independent*
Wealth at death £185,000: resworn probate, 20 Oct 1996, *CGPLA Eng. & Wales*

Birley, Sir Oswald Hornby Joseph (1880–1952), painter, was born on 31 March 1880 in Auckland, New Zealand, the son of Hugh Francis Birley, of St Asaph, north Wales, and his wife, Elizabeth, daughter of George McCorquodale, of Newton-le-Willows, Lancashire, while his parents were on a world tour. He was their only child and his father was determined to ensure the development of his son's artistic talent which had shown itself at an early age. He was educated at Harrow School and then, in 1897, was taken by his father to Dresden, Munich, and Florence. In 1898 he went up to Trinity College, Cambridge, and then to Paris in 1901 where he studied under Marcel Baschet at the Académie Julian and exhibited regularly at the Salon until 1904. In 1905 he visited Madrid, staying there for almost a year and executing a series of copies from Velázquez which presented him with an ideal and helped him to formulate his style.

From 1906 Birley was working in London, rapidly establishing a reputation as a portrait painter and exhibiting his portraits at the Royal Academy from 1904 and almost every year thereafter until 1945. In 1907 he was one of the co-founders of the Modern Society of Portrait Painters, exhibiting alongside his friends and principal rivals, Glyn Philpot and Gerald Kelly, both of whose portraits he painted about this time (both National Portrait Gallery, London). From an artistic viewpoint, much of his best work, including interiors such as *Room at James Pryde's* (1914; sold Christies, Charleston Manor, Sussex, 3 October 1980, lot 25), was executed during this period.

In 1914 Birley enlisted in the Royal Fusiliers with whom he served until 1915 when he was transferred to the intelligence corps, flying as an observer with the Royal Flying Corps. He became a captain in 1916 and received the MC in 1917. In 1921 he married Rhoda Vava Mary Lecky Pike (*d.* 1981), daughter of Robert Lecky Pike, of Kilnock, co. Carlow (they had one daughter and one son), and the following year moved to 62 Wellington Road, St John's Wood, London, which had been built for him by Clough Williams-Ellis.

Sir Oswald Hornby Joseph Birley (1880–1952), self-portrait, 1920

In the 1920s Birley's painting began to change rapidly, the artist using coarser brushwork and his approach becoming increasingly literal, but this had no discernible effect on his burgeoning career as a society portraitist. He received his first royal commission, a portrait of George V for the board of the National Museum of Wales in 1928; and thereafter he was to paint virtually every member of the royal family including Queen Mary and George VI (1945), and Queen Elizabeth, Elizabeth II, and Prince Philip (1949). He painted Stanley Baldwin twice (1928, Goldsmiths' Company; 1939, formerly Carlton Club, London), Neville Chamberlain (1933, City of Birmingham Museum and Art Gallery), a bluff portrait of Ernest Rutherford (1932) for the Royal Society, and, as well, a large *Conversation Piece* (1937) for *The Times*. A series of painting travels included, besides Europe, visits to the United States (1922 and subsequently); Mexico in 1926, where he painted President Plutarco Calles; India (1927 and subsequent visits), which produced some of his more inspired 'off-duty' work; and Siam in 1929, where he painted the king and queen.

In 1943, while serving with the Sussex Home Guard, Birley lost the sight of an eye in an accident when a weapon exploded, but he adapted himself with great patience to his partial loss of vision. He painted most of the statesmen and military leaders of the war, particularly a series for the Royal Naval College, Greenwich, of George VI and his admirals, and four portraits of Winston Churchill with whom he sometimes painted in the south of France.

Birley, who was a member of the Royal Society of Portrait Painters from 1912 and latterly its vice-president, was knighted in 1949. In 1951 an exhibition of his work, ranging over half a century, was held at the Royal Institute Galleries in London. A year later, after a final visit to the United States and a long period of increasingly poor health, he died at his London home on 6 May 1952. He was buried in the country churchyard at Westdean, near his Sussex home of Charleston Manor. The house and garden subsequently became well known for an annual festival of music and the arts organized by his widow, herself an amateur painter, until shortly before her death in 1981.

Captain Birley, as he continued to call himself, was indeed described by *The Times* (7 May 1952) as looking more like a soldier than a painter. Exceptionally handsome, he had immense charm which must in no small degree have accounted for the success of his portrait practice. Although a number of obituaries expressed surprise that he had never been elected a member of the Royal Academy, it was presumably for the same reasons that none of his work was ever acquired by the Tate Gallery or any of the major municipal art collections. In addition to the collections already mentioned, however, his portraits are also found in the Scottish National Portrait Gallery, Edinburgh (*Lord Reith*, 1933) and the Imperial War Museum, London.   ROBIN GIBSON

Sources *DNB* · *Sir Oswald Birley M.C.* (1980) [sale catalogue for Charleston Manor, Christies, 13 Oct 1980] · *The Times* (7 May 1952) · *WWW* · G. Kelly, *The Times* (11 May 1952) · A. Jarman and others, eds., *Royal Academy exhibitors, 1905–1970: a dictionary of artists and their work in the summer exhibitions of the Royal Academy of Arts*, 1 (1973) · *CGPLA Eng. & Wales* (1952) · *The Times* (25 June 1981) · personal knowledge (1971) [*DNB*]

Likenesses O. Birley, self-portrait, oils, 1903; Christies, 3 Oct 1980 · O. Birley, self-portrait, oils, 1905; Christies, 3 Oct 1980 · O. Birley, self-portrait, oils, 1915, Musée de l'Art Moderne, Paris · O. Birley, self-portrait, oils, 1920, priv. coll. [*see illus.*] · C. Beaton, group photograph, *c.*1937, NPG · O. Birley, self-portrait, oils, 1942; photograph, NPG · C. Sheridan, bronze head; Christies, 3 Oct 1980

Wealth at death £52,506 8*s*. 11*d*.: probate, 28 Aug 1952, *CGPLA Eng. & Wales*

Birley, Sir Robert (1903–1982), headmaster and educational administrator, was born on 14 July 1903 at Midnapore, India, the only son and elder child of Leonard Birley CSI CIE (1875–1951) of the Indian Civil Service (Bengal), and his first wife, Grace Dalgleish, younger daughter of Maxwell Smyth, indigo planter, formerly of Moffat, Dumfriesshire. His mother died when he was three and he was brought up by his paternal grandparents in Bournemouth. He was educated at Rugby School (1917–22) where he specialized in history and soon developed a taste for exploring its byways and oddities, which was stimulated by a tour of Europe between school and university, roaming about Italy, Germany, and Czechoslovakia. By a series of chances he had generally escaped external examinations, and this was to colour his approach to education later on. He went to Balliol College, Oxford (1922–5, Brackenbury scholar in history), where he won the Gladstone memorial prize (1924) and obtained first-class honours in modern history (1925). Balliol nurtured the strong idealism in Birley's character.

Sir Robert Birley (1903–1982), by unknown photographer

On leaving Oxford, Birley joined the staff at Eton College, where he remained from 1926 to 1935, and married, in 1930, Elinor Margaret, daughter of Eustace Corrie Frere, architect; they had two daughters, Julia (1931–1978) and Rachael (*b.* 1935). At Eton he made an immediate impact as an inspiring history teacher. He also startled some of the staff by putting the case for the strikers in the general strike of 1926 and organizing relief for the unemployed of Slough in 1931. He developed a lifelong absorption in the magnificent college library, from which he obtained much of his large store of often esoteric knowledge. He taught mainly the cleverer boys, introducing them to adult modes of thought and awakening their aesthetic sense. In all he made such an impression that on the retirement of C. A. Alington as headmaster in 1933 Birley was seriously suggested by some as his successor. But the post went to an older man, Claude Elliott, and soon Birley was made the headmaster of Charterhouse School, a post he held from 1935 to 1947.

As a young liberal-minded headmaster Birley had a stimulating effect in the school, and brought it into closer touch with the world of affairs. He believed that a headmaster should do as much teaching as possible. In addition to the contact with the pupils that this afforded, Birley and his wife encouraged individual boys, particularly those whom life was not treating well, with private hospitality, both in the school and at their holiday home in Somerset. Soon Charterhouse had to be guided through the war, and Birley stoutly resisted all pressures to remove it from Godalming.

Birley's public spirit made him a prominent member of

the Headmasters' Conference. In 1942 he was appointed as its member on the government committee set up under Lord Fleming to bridge the gap between private and state education. He contributed much to the final report, and at the end of the war his reputation was such that he was appointed educational adviser to the military governor, Allied Control Commission for Germany (1947–9). In Germany, Birley worked for reconciliation by bringing people together. He must be given a generous share of the credit for rebuilding the German educational system. He also played a leading part in setting up the Königswinter conferences, the first of which was held in 1950, by which Anglo-German understanding was strengthened and sustained.

In 1949 Birley became headmaster at Eton, where he remained until 1963. During his first term there he gave the Reith lectures, which were not a success. Historian that he was, he had a deep understanding of the historical role of Eton and a subtle appreciation of its special character. Birley was not a reforming headmaster, but under him respect grew for the intellect and the arts, and the teaching of science was improved and modernized. He realized the need for technologists in the second half of the twentieth century, and he felt that ideally they should be literate, go to church, and know Greek.

Birley soon became the most influential public school headmaster of his generation and he occupied the chair of the Headmasters' Conference for four years. He saw the main purpose of education as the encouragement of independent thought. The leisurely Eton education of his day, with its late specialization and freedom from the tyranny of the A level syllabus, admirably suited this approach. However, towards the end of Birley's time some parents grew restive and there was a growing demand for paper qualifications, which he was unable to resist.

The next phase of Birley's life was as remarkable as it was unexpected. On a visit to South Africa, Birley's crusading zeal was aroused by the political and racial constraints in that country. He left Eton to become visiting professor of education at the University of the Witwatersrand (1964–7). Tirelessly and single-mindedly he and his wife worked in their favourite cause, freedom of the spirit against repression and injustice. Their presence heartened liberals throughout South Africa and they made innumerable friends among both white and black people.

Birley filled one more important post on his return from South Africa, that of professor and head of the department of social science and the humanities at the City University, London (1967–71).

6 feet 6 inches in height, clumsy and unathletic, with a shy smile and an increasing stoop, Birley was an imposing and compelling figure, particularly in his cassock and bands as headmaster of Eton. Incapable of small talk, he would launch into the serious topic of the moment with excited earnestness, livened by a keen sense of the absurd and a mischievousness which never lapsed into irresponsibility. Anyone so sure of his own rectitude could not fail to have his detractors, but his natural goodness and lofty ideals won the respect of most and the devotion of many. His effect on the moral and intellectual climate of his time was immense.

Birley was given many honours in his life, including honorary doctorates (one of them an Oxford DCL, 1972) at eight universities. He was appointed CMG (1950) and KCMG (1967) but not to the honour to which his talents and sense of service were perhaps best suited, namely a life peerage. He became an honorary fellow of Balliol in 1969. He died on 22 July 1982 at Somerton in Somerset.

M. A. NICHOLSON, rev.

Sources A. Hearnden, *Red Robert: a life of Robert Birley* (1984) · D. Astor and M. Benson, eds., *Robert Birley, 1903–1982* (1985) · A. Hearnden, ed., *The British in Germany* (1978) · *Eton College Chronicle* (Sept 1963) · *Eton College Chronicle* (Sept 1982) · personal knowledge (1990)
Archives Borth. Inst., political and research papers relating to South Africa · City University Library, London, corresp. and papers | FILM BFI NFTVA, current affairs footage
Likenesses photograph, Eton College [*see illus.*]
Wealth at death £47,923: probate, 15 Nov 1982, *CGPLA Eng. & Wales*

Birmingham family (*per. c.*1135–*c.*1300), gentry, were lords of Birmingham, Warwickshire, Hoggeston, Buckinghamshire, and Shutford, Oxfordshire, and were important tenants and retainers of the lords of Dudley. The earliest known member of the family is William [i] of Birmingham (*fl.* 1135), who may have been of Norman origins, but his son **Peter of Birmingham** (*d.* before 1174) is the first about whom much is known. Peter occurs as a witness to a charter of Henry, duke of Normandy, the future Henry II, granting rights to the bishop of Lichfield in 1153/4. Peter is described as steward of Dudley, and was probably representing his master Gervase Pagnell. In 1166 it was recorded that Peter was holding nine knights' fees of Gervase, making him easily the greatest of the tenants of the honour of Dudley. The lands which made up these fees comprised at least ten manors, all but Hoggeston within a few miles of Dudley. Also in 1166 Peter was granted a royal charter of confirmation for a market at Birmingham, adjacent to his castle there. The castle was presumably on the same site as the later manor house, but archaeological excavation has not confirmed this. In 1168 Peter appears in the pipe roll accounting for the pannage of Cannock Forest, Staffordshire, and the following year was supervising work on the bridge at Newcastle under Lyme, Staffordshire. He died before 1174 and was succeeded by his son **William** [ii] **of Birmingham** (*fl.* 1174–1210), often styled William fitz Peter. Another son, Hugh fitz Peter (*fl.* 1174–1210), was granted lands at Bushbury, Upper Penn, and Rushall, Staffordshire, held from his brother as one and a half knights' fees. It is possible that the Robert of Bermingham who was a follower of Earl Richard fitz Gilbert (Strongbow) during the conquest of Ireland in 1169–71 and was granted land at Tethmory, Offaly, was also Peter's son, but this cannot be proved.

During the 1174 uprising against Henry II Gervase Pagnell rebelled, but, in a notable example of a principal tenant turning against his nominal lord, William fitz Peter commanded a party of knights garrisoning the motte of

Warwick Castle for the king. William married Margery de Malpas, whose family were tenants of the earls of Chester, and through her acquired land in Cheshire. In 1191 he went on the third crusade. William fitz Peter was succeeded by his eldest son, Brian of Birmingham (*fl. c.*1222), but Brian died soon after his father leaving no children of his own and was in turn succeeded by his brother **William** [iii] **of Birmingham** (*fl.* 1222–1242). William [iii] and a third brother, Henry of Birmingham, were in litigation regarding demesne land at Morfe, Staffordshire, which Henry subsequently held from his brother as a quarter of a knight's fee. William [iii] married Sybil de Colville and through her acquired two small manors in Buckinghamshire and Berkshire. The marriage produced at least four sons: **William** [iv] **of Birmingham** (*fl.* 1242–1263), who succeeded his father; Brian (*fl.* 1254–1262); Robert (*fl.* 1252–1262); and Roger (*fl.* 1262). Brian was a knight, but Robert and Roger were clerics, respectively rectors of Hoggeston and Enville in Staffordshire. William [iv], Brian, and Robert all accompanied Henry III on the 1254 expedition to Gascony. William [iv] married Maud of Gatcombe (*fl.* 1242–1283) whose dowry was Shutford, Oxfordshire. In 1249 he received a life exemption from serving on assizes, juries, or recognitions, an acknowledgement of favour and enhanced status; and it is probably to his lifetime that the impressive masonry work found during excavation of the site of the manor house at Birmingham belongs. In 1262 he was impleaded by Roger de Somery, lord of Dudley, regarding the extent of the services owed for his lands. William was a supporter of Simon de Montfort, marrying his son, **William** [v] **of Birmingham** (*d.* 1265), to Isabel of Astley, the daughter of Montfort's steward Thomas of Astley, and the granddaughter of Arnold du Bois, another Montfort associate. William [v] fought for Montfort at Evesham on 4 August 1265 where he was killed with many others of Montfort's household knights. His demesne lands and the wardship of his infant son **William** [vi] **of Birmingham** (*c.*1260–1302) were granted by Henry III to Roger de Clifford, but both lands and child were subsequently redeemed under the terms of the dictum of Kenilworth by Roger de Somery.

William [vi] reached his majority by 1283 but suffered huge financial difficulties. His grandmother and stepfather had life interests in a substantial part of his demesne land, he was indebted to his former guardian Roger de Somery for redemption moneys paid on his behalf, and some redemption fines had never been paid. Small wonder that he sought to avoid the burdens of knighthood; but in 1286 he was judged to have evaded and was fined accordingly. Bowing to the inevitable, he was dubbed knight and in 1297 fought in the Gascony campaign where he was captured and eventually ransomed. He died in 1302, still burdened by debt.

Dugdale refers to a seal, which he claimed to be that of Peter of Birmingham, showing a shield of arms, a bend lozenge on a plain field. The arms which his descendants bore during the thirteenth century were azure a bend lozenge or, and if they were indeed borne by Peter he would be one of the earliest examples of an armigerous knight.

The Birmingham family were active patrons of commerce. In 1189 another confirmation charter was secured for the market at Birmingham, and by the end of the twelfth century there are already indications that it was growing into a small town. In 1232 the townsmen came to an agreement with William [iii] of Birmingham regarding rents and labour services; and in 1250 William [iv] was granted confirmation for a three-day spring fair held at the town. By the second half of the thirteenth century Birmingham was recognizably a borough with burgesses, bailiffs, a court, and bounds which set it apart from the manorial lands of its founders. The relationship between a leading family of knights and an urban foundation is rare, and marks out the Birminghams as highly enterprising—an enterprise that may account for the abandonment of their Dudley allegiance for the king in 1174 and for Montfort in 1265.   RICHARD DACE

Sources *Chancery records* · *Pipe rolls* · Birm. CL, MS 735/8–10 · 'Birmingham moat', *Transactions of the Birmingham Archaeological Society*, 89 (1980)

Birmingham, John (1816–1884), astronomer, was a country gentleman residing at Millbrook, near Tuam, co. Galway, Ireland, whose attention was directed to astronomy by his discovery of a remarkable new star in Corona Borealis on 12 May 1866. In 1872, at the suggestion of the Revd T. W. Webb, he undertook a revision and extension of Schjellerup's *Catalogue of Red Stars*. In all he included 658 such objects reobserved with a 4½ inch refractor and a magnifying power of 53. The spectra of several, as described by previous authorities, were added. This work was presented to the Royal Irish Academy on 26 June 1876, and published as 'The red stars: observations and catalogue' (*Transactions of the Royal Irish Academy*, 26, 1879, 249–354). Its merit was acknowledged by the bestowal of the Cunningham medal early in 1884. Birmingham was engaged in further revising and extending it at the time of his death.

Birmingham was unmarried, a pious Catholic, liberal, kindly, and unassuming. He possessed considerable linguistic accomplishments, had travelled in most parts of Europe, and was in correspondence with several foreign astronomers, notably with Father Secchi of Rome. He held for some time the post of inspector under the board of works. On 22 May 1881 he discovered a deep red star in Cygnus, which proved strikingly variable, and became known by his name. He published articles on meteor showers, on the transit of Venus, and on sunspots. He also wrote on the geology of co. Galway for the *Journal of the Geological Society of Dublin*. His only separate publication was a small poetical work of a controversial character entitled *Anglicania, or, England's Mission to the Celt* (1863). He died, after an attack of jaundice, at Millbrook on 7 September 1884.   A. M. CLERKE, *rev.* JOSEPH GROSS

Sources *The Athenaeum* (20 Sept 1884), 376 · *Tuam News* (12 Sept 1884) · *Catalogue of scientific papers*, Royal Society, 19 vols. (1867–1925) · J. C. Poggendorff and others, eds., *Biographisch-literarisches Handwörterbuch zur Geschichte der exacten Wissenschaften*, 3 (Leipzig, 1898)

Birmingham, Peter of (*d.* before 1174). *See under* Birmingham family (*per. c.*1135–*c.*1300).

Birmingham, William of (*fl.* 1174–1210). *See under* Birmingham family (*per. c.*1135–*c.*1300).

Birmingham, William of (*fl.* 1222–1242). *See under* Birmingham family (*per. c.*1135–*c.*1300).

Birmingham, William of (*d.* 1265). *See under* Birmingham family (*per. c.*1135–*c.*1300).

Birmingham, William of (*fl.* 1242–1263). *See under* Birmingham family (*per. c.*1135–*c.*1300).

Birmingham, Sir William of (*c.*1260–1302). *See under* Birmingham family (*per. c.*1135–*c.*1300).

Birnie, Alexander [*pseud.* Cock of the Steeple] (1826–1862), journalist, was born in Moray; nothing is known about his parents. At an early age he went to England, and became a Baptist minister in Preston. During a period of major labour strikes in the town he wrote several letters to local journals, commenting on events. At some point he married and had several children.

In 1860 Birnie walked to Falkirk, arriving in the town penniless. He eventually found employment as a painter at the town's Carron works. During this period he began to write journalistic notes, signing himself Cock of the Steeple. Following dismissal from the Carron works for intemperance, he eventually became a member of the regular staff of the *Falkirk Advertiser*. In 1861 he started the *Falkirk Liberal* as an organ of the feuars of Falkirk. It was published at ½d. per copy, and printed in Stirling. It rapidly collapsed.

Devastated by the blow, Birnie made his way to Edinburgh, apparently in the hope of finding work. On being robbed of the little money he had, he resolved to commit suicide, and made an unsuccessful attempt to poison himself with laudanum. He then set off on foot for Newcastle, all the while making daily entries in a journal. In March 1862 he was found in Morpeth, where he had lain in a stack of straw for two weeks without food or drink. He died on 25 March soon after being moved to the local workhouse hospital. In his final diary entry he requested that a selection of his articles might be published and sold on behalf of his family, but this was never carried out, although a subscription was raised for their assistance.

G. B. SMITH, *rev.* DOUGLAS BROWN

Sources Boase, *Mod. Eng. biog.* · *GM*, 3rd ser., 12 (1862), 654–5 · *Falkirk Herald* (March 1862) · *Newcastle Chronicle* (March 1862) · d. cert.

Birnie, Sir Richard (*c.*1760–1832), police magistrate, was a native of Banff, Scotland. After serving his apprenticeship to a saddler he went to London, where he found work in the Haymarket with Macintosh & Co., saddlers and harness makers to the royal family. Having on one occasion been called upon by chance to attend the prince of Wales, he did his work so satisfactorily that on subsequent occasions the prince used to ask that the 'young Scotchman' might be sent to him. The patronage of the prince secured his advancement with the firm, and he was made foreman and eventually a partner. Through his marriage with the daughter of a wealthy baker of Oxenford Street, London, he also obtained a considerable fortune, including a cottage with adjoining land at Acton, Middlesex.

After his marriage Birnie rented a house in the parish of St Martin-in-the-Fields, London, and immediately began to distinguish himself by his activity in parochial affairs, serving successively, as he himself said, 'every parochial office except that of watchman and beadle'. In 1805 he was appointed churchwarden, and, along with his colleague and the vicar, he established a number of almshouses for elderly parishioners in Pratt Street, Camden Town. He enrolled in the Royal Westminster volunteers, in which he became a captain. At the special request of the duke of Northumberland Birnie was placed in the commission of the peace for St Martin's parish and from this time he began to frequent the Bow Street police court, to familiarize himself with magisterial duties. In the absence of the stipendiary magistrates he sometimes presided on the bench, and with such efficiency that he was at length appointed police magistrate at Union Hall, from which he was a few years afterwards promoted to the Bow Street office, a position which he had long desired.

In February 1820 Birnie headed the police officers in the arrest of the Cato Street conspirators. In the absence of the soldiers (who failed, as they had been ordered, to turn out at a moment's notice), he took the responsibility of making an immediate attempt to capture the band, before they were fully prepared and armed. According to a contemporary account, he 'exposed himself everywhere, encouraging officers to do their duty, while the balls were whizzing about his head'. He was greatly offended when Sir Robert Baker was appointed to the post of chief magistrate following the death of Sir Nathaniel Conant. In August 1821 at the funeral of Queen Caroline he took it upon himself to read the Riot Act, which Baker had thought unnecessary. His action found favour with the ministry and, when Baker resigned shortly afterwards, Birnie was appointed to succeed him and knighted. During his term of office he was held in high respect by the ministers in power and frequently consulted by them. He also retained throughout life the special favour of George IV. He died in Bow Street, London, on 29 April 1832 and was buried on 6 May in the church of St Martin-in-the-Fields. He was survived by his wife and a son and two daughters.

T. F. HENDERSON, *rev.* CATHERINE PEASE-WATKIN

Sources *GM*, 1st ser., 102/1 (1832), 470–71 · *Annual Register* (1832), 198–9
Likenesses W. Say, mezzotint, pubd 1819 (after J. Green), BM, NPG · H. B., lithograph, 1829, NPG

Birnie, William (1563–1619), Church of Scotland minister, was the only son of William Birnie (*d. c.*1565) of Birnie, probably a merchant, and his wife, Margaret Fraser of Philorth (later named Fraserburgh), mistress of the mint under Mary, queen of Scots. He was educated at the University of St Andrews from 1584, graduating MA in 1588, and was subsequently a student of divinity (*c.*1592–5) at the University of Leiden.

Birnie had returned to Scotland by 25 January 1596, at which date he was an expectant minister of the presbytery of Edinburgh. It was probably during this period that he married Elizabeth, daughter of John Lindsay, minister of Carstairs, in the presbytery of Lanark. The couple had two daughters and three sons, the eldest of whom, John, was born in 1600. Elizabeth's uncle Robert Lindsay was minister of Lanark, and on his death in December 1597 Birnie succeeded to his benefice.

Birnie was a commissioner to the general assembly of 1602, and was appointed master and economus of the hospital and almshouse of St Leonard's, Lanark, the following year. In 1606 he accepted the office of constant moderator of the presbytery of Lanark, and as commissioner to the assemblies of 1608 and 1610 he supported the king's further plans to impose an episcopal polity on the kirk. Such support did not go unnoticed, and in 1609 Archbishop John Spottiswood of Glasgow recommended 'his Majesties favour … to Mr William Birnie … whose dispositioun your Lordship kens to his Majesties service' (Calderwood, 7.8). Birnie served on the court of high commission for the province of Glasgow from 1610, and was reappointed when the two courts were united in 1615. In 1612 his efforts were rewarded with an appointment to the benefice of Ayr, because the king had 'a mynd to prefer him also to be Deane of our Chapell Royall [at Stirling]', and 'Air is a church thereupon depending' (Botfield, 1.282). Within two years, however, James had resolved to unite the latter office with the bishopric of Galloway, and Birnie was required to surrender the deanery in return for the revenues of the vicarages of Ayr and Alloway.

A man of many parts Birnie was the author of *The Blame of Kirk-Buriall, Tending to Perswade Cemeteriall Civilitie* (1606), a work which deprecated interment within the kirk. He was also an athlete and swordsman of some renown, who—besides 'being obliged many times' to step between feuding parishioners—'was so agile that he could make the salmon's leap by stretching himself on the grass [and] leaping to his feet' (*Fasti Scot.*, 3.7).

Inevitably, Birnie's support for royal policy attracted the ire of the presbyterian party within the kirk, and accusations that he sought preferment and worldly comforts at the expense of others were not entirely unjustified. It was certainly true that his various pensions augmented his stipend by £1000 Scots. Yet, as with the tiends of Alloway, little of the income reached his purse. Despite such criticisms Birnie was highly regarded by his congregation as a 'pleasant [and] pious' minister, who was 'charitable, even above his estate'. The elegiac notion that he 'waited on his charge with care and pains, At Air, on little hope and smaller gains' (*Fasti Scot.*, 3.7) was probably a more accurate reflection of his pastoral concern and personal wealth. He died at Ayr on 19 January 1619.

VAUGHAN T. WELLS

Sources D. Calderwood, *The history of the Kirk of Scotland*, ed. T. Thomson and D. Laing, 8 vols., Wodrow Society, 7 (1842–9), vols. 6–8 · *Fasti Scot.*, new edn, vol. 3 · R. Botfield, ed., *Original letters relating to the ecclesiastical affairs of Scotland*, 1 (1841) · C. Rogers, *History of* the Chapel Royal of Scotland (1882) · Anderson, *Scot. nat.* · *The autobiography and diary of Mr James Melvill*, ed. R. Pitcairn, Wodrow Society (1842)

Birrel, Robert (*fl.* 1567–1605), diarist, was a burgess of Edinburgh. His 'Diary, containing Divers passages of Staite, and Uthers Memorable Accidents, from the 1532 yeir of our Redemption, till ye Beginning of the yeir 1605' was published in 1798 in *Fragments of Scottish History*, edited by Sir John Graham Dalyell. There is not much minuteness in the record of events until about 1567, when Birrel probably began to keep a note of them. There is no evidence in the 'Diary' regarding the political or religious views of the writer, facts being simply recorded as they happened, without comment or any apparent bias of opinion. There is some evidence that the work was intended for publication, the writer having apparently taken some trouble to collect his facts. In the seventeenth century a considerable part of it was incorporated by Sir James Balfour in his *Annals*. The original manuscript was deposited in the library of the Faculty of Advocates.

T. F. HENDERSON, *rev.* J. K. MᶜGINLEY

Sources J. G. Dalyell, ed., *Fragments of Scottish history* (1798) · *The historical works of Sir James Balfour*, ed. J. Haig, 4 vols. (1824–5) **Archives** BL, diary, Harley MS 6371

Birrell, Augustine (1850–1933), politician and author, was born at Wavertree, near Liverpool, on 19 January 1850, the younger son of Charles Morton Birrell, a Baptist minister, and Harriet Jane Grey, daughter of Henry *Grey, Free Church of Scotland minister. Though he later became an agnostic, he always retained a deep respect for the Liberal nonconformist tradition of his Liverpool upbringing. He left Amersham Hall School, Caversham, in 1866 to become an articled clerk in a Liverpool solicitor's office, when a lucky legacy allowed him to study law at Trinity Hall, Cambridge, where he earned a good second-class degree in 1872. He was called to the bar by the Inner Temple at twenty-five, earning a solid living which enabled him in 1878 to marry Margaret, daughter of Archibald *Mirrielees [see under Muir, Andrew (1817–1899)]. She died after only 'a twelve-month's bliss', as Birrell sadly remarked. His younger sister looked after him for the next nine years while he developed both his law practice and his literary skills.

Birrell's legal career was by no means undistinguished—he took silk in 1895, and for three years from 1896 was professor of law at University College, London. He also acquired a considerable reputation as an essayist and literary critic, especially with his two small volumes of *Obiter dicta* (1884, 1887), which aimed to remind his readers 'of books they once had by heart, and of authors they must ever love' (*Obiter dicta*, 2nd ser., 1896, vi). His witty and elegant essays on writers he admired, such as Milton, Pope, Carlyle, and Dr Johnson, revealed his passion for literature and his intellectual versatility. He had collected more than 10,000 books for his library by the time he was fifty, observing in his essay 'Book-buying' that 'the man who has a library of his own collection is able to

Augustine Birrell (1850–1933), by Sir William Orpen, 1909

contemplate himself objectively' (*Obiter dicta*, 2nd ser., 1896, 264).

Liberal politician Birrell was a charming, intelligent, and tolerant man, whose genial cynicism concealed an unexpected shyness and vastly more ability than his critics allowed. Lytton Strachey later observed: 'He was decidedly a Victorian product. Large and tall and oddly like Thackeray to look at—with spectacles and sharp big nose' (M. Holroyd, *Lytton Strachey*, 2.230). In 1888 he married Eleanor Mary Bertha (*d.* 1915), widow of Lionel Tennyson (younger son of the poet laureate), and daughter of the poet Frederick Locker-*Lampson. They were happily married for twenty-seven years, bringing up two sons and sharing keen interests in literature and politics. Domestic contentment provided a secure base from which to launch Birrell's political career. After unsuccessful attempts to enter parliament in 1885 and 1886, he won a by-election as Liberal member for West Fife in 1889, and established himself in the 1890s as a devoted follower of Gladstone's last Liberal government. At the 1900 general election he unsuccessfully stood for the North-East division of Manchester, and was out of parliament until his return for North Bristol at the 1906 election, which resulted in a landslide Liberal victory.

For the next ten years Birrell was a minister in the cabinets of Campbell-Bannerman and H. H. Asquith, where he contributed significantly to the reforming achievements of Britain's last Liberal governments before war transformed the political scene and the Labour Party replaced the Liberals as the party of the left. Sir Charles Mallet

observed in *The Times* (22 November 1933) that Birrell was a master of debate who delighted audiences by his eloquence and moved them deeply by his strong conviction: 'few men at the end of 1906 enjoyed a greater reputation in the House of Commons'. His challenge as president of the Board of Education in 1906 was to amend the controversial 1902 Education Act, which was deemed by nonconformists and Liberals to favour Church of England elementary schools. His Education Bill of 1906 was intended to restore equal educational treatment but could satisfy neither the English Anglicans and Irish Catholics in the House of Commons nor the permanent Conservative majority in the House of Lords. It was withdrawn after its inevitable mutilation in the upper house, but the delicate negotiations between rival religious denominations demonstrated his superb skills as an adept diplomat and sensitive conciliator, reinforced by his tolerance and humour.

Chief secretary for Ireland Birrell's political reputation rests primarily on his substantial achievements as chief secretary for Ireland in the first six years of his tenure, from 1907 to 1912. He reluctantly succeeded James Bryce, with no idea that he was 'doomed to last nine long years, two years being the average' in that peculiarly difficult post (A. Birrell, *Things Past Redress*, 1937, 194). Sir Henry Robinson, the vice-president of the Local Government Board, considered Birrell's term in office 'infinitely more momentous and prolific in legislative reforms' than that of any of his predecessors, with fifty-six measures passed through parliament, in areas such as working-class housing, public health, and conditions in schools (Robinson, 189). He was conscientious and energetic in dealing with the routine problems of the Irish government within Ireland and he also frequently attended the House of Commons, where he made an impressive number of effective speeches on Irish business. He rapidly won and retained the confidence and respect of the Irish nationalist leaders John Redmond and John Dillon; this was absolutely crucial in 1907–11, when Irish home rule was low on the list of Liberal priorities. The Liberal government needed to abolish the veto power of the House of Lords before it could pass a third home rule Bill for Ireland, and from 1906 to 1910 it was fully occupied with a radical programme of social reform for Britain. He was notably successful in his holding operation on home rule, which meant walking the uneasy tightrope between Irish nationalist aspirations and Liberal intentions.

Birrell achieved a significant programme of vital reforms for Ireland as a prelude to ultimate self-government. His solution to the Irish university question resolved a problem which had bedevilled Anglo-Irish politics for decades. The Catholic majority in Ireland had long been deprived of a Catholic teaching university, but the Presbyterians and Anglicans were opposed to a nonsectarian national university. Birrell's tolerance and negotiating skills helped to construct a careful compromise in the 1908 Irish Universities Act, which created two independent teaching universities in addition to the historic Trinity College; the new National University of Ireland for

Catholics amalgamated the constituent colleges of Dublin, Galway, and Cork, while the Presbyterian Queen's College became Queen's University, Belfast. Dillon acclaimed the act as one of the greatest services ever rendered to the Irish nation by an English statesman.

Birrell's second major achievement was the 1909 Land Act, all the more notable in a period when the Lords were deliberately wrecking key Liberal measures as this one attacked wealthy Irish landlords. The new legislation introduced the principle of compulsory purchase in congested areas, and increased Treasury support for land purchase, though not so far as Birrell had hoped. It had to be another compromise because of the bill's inevitable transformation in the Lords, but as he claimed in parliament, 'I got the most I could' (*Hansard 5C*, 16 Aug 1911). The new Land Act was crucial for two reasons. The financial machinery of the 1903 Land Purchase Act, which transferred estates from landlords to tenants, was collapsing from lack of funds, causing a campaign of agrarian violence between 1907 and 1909. His solution to agrarian violence was not the coercion and repression of poverty-stricken peasants and political agitators, but reform of the defective land purchase scheme. The Conservative Party clamoured for the re-imposition of repressive measures, but coercion violated his fundamental Liberal principles and he rode the storm of abuse in press and parliament with courage. Even in its amended form the 1909 Land Act was a considerable achievement in the circumstances, since it accelerated land purchase and reduced agrarian violence.

Third, Birrell ensured that an Irish home rule bill was finally introduced into parliament in April 1912 and that it had the support of the Irish nationalists. H. W. Massingham paid warm tribute in *The Nation* (6 April 1912) to Birrell's impressive feat in holding the fort 'stoutly and warily' until the 1911 Parliament Act ended the Lords' veto: 'without a wise, tactful, forbearing, and sympathetic Irish Secretary, the links [with Irish Nationalism] would have snapped'. Had Birrell's resignation been accepted in 1912, as he wished, this would have been his enduring political epitaph. Instead, his political career ended tragically when he accepted the blame for the 1916 Easter rising, which has haunted his reputation ever since. There was a watershed in Birrell's career about 1912, when his public career and private life suffered an agonizing decline, for reasons largely beyond his own control. From 1911 he was increasingly eager to leave the Irish Office because his beloved wife had an inoperable brain tumour which finally caused insanity. The result was for him a profound private agony, known only to his family, which affected his capacity for effective work from 1913 until her death in March 1915. This severe personal strain undoubtedly contributed to the uncharacteristic combination of excessive zeal and indecision which marked his response to the Dublin industrial agitation of 1913. When the militant trade union leader James Larkin reduced the city to chaos, Birrell was condemned by both Labour and Liberal critics for an acrimonious prosecution of Larkin and an excessive sentence of imprisonment.

Birrell became increasingly ineffective as Irish secretary after the introduction of the Home Rule Bill in April 1912, but Asquith refused to accept his resignation on several occasions. His position became almost intolerable after the Ulster protestants threatened civil war rather than accept a home rule bill for a united Ireland. In November 1913 Lloyd George persuaded the cabinet to accept temporary exclusion from the bill of the predominantly protestant Ulster counties to meet these threats. Though Birrell accepted that such a decision was politically expedient, it conflicted with his own preference for a united Ireland and with his long-standing commitment to the Irish nationalists. But the prime minister persuaded him to remain at his unwelcome post out of a deep sense of public duty and a dual loyalty to Asquith and the Irish nationalists. From November 1913 supreme control of home rule policy passed almost entirely into the hands of Asquith, Lloyd George, and Winston Churchill, while Birrell played little more than a reluctant, passive role and was available as the scapegoat when policies misfired. The blame for weaknesses in the wider home rule policy from 1913, for the vacillation over the treatment of Ulster, for the Curragh fiasco, and for the disaster of 1916, should be shared with Asquith, Lloyd George, the Liberal cabinet, and the Unionist opposition.

Birrell accepted public responsibility for the Liberal government's inadequate and belated responses to the escalating crises from 1913. He failed to prevent the formation of rival private armies in the north and the south in defiance of the government, and refused to prosecute the Ulster protestant leaders who were threatening civil war. His problems were vastly increased by the unreliability of the Royal Irish Constabulary reports and the espionage networks, while he feared that coercion would inflame popular passions, with no certain deterrent effect. He was also condemned for taking harsher steps against the national volunteers in the south of Ireland than the Ulster Volunteer Force in the north. He did not prosecute the protestant ringleaders of the gun-running operation at Larne in April 1914 because arrests might have accelerated Ulster's plans for civil war. But when the nationalists attempted their own large-scale gun-running coup at Howth in July 1914, troops killed three civilians in an unarmed crowd.

The Easter rising In the terrible years between 1914 and 1916 Birrell's hopes for Irish home rule seemed doomed because the bill became non-operational in wartime, and the Ulster protestant obstacle was shelved rather than solved. While his wife was slowly dying, he remained in a thankless and impossible position, as several letters of resignation bore witness. He attracted the most damning criticism of all in his final year at the Irish Office because he did not anticipate and prevent the Dublin Easter rising in 1916, which changed the course of Irish history. He was almost universally condemned for the government's failure either to counter the growth of Irish militant separatism or to recognize the shift in nationalist sympathies away from Redmond's Home Rule Party after it supported the First World War. He certainly underestimated the potential danger from the Irish Republican Brotherhood and the Irish Volunteers because their numbers seemed small, the Irish intelligence system was woefully inadequate, and he feared government repression would itself provoke violence. Moreover, he did not take seriously the possibility that Irish rebels might welcome martyrdom in a rising doomed to defeat, nor could he anticipate that British executions of the leaders would help create those martyrs. Immediately after the rising Asquith finally accepted his resignation, two years too late, having refused all earlier offers. In his resignation speech in the House of Commons (*Hansard 5C*, 82.31–5, 3 May 1916), Birrell publicly accepted full blame for the rising, consoled only by the thought that his wife's death in 1915 had spared her this humiliation. The subsequent report (26 June 1916) of the royal commission on the rebellion in Ireland placed primary responsibility on him as the administrative head of the government in Ireland.

Birrell spent his retirement from politics from 1916 to 1933 at 70 Elm Park Road, Chelsea, surrounded by his family including his two sons, Tony and Frankie. He wrote two more volumes of collected essays, a sketch of his father-in-law, Frederick Locker-Lampson, and his own memoir, *Things Past Redress* (1937). In dictionaries of quotations some of his witty epigrams achieved fame as 'Birrellisms'—such as 'That great dust-heap called history' (Ó Broin, *The Chief Secretary*, 205). At the age of eighty-one he was still, according to Tom Clarke, 'a very sprightly luncheoneer … a snappy 81' (T. Clarke, *My Lloyd George Diary*, 1939, 120). In old age he was saddened by the dramatic decline of the Liberal Party as well as by the collapse of his hopes for a home rule Ireland. He died in Chelsea, probably at home on 20 November 1933, followed a year later by his son Frankie. Birrell would not have been surprised that after his death he was generally condemned by the English, who blamed him for the Easter rising but cared little about his achievements in Ireland from 1907 to 1912. Irish historians and writers have generally taken a more balanced view of his career; Piaras Beaslai's judgement of Birrell as 'one of the best and most successful of Irish Chief Secretaries' is justified at least up to 1912 (P. Beaslai, *Michael Collins*, 1937, 42). PAT JALLAND

Sources P. Jalland, 'A liberal chief secretary and the Irish question: Augustine Birrell, 1907–1914', *HJ*, 19 (1976), 421–51 • L. Ó Broin, *The chief secretary: Augustine Birrell in Ireland* (1969) • P. Jalland, *The liberals and Ireland: the Ulster question in British politics to 1914* (1980) • A. Birrell, *Things past redress* (1937) • *DNB* • L. Ó Broin, *Dublin Castle and the 1916 rising: the story of Sir Matthew Nathan* (1966) • H. Robinson, *Memories: wise and otherwise* (1923) • A. Birrell, *Obiter dicta*, 2nd ser. (1896) • D. Gwynn, *The life of John Redmond* (1932) • C. Mallet, *The Times* (22 Nov 1933) • H. W. Massingham, *The Nation* (6 April 1912)

Archives Bodl. Oxf., corresp. and papers as chief secretary for Ireland • U. Lpool L., family corresp. and papers | BL, letters to Sir Henry Campbell-Bannerman, Add. MSS 41235–41240 • BL, corresp. with Lord Herbert Gladstone, Add. MSS 46056–46081 • BL, letters, mainly to H. G. Hutchinson, Add. MS 49382 • BL, corresp. with Lord Ripon, Add. MS 43542 • Bodl. Oxf., corresp. with Herbert Asquith • Bodl. Oxf., letters to Bertram Dobell • Bodl. Oxf., letters to J. L. L. Hammond • Bodl. Oxf., letters to Lewis Harcourt • Bodl. Oxf., letters to members of the Lewis family • Bodl. Oxf., letters to Andrew Philip Magill • Bodl. Oxf., letters to Sir Matthew Nathan • Ches. & Chester ALSS, letters to Rhoda Broughton • HLRO, corresp. with

David Lloyd George, etc. • HLRO, letters to Herbert Samuel • King's AC Cam., letters to Oscar Browning • LPL, corresp. with Randall Thomas Davidson • NL Ire., letters to A. S. Green • NL Ire., letters to John Redmond • NL Scot., letters to A. C. Cunningham • NL Scot., corresp. mainly with Lord Rosebery • NRA Scotland, priv. coll., letters to Lord Aberdeen • NRA Scotland, priv. coll., corresp. with John Ewart • Queen Mary College, London, letters to Katherine Lyttelton • TCD, corresp. with John Dillon • TCD, corresp. with William Starkie • U. Leeds, Brotherton L., letters to Edmund Gosse • U. Leeds, Brotherton L., letters to Clement Shorter • U. Newcastle, Robinson L., corresp. with Walter Runciman • U. Newcastle, Robinson L., letters to C. P. Trevelyan

Likenesses Elliott & Fry, photograph, 1880–89, NPG • B. Stone, photographs, 1899, NPG • W. Orpen, chalk drawing, 1909, NPG • W. Orpen, oils, 1909, Hugh Lane Gallery of Modern Art, Dublin [*see illus.*] • E. Kapp, drawing, 1913, Barber Institute of Fine Arts, Birmingham • A. McEvoy, oils, 1918, National Gallery of Canada, Ottawa • O. Edis, autochrome, *c.*1925, NPG • R. Schwabe, chalk drawing, 1927, NPG • R. Fry, oils, 1928, Trinity Hall, Cambridge • H. Coster, photograph, 1930–39, NPG • O. Edis, photograph, NPG • H. Furniss, ink drawings, NPG • R. G. Jenning, print, BM, NPG • D. Low, pencil drawing, NPG • W. Orpen, oils, NG Ire. • Spy [L. Ward], watercolour cartoon, NPG; repro. in *VF* (18 Jan 1906) • H. J. Whitlock & Sons, photograph, NPG

Wealth at death £25,499 7*s.* 9*d.*: probate, 29 Jan 1934, *CGPLA Eng. & Wales*

Birrell, John (1836–1901), orientalist, was born at Drumeldrie, Newburn parish, near St Andrews, on 21 October 1836, the elder of two sons of Hugh Birrell, architect, and his wife, Margaret Smith. His brother, George, an architect, died in 1876. After attending the parish school and Madras College, St Andrews, Birrell entered St Andrews University as first bursar in 1852, and after distinguishing himself in classics and mathematics graduated MA in 1856. With thoughts of the Indian Civil Service, he passed the next two years at the University of Halle as pupil of the orientalist Emil Roediger. After the Indian mutiny he altered his plans, and trained from 1859 to 1862 at St Mary's College, St Andrews, for the ministry of the Church of Scotland.

Birrell was licensed as a preacher on 14 August 1862 by St Andrews presbytery, and for two years held the post of tutor at the College Hall, St Andrews. In 1863 he became assistant to Dr Robertson at St Mungo's Cathedral, Glasgow, and in June 1864 he was presented by the senatus of St Andrews, then patrons of the living, to the parish of Dunino adjoining that of St Andrews, which he retained until 1872. He was there able to continue in academic life. He was examiner in classics at St Andrews (1862–6) and for some years assisted John Cook, professor of church history. On 7 June 1871 he was appointed by the crown to the chair of Hebrew and oriental languages in St Mary's College, St Andrews, to which he was admitted on 4 November, and proved himself a painstaking, broad-minded, and lucid teacher. On 3 June 1874 Birrell married Elizabeth (*d.* 13 April 1943), daughter of James Wallace, a farmer, of The Brake, Dunino; they had five children (Hugh, Agnes, James Wallace, and twins John and Elizabeth).

Birrell's abilities were widely recognized. He received an honorary DD from Edinburgh University in 1878, and he was a member of the Old Testament revision committee (1874–84). He was the first chairman of the St Andrews school board, and held the position for fifteen years. As examiner of secondary schools in Scotland from 1876 to 1886, he originated and carried out with great success the scheme (afterwards superseded by the system of leaving certificates) of university local examinations at St Andrews. Birrell died at St John's, St Andrews, on 31 December 1901, after a prolonged illness, and was buried in the cathedral burying-ground of the city.

T. W. BAYNE, *rev.* R. S. SIMPSON

Sources *Fasti Scot.*, 5.198; 7.427; 8.718 • *The Times* (2 Jan 1902), 4e • *WWW, 1897–1915* • *Annual Register* (1902) • P. Schaff and S. M. Jackson, *Encyclopedia of living divines and Christian workers of all denominations in Europe and America: being a supplement to Schaff-Herzog encyclopedia of religious knowledge* (1887) • J. M. Anderson, ed., *The matriculation roll of the University of St Andrews, 1747–1897* (1905) • *CCI* (1902)

Wealth at death £2279 6s. 4d.: confirmation, 7 March 1902, *CCI*

Birsay. For this title name *see* Leslie, Sir Harald Robert, Lord Birsay (1905–1982).

Birt, William Radcliff (1804–1881), meteorologist and astronomer, was born on 15 July 1804 in Southwark, London, of unknown parentage. Although without the advantages of birth, independent means, or known education, he married, and made his way into the scientific community.

Birt's notices on variable stars and meteorology between about 1830 and 1832 impressed Sir John Herschel to pay him from a small British Association for the Advancement of Science (BAAS) grant in 1839–43 to compute barometric fluctuations to trace the magnitude, direction, and velocity of atmospheric pressure waves. This proved a vast and laborious calculation, and Herschel withdrew in 1843 from all but supervision after announcing two of an eventual three waves identified by Birt (*DSB*, 2.147). Between 1844 and 1848 Birt was entrusted by the BAAS with further analysis, and produced annual reports and articles. This theoretical investigation was abandoned when the data could not be made to fit the theory (Jankovic, 36–7). He published the well-reviewed *Hurricane Guide* (1850) and *Handbook on the Laws of Storms* (1853; 2nd edn, 1878) which offered a barometric method for seamen to forecast and more safely navigate cyclonic storms. After failing to secure posts at the Cape, Madras, and Kew observatories, in 1849 he reported at length to the association on their Kew observations of atmospheric electricity. This led in November 1849 to a post at Kew, but in June 1850 his protest that the work was menial was misunderstood as resignation, and to his chagrin he fell out with the BAAS management and had to leave (Jankovic, 37).

After the BAAS Oxford meeting in 1847 Birt was with the distinguished group which stayed two nights at John Lee's Hartwell House, and during the next six years, with other 'Hartwell Synod' observers, very regularly reported to the BAAS on luminous meteors. Elected FRAS in 1859, he borrowed a 2.75 inch refractor and started systematic observations of sunspots and lunar features.

In 1860 Lee sundered the Royal Astronomical Society (RAS) by canvassing the ballot and snatching the 1861–3 presidency from the astronomer royal, G. B. Airy. In 1861

Lee encouraged Birt to petition the Treasury for the 'favour' of an annual pension on the grounds that his lack of means for an efficient stand and micrometer interfered with the research of an able man of science. Birt drew up the 'Memorial' himself, noting that 'As a Public Lecturer on Natural Science including Astronomy, and not holding a Public appointment … his income is very limited and uncertain'. He needed Herschel's to be the first signature. However, Sir John amended and initialled two careful caveats, one being a claim that Birt's work on atmospheric waves 'resulted from his previous work for Sir John', a modest claim to which Sir John appended 'I cannot say'. The memorial was withdrawn (Birt, 'Memorial', Birt MSS).

In 1862 John Phillips (1800–1874) renewed his 1852 proposal to the BAAS to remedy the lack of a reliable and comprehensive map of the moon to supersede Beer and Madler's 37 inch map of 1836. He proposed new methods for co-operation by observers with 6 inch telescopes to study the physical nature of the moon and map it to a scale of 100 inches, the largest outline Warren De La Rue could achieve photographically. He obtained the backing of the Royal Society. Birt responded promptly, was given free access to Admiral Smyth's famed 5.9 inch refractor at Hartwell, and from 1863, as secretary of the Lunar Committee for Mapping the Surface of the Moon, collated the observations of eleven regular and twenty-four other observers and issued annual reports during 1864–9; but he proposed the scale to be 200 inches. Lee initiated Birt's second proposal that year, an 'extension of lunar nomenclature' to name or rename for posterity a list of lunar features after English astronomers. Admiral Smyth sent a copy to Airy with three huge black exclamation marks on the top. Birt used a borrowed 13 inch Newtonian at his home, and the 5.9 inch for fine detail. He discovered a feature in the crater Plato and named it Hartwell ledge. Even less discreetly Birt named a crater after RAS benefactor Mrs Jackson-Gwilt, and two after his cousins the Gwilt brothers.

Birt's original work as an astronomer under the notice of potential patrons earned him considerable reputation as the BAAS's expert on storms and atmospheric phenomena, then as a selenographer. His aim was not precise positions, but co-ordination of minute scrutiny. Only four of 160 portions of the 200 inch map were completed, which identified 443 physical features of a total of 2099 registered. His incomplete mapping and nomenclature were partly used by Edmund Nieson (1876), and definitively superseded by S. A. Saunder and Mary A. Blagg (1913). Apart from three minor books on his lunar observations (1869–74), he published many articles on atmospheric physics and phenomena, variable stars, sunspots, solar rotation, and zodiacal light in *Monthly Notices* (1830–73), *Philosophical Magazine* (1842–80), the *English Mechanic*, and *Astronomical Register*, and his last article, 'Lunar physics', appeared in the *Observatory* when he was seventy-seven years of age. Birt was unfortunate with his patrons. Despite long service to the BAAS it declined a small grant in 1857. Herschel snubbed his claim in 1863 when Dr Lee had riven the RAS and so could do Birt no good. Undaunted, and surely in part response, Birt doubled the size of the moon map. When Lee died in 1866, Birt built a small observatory for £90 to house a borrowed 4.5 inch refractor. But in 1870 the BAAS considered the extent and slowness of mapping unsuitable for further assistance. This led him to form a Lunar Committee to publish a catalogue of the alterations accumulated to Madler's map; Phillips and a number of RAS members subscribed. In 1882 the BAAS formally abandoned a scheme which could not survive his death. However, by his selenography, and particularly by his observations which stimulated a debate on observed changes on the floors of craters Plato and Linne, Birt left a lasting mark on astronomy.

In poor health since 1873, Birt had to stop observing in 1877, but established and became the first president of the Selenographical Society. His scheme for the great lunar map and catalogue was unrealizable, his powers spent, and in 1879 he gave his twelve-volume manuscript of the lunar catalogue to the RAS, which society had not invited him to serve on its council. In that year he published a second edition of his *Table-Moving and Spirit-Rapping Solved* (1853). Birt died of a stroke on 14 December 1881 at 4 Leyspring Terrace, Leytonstone, Essex, his son recording him as a 'gentleman'. ROGER HUTCHINS

Sources d. cert. · *Monthly Notices of the Royal Astronomical Society*, 42 (1881–2), 142–4 · *DSB*, 2.147 [incl. bibliography] · Boase, *Mod. Eng. biog.* [incl. bibliography] · C. L. F. André, *L'astronomie pratique et les observatoires en Europe et en Amérique*, 1: *Angleterre* (Paris, 1874), 164–5 · *Astronomical Register* (1863–85) · *Report of the British Association for the Advancement of Science* (1859–70) · Reports of the Selenographic Committee of the British Association for the Advancement of Science, 1863–9 · W. R. Birt, 'On the extension of lunar nomenclature', *Monthly Notices of the Royal Astronomical Society*, 24 (1863–4), 19–20 [text refers to CUL, RGO 6 381, 628] · A. M. Clerke, 'Planets and satellites', *A popular history of astronomy during the nineteenth century*, 2nd edn (1887), 310–21 · R. Hutchins, 'Professor John Phillips at Oxford, 1853–74; catalyst for the University observatory', additional option thesis, U. Oxf., 1992, 17–22, 28–32 · J. Morrell and A. Thackray, *Gentlemen of science: early years of the British Association for the Advancement of Science* (1981) · J. C. Poggendorff and others, eds., *Biographisch-literarisches Handwörterbuch zur Geschichte der exacten Wissenschaften*, 3 (Leipzig, 1898) [for list of articles] · RAS, Hartwell MSS 37; Birt MSS · *Catalogue of scientific papers*, Royal Society, 19 vols. (1867–1925) [lists 81 papers: 1830–75] · CUL, Royal Greenwich Observatory papers · W. R. Birt and J. Phillips, correspondence, 1845–69, Oxf. U. Mus. NH, John Phillips Archive · T. E. R. Phillips and W. H. Steavenson, eds., *Hutchinson's splendour of the heavens* (1929), 258 · V. Jankovic, 'Ideological crests versus empirical troughs: John Herschel's and William Radcliffe Birt's research on atmospheric waves, 1843–50', *British Journal for the History of Science*, 31 (1998), 21–40
Archives RAS, MSS | Bucks. RLSS, corresp. with John Lee · Inst. EE, letters to Sir Francis Rolands · LPL, corresp. with John Lee · Oxf. U. Mus. NH, John Phillips Archive, letters to John Phillips · RAS, letters to John Lee · RS, corresp. with John Herschel
Likenesses photograph, 1867, RAS, MS Add. 90 Jackson-Gwilt, 51

Birtwistle, Thomas (1833–1912), trade unionist and factory inspector, was born at Great Harwood, Lancashire, on 16 October 1833, the son of Jonathan Birtwistle, a calico printer, and Ann Birtwistle, a hand-loom weaver. Put to the hand-loom at the age of six, he became a power-loom weaver when he was fourteen and married a fellow weaver, Ellen Butterworth (who predeceased him), when he was twenty. Despite only a rudimentary formal education, Birtwistle showed a natural facility for mathematics, and became expert at calculating the complex piece-rates which formed the basis of a cotton weaver's wages. It was this rare ability which led to his involvement in the nascent trade union movement of the north Lancashire weaving towns during the later 1850s.

The aim of the early cotton weavers' unions, which Birtwistle later pursued consistently, was to secure an agreed list of weaving piece-rates from the leading employers and to enforce its uniform observance throughout the weaving districts. For this purpose, close co-operation between weavers' organizations in the different towns was essential. Having become a leading figure in his local union during the 1858 lock-out at Great Harwood, Birtwistle was elected to the council of the newly established North-East Lancashire Powerloom Weavers' Association (the so-called 'first amalgamation') during subsequent strikes at Padiham (1859) and Colne (1860), and in February 1861 he was appointed its full-time secretary, a post which he held for the next thirty-one years.

Birtwistle's union career could hardly have begun at a less opportune time. The year-long Colne strike had ended in defeat, and the cotton famine of the early 1860s caused a sharp decline in the amalgamation's membership. However, it escaped complete collapse, and the subsequent revival and expansion of cotton weavers' unionism owed much to Birtwistle's quiet, pragmatic persistence. Growth was slow and erratic, none the less: the industry-wide lock-out during the depression of 1878 demonstrated yet again both the fragility of inter-union co-operation and the hostility of many employers to collective bargaining. The Northern Counties Amalgamated Weavers' Association of 1884 (the 'second amalgamation') eventually provided the strong central organization the weavers needed for effective wage negotiations. Birtwistle served as its secretary during its early months, and although he was later overshadowed by the association's more assertive president, David Holmes, he had the ultimate satisfaction of negotiating the first uniform weaving price-list for the cotton industry in 1892.

Birtwistle's role in trade union history went far beyond brokering intricate back-stage deals between high-handed employers and truculent local union officials in Lancashire's smaller mill-towns. He represented the first amalgamation at the Trades Union Congress from 1872, served continuously on its parliamentary committee between 1875 and 1889, and took his turn as its chairman in 1882. Along with his younger counterpart, James Mawdsley, the spinners' leader, Birtwistle helped to forge the alliance between coal and cotton unions which largely determined the TUC's cautious and 'anti-political' stance in the 1880s and 1890s. Finally, he was a leading figure in the cotton workers' repeated attempts to extend the scope of the Factory Acts. Beginning with the nine-hours movement, Birtwistle successfully developed the art of lobbying local MPs which extracted favourable legislation from both Conservative and Liberal administrations in the 1870s and 1880s. As secretary of the United Textile Factory Workers' Association, he was mainly responsible for securing—in collaboration with Sir Henry James, the Unionist MP for Bury (later Lord James of Hereford)—the Factory Acts extensions of 1889 (which regulated the unhealthy practice of 'steaming' to increase the humidity of cotton-weaving factories) and 1891 (which obliged employers to provide their weavers with detailed printed 'particulars' of each piece of work they received). At the same time, he became increasingly hostile to the idea—frequently mooted at the TUC in the late 1880s—of a legally-enforced eight-hour working day, on the grounds that it would either lead to lower wages or damage the cotton industry's international competitiveness.

Birtwistle's growing importance in industrial affairs, both locally and nationally, earned him public recognition in the course of the 1880s. He was appointed to the royal commission on the depression of trade and industry in 1885, and became one of the country's first working-class JPs in the same year. In the immediate aftermath of the third reform act there were suggestions that he might stand as a 'labour' candidate for a Lancashire constituency; but his well-known Conservative sympathies were at odds with the predominant radical-Liberal tendencies of the weaving communities. In June 1892, however, he surprised his fellow union leaders (and offended some) by accepting a government appointment as a factory inspector, with specific responsibility for implementing the 'particulars clause' of the 1891 Factory Act. Although this was an appropriate and adventurous appointment, given his long experience of the intricacies of piece-rates in the cotton industry, the suspicion remained that it was a political reward for services rendered to class collaboration in general, and to Lancashire Conservatism in particular. Despite this, his subsequent work as a factory inspector seems to have given satisfaction to his superiors and to employers and workers alike in the cotton industry.

Birtwistle retired as an inspector on reaching his seventieth birthday in 1903, and died at his home, 17 St James's Street, Accrington, on 22 March 1912; he was buried in Accrington cemetery on the 26th. He was survived by his second wife, Mary. By that time, although he was still something of a local celebrity, the details of his earlier record as a union leader had been effectively written out of the weavers' collective memory. Nevertheless, to have linked the worlds of Joseph Raynor Stephens (1805–1879) and David Shackleton (1863–1938), as Birtwistle did, was no mean achievement; and few careers better illustrate the extent to which British trade unions gained recognition, respectability, and responsibility during the second half of the nineteenth century.   DUNCAN BYTHELL

Sources *Accrington Division Gazette* (23 March 1912) · *Accrington Observer* (23 March 1912) · *Cotton Factory Times* (1885) · *Cotton Factory Times* (1892) · *Annual Report* [Trades Union Congress] (1872–92) · A. Bullen, *The Lancashire Weavers' Union* (1984) · H. A. Clegg, A. Fox, and A. F. Thompson, *A history of British trade unions since 1889*, 1 (1964) · 'Royal commission on labour', *Parl. papers* (1892), vol. 34, C. 6708 · E. Hopwood, *The Lancashire weavers' story* (1969) · H. A. Turner, *Trade union growth, structure, and policy: a comparative study of the cotton unions* (1962) · B. C. Roberts, *The T. U. C., 1868–1921* (1958) · J. A. Jowitt and A. J. McIvor, eds., *Employers and labour in the English textile industries, 1850–1939* (1988) · S. J. Webb, B. P. Webb, and R. A. Peddie, *The history of trade unionism* (1894) · parish register (baptism), Lancashire, Great Harwood, St Bartholomew, 17 Nov 1833 · parish register (marriage), Lancashire, Great Harwood, St Bartholomew, 1 July 1854 · census returns, 1871, 1881, 1891 · d. cert.
Likenesses photograph, 1890, Accrington Public Library, local studies section · photograph, repro. in *Accrington Observer*, 8
Wealth at death £334: probate, 26 April 1912, *CGPLA Eng. & Wales*

Bisbie [Bisby], **Nathaniel** (1635–1695), Church of England clergyman, was born on 5 June 1635, the son of the Revd John Bisbie (d. 1648x50), perpetual curate of Tipton, Staffordshire, and his wife, Margaret Hoo, daughter of Anthony Hoo of Bradeley Hall in the same county. John Bisbie was ejected from a prebend in Lichfield Cathedral about 1644, but by 1648 was in place as curate of Edstaston, Shropshire; at the time that John Bisbie made his will, on 30 October 1648, Nathaniel had three brothers and two sisters, as also a stepbrother and a stepmother.

Nathaniel Bisbie was elected student of Christ Church, Oxford, from Westminster School, in 1654; he graduated BA in 1658 and MA in 1660, accumulating his degrees in divinity on 7 June 1668 (incorporated at Cambridge in 1669). At the Restoration he was presented by Sir Robert Cordell to the rectory of Long Melford, Suffolk, worth £300 a year according to Thomas Hearne. Bisbie was then, says Anthony Wood, 'esteemed an excellent preacher and a zealous person for the church of England' (Wood, *Ath. Oxon.* 4.640). He married Elizabeth Wall, daughter of John Wall of Radwater Grange, Essex, in 1672, and they apparently had many children.

Bisbie published a number of sermons, three of which were originally delivered at the assizes at Bury St Edmunds in 1681 and 1684. These were spent largely in attacking what he saw as the unholy alliance between Jesuits and puritans to undermine church and state—a not uncommon theme in loyalist propaganda in those years. Bisbie refused to take the oath of allegiance to William and Mary, and as a nonjuror was deprived of his rectory of Long Melford in February 1690. He continued to write after losing his living and contributed two works to the controversy over Humphrey Hody's anti-nonjuror tract, *The Unreasonableness of a Separation from the New Bishops* (1691). In *An Answer to a Treatise out of Ecclesiastical History* (1691), Bisbie argued that Hody's reasoning would have justified obeying the usurping Novatian bishops under Constantine. He died at Long Melford on 14 May 1695, about five in the afternoon, and was buried there two days later.   A. B. GROSART, *rev.* EDWARD VALLANCE

Sources Foster, *Alum. Oxon.* · *Remarks and collections of Thomas Hearne*, ed. C. E. Doble and others, 2, OHS, 7 (1886), 68 · *DNB* · *Walker rev.*, 303 · T. Wagstaffe, letter to T. Hearne, 25 Oct 1714, Bodl. Oxf., MS Rawl., letters 17, fol. 35 · Wood, *Ath. Oxon.*, new edn, 4.640 · Venn, *Alum. Cant.*
Archives Bodl. Oxf., MS Rawl., letters 17, fol. 35
Wealth at death 'impoverished' due to loss of living and large family: *Remarks and collections of Thomas Hearne*, vol. 2, p. 68

Bischoff, James (*bap.* 1775, *d.* 1845), merchant and writer, was baptized on 15 November 1775 at Call Lane Arian Independent chapel, Leeds, the younger son of the six children of George Bischoff (1737–1812), a merchant, and his second wife, Elizabeth, the daughter of John Crompton of Gainsborough and the widow of William Whitaker of Leeds. James Bischoff's grandfather, of German extraction but born in Basel, had settled in Leeds around 1715. The family prospered in the chief centre of the West Riding wool textile industry, and in 1782 they were reckoned to be the second largest cloth export house in Leeds.

Nothing is known of Bischoff's education and training, but he was, like so many of his forebears and members of his wife's family, occupied as a cloth merchant in Leeds at the turn of the eighteenth century. In 1802 he married Margaret, the daughter of David Stansfeld, a prosperous Leeds cloth merchant. Her maternal grandfather, Thomas Wolrich, another leading merchant in the town, had collected a notable series of statistics relating to the cloth industry in the early 1770s. Bischoff had ample access to these papers; perhaps they inspired him to begin his own tireless researches into, and defence of, the industry. He first came to public notice in 1816 with a series of letters in the *Leeds Mercury*, the *Farmer's Journal*, and the *Gentleman's Magazine* opposing the imposition of a duty of 6d. per pound on imported wool, nevertheless levied between 1820 and 1824 as a measure to relieve the distressed British agricultural sector. An advocate of free trade, he was appointed one of the deputies from the West Riding to a series of meetings in London to promote the repeal of the wool duty. He was prominent in collecting statistics to support their case, and published two pamphlets, *Reasons for the Immediate Repeal of the Tax on Foreign Wool* (1819) and *Observations* (1820) on the *Report of the Earl of Sheffield to the Meeting at Lewes Wool Fair, July 20, 1820*. In 1824 the duty was reduced to a nominal 1d. in the pound, and, in a move to placate the agricultural interest, exports of wool (there were very few as imports burgeoned) were allowed for the first time for centuries on the payment of the same negligible rate. In the following year Bischoff was consulted by William Huskisson, president of the Board of Trade, about a reduction of duties on foreign manufactured goods. Bischoff advocated free trade, views he again propounded in his evidence to the House of Lords committee on the British wool trade in 1828.

By the early 1820s Bischoff was living in London, working as a merchant and insurance broker. After 1824 he was prominent in the affairs of the Van Diemen's Land Company. With a nominal capital of £1 million (10,000 shares of £100 each), and supported by several members of parliament, it was one of the many speculative companies launched in the boom of 1823–5. Bischoff was its managing director. By 1831 it had acquired 350,000 acres of good sheep land in north-west Tasmania, where Mount Bischoff is named after him. Although it seems that he had never been there, he wrote *A Sketch of the History of Van Diemen's Land* (1832). Four years later, he published an essay on marine insurance.

Bischoff's most important work, however, was his compilation *A comprehensive history of the woollen and worsted manufactures, and the natural and commercial history of sheep, from the earliest records to the present period* (1842). It brought together, in two volumes, a multitude of material about the wool textile industry, especially those statistics and papers relating to his own activities surrounding the duty in wool. Together with John James's *History of the Worsted Manufacture in England from the Earliest Times* (1857), it provides a mine of information about the evolution of Britain's premier industry and its principal raw material, wool. Bischoff's last publication was a pamphlet inveighing against foreign tariffs, originally printed as a series of articles appearing in the *Leeds Mercury* between October and February 1843. He died on 8 February 1845 at his home, 20 Highbury Terrace, Highbury, Middlesex, leaving a family of three sons (the youngest of them was in partnership with his father) and four daughters.

R. G. WILSON

Sources R. V. Taylor, ed., *The biographia Leodiensis, or, Biographical sketches of the worthies of Leeds* (1865), 409–11 · J. Bischoff, *A comprehensive history of the woollen and worsted manufactures*, 2 vols. (1842) · J. Bischoff, *A sketch of the history of Van Diemen's Land* (1832) · J. Risby, ed., 'Pedigrees and arms of Leeds families', 1892, Leeds City Reference Library, 54 · *GM*, 2nd ser., 23 (1845), 443 · d. cert. · will, PRO, PROB 11/2017, sig. 361

Bischoffsheim, Henri Louis [Henry Louis] (1829–1908), financier, was born in Amsterdam, the younger of the two sons of Louis Raphael Bischoffsheim (1800–1873), banker, and his wife, Amélie, *née* Goldschmidt. His grandfather, Raphael Nathan, had migrated to Mainz in the eighteenth century from Bischofsheim on the River Tauber in Baden, and thereafter he took the name of Bischoffsheim. He became president of the Jewish community in Mainz. His elder son Louis Raphael Bischoffsheim established a bank in Amsterdam with branches in Paris, London, and Antwerp. Paris later became his headquarters. Raphael Nathan's younger son, Raphael Jonathan, settled in Belgium, where he opened banking houses which rendered financial services to the Belgian government of such magnitude that after his death the street on which he lived in Brussels was renamed boulevard Bischoffsheim. He became a senator and was father-in-law of Baron Maurice de Hirsch.

Louis Raphael's elder son Raphael Louis settled in Paris, where he became a prominent and successful banker. He was also deeply interested in astronomy and founded one of the foremost observatories in France, close to Nice. Henri Louis, the younger son, went to London in 1849 to serve in the London branch of his father's business, which had been founded in 1836. The branch was under the management of his uncle, S. H. Goldschmidt, who subsequently retired to Paris and became in 1882 president of the Alliance Israelite. During his life in England Bischoffsheim was known as Henry. In 1856 he married Clarissa, one of 'seven beautiful daughters' of J. Biedermann of Vienna, four of whom married prominent figures in the City of London (*The Times*, 12 March 1908). The Bischoffsheims had two daughters, one of whom, Ellen (1857–

1933), became countess of Desart and the first female senator of the Irish Free State. Like her parents, she was very active in Jewish philanthropy. The second daughter married Sir Maurice Fitzgerald, knight of Kerry and equerry to the duke of Connaught.

On his father's death in 1873 Henry separated from the Paris firm and settled into business, still in association with Goldschmidt, as a successful merchant banker. Until the mid-1870s when Bischoffsheim's business activities slackened, he carried on wide-ranging international financial operations from offices at 31 Throgmorton Street under the title of Bischoffsheim and Goldschmidt. The firm's success in the mid-nineteenth century, according to his *Times* obituary, owed much to 'Mr Bischoffsheim's sanguine and energetic temperament' (*The Times*, 12 March 1908). Such an account, however, fails to bring out the controversial nature of the foreign loans with which Bischoffsheim and Goldschmidt became associated early in their partnership. The firm's involvement in the Honduras loan of 1867 was especially notorious. 'Bischoffsheims saw its chance for a killing and had few if any compunctions about taking it' (Kynaston, 270). This was one of the episodes investigated in March 1875 by the select committee on loans to foreign states, and it was undoubtedly the case that between 1866 and 1875, when the market in foreign loans reached its peak, 'their transactions were on an extraordinary scale' (Emden, 537). From *c*.1874 Bischoffsheim took little part in the affairs of the firm; although he still attended his office for a few hours on most days of the week and gave advice, he initiated no transactions. By this time Sir Ernest Cassel was a successful manager in the firm.

Bischoffsheim occupied his semi-retirement with a glittering social life and with philanthropy, in both of which his wife was his close partner. She was an active and distinguished hostess and was said to have won the favourable regard of Queen Victoria (*The Times*, 12 March 1908). The couple gained the society nickname of the 'Bischs', and were known for the splendour of their entertainment at their London home, Bute House, South Audley Street, and their country estate, Manor House, at Stanmore, Middlesex. On these occasions 'Mrs Bischoffsheim played her part as hostess with a distinction and brilliancy which was natural to her; her husband was as unassuming as he was generous' (ibid.). Bischoffsheim also owned a stud farm, The Severals, at Newmarket.

The couple were generous donors to charity, especially to Jewish charity. 'That he accumulated a considerable fortune is a fact well-known, and even more notable is the generous use to which he put his wealth, of which he devoted large sums to general and communal purposes', noted the *Jewish Chronicle* after his death. 'No movement of importance has gone forward in the community to which Mr Bischoffsheim did not contribute munificently and readily' (*Jewish Chronicle*, 13 March 1908). He was also actively involved on the committee of the Jews' Free School, the council of the Anglo-Jewish Association, the Roumanian Committee, and as a trustee of the Jewish

Convalescent Home, Hampstead. He was one of the founders of the Imperial Cancer Research Fund, and was the founder and sole owner of the Metropolitan Hospital Ambulances, which were established in various parts of London to provide first aid. The cost of constructing the children's wing of the Jewish Convalescent Home, which was established by his cousin Baroness de Hirsch, was also borne by Bischoffsheim. Together with his wife he founded the Daneswood Sanatorium at Woburn Sands, Bedfordshire, for Jewish consumptives.

The Bischoffsheims celebrated their golden wedding anniversary in 1906 by giving a total of £100,000 to charity. The largest sum—£40,000—was given to the Imperial Cancer Research Association, £10,000 each to the Daneswood Sanatorium and to King Edward VII's Sanatorium; a further £10,000 went to various Jewish charities. Although the public credit for these philanthropic activities often went to Bischoffsheim alone, the initiative often lay equally with his wife. She was active as vice-president of the Union of Jewish Women, served as a committee member of the Jews' Infant Schools and the Ladies West End Charity and of various hospitals, dispensaries and help societies. Bischoffsheim was also in his later years treasurer of the Twentieth Century League, founder of the Twentieth Century Club, and chairman of the committee formed to raise funds for the enlargement of the Stepney Jewish Free School.

Bischoffsheim died at Bute House, 75 South Audley Street, Mayfair, London on 11 March 1908 and was buried at the Golders Green cemetery of the West London Synagogue. Survived by his wife, he was described by the *Jewish Chronicle* as

> an ideal type of the rich Jew. He gathered his vast wealth by means at which the sternest moralist could set no cavil, he took a pride and a pleasure in distributing huge amounts of it with an unsparing hand, an example to Jews of what a rich Jew should be, an example to the world of what a rich Jew can be.

His obituarist added: 'Both in public and private life Mr Bischoffsheim was a man of exceedingly simple manners, and the natural amiability of his disposition was never spoilt by success' (*Jewish Chronicle*, 13 March 1908).

PAT THANE

Sources *The Times* (12 March 1908) · *Jewish Chronicle* (13 March 1908) · *Jewish Chronicle* (20 March 1908) [account of funeral] · D. Kynaston, *The City of London*, 1 (1994) · P. H. Emden, *Jews of Britain: a series of biographies* (1944) · *WWW, 1897–1915* · d. cert.
Wealth at death £1,622,332 8s. 8d.: resworn probate, 2 May 1908, *CGPLA Eng. & Wales*

Biscoe, Cecil Earle Tyndale- (1863–1949), missionary and educationist, was born on 9 February 1863 at Holton Park, Wheatley, Oxfordshire, the son of William Earle Tyndale (1813–1895), a landowner, and his wife, Elizabeth Carey (d. 1891), daughter of Albert Glass Sandeman, founder of Geo. G. Sandeman Sons & Co., the port importing company. His father changed his surname to Biscoe on inheriting Holton Park. Tyndale was added in the following generation. Cecil was the fourth child in a family of seven sons and one daughter. A connection with Rhodesia was established by his much admired younger brother Edward, a naval officer who had joined the Rhodes expedition to Mashonaland and hoisted the flag at Fort Salisbury.

Tyndale-Biscoe's sufferings as a small boy at Bradfield College, including a near rape by older pupils, set the pattern for his defence of the underdog and his fight against the devil. At Jesus College, Cambridge, he coxed the winning university crew in 1884, and the college winner of the Grand Challenge Cup at Henley in 1886. Although he weighed only 8 stone, he won the college pairs with the great Steve Fairbairn, whose apophthegm, 'As you meet your stretcher so you will meet your God', he employed and adapted (*Tyndale-Biscoe of Kashmir*, 4). An undistinguished BA (1886) was followed by ordination as deacon and priest in the Church of England. Several curacies, latterly in the Whitechapel slums, led to his appointment to the Church Missionary Society mission school in Kashmir in 1890. In 1891 he married Blanche Violet (d. 1947), daughter of the Revd Richard Bennet Burges. They had three sons and one daughter.

The physical and moral squalor of Kashmiri society, a depressed Muslim majority dominated by a venal Hindu élite, gave Tyndale-Biscoe many devils to fight. Its unreliable princely house was monitored by the resident, from 1906 to 1909 Curzon's protégé Sir Francis Younghusband, one of Tyndale-Biscoe's imperialist heroes and friends (a group that included Lord Roberts, Lord Baden-Powell, and General Dunsterville, the model for Kipling's Stalky). Younghusband's preoccupation was with protecting the frontier of Kashmir, the largest of the princely states; Tyndale-Biscoe's was its moral regeneration through a systematic assault on its caste culture and the development of public service ideals inspired by Christian example. Ignoring his missionary critics, he never pursued conversions. A robust imperialist, he was an early supporter of Churchill's India Defence League, and believed Indian society had a long moral apprenticeship to serve before achieving any conceivable political independence.

Tyndale-Biscoe rated intellectual cleverness in his pupils below what he called 'soul', a compound of elements ranging from honesty and pluck to 'colour of heart'. Boxing and boating were only two of the disciplines he insisted on, but his emphasis on physical activity was no simple replication of upper-class Edwardian athleticism. His early scholars were grown men, Brahmans exempted from physical labour by caste status, and habituated to ascribed superiority. Gainful employment, however, depended on the achieved status the school could dispense, and Tyndale-Biscoe exploited this tension with aggressive and inventive good humour.

Tyndale-Biscoe's Hindu and Muslim masters, armed with single sticks, enforced contact between bare feet and polluting leather at the first game of football, and the principal himself gave painful instruction on the advantages of manly self-defence. Parents who jibbed at the low-caste skill of swimming paid stiffer fees. From rowing, like English gentlemen, Brahmans graduated to paddling racing shikaras, like coolies; penalties for dishonesty and sexual depravity were public and severe. Physically competent and collectively co-ordinated, the boys were mobilized in public service, from cleaning alleys to saving lives during the frequent floods, fires, and cholera epidemics.

Over fifty-seven years Tyndale-Biscoe expanded the foundation to some 1800 pupils in six schools, one of them for girls. The central school became a show-piece for important visitors. In recognition of his educational achievements Tyndale-Biscoe received the kaisar-i-Hind gold medal (1912) and bar (1929). At independence fourteen old boys were ministers in the new government of Kashmir under the prime minister, Sheikh Abdullah.

Tyndale-Biscoe left Kashmir for Southern Rhodesia in 1947, distressed but not surprised by the communal violence imperialist die-hards had predicted from British withdrawal. He died at Purbeck, Dorset Road, Avondale, Salisbury, Rhodesia, on 1 August 1949, and was buried in Salisbury. GERALD STUDDERT-KENNEDY

Sources *Tyndale-Biscoe of Kashmir: an autobiography* (1951) · G. Studdert-Kennedy, *British Christians, Indian nationalists and the raj* (1991), 157–62 · G. Studdert-Kennedy, 'The Christian imperialism of the die-hard defenders of the raj, 1926–35', *Journal of Imperial and Commonwealth History*, 18 (1990), 342–62 · C. E. Tyndale-Biscoe, *Kashmir in sunlight and shade* (1925) · E. D. Tyndale-Biscoe, *Fifty years against the stream, 1880–1930* (1930) · CGPLA Eng. & Wales (1950) · J. A. Mangan, *The games ethic and imperialism* (1987)
Archives Jesus College, Cambridge, drawings and watercolour sketches
Likenesses C. Quien, bronze bust, Jesus College, Cambridge · photograph, repro. in Tyndale-Biscoe, *Tyndale-Biscoe of Kashmir*, 48
Wealth at death £919 3s. 6d.—(in England): probate, 27 Oct 1950, CGPLA Eng. & Wales

Biscoe [Bisco], **John** (1605/6–1679), clergyman and ejected minister, was born in High Wycombe, the son of Robert Biscoe (1572–1630), yeoman of High Wycombe, and his second wife, Susan Lane (d. 1648?), of Northdeane in Hughenden, Buckinghamshire. He is to be distinguished from his first cousin and namesake, John Biscoe, a lieutenant-colonel in the parliamentarian army, who was MP for Amersham in the protectorate parliament of 1658–9, a colleague in exile of Edmund Ludlow, and a military conspirator against the restored monarchy.

John Biscoe of High Wycombe attended Oxford, matriculating from New Inn Hall on 20 June 1623 aged seventeen and graduating BA on 1 February 1627. After leaving Oxford he may have served as a lecturer at St Helen's, Abingdon. According to Anthony Wood, having been educated in the principles of 'precise' religion, Biscoe 'closed with the presbyterians in time of their rebellion and took the covenant' (Wood, *Ath. Oxon.*, 3.1198). On 16 March 1643 the House of Commons named him for the chaplaincy of St Thomas's Hospital, Southwark, in the place of the sequestered Benjamin Spencer, an appointment confirmed by the House of Lords on 23 March. The following month the Lords ordered that of the £50 or £60 per annum income of the post £30 should be paid to Spencer's wife and children, but on 16 August this was rescinded and it was ordered that Biscoe be paid the full amount.

In 1647 Biscoe issued *The Glorious Mystery of Gods Mercy*, prefaced 'To the congregation of faithful ones, in Thomas

Southwark', a work which reflects the preoccupation then prevalent with spiritual religion: love, the author wrote, 'makes heaven upon earth: they that love spiritually do dwell in God, and God in them' (sig. A4). Biscoe was still 'minister of the gospel in Thomas Southwark' when he issued *The Grand Triall of True Conversion* with a preface by Joseph Caryl dated 7 July 1655. A dedication by the author to Thomas Andrews, alderman and president of the hospital, recalls 'your special favour and bounty to myself'. In this work Biscoe set out to unravel two mysteries, 'of iniquity working in Man's thoughts by corrupt nature', and 'of holiness working in the thoughts of sanctified persons' (Bisco, *Grand Triall*, foreword).

On 25 November 1657 Biscoe was admitted to the vicarage of St Helen's Abingdon, in succession to John Tickell; unlike his predecessor Biscoe appears not to have sought to interfere in, or to profit from, the vicarage of St Nicholas's in the town, a living separated from that of St Helen's by a commission of 1650. He was nevertheless ejected from the benefice in 1660, a successor being instituted on 3 April 1661 on the presentation of the crown. Edmund Calamy states that he then returned to Southwark, acting as a lecturer of St George's, but was removed the following year.

John Biscoe married twice. His first wife's name was Margaret (d. 1666), and they are probably the John Biscoe and Margaret Davenporte who married at High Wycombe on 10 November 1628, a year and a half after his graduation. Margaret was surely the mother of the Samuel Biscoe, listed as the son of a minister, who matriculated at New Inn Hall, Oxford, on 6 June 1660. It seems fairly certain that after the Restoration the couple settled for some years in Uxbridge, Middlesex, where Margaret was buried on 19 September 1666. Their eldest child was Robert Biscoe, a citizen and leatherseller of London; perhaps another was Richard Biscoe or Buscold, 'a rich tanner' who in 1669 was sheltering Hezekiah Woodward, a dissenting minister, at Uxbridge (Turner, 1.90). Richard was licensed for his house there in 1672, but in the same year John Biscoe received a licence as a congregationalist preacher at his house at West Wycombe in his native Buckinghamshire. Another son, John, was living when his father drew up his will on 23 March 1675. John Biscoe the elder died in 1679 and was buried at High Wycombe on 9 June, 'to the great lamentation of the brethren' as Wood reported it (Wood, *Ath. Oxon.*, 3.1198). His second wife, Mary (d. 1684), outlived him; she was buried, also at High Wycombe, on 7 October 1684.   STEPHEN WRIGHT

Sources Wood, *Ath. Oxon.*, new edn, 3.1198 · J. Bisco, *The glorious mystery of Gods mercy* (1647) · J. Bisco, *The grand triall of true conversion* (1655) · *Calamy rev.* · J. C. C. Smith, *Pedigree of the family of Biscoe* (1887) · *IGI* · G. L. Turner, ed., *Original records of early nonconformity under persecution and indulgence*, 1 (1911), 90

Biscoe, John (*bap.* 1794, *d.* 1843), merchant navy officer and explorer, was baptized in Enfield on 28 June 1794, the third son and youngest child of Thomas Biscoe of Waltham Abbey and his wife, Ann Tibbs. Nothing is known of his early years, but on leaving school he became a clerk. On 11 March 1812 he volunteered for the *San Domingo* (74 guns), probably to avoid being pressed into the navy, and he served off North America. On 4 January 1813, as volunteer first class, he entered the brig *Colibri* (16 guns), which was lost off South Carolina in a hurricane. In 1813–15 he was midshipman, quartermaster, and acting master in the *Moselle* (16 guns) in the West Indies and off the coast of the United States. Captain John Moberley of the *Moselle* said of him, 'keeps a good reckoning, is attentive and promises to make a good officer' (PRO, ADM/6/177/2634). Biscoe was later to name a mountain after Moberley.

Nothing is known about Biscoe's employment from 1815 to 1830, when Messrs C., H., and G. Enderby, oil merchants in the City, proposed an Antarctic sealing voyage, and appointed him master of the brig *Tula* (150 tons)—which was not a good sea boat—with the cutter *Lively* and twenty-nine men and boys in all. The two ships left the River Thames on 10 July 1830 and returned in January 1833. Biscoe called at the Falkland Islands for refreshment, searched in vain for the 'Aurora Islands', and between 17 and 31 December 1830 examined the South Sandwich Islands as best he could. On 24–25 February 1831, in lat. 65°57′ S, long. 47°20′ E, Biscoe discovered Enderby Land, which he named after his employers, sighting black mountain tops showing through the ice-cap. His landfall was probably the Tange peninsula. He charted Cape Ann (named after his mother) and mounts Charles, Henry, George, and Gordon (named after the Enderbys), and Mount Codrington. At a cost to the health of the crew and himself, he persisted off the coast for a month, trying to make a fuller chart. When he reached Hobart Town on 9 May 1831, all save four men were ill with scurvy.

In a second season Biscoe visited New Zealand and the Chatham Islands, and then made for South Shetland. On 15–16 February 1832 he discovered Adelaide Island; then he sighted Alexander Land, charted the Pitt Islands and Anvers Island, and called at South Shetland. He returned home from the Falklands after most of his crew, who could stand no more of the Antarctic, had deserted and he had had to use his own funds to secure supplies. His voyage was outstanding for his persistence and seamanship, and his charts are of high quality, despite his poor equipment; in 1833 he was awarded the royal premium of the Royal Geographical Society and was honoured by the French Geographical Society. He was proposed as an 'ordinary member without payment of fees' of the RGS, a testimony to his geographical achievement and to his poverty. He applied in vain to the Admiralty for his master's warrant.

In 1833 Biscoe was appointed by the Enderbys to the *Hopefull* and the *Rose* for a similar expedition, but resigned before sailing. In 1834–6 he was in the West Indies trade, and in 1837 sailed from London for Hobart Town, commanding the *Superb* (345 tons). There he became master of the *Emma*, a brig of 122 tons. In 1839, at Campbell Island, he met John Balleny and on a sealing voyage (also in 1839) he penetrated what was later named the Ross Sea to lat. 75° S, probably on the Pennell Bank, before its 'discovery' by James Clark Ross. In 1839–41 Biscoe commanded the *Marian Watson* and the *Trugenina*, trading out of Sydney.

Biscoe's health was failing and there was a subscription, to which Sir John Franklin was a leading contributor, for his return to England. He embarked on the *Janet Izatt*, but the hardships of his exploring voyages had broken his health and he died at sea or in a port somewhere between Sydney and London at some time between February and June 1843. More precise information cannot be obtained since the ship's log was destroyed. He left his wife, Emma Crowe (the daughter of a Hackney bootmaker, whom he had married on 8 September 1836 in Whitechapel), a daughter, and three sons in extreme poverty. Among those who subscribed for their relief was Queen Adelaide, after whom Biscoe had named an island in the Antarctic. His eldest son, William John Dawson, was given a charity place at the Greenwich Hospital school and in 1901 his daughter, Emily, was given a civil-list pension of £30 for her father's services to geography. Biscoe was the first to chart portions of the Antarctic continent and, despite limited means and difficult conditions, contributed significantly to Antarctic exploration.

A. G. E. JONES, *rev.* ELIZABETH BAIGENT

Sources A. Savours, 'John Biscoe, master mariner, 1794–1843', *Polar Record*, 21 (1982–3), 485–91 • A. E. E. Jones, 'John Biscoe, 1794–1843', *Mariner's Mirror*, 50 (1964), 271–81 • A. E. E. Jones, 'The voyage of the *Hopefull* and the *Rose*, 1833–4', *Mariner's Mirror*, 51 (1965), 233–42 • A. E. E. Jones, 'John Biscoe's voyage round the world, 1830–33', *Mariner's Mirror*, 57 (1971), 41–62 • A. Savours, *Australian dictionary of biography*, 1 • A. G. E. Jones, 'John Biscoe's training as a master mariner', *Local Historian*, 8/5 (1969), 160–66 • J. Cumpston, 'The Antarctic landfalls of John Biscoe, 1831', *GJ*, 129 (1963), 175–84 **Archives** BL, journal, Add. MS 15716 • RGS, journals

Biscoe, Richard (1687/8–1748), theologian, of unknown parents, was educated for the nonconformist ministry at Samuel Benion's academy, Shrewsbury, from about 1706 until Benion's death in 1708, and later at Leiden University. He was ordained on 19 December 1716 at the Old Jewry meeting-house, London, by nine ministers including Edmund Calamy III, who gave the charge which was subsequently published. He was minister of the Presbyterian meeting, Newington Green, Middlesex, from at least 1714. Walter Wilson suggests he was there from 1708, presumably as assistant to John Russell who died in 1714. Dudley Ryder, the future lord chief justice, who heard him preach in October 1716 and again in December, thought him 'a very dull preacher'. 'Mr Biscoe does not become the pulpit well at all. He has a very dull manner of delivery and has a very simple air in it' (*Diary of Dudley Ryder*, 355, 372). He resigned from Newington Green on 25 December 1727, conformed, and was ordained deacon, the date of his subscription being 8 January 1728. He was presented to the rectory of St Martin Outwich, London, on 27 February. In 1729 he was admitted MA by Magdalene College, Cambridge, by royal mandate.

Biscoe wrote to Bishop Edmund Gibson in 1733 with comments on Gibson's proposals for church reform. In 1736 he was chosen to preach the Boyle lectures, evidence of his reputation for learning, which he delivered in a series of twenty-four sermons over three years in the parish church of St Mary-le-Bow, London. He may have been the author of the *Remarks* on Benjamin Hoadley's *Plain Account of the Nature … of the Lord's Supper* (1735); if so he already had a reputation as a controversialist. In 1736 he was appointed to the prebendary of Ealdstreet, and collated to his stall in St Paul's Cathedral on 19 October. He published his Boyle lectures as *The History of the Acts of the Holy Apostles … Consider'd as Full Evidence of the Truth of Christianity* (1742). It was translated into German and published at Magdeburg in 1751. According to William Orme, although the biblical critic John Lightfoot had collected a great deal of material on the same subject it was 'better digested' by Biscoe (Orme, 47–8). Philip Doddridge thought highly of the work as demonstrating 'in the most convincing manner how incontestably the Acts of the Apostles demonstrate the truth of christianity' (Allibone, *Dict.*, 1.194). Biscoe was presented to the vicarage of North Weald Bassett, near Epping in Essex, on 5 April 1738 by the bishop of London. He held both his livings until his death at North Weald Bassett on 8 June 1748, at the age of sixty. He was buried in the church there on 12 June 1748.

DAVID L. WYKES

Sources appendix 3, 'Sketch of the history and antiquities of Stoke Newington', *Antiquities in Middlesex and Surrey* (1790), no. 9 [2/2] of *Bibliotheca topographica Britannica*, ed. J. Nichols (1780–1800), 49–50 • J. Toulmin, *An historical view of the state of the protestant dissenters in England* (1814), 442 • E. Calamy, *An historical account of my own life, with some reflections on the times I have lived in, 1671–1731*, ed. J. T. Rutt, 2nd edn, 2 (1830), 364, 504 • 'An account of the dissenting academies from the Restoration of Charles the Second', DWL, MS 24.59, p. 29 • Venn, *Alum. Cant.* • Allibone, *Dict.* • W. Orme, *Bibliotheca biblica* (1824) • *The diary of Dudley Ryder, 1715–1716*, ed. W. Matthews (1939), 355, 372 • C. W. F. Goss, *The parish and church of St Martin Outwich, London* (1929), 26 • P. Morant, *The history and antiquities of the county of Essex*, 1 (1768), 152 • *DNB* • monumental inscription, 1748, North Weald Bassett church, Essex • parish register (burial), 12/6/1748, North Weald Bassett church, Essex

Bishop, Ann (1899–1990), parasitologist, was born on 19 December 1899 at 43 Derby Street, Hulme, Manchester, the first of the two children of James Kimberley Bishop, cabinet-maker, and his wife, Eileen, daughter of George Ginger, builder, and his wife, Mary. Ann Bishop's grandfather Joseph Bishop set up a successful cabinet-making business in Manchester soon after his marriage to Ann Kimberley. When Joseph died, his two young sons were left to help their mother to run the business. The elder, James, appreciated his mother's ability; he had high moral standards, read widely, and believed that the best thing a father could give to a child was the chance to train for a profession. Ann owed to him her own tough, independent approach to life and the opportunity of a good education (unusual for a woman at the time).

Ann was taught privately at home until she was seven years old, then at the Fielden School (1909–12) and the Manchester High School for Girls (1912–18). In 1918 she

Ann Bishop (1899–1990), by Walter Bird

signed on for the ordinary BSc course at Manchester University, choosing chemistry, botany, and zoology for her first-year subjects. She was aware that such a selection would be unlikely to get her a job in the chemical industry; but she had found books by Darwin, Huxley, and Wallace among her father's collection and was determined to learn some biology. Zoology was her immediate interest, and she registered for the honours course, with Professor S. J. Hickson in the school of zoology. There, Geoffrey Lapage fired her with a desire to study the microscopic parasites that cause malaria and other human and animal diseases. Her second subject, on Hickson's advice, was organic chemistry, which in Manchester was tailored to the dyestuffs industry; later, when Ann's interests had turned to chemotherapy, she found this training very useful. She graduated with honours in 1921 and was awarded the John Dalton natural history prize. She stayed for a further year and was awarded an MSc for work on the beautiful, free-swimming microscopic ciliates that she found in ponds during walks in the north Cheshire countryside. She cultivated them in the laboratory and studied their division and conjugation.

Determination in the face of male competition secured Ann a part-time teaching post in the zoology department at Cambridge University. In 1922 she entered Girton College, which was to be her home for many years. She became a Yarrow fellow of the college in 1932. Life was not always comfortable in the male-dominated atmosphere of

Cambridge (she was forced to sit on the first-aid box at departmental tea, while the men occupied the table), but she continued with her work on ciliates and presented a successful PhD thesis in 1926.

A meeting with Clifford Dobell, protozoologist to the Medical Research Council, led to Ann being invited to work with him at the National Institute for Medical Research at Hampstead, London. Dobell was trying to cultivate the amoebae that cause human dysentery, and his teaching (which Ann described as 'rigorous') had a profound effect. She began to investigate the use of cultures to study the way in which drugs used for the treatment of human disease acted on the isolated parasites. In 1929, with a Beit fellowship, Ann returned to Cambridge to work with David Keilin at the Molteno Institute; she remained there, with a succession of Medical Research Council appointments, for the rest of her working life. She made cultures of malaria parasites and used them to test many new chemical compounds. At the time this unit was one of the very few laboratories in the world studying malaria and its treatment. In 1941 she submitted her work on flagellates and amoebae for a Cambridge ScD degree. She was awarded the titular degree, as women were not yet members of the university. She was appointed director of the unit in 1948.

Ann was interested in observations made at the turn of the twentieth century that trypanosomes that cause sleeping sickness could become resistant to treatment with arsenic compounds. Using her culture techniques, Ann showed that malaria parasites would also develop resistance after prolonged exposure to drugs, and were still resistant after passage through the mosquitoes that transmitted them. This gave a clear warning of trouble to come: resistance to treatment in the field was reported from Malaya in 1950. Ann's experiments, in the days before parasites could be preserved by freezing, demanded meticulous care and late hours, and they ruled her life. She preferred to work alone or with one or two trusted colleagues and, like her master, Dobell, poured scorn on researchers who sat at desks and never got their hands dirty. She was elected FRS in 1959.

Ann saw the need for parasitologists to co-operate more closely, and was the moving spirit in the formation of the parasitology group of the Institute of Biology: it began with a grant of £5 and the promise of secretarial assistance; Ann helped with the finances by taking a collection in a pudding basin after the meetings. The group was so successful that in 1960 it became the British Society for Parasitology, and developed into one of the leading international scientific societies.

Ann Bishop was, at heart, a private person. Although she worked on tropical disease, she did not travel very much, but until bound by arthritis, was a tireless walker. She did a great deal for Girton, where she lived as a research fellow until she retired in 1967, when she became a life fellow. She wrote no more scientific papers, but took a keen interest in the British Society for Parasitology and the activities of her friends and former students. She died after a brief attack of pneumonia on 7 May 1990, and a memorial service was held for her on 1 June in the chapel at Girton, where a memorial plaque was erected.

L. G. GOODWIN

Sources autobiographical notes, RS · L. G. Goodwin and K. Vickerman, *Memoirs FRS*, 38 (1992), 29–39 · *The Times* (22 May 1990) · *The Guardian* (17 May 1990) · *The Telegraph* (22 May 1990) · *CGPLA Eng. & Wales* (1990) · b. cert. · Girton Cam.
Likenesses photograph, 1962, repro. in Goodwin and Vickermann, *Memoirs FRS* · W. Bird, photograph, RS [*see illus.*]
Wealth at death £169,938: probate, 4 Sept 1990, *CGPLA Eng. & Wales*

Bishop [*née* Riviere], **Anna** (1810–1884), singer, was the daughter of Daniel Valentine Riviere (1780–1854), a drawing master of Huguenot descent, and his wife, Henrietta Thunder. William *Riviere, Robert *Riviere and Henry Parsons *Riviere. were her brothers. She was born in London on 9 January 1810, and as a child she studied the piano with Ignaz Moscheles. In 1824 she entered the Royal Academy of Music, where she soon distinguished herself by her singing. She made her professional début at the Ancient Concerts on 20 April 1831, and on 9 July she married the composer Henry Rowley *Bishop (1786–1855), who had formerly been her singing teacher. Her reputation quickly grew, and she took a prominent part in the concerts at Vauxhall, where her husband was music director, at the Lenten oratorios, and at provincial music festivals. Her repertory consisted of sacred music and English songs, but she was persuaded by Nicholas Bochsa, the harpist with whom she and her husband toured, to extend her performances to include Italian opera. In 1839, accompanied by Bochsa, but without her husband, she undertook a provincial tour which included Dublin and Edinburgh and ended in London in July. Four weeks after their return to London she abandoned her husband and three children, and eloped with Bochsa to Hamburg.

For the next four years Madame Bishop (as she was henceforth known) travelled widely on the continent with Bochsa, visiting all the principal towns outside France (where Bochsa, a bigamist and forger, was wanted by the authorities), including St Petersburg and Kazan, where they stayed during 1840–41; during this period she sang at some 260 concerts. Between 1843 and 1846 she sang in about twenty operas at San Carlo, Naples. She was well received by her audiences, although Verdi remained unmoved.

In 1846 Madame Bishop and Bochsa returned to England, where she sang Isoline in Balfe's *The Lady of Artois* to critical acclaim. The following year they went to Dublin and on to New York, where on 12 July 1847 she appeared at a private reception held in her honour. They then undertook a lengthy tour encompassing Mexico, Cuba, and California, and returned to New York in 1850. On 1 November 1852 Madame Bishop produced and sang in the first American performance of Flotow's *Martha* at Niblo's Garden. In 1854 she was in California, and the following year in Sydney, Australia. Bochsa died there on 6 January 1856, and she went on to tour Chile, Argentina, and Brazil before returning to New York in 1858. There she married a

Anna Bishop (1810–1884), by D. J. Pound, pubd 1859 (after John Jabez Edwin Mayall)

diamond merchant, Martin Schultz, Sir Henry Bishop having died in 1855. She spent the 1858–9 season in London, then embarked on another extensive tour of North and Central America. In 1866 she left California across the Pacific, but on 19 February the ship in which she was travelling was wrecked on a coral reef; she lost all her music, jewellery, and clothes in the wreck. After a month in a small boat she and her husband reached land, and, undaunted, she resumed her tour in Manila, proceeded to Hong Kong, Singapore, China, and India, and arrived in England by way of Australia. She returned to New York, and undertook another world tour between 1874 and 1876. She finally settled in New York, where she made her last public appearance on 22 April 1883, and where she died on 18 or 19 March 1884.

A woman of middle size, with large, lustrous eyes, Anna Bishop was one of the most popular English singers of the period. She had great technical mastery over her high soprano voice, but was a somewhat unsympathetic singer. A member of many musical societies around the world, she was extremely popular in the United States, and was one of the most widely travelled performers of the century.

W. B. SQUIRE, *rev.* J. GILLILAND

Sources *New Grove* · P. M. Tayler, 'Isaac Riviere, gunsmith (1781–1851), his life, ancestors and descendants', 1989, Society of Genealogists' Library, London · J. D. Brown, *Biographical dictionary of musicians: with a bibliography of English writings on music* (1886) · J. N. Ireland, *Records of the New York stage, from 1750 to 1860*, 2 vols. (1866–7) · *The Times* (24 March 1884) · *Musical World* (2 May 1839), 11 · *Musical World* (11 July 1839), 179–82 · *Musical World* (8 Aug 1839), 235 · D. Hyde, *New-found voices: women in nineteenth-century English music* (1984) · Brown & Stratton, *Brit. mus.* · W. W. Cazalet, *History of the*

Royal Academy of Music (1854) • S. D'Amico, ed., *Enciclopedia dello spettacolo*, 11 vols. (Rome, 1954–68) • *Baker's biographical dictionary of musicians*, rev. N. Slonimsky, 7th edn (1984) • Boase, *Mod. Eng. biog.* • *IGI*

Likenesses D. J. Pound, stipple and line engraving, pubd 1859 (after J. J. E. Mayall), NPG [*see illus.*] • prints, Harvard TC

Bishop, Bridget (*d.* 1692). *See under* Salem witches and their accusers (*act.* 1692).

Bishop, Caroline Garrison (1846–1929), promoter of kindergarten education, was born on 18 October 1846 at St Leonards, Heavitree, Devon, daughter of the Revd Francis Bishop, minister in the Unitarian church, and his first wife, Lavinia, daughter of Isaac Solly. Her mother died when she was six and her father remarried. Caroline subsequently had a stepbrother and stepsister for whose care she was given responsibility. Caroline's second name reflects her father's admiration for William Lloyd Garrison, the founder of the anti-slavery movement in America. When the family moved to Liverpool Caroline came into contact with runaway slaves who visited their house and the family took part in bazaars to raise funds for the cause.

At the age of eleven Caroline Bishop was sent to a school at Rödelheim, near Frankfurt am Main. The school, housed in an old castle, was recommended to her maternal aunt, Charlotte Manning, by Florence Nightingale. It was happily remembered and she gained a facility in the German language which was to prove invaluable for her career as a Froebelian. After two years, in 1859, she returned to England and attended a school at Knutsford (the village which was the model for Mrs Gaskell's *Cranford*), and was a fellow pupil of one of the author's daughters. She subsequently moved to London in the early 1860s to continue her studies at 32 Tavistock Place under the two Praetorius sisters, who had taken over the kindergarten and school established by Bertha and Johannes Ronge in 1853. This formed her introduction to the Froebelian ideas which were to motivate her lifelong educational work. Her friendship with her step-cousin, Elizabeth Adelaide Manning, developed at this period and Caroline introduced her to the Froebel Society; Adelaide subsequently became its honorary secretary and treasurer.

During the early 1870s Caroline went to Berlin to continue her studies in education, staying with relatives of her mother. On her return to England she spent two years as governess to four of the younger children of George MacDonald in their home at Tudor Lodge, Albert Street, Regent's Park, forming friendships with both her charges and their father. '"Well, Bunny!" was George MacDonald's greeting to her years later, after a lecture in Birmingham' (Last, 222).

In 1873 the school management committee of the London school board recommended the appointment of an instructor in 'Kinder Garten [*sic*] exercises'. Caroline Bishop was duly appointed in October 1873 at a salary of £100 p.a. plus travelling expenses. The success of the classes, which began in January 1874, was so considerable that it was necessary to restrict them to pupil-teachers in the five training centres. The emphasis in the twelve-week course was on the practical aspects of kindergarten education but the initial results were poor; only ninety-three passed the two-hour examination out of 199 candidates. Eleanor Heerwart, lecturer in kindergarten at Stockwell Training College, advised the board to concentrate on training head teachers and their assistants adequately in kindergarten principles before attempting to introduce Froebelian ideas throughout its infants' schools. Classes were subsequently arranged for them at various centres and the requirement that they should attend was strictly enforced. Inspectors were to report on schools where the exercises had not been introduced or were inadequately presented. Other duties of the post included visiting schools to advise on methods and the establishment of model kindergartens in three infants' schools. Caroline Bishop remained as instructor until 1877. By then the board was insisting that every infants' school should have at least one teacher trained in kindergarten methods and the Froebel Gifts and Occupations had been introduced into nearly all London infants' schools.

Caroline Bishop attended the preliminary meeting of the Froebel Society at the Kensington home of Fraulein Beata Doreck in November 1874 and became a member of the committee in 1878. She supported the attempts of the Froebel Society to establish its own central kindergarten and training institution. In 1879 she returned to Germany to continue her studies at the Pestalozzi-Froebel House in Berlin, under the principal Fraulein Annette Schepel. When she returned to London she was appointed to the post of principal of the Tavistock Place Training College. This new venture by the Froebel Society in training teachers in a specifically Froebelian, non-denominational college was not to prove a success. Disagreements with the society led her to resign after two years, and she returned to Berlin where she took charge of the Pestalozzi-Froebel House in Fraulein Schepel's absence.

Caroline Bishop returned to England in 1883 with Herr and Frau Schrader and Fraulein Schepel, and met Miss Emily Last, later her biographer and close colleague. She moved to Edgbaston where she took over a kindergarten, which she ran for twenty-three years, adding a transition class, schoolrooms, and a training college to the original kindergarten. Emily Last joined her staff in 1886 and the training college became residential in 1894 when premises at 18 Harborne Road, Edgbaston, became available. The Edgbaston Froebel College, School and Kindergarten was the culmination of Caroline Bishop's work to promote Froebelian education, and Emily Last's memoir of her contains many examples of her influence on a succession of children and students. Students trained at the Edgbaston college supplied many of the superintendents for the Greet Free Kindergarten in Birmingham, which opened in 1904 with funds provided by Mr and Mrs Barrow Cadbury, and supported by Miss Bishop. One former pupil remembered her as a disciplinarian: 'Her "Put back your chair. Stand," was enough to bring the most hardened offender to a sense of the enormity of his transgression. But I don't think any child was frightened' (Last, 94). A past student described her as 'short of stature, with her large and piercing blue eyes' (ibid., 95), while another recalled her 'vigorous geniality' (ibid., 75). A common theme is her leadership: 'She took us all, younger or older, a jumble lot, many of us much cumbered with cares of self, and showed us the deeper things of life' (ibid., 71–2). Her pamphlet *Life in the Kindergarten* (1895) was reprinted in *Child Life* (16, 1914) and her paper to the Froebel Society, 'Ideals of training for Froebelian teachers', appeared in the third volume of *Child Life* (1901).

When she retired in 1906 Caroline Bishop moved to Knighton, a suburb of Leicester, and became manager of Medway Street infants' school. From 1910 to 1913 she served as a Guardian of the Poor in the Newton ward of Leicester and sat on the children's committee, which dealt with issues such as emigration and adoption of children and visiting arrangements with parents. She supported the proposal that relieving officers should be required to report on the physical condition of children under school age whose parents were in receipt of outdoor relief. When her health began to fail in 1923 Caroline Bishop, who was unmarried, moved to Felden, Boxmoor, in Hertfordshire, to live with Emily Last at Dew Green Cottage, and died there on 12 December 1929.

JANE READ

Sources E. Last, *Memoir of Caroline Garrison Bishop* (1936) · minutes, LMA · 'School management committee minutes', LMA, London School Board MSS · I. M. Lilley, 'The dissemination of Froebelian doctrines and methods in the English system of elementary education, 1854–1914', MA diss., U. Lond., 1963 · Minutes I, Froebel Society, National Froebel Foundation, London · Minutes II, Froebel Society, National Froebel Foundation, London · T. Spalding, *The work of the London School Board* (1900) · E. R. Murray, *A story of infant schools and kindergartens* (1912) · education committee minutes, Borough of Leicester · minute book, 1909–1910, Leicester Poor Law Union · minute book, children's committee, 1910–1948, Leicester Poor Law Union · E. M. Lawrence, ed., *Friedrich Froebel and English education* (1952) · J. Liebschner, *Foundations of progressive education* (1991) · *Birmingham Mail* (24 July 1936) · b. cert. · d. cert.
Likenesses photographs, 1905–23, repro. in Last, *Memoir*
Wealth at death £2085 9s. 11d.: probate, 27 Jan 1930, CGPLA Eng. & Wales

Bishop, Edmund (1846–1917), liturgical scholar and ecclesiastical historian, was born at Bridgetown, in Berry Pomeroy, near Totnes, Devon, on 17 May 1846, the youngest child of Michael Bishop (1802–1851), an innkeeper, and his wife, Susanna Quick (1804–1863). He had his early schooling in the grammar school at Ashburton (where a master taught him the habit of keeping notebooks of his reading), and at the age of thirteen he was sent for two years to a school at Vilvorde, near Brussels, where he strengthened his Latin and carried further his school Greek, as well as becoming bilingual in French and English. He then attended a private school at Mansion House, Exeter, and here, apparently, he taught himself ecclesiastical history by tracking Gibbon's references. He served as amanuensis to Thomas Carlyle, and at the same time was given his own copy of August Potthast's (1824–1898) learned *Bibliotheca historica medii aevi*, just published in 1862: this he devoured.

In 1864 Bishop joined the civil service as a clerk in the education department, where he served until 1885. During those years he was a regular reader at the British Museum, before and after office hours (which were then eleven to five o'clock), and he systematically examined manuscripts on a large scale. In 1877 he discovered in the British Museum the *Collectio Britannica*, an important document in canon law which contained some 300 papal letters of the fifth to the eleventh centuries, most of them previously unknown. Lacking a ready means of publishing the work in England he presented it to the prestigious scholarly series Monumenta Germaniae Historica: 'taken it for all in all, it is the *Monumenta* that has set up for all Western historical scholarship the ideal of the critical text' (Knowles, *Historical Enterprises*, 96). In 1880, writing in the scholarly journal *Neues Archiv*, the brilliant younger scholar Paul Ewald, who had edited the letters of Gregory the Great and who introduced the collection of papal letters edited by Bishop, signalled this remarkable find and praised the 'infinite pains … thorough palaeographical knowledge … brilliant conjectures … and surety of the restitutions of passages unintelligibly corrupt' that marked Bishop's work (*DNB*). Bishop had thus earned a reputation as a medieval historian, and he was accepted into the circle of distinguished Monumenta historians.

In collaboration with the learned Benedictine scholar Dom Suitbert Bäumer of Beuron Abbey (1845–1894), Bishop began to publish original scholarship on the history of the missal and breviary, and especially the mass book and the sixth-century collection the *Gelasianum*, sharply critical of the then highly regarded work of the theologian Pierre Batiffol (1861–1929) and the historian-archaeologist Louis Duchesne (1843–1922). Bishop also collaborated with Dom Francis Gasquet in more polemical work on the history and role of the Catholic church in England before the Reformation, particularly of the black monks, and with the Revd Richard Stanton of the London Oratory (d. 1901), in the collections that were the basis for Stanton's *Menology* (printed in 1887 and 1892). Strongly influenced by Lord Acton and his *Home and Foreign Review*, Bishop was received into the Church of Rome in 1867 and was attracted to the attempted revival of monastic ideals at Downside Priory. His retirement from the civil service in 1885 (on a grossly inadequate retirement pension) was in part predicated upon his being received into the Downside Benedictine community, where he went in 1886; but his intentions were thwarted for reasons, largely, of health. However, he stayed on at Downside until 1889, and nearly every year of his life he spent several months there. For half a dozen years until 1901 Bishop resided and worked with Gasquet in a house near the British Museum, contributing greatly to the accuracy of historical studies on which Gasquet's reputation as a scholar was made, especially with *Henry VIII and the English Monasteries* (1888–9) and *Edward VI and the Book of Common Prayer* (3rd edn, 1891), which is identified as a joint work. In 1908 Gasquet and Bishop together edited and published the Bosworth psalter, now Add. MS 37517 in the British Library.

Bishop wrote many articles that appeared in Catholic

periodicals, and he maintained a voluminous private correspondence, one that often involved answering requests for information. Bishop's replies at times were treatises involving days of labour; thus Dom Cuthbert Butler (1858–1934), the second abbot of Downside, who knew him well, comments in the *Dictionary of National Biography* that 'the amount of his work thus buried in the books of others cannot be estimated'. One must add his collaboration with Gasquet over a period of many years, with Bäumer on the history of the breviary, and with Dom André-Marie Wilmart (1876–1941), the magisterial Benedictine historian of Christian Latin literature. Further, Bishop helped to found and establish the Henry Bradshaw Society, and his influence upon the intellectual and religious climate of Downside Abbey, and upon the liturgical renascence in the Roman Catholic and Anglican churches, was very great. At the heart of the modernist crisis, Bishop, by virtue of his friendship with Baron von Hügel and others involved, and still more because of his original research on liturgical and doctrinal history, had great sympathy for the position of the layman in the contemporary Roman Catholic church. During the climactic years following 1903 (when five of Loisy's books were put on the Index, and the elevation of Pius X to the papacy brought criticism of the modernism movement out into the open), Bishop and other laymen lived through troubled times. A number of the clergy were excommunicated, but for the most part laymen like von Hügel and Bishop were not touched. Bishop felt great compassion for and indeed gratitude to Loisy, and in 1908 he wrote, 'I am an irredeemable modernist from long before the days when modernism was thought of' (Abercrombie, *Edmund Bishop*, 382). Yet the implied sense for Bishop was always inclusive of loyalty to the Catholic church, as it was for von Hügel and Lord Acton.

For the last fifteen years of his life Bishop was much enfeebled in health and lived with his sister in Barnstaple, Devon; he died there, unmarried, of heart disease at Caburn, Park Lane, on 19 February 1917. In 1918 Bishop's papers on the liturgy and religious life of the Western church were collected and published posthumously under the title of *Liturgica historica*, with the aid of Dom Hugh Connolly and Kenneth Sisam.

As early as 1880 Bishop had been prophetically praised by Paul Riant as 'un savant de premier ordre. … Il y a, en lui, l'étoffe d'un Montfaucon ou d'un Mabillon' (Abercrombie, *Edmund Bishop*, 101). His work still stands as the foundation for present-day scholarship on such questions as Alcuin as liturgist, or Anglo-Saxon as well as medieval Latin ecclesiastical manuscripts, and one must always bear in mind Knowles's characterization of him as 'one of the last great English autodidacts' (in his foreword to the biography by Abercrombie, page xi). He was a pioneering scholar in liturgical history, and he was (again in Knowles's words) 'an intuitive genius who was able also to say on many things the last word'; his 'ideas and influence have penetrated and germinated and are still working over the whole field in which they were pioneers' (Knowles, 'Foreword', xi). R. J. SCHOECK

Sources N. J. Abercrombie, *The life and work of Edmund Bishop* (1959) · *DNB* · N. J. Abercrombie, 'Edmund Bishop', *New Catholic encyclopedia* (1967–89) · H. Leclercq, 'Edmond Bishop', *Dictionnaire d'archéologie chrétienne et de liturgie*, ed. F. Cabrol and H. Leclercq, 9/2 (Paris, 1930), cols. 1729–1749, esp. 1735–6 · R. J. Schoeck, review, *Victorian Studies*, 4 (1960–61), 79–81 · G. Dix, *The shape of the liturgy* (1945) · F. L. Cross, ed., *Oxford dictionary of the Christian church*, 3rd edn, ed. E. A. Livingstone (1997) · A. R. Vidler, *A variety of Catholic modernists* (1970), 134–52 · D. Knowles, *Great historical enterprises* (1963) · b. cert. · d. cert. · D. Knowles, foreword, in N. J. Abercrombie, *The life and work of Edmund Bishop* (1959)
Archives Beuron Abbey, Hohenzollern, Germany, corresp. · BL, liturgical collections, Add. MSS 36598–36602 · Downside Abbey, near Bath, archives, corresp. and papers · London Oratory, corresp. · monastery of Solesmes, Sarthe, France, correspondence · Westcountry Studies Library, Exeter, calendar of saints | BL, corresp. with Sir Sydney Cockerell, Add. MS 52706 · Lincs. Arch., letters to J. H. Srawley
Likenesses photograph (in later years), repro. in Abercrombie, *Edmund Bishop*
Wealth at death £202 6s. 1d.: probate, 4 March 1917, *CGPLA Eng. & Wales*

Bishop, George (*d.* 1668), government official and religious writer, was born in Bristol, probably the son of Thomas Bishop, brewer, who became a freeman of the city in 1612. A local and London administrator as well as a New Model Army captain during the civil wars, Bishop is significant because he possessed the organizational and literary skills that proved invaluable to the establishment of the Quaker movement in seventeenth-century Bristol. A man of evident education and a skilled publicist, Bishop wrote more than thirty Quaker tracts. Rich in apocalyptic imagery and Jeremianic in tone, his arguments are grounded in scripture, early church history, politics, and natural reason. His religious ideas are infused with republican sentiments that distrust power wielded by monarchs and clerics alike.

In 1648 Bishop married Elizabeth (*d.* 1658), daughter of William Canne, mayor of Bristol and a powerful local figure. His father-in-law's influence may have kept Bishop out of harm's way during his early years of organizing and publishing on the Quakers' behalf. The Bishops' only surviving child, Elizabeth (1655–1724), married the Quaker writer Richard Vickris in 1672 and raised eight or nine children at Firgrove, the Vickris estate in Chew Magna, Somerset.

During the civil wars Bishop fought with the parliamentary army, and evidently was the politically radical Captain Bishop who in the army debates at Putney in 1647 advocated regicide, attributing the kingdom's difficulties to Charles I, 'that man of blood'. His appointment in 1650 as secretary to the committee for examinations of the republican council of state brought him to London, where he and Thomas Scott headed the intelligence operation and skilfully countered royalist conspiracy. Bishop's reports disclose an intense, perhaps overstated, concern for the fragile Commonwealth, which in his estimation had 'clouds darkening over it'. After Oliver Cromwell became lord protector, Bishop, who had criticized what he regarded as kingly ambitions, gradually turned over his duties to John Thurloe and retired to Bristol, where he unsuccessfully stood for parliament in 1654.

Bishop's association with the Quakers followed the visit of itinerant preachers John Audland and John Camm to Bristol in 1654. His conversion sharpened his criticism of national and local politicians, who in turn questioned his integrity. Bishop soon abandoned the 'exalted' demeanour that troubled his brethren, and his organizational skills made him an invaluable member of the emerging movement. His early tracts, including *The Cry of Blood* (1656) and *The Throne of Truth* (1657), provide insight into the early Quakers' denunciation of the Presbyterian settlement, and their own vociferous performances of protest, which frequently resulted in violence and arrest. In 1656 his Bristol neighbour Captain Edward Pyot and other imprisoned Quakers forwarded Bishop accounts of their experiences, which he published in *The West Answering to the North* (1656), a work formerly credited to George Fox. As a Quaker spokesman Bishop denounced the protectorate's ambiguous religious and social policy, which reflected a growing weariness with radical sectarianism. In 1659, when for a brief time it seemed that reforms would be legislated, Bishop petitioned the recalled Rump Parliament to support 'The Good Old Cause'.

After the Commonwealth fell in the following year, Bishop continued his advocacy for religious liberty, conveying a welcome from the Quakers when the king visited Bristol, and publicizing their religious beliefs and peaceful intentions. Although Charles II had initially promised toleration to nonconformists, Bishop anticipated the legal prescriptions of the Clarendon code and the 1662 Quaker Act. In *To thee Charles Stuart King of England* (1660) he warned the king that, like King David, he must govern the faithful justly lest he repeat the disaster that had toppled 'the other chaff before thee'.

Bishop was subsequently arrested on several occasions for attending illegal religious meetings and refusing to give surety of good behaviour. As the Quakers grew quieter in their response to religious intolerance, he advocated passive resistance to state regulation of religious worship. His *Illumination to Open the Eyes of Papists* (1661), reflective of the contemporary interest in scientific discourse, argues that moral restraints on conscience are ineffective since force 'can reach no further than to that which is of the same Nature with it. A thing cannot be extended beyond its Principle' (p. 10). Bishop's best-known work, *New England Judged* (1661, 1667, 1703), compiled from firsthand reports conveyed to Bristol, is a standard account of the puritans' persecution of Quakers in colonial America. Bishop's widely read account may well be the Quaker text to which Hawthorne alluded in *The Scarlet Letter*.

Bishop died in Bristol in November 1668. A state official commented on the unusually large gathering of 'that sect' who attended the burial of their 'archbishop' near Redcliff parish; the turn-out fittingly symbolized George Bishop's contribution to the establishment of Quakerism in Bristol.   MARYANN S. FEOLA

Sources M. Feola, *George Bishop: seventeenth century soldier turned Quaker* (1996) · *Original letters and papers of state addressed to Oliver Cromwell ... found among the political collections of Mr John Milton*, ed. J. Nickolls (1743) · *CSP dom.* · 'Dictionary of Quaker biography', RS Friends, Lond. [card index] · Bodl. Oxf., MSS Rawl. · Bodl. Oxf., MSS Tanner · supplement of the quarterly meeting, births, 1653–1784, Bristol RO · quarterly meeting of burials, 1651–77, Bristol RO · C. Horle, ed., A. R. Barclay MS, RS Friends, Lond. · RS Friends, Lond., Etting papers · U. Lond., Institute of Historical Research, Longleat-Whitelocke MSS · H. Barbour and A. O. Roberts, eds., *Early Quaker writings, 1650–1700* (1973) · C. Hill, *The experience of defeat: Milton and some contemporaries* (1984) · R. Mortimer, *Early Bristol Quakerism* (1967) · alehouse licence book, Bristol RO · will, PRO, PROB 12/45, 43

Archives BL, Stowe MSS · Bodl. Oxf., MSS Rawl. · Bodl. Oxf., Tanner MSS · RS Friends, Lond., the original record of sufferings · U. Lond., Institute of Historical Research, Longleat-Whitelocke MSS

Wealth at death property in Bristol: will, PRO, PROB 12/45, 43

Bishop, George (1785–1861), astronomer, was born on 21 August 1785 at Leicester. At the age of eighteen he entered a British wine-making business in London, and later became its proprietor. He expanded the business to the extent that the excise returns were said to exhibit half of all home-made wines as being of his manufacture. Bishop was not educated as a scientist; his scientific career may be said to date from his admission to the Astronomical Society in 1830. Ample and reliable means by that time enabled him to pursue the science he enjoyed. He took lessons in algebra from Augustus De Morgan with a view to reading the *Mécanique céleste* of Pierre Laplace, and acquired, when nearly fifty, enough mathematical knowledge to enable him to comprehend the scope of its methods. In 1836 he realized a long-cherished desire by erecting an observatory near his home at South Villa, Regent's Park, London. No expense was spared in its equipment, and the excellence of the equatorial furnished by Dollond (with an aperture of 7 inches) confirmed his resolve to pursue at his observatory serious science, not mere amusement.

Bishop employed the best observers. W. R. Dawes conducted his noted investigations of double stars at South Villa between 1839 and October 1844, when John Russell Hind took over. From the time that Hencke's detection of Astraea (8 December 1845) showed a prospect of success in the search for new planets, the resources of Bishop's observatory were turned in that direction, and with conspicuous results. Between 1847 and 1854 Hind discovered ten small planets, and Marth one, making a total of eleven asteroids dating from South Villa. The ecliptic charts undertaken by Hind to further the search were continued, after his appointment in 1853 as superintendent of the *Nautical Almanac*, by Norman Pogson, Vogel, Marth, and Talmage successively, under his general supervision. They included all stars down to the eleventh magnitude inclusive, and extended over a zone of three degrees on each side of the ecliptic. Seventeen of the twenty-four hours were engraved when the observatory was broken up on the death of its owner.

A testimonial was awarded to Bishop by the Royal Astronomical Society on 14 January 1848 'for the foundation of an observatory leading to various astronomical discoveries', and presented to him, with a warmly commendatory address, by Sir John Herschel on 11 February. Bishop acted as secretary (1833–9) and as treasurer (1840–57) to the society, and was chosen president in two successive years (1857 and 1858), although his poor health prevented him from taking the chair. He was elected a fellow of the Royal Society (9 June 1848), was also a fellow of the Society of Arts, and sat for some years on the council of University College. He published in 1852 *Astronomical Observations taken at the Observatory, South Villa, Regent's Park, during the Years 1839–51*, including a catalogue of double stars observed by Dawes and Hind, with valuable 'historical and descriptive notes' by the latter, and observations of new planets and comets and of the temporary star discovered by Hind in Ophiuchus on 27 April 1848. After a long period of illness he died at South Villa on 14 June 1861. After his death the instruments and dome were removed to the home of his son George Bishop, at Twickenham, where the same system of work was pursued under the continued supervision of Hind.

A. M. CLERKE, rev. JOSEPH GROSS

Sources *Monthly Notices of the Royal Astronomical Society*, 22 (1861–2), 104–6 · C. L. F. André, *L'astronomie pratique et les observatoires en Europe et en Amérique*, 1: *Angleterre* (Paris, 1874) · *Annual Register* (1861) · *DSB* · J. North, *The Fontana history of astronomy and cosmology* (1994) · *CGPLA Eng. & Wales* (1861)
Likenesses H. G. May, marble bust, 1866, RAS · photograph, RS · portrait, Tallotype Gallery, Brighton
Wealth at death £140,000: probate, 16 Oct 1861, *CGPLA Eng. & Wales*

Bishop, Sir Harold (1900–1983), broadcasting engineer, was born on 29 October 1900, at 57 Rosebery Road, Clapham, London, the third son of Henry Thomas Bishop, a builder, and his wife, Mary Ann Ellis. He was educated at Alleyn's School, Dulwich, and on leaving school took an apprenticeship with Argus Engineering Co. Ltd in London, while studying at the City and Guilds College. He was awarded a BSc in engineering by the University of London in 1920. He joined the civil service, working as an assistant engineer at the office of works for two years before joining the Marconi Wireless Telegraph Co. Ltd in 1922. He was put in charge of the transmitter at the 2LO experimental broadcasting station at Marconi House in the Strand, London, and when the BBC was formed Bishop was offered a job in May 1923 as maintenance engineer, in charge of all the transmitting stations and studio centres in the southern half of England. In 1925 he married Madge Adeline, daughter of Frank Harry Vaus; they had one son and two daughters.

At the BBC one of Bishop's responsibilities was outside broadcasting, and he was in charge of the technical arrangements for George V's first broadcast, on 23 April 1924, from the British Empire Exhibition at Wembley, which was heard by over 10 million people. He was also involved in the early days of schools broadcasting, as one of the BBC engineers who took part in the experiments in Kent in 1927, and he worked on ways of improving the poor reception about which many schools complained. He was promoted to assistant chief engineer in 1929. With the worsening international situation in the mid-1930s, the government set up a technical subcommittee of the imperial defence committee in 1935 to draw up a plan for broadcasting in the event of the outbreak of war. Bishop sat on this committee, which considered the problem that broadcasting might help enemy aircraft by guiding them to bombing targets. It was important that broadcasting should be able to continue during air attacks. The system proposed was to have two groups of medium-wave transmitters, with several working on each wavelength at any given time, so that when an aircraft came within range of one transmitter it could be closed down on the orders of Fighter Command, but broadcasting could continue from other transmitters using the same wavelength. The government approved the plan in 1938, and by 1939 the necessary equipment had been installed at all the transmitters. The system worked well, and only once were all the transmitters closed down simultaneously. In order to broadcast news and information to other countries during the war, including enemy countries, the BBC set up three new short-wave broadcasting stations, and Bishop became an expert on this, and was called on after the war to advise the Swedish board of telegraphs on the design and operation of a short-wave station.

Promoted to assistant controller in October 1939, and controller in 1943, in 1952 Bishop became director of technical services, a title that was redesignated director of engineering in 1956. He was knighted in 1955. In these years he played an important part representing the BBC at international conferences, and he travelled extensively, keeping a close eye on developments abroad, especially in America. The most important development in the 1950s was colour television, and Bishop attended meetings of the Comité Consultatif International de Radiocommunications study group on colour television. With competition from ITV, it was especially important for the BBC to keep abreast of developments, and as a result of Bishop's report to the governors of the BBC in 1960 showing that the BBC led the way in research and development of colour television in Britain, it was decided to spend £100,000 on 625-line colour tests, in order to maintain this lead. He was active in the Institution of Electrical Engineers, as vice-president from 1948 to 1953, and president 1953–4, and with Sir Noel Ashbridge he delivered 'Television', the Faraday lecture in 1948. He was president of the Royal Television Society from 1961 to 1962.

A brilliant engineering administrator, Bishop was involved in all the important developments in broadcasting from the beginning, when he was one of a total engineering staff of four. He retired on 10 May 1963, forty years to the day after joining the BBC. He was elected the first president of the new Institution of Electrical and Electronic Technical Engineers in 1965, serving until 1969.

Bishop died on 22 October 1983 at 42 Mill Road, Worthing, Sussex. He was buried on 26 October after a funeral at St Mary's Church, West Chillington.

ANNE PIMLOTT BAKER

Sources A. Briggs, *The history of broadcasting in the United Kingdom*, rev. edn, 5 vols. (1995), vols. 1–3, 5 · E. Pawley, *BBC engineering, 1922–1972* (1972) · H. Bishop, 'The war-time activities of the engineering division of the BBC', *Journal of the Institute of Electrical Engineers*, 94, pt. 3 A (1947), 169–85 · *The Times* (26 Oct 1983) · *WW* · BBC WAC · b. cert. · d. cert. · *CGPLA Eng. & Wales* (1983)

Archives BBC WAC, engineering archives | SOUND BL NSA, current affairs recording

Likenesses photograph, repro. in *The Times* · photograph, repro. in Pawley, *BBC engineering*, pl. 17

Wealth at death £213,596: probate, 29 Dec 1983, *CGPLA Eng. & Wales*

Bishop, Sir Henry Rowley (1786–1855), composer, the son of Samuel Bishop, a watchmaker and later haberdasher, and his wife, Elizabeth, *née* Wigley, was born at 83 Great Portland Street, London, on 18 November 1786. His early education was at Dr Barrow's academy at 8 Soho Square. By the time he was thirteen he was working with his cousin Charles Wigley as a music-seller at 6 Spring Gardens, Charing Cross. His first publications, songs and piano pieces, were issued by this firm in the years 1800 to 1803. When he was about sixteen it was decided that he should go to Newmarket to train as a jockey, but his patron, the racehorse owner Thomas Panton, considered him better suited to the study of music and paid for a course of instruction with the successful opera composer and theoretician Francesco Bianchi. At the same time Bishop continued to compose, and his first stage work, *Angelina*, written in collaboration with Gesualdo Lanza, was performed at the Theatre Royal, Margate, on 30 August 1804. This was followed by music for a number of ballets at the King's Theatre and Drury Lane. Of these, *Tamerlan et Bajazet*, given at the King's Theatre in 1806, was so successful that Bishop obtained a permanent engagement and began to produce the adaptations, compilations, and occasional pieces that were to occupy him constantly for the next thirty years. At this period he also produced a few instrumental compositions, including the first movement of a symphony (1805) and a concertante for flute, oboe, bassoon, violin, and double bass (1807). His great success of these years, however, was his first full-length opera, *The Circassian Bride*, which was very well received at its première at Drury Lane on 23 February 1809; but the following night the theatre burnt down and the score was destroyed. Nevertheless, Bishop quickly rewrote portions of it for publication as 'Overture, Songs, and Duets'. Just over a month after the opening of *The Circassian Bride*, on 30 April 1809, he married one of the cast, Elizabeth Sarah Lyon (1787–1831), with whom he had two sons and a daughter.

After a short period attempting to establish a teaching practice in Bedford the Bishops returned to London for the production at the Lyceum Theatre on 13 March 1810 of Bishop's second three-act opera, *The Maniac, or, The Swiss Banditti*, to a libretto by Samuel J. Arnold, in which Elizabeth Bishop sang a leading role. The opera's successful run of twenty-six performances secured Bishop the offer of a three-year engagement as composer and music director at Covent Garden. During the next three seasons, beginning with *The Knight of Snowdoun*, a three-act musical drama based on Scott's *The Lady of the Lake*, on 5 February 1811, he contributed or arranged varying quantities of music for a host of productions, ranging from burletta to 'operatic drama'. His compositions and arrangements were highly

Sir Henry Rowley Bishop (1786–1855), by Samuel William Reynolds senior, pubd 1822 (after Thomas Foster, 1821)

successful with the public and many of them enjoyed wide currency outside the theatre in publications that were issued immediately after the works had been staged. At the expiration of his initial contract Bishop's engagement was renewed for a further five years, and he continued his routine of providing whatever music was required for the theatre's productions. Among his successes at that time was his contribution to Pocock's *The Miller and his Men*, first performed on 21 October 1813 and revived with additions the following year, and the nine numbers he wrote for the same author's *For England, Ho!*, produced on 15 December 1813. During this five-year period Bishop composed or contributed to the music of some forty productions, including incidental music for *A Midsummer Night's Dream*, the first of a series of Shakespeare adaptations with which he was involved. Individual numbers from these works, such as the glees 'Our Ship in Port' (*For England, Ho!*) and 'The Chough and Crow' (*Guy Mannering*, 11 March 1816), gained lasting popularity.

Despite his heavy commitment to Covent Garden, Bishop became a founder member of the Philharmonic Society in 1813, for which he composed and directed an overture in E at a concert on 26 May 1817. He also found time to compose a string quartet in 1816, though he did not publish it, and for George Thompson of Edinburgh he set Burns's *The Jolly Beggars* in 1817. His engagement at Covent Garden continued for another six years, during which he contributed to some thirty productions, beginning with very free adaptations of *The Barber of Seville* (combining Paisiello's and Rossini's music with his own) on 13

October 1818, and Mozart's *The Marriage of Figaro* on 6 March 1819. Bishop later claimed that it gave him pain to incorporate his own music into these pieces, 'which only the nature of my engagement with the theatre would have obliged me to do—and that their having been inserted into Mozart's or Rossini's operas was contrary to my opinion and wholly against my will' (Northcott, 34). Among the plays for which he provided music were adaptations of Shakespeare's *Macbeth* and *The Comedy of Errors* (1819), *Twelfth Night* (1820), *The Tempest*, *Two Gentlemen of Verona*, and *2 Henry IV* (1821), and *As You Like It* (1824), as well as the usual mixture of other plays, occasional pieces, and operas. A three-act musical drama, *The Law of Java*, produced on 11 May 1822, contained a piece, 'Mynheer van Dunck', that became especially popular as a separate number (a particular favourite with W. E. Gladstone, who used to sing it at parties). But Bishop's most lasting success was the ballad 'Home, Sweet Home', from *Clari, or, The Maid of Milan*, given its première on 8 May 1823; this piece was, according to the title-page of its first edition, 'composed and partly founded on a Sicilian air by Henry R. Bishop'. It was made especially popular by Jenny Lind in the second half of the century and remains one of the best-known of nineteenth-century ballads.

In addition to his work at Covent Garden, Bishop was music director at the King's Theatre in 1816 and 1817, and in 1819 and 1820 he managed the so-called oratorios, a series of mixed concerts given in the opera houses during Lent, when the theatres were closed for stage productions. He made three visits to Paris in 1814, 1816, and 1822. From 20 January to 5 October 1820 he was in Dublin, directing performances at the Rotunda (Theatre Royal), and he was awarded the freedom of the Irish capital on 21 August. By the 1820s Bishop's music had become widely popular, and numbers from his stage works began to provide material for other musicians to compose variations, fantasias, and similar pieces; the indefatigable John Weippert based seven of his numerous sets of quadrilles on items from Bishop's celebrated operas during these years.

Bishop's employment at Covent Garden came to an end in 1824 after a dispute over his salary. In November 1824 his adaptation of Weber's *Der Freischütz* was given at Drury Lane, and he accepted R. W. Elliston's offer of an engagement there in the following year. His first major piece in the new house was a three-act opera, *The Fall of Algiers*, which was given its première on 19 January 1825. This was followed during the rest of the year by a heterogeneous mixture of pieces, similar to those he had produced at Covent Garden: incidental music to two historical dramas, *Masaniello* and *William Tell* (foreshadowing Auber and Rossini respectively by several years), music for an English adaptation of Goethe's *Faust*, and a 'spectacle' entitled *The Coronation of Charles X*. The news that Weber was writing an opera for Covent Garden, where he was to direct it himself in 1826, led the management of Drury Lane to commission Bishop to write a counter-attraction, *Aladdin*, a 'romantic fairy opera', which opened on 29 April, shortly after Weber's *Oberon*. Although Bishop took

unusual care over its composition and attempted musically to meet his rival on his own ground, it did not seriously challenge Weber's opera. Further routine pieces followed before Bishop left his post at Drury Lane a couple of years later, but he continued to provide similar fare for the London stage for the next decade. From 1830 to 1833 he was music director at Vauxhall Gardens, for which he had earlier written his cantata *Waterloo* (1826). During this period he composed a number of short dramatic pieces, in conjunction with the librettist Fitzball, for performance at the gardens, beginning with the 'vaudeville opera' *Under the Oak*, and the 'nautical burletta' *Adelaida, or, The Royal William* in 1830, and concluding with the one-act operettas *The Magic Fan*, *The Bottle of Champagne*, and *The Sedan Chair* in 1832.

On 9 July 1831, shortly after the death of his first wife, Bishop married his former singing pupil Anna Riviere (1810–1884) [*see* Bishop, Anna], with whom he had two daughters and a son. During the next few years they made several concert tours in the provinces, where Anna Bishop acquired a high reputation as a performer of sacred music and English song; they were accompanied on these tours by the harpist Nicholas Bochsa, with whom she absconded to Hamburg in 1839.

A departure from Bishop's usual activities was the composition of his sacred cantata *The Seventh Day*, commissioned and performed by the Philharmonic Society on 3 March 1834. In this work Bishop forsook his usually Italianate style for that of Spohr, whose *The Last Judgement* had just begun to captivate English musicians; but it was not a success. A 'scena', *The Departure from Paradise*, performed at the Philharmonic on 6 June 1836, was equally unsuccessful, notwithstanding its performance by the celebrated soprano Maria Malibran. A third sacred composition, *The Fallen Angel*, was performed as his exercise for the degree of BMus at Oxford on 10 June 1839, but it too failed to secure further performances. The texts of all three of these works were taken from Milton's *Paradise Lost*. During the 1830s Bishop's contributions to the London theatres declined in number, and they ceased altogether at about the time of the breakdown of his marriage. His last work for the theatre, written for Covent Garden, where he had been engaged by Lucia Vestris as music director for the 1840–41 season, was the 'allegorical and national masque' *The Fortunate Isles, or, The Triumphs of Britannia*, given on 12 February 1840 to celebrate Queen Victoria's marriage. Over a period of thirty-six years Bishop had composed, contributed to, or arranged around 130 stage works; selections from some 70 of them were published, and Frederick Corder calculated that these volumes contain 48 overtures, 190 airs and ballads, 53 display songs, 73 duets and trios, 150 glees and ensemble pieces, and 340 melodramas, marches, and ballet airs. In 1840 the composer published his collected glees, trios, quartets, quintets, and choruses in eight large volumes dedicated to the 'Glee and Choral Societies of Great Britain'.

On 1 June 1842, at Prince Albert's suggestion, Bishop was knighted, and a fortnight later he was appointed a chevalier of the Légion d'honneur. In November 1841 he had been elected to the Reid professorship of music at Edinburgh University, but he resigned the chair, after having given only two lectures, in December 1843. In 1842 he became permanent conductor of the Ancient Concerts, which he had conducted periodically since 1840, and for which he provided many arrangements and additional accompaniments (twenty volumes of which survive in the British Library); he retained this post until the series was discontinued in 1848. In that year he succeeded William Crotch as Heather professor of music at Oxford. His last substantial composition was an ode for the installation of the earl of Derby as chancellor of the university, in 1853, and on 22 June 1854 he became a Doctor of Music of the university. In connection with his Oxford appointment he wrote a *Syllabus of a Course of 6 Lectures on ... Vocal Music ... in the 17th and 18th Centuries*, published in 1848, and left a manuscript of 'Lectures on the history of music', written shortly afterwards. At this period he often lectured on music and was much involved in arranging and editing. He edited Handel's chamber duets and cantatas for the London Handel Society and collaborated with Charles Mackay on a series of English national songs.

During his last years Bishop was in poor health, and in March 1855 it was decided that an operation was required to ameliorate his condition. On 24 April he made his will, in which the value of his estate was given 'as not exceeding £200'. He died at his house at 13 Cambridge Street, Hyde Park, on Monday evening, 30 April 1855; a postmortem certified that he died from 'cancer (scirrhus) of bladder and atrophy of kidney'. He was buried on 5 May at Marylebone cemetery, Finchley Road, where a monument to his memory (with incorrect years of birth and death) was later erected by public subscription.

CLIVE BROWN

Sources R. Northcott, *The life of Sir Henry R. Bishop* (1920) · *The Athenaeum* (5 May 1855), 520–21 · F. J. W. C., 'Sir Henry R. Bishop', *MT*, 36 (1895), 662–6 [incl. summary of Bishop's lost MS 'List of the musical compositions of Henry R. Bishop', 1841] · G. A. Macfarren, 'Bishop's glees [pt 1]', *MT*, 11 (1863–5), 257–9 · G. A. Macfarren, 'Bishop's glees [pt 2]', *MT*, 12 (1865–7), 5–7 · 'Henry Rowley Bishop', *Monthly Musical Record*, 10 (1880), 73, 88, 104 · D. Baptie, *Sketches of the English glee composers: historical, biographical and critical (from about 1735–1866)* [1896], 105 · F. Corder, 'The works of Sir Henry Bishop', *Musical Quarterly*, 4 (1918), 78 · T. Fawcett, 'Bishop and Aladdin', *MT*, 113 (1972), 1076–7 · N. Temperley and B. Carr, 'Bishop, Sir Henry R(owley)', *New Grove* · *IGI*

Archives BL, letters to Charles Mackay, Add. MS 29905 · U. Edin. L., letters to H. B. Peacock

Likenesses attrib. G. B. Harlow, oils, *c*.1810, NPG · G. H. Harlow (?), *c*.1810, NPG · portraits, 1810?–1830?, repro. in Northcott, *Life* · attrib. I. Pocock, oils, 1813, NPG · I. Pocock, painting, 1813, NPG · B. Hall, engraving, 1820? · S. W. Reynolds, mezzotint print, 1822 (after T. Foster), BM, NPG · S. W. Reynolds senior, mezzotint, pubd 1822 (after T. Foster, 1821), BM, NPG [*see illus.*] · Wageman, portrait, 1825? · T. Foster, portrait, 1830?

Wealth at death under £200: Northcott, *Life of Sir Henry R. Bishop*, 120

Bishop [*née* Bird], **Isabella Lucy** (1831–1904), traveller, was born on 15 October 1831 at Boroughbridge Hall, Yorkshire, the home of her maternal grandmother. She was the elder daughter of the Revd Edward Bird (*d*. 1858) and his second

Isabella Lucy Bishop [Bird] (1831–1904), by Elliott & Fry [detail]

wife, Dora, the daughter of the Revd Marmaduke Lawson. The Birds were prosperous middle-class evangelical Christians. Having abandoned a career at the Calcutta bar, Isabella's father took holy orders at the age of thirty-eight. After his curacy at Boroughbridge, he held the livings of Tattenhall, Cheshire (1834–42), St Thomas's, Birmingham (1842–8), where he met such sustained opposition to his ministry that his health suffered, and Wyton, Buckinghamshire (1848–58). Mrs Bird and her daughters Isabella and Henrietta then moved to Edinburgh.

From an early age Isabella had been recommended an open-air life as a cure for her spinal complaint, nervous headaches, and insomnia, ills exacerbated, or perhaps caused, by her sensitive temperament. So she rode as much as her back would allow, visited the United States and Canada in 1854 and 1857, and later toured the western highlands of Scotland. But her health grew worse, and, after Mrs Bird's death in 1868 and Henrietta's decision to settle on the island of Mull, she reached a crisis. Although devoted to her sister, Isabella could not face Mull's 'unendurable climate', and in 1872 she sailed for New Zealand, Australia, and the Sandwich Islands.

In Hawaii, where women rode astride, Isabella abandoned the side saddle and henceforth could ride anywhere, on any mount, in perfect comfort. On hearing that the air of the Colorado Rockies was good for invalids, she went in 1873 to Estes Park, a valley high in the mountains. *A Lady's Life in the Rocky Mountains* (1879) records a four-week tour alone on horseback over snow-covered slopes. She writes of a thirty-hour day with a gang of cowboys herding cattle: 'with something of "a High tally ho in the morning" away we went at a hard gallop downhill … Our leader said I was a good cattle man and that he had forgotten a lady was of the party' (*A Lady's Life*, 147). At Estes Park she met Jim Nugent, 'Rocky Mountain Jim', a trapper and hunter, who bore scars from a native arrow and a grizzly bear. He was intelligent and well read, excellent company when sober, dangerous when drunk. The pious middle-aged spinster found him fascinating, and surprisingly he was drawn to her. Their friendship developed rapidly. Something of its intensity may be guessed from her letters to Henrietta, which, severely edited, were published in *A Lady's Life*. Nearly a hundred years later examination of their full text revealed how deeply Isabella cared for her desperado and how fully he responded: but the gulf between them was too wide to be bridged. By the next spring she was back in Scotland, and a few months later Jim Nugent was dead, shot in a quarrel.

Six Months in the Sandwich Islands was launched in 1875 by John Murray, who became Isabella's life-long friend and the publisher of all her books. In 1876 she received a proposal of marriage from John Bishop, an Edinburgh doctor ten years her junior. Unwilling to become an invalid wife, she fled to recoup her health in the Far East. *Unbeaten Tracks in Japan* (1880) records how she rode pack horses into Hokkaido and spent several nights among the Hairy Ainu, afterwards assuring Henrietta that nothing occurred that could 'offend the most fastidious sense of delicacy' (*Unbeaten Tracks*). From Japan she sailed to Hong Kong and Canton (Guangzhou), and thence to Saigon and Singapore. Her lively letters to Henrietta were incorporated into *The Golden Chersonese* (1883).

Henrietta died in 1880. Prostrated by grief, Isabella accepted John Bishop's repeated proposal, and they were married in February 1881, the bride in deepest mourning and on the verge of a nervous breakdown. A skilled doctor and a supremely unselfish man, Bishop nursed her back to health and sanity, and the marriage prospered until his death in 1886. Isabella resolved to travel again, not for her own health or amusement, but to visit medical missions in remote lands. She studied practical medicine at St Mary's Hospital, London, and was baptized in a ceremony of total immersion in which she dedicated herself to the cause of missions (but did not become a Baptist).

In February 1889 Isabella Bishop set out for India, where she visited medical missions in the care of the Church Missionary Society, but made time for an adventurous ride in Ladakh, which she described in *Among the Tibetans* (1894). Her next project was to ride across little known parts of Turkey and Persia, to visit Christian outposts and the ancient communities of the Armenians and Nestorians in Kurdistan. She fell in with Major Herbert Sawyer of the Indian army. Her reputation as a traveller must have preceded her, for the tough officer of thirty-eight agreed to set off with the widow of sixty (said to be in poor health). On 21 January 1890 they left Baghdad for Tehran on the roughest journey in her experience. It took them forty-five days, through driving and drifting snow, sheltering at night in overcrowded and filthy caravanserai. So impressed was Sawyer with his companion's courage and efficiency that he took her with him on his official journey among the Bakhtiari tribespeople of south-west Persia. 'Very hot and the atmosphere thievish', was Major Sawyer's verdict, as they rode for three months over wild country: he only once mentions his companion, 'when Mrs Bishop was so threatened with up-raised sticks and shouts that she had to draw her revolver' (Sawyer, 67). Isabella helped him in his survey work, and, with her medicine chest (presented by Burroughs and Wellcome), tended the local people. Three months completed Sawyer's work, and they parted good friends. She rode north for the Black Sea to end a journey recorded in *Travels in Persia and Kurdistan* (1891).

By 1890 Mrs Bishop's fame was fully established. She addressed the British Association in 1891, 1892, and 1898, and was made fellow of the Scottish Geographical Society in 1891 and of the Royal Geographical Society, to which no lady had previously been admitted, in 1892. She had earlier declined to speak at the RGS, remarking, 'it seems scarcely consistent in a society which does not recognise the work of women to ask women to read a paper'. However, she was annoyed when her comment was made public in support of arguments for the admission of women (letter of 6 June 1893, in Birkett, 223).

In January 1894 Mrs Bishop left England for Korea. She explored the Han River and crossed the Diamond mountains to the east coast of the peninsula. After a visit to Chinese Manchuria she went up the Yangtze (Yangzi), through Szechwan (Sichuan), to the Tibetan border, spending fifteen months and travelling 8000 miles in China alone. She returned to Britain in 1897 and published *Korea and her Neighbours* (1898) and *The Yangtse Valley and Beyond* (1899). The public was disappointed in her last book, but it recounted the most remarkable of her journeys.

Mrs Bishop was planning another visit to China when she fell really ill, and on 7 October 1904 she died at her home, 16 Melville Street, Edinburgh; she was buried in the Dean cemetery. How did she achieve so much? John Bishop diagnosed the appetite of a tiger and the digestion of an ostrich. She was a complex mixture of frailty and fortitude. Marianne North found her, in 1882, a 'very solid and substantial little person, short but broad, very decided and measured in her way of speaking'. Her decision and determination made her the most notable woman traveller of her time, setting standards which any traveller, man or woman, would be proud to attain.

DOROTHY MIDDLETON

Sources D. Middleton, *Victorian lady travellers* (1965) · H. A. Sawyer, *A reconnaissance in the Bakhtiari country, south-west Persia* (1891) · D. Birkett, *Spinsters abroad* (1989) · M. North, *Recollections of a happy life: being the autobiography of Marianne North*, ed. Mrs J. A. Symonds, 2 vols. (1892) · A. M. Stoddart, *The life of Isabella Bird (Mrs Bishop)* (1906) · *The Times* (10 Oct 1904) · *CGPLA Eng. & Wales* (1904)

Archives Royal Scottish Geographical Society, Glasgow, papers | NL Ire., letters to A. S. Green · NL Scot., letters to J. S. Blackie · RGS, corresp. with Royal Geographical Society
Likenesses Elliott & Fry, photograph, RGS [*see illus.*] · two photographs, repro. in Middleton, *Victorian lady travellers* · wood-engraving, NPG; repro. in *ILN* (27 June 1891)
Wealth at death £33,408 14*s.* 3*d.*: probate, 12 Dec 1904, *CGPLA Eng. & Wales*

Bishop, John (1664/5–1737), organist and composer, was seventy-two at the time of his death, and so was probably born in late 1664 or in 1665, quite possibly in Gloucester, where from 1679 to 1685 he was a chorister at the cathedral. Nothing is known of his parents. According to Hawkins, Bishop was a pupil of Daniel Roseingrave, but if so, it would have to have been during the period 1679–81, when Roseingrave was organist of Gloucester and not, as Hawkins says, Salisbury, which latter post he held from 1692 to 1698.

In 1687 Bishop became a lay clerk at King's College, Cambridge, and, within a year, master of the choristers as well. In 1696 he was appointed organist of Winchester College in succession to Jeremiah Clarke and, in June 1697, he also became a lay vicar at the cathedral. Some thirty years later, on 29 June 1729, he succeeded Vaughan Richardson as organist and master of the choristers, holding both posts, together with that at the college, until his death. Though he evidently faced a younger and better player (James Kent) in the competition for this latter appointment, it was, said Hayes, his 'age and amiable disposition', not to mention 'some misfortunes in his family', which 'inclined the Dean and Chapter to decide the contest wholly in his favour' (Hayes, v).

As a composer Bishop is of no great interest, and much of his music (almost entirely sacred) survives only in manuscript. His most substantial work, a service in D, is to be found complete only in Christ Church, Oxford, but there are copies of the morning canticles elsewhere. A *Sett of New Psalm Tunes* first printed in 1710 was clearly intended for parish use; reissued 'with variety of anthems' in 1722 and again in 1730, it also has a 1725 supplement containing another twelve similar pieces. His Latin graces for the use of Winchester College were published by Hayes in 1780. His only instrumental music, a set of airs and sonatas for two flutes printed for the author in December 1700, does not survive. Bishop died in Winchester on 19 December 1737 and was buried on 22 December on the west side of the college cloister, where his memorial (transcribed by Hayes) speaks of an honest and upright life, his gentle manners, and faithful service over forty years.

H. DIACK JOHNSTONE

Sources H. W. Shaw, *The succession of organists of the Chapel Royal and the cathedrals of England and Wales from c.1538* (1991) · J. Hawkins, *A general history of the science and practice of music*, new edn, 3 vols. (1853); repr. in 2 vols. (1963) · P. Hayes, ed., *Harmonia Wiccamica* (1780) · *New Grove* · I. Spink, *Restoration cathedral music, 1660–1714* (1995) · N. Temperley, *The music of the English parish church*, 2 vols. (1979) · B. Matthews, *The organs and organists of Winchester Cathedral* (1967) · W. C. Smith, *A bibliography of the musical works published by John Walsh … 1695–1720* (1948); repr. (1968) · S. Eward, *No fine but a glass of wine: cathedral life at Gloucester in Stuart times* (1985)

Bishop, John (1797–1873), surgeon, the fourth son of Samuel Bishop, of Pimperne, Dorset, was born on 15 September 1797 and educated at the grammar school at Childe Okeford in Dorset. It was originally intended that he should have a career in the legal profession, but this came to nothing and for many years he led the life of a country gentleman. When he was about twenty-five years old he was persuaded by his cousin, John Tucker, a surgeon of Bridport, to enter the medical profession. After a short time working with Tucker at Bridport, he moved to London and studied at St George's Hospital under Sir Everard Home. He also attended the lectures of Sir Charles Bell, George James Guthrie, and George Pearson, and he was a regular attendant at the chemistry courses which were delivered at the Royal Institution. Bishop became a member of the Royal College of Surgeons in 1824 and an honorary fellow in 1843. He was an elected member of the college council (1849–61), and in 1852 he became president of the Medical Society of London.

Bishop soon acquired a reputation as a careful and skilled observer. This secured him the offices of senior surgeon to the Islington Dispensary and surgeon to the Northern and St Pancras dispensaries and to the Drapers' Benevolent Institution. In 1844 he contributed a paper to the *Philosophical Transactions of the Royal Society*, on the physiology of the human voice. In the same year he was elected a fellow of the Royal Society, and he became a corresponding member of the medical societies of Berlin and Madrid. The Royal Academy of Science of Paris awarded him two prizes for his memoirs entitled 'The human and comparative anatomy and physiology of voice'; *Experimental Researches into the Physiology of the Human Voice* appeared in 1836. Bishop was also the author of *On Articulate Sounds* (1851) and *Researches into the Pathology and Treatment of Deformities in the Human Body* (1852). These works were considered remarkable for their careful examinations and for the mathematical demonstrations given of each theory advanced. Bishop contributed the articles 'Larynx', 'Motion', and 'Voice' to Robert Bentley Todd's *Cyclopaedia of Anatomy and Physiology*. He delivered the Hunterian oration at the Royal College of Surgeons in 1861, but was not considered to be an eloquent or fluent speaker.

Bishop was a man of varied attainments; he was knowledgeable about continental as well as English literature, and up until a few months of his death he was deeply interested in the progress of science. In later years his health began to fail: he lost an eye, and broke an arm while trying to apprehend a pick-pocket in London's Regent Street. Bishop, who was married twice, died on 29 September 1873 at Strangeways House, Marnhull, Dorset, within a few miles of his birthplace; he left a widow, Sarah Hilton Bishop, but no children.

ROBERT HUNT, rev. CHRISTIAN KERSLAKE

Sources *PRS*, 21 (1872–3), 5 · *BMJ* (11 Oct 1873), 450 · D. Rockey, *Speech disorder in 19th century Britain* (1980) · *CGPLA Eng. & Wales* (1873) · V. G. Plarr, *Plarr's Lives of the fellows of the Royal College of Surgeons of England*, rev. D'A. Power, 2 vols. (1930) · Z. Cope, *The Royal College of Surgeons of England: a history* (1959)
Wealth at death under £6000: probate, 14 Nov 1873, *CGPLA Eng. & Wales*

Bishop, Dame (**Margaret**) **Joyce** (1896–1993), headmistress, was born on 28 July 1896 at The Glen, Oxford Road, Moseley, King's Norton, Worcestershire, the second of three children of Charles Benjamin Bishop, lacquer manufacturer and owner of a silver plating business, and his wife, Amy Stewart, *née* Tindall. From a solid middle-class churchgoing background, the family believed in the importance of educating girls and the development of a sense of personal commitment to society. Her early education was interrupted by serious illness, and she was taught at home until she was nine. From an early age her interest in literature was encouraged and after Edgbaston high school she went in 1915 to read English at Lady Margaret Hall, Oxford. Oxford in wartime was a difficult place, although Bishop contributed regularly to college dramatic productions along with her academic studies, enjoying her time there. Because she was taken ill during her final examinations her degree results were not distinguished (she was awarded a third-class degree in 1918). However, personal recommendations from her tutors enabled her to obtain her first teaching post at Hertfordshire and Essex high school. Her next appointment, in 1924, took her as headmistress to Holly Lodge high school, Smethwick (where she succeeded her elder sister, Phyllis Mabel, born in 1891) in one of the poorest and most heavily industrial areas near Birmingham, where she remained for eleven years. When she first arrived the school was only two years old and still incomplete. Here she developed her ideas on the importance of an academic education available regardless of parental income as the way to develop the full potential of girls. This conviction remained central to her work throughout her career.

In 1935 Bishop became headmistress of the Godolphin and Latymer School, Hammersmith, west London, remaining there for twenty-eight years. This was a well established, endowed girls' school with about 40 per cent of scholarship places. Here she found that, freed from having to battle for what she wanted as she had done at Holly Lodge, she was able to turn her formidable energies into other channels and develop strategic plans for the school. In addition she became an active member of the Association of Headmistresses. The threat of war led her to decide on evacuation for the whole school in September 1939, eventually to Newbury, Berkshire. However, after two years it was finally decided that school life would be more satisfactory in London, and by July 1943 all the students and staff had returned. The next challenge facing Bishop and the governors, that of the Butler Education Act of 1944, was met with the decision that Godolphin should take aided status. As a result fees were abolished for all, while the school remained selective and academic, continuing, in Bishop's words, 'to foster scholarship and sound learning'. Throughout her career as headmistress she inspired deep loyalties among both staff and pupils, and many remained immensely grateful for the opportunities she opened to them. At the same time she continued to expand her interests outside the school and became

Dame (Margaret) Joyce Bishop (1896–1993), by Walter Bird, 1963

involved in a number of working parties and committees at a national level. One of the most far reaching concerned the recruitment of women into teaching. She joined a government working party which reported in 1949 to the Ministry of Education with wide ranging recommendations designed to attract more women entrants. A pioneer herself in her recruitment of both married and part-time women teachers at Godolphin, she was involved in follow-up research to reverse the shortages created by the shrinking number of unmarried graduate teachers, particularly in girls' grammar schools. This report was presented to the Association of Headmistresses and the Association of Assistant Mistresses in 1961. Both these reports contributed to the growing debate changing the climate of opinion about professional women working outside the home. Bishop's words on the subject of the 'vanishing spinster' in 1962 were widely reported.

Bishop's contribution to the Association of Headmistresses was recognized when she became chairman in 1951–2. Her keynote speeches to the annual conferences in these years reflected her educational principles, which were essentially practical rather than original. School 'must be a place where [the pupil] develops her intellectual gifts for the fulfilment of herself, and for the service of God and one where she learns to know that in that service lies perfect freedom' (report of 1951 Headmistresses' Conference, 11: U. Warwick Mod. RC, MSS 18, Association of Headmistress, TBN 27). From this period too, the invitations to sit on committees and governing bodies increased. Her formidable energy enabled her to combine the direction of her school with her outside interests. Among other bodies she served on the Secondary Schools Examination Council and the National Advisory Council for the Training and Supply of Teachers. On her retirement from Godolphin in 1963 she was made a DBE in recognition of her services to education (having already been made CBE in 1953).

Bishop continued to develop her interests in education long into retirement. She was supervising tutor of postgraduate teaching students at King's College, London, for ten years. A passionate opponent of comprehensive education and combative supporter of grammar schools, she made a major contribution to the effort to raise substantial bursary funds when Godolphin became independent in 1977 in reaction to local reorganization. Between 1958 and 1984 she served as a governor of the Royal Ballet School, taking particular interest in the academic education of the young dancers. For many years she was closely associated with the Froebel College, Roehampton, which trained teachers for primary schools, and its associated school, Ibstock Place, becoming chairman of the governors of the Froebel College in 1964. Minutes of governors' meetings indicate an incisive mind at work, able to present clear summaries for consideration: her style was direct and unpompous. Her main interests were in management and the welfare of the student body. In the 1970s, with the reduction in teacher training numbers, the college faced major reorganization and amalgamation, which Bishop strongly opposed. She favoured continuing independence for the college. However, the weight of government policy led to the plans being accepted in 1977. Bishop made her final appearance at the governing body in 1979.

Bishop's energy and good health continued well into her retirement. Her interest in people and her capacity for making friends and networking were facilitated by her companion and housekeeper, Elizabeth Ellett, whose loyalty over fifty years liberated Bishop from domestic chores, enabling her to develop a multi-faceted career while at the same time enjoying a well organized home life. Her dinner parties became legendary: carefully constructed occasions for introducing like minds or sparking controversy. She died of bronchopneumonia at Queen Mary's University Hospital, Roehampton, on 7 June 1993, and was buried at Putney Vale cemetery. A memorial service was held in St Margaret's Church, Westminster, on 4 October 1993.   CAROLINE M. K. BOWDEN

Sources S. Rose, *Portrait of a headmistress: Dame Joyce Bishop* (1984) · *WWW*, 1991–5 · *The Times* (15 June 1993) · *The Independent* (16 June 1993) · b. cert. · d. cert. · Godolphin and Latymer School, London, archives · University of Surrey, Roehampton, London, Froebel College, archives · U. Warwick Mod. RC, Association of Headmistresses papers · private information (2004) [E. Ellett and others] · C. Avent and H. Pipe, eds., *Lady Margaret Hall register, 1879–1990* (1990) · CGPLA Eng. & Wales (1993)

Archives Godolphin and Latymer School, London · University of Surrey, Roehampton, London, Froebel Institute | U. Warwick Mod. RC, Association of Headmistresses MSS · University of Surrey, Roehampton, London

Likenesses W. Bird, photograph, 1963, NPG [*see illus.*] · W. Narroway, portrait, c.1976, Froebel Institute, Priory Lane, London, Templeton House · photograph, repro. in *The Times* · photographs, priv. coll.

Wealth at death £426,463: probate, 15 Sept 1993, CGPLA Eng. & Wales

Bishop, Matilda Ellen (1842–1913), college head, was born at Tichborne, Hampshire, on 12 April 1842, elder daughter of Alfred Caesar Bishop (1811–1885), a scholarly clergyman who throughout most of Matilda's early life held the living of Martyr Worthy, near Winchester, and his wife, Lucy Wedderburne. Her father was considered a conscientious incumbent, though he augmented his income by preparing young men for Oxford and the army, and still found time to ride to hounds. She taught in his Sunday school from the age of eleven. Matilda was educated at a seminary for young ladies in Brighton, where she was obliged to learn long passages of the Bible by heart, and was given an excellent grounding in French by a 'gifted although very ill-tempered French lady'. At sixteen she was sent to Queen's College, Harley Street, where she fell deeply under the influence of the Revd F. D. Maurice, whose lectures in literature and history had a strong religious bias. Matilda described him as 'the greatest man I have ever known, the strongest influence of my girlhood, intellectual and spiritual, with a mysterious power, too sacred for analysis' (Luxton, 12). This near-idolatry characterized her attitude to the clergy of the Church of England. She experienced it again with almost equal intensity during her principalship of Royal Holloway College, when she idolized Archbishop Benson, one of the governors, whom she described as a man whose wishes were her commands.

A broken engagement to a young man whose name she suppressed and a period spent keeping house for her father between his widowhood and his second marriage preceded Miss Bishop's teaching career. In 1875 she became an assistant mistress at Oxford High School for Girls, of which the headmistress was Ada Benson, the archbishop's sister. From 1877 to 1879 she was headmistress of Chelsea high school, and headmistress of Oxford high school from 1879 to 1887. Her appointment as principal of the newly founded Royal Holloway College in 1887 gave her the opportunity to set high academic standards and create social traditions in a women's college which was unique in the opulence of its buildings and the generosity of its endowment.

Miss Bishop's connection with Oxford encouraged her to arrange that students of the Royal Holloway College should take the Oxford degree examinations, though the successful candidates were given only notification of the class they would have attained, since Oxford did not admit women to its degrees until 1920. Initially she had taken the view that lack of a degree was 'no sort of disadvantage' to women seeking teaching posts, and she remained unconvinced 'whether in the long run women's education can be developed best by following the exact lines of men's education' (Bishop to Bertha Johnson, 15 Jan 1895, Johnson MSS). So her policy on degrees was undertaken in a context of some internal uncertainty. However, students of the college were also entered for London University degree examinations, and successful candidates were awarded degrees, to which London University had admitted women in 1878. At this period London University was an examining and degree-giving body, but not a teaching university. When it prepared to metamorphose itself into a teaching university Miss Bishop expressed the opinion that the Royal Holloway College would do well to seek admission as a constituent school of London University, a forward-looking policy which was followed in the next principalship.

Miss Bishop created at the college a social tradition in which formality and good manners were happily blended with a lack of class-consciousness unusual at this period. The hard work which high academic standards necessitated, however, led Miss Bishop to impose a level of discipline which one of her staff considered more appropriate to a school than to a college: 'Noise was an agony to her, and order and neatness a passion, so there was naturally more sense of restraint than youth could quite bear. It was not easy for her to cease to be the schoolmistress and to realize that if the students were to be transformed from schoolgirls into women it was to be done by treating their immaturity as maturity' (Faithfull, 92–3).

Miss Bishop was a typical member of the first generation of women's college principals; they were cultivated women rather than intellectuals. Though Miss Bishop was dedicated to the ideal of higher education for women, even greater was her dedication to the Church of England. In 1897 she resigned the principalship of the Royal Holloway College when the governors required her to introduce nonconformist services in the college chapel on alternate Sundays. In accordance with her conviction that Anglicanism was the 'true religion', she had arranged that nonconformist students should attend churches or chapels of their own denominations in the vicinity, despite the founder's stipulation that the college should be non-denominational. Her departure was regretted by students and alumnae alike.

In 1899 Miss Bishop was appointed principal of the newly founded St Gabriel's Church of England Training College for Women Teachers in Camberwell, London, a post eminently suited to her abilities and convictions. She died in office at the college on 1 July 1913, having suffered for some time from a weak heart and ignored warnings of the dangers of overwork.

A portrait of Miss Bishop by James Shannon, housed in the dining hall of the Royal Holloway College, shows a slender, dignified woman with black hair and fine dark eyes. Whereas photographs of Miss Bishop show a tense, gaunt face, expressive of the troubles of an overactive conscience, Shannon's flattering image gives the subject tranquillity and grace.   CAROLINE BINGHAM

Sources A. Luxton, *Matilda Ellen Bishop, a memoir* (1914) · M. J. Powell, ed., *The Royal Holloway College, 1887–1937* (privately printed, Egham, [1937]) · L. Faithfull, *In the house of my pilgrimage* (1924) · M. Pick, 'Social life at Royal Holloway College, 1889–1939', typescript, Royal Holloway College, Egham, Surrey · C. Bingham, *The*

history of Royal Holloway College, 1886–1986 (1987) · b. cert. · d. cert. · St Anne's College, Oxford, Johnson MSS
Archives Royal Holloway College, Egham, Surrey, minutes of governors' meetings · Royal Holloway College, Egham, Surrey, Royal Holloway College Association, college letters
Likenesses J. J. Shannon, oils, 1897, Royal Holloway College, Egham, Surrey · photographs, Royal Holloway College, Egham, Surrey
Wealth at death £6536 3s. 0d.: probate, 29 July 1913, CGPLA Eng. & Wales

Bishop, Richard Evelyn Donohue [Dick] (1925–1989), mechanical engineer and naval architect, was born on 1 January 1925 in Lewisham, London, the elder son (there were no daughters) of Norman Richard Bishop, chief accountant and director of Tar Residuals Ltd, and his wife, Dorothy Mary Wood, teacher of French. His father, through self-education, obtained the London external degrees of bachelor of commerce and PhD (1944) and in 1949 was ordained a priest in the Church of England. Dick Bishop's early years were spent in Catford, London, in a family whose main interests were music and the church. He attended Roan School for Boys, Greenwich, and left in 1943 with a burning desire to join the Royal Navy but no great ambition to go to university. He volunteered as an ordinary seaman in the Royal Naval Volunteer Reserve and impressed the authorities by the results of examinations taken while he was training. Subsequently a series of psychological tests indicated that he would make an engineer in the Fleet Air Arm. In mid-1944 he emerged from training with a first-class certificate of competency, as an air engineering officer, and was posted to a squadron.

Having become an engineer by accident and acquired a great interest in technology, after leaving the navy in 1946 Bishop entered University College, London, where he graduated with a first-class honours BSc (Eng.) and a diploma with distinction in 1949. Before leaving in 1949 for Stanford University, California, as a Commonwealth Fund fellow to work under the supervision of J. N. Goodier, he married Jean (Liz), elder daughter of Hector Cross Buchanan Paterson, bank clerk; they had a daughter and a son. Bishop obtained his PhD in 1951 with a thesis entitled 'The analysis of elastic wave propagation'.

Bishop returned to England and was employed by the Ministry of Supply as a senior scientific officer (1951–2). He then moved to the University of Cambridge on his appointment as an engineering demonstrator in 1952. He became a fellow of Pembroke College (1954) and a university lecturer (1955). His lifelong fascination for engineering and vibration, rather than his earlier commitment to applied mechanics and wave motions, was fostered in the Cambridge Engineering Laboratory. He returned to his old department at University College, London, and was its departmental head (1957–77), a Kennedy professor of mechanical engineering (1957–81), and a research professor (1977–81). He laid the foundations of modern rotor dynamics theory; devised the first successful method of balancing flexible shafts; and made significant advances in knowledge about the instability of high-speed rolling-stock, aircraft resonance testing, torsional oscillating of rotating machinery caused by gear eccentricity, structural self-excitation by shedding of entrained vortices, measurement of forces transmitted by the human knee, and various aspects of ships' structural behaviour in waves based on hydroelasticity theory. In technical matters he was a man of vision, having the ability to simplify a complex dynamics problem to a discussion of fundamental principles. An excellent communicator, he wrote seven books and well over 200 papers. In 1981, surprisingly, he moved from research into administration, as vice-chancellor and principal of Brunel University in Middlesex. Through his stress on academic excellence and scholarship, he successfully reorganized the apparatus of Brunel and changed its culture, laying the foundation of a flourishing university.

Bishop's fine clear mind brought him significant achievements and honours in the scientific world. He was a fellow of the Royal Society (1980) and appointed a vice-president and member of its council (1986–8). He was a fellow of the Royal Academy of Engineering (1977) and was appointed CBE in 1979. He received the Thomas Hawksley (Institution of Mechanical Engineers, 1965), Krizik (Czechoslovak Academy of Science, 1969), Rayleigh (British Acoustical Society, 1972), and the William Froude (Royal Institution of Naval Architects, 1988) gold medals; the Skoda silver (1967) and Anniversary (1980) medals; the Archibald Head (University College, London, 1948) and Royal Institution of Naval Architects (1980) bronze medals; and the George Stephenson (1959) and Clayton (1972) prizes of the Institution of Mechanical Engineers.

Bishop was a severe critic and yet the staunchest of supporters. He thrived on technical discussion and debate—not argument—though at times this fine distinction depended on the sensitivity of the listener/combatant. By his probing he stimulated others, but he caused resentment in many, especially when he questioned the professionalism of engineers and engineering practices. He was an independent, innovative research engineer who spoke his mind on technical matters. An earnest man who from his late twenties had a head of distinguishing white hair, he loved sailing and was always active. He died in Portsmouth on 12 September 1989 from the effects of a hepatic abscess and septicaemia. After cremation at Portchester crematorium, his ashes were interred in the memorial garden of Portsmouth Cathedral.

W. Geraint Price, rev.

Sources W. G. Price, *Memoirs FRS*, 40 (1994), 1–29 · *CGPLA Eng. & Wales* (1989) · personal knowledge (1996)
Likenesses portrait, repro. in Price
Wealth at death £290,320: administration with will, 6 Nov 1989, *CGPLA Eng. & Wales*

Bishop, Samuel (1731–1795), headmaster and poet, was born in St John Street, London, on 21 September 1731, the eldest son of George Bishop, who came from Hollway, near Cattistock, in Dorset, and Mary, daughter of Samuel Palmer of Southover, near Lewes, in Sussex. He was entered at Merchant Taylors' School, London, on 6 June 1743, where he was a keen and able student. In June 1750 he was elected to St John's College, Oxford, and matriculated in July. Educated under Dr Thomas Fry he was elected a fellow of his college in June 1753, and in the following April he graduated BA. Not long afterwards he was ordained curate of Headley in Surrey, and he lived either in that village or at Oxford until 1758, when he took his MA degree.

On 26 July 1758 Bishop was appointed third undermaster of his old school. He served as curate of St Mary Abchurch and then as lecturer of St Christopher-le-Stocks, both in London; he was also chaplain to John Warren, bishop of Bangor. In 1763, at St Augustine with St Faith, Watling Street, he married one of his mother's relatives, Mary, daughter of Joseph Palmer of Old Malling, near Lewes, and they settled in Scots Yard, Bush Lane, London. He rose to the second under-mastership on 11 February 1772, the first under-mastership on 12 August 1778, and was elected headmaster on 22 January 1783. He and his wife and daughter Mary (*bap.* 1763) moved to Suffolk Lane, next to the school, and he also took a house in Golders Green for the sake of his deteriorating health. He was presented to the rectory of Ditton in Kent, and on 1 March 1789 was rewarded for his long service to the school with the living of St Martin Outwich in London.

Opinions varied on Bishop's success as headmaster. Eulogized by one pupil, Harry Bristow Wilson, in his history of the school, Bishop was portrayed as a mild, affectionate, and inspiring schoolmaster. His memorialist, Thomas Clare, wrote of his desire to avoid any unnecessary severity in maintaining discipline, but another pupil, Charles Matthews, described Bishop and his under-master, John Rose, as 'cruel tyrants' (Farr, 58–9). Matthews related how the boys threatened rebellion following a particularly vicious bout of flogging by Rose, and thereby forced Bishop to end all flogging in the school. Bishop's pupils were certainly not afraid of ridiculing him, for Matthews recorded how a favourite sport was to shoot paper darts into his oversize powdered wig so that it resembled 'a fretful porcupine' (Draper, 112). Bishop, however, was a diligent headmaster and devoted his holidays to school work.

Bishop was a prolific and able poet but published only some of his compositions during his lifetime; they included the anonymous 'Ode to the Earl of Lincoln on the Duke of Newcastle's Retirement' (1762), said to have been prompted by the connection of Bishop's future wife's family with the duke, and a collection of Latin and English poems in the *Feriae poeticae* (1766). The majority of his poems were published after his death as *Poetical Works of the Rev. Samuel Bishop, A.M.* (2 vols., 1796), with a life of the author by Thomas Clare. A second edition was issued in 1800 and a third in 1802. His subjects are primarily domestic and familiar, and testify to a very contented marriage and home life. Southey said of Bishop that 'no other poet crowds so many syllables into a verse … His domestic poems breathe a Dutch spirit—by which I mean a very amiable and happy feeling of domestic duties and enjoyments' (*Southey's Common-place Book*, 4.308–9). He also wrote essays and poems for 'The Ladies Club' in the *Public*

Ledger and published a sermon on the anniversary of Henry Raine's charity.

Bishop died on 17 November 1795, worn out by physical suffering caused by gout and water on the chest; he was buried at St Martin Outwich. He was survived by his wife, who subsequently married Bishop's memorialist, the Revd Thomas Clare, later vicar of St Bride's, Fleet Street. A volume of Bishop's sermons on practical subjects appeared in 1798.   W. P. COURTNEY, *rev.* S. J. SKEDD

Sources T. Clare, 'Memoirs of the life of the author', in *The poetical works of the Rev. Samuel Bishop*, 2 vols. (1796) · H. B. Wilson, *The history of Merchant-Taylors' School*, 2 vols. (1814) · C. J. Robinson, ed., *A register of the scholars admitted into Merchant Taylors' School, from AD 1562 to 1874*, 2 vols. (1882–3) · F. W. M. Draper, *Four centuries of Merchant Taylors' School, 1561–1961* (1962) · Foster, *Alum. Oxon.* · *GM*, 1st ser., 65 (1795), 972, 994, 1052 · W. C. Farr, ed., *Merchant Taylors' School: its origins, history and present surroundings* (1929) · will, PRO, PROB 11/1270, fols. 30r–31r · *IGI* · *Southey's common-place book*, ed. J. W. Warter, 4 vols. (1849–51)
Likenesses H. D. Thielcke, stipple, pubd 1814 (after Clarkson), BM, NPG · C. Townley, stipple (after G. Dance), BM, NPG; repro. in *The poetical works of the Rev. Samuel Bishop*
Wealth at death bequeathed £500–£800 in annuities, etc.; also property: will, PRO, PROB 11/1270, fols. 30r–31r

Bishop, William (*c.*1554–1624), Roman Catholic bishop, was born at Brailes, Warwickshire, the eldest son of John Bishop (*c.*1509–1601) and Helen Onsley (*d.* 1588). His family was armigerous and came originally from Yorkshire; they remained on the same estate at Brailes, faithful to Catholicism, until 1830. He was sent to Oxford at the age of sixteen, probably to Gloucester Hall or Lincoln College. He went down without taking a degree and is recorded next at the English seminary then at Rheims, which he left on 16 February 1579 for Rome, where he continued his studies at the English College. He was ordained in Rome in September 1581 and was then sent back to Rheims, and thence on the mission to England.

When Bishop landed at Rye with two other priests he was immediately captured. He was able to tell the officials at the port that he was a merchant, but when asked next what he traded in he had no answer ready and was arrested. As Godfrey Anstruther comments: 'he seems to have had something of the simplicity of the dove' (Anstruther, 1.38). He was committed to the Marshalsea and was condemned to death in 1583 on the false charge of plotting the death of the queen. He certainly came very close to death at this point, but the government wished to avoid too many martyrdoms, largely to improve its relations with France, and so Bishop and a number of other priests were, in 1585, loaded into a boat and dropped off on the coast of France. He went to Paris and enrolled as a student at the Sorbonne, where he eventually took the degree of doctor of divinity. Throughout his subsequent career his ideas were strongly influenced by mildly Gallican or 'Sorbonnist' ideas, especially on matters of papal power, the independence of national churches, and the rights of the secular clergy. When the persecution in England abated somewhat he returned to resume his work there as a missionary priest, leaving Rheims on 15 May 1591.

Bishop gradually grew to prominence on the English

William Bishop (*c.*1554–1624), by unknown artist

mission among the secular clergy, who were at this time developing a hostility towards what they saw as the excessive influence of the Society of Jesus on their arrangements in England and on the wider politics of the mission, especially in terms of the relations of Catholics with the queen. In 1598 the pope was persuaded by the Jesuits to appoint George Blackwell, a secular priest, as archpriest or head of the mission in England. This immediately inflamed a section of the secular clergy and they deputed Bishop and Robert Charnock to go to Rome to appeal against this appointment. So began the archpriest or appellant controversy, which rumbled on for the rest of Elizabeth's reign. Bishop and Charnock arrived in Rome on 11 December 1598 and were almost immediately arrested at the behest of Robert Parsons, the leading English Jesuit, who saw them as factious and unrepresentative of Catholic opinion. They were put on trial, and Bishop was now banished again, this time by the pope from Rome, with the additional exclusion that he should not return to England. Bishop was as much affected by the pope's ban as he had been by the queen's, and after the papal position on the appellants had softened he was back in England, by 31 January 1603, when he headed a list of thirteen Catholic priests who made a profession of loyalty to the queen. This was in itself an action which was part of the archpriest controversy, in that it was intended to highlight the disloyalty of the Jesuits. Despite this declaration of obedience he was arrested in England again in 1603, shortly after the accession of James I, but was soon released.

Bishop seems to have worked largely as a missionary

priest in his own area, the midlands. He was reported as being in Herefordshire in 1605, when he was staying at Trevil Park with a Francis Bishop, who was perhaps a kinsman, and in Oxfordshire in 1610. About this time a government spy described him as 'tall of stature, flaxen hair, broad-faced, somewhat pale, somewhat gross, an enemy of the Jesuits' (Anstruther, 1.38). It was during the reign of James I that Bishop wrote his five contributions to the polemical literature of the time, mainly in answer to the anti-Catholic writings of the protestants William Perkins and George Abbot. As a controversialist Bishop was thorough and disputatious, but hardly original or lively. Bishop was imprisoned for a third time in England in 1611, but refused to take the oath of allegiance, although his reason for doing so was not because he supported papal power in temporals (which in taking the oath he would have denied), but because he did not wish to alienate the pope from the secular clergy and thus strengthen the Jesuits. On his release from prison Bishop went again to Paris, where he became a member of Arras College, which was a new postgraduate society for the English secular clergy. Here his Sorbonnist tendencies were reinforced, and he continued to study and write.

The death of the last surviving Marian bishop, Thomas Goldwell, in 1585, who in any case had not exercised his office since the accession of Elizabeth I, had left the English Catholics without a bishop. The appointment of Blackwell as archpriest, against which Bishop had struggled so hard, had been an attempt to overcome the problem. But the obvious solution was to appoint a new English bishop. When the third archpriest died in 1621 this point was successfully raised in Rome and the pope, who now favoured the English seculars, chose William Bishop as the first post-Reformation bishop to the English. Few can have had such perfect revenge on their professional rivals as Bishop, for his appointment represented the final triumph of the anti-Jesuit appellants. Bishop took as his see Chalcedon, a Greek city *in partibus infidelium*. So started the tradition, later enshrined in English law, by which Catholic bishops avoided English sees in their titles. According to Peter Heylin the story was that the Jesuits persuaded James I to object to the pope's giving the new bishop an English title, and so it was through their jealous machinations that the curious foreign designation was adopted (Heylin, 2.96-7). In truth, however, it would have been needlessly provocative to have used an English diocese, and perhaps also geographically confusing, since Bishop's faculties extended to the whole country. The appointment, however, did not have the effect of reuniting the English Catholics, although this became clearer during the period of Bishop's successor.

Bishop was consecrated in Paris on 4 June 1623 and set out for England on 29 July, arriving at midnight on the coast of Kent after a three-day voyage. At nearly seventy years old he then walked 13 miles until he reached a Catholic safe house. His term in office was brief. He had time to appoint a chapter and to travel around administering the sacrament of episcopal confirmation, which the country

had been deprived of for so long. He also entered into conflict with the Scots, over whom his jurisdiction was at first claimed to extend. But before he could begin a projected visitation of his flock he died, on 13 April 1624, at Bishop's Court, or Hall, Essex, the home of the courtier Sir Basil Brook. He may have been buried at St Pancras, Middlesex.

PETER HOLMES

Sources G. Anstruther, *The seminary priests*, 4 vols. (1969-77) · Gillow, *Lit. biog. hist.* · J. Pitts, *De illustribus Angliae scriptoribus* (1619) · Wood, *Ath. Oxon.*, new edn, 2.358 · *DNB* · *The letters and memorials of William, Cardinal Allen (1532-1594)*, ed. T. F. Knox (1882), vol. 2 of *Records of the English Catholics under the penal laws* (1878-82) · T. G. Law, ed., *The archpriest controversy: documents relating to the dissensions of the Roman Catholic clergy, 1597-1602*, 2 vols., CS, new ser., 56, 58 (1896-8), index · W. Dugdale, *The antiquities of Warwickshire illustrated*, rev. W. Thomas, 2nd edn, 2 vols. (1730), 554 · *Dodd's Church history of England*, ed. M. A. Tierney, 5 vols. (1839-43), vol. 4, pp. cclxix, cclxxx · W. Camden, *The visitation of the county of Warwick in the year 1619*, ed. J. Fetherston, Harleian Society, 12 (1877) · W. H. Rylands, ed., *The visitation of the county of Warwick ... 1682 ... 1683*, Harleian Society, 62 (1911) · *VCH Warwickshire*, 5.25 · A. Woodward, *Memories of Brailes* (1988), 34 · P. Heylin, *Examen historicum* (1659), 2.96-7 · A. G. Petti, ed., *Recusant documents from the Ellesmere manuscripts, 1577-1715*, Catholic RS, 60 (1968), 19-23 · A. F. Allison and D. M. Rogers, eds., *The contemporary printed literature of the English Counter-Reformation between 1558 and 1640*, 2 (1994), 16-18 · M. C. Questier, *Newsletters from the archpresbyterate of George Birkhead*, CS, 5th ser., 12 (1998)

Archives Inner Temple, London, papers

Likenesses stipple, pubd 1810, NPG · portrait, Archbishop's House, Westminster [*see illus.*] · portrait, repro. in *Laity's Directory* (1810) · print, repro. in T. Scot, *Vox populi* (1644)

Bishop, William Avery [Billy] (**1894–1956**), air force officer and businessman in Canada, was born at Owen Sound, Ontario, Canada, on 8 February 1894, the third of four children of William Avery Bishop, lawyer, and his wife, Margaret Louise Green (*b. c.*1855), daughter of William Green MD. His father's family were a blend of United Empire loyalists and Pennsylvania Dutch, while his mother's was recently arrived from Ireland.

Bishop earned notoriety as one of the highest scoring fighter aces of the First World War, and as a terrible flier. Both qualities were demonstrated in his early years. His father's offer of 25 cents for every squirrel shot in their backyard fruit trees quickly revealed a keen eye for leading a small target and economical shooting. Young Billy was soon down to 'one bullet–one squirrel' and his father many dollars poorer. His first attempt to fly a home-built glider off the roof of the family house ended in a crash, not the last he walked away from.

After attending Owen Sound high school, Bishop entered the Royal Military College of Canada in 1911, where he was a less than stellar student. He was on the verge of being expelled for cheating in exams in 1914 when his military career was saved by the war. Commissioned into the cavalry, he was sent overseas with the 7th Canadian mounted rifles in the spring of 1915. It was while training in southern England that he was smitten again by the urge to fly. Not being shy, he went straight to the War Office to see Lord Hugh Cecil, who was in charge of recruiting for the Royal Flying Corps. When told that he

William Avery Bishop (1894–1956), by William Rider-Rider, 1917

would have to wait six months for pilot training, he immediately joined the Royal Flying Corps as an observer. He made his first flight with 21st squadron on 1 September 1915.

Bishop's squadron, equipped with lumbering RE7 bomber–reconnaissance aircraft, deployed to France in January 1916. Fortunately he was on convalescent leave when his squadron was decimated during the Somme offensive the following summer. In hospital he was visited by Lady St Helier, whose passing acquaintance with his father was recalled by the appearance of Bishop's name on the list of new patients. 'Granny' St Helier became a fast friend and provided him with an entrée into British society.

After a brief convalescence in Canada, Bishop enlisted Lady St Helier in his quest for pilot training, which was finally granted in September 1916. A keen learner, he remained a questionable pilot. The crash landing at the end of his first solo flight was simply the first of what became known to many as 'Bishop landings'. Although his flying skills improved over time, his reckless handling of finely balanced and often unstable fighters probably contributed to his success—and survival.

After a brief stint in home defence squadrons, Bishop arrived at 60th squadron Royal Flying Corps in France on 17 March 1917; a week later he recorded his first kill, an Albatross DIII fighter. He quickly established himself as cold and gifted hunter. He had exceptionally good eyesight and usually saw his prey long before it saw him. That, along with his remarkable marksmanship, allowed him to shoot most of his victims down with a single pass and a few well placed bullets. These latter typically went into the enemy pilot. By the end of April 1917 Bishop had fourteen official victories, and a German bounty on his head. Flying and fighting went on at a frantic pace. On 2 May 1917 he flew four patrols, shot down two aircraft, forced a third to land—giving him three 'kills' for the day—and engaged nineteen other enemy aircraft. He would have accounted for more enemy machines but he kept running out of ammunition or his guns jammed.

Success in the air meant that Bishop, always an individualist, was soon allowed to fly alone. He did so at dawn on 2 June 1917, when he set out to attack a German aerodrome near Cambrai. He strafed the parked aircraft and claimed three enemy fighters as they struggled to get airborne. He arrived back at his airfield with his Nieuport stitched with bullet holes. For this daring solo effort he was awarded the Victoria Cross by the king on 11 August 1917, receiving at the same time the Military Medal and being made a DSO. A bar to his DSO was awarded a week later. He then left for a prolonged public relations and recruiting tour of Canada.

While at home Bishop married on 17 October 1917 a long-time friend, Margaret Eaton Burden, daughter of C. E. Burden of Toronto, a union that produced a son and a daughter. While on leave he also found time to write a memoir of his exploits, *Winged Warfare*, which was published in 1918.

Bishop returned to France in May 1918 in command of his own squadron, 85, with fifty-four kills to his credit and a burning passion to add to the score. Over the next six weeks he shot down a further eighteen enemy aircraft, and was well on the way to becoming the highest scoring ace of the war, on either side. On his last day of aerial combat, 19 June 1918, he was credited with the destruction of five machines, which earned him the DFC. In the end, Bishop was the third highest scoring allied fighter ace of the war, and second only to Edward (Mick) Mannock among the aces of the British empire. He was officially credited with destroying seventy-two enemy machines, one less than Mannock and only three behind France's René Fonck. Had his seven other claims been credited, Bishop would rank second only to Germany's Manfred von Richtofen, the famous Red Baron.

To save this imperial icon from the fate of so many pilots, Bishop was recalled from France in late June 1918. Promoted to lieutenant-colonel, he was assigned to command the 'Canadian wing', two squadrons preparing to operate in support of the Canadian corps, and to help create a Canadian air force.

When the war ended in November Bishop resigned from the service and went into the flying business in Britain with William Barker, another Canadian fighter ace. When a crash in 1920 affected Bishop's vision so that he was unable to fly again, the company dissolved. Bishop remained in Britain where he moved easily within society, playing polo, counting among his intimates Winston Churchill, and publishing *Flying Squad* in 1926. He also did well in business—in which it was said he 'had the face of an angel and the mind of a murderer'—at least until the stock market crash of 1929. Unable to sustain his lifestyle, Bishop returned to Canada to work for an oil company. In 1931 he was made an honorary group captain of the Royal Canadian Air Force and, during the war, in the honorary rank of air marshal, was appointed director of recruiting. In 1945 he published *Winged Peace*.

Diligence and commitment to the Royal Canadian Air Force during the Second World War took a toll on Bishop's health and he took an early retirement from the oil business in 1952. He never recovered and died quietly in his sleep in Palm Beach, Florida, on 10 September 1956.

Bishop remains a well-known and somewhat controversial figure. No German evidence corroborating his attack on an airfield (claimed to be Estourmel) on 2 June 1917 has ever been found, although German aerodrome records are unusually complete. Moreover, as with most other First World War aces, many of his kills were awarded on his word alone. Doubts about this most famous Canadian hero prompted the Canadian National Film Board documentary *The Kid who Couldn't Miss* (1982) which portrayed Bishop as a cold-blooded killer and an ambitious liar and caused a national scandal. A kinder and more popular treatment, the one-man play *Billy Bishop Goes to War*, was well received both in theatres and in a television film version during the 1980s and 1990s. It served to keep Bishop, the essential hero of 1917, in the public eye until the end of the century.   MARC MILNER

Sources W. A. Bishop, *The courage of the early morning: a son's biography of a famous father* (1965) · *Who's who in Canada* (1949–51)
Archives FILM BFI NFTVA, documentary footage · BFI NFTVA, news footage
Likenesses W. Rider-Rider, photograph, 1917, NA Canada [*see illus.*] · R. Speller, group portrait, photograph, 1942, Hult. Arch.

Bissait, Baldred. *See* Bisset, Baldred (*c.*1260–1311?).

Bisse, Philip (*bap.* **1666**, *d.* **1721**), bishop of Hereford, was baptized on 28 May 1666 at Oldbury on the Hill, Gloucestershire, the elder son of the Revd John Bisse (*c.*1638–1686), rector of the parish, and his wife, Joyce Gyles. He was a cousin of Robert Harley, through whose patronage he no doubt won his later promotion to the episcopal bench. His brother Thomas *Bisse (1675–1731) was notable for his part in founding the Three Choirs festival. Philip entered Winchester College in 1682, where, though the college visitor later disallowed it, his family claimed for him special privileges as one of the founder's numerous kin. In June 1686 he entered New College, Oxford, where he graduated BA in 1690 and proceeded MA on 15 January 1694; he became a fellow and subsequently BD and DD (29 January 1706). On 13 February 1706 he was elected a fellow of the Royal Society. In October 1710 he was consecrated bishop of St David's, and in September 1713 he was enthroned bishop of Hereford.

As for patronage, Bisse had already improved his position in 1704 by marrying Bridget Osborne (1661–1718), daughter of Thomas Osborne, first duke of Leeds, formerly lord treasurer of Charles II, and widow of Charles fitz-Charles, earl of Plymouth, the king's illegitimate son. Bisse was her chaplain, and perhaps for this reason news of the marriage was not published until 1706. Described as Robert Harley's 'urbane and socially-minded cousin, whose talents as a genial matchmaker for the aristocratic young were unsurpassed' (Bennett, 141), Bisse gave him, as a moderate Hanover tory, political support. As earl of Oxford and treasurer, Harley repaid this by having him preferred to his two bishoprics in 1710 and 1713 respectively. In return Bisse supported Harley, even through his impeachment, by frequent attendance in the House of Lords until at least 1719, and also by often acting as proxy for Bishop George Hooper of Bath and Wells. In ecclesiastical politics, too, like John Robinson, bishop successively

Philip Bisse (*bap.* 1666, *d.* 1721), attrib. Thomas Hill, 1719

of Bristol and London, and like Hooper, Bisse was a moderate in the Harleian mould. Certainly as bishop of St David's he was a prominent member of a small inner group of six tory bishops in convocation in 1710. Chosen by them to bear a message to the queen, he was noted to have managed his business so well that the queen 'was pleased to send us a message in writing' (Sykes, 1.130). In 1714 some thought that his political and ecclesiastical activity betrayed a reputation for angling, like others, for further preferment to the archbishopric of York when it fell vacant on John Sharp's death; and a contemporary noted that 'our friend the bishop of Hereford never at first desired a bishopric so much as he now does a better' (*Portland MSS*, 178).

Despite his political connections Bisse was an exemplary diocesan bishop. He undertook his episcopal duties with efficiency and care of the highest order. The articles for his primary visitation, originally planned for 1714 but postponed until 1716, displayed an unusual thoroughness. They were presented in a new format, and copied by his successors; and there were special new sections on charities, and enquiries into peculation and overzealousness of his diocesan officers. In 1718 he introduced a new investigation into the use and abuse of diocesan charitable investments. Moreover not only was Bisse enthroned in person at a time when many bishops used proxies, but he also himself regularly conducted the ordinations in Hereford Cathedral. Seven out of the eleven ordinations he undertook were held there and only one was outside the diocese—at Duke Street Chapel, Westminster, soon after he became bishop. Furthermore he impressed many by extensively refurbishing the cathedral and the bishop's palace. He died at Westminster on 6 September 1721, and was buried in Hereford Cathedral on 11 September. His only published works were a few sermons. He may have been a political schemer and an artful manipulator of patronage, but, more important, he was a dedicated and efficient diocesan bishop. WILLIAM MARSHALL

Sources *Fasti Angl.* (Hardy), 1.304, 473 · Foster, *Alum. Oxon.* · *A catalogue of all graduates … in the University of Oxford, between … 1659 and … 1850* (1851) · Glos. RO, P114/2 IN 1/1 · Bodl. Oxf., MS Oxf. dioc. d106 · Bishop's registers, 1709–23, Herefs. RO · W. M. Marshall, 'The administration of the dioceses of Hereford and Oxford, 1660–1760', PhD diss., University of Bristol, 1979 · T. F. Kirby, *Winchester scholars: a list of the wardens, fellows, and scholars of … Winchester College* (1888) · N. Sykes, *William Wake, archbishop of Canterbury*, 2 vols. (1957) · A. L. Moir, *The bishops of Hereford* (1964) · G. V. Bennett, *The tory crisis in church and state: the career of Francis Atterbury, bishop of Rochester* (1975) · IGI · *The manuscripts of his grace the duke of Portland*, 10 vols., HMC, 29 (1891–1931), vol. 7, p. 178 · *DNB* · Burke, *Peerage* (1933)

Likenesses attrib. T. Hill, oils, 1719, New College, Oxford [*see illus.*] · G. Vertue, line engraving, 1719 (after T. Hill), BM, NPG · portrait, bishop's palace, Hereford

Bisse, Thomas (1675–1731), Church of England clergyman and founder of the Three Choirs festival, was baptized on 6 April 1675 at Oldbury on the Hill, Gloucestershire, one of two sons of John Bisse (c.1638–1686), rector of that parish, and his wife, Joyce Gyles. Bisse came from a Somerset clerical family of long standing and, at times, distinction. His elder brother, Philip *Bisse (bap. 1666, d. 1721), was bishop of Hereford (1713–21). Thomas entered Corpus Christi College, Oxford, in 1691, and later became a fellow; he graduated BA in 1695, and proceeded MA in 1698, BD in 1708 and DD in 1712. He was ordained deacon at Oxford on 4 June 1699. In 1715 he was preacher at the Rolls Chapel, London.

On becoming bishop of Hereford in 1713 Philip Bisse appointed Thomas to a prebend in Hereford Cathedral and to the incumbency of Cradley and part of Ledbury. There is evidence of non-residence at least until 1716, when his Cradley churchwardens acidly noted that Bisse was always in London. But in that year his brother promoted him to the chancellorship of the cathedral and to the prebend of Colwall in place of the nonjuring John Harvey, who had been deprived of both. In the same year Bisse also succeeded Harvey as rector of Weston under Penyard, Herefordshire, where he added a brewhouse to the parsonage. He held his chancellorship, the two prebends, and all his Hereford livings until his death, but his parishes were well tended by curates in his absence.

Besides these offices Bisse is chiefly remembered in musical circles as the instigator in 1724 of the Three Choirs festival, which survived to become the oldest musical festival in the country. Before moving to Herefordshire he had been much impressed by the annual charity services for the Corporation of the Sons of the Clergy in London (founded in 1655); these took the form of a choral service and an appropriate sermon, one of which Bisse had preached at St Paul's. On his arrival in Herefordshire he became an enthusiastic supporter of the existing occasional meetings of the three cathedral choirs of Hereford, Gloucester, and Worcester, and at Bisse's suggestion these meetings were put on a regular footing, possibly in 1716 or 1717, and certainly by 1724; each cathedral took a turn every three years, and there was a sermon in support of the orphans of clergy in the three dioceses. Nowadays the sermon is preached on the Sunday preceding the festival.

Bisse was regarded as an eloquent preacher. Among the subjects of his published sermons are defence of episcopacy and charity schools, but perhaps the most notable are *The Beauty of Holiness in the Common Prayer* (1716), *A Rationale on Cathedral Worship or Choir-Service* (1720), and *Musick the Delight of the Sons of Men*, the last preached at the Three Choirs festival in 1726. He also published two Latin poems, *Lusus poetica olim conscripti* (1720) and *Microscopium* (1721). He died on 22 April 1731. It is not known whether he was married. WILLIAM MARSHALL

Sources Foster, *Alum. Oxon.* · *A catalogue of all graduates … in the University of Oxford, between … 1659 and … 1850* (1851) · *Fasti Angl.* (Hardy), vol. 1 · E. Blom, *Music in England* (1942) · Grove, *Dict. mus.* (1954) · W. M. Marshall, 'The administration of the dioceses of Hereford and Oxford, 1660–1760', PhD diss., University of Bristol, 1979 · episcopal registers; visitation returns, Herefs. RO, Hereford diocese · A. T. Bannister, *Diocese of Hereford, institutions, 1539–1900* (1923) · parish register, Oldbury on the Hill, Glos. RO, P114/2 IN 1/1

Bisset [Bissait], **Baldred** (c.1260–1311?), ecclesiastic, is best known for advocating the cause of Scottish independence before Pope Boniface VIII in 1301. Traditionally believed to originate in Stirlingshire, Bisset may have been related to William Biset, lord of Upsettlington, Berwickshire, who was constable of Stirling Castle in 1306 under Edward I and briefly a Stirlingshire landholder during the reign of Robert I.

According to David Buchanan, writing in the first half of the seventeenth century, Bisset attended school in Stirling, studied philosophy at St Andrews, and furthered his studies in France. But no contemporary evidence supports such a claim, and the first reliable record places him in Bologna in 1277, when he was styled *Dominus*; he was called 'Master' by 1284 and most probably graduated as doctor of civil law, since he was described as *Dottor di Legge* ('Doctor of law') in 1305.

Bisset pursued a career in the Scottish church in the 1280s. He was a canon of Caithness by August 1284, and was rector of Kinghorn in St Andrews diocese by 19 September 1289. He apparently remained in possession of the Kinghorn living until his replacement, some time between 1296 and 1301, by an English cleric, Peter of Dunwich. He learned of this while in Bologna, and appealed directly to Rome late in 1304, and by proxy at the diocesan court of St Andrews shortly thereafter.

Before his return to Bologna, Bisset held a key position in diocesan administration as official of St Andrews, presiding over the bishop's ordinary court during the episcopate of William Fraser (1280–97). He appears in this office before October 1282 and continued to hold it until some time in 1289. During the same decade he took part in litigation between the sees of York and Durham, apparently supporting the latter. Little is known of his career during the 1290s, though he may well have taught law in Bologna.

Bisset's most enduring legacy, however, was as spokesman for the Scottish cause at the papal curia in 1301, while John Soulis was acting as guardian for the exiled King John, who had been forced to abdicate in 1296. After Boniface VIII had addressed his bull *Scimus, fili* to Edward I in 1299, claiming papal supremacy over Scotland, the English king, in his reply of 1301, adduced historical evidence to support his right to the overlordship of Scotland. Edward's letter included references to legendary material derived from Geoffrey of Monmouth, which inspired a reply in kind.

The Scottish government appointed Master William Frere, archdeacon of Lothian, to lead a commission that included Bisset and Master William of Eaglesham. The three Scottish proctors worked on a reply to Edward's letter in July 1301. Three separate drafts of an informal version, known somewhat misleadingly as the 'Instructions', were composed. Two of these survive as full texts in fifteenth-century manuscripts of an appendix to John Fordun's *Chronica gentis Scotorum* and of Walter Bower's *Scotichronicon*. A briefer version, known as the *Processus* ('Pleading'), also survives, though there is no evidence it was ever presented in court; in any case, Boniface reversed his previous support for the Scottish side in August 1302.

Bisset may well have been the principal author of the 'Instructions' and 'Pleading', as a number of early Scottish chronicles suggest. The author shows himself a skilful polemicist with a good knowledge of canon and civil law and well informed about thirteenth-century Anglo-Scottish relations. To counter Edward's argument from the legendary history of the Britons, Bisset adapts a legend that traced Scottish origins back to Scota, daughter of the Egyptian pharaoh, and her husband, Gaythelos, a Greek prince. At the same time, Bisset was sophisticated enough to argue that recent history provides evidence that is more relevant and better documented than that of the remote past.

Bisset returned to Bologna after his activities in the papal curia and was appointed vicar-general there to Bishop Hubert by April 1305. He seems to have spent most of his remaining life on the continent, where he occasionally appeared at Avignon. But he went on an embassy to Lanercost, to meet with Edward I late in 1306, after Robert I's usurpation of the throne; Bisset's purpose is unclear, but he may have sought to negotiate against Bruce's interests. Bisset's last important activity was to lead the defence of Boniface VIII in a posthumous trial in the consistory at Avignon. He was still alive on 27 April 1311, when he was mentioned in a record of Pope Clement V, and probably died soon thereafter.   R. James Goldstein

Sources W. Bower, *Scotichronicon*, ed. D. E. R. Watt and others, new edn, 9 vols. (1987–98), vol. 6, pp. 99, 133–89, 257–88, 291, 417 · D. E. R. Watt, *A biographical dictionary of Scottish graduates to AD 1410* (1977), 49–51 · R. J. Goldstein, *The matter of Scotland: historical narrative in medieval Scotland* (1993), 66–78 · R. J. Goldstein, 'The Scottish mission to Boniface VIII in 1301: a reconsideration of the context of the *Instructiones* and *Processus*', *SHR*, 70 (1991), 1–15 · E. L. G. Stones, ed. and trans., *Anglo-Scottish relations, 1174–1328: some select documents*, 2nd edn, OMT (1970), 49–51 · G. W. S. Barrow, *Robert Bruce and the community of the realm of Scotland*, 3rd edn (1988), 116–19 · D. Buchanan, *De scriptoribus Scotis libri duo*, ed. D. Irving, Bannatyne Club, 55 (1837) · R. Brentano, *York metropolitan jurisdiction and papal judges delegate, 1279–1296* (1959), 159–60, 233–4 · *Johannis de Fordun Chronica gentis Scotorum / John of Fordun's Chronicle of the Scottish nation*, ed. W. F. Skene, trans. F. J. H. Skene, 2 vols. (1871–2)

Bisset, Charles (1717–1791), physician and military engineer, was born at Glenalbert, near Dunkeld, Perthshire, the son of a lawyer who specialized in Scots law. He studied medicine in Edinburgh and in 1740 was appointed second surgeon of the military hospital, Jamaica. He later served on board Admiral Vernon's fleet, by some accounts as a naval surgeon and by others as surgeon of one of the marine regiments subsequently disbanded. After spending five years in the West Indies and America he returned home in 1745 owing to ill-health.

In May 1746 Bisset obtained an ensigncy in the 42nd highlanders, then commanded by Lord John Murray, with which he served in the unsuccessful attack on the French coast near L'Orient, in September that same year. After spending the winter with his regiment at Limerick, he accompanied it to the Low Countries, where it was first engaged at Sandberg, near Hulst, in Dutch Flanders, in April 1747. Military sketches of this affair and of the defences of Bergen-op-Zoom, drawn by him, having been submitted by Lord John Murray to the duke of Cumberland, Bisset was ordered to the latter fortress to prepare reports of the progress of the siege. For his brave and skilful performance of this duty he was recommended by the duke of Cumberland for the post of engineer-extraordinary in the brigade of engineers attached to the army. Bisset served in this capacity for the remainder of the war. At the peace of 1748 the engineer brigade was broken up, and Bisset was placed on half-pay as a lieutenant. In 1751 he published an essay entitled *The Theory and Construction of Fortifications*, based on his military experiences.

Bisset returned to the profession of medicine, and went into practice at the village of Skelton, in Cleveland, Yorkshire, where he built up a lucrative practice. In 1765 he took his MD at St Andrews University. He was the author of a variety of medical publications. In 1755 he published his *Treatise on Scurvy*, which he dedicated to the lords of the Admiralty. In this he recommended the consumption of alcohol for the prevention of scurvy, contrary to the teachings of James Lind. In 1762 he published *An Essay on the Medical Constitution of Great Britain*, a manuscript of which he presented to the Leeds Infirmary. His publication *Medical Essays and Observations* (1766) was subsequently translated into German and Italian.

Bisset also wrote on non-medical topics, among them politics and naval tactics. A manuscript treatise by him entitled *Permanent and Temporary Fortifications and the Attack and Defence of Temporary Defensive Works*, which is dedicated to George, prince of Wales, and dated 1778, is preserved in the British Library (Add. MS 19695). Some contemporaries, perturbed by his proficiency in both military and medical subjects, questioned the authenticity of his medical qualifications. In reply Bisset published a rejoinder in which he outlined his medical qualifications and experience. A copy of William Cullen's *First Lines of Practice of Physic*, with numerous manuscript notes by him, was preserved in the library of the London Medical Society.

Bisset was thin in person and of weakly habit. His correspondence with Dr John Coakley Lettsom gives some insight into his character. He was married, and retired to Knayton, near Thirsk in Yorkshire, where he died in 1791. He was buried at Leake church. His wife, Ann, died on 31 August 1810, aged seventy-six.

H. M. CHICHESTER, rev. CLAIRE E. J. HERRICK

Sources 'Dr Charles Bisset of Knayton, Thirsk', *Medical Bookman and Historian*, 2 (1948), 165 · J. J. Keevil, J. L. S. Coulter, and C. Lloyd, *Medicine and the navy, 1200–1900*, 3: *1714–1815* (1961), 303 · *Memoirs of the life and writings of the late John Coakley Lettsom*, ed. T. J. Pettigrew, 3 vols. (1817), vol. 3, pp. 303–37 · *GM*, 1st ser., 61 (1791), 598, 965–6 · R. Cannon, ed., *Historical record of the forty-second, or the royal highland regiment of foot* (1845)

Archives BL, Add. MS 19695 · Royal College of Physicians and Surgeons of Glasgow

Bisset, James (1762?–1832), artist and writer of verse, was born in Perth. He received his early education at a dame-school. He developed early a love of art and literature and from the age of nine began regularly to take the *Gentleman's Magazine* with the help of pocket money supplied by an indulgent uncle.

At the age of fifteen Bisset became an artist's apprentice at Birmingham. In the *Birmingham Directory* of 1785 his name appears as miniature painter, Newmarket, and in 1797 as fancy painter, New Street. In the latter premises he established a museum and shop for the sale of curiosities. He was also a coiner of medals, and was permitted to use the designation medallist to his majesty. On the title-page of one of his books he advertised medallions of their majesties and of several leading statesmen, and a medal commemorating the death and victory of Nelson. Bisset also had great facility in composing amusing and grandiloquent verses on the topics of the day; while he obtained a considerable profit from their sale, they served to attract customers to his museum and to advertise his medals. Among his earlier volumes of verse were *The Orphan Boy*, *Flights of Fancy*, *Theatrum oceani*, *Songs of Peace* (1802), and *The patriotic clarion, or, Britain's call to glory: original songs written on the threatened invasion* (1803). The last was dedicated by permission to the duke of York, and the presentation copy to George III with Bisset's inscription is in the British Library. One of his most notable works is his *Poetic survey round Birmingham, with a brief description of the different curiosities and manufactures of the place, accompanied with a magnificent directory, with the names and professions, &c. superbly engraved in emblematic plates* (1800). A second edition of the *Directory* appeared in 1808, with several additional plates, but without the *Poetic Survey*. In 1804 he published *Critical Essays on the Dramatic Essays of the Young Roscius*. In Birmingham he belonged to the Minerva Club, consisting of twelve members, nicknamed the Apostles, who met at the Leicester Arms to discuss political subjects. A picture of the members was painted by the Prussian artist Eckstein; Bisset, as the oldest surviving member, fell heir to it.

In 1813 Bisset moved to Leamington, where he had opened a museum, newsroom, and picture gallery in the preceding year. A *Picturesque Guide to Leamington*, enlivened by stray scraps of verse, was published by him in 1814, followed by *Comic Strictures on Birmingham's Fine Arts and Conversaziones, by an Old Townsman*, in 1829. His verses also appeared occasionally in the *Gentleman's Magazine*. He boasted that he had sold over 100,000 of his different works, and that many had reached the fifteenth and sixteenth editions. He died at Leamington on 17 August 1832, and was buried there, where a monument was erected by his friends to his memory. Bisset's collection of pictures, which included several celebrated paintings, as well as some pieces by himself, was sold by auction after his death.

T. F. HENDERSON, rev. MICHAEL MARKER

Sources D. Foskett, *A dictionary of British miniature painters*, 2 vols. (1972) · Bénézit, *Dict.*, 4th edn · *Mr Bisset goes to Stratford: an extract from the diary*, ed. P. Morgan (1965) · J. A. Langford, ed., *A century of Birmingham life … 1741–1841* (1868) · *GM*, 1st ser., 102/2 (1832), 648–50 · R. K. Dent, *Old and new Birmingham: a history of the town and its people*, 3 vols. (1879–80) · J. Bisset, *A poetic survey round Birmingham, with a brief description of the different curiosities and manufactures of the place, accompanied with a magnificent directory, with the names and professions, &c., superbly engraved in emblematic plates* (1800)

Archives Warks. CRO, memoirs and other papers

Bisset, James (1795–1872), scholar, was the son of George Bisset and his wife, Mary Adamson. He was born on 20 April 1795 in the parish of Udny in Aberdeenshire, where his father was parish schoolmaster and headmaster of a private academy and boarding-school. James was the second son of a large family; one brother, Thomas, became vicar of Pontefract (1865–78), another, Charles, was incumbent of Upholland in Wigan (1844–81), and a third attained the rank of colonel in the East India Company's service. Bisset was well trained by his father, and then proceeded to Marischal College, Aberdeen.

At the early age of seventeen, as a result of the death of his father, Bisset was obliged to assume all the responsibilities of schoolteaching, and of educating his younger brothers and sisters. Like his father he developed remarkable teaching ability, and his private school became celebrated. Many of the local gentry were educated by him, and several of his pupils became men of mark, among them Sir James Outram and J. C. Robertson, the ecclesiastical historian. He was aided by very able assistants; Dr James Melvin, afterwards rector of Aberdeen grammar school, and Dr Adam Thom, sometime recorder of the Hudson's Bay Company, were both members of his staff. He qualified himself for the ministry of the Church of Scotland, studying divinity at the universities of Aberdeen and Edinburgh. In 1826 he became minister of the small parish of Bourtie, Aberdeenshire. The duties of his limited parochial charge left him leisure to continue his philological studies, for he was known as an elegant Latinist. His repute as a scholar was not, however, sustained by any publication of permanent value. In 1850 the degree of DD was conferred upon him by the University of Aberdeen.

Bisset was twice married: first, in 1829, to Mary Bannerman (d. 1836), eldest daughter of the Revd Robert Lessel of Inverurie; and second, in 1840, to Elizabeth Sinclair, daughter of the Revd William Smith of Bowes. Bisset had four daughters and one son from his first marriage, and one daughter and two sons from his second.

Bisset became an ardent politician on what was called the 'constitutional side', and ecclesiastically was a prominent figure in the prolonged conflict within and without the church courts which terminated in the founding of the Free Church of Scotland. Bisset did not support the secession headed by Thomas Chalmers, Robert Candlish, and Thomas Guthrie. In 1862 he was chosen moderator of the general assembly of the Church of Scotland. He died at Bourtie on 8 September 1872.

A. B. GROSART, rev. M. C. CURTHOYS

Sources Fasti Scot. · Boase, Mod. Eng. biog. · private information (1885)
Wealth at death £1728 0s. 4d.: inventory, 11 Oct 1872, NA Scot., SC 1/36/71/432

Bisset, Sir John (1774–1854), commissariat officer, was born in Perth. He served in the commissariat (the civil department, which provided the army with transport, food, and forage, and kept the stores) in Britain from 1795 to 1800, in Germany from May 1800 to June 1802, in Britain again from 1802 to 1806, in South America in 1806–7, and at the Scheldt in 1809. He was commissary-general from 31 July 1811 until 1819, when he was placed on half pay. He had charge of the commissariat of Wellington's army at a crucial period of the Peninsular War, before and after the battle of Salamanca. Bisset, who was made a knight bachelor and knight commander of the Royal Guelphic Order in 1832 and KCB in August 1850, was granted a pension of £550. He published Memoranda Regarding the Duties of the Commissariat on Field Service Abroad (1846). He died at Perth, where he had resided for many years, on 3 April 1854.

H. M. CHICHESTER, rev. DAVID GATES

Sources Boase, Mod. Eng. biog. · GM, 2nd ser., 41 (1854), 558 · J. Bisset, Memoranda regarding the duties of the commissariat on field service abroad (1846) · D. Gates, The Spanish ulcer: a history of the Peninsular War (1986) · A. B. Rodger, The war of the second coalition: 1798–1801, a strategic commentary (1964) · S. G. P. Ward, Wellington's headquarters: a study of the administrative problems in the Peninsula, 1809–14 (1957)
Archives NL Scot., divisional letter-book · NL Scot., letters to quartermasters-general · U. Southampton L., corresp. as commissary-general | BL, corresp. with John Charles Herries, Add. MS 57377 · U. Nott. L., corresp. with Lord William Bentinck and Lieutenant-General Maitland · W. Sussex RO, letters to duke of Richmond

Bisset, Patrick (fl. 1549–1577). See under Bisset, Peter (supp. fl. 1401).

Bisset, Peter (supp. fl. 1401), canonist, is said to have studied at St Andrews University. According to Thomas Dempster, and by other authors who followed his lead, Bisset was a professor of canon law at Bologna in 1401, and wrote treatises entitled 'De irregularitate liber unus' and 'Lectiones seriales liber unus'. But evidence, apart from Dempster's say-so, is lacking, and a death date of 1568 has also been suggested. Bisset has been confused with Pietro *Bizzarri,

whose Varia opuscula, published at Venice in 1565, show that he had recently visited Scotland and contacted George Buchanan and Andrew Melville, among others. In all probability Peter Bisset never existed, whereas there is sound evidence for the life of **Patrick Bisset** (fl. 1549–1577), who was born in Lessendrum, Drumblade parish, Aberdeenshire, an estate which he reacquired in 1563. He was possibly the son of Patrick Bisset of Lessendrum who died in battle at Corrichie under the Catholic earl of Huntly in 1562. Probably an arts graduate of Aberdeen University, Bisset was received as a burgess in Edinburgh in 1549. On 22 September 1554 he is recorded as a merchant visiting Paris, where he bought books from the publisher Michel de Vascosan. In that same year he is found selling wine from Anjou in Edinburgh, where he furnished wine to the English ambassador in 1565. In 1557 he entered into obligations with Timotheo Cagnioli, an Italian banker in Edinburgh, along with Leslie of Balquhair and Menzies, provost of Aberdeen. In 1574 he occupied the house of Sebastien Davelourt, a Frenchman who had been a member of Queen Mary's household, and was witness to a deed at Gight in 1577, after which date he disappears from record.

JOHN DURKAN

Sources Thomae Dempsteri Historia ecclesiastica gentis Scotorum, sive, De scriptoribus Scotis, ed. D. Irving, rev. edn, 2, Bannatyne Club, 21 (1829), 95 · S. Menchi, 'Bizzarri, Pietro', Dizionario biografico degli Italiani, ed. A. M. Ghisalberti, 10 (Rome, 1968), 738–41 · Register of deeds, NA Scot., RD1/2, fols. 43, 48 · Register of deeds, NA Scot., RD1/6, fol. 227 · C. B. B. Watson, ed., Roll of Edinburgh burgesses and guild-brethren, 1406–1700, Scottish RS, 59 (1929) · R. Adams, ed., Bailies' accounts, 1544–1566 (1899), vol. 1 of Edinburgh records: the burgh accounts, 2, 67, 291, 479 · M. Livingstone, D. Hay Fleming, and others, eds., Registrum secreti sigilli regum Scotorum / The register of the privy seal of Scotland, 6 (1963), no. 2764 · J. M. Thomson and others, eds., Registrum magni sigilli regum Scotorum / The register of the great seal of Scotland, 11 vols. (1882–1914), vol. 4, no. 2740 · J. B. Paul, ed., Compota thesaurariorum regum Scotorum / Accounts of the lord high treasurer of Scotland, 11 (1916), 142 · A. Parent, Les métiers du livre à Paris au XVIe siècle, 1539–1560 (1974), 158 · Tanner, Bibl. Brit.-Hib., 102

Bisset, Robert (1758/9–1805), historian and novelist, was one of the leading anti-Jacobin writers during the era of the French Revolution. Little is known of his life beyond his published works. His first production, appearing in 1793–4 (with a second edition in 1799), was a new edition of The Spectator, to which he prefixed biographies of the authors. In 1796 he graduated as doctor of laws from the University of Edinburgh, and in the same year he published a Sketch of Democracy, the aim of which was to show, by a survey of the democratic states of ancient times, that democracy is a vicious form of government. His next work, The Life of Edmund Burke (1798; 2nd edn, 1800), was well received, but his militantly conservative sentiments are most evident in his many contributions to the Anti-Jacobin Review. Over the period 1798 to 1800 Bisset produced more articles for that magazine than anyone save its editor, John Gifford. He has been called the Review's 'pacesetter' (de Montluzin, 58), and as such Bisset has a strong claim to be thought of as having set the standard for the whole loyalist campaign of the 1790s and early 1800s.

Bisset edited the short-lived *Historical, Biographical, Literary, and Scientific Magazine* in 1799, and then produced two vociferously anti-Jacobin novels, *Douglas, or, The Highlander* (1800) and *Modern Literature* (1804). His chief targets here, as well as avowedly radical writers such as Thomas Paine, William Godwin, and Mary Wollstonecraft, were contemporary novelists who, in Bisset's opinion, undermined the morals, piety, and loyalty of an all too susceptible readership. Also in 1804 Bisset published, in six volumes, *A History of the Reign of George the Third, to the Termination of the Late War*, to which he prefixed 'a view of the progressive improvement of England, in prosperity and strength, to the accession of his Majesty'. (Volume 7, by an anonymous author, was published in 1820.) The work was generally praised and, surprisingly, was applauded for its impartiality. Three pamphlets are attributed to Bisset by manuscript notes in the British Library copies: *A Defence of the Slave Trade* (1804), *A Plain Reply to the Pamphlet calling itself 'A Plain Answer'* (1804), and *Essays on the Slave Trade* (1805). By 1796 he was living in Chelsea, and at the time of his death in 1805 at the age of forty-six he was master of an academy in Sloane Street. His death, at his home in Sloane Terrece, is said to have been caused by 'chagrin under embarrassed circumstances' (*GM*).   A. H. BULLEN, rev. M. O. GRENBY

Sources *GM*, 1st ser., 75 (1805), 494 • E. L. de Montluzin, *The anti-Jacobins, 1798–1800: the early contributors to the 'Anti-Jacobin Review'* (1988), 57–9 • Watt, *Bibl. Brit.* • D. Laing, ed., *A catalogue of the graduates … of the University of Edinburgh*, Bannatyne Club, 106 (1858), 259 • *BL cat.*

Bisset, William (1669/70–1747), Church of England clergyman and pamphleteer, was the son of William Bissett of Middlesex. His father was a royalist, but Bisset claimed he was not rewarded for his devotion to the crown. After being educated at Westminster School as a king's scholar (*c*.1684), he went in 1687 to Trinity College, Cambridge, where he was elected a scholar in 1688 and took his BA degree in 1691. Having taken orders, he was for some time in charge of the parish of Iver, Buckinghamshire. From the start of his career he was a pugnacious clergyman. While at Iver he married, and his wife brought him some money. With this he set up a coach, which gave his enemies occasion to make many sneers at his foolish ostentation in the pamphlet war he afterwards engaged in. He defended himself in the second part of *The Modern Fanatick* by declaring that he bought this 'leathern conveniency' in order to enable himself to fulfil an engagement to preach three times a week in a neighbouring parish. During this period of his life he appears to have been industrious in his clerical work. He became rector of Whiston, Northamptonshire, in 1697. Having been elected elder brother of the hospital church of St Katharine by the Tower in 1699, he resided much in London, leaving his wife and children at Whiston.

The first of the books for which Bisset is remembered, *Plain English*, was published in 1705. It was the text of his sermon before the Society for the Reformation of Manners, which he had been asked to preach as a substitute at the last moment. To the astonishment of all, he attacked the society for wanting to quieten the people rather than

reform them; he also criticized its prosecution of poor sinners, rather than the affluent and prominent. The tract caused a controversy in which Isaac Sharpe responded with *Plain English Made Plainer*, but Bisset produced six editions of the work. As a low-churchman and a whig he was offended by Dr Sacheverell's sermon at St Paul's on 5 November 1709, and at once preached and published a reply to it. He followed up this attack in a pamphlet entitled *The Modern Fanatick*, which appeared in 1710. In it he raked up Sacheverell's family background, and published stories of Sacheverell's debts to besmirch his character. Nevertheless *The Modern Fanatick* ran through eleven editions in 1710 alone. The pamphlet stimulated many replies, and among them one by Dr W. King. Bisset responded by publishing a second part of *The Modern Fanatick* in February 1711, and a third part followed in May 1714. William Cole, in his manuscript 'Athenæ Cantabrigienses', described him as 'almost a madman' (Cole MSS), yet the character of the pamphlets put forth by both sides in this controversy is little proof of the sanity of any of the parties concerned in it. A more recent historian has called him a 'muckraker' (Holmes, 14). Bisset was the champion of an unpopular cause. He fought with courage, and bad as his weapons were, they were of much the same kind as those used against him. There is no reason to doubt the truth of his assertion that he was constantly mobbed and insulted, especially by Sacheverell's 'female proselytes'. He also declares that there were three attempts on his life. He deserves credit for having raised an indignant protest against the cruel floggings then often inflicted on soldiers. A probably exaggerated account of the flogging of a man and his wife is given in the collective edition of the *Fanatick* tracts. He was made chaplain to Queen Caroline. He died on 7 November 1747.

WILLIAM HUNT, rev. WILLIAM GIBSON

Sources W. Bisset, *The modern fanatick*, 3 parts (1710–14) • Venn, *Alum. Cant.* • D. W. R. Bahlman, *The moral revolution of 1688* (1957) • A. T. Scudi, *The Sacheverell affair* (1939) • G. Holmes, *The trial of Dr Sacheverell* (1973) • *GM*, 1st ser., 17 (1747), 545 • BL, Cole MSS • *Old Westminsters*, vols. 1–2 • Nichols, *Lit. anecdotes*

Bisset, William (1758–1834), Church of Ireland bishop of Raphoe, was born on 27 October 1758, the son of the Revd Dr Alexander Bisset (*d.* 1782), chancellor of Armagh, into a family from Lessendrum, Drumblade, near Huntly, Aberdeenshire. Like his father, William was educated at Westminster School, where he was admitted a king's scholar in 1771, and at Christ Church, Oxford, where he matriculated on 16 April 1775, and was elected a scholar in the same year; he graduated BA (4 November 1779), and MA (7 February 1782). In 1784 he was presented to the rectory of Dunbin, co. Louth, which he resigned upon his collation on 31 January 1791 to the prebend of Loughgall, or Levalleaglish, in the cathedral church of Armagh. In 1794 he became rector of Clonmore, and on 29 September 1804 was collated to the archdeaconry of Ross, in the united episcopate of Cork, Cloyne, and Ross. In 1807 he resigned as prebend of Loughgall in order to become rector of Donoghmore, and was appointed in 1812 to the rectory of Loughgilly. All his preferments, with the exception of the archdeaconry of Ross, were within the diocese of Armagh. In August 1817 he was appointed to the chancellorship of Armagh, thus succeeding his father after an interval of twenty-five years.

In June 1822 Bisset was promoted by Marquess Wellesley, lord lieutenant of Ireland, to the bishopric of Raphoe. His administration of the diocese, which met with general approval, included the building of several churches and improvements to the palace at Raphoe. Bisset also made up the deficit in funds when the parliamentary grant was withdrawn from the Association for Discountenancing Vice. He was later pressed to become archbishop of Dublin following the death of William Magee in August 1831, but declined on the grounds of ill health. Bisset was married but nothing is known of his wife except that she predeceased him. He died on 5 September 1834, while on a visit to his nephew at Lessendrum. His clergy erected to his memory a monument in Raphoe Cathedral, with an inscription by W. Archer Butler. At his death the see of Raphoe became annexed to that of Derry.

ARTHUR H. GRANT, rev. PHILIP CARTER

Sources H. Cotton, *Fasti ecclesiae Hibernicae*, 1–5 (1845–60) • Foster, *Alum. Oxon.* • *St James's Chronicle* (16 Sept 1834)
Likenesses T. Lawrence, oils, *c.*1827, Christ Church Oxf.

Bitton, William. *See* Button, William (*d.* 1264); Button, William (*d.* 1274).

Bix, Angel (1645/6–1695), Franciscan friar, was born in London; the surname may be the same as Biss. In 1655 a Brigit Biss was the mother of a Poor Clare nun named Margaret Figg in Flanders; Bix may have been a relative of hers as he later gave devoted service as chaplain to the Poor Clares in that area. When he died in 1695 it was said that he was forty-nine years old, having spent twenty-nine years as a Franciscan and twenty-three as a priest; he was therefore ordained about 1672.

Nothing is now known of Bix's early years and education, nor of his entry into the Franciscan order; however, a gifted preacher, his subsequent priestly life was divided among England, northern France, and the southern Netherlands. The English Franciscan chapter held at Somerset House in London in 1677 asked him to go to Aire-sur-la-Lys, south of St Omer, to supply for the chaplain to the Poor Clares there, Joachim St Ann. In 1680 the chapter was held in Bruges, and Bix was reappointed to Aire; at the chapter held in York a year later he was transferred as chaplain to the Poor Clares in Bruges. In 1684 he was recalled to the mission in England, and was succeeded at Bruges by Joseph Woodward.

Three years later, with James II on the throne, Bix was stationed as preacher at the new friary beside the arches at Lincoln's Inn Fields in London, and became chaplain to the Spanish ambassador. Still there in 1688 he was elected titular guardian of the vacated Canterbury friary, which post gave him a vote in chapter. In the same year he published *A sermon on the passion … preach'd before her majesty the queen dowager in her chappel at Sommerset House upon Good Fryday, 13 April 1688*. However, on the same day that the prince of Orange landed in Devon, on 4 November, a mob attacked the friary. James was asked to send soldiers to protect the friars but after his own flight the following month he had to tell the friars to vacate their residence beside the arches. Three or four years later, when it had been repaired at the friars' own expense, it became the residence of the Portuguese ambassador; once the friars' ten-year lease expired they had no more to do with it.

Bix left London for the continent in 1688 and in 1690 was again chaplain to the Poor Clares at Aire, and later to the third order sisters in the ancient palace at Princenhoff in Bruges. He returned to England about 1692, and in 1693 was the *praeses* or local superior at Osmotherley in Yorkshire; two years later he was at York itself. He died at Durham on 15 January 1695.

IGNATIUS FENNESSY

Sources R. Trappes-Lomax, ed., *The English Franciscan nuns, 1619–1821, and the Friars Minor of the same province, 1618–1761*, Catholic RS, 24 (1922) • J. C. H. Aveling, *Catholic recusancy in the city of York, 1558–1791*, Catholic RS, monograph ser., 2 (1970) • T. H. Clancy, *English Catholic books, 1641–1700: a bibliography*, rev. edn (1996) • Gillow, *Lit. biog. hist.*, vol. 1 • Father Thaddeus [F. Hermans], *The Franciscans in England, 1600–1850* (1898) • G. Oliver, *Collections illustrating the history of the Catholic religion in the counties of Cornwall, Devon, Dorset, Somerset, Wilts, and Gloucester* (1857) • DNB

Bizzarri [Bizari], **Pietro** (*b.* 1525, *d.* in or after 1586), historian and spy, was born probably in Sassoferrato Castello (Marche), Italy, the son of Antonio Bizzarri, a soldier who died in 1528. He must also have lived in Perugia, hence his common description as *Perusinus*. He was sent to Venice for an excellent education in classical letters. There in his eighteenth year (1542–3) he was converted to protestantism, perhaps under the influence of Bernardino Ochino and the writings of Erasmus. Now devoted to evangelical reform, Bizzarri left Italy in the summer of 1545 for Germany, settling first in Nuremberg, and then in Wittenberg, where he sought his spiritual guide, Philip Melanchthon, with whom he planned to study. However, Charles V's victory at Muhlberg (1547) resulted in Bizzarri abandoning Germany, and after stopping briefly at several German universities he eventually crossed the channel to England, where he was resident from 1549.

What drove Bizzarri to England is unknown, although it is probable that other Italians who had adopted reformed beliefs, such as Ochino and Pietro Martire Vermigli, and the German Martin Bucer, had much to do with his decision. The intervention of powerful friends is clear from the young man's career: in July 1549 he was named a fellow of St John's College, Cambridge, by the royal visitors. This appointment was, however, brief. The death of Bucer in February 1551 and Bizzarri's increasingly close relations with Francis Russell resulted in his resigning his fellowship to follow Russell to court, perhaps as his secretary and Italian tutor, hoping to build a career as a poet and courtier. Unfortunately, the death of the king and the accession of Mary exploded Bizzarri's ambitions and drove him back to the continent.

Bizzarri next appears in Venice in December 1558 complimenting Elizabeth I on her accession. Subsequently he returned to England, where he dedicated a beautiful manuscript, *De principe tractatus*, to the queen. In return for this treatise—essentially a collection of common-places on the ideal ruler, heavily influenced by Erasmian eirenic principles—he received a pension from the crown and the living of Alton Pancras, Dorset, from Bishop Jewel of Salisbury, through the mediation of Archbishop Parker, whom Bizzarri had certainly known at Cambridge. Moreover, he seems to have re-established his connection with Russell, now earl of Bedford. In February 1564 Bedford was appointed governor of Berwick and took Bizzarri north with him. Consequently, Bizzarri became associated with the court of Mary Stuart, and in the hope of acquiring the patronage of the Scottish queen as well he presented to her a Latin treatise, *De bello et pace*. This is a much more original tract than the one which he presented to Elizabeth. Bizzarri had himself seen and experienced the effects of civil and foreign conflict, both in England and on the continent, and this gives urgency to his discussion of the horrors that result from war. Peace, he argues, should be the highest ambition of any ruler, since peace is Christ's message. War, by contrast, is an affront to God, causing true religion to be neglected and making resistance to the Turks impossible.

For some reason Bizzarri left Scotland almost immediately afterwards, requesting permission from William Cecil on 12 June 1564 to settle on the continent with the continuation of his pension. That summer he left for Venice, but stopped for the autumn in Padua, where he engaged in informal studies. It is also at this time that Bizzarri began his lifelong career as an intelligencer, passing political and diplomatic information to Cecil. Although there is no clear evidence, it is possible that Bizzarri had been used at the Scottish court as an agent, and that it was Cecil who encouraged him to settle in Venice to collect and transmit information at a time when no Venetian ambassador was resident in England.

Bizzarri also frequented the literary circles of Venice. He solicited poems in praise of Elizabeth for his first volume, *Varia opuscula*, printed by Aldus in 1565, which not only contained his earlier poems to English courtiers but also included the works dedicated to Elizabeth and Mary Stuart. Also, in 1566 Bizzarri edited and had printed *La santa*, a comedy by his fellow Italian exile in England, Mario Cardoini. This productive period in Venice also included the completion of his *Historia della guerra fatta in Ungheria*, which follows the events of the current Turkish-imperial confrontation in Hungary, written in an almost journalistic style.

Bizzarri, however, fled Venice almost immediately afterwards, and had the book printed at Lyons in 1568, dedicated to Bedford. Perhaps a warning from the Inquisition forced him from Italy, or Cecil may have ordered his return as a result of the flight to England of Mary Stuart, whom Bizzarri had praised and briefly served. From April 1570 until August 1572 Bizzarri was again in England, apparently in the service of Bedford. During his absence from Venice he seems to have arranged for another informer, della Roche, to send reports on European affairs, implying that he managed information for Cecil as well as collecting it. Leaving England again for Venice, Bizzarri travelled by way of Paris and found himself in danger that August during the St Bartholomew's day massacre. He sought refuge with the English ambassador, Sir Francis Walsingham, beginning a lasting association not only with the ambassador but also with Hubert Languet, and through him with Philip Sidney, with whom Bizzarri would engage in correspondence.

Once safely able to flee Paris, Bizzarri travelled to Basel, where he had printed by February 1573 a work prepared in London, his *Cyprium bellum*—Cyprus had just been conquered by the Turks. To this he added a Latin translation of his earlier history of the Hungarian war, now entitled *Pannonicum bellum*, which he dedicated to the Elector August of Saxony, probably on the advice of his new friend, Languet, who was August's representative in Paris. Bizzarri then travelled to Dresden, where the elector honoured him with an annual pension of 100 thalers.

Bizzarri then began to function as an intelligencer for August of Saxony as well, with a first report from Augsburg sent in April. In September 1573 Bizzarri's pension was increased by 50 thalers, and the Italian enjoyed a comfortable, secure income for the first time, acquiring a large house in Nuremberg. He even attempted to arrange a marriage with the eighteen-year-old daughter of his former fellow Italian protestant exile in England, Pietro Martire Vermigli, although the negotiations failed.

Bizzarri remained in Augsburg until early 1576 when he is found in Cologne. Beginning in 1575–6 he also sent intelligence reports to Walsingham, a practice he continued for the rest of his career. Although Cecil still received reports, they became less frequent than those to Walsingham or August. From his base in Cologne, Bizzarri travelled widely in Germany, but by January 1578 he was established in Antwerp, where he frequented the circle of the printer Christopher Plantin. It was Plantin who in 1579 printed Bizzarri's most ambitious work, his immense history of Genoa (*Senatus populique Genuensis … historiae atque annales*). Unfortunately, despite having personally presented his work, Bizzarri was refused any reward. The senate had been prejudiced against the history by Uberto Foglietta, the city's official historian, who denounced its style and suggested parts were heretical. Although he importuned the republic for years after, Bizzarri received nothing for this monumental piece of scholarship, which was later placed on the index of prohibited books.

Despite this failure, Bizzarri continued to write histories for Plantin's press. In 1583 appeared his Persian history, *Rerum Persicarum historia*, dedicated to August of Saxony, although two presentation copies were also sent to England: one for the queen and one for Walsingham. Bizzarri left for Dresden to present the book, and narrowly escaped death when his ship was captured on the Rhine by Catholic soldiers. Nevertheless, the voyage was a success: August generously granted Bizzarri 100 thalers and increased his pension. On 11 July he returned to Antwerp, where he produced his last work, *De quattuor monarchiis*, and sent it to Frankfurt for printing. Unfortunately, the work was lost and no trace of it remains.

In August 1585, although very ill, Bizzarri was forced to flee the Spanish armies of Alessandro Farnese, first to Dordrecht and then to England, where he was resident by February 1586; but the death of August of Saxony in that year drew him back to Dresden to plead for continuation of his pension. From Saxony Bizzarri returned to the Netherlands, where from The Hague on 23 November 1586 he wrote his last letter to Cecil. He must have died soon after, since no further trace of him survives.

KENNETH R. BARTLETT

Sources M. Firpo, *Pietro Bizzarri, esule italiano del cinquecento* (Turin, 1971) · S. Menchi, 'Bizzarri, Pietro', *Dizionario biografico degli Italiani*, ed. A. M. Ghisalberti, 10 (Rome, 1968) · E. Cochrane, *Historians and historiography in the Italian Renaissance* (Chicago, 1981), 244–5, 355–6 · D. Woolf, ed., *A global encyclopedia of historical writing* (1998), 1.93 · K. Bartlett, *The English in Italy, 1525–1558: a study in culture and politics* (1991), 95–8
Archives PRO, state papers, foreign, letters · PRO, Hatfield MSS, letters · University of Basel, letters

Blaauw, William Henry (1793–1870), antiquary, was born on 25 May 1793 in Queen Anne Street, Marylebone, Middlesex, the only son of William Blaauw (1748–1808), an immigrant from Amsterdam, and his second wife, Louisa (*d.* 1812), daughter of Christopher Puller of Woodford, Essex. He was educated at school in Sunbury and then at Eton College and privately before going to Christ Church, Oxford, where he gained a first-class BA in classics in 1815 and proceeded MA in 1818. On 24 June 1825 he married Harriet, daughter of John King MP and under-secretary of state, but she died in 1828; both daughters of the marriage died young. His second wife, whom he married at St Marylebone on 16 June 1832, was Margaret Emily (1798/9–1881), daughter of Sir John St Leger Gillman, bt, of Curraheen, co. Cork; their elder son died young, and a son and a daughter survived him. His first wife's marriage settlement gave Blaauw an annual income of £1000 for life.

Between 1827 and 1837 Blaauw lived at 24 Lower Brook Street, St George's Hanover Square, London. In 1834 he purchased a 39 acre estate in Newick, Sussex, and after greatly enlarging the farmhouse on the estate, Beechland, he took up residence there in 1837. As a country gentleman, Blaauw extended his estate by judicious purchases, sat on the bench, and served in the lieutenancy. The distant view of the battlefield of Lewes inspired him to study the upheavals of Henry III's reign and in 1844 to publish *The Barons' War*, which drew extensively on chronicles then only in manuscript. As many as 120 years later R. F. Treharne considered that it 'is still the only account of the baronial reform movement as such, and remains a work of great perception and value today' (*The Battle of Lewes, 1264*, 1964, 121).

The Barons' War brought Blaauw to the attention of those active in organized historical scholarship. He was known as a very valuable supporter of the Archaeological Institute of Great Britain and Ireland from its first congress (1845). He was elected a fellow of the Society of Antiquaries in 1850 and also of the Royal Geographical Society, and he served as a council member of the Camden Society from 1848 and as the society's treasurer from 1862. Nearer

home, he was a founder of the Sussex Archaeological Society in 1846, its first secretary until 1859, and the first editor of *Sussex Archaeological Collections* (1847–58). As a gentleman and scholar of independent means, he made the society possible by providing the bridge both to the national societies, and between the Sussex gentry and nobility and the lesser professional men of Lewes, such as Mark Antony Lower, who were the other prime movers.

Blaauw did not again produce sustained research to match *The Barons' War*, although he was preparing a revision at the time of his death (edited by C. H. Pearson, 1871). All his contributions to *Sussex Archaeological Collections* (as also to the *Archaeological Journal*) were based on a single or a few documents, or described one antiquity, and they ended in 1861. His public service culminated in the office of high sheriff in 1859. A portrait in middle age suggests a man of medium height and build, clean shaven and balding. An obituary referred to a melancholy illness which had long precluded any exertion. Blaauw died on 26 April 1870 at Beechland and was buried on 3 May in the churchyard at Newick.

JOHN H. FARRANT

Sources *Sussex Archaeological Collections*, 22 (1870), ix–xi · *Sussex Agricultural Express* (30 April 1870), 6 · *Sussex Agricultural Express* (7 May 1870), 6 · Burke, *Gen. GB* · E. Sussex RO, SAS Acc 1357; SAS/FB 672–80; AMS 6293 · Sussex Archaeological Society Library, Lower MSS, BLA 1–39 · L. F. Salzman, 'The history of the Sussex Archaeological Society', *Sussex Archaeological Collections*, 85 (1946), 1–76 · Foster, *Alum. Oxon.*
Archives Sussex Archaeological Society Library | Sussex Archaeological Society Library, Lower MSS, BLA 1–39
Likenesses W. Beechey, oils, 1811, Eton · Mulready, portrait, Sussex Archaeological Library
Wealth at death under £40,000: probate, 4 July 1870, *CGPLA Eng. & Wales*

Blacader, Robert. See Blackadder, Robert (*c.*1445–1508).

Blacater, Adam. See Blackadder, Adam (*supp. fl.* 1319).

Blachford. For this title name *see* Rogers, Frederic, Baron Blachford (1811–1889).

Blachford [*née* Tighe], **Theodosia** (*c.*1745–*c.*1817), philanthropist, was the only daughter of four children born to William Tighe MP and his first wife, Lady Mary Bligh, granddaughter of the first earl of Darnley, of Rosanna, co. Wicklow, Ireland. Her mother died while she was young, and Theodosia spent her youth looking after her father, who suffered from gout. It was through reading to him from his library that she educated herself. In 1770 Theodosia married William Blachford (*c.*1730–1773), a landowner, clergyman of the Church of Ireland, and the librarian of St Patrick's Library in Dublin. She was widowed in 1773, the mother of two children, a boy and a girl. She believed that the education of children was the primary duty of women, and educated her children at home before sending her son to Eton College when he was twelve years old. Her daughter, the poet Mary *Tighe (1772–1810), was the author of *Psyche* (1805).

About 1761, when Theodosia was almost seventeen, she experienced what she regarded as a spiritual awakening from which she resolved to 'renounce the world, leave all' (Wicklow MS 4810). About 1775 she became interested in

Methodism and corresponded with Agnes Smith. John Wesley was to note in correspondence to the Revd Henry Moore in June 1788 that, 'Mrs. Blachford is one of our jewels, I love her much' (Crookshank, 142). Blachford educated poor girls and penned a number of tracts. She translated the *Life* of Jeanne de Chantal, founder of the Visitation order, into English. She was influenced by the author and religious mystic William Law, who about 1740 had established a small community in Northamptonshire which was dedicated to pious reflection and to charitable works. For Theodosia philanthropy and faith were inextricably linked. She was associated with a number of charities in Dublin, and was instrumental in establishing the Female Orphan House in 1790 and founding the House of Refuge in Baggot Street, Dublin, in 1802. Theodosia died about 1817, and her burial place remains unrecorded.

MARIA LUDDY

Sources NL Ire., Wicklow MSS, MS 4810 · NL Ire., Wicklow MS 3575 · C. H. Crookshank, *Memorable women of Irish Methodism in the last century* (1882), 140–50

Archives NL Ire., Wicklow MSS, 'account of Mrs Blachford copied from a manuscript in her own handwriting', MSS 4810, 3575

Black, Adam (1784–1874), publisher and politician, was born on 20 February 1784 at 7 Charles Street, Edinburgh, the second of the three sons of Charles Black (1755/6–1826), master builder, and his wife, Isabella Nicol (1757/8–1847) of Drygrange Farm near Melrose.

Education, early life, and bookselling After initially attending a school in the Pleasance, Edinburgh, Black was sent to the Edinburgh high school in October 1791. His progress was hampered by the need to help at home. He attended Greek and Latin classes at Edinburgh University in 1798–9, again without much profit. In March 1799 he began an apprenticeship with John Fairbairn, an Edinburgh bookseller, a period he described as 'a dreary, disgusting servitude, in which I wasted five of the best years of my life' (Nicolson, 18). At this time he also served in the Edinburgh Volunteers. In 1804 Black took employment as an assistant at Lackington, Allen & Co., the 'Temple of the Muses', in Finsbury, London, and stayed there for over two years. He was subjected to a thorough drilling, the hardships of which he would recount to his own employees in later life.

Having returned to Edinburgh, Black married Isabella, daughter of James Tait, an Edinburgh builder, on 4 June 1817. Her brother, William Tait (1793–1864), was later well known as the publisher of *Tait's Edinburgh Magazine*. Adam and Isabella had four sons and five daughters who lived to survive their father. Black set up in business on his own account, and by the time he moved his shop into the old General Post Office premises on the North Bridge in 1823 he had begun to be recognized as one of the principal booksellers in Edinburgh. He took his nephew, Charles Black, into partnership, thereby establishing the house of A. and C. Black. With the collapse of Archibald Constable & Co. in 1827 and Black's acquisition from them of the copyright to the *Encyclopaedia Britannica*, he moved his business into the first rank of publishers. In addition A. and C. Black became the Edinburgh distributing agents

Adam Black (1784–1874), by unknown engraver, pubd 1885

of the important whig–Liberal periodical the *Edinburgh Review*. In 1830 he began to issue the seventh edition of the *Encyclopaedia*, and by 1837 the firm of A. and C. Black was its sole proprietor. An eighth edition was completed in 1861 and a ninth was in preparation at the time of his death. Black also contributed articles to the *Encyclopaedia*. His firm consolidated its position still further in 1851 by purchasing the remainder of the copyright on Sir Walter Scott's works. These were then published in a variety of editions, the popular sixpenny edition of Scott's novels with particular success. At this time also Black moved to new, extensive premises on the other side of the North Bridge.

Role in Liberal politics in Edinburgh From the period of his return from London, and at some risk at that time to his business prospects, Black was also active as a Liberal reformer in Edinburgh politics. His initial power-base was the Edinburgh Merchant Company, of which he served two terms as assistant and one, from 1831, as master. Black was consulted by the Parliament House whigs on whether the mercantile community of the city would support the reformers' landmark protest meeting eventually held in the Pantheon in December 1820. In 1822 he moved and carried a series of resolutions in the Merchant Company welcoming Lord Advocate William Rae's proposals to open up the system of burgh administration but at the same time attacking them for not addressing the root of the problem. This early example shows the direction his political activity was to take, namely that of pressing for limited constitutional and civil reform.

In addition to pressure for burgh reform Black was

instrumental in getting the Merchant Company to petition against the Test and Corporation Acts, which imposed civil disabilities on religious dissenters. Black was himself a prominent voluntary dissenter and later a member of the Voluntary Church Association for the diffusion of voluntary principles. He also used his influence with the Merchant Company to support the movement for city improvement which resulted in the development of the George IV Bridge and Johnston Terrace areas round the castle. Black was a governor of the Merchant Maiden Hospital and was active in the 1820s in various positions, including that of chairman, in the Edinburgh chamber of commerce.

With this record of public activity behind him Black went on to take a prominent role in the demonstrations called in Edinburgh to press for parliamentary reform in 1831 and 1832. He was convener of the first Liberal committee set up after the passage of the Reform Bill to support the two whig candidates for Edinburgh, Francis Jeffrey and James Abercromby, at the election of December 1832. In 1833 Black was himself elected to the reformed town council and became city treasurer. Finding the city bankrupt and deeply in debt, in the following three years he laid the basis of the settlement with the city's creditors which was completed by his successor as treasurer, Duncan McLaren. Black refused to stand for re-election in 1836, but by late 1840 he was again a member and was then the loser in a very bitter contest for the provostship with Sir James Forrest, also a Liberal. The campaign against Black was explicitly based on objections to his voluntary religious beliefs, and his eventual election as lord provost in 1843, in the changed religious atmosphere immediately surrounding the Disruption of that year, was seen as a triumph for unsectarian principles. He was re-elected in 1846 and left office and the council in 1848, before the end of his second term. At this time he declined the offer of a knighthood. Black himself described his main achievement as demonstrating that the interests of the whole community could be safely entrusted to a voluntary dissenter.

Other public activities and parliamentary career Overlapping with these years during which he held civic office, Black was also active in other roles. In 1839 he became a director of the Edinburgh Zoological Gardens Association and was elected the first president of the Philosophical Institution at its foundation in 1845. As provost he was an *ex officio* director of the Edinburgh Water Company, and as a leading shareholder in the Edinburgh and Leith Gas Company he was its chairman for a period from 1846. His spirit of religious tolerance found expression in his chairmanship from 1846 to 1848 of the Edinburgh Cemetery Company, which was set up to facilitate Sunday burials, especially important to working people, in the face of opposition from the sabbatarian party.

Adam Black owes his significance beyond his contribution to the development of reformed municipal government in Edinburgh to his involvement with the parliamentary politics of the city. His position as link man

between leading whig lawyers and the business community in Edinburgh was enhanced by the contacts he formed with nationally prominent figures, especially whigs, through being agent for the *Edinburgh Review* and publisher of the *Encyclopaedia Britannica*.

One of these was T. B. Macaulay, whose candidature for the city at a by-election in 1839 Black suggested to the Liberal committee. For the next eight years Black was the major channel of communication between Macaulay and his constituency. Seen through the eyes of Duncan McLaren it was at this time in the early 1840s that Black chose to remain true to his whig roots, especially on the subject of corn law repeal, and began to find himself at odds with more 'advanced' Liberals. Although personally in favour of immediate and total repeal, Black, unlike McLaren, remained loyal to whigs such as Macaulay, who were trying to find a compromise based on a fixed duty. A further source of division between Black and more radical Liberals and voluntary dissenters was his opposition to attempts to repeal the grant to the Roman Catholic college at Maynooth in Ireland. This issue had been made into a *cause célèbre* by the Peel government's decision to increase the grant and make it permanent in 1845. Black's position was that it was unfair to select this particular grant for withdrawal while public money was still given to other religious institutions.

At the general election of 1847 Black gave public expression to his mortification at Macaulay's defeat in Edinburgh. This result was in large measure caused by Macaulay's positions, similar to those of Black, on issues such as corn law repeal and Maynooth. At the next general election (1852) Black took the lead in getting Macaulay again returned for Edinburgh, a candidacy which Macaulay himself made a point of taking no step to further. The election also saw the defeat of Black's former town council colleague Duncan McLaren.

On Macaulay's retirement in early 1856 Black was elected in his place. Although his partner, Charles, had died in 1854, Black was now relieved of the pressure of running his business by the participation of his sons. He identified his support as coming from the whigs, the Roman Catholics (because of his position on Maynooth), the publicans, and the *Scotsman* newspaper. A combination of radical Liberals, Conservatives, and many voluntary dissenters (despite Black being one of their number) gathered round his opponent, Francis Brown-Douglas. One of the leaders of this anti-whig grouping was again Duncan McLaren.

Black was re-elected twice for Edinburgh, in 1857 and 1859, and sat in parliament until his defeat at the general election of 1865. Especially in the latter part of his parliamentary career he found himself more and more out of step with the increasingly powerful advanced or 'independent' Liberals in Edinburgh led by Duncan McLaren, who came top of the poll in 1865. To them, his earlier offences were compounded by his reluctance to further extend the franchise and a willingness to compromise on the still unsolved problem of the Edinburgh annuity tax.

Black was comfortable with the prevailing Palmerstonian unwillingness to engage in electoral reform. He voted against the Disraeli–Derby Reform Bill in 1859, against lowering the franchise to £6 as proposed in the Liberal government's bill of 1860, and more than once against Baines's Borough Franchise Bill. Black believed that the franchise was a duty to be exercised in the interests of others rather than a right. During the 1859 election he commented on the tyranny and oppression prevalent in some trades, which he implied made their members unfit to be electors. Together with his position on the franchise, these comments were held to have particularly offended new, mostly working-class electors who had come onto the register by 1865.

Black's acceptance of Lord Advocate Moncreiff's bill to reform the Edinburgh annuity tax was, in McLaren's opinion, even more important than the franchise question in bringing about his defeat. He had long been associated with the movement to abolish this tax, raised to support the city's established clergy. In the 1830s he had been recognized as an authority on the subject of ecclesiastical revenues in the city, and had produced a report which had provided ammunition for agitation against the tax. His brother-in-law, William Tait, though an established churchman, had been imprisoned for four days for non-payment. In 1860, however, Black had abandoned a bill of his own and with it the principle of total abolition, and had compromised on Moncreiff's which, while it lowered the tax, made it perpetual. In 1865 McLaren was therefore able to draw on the support of those who continued to press for the tax's total removal.

Black's parliamentary career was also marked by his interest in educational matters. He was partially successful in his attempt to ensure that the Scottish Universities Act of 1858 preserved the part played by the Edinburgh town council in the management of Edinburgh University. Untypically for a voluntary he supported the giving of state aid to the ragged schools. In 1864 he was appointed to the Argyll commission of inquiry into education in Scotland. For Black the 'religious difficulty' did not exist and he was consistently in favour of an unsectarian, national educational system.

Final years After his defeat Black continued to travel, visiting Spain and Wiesbaden, the latter for his health. He had also been in 1863 to Italy, where he met the pope. He continued to be interested in his own firm until his retirement in favour of his sons in 1870. Black also acted as chairman of the Edinburgh and Leith Shipping Company, and participated in the management of other companies, such as the Union Bank, in this period. When not attending to business he spent the greater part of his time at his country house at Prior Bank, near Melrose.

At eighty Black was variously described as having an elastic and wiry frame, good features marked by the effects of smallpox, and a firm nose and mouth, 'altogether the form and face of a strong man, physically and mentally, eminently healthy, capable, trustworthy' (Nicolson, 256). His strict religion, which included daily religious observances at home, was not at all marked by intolerance or sanctimoniousness. Black could relish a good joke.

Adam Black died at his Edinburgh home, 38 Drummond Place, on 24 January 1874, and was buried in the Warriston cemetery, Edinburgh, on 28 January. His wife survived him. Three years later a statue in his memory was placed in East Princes Street Gardens. This had been proposed in 1854 but turned down by Black himself on the grounds that statues should not be put up to those still alive. It is likely that the vein of shyness in his temperament played just as big a role as any such principle. Black may have seen himself as the link man, the facilitator, for the whigs in Edinburgh in their struggle to achieve moderate constitutional and civic reform. He himself, however, was a central figure in mid-nineteenth century Scottish politics whose political fate mirrored that of the whigs to whom he remained so loyal. In the vanguard of Liberalism up until the 1830s, he subsequently, by standing still and continuing to concentrate on the limited whig reform agenda of civil, religious, and commercial freedom, slowly found himself left behind as those such as Duncan McLaren moved on to forge an independent Liberalism. This drew strength from those interested in more franchise reform and involved in the Edinburgh trades union movement, people with whom Adam Black publicly said he was out of sympathy. He refused to 'bow popularly low' (*The Scotsman*, 26 Jan 1874) and, like Macaulay before him in 1847, paid the price electorally.

GORDON F. MILLAR

Sources A. Nicolson, ed., *Memoirs of Adam Black* (1885) · *The Scotsman* (26 Jan 1874) · *The Scotsman* (29 Jan 1874) · B. W. Crombie and W. S. Douglas, *Modern Athenians: a series of original portraits of memorable citizens of Edinburgh* (1882), 179–82 · J. B. Mackie, *The life and work of Duncan McLaren*, 2 vols. (1888) · J. D. Marwick, *A retrospect* (privately printed, Glasgow, 1905) · *The Times* (26 Jan 1874) · *Glasgow Herald* (26 Jan 1874) · *Men of the time* (1872), 107–8 · G. O. Trevelyan, *The life and letters of Lord Macaulay*, 2 vols. (1876); repr. in one vol. (1978) · WWBMP, 1.35 · J. Foster, *Members of parliament, Scotland … 1357–1882*, 2nd edn (privately printed, London, 1882), 28 · DNB · EdinR, 196 (1902), 275–318, esp. 291 · *Encyclopaedia Britannica*, 11th edn (1910–11), vol. 4, p. 18
Archives Mitchell L., Glas., Glasgow City Archives, corresp. with John Strang · NL Scot., corresp. with Henry Cockburn, MS 823 · U. Cal., Los Angeles, corresp. with Richard Cobden · U. St Andr., corresp. with James Forbes · U. Texas, corresp. with W. M. Thackeray
Likenesses J. W. Gordon, portrait, 1847–8, City Chambers, Edinburgh · B. W. Crombie, caricature, coloured etching, 1848, NPG · J. Hutchison, bronze statue, 1877, East Princes Street Gardens, Edinburgh · W. Stewart, lithograph, BM · chalk drawing, Scot. NPG · drawing, repro. in Crombie and Douglas, *Modern Athenians*, no. 48 · engraving, repro. in Nicolson, ed., *Memoirs of Adam Black* [see illus.] · photographic or drawing, repro. in Nicolson, ed., *Memoirs* · stipple and line engraving, NPG
Wealth at death £48,350 10s. 4d.: confirmation, 28 March 1874, NA Scot., SC 70/1/167/509–525

Black, Alexander (1789–1864), Free Church of Scotland minister and theologian, was born in Aberdeen on 18 January 1789, where his father was a gardener. Educated at the grammar school and at Marischal College, Aberdeen, Black's initial interest in medicine gave way to the study of divinity. Licensed by the presbytery of Aberdeen in February 1814, Black was at first assistant to Dr James Ross,

East Church, Aberdeen. He was a candidate for the divinity chair in King's College, Aberdeen, in 1817. When Duncan Mearns was preferred, Black succeeded him as minister of Tarves, Aberdeenshire, where he was ordained on 1 April 1818. He married, on 9 November 1826, Rachel (*d.* 1839/40), daughter of Alexander Booth, a merchant of Aberdeen; the couple had two sons and a daughter.

Black received appointment as professor of divinity in Marischal College in 1831, having received the degree of DD there in 1824. A formidable linguist, able to converse in nineteen languages and correspond in twelve, he was a natural choice as a member of a mission of inquiry to the Jews in 1839. His colleagues were Alexander Keith and two young ministers, R. M. McCheyne and A. A. Bonar. The rigours of travel in the Holy Land, exemplified by Black's fall from a camel, persuaded the senior members of the party to opt out of the later stages of the journey. Their return home, via the Danube, came to a halt at Pest in Hungary, where illness prostrated them. These mishaps were later seen as providential and led in time to the establishment of a mission to the Jews in Pest. However, misfortune had not finished with Black, who returned to Scotland to find his wife on her deathbed.

At the Disruption of 1843 Black adhered to the Free Church and was appointed professor of biblical exegesis in New College, Edinburgh, where he remained until his retirement in 1857. For whatever reason, his tenure at New College was deemed a disappointment: despite his prominent position Black was not subsequently included in the pantheon of Free Church ministers, *Disruption Worthies* (1881). It may have been that, as an obituary stated, 'The very fulness of his resources was the chief cause of his comparative unacceptability as a preacher and a professor' (*Aberdeen Journal*). Certainly, his considerable knowledge was not transmitted in any publication of note. In his final years Black occupied himself with the study of Chinese. He died at his home, 16 Claremont Crescent, Edinburgh, on 27 January 1864, after failing to recover from injuries received in a fall; he was buried in Warriston cemetery, Edinburgh, on 30 January.

LIONEL ALEXANDER RITCHIE

Sources *Aberdeen Journal* (3 Feb 1864) • *Free Church of Scotland Monthly Record*, new ser., 20 (March 1864) • *The Witness* (30 Jan 1864) • *Fasti Scot.* · A. A. Bonar and R. M. McCheyne, *Narrative of a mission of inquiry to the Jews from the Church of Scotland in 1839* (1842) • A. A. Bonar, *Memoir and remains of the Rev. Robert Murray McCheyne* (1844) • D. Brown, *Life of the late John Duncan LL.D.* (1872), 301–13 • H. Watt, *New College, Edinburgh: a centenary history* (1946) • DNB
Likenesses photograph, repro. in Watt, *New College, Edinburgh*
Wealth at death £4525 5s. 1d.: inventory, 9 June 1864, NA Scot., SC 70/1/121, 233

Black, Clementina Maria (1853–1922), political activist, suffragist, and writer, was born on 27 July 1853 in Brighton, the eldest girl in the family of five daughters and three sons of David Black, solicitor, town clerk, and coroner of Brighton, and his wife, Clara Maria (*d.* 1875/6), daughter of George *Patten, portrait painter to the prince consort. Educated at home, mainly by her mother, she became fluent in French and German.

When Clementina Black was twenty-two her mother

Clementina Maria Black (1853–1922), by unknown photographer, pubd 1912

died, leaving her to look after the family, including an invalid father. A teaching job added to her duties, but she began to write short stories. These were followed by her first novel, *A Sussex Idyll* (1877), and a three-volume novel, *Orlando* (1879). In the 1880s she and her sisters (one of whom was Constance *Garnett) moved to Fitzroy Street, London. Here she divided her time between private studies (which included work on social problems) at the British Museum Library, literary work, and lecturing on eighteenth-century literature. She began associating with both Marxist and Fabian intellectual socialists and was a friend of the Marx family.

Ill health forced Black abroad in 1885 and she returned to England to the Trafalgar Square riots of 1886. This event made her determined to become actively involved in social issues. She promoted the idea of a consumers' league, whose members would purchase only from firms paying decent wages, and advocated closer ties between trade union and co-operative societies. In 1886 she became secretary to the Women's Protective and Provident League (founded by Emma Patterson), and as a delegate to the 1888 Trades Union Congress initiated an equal pay resolution. She resigned in 1889 after becoming actively involved in the match girls' strike in London's East End. Convinced that a more radical, militant approach to women's trade unionism was needed, she became one of the founders of the Women's Trade Union Association (WTUA) in the East End in 1889, supported by John Burns and H. H. Champion, well-known socialists, and served as secretary until 1891.

The failure of the WTUA in 1894 led to the formation of the Women's Industrial Council (WIC), a new kind of organization which sent out its mainly middle-class women investigators to see for themselves conditions of working women, after which they wrote reports in an attempt to influence public opinion and government policy. Clementina Black became editor of its journal, the *Women's Industrial News*, in 1895 and later president of the WIC. She became increasingly active as a speaker and writer on problems facing women workers. She saw low pay as the root of the problem, and from 1896 began to campaign for a legal minimum wage. She was concerned with the plight of women home workers (usually widows or wives of casual labourers), especially in the tailoring trade in east and south London. She was on the executive committee of the National Anti-Sweating League and one of the organizers of the *Daily News* sweated industries exhibition of 1906. Her two books, *Sweated Industry and the Minimum Wage* (1907) and *Makers of our Clothes: a Case for Trade Boards* (which she wrote jointly with C. Meyer, 1909) were powerful works of propaganda. The Trade Boards Act was passed in 1909, but her stand on the legal minimum wage caused a split within the WIC and she resigned, though later returned as its president. Her interest in improving conditions for working women remained, and she edited *Married Women's Work* (1915), the findings of the WIC's inquiry into the effect of industrial employment on married women. In 1918 she wrote on ways of improving housing and housekeeping so that women could be freed for employment.

A non-militant suffragist, Black inaugurated the suffrage declaration of 1906 which was signed by thousands. Representing the WIC, she was one of twenty-one distinguished women who met the prime minister (Asquith) in 1910 during the campaign for the Conciliation Bill which, if passed, would have allowed limited women's suffrage. She realized that, without the vote, women had no power to legislate against poor working and social conditions. She became one of the vice-presidents of the London Society for Women's Suffrage in 1913 and was acting editor of the *Common Cause*. She was a well-known author in her day, writing fiction, biographies, translations, and even plays for children. One novel, *An Agitator* (1894), was described by Eleanor Marx as a realistic account of the British working-class movement, but her other fiction avoided social concerns. A non-revolutionary socialist, she believed in legislative action. A deceptively fragile and refined appearance belied her dedication and untiring industry in the cause of justice for women. Her cheerful disposition, sympathy, and tact made her popular. In recognition of her endeavours on behalf of women, she was granted a civil-list pension of £75 a year in 1913.

Unmarried, Black took her niece Gertrude Speedwell, daughter of her brother Arthur, into her house when Arthur and his wife committed suicide, and brought her up herself. Clementina Black died at 22 Westmoreland Road, Barnes, Surrey, on 19 December 1922.

JANET E. GRENIER

Sources M. Cameron, 'Clementina Black: a character sketch', *Young Woman*, 1 (1892–3), 315–16 · L. Glage, *Clementina Black, a study in social history and literature* (1981) · E. Mappen, *Helping women at work: the Women's Industrial Council, 1889–1914* (1985) · L. P. Hume, *The National Union of Women's Suffrage Societies, 1897–1914* (1982) · A. J. R., ed., *The suffrage annual and women's who's who* (1913) · C. Collette, *For labour and for women: the Women's Labour League, 1906–1918* (1989) · *The Times* (20 Dec 1922) · *Daily Chronicle* [London] (20 Dec 1922) · *Westminster Gazette* (20 Dec 1922) · C. Tsuzuki, *The life of Eleanor Marx, 1855–1898* (1967) · b. cert.

Archives BLPES, Women's Industrial Council MSS · Trades Union Congress Library, London, Gertrude Tuckwell MSS

Likenesses photograph, pubd 1912, Women's Library [*see illus.*] · photograph, repro. in *Daily Chronicle*

Wealth at death £81 16s. 11d.: probate, 26 June 1923, CGPLA Eng. & Wales

Black, Sir Cyril Wilson (1902–1991), property developer and politician, was born on 8 April 1902 at 11 Langham Mansions, Kensington, London, one of four sons (three surviving) and two daughters of Robert Wilson Black (1871–1951), property developer, of 11 Langham Mansions, and his wife, Annie Louise (*b*. 1880), elder daughter of Lieutenant-Colonel Sir Jonathan North, mayor of Leicester in 1914–18, of Glebe Mount, Oadby, Leicester. Both parents were devout Baptists. His father was both assiduous and astute in building up a family fortune, which amounted to more than £2 million at his death.

Black's upbringing was austere; it would, indeed, be reasonable to call it severe. The house was teetotal, and nicotine was prohibited. Regular church attendance was mandatory. Striving for riches and success, however, was encouraged. Robert Black was not disposed to bestow on his son any financial advantages accruing from his own wealth. The one major monetary outlay he was prepared to make was on the boy's education, and it can reasonably be supposed that he was pleased when, eventually, Black followed him into the business of property development, having trained as a chartered surveyor. He must have been even more pleased when, before he was forty, his son had made himself a millionaire through his own unstinting efforts. Many youngsters might have rebelled against the strictness of this upbringing, but Black revelled in it and, to the end of his days, held fast to its principles. During the twenty years in which he served in the House of Commons—from 1950 to 1970—even his most virulent enemies (and he had many) could find no chink in his moral armour.

Black was educated at King's College School, and went on to train at the Royal Institute of Chartered Surveyors. He quickly—in his twenties—began to put his technical training to effective commercial use, and when he married (Dorothy) Joyce (*b*. 1908/9), daughter of Thomas Birkett, boot manufacturer, of Wigston Hall, Leicester, on 6 March 1930, he was a coming man in the property world. However, he was driven by much more than financial ambition. From his youth he threw himself into public work (which he listed as a recreation rather than as a vocation). He saw political activity as the best means of achieving moral ends. He began with local politics, and became a member of Wimbledon borough council in 1942, and was its mayor from 1945 to 1946 and 1946 to 1947. He became member of Surrey county council in 1943, was elected chairman from 1956 to 1959, and served until 1965. In that year he also became a member of Merton borough council, and was mayor of Merton from 1965 to 1966. His energy was titanic, and a résumé of his political career only hints at its strength. At one time he was a director of more than fifty companies, but still found time to give efficient devotion to his favourite causes: the advocacy of

Sir Cyril Wilson
Black (1902–1991),
by Walter Bird,
1959

temperance, the censorship of what he considered pornography, and the development of a morally uplifting educational system.

When Black entered the House of Commons in 1950, as Conservative MP for Wimbledon, allies and opponents alike found him completely immoveable on his chosen subjects. He was already prominent in the temperance movement and chairman of the Temperance Permanent Building Society. He had acquired a chain of alcohol-free hotels through a family company; when, in 1981, the directors decided to apply for a drinks licence, he resigned, and sold his shares. He was also, at various times, involved in the Boys' Brigade and the Girls' Brigade, a governor of a number of schools (including his own), a member of the South-West Metropolitan Regional Hospital Board, and an enthusiastic lay preacher.

In the House of Commons, however, Black met with virtually no success. He campaigned against the liberalization of divorce law, and the relaxation of licensing laws, and failed. He fought for the return of the birch as an instrument of criminal punishment, and for stricter control of immigration, but this latter subject had already been taken up by more formidable politicians. He was, however—paradoxical though it seemed to his critics—a keen supporter of the United Nations Association, and a governor of a Roman Catholic Ursuline convent in his constituency. There were, then, limits to his intolerance, and he was a man who strove mightily to do good. Nevertheless, he was not an easy man to like. His successful prosecution for libel of the *Socialist Leader*, for calling him a racist, and his unsuccessful attacks on the publication of *Lady Chatterley's Lover* and *Last Exit to Brooklyn*, set him firmly against the tide of his times. In private he could be a reasonable, if over-earnest, conversationalist. But, as he went about his multifarious activities, with a permanent half-sneer on his face, and as he thundered in public against what he called decadence, he was a voice calling in the lonely wilderness. The sole consolation he received, outside his own circles, was the knighthood bestowed upon him on Harold Macmillan's recommendation in 1959. He retired as MP for Wimbledon in 1970, although

he remained active in various causes thereafter. He died in Cheam, Surrey, on 29 October 1991; he was survived by his wife, two daughters, and a son. PATRICK COSGRAVE

Sources *The Times* (31 Oct 1991) · *The Independent* (2 Nov 1991) · *WWW* · Burke, *Peerage* · Burke, *Gen. GB* · Kelly, *Handbk* · b. cert. · m. cert. · personal knowledge (2004) · *CGPLA Eng. & Wales* (1992) **Likenesses** W. Bird, photograph, 1959, NPG [*see illus.*] · photograph, repro. in *The Times* · photograph, repro. in *The Independent* **Wealth at death** £1,600,226: probate, 1992, *CGPLA Eng. & Wales*

Black, David (*c.*1546–1603), Church of Scotland minister, was probably born in Perth, the son of Henry Black (*d.* before 1594), a burgess of the city. He matriculated as a student in St Salvator's College at the University of St Andrews in 1561, when he is likely to have been aged about fifteen. Although there is no record of his graduation as MA, he must have completed the full arts course over four years, as he was always given the title Mr. On completing his studies he followed the career of a schoolmaster in England, where he lived for about seventeen years, and where he was given rights of citizenship. In the early 1580s he was living with his wife, Katherine Prattie, in the parsonage of Kilkhampton in Cornwall, as the guest of the incumbent Eusebius Paget. The patronage of the parish was in the hands of Sir Richard Grenville, who was apparently briefly converted to puritanism by Paget and Black but who later turned against them. Paget, an eloquent preacher and writer, had before his presentation to Kilkhampton in 1580 been on one occasion deprived for nonconformity. In Black he found a kindred spirit.

On 9 November 1584 Black appeared before Bishop Woolton of Exeter, who was acting on behalf of the high commission witnesses. The bishop gave evidence that Black had, privately in Grenville's house and publicly in the church of Kilkhampton at the time of service, expounded the scriptures without ecclesiastical authority, conducted other religious services, and made accusations against the practices of the Church of England. Black was ordered to appear before the high commission in London on 26 November 1584. From the articles then put forward against him it appears that he had criticized the Book of Common Prayer, claimed that there ought not to be bishops in the Church of England, did not pray for the queen, and did not acknowledge her as the supreme head of the church. He was said to be 'a common inveygher against the state ecclesiasticall of this realme and the members therof' (Ritchie, 522). In 1583 Archbishop John Whitgift had launched a campaign against puritan clergy, requiring subscription to three articles, of which the second declared 'That the Book of Common Prayer and of ordering bishops, priests and deacons containeth nothing in it contrary to the word of God' (Collinson, 245). It was therefore unsurprising that Black should now consider returning to Scotland.

At this time a number of ministers also arrived in London who had fled from Scotland, following attempts by the government there to restore episcopacy and assert royal supremacy over the church. Among them was Black's contemporary at St Andrews University, Andrew Melville, who had recently been called before the privy council for alleged treasonable statements made in sermons and had been sentenced to imprisonment for declining the council's jurisdiction in the matter. It is reasonable to assume that Black met with Melville in London, and that together they discussed the possibility of Black's returning to Scotland. It is not known how Black was treated by the high commission, but on 13 May 1587 he signed a declaration undertaking to conform to the Church of England during his residence in England, and apologized for remarks he had made about the archbishop of Canterbury.

In 1590 Black, 'be the cairfull procurement' of Andrew Melville at the general assembly, was appointed minister of St Andrews (*Autobiography and Diary of … Melvill*, 293). On 11 November of that year he was unanimously chosen by the St Andrews kirk session as their pastor and minister. His settlement in St Andrews did not run smoothly. He found at the end of his first year that the work was too demanding for one minister and he withdrew from his charge. In April 1593 the general assembly required that he return and nominated Robert Wallace as his colleague. By 19 September 1593 Black and Wallace had accepted this decision and required that pastoral responsibilities be divided equally between them. Black gave early indication of his rigorous plans for the exercise of ecclesiastical discipline by requiring in this matter from the outset the full support of the magistrates. Emphasis was placed on eradicating fornication, on enforcing strict sabbath observance, and on providing adequately for the poor. As a member of presbytery Black exhibited a similar diligence in calling upon his non-resident ministerial brethren to return to their charges and to fulfil their responsibilities. His 'singular fidelitie and diligence in the ministrie' won for him the unstinted praise of like-minded colleagues (*Autobiography and Diary of … Melvill*, 293).

Not unexpectedly Black's emphasis on discipline made him enemies. He had a hard struggle with both the kirk session and the town council in the early years of his ministry to gain acceptance for his programme of moral reform, and in addition he incurred the ill will of individual citizens. One of those was William Balfour, who feared eviction from a house in the abbey grounds, which had been designated as a manse for Black. According to James Melvill, Balfour was one of a group of malcontents who reported to James VI 'calumnious informationes' against Black (*Autobiography and Diary of … Melvill*, 323), who was consequently summoned before the king for alleged defamatory remarks made from the pulpit against earlier monarchs. Black declined the king's jurisdiction in the matter, and maintained that he ought to answer for what he said from the pulpit in an ecclesiastical court. After a somewhat heated discussion and a private explanation by Black to James of what he had said about the latter's mother, the matter was resolved. Subsequently Black and Balfour were reconciled.

This incident in no way restricted Black's moral reforming activities, nor did it end the monitoring of his pulpit pronouncements. His reputation in England as an outspoken critic of the establishment there had apparently followed him to Scotland and his pulpit pronouncements were reported to English agents. At the end of October 1596, for instance, Black was reported to have declared that the queen of England was an atheist and that the religion professed in England was but a show. By 12 November James had taken action against Black, who was summoned to appear before the king and his council. A council of ministers objected to the king's action, but James was determined that Black should answer the charges against him, which included derogatory statements made against King James, his queen, and kings in general. At a time when relations between king and church were frequently strained, James was anxious to hold ministers responsible for the political content of their sermons, to reassure Queen Elizabeth of the strength and stability of his rule, and to restrict ministers' attempts to reserve matters that were in the first instance ecclesiastical for the jurisdiction of the church's courts. This last point was set out by Black and other ministers in a written declinature submitted before he appeared in front of king and council. In the presence of the council he again declined its authority, maintaining that he was answerable to a church court for what he said in the pulpit. In taking this position he was confident of the support of the commissioners of the general assembly. King James, however, regarded Black's stance as a flagrant challenge to his right to rule. He was determined to act quickly and decisively, well aware that his action against Black was being reported to Burghley.

Black was publicly summoned to appear again before the council. Most of those who had submitted written evidence described him 'as an unquiet and restless spirited man, a sower of sedition and discord … though one added that by some of the town he was reputed good, quiet and honest' (*CSP Scot.*, 1595–7, 382). But although Black had obtained favourable testimonials from the provost and bailies of St Andrews, from the kirk session, and from the university, the king and council declared themselves competent judges, as the accusations were treasonable and seditious, and on 9 December he was convicted and ordered to go into ward, 'in a part by north the North Water' (the area of Kincardine across the North Esk) at his own expense until the king had decided what to do with him (*Reg. PCS*, 1592–9, 340). Queen Elizabeth, who had been kept fully informed, wrote to James expressing her gratitude and her confidence in leaving to him the punishment of Black, whose name she disdained to mention.

Early in the new year there were repeated appeals to the king to allow Black to return to his charge, as he had complied with the king's wishes, but to no avail. In July 1597 he was debarred by the king from returning to St Andrews, but permitted to settle in a rural parish. That year he was translated and admitted to the parish of Arbirlot in Forfarshire, left vacant by the translation of George Gladstanes to St Andrews. On 15 May 1598 Black was presented to the vicarage by the crown. He died, according to Calderwood, on 12 January 1603 in Dundee; his friend John Johnston, writing from St Andrews to Caspar Waser in Zürich on 29 January 1603, gave 5 January as the date of his death. He was survived by his wife and their daughter.

Such colleagues as Andrew Melville, James Melvill, and John Johnston, who held Black in high esteem, wrote laudatory Latin verses in his memory. They were followed in their appreciation by presbyterian historians from the seventeenth to the nineteenth centuries. But other writers have stressed that what was central to this controversy was not so much the question of the truth of the accusations brought against David Black, as of the right of the king and council to be his judges, and the judges of what ministers expounded in their pulpits.

JAMES K. CAMERON

Sources CSP Scot., 1595–7 · Reg. PCS, 1st ser., vol. 5 · LPL, cartae miscellaneae, 12.16 · LPL, Fairhurst MSS, MS 3471, fol. 27 · The autobiography and diary of Mr James Melvill, ed. R. Pitcairn, Wodrow Society (1842) · D. H. Fleming, ed., Register of the minister, elders, and deacons of the Christian congregation of St Andrews, 2, Scottish History Society, 7 (1890) · T. Thomson, ed., Acts and proceedings of the general assemblies of the Kirk of Scotland, 3 pts, Bannatyne Club, 81 (1839–45), pts 2–3, p. 45 · D. Calderwood, The history of the Kirk of Scotland, ed. T. Thomson and D. Laing, 8 vols., Wodrow Society, 7 (1842–9), vols. 5–6 · J. Row, The history of the Kirk of Scotland, from the year 1558 to August 1637, ed. D. Laing, Wodrow Society, 4 (1842) · The Warrender papers, ed. A. I. Cameron, 2, Scottish History Society, 3rd ser., 19 (1932) · C. I. A. Ritchie, 'Sir Richard Grenville and the puritans', EngHR, 77 (1962), 518–23 · P. Collinson, The Elizabethan puritan movement (1967) · T. M'Crie, The life of Andrew Melville, new edn (1856) · A. R. Macdonald, The Jacobean kirk, 1567–1625: sovereignty, polity and liturgy (1998) · Fasti Scot. · J. M. Anderson, ed., Early records of the University of St Andrews, Scottish History Society, 3rd ser., 8 (1926) · Letters of John Johnston, c.1565–1611 and Robert Howie, c.1565–c.1645, ed. J. K. Cameron (1963)

Archives LPL

Wealth at death had inherited land from father: act book of the commissariot of St Andrews, 18 July 1594, quoted M'Crie, Life of Andrew Melville, 443

Black, Dora Winifred. See Russell, Dora Winifred (1894–1986).

Black, Edward (1900–1948), film producer, was born on 18 August 1900 at 90 Hensham Road, Birmingham, one of three sons of George Black, then a house-painter, and his wife, Mary Davies. His father, subsequently an actor and stage carpenter, gave up his job as property master at the Theatre Royal, Birmingham, to run a hand-cranked children's roundabout, a touring waxworks, and then a cinematograph film show. In 1905 he rented a Presbyterian chapel in Sunderland and turned it into the Monkwearmouth Picture Hall, one of the first permanent cinemas in Britain. When George Black died in 1910 he had eight cinemas in operation and Edward was able to help his brothers, including George *Black, to run the expanding circuit.

In 1928 the Black brothers' cinemas were taken over by the General Theatre Corporation, which was itself quickly swallowed by the Gaumont-British Picture Corporation. Black was employed as a circuit manager but in 1930 he switched to the production side of the corporation, becoming assistant production manager at the Gainsborough studios in Islington. By 1936 he had become producer in chief, responsible for the production of around six films a year. The following year, the main Gaumont-British studio at Lime Grove, Shepherd's Bush, which was making heavy losses, was closed down, but Black's efficient Gainsborough unit continued to operate, turning out popular comedies like Oh Mr Porter (1937) and thrillers such as The Lady Vanishes (1938). When war broke out in September 1939, the Islington studio—a converted power station with a huge chimney—was considered too vulnerable to German bombs and Black moved the Gainsborough team into Lime Grove. There he produced highly successful films such as Millions Like Us (1943) and The Man in Grey (1943).

Black's strategy was to build up a stable of stars and to put out a balanced production programme consisting of comedies, musicals, melodramas, thrillers, and serious war films. However, the phenomenal success of The Man in Grey in 1943 destroyed the power balance at the studio. The nominal head of production at Gainsborough, Maurice Ostrer, was a director of Gaumont-British and the brother of its chairman, Isidore Ostrer (though by 1943 the company was in the process of being transferred to the Rank Organisation). Maurice Ostrer decided that the success of The Man in Grey proved that Gainsborough had hit on a winning formula and henceforth the studio should concentrate entirely on costume melodrama. Black disagreed and when he was overruled, left to act as a producer for Alexander Korda.

Black's tenacity was tested to the limit in producing Korda's unwieldy historical epic, Bonnie Prince Charlie (1948), and he died of lung cancer on 30 November 1948 at his home, Flat 60, Fairacres, Roehampton, Putney. He was only forty-eight. His widow, Frances Clementine Black, survived him. Together the couple had two daughters. An indefatigable worker, Black was respected by actors, writers, directors, and technicians. He fostered the careers of Margaret Lockwood, Phyllis Calvert, Michael Redgrave, Stewart Granger, and James Mason, giving them the opportunity to develop as popular British film stars. He also encouraged the development of a talented scriptwriting team, ensuring that Gainsborough films were based on original scripts rather than adaptations of novels and stage plays. James Mason, who regarded producers as his natural enemies, made an exception for Black, whom he respected and saw as largely responsible for the success of Gainsborough as a studio. Sidney Gilliat, who worked under Black as scriptwriter and director, pointed out that he had 'the longest and most financially successful run any producer in Britain has ever had' (Brown, 112). Black staunchly protected Gilliat from studio politics while he was making his first film as a solo director, Waterloo Road (1944). Gilliat admired his unflappability and described him as 'a man to go tiger shooting with' (ibid., 111). He was the sort of efficient but imaginative producer the British film industry sorely needed.

ROBERT MURPHY

Sources O. Baldwin, 'These people make British pictures: Edward Black', Picturegoer (26 Aug 1939), 12–13 · G. Brown, Launder and Gilliat (1977) · A. Wood, Mr Rank: a study of J. Arthur Rank and British films (1952) · R. Murphy and S. Aspinall, eds., Gainsborough melodrama (1983) · J. Mason, Before I forget (1981) · CGPLA Eng. & Wales (1949) · b. cert. · d. cert.

Wealth at death £80,577 8s. 3d.: probate, 5 April 1949, CGPLA Eng. & Wales

Black, George (1890–1945), theatre manager and impresario, was born on 20 April 1890 at 3 Court, 7 Sutton Street, Birmingham, one of three sons of George Black, then a house-painter, and his wife, Mary Davies. In the late 1890s his father gave up a post as property master at the Theatre Royal, Birmingham, to tour the fairgrounds with a waxworks show, and George's first job was to collect the admission money. In 1905 the waxworks were exchanged for one of Robert Paul's Animatographs, an early cinema projector. Rather than touring, Black senior decided to settle down in Sunderland, his home town, turning a deconsecrated chapel into the Monkwearmouth Picture Hall, one of the first permanent cinemas in Britain. George worked the projector and sang songs in between the shows. The cinema prospered and more were bought. His father died in 1910 but George and his brothers Alfred and Edward *Black built up a circuit of thirteen cinemas. In 1919 they sold them for £280,000 but immediately set about establishing another circuit. In 1928 this too was sold, to Sir Walter Gibbons's conglomerate, the General Theatre Corporation (GTC), but George insisted on being given a seat on the board of directors. By the end of the year GTC had been swallowed by a rival, the Gaumont-British Picture Corporation, and Black was the only one of the original directors to retain his position. He was given charge of GTC's non-cinema interests—twelve provincial music-halls and the London Palladium.

With the support of Val *Parnell, a young showman who had worked as a booker for the London Theatres of Variety circuit, which had also been taken over by GTC, Black sought to revive music-hall as a popular form of entertainment. He argued that there was still a demand for live entertainment but that people were deserting the music-halls because they were dirty, old-fashioned, and badly run. He showed how the trend might be reversed by producing imaginative and lavishly mounted variety programmes at the London Palladium which filled the 2200 seat theatre to capacity. In November 1932 he expanded his operations when Gaumont-British bought a controlling interest in Moss Empires, the largest surviving circuit of music-halls. Black was able to combine his GTC halls with the thirty-odd Moss Empires—which included the Leicester Square Hippodrome and the Holborn Empire. This meant that the London Palladium was at the apex of a substantial circuit of live entertainment venues.

The Crazy Gang, the mainstay of the Palladium between 1932 and 1940, was essentially the brainchild of Val Parnell, but it was the powerful personality of George Black that managed to exert a measure of discipline over this anarchic team of zany comedians whose practical jokes often threatened to disrupt the smooth running of the Palladium. During the war, Black evolved a different strategy for the Palladium, presenting shows such as *Garrison Theatre* and *Happy and Glorious* designed to fit the different phases of the war. *Happy and Glorious*, starring Tommy Trinder, was the longest lasting show in the Palladium's history, and was still running early in 1945 at the time of Black's death.

George Black was married to Hannah Mary Gibson, known as May Gibson, an actress who appeared in *Dick Whittington* at the Palladium in 1914, long before Black's involvement with the hall. They had two sons, George and Alfred, and a daughter, Pauline Mary. The sons followed in their father's footsteps as theatrical impresarios, though they were also involved in film production and in the setting up of Tyne Tees Television.

A man of decided views, George Black was once described (by lyric writer Henry Purcell) as 'a virile hurricane blowing across the stage, sweeping away all nonsense' (Bevan, 83). He was an outspoken critic of theatrical agents for their failure to foster new talent, and also of the BBC, which he regarded as a parasite sucking away his artists and his audiences. Nevertheless, he made few enemies and is generally regarded, along with C. B. Cochran, as one of the last great showmen committed to live entertainment. Black died at 40 Upper Grosvenor Street, London, on 4 March 1945.   ROBERT MURPHY

Sources I. Bevan, *Top of the bill: the story of the London Palladium* (1952) · P. Pilton, *Every night at the London Palladium* (1976) · G. J. Mellor, *The northern music hall* (1970) · *Kinematograph Weekly* (26 Jan 1928), 37 · *Kinematograph Weekly* (22 March 1928), 78 · *Kinematograph Weekly* (17 May 1928), 48 · *Kinematograph Weekly* (13 Sept 1928), 75 · *Kinematograph Weekly* (17 Nov 1932), 32 · *Motion Picture Herald* (10 March 1945) · b. cert. · d. cert. · CGPLA Eng. & Wales (1945) · will, proved, Durham, 9 July 1945

Wealth at death £160,653 6s. 10d.: probate, 9 July 1945, CGPLA Eng. & Wales

Black, Sir Harold (1914–1981), civil servant, was born at 10 Burmah Street, Belfast, on 9 April 1914, the elder son of Alexander Black (1879–1946), a clerk and warehouseman in a local linen business and later a company director, and his wife, Emily Adelaide Cordner (1883–1949). He was educated at St Jude's public elementary school in his native city, before leaving it in September 1927 to enter one of the province's leading grammar schools, the Royal Belfast Academical Institution (well known locally as Inst).

On completing his education at Inst in April 1933 Black sought to obtain, like so many young Ulstermen of that generation, a foothold in a secure career. He first competed for, and was offered, a position in the Northern Bank, but opted instead to take up a place in the Northern Ireland civil service, having obtained ninth place in the clerical grade examination of 1934. He married on 4 September 1940 Margaret Saxton (1909–1991), with whom he had a son and a daughter.

Black rose steadily but unobtrusively through the ranks of the service, and with his appointment as assistant secretary to the cabinet in 1959 he moved into a post right at the centre of affairs. Although he left the cabinet office temporarily in 1963 on the appointment of Terence O'Neill as prime minister, gaining wider experience as director of establishments in the ministry of finance, he returned to Stormont Castle in 1965 to succeed Sir Cecil Bateman as secretary to the cabinet and clerk of the privy council. Thereafter he was to be a key adviser to the last three prime ministers of Northern Ireland, Terence O'Neill, James Chichester-Clark, and Brian Faulkner. Thus he accompanied Northern Ireland's political leaders to crucial and difficult encounters with British ministers at the Home Office and 10 Downing Street as events in his native province progressively overtook the provincial administration. After James Callaghan's crisis visit in October 1969 he served on the steering committee which co-ordinated the work of groups concerned with detailed changes in housing, policing, public administration, and other areas. At this difficult and testing time it was helpful to all concerned that Black had won the trust and confidence of Sir Philip Allen and other senior officials at the Home Office. Unflustered, reliable, and infinitely discreet, he was indeed during this crisis 'a man for all seasons'. He received a knighthood in 1970.

With the imposition of direct rule in March 1972 Black joined the head of the Northern Ireland civil service, Sir David Holden, and deputy secretary to the cabinet, Kenneth Bloomfield, in a small local team at Stormont Castle working closely with incoming Whitehall officials to ensure the continuing smooth government of the province. His last task as a civil servant was to prepare the way for the appointment of a devolved Northern Ireland executive in 1974; at that point, after almost forty years of service, he decided to leave to others the task of serving the new local administration (which was in any event to be short-lived).

Thereafter Black's work from 1976 to 1979 as chairman of an influential review group on legislation and services for children and young people in Northern Ireland showed that he had much to contribute to society in a private capacity. The Black report published in December 1979 established principles and objectives reflected to varying extents in subsequent developments. Black's relatively early death on 19 January 1981 of a coronary thrombosis at his home, 19 Rosepark, Dundonald, Belfast, was therefore a real loss to his native province. He was cremated, and his ashes were interred at St Elizabeth's parish church in Dundonald.

Short and dapper in appearance, and gazing out from behind serious spectacles, Black could too easily be summed up on brief acquaintance as a typical self-effacing bureaucrat. For those who knew him better, the rakish angle at which he wore his hat and the lightness of step surviving in a member of a celebrated school sprint relay team pointed to a much richer personality. Always interested in photography, he was to become in later years a passionate and enthusiastic yachtsman. On a celebratory occasion, and after one or two Irish 'jars' his personality would open like a flower, becoming almost skittish. His closest colleagues loved and admired him for his loyalty and generosity; for he always embraced blame and distributed credit to others.   KENNETH BLOOMFIELD

Sources WWW · *Belfast Telegraph* (21 Jan 1981) · *The Times* (22 Jan 1981) · private information [P. Black, son; R. J. S. Wilson, colleague] · personal knowledge (2004) · school records, Royal Belfast Academical Institution · civil registration and church records, Ulster Historical Foundation, Belfast
Wealth at death £90,397: probate, 12 March 1981, *CGPLA NIre.*

Black, James (1788/9–1867), physician, the son of William Black, merchant, and his wife, Janet, *née* Douglas, was born in Scotland and admitted a licentiate of the Royal

College of Surgeons of Edinburgh in 1808. He then entered the Royal Navy and at the end of the Napoleonic wars retired on half pay. After beginning practice at Newton Stewart, he shortly afterwards moved to Bolton, where he lived until 1839. From that date to 1848 he practised at Manchester. He then returned to Bolton, where he stayed until 1856. Black became MD at Glasgow in 1820; LRCS, London, in 1823; and FRCP in 1860. He was for some time physician to the Bolton Infirmary and Dispensary, and to the Manchester Union Hospital. While practising in Manchester he also lectured on forensic medicine at the Royal School of Medicine. He was sometime president of the Manchester Geological Society, and he was an original member of the British Association (1831); he was also elected FGS (1838) and FRSE (1857).

Black wrote a number of medical works, and also published several papers on geological subjects and antiquarian matters. In 1837 he published in the *Transactions of the Provincial Medical and Surgical Association* a paper entitled 'A medico-topographical, geological, and statistical sketch of Bolton and its neighbourhood'. On the establishment of a free library in Bolton, Black was chosen as a member of its committee and he published *A few words in aid of literature and science, on the occasion of opening the public library, Bolton* (1853).

Black, who was married to Jane Galt, eventually moved to Edinburgh, where he died at his home, 2 George Square, on 30 April 1867, aged seventy-eight; he was survived by his wife.   C. W. SUTTON, *rev.* PATRICK WALLIS

Sources W. I. Addison, *A roll of graduates of the University of Glasgow from 31st December 1727 to 31st December 1897* (1898) · Munk, *Roll* · P. A. Whittle, *Bolton-le-Moors and the townships in the parish* (1855) · *GM*, 4th ser., 3 (1867), 826 · *BMJ* (25 May 1867) · *Proceedings of the Geological Society* (1868), 38 · Boase, *Mod. Eng. biog.* · d. cert.

Black, John (*d.* 1566), Dominican friar, was a member of a prominent Aberdeen family. He was procurator of the Aberdeen Blackfriars between 1544 and 1550, before becoming preacher to Archbishop Hamilton of St Andrews and confessor to Mary, queen of Scots. During the 1550s he was an apologist for Roman Catholicism and was associated with a group of Catholic reformers within the Scottish church. In 1559 he taught theology in St Andrews. In Edinburgh in 1561 he disputed with John Willock, a renegade Dominican friar, on transubstantiation and the real presence in the eucharist. In August 1561 Black was attached to the queen's household and officiated in her private chapel at Holyrood. He acted as a channel of communication between the queen and certain conservative Edinburgh burgesses, and may have facilitated secret contacts between Mary and her supporters outside Scotland.

Black was regarded as a dangerous Catholic influence. A campaign of slander alleging fornication was mounted against him in Edinburgh, and in February 1566 he was seriously assaulted by Edinburgh men who were subsequently implicated in the murder of David Riccio. Simultaneous rumours of association between Black and Riccio, and of the promotion of a Catholic revival planned by the queen, are given credit by Black's own murder on the same night as Riccio, on 9 March 1566. Black was credited in the eighteenth century with the authorship of *De reali praesentia corporis Christi in sacramento altaris tractatus*; *Acta colloquii sui cum Johanne Willoxio impio apostata collega Johannis Knoxii*; *Monitorium ad apostatas*; and *Conciones et piissima*. These works are not known to survive.

ALLAN WHITE

Sources D. McRoberts, ed., *Essays on the Scottish Reformation, 1513–1625* (1962), 195, 199, 201, 316, 391–2 · J. Durkan, 'Critical review of John Knox', in *John Knox's History of the Reformation in Scotland*, ed. W. C. Dickinson, 2 vols. (1949) · J. Durkan, 'John Knox's *History of the Reformation in Scotland*', *Innes Review*, 1 (1950), 158–61 [review] · J. Durkan and A. Ross, 'Early Scottish libraries', *Innes Review*, 9 (1958), 5–167, esp. 76 · burgh court books, City Archives, Aberdeen, no. 17, 239; no. 20, 346 · J. D. Marwick, ed., *Extracts from the records of the burgh of Edinburgh, AD 1557–1571*, [3], Scottish Burgh RS, 4 (1875), 133 · R. Pitcairn, ed., *Ancient criminal trials in Scotland*, 1, Bannatyne Club, 42 (1833), pt 1, p. 475 · H. Robinson, ed. and trans., *The Zurich letters, comprising the correspondence of several English bishops and others with some of the Helvetian reformers, during the early part of the reign of Queen Elizabeth*, 1, Parker Society, 7 (1842), 99 · CSP Scot., 1588–93, 267 · M. Lynch, *Edinburgh and the Reformation* (1981), 37, 76, 99, 114–15, 175–6 · J. Quétif and J. Echard, *Scriptores ordinis praedicatorum recensiti*, 2 (Paris, 1721), 182 · A. Ross, 'Some notes on the religious orders in pre-Reformation Scotland', *Essays on the Scottish Reformation, 1513–1625*, ed. D. McRoberts (1962), 185–244 · J. Durkan, 'The cultural background in sixteenth-century Scotland', *Essays on the Scottish Reformation, 1513–1625*, ed. D. McRoberts (1962) · A. Ross, 'Reformation and repression', *Essays on the Scottish Reformation, 1513–1625*, ed. D. McRoberts (1962), 371–414

Black, John (1783–1855), journalist and newspaper editor, was born on 7 November 1783 in a poor cottage on a farm called Burnhouses, 4 miles north of Duns in Berwickshire. His father, Ebenezer Black, had been a pedlar in Perthshire, but in the decline of life he accepted employment at Burnhouses, and married Janet Gray, another worker on the farm. Four years after the marriage Janet was left a widow with one daughter and a son, John, and before the boy reached the age of twelve, his mother and sister had died. He was taken in by his mother's brother John Gray, a labourer on the same farm, who sent him to the parish school at Duns. Black gained there a knowledge of English, Latin, and Greek. He made many friends at Duns, among them James Gray, poet and missionary, and James Cleghorn, actuary. At the age of thirteen Black was articled by his uncle to Mr Turnbull, a writer of Duns, with whom he remained until 1800. During this time he borrowed extensively from the subscription library in the town, and formed a very creditable collection of his own, beginning the habit of book collecting that was to become so important in his adult life. He accepted a well-paid clerkship in the branch bank of the British Linen Company, but was obliged to leave the town on account of a practical joke played upon one of the 'respectabilities'.

Black found a situation in Edinburgh in the office of Mr Selkrig, an accountant, who allowed his clerk time to attend classes at the university. Black's official duties were strictly performed, his attendance in the lecture-rooms never failed, and he undertook any remunerative work that was offered, notably some translations from the German for Sir David Brewster's *Edinburgh Cyclopaedia*. He met with an intellectual companion in William Mudford, the

son of a London shopkeeper. *Cobbett's Weekly Political Register* was then a popular serial, and there Black and Mudford engaged in another 'battle of the books', the former defending ancient classical study, the latter insisting on the acquisition of modern learning as better.

In Edinburgh the hot-tempered Black is reported to have delivered a dozen challenges before he was thirty years old. His schoolfellow James Gray was now classical master at Edinburgh high school, and exercised a moderating influence upon him. In 1809 Black became engaged to a lady from Carlisle, but broke off the engagement when an expected increase of income did not materialize. This seemed to have had a demoralizing effect upon Black. He fell into low company and bad habits, quarrelled with his employer, from whom he was receiving a salary of £150 a year, and distressed his best friends.

William Mudford was then in London and editor of the *Universal Magazine*, to which Black contributed articles on the Italian drama and on German literature from 1807 to 1809. It was through Mudford's persuasion that Black left Edinburgh for London in 1810. Charles Mackay gives as a doubtful statement of Black himself, that he walked with a few pence in his pocket all the way from Berwickshire to London, subsisting on the hospitality of farmers. He carried a letter of introduction to Robert Hartley Cromek, engraver and publisher, who received him at once into his friendly home. Three months after his arrival in London Black was engaged as a reporter and translator of foreign correspondence by James Perry, who, with an assistant master at Charterhouse School named Gray, had in 1789 become the proprietor of the *Morning Chronicle*. Black's longer translations included *Humboldt's Political Essay on New Spain* (4 vols., 1811–12), *Travels in Norway and Lapland, by Leopold von Buch* (1813), *Berzelius on a System of Mineralogy*, and *Schlegel's Lectures on Dramatic Literature* (1814).

Black's first marriage, in December 1812, was to the mistress of a London friend, after a five-month courtship promoted and encouraged by the duplicitous pair. The union was extremely unhappy, as his wife made no pretence of love for him, and in the space of two months she had involved him in debt, sold some of his furniture, and clandestinely renewed acquaintance with her former lover. In February 1813 she left Black, and in 1814 he sought a divorce. An arrangement was made that she should go to Scotland and be domiciled there long enough to sue for a divorce on her petition. The project, however, failed, the proof of domicile of both parties not being deemed adequate by the court. Black, in full expectation of a divorce, had offered marriage to an old friend, a 'Miss Cromeck', possibly a relative of his former employer who became his housekeeper and bore the name of Mrs Black. The undivorced wife continued to extract money from her husband, and this persecution went on for many years. This episode in Black's life explains the disorganization of his official labours which led to a quarrel with James Perry, but due explanation being given, the breach was healed. In 1817 Perry's health was giving way, and the functions of editor gradually devolved on Black.

The *Morning Chronicle* was the most uncompromising of

all the opposition papers, and Black maintained its position, greatly assisted by the counsels of James Mill. John Stuart Mill wrote of Black:

> I have always considered Black as the first journalist who carried criticism & the spirit of reform into the details of English institutions. Those who are not old enough to remember those times can hardly believe what the state of public discussion then was. People now & then attacked the Constitution & the boroughmongers but none thought of censuring the law or the courts of justice & to say a word against the unpaid magistracy was a sort of blasphemy. Black was the writer who carried the warfare into these subjects … And by doing this he broke the spell. (Later Letters, 978–80)

Black's methods were also admired by Jeremy Bentham, who called him 'the greatest publicist yet produced in Great Britain' (Escott, 159). At the outset of his editorial career Black attracted much public attention by his determined condemnation of the conduct of the authorities in the Peterloo massacre (16 August 1819), and he was denigrated for this by Cobbett's *Register* as 'Doctor Black the feel-osopher'. In the matter of Queen Caroline's trial the *Chronicle* leaned to the unpopular side, deeming the queen guilty, and the circulation of the paper was greatly diminished.

In 1821 Perry died, and his executors sold for £42,000 the newspaper which thirty years before had been bought for £150. Black retained his post of editor, but the new proprietor, William Innell Clement, owner also of *The Observer* and of *Bell's Life*, had not the public spirit of his predecessor, and the paper began to decline in commercial terms. In 1834 it was again sold, for the sum of £16,500, to Sir John Easthope and two partners. *The Times* had outdistanced the *Chronicle* when, by shifting its politics in 1835 to support Sir Robert Peel's tory ministry, it caused great numbers of its whig subscribers to abandon it and support the *Chronicle*. This was a turn of events that greatly pleased Black, as his rivalry with Sterling of *The Times* had been intense, and may have suggested the battles of Pott and Slurk in *The Pickwick Papers*.

In November 1835 Black demonstrated that his hot temper and keen sense of honour had not been characteristics merely of his youth, as he fought a duel with John Arthur Roebuck. The latter had published a pamphlet in which cowardice was attributed to the editor of the *Chronicle*. Although shots were fired at the meeting, no one was injured.

When Lord Melbourne returned to office (8 April 1835) he found a useful ally and a congenial companion in Black, who supported the ministry with all his powers, and wrote some especially vigorous articles against Sir Robert Peel in 1839. During his next administration, Melbourne professed a desire to serve Black, who declined the offer on the ground that he 'lived happily on his income'. 'Then by — I envy you', said the peer, 'and you're the only man I ever did.' Black did not get on quite so well with Lord Palmerston. He once exasperated the busy foreign secretary by launching out into half an hour's dissertation on the ethnological peculiarities of the Finnish, when the business of the interview was simply to know what the government meant to do at a certain crisis in foreign

affairs. Lord Brougham was very intimate with 'Dear Doctor', as he styled Black, a title derisively applied by Cobbett, and so distasteful to Black.

It was Black's great pleasure to encourage the ambitions of the young writers around him, and among others those of Charles Dickens, who began his literary career as a reporter for the *Chronicle*. As late as the year of his death, Dickens remembered Black as 'my first hearty out-and-out appreciator' (Forster, 1.65).

Latterly there was thought to be a decline of energy in the management of the paper, and in 1843 Black received an intimation that his resignation would be accepted. Black, who was now sixty years old, had saved no money, and had to part with his beloved library of some 30,000 volumes. This product of a lifetime's book collecting had not always been augmented in the most straightforward manner. As James Grant puts it:

> it was an essential part of his creed that no book which he borrowed from a friend should ever be returned … The truth was that Mr Black never could part with any books that ever came into his possession,—no matter by what means, or under what circumstances. (Grant, 1.285–7)

His rooms had reputedly been so full of books that he and his second wife had occasionally been 'obliged to creep into bed at the end, both sides being blocked up with dusty volumes of divinity and politics' (*Men of the time*).

After the difficult auction of his library, friends and admirers rallied round Black and a sum, to which the proprietors of the *Chronicle* contributed, was raised sufficient to buy him an annuity of £150. His old friend Walter Coulson placed a comfortable cottage at Snodland, near Maidstone, at his disposal, and there Black passed the remaining twelve years of his life in the study of Greek, and in the practice of gardening. Black's Newfoundland dogs Cato and Plutus were as well known as himself; one of them rescued from the Thames a boy who subsequently attained a seat on the judicial bench. James Grant described Black in his latter years as having 'the blunt and bluff appearance of a thickset farmer … never seen in the streets without being accompanied by a large mastiff (? Newfoundland), and a robust stick in his hand'. He died on 15 June 1855 at Birling, near Town Malling in Kent.

ROBERT HARRISON, rev. M. CLARE LOUGHLIN-CHOW

Sources J. Grant, *The newspaper press: its origin, progress, and present position*, 3 vols. (1871–2) · C. Mackay, *Forty years' recollections of life, literature and public affairs, from 1830–1870*, 2 vols. (1877) · F. K. Hunt, *The fourth estate: contributions towards a history of newspapers, and of the liberty of the press*, 2 vols. (1850) · *Men of the time* (1885) · T. H. S. Escott, *Masters of English journalism* (1911) · Boase, *Mod. Eng. biog.* · Irving, *Scots.* · J. Forster, *The life of Charles Dickens*, ed. J. W. T. Ley (1928) · *ILN* (7 July 1855), 13–14 · *The later letters of John Stuart Mill, 1849–1873*, ed. F. E. Mineka and D. N. Lindley, 4 vols. (1972), vols. 14–17 of *The collected works of John Stuart Mill*, ed. J. M. Robson and others (1963–91), vol. 2 · bap. reg. Scot.

Likenesses W. H. Worthington, line engraving, pubd 1835, NPG · W. H. Worthington, oils, Scot. NPG

Black, Sir John Paul (1895–1965), motor vehicle manufacturer, was born on 10 February 1895 at Kingston upon Thames, the fourth son of John George Black, an official at the Public Record Office, and Ellan Elizabeth Marion, *née*

Smith. Black was educated locally and studied law, which brought out an aptitude for clear-cut decisions that was further developed in the First World War, during which he attained the rank of captain. In 1919 Black was recruited by the Hillman motor car marque in Coventry. He soon became joint managing director, with Spencer Wilks. Their success led to Hillman's being taken over by Rootes Ltd, a move which prompted both to resign in 1929.

Black joined the Standard Motor Company the same year, at the invitation of its founder, Reginald Maudslay. The marque was in dire financial straits and Black, who became general manager in 1930, set about restoring the company's fortunes. He ended the costly in-house manufacture of components and started to introduce mass production techniques. Black also brought in Edward Grinham from Humber as chief engineer; he was able to interpret Black's ideas for stylish and competitively priced models, especially in the Flying Standard series. By 1939 total car production had reached 50,000 units a year, making Standard Coventry's largest motor car manufacturer and earning the marque a place in the 'Big Six' league of leading British-based producers. Although Black did not officially become managing director until Maudslay's death in December 1934, he was effectively in command from the start.

In 1936 Standard was invited to join the Baldwin government's 'shadow' rearmament scheme, in which Black was an enthusiastic participant. He took charge of two aero-engine 'shadow' factories, the second of which, at Banner Lane, was the largest in Coventry. Black also succeeded Lord Austin, in 1940, in the chairmanship of the overseeing 'shadow' joint aero-engine committee. Standard's substantial contribution to the war effort totalled 20,000 Bristol Hercules aero-engines, 54,000 aero-carburettors, 417,000 cylinders, 1066 De Havilland Mosquito fighter–bombers (14 per cent of the total built), and numerous Oxford trainer aircraft. Black was rewarded with a knighthood in 1943.

Black was astute enough to recognize that Standard could benefit from its wartime activities. He successfully negotiated with the authorities to take over the two aero-engine 'shadow' factories. The Banner Lane facility provided an ideal venue for tractor production, with Black succeeding in his bid to link up with Harry Ferguson. The other component of Black's post-war strategy was the Vanguard motor car, which was a major contributor to the Attlee government's 'export or die' strategy between 1949 and 1951. But, as foreign competition intensified, the Vanguard's limitations in overseas conditions led to falling sales.

Black took Standard in another direction when, in 1944, at his urging, the bankrupt Triumph Motor Company was acquired. Seeking a more glamorous image in keeping with his personality, Black was behind the development of the TR sports car range, though he had left Standard before its success came. In many ways Black lost his touch after 1945. Before the war, he had adopted a vigorous anti-trade union stance, but after the war he completely reversed his labour policy by paying higher wages than was the norm in Coventry and handing greater influence to shop stewards. The inevitable outcome adversely affected Standard's competitive position and profits—the year before Black's resignation profits per unit were down to £13, under one-third of the amount made by Ford at Dagenham.

In fact, it was the tractor division which sustained Standard-Triumph. In 1948 more tractors were being produced than cars and by the early 1950s about 70 per cent of the profits were derived from Banner Lane.

But all was not well between Black and Ferguson; Black resented Ferguson's relegation of Standard-Triumph to contractor status rather than seeing the marque as an equal partner. At the heart of the bickering lay Black's jealousy at the huge personal rewards accruing to Ferguson. The latter tried to redress the balance by offering Black some shares in his company, but withdrew his proposal when Black insisted on a 50 per cent holding.

Black's decisions grew increasingly questionable and he eventually lost the confidence of the Standard-Triumph board. Black let Fisher and Ludlow, his company's main body suppliers, fall into the hands of the British Motor Corporation. Then, after the board agreed that the tractor contract would not be renewed following Ferguson's shock merger with the Canadian firm, Massey-Harris, Black concluded a twelve-year deal with the new Massey-Ferguson organization.

At Christmas 1953 Black became chairman of Standard-Triumph, but his position was far from secure. After he threatened to fire the revered Grinham, the board used the excuse of an accident Black was involved in as a passenger in a TR prototype as a convenient public excuse to force his resignation.

Outside his work, Black led the life of a playboy, being a keen golfer, yachtsman, and skier. In the 1930s he ordered a luxury company bungalow to be constructed at Harlech Bay in Wales, which was part of his resignation settlement. He bought a nearby farm and retired there to raise sheep and cattle. He was married twice, first, in 1921, to Daisy Hillman, daughter of William Hillman, owner of the Hillman Company. This marriage was dissolved after his wife left him and in 1943 he married again, his bride being Alison Joan Pears, daughter of the bishop of Hansworth. This second union produced three sons.

Black died suddenly on Christmas eve 1965 in Cheadle Royal Hospital in Cheshire. A memorial service in Coventry Cathedral was well attended by industrialists and shop-floor workers. Despite being reputedly the second highest paid executive in the motor industry when he resigned, Black left only £33,825, a sum which reflected his colourful and extravagant lifestyle.

STEVEN MOREWOOD

Sources S. Morewood, *Pioneers and inheritors: top management in the Coventry motor industry, 1896–1972* (1990) • b. cert. • *WWW* • K. Richardson, *Twentieth-century Coventry* (1972) • D. Thoms and T. Donnelly, *The motor car industry in Coventry since the 1890s* (1985) • J. R. Davy, *The Standard car, 1903–1963* (1967) • D. Thoms, *War, industry and society: the midlands, 1939–1945* (1989) • d. cert. • *Coventry Evening Telegraph* (29 Dec 1965)

Black, Joseph (1728–1799), chemist and physician, was born on 16 April 1728 in Bordeaux, the sixth of twelve children of John Black, an Ulsterman who was a factor in the wine trade, and his wife, Margaret Gordon (d. 1747). Black's brothers all became manufacturers or tradesmen of various kinds and all were unsuccessful in business. Black alone became an academic and, being financially astute, was often called upon to assist his impoverished siblings.

Early years and education Black was first educated at home but at the age of twelve he was sent to school in Belfast. In 1744 he went to Glasgow University to continue his education, entering (as was then usual) the arts class. After five years he was prevailed upon by his father to study a subject which would lead to a profession. He chose medicine, coming under the influence of William Cullen (1710–1790), who had been appointed to a lectureship in chemistry in 1747. Black did not, however, graduate from Glasgow, for in 1752 he transferred to Edinburgh University where medical teaching had a higher reputation and was better established. For graduation, a thesis had to be produced. Black took this work very seriously (not all students did) and he involved himself in chemical experiments on alkalis. Causticity, the property produced when alkaline earths such as chalk are roasted in a lime kiln, had been a matter of considerable discussion by medical professors at Edinburgh University. Because he did not wish to become embroiled in their specific quarrels, Black conducted his research on a substance similar to limestone, magnesia alba. He initially believed that this substance was simply another progenitor of quicklime and lime water and his research started with limited aspirations. It led, however, to a new theory of causticity and, later, to the first chemical identification of a gas. After heating a weighed quantity of the magnesia alba, Black noticed that the weight of the substance which remained was less than that of the original white powder. The weight lost could be replaced by reacting the product with potash in solution. The potash must have contained the gas which was driven off, which Black called fixed air. Black offered his thesis in 1754 and graduated MD. He then extended his work to experiments on limestone and he showed in a paper presented to the Philosophical Society in 1755 and published one year later in a refined paper that fixed air could be distinguished from the air which makes up the atmosphere. The series of experiments by which he arrived at this conclusion are the most important experiments which Black conducted. He confirmed the view of his teacher, Charles Alson, that when lime is produced by roasting chalk the caustic properties acquired by

Joseph Black (1728–1799), by Sir Henry Raeburn, c.1790

the former do not derive from the absorption of fiery particles from the heating process but are a property of the lime itself.

In experiments similar to those previously performed for his thesis, Black showed that both chalk and lime combine with the same quantity of acid to form salts, and that a given weight of chalk can be recovered by forming lime and then reacting this with a solution of potash. The explanation is the same in both cases: the lime combines with air contained in the alkali. He then considered a paradox. Lime in solution should combine with air dissolved in water to form a small amount of chalk as an insoluble precipitate, but this does not happen; one explanation might be that on solution of the lime, the air might be driven off. Black tested this by placing two vessels under a bell jar, then reducing the pressure with an air pump. He observed that the same quantity of air bubbles off from both liquids. Clearly this explanation is not tenable. The air in the lime solution was not the sort which formed a chalk precipitate. This 'fixed' air and atmospheric air are not chemically the same. Black was the first to show, decisively, that gases can be differentiated in the same way as can solids and liquids.

Glasgow, 1756–1766, and early teaching The elderly and poorly regarded Edinburgh professor of chemistry, Andrew Plummer, died in 1756 and Black's former Glasgow teacher, Cullen, was appointed in his place. This allowed Black to apply for the Glasgow lectureship. He was successful and later he was elevated to the title of professor. His main research interests in Glasgow were conducted on the properties of heat, interests probably inherited from Cullen's own work. Black considered the phenomenon of heat transfer to or from a body on liquefaction or solidification, evaporation or condensation, which he noticed could occur without a change in temperature being registered on a thermometer. He had been intrigued that when snow melts to form ice it does so over a period of time, not instantaneously. Black introduced the term 'latent heat', that being the quantity of heat which needed to be supplied to the snow before it would melt. He also discovered that different bodies have different capacities for heat: when equal volumes of mercury and water at different temperatures were mixed, the temperature of the mixture at equilibrium was found to be closer to the initial temperature of the water than that of the mercury. This led to a concept of 'specific heat'. Black never published his findings on heat, though he presented some of the results to the Literary Society in Glasgow in 1762 and he taught his ideas to his students throughout his long teaching career.

Also working on heat experiments at Glasgow, though apparently somewhat independently, was James Watt (1736–1819), then mathematical instrument maker to the university. The two men became lifelong friends and Watt was able to supply Black with furnishings for his laboratory. Black formally formed a partnership with Watt, along with Alexander Wilson (1714–1786), a typefounder who later became professor of astronomy. Black was to help finance Watt's early endeavours at Glasgow, debts which were not repaid for several years. From 1766, when Black moved to Edinburgh, they were never again to live in the same place but kept up a lively and informative correspondence.

Black's reputation as an inspired teacher of chemistry began to grow in his early years at Glasgow and later at Edinburgh, attracting numbers of foreign students to undertake courses. Although formally part of the medical curriculum, many more students attended the lectures than ever intended to graduate in medicine. Chemistry was a rapidly developing subject and Black's audience included many who wanted to experience the intellectual stimulation which it provided. A significant proportion had not even matriculated; all that was necessary was to pay the 3 guinea fee for the mid-November to mid-May course comprising about 120 lectures. At Edinburgh, only about 20 per cent of those following medical lectures would graduate as doctors of medicine. Black did not vary the basic structure of the lecture series throughout his teaching career. Introductory lectures consisted of definitions and an outline history of chemistry. Following this there were four sections: the general effects of heat (expansion, fluidity, and inflammation); the general effects of mixture; chemical apparatus; and the 'chemical history' of bodies. This last, and largest, section was divided into salts, earths, inflammable substances, metals, and waters. Though the content of the lectures was to some extent kept up to date by intelligence provided by Black's wide circle of correspondents and his own reading, the course must have seemed to be very dated by the

time he retired. Nevertheless, his reputation as an accomplished lecturer, combined with his skill at performing lecture demonstrations, did not dim even when he was close to retirement. The lectures were published after Black's death (as well as the British edition there were German and American ones) in a somewhat restructured form, the editor being John Robison, professor of natural philosophy at Edinburgh. Robison initially considered his task as an act of piety, though he became disillusioned before long with Black's outmoded approach.

Chemical consultancy After he had taught for only a few years at Glasgow efforts were made to attract Black back to Edinburgh. In a complex series of moves which involved his former teacher, Cullen, the chair of medicine and chemistry was vacated and Black was appointed to it. Curiously, the move to Edinburgh marked the end of Black's researches into fundamental chemical concepts. It was not the end of his experimental work, however; it is clear that he spent considerable periods of time in his laboratory. His work was largely directed to investigations which would improve industrial processes and benefit public health. At Glasgow, he had provided metal analyses of minerals for landowners anxious to exploit their estates. This was all part of a drive towards 'improvement', a process which had started early in the eighteenth century in Scotland following the Act of Union of 1707. An early form of financial assistance had been made available from the board of trustees for manufactures in Scotland, established by the government, whereby an annual sum of money was set aside initially to encourage the coarse woollen industry. The scope of assistance was increased and from 1727 help was made available for the herring, linen, and woollen industries. Black and his colleagues were involved in proposals put to the board and in adjudicating proposals of others made to it. A particularly important commodity to Scotland was linen. A crisis had arisen in the 1750s when the price of the agent used for bleaching, caustic potash, rose sharply. The alternative, sour milk, was slow reacting and less effective. Black's colleague, the professor of materia medica, Francis Home, was awarded a premium by the board for proposing dilute sulphuric acid, though it was considered by many to have a destructive effect on the fabric. Black set out to discover cheaper ways of making caustic potash, and showed that kelp, a form of seaweed commonly found around Scottish islands, could be economically turned into the alkali. For this, he was awarded a premium in 1783. Somewhat earlier, Black had sought an alternative means of alkali production by chemical reaction. He had the idea about 1766 that lime and common salt might react to produce soda. This was taken up with enthusiasm by Watt and John Roebuck, a manufacturer of vitriol and leading industrial chemist. The reactants were formed into bricks or cakes and from these walls were built. After a few months, crystals of mild alkali (soda) were formed on the surface and could be scraped off, but the yield was low and the time needed for reaction long. Black seems to have realized the limitations of the process from an early date, but all the same experiments continued until well into the 1780s, with Black playing an unenthusiastic role.

As assessors for the board of manufactures, Black and the geologist James Hutton, a friend who shared many of Black's scientific interests, were asked in 1783 to adjudicate the effectiveness of a new design of furnace for the production of pig iron by a founder in Leith. Though the furnace was not a success, they took significant pains in their judgement and the episode illustrates the efforts being made in Scotland, with the help of the intellectual community, to establish innovative processes for the promotion of industry. A further example, in which Black's economic as well as his technical assessment was important, was the advice he gave to Archibald Cochrane, earl of Dundonald. Lord Dundonald had discovered that if ships' hulls were coated with tar the destructive effect of worms eating their way through the wood could be considerably lessened. He had established a tar works at Culross, on the Firth of Forth, to produce tar by the distillation of coal in closed vessels. Dundonald's business skills were not sophisticated enough: though the process seemed to be potentially profitable, he had immediate financial problems. Black was called in as a consultant to check the technological and financial viability of the scheme. His estimates took many factors into account including the significant one of whether or not the country was in a state of war—in time of war the demand for tar would be much greater and its value higher. He also considered increased profitability which would derive from selling the by-products of the process—varnish from the resin, coke which might be used for iron production in the nearby Carron iron works, and so on. Dundonald was guided by Black to proceed and applied to parliament for an extension to his patent. The advice proved correct and by 1788 Dundonald's British Tar Company was yielding a clear annual profit of £5000. Referring to this success, Sir John Dalrymple, solicitor to the board of excise (and entrepreneur himself) described Black as 'the best judge, perhaps in Europe, of such inventions' (Dalrymple, 6).

Black's correspondence reveals a wide range of topics on which he was approached to offer advice. In addition to those mentioned already, these included sugar refining, ceramic glazing, dyeing, brewing, metal corrosion, salt extraction, glass making, vinegar manufacture, the properties of materials, and water analysis. This last was at the request of the Edinburgh and Leith authorities who were anxious about the quality of the water supply being provided from various sources. For this work Black devised a delicate balance for weighing small quantities of solid matter derived from the water samples which he was sent.

Medicine Black had originally trained as a physician and he practised, to a very limited extent, throughout his career; he mentions that private patients were occupying him from as early as February 1753. Only the most famous of his patients are known. He advised Walter Scott, father of the future author Sir Walter Scott (1771–1832), that his son might contract consumption if his tuberculous nurse were not dismissed. Both Edinburgh philosophers, Adam Ferguson and David Hume, consulted Black, and it was he who appreciated the incurable nature of Hume's last illness (other physicians had not) and who informed him of its fatal consequences. Black laid great stress on the benefits of fresh air, exercise (he rode for this reason), and a plain diet including milk and vegetables.

Black was closely involved in the two major Scottish medical institutions of his time, the Royal Infirmary of Edinburgh and the Royal College of Physicians of Edinburgh. He served as a manager to the infirmary on four occasions between 1771 and 1794, his responsibilities being to make regular inspections and to report these to the board. He also acted, briefly, as physician to the infirmary. Black was admitted a member of the Faculty of Physicians and Surgeons of Glasgow in 1757, and as a fellow of the Edinburgh Royal College in 1767. He played a significant role in the life of the college, serving as its president from 1788 to 1790. He was a member of the revision committee for the sixth, seventh, and eighth editions of the college's *Pharmacopoeia Edinburgensis* of 1774, 1783, and 1794, taking particular interest in mercurial and antimonial preparations. Black was appointed principal physician to George III in Scotland (though the king never, in fact, visited Scotland). He was a founding fellow of the Royal Society of Edinburgh and was elected a member of the Imperial Academy of St Petersburg, the Société Royale de Médecine and the Académie Royale des Sciences of France. Catherine the Great tried unsuccessfully to persuade him to teach in St Petersburg.

Final years and reputation Black ceased teaching in 1796, handing over to his chosen successor, Thomas Charles Hope (1766–1844), son of John Hope (1725–1786), professor of botany. Towards the end of his career the aspect of his teaching which seemed particularly behind the times was his approach to combustion. Through most of the eighteenth century, the accepted explanation of burning was offered by the phlogiston theory, propounded in the previous century. Phlogiston was said to be an invisible, weightless substance which was given off when inflammable substances were burned or metals calcined. When Black's contemporary Henry Cavendish (1731–1810) discovered hydrogen in 1766 some considered this to be pure phlogiston. On the other hand, the chemist (and religious dissenter) Joseph Priestley (1733–1804), on heating the calx of mercury found that a gas was produced which strongly supported burning and living systems. He believed this to be atmospheric air without its phlogiston component ('dephlogisticated air'). At the same time the French chemist Antoine-Laurent Lavoisier, produced and studied the gas and suggested that it was a chemical species which he called *oxigène*. This theory, which he developed in a sophisticated way, was formulated by 1777 and it gradually overturned the phlogiston theory. Black was very slow to accept this changed view—certainly he was not yet won over in the mid 1780s, though by 1790, in a letter to Lavoisier, he wrote that he had:

> been habituated 30 years to believe and teach the doctrine of Phlogiston … I felt much aversion to the new system … This aversion however proceeded from the power of habit alone

has gradually subsided … Your plan … is infinitely better supported than the former Doctrine. (Black to Lavoisier, 24 Oct 1790, Archives Nationales, Paris, Lavoisier MSS, letters and notes 1770–1794)

Black's students had, however, been discussing enthusiastically the new theory five years earlier in their own chemical society (which is thought to be the first of its kind).

Though Black was slow to accept this most significant of chemical theories, his popularity as a lecturer did not wane, with classes of well over 200 students regularly subscribing each year. Attending with the students were well-established chemists who wanted to hear Black describe the seminal experiments which he had performed many years earlier ('the historian of his own discoveries' as Henry Brougham put it). For those who did not require as rigorous a programme Black put on more popular courses. James Boswell (1740–1795) attended one such series for members of the legal profession in 1775. Though Black's fame was widespread, this did not arise from self-promotion. He steadfastly refused to publish his work, though urged to do so by his friends. As Robison put it 'Dr Black was perhaps … too severe in his observations on the hurried publications of some chemists, which he called slovenly, and to consider as literary manufacture for profit'. He wrote only two really significant papers for publication: the MD thesis (in Latin), *De humore acido a cibis orto, et magnesia alba* (1754), and the much developed further paper, 'Experiments upon magnesia alba, quicklime, and some other alcaline substances' in *Essays and Observations, Physical and Literary* (1756). He published nothing on heat, though a pirated version of his lectures on the subject appeared anonymously, *An Enquiry into the General Effects of Heat* (1770). A number of letters written by Black were published by their recipients in his lifetime, which annoyed him. A letter to the president of the Royal Society on the subject of the effect of having boiled water on its freezing point was published in *Philosophical Transactions* (1775), as was a letter on the temperature of mercurial congelation (1783). The *Transactions of the Royal Society of Edinburgh* for 1794 includes a paper by Black on the analysis of some hot springs in Iceland.

Black had a thin and pale physique. He frequently complained about his poor health and took care of himself, renting houses on the edge of Edinburgh for long summer breaks. He disliked travelling and avoided it as much as possible; many eminent men of the day seemed happy enough to come to Edinburgh in order to call on him. Black was sociable in the manner of his day, attending a variety of dining clubs regularly with male friends, the circle including Cullen, Hutton, Hume, Smith, Ferguson, and the eccentric Lord Monboddo. Black could play the flute, sing, and draw skilfully. Though he never married, he appears to have enjoyed the company of intelligent women. After what may have been a heart attack he died on 6 December 1799 at Nicolson Street, Edinburgh, and was buried on 13 December in Greyfriars churchyard.

In the second half of the eighteenth century Black was widely known throughout the academic communities of Europe and North America. He helped to maintain and develop the reputation of the Edinburgh medical school as the leading place of study of its age. On the other hand, he had a conservative outlook and did not encourage practical skills among his students. No research school was to develop at Edinburgh, and after Black's death there was a relative decline in its status. He had no pupils who became major chemists but he stimulated many students to become competent ones. His own significance as a chemist lies in the work of a few years in the 1750s. His meticulous quantitative technique and his logical mind led to the first chemical characterization of a gas. Other chemists, using similar methods, followed, discovering more and more new species. Black can be seen as the modest initiator of the age of pneumatic chemistry. His work on theoretical concepts of heat was also of great importance and was widely acclaimed. The influence of this on Watt's development of more efficient steam engines is difficult to assess. Watt was anxious to assert that his practical work was independent of Black's ideas on latent heat.

Important though his conceptual work was, Black's contribution to Scottish industrialization and teaching must be properly recognized. When he was born in 1728, industry in the country was in an embryonic state and the youthful medical school, established only two years earlier, regarded chemistry purely in terms of its pharmaceutical applications. At the time of his death seventy-one years later Scottish industry was poised for its great leap forward in the nineteenth century and chemistry had become recognized as an independent subject. Black had much to do with both these changes.

R. G. W. ANDERSON

Sources *Lectures on the elements of chemistry … by the late Joseph Black, MD … now published from his manuscripts by John Robison, LLD* (1803) • A. L. Donovan, *Philosophical chemistry in the Scottish Enlightenment* (1975) • W. Ramsay, *The life and letters of Joseph Black, MD* (1918) • *Partners in science: letters of James Watt and Joseph Black*, ed. E. Robinson and D. McKie (1970) • A. D. C. Simpson, ed., *Joseph Black, 1728–1799* (1982) • J. G. Fyffe and R. G. W. Anderson, *Joseph Black: a bibliography* (1992) • R. G. W. Anderson, *The Playfair collection and the teaching of chemistry at the University of Edinburgh, 1713–1858* (1978) • H. Guerlac, 'Joseph Black and fixed air', *Isis*, 48 (1957), 124–51, 433–56 • A. Clow and N. L. Clow, *The chemical revolution* (1952) • A. E. Musson and E. Robinson, *Science and technology in the industrial revolution* (1969) • A. Kent, ed., *An eighteenth century lectureship in chemistry: essays and bicentenary addresses relating to the chemistry department, 1747, of Glasgow University* (1950) • H. Riddell, 'The great chemist Joseph Black, his Belfast friends and family connections', *Proceedings of the Belfast Natural History and Philosophical Society*, 3 (1920), 49–88 • D. McKie, ed., *Thomas Cochrane, notes from Doctor Black's lectures on chemistry, 1767/8* (1966) • J. Dalrymple, *Addresses and proposals on the subject of the coal, tar, and iron branches of trade* (1784) • U. Edin. L., MS gen 873/vii, fol. 22 • PRO NIre., MS T 1073, no. 1 • A. Doig, 'Joseph Black: a remarkable physician', *Joseph Black: a commemorative symposium*, ed. A. D. C. Simpson (1982), 37–41 • *Edinburgh Evening Courant* (14 Dec 1799)

Archives BL, Add. MS 52496 • Historical Society of Pennsylvania, Philadephia, papers • Hunt. L., letters • JRL, lecture notes • National Museums of Scotland, Edinburgh, The Playfair Collection • NL Scot., lecture • NRA, priv. coll., letters • NRA, priv. coll., papers • Royal College of Physicians of Edinburgh • Royal Pharmaceutical Society of Great Britain, London, lecture notes • Sci. Mus., lecture notes • U. Edin. L., corresp. and papers • U. Lpool L., lecture notes • U. Wales, Aberystwyth, lecture notes • UCL, lecture notes • University of Toronto, Thomas Fisher Rare Book Library, lecture notes · University of Wisconsin, Madison, lecture notes · Wellcome L., lecture notes | Birm. CA, corresp. with James Watt · NRA Scotland, priv. coll., corresp. with William Creech

Likenesses T. Cochrane, pencil and ink sketches, 1767–8, Strathclyde University, Andersonian Library, lecture notes of 1767 or 1768 · D. Martin, c.1770, U. Edin. · J. Kay, etchings, 1787, BM, NPG; repro. in J. Kay, *A series of original portraits*, 1 (1838), facing p. 54 · D. Martin, oils, 1787, Scot. NPG; on loan from the Royal Medical Society, Edinburgh · J. Tassie, wax and glass paste medallions, 1788, NPG, Scot. NPG · H. Raeburn, oils, c.1790, U. Glas. [*see illus.*] · J. Beugo, stipple (after J. Brown), BM · Robertson, line engraving (after Thornton), BM · J. Rogers, stipple (after H. Raeburn), BM, NPG; repro. in Chambers, *Scots.* · Wedgwood, medallion (after J. Tassie), Scot. NPG · chalk drawing, Scot. NPG

Wealth at death approx. £18,415: U. Edin. L., MS gen 873/vii, fol. 22, 16 Feb 1799

Black, Mary (c.1737–1814), artist, was born in London, the first of two children of Thomas Black (d. 1777), the son of a Northamptonshire gentleman, and his wife, Mary. He was a competent portrait, genre, and drapery painter, reputed to have been a member of the St Martin's Lane Academy. An assistant to Allan Ramsay in the early 1760s and supported by Joshua Reynolds, Mary Black initially copied works of old masters 'with the utmost fidelity and spirit', reproducing for its owner, the second earl of Godolphin, a painting by Teniers 'comprising above a hundred figures' (*GM*). Ambitious to establish herself as a portraitist she received a prestigious commission, while still in her twenties, to paint Dr James Mounsey (or Monsey) of Rammerscales, a physician at the Russian court, and his cousin Dr Messenger Monsey; she was also engaged to produce copies of these works for the sitters to exchange. None the less only the three-quarters-length portrait of Messenger Monsey, formerly attributed to her father and now at the Royal College of Physicians, London, is known. Painted in 1764 it shows the seventy-year-old sitter in a contemplative pose with an open book resting, face down, on his knee. Although Mounsey recognized in a letter to his cousin that 'she has merit in the picture' and that the artist 'was in hopes to have had ½ Reynolds price' Messenger Monsey proved unwilling to pay for the work (Harris, 535). Monsey never received the portrait and it remained in the artist's collection. Black produced a mezzotint portrait of her sister Clara, who was also an artist, and a portrait of Abigaël Drummond, recorded in an engraving by James Watson, as well as oil portraits of Charles and Caroline Wyndham as children, both signed.

Black exhibited at the Society of Artists in 1768, where she was listed, like her more famous female colleague Catherine Read, as a 'crayon painter'. She exhibited the half-length *Portrait of a Gentleman*, in oil, and three portraits 'in crayon' of young ladies (Graves, *Soc. Artists*, 34); she was elected an honorary member of the Society of Artists shortly thereafter. Later in life she worked exclusively as a portraitist and art teacher, instructing a wealthy and aristocratic clientele. According to her obituary she considered that 'she was more likely to acquire independence by teaching' (*GM*). Thus, while she had displayed her work publicly, like so many women artists she found success not on the open market but, foremost, within polite society. Her obituary emphasizes that 'she was protected by

some of the first people in this country, who esteemed her for her good sense, and the propriety of her conduct, as well as for her skill and taste in the Fine Arts' (ibid.).

Financially successful and independent—she kept liveried servants and a carriage—Black remained unmarried and lived in the family residence, 1 Bolton Street, Piccadilly, until her sudden death there on 24 November 1814. She left 'a house literally crammed with pictures, valuable china and other objects of vertu' (Walford, 10). Administration of her will, which contains three codicils, was granted to her nephew Thomas Walford and his wife, Mary, on 3 December 1814. She was interred in her family's vault in Grosvenor Chapel, South Audley Street, London.

ANGELA ROSENTHAL

Sources F. Harris, 'Mary Black and the portrait of Dr Monsey', *Burlington Magazine*, 135 (Aug 1993), 534–6 · F. Walford, *A short memoir of Miss Mary Black* (1876) · *GM*, 1st ser., 85/1 (1815), 89 · E. C. Clayton, *English female artists*, 2 vols. (1876), 1.366 · W. T. Whitley, *Artists and their friends in England, 1700–1799*, 2 vols. (1928); repr. (1968) · Waterhouse, *18c painters* · Graves, *Soc. Artists* · G. Wolstenholme and D. Piper, *The Royal College of Physicians of London: portraits*, 2 vols. (1964–77), 1.308 · C. Petteys and others, eds., *Dictionary of women artists: an international dictionary of women artists born before 1900* (1985) · G. Meissner, ed., *Allgemeines Künstlerlexikon: die bildenden Künstler aller Zeiten und Völker*, [new edn, 34 vols.] (Leipzig and Munich, 1983–) · M. Pointon, *Strategies for showing: women, possession, and representation in English visual culture, 1665–1800* (1997), 139 · will, PRO, PROB 11/1031, sig. 200 [Thomas Black] · will, PRO, PROB 11/1562, sig. 639

Wealth at death substantial: Harris, 'Mary Black', 535; will, PRO, PROB 11/1562, sig. 639

Black, Matthew (1908–1994), biblical scholar, was born in Kilmarnock on 3 September 1908, the son of James Black (1888–1960), engineer's patternmaker, and his wife, Helen, *née* Currie (1889–1985), hosiery worker. He was educated at Kilmarnock Academy and Glasgow University, graduating with first-class honours in classics in 1930 and second-class honours in philosophy in 1931. He studied for the ministry, and took his BD in 1934 with distinction in Old Testament. He followed the Scottish scholar's path to Germany, and gained his DPhil from Bonn in 1937 for an edition, with English translation (published 1938), of the *Rituale Melchitarum*, a collection of early Christian Palestinian texts, mainly in Aramaic. From 1935 to 1937 he was also assistant to the professor of Hebrew in Glasgow, and then moved to Manchester as lecturer in Semitic languages. There Professor Thomas Walter Manson showed him the need to approach the New Testament from its Jewish background, rather than from classical Greek, and from this stemmed his prodigious work thereafter.

On 16 June 1938 Black married Ethel Mary (b. 1915), a catering manageress and the daughter of Lieutenant-Commander A. T. Hall of the Royal Indian Navy. They spent their honeymoon in Bonn. A year later he was appointed lecturer in biblical criticism at Aberdeen. The wartime church needed ministers, and in 1942 he accepted a call to the parish of Dunbarney, near Perth, where he was also officiating chaplain to the forces and to a German prisoner of war camp. Scholarship was not abandoned, and his *Aramaic Approach to the Gospels and Acts* (1946, 1954, 1967) earned him his Glasgow DLitt in 1944.

Matthew Black (1908–1994), by Walter Bird, 1965

With the war over, Black felt free to return to academe, and became lecturer in New Testament in Leeds (1947–52). In 1952 he went to the chair of biblical criticism in Edinburgh. There he might have stayed, had not Principal Malcolm Knox been determined to get a distinguished scholar for the chair of biblical criticism in St Andrews. Black was offered not only the chair but the principalship of St Mary's College. He took many soundings before accepting. From 1954 until he retired in 1978 his name was inseparable from that of St Mary's. Under his aegis the college attracted postgraduates from all over the world, and not only in New Testament. He was generous in the time he gave to his own research students and in furthering their careers, just as he was always generous in encouragement of his junior colleagues. He was a formidable figure in the politics of the university, always for the good of St Mary's and the teaching of theology. He saw that in the expanding universities of the 1960s divinity faculties too had to expand or disappear. Theology had been taught largely to church candidates, and the BD was a second degree. St Andrews defied opposition from the other Scottish faculties, introduced a first degree in theology, and began to open divinity courses to students of other faculties. In due course the others followed.

Black's own scholarly work was untiring. He quickly engaged with the Dead Sea scrolls, and his critical and sober judgement in *The Scrolls and Christian Origins* (1961, 1983) was much valued. For twenty-three years he edited *New Testament Studies*, and for ten was chairman for the Peshitta Project of Leiden. He had a long association with the United Bible Societies' *Greek New Testament* (1966), of which he was an editor. He edited the new *Peake's Commentary on the Bible* (1962), and was initially responsible for the updating of Schürer's *History of the Jewish People in the Age of Jesus Christ* (1973–87). He lectured in the United States, Europe, and the antipodes. His lifelong interest in the Son of Man title in the gospels lay behind his last book, an edition of *The Book of Enoch* (1985), published after his retirement. The critical reception of this discouraged him. He was a perfectionist, of whom it was said 'His self-criticism is unsparing, and sometimes melancholy' (Watson). Unlike some scholars, he did not separate his personal faith from his scholarly quest—an integrity which added to the perturbation of his spirit.

Black was elected a fellow of the British Academy in 1955, and awarded its Burkitt medal in 1962. In 1977 he became a fellow of the Royal Society of Edinburgh. He had the rare distinction of being president both of the Society for Old Testament Studies and of Studiorum Novi Testamenti Societas. Honorary degrees were given by Glasgow, Cambridge, Münster, Queen's (Ontario), and St Andrews. He was a loyal churchman, an elder in his parish church. In 1968–9 he was moderator of the presbytery of St Andrews. But the church had its conflicts, which did not always strengthen his faith. He once asked 'Should I go to church when all that happens is that my adrenalin goes up?' (personal knowledge). He was chaplain to the Royal and Ancient Golf Club and played golf himself. Where he relaxed was in his family. He was generous to his own parents when his father, a skilled patternmaker in the Clyde shipyards, knew unemployment. In the calm wisdom of his wife, Ethel, his quick-firing temperament found its perfect complement. He found much joy in the doings of his children, Harvey and Elizabeth, and, in time, in his grandchildren. His last years were clouded by ill health and the dread of failing powers. He died at his home, St Michael's, 40 Buchanan Gardens, St Andrews, of cardiac failure on 2 October 1994. He was cremated at Dundee crematorium on 6 October and a memorial service was held in the collegiate church of St Salvator, St Andrews, on 29 October. He was survived by his wife.

JAMES A. WHYTE

Sources personal knowledge (2004) · private information (2004) · *WWW*, 1991–5 · *Fasti Scot.*, vols. 9 and 10 · *The Scotsman* (14 Oct 1994) · *The Times* (15 Oct 1994) · *The Independent* (1 Nov 1994) · W. McKane, 'Matthew Black', *PBA*, 90 (1996), 283–94 · J. S. Watson, 'Matthew Black, principal of St Mary's', *Alumnus Chronicle* [U. St Andr.], 69 (June 1978), 26–7

Archives U. St Andr. | SOUND BL NSA, performance recordings

Likenesses W. Bird, photograph, 1965, NPG [*see illus.*] · photograph, repro. in *The Times* · photograph, repro. in *The Scotsman* · portrait, U. St Andr.

Wealth at death £166,055.26: confirmation, 6 Dec 1994, NA Scot., SC/CO 801/86

Black, Max (1909–1988), philosopher, was born on 24 February 1909 in Baku, Russia, the first of four children of Lionel Black (formerly Tcherny; 1885–1960), merchant, and Sophia Divinska (d. c.1970). Sir Misha *Black was his younger brother. The family migrated to England in 1912

to enjoy greater religious freedom and educational opportunities. Black was a brilliant student and was awarded scholarships, first to Dame Alice Owen's School, Islington, then to Queens' College, Cambridge, where in 1930 he received a BA in mathematics. While at Cambridge he worked with F. P. Ramsey and attended the classes of G. E. Moore and Ludwig Wittgenstein, both of whom extensively influenced his later work. He also began attending meetings of the Cambridge Moral Sciences Club and the Aristotelian Society. The following year he studied at the University of Göttingen. His first book, *The Nature of Mathematics*, appeared in 1933.

Black then taught (1931–6) as mathematics master at the Royal Grammar School, Newcastle upon Tyne. On 21 August 1933 he married Michal (or Mabel) Landesberg (1911–1985) a clerk, daughter of Hyman Landesberg, a provision dealer; they had a daughter and a son. From 1936 to 1940 he was a lecturer and tutor in mathematics at the University of London Institute of Education; in 1939, with a thesis entitled 'The theories of logical positivism', he was awarded a PhD in mathematical logic, working with Susan Stebbing, and in 1955 a DLitt in philosophy, by the University of London.

In 1940 Black was appointed professor of philosophy in the University of Illinois; he and his family then settled in Urbana, Illinois, USA. In 1946 he was appointed professor of philosophy at Cornell University, Ithaca, New York. Black helped make Cornell one of the outstanding philosophical schools in the United States, and he also helped introduce the work of Wittgenstein to American philosophical circles. He was appointed Susan Linn Sage professor of philosophy and humane letters in 1954, becoming professor emeritus in 1977. He served as director of the Cornell Society for the Humanities (1965–70) and as senior member of the program in science, technology, and society from 1971 until his death.

Black taught himself chess at an early age, competed for a time in tournaments, and occasionally staged exhibitions of blindfold chess and matches against several opponents. He was an excellent teacher, with a great interest in the principles of pedagogy, pointing out that one cannot teach students if one has not succeeded in getting them interested. He lectured all over the world, and gave the Tarner lectures at Cambridge in 1976. He was co-editor of the *Journal of Symbolic Logic* (1945–51), editor of the *Philosophical Review* for several terms from 1950 on, and editor of the Cornell University Press Contemporary Philosophy Series from 1956. He was a fellow of the American Academy of Arts and Sciences, president of the American Philosophical Association (1958), and president of the Institut International de Philosophie (1981–4).

Black wrote eleven books, edited or co-edited eight others, and published about 200 articles and 50 reviews. Starting from a solid training in mathematics and natural science Black rapidly developed an overriding interest in logic and philosophy, and became an acknowledged expert in philosophy of language. He was fascinated all his life by language:

In spite of an impressive amount of work on language by linguists, literary critics, psychologists, and philosophers, language still remains a mystery. It remains wonderful that mere puffs of wind should allow men to discover what they think and feel, to share their attitudes and plans, to anticipate the future and learn from the past, and to create lasting works of art. (M. Black, *The Importance of Language*, 1962, xi)

His curiosity about language, reflected further in *The Labyrinth of Language* (1968), was combined with an intense interest in other matters, and he had important things to say in nearly every branch of philosophy.

Seven of Black's books are collections of his essays, all written with wit and humour in an urbane, lucid, graceful style largely free from technicalities. He was fascinated by puzzles of all kinds, especially those that seem incapable of any solution, and had a special talent for thinking up examples. Black was not one of those rare thinkers who establish or transform a whole field of enquiry, but he was none the less a first-rate thinker with an acute and original mind who made important contributions to a very wide range of subjects. These include his pioneering work on vagueness and what he later called 'loose concepts'; his fascination with metaphor, which took him into the areas of literary criticism and the understanding of poetry; and his contributions to the understanding of scientific method and of what a definition of scientific method would consist. He developed this out of his account of what he called 'range definition', which involves abandoning the search for a set of necessary and sufficient conditions in favour of identifying 'a set of overlapping and interacting criteria', and combining this with '[taking] seriously the organic and historical aspects of science' and treating '"scientific method" as a historical expression meaning ... "those procedures which, as a matter of historical fact, have proved most fruitful in the acquisition of systematic and comprehensive knowledge"' (*Problems of Analysis*, 1954, 13). He also did fundamental work on the logical paradoxes, the concepts of definition, implication, presupposition, and justification, the justification of logical axioms, and the justification of inductive inference. One distinctive contribution in this last area was his argument that inductive arguments can be self-supporting without being circular and without presupposing any fundamental principle of induction (ibid., chap. 11). He attempted to clarify the concept of a model and introduced the notion of an 'archetype', which he defined as 'a systematic repertoire of ideas by means of which a given thinker describes, by *analogical extension*, some domain to which those ideas do not immediately and literally apply' (M. Black, *Models and Metaphors*, 1962, 241) He went on to 'diagnose ... the part played in scientific method by models and archetypes', and to trace out the consequences that follow for the relations between the sciences and the humanities. 'Perhaps', he conjectured, 'every science must start with metaphor and end with algebra; and perhaps without the metaphor there would never have been any algebra. ... For science, like the humanities, like literature, is an affair of the imagination' (ibid., 242–3).

Black's *magnum opus* was *A Companion to Wittgenstein's 'Tractatus'* (1964), an essential work on the early Wittgenstein, in which he provided independent discussions of such concepts as facts, propositions, probability, and logical truth. He said: 'There can be no question here of any "definitive" reading: since my own views have oscillated while I was writing, I cannot be confident that my final judgement has always been the best' (M. Black, *A Companion to Wittgenstein's 'Tractatus'*, 1964, vii). And later on he referred to it, and 'several later essays in which [he] partially discharged [his] great debt to Wittgenstein's provocations, [as] both expository and critical' (M. Black, *Perplexities*, 1990, 2–3).

Describing his work early on as linguistic analysis, Black later came to conceive of it as conceptual clarification, and he developed an interest in questions of rationality and reasonableness, conjoined with an attempt to work out the rudiments of a theory of practical reasoning and the concept of humaneness. Throughout his career he provided incisive critical comment on the work of many of his own best-known contemporaries. He characterized his own work and interests as 'an intermittent tension between interest in finding good reasons and sound arguments … and … a standing conviction that a single fruitful idea is worth a hundred syllogisms'. 'My concern', he said, 'is … with concepts, hidden rules of usage, and the non-verbal realities or fictions designated. The elusive character of fundamental concepts partly accounts for the imperfection of much philosophical as well as popular argument' (M. Black, *The Prevalence of Humbug*, 1983, 13, 15).

Black, though he 'never … belonged to any philosophical school' (*Perplexities*, 8), none the less confessed 'to a strong belief that common-sense convictions … are more likely to be right than the skeptical objections of even the greatest philosophers' (*The Prevalence of Humbug*, 15–16). Early in his career he was greatly interested in the work of the logical positivists, but he soon lost patience with their attempts to erect a rigid ideology out of their philosophical ideas and to legislate philosophical problems out of existence by the application of strict criteria. In his view philosophical questions are too subtle and complex to be dealt with summarily by such 'high priori methods', and need to be dealt with by careful consideration of context and reflection on multiple considerations. In his later life, along with his reflections on humaneness and reasonableness, he was led more into moral theory, in which he had previously done little. About 1950 he said that 'the task of the moral philosopher is to solve the moral problems of his society', but he did nothing for quite a while to amplify this idea. His yet unworked out moral philosophy emphasized '"fellow feeling" and respect for the integrity of other human beings', and he said his 'moral position can be crystallized in the defeasible maxim, "Do no harm"' (*Perplexities*, 8). If he had lived longer he would no doubt have come to see the weakness of this as a crystallization of a 'moral position'. Yet he was not given the opportunity to work out a moral philosophy, supposing he had any such aim in mind.

So, with no attempt to generate a system of philosophy and with studied avoidance of paradox, Black worked with enormous skill and facility on problems that especially intrigued him, which then turned out to have applications to various and diverse large subjects. His writing was often enlivened by a trenchant wit, and he observed that 'it is a well-kept secret that philosophical investigation, like music, can be enjoyable' (*Perplexities*).

Black was Jewish, but did not profess any religious belief or belong to any organized religious congregation. He spent considerable time in Israel teaching and lecturing, and later in life he and his wife seriously considered settling there.

Max Black was of medium height, and in middle age was bald and wore thick glasses. He was an inveterate pipe smoker and had a friendly though sometimes very intense manner, a keen sense of humour, and an incisive wit; he was fond of telling stories and anecdotes, and was always ready for conversation or discussion on practically any topic connected with his main interests. In addition to chess, he enjoyed playing ping-pong, was an accomplished pianist, and had a keen interest in both the visual and the musical arts. One of his special abilities was his uncanny and distinctly unusual capacity to provide objective and accurate assessments of the professional abilities of people, altogether independent of his feelings of regard for them. He died in Ithaca, New York, on 27 August 1988 from a heart attack suffered following surgery for cancer, and, in accordance with his wishes, his body was cremated and the ashes scattered. As one contemporary of note observed, 'His relentless rationality deserves the enduring respect of all' (Ruth Barcan Marcus, private communication, 13 Dec 1998).

MARCUS G. SINGER

Sources personal knowledge (2004) · private information (2004) · M. Black, 'The articulation of concepts', *Philosophers on their own work* (1985), 12.9–41 [incl. most complete list of pubns available] · *Who was who in America*, 9 (1989) · *Who's who in America*, 43rd edn (1984–5) · memorial notice, *Proceedings and Addresses of the American Philosophical Association*, 64 (1991), 61–2 · R. B. Marcus, 'Max Black (1909–1988)', *Dialectica*, 44/1–2 (1990), 5–8 · N. Garver, 'Black, Max', *The encyclopedia of philosophy*, ed. P. Edwards (1967), 318–19 · J. Kaminsky, 'Black, Max', *Thinkers of the twentieth century: a biographical, bibliographical and critical dictionary*, ed. E. Devine (1983), 83–4 · 'Max Black', *Memorial Statements, Cornell University Faculty* (1988–9), 12–18 · J. O. Urmson, ed., *The concise encyclopedia of philosophy and Western philosophers* (1960) · N. Malcolm, *Ludwig Wittgenstein: a memoir* (1958) · G. H. von Wright, 'Biographical sketch', in N. Malcolm, *Ludwig Wittgenstein: a memoir* (1958), 1–22 · G. E. Moore, 'Wittgenstein's lectures in 1930–33 [pt 1]', *Mind*, new ser., 63 (1954), 1–15 · F. P. Ramsey, *The foundations of mathematics*, ed. R. B. Braithwaite (1931) · *ANB* · m. cert.
Archives Cornell University, Ithaca, New York, Carl A. Kroch Library, MSS 14/21/2466 | CUL, corresp. with Charles Ogden
Likenesses photographs, priv. coll.

Black, Sir Misha (1910–1977), architect and industrial designer, was born on 16 October 1910 in Baku, Russia, the second of the three sons (there was also a daughter) of Lionel Tcherny (1885–1960), merchant, and his wife, Sophia Divinska (*d. c.*1970), who took him at the age of eighteen months to London. His elder brother was the philosopher

Sir Misha Black (1910–1977), by Gordon Lawson

Max *Black. Lionel Tcherny changed his name to Black in 1911–12 and his son Moisey became Misha. Black received his early education at the Dame Alice Owen School in Islington. He went on to take evening classes at the Central School of Arts and Crafts in London and studied briefly in Paris in 1928.

In spite of this modest education Black ended his life as a professor emeritus of the Royal College of Art (from 1975), a trustee of the British Museum (from 1968), an honorary doctor of technology of Bradford University, and an internationally recognized authority on the teaching and practice of industrial design. He arrived at these distinctions by a circuitous route, for industrial design was an unknown, untaught subject when he was born.

Black began his career at the age of seventeen, designing posters and exhibition stands. It was about this time that he met Lucy Rossetti, the great-niece of Dante Gabriel Rossetti. The two studied together under Hans Kiesewelter and worked for Messrs Wickham and Arundell Display Ltd. They set up a partnership and set about designing what Black called 'stomach fillers' such as book-plates, book jackets, posters, and exhibition stands, under the name Studio Z. They conducted these youthful freelance activities from an attic overlooking Seven Dials. The partnership lasted about a year, after which Black carried on working alone until 1934, when he joined Milner and Thomas Gray and others in the Industrial Design Partnership. His early designs included television and radio sets for E. K. Cole Ltd and the redesign of the Kardomah cafés in London and Manchester. It was through his work on commercial display stands that he eventually became a leader in the field of exhibition design working as co-ordinating designer for the 1938 Modern Architectural Research (MARS) Group exhibition *New architecture* and as interior designer for the British pavilion at the 1939 New York World's Fair. In 1935 he married Helen Lillian, daughter of Frank Foster Evans, engineer, with whom he had one son and one daughter (the marriage was dissolved in 1952).

From 1940 to 1945 Black was principal exhibition architect to the Ministry of Information. In 1946 he designed the 'Birth of an Egg Cup' exhibit at the 'Britain Can Make It' exhibition at the Victoria and Albert Museum, but his real chance came in 1951 at the Festival of Britain south bank exhibition, of which he was co-ordinating architect for the upstream section, co-ordinating designer for the Dome of Discovery, and co-architect of the Regatta restaurant and the Bailey Bridge. Thereafter he was endlessly busy as architect, designer, or consultant, having formed in 1946, at the instigation of Marcus Brumwell and Herbert Read, his lifelong partnership with Milner Gray, which they cleverly called Design Research Unit (DRU), thereby winning national and international standing as the leading design consultancy in Britain. Although the DRU practice ranged across the whole spectrum of design, Black's own leanings were towards blending art with technics and bridging the gap between industrial and engineering design, particularly in the field of public transport. This led him to consultancies with British Rail, London Transport for whom he designed the stations and trains of the Victoria Line, the Orient Line, British Overseas Airways Corporation, Beagle Aircraft, and the Hong Kong rapid transport system, among others. He went on to become a partner in the architectural practice Black, Bayes, and Gibson, architects, between 1963 and 1977, with whom he designed the Charles Clare pavilion for small mammals at London Zoo.

Black was also active in many societies and public bodies. In 1933, again with Milner Gray, he had been a founder member of the British Society of Industrial Artists and in 1954–6 he was its president, an experience which together with his many foreign friendships led him to become a prime mover in the establishment of the International Council of Societies of Industrial Design, the first meeting of which was held in London in 1957 and of which Black was president from 1959 to 1961.

Black married for a second time in 1955; his new wife was Edna Joan, daughter of George Septimus Fairbrother, engineer, with whom he had one son. That year he also acquired another string to his bow and one that brought him almost more acclaim worldwide than had his widespread professional practice, for it was in that year that he was appointed professor of industrial design at the Royal College of Art, a chair he held until his retirement in 1975. Although Black never himself went to a university, his arrival at the Royal College of Art soon gave academic authority to the profession he had adopted and he became in great demand as a writer and lecturer. His mastery of language was a joy to witness, developing as it did from early pretentiousness to such clarity of thought and expression as to leave audiences eating out of his hand. No one could sum up a debate or seminar or conference more precisely or punctiliously, thereby sending everyone home comforted that some wisdom had transpired. It was indeed for his wisdom that he was picked for membership of all manner of organizations such as the Council of Industrial Design (1955–64), the Design and Industries' Association, the National Advisory Council on Art Education (1959–72), the advisory council to the Science Museum (from 1966), the Faculty of Royal Designers for Industry, of which he was master in 1973–4, the British Association for the Advancement of Science, and even the National Union of Students, which offered him honorary membership in 1967. He was appointed OBE in 1946 (he was naturalized in 1950, whereupon the OBE was reissued) and knighted in 1972. He became RDI in 1957.

Misha Black wrote on design throughout his career, giving lectures and writing in the popular and design press, and contributing to design manuals. His best-known works are *Exhibition Design* (1950) and *Public Interiors* (1960). He died in London on 11 August 1977. The British Architectural Library holds a number of his drawings.

PAUL REILLY, rev. KAYE BAGSHAW

Sources personal knowledge (1986) · private information (1986) · A. Blake, *Misha Black* (1984) · A. Blake, ed., *The Black papers on design* (1983) · C. Naylor, ed., *Contemporary designers*, 2nd edn (1990) · *CGPLA Eng. & Wales* (1977)

Archives V&A, MSS

Likenesses G. Lawson, portrait, Royal College of Art [*see illus.*]

Wealth at death £119,665: probate, 26 Oct 1977, *CGPLA Eng. & Wales*

Black, Patrick (1813–1879), physician, was born in Aberdeen on 22 August 1813, the second son of Lieutenant-Colonel Patrick Black (*d.* 1819/20), of the Bengal army, and his wife, Jane Young. Black, like his father, was named after his ancestor Sir Patrick Dun, a former president of the King and Queen's College of Physicians in Ireland. Black's father died when he was only six years old, and after an early education in Aberdeenshire the family moved to London, in 1825, where Black went to Mr Roberts's school at Chelsea. Black attended Eton College between 1828 and 1830, and his subsequent failure at his first attempt to gain entry to Christ Church, Oxford, encouraged him to work harder, so that he spent six months in Paris studying anatomy, toxicology, and medical jurisprudence before matriculating from Christ Church on 10 November 1831. He graduated BA in 1835 and began his medical studies at St Bartholomew's Hospital, London. He graduated BM (1838) and DM (1844) from Oxford. He was elected assistant physician to St Bartholomew's Hospital in 1842, and became warden of the medical school (1851–6), physician to the hospital in 1860, and lecturer on medical jurisprudence (1855–61) and on medicine (1861–78). He was elected fellow of the Royal College of Physicians in 1845 and was later its censor.

During the cholera outbreak in London in 1854 Black took charge of the cholera wards at St Bartholomew's Hospital. In 1855 he delivered the Croonian lectures at the Royal College of Physicians, on the forces of the circulation. Black was appointed examiner for the Oxford medical degree in 1874, and he also held positions as physician to Christ's Hospital, the Marine Society, the Royal Naval Hospital on the *Dreadnought*, and was a director of the Clerical, Medical and General Life Assurance Company.

The most significant part of Black's association with St Bartholomew's was his appointment as its first administrator of chloroform from 1852 to 1856. During this period he published *Chloroform; how Shall we Ensure Safety in its Administration?* (1855), which examines the exact source of danger in the administration of chloroform. In this pamphlet he expresses indebtedness to the writings of John Snow but differs in his interpretation of the cause of death from chloroform. Snow argued that death followed the paralysis of the heart after chloroform had been inhaled in too concentrated a form; Black believed it to be due to asphyxia—the chloroform being too pungent to be breathed in the first moments of administration—and referred to numerous fatal cases in support of his theory. He had presented these views in a paper read to the Abernethian Society in 1854, of which he was president for several years. Debates surrounding the probable cause of chloroform fatalities were intense during this period, and Black's pamphlet represents some of the then commonly held views.

Black was a tall and handsome man, and was respected and loved by his family and many friends. He married in November 1843 Julia Louisa Mark, daughter of William Mark, HM counsel at Malaga, and their marriage was noted by his friends to be a happy and fulfilling one, even though the couple sadly lost two sons within the space of two years—one from a wasting disease and the second in the *Eurydice* disaster. Black was a careful observer, a just reasoner, well read in medicine and literature, and a physician who, as one of his patients remarked, hastened no one into the grave; yet he never attained a large medical practice. His contemporaries suggested that the reason for this was his strong scepticism of the value of therapeutics and a lack of interest in the new methods of physical examination and clinical enquiry. His practice of medicine was more akin to the traditions of the late eighteenth century, rather than the rapidly developing medicine of the 1860s and 1870s. As a result he questioned such practices as the value of quinine as a remedy for malaria and the use of lime juice in the treatment of scurvy. It was a trait which prevented him from totally fulfilling his promise. Another reason may have been the fact that 'he was a man of considerable property' (*DNB*). Nevertheless, he was sound in his judgement of character, firm in his friendship, and universal in his kindness.

In spite of a talent for original and lucid writing Black wrote little. He revised the Latin part of the *Nomenclature of Diseases* (1867) for the Royal College of Physicians, and his writings included *An Address to Students* (1852), *Respiration, or, Why do we Breathe?* (1876), *Scurvy in high latitudes; an attempt to explain the cause of the 'medical failure' of the Arctic expedition of 1875–6* (1876), and *An essay of the use of the spleen with an episode of the spleen's marriage; a physiological love-story* (1876).

On 12 October 1879, after several months of illness during which he had gained pain relief from morphia, Black died from pancreatic cancer at his home, 11 Queen Anne Street, Cavendish Square, London, leaving an estate valued at under £60,000. His personal appearance, character, and manner of teaching were recorded in a Latin poem dedicated to him in 1876 by Robert Bridges (1844–1930), a former house physician and later poet laureate. It was a lasting mark of esteem from one of his many friends. He was survived by his wife. STEPHANIE J. SNOW

Sources R. Southey, *St Bartholomew's Hospital Reports*, 15 (1879), xxix–xl · J. L. Thornton, 'Patrick Black (1813–1879), first "administrator of chloroform" at St Bartholomew's Hospital, London', *Anaesthesia*, 10 (1955), 70–73 · R. Bridges, *Carmen elegiacum* (1876); repr. (1877) · *The Lancet* (18 Oct 1879), 595–6 · *CGPLA Eng. & Wales* (1879) · parish register (births and baptisms), 22 Aug 1813, Aberdeen · *DNB* · Munk, *Roll* · Foster, *Alum. Oxon.*
Archives St Bartholomew's Hospital, stethoscopes
Likenesses photograph, *c.*1860–1869, St Bartholomew's Hospital, London archives, Junior Contemporary Club
Wealth at death under £60,000: probate, 5 Nov 1879, *CGPLA Eng. & Wales*

Black, Robert (1752–1817), minister of the Presbyterian General Synod of Ulster, was the eldest son of Valentine Black, a farmer at Mullabrack, co. Armagh. In 1770 he entered the class of ethics under Dr Thomas Reid at Glasgow University. He was licensed by the Armagh presbytery, declined in 1776 a call to Keady, co. Armagh, and in the following year, on the death of Alexander Colville MD, the non-subscribing minister of Dromore, co. Down, he accepted the call of this congregation, which returned to the jurisdiction of the General Synod of Ulster. Black was ordained at Dromore by the Armagh presbytery on 28 June 1777. On 15 February 1782 he attended the convention of Irish volunteers at Dungannon as Captain Robert Black (Dromore first company) and seconded the resolution adopted in favour of Catholic emancipation. He attended also the second great Dungannon convention, on 8 September 1783, when his eloquence attracted the attention of Frederick Augustus, earl of Bristol and bishop of Derry, and of Robert Moore of Molenan, near Londonderry. Hence his call to First Derry, where he was installed by the Londonderry presbytery on 7 January 1784 as colleague to David Young. Black, whom contemporaries described as a handsome man of dark complexion, aquiline features, and a commanding presence, married his cousin Margaret Black (*d.* 1824).

On 2 December 1788 Black was elected synod agent for the *regium donum* (the small royal bounty paid to Irish Presbyterian ministers since the reign of Charles II), in succession to James Laing. He delivered an applauded oration at the centenary commemoration (7 December 1788) of the closing of the gates of Londonderry, an occasion which was (unusually) celebrated by both religious traditions. As agent for the royal bounty he exerted himself to secure its augmentation; in 1792, through the influence of the earl of Charlemont, Henry Grattan, and Colonel Stewart of

Killymoon, the Irish parliament added £500 a year to the grant. In gratitude for his services the synod, in 1793, presented Black with a piece of plate.

The seditious tendencies that began to appear in the volunteer movement in the early 1790s alarmed Black and he delivered a solemn warning against them in a speech at a meeting of the parishioners of Templemore, held in Londonderry Cathedral on 14 January 1793. He never, however, receded from the positions he had taken in favour of parliamentary reform and Catholic emancipation. In the rising of 1798 he was strongly on the side of constituted authority and had great influence as the friend and correspondent of Lord Castlereagh. One form in which this influence was exercised was a further increase of the *regium donum*, which from 1804 was distributed in three classes (£100, £75, and £50), the agent being henceforth appointed not by the synod but by the government. Black held this office until his death and did not scruple to use the power it gave him. Opponents called him 'the unmitred bishop' and 'chief consul of the general synod'. In 1800 or 1801 the degree of DD was sent him by an American college. As a speaker he had no equal in his day.

In theology Black was suspected of the heresy of not believing in the divinity of Christ, a view which seemed to be confirmed when, in 1804, he endeavoured to secure as his colleague William Porter, whose Arianism was openly known. Black's local prestige was impaired by the circumstances of Castlereagh's defeat at the County Down election of 1805, but his influence at Dublin Castle was equally strong with all ministries. In 1809 the synod publicly thanked him for his exertions in procuring the act of parliament incorporating the widows' fund. In 1813 his controversy with William Steel Dickson, who was implicated in the rising of 1798, was ended by a synodical resolution declaring that words in a previous resolution (1799), complained of by Dickson, had been 'inaccurately used'. Black's influence, however, was still powerful enough to cause the expulsion of an elder who, in the course of debate, had laid charges against him in connection with the bounty; he published an account of these proceedings in 1814. Black was opposed to the establishment of the Belfast Academical Institution (opened 1814), which, it was hoped, would develop into a college for training Presbyterian ministers. At the synod of 1815, in Black's absence, a resolution was passed in the institution's favour, and in the same year the government made it an annual grant of £1500. The grant was withdrawn on political grounds the following year after some of the managers were accused of drinking disloyal toasts on St Patrick's day, and Black vainly endeavoured, in two successive years, to obtain the permanent rescinding of the synod's resolution. His defeat was softened by a less than successful public dinner that was given by his admirers in Belfast.

Black outlived his power and popularity. His ambition could not brook repulses; his temperament alternated between geniality and gloom. Loss of leadership unhinged his spirit and he threw himself over the railing of Londonderry Bridge and was drowned in the Foyle on the evening of 4 December 1817. His body later disappeared from its grave. He was survived by his wife, who died in April 1824, and by three sons and two daughters.

ALEXANDER GORDON, rev. A. T. Q. STEWART

Sources *Records of the General Synod of Ulster, from 1691 to 1820*, 3 vols. (1890–98) · PRO NIre., Presbyterian records · T. Witherow, *Historical and literary memorials of presbyterianism in Ireland, 1731–1800* (1880), 226–75 · W. T. Latimer, *A history of the Irish Presbyterians* [1893] · J. S. Reid and W. D. Killen, *History of the Presbyterian church in Ireland*, 3 (1853) · *A history of congregations in the Presbyterian Church in Ireland, 1610–1982*, Presbyterian Church in Ireland (1982) · J. S. Reid, *History of congregations of the Presbyterian church in Ireland*, ed. W. D. Killen (1886) · J. McConnell and others, eds., *Fasti of the Irish Presbyterian church, 1613–1840*, rev. S. G. McConnell, 2 vols. in 12 pts (1935–51) · W. S. Dickson, *A narrative of the confinement and exile of William Steel Dickson, D. D.* (1812) · J. M. Barkley, *A short history of the Presbyterian church in Ireland* (1959)

Archives PRO NIre., corresp. with Lord Castlereagh

Likenesses caricature sketch (*Election squibs*), repro. in F. Holmes, *Our Irish Presbyterian heritage* (1985), 96

Black, Sir Robert Brown [Robin] (1906–1999), colonial administrator, was born at 1 Ponton Street, Edinburgh, on 3 June 1906, the son of Robert Black, superintendent of a boys' home, and his wife, Catherine, *née* Bonar. From childhood onwards he was known as Robin. From George Watson's College, Edinburgh (1912–24), he went on to Edinburgh University, where he graduated in 1928, with history as his main subject. His father encouraged his inclination to follow a Scottish tradition by making his career overseas. He declined an offer of an appointment in the Indian Civil Service, and joined the Malayan civil service in 1930. At that time the colonial administrative service was entering a period of rapid change. Unification facilitated promotion by transfer. In the post-war period the service modernized its working procedures, particularly in central government ('secretariat') contexts. Both trends were important factors in shaping Black's career.

On first arrival in Malaya, Black was appointed temporarily to be private secretary to the governor, and noted that Sir Cecil Clementi's hauteur was unhelpful in his dealings with the local community. He then asked for a posting to the co-operative department to pursue his particular interest in economics. In 1937 he married (Elsie) Anne Stevenson (*d*. 1986), who, like himself, came from Edinburgh; they had two daughters. In 1939 he was transferred to Trinidad, but at the outbreak of war returned to Malaya, where he was commissioned in the intelligence corps and was employed in organizing guerrilla forces to oppose the Japanese. From 1942 he was a prisoner of war in Japan, an experience which left bitter memories.

In the reconstruction after the war North Borneo (later Sabah) had to make a transition from pre-war chartered company rule to a crown colony regime. Black was selected, in preference to more senior members of the Malayan civil service, for the post of deputy chief secretary. His competence in those duties led to his transfer in 1952 to the much more senior position of colonial secretary, Hong Kong, which he held for three years (1952–5). The governor, Sir Alexander Grantham, had a low opinion of the central government as pompous, ponderous, and lost in detail. In addition to remedying this situation Black

had, soon after his arrival, to act as governor during Grantham's leave and to deal with some difficult problems.

Thus far Black had risen steadily to the upper level of the colonial service by his ability to deal calmly but very effectively with the improvement of the machinery of government. His promotion as governor of Singapore (1955–7) brought him face to face with local political leaders who had come to power only recently but were in a hurry to implement programmes of change leading to the end of colonial rule. He reacted with characteristic steadiness in dealing with volatile figures such as David Marshall, the first chief minister, and with the threat of serious disorder.

In 1958 Black returned to Hong Kong to begin a six-year term (1958–64) as governor. Neither the influential business community nor the communist regime in China favoured a rapid advance towards self-government in Hong Kong, such as had been planned immediately after the war, and so these plans were abandoned. A *Daily Telegraph* obituary described Black as 'a somewhat old-fashioned figure of calm imperial authority … not much given to reform' (*Daily Telegraph*, 2 Nov 1999). But he possessed a subtler understanding than that opinion suggests. In dealings with the communist government of China, then subject to the extremes of the 'great leap forward', he felt that he should show 'unremitting vigilance and intelligent anticipation' while 'avoiding any involvement in its domestic politics' (transcript of interview, 1987, Bodl. RH). Here the problem was that the Kuomintang, supported by the USA, still hoped to regain its position in China, and used Hong Kong as its outpost. But Black was able to negotiate successful cross-border arrangements with Guangzhou (Canton) to secure the Hong Kong water supply from the mainland. In domestic affairs Black combined 'constant vigilance and a firm stance' (ibid.) with a realization that colonial government would only be acceptable if it adopted progressive social policies. The waves of refugees from China, at first restrained and then encouraged by the Chinese authorities, were not all sent back, and their needs were met by a programme of housing construction and public health measures, though Black's repeated appeals to an indifferent government in London for financial aid for these purposes evoked little response. In educational development, especially at university level, he also played an active part, which was recognized by his honorary appointment as chancellor of both the English and Chinese universities. Through it all he had also to retain the confidence and support of the local community, at all levels, for costly social programmes. In retirement Black paid tribute to the sheer practical good sense of the Hong Kong Chinese as the bulwark of the colonial government. He had grasped this essential point and built upon it.

Black was appointed MBE (Military) in 1948, OBE in 1949, CMG in 1953, KCMG in 1955, and GCMG in 1962. In a long retirement he was a member of the Commonwealth War Graves Commission (1964–82) and chairman of the Clerical Medical and General Life Assurance Society (1975–8). A fit and athletic figure, quiet in manner but also jovial on occasion, he was a mountaineer in his younger days; later, walking and fishing were his hobbies. He died in Dunedin Hospital, Reading, on 29 October 1999 and was survived by his two daughters.   J. M. GULLICK

Sources interview (transcript), 1987, Bodl. RH, MS Ind. Ocn.s.348 · Bodl. RH, Heussler MSS · *The Times* (9 Dec 1999) · *The Scotsman* (18 Nov 1999) · *Daily Telegraph* (2 Nov 1999) · *The Independent* (9 Nov 1999) · *WW* (1998) · Burke, *Peerage* · records, George Watson's College, Edinburgh · records, U. Edin. · R. Heussler, *British rule in Malaya: the Malayan civil service* (1981) · b. cert.
Archives Bodl. RH, interviews, 1987, MS Ind. Ocn.s.348 [transcript] | Bodl. RH, Heussler MSS, corresp. with R. Heussler
Likenesses photograph, 1955, repro. in *Daily Telegraph* · photograph, 1955, repro. in *The Independent*
Wealth at death £899,282: probate, 4 April 2000, *CGPLA Eng. & Wales*

Black, William (1749/50–1829), physician and writer on medicine, was born in Ireland of unknown parentage. He studied medicine, first at Edinburgh, then from 1771 at the University of Leiden, gaining his MD there in 1772 with a dissertation on fevers, dedicated to his fellow students at Edinburgh. Black's first publication, in 1781, was on smallpox and the arguments for inoculation at a time when concern was being voiced over the prevalence of this disease among children of the expanding industrial towns. He next published *A Historical Sketch of Medicine and Surgery … with a Chronological Chart of … Authors* (1782). Black was licensed by the Royal College of Physicians in 1787, after which he moved to Piccadilly, Westminster, where he practised.

Black did not rise to eminence as a physician, but he was one of the first writers in England to apply statistics, previously employed in politics and commerce, to medicine. Having delivered the annual oration before the Medical Society of London, he expanded his lecture into a volume entitled *A comparative view of the mortality of the human species at all ages, and of diseases and casualties, with charts and tables* (1788). Before the edition was even half sold he cancelled the remainder and brought out a corrected edition as *An Arithmetical and Medical Analysis of the Diseases and Mortality of the Human Species* (1789). His purpose was to show that births, mortalities, diseases, and casualties could be subjected to arithmetical proof, to construct for the benefit of the progress of medicine a 'medical arithmetic', a phrase suggested by the 'political arithmetic' of Sir William Petty. His efforts had considerable importance in their day although they were eventually eclipsed by later workers in the same field. Events in revolutionary France led him to publish anti-French pamphlets in 1792 and 1796.

Observations on two to three thousand cases at Bethlem Hospital, provided by a member of Bethlem's staff and added to an expanded chapter from the *Arithmetical … Analysis*, provided the substance of Black's *Dissertation on Insanity* (1810). Black retired to live in Hammersmith, Middlesex, where he died in December 1829. There is no evidence that he ever married; administration of his modest estate was granted to his widowed sister, Jane Elliott.

                                J. F. PAYNE, *rev.* ANITA MCCONNELL

Sources M. Neuburger, 'Francis Clifton and William Black: eighteenth century critical historians of medicine', *Journal of the History of Medicine and Allied Sciences*, 5 (1950), 44–9 · *GM*, 1st ser., 100/1 (1830), 90 · R. W. Innes Smith, *English-speaking students of medicine at the University of Leyden* (1932), 23 · administration, PRO, PROB 6/206, fol. 186
Likenesses R. Stanier, stipple, pubd 1790, BM, NPG
Wealth at death under £1500: administration, PRO, PROB 6/206, fol. 186

Black, William (1841–1898), journalist and novelist, was born at Glasgow on 9 November 1841, the son of James Black (*d.* 1855), a merchant. After receiving his education at various private schools, he studied landscape painting for a short time in the Glasgow School of Art, but, becoming connected with the *Glasgow Citizen*, gradually exchanged art for journalism. His contributions to the *Citizen* included sketches of the most eminent literary men of the day.

In 1864 Black published his first novel, *James Merle: an Autobiography*, which was a total failure. In the same year, after an unhappy love affair with an actress, he went to London and built up a reputation as a contributor to the magazines. He married a German woman, Augusta Wenzel, on 8 April 1865. She died in May 1866, and left him a son, who died in 1871. In 1865 he became connected with the *Morning Star*, and in the following year went to Germany as its correspondent in the Franco-Prussian War. As he himself admitted, he had no special qualification for the part except for a smattering of German. During most of the very short campaign he was under arrest on suspicion of being a spy, but the observations he made in the Black Forest aided the success of his third novel, *In Silk Attire* (1869), partly set there. He had already, in 1867, produced *Love or Marriage*, which was unpopular on account of its discussion of delicate social questions, and which he spoke of later as 'fortunately out of print'. The success of *In Silk Attire* helped *Kilmeny* (1870), a story equally delightful for its sketches of artistic life in London and its rural scenery, and *A Monarch of Mincing Lane*; but the author's first real triumph was won by *A Daughter of Heth* (1871). Here he was most fortunate in his subject, depicting the transformations and tragic adventures of a lively French girl, a coquette, transplanted into a Scottish puritan family. *The Strange Adventures of a Phaeton* (1872) was even more successful, and introduced what became Black's special characteristic: so thorough a combination of scenes of actual experience in travel and sport with fictitious adventures that readers sometimes hardly knew whether they were reading a book of travel or a novel. After the interruption of publication of the *Morning Star* Black became connected with the *Daily News* in 1870, and was for some time assistant editor, but retired from journalism upon gaining an assured position as a novelist. In 1874 *A Princess of Thule* thoroughly confirmed his reputation. It was very popular in both England and America and was translated into German, Russian, and Swedish; Queen Victoria even had an imaginary portrait of the heroine painted for her private collection. Both in this book and in *Madcap Violet* (1876), as previously in *A Daughter of Heth*, the delineation of young female characters was particularly successful. In 1874 Black married Eva Simpson, the daughter of a journalist.

Black was a very entertaining author, and continued to maintain his popularity to the end of an active career, although he never regained the level of the best work of his middle period. The most remarkable of his later novels were *Macleod of Dare* (1878), the story of a highland chief who discovers London; *Sunrise* (1880), a controversial picture of international socialism; and *Judith Shakespeare* (1884), a romance about the dramatist's daughter. He also wrote the study on Goldsmith in the English Men of Letters series (1878). A collected edition of his works in twenty-six volumes appeared between 1892 and 1894. Although lacking in extraordinary incidents or situations and in subtlety, his novels were built on precise and exhaustive descriptions which won the admiration of many readers, among whom was Ruskin, who commended warmly their closely observed picturesqueness.

Black was wealthy enough to spend most of his time in travelling and yachting, and his amusements helped to provide material for his novels. His permanent residence was Paston House, 1 Paston Place, Brighton, where he was a liberal host. He died at his home after a short illness, on 10 December 1898. He was buried on 15 December within a few yards of Sir Edward Burne-Jones in Rottingdean churchyard. A William Black memorial lighthouse tower, designed by William Leiper RSA and erected on Duart Point in the Sound of Mull, was lit for the first time on 13 May 1901.   RICHARD GARNETT, *rev.* S. R. J. BAUDRY

Sources *The Times* (12 Dec 1898) · *Daily News* (12 Dec 1898) · *Daily News* (16 Dec 1898) · *Glasgow Herald* (12 Dec 1898) · *The Athenaeum* (17 Dec 1898) · J. Sutherland, *The Longman companion to Victorian fiction* (1988) · S. J. Kunitz and H. Haycraft, eds., *British authors of the nineteenth century* (1936) · A. T. C. Pratt, ed., *People of the period: being a collection of the biographies of upwards of six thousand living celebrities*, 2 vols. (1897) · R. Cochrane, *The treasury of modern biography* (1878) · L. C. Sanders, *Celebrities of the century: being a dictionary of men and women of the nineteenth century* (1887) · d. cert.
Archives BL, letters as sponsor to the Royal Literary Fund, loan no. 96 · NL Scot., corresp. and literary MSS · Princeton University Library, New Jersey, corresp. and literary MSS | BL, letters to G. L. Craik, Add. MS 61895 · BL, letters to Macmillan & Co., Add. MS 54929 · Hunt. L., corresp. and literary MSS · NL Scot., letters to William Blackwood & Sons · U. Edin. L., letters to James Halliwell-Phillipps
Likenesses oil study for *A knight of the seventeenth century*, c.1877, Scot. NPG · Barraud, photograph, NPG; repro. in *Men and Women of the Day*, 3 (1890) · J. J. Cade, stipple, NPG; repro. in *Eclectic Magazine* · Elliott & Fry, photogravure, NPG · Lock & Whitfield, photograph, NPG; repro. in T. Cooper and others, *Men of mark: a gallery of contemporary portraits*, 2 (1877) · Maclure & McDonald, chromolithograph, NPG · P. Naumann & R. Taylor & Co., wood-engraving (*Our literary contributors—past and present*), BM; repro. in *ILN* (1892) · J. Pettie, oils, Scot. NPG · Spy [L. Ward], chromolithograph caricature, NPG; repro. in *VF* (21 Feb 1891)
Wealth at death £29,625 13s. 6d.: probate, 21 Jan 1899, *CGPLA Eng. & Wales*

Black, William Henry (1808–1872), antiquary, the eldest son of John Black of Kintore, in Aberdeenshire, was born on 7 May 1808. His mother's family, the Langleys, who owned estates in Oxfordshire and Buckinghamshire, influenced his strong religious opinions and formed his taste for antiquarian pursuits. He was educated at a private school, and at seventeen years of age became a tutor among families living at Tulse Hill, London, and the surrounding neighbourhood. His first publications were catalogues of the Arundel manuscripts at the College of Arms (1829) and of Colfe's Library at Lewisham (1831) for the Leathersellers' Company. He contributed to Samuel Bentley's *Excerpta historica* (1831) and to Sir Richard Colt Hoare's *A History of Modern Wiltshire* (1822–44). He was in Oxford between 1831 and 1833 compiling the justly esteemed catalogue, published in 1845, of the Ashmole manuscripts, now in the Bodleian Library. As a reader at the British Museum in London he became acquainted with many literary men, through whose influence in 1834 he obtained a situation in the Record Commission. He claimed to be the first on the scene to save some of the records during the burning of the houses of parliament in the same year, while he was living in Lambeth. At the Record Commission he helped to train transcribers of records, and to revise Rymer's *Foedera*, and edited without completing the *Docquets of Letters Patent Charles I*, which was eventually published after his death.

In 1840 Black was appointed assistant keeper in the newly established Public Record Office, where among other duties he compiled inventories of the Pells Office records and reported on the Treasury records. He suffered from poor health and thought his eyesight was damaged when attempting to salvage records soaked with sewage in a flood at Treasury Chambers. A strong sabbatarian, his service was terminated in 1853 because of his refusal to work on Saturdays and his work at the Treasury ceased the following year.

Black was a prolific contributor to the journals of antiquarian societies. He issued numerous pamphlets on biblical history, edited three volumes of early English poetry for the Percy Society, and had articles in most issues of the *British Archaeological Association Journal* from 1846 to 1872. His edition of the Antonine itinerary in preparation for the Rolls Series was never published.

Black was elected fellow of the Society of Antiquaries of London in 1858 and served on the council. Several communications between 1861 and 1871 were reported in the society's *Proceedings*, of which the first, on his discovery of Holbein's will, aroused considerable interest. He was also one of the earliest members of the British Archaeological Association, the Surrey, London and Middlesex, and Wiltshire Archaeological societies, and the founder of the Chronological Institute of London, the Palestine Archaeological Association, and the Anglo-Biblical Institute, besides being a member of the Camden Society. As a conscientious and painstaking antiquary, he was highly regarded by his contemporaries.

In 1840 Black was ordained minister of a small congregation of Seventh-Day Baptists, whose chapel was in Mill Yard, Leman Street, Whitechapel, until 1885. He lived in the minister's house at 15 Mill Yard. He associated the church with the Unitarians, but his stress on the Old Testament led to a charge of secret Judaism. He was constantly involved in litigation and in 1851 had heavy damages awarded against him for libelling a fellow Baptist minister. Black was married three times. With his first wife, whose name is not known, he had three daughters. In 1841 he married Mary Anne (d. 1843), daughter of Benjamin Noakes, doctor of medicine. Later he married Harriot (d. 1861), daughter of William Slater, formerly a minister at Mill Yard. Black's daughter Theodora married William Mead Jones, his own successor as pastor. He died on 12 April 1872 in Mill Yard.   BERNARD NURSE

Sources DNB · J. D. Cantwell, *The Public Record Office, 1838–1958* (1991) · F. H. A. Micklewright, 'A congregation of sabbatarian and Unitarian Baptists', *N&Q*, 191 (1946), 95–9 · 'Some further notes on Mill Yard meeting house', *N&Q*, 191 (1946), 137–40, 161–3, 185–9 · R. W. Hunt, ed., *A summary catalogue of Western manuscripts in the Bodleian Library at Oxford*, 1 (1953) · *CGPLA Eng. & Wales* (1872) · record book of Mill Yard Seventh Day General Baptist Church, library of the Seventh Day Baptist Historical Society, Janesville, Wisconsin, USA [copy in Dr Williams's Library, London]
Archives Bodl. Oxf., notes and papers relating to Ashmole MSS · Bodl. Oxf., papers · Chetham's Library, Manchester, journal · CUL, memorials of Seventh-Day Baptists · Harvard U., Houghton L., notes · JRL, papers · Magd. Oxf., papers relating to the 'Maudelyne grace' · PRO, 1/12/8 · U. Cal., Berkeley, Bancroft Library, notes on literary and historical works · Yale U., Beinecke L., papers | BL, corresp. with Sir Frederic Madden, Eg MSS 2838–2842 · Bodl. Oxf., letters to Sir Thomas Phillipps · U. Edin., letters to James Halliwell-Phillipps
Likenesses engraving, 1856, PRO, 8/56
Wealth at death under £1500: administration with will, 17 May 1872, *CGPLA Eng. & Wales*

Blackaby, Frank Thomas (1921–2000), economist and peace campaigner, was born on 25 October 1921 at Milton under Wychwood, Gloucestershire, the second child and only son of the Revd Edgar Percival Blackaby (1883–1977) and his wife, Muriel Ruth Hawkins (1884–1977). His parents, both Baptists, met in India, where his father was serving as a minister and his mother as a medical missionary. In 1917 they were married in India, where Frank's sister was born in 1918. The family returned to England, where after a few years in Gloucestershire they moved to Willingham, near Cambridge, living always on the very small income of a Baptist minister. The children attended the village school, from which Frank went on to the Perse School, Cambridge, in 1931 and then, in 1939, to Emmanuel College, Cambridge, where he took a first in part one of the classical tripos in 1940.

Blackaby's education was interrupted by the war. Determined to be a conscientious objector doing social work, he made an uncompromising statement of his beliefs to the authorities. It began:

> I believe that Christ, by his word and by his life and death, taught that the power of love alone could overcome the power of individual and social sin. I, as a Christian, am committed to try to show forth that love, however imperfectly; and though I may have to compromise with methods in social life which fall short of it, I can never cooperate in a method which utterly denies it, as does war. (private information)

Granted exemption from military service, he served in the Friends' Ambulance Unit in Egypt, Palestine, and the Dodecanese Islands, followed by two post-war years in those islands with the United Nations Relief and Rehabilitation Administration (UNRRA). During this period he lost his Christian faith. Back at Cambridge in 1947 he turned to economics, believing it had potential for improving the world. Having taken a first in part two of the economics tripos in 1949 he worked from 1950 to 1957 as an economic assistant in the Treasury information division and then for a year as assistant secretary of the council for prices, productivity, and incomes.

In 1958 Blackaby moved to the National Institute for Economic and Social Research (NIESR) to be assistant editor of its *Economic Review*, which was being launched to provide the public for the first time with regular economic forecasts of the kind produced within Whitehall as a guide to macro-economic policy. In 1962 he became its editor, a position that he held until 1968, when he went to join the Stockholm International Peace Research Institute (SIPRI), which had just been established by the Swedish government. He edited the first two issues of the SIPRI *Yearbook of Armaments and Disarmament* (1969) and he was leader of a most able team that produced SIPRI's study *The Arms Trade with the Third World* (1971). In 1971 he returned to the NIESR, as deputy director, and there, besides taking part in the running of the institute, he organized, edited, and contributed to four studies: *An Incomes Policy for Britain* (1972), *British Economic Policy, 1960–74* (1978), *Deindustrialisation* (1979), and *The Future of Pay Bargaining* (1980). In 1981 he returned to Stockholm, as director of SIPRI, and remained there until he retired, in 1986.

In retirement Blackaby turned his energies to campaigning for peace. He was a member of the British-American Security Information Society, the British National Peace Council, and the World Disarmament Campaign; he was treasurer of the British Pugwash movement; he wrote a history of SIPRI's first thirty years (1996); and he was a resolute participant in demonstrations and representations to governments. In protest against France's resumption of nuclear tests in September 1995 he initiated a campaign for a boycott of French wine by demonstrating with placards outside the French embassy and pouring French wine into a dustbin while handing out other wine.

Blackaby married first, on 27 October 1961, Elizabeth Brock, *née* Partington, (b. 1923/4), a social worker, with whom he had one son, Mark, and from whom he was divorced on 30 October 1975; on 31 December 1975 he married the economist Mary Mildred Acland-Hood (b. 1941), widow of Toby Hodder-Williams (d. 1969), who retained her maiden name and with whom he had a daughter, Susan, and a son, John.

Frank Blackaby died, of cancer, on 18 May 2000 in Guy's Hospital, London, and was buried on 26 May in woodland at his wife's family home, Wootton House, near Glastonbury, Somerset. He was a man of conscience who sought to improve the world through economics and peace research. To that task he applied his unusual skill in deploying words and statistics with didactic clarity.

ROBERT NEILD

Sources *The imperial calendar and civil service list* · private information (2004) [M. Acland-Hood] · personal knowledge (2004) · *The Guardian* (20 May 2000) · b. cert. · m. cert. [E. Brock] · m. cert. [M. Acland-Hood] · d. cert. · divorce certificate
Likenesses photograph, repro. in *The Guardian*

Blackadder [Blacater], **Adam** (*supp. fl.* **1319**), supposed author, is said by Thomas Dempster, writing in the early seventeenth century, to have taught philosophy at Cracow and Bologna before settling in Paris, where he was rector of the university and head of the Collège de Tournai. With a precision which he does nothing to explain, Dempster states that Blackadder flourished in 1319. He allegedly wrote 'Dissertatio pro Alexandro Magno contra T. Livii locum ex decad. I. lib. IX', said to have been published at Lyons. None of this has been confirmed by subsequent research. There is no record of Blackadder at either Bologna or Paris; his supposed work on Livy cannot be traced; and he cannot have taught in Cracow at the time Dempster suggests, since the university there was not founded until 1364. It is possible that he owes his shadowy existence to confusion with the Adam Blackadder who was prior of Coldingham from 1528 to 1541 and thereafter commendator of Dundrennan. This Adam Blackadder matriculated at St Andrews in 1532, but there is otherwise no indication that he had an academic career. In any case, Dempster's unreliability makes even this supposed confusion of identity quite uncertain. J. H. BURNS

Sources *Thomae Dempsteri Historia ecclesiastica gentis Scotorum, sive, De scriptoribus Scotis*, ed. D. Irving, rev. edn, 1, Bannatyne Club, 21 (1829), 124 · G. Mackenzie, *The lives and characters of the most eminent writers of the Scots nation*, 1 (1708), 420–22 · M. Dilworth, 'Coldingham Priory and the Reformation', *Innes Review*, 23 (1972), 115–37, esp. 125–6

Blackadder, Adam (*b.* **1659**, *d.* in or after **1696**), merchant and writer on covenanting, was probably born in the parish of Troqueer, near Dumfries, the second son of John *Blackadder (1615/1623?–1686), the minister there, and his wife, Janet Haining (*d.* 1688). Among his brothers were Dr William *Blackadder (1647–1696) and John *Blackadder (1664–1729). As his father was a prominent covenanting minister (one of Howie's 'Scots worthies'), who was constantly harassed and pursued by the authorities, Blackadder's childhood was turbulent. In 1662 his father was expelled from his parish with the restoration of episcopacy, and the family moved to Barndennock in the parish of Glencairn. In 1666, while Blackadder's father was fortunately away, soldiers sent by the bishop of Galloway raided the family house at night, confiscating John Blackadder's books and sermons, and pillaging the house. Blackadder was forced to hold a candle to assist the men in their search. He managed to escape and fled to a nearby town, where he collapsed on a doorstep and was taken in by the owners of the house when he told them his father's name. After this the family was dispersed for safety.

The young Blackadder was raised to be a merchant, and is next heard of in Stirling in November 1674, when, still an apprentice, he was arrested for allegedly refusing to sign the 'Black bond' and for attending conventicles. He was kept in prison for five weeks, after which he was released as a result of petitions to the privy council made by his elder brother, William. He was subsequently imprisoned twice more, in Fife and Blackness, in the latter place for attending his father's conventicle near Borrowstounness, Linlithgowshire, where twenty-six children were baptized.

About 1675 Blackadder went to Sweden, where he lived as a merchant for the next nine years. While there he married a Swedish woman, whose name is unknown, whom he converted from Lutheranism to presbyterian Calvinism. This put both Blackadder and his wife in danger, as the penalty for a Swede making such a conversion was death. The couple lived for a while under the protection of the Dutch ambassador in Stockholm; they then left for Scotland, and arrived in Dunbar in late 1684. After visiting his father, who was at that time in the Bass Rock prison, Blackadder went to Edinburgh, where he settled at the close of 1684, again as a merchant.

On 26 March 1696 Blackadder subscribed £100 to the Darien scheme as factor for his brother Captain John Blackadder (or Blackader). He is known to have supported the Darien venture in various tracts, and he also wrote pamphlets on the political state of Scotland. He later wrote an account of his father's sufferings and his own experiences during the persecutions of the late seventeenth century, which he sent to the great Presbyterian historian Robert Wodrow. This account was subsequently used by other writers as a source for works about the persecutions, including Andrew Crichton and John Howie. Blackadder probably lived in Edinburgh for the rest of his life; the date of his death is unknown.

ALEXANDER DU TOIT

Sources Anderson, *Scot. nat.*, 1.312 · *Memoirs of Rev. John Blackader*, ed. A. Crichton (1823), 328–38 · J. Howie and W. H. Carlaw, *The Scots worthies* (1885), 481–502 · *Fasti Scot.*, new edn, 2.302 · R. Wodrow, *The history of the sufferings of the Church of Scotland from the Restoration to the revolution*, ed. R. Burns, 3 (1829), 264–6 · A. Crichton, *The life and diary of Lt. Col John Blackader* (1824) · *The Darien papers* (1848), 384
Archives BL, Lansdowne collection

Blackadder, John (1615/1623?–1686), Church of Scotland minister, was perhaps born in December 1615 or in 1623, the son of John Blackadder of Inzievar, of the families of Blackadder of Blairhall and Tulliallan, and his wife, Helen, daughter of Robert *Pont (1524–1606), minister of St Cuthbert, near Edinburgh. In 1640 or 1646 he married Janet (*d.* 1688), daughter of Homer Haining, merchant of Dumfries. He was a distinguished student at the University of Glasgow, where his uncle John *Strang (1583/4–1654) was principal, and from where he graduated MA in 1650. Unanimously called to the parish of Troqueer, near Dumfries, in 1652, he was ordained on 7 June 1653. Blackadder is said to have worked hard to restore church discipline and reform his flock during this turbulent period. However, following the restoration of episcopacy in 1662, he was deprived of his charge and temporarily imprisoned in Edinburgh.

Blackadder then retired with his wife and family to Glencairn, Dumfriesshire, and other places. As one of the deprived ministers who believed that the civil government could not revoke their right to preach, he strove to maintain presbyterianism by preaching at conventicles together with other respected preachers, such as John Welsh, Alexander Peden, and Donald Cargill. The records of the privy council show that letters for his apprehension were issued four times between 1666 and 1677, but Blackadder remained at large. On one occasion, when he delivered a sermon at Kinkell, near St Andrews, the people crowded to hear him, notwithstanding the absolute commands of Archbishop James Sharp (himself a former presbyterian). When the irate archbishop ordered the provost to march out the militia to disperse the congregation, he was told it was impossible, as the militia had gone there as worshippers.

Outlawed, and with a reward offered for his body, in 1678 Blackadder fled to Rotterdam, where he apparently helped to heal differences between the presbyterian incumbents of the Scottish kirk, the moderate Robert Fleming and the more extreme Robert McWard. He was back in Edinburgh in June 1679, though he seems to have returned briefly to the Netherlands, where in 1680 his eldest son, William *Blackadder (1647–1696), enrolled at the University of Leiden. On 5 April 1681 he was seized in Edinburgh, examined before the privy council, and sent to the Bass Rock. After four years of rigid imprisonment his health finally gave way. In December 1685 the privy council gave permission for him to leave, on condition of his confining himself to Edinburgh, but it was too late, and he died on the Bass in January 1686. He was buried in the churchyard at North Berwick, where a dedicatory tombstone was erected in the nineteenth century. He was survived by his wife, who died on 9 November 1688 and was buried the next day at Greyfriars, Edinburgh, and by at least four of his five sons and two daughters: William, Adam *Blackadder (b. 1659, d. in or after 1696), John *Blackadder (1664–1729), and Elizabeth, who in 1687 married James Young, writer, of Edinburgh.

A. B. GROSART, rev. GINNY GARDNER

Sources Fasti Scot., 2.302 • T. McCrie, ed., The Bass Rock (1848), 350–61 • R. Wodrow, The history of the sufferings of the Church of Scotland from the Restauration to the revolution, 2 vols. (1721–2) • Anderson, Scot. nat. • DSCHT • Select passages from the diary and letters of the late John Blackadder, Esq. formerly lieutenant colonel of the XXVIth or Cameronian regiment of foot, and afterwards deputy governor of Stirling Castle, ed. J. Newton (1806), i–xiii • I. B. Cowan, The Scottish covenanters, 1660–1688 (1976) • W. Steven, The history of the Scottish church, Rotterdam (1832, 1833)

Archives NL Scot., life and memoirs [copy]

Blackadder [Blackader], **John** (1664–1729), army officer, was the fifth son of John *Blackadder the elder (1615/1623?–1686) and his wife, Janet Haining (d. 1688), and was born in the parish of Glencairn, Dumfriesshire, on 14 September 1664. William *Blackadder (1647–1696) and Adam *Blackadder (b. 1659, d. in or after 1696) were his elder brothers. Notwithstanding the persecution suffered by his father, the son, after receiving from him the foundations of a classical education, attended the courses of humanity and philosophy in the University of Edinburgh, but did not matriculate. He acquired at an early period

strong Calvinistic convictions and strict and stern views of conduct and duty. When the regiment raised by the covenanting Cameronians (later the 26th foot) was raised by James Douglas, earl of Angus (d. 1692), in 1689, Blackadder volunteered into it as a cadet at the pay of 6d. a day. Probably through his intimacy with the commander, Colonel William Cleland, who was an old college acquaintance, he was in a few months promoted lieutenant. The regiment, by the remarkable stand it made against the highlanders at Dunkeld, played a prominent role in quelling the rising.

Soon afterwards Blackadder embarked with his regiment for Flanders, where he served in all the principal sieges and battles until the treaty of Ryswick in 1697. At winter quarters in Maastricht in December 1691 he was court-martialled for killing Lieutenant Robert Murray in a duel. However, in May 1692 he was pardoned by King William and restored to his position in the regiment. In January 1693 he was promoted captain. After the treaty of Ryswick the Cameronians remained in Holland with the Scots brigade on Dutch pay and were later garrisoned at Perth.

Following a period in London negotiating over arrears of pay, Blackadder rejoined his regiment at Perth in August 1701. Here he began a courtship of Anne, daughter of James Callender of Craigforth, near Stirling. They were married on 4 February 1702. On the resumption of war in 1702 the Cameronians were ordered to Holland and it became the practice of Anne to reside within the Dutch border towns during this and subsequent campaigns.

Blackadder served in all Marlborough's campaigns. In 1704 he was wounded at the battle of Blenheim, where his regiment suffered heavy losses in the assault on Blenheim village. He was promoted major in October 1705 and was present at Ramillies (1706) and Oudenarde (1708), and at the siege of Lille he was wounded twice while in command of a force of 400 grenadiers in an attempt to breach the French fortifications.

Blackadder also fought at Malplaquet (1709), where the vacancy caused by the death of Colonel Cranston led to his promotion to lieutenant-colonel and command of the regiment. Blackadder commanded the Cameronians until October 1711, shortly before the treaty of Utrecht, when he sold his colonelcy to George, fifth Lord Forrester, of the Scots Greys, for £2600. Thus ended twenty-two years of active service with the regiment.

Blackadder returned to Scotland, taking up residence in Edinburgh, and afterwards at Craigforth, Stirling. He occupied much of his attention with ecclesiastical affairs, becoming an elder of the College Church, Edinburgh, and a member of the Society for Promoting Christian Knowledge, and of the general assembly of the Church of Scotland. At the Jacobite rising of 1715, he was appointed colonel of the regiment raised by the city of Glasgow, which he posted at the bridge of Stirling to guard against an attack of the highlanders who, however, were defeated at the battle of Sheriffmuir. In consideration of his services during the rising he was, in March 1717, appointed deputy governor of Stirling Castle. He died on 31 August 1729, presumably at Craigforth, and was buried in the West Church of Stirling, where a marble tablet was erected to his memory. He had no children but was survived by his wife, Anne, who later married Sir James Campbell, bt, of Ardinglas, formerly an officer with the Scots troop of life guards. Blackadder's diaries, extracts of which together with a life were published in 1824, remain a source of information for historians of the period. Although written as a spiritual record of his experiences, they shed some light on Marlborough's campaigns in the early eighteenth century.

T. F. HENDERSON, *rev.* JONATHAN SPAIN

Sources *The life and diaries of Lieut. Col. John Blackadder*, ed. A. Chrichton (1824) · C. Dalton, ed., *English army lists and commission registers, 1661–1714*, 6 vols. (1892–1904) · S. H. F. Johnston, *The history of the Cameronians*, 4 vols. (1957–71) · R. E. Scouller, *The armies of Queen Anne* (1966) · J. C. R. Childs, *The Nine Years' War and the British army, 1688–1697: the operations in the Low Countries* (1991) · D. Chandler, *Marlborough as military commander* (1973)
Likenesses oils, Scot. NPG

Blackadder [Blackader], **Robert** (*d.* in or before **1468**), landowner, is described by Andrew Crichton, in his account of the ancestry of the seventeenth-century covenanter John Blackadder, as having been 'remarkable for courage and daring enterprise' on the Anglo-Scottish borders in the fifteenth century (Crichton, 2). Crichton, who was clearly drawing on a manuscript family history, wrongly names Robert as Cuthbert in a report of his life and exploits which is only sometimes, and then probably coincidentally, reliable. Record evidence shows that Blackadder took his name from Blackadder in Berwickshire, where in 1452 the estate he had once held of the earl of March was granted to him in free barony by James II. Thereafter he received occasional payments for services to the crown, most notably in 1464, when he was one of three envoys paid for going to England to negotiate a truce; on 11 October of that year he was present in parliament at Edinburgh. He probably died in or shortly before 1468, when Adam Blackadder, presumably his son, received sasine of Blackadder.

Crichton, however, attributes to Blackadder a conspicuous role in the defence of the Scottish borders against English attacks and also participation in a campaign into England which ended in a battle—assumed by Crichton to have been that of Bosworth—where he and three of his sons were killed. There is no doubt that Blackadder Castle was involved in the Anglo-Scottish campaigns of the early 1480s, for it was garrisoned by twenty men in 1481 and in the following year the lands around it were devastated by Richard of Gloucester's invading army. And it is equally well established that a Scottish force fought for Henry Tudor at Bosworth, under the leadership of Sir Alexander Bruce of Earlshall. But Robert Blackadder was certainly dead long before 1485, while Adam Blackadder and such other likely members of his family as can be identified as having been active then were still active for years afterwards. Consequently the contribution of the Blackadders

to these events would appear to have occupied an indistinct point somewhere between marginality and non-existence.

HENRY SUMMERSON

Sources *Memoirs of Rev. John Blackader*, ed. A. Crichton, 2nd edn (1826) · J. M. Thomson and others, eds., *Registrum magni sigilli regum Scotorum / The register of the great seal of Scotland*, 11 vols. (1882–1914), vol. 2 · G. Burnett and others, eds., *The exchequer rolls of Scotland*, 6–7 (1883–4); 9–10 (1886–7) · N. Macdougall, *James III: a political study* (1982) · P. G. B. McNeill and H. L. MacQueen, eds., *Atlas of Scottish history to 1707* (1996), 119 · G. Ridpath and P. Ridpath, *The border history of England and Scotland*, new edn (1848), 305

Blackadder [Blacader], **Robert** (*c.*1445–1508), administrator and archbishop of Glasgow, may have been born in Berwickshire; he was the brother of Sir Patrick Blackadder of Tulliallan, Fife. He determined as BA at the University of St Andrews in 1462, was admitted to the faculty of arts at the University of Paris in 1464, and graduated MA there in 1465. A study of his seven visits to Rome from 1471 onwards, and especially after his admission as protonotary apostolic in 1476, shows him to have been a strong and forceful pursuer of causes for James III, James IV, and for himself at the papal curia, despite the debts he incurred with the apostolic camera as he sought to annex the precentorship of Dunkeld, the archdeaconry of St Andrews, and the archdeaconry of Aberdeen to his rectory of Lasswade, Edinburghshire, before being provided to the see of Aberdeen on 14 July 1480. He was transferred unconsecrated to Glasgow on 19 March 1483; the cathedral chapter there had already elected George Carmichael to the see by 13 February 1483, but this election was annulled by the pope, and Blackadder was consecrated in Rome between 13 and 30 April 1483.

Blackadder, conscious of the ancient traditions of Glasgow as a *filia specialis* of the Holy See, deeply resented being subject to the jurisdiction of William Scheves (*d.* 1497) when St Andrews was raised to the primacy of the Scottish church in 1487, and with his diocese he was formally exempted from its jurisdiction by Innocent VIII (*r.* 1484–92) on 25 May 1488. Backed by a strong plea from James IV, whom Blackadder had supported in his rebellion against his father in 1488, Glasgow was raised to archiepiscopal and metropolitan, but not primatial status on 9 January 1492—a situation which could only deepen the rift between the two metropolitan jurisdictions. Nevertheless, Blackadder remained an active, hardworking participant in the daily government of the realm. He was one of James III's representatives at the coronation of Henry VII at Westminster in 1485 and visited Spain twice, in 1495 and 1496, to seek a bride for James IV. He helped to negotiate the terms of the marriage settlement between James IV and Margaret Tudor, and performed their marriage ceremony in Holyrood Abbey on 8 August 1503.

A learned, orthodox archbishop, Blackadder also devoted much time and energy to his cathedral, refashioning its choir and transepts and extending a project to provide a proper setting for the shrine of St Kentigern, besides building a chapel at Culross, where St Kentigern was thought to have been educated. In February 1508 he set off on a pilgrimage to Jerusalem. In June, having got to Venice, he made his will, leaving most of his goods and money for the completion of his building projects in Glasgow, to religious orders to preach the gospel throughout his archdiocese, and to the poor. But on 28 July 1508 he died at sea between Venice and Jaffa with twenty-six other pilgrims, almost certainly from typhoid or cholera, and never reached Jerusalem. He was probably buried at sea on the day of his death or soon after.

LESLIE J. MACFARLANE

Sources Vatican Archives, Fondo Borghese, vol. 880, ser. 1, fols. 390r–310r · *CEPR letters*, vols. 14–15, 17 · C. Innes, ed., *Registrum episcopatus Glasguensis*, 2 vols., Bannatyne Club, 75 (1843), nos. 457–8, 460–63 · A. Theiner, *Vetera monumenta Hibernorum et Scotorum historiam illustrantia* (Rome, 1864), nos. 852, 885, 889 · A. I. Cameron, ed., *The apostolic camera and Scottish benefices, 1418–1488* (1934) · A. I. Dunlop, ed., *Acta facultatis artium universitatis Sanctiandree, 1413–1588*, St Andrews University Publications, 56 (1964), 148 · A. L. Gabriel and G. C. Boyce, eds., *Auctarium chartularii universitatis Parisiensis*, 6 (Paris, 1964) · *APS*, 1424–1567 nos. 213, 232–3 · L. J. Macfarlane, 'The elevation of the diocese of Glasgow into an archbishopric in 1492', *Innes Review*, 43 (1992), 99–118 · J. M. Thomson and others, eds., *Registrum magni sigilli regum Scotorum / The register of the great seal of Scotland*, 11 vols. (1882–1914), vol. 2, no. 2723 · *CSP Venice, 1202–1509*, nos. 568, 604, 615, 774, 903–4, 909 · J. Durkan, 'Archbishop Robert Blackadder's will', *Innes Review*, 23 (1972), 138–48 · *CSP Spain, 1485–1509*, nos. 103–4 · D. McRoberts, 'Scottish pilgrims to the Holy Land', *Innes Review*, 20 (1969), 80–106 · T. M. Chalmers, 'The king's council, patronage, and governance of Scotland, 1460–1513', PhD diss., U. Aberdeen, 1982

Wealth at death considerable; left benefactions well over £1000 Scots: notarial copy of will, *Bolletino dell' Istituto*, vol. 1, pp. 169–78

Blackadder, William (1647–1696), physician and plotter, was the eldest son of John *Blackadder the elder (1615/1623?–1686), and his wife, Janet Haining (d. 1688); Adam *Blackadder (b. 1659, d. in or after 1696) and John *Blackadder (1664–1729) were among his brothers. Admitted to Edinburgh University in 1665, he graduated in 1668. In 1674 he secured the release of one of his brothers, who had been imprisoned by the provost of Stirling for not taking the prescribed oaths and for attending conventicles. On 14 July 1675 he was apprenticed to Patrick Hepburn, an apothecary in Edinburgh. Blackadder then studied medicine at Leiden, where he graduated MD on 24 August 1680. While in the United Provinces he made the acquaintance of many Scottish exiles, aided perhaps by his father's reputation as a presbyterian divine.

In 1685 Blackadder joined the earl of Argyll's expedition to Scotland. On 6 May, with three ships anchored off Orkney, he was sent ashore with Argyll's secretary, William Spence, in order to find a pilot and to gather intelligence. He was captured in Kirkwall and ordered to be taken to Edinburgh for examination by the privy council. On 6 June he landed at Leith and managed to signal to his sister to destroy any incriminating evidence in his lodgings. He remained in prison for over a year, until he was able to write to Pensionary Fagel in the United Provinces, a former patient, who sent for James II's envoy and asked him to release Blackadder as a naturalized Dutchman.

In 1688 Blackadder was sent by the prince of Orange into Edinburgh, but he was arrested by the governor and sent

for trial. He was freed following the revolution and on 3 January 1690 was appointed physician to the army in Scotland. He was also appointed a physician in ordinary to William III. He seems to have spent most of his time in Edinburgh. On 6 February 1691 he married Marion (b. after 1660, d. in or after 1698), eldest legitimate daughter of James Hunter of Muirhouse, advocate. By order of Edinburgh council on 29 September 1693 he was named a burgess of the city, reference being made to his apprenticeship under Sir Patrick Hepburn. Blackadder was elected a fellow of the Royal College of Physicians of Edinburgh in 1695, but he died the following year; he was buried on 27 October 1696 in Greyfriars, Edinburgh. His wife survived him and married William Walkinshaw on 14 September 1698.

STUART HANDLEY

Sources R. W. Innes Smith, *English-speaking students of medicine at the University of Leyden* (1932), 23 · *Memoirs of the Rev. John Blackadder*, ed. A. Crichton, 2nd edn (1826), 295–301 · *The life and diary of Lieutenant-Colonel John Blackader*, ed. A. Crichton (1824), 13, 19 · J. Willcock, *A Scots earl in covenanting times* (1907) · D. Laing, ed., *A catalogue of the graduates … of the University of Edinburgh*, Bannatyne Club, 106 (1858), 95 · H. Paton, ed., *Register of interments in the Greyfriars burying-ground, Edinburgh, 1658–1700*, Scottish RS, 26 (1902), 57 · H. Paton, ed., *The register of marriages for the parish of Edinburgh, 1595–1700*, Scottish RS, old ser., 27 (1905), 64 · C. B. B. Watson, ed., *Roll of Edinburgh burgesses and guild-brethren, 1406–1700*, Scottish RS, 59 (1929), 60 · C. B. B. Watson, *Register of Edinburgh apprentices, 1666–1700*, Scottish RS, 60 (1929), 9 · C. Dalton, ed., *English army lists and commission registers, 1661–1714*, 3 (1896), 161

Blackader, Cuthbert. *See* Blackadder, Robert (d. in or before 1468).

Blackall, John (1771–1860), physician, was born in St Paul's Street, Exeter, on 24 December 1771, the sixth son of the Revd Theophilus Blackall (d. 1781), and his wife, Elizabeth Ley, and great-grandson of Bishop Ofspring Blackall. He was educated at Exeter grammar school, from where he matriculated on 25 May 1789 at Balliol College, Oxford. He graduated BA in 1793, MA in 1796, MB in 1797, and MD on 2 March 1801. Immediately after taking his first degree he began to study medicine at St Bartholomew's Hospital, London, and it was in its wards, while working as the clinical clerk of John Latham, that he made the observations on albuminuria which were afterwards described and enlarged in his treatise on dropsies.

In 1797 Blackall settled in his native city of Exeter and on 1 June in that year he was chosen physician to the Devon and Exeter Hospital. As a young man, however, he felt eclipsed in his practice by Hugh Downman, Bartholomew Parr, and George Daniell, and in 1801 he resigned his hospital appointment and settled at Totnes. There he worked hard, often riding 60 miles a day, and built an extensive practice. His reputation increased, and in 1807 he returned to Exeter, where he was elected physician to the Devon and Exeter Hospital for the second time. In 1812 he was also appointed physician to St Thomas's Lunatic Asylum, which was later to be relocated and developed as the Exe Vale Hospital, Wonford.

In 1813 Blackall published his well-known and admirable *Observations on the Nature and Cure of Dropsies*. The work almost coincided with that of William Wells, who in 1812 published a paper entitled 'Observations on the dropsy which succeeds scarlet fever'. Richard Bright, whose name was to become attached eponymously to kidney disease, did not publish the first of his classic works on the subject until 1827. In it he paid generous tribute to Blackall. However, unlike Bright neither Wells nor Blackall had appreciated the full significance of abnormal appearances of the kidneys in those of their patients on whom post-mortem examinations had been carried out. Nevertheless, Blackall's book made clear the relation between dropsy (accumulation of serous fluid in the cavities and tissues of the body) and the presence of albumen in the urine (albuminuria). He made the important observation that mercurial drugs damaged the kidneys and caused dropsy. An appendix described a number of cases of angina pectoris, which had begun to attract attention after William Heberden's observations in 1802.

Blackall was admitted a candidate of the Royal College of Physicians on 22 December 1814, and a fellow on 22 December 1815. His progress from this period was rapid and uninterrupted, and for many years he had an extensive and lucrative practice in the west of England, especially since the death of George Daniell. According to Thomas Shapter his diagnostic powers were of the highest order, and as a consulting practitioner no one more entirely won the esteem of his professional colleagues.

Blackall married Laura Barnes (1773–1862) on 30 August 1806, and they had four sons: John Ofspring, who was drowned in the River Exe, aged seventeen; Theophilus and Henry, who also both predeceased their father; and Thomas MD, who was to outlive him. Blackall retained his strength and faculties to an advanced age, and he did not give up private practice until he was eighty years old. He died at his home, 13 Southernhay West, Exeter, on 10 January 1860, and his burial in Holy Trinity churchyard was attended by a large body of relations and friends and the whole of the medical profession in Exeter.

G. C. BOASE, rev. ALICK CAMERON

Sources T. Shapter, 'The late John Blackall', *BMJ* (1860), 75–6 · Munk, *Roll* · P. de la Garde, *Address to district branch of British Medical Association, Exeter* (1 Dec 1871) · D. Berry and C. Mackenzie, eds., *Richard Bright, 1789–1858* (1992), 144–6, 150, 176, 187 · L. Fine and V. English, 'John Blackall', *American Journal of Nephrology*, 14 (1994), 371–6 · Foster, *Alum. Oxon.* · Burnet-Morris Index, Westcountry Studies Library, Exeter
Likenesses S. Cousins, mezzotint, pubd 1844 (after R. R. Reinagle), BM, NPG · R. R. Reinagle, oils, *c*.1850, RCP Lond. · portrait (after R. R. Reinagle), Royal Devon and Exeter Healthcare NHS trust
Wealth at death £60,000: probate, 21 Feb 1860, *CGPLA Eng. & Wales*

Blackall, Ofspring (*bap.* 1655, *d.* 1716), bishop of Exeter and religious controversialist, was born in London and baptized on 26 April 1655 at St Gregory by Paul's, the son of Thomas Blackall (*bap.* 1621, *d.* 1688), freeman of the Haberdashers' Company and later alderman of the City of London, and his wife, Martha (*bap.* 1625, *d.* 1701?), daughter of Charles Ofspring, rector of St Antholin, Budge Row,

Ofspring Blackall (*bap.* 1655, *d.* 1716), by George Vertue, 1722 (after Michael Dahl, *c*.1715)

and trier of the second presbyterian classis (or eldership) of London. Blackall's father owned land in several counties as well as property in the city, and although he conformed to the established church may have retained some puritan sympathies. During Blackall's youth his parents resided in Lordshold Manor, an 'ancient brick house' in Dalston, Middlesex (*VCH Middlesex*, 10.89). He was educated in nearby Hackney, perhaps at the free school of which Robert Skingle was master, before being admitted as a pensioner to St Catharine's College, Cambridge, on 26 April 1671. He graduated BA in 1675, proceeded MA in 1678, and was elected in 1679 (by the interest, it was rumoured, of William Wake) to a fellowship, which he resigned in 1687. He was ordained deacon on 11 March 1677 and priest on 19 December 1680. The university awarded him the degree of DD in 1700.

On 14 January 1690 Blackall was instituted to the rectory of South Ockendon, Essex; he resigned this for the rectory of St Mary Aldermary, London, to which he was presented by the dean and chapter of St Paul's on 6 November 1694. He also held the city lectureships of St Olave Jewry from

1695 to 1698, and St Dunstan-in-the-West from 1698. He was appointed chaplain to William and Mary, although it was later alleged that he had been a nonjuror and had refused to swear allegiance to the new monarchs for two years.

Blackall came to public prominence in 1699 when he engaged in a controversy with the Irish deist and pamphleteer John Toland. In his *Life of John Milton* (1699), Toland had disputed Charles I's authorship of *Eikon basilike*. In a brief aside Toland remarked that if such a recent deception could remain undiscovered, it was not surprising that the dubious authorship of some ancient Christian writings had likewise gone undetected. Blackall understood that Toland had slyly insinuated that parts of the New Testament were forgeries. In a sermon before the House of Commons on 30 January 1699, Blackall called on the Commons to act against this denial of the authenticity of the revelation of God, which if left unchecked would undermine public morality as well as Christian doctrine. Toland replied with *Amyntor, or, A Defence of Milton's Life* (1699), which attacked Blackall in a highly personal manner and accused him of theological ignorance. Toland disingenuously claimed he had disputed the authenticity not of the New Testament, but of 'spurious' apocryphal Christian works, of which he provided an extensive catalogue. Blackall's response, *Mr Blackall's Reasons for not Replying to a Book Lately Published Entituled Amyntor* (1699), ably demonstrated that Toland's words should most naturally have been taken to have referred to the New Testament, but Blackall nevertheless acknowledged Toland's apparent retraction. Blackall's altercation with Toland had brought him to prominence as a defender of revealed religion against the attacks of the deists. Consequently he was chosen to deliver the Boyle lectures in 1700. These consisted of seven sermons, which he preached at St Paul's Cathedral, on the theme 'The sufficiency of a standing revelation'.

Ten years after his exchange with Toland, Blackall found himself embroiled in controversy again, this time with a fellow clergyman. On 8 March 1709, the anniversary of Queen Anne's accession, Blackall preached a sermon before the queen in St James's Chapel, on the text Romans 13: 4. It was later published, with the title *The Divine Institution of Magistracy* (1709). Its themes echoed those of a sermon which Blackall had preached on the same occasion in 1705, at St Dunstan's, and which had also been published. It was a strong attack on the doctrines of popular sovereignty and the right of resistance, in which Blackall maintained that the magistrate's authority was a 'Portion of the Divine Authority … entrusted with him by God' (p. 3). It also maintained the independent *jure divino* basis of clerical authority in spiritual matters. Benjamin Hoadly, in *Some Considerations Humbly Offered to the … Bishop of Exeter* (1709), took offence to both sermons, which, he alleged, condemned the revolution of 1688–9. Hoadly claimed that the revolution had involved resistance to James II, but that such resistance was justified by the necessity of self-preservation. Blackall, in *The Lord Bishop of Exeter's Answer*

to Mr Hoadly's Letter, dismissed Hoadly's premise that civil authority derived from an original contract. He undertook to reply again to Hoadly only if he kept to issues of scriptural interpretation, and avoided speculations concerning matters such as an alleged 'State of Nature' about which the scriptures were silent. Hoadly's subsequent *Humble Reply* failed to comply with Blackall's conditions, and he did not therefore respond to it. The numerous pamphlets which were published on either side during the ensuing controversy included an anonymous work in support of Blackall, entitled *The Best Answer Ever was Made* (1709), by the Irish nonjuror and formidable controversialist Charles Leslie. As Blackall was by now a bishop, Hoadly's attack on him was later cited to justify the forthright treatment Hoadly received in the Bangorian controversy, after he himself had been elevated to the episcopal bench.

Ironically Blackall's same accession-day sermon of 1705, *The Subjects Duty*, had been attacked on its first publication by tory patriarchalist writers, who accused him of being a republican. The anonymous work *An essay upon government: wherein the republican schemes reviv'd by Mr. Lock, Dr. Blackal &c. are fairly consider'd and refuted* (1705), as well as linking Blackall's name with that of John Locke, took Blackall to task for contending that the precise form of government in any nation was a matter of human, and not divine, institution. Blackall suffered further abuse in a pamphlet entitled *Dr Blackall's Offspring* (1705).

Despite being attacked from both sides Blackall was considered by contemporaries to have distinct high-church and tory principles. Gilbert Burnet went so far as to judge that, although Blackall claimed to be loyal to the government, 'his notions were all on the other side', that is, the Jacobite side, and that he 'seemed to condemn the Revolution, and all that had been done pursuant to it' (*Bishop Burnet's History of his Own Time*, ed. G. Burnet and T. Burnet, 2 vols., 1724–34, 2.488). In fact Blackall was a consistent 'revolution tory' and maintained the high-church doctrines of passive obedience and non-resistance to sovereign powers, while denying the Filmerian tenet of divine hereditary right. By holding that sovereignty was always absolute, but that it belonged in the English constitution to the monarch in parliament, Blackall was articulating an important theory by which tories reconciled themselves to the revolution.

Blackall was nominated to the bishopric of Exeter by the personal determination of Queen Anne, upon the recommendation of John Sharp, archbishop of York, but without the knowledge of her ministers, whose politically expedient recommendations the queen, mindful of the royal prerogative, deemed insufficiently orthodox. It was consequently remarked wittily that he was the 'queen's bishop'. He was consecrated at Lambeth on 8 February 1708. In order to supplement his episcopal revenues he was permitted to hold, in addition to his bishopric, the deanery of St Borian, Cornwall, the rectory of Shorbrook, Devon, and the offices of archdeacon and treasurer of Exeter. He was a diligent bishop in his diocese, and he was also instrumental in the institution of charity schools in Exeter. He lived to see the establishment of two such schools for boys and two for girls, of fifty pupils each.

During his lifetime Blackall's reputation as a preacher was considerable, and a reading of his posthumously published *Works* (2 vols., 1723, edited by Blackall's friend, William Dawes, archbishop of York) shows that it was justified. His greatest literary work was a series of eighty-seven sermons issued as *Discourses on the Sermon on the Mount*. These sermons are both expository and pastoral, and while written in an uncomplicated style, are far from superficial and betray a considerable erudition. However the great magnitude of the work perhaps hindered its reception, and despite its literary and theological merits it receded into relative obscurity.

Blackall married Anne Dillingham (*d.* 1762) of London, probably the daughter of James and Elizabeth Dillingham. Seven of their children—Theophilus, John, Charles Ofspring, Elizabeth, Ann, Mary, and Jane—survived the death of their father on 29 November 1716 in Exeter. Blackall had fallen from a horse in the spring of that year, and as a consequence he suffered a long and painful illness during which he developed gangrene. An earnest account of Blackall's life and death, and particularly of the sufferings of his final illness, can be found in William Dawes's preface to Blackall's *Works*. Blackall was buried on 2 December in Exeter Cathedral, on the south side of the choir. In accordance with his will, no funeral sermon was preached, and his grave was not marked by any monument or inscription.

ANDREW STARKIE

Sources Venn, *Alum. Cant.* · G. Oliver, *Lives of the bishops of Exeter, and a history of the cathedral* (1861) · R. Polwhele, *The history of Devonshire*, 3 vols. (1793–1806), vol. 1, pp. 312–13 · G. Hennessy, *Novum repertorium ecclesiasticum parochiale Londinense, or, London diocesan clergy succession from the earliest time to the year 1898* (1898), 130 · *VCH Middlesex*, 10.89, 118 · BL Add. MS 4224, fol. 302 · J. R. Woodhead, *The rulers of London, 1660–1689* (1965), 32 · M. M. Goldsmith, '"Our Great Oracle, Mr Lock": Locke's political theory in the early eighteenth century', *Eighteenth-Century Life*, 16 (1992), 60–75 · D. Lysons, *The environs of London*, 4 vols. (1792–6), vol. 2, p. 463 · B. Clarke, *Glimpses of ancient Hackney and Stoke Newington* (1986), 242–3 · W. Robinson, *The history and antiquities of the parish of Hackney*, 2 vols. (1842), vol. 1, pp. 263–4; vol. 2, pp. 25, 40 · R. Simpson, *Memorials of St John at Hackney*, 3 pts (1882), 40 · J. L. Chester and G. J. Armytage, eds., *The parish registers of St Antholin, Budge Row … and of St John the Baptist on Wallbrook*, Harleian Society, register section, 8 (1883), 79 · *The registers of baptisms, marriages, and burials of the city of Exeter*, 1, ed. W. U. Reynell-Upham and H. Tapley-Soper, Devon and Cornwall RS (1910), 161 · I. W. Archer, *The history of the Haberdashers' Company* (1991), 240

Likenesses G. Vertue, line engraving, 1722 (after M. Dahl, *c.*1715), NPG [*see illus.*] · M. Dahl, oils, Bishop's Palace, Exeter · J. Sturt, line engraving (after M. Dahl), BM, NPG; repro. in O. Blackall, *Fourteen sermons*, 2nd edn (1706)

Blackall, Samuel (*bap.* **1737**, *d.* **1792**), Church of England clergyman, was baptized at Exminster, Devon, on 24 February 1737, the son of Theophilus Blackall (*d.* 1757), chancellor of the diocese of Exeter, and his wife, Phillippa Cooke; his paternal grandfather was Ofspring *Blackall, bishop of Exeter. Having been educated at Tiverton under Mr Dadds he was admitted as pensioner at Emmanuel College, Cambridge, on 29 October 1755. He graduated BA (as

twelfth wrangler) in 1760, proceeded MA in 1763 and BD in 1770, and was made fellow of his college in 1772. He was ordained deacon in London on 1 June 1760.

Blackall was described as a lively, clever, musical man who was a good rower, played the harpsichord well and sang, and was good at drawing and etching. In appearance he was dark and short, with a rather ugly face, and he suffered with a lame leg. He was one of those who in 1771–2 were involved with the Feathers tavern petition, which sought to end the requirements regarding subscription to the Thirty-Nine Articles. In 1772 he published *A letter to Dr Hallifax, upon the subject of his three discourses preached before the University of Cambridge, occasioned by an attempt to abolish subscription to the XXXIX Articles*. Samuel Hallifax, then a fellow of Trinity Hall, Cambridge, responded dismissively to Blackall in the preface to the 1772 (third) edition of his controversial *Three Sermons*, whose contents were mentioned in the title of Blackall's tract, merely observing that he held it a duty to himself 'not to render an enemy considerable by opposition, whose malice may most effectually be disarmed by contempt' (Hallifax, xi). The disagreement between the two men was continued in the letter pages of the *Gentleman's Magazine*, where both parties, but especially Blackall, found articulate defenders. 'M.X.' accused Blackall of Socinianism in one letter, prompting 'L.S.', 'C.D.', and 'L.L.B.' to write in Blackall's defence; L.S. asserted that such a charge could only be the invention of slander, and went on to explain that 'I never knew any divine more earnest in the defence of Christianity against the objections of infidels, or a warmer advocate for the fundamental articles of our faith, as well as for the essentials of church discipline' (*GM*, 43.69). Certainly Blackall, unlike Theophilus Lindsey, remained in the Church of England after the failure of the Feathers tavern petition.

In 1786 Blackall was appointed rector of Loughborough, Leicestershire, an Emmanuel College living, which he held until his death, on 6 May 1792, at Bristol Hotwells. He never married, and left most of his possessions to his sister Anne, whose husband, Archdeacon Barnes, was Blackall's executor. Ann inherited £1200 in old South Sea Company stocks, together with the leases of Blackall's house and land in Sidmouth, Devon, and his stables there; she was instructed to bequeath this inheritance, in turn, to her children. Blackall left his nephews Samuel and John *Blackall (the sons of his late brother Theophilus) all his books, manuscripts, and drawing and mathematical instruments, and 20 guineas apiece. Blackall was buried at the parish church of Sidmouth, where a memorial was put up in his name. He specially wished to be buried at Sidmouth because it was 'a place in which he had taken great delight when living' (*N&Q*, 8.55).

EMMA MAJOR

Sources Venn, *Alum. Cant.*, 1/4 · will, PRO, PROB 11/1219, sig. 317 · *GM*, 1st ser., 26 (1756), 563 · *GM*, 1st ser., 27 (1757), 531 · *GM*, 1st ser., 42 (1772), 265, 446, 516, 572 · *GM*, 1st ser., 43 (1773), 69 · *GM*, 1st ser., 50 (1780), 225 · *GM*, 1st ser., 62 (1792), 483 · S. Hallifax, *Three sermons preached before the University of Cambridge, occasioned by an attempt to abolish subscription to the XXXIX articles of religion*, 3rd edn (1772) · ESTC · *N&Q*, 6th ser., 7 (1883), 369 · *N&Q*, 6th ser., 8 (1883), 55 · DNB · IGI

Wealth at death approx. £1260; plus property in Sidmouth: will, PRO, PROB 11/1219, sig. 317

Black Baron, the. *See* Monro, Robert, of Foulis (*d.* 1633).

Blackbeard. *See* Teach, Edward (*d.* 1718).

Blackborne, Robert (*c.*1620–1701), naval official, was described by a herald as belonging to an armigerous family, with a Yorkshire father and Lancashire grandfather. It has been suggested that he was an apprentice in London, possibly the namesake made free of the Merchant Taylors' Company by patrimony of his father, William, in 1638. It is more likely that he was bred as a clerk, and he may have been the son (or kinsman) of Walter Blackborne, who was appointed overseer of the East India Company's cordage works at Woolwich in 1633, at £80 per annum, and seconded to supply the Navy Office the following year. Blackborne also had Devon connections, and was possibly related to the Robert Blackborne who was master of the *Robert* of Fawley in 1641.

Blackborne first appears as clerk to the parliamentary navy commissioners early in 1643. He proved a capable administrator and in October 1648 served as joint secretary to the parliamentary commissioners, among them Sir Henry Vane, negotiating with Charles I in the Isle of Wight. From 1650 or earlier he served the Rump's navy committee, and was solicitor to the commissioners of customs. He was appointed secretary to the customs commissioners in 1652, and at the end of the year became secretary to the admiralty and navy commissioners, holding both posts until the Restoration. These important positions placed him at the heart of naval affairs and customs revenues throughout the decade, with an estimated income of at least £500 a year. His correspondence reveals an energetic, respected, and efficient administrator. He lived in official quarters in Scotland Yard, off Whitehall, for which he could afford to pay a substantial entry-fine of £250 for a lease of fourteen years. His wife is first mentioned in 1656, though her name and the date of their marriage are both unknown; she was the aunt of Will Hewer, Pepys's trusted assistant, and possibly shared his surname.

Blackborne was a radical puritan, hailed as a 'dear friend' by Cromwell's chaplain, Hugh Peter (PRO, SP 18/103/72), and he acted as spiritual confessor to some of the officers. He was delighted when Cromwell expelled parliament in April 1653, and gave a Fifth Monarchist colleague a glowing account of the first weeks of Barebone's Parliament, which succeeded it. He readily accepted the protectorate, however, and laboured to persuade puritan naval commanders to do likewise. Blackborne remained in service during all the upheavals of 1659–60, until the Restoration ended his naval career. In March 1660 he confessed that the prospect of the king's return filled him with dismay, though in official correspondence he acknowledged that the nation was longing for it. By early April he was ready to accept the inevitable, and to speak of Charles in positive terms. Pepys noted that he was now willing to bend to the times and drink healths, but it is unlikely that he would have been prepared or allowed to serve the restored monarchy, and his admiralty post was given to William Coventry in July. Blackborne was reappointed as secretary to the new customs commissioners, however, and his experience and expertise soon opened up further opportunities. He had been made free of the East India Company as early as 1650, for services he had rendered through the Navy Office, and in December 1666 he was made secretary to the company, an appointment he was to hold for over thirty years, until 1700.

In the immediate aftermath of the Restoration, Blackborne was a valuable mentor to Pepys on Admiralty matters, and their families were on friendly terms. After a dinner party in October 1660 Pepys decided that Mrs Blackborne was 'a very high dame and a costly one' (Pepys, 1.268), but he continued to respect Blackborne, who for his part aired his views very frankly. In the course of a fascinating conversation on 9 November 1663 he defended the nonconformist clergy and Cromwellian officers, declared religious toleration essential to preserve the nation, and dismissed the bishops as generally despised. He also deplored the influence of hardline cavaliers, arguing that the king would have been more secure under a negotiated Restoration settlement. Blackborne condemned Monck, Lawson, and Penn as hypocrites for serving the monarchy, and while mocking the religious excesses of the Barebone's era remained clearly sympathetic to the Cromwellian regime. He assured Pepys, however, that he would always live quietly under the king, praying for God to enlighten him. The conversation was terminated by loud singing in the next room, but their friendship endured; many years later, in 1690, Blackborne stood bail for Pepys when he was imprisoned in the Gatehouse by the suspicious new government of William III.

Little is known of Blackborne's later years, apart from his diligent service with the East India Company. In 1667 the Treasury commissioners commended his role in handling the company's loan to the crown, though in 1668 he was twice examined by the House of Lords over an allegedly 'scandalous libel' issued by the company and bearing his signature (*Eighth Report*, HMC, appx 1, 167–8). A son, Samuel, was licensed to travel abroad in 1680. Blackborne owned landed property at Leake Chantry, and in 1695, when he was described as a widower, he was assessed for property worth £600 in St Andrew Undershaft, London. He died in the first half of 1701. His younger brother James was a prize officer and later surveyor of customs in Plymouth from 1654 to 1679, and other kin served as tax and customs officials in Devon.

BERNARD CAPP

Sources G. E. Aylmer, *The state's servants: the civil service of the English republic, 1649–1660* (1973) · B. Capp, *Cromwell's navy: the fleet and the English revolution, 1648–1660* (1989) · S. R. Gardiner and C. T. Atkinson, eds., *Letters and papers relating to the First Dutch War, 1652–1654*, 6 vols., Navy RS, 13, 17, 30, 37, 41, 66 (1898–1930) · Pepys, *Diary*, vols. 1–4, 9–10 · *CSP dom.*, 1643–1700 · *CSP col.*, vols. 8, 9, 15–18 · *Eighth report*, 1, HMC, 7 (1907–9) · W. A. Shaw, ed., *Calendar of treasury books*, 2–5, PRO (1905–11) · E. B. Sainsbury, ed., *A calendar of the court minutes … of the East India Company*, 11 vols. (1907–38) · will, PRO, PROB 11/461, sig. 90

Archives PRO, official corresp. and state papers

Blackbourne, John (1683–1741), bishop of the nonjuring Church of England, was the son of Thomas Blackbourne. He was educated at a school in Audley, Cheshire, and from May 1697 at Trinity College, Cambridge, where he graduated BA in 1701 and MA in 1705. His refusal to recognize the revolutionary settlement and to swear an oath of allegiance to William and Mary excluded him from clerical preferment.

Blackbourne then moved to Little Britain in the City of London, where,

> almost lost to the world and hid amongst old books … [he] lived a very exemplary, good life, and studied hard, endeavouring to be useful to mankind, both as a scholar and divine. To keep himself independent, he became corrector of the press to Mr. Bowyer, printer, and was, indeed, one of the most accurate of any that ever took upon him that laborious employ. (Nichols, 1.252–3)

In London he attracted a small religious community and regularly performed secret nonjuring services in an unofficial chapel at Gray's Inn. He was powerfully recommended to the exiled Stuart court in Rome by Lord Winchilsea, whose patronage was crucial for a number of nonjurors in London. In his presence, Blackbourne was consecrated as a nonjuring bishop on 6 May 1725 by the nonjuring prelates Nathaniel Spinckes and Henry Gandy, and later took part himself in the consecration of Richard Rawlinson on 25 March 1728.

In the 1720s Blackbourne became the leading figure among the group of nonjurors that, in respect to liturgical questions and the Book of Common Prayer, adhered to the practice of the Restoration church. He exemplified these principles (in, for example, his refusal to use the mixed chalice) in the biographical account of his friend, *The Life of the R. Reverend Mr. Nathanael Spinckes* (1731). The group came to be known as the nonusagers, in contradistinction to the usagers, who emphasized the importance of tradition in doctrinal questions and wished to introduce chiefly into their eucharistic liturgy certain changes, based on their knowledge of the ancient church and the first Book of Common Prayer (1549). The two parties remained separate, each consecrating several bishops, from the year 1718 to 1732, when a reconciliation was attempted. Blackbourne, however, 'the most violent opponent of that scheme of conciliation' (Broxap, 226), still refused to relinquish the use of the communion office of the Anglican church. He lost more and more influence within the nonjuring sect, but continued to lead a small separate community, the extreme nonusagers, which ceased to exist with his death.

Apart from his press corrections for the leading London printer William Bowyer, Blackbourne also edited several religious books and published a four-volume edition of the works of Francis Bacon (1730), which apparently contributed to the fact that he was well off compared to other nonjurors, leaving several hundred pounds to his wife, Philadelphia (c.1680–1751), and fellow brethren. He died in London on 17 November 1741, and was buried in Islington churchyard four days later. His library of about 1500 books was sold by auction in February 1743.

CHRISTOPH V. EHRENSTEIN

Sources Venn, *Alum. Cant.*, 1/1.160 · PRO, PROB 11/714, fols. 44–5 · H. Broxap, *The later nonjurors* (1924) · Bodl. Oxf., MS Rawl. D. 835 [nonjuror varia] · J. Nichols, *Biographical and literary anecdotes of William Bowyer, printer, FSA, and of many of his learned friends* (privately printed, London, 1782) · J. C. Findon, 'The nonjurors and the Church of England, 1689–1716', DPhil diss., U. Oxf., 1978 · Bodl. Oxf., MS Rawl. C. 1192, fol. 71 · *Bibliotheca Blackbourniana, or, A catalogue of the library of the reverend and learned Mr. John Blackbourne lately deceased* [1743] · J. D. Smith, *The eucharistic doctrine of the later nonjurors: a revisionist view of the eighteenth-century usage controversy* (2000)
Archives Bodl. Oxf., MS Rawl.
Wealth at death at least £170 was to be distributed to friends; he was also owed £550; library of approx. 1500 books: PRO, PROB 11/714, fol. 45

Blackburn, Colin, Baron Blackburn of Killearn (1813–1896), judge, was born in Levenside, Dunbartonshire, on 18 May 1813, the second eldest son of John Blackburn (1756–1840) of Killearn, a Jamaican proprietor, and Rebecca Leslie (b. 1788), daughter of the Revd Dr Gillies. He was educated at Edinburgh Academy and Eton College, before going to Trinity College, Cambridge. Having 'come up after being idle at Eton to be idle again at Cambridge', he was fortunate in having as his tutor at Trinity, not William Whewell, who would never have encouraged him to study, but George Peacock, who 'saw merit in Blackburn's mathematical paper' and 'advised him to cultivate what he saw were his talents and he did' (Trinity College, Cambridge, Add. MS b.49.199). A very serious student, he became a first-class mathematician, graduating as eighth wrangler in 1835. Two younger brothers, Hugh *Blackburn (1823–1909) and Robert Bogle Blackburn (1821–1875), shared this academic pedigree: the former became professor of mathematics at Glasgow University, the latter an advocate and later sheriff of Stirlingshire.

Blackburn was admitted a student at Lincoln's Inn in April 1835, but he later migrated to the Inner Temple and was called to the bar on 23 November 1838. He joined the northern circuit. His early career was that of a relatively briefless barrister, without legal or political connections. Publicly he never expressed political views, although his older brother, Peter Blackburn (1811–1870), was the liberal conservative member for Stirlingshire in the parliaments of 1855 to 1865. His appearance, with his burly figure, strong face, and round bullet head, was not prepossessing. Moreover, as Ballantine observed, 'a scotch accent does not improve a naturally harsh voice and his demeanour can scarcely be termed graceful or his manner pleasant' (Ballantine, 248). He was the antithesis of the suave advocate: his humour was dry, his personality grave. He studied 'human nature' in '*Coke upon Littleton* without assistance from haunts of revelry'; a confirmed bachelor, he was never 'a ladies' man' (ibid., 332, 248).

It took many years for Blackburn's legal talents to be recognized. His ability to distil principle from raw case law became known with the publication of his much praised treatise on Sale (1845) which led to his appearing as a junior in some heavy mercantile cases. During these years of obscurity he would be seen in the back row of the queen's bench and the exchequer chamber, with Thomas Flower Ellis, T. B. Macaulay's great friend, listening to arguments and judgments which they reported in eight volumes as Ellis and Blackburn and one as Ellis, Blackburn, and Ellis.

On 27 June 1859 Blackburn, who had never taken silk, was appointed a judge of the queen's bench by the lord chancellor, Lord Campbell, in succession to Sir William Erle, who had been appointed chief justice of the common pleas. He was invested with the coif on 2 November and knighted on 24 April 1860. His appointment was greeted with consternation by the profession. Campbell recorded in his diary the great disgrace he incurred

> by disposing of [my] judicial patronage on the principle *detur digniori* … whereas several Whig Queen's Counsel, M.P.'s, were considering which of them would be the man, not dreaming that they could all be passed over. They got me well abused in the 'Times' and other newspapers, but Lyndhurst has defended me gallantly in the House of Lords. (Hardcastle, 372–3)

Blackburn's judicial career was a vindication of Campbell's bold appointment. In the course of his seventeen years in the queen's bench from 1859 to 1876, he came to be recognized as one of the ablest judges in a strong court. He was an excellent *nisi prius* judge, very hard-working, sober in judgment, and fair-minded. There was, said Serjeant Ballantine, 'no one before whom I would sooner have practised' (Ballantine, 333). Blackburn's manner on the bench was said to be 'harsh and uncongenial, but it was soon found that this was only his surface deportment' (ibid.). He was a compassionate man.

As a judge, Blackburn rarely excited controversy. The one time his conduct was questioned arose from his charge to the grand jury in June 1868 in the trial of Edward Eyre, governor of Jamaica, who had been indicted for acts of oppression in suppressing an insurrection of black rioters in Jamaica and in executing its supposed ringleader, George William Gordon. After the grand jury had refused to return a bill of indictment, the chief justice, Sir Alexander Cockburn, questioned in open court Blackburn's direction that removing Gordon from 'Kingston into the proclaimed district for the purpose of subjecting him to martial law was legally justifiable', and that the execution of Gordon was justifiable if Eyre

> *bona fide* thought … that it was really necessary and proper for the purpose of checking [the insurrection] that Gordon … should be summarily tried, and that it was of importance that he, as the head of the insurrection, should be made an example of at once, in order to stop the insurrection. (*Annual Register*, 1868, pt 2, 214)

The chief justice, who had given a different charge in the earlier case of *R. v. Nelson and Brand* (1867), suggested that the queen's bench judges whom Blackburn had consulted before delivering his charge did not realize that he would so direct the jury.

In 1875 Blackburn became a justice of the newly constituted high court of judicature, and a year later was appointed to serve as one of the two lords of appeal in ordinary, offices created by the Appellate Jurisdiction Act of 1876. This time his appointment was not greeted with consternation by the legal profession but was applauded. His judgments in the queen's bench had demonstrated his profound knowledge of the principles of the common law. They continue to be read with admiration and cited as authoritative, notably his judgment in *Taylor v. Caldwell* (1863) which did much to formulate what modern lawyers call the doctrine of 'frustration of purpose' and demonstrates Blackburn's considerable command of civilian sources. The defendants had agreed to let the plaintiffs have the use of the Surrey Gardens and Music Hall on four specific days for the purpose of giving concerts and fêtes. Before the date of the first concert the Music Hall was destroyed by fire. The question which the court had to decide was whether the loss which the plaintiffs had sustained should fall upon the defendants. The court, whose judgment Blackburn delivered, held that it should not. The defendants' promise was not an absolute one. It was an implied condition of the contract that the Music Hall should continue to be in existence. Both parties would be excused if 'performance becomes impossible from the perishing of the thing without default of the contractor'. He pointed out that this principle was not novel; contracts had been discharged where performance was dependent on the existence of specific goods or the life of a human being, just as they were in Roman law (the *Digest*) and contemporary civil law (Pothier's 'celebrated *Traité du contrat de vente*').

Robust common sense as well as legal learning were the hallmarks of Blackburn's judgments and speeches in the House of Lords. In *Orr-Ewing v. Colquhoun* (1877) he was 'not inclined to reject the evidence of practical men as to a fact, merely because they [gave] a bad theoretical reason for it, and [he was] not able to furnish the right one'. In *Foakes v. Beer* (1884) Blackburn, alone of the peers, accepted that 'prompt payment of a part payment of their demand may be more beneficial to [creditors] than it would be to insist on their rights and enforce payment of the whole'. There are many other notable decisions, among them *Pharmaceutical Society v. London and Provincial Supply Association* (1880) (important for his dictum that a corporation can be sued for a libel or convicted for committing a nuisance) and *Erlanger v. New Sombrero Phosphate Co.* (1878) (discussing the fiduciary duties of company promoters and the principles determining rescission of contracts).

Blackburn was a member of the royal commission on the courts of law (1867) and on the stock exchange (1877), and chaired that on the draft criminal code (1878). In 1877 he became an honorary bencher of the Inner Temple.

After his retirement in December 1886, Blackburn rarely spoke in the house, possibly because he was 'a victim to that sad disease which often attacks the strongest brains' (Manson, 263). His remaining years were lived quietly on his Scottish estate, Doonholm, Alloway, Ayrshire, where he died on 8 January 1896.

GARETH H. JONES

Sources *The Times* (10 Jan 1896) · *Solicitors' Journal*, 40 (1895–6), 190–91 · Boase, *Mod. Eng. biog.* · E. W. D. Manson, *Builders of our law* *during the reign of Queen Victoria* (1895) · W. Ballantine, *Some experiences of a barrister's life*, 2nd–5th edns (1882) · March 1870, Trinity Cam., Add. MS b.49 · *Life of John, Lord Campbell, lord high chancellor of Great Britain*, ed. Mrs Hardcastle, 2 vols. (1881) · B. Semmel, *The Governor Eyre controversy* (1962)

Archives Trinity Cam.
Likenesses G. Aikman, engraving, 1888, Trinity Cam. · London Stereoscopic Co., carte-de-viste, NPG
Wealth at death £139,965 13s. 4d.: confirmation, 31 Jan 1896, *CCI*

Blackburn, Helen (1842–1903), campaigner for women's rights, was born at Knightstown, Valentia Island, co. Kerry, Ireland, on 25 May 1842. She had one brother, and was the only surviving daughter of Bewicke Blackburn (1811–1897), civil engineer and manager of the knight of Kerry's slate quarries on Valentia from 1837, and Isabella, youngest daughter of Humble Lamb of Ryton Hall, co. Durham, and a descendant of the brother of John Knox. Her father was an ingenious inventor whose designs included the Blackburn steam car (1877), which anticipated the modern automobile. He claimed descent from Thomas Coventry, lord keeper and chancellor during the reign of Charles I. Until 1859, when the family moved to London, Helen spent a happy childhood on Valentia, developing a talent for watercolour landscape painting, which she was forced to abandon because of the onset of eyesight trouble at the age of twenty-three. She turned to literary pursuits, and although the reasons for her subsequent interest in feminism are unknown, she began to write articles for the *Englishwoman's Review* and other papers.

Helen Blackburn's outstanding contribution to the Victorian women's movement centred on two key issues: suffrage and women's employment. Much respected for her organizational skills, she was secretary of the London-based Central Committee of the National Society for Women's Suffrage (1874–80), helping to organize the great demonstrations of 1880; secretary of the Bristol and West of England Society for Women's Suffrage (1880–95); assistant secretary of the reorganized central committee (1888–95); and honorary secretary of the Central and East of England Society for Women's Suffrage from 1897. While working for the Bristol society, a donation of £1000 funded her for three years of organizational work in south and west Wales and the west country, during which time she embarked upon a series of exhausting lecture tours, spreading the suffrage 'gospel'. Also in Bristol, which was an important centre for feminist activity, she became actively involved with the National Union of Working Women, representing it as a suffrage advocate at the TUC in 1881, and promoted the work of the newly founded West Bristol Women's Liberal Association, in which suffrage and Liberalism were intertwined.

Helen Blackburn's greatest contribution to the women's movement was, arguably, as noted author and historian. Her *Women's suffrage: a record of the women's suffrage movement in the British Isles, with biographical sketches of Miss Becker* (1902) is an invaluable history of the Victorian campaign, its antecedents, organizational development, and personalities. She was the author of several well-

Helen Blackburn (1842–1903), by Elizabeth S. Guinness

argued suffrage pamphlets, and compiled the annual *Women's Suffrage Calendar* (1886–99) and *A Handbook for Women Engaged in Social and Political Work* (1881, 1895), an encyclopaedic compendium of information. Her writings epitomized the British movement's grasp of detail and meticulous marshalling of facts, and its understanding of the need for sound rational argument to counter entrenched prejudice and opposition to the cause. Her literary talents were put to further use as editor (1880–90) and joint editor (1890–95) of the *Englishwoman's Review*, a feminist journal founded and financially supported by Jessie Boucherett, with whom she shared a common interest in women's employment.

Blackburn once agreed with J. S. Mill that 'The power of earning is essential to the dignity of a woman if she has not independent property' (*Englishwoman's Review*, June 1877). Liberal individualism and the opportunity for women to enter all occupations hitherto denied them were the central tenets of the Society for Promoting the Employment of Women, on whose executive committee she served for a number of years. But while a belief in an unfettered labour market suited the needs of middle-class women who wanted to work, the position of working-class women in industry and the thorny question of protective legislation suggested a different analysis. Increasingly out of tune with those feminists who called for state intervention to 'protect' women workers, Blackburn approved of legislation which regulated health and safety matters, but argued that other restrictions which applied only to women placed them at an economic disadvantage in the labour market, and diminished their self-reliance and self-respect. In order to propagate these views she wrote, with Jessie Boucherett, *The Condition of Working Women and the Factory Acts* (1896), and, with Nora Vynne, *Women under the Factory Act* (1903), and helped to found the Freedom of Labour Defence Committee in 1899. She was acknowledged by the labour movement to be a formidable opponent, and the supporters of each new Factory Act had to calculate the strength of her opposition.

Blackburn retained her love for her native Ireland, albeit as a staunch unionist. A friend of the Irish Women's Suffrage and Local Government Association, she was also honorary treasurer of the Society for School and University Education for Women in Ireland, formed in 1879, and edited *A Handy Book of Reference for Irishwomen* (1888). In 1895 she gave up public work to nurse her father until his death in 1897.

A keen antiquarian, Blackburn presented a series of historical portraits of notable women, originally shown at the International Exhibition at Chicago in 1883, to the women's hall at University College, Bristol (it was subsequently lost), and also bequeathed her fine library of periodicals, pamphlets, and books on women's questions to Girton College, Cambridge. Although tremendously influential through her writings and organizational work, Helen Blackburn was none the less personally diffident and self-effacing: there is almost no reference to her own distinguished career in any of her books. She died at her home, 18 Grey Coat Gardens, Westminster, on 11 January 1903, and was buried on 14 January at Brompton cemetery. A loan fund for training young women was established in her memory in 1905 and administered by the Society for Promoting the Employment of Women. At her death, there were warm tributes at home and overseas in recognition of a prodigious worker for the cause of women's rights.   LINDA WALKER

Sources *Englishwoman's Review*, 34 (1903), 1–5 · *Englishwoman's Review*, 34 (1903), 73–85 · *Englishwoman's Review*, 36 (1905), 45–6 · *The Times* (12 Jan 1903) · *Women's Suffrage Journal* (1874–90) · *Englishwoman's Review* (1875 1905) · H. Blackburn, *Women's suffrage: a record of the women's suffrage movement in the British Isles* (1902) · *Englishwoman's Yearbook and Directory* (1899) · CGPLA Eng. & Wales (1903) · will, proved, London, 10 Feb 1903
Archives Girton Cam., memorial library of books, pamphlets, periodicals, annual reports · Women's Library, London, autograph letters collection
Likenesses E. S. Guinness, crayon, University College, Bristol, formerly Women's Hall · E. S. Guinness, drawing, Girton Cam. [*see illus.*] · photograph, repro. in *Englishwoman's Review* (15 April 1903)
Wealth at death £806 16s. 10d.: probate, 10 Feb 1903, CGPLA Eng. & Wales

Blackburn, Hugh (1823–1909), mathematician and college administrator, was born on 2 July 1823 at Craigflower in Fife, the seventh and youngest son of the eight children of John Blackburn (1756–1840), Glasgow sugar merchant, and his wife, Rebecca Leslie (*b.* 1788), daughter of Dr Colin

Gillies (1748–1810), a minister in the Church of Scotland, and his wife, Isabella (*d.* 1833).

Hugh's father made a fortune in Jamaica and returned to Glasgow in 1810, married in the following year, and built Killearn House, an elegant mansion on the banks of the Blane. He supported his large family as well as numerous natural descendants of mixed race either left in Jamaica or resettled in Nova Scotia (to his friends he was known as Bluebeard). Hugh's mother was a grandniece of the mathematician Colin MacLaurin (1698–1746). His eldest brother, Peter Blackburn (1811–1870), became Conservative MP for Stirlingshire (1859–65), while the second eldest, Colin *Blackburn (1813–1896), became a queen's bench judge and was elevated to the peerage.

Killearn House was a centre of gaiety and family activity while Hugh was growing up. The Wedderburns (one of Scotland's most distinguished families, and distantly related) were visitors, including the young Jemima Wedderburn and her first cousin James Clerk-Maxwell. Hugh was a quiet, studious youth with an interest in conducting experiments. He possessed a four-volume set of Charles Hutton's *Mathematical Recreations*, chock-full of games and practical devices. Optics fascinated him and he experimented with photography, though his progress was hampered by a lack of interest in chemistry.

Hugh attended Edinburgh Academy (1831–6), where he was taught by the classics scholar George Ferguson, and then Eton College for his upper school education (1836–41), being admitted to Trinity College, Cambridge, as a pensioner on 3 December 1840. In his first term in October 1841 he became a close friend of William Thomson (1824–1907). In the middle of winter they went outdoor swimming together and spent evenings reading *Faust*. In Blackburn's rooms they swung on 'Blackburn's pendulum', an ingenious device with a double suspension, which could oscillate in planes at right angles to each other. Blackburn gained a Trinity scholarship in 1843 and for ten months (1844–5) was a member of the Cambridge Apostles.

In the mathematical tripos of 1845 Blackburn graduated fifth wrangler. He was elected a fellow of Trinity in the tight competition of 1846; he was a clear choice for a fellowship, while the seniority of Trinity vacillated between the senior wrangler and the senior classic of that year. Blackburn intended a career in the law and on 2 November 1847 was admitted at the Inner Temple, but afterwards an academic career loomed, and he formally withdrew on 8 May 1849 without being called to the bar. Following the tripos, William Thomson had written to his father, James, professor of mathematics at Glasgow: 'I wish you could hear of a professorship for him at a Scotch University. I think if there were any more professorships in Natural Philosophy he would answer exceedingly well' (S. P. Thompson, *The Life of Lord Kelvin*, 2 vols., 1910, 1.93). Four years later, James Thomson died, and Blackburn was appointed to his chair and took up duties on 23 April 1849.

On 12 June 1849, at St John's Episcopal Chapel, Edinburgh, Hugh Blackburn married Jemima Wedderburn (1823–1909) [*see* Blackburn, Jemima] his childhood visitor, youngest daughter of James Wedderburn (1782–1822), solicitor-general for Scotland in 1816, and his wife, Isabella Clerk (1789–1865) of Penicuik (another daughter, Jean, married Hugh's brother Peter). In 1855 they built Roshven House on Loch Ailort in Moidart and invariably spent their summers at this remote property. It became a meeting place for many notables in the sciences and the arts (Jemima Blackburn was a noted book illustrator). Sailing from Skye on one occasion, Thomson took his yacht *Lalla Rookh* to Loch Ailort in the company of Hermann von Helmholtz, who was impressed by the friendly and relaxed atmosphere of the Blackburns' home. Around their dinner table could be found all shades of political and religious affiliation. Hugh was a devout Christian and apolitical, while Jemima's atheism was coupled with a stout defence of Disraeli's brand of toryism. Outwardly an upright Victorian paterfamilias, Blackburn loved to spend time with his children: William (named after godfather William Thomson), Margaret, Hugh, and Alan. The Blackburns were prodigious travellers: Algeria, Spain, Italy, Corfu, Greece, and Iceland (in the company of Anthony Trollope) were all visited, where their largely unplanned expeditions progressed at a leisurely pace.

William Thomson never wavered in his admiration of Blackburn's mathematical ability and frequently consulted him. In reading James Clerk-Maxwell's work Blackburn was able to offer useful critical advice. Blackburn himself published remarkably little. He wrote a single paper (on astronomy) while at Cambridge (published in the *Cambridge and Dublin Mathematical Journal*, 1, 1846) and in 1854 revised a popular edition of George Biddell Airy's *Treatise on Trigonometry*. In collaboration with Thomson he edited an edition (1871) of Newton's *Principia*. Blackburn's mathematical interest lay in its applications to the natural world, in which his broad span covered botany, geology, marine biology, and ornithology. He was in the tradition of the natural philosopher, but one with a gift for analysing detail and a ready eye for flaws in a scientific argument. He was not a pure mathematician but Arthur Cayley, who had recommended him for the Glasgow chair, knew him as a maker of geometrical models.

Blackburn's mathematical classes grew large, rising from ninety when he began at Glasgow to three or four hundred when he stepped down. In 1871–4 he was joined by Thomas Muir (1844–1934), who acted as his assistant. Generations of Glasgow students could thank him for the firm grounding in mathematics which he imparted. Yet Blackburn had all the necessary qualities for teaching save one: he was unable to instil student discipline. His explanations were models of logical exposition and he presented them with the lucidity of a cultured man, but in his boisterous lecture room this mastery often counted for little. As the air grew thick with flying paper darts, Blackburn retreated to his chair hoping for calm but powerless to effect it.

Blackburn contributed to the administration of the university. His love of order, bordering on pedantry at times, found another outlet. He was clerk of faculty or, as he styled himself, *Clericus Collegii Glasuensis*. In this role he allowed no wastage and kept the college servants firmly in line (and the mathematical staff too, it was whispered). He took an unusually keen interest in university regalia and academic dress, and brought out a short constitutional history of Glasgow University with remarks on the 1858 Universities (Scotland) Bill.

Blackburn retired from Glasgow in 1879 on account of growing deafness. It was a cruel blow as he was passionately fond of music. Before the affliction he used to collect highland stories and songs about Moidart, particularly those connected with the Jacobite rebellion of the '45. In 1885 he was awarded the LLD for his services to the university. In retirement he lived at Roshven, where he spent his days with his books and involved in photography, cultivating his property, and researching the Blackburn genealogy. His passion for excruciating detail never left him. If a book had no index, he made one. Roshven was made more isolated by all of his clocks being set to 'Blackburn time'. He remained astute, and his argument to the House of Lords explaining reasons why the railway line should avoid his property, based on the sensible grounds that Loch Ailort was unsuitable as a harbour, was masterful.

Hugh Blackburn died on 9 October 1909 at his estate, two months after Jemima. He is buried in Roshven graveyard on the family estate. He was a man of ingenuity and wide-ranging capabilities who made a valuable contribution to the well-being of the University of Glasgow and was an intimate of an illustrious group of British scientists.   A. J. CRILLY

Sources R. Fairley, *Jemima* (1988) · *The Times* (12 Oct 1909) · *Nature*, 81 (1909), 522–3 · D. Murray, *Memories of the old college of Glasgow: some chapters in the history of the university* (1927) · L. Campbell and W. Garnett, *The life of James Clerk Maxwell* (1882) · C. Smith and M. N. Wise, *Energy and empire: a biographical study of Lord Kelvin* (1989) · L. Koenigsberger, *Hermann von Helmholtz* (1906) · *The parish of Killearn*, Killearn Trust (1988) · M. Stuart, *Scottish family history* (1930) · W. Nimmo, *The history of Stirlingshire*, 3rd edn, 2 (1880) · *Fasti Scot.* · Venn, *Alum. Cant.* · private information (2004) · d. cert.
Archives priv. coll. | CUL, Kelvin MSS · U. Glas., Kelvin MSS
Likenesses J. Blackburn, portrait, 1889, repro. in Fairley, *Jemima*, 87 · J. Blackburn, bust, U. Glas., Hunterian Museum

Blackburn [*née* Wedderburn], **Jemima** (1823–1909), painter and illustrator, was born on 1 May 1823 at 31 Heriot Row, Edinburgh, the youngest of the six children of James Wedderburn (1782–1822), solicitor-general for Scotland, and Isabella Clerk (1789–1865). Her early childhood was overshadowed by the death of her father (before her birth) and beset by intermittent illness. She was encouraged to draw by her doctor, the distinguished John Abercrombie, and although she seems to have received no artistic training and little formal education, Jemima Wedderburn lived in vibrant intellectual surroundings which moulded her remarkable, enquiring mind. (As a child she used to skin mice so as to find out how their muscles worked.) Her cousin the physicist James Clerk Maxwell moved to 31 Heriot Row after the death of his mother and the close friendship that developed was vital and stimulating to both. The physician Henry Acland introduced her to John Ruskin who took a keen interest in her work, even thinking of her, according to a letter from Effie Ruskin, 'as the best artist he knows' (Lutyens, 113–14). Sir Edwin Landseer claimed that in the drawing of animals he had nothing to teach her (G. Du Maurier, *The Young George Du Maurier: a Selection of his Letters*, 1860–67, appendix, 287). On 12 June 1849 Wedderburn married Hugh *Blackburn (1823–1909), professor of mathematics at Glasgow University. Outside term they stayed at Ardmillan House in Ayrshire until, in 1853, they purchased the estate of Roshven lying on the remote north coast of Moidart in the west highlands. It was there that her best work was accomplished. She often painted ambitious compositions, such as the magnificent watercolour *Building a Haystack* (*c*.1857), and she has come to be regarded as one of Scotland's first major women artists of the modern period (MacDonald, 113). Blackburn kept a visual journal (Christies, 1 December 1994, dispersed) from the age of twelve, describing the day's activities. Each entry contained at least one drawing or painting and described the circles in which she moved, her wide travels, and life on a Victorian west highland estate. Her work grew in popularity and she became much sought after as an illustrator of books and periodicals, *The History of Thomas Thumb* (1855) and *The Cat's Pilgrimage* (1870) being perhaps the most attractive. Blackburn had always held a keen interest in natural history and Charles Darwin acknowledged that it was she who first recorded how the young cuckoo ejects its rivals from the nest (Darwin, *Origin of Species*, 6th edn, 1882). In 1862 she produced *Birds from Nature*, a volume of bird illustrations painted from life which immediately placed her in the first rank of Victorian ornithological illustrators. The book was reissued in 1868 in an enlarged edition, though only six copies were coloured, a fact which undoubtedly has led to her lack of recognition.

Blackburn travelled widely, visiting countries from Egypt to Iceland, the latter visited in a party which included Anthony Trollope with whom she produced an idiosyncratic account of their adventures: *How the Mastiffs Went to Iceland* (1878). With much taste and judgement, the Blackburns turned Roshven into one of the most beautiful estates on the west coast and for a time it became a summer destination for many of the most distinguished scientists and artists of the age, in particular Hugh Blackburn's closest friend, the physicist and mathematician William Thomson, Lord Kelvin, and the German physiologist and physicist Hermann von Helmholtz. Her artistic and intellectual powers diminished by senile dementia, Jemima Blackburn died on 9 August 1909. Her husband, who was two months and one day younger, survived her by exactly two months. They were buried in the private graveyard at Roshven. The National Portrait Gallery and British Museum, London, the National Gallery of Scotland, Edinburgh, and the Royal Library, Windsor, hold collections of her works.   ROB FAIRLEY

Sources Wedderburn family MSS · R. Fairley, *Jemima: the paintings and memoirs of a Victorian lady* (1988) · R. Fairley, *Blackburn's 'Birds'* (1993) · M. Lutyens, *Millais and the Ruskins* (1967) · D. Macmillan, *Scottish art, 1460–1990* (1990) · M. MacDonald, *Scottish art* (2000)

Blackburn, Joseph (*fl.* 1752–1777), portrait painter, is of obscure origins: nothing is known of his birth, parents,

geographical area of origin, or education. His career is documented primarily by about seventy signed portraits painted between 1752 and 1777 in Bermuda, New England, Ireland, and the west of England. An equal number of portraits, mainly of New England subjects, are attributed to him.

Blackburn is first documented in 1752–3, when he painted about two dozen portraits in Bermuda. His portrait style, already fully developed, derives from paintings by earlier eighteenth-century English portrait painters. In 1754 he painted about six portraits in Rhode Island, after which the Newport merchant Thomas Vernon recommended him to James Boutineau of Boston as 'late from the Island of Bermuda a Limner by profession … being possess'd with the agreeable qualities of great modesty, good sence & genteel behaviour' (MS letter, 25 Nov 1754, Newport, Rhode Island, Historical Society). In Boston Blackburn was very successful, and painted half of his known portraits there between 1755 and 1759. The sitters were merchants, public officials, and military men, and members of their families. The portraits primarily depict single figures, although he occasionally painted paired or group portraits. Mary Cary Russell praised his ability to paint 'such extreem fine lace and satten besides taking so exact a likeness' (MS letter, *c*.1757, Morgan and Foote, 69). Some compositions indicate familiarity with specific portraits by Sir Godfrey Kneller and Thomas Hudson.

In 1760 and 1761 Blackburn painted about twenty portraits in Portsmouth, New Hampshire, where he was last documented on 12 July 1762 by a payment for a portrait. He was in England by January 1764. His last fifteen portraits were painted in the British Isles, primarily in the west of England. The earliest, however, is his *Portrait of a Young Girl Holding a Dublin Lottery Ticket* (1767; National Gallery of Ireland, Dublin). His last, of Hugh Jones, agent to the Morgan family of Tredegar, Monmouth, was painted in 1777 (Worcester Art Museum, Massachusetts). Nothing is known of Blackburn's death or burial. He has at times been confused with the Norwich painter John Blackburn, who exhibited in London in 1769–75; that artist, however, was in Rome in 1760–65. Blackburn's Boston portraits were a major influence on the work of John Singleton Copley. The American novelist Kenneth Roberts included Blackburn as a character in his historical novel *Northwest Passage* (1937).   ELLEN G. MILES

Sources L. Park, *Joseph Blackburn: a colonial portrait painter, with a descriptive list of his works* (1923) · J. H. Morgan and H. W. Foote, *An extension of Lawrence Park's descriptive list of the work of Joseph Blackburn* (1937) · L. Dresser, 'The background of colonial American portraiture: some pages from a European notebook', *Proceedings of the American Antiquarian Society*, 76 (1966), 19–58 · W. B. Stevens jr, 'Joseph Blackburn and his Newport sitters, 1754–1756', *Newport History*, 40 (1967), 95–107 · E. A. R. Ackroyd, 'Joseph Blackburn, limner, in Portsmouth', *Historical New Hampshire*, 30 (1975), 231–43 · A. Oliver, 'The elusive Mr. Blackburn', *Sibley's heir: a volume in memory of Clifford Kenyon Shipton* (1982), 379–91 · L. P. Jones, *Notes on the Jones family of Bermuda* (1947) · H. T. Watlington, 'The portraits in the [Tucker] house', *Bermuda Historical Quarterly*, 10 (1953), 58–61 · C. Rebora, P. Staiti, E. E. Hirshler, T. Stebbins jr, and C. Troyen, *John Singleton Copley in America* (1995) · T. Vernon, MS letter, Historical Society, Newport, Rhode Island, 25 Nov 1754

Blackburn, Robert (1885–1955), aircraft designer and manufacturer, was born on 26 March 1885 at Kirkstall near Leeds, the eldest of three sons of George William Blackburn, an engineer, and his wife, Kate, *née* Naylor. His career was influenced by his engineering background— George Blackburn was works manager of William Green & Sons, lawnmower and steamroller manufacturers—and by the world's first heavier-than-air flight by the Wright brothers in 1903. He attended Leeds modern school and gained an honours degree in engineering at Leeds University; he became an associate member of the Institution of Civil Engineers in 1906, and was given practical experience at his father's firm.

Blackburn considered the company's methods old-fashioned and went to the continent to study new techniques. In France he saw Wilbur Wright fly, and this proved the catalyst for his future career. He began to design an aircraft in Paris during that year (1908) and when he returned home his father set him up with a workshop in Benson Street, Leeds. There the first Blackburn aircraft, a monoplane powered by a 35 hp Green engine, was built. He had it transported to Marske by the Sea on the Yorkshire coast, where he taxied it along the sands at increasing speeds, eventually becoming airborne. Although the machine side-slipped into the ground and was wrecked, Blackburn had achieved his initial ambition and his second monoplane was more successful. Within three years he had proved himself as designer, builder, and pilot. By June 1914 he had become a manufacturer, founding his own company, the Blackburn Aeroplane and Motor Company. He was twice married, first to Jessica Tryphena Thompson on 31 October 1914; they had three sons and two daughters. This marriage was dissolved on 23 March 1936. His second wife was Phyllis Margaret Kirton, whom he married on 9 April 1936; they had two daughters. Both wives survived him.

Blackburn's genius for organizing large-scale production showed itself during the First World War, when the company received Admiralty and War Office orders and through subcontracting arrangements proved itself capable of undertaking aircraft work of every kind. In January 1920 he was made OBE for services in connection with the war.

During 1915 Blackburn had sponsored two important developments for his company—the acquisition of an airfield and slipway at Brough, by the River Humber, and a decision to specialize in naval aircraft design and manufacture. In post-war years he demonstrated his organizational skill overseas, setting up, at the Greek government's invitation in 1925, a national aircraft factory near Athens. For this he was awarded the gold cross of the order of the Redeemer.

During the Second World War Blackburn's Brough works, to which all manufacturing had been transferred in 1936, built 1700 Fairey Swordfishes and 700 Barracudas—in addition to its own Skuas and Rocs—for the Royal Navy, plus Bothas for the RAF, and co-operated with the Clydeside shipbuilders Dennys of Dumbarton in building Sunderland flying boats. A 1948 amalgamation with General Aircraft led to production of the Beverley heavy freighter for the RAF, and Blackburn saw one of these on show at the Society of British Aerospace Companies' display only a few days before his death in Exeter from a heart attack on 10 September 1955.

In 1950 the Royal Aeronautical Society had made Blackburn an honorary fellow, and in 1953, when he went to live in Branscombe, Devon, in semi-retirement, he proudly said at a dinner given in his honour that 274 of his employees had served for twenty-one years. A friendly, unpretentious but determined man, who remained based in Yorkshire throughout his career, Blackburn inspired such loyalty; his original belief in the future of aviation never wavered. HUMPHREY WYNN

Sources R. Blackburn, autobiographical memoir, Royal Aeronautical Society Library · C. G. Grey, 'Biography of Robert Blackburn', Royal Aeronautical Society Library · H. Wynn, 'Blackburn, Robert', *DBB* · private information (2004) · *Flight* · *The Aeroplane* · b. cert. · C. G. Grey, 'The history of Blackburn aircraft', Royal Aeronautical Society
Archives Royal Aeronautical Society Library, autobiographical memoir
Likenesses B. Adams, oils, Royal Aero Club
Wealth at death £131,785—gross: Wynn, 'Blackburn, Robert'

Blackburn, William (1750–1790), surveyor and architect, was born in Southwark, the son of a tradesman of St John's Horsleydown, probably the John Blackburn who on 15 November 1749 married Eleanor Howell of that parish. His mother, said to be a native of Spain, died in his infancy. Though apprenticed to a surveyor, Blackburn was essentially self-educated. In 1769 he competed for the Dublin royal exchange. He entered the Royal Academy Schools in 1772, and obtained a silver medal in 1773 for the best drawing of the interior of Wren's St Stephen Walbrook. In 1775 he exhibited drawings of minor buildings 'designed for a gentleman in Surrey'.

Blackburn's great opportunity arose from the 1779 Penitentiary Act, which permitted imprisonment to replace transportation: solitary confinement was to induce remorse, and hard labour to provide correction. In 1782 he won the subsequent competition for a national male penitentiary house to accommodate 600, out of a field of sixty-three entries which included designs by John Soane, Thomas Hardwick, and Thomas Baldwin. It was he who 'first turned prison design into a kind of technology, translating the doctrine of reform into the practicalities of construction' (Evans, 118). Financial exigencies prevented the construction of his prize design (now lost), but the ideas embodied in the Penitentiary Act were extensively implemented by local authorities under the 1784 Gaols Acts; Blackburn secured many of their commissions and began 'to develop prison design into a kind of moral geography' (ibid., 142). By 1787 he was regarded as the leading authority in the country on prison design.

According to a report of 1826, the plan of Liverpool borough gaol (1786–9; dem. 1855) resembled Blackburn's original proposal. The 1784 legislation required such local prisons to be divided into 'distinct apartments' for various classes of prisoner, graded by sex and delinquency.

Designed for 270 inmates—huge by contemporary standards—Liverpool gaol's six free-standing radial blocks were all externally visible from the gaoler's house at the hub. John Howard praised it when under construction: 'with a view to security, health, reformation and convenience, I apprehend, it will be one of the first borough gaols in the kingdom' (Howard, 206). Blackburn had in each of his prisons to resolve the problem of reconciling these prerequisites. To achieve security he established a patrollable zone between the cell blocks and the perimeter wall, itself designed so as to afford no internal foothold. He told Jeremy Bentham that his stone walls were too massive to break through, and undermining was blocked by a water trap. His radial plans, perhaps influenced by contemporary French circular forms, facilitated maintenance of order. Fragmentation of the structure facilitated the ventilation then regarded as essential to prevent 'gaol fever', typhus or typhoid; furthermore—as in his Gloucester gaol and 'houses of correction'—the structure was punctured by air holes in walls, floors, and ceilings, the cell blocks being elevated on piers or arcades. His gaols were further characterized by a severe flat-roofed entrance lodge that provided a platform for executions. Blackburn was the originator of a type of architecture in which the formal traditional elements were 'sublimated to the requirements of reform' (Evans, 181). John Howard regarded Blackburn as the only man capable of delineating upon paper his ideas of what a prison ought to be.

In addition to executing or beginning gaols in Gloucestershire (the county gaol, 1788–91, and four houses of correction, 1787–91) and at Oxford (county gaol, *c.*1785, and city gaol, 1786–9; dem. 1879), Liverpool (1786–7; dem. 1855), Ipswich (1786–90), Salford (New Bayley, 1787–90; dem. *c.*1872), Preston (house of correction, 1789), Monmouth (1788–90), Dorchester (1789–95), Exeter (1789–95; dem. 1853), Lewes (house of correction, 1789–93; dem. 1967), Stafford (*c.*1789–93), and Shrewsbury (1789–93), Blackburn prepared designs for gaols at Bedford and Lancaster Castle. He is said to have planned the gaol at Limerick (*c.*1789), and designed improvements to the Dublin Newgate (dem. *c.*1880). For the Bristol Unitarians he designed the chapel at Lewin's Mead (1788–91) and in September 1790 he surveyed the cathedral at Exeter. As surveyor to the Watermen's Company from 1776, he designed their hall in St Mary-at-Hill, London (1778–80). Blackburn also designed houses both on his account and for others: a villa at Denmark Hill (1785–6), 'perhaps the finest house' in South Lambeth (Survey of London, 146), provided a model for others close by. He worked consistently within the classical tradition, influenced by Robert Adam, employing such features as a rusticated ground floor, lunettes, and continuous sill-courses generally throughout his *œuvre*. He was surveyor to St Thomas's Hospital and Guy's Hospital (alterations *c.*1788) in his native Southwark. His design for rebuilding Hackney church, Middlesex, was set aside by his death.

Corpulent in figure, medium in height, Presbyterian in religion, Blackburn was noted, according to an obituary, for his candour and modesty. He married a Quaker, Lydia, daughter of Joshua Hobson, a Southwark builder, on 2 February 1783 at St Olave's, Southwark. He died suddenly on 28 October 1790 at Preston, Lancashire, as he was on his way to Glasgow to discuss a proposal for a new prison there. He was buried in Bunhill Fields, London. His wife survived him with a son and two daughters; a second son was born posthumously. Blackburn owned leasehold and freehold property, and left his family in comfortable circumstances. His brother-in-law William Hobson completed several of his undertakings. **M. H. PORT**

Sources Colvin, *Archs.* · *DNB* · PRO, PROB 11/1200, fol. 5 · *GM*, 1st ser., 60 (1790), 1053 · R. Evans, *The fabrication of virtue: English prison architecture, 1750–1840* (1982) · J. R. S. Whiting, *Prison reform in Gloucestershire, 1776–1820* (1979) · M. B. Weinstock, 'Dorchester model prison', *Proceedings of the Dorset Natural History and Archaeological Society*, 78 (1956), 94–5 · register, St Olave's, Southwark, 1783, LMA [marriage] · births register, St Thomas Presbyterian Chapel Southwark, PRO, RG4/4513, nos. 25–7 · *The parish of St Mary, Lambeth*, 2 (1956), 146–50 · J. Edwards, *A companion from London to Brighthelmston*, pt 1 (1801), 17 · W. Ison, *The Georgian buildings of Bristol* (1952), 81–4 and pl. 13a · H. Humpherus, *History of the origin and progress of the Company of Watermen*, 2 [n.d.], 321, 332, 340–41 · J. Howard, *An account of the principal lazarettos in Europe* (1791) · C. Davies, 'Skilled boatmen of the Thames', *Country Life*, 156 (14 Nov 1974), 1488–9 · *VCH Staffordshire*, 6.204 · H. Rosenau, *Social purpose in architecture* (1970), 84

Archives Dorset RO, plans and specifications for Dorchester gaol · Glos. RO, plans and working drawings of county gaol and the four bridewells

Wealth at death legacies totalling £5100; annuities of £50 p.a.; leasehold and freehold property: will, 2 Oct 1790, PRO, PROB 11/1200, fol. 5

Blackburne, Anna (1726–1793), botanist, was the fifth of nine children of John *Blackburne (*bap.* 1694, *d.* 1786), horticulturist, and Catherine Ashton (1701–1740). She was born at and grew up at Orford Hall, north of Warrington, Lancashire, in an area where her family had held estates for three generations. Following the early death of her mother Anna took on central responsibilities at Orford Hall and also joined her father in scientific activities. John Blackburne established an extensive, much-admired garden that was filled with aquatic plants, fruits, hardy exotics, and hothouse specimens such as pineapples. Anna developed a well-known natural history collection. She did not marry, but was widely known as Mrs Blackburne. For many decades she received visitors such as the naturalists Thomas Pennant and Peter Simon Pallas, corresponded widely with naturalists at home and abroad, and exchanged plants, rare seeds, and natural history specimens with them. When the German naturalist and traveller Johann Reinhold Forster was tutor in natural science at the educationally progressive Warrington Academy, 1767–70, he regularly dined at Orford Hall and read his entomology lectures to her.

Anna Blackburne taught herself Latin so that she could study the Linnaean classification system. In his *System of Vegetables* Erasmus Darwin called her 'learned and ingenious'. On 29 July 1771 she wrote to Linnaeus in Uppsala and offered to send him North American birds and insects collected by one of her brothers, Ashton Blackburne, near New York. Linnaeus replied that he knew of her already, as one of 'three botanical ladies' who 'disputed in 1769 with and triumphed over the botanist in the physic garden at Oxford about the geranium' (Wystrach, 153). The two corresponded in the early 1770s; Linnaeus praised her as 'a true naturalist whose esteem I covet' (ibid., 155).

At Orford Hall, Anna Blackburne assembled a large and notable museum of natural history that contained specimens of plants, birds, shells, insects, fish, and minerals. Her collection rivalled the museums of natural history established by her cousin Sir Ashton Lever in Manchester and London. After her father's death, in 1787 she moved to Fairfield, a new house closer to Warrington, in which one large room was designed for her collection of birds and other natural curiosities. She planned to organize the garden according to the Linnaean system but ill health interfered with the project. She died on 30 December 1793, and was buried in the family plot at Winwick, Lancashire. The *Gentleman's Magazine* obituary celebrated her as 'sincere and hospitable, of open, candid, and unaffected manners, with a truly good heart, and a clear head'. The plant genus *Blackburnia* an Australian shrub, and the Blackburnian warbler (*Dendroica fusca*) were named in her honour by Pennant and Forster. Bequests to her family and various charities totalled some £12,000.   ANN B. SHTEIR

Sources V. P. Wystrach, 'Anna Blackburne (1726–1793)—a neglected patroness of natural history', *Journal of the Society for the Bobliography of Natural History*, 8 (1976–8?), 148–68 • *GM*, 1st ser., 64 (1794), 180 • will, PRO, PROB 11/1241, sig. 62
Likenesses Winstanley, group portrait (aged fifteen; with her family), repro. in J. P. Rylands, *Hale Hall, with notes on the family of Ireland Blackburne* (1881) • silhouette, repro. in J. Kendrick, *Profiles of Warrington worthies*, 2nd edn (1854), fig. 2
Wealth at death over £12,000: will, PRO, PROB 11/1241, sig. 62

Blackburne, Francis (1705–1787), Church of England clergyman and religious controversialist, was born at Richmond, Yorkshire, on 9 June 1705, the elder son of Francis Blackburne (*bap.* 1680?, *d.* 1708/9?), a businessman and alderman, and his wife, Alice (*b. c.*1670), the elder daughter of Dr Thomas *Comber, dean of Durham, and Alice Thornton. His father died at the age of twenty-nine, and his mother later married William Kirkby of Ashlack, Lancashire, to which the family moved. He was educated at schools in Kendal, Hawkshead, and Sedbergh, after which he spent a year studying with his maternal uncle, Thomas Comber, of East Newton, Yorkshire. He was admitted in May 1723 at St Catharine's College, Cambridge, where he became conduit or chaplain-fellow when ordained on 12 March 1728 by Bishop Green of Ely. He graduated BA in 1727, and MA in 1733. He was refused a fellowship of his college by its conservative fellows, who strongly disliked the firmly Lockean politico-theology which Blackburne had quickly imbibed when advised to read Locke on government on going up to Cambridge. He left Cambridge for East Newton, where he lived until 1739, having been taken ill with a nervous disorder which he overcame by taking up fox-hunting and other field sports. He was ordained priest by Bishop Gooch of Norwich at Ely Chapel, Holborn, on 18 March 1739 in order to qualify for the rectory of Richmond, which had been promised to

him on the first vacancy. After taking up the rectory he resided in Richmond until his death. On 30 August 1744 he married Hannah Elsworth, *née* Hotham (1713–1799), the widow of Joshua Elsworth, with whom she had had three children, one of whom, Hannah, later married Theophilus Lindsey, the founder of Unitarianism.

It was at Richmond that Blackburne began seriously to read. In 1742 he became chaplain to Henry D'Arcy of Sedbury, near Richmond. He was collated to the archdeaconry of Cleveland in 1750, and in August that year he was given the prebend of Bilton by Archbishop Hutton, to whom he was titular chaplain. His liberal principles prevented him from taking any further preferment since he had made up his mind never again to subscribe to the Thirty-Nine Articles. In an apology published in 1750 he defended John Jones's *Free and Candid Disquisitions Relating to the Church of England* (1749), denying that he had any part in their composition, though he had seen the work in manuscript. In 1752 he anonymously published a controversial attack on Bishop Joseph Butler's 1751 charge, *A Serious Inquiry into the Use and Importance of External Religion*, in which he accused Butler of coming close to Roman Catholicism on the matter. This was first printed with Blackburne's name in 1767 in *Pillars of Priestcraft and Orthodoxy Shaken*, a collection edited by the dissenting minister and controversialist Richard Baron.

Blackburne supported the mortalism of his Cambridge friend and contemporary Edmund Law in a tract called *No Proof in the Scriptures of an Intermediate State* (1755). This stated the heterodox belief that the soul, which was not naturally immortal, but was made so by Christ, passed into a state of sleep between death and the resurrection into eternal life. This restatement of a doctrine which had been held by several of the civil war sects provoked a minor controversy in the 1750s and 1760s, and it related to Blackburne's increasing interest in the incendiary politico-theology of the mid-seventeenth century. A further contribution to the debate, *A Historical View of the Controversy Concerning an Intermediate State*, appeared in 1765, of which a second, much enlarged edition appeared in 1772. This brought him into collision with Bishop William Warburton on the matter, and Blackburne considered his own 'masterpiece' to be his response to Warburton's ire, *Remarks on Dr. Warburton's Account of the Sentiments of the Jews Concerning the Soul*. Blackburne played a leading role in the controversy over subscription to the Thirty-Nine Articles which convulsed Cambridge in the 1760s and 1770s, an engagement which also saw him on Law's side. In 1758 he had argued, in *Remarks on the Rev. Dr. Powell's Sermon in Defence of Subscription*, against what he considered to be the casuistry which would permit subscription to articles to be made with a considerable latitude of meaning. This led him to write his best-known work, the *Confessional, or, A full and free inquiry into the right, utility, and success of establishing confessions of faith and doctrine in protestant churches*, which appeared in May 1766, but which had been in preparation for some years before. Nathaniel Lardner, the dissenting divine and a fellow church historian, had long wanted Blackburne to go into print on the matter, and it was the bibliophile and philanthropist Thomas Hollis, a champion of the commonwealth tradition in English political thought, who finally persuaded him to publish the manuscript. Andrew Millar published the work anonymously; a second edition appeared in 1767, and a third, enlarged edition in 1770. The work took the form of a decidedly polemical account of the history of the Church of England, in which Blackburne attacked those who defended subscription to Calvinist articles according to their own lax interpretations; he denounced orthodoxy as a man of straw. He was particularly critical of Laud's Arminian interpretation of the articles, and he lamented that conditions of service in the church required of honest men that they confront the dilemma of 'subscribe or starve'. A lively controversy arose; it has been calculated that orthodox responses to the *Confessional*, largely supported by Archbishop Thomas Secker who despised Blackburne for his attack on Butler, amounted to enough to fill ten volumes. In 1772 a petition was drawn up at the Feathers tavern in London, which belonged to Peterhouse, in support of Blackburne's proposal that a private statement of faith, of the sort sworn by his own son at Cambridge, should be substituted for subscription to the articles. The petition was signed by some 200 people: it was rejected by the House of Commons by 217 votes to 71.

Theophilus Lindsey, the husband of Blackburne's stepdaughter, and Dr John Disney, who married his elder daughter, Jane, were deeply involved in the debate, and both of them shortly afterwards left the Church of England in favour of the new denomination which they founded: Unitarianism. Blackburne was widely supposed to share their views, and his sincerity on the doctrine of the Trinity was questioned accordingly. On Disney's secession, Blackburne drew up a paper called 'An answer to the question, why are not you a Socinian?', in the course of which he denounced '*rational Christianity*, the foster father of modern infidelity'. He also declared himself to be a Calvinist of 'the largest and most liberal sort'. This was later published as an appendix to the introductory 'Life' with which his son, also named Francis, prefaced an edition of his works in 1804–5. Blackburne continued to emphasize his opposition to tests, but it was pointed out that he was no clerical careerist since his preferments produced only £150 a year, and he had declined an offer to succeed Samuel Chandler at the fashionable dissenting chapel in London, the Old Jewry, at a salary of £400.

Blackburne abandoned plans to publish a life of Luther, on which he had undertaken considerable amounts of research, in favour of an act of personal piety, writing instead a two-volume life of his friend and patron Hollis, which appeared, together with many rich engravings, in 1780. This anonymously published work takes the form of a memorial to the radical tradition whose values Hollis had venerated and encouraged, both in England and in America, and whose extremely liberal religious views were admired but not shared by Blackburne. A figure central to this tradition, John Milton, had been defended by Blackburne in his *Remarks on Johnson's Life of Milton* (1780). Blackburne began to lose his sight in 1784, and he resorted

to the use of an amanuensis. In 1787 he performed his thirty-eighth visitation of Cleveland, and he died peacefully in his chair at home in Richmond on 7 August 1787. He left his wife, who died on 23 August 1799, and four children: Jane, married to Dr Disney; Francis, vicar of Brignal; Sarah, married to the Revd John Hall, vicar of Chew Magna; and William, a physician in London. A son Thomas had died aged thirty-three in Durham in 1782.

Blackburne's *Works, Theological and Miscellaneous*, together with a detailed memoir, were edited by his son and published by Benjamin Flower, a radical Cambridge publisher, in seven volumes. Besides the works mentioned above, they contain his charges as archdeacon, which reveal his marked antipathy towards Roman Catholicism, to which he was not at all prepared to extend full toleration and of which denomination he was a very firm critic. A large number of miscellaneous pamphlets comprise the remaining volumes.   B. W. YOUNG

Sources F. Blackburne, 'Life of Francis Blackburne', in *The works, theological and miscellaneous of … Francis Blackburne*, ed. F. Blackburne, 7 vols. (1804–5), vol. 1 • L. Stephen, *History of English thought in the eighteenth century*, 2 vols. (1876) • B. W. Young, *Religion and Enlightenment in eighteenth-century England: theological debate from Locke to Burke* (1998) • C. Haydon, *Anti-Catholicism in eighteenth-century England, c. 1714–80: a political and social study* (1993) • D. Griffin, *Regaining paradise* (1986) • C. Robbins, *The eighteenth-century commonwealthman* (1959) • N. T. Burns, *Christian mortalism from Tyndale to Milton* (1972) • A. Patterson, *Early modern liberalism* (1997) • GM, 1st ser., 57 (1787), 743 • GM, 1st ser., 69 (1799), 726 • DNB • IGI

Archives DWL, corresp. | DWL, letters to Theophilus Lindsey

Likenesses G. Cuitt, oils, St Catharine's College, Cambridge • Schiavonetti, stipple, NPG • engraving, repro. in Blackburne, ed., *Works theological and miscellaneous*, vol. 1 • oils, St Catharine's College, Cambridge

Blackburne, Francis (1782?–1867), judge, was born at Great Footstown, co. Meath, almost certainly on 11 November 1782, though one source gives his year of birth as 1780. He was the fourth son of Richard Blackburne of Footstown, and his wife, Elizabeth, daughter of Francis Hopkins of Darvistown, co. Meath. He was educated at the village school at Dunshaughlin, co. Meath, and subsequently at the school of the Revd William White in Dublin, where the Blackburne family had moved, apprehensive of being attacked in their rural home during a period of agrarian disturbance. Blackburne entered Trinity College, Dublin, in July 1798, where he acquired numerous distinctions; he became a scholar in 1801 and graduated BA in 1803. In 1809 he married Jane, only daughter of William Martley of Ballyfallon, co. Meath. They had fourteen children, five of whom survived him.

Blackburne entered the King's Inns, Dublin, in 1801, and entered Lincoln's Inn in London in 1803. He was called to the Irish bar in 1805 and joined the home circuit. He specialized in chancery matters, though not to the exclusion of common-law work, and became a king's counsel in 1822. He became third serjeant in 1826 and second serjeant in 1830. In 1822–4, while still a member of the bar, he acted as a special judge in the city and county of Limerick, pursuant to an appointment under the Insurrection Act, and helped to restore order at a turbulent time. When Earl Grey became prime minister in 1830, Blackburne, though known to be a tory, was appointed as attorney-general for Ireland, with a view to the Irish administration having a broad political base. He continued in that office until 1835, under Grey and during the initial short administrations of Melbourne and Peel. He was in charge of the government's legal responses to the campaigns of Daniel O'Connell and the disorder associated with Orangeism and tithe issues.

Blackburne was reappointed by Peel as attorney-general in 1841, and he became master of the rolls in 1842. In January 1846 he was appointed chief justice of the queen's bench, in which capacity he presided over the trials of William Smith O'Brien and other leaders of the 1848 rebellion. During the first government of Lord Derby (who, as Lord Stanley, had been chief secretary for Ireland between 1830 and 1833, during part of Blackburne's initial period of office as attorney-general), between February and December 1852, Blackburne was lord chancellor of Ireland. In 1852 he was appointed as one of the commissioners of national education, but he retired in the following year in objection to a perceived diminution in religious instruction in national schools. He was for some years vice-chancellor of Dublin University.

In 1856 Blackburne was appointed by Lord Palmerston as lord justice of appeal in Ireland. Two years later he was invited by Lord Derby again to become lord chancellor, but he declined on account of his advanced age and failing health. He changed his mind, however, and decided to accept Derby's offer but was told that the position had been offered to and accepted by Joseph Napier. On the last accession to power of Lord Derby in 1866, Blackburne consented to accept the position, to facilitate other appointments that Derby wished to make. He resigned with some ill feeling in March 1867, at Derby's request. Blackburne's son and biographer remarks that his party loyalty had compelled him to accept Derby's invitation in the first place. In May 1867 he declined an offer of a baronetcy, perhaps having hoped for a peerage.

In private character Blackburne was generous and urbane. As a lawyer he possessed extraordinary powers of mental concentration, wide experience, and profound acquaintance with every branch of law and equity. He had a dignified and courteous manner, a distinct and melodious voice, and fluent delivery. He resided in Dublin at Leinster Street and then at 34 Merrion Square; and also near Dublin at Roebuck Hall and then Rathfarnham Castle, co. Dublin, a substantial Elizabethan castle which he had bought in 1847. He died there on 17 September 1867 and was buried in Mount Jerome cemetery, Dublin.

G. B. Smith, *rev.* Daire Hogan

Sources E. Blackburne, *Life of Francis Blackburne* (1874) · F. E. Ball, *The judges in Ireland, 1221–1921*, 2 vols. (1926) · D. Hogan, '"Vacancies for their friends": judicial appointments in Ireland, 1866–1867', *Brehons, serjeants, and attorneys: studies in the history of the Irish legal profession*, ed. D. Hogan and W. N. Osborough (1990), 211–29
Archives TCD, corresp. | Lpool RO, letters to fourteenth earl of Derby
Likenesses J. Kirkwood, stipple, pubd 1844 (after C. Grey), NG Ire., NPG; repro. in *Dublin University Magazine* (24 Oct 1844) · C. H. Jeens, line print, 1874, BM; repro. in Blackburne, *Life of Francis*

Blackburne · T. A. Jones, oils, 1875 (after S. C. Smith the elder), King's Inns, Dublin · G. Sanders, mezzotint (after S. C. Smith), NG Ire. · S. C. Smith, portrait, King's Inns, Dublin
Wealth at death under £80,000: probate, 11 Oct 1867, *CGPLA Ire.*

Blackburne, John (*bap.* 1694, *d.* 1786), horticulturist, baptized on 13 September 1694 at Warrington parish church, was born at Orford Old Hall, near Warrington where his father, Jonathan Blackburne (1646–1724), owned a country estate. His mother was the widowed Anne Lockwood, *née* Chilton (1655×7–1732). Nothing is known of his education or early years. His wife, Catherine, *née* Ashton (1701–1740), whom he married about 1719, was related to Sir Ashton Lever. Hamlet Winstanley painted a memorial portrait, showing her with her husband and eight of their children, in 1741. Their daughter Anna *Blackburne made an extensive museum collection of birds, minerals, and insects. Their son, John Blackburne, became mayor of Liverpool; a grandson, again named John Blackburne, was member of parliament for Lancashire. A magistrate in Warrington, Blackburne held the office of deputy lieutenant for the county of Lancashire, and later purchased the lordship of the manor of Warrington.

John Blackburne was described by his friend Thomas Pennant as 'another Evelyn' (*Tour in Scotland*, 1.12), on account of his passion for horticulture and rural improvement. Though he seldom travelled far afield, he acquired many North American plants through his sponsorship of the collector John Bartram in partnership with Peter Collinson and Richard Richardson. The naturalist Johann Reinhold Forster commemorated him and his daughter Anna by naming a genus *Blackburnia*. Blackburne is also known for his achievement in producing pineapple fruits in his stove, and for successfully growing the fan palm *Sabal blackburniana*, named for him by Thomas Glazebrook. In 1779 his gardener Adam Neal published a catalogue of the living plant collections at Orford Hall which confirmed Blackburne's reputation as Lancashire's leading horticulturist. Blackburne died on 20 December 1786 at Orford Hall, aged ninety-two, and was buried at St Oswald's parish church, Winwick.   J. R. Edmondson

Sources W. Beamont, *Hale and Orford: an account of two old Lancashire houses* (1886), 175–237 · *GM*, 1st ser., 57 (1787), 204 · W. Beamont, *Annals of the lords of Warrington and Bewsey, from 1587 to 1833* (1873), 103–18 · H. E. Blackburne, *Hale Hall, with notes on the family of Ireland Blackburne* (1881) [privately printed, Liverpool] · H. Wells, *A short history of Orford Hall* (1996) · J. P. Rylands, 'Grant of the arms of Green and Aspinwall as quarterings to John Blackburne', *The Genealogist*, new ser., 34 (1917–18), 87–8 · A. Neal, *A catalogue of the plants in the garden of J. Blackburne Esq. at Orford, Lancashire* (1779) · J. Edmondson and G. Rowley, 'John Blackburne of Orford Hall and his cultivated succulents', *Bradleya*, 16 (1998), 14–24 · *Extracts from the literary and scientific correspondence of Richard Richardson*, ed. D. Turner (1835) · N. T. Barton, 'Historical gleanings of Bolton and district', *Chamber Hall and other old property in Bolton* (1882), chap. 13 · T. Pennant, *A tour in Scotland and voyage to the Hebrides, 1772*, 1 (1774) · J. H. Harvey, 'A Scottish botanist in London in 1766', *Garden History*, 9/1 (1981), 40–75 · J. C. Lettsom, *Memoir of John Fothergill, M.D.* (1783) · W. Beamont, *Memoir of Hamlet Winstanley, formerly of Warrington, artist* (1883)
Archives Bodl. Oxf., letters to Richard Richardson · Linn. Soc., letters to John Ellis · Liverpool Museum, department of botany,

notes on John Blackburne and Anna Blackburne • Lpool RO, Wakefield MSS • NL Wales, additions to Kendrick's *Warrington worthies*

Blackburne, Joseph Henry (1841–1924), chess player, was born in or near Hulme, Manchester, on 10 December 1841, the son of Joseph Blackburne, a Quaker bookkeeper and temperance reformer (not a path taken by his son), and his wife, Anne Pritchard. Educated locally, he entered the hosiery business. Quite a proficient draughts player as a boy, the visit of the young American chess player Paul Morphy to England in 1857–9 turned Blackburne's attention (late in the day for a leading player) to chess. He was encouraged by Bernard Horwitz, whom he beat to win first prize in the Manchester chess club's tournament of 1861–2, and competed in the London international tournament of 1862, where he scored only four games in a field of fourteen competitors, yet defeated the redoubtable Wilhelm Steinitz. During this tournament he gave his first blindfold display, conducting ten games at the same time, winning five, drawing three, and losing two, a foretaste of his remarkable success in this branch of chess playing.

For the next forty years Blackburne was a constant competitor in international chess tournaments. He abandoned his work in the hosiery business, and supported himself financially by public chess displays. He won several major tournaments—including those in London (1869, 1876, and 1886) and Berlin (1881)—and was runner-up at others, such as the 1873 Vienna tournament, when the Germans nicknamed him the Black Death and 'the man with the iron nerves', and when he was beaten only by Steinitz. His rivalry with the latter was acute enough that he was said to have responded to being spat at by Steinitz in 1867 by defenestrating him. In tournament games he could vanquish such players as Anderssen, Steinitz, Chigorin, Lasker, and Nimzowitsch, the last in 1914 when he was seventy-two, often by unexpected recoveries from behind, although they would be too much for him in matches. The formation of the British Chess Federation in 1904 led to his competing in the British championship tournaments; he never won this title, although he had been awarded it in more informal circumstances back in 1869. He tied with F. D. Yates at the Chester tournament of 1914, but resigned the title to Yates in the following winter as ill health prevented him from playing off the tie.

From the time of his first entry into the chess arena Blackburne made a feature of simultaneous displays, both with and without sight of the board, travelling all over England for this purpose (and as far as Cuba and Australia) until the last few years of his life. At one time he frequently walked the sixty-odd miles from his home to the south coast, halting at intermediate towns where displays had been arranged. He was 'the quickest solver of problems known' (Hoffer, 764). 'The finest player this country has ever produced', of international stature throughout an exceptionally long career, 'he never kept his reputation in a glass case (as Staunton did)' (*The Times*, 14), but was ready to play some two thousand games every year against all and sundry, unashamedly swigging whisky the while. He was married twice: first, to Beatrice Lapham; second,

by 1877, to Mary Jane Fox (1840/41–1922), with whom he had a son.

Blackburne was the most popular figure in the English chess world from the moment that he took up chess professionally, as indicated by the subscription raised for his benefit when he completed fifty years of chess playing in 1911, administered by Sir John Thursby, which produced £100 per annum until Blackburne's death. He was badly shaken by a near miss by a bomb in 1918. When the great players of the world met for the London tournament of 1922 he was too ill to attend. In the autumn of that year J. R. Capablanca, the world champion, visited him at his bedside. He lingered after a stroke until 1 September 1924, dying at Lewisham. He was buried three days later in Ladywell cemetery, Lewisham, in the same grave as his second wife, who had died in 1922.

E. S. TINSLEY, rev. JULIAN LOCK

Sources *British Chess Magazine*, 44 (1924), 393–402 • *The Times* (2 Sept 1924), 13–14 • D. Hooper and K. Whyld, *The Oxford companion to chess*, 2nd edn (1992), 42–3 • J. H. Blackburne, *Mr Blackburne's games at chess*, ed. P. A. Graham (1899); facs. edn with introduction by D. Hooper (1979) • P. W. Sergeant, *A century of British chess* (1934) • R. N. Coles, *Battles-royal of the chessboard* (1948) • K. Matthews, *British chess* (1948) • W. H. Cozens, 'Half a century back', *British Chess Magazine*, 94 (1974), 387–93 • L. Hoffer, 'The chess masters of today', *Fortnightly Review*, 46 (1886), 753–65 • F. Reinfeld, *Treasury of British chess masterpieces* (1950) • F. Reinfeld, *British chess masters past and present* (1947) • private information (1937) • personal knowledge (1937) • census returns, 1881 • W. Wall, 'Joseph Blackburne', www.geocities.com/siliconvalley/lab/7378/black.htm, Jan 2003
Likenesses A. Rosenbaum, group portrait, oils, 1880 (*Chess players*), NPG • Ape [C. Pellegrini], caricature, chromolithograph, NPG; repro. in *VF* (2 June 1888) • photograph, repro. in Cozens, 388 • photograph, repro. in Cozens, facing p. 393

Blackburne, Lancelot (1658–1743), archbishop of York, was born on 10 December 1658 in London, the son of Richard Blackburne, a gentleman of London, and the brother of Richard *Blackburne. He was educated at Westminster School, which he entered as a king's scholar in 1671. On leaving Westminster he was admitted to Christ Church, Oxford, matriculating on 20 October 1676, and was also that year elected a student (fellow) of the college. He graduated BA in 1680, and in 1681, having been ordained, went to the West Indies. He received permission to proceed MA *in absentia*, which he did by a decree of convocation on 28 January 1684. He was at that time at Nevis, in the king's service. The precise nature of Blackburne's services to the crown remains obscure. A list of payments for 'Secret Services' of Charles II in 1681 notes that £20 was paid 'To Launcelott Blackburne, clerk, bounty, for his transportation to Antego' (Akerman, 42).

Having returned from his travels, Blackburne married Catherine (*c*.1646–1726), daughter of William Talbot of Stourton Castle, Staffordshire, and widow of Walter Littleton of Lichfield, Staffordshire, on 2 September 1684 at the Savoy Chapel. She was the elder sister of William *Talbot, later bishop successively of Oxford, Salisbury, and Durham. There is no indication in Blackburne's will that the couple had any children.

Three months after his marriage Blackburne was presented to the rectory of Camerton, Somerset, on 26

Lancelot Blackburne (1658–1743), by Isaac Seeman, 1726

November 1684. Though himself a whig, he cultivated the patronage of Jonathan Trelawny, the high-church bishop of Exeter, and was rewarded with a canonry at Exeter in 1691, the first of several preferments in the diocese that also included the rectory of Calstock, Cornwall, in 1697, and the vicarage of Alternon, Cornwall, in 1699. He was appointed subdean of Exeter on 9 January 1695, and in this capacity wrote to Bishop Trelawny recounting the evidence given at a witch trial at Exeter in 1696 (a copy of the letter is printed in *N&Q*). He was not without enemies in Exeter, however, and despite the support of influential friends was forced to resign his subdeanery in 1702 following allegations of a scandal, the nature of which is uncertain. Francis Atterbury wrote to Trelawny in support of Blackburne in October 1703, noting that:

> his enemies have been so industrious in spreading and fixing that black scandal, that he would find but a very cold and mortifying reception here, till his friends have made a little way for him, by removing men's prejudices, and clearing up matters to his service.   (*Miscellaneous Works*, 1.253)

His position had, however, improved sufficiently that following the death of his successor he was reinstalled as subdean on 27 July 1704. During his time as subdean Blackburne came to the notice of the dean of Exeter, William Wake. On Wake's elevation to the bishopric of Lincoln in 1705, Blackburne was appointed his successor as dean. Blackburne maintained the favour of the ministry by keeping a watchful eye on the local gentry who were thought to be disaffected to the government. In 1715 he added to his growing collection of preferments by becoming archdeacon of Cornwall.

After Wake had been translated to Canterbury, Blackburne continued to benefit from the patronage of the new archbishop. Wake nominated Blackburne to accompany

George I as the king's chaplain on his visit to Hanover in 1716. This was an important appointment, and the position came to be seen as the precursor to elevation to the bench of bishops. In 1717 Blackburne was duly elevated to the bishopric of Exeter, although he did not succeed in obtaining 'a prebend of Westminster when one should fall vacant' which he had requested so that he might have a convenient house when attending parliament (Sykes, 150). He took his parliamentary duties seriously and was a strong supporter of the whig government in parliament, siding, for example, with the ministry and against his erstwhile patron Wake in voting for the bill introduced by James Stanhope, Earl Stanhope, for the repeal of the Occasional Conformity and Schism Acts in December 1718. He was appointed lord high almoner in 1723. It was no doubt Blackburne's political loyalties which recommended him to Edmund Gibson, bishop of London and Walpole's ecclesiastical adviser, by whose influence he was translated on 19 October 1724 to the archbishopric of York, a position he held for the remainder of his life.

While Blackburne was assiduous in executing his political duties, he was less diligent in performing his spiritual functions. During his tenure at York he appears to have conducted no confirmations. Initially he did ordain in person, although he did so only in July, August, and September, during his summer residence at Bishopthorpe, and after 1733 he ceased to ordain in person at all, but gave candidates letters dimissory to be ordained by other bishops. He attended instead to political matters, civil and ecclesiastical, and kept a Westminster residence in Downing Street. He did, however, take seriously the exercise of his ecclesiastical patronage, particularly in promoting the interests of loyal whigs, and he also resorted to the courts to defend the prerogatives and interests of the archbishopric of York against encroachments. His undoubted presence as a court bishop, moreover, gives credibility to the story which attributes to the archbishop's influence the rise of Joseph Butler, the moral philosopher and future bishop, from ecclesiastical obscurity. Butler had given up his preachership at the Rolls Chapel and had for ten years ministered in the northern parish of Stanhope. It is said that Queen Caroline enquired of Blackburne whether Butler was not dead, to which he is supposed to have replied, 'No, madam, he is not *dead*, but *buried*', thereby prompting the queen to appoint him her clerk of the closet, or private chaplain.

Unfortunately, however, Blackburne's reputation, both during his lifetime and subsequently, has been characterized, whether justifiably or not, more by unverifiable rumour and scandal than by his political and ecclesiastical accomplishments. A story was told that while in the West Indies he had served on a buccaneering expedition against the Spanish, and took his part of the booty. It was said that one old buccaneer returned to England and asked after his old chum Blackburne, only to be told he was now archbishop of York. Another story, recounted by James Granger, also illustrates the very worldly reputation which Blackburne enjoyed. The archbishop, it was alleged, was conducting a visitation to St Mary's Church in Nottingham. It was said that Blackburne 'had ordered some of the … attendants, to bring him pipes and tobacco, and some liquor into the vestry for his refreshment after the *fatigue of confirmation*'. The rector of the church, hearing of the orders, 'remonstrated with the archbishop upon the impropriety of his conduct' and told Blackburne that 'his vestry should not be converted into a smoking-room' (Malcolm, 199). The apparent failure of Blackburne to perform any confirmations while archbishop of York, however, calls into question the reliability of this account.

Blackburne was also alleged to have fathered Thomas *Hayter, bishop of Norwich. Horace Walpole described Hayter as:

> natural son of Blackbourn, the jolly old Archbishop of York, who had all the manners of a man of quality, though he had been a buccaneer, and was a clergyman; but he retained nothing of his first profession, except his seraglio. (Walpole, *Memories*, 1.74–5)

It must be acknowledged that Blackburne was particularly munificent in showering preferments on Hayter, a younger man, and that Hayter inherited a large portion of Blackburne's considerable estate. An item in the *Quarterly Review* (1822) pretended to demonstrate that Blackburne was not Hayter's father by citing Hayter's baptismal entry in the parish register of Chagford, Devon, for 17 November 1702; it reads 'son of George Hayter, Rector of this parish, and of Grace, his wife', although this can hardly be said definitively to settle the question.

Soon after his death Blackburne was the subject of a piece of scurrilous and satirical verse entitled *Priest-Craft and Lust, or, Lancelot to his Ladies, an Epistle from the Shades* (1743), which had him lamenting:

> No longer thro' the Town I range with raging Flame
> To seek the Virgin Nymph or married Dame.
> (p. 4)

It was also wittily said, concerning his reputation for carnality, that 'he gained more hearts than souls' (Noble, 3.69). The archbishop also featured in a satirical poem of 1737 entitled *First Oars to L—m—th*, which portrayed Blackburne competing against his fellow bishops Edmund Gibson and Benjamin Hoadly for the archbishopric of Canterbury.

It was contended that Blackburne was favoured by the first two Georges because of the laxity of his moral precepts. One rumour suggested that Blackburne was rewarded with the archbishopric of York for secretly marrying George I to his mistress the duchess of Kendal. Horace Walpole alleged that Blackburne, talking with Queen Caroline in the presence of Sir Robert Walpole, had remarked, 'Madam, I am glad you like the king's new mistress, Lady Yarmouth; it shews you are a sensible woman, your Majesty having no objection for your husband to divert himself' (*Works of … Sir Charles Hanbury Williams*, 2.135). The controversial archbishop has even been charged with the evidently groundless allegations that he was the father of Francis Blackburne, the heterodox author of the *Confessional*, and that Dick Turpin was his butler at Bishopthorpe. It is at this distance of time impossible to make definitive judgements about the veracity of the numerous allegations levelled against Blackburne. They must therefore be thought to illustrate the reputation rather than the reality of the man.

Blackburne was the author of several published sermons: one given before Queen Mary, entitled *The Unreasonableness of Anger* (1694); two before Queen Anne, *The Mystery of Godliness* (1706) and *The Blessedness of Suffering Persecution for Righteousness Sake* (1709); two before the mayor and aldermen of the City of London (1697, 1715); a Latin sermon before convocation (1714); and a sermon before the House of Commons on the anniversary of the martyrdom of Charles I (1716), in which he took the opportunity to liken the Jacobites to the regicides. He also published a pastoral letter addressed to the bishops of the province of York, which is annexed to a sermon of Lewis Stephens published in 1727. His wife, Catherine, died in 1726 and was buried on 11 June in the middle chancel of St Margaret's Church, Westminster. Blackburne himself died on 23 March 1743 at a time of severe weather. As Horace Walpole records it, 'his ancient Grace of York' died of one of the 'epidemical distempers' which accompanied ten days of 'snows, north-east winds, and blue plagues' (Walpole, *Memories*, 1.235). He was buried on 1 April 1743 in St Margaret's, Westminster, near his wife.

ANDREW STARKIE

Sources H. Walpole, *Memories of the last ten years of the reign of George the Second*, ed. Lord Holland, 1 (1822), 74–5 · *A biographical history of England, from the revolution to the end of George I's reign: being a continuation of the Rev. J. Granger's work*, ed. M. Noble, 3 (1806), vol. 3, pp. 68–9 · A. Tindal Hart, *Ebor* (1986), 142 · Foster, *Alum. Oxon.* · *Old Westminsters*, 1.93–4 · *The letters of Horace Walpole, earl of Orford*, ed. P. Cunningham, 9 vols. (1861–6), vol. 1, p. 235 · *The miscellaneous works of Bishop Atterbury*, ed. J. Nichols, 5 vols. (1789–98), vol. 1, p. 253 · J. P. Malcolm, *Letters between the Rev. James Granger …* (1805), 199 · *The works of … Sir Charles Hanbury Williams*, ed. E. Jefferey, 3 vols. (1822), vol. 2, p. 135 · burial register, St Margaret's, Westminster, Westminster RO · M. E. C. Walcott, *The history of the parish church of Saint Margaret, in Westminster* (1847), 47 · N. Sykes, *Church and state in England in the XVIII century* (1934), 150 · G. Oliver, *Lives of the bishops of Exeter, and a history of the cathedral* (1861), 160–61 · *Priest-craft and lust, or, Lancelot to his ladies, an epistle from the shades* (1743) · J. Y. Akerman, ed., *Moneys received and paid for secret services of Charles II and James II from 30th March 1679 to 25th December 1688*, CS, 52 (1851), 42 · *N&Q*, 11 (1855), 498–9 · *QR*, 27 (1822), 186–7 · PRO, PROB 11/725, fols. 387v–393r

Likenesses I. Seeman, oils, 1726, Bishopthorpe Palace, York [*see illus.*] · G. Vertue, line engraving, 1727 (after I. Seeman), BM, NPG; versions, Bishop's Palace, Exeter; Christ Church Oxf. · mezzotint (after unknown artist), NPG

Wealth at death see will, PRO, PROB 11/725, fols. 387v–393r

Blackburne, Richard (1651/2–1716), physician and writer, was born in London, the son of Richard Blackburne and the older brother of Lancelot *Blackburne. He entered Trinity College, Cambridge, as a pensioner in 1665 under Thomas Gale. He became a scholar of the college in 1668 and graduated BA in 1670. In May 1676, at the age of twenty-four, he took the degree of MD from Leiden University. His thesis, on the formation of the blood, was published as *Disputatio medica inauguralis de sanguificatione* (1676).

Blackburne returned to London, where he assisted John

Aubrey in producing a supplement to the prose autobiography of Thomas Hobbes soon after the philosopher's death in December 1679. In February 1680 Aubrey described Blackburne to Anthony Wood as one of 'the best scholars in London of his age, & *philo* Hobbist' as well as a 'mighty read man' who 'hath harried all Mr Hobbes's adversaries' (Bodl. Oxf., MS Ballard 14, fol. 125). Initially Aubrey enlisted Blackburne to be his 'Aristarchus', providing editorial advice. Aubrey however soon relinquished his notes and control of the project to Blackburne, who organized Aubrey's manuscripts and began to produce a Latin translation of the supplement. At first Aubrey was pleased with Blackburne's 'delicate style'. He wrote to Wood that 'it was as if Mr Hobbes's soule were come into his body'. However Aubrey also complained that 'the Dr is a great Judge & consequently magisteriall: he is much against minuteness' (Bodl. Oxf., MS Tanner 456a, fol. 23). A serious disagreement developed between Blackburne and Aubrey on the nature of the biography. Blackburne and his advisers, John Dryden and Lord John Vaughan, advocated what Aubrey disparaged as a panegyric 'High Style'. Aubrey objected to the omission of small details, such as Hobbes's having been a page. A disgruntled but prescient Aubrey wrote to Wood that 'The Dr says I am too minute; but a hundred yeare hence that minuteness will be gratefull' (Bodl. Oxf., MS Wood F39, fol. 340). Aubrey's dissatisfaction with Blackburne's treatment of Hobbes apparently spurred him to begin writing his *Brief Lives*, in which his own biographical ideas and concern with detail was fully expressed. Blackburne's *Vitae Hobbianae auctarium* was completed by September 1680, giving an unusually positive view of the controversial philosopher's achievements. It included a list of Hobbes's friends and detailed bibliographies of his works and those of his critics and admirers. Although Aubrey was not entirely happy with the finished product, an English translation was projected, although it was never produced. The work does, however, form the basis for the English biographical introduction to *The Moral and Political Works of Thomas Hobbes of Malmesbury* (1750). Blackburne's biography appeared in the materials published by William Crooke in 1681 under the title *Thomae Hobbes Angli Malmesburiensis philosophi vita*. This was probably edited by Blackburne and was dedicated to Hobbes's patron, William Cavendish, earl of Devonshire. It contained verses by Abraham Cowley, Ralph Bathurst, and one incorrectly attributed to Aubrey. Blackburne supplied a preface to three works: Hobbes's Latin prose autobiography, *Thomii Hobbes Malmesburiensis vita*, Blackburne's much longer *Vitae* and finally Hobbes's Latin verse autobiography. The work ran to a second edition in 1682.

The dispute over the biography did not appear to ruin Blackburne's and Aubrey's friendship. In 1681 they co-operated over an attempt to promote the medicinal chalybeate springs at Seend, near Devizes in Wiltshire, which Aubrey had discovered in 1665. Blackburne, who practised annually at Tunbridge Wells, worded an advertisement celebrating the virtues of the waters. These efforts were unsuccessful—the springs were not regularly frequented until after 1688. On 25 June 1685 Blackburne became an honorary fellow of the Royal College of Physicians. He was admitted as a full fellow at the extraordinary *comitia* of 12 April 1687 under the new charter granted to the college by James II. Blackburne became a censor of the college in 1688. The revolution of 1688 brought the validity of the new charter, and the position of the new fellows, into question. Blackburne took a leading role in representing the 'new' college in the disputes which resulted in 1689. A sometimes severe critic of the college authorities, Blackburne was a vocal presence at college meetings, being fined on several occasions for 'unseasonable Speaking' and 'unseemly Language' (annals, RCP Lond., 5.127, 6.9). In October 1690 he pointed out the technical illegality of one of the new college statutes which prevented the admission of any physician who had practised any less liberal art or had served an apprenticeship in a shop. The statute conflicted with the college's stated duty to reject only for lack of due learning and skill and, as a result of Blackburne's protest, it was withdrawn. In July 1695 Blackburne was part of a group which refused to contribute funds for the establishment of a charitable dispensary (a measure which could also be seen as an attack upon the apothecaries' trade). Later in the same year he was also one of the fellows who refused to contribute a £50 bond to observe the statutes of the college. From 1706 Blackburne is described in the fellows' list as living in 'the country' and then from 1709 in Epsom. His will (made in 1714) suggests that he was at that time resident in the village of Sutton in Surrey, where he died in 1716. He was buried in Sutton churchyard on 30 May.   JON PARKIN

Sources M. Hunter, *John Aubrey and the realm of learning* (1975), 60, 77–80, 109, 179 · A. Powell, *John Aubrey and his friends*, rev. edn (1963), 178–9 · H. J. Cook, *The decline of the old medical regime in Stuart London* (1986), 220–22, 235, 237 · Munk, *Roll*, 1.451–2 · G. Clark and A. M. Cooke, *A history of the Royal College of Physicians of London*, 1 (1964), 361, 369 · J. Britton, *Memoir of John Aubrey* (1845), 17 · Venn, *Alum. Cant.* · W. W. Rouse Ball and J. A. Venn, eds., *Admissions to Trinity College, Cambridge*, 2 (1913), 472 · annals, RCP Lond., vols. 4–7 · D. Tylden-Wright, *John Aubrey: a life* (1991), 215–17 · J. B. Kite, *A study of the works and reputation of John Aubrey: with emphasis on his 'Brief lives'* (1993), 108–9 · PRO, PROB 11/552, sig. 113 · parish register, burial, Sutton, Sutton Central Library, P42/1/1, 30 May 1716 · J. Aubrey, letters to Anthony Wood, Bodl. Oxf., MS Aubrey 9, fols. 25v, 28v, 55r · J. Aubrey, letters to A. Wood, Bodl. Oxf., MS Ballard 14, fols. 125, 127, 131 · J. Aubrey, letters to A. Wood, Bodl. Oxf., MS Tanner 456a · J. Aubrey, letters to A. Wood, Bodl. Oxf., MS Wood F. 39, fols. 340v, 344r, 345v, 347v, 350r, 351v, 354v, 362r, 397r

Wealth at death see will, PRO, PROB 11/552, sig. 113

Blackburne, Sir William (1764–1839), army and political officer in India, was appointed to the Madras army as a cadet of native infantry in 1782, arrived at Madras in June 1783, and in 1784 served with the force employed under Colonel Fullarton in the campaign against the Poligars in Madura and Tinnevelly. He subsequently served in the campaign which ended in the defeat of Tipu Sultan in 1792. His proficiency as a linguist led to his being employed in 1787 as Maratha interpreter at Tanjore during the inquiry into the succession to the Tanjore raj, and he was for some years Maratha interpreter under the British resident at Tanjore. In 1801, having attained the rank of captain, he was appointed resident at the Tanjore court, and held that office until he left India in 1823.

Very shortly after his appointment as resident, Blackburne had to take the field at the head of his escort and of the raja's troops to repel two invasions of the province by insurgents from the adjoining districts. This he achieved with great skill, and the neighbouring province of Ramnad was recovered. In 1804 he exposed extensive frauds and oppression by the indigenous officials in Tanjore, the civil administration of which was under officials independent of the resident. He was employed subsequently by the Madras government to remodel the administration both in Tanjore and in the princely state of Pudukkottai, and was twice sent on special missions to Travancore. His political services gained the approval of Lord Wellesley and of successive governors of Madras, including Sir Thomas Munro. Blackburne, then a major-general, was knighted in 1838. He died at his house in Portland Place, London, on 16 October 1839, survived by his wife.   A. J. ARBUTHNOT, rev. JAMES FALKNER

Sources J. Philippart, East India military calendar, 3 vols. (1823–6) · East-India Register · GM, 2nd ser., 13 (1840), 92
Wealth at death under £45,000: GM

Blacker, Carlos Paton (1895–1975), psychiatrist and eugenicist, was born on 8 December 1895 in Paris, the elder of the two sons of Carlos Blacker and Caroline Frost. His father, a gentleman of independent means, was descended on his maternal side from a prominent Peruvian political family, and one of Blacker's cousins, Pedro Beltran, served for a time as prime minister of Peru. Blacker's mother was the daughter of a Confederate general from St Louis who gained some distinction during the American Civil War. French was C. P. Blacker's first language and he remained bilingual throughout his life. Both Blacker and his brother were educated at Eton College, which Blacker left to serve as an officer in the Coldstream Guards from 1915 to 1919. He was wounded, and decorated with the Military Cross. Blacker's experiences during the First World War, in which his brother was killed, had an enduring impact on him and contributed to a falling away from his Roman Catholic origins and to his decision to practise psychiatry. During his last years Blacker returned in his mind to the war, writing an extensive account (unpublished) of his life in the trenches.

Following the war Blacker entered Balliol College, Oxford, graduating in 1922 with distinction in natural science and zoology. While at Oxford Blacker represented the university at foils and was captain of the boxing club from 1920 to 1922, establishing a pattern of vigorous physical activity that saw him still running 5 miles a day or plunging into icy waters for a swim when in his mid-sixties. Blacker, in 1923, married Helen Maude, the daughter of Major A. J. Pilkington, whose family was living in Florence at the time. From 1922 to 1925 he trained for medicine at Guy's Hospital, London, and obtained his MB (1927) and later his MD (1931) from Oxford. From 1927 to 1936 he was registrar of psychological medicine at Guy's. He left to join the psychiatric staff of the Maudsley Hospital, London, where, with the Second World War years

excepted, he spent much of the remainder of his clinical career, retiring in 1960. Blacker's many professional publications included Human Values in Psychological Medicine (1933), Voluntary Sterilization (1934), and The Chances of Morbid Inheritance (1934). Immediately upon the outbreak of war in 1939 Blacker rejoined the Coldstream Guards as a regimental medical officer, was evacuated at Dunkirk and was awarded the George Medal for his gallantry in rescuing a wounded fellow officer from a minefield in which two men had already been killed. In 1942 he was seconded to the Ministry of Health as adviser on population and medico-social problems to undertake a comprehensive survey of psychiatric facilities required in the post-war period. His important report, Neurosis and the Mental Health Services (1946), provided guidelines for both in-patient and out-patient psychiatric requirements, including special child psychiatric facilities, developed by the new National Health Service.

Blacker's appointment to the Ministry of Health was an acknowledgement of the reputation he enjoyed in the inter-war years not only as a psychiatrist but as an influential authority on the eugenic aspects of birth control and population. His interests in the social consequences of human heredity and variability, which led him to eugenics in the 1920s, were stimulated by his biological studies at Oxford and his reading of Sir Francis Galton, whose broad goals of eugenic improvement Blacker sought to advance as general secretary of the Eugenics Society from 1931 to 1952. Under Blacker the Eugenics Society was transformed from an unfocused, amateur propaganda agency dabbling uncertainly in the newly emerging areas of birth control and genetics, into a quasi-professional research foundation committed to family planning and the serious study of population problems.

Blacker's interest in birth control began when he was a medical student at Guy's Hospital. He was distressed by the large number of poor female clinic patients desperate for help in avoiding further pregnancies. He complained of the medical profession's irresponsible hostility to birth control and warned that unless doctors began to take an interest in the field it would be pre-empted by non-medical people like Marie Stopes with her 'flowery and highly-coloured books'. The publication of Birth Control and the State (1926) was the first of Blacker's many books and articles advocating the medicalization of contraception and pointing out its great value for the improvement of physical, mental, and 'racial' health. He was instrumental in founding the birth control investigation committee (BCIC) in 1927 composed of scientists and doctors committed to studying the medical and sociological effects of contraception. Blacker also persuaded a reluctant Eugenics Society to endorse birth control as a eugenic weapon and to finance the BCIC as well as the unique, decade-long efforts of the Oxford zoologist, John Baker, to find a simple, reliable contraceptive for use by the most populous and, allegedly, eugenically least desirable sectors of society.

In his ultimately vain efforts to win for eugenics the

scientific credibility and respectability he believed it deserved as an instrument of rational demographic planning and social improvement, Blacker recruited prominent scientists, social scientists, and physicians to the cause. As an advocate of a more liberal minded, scientific, reform eugenics, Blacker persuaded the Eugenics Society, sometimes under threat of his own resignation, to forge alliances with the National Birth Control Association, later the Family Planning Association (FPA), and with new demographic research groups such as the population investigation committee (PIC) and population and economic planning, all of which the Eugenics Society agreed not only to finance, but, in the case of the PIC and FPA, to house for a time in the society's offices in Eccleston Square. Blacker served for several years as honorary secretary of the PIC.

The close ties that Blacker fashioned between eugenics, birth control, and population studies in the 1930s culminated in 1944 in the achievement of one of his long-term goals, the appointment of the royal commission on population (1949), whose ranks, from chairman down, contained a number of prominent eugenicists. Blacker hoped that their role on the prestigious commission would revive the scientific credibility of a eugenics movement tainted by its association with the race hygiene policies of the Nazis. But he acknowledged in a brief history, *Eugenics: Galton and after*, published in 1952 to coincide with his resignation as general secretary of the Eugenics Society, that his efforts had failed.

Following his resignation, Blacker became increasingly involved in international population issues, serving as the first chairman of the Simon Population Trust and playing an important role as an ally of Margaret Sanger in the founding of the International Planned Parenthood Federation in 1952. He brought to the often tempestuous international conferences many of the qualities of patience, courtesy, good humour, and compromise that made it possible for him to work so successfully throughout his life with the many difficult and contentious people who populated the birth control and eugenics movements. Tall, spare, and determined, he was to some a formidable, efficient, rather distant person who remained every inch an old Etonian and ex-Coldstream Guards officer. But to his close friends, who called him 'Pip', Blacker was warm, generous, and unfailingly loyal and supportive.

As a consulting psychiatrist to the merged Bethlem Royal and Maudsley Hospital Blacker continued to see patients at a weekly clinic until shortly before his death. As he lay dying in 1975 the Eugenics Society, which had awarded him the Galton medal in 1957, sent him a silver Galton plate commemorating his many years of service to the cause. He died before he could see it of a cerebral thrombosis on 21 April 1975 at the Royal Surrey County Hospital in Guildford, survived by his wife, one son, and two daughters. He was buried at Shamley Green, Surrey.

RICHARD A. SOLOWAY

Sources R. A. Soloway, *Demography and degeneration: eugenics and the declining birthrate in twentieth-century Britain* (1990) · Munk, *Roll* · G. C. L. Bertram, 'Dr C. P. Blacker', *Bulletin of the Eugenics Society*, 7

(1975), 61–3 · *The Lancet* (10 May 1975) · *The Times* (26 April 1975) · *Daily Telegraph* (24 April 1975) · WWW · d. cert. · E. Lemon, ed., *The Balliol College register, 1916–1967*, 4th edn (privately printed, Oxford, 1969)

Archives Wellcome L., papers relating to secretaryship of Eugenics Society · Wellcome L., further papers | BL, corresp. with Havelock Ellis, Add. MS 70540 · Bodl. Oxf., corresp. with John Randall Baker · Rice University, Houston, Texas, Woodson Research Center, corresp. with Sir Julian Huxley

Wealth at death £94,735: probate, 17 Feb 1976, CGPLA Eng. & Wales

Blacker, George Dacre (1791–1871), Church of Ireland clergyman, was the elder son of James Blacker, a Dublin magistrate, and was born in Dublin. He entered Trinity College, Dublin, in 1806, was elected a scholar in 1809, and proceeded BA in 1811 and MA in 1858. He was for several years curate of St Andrew's, Dublin, chaplain of the city corporation, and rector of Taghadoe. In 1840 he became vicar of Maynooth and a prebendary in St Patrick's Cathedral. Blacker wrote several local historical works including the *Castle of Maynooth* (1853) and *A Record of Maynooth Church* (1867), which were printed for private circulation. He was also the author of *Types and Prophecies Relating to Messiah* (1829). He died unmarried at his home, The Glebe, Maynooth, co. Kildare, on 23 May 1871, and was buried on 27 May in the Leinster mausoleum, by Maynooth parish church. [ANON.], *rev.* DAVID HUDDLESTON

Sources *Irish Ecclesiastical Gazette* (21 June 1871), 131–2 · H. Cotton, *Fasti ecclesiae Hibernicae*, 2 (1848), 168 · H. Cotton, *Fasti ecclesiae Hibernicae*, 6 (1878), 62 · [J. H. Todd], ed., *A catalogue of graduates who have proceeded to degrees in the University of Dublin, from the earliest recorded commencements to ... December 16, 1868* (1869), 47 · Burtchaell & Sadleir, *Alum. Dubl.*, 2nd edn · private information (1885)

Wealth at death under £3000: probate, 30 Aug 1871, CGPLA Ire.

Blacker, Sir George Francis (1865–1948), obstetrician, was born in Dublin on 23 October 1865, the fourth child of Commissary-Major-General Latham William Blacker (1829–1916), who came from a military and landed family in co. Tyrone, and his wife, Harriette de Maine (d. 1908), daughter of Captain John Bagot-Smith. Little is known about Blacker's childhood except that between the ages of thirteen and seventeen he was educated in England, at Cheltenham College. He retained a lifelong affection for his school, and later in life held office as president of the Old Cheltonian Society.

After matriculation Blacker became a student at University College, London, attending first the faculty of arts (1883–5) and then the faculty of medicine (1885–6 and 1891–2), where he proved to be a gifted scholar. He won an exhibition and gold medals in his intermediate examinations in July 1888 and achieved a first-class pass in the London MB examinations in 1891, when he was also awarded a gold medal; he went on to win a further two gold medals in the MD examination in 1893. Obstetrics and gynaecology became Blacker's speciality and although at the time obstetricians were classed as physicians (he was elected fellow of the Royal College of Physicians in 1902), Blacker continued to pursue the surgical side of his specialism. In 1890 he was elected Atkinson-

Morley surgical scholar at University College Hospital, and in 1891 he took his surgical fellowship (FRCS).

Except for the period of the First World War, when he served as a captain with the Royal Army Medical Corps (he was mentioned twice in dispatches), Blacker devoted his working life to his own teaching hospital. His first appointments at University College Hospital were very junior but they marked the beginning of a distinguished career; by 1893 he was elected assistant obstetric physician, he was appointed obstetric physician in 1900, and physician in 1927. However, his foremost interest was in medical education and it was in this sphere that Blacker made his greatest contribution. During his first tenure as dean of the medical school, from 1912 to 1915, he supported the report of the 1913 royal commission on university education in London, and advocated the creation of full-time medical professorships. His second term as dean, from 1917 to 1926, proved most eventful for University College Hospital was one of the medical schools to respond to a government initiative by reforming its system of teaching. Not only was Blacker responsible for developing the new clinical unit system but when the Rockefeller Foundation donated gifts to the hospital, in excess of £1 million in support of this and other projects, he gained wide recognition for his invaluable administrative services.

During the early 1920s Blacker became involved in the professional debate concerning the reform of obstetric teaching. This had been initiated by T. Watts Eden at the Royal Society of Medicine while Blacker was president of its obstetrics and gynaecology section (1917–18). For his part Blacker upheld proposals which advocated the extension of midwifery teaching facilities to all medical students in London, and the establishment of four or more new centres where tuition and practical experience could be gained in all aspects of midwifery, gynaecology, and maternal and child welfare.

In addition to his teaching and practice, at various times Blacker acted as an examiner in midwifery to the universities of London, Liverpool, and New Zealand. He was also a keen committee man, and during his membership of the Obstetrical Society of London (1893–1907) and of the obstetrics and gynaecology section of the Royal Society of Medicine (1907–48) he sat on a great number of them. These activities left him little time for writing but he did make occasional contributions to medical journals and was noted for editing the seventh edition of Galabin's renowned text, *Practice of Midwifery*, published in 1910. He also took a keen interest in the use of radium in gynaecology and, in 1929, was president of the Radium Institute at Mount Vernon Hospital.

Blacker was appointed CBE in 1920, and was knighted in 1923. He married Shirley Elvina (b. 1879/80), second daughter of Canon Thomas James Bowen, at St Mary's Church, Tormarton, Gloucestershire, on 8 November 1904; their only child, George Patrick Demaine (1906–1974), was born two years later. Blacker was apparently an energetic and cheerful man, whose leisure activities included fishing and, on retirement, working with the British Red Cross

Society. In all other respects he led a quiet and modest life, retiring first to Shedfield in Hampshire in the early 1930s before finally settling at Frensham in Surrey in 1940. He died, of a heart attack, at his home, Oak Hill Cottage, Frensham, on 21 May 1948.   SUSAN L. COHEN

Sources *BMJ* (29 May 1948), 1053 · W. R. Merrington, *University College Hospital and its medical school: a history* (1976) · D'A. Power and W. R. Le Fanu, *Lives of the fellows of the Royal College of Surgeons of England, 1930–1951* (1953), 83–4 · *The Times* (25 May 1948), 7 · *WWW, 1941–50* · *The Lancet* (18 Aug 1888), 350 · *BMJ* (28 Nov 1891), 1177 · *The Lancet* (5 June 1948), 890 · J. M. M. Kerr, R. W. Johnstone, and M. H. Phillips, *Historical review of British obstetrics and gynaecology, 1800–1950* (1954) · Munk, *Roll* · m. cert. · d. cert. · Burke, *Gen. Ire.* (1976), 113–14 · *CGPLA Eng. & Wales* (1948)
Archives Royal Society of Medicine, London, reports of the Obstetrical Society of London
Likenesses photograph, repro. in *The Lancet* (5 June 1948), 890
Wealth at death £44,470 12s. 2d.: probate, 25 Aug 1948, *CGPLA Eng. & Wales*

Blacker, (Latham Valentine) Stewart (1887–1964), soldier and inventor of armaments, was born on 1 October 1887 at The Beeches, Grappenhall, near Warrington, Cheshire, the son of Major Latham Charles Miller Blacker who came of a soldiering family, and his wife, Emily Violet Mattie. One of his ancestors was Valentine Blacker (1778–1823), who was instrumental in mapping Mount Everest. Educated at Cheltenham College (1899–1900) and at Bedford School, he went to the Royal Military College at Sandhurst, and then followed his father into the Indian army, serving first in India, and later in Afghanistan, Turkestan, and Russia. Although without special engineering training, Blacker early on showed an aptitude for armaments design, and in 1905 was associated with developing the 3.5 inch infantry mortar. He became keen on flying, and in 1911 obtained his flying certificate (no. 121). During his service abroad he was awarded many medals and clasps, and was frequently mentioned in dispatches.

When war broke out in 1914 Blacker got himself transferred from the Indian army to the Royal Flying Corps. As a pilot he was first shot down in France in 1915 and severely wounded. He was again seriously wounded in 1916 and 1917. After the war he decided to concentrate on developing special weapons at his own expense without help from the services; it was his proud boast to be the country's sole private inventor of armaments.

In 1920 Blacker was appointed OBE, and from 1924 to 1928 he was on the Imperial General Staff. On 15 February 1927 he married Lady Doris (b. 1900), only daughter of William Robert Wellesley Peel, the first Earl Peel; they had twin sons and two daughters. At his mansion in Liss, Hampshire, he set up a modern workshop for the manufacture of his devices and a firing range for trying them out. In 1933 Blacker joined the first expedition to fly over Mount Everest. This led to his writing *First over Everest* (1933), the last of his three books, and to the award of the Paris Geographical Society's gold medal.

The Second World War found Blacker with the rank of lieutenant-colonel in the Territorial Army, but obviously unfit for further service overseas. He therefore concentrated on his projects for developing weapons. His first interest had been in trying to devise an anti-tank weapon for use by the infantry. What was needed was a projector for a bomb containing high explosive of the plastic variety, which would plaster on to the tank so as to secure the comparatively large area of contact required to blow a hole on detonation. Such a bomb was much too large to be fired through any barrel, so Blacker adopted the simple solution of making the barrel a part of the bomb and firing the entire unit from a spigot.

Before the war neither the anti-tank Blacker bombard, as he called it, nor any of his other weapons had been adopted by the army. However, when the war had started Blacker, complete with eyeglass and leggings, approached everyone he knew at the War Office to do something about them. A new section of military intelligence research (MIRc) had recently been formed there to develop special weapons, and Blacker was referred to the head of it, Major R. Millis Jefferis. Jefferis, always receptive to new ideas, welcomed Blacker's invention and arranged for his bombard to be perfected and put into production. It was modified for the Royal Navy as the anti-submarine Hedgehog.

The PIAT, based on one of Blacker's experimental guns, became one of the most successful British anti-tank weapons, and destroyed many German tanks. Carrying on with his spigot principle, Blacker had developed a spigot gun which could be fired from the shoulder, a spring taking up the recoil so that it did not affect the firer. Jefferis was experimenting with what were known as hollow-charge rounds. A high explosive charge carried in a bomb would be focused by a cone, so that on contact with the target and detonation a small hole would be driven through heavy armour plate. This hollow charge weighed 2 lbs, and Jefferis wanted to equip infantrymen to fire it from the shoulder. The PIAT, based on Blacker's spring gun, proved to be the answer and Blacker received an inventor's award of £25,000.

Blacker was the perfect example of a gentleman, always courteous and understanding. He had a remarkable brain, was very persuasive, acquired vast knowledge on developing armaments, and was an ingenious inventor. He died at his home, Cold Hayes, Liss, Hampshire, on 19 April 1964, and was survived by his wife.   STUART MACRAE, *rev.*

Sources S. Macrae, *Winston Churchill's toyshop* (1971) · personal knowledge (1981) · *The Times* (20 April 1964) · *WWW* · Burke, *Peerage* (1980) · b. cert. · m. cert. · d. cert. · *CGPLA Eng. & Wales* (1964)
Archives FILM BFI NFTVA, documentary footage · BFI NFTVA, news footage
Wealth at death £56,255: probate, 2 Sept 1964, *CGPLA Eng. & Wales*

Blacker, Valentine (1778–1823), army officer in the East India Company, was born on 19 October 1778. He obtained his commission in the Madras cavalry in 1798, and served as a cornet in the Mysore campaign of 1799, with a troop of cavalry of the nizam's contingent. A year later he was employed in Wainad as aide-de-camp to Colonel Stevenson, and subsequently served with his regiment in the southern provinces of the Madras presidency under Colonel Agnew, by whom he was thanked in dispatches for

having surprised a party of the enemy and for a successful charge with the troop of cavalry under his command. The remainder of his military service was in the quartermaster-general's department, of which he became head in 1810. In 1815 he served with the army of reserve under Lieutenant-General Sir Thomas Hislop, and in 1817 under him with the army of the Deccan at the battle of Mehidpur and the other operations in the Deccan. His services at Mehidpur and the reconnaissances made by him before the battle were specially brought to the notice of the governor-general. He was made CB in 1823.

Blacker was subsequently appointed surveyor-general of India, and on returning to Europe in 1821 was thanked in general orders by the commander-in-chief of the Madras army for his eminent and scientific services as quartermaster-general of the army of Fort St George during a period of ten years. In 1821 he published his *Memoir of the operations of the British army in India during the Mahratta War of 1817, 1818, 1819*. Blacker died at Calcutta in 1823.

A. J. ARBUTHNOT, *rev.* JAMES LUNT

Sources V. Blacker, *Memoir of the operations of the British army in India during the Mahratta War of 1817, 1818, 1819* (1821) · BL OIOC · Fortescue, *Brit. army*, vol. 11 · E. G. Phythian-Adams, *The Madras regiment, 1758–1958* (1958)
Archives BL, memoir of the Anglo-Maratha wars, Add. MS 23754 · Duke U., Perkins L., letter-book

Blackerby, Richard (1574–1648), preacher, was born in Worlington in Suffolk, the second son of Thomas Blackerby. He was prepared for a career in the ministry by his pious upbringing and education at Bury St Edmunds and then Trinity College, Cambridge, where he matriculated at Easter 1587. For nine years he spent most of his time in Cambridge, where he graduated BA, probably in 1590, and gained a reputation for great skill in Latin, Greek, and especially Hebrew. His abilities were such that in later years famous divines would send him scriptural problems of a linguistic nature. While still at college Blackerby experienced a religious crisis that seems to have been inspired by the preaching of William Perkins which, as Samuel Clark reports, left Blackerby 'truly converted, but he lay some years in great distress of Conscience, and much perplexity of Spirit' (Clark, 57). His father brought him home temporarily in the hope that a change of air would relieve his melancholy, but relief only came on Blackerby's return to Cambridge, during which journey he experienced reconciliation to Christ and 'that Peace of Conscience (so well grounded, and so clearly evidenced) that he never lost it to his dying day' (Clark, 58).

Blackerby's ecclesiastical scruples prevented him from pursuing a career as a beneficed minister and he was never ordained. His subsequent career was governed by the desire to work as much like a pastoral minister as was possible without subscribing. After leaving Cambridge he became the chaplain of Sir Thomas Jermyn of Rushbrook in Suffolk, and then lived with Sir Edward Lewknor of Denham, also in Suffolk, presumably in a similar role. The minister of Denham was Robert Pricke (*d.* 1607), whose daughter Sarah Blackerby married in or before 1600; their elder daughters Susan and Margaret were baptized there respectively in June 1601 and June 1603, and a third, Martha, was mentioned in her grandfather's will of November 1607. From Denham, Blackerby went to Feltwell in Norfolk as the minister. He managed to keep his place there for some time but was eventually forced to move. About 1603 he found a new home at Ashen, Essex, near the Suffolk border, and he spent the next twenty-three years teaching young men who boarded with him. His pupils were a mixture of the sons of local gentlemen, tradesmen, and yeomen, and students fresh from university who required preparation for the ministry. This kind of ministerial 'finishing school' had been a common feature of godly education from the time of Richard Greenham's Elizabethan version in Dry Drayton. Blackerby covered Hebrew, scriptural study, divinity, and other topics pertinent to the ministry. Among his pupils were Nicholas Bernard, the biographer of Archbishop Ussher, Samuel Stone, Samuel *Fairclough (1594–1677), and Christopher Burrell (d. 1660); the last two married Blackerby's daughters.

Paternal and educational responsibilities were not permitted to hold Blackerby back from pursuing his vocation as a preacher along the Stour valley. Blackerby played a cat-and-mouse game with the ecclesiastical authorities, exploiting the fact that his home was within the range of several counties and moving between them as he was suspended. Like other contemporary preachers he seems to have drawn upon his own experience of the agonies of conscience to induce in his audience a version of the same struggle; as Clark reports, 'He was a mighty man in wounding Consciences by the Sword of the Spirit, and in healing them by the Blood of Jesus' (Clark, 59). His preaching style was unusual, concentrating on scriptural interpretation and adding short spiritual observations. He was a powerful preacher, and left Daniel Rogers, minister of Wethersfield in Essex, unable to come into his presence without trembling because of the 'Divine Majesty and Holiness which seemed to shine in him' (Clark, 65). He tempered his authority with a certain gentleness, or, as Clark puts it, 'His reproofs were truly, as one well expresses, Nailes dipt in Oil, driven with power into the inmost of the heart, and received with acceptation, because of the overcoming kindness they were accompanied with' (Clark, 61).

As well as preaching Blackerby visited individual families for prayer and exhortation. By his own estimation he was the 'Spiritual Father' to more than 2000 people. Samuel Clark (whose tendency to emphasize the moderation of his subjects should perhaps be borne in mind) reports that Blackerby never swerved from his unwillingness to subscribe, but conformed to the Church of England as far as was possible, bringing his family to common prayer on the sabbath and on weekdays, and conducting himself with great reverence. Blackerby had a keen interest in scriptural prophecies, and was one of the first of those in his locale who came to believe in God's intention to convert the Jews. He was opposed in this by two senior Essex preachers, John Rogers and Stephen Marshall, but he

eventually managed to persuade them both of the truth of his opinion. As a preacher, teacher, and disputant, Blackerby was clearly an important figure in one of the most staunchly puritan regions of England.

About 1629 Blackerby went to live with his son-in-law, Christopher Burrell, who in 1623 had been presented by Sir Nathaniel Barnardiston to the rectory of Great Wratting, Suffolk. Blackerby continued to preach, albeit on a somewhat reduced scale, and lectured regularly at Gastingthorpe in Essex until the end of his life. Burrell was deprived in 1638, and among the articles exhibited later against William Procter, vicar of Stradishall, and Mark Reynolds, rector of Wixoe, before the Suffolk committee for scandalous ministers was that they had opposed the preaching of Blackerby and his sons-in-law. The 1640s brought better times for all three. Blackerby's final home was Great Thurlow, where he was interim minister by 1645 and where he died in 1648. Blackerby has left no literary remains. He was the author of three spiritual diaries in Greek, Latin, and English, but they seem to have been destroyed in a fire.   JASON YIANNIKKOU

Sources S. Clark [S. Clarke], *The lives of sundry eminent persons in this later age* (1683), 57–65, 159 • Venn, *Alum. Cant.* • T. Webster, *Godly clergy in early Stuart England: the Caroline puritan movement, c.1620–1643* (1997) • *Walker rev.*, 331, 341–2 • [S. H. A. Hervey], *Denham parish registers, 1539–1850* (1904), 5, 117, 274 • C. Holmes, ed., *The Suffolk committee for scandalous ministers, 1644–1646*, Suffolk Records Society, 13 (1970), 53–4, 89
Likenesses F. H. Van Hove, line engraving, BM, NPG; repro. in Clark, *Lives*

Blacket, Joseph (1786–1810), poet, was born at Tunstall, a Yorkshire village 2 miles from Catterick, the eleventh of twelve children of a day labourer employed by Sir John Lawson, bt, widely admired for his aid to the neighbouring poor. He was taught free by the village schoolmistress until seven, and then by a master until eleven.

In 1797 Blacket's brother John, a ladies' shoemaker in London, offered him work as his apprentice, and he reached the capital by wagon in ten days. He was devoted to books, and before he was fifteen had read Josephus, Eusebius's *Ecclesiastical History*, and Foxe's *Martyrs.* A visit to the theatre to see Kemble play Richard III attracted him to Shakespeare. In 1804 he married the sister of his brother's wife, but she died of consumption in 1807 leaving an infant daughter, Mary. Desolate and poor, Blacket turned for consolation to composing poetry and dramatic verse.

Blacket's first patron was his printer, William Marchant, who set up his poetry for nothing, and in the autumn of 1808 passed his manuscripts to Mr S. J. Pratt. Pratt was at once struck by Blacket's genius and drew a detailed parallel between him and Bloomfield, whose muse had been cherished by Capel Lofft. Pratt became Blacket's patron and promoted him as a literary rarity. *Specimens of the Poetry of Joseph Blacket* (1809) was a private edition for limited circulation to which the duchess of Leeds, and numerous other people, subscribed.

Meanwhile ill health compelled Blacket to relinquish his trade. Friends enabled him to take a sea voyage to his brother-in-law, John Dixon, gamekeeper of Sir Ralph Milbanke, at Seaham, co. Durham, in August 1809. There Milbanke, his wife, and his daughter Anne Isabella (later Lady Byron), interested themselves in him. Blacket attempted drama in a tragedy, *The Earl of Devon*. He died of consumption on 23 August 1810 and was buried in Seaham churchyard. A plain monument bears the concluding lines of his own poem, 'Reflections at Midnight', written in 1802. Gifts from friends covered funeral expenses leaving £97 10s. for the benefit of his child (Pratt, 101).

Pratt collected and published his *Remains* (1811) with a rather fulsome memoir based on his own acquaintance and the poet's letters to his brother, his mother, and his fellow poet Bloomfield. Byron satirized him in *English Bards and Scotch Reviewers* (ll. 765–70), and wrote a facetious, heartless *Epitaph* on the 'shoemaker poet'.

JAMES MEW, *rev.* JOHN D. HAIGH

Sources [J. Blacket], *The remains of Joseph Blacket*, ed. S. J. Pratt, 2 vols. (1811) · *Lord Byron: the complete poetical works*, ed. J. J. McGann, 2 (1980), ll. 765–70, and *Epitaph for Mr Joseph Blackett, late poet and shoemaker*, 338 · *GM*, 1st ser., 81/2 (1811), 337–41 · *Monthly Review*, new ser., 66 (1811), 392 · *Monthly Review*, new ser., 59 (1809), 100–01
Archives Bodl. Oxf., letters, with verses, to Lady Byron
Likenesses H. R. Cook, stipple (after print by J. J. Masquerier), BM, NPG; repro. in *Remains of Joseph Blacket* (1811)
Wealth at death very poor; died with insufficient funds to cover his funeral expenses: *Remains*, ed. Pratt

Blackett, Sir Basil Phillott (1882–1935), civil servant, was born on 8 January 1882 at Calcutta, the eldest son of missionaries, the Revd William Russell Blackett (then principal of a theological college and between 1885 and 1891 vicar of Holy Trinity Church, Nottingham) and his wife, Grace Anne Phillott. His father died in 1893, leaving his family in straitened circumstances. Blackett won scholarships to Marlborough and to University College, Oxford, where he took a first in *literae humaniores* in 1904. In the same year he sat the civil service examination, intending to go to India, but being placed first, he chose the Treasury. He married on 12 August 1905 Marion Enid, daughter of David Provan Graham, of Glasgow. Between 1909 and 1911 he was private secretary to the financial secretary, Charles Hobhouse. In 1911 he was promoted to first class clerk and during 1913–14 he was secretary to the royal commission on Indian finance and currency.

As a specialist in banking and currency, Blackett, with Sir John Bradbury, gave Treasury advice on the handling of the financial crisis that greeted the outbreak of war in 1914. In October that year he joined Sir George Paish in a mission to the USA to seek a solution to the shortage of sterling which was affecting the finance of American cotton exporters and the repayment of their London debts. By 1915 it was the allies who needed to borrow, and in the autumn Blackett returned to the USA as British Treasury member of the Anglo-French financial mission which negotiated a $500 million issue of bonds to finance allied war purchases. In 1917 he was briefly a member of the National War Savings Committee, before going to the USA in July to help Hardman Lever (joint financial secretary and British assistant commissioner for finance) manage

British dollar finance and day-to-day relations with the United States treasury.

In October 1919 the Treasury was reorganized and, on Bradbury's recommendation, Blackett was appointed its first controller of finance. Controllers advised chancellors directly and Blackett had wide responsibilities, including those for revenue, annual estimates, presentation of the public accounts, debt management, borrowing, banking, currency, foreign exchange, reparations, war debts, and financial relations with the dominions and foreign countries. He held the post for three years, seeking a return to 'sound finance', while (unsuccessfully) trying to avoid a deflationary crisis. Monetary control was reasserted, the public finances adjusted to peace, external market debt largely repaid, and the post-war boom broken. In December 1919 the government accepted the orthodox monetary, fiscal, and borrowing policies recommended by the Cunliffe committee. That autumn, and in the spring of 1920, against strong ministerial opposition, Treasury bill rates were raised so that bank rate could become effective and play its part in deflating the economy. Although a substantial surplus was already in prospect for 1920/21, taxation was sharply increased in the budget of April 1920 to make funds available for the repayment of short-term debt. Believing that funding was impossible when private demand for credit was so strong, in the first few months of 1920 Blackett was attracted by a levy on wartime accumulations of wealth to repay short-term debt. In June the tax was rejected by a cabinet fearful that it might create a financial panic. In April 1921 he was responsible for a funding loan, which managed at the same time to be both costly and a failure.

Overseas, Blackett believed that the UK should repay its wartime debts, not from a budget surplus, but by converting the obligations into sterling when the exchange rate was strong. Thus, from the autumn of 1919, while negotiating the funding of the debt to the US treasury, he pressed for options for early and flexible repayment. Frustrated by the American attitude, in February 1920 he began to argue that the UK, while recognizing the debt it owed to the USA, should forgive the debts the allies owed it. The cabinet considered the policy politically insupportable, but two years later the debate fathered the policy of the Balfour note, whose dispatch Blackett strongly opposed. The recognition that continental Europe's intergovernmental debts and reparations could not be paid and were retarding recovery underlay Blackett's advice to ministers, his approach to the many post-war international conferences, and the reparations schemes, including the London schedule of payments, which he designed.

At the end of 1922 Blackett became the finance member of the viceroy's executive council in India. He was both orthodox and a reformer. To cover a budget deficit he doubled the salt duty, fuelling political unrest, but with good monsoons and expenditure cuts it was the beginning of surpluses on revenue account and external debt repayment. He abolished the unpopular provincial contribution to central government; took the finances of the railways out of the central budget; and ended the unpopular cotton excise duties. After the Hilton Young commission reported in 1926, Blackett had to accept a gold exchange standard in place of the gold standard he preferred, and clashed with the Bombay cotton mill interests when he fixed the rupee at 1s. 6d. His departure from India in April 1928 was clouded by the legislative assembly's refusal to accept the governance and ownership provisions the government felt necessary before establishing a reserve bank.

In 1929 Blackett was elected to the court of the Bank of England and appointed government-approved chairman and director respectively of Imperial and International Communications and Cable and Wireless. He also became a British alternate member of the Young committee (on German reparations), chairman of the colonial development advisory committee and (in 1930) a director of De Beers Consolidated Mines. One of the new breed of non-bankers recruited by Montagu Norman, Blackett was active in the bank and, after sterling left gold in 1931, a member of the bank's special committee on foreign exchange. Although his role at the bank would traditionally have demanded discreet silence, he publicly advocated new solutions for the depression, notably in planning and the replacement of an exchange rate fixed to the gold price by a rate chosen to provide internal price stability: in 1932 he presented these views in *Planned Money*.

In 1931 Blackett helped to establish a new research body, Political and Economic Planning, and became its first chairman. He proved an ineffective leader and resigned at the end of 1932 after his own insistence on an imperial approach had clashed with the more internationalist views of the majority of the directorate. Also in 1932 he served on an Economic Advisory Council committee on international economic policy, which considered the programme for the World Economic Conference of 1933. In April 1932, having failed to be adopted as the official candidate, he fought a by-election at Marylebone as an independent Conservative, arguing that parliament needed members with financial experience. He lost narrowly, despite support from elder statesmen and the Liberal Party. In the same month he resigned as chairman of Imperial and International Communications, where he had clashed with his board over personalities and the management structure.

Blackett was energetic with a strong intelligence and great power of concentration. However, his career—in the post-war Treasury, in India, and as chairman of Imperial and International Communications—was marked by episodes of poor judgement which came, in the words of the headmaster of Marlborough, from seeking a 'simplicity of realization which the contradictions and contingencies of life keep beyond our grasp' (*The Marlburian*, 165). He was initiated into the freemasons in 1921 and was nominated as grand treasurer of English freemasons for 1933. He was president of the British Social Hygiene Council (formerly the National Council for Combating Venereal Diseases). His first marriage ended in divorce and on 14 December 1920 he married Beatrice, daughter of Edward H. Bonner of New York. He had no children. He was appointed CB in 1915, KCB in 1921, and KCSI in 1926. He died in the Deutschhaus Klinik, Marburg, on 15 August 1935 as a result of a motor accident on his way to lecture at the University of Heidelberg. A window in the west wall of the north transept of Durham Cathedral preserves his memory.   JEREMY WORMELL

Sources Treasury files, PRO · *WWW* · *The Economist* (1923–32) · *The Times* (1923–32) · *The Times* (16 Aug 1935) · *Daily Telegraph* (Jan–June 1932) · H. Barty-King, *Girdle round the earth: the story of Cable and Wireless and its predecessors* (1979), chaps. 8–9 · *The Marlburian*, 70 (Oct 1935) · The Library and Museum of Freemasonry, London · *University College Record* [Oxford] (1935) · *DNB* · Burke, *Peerage* (1924) · G. C. Peden, *The treasury and British public policy, 1906–1959* (2000) · *The collected writings of John Maynard Keynes*, ed. D. Moggridge and E. Johnson, 30 vols. (1971–89), vols. 1, 11–12, 15–18 · J. Pinder, ed., *Fifty years of political and economic planning* (1981)
Archives BL OIOC, corresp. and papers, MSS Eur. E 238, F 118 | BL OIOC, letters to Lord Reading · NA Scot., corresp. with Lord Lothian · PRO, Treasury files, esp. classes T160, T170, T172
Likenesses W. Stoneman, two photographs, 1921–31, NPG · D. Low, pencil caricature, NPG · photographs, repro. in Barty-King, *Girdle round the earth*, 43 · portrait, repro. in *The Times* (16 Aug 1935)
Wealth at death £43,632 2s. 1d.: probate, 30 Sept 1935, CGPLA Eng. & Wales

Blackett, Sir Edward, second baronet (1649–1718). *See under* Blackett, Sir William, first baronet (1621–1680).

Blackett, Patrick Maynard Stuart, Baron Blackett (1897–1974), physicist and government and military adviser, was born on 18 November 1897 at Kensington, London, the only son and the second of three children of Arthur Stuart Blackett (1865–1922), stockbroker, and his wife, Caroline Frances (1868–1954), daughter of Major Charles Maynard RA, a veteran of the Indian mutiny.

Education and marriage Blackett received his early education at a preparatory school in High Street, Guildford, from 1907 and entered Royal Naval College at Osborne in 1910, moving on to Royal Naval College at Dartmouth in 1912, as was customary for naval cadets. When war broke out in August 1914 he and other cadets were immediately sent into action, and he participated in the battle of the Falkland Islands in 1914 and the battle of Jutland in 1916. Promoted to lieutenant in May 1918, he resigned from the navy shortly after January 1919 when the Admiralty sent him to Cambridge along with other officers whose study had been interrupted in 1914. He completed part one of the mathematics tripos in May 1919 and part two of the natural sciences tripos (physics) in 1921, graduating with first-class honours that year. He was elected to a Bye fellowship at his college, Magdalene, and in autumn 1921 he became a research student under Ernest Rutherford at the Cavendish Laboratory.

In 1923 Blackett was elected a fellow of King's College, a position that he held until 1933, to which he added a university lectureship in 1930. He spent the academic year 1924–5 with the physicist James Franck in Göttingen during the second of a two-year tenureship of the Moseley research fellowship of the Royal Society. In March 1924 he married Costanza (or Constanza; b. 1899), daughter of Eugenio Bayon, an Italian. Their daughter, Giovanna, was

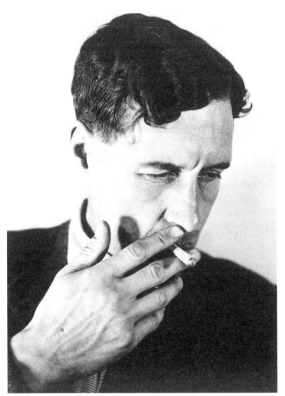

Patrick Maynard Stuart Blackett, Baron Blackett (1897–1974), by Lucia Moholy, 1936

born in 1926 and their son, Nicolas (or Nicholas) Maynard, in 1928.

Subatomic physics, 1921–1938 During the Cambridge and Göttingen years Blackett established solid credentials as an experimental nuclear physicist in work that led to the award of the Nobel prize in physics in 1948. He was enthusiastic about the rapidly developing theory of quantum mechanics; his experimental researches addressed fundamental questions within a broad theoretical context. In the widely admired essay on 'The craft of experimental physics', he emphasized that 'the experimental physicist must be enough of a theorist to know what experiments are worth doing and enough of a craftsman to be able to do them. He is only preeminent in being able to do both' (in *University Studies*, ed. H. Wright, 1933, 67).

At the Cavendish Blackett, like many of his fellow researchers, was put to work by Rutherford counting the microscopic scintillations that provided evidence of the expulsion of protons from atomic nuclei targeted with fast alpha particles. From the scintillation work Blackett estimated that a million alpha particles fired into nitrogen should result in about twenty disintegration protons. Rutherford was also interested in using the cloud chamber as a detector in which vapour condenses on ionized particles during the expansion of gas. By developing an automatic cloud chamber Blackett, in the summer of 1924, obtained 23,000 photographs showing 415,000 tracks of ionized particles, of which eight tracks were of a strikingly different type. These showed the path of a proton ejected from a recoiling nitrogen nucleus and the capture of the alpha particle by the nitrogen nucleus, creating an isotope of oxygen. Blackett's classic paper, published in the *Proceedings of the Royal Society* in 1925, included photographs that have been widely reprinted ever since.

While in Berlin in 1930 Blackett met Bruno Rossi, who was studying ways to use the Geiger–Müller counter to detect charged particles in cosmic radiation. Rossi arranged for Giuseppe P. S. Occhialini to visit Blackett at the Cavendish in order to learn cloud chamber techniques. Blackett and Occhialini soon developed a counter controlled cloud chamber in which the expansion of the chamber was triggered by the passage of charged particles through the plane of the chamber.

In late 1932 Carl D. Anderson, a physicist at the California Institute of Technology, published his discovery of a positively charged particle with a mass smaller than the proton. In March 1933 Anderson suggested that the particle was a positively charged electron (positron). By that time, in February 1933, Blackett and Occhialini had communicated to the Royal Society the results of 700 automatic expansions resulting in 500 tracks of cosmic ray particles, of which fourteen tracks were evidence for the existence of a positive electron. In contrast to Anderson's 1932 paper, they explicitly associated the new particle with Cambridge physicist P. A. M. Dirac's recent formulation of quantum mechanics that predicted pair production of an electron and an anti-electron. Later Blackett questioned new reports by Anderson and S. H. Neddermeyer that they had identified a particle heavier than the electron in the penetrating cosmic rays. However, by 1938 he had accepted the interpretation of what came to be called the mu-meson (muon).

In 1933, the year that Blackett was elected FRS, he moved to Birkbeck College in London in order to head his own laboratory. In co-ordination with Metropolitan-Vickers in Manchester he designed a large electromagnet for use with the cloud chamber. Blackett set up his equipment 100 feet below ground at an unused platform in Holborn tube station, attracting the attention of science journalists who compared his investigations to those of Sherlock Holmes. In 1937 he succeeded William Lawrence Bragg as Langworthy professor of physics at the University of Manchester. From 1937 to 1953 he built an international physics school with expanding student enrolments; distinguished foreign visitors, some of them refugees from Europe; and intersecting research programmes that came to include the work of D. R. Hartree and Léon Rosenfeld in theoretical physics; J. G. Wilson, G. D. Rochester, L. Jánossy, and C. C. Butler in cosmic ray physics; and Bernard Lovell in radio astronomy.

Military research and political involvements, 1935–1948 From the 1930s onwards, Blackett's attention focused equally on military and political matters. While in London in 1935 he joined a committee chaired by Henry T. Tizard that advised the Air Ministry to give high priority to the development of radar for defence against enemy air attack. This argument prevailed over the objections of

Frederick A. Lindemann, who was to become Winston Churchill's scientific adviser in 1939. At the outbreak of war Blackett joined the instrument section of the Royal Aircraft Establishment where he worked with H. J. J. Braddick on the design of the Mark 14 bombsight. This instrument eliminated the need for a level bombing run at the time of bomb release.

In August 1940 Blackett became scientific adviser to General Frederick A. Pile, the commander-in-chief of anti-aircraft command. Blackett organized a group of scientists to study the operational use of radar sets, guns, and mechanical calculators, resulting in improved accuracy of anti-aircraft fire during the battle of Britain. Joining the coast command in March 1941, he headed a group that recalculated the depth settings for anti-submarine explosives, and applied mathematical techniques (Poisson's distribution) to settle tactical and strategic arguments within the command. At the Admiralty from January 1942 to the summer of 1945 Blackett, and 'Blackett's circus', as it became known, exerted a major influence on the British battle against U-boats, and brought about significant improvement in the use of airborne radar for finding German submarines that were sinking Allied merchant ships.

Two reports that Blackett drafted in 1941 on the organization and methodology of operational research enjoyed broad circulation in Great Britain and elsewhere, appearing later in his *Studies of War* (1962). By the late 1950s Blackett was expressing misgivings about the teaching of operational research as an academic speciality, especially the use of game theory, which he considered practically inadequate and morally suspect in its application to warfare. On the other hand he was optimistic, like some other veterans of operational research, about the use of operational research in industry.

During 1942–3 Blackett incensed some members of the government and the Air Ministry by arguing against Lindemann's recommendation for saturation bombing and the targeting of civilian housing in German cities. He was also the sole dissenting member in June 1941 from the finding of the Maud committee that an atomic bomb could be produced by 1943 at a cost of £5 million; instead, he recommended that the project should be co-ordinated with work in the USA, as indeed subsequently occurred. Again during 1945–7, when appointed to the advisory committee on atomic energy, his views diverged from majority opinion as he opposed British development of atomic weapons and argued for a neutralist foreign policy. Having failed to influence government policy, Blackett circulated his opinions, first in the Fabian Society publication *The Atom and the Charter* (1946) and then in the widely read book *Military and Political Consequences of Atomic Energy* (1948), published in the United States under the title *Fear, War and the Bomb*. This book excited considerable criticism for its sympathetic treatment of Soviet objections to American plans for international control of atomic energy, for its suspicion of American post-war global ambitions, for its criticism of British bombing strategy during the war, and for its debunking of claims that bombs alone could win a war.

Post-war activities in science and politics During the immediate post-war years, as Blackett returned to the problem of the origins and distribution of cosmic radiation, he revived the hypothesis that the magnetic fields of the sun, stars, and the earth are a fundamental property of their rotating mass. His presentation in May 1947 of a simple equation involving Newton's constant of universal graviation and the speed of light led journalists to compare his work with Einstein's theory of relativity.

While marshalling evidence for his theory from the fields of quantum electrodynamics, astronomy, and geophysics, Blackett developed a magnetometer of great sensitivity and precision in order to measure a predicted magnetic effect on the order of 10^{-8} Gauss for experimental cylinders. In 1952 he communicated his negative results to the Royal Society, as well as the failure of other lines of evidence to confirm his hypothesis. He offered a masterful account of his geomagnetic theory and of the operation of his magnetometer, noting its suitability for measuring remanent magnetism in sedimentary rocks that might corroborate the hypothesis of continental drift. He built up a research group for studying rock magnetism, first at Manchester and then at Imperial College, where he moved from Manchester in 1953. After a decade of fostering geophysical research, much of it led by Edward Bullard, Stanley Runcorn, and J. A. Clegg, Blackett initiated a Royal Society discussion meeting on continental drift in March 1964 that had a great impact on the acceptance of the hypothesis of continental drift and the development of the theory of plate tectonics.

During the 1940s and 1950s Blackett was a forceful advocate of university expansion and government funding of research and development. He was a member of the Barlow committee (1945–6), the council and the research grants committee of the Department of Scientific and Industrial Research (1956–1960), and the National Research Development Corporation (1949–64), where he pushed for the development of the computer industry. He was dean of the faculty of science (1948–50) and pro-vice-chancellor (1950–52) at Manchester; dean of the Royal College of Science (1955–60) and pro-rector (1961–4) in London. After formally retiring from Imperial College and the University of London in September 1965 Blackett served as president of the Royal Society from 1965 to 1970.

Blackett had longstanding Fabian and socialist political allegiances, dating from his undergraduate years at Magdalene College. His conception of laboratory organization emphasized co-operation and teamwork. As he told Brian Connell of Anglia Television in 1971, a good laboratory is a place where ordinary people do first-class work. He was an active member and president (1943–6) of the trade unionist British Association of Scientific Workers. The grandson of a vicar, he respected religious observances that were established social customs, but described himself as agnostic or atheist.

Blackett felt more at home in London than in Cambridge, declining in 1953 to be considered as a candidate to succeed Bragg as director of the Cavendish Laboratory. During 1939–40 he was part of the London based Tots and Quots political dining club organized by Solly Zuckermann. From 1953 to 1963 he met a group of scientists hosted by J. R. M. Brumwell, and including J. D. Bernal and C. P. Snow among others, who advised Hugh Gaitskell, as leader of the Labour Party, and then Harold Wilson and his shadow minister for education, Richard Crossman. The expansion of science and technology became a main platform of the Labour Party in the 1964 general election.

Blackett first travelled to India in 1947, and increasingly became concerned with improving living conditions in poorer countries of the world through applications of science and technology. His sympathetic attitude toward the Soviet Union was based largely in his optimism that socialism and science could improve human welfare. Blackett was appointed CH in 1965 and OM in 1967. He never took a PhD, but he held twenty honorary degrees and was an honorary member of academic or other institutions in eleven countries, including the Soviet Union and China. In 1969 he was created a life peer, an honour that he had declined five years earlier. Sir Edward Bullard recalled Blackett's quip that, at any rate, he had remained Mr Blackett until after he retired (Bullard, 370).

Tall and handsome, Blackett was a powerful and versatile figure in British scientific and governmental circles. He was a problem solver who was willing to take responsibility and to assess responsibility. 'Never say "They"', he cautioned a friend, 'it's a sign of frustration and woolly thinking and will get you nowhere' (Hodgkin and others, 137). He believed that science, clear thinking, and good will could win the day. He died in London on 13 July 1974.

MARY JO NYE

Sources B. Lovell, *Memoirs FRS*, 21 (1975), 1–115 · A. Hodgkin and others, 'Memorial meeting for Lord Blackett … at the Royal Society of London on 31 October 1974', *Notes and Records of the Royal Society*, 29 (1974–5), 135–62 · E. Bullard, 'Patrick Blackett: an appreciation', *Nature*, 250 (1974), 370 · transcript of interview with Brian Connell, Anglia TV, 4 Oct 1971, RS · notes on interview of Patrick Blackett with John Heilbron, 17 Dec 1962; and transcript of interview of Carl Anderson with Charles Weiner, 30 June 1966, American Institute of Physics, College Park, Maryland, Niels Bohr Library, Archive of sources for the history of quantum mechanics · *Annual Report of the Council* [King's College, Cambridge] (1974) · J. A. Hughes, 'The radioactivists: community, controversy, and the rise of nuclear physics', PhD diss., U. Cam., 1993 · R. E. Rider, 'Operational research', *Companion encyclopedia of the history and philosophy of the mathematical sciences*, ed. I. Grattan-Guinness (1993), 837–42 · M. Fortun and S. S. Schweber, 'Scientists and the legacy of World War II: the case of operations research (OR)', *Social Studies of Science*, 23 (1993), 595–642 · RS, Blackett MSS · private information (2004) [Giovanna Bloor and Nicolas Blackett] · *CGPLA Eng. & Wales* (1975)

Archives American Institute of Physics, College Park, Maryland, Niels Bohr Library, archive of sources for the history of quantum mechanics · RS, corresp. and papers | BL, corresp. with Society of Authors, Add. MSS 63214 · Bodl. Oxf., corresp. with Sir Rudolph Peierls and corresp. relating to Society for the Protection of Science and Learning · CAC Cam., corresp. with A. V. Hill · CUL, corresp. with Lord Rutherford · ICL, corresp. with Lord Jackson; corresp. with Herbert Dingle; corresp. with J. D. McGee · IWM, corresp. with Sir Henry Tizard · King's Lond., Liddell Hart C., corresp. with Sir B. H. Liddell Hart · Rice University, Houston, Texas, Woodson Research Center, corresp. with Sir Julian Huxley · Sci. Mus., corresp. with Stanley Gill · U. Glas., corresp. with Sir Edward Bullard · U. Leeds, Brotherton L., corresp. with Edward Stoner · U. Nott. L., corresp. with Robert Peers · U. Sussex, letters to J. G. Crowther · University of Copenhagen, Niels Bohr Institute for Astronomy, Physics, and Geophysics, corresp. with Niels Bohr | FILM BFI NFTVA, interview by Brian Connell, Anglia TV, 4 Oct 1975 · BFI NFTVA, news footage | SOUND BL NSA, documentary recordings

Likenesses photograph, 1932, RS, Blackett MSS · L. Moholy, photograph, 1936, NPG [*see illus.*] · W. Stoneman, four photographs, 1942, NPG · photographs, 1943–50, Hult. Arch. · D. Low, chalk caricature, 1949, NPG · E. Levy, oils, 1956, NPG · C. Rogers, oils, 1965, ICL · W. Bird, photograph, 1966, NPG · W. Evans, oils, 1970, RS · H. Coster, photographs, NPG · J. Epstein, bronze head, priv. coll.; replica, ICL · L. M. Graf, photograph, RS, Blackett MSS · D. Low, pencil sketches, NPG · R. Mayne, photograph, NPG

Wealth at death £27,286: probate, 13 Jan 1975, *CGPLA Eng. & Wales*

Blackett, Sir William, first baronet (1621–1680), merchant and mine owner, was born on 1 May 1621 and baptized at Gateshead although his family was based at Hamsterley, 6 miles west of Bishop Auckland in the county palatine of Durham. He was the third son of William Blackett (1593–1648) and his first wife, Isabella (d. 1666), daughter of William Crook of Wolsingham. The Blacketts were minor gentry who claimed kin with the old family Blacket of Woodcroft, whose right to arms was recognized in the Durham visitation of 1575. The nature of William Blackett senior's business is unknown but it was profitable. By 1631 he had married his eldest son, Christopher, to the heir of Thomas Fenwick of West Matfen, Northumberland, and he procured the admission of his two younger sons, Edward and William, to the exclusive Newcastle Company of Merchant Adventurers.

Newcastle was prospering from its position in the centre of the largest coal-producing district in the world, employing 10,000 workmen in the mines and exporting over 450,000 tons of coal to London in 1633–4. The coal trade on the Tyne was controlled by a small company called the Hostmen. The other trade in the town was controlled by the Company of Merchant Adventurers, in which William Blackett was apprenticed in 1636. This was a year of plague, and the town soon suffered other difficulties. The Scots, protesting at the episcopal policy of Charles I, were allowed into the town by a sympathetic mayor in August 1640, and departed only in August 1641. The royalists then held the town, with the consequence that in January 1643 parliament blockaded it, bringing economic life almost to a standstill until October 1644 when it was stormed by the Scots, then allied to parliament. During these years William Blackett's elder brother Edward was establishing a base in the Low Countries, where much of the trading of the Merchant Adventurers was done, and he acted as an agent for many of them. William himself obtained his freedom of the company after nine years' apprenticeship on 20 June 1645, and within three weeks he had married Elizabeth (*bap.* 1617, *d.* 1674), the daughter of Michael Kirkley and his wife, Elizabeth, *née* Chapman, who was connected to the Andersons and

Sir William Blackett, first baronet (1621–1680), by Peter Cross

the Bonners among the ruling families in the town. In 1648 his kinsman Robert Lilburne was governor of the town and Blackett was elected a common councillor. The following October his first son, Edward [see below], was born.

Although Blackett inclined to royalism, his family links with the new parliamentarian order must have helped his growing trade. So did the assistance of his brother Edward in Amsterdam. Blackett soon joined the Eastland Company, which had sole rights to trade in the Baltic. He traded with Denmark and by 1659 he had interests in the whaling and fishing trade as far away as Greenland. Later in his life he was trading lead, coal, salt, butter, and barrels of salmon to Sweden, Amsterdam, Rotterdam, and Rouen, and bringing back iron, timber, pitch, tar, peas, beans, and brass ware. It is said that his breakthrough came when he had ventured extravagantly on a cargo of flax, the trade in which was highly speculative. His later success in the coal and then the lead industries, and his immense wealth at his death, are explained by his stupendous success in seaborne trade during the difficult years of the Commonwealth.

Although Blackett and his brother Edward had started business as maritime merchants, they next turned their attention to coal ownership, the business of their kinsmen the Andersons, Chapmans, Bonners, Kirkleys, and Lilburnes. The two brothers were admitted on 15 November 1652 to the forty members of the Company of Hostmen, and they embarked upon the lucrative trade of acting as agents or 'fitters' for other coal owners who were not Hostmen. Edward died young but Blackett became the business adviser of Charles Howard (later first earl of Carlisle) in relation to his mines. During the year ending 25 June 1659 the coal carried from Newcastle and Sunderland to English ports approached 600,000 tons, of which by far the greatest part came out of the Tyne. The following year, with the Restoration, Blackett was elected the town's sheriff (in effect deputy mayor). He became a commissioner of assessment and a captain in the militia, and was elected an alderman. His commercial enterprises as a merchant, mine owner, and fitter were now on such a scale that he had difficulty finding the coinage to pay his men and so, until 1672, he minted his own copper farthing token with the arms of Blackett on the face.

The picture that emerges is of a man of public trust. In February 1662 Blackett attended the general meeting of the Eastland Company in London on behalf of the Newcastle members. He acted on behalf of the Newcastle Merchant Adventurers when their dispute with the London Merchant Adventurers was heard by the royal council in February 1664, when a compromise between the two companies was being discussed in London in April of that year, and in York in September. He was elected governor of the Hostmen in the years 1662–3 and 1667–8, and mayor of the town in 1666. That year he had to deal with the refusal of the keelmen (on the grounds of poverty) to pay the new hearth tax. He solved the problem by assuring them that the tax was voluntary. He was elected one of the MPs for Newcastle on 3 December 1673 and nine days later was created a baronet, but he attended the House of Commons not out of political ambition but more out of duty to the town, which paid him 13s. 4d. per day for it. His only recorded speech was in successful opposition to the proposal for a ballast shore at Shields, which might upset the existing arrangements for the loading of coal at Newcastle.

Blackett's material success was overshadowed by the death of his wife, Elizabeth, who was buried on 7 April 1674. She had borne him eleven children of whom seven were surviving. The eldest son, Edward, was now twenty-five and imminently to be married. On 28 April 1674 Blackett settled upon him his 'West Water estate', lying between Haydon Bridge and Haltwhistle in Northumberland, but he reserved the lead mines to himself. For centuries lead had been dug and smelted in the moorlands nearby. Blackett had bought lead-bearing land and had taken leases from the bishop of Durham and Sir Francis Ratcliffe and he brought economies of scale and new smelting methods to the industry. He had no partners with him, but his two large smelt-mills at Dukesfield and Planking attracted ore both from his own lead mines and from other mines as far away to the south as Dufton in Westmorland and Lune-Head in Yorkshire. From Newcastle the lead was exported as Blackett's own cargoes.

In 1674 or 1675 Blackett married Margaret (bap. 1631, d. 1709/10), daughter of Henry Cocke of a leading Newcastle merchant family, and widow of John Rogers. Sir William, who had low-church sympathies (he had appointed Nathaniel Burnand, the excluded vicar of Brampton, to be minister to the miners of Alston Moor), had hitherto lived quite modestly. But his new wife gave him a taste for splendour. His largest extravagance was the acquisition of the Gray Friars mansion in Pilgrim Street, Newcastle, in 1675 from Sir Francis Anderson, his fellow MP for the town. It was where the king had been lodged after his surrender to the Scots at Newark in 1646: 'a princely house, and very stately and magnificent, being supposed to be the most so of any house in the whole kingdom within a walled town' (Brand, 341). In 1679 he was re-elected MP for the town in March and again in October, but his declining health allowed him little activity in the Commons. In his will, made on 9 March 1680, Sir William left the staggering sum of £1000 for 'my funeral expenses and for mourning for my wife and for all my children and grandchildren' (will). Other provisions suggest that relations with his new wife were poor, and he favoured most his 22-year-old third son, William *Blackett, who was appointed sole executor and received the residue of the estate. The two elder sons also received a substantial share of his land, lead mines, and interests in coal mines, entailed for their male descendants, with remainders over to the others in default of male heirs.

Sir William Blackett died in Newcastle on 16 May 1680 and was buried in great pomp in St Nicholas's Church. His wife survived him by thirty years. His son Michael died an alderman, but childless, on 26 April 1683, and the property that his father left him accrued to add to his two brothers' considerable wealth. Sir Edward was soon building Newby Hall near Ripon, and Sir William (as he became) was soon building Wallington in Northumberland. As his descendant Sir Charles Otto Trevelyan wrote in 1932 (*Country Life*, 22 July 1918), 'the first Sir William was rich enough to make two elder sons'.

His son **Sir Edward Blackett**, second baronet (1649–1718), landowner, was born on 22 October 1649 at Newcastle. He was entered as a Merchant Adventurer on 23 January 1673 and a Hostman in 1684, but there is no evidence that he concerned himself in business any more than was essential after he had received a large part of the coal and lead mining interests that his father had built up in Northumberland and co. Durham. The first part of this, the West Water estate, part of his marriage settlement of 28 April 1674, comprised an assortment of lead-rich lands lying west of Hexham, including Willimontswick and Fallowfield and the tithes of Haltwhistle, but excluding the choice lead mines of Fallowfield, which his father was working for himself. His bride was Mary, heir of Thomas Norton of Langthorne, Yorkshire, which they soon inherited and to which they moved from remote Willimontswick. However, their child, William, died after birth and his mother died soon afterwards. Edward married, in 1676, Mary (c.1657–1698), heir of the late Sir John Yorke of Gouldthwaite, Yorkshire; they had twelve children before her death in November 1698. A year after their marriage, on 13 November 1677, Edward acquired the manor of Newby, near Ripon in Yorkshire, and the building and beautifying of Newby Hall and its gardens became his passion. In 1697 Celia Fiennes reported on her visit to a thoroughly finished new house: 'He has a great state …

this was the finest house I saw in Yorkshire' (*The Journeys of Celia Fiennes*, 1983, 106).

Edward Blackett was serving as sheriff of Northumberland in 1679–80 when he inherited his father's baronetcy and another share of his father's wealth in coal and lead mines. Although he purchased some more land to add to the West Water estate, his business interests, mostly in the lead mines and in exportation of lead, were left for the large part to his cousin John Blackett and his agent James Meaburne, to whom he constantly complained about lack of money. His friend and neighbour in Yorkshire, John Aislabie MP of Studley Royal, a lord of the Admiralty, was badgered into obtaining a captain's commission and the command of a ship for Blackett's second son, Edward; his third son, John, was set up in trade at Rotterdam.

Sir Edward was a sociable man—travellers in Yorkshire were often detained at Newby. He kept a house in York and, at least after he entered parliament, a house in Dartmouth Street, London. He was elected MP for the borough of Ripon in 1689 after a contest with the local family of Jennings, who regarded the nomination as theirs. His political stand was that of a moderate. He had been vigorous in levying fines against recusants when he had been sheriff of Northumberland, but he was not prepared to declare the throne vacant after the flight of James II in 1688. When he was elected MP for the county of Northumberland in 1698, he was regarded as a tory.

On 21 October 1699 Sir Edward married again; his third wife was Diana (d. 1713), daughter of George Booth, Baron Delamer, and widow of Sir Ralph Delaval of Seaton Delaval. His wife's only daughter, Diana, was married two months later, at the age of thirteen, to Sir Edward's eldest son, William, with a portion of £8000 charged upon the Seaton Delaval estate. Sir Edward died in London on 22 April 1718; his body was taken back for burial in Ripon Minster, where it lies under a stately monument, with his effigy, representing him as rather portly, lying between those of his first two wives. His will made lavish provision for his dependants, and made no allowance for his shortage of cash. His late son William's debts had not been paid, and there was money outstanding on his daughters' marriage portions, as well as the mortgage on Newby. He appointed his son John to be his sole executor, and the will was disputed. By the time that matters had been resolved in 1723, the debts and liabilities of his estate totalled £13,365.

MARK BLACKETT-ORD

Sources Northumbd RO, Newcastle upon Tyne, Blackett (Matfen) papers, ZBL 30, 189–95, 261, 264, 269, 273 · M. Blackett, letter-book, CUL, Add. 91 and DD vii 26 · *Diary of Sir Walter Blackett bt* (1883) · [J. R. Boyle and F. W. Dendy], eds., *Extracts from the records of the merchant adventurers of Newcastle-upon-Tyne*, 2 vols., SurtS, 93, 101 (1895–9) · F. W. Dendy, ed., *Extracts from the records of the Company of Hostmen of Newcastle-upon-Tyne*, SurtS, 105 (1901) · will, U. Durham · H. Conyers Surtees, *History of the parishes of Hamsterley and Lynesack and Softley* (1926) · R. Howell, *Newcastle upon Tyne and the puritan revolution: a study of the civil war in north England* (1967) · J. V. Nef, *Rise of the British coal industry* (1932) · R. Welford, *Men of mark 'twixt Tyne and Tweed*, 3 vols. (1895) · *A history of Northumberland*, Northumberland County History Committee, 15 vols. (1893–1940) · HoP, *Commons, 1660–90*, vol. 1 · J. Brand, *The history and antiquities of the town and* *county of the town of Newcastle upon Tyne*, 2 vols. (1789) · parish register, Gateshead, 13 May 1621 [baptism] · memorial, Ripon Cathedral [Sir Edward Blackett]

Archives Northumbd RO, Newcastle upon Tyne, corresp. and papers

Likenesses British school, miniature, Wallington, Northumberland · P. Cross, miniature, Wallington, Northumberland [*see illus.*]

Wealth at death immense wealth: will, U. Durham L.; schedule of assets and liabilities after administration of estate, Blackett (Matfen) corresp. and papers, Northumbd RO, Newcastle upon Tyne

Blackett, Sir William, first baronet (1657–1705), landowner and mine owner, was born at Newcastle upon Tyne on 5 April 1657. He was the eighth child and third surviving son of Sir William *Blackett, also first baronet (1621–1680), and his first wife, Elizabeth (*bap.* 1617, *d.* 1674), daughter of Michael Kirkley and his wife, Elizabeth, daughter of Matthew Chapman MP. Sir William Blackett senior was the first to exploit the lead mines of the northern Pennines on a large scale, and William junior was his favourite son. By the age of seventeen the son was involved in the management of the mines, especially when his father was absent on parliamentary business at Westminster. On 9 March 1680, when he was still only twenty-two, he was named as sole executor of his father's will. When his father died on 16 May he received the huge mansion known as Grayfriars in Pilgrim Street, Newcastle, some of his father's coalmines, and most of his lead-mining interests.

William Blackett junior had already become a freeman of Newcastle in 1678 and a freeman of the Merchant Adventurers (who controlled the town's trade) in 1679, and in 1680 he was a commissioner for assessment for Newcastle and a sub-farmer of coal duties. At Michaelmas 1683, aged twenty-six, he was elected mayor, though he had not held the customary prior office of sheriff. His office took him to London, with another alderman, to secure the replacement for the town's recently surrendered charter. The duke of Newcastle commented that they were 'Very rich and of great reputation for understanding and honesty' (*CSP dom.*).

On 4 January 1685 Blackett was elected governor of the Hostmen, the small fraternity that controlled the Tyne coal trade. On the 23rd of the same month he was created a baronet. Four days later he married Julia (1667 1722), the seventeen-year-old daughter of Sir Christopher Conyers and the granddaughter of Viscount Lumley of Lumley Castle. Two months later he was elected MP for the town in James II's first parliament. He opposed the royal policy which was to control the boroughs. The king removed him from the town council, together with the mayor, the sheriff, six other aldermen, and fifteen of the common council, on Christmas eve 1687. But by October 1688 the king was alarmed at the strength of opposition in the country as a whole, and one of his conciliatory acts was to restore Sir William to the corporation, on the advice of the duke of Newcastle. It was too late; William of Orange landed in November and the king's remaining support collapsed across England. The town elected Sir William on

10 January as its MP for the Convention Parliament without a candidate standing against him. He was pricked as high sheriff of Northumberland for the ensuing year.

These public events did not slow the expansion of Blackett's mining business, and in particular his negotiation to acquire the two Northumbrian estates of the arrogant but pitifully spendthrift Sir John Fenwick. One was the regality or lordship of Hexham Priory, which had been granted to the Fenwicks in 1632, and which included the freeholds of the Blackett lead mines at Allendale. The other estate was that around the medieval tower of the Fenwicks at Wallington, near Cambo, in north Northumberland. The purchase was concluded with the Fenwicks and their mortgagees (after some tortuous conveyancing) in December 1689. Sir William paid £4000 down and an annuity of £2000 per annum for the lives of Sir John and his wife, Lady Mary.

Sir William developed the Allendale mines and added to them a lease of all the mines in adjoining Weardale owned by the bishop of Durham, extending 21 miles from Harperley to Kilhope at the head of the dale, at a royalty of one-ninth of the ore. He pulled down the medieval tower at Wallington and built a new house on the site, with four ranges 120 feet long around a central courtyard. The ground plan survives today in the existing house, but the internal arrangements were primitive and contrasted with the lavish modernity of the house that his elder brother Sir Edward was building at Newby Park in Yorkshire. But the explanation is simple: Sir William was a townsman. In all official documents he styled himself 'of Newcastle'. He added north and south wings to Grayfriars, for his family had reached seven children.

Blackett was idolized in Newcastle, where he was mayor of the town again in 1698 and re-elected its MP in 1695, 1698, and 1705. In parliament he supported William III. In 1696 this led to his voting for the bill of attainder against Sir John Fenwick for his offensive Jacobitism. The government appreciated Sir William's abilities and in 1699 the chancellor of the exchequer, Sir Charles Montagu (the inventor of the national debt, and later earl of Halifax), asked him to join the Treasury board, displacing Sir Stephen Fox. Sir William declined, excusing himself because of his concerns in the north.

Sir William died in London on 2 December 1705 and was buried magnificently on 29 December at St Nicholas's, Newcastle. The bulk of his wealth was left to his son William, then aged fifteen. On the latter's death the lead mines of Allendale and the adjoining Pennines descended through this William's sister Lady Wentworth, and became the Blackett-Beaumont mines. The Cambo and Wallington estate was left by the same William to the son of another of his sisters, Lady Calverley, on condition he married William's illegitimate daughter Elizabeth. From them it descended to the Trevelyans, and even in its depleted state in 1941 was still the largest property ever given to the National Trust.   MARK BLACKETT-ORD

Sources R. Welford, *Men of mark 'twixt Tyne and Tweed*, 3 vols. (1895) · G. Hampson, 'Blackett, Sir William', HoP, *Commons, 1660–*

90 • A. Raistrick and B. Jennings, *A history of lead mining in the Pennines* (1965) • Robert Dale's family tree, Northumbd RO, Newcastle upon Tyne, ZBL 194 • *A history of Northumberland*, Northumberland County History Committee, 15 vols. (1893–1940), vols. 4, 10, 13 • [J. R. Boyle and F. W. Dendy], eds., *Extracts from the records of the merchant adventurers of Newcastle-upon-Tyne*, 1 (1895), SurtS, 93 (1895) • M. Blackett, letters, CUL, Add. MS 91.DD.vii.26 • *CSP dom.*, 1684–5, 205 • R. Trevelyan, *Wallington* (1994) • parish register, Newcastle, St Nicholas's, 29 Dec 1705 [burial]

Archives Northumbd RO, Newcastle upon Tyne, Blackett MSS, ZBL 194

Likenesses J. Riley?, portrait, Wallington, Northumberland

Blackfish [Cottawamago, Mkahdaywaymayqua] (**1729?–1779**), leader of the Shawnee Indians, was born probably about 1729 in the Shawnee territory in the Ohio River valley. Of unknown parentage, Blackfish, or Cottawamago or Mkahdaywaymayqua, appears in the historical record in 1777 as the war chief of the Chillicothe division of the Shawnee.

Shawnee relations with the British and American colonists in the second half of the eighteenth century were among the most turbulent Anglo-American Indian relationships. The Shawnee were allies of France in the French and Indian War, fighting both alongside French troops and in raiding parties that ravaged the colonial American frontier. Outraged that their French allies ceded Shawnee lands to the British at the peace of Paris in 1763, they, like many of the Ohio tribes, conducted their own battle against the British troops and colonial settlements in what became known as the Pontiac War (1763–6). Able to defeat British and American troops on open ground but unable to lay effective siege to the major forts such as those at Niagara, Pittsburgh, and Detroit, the American Indian tribes agreed to a shaky peace. The British attempted to ease American Indian anger by regulating trade and preventing further white settlement in the interior, but lack of commitment and unruly colonists frustrated such plans. In 1772 the British government recognized that an estimated 30,000 families were living in the Ohio region illegally, 5000 of which had arrived in 1772 (Sosin, 203). On the eve of the American War of Independence, British authority in the interior had effectively collapsed, leaving the individual colonies to handle their own expansion and the skirmishes and wars that followed it. In 1774 'Lord Dunmore's War' erupted between the Virginians and the Shawnee, the war being named after the governor of Virginia, John Murray, fourth earl of Dunmore. The Shawnee were once again defeated, losing further territories including Kentucky.

Blackfish and his followers refused to recognize these territorial losses, and the eruption of war between Britain and its North American colonies in 1775 provided an opportunity for his people to strike back at the colonial trespassers. Finding support from the British based at Detroit, Blackfish orchestrated raids on settlements across the Ohio region in 1777 in an attempt to drive the American garrisons away from their principal Kentucky forts, Harrodsburg, Boonesborough, and St Asaph's. Without artillery, Blackfish and his companions were unable to meet their goals. Nevertheless they managed to severely disrupt the frontier, destroying outlying settlements and capturing colonists.

The most celebrated captive was the legendary Daniel Boone, who was taken by a group of Shawnee warriors under Blackfish's command. Many of Boone's companions spent their last days enduring physical torture and death, but Boone luckily experienced the kinder side of Shawnee captivity and was given to a family that had lost a son. According to tradition, his adoptive father was Blackfish. Boone, renamed Shetowee or Big Turtle (Thwaites, 148), clearly gained the interest of Blackfish, who gave him increased freedom throughout the winter and spring and refused the £100 ransom of the British at Detroit in March 1778. Boone himself later remarked that 'the Shawnee king [Blackfish] took great notice of me, and treated me with profound respect, and entire friendship' (Jillson, 25).

In June 1778 Boone escaped to Boonesborough, where he warned the inhabitants of an imminent Shawnee attack. That summer was spent preparing the decaying fort. On 7 September Blackfish appeared at the head of a force of about four hundred men, which included Shawnee, Delaware, Cherokee, and Mingo warriors as well as whites. According to Boone, Blackfish wept at the prospect of facing his adoptive son in combat. Whether Boone's claim is true or not, Blackfish attempted unsuccessfully to persuade the colonists to abandon the fort during two days of negotiations. When negotiations broke down, the American Indian force laid an unsuccessful siege to the fort for a further nine days before withdrawing.

In the following spring the American colonists went on to the offensive and attacked the Shawnee heartland. In the night of 29–30 May Colonel John Bowman led a force of several hundred men against Chillicothe while most of its warriors were away. Blackfish led the remaining warriors against the attackers but was severely wounded in his right leg. Although the attackers were repelled the next day, the wound ultimately proved fatal and Blackfish died in Chillicothe either in the following summer or autumn, 1779.

TROY O. BICKHAM

Sources J. Sugden, 'Blackfish', *ANB* • W. R. Jillson, *The Boone narrative* (1932) • R. G. Thwaites, *Daniel Boone* (1902) • J. Bakeless, *Daniel Boone: master of the wilderness* (1939) • G. W. Ranck, *Boonesborough* (1901) • J. M. Faragher, *Daniel Boone: the life and legend of an American pioneer* (1992) • C. G. Calloway, *The American Revolution in Indian country: crisis and diversity in Native American communities* (1995) • J. M. Sosin, *Whitchall and the wilderness: the middle west in British colonial policy, 1760–1775* (1961)

Archives Wisconsin Historical Society, Madison, Draper MSS

Blackhall, Andro (1535/6–1609), composer, is earliest known as a canon of the Augustinian abbey of Holyrood, Edinburgh. Following the dissolution of the monastery during the Scottish Reformation of 1559/60 he pursued a career in the reformed church as minister in the nearby churches of Liberton (appointed 1564), Ormiston (1568), Cranstoun (1570/71), and finally Inveresk and Musselburgh (1574), and in 1586 he was an assembly commissioner trying the offences of the ministry of Lothian.

Blackhall's surviving music for the reformed church ranges from simple four-part settings of Psalms 68, 76, and 121 and the canticles 'Ane Prayer' and 'The Humble Suit of a Sinner' to three more elaborate five-part polyphonic settings of psalms, all preserved in the Wode partbooks. These latter pieces imply close connections with the Scottish court: Psalm 101 (1569) was 'giffin in propyne [tribute] to the king' (the three-year-old James VI), Psalm 128 (1573) was written for a dynastic wedding masterminded by the regent Morton and linking the Mar and Angus families, and Psalm 43 ('Judge and revenge my cause, O Lord, from them that evill be', significantly with a Sarum 'miserere' as cantus firmus) was personally commissioned by Morton in 1579 to enlist royal support for the destruction of the Catholic house of Hamilton. Other psalm settings, including an imitative five-part setting 'in reports' of Psalm 18 in 'The art of music' (an anonymous Scottish treatise on composition, c.1579), Psalm 130 in Davidson's 'Some helpes for young schollers' (1602), and other psalms 'in reports' in Edward Millar's 1635 psalter, are probably Blackhall's work. He may even have helped compose the twelve Scottish common tunes for psalms, while the reference by the Catholic satirist Nicol Burne to singing 'bass to Blackhall' suggests that his name was synonymous with psalm setting. The Wode partbooks also preserve Blackhall's only surviving secular music, a beautiful four-part song 'About the Banks of Helicon', which matches the complex Helicon stanza beloved of James VI's Castalian band of poets. The title makes reference to the lyric 'The Banks of Helicon' and the longer allegorical poem *The Cherrie and the Slae* (which begins 'About ane bank …') by the pre-eminent Castalian Alexander Montgomerie, while Thomas Wode also cites a poem by Sir Richard Maitland as suiting Blackhall's music.

With his spouse, Janet Wright, and son Andrew, Blackhall received several royal gifts, which included a personal grant from James VI of 300 merks to finance a music school in Musselburgh. However, in October 1593 Blackhall applied to the Lothian and Tweeddale synod for relief on account of his great age. As he was actually only fifty-seven at the time, his penury may have been due to the notoriously inadequate stipends paid to reformed ministers and the profligacy of his son, who by 1627 was found to have 'sauld and disponit' the royal pension for the music school. Blackhall's memorial inscription in St Michael's cemetery, Inveresk, states that he was seventy-three when he died at Inveresk, Musselburgh, on 31 January 1609. **D. JAMES ROSS**

Sources D. J. Ross, *Musick fyne: Robert Carver and the art of music in 16th-century Scotland* (1993) · H. S. P. Hutchison, 'The St Andrews psalter: transcription and critical study of Thomas Wode's psalter', DMus diss., U. Edin., 1957 · *Fasti Scot.* · K. Elliott, 'Music in Scotland, 1500–1700', PhD diss., U. Cam., 1960 · K. Elliott and H. M. Shire, eds., *Music of Scotland, 1500–1700*, 3rd edn, Musica Britannica, 15 (1975) · K. Elliott, 'Another of Thomas Wode's missing parts', *Innes Review*, 39 (1988), 151–5 · G. Monro, 'The Scottish Reformation and its consequences', in I. W. Preece, *Our awin Scottis use: music in the Scottish church up to 1603* (2000), 273–303 · K. Elliott, 'Some helpes for young schollers', *The Renaissance in Scotland: studies in literature, religion, history, and culture offered to John Durkan*, ed. A. MacDonald and others (1994), 264–75 · K. Elliott, *Fourteen psalm-settings of the early reformed church in Scotland* (1960) · C. H. Haws, *Scottish parish clergy at the Reformation, 1540–1574*, Scottish RS, new ser., 3 (1972) · J. D. Maynard, 'An anonymous Scottish treatise', PhD diss., Indiana University, 1961 · J. Cranstoun, ed., *Satirical poems of the time of the Reformation*, 2 vols. in 4 pts, STS, 20, 24, 28, 30 (1891–3) · memorial, St Michael's cemetery, Inveresk, Lothian

Blackhall [Blakhal], **Gilbert** (d. **1671**), Roman Catholic priest, was evidently descended from the Blackhalls of Barra, Aberdeenshire, though his parentage is unknown. His brother George (d. 1656) was a merchant who became a Jesuit coadjutor (lay brother) in Spain. Gilbert served as a soldier on the continent before, in 1626, enrolling in the Scots College in Rome, where he was ordained as a priest on 30 March 1630. The following year, on the recommendation of a cousin, he became confessor to Lady Isabelle Hay, eldest daughter of the earl of Erroll, in Paris. With the support of the viceroy of the Spanish Netherlands, the infanta, Clara Eugenia, Blackhall arranged her settlement in a house of aristocratic canonesses in Mons in 1637. He then travelled through England to Scotland, arriving there in August 1637, and took up work as a missionary priest in Aberdeenshire. Basing himself in Aboyne Castle (from July 1638) he served as priest to the widowed Lady Aboyne (Sophia Hay, sister of his former charge), as well as ministering to Catholic households between Aboyne and Aberdeen, and between Aberdeen and Strathbogie (Huntly). The outbreak of the covenanters' rebellion against Charles I had intensified persecution of Roman Catholics, and to the dangers of the situation were added the complications of bitter disputes between Jesuits and secular priests like Blackhall. The unsettled times also forced him, not unwillingly, into the role of Lady Aboyne's military adviser, organizing the defence of her castle against highland raiders. 'Know that I was a soldier befor you could weepe your owne nose' (Blakhal, 85), he contemptuously told the captain of a gang of Camerons after disarming his men.

Shortly before her death early in 1642 Lady Aboyne entrusted Blackhall with ensuring that her only surviving child, Henrietta Gordon, was brought up as a Catholic and not perverted to protestantism. This he undertook with his customary tenacity. He visited the girl's grandmother, the dowager Lady Huntly, in France, in 1643 but she refused to help, whereupon the obscure priest boldly approached Anne of Austria, queen of France, and through her obtained a letter from Louis XIII to the marquess of Huntly, Henrietta's guardian, promising her a position at court. Back in Scotland, however, he found Huntly unwilling to help, and that Henrietta had converted to protestantism. None the less he managed to persuade her to allow him to smuggle her to France and Roman Catholicism.

In his *Narration*, a lively narrative of his services, which he completed in 1653 and addressed to Henrietta at the French court, Blackhall complains of the lack of thanks he had received from his three ladies. Both Isabelle Hay and Henrietta Gordon had conceived a hearty dislike of him through his well-meant meddling in their lives—and

Lady Aboyne had inconveniently died. In between his complaints Blackhall provides valuable glimpses of a robust and energetic Roman Catholic priest at large in covenanting Scotland. His swaggering boldness and liking for drink and song, no doubt legacies of his military past, on occasion helped to deflect suspicion from him when he was in danger of detection. He served briefly as principal of the Scots College in Paris in 1653, but nothing further is known of him except that he visited Scotland about 1668 and died in Paris on 1 July 1671.   DAVID STEVENSON

Sources G. Blakhal, *A breiffe narration of the services done to three noble ladyes*, ed. J. Stuart (1844) · D. Stevenson, 'A priest and his ladies', *King or covenant?* (1996), 49–63 · A. Morison, *The Blackhalls of that ilk and Barra* (1905) · B. M. Halloran, *The Scots College, Paris, 1603–1792* (1997) · M. V. Hay, *The Blairs papers, 1603–1660* (1929), 106, 108 · D. Mathew, 'Catholicism in the north east', *Scotland under Charles I* (1955) · A. F. B. Roberts, 'The role of women in Scottish Catholic survival', *SHR*, 70 (1991), 129–50

Blackie, John (1782–1874), publisher, was born at Old Wynd, Glasgow, on 27 October 1782, the first child of John Blackie (b. 1762), tobacco spinner of Glasgow, and Agnes Burrell (b. 1760), who had married in 1781. Childhood memory survives only in Blackie's own words that he was 'very little at school after six years of age'. As American independence reduced the Glasgow-dominated European tobacco trade, Blackie was apprenticed, aged eleven, to a master weaver. At eighteen he was a journeyman with another, John Duncan.

On 31 December 1804 Blackie married Duncan's daughter, Catharine (1777–1847). Nelson's victory at Trafalgar dispelled fear of Napoleonic invasion, but development of power-looms brought new worries. In 1805 a son was born and Blackie abandoned weaving to join W. D. and A. Brownlie, publishers. For them he sold books in cheap monthly parts, as a colporteur.

Unexpectedly, retiring in 1807, the Brownlies offered their business to Blackie. Acceptance became possible through the generosity of Walter Graham, a Glasgow merchant. Mrs Graham had befriended Blackie before his marriage, and her husband stood as guarantor for payment. The friendship prospered, and later, in 1816, a second (surviving) son was baptized Walter Graham Blackie.

Meanwhile Blackie entered partnership in 1809 with William Sommerville and Archibald Fullarton, former Brownlies employees, later joined by another, Edward Khull, a printer. In 1816 they erected a five-storey building in the city: ground-floor printing works, with bindery, warehouse, and offices above. Operations were divided in 1819 between Glasgow and Edinburgh; subsequently numerous reorganizations took place. Sommerville left in 1821: Khull became independent but still printed for Blackie. John Blackie junior became publishing partner in Blackie & Son, Glasgow: young Walter was learning printing under Khull. In 1826 Khull finally left, and in 1829 Blackie bought the valuable business at Villafield of Andrew and J. M. Duncan, university printers and successors to the Foulis brothers, famous throughout Europe in the eighteenth century. His younger son, only twenty-one,

with stout parental confidence, led a new firm, W. G. Blackie & Co., printers, Villafield.

Although the original partners had disagreed, Sommerville and Blackie always intended to publish books. Before Sommerville left, a substantial list included religious, historical, and travel works; literature, notably Richardson's four-volume *Pamela*; and yet another to join the myriad editions of Burns's *Poems*. By 1842 all three of Blackie's sons were partners. Throughout the changes Blackie himself controlled finance, and his remarkable skills never failed, despite his lack of schooling.

Those skills went beyond financial management. Blackie travelled throughout Britain, later crossing the Atlantic, visiting paper, cloth, and board mills; renewing plant and stocks. He assessed manuscripts with technical comprehension; appointed marketing and distribution agents; supervised quality control in factory and offices. Blackie never relaxed from self-imposed responsibilities, driven sometimes by determination to banish sadness. A devout man, concerned in matters of the established church, and later the Free Church, he was greatly disturbed by the Disruption of 1843, and in 1847 by the death of his first wife.

Blackie's private time and money were much devoted to ailing relations; he invested shrewdly in property and the stock market, becoming, in 1850, a director of the Clydesdale Bank. On 4 November of that year he married Margaret Ferguson, née Frame, a widow. She survived him. A natural manager, Blackie worried over working conditions and the welfare and health of his employees. He eschewed popularity. His understanding of difficulties in the lives of others had grown out of the humble beginning and order of his own: his employees developed reciprocal understanding, and devotion to him.

Blackie died at his home, 20 Kew Terrace, Glasgow, on 16 June 1874. The business he founded was carried on successfully by his son Walter Graham Blackie, who was eventually succeeded by *his* son John Alexander *Blackie (1850–1918); it developed for generations as Blackie & Son. It became renowned among the great Scottish printers and publishers for nearly 200 years. Another grandson, Walter W. Blackie, wrote of him with affectionate pride, and of 'the impression that he was rather an exceptional man, a blend of a Saint, a Superman, and a Right-Good-Sort' (W. W. Blackie, *John Blackie, Senior*, 74).

PETER NEWBOLT

Sources W. W. Blackie, *John Blackie, senior (1782–1874)* (privately printed, 1933) · W. W. Blackie, *A Scottish student in Leipzig, being letters of W. G. Blackie, his father and his brothers (1839–1840)* (privately printed, 1932) · W. W. Blackie, *Walter Graham Blackie, Ph.D., LL.D. (1816–1906)* (privately printed, 1936) · A. A. C. Blackie, *Blackie & Son (1809–1859), a short history of the firm* (1959) · P. Newbolt, *G. A. Henty (1832–1902): a bibliographical study* (1996) · private information (2004) [family: Simonette Rattenbury, Ruth Currie] · m. reg. Scot. [both marriages] · NA Scot., SC 36/48/74/628–637
Likenesses W. Bonnar, oils, 1839, repro. in Blackie, *Scottish student in Leipzig*, frontispiece · K. Macleay, watercolour, 1853, repro. in Blackie, *John Blackie, senior*, frontispiece
Wealth at death £25,346 7s. 8d.: confirmation, 8 Sept 1874, NA Scot., SC 36/48/74/628–637

Blackie, John Alexander (1850–1918), printer and publisher, was born in Glasgow on 7 March 1850, the elder son of Dr Walter Graham Blackie (1816–1906) of Glasgow, and his wife, Marion Brodie (b. 1822); he was the eldest grandchild of John *Blackie (1782–1874), founder of the Scottish printing and publishing firm, for generations known as Blackie & Son. John Alexander (Jack) was educated at the Glasgow Academy, and from 1863 to 1864 at Professor Hirsch's school at Canstadt, Württemberg, Germany. He entered the family business in 1869, and became a partner in 1876. In 1884 he visited Australia on business, where he met his future wife, Sarah Gemmell (1859–1910), the daughter of Hugh Gemmell of Ayr and his Dutch wife, Simonette Christiani, Baroness van Oukema. They were married on 11 February 1885 in Melbourne, and had one son and two daughters.

Blackie's academic ability and technical skills combined with an unusual degree of imagination and vision to make him a great publisher. He first negotiated rights in an important series of educational works, and after a few years in school book publishing was appointed by his father to institute a department for school rewards and children's books in general. He saw things on a grand scale and built a solid and successful juvenile list of a quality unmatched in his time. Simultaneously his mind delighted in the complex and multifarious details of commercial printing and binding. No other family member displayed comparable literary discrimination and editorial ability in his own field, coupled, unusually, with practical understanding and enjoyment of mechanical processes, qualities which suited him ideally to plan the physical production of books. His choice of authors for children was intelligent and imaginative, headed by the talents of G. A. Henty, whom he developed into a household name.

With his wide technical knowledge Blackie revolutionized production methods, inventing a unique system of mass production so ingenious that constructional uniformities were disguised at the time by rich variations in book design, and were fully comprehended only seventy-five years after his death. Consequent reduction of factory costs and bulk buying of materials gave him the edge over rival publishers. His books were consistently praised by parents, teachers, reviewers, and educationists alike.

Blackie had a talent for communication, made friends easily, and was blessed with charm and a persuasive nature. He was lucky to have a staff writer, Thomas Archer, who introduced him to some authors, including Henty. His uncle Robert Blackie, in charge of the 'art department' in his father's day, continued to manage it until the appointment in 1892 of the designer Talwin Morris. Almost at once Blackies became patrons of an art nouveau movement more famous in Europe than in Britain, ultimately known as the 'Glasgow style', and associated with Charles Rennie Mackintosh. By the time Blackie succeeded his father as chairman in 1906, school books and children's books were the main output of the firm. A very wide range of 'juvenile' publications, including the Blackie children's annuals and other ventures, was Jack

Blackie's responsibility: his brother Walter looked after educational texts, and the two men shared some general publishing.

Today Jack Blackie might be called a workaholic: his niece, Agnes Blackie, later the firm's historian, wrote that 'business was always his interest, to the extent that nothing bored him so much as a holiday from it' (A. A. C. Blackie, 47). His granddaughter was told by her mother that he was very radical and supported trade unions, believing them essential to a fair deal for workers. She also noted that he enjoyed photographing formal family groups—to the 'boredom of the sitters'. In 1916 Jack's spirit was shattered by the death of his only son on the Somme. He never recovered from the blow, and died, at his home, 6 Victoria Circus, Kelvinside, Glasgow, just after armistice day, on 17 November 1918. He was buried in Glasgow. PETER NEWBOLT

Sources W. W. Blackie, *A Scottish student in Leipzig, being letters of W. G. Blackie, his father and his brothers (1839–1840)* (privately printed, 1932) · A. A. C. Blackie, *Blackie & Son (1809–1859), a short history of the firm* (1959) · P. Newbolt, *G. A. Henty (1832–1902): a bibliographical study* (1996) · private information (2004) [family: Simonette Rattenbury, Ruth Currie] · bap. reg. Scot. · d. cert.
Likenesses photograph, U. Glas.; repro. in Newbolt, *G. A. Henty*

Blackie, John Stuart (1809–1895), university teacher and writer, was born on 28 July 1809 in Charlotte Street, Glasgow, the eldest son of Alexander Blackie (bap. 1780, d. 1856), banker, and Helen (1783–1819), daughter of William Stodart of Hamilton and his wife, Christina. In that year his father moved as manager of the Commercial Bank to Aberdeen, where Blackie was educated at Merson's academy, a private subscription school, and at Marischal College (1821–4), where he attended the Greek class. Intended by his father for law, he was placed in an advocate's office, but, with a preference for theology, he went to Edinburgh to complete an arts course, including Greek, which he pursued in 1825–6, but without graduating.

Preparing for entry to a divinity hall, Blackie returned to Aberdeen to study theology for two years with a view to entering the ministry. A decisive change in his plans resulted from his being sent to Germany in April 1829, studying in Göttingen under scholars including Ottfried Müller, and subsequently in Berlin with Boeckh and Schleiermacher. He also developed an enthusiasm for the long walks which were to become characteristic of his whole life. With two friends he travelled to Italy, adding facility in the language to his good knowledge of German. In Rome, with introductions to well-known scholars, in particular the Prussian diplomat Baron Christian von Bunsen, who became a great friend, he became interested in archaeology and art, and through contact with a Greek student learned also to speak modern Greek, becoming particularly fascinated by the accentuation, which differed so much from the traditional pronunciation of the ancient tongue.

On his return to Britain in 1831, when Blackie began to study for the Scottish bar, his enthusiasm for both the church and the law was waning, though he was admitted

John Stuart Blackie (1809–1895), by Sir George Reid, 1893

to the Faculty of Advocates in 1834, in which year he published his first substantial work, a translation of *Faust* which was commended by Carlyle. He began a series of articles, often on German literature, in literary periodicals, and joined Edinburgh's Speculative and Juridical societies, which helped him become well known in intellectual circles.

About this time the Liberal MP for Aberdeen, Alexander Bannerman, who was a close friend of Blackie's father, was pressing for the institution of a chair of humanity at Aberdeen, which alone of the Scottish universities did not have one. When in 1839 this was ratified, Blackie was appointed as its first incumbent, giving rise to vocal criticism of this being a 'whig job'. Before he could be installed, Blackie was required to subscribe to the Westminster confession of faith, and though consenting to sign he nevertheless expressed reservations, declaring that his agreement was 'in reference to university offices and duties merely'. The presbytery then attempted to annul the appointment, and Blackie had to raise an action first against the senatus, then the presbytery. The affair dragged on for two years before his installation was confirmed.

Meanwhile Blackie returned to Edinburgh, and became the suitor of Eliza Wyld (*bap.* 1819, *d.* 1908), but found her father opposed to the match. By the time his Aberdeen chair was ratified, Mr Wyld relented, and the couple were married on 19 April 1842. It was a long and happy (though childless) marriage. During his eleven years at Aberdeen Blackie applied himself strenuously to university reform, since

> the whole style of academical learning seemed so juvenile and pedantic ... I had to sit down in a sort of intellectual Botany Bay, and teach raw country lads and little boys to blunder through Latin sentences, in the human meaning and purport of which they seemed incapable of taking any interest. (*Notes of a Life*, 129)

In addition to university teaching, he embarked upon his noted popular lectures on a variety of subjects, delivered mainly extempore, which he found more effective than formal reading.

In 1850 Blackie published his verse translation of Aeschylus's tragedies, and he seized the opportunity of succeeding to the Edinburgh Greek chair, when, as he put it bluntly, 'Dunbar [his predecessor] should retire from Greek, or the world, or from both together'. He was appointed Greek professor in 1852, and 'exchanged Latin for Greek, copper for gold'. His inaugural lecture was entitled 'Classical literature in its relation to the nineteenth century'. Again he campaigned for reform, instituting an entrance examination, the introduction of a tutorial system, and the appointment of assistants. He published a short volume on his favourite subject of the pronunciation of Greek, lambasting the Oxford style 'case-hardened in ignorance, prejudice, and pedantry' (*Letters*, 395). In 1857 his *Lays and Legends of Ancient Greece* was published.

In 1866 Blackie's substantial four-volume translation and commentary on the *Iliad* appeared. Among its often idiosyncratic notes, that on a minor figure, Agamede, had an interesting sequel. Blackie saw her as 'prophetic of Florence Nightingale', and concluded that 'a field of activity which has recently been claimed for the sex by English aspiration and American example should develop into the systematic instruction of women in certain departments of the medical art'. At that very time, Sophia Jex-Blake was prosecuting her case for women's medical education in America, having also visited Edinburgh. When in 1869 she made her first attempt to enrol in the university, through the support of David Masson, professor of English, she gained an introduction to Blackie, who showed her his note, and was one of her most prominent supporters in the angry debates which ensued in senate. When the women were barred by an angry mob in the 'Surgeons' Hall riot' of 1870, Blackie observed to her 'Ye can now say ye've fought with wild beasts at Ephesus', and on their ultimate victory he composed a Greek triumphal ode for one of the first graduates at a meeting of the Hellenic Society which he formed in Edinburgh, as he had earlier done in Aberdeen. Subsequently, the women's bronze class medal in the Medical College for Women pictured Homer's Agamede, doubtless at Blackie's suggestion.

There was nothing Blackie liked better than to espouse a cause and pursue it with unflagging commitment. He was a proponent of the new fine art chair (1873), and his passion for modern Greek led to the foundation of a theological fellowship for residence in Greece. (He himself had made the first of his journeys there in 1853.) He was active in support of the establishment of student halls of residence. Above all, he threw himself into fund-raising for a chair of Celtic from the 1870s until its establishment in 1882, almost single-handedly setting about raising the £12,000 required by lecturing, hectoring, cajoling, almost compelling people (from Queen Victoria downwards) to contribute. He had been appalled by the plight of highland crofters, and became fired with enthusiasm for Gaelic, publishing *The Gaelic Language* in 1864, followed by *Lays of the Highlands and Islands* (1871), *The Language and Literature of the Highlands* (1876), and *Altavona … from my Life in the Highlands* (1882). Mention might be made here too of his *Life of Robert Burns* (1887) and *Scottish Song* (1889). Blackie's writings on Scotland made him an important figure in the historicist movement there.

Blackie's early enthusiasm for German student life had already resulted in publication of a collection of student songs (*Musa Burschicosa*, 1869) and *War Songs of the Germans* (1870), and he wrote the preface and contributed a number of his own songs to the once very popular, and much reprinted, *Scottish Students' Song Book* (1891). One song in the 1891 volume is about Blackie himself, by his Sanskrit colleague Julius Eggeling, 'A Famous Scotch Professor', celebrating Blackie's visit to Egypt aged seventy, when—characteristically—he mounted a pyramid to sing 'Scots wha hae'. He was nothing if not the archetype of the perfervid Scot, and there was an undoubted coolness in his relations with 'those sleek Hellenists on the banks of the Cam and Isis', as he once remarked, and he argued for a separate Scottish parliament, against 'the multitudinous babblement and insolent centralisation' of Westminster (Kennedy, 111, 216). In 1867 he had engaged in a notorious two-day debate in the George Street Music Hall with Ernest Jones on democracy, when he attacked the Reform Bill, haranguing for nearly three hours.

As a teacher, Blackie was not entirely successful. One writer of memoirs commented 'he did everything well, except what he was paid to do, viz. teach Greek to his students' (D. T. Holmes, *Literary Tours in the Highlands and Islands of Scotland*, 1909, 56), who soon learned how to divert their professor to politics, Scottish song, or the like, and his classes were frequently rowdy. After an uproarious lecture, he could be seen striding cheerfully down the Bridges from Old College playing on imaginary bagpipes. He enjoyed his persona as a flamboyant eccentric, and with his long white hair and in his regular dress—a plaid thrown over his shoulders, a long stick, and a soft hat with a broad band—he was a familiar figure to the citizens. One well-known anecdote relates his posting of a notice that he was unable to meet 'his classes', which students adjusted by deleting the 'c'; waiting to see how the professor would react, they saw him study the notice, and imperiously delete further the 'l'. The story may be apocryphal, however, since the same tale was told of an earlier Edinburgh professor, W. E. Aytoun, and Blackie himself denied it.

Even after his retirement Blackie continued to lecture with gusto and good humour throughout Scotland, and was widely admired. He remained also an indefatigable traveller, last visiting Greece in 1891. Not until 1894, when he was attacked with asthma, did his health deteriorate somewhat, and his last public appearance was at the opening of the university session in October of that year. He died at his home at 9 Douglas Crescent on 2 March 1895, and after the public funeral service at St Giles was buried in the Dean cemetery four days later. It was a raw, drizzling day, yet the streets were lined with mourners along the route via Princes Street, and the cortège bore wreaths from persons as diverse as the prime minister and Sir Henry Irving. *The Scotsman* devoted nearly a whole page to his obituary, and the muse of notorious 'poet and tragedian' William McGonagall was stirred to compose a funeral ode, to be found in his *Last Poetic Gems*. David Masson in a tribute referred to his 'almost childlike innocence of heart and a seraphic kind of goodness' (Duncan, 202).

In addition to the works mentioned above, Blackie published prolifically on Greek, Scottish, religious, philosophical, and political topics. A. Stodart Walker collected and published from manuscript 'random thoughts on life, character, literature, and general economics' in *The Day-Book of John Stuart Blackie* (1901), and also compiled a selection of his poems (1896).   E. KERR BORTHWICK

Sources A. M. Stoddart, *John Stuart Blackie*, 2 vols. (1895) · H. A. Kennedy, *Professor Blackie, his sayings and doings* (1895) · *The letters of John Stuart Blackie to his wife*, ed. A. S. Walker (1909) · *Notes of a life, by John Stuart Blackie*, ed. A. S. Walker (1910) · J. G. Duncan, *The life of Professor John Stuart Blackie* (1895) · *The day-book of John Stuart Blackie*, ed. A. S. Walker, 2nd edn (1902) · E. K. Borthwick, 'A famous Scotch professor', *University of Edinburgh Journal*, 33 (1987–8), 101–5 **Archives** Harvard U., Houghton L. · NL Scot., corresp. and papers; letters relating to his publications · U. Edin. L., corresp. and papers | BL, corresp. with Mary Gladstone, Add. MS 46251 · BL, corresp. with W. E. Gladstone, Add. MS 44107 · British School at Athens, corresp. with G. Finlay · Mitchell L., Glas., Glasgow City Archives, letters to Sir William Stirling-Maxwell · NL Scot., corresp. with Blackwoods · NL Scot., letters to John Hill Burton · NL Scot., corresp. with Henry Drummond · NL Scot., letters to Alexander Campbell Frazer · NL Scot., corresp. incl. with Sir Patrick Geddes · NL Scot., letters, incl. to Charles Gray · NL Scot., letters to Alan Reid · NL Scot., corresp. with Lord Rosebery · U. Edin. L., letters to Sir A. Geikie · U. Reading L., letters to Macmillans **Likenesses** W. Brodie, plaster bust, 1863, Scot. NPG · J. Archer, oils, 1874, Royal Scot. Acad. · G. Webster, statuette, 1874, repro. in Duncan, *Life of professor John Stuart Blackie*, 15 · portrait, 1877 (after photograph by D. Macara), U. Edin., classics department · J. H. Lorimer, oils, exh. RA 1881, U. Edin., Old College · W. B. Hole, etching on paper, 1882, Scot. NPG · W. Hole, etching, pubd 1884, NPG · Barraud, photograph, 1890, NPG · D. W. Stevenson, waxed plaster bust, 1890, Scot. NPG · G. Reid, oils, 1893, Scot. NPG [*see illus.*] · Cassell, Petter & Galpin, lithograph, NPG · W. & D. Darney, photograph, NPG · Elliott & Fry, carte-de-visite, NPG · Hahnisch, lithograph, BM · S. Macdonald, oils, NPG · J. Moffat, carte-de-visite, NPG **Wealth at death** £4988: NA Scot.

Blackie, Margery Grace (1898–1981), homoeopathic physician, was born on 4 February 1898 at Redbourn, Hertfordshire. She was the youngest of ten children of Robert Blackie (*c.*1852–1936), a man of independent means, and his wife, Elizabeth (*d.* 1941), daughter of Rowland Rees, civil engineer and architect. Her mother's family were ardent supporters of homoeopathy and Elizabeth's sister

Margery Grace Blackie (1898–1981), by Mayotte Magnus, 1977

Katherine married James Compton Burnett, an eminent homoeopathic physician and father of the novelist Ivy Compton Burnett.

In 1911 the Blackie family moved to London where Margery attended the Haberdashers' Aske's School for Girls in Acton. At an early age she determined upon a medical career and in 1917 entered the London School of Medicine for Women. She was by no means a brilliant student. Her path to qualification included several failed examinations. In 1923 she eventually qualified as a licenciate of the Royal College of Physicians and a member of the Royal College of Surgeons. Three years later she passed, at the second attempt, the examination for the London University degree of MB BS. However within two years she proceeded MD at the early age of thirty.

Immediately after qualification Blackie became resident medical officer at the London Homoeopathic Hospital, where she added to the knowledge of the homoeopathy she had gained from her family. She came under the particular influence of Douglas Borland and John Weir, who were two of the first British doctors to study under James Tyler Kent in the United States. She never deviated from her devotion to his principles, and his advocacy of the use of high potency remedies. After the completion of her residency in 1926 Blackie had opened a practice at 10 Drayton Gardens, Fulham, but also resurrected a defunct homoeopathic dispensary at 68B Fulham Road. Although she always regarded herself as a general practitioner she continued to work at the hospital, becoming assistant physician to the children's department in 1929 and, years

later, physician in charge of out-patients. At the end of the decade she moved to 18 Thurloe Street, Kensington, where she remained for the rest of her working life in partnership with Helen Banks (d. 1971).

Blackie kept up to date with developments in medicine, and was respected by her medically more conventional colleagues, consulting them whenever she thought it necessary. She was a remarkable homoeopath, who attracted patients from all over the country and, indeed, the world. Her ability was recognized in 1969 when she was appointed physician to the queen in succession to Sir John Weir. Although her prime concern was always the welfare of the patient she came to recognize the need for research that would demonstrate the effectiveness of homoeopathy. In 1971 she founded the Blackie Foundation Trust to encourage education and research.

In 1965, having already served as president, Blackie was appointed dean of the Faculty of Homoeopathy. She reorganized teaching and ran three week-long courses per year. These grew from small beginnings to serve up to one hundred students per course. She did not hesitate to write personally to doctors who she thought would become good homoeopaths, to encourage them to attend. She was persistent in her pressure upon those she wanted as lecturers so that few ultimately refused her. At her own expense she entertained students to a fork supper at Thurloe Street and to a dinner at a Bloomsbury hotel. A number of these students on each course would be selected to attend her surgery at Thurloe Street, where she would demonstrate her methods leading to the selection of a remedy. She always emphasized the advantage of bringing the patient from the waiting room herself, because so much knowledge could be gained from the patient's attitude and from a handshake. She also unwittingly demonstrated her instinctive ability to select the appropriate remedy.

Blackie was a lifelong devout evangelical Christian, greatly influenced in adult life by the Congregational ministers at the Westminster Chapel. She always regarded herself as on call but her long friendship with Musette Majendie, whose home was Hedingham Castle in Essex, enabled her to spend her limited leisure time watching birds, playing croquet and bridge, and solving jigsaw puzzles. Her summer holidays were spent with her friends at Aviemore. While she gave many lectures (a selection of which was published posthumously under the title *Classical Homoeopathy*, 1986) she wrote very little and published only one book. *The Patient, not the Cure* was published in 1975 and was an anecdotal summary of her ideas on homoeopathy. In later life Blackie contracted and recovered from rheumatoid arthritis, but a broken hip eventually led to her retirement in 1980. She resigned from her appointment as physician to the queen in June 1979. She received the honour of CVO in recognition of her devoted service to the royal family. Blackie spent her final year at Hedingham, becoming increasingly frail, although her bedside reading remained what it had always been, the Bible and Kent's *Homeopathic materia medica*, which sum up her main interests in life.

Blackie had an excellent memory for names. She was polite and meticulous about punctuality, although delays such as traffic jams were accepted with patience. Always well dressed she evolved and kept to her own smart bright style with the assistance of Peter Crown of La Chasse, a London fashion house. Margery Blackie died peacefully of a stroke on 24 August 1981 and was buried on 29 August at Castle Hedingham.   BERNARD LEARY

Sources C. Babington Smith, *Champion of homoeopathy* (1986) · *British Homoeopathic Journal*, 71/1 (1982), 1–8 · 'In memoriam: Dr Margery Blackie', *British Homoeopathic Journal*, 71/2 (1982), 69–71 · private information (2004) [Blackie Foundation Trust] · *Medical Directory* (1962)
Archives Blackie Foundation Trust, London · priv. coll. | FILM British Homoeopathic Association Library, London | SOUND Faculty of Homoeopathy Tape Library
Likenesses M. Magnus, photograph, 1977, NPG [*see illus.*] · P. Gunn, oils, Blackie Foundation Trust · photographs, Blackie Foundation Trust
Wealth at death £284,891: probate, 7 April 1982, *CGPLA Eng. & Wales*

Blacking, John Anthony Randoll (1928–1990), social anthropologist and ethnomusicologist, was born on 22 October 1928 in Guildford, Surrey, the elder child and only son of William Henry Randoll Blacking, ecclesiastical architect, and his wife, (Josephine) Margaret Newcombe Waymouth. The family moved to 21 The Close, Salisbury, in 1930. Blacking attended Salisbury Cathedral school (1934–42) where, as a chorister and pianist, he showed early musical promise. Attendance at Sherborne School, Dorset (1942–7), was followed by a commission in the Coldstream Guards and active service in Malaya (1947–9). The plight of the aboriginal peoples caught up in the conflict moved him deeply, and on his release from national service he went to King's College, Cambridge, to read archaeology and anthropology. While there, he was active in artistic life as a pianist and actor, and as a performer and promoter of contemporary music. He obtained second classes (division one in part one and division two in part two) in his tripos (1952 and 1953).

Blacking began to use his musical and anthropological talents in a variety of ways. For a time he considered becoming a professional pianist, he worked as a social worker in the East End of London, and he spent a summer studying ethnomusicology in Paris. In October 1953 he was invited by the Colonial Office to return to Malaya as assistant adviser on aboriginal peoples, which he did, only then to learn that his role was to provide the intelligence that would enable the forced removal of the forest peoples, all of whom were apparently suspected of being (or harbouring) terrorists. He refused, resigning after only six days.

Blacking took a post as a musicologist at the International Library of African Music at Roodepoort, near Johannesburg, South Africa, in 1954. In this capacity he carried out field studies in Zululand and Mozambique, and among the Venda and Gwembe Tonga peoples. In 1955 he married Brenda Eleonora, daughter of Herman Wilhelm Friedrich Gebers, a farmer. They had a son and four daughters, two of whom died in childhood (1956 and

1963). In 1959 Blacking took up a lectureship in social anthropology and African government at the University of Witwatersrand, Johannesburg, becoming professor and head of the department in 1965. Witwatersrand awarded him a PhD in 1965 and a DLitt in 1972. His principal publications during this period included (as editor) *Black Background: the Childhood of a South African Girl* (1964) and (as author) *Venda Children's Songs: a Study in Ethnomusicological Analysis* (1967). A man of forceful personality and an enthusiastic evangelist in promoting understanding between people, and between people and the institutions they create, Blacking set up courses in African music and Asian studies, and took an increasingly outspoken role in anti-apartheid politics, which eventually led him to clash with the authorities. He was prosecuted under the notorious Immorality Act, which forbade sexual relations between people of different colours.

In 1969 Blacking left South Africa with Zureena Rukshana Desai, a medical doctor, with whom he was later to have four daughters. She was the daughter of Suliman Mohamed Desai, a company director. After his divorce in 1975, he and Zureena were married in 1978. Offered a choice of chairs in Britain and the United States, he chose, after a short spell as professor of anthropology at Western Michigan University, Kalamazoo, to take up in 1970 the first appointment to the chair of social anthropology at the Queen's University of Belfast. This was at the very height of the 'troubles' in Northern Ireland, in which he saw many parallels with Malaya and South Africa. It was with a sense of mission that he guided the department from modest beginnings in 1970 to become one of the largest in the British Isles and an internationally recognized centre of ethnomusicology. His most influential book, *How Musical is Man?* (1974), stressed the importance of identifying the structural relationships between patterns of musical organization and those of social life. It argued that the human potential for musical creativity had been stifled in the West by an élitist conception of musical ability, whereas in pre-industrial societies everyone was an active musician. The book was soon published in paperback and was translated into several languages. It brought students of ethnomusicology to Belfast from all over the world.

Blacking was a handsome man, tall and fair with clear blue eyes and the lean, broad-shouldered frame of a rugby player. He frequently wore his regiment of guards tie, which gave him a rather formal and military air that contrasted with the rebellious and iconoclastic things he often said. His impact upon an audience was both physical and intellectual. A gifted lecturer, always at his best playing to an audience, he could, and did, teach anything in the syllabus with authority and flair. He served in various capacities on the committees of the International Folk Music Council, the Royal Anthropological Institute, the Social Science Research Council, the Council for National Academic Awards, and the British Council, and gave dozens of guest lectures and addresses, but yet still found the time to do voluntary work for homeless, handicapped, and unemployed people as a council member in local charitable organizations. He regularly gave solo piano recitals at the university's lunchtime concerts. A man of great verve, wide interests, and an abiding belief in the creative genius of all humanity, he was constantly active. He believed that human beings were inherently musical and that music was an important means of communication across cultural boundaries.

In 1984 Blacking was elected to the Royal Irish Academy. He was awarded the Rivers memorial medal of the Royal Anthropological Institute (1986) and the Koizumi Fumio prize in Tokyo (1989). His last works included a six-part series, *Dancing*, for Independent Television, and a book on the ethnomusicological work of the Australian composer Percy Grainger, *A Commonsense View of All Music* (1987). Blacking died of cancer in Belfast on 24 January 1990. A posthumous collection of his essays on ethnomusicology, together with an extended biographical introduction and a full list of his works, was published in 1995.

REGINALD BYRON, *rev.*

Sources *Newsletter* [Queen's University, Belfast] (March 1990) · *Annals of the Association of Social Anthropologists of the Commonwealth* (1990) · *The Guardian* (30 Jan 1990) · *Journal of Comparative Family Studies*, 22/3 (autumn 1991) · private information (1996) · R. Byron, 'The ethnomusicology of John Blacking', in *Music, culture, and experience: selected papers of John Blacking*, ed. R. Byron (1995), 1–28 **Archives** Queen's University, Belfast

Blackley, William Lewery (1830–1902), Church of England clergyman and social reformer, was born at Dundalk, Ireland, on 30 December 1830. He was the second son of Travers Robert Blackley of Dublin and Bohogh, co. Roscommon, and Eliza, daughter of Colonel Lewery, who was taken prisoner by the French at Verdun. His maternal grandfather was Travers Hartley, MP for Dublin City (1776–90) and governor of the Bank of Ireland. In 1843–5 Blackley, together with his brother John, was sent to a school in Brussels kept by Dr Carl Friedlander, a Polish political refugee. There he became proficient in French, German, and other languages. In 1847 he entered Trinity College, Dublin, was awarded his BA in 1850 and his MA in 1854, and took holy orders. In 1854 he became curate of St Peter's, Southwark, London. An attack of cholera compelled him to leave London. From 1855 to 1867 he was in charge of two parishes at Frensham near Farnham, Surrey. He was rector of North Waltham, Hampshire (1867–83), and from 1883 to 1889 of King's Somborne with Little Somborne (to which was added Upper Eldon in 1885). In 1883 he was made honorary canon of Winchester.

In 1855 Blackley married Amelia Jeanne Josephine, second daughter of his teacher in Brussels, Carl Friedlander. They had one son who died in infancy and two daughters who, with his widow, survived him. He is best-known as an early proponent of national insurance for sickness and old age. As a parish priest he became keenly interested in social questions. He devised a scheme for the statutory enforcement of personal saving. He elaborated it in an essay published in November 1878 in the journal *Nineteenth Century* entitled 'National provident insurance, a

William Lewery Blackley (1830–1902), by unknown photographer, pubd 1891

cheap, practical and popular way of preventing pauperism'. Thereafter he promoted it tirelessly, with the active support of his wife and also, from 1880, of the National Providence League, over which the earl of Shaftesbury presided. He was also an advocate of temperance. He was an elegant and humorous speaker, and audiences were readily attracted to his plans. His views on the prevention of pauperism were further disseminated in his books, which included: *How to Teach Domestic Economy* (1879), *Collected Essays on the Prevention of Pauperism* (1880), *Social Economy Reading Book, Adapted to the New Code* (1881), *Thrift and Independence: a Word for Working-Men* (1884), and *Old Age Pensions* (1900).

The essence of Blackley's national insurance scheme was that all persons between the ages of eighteen and twenty-one should subscribe £10 to a national fund, which would accrue interest. In return, 'wage-earners' (as distinct from 'wage-payers and leisured and salary earners') would receive 8s. per week in time of sickness until the age of seventy, then 4s. per week as an old-age pension from the age of seventy. The scheme was widely discussed in political circles and was the subject of a House of Commons select committee on national provident insurance during 1885–7. Though the scheme attracted much support, the committee disliked its compulsory character, which undermined the principle of self-help, and believed that friendly societies provided adequately for the needs of working people. It also concluded, rightly, that the proposed benefits could not be sustained by the proposed contributions, and that those who most needed such a scheme, in particular poorer women, could not afford larger contributions. Blackley acknowledged this weakness and thereafter advocated this method of provision for old-age pensions only. However, his calculations continued to be excessively optimistic and the popularity of his scheme waned after the publication of the *Report of the Select Committee*. He had also incurred the wrath of the leading institutions of working-class saving, the friendly societies, by his sweeping and sometimes unfair criticisms of their operations, and they campaigned against his proposals. On the other hand, he had stimulated a debate in Britain about new forms of state provision for the poor, especially the aged poor, similar to debates which were emerging in most industrially developed countries at the time. It led to the development of more realistic proposals in Britain, and to the introduction of the first wholly state-financed old-age pensions in 1908 and of national health insurance in 1911. He believed that he had personally persuaded Bismarck to introduce the first national insurance scheme in the world in Germany in 1884, but it is unlikely that his was the major source of inspiration.

Blackley's success was less equivocal in 1887 when, as director of the Clergy Mutual Insurance Company, proposals which he made to the church congress led to the formation of the first clergy pension scheme and to the creation of a society for ecclesiastical fire insurance. In 1889 he became vicar of St James-the-Less, Vauxhall Bridge Road, in a poor district of London. He was a capable parish organizer and there he enlarged the schools and built a parish hall and a vicarage.

Blackley died, after a brief illness, at his home, 79 St George's Square, London, on 25 July 1902. Brasses were put up to his memory in the churches of St James-the-Less, North Waltham, and Frensham. His publications, in addition to those already mentioned, included: *The Frithiof Saga, or, Lay of Frithiof*, a translation from the Swedish of Esaia Tegner (1857; New York edn, 1867; illustrated edn, 1880); with Dr Friedlander, *A Practical Dictionary of the German and English Languages* (1866; pocket edn, 1876); and *Word Gossip* (1869), a series of popular essays on words and their peculiarities. He was also joint editor, with James Hawes, of the *Critical English Testament* (3 vols., 1866). His *Collected Essays* (1880) was reissued in 1906 under the title *Thrift and National Insurance as a Security Against Pauperism*, with a preface by his widow.

W. B. OWEN, *rev.* PAT THANE

Sources P. M. Williams, 'The development of old age pensions policy in Great Britain, 1878–1925', PhD diss., London School of Economics, 1970 · W. L. Blackley, *Thrift and national insurance as a security against pauperism* (1906) [memoirs in preface and first section] · *The Times* (26 July 1902)
Likenesses photograph, pubd 1891, NPG [*see illus.*]
Wealth at death £10,339 18s. 6d.: probate, 17 Sept 1902, CGPLA Eng. & Wales

Blacklo, Thomas. *See* White, Thomas (1592/3–1676).

Blacklock, Thomas (1721–1791), poet and writer, was born on 10 November 1721 in Annan, Dumfriesshire, the son of John Blacklock (*d.* 1740), a bricklayer from Cumberland, and his wife, Ann, the daughter of Richard Rae, a cattle dealer. In early infancy Blacklock lost his sight owing to smallpox. Despite this misfortune the attentions of his father and friends engendered in him an interest in languages and literature, particularly poetry. In 1740 his father was killed while trying to repair a malt kiln. Richard Hewitt, a young boy from Rockcliff in Cumberland, then came to be educated and to attend Thomas as his guide and reader.

John Stevenson, an Edinburgh physician, became

Thomas Blacklock (1721–1791), by William Bonnar

Blacklock's benefactor and enabled him to attend a grammar school in Edinburgh. Because of the Jacobite rising of 1745 Blacklock returned to Dumfries to live with his sister and her husband. Blacklock's first book, *Poems on Several Occasions*, was published in Glasgow in 1746: the poems ranged from one written before he was twelve to two odes about the disturbances. This book was reprinted with a life by Gilbert Gordon after Blacklock resumed his studies at the University of Edinburgh. He studied philosophy and then divinity, and continued his interest in languages including French, Greek, Latin, and Italian.

David Hume exhorted his friends and acquaintances to support Blacklock by purchasing his *Poems*. In 1754, in order to retain his position as keeper of the Faculty of Advocates library, Hume used the tactic of a token transfer of his salary to Blacklock.

Joseph Spence, prebendary at Durham, wrote a short life of Blacklock which was attached to a reprint of the 1754 edition of the *Poems*. Spence attempted an analysis of Blacklock's treatment of visible objects, and after Spence met Blacklock the account was amended for publication with an expanded edition of the *Poems* (1756). Spence made great efforts to ensure that the publication was supported by a long and prestigious list of subscribers.

In 1759, after Blacklock abandoned his hopes of lecturing in the University of Edinburgh, he was licensed to preach by the presbytery of Dumfries. In 1760 the earl of Selkirk proposed to place him as minister of the church at Kirkcudbright but the parishioners were resistant to church patronage and judged that Blacklock's blindness made him unfit to be their spiritual leader. Legal opinion was sought and the case aroused interest throughout the country. There were many delays before he was ordained on 22 April 1762. On 4 April Blacklock had married Sarah Johnston (1732–1808), daughter of a Dumfries surgeon. At his ordination Blacklock had to make his way through jeering crowds. The stress of the occasion was such that later in the day he appeared to be in a state of altered consciousness. The disputations continued and the kirk session refused to work with him. A local man even threatened to kill him. Eventually an agreement was reached whereby, in return for an annuity, Blacklock demitted the charge in 1765.

Blacklock and his wife then moved to Edinburgh and established a boarding-house for young gentlemen studying at the university or associated with the Royal College of Physicians of Edinburgh. Young men from Europe and America as well as from the British Isles boarded and studied with Blacklock and also on occasion acted as his amanuensis. Several students later achieved eminence and kept in touch with the man who had influenced their careers. When Samuel Johnson met Blacklock the two men compared the difficulties and enjoyment of compiling a dictionary with those experienced when writing poetry. The discussion was noted by James Boswell, but led to a request by Blacklock that the account be corrected. Although Blacklock's comment was acknowledged in a later publication, Boswell maintained that a written record was superior to one of memory (Boswell). Blacklock was also acquainted with the young Walter Scott, who appreciated his guidance and made use of his library.

Blacklock produced *An Essay on Universal Etymology* (1756), where the general principles of grammar and the definitions of the parts of speech were given in verse followed by illustrative notes in prose. In 1760 and 1762 Blacklock's work was published in the two-volume *A Collection of Original Poems. By the Rev. Mr Blacklock and other Scotch Gentlemen*. Blacklock was highly respected and his literary opinion was sought by his contemporaries. Throughout his life he produced poems, reviews, articles, sermons, translations, and other prose works. His writings were to be found in journals such as the *Edinburgh Magazine and Review*. Blacklock was encouraged to express his support of James Beattie's criticism of Hume's writings (*Edinburgh Courant*, 1770). In 1781 a small collection of pieces of scripture in verse-form 'to be sung in churches' was approved by the general assembly of the Church of Scotland. An amended version of Blacklock's paraphrase of part of Ecclesiastes 12 was included. His work also included an extensive and detailed article on blindness for the second edition of the *Encyclopaedia Britannica* (1783). Blacklock occasionally wrote satirical verses but usually consigned them to the flames soon after their composition. 'Pistapolis', an astonishing poetic diatribe lampooning those in Kirkcudbright who had rejected him, survived but remained unpublished until 1907.

In 1767, on the recommendation of James Beattie, Blacklock was awarded an honorary DD by Marischal College, Aberdeen. By 1768 he had communicated to Beattie his intention of compiling a collection of Scottish music and poetry with a view to publication. In October 1779 his (more general) 'Discourse on national musick' appeared in the *Scots Magazine*. Although Blacklock rarely wrote in the Scots vernacular he did not follow the fashion that it should be disregarded, and when he became aware of the poems of Robert Burns he indicated his wish to subscribe for their first publication. After receiving a copy of the 'Kilmarnock Edition' of Burns's poems he advised Burns that he should come to Edinburgh and produce a second enlarged edition. This advice from someone of Blacklock's literary standing resulted (according to Burns himself) in Burns's abandoning his planned journey to Jamaica. Blacklock introduced Burns to many influential people and was active in winning support for an Edinburgh edition of Burns's poems. Burns soon began to collaborate with Blacklock, Beattie, and William Tytler of Woodehouselee in their project to collect the songs and music of Scotland (published by James Johnson as *The Scots Musical Museum*, 6 vols., 1787–1803).

Blacklock was an accomplished musician and composer, and advocated that blind children should learn music precisely rather than play by ear. He made recommendations about the manner of treatment and the means of education of blind children and adults, and applied his mind to the invention of techniques and devices for the education of the blind. When Blacklock became aware of the new methods of educating blind children being developed in Paris by M. Haüy at the Institut des Jeunes Aveugles he requested a sample of the raised type used to help the children to print and learn to read. Although communication between the countries was disrupted by the onset of the French Revolution, Blacklock received a copy of the book containing the raised text and began translating it into English as *An Essay on the Education of the Blind*. Blacklock determined that an institution similar to that in Paris should be set up in Edinburgh so that blind children and adults could be educated and earn their living with dignity. Blacklock died at his home in Chapel Street, Edinburgh, on 7 July 1791, after contracting a fever. He was buried in the churchyard of St Cuthbert's Chapel of Ease, Edinburgh, on 11 July. His ambition to establish an institution to educate blind people was realized through the efforts of his friend David Miller (also blind) and the Revd David Johnston. The Society for the Relief of the Indigent Blind was established in 1793, two years after the first such institution in Britain had been formed in Liverpool.

Editions of Blacklock's work continued to be published after his death and in 1793 a new edition of his *Poems* was published together with *An Essay on the Education of the Blind* and a life by Henry Mackenzie. Many of Blacklock's sermons remain in manuscript form.

EUNICE MCALPINE SMITH

Sources T. Blacklock, *Poems on several occasions, to which is prefix'd, an account of the life, character, and writings, of the author, by the Reverend Mr Spence* (1756) • F. Miller, *A bibliography of the parish of Annan* (1925), 11–15 • T. Blacklock, *Poems by the late Reverend Dr. Thomas Blacklock; together with an essay on the education of the blind, to which is*

prefixed a new account of the life and writings of the author (1793) ·
J. Robison, 'Bi-centenary of Dr. Thomas Blacklock', *Transactions of
the Dumfriesshire and Galloway Natural History and Antiquarian Society*,
3 (1934–5), 205–11 · C. Rodgers, *The book of Robert Burns: genealogical
and historical memoirs*, 3 vols., Grampian Club (1889) · H. Duncan,
'Blacklock, Thomas', *Edinburgh Encyclopaedia*, ed. D. Brewster (1811),
560–63 · W. Forbes, *An account of the life and writings of James Beattie*, 2
vols. (1806) · *The letters of David Hume*, ed. J. Y. T. Greig, 2 vols. (1932) ·
Memoirs of the life, writings, and correspondence of William Smellie, ed.
R. Kerr (1996) [with a new introduction by R. B. Sher] · J. Boswell,
The life of Samuel Johnson, ed. P. Fitzgerald, new edn, 3 (1888), 494–6 ·
T. Blacklock, 'Blind', *Encyclopaedia Britannica*, 2nd edn, 2 (1778–83),
1188–1204 · *The papers of Benjamin Franklin*, ed. L. W. Labaree, 12
(1968), 197–8 · chapel record book, St Cuthbert's Chapel of Ease,
parish of St Cuthbert's, Edinburgh, 1791 · OPR index (marriage),
parish of Dumfries, 1762, 821/5, p. 175 · *Williamson's directory for the
city of Edinburgh, Canongate, Leith and suburbs* [several vols. covering
1773–90]
Archives BL, corresp., Add. MS 21509, fol. 44 · Burns Museum,
Alloway, Ayrshire, corresp. · Royal Blind Asylum and School, Edinburgh · Society of Antiquaries, Edinburgh, corresp. · U. Edin. L.,
lecture notes · V&A | Birm. CA, facsimile of Dodsley letter-book ·
Bodl. Oxf., corresp. · Broughton House, Kirkcudbright, MSS collection · Dalhousie University, James Dinwiddie fonds, MS-2-
726 · Ewart Library, Dumfries, Frank Miller collection · Kirkcud-
bright Museum, Town Council Minutes · NL Scot., Fettercairn
MSS, corresp. with James Beattie · Savings Banks Museum, Ruth-
well, Dumfriesshire, Duncan archive · U. Aberdeen, corresp. with
James Beattie · U. Edin. L., diary of Benjamin Rush [microfilm] ·
U. Nott. L., corresp. of Joseph Spence · Yale U., Beinecke L., James
Marshall and Marie-Louise Osborn Collection, corresp. with
J. Spence · Yale U., Beinecke L., Boswell MSS, corresp. · Kilravock,
Inverness-shire, corresp. with David Hume
Likenesses J. Edgar, wash drawing, *c*.1854, Burns' Club, Irvine ·
W. Bonnar, oil on millboard (after engraving by W. & F. Holl), Scot.
NPG · W. Bonnar, oils, Scot. NPG [*see illus.*] · W. & F. Holl, stipple
(after oils by W. Bonnar), NPG · W. & F. Holl, stipple engraving
(after unknown portrait), repro. in J. Wilson and R. Chalmers, *The
land of Burns*, 2 vols. (1840), coverplate · wash drawing, Scot. NPG

Blacklock, William James (1816–1858), landscape painter
and lithographer, was born on 3 March 1816 in Shoreditch,
London, the second of the five children of James Blacklock (1782–1823), bookseller and publisher, and Mary Ann
Pearson (1784–1853). In 1818 the family moved to Cumwhitton, Cumberland, where the Blacklock family had
been farmers and property owners since the 1730s. James
Blacklock was a friend of Charles Thurnam, a publisher,
bookseller, and printer in nearby Carlisle, and William
was apprenticed under him as a boy along with George
Routledge, the future London publisher. In 1833 William
first exhibited at the decade-old Academy of Art, Carlisle,
and was described as a 'rising artist' with a 'feeling for
nature and a correctness of taste' (*Carlisle Journal*, 2 Nov
1833). In 1836 he moved to London and first exhibited four
pictures at the Royal Academy of Arts. J. Robinson of London published a series of his engraved views of the new
Newcastle–Carlisle railway in 1838, as well as *Sketches in
Norway* in 1841 with Blacklock's engravings after studies
by Bruce Skinner. Blacklock showed thirty-six pictures at
the Royal Academy, four at the British Institution, and
eleven at the Society of British Artists from 1836 to 1855.
Garnering the praise of the contemporary landscapists
J. M. W. Turner, David Roberts, and Thomas Creswick, he
developed a picturesque style likened by contemporaries

to the works of William Mulready, and gained the patronage of William Gladstone, who bought *Lanercost Abbey* in
1847. In the same year Blacklock's *Calder Abbey* was
selected by a prize-holder in the London Art Union. The
Scottish artist and head of the Newcastle School of Art,
William Bell Scott (1811–1890), introduced him to the
important Tyneside lead manufacturer and art collector
James Leathart (1820–1895), who bought several paintings
in the 1850s and brought Blacklock to the notice of the
industrialist and collector William Armstrong (1810–
1900). In 1850 Blacklock moved back to Cumwhitton
owing to ill health and failing eyesight, establishing a studio at Stanwix. By this time he was regarded as '*the* painter
of Cumberland' and more specifically 'the painter *par
excellence* of lake and mountain scenery, border tower and
heath-clad waste' (*Carlisle Journal*, 21 Feb 1851, 23 June
1855). By late 1854 Blacklock's career had become seriously threatened by illness and loss of vision in one eye,
and in the next year he gave up work and his youngest
brother, Thomas, consigned him to the Crichton Institution in Dumfries. According to medical records, he died
there on 12 March 1858 of general paralysis of the insane,
or syphilis, after much mental deterioration; he was buried on 16 March at Cumwhitton. The *Art Journal* obituary
described him as a 'truthful and unpretending artist, who
wooed nature rather than popular favour' (*Art Journal*, 1
May 1858). Over thirty oils and watercolours are in the
Tullie House Museum and Art Gallery, Carlisle. There are
works in the British Museum, the Victoria and Albert
Museum, and the National Gallery of Ireland; drawings
executed while in the Crichton Institution are at Edinburgh University Library.   JASON ROSENFELD

Sources private information (2004) [J. E. B. Lee] · *Glasgow Evening
News* (25 July 1900) · *Art Journal*, 20 (1858), 157 · G. Grigson, 'A
painter of the real Lakeland', *Country Life*, 156 (1974), 24–6 · *Carlisle
Journal* (2 Nov 1833) · *Carlisle Journal* (9 Nov 1833) · *Carlisle Journal* (14
Dec 1844) · *Carlisle Journal* (11 Sept 1847) · *Carlisle Journal* (9 June
1848) · *Carlisle Journal* (17 Nov 1848) · *Carlisle Journal* (21 Feb 1851) ·
Carlisle Journal (21 May 1852) · *Carlisle Journal* (23 June 1855) · *Carlisle
Journal* (19 March 1858) · *Carlisle Journal* (23 April 1858) · archives,
Tullie House Museum and Art Gallery, Carlisle · D. Child, *Painters in
the northern counties of England and Wales* (1994) · Wood, *Vic. painters*,
3rd edn · Marshall Hall Association, *Artists of Cumbria* (1979) · *Cumberland artists, 1700–1900* (1971) [exhibition catalogue, Carlisle City
Art Gallery, 1971] · L. Binyon, *Catalogue of drawings by British artists
and artists of foreign origin working in Great Britain*, 4 vols. (1898–1907),
vol. 1, p. 123 · Redgrave, *Artists* · S. H. Pavière, *A dictionary of Victorian
landscape painters* (1968) · M. H. Grant, *A dictionary of British landscape
painters, from the 16th century to the early 20th century* (1952) · Graves,
RA exhibitors · J. Johnson, ed., *Works exhibited at the Royal Society of
British Artists, 1824–1893, and the New English Art Club, 1888–1917*, 2
vols. (1975) · *DNB* · E. Kilmurray, *Dictionary of British portraiture*, 3
(1981) · medical records, Crichton Institution, Dumfries · parish
register, 1816, Shoreditch, St Leonard
Archives priv. coll., works, letters, documents, John Edward
Blacklock Lee collection · St Deiniol's Library, Hawarden · Tullie
House Museum and Art Gallery, Carlisle · U. Edin. | University of
British Columbia, Leathart letters collection
Likenesses T. H. Carrick, watercolour on marble miniature,
Tullie House Museum and Art Gallery, Carlisle · T. Heathfield,
watercolour on marble miniature, Carlisle City Art Gallery
Wealth at death under £200: administration, 3 June 1858, *CGPLA
Eng. & Wales*

Blackman, Frederick Frost (1866–1947), plant physiologist, was born at Lambeth, London, on 25 July 1866, the eldest son and third child of Frederick Blackman, surgeon, and his wife, Catherine Elizabeth Frost. Interested in plants from an early age, he started a herbarium during his schooldays at Mill Hill. However, on leaving school in 1883 he began medical studies at St Bartholomew's Hospital. He graduated BSc (London) in 1885 while still at the hospital, and became so interested in the chemistry of vital processes that in 1887 he abandoned medicine and went to read science at St John's College, Cambridge. There he was placed in the first class of both parts of the natural sciences tripos (1889, 1891). This success was repeated by two of his brothers who followed him to St John's, one of whom, Vernon Herbert *Blackman (1872–1967), became professor of plant physiology at Imperial College. In 1891 Blackman was appointed to a demonstratorship in the Cambridge botany school, becoming lecturer in 1897 and reader in 1904; he remained there until his retirement in 1936. In 1917 he married Elsie Chick, daughter of Samuel Chick, and sister of the physiologist Dame Harriette Chick (1875–1977). The couple later had a son.

Blackman's chief published contributions, which are few in number, are in two series of papers. The first series, entitled Experimental Researches in Vegetable Assimilation and Respiration, began in 1895; the second, Analytical Studies in Plant Respiration, in 1928.

Blackman's first paper described an elaborate apparatus for determining simply and precisely the amount of carbon dioxide in small samples of a gaseous mixture such as air. With this he was able to show conclusively, for the first time, that the bulk of the exchange of carbon dioxide between foliage and the air was via the stomata. In 1904 his student Miss G. L. C. Matthaei showed that at high intensities of illumination the rate of photosynthesis is determined by chemical (now called 'Blackman') and not by photochemical reactions. In April 1905 his seminal paper 'Optima and limiting factors' appeared in *Annals of Botany*. It revealed Blackman as a pioneer in the application of physico-chemical ideas to biological problems while still realizing that, although research might show how far the recorded optima are metabolic truths rather than artefacts of experimentation, physico-chemical finality was unlikely to be achieved. Blackman's belief that vital phenomena were amenable to physico-chemical analysis was advanced more boldly in his presidential address to the botany section at the meeting of the British Association in 1908. He pleaded for a dynamic general physiology of plants in terms of reaction velocity, complaining that the prevalent view, 'that every change in which protoplasm takes part is a case of *reaction of an irritable living substance to a stimulus*' overflowed its 'legitimate bounds and swamped the development of physical-chemical concepts' (Briggs, *Obits. FRS*, 656).

As reader in botany from 1906, Blackman built up a vigorous school of research. This was partly due to his teaching, which attracted many to the subject, and partly due to his ability to inspire those working under his guidance.

From 1918 onwards the work of Blackman's many research students was focused on the application of his dynamic approach to problems connected with respiration in plants. Thus, in 1928 he presented to the Royal Society results of experiments on the effect of change in the partial pressure of oxygen. He advanced the view that the products of glycolysis were used for the formation of carbohydrates at a rate which was reduced by lowering the supply of oxygen, by a process he called oxidative anabolism. In these experiments Blackman showed his ability to organize a complicated set of data and to produce a plausible interpretation of all the quantitative variations. This interpretation was considerably expanded in his last paper, which was published after his death with the assistance of J. Baker, another of his research students.

Blackman made contributions to other aspects of life in Cambridge. He helped greatly in the administration of the botany school and in planning its extension in 1933 (which came too late for him to be appointed first professor of plant physiology). Among his services to the university was his long membership of the Fitzwilliam Museum syndicate. Reflecting his interest in the design of apparatus, so crucial to his experiments, he was a member of the board of the Cambridge Instrument Company from 1901 to 1936. He was much involved with St John's College, of which he became a fellow in 1895, where he lived as a bachelor until 1917, and which he served as steward from 1908 to 1914. His contributions often arose from his breadth of outlook; he combined a critical and candid intelligence with wide-ranging interests which included the arts as well as the sciences.

Blackman was elected FRS in 1906, was awarded a royal medal in 1921, and was Croonian lecturer in 1923. He died at his home, Upper Cross, Storey's Way, Cambridge, on 30 January 1947; he was survived by his wife.

G. E. BRIGGS, *rev.* PAOLO PALLADINO

Sources G. E. Briggs, *Obits. FRS*, 5 (1945–8), 651–8 · G. E. Briggs, 'Blackman, Frederick Frost', *DSB* · B. Thomason, 'The new botany in Britain, 1870–1914', PhD diss., University of Manchester, 1987 · *WWW* · Venn, *Alum. Cant.* · *CGPLA Eng. & Wales* (1947)
Archives BL | BL, corresp. with Sir Sydney Cockerell, Add. MS 52707
Likenesses F. A. de Biden Footner, 1924, priv. coll. · H. Lamb, oils, 1937, U. Cam., department of botany · D. G. Lillie, double portrait, caricature, watercolour (with Sir Arthur Tansley), NPG
Wealth at death £53,284 2s. 3d.: probate, 9 Aug 1947, *CGPLA Eng. & Wales*

Blackman, Geoffrey Emett (1903–1980), agricultural scientist, was born on 17 April 1903 at 58 Scarsdale Villas, Kensington, London. He was the eldest of the three children of the cytologist and plant physiologist Vernon Herbert *Blackman (1872–1967), then an assistant in the British Museum (Natural History), and Edith Delta (1876/7–1940), daughter of Joseph and Rebecca Ann Emett of Mangotsfield, Gloucestershire. Blackman began his schooling in Leeds, where his father was professor of botany from 1907. Following his father's return to London as professor of plant physiology and pathology at Imperial College, he attended King's College School, Wimbledon, before entering St John's College, Cambridge. Blackman graduated second class in both parts of the natural sciences tripos (1924 and 1926). He was also a good sportsman, a jazz fan, and president of the dance club.

Blackman's interest in biology started very early. He grew up surrounded by renowned biologists including his uncle Frederick Frost *Blackman (1866–1947), his aunt Dame Harriette *Chick (1875–1977), and Sir Arthur *Tansley (1871–1955), a close friend of the family. In Cambridge he became interested in the applications of mathematical statistics to biological problems through his teacher G. E. Briggs. This interest was furthered in 1926 during Blackman's five months as a student worker in the Rothamsted Experimental Station under Ronald Fisher and Bernard Keen, studying the effects of fertilizers on plant growth in the field laboratory. His father, considering his performance in Cambridge poor, then advised Blackman to go into industry rather than try to follow an academic career. Thus, in 1927, he joined Imperial Chemical Industries (ICI). There he worked under Frederick Keeble, director of the agricultural research station at Jealott's Hill. Blackman eventually headed the station's botany section, working in particular on the effects of fertilizers and poisonous substances on the ecological interactions between different plant species, thereby laying the foundations of the study of selective herbicides. Some of this work was publicized in articles in the *Gardeners' Chronicle*. Blackman later became an assistant scientific editor of the *Chronicle*.

On 8 October 1931 Blackman married Audrey Babette Seligman (*b.* 1906/7), sculptress, with whom he shared many interests, including the collection of British watercolour paintings. She was the daughter of Richard Joseph Simon Seligman, chemical engineer and director of APV Ltd, manufacturers of machinery for the food trade, on whose board Blackman sat from 1930. They had no children.

During his time at ICI Blackman developed his hobby of gardening, in which he became a great expert—well known for his gardens on acid soils. He also became passionately fond of mountains and winter sports, making regular visits to the Alps until he was over seventy.

During the first half of the 1930s Blackman grew increasingly frustrated with routine testing at ICI, and with the secrecy surrounding the composition of the compounds involved, which, he argued, kept him from designing satisfactory experiments. He sought employment elsewhere, and in 1935 was appointed to a lectureship in the department of biology at Imperial College, then still headed by his father. While the department was very interested in the agricultural applications of its work, Blackman was very sensitive about having started his scientific career in industry, and, therefore, turned his attention increasingly to ecological experiments in natural habitats. However, the time spent in Rothamsted and at Jealott's Hill left its mark. The statistical methods he and A. J. Rutter deployed in their work on the autecology of the bluebell and on the dispersion of plants were pioneering, as was their application to native vegetation of techniques of plant growth analysis then being used by agricultural scientists in Cambridge and Rothamsted. Significantly, Blackman remained uninterested in experimental work on the mechanisms of photosynthesis, nutrient absorption, and intermediate metabolism, which his colleagues believed to be fundamentally important to understand plant growth.

Blackman's agricultural work before moving to Imperial College also facilitated his efforts to establish a role for biologists in the war effort. He was centrally involved in moving the Association of Applied Biologists, the Society of Experimental Biology, and the British Ecological Society to support the establishment of the biology war committee, of which he was the secretary from 1942 to 1946. He also supervised research under the aegis of the Agricultural Research Council on many agricultural problems, including the possible use of selective herbicides, and the introduction of new crops such as oilseed rape, maize, and flax to compensate for lost imports. His involvement with the war effort also cemented his friendship with Sir Henry Tizard who, after being elected president of Magdalen College, Oxford, was instrumental in persuading Blackman to apply for an Oxford chair.

Appointed to the Sibthorpian chair in rural economy in 1945, Blackman was quick to change the emphasis of the department. This was reflected in its name which he changed first to the department of agriculture and subsequently to the department of agricultural science. Teaching and research changed in line with this transformation to reflect the needs of students less interested in becoming farm managers than in embarking on a scientific career. By 1950 the team of collaborators Blackman had drawn together during the war was unified in the Agricultural Research Council unit of agronomy, and was engaged in important research on the physiology of plant hormones and plant growth, the kind of work he had disdained at Imperial College. Blackman's persistent reservations about scientific work in industry, together with criticism from colleagues in Oxford, also resulted in a determined avoidance of any close relationship with the agricultural industry. Some members of the unit who disagreed with these developments eventually succeeded in 1960 in establishing, under the aegis of the Agricultural Research Council, a separate Weed Research Organization at Letcombe.

During the 1950s Blackman became less actively involved in research and more interested in the wider activities of both St John's College and the university, particularly the management of the university parks and the university botanic garden. He also expanded his advisory and administrative activities outside Oxford; these included supervision of the organization of the Malaysian Rubber Research Institute and chairing the section on production and processes of the International Biological Programme. He retired from his professorship in 1970 and was invited to join the committee set up by the United States National Academy of Sciences to report to Congress on the controversial use of herbicides in Vietnam for military purposes. In spite of his age and the dangers involved he took a very active part in the committee's surveys, and was only disappointed that there was no support for more detailed investigations of the herbicides' effects.

Blackman was elected to the Royal Society in 1959, and served on its council and as vice-president (1967–8). He was elected to the Royal Swedish Academy of Agriculture (1963), to an honorary fellowship of Imperial College (1968), and as honorary councillor of the Superior Scientific Circle of Spain (1968). An annual Blackman lecture, at Oxford, was created in his honour. Blackman died at 29 Norman Avenue, Abingdon, on 8 February 1980 after a short illness. He was survived by his wife.

J. L. HARLEY, *rev.* PAOLO PALLADINO

Sources J. L. Harley, *Memoirs FRS*, 27 (1981), 45–82 · *The Times* (12 Feb 1980) · *The Times* (16 Feb 1980) · private information (1981) · personal knowledge (1981) · b. cert. · m. cert. · d. cert. · d. cert. [Vernon Herbert Blackman] · m. cert. [Edith Delta Blackman] · 'Blackman, Vernon Herbert', *DNB*
Archives Bodl. Oxf., corresp. and papers
Wealth at death £114,599: probate, 12 May 1980, *CGPLA Eng. & Wales*

Blackman, Vernon Herbert (1872–1967), cytologist and plant physiologist, was born on 8 January 1872 at 4 York Road, Lambeth, London. He was the sixth child and third son in a family of ten. His father, Frederick Blackman, was a medical practitioner, and his mother, Catherine Elizabeth, was the daughter of Charles Maynard Frost, medical superintendent of Portland prison. His eldest brother was Frederick Frost *Blackman (1866–1947).

In 1889, having attended the City of London and King's College schools, Blackman entered St Bartholomew's Hospital medical school, as his father and older brothers had done before him. The pre-clinical courses stimulated his interest in biological sciences and so, in 1892, again following the example of his brothers, he interrupted his medical studies and went to read botany at St John's College, Cambridge.

In late nineteenth-century Britain the established members of the botanical profession remained largely absorbed by classification of plants. However, in Germany botanists had already begun to investigate the mechanisms by which plants grow, both as communities and as individuals. From the 1860s onwards Ernst Haeckel began to develop ecological concepts, while Julius von Sachs and others investigated the internal physiology of the plant. By the 1890s these new ideas had spread to Cambridge, and so, although much of his botanical training there was taxonomic, Blackman received a course of lectures on physiology from Francis Darwin and was able to familiarize himself with the latest German work in cytology and plant physiology. Moreover, his elder brother, Frederick, with whom he shared rooms in St John's College, had been appointed to a demonstratorship in the botany school in 1891 and by 1895 had begun work on respiration in plants. Blackman began his own investigation into the process of fertilization in *Pinus sylvestris* while still an undergraduate. Having obtained first classes in both parts of the tripos he graduated in 1895 and then spent a year in

Vernon Herbert Blackman (1872–1967), by Walter Stoneman, 1944

Strasburger's laboratory in Bonn, presumably extending his work on fertilization. Strasburger was one of the leading cytologists of the time, but also worked extensively on the processes of water transportation in plants.

Through his acquaintances in both Cambridge and Bonn Blackman was in contact with the latest work on physiology, but for fifteen years after his return from Germany in 1896 his research interests were dominated by cytology. In 1896 he was appointed to an assistantship at the British Museum (Natural History), where he was responsible for the fungal collections. After publishing his first article, 'On the cytological features of fertilization and related phenomena in *Pinus sylvestris*', in 1898, he concentrated on work with fungi, and especially on the alternation of generations in the rust fungi. When his friend A. G. Tansley became editor of the newly established *New Phytologist* Blackman was a frequent contributor of notes and reviews. He also taught in the University of London from time to time; his lectures included a course on vegetable physiology at University College. In the course of his work at the museum Blackman also met his future wife, Edith Delta Emett (1876/7–1940), who was employed to make wax models of plants and animals. They were married on 6 June 1901. She was the daughter of Joseph Emett, an accountant.

The keeper of botany under whom Blackman had originally been employed at the museum had not objected to his spending much of his time on research, but his successor, Alfred Rendle, took a different view. Blackman began to look for another post, and in 1907 became the first professor of botany at the University of Leeds. It was a small department, and he seems to have initiated little research while he held the chair. However, it was during his time at Leeds that he came to the conclusion that progress in elucidating the internal workings of the plant would depend upon chemical explanations, and that he could make no further progress with cytological methods. Consequently he turned to physiology, and in 1911 returned to London as the first professor of plant physiology and pathology at the Imperial College of Science and Technology. Nevertheless it was his cytological work which had established Blackman as a leading figure in British botany, and which was largely responsible for his election as FRS in 1913.

Blackman's return to London signalled the beginning of a new phase in his researches—into practical rather than theoretical problems. Blackman was one of the first scientists to benefit from the decision to use public money for scientific research—especially research likely to benefit agriculture. The decision led to the establishment of several research institutes including the Institute of Plant Physiology, which was set up at Imperial College under Blackman's direction. Increasingly interested in plant growth, in 1919 Blackman made his greatest individual contribution to the field with a paper published in the *Annals of Botany*, which compared plant growth to the rate of interest earned by a business. He argued that the important figure was the increase in weight per existing unit of weight per unit of time. This he called the efficiency index, which represented the efficiency of the plant as a producer of new material. This concept, later termed the relative growth rate, was basic to plant growth analysis, and much subsequent work in Blackman's department during the 1920s and 1930s was concerned with fitting mathematical functions to experimental data.

In the inter-war years Blackman's main role was to facilitate and guide the work of a large and successful group as the funds available for research increased. He was head of Imperial College's botany department from 1929. His department and research institute had connections with other establishments, and so he was also involved in studies of plant nutrition at Rothamsted, and of chemical changes in stored apples with the fruit research station at East Malling, Kent. During this period Blackman served on a number of committees, including the advisory council of the Department of Scientific and Industrial Research, the board of the National Fruit and Cider Institute, the Water Pollution Board, the board of the Forest Products Research Station, and the governing bodies of Rothamsted Experimental Station, the John Innes Horticultural Institution, and East Malling Research Station. He was also on the first editorial board of the *Biochemical Journal*, and for twenty-five years (1922–47) edited the *Annals of Botany*.

In 1937 Blackman retired as head of the botany department and visited India, where he received honorary degrees from the universities of Allahabad and Benares. He continued in charge of the research institute at Imperial College until 1942, and as late as 1951 was the joint author of a paper in the *Annals of Botany*. His connection with the East Malling Research Station was severed only in 1960 when he was eighty-eight, and his work there was commemorated by a portrait and the Blackman scholarship for applied botany.

Portraits of Blackman reveal a lean featured and heavily moustached face, and he was said to be a fastidious, neat, courteous, and perhaps rather shy man, well known for his insistence on clarity of expression and grammatical accuracy in scientific writing. This was an interest he carried with him into retirement: he became involved with the English Association, and acted as its treasurer between 1953 and 1959.

Blackman's first wife, Edith, died in 1940. They had a daughter and two sons, the elder of whom, Geoffrey Emett *Blackman, also became a plant physiologist. On 29 December 1941 Blackman married Thérèse Elizabeth (b. 1904/5), daughter of Sydney Glyde Stephen Panisset, a director of chemical research. She was initially one of his students, and later his secretary. She cared for him over the last quarter century of his life at their home, 17 Berkeley Place, Wimbledon, London, a house in which he lived for over fifty years. He died on 1 October 1967 at 48 Murray Road, Wimbledon, and was cremated. He was survived by his second wife.   PAUL BRASSLEY

Sources H. K. Porter, *Memoirs FRS*, 14 (1968), 37–60 · *DNB* · W. Brown, 'Vernon Herbert Blackman', *Annals of Botany*, new ser., 32 (1968), 233–5 · R. Hunt, *Plant growth curves* (1982) · b. cert. · m. certs. · d. cert. · *The Times* (3 Oct 1967) · V. H. Blackman, 'The compound interest law and plant growth', *Annals of Botany*, 33 (1919), 353–60

Likenesses W. Stoneman, photograph, 1944, NPG [*see illus.*] · A. Blackman, bronze bust, 1953, ICL · R. Lewis, portrait, 1957, East Malling Research Station, West Malling, Kent; repro. in Brown, 'Vernon Herbert Blackman', 233 · photograph, repro. in Porter, *Memoirs FRS*

Wealth at death £43,623: probate, 1 Jan 1968, *CGPLA Eng. & Wales*

PICTURE CREDITS

Belle, Dido Elizabeth (*b. c.*1763, *d.* in or after 1794)—from the collection of the Earl of Mansfield, Scone Palace, Perth

Bellingham, John (1770–1812)—© National Portrait Gallery, London

Bellman, Sir (Charles) Harold (1886–1963)—© National Portrait Gallery, London

Belloc, (Joseph) Hilaire Pierre René (1870–1953)—© National Portrait Gallery, London

Bellows, John Thomas (1831–1902)—© National Portrait Gallery, London

Beloff, Max, Baron Beloff (1913–1999)—Getty Images – Sydney O'Meara

Belsham, Thomas (1750–1829)—by permission of Dr Williams's Library

Belzoni, Giovanni Battista (1778–1823)—© National Portrait Gallery, London

Benbow, John (1653?–1702)—National Maritime Museum, London; photograph National Portrait Gallery, London

Benedict, Sir Julius (1804–1885)—© National Portrait Gallery, London

Benett, Etheldred (1775–1845)—Norwich Castle Museum & Art Gallery

Benjamin, Arthur Leslie (1893–1960)—© National Portrait Gallery, London

Benjamin, (Thomas) Brooke (1929–1995)—© The Royal Society

Benlowes, Edward (1602–1676)—© National Portrait Gallery, London

Benn, Sir Ernest John Pickstone, second baronet (1875–1954)—Witt Library, Courtauld Institute of Art, London

Benn, Sir John Williams, first baronet (1850–1922)—Guildhall Art Gallery, Corporation of London

Benn, William Wedgwood, first Viscount Stansgate (1877–1960)—© National Portrait Gallery, London

Bennelong (*c.*1765–1813)—by permission of the National Library of Australia / The Rex Nan Kivell Collection NK3946

Bennet, Henry, first earl of Arlington (*bap.* 1618, *d.* 1685)—private collection. Photograph: Photographic Survey, Courtauld Institute of Art, London

Bennett, Alfred Rosling (1850–1928)—© National Portrait Gallery, London

Bennett, (Enoch) Arnold (1867–1931)—© National Portrait Gallery, London

Bennett, Donald Clifford Tyndall (1910–1986)—© National Portrait Gallery, London

Bennett, George John (1800–1879)—© National Portrait Gallery, London

Bennett, George Macdonald (1892–1959)—Godfrey Argent Studios / Royal Society

Bennett, Jack Arthur Walter (1911–1981)—photograph reproduced by courtesy of The British Academy

Bennett, (Nora Noel) Jill (1929?–1990)—© Patrick Procktor

Bennett, Sir John (1814–1897)—© National Portrait Gallery, London

Bennett, Richard Bedford, Viscount Bennett (1870–1947)—© National Portrait Gallery, London

Bennett, William Henry (1855–1920)—© National Portrait Gallery, London

Bennett, William James Early (1804–1886)—Ashmolean Museum, Oxford

Bennett, Sir William Sterndale (1816–1875)—© National Portrait Gallery, London

Benson, Ada (1840–1882)—from the archives of Bedford High School; reproduced with permission

Benson, Arthur Christopher (1862–1925)—© Fitzwilliam Museum, University of Cambridge

Benson, Edward White (1829–1896)—reproduced by kind permission of His Grace the Archbishop of Canterbury and the Church Commissioners. Photograph: Photographic Survey, Courtauld Institute of Art, London

Benson, Sir Francis Robert (1858–1939)—© National Portrait Gallery, London

Benson, George (1699–1762)—by permission of Dr Williams's Library

Benson, Ivy (1913–1993)—V&A Images, The Victoria and Albert Museum; collection National Portrait Gallery, London

Benson, Joseph (1749–1821)—© National Portrait Gallery, London

Benson, Margaret Jane (1859–1936)—by permission of the Linnean Society of London

Benson, Martin (1689–1752)—unknown collection / Christie's; photograph National Portrait Gallery, London

Benson, Mary Eleanor (1863–1890)—© National Portrait Gallery, London

Benson, Robert Hugh (1871–1914)—© National Portrait Gallery, London

Benson, Samuel Herbert (1854–1914)—from The History of Advertising Trust Archive

Benson, Stella (1892–1933)—© Estate of C. J. Orde

Bent, Sir Thomas (1838–1909)—La Trobe Picture Collection, State Library of Victoria

Bentham, George (1800–1884)—by permission of the Linnean Society of London; photograph National Portrait Gallery, London

Bentham, Jeremy (1748–1832)—© National Portrait Gallery, London

Bentham, Samuel (1757–1831)—© National Portrait Gallery, London

Bentinck, Lord (William) George Frederic Cavendish-Scott- (1802–1848)—© National Portrait Gallery, London

Bentinck, Hans Willem, first earl of Portland (1649–1709)—© National Portrait Gallery, London

Bentinck, John Albert (1737–1775)—© National Maritime Museum, London

Bentinck, (William) John Cavendish-Scott- [Lord John Bentinck], fifth duke of Portland (1800–1879)—unknown collection; photograph Sotheby's Picture Library, London / National Portrait Gallery, London

Bentinck, Margaret Cavendish [Lady Margaret Cavendish Harley], duchess of Portland (1715–1785)—© National Portrait Gallery, London

Bentinck, Victor Frederick William Cavendish- [Bill Bentinck], ninth duke of Portland (1897–1990)—© National Portrait Gallery, London

Bentinck, William Henry Cavendish Cavendish-, third duke of Portland (1738–1809)—Bristol Museums and Art Gallery

Bentinck, Lord William Henry Cavendish- (1774–1839)—private collection

Bentine, Michael (1922–1996)—Rex Features

Bentley, Derek William (1933–1953)—Getty Images – Hulton Archive

Bentley, Edmund Clerihew (1875–1956)—© National Portrait Gallery, London

Bentley, Elizabeth (*bap.* 1767, *d.* 1839)—© National Portrait Gallery, London

Bentley, John Francis (1839–1902)—© National Portrait Gallery, London

Bentley, Nicolas Clerihew (1907–1978)—© National Portrait Gallery, London

Bentley, Richard (1662–1742)—The Master and Fellows, Trinity College, Cambridge

Bentley, Richard (1794–1871)—© National Portrait Gallery, London

Bentley, Walter Owen (1888–1971)—© reserved; collection Science & Society Picture Library; photograph National Portrait Gallery, London

Bentwich, Norman de Mattos (1883–1971)—© National Portrait Gallery, London

Beresford, Charles William de la Poer, Baron Beresford (1846–1919)—© National Portrait Gallery, London

Beresford, Jack (1899–1977)—Getty Images – Hulton Archive

Beresford, John (1738–1805)—© National Portrait Gallery, London

Beresford, Lord John George de la Poer (1773–1862)—private collection. Photograph: Photographic Survey, Courtauld Institute of Art, London

Beresford, Louisa Anne, marchioness of Waterford (1818–1891)—private collection. Photograph: Photographic Survey, Courtauld Institute of Art, London

Beresford, William Carr, Viscount Beresford (1768–1854)—V&A Images, The Victoria and Albert Museum

Berington, Joseph (1743–1827)—© National Portrait Gallery, London

Beriosova, Svetlana (1932–1998)—Corbis

Berkeley, George (1685–1753)—© National Portrait Gallery, London

Berkeley, Sir Lennox Randal Francis (1903–1989)—© National Portrait Gallery, London

Berkeley, Sir Robert (1584–1656)—© National Portrait Gallery, London

Berkeley, Sir William (1639–1666)—© National Maritime Museum, London, Greenwich Hospital Collection

Berlin, Sir Isaiah (1909–1997)—© Lucinda Douglas-Menzies; collection National Portrait Gallery, London

Berlin, Sven Paul (1911–1999)—© News International Newspapers Ltd

Berlioz, (Louis) Hector (1803–1869)—Getty Images – Hulton Archive

Bernal, (John) Desmond (1901–1971)—© Wolfgang Suschitzky / National Portrait Gallery, London

Bernard, Sir Francis, first baronet (1712–1779)—Christ Church, Oxford

Bernard, Mountague (1820–1882)—© National Portrait Gallery, London

Bernard, Richard (*bap.* 1568, *d.* 1641)—© National Portrait Gallery, London

Bernhardt, Sarah Henriette Rosine (1844–1923)—private collection

Berni, Aldo (1909–1997)—Bristol Evening Post

Bernstein, Sidney Lewis, Baron Bernstein (1899–1993)—© National Portrait Gallery, London

Berry, Sir Graham (1822–1904)—© National Portrait Gallery, London

Berry, Mary (1763–1852)—private collection. Photograph: Photographic Survey, Courtauld Institute of Art, London

Berry, Sidney Malcolm (1881–1961)—© National Portrait Gallery, London

Berthoud, Sir Eric Alfred (1900–1989)—© National Portrait Gallery, London

Bertie, Francis Leveson, first Viscount Bertie of Thame (1844–1919)—© Crown copyright in photograph: UK Government Art Collection

Bertie, Peregrine, thirteenth Baron Willoughby of Willoughby, Beck, and Eresby (1555–1601)—The Trustees of the Grimsthorpe and Drummond Castle Trust Ltd. Photograph: Photographic Survey, Courtauld Institute of Art, London

Bertie, Robert, first earl of Lindsey (1582–1642)—© reserved

Besant, Annie (1847–1933)—© National Portrait Gallery, London

Besse, Antonin (1877–1951)—courtesy of St Antony's College, Oxford

Bessemer, Sir Henry (1813–1898)—© National Portrait Gallery, London

Betham, William (1749–1839)—© National Portrait Gallery, London

Bethel, Slingsby (*bap.* 1617, *d.* 1697)—© Copyright The British Museum

Bethell, Richard, first Baron Westbury (1800–1873)—by kind permission of the Masters of the Bench of the Honourable Society of the Middle Temple. Photograph: Photographic Survey, Courtauld Institute of Art, London